INDEX OF ECONOMIC ARTICLES
In Journals and Collective Volumes

Index of
Economic Articles

IN JOURNALS AND COLLECTIVE VOLUMES

Volume XXVII · 1985

Part One—Subject Index

Prepared under the auspices of

THE JOURNAL OF ECONOMIC LITERATURE

of the

AMERICAN ECONOMIC ASSOCIATION

JOHN PENCAVEL

Managing Editor

MOSES ABRAMOVITZ

Associate Editor

DRUCILLA EKWURZEL

Associate Editor

ASATOSHI MAESHIRO

Editorial Consultant

MARY KAY AKERMAN

Assistant Editor

NASHVILLE, TENNESSEE
AMERICAN ECONOMIC ASSOCIATION
1989

Student Classifiers: A'Amer Farooqi, Nayyer Hussain, Edgar L. Zamalloa, and Lorena M. Zamalloa.

Library of Congress Catalog Card Number: 61–8020
International Standard Book Number: 0–917290–16–X
International Standard Serial Number: 0536–647X
Printed in the United States of America

TABLE OF CONTENTS

INTRODUCTORY DISCUSSION

This volume of the *Index* lists, both by subject category and by author, articles in major economic journals and in collective volumes published during the year 1985. The articles listed include all articles published in English or with English summaries in the journals and books identified in the following sections. Part One includes the Subject Index of Articles in Journals and Collective Volumes, and Part Two consists of an alphabetical Author Index of all the articles indexed in Part One.

Relationship to JEL

This *Index* is prepared largely as an adjunct to the bibliographic activities of the *Journal of Economic Literature (JEL)*. Economies of joint production are pursued throughout the production process. Journals included are those indexed in the *JEL* quarterly; collective volumes are selected from the annotated 1985 books; the classification system is a more detailed version of the *JEL* system.

Journals Included

The 298 journals listed represent, in general, those journals that we believe will be most helpful to research workers and teachers of economics. These journals are listed below on page x.

Generally, articles, notes, communications, comments, replies, rejoinders, as well as papers and formal discussions in proceedings and review articles have been indexed. There are some exceptions; only articles in English or with English summaries are included—this practice results in a slightly reduced coverage compared with the *JEL* quarterly. Articles lacking author identification are omitted, as are articles without economic content. Identical articles appearing in two different journals in 1985 are listed from both sources. The journal issues included usually fall within a single volume. When a volume of a journal overlaps two calendar years, for example, Fall 1984 to Summer 1985, we include the issues from the two volumes relating to 1985 as best we can determine.

Collective Volumes

The collective volumes consist of the following:
1. *Festschriften*
2. Conference publications with individual papers
3. Collected essays, original, by one or more authors
4. Collected essays, reprinted, by one or more authors
5. Proceedings volumes
6. Books of readings

All original articles in English are indexed with the exception of unsigned articles or articles without economic content. Reprinted articles are included on the basis that a researcher would be interested in knowing about another source of the article. The original publication dates are shown in italics on the citations of reprinted articles. Excerpts are not included. The same article appearing for the first time in different collective volumes in the same year is cited from both publications.

In the article citation, reference to the book in which the article appears is by author or editor of the volume. If the same person or persons wrote or edited more than one book included in the 1982 *Index*, it is indicated by a I or II appearing in both the source given in the article citation and the bibliographic reference in the book listing. If the same person wrote one book and edited another in 1985, the specification of "ed" in the reference indicates which book is being cited.

The collective volumes are listed alphabetically by author or editor beginning on page xvi and include a full bibliographic reference. If there is more than one edition, the publisher cited is the one on the copy the *JEL* received, usually the American publisher.

Arrangement

The *Index* consists of two parts:
1. A Subject Index in which the articles are arranged by subject.
2. An Author Index.

Part One—Subject Index

In Part One, all articles are listed alphabetically by first author under each 4-digit subject category. Joint authors are listed up to three; beyond that, only the first author is listed, followed by *et al.*

There is one exception to the alphabetical author arrangement. In the 0322 category, a subdivision of **History of Thought** entitled **Individuals**, the arrangement is first alphabetical by the individual discussed in the article and then alphabetical by the article's author.

Articles with empirical content or discussing a particular geographic area carry a geographic descriptor (see discussion below).

Classification System

The classification system is an expansion of the 3-digit classification system used in the *Journal of Economic Literature* to a 4-digit system with slightly over 300 subcategories. The classification system, itself, is shown beginning on page xxxiv (Part One). In most cases the classification heading is self-explanatory; however, in some cases notes have been added to clarify the coverage or indicate alternative subject classifications. The basic approach in classification is from the point of view of the researcher rather than the teacher; course content does not necessarily coincide with subfields of our classification system. In all cases where there are two or more 4-digit classifications under a 3-digit category, there is a zero classification; in most instances this is labeled "General." The zero or general category has been used both as an inclusive and a residual category. For example, an article discussing *all* aspects of international trade theory appears in the general category. There are also some articles that do not fall in any of the individual subcategories, and these, too, are classified in the general or zero category.

The criterion used in the classifying process is whether persons interested in this topic would wish to have the article drawn to their attention. With the advent of the online ECONOMIC LITERATURE INDEX on DIALOG, the interpretation of "interest" has broadened slightly to include cross-classifications that indicate the subject matter, particularly in such categories as industry studies or occupational designations. Over half of the articles are classified in more than one subcategory. From time to time, we find it desirable to add subject classifications as particular topics become prominent or to change subject headings to make them more descriptive of the contents of the category.

Geographic Descriptors

Geographic descriptors appear in brackets at the end of any article entry in the Subject Index where the article cites data from or refers to a particular country or area. Research workers interested in these countries thus are made aware of the empirical content in the article. The descriptors used are countries or broader areas, such as southeast Asia (S. E. Asia); articles referring to cities or regions within a country are classified under the country. In general, the country name is written out in full with some adaptations and abbreviations, *e.g.,* U.S. is used for United States, U.K. for United Kingdom, and U.S.S.R. for Union of Soviet Socialist Republics. Abbreviations include: W. for West, E. for East, S. for South, N. for North. A shortened name such as W. Germany is used rather than the correct, but longer, Federal Republic of Germany. When broader regions are used as descriptors, the article may or may not refer to the full unit. For example, OECD has been used at times when most, but not all, of the OECD member countries are referred to.

Index volumes prior to 1979 sometimes did not include geographic descriptors on articles listed under subject categories 1210, 1211, 1220, 1221, 1230, 1240, and 1241, involving general or comparative economic country studies. In the 1979 *Index* and later volumes, these articles carry geographic descriptors in order to facilitate online identification in the ECONOMIC LITERATURE INDEX on DIALOG. Because the descriptor fields are limited to five, very general descriptors, such as LDCs (developing countries) and MDCs (developed countries), are often used on articles.

The fact that an article carries a geographic descriptor does not necessarily preclude its being primarily theoretical in nature. Any theoretical article drawing on empirical data to demonstrate its findings will carry a geographic descriptor.

Topical Guide to the Classification System

At the end of Part One there is an alphabetical listing of standard economic terms and concepts. References are to the appropriate 4-digit classification numbers, not to page numbers.

Part Two—Author Index

Part Two consists of an alphabetical Author Index in which citations appear under each author (up to three) of an article. Wherever possible the full first name and middle initial or middle name(s) are used. Wherever it could be definitely ascertained, articles by the same person are grouped together with only one listing of the name. Authors' first names and initials are listed differently in various journals and books; for example, an individual may be identified as John L. Smith, J. L. Smith, or John Smith. Thus, despite our best efforts, we were left in doubt in several instances. Joint authors are listed up to three; beyond that, only the first author is listed, followed by *et al.* Under each author, articles are listed alphabetically. Names carrying prefixes are alphabetized according to the first *capitalized* letter, with occasional exceptions following national practices. Thus, van Arkadie would appear under A and D'Alabro under D.

LIST OF JOURNALS INDEXED 1985

Accounting Review, Vol. 60.

Acta Oeconomica, Vol. 34; Vol. 35.

L'Actualité Economique, Vol. 61.

African Economic History, Issue no. 14.

Agricultural Economics Research, Vol. 37.

American Economic Review, Vol. 75.
Includes American Economic Association Papers and Proceedings of the annual meeting in 75(2).

American Economist, Vol. 29.

American Historical Review, Vol. 90.

American Journal of Agricultural Economics, Vol. 67.
Title changed from Journal of Farm Economics in 1968.

American Journal of Economics and Sociology, Vol. 44.

American Political Science Review, Vol. 79.

American Real Estate and Urban Economics Association Journal, Vol. 13.

Annales de l'INSEE, Issue nos. 57–60.

Annals of Public and Co-operative Economy, Vol. 56.

Annals of Regional Science, Vol. 19.

Antitrust Bulletin, Vol. 30.

Applied Economics, Vol. 17.

ACES Bulletin (Association for Comparative Economic Studies Bulletin). See Comparative Economic Studies.

Atlantic Economic Journal, Vol. 13.

Aussenwirtschaft, Vol. 40.

Australian Bulletin of Labour, Vol. 11, Issue nos. 2–4; Supplement; Vol. 12, Issue no. 1.

Australian Economic History Review, Vol. 25.
Title changed from Business Archives and History in 1967; prior to 1962 entitled Bulletin of the Business Archives Council of Australia.

Australian Economic Papers, Vol. 24.

Australian Economic Review, Issue nos. 69–72.

Australian Journal of Agricultural Economics, Vol. 29.

Australian Tax Forum, Vol. 2.

Banca Nazionale del Lavoro—Quarterly Review, Issue nos. 152–155.

Bancaria, Vol. 41.

Bangladesh Development Studies, Vol. 13, Issue nos. 3–4.

British Journal of Industrial Relations, Vol. 23.

British Review of Economic Issues, Vol. 7

Brookings Papers on Economic Activity, Issue nos. 1–2, 1985.

Bulletin of Economic Research, Vol. 37, Issue nos. 1–3.
Title changed from Yorkshire Bulletin of Economic and Social Research in 1971.

Bulletin of Indonesian Economic Studies, Vol. 21.

Bulletin for International Fiscal Documentation, Vol. 39.

Business Economics, Vol. 20.

Business History Review, Vol. 59.
Title changed from Bulletin of the Business Historical Society in 1954.

Cahiers Économiques de Bruxelles, Issue nos. 105–108.

Cambridge Journal of Economics, Vol. 9.

Canadian Journal of Agricultural Economics, Vol. 32, Workshop Proceedings; Vol. 32, Annual Meeting Proceedings; Vol. 33.

Canadian Journal of Development Studies, Vol. 6.

Canadian Journal of Economics, Vol. 18.

Canadian Public Policy, Vol. 11; Supplement.

Carnegie–Rochester Conference Series on Public Policy, Vols. 22–23.
Vols. 1–17 were listed as supplements to the Journal of Monetary Economics.

Cato Journal, Vol. 4, Issue no. 3; Vol. 5, Issue nos. 1–2.

Cepal Review, Issue nos. 25–27.

Challenge, Vol. 27, Issue no. 6; Vol. 28, Issue nos. 1–5.

Chinese Economic Studies, Vol. 18, Issue nos. 2–4; Vol. 19, Issue no. 1.

Colección Estudios CIEPLAN, Issue nos, 16–18.

Comparative Economic Studies, Vol. 26.
Title changed from ACES Bulletin in 1985.

Conflict Management and Peace Science, Vol. 8, Issue no. 2; Vol. 9, Issue no. 1.
Title changed from Journal of Peace Science in 1979–80.

Contemporary Policy Issues, Vol. 3, Issue nos. 2–5.

Cuadernos de Economia, Vol. 22.

Czechoslovak Economic Digest, Issue nos. 1–8, 1985.

Czechoslovak Economic Papers, Issue no. 23

Demography, Vol. 22.

Desarrollo Económico, Vol. 24, Issue no. 96; Vol. 25, Issue nos. 97–99.

Developing Economies, Vol. 23.

Eastern Economic Journal, Vol. 11.

Eastern European Economics, Vol. 23, Issue no. 3–4; Vol. 24, Issue nos. 1–2.

Econometric Reviews, Vol. 4.

Econometrica, Vol. 53.

Economia (Portuguese Catholic University), Vol. 9.

Economia Internazionale, Vol. 38.

Economia e Lavoro, Vol. 19.

Economía et Política, Vol. 2.

Economic Analysis and Workers' Management, Vol. 19.

Economic Computation and Economic Cybernetics Studies and Research, Vol. 20.
Title changed from Studii și Cercetări Economicè in 1974. Changed from issue numbers to volume numbers in 1978.

Economic Development and Cultural Change, Vol. 33, Issue nos. 2–4; Vol. 34, Issue no. 1.

Economic Forum, Vol. 5, Issue no. 2.
Title changed from Intermountain Economic Review in 1979.

Economic Geography, Vol. 61.

Economic History Review, Vol. 38.

Economic Inquiry, Vol. 23.
Title changed from Western Economic Journal in 1974.

Economic Journal, Vol. 95; Supplement.

Economic Modelling, Vol. 2.

Economic Notes, Issue nos. 1–3, 1985.

Economic Record, Vol. 61.

Economic and Social Review, Vol. 16, Issue nos. 2–4; Vol. 17, Issue no. 1.

Economic Studies Quarterly, Vol. 36.

Economica, Vol. 52.
Title changed from Economica, N.S. in 1974.

Económica, Vol. 31.

Economics of Education Review, Vol. 4.

Economics and Philosophy, Vol. 1.

Economics of Planning, Vol. 19.

Économie Appliquée, Vol. 38.

Économies et Sociétés, Vol. 19.

De Economist, Vol. 133.

Ekonomiska Samfundets Tidskrift, Vol. 38.

Empirica, Vol. 12.

Empirical Economics, Vol. 10.

Energy Economics, Vol. 7.

Energy Journal, Vol. 6.

European Economic Review, Vols. 27–29.

European Review of Agricultural Economics, Vol. 12.

Explorations in Economic History, Vol. 22.
Title changed from Explorations in Entrepreneurial History in 1969–70.

Federal Reserve Bank of Dallas Economic Review, January, March, May, July, September, November, 1985.

Federal Reserve Bank of Minneapolis Quarterly Review, Vol. 9.

Federal Reserve Bank of New York Quarterly Review, Vol. 10.

Federal Reserve Bank of Richmond Economic Review, Vol. 71.

Federal Reserve Bank of San Francisco Economic Review, Issue nos. 1–4, 1985.

Federal Reserve Bank of St. Louis Review, Vol. 67.

Federal Reserve Bulletin, Vol. 71.

Finance, Vol. 6.

Finance and Development, Vol. 22.

Financial Review, Vol. 20.

Fiscal Studies, Vol. 6.

Food Research Institute Studies, Vol. 19, Issue no. 3.

Foreign Affairs, Vol. 63, Issue nos. 3–5; Vol. 64, Issue no. 1.

Giornale degli Economisti e Annali di Economia, Vol. 44.

Greek Economic Review, Vol. 7.

Growth and Change, Vol. 16.

History of Political Economy, Vol. 17.

Hitotsubashi Journal of Economics, Vol. 26.

Hong Kong Economic Papers, Issue no. 16.

Housing Finance Review, Vol. 4.

Ifo-Studien, Vol. 31.

Indian Economic Journal, Vol. 31, Issue nos. 3–4; Vol. 32, Issue nos. 1–2.

Indian Economic Review, Vol. 20.

Industrial and Labor Relations Review, Vol. 38, Issue nos. 2–4; Vol. 39, Issue no. 1.

Industrial Relations, Vol. 24.

Industry and Development, Issue nos. 14–15.

Inquiry, Vol. 22.

International Economic Review, Vol. 26.

International Journal of Industrial Organization, Vol. 3.

International Journal of Social Economics, Vol. 12.

International Journal of Transport Economics, Vol. 12.

International Labour Review, Vol. 124.

International Monetary Fund Staff Papers, Vol. 32; Supplement.

International Organization, Vol. 39.

Irish Journal of Agricultural Economics and Rural Sociology, Vol. 10, Issue no. 2.

Jahrbücher für Nationalökonomie und Statistik, Vol. 200.

Journal of Accounting and Economics, Vol. 7.

Journal of Accounting Research, Vol. 23; Supplement.

Journal of the American Statistical Association, Vol. 80.

Journal of Bank Research, Vol. 15, Issue no. 4; Vol. 16, Issue nos. 1–3.

Journal of Banking and Finance, Vol. 9.

Journal of Behavioral Economics, Vol. 14.

Journal of Business, Vol. 58.

Journal of Business and Economic Statistics, Vol. 3.

Journal of Common Market Studies, Vol. 23, Issue nos. 3–4; Vol. 24, Issue nos. 1–2.

Journal of Comparative Economics, Vol. 9.

Journal of Consumer Research, Vol. 11, Issue no. 4; Vol. 12, Issue nos. 1–3.

Journal of Cultural Economics, Vol. 9; Supplement.

Journal of Developing Areas, Vol. 19, Issue nos. 2–4; Vol. 20, Issue no. 1.

Journal of Development Economics, Vols. 17–19.

Journal of Development Studies, Vol. 21, Issue nos. 2–4; Vol. 22, Issue no. 1.

Journal of Econometrics, Vols. 27–30.

Journal of Economic Behavior and Organization, Vol. 6.

Journal of Economic Development, Vol. 10.

Journal of Economic Dynamics and Control, Vol. 9.

Journal of Economic Education, Vol. 16.

Journal of Economic History, Vol. 45.

Journal of Economic Issues, Vol. 19.

Journal of Economic Literature, Vol. 23.

Journal of Economic and Social Measurement, Vol. 13.
Title changed from **Review of Public Data Use** in 1985.

Journal of Economic Studies, Vol. 12.

Journal of Economic Theory, Vols. 35–37.

Journal of Economics and Business, Vol. 37.
Title changed from **Economics and Business Bulletin** in 1972–73.

Journal of Energy and Development, Vol. 10, Issue no. 2; Vol. 11, Issue no. 1.

Journal of Environmental Economics and Management, Vol. 12.

Journal of European Economic History, Vol. 14.

Journal of Finance, Vol. 40.

Journal of Financial Economics, Vol. 14.

Journal of Financial and Quantitative Analysis, Vol. 20.

Journal of Financial Research, Vol. 8.

Journal of Futures Markets, Vol. 5.

Journal of Health Economics, Vol. 4.

Journal of Human Resources, Vol. 20.

Journal of Industrial Economics, Vol. 33, Issue nos. 3–4; Vol. 34, Issue nos. 1–2.

Journal of International Economics, Vols. 18–19.

Journal of International Money and Finance, Vol. 4.

Journal of Labor Economics, Vol. 3.

Journal of Labor Research, Vol. 6.

Journal of Law and Economics, Vol. 28.

Journal of Law, Economics, and Organization, Vol. 1.

Journal of Macroeconomics, Vol. 7.

Journal of Mathematical Economics, Vol. 14.

Journal of Monetary Economics, Vols. 15–16.

Journal of Money, Credit and Banking, Vol. 17.

Journal of Policy Analysis and Management, Vol. 4, Issue nos. 2–4; Vol. 5, Issue no. 1.

Journal of Policy Modeling, Vol. 7.

Journal of Political Economy, Vol. 93.

Journal of Portfolio Management, Vol. 11, Issue nos. 2–4; Vol. 12, Issue no. 1.

Journal of Post Keynesian Economics, Vol. 7, Issue nos. 2–4; Vol. 8, Issue no. 1.

Journal of Public Economics, Vols. 26–28.

Journal of Quantitative Economics, Vol. 1.

Journal of Regional Science, Vol. 25.

Journal of Research in Islamic Economics, Vol. 2, Issue no. 2; Vol. 3, Issue no. 1.

Journal of Risk and Insurance, Vol. 52.

Journal of the Royal Statistical Society, Series A, Vol. 148.

Journal for Studies in Economics and Econometrics, Issue nos. 21–23.

Journal of Transport Economics and Policy, Vol. 19.

Journal of Urban Economics, Vols. 17–18.

Journal of World Trade Law, Vol. 19.

Kansantaloudellinen Aikakauskirja, Vol. 81.

Keio Economic Studies, Vol. 22, Issue no. 1.

Kobe University Economic Review, Issue no. 31.

Konjunkturpolitik, Vol. 31.

Kredit und Kapital, Vol. 18, Issue nos. 2–4.

Kyklos, Vol. 38.

Labor History, Vol. 26.

Land Economics, Vol. 61.

Law and Contemporary Problems, Vol. 48.

Liiketaloudellinen Aikakauskirja, Vol. 34.

Lloyds Bank Review, Issue nos. 156–158.

Logistics and Transportation Review, Vol. 21.

Managerial and Decision Economics, Vol. 6.

Manchester School of Economics and Social Studies, Vol. 53.
Title changed from **The Manchester School** in 1939; prior to 1932 entitled **The Manchester School of Economics, Commerce and Administration.**

Margin, Vol. 17, Issue nos. 2–4; Vol. 18, Issue no. 1.

Marine Resource Economics, Vol. 1, Issue nos. 3–4; Vol. 2, Issue nos. 1–2.

Marketing Science, Vol. 4.

Matekon, Vol. 21, Issue nos. 3–4; Vol. 22, Issue nos. 1–2.
   Title changed from Mathematical Studies in Economics and Statistics in the USSR and Eastern Europe in 1969.

Mathematical Social Sciences, Vols. 9–10.

Metroeconomica, Vol. 37.

METU—Studies in Development, Vol. 12.

Michigan Law Review, Vol. 83, Issue nos. 4–8; Vol. 84, Issue nos. 1–3.

Mondo Aperto, Vol. 39.

Monthly Labor Review, Vol. 108.

National Institute Economic Review, Issue nos. 111–114.

National Tax Journal, Vol. 38.

National Westminster Bank Quarterly Review, February, May, August, November, 1985.

Nationaløkonomisk Tidsskrift, Vol. 123.

Natural Resources Journal, Vol. 25; Supplement.

New England Economic Review, January/February, March/April, May/June, July/August, September/October, November/December, 1985.

OECD Economic Studies, Issue nos. 4–5, 1985.

Osaka Economic Papers, Vol. 34, Issue nos. 3–4.

Oxford Bulletin of Economics and Statistics, Vol. 47.
   Title changed from Bulletin Oxford University Institute of Economics and Statistics in 1973. Prior to 1972 entitled Bulletin of the Institute of Economics and Statistics.

Oxford Economic Papers, Vol. 37

Oxford Review of Economic Policy, Vol. 1.

Pakistan Development Review, Vol. 24.

Pakistan Economic and Social Review, Vol. 23.

Pakistan Journal of Applied Economics, Vol. 4.

Philippine Economic Journal, Vol. 24.

Philippine Review of Economics and Business, Vol. 22.

Policy Review, Issue nos. 31–34.

Policy Sciences, Vol. 18.

Politica Economica, Vol. 1.

Population and Development Review, Vol. 11.

Population Studies, Vol. 39.

Problems of Economics, Vol. 27, Issue nos. 9–12; Vol. 28, Issue nos. 1–8.

Public Budgeting and Finance, Vol. 5.

Public Choice, Vols. 45–47.

Public Finance, Vol. 40.

Public Finance Quarterly, Vol. 13.

Quarterly Journal of Business and Economics, Vol. 24.
   Title changed from Nebraska Journal of Economics and Business in 1983.

Quarterly Journal of Economics, Vol. 100; Supplement.

Quarterly Review of Economics and Business, Vol. 25.

Rand Journal of Economics, Vol. 16.
   Title changed from Bell Journal of Economics in 1984.

Recherches Economiques de Louvain, Vol. 51.

Regional Science Perspectives, Vol. 15.

Regional Science and Urban Economics, Vol. 15.

Regional Studies, Vol. 19.

Review of Black Political Economy, Vol. 13, Issue no. 4; Vol. 14, Issue nos. 1–3.

Review of Economic Conditions in Italy, Issue nos. 1–3, 1985.

Review of Economic Studies, Vol. 52.

Review of Economics and Statistics, Vol. 67.
   Title changed from The Review of Economic Statistics in 1948.

Review of Income and Wealth, Vol. 31.

Review of Industrial Organization, Vol. 2.

Review of Marketing and Agricultural Economics, Vol. 53.

Review of Public Data Use.
   See Journal of Economic and Social Measurement.

Review of Radical Political Economics, Vol. 17.

Review of Regional Studies, Vol. 15.

Review of Social Economy, Vol. 43.

Revista Española de Economia, Vol. 2.

Revue d'Economie Industrielle, Issue no. 31.

Revue d'Economie Politique, Vol. 95.

Revue Économique, Vol. 36.

Ricerche Economiche, Vol. 39.

Rivista Internazionale di Scienze Economiche e Commerciali, Vol. 32.

Rivista di Politica Economia, Vol. 19; Supplement.

Scandinavian Economic History Review, Vol. 33.

Scandinavian Journal of Economics, Vol. 87.
Title changed from Swedish Journal of Economics in 1976; prior to 1965 entitled Ekonomisk Tidskrift.

Schweizerische Zeitschrift für Volkswirtschaft und Statistik, Vol. 121.

Science and Society, Vol. 49.

Scottish Journal of Political Economy, Vol. 32.

Singapore Economic Review, Vol. 30.
Title changed from Malayan Economic Review in 1983.

Social Choice and Welfare, Vol. 1, no. 4; Vol. 2.

Social and Economic Studies, Vol. 34.

Social Science Quarterly, Vol. 66.

Social Security Bulletin, Vol. 48.

South African Journal of Economics, Vol. 53.

Southern Economic Journal, Vol. 51, Issue nos. 3–4; Vol. 52, Issue nos. 1–2.

Southern Journal of Agricultural Economics, Vol. 17.

Soviet and Eastern European Foreign Trade, Vol. 21.

Soviet Economy, Vol. 1.

Statistica, Vol. 45.

Statistical Journal, Vol. 3.

Studi Economici, Vol. 40.

Survey of Current Business, Vol. 65.

Tijdschrift Voor Economie en Management, Vol. 30.
Title changed from Tijdschrift voor Economie in 1975.

Urban Studies, Vol. 22.

Water Resources Research, Vol. 21.

Weltwirtschaftliches Archiv, Vol. 121.

Western Journal of Agricultural Economics, Vol. 10.

World Development, Vol. 13.

World Economy, Vol. 8.

Yale Journal on Regulation, Vol. 2, Issue no. 2; Vol. 3, Issue no. 1.

Yale Law Journal, Vol. 94, Issue nos. 3–8; Vol. 95, Issue nos. 1–2.

Zeitschrift für die gesamte Staatswissenschaft, Vol. 141.

Zeitschrift für Nationalökonomie, Vol. 45.

Zeitschrift für Wirtschafts- und Socialwissenschaften, Vol. 105.

LIST OF COLLECTIVE VOLUMES INDEXED 1985

ABEL, CHRISTOPHER AND LEWIS, COLIN M., eds. *Latin America, Economic Imperialism and the State: The Political Economy of the External Connection from Independence to the Present.* Institute of Latin American Studies Monographs, no. 13. London and Dover, N.H.: Athlone Press for the University of London, Institute of Latin American Studies, 1985.

ADAMS, F. GERARD, ed. *Industrial Policies for Growth and Competitiveness:* Volume II. *Empirical Studies.* Wharton Econometric Studies Series. Lexington, Mass., and Toronto: Heath, Lexington Books, 1985.

ADAMS, JOHN, ed. *The Contemporary International Economy: A Reader.* Second edition. New York: St. Martin's Press, [1979] 1985.

AHMED, IFTIKHAR, ed. *Technology and Rural Women: Conceptual and Empirical Issues. London; Boston and Sydney: Allen & Unwin,* 1985.

AIDA, S., ET AL. *The Science and Praxis of Complexity: Contributions to the Symposium Held at Montpellier, France, 9–11 May, 1984.* Tokyo: United Nations University, 1985.

ALIPRANTIS, C. D.; BURKINSHAW, O. AND ROTHMAN, N. J., eds. *Advances in Equilibrium Theory: Proceedings of the Conference on General Equilibrium Theory held at Indiana University–Purdue University at Indianapolis, USA, February 10–12, 1984.* Lecture Notes in Economics and Mathematical Systems series, vol. 244. New York; Berlin and Tokyo: Springer, 1985.

ANDERSON, E. J. AND PHILPOTT, A. B., eds. *Infinite Programming: Proceedings of an International Symposium on Infinite Dimensional Linear Programming, Churchill College, Cambridge, United Kingdom, September 7–10, 1984.* Lecture Notes in Economics and Mathematical Systems series, vol. 259. New York; Heidelberg and Tokyo: Springer, 1985.

ANDO, ALBERT, ET AL., eds. *Monetary Policy in Our Times: Proceedings of the First International Conference Held by the Institute for Monetary and Economic Studies of the Bank of Japan.* Cambridge, Mass., and London: MIT Press, 1985.

ARENA, R., ET AL. *Production circulation et monnaie.* Transformation de l'Appareil Productif et Structuration de l'Espace Social. Travaux et Recherches du Laboratoire Associé, no. 301. Paris: Presses Universitaires de France in cooperation with the University of Nice and the Comité Doyen Jean Lépine, 1985.

ARESTIS, PHILIP AND SKOURAS, THANOS, eds. *Post Keynesian Economic Theory: A Challenge to Neoclassical Economics.* Sussex: Harvester Press, Wheatsheaf Books; Armonk, N.Y.: Sharpe, 1985.

ARGY, VICTOR E. AND NEVILLE, JOHN W., eds. *Inflation and Unemployment: Theory, Experience and Policy-Making.* London; Boston and Sydney: Allen & Unwin, 1985.

ARHIN, KWAME; HESP, PAUL AND VAN DER LAAN, LAURENS, eds. *Marketing Boards in Tropical Africa.* Monographs from The African Studies Centre, Leiden series. London; Boston and Melbourne: Routledge and Kegan Paul, KPI, 1985.

ARNDT, SVEN W.; SWEENEY, RICHARD J. AND WILLETT, THOMAS D., eds. *Exchange Rates, Trade, and the U.S. Economy.* Washington, D.C.: American Enterprise Institute; Cambridge, Mass.: Harper & Row, Ballinger, 1985.

ARROW, KENNETH J. *Collected Papers of Kenneth J. Arrow.* Volume 5. *Production and Capital.* Cambridge, Mass., and London: Harvard Unviersity Press, Belknap Press, 1985. (I)

ARROW, KENNETH J. *Collected Papers of Kenneth J. Arrow.* Volume 6. *Applied Economics.* Cambridge, Mass., and London: Harvard Univeristy Press, Belknap Press, 1985. (II)

ARROW, KENNETH J. AND HONKAPOHJA, SEPPO, eds. *Frontiers of Economics.* Oxford and New York: Blackwell, 1985.

ASTON, T. H. AND PHILPIN, C. H. E., eds. *The Brenner Debate: Agrarian Class Structure and Economic Development in Pre-industrial Europe.* Past and Present Publications series. Cambridge; New York and Sydney: Cambridge University Press, 1985.

ATACK, JEREMY, ed. *Business and Economic History, second series.* Volume 14. Champaign: University of Illinois, 1985.

ATKINSON, G. B. J., ed. *Developments in Economics. An Annual Review, vol. 1.* Lancashire, England: Causeway Press; distributed in the U.S. by Sheridan House, Dobbs Ferry, N.Y., 1985.

AUBIN, J.-P.; SAARI, D. AND SIGMUND, K., eds. *Dynamics of Macrosystems: Proceedings of a Workshop on the Dynamics of Macrosystems Held at the International Institute for Applied Systems Analysis (IIASA), Laxenburg, Austria, September 3–7, 1984.* Lecture Notes in Economics and Mathematical Systems series, vol. 257. New York; Berlin and Tokyo: Springer, 1985.

AUERBACH, ALAN J. AND FELDSTEIN, MARTIN, eds. *Handbook of Public Economics.* Volume 1. Handbooks in Economics series, no. 4. New York and Oxford: North-Holland; distributed in the U.S. and Canada by Elsevier Science, N.Y., 1985.

AUGENBLICK, JOHN, ed. *Public Schools: Issues in Budgeting and Financial Management.* New Brunswick, N.J., and Oxford: Transaction Books, 1985.

BAILY, MARY ANN AND CIKINS, WARREN I., eds. *The Effects of Litigation on Health Care Costs.* Washington, D.C.: Brookings Institution, 1985.

BALASSA, BELA. *Change and Challenge in the World Economy.* New York: St. Martin's Press, 1985.

BANDYOPADHYAY, R. AND KHANKHOJE, D. P., eds. *Finance and Development.* Pune, India: National Institute of Bank Management, 1985.

BAPNA, ASHOK, ed. *One World One Future: New International Strategies for Development.* New York; Eastbourne, U.K.; Toronto and Sydney: Praeger, 1985.

BATTEN, DAVID F. AND LESSE, PAUL F., eds. *New Mathematical Advances in Economic Dynamics.* New York: New York University Press, 1985.

BEAN, PHILIP; FERRIS, JOHN AND WHYNES, DAVID, eds. *In Defence of Welfare.* Social Science Paperbacks. London and New York: Tavistock; Bungay, U.K.: Clay, Chaucer Press, 1985.

BENJAMIN, ROGER AND ELKIN, STEPHEN L., eds. *The Democratic State* Studies in Government and Public Policy series. Lawrence: University Press of Kansas, 1985.

BERGMANN, THEODOR AND OGURA, TAKEKAZU B., eds. *Cooperation in World Agriculture: Experiences, Problems and Perspectives.* Tokyo: Food and Agriculture Policy Research Centre; distributed by Maruzen, Tokyo, 1985.

BERGSTEN, C. FRED, ed. *Global Economic Imbalances.* Special Reports series, no. 4. Washington, D.C.: Institute for International Economics, 1985.

BERNARDO, J. M., ET AL., eds. *Bayesian Statistics 2: Proceedings of the Second Valencia International Meeting, September 6/10, 1983.* Amsterdam; New York and Oxford: Elsevier Science, North-Holland; Valencia, Spain: Valencia University Press, 1985.

BETSEY, CHARLES L.; HOLLISTER, ROBINSON G., JR. AND PAPAGEORGIOU, MARY R., eds. *Youth Employment and Training Programs: The YEDPA Years.* Washington, D.C.: National Academy Press, 1985.

BHAGWATI, JAGDISH N. *Dependence and Interdependence.* Edited by GENE GROSSMAN. Essays in Development Economics series, vol. 2. Cambridge, Mass.: MIT Press; Oxford, England: Blackwell, 1985. (I)

BHAGWATI, JAGDISH N. *Wealth and Poverty.* Edited by GENE GROSSMAN. Essays in Development Economics series, vol. 1. Cambridge, Mass.: MIT Press; Oxford: Blackwell, 1985. (II)

BHANDARI, JAGDEEP S., ed. *Exchange Rate Management under Uncertainty.* Cambridge, Mass., and London: MIT Press, 1985.

BJERKHOLT, OLAV AND OFFERDAL, ERIK, eds. *Macroeconomic Prospects for a Small Oil Exporting Country.* International Studies in Economics and Econometrics series, vol. 11. Dordrecht; Hingham, Mass., and Lancaster: Kluwer Academic, Nijhoff, 1985.

BLOCK, WALTER; BRENNAN, GEOFFREY AND ELZINGA, KENNETH, eds. *Morality of the Market: Religious and Economic Perspectives.* Vancouver: Fraser Institute, 1985.

[BLOOMFIELD, ARTHUR I.] *International Financial Markets and Capital Movements: A Symposium in Honor of Arthur I. Bloomfield.* Edited by WILFRED J. ETHIER AND RICHARD C. MARSTON. Essays in International Finance series, no. 157. Princeton, N.J.: Princeton University, Department of Economics, International Finance Section, 1985.

BOAZ, DAVID AND CRANE, EDWARD H., eds. *Beyond the Status Quo: Policy Proposals for America.* Washington, D.C.: Cato Institute, 1985.

BORJAS, GEORGE J. AND TIENDA, MARTA, eds. *Hispanics in the U.S. Economy.* Institute for Research on Poverty Monograph Series. Orlando; London; Toronto and Sydney: Harcourt Brace Jovanovich, Academic Press, 1985.

BORNSTEIN, MORRIS, ed. *Comparative Economic Systems: Models and Cases.* Fifth edition. Irwin Publications in Economics series. Homewood, Ill.: Irwin, [1965...1979] 1985.

BROWN, ROY CHAMBERLAIN, ed. *Quantity and Quality in Economic Research.* Volume I. Lanham, Md., and London: University Press of America, 1985.

BUCKLEY, PETER J. AND CASSON, MARK. *The Economic Theory of the Multinational Enterprise: Selected Papers.* New York: St. Martin's Press; London: Macmillan Press, 1985.

BUITER, WILLEM H. AND MARSTON, RICHARD C., eds. *International Economic Policy Coordination.* Cambridge; New York and Sydney: Cambridge University Press, 1985.

CAGAN, PHILLIP AND SOMENSATTO, EDUARDO, eds. *Essays in Contemporary Economic Problems, 1985: The Economy in Deficit.* Contemporary Economic Problems Series, vol. 8. Washington, D.C., and London: American Enterprise Institute, 1985.

CAMPBELL, RICHMOND AND SOWDEN, LANNING, eds. *Paradoxes of Rationality and Cooperation: Prisoner's Dilemma and Newcomb's Problem.* Vancouver: University of British Columbia Press, 1985.

CARAVALE, GIOVANNI A., ed. *The Legacy of Ricardo.* Oxford and New York: Blackwell, 1985.

CARLINE, DEREK, ET AL. *Labour Economics.* Surveys in Economics series. London and New York: Longman, 1985.

CASSEN, ROBERT, ed. *Soviet Interests in the Third World.* London: Royal Institute of International Affairs; London; Beverly Hills and New Delhi: Sage, 1985.

CERNEA, MICHAEL M., ed. *Putting People First: Sociological Variables in Rural Development.* New York; Oxford; Toronto and Hong Kong: Oxford University Press for the World Bank, 1985.

CHAN, JAMES L., ed. *Research in Governmental and Non-Profit Accounting.* Volume 1. A Research Annual. Greenwich, Conn., and London: JAI Press, 1985.

CHRISTIANSON, JON B. AND SMITH, KENNETH R., eds. *Current Strategies for Containing Health Care Expenditures: A Summary of their Potential, Performance and Prevalence.* Health Systems Management series, vol. 18. New York: Spectrum, Medical & Scientific Books, 1985.

CHUBB, JOHN E. AND PETERSON, PAUL E., eds. *The New Direction in American Politics.* Washington, D.C.: Brookings Institution, 1985.

CIRIACY-WANTRUP, S. V. *Natural Resource Economics: Selected Papers.* Edited by RICHARD C. BISHOP AND STEPHEN O. ANDERSEN. Boulder, Colo., and London: Westview Press, 1985.

CLARK, SHIRLEY M. AND LEWIS, DARRELL R., eds. *Faculty Vitality and Institutional Productivity: Critical Perspectives for Higher Education.* New York and London: Columbia University, Teachers College Press, 1985.

CLARK, TERRY NICHOLS, ed. *Research in Urban Policy.* Volume 1. *Coping with Urban Austerity.* A Research Annual. Greenwich, Conn., and London: JAI Press, 1985.

COCKLE, PAUL, ed. *Public Expenditure Policy, 1985–86.* New York: St. Martin's Press, 1985.

COE, RICHARD D. AND WILBER, CHARLES K., eds. *Capitalism and Democracy: Schumpeter Revisited.* Notre Dame: University of Notre Dame Press, 1985.

CONKLIN, DAVID W. AND COURCHENE, THOMAS J., eds. *Canadian Trade at a Crossroads: Options for New International Agreements.* Ontario Economic Council Special Research Report series. Toronto: Ontario Economic Council, 1985.

CONNOLLY, MICHAEL B. AND MCDERMOTT, JOHN, eds. *The Economics of the Caribbean Basin.* New York; Eastbourne, U.K.; Toronto and Sydney: Praeger, 1985.

CONNOR, WALKER, ed. *Mexican-Americans in Comparative Perspective.* Washington, D.C.: Urban Institute Press, 1985.

CORDEN, W. MAX. *Protection, Growth and Trade: Essays in International Economics.* Oxford and New York: Blackwell, 1985.

COURCHENE, THOMAS J.; CONKLIN, DAVID W. AND COOK, GAIL C. A., eds. *Ottawa and the Provinces: The Distribution of Money and Power*. Volume 1. Federal–Provincial Relations Series. Toronto: Ontario Economic Council, 1985.

COURCHENE, THOMAS J.; CONKLIN, DAVID W. AND COOK, GAIL C. A., eds. *Ottawa and the Provinces: The Distribution of Money and Power*. Volume 2. Federal–Provincial Relations Series. Toronto: Ontario Economic Council, 1985.

CREW, MICHAEL A., ed. *Analyzing the Impact of Regulatory Change in Public Utilities*. Lexington, Mass., and Toronto: Heath, Lexington Books, 1985.

CROSS, MICHAEL, ed. *Managing Workforce Reduction: An International Survey*. New York; Eastbourne, U.K.; Toronto and Sydney: Praeger, 1985.

CUMMINGS, L.L. AND STAW, BARRY M., eds. *Research in Organizational Behavior: An Annual Series of Analytical Essays and Critical Reviews*. Volume 7. Greenwich, Conn., and London: JAI Press, 1985.

CURRIE, DAVID, ed. *Advances in Monetary Economics*. London; Sydney and Dover, N.H.: Croom Helm, 1985.

CZINKOTA, MICHAEL R. AND MARCIEL, SCOT, eds. *U.S.–Arab Economic Relations: A Time of Transition*. New York; Eastbourne, U.K.; Toronto and Sydney: Praeger, 1985.

DAMJANOVIC, MIJAT AND VOICH, DAN, JR., eds. *The Impact of Culture-based Value Systems on Management Policies and Practices: Yugoslav and United States Issues and Viewpoints*. Comparative Policy Studies. New York; Eastbourne, U.K.; Toronto and Sydney: Praeger, 1985.

DAUGHETY, ANDREW F., ed. *Analytical Studies in Transport Economics*. Cambridge; New York and Sydney: Cambridge University Press, 1985.

DAVID, MARTIN AND SMEEDING, TIMOTHY, eds. *Horizontal Equity, Uncertainty, and Economic Well-Being*. NBER Studies in Income and Wealth series, vol. 50. Chicago and London: University of Chicago Press, 1985.

DAVIES, H. R. J., ed. *Natural Resources and Rural Developments in Arid Lands: Case Studies from Sudan*. Tokyo: United Nations University, 1985.

DAVIS, KINGSLEY, ed. *Contemporary Marriage: Comparative Perspectives on a Changing Institution*. In association with AMYRA GROSSBARD-SCHECHTMAN. New York: Russell Sage Foundation, 1985.

DAVIS, TED J., ed. *Proceedings of the Fifth Agriculture Sector Symposium: Population and Food*. Washington, D.C.: World Bank, 1985.

DEACON, ROBERT T. AND JOHNSON, M. BRUCE, eds. *Forestlands: Public and Private*. Foreword by B. DELWORTH GARDNER. Pacific Studies in Public Policy series. San Francisco: Pacific Institute for Public Policy Research; Cambridge, Mass.: Harper & Row, Ballinger, 1985.

DEMYANOV, V. F. AND PALLASCHKE, D., eds. *Nondifferentiable Optimization: Motivations and Applications. Proceedings of an IIASA (International Institute for Applied Systems Analysis) Workshop on Nondifferentiable Optimization held at Sopron, Hungary, September 17–22, 1984*. Lecture Notes in Economics and Mathematical Systems series, no. 255. New York; Heidelberg and Tokyo: Springer, 1985.

DENNIS, BARBARA D., ed. *Industrial Relations Research Association: Proceedings of the 1985 Spring Meeting, April 18–19, 1985, Detroit, Michigan*. Madison, Wisc.: Industrial Relations Research Association, 1985.

DIDSBURY, HOWARD F., JR., ed. *The Global Economy: Today, Tomorrow, and the Transition*. Bethesda, Md.: World Future Society; distributed by Westview Press, Boulder, Colo., 1985.

DOMMEN, EDWARD AND HEIN, PHILIPPE, eds. *States, Microstates and Islands*. London; Sydney and Dover, N.H.: Croom Helm, 1985.

DONGES, JUERGEN B., ed. *The Economics of Deep-Sea Mining*. New York; Berlin and Toyko: Springer, 1985.

DORAN, CHARLES F. AND SIGLER, JOHN H., eds. *Canada and the United States: Enduring Friendship, Persistent Stress*. American Assembly, Columbia University, and Council on Foreign Relations series. Englewood Cliffs, N.J.: Prentice-Hall, Spectrum, 1985.

DRYSDALE, PETER AND SHIBATA, HIROFUMI, eds. *Federalism and Resource Development: The Austra-*

lian Case. Sydney; London and Boston: Allen & Unwin in association with Australian National University, Australia–Japan Research Centre, Canberra, 1985.

DUNNING, JOHN H., ed. *Multinational Enterprises, Economic Structure and International Competitiveness.* Wiley/IRM Series on Multinationals. Chichester; New York; Brisbane and Toronto: Wiley, 1985.

DURAN, ESPERANZA, ed. *Latin America and the World Recession.* Cambridge; New York and Sydney: Cambridge University Press in association with The Royal Institute of International Affairs, 1985.

ECONOMIC COUNCIL OF CANADA. *Towards Equity: Proceedings of a Colloquium on the Economic Status of Women in the Labour Market, November 1984.* Ottawa: Supply and Services Canada; distributed by Canadian Government Publishing Centre, 1985.

EICHNER, ALFRED S. *Toward a New Economics: Essays in Post-Keynesian and Institutionalist Theory.* Armonk, N.Y.: Sharpe, 1985.

EISENSTADT, SHMUEL N. AND AHIMEIR, ORA, eds. *The Welfare State and Its Aftermath.* Totowa, N.J.: Barnes & Noble Books, 1985.

EMPLOYEE BENEFIT RESEARCH INSTITUTE. *Medicare Reform: The Private-Sector Impact.* EBRI–ERF Policy Forum series. Washington, D.C.: Author, 1985.

ENGELS, WOLFRAM AND POHL, HANS, eds. *German Yearbook on Business History, 1984.* Translated by EILEEN MARTIN AND ANNE WEGNER. New York; Heidelberg and Tokyo: Springer, 1985.

ERDILEK, ASIM, ed. *Multinationals as Mutual Invaders: Intra-industry Direct Foreign Investment.* New York: St. Martin's Press, 1985.

ESKRIDGE, WILLIAM N., JR., ed. *A Dance Along the Precipice: The Political and Economic Dimensions of the International Debt Problem.* Lexington, Mass., and Toronto: Heath, Lexington Books, 1985.

EVANS, PETER B.; RUESCHEMEYER, DIETRICH AND SKOCPOL, THEDA, eds. *Bringing the State Back In.* Cambridge; New York and Sydney: Cambridge University Press, 1985.

EVANS, PETER; RUESCHEMEYER, DIETRICH AND STEPHENS, EVELYN HUBER, eds. *States versus Markets in the World-System.* Political Economy of the Sorld-System Annuals series, vol. 8. Beverly Hills; London and New Delhi: Sage, 1985.

FANDEL, GÜNTER AND SPRONK, JAAP, eds. *Multiple Criteria Decision Methods and Applications: Selected Readings of the First International Summer School, Acireale, Sicily, September 1983.* In collaboration with BENEDETTO MATARAZZO. Berlin; New York and Tokyo: Springer, 1985.

FEDERAL HOME LOAN BANK OF SAN FRANCISCO. *Solving the Mortgage Menu Problem: Proceedings of the Tenth Annual Conference, December 11–12, 1984, San Francisco, California.* San Francisco: Author, 1985.

FEDERAL RESERVE BANK OF ATLANTA. *How to Compete Beyond the 1980s: Perspectives from High Performance Companies: Conference Proceedings.* Westport, Conn., and London: Greenwood Press, Quorum Books, 1985. (I)

FEDERAL RESERVE BANK OF ATLANTA. *Interstate Banking: Strategies for a New Era—Conference Proceedings Sponsored by Federal Reserve Bank of Atlanta.* Westport, Conn., and London: Greenwood Press, Quorum Books, 1985. (II)

FEIWEL, GEORGE R., ed. *Issues in Contemporary Macroeconomics and Distribution.* Albany: State University of New York Press, 1985. (I)

FEIWEL, GEORGE R., ed. *Issues in Contemporary Microeconomics and Welfare.* Albany: State University of New York Press, 1985. (II)

FERRARA, PETER J., ed. *Social Security: Prospects for Real Reform.* Washington, D.C.: Cato Institute, 1985.

FIENBERG, STEPHEN E.; MARTIN, MARGARET E. AND STRAF, MIRON L., eds. *Sharing Research Data.* Washington, D.C.: National Academy Press, 1985.

FISHER, BART S. AND HARTE, KATHLEEN M., eds. *Barter in the World Economy.* New York; Eastbourne, U.K.; Toronto and Sydney: Praeger, 1985.

FØRSUND, FINN R. AND HONKAPOHJA, SEPPO, eds. *Limits and Problems of Taxation.* New York: St. Martin's Press, 1985.

FORTE, FRANCESCO AND PEACOCK, ALAN, eds. *Public Expenditure and Government Growth*. Oxford and New York: Blackwell, 1985.

FRETZ, DEBORAH; STERN, ROBERT AND WHALLEY, JOHN, eds. *Canada/United States Trade and Investment Issues*. Ontario Economic Council Special Research Report. Canadian Trade at a Crossroads Series. Toronto: Ontario Economic Council; distributed by University of Toronto Press, Toronto, Hertfordshire, U.K., and Buffalo, 1985.

FRIEDMAN, BENJAMIN M., ed. *Corporate Capital Structures in the United States*. National Bureau of Economic Research Project Report series. Chicago and London: University of Chicago Press, 1985.

GAERTNER, WULF AND WENIG, ALOIS, eds. *The Economics of the Shadow Economy: Proceedings of the International Conference on the Economics of the Shadow Economy Held at the University of Bielefeld, West Germany, October 10–14, 1983*. Studies in Contemporary Economics series, vol. 15. New York; Berlin and Tokyo: Springer, 1985.

GALENSON, WALTER, ed. *Foreign Trade and Investment: Economic Development in the Newly Industrializing Asian Countries*. Madison and London: University of Wisconsin Press, 1985.

GARDNER, BRUCE L., ed. *U.S. Agricultural Policy: The 1985 Farm Legislation*. AEI Symposia series, no. 85C. Washington, D.C.: American Enterprise Institute for Public Policy Research, 1985.

GAUHAR, ALTAF, ed. *Regional Integration: The Latin American Experience*. London: Third World Foundation for Social and Economic Studies; Boulder, Colo.: Westview Press, 1985.

GEROSKI, P. A.; PHLIPS, L. AND ULPH, A., eds. *Oligopoly, Competition and Welfare*. Oxford and New York: Blackwell in cooperation with the *Journal of Industrial Economics*, 1985.

GINZBERG, ELI. *Understanding Human Resources: Perspectives, People, and Policy*. Lanham, Md., and London: University Press of America, Abt Books, 1985.

GINZBERG, ELI, ed. *The U.S. Health Care System: A Look to the 1990s*. Conservation of Human Resources Series, no. 26. Totowa, N.J.: Littlefield, Adams; Rowman and Allanheld, 1985.

GLAZER, NATHAN, ed. *Clamor at the Gates: The New American Immigration*. San Francisco: ICS Press, 1985.

GOMES, P. I., ed. *Rural Development in the Caribbean*. New York: St. Martin's Press; London: Hurst, 1985.

VAN GOOL, W. AND BRUGGINK, J. J. C., eds. *Energy and Time in the Economic and Physical Sciences: Papers and Comments, Workshop Wolfheze, the Netherlands, June 1984*. With the cooperation of J. A. OVER AND J. L. SWEENEY. Amsterdam and Oxford: North-Holland; distributed in the U.S. and Canada by Elsevier Science, New York, 1985.

GRAMLICH, EDWARD M. AND YSANDER, BENGT-CHRISTER, eds. *Control of Local Government*. IUI Conference Reports series, 1985:1. Stockholm: Industrial Institute for Economic and Social Research; distributed by Almqvist & Wiksell International, Stockholm, 1985.

GRANT, MARCUS, ed. *Alcohol Policies*. WHO Regional Publications, European Series, no. 18. Copenhagen: World Health Organization Regional Office for Europe, 1985.

GRANT, WYN, ed. *The Political Economy of Corporatism*. Sociology, Politics and Cities series. New York: St. Martin's Press, 1985.

GRAUER, M.; THOMPSON, M. AND WIERZBICKI, A. P., eds. *Plural Rationality and Interactive Decision Processes: Proceedings of an IIASA (International Institute for Applied Systems Analysis) Summer Study on Plural Rationality and Interactive Decision Processes Held at Sopron, Hungary, August 16–26, 1984*. Lecture Notes in Economics and Mathematical Systems series, vol. 248. New York; Berlin and Tokyo: Springer, 1985.

GREENAWAY, DAVID, ed. *Current Issues in International Trade: Trade and Policy*. New York: St. Martin's Press; London: Macmillan, 1985.

GRIFFITH-JONES, STEPHANY AND HARVEY, CHARLES, eds. *World Prices and Development*. Aldershot, U.K., and Brookfield, Vt.: Gower, 1985.

GUISINGER, STEPHEN E., ET AL. *Investment Incentives and Performance Requirements: Patterns of International Trade, Production, and Investment*. New York; Eastbourne, U.K.; Toronto and Sydney: Praeger, 1985.

GUSTAVSSON, BENGTOVE; KARLSSON, JAN CH. AND RAFTEGARD, CURT. *Work in the 1980s: Emancipation and Derogation. Papers from the Karlstad Symposium on Work.* Brookfield, Vt., and Aldershot, U.K.: Gower, 1985.

GUTOWSKI, ARMIN; ARNAUDO, A. A. AND SCHARRER, HANS-ECKART, eds. *Financing Problems of Developing Countries: Proceedings of a Conference Held by the International Economic Association in Buenos Aires, Argentina.* New York: St. Martin's Press, 1985.

HABERLER, GOTTFRIED. *Selected Essays of Gottfried Haberler.* Edited by ANTHONY Y. C. KOO. Cambridge, Mass., and London: MIT Press, 1985.

HAHN, FRANK. *Money, Growth and Stability.* Cambridge, Mass.: MIT Press; London: Blackwell, 1985.

HAIMES, YACOV Y. AND CHANKONG, VIRA, eds. *Decision Making with Multiple Objectives: Proceedings of the Sixth International Conference on Multiple-Criteria Decision Making Held at the Case Western Reserve University, Cleveland, Ohio, USA, June 4–8, 1984.* Lecture Notes in Economics and Mathematical Systems series, vol. 242. New York; Berlin and Tokyo: Springer, 1985.

HARCOURT, G. C., ed. *Keynes and His Contemporaries: The Sixth and Centennial Keynes Seminar Held at the University of Kent at Canterbury, 1983.* New York: St. Martin's Press; London: Macmillan, 1985.

HARKER, PATRICK T., ed. *Spatial Price Equilibrium: Advances in Theory, Computation and Application: Papers Presented at the Thirty-First North American Regional Science Association Meeting Held at Denver, Colorado, USA, November 1984.* Lecture Notes in Economics and Mathematical Systems series, vol. 249. New York; Berlin and Tokyo: Springer, 1985.

HARRISS, C. LOWELL, ed. *Control of Federal Spending: Proceedings of the Academy of Political Science.* New York: Academy of Political Science, 1985.

HARTMANN, HEIDI I., ed. *Comparable Worth: New Directions for Research.* Washington, D.C.: National Academy Press, 1985.

HAUSMAN, JERRY A. AND WISE, DAVID A., eds. *Social Experimentation.* National Bureau of Economic Research Conference Report. Chicago and London: University of Chicago Press, 1985.

HAWDON, DAVID, ed. *The Changing Structure of the World Oil Industry.* London; Sydney and Dover, N.H.: Croom Helm, 1985.

HEALEY, DEREK T.; JARRETT, FRANK G. AND MCKAY, JENNIFER M., eds. *The Economics of Bushfires: The South Australian Experience.* Adelaide: Centre for South Australian Economic Studies; Melbourne: Oxford University Press, 1985.

HECKMAN, JAMES J. AND SINGER, BURTON, eds. *Longitudinal Analysis of Labor Market Data.* Econometric Society Monographs series, no. 10. Cambridge; New York and Sydney: Cambridge University Press, 1985.

[HEIDHUES, THEODOR] *Agriculture and International Relations: Analysis and Policy. Essays in Memory of Theodor Heidhues.* Edited by HARTWIG DE HAEN, GLENN L. JOHNSON, AND STEFAN TANGERMANN. New York: St. Martin's Press, 1985.

HENDERSHOTT, PATRIC H., ed. *The Level and Composition of Household Saving.* Cambridge, Mass.: Harper & Row, Ballinger, 1985.

HINSHAW, RANDALL, ed. *Global Economic Priorities.* New Brunswick, N.J., and Oxford: Transaction Books, 1985.

HOCHMUTH, MILTON AND DAVIDSON, WILLIAM, eds. *Revitalizing American Industry: Lessons from Our Competitors.* Cambridge, Mass.: Harper & Row, Ballinger, 1985.

HOJMAN, DAVID E., ed. *Chile after 1973: Elements for the Analysis of Military Rule.* Monograph Series, no. 12. Liverpool: University of Liverpool, Centre for Latin American Studies, 1985.

HONT, ISTVAN AND IGNATIEFF, MICHAEL, eds. *Wealth and Virtue: The Shaping of Political Economy in the Scottish Enlightenment.* Paperback reprint. King's College Research Centre Projection on Political Economy and Society, 1750–1850 series. Cambridge; New York and Sydney: Cambridge University Press, [1983] 1985.

HUDSON, RAY AND LEWIS, JIM, eds. *Uneven Development in Southern Europe: Studies of Accumulation, Class, Migration and the State.* London and New York: Methuen, 1985.

HUTCHINSON, BRUCE G.; NIJKAMP, PETER AND BATTY, MICHAEL, eds. *Optimization and Discrete Choice in Urban Systems: Proceedings of the International Symposium on New Directions in Urban Systems Modelling Held at the University of Waterloo, Canada, July 1983*. Lecture Notes in Economics and Mathematical Systems series, vol. 247. New York; Berlin and Tokyo: Springer, 1985.

INMAN, ROBERT P., ed. *Managing the Service Economy: Prospects and Problems. Essays Commissioned for the Inaugural Conference of the Fishman–Davidson Center for the Study of the Service Sector, Wharton School, University of Pennsylvania*. Cambridge; New York and Sydney: Cambridge University Press, 1985.

INTERNATIONAL FISCAL ASSOCIATION. *The Assessment and Collection of Tax from Non-residents*. Studies on International Fiscal Law, vol. 70a. Deventer, the Netherlands; Hingham, Mass.; London and Frankfurt: Kluwer, 1985. (I)

INTERNATIONAL FISCAL ASSOCIATION. *International Double Taxation of Inheritances and Gifts*. Studies on International Fiscal Law, vol. 70b. Deventer, the Netherlands; Hingham, Mass.; London and Frankfurt: Kluwer, 1985. (II)

ISLAM, RIZWANUL, ed. *Strategies for Alleviating Poverty in Rural Asia*. Dhaka: Bangladesh Institute of Development Studies; Bangkok: International Labour Organisation Asian Employment Programme, 1985.

JAMES, JEFFREY AND WATANABE, SUSUMU, eds. *Technology, Institutions and Government Policies*. New York: St. Martin's Press, 1985.

JANSEN, GIJSBERTUS R. M.; NIJKAMP, PETER AND RUIJGROK, CEES J., eds. *Transportation and Mobility in an Era of Transition*. Studies in Regional Science and Urban Economics series, vol. 13. Amsterdam and Oxford: North-Holland; distributed in the U.S. and Canada by Elsevier Science, New York, 1985.

JERVE, ALF MORTEN, ed. *Pakistan: Country Study and Norwegian Aid Review*. Fantoft, Norway: Chr. Michelsen Institute, Department of Social Science and Development, Development Research and Action Programme, 1985.

JHA, L. K. *Growth, Inflation and Other Issues* New Delhi: Allied; Riverdale, Md.: Riverdale, 1985.

[JOHANSEN, LEIF] *Production, Multi-sectoral Growth and Planning: Essays in Memory of Leif Johansen*. Edited by FINN R. FORSUND, MICHAEL HOEL, AND SVEIN LONGVA. Contributions to Economic Analysis series, no. 154. Amsterdam; New York and Oxford: North-Holland; distributed in the U.S. and Canada by Elsevier Science, New York, 1985.

JONES, DEREK C. AND SVEJNAR, JAN, eds. *Advances in the Economic Analysis of Participatory and Labor-Managed Firms*. A Research Annual, vol. 1. Greenwich, Conn., and London: JAI Press, 1985.

JONES, RONALD W. AND KENEN, PETER B., eds. *Handbook of International Economics. Volume 2*. New York; Amsterdam and Oxford: North-Holland distributed in U.S. and Canada by Elsevier Science, New York, 1985.

JORDAN, ROBERT S., ed. *The United States and Multilateral Resource Management*. New York; Eastbourne, U.K.; Toronto and Sydney: Praeger, 1985.

JORGE, ANTONIO; SALAZAR-CARRILLO, JORGE AND DIAZ-POU, FRANK, eds. *External Debt and Development Strategy in Latin America*. New York; Oxford; Toronto and Sydney: Pergamon Press, 1985.

JUNGENFELT, KARL AND HAGUE, DOUGLAS [SIR], eds. *Structural Adjustment in Developed Open Economies*. New York: St. Martin's Press, 1985.

JURIS, HERVEY; THOMPSON, MARK AND DANIELS, WILBUR, eds. *Industrial Relations in a Decade of Economic Change*. Industrial Relations Research Association Series. Madison, Wisc.: Industrial Relations Research Association, 1985.

KAUSHIK, S. K., ed. *The Debt Crisis and Financial Stability: The Future. Proceedings of a Conference held at Pace University, New York City, in March 1985*. New York: Pace University, 1985.

KAY, JOHN, ed. *The Economy and the 1985 Budget*. Oxford: Blackwell, 1985.

KAYNAK, ERDENER, ed. *Global Perspectives in Marketing*. New York; Eastbourne, U.K.; Toronto and Sydney: Greenwood Press, Praeger, 1985. (I)

KAYNAK, ERDENER, ed. *International Business in the Middle East*. De Gruyter Studies in Organization series, no. 5. Berlin and New York: De Gruyter, 1985. (II)

KEELER, THEODORE E., ed. *Research in Transportation Economics*. A Research Annual series, vol. 2. Greenwich, Conn., and London: JAI Press, 1985.

KENNEDY, LÍAM AND OLLERENSHAW, PHILIP, eds. *An Economic History of Ulster, 1820–1939*. Manchester, U.K., and Dover, N.H.: Manchester University Press, 1985.

KHAN, MUHAMMAD AKRAM. *Challenge of Islamic Economics*. Lahore, Pakistan: All-Pakistan Islamic Education Congress, 1985.

KIDD, ALAN J. AND ROBERTS, K. W. *City, Class and Culture: Studies of Social Policy and Cultural Production in Victorian Manchester*. Manchester, U.K., and Dover, N.H.: Manchester University Press; distributed in N. America by St. Martin's Press, New York, 1985.

KIM, KWAN S. AND RUCCIO, DAVID F., eds. *Debt and Development in Latin America*. Notre Dame, Ind.: University of Notre Dame Press, 1985.

KINDLEBERGER, CHARLES P. *Keynesianism vs. Monetarism and Other Essays in Financial History*. London; Boston and Sydney: Allen & Unwin, 1985.

KIPNIS, KENNETH AND MEYERS, DIANA T., eds. *Economic Justice: Private Rights and Public Responsibilities*. An AMINTAPHIL Volume. Totowa, N.J.: Littlefield, Adams; Rowman & Allanheld, 1985.

KIRZNER, ISRAEL M. *Discovery and the Capitalist Process*. Chicago and London: University of Chicago Press, 1985.

KLEIN, RUDOLF AND O'HIGGINS, MICHAEL, ed. *The Future of Welfare*. Oxford and New York: Blackwell, 1985.

KNEESE, ALLEN V. AND SWEENEY, JAMES L., eds. *Handbook of Natural Resource and Energy Economics*. Volume 1. Handbooks in Economics series, vol. 6. Amsterdam and Oxford: North-Holland; distributed in North America by Elsevier Science, New York, 1985.

KNEESE, ALLEN V. AND SWEENEY, JAMES L., eds. *Handbook of Natural Resource and Energy Economics*. Volume 2. Handbooks in Economics series, vol. 6. Amsterdam and Oxford: North-Holland; distributed in North America by Elsevier Science, New York, 1985.

KONECCI, EUGENE B. AND KUHN, ROBERT LAWRENCE, eds. *Technology Venturing: American Innovation and Risk-Taking*. New York; Eastbourne, U.K.; Toronto and Melbourne: Praeger, 1985.

KOOPMANS, TJALLING C. *Scientific papers of Tjalling C. Koopmans*. Volume 2. With a foreword by HERBERT E. SCARF. Cambridge, Mass., and London: MIT Press, 1985.

KOSLOWSKI, PETER, ed. *Economics and Philosophy*. Series Civitas Resultate, vol. 7. Tübingen: Mohr (Siebeck), 1985.

KREISBERG, PAUL H., ed. *American Hostages in Iran: The Conduct of a Crisis*. Council on Foreign Relations Books. New Haven and London: Yale University Press, 1985.

KRISHNAMURTY, K. AND PANDIT, V. *Macroeconometric Modelling of the Indian Economy: Studies on Inflation and Growth*. Foreword by LAWRENCE R. KLEIN. Delhi: Hindustan, 1985.

KUBURSI, ATIF A. AND NAYLOR, THOMAS, eds. *Co-operation and Development in the Energy Sector: The Arab Gulf States and Canada*. Proceedings of a Symposium on the Energy Sector Co-sponsored by the Petroleum Information Committee of the Arab Gulf States and McMaster University, Canada, and held at McMaster University, 16–17 May 1984. London; Sydney and Dover, N.H.: Croom Helm, 1985.

KURY, CHANNING, ed. *Enclosing the Environment: NEPA's Transformation of Conservation into Environmentalism: Natural Resources Journal, 25th Anniversary Anthology*. Albuquerque: University of New Mexico School of Law, 1985.

LAKSHMANAN, T. R. AND JOHANSSON, B., eds. *Large-Scale Energy Projects: Assessment of Regional Consequences. An International Comparison of Experiences With Models and Methods*. Studies in Regional Science and Urban Economics series, vol. 12. Amsterdam; New York and Oxford: North-Holland; distributed in the U.S. and Canada by Elsevier Science, New York, 1985.

LANE, JAN-ERIK, ed. *State and Market: The Politics of the Public and the Private.* SAGE Modern Politics Series, vol. 9. Beverly Hills; London and New Delhi: SAGE, 1985.

LANGDON, RICHARD AND ROTHWELL, ROY, eds. *Design and Innovation: Policy and Management.* New York: St. Martin's Press, 1985.

LAVE, CHARLES A., ed. *Urban Transit: The Private Challenge to Public Transportation.* Foreword by JOHN MEYER. Pacific Studies in Public Policy series. San Francisco: Pacific Institute for Public Policy Research; Cambridge, Mass.: Harper & Row, Ballinger, 1985.

LAWSON, TONY AND PESARAN, HASHEM, eds. *Keynes' Economics: Methodological Issues.* Armonk, N.Y.: Sharpe, 1985.

LEA, JOHN P. AND COURTNEY, JOHN M., eds. *Cities in Conflict: Studies in the Planning and Management of Asian Cities.* Washington, D.C.: World Bank, 1985.

LEAB, DANIEL J., ed. *The Labor History Reader.* The Working Class in American History series. Urbana: University of Illinois Press, 1985.

LEONTIEF, WASSILY. *Essays in Economics: Theories, Theorizing, Facts, and Policies.* Reprint. New Brunswick, N.J., and Oxford: Transaction Books, [1966, 1977] 1985.

[LEVCIK, FRIEDRICH] *Socialist Economy and Economic Policy: Essays in Honour of Friedrich Levcik.* Edited by G. FINK. Studien über Wirtschafts- und Systemverglerche, Band 13. Vienna and New York: Springer, 1985.

LEVINE, CHARLES H., ed. *The Unfinished Agenda for Civil Service Reform: Implications of the Grace Commission Report.* Brookings Dialogues on Public Policy series. Washington, D.C.: Brookings Institution, 1985.

LEVINSON, PINCHAS AND LANDAU, PINCHAS, eds. *The Israel Economic and Business Review: 1985.* With an introduction by ZVI SUSSMAN. Boulder, Colo.: Westview Press; Jerusalem: *Israel Economist* and *Jerusalem Post,* 1985.

LEWIN, MARION EIN, ed. *The Health Policy Agenda: Some Critical Questions.* AEI Studies in Health Policy series, no. 427. Washington, D.C.: American Enterprise Institute for Public Policy Research, 1985.

LEWIS, STEPHEN R., JR., ed. *Henry George and Contemporary Economic Development.* Williamstown, Mass.: Williams College, 1985.

LIM, DAVID, ed. *Asian–Australia Trade in Manufactures.* Melbourne: Longman Cheshire, 1985.

LINDBERG, LEON N. AND MAIER, CHARLES S., eds. *The Politics of Inflation and Economic Stagnation: Theoretical Approaches and International Case Studies.* Washington, D.C.: Brookings Institution, 1985.

LINZ, SUSAN J., ed. *The Impact of World War II on the Soviet Union.* Totowa, N.J.: Rowman and Allanheld, 1985.

LIPSKY, DAVID B., ed. *Advances in Industrial and Labor Relations.* A Research Annual series, vol. 2. Greenwich, Conn., and London: JAI Press, 1985.

LUNDAHL, MATS, ed. *The Primary Sector in Economic Development: Proceedings of the Seventh Arne Ryde Symposium, Frostavallen, August 29–30, 1983.* New York: St. Martin's Press, 1985.

MACHIN, HOWARD AND WRIGHT, VINCENT, eds. *Economic Policy and Policy-making under the Mitterrand Presidency: 1981–84.* New York: St. Martin's Press, 1985.

MACPHERSON, C. B. *The Rise and Fall of Economic Justice and Other Essays.* Oxford and New York: Oxford University Press, 1985.

MĄCZAK, ANTONI; SAMSONOWICZ, HENRYK AND BURKE, PETER, eds. *East–Central Europe in Transition: From the Fourteenth to the Seventeenth Century.* Studies in Modern Capitalism series. Cambridge; New York and Sydney: Cambridge University Press; Paris: Editions de la Maison des Sciences de l'Homme, 1985.

[MAGDOFF, HARRY AND SWEEZY, PAUL] *Rethinking Marxism: Struggles in Marxist Theory. Essays for Harry Magdoff and Paul Sweezy.* Edited by STEPHEN RESNICK AND RICHARD WOLFF. Brooklyn, N.Y.: Autonomedia, 1985.

MAITAL, SHLOMO AND LIPNOWSKI, IRWIN, eds. *Macroeconomic Conflict and Social Institutions.* Cambridge, Mass.: Harper & Row, Ballinger, 1985.

MANNE, A. S., ed. *Economic Equilibrium: Model Formulation and Solution.* Mathematical Programming Study series, no. 23. Amsterdam and Oxford: North-Holland; distributed in the U.S. and Canada by Elsevier Science, New York, 1985.

MARX, ANNA VANNINI, ed. *Credito, Banche e Investimenti: Secoli XIII–XX.* Instituto Internazionale de Storia Economica, F. Datini, Pubblicazioni Serie II—Atti Delle "Settimane di Studio" e Altri Convegni. Florence: Le Monnier, 1985.

MASSEY, DOREEN AND MEEGAN, RICHARD, eds. *Politics and Method: Contrasting Studies in Industrial Geography.* New York and London: Methuen, 1985.

MATHEWS, RUSSELL, ET AL. *Australian Federalism, 1981.* Canberra: Australian National University, Centre for Research on Federal Financial Relations; distributed by ANUTECH, Canberra, 1985.

MATTHEWS, R. C. O., ed. *Economy and Democracy.* New York: St. Martin's Press, 1985.

[McGOWAN, JOHN J.] *Antitrust and Regulation: Essays in Memory of John J. McGowan.* Edited by FRANKLIN M. FISHER. Cambridge, Mass., and London: MIT Press, 1985.

McKELVEY, JEAN T., ed. *The Changing Law of Fair Representation.* Ithaca, N.Y.: Cornell University, New York State School of Industrial and Labor Relations, ILR Press, 1985.

MEHRAN, HASSANALI, ed. *External Debt Management: Papers Presented at a Seminar Organized by the IMF Institute and the Central Banking Department of the International Monetary Fund, Held in Washington in December 1984.* Washington, D.C.: International Monetary Fund, 1985.

MEIER, HENRI B., ed. *The Swiss Equity Market: A Guide for Investors.* Westport, Conn.: Greenwood Press, Quorum Books, 1985.

MELITZ, JACQUES AND WYPLOSZ, CHARLES, eds. *The French Economy: Theory and Policy.* Westview Special Studies series. Boulder, Colo., and London: Westview Press, 1985.

MELLOR, JOHN W. AND DESAI, GUNVANT M., eds. *Agricultural Change and Rural Poverty: Variations on a Theme by Dharm Narain.* Baltimore and London: Johns Hopkins University Press for the International Food Policy Research Institute, 1985.

MENDELL, JAY S., ed. *Nonextrapolative Methods in Business Forecasting: Scenarios, Vision, and Issues Management.* Westport, Conn., and London: Greenwood Press, Quorum, 1985.

[MENGES, GUNTER] *Contributions to Econometrics and Statistics Today: In Memoriam Günter Menges.* Edited by HANS SCHNEEWEISS AND HEINRICH STRECKER. New York; Berlin and Tokyo: Springer, 1985.

DE MÉNIL, GEORGES AND WESTPHAL, UWE, eds. *Stabilization Policy in France and the Federal Republic of Germany.* Contributions to Economic Analysis series, no. 153. Amsterdam; New York and Oxford: North-Holland; distributed in the U.S. and Canada by Elsevier Science, New York, 1985.

MESA-LAGO, CARMELO, ed. *The Crisis of Social Security and Health Care: Latin American Experiences and Lessons.* Latin American Monograph and Document Series, no. 9. Pittsburgh: University of Pittsburgh, Center for Latin American Studies, 1985.

MEYER, F. V., ed. *Prospects for Recovery in the British Economy.* London; Sydney and Dover, N.H.: Croom Helm, 1985.

MEYER, JACK A., ed. *Incentives vs. Controls in Health Policy: Broadening the Debate.* American Enterprise Institute Studies in Health Policy, no. 417. Washington, D.C., and London: American Enterprise Institute for Public Policy Research, 1985.

MOKYR, JOEL, ed. *The Economics of the Industrial Revolution.* Totowa, N.J.: Littlefield, Adams; Rowman and Allanheld, 1985.

MONGIA, J. N., ed. *India's Economic Development Strategies, 1951–2000 A.D.* Dordrecht, the Netherlands, and Hingham, Mass.: Kluwer Academic, Reidel; New Delhi: Allied Publishers Private, 1985.

MORAN, THEODORE H., ed. *Multinational Corporations: The Political Economy of Foreign Direct Investment.* Lexington, Mass., and Toronto: Heath, Lexington Books, 1985.

MORENO FRANGINALS, MANUEL; MOYA PONS, FRANK AND ENGERMAN, STANLEY L., eds. *Between Slavery and Free Labor: The Spanish-Speaking Caribbean in the Nineteenth Century.* Johns Hopkins Studies in Atlantic History and Culture series. Baltimore and London: Johns Hopkins University Press, 1985.

MORRIS, DEREK, ed. *The Economic System in the UK*. Third edition. Oxford; New York; Toronto and Delhi: Oxford University Press, [1977, 1979] 1985.

MORSS, ELLIOTT R. AND GOW, DAVID D., eds. *Implementing Rural Development Projects: Lessons from AID and World Bank Experiences*. Boulder, Colo., and London: Westview Press, 1985.

MUKHOPADHYAY, SWAPNA AND CHEE, PENG LIM, eds. *Development and Diversification of Rural Industries in Asia*. Human Resource Mobilization Programme Publications series. Kuala Lumpur, Malaysia: Asian and Pacific Development Centre, 1985. (I)

MUKHOPADHYAY, SWAPNA AND CHEE, PENG LIM, eds. *The Rural Non-farm Sector in Asia*. Human Resource Mobilization Programme Publications. Kuala Lumpur, Malaysia: Asian and Pacific Development Centre, 1985. (II)

MUSGRAVE, PEGGY B., ed. *Mexico and the United States: Studies in Economic Interaction*. Westview Special Studies in International Economics series. Boulder, Colo., and London: Westview Press, 1985.

NANTO, DICK K., ed. *Japan's Economy and Trade with the United States: Selected Papers Submitted to the Subcommittee on Economic Goals and Intergovernmental Policy of the Joint Economic Committee, Congress of the United States*. 99th Congress, 1st Session, Joint Committee Print. Washington, D.C.: U.S. Government Printing Office, 1985.

NEGRINE, RALPH M., ed. *Cable Television and the Future of Broadcasting*. New York: St. Martin's Press, 1985.

NEWFARMER, RICHARD S., ed. *Profits, Progress and Poverty: Case Studies of International Industries in Latin America*. Notre Dame, Ind.: Unitersity of Notre Dame Press, 1985.

NIBLOCK, TIM AND LAWLESS, RICHARD, eds. *Prospects for the World Oil Industry. Proceedings of a Symposium on the Energy Economy Cosponsored by the Petroleum Information Committee of the Arab Gulf States and the University of Durham, England, and held in Durham, 9–10 May, 1984*. Dover, N.H.; London and Sydney: Croom Helm, 1985.

NIEHAUS, RICHARD J., ed. *Human Resource Policy Analysis: Organizational Applications*. New York; Eastbourne, U.K.; Toronto and Sydney: Praeger, 1985.

NOAM, ELI M , ed *Video Media Competition: Regulation, Economics, and Technology*. Columbia Studies in Business, Government, and Society series. New York: Columbia University Press, 1985.

NOLL, ROGER G., ed. *Regulatory Policy and the Social Sciences*. California Series on Social Choice and Political Economy. Berkeley and London: University of California Press, 1985.

OFFE, CLAUS. *Disorganized Capitalism: Contemporary Transformations of Work and Politics*. Edited by JOHN KEANE. Studies in Contemporary German Social Thought series. Cambridge, Mass.: MIT Press, 1985.

OHKAWA, KAZUSHI AND RANIS, GUSTAV, eds. *Japan and the Developing Countries: Comparative Analysis*. With LARRY MEISSNER. Oxford and New York: Blackwell on behalf of the International Development Center of Japan and the Economic Growth Center of Yale University, 1985.

PARROTT, BRUCE, ed. *Trade, Technology, and Soviet–American Relations*. CSIS Publication Series on the Soviet Union in the 1980s. Bloomington: Indiana University Press in association with the Center for Strategic and International Studies, Georgetown University, Washington, D.C., 1985.

PAUL, ELLEN FRANKEL; PAUL, JEFFREY AND MILLER, FRED D., JR., eds. *Ethics and Economics*. Oxford and New York: Blackwell for the Bowling Green State University, Social Philosophy and Policy Center, 1985.

[PAZNER, ELISHA] *Social Goals and Social Organization: Essays in Memory of Elisha Pazner*. Edited by LEONID HURWICZ, DAVID SCHMEIDLER, AND HUGO SONNENSCHEIN. Cambridge; New York and Sydney: Cambridge University Press, 1985.

[PEACOCK, ALAN] *Public Choice, Public Finance and Public Policy: Essays in Honour of Alan Peacock*. Edited by DAVID GREENAWAY AND G. K. SHAW. Oxford and New York: Blackwell, 1985.

PECHMAN, JOSEPH A., ed. *A Citizen's Guide to the New Tax Reforms: Fair Tax, Flat Tax, Simple Tax*. Totowa, N.J.: Littlefield, Adams; Rowman and Allanheld, 1985. (I)

PECHMAN, JOSEPH A., ed. *The Promise of Tax Reform.* American Assembly, Columbia University, series. Englewood Cliffs, N.J.: Prentice-Hall, Spectrum Books, 1985. (II)

PECK, ANNE E., ed. *Futures Markets: Regulatory Issues.* AEI Studies in Government Regulation. Washington, D.C.: American Enterprise Institute for Public Policy Research, 1985. (I)

PECK, ANNE E., ed. *Futures Markets: Their Economic Role.* AEI Studies in Government Regulation series. Washington, D.C.: American Enterprise Institute for Public Policy Research, 1985. (II)

PEETERS, THEO; PRAET, PETER AND REDING, PAUL, eds. *International Trade and Exchange Rates in the Late Eighties.* Amsterdam and Oxford: North-Holland; distributed in the U.S. and Canada by Elsevier Science, N.Y., 1985.

PENNINGS, JOHANNES M., ET AL. *Organizational Strategy and Change.* Jossey-Bass Management Series and Jossey-Bass Social and Behavioral Science Series. San Francisco and London: Jossey-Bass, 1985.

PERRY, ELIZABETH J. AND WONG, CHRISTINE, eds. *The Political Economy of Reform in Post-Mao China.* Harvard Contemporary China Series, no. 2. Cambridge, Mass., and London: Harvard University Council on East Asian Studies; distributed by Harvard University Press, Cambridge, Mass., 1985.

PETERSON, PAUL E., ed. *The New Urban Reality.* Washington, D.C.: Brookings Institution, 1985.

PIGGOTT, JOHN AND WHALLEY, JOHN, eds. *New Developments in Applied General Equilibrium Analysis.* Cambridge; New York and Melbourne: Cambridge University Press, 1985.

PITT, JOSEPH C., ed. *Change and Progress in Modern Science: Papers Relating To and Arising from the Fourth International Conference on History and Philosophy of Science, Blacksburg, Virginia, November, 1982.* University of Western Ontario Series in Philosophy of Science, vol. 27. Dordrecht, the Netherlands; Boston and Lancaster: Reidel; distributed in the U.S. and Canada by Kluwer Academic, Hingham, Mass., 1985.

PLATT, D. C. M. AND DI TELLA, GUIDO, eds. *Argentina, Australia and Canada: Studies in Comparative Development, 1870–1965.* New York: St. Martin's Press, 1985.

PONSTEIN, JACOB, ed. *Convexity and Duality in Optimization: Proceedings of the Symposium on Convexity and Duality in Optimization, Held at the University of Groningen, the Netherlands, June 22, 1984.* Lecture Notes in Economics and Mathematical Systems series, vol. 256. New York; Berlin and Tokyo: Springer, 1985.

POOLE, ROBERT W., JR., ed. *Unnatural Monopolies: The Case for Deregulating Public Utilities.* Lexington, Mass., and Toronto: Heath, Lexington Books, 1985.

PORTER, A. N. AND HOLLAND, R. F., eds. *Money, Finance and Empire, 1790–1960.* London: Cass; distributed in the United States by Biblio Distribution Center, Totowa, N.J., 1985.

PRATT, JOHN W. AND ZECKHAUSER, RICHARD J., eds. *Principals and Agents: The Structure of Business.* Harvard Business School Research Colloquium series. Boston: Harvard Business School Press, 1985.

PREEG, ERNEST H., ed. *Hard Bargaining Ahead: U.S. Trade Policy and Developing Countries.* Overseas Development Council, U.S.–Third World Policy Perspectives series, no. 4. New Brunswick, N.J., and Oxford: Transaction Books, 1985.

QUIGLEY, JOHN M. AND RUBINFELD, DANIEL L., eds. *American Domestic Priorities: An Economic Appraisal.* California Series in Real Estate, Economics, and Finance. Berkeley and London: University of California Press, 1985.

RAJ, K. N., ET AL., eds. *Essays on the Commercialization of Indian Agriculture.* Oxford; New York; Toronto and Delhi: Oxford University Press for the Centre for Development Studies, Trivandrum, 1985.

[RECKTENWALD, HORST CLAUS] *Public Sector and Political Economy Today: Essays in Honour of Horst Claus Recktenwald.* Edited by HORST HANUSCH, KARL W. ROSKAMP, AND JACK WISEMAN. Stuttgart and New York: Fischer, 1985.

RICCI, PAOLO F., ed. *Principles of Health Risk Assessment.* Englewood Cliffs, N.J.: Prentice-Hall, 1985.

RICHARDSON, HARRY W. AND TUREK, JOSEPH H., eds. *Economic Prospects for the Northeast.* Philadelphia: Temple University Press, 1985.

RINNOOY KAN, ALEXANDER H. G., ed. *New Challenges for Management Research*. Advanced Series in Management, vol. 9. Amsterdam; New York and Oxford: North-Holland; distributed in the U.S. and Canada by Elsevier Science, New York, 1985.

ROBERTS, BRYAN; FINNEGAN, RUTH AND GALLIE, DUNCAN, eds. *New Approaches to Economic Life. Economic Restructuring: Unemployment and the Social Division of Labour*. Manchester, U.K., and Dover, N.H.: Manchester University Press, 1985.

ROBERTS, GERALD, ed. *Guide to World Commodity Markets*. Fourth edition. London: Kogan Page; New York: Nichols in association with *The Economist Newspaper*, Economist Books, [1977 . . .1982] 1985.

ROCKWELL, LLEWELLYN H., JR., ed. *The Gold Standard: An Austrian Perspective*. Introduction by LELAND B. YEAGER. Lexington, Mass., and Toronto: Heath, Lexington Books, 1985.

RODE, REINHARD AND JACOBSEN, HANNS-D., eds. *Economic Warfare or Detente: An Assessment of East–West Relations in the 1980s*. International Perspectives on Security Series, no. 1. Boulder, Colo., and London: Westview Press, 1985.

ROSE, RICHARD. *Public Employment in Western Nations*. With EDWARD PAGE ET AL. Cambridge; New York and Sydney: Cambridge University Press, 1985.

ROSE, TORE, ed. *Crisis and Recovery in Sub-Saharan Africa*. Development Centre Seminars, vol. 1. Paris: Organisation for Economic Co-operation and Development, Development Centre, 1985.

ROSENBERG, NATHAN AND FRISCHTAK, CLAUDIO, eds. *International Technology Transfer: Concepts, Measures, and Comparisons*. New York; Eastbourne, U.K.; Toronto and Sydney: Praeger, 1985.

[ROSSIER, EDOUARD] *Optimalite et Structures, Etudes en Hommage a Edouard Rossier (Optimality and Structures: Selected Papers in Honour of Edouard Rossier)*. Edited by GILBERT RITSCHARD AND DANIEL ROYER. Preface by PETER TSCHOPP. Paris: Economica; distributed by Diffuseur G. Vermette, Boucheville, Quebec, 1985.

ROTH, ALVIN E., ed. *Game-Theoretic Models of Bargaining*. Cambridge; New York and Sydney: Cambridge University Press, 1985.

ROWLAND, KENDRITH M. AND FERRIS, GERALD R., eds. *Research in Personnel and Human Resources Management*. Volume 3. A Research Annual. Greenwich, Conn., and London: JAI Press, 1985.

RUGMAN, ALAN M. AND EDEN, LORRAINE, eds. *Multinationals and Transfer Pricing*. New York: St. Martin's Press, 1985.

SAITH, ASHWANI, ed. *The Agrarian Question in Socialist Transitions*. London: Cass, distributed in the U.S. by Biblio Distribution Centre, Totowa, N.J., 1985.

SALAZAR-CARRILLO, JORGE AND DE ALONSO, IRMA TIRADO, eds. *Foreign Debt and the Strategy of Development in the Caribbean Basin*. IESCARIBE Research Summaries series, no. 3. Miami: Florida International University, Latin-American and Caribbean Center, 1985.

SALAZAR-CARRILLO, JORGE AND FENDT, ROBERTO, JR., eds. *The Brazilian Economy in the Eighties*. New York; Toronto; Sydney and Paris: Pergamon Press, 1985.

SAMLI, A. COSKUN, ed. *Technology Transfer: Geographic, Economic, Cultural, and Technical Dimensions*. Westport, Conn., and London: Greenwood Press, Quorum Books, 1985.

SARGENT, THOMAS J., ed. *Energy, Foresight, and Strategy*. Washington, D.C.: Resources for the Future, 1985.

SAUNDERS, CHRISTOPHER T., ed. *East–West Trade and Finance in the World Economy: A New Look for the 1980s*. New York: St. Martin's Press, 1985.

SAVONA, PAOLO AND SUTIJA, GEORGE, eds. *Eurodollars and International Banking*. New York: St. Martin's Press, 1985.

SCHEFFLER, RICHARD M. AND ROSSITER, LOUIS F., eds. *Advances in Health Economics and Health Services Research*. Volume 6. *Biased Selection in Health Care Markets*. A Research Annual. Greenwich, Conn., and London: JAI Press, 1985.

SCHMANDT, JURGEN AND RODERICK, HILLARD, eds. *Acid Rain and Friendly Neighbors: The Policy Dispute Between Canada and the United States*. Duke Press Policy Studies series. Durham, N.C.: Duke University Press, 1985.

SCHORR, PHILIP, ed. *Critical Cornerstones of Public Administration*. Boston: Oelgeschlager, Gunn & Hain, 1985.

SCHWALBACH, JOACHIM, ed. *Industry Structure and Performance*. Introduction by FREDERIC M. SCHERER. Berlin: Bohn, Sigma, 1985.

SCOTT, ANTHONY, ed. *Progress in Natural Resource Economics: Essays in Resource Analysis by Members of the Programme in Natural Resource Economics (PNRE) at the University of British Columbia*. With the assistance of JOHN HELLIWELL, TRACY LEWIS, AND PHILIP NEHER. Oxford; New York; Toronto and Delhi: Oxford University Press, 1985.

SCOTT, BRUCE R. AND LODGE, GEORGE C., eds. *U.S. Competitiveness in the World Economy*. Boston: Harvard Business School Press, 1985.

SCUTT, JOCELYNNE A., ed. *Poor Nation of the Pacific? Australia's Future?* Australian Institute of Political Science Publications series. Sydney; London and Boston: Allen & Unwin, 1985.

SEWELL, JOHN W.; FEINBERG, RICHARD E. AND KALLAB, VALERIANA, eds. *U.S. Foreign Policy and the Third World: Agenda 1985–86*. Overseas Development Council Series, Policy Perspectives, no. 3. New Brunswick, N.J., and Oxford: Transaction Books, 1985.

SHADOW OPEN MARKET COMMITTEE. *Policy Statement and Position Papers, September 22–23, 1985*. Rochester: University of Rochester, Graduate School of Management, Center for Research in Government Policy and Business, 1985.

SHISHIDO, TOSHIO AND SATO, RYUZO, eds. *Economic Policy and Development: New Perspectives*. Dover, Mass.: Auburn House; London and Sydney: Croom Helm, 1985.

SKULLY, MICHAEL T., ed. *Financial Institutions and Markets in the Southwest Pacific: A Study of Australia, Fiji, New Zealand and Papua, New Guinea*. New York: St. Martin's Press, 1985.

SMITH, BRUCE L. R., ed. *The State of Graduate Education*. Brookings Dialogues on Public Policy series. Washington, D.C.: Brookings Institution, 1985.

SMITH, MICHAEL, ET AL. *Asia's New Industrial World*. London and New York: Methuen, 1985.

SMITH, ROBERT B., ed. *Handbook of Social Science Methods*. Volume 3. *Quantitative Methods: Focused Survey Research and Causal Modeling*. New York; Eastbourne, U.K.; Toronto and Hong Kong: Praeger, 1985.

SMITH, STEVE, ed. *International Relations: British and American Perspectives*. Oxford and New York: Blackwell in association with British International Studies Association, 1985.

SMYSHLYAEV, A., ed. *Input–Output Modeling: Proceedings of the Fifth IIASA (International Institute for Applied Systems Analysis) Task Force Meeting on Input–Output Modeling Held at Laxenburg, Austria, October 4–6, 1984*. Lecture Notes in Economics and Mathematical Systems series, vol. 251. New York; Heidelberg and Tokyo: Springer, 1985.

[SPRY, IRENE M.] *Exploration in Canadian Economic History: Essays in Honour of Irene M. Spry*. Edited by DUNCAN CAMERON. Ottawa: University of Ottawa Press, 1985.

STAHL, KONRAD, ed. *Microeconomic Models of Housing Markets*. Lecture Notes in Economics and Mathematical Systems series, vol. 239. New York; Berlin and Tokyo: Springer, 1985.

STAUFFER, ROBERT B., ed. *Transnational Corporations and the State*. Sydney: University of Sydney, Transnational Corporations Research Project, 1985.

STENT, ANGELA E., ed. *Economic Relations with the Soviet Union: American and West German Perspectives*. Westview Special Studies on the Soviet Union and Eastern Europe series. Boulder, Colo., and London: Westview, 1985.

STERN, ROBERT M., ed. *Trade and Investment in Services: Canada/U.S. Perspectives*. Ontario Economic Council Special Research Report, Canadian Trade at a Crossroads Series. Toronto: Ontario Economic Council, 1985.

STOREY, D. J., ed. *Small Firms in Regional Economic Development: Britain, Ireland and the United States*. Cambridge; New York and Melbourne: Cambridge University Press, 1985.

SWEENEY, GERRY, ed. *Innovation Policies: An International Perspective*. New York: St. Martin's Press, 1985.

TAITTE, W. LAWSON, ed. *Our Freedom: Rights and Responsibilities*. Introduction by ANDREW R. CECIL. Andrew R. Cecil Lectures on Moral Values in a Free Society, vol. 6. Dallas: University of Texas Press; distributed by the University of Texas Press Services, Austin, 1985.

TAKAMIYA, SUSUMU AND THURLEY, KEITH, eds. *Japan's Emerging Multinationals: An International Comparison of Policies and Practices.* Foreword by HERBERT A. SIMON. Tokyo: University of Tokyo Press, 1985.

TERNY, GUY AND CULYER, A. J., eds. *Public Finance and Social Policy: Proceedings of the 39th Congress of the International Institute of Public Finance Budapest, Hungary, 1983.* Detroit: Wayne State University Press, 1985.

THWAITES, A. T. AND OAKEY, R. P., eds. *The Regional Economic Impact of Technological Change.* New York: St. Martin's Press, 1985.

TINBERGEN, JAN. *Production, Income and Welfare: The Search for an Optimal Social Order.* Lincoln and London: University of Nebraska Press; Brighton, U.K.: Harvester Press, Wheatsheaf Books, 1985.

TOLLIDAY, STEVEN AND ZEITLIN, JONATHAN, eds. *Shop Floor Bargaining and the State: Historical and Comparative Perspectives.* Cambridge; New York and Sydney: Cambridge University Press, 1985.

UNITED NATIONS CONFERENCE ON TRADE AND DEVELOPMENT. *Operation and Effects of the Generalized System of Preferences: Seventh and Eighth Reviews. Selected Studies Submitted to the Special Committee on Preferences at Its Eleventh Session, Geneva, 3–11 May 1982 and at Its Twelfth Session, Geneva, 24 April–4 May 1984.* New York: United Nations, 1985.

UTRECHT, ERNST, ed. *Transnational Corporations and Export-Oriented Industrialization.* Transnational Corporations in South-East Asia and the Pacific series, vol. 7. Sydney: University of Sydney, Transnational Corporations Research Project, 1985.

VERNON, RAYMOND. *Exploring the Global Economy: Emerging Issues in Trade and Investment.* Cambridge, Mass.: Harvard University Center for International Affairs; Lanham, Md.: University Press of America, 1985.

VICARELLI, FAUSTO, ed. *Keynes's Relevance Today.* English Translation. Philadelphia: University of Pennsylvania Press, [1983] 1985.

WADHVA, CHARAN D. AND ASHER, MUKUL G., eds. *ASEAN–South Asia Economic Relations.* Singapore: Institute of Southeast Asian Studies, ASEAN Economic Research Unit in collaboration with the Indian Council for Research on International Economic Relations and the Marga Institute, 1985.

WALTER, INGO, ed. *Deregulating Wall Street: Commercial Bank Penetration of the Corporate Securities Market.* Wiley Professional Banking and Finance Series. New York; Chichester; Toronto and Brisbane: Wiley, 1985.

WATTEL, HAROLD L., ed. *The Policy Consequences of John Maynard Keynes.* Armonk, N.Y.: Sharpe, 1985.

WEINBLATT, JIMMY, ed. *The Economics of Export Restrictions: Free Access to Commodity Markets and the NIEO.* Westview Special Studies in International Economics series. Boulder, Colo., and London: Westview Press, 1985.

[WEINTRAUB, ROBERT E.] *Monetary Policy and Monetary Regimes: A Symposium Dedicated to Robert E. Weintraub.* Edited by KARL BRUNNER, ET AL. Center Symposia Series, no. CS–17. Rochester: University of Rochester, Graduate School of Management, Center for Research in Government Policy & Business, 1985.

WEISERBS, D., ed. *Industrial Investment in Europe: Economic Theory and Measurement.* International Studies in Economics and Econometrics, vol. 12. Dordrecht, the Netherlands: Nijhoff; distributed in the U.S. and Canada by Kluwer Academic, Hingham, Mass., 1985.

WELLS, NICHOLAS, ed. *Pharmaceuticals among the Sunrise Industries.* New York: St. Martin's Press, 1985.

WESTCOTT, G.; SVENSSON, P.-G. AND ZOLLNER, H. F. K., eds. *Health Policy Implications of Unemployment.* Copenhagen: World Health Organization, Regional Office for Europe, 1985.

WIONCZEK, MIGUEL S., ed. *Politics and Economics of External Debt Crisis: The Latin American Experience.* In collaboration with LUCIANO TOMASSINI. Westview Special Studies on Latin America and the Caribbean series. Boulder, Colo., and London: Westview Press, 1985.

WISE, DAVID A., ed. *Pensions, Labor, and Individual Choice*. National Bureau of Economic Research Project Report series. Chicago and London: University of Chicago Press, 1985.

WONG, KWAN-YIU AND CHU, DAVID K.Y., eds. *Modernization in China: The Case of the Shenzhen Special Economic Zone*. Oxford; New York; Toronto and Hong Kong: Oxford University Press, 1985.

WOODWORTH, WARNER; MEEK, CHRISTOPHER AND WHYTE, WILLIAM FOOTE, eds. *Industrial Democracy: Strategies for Community Revitalization*. Sage Focus Editions series, no. 73. Beverly Hills; London and New Delhi: Sage, 1985.

WORRALL, JOHN D. AND APPEL, DAVID, eds. *Workers' Compensation Benefits: Adequacy, Equity, and Efficiency*. Ithaca, N.Y.: Cornell University, New York State School of Industrial and Labor Relations, ILR Press, 1985.

WORSWICK, G. D. N., ed. *Education and Economic Performance*. National Institute of Economic and Social Research, Policy Studies Institute, and Royal Institute of International Affairs Joint Studies in Public Policy series, no. 9. Aldershot, U.K., and Brookfield, Vt.: Gower, 1985.

YAMEY, BASIL S.; SANDOR, RICHARD L. AND HINDLEY, BRIAN. *How Commodity Futures Markets Work*. Thames Essay, no. 42. London: Trade Policy Research Centre, 1985.

YOCHELSON, JOHN N., ed. *The United States and the World Economy: Policy Alternatives for New Realities*. Assisted by CATHERINE STIRLING. Westview Special Studies in International Economics and Business series. Boulder, Colo., and London: Westview Press in cooperation with Center for Strategic and International Studies, Georgetown University, 1985.

YOUDI, R. VESITULUTA AND HINCHLIFFE, KEITH, eds. *Forecasting Skilled-Manpower Needs: The Experience of Eleven Countries*. Paris: Unesco, International Institute for Educational Planning, 1985.

YOUNG, H. PEYTON, ed. *Cost Allocation: Methods, Principles, Applications*. Amsterdam and Oxford: North-Holland; distributed in the U.S. and Canada by Elsevier Science, New York, 1985.

YUI, TSUNEHIKO AND NAKAGAWA, KEIICHIRO, eds. *Business History of Shipping: Strategy and Structure: The International Conference on Business History 11, Proceedings of the Fuji Conference*. Tokyo: University of Tokyo Press; distributed by Columbia University Press, New York, 1985.

ZERBE, RICHARD O., JR., ed. *Normative Law and Economics*. Research in Law and Economics, vol. 7. Greenwich, Conn., and London: JAI Press, 1985.

ZIJLSTRA, JELLE *Jelle Zijlstra: A Central Banker's View: Selected Speeches and Articles*. Edited by C. GOEDHART ET AL. Financial and Monetary Policy Studies series, vol. 10. Dordrecht, the Netherlands: Martinus Nijhoff; distributed in the U.S. and Canada by Kluwer Academic, Hingham, Mass., 1985.

ZUKIN, SHARON, ed. *Industrial Policy: Business and Politics in the United States and France*. New York; Eastbourne, U.K.; Toronto and Sydney: Praeger, 1985.

CLASSIFICATION SYSTEM

Subject Index of Articles
in Current Periodicals and Collective Volumes

Abbreviated titles for journals are the same as those used in the *Journal of Economic Literature*. Full titles of journals may be found on pages x–xv.

Books have been identified by author or editor (noted *ed.*). In rare cases where two books by the same author appear, volumes are distinguished by I or II after the name. In some cases there appear two books by the same person, once as author, once as editor. These may be distinguished by *ed.* noted for the edited volume. Full titles and bibliographic references for books may be found on pages xvi–xxxii.

Geographic Descriptors when appropriate appear in brackets at the end of the article citation.

000 General Economics; Theory; History; Systems

010 GENERAL ECONOMICS

011 General Economics

0110 General

Anderson-Courtney, Linda D. *Journal of Econometrics* Subject Index Volumes 21–30, 1983–1985. *J. Econometrics*, December 1985, *30*(3), pp. 475–543.

Anderton, Charles H. A Selected Bibliography of Arms Race Models and Related Subjects. *Conflict Manage. Peace Sci.*, Spring 1985, *8*(2), pp. 99–122.

Boulding, Kenneth E. Thoughts in Verse on Contributions to the Symposium. In *Aida, S., et al.*, 1985, pp. 375–80.

Burns, Arthur F. An Economist's Perspective over 60 Years. *Challenge*, January/February 1985, *27*(6), pp. 17–25. [G: U.S.]

Clark, Robert Emmet. Recollections of the Origins of the Natural Resources Journal. *Natural Res. J.*, January 1985, *25*(1), pp. 1–5. [G: U.S.]

Coats, A. W. The American Economic Association and the Economics Profession. *J. Econ. Lit.*, December 1985, *23*(4), pp. 1697–1727. [G: U.S.]

Dalkir, Serdar. A Note on Interest and Value as Inspired by Aristophanes. *METU*, 1985, *12*(3/4), pp. 353–57.

Ekwurzel, Drucilla and Saffran, Bernard. Online Information Retrieval for Economists—The Economic Literature Index. *J. Econ. Lit.*, December 1985, *23*(4), pp. 1728–63. [G: U.S.]

Giarini, Orio. The Consequences of Complexity in Economics: Vulnerability, Risk, and Rigidity Factors in Supply. In *Aida, S., et al.*, 1985, pp. 133–45.

Gopal, M. H. Criteria for Assessing Current Research in Social Sciences in Indian Universities. *Indian Econ. J.*, Apr.-June 1985, *32*(4), pp. 45–54. [G: India]

Guitton, Henry. Les problèmes insolubles. (Insoluble Problems. With English summary.) *Rivista Int. Sci. Econ. Com.*, May 1985, *32*(5), pp. 421–25.

Gunning, James Patrick. Piaget and Social Economy [The Social Economy—Analogue of Piaget's Development of Knowledge]. *Rev. Soc. Econ.*, December 1985, *43*(3), pp. 371–79.

Hirschleifer, Jack. The Expanding Domain of Economics. *Amer. Econ. Rev.*, December 1985, *75*(6), pp. 53–68.

Jeremy, David J. A Gallery of Distinguished Individuals: *The Biographical Dictionary of American Business Leaders*: A Review Article. *Bus. Hist. Rev.*, Summer 1985, *59*(2), pp. 278–83.

Laband, David N. A Note on Imperfections in the Distribution of Economic Knowledge. *Eastern Econ. J.*, April-June 1985, *11*(2), pp. 161–66. [G: U.S.]

Laband, David N. A Ranking of the Top Canadian Economics Departments by Research Productivity of Graduates. *Can. J. Econ.*, November 1985, *18*(4), pp. 904–07. [G: Canada]

Laband, David N. An Evaluation of "50 Ranked" Economics Departments—By Quantity and Quality of Faculty Publications and Graduate Student Placement and Research Success. *Southern Econ. J.*, July 1985, *52*(1), pp. 216–40. [G: U.S.]

Laband, David N. Publishing Favoritism: A Critique of Department Rankings Based on Quantitative Publishing Performance. *Southern Econ. J.*, October 1985, *52*(2), pp. 510–15.

Laband, David N. and Sophocleus, John P. Revealed Preference for Economics Journals: Citations as Dollar Votes. *Public Choice*, 1985, *46*(3), pp. 317–24.

Laband, David N. and Sophocleus, John P. The Determinants of Article Popularity: Preliminary Results. *Atlantic Econ. J.*, December 1985, *13*(4), pp. 80. [G: U.S.]

Lagus, Kalevi. Kirjallisuutta kautta aikain. Poimintoja ja muistikuvia. (Book Reviews in the Finnish Economic Journal, 1905–1985. With English summary.) *Kansant. Aikak.*, 1985, *81*(1), pp. 20–24. [G: Finland]

Leontief, Wassily. Essays in Economics: Theories, Theorizing, Facts, and Policies: Introduction. In *Leontief, W.*, 1985, pp. ix–xii.

Leontief, Wassily. When Should History Be Written Backwards? In *Leontief, W.*, 1985, pp. 12–21.

Levan-Lemesle, Lucette. Guillaumin, éditeur d'économie politique 1801–1864. (With En-

3

glish summary.) *Revue Écon. Polit.*, Mar.–Apr. 1985, *95*(2), pp. 134–49.

Lindbeck, Assar. The Prize in Economic Science in Memory of Alfred Nobel. *J. Econ. Lit.*, March 1985, *23*(1), pp. 37–56.

Mabry, Rodney H. and Sharplin, Arthur D. The Relative Importance of Journals Used in Finance Research. *J. Finan. Res.*, Winter 1985, *8*(4), pp. 287–96.

McCloskey, Donald N. Economical Writing. *Econ. Inquiry*, April 1985, *23*(2), pp. 187–222.

Moulton, Edward C. South Asian Studies in Canada: A State of the Discipline Review. *Can. J. Devel. Stud.*, 1985, *6*(1), pp. 129–45.
[G: Canada; Asia]

Palmer, Jan. The Production of Economic Knowledge: A Second Look. *Quart. Rev. Econ. Bus.*, Winter 1985, *25*(4), pp. 107–08. [G: U.S.]

Peebles, Gavin. Recent Books from China: A Review Article. *Comparative Econ. Stud.*, Winter 1985, *27*(4), pp. 53–66. [G: China]

Riha, Tomas. German Political Economy: The History of an Alternative Economics. *Int. J. Soc. Econ.*, 1985, *12*(3/4/5/), pp. 1–252.
[G: Germany]

Salda, Anne C. M. The International Monetary Fund, 1984: A Selected Bibliography. *Int. Monet. Fund Staff Pap.*, Suppl. Dec. 1985, *32*, pp. 749–87.

Samuelson, Paul A. Succumbing to Keynesianism. *Challenge*, January/February 1985, *27*(6), pp. 4–11. [G: U.S.]

Simpson, James R. and Steele, John T. Institutional Affiliation of Contributors to the *American Journal of Agricultural Economics*, 1973-83. *Amer. J. Agr. Econ.*, May 1985, *67*(2), pp. 325–27.

Smithin, John Nicholas. The Market Mechanism versus the Historical Process as the Source of Economic Controversy. *Econ. Notes*, 1985, (1), pp. 169–76.

Solterer, Joseph. Elementary Motions: A Response [The Social Economy—Analogue of Piaget's Development of Knowledge]. *Rev. Soc. Econ.*, December 1985, *43*(3), pp. 380–83.

Spellman, William E. and Borum, Bradley. A Backward Glance at the AEA Presidents. *Amer. Econ.*, Fall 1985, *29*(2), pp. 27–40.
[G: U.S.]

Stone, Richard. Bibliography of Richard Stone's Works, 1936–1984. *Scand. J. Econ.*, 1985, *87*(1), pp. 33–43.

Thanawala, Kishor. What Is Social Economics? *Int. J. Soc. Econ.*, 1985, *12*(6/7), pp. 34–40.

Throsby, David and Withers, Glenn. What Price Culture? *J. Cult. Econ.*, December 1985, *9*(2), pp. 1–34. [G: Australia]

Vernon, Raymond. Swan Song. *J. Policy Anal. Manage.*, Summer 1985, *4*(4), pp. 573–81.

Weintraub, Sidney. A Jevonian Seditionist: A Mutiny to Enhance the Economic Bounty? *J. Post Keynesian Econ.*, Summer 1985, *7*(4), pp. 510–29.

Zahka, William J. A Backward Glance at the AEA Presidents: Comment. *Amer. Econ.*, Fall 1985, *29*(2), pp. 40–41. [G: U.S.]

0112 Role of Economics; Role of Economists

Andersen, Stephen O. Natural Resource Economics: Biographical Sketch. In *Ciriacy-Wantrup, S. V.*, 1985, pp. 7–17.

Armour, Leslie. The Economist and Moral Values. *Int. J. Soc. Econ.*, 1985, *12*(6/7), pp. 41–53.

Booth, Alan. Economists and Points Rationing in the Second World War. *J. Europ. Econ. Hist.*, Fall 1985, *14*(2), pp. 297–317. [G: U.K.]

Brandl, John E. Distilling Frenzy from Academic Scribbling: How Economics Influences Politicians. *J. Policy Anal. Manage.*, Spring 1985, *4*(3), pp. 344–53. [G: U.S.]

Breton, Yves. Les économistes libéraux français de la période 1840–1914, précurseurs des théoriciens actuels du marche politique et de la bureaucratie? (With English summary.) *Revue Écon. Polit.*, Mar.–Apr. 1985, *95*(2), pp. 150–67. [G: France]

Broder, Josef M. The Southern Agricultural Economics Association and Resident Instruction. *Southern J. Agr. Econ.*, July 1985, *17*(1), pp. 7–14. [G: U.S.]

Bronfenbrenner, Martin. Pity the Country Specialist! *Rivista Int. Sci. Econ. Com.*, April 1985, *32*(4), pp. 297–303.

Brunner, Karl. Ideology and Analysis in Macroeconomics: Comment. In *Koslowski, P., ed.*, 1985, pp. 208–18.

Brunner, Karl. The Limits of Economic Policy. *Schweiz. Z. Volkswirtsch. Statist.*, September 1985, *121*(3), pp. 213–36.

Cairncross, Alec. Economics in Theory and Practice. *Amer. Econ. Rev.*, May 1985, *75*(2), pp. 1–14.

Conner, J. Richard. Observations on Changes in Factors Influencing Agricultural Economics and Some Implications for the Profession. *Southern J. Agr. Econ.*, July 1985, *17*(1), pp. 1–6. [G: U.S.]

Davis, Carlton G. Human Capital Needs of Black Land-Grant Institutions: Discussion. *Southern J. Agr. Econ.*, July 1985, *17*(1), pp. 71–73.
[G: U.S.]

Dwyer, Larry. Scientific Rationality, Value Judgments, and Economic Advice. *Australian Econ. Pap.*, June 1985, *24*(44), pp. 169–84.

Eichner, Alfred S. Towards an Empirically Valid Economics. *Eastern Econ. J.*, Oct.-Dec. 1985, *11*(4), pp. 437–49.

Etzioni, Amitai. Making Policy for Complex Systems: A Medical Model for Economics. *J. Policy Anal. Manage.*, Spring 1985, *4*(3), pp. 383–95.

Filippello, A. Nicholas. Where Do Business Economists Go from Here? *Bus. Econ.*, January 1985, *20*(1), pp. 12–16.

Gitlow, Abraham L. Economics Seen Darkly in a Political Mirror. *Rivista Int. Sci. Econ. Com.*, January 1985, *32*(1), pp. 87–98. [G: U.S.; LDCs]

Goddard, E. The Future Role of the Agricultural Economist in Outlook Preparation. *Can. J. Agr. Econ.*, August 1985, *32*, pp. 86–99.

Gordon, Wendell. Economists Should Tell It Like It Is: Remarks upon Receipt of the Veblen–Commons Award. *J. Econ. Issues*, June 1985, *19*(2), pp. 305–09. **[G: U.S.]**

Griffin, Robert A. A Communicative Study of the Dissenting Views of John Maynard Keynes and Thorstein Veblen on the Treaty of Versailles. *Revue Écon. Polit.*, Mar.–Apr. 1985, *95*(2), pp. 174–88.

Guedry, Leo J., Jr. Teaching, Research, and Extension Programs at Predominantly Black Land-Grant Institutions: Discussion. *Southern J. Agr. Econ.*, July 1985, *17*(1), pp. 43–45. **[G: U.S.]**

Hardaker, J. Brian. Beliefs and Values in Agricultural Economics Research. *Australian J. Agr. Econ.*, August 1985, *29*(2), pp. 97–106.

Harris, Harold M., Jr. Role of the Southern Agricultural Economics Association in Extension: Discussion. *Southern J. Agr. Econ.*, July 1985, *17*(1), pp. 27–29. **[G: U.S.]**

Hemenway, David. "Seek Simplicity and Distrust It": Assumptions of Microeconomics. *J. Policy Anal. Manage.*, Winter 1985, *4*(2), pp. 262–66.

Hollis, Martin. The Emperor's Newest Clothes [The Rhetoric of Economics]. *Econ. Philos.*, April 1985, *1*(1), pp. 128–33.

Jha, L. K. Economic Theorems and Human Problems. In *Jha, L. K.*, 1985, pp. 187–202.

Kitromilides, Y. The Formation of Economic Policy: A Question for Economists? In *Arestis, P. and Skouras, T., eds.*, 1985, pp. 7–23.

Knutson, Ronald D. Role of the Southern Agricultural Economics Association in Extension. *Southern J. Agr. Econ.*, July 1985, *17*(1), pp. 17–25. **[G: U.S.]**

Kohl, David M. The Southern Agricultural Economics Association and Resident Instruction: Discussion. *Southern J. Agr. Econ.*, July 1985, *17*(1), pp. 15–16. **[G: U.S.]**

Leijonhufvud, Axel. Ideology and Analysis in Macroeconomics. In *Koslowski, P., ed.*, 1985, pp. 182–207.

Leontief, Wassily. The Decline and Rise of Soviet Economic Science. In *Leontief, W.*, 1985, pp. 223–36.

Leontief, Wassily. Theoretical Assumptions and Nonobserved Facts. In *Leontief, W.*, 1985, pp. 272–82.

Lombardi, S. At the Roots of the Crisis in Economic Theory. *Econ. Int.*, Aug./Nov. 1985, *38*(3/4), pp. 323–50.

McCloskey, Donald N. Sartorial Epistemology in Tatters: A Reply [The Rhetoric of Economics]. *Econ. Philos.*, April 1985, *1*(1), pp. 134–37.

Meier, Alfred and Mettler, Daniel. Auf der Suche nach einem neuen Paradigma der Wirtschaftspolitik. (Toward a New Paradigm of Economic Policy. With English summary.) *Kyklos*, 1985, *38*(2), pp. 171–99.

Michaelis, Lynn O. The Business Economist at Work: Weyerhaeuser Co. *Bus. Econ.*, July 1985, *20*(3), pp. 58–60. **[G: U.S.]**

Naqvi, Syed Nawab Haider. The Importance of Being Defunct. *Pakistan Devel. Rev.*, Autumn-Winter 1985, *24*(3/4), pp. 211–34. **[G: Pakistan; India]**

Nathan, Richard P. Research Lessons from the Great Society. *J. Policy Anal. Manage.*, Spring 1985, *4*(3), pp. 422–26.

Olsen, Erling. Finansiel Know-How. (Financial Know-How. With English summary.) *Nationaløkon. Tidsskr.*, 1985, *123*(3), pp. 377–88.

Paris, Donald G. The Business Economist at Work: Caterpillar Tractor Co. *Bus. Econ.*, October 1985, *20*(4), pp. 50–51. **[G: U.S.]**

Parks, Alfred L. and Robbins, Richard D. Human Capital Needs of Black Land-Grant Institutions. *Southern J. Agr. Econ.*, July 1985, *17*(1), pp. 61–69. **[G: U.S.]**

Powell, Roy A.; Jensen, Rodney C. and West, Guy R. Responsibility and Objectivity in Economic Research. *Rev. Marketing Agr. Econ.*, April 1985, *53*(1), pp. 32–33.

Ross, Howard N. John Blair and Monopoly. *Antitrust Bull.*, Winter 1985, *30*(4), pp. 997–1009. **[G: U.S.]**

Shishido, Toshio. Economic Policy and Development: New Perspectives: Introduction. In *Shishido, T. and Sato, R., eds.*, 1985, pp. xi–xv.

Smith, James F. Union Carbide Corporation. *Bus. Econ.*, April 1985, *20*(2), pp. 55–57. **[G: U.S.]**

Solow, Robert M. Economic History and Economics. *Amer. Econ. Rev.*, May 1985, *75*(2), pp. 328–31.

Stein, Herbert. Are Economists Getting a Bum Rap? *Southern Econ. J.*, April 1985, *51*(4), pp. 975–82. **[G: U.S.]**

Streeten, Paul. In Memory of Thomas Balogh. *World Devel.*, April 1985, *13*(4), pp. 465–66.

Sufrin, Sidney C. Philosophical Foundations. An Essay in Economic Pragmatism. *Rivista Int. Sci. Econ. Com.*, June 1985, *32*(6), pp. 525–49.

Williams, Thomas T. and Williamson, Handy, Jr. Teaching, Research, and Extension Programs at Predominantly Black Land-Grant Institutions. *Southern J. Agr. Econ.*, July 1985, *17*(1), pp. 31–41. **[G: U.S.]**

0113 Relation of Economics to Other Disciplines

Albert, Hans. On Using Leibniz in Economics: Comment. In *Koslowski, P., ed.*, 1985, pp. 68–78.

Allen, Peter M. Towards a New Science of Complex Systems. In *Aida, S., et al.*, 1985, pp. 268–97.

Ault, David E. and Rutman, Gilbert L. Freedom and Regulation: An Anthropological Critique of Free Market Ideology: Comment. In *Zerbe, R. O., Jr., ed.*, 1985, pp. 149–56.

Baepler, Richard. The Concept of Economic Justice in Religious Discussion: Comment. In *Block, W.; Brennan, G. and Elzinga, K., eds.*, 1985, pp. 482–89.

Baum, Sandra R. Moral Philosophy, Cognitive Psychology and Economic Theory. *Eastern Econ. J.*, Oct.-Dec. 1985, *11*(4), pp. 422–36.

Bilmes, Jack. Freedom and Regulation: An Anthropological Critique of Free Market Ideology: Rejoinder. In *Zerbe, R. O., Jr., ed.*, 1985, pp. 157–59.

Bilmes, Jack. Freedom and Regulation: An Anthropological Critique of Free Market Ideology. In *Zerbe, R. O., Jr., ed.*, 1985, pp. 123–47.

Block, Walter. Theological Perspective on Economics: Comment. In *Block, W.; Brennan, G. and Elzinga, K., eds.*, 1985, pp. 67–96.
[G: Selected Countries]

Block, Walter; Brennan, Geoffrey and Elzinga, Kenneth G. Morality of the Market: Religious and Economic Perspectives: Preface. In *Block, W.; Brennan, G. and Elzinga, K., eds.*, 1985, pp. xv–xxv.

Boulding, Kenneth E. Learning by Simplifying Complexity: How to Turn Data into Knowledge. In *Aida, S., et al.*, 1985, pp. 25–34.

Buchanan, James M. Political Economy and Social Philosophy. In *Koslowski, P., ed.*, 1985, pp. 19–32.

Coelho, Philip R. P. An Examination into the Causes of Economic Growth: Status as an Economic Good. In *Zerbe, R. O., Jr., ed.*, 1985, pp. 89–116.

Cooper, John W. Theological Perspective on Economics: Comment. In *Block, W.; Brennan, G. and Elzinga, K., eds.*, 1985, pp. 59–66.

Costa de Beauregard, Olivier. Quanta and Relativity, Cosmos and Consciousness. In *Aida, S., et al.*, 1985, pp. 153–69.

Dadkhah, Kamran M. The Case of Erudite Economists. *J. Polit. Econ.*, December 1985, *93*(6), pp. 1268–71.

Danzin, André. The Pervasiveness of Complexity: Common Trends, New Paradigms, and Research Orientations. In *Aida, S., et al.*, 1985, pp. 69–80.

Davis, J. Rules Not Laws: Outline of an Ethnographic Approach to Economics. In *Roberts, B.; Finnegan, R. and Gallie, D., eds.*, 1985, pp. 502–11.

Dumont, Louis. The Economic Mode of Thought in an Anthropological Perspective. In *Koslowski, P., ed.*, 1985, pp. 251–61.

Etzioni, Amitai. Making Policy for Complex Systems: A Medical Model for Economics. *J. Policy Anal. Manage.*, Spring 1985, *4*(3), pp. 383–95.

Faber, Malte and Proops, John L. R. Interdisciplinary Research between Economists and Physical Scientists: Retrospect and Prospect. *Kyklos*, 1985, *38*(4), pp. 599–616.

Fiorina, Morris P. Group Concentration and the Delegation of Legislative Authority. In *Noll, R. G., ed.*, 1985, pp. 175–97.

Forte, Francesco. Political Economy and Social Philosophy: Comment. In *Koslowski, P., ed.*, 1985, pp. 33–36.

Frey, Bruno S. Economics and Philosophy: A Conference Summary. In *Koslowski, P., ed.*, 1985, pp. 269–71.

Gleizal, J.-J. Critique du droit et théorie de la régulation. (Critique of Law and the Theory of Regulation. With English summary.) *Écon. Soc.*, January 1985, *19*(1), pp. 91–101.

van Gool, W. Physics, Thermodynamics, Economics, Energy Analysis, and Time. In *van Gool, W. and Bruggink, J. J. C., eds.*, 1985, pp. 149–53.

Hannon, B. M. Time Value in Ecosystems. In *van Gool, W. and Bruggink, J. J. C., eds.*, 1985, pp. 261–85.

Hartwell, R. Max. Economic History and Philosophy. In *Koslowski, P., ed.*, 1985, pp. 80–87.

Hartwell, R. Max. The Economic Mode of Thought in an Anthropological Perspective. In *Koslowski, P., ed.*, 1985, pp. 262–64.

Heyne, Paul. The Concept of Economic Justice in Religious Discussion. In *Block, W.; Brennan, G. and Elzinga, K., eds.*, 1985, pp. 463–82.

Hirschman, Albert O. Against Parsimony: Three Easy Ways of Complicating Some Categories of Economic Discourse. *Econ. Philos.*, April 1985, *1*(1), pp. 7–21.

James, Jeffrey and Gutkind, Efraim. Attitude Change Revisited: Cognitive Dissonance Theory and Development Policy. *World Devel.*, Oct./Nov. 1985, *13*(10/11), pp. 1139–49.

Kambartel, Friedrich. Where Is More Fog—In Philosophy or in Economics? In *Koslowski, P., ed.*, 1985, pp. 272–74.

Kolm, Serge-Christophe. Must One Be Buddhist to Grow? An Analysis of the Cultural Basis of Japanese Productivity. In *Koslowski, P., ed.*, 1985, pp. 221–42.

Koopmans, Tjalling C. Economics among the Sciences. In *Koopmans, T. C.*, 1985, pp. 237–49.

Koslowski, Peter. Economy Principle, Maximizing, and the Co-ordination of Individuals in Economics and Philosophy. In *Koslowski, P., ed.*, 1985, pp. 39–67.

Koslowski, Peter. Philosophy and Economics: An Introduction. In *Koslowski, P., ed.*, 1985, pp. 1–16.

Küng, Emil. Beyond Economic Man: Humanistic Economics: Comment. In *Koslowski, P., ed.*, 1985, pp. 121–23.

Laborit, Henri. The Complexity of Interdependence in Living Systems. In *Aida, S., et al.*, 1985, pp. 146–52.

Laudan, Larry. Kuhn's Critique of Methodology. In *Pitt, J. C., ed.*, 1985, pp. 283–99.

Le Moigne, Jean-Louis. The Intelligence of Complexity. In *Aida, S., et al.*, 1985, pp. 35–61.

Leijonhufvud, Axel. Buddhist Values and Japanese Growth: Comment. In *Koslowski, P., ed.*, 1985, pp. 243–47.

Leontief, Wassily. Mathematics in Economics. In *Leontief, W.*, 1985, pp. 22–44.

Leontief, Wassily. Note on the Pluralistic Interpretation of History and the Problem of Interdisciplinary Co-operation. In *Leontief, W.*, 1985, pp. 3–11.

Lichtenstein, Peter M. Radical Liberalism and Radical Education: A Synthesis and Critical Evaluation of Illich, Freire, and Dewey. *Amer. J. Econ. Soc.*, January 1985, *44*(1), pp. 39–53.

Lindenberg, Siegwart. Rational Choice and Sociological Theory: New Pressures on Economics as a Social Science. *Z. ges. Staatswiss. (JITE)*, June 1985, *141*(2), pp. 244–55.

Luhmann, Niklas. Complexity and Meaning. In *Aida, S., et al.*, 1985, pp. 99–104.

Lutz, Mark A. Beyond Economic Man: Humanistic Economics. In *Koslowski, P., ed.*, 1985, pp. 91–120.

MacLennan, Carol. A Wide Angle on Regulation: Comment. In *Noll, R. G., ed.*, 1985, pp. 160–71. [G: U.S.]

Macpherson, C. B. The Economic Penetration of Political Theory: Some Hypotheses. In *Macpherson, C. B.*, 1985, pp. 101–19.

Morin, Edgar. On the Definition of Complexity. In *Aida, S., et al.*, 1985, pp. 62–68.

Nader, Laura and Nader, Claire. A Wide Angle on Regulation: An Anthropological Perspective. In *Noll, R. G., ed.*, 1985, pp. 141–60. [G: U.S.]

Ogus, Anthony. Legislation, the Courts and the Demand for Compensation. In *Matthews, R. C. O., ed.*, 1985, pp. 151–67.

Opp, Karl-Dieter. Sociology and Economic Man. *Z. ges. Staatswiss. (JITE)*, June 1985, *141*(2), pp. 213–43.

Optiz, Edmund A. *The Christian Century* on Religion and Society: Reply. In *Block, W.; Brennan, G. and Elzinga, K., eds.*, 1985, pp. 150–56.

Optiz, Edmund A. *The Christian Century* on Religion and Society. In *Block, W.; Brennan, G. and Elzinga, K., eds.*, 1985, pp. 119–42.

Ploman, Edward W. The Science and Praxis of Complexity: Introduction. In *Aida, S., et al.*, 1985, pp. 7–22.

Pribram, Karl H. Complexity and Causality. In *Aida, S., et al.*, 1985, pp. 119–32.

Prigogine, Ilya. New Perspectives on Complexity. In *Aida, S., et al.*, 1985, pp. 107–18.

Proops, John L. R. Thermodynamics and Economics: From Analogy to Physical Functioning. In *van Gool, W. and Bruggink, J. J. C., eds.*, 1985, pp. 155–74.

Riker, William H. Group Concentration and the Delegation of Legislative Authority: Comment. In *Noll, R. G., ed.*, 1985, pp. 197–99.

Rowley, Charles K. The Relationship between Economics, Politics and the Law in the Formation of Public Policy. In *Matthews, R. C. O., ed.*, 1985, pp. 127–50.

Slovic, Paul; Fischhoff, Baruch and Lichtenstein, Sarah. Regulation of Risk: A Psychological Perspective. In *Noll, R. G., ed.*, 1985, pp. 241–78. [G: U.S.]

Thisayakorn, Nopharatna. Perspectives on Statistics for Qualifying Research. In *Brown, R. C., ed.*, 1985, pp. 413–23.

de Vries, Bert. Energy and Time in the Economic and Physical Sciences. In *van Gool, W. and Bruggink, J. J. C., eds.*, 1985, pp. 381–83.

Wall, James M. *The Christian Century* on Religion and Society: Comment. In *Block, W.; Brennan, G. and Elzinga, K., eds.*, 1985, pp. 143–50.

Winett, Richard A. Regulation of Risk: Comment. In *Noll, R. G., ed.*, 1985, pp. 278–83. [G: U.S.]

Witt, Ulrich. Economic Behavior and Biological Evolution: Some Remarks on the Sociobiology Debate. *Z. ges. Staatswiss. (JITE)*, September 1985, *141*(3), pp. 365–89.

Wogaman, J. Philip. Theological Perspective on Economics: Reply. In *Block, W.; Brennan, G. and Elzinga, K., eds.*, 1985, pp. 97–101.

Wogaman, J. Philip. Theological Perspective on Economics. In *Block, W.; Brennan, G. and Elzinga, K., eds.*, 1985, pp. 35–59.

Worrall, John. Scientific Discovery and Theory-Confirmation. In *Pitt, J. C., ed.*, 1985, pp. 301–31.

Zerbe, Richard O., Jr. Is the Attempt to Gain Status a Zero-Sum Game? In *Zerbe, R. O., Jr., ed.*, 1985, pp. 117–121.

Zsolnai, Laszlo and Kiss, István N. Different Dissolutions of the Man-and-World Problem. In *Grauer, M.; Thompson, M. and Wierzbicki, A. P., eds.*, 1985, pp. 75–82.

0114 Relation of Economics to Social Values

Arif, Muhammad. Toward a Definition of Islamic Economics: Some Scientific Considerations. *J. Res. Islamic Econ.*, Winter 1985, *2*(2), pp. 87–103.

Armour, Leslie. The Economist and Moral Values. *Int. J. Soc. Econ.*, 1985, *12*(6/7), pp. 41–53.

Baepler, Richard. The Concept of Economic Justice in Religious Discussion: Comment. In *Block, W.; Brennan, G. and Elzinga, K., eds.*, 1985, pp. 482–89.

Bennett, John C. Morality of the Market: Religious and Economic Perspectives: Overview. In *Block, W.; Brennan, G. and Elzinga, K., eds.*, 1985, pp. 547–66.

Bergsten, Gordon S. On the Role of Social Norms in a Market Economy. *Public Choice*, 1985, *45*(2), pp. 113–37.

Berns, Walter. Religion, Ethics and Politics in the 1980s: Comment. In *Block, W.; Brennan, G. and Elzinga, K., eds.*, 1985, pp. 524–31.

Biddle, Jeff E. Veblen, Twain, and the Connecticut Yankee: A Note. *Hist. Polit. Econ.*, Spring 1985, *17*(1), pp. 97–107.

Blandy, Richard. Soft Science. *Econ. Rec.*, December 1985, *61*(175), pp. 693–706.

Block, Walter. Theological Perspective on Economics: Comment. In *Block, W.; Brennan, G. and Elzinga, K., eds.*, 1985, pp. 67–96. [G: Selected Countries]

Block, Walter; Brennan, Geoffrey and Elzinga, Kenneth G. Morality of the Market: Religious and Economic Perspectives: Preface. In *Block, W.; Brennan, G. and Elzinga, K., eds.*, 1985, pp. xv–xxv.

Boulding, Kenneth E. Markets and Majorities,

Morals and Madness: An Essay on Religion and Institutional Choice: Comment. In *Block, W.; Brennan, G. and Elzinga, K., eds.,* 1985, pp. 251–61. **[G: U.S.]**

Brennan, Geoffrey. Markets and Majorities, Morals and Madness: An Essay on Religion and Institutional Choice. In *Block, W.; Brennan, G. and Elzinga, K., eds.,* 1985, pp. 233–48.

Buchanan, James M. The Moral Dimension of Debt Financing. *Econ. Inquiry,* January 1985, *23*(1), pp. 1–6.

Caffè, Federico. Il neoliberismo contemporaneo e l'eredità intellettuale di Francesco Ferrara. (The New Laissez-Faire in Contemporary Economics and the Intellectual Heritage of Francesco Ferrara. With English summary.) *Rivista Int. Sci. Econ. Com.,* January 1985, *32*(1), pp. 51–62.

Cecil, Andrew R. Economic Freedom: The Rights and Responsibilities of the Entrepreneur in Our Mixed Economy. In *Taitte, W. L., ed.,* 1985, pp. 147–200.

Cooper, John W. Theological Perspective on Economics: Comment. In *Block, W.; Brennan, G. and Elzinga, K., eds.,* 1985, pp. 59–66.

Crotty, James R. and Stormes, James R. The Bishops on the U.S. Economy. *Challenge,* March/April 1985, *28*(1), pp. 36–41.

Dwyer, Larry. Scientific Rationality, Value Judgments, and Economic Advice. *Australian Econ. Pap.,* June 1985, *24*(44), pp. 169–84.

Elzinga, Kenneth G. Religion, Culture, and Technology: Comment. In *Block, W.; Brennan, G. and Elzinga, K., eds.,* 1985, pp. 322–29.

Falkena, H. B. On Hayek's Philosophy of Limited Government and the Economic Order (Review Article). *S. Afr. J. Econ.,* December 1985, *53*(4), pp. 366–80.

Faulhaber, Robert W. Of Power and Authority, People and Democracy. *Rev. Soc. Econ.,* October 1985, *43*(2), pp. 193–211.

Frankel, S. Herbert. Capitalism and the Jews: Comment. In *Block, W.; Brennan, G. and Elzinga, K., eds.,* 1985, pp. 429–42.

Friedman, David. Religion, Culture, and Technology: Comment. In *Block, W.; Brennan, G. and Elzinga, K., eds.,* 1985, pp. 313–21.

Friedman, Milton. Capitalism and the Jews. In *Block, W.; Brennan, G. and Elzinga, K., eds.,* 1985, pp. 401–18.

Friedman, Milton. Capitalism and the Jews: Reply. In *Block, W.; Brennan, G. and Elzinga, K., eds.,* 1985, pp. 443–46.

Gauthier, David. Bargaining and Justice. In *Paul, E. F.; Paul, J. and Miller, F. D., Jr., eds.,* 1985, pp. 29–47.

Gibbard, Allan. What's Morally Special about Free Exchange. In *Paul, E. F.; Paul, J. and Miller, F. D., Jr., eds.,* 1985, pp. 20–28.

Gitlow, Abraham L. Economics Seen Darkly in a Political Mirror. *Rivista Int. Sci. Econ. Com.,* January 1985, *32*(1), pp. 87–98. **[G: U.S.; LDCs]**

Hägerstrand, Torsten. Time-Geography: Focus on the Corporeality of Man, Society, and Envi-

ronment. In *Aida, S., et al.,* 1985, pp. 193–216.

Harsanyi, John C. Rule Utilitarianism, Equality, and Justice. In *Paul, E. F.; Paul, J. and Miller, F. D., Jr., eds.,* 1985, pp. 115–27.

Heyne, Paul. The Concept of Economic Justice in Religious Discussion. In *Block, W.; Brennan, G. and Elzinga, K., eds.,* 1985, pp. 463–82.

Hickerson, Steven R. Justice and the Social Economist: An Instrumentalist Interpretation. *Int. J. Soc. Econ.,* 1985, *12*(6/7), pp. 90–103.

Hofstede, Geert. National Cultures and Organizational Cultures. *Liiketaloudellinen Aikak.,* 1985, *34*(1), pp. 3–19.
[G: Selected Countries]

Horn, Walter. Libertarianism and Private Property in Land: Compensatory Payments by Landholders Are Required by Both Utility and Justice. *Amer. J. Econ. Soc.,* January 1985, *44*(1), pp. 67–80.

Karsten, Siegfried G. Eucken's 'Social Market Economy' and Its Test in Post-war West Germany: The Economist as Social Philosopher Developed Ideas that Parallelled Progressive Thought in America. *Amer. J. Econ. Soc.,* April 1985, *44*(2), pp. 169–83. **[G: W. Germany]**

Khan, Shahrukh Rafi. Islamic Economics: A Note on Methodology. *J. Res. Islamic Econ.,* Winter 1985, *2*(2), pp. 83–85.

Kneese, Allen V. and Schulze, William D. Ethics and Environmental Economics. In *Kneese, A. V. and Sweeney, J. L., eds. Vol. 1,* 1985, pp. 191–220.

Kolm, Serge-Christophe. Must One Be Buddhist to Grow? An Analysis of the Cultural Basis of Japanese Productivity. In *Koslowski, P., ed.,* 1985, pp. 221–42.

Küng, Emil. Beyond Economic Man: Humanistic Economics: Comment. In *Koslowski, P., ed.,* 1985, pp. 121–23.

Leijonhufvud, Axel. Buddhist Values and Japanese Growth: Comment. In *Koslowski, P., ed.,* 1985, pp. 243–47.

Levine, Aaron. Capitalism and the Jews: Comment. In *Block, W.; Brennan, G. and Elzinga, K., eds.,* 1985, pp. 419–29.

Lutz, Mark A. Beyond Economic Man: Humanistic Economics. In *Koslowski, P., ed.,* 1985, pp. 91–120.

Lutz, Mark A. Pragmatism, Instrumental Value Theory and Social Economics. *Rev. Soc. Econ.,* October 1985, *43*(2), pp. 140–72. **[G: U.S.]**

Macpherson, C. B. The Rise and Fall of Economic Justice. In *Macpherson, C. B.,* 1985, pp. 1–20.

Maritain, Jacques. A Society without Money. *Rev. Soc. Econ.,* April 1985, *43*(1), pp. 73–83.

Marshall, Ray. Labor in a Free Society. In *Taitte, W. L., ed.,* 1985, pp. 203–33.

Martin, David A. R. H. Tawney's Normative Economic History of Capitalism. *Rev. Soc. Econ.,* April 1985, *43*(1), pp. 84–102.

McLean, Murdith R. From Theology to Social Decisions—and Return: Comment. In *Block,*

W.; *Brennan, G. and Elzinga, K., eds.*, 1985, pp. 201–09.

van Meerhaeghe, Marcel A. G. Right and Left—Ideology and Welfare State. *Rivista Int. Sci. Econ. Com.*, March 1985, *32*(3), pp. 263–70.

Meiselman, David I. Markets and Majorities, Morals and Madness: An Essay on Religion and Institutional Choice: Comment. In *Block, W.; Brennan, G. and Elzinga, K., eds.*, 1985, pp. 248–51.

Mishan, Ezra J. Religion, Culture, and Technology: Reply. In *Block, W.; Brennan, G. and Elzinga, K., eds.*, 1985, pp. 330–40.

Mishan, Ezra J. Religion, Culture, and Technology. In *Block, W.; Brennan, G. and Elzinga, K., eds.*, 1985, pp. 279–312.

Norman, Edward R. Religion, Ethics and Politics in the 1980s. In *Block, W.; Brennan, G. and Elzinga, K., eds.*, 1985, pp. 511–23.

Novak, Michael. Morality of the Market: Religious and Economic Perspectives: Overview. In *Block, W.; Brennan, G. and Elzinga, K., eds.*, 1985, pp. 567–87. [G: U.S.]

O'Connor, James. Capital, Crisis, Class Struggle. In *[Magdoff, H. and Sweezy, P.]*, 1985, pp. 273–93.

Optiz, Edmund A. *The Christian Century* on Religion and Society. In *Block, W.; Brennan, G. and Elzinga, K., eds.*, 1985, pp. 119–42.

Optiz, Edmund A. *The Christian Century* on Religion and Society: Reply. In *Block, W.; Brennan, G. and Elzinga, K., eds.*, 1985, pp. 150–56.

Phillipson, Nicholas. Adam Smith as Civic Moralist. In *Hont, I. and Ignatieff, M., eds.*, 1985, pp. 179–202.

Plant, Raymond. The Very Idea of a Welfare State. In *Bean, P.; Ferris, J. and Whynes, D., eds.*, 1985, pp. 3–30. [G: U.K.]

Podunavac, Milan. Culture-Based Value Systems in Yugoslavia. In *Damjanovic, M. and Voich, D., Jr., eds.*, 1985, pp. 39–63.
[G: Yugoslavia]

Robertson, John. The Scottish Enlightenment at the Limits of the Civic Tradition. In *Hont, I. and Ignatieff, M., eds.*, 1985, pp. 137–78.

Scaperlanda, Anthony. Is Neo-Humanistic Economics the New Paradigm for Social Economists? *Rev. Soc. Econ.*, October 1985, *43*(2), pp. 173–80.

Schlicht, Ekkehart. The Shadow Economy and Morals: A Note. In *Gaertner, W. and Wenig, A., eds.*, 1985, pp. 265–71.

Sen, Amartya. The Moral Standing of the Market. In *Paul, E. F.; Paul, J. and Miller, F. D., Jr., eds.*, 1985, pp. 1–19.

Shenfield, Arthur A. From Theology to Social Decisions—and Return: Comment. In *Block, W.; Brennan, G. and Elzinga, K., eds.*, 1985, pp. 196–200.

Shinn, Roger L. From Theology to Social Decisions—and Return. In *Block, W.; Brennan, G. and Elzinga, K., eds.*, 1985, pp. 175–95.

Simon, Herbert A. My Life Philosophy. *Amer. Econ.*, Spring 1985, *29*(1), pp. 15–20.

Stevenson, Rodney. Corporate Power and the Scope of Economic Analysis. *J. Econ. Issues*, June 1985, *19*(2), pp. 333–41.

Sufrin, Sidney C. Philosophical Foundations. An Essay in Economic Pragmatism. *Rivista Int. Sci. Econ. Com.*, June 1985, *32*(6), pp. 525–49.

Wall, James M. *The Christian Century* on Religion and Society: Comment. In *Block, W.; Brennan, G. and Elzinga, K., eds.*, 1985, pp. 143–50.

Waterman, Anthony. Religious Belief and Political Bias. In *Block, W.; Brennan, G. and Elzinga, K., eds.*, 1985, pp. 3–20.

Watkins, John. Second Thoughts on Self-interest and Morality. In *Campbell, R. and Sowden, L., eds.*, 1985, pp. 59–74.

Watts, Michael. Economic Policy and the Lives of Contemplation, Civic Humanism, Collectivism and Individualism. *Int. J. Soc. Econ.*, 1985, *12*(6/7), pp. 54–67.

Wingren, Gustaf. Everyday Life in Europe and the Effect of the 'Protestant Work Ethic.' In *Gustavsson, B.; Karlsson, J. C. and Raftegard, C.*, 1985, pp. 139–47.

Wogaman, J. Philip. Theological Perspective on Economics: Reply. In *Block, W.; Brennan, G. and Elzinga, K., eds.*, 1985, pp. 97–101.

Wogaman, J. Philip. Theological Perspective on Economics. In *Block, W.; Brennan, G. and Elzinga, K., eds.*, 1985, pp. 35–59.

Wootton, Barbara. The Moral Basis of the Welfare State. In *Bean, P.; Ferris, J. and Whynes, D., eds.*, 1985, pp. 31–45. [G: U.K.]

Yeager, Leland B. Rights, Contract, and Utility in Policy Espousal. *Cato J.*, Spring/Summer 1985, *5*(1), pp. 259–94.

Zsolnai, Laszlo and Kiss, István N. Different Dissolutions of the Man-and-World Problem. In *Grauer, M.; Thompson, M. and Wierzbicki, A. P., eds.*, 1985, pp. 75–82.

0115 Methods Used by Economists

Batten, David F. New Mathematical Advances in Economic Dynamics: Introduction. In *Batten, D. F. and Lesse, P. F., eds.*, 1985, pp. 1–12.

Baumol, William J. On Method in U.S. Economics a Century Earlier. *Amer. Econ. Rev.*, December 1985, *75*(6), pp. 1–12. [G: U.S.]

Bruggink, J. J. C. The Theory of Economic Growth and Thermodynamical Laws. In *van Gool, W. and Bruggink, J. J. C., eds.*, 1985, pp. 135–45.

Caplovitz, David. Concepts, Indices and Contexts. In *Smith, R. B., ed.*, 1985, pp. 193–240. [G: U.S.]

Christ, Carl F. Early Progress in Estimating Quantitative Economic Relationships in America. *Amer. Econ. Rev.*, December 1985, *75*(6), pp. 39–52. [G: U.S.]

Faber, Malte. A Biophysical Approach to the Economy Entropy, Environment and Resources. In *van Gool, W. and Bruggink, J. J. C., eds.*, 1985, pp. 315–37.

Leontief, Wassily. Mathematics in Economics. In

011 General Economics

Leontief, W., 1985, pp. 22–44.

Ploman, Edward W. The Science and Praxis of Complexity: Introduction. In *Aida, S., et al.*, 1985, pp. 7–22.

Proops, John L. R. Thermodynamics and Economics: From Analogy to Physical Functioning. In *van Gool, W. and Bruggink, J. J. C., eds.*, 1985, pp. 155–74.

Smith, Robert B. A Handbook of Social Science Methods: Introduction: Linking Quality and Quantity. In *Smith, R. B., ed.*, 1985, pp. 1–51.

012 Teaching of Economics

0120 Teaching of Economics

Amsler, Christine E. A Survey of Ten Money and Banking Textbooks. *J. Econ. Educ.*, Fall 1985, *16*(4), pp. 313–18.

Anderson, Oliver D. How to Teach Economics—Take Two: A Mathematician (?) Stakes His Claim. In *Brown, R. C., ed.*, 1985, pp. 357–59.

Blank, Steven C. A Decade of Change in Agricultural Economics Programs, 1975–84. *Western J. Agr. Econ.*, December 1985, *10*(2), pp. 375–81. [G: U.S.]

Blank, Steven C. Effectiveness of Role Playing, Case Studies, and Simulation Games in Teaching Agricultural Economics. *Western J. Agr. Econ.*, July 1985, *10*(1), pp. 55–62. [G: U.S.]

Bond, Patrick. A Student's Appreciation of Sidney Weintraub. *J. Post Keynesian Econ.*, Summer 1985, *7*(4), pp. 530–32.

Brandis, Royall. The Principles of Economics Course: A Historical Perspective. *J. Econ. Educ.*, Fall 1985, *16*(4), pp. 277–80.

Broder, Josef M. The Southern Agricultural Economics Association and Resident Instruction. *Southern J. Agr. Econ.*, July 1985, *17*(1), pp. 7–14. [G: U.S.]

Bronfenbrenner, Martin. Economic Education in Japan at the University Level. *J. Econ. Educ.*, Fall 1985, *16*(4), pp. 269–72. [G: Japan]

Case, Karl E. and Fair, Ray C. Macro Simulations for PCs in the Classroom. *Amer. Econ. Rev.*, May 1985, *75*(2), pp. 85–90. [G: U.S.]

Charkins, R. J.; O'Toole, Dennis M. and Wetzel, James N. Linking Teacher and Student Learning Styles with Student Achievement and Attitudes. *J. Econ. Educ.*, Spring 1985, *16*(2), pp. 111–20. [G: U.S.]

Chizmar, John F., et al. "Give and Take," Economics Achievement, and Basic Skills Development. *J. Econ. Educ.*, Spring 1985, *16*(2), pp. 99–110.

Clark, Ronald L. and Sweeney, Robert B. Admission to Accounting Programs: Using a Discriminant Model as a Classification Procedure. *Accounting Rev.*, July 1985, *60*(3), pp. 508–18.

Cottrell, Allin. Keynesianism and the Natural Rate of Unemployment: A Problem in Pedagogy. *J. Post Keynesian Econ.*, Winter 1984–85, *7*(2), pp. 263–68.

Crum, William F. and Garner, Don E. 1983 Survey of Doctoral Programs in Accounting in the United States and Canada. *Accounting Rev.*, July 1985, *60*(3), pp. 519–25.

Daly, Herman E. The Circular Flow of Exchange Value and the Linear Throughput of Matter-Energy: A Case of Misplaced Concreteness. *Rev. Soc. Econ.*, December 1985, *43*(3), pp. 279–97.

Davis, James A. Statistical Inference with Proportions. In *Smith, R. B., ed.*, 1985, pp. 336–66.

Debertin, David L. Developing Realistic Agricultural Production Functions for Use in Undergraduate Classes. *Southern J. Agr. Econ.*, December 1985, *17*(2), pp. 207–14.

Drèze, Jacques H. Econometrics in the General Economics Curriculum: Teachers in a Quandry? *Tijdschrift Econ. Manage.*, 1985, *30*(3–4), pp. 445–52. [G: Belgium]

Field, William J.; Wachter, Daniel R. and Catanese, Anthony V. Alternative Ways to Teach and Learn Economics: Writing, Quantitative Reasoning, and Oral Communication. *J. Econ. Educ.*, Summer 1985, *16*(3), pp. 213–17.

Guedry, Leo J., Jr. Teaching, Research, and Extension Programs at Predominantly Black Land-Grant Institutions: Discussion. *Southern J. Agr. Econ.*, July 1985, *17*(1), pp. 43–45. [G: U.S.]

Hallagan, William S. and Donnelly, John. An Integrated Modular Approach to Teaching Introductory Economics. *J. Econ. Educ.*, Spring 1985, *16*(2), pp. 129–34. [G: U.S.]

Hansen, Harlan S. The Economics of Early Childhood Education in Minnesota. *J. Econ. Educ.*, Summer 1985, *16*(3), pp. 219–24. [G: U.S.]

Hansen, Richard B.; McCormick, Ken and Rives, Janet M. The Aggregate Demand Curve and Its Proper Interpretation. *J. Econ. Educ.*, Fall 1985, *16*(4), pp. 287–96.

Harrell, Adrian; Caldwell, Charles and Doty, Edwin. Within-Person Expectancy Theory Predictions of Accounting Students' Motivation to Achieve Academic Success. *Accounting Rev.*, October 1985, *60*(4), pp. 724–35. [G: U.S.]

Honig, Solomon. Comparisons between Estimated and Simulated Phillips Curve: A Computer–Student Interaction. In *Brown, R. C., ed.*, 1985, pp. 361–74.

Honko, Jaakko. Liiketaloustieteen tutkimuksen ja opetuksen keskeisiä Kysymyksiä. (Key Questions in Managerial and Business Economics Research and Teaching. With English summary.) *Liiketaloudellinen Aikak.*, 1985, *34*(1), pp. 20–31. [G: Finland]

Jackstadt, Stephen L.; Brennan, Jerry and Thompson, Scott. The Effect of Introductory Economics Courses on College Students' Conservatism. *J. Econ. Educ.*, Winter 1985, *16*(1), pp. 37–51. [G: U.S.]

Johnson, Steven B. The Economic Function of Doctoral Programs in Accounting: Alternative Theories and Educational Implications. *Ac-*

counting Rev., October 1985, 60(4), pp. 736–43.

Khan, Muhammad Akram. Teaching Islamic Economics at University Level. In Khan, M. A., 1985, pp. 72–91.

Kohl, David M. The Southern Agricultural Economics Association and Resident Instruction: Discussion. Southern J. Agr. Econ., July 1985, 17(1), pp. 15–16. [G: U.S.]

Kumar, Binod. On Teaching of Statistics. In Brown, R. C., ed., 1985, pp. 381–85.

Lee, Joe Won and Kidane, Amdetsion. The Adequacy of Coverage of Statistics in Business Schools for Statistical Literacy: A Case Study. In Brown, R. C., ed., 1985, pp. 375–79.

Levan-Lemesle, Lucette. Innovations et institutions: Le Conservatoire des Arts et Métiers et la Faculté de Droit de Paris. (Innovations and Institutions: The Conservatory of Arts and Trades and the Law School of Paris. With English summary.) Écon. Soc., October 1985, 19(10), pp. 107–19. [G: France]

Lewis, Darrell R.; Dalgaard, Bruce R. and Boyer, Carol M. Cost Effectiveness of Computer-assisted Economics Instruction. Amer. Econ. Rev., May 1985, 75(2), pp. 91–96.

Locke, Robert R. Business Education in Germany: Past Systems and Current Practice. Bus. Hist. Rev., Summer 1985, 59(2), pp. 232–53. [G: W. Germany]

Lumsden, Keith and Scott, Alex. Public Funding of Universities: Effects on Economics I Students. In [Peacock, A.], 1985, pp. 105–24. [G: U.K.]

Martin, David A. and Bender, David S. "Trade-Offs," Field Dependence/Independence, and Sex-based Economics Comprehension Differences. J. Econ. Educ., Winter 1985, 16(1), pp. 62–70. [G: U.S.]

Maxwell, Nan L. Survey of Labor Economics Textbooks. J. Econ. Educ., Spring 1985, 16(2), pp. 147–56.

McGrath, Eileen L. and Tiemann, Thomas K. Introducing Empirical Exercises into Principles of Economics. J. Econ. Educ., Spring 1985, 16(2), pp. 121–27. [G: U.S.]

Mortensen, Peter S. The Art of Planning a Course in Applied Statistics for Business and Economics. In Brown, R. C., ed., 1985, pp. 387–94.

Policano, Andrew J. The Current State of Macroeconomics: A View from the Textbooks. J. Monet. Econ., May 1985, 15(3), pp. 389–97.

Post, Gerald V. Microcomputers in Teaching Economics. J. Econ. Educ., Fall 1985, 16(4), pp. 309–12.

Rowley, J. C. Robin and Jain, Renuka. Confirmation, Explanation and Criticism—Three Interacting Themes of Basic Courses in Econometrics. In Brown, R. C., ed., 1985, pp. 395–411.

Sass, Steven A. The Managerial Ideology in Collegiate Business Education. In Atack, J., ed., 1985, pp. 199–212.

Siegfried, John J. and Raymond, Jennie E. Economics Student and Faculty Attitudes on the Purpose of Undergraduate Education. J. Econ.

Educ., Winter 1985, 16(1), pp. 71–78. [G: U.S.]

Snellings, Eleanor C. "Real" Principles of Economics for the Real World. Atlantic Econ. J., December 1985, 13(4), pp. 79. [G: U.S.]

Strecker, Mary F. Selected Teaching and Learning Aids in the Area of Governmental and Nonprofit Accountability. Public Budg. Finance, Spring 1985, 5(1), pp. 100–106. [G: U.S.]

Sumansky, John M. Computer Applications in Pre-college Economics. Amer. Econ. Rev., May 1985, 75(2), pp. 80–84. [G: U.S.]

Umapathy, Srinivasan. Teaching Behavioral Aspects of Performance Evaluation: An Experiential Approach. Accounting Rev., January 1985, 60(1), pp. 97–108. [G: U.S.]

Walstad, William and Watts, Michael. Teaching Economics in the Schools: A Review of Survey Findings. J. Econ. Educ., Spring 1985, 16(2), pp. 135–46. [G: U.S.]

Watts, Michael. A Statewide Assessment of Pre-college Economic Understanding and DEEP. J. Econ. Educ., Summer 1985, 16(3), pp. 225–37. [G: U.S.]

Watts, Michael. Errata: [A Statewide Assessment of Precollege Economic Understanding and DEEP]. J. Econ. Educ., Fall 1985, 16(4), pp. 286. [G: U.S.]

Watts, Michael. School District Inputs and Biased Estimation of Educational Production Functions. J. Econ. Educ., Fall 1985, 16(4), pp. 281–85. [G: U.S.]

Wells, Paul. The Aggregate Supply Curve: Keynes and Downwardly Sticky Money Wages. J. Econ. Educ., Fall 1985, 16(4), pp. 297–304.

Wetzstein, Michael E. and Broder, Josef M. The Economics of Effective Teaching. J. Econ. Educ., Winter 1985, 16(1), pp. 52–59.

Whitehead, David J. The Training of Economics Teachers in England and Wales. J. Econ. Educ., Fall 1985, 16(4), pp. 254–68. [G: U.K.]

Williams, Thomas T. and Williamson, Handy, Jr. Teaching, Research, and Extension Programs at Predominantly Black Land-Grant Institutions. Southern J. Agr. Econ., July 1985, 17(1), pp. 31–41. [G: U.S.]

Wilson, R. G. and Hadwin, J. F. Economic and Social History at Advanced Level. Econ. Hist. Rev., 2nd Ser., November 1985, 38(4), pp. 548–68.

Wood, William C. The Educational Potential of News Coverage of Economics. J. Econ. Educ., Winter 1985, 16(1), pp. 27–35.

Wood, William C. The Price Level in Principles of Macroeconomic: A Review Essay. Amer. Econ., Spring 1985, 29(1), pp. 80–84.

Yamane, Eiji. Economic Education in Japan at the Precollege Level. J. Econ. Educ., Fall 1985, 16(4), pp. 273–76. [G: Japan]

Yano, Makoto. Competitive Equilibria on Turnpikes in a McKenzie Economy, II: An Asymptotic Turnpike Theorem. Int. Econ. Rev., October 1985, 26(3), pp. 661–69.

020 GENERAL ECONOMIC THEORY

0200 General Economic Theory

Arrow, Kenneth J. and Honkapohja, Seppo. Frontiers of Economics: Introduction. In *Arrow, K. J. and Honkapohja, S., eds.*, 1985, pp. 1–27.

Barry, Norman P. In Defense of the Invisible Hand. *Cato J.*, Spring/Summer 1985, 5(1), pp. 133–48.

Batten, David F. New Mathematical Advances in Economic Dynamics: Introduction. In *Batten, D. F. and Lesse, P. F., eds.*, 1985, pp. 1–12.

Baum, Sandra R. Moral Philosophy, Cognitive Psychology and Economic Theory. *Eastern Econ. J.*, Oct.-Dec. 1985, 11(4), pp. 422–36.

Bookstaber, Richard and Langsam, Joseph. Predictable Behavior: Comment [The Origin of Predictable Behavior]. *Amer. Econ. Rev.*, June 1985, 75(3), pp. 571–75.

Cencini, Alvaro. La teoria quantica della produzione. (With English summary.) *Econ. Polít.*, August 1985, 2(2), pp. 215–43.

Chase, Richard X. A Theory of Socioeconomic Change: Entropic Processes, Technology, and Evolutionary Development. *J. Econ. Issues*, December 1985, 19(4), pp. 797–823.

Cohen, Suleiman I. The Controversial Debate on Development Economics: An Opinion. *Pakistan Devel. Rev.*, Spring 1985, 24(1), pp. 61–76.

Cowen, Tyler and Fink, Richard H. Inconsistent Equilibrium Constructs: The Evenly Rotating Economy of Mises and Rothbard. *Amer. Econ. Rev.*, September 1985, 75(4), pp. 866–69.

Cross, Melvin L. Are the Bishops Taking Us Back to Adam Smith? *Can. Public Policy*, December 1985, 11(4), pp. 745–48.

Daly, Herman E. The Circular Flow of Exchange Value and the Linear Throughput of Matter-Energy: A Case of Misplaced Concreteness. *Rev. Soc. Econ.*, December 1985, 43(3), pp. 279–97.

Debreu, Gerard and Koopmans, Tjalling C. Additively Decomposed Quasiconvex Functions. In *Koopmans, T. C.*, 1985, pp. 273–310.

Demaria, Giovanni. Il problema della datità in economia. (The Problem of Economic and Extraeconomic Assumptions. With English summary.) *Rivista Int. Sci. Econ. Com.*, January 1985, 32(1), pp. 5–38.

Dore, M. H. I. On the Concept of Equilibrium. *J. Post Keynesian Econ.*, Winter 1984–85, 7(2), pp. 193–206.

Dow, Alexander and Dow, Sheila C. Animal Spirits and Rationality. In *Lawson, T. and Pesaran, H., eds.*, 1985, pp. 46–65.

Drugman, B. A nouveau sur la question de la régulation. Economie politique, Marxisme et... crise: quelle alternative réelle? (Theory of Regulation Revisited. Political Economy, Marxism and Crisis: Is There a Real Alternative? With English summary.) *Écon. Soc.*, January 1985, 19(1), pp. 29–64.

Duménil, G. and Lévy, D. The Classicals and the Neoclassicals: A Rejoinder. *Cambridge J. Econ.*, December 1985, 9(4), pp. 327–45.

Earl, Peter E. and Kay, Neil M. How Economists Can Accept Shackle's Critique on Economic Doctrines without Arguing Themselves out of Their Jobs. *J. Econ. Stud.*, 1985, 12(1/2), pp. 34–48.

Eichner, Alfred S. Toward a New Economics: Introduction. In *Eichner, A. S.*, 1985, pp. 3–9.

Eichner, Alfred S. Towards an Empirically Valid Economics. *Eastern Econ. J.*, Oct.-Dec. 1985, 11(4), pp. 437–49.

Etzioni, Amitai. Encapsulated Competition. *J. Post Keynesian Econ.*, Spring 1985, 7(3), pp. 287–302.

Feiwel, George R. Issues in Contemporary Microeconomics and Welfare: Preface. In *Feiwel, G. R., ed. (II)*, 1985, pp. xiii–xxviii.

Feiwel, George R. Some Sources of Disagreements in Economics. *Rivista Int. Sci. Econ. Com.*, April 1985, 32(4), pp. 305–22.

Ford, J. L. Shackle's Theory of Decision Making under Uncertainty: Synopsis and Brief Appraisal. *J. Econ. Stud.*, 1985, 12(1/2), pp. 59–69.

Friedman, Daniel. Experimental Economics: Comment. *Amer. Econ. Rev.*, March 1985, 75(1), pp. 264.

Garrison, Roger W. Predictable Behavior: Comment [The Origin of Predictable Behavior]. *Amer. Econ. Rev.*, June 1985, 75(3), pp. 576–78.

Gnanadoss, B. The Concept of Field in Economic Analysis. *Indian Econ. J.*, Apr.-June 1985, 32(4), pp. 75–79.

Goodwin, Richard. A Personal Perspective on Mathematical Economics. *Banca Naz. Lavoro Quart. Rev.*, March 1985, (152), pp. 3–13.

Gutman, Pablo. Teoría económica y problemática ambiental: un diálogo difícil. (With English summary.) *Desarrollo Econ.*, April–June 1985, 25(97), pp. 46–70.

Hahn, Frank. In Praise of Economic Theory. In *Hahn, F.*, 1985, pp. 10–28.

Hahn, Frank. Money and General Equilibrium. In *Hahn, F.*, 1985, pp. 31–45.

Haltiwanger, John C. and Waldman, Michael. Rational Expectations and the Limits of Rationality: An Analysis of Heterogeneity. *Amer. Econ. Rev.*, June 1985, 75(3), pp. 326–40.

Hamilton, James D. and Whiteman, Charles H. The Observable Implications of Self-fulfilling Expectations. *J. Monet. Econ.*, November 1985, 16(3), pp. 353–73.

Harris, Donald J. Value, Exchange and Capital. In *[Magdoff, H. and Sweezy, P.]*, 1985, pp. 151–83.

Heiner, Ronald A. Experimental Economics: Comment. *Amer. Econ. Rev.*, March 1985, 75(1), pp. 260–63.

Heiner, Ronald A. Predictable Behavior: Reply [The Origin of Predictable Behavior]. *Amer. Econ. Rev.*, June 1985, 75(3), pp. 579–85.

Hey, John D. The Possibility of Possibility. *J. Econ. Stud.*, 1985, *12*(1/2), pp. 70–88.

Hirschman, Albert O. Against Parsimony: Three Easy Ways of Complicating Some Categories of Economic Discourse. *Econ. Philos.*, April 1985, *1*(1), pp. 7–21.

Hodgson, Geoffrey M. Persuasion, Expectations and the Limits to Keynes. In *Lawson, T. and Pesaran, H., eds.*, 1985, pp. 10–45.

Hodgson, Geoffrey M. The Rationalist Conception of Action. *J. Econ. Issues,* December 1985, *19*(4), pp. 825–51.

Honkapohja, Seppo. Rationaaliset odotukset kansantaloustieteessä: Johdanto kirjallisuuteen. *Kansant. Aikak.*, 1985, *81*(2), pp. 238.

Jha, L. K. Economic Theorems and Human Problems. In *Jha, L. K.*, 1985, pp. 187–202.

Kanel, Don. Institutional Economics: Perspectives on Economy and Society. *J. Econ. Issues,* September 1985, *19*(3), pp. 815–28.

Katzner, Donald W. Alternatives to Equilibrium Analysis. *Eastern Econ. J.*, Oct.-Dec. 1985, *11*(4), pp. 404–21.

Kompas, Thomas Frank. Traditional Notions of Equilibrium Reconsidered. *Eastern Econ. J.*, Oct.-Dec. 1985, *11*(4), pp. 361–72.

Koopmans, Tjalling C. Note on a Social System Composed of Hierarchies with Overlapping Personnel. In *Koopmans, T. C.*, 1985, pp. 1–11.

Koopmans, Tjalling C. and Montias, John Michael. On the Description and Comparison of Economic Systems. In *Koopmans, T. C.*, 1985, pp. 29–80.

Leontief, Wassily. Composite Commodities and the Problem of Index Numbers. In *Leontief, W.*, 1985, pp. 126–50.

Leontief, Wassily. Mathematics in Economics. In *Leontief, W.*, 1985, pp. 22–44.

Leontief, Wassily. The Problem of Quality and Quantity in Economics. In *Leontief, W.*, 1985, pp. 45–57.

Leontief, Wassily. The Significance of Marxian Economics for Present-Day Economic Theory. In *Leontief, W.*, 1985, pp. 72–83.

Leontief, Wassily. Theoretical Assumptions and Nonobserved Facts. In *Leontief, W.*, 1985, pp. 272–82.

Loasby, Brian J. Profit, Expectations and Coherence in Economic Systems. *J. Econ. Stud.*, 1985, *12*(1/2), pp. 21–33.

Lombardi, S. At the Roots of the Crisis in Economic Theory. *Econ. Int.*, Aug./Nov. 1985, *38*(3/4), pp. 323–50.

Meier, Alfred and Mettler, Daniel. Auf der Suche nach einem neuen Paradigma der Wirtschaftspolitik. (Toward a New Paradigm of Economic Policy. With English summary.) *Kyklos*, 1985, *38*(2), pp. 171–99.

Polkinghorn, Bette. A Communication: An Unpublished Letter of J. B. Say. *Eastern Econ. J.*, April-June 1985, *11*(2), pp. 167–70.

Quandt, Richard E. Concepts and Structures in Disequilibrium Models. *Rivista Int. Sci. Econ. Com.*, March 1985, *32*(3), pp. 207–32.

van Raaij, W. Fred. Attribution of Causality to Economic Actions and Events. *Kyklos*, 1985, *38*(1), pp. 3–19.

Robinson, Joan. The Theory of Normal Prices and Reconstruction of Economic Theory. In *Feiwel, G. R., ed. (I),* 1985, pp. 157–65.

Russell, Thomas and Thaler, Richard. The Relevance of Quasi Rationality in Competitive Markets. *Amer. Econ. Rev.*, December 1985, *75*(5), pp. 1071–82.

Sakakibara, Kenichi. Another Example of "Sunspots" Equilibrium. *Econ. Stud. Quart.*, December 1985, *36*(3), pp. 252–55.

Salvati, Michele. Diversità e mutamento: osservazioni inconcludenti sul modello degli economisti. (With English summary.) *Econ. Polit.*, August 1985, *2*(2), pp. 249–92.

Sato, Ryuzo. The Invariance Principle and Income– Wealth Conservation Laws: Application of Lie Groups and Related Transformations. *J. Econometrics*, Oct./Nov. 1985, *30*(1/2), pp. 365–89.

Sawyer, Malcolm C. The Economics of Michal Kalecki. *Eastern Europ. Econ.*, Spring-Summer 1985, *23*(3–4), pp. 1–319.

Shepherd, A. Ross. A Comment on Lerner's "Extortion Tax" Plan [Lerner's Contribution to Economics]. *J. Econ. Lit.*, September 1985, *23*(3), pp. 1192.

Smith, Vernon L. Experimental Economics: Reply. *Amer. Econ. Rev.*, March 1985, *75*(1), pp. 264–72.

Stegman, Trevor R. On the Rationality of the Rational Expectations Hypothesis. *Australian Econ. Pap.*, December 1985, *24*(45), pp. 350–55.

Stewart, Ian G. Political Economy, Classical and Modern: Review Article. *Scot. J. Polit. Econ.*, November 1985, *32*(3), pp. 343–46.

Stiglitz, Joseph E. Information and Economic Analysis: A Perspective. *Econ. J.*, Supplement 1985, *95*, pp. 21–41.

Sugden, Robert. Why Be Consistent? A Critical Analysis of Consistency Requirements in Choice Theory. *Economica*, May 1985, *52*(206), pp. 167–83.

Summers, Lawrence H. On Economics and Finance. *J. Finance*, July 1985, *40*(3), pp. 633–35.

Teboul, René. Le circuit comme représentation de l'espace économique (une relecture de l'oeuvre de Pierre de Boisguillebert). (With English summary.) *Revue Écon. Polit.*, Mar.–Apr. 1985, *95*(2), pp. 117–33.

Van Moeseke, Paul. Socio-economic Interface and Social Income. *Math. Soc. Sci.*, June 1985, *9*(3), pp. 263–73.

Vickers, Douglas. On Relational Structures and Non-equilibrium in Economic Theory. *Eastern Econ. J.*, Oct.-Dec. 1985, *11*(4), pp. 384–403.

Wagener, Hans-Jürgen. Structural Change and International Economic Comparisons. In *[Levcik, F.]*, 1985, pp. 83–95.

021 General Equilibrium and Disequilibrium Theory

0210 General Equilibrium and Disequilibrium Theory

Aghion, Philippe. On the Generic Inefficiency of Differentiable Market Games. *J. Econ. Theory*, October 1985, *37*(1), pp. 126–46.

Aliprantis, C. D.; Brown, Donald J. and Burkinshaw, O. Examples of Excess Demand Functions on Infinite-Dimensional Commodity Spaces. In *Aliprantis, C. D.; Burkinshaw, O. and Rothman, N. J., eds.*, 1985, pp. 131–43.

Allen, Beth. The Existence of Fully Rational Expectations Approximate Equilibria with Noisy Price Observations. *J. Econ. Theory*, December 1985, *37*(2), pp. 213–53.

Allen, Beth. The Existence of Rational Expectations Equilibria in a Large Economy with Noisy Price Observations. *J. Math. Econ.*, 1985, *14*(1), pp. 67–103.

Anderson, Robert M. Strong Core Theorems with Nonconvex Preferences. *Econometrica*, November 1985, *53*(6), pp. 1283–94.

Anderson, Robert M. and Sonnenschein, Hugo. Rational Expectations Equilibrium with Econometric Models. *Rev. Econ. Stud.*, July 1985, *52*(3), pp. 359–69.

Araujo, Aloisio. Lack of Pareto Optimal Allocations in Economies with Infinitely Many Commodities: The Need for Impatience. *Econometrica*, March 1985, *53*(2), pp. 455–61.

Araujo, Aloisio. Regular Economies and Sets of Measure Zero in Banach Spaces. *J. Math. Econ.*, 1985, *14*(1), pp. 61–66.

Armstrong, Thomas E. Remarks Related to Finitely Additive Exchange Economies. In *Aliprantis, C. D.; Burkinshaw, O. and Rothman, N. J., eds.*, 1985, pp. 185–204.

Arrow, Kenneth J. The Potentials and Limits of the Market in Resource Allocation. In *Feiwel, G. R., ed. (II)*, 1985, pp. 107–24.

Aumann, Robert J. An Axiomatization of the Nontransferable Utility Value. *Econometrica*, May 1985, *53*(3), pp. 599–612.

Aumann, Robert J. On the Non-transferable Utility Value: A Comment on the Roth–Shafer Examples [Values for Games without Side Payments: Some Difficulties with Current Concepts] [On the Existence and Interpretation of Value Allocations]. *Econometrica*, May 1985, *53*(3), pp. 667–77.

Aumann, Robert J. Repeated Games. In *Feiwel, G. R., ed. (II)*, 1985, pp. 209–42.

Baldone, Salvatore. Durable Capital Inputs: Conditions for Prices Ratios to Be Invariant to Profit-Rate Changes: A Comment. *Z. Nationalökon.*, 1985, *45*(4), pp. 409–20.

Barrados, John P. Conceptualization of Behavior in the Traditional Neoclassical General Price Theory. *Atlantic Econ. J.*, July 1985, *13*(2), pp. 81.

Beato, Paulina and Mas-Colell, Andreu. On Marginal Cost Pricing with Given Tax-Subsidy Rules. *J. Econ. Theory*, December 1985, *37*(2), pp. 356–65.

Benhabib, Jess and Nishimura, Kazuo. Competitive Equilibrium Cycles. *J. Econ. Theory*, April 1985, *35*(2), pp. 284–306.

Bergstrom, Theodore C. and Varian, Hal R. When Do Market Games Have Transferable Utility? *J. Econ. Theory*, April 1985, *35*(2), pp. 222–33.

Berliant, Marcus. An Equilibrium Existence Result for an Economy with Land. *J. Math. Econ.*, 1985, *14*(1), pp. 53–56.

Bigelow, John P. Experts against Adverse Selection: A Note on the Existence of Equilibrium with Costly Appropriable Information. *J. Econ. Theory*, December 1985, *37*(2), pp. 379–93.

Boggio, L. On the Stability of Production Prices. *Metroecon.*, October 1985, *37*(3), pp. 241–67.

Boyer, Marcel and Moreaux, Michel. La convergence d'équilibres stratégiques en prix-quantités vers l'équilibre concurrentiel. (Convergence of Prices–Quantity Strategic Equilibria towards Competitive Equilibrium. With English summary.) *L'Actual. Econ.*, December 1985, *61*(4), pp. 411–27.

Brown, Donald J. and Heal, Geoffrey M. The Optimality of Regulated Pricing: A General Equilibrium Analysis. In *Aliprantis, C. D.; Burkinshaw, O. and Rothman, N. J., eds.*, 1985, pp. 43–54.

Coles, Jeffrey Link. Equilibrium Turnpike Theory with Constant Returns to Scale and Possible Heterogeneous Discount Factors. *Int. Econ. Rev.*, October 1985, *26*(3), pp. 671–79.

Cooper, Russel J.; McLaren, Keith R. and Powell, Alan A. Short-run Macroeconomic Closure in Applied General Equilbrium Modelling: Experience from ORANI and Agenda for Further Research. In *Piggott, J. and Whalley, J., eds.*, 1985, pp. 411–40. [G: Australia]

Costa, Giacomo. Time in Ricardian Models: Some Critical Observations and Some New Results. In *Caravale, G. A., ed.*, 1985, pp. 59–83.

Cox, John C.; Ingersoll, Jonathan E., Jr. and Ross, Stephen A. An Intertemporal General Equilibrium Model of Asset Prices. *Econometrica*, March 1985, *53*(2), pp. 363–84.

van Daal, J.; Henderiks, R. E. D. and Vorst, A. C. F. On Walras' Model of General Economic Equilibrium. *Z. Nationalökon.*, 1985, *45*(3), pp. 219–44.

DasGupta, Swapan. A Local Analysis of Stability and Regularity of Stationary States in Discrete Symmetric Optimal Capital Accumulation Models. *J. Econ. Theory*, August 1985, *36*(2), pp. 302–18.

Dehez, Pierre. Monopolistic Equilibrium and Involuntary Unemployment. *J. Econ. Theory*, June 1985, *36*(1), pp. 160–65.

Dierker, Egbert; Guesnerie, Roger and Neuefeind, Wilhelm. General Equilibrium When Some Firms Follow Special Pricing Rules. *Econometrica*, November 1985, *53*(6), pp. 1369–93.

Diewert, W. E. The Measurement of Waste and Welfare in Applied General Equilibrium Models. In *Piggott, J. and Whalley, J., eds.*, 1985, pp. 42–103.

Drèze, Jacques H. (Uncertainty and) the Firm in General Equilibrium Theory. *Econ. J.*, Supplement 1985, *95*, pp. 1–20.

Drèze, Jacques H. Labor Management and General Equilibrium. In *Jones, D. C. and Svejnar, J., eds.*, 1985, pp. 3–20.

Duffie, Darrell and Huang, Chi-fu. Implementing Arrow–Debreu Equilibria by Continuous Trading of Few Long-lived Securities. *Econometrica*, November 1985, *53*(6), pp. 1337–56.

Duffie, Darrell and Shafer, Wayne. Equilibrium in Incomplete Markets: I—A Basic Model of Generic Existence. *J. Math. Econ.*, 1985, *14*(3), pp. 285–300.

Dumitrescu, T. Some Aspects of Modelling the Economic Equilibrium. *Econ. Computat. Cybern. Stud. Res.*, 1985, *20*(1), pp. 15–22.

Dye, Ronald A. Costly Contract Contingencies. *Int. Econ. Rev.*, February 1985, *26*(1), pp. 233–50.

Eaves, B. Curtis. Finite Solution of Pure Trade Markets with Cobb-Douglas Utilities. In *Manne, A. S., ed.*, 1985, pp. 226–39.

Emmons, David W. and Scafuri, Allen J. Value Allocations: An Exposition. In *Aliprantis, C. D.; Burkinshaw, O. and Rothman, N. J., eds.*, 1985, pp. 55–78.

Emmons, David W. and Yannelis, Nicholas C. On Perfectly Competitive Economies: Loeb Economies. In *Aliprantis, C. D.; Burkinshaw, O. and Rothman, N. J., eds.*, 1985, pp. 145–72.

Esteban Marquillas, Joan M. Una caracterización del núcleo en economías de generaciones sucesivas. (With English summary.) *Revista Española Econ.*, 1985, *2*(1), pp. 3–17.

Fujimoto, Takao; Herrero, Carmen and Villar, Antonio. A Sensitivity Analysis in a Nonlinear Leontief Model. *Z. Nationalökon.*, 1985, *45*(1), pp. 67–71.

Gabszewicz, Jean Jaskold. Imperfect Competition in General Equilibrium: An Overview of Recent Work: Comment. In *Arrow, K. J. and Honkapohja, S., eds.*, 1985, pp. 150–69.

Ginsburgh, Victor; Papageorgiou, Yorgo and Thisse, Jacques-François. On Existence and Stability of Spatial Equilibria and Steady-States. *Reg. Sci. Urban Econ.*, June 1985, *15*(2), pp. 149–58.

Gretsky, Neil E. and Ostroy, Joseph M. Thick and Thin Market Nonatomic Exchange Economies. In *Aliprantis, C. D.; Burkinshaw, O. and Rothman, N. J., eds.*, 1985, pp. 107–29.

Guesnerie, Roger and Hart, Oliver D. Welfare Losses Due to Imperfect Competition: Asymptotic Results for Cournot Nash Equilibria with and without Free Entry. *Int. Econ. Rev.*, October 1985, *26*(3), pp. 525–45.

Hahn, Frank. Equilibrium with Transaction Costs. In *Hahn, F.*, 1985, pp. 75–104.

Hahn, Frank. Exercises in Conjectural Equilibria. In *Hahn, F.*, 1985, pp. 159–80.

Hahn, Frank. On the Stability of Pure Exchange Equilibrium. In *Hahn, F.*, 1985, pp. 192–201.

Hahn, Frank. On Equilibrium with Market-Dependent Information. In *Hahn, F.*, 1985, pp. 377–87.

Hahn, Frank. On Non-Walrasian Equilibria. In *Hahn, F.*, 1985, pp. 131–58.

Hahn, Frank. On Some Propositions of General Equilibrium Analysis. In *Hahn, F.*, 1985, pp. 183–91.

Hahn, Frank. On Transaction Costs, Inessential Sequence Economies and Money. In *Hahn, F.*, 1985, pp. 105–27.

Hahn, Frank. The General Equilibrium Theory of Money: A Comment. In *Hahn, F.*, 1985, pp. 46–55.

Hahn, Frank. The Rate of Interest and General Equilibrium Analysis. In *Hahn, F.*, 1985, pp. 56–74.

Hahn, Frank and Negishi, Takashi. A Theorem on Non-tâtonnement Stability. In *Hahn, F.*, 1985, pp. 202–09.

Hahn, Frank H. Fix-Price Models: A Survey of Recent Empirical Work: Comment. In *Arrow, K. J. and Honkapohja, S., eds.*, 1985, pp. 368–78.

Hands, Douglas W. The Structuralist View of Economic Theories: A Review Essay: The Case of General Equilibrium in Particular. *Econ. Philos.*, October 1985, *1*(2), pp. 303–35.

Harris, Christopher J. Existence and Characterization of Perfect Equilibrium in Games of Perfect Information. *Econometrica*, May 1985, *53*(3), pp. 613–28.

Harris, Curtis C., Jr. and Nadji, Mehrzad. The Spatial Content of the Arrow–Debreu General Equilibrium System. *J. Reg. Sci.*, February 1985, *25*(1), pp. 1–10.

Harris, Milton and Townsend, Robert M. Allocation Mechanisms, Asymmetric Information and the 'Revelation Principle.' In *Feiwel, G. R., ed. (II)*, 1985, pp. 379–94.

Hart, Oliver D. Imperfect Competition in General Equilibrium: An Overview of Recent Work. In *Arrow, K. J. and Honkapohja, S., eds.*, 1985, pp. 100–149.

Hirota, Masayoshi. Global Stability in a Class of Markets with Three Commodities and Three Consumers. *J. Econ. Theory*, June 1985, *36*(1), pp. 186–92.

Hosoda, Eiji. On the Classical Convergence Theorem. *Metroecon.*, June 1985, *37*(2), pp. 157–74.

Huang, Chi-fu. Information Structure and Equilibrium Asset Prices. *J. Econ. Theory*, February 1985, *35*(1), pp. 33–71.

Hurwicz, Leonid. Information and Incentives in Designing Non-wasteful Resource Allocation Systems. In *Feiwel, G. R., ed. (II)*, 1985, pp. 125–68.

Ichiishi, Tatsuro. Management versus Ownership, II. *Europ. Econ. Rev.*, March 1985, *27*(2), pp. 115–38.

James, John A. New Developments in the Application of General Equilibrium Models to Economic History. In *Piggott, J. and Whalley, J., eds.*, 1985, pp. 441–65.

John, Reinhard. A Remark on Conjectural Equilibria. *Scand. J. Econ.*, 1985, *87*(1), pp. 137–41.

John, Reinhard and Ryder, Harl E. On the Second Optimality Theorem of Welfare Economics. *J. Econ. Theory*, June 1985, *36*(1), pp. 176–85.

Johnsen, Thore H. and Donaldson, John B. The Structure of Intertemporal Preferences under Uncertainty and Time Consistent Plans. *Econometrica*, November 1985, *53*(6), pp. 1451–58.

Jordan, J. S. Learning Rational Expectations: The Finite State Case. *J. Econ. Theory*, August 1985, *36*(2), pp. 257–76.

Kats, Amoz and Tauman, Yair. Coalition Production Economies with Divisible and Indivisible Inputs: Asymptotic Results. *J. Math. Econ.*, 1985, *14*(1), pp. 19–42.

Kehoe, Timothy J. A Numerical Investigation of Multiplicity of Equilibria. In *Manne, A. S., ed.*, 1985 , pp. 240–58.

Kehoe, Timothy J. Multiplicity of Equilibria and Comparative Statics. *Quart. J. Econ.*, February 1985, *100*(1), pp. 119–47.

Kehoe, Timothy J. The Comparative Statics Properties of Tax Models. *Can. J. Econ.*, May 1985, *18*(2), pp. 314–34.

Kehoe, Timothy J. and Levine, David K. Comparative Statics and Perfect Foresight in Infinite Horizon Economies. *Econometrica*, March 1985, *53*(2), pp. 433–53.

Keiding, Hans. On the Existence of Equilibrium in Social Systems with Coordination. *J. Math. Econ.*, 1985, *14*(2), pp. 105–11.

Kennan, Donald and Rader, Trout. Market Dynamics and the Law of Demand. *Econometrica*, March 1985, *53*(2), pp. 465–71.

Khan, M. Ali. On Extensions of the Cournot–Nash Theorem. In *Aliprantis, C. D.; Burkinshaw, O. and Rothman, N. J., eds.*, 1985, pp. 79–106.

Khan, M. Ali and Vohra, Rajiv. On the Existence of Lindahl Equilibria in Economies with a Measure Space of Non-transitive Consumers. *J. Econ. Theory*, August 1985, *36*(2), pp. 319–32.

Kirman, Alan P. Organisation et communication dans les marchés. (Organization and Communication in Markets. With English summary.) *Écon. Appl.*, 1985, *38*(3/4), pp. 597–609.

Koopmans, Tjalling C. Concepts of Optimality and Their Uses. In *Koopmans, T. C.*, 1985, pp. 191–208.

Koopmans, Tjalling C. Is the Theory of Competitive Equilibrium with It? In *Koopmans, T. C.*, 1985, pp. 181–85.

Kornai, János. Fix-Price Models: A Survey of Recent Empirical Work: Comment. In *Arrow, K. J. and Honkapohja, S., eds.*, 1985, pp. 379–90.

van der Laan, Gerard. The Computation of General Equilibrium in Economies with a Block Diagonal Pattern. *Econometrica*, May 1985, *53*(3), pp. 658–65.

Laffont, Jean-Jacques. Fix-Price Models: A Survey of Recent Empirical Work. In *Arrow,*

K. J. and Honkapohja, S., eds., 1985, pp. 328–67.

Laffont, Jean-Jacques. Incitations dans les procédures de planification. (Incentives in Planning Procedures. With English summary.) *Ann. INSEE*, Apr.-June 1985, (58), pp. 3–37.

Laffont, Jean-Jacques. On the Welfare Analysis of Rational Expectations Equilibria with Asymmetric Information. *Econometrica*, January 1985, *53*(1), pp. 1–29.

Laitner, John P. Stationary Equilibrium Transition Rules for an Overlapping Generations Model with Uncertainty. *J. Econ. Theory*, February 1985, *35*(1), pp. 83–108.

Madden, Paul. Uniqueness of Non-Walrasian Equilibrium in the Macroeconomic Model with Decreasing or Increasing Returns. *Rev. Econ. Stud.*, October 1985, *52*(4), pp. 703–13.

Mäler, Karl-Göran. Welfare Economics and the Environment. In *Kneese, A. V. and Sweeney, J. L., eds. Vol. 1*, 1985, pp. 3–60.

Mas-Colell, Andreu. Pareto Optima and Equilibria: The Finite Dimensional Case. In *Aliprantis, C. D.; Burkinshaw, O. and Rothman, N. J., eds.*, 1985, pp. 25–42.

Mehra, Rajnish and Prescott, Edward C. The Equity Premium: A Puzzle. *J. Monet. Econ.*, March 1985, *15*(2), pp. 145–61.

Mendelson, Haim. Random Competitive Exchange: Price Distributions and Gain from Trade. *J. Econ. Theory*, December 1985, *37*(2), pp. 254–80.

Moussa, Hassouna and Murota, Takeshi. Social Value of Public Information Re-examined. *J. Econ. Behav. Organ.*, September 1985, *6*(3), pp. 249–74.

Nguyen, Trien T. General Equilbrium with Price Rigidities. In *Piggott, J. and Whalley, J., eds.*, 1985, pp. 396–410.

Nicola, Pier Carlo. Sulla introduzione di unamoneta nell'equilibrio generale. (With English summary.) *Econ. Polít.*, April 1985, *2*(1), pp. 11–30.

al-Nowaihi, A. and Levine, Paul. The Stability of the Cournot Oligopoly Model: A Reassessment. *J. Econ. Theory*, April 1985, *35*(2), pp. 307–21.

Okuda, Hidesuke and Shitovitz, Benyamin. Core Allocations and the Dimension of the Cone of Efficiency Price Vectors. *J. Econ. Theory*, February 1985, *35*(1), pp. 166–71.

Pagan, Adrian R. and Shannon, John H. Sensitivity Analysis for Linearized Computable General Equilibrium Models. In *Piggott, J. and Whalley, J., eds.*, 1985, pp. 104–18.

Piggott, John R. New Developments in Applied General Equilibrium Analysis: Introduction. In *Piggott, J. and Whalley, J., eds.*, 1985, pp. 1–24.

ten Raa, Thijs and Berliant, Marcus. General Competitive Equilibrium of the Spatial Economy: Two Teasers. *Reg. Sci. Urban Econ.*, November 1985, *15*(4), pp. 585–90.

Rashid, Salim. Envy Stimulates Competition. *Econ. Notes*, 1985, (2), pp. 171–74.

Rashid, Salim. Nonstandard Analysis and Infinite

Economies: The Cournot–Nash Solution. **In** *Aliprantis, C. D.; Burkinshaw, O. and Rothman, N. J., eds.,* 1985, pp. 173–84.

Robinson, Clark and Suchanek, Gerry L. On the Design of Optimal Mechanisms for the Arrow–Hahn–McKenzie Economy. *Public Choice,* 1985, *47*(2), pp. 313–35.

Rust, John. Stationary Equilibrium in a Market for Durable Assets. *Econometrica,* July 1985, *53*(4), pp. 783–805.

Safra, Zvi. Existence of Equilibrium for Walrasian Endowment Games. *J. Econ. Theory,* December 1985, *37*(2), pp. 366–78.

Sancho, Ferran. Propiedades del núcleo en economías estocásticas. (With English summary.) *Revista Española Econ.,* 1985, *2*(1), pp. 19–34.

Silvestre, Joaquim. Voluntary and Efficient Allocations Are Walrasian. *Econometrica,* July 1985, *53*(4), pp. 807–16.

Simonovits, András. Dynamic Adjustment of Supply under Buyers' Forced Substitution. *Z. Nationalökon.,* 1985, *45*(4), pp. 357–72.

Sonnenschein, Hugo. Imperfect Competition in General Equilibrium: An Overview of Recent Work: Comment. **In** *Arrow, K. J. and Honkapohja, S., eds.,* 1985, pp. 170–77.

Spear, Stephen E. Rational Expectations in the Overlapping Generations Model. *J. Econ. Theory,* April 1985, *35*(2), pp. 251–75.

Srivastava, Sanjay. Pure Strategy Nash Equilibria with Continuous Objectives. *J. Econ. Theory,* June 1985, *36*(1), pp. 26–35.

Stacchetti, Ennio. Analysis of a Dynamic, Decentralized Exchange Economy *J. Math. Econ.,* 1985, *14*(3), pp. 241–59.

Stahl, Dale O., II. Relaxing the Sure-Solvency Conditions in Temporary Equilibrium Models. *J. Econ. Theory,* October 1985, *37*(1), pp. 1–18.

Stahl, Dale O., II and Alexeev, Michael. The Influence of Black Markets on a Queue-rationed Centrally Planned Economy. *J. Econ. Theory,* April 1985, *35*(2), pp. 234–50.

Stephan, Gunter. Competitive Finite Value Prices: A Complete Characterization. *Z. Nationalökon.,* 1985, *45*(1), pp. 35–45.

Tillmann, Georg. Existence and Stability of Rational Expectation-Equilibria in a Simple Overlapping Generation Model. *J. Econ. Theory,* August 1985, *36*(2), pp. 333–51.

Tobin, Roger L. General Spatial Price Equilibria: Sensitivity Analysis for Variational Inequality and Nonlinear Complementarity Formulations. **In** *Harker, P. T., ed.,* 1985, pp. 158–95.

Trujillo, José A. Rational Responses and Rational Conjectures. *J. Econ. Theory,* August 1985, *36*(2), pp. 289–301.

Weintraub, E. Roy. Appraising General Equilibrium Analysis. *Econ. Philos.,* April 1985, *1*(1), pp. 23–37.

Weintraub, E. Roy. Joan Robinson's Critique of Equilibrium: An Appraisal. *Amer. Econ. Rev.,* May 1985, *75*(2), pp. 146–49.

Werner, Jan. Equilibrium in Economies with In-complete Financial Markets. *J. Econ. Theory,* June 1985, *36*(1), pp. 110–19.

Whalley, John. Hidden Challenges in Recent Applied General Equilibrium Exercises. **In** *Piggott, J. and Whalley, J., eds.,* 1985, pp. 25–41.

Whalley, John and White, Philip M. A Decomposition Algorithm for General Equilibrium Computation with Application to International Trade Models: A Correction. *Econometrica,* May 1985, *53*(3), pp. 679.

Wiegard, Wolfgang. Die Algorithmen von Scarf und Merrill zur numerischen Berechnung allgemeiner Gleichgewichte. Eine Einführung mit Beispielen aus der Steuerpolitik. (With English summary.) *Z. Wirtschaft. Sozialwissen.,* 1985, *105*(6), pp. 709–41.

Wilson, Robert B. Efficient Trading. **In** *Feiwel, G. R., ed. (II),* 1985, pp. 169–208.

Wolfstetter, Elmar. Optimale Arbeitsverträge bei asymmetrischer Information: Ein Beitrag zur Theorie der Arbeitslosigkeit. (With English summary.) *Z. Wirtschaft. Sozialwissen.,* 1985, *105*(4), pp. 433–58.

Yannelis, Nicholas C. Value and Fairness. **In** *Aliprantis, C. D.; Burkinshaw, O. and Rothman, N. J., eds.,* 1985, pp. 205–35.

022 Microeconomic Theory

0220 General

Adler, Moshe. Stardom and Talent. *Amer. Econ. Rev.,* March 1985, *75*(1), pp. 208–12.

Akerlof, George A. and Yellen, Janet L. Can Small Deviations from Rationality Make Significant Differences to Economic Equilibria? *Amer. Econ. Rev.,* September 1985, *75*(4), pp. 708–20.

Allen, Beth. The Existence of Fully Rational Expectations Approximate Equilibria with Noisy Price Observations. *J. Econ. Theory,* December 1985, *37*(2), pp. 213–53.

Anderson, Robert M. and Sonnenschein, Hugo. Rational Expectations Equilibrium with Econometric Models. *Rev. Econ. Stud.,* July 1985, *52*(3), pp. 359–69.

Arrow, Kenneth J.; Levhari, David and Sheshinski, Eytan. A Production Function for the Repairman Problem. **In** *Arrow, K. J. (I),* 1985, pp. 443–55.

Aubin, Jean-Pierre and Frankowska, Halina. Heavy Viable Trajectories of Controlled Systems. **In** *Aubin, J.-P.; Saari, D. and Sigmund, K., eds.,* 1985, pp. 148–67.

Aumann, Robert J. and Maschler, Michael. Game Theoretic Analysis of a Bancruptcy Problem from the Talmud. *J. Econ. Theory,* August 1985, *36*(2), pp. 195–213.   **[G: Israel]**

d'Autume, Antoine. Prix, taux de profit et étalons. (With English summary.) *Revue Écon. Polit.,* January–February 1985, *95*(1), pp. 27–50.

Barrados, John P. Conceptualization of Behavior in the Traditional Neoclassical General Price Theory. *Atlantic Econ. J.,* July 1985, *13*(2), pp. 81.

Barzel, Yoram. Transaction Costs: Are They Just Costs? *Z. ges. Staatswiss. (JITE)*, March 1985, *141*(1), pp. 4–16.

Benhabib, Jess and Nishimura, Kazuo. Competitive Equilibrium Cycles. *J. Econ. Theory*, April 1985, *35*(2), pp. 284–306.

Benson, Bruce L. Free Market Congestion Tolls: A Correction [Spatial Price Theory and an Efficient Congestion Toll Established by the Free Market]. *Econ. Inquiry*, April 1985, *23*(2), pp. 361–62.

Bhagwati, Jagdish N. Splintering and Disembodiment of Services and Developing Nations. In *Bhagwati, J. N. (II)*, 1985, pp. 92–103.
[G: LDCs; U.S.; U.K.]

Boggio, L. On the Stability of Production Prices. *Metroecon.*, October 1985, *37*(3), pp. 241–67.

Bray, Margaret. Rational Expectations, Information and Asset Markets: An Introduction. *Oxford Econ. Pap.*, June 1985, *37*(2), pp. 161–95.

Burt, Robert A. Enforcing Rules on Oneself: Commentary. *J. Law, Econ., Organ.*, Fall 1985, *1*(2), pp. 381–83.

Campbell, Richmond. Paradoxes of Rationality and Cooperation: Prisoner's Dilemma and Newcomb's Problem: Background for the Uninitiated. In *Campbell, R. and Sowden, L., eds.*, 1985, pp. 3–41.

Carter, Michael R. A Wisconsin Institutionalist Perspective on Microeconomic Theory of Institutions: The Insufficiency of Pareto Efficiency. *J. Econ. Issues*, September 1985, *19*(3), pp. 797–813.

Chateauneuf, Alain. On the Existence of a Probability Measure Compatible with a Total Preorder on a Boolean Algebra. *J. Math. Econ.*, 1985, *14*(1), pp. 43–52.

Corchón, Luis. Economía neoclásica: conceptos y avances recientes. (With English summary.) *Revista Española Econ.*, 1985, *2*(1), pp. 153–63.

D'Agata, Antonio. Produzione congiunta e ordine de fertilità: una nota. (With English summary.) *Econ. Polít.*, August 1985, *2*(2), pp. 245–48.

Davis, Lawrence H. Is the Symmetry Argument Valid? In *Campbell, R. and Sowden, L., eds.*, 1985, pp. 255–63.

Davis, Lawrence H. Prisoners, Paradox, and Rationality. In *Campbell, R. and Sowden, L., eds.*, 1985, pp. 45–59.

Dooley, Peter C. Alfred Marshall: Fitting the Theory to the Facts. *Cambridge J. Econ.*, September 1985, *9*(3), pp. 245–55.

Dow, Sheila C. Microfoundations: A Diversity of Treatments. *Eastern Econ. J.*, Oct.-Dec. 1985, *11*(4), pp. 342–60.

Dye, Ronald A. Costly Contract Contingencies. *Int. Econ. Rev.*, February 1985, *26*(1), pp. 233–50.

Eells, Ellery. Causality, Decision, and Newcomb's Paradox. In *Campbell, R. and Sowden, L., eds.*, 1985, pp. 183–213.

Feiwel, George R. Some Perceptions and Tensions in Microeconomics: A Background. In *Feiwel, G. R., ed. (II)*, 1985, pp. 1–104.

Frey, Bruno S. Transaction Costs: Are They Just Costs? Comment. *Z. ges. Staatswiss. (JITE)*, March 1985, *141*(1), pp. 17–20.

Friedman, Daniel. Experimental Economics: Comment. *Amer. Econ. Rev.*, March 1985, *75*(1), pp. 264.

Gauthier, David. Maximization Constrained: The Rationality of Cooperation. In *Campbell, R. and Sowden, L., eds.*, 1985, pp. 75–93.

Gibbard, Allan and Harper, William L. Counterfactuals and Two Kinds of Expected Utility. In *Campbell, R. and Sowden, L., eds.*, 1985, pp. 133–58.

Gottfries, Nils. Multiple Perfect Foresight Equilibriums and Convergence of Learning Processes. *J. Money, Credit, Banking*, February 1985, *17*(1), pp. 111–17.

Gourieroux, Christian and Laroque, Guy. The Aggregation of Commodities in Quantity Rationing Models. *Int. Econ. Rev.*, October 1985, *26*(3), pp. 681–99.

Hänchen, Thomas and von Ungern-Sternberg, Thomas. Information Costs, Intermediation and Equilibrium Price. *Economica*, November 1985, *52*(208), pp. 407–19.

Hardin, Russell. Individual Sanctions, Collective Benefits. In *Campbell, R. and Sowden, L., eds.*, 1985, pp. 339–54.

Harris, Christopher J. A Characterisation of the Perfect Equilibria of Infinite Horizon Games. *J. Econ. Theory*, October 1985, *37*(1), pp. 99–125.

Harsanyi, John C. Rule Utilitarianism, Equality, and Justice. In *Paul, E. F.; Paul, J. and Miller, F. D., Jr., eds.*, 1985, pp. 115–27.

Heiner, Ronald A. Experimental Economics: Comment. *Amer. Econ. Rev.*, March 1985, *75*(1), pp. 260–63.

Herriott, Scott R.; Levinthal, Daniel and March, James G. Learning from Experience in Organizations. *Amer. Econ. Rev.*, May 1985, *75*(2), pp. 298–302.

Hochman, Harold M. and Nitzan, Shmuel. Concepts of Extended Preference. *J. Econ. Behav. Organ.*, June 1985, *6*(2), pp. 161–76.

Horgan, Terence. Counterfactuals and Newcomb's Problem. In *Campbell, R. and Sowden, L., eds.*, 1985, pp. 159–82.

Horgan, Terence. Newcomb's Problem: A Stalemate. In *Campbell, R. and Sowden, L., eds.*, 1985, pp. 223–34.

Hosoda, Eiji. On the Classical Convergence Theorem. *Metroecon.*, June 1985, *37*(2), pp. 157–74.

Huang, Chi-fu. Information Structures and Viable Price Systems. *J. Math. Econ.*, 1985, *14*(3), pp. 215–40.

Hurwicz, Leonid. Information and Incentives in Designing Non-wasteful Resource Allocation Systems. In *Feiwel, G. R., ed. (II)*, 1985, pp. 125–68.

Iverson, G. and Falmagne, J.-C. Statistical Issues in Measurement. *Math. Soc. Sci.*, October 1985, *10*(2), pp. 131–53.

Jackson, Frank and Pargetter, Robert. Where the Tickle Defense Goes Wrong. In *Campbell,*

R. and Sowden, L., eds., 1985, pp. 214–19.

Jordan, J. S. Learning Rational Expectations: The Finite State Case. *J. Econ. Theory*, August 1985, *36*(2), pp. 257–76.

Kanbur, S. M. R. Corrigendum [Increases in Risk with Kinked Payoff Functions]. *J. Econ. Theory*, April 1985, *35*(2), pp. 399.

Karni, Edi. Increasing Risk with State-Dependent Preferences. *J. Econ. Theory*, February 1985, *35*(1), pp. 172–77.

Katz, Michael L. and Shapiro, Carl. Network Externalities, Competition, and Compatibility. *Amer. Econ. Rev.*, June 1985, *75*(3), pp. 424–40.

Knez, Peter; Smith, Vernon L. and Williams, Arlington W. Individual Rationality, Market Rationality, and Value Estimation. *Amer. Econ. Rev.*, May 1985, *75*(2), pp. 397–402.

Krouse, Clement G. Competition and Unanimity Revisited, Again. *Amer. Econ. Rev.*, December 1985, *75*(5), pp. 1109–14.

Laffont, Jean-Jacques. On the Welfare Analysis of Rational Expectations Equilibria with Asymmetric Information. *Econometrica*, January 1985, *53*(1), pp. 1–29.

Lambert, David K. and McCarl, Bruce A. Risk Modeling Using Direct Solution of Nonlinear Approximations of the Utility Function. *Amer. J. Agr. Econ.*, November 1985, *67*(4), pp. 846–52.

Leininger, Wolfgang. Rawls' Maximin Criterion and Time-Consistency: Further Results. *Rev. Econ. Stud.*, July 1985, *52*(3), pp. 505–13.

Leonard, Herman B. and Zeckhauser, Richard J. Financial Risk and the Burden of Contracts. *Amer. Econ. Rev.*, May 1985, *75*(2), pp. 375–80.

Leontief, Wassily. Introduction to a Theory of the Internal Structure of Functional Relationships. In *Leontief, W.*, 1985, pp. 151–65.

Levine, A. Lawrence. Sraffa's *Production of Commodities by Means of Commodities*, Returns to Scale, Relevance, and Other Matters: A Note. *J. Post Keynesian Econ.*, Spring 1985, *7*(3), pp. 342–49.

Lewis, Alain A. The Minimum Degree of Recursively Representable Choice Functions. *Math. Soc. Sci.*, October 1985, *10*(2), pp. 179–88.

Lewis, David. Prisoners' Dilemma Is a Newcomb Problem. In *Campbell, R. and Sowden, L., eds.*, 1985, pp. 251–55.

Matsuyama, Kiminori. Chernoff's Dual Axiom, Revealed Preference, and Weak Rational Choice Functions. *J. Econ. Theory*, February 1985, *35*(1), pp. 155–65.

Matthews, Steven and Postlewaite, Andrew. Quality Testing and Disclosure. *Rand J. Econ.*, Autumn 1985, *16*(3), pp. 328–40.

McClennen, Edward F. Prisoner's Dilemma and Resolute Choice. In *Campbell, R. and Sowden, L., eds.*, 1985, pp. 94–104.

Meyer, Jack and Ormiston, Michael B. Strong Increases in Risk and Their Comparative Statics. *Int. Econ. Rev.*, June 1985, *26*(2), pp. 425–37.

Moran, R. Allen. Queues: The Economic Theory of Screening and Human Service Productivity. *Southern Econ. J.*, October 1985, *52*(2), pp. 492–99.   [G: U.S.]

Nozick, Robert. Newcomb's Problem and Two Principles of Choice. In *Campbell, R. and Sowden, L., eds.*, 1985, pp. 107–33.

Osborne, Martin J. The Role of Risk Aversion in a Simple Bargaining Model. In *Roth, A. E., ed.*, 1985, pp. 181–213.

Papageorgiou, Yorgo and Thisse, Jacques-François. Agglomeration as Spatial Interdependence between Firms and Households. *J. Econ. Theory*, October 1985, *37*(1), pp. 19–31.

Ranade, Ravindra R. Rationalisable Choice Functions: An Alternative Characterisation. *J. Quant. Econ.*, July 1985, *1*(2), pp. 265–72.

Riordan, Michael H. and Williamson, Oliver E. Asset Specificity and Economic Organization. *Int. J. Ind. Organ.*, December 1985, *3*(4), pp. 365–78.

Roemer, John E. Equality of Talent. *Econ. Philos.*, October 1985, *1*(2), pp. 151–88.

Roth, Alvin E. The College Admissions Problem Is Not Equivalent to the Marriage Problem. *J. Econ. Theory*, August 1985, *36*(2), pp. 277–88.

Runde, J. H. and Torr, C. S. W. Divergent Expectations and Rational Expectations. *S. Afr. J. Econ.*, September 1985, *53*(3), pp. 217–25.

Ryder, Harl E. Heterogeneous Time Preferences and the Distribution of Wealth. *Math. Soc. Sci.*, February 1985, *9*(1), pp. 63–76.

Saari, Donald G. The Representation Problem and the Efficiency of the Price Mechanism. *J. Math. Econ.*, 1985, *14*(2), pp. 135–67.

Schefold, Bertram. Cambridge Price Theory: Special Model or General Theory of Value? *Amer. Econ. Rev.*, May 1985, *75*(2), pp. 140–45.

Schelling, Thomas C. Enforcing Rules on Oneself. *J. Law, Econ., Organ.*, Fall 1985, *1*(2), pp. 357–74.

Schultze, Charles L. Microeconomic Efficiency and Nominal Wage Stickiness. *Amer. Econ. Rev.*, March 1985, *75*(1), pp. 1–15.

Scitovsky, Tibor. Pricetakers' Plenty: A Neglected Benefit of Capitalism. *Kyklos*, 1985, *38*(4), pp. 517–36.

Sen, Amartya. Goals, Commitment, and Identity. *J. Law, Econ., Organ.*, Fall 1985, *1*(2), pp. 341–55.

Seton, Francis. Corrigendum [A Quasi-competitive Price Basis for Intersystem Comparisons of Economic Structure and Performance]. *J. Compar. Econ.*, March 1985, *9*(1), pp. 123.   [G: Kenya; U.S.S.R.; Japan; U.K.; U.S.]

Smith, V. Kerry. Supply Uncertainty, Option Price, and Indirect Benefit Estimation. *Land Econ.*, August 1985, *61*(3), pp. 303–07.

Smith, Vernon L. Experimental Economics: Reply. *Amer. Econ. Rev.*, March 1985, *75*(1), pp. 264–72.

Sobel, Jordan Howard. Not Every Prisoner's Dilemma Is a Newcomb Problem. In *Campbell, R. and Sowden, L., eds.*, 1985, pp. 263–74.

Sobel, Jordan Howard. Utility Maximizers in Iterated Prisoner's Dilemmas. In *Campbell, R. and Sowden, L., eds.*, 1985, pp. 306–19.

Stahl, Dale O., II. Bankruptcies in Temporary Equilibrium Forward Markets with and without Institutional Restrictions. *Rev. Econ. Stud.*, July 1985, 52(3), pp. 459–71.

Stahl, Konrad. Existence of Equilibria in Spatial Economies: Presentation. *Reg. Sci. Urban Econ.*, June 1985, 15(2), pp. 143–47.

Stephan, Gunter. Competitive Finite Value Prices: A Complete Characterization. *Z. Nationalökon.*, 1985, 45(1), pp. 35–45.

Sugden, Robert. Why Be Consistent? A Critical Analysis of Consistency Requirements in Choice Theory. *Economica*, May 1985, 52(206), pp. 167–83.

Tillmann, Georg. Existence and Stability of Rational Expectation-Equilibria in a Simple Overlapping Generation Model. *J. Econ. Theory*, August 1985, 36(2), pp. 333–51.

Trujillo, José A. Rational Responses and Rational Conjectures. *J. Econ. Theory*, August 1985, 36(2), pp. 289–301.

Viscusi, W. Kip. Are Individuals Bayesian Decision Makers? *Amer. Econ. Rev.*, May 1985, 75(2), pp. 381–85.

Wilde, Keith D.; LeBaron, Allen D. and Israelsen, L. Dwight. Knowledge, Uncertainty, and Behavior. *Amer. Econ. Rev.*, May 1985, 75(2), pp. 403–08.

Winston, Gordon C. The Reasons for Being of Two Minds: A Comment [Enforcing Rules on Oneself]. *J. Law, Econ., Organ.*, Fall 1985, 1(2), pp. 375–79.

Woods, John Edward. Exercises in Relative Price Variance. *Giorn. Econ.*, Mar.-Apr. 1985, 44(3–4), pp. 135–52.

0222 Theory of the Household (consumer demand)

Abel, Andrew B. Precautionary Saving and Accidental Bequests. *Amer. Econ. Rev.*, September 1985, 75(4), pp. 777–91. **[G: U.S.]**

Albanese, Paul J. Opening the Preferences: A Socio-Economic Research Agenda: Comments. *J. Behav. Econ.*, Winter 1985, 14, pp. 207–08.

Anderson, Gary M. and Brown, Pamela J. Heir Pollution: A Note on Buchanan's 'Laws of Succession' and Tullock's 'Blind Spot.' *Int. Rev. Law Econ.*, June 1985, 5(1), pp. 15–23.

Anderson, William A. Indivisibility, Irreversibility, and the Demand for Consumer Durables. *J. Macroecon.*, Summer 1985, 7(3), pp. 363–80.

Arrow, Kenneth J. and Kurz, Mordecai. Optimal Consumer Allocation over an Infinite Horizon. In *Arrow, K. J. (I)*, 1985, pp. 307–31.

Attfield, Clifford L. F. and Browning, Martin J. A Differential Demand System, Rational Expectations and the Life Cycle Hypothesis. *Econometrica*, January 1985, 53(1), pp. 31–48. **[G: U.K.]**

Balasko, Yves. Preferences, Price Expectations and Speculation. In *[Rossier, Edouard]*, 1985, pp. 1–16.

Barnett, William A. and Lee, Yul W. The Global Properties of the Miniflex Laurent, Generalized Leontief, and Translog Flexible Functional Forms. *Econometrica*, November 1985, 53(6), pp. 1421–37.

Basmann, R. L., et al. On Deviations between Neoclassical and GFT-Based True Cost-of-Living Indexes Derived from the Same Demand Function System. *J. Econometrics*, Oct./Nov. 1985, 30(1/2), pp. 45–66.

Basu, Kaushik. Poverty Measurement: A Decomposition of the Normalization Axion [Cardinal Utility, Utilitarianism and a Class of Invariance Axioms in Welfare Analysis] [Poverty: An Ordinal Approach to Measurement]. *Econometrica*, November 1985, 53(6), pp. 1439–43.

Bawa, Vijay S., et al. On Determination of Stochastic Dominance Optimal Sets. *J. Finance*, June 1985, 40(2), pp. 417–31.

Beals, Richard and Koopmans, Tjalling C. Maximizing Stationary Utility in a Constant Technology. In *Koopmans, T. C.*, 1985, pp. 13–27.

Benabou, Roland. Le modèle d'optimisation dynamique de la consommation et de l'offre de travail: un test sur données françaises. (The Model of Dynamic Optimisation on Consumption and Labour Supply: A Test on French Data. With English summary.) *Ann. INSEE*, Jan.-Mar. 1985, (57), pp. 75–97. **[G: France]**

Benjamini, Yael and Maital, Shlomo. Optimal Tax Evasion and Optimal Tax Evasion Policy: Behavioral Aspects. In *Gaertner, W. and Wenig, A., eds.*, 1985, pp. 245–64. **[G: Israel]**

Bennett, Jeff W. and Smith, Ben. The Estimation of Indifference Maps by Expected Utility Analysis. *Amer. J. Agr. Econ.*, November 1985, 67(4), pp. 833–38.

Bergman, Yaacov Z. Time Preference and Capital Asset Pricing Models. *J. Finan. Econ.*, March 1985, 14(1), pp. 145–59.

Bergstrom, Theodore C. and Varian, Hal R. When Do Market Games Have Transferable Utility? *J. Econ. Theory*, April 1985, 35(2), pp. 222–33.

Bernheim, B. Douglas; Shleifer, Andrei and Summers, Lawrence H. The Strategic Bequest Motive. *J. Polit. Econ.*, December 1985, 93(6), pp. 1045–76. **[G: U.S.]**

Bingen, Georges and Dewatripont, Mathias. Vérification empirique de la théorie du consommateur: quelques testes emboîtés et non emboîtés. (With English summary.) *Cah. Écon. Bruxelles*, 1st Trimester 1985, (105), pp. 3–40. **[G: Belgium]**

Blackorby, C. and Donaldson, D. Consumers' Surpluses and Consistent Cost–Benefit Tests. *Soc. Choice Welfare*, March 1985, 1(4), pp. 251–62.

Blinder, Alan S. and Rosen, Harvey S. Notches. *Amer. Econ. Rev.*, September 1985, 75(4), pp. 736–47.

Border, K. C. More on Harsanyi's Utilitarian Cardinal Welfare Theorem. *Soc. Choice Welfare*, March 1985, 1(4), pp. 279–81.

Bordley, Robert F. Relating Elasticities to

Changes in Demand. *J. Bus. Econ. Statist.*, April 1985, *3*(2), pp. 156–58.

Bridges, Douglas S. Representing Interval Orders by a Single Real-valued Function. *J. Econ. Theory*, June 1985, *36*(1), pp. 149–55.

Browning, Martin J.; Deaton, Angus and Irish, Margaret. A Profitable Approach to Labor Supply and Commodity Demands over the Life-Cycle. *Econometrica*, May 1985, *53*(3), pp. 503–43.   [G: U.K.]

Bucovetsky, S. Erratum: Price Dispersion and Stockpiling by Consumers. *Rev. Econ. Stud.*, January 1985, *52*(1), pp. 171.

Byrnes, Patrica; Grosskopf, Shawna and Hayes, Kathy J. How 'Exact' are Exact Measures of Welfare Loss? *Appl. Econ.*, December 1985, *17*(6), pp. 1071–81.   [G: U.S.]

Cheng, Leonard. Inverting Systems of Demand Functions. *J. Econ. Theory*, October 1985, *37*(1), pp. 202–10.

Chiappori, Pierre-André. Distribution of Income and the "Law of Demand." *Econometrica*, January 1985, *53*(1), pp. 109–27.
[G: Selected Countries]

Clark, Stephen A. A Complementary Approach to the Strong and Weak Axioms of Revealed Preference. *Econometrica*, November 1985, *53*(6), pp. 1459–63.

Clark, Stephen A. Consistent Choice under Uncertainty. *J. Math. Econ.*, 1985, *14*(2), pp. 169–85.

Cohn, Michael B. A Graphical Explanation of the Pareto Rate of Substitution as Mentioned by Hicks in *Value and Capital*. *Indian Econ. J.*, Apr.-June 1985, *32*(4), pp. 17–18.

Cooter, Robert D. and Rappoport, Peter. Reply to I. M. D. Little's Comment [Were the Ordinalists Wrong about Welfare Economics?]. *J. Econ. Lit.*, September 1985, *23*(3), pp. 1189–91.

Coursey, Don L. A Normative Model of Behavior Based upon an Activity Hierarchy. *J. Cons. Res.*, June 1985, *12*(1), pp. 64–73.

Cowell, Frank A. Public Policy and Tax Evasion: Some Problems. In *Gaertner, W. and Wenig, A., eds.*, 1985, pp. 273–84.

Danilov, V. I. The Structure of Binary Rules for Aggregating Preferences. *Matekon*, Summer 1985, *21*(4), pp. 44–65.

Deacon, Robert T. and Sonstelie, Jon. Rationing by Waiting and the Value of Time: Results from a Natural Experiment. *J. Polit. Econ.*, August 1985, *93*(4), pp. 627–47.   [G: U.S.]

Delforce, Robert J. and Hardaker, J. Brian. An Experiment in Multiattribute Utility Theory. *Australian J. Agr. Econ.*, December 1985, *29*(3), pp. 179–98.   [G: Australia]

DeSalvo, Joseph S. A Model of Urban Household Behavior with Leisure Choice. *J. Reg. Sci.*, May 1985, *25*(2), pp. 159–74.

Diewert, W. E. and Parkan, C. Tests for the Consistency of Consumer Data. *J. Econometrics*, Oct./Nov. 1985, *30*(1/2), pp. 127–47.

DiMasi, J. A. and Schap, David. The Appropriate Specification of Constant Elasticity Demand

Functions. *Soc. Choice Welfare*, September 1985, *2*(2), pp. 89–94.

Dooley, Peter C. Giffen's Hint? *Australian Econ. Pap.*, June 1985, *24*(44), pp. 201–05.

Dugger, William M. The Analytics of Consumption Externalities. *Rev. Soc. Econ.*, October 1985, *43*(2), pp. 212–33.

Ebert, U. On the Relationship between the Hicksian Measures of Change in Welfare and the Pareto Principle. *Soc. Choice Welfare*, March 1985, *1*(4), pp. 263–72.

Eckstein, Zvi; Eichenbaum, Martin S. and Peled, Dan. The Distribution of Wealth and Welfare in the Presence of Incomplete Annuity Markets. *Quart. J. Econ.*, August 1985, *100*(3), pp. 789–806.

Eells, Ellery. Where the Tickle Defense Goes Wrong: Reply. In *Campbell, R. and Sowden, L., eds.*, 1985, pp. 219–23.

Ekelund, Robert B., Jr. and Hébert, Robert F. Consumer Surplus: The First Hundred Years. *Hist. Polit. Econ.*, Fall 1985, *17*(3), pp. 419–54.

Epstein, Larry G. Decreasing Risk Aversion and Mean-Variance Analysis. *Econometrica*, July 1985, *53*(4), pp. 945–61.

Epstein, Larry G. and Yatchew, Adonis John. Non-parametric Hypothesis Testing Procedures and Applications to Demand Analysis. *J. Econometrics*, Oct./Nov. 1985, *30*(1/2), pp. 149–69.

Etzioni, Amitai. Opening the Preferences: A Socio-economic Research Agenda. *J. Behav. Econ.*, Winter 1985, *14*, pp. 183–205.

Fauvel, Yvon. Théorie du cycle de vie et rentes publiques. (Life Cycle Theory and Public Pension Plans. With English summary.) *L'Actual. Econ.*, June 1985, *61*(2), pp. 220–38.

Fishburn, Peter C. Nontransitive Preference Theory and the Preference Reversal Phenomenon. *Rivista Int. Sci. Econ. Com.*, January 1985, *32*(1), pp. 39–50.

Frank, Robert H. The Demand for Unobservable and Other Nonpositional Goods. *Amer. Econ. Rev.*, March 1985, *75*(1), pp. 101–16.
[G: U.S.]

Freeman, A. Myrick, III. Supply Uncertainty, Option Price, and Option Value. *Land Econ.*, May 1985, *61*(2), pp. 176–81.

Freeman, A. Myrick, III. The Sign and Size of Option Value: Reply. *Land Econ.*, February 1985, *61*(1), pp. 78.

Goering, Patricia A. Effects of Product Trial on Consumer Expectations, Demand, and Prices. *J. Cons. Res.*, June 1985, *12*(1), pp. 74–82.

Gowdy, John M. Utility Theory and Agrarian Societies. *Int. J. Soc. Econ.*, 1985, *12*(6/7), pp. 104–17.

Green, Richard C. and Srivastava, Sanjay. Risk Aversion and Arbitrage. *J. Finance*, March 1985, *40*(1), pp. 257–68.

Hahn, Frank. Savings and Uncertainty. In *Hahn, F.*, 1985, pp. 341–47.

Hansen, Gerd. Die Nachfrage nach nichtdauerhaften Gütern—Eine Schätzung anhand des "Almost-Ideal-Demand-System." (The Demand for Nondurables: An Example of the Al-

most-Ideal-Demand System. With English summary.) *Jahr. Nationalökon. Statist.*, January 1985, *200*(1), pp. 27–40.
[G: W. Germany]

Harris, Richard and Wildasin, David E. An Alternative Approach to Aggregate Surplus Analysis. *J. Public Econ.*, April 1985, *26*(3), pp. 289–302.

Hayashi, Fumio. The Effect of Liquidity Constraints on Consumption: A Cross-sectional Analysis. *Quart. J. Econ.*, February 1985, *100*(1), pp. 183–206.
[G: U.S.]

Hayashi, Fumio. The Permanent Income Hypothesis and Consumption Durability: Analysis Based on Japanese Panel Data. *Quart. J. Econ.*, November 1985, *100*(4), pp. 1083–1113.
[G: Japan]

Helms, L. Jay. Errors in the Numerical Assessment of the Benefits of Price Stabilization. *Amer. J. Agr. Econ.*, February 1985, *67*(1), pp. 93–100.

Helms, L. Jay. Expected Consumer's Surplus and the Welfare Effects of Price Stabilization. *Int. Econ. Rev.*, October 1985, *26*(3), pp. 603–17.

Holden, K. and Peel, D. A. Surprises in the Consumption Function, Incomplete Current Information, and Moving Average Errors: A Note [Stochastic Implications of the Life Cycle Permanent Income Hypothesis: Theory and Evidence]. *Econ. J.*, March 1985, *95*(377), pp. 183–88.
[G: U.K.]

Horowitz, Joel. Random Utility Travel Demand Models. In *Jansen, G. R. M.; Nijkamp, P. and Ruijgrok, C. J., eds.*, 1985, pp. 141–55.

Johnsen, Thore H. and Donaldson, John B. The Structure of Intertemporal Preferences under Uncertainty and Time Consistent Plans. *Econometrica*, November 1985, *53*(6), pp. 1451–58.

Johnson, Frederick I. The Imprecision of Traditional Welfare Measures in Empirical Applications. *Appl. Econ.*, October 1985, *17*(5), pp. 923–32.

Johnson, William R. The Economics of Copying. *J. Polit. Econ.*, February 1985, *93*(1), pp. 158–74.

Jones, H. G. Consumer Behaviour. In *Morris, D., ed.*, 1985, pp. 29–52.
[G: U.K.]

Kaempfer, William H. and Brastow, Raymond T. The Effect of Unit Fees on the Consumption of Quality. *Econ. Inquiry*, April 1985, *23*(2), pp. 341–48.

Kapteyn, Arie. Utility and Economics. *De Economist*, 1985, *133*(1), pp. 1–20.

Késenne, Stefan. Substitution in Consumption: A Reply. *Europ. Econ. Rev.*, April 1985, *27*(3), pp. 395–96.
[G: Belgium]

Kohli, Ulrich. Inverse Demand and Anti-Giffen Goods. *Europ. Econ. Rev.*, April 1985, *27*(3), pp. 397–404.

Koopmans, Tjalling C. Representation of Preference Orderings over Time. In *Koopmans, T. C.*, 1985, pp. 103–24.

Koopmans, Tjalling C. Representation of Preference Orderings with Independent Components of Consumption. In *Koopmans, T. C.*, 1985, pp. 81–102.

Kooreman, Peter. Substitution in Consumption; An Application to the Allocation of Time: A Comment. *Europ. Econ. Rev.*, April 1985, *27*(3), pp. 391–94.
[G: Belgium]

Koskela, Erkki and Virén, Matti. Consumption Function, Labour Supply Rationing and Borrowing Constraints. *Oxford Econ. Pap.*, September 1985, *37*(3), pp. 500–509.
[G: Finland]

Kunreuther, Howard; Sanderson, Warren and Vetschera, Rudolf. A Behavioral Model of the Adoption of Protective Activities. *J. Econ. Behav. Organ.*, March 1985, *6*(1), pp. 1–15.
[G: U.S.]

LaFrance, Jeffrey T. Linear Demand Functions in Theory and Practice. *J. Econ. Theory*, October 1985, *37*(1), pp. 147–66.

Lau, Laurence J. The Technology of Joint Consumption. In *Feiwel, G. R., ed. (II)*, 1985, pp. 484–504.

Leigh, J. Paul. Divorce as a Risky Prospect. *Appl. Econ.*, April 1985, *17*(2), pp. 309–20.
[G: U.S.]

Levine, David K. A Simple Durable Goods Model. *Quart. J. Econ.*, August 1985, *100*(3), pp. 775–88.

Lewbel, Arthur. A Unified Approach to Incorporating Demographic or Other Effects into Demand Systems. *Rev. Econ. Stud.*, January 1985, *52*(1), pp. 1–18.

Lewis, Barry L. and Bell, Jan. Decisions Involving Sequential Events: Replications and Extensions. *J. Acc. Res.*, Spring 1985, *23*(1), pp. 228–39.
[G: U.S.]

Little, Ian M. D. Were the Ordinalists Wrong about Welfare Economics? A Comment. *J. Econ. Lit.*, September 1985, *23*(3), pp. 1186–88.

Machina, Mark J. Stochastic Choice Functions Generated from Deterministic Preferences over Lotteries. *Econ. J.*, September 1985, *95*(379), pp. 575–94.

Maclean, Douglas. Rationality and Equivalent Redescriptions. In *Grauer, M.; Thompson, M. and Wierzbicki, A. P., eds.*, 1985, pp. 83–94.

Malakooti, B. A Nonlinear Multi-attribute Utility Theory. In *Haimes, Y. Y. and Chankong, V., eds.*, 1985, pp. 190–200.

Mehrez, Abraham and Gafni, Amiram. A Note on an Application of the Trade-off Method in Evaluating a Utility Function. *Managerial Dec. Econ.*, September 1985, *6*(3), pp. 191–92.

Monticelli, Carlo. Lo stock ottimale di beni di consumo durevoli in condizioni di incertezza. (The Optimal Stock of Consumer Durables under Uncertainty. With English summary.) *Ricerche Econ.*, July-Sept. 1985, *39*(3), pp. 357–77.

Moulin, Hervé. Choice Functions over a Finite Set: A Summary. *Soc. Choice Welfare*, September 1985, *2*(2), pp. 147–60.

Nairay, Alain. Recoverability of Uzawa Utility Functionals under Asset Price Lognormality.

J. Econ. Dynam. Control, October 1985, 9(2), pp. 241–50.

Nieswiadomy, Michael. A Technique for Comparing the Elasticities of Linear Demand and Supply Curves. *Atlantic Econ. J.*, December 1985, 13(4), pp. 68–70.

Nozick, Robert. Interpersonal Utility Theory. *Soc. Choice Welfare*, December 1985, 2(3), pp. 161–79.

Perloff, Jeffrey M. and Salop, Steven C. Equilibrium with Product Differentiation. *Rev. Econ. Stud.*, January 1985, 52(1), pp. 107–20.

Persky, A. L. An Inferior Good and a Novel Indifference Map. *Amer. Econ.*, Spring 1985, 29(1), pp. 67–69.

Plummer, Mark L. The Sign and Size of Option Value: Comment. *Land Econ.*, February 1985, 61(1), pp. 76–77.

Pollak, Robert A. A Transaction Cost Approach to Families and Households. *J. Econ. Lit.*, June 1985, 23(2), pp. 581–608.

Quirk, James. Consumer Surplus under Uncertainty: An Application to Dam–Reservoir Projects. *Water Resources Res.*, September 1985, 21(9), pp. 1307–12.

Raiffa, Howard. Back from Prospect Theory to Utility Theory. In *Grauer, M.; Thompson, M. and Wierzbicki, A. P., eds.*, 1985, pp. 100–113.

Rao, T. V. S. Ramamohan. Efficient Choice of the Quality of Product. *Rivista Int. Sci. Econ. Com.*, July-Aug. 1985, 32(7–8), pp. 609–23.

Rashid, Salim. Envy Stimulates Competition. *Econ. Notes*, 1985, (2), pp. 171–74.

Ray, Dipankar. Can the Friedman–Savage Case Be Due to the Cost of Information? *Math. Soc. Sci.*, June 1985, 9(3), pp. 275–85.

Revier, Charles F. and McKean, John R. Derivation of Slutsky Compensated Demand Functions. *Amer. Econ.*, Spring 1985, 29(1), pp. 53–59.

Rosenberg, Alexander. Prospects for the Elimination of Tastes from Economics and Ethics. In *Paul, E. F.; Paul, J. and Miller, F. D., Jr., eds.*, 1985, pp. 48–68.

Ryder, Harl E. Heterogeneous Time Preferences and the Distribution of Wealth. *Math. Soc. Sci.*, February 1985, 9(1), pp. 63–76.

Samuelson, Larry. On the Independence from Irrelevant Alternatives in Probabilistic Choice Models. *J. Econ. Theory*, April 1985, 35(2), pp. 376–89.

Sandmo, Agnar. The Effects of Taxation on Savings and Risk Taking. In *Auerbach, A. J. and Feldstein, M., eds.*, 1985, pp. 265–311.

Scarsini, Marco. Stochastic Dominance with Pairwise Risk Aversion. *J. Math. Econ.*, 1985, 14(2), pp. 187–201.

Segal, Uzi. On the Separability of the Quasi Concave Closure of an Additively Separable Function. *J. Math. Econ.*, 1985, 14(2), pp. 129–34.

Seo, Fumiko. Multiattribute Utility Analysis and Collective Choice: A Methodological Review. In *Haimes, Y. Y. and Chankong, V., eds.*, 1985, pp. 170–89.

Simmons, P. Consumption Constraints, Uncertain Income Streams and the Life Cycle Model. *Rech. Écon. Louvain*, 1985, 51(2), pp. 175–80.

Skinner, Jonathan S. The Effect of Increased Longevity on Capital Accumulation. *Amer. Econ. Rev.*, December 1985, 75(5), pp. 1143–50. [G: U.S.]

Skinner, Jonathan S. Variable Lifespan and the Intertemporal Elasticity of Consumption. *Rev. Econ. Statist.*, November 1985, 67(4), pp. 616–23. [G: U.S.]

Spiegel, Uriel and Templeman, Joseph. Interdependent Utility and Cooperative Behavior. *J. Compar. Econ.*, September 1985, 9(3), pp. 314–28.

Sproule, Robert A. An Optimal Allocation of Labor Supply and Savings under Interest-Rate Uncertainty: An Extension. *Bull. Econ. Res.*, May 1985, 37(2), pp. 115–22.

van de Stadt, Huib; Kapteyn, Arie and van de Geer, Sara. The Relativity of Utility: Evidence from Panel Data. *Rev. Econ. Statist.*, May 1985, 67(2), pp. 179–87. [G: Netherlands]

Sullivan, Dennis H. Simultaneous Determination of Church Contributions and Church Attendance. *Econ. Inquiry*, April 1985, 23(2), pp. 309–20. [G: U.S.]

Thaler, Richard. Mental Accounting and Consumer Choice. *Marketing Sci.*, Summer 1985, 4(3), pp. 199–214.

Thistle, Paul D. An Experimental Study of Consumer Demand Using Rats: Comment. *J. Behav. Econ.*, Summer 1985, 14(2), pp. 115–19.

Tinbergen, Jan. Measurability of Utility (or Welfare). *De Economist*, 1985, 133(3), pp. 411–14.

Vázquez, Andrés. Geometrical Analysis of the Arc Price Elasticity of Demand and the Change in Total Revenue. *Can. J. Agr. Econ.*, November 1985, 33(3), pp. 387–95.

Vázquez, Andrés. Geometrical Measurement of the Elasticity of Demand and the Elasticities of Total Revenue. *Giorn. Econ.*, Nov.-Dec. 1985, 44(11–12), pp. 657–65.

Vincke, Philippe. Multiattribute Utility Theory as a Basic Approach. In *Fandel, G. and Spronk, J., eds.*, 1985, pp. 27–40.

Wagneur, Edouard. Budget et systèmes mixtes de demande. (Budget and Mixed Demand Systems. With English summary.) *L'Actual. Econ.*, December 1985, 61(4), pp. 489–506.

Watkins, John. Second Thoughts on Self-interest and Morality. In *Campbell, R. and Sowden, L., eds.*, 1985, pp. 59–74.

Wernerfelt, Birger. Brand Loyalty and User Skills. *J. Econ. Behav. Organ.*, December 1985, 6(4), pp. 381–85.

Weymark, John A. Money-Metric Utility Functions. *Int. Econ. Rev.*, February 1985, 26(1), pp. 219–32.

Wierzbicki, Andrzej. Negotiation and Mediation in Conflicts: II. Plural Rationality and Interactive Decision Processes. In *Grauer, M.; Thompson, M. and Wierzbicki, A. P., eds.*, 1985, pp. 114–31.

Witt, Ulrich. Economic Behavior and Biological

Evolution: Some Remarks on the Sociobiology Debate. *Z. ges. Staatswiss. (JITE)*, September 1985, *141*(3), pp. 365–89.

Wolff, Reiner. On a Family of Utility Functions as a Basis of Separable Demand. *Z. Nationalökon.*, 1985, *45*(2), pp. 171–77.

Zamagni, Stefano. Quale spazio fra punto e funzione di domanda? Alcune note preliminari. (Between the Point of Demand and the Demand Function: Some Preliminary Notes. With English summary.) *Rivista Int. Sci. Econ. Com.*, April 1985, *32*(4), pp. 343–57.

0223 Theory of Production

Abel, Andrew B. A Stochastic Model of Investment, Marginal q and the Market Value of the Firm. *Int. Econ. Rev.*, June 1985, *26*(2), pp. 305–22.

Abel, Andrew B. Inventories, Stock-Outs and Production Smoothing. *Rev. Econ. Stud.*, April 1985, *52*(2), pp. 283–93.

Anderson, Simon. Product Choice with Economies of Scope. *Reg. Sci. Urban Econ.*, June 1985, *15*(2), pp. 277–94.

Andersson, Roland and Bohman, Mats. Short- and Long-run Marginal Cost Pricing: On Their Alleged Equivalence. *Energy Econ.*, October 1985, *7*(4), pp. 279–88.

Arrow, Kenneth J. Comment on Duesenberry's "Portfolio Approach to the Demand for Money and Other Assets." In *Arrow, K. J. (II)*, 1985, pp. 9–14.

Arrow, Kenneth J. Informational Structure of the Firm. *Amer. Econ. Rev.*, May 1985, *75*(2), pp. 303–07.

Arrow, Kenneth J. Optimal Capital Adjustment. In *Arrow, K. J. (I)*, 1985, pp. 120–39.

Arrow, Kenneth J. Optimal Capital Policy with Irreversible Investment. In *Arrow, K. J. (I)*, 1985, pp. 241–60.

Arrow, Kenneth J. Optimal Capital Policy, the Cost of Capital, and Myopic Decision Rules. In *Arrow, K. J. (I)*, 1985, pp. 181–90.

Arrow, Kenneth J. and Levhari, David. Uniqueness of the Internal Rate of Return with Variable Life of Investment. In *Arrow, K. J. (I)*, 1985, pp. 373–81.

Arrow, Kenneth J.; Levhari, David and Sheshinski, Eytan. A Production Function for the Repairman Problem. In *Arrow, K. J. (I)*, 1985, pp. 443–55.

Artus, Patrick. Rationnement de crédit et réactions des entreprises. (Credit Rationing and Firms' Reactions. With English summary.) *Revue Écon.*, November 1985, *36*(6), pp. 1207–46. [G: France]

Arvan, Lanny and Moses, Leon N. A Model of the Firm in Time and Space. *J. Econ. Dynam. Control*, September 1985, *9*(1), pp. 77–100.

Ashley, Richard A. and Orr, Daniel. Further Results on Inventories and Price Stickiness. *Amer. Econ. Rev.*, December 1985, *75*(5), pp. 964–75.

Austen-Smith, M. David and Jenkins, Stephen P. A Multiperiod Model of Nonprofit Enter-

prises. *Scot. J. Polit. Econ.*, June 1985, *32*(2), pp. 119–34. [G: U.K.]

d'Autume, Antoine and Michel, Philippe. Future Investment Constraints Reduce Present Investment. *Econometrica*, January 1985, *53*(1), pp. 203–06.

Bartoli, Gloria and Lecaldano Sasso la Terza, Edoardo. Microeconomic Foundations of Aggregate Behaviour of Firms in Kalecki and Some of His Followers. *Econ. Notes*, 1985, (1), pp. 43–62.

Beato, Paulina and Mas-Colell, Andreu. On Marginal Cost Pricing with Given Tax-Subsidy Rules. *J. Econ. Theory*, December 1985, *37*(2), pp. 356–65.

Behrens, Peter. The Firm as a Complex Institution. *Z. ges. Staatswiss. (JITE)*, March 1985, *141*(1), pp. 62–75.

Beker, Víctor A. La inflexibilidad descendente de los precios y la teoría de la empresa. (Price Inflexibility and the Theory of the Firm. With English summary.) *Económica (La Plata)*, Jan.-Apr. 1985, *31*(1), pp. 3–19.

Bernstein, Michael A. The Methodological Resolution of the Cambridge Controversies: A Comment. *J. Post Keynesian Econ.*, Summer 1985, *7*(4), pp. 607–11.

Bhagwati, Jagdish N. The Choice of Technology. In *Bhagwati, J. N. (II)*, 1985, pp. 231–36.

Biddle, Gary C. and Steinberg, Richard. Common Cost Allocation in the Firm. In *Young, H. P., ed.*, 1985, pp. 31–54.

Biswas, Tapan. Factor-Supply Responses and the Gross-Substitute System. *Math. Soc. Sci.*, April 1985, *9*(2), pp. 183–87.

Black, J. M. and Bulkley, George. Wage-Employments Contracts When There Is a Constraint on the Firm's Profit Level in Each State. *Scot. J. Polit. Econ.*, November 1985, *32*(3), pp. 328–32.

Blair, Roger D. and Kaserman, David L. Unanswered Questions about Franchising: Reply. *Southern Econ. J.*, January 1985, *51*(3), pp. 933–36.

Blitch, Charles P. The Genesis of Chamberlinian Monopolistic Competition Theory: Addendum [The Origin and Early Development of Monopolistic Competition Theory]. *Hist. Polit. Econ.*, Fall 1985, *17*(3), pp. 395–400.

de Boer, P. M. C. and Donkers, H. W. J. On the Relationship between Input–Output Production Coefficients and the CES Production Function. *Z. Nationalökon.*, 1985, *45*(3), pp. 331–35.

Bosworth, Derek and Pugh, Clive. Optimal Capital Utilisation and Shiftworking. *Scand. J. Econ.*, 1985, *87*(4), pp. 658–67.

Bowles, Samuel. The Production Process in a Competitive Economy: Walrasian, Neo-Hobbesian, and Marxian Models. *Amer. Econ. Rev.*, March 1985, *75*(1), pp. 16–36.

Briys, Eric P. and Eeckhoudt, Louis. Relative Risk Aversion in Comparative Statics: Comment. *Amer. Econ. Rev.*, March 1985, *75*(1), pp. 281–83.

Brock, William A. and Dechert, W. D. Dynamic

Ramsey Pricing. *Int. Econ. Rev.*, October 1985, *26*(3), pp. 569–91.

Brown, Murray and Wolfstetter, Elmar. Under- and Overemployment in Optimal Layoff Contracts. *Z. Nationalökon.*, 1985, *45*(2), pp. 101–14.

Caravani, Paolo and De Luca, Alessandro. Aggregazione settoriale: una applicazione al modello sraffiano di produzione semplice. (Sectoral Aggregation: An Application to the Sraffian Model of Simple Production. With English summary.) *Ricerche Econ.*, July-Sept. 1985, *39*(3), pp. 293–317.

Charnes, A., et al. Foundations of Data Envelopment Analysis for Pareto–Koopmans Efficient Empirical Production Functions. *J. Econometrics*, Oct./Nov. 1985, *30*(1/2), pp. 91–107.

Chavas, Jean-Paul and Pope, Rulon D. Price Uncertainty and Competitive Firm Behavior: Testable Hypotheses from Expected Utility Maximization. *J. Econ. Bus.*, August 1985, *37*(3), pp. 223–35.

Chen, K. C. and Scott, Louis O. Uncertain Inflation and the Input–Output Choices of Competitive Firms. *Quart. Rev. Econ. Bus.*, Autumn 1985, *25*(3), pp. 48–54.

Clarke, Richard N. Certainty-Equivalence and the Theory of the Firm under Uncertainty. *Int. Econ. Rev.*, June 1985, *26*(2), pp. 323–29.

Cohen, Avi J. Issues in the Cambridge Controversies [The Methodological Resolution of the Cambridge Controversies]. *J. Post Keynesian Econ.*, Summer 1985, *7*(4), pp. 612–15.

Collins, William H.; Collins, Carol B. and Gulati, Unmesh C. A Mathematical Model for Desired Capital– Catastrophe Theory. *Indian Econ. J.*, Apr.-June 1985, *32*(4), pp. 62–74.

Cooper, Russell. Worker Asymmetric Information and Employment Distortions. *J. Lab. Econ.*, April 1985, *3*(2), pp. 188–208.

Crampes, Claude and Moreaux, Michel. Intégration verticale et rendements décroissants. (Vertical Integration and Decreasing Returns. With English summary.) *Revue Écon.*, July 1985, *36*(4), pp. 669–85.

Diewert, W. E. Transfer Pricing and Economic Efficiency. **In** *Rugman, A. M. and Eden, L., eds.*, 1985, pp. 47–81.

Dixon, Huw. Strategic Investment in an Industry with a Competitive Product Market. *J. Ind. Econ.*, June 1985, *33*(4), pp. 483–99.

Dow, Gregory K. Internal Bargaining and Strategic Innovation in the Theory of the Firm. *J. Econ. Behav. Organ.*, September 1985, *6*(3), pp. 301–20.

Drèze, Jacques H. Labor Management and General Equilibrium. **In** *Jones, D. C. and Svejnar, J., eds.*, 1985, pp. 3–20.

Eccles, Robert G. Transfer Pricing as a Problem of Agency. **In** *Pratt, J. W. and Zeckhauser, R. J., eds.*, 1985, pp. 151–86.

Eckel, Catherine C. and Vining, Aidan R. Elements of a Theory of Mixed Enterprise. *Scot. J. Polit. Econ.*, February 1985, *32*(1), pp. 82–94.

Eden, Lorraine. The Microeconomics of Transfer Pricing. **In** *Rugman, A. M. and Eden, L., eds.*, 1985, pp. 13–46.

Edwards, J. S. S. and Keen, M. J. Taxes, Investment and Q. *Rev. Econ. Stud.*, October 1985, *52*(4), pp. 665–79.

Eichner, Alfred S. Micro Foundations of the Corporate Economy. **In** *Eichner, A. S.*, 1985, pp. 28–74.

Endres, Alfred. Tie-in Financing and Pragmatic Price Discrimination. *Metroecon.*, February 1985, *37*(1), pp. 119–33.

Englmann, Frank C. Pasinetti on the Choice of Technique: A Note. *Cambridge J. Econ.*, March 1985, *9*(1), pp. 85–88.

Epstein, Larry G. and Yatchew, Adonis John. The Empirical Determination of Technology and Expectations: A Simplified Procedure. *J. Econometrics*, February 1985, *27*(2), pp. 235–58. [G: U.S.]

Estrin, Saul. Self-managed and Capitalist Behavior in Alternative Market Structures. **In** *Jones, D. C. and Svejnar, J., eds.*, 1985, pp. 71–86.

Eswaran, Mukesh and Kotwal, Ashok. A Theory of Contractual Structure in Agriculture. *Amer. Econ. Rev.*, June 1985, *75*(3), pp. 352–67.

Faini, Riccardo and Schiantarelli, Fabio. A Unified Framework for Firms' Decisions Theoretical Analysis and Empirical Application to Italy 1970–1980. **In** *Weiserbs, D., ed.*, 1985, pp. 51–74. [G: Italy]

Faini, Riccardo and Schiantarelli, Fabio. Oligopolistic Models of Investment and Employment Decisions in a Regional Context: Theory and Empirical Evidence from a Putty–Clay Model. *Europ. Econ. Rev.*, March 1985, *27*(2), pp. 221–42. [G: Italy]

Färe, Rolf and Grosskopf, Shawna. Nonparametric Cost Approach to Scale Efficiency. *Scand. J. Econ.*, 1985, *87*(4), pp. 594–604.

Farmer, Roger E. A. Implicit Contracts with Asymmetric Information and Bankruptcy: The Effect of Interest Rates on Layoffs. *Rev. Econ. Stud.*, July 1985, *52*(3), pp. 427–42. [G: U.S.]

Fooladi, Iraj. A General Theory of the Competitive Firm under Undercertainty. *Atlantic Econ. J.*, September 1985, *13*(3), pp. 41–49.

Formby, John P. and Millner, Edward L. The Convergence of Utility and Profit Maximization. *Southern Econ. J.*, April 1985, *51*(4), pp. 1174–85.

Førsund, Finn R. Frontier Production Functions: Comment. *Econometric Rev.*, 1985-86, *4*(2), pp. 329–34.

Førsund, Finn R.; Hjalmarsson, Lennart and Eitrheim, Øyvind. An Intercountry Comparison of Cement Production: The Short-run Production Function Approach. **In** *[Johansen, L.]*, 1985, pp. 11–42. [G: Norway; Sweden; Denmark; Finland]

Førsund, Finn R. and Jansen, Eilev S. The Interplay between Sectoral Models Based on Micro Data and Models for the National Economy. **In** *[Johansen, L.]*, 1985, pp. 109–25.

Frantz, Roger S. Symposium on Decision Making in the Firm: An Introduction. *J. Behav. Econ.*,

Winter 1985, *14*, pp. 1–4.

Frantz, Roger S. X-Efficiency Theory and Its Critics. *Quart. Rev. Econ. Bus.*, Winter 1985, *25*(4), pp. 38–58.

Frantz, Roger S. and Galloway, Fred. A Theory of Multidimensional Effort Decisions. *J. Behav. Econ.*, Winter 1985, *14*, pp. 69–82.

Fraser, R. W. Uncertainty and the Theory of Mark-up Pricing. *Bull. Econ. Res.*, January 1985, *37*(1), pp. 55–64.

Fratrik, Mark R. and Lafferty, Ronald N. Unanswered Questions about Franchising: Comment [Optimal Franchising]. *Southern Econ. J.*, January 1985, *51*(3), pp. 927–32.

Frech, H. E., III. The Property Rights Theory of the Firm: Some Evidence from the U.S. Nursing Home Industry. *Z. ges. Staatswiss. (JITE)*, March 1985, *141*(1), pp. 146–66.
[G: U.S.]

Freixas, Xavier and Laffont, Jean-Jacques. Average Cost Pricing versus Marginal Cost Pricing under Moral Hazard. *J. Public Econ.*, March 1985, *26*(2), pp. 135–46.

Fudenberg, Drew and Tirole, Jean. Preemption and Rent Equilization in the Adoption of New Technology. *Rev. Econ. Stud.*, July 1985, *52*(3), pp. 383–401.

Furubotn, Eirik G. Codetermination, Productivity Gains, and the Economics of the Firm. *Oxford Econ. Pap.*, March 1985, *37*(1), pp. 22–39.

Gäfgen, Gérard. The Property Rights Theory of the Firm: Some Evidence from the U.S. Nursing Home Industry: Comment. *Z. ges. Staatswiss. (JITE)*, March 1985, *141*(1), pp. 167–69.

Gale, Douglas and Hellwig, Martin F. Incentive-Compatible Debt Contracts: The One-Period Problem. *Rev. Econ. Stud.*, October 1985, *52*(4), pp. 647–63.

Gapinski, James H. Do the Nonprofit Performing Arts Optimize? The Moral from Shakespeare. *Quart. Rev. Econ. Bus.*, Summer 1985, *25*(2), pp. 27–37.
[G: U.K.]

Garen, John E. Worker Heterogeneity, Job Screening, and Firm Size. *J. Polit. Econ.*, August 1985, *93*(4), pp. 715–39.
[G: U.S.]

Gilad, B.; Kaish, S. and Loeb, Peter D. A Theory of Surprise and Business Failure. *J. Behav. Econ.*, Winter 1985, *14*, pp. 35–55.

Glazer, Amihai. The Advantages of Being First. *Amer. Econ. Rev.*, June 1985, *75*(3), pp. 473–80.
[G: U.S.]

Goisis, Gianandrea. Domanda variabile, prezzi dei fattori e scelta degli assetti produttivi: alcuni recenti contributi. (Variability of Demand, Prices of Inputs and Choice of Technologies: Some Recent Contributions. With English summary.) *Rivista Int. Sci. Econ. Com.*, May 1985, *32*(5), pp. 467–80.

Goldberg, Victor P. Production Functions, Transactions Costs and the New Institutionalism. In *Feiwel, G. R., ed. (II)*, 1985, pp. 395–402.

van Gool, W. Towards a Physical Interpretation of Production Functions. In *van Gool, W. and Bruggink, J. J. C., eds.*, 1985, pp. 247–56.

Gordon, Roger H. Taxation of Corporate Capital Income: Tax Revenues versus Tax Distortions. *Quart. J. Econ.*, February 1985, *100*(1), pp. 1–27.

Gorman, Ian E. Conditions for Economies of Scope in the Presence of Fixed Costs. *Rand J. Econ.*, Autumn 1985, *16*(3), pp. 431–36.

Gramm, Warren S. Behavioral Elements in the Theory of the Firm: An Historical Perspective. *J. Behav. Econ.*, Winter 1985, *14*, pp. 21–34.

Grant, Dwight. Theory of the Firm with Joint Price and Output Risk and a Forward Market. *Amer. J. Agr. Econ.*, August 1985, *67*(3), pp. 630–35.

Greene, William H. Frontier Production Functions: Comment. *Econometric Rev.*, 1985-86, *4*(2), pp. 335–38.

Gronchi, Sandro. Un tasso interno di rendimento generalizzato. (With English summary.) *Econ. Polit.*, April 1985, *2*(1), pp. 55–80.

Groves, Theodore. The Impossibility of Incentive-Compatible and Efficient Full Cost Allocation Schemes. In *Young, H. P., ed.*, 1985, pp. 95–100.

Gui, Benedetto. Limits to External Financing: A Model and an Application to Labor-Managed Firms. In *Jones, D. C. and Svejnar, J., eds.*, 1985, pp. 107–20.

Halevi, Joseph. Switching and Employment. *Eastern Econ. J.*, July-Sept. 1985, *11*(3), pp. 229–34.

Hallagan, William S. and Joerding, Wayne. Polymorphism in Competitive Strategies: Trading Stamps. *J. Econ. Bus.*, February 1985, *37*(1), pp. 1–17.

Haller, Hans. Separation of Ownership and Labour: Welfare Considerations. *Z. Nationalökon.*, 1985, *45*(3), pp. 245–65.

Hamlin, Alan P. and Heathfield, D. F. Capital Utilization and Investment in a "Mixed" Economy. In *Weiserbs, D., ed.*, 1985, pp. 319–40.

Haruna, Shoji. A Unified Theory of the Behaviour of Profit-maximising, Labour-managed and Joint-Stock Firms Operating under Uncertainty: A Comment. *Econ. J.*, December 1985, *95*(380), pp. 1093–94.

Helpman, Elhanan. Multinational Corporations and Trade Structure. *Rev. Econ. Stud.*, July 1985, *52*(3), pp. 443–57.

van den Heuvel, P. Engineering Production Functions: A General Framework. In *van Gool, W. and Bruggink, J. J. C., eds.*, 1985, pp. 223–37.

Hey, John D. A Dynamic Model of the Competitive Firm with a Forward Market. *J. Econ. Stud.*, 1985, *12*(3), pp. 21–35.

Hey, John D. A Unified Theory of the Behaviour of Profit-maximising, Labour-managed and Joint-Stock Firms Operating under Uncertainty: A Rejoinder. *Econ. J.*, December 1985, *95*(380), pp. 1095.

Hey, John D. Relative Risk Aversion in Comparative Statics: Comment. *Amer. Econ. Rev.*, March 1985, *75*(1), pp. 284–85.

Holmström, Bengt R. and Weiss, Laurence M. Managerial Incentives, Investment, and Aggregate Implications: Scale Effects. *Rev. Econ. Stud.*, July 1985, 52(3), pp. 403–25.

Honda, Yuzo. Downside Risk and the Competitive Firm. *Metroecon.*, June 1985, 37(2), pp. 231–40.

Honkapohja, Seppo and Kanniainen, Vesa. Adjustment Costs, Optimal Capacity Utilization, and the Corporation Tax. *Oxford Econ. Pap.*, September 1985, 37(3), pp. 486–99.

Horowitz, Ira. The Risk-averse Price-taking Firm: A Partial Synthesis. *Quart. J. Bus. Econ.*, Summer 1985, 24(3), pp. 30–40.

Horstmann, Ignatius J.; MacDonald, Glenn M. and Slivinski, Alan D. Patents as Information Transfer Mechanisms: To Patent or (Maybe) Not to Patent. *J. Polit. Econ.*, October 1985, 93(5), pp. 837–58.

Huffman, Gregory W. Adjustment Costs and Capital Asset Pricing. *J. Finance*, July 1985, 40(3), pp. 691–705.

Hughes, Edward and McFetridge, Donald G. A Theoretical Analysis of Incremental Investment Incentives with an Application to the Case of Industrial R and D. *J. Public Econ.*, August 1985, 27(3), pp. 311–29.

Hurter, Arthur P., Jr. and Martinich, Joseph S. Input Price Uncertainty and the Production-location Decision: A Critique and Synthesis. *Reg. Sci. Urban Econ.*, November 1985, 15(4), pp. 591–96.

Ichiishi, Tatsuro. Management versus Ownership, II. *Europ. Econ. Rev.*, March 1985, 27(2), pp. 115–38.

Ireland, Norman J. and Law, Peter J. Maximum Returns Firms and Codetermination. In *Jones, D. C. and Svejnar, J., eds.*, 1985, pp. 21–40.

Johnson, William R. The Social Efficiency of Fixed Wages. *Quart. J. Econ.*, February 1985, 100(1), pp. 101–18.

Jordan, W. John. Capacity Costs, Heterogeneous Users, and Peak-Load Pricing [Heterogeneous Users and the Peak-load Pricing model]. *Quart. J. Econ.*, November 1985, 100(4), pp. 1335–37.

Kahn, Charles M. Optimal Severance Pay with Incomplete Information. *J. Polit. Econ.*, June 1985, 93(3), pp. 435–51.

Kahn, Charles M. and Scheinkman, José A. Optimal Employment Contracts with Bankruptcy Constraints. *J. Econ. Theory*, April 1985, 35(2), pp. 343–65.

Karlson, Stephen H. Spatial Competition with Location-dependent costs. *J. Reg. Sci.*, May 1985, 25(2), pp. 201–14.

Katz, Eliakim. Relative Risk Aversion in Comparative Statics: Reply. *Amer. Econ. Rev.*, March 1985, 75(1), pp. 286–87.

Kemp, Murray C.; van Long, Ngo Van and Tawada, Makoto. Sharp Points in Production Surfaces. *Oxford Econ. Pap.*, September 1985, 37(3), pp. 375–81.

Klodt, Henning. Kapitalgebundener technischer Fortschritt: Ein Überblick. (Embodied Technical Change: A Survey. With English summary.) *Weltwirtsch. Arch.*, 1985, 121(1), pp. 151–70.

Kohli, Ulrich. Technology and Public Goods. *J. Public Econ.*, April 1985, 26(3), pp. 379–400.

Kollintzas, Tryphon and Thorn, Richard S. The Generalized User Cost of Capital. *Public Finance Quart.*, October 1985, 13(4), pp. 355–74.

Le Bas, Christian. La diffusion de l'innovation interne a la firme: Un survol de littérature et un modèle d'apprentissage technoligique. (The Intra-firm Diffusion of Innovation: A Survey and a Model of Technological Learning. With English summary.) *Revue Écon.*, September 1985, 36(5), pp. 873–95.

Leibenstein, Harvey. On Relaxing the Maximization Postulate. *J. Behav. Econ.*, Winter 1985, 14, pp. 5–20.

Lensberg, Terje. Bargaining and Fair Allocation. In *Young, H. P., ed.*, 1985, pp. 101–16.

Lesourd, Jean-Baptiste. Energy and Resources as Production Factors in Process Industries. *Energy Econ.*, July 1985, 7(3), pp. 138–44.

Levine, David K. A Simple Durable Goods Model. *Quart. J. Econ.*, August 1985, 100(3), pp. 775–88.

Levy, Santiago. Factor Demand Functions for Constant Returns to Scale Technologies. *Southern Econ. J.*, January 1985, 51(3), pp. 860–67.

Lichtenstein, Peter M. Neoclassical and Marxian Theories of Capitalist Organizations: Prospects for a Post-Keynesian Challenge. *Econ. Forum*, Winter 1985-1986, 15(2), pp. 35–50.

Lipman, Barton L. Dynamic Behavior of a Firm Subject to Stochastic Regulatory Review: A Comment. *Int. Econ. Rev.*, June 1985, 26(2), pp. 511–16.

Loasby, Brian J. Profit, Expectations and Coherence in Economic Systems. *J. Econ. Stud.*, 1985, 12(1/2), pp. 21–33.

Lopez, Ramon E. Structural Implications of a Class of Flexible Functional Forms for Profit Functions. *Int. Econ. Rev.*, October 1985, 26(3), pp. 593–601.

MacDonald, Glenn M. and Markusen, James R. A Rehabilitation of Absolute Advantage. *J. Polit. Econ.*, April 1985, 93(2), pp. 277–97.

Mai, Chao-cheng. Optimum Location and Theory of the Firm under a Regulatory Constraint. *J. Reg. Sci.*, August 1985, 25(3), pp. 453–61.

Maital, Shlomo and Roll, Yaakov. Solving for 'X': Theory & Measurement of Allocative and X-Efficiency at the Plant Level. *J. Behav. Econ.*, Winter 1985, 14, pp. 99–116.

Malcomson, James M. Capital Utilization and Empirical Analysis. In *Weiserbs, D., ed.*, 1985, pp. 341–50.

Margolis, Stephen E. The Excess Capacity Controversy: A Critique of Recent Criticism. *Econ. Inquiry*, April 1985, 23(2), pp. 265–75.

Martin, Robert E. Random Capital Service in Labor-managed and Profit-maximizing Firms. *J. Compar. Econ.*, September 1985, 9(3), pp. 296–313.

Mathur, V. K. Location Theory of the Firm under Price Uncertainty: Some New Conclusions. *Reg. Sci. Urban Econ.*, November 1985, 15(4), pp. 597–98.

Mayer, Colin and Meadowcroft, Shirley A. Equity Rates of Return in the UK—Evidence from Panel Data. In *Weiserbs, D., ed.*, 1985, pp. 351–86. **[G: U.K.]**

McCain, Roger A. The Economics of a Labor-Managed Enterprise in the Short Run: An "Implicit Contracts" Approach. In *Jones, D. C. and Svejnar, J., eds.*, 1985, pp. 41–53.

McDonald, Robert L. and Siegel, Daniel R. Investment and the Valuation of Firms When There Is an Option to Shut Down. *Int. Econ. Rev.*, June 1985, *26*(2), pp. 331–49.

Miller, Ellen M. Pass-through Lags in Fuel Adjustment Clauses and Firm Performance. *Atlantic Econ. J.*, December 1985, *13*(4), pp. 91–92.

Miller, Merton H and Upton, Charles W. A Test of the Hotelling Valuation Principle. *J. Polit. Econ.*, February 1985, *93*(1), pp. 1–25. **[G: U.S.]**

Mitchell, William F. and Watts, Martin. Efficiency under Capitalist Production: A Critique and Reformulation. *Rev. Radical Polit. Econ.*, Spring and Summer 1985, *17*(1/2), pp. 212–20.

Miyazaki, Hajime and Neary, Hugh M. Output, Work Hours and Employment in the Short Run of a Labour-managed Firm. *Econ. J.*, December 1985, *95*(380), pp. 1035–48.

Moene, Karl Ove. Shopping for an Investment Good. *Int. Econ. Rev.*, June 1985, *26*(2), pp. 351–63.

Morris, Derek J. The Behaviour of Firms. In *Morris, D., ed.*, 1985, pp. 53–85. **[G: U.K.]**

Morrison, Catherine J. On the Economic Interpretation and Measurement of Optimal Capacity Utilization with Anticipatory Expectations. *Rev. Econ. Stud.*, April 1985, *52*(2), pp. 295–310. **[G: U.S.]**

Muet, Pierre-Alain. A Unified Framework for Firm's Decisions: Theoretical Analysis and Empirical Application to Italy 1970–1981: Comment. In *Weiserbs, D., ed.*, 1985, pp. 75–79. **[G: Italy]**

Mulligan, James G. A Stochastic Production Function for Machine Repair [A Microeconomic Production Function] [Returns to Scale and Substitutability in the Repairman Problem]. *Appl. Econ.*, June 1985, *17*(3), pp. 559–66.

Ng, Yew-Kwang. A Micro–Macroeconomic Analysis Based on a Representative Firm: Progress Report. In *Feiwel, G. R., ed. (I)*, 1985, pp. 216–32.

Nicodano, Giovanna. Decisioni d'investimento e di finanziamento dell'impresa: un'integrazione formale. (Investment and Financing Decisions of the Firm: A Formal Integration. With English summary.) *Ricerche Econ.*, July-Sept. 1985, *39*(3), pp. 378–97.

Nieswiadomy, Michael. A Technique for Comparing the Elasticities of Linear Demand and Supply Curves. *Atlantic Econ. J.*, December 1985, *13*(4), pp. 68–70.

O'Hara, Maureen. Technology and Hedging Behavior: A Proof of Hicks' Conjecture. *Amer. Econ. Rev.*, December 1985, *75*(5), pp. 1186–90.

Olsen, Randall J. Frontier Production Functions: Comment. *Econometric Rev.*, 1985-86, *4*(2), pp. 339–43.

Papagni, Erasmo. Produzione con costi d'aggiustamento: l'approccio duale. (With English summary.) *Stud. Econ.*, 1985, *40*(26), pp. 87–116.

Pope, Rulon D. and Chavas, Jean-Paul. Producer Surplus and Risk. *Quart. J. Econ.*, Supp. 1985, *100*, pp. 853–69.

Precious, Mark. Demand Constraints, Rational Expectations and Investment Theory. *Oxford Econ. Pap.*, December 1985, *37*(4), pp. 576–605.

Putterman, Louis. On the Interdependence of Labor Supplies in Producers' Cooperatives. In *Jones, D. C. and Svejnar, J., eds.*, 1985, pp. 87–105.

ten Raa, Thijs. Closedness of Production Sets. *Z. Nationalökon.*, 1985, *45*(2), pp. 155–60.

Reinganum, Jennifer F. A Two-Stage Model of Research and Development with Endogenous Second-Mover Advantages. *Int. J. Ind. Organ.*, September 1985, *3*(3), pp. 275–92.

Reinwald, Thomas P. The Genesis of Chamberlinian Monopolistic Competition Theory: Addendum—A Comment [The Origin and Early Development of Monopolistic Competition Theory]. *Hist. Polit. Econ.*, Fall 1985, *17*(3), pp. 400–402.

Rossana, Robert J. Delivery Lags and Buffer Stocks in the Theory of Investment by the Firm. *J. Econ. Dynam. Control*, October 1985, *9*(2), pp. 153–93.

Rozen, Marvin E. Maximizing Behavior: Reconciling Neoclassical and X-Efficiency Approaches. *J. Econ. Issues*, September 1985, *19*(3), pp. 661–85.

Russell, R. Robert. Measures of Technical Efficiency. *J. Econ. Theory*, February 1985, *35*(1), pp. 109–26.

Salvadori, Neri. Switching in Methods of Production and Joint Production. *Manchester Sch. Econ. Soc. Stud.*, June 1985, *53*(2), pp. 156–78.

Salvadori, Neri. Was Sraffa Making No Assumption on Returns? *Metroecon.*, June 1985, *37*(2), pp. 175–86.

Samuelson, Larry. Transfer Pricing in Exhaustible Resource Markets. In *Rugman, A. M. and Eden, L., eds.*, 1985, pp. 98–116.

Schmidt, Peter. Frontier Production Functions: Reply. *Econometric Rev.*, 1985-86, *4*(2), pp. 353–55.

Schmidt, Peter. Frontier Production Functions. *Econometric Rev.*, 1985-86, *4*(2), pp. 289–328.

Schwalbach, Joachim. Multi-plant Operation Economies in the West German Beer and Cement Industries. In *Schwalbach, J., ed.*, 1985, pp. 167–95. **[G: W. Germany]**

Scott, Kenneth E. The Firm as a Complex Institution: Comment. *Z. ges. Staatswiss. (JITE)*, March 1985, *141*(1), pp. 76–79.

Segerson, Kathleen and Mount, Timothy D. A Non-homothetic Two-Stage Decision Model

Using AIDS. *Rev. Econ. Statist.*, November 1985, 67(4), pp. 630–39.   [G: U.S.]

Seidmann, Daniel J. Target Buffer Stocks. *Europ. Econ. Rev.*, March 1985, 27(2), pp. 165–82.

Seierstad, Atle. Properties of Production and Profit Functions Arising from the Aggregation of a Capacity Distribution of Micro Units. In *[Johansen, L.]*, 1985, pp. 65–85.

Shieh, Yeung-Nan. A Note on the Clarke and Shrestha Linear Space Model [Location and Input Mix Decisions for Energy Facilities]. *Reg. Sci. Urban Econ.*, February 1985, 15(1), pp. 131–35.

Shubik, Martin. The Cooperative Form, the Value, and the Allocation of Joint Costs and Benefits. In *Young, H. P., ed.*, 1985, pp. 79–94.

Sibley, David S. Response to Lipman and Further Results [Dynamic Behavior of a Firm Subject to Stochastic Regulatory Review]. *Int. Econ. Rev.*, June 1985, 26(2), pp. 517–20.

Silva, Francesco. Qualcosa di nuovo nelle teoria dell'impresa? (With English summary.) *Econ. Polit.*, April 1985, 2(1), pp. 95–134.

Singleton, Kenneth J. Adjustment Costs and Capital Asset Pricing: Discussion. *J. Finance*, July 1985, 40(3), pp. 705–09.

Solow, Robert M. Leif Johansen's Contributions to the Theory of Production, Planning, and Multisectoral Growth. In *[Johansen, L.]*, 1985, pp. 1–9.

Spronk, Jaap. Financial Planning with Conflicting Objectives. In *Fandel, G. and Spronk, J., eds.*, 1985, pp. 269–88.

Spulber, Daniel F. Risk Sharing and Inventories. *J. Econ. Behav. Organ.*, March 1985, 6(1), pp. 55–68.

Stagni, Anna. Sistemi dinamici di domanda di fattori: un'applicazione agli impieghi di energia nell'industria italiana. (Dynamic Factor Demand Systems: An Application to Energy Inputs in the Italian Industry. With English summary.) *Ricerche Econ.*, Jan.-Mar. 1985, 39(1), pp. 5–28.   [G: Italy]

Standaert, Stan. Neary and Roberts on Le Chatelier Properties of Spill-over Effects: A Correction [The Theory of Household Behaviour under Rationing]. *Europ. Econ. Rev.*, December 1985, 29(3), pp. 381–86.

Steedman, Ian. On the 'Impossibility' of Hicks-Neutral Technical Change. *Econ. J.*, September 1985, 95(379), pp. 746–58.

Steedman, Ian. On Input 'Demand Curves.' *Cambridge J. Econ.*, June 1985, 9(2), pp. 165–72.

Stiglitz, Joseph E. Credit Markets and the Control of Capital. *J. Money, Credit, Banking*, May 1985, 17(2), pp. 133–52.

Tarling, Roger and Wilkinson, Frank. Mark-up Pricing, Inflation and Distributional Shares: A Note. *Cambridge J. Econ.*, June 1985, 9(2), pp. 179–85.

Tinbergen, Jan. Production Functions: Research Lacunae. In *Tinbergen, J.*, 1985, pp. 56–65.

Tinbergen, Jan. Technology and Production Functions. *Rivista Int. Sci. Econ. Com.*, February 1985, 32(2), pp. 107–17.

Tinbergen, Jan and Wegner, Eckhard. On a Macroeconomic Model of Income Formation. In *Tinbergen, J.*, 1985, pp. 69–77.
                    [G: Switzerland]

Tobin, Roger L. and Friesz, Terry L. A New Look at Spatially Competitive Facility Location Models. In *Harker, P. T., ed.*, 1985, pp. 1–19.

Tomiyama, Ken. Two-Stage Optimal Control Problems and Optimality Conditions. *J. Econ. Dynam. Control*, November 1985, 9(3), pp. 317–37.

Ulph, A. Equity Rates of Return in the U.K.; Evidence from Panel Data: Comment. In *Weiserbs, D., ed.*, 1985 , pp. 387–89.   [G: U.K.]

Vanek, Jaroslav. The Participatory Economy. In *Bornstein, M., ed.*, 1985, pp. 131–40.

Vickers, John. Delegation and the Theory of the Firm. *Econ. J.*, Supplement 1985, 95, pp. 138–47.

Vickrey, William. The Fallacy of Using Long-run Cost for Peak-Load Pricing [Heterogeneous Users and the Peak-load Pricing model]. *Quart. J. Econ.*, November 1985, 100(4), pp. 1331–34.

Virén, Matti. Determination of Employment with Wage and Price Speculation. *Scand. J. Econ.*, 1985, 87(3), pp. 537–53.   [G: Finland]

White, Harrison C. Agency as Control. In *Pratt, J. W. and Zeckhauser, R. J., eds.*, 1985, pp. 187–212.

Woods, John Edward. On the Representation of Technology. *Metroecon.*, October 1985, 37(3), pp. 331–45.

Yatchew, Adonis John. Frontier Production Functions: Comment. *Econometric Rev.*, 1985-86, 4(2), pp. 345–52.

Young, H. Peyton. Methods and Principles of Cost Allocation. In *Young, H. P., ed.*, 1985, pp. 3–29.   [G: U.K.; Sweden]

Young, H. Peyton. Producer Incentives in Cost Allocation. *Econometrica*, July 1985, 53(4), pp. 757–65.

Zalai, Ernő. Joint Production and Labour Values. *Acta Oecon.*, 1985, 35(3–4), pp. 327–36.

0224 Theory of Factor Distribution and Distributive Shares

Addi, Lahouari. Le statut de la rente chez Sraffa: contribution a un débat recent. (Sraffa's Status of Rent: Contribution to a Recent Debate. With English summary.) *Revue Écon.*, May 1985, 36(3), pp. 579–601.

Afxentiou, P. C. Opportunity Costs and Collective Bargaining. *S. Afr. J. Econ.*, December 1985, 53(4), pp. 381–92.

Baldone, Salvatore. Durable Capital Inputs: Conditions for Prices Ratios to Be Invariant to Profit-Rate Changes: A Comment. *Z. Nationalökon.*, 1985, 45(4), pp. 409–20.

Bronfenbrenner, Martin. Marginal Productivity, a Rehabilitation. In *Feiwel, G. R., ed. (I)*, 1985, pp. 366–77.

Casarosa, Carlo. The 'New View' of the Ricardian Theory of Distribution and Economic Growth.

In *Caravale, G. A., ed.*, 1985, pp. 45–58.

Gehrels, Franz. Allocations, Outputs and Rentals in General Equilibrium with a Limiting Factor. *Rivista Int. Sci. Econ. Com.*, April 1985, 32(4), pp. 323–41.

Goldstein, Jonathan P. The Cyclical Profit Squeeze: A Marxian Microfoundation. *Rev. Radical Polit. Econ.*, Spring and Summer 1985, 17(1/2), pp. 103–28.

Grubb, David B. Ability and Power over Production in the Distribution of Earnings. *Rev. Econ. Statist.*, May 1985, 67(2), pp. 188–94. [G: W. Europe; U.S.; Australia]

Niccoli, Alberto. Efficiency of Microeconomic Income Distribution and Global Productivity Differentials. *Rivista Polit. Econ.*, Suppl. Dec. 1985, 76, pp. 65–119. [G: Italy]

Sánchez Chóliz, Julio. Eficiencia y control en las innovaciones. (With English summary.) *Revista Española Econ.*, 1985, 2(2), pp. 291–305.

Tinbergen, Jan. Production Functions with Several Factors. In *Tinbergen, J.*, 1985, pp. 20–24. [G: U.S.]

Tinbergen, Jan. Theories of Income Distribution in Developed Countries. In *Feiwel, G. R., ed. (I)*, 1985, pp. 335–65. [G: U.S.]

Tinbergen, Jan and Kol, Jacob. Market-Determined and Residual Incomes—Some Dilemmas. In *Tinbergen, J.*, 1985, pp. 3–19. [G: U.S.; Japan]

0225 Theory of Firm and Industry under Competitive Market Structures

Afxentiou, P. C. The Envelope Curve and Market Structure: A Note. *S. Afr. J. Econ.*, March 1985, 53(1), pp. 85–89.

Amigues, Jean-Pierre. Ressource épuisable contre ressource renouvelable: le cas du gravier et du vin dans le Bordelais. (Exhaustible Resources versus Non Exhaustible Resources: The Case of Gravel and Vineyard in the Bordelais. With English summary.) *L'Actual. Econ.*, March 1985, 61(1), pp. 5–23. [G: France]

Beckmann, Martin J. A Model of Perfect Competition in Spatial Markets. *Rivista Int. Sci. Econ. Com.*, May 1985, 32(5), pp. 413–19.

Boyer, Marcel and Moreaux, Michel. L'équilibre concurrentiel comme limite de suites d'équilibres stratégiques de Stackelberg. (Competitive Equilibrium as the Limit of a Series of Stackelberg Strategic Equilibria. With English summary.) *L'Actual. Econ.*, September 1985, 61(3), pp. 299–315.

Boyer, Marcel and Moreaux, Michel. La convergence d'équilibres stratégiques en prix-quantités vers l'équilibre concurrentiel. (Convergence of Prices–Quantity Strategic Equilibria towards Competitive Equilibrium. With English summary.) *L'Actual. Econ.*, December 1985, 61(4), pp. 411–27.

Caron-Salmona, Hélène. Equilibre sur le marché d'un bien en information imparfaite: une analyse de la littérature. (Commodity Market Equilibrium with Imperfect Information: A Survey of the Literature. With English sum-

mary.) *Écon. Appl.*, 1985, 38(3/4), pp. 637–61.

Chavas, Jean-Paul. On the Theory of the Competitive Firm under Uncertainty When Initial Wealth Is Random. *Southern Econ. J.*, January 1985, 51(3), pp. 818–27.

Chavas, Jean-Paul and Pope, Rulon D. Price Uncertainty and Competitive Firm Behavior: Testable Hypotheses from Expected Utility Maximization. *J. Econ. Bus.*, August 1985, 37(3), pp. 223–35.

Connolly, Robert A. and Schwartz, Steven. The Intertemporal Behavior of Economic Profits. *Int. J. Ind. Organ.*, December 1985, 3(4), pp. 379–400. [G: U.S.]

Copes, Parzival. The Market as a Commons: Open Access vs. Price Adjustment. *De Economist*, 1985, 133(2), pp. 225–31.

Demange, Gabrielle and Ponssard, Jean-Pierre. Asymmetries in Cost Structures and Incentives towards Price Competition. *Int. J. Ind. Organ.*, March 1985, 3(1), pp. 85–100.

Economides, Nicholas S. A Note on Equilibrium in Price–Quality Competition. *Greek Econ. Rev.*, August 1985, 7(2), pp. 179–86.

Glazer, Amihai. The Advantages of Being First. *Amer. Econ. Rev.*, June 1985, 75(3), pp. 473–80. [G: U.S.]

Glick, Reuven and Wihlborg, Clas. Price Determination in a Competitive Industry with Costly Information and a Production Lag. *Rand J. Econ.*, Spring 1985, 16(1), pp. 127–40.

Gordon, Scott and Stegemann, Klaus. The Market as a Commons: Is Catching Customers Like Catching Fish? *De Economist*, 1985, 133(2), pp. 218–24.

Guesnerie, Roger and Hart, Oliver D. Welfare Losses Due to Imperfect Competition: Asymptotic Results for Cournot Nash Equilibria with and without Free Entry. *Int. Econ. Rev.*, October 1985, 26(3), pp. 525–45.

Hashimoto, Hideo. A Spatial Nash Equilibrium Model. In *Harker, P. T., ed.*, 1985, pp. 20–40.

Holler, Manfred J. The Theory of Contestable Markets: Comment [Contestable Markets: An Uprising in the Theory of Industry Structure]. *Bull. Econ. Res.*, January 1985, 37(1), pp. 65–67.

Jadresić, Estaban. Una revisión de los modelos de formación de precios. (With English summary.) *Cuadernos Econ.*, December 1985, 22(67), pp. 419–41.

Leontief, Wassily. Delayed Adjustment of Supply and Partial Equilibrium. In *Leontief, W.*, 1985, pp. 166–74.

Mas-Colell, Andreu. La libre entrada y la eficiencia económica: un análisis de equilibrio parcial. Corrección. (With English summary.) *Revista Española Econ.*, 1985, 2(2), pp. 389.

Mas-Colell, Andreu. La libre entrada y la eficiencia económica: Un análisis de equilibrio parcial. (Free Entry and Economic Efficiency: A Partial Equilibrium Analysis. With English summary.) *Revista Española Econ.*, 1985, 2(1), pp. 135–52.

Mazón, Cristina. Un modelo de información imperfecta en el que se envían anuncios por correo. (With English summary.) *Revista Española Econ.*, 1985, 2(1), pp. 35–48.

Novshek, William. Perfectly Competitive Markets as the Limits of Cournot Markets. *J. Econ. Theory*, February 1985, 35(1), pp. 72–82.

Orosel, Gerhard O. Infinite Horizon Rational Expectations Equilibrium in a Competitive Market for an Exhaustible Resource. *Int. Econ. Rev.*, October 1985, 26(3), pp. 701–20.

Rodriguez, Alvaro. Entry and Price Dynamics in a Perfect Foresight Model. *J. Econ. Dynam. Control*, November 1985, 9(3), pp. 251–71.

Telser, Lester G. Cooperation, Competition, and Efficiency. *J. Law Econ.*, May 1985, 28(2), pp. 271–95.

0226 Theory of Firm and Industry under Imperfectly Competitive Market Structures

Afxentiou, P. C. The Envelope Curve and Market Structure: A Note. *S. Afr. J. Econ.*, March 1985, 53(1), pp. 85–89.

Andersen, Torben M. Price Dynamics under Imperfect Information. *J. Econ. Dynam. Control*, November 1985, 9(3), pp. 339–61.

Appelbaum, Elie and Lim, Chin. Contestable Markets under Uncertainty. *Rand J. Econ.*, Spring 1985, 16(1), pp. 28–40.

Arrow, Kenneth J. and Nerlove, Marc. Optimal Advertising Policy under Dynamic Conditions. In *Arrow, K. J. (I)*, 1985, pp. 140–56.

Arvan, Lanny. Some Examples of Dynamic Cournot Duopoly with Inventory. *Rand J. Econ.*, Winter 1985, 16(4), pp. 569–78.

Arvan, Lanny and Moses, Leon N. A Model of the Firm in Time and Space. *J. Econ. Dynam. Control*, September 1985, 9(1), pp. 77–100.

Ashley, Richard A. and Orr, Daniel. Further Results on Inventories and Price Stickiness. *Amer. Econ. Rev.*, December 1985, 75(5), pp. 964–75.

d'Aspremont, Claude and Gabszewicz, Jean Jaskold. Quasi-monopolies. *Economica*, May 1985, 52(206), pp. 141–51.

d'Aspremont, Claude and Jacquemin, Alexis. Measuring the Power to Monopolize: A Simple-Game-Theoretic Approach. *Europ. Econ. Rev.*, February 1985, 27(1), pp. 57–74.

Bamón, Rodrigo and Frayssé, Jean. Existence of Cournot Equilibrium in Large Markets. *Econometrica*, May 1985, 53(3), pp. 587–97.

Basile, Liliana and Salvadori, Neri. Kalecki's Pricing Theory. *J. Post Keynesian Econ.*, Winter 1984–85, 7(2), pp. 249–62.

Benoit, Jean-Pierre. Innovation and Imitation in a Duopoly. *Rev. Econ. Stud.*, January 1985, 52(1), pp. 99–106.

Berck, Peter and Perloff, Jeffrey M. A Dynamic Analysis of Marketing Orders, Voting, and Welfare. *Amer. J. Agr. Econ.*, August 1985, 67(3), pp. 487–96.

Bergstrom, Theodore C. and Varian, Hal R. When Are Nash Equilibria Independent of the Distribution of Agents' Characteristics? *Rev.*

Econ. Stud., October 1985, 52(4), pp. 715–18.

Bhagwati, Jagdish N. and Sihag, Balabir S. Dual Markets, Rationing and Queues. In *Bhagwati, J. N. (II)*, 1985, pp. 205–09.

Bhattacharya, Gautam. Strategic Learning and Entry-Equilibrium. *J. Econ. Dynam. Control*, October 1985, 9(2), pp. 195–223.

Blair, Roger D.; Cooper, Thomas E. and Kaserman, David L. A Note on Vertical Integration as Entry. *Int. J. Ind. Organ.*, June 1985, 3(2), pp. 219–29.

Blitch, Charles P. The Genesis of Chamberlinian Monopolistic Competition Theory: Addendum [The Origin and Early Development of Monopolistic Competition Theory]. *Hist. Polit. Econ.*, Fall 1985, 17(3), pp. 395–400.

Bonanno, Giacomo and Zeeman, E. Christopher. Limited Knowledge of Demand and Oligopoly Equilibria. *J. Econ. Theory*, April 1985, 35(2), pp. 276–83.

Borenstein, Severin. Price Discrimination in Free-Entry Markets. *Rand J. Econ.*, Autumn 1985, 16(3), pp. 380–97.

Boyer, Marcel and Moreaux, Michel. L'équilibre concurrentiel comme limite de suites d'équilibres stratégiques de Stackelberg. (Competitive Equilibrium as the Limit of a Series of Stackelberg Strategic Equilibria. With English summary.) *L'Actual. Econ.*, September 1985, 61(3), pp. 299–315.

Boyer, Marcel and Moreaux, Michel. La convergence d'équilibres stratégiques en prix-quantités vers l'équilibre concurrentiel. (Convergence of Prices–Quantity Strategic Equilibria towards Competitive Equilibrium. With English summary.) *L'Actual. Econ.*, December 1985, 61(4), pp. 411–27.

Brander, James A. and Spencer, Barbara J. Tacit Collusion, Free Entry, and Welfare. *J. Ind. Econ.*, March 1985, 33(3), pp. 277–94.

Brennan, Geoffrey; Buchanan, James M. and Lee, Dwight R. On Monopoly Price: Reply. *Kyklos*, 1985, 38(2), pp. 274–75.

Bresnahan, Timothy F. and Reiss, Peter C. Dealer and Manufacturer Margins. *Rand J. Econ.*, Summer 1985, 16(2), pp. 253–68. [G: U.S.]

Brock, William A. and Dechert, W. D. Dynamic Ramsey Pricing. *Int. Econ. Rev.*, October 1985, 26(3), pp. 569–91.

Brock, William A. and Scheinkman, José A. Price Setting Supergames with Capacity Constraints. *Rev. Econ. Stud.*, July 1985, 52(3), pp. 371–82.

Bucovetsky, S. Erratum: Price Dispersion and Stockpiling by Consumers. *Rev. Econ. Stud.*, January 1985, 52(1), pp. 171.

Bulow, Jeremy I.; Geanakoplos, John D. and Klemperer, Paul D. Holding Idle Capacity to Deter Entry [The Role of Investment in Entry Deterrence]. *Econ. J.*, March 1985, 95(377), pp. 178–82.

Bulow, Jeremy I.; Geanakoplos, John D. and Klemperer, Paul D. Multimarket Oligopoly: Strategic Substitutes and Complements. *J. Polit. Econ.*, June 1985, 93(3), pp. 488–511.

Campbell, Robert B. and Turnovsky, Stephen J. An Analysis of the Stabilizing and Welfare Effects of Intervention in Spot and Futures Markets. *J. Public Econ.*, November 1985, *28*(2), pp. 165–209.

Cheng, Leonard. Comparing Bertrand and Cournot Equilibria: A Geometric Approach [Price and Quantity Competition in a Differentiated Duopoly]. *Rand J. Econ.*, Spring 1985, *16*(1), pp. 146–52.

Choi, Eun Kwan; Menezes, Carmen F. and Tressler, John H. A Theory of Price-fixing Rings. *Quart. J. Econ.*, May 1985, *100*(2), pp. 465–78.

Clapp, John M. Quantity Competition in Spatial Markets with Incomplete Information. *Quart. J. Econ.*, May 1985, *100*(2), pp. 519–28.

Colander, David C. Some Simple Geometry of the Welfare Loss from Competitive Monopolies. *Public Choice*, 1985, *45*(2), pp. 199–206.

Cooper, Russell and Ross, Thomas W. Monopoly Provision of Product Quality with Uninformed Buyers. *Int. J. Ind. Organ.*, December 1985, *3*(4), pp. 439–49.

Crampes, Claude and Moreaux, Michel. Intégration verticale et rendements décroissants. (Vertical Integration and Decreasing Returns. With English summary.) *Revue Écon.*, July 1985, *36*(4), pp. 669–85.

Crémer, Jacques and McLean, Richard P. Optimal Selling Strategies under Uncertainty for a Discriminating Monopolist When Demands Are Interdependent. *Econometrica*, March 1985, *53*(2), pp. 345–61.

Cresta, Jean-Paul. Tarification sur un marché monopolistique avec sélection adverse. (With English summary.) *Revue Écon. Polit.*, July-August 1985, *95*(4), pp. 397–413.

Crew, Michael A. and Kleindorfer, Paul R. Governance Structures for Natural Monopoly: A Comparative Institutional Assessment. *J. Behav. Econ.*, Winter 1985, *14*, pp. 117–40.

Daughety, Andrew F. Reconsidering Cournot: The Cournot Equilibrium Is Consistent. *Rand J. Econ.*, Autumn 1985, *16*(3), pp. 368–79.

Davidson, Carl and Martin, Lawrence W. General Equilibrium Tax Incidence under Imperfect Competition: A Quantity-setting Supergame Analysis. *J. Polit. Econ.*, December 1985, *93*(6), pp. 1212–23.

Davies, Glyn. The Revolution in Monopoly Theory: Reply. *Lloyds Bank Rev.*, July 1985, (157), pp. 37–38.

DeJong, Douglas V.; Forsythe, Robert and Lundholm, Russell J. Ripoffs, Lemons, and Reputation Formation in Agency Relationships: A Laboratory Market Study. *J. Finance*, July 1985, *40*(3), pp. 809–20.

Demange, Gabrielle and Ponssard, Jean-Pierre. Asymmetries in Cost Structures and Incentives towards Price Competition. *Int. J. Ind. Organ.*, March 1985, *3*(1), pp. 85–100.

Deneckere, Raymond and Davidson, Carl. Incentives to Form Coalitions with Bertrand Competition. *Rand J. Econ.*, Winter 1985, *16*(4), pp. 473–86.

Denzau, Arthur T.; Kats, Amoz and Slutsky, S. Multi-agent Equilibria with Market Share and Ranking Objectives. *Soc. Choice Welfare*, September 1985, *2*(2), pp. 95–117.

Donsimoni, Marie-Paule. Stable Heterogeneous Cartels. *Int. J. Ind. Organ.*, December 1985, *3*(4), pp. 451–67.

Easley, David; Masson, Robert T. and Reynolds, Robert J. Preying for Time. *J. Ind. Econ.*, June 1985, *33*(4), pp. 445–60.

Eaton, B. Curtis and Wooders, Myrna Holtz. Sophisticated Entry in a Model of Spatial Competition. *Rand J. Econ.*, Summer 1985, *16*(2), pp. 282–97.

Economides, Nicholas S. A Note on Equilibrium in Price–Quality Competition. *Greek Econ. Rev.*, August 1985, *7*(2), pp. 179–86.

Eswaran, Mukesh and Lewis, Tracy R. Exhaustible Resources and Alternative Equilibrium Concepts. *Can. J. Econ.*, August 1985, *18*(3), pp. 459–73.

Feinberg, Robert M. and Sherman, Roger. An Experimental Investigation of Mutual Forbearance by Conglomerate Firms. In *Schwalbach, J., ed.*, 1985, pp. 139–66.

Feldman, David and Tower, Edward. Errata: Profitable Destabilizing Speculation as Intertemporal Price Discrimination. *Amer. Econ.*, Spring 1985, *29*(1), pp. 84.

Fershtman, Chaim. Managerial Incentives as a Strategic Variable in Duopolistic Environment. *Int. J. Ind. Organ.*, June 1985, *3*(2), pp. 245–53.

Fisher, Franklin M. Can Exclusive Franchises Be Bad? In *[McGowan, J. J.]*, 1985, pp. 153–71.

Fisher, Franklin M. The Social Costs of Monopoly and Regulation: Posner Reconsidered. *J. Polit. Econ.*, April 1985, *93*(2), pp. 410–16. [G: U.S.]

Frayssé, Jean and Moreaux, Michel. Collusive Equilibria in Oligopolies with Finite Lives. *Europ. Econ. Rev.*, February 1985, *27*(1), pp. 45–55.

Fudenberg, Drew and Tirole, Jean. Preemption and Rent Equilization in the Adoption of New Technology. *Rev. Econ. Stud.*, July 1985, *52*(3), pp. 383–401.

Gabszewicz, Jean Jaskold. Imperfect Competition in General Equilibrium: An Overview of Recent Work: Comment. In *Arrow, K. J. and Honkapohja, J., eds.*, 1985, pp. 150–69.

Gal-Or, Esther. Differentiated Industries without Entry Barriers. *J. Econ. Theory*, December 1985, *37*(2), pp. 310–39.

Gal-Or, Esther. First Mover and Second Mover Advantages. *Int. Econ. Rev.*, October 1985, *26*(3), pp. 649–53.

Gal-Or, Esther. Information Sharing in Oligopoly. *Econometrica*, March 1985, *53*(2), pp. 329–43.

Gardner, R. Rationing, Bargaining, and Voting in 2-Sided Markets? *Soc. Choice Welfare*, May 1985, *2*(1), pp. 39–48.

Geroski, P. A.; Phlips, Louis and Ulph, A. Oligopoly, Competition and Welfare: Some Recent Developments. *J. Ind. Econ.*, June 1985, 33(4), pp. 369–86.   [G: U.S.; U.K.]

Geroski, P. A.; Phlips, Louis and Ulph, A. Oligopoly, Competition and Welfare: Some Recent Developments. In *Geroski, P. A.; Phlips, L. and Ulph, A., eds.*, 1985, pp. 1–18.

Ghemawat, Pankaj and Nalebuff, Barry. Exit. *Rand J. Econ.*, Summer 1985, 16(2), pp. 184–94.

Ghemawat, Pankaj and Spence, A. Michael. Learning Curve Spillovers and Market Performance. *Quart. J. Econ.*, Supp. 1985, 100, pp. 839–52.

Glick, Mark. Monopoly or Competition in the U.S. Economy? *Rev. Radical Polit. Econ.*, Winter 1985, 17(4), pp. 121–27.   [G: U.S.]

Glick, Reuven and Wihlborg, Clas. Price and Output Adjustment, Inventory Flexibility, and Cost and Demand Disturbances. *Can. J. Econ.*, August 1985, 18(3), pp. 566–73.

Goldstein, Jonathan P. The Cyclical Profit Squeeze: A Marxian Microfoundation. *Rev. Radical Polit. Econ.*, Spring and Summer 1985, 17(1/2), pp. 103–28.

Gould, John P. and Verrecchia, Robert E. The Information Content of Specialist Pricing. *J. Polit. Econ.*, February 1985, 93(1), pp. 66–83.

Graeser, Paul. Rationality, Rent, and the Marginal Customer. *Atlantic Econ. J.*, December 1985, 13(4), pp. 81.

Greenhut, Melvin L.; Ohta, Hiroshi and Sailors, Joel. Reverse Dumping: A Form of Spatial Price Discrimination. *J. Ind. Econ.*, December 1985, 34(2), pp. 167–81.

Greenhut, Melvin L., et al. An Anomaly in the Service Industry: The Effect of Entry on Fees. *Econ. J.*, March 1985, 95(377), pp. 169–77.

Guesnerie, Roger and Hart, Oliver D. Welfare Losses Due to Imperfect Competition: Asymptotic Results for Cournot Nash Equilibria with and without Free Entry. *Int. Econ. Rev.*, October 1985, 26(3), pp. 525–45.

Hahn, Frank. Excess Capacity and Imperfect Competition. In *Hahn, F.*, 1985, pp. 348–63.

Hahn, Frank. Uncertainty and the Cobweb. In *Hahn, F.*, 1985, pp. 210–28.

Hallagan, William S. and Joerding, Wayne. Equilibrium Price Dispersion [The Theory of Sales: A Simple Model of Equilibrium Price Dispersion with Identical Agents]. *Amer. Econ. Rev.*, December 1985, 75(5), pp. 1191–94.

Hannesson, Rögnvaldur. The Effects of a Fishermen's Monopoly in the Market for Unprocessed Fish. *Marine Resource Econ.*, 1985, 2(1), pp. 75–85.

Harpaz, Giora. Learning by a Dominant Firm. *Managerial Dec. Econ.*, March 1985, 6(1), pp. 59–63.

Harris, Christopher J. and Vickers, John. Patent Races and the Persistence of Monopoly. In *Geroski, P. A.; Phlips, L. and Ulph, A., eds.*, 1985, pp. 93–113.

Harris, Christopher J. and Vickers, John. Patent Races and the Persistence of Monopoly. *J. Ind. Econ.*, June 1985, 33(4), pp. 461–81.

Harris, Jeffrey. Competition and Equilibrium as a Driving Force in the Health Services Sector: Comment. In *Inman, R. P., ed.*, 1985, pp. 268–72.

Harrison, Glenn W. and McKee, Michael. Monopoly Behavior, Decentralized Regulation, and Contestable Markets: An Experimental Evaluation. *Rand J. Econ.*, Spring 1985, 16(1), pp. 51–69.

Hart, Oliver D. Imperfect Competition in General Equilibrium: An Overview of Recent Work. In *Arrow, K. J. and Honkapohja, S., eds.*, 1985, pp. 100–149.

Hart, Oliver D. Monopolistic Competition in the Spirit of Chamberlin: A General Model. *Rev. Econ. Stud.*, October 1985, 52(4), pp. 529–46.

Hart, Oliver D. Monopolistic Competition in the Spirit of Chamberlin: Special Results. *Econ. J.*, December 1985, 95(380), pp. 889–908.

Hashimoto, Hideo. A Spatial Nash Equilibrium Model. In *Harker, P. T., ed.*, 1985, pp. 20–40.

Helwege, Ann and Hendricks, Ann. Contestability and Creative Destruction: Two Approaches to Monopoly. *Rev. Ind. Organ.*, 1985, 2(3), pp. 218–30.

Higani, Yoshiro. On the 'Exclusion Theorem.' *Reg. Sci. Urban Econ.*, August 1985, 15(3), pp. 449–58.

Holler, Manfred J. The Theory of Contestable Markets: Comment [Contestable Markets: An Uprising in the Theory of Industry Structure]. *Bull. Econ. Res.*, January 1985, 37(1), pp. 65–67.

Holt, Charles A. An Experimental Test of the Consistent-Conjectures Hypothesis. *Amer. Econ. Rev.*, June 1985, 75(3), pp. 314–25.

Horstmann, Ignatius J. and Slivinski, Alan D. Location Models as Models of Product Choice. *J. Econ. Theory*, August 1985, 36(2), pp. 367–86.

Hurter, Arthur P., Jr. and Lederer, Phillip J. Spatial Duopoly with Discriminatory Pricing. *Reg. Sci. Urban Econ.*, November 1985, 15(4), pp. 541–53.

Ilmakunnas, Pekka. Conjectural Variations, Risk Aversion and Price–Cost Margins. *Z. Nationalökon.*, 1985, 45(1), pp. 73–80.

Ireland, Norman J. Product Diversity and Monopolistic Competition under Uncertainty. *J. Ind. Econ.*, June 1985, 33(4), pp. 501–13.

Ireland, Norman J. Product Diversity and Monopolistic Competition under Uncertainty. In *Geroski, P. A.; Phlips, L. and Ulph, A., eds.*, 1985, pp. 133–45.

Ireland, Norman J. and Stoneman, Paul L. Order Effects, Perfect Foresight and Intertemporal Price Discrimination. *Rech. Écon. Louvain*, 1985, 51(1), pp. 7–20.

Jadresić, Esteban. Una revisión de los modelos de formación de precios. (With English summary.) *Cuadernos Econ.*, December 1985, 22(67), pp. 419–41.

Jeuland, Abel P. and Narasimhan, Chakravarthi. Dealing—Temporary Price Cuts—by Seller as a Buyer Discrimination Mechanism. *J. Bus.*,

July 1985, *58*(3), pp. 295–308.

Judd, Kenneth L. Credible Spatial Preemption. *Rand J. Econ.*, Summer 1985, *16*(2), pp. 153–66.

Judd, Kenneth L. and Petersen, Bruce C. Dynamic Limit Pricing: A Reformulation. *Rev. Ind. Organ.*, 1985, *2*(2), pp. 160–77.

Kalai, Ehud and Stanford, William. Conjectural Variations Strategies in Accelerated Cournot Games. *Int. J. Ind. Organ.*, June 1985, *3*(2), pp. 133–52.

Katz, Michael L. and Shapiro, Carl. On the Licensing of Innovations. *Rand J. Econ.*, Winter 1985, *16*(4), pp. 504–20.

Kim, Jae-Cheol. The Market for "Lemons" Reconsidered: A Model of the Used Car Market with Asymmetric Information. *Amer. Econ. Rev.*, September 1985, *75*(4), pp. 836–43.

Kim, Ki Hang and Roush, Fred W. Price Adjustment in an Economy with Markov Disturbance. *Math. Soc. Sci.*, December 1985, *10*(3), pp. 263–67.

Kuenne, Robert E. Oligopoly under Rivalrous Consonance: An Exploration of Phantom Objective Functions and Some Algorithmic Considerations. *Rivista Int. Sci. Econ. Com.*, May 1985, *32*(5), pp. 393–411.

Kuenne, Robert E. The Oligopolistic Industry under Rivalrous Consonance with Target-Rate-of-Return Objectives. In *Feiwel, G. R., ed. (II),* 1985, pp. 281–308.

Kumar, K. Ravi and Satterthwaite, Mark A. Monopolistic Competition, Aggregation of Competitive Information, and the Amount of Product Differentiation. *J. Econ. Theory*, October 1985, *37*(1), pp. 32–54.

Kunreuther, Howard and Pauly, Mark V. Market Equilibrium with Private Knowledge: An Insurance Example. *J. Public Econ.*, April 1985, *26*(3), pp. 269–88.

Kurz, Mordecai. Cooperative Oligopoly Equilibrium. *Europ. Econ. Rev.*, February 1985, *27*(1), pp. 3–24.

Kurz, Mordecai. Reconsideration of Duopoly Theory: A Co-operative Perspective. In *Feiwel, G. R., ed. (II),* 1985, pp. 245–80.

Laffond, Gilbert and Lesourne, Jacques. Market Dynamics with Search Processes and Information Costs. *Écon. Appl.*, 1985, *38*(3/4), pp. 739–65.

Laffont, Jean-Jacques and Moreaux, Michel. Large-Market Cournot Equilibria in Labour-managed Economies. *Economica*, May 1985, *52*(206), pp. 153–65.

Landsberger, Michael and Meilijson, Isaac. Intertemporal Price Discrimination and Sales Strategy under Incomplete Information. *Rand J. Econ.*, Autumn 1985, *16*(3), pp. 424–30.

Lawler, Kevin. The Revolution in Monopoly Theory: Comment. *Lloyds Bank Rev.*, July 1985, (157), pp. 36–37.

Lee, Frederic S. "Full Costx" Prices, Classical Price Theory, and Long Period Method Analysis: A Critical Evaluation. *Metroecon.*, June 1985, *37*(2), pp. 199–219.

Lee, Frederic S. "Kalecki's Pricing Theory": Two Comments. *J. Post Keynesian Econ.*, Fall 1985, *8*(1), pp. 145–48.

Levin, Dan. Taxation within Cournot Oligopoly. *J. Public Econ.*, August 1985, *27*(3), pp. 281–90.

Lewbel, Arthur. Bundling of Substitutes or Complements. *Int. J. Ind. Organ.*, March 1985, *3*(1), pp. 101–07.

Li, Lode. Cournot Oligopoly with Information Sharing. *Rand J. Econ.*, Winter 1985, *16*(4), pp. 521–36.

Lovell, C. A. Knox and Wertz, Kenneth L. Third Degree Price Discrimination in Imperfectly Sealed Markets. *Atlantic Econ. J.*, July 1985, *13*(2), pp. 1–11.

MacLeod, W. Bentley. A Theory of Conscious Parallelism. *Europ. Econ. Rev.*, February 1985, *27*(1), pp. 25–44.

MacLeod, W. Bentley. On the Non-existence of Equilibria in Differentiated Product Models. *Reg. Sci. Urban Econ.*, June 1985, *15*(2), pp. 245–62.

MacLeod, W. Bentley. On Adjustment Costs and the Stability of Equilibria. *Rev. Econ. Stud.*, October 1985, *52*(4), pp. 575–91.

Margolis, Stephen E. The Excess Capacity Controversy: A Critique of Recent Criticism. *Econ. Inquiry*, April 1985, *23*(2), pp. 265–75.

McElroy, F. William. The Welfare Economics of Dominant-Firm Acquisitions. *Z. Nationalökon.*, 1985, *45*(2), pp. 115–40.

Mendelson, Haim. Ripoffs, Lemons, and Reputation Formation in Agency Relationships: A Laboratory Market Study: Discussion. *J. Finance*, July 1985, *40*(3), pp. 820–23.

de Meza, David. A Stable Cournot–Nash Industry Need Not Be Quasi-competitive. *Bull. Econ. Res.*, May 1985, *37*(2), pp. 153–56.

Miller, Ross M. and Plott, Charles R. Product Quality Signaling in Experimental Markets. *Econometrica*, July 1985, *53*(4), pp. 837–72.

Mirakhor, Abbas and Khalili, A. Optimum Location and the Theory of Production: An Extension. *Reg. Sci. Persp.*, 1985, *15*(1), pp. 63–74.

Mirman, Leonard J.; Tauman, Yair and Zang, Israel. Monopoly and Sustainable Prices as a Nash Equilibrium in Contestable Markets. In *Feiwel, G. R., ed. (II),* 1985, pp. 328–39.

Mirman, Leonard J.; Tauman, Yair and Zang, Israel. Supportability, Sustainability, and Subsidy-free Prices. *Rand J. Econ.*, Spring 1985, *16*(1), pp. 114–26.

Mixon, J. Wilson and Uri, Noel D. On the Optimal Pricing Policy of a Dominant Firm. *Indian Econ. J.*, Oct.-Nov. 1985, *33*(2), pp. 131–34.

Moorthy, K. Sridhar. Cournot Competition in a Differentiated Oligopoly. *J. Econ. Theory*, June 1985, *36*(1), pp. 86–109.

Mork, Knut Anton. Flexibility in Intercommodity Substitution May Sharpen Price Fluctuations. *Quart. J. Econ.*, May 1985, *100*(2), pp. 447–63.

Murray, Sean. On Monopoly Price: A Comment. *Kyklos*, 1985, *38*(2), pp. 268–73.

Nakao, Takeo. The Effects of Demonopolization on Economic Growth. *Can. J. Econ.*, August

1985, *18*(3), pp. 622–35.

Neary, Hugh M. The Labour-managed Firm in Monopolistic Competition. *Economica*, November 1985, *52*(208), pp. 435–47.

Nelson, Carl H. and McCarl, Bruce A. Including Imperfect Competition in Spatial Equilibrium: A Reply. *Can. J. Agr. Econ.*, March 1985, *33*(1), pp. 113–14.

Neumann, Manfred; Böbel, Ingo and Haid, Alfred. Domestic Concentration, Foreign Trade, and Economic Performance. *Int. J. Ind. Organ.*, March 1985, *3*(1), pp. 1–19.
[G: W. Germany]

Neven, Damien J. Two Stage (Perfect) Equilibrium in Hotelling's Model. *J. Ind. Econ.*, March 1985, *33*(3), pp. 317–25.

Neven, Damien J. and Phlips, Louis. Discriminating Oligopolists and Common Markets. *J. Ind. Econ.*, December 1985, *34*(2), pp. 133–49.

Novshek, William. On the Existence of Cournot Equilibrium. *Rev. Econ. Stud.*, January 1985, *52*(1), pp. 85–98.

Novshek, William. Perfectly Competitive Markets as the Limits of Cournot Markets. *J. Econ. Theory*, February 1985, *35*(1), pp. 72–82.

al-Nowaihi, A. and Levine, Paul. The Stability of the Cournot Oligopoly Model: A Reassessment. *J. Econ. Theory*, April 1985, *35*(2), pp. 307–21.

Ohlson, James A. Ex Post Stockholder Unanimity: A Complete and Simplified Treatment. *J. Banking Finance*, September 1985, *9*(3), pp. 387–99.

Oren, Shmuel S.; Smith, Stephen S. and Wilson, Robert B. Capacity Pricing. *Econometrica*, May 1985, *53*(3), pp. 545–66.

Palfrey, Thomas R. Uncertainty Resolution, Private Information Aggregation, and the Cournot Competitive Limit. *Rev. Econ. Stud.*, January 1985, *52*(1), pp. 69–83.

de Palma, André, et al. The Principle of Minimum Differentiation Holds under Sufficient Heterogeneity. *Econometrica*, July 1985, *53*(4), pp. 767–81.

Perloff, Jeffrey M. and Salop, Steven C. Equilibrium with Product Differentiation. *Rev. Econ. Stud.*, January 1985, *52*(1), pp. 107–20.

Perry, Martin K. and Groff, Robert H. Resale Price Maintenance and Forward Integration into a Monopolistically Competitive Industry. *Quart. J. Econ.*, November 1985, *100*(4), pp. 1293–1311.

Perry, Martin K. and Porter, Robert H. Oligopoly and the Incentive for Horizontal Merger. *Amer. Econ. Rev.*, March 1985, *75*(1), pp. 219–27.

Peters, Michael. Immobility, Rationing and Price Competition. *Rev. Econ. Stud.*, October 1985, *52*(4), pp. 593–604.

Phillips, Almarin and Roberts, Gary L. Borrowing from Peter to Pay Paul: More on Departures of Price from Marginal Cost. In *[McGowan, J. J.]*, 1985 report, pp. 299–307.

Pöll, Günther. Introduction to the Sustainability Analysis of Contested Markets and the Multi-

product Firm: A Graphical Exposition. *Z. ges. Staatswiss. (JITE)*, September 1985, *141*(3), pp. 413–34.

Rao, T. V. S. Ramamohan. Efficient Choice of the Quality of Product. *Rivista Int. Sci. Econ. Com.*, July-Aug. 1985, *32*(7–8), pp. 609–23.

Rees, Ray. Cheating in a Duopoly Supergame. *J. Ind. Econ.*, June 1985, *33*(4), pp. 387–400.

Rees, Ray. Cheating in a Duopoly Supergame. In *Geroski, P. A.; Phlips, L. and Ulph, A., eds.*, 1985, pp. 19–32.

Reinganum, Jennifer F. and Stokey, Nancy L. Oligopoly Extraction of a Common Property Natural Resource: The Importance of the Period of Commitment in Dynamic Games. *Int. Econ. Rev.*, February 1985, *26*(1), pp. 161–73.

Reinwald, Thomas P. The Genesis of Chamberlinian Monopolistic Competition Theory: Addendum—A Comment [The Origin and Early Development of Monopolistic Competition Theory]. *Hist. Polit. Econ.*, Fall 1985, *17*(3), pp. 400–402.

Riley, John G. Competition with Hidden Knowledge. *J. Polit. Econ.*, October 1985, *93*(5), pp. 958–76.

Riordan, Michael H. Imperfect Information and Dynamic Conjectural Variations. *Rand J. Econ.*, Spring 1985, *16*(1), pp. 41–50.

Rob, Rafael. Equilibrium Price Distributions. *Rev. Econ. Stud.*, July 1985, *52*(3), pp. 487–504.

Roberts, Kevin. Cartel Behaviour and Adverse Selection. In *Geroski, P. A.; Phlips, L. and Ulph, A., eds.*, 1985, pp. 33–45.

Roberts, Kevin. Cartel Behaviour and Adverse Selection. *J. Ind. Econ.*, June 1985, *33*(4), pp. 401–13.

Rochet, Jean-Charles. Bilateral Monopoly with Imperfect Information. *J. Econ. Theory*, August 1985, *36*(2), pp. 214–36.

Rochet, Jean-Charles. The Taxation Principle and Multi-time Hamilton–Jacobi Equations. *J. Math. Econ.*, 1985, *14*(2), pp. 113–28.

Rodriguez, Alvaro. Entry and Price Dynamics in a Perfect Foresight Model. *J. Econ. Dynam. Control*, November 1985, *9*(3), pp. 251–71.

Romano, Richard E. and Berg, Sanford V. The Identification of Predatory Behavior in the Presence of Uncertainty. *Int. J. Ind. Organ.*, June 1985, *3*(2), pp. 231–43.

Rubinstein, Ariel and Wolinsky, Asher. Equilibrium in a Market with Sequential Bargaining. *Econometrica*, September 1985, *53*(5), pp. 1133–50.

Rust, John. Stationary Equilibrium in a Market for Durable Assets. *Econometrica*, July 1985, *53*(4), pp. 783–805.

Saari, Donald G. Iterative Price Mechanisms. *Econometrica*, September 1985, *53*(5), pp. 1117–31.

Sakai, Yasuhiro. The Value of Information in a Simple Duopoly Model. *J. Econ. Theory*, June 1985, *36*(1), pp. 36–54.

Sappington, David E. M. and Wernerfelt, Birger. To Brand or Not to Brand? A Theoretical and Empirical Question. *J. Bus.*, July 1985, 58(3), pp. 279–93.   [G: U.S.]

Satterthwaite, Mark A. Competition and Equilibrium as a Driving Force in the Health Services Sector. In *Inman, R. P., ed.*, 1985, pp. 239–67.

Saunders, Ronald S. Learning by Doing and Dominant Firm Pricing Strategy. *Rev. Ind. Organ.*, 1985, 2(1), pp. 32–39.

Schap, David. X-Inefficiency in a Rent-seeking Society: A Graphical Analysis. *Quart. Rev. Econ. Bus.*, Spring 1985, 25(1), pp. 19–27.

Schöler, Klaus. The Welfare Effects of Spatial Competition under Sequential Market Entry. *Southern Econ. J.*, July 1985, 52(1), pp. 265–73.

Schulz, Norbert and Stahl, Konrad. Localisation des oligopoles et marchés du travail locaux. (Oligopolistic Industry Location and Local Labor Markets. With English summary.) *Revue Écon.*, January 1985, 36(1), pp. 103–34.

Schulz, Norbert and Stahl, Konrad. On the Non-existence of Oligopolistic Equilibria in Differentiated Products Spaces. *Reg. Sci. Urban Econ.*, June 1985, 15(2), pp. 229–43.

Schwartz, Alan and Wilde, Louis L. Product Quality and Imperfect Information. *Rev. Econ. Stud.*, April 1985, 52(2), pp. 251–62.

Scotchmer, Suzanne. Two-tier Pricing of Shared Facilities in a Free-Entry Equilibrium. *Rand J. Econ.*, Winter 1985, 16(4), pp. 456–72.

Scott, Frank A., Jr. and Morrell, Stephen O. Two-Part Pricing for a Multi-product Monopolist. *Econ. Inquiry*, April 1985, 23(2), pp. 295–307.

Shaffer, Sherrill. Price Leadership without Collusion. *Australian Econ. Pap.*, June 1985, 24(44), pp. 210–13.

Shubik, Martin. The Many Approaches to the Study of Monopolistic Competition. *Europ. Econ. Rev.*, February 1985, 27(1), pp. 97–114.

Simon, Marilyn J.; Wolf, Robert G. and Perloff, Jeffrey M. Product Safety, Liability Rules and Retailer Bankruptcy. *Southern Econ. J.*, April 1985, 51(4), pp. 1130–41.

Smith, Janet K. and Smith, Richard L. A Theory of *Ex Post* versus *Ex Ante* Price Determination. *Econ. Inquiry*, January 1985, 23(1), pp. 57–67.

Smith, Tony E. and Friesz, Terry L. Spatial Market Equilibria with Flow-Dependent Supply and Demand: The Single Commodity Case. *Reg. Sci. Urban Econ.*, June 1985, 15(2), pp. 181–218.

Sonnenschein, Hugo. Imperfect Competition in General Equilibrium: An Overview of Recent Work: Comment. In *Arrow, K. J. and Honkapohja, S., eds.*, 1985, pp. 170–77.

Spatt, Chester S. and Sterbenz, Frederic P. Learning, Preemption, and the Degree of Rivalry. *Rand J. Econ.*, Spring 1985, 16(1), pp. 84–92.

Srinagesh, P. Non-linear Prices with Heterogeneous Consumers and Uncertain Demand. *Indian Econ. Rev.*, July-Dec. 1985, 20(2), pp. 299–315.

Srivastava, Sanjay. Pure Strategy Nash Equilibria with Continuous Objectives. *J. Econ. Theory*, June 1985, 36(1), pp. 26–35.

Stahl, Dale O., II. Relaxing the Sure-Solvency Conditions in Temporary Equilibrium Models. *J. Econ. Theory*, October 1985, 37(1), pp. 1–18.

Turnovsky, Stephen J. and Campbell, Robert B. The Stabilizing and Welfare Properties of Futures Markets: A Simulation Approach. *Int. Econ. Rev.*, June 1985, 26(2), pp. 277–303.

von Ungern-Sternberg, Thomas and von Weizsäcker, Carl Christian. The Supply of Quality on a Market for "Experience Goods." *J. Ind. Econ.*, June 1985, 33(4), pp. 531–51.

von Ungern-Sternberg, Thomas and von Weizsäcker, Carl Christian. The Supply of Quality on a Market for "Experience Goods." In *Geroski, P. A.; Phlips, L. and Ulph, A., eds.*, 1985, pp. 163–72.

Ushio, Yoshiaki. Approximate Efficiency of Cournot Equilibria in Large Markets. *Rev. Econ. Stud.*, October 1985, 52(4), pp. 547–56.

Varian, Hal R. Price Discrimination and Social Welfare. *Amer. Econ. Rev.*, September 1985, 75(4), pp. 870–75.

Veall, Michael R. On Product Standardization as Competition Policy. *Can. J. Econ.*, May 1985, 18(2), pp. 416–25.

Vives, Xavier. On the Efficiency of Bertrand and Cournot Equilibria with Product Differentation. *J. Econ. Theory*, June 1985, 36(1), pp. 166–75.

Ware, Roger. Inventory Holding as a Strategic Weapon to Deter Entry. *Economica*, February 1985, 52(205), pp. 93–101.

Waterson, Michael. Locational Mobility and Welfare. *Econ. J.*, September 1985, 95(379), pp. 774–77.

Watson, John Keith. A Behavioral Analysis of Negative Price Reactions in Spatial Markets. *Southern Econ. J.*, January 1985, 51(3), pp. 882–85.

Weinberg, Jakob. Bertrand Oligopoly in a Spatial Context: The Case of Quantity Independent Transportation Costs. *Reg. Sci. Urban Econ.*, June 1985, 15(2), pp. 263–75.

Weskamp, Anita. Existence of Spatial Cournot Equilibria. *Reg. Sci. Urban Econ.*, June 1985, 15(2), pp. 219–27.

Wolf, Robert G. Monopsonistically/Monopolistically Competitive Regional Development: Public Correction of Market Outcomes. *J. Urban Econ.*, May 1985, 17(3), pp. 263–79.

Yamey, Basil S. Deconcentration as Antitrust Policy: The Rise and Fall of the Concentration Ratio. *Rivista Int. Sci. Econ. Com.*, February 1985, 32(2), pp. 119–40.

Yang, Chin-Wei. Including Imperfect Competition in Spatial Equilibrium Models: A Comment. *Can. J. Agr. Econ.*, March 1985, 33(1), pp. 111–12.

Yarrow, George K. Welfare Losses in Oligopoly and Monopolistic Competition. *J. Ind. Econ.*, June 1985, 33(4), pp. 515–29.

Yarrow, George K. Welfare Losses in Oligopoly

and Monopolistic Competition. In *Geroski, P. A.; Phlips, L. and Ulph, A., eds.*, 1985, pp. 147–61.

Ziemes, Georg. The Averch/Johnson Effect in a Simple Oligopoly Model. *Z. ges. Staatswiss. (JITE)*, September 1985, *141*(3), pp. 444–51.

Zigiotti, Ermanno. Incertezza probabilistica, rischi assicurabili e integrazione verticale. (Probabilistic Uncertainty, Insurable Risks, and Vertical Integration. With English summary.) *Giorn. Econ.*, May-June 1985, *44*(11–12), pp. 301–12.

0227 Theory of Auction Markets

Burns, Penny. Market Structure and Buyer Behaviour: Price Adjustment in a Multi-object Progressive Oral Auction. *J. Econ. Behav. Organ.*, September 1985, *6*(3), pp. 275–300.

Cox, James C.; Smith, Vernon L. and Walker, James M. Experimental Development of Sealed-Bid Auction Theory: Calibrating Controls for Risk Aversion. *Amer. Econ. Rev.*, May 1985, *75*(2), pp. 160–65.

Crémer, Jacques and McLean, Richard P. Optimal Selling Strategies under Uncertainty for a Discriminating Monopolist When Demands Are Interdependent. *Econometrica*, March 1985, *53*(2), pp. 345–61.

Feinstein, Jonathan S.; Block, Michael K. and Nold, Frederick C. Asymmetric Information and Collusive Behavior in Auction Markets. *Amer. Econ. Rev.*, June 1985, *75*(3), pp. 441–60.

Gilley, Otis W. and Karels, Gordon V. The Number of Competitors and Bid Prices: Comment. *Southern Econ. J.*, January 1985, *51*(3), pp. 921–23. [G: U.S.]

Hansen, Robert G. Auctions with Contingent Payments. *Amer. Econ. Rev.*, September 1985, *75*(4), pp. 862–65.

Hansen, Robert G. Empirical Testing of Auction Theory. *Amer. Econ. Rev.*, May 1985, *75*(2), pp. 156–59.

Harstad, Ronald M. and Levin, Dan. A Class of Dominance Solvable Common-Value Auctions. *Rev. Econ. Stud.*, July 1985, *52*(3), pp. 525–28.

Isaac, R. Mark and Walker, James M. Information and Conspiracy in Sealed Bid Auctions. *J. Econ. Behav. Organ.*, June 1985, *6*(2), pp. 139–59.

Kobrin, Paul. Joint Bidding, Collusion, and Bid Clustering in Competitive Auctions: Comment. *Southern Econ. J.*, April 1985, *51*(4), pp. 1216–18.

Kuhlman, John M. and Johnson, Stanley R. The Number of Competitors and Bid Prices: Reply. *Southern Econ. J.*, January 1985, *51*(3), pp. 924–26. [G: U.S.]

Kyle, Albert S. Continuous Auctions and Insider Trading. *Econometrica*, November 1985, *53*(6), pp. 1315–35.

Maskin, Eric S. and Riley, John G. Auction Theory with Private Values. *Amer. Econ. Rev.*, May 1985, *75*(2), pp. 150–55.

Milgrom, Paul R. The Economics of Competitive Bidding: A Selective Survey. In *[Pazner, E.]*, 1985, pp. 261–89.

Robinson, Marc S. Collusion and the Choice of Auction. *Rand J. Econ.*, Spring 1985, *16*(1), pp. 141–45.

Smith, James L. Joint Bidding, Collusion, and Bid Clustering in Competitive Auctions: Reply. *Southern Econ. J.*, April 1985, *51*(4), pp. 1219–20.

Wilson, Robert B. Incentive Efficiency of Double Auctions. *Econometrica*, September 1985, *53*(5), pp. 1101–15.

0228 Agent Theory

Arrow, Kenneth J. The Economics of Agency. In *Pratt, J. W. and Zeckhauser, R. J., eds.*, 1985, pp. 37–51.

Bhattacharya, Sudipto and Pfleiderer, Paul. Delegated Portfolio Management. *J. Econ. Theory*, June 1985, *36*(1), pp. 1–25.

Campbell, Tim S. and Kracaw, William A. The Market for Managerial Labor Services and Capital Market Equilibrium. *J. Finan. Quant. Anal.*, September 1985, *20*(3), pp. 277–97.

Clark, Robert C. Agency Costs versus Fiduciary Duties. In *Pratt, J. W. and Zeckhauser, R. J., eds.*, 1985, pp. 55–79.

Cooper, Russell and Ross, Thomas W. Product Warranties and Double Moral Hazard. *Rand J. Econ.*, Spring 1985, *16*(1), pp. 103–13.

DeJong, Douglas V.; Forsythe, Robert and Lundholm, Russell J. Ripoffs, Lemons, and Reputation Formation in Agency Relationships: A Laboratory Market Study. *J. Finance*, July 1985, *40*(3), pp. 809–20.

DeJong, Douglas V., et al. A Laboratory Investigation of the Moral Hazard Problem in an Agency Relationship. *J. Acc. Res.*, Supp. 1985, *23*, pp. 81–120. [G: U.S.]

Easterbrook, Frank H. Insider Trading as an Agency Problem. In *Pratt, J. W. and Zeckhauser, R. J., eds.*, 1985, pp. 81–100.

Eccles, Robert G. Transfer Pricing as a Problem of Agency. In *Pratt, J. W. and Zeckhauser, R. J., eds.*, 1985, pp. 151–86.

Fellingham, John C.; Newman, D. Paul and Suh, Yoon S. Contracts without Memory in Multiperiod Agency Models. *J. Econ. Theory*, December 1985, *37*(2), pp. 340–55.

Haller, Hans. The Principal–Agent Problem with a Satisficing Agent. *J. Econ. Behav. Organ.*, December 1985, *6*(4), pp. 359–79.

Holmström, Bengt R. The Provision of Services in a Market Economy. In *Inman, R. P., ed.*, 1985, pp. 183–213.

Kanodia, Chandra S. Stochastic Monitoring and Moral Hazard. *J. Acc. Res.*, Spring 1985, *23*(1), pp. 175–93.

Lambert, Richard A. Variance Investigation in Agency Settings. *J. Acc. Res.*, Autumn 1985, *23*(2), pp. 633–47.

Maskin, Eric S. and Riley, John G. Input versus Output Incentive Schemes. *J. Public Econ.*, October 1985, *28*(1), pp. 1–23.

Mendelson, Haim. Ripoffs, Lemons, and Reputation Formation in Agency Relationships: A Laboratory Market Study: Discussion. *J. Finance,* July 1985, *40*(3), pp. 820–23.

Mikkelson, Wayne H. and Ruback, Richard S. Takeovers and Managerial Compensation: A Discussion [Merger Decisions and Executive Stock Ownership in Acquiring Firms] [Agency Theory, Managerial Welfare, and Takeover Bid Resistance]. *J. Acc. Econ.,* April 1985, *7*(1–3), pp. 233–38.

Penno, Mark. Informational Issues in the Financial Reporting Process. *J. Acc. Res.,* Spring 1985, *23*(1), pp. 240–55.

Postlewaite, Andrew. The Provision of Services in a Market Economy: Comment. In *Inman, R. P., ed.,* 1985, pp. 214–16.

Pratt, John W. and Zeckhauser, Richard J. Principals and Agents: An Overview. In *Pratt, J. W. and Zeckhauser, R. J., eds.,* 1985, pp. 1–35.

Radner, Roy. Repeated Principal–Agent Games with Discounting. *Econometrica,* September 1985, *53*(5), pp. 1173–98.

Rees, Ray. The Theory of Principal and Agent: Part 2. *Bull. Econ. Res.,* May 1985, *37*(2), pp. 75–95.

Rees, Ray. The Theory of Principal and Agent: Part 1. *Bull. Econ. Res.,* January 1985, *37*(1), pp. 3–26.

Riley, John G. Competition with Hidden Knowledge. *J. Polit. Econ.,* October 1985, *93*(5), pp. 958–76.

Rogerson, William P. Repeated Moral Hazard. *Econometrica,* January 1985, *53*(1), pp. 69–76.

Rogerson, William P. The First-Order Approach to Principal–Agent Problems. *Econometrica,* November 1985, *53*(6), pp. 1357–67.

Shen, T. Y. Worker Motivation and X-Efficiency. *Kyklos,* 1985, *38*(3), pp. 392–411.

Singh, Nirvikar. Monitoring and Hierarchies: The Marginal Value of Information in a Principal–Agent Model. *J. Polit. Econ.,* June 1985, *93*(3), pp. 599–609.

Stiglitz, Joseph E. Credit Markets and the Control of Capital. *J. Money, Credit, Banking,* May 1985, *17*(2), pp. 133–52.

White, Harrison C. Agency as Control. In *Pratt, J. W. and Zeckhauser, R. J., eds.,* 1985, pp. 187–212.

Yarbrough, Beth V. and Yarbrough, Robert M. Free Trade, Hegemony, and the Theory of Agency. *Kyklos,* 1985, *38*(3), pp. 348–64.

Young, S. Mark. A Laboratory Investigation of the Moral Hazard Problem in an Agency Relationship: Discussion. *J. Acc. Res.,* Supp. 1985, *23,* pp. 121–23.

0229 Microeconomics of Intertemporal Choice

Diamond, Peter A. The Economics of Saving: A Survey of Recent Contributions: Comment. In *Arrow, K. J. and Honkapohja, S., eds.,* 1985, pp. 295–306. [G: U.S.]

Judd, Kenneth L. Redistributive Taxation in a Simple Perfect Foresight Model. *J. Public Econ.,* October 1985, *28*(1), pp. 59–83.

King, Mervyn. The Economics of Saving: A Survey of Recent Contributions. In *Arrow, K. J. and Honkapohja, S., eds.,* 1985, pp. 227–94.

Koopmans, Tjalling C. Representation of Preference Orderings over Time. In *Koopmans, T. C.,* 1985, pp. 103–24.

Kurz, Mordecai. Heterogeneity in Savings Behavior: A Comment. In *Arrow, K. J. and Honkapohja, S., eds.,* 1985, pp. 307–27. [G: U.S.]

Monticelli, Carlo. Lo stock ottimale di beni di consumo durevoli in condizioni di incertezza. (The Optimal Stock of Consumer Durables under Uncertainty. With English summary.) *Ricerche Econ.,* July-Sept. 1985, *39*(3), pp. 357–77.

Nicola, Pier Carlo. Sulla introduzione di una moneta nell'equilibrio generale. (With English summary.) *Econ. Polít.,* April 1985, *2*(1), pp. 11–30.

Precious, Mark. Demand Constraints, Rational Expectations and Investment Theory. *Oxford Econ. Pap.,* December 1985, *37*(4), pp. 576–605.

Singleton, Kenneth J. Testing Specifications of Economic Agents' Intertemporal Optimum Problems in the Presence of Alternative Models. *J. Econometrics,* Oct./Nov. 1985, *30*(1/2), pp. 391–413. [G: U.S.]

Skinner, Jonathan S. Variable Lifespan and the Intertemporal Elasticity of Consumption. *Rev. Econ. Statist.,* November 1985, *67*(4), pp. 616–23. [G: U.S.]

Ströbele, Wolfgang. An Economist's Definition of the Energy Problem: On the Optimal Intertemporal Allocation of Exergy. In *van Gool, W. and Bruggink, J. J. C., eds.,* 1985, pp. 61–78.

Zee, Howell H. An Efficient Method of Calculating the Impact of Finite Tax Changes in an Intertemporal Framework. *Atlantic Econ. J.,* December 1985, *13*(4), pp. 26–33.

023 Macroeconomic Theory

0230 General

Adam, M. C. and Ginsburgh, Victor. The Effects of Irregular Markets on Macroeconomic Policy: Some Estimates for Belgium. *Europ. Econ. Rev.,* October 1985, *29*(1), pp. 15–33. [G: Belgium]

Adolph, Brigitte and Wolfstetter, Elmar. Pareto-Verbessernde Fiskalpolitik im allgemeinen Gleichgewicht bei rationalen Erwartungen. (With English summary.) *Z. Wirtschaft. Sozialwissen.,* 1985, *105*(1), pp. 51–63.

Aiyagari, S. Rao. Observational Equivalence of the Overlapping Generations and the Discounted Dynamic Programming Frameworks for One-Sector Growth. *J. Econ. Theory,* April 1985, *35*(2), pp. 201–21.

Aiyagari, S. Rao and Gertler, Mark. The Backing of Government Bonds and Monetarism. *J. Monet. Econ.,* July 1985, *16*(1), pp. 19–44.

Akerlof, George A. and Yellen, Janet L. A Near-rational Model of the Business Cycle, with Wage and Price Intertia. *Quart. J. Econ.*, Supp. 1985, *100*, pp. 823–38.

Andersen, Torben M. Uncoordinated Prices and Monetary Policy. *Revue Écon.*, November 1985, *36*(6), pp. 1247–70.

Anyadike-Danes, M. K. Dennis Robertson and Keynes's General Theory. In *Harcourt, G. C., ed.*, 1985, pp. 105–23.

Arestis, P. and Skouras, Thanos. Post-Keynesian Economic Theory: Introduction. In *Arestis, P. and Skouras, T., eds.*, 1985, pp. 1–5.

Aschauer, David Alan and Greenwood, Jeremy. Macroeconomic Effects of Fiscal Policy. *Carnegie-Rochester Conf. Ser. Public Policy*, Autumn 1985, *23*, pp. 91–138.

Asimakopulos, Athanasios. The Foundations of Unemployment Theory: A Comment. *J. Post Keynesian Econ.*, Spring 1985, *7*(3), pp. 352–62.

d'Autume, Antoine and Michel, Philippe. Épargne, investissement et monnaie dans une perspective intertemporelle. (Saving, Investment, and Money in an Intertemporal Setting. With English summary.) *Revue Écon.*, March 1985, *36*(2), pp. 243–90.

Azariadis, Costas and Cooper, Russell. Nominal Wage–Price Rigidity as a Rational Expectations Equilibrium. *Amer. Econ. Rev.*, May 1985, *75*(2), pp. 31–35.

Backus, David and Driffill, John. Inflation and Reputation. *Amer. Econ. Rev.*, June 1985, *75*(3), pp. 530–38.

Backus, David and Driffill, John. Rational Expectations and Policy Credibility Following a Change in Regime. *Rev. Econ. Stud.*, April 1985, *52*(2), pp. 211–21.

Balasko, Yves and Royer, Daniel. Effective Demand Failures Revisited. *Scand. J. Econ.*, 1985, *87*(3), pp. 521–36.

Barrère, Christian. Prix réels et prix monétaires. (Real Prices and Monetary Prices. With English summary.) *Écon. Appl.*, 1985, *38*(1), pp. 265–97.

Bartlett, Bruce. Supply-Side Economics: Theory and Evidence. *Nat. Westminster Bank Quart. Rev.*, February 1985, pp. 18–29. [G: U.S.]

Bartmann, Hermann and John, Klaus-Dieter. Entscheidungen, Erwartungen und Kontrakte bei Unsicherheit. Eine postkeynesianische Sicht. (Decisions, Expectations and Contracts under Uncertainty: A Post-Keynesian View. With English summary.) *Jahr. Nationalökon. Statist.*, May 1985, *200*(3), pp. 217–28.

Bartoli, Gloria and Lecaldano Sasso la Terza, Edoardo. Microeconomic Foundations of Aggregate Behaviour of Firms in Kalecki and Some of His Followers. *Econ. Notes*, 1985, (1), pp. 43–62.

Bausor, Randall. Conceptual Evolution in Economics: The Case of Rational Expectations. *Eastern Econ. J.*, Oct.-Dec. 1985, *11*(4), pp. 297–308.

Beenstock, Michael; Dalziel, Alan and Warburton, Peter J. Aggregate Investment and Output in the U.K. In *Weiserbs, D., ed.*, 1985, pp. 117–36. [G: U.K.]

Begg, David K. H. Macroeconomic Policy Design in an Interdependent World: Comment. In *Buiter, W. H. and Marston, R. C., eds.*, 1985, pp. 268–71.

Benassy, Jean-Pascal. A Non-Walrasian Model of Employment with Partial Price Flexibility and Indexation. In *Feiwel, G. R., ed. (I)*, 1985, pp. 184–96.

Benavie, Arthur. Monetary-Fiscal Policy under Rational Expectations in a Lucas–Rapping Macromodel. *Atlantic Econ. J.*, December 1985, *13*(4), pp. 1–9.

Benhabib, Jess and Nishimura, Kazuo. Competitive Equilibrium Cycles. *J. Econ. Theory*, April 1985, *35*(2), pp. 284–306.

Bental, Benjamin; Ben-Zion, Uri and Wenig, Alois. Macroeconomic Policy and the Shadow Economy. In *Gaertner, W. and Wenig, A., eds.*, 1985, pp. 179–93.

Beraud, Alain and Etner, François. Quasi-demande et demande effectif: une note pedagogique. (Quasi-demand and Effective Demand: A Pedagogic Note. With English summary.) *Revue Écon.*, July 1985, *36*(4), pp. 797–816.

Blad, Michael and Kirman, Alan P. L'évolution à long terme d'un modéle d'équilibre avec rationnement. (With English summary.) *Revue Écon. Polit.*, Nov.-Dec. 1985, *95*(6), pp. 795–808.

Blanchard, Olivier J. Debt, Deficits, and Finite Horizons. *J. Polit. Econ.*, April 1985, *93*(2), pp. 223–47.

Boddy, Raford. Demand Distribution and Productivity Decline. *Econ. Forum*, Winter 1985-1986, *15*(2), pp. 15–20.

Booth, Alan. The "Keynesian Revolution" and Economic Policy-making: A Reply. *Econ. Hist. Rev., 2nd Ser.*, February 1985, *38*(1), pp. 101–06.

Boschen, John F. Employment and Output Effects of Observed and Unobserved Monetary Growth. *J. Money, Credit, Banking*, May 1985, *17*(2), pp. 153–63. [G: U.S.]

Boskin, Michael J. A Longer-term Perspective on Macroeconomics and Distribution: Time, Expectations, and Incentives. In *Feiwel, G. R., ed. (I)*, 1985, pp. 444–58.

Brazelton, W. Robert. Aggregate Supply Once More: A Reply to a Rejoinder. *Amer. Econ.*, Spring 1985, *29*(1), pp. 70–72.

Bricall, Josep M. Sur la demande effective et la crise. (On Effective Demand and Crisis. With English summary.) *Écon. Soc.*, August 1985, *19*(8), pp. 99–116.

Bródy, Andras; Martinás, Katalin and Sajó, Konstantin. An Essay in Macroeconomics. *Acta Oecon.*, 1985, *35*(3–4), pp. 337–43.

Brown-Collier, Elba K. Methodology and the Practice of Economics: A Critique of Patinkin's Interpretation of Keynes. *Eastern Econ. J.*, Oct.-Dec. 1985, *11*(4), pp. 373–83.

Brunner, Karl. Ideology and Analysis in Macroeconomics: Comment. In *Koslowski, P., ed.*, 1985, pp. 208–18.

Buck, Andrew J. An Empirical Note on the Foundations of Rational Expectations. *J. Post Keynesian Econ.*, Spring 1985, 7(3), pp. 311–23.   [G: W. Germany]

Buffie, Edward F. Price–Output Dynamics, Capital Inflows and Real Appreciation. *Oxford Econ. Pap.*, December 1985, 37(4), pp. 529–51.

Burmeister, Edwin. On the Assumption of Convergent Rational Expectations. In *Feiwel, G. R., ed. (I)*, 1985, pp. 258–69.

Burns, Michael E. and Mitchell, William F. Real Wages, Unemployment and Economic Policy in Australia. *Australian Econ. Pap.*, June 1985, 24(44), pp. 1–23.   [G: Australia]

Butos, William N. Hayek and General Equilibrium Analysis. *Southern Econ. J.*, October 1985, 52(2), pp. 332–43.

Calvo, Guillermo A. Macroeconomic Implications of the Government Budget: Some Basic Considerations. *J. Monet. Econ.*, January 1985, 15(1), pp. 95–112.

Caprara, Ugo. Opinioni e teorie di John Maynard Keynes nella interpretazione di un economista aziendale. (Opinions and Theories of John Maynard Keynes as Interpreted by a Professor of Business Economics. With English summary.) *Rivista Int. Sci. Econ. Com.*, February 1985, 32(2), pp. 167–82.

Cartelier, Jean. Théorie de la valeur ou hétérodoxie monétaire: les termes d'un choix. (Value Theory and Monetary Heterodoxy: The Crucial Choice. With English summary.) *Écon. Appl.*, 1985, 38(1), pp. 63–82.

Carvalho, Fernando. Alternative Analyses of Short and Long Run in Post Keynesian Economics. *J. Post Keynesian Econ.*, Winter 1984–85, 7(2), pp. 214–34.

Cebula, Richard J. Money Multipliers and the Slopes of IS and LM: Comment. *Southern Econ. J.*, January 1985, 51(3), pp. 906–08.

Chiarella, Carl. Analysis of the Effects of Time Lags and Nonlinearities in a Macroeconomic Model Incorporating the Government Budget Constraint. In *Batten, D. F. and Lesse, P. F., eds.*, 1985, pp. 131–52.

Chick, Victoria. Keynesians, Monetarists and Keynes: The End of the Debate—or a Beginning? In *Arestis, P. and Skouras, T., eds.*, 1985, pp. 79–98.

Chick, Victoria. Time and the Wage-Unit in the Method of *The General Theory:* History and Equilibrium. In *Lawson, T. and Pesaran, H., eds.*, 1985, pp. 195–208.

Chiesa, Gabriella. Oil Shock, Saving, Investment and Trade Balance: The Role of Short Run Rigidity versus Long Run Flexibility. An Intertemporal Approach. *Econ. Int.*, February 1985, 38(1), pp. 1–20.

Chisari, Omar O. Growth, Inflation and Rules of Active and Passive Mark-up Factor. *Econ. Notes*, 1985, (2), pp. 57–67.

Choudhri, Ehsan U. and Ferris, J. Stephen. Wage and Price Contracts in a Macro Model with Information Costs. *Can. J. Econ.*, November 1985, 18(4), pp. 766–83.

Clark, Simon J. The Effects of Government Expenditure on the Term Structure of Interest Rates: A Comment. *J. Money, Credit, Banking*, August 1985, 17(3), pp. 397–400.

Colander, David C. and Koford, Kenneth J. Externalities and Macroeconomic Policy. In *Maital, S. and Lipnowski, I., eds.*, 1985, pp. 17–38.

Cooley, Thomas F. Individual Forecasting and Aggregate Outcomes: A Review Essay. *J. Monet. Econ.*, March 1985, 15(2), pp. 255–66.

Cooley, Thomas F. and LeRoy, Stephen F. Atheoretical Macroeconometrics: A Critique. *J. Monet. Econ.*, November 1985, 16(3), pp. 283–308.

Corden, W. Max. Booming Sector and Dutch Disease Economics: Survey and Consolidation. In *Corden, W. M.*, 1985, pp. 246–68.

Corden, W. Max. Macroeconomic Policy Interaction under Flexible Exchange Rates: A Two-Country Model. *Economica*, February 1985, 52(205), pp. 9–23.

Corden, W. Max and Neary, J. Peter. Booming Sector and De-industrialization in a Small Open Economy. In *Corden, W. M.*, 1985, pp. 225–45.

Cosimano, Thomas F. Erratic Monetary Policy and Price Variability. *J. Macroecon.*, Summer 1985, 7(3), pp. 313–31.

Cottrell, Allin. Keynesianism and the Natural Rate of Unemployment: A Problem in Pedagogy. *J. Post Keynesian Econ.*, Winter 1984–85, 7(2), pp. 263–68.

Currie, David and Levine, Paul. Macroeconomic Policy Design in an Interdependent World. In *Buiter, W. H. and Marston, R. C., eds.*, 1985, pp. 228–68.

Currie, David and Levine, Paul. Simple Macropolicy Rules for the Open Economy. *Econ. J.*, Supplement 1985, 95, pp. 60–70.

Dadkhah, Kamran M. and Valbuena, Santiago. Non-nested Test of New Classical vs Keynesian Models: Evidence from European Economies. *Appl. Econ.*, December 1985, 17(6), pp. 1083–98.   [G: France; Italy; W. Germany; Spain]

Darity, William A., Jr. On Involuntary Unemployment and Increasing Returns. *J. Post Keynesian Econ.*, Spring 1985, 7(3), pp. 363–72.

Darrat, Ali F. The Monetarist versus the New Classical Economics and the Money Unemployment Linkage: Some European Evidence. *Quart. J. Bus. Econ.*, Summer 1985, 24(3), pp. 78–91.   [G: U.K.; Italy; W. Germany]

Davidson, Paul. Liquidity and Not Increasing Returns Is the Ultimate Source of Unemployment Equilibrium. *J. Post Keynesian Econ.*, Spring 1985, 7(3), pp. 373–84.

Davidson, Paul. Sidney Weintraub—An Economist of the Real World. *J. Post Keynesian Econ.*, Summer 1985, 7(4), pp. 533–39.

Dawson, Alistair. Comment upon a New-Classical Model of the Postwar UK. *Appl. Econ.*, April 1985, 17(2), pp. 257–61.   [G: U.K.]

Day, Richard H. and Shafer, Wayne. Keynesian

Chaos. *J. Macroecon.*, Summer 1985, 7(3), pp. 277–95.

Dehez, Pierre. Monopolistic Equilibrium and Involuntary Unemployment. *J. Econ. Theory*, June 1985, *36*(1), pp. 160–65.

Delbono, Flavio. Equazioni fondamentali e teoria quantitativa nel "Treatise on Money" di J. M. Keynes: Una nota. (With English summary.) *Stud. Econ.*, 1985, *40*(26), pp. 65–85.

Delbono, Flavio. On the Determination of Effective Demands in Benassy's Model. *Econ. Notes*, 1985, (3), pp. 115–20.

Diamond, Peter A. and Yellin, Joel. The Distribution of Inventory Holdings in a Pure Exchange Barter Search Economy. *Econometrica*, March 1985, *53*(2), pp. 409–32.

Dotsey, Michael. Controversy over the Federal Budget Deficit: A Theoretical Perspective. *Fed. Res. Bank Richmond Econ. Rev.*, Sept./Oct. 1985, *71*(5), pp. 3–16.

Drèze, Jacques H. Second-best Analysis with Markets in Disequilibrium: Public Sector Pricing in a Keynesian Regime. *Europ. Econ. Rev.*, December 1985, *29*(3), pp. 263–301.

Drobny, Andres and Klonis, Dimitris C. Equilibrium and Disequilibrium Macro Models: A Note on Price Inertia. *Greek Econ. Rev.*, December 1985, 7(3), pp. 268–77.

Ducos, G. Modèle macroéconomique de déséquilibre avec dé lais d'attente. (A Macro-disequilibrium Model with Waiting Delays. With English summary.) *L'Actual. Econ.*, September 1985, *61*(3), pp. 316–29.

Eckalbar, John C. Inventories in a Dynamic Macro Model with Flexible Prices. *Europ. Econ. Rev.*, March 1985, *27*(2), pp. 201–19.

Eden, Benjamin. Indexation and Related Issues: A Review Essay. *J. Monet. Econ.*, September 1985, *16*(2), pp. 259–66.

Edwards, J. R. Effective Demand Failure: Critique of an Anti-monetary Theory. *S. Afr. J. Econ.*, June 1985, *53*(2), pp. 124–40.

Eichner, Alfred S. Micro Foundations of the Corporate Economy. In *Eichner, A. S.*, 1985, pp. 28–74.

Eichner, Alfred S. Post-Keynesian Theory and Empirical Research. In *Eichner, A. S.*, 1985, pp. 176–99.

Eichner, Alfred S. Stagflation: Explaining the Inexplicable. In *Eichner, A. S.*, 1985, pp. 113–50. [G: U.S.]

Eichner, Alfred S. The New Paradigm and Macrodynamic Modeling. In *Eichner, A. S.*, 1985, pp. 151–75.

Ellis, Christopher J. and Fender, John. Wage Bargaining in a Macroeconomic Model with Rationing. *Quart. J. Econ.*, August 1985, *100*(3), pp. 625–50.

Estrin, Saul and Holmes, Peter. Uncertainty, Efficiency, and Economic Planning in Keynesian Economics. *J. Post Keynesian Econ.*, Summer 1985, 7(4), pp. 463–73.

Evans, George. Bottlenecks and the Phillips Curve: A Disaggregated Keynesian Model of Inflation, Output, and Unemployment. *Econ. J.*, June 1985, *95*(378), pp. 345–57.

Evans, George. Expectational Stability and the Multiple Equilibria Problem in Linear Rational Expectations Models. *Quart. J. Econ.*, November 1985, *100*(4), pp. 1217–33.

Evans, Paul. Do Large Deficits Produce High Interest Rates? *Amer. Econ. Rev.*, March 1985, *75*(1), pp. 68–87. [G: U.S.]

Fackler, James S. An Empirical Analysis of the Markets for Goods, Money, and Credit. *J. Money, Credit, Banking*, February 1985, *17*(1), pp. 28–42. [G: U.S.]

Falkinger, Josef. Änderungen des Konsum- und Sparverhaltens als positive oder negative Signale für Investitionen und Wachstum. Einige Anmerkungen zu einem Beitrag von Karl Georg Zinn. (Shifts in Consumption and Saving Behaviour as Positive or Negative Signals for Investment and Growth. With English summary.) *Konjunkturpolitik*, 1985, *31*(6), pp. 336–47.

Fane, George. A Derivation of the IS-LM Model from Explicit Optimizing Behavior. *J. Macroecon.*, Fall 1985, 7(4), pp. 493–508.

Favereau, Olivier. L'incertain dans la "révolution keynésienne": l'hypothèse Wittgenstein. (Uncertainty in the Keynesian Revolution: The Wittgenstein Hypothesis. With English summary.) *Écon. Soc.*, March 1985, *19*(3), pp. 29–72.

Favero, Carlo. Antilopi o cicogne? Un'analisi critica delle verifiche empiriche della teoria della neutralità della politica economica. (Antelopes or Storks? A Critical Analysis of the Empirical Tests of the Economic Policy Neutrality Theory. With English summary.) *Giorn. Econ.*, July-Aug. 1985, *44*(7–8), pp. 427–44. [G: Italy]

Fazzari, Steven M. Keynes, Harrod, and the Rational Expectations Revolution. *J. Post Keynesian Econ.*, Fall 1985, *8*(1), pp. 66–80.

Feiwel, George R. Issues in Contemporary Macroeconomics and Distribution: Preface. In *Feiwel, G. R.*, ed. (I), 1985, pp. xiii–xxviii.

Feiwel, George R. Quo Vadis Macroeconomics? Issues, Tensions and Challenges. In *Feiwel, G. R.*, ed. (I), 1985, pp. 1–100.

Ferguson, J. David and Hart, William R. The Implications of Spillover for the Design of Monetary Policy: An Empirical Analysis of Income and Price Determination in Nonclearing Markets. *Amer. Econ. Rev.*, December 1985, *75*(5), pp. 1133–42. [G: U.S.]

Fischer, Stanley. Supply Shocks, Wage Stickiness, and Accommodation. *J. Money, Credit, Banking*, February 1985, *17*(1), pp. 1–15.

Flaschel, Peter. Macroeconomic Dynamics and Effective Demand. Some Corrections. *Metroecon.*, June 1985, *37*(2), pp. 135–56.

Flood, Robert P. and Hodrick, Robert J. Optimal Price and Inventory Adjustment in an Open-Economy Model of the Business Cycle. *Quart. J. Econ.*, Supp. 1985, *100*, pp. 887–914.

Fluet, Claude. Bénassy et al macroéconomie du déséquilibre. (With English summary.) *L'Actual. Econ.*, June 1985, *61*(2), pp. 239–51.

Fornero, Elsa. La disoccupazione nei modelli di

equilibrio non walrasiano. (With English summary.) *Econ. Polit.*, December 1985, *2*(3), pp. 421–68.

Fratianni, Michele and Nabli, Mustapha. Inflation and Output with Rational Expectations in Open Economies. *Weltwirtsch. Arch.*, 1985, *121*(1), pp. 33–52. [G: Belgium; France; W. Germany; Italy; Netherlands]

Friedman, Benjamin M. Recent Perspectives in and on Macroeconomics. In *Feiwel, G. R., ed.* (*I*), 1985, pp. 270–86. [G: U.S.]

Frisch, Helmut. Real and Nominal Shocks in an Open Economy Model with Wage Contracts. *Giorn. Econ.*, July–Aug. 1985, *44*(7–8), pp. 347–73.

Fukiharu, Toshitaka. Static Macroeconomics from the Neoclassical Viewpoint. *Kobe Univ. Econ.*, 1985, (31), pp. 33–52.

Fusfeld, Daniel R. Keynes and the Keynesian Cross: A Note. *Hist. Polit. Econ.*, Fall 1985, *17*(3), pp. 385–89.

Galli, Giampaolo. International Coordination in the Design of Macroeconomic Policies: Comment. *Europ. Econ. Rev.*, June–July 1985, *28*(1–2), pp. 83–87. [G: OECD]

Gapinski, James H. Capital Malleability, Macro Performance, and Policy Effectiveness. *Southern Econ. J.*, July 1985, *52*(1), pp. 150–66.

German, Israel. Disequilibrium Dynamics and the Stability of Quasi Equilibria. *Quart. J. Econ.*, August 1985, *100*(3), pp. 571–96.

Geweke, John. Macroeconometric Modeling and the Theory of the Representative Agent. *Amer. Econ. Rev.*, May 1985, *75*(2), pp. 206–10.

Ghosh, Dilip K. and Elyasiani, Elyas. Money Multipliers and the Slopes of IS-LM: Comment. *Southern Econ. J.*, January 1985, *51*(3), pp. 909–15.

Ginsburgh, Victor, et al. Macroeconomic Policy in the Presence of an Irregular Sector. In *Gaertner, W. and Wenig, A., eds.*, 1985, pp. 194–217.

Goldstein, Jonathan P. Pricing, Accumulation, and Crisis in Post Keynesian Theory. *J. Post Keynesian Econ.*, Fall 1985, *8*(1), pp. 121–34.

Gottfries, Nils. Multiple Perfect Foresight Equilibriums and Convergence of Learning Processes. *J. Money, Credit, Banking*, February 1985, *17*(1), pp. 111–17.

Gourieroux, Christian and Laroque, Guy. The Aggregation of Commodities in Quantity Rationing Models. *Int. Econ. Rev.*, October 1985, *26*(3), pp. 681–99.

Grandmont, Jean-Michel. On Endogenous Competitive Business Cycles. *Econometrica*, September 1985, *53*(5), pp. 995–1045.

Green, Christopher J. Permanent Income, Budget Constraints and Overshooting in Simple Aggregate Models. *Manchester Sch. Econ. Soc. Stud.*, September 1985, *53*(3), pp. 231–40.

Gregory, Allan W. and Veall, Michael R. A Lagrange Multiplier Test of the Restrictions for a Simple Rational Expectations Model. *Can. J. Econ.*, February 1985, *18*(1), pp. 94–105. [G: Canada]

Gröschel, Ulrich. Risikobewältigung durch Güter- und Arbeitsmarktkontrakte. (Contracts on Labour and Commodity Markets and the Allocation of Risk. With English Summary.) *Konjunkturpolitik*, 1985, *31*(4/5), pp. 300–317.

Guido, Vinicio. Sull'esistenza dell'equilibrio temporaneo in economie monetarie con produzione. (With English summary.) *Econ. Polit.*, December 1985, *2*(3), pp. 403–20.

Guiso, Luigi. Crowding-out and Rational Expectations. *Giorn. Econ.*, May–June 1985, *44*(5–6), pp. 239–57.

Haberler, Gottfried. Mr. Keynes' Theory of the "Multiplier": A Methodological Criticism. In *Haberler, G.*, 1985, pp. 553–60.

Haberler, Gottfried. Notes on Rational and Irrational Expectations. In *Haberler, G.*, 1985, pp. 603–17.

Haberler, Gottfried. The General Theory after Ten Years and Sixteen Years Later. In *Haberler, G.*, 1985, pp. 581–602.

Haberler, Gottfried. The Pigou Effect Once More. In *Haberler, G.*, 1985, pp. 573–80.

Haberler, Gottfried. The World Economy, Macroeconomic Theory and Policy—Sixty Years of Profound Change. In *Haberler, G.*, 1985, pp. 429–50.

Hahn, Frank. Some Keynesian Reflections on Monetarism. In *Vicarelli, F., ed.*, 1985, pp. 1–20.

Hahn, Frank H. Fix-Price Models: A Survey of Recent Empirical Work: Comment. In *Arrow, K. J. and Honkapohja, S., eds.*, 1985, pp. 368–78.

Halevi, Joseph. Effective Demand, Capacity Utilization and the Sectoral Distribution of Investment. *Écon. Soc.*, August 1985, *19*(8), pp. 25–45.

Hamada, Koichi. Macroeconomic Policy Design in an Interdependent World: Comment. In *Buiter, W. H. and Marston, R. C., eds.*, 1985, pp. 271–73.

Hamouda, Omar F. The Evolution of Hicks' Theory of Money. *Bull. Econ. Res.*, May 1985, *37*(2), pp. 131–51.

Hansen, Jørgen Drud. Statsgaeld og økonomisk politik. (Public Deficits and the Targets of Economic Policy. With English summary.) *Nationaløkon. Tidsskr.*, 1985, *123*(1), pp. 32–49.

Hansson, Björn. Keynes's Notion of Equilibrium in the *General Theory*. *J. Post Keynesian Econ.*, Spring 1985, *7*(3), pp. 332–41.

Haque, M. Badrul. Monetary Policy and Its Effects on Inflation. *Revue Écon.*, November 1985, *36*(6), pp. 1271–99.

Harcourt, G. C. Post-Keynesianism: Quite Wrong and/or Nothing New. In *Arestis, P. and Skouras, T., eds.*, 1985, pp. 125–45.

Harcourt, G. C. and O'Shaughnessy, T. J. Keynes's Unemployment Equilibrium: Some Insights from Joan Robinson, Piero Sraffa and Richard Kahn. In *Harcourt, G. C., ed.*, 1985, pp. 3–41.

Hénin, Pierre-Yves and Michel, Philippe. L'extension du modèle IS-LM aux différents régimes d'équilibre avec rationnement. (An Extension of the IS-LM Model under Alternative Regimes of Equilibrium with Rationing. With English summary.) *Revue Écon.*, July 1985, *36*(4), pp. 643–67.

Hicks, John. Keynes and the World Economy. In *Vicarelli, F., ed.*, 1985, pp. 21–27.

Hillier, Brian. Rational Expectations, the Government Budget Constraint, and the Optimal Money Supply. *J. Macroecon.*, Winter 1985, *7*(1), pp. 39–50.

Holland, A. Steven. Rational Expectations and the Effects of Monetary Policy: A Guide for the Uninitiated. *Fed. Res. Bank St. Louis Rev.*, May 1985, *67*(5), pp. 5–11.

Hong, Kyttack. Macroeconomic Dynamics in a Financially Repressed Economy. *J. Econ. Devel.*, July 1985, *10*(1), pp. 169–94. [G: LDCs]

Honkapohja, Seppo. Rational Expectations Models in Macroeconomics: Comment. In *Arrow, K. J. and Honkapohja, S., eds.*, 1985, pp. 426–36.

Honkapohja, Seppo and Ito, Takatoshi. On Macroeconomic Equilibrium with Stochastic Rationing. *Scand. J. Econ.*, 1985, *87*(1), pp. 66–88.

Howitt, Peter. Transaction Costs in the Theory of Unemployment. *Amer. Econ. Rev.*, March 1985, *75*(1), pp. 88–100.

Hutchison, Terence W. Philosophy and Economic Policy. In *Koslowski, P., ed.*, 1985, pp. 161–73.

Ilmakunnas, Pekka and Tsurumi, Hiroki. Testing the Lucas Hypothesis on Output Inflation Trade-offs. *J. Bus. Econ. Statist.*, January 1985, *3*(1), pp. 43–53. [G: U.S.]

Jansen, Dennis W. Real Balances in an Ad Hoc Keynesian Model and Policy Ineffectiveness: A Note. *J. Money, Credit, Banking*, August 1985, *17*(3), pp. 378–86.

Kamath, Shyam J. Monetary Aggregates, Income and Causality in a Developing Economy. *J. Econ. Stud.*, 1985, *12*(3), pp. 36–53. [G: India]

Kano, Masao. Money, Financial Assets and Pasinetti's Theory of Profit. (In Japanese. With English summary.) *Econ. Stud. Quart.*, August 1985, *36*(2), pp. 169–77.

Kelly, Christopher M. A Cautionary Note on the Interpretation of Long-run Equilibrium Solutions in Conventional Macro Models [Economic Modelling of the Aggregate Time Series Relationship between Consumers' Expenditure and Income in the United Kingdom] [Serial Correlation as a Convenient Simplification, Not a Nuisance]. *Econ. J.*, December 1985, *95*(380), pp. 1078–86.

Kindleberger, Charles P. Collective Memory vs. Rational Expectations: Some Historical Puzzles in Macro-Economic Behavior. In *Kindleberger, C. P.*, 1985, pp. 129–38.

Kirchgässner, Gebhard. Ist "rationale" Wirtschaftspolitik möglich? Zu den Auswirkungen der Theorie rationaler Erwartungen und der ökonomischen Theorie der Politik auf die Theorie der Wirtschaftspolitik. (Is There a Real Possibility for "Rational" Economic Policy making? With English Summary.) *Konjunkturpolitik*, 1985, *31*(4/5), pp. 209–37.

Kooiman, Peter and Kloek, Teun. An Empirical Two Market Disequilibrium Model for Dutch Manufacturing. *Europ. Econ. Rev.*, December 1985, *29*(3), pp. 323–54. [G: Netherlands]

Kornai, János. Fix-Price Models: A Survey of Recent Empirical Work: Comment. In *Arrow, K. J. and Honkapohja, S., eds.*, 1985, pp. 379–90.

Kregel, J. A. Constraints on the Expansion of Output and Employment: Real or Monetary? *J. Post Keynesian Econ.*, Winter 1984–85, *7*(2), pp. 139–52.

Kregel, J. A. Hamlet without the Prince: Cambridge Macroeconomics without Money. *Amer. Econ. Rev.*, May 1985, *75*(2), pp. 133–39.

Kregel, J. A. Harrod and Keynes: Increasing Returns, the Theory of Employment and Dynamic Economics. In *Harcourt, G. C., ed.*, 1985, pp. 66–88.

Kregel, J. A. Sidney Weintraub's Macrofoundations of Microeconomics and the Theory of Distribution. *J. Post Keynesian Econ.*, Summer 1985, *7*(4), pp. 540–58.

Krishna Rao, Ch. A. and Ratnam, C. The IS–LM Curves Revisited with the Aid of Geometry of International Trade: A Comment. *Indian Econ. J.*, Jan.-Mar. 1985, *32*(3), pp. 90–91.

Kurz, Heinz D. Effective Demand in a "Classical" Model of Value and Distribution: The Multiplier in a Sraffian Framework. *Manchester Sch. Econ. Soc. Stud.*, June 1985, *53*(2), pp. 121–37.

Laffont, Jean-Jacques. Fix-Price Models: A Survey of Recent Empirical Work. In *Arrow, K. J. and Honkapohja, S., eds.*, 1985, pp. 328–67.

Lang, Harald. Expectations and the Neutrality of Money: A Comment. *J. Econ. Theory*, August 1985, *36*(2), pp. 392–93.

Langer, Gary F. Kalecki and the Keynesians. *Econ. Forum*, Winter 1985-1986, *15*(2), pp. 21–34.

Larceneux, A. Keynes et Ricardo: une synthe est-elle possible? (Keynes and Ricardo: The Impossible Synthesis. With English summary.) *Écon. Soc.*, August 1985, *19*(8), pp. 7–23.

Lee, S. Y. and Li, W. K. The Lead-Lag Relationship of Money, Income, and Prices in Malaysia. *Singapore Econ. Rev.*, April 1985, *30*(1), pp. 68–76. [G: Malaysia]

Leijonhufvud, Axel. Ideology and Analysis in Macroeconomics. In *Koslowski, P., ed.*, 1985, pp. 182–207.

Lempinen, Urho. Keynesiläinen kansantalous, rationaaliset taloudenpitäjät ja suhdannevaihtelut. (Rational Agents and the Keynesian Economy: Some Results in Business Cycle Theory. With English summary.) *Kansant. Aikak.*, 1985, *81*(2), pp. 150–59.

Léonard, Jacques. Minsky entre Keynes et Hayek: Une autre lecture de la crise. (Minsky between Keynes and Hayek: A New Interpretation of the Crisis. With English summary.) *Écon. Soc.*, August 1985, *19*(8), pp. 117–44.

Leontief, Wassily. Postulates: Keynes's *General Theory* and the Classicists. In *Leontief, W.*, 1985, pp. 93–103.

Leontief, Wassily. Theoretical Note on Time-Preference, Productivity of Capital, Stagnation, and Economic Growth. In *Leontief, W.*, 1985, pp. 175–84.

Lissner, Will. A New School of Economic Theorists: The 'New Classical Economists.' *Amer. J. Econ. Soc.*, April 1985, *44*(2), pp. 255–56.

Madden, Paul. Uniqueness of Non-Walrasian Equilibrium in the Macroeconomic Model with Decreasing or Increasing Returns. *Rev. Econ. Stud.*, October 1985, *52*(4), pp. 703–13.

Mahloudji, Farhad. Hicks and the Keynesian Revolution. *Hist. Polit. Econ.*, Summer 1985, *17*(2), pp. 287–307.

Maier-Rigaud, Gerhard. Durch statisches Denken zur stationären Wirtschaft. (Through Static Economics to a Stationary Economy. With English summary.) *Konjunkturpolitik*, 1985, *31*(1/2), pp. 1–33.   [G: W. Germany]

Mangum, Stephen L. Time and Post-Keynesian Thought. *Econ. Forum*, Winter 1985-1986, *15*(2), pp. 51–63.

Mankiw, N. Gregory. Small Menu Costs and Large Business Cycles: A Macroeconomic Model. *Quart. J. Econ.*, May 1985, *100*(2), pp. 529–38.

Marini, Giancarlo. Built-in Flexibility of Taxation, Public Spending Rules and Stabilisation Policy. *Econ. Notes*, 1985, (2), pp. 5–21.

Marini, Giancarlo. Intertemporal Substitution and the Role of Monetary Policy. *Econ. J.*, March 1985, *95*(377), pp. 87–100.

Maussner, Alfred. Ineffektivität der Wirtschaftspolitik bei "rationalen Erwartungen"? Ein Kommentar mit anderen Argumenten für eine unzureichend begründete These. (Ineffectiveness of Economic Policy under "Rational Expectations"? A Commentary with Different Arguments for an Insufficient Founded Thesis. With English summary.) *Kredit Kapital*, 1985, *18*(2), pp. 217–29.

McAuliffe, Robert E. The Rational Expectations Hypothesis and Economic Analysis. *Eastern Econ. J.*, Oct.-Dec. 1985, *11*(4), pp. 331–41.

McCombie, J. S. L. Economic Growth, the Harrod Foreign Trade Multiplier and the Hicks Super-multiplier. *Appl. Econ.*, February 1985, *17*(1), pp. 55–72.   [G: OECD]

McDonald, Ian M. Market Power and Unemployment. *Int. J. Ind. Organ.*, March 1985, *3*(1), pp. 21–35.

McGee, Robert T. and Stasiak, Richard T. Does Anticipated Monetary Policy Matter? Another Look. *J. Money, Credit, Banking*, February 1985, *17*(1), pp. 16–27.   [G: U.S.]

Ménard, Claude. Le keynésianisme: naissance d'une illusion. (Keynesianism: The Genesis of an Illusion. With English summary.) *Écon. Soc.*, March 1985, *19*(3), pp. 3–27.

Meyer, Paul A. Money Multipliers and the Slopes of IS-LM: Reply. *Southern Econ. J.*, January 1985, *51*(3), pp. 916–20.

de Meza, David and Perlman, Morris. Increasing Returns and the Foundation of Unemployment Theory. *J. Post Keynesian Econ.*, Spring 1985, *7*(3), pp. 385–94.

Miller, Marcus and Salmon, Mark. Dynamic Games and the Time Inconsistency of Optimal Policy in Open Economies. *Econ. J.*, Supplement 1985, *95*, pp. 124–37.

Minsky, Hyman P. An Introduction to Post-Keynesian Economics. *Econ. Forum*, Winter 1985-1986, *15*(2), pp. 1–13.

Minsky, Hyman P. The Financial Instability Hypothesis: A Restatement. In *Arestis, P. and Skouras, T., eds.*, 1985, pp. 24–55.

Minsky, Hyman P. The Legacy of Keynes. *J. Econ. Educ.*, Winter 1985, *16*(1), pp. 5–15.

Mitchell, Douglas W. Expected Inflation and Interest Rates in a Multi-asset Model: A Note. *J. Finance*, June 1985, *40*(2), pp. 595–99.

Mondello, Gérard. Étude de la liaison monnaie-revenu demande effective: les théories de Thomas Tooke et J. M. Keynes. (A Study about the Links between Money-Income-Effective Demand: The Theories of T. Tooke and J. M. Keynes. With English summary.) *Revue Écon.*, May 1985, *36*(3), pp. 509–54.

Moore, Michael J. Demand Management with Rationing. *Econ. J.*, March 1985, *95*(377), pp. 73–86.

Mork, Knut Anton. Factor Substitution, Rational Expectations, and the Effects of Commodity Price Shocks on Employment and Investment. *Econ. Inquiry*, July 1985, *23*(3), pp. 507–24.

Moro, Beniamino. Una generalizzazione del modello IS-LM. (With English summary.) *Econ. Polit.*, December 1985, *2*(3), pp. 365–401.

Mott, Tracy. Kalecki's Principle of Increasing Risk and the Relation among Mark-up Pricing, Investment Fluctuations, and Liquidity Preference. *Econ. Forum*, Winter 1985-1986, *15*(2), pp. 65–76.

Negishi, Takashi. Non-Walrasian Foundations of Macroeconomics. In *Feiwel, G. R., ed. (I)*, 1985, pp. 169–83.

Nell, Edward. Jean Baptiste Marglin: A Comment on 'Growth, Distribution and Inflation.' *Cambridge J. Econ.*, June 1985, *9*(2), pp. 173–78.

Neumann, Manfred J. M. and von Hagen, Jürgen. Inflation and Relative Price Risk. *Z. Wirtschaft. Sozialwissen.*, 1985, *105*(2/3), pp. 169–92.   [G: W. Germany]

Nickerson, David. A Theorem on Policy Neutrality. *Europ. Econ. Rev.*, August 1985, *28*(3), pp. 331–45.

Nickerson, David. Optimal Monetary Policy with a Flexible Price-setting Rule. *Kredit Kapital*, 1985, *18*(3), pp. 289–98.

Nordhaus, William. International Coordination in the Design of Macroeconomic Policies: Comment. *Europ. Econ. Rev.*, June-July 1985, *28*(1–2), pp. 89–92.   [G: OECD]

Otani, Kiyoshi. Rational Expectations and Non-neutrality of Money. *Weltwirtsch. Arch.*, 1985, *121*(2), pp. 203–16.

Owen, Robert F. A Two-Country Disequilibrium

Model. *J. Int. Econ.*, May 1985, *18*(3/4), pp. 339–55.

Parguez, Alain. La monnaie, les déficits et la crise: dans le circuit dynamique l'effect d'éviction est un mythe. (Money, Deficits and Crisis: In the Dynamic Circuit of Money, Crowding-out Effects Are Just a Myth. With English summary.) *Écon. Soc.*, August 1985, *19*(8), pp. 229–51.

Pasinetti, Luigi. The Difficulty, and Yet the Necessity, of Aiming at Full Employment: A Comment [Involuntary Unemployment in the Long Run: Pasinetti's Formulation of the Keynesian Argument—A Review Article]. *J. Post Keynesian Econ.*, Winter 1984–85, *7*(2), pp. 246–48.

Peel, D. A. Global Capital Markets and the Impact of Changes in the Money Stock on Real Activity. *J. Macroecon.*, Fall 1985, *7*(4), pp. 577–82.

Peston, Maurice. The Efficacy of Macroeconomic Policy. In *[Peacock, A.]*, 1985, pp. 125–48.

Phaneuf, Louis. Rigidités de prix contractuelles, anticipations rationnelles et cycle économique. (Contractual Price Rigidities, Rational Expectations and the Business Cycle. With English summary.) *L'Actual. Econ.*, June 1985, *61*(2), pp. 252–73.

Pissarides, Christopher A. Taxes, Subsidies, and Equilibrium Unemployment. *Rev. Econ. Stud.*, January 1985, *52*(1), pp. 121–33.

Policano, Andrew J. The Current State of Macroeconomics: A View from the Textbooks. *J. Monet. Econ.*, May 1985, *15*(3), pp. 389–97.

Poulon, Frédéric. Réponses de la théorie du circuit à quelques questions relatives au temps, à l'équilibre macro-économique et au libre-échange. (The Theory of Circuits Answers Questions Concerning Concepts of Time, Macroeconomic Equilibrium and Free Trade. With English summary.) *Écon. Soc.*, August 1985, *19*(8), pp. 69–84.

Reid, Gavin C. Keynes versus the Classics: Fluctuations and Growth. *Scot. J. Polit. Econ.*, November 1985, *32*(3), pp. 315–27.

Robinson, Joan. Ideology and Logic. In *Vicarelli, F.*, *ed.*, 1985, pp. 73–98.

Rogers, C. A Critique of Clower's Dual Decision Hypothesis. *S. Afr. J. Econ.*, June 1985, *53*(2), pp. 111–23.

Rollings, N. The "Keynesian Revolution" and Economic Policy-making: A Comment. *Econ. Hist. Rev., 2nd Ser.*, February 1985, *38*(1), pp. 95–100. **[G: U.K.]**

Rose, Hugh. A Policy Rule for 'Say's Law' in a Theory of Temporary Equilibrium. *J. Macroecon.*, Winter 1985, *7*(1), pp. 1–17.

Rothschild, Kurt W. Der Multiplikator in der offenen Wirtschaft. (The Multiplier in an Open Economy. With English summary.) *Jahr. Nationalökon. Statist.*, November 1985, *200*(6), pp. 637–43.

Runde, J. H. and Torr, C. S. W. Divergent Expectations and Rational Expectations. *S. Afr. J. Econ.*, September 1985, *53*(3), pp. 217–25.

Salant, Walter S. *Keynes and the Modern World: A Review Article. J. Econ. Lit.*, September

1985, *23*(3), pp. 1176–85.

Samuelson, Paul A. Succumbing to Keynesianism. *Challenge*, January/February 1985, *27*(6), pp. 4–11. **[G: U.S.]**

Sargent, Thomas J. and Wallace, Neil. Interest on Reserves. *J. Monet. Econ.*, May 1985, *15*(3), pp. 279–90.

Sawyer, Malcolm C. Towards a Post-Kaleckian Macroeconomics. In *Arestis, P. and Skouras, T.*, *eds.*, 1985, pp. 146–79.

Scarth, William M. A Note on Non-uniqueness in Rational Expectations Models. *J. Monet. Econ.*, March 1985, *15*(2), pp. 247–54.

Scherf, Wolfgang. Budgetmultiplikatoren. Eine Analyse der fiskalischen Wirkungen konjunkturbedingter und antizyklischer Defizite. (Budgetary Multiplier Effects of Cyclically Conditioned and Anticyclical Deficits. With English summary.) *Jahr. Nationalökon. Statist.*, July 1985, *200*(4), pp. 349–63. **[G: W. Germany]**

Schultze, Charles L. Microeconomic Efficiency and Nominal Wage Stickiness. *Amer. Econ. Rev.*, March 1985, *75*(1), pp. 1–15.

Seccareccia, Mario S. The Role of Saving and Financial Acquisition in the Process of Capital Formation under Policies of Austerity: The Case of Canada. *Écon. Soc.*, August 1985, *19*(8), pp. 253–71. **[G: Canada]**

Shah, Anup R. A Macro Model with Trade Unions. *J. Macroecon.*, Spring 1985, *7*(2), pp. 175–94.

Shapiro, Nina. Involuntary Unemployment in the Long Run: Pasinetti's Formulation of the Keynesian Argument—A Review Article. *J. Post Keynesian Econ.*, Winter 1984–85, *7*(2), pp. 235–45.

Sheehan, Richard G. Money, Anticipated Changes, and Policy Effectiveness. *Amer. Econ. Rev.*, June 1985, *75*(3), pp. 524–29. **[G: U.S.]**

Siegel, Jeremy J. Money Supply Announcements and Interest Rates: Does Monetary Policy Matter? *J. Monet. Econ.*, March 1985, *15*(2), pp. 163–76.

Simonovits, András. Dynamic Adjustment of Supply under Buyers' Forced Substitution. *Z. Nationalökon.*, 1985, *45*(4), pp. 357–72.

Skott, Peter. Increasing Returns and Involuntary Unemployment: Is There a Connection? *J. Post Keynesian Econ.*, Spring 1985, *7*(3), pp. 395–402.

Smithin, John Nicholas. The Definition of Involuntary Unemployment in Keynes' *General Theory*: A Note. *Hist. Polit. Econ.*, Summer 1985, *17*(2), pp. 219–22.

Snippe, Jan. On the Integration of Spending and Portfolio Decisions and the Coordination Problem in Macroeconomic Analysis. *Metroecon.*, October 1985, *37*(3), pp. 293–305.

Snippe, Jan. On the Scope of Hydraulic Macroeconomics: Some Reflections on Alan Coddington's Keynesian Economics. *De Economist*, 1985, *133*(4), pp. 467–83.

Sondermann, Dieter. Keynesian Unemployment as Non-Walrasian Equilibria. In *Feiwel, G. R.*, *ed. (I)*, 1985, pp. 197–215.

Sorensen, Peter Birch. Det monetaristiske syn på stabiliseringspolitikken. (A Macro-economic Model of Explaining Monetarist Assumptions in Stabilization Policy. With English summary.) *Nationaløkon. Tidsskr.*, 1985, *123*(1), pp. 64–76.

Spear, Stephen E. Rational Expectations in the Overlapping Generations Model. *J. Econ. Theory*, April 1985, *35*(2), pp. 251–75.

Sprumont, Yves. Multiplicateur keynésien et interdépendance des secteurs de production. (Keynesian Multipliers and Interdependence of Production Sectors. With English summary.) *Ann. INSEE*, Jan.-Mar. 1985, (57), pp. 27–50.

Standaert, Stan. Neary and Roberts on Le Chatelier Properties of Spill-over Effects: A Correction [The Theory of Household Behaviour under Rationing]. *Europ. Econ. Rev.*, December 1985, *29*(3), pp. 381–86.

Stockton, David J. and Glassman, James E. The Theory and Econometrics of Reduced-Form Nominal Income and Price Equations. *Southern Econ. J.*, July 1985, *52*(1), pp. 103–21.

Sundararajan, V. Debt–Equity Ratios of Firms and Interest Rate Policy: Macroeconomic Effects of High Leverage in Developing Countries. *Int. Monet. Fund Staff Pap.*, September 1985, *32*(3), pp. 430–74.

Sylos Labini, Paolo. The *General Theory:* Critical Reflections Suggested by Some Important Problems of Our Time. In *Vicarelli, F., ed.,* 1985, pp. 126–54.

Sylos Labini, Paolo. Weintraub on the Price Level and Macroeconomics. *J. Post Keynesian Econ.*, Summer 1985, *7*(4), pp. 559–74.

Taylor, John B. International Coordination in the Design of Macroeconomic Policy Rules. *Europ. Econ. Rev.*, June-July 1985, *28*(1–2), pp. 53–81.   [G: OECD]

Taylor, John B. Rational Expectations Models in Macroeconomics. In *Arrow, K. J. and Honkapohja, S., eds.,* 1985, pp. 391–425.

Taylor, Lance. A Stagnationist Model of Economic Growth. *Cambridge J. Econ.*, December 1985, *9*(4), pp. 383–403.

Taylor, Lance and O'Connell, Stephen A. A Minsky Crisis. *Quart. J. Econ.*, Supp. 1985, *100*, pp. 871–85.

Thornton, Daniel L. and Batten, Dallas S. Lag-Length Selection and Tests of Granger Causality between Money and Income. *J. Money, Credit, Banking*, May 1985, *17*(2), pp. 164–78.

Tobin, James. Cycles in Macroeconomic Theory. *Indian Econ. Rev.*, Jan.-June 1985, *20*(1), pp. 1–24.

Tobin, James. La teoria macreconomica in discussione. (Macreconomics under Debate. With English summary.) *Bancaria*, January 1985, *41*(1), pp. 13–31.

Tobin, James. Theoretical Issues in Macroeconomics. In *Feiwel, G. R., ed. (I),* 1985, pp. 103–33.

Torr, C. S. W. Involuntary Unemployment and Equilibrium. *S. Afr. J. Econ.*, March 1985, *53*(1), pp. 82–84.

Tramontana, Antonino. The Wealth Effect of the Public Debt: A Macroeconomic Approach. *Econ. Notes*, 1985, (1), pp. 71–103.

Vallageas, Bernard. Les circuits dans les analyses de Marx, Boehm-Bawerk, Hayek et Keynes. (Circuits in the Analyses of Marx, Boehm-Bawerk, Hayek and Keynes. With English summary.) *Écon. Soc.*, August 1985, *19*(8), pp. 47–68.

Venieris, Yiannis P. and Gupta, Dipak K. Macro Interactions in a Social System: A Case Study of Great Britain. *Southern Econ. J.*, January 1985, *51*(3), pp. 681–96.   [G: U.K.]

Vicarelli, Fausto. Leggi di natura e politica economica: considerazioni sui fondamenti teorici della nuova macroeconomia classica. (Natural Laws and Economic Policy: on the Theoretical Foundations of the New Classical Macroeconomics. With English summary.) *Polit. Econ.*, April 1985, *1*(1), pp. 7–36.

Villacís González, José. La teoria macroeconómica de German Bernácer. (With English summary.) *Economia (Portugal)*, October 1985, *9*(3), pp. 431–46.

Wallace, Myles S. Fiscal Expansion and Falling Interest Rates? Another Case against Crowding Out. *Econ. Notes*, 1985, (1), pp. 162–68.

Wan, Henry Y., Jr. The New Classical Economics—A Game-theoretic Critique. In *Feiwel, G. R., ed. (I),* 1985, pp. 235–57.

Wasserfallen, Walter. Forecasting, Rational Expectations and the Phillips-Curve: An Empirical Investigation. *J. Monet. Econ.*, January 1985, *15*(1), pp. 7–27.   [G: Switzerland]

Weiss, Laurence M. Rational Expectations Models in Macroeconomics: Comment. In *Arrow, K. J. and Honkapohja, S., eds.,* 1985, pp. 437–44.

Weitzman, Martin L. Increasing Returns and the Foundations of Unemployment Theory: An Explanation. *J. Post Keynesian Econ.*, Spring 1985, *7*(3), pp. 403–09.

Weitzman, Martin L. The Simple Macroeconomics of Profit Sharing. *Amer. Econ. Rev.*, December 1985, *75*(5), pp. 937–53.

Wible, James R. An Epistemic Critique of Rational Expectations and the Neoclassical Macroeconomic Research Program. *J. Post Keynesian Econ.*, Winter 1984–85, *7*(2), pp. 269–81.

Wilson, T. Dennis Robertson and Keynes's General Theory: Comment. In *Harcourt, G. C., ed.,* 1985, pp. 124–28.

Wiseman, Jack. Philosophy and Economic Policy: Comment. In *Koslowski, P., ed.,* 1985, pp. 174–81.

Witte, Willard E. and Bhandari, Jagdeep S. Monetary Disturbances, Inventory Fluctuations and the Level of Sales: A Theoretical and Empirical Analysis. *Southern Econ. J.*, April 1985, *51*(4), pp. 1151–61.   [G: U.S.]

Wohltmann, Hans-Werner. On the Controllability of Continuous-Time Macroeconomic Models. *Z. Nationalökon.*, 1985, *45*(1), pp. 47–66.

Wood, William C. The Price Level in Principles of Macroeconomic: A Review Essay. *Amer.*

Econ., Spring 1985, *29*(1), pp. 80–84.

Wren-Lewis, Simon. Expectations in Keynesian Econometric Models. In *Lawson, T. and Pesaran, H., eds.*, 1985, pp. 66–79.

Zarnowitz, Victor. Recent Work on Business Cycles in Historical Perspective: A Review of Theories and Evidence. *J. Econ. Lit.*, June 1985, *23*(2), pp. 523–80. **[G: U.S.]**

Zinn, Karl Georg. Wachstum, Zeitallokation und die Grenzen der Geldvermögenspräferenz. (Growth, Allocation of Time, and the Limits to the Preference for Money Capital-Accumulation. With English summary.) *Konjunkturpolitik*, 1985, *31*(1/2), pp. 34–51.

0232 Theory of Aggregate Demand: Consumption

Anderson, William A. Indivisibility, Irreversibility, and the Demand for Consumer Durables. *J. Macroecon.*, Summer 1985, *7*(3), pp. 363–80.

Arestis, P. Is There Any Crowding-out of Private Expenditure by Fiscal Actions? In *Arestis, P. and Skouras, T., eds.*, 1985, pp. 99–124.

Aschauer, David Alan. Fiscal Policy and Aggregate Demand. *Amer. Econ. Rev.*, March 1985, *75*(1), pp. 117–27. **[G: U.S.]**

Barbour, G. Jeffrey; Beladi, Hamid and Severson, Robert F. Empirical Testing of the Life Cycle Hypothesis. *Atlantic Econ. J.*, December 1985, *13*(4), pp. 71–74. **[G: U.S.]**

Beraud, Alain and Etner, François. Quasi-demande et demande effectif: une note pedagogique. (Quasi-demand and Effective Demand: A Pedagogic Note. With English summary.) *Revue Econ.*, July 1985, *36*(4), pp. 797–816.

Bernanke, Ben. Adjustment Costs, Durables, and Aggregate Consumption. *J. Monet. Econ.*, January 1985, *15*(1), pp. 41–68. **[G: U.S.]**

Blinder, Alan S. and Deaton, Angus. The Time Series Consumption Function Revisited. *Brookings Pap. Econ. Act.*, 1985, (2), pp. 465–511. **[G: U.S.]**

Borpujari, Jitendra G. Savings Generation and Financial Programming in a Basic Need Constrained Developing Economy. In *Gutowski, A.; Arnaudo, A. A. and Scharrer, H.-E., eds.*, 1985, pp. 59–82. **[G: India]**

Chiappori, Pierre-André. Distribution of Income and the "Law of Demand." *Econometrica*, January 1985, *53*(1), pp. 109–27.
[G: Selected Countries]

Diamond, Peter A. The Economics of Saving: A Survey of Recent Contributions: Comment. In *Arrow, K. J. and Honkapohja, S., eds.*, 1985, pp. 295–306. **[G: U.S.]**

El-Beblawi, Hazem. Oil Surplus Funds: The Impact of the Mode of Placement. In *Gutowski, A.; Arnaudo, A. A. and Scharrer, H.-E., eds.*, 1985, pp. 210–33. **[G: LDCs; OPEC]**

Fauvel, Yvon. Théorie du cycle de vie et rentes publiques. (Life Cycle Theory and Public Pension Plans. With English summary.) *L'Actual. Econ.*, June 1985, *61*(2), pp. 220–38.

Fichtenbaum, Rudy. Consumption and the Distribution of Income. *Rev. Soc. Econ.*, October

1985, *43*(2), pp. 234–44.

Flavin, Marjorie. Excess Sensitivity of Consumption to Current Income: Liquidity Constraints or Myopia? *Can. J. Econ.*, February 1985, *18*(1), pp. 117–36. **[G: U.S.]**

Green, Christopher J. Permanent Income, Budget Constraints and Overshooting in Simple Aggregate Models. *Manchester Sch. Econ. Soc. Stud.*, September 1985, *53*(3), pp. 231–40.

Hall, Robert E. The Time Series Consumption Function Revisited: Comment. *Brookings Pap. Econ. Act.*, 1985, (2), pp. 512–13. **[G: U.S.]**

Hansen, Richard B.; McCormick, Ken and Rives, Janet M. The Aggregate Demand Curve and Its Proper Interpretation. *J. Econ. Educ.*, Fall 1985, *16*(4), pp. 287–96.

Hason, Zubair. Macro Consumption Function in an Islamic Framework: Comment. *J. Res. Islamic Econ.*, Winter 1985, *2*(2), pp. 79–81.

Holden, K. and Peel, D. A. Surprises in the Consumption Function, Incomplete Current Information, and Moving Average Errors: A Note [Stochastic Implications of the Life Cycle Permanent Income Hypothesis: Theory and Evidence]. *Econ. J.*, March 1985, *95*(377), pp. 183–88. **[G: U.K.]**

Hubbard, R. Glenn. The Time Series Consumption Function Revisited: Comment. *Brookings Pap. Econ. Act.*, 1985, (2), pp. 514–19.
[G: U.S.]

Iqbal, Munawar. Zakah, Moderation and Aggregate Consumption in an Islamic Economy. *J. Res. Islamic Econ.*, Summer 1985, *3*(1), pp. 45–61.

Jones, H. G. Consumer Behaviour. In *Morris, D., ed.*, 1985, pp. 29–52. **[G: U.K.]**

King, Mervyn. The Economics of Saving: A Survey of Recent Contributions. In *Arrow, K. J. and Honkapohja, S., eds.*, 1985, pp. 227–94.

Koskela, Erkki and Virén, Matti. On the Role of Inflation in Consumption Function. *Weltwirtsch. Arch.*, 1985, *121*(2), pp. 252–60.
[G: U.K.]

Kurz, Mordecai. Heterogeneity in Savings Behavior: A Comment. In *Arrow, K. J. and Honkapohja, S., eds.*, 1985, pp. 307–27. **[G: U.S.]**

Mahdi, S. Iqbal. Macro Consumption Function in an Islamic Framework. *J. Res. Islamic Econ.*, Winter 1985, *2*(2), pp. 73–77.

Mamalakis, Markos J. Financial Services and the Debt Problem in Latin America. In *Jorge, A.; Salazar-Carrillo, J. and Diaz-Pou, F., eds.*, 1985, pp. 29–37. **[G: Latin America]**

Mankiw, N. Gregory; Rotemberg, Julio J. and Summers, Lawrence H. Intertemporal Substitution in Macroeconomics. *Quart. J. Econ.*, February 1985, *100*(1), pp. 225–51.
[G: U.S.]

Mankiw, N. Gregory and Shapiro, Matthew D. Trends, Random Walks, and Tests of the Permanent Income Hypothesis. *J. Monet. Econ.*, September 1985, *16*(2), pp. 165–74.

Monticelli, Carlo. La teoria della funzione del consumo con aspettative razionali e il caso italiano. (With English summary.) *Stud. Econ.*,

1985, *40*(26), pp. 15–39. **[G: Italy]**

Otani, Kiyoshi. Effects of Fiscal Policy on Consumption in a Neoclassical Intertemporal Optimization Model. *Econ. Stud. Quart.*, December 1985, *36*(3), pp. 193–208.

Pellanda, Anna. Riflessioni sul risparmio desunte da tre scadenze secolari: 1734, 1836, 1936. (Reflections on Savings from Three Centennial Dates: 1734, 1836, 1936. With English summary.) *Rivista Int. Sci. Econ. Com.*, April 1985, *32*(4), pp. 375–88.

Royer, Daniel. A Note on Disequilibrium Dynamics in a Simple Macroeconomic Model. In *[Rossier, Edouard]*, 1985, pp. 59–67.

Sandmo, Agnar. The Effects of Taxation on Savings and Risk Taking. In *Auerbach, A. J. and Feldstein, M., eds.*, 1985, pp. 265–311.

Seater, John J. and Mariano, Roberto S. New Tests of the Life Cycle and Tax Discounting Hypotheses. *J. Monet. Econ.*, March 1985, *15*(2), pp. 195–215. **[G: U.S.]**

Seidman, Laurence S. A General Equilibrium Critique of Feldstein's Social Security Estimate. *Eastern Econ. J.*, April-June 1985, *11*(2), pp. 101–05. **[G: U.S.]**

Simmons, P. Consumption Constraints, Uncertain Income Streams and the Life Cycle Model. *Rech. Écon. Louvain*, 1985, *51*(2), pp. 175–80.

Sproule, Robert A. An Optimal Allocation of Labor Supply and Savings under Interest-Rate Uncertainty: An Extension. *Bull. Econ. Res.*, May 1985, *37*(2), pp. 115–22.

Takayama, Akira. Permanent Income Hypothesis: An Optimal Control Theory Approach to a Classical Macro Thesis. *J. Macroecon.*, Summer 1985, *7*(3), pp. 347–62.

Testi, Angela. Alcune considerazioni sul ruolo della ricchezza nella funzione aggregata del consumo. (Analysis of the Role of Wealth in the Consumption Function. With English summary.) *Econ. Int.*, February 1985, *38*(1), pp. 91–120. **[G: Italy]**

Vicarelli, Fausto. From Equilibrium to Probability: A Reinterpretation of the Method of the *General Theory*. In *Vicarelli, F., ed.*, 1985, pp. 155–77.

Zamagni, Stefano. Quale spazio fra punto e funzione di domanda? Alcune note preliminari. (Between the Point of Demand and the Demand Function: Some Preliminary Notes. With English summary.) *Rivista Int. Sci. Econ. Com.*, April 1985, *32*(4), pp. 343–57.

0233 Theory of Aggregate Demand: Investment

Arestis, P. Is There Any Crowding-out of Private Expenditure by Fiscal Actions? In *Arestis, P. and Skouras, T., eds.*, 1985, pp. 99–124.

Arrow, Kenneth J. and Kurz, Mordecai. Optimal Growth with Irreversible Investment in a Ramsey Model. In *Arrow, K. J. (I)*, 1985, pp. 401–17.

Artus, Patrick. Inventory Investment, Investment and Employment with Uncertain Demand. *Empirical Econ.*, 1985, *10*(3), pp. 177–200. **[G: France]**

Artus, Patrick and Muet, Pierre-Alain. Investment, Output and Labor Constraints, and Financial Constraints: The Estimation of a Model with Several Regimes. In *Weiserbs, D., ed.*, 1985, pp. 25–44. **[G: France]**

Ashley, Richard A. and Orr, Daniel. Further Results on Inventories and Price Stickiness. *Amer. Econ. Rev.*, December 1985, *75*(5), pp. 964–75.

Asimakopulos, Athanasios. Finance, Saving and Investment in Keynes's Economics: A Comment. *Cambridge J. Econ.*, December 1985, *9*(4), pp. 405–07.

d'Autume, Antoine and Michel, Philippe. Épargne, investissement et monnaie dans une perspective intertemporelle. (Saving, Investment, and Money in an Intertemporal Setting. With English summary.) *Revue Écon.*, March 1985, *36*(2), pp. 243–90.

d'Autume, Antoine and Michel, Philippe. Future Investment Constraints Reduce Present Investment. *Econometrica*, January 1985, *53*(1), pp. 203–06.

Caplin, Andrew S. The Variability of Aggregate Demand with (S, s) Inventory Policies. *Econometrica*, November 1985, *53*(6), pp. 1395–1409.

Cebula, Richard J. The 'Crowding Out' Effect of Fiscal Policy: Correction [An Empirical Analysis of the "Crowding Out" Effect of Fiscal Policy in the United States and Canada]. *Kyklos*, 1985, *38*(3), pp. 435–37.

Diamond, Peter A. and Yellin, Joel. The Distribution of Inventory Holdings in a Pure Exchange Barter Search Economy. *Econometrica*, March 1985, *53*(2), pp. 409–32.

Dow, Alexander and Dow, Sheila C. Animal Spirits and Rationality. In *Lawson, T. and Pesaran, H., eds.*, 1985, pp. 46–65.

Eckalbar, John C. Inventories in a Dynamic Macro Model with Flexible Prices. *Europ. Econ. Rev.*, March 1985, *27*(2), pp. 201–19.

Eckalbar, John C. Inventory Fluctuations in a Disequilibrium Macro Model. *Econ. J.*, December 1985, *95*(380), pp. 976–91.

Fortune, J. Neill. Manufacturers' Aggregate Inventory Accumulation and Unfilled Orders. *J. Post Keynesian Econ.*, Spring 1985, *7*(3), pp. 324–31. **[G: U.S.]**

Gronchi, Sandro. Un tasso interno di rendimento generalizzato. (With English summary.) *Econ. Polít.*, April 1985, *2*(1), pp. 55–80.

Hartman, Richard. Uncertainty in Future Government Spending and Investment. *Quart. J. Econ.*, November 1985, *100*(4), pp. 1339–47.

Ilzkovitz, Fabienne. Les déterminants des investissements des entreprises en Belgique. (With English summary.) *Cah. Écon. Bruxelles*, 4th Trimester 1985, (108), pp. 487–545. **[G: Belgium]**

Ingham, A. Aggregate Investment and Output in the U.K.: Comment. In *Weiserbs, D., ed.*, 1985, pp. 137–43. **[G: U.K.]**

Judd, Kenneth L. Short-run Analysis of Fiscal Policy in a Simple Perfect Foresight Model. *J. Polit. Econ.*, April 1985, *93*(2), pp. 298–319.

Kopcke, Richard W. The Determinants of Investment Spending. *New Eng. Econ. Rev.*, July/August 1985, pp. 19–35. [G: U.S.]

Kurz, Heinz D. Effective Demand in a "Classical" Model of Value and Distribution: The Multiplier in a Sraffian Framework. *Manchester Sch. Econ. Soc. Stud.*, June 1985, 53(2), pp. 121–37.

Larkins, Daniel. Comment on Aggregate Inventory Behavior: Response to Uncertainty and Interest Rates. *J. Post Keynesian Econ.*, Fall 1985, 8(1), pp. 149–50.

Lawrence, Colin and Siow, Aloysius. Interest Rates and Investment Spending: Some Empirical Evidence for Postwar U.S. Producer Equipment, 1947—1980. *J. Bus.*, October 1985, 58(4), pp. 359–75. [G: U.S.]

Mehdizadeh, Mostafa. The Effect of Liquid Assets on the Consumption Function of a Less Developed Economy, a Note. *Amer. Econ.*, Spring 1985, 29(1), pp. 78–79. [G: Iran]

Moene, Karl Ove. Fluctuations and Factor Proportions: Putty–Clay Investments under Uncertainty. In *[Johansen, L.]*, 1985, pp. 87–108.

Nicodano, Giovanna. Struttura finanziaria e decisioni d'investimento: una verifica econometrica. (Financial Structure and Investment Decisions: An Econometric Model. With English summary.) *Giorn. Econ.*, Mar.-Apr. 1985, 44(3–4), pp. 179–207. [G: Italy]

Patterson, Kerry D. Income Adjustments and the Role of Consumers' Durables in Some Leading Consumption Functions. *Econ. J.*, June 1985, 95(378), pp. 469–79. [G: U.K.]

Plasmans, Joseph. Investment, Output and Labor Constraints, and Financial Constraints: The Estimation of a Model with Several Regimes: Comment. In *Weiserbs, D., ed.*, 1985, pp. 45–49. [G: France]

Seidmann, Daniel J. Target Buffer Stocks. *Europ. Econ. Rev.*, March 1985, 27(2), pp. 165–82.

Snippe, Jan. Finance, Saving and Investment in Keynes's Economics. *Cambridge J. Econ.*, September 1985, 9(3), pp. 257–69.

Sterman, John D. A Behavioral Model of the Economic Long Wave. *J. Econ. Behav. Organ.*, March 1985, 6(1), pp. 17–53. [G: U.S.]

Wisley, T. O. and Johnson, Stanley R. An Evaluation of Alternative Investment Hypotheses Using Non-nested Tests. *Southern Econ. J.*, October 1985, 52(2), pp. 422–30. [G: U.S.]

Zinn, Karl Georg. Investitionstheoretische Implikationen einer sättigungsorientierten Erklärung von Stagnation und Arbeitslosigkeit. Replik. (Implications of a Demand Side Explanation of Stagnation Concerning the Investment Function. With English summary.) *Konjunkturpolitik*, 1985, 31(6), pp. 348–60.

0234 Theory of Aggregate Supply

Andersen, Torben M. Price and Output Responsiveness to Nominal Changes under Differential Information. *Europ. Econ. Rev.*, October 1985, 29(1), pp. 63–87.

Arnott, Richard J. and Stiglitz, Joseph E. Labor Turnover, Wage Structures, and Moral Hazard: The Inefficiency of Competitive Markets. *J. Lab. Econ.*, October 1985, 3(4), pp. 434–62.

Arrow, Kenneth J. Some Tests of the International Comparisons of Factor Efficiency with the CES Production Function: Reply. In *Arrow, K. J. (I)*, 1985, pp. 236–40. [G: Selected Countries]

Arrow, Kenneth J. The Measurement of Real Value Added. In *Arrow, K. J. (I)*, 1985, pp. 456–75.

Arrow, Kenneth J., et al. Capital–Labor Substitution and Economic Efficiency. In *Arrow, K. J. (I)*, 1985, pp. 50–103. [G: Selected Countries]

Artus, Patrick. Inventory Investment, Investment and Employment with Uncertain Demand. *Empirical Econ.*, 1985, 10(3), pp. 177–200. [G: France]

Asimakopulos, Athanasios. "Long-Period Employment" in *The General Theory. J. Post Keynesian Econ.*, Winter 1984–85, 7(2), pp. 207–13.

Asimakopulos, Athanasios. The Foundations of Unemployment Theory: A Comment. *J. Post Keynesian Econ.*, Spring 1985, 7(3), pp. 352–62.

Bartoli, Gloria and Lecaldano Sasso la Terza, Edoardo. Microeconomic Foundations of Aggregate Behaviour of Firms in Kalecki and Some of His Followers. *Econ. Notes*, 1985, (1), pp. 43–62.

Beraud, Alain and Etner, François. Quasi-demande et demande effectif. une note pedagogique. (Quasi-demand and Effective Demand: A Pedagogic Note. With English summary.) *Revue Econ.*, July 1985, 36(4), pp. 797–816.

Bernstein, Michael A. The Methodological Resolution of the Cambridge Controversies: A Comment. *J. Post Keynesian Econ.*, Summer 1985, 7(4), pp. 607–11.

Bosworth, Derek and Westaway, A. J. The Theory and Measurement of Capital Utilisation and Its Role in Modelling Investment. In *Weiserbs, D., ed.*, 1985, pp. 291–317. [G: U.K.]

Brocato, Joe. Persistence under Alternative Forms of the Lucas Supply Function: Implications for the Lucas–Sargent Price Confusion Hypothesis and Barro-Type Money Models. *Quart. Rev. Econ. Bus.*, Spring 1985, 25(1), pp. 28–39. [G: U.S.]

Brown, Murray and Wolfstetter, Elmar. A Micro Theory of Layoffs and Involuntary Unemployment. *Metroecon.*, February 1985, 37(1), pp. 1–19.

Buccellato, Claudio. Production, Reproduction and Exchange in Multi-sector Systems. *Rivista Int. Sci. Econ. Com.*, July-Aug. 1985, 32(7–8), pp. 705–22.

Calmfors, Lars. Trade Unions, Wage Formation and Macroeconomic Stability—An Introduction. *Scand. J. Econ.*, 1985, 87(2), pp. 143–59. [G: W. Europe; U.S.]

Calmfors, Lars and Horn, Henrik. Classical Unemployment, Accommodation Policies and Adjustment of Real Wages. *Scand. J. Econ.*, 1985, 87(2), pp. 234–61.

Caravani, Paolo and De Luca, Alessandro. Aggregazione settoriale: una applicazione al modello sraffiano di produzione semplice. (Sectoral Aggregation: An Application to the Sraffian Model of Simple Production. With English summary.) *Ricerche Econ.*, July-Sept. 1985, 39(3), pp. 293–317.

Carlberg, Michael. Makroökonomische Effekte einer Arbeitszeitverkürzung. (With English summary.) *Z. Wirtschaft. Sozialwissen.*, 1985, 105(1), pp. 17–32.

Cencini, Alvaro. Moneta e produzione. (With English summary.) *Stud. Econ.*, 1985, 40(25), pp. 105–29.

Cencini, Alvaro. Moneta e produzione: Replica. (With English summary.) *Stud. Econ.*, 1985, 40(25), pp. 143–49.

Chacholiades, Miltiades. Circulating Capital in the Theory of International Trade. *Southern Econ. J.*, July 1985, 52(1), pp. 1–22.

Cohen, Avi J. Issues in the Cambridge Controversies [The Methodological Resolution of the Cambridge Controversies]. *J. Post Keynesian Econ.*, Summer 1985, 7(4), pp. 612–15.

Costabile, Lilia. Credit Creation, Capital Formation and Abstinence in the Approach of D. H. Robertson. In *Arena, R., et al.*, 1985, pp. 265–86.

Dar, Atul and DasGupta, Swapan. The Estimation of Production Functions: The CRES and CDE Approaches Applied to U.S. Manufacturing Data—A Comparative Study. *Appl. Econ.*, June 1985, 17(3), pp. 437–49.   [G: U.S.]

Darity, William A., Jr. On Involuntary Unemployment and Increasing Returns. *J. Post Keynesian Econ.*, Spring 1985, 7(3), pp. 363–72.

Darrat, Ali F. 'Efficient' Market Testing of the Expectations-adjusted Supply Function Hypothesis for Italy. *Appl. Econ.*, December 1985, 17(6), pp. 1065–70.   [G: Italy]

Darrat, Ali F. Anticipated Money and Real Output in Italy: Some Tests of a Rational Expectations Approach. *J. Post Keynesian Econ.*, Fall 1985, 8(1), pp. 81–90.   [G: Italy]

Darrat, Ali F. Inflationary Surprises and Real Economic Activity in Germany: Some Tests Based on 'Efficient Market' Expectations. *Kredit Kapital*, 1985, 18(2), pp. 230–39.
[G: W. Germany]

Darrat, Ali F. Unanticipated Inflation and Real Output: The Canadian Evidence. *Can. J. Econ.*, February 1985, 18(1), pp. 146–55.
[G: Canada]

Davidson, Lawrence S. and Hafer, R. W. Relative Price Variability: Evidence from Supply and Demand Events. *J. Monet. Econ.*, May 1985, 15(3), pp. 333–41.   [G: U.S.]

Davidson, Paul. Liquidity and Not Increasing Returns Is the Ultimate Source of Unemployment Equilibrium. *J. Post Keynesian Econ.*, Spring 1985, 7(3), pp. 373–84.

De Vroey, Michel. La théorie du salaire de Marx: une critique hétérodoxe. (Marx's Theory of

Wages: An Heterodox Criticism. With English summary.) *Revue Écon.*, May 1985, 36(3), pp. 451–80.

Drazen, Allan. Cyclical Determinants of the Natural Level of Economic Activity. *Int. Econ. Rev.*, June 1985, 26(2), pp. 387–97.

Drazen, Allan. State Dependence in Optimal Factor Accumulation. *Quart. J. Econ.*, May 1985, 100(2), pp. 357–72.

Driscoll, Michael J.; Mullineux, A. W. and Sen, Somnath. Testing the Rational Expectations and Structural Neutrality Hypotheses: Some Further Results for the U.K. *Empirical Econ.*, 1985, 10(1), pp. 51–58.   [G: U.K.]

Farmer, Roger E. A. Implicit Contracts with Asymmetric Information and Bankruptcy: The Effect of Interest Rates on Layoffs. *Rev. Econ. Stud.*, July 1985, 52(3), pp. 427–42.
[G: U.S.]

Fethke, Gary. The Conformity of Wage-Indexation Models with "Stylized Facts." *Amer. Econ. Rev.*, September 1985, 75(4), pp. 856–61.   [G: Canada; W. Germany; Japan; U.K.; U.S.]

Fischer, Stanley. Supply Shocks, Wage Stickiness, and Accommodation. *J. Money, Credit, Banking*, February 1985, 17(1), pp. 1–15.

Førsund, Finn R. and Jansen, Eilev S. The Interplay between Sectoral Models Based on Micro Data and Models for the National Economy. In *[Johansen, L.]*, 1985, pp. 109–25.

Fukushima, Takashi. Price–Output Response Is Always Normal Despite Factor Market Distortions. *Econ. Stud. Quart.*, December 1985, 36(3), pp. 247–51.

Gelauff, George M. M.; Wennekers, Sander R. M. and de Jong, André H. M. A Putty-Clay Model with Three Factors of Production and Partly Endogenous Technical Progress. *De Economist*, 1985, 133(3), pp. 327–51.
[G: Netherlands]

Ghosh, Dipak. A Disequilibrium Interpretation of Kaldor's Technical Progress Function. *Bull. Econ. Res.*, January 1985, 37(1), pp. 69–73.

Graziani, Augusto. Moneta e produzione: Commento. (With English summary.) *Stud. Econ.*, 1985, 40(25), pp. 131–42.

Grellet, Gérard. La monnaie est-elle à l'origine du chômage? (Is Money Generating Unemployment? With English summary.) *Écon. Appl.*, 1985, 38(1), pp. 301–08.

Guibert, Bernard. Théorie naive des ensembles capitalistes. (A Naive Theory of the Capitalist Sets. With English summary.) *Revue Écon.*, May 1985, 36(3), pp. 481–508.

Hamlin, Alan P. and Heathfield, D. F. Capital Utilization and Investment in a "Mixed" Economy. In *Weiserbs, D., ed.*, 1985, pp. 319–40.

Harvey, Philip. The Value-creating Capacity of Skilled Labor in Marxian Economics. *Rev. Radical Polit. Econ.*, Spring and Summer 1985, 17(1/2), pp. 83–102.

Horn, Gustav and Möller, Joachim. Keynesianische oder Klassische Arbeitslosigkeit in der Bundesrepublik Deutschland? Empirische überprüfung eines Mengenrationierungsmo-

dells mittels Kalman–Verfahren für den Zeitraum 1970–1982. (Keynesian or Classical Unemployment in the Federal Republic of Germany? Empirical Test of a Quantity Rationing Model Applying the Kalman Approach with Data from 1970 to 1982. With English summary.) *Ifo-Studien*, 1985, *31*(3), pp. 203–38.
[G: W. Germany]

Humphrey, Thomas M. The Early History of the Phillips Curve. *Fed. Res. Bank Richmond Econ. Rev.*, Sept./Oct. 1985, *71*(5), pp. 17–24.

Ihori, Toshihiro and Kurosaka, Yoshio. Fiscal Policies, Government's Deficits and Capital Formation. *Econ. Stud. Quart.*, August 1985, *36*(2), pp. 106–20.

Jadresić, Estaban. Una revisión de los modelos de formación de precios. (With English summary.) *Cuadernos Econ.*, December 1985, *22*(67), pp. 419–41.

Jonung, Lars. Classical Unemployment, Accommodation Policies and Adjustment of Real Wages: Comment. *Scand. J. Econ.*, 1985, *87*(2), pp. 262–66.

Jung, Woo S. Output–Inflation Tradeoffs in Industrial and Developing Countries. *J. Macroecon.*, Winter 1985, *7*(1), pp. 101–13. [G: LDCs; MDCs]

Kagawa, Akio and Kuga, Kiyoshi. Some Fundamentals of the Implicit Contract Theory. *Econ. Stud. Quart.*, April 1985, *36*(1), pp. 81–86.

Katsoulacos, Y. The Effect of Innovation in the Long-run: Ricardo and the Traverse. *Greek Econ. Rev.*, December 1985, *7*(3), pp. 242–54.

Khan, Ashfaque H. and Ahmad, Mushtaq. Real Money Balances in the Production Function of a Developing Country. *Rev. Econ. Statist.*, May 1985, *67*(2), pp. 336–40. [G: Pakistan]

Layard, Richard. Classical Unemployment, Accommodation Policies and Adjustment of Real Wages: Comment. *Scand. J. Econ.*, 1985, *87*(2), pp. 267–69.

Leontief, Wassily. Delayed Adjustment of Supply and Partial Equilibrium. In *Leontief, W.*, 1985, pp. 166–74.

Leontief, Wassily. The Fundamental Assumption of Mr. Keynes's Monetary Theory of Unemployment. In *Leontief, W.*, 1985, pp. 87–92.

Levačić, Rosalind. Supply Side Economics. In *Atkinson, G. B. J.*, *ed.*, 1985, pp. 133–53.
[G: U.K.]

Levine, A. Lawrence. Sraffa's *Production of Commodities by Means of Commodities*, Returns to Scale, Relevance, and Other Matters: A Note. *J. Post Keynesian Econ.*, Spring 1985, *7*(3), pp. 342–49.

Lindbeck, Assar and Snower, Dennis J. Explanations of Unemployment. *Oxford Rev. Econ. Policy*, Summer 1985, *1*(2), pp. 34–59.

Malcomson, James M. Capital Utilization and Empirical Analysis. In *Weiserbs, D.*, *ed.*, 1985, pp. 341–50.

de Meza, David and Perlman, Morris. Increasing Returns and the Foundation of Unemployment

Theory. *J. Post Keynesian Econ.*, Spring 1985, *7*(3), pp. 385–94.

Moene, Karl Ove. Fluctuations and Factor Proportions: Putty–Clay Investments under Uncertainty. In *[Johansen, L.]*, 1985, pp. 87–108.

Montgomery, Edward and Shaw, Kathryn. Longterm Contracts, Expectations and Wage Inertia. *J. Monet. Econ.*, September 1985, *16*(2), pp. 209–26.

Mork, Knut Anton. Flexibility in Intercommodity Substitution May Sharpen Price Fluctuations. *Quart. J. Econ.*, May 1985, *100*(2), pp. 447–63.

Myatt, Anthony. The Adverse Supply-Side Effects of High Interest Rates and Procyclical Real Wage Movements. *J. Macroecon.*, Spring 1985, *7*(2), pp. 237–46.

Neldner, Manfred. Die volkswirtschaftliche Produktivität des Geldes. Theoretische Überlegungen und einige empirische Ergebnisse für die Bundesrepublik Deutschland. (The Productivity of Money: Theoretical Remarks and Empirical Findings for West Germany. With English summary.) *Jahr. Nationalökon. Statist.*, July 1985, *200*(4), pp. 364–80.
[G: W. Germany]

Ng, Yew-Kwang. A Micro–Macroeconomic Analysis Based on a Representative Firm: Progress Report. In *Feiwel, G. R.*, *ed. (I)*, 1985, pp. 216–32.

Nickell, Stephen. Understanding Unemployment. *Empirica*, 1985, *12*(2), pp. 147–61.

Persson, Håkan. A Version of the MSG-Model with Putty–Clay and Vintage Technology. In *[Johansen, L.]*, 1985, pp. 163–85.

Rankin, Neil. Debt Neutrality in Disequilibrium. In *Currie, D.*, *ed.*, 1985, pp. 17–40.

Salanti, Andrea. Prices of Production, Market Prices, and the Analysis of the Choice of Techniques. *Metroecon.*, February 1985, *37*(1), pp. 97–117.

Salituro, Bruno. La teoria dei contratti impliciti, la rigidità salariale e la disoccupazione involontaria: una sintesi dei risultati. (With English summary.) *Econ. Polit.*, April 1985, *2*(1), pp. 31–53.

Salvadori, Neri. Switching in Methods of Production and Joint Production. *Manchester Sch. Econ. Soc. Stud.*, June 1985, *53*(2), pp. 156–78.

Seierstad, Atle. Properties of Production and Profit Functions Arising from the Aggregation of a Capacity Distribution of Micro Units. In *[Johansen, L.]*, 1985, pp. 65–85.

Sheffrin, Steven M. Accommodation, Supply Shocks, and Sluggish Real Wages. *J. Macroecon.*, Summer 1985, *7*(3), pp. 333–46.

Skott, Peter. Increasing Returns and Involuntary Unemployment: Is There a Connection? *J. Post Keynesian Econ.*, Spring 1985, *7*(3), pp. 395–402.

Solow, Robert M. Leif Johansen's Contributions to the Theory of Production, Planning, and Multisectoral Growth. In *[Johansen, L.]*, 1985, pp. 1–9.

Steedman, Ian. On the 'Impossibility' of Hicks-

Neutral Technical Change. *Econ. J.*, September 1985, 95(379), pp. 746–58.

Stemp, Peter J. The Effects on the Economy of Changing Unemployment Benefits and Pensions. *Australian Econ. Pap.*, June 1985, 24(44), pp. 127–41. [G: Australia]

Țigănescu, E. and Oprescu, G. Fundamental Correlations in the Macroeconomic System Efficiency—Profitableness. *Econ. Computat. Cybern. Stud. Res.*, 1985, 20(3), pp. 21–26.

Tinbergen, Jan. Constraints on Production Functions: Essential vs. Non-essential Factors. In *Tinbergen, J.*, 1985, pp. 25–34. [G: U.S.]

Tinbergen, Jan. Counterproduction. In *Tinbergen, J.*, 1985, pp. 35–42.

Tinbergen, Jan. Production Functions with Several Factors. In *Tinbergen, J.*, 1985, pp. 20–24. [G: U.S.]

Tinbergen, Jan. Production Functions: Research Lacunae. In *Tinbergen, J.*, 1985, pp. 56–65.

Tinbergen, Jan and Kol, Jacob. Market-Determined and Residual Incomes—Some Dilemmas. In *Tinbergen, J.*, 1985, pp. 3–19. [G: U.S.; Japan]

Venables, Anthony J. The Economic Implications of a Discrete Technical Change. *Oxford Econ. Pap.*, June 1985, 37(2), pp. 230–48.

Vincens, Jean. Réel, nominal, monétaire: Keynes et les salaires relatifs. (Real, Nominal and Monetary: Keynes and Relative Wages. With English summary.) *Écon. Appl.*, 1985, 38(1), pp. 237–64.

Virén, Matti. Determination of Employment with Wage and Price Speculation. *Scand. J. Econ.*, 1985, 87(3), pp. 537–53. [G: Finland]

Weitzman, Martin L. Increasing Returns and the Foundations of Unemployment Theory: An Explanation. *J. Post Keynesian Econ.*, Spring 1985, 7(3), pp. 403–09.

Wells, Paul. The Aggregate Supply Curve: Keynes and Downwardly Sticky Money Wages. *J. Econ. Educ.*, Fall 1985, 16(4), pp. 297–304.

van Wijnbergen, Sweder. Optimal Capital Accumulation and the Allocation of Investment between Traded and Nontraded Sectors in Oil-producing Countries. *Scand. J. Econ.*, 1985, 87(1), pp. 89–101. [G: LDCs]

Woods, John Edward. Exercises in Relative Price Variance. *Giorn. Econ.*, Mar.-Apr. 1985, 44(3–4), pp. 135–52.

Woods, John Edward. Okishio's Theorem and Fixed Capital. *Metroecon.*, June 1985, 37(2), pp. 187–97.

Wörgötter, Andreas. Supply Shocks, Stagflation and Wage Restraint. *Econ. Notes*, 1985, (2), pp. 38–56.

Yu, Eden S. H. and Ingene, Charles A. Resource Allocation with Factor Price Differentials under Price Uncertainty. *Southern Econ. J.*, October 1985, 52(2), pp. 460–70.

0235 Theory of Aggregate Distribution

Afxentiou, P. C. Opportunity Costs and Collective Bargaining. *S. Afr. J. Econ.*, December 1985, 53(4), pp. 381–92.

Aizenman, Joshua. Wage Flexibility and Openness. *Quart. J. Econ.*, May 1985, 100(2), pp. 539–50.

Al-Jarhi, Mabid Ali. Towards an Islamic Macro Model of Distribution: A Comparative Approach. *J. Res. Islamic Econ.*, Winter 1985, 2(2), pp. 1–29.

Appelbaum, Eileen. Employment and the Distribution of Earned Income. *J. Post Keynesian Econ.*, Summer 1985, 7(4), pp. 594–602.

Arrow, Kenneth J. Optimal Capital Adjustment. In *Arrow, K. J. (I)*, 1985, pp. 120–39.

Basile, Liliana and Salvadori, Neri. Kalecki's Pricing Theory. *J. Post Keynesian Econ.*, Winter 1984–85, 7(2), pp. 249–62.

Baslé, M. Profitabilité, accumulation-répartition, et régulation d'ensemble: propositions de synthèse et premie application au cas de la France. (Profitability, Accumulation-Repartition, and Global Regulation. Some Propositions for Synthetic Analysis and a First Application in the French Case. With English summary.) *Écon. Soc.*, January 1985 cf, 19(1), pp. 131–76. [G: France]

Bhaduri, Amit. L'accumulation du capital: temps logique et temps historique. (Capital Accumulation: Logical and Historical Time. With English summary.) *Écon. Appl.*, 1985, 38(2), pp. 453–69.

Boskin, Michael J. A Longer-term Perspective on Macroeconomics and Distribution: Time, Expectations, and Incentives. In *Feiwel, G. R., ed. (I)*, 1985, pp. 444–58.

Bowles, Samuel and Gintis, Herbert. The Labor Theory of Value and the Specificity of Marxian Economics. In *[Magdoff, H. and Sweezy, P.]*, 1985, pp. 31–44.

Brandis, Royall. Distribution Theory: Scientific Analysis or Moral Philosophy? *J. Econ. Issues*, December 1985, 19(4), pp. 867–78.

Casarosa, Carlo. The 'New View' of the Ricardian Theory of Distribution and Economic Growth. In *Caravale, G. A., ed.*, 1985, pp. 45–58.

Chacholiades, Miltiades. Circulating Capital in the Theory of International Trade. *Southern Econ. J.*, July 1985, 52(1), pp. 1–22.

Drazen, Allan. State Dependence in Optimal Factor Accumulation. *Quart. J. Econ.*, May 1985, 100(2), pp. 357–72.

Edel, Kim and Edel, Matthew. Dialogue, Utopia and the Division of Labor: Reflections on Some Themes by Harry Magdoff. In *[Magdoff, H. and Sweezy, P.]*, 1985, pp. 83–98.

Fazi, Elido and Salvadori, Neri. The Existence of a Two-Class Economy in a General Cambridge Model of Growth and Distribution. *Cambridge J. Econ.*, June 1985, 9(2), pp. 155–64.

Fichtenbaum, Rudy. Consumption and the Distribution of Income. *Rev. Soc. Econ.*, October 1985, 43(2), pp. 234–44.

Franke, Reiner. On the Upper- and Lower-Bounds of Workers' Propensity to Save in a Two-Class Pasinetti Economy. *Australian Econ. Pap.*, December 1985, 24(45), pp. 271–77.

Fuhrmann, Wilfried. Tatsächliche und erwartete Nominallohnsatzänderungen in einem einfachen keynesianischen Modell. (Actual and Expected Changes of the Nominal Wage Rate in a Simple Keynesian Model. With English summary.) *Jahr. Nationalökon. Statist.*, March 1985, *200*(2), pp. 137–52.

George, Donald A. R. Wage-Earners' Investment Funds in the Long Run. *Econ. Anal. Worker's Manage.*, 1985, *19*(1), pp. 13–28.

Giannola, A. Some Notes on Income Distribution, Activity Levels and the Structure of Interest Rates in a Pure Credit Economy. In *Arena, R., et al.*, 1985, pp. 179–90.

Goldstein, Jonathan P. The Cyclical Profit Squeeze: A Marxian Microfoundation. *Rev. Radical Polit. Econ.*, Spring and Summer 1985, *17*(1/2), pp. 103–28.

Graziani, Augusto. Monnaie, intérêt dépense publique. (Money, Interest and Government Spending. With English summary.) *Écon. Soc.*, August 1985, *19*(8), pp. 209–27.

Hahn, Frank. Equilibrium Dynamics with Heterogeneous Capital Goods. In *Hahn, F.*, 1985, pp. 243–60.

Hallwirth, Volker. Reallohn und Beschäftigung—Ein Ansatz zum Test der klassischen Grenzproduktivitätstheorie der Arbeit. (The Marginal Productivity Relationship of Wages and Employment—A Specification of an Empirical Test. With English summary.) *Jahr. Nationalökon. Statist.*, March 1985, *200*(2), pp. 153–72. [G: W. Germany]

Harvey, Philip. The Value-creating Capacity of Skilled Labor in Marxian Economics. *Rev. Radical Polit. Econ.*, Spring and Summer 1985, *17*(1/2), pp. 83–102.

Hasan, Zubair. Determination of Profit and Loss Sharing Ratios in Interest-Free Business Finance. *J. Res. Islamic Econ.*, Summer 1985, *3*(1), pp. 13–29.

Horvat, Branko. *Structural Change and Economic Growth:* Review Article. *Econ. Anal. Worker's Manage.*, 1985, *19*(3), pp. 327–32.

Koopmans, Tjalling C. Examples of Production Relations Based on Microdata. In *Koopmans, T. C.*, 1985, pp. 209–36.

Kregel, J. A. Post-Keynesian Distribution Theory in Relation to Growth and Technical Progress. *Écon. Appl.*, 1985, *38*(2), pp. 375–88.

Kregel, J. A. Sidney Weintraub's Macrofoundations of Microeconomics and the Theory of Distribution. *J. Post Keynesian Econ.*, Summer 1985, *7*(4), pp. 540–58.

Kurz, Heinz D. Effective Demand in a "Classical" Model of Value and Distribution: The Multiplier in a Sraffian Framework. *Manchester Sch. Econ. Soc. Stud.*, June 1985, *53*(2), pp. 121–37.

Lebowitz, Michael A. The Theoretical Status of Monopoly Capital. In *[Magdoff, H. and Sweezy, P.]*, 1985, pp. 185–203.

Lee, Frederic S. "Kalecki's Pricing Theory": Two Comments. *J. Post Keynesian Econ.*, Fall 1985, *8*(1), pp. 145–48.

Leontief, Wassily. The Pure Theory of the Guaranteed Annual Wage Contract. In *Leontief, W.*, 1985, pp. 108–15.

Lianos, Theodore P. A Note on Three Theories of the Relative Share of Labor. *Greek Econ. Rev.*, April 1985, *7*(1), pp. 82–84.

Lippi, Marco. Ancora su valore e costa reale in Marx: risposta alle critiche di petri. (Value and Real Cost in Marx Once Again. With English summary.) *Rivista Int. Sci. Econ. Com.*, July-Aug. 1985, *32*(7–8), pp. 635–59.

McCallum, John. Wage Gaps, Factor Shares and Real Wages. *Scand. J. Econ.*, 1985, *87*(2), pp. 436–59. [G: U.S.; W. Europe; Japan; Canada]

Morris, Jacob. Value Relations and Divisions within the Working Class: A Comment. *Sci. Soc.*, Summer 1985, *49*(2), pp. 214–20.

Moseley, Fred. The Rate of Surplus Value in the Postwar U.S. Economy: A Critique of Weisskopf's Estimates. *Cambridge J. Econ.*, March 1985, *9*(1), pp. 57–79. [G: U.S.]

Naples, Michele I. Dynamic Adjustment and Long-run Inflation in a Marxian Model. *J. Post Keynesian Econ.*, Fall 1985, *8*(1), pp. 97–112.

Naqvi, K. A. Towards an Islamic Macro Model of Distribution: A Comparative Approach: Comment. *J. Res. Islamic Econ.*, Winter 1985, *2*(2), pp. 67–71.

Nikaido, Hukukane. Dynamics of Growth and Capital Mobility in Marx's Scheme of Reproduction. *Z. Nationalökon.*, 1985, *45*(3), pp. 197–218.

Nuñez Miñana, Horacio. Distribución del ingreso y crecimiento económico: una propuesta de integracion de diferentes tradiciones. (Income Distribution and Economic Growth: An Integrated Proposal of Different Traditions. With English summary.) *Económica (La Plata)*, May-Dec. 1985, *31*(2–3), pp. 171–221.

O'Connell, Joan. Undistributed Profits and the Pasinetti and Dual Theorems. *J. Macroecon.*, Winter 1985, *7*(1), pp. 115–19.

Parker, Ian. Harold Innis: Staples, Communications, and the Economics of Capacity, Overhead Costs, Rigidity, and Bias. In *[Spry, I. M.]*, 1985, pp. 73–93.

van der Ploeg, Frederick. Classical Growth Cycles. *Metroecon.*, June 1985, *37*(2), pp. 221–30.

Prebisch, Raúl. Power Relations and Market Laws. In *Kim, K. S. and Ruccio, D. F., eds.*, 1985, pp. 9–31.

Resnick, Stephen A. and Wolff, Richard D. A Marxian Reconceptualization of Income and its Distribution. In *[Magdoff, H. and Sweezy, P.]*, 1985, pp. 319–44.

Rothschild, Kurt W. Some Notes on Weintraub's Eclectic Theory of Income Shares. *J. Post Keynesian Econ.*, Summer 1985, *7*(4), pp. 575–93. [G: Austria]

Rowthorn, Bob and Harris, Donald J. The Organic Composition of Capital and Capitalist Development. In *[Magdoff, H. and Sweezy, P.]*, 1985, pp. 345–57.

Tarling, Roger and Wilkinson, Frank. Mark-up Pricing, Inflation and Distributional Shares: A

Note. *Cambridge J. Econ.*, June 1985, 9(2), pp. 179–85.

Violi, Roberta. Sentiero di traversa e convergenza. (Traverse Path and Convergence. With English summary.) *Giorn. Econ.*, Mar.-Apr. 1985, 44(3–4), pp. 153–78.

de Vivo, Giancarlo. Robert Torrens and Ricardo's 'Corn-Ratio' Theory of Profits. *Cambridge J. Econ.*, March 1985, 9(1), pp. 89–92.

Wadensjö, Eskil. Wage Gaps, Factor Shares and Real Wages: Comment. *Scand. J. Econ.*, 1985, 87(2), pp. 460–62. [G: U.S.; W. Europe; Japan]

Weintraub, Sidney. Aggregate Income Distribution Theory. In *Vicarelli, F., ed.*, 1985, pp. 178–203.

Weisskopf, Thomas E. The Rate of Surplus Value in the Postwar U.S. Economy: A Response to Moseley's Critique. *Cambridge J. Econ.*, March 1985, 9(1), pp. 81–84. [G: U.S.]

Woods, John Edward. Okishio's Theorem and Fixed Capital. *Metroecon.*, June 1985, 37(2), pp. 187–97.

0239 Macroeconomics of Intertemporal Choice

Bental, Benjamin. Welfare Analysis of Income Distributions: A Neoclassical Approach. In *Maital, S. and Lipnowski, I., eds.*, 1985, pp. 153–61.

Blanchard, Olivier J. and Sachs, Jeffrey. Anticipations, Recessions and Policy; An Intertemporal Disequilibrium Model. In *Melitz, J. and Wyplosz, C., eds.*, 1985, pp. 117–44.

Chappell, David. On Optimal Economic Growth with Intertemporally Dependent Preferences. *Indian Econ. J.*, Apr.-June 1985, 32(4), pp. 29–38.

Esteban Marquillas, Joan M. Una caracterización del núcleo en economías de generaciones sucesivas. (With English summary.) *Revista Española Econ.*, 1985, 2(1), pp. 3–17.

Fane, George. A Derivation of the IS-LM Model from Explicit Optimizing Behavior. *J. Macroecon.*, Fall 1985, 7(4), pp. 493–508.

Kouri, Pentti. Anticipations, Recessions and Policy; An Intertemporal Disequilibrium Model: Comments. In *Melitz, J. and Wyplosz, C., eds.*, 1985, pp. 147–48.

Leontief, Wassily. Theoretical Note on Time-Preference, Productivity of Capital, Stagnation, and Economic Growth. In *Leontief, W.*, 1985, pp. 175–84.

Masson, P. R. The Sustainability of Fiscal Deficits. *Int. Monet. Fund Staff Pap.*, December 1985, 32(4), pp. 577–605.

Rankin, Neil. Debt Neutrality in Disequilibrium. In *Currie, D., ed.*, 1985, pp. 17–40.

024 Welfare Theory

0240 General

Akiyama, Shigeru and Kawai, Masahiro. Welfare Implications of Commodity Price Stabilization with Partially Flexible Production, Private Storage and Buffer-Stock Costs. *Weltwirtsch. Arch.*, 1985, 121(2), pp. 261–79.

Apps, Patricia. The Relative Deprivation Curve and Its Applications: Comment. *J. Bus. Econ. Statist.*, April 1985, 3(2), pp. 169–71. [G: Australia]

Armstrong, Thomas E. Precisely Dictatorial Social Welfare Functions: Erratum and Addendum to 'Arrows Theorem with Restricted Coalition Algebras.' *J. Math. Econ.*, 1985, 14(1), pp. 57–59.

Arrow, Kenneth J. Criteria for Social Investment. In *Arrow, K. J. (I)*, 1985, pp. 200–214.

Arrow, Kenneth J. Discounting and Public Investment Criteria. In *Arrow, K. J. (I)*, 1985, pp. 215–35.

Arrow, Kenneth J. Distributive Justice and Desirable Ends of Economic Activity. In *Feiwel, G. R., ed. (I)*, 1985, pp. 134–56.

Arrow, Kenneth J. The Social Discount Rate. In *Arrow, K. J. (I)*, 1985, pp. 382–400.

Arrow, Kenneth J. Uncertainty and the Welfare Economics of Medical Care. In *Arrow, K. J. (II)*, 1985, pp. 15–50.

Arrow, Kenneth J. and Kurz, Mordecai. Optimal Public Investment Policy and Controllability with Fixed Private Savings Ratio. In *Arrow, K. J. (I)*, 1985, pp. 332–72.

Arrow, Kenneth J. and Lind, Robert C. Uncertainty and the Evaluation of Public Investment Decisions. In *Arrow, K. J. (I)*, 1985, pp. 418–39.

Arrow, Kenneth J. and Lind, Robert C. Uncertainty and the Evaluation of Public Investment Decisions: Reply. In *Arrow, K. J. (I)*, 1985, pp. 440–42.

d'Aspremont, Claude. Axioms for Social Welfare Orderings. In *[Pazner, E.]*, 1985, pp. 19–76.

Auerbach, Alan J. The Theory of Excess Burden and Optimal Taxation. In *Auerbach, A. J. and Feldstein, M., eds.*, 1985, pp. 61–127.

Aumann, Robert J. On the Non-transferable Utility Value: A Comment on the Roth–Shafer Examples [Values for Games without Side Payments: Some Difficulties with Current Concepts] [On the Existence and Interpretation of Value Allocations]. *Econometrica*, May 1985, 53(3), pp. 667–77.

Basu, Kaushik. Poverty Measurement: A Decomposition of the Normalization Axion [Cardinal Utility, Utilitarianism and a Class of Invariance Axioms in Welfare Analysis] [Poverty: An Ordinal Approach to Measurement]. *Econometrica*, November 1985, 53(6), pp. 1439–43.

Baye, Michael R. A Note on Price Stability and Consumers' Welfare. *Econometrica*, January 1985, 53(1), pp. 213–16.

Bergsten, Gordon S. On the Role of Social Norms in a Market Economy. *Public Choice*, 1985, 45(2), pp. 113–37.

Berrebi, Z. M. and Silber, Jacques. The Gini Coefficient and Negative Income: A Comment. *Oxford Econ. Pap.*, September 1985, 37(3), pp. 525–26.

Blackorby, C. and Donaldson, D. Consumers' Surpluses and Consistent Cost–Benefit Tests.

Soc. Choice Welfare, March 1985, *1*(4), pp. 251–62.

Blankart, Charles. Market and Non-market Alternatives in the Supply of Public Goods: General Issues. In *Forte, F. and Peacock, A., eds.*, 1985, pp. 192–202.

Blaug, Mark. Marginal Cost Pricing: No Empty Box. In *[Peacock, A.]*, 1985, pp. 15–30.

Border, K. C. More on Harsanyi's Utilitarian Cardinal Welfare Theorem. *Soc. Choice Welfare*, March 1985, *1*(4), pp. 279–81.

Bös, Dieter. Income Taxation, Public Sector Pricing and Redistribution. In *Førsund, F. R. and Honkapohja, S., eds.*, 1985, pp. 68–85.

Brander, James A. and Spencer, Barbara J. Ramsey Optimal Two Part Tariffs: The Case of Many Heterogeneous Groups. *Public Finance*, 1985, *40*(3), pp. 335–46.

Brennan, Goeffrey and Walsh, Cliff. Private Markets in (Excludable) Public Goods: A Reexamination [Private Markets in Public Goods (or Qualities)]. *Quart. J. Econ.*, August 1985, *100*(3), pp. 811–19.

Broome, John. The Economic Value of Life. *Economica*, August 1985, *52*(207), pp. 281–94.

Broome, John. The Welfare Economics of the Future: A Review. *Soc. Choice Welfare*, December 1985, *2*(3), pp. 221–34.

Browning, Edgar K. A Critical Appraisal of Hausman's Welfare Cost Estimates. *J. Polit. Econ.*, October 1985, *93*(5), pp. 1025–34. [G: U.S.]

Byrnes, Patrica; Grosskopf, Shawna and Hayes, Kathy J. How 'Exact' are Exact Measures of Welfare Loss? *Appl. Econ.*, December 1985, *17*(6), pp. 1071–81. [G: U.S.]

Carens, Joseph H. Compensatory Justice and Social Institutions. *Econ. Philos.*, April 1985, *1*(1), pp. 39–67.

Chakravarty, Satya R.; Dutta, Bhaskar and Weymark, John A. Ethical Indices of Income Mobility. *Soc. Choice Welfare*, May 1985, *2*(1), pp. 1–21.

Chen, Chau-Nan; Tsuar, Tien-Wang and Rhai, Tong-Shieng. The Gini Coefficient and Negative Income: Reply. *Oxford Econ. Pap.*, September 1985, *37*(3), pp. 527–28.

Cima, Lawrence R. and Cotter, Patrick S. The Coherence of the Concept of Limited Government. *J. Policy Anal. Manage.*, Winter 1985, *4*(2), pp. 266–69.

Ciriacy-Wantrup, S. V. The Economics of Environmental Policy. In *Ciriacy-Wantrup, S. V.*, 1985, pp. 39–50.

Cooter, Robert D. and Rappoport, Peter. Reply to I. M. D. Little's Comment [Were the Ordinalists Wrong about Welfare Economics?]. *J. Econ. Lit.*, September 1985, *23*(3), pp. 1189–91.

Cornes, Richard and Sandler, Todd. On the Consistency of Conjectures with Public Goods. *J. Public Econ.*, June 1985, *27*(1), pp. 125–29.

Cornes, Richard and Sandler, Todd. The Simple Analytics of Pure Public Good Provision. *Economica*, February 1985, *52*(205), pp. 103–16.

Cowell, Frank A. 'A Fair Suck of the Sauce Bottle' or What Do You Mean by Inequality? *Econ.*

Rec., June 1985, *61*(173), pp. 567–79.

Cowell, Frank A. Measures of Distributional Change: An Axiomatic Approach. *Rev. Econ. Stud.*, January 1985, *52*(1), pp. 135–51.

Cowen, Tyler. Public Goods Definitions and Their Institutional Context: A Critique of Public Goods Theory. *Rev. Soc. Econ.*, April 1985, *43*(1), pp. 53–63.

Ebert, U. On the Relationship between the Hicksian Measures of Change in Welfare and the Pareto Principle. *Soc. Choice Welfare*, March 1985, *1*(4), pp. 263–72.

Ekelund, Robert B., Jr. and Hébert, Robert F. Consumer Surplus: The First Hundred Years. *Hist. Polit. Econ.*, Fall 1985, *17*(3), pp. 419–54.

Elster, Jon. Weakness of Will and the Free-Rider Problem. *Econ. Philos.*, October 1985, *1*(2), pp. 231–65.

Fine, Ben. A Note on the Measurement of Inequality and Interpersonal Comparability. *Soc. Choice Welfare*, March 1985, *1*(4), pp. 273–77.

Gallagher, David R. and Smith, V. Kerry. Measuring Values for Environmental Resources under Uncertainty. *J. Environ. Econ. Manage.*, June 1985, *12*(2), pp. 132–43.

Gauthier, David. Bargaining and Justice. In *Paul, E. F.; Paul, J. and Miller, F. D., Jr., eds.*, 1985, pp. 29–47.

Gibbard, Allan. What's Morally Special about Free Exchange. In *Paul, E. F.; Paul, J. and Miller, F. D., Jr., eds.*, 1985, pp. 20–28.

Gowdy, John M. Utility Theory and Agrarian Societies. *Int. J. Soc. Econ.*, 1985, *12*(6/7), pp. 104–17.

Gunning, James Patrick. Piaget and Social Economy [The Social Economy—Analogue of Piaget's Development of Knowledge]. *Rev. Soc. Econ.*, December 1985, *43*(3), pp. 371–79.

Hahn, Frank. On Optimum Taxation. In *Hahn, F.*, 1985, pp. 364–76.

Hammond, Peter. Welfare Economics. In *Feiwel, G. R., ed. (II)*, 1985, pp. 405–34.

Harris, Richard and Wildasin, David E. An Alternative Approach to Aggregate Surplus Analysis. *J. Public Econ.*, April 1985, *26*(3), pp. 289–302.

Harsanyi, John C. Rule Utilitarianism, Equality, and Justice. In *Paul, E. F.; Paul, J. and Miller, F. D., Jr., eds.*, 1985, pp. 115–27.

Haveman, Robert H. Does the Welfare State Increase Welfare? Reflections on Hidden Negatives and Observed Positives. *De Economist*, 1985, *133*(4), pp. 445–66. [G: U.S.; Netherlands]

Hayes, Kathy J. and Grosskopf, Shawna. Measuring the Welfare Loss of Pension Mandates: A Methodology and Example. *Public Finance Quart.*, January 1985, *13*(1), pp. 47–62. [G: U.S.]

Head, John G. and Brennan, Geoffrey. Free Provision, Tax Limits and Fiscal Reform. In *[Recktenwald, H. C.]*, 1985, pp. 193–207.

Helms, L. Jay. Expected Consumer's Surplus and the Welfare Effects of Price Stabilization. *Int.*

Econ. Rev., October 1985, *26*(3), pp. 603–17.

Hickerson, Steven R. Justice and the Social Economist: An Instrumentalist Interpretation. *Int. J. Soc. Econ.*, 1985, *12*(6/7), pp. 90–103.

Hirshleifer, J. From Weakest-Link to Best-Shot: Correction. *Public Choice*, 1985, *46*(2), pp. 221–23.

Hochman, Harold M. and Nitzan, Shmuel. Concepts of Extended Preference. *J. Econ. Behav. Organ.*, June 1985, *6*(2), pp. 161–76.

Hurwicz, Leonid. Social Goals and Social Organization: A Perspective. In *[Pazner, E.]*, 1985, pp. 1–16.

Ihori, Toshihiro. Liability Rules and the Iterative Process. *Econ. Stud. Quart.*, April 1985, *36*(1), pp. 15–22.

Johnson, Frederick I. The Imprecision of Traditional Welfare Measures in Empirical Applications. *Appl. Econ.*, October 1985, *17*(5), pp. 923–32.

Jorgenson, Dale W. Efficiency versus Equity in Economic Policy Analysis. *Amer. Econ.*, Spring 1985, *29*(1), pp. 5–14.

Jorgenson, Dale W. and Slesnick, Daniel T. Efficiency versus Equity in Natural Gas Price Regulation. *J. Econometrics*, Oct./Nov. 1985, *30*(1/2), pp. 301–16. **[G: U.S.]**

Kakwani, Nanak. Measurement of Welfare with Applications to Australia. *J. Devel. Econ.*, August 1985, *18*(2–3), pp. 429–61.
[G: Australia]

Kakwani, Nanak. The Relative Deprivation Curve and Its Applications: Reply. *J. Bus. Econ. Statist.*, April 1985, *3*(2), pp. 171–73.
[G: Australia]

Kelsey, D. The Liberal Paradox: A Generalisation. *Soc. Choice Welfare*, March 1985, *1*(4), pp. 245–50.

Kneese, Allen V. and Schulze, William D. Ethics and Environmental Economics. In *Kneese, A. V. and Sweeney, J. L., eds. Vol. 1*, 1985, pp. 191–220.

Kohli, Ulrich. Technology and Public Goods. *J. Public Econ.*, April 1985, *26*(3), pp. 379–400.

van de Kragt, Alphons J. C.; Orbell, John and Dawes, Robyn M. Reply [The Minimal Contributing Set as a Solution to Public Goods Problems]. *Amer. Polit. Sci. Rev.*, September 1985, *79*(3), pp. 823–24.

Kula, Erhun. The Social Time Preference Rate for Portugal. *Economia (Portugal)*, October 1985, *9*(3), pp. 447–66. **[G: Portugal]**

LaFrance, Jeffrey T. Linear Demand Functions in Theory and Practice. *J. Econ. Theory*, October 1985, *37*(1), pp. 147–66.

Lambert, Peter J. Social Welfare and the Gini Coefficient Revisited. *Math. Soc. Sci.*, February 1985, *9*(1), pp. 19–26.

Lane, Jan-Erik. State and Market: The Politics of the Public and the Private: Introduction: Public Policy or Markets? The Demarcation Problem. In *Lane, J.-E., ed.*, 1985, pp. 3–52.

Le Breton, M.; Trannoy, A. and Uriarte, J. R. Topological Aggregation of Inequality Preorders. *Soc. Choice Welfare*, September 1985, *2*(2), pp. 119–29.

Leininger, Wolfgang. Rawls' Maximin Criterion and Time-Consistency: Further Results. *Rev. Econ. Stud.*, July 1985, *52*(3), pp. 505–13.

Little, Ian M. D. Were the Ordinalists Wrong about Welfare Economics? A Comment. *J. Econ. Lit.*, September 1985, *23*(3), pp. 1186–88.

Mäler, Karl-Göran. Welfare Economics and the Environment. In *Kneese, A. V. and Sweeney, J. L., eds. Vol. 1*, 1985, pp. 3–60.

Matsuyama, Kiminori. Chernoff's Dual Axiom, Revealed Preference, and Weak Rational Choice Functions. *J. Econ. Theory*, February 1985, *35*(1), pp. 155–65.

McCaleb, Thomas S. and Wagner, Richard E. The Experimental Search for Free Riders: Some Reflections and Observations. *Public Choice*, 1985, *47*(3), pp. 479–90.

McCarl, Bruce A. and Brokken, Ray F. An Economic Analysis of Alternative Grazing Fee Systems. *Amer. J. Agr. Econ.*, November 1985, *67*(4), pp. 769–78.

de Meza, David and Gould, J. R. Free Access vs Private Ownership: A Comparison [Free Access vs Private Ownership as Alternative Systems for Managing Common Property]. *J. Econ. Theory*, August 1985, *36*(2), pp. 387–91.

van Mierlo, Hans J. G. A. Improvement of Public Provision of Goods and Services. In *Lane, J.-E., ed.*, 1985, pp. 53–69.

Mishan, Ezra J. Consistency in the Valuation of Life: A Wild Goose Chase? In *Paul, E. F.; Paul, J. and Miller, F. D., Jr., eds.*, 1985, pp. 152–67.

Moulin, Hervé. From Social Welfare Ordering to Acyclic Aggregation of Preferences. *Math. Soc. Sci.*, February 1985, *9*(1), pp. 1–17.

Moulin, Hervé. The Separability Axiom and Equal-sharing Methods. *J. Econ. Theory*, June 1985, *36*(1), pp. 120–48.

Musgrave, Richard A. A Brief History of Fiscal Doctrine. In *Auerbach, A. J. and Feldstein, M., eds.*, 1985, pp. 1–59.

Nerlove, Marc; Razin, Assaf and Sadka, Efraim. Population Size: Individual Choice and Social Optima. *Quart. J. Econ.*, May 1985, *100*(2), pp. 321–34.

Ng, Yew-Kwang. Equity and Efficiency vs. Freedom and Fairness: An Inherent Conflict. *Kyklos*, 1985, *38*(4), pp. 495–516. **[G: China]**

Ng, Yew-Kwang. Some Fundamental Issues in Social Welfare. In *Feiwel, G. R., ed. (II)*, 1985, pp. 435–69.

Ng, Yew-Kwang. The Utilitarian Criterion, Finite Sensibility, and the Weak Majority Preference Principle. A Futher Analysis [Bentham or Bergson? Finite Sensibility, Utility Functions and Social Welfare Functions] [Bentham or Nash? On the Acceptable Form of Social Welfare Functions]. *Soc. Choice Welfare*, May 1985, *2*(1), pp. 37–38.

Nozick, Robert. Interpersonal Utility Theory. *Soc. Choice Welfare*, December 1985, *2*(3), pp. 161–79.

Oates, Wallace E. The Public Sector in Economics: An Analytical Chameleon. In *[Reckten-wald, H. C.]*, 1985, pp. 45–58.

Pope, Rulon D. and Chavas, Jean-Paul. Producer Surplus and Risk. *Quart. J. Econ.*, Supp. 1985, *100*, pp. 853–69.

Quirk, James. Consumer Surplus under Uncertainty: An Application to Dam–Reservoir Projects. *Water Resources Res.*, September 1985, *21*(9), pp. 1307–12.

Rapoport, Amnon. Provision of Public Goods and the MCS Experimental Paradigm. *Amer. Polit. Sci. Rev.*, March 1985, *79*(1), pp. 148–55.

Riley, Jonathan. On the Possibility of Liberal Democracy. *Amer. Polit. Sci. Rev.*, December 1985, *79*(4), pp. 1135–51.

Ritz, Zvi. Restricted Domains, Arrow Social Welfare Functions and Noncorruptible and Nonmanipulable Social Choice Correspondences: The Case of Private and Public Alternatives. *J. Econ. Theory*, February 1985, *35*(1), pp. 1–18.

Roberts, Russell D. A Taxonomy of Public Provision: Reply. *Public Choice*, 1985, *47*(1), pp. 311–12.

Roberts, Russell D. A Taxonomy of Public Provision. *Public Choice*, 1985, *47*(1), pp. 267–303.

Roemer, John E. Equality of Talent. *Econ. Philos.*, October 1985, *1*(2), pp. 151–88.

Ross, Thomas W. Extracting Regulators' Implied Welfare Weights: Some Further Developments and Applications. *Quart. Rev. Econ. Bus.*, Autumn 1985, *25*(3), pp. 72–84. [G: U.S.]

Russell, R. Robert. A Note on Decomposable Inequality Measures. *Rev. Econ. Stud.*, April 1985, *52*(2), pp. 347–52.

Sen, Amartya. *Social Choice and Justice*: A Review Article. *J. Econ. Lit.*, December 1985, *23*(4), pp. 1764–76.

Sen, Amartya. A Sociological Approach to the Measurement of Poverty: A Reply [Poor, Relatively Speaking]. *Oxford Econ. Pap.*, December 1985, *37*(4), pp. 669–76.

Sen, Amartya. Goals, Commitment, and Identity. *J. Law, Econ., Organ.*, Fall 1985, *1*(2), pp. 341–55.

Sen, Amartya. The Moral Standing of the Market. In *Paul, E. F.; Paul, J. and Miller, F. D., Jr., eds.*, 1985, pp. 1–19.

Solterer, Joseph. Elementary Motions: A Response [The Social Economy—Analogue of Piaget's Development of Knowledge]. *Rev. Soc. Econ.*, December 1985, *43*(3), pp. 380–83.

Spiegel, Uriel and Templeman, Joseph. Interdependent Utility and Cooperative Behavior. *J. Compar. Econ.*, September 1985, *9*(3), pp. 314–28.

Strnad, Jeff. The Structure of Continuous-valued Neutral Monotonic Social Functions. *Soc. Choice Welfare*, December 1985, *2*(3), pp. 181–95.

Sugden, Robert. Consistent Conjectures and Voluntary Contributions to Public Goods: Why the Conventional Theory Does Not Work. *J. Public Econ.*, June 1985, *27*(1), pp. 117–24.

Sugden, Robert. Liberty, Preference, and Choice. *Econ. Philos.*, October 1985, *1*(2), pp. 213–29.

Suzumura, Kotaro and Sato, Kimitoshi. Equity and Efficiency in the Public Goods Economy: Some Counterexamples. *Hitotsubashi J. Econ.*, June 1985, *26*(1), pp. 59–82.

Svensson, L.-G. The Utilitarian Criterion, Finite Sensibility, and the Weak Majority Preference Principle. A Futher Analysis [Bentham or Bergson? Finite Sensibility, Utility Functions and Social Welfare Functions] [Bentham or Nash? On the Acceptable Form of Social Welfare Functions]. *Soc. Choice Welfare*, May 1985, *2*(1), pp. 23–35.

Tesfatsion, L. Fair Division with Uncertain Needs and Tastes. *Soc. Choice Welfare*, December 1985, *2*(4), pp. 295–309.

Tinbergen, Jan. On Collective and Part-Collective Goods. In *Tinbergen, J.*, 1985, pp. 43–55.

Tinbergen, Jan. Some Neglected Determinants of Welfare Functions. In *Tinbergen, J.*, 1985, pp. 131–42.

Tinbergen, Jan. The Dynamic Welfare Maximum. In *Tinbergen, J.*, 1985, pp. 145–57.

Tinbergen, Jan. The Measurement of Social Welfare. In *Tinbergen, J.*, 1985, pp. 113–22.

Tinbergen, Jan. Two Approaches to Quantify the Concept of Equitable Income Distribution. In *Tinbergen, J.*, 1985, pp. 101–10.

Townsend, Peter. A Sociological Approach to the Measurement of Poverty—A Rejoinder [Poor, Relatively Speaking]. *Oxford Econ. Pap.*, December 1985, *37*(4), pp. 659–68.

Usher, Dan. A Taxonomy of Public Provision: Comment. *Public Choice*, 1985, *47*(1), pp. 305–10.

Usher, Dan. The Value of Life for Decision Making in the Public Sector. In *Paul, E. F.; Paul, J. and Miller, F. D., Jr., eds.*, 1985, pp. 168–91.

Varian, Hal R. Dworkin on Equality of Resources [What Is Equality? Part 1: Equality of Welfare] [What Is Equality? Part 2: Equality of Resources]. *Econ. Philos.*, April 1985, *1*(1), pp. 110–25.

van der Veen, Robert J. and Van Parijs, Philippe. Entitlement Theories of Justice: From Nozick to Roemer and Beyond. *Econ. Philos.*, April 1985, *1*(1), pp. 69–81.

Weller, Dietrich. Fair Division of a Measurable Space. *J. Math. Econ.*, 1985, *14*(1), pp. 5–17.

Wilson, Thomas. The Unwithered Welfare State. In *[Peacock, A.]*, 1985, pp. 78–93. [G: U.K.]

Zajac, Edward E. Perceived Economic Justice: The Example of Public Utility Regulation. In *Young, H. P., ed.*, 1985, pp. 119–53.

0242 Allocative Efficiency Including Theory of Cost/Benefit

Adolph, Brigitte and Wolfstetter, Elmar. Pareto-Verbessernde Fiskalpolitik im allgemeinen Gleichgewicht bei rationalen Erwartungen. (With English summary.) *Z. Wirtschaft. So-*

zialwissen., 1985, *105*(1), pp. 51–63.

Aghion, Philippe. On the Generic Inefficiency of Differentiable Market Games. *J. Econ. Theory*, October 1985, *37*(1), pp. 126–46.

Akerlof, George A. and Yellen, Janet L. Can Small Deviations from Rationality Make Significant Differences to Economic Equilibria? *Amer. Econ. Rev.*, September 1985, *75*(4), pp. 708–20.

Araujo, Aloisio. Lack of Pareto Optimal Allocations in Economies with Infinitely Many Commodities: The Need for Impatience. *Econometrica*, March 1985, *53*(2), pp. 455–61.

Arnott, Richard J. and Stiglitz, Joseph E. Labor Turnover, Wage Structures, and Moral Hazard: The Inefficiency of Competitive Markets. *J. Lab. Econ.*, October 1985, *3*(4), pp. 434–62.

Arrow, Kenneth J. Economic Welfare and the Allocation of Resources for Invention. In *Arrow, K. J. (I)*, 1985, pp. 104–19.

Arrow, Kenneth J. The Potentials and Limits of the Market in Resource Allocation. In *Feiwel, G. R., ed. (II)*, 1985, pp. 107–24.

Arrow, Kenneth J. and Kurz, Mordecai. Optimal Consumer Allocation over an Infinite Horizon. In *Arrow, K. J. (I)*, 1985, pp. 307–31.

Arrow, Kenneth J. and Kurz, Mordecai. Optimal Public Investment Policy and Controllability with Fixed Private Savings Ratio. In *Arrow, K. J. (I)*, 1985, pp. 332–72.

Azariadis, Costas and Cooper, Russell. Predetermined Prices and the Allocation of Social Risks. *Quart. J. Econ.*, May 1985, *100*(2), pp. 495–518.

Bandyopadhyay, Taradas. Pareto Optimality and the Decisive Power Structure with Expansion Consistency Conditions. *J. Econ. Theory*, April 1985, *35*(2), pp. 366–75.

Beato, Paulina and Mas-Colell, Andreu. On Marginal Cost Pricing with Given Tax-Subsidy Rules. *J. Econ. Theory*, December 1985, *37*(2), pp. 356–65.

Bénard, Jean. Capital Humain et Optimum de Second Rang. Le Cas des Dépenses de Sante. In *Terny, G. and Culyer, A. J., eds.*, 1985, pp. 319–35.

Bental, Benjamin. Is Capital Mobility Always Desirable? A Welfare Analysis of Portfolio Autarky in a Growing Economy. *Int. Econ. Rev.*, February 1985, *26*(1), pp. 203–12.

Berlage, L. and Renard, R. The Discount Rate in Cost–Benefit Analysis and the Choice of a Numeraire. *Oxford Econ. Pap.*, December 1985, *37*(4), pp. 691–99.

Blaug, Mark. Marginal Cost Pricing: No Empty Box. In *[Peacock, A.]*, 1985, pp. 15–30.

Bockstael, Nancy E. and Strand, Ivar E. Distributional Issues and Nonmarket Benefit Measurement. *Western J. Agr. Econ.*, December 1985, *10*(2), pp. 162–69.   [G: U.S.]

Brock, William A. and Dechert, W. D. Dynamic Ramsey Pricing. *Int. Econ. Rev.*, October 1985, *26*(3), pp. 569–91.

Brock, William A. and Scheinkman, José A. Price Setting Supergames with Capacity Constraints.

Rev. Econ. Stud., July 1985, *52*(3), pp. 371–82.

Brown, Donald J. and Heal, Geoffrey M. The Optimality of Regulated Pricing: A General Equilibrium Analysis. In *Aliprantis, C. D.; Burkinshaw, O. and Rothman, N. J., eds.*, 1985, pp. 43–54.

Burrows, Paul. Efficiency Levels, Efficiency Gains and Alternative Nuisance Remedies. *Int. Rev. Law Econ.*, June 1985, *5*(1), pp. 59–71.

Calvo, Guillermo A. The Inefficiency of Unemployment: The Supervision Perspective. *Quart. J. Econ.*, May 1985, *100*(2), pp. 373–87.

Campbell, Robert B. and Turnovsky, Stephen J. An Analysis of the Stabilizing and Welfare Effects of Intervention in Spot and Futures Markets. *J. Public Econ.*, November 1985, *28*(2), pp. 165–209.

Carter, Michael R. A Wisconsin Institutionalist Perspective on Microeconomic Theory of Institutions: The Insufficiency of Pareto Efficiency. *J. Econ. Issues*, September 1985, *19*(3), pp. 797–813.

Cass, David. Optimality with Unbounded Numbers of Households: I—Overlapping (or Overlapping-Generations) Structure and the First Basic Theorem of Welfare. In *[Rossier, Edouard]*, 1985, pp. 17–42.

Colander, David C. Some Simple Geometry of the Welfare Loss from Competitive Monopolies. *Public Choice*, 1985, *45*(2), pp. 199–206.

Collinge, Robert A. Toward 'Privatization' of Public Sector Output: Decentralized Contracting for Public and Private Goods. *J. Public Econ.*, August 1985, *27*(3), pp. 371–87.

Copes, Parzival. The Market as a Commons: Open Access vs. Price Adjustment. *De Economist*, 1985, *133*(2), pp. 225–31.

Copp, David. Morality, Reason, and Management Science: The Rationale of Cost–Benefit Analysis. In *Paul, E. F.; Paul, J. and Miller, F. D., Jr., eds.*, 1985, pp. 128–51.

Corcoran, William J. and Karels, Gordon V. Rent-seeking Behavior in the Long-run. *Public Choice*, 1985, *46*(3), pp. 227–46.

Coughlin, P. J. and Palfrey, Thomas R. Pareto Optimality in Spatial Voting Models. *Soc. Choice Welfare*, March 1985, *1*(4), pp. 307–19.

Crawford, Vincent P. Efficient and Durable Decision Rules: A Reformulation. *Econometrica*, July 1985, *53*(4), pp. 817–35.

Crocker, Keith J. and Snow, Arthur. The Efficiency of Competitive Equilibria in Insurance Markets with Asymmetric Information. *J. Public Econ.*, March 1985, *26*(2), pp. 207–19.

Diewert, W. E. A Dynamic Approach to the Measurement of Waste in an Open Economy. *J. Int. Econ.*, November 1985, *19*(3/4), pp. 213–40.

Diewert, W. E. The Measurement of Waste and Welfare in Applied General Equilibrium Models. In *Piggott, J. and Whalley, J., eds.*, 1985, pp. 42–103.

Dinwiddy, Caroline and Teal, Francis. Shadow

Prices and Cost-Benefit Rules for Non-traded Commodities in a Second Best Economy. *Oxford Econ. Pap.*, December 1985, *37*(4), pp. 683–90.

Dobbs, Ian M. Shadow Prices, Consistency and the Value of Life. *J. Public Econ.*, July 1985, *27*(2), pp. 177–93.

Drèze, Jacques H. Second-best Analysis with Markets in Disequilibrium: Public Sector Pricing in a Keynesian Regime. *Europ. Econ. Rev.*, December 1985, *29*(3), pp. 263–301.

Eckstein, Zvi; Eichenbaum, Martin S. and Peled, Dan. Uncertain Lifetimes and the Welfare Enhancing Properties of Annuity Markets and Social Security. *J. Public Econ.*, April 1985, *26*(3), pp. 303–26.

Field, Barry C. The Optimal Commons. *Amer. J. Agr. Econ.*, May 1985, *67*(2), pp. 364–67.

Geroski, P. A.; Phlips, Louis and Ulph, A. Oligopoly, Competition and Welfare: Some Recent Developments. *J. Ind. Econ.*, June 1985, *33*(4), pp. 369–86.　　　　[G: U.S.; U.K.]

Goodman, John C. and Porter, Philip K. Majority Voting and Pareto Optimality. *Public Choice*, 1985, *46*(2), pp. 173–86.

Gordon, Scott and Stegemann, Klaus. The Market as a Commons: Is Catching Customers Like Catching Fish? *De Economist*, 1985, *133*(2), pp. 218–24.

Górecki, H., et al. Decision Support Based on the Skeleton Method—The HG Package. In *Grauer, M.; Thompson, M. and Wierzbicki, A. P., eds.*, 1985, pp. 269–80.

Guesnerie, Roger and Hart, Oliver D. Welfare Losses Due to Imperfect Competition: Asymptotic Results for Cournot Nash Equilibria with and without Free Entry. *Int. Econ. Rev.*, October 1985, *26*(3), pp. 525–45.

Haller, Hans. Separation of Ownership and Labour: Welfare Considerations. *Z. Nationalökon.*, 1985, *45*(3), pp. 245–65.

Harford, Jon D. and Park, Keehwan. Resource Allocation under Production Uncertainty: Closed Economy vs. Open Economy. *Atlantic Econ. J.*, July 1985, *13*(2), pp. 38–43.

Harris, Milton and Townsend, Robert M. Allocation Mechanisms, Asymmetric Information and the 'Revelation Principle.' In *Feiwel, G. R., ed. (II)*, 1985, pp. 379–94.

Hau, Timothy Doe-Kwong. A Hicksian Approach to Cost–Benefit Analysis with Discrete-Choice Models. *Economica*, November 1985, *52*(208), pp. 479–90.

Hausman, Jerry A. and Wise, David A. Technical Problems in Social Experimentation: Cost versus Ease of Analysis. In *Hausman, J. A. and Wise, D. A., eds.*, 1985, pp. 187–208.
　　　　[G: U.S.]

Higgins, Richard S.; Shughart, William F., II and Tollison, Robert D. Free Entry and Efficient Rent Seeking. *Public Choice*, 1985, *46*(3), pp. 247–58.

Hurwicz, Leonid. Information and Incentives in Designing Non-wasteful Resource Allocation Systems. In *Feiwel, G. R., ed. (II)*, 1985, pp. 125–68.

Jadlow, Joseph M. Monopoly Rent Seeking under Conditions of Uncertainty. *Public Choice*, 1985, *45*(1), pp. 73–87.

John, Reinhard and Ryder, Harl E. On the Second Optimality Theorem of Welfare Economics. *J. Econ. Theory*, June 1985, *36*(1), pp. 176–85.

Jones, H. G. Principles of Resource Allocation. In *Morris, D., ed.*, 1985, pp. 747–70.

Kim, Ki Hang and Roush, Fred W. The Liberal Paradox and the Pareto Set. *Math. Soc. Sci.*, February 1985, *9*(1), pp. 45–51.

Kirzner, Israel M. Taxes and Discovery: An Entrepreneurial Perspective. In *Kirzner, I. M.*, 1985, pp. 93–118.

Kohn, Robert E. A General Equilibrium Analysis of the Optimal Number of Firms in a Polluting Industry. *Can. J. Econ.*, May 1985, *18*(2), pp. 347–54.

Kohn, Robert E. and Aucamp, Donald C. Lower Level Inefficiencies as Second Best Correctives. *Public Finance*, 1985, *40*(2), pp. 220–29.　　　　[G: U.S.]

Koopmans, Tjalling C. Concepts of Optimality and Their Uses. In *Koopmans, T. C.*, 1985, pp. 191–208.

Laffont, Jean-Jacques. Incitations dans les procédures de planification. (Incentives in Planning Procedures. With English summary.) *Ann. INSEE*, Apr.-June 1985, (58), pp. 3–37.

Laffont, Jean-Jacques. On the Welfare Analysis of Rational Expectations Equilibria with Asymmetric Information. *Econometrica*, January 1985, *53*(1), pp. 1–20.

Laffont, Jean-Jacques and Rochet, Jean-Charles. Price-Quantity Duality in Planning Procedures. *Soc. Choice Welfare*, December 1985, *2*(4), pp. 311–22.

Laine, Charles R. Distribution of Jointly Owned Private Goods by the Demand-revealing Process: Applications to Divorce Settlements and Estate Administration. *Public Choice*, 1985, *47*(3), pp. 437–57.

Lorenz, Wilhelm. Drei neoklassische Modelle der Diskriminierung. Eine vergleichende Darstellung. (With English summary.) *Z. Wirtschaft. Sozialwissen.*, 1985, *105*(4), pp. 459–79.

Marchand, Maurice; Mintz, Jack and Pestieau, Pierre. Public Production and Shadow Pricing in a Model of Disequilibrium in Labour and Capital Markets. *J. Econ. Theory*, August 1985, *36*(2), pp. 237–56.

Mas-Colell, Andreu. Pareto Optima and Equilibria: The Finite Dimensional Case. In *Aliprantis, C. D.; Burkinshaw, O. and Rothman, N. J., eds.*, 1985, pp. 25–42.

McElroy, F. William. The Welfare Economics of Dominant-Firm Acquisitions. *Z. Nationalökon.*, 1985, *45*(2), pp. 115–40.

McGuire, Martin C. and Groth, Carl H., Jr. A Method for Identifying the Public Good Allocation Process within a Group. *Quart. J. Econ.*, Supp. 1985, *100*, pp. 915–34.

Morey, Edward R. Characteristics, Consumer Surplus, and New Activities: A Proposed Ski

Area. *J. Public Econ.*, March 1985, *26*(2), pp. 221–36. **[G: U.S.]**

Morey, Richard C.; Capettini, Robert and Dittman, David A. Pareto Rate Setting Strategies: An Application to Medicaid Drug Reimbursement. *Policy Sci.*, September 1985, *18*(2), pp. 169–200. **[G: U.S.]**

Moussa, Hassouna and Murota, Takeshi. Social Value of Public Information Re-examined. *J. Econ. Behav. Organ.*, September 1985, *6*(3), pp. 249–74.

Nanda, Shibanarayan. More on Externality in the Fishery: A Discussion of Economic Efficiency. *Indian Econ. J.*, Apr.-June 1985, *32*(4), pp. 19–28.

Neary, Hugh M. The Labour-managed Firm in Monopolistic Competition. *Economica*, November 1985, *52*(208), pp. 435–47.

Negishi, Takashi. Advertising and the Social Imbalance between Private and Public Goods. *Rivista Int. Sci. Econ. Com.*, January 1985, *32*(1), pp. 64–70.

Nijkamp, Peter and Voogd, Henk. An Informal Introduction to Multicriteria Evaluation. In *Fandel, G. and Spronk, J., eds.*, 1985, pp. 61–84.

Okuda, Hidesuke and Shitovitz, Benyamin. Core Allocations and the Dimension of the Cone of Efficiency Price Vectors. *J. Econ. Theory*, February 1985, *35*(1), pp. 166–71.

Page, Talbot and Ricci, Paolo F. A Cost–Benefit Perspective for Risk Assessment. In *Ricci, P. F., ed.*, 1985, pp. 37–65.

Pazner, Elisha A. Pitfalls in the Theory of Fairness. In *[Pazner, E.]*, 1985, pp. 321–29.

Pazner, Elisha A. and Schmeidler, David. A Difficulty in the Concept of Fairness. In *[Pazner, E.]*, 1985, pp. 293–296.

Pazner, Elisha A. and Schmeidler, David. Egalitarian Equivalent Allocations: A New Concept of Economic Equity. In *[Pazner, E.]*, 1985, pp. 341–57.

Peters, Wolfgang. Can Inefficient Public Production Promote Welfare? *Z. Nationalökon.*, 1985, *45*(4), pp. 395–407.

Piron, Robert. Fair Outcome/Fair Process [Applied Fairness Theory and Rationing Policy]. *Amer. Econ. Rev.*, September 1985, *75*(4), pp. 878–80.

Postlewaite, Andrew. Implementation via Nash Equilibria in Economic Environments. In *[Pazner, E.]*, 1985, pp. 205–28.

Price, Colin and Nair, C. T. S. Social Discounting and the Distribution of Project Benefits. *J. Devel. Stud.*, July 1985, *21*(4), pp. 525–32.

Putterman, Louis and DiGiorgio, Marie. Choice and Efficiency in a Model of Democratic Semicollective Agriculture. *Oxford Econ. Pap.*, March 1985, *37*(1), pp. 1–21.

Ray, Ranjan. Evaluating Expenditure Inequality Using Alternative Social Welfare Functions: A Case Study of Rural India. *Indian Econ. Rev.*, July-Dec. 1985, *20*(2), pp. 171–90. **[G: India]**

Reynolds, R. Larry. The Regulation of Regulation. *J. Econ. Issues*, March 1985, *19*(1), pp. 103–10.

Robinson, Clark and Suchanek, Gerry L. On the Design of Optimal Mechanisms for the Arrow–Hahn–McKenzie Economy. *Public Choice*, 1985, *47*(2), pp. 313–35.

Rogerson, William P. Repeated Moral Hazard. *Econometrica*, January 1985, *53*(1), pp. 69–76.

Rosenband, Leonard N. Productivity and Labor Discipline in the Montgolfier Paper Mill, 1780–1805. *J. Econ. Hist.*, June 1985, *45*(2), pp. 435–43. **[G: France]**

Saari, Donald G. The Representation Problem and the Efficiency of the Price Mechanism. *J. Math. Econ.*, 1985, *14*(2), pp. 135–67.

Sakai, Yasuhiro. The Value of Information in a Simple Duopoly Model. *J. Econ. Theory*, June 1985, *36*(1), pp. 36–54.

Schap, David. X-Inefficiency in a Rent-seeking Society: A Graphical Analysis. *Quart. Rev. Econ. Bus.*, Spring 1985, *25*(1), pp. 19–27.

Scotchmer, Suzanne. Hedonic Prices and Cost/Benefit Analysis. *J. Econ. Theory*, October 1985, *37*(1), pp. 55–75.

Scotchmer, Suzanne. Profit-maximizing Clubs. *J. Public Econ.*, June 1985, *27*(1), pp. 25–45.

Sharir, Shmuel. A Note on the Measurement of Welfare Changes Due to a Merger. *Scot. J. Polit. Econ.*, February 1985, *32*(1), pp. 107–10.

Silvestre, Joaquim. Voluntary and Efficient Allocations Are Walrasian. *Econometrica*, July 1985, *53*(4), pp. 807–16.

Stephan, Gunter. Competitive Finite Value Prices: A Complete Characterization. *Z. Nationalökon.*, 1985, *45*(1), pp. 35–45.

Suzumura, Kotaro and Sato, Kimitoshi. Equity and Efficiency in the Public Goods Economy: Some Counterexamples. *Hitotsubashi J. Econ.*, June 1985, *26*(1), pp. 59–82.

Telser, Lester G. Cooperation, Competition, and Efficiency. *J. Law Econ.*, May 1985, *28*(2), pp. 271–95.

Thomson, William and Varian, Hal R. Theories of Justice Based on Symmetry. In *[Pazner, E.]*, 1985, pp. 107–29.

Tisdell, Clement A. Conceptual Issues in the Measurement of Economic and Productive Efficiencies. *S. Afr. J. Econ.*, March 1985, *53*(1), pp. 55–66.

Tsuneki, Atsushi. On the Choice of Large Projects: A Generalization. *Can. J. Econ.*, August 1985, *18*(3), pp. 660–64.

Tullock, Gordon. Back to the Bog. *Public Choice*, 1985, *46*(3), pp. 259–63.

Turnovsky, Stephen J. and Campbell, Robert B. The Stabilizing and Welfare Properties of Futures Markets: A Simulation Approach. *Int. Econ. Rev.*, June 1985, *26*(2), pp. 277–303.

Usategui Díaz de Otalora, José M. Congestión desigual y eficiencia. (With English summary.) *Revista Española Econ.*, 1985, *2*(1), pp. 73–87.

Warr, Peter G. Sub-optimal Saving and the Shadow Price of Labor: The Public Good Argument. *J. Devel. Econ.*, April 1985, *17*(3), pp. 239–57.

Waterson, Michael. Locational Mobility and Welfare. *Econ. J.*, September 1985, *95*(379), pp. 774–77.

Weber, Shlomo and Zamir, Shmuel. Proportional Taxation: Nonexistence of Stable Structures in an Economy with a Public Good [Second Best Taxation as a Game]. *J. Econ. Theory*, February 1985, *35*(1), pp. 178–85.

Weller, Dietrich. Fair Division of a Measurable Space. *J. Math. Econ.*, 1985, *14*(1), pp. 5–17.

Weymark, John A. Majority-Rule Directions of Income Tax Reform and Second-Best Optimality. In *Førsund, F. R. and Honkapohja, S., eds.*, 1985, pp. 96–115.

Weymark, John A. Remarks on the First Welfare Theorem with Nonordered Preferences. *J. Econ. Theory*, June 1985, *36*(1), pp. 156–59.

Willett, Thomas D. and Flacco, Paul R. The Reallocation Effects of Exchange Rate Fluctuations under Uncertainty with Efficient Speculation. In *Arndt, S. W.; Sweeney, R. J. and Willett, T. D., eds.*, 1985, pp. 145–52.

Wilson, Robert B. Efficient Trading. In *Feiwel, G. R., ed. (II)*, 1985, pp. 169–208.

Wilson, Robert B. Incentive Efficiency of Double Auctions. *Econometrica*, September 1985, *53*(5), pp. 1101–15.

Yamada, Masatoshi. More on Production Efficiency in the Optimal Tax Economy. *Econ. Stud. Quart.*, April 1985, *36*(1), pp. 87–90.

Yannelis, Nicholas C. Value and Fairness. In *Aliprantis, C. D.; Burkinshaw, O. and Rothman, N. J., eds.*, 1985, pp. 205–35.

0243 Redistribution Analyses

Abel, Andrew B. Precautionary Saving and Accidental Bequests. *Amer. Econ. Rev.*, September 1985, *75*(4), pp. 777–91. [G: U.S.]

Anderson, Gary M. and Brown, Pamela J. Heir Pollution: A Note on Buchanan's 'Laws of Succession' and Tullock's 'Blind Spot.' *Int. Rev. Law Econ.*, June 1985, *5*(1), pp. 15–23.

Baepler, Richard. The Concept of Economic Justice in Religious Discussion: Comment. In *Block, W.; Brennan, G. and Elzinga, K., eds.*, 1985, pp. 482–89.

Bernheim, B. Douglas; Shleifer, Andrei and Summers, Lawrence H. The Strategic Bequest Motive. *J. Polit. Econ.*, December 1985, *93*(6), pp. 1045–76. [G: U.S.]

Bhagwati, Jagdish N. Class Structure, Poverty and Redistribution. In *Bhagwati, J. N. (II)*, 1985, pp. 167–69.

Bhagwati, Jagdish N. Education, Class Structure and Income Equality. In *Bhagwati, J. N. (II)*, 1985, pp. 170–204. [G: India]

Bös, Dieter. Income Taxation, Public Sector Pricing and Redistribution. In *Førsund, F. R. and Honkapohja, S., eds.*, 1985, pp. 68–85.

Bös, Dieter and Tillmann, Georg. An 'Envy Tax': Theoretical Principles and Applications to the German Surcharge on the Rich. *Public Finance*, 1985, *40*(1), pp. 35–63.

Buchanan, James M. The Ethical Limits of Taxation. In *Førsund, F. R. and Honkapohja, S., eds.*, 1985, pp. 4–16.

Burgat, Paul and Jeanrenaud, Claude. Consequences d'une perequation tarifaire spatiale du point de vue du bien-etre et de la redistribution des revenus. (Consequences of Interregional Cross Subsidization with Regard to Welfare and Redistribution. With English summary.) *Public Finance*, 1985, *40*(1), pp. 64–81.

Cavaco-Silva, Anibal A. Forced Loans: Tax Element, Equity and Effects on Consumption. In *[Peacock, A.]*, 1985, pp. 51–66.

Christiansen, Vidar. The Choice of Excise Taxes When Savings and Labour Decisions Are Distorted. *J. Public Econ.*, October 1985, *28*(1), pp. 95–110.

Coelho, Philip R. P. An Examination into the Causes of Economic Growth: Status as an Economic Good. In *Zerbe, R. O., Jr., ed.*, 1985, pp. 89–116.

Coleman, Jules L. Market Contractarianism and the Unanimity Rule. In *Paul, E. F.; Paul, J. and Miller, F. D., Jr., eds.*, 1985, pp. 69–114.

Conrad, Robert F. and Gillis, Malcolm. Progress and Poverty in Developing Countries: Rents and Resource Taxation. In *Lewis, S. R., Jr., ed.*, 1985, pp. 25–47.

Cowell, Frank A. Public Policy and Tax Evasion: Some Problems. In *Gaertner, W. and Wenig, A., eds.*, 1985, pp. 273–84.

Eckart, Wolfgang and Schulz, Norbert. Distributional Equity and Two-part Tariffs. *Z. ges. Staatswiss. (JITE)*, June 1985, *141*(2), pp. 301–11.

Eckstein, Zvi; Eichenbaum, Martin S. and Peled, Dan. The Distribution of Wealth and Welfare in the Presence of Incomplete Annuity Markets. *Quart. J. Econ.*, August 1985, *100*(3), pp. 789–806.

Fernández-Diaz, Andrés. Consequences of Budgetary Restraint for Social Policy. In *Terny, G. and Culyer, A. J., eds.*, 1985, pp. 171–82.

Gilani, Shaukat J. The Qur'an on Charitable Giving and Contemporary Social Values. *J. Res. Islamic Econ.*, Summer 1985, *3*(1), pp. 63–72.

Goodman, Wolfe D. International Double Taxation of Inheritances and Gifts: General Report. In *International Fiscal Association (II)*, 1985, pp. 15–61. [G: OECD]

Grewal, Bhajan and Mathews, Russell L. Federalism, Locational Surplus and the Redistributive Role of Subnational Governments. In *Terny, G. and Culyer, A. J., eds.*, 1985, pp. 355–70.

Hansson, Ingemar. Tax Evasion and Government Policy. In *Gaertner, W. and Wenig, A., eds.*, 1985, pp. 285–300.

Helms, L. Jay. Errors in the Numerical Assessment of the Benefits of Price Stabilization. *Amer. J. Agr. Econ.*, February 1985, *67*(1), pp. 93–100.

Herber, Bernard P. The State and Distribution: A Historical Look at Egalitarianism in the United States. In *[Recktenwald, H. C.]*, 1985, pp. 333–45. [G: U.S.]

Heyne, Paul. The Concept of Economic Justice in Religious Discussion. In *Block, W.; Bren-*

nan, G. and Elzinga, K., eds., 1985, pp. 463–82.

Ihori, Toshihiro. On the Welfare Cost of Permanent Inflation. *J. Money, Credit, Banking,* May 1985, *17*(2), pp. 220–31.

Jorgenson, Dale W. and Slesnick, Daniel T. General Equilibrium Analysis of Economic Policy. In *Piggott, J. and Whalley, J.,* eds., 1985, pp. 293–370. [G: U.S.]

Judd, Kenneth L. Redistributive Taxation in a Simple Perfect Foresight Model. *J. Public Econ.,* October 1985, *28*(1), pp. 59–83.

Keenan, Donald C. and Rubin, Paul H. The Limits of the Equity–Efficiency Tradeoff. *Public Choice,* 1985, *47*(3), pp. 425–36.

Lambert, Peter J. On the Redistributive Effect of Taxes and Benefits. *Scot. J. Polit. Econ.,* February 1985, *32*(1), pp. 39–54. [G: U.K.; U.S.]

Le Grand, Julian. On Measuring the Distributional Impact of Public Expenditure. In *Terny, G. and Culyer, A. J.,* eds., 1985, pp. 197–208.

Lermer, George and Stanbury, W. T. Measuring the Cost of Redistributing Income by Means of Direct Regulation. *Can. J. Econ.,* February 1985, *18*(1), pp. 190–207. [G: Canada]

Lewis, Stephen R., Jr. Progress and Poverty in Developing Countries: Rents and Resource Taxation: Comments. In *Lewis, S. R., Jr.,* ed., 1985, pp. 49–51.

Lindbeck, Assar. Redistribution Policy and the Expansion of the Public Sector. *J. Public Econ.,* December 1985, *28*(3), pp. 309–28.

Macleod, Alistair M. Economic Inequality: Justice and Incentives. In *Kipnis, K. and Meyers, D. T.,* eds., 1985, pp. 176–89.

Macpherson, C. B. Property as Means or End. In *Macpherson, C. B.,* 1985, pp. 86–91.

Macpherson, C. B. The Rise and Fall of Economic Justice. In *Macpherson, C. B.,* 1985, pp. 1–20.

Meltzer, Allan H. and Richard, Scott F. A Positive Theory of In-Kind Transfers and the Negative Income Tax. *Public Choice,* 1985, *47*(1), pp. 231–65.

Musgrave, Richard A. Death and Taxes. In *[Recktenwald, H. C.],* 1985, pp. 149–55.

Musgrave, Richard A. Public Finance and Distributive Justice. In *[Peacock, A.],* 1985, pp. 1–14.

Naqvi, Syed Nawab Haider and Qadir, Asghar. Incrementalism and Structural Change: A Technical Note. *Pakistan Devel. Rev.,* Summer 1985, *24*(2), pp. 87–102.

Nelson, William. Rights, Responsibilities and Redistribution. In *Kipnis, K. and Meyers, D. T.,* eds., 1985, pp. 95–107.

Okun, Arthur M. Rewards in a Market Economy. In *Bornstein, M.,* ed., 1985, pp. 41–47.

Pazner, Elisha A. Pitfalls in the Theory of Fairness. In *[Pazner, E.],* 1985, pp. 321–29.

Pazner, Elisha A. Recent Thinking on Economic Justice. In *[Pazner, E.],* 1985, pp. 297–309.

Pazner, Elisha A. and Schmeidler, David. Egalitarian Equivalent Allocations: A New Concept of Economic Equity. In *[Pazner, E.],* 1985, pp. 341–57.

Pazner, Elisha A. and Schmeidler, David. Social Contact Theory and Ordinal Distributive Equity. In *[Pazner, E.],* 1985, pp. 311–19.

Persson, Mats and Wissén, Pehr. Redistributional Aspects of Tax Evasion. In *Førsund, F. R. and Honkapohja, S.,* eds., 1985, pp. 33–51.

Persson, Torsten. Deficits and Intergenerational Welfare in Open Economies. *J. Int. Econ.,* August 1985, *19*(1/2), pp. 67–84.

Rasler, Karen A. and Thompson, William R. War Making and State Making: Governmental Expenditures, Tax Revenues, and Global Wars. *Amer. Polit. Sci. Rev.,* June 1985, *79*(2), pp. 491–507. [G: U.S.; U.K.; France; Japan]

Rosenberg, Alexander. Prospects for the Elimination of Tastes from Economics and Ethics. In *Paul, E. F.; Paul, J. and Miller, F. D., Jr.,* eds., 1985, pp. 48–68.

Rueschemeyer, Dietrich and Evans, Peter B. The State and Economic Transformation: Toward an Analysis of the Conditions Underlying Effective Intervention. In *Evans, P. B.; Rueschemeyer, D. and Skocpol, T.,* eds., 1985, pp. 44–77.

Shughart, William F., II and Tollison, Robert D. The Positive Economics of Antitrust Policy: A Survey Article. *Int. Rev. Law Econ.,* June 1985, *5*(1), pp. 39–57. [G: U.S.]

Stark, Oded. On Private Charity and Altruism. *Public Choice,* 1985, *46*(3), pp. 325–32.

Thomson, William and Varian, Hal R. Theories of Justice Based on Symmetry. In *[Pazner, E.],* 1985, pp. 107–29.

Tinbergen, Jan. Some Remarks on the Optimal Tax System. In *Tinbergen, J.,* 1985, pp. 158–67.

Tuomala, Matti. Optimal Degree of Progressivity under Income Uncertainty. In *Førsund, F. R. and Honkapohja, S.,* eds., 1985, pp. 86–95.

Weiss, Jeffrey H. Can Donations Reduce a Donor's Welfare? *Public Choice,* 1985, *47*(2), pp. 337–47.

Whynes, David. Markets and Neo-liberal Political Economy. In *Bean, P.; Ferris, J. and Whynes, D.,* eds., 1985, pp. 99–121. [G: U.K.]

Wolfson, Dirk J. Criteria in Engineering Social Justice. In *Terny, G. and Culyer, A. J.,* eds., 1985, pp. 185–96.

Zerbe, Richard O., Jr. Is the Attempt to Gain Status a Zero-Sum Game? In *Zerbe, R. O., Jr.,* ed., 1985, pp. 117–121.

0244 Externalities

Arrow, Kenneth J. and Fisher, Anthony C. Environmental Preservation, Uncertainty, and Irreversibility. In *Arrow, K. J. (II),* 1985, pp. 165–73.

Barzel, Yoram. Transaction Costs: Are They Just Costs? *Z. ges. Staatswiss. (JITE),* March 1985, *141*(1), pp. 4–16.

Becker, Lawrence C. Property Rights and Social Welfare. In *Kipnis, K. and Meyers, D. T.,* eds., 1985, pp. 71–86.

Bohanon, Cecil E. Externalities: A Note on Avoiding Confusion. *J. Econ. Educ.*, Fall 1985, *16*(4), pp. 305–07.

Ciriacy-Wantrup, S. V. "Common Property" as a Concept in Natural Resources Policy. In *Ciriacy-Wantrup, S. V.*, 1985, pp. 25–37. [G: U.S.]

Cornes, Richard and Sandler, Todd. Externalities, Expectations, and Pigouvian Taxes. *J. Environ. Econ. Manage.*, March 1985, *12*(1), pp. 1–13.

Cory, Dennis C. Congestion Costs and Quality-adjusted User Fees: A Methodological Note. *Land Econ.*, November 1985, *61*(4), pp. 452–55.

De Alessi, Louis. Property Rights and the Judiciary. *Cato J.*, Winter 1985, *4*(3), pp. 805–11. [G: U.S.]

Dragun, Andrew K. Property Rights and Pigovian Taxes. *J. Econ. Issues*, March 1985, *19*(1), pp. 111–22.

Dugger, William M. The Analytics of Consumption Externalities. *Rev. Soc. Econ.*, October 1985, *43*(2), pp. 212–33.

Frey, Bruno S. Transaction Costs: Are They Just Costs? Comment. *Z. ges. Staatswiss. (JITE)*, March 1985, *141*(1), pp. 17–20.

Harrison, Glenn W. and McKee, Michael. Experimental Evaluation of the Coase Theorem. *J. Law Econ.*, October 1985, *28*(3), pp. 653–70.

Horn, Walter. Coase's Theorem and the Speculative Withholding of Land. *Land Econ.*, May 1985, *61*(2), pp. 208–12.

Katz, Michael L. and Shapiro, Carl. Network Externalities, Competition, and Compatibility. *Amer. Econ. Rev.*, June 1985, *75*(3), pp. 424–40.

Knetsch, Jack L. Values, Biases and Entitlements. *Ann. Reg. Sci.*, July 1985, *19*(2), pp. 1–9.

Koenig, Evan F. Indirect Methods for Regulating Externalities under Uncertainty. *Quart. J. Econ.*, May 1985, *100*(2), pp. 479–93.

Levin, Dan. Taxation within Cournot Oligopoly. *J. Public Econ.*, August 1985, *27*(3), pp. 281–90.

Liebeler, Wesley J. A Property Rights Approach to Judicial Decision Making. *Cato J.*, Winter 1985, *4*(3), pp. 783–804. [G: U.S.]

McGartland, Albert M. and Oates, Wallace E. Marketable Permits for the Prevention of Environmental Deterioration. *J. Environ. Econ. Manage.*, September 1985, *12*(3), pp. 207–28. [G: U.S.]

Mestelman, Stuart. Externality Control, Income Distribution, and Social Choice. *Public Finance*, 1985, *40*(1), pp. 93–113.

Meyers, Diana T. Property Rights and Social Welfare: Comment: A Sketch of a Rights Taxonomy. In *Kipnis, K. and Meyers, D. T., eds.*, 1985, pp. 87–94.

Norton, Roger D. and Patrick, Robert H. A Note on Prudencio's Experimental Tests of the Coase Propositions [The Voluntary Approach to Externality Problems: An Experimental Test]. *J. Environ. Econ. Manage.*, March 1985, *12*(1), pp. 96–100.

Prince, Raymond. A Note on Environmental Risk and the Rate of Discount: Comment. *J. Environ. Econ. Manage.*, June 1985, *12*(2), pp. 179–80.

Prudencio, Yves Coffi. On Tests of the Coase Propositions: A Reply [The Voluntary Approach to Externality Problems: An Experimental Test]. *J. Environ. Econ. Manage.*, June 1985, *12*(2), pp. 193.

Saari, Donald G. The Representation Problem and the Efficiency of the Price Mechanism. *J. Math. Econ.*, 1985, *14*(2), pp. 135–67.

Samuelson, William. A Comment on the Coase Theorem. In *Roth, A. E., ed.*, 1985, pp. 321–39.

Scott, Anthony D. and Johnson, James. Property Rights: Developing the Characteristics of Interests in Natural Resources. In *Scott, A., ed.*, 1985, pp. 376–403. [G: Canada; U.S.]

Siebert, Horst. Spatial Aspects of Environmental Economics. In *Kneese, A. V. and Sweeney, J. L., eds. Vol. 1*, 1985, pp. 125–64.

Smith, Vernon L. Property Rights: Developing the Characteristics of Interests in Natural Resources: Comment. In *Scott, A., ed.*, 1985, pp. 403–21. [G: Canada; U.S.]

Spulber, Daniel F. Effluent Regulation and Long-run Optimality. *J. Environ. Econ. Manage.*, June 1985, *12*(2), pp. 103–16.

Wijkander, Hans. Correcting Externalities through Taxes On/Subsidies to Related Goods. *J. Public Econ.*, October 1985, *28*(1), pp. 111–25.

Wittman, Donald. Pigovian Taxes Which Work in the Small-Number Case. *J. Environ. Econ. Manage.*, June 1985, *12*(2), pp. 144–54.

Wittman, Donald. Should Compensation Be Based on Costs or Benefits? *Int. Rev. Law Econ.*, December 1985, *5*(2), pp. 173–85. [G: U.S.]

Wolfson, Dirk J. Criteria in Engineering Social Justice. In *Terny, G. and Culyer, A. J., eds.*, 1985, pp. 185–96.

025 Social Choice

0250 General

Anderson, Gary M. and Brown, Pamela J. Heir Pollution: A Note on Buchanan's 'Laws of Succession' and Tullock's 'Blind Spot.' *Int. Rev. Law Econ.*, June 1985, *5*(1), pp. 15–23.

Armentano, D. T. Efficiency, Liberty, and Antitrust Policy [Public Choice and Antitrust]. *Cato J.*, Winter 1985, *4*(3), pp. 925–32. [G: U.S.]

Arneson, Richard J. Marxism and Secular Faith. *Amer. Polit. Sci. Rev.*, September 1985, *79*(3), pp. 627–40.

Becker, Lawrence C. Property Rights and Social Welfare. In *Kipnis, K. and Meyers, D. T., eds.*, 1985, pp. 71–86.

Benditt, Theodore M. The Demands of Justice: The Difference that Social Life Makes. In *Kipnis, K. and Meyers, D. T., eds.*, 1985, pp. 108–20.

Davidson, James Dale. The Balanced Budget Amendment: A Truly Marginal Reform. In *Boaz, D. and Crane, E. H., eds.*, 1985, pp. 13–28. [G: U.S.]

Denzau, Arthur T.; Kats, Amoz and Slutsky, S. Multi-agent Equilibria with Market Share and Ranking Objectives. *Soc. Choice Welfare*, September 1985, 2(2), pp. 95–117.

Elkin, Stephen L. Regulation as a Political Question. *Policy Sci.*, March 1985, 18(1), pp. 95–108.

Elzinga, Kenneth G. Public Choice and Antitrust: A Comment. *Cato J.*, Winter 1985, 4(3), pp. 917–23. [G: U.S.]

Frey, Bruno S. State and Prospect of Public Choice: A European View. *Public Choice*, 1985, 46(2), pp. 141–61.

Gewirth, Alan. Economic Justice: Concepts and Criteria. In *Kipnis, K. and Meyers, D. T., eds.*, 1985, pp. 7–32.

Gould, Carol C. Economic Justice, Self-management, and the Principle of Reciprocity. In *Kipnis, K. and Meyers, D. T., eds.*, 1985, pp. 202–16.

Gwaltney, Marilyn. The Demands of Justice: The Difference that Social Life Makes: Comment: Actual and Potential Demands of Justice. In *Kipnis, K. and Meyers, D. T., eds.*, 1985, pp. 125–29.

Held, Virginia. Economic Justice: Concepts and Criteria: Comment: Reason and Economic Justice. In *Kipnis, K. and Meyers, D. T., eds.*, 1985, pp. 33–41.

Hont, Istvan and Ignatieff, Michael. Needs and Justice in the *Wealth of Nations:* An introductory Essay. In *Hont, I. and Ignatieff, M., eds.*, 1985, pp. 1–44.

Ingberman, Daniel E. Running against the Status Quo: Institutions for Direct Democracy Referenda and Allocations over Time. *Public Choice*, 1985, 46(1), pp. 19–43.

Koslowski, Peter. Philosophy and Economics: An Introduction. In *Koslowski, P., ed.*, 1985, pp. 1–16.

Landesman, Bruce M. The Demands of Justice: The Difference that Social Life Makes: Comment: Justice:Cosmic or Communal? In *Kipnis, K. and Meyers, D. T., eds.*, 1985, pp. 121–24.

Macleod, Alistair M. Economic Inequality: Justice and Incentives. In *Kipnis, K. and Meyers, D. T., eds.*, 1985, pp. 176–89.

Martin, Rex. Poverty and Welfare in Rawl's Theory of Justice: On the Just Response to Needs. In *Kipnis, K. and Meyers, D. T., eds.*, 1985, pp. 161–75.

Meyers, Diana T. Property Rights and Social Welfare: Comment: A Sketch of a Rights Taxonomy. In *Kipnis, K. and Meyers, D. T., eds.*, 1985, pp. 87–94.

Nelson, William. Rights, Responsibilities and Redistribution. In *Kipnis, K. and Meyers, D. T., eds.*, 1985, pp. 95–107.

Noll, Roger G. Government Regulatory Behavior: A Multidisciplinary Survey and Synthesis. In *Noll, R. G., ed.*, 1985, pp. 9–63.

Oates, Wallace E. The Public Sector in Economics: An Analytical Chameleon. In *[Recktenwald, H. C.]*, 1985, pp. 45–58.

Offe, Claus. Disorganized Capitalism: Introduction. In *Offe, C.*, 1985, pp. 1–9.

Plotnick, Robert D. and Winters, Richard F. A Politico-economic Theory of Income Redistribution. *Amer. Polit. Sci. Rev.*, June 1985, 79(2), pp. 458–73. [G: U.S.]

Riker, William H. Group Concentration and the Delegation of Legislative Authority: Comment. In *Noll, R. G., ed.*, 1985, pp. 197–99.

Rowley, Charles K. The Relationship between Economics, Politics and the Law in the Formation of Public Policy. In *Matthews, R. C. O., ed.*, 1985, pp. 127–50.

Schwarz, Michiel and Thompson, Michael. Beyond the Politics of Interest. In *Grauer, M.; Thompson, M. and Wierzbicki, A. P., eds.*, 1985, pp. 22–36.

Sen, Amartya. *Social Choice and Justice*: A Review Article. *J. Econ. Lit.*, December 1985, 23(4), pp. 1764–76.

Simon, Herbert A. Human Nature in Politics: The Dialogue of Psychology with Political Science. *Amer. Polit. Sci. Rev.*, June 1985, 79(2), pp. 293–304.

Skocpol, Theda. Bringing the State Back In: Strategies of Analysis in Current Research. In *Evans, P. B.; Rueschemeyer, D. and Skocpol, T., eds.*, 1985, pp. 3–37.

Tollison, Robert D. Public Choice and Antitrust. *Cato J.*, Winter 1985, 4(3), pp. 905–16. [G: U.S.]

Vessillier, Elisabeth and Vedie, Henri-Louis. Justice Sociale et Objectifs de Politique Sociale. (With English summary.) In *Terny, G. and Culyer, A. J., eds.*, 1985, pp. 83–91.

Wellman, Carl. Bibliographic Essay: Welfare Rights. In *Kipnis, K. and Meyers, D. T., eds.*, 1985, pp. 229–45.

0251 Social Choice Theory

Aizerman, M. A. New Problems in the General Choice Theory. Review of a Research Trend. *Soc. Choice Welfare*, December 1985, 2(4), pp. 235–82.

Albert, Hans. On Using Leibniz in Economics: Comment. In *Koslowski, P., ed.*, 1985, pp. 68–78.

Armstrong, Thomas E. Precisely Dictatorial Social Welfare Functions: Erratum and Addendum to 'Arrows Theorem with Restricted Coalition Algebras.' *J. Math. Econ.*, 1985, 14(1), pp. 57–59.

d'Aspremont, Claude. Axioms for Social Welfare Orderings. In *[Pazner, E.]*, 1985, pp. 19–76.

Aumann, Robert J. On the Non-transferable Utility Value: A Comment on the Roth–Shafer Examples [Values for Games without Side Payments: Some Difficulties with Current Concepts] [On the Existence and Interpretation of Value Allocations]. *Econometrica*, May 1985, 53(3), pp. 667–77.

Axelrod, Robert. The Emergence of Cooperation

among Egoists. In *Campbell, R. and Sowden, L., eds.*, 1985, pp. 320–39.

Baigent, Nick. Anonymity and Continuous Social Choice. *J. Math. Econ.*, 1985, *14*(1), pp. 1–4.

Bandyopadhyay, Taradas. Pareto Optimality and the Decisive Power Structure with Expansion Consistency Conditions. *J. Econ. Theory*, April 1985, *35*(2), pp. 366–75.

Banks, Jeffrey S. Sophisticated Voting Outcomes and Agenda Control. *Soc. Choice Welfare*, March 1985, *1*(4), pp. 295–306.

Barro, Robert J. Federal Deficits, Interest Rates, and Monetary Policy: Comment. *J. Money, Credit, Banking*, Pt. 2, Nov. 1985, *17*(4), pp. 682–85.   [G: U.S.]

Becker, Gary S. Public Policies, Pressure Groups, and Dead Weight Costs. *J. Public Econ.*, December 1985, *28*(3), pp. 329–47.

Bendor, Jonathan and Moe, Terry M. An Adaptive Model of Bureaucratic Politics. *Amer. Polit. Sci. Rev.*, September 1985, *79*(3), pp. 755–74.

Berg, Sven. Paradox of Voting under an Urn Model: The Effect of Homogeneity. *Public Choice*, 1985, *47*(2), pp. 377–87.

Bernhardt, M. Daniel and Ingberman, Daniel E. Candidate Reputations and the 'Incumbency Effect.' *J. Public Econ.*, June 1985, *27*(1), pp. 47–67.

Blinder, Alan S. Federal Deficits, Interest Rates, and Monetary Policy: Comment. *J. Money, Credit, Banking*, Pt. 2, Nov. 1985, *17*(4), pp. 685–89.

Blinder, Alan S. Rationality, Causality, and the Relation between Economic Conditions and the Popularity of Parties: Comment. *Europ. Econ. Rev.*, June-July 1985, *28*(1–2), pp. 269–72.   [G: W. Germany]

Booth, Alison L. The Free Rider Problem and a Social Custom Model of Trade Union Membership. *Quart. J. Econ.*, February 1985, *100*(1), pp. 253–61.

Border, K. C. More on Harsanyi's Utilitarian Cardinal Welfare Theorem. *Soc. Choice Welfare*, March 1985, *1*(4), pp. 279–81.

Bordley, Robert F. A Precise Method for Evaluating Election Schemes. *Public Choice*, 1985, *46*(2), pp. 113–23.

Bordley, Robert F. Using Factions to Estimate Preference Intensity: Improving upon One Person/One Vote. *Public Choice*, 1985, *45*(3), pp. 257–68.

Bös, Dieter. Public Sector Pricing. In *Auerbach, A. J. and Feldstein, M., eds.*, 1985, pp. 129–211.

Boulding, Kenneth E. Markets and Majorities, Morals and Madness: An Essay on Religion and Institutional Choice: Comment. In *Block, W.; Brennan, G. and Elzinga, K., eds.*, 1985, pp. 251–61.   [G: U.S.]

Brady, Henry E. and Sniderman, Paul M. Attitude Attribution: A Group Basis for Political Reasoning. *Amer. Polit. Sci. Rev.*, December 1985, *79*(4), pp. 1061–78.   [G: U.S.]

Brams, Steven J. and Fishburn, Peter C. Comment: The Problem of Strategic Voting under

Approval Voting. *Amer. Polit. Sci. Rev.*, September 1985, *79*(3), pp. 816–18.

Brams, Steven J. and Fishburn, Peter C. Rejoinder: The Problem of Strategic Voting under Approval Voting. *Amer. Polit. Sci. Rev.*, September 1985, *79*(3), pp. 819.

Braybrooke, David. The Insoluble Problem of the Social Contract. In *Campbell, R. and Sowden, L., eds.*, 1985, pp. 277–306.

Brennan, Geoffrey. Markets and Majorities, Morals and Madness: An Essay on Religion and Institutional Choice. In *Block, W.; Brennan, G. and Elzinga, K., eds.*, 1985, pp. 233–48.

Brennan, Geoffrey and Lomasky, Loren E. The Impartial Spectator Goes to Washington: Toward a Smithian Theory of Electoral Behavior. *Econ. Philos.*, October 1985, *1*(2), pp. 189–211.

Breton, Albert and Galeotti, Gianluigi. Is Proportional Representation Always the Best Electoral Rule? *Public Finance*, 1985, *40*(1), pp. 1–16.   [G: Canada]

Brunk, Gregory C. Congressional Rationality and Spatial voting. *Public Choice*, 1985, *45*(1), pp. 3–17.   [G: U.S.]

Buchanan, James M. Political Economy and Social Philosophy. In *Koslowski, P., ed.*, 1985, pp. 19–32.

Campbell, D. E. Impossibility Theorems and Infinite Horizon Planning. *Soc. Choice Welfare*, December 1985, *2*(4), pp. 283–93.

Cartwright, Phillip A.; DeLorme, Charles D., Jr. and Wood, Norman J. The By-Product Theory of Revolution: Some Empirical Evidence. *Public Choice*, 1985, *46*(3), pp. 265–74.   [G: Asia; Africa]

Chappell, Henry W., Jr. and Keech, William R. The Political Viability of Rule-based Monetary Policy. *Public Choice*, 1985, *46*(2), pp. 125–40.   [G: U.S.]

Colander, David C. Some Simple Geometry of the Welfare Loss from Competitive Monopolies. *Public Choice*, 1985, *45*(2), pp. 199–206.

Coleman, Jules L. Market Contractarianism and the Unanimity Rule. In *Paul, E. F.; Paul, J. and Miller, F. D., Jr., eds.*, 1985, pp. 69–114.

Corcoran, William J. and Karels, Gordon V. Rent-seeking Behavior in the Long-run. *Public Choice*, 1985, *46*(3), pp. 227–46.

Cornwell, Elmer E. Comments [Constitutional Change and Agenda Control] [Demographic Factors Affecting Constitutional Decisions: The Case of Municipal Charters]. *Public Choice*, 1985, *47*(1), pp. 219–29.   [G: U.S.]

Coughlin, P. J. and Palfrey, Thomas R. Pareto Optimality in Spatial Voting Models. *Soc. Choice Welfare*, March 1985, *1*(4), pp. 307–19.

Cremer, Helmuth; de Kerchove, Anne-Marie and Thisse, Jacques-François. An Economic Theory of Public Facilities in Space. *Math. Soc. Sci.*, June 1985, *9*(3), pp. 249–62.

Cuzán, Alfred G. and Heggen, Richard J. Expenditures and Votes: In Search of Downward-sloping Curves in the United States and Great

Britain. *Public Choice*, 1985, *45*(1), pp. 19–34. [G: U.S.]

Danilov, V. I. The Structure of Binary Rules for Aggregating Preferences. *Matekon*, Summer 1985, *21*(4), pp. 44–65.

Denzau, Arthur T. Constitutional Change and Agenda Control. *Public Choice*, 1985, *47*(1), pp. 183–217. [G: U.S.]

Denzau, Arthur T. and Mackay, Robert J. Tax Systems and Tax Shares. *Public Choice*, 1985, *45*(1), pp. 35–47.

Denzau, Arthur T.; Riker, William H. and Shepsle, Kenneth A. Farquharson and Fenno: Sophisticated Voting and Home Style. *Amer. Polit. Sci. Rev.*, December 1985, *79*(4), pp. 1117–34.

DiMasi, J. A. and Schap, David. The Appropriate Specification of Constant Elasticity Demand Functions. *Soc. Choice Welfare*, September 1985, *2*(2), pp. 89–94.

Donnenfeld, S. and Weber, S. Lobbying for Tariffs and the Cost of Protection. *Rech. Écon. Louvain*, 1985, *51*(1), pp. 21–27.

Dutta, Bhaskar and Pattanaik, K. On Enforcing Socially Best Alternatives of Binary Group Decision Rules. *Soc. Choice Welfare*, March 1985, *1*(4), pp. 283–93.

Dwyer, Gerald P., Jr. Federal Deficits, Interest Rates, and Monetary Policy. *J. Money, Credit, Banking*, Pt. 2, Nov. 1985, *17*(4), pp. 655–81. [G: U.S.]

Elster, Jon. Weakness of Will and the Free-Rider Problem. *Econ. Philos.*, October 1985, *1*(2), pp. 231–65.

Feldman, Allan M. A Model of Majority Voting and Growth in Government Expenditure. *Public Choice*, 1985, *46*(1), pp. 3–17. [G: U.S.]

Fiorina, Morris P. Group Concentration and the Delegation of Legislative Authority. In *Noll, R. G., ed.*, 1985, pp. 175–97.

Fishburn, Peter C. and Gehrlein, William V. The Power of a Cohesive Subgroup within a Voting Body. *Soc. Choice Welfare*, December 1985, *2*(3), pp. 197–206.

Forte, Francesco. Competitive Democracy and Fiscal Constitution. *Atlantic Econ. J.*, September 1985, *13*(3), pp. 1–11.

Forte, Francesco. Political Economy and Social Philosophy: Comment. In *Koslowski, P., ed.*, 1985, pp. 33–36.

Gallástegui, Inmaculada. Aspectos básicos de los modelos de elección discreta en economía. (With English summary.) *Revista Española Econ.*, 1985, *2*(2), pp. 187–202.

Gandhi, Devinder K.; Hausmann, Robert, Jr. and Saunders, Anthony. On Syndicate Sharing Rules for Unanimous Project Rankings. *J. Banking Finance*, December 1985, *9*(4), pp. 517–34.

Gardner, R. Rationing, Bargaining, and Voting in 2-Sided Markets? *Soc. Choice Welfare*, May 1985, *2*(1), pp. 39–48.

Gauthier, David. Maximization Constrained: The Rationality of Cooperation. In *Campbell, R. and Sowden, L., eds.*, 1985, pp. 75–93.

Gehrlein, William V. The Condorcet Criterion and Committee Selection. *Math. Soc. Sci.*, December 1985, *10*(3), pp. 199–209.

Glazer, Amihai and Robbins, M. How Elections Matter: A Study of U.S. Senators. *Public Choice*, 1985, *46*(2), pp. 163–72. [G: U.S.]

Gonzalez, Rodolfo A. and Mehay, Stephen L. Bureaucracy and the Divisibility of Local Public Output. *Public Choice*, 1985, *45*(1), pp. 89–101. [G: U.S.]

Goodman, John C. and Porter, Philip K. Majority Voting and Pareto Optimality. *Public Choice*, 1985, *46*(2), pp. 173–86.

Greenberg, Joseph and Weber, Shlomo. Consistent δ-Relative Majority Equilibria. *Econometrica*, March 1985, *53*(2), pp. 463–64.

Greenberg, Joseph and Weber, Shlomo. Multiparty Equilibria under Proportional Representation. *Amer. Polit. Sci. Rev.*, September 1985, *79*(3), pp. 693–703.

Hammond, Thomas H. and Horn, Jeffrey H. 'Putting One Over on the Boss': The Political Economy of Strategic Behavior in Organizations. *Public Choice*, 1985, *45*(1), pp. 49–71.

Hardin, Russell. Individual Sanctions, Collective Benefits. In *Campbell, R. and Sowden, L., eds.*, 1985, pp. 339–54.

Harris, Christopher J. An Alternative Solution to Rubinstein's Model of Sequential Bargaining under Incomplete Information. *Econ. J.*, Supplement 1985, *95*, pp. 102–12.

Harrison, Glenn W. and McKee, Michael. Experimental Evaluation of the Coase Theorem. *J. Law Econ.*, October 1985, *28*(3), pp. 653–70.

Henriet, D. The Copeland Choice Function. An Axiomatic Characterization. *Soc. Choice Welfare*, May 1985, *2*(1), pp. 49–63.

Higgins, Richard S.; Shughart, William F., II and Tollison, Robert D. Free Entry and Efficient Rent Seeking. *Public Choice*, 1985, *46*(3), pp. 247–58.

Hill, Jeffrey S. Why So Much Stability? The Impact of Agency Determined Stability. *Public Choice*, 1985, *46*(3), pp. 275–87. [G: U.S.]

Holcombe, Randall G. and Caudill, Steven B. Tax Shares and Government Spending in a Median Voter Model. *Public Choice*, 1985, *46*(2), pp. 197–205.

Homann, Karl. Types of Rationality versus Theory of Rationality. In *Koslowski, P., ed.*, 1985, pp. 141–56.

Jadlow, Joseph M. Monopoly Rent Seeking under Conditions of Uncertainty. *Public Choice*, 1985, *45*(1), pp. 73–87.

Jain, Satish K. A Direct Proof of Inada–Sen–Pattanaik Theorem on Majority Rule. *Econ. Stud. Quart.*, December 1985, *36*(3), pp. 209–15.

Johnson, Ronald N. Retail Price Controls in the Dairy Industry: A Political Coalition Argument. *J. Law Econ.*, April 1985, *28*(1), pp. 55–75.

Kalai, Ehud and Samet, Dov. Monotonic Solutions to General Cooperative Games. *Econometrica*, March 1985, *53*(2), pp. 307–27.

Kayaalp, Orhan. Public-Choice Elements of the Italian Theory of Public Goods. *Public Finance*,

1985, *40*(3), pp. 395–410.   [G: Italy]

Keech, William R. and Simon, Carl P. Electoral and Welfare Consequences of Political Manipulation of the Economy. *J. Econ. Behav. Organ.*, June 1985, *6*(2), pp. 177–202.

Keenan, Donald C. and Rubin, Paul H. The Limits of the Equity–Efficiency Tradeoff. *Public Choice*, 1985, *47*(3), pp. 425–36.

Kelsey, D. Acyclic Choice and Group Veto. *Soc. Choice Welfare*, September 1985, *2*(2), pp. 131–37.

Kelsey, D. The Liberal Paradox: A Generalisation. *Soc. Choice Welfare*, March 1985, *1*(4), pp. 245–50.

Kim, Ki Hang and Roush, Fred W. Consistent Social Choice Functions and Systems of Distinct Representatives. *Math. Soc. Sci.*, February 1985, *9*(1), pp. 27–34.

Kim, Ki Hang and Roush, Fred W. The Liberal Paradox and the Pareto Set. *Math. Soc. Sci.*, February 1985, *9*(1), pp. 45–51.

Kirschgässner, Gebhard. Causality Testing of the Popularity Function: An Empirical Investigation for the Federal Republic of Germany, 1971–1982. *Public Choice*, 1985, *45*(2), pp. 155–73.   [G: W. Germany]

Korhonen, Pekka J. A Principle for Solving Qualitative Multiple-Criteria Problems. In *Grauer, M.; Thompson, M. and Wierzbicki, A. P.*, eds., 1985, pp. 281–95.

Koslowski, Peter. Economy Principle, Maximizing, and the Co-ordination of Individuals in Economics and Philosophy. In *Koslowski, P.*, ed., 1985, pp. 39–67.

Krier, James E. and Gillette, Clayton P. The Un-easy Case for Technological Optimism. *Mich. Law Rev.*, December 1985, *84*(3), pp. 405–29.

Laband, David N. and Haughton, Jonathan. Toward an Economic Theory of Voluntary Resignation by Dictators. *Int. Rev. Law Econ.*, December 1985, *5*(2), pp. 199–207.

Laine, Charles R. Distribution of Jointly Owned Private Goods by the Demand-revealing Process: Applications to Divorce Settlements and Estate Administration. *Public Choice*, 1985, *47*(3), pp. 437–57.

Lee, Dwight R. Marginal Lobbying Cost and the Optimal Amount of Rent Seeking. *Public Choice*, 1985, *45*(2), pp. 207–13.

Lee, Dwight R. Reverse Revenue Sharing: A Modest Proposal. *Public Choice*, 1985, *45*(3), pp. 279–89.

Leininger, Wolfgang. Rawls' Maximin Criterion and Time-Consistency: Further Results. *Rev. Econ. Stud.*, July 1985, *52*(3), pp. 505–13.

Leonard, John and Prinzinger, Joseph. Vote Maximization by International Predation. *Atlantic Econ. J.*, December 1985, *13*(4), pp. 90.

Lerer, Ehud and Nitzan, Shmuel. Some General Results on the Metric Rationalization for Social Decision Rules. *J. Econ. Theory*, October 1985, *37*(1), pp. 191–201.

Lewis, Alain A. On Effectively Computable Realizations of Choice Functions. *Math. Soc. Sci.*, August 1985, *10*(1), pp. 43–80.

Lipton, Michael. The Prisoners' Dilemma and Coase's Theorem: A Case for Democracy in Less Developed Countries? In *Matthews, R. C. O.*, ed., 1985, pp. 49–109.

Lui, Francis T. An Equilibrium Queuing Model of Bribery. *J. Polit. Econ.*, August 1985, *93*(4), pp. 760–81.

Macpherson, C. B. The Rise and Fall of Economic Justice. In *Macpherson, C. B.*, 1985, pp. 1–20.

Maskin, Eric S. The Theory of Implementation in Nash Equilibrium: A Survey. In *[Pazner, E.]*, 1985, pp. 173–204.

Matsumoto, Yasumi. Non-binary Social Choice: Revealed Preferential Interpretation. *Economica*, May 1985, *52*(206), pp. 185–94.

Matsuyama, Kiminori. Chernoff's Dual Axiom, Revealed Preference, and Weak Rational Choice Functions. *J. Econ. Theory*, February 1985, *35*(1), pp. 155–65.

McCaleb, Thomas S. and Wagner, Richard E. The Experimental Search for Free Riders: Some Reflections and Observations. *Public Choice*, 1985, *47*(3), pp. 479–90.

McCubbins, Mathew D. and Schwartz, Thomas. The Politics of Flatland. *Public Choice*, 1985, *46*(1), pp. 45–60.

McGuire, Martin C. and Groth, Carl H., Jr. A Method for Identifying the Public Good Allocation Process within a Group. *Quart. J. Econ.*, Supp. 1985, *100*, pp. 915–34.

McKelvey, Richard D. and Ordeshook, Peter C. Elections with Limited Information: A Fulfilled Expectations Model Using Contemporaneous Poll and Endorsement Data as Information Sources. *J. Econ. Theory*, June 1985, *36*(1), pp. 55–85.

McLean, Murdith R. From Theology to Social Decisions—and Return: Comment. In *Block, W.; Brennan, G. and Elzinga, K.*, eds., 1985, pp. 201–09.

Meiselman, David I. Markets and Majorities, Morals and Madness: An Essay on Religion and Institutional Choice: Comment. In *Block, W.; Brennan, G. and Elzinga, K.*, eds., 1985, pp. 248–51.

Meltzer, Allan H. and Richard, Scott F. A Positive Theory of In-Kind Transfers and the Negative Income Tax. *Public Choice*, 1985, *47*(1), pp. 231–65.

Merrill, Samuel, III. A Statistical Model for Condorcet Efficiency Based on Simulation under Spatial Model Assumptions. *Public Choice*, 1985, *47*(2), pp. 389–403.

Mestelman, Stuart. Externality Control, Income Distribution, and Social Choice. *Public Finance*, 1985, *40*(1), pp. 93–113.

Moulin, Hervé. Choice Functions over a Finite Set: A Summary. *Soc. Choice Welfare*, September 1985, *2*(2), pp. 147–60.

Moulin, Hervé. Egalitarianism and Utilitarianism in Quasi-linear Bargaining. *Econometrica*, January 1985, *53*(1), pp. 49–67.

Moulin, Hervé. From Social Welfare Ordering to Acyclic Aggregation of Preferences. *Math. Soc. Sci.*, February 1985, *9*(1), pp. 1–17.

Moulin, Hervé. The Separability Axiom and Equal-sharing Methods. *J. Econ. Theory*, June 1985, *36*(1), pp. 120–48.

Muller, Eitan and Satterthwaite, Mark A. Strategy-proofness: The Existence of Dominant-Strategy Mechanisms. In *[Pazner, E.]*, 1985, pp. 131–71.

Naert, Frank. The Political Economy of Pressure Groups. *Econ. Scelte Pubbliche/J. Public Finance Public Choice*, 1985, (1), pp. 55–63.

Newman, Bruce I. and Sheth, Jagdish N. A Model of Primary Voter Behavior. *J. Cons. Res.*, September 1985, *12*(2), pp. 178–87. [G: U.S.]

Ng, Yew-Kwang. Some Fundamental Issues in Social Welfare. In *Feiwel, G. R., ed. (II)*, 1985, pp. 435–69.

Ng, Yew-Kwang. The Utilitarian Criterion, Finite Sensibility, and the Weak Majority Preference Principle. A Futher Analysis [Bentham or Bergson? Finite Sensibility, Utility Functions and Social Welfare Functions] [Bentham or Nash? On the Acceptable Form of Social Welfare Functions]. *Soc. Choice Welfare*, May 1985, *2*(1), pp. 37–38.

Niemi, Richard G. Reply: The Problem of Strategic Voting under Approval Voting. *Amer. Polit. Sci. Rev.*, September 1985, *79*(3), pp. 818–19.

Niemi, Richard G. and Gretlein, Rodney J. A Precise Restatement and Extension of Black's Theorem on Voting Orders. *Public Choice*, 1985, *47*(2), pp. 371–76.

Nijkamp, Peter and Voogd, Henk. An Informal Introduction to Multicriteria Evaluation. In *Fandel, G. and Spronk, J., eds.*, 1985, pp. 61–84.

Nitzan, Shmuel. The Vulnerability of Point-Voting Schemes to Preference Variation and Strategic Manipulation. *Public Choice*, 1985, *47*(2), pp. 349–70.

Noam, Eli M. A Local Regulator's Rewards for Conformity in Policy. *Public Choice*, 1985, *45*(3), pp. 291–302. [G: U.S.]

Oppenheimer, Joe A. Public Choice and Three Ethical Properties of Politics. *Public Choice*, 1985, *45*(3), pp. 241–55.

Palfrey, Thomas R. and Rosenthal, Howard. Voter Participation and Strategic Uncertainty. *Amer. Polit. Sci. Rev.*, March 1985, *79*(1), pp. 62–78.

Pasour, E. C., Jr. The Public Interest and Rent Seeking. *Public Choice*, 1985, *47*(3), pp. 527–29.

Pazner, Elisha A. Recent Thinking on Economic Justice. In *[Pazner, E.]*, 1985, pp. 297–309.

Pazner, Elisha A. and Schmeidler, David. Social Contact Theory and Ordinal Distributive Equity. In *[Pazner, E.]*, 1985, pp. 311–19.

Pazner, Elisha A. and Wesley, Eugene. Cheatproofness Properties of the Plurality Rule in Large Societies. In *[Pazner, E.]*, 1985, pp. 331–40.

Pecquet, Gary M. The Effects of Voter Mobility on Agenda Controllers. *Public Choice*, 1985, *45*(3), pp. 269–78.

Poljak, Svatoplukk and Turzík, Daniel. Social In-

fluence Models with Ranking Alternatives and Local Election Rules. *Math. Soc. Sci.*, October 1985, *10*(2), pp. 189–98.

Poole, Keith T. and Romer, Thomas. Patterns of Political Action Committee Contributions to the 1980 Campaigns for the United States House of Representatives. *Public Choice*, 1985, *47*(1), pp. 63–111. [G: U.S.]

Putterman, Louis and DiGiorgio, Marie. Choice and Efficiency in a Model of Democratic Semicollective Agriculture. *Oxford Econ. Pap.*, March 1985, *37*(1), pp. 1–21.

Repullo, Rafael. Implementation in Dominant Strategies under Complete and Incomplete Information. *Rev. Econ. Stud.*, April 1985, *52*(2), pp. 223–29.

Riley, Jonathan. On the Possibility of Liberal Democracy. *Amer. Polit. Sci. Rev.*, December 1985, *79*(4), pp. 1135–51.

Ritz, Zvi. Restricted Domains, Arrow Social Welfare Functions and Noncorruptible and Nonmanipulable Social Choice Correspondences: The Case of Private and Public Alternatives. *J. Econ. Theory*, February 1985, *35*(1), pp. 1–18.

Rowley, Charles K. and Elgin, Robert. Towards a Theory of Bureaucratic Behaviour. In *[Peacock, A.]*, 1985, pp. 31–50.

Saari, Donald G. Price Dynamics, Social Choice, Voting Methods, Probability and Chaos. In *Aliprantis, C. D.; Burkinshaw, O. and Rothman, N. J., eds.*, 1985, pp. 1–24.

Sandler, Todd; Sterbenz, Frederic P. and Tschirhart, John. Uncertainty and Clubs. *Economica*, November 1985, *52*(208), pp. 467–77.

Schap, David. X-Inefficiency in a Rent-seeking Society: A Graphical Analysis. *Quart. Rev. Econ. Bus.*, Spring 1985, *25*(1), pp. 19–27.

Schofield, N. Anarchy, Altruism and Cooperation: A Review. *Soc. Choice Welfare*, December 1985, *2*(3), pp. 207–19.

Scotchmer, Suzanne. Profit-maximizing Clubs. *J. Public Econ.*, June 1985, *27*(1), pp. 25–45.

Seitz, Steven Thomas. Fuzzy Modeling and Conflict Analysis. *Conflict Manage. Peace Sci.*, Fall 1985, *9*(1), pp. 53–67.

Seo, Fumiko. Multiattribute Utility Analysis and Collective Choice: A Methodological Review. In *Haimes, Y. Y. and Chankong, V., eds.*, 1985, pp. 170–89.

Shelley, Fred M. Voting Power in a System of Compound Majority Rule. *Math. Soc. Sci.*, June 1985, *9*(3), pp. 287–91.

Shenfield, Arthur A. From Theology to Social Decisions—and Return: Comment. In *Block, W.; Brennan, G. and Elzinga, K., eds.*, 1985, pp. 196–200.

Shinn, Roger L. From Theology to Social Decisions—and Return. In *Block, W.; Brennan, G. and Elzinga, K., eds.*, 1985, pp. 175–95.

Shughart, William F., II and Tollison, Robert D. The Cyclical Character of Regulatory Activity. *Public Choice*, 1985, *45*(3), pp. 303–11. [G: U.S.]

Sisk, David E. Rent-seeking, Noncompensated Transfers, and Laws of Succession: A Property

Rights View. *Public Choice*, 1985, *46*(1), pp. 95–102.

Sjoblom, Kriss. Voting for Social Security. *Public Choice*, 1985, *45*(3), pp. 225–40. **[G: U.S.]**

Skorkupski, John. Utilitarianism and Contractualism. **In** *Koslowski, P., ed.*, 1985, pp. 275–77.

Smith, V. Kerry. A Theoretical Analysis of the "Green Lobby." *Amer. Polit. Sci. Rev.*, March 1985, *79*(1), pp. 132–47. **[G: U.S.]**

Snidal, Duncan. Coordination versus Prisoners' Dilemma: Implications for International Cooperation and Regimes. *Amer. Polit. Sci. Rev.*, December 1985, *79*(4), pp. 923–42.

Snidal, Duncan. The Limits of Hegemonic Stability Theory. *Int. Organ.*, Autumn 1985, *39*(4), pp. 579–614.

Stark, Oded. On Private Charity and Altruism. *Public Choice*, 1985, *46*(3), pp. 325–32.

Strnad, Jeff. The Structure of Continuous-valued Neutral Monotonic Social Functions. *Soc. Choice Welfare*, December 1985, *2*(3), pp. 181–95.

Sturm, Peter H. Rationality, Causality, and the Relation between Economic Conditions and the Popularity of Parties: Comment. *Europ. Econ. Rev.*, June-July 1985, *28*(1–2), pp. 273–77. **[G: W. Germany]**

Sugden, Robert. Liberty, Preference, and Choice. *Econ. Philos.*, October 1985, *1*(2), pp. 213–29.

Svensson, L.-G. The Utilitarian Criterion, Finite Sensibility, and the Weak Majority Preference Principle. A Futher Analysis [Bentham or Bergson? Finite Sensibility, Utility Functions and Social Welfare Functions] [Bentham or Nash? On the Acceptable Form of Social Welfare Functions]. *Soc. Choice Welfare*, May 1985, *2*(1), pp. 23–35.

Tideman, T. Nicolaus. Remorse, Elation, and the Paradox of Voting. *Public Choice*, 1985, *46*(1), pp. 103–06.

Tullock, Gordon. Back to the Bog. *Public Choice*, 1985, *46*(3), pp. 259–63.

Tumlir, Jan. Who Benefits from Discrimination? *Schweiz. Z. Volkswirtsch. Statist.*, September 1985, *121*(3), pp. 249–58.

van Velthoven, Ben and van Winden, Frans A. A. M. Towards a Politico-economic Theory of Social Security. *Europ. Econ. Rev.*, March 1985, *27*(2), pp. 263–89.

Vossenkuhl, Wilhelm. Types of Rationality and Economic Action. **In** *Koslowski, P., ed.*, 1985, pp. 126–40.

Waterman, Anthony. Religious Belief and Political Bias. **In** *Block, W.; Brennan, G. and Elzinga, K., eds.*, 1985, pp. 3–20.

Watkins, John. Second Thoughts on Self-interest and Morality. **In** *Campbell, R. and Sowden, L., eds.*, 1985, pp. 59–74.

Willner, Johan. Professional Associations and Their Members: A Study of the Market for Professional Services When Ability and Size Are Independent. *Int. J. Ind. Organ.*, June 1985, *3*(2), pp. 179–95.

Wiseman, Jack. Economic Efficiency and Effi-

cient Public Policy. **In** *[Recktenwald, H. C.]*, 1985, pp. 33–44.

Wriglesworth, John L. Respecting Individual Rights in Social Choice. *Oxford Econ. Pap.*, March 1985, *37*(1), pp. 100–117.

0252 Social Choice Studies: Voting, Committees, etc.

Aitkin, Don. Taxation and Policy Change: A Median Voter Model for Australia 1968–69 to 1981–82: Comment. *Australian Econ. Rev.*, 3rd Quarter, Spring 1985, (71), pp. 34–35. **[G: Australia]**

Anderson, Gary M. and Tollison, Robert D. Ideology, Interest Groups, and the Repeal of the Corn Laws. *Z. ges. Staatswiss. (JITE)*, June 1985, *141*(2), pp. 197–212. **[G: U.K.]**

Aranson, Peter H. Judicial Control of the Political Branches: Public Purpose and Public Law. *Cato J.*, Winter 1985, *4*(3), pp. 719–82. **[G: U.S.]**

Aranson, Peter H. and Ordeshook, Peter C. Public Interest, Private Interest, and the Democratic Polity. **In** *Benjamin, R. and Elkin, S. L., eds.*, 1985, pp. 87–177.

Auerbach, Robert D. Politics and the Federal Reserve. *Contemp. Policy Issues*, Fall 1985, *3*(5), pp. 43–58. **[G: U.S.]**

Basevi, Giorgio. The Effects of Economic Structure and Policy Choices on Macroeconomic Outcomes in Ten Industrial Countries: Comments. **In** *Melitz, J. and Wyplosz, C., eds.*, 1985, pp. 301–02. **[G: Selected OECD]**

Becker, Gary S. Pressure Groups and Political Behavior. **In** *Coe, R. D. and Wilber, C. K., eds.*, 1985, pp. 120–46.

Bendor, Jonathan and Moe, Terry M. An Adaptive Model of Bureaucratic Politics. *Amer. Polit. Sci. Rev.*, September 1985, *79*(3), pp. 755–74.

Bendor, Jonathan; Taylor, Serge and Van Gaalen, Roland. Bureaucratic Expertise versus Legislative Authority: A Model of Deception and Monitoring in Budgeting. *Amer. Polit. Sci. Rev.*, December 1985, *79*(4), pp. 1041–60.

Benjamin, Roger and Duvall, Raymond. The Capitalist State in Context. **In** *Benjamin, R. and Elkin, S. L., eds.*, 1985, pp. 19–57.

Bergsten, Gordon S. On the Role of Social Norms in a Market Economy. *Public Choice*, 1985, *45*(2), pp. 113–37.

Black, Stanley W. The Effects of Economic Structure and Policy Choices on Macroeconomic Outcomes in Ten Industrial Countries: Reply to Basevi. **In** *Melitz, J. and Wyplosz, C., eds.*, 1985, pp. 307. **[G: Selected OECD]**

Black, Stanley W. The Effects of Economic Structure and Policy Choices on Macroeconomic Outcomes in Ten Industrial Countries. **In** *Melitz, J. and Wyplosz, C., eds.*, 1985, pp. 279–300. **[G: Selected OECD]**

Borooah, Vani K. The Interaction between Economic Policy and Political Performance. **In** *Matthews, R. C. O., ed.*, 1985, pp. 20–48. **[G: U.K.]**

Bowles, Samuel. State Structures and Political Practices: A Reconsideration of the Liberal Democratic Conception of Politics and Accountability. In *Coe, R. D. and Wilber, C. K., eds.*, 1985 , pp. 147–90.

Brady, Henry E. and Sniderman, Paul M. Attitude Attribution: A Group Basis for Political Reasoning. *Amer. Polit. Sci. Rev.*, December 1985, *79*(4), pp. 1061–78. [G: U.S.]

Braybrooke, David. Contemporary Marxism on the Autonomy, Efficacy, and Legitimacy of the Capitalist State. In *Benjamin, R. and Elkin, S. L., eds.*, 1985, pp. 59–86.

Brennan, Geoffrey. Taxation and Policy Change: A Median Voter Model for Australia 1968–69 to 1981–82. *Australian Econ. Rev.*, 3rd Quarter, Spring 1985, (71), pp. 20–33.
[G: Australia]

Brera, Paolo. Social Partnership and Economic Growth. Austria and Sweden after the Oil Shocks. *Ricerche Econ.*, Apr.-June 1985, *39*(2), pp. 201–20. [G: Austria; Sweden]

Breton, Albert and Galeotti, Gianluigi. Is Proportional Representation Always the Best Electoral Rule? *Public Finance*, 1985, *40*(1), pp. 1–16. [G: Canada]

Cairns, Robert D. Rent Seeking, Deregulation and Regulatory Reform. *Can. Public Policy*, September 1985, *11*(3), pp. 591–601.
[G: Canada]

Cartwright, Phillip A. and DeLorme, Charles D., Jr. The Unemployment–Inflation–Voter Utility Relationship in the Political Business Cycle: Some Evidence. *Southern Econ. J.*, January 1985, *51*(3), pp. 898–905. [G: U.S.]

Cassing, James H. and Hillman, Arye L. Political Influence Motives and the Choice between Tariffs and Quotas. *J. Int. Econ.*, November 1985, *19*(3/4), pp. 279–90.

Cawson, Alan. Corporatism and Local Politics. In *Grant, W., ed.*, 1985, pp. 126–47.
[G: U.K.]

Chappell, Henry W., Jr. and Keech, William R. A New View of Political Accountability for Economic Performance. *Amer. Polit. Sci. Rev.*, March 1985, *79*(1), pp. 10–27. [G: U.S.]

Chubb, John E. The Political Economy of Federalism. *Amer. Polit. Sci. Rev.*, December 1985, *79*(4), pp. 994–1015.

Cima, Lawrence R. and Cotter, Patrick S. The Coherence of the Concept of Limited Government. *J. Policy Anal. Manage.*, Winter 1985, *4*(2), pp. 266–69.

Clark, Terry Nichols. Choose Austerity Strategies that Work for You. In *Clark, T. N., ed.*, 1985, pp. 71–88. [G: U.S.]

Coe, Richard D. and Wilber, Charles K. Schumpeter Revisited: An Overview. In *Coe, R. D. and Wilber, C. K., eds.*, 1985, pp. 1–59.

Cornwell, Elmer E. Comments [Constitutional Change and Agenda Control] [Demographic Factors Affecting Constitutional Decisions: The Case of Municipal Charters]. *Public Choice*, 1985, *47*(1), pp. 219–29. [G: U.S.]

Coughlin, Cletus C. Domestic Content Legislation: House Voting and the Economic Theory of Regulation. *Econ. Inquiry*, July 1985, *23*(3), pp. 437–48. [G: U.S.]

Danziger, James N. Leaders, Perceptions and Policy under Austerity. In *Clark, T. N., ed.*, 1985, pp. 89–93. [G: Denmark; U.S.]

Delforce, Robert J. and Hardaker, J. Brian. An Experiment in Multiattribute Utility Theory. *Australian J. Agr. Econ.*, December 1985, *29*(3), pp. 179–98. [G: Australia]

Denzau, Arthur T. Constitutional Change and Agenda Control. *Public Choice*, 1985, *47*(1), pp. 183–217. [G: U.S.]

Denzau, Arthur T.; Riker, William H. and Shepsle, Kenneth A. Farquharson and Fenno: Sophisticated Voting and Home Style. *Amer. Polit. Sci. Rev.*, December 1985, *79*(4), pp. 1117–34.

Dobra, John L. and Eubank, William Lee. Political Survivorship: An Interest Group Perspective. *Southern Econ. J.*, April 1985, *51*(4), pp. 1038–52. [G: U.S.]

Dutter, Lee E. An Application of the Multicandidate Calculus of Voting in the 1972 and 1976 German Federal Elections. *Public Choice*, 1985, *47*(2), pp. 405–24. [G: W. Germany]

Eberts, Paul R. and Kelly, Janet M. How Mayors Get Things Done: Community Politics and Mayors' Initiatives. In *Clark, T. N., ed.*, 1985, pp. 39–70. [G: U.S.]

Elkin, Stephen L. Pluralism in Its Place: State and Regime in Liberal Democracy. In *Benjamin, R. and Elkin, S. L., eds.*, 1985, pp. 179–211.

Elliott, E. Donald; Ackerman, Bruce A. and Millian, John C. Toward a Theory of Statutory Evolution: The Federalization of Environmental Law. *J. Law, Econ., Organ.*, Fall 1985, *1*(2), pp. 313–40. [G: U.S.]

Evans, Peter B.; Rueschemeyer, Dietrich and Skocpol, Theda. On the Road toward a More Adequate Understanding of the State. In *Evans, P. B.; Rueschemeyer, D. and Skocpol, T., eds.*, 1985, pp. 347–66.

Ferejohn, John A. The State in Politics: Comment. In *Noll, R. G., ed.*, 1985, pp. 105–10.

Ferejohn, John A. and Fiorina, Morris P. Incumbency and Realignment in Congressional Elections. In *Chubb, J. E. and Peterson, P. E., eds.*, 1985, pp. 91–115. [G: U.S.]

Figueroa, Mark. An Assessment of Overvoting in Jamaica. *Soc. Econ. Stud.*, September 1985, *34*(3), pp. 71–106. [G: Jamaica]

Flowers, Marilyn R. Public Choice and the Flat Tax. *Cato J.*, Fall 1985, *5*(2), pp. 625–28.
[G: U.S.]

Forte, Francesco. Control of Public-Spending Growth and Majority Rule. In *Forte, F. and Peacock, A., eds.*, 1985, pp. 132–42.

Forte, Francesco. The Theory of Social Contract and the EEC. In *[Peacock, A.]*, 1985, pp. 149–66.

Frendreis, John P. and Waterman, Richard W. PAC Contributions and Legislative Behavior: Senate Voting on Trucking Deregulation. *Soc. Sci. Quart.*, June 1985, *66*(2), pp. 401–12.
[G: U.S.]

Frey, Bruno S. The Political Economy of Protection. In *Greenaway, D., ed.*, 1985, pp. 139–57. **[G: OECD]**

Gonzalez, Rodolfo A. and Mehay, Stephen L. Bureaucracy and the Divisibility of Local Public Output. *Public Choice*, 1985, *45*(1), pp. 89–101. **[G: U.S.]**

Gramlich, Edward M. Excessive Government Spending in the U.S.: Facts and Theories. In *Gramlich, E. M. and Ysander, B.-C., eds.*, 1985, pp. 29–73. **[G: U.S.]**

Grant, Wyn. The Political Economy of Corporatism: Introduction. In *Grant, W., ed.*, 1985, pp. 1–31.

Hamlin, Alan P. The Political Economy of Constitutional Federalism. *Public Choice*, 1985, *46*(2), pp. 187–95.

Hann, Danny. Political and Bureaucratic Pressures on U.K. Oil Taxation Policy. *Scot. J. Polit. Econ.*, November 1985, *32*(3), pp. 278–95. **[G: U.K.]**

Hansen, John Mark. The Political Economy of Group Membership. *Amer. Polit. Sci. Rev.*, March 1985, *79*(1), pp. 79–96.

Hansen, Susan B. Citizen Preferences and Participatory Roles: Comment. In *Clark, T. N., ed.*, 1985, pp. 263–67. **[G: U.S.]**

Heberlein, Thomas A. Some Observations on Alternative Mechanisms for Public Involvement: The Hearing, Public Opinion Poll, the Workshop and the Quasi-experiment. In *Kury, C., ed.*, 1985, pp. 106–21.

Hibbs, Douglas A., Jr. Inflation, Political Support, and Macroeconomic Policy. In *Lindberg, L. N. and Maier, C. S., eds.*, 1985, pp. 175–95. **[G: OECD]**

Hymans, Saul H. Median Voter Models and the Growth of Government Services. In *Gramlich, E. M. and Ysander, B.-C., eds.*, 1985, pp. 75–89. **[G: U.S.]**

Inglehart, Ronald. Aggregate Stability and Individual-Level Flux in Mass Belief Systems: The Level of Analysis Paradox. *Amer. Polit. Sci. Rev.*, March 1985, *79*(1), pp. 97–116. **[G: OECD]**

Isermann, Heinz. Interactive Group Decision Making by Coalitions. In *Grauer, M.; Thompson, M. and Wierzbicki, A. P., eds.*, 1985, pp. 202–11.

Jackson, Peter M. Economy, Democracy and Bureaucracy. In *Matthews, R. C. O., ed.*, 1985, pp. 168–203.

Jacobson, Gary C. Money and Votes Reconsidered: Congressional Elections, 1972–1982. *Public Choice*, 1985, *47*(1), pp. 7–62. **[G: U.S.]**

Jacobson, Gary C. The Republican Advantage in Campaign Finance. In *Chubb, J. E. and Peterson, P. E., eds.*, 1985, pp. 143–73. **[G: U.S.]**

Johnson, Linda L. The Effectiveness of Savings and Loan Political Action Committees. *Public Choice*, 1985, *46*(3), pp. 289–304. **[G: U.S.]**

Jones, Melinda. The Politics of Tax Reform. *Australian Tax Forum*, Winter 1985, *2*(2), pp. 147–60. **[G: Australia]**

Kau, James B. and Rubin, Paul H. The Specifica-

tion of Models of Campaign Finance: Comments [Money and Votes Reconsidered: Congressional Elections, 1972–1982] [Patterns of Political Action Committee Contributions to the 1980 Campaigns for the United States House of Representatives]. *Public Choice*, 1985, *47*(1), pp. 113–19. **[G: U.S.]**

Kiewiet, D. Roderick and Rivers, Douglas. The Economic Basis of Reagan's Appeal. In *Chubb, J. E. and Peterson, P. E., eds.*, 1985, pp. 69–90. **[G: U.S.]**

Kirby, Michael J. L. Complexity, Democracy, and Governance. In *Aida, S., et al.*, 1985, pp. 329–37.

Kirchgässner, Gebhard. Rationality, Causality, and the Relation between Economic Conditions and the Popularity of Parties: An Empirical Investigation for the Federal Republic of Germany, 1971-1982. *Europ. Econ. Rev.*, June-July 1985, *28*(1–2), pp. 243–68. **[G: W. Germany]**

Knoke, David. Citizen Preferences and Participatory Roles: Comments. In *Clark, T. N., ed.*, 1985, pp. 259–62. **[G: U.S.]**

Laband, David N. Federal Budget Cuts: Rejoinder [Federal Budget Cuts: Bureaucrats Trim the Meat, Not the Fat]. *Public Choice*, 1985, *45*(2), pp. 221–22.

Ladd, Helen F. and Wilson, Julie Boatright. Proposition 2½: Explaining the Vote. In *Clark, T. N., ed.*, 1985, pp. 199–243. **[G: U.S.]**

Lane, Jan-Erik. State and Market: The Politics of the Public and the Private: Introduction: Public Policy or Markets? The Demarcation Problem. In *Lane, J.-E., ed.*, 1985, pp. 3–52.

Lee, Dwight R. Reverse Revenue Sharing: A Modest Proposal. *Public Choice*, 1985, *45*(3), pp. 279–89.

Levy, Frank. Happiness, Affluence, and Altruism in the Postwar Period. In *David, M. and Smeeding, T., eds.*, 1985, pp. 7–29. **[G: U.S.]**

Lindbeck, Assar. Redistribution Policy and the Expansion of the Public Sector. *J. Public Econ.*, December 1985, *28*(3), pp. 309–28.

Lomasky, Loren E. Is Social Security Politically Untouchable? *Cato J.*, Spring/Summer 1985, *5*(1), pp. 157–75. **[G: U.S.]**

Lowi, Theodore J. The State in Politics: The Relation between Policy and Administration. In *Noll, R. G., ed.*, 1985, pp. 67–105.

Lubinsky, R. Policy, Power and Order—The Persistence of Economic Problems in Capitalist States (Review Note). *S. Afr. J. Econ.*, September 1985, *53*(3), pp. 297–301.

Lundahl, Mats. Government and Inefficiency in the Haitian Economy: The Nineteenth Century Legacy. In *Connolly, M. B. and McDermott, J., eds.*, 1985, pp. 175–218. **[G: Haiti]**

Lyons, William. Commentary: Urban Politics and Fiscal Strain. In *Clark, T. N., ed.*, 1985, pp. 95–98. **[G: Denmark; U.S.]**

Malaska, Pentti. Outline of a Policy for the Future. In *Aida, S., et al.*, 1985, pp. 338–54.

Marable, Manning. Black Power in Chicago: An Historical Overview of Class Stratification and

Electoral Politics in a Black Urban Community. *Rev. Radical Polit. Econ.*, Fall 1985, *17*(3), pp. 157–82. **[G: U.S.]**

Marlow, Michael L. Federal Budget Cuts: Bureaucrats Trim the Meat, Not the Fat: Comment. *Public Choice*, 1985, *45*(2), pp. 215–19.

Martelli, Paolo. Legislative Choice and Public-Spending Growth. In *Forte, F. and Peacock, A., eds.*, 1985, pp. 37–51.

Martin, John P. The Effects of Economic Structure and Policy Choices on Macroeconomic Outcomes in Ten Industrial Countries: Comments. In *Melitz, J. and Wyplosz, C., eds.*, 1985, pp. 303–05. **[G: Selected OECD]**

Maser, Steven M. Demographic Factors Affecting Constitutional Decisions: The Case of Municipal Charters. *Public Choice*, 1985, *47*(1), pp. 121–62. **[G: U.S.]**

Mashaw, Jerry L. Prodelegation: Why Administrators Should Make Political Decisions. *J. Law, Econ., Organ.*, Spring 1985, *1*(1), pp. 81–100. **[G: U.S.]**

McCaleb, Thomas S. Public Choice Perspectives on the Flat Tax Follies. *Cato J.*, Fall 1985, *5*(2), pp. 613–24. **[G: U.S.]**

Mehay, Stephen L. and Gonzalez, Rodolfo A. Economic Incentives under Contract Supply of Local Government Services. *Public Choice*, 1985, *46*(1), pp. 79–86. **[G: U.S.]**

van Mierlo, Hans J. G. A. Improvement of Public Provision of Goods and Services. In *Lane, J.-E., ed.*, 1985, pp. 53–69.

Miller, Gary J. Progressive Reform as Induced Institutional Preferences [Demographic Factors Affecting Constitutional Decisions: The Case of Municipal Charters]. *Public Choice*, 1985, *47*(1), pp. 163–81. **[G: U.S.]**

Moe, Terry M. Control and Feedback in Economic Regulation: The Case of the NLRB. *Amer. Polit. Sci. Rev.*, December 1985, *79*(4), pp. 1094–116. **[G: U.S.]**

Mounts, Wm. Stewart, Jr.; Sowell, Clifford and Lindley, James T. Rent-seeking over Time: The Continuity of Capture. *Public Choice*, 1985, *46*(1), pp. 87–94. **[G: U.S.]**

Mouritzen, Poul Erik. Local Resource Allocation: Partisan Politics or Sector Politics. In *Clark, T. N., ed.*, 1985, pp. 3–17. **[G: Denmark]**

Mueller, Dennis C. and Murrell, Peter. Interest Groups and the Political Economy of Government Size. In *Forte, F. and Peacock, A., eds.*, 1985, pp. 13–36. **[G: OECD]**

Newman, Bruce I. and Sheth, Jagdish N. A Model of Primary Voter Behavior. *J. Cons. Res.*, September 1985, *12*(2), pp. 178–87. **[G: U.S.]**

Noam, Eli M. A Local Regulator's Rewards for Conformity in Policy. *Public Choice*, 1985, *45*(3), pp. 291–302. **[G: U.S.]**

Oates, Wallace E. Fiscal Limitations: An Assessment of the U.S. Experience. In *Gramlich, E. M. and Ysander, B.-C., eds.*, 1985, pp. 91–136. **[G: U.S.]**

Offe, Claus. Legitimation Through Majority Rule? In *Offe, C.*, 1985, pp. 259–99.

Offe, Claus. The Attribution of Public Status to Interest Groups. In *Offe, C.*, 1985, pp. 221–58. **[G: W. Germany]**

Offe, Claus. The Divergent Rationalities of Administrative Action. In *Offe, C.*, 1985, pp. 300–316.

Offe, Claus and Hinrichs, Karl. The Political Economy of the Labour Market. In *Offe, C.*, 1985, pp. 10–51.

Offe, Claus and Wiesenthal, Helmut. Two Logics of Collective Action. In *Offe, C.*, 1985, pp. 170–220.

Ohkawa, Masazo. The Role of Political Parties and Executive Bureaucrats in Governmental Budget-Making—The Case of Japan. In *[Recktenwald, H. C.]*, 1985, pp. 123–34. **[G: Japan]**

Ostrom, Charles W., Jr. and Simon, Dennis M. Promise and Performance: A Dynamic Model of Presidential Popularity. *Amer. Polit. Sci. Rev.*, June 1985, *79*(2), pp. 334–58. **[G: U.S.]**

Owen, Bruce M. Interest Groups and the Political Economy of Regulation. In *Meyer, J. A., ed.*, 1985, pp. 26–52. **[G: U.S.]**

Palda, K. Filip and Palda, Kristian S. Ceilings on Campaign Spending: Hypothesis and Partial Test with Canadian Data. *Public Choice*, 1985, *45*(3), pp. 313–31. **[G: Canada]**

Parent, Wayne and Shrum, Wesley. Critical Electoral Success and Black Voters Registration: An Elaboration of the Voter Consent Model. *Soc. Sci. Quart.*, September 1985, *66*(3), pp. 695–703. **[G: U.S.]**

Peltzman, Sam. An Economic Interpretation of the History of Congressional Voting in the Twentieth Century. *Amer. Econ. Rev.*, September 1985, *75*(4), pp. 656–75. **[G: U.S.]**

Poole, Keith T. and Daniels, R. Steven. Ideology, Party, and Voting in the U.S. Congress, 1959–1980. *Amer. Polit. Sci. Rev.*, June 1985, *79*(2), pp. 373–99.

Primeaux, Walter J., Jr. and Mann, Patrick C. Voter Power and Electricity Prices. *Public Choice*, 1985, *47*(3), pp. 519–25. **[G: U.S.]**

Rainwater, Lee. Happiness, Affluence, and Altruism in the Postwar Period: Comment. In *David, M. and Smeeding, T., eds.*, 1985, pp. 29–33. **[G: U.S.]**

Rapoport, Amnon and Golan, Esther. Assessment of Political Power in the Israeli Knesset. *Amer. Polit. Sci. Rev.*, September 1985, *79*(3), pp. 673–92.

Rizzo, Ilde. Regional Disparities and Decentralization as Determinants of Public-Sector Expenditure Growth in Italy (1960–81). In *Forte, F. and Peacock, A., eds.*, 1985, pp. 65–82. **[G: Italy]**

Robertson, John D. Economic Issues and the Probability of Forming Minority Coalition Cabinets. *Soc. Sci. Quart.*, September 1985, *66*(3), pp. 687–94. **[G: W. Europe]**

Rodgers, William. The Political Process: Market Place or Battleground? In *Matthews, R. C. O., ed.*, 1985, pp. 110–26.

Rolnick, Arthur J. Research Activities and Budget Allocations among Federal Reserve Banks:

Comment. *Public Choice*, 1985, *45*(2), pp. 193–95.

Rueschemeyer, Dietrich and Evans, Peter B. The State and Economic Transformation: Toward an Analysis of the Conditions Underlying Effective Intervention. In *Evans, P. B.; Rueschemeyer, D. and Skocpol, T., eds.*, 1985, pp. 44–77.

Rustici, Thomas. A Public Choice View of the Minimum Wage. *Cato J.*, Spring/Summer 1985, *5*(1), pp. 103–31.   [G: U.S.; Puerto Rico]

Samuels, Warren J. A Critique of *Capitalism, Socialism, and Democracy.* In *Coe, R. D. and Wilber, C. K., eds.*, 1985, pp. 60–119.

Samuels, Warren J. Some Considerations Which May Lead Lawmakers to Modify a Policy When Adopting It as Law: Comment. *Z. ges. Staatswiss. (JITE)*, March 1985, *141*(1), pp. 58–61.

Schmitter, Philippe C. Neo-corporatism and the State. In *Grant, W., ed.*, 1985, pp. 32–62.

Shaw, Jane. Breaking New Ground: Public Choice Economists Explain Why Government Doesn't Work. *Policy Rev.*, Summer 1985, (33), pp. 77–80.   [G: U.S.]

Shepsle, Kenneth A. and Weingast, Barry R. Policy Consequences of Government by Congressional Subcommittees. In *Harriss, C. L., ed.*, 1985, pp. 114–31.   [G: U.S.]

Shughart, William F., II and Tollison, Robert D. Legislation and Political Business Cycles. *Kyklos*, 1985, *38*(1), pp. 43–59.   [G: U.S.]

Skovsgaard, Carl-Johan. Budget-Making and Fiscal Austerity: A Case Study of Danish Local Government. In *Clark, T. N., ed.*, 1985, pp. 19–37.   [G: Denmark]

Smith, Steven S. New Patterns of Decisionmaking in Congress. In *Chubb, J. E. and Peterson, P. E., eds.*, 1985, pp. 203–33.   [G: U.S.]

Smith, V. Kerry. A Theoretical Analysis of the "Green Lobby." *Amer. Polit. Sci. Rev.*, March 1985, *79*(1), pp. 132–47.   [G: U.S.]

Strom, Kaare. Party Goals and Government Performance in Parliamentary Democracy. *Amer. Polit. Sci. Rev.*, September 1985, *79*(3), pp. 738–54.   [G: W. Europe]

Summers, Robert S. Some Considerations Which May Lead Lawmakers to Modify a Policy When Adopting It as Law. *Z. ges. Staatswiss. (JITE)*, March 1985, *141*(1), pp. 41–57.

Toma, Eugenia Froedge and Toma, Mark. Research Activities and Budget Allocations among Federal Reserve Banks: Reply. *Public Choice*, 1985, *45*(2), pp. 197–98.

Toma, Eugenia Froedge and Toma, Mark. Research Activities and Budget Allocations among Federal Reserve Banks. *Public Choice*, 1985, *45*(2), pp. 175–91.   [G: U.S.]

Turk, Herman and Zucker, Lynne G. Structural Bases of Minority Effects on Majority-supported Change. *Soc. Sci. Quart.*, June 1985, *66*(2), pp. 365–85.   [G: U.S.]

Uslaner, Eric M. and Conway, M. Margaret. The Responsible Congressional Electorate: Watergate, the Economy, and Vote Choice in 1974. *Amer. Polit. Sci. Rev.*, September 1985, *79*(3), pp. 788–803.   [G: U.S.]

Verbon, Harry A. A. and van Winden, Frans A. A. M. Public Pensions and Political Decision-making. *De Economist*, 1985, *133*(4), pp. 527–44.   [G: Netherlands]

Wade, L. L. Tocqueville and Public Choice. *Public Choice*, 1985, *47*(3), pp. 491–508.   [G: U.S.]

Wade, Robert. The Market for Public Office: Why the Indian State Is Not Better at Development. *World Devel.*, April 1985, *13*(4), pp. 467–97.

Weale, Albert. Why Are We Waiting? The Problem of Unresponsiveness in the Public Social Services. In *Klein, R. and O'Higgins, M., ed.*, 1985, pp. 150–65.   [G: U.K.]

Weir, Margaret and Skocpol, Theda. State Structures and the Possibilities for "Keynesian" Responses to the Great Depression in Sweden, Britain, and the United States. In *Evans, P. B.; Rueschemeyer, D. and Skocpol, T., eds.*, 1985, pp. 107–63.   [G: U.K.; U.S.; Sweden]

Wengert, Norman. Citizen Participation: Practice in Search of a Theory. In *Kury, C., ed.*, 1985, pp. 68–85.

White, Eugene Nelson. Voting for Costly Regulation: Evidence from Banking Referenda in Illinois, 1924. *Southern Econ. J.*, April 1985, *51*(4), pp. 1084–98.   [G: U.S.]

Wildavsky, Aaron. Budgets as Social Orders. In *Clark, T. N., ed.*, 1985, pp. 183–97.

Wildavsky, Aaron. The Logic of Public Sector Growth. In *Lane, J.-E., ed.*, 1985, pp. 231–70.

Williamson, John. International Agencies and the Peacock Critique. In *[Peacock, A.]*, 1985, pp. 167–75.

Wilson, L. S. The Socialization of Medical Insurance in Canada. *Can. J. Econ.*, May 1985, *18*(2), pp. 355–76.   [G: Canada]

Winch, Donald. Adam Smith's 'Enduring Particular Result': A Political and Cosmopolitan Perspective. In *Hont, I. and Ignatieff, M., eds.*, 1985, pp. 253–69.

Wright, John R. PACs, Contributions, and Roll Calls: An Organizational Perspective. *Amer. Polit. Sci. Rev.*, June 1985, *79*(2), pp. 400–414.   [G: U.S.]

Wright, John R. and Goldberg, Arthur S. Risk and Uncertainty as Factors in the Durability of Political Coalitions. *Amer. Polit. Sci. Rev.*, September 1985, *79*(3), pp. 704–18.

Zardkoohi, Asghar. On the Political Participation of the Firm in the Electoral Process. *Southern Econ. J.*, January 1985, *51*(3), pp. 804–17.   [G: U.S.]

Zeleny, Milan. Spontaneous Social Orders. In *Aida, S., et al.*, 1985, pp. 312–28.

026 Economics of Uncertainty and Information; Game Theory and Bargaining Theory

0260 General

Backus, David and Driffill, John. Rational Expectations and Policy Credibility Following a

Change in Regime. *Rev. Econ. Stud.*, April 1985, *52*(2), pp. 211–21.

Blazenko, George. The Design of an Optimal Insurance Policy: Note. *Amer. Econ. Rev.*, March 1985, *75*(1), pp. 253–55.

Crocker, Keith J. and Snow, Arthur. A Simple Tax Structure for Competitive Equilibrium and Redistribution in Insurance Markets with Asymmetric Information. *Southern Econ. J.*, April 1985, *51*(4), pp. 1142–50.

Davis, Lawrence H. Is the Symmetry Argument Valid? In *Campbell, R. and Sowden, L., eds.*, 1985, pp. 255–63.

Davis, Lawrence H. Prisoners, Paradox, and Rationality. In *Campbell, R. and Sowden, L., eds.*, 1985, pp. 45–59.

Gal-Or, Esther. Information Sharing in Oligopoly. *Econometrica*, March 1985, *53*(2), pp. 329–43.

Geroski, P. A.; Phlips, Louis and Ulph, A. Oligopoly, Competition and Welfare: Some Recent Developments. *J. Ind. Econ.*, June 1985, *33*(4), pp. 369–86.   [G: U.S.; U.K.]

Green, Jerry R. Differential Information, the Market and Incentive Compatibility. In *Arrow, K. J. and Honkapohja, S., eds.*, 1985, pp. 178–99.

Haltiwanger, John C. and Waldman, Michael. Rational Expectations and the Limits of Rationality: An Analysis of Heterogeneity. *Amer. Econ. Rev.*, June 1985, *75*(3), pp. 326–40.

Holmström, Bengt R. Differential Information, the Market and Incentive Compatability: Comment. In *Arrow, K. J. and Honkapohja, S., eds.*, 1985, pp. 200–212.

Lewis, David. Prisoners' Dilemma Is a Newcomb Problem. In *Campbell, R. and Sowden, L., eds.*, 1985, pp. 251–55.

Myerson, Roger B. Bayesian Equilibrium and Incentive-Compatibility: An Introduction. In *[Pazner, E.]*, 1985, pp. 229–59.

Palfrey, Thomas R. Uncertainty Resolution, Private Information Aggregation, and the Cournot Competitive Limit. *Rev. Econ. Stud.*, January 1985, *52*(1), pp. 69–83.

Riley, John G. Differential Information, the Market and Incentive Compatability: Comment. In *Arrow, K. J. and Honkapohja, S., eds.*, 1985, pp. 213–26.

Rubinstein, Ariel. A Bargaining Model with Incomplete Information about Time Preferences. *Econometrica*, September 1985, *53*(5), pp. 1151–72.

Sobel, Jordan Howard. Not Every Prisoner's Dilemma Is a Newcomb Problem. In *Campbell, R. and Sowden, L., eds.*, 1985, pp. 263–74.

Spatt, Chester S. and Sterbenz, Frederic P. Learning, Preemption, and the Degree of Rivalry. *Rand J. Econ.*, Spring 1985, *16*(1), pp. 84–92.

Wilson, Robert B. Efficient Trading. In *Feiwel, G. R., ed. (II)*, 1985, pp. 169–208.

0261 Theory of Uncertainty and Information

Admati, Anat R. A Noisy Rational Expectations Equilibrium for Multi-asset Securities Mar-

kets. *Econometrica*, May 1985, *53*(3), pp. 629–57.

Allen, Beth. The Existence of Fully Rational Expectations Approximate Equilibria with Noisy Price Observations. *J. Econ. Theory*, December 1985, *37*(2), pp. 213–53.

Andersen, Torben M. Price Dynamics under Imperfect Information. *J. Econ. Dynam. Control*, November 1985, *9*(3), pp. 339–61.

Anderson, Robert M. and Sonnenschein, Hugo. Rational Expectations Equilibrium with Econometric Models. *Rev. Econ. Stud.*, July 1985, *52*(3), pp. 359–69.

Appelbaum, Elie and Lim, Chin. Contestable Markets under Uncertainty. *Rand J. Econ.*, Spring 1985, *16*(1), pp. 28–40.

Arnott, Richard J. and Stiglitz, Joseph E. Labor Turnover, Wage Structures, and Moral Hazard: The Inefficiency of Competitive Markets. *J. Lab. Econ.*, October 1985, *3*(4), pp. 434–62.

Arrow, Kenneth J. Informational Structure of the Firm. *Amer. Econ. Rev.*, May 1985, *75*(2), pp. 303–07.

Arrow, Kenneth J. The Implications of Transaction Costs and Adjustment Lags in Health Insurance [Uncertainty and the Welfare Economics of Medical Care]. In *Arrow, K. J. (II)*, 1985, pp. 51–55.

Arrow, Kenneth J. Uncertainty and the Welfare Economics of Medical Care. In *Arrow, K. J. (II)*, 1985, pp. 15–50.

Arrow, Kenneth J.; Harris, Theodore E. and Marschak, Jacob. Optimal Inventory Policy. In *Arrow, K. J. (I)*, 1985, pp. 25–49.

Azariadis, Costas and Cooper, Russell. Predetermined Prices and the Allocation of Social Risks. *Quart. J. Econ.*, May 1985, *100*(2), pp. 495–518.

Bacharach, Michael. Some Extensions of a Claim of Aumann in an Axiomatic Model of Knowledge. *J. Econ. Theory*, October 1985, *37*(1), pp. 167–90.

Baron, David P. Regulation of Prices and Pollution under Incomplete Information. *J. Public Econ.*, November 1985, *28*(2), pp. 211–31.

Battalio, Raymond C.; Kagel, John H. and MacDonald, Don N. Animals' Choices over Uncertain Outcomes: Some Initial Experimental Results. *Amer. Econ. Rev.*, September 1985, *75*(4), pp. 597–613.

Bhandari, Jagdeep S. Informational Regimes, Economic Disturbances, and Exchange Rate Management. In *Bhandari, J. S., ed.*, 1985, pp. 126–53.

Bhattacharya, Sudipto and Pfleiderer, Paul. Delegated Portfolio Management. *J. Econ. Theory*, June 1985, *36*(1), pp. 1–25.

Bigelow, John P. Experts against Adverse Selection: A Note on the Existence of Equilibrium with Costly Appropriable Information. *J. Econ. Theory*, December 1985, *37*(2), pp. 379–93.

Bookstaber, Richard and Langsam, Joseph. Predictable Behavior: Comment [The Origin of Predictable Behavior]. *Amer. Econ. Rev.*, June 1985, *75*(3), pp. 571–75.

Boulding, Kenneth E. Learning by Simplifying Complexity: How to Turn Data into Knowledge. In *Aida, S., et al.*, 1985, pp. 25–34.

Boyer, Marcel and Dionne, Georges. Sécurité routière: responsabilité pour négligence et tarification. Road Safety: Liability for Negligence and Pricing. With English summary.) *Can. J. Econ.*, November 1985, *18*(4), pp. 814–30.

Bray, Margaret. Rational Expectations, Information and Asset Markets: An Introduction. *Oxford Econ. Pap.*, June 1985, *37*(2), pp. 161–95.

Briys, Eric P. and Eeckhoudt, Louis. Relative Risk Aversion in Comparative Statics: Comment. *Amer. Econ. Rev.*, March 1985, *75*(1), pp. 281–83.

Briys, Eric P. and Loubergé, Henri. On the Theory of Rational Insurance Purchasing: A Note. *J. Finance*, June 1985, *40*(2), pp. 577–81.

Brown, Murray and Wolfstetter, Elmar. A Micro Theory of Layoffs and Involuntary Unemployment. *Metroecon.*, February 1985, *37*(1), pp. 1–19.

Bucovetsky, S. Erratum: Price Dispersion and Stockpiling by Consumers. *Rev. Econ. Stud.*, January 1985, *52*(1), pp. 171.

Buttler, Günter and Heinlein, Werner. Untersuchungen zuer empirischen Evidenz ökonomischer Spekulationstheorien. (Empirical Evidence of Economic Theories of Speculation. With English summary.) *Jahr. Nationalökon. Statist.*, September 1985, *200*(5), pp. 486–507.

Caron-Salmona, Hélène. Equilibre sur le marché d'un bien en information imparfaite: une analyse de la littérature. (Commodity Market Equilibrium with Imperfect Information: A Survey of the Literature. With English summary.) *Écon. Appl.*, 1985, *38*(3/4), pp. 637–61.

Chang, Yang-Ming and Ehrlich, Issac. Insurance, Protection from Risk, and Risk-bearing. *Can. J. Econ.*, August 1985, *18*(3), pp. 574–86.

Chateauneuf, Alain. On the Existence of a Probability Measure Compatible with a Total Preorder on a Boolean Algebra. *J. Math. Econ.*, 1985, *14*(1), pp. 43–52.

Chatterjee, Kalyan. Disagreement in Bargaining: Models with Incomplete Information. In *Roth, A. E., ed.*, 1985, pp. 9–26.

Chavas, Jean-Paul. On the Theory of the Competitive Firm under Uncertainty When Initial Wealth Is Random. *Southern Econ. J.*, January 1985, *51*(3), pp. 818–27.

Choudhri, Ehsan U. and Ferris, J. Stephen. Wage and Price Contracts in a Macro Model with Information Costs. *Can. J. Econ.*, November 1985, *18*(4), pp. 766–83.

Clapp, John M. Quantity Competition in Spatial Markets with Incomplete Information. *Quart. J. Econ.*, May 1985, *100*(2), pp. 519–28.

Clark, Stephen A. Consistent Choice under Uncertainty. *J. Math. Econ.*, 1985, *14*(2), pp. 169–85.

Cochran, Mark J.; Robison, Lindon J. and Lodwick, Weldon. Improving the Efficiency of Stochastic Dominance Techniques Using Convex Set Stochastic Dominance. *Amer. J. Agr. Econ.*, May 1985, *67*(2), pp. 289–95.

[G: U.S.]

Collender, Robert N. and Zilberman, David. Land Allocation under Uncertainty for Alternative Specifications of Return Distributions. *Amer. J. Agr. Econ.*, November 1985, *67*(4), pp. 779–86.

Colson, Gerard. Theories of Risk and MCDM. In *Fandel, G. and Spronk, J., eds.*, 1985, pp. 171–96.

Cooper, Russell and Ross, Thomas W. Product Warranties and Double Moral Hazard. *Rand J. Econ.*, Spring 1985, *16*(1), pp. 103–13.

Costa de Beauregard, Olivier. Quanta and Relativity, Cosmos and Consciousness. In *Aida, S., et al.*, 1985, pp. 153–69.

Cowell, Frank A. The Economic Analysis of Tax Evasion. *Bull. Econ. Res.*, September 1985, *37*(3), pp. 163–93.

Crawford, Vincent P. Efficient and Durable Decision Rules: A Reformulation. *Econometrica*, July 1985, *53*(4), pp. 817–35.

Crémer, Jacques and McLean, Richard P. Optimal Selling Strategies under Uncertainty for a Discriminating Monopolist When Demands Are Interdependent. *Econometrica*, March 1985, *53*(2), pp. 345–61.

Crémer, Jacques and Riordan, Michael H. A Sequential Solution to the Public Goods Problem. *Econometrica*, January 1985, *53*(1), pp. 77–84.

Crocker, Keith J. and Snow, Arthur. The Efficiency of Competitive Equilibria in Insurance Markets with Asymmetric Information. *J. Public Econ.*, March 1985, *26*(2), pp. 207–19.

Danzin, André. The Pervasiveness of Complexity: Common Trends, New Paradigms, and Research Orientations. In *Aida, S., et al.*, 1985, pp. 69–80.

Denton, Frank T. The Effect of Professional Advice on the Stability of a Speculative Market. *J. Polit. Econ.*, October 1985, *93*(5), pp. 977–93.

Dionne, Georges and Lasserre, Pierre. Adverse Selection, Repeated Insurance Contracts and Announcement Strategy. *Rev. Econ. Stud.*, October 1985, *52*(4), pp. 719–23.

Drèze, Jacques H. (Uncertainty and) the Firm in General Equilibrium Theory. *Econ. J.*, Supplement 1985, *95*, pp. 1–20.

Duffie, Darrell and Shafer, Wayne. Equilibrium in Incomplete Markets: I—A Basic Model of Generic Existence. *J. Math. Econ.*, 1985, *14*(3), pp. 285–300.

Dupey, Pradeep and Kaneko, Mamoru. Information Patterns and Nash Equilibria in Extensive Games—II. *Math. Soc. Sci.*, December 1985, *10*(3), pp. 247–62.

Dye, Ronald A. Costly Contract Contingencies. *Int. Econ. Rev.*, February 1985, *26*(1), pp. 233–50.

Earl, Peter E. and Kay, Neil M. How Economists Can Accept Shackle's Critique on Economic Doctrines without Arguing Themselves out of Their Jobs. *J. Econ. Stud.*, 1985, *12*(1/2), pp. 34–48.

Eckstein, Zvi; Eichenbaum, Martin S. and Peled, Dan. The Distribution of Wealth and Welfare in the Presence of Incomplete Annuity Markets. *Quart. J. Econ.*, August 1985, *100*(3), pp. 789–806.

Eckstein, Zvi; Eichenbaum, Martin S. and Peled, Dan. Uncertain Lifetimes and the Welfare Enhancing Properties of Annuity Markets and Social Security. *J. Public Econ.*, April 1985, *26*(3), pp. 303–26.

Edmonds, James A. and Reilly, John. Time and Uncertainty: Analytic Paradigms and Policy Requirements. In *van Gool, W. and Bruggink, J. J. C., eds.*, 1985, pp. 287–313.

Eeckhoudt, Louis; Lebrun, T. and Sailly, J. C. Risk-aversion and Physicians' Medical Decision-making. *J. Health Econ.*, September 1985, *4*(3), pp. 273–81.

Eells, Ellery. Causality, Decision, and Newcomb's Paradox. In *Campbell, R. and Sowden, L., eds.*, 1985, pp. 183–213.

Endres, Alfred. Tie-in Financing and Pragmatic Price Discrimination. *Metroecon.*, February 1985, *37*(1), pp. 119–33.

Epstein, Larry G. Decreasing Risk Aversion and Mean-Variance Analysis. *Econometrica*, July 1985, *53*(4), pp. 945–61.

Estrin, Saul and Holmes, Peter. Uncertainty, Efficiency, and Economic Planning in Keynesian Economics. *J. Post Keynesian Econ.*, Summer 1985, *7*(4), pp. 463–73.

Farmer, Roger E. A. Implicit Contracts with Asymmetric Information and Bankruptcy: The Effect of Interest Rates on Layoffs. *Rev. Econ. Stud.*, July 1985, *52*(3), pp. 427–42. [G: U.S.]

Farrell, Joseph and Saloner, Garth. Standardization, Compatability, and Innovation. *Rand J. Econ.*, Spring 1985, *16*(1), pp. 70–83.

Feinstein, Jonathan S.; Block, Michael K. and Nold, Frederick C. Asymmetric Information and Collusive Behavior in Auction Markets. *Amer. Econ. Rev.*, June 1985, *75*(3), pp. 441–60.

Feldman, David and Tower, Edward. Errata: Profitable Destabilizing Speculation as Intertemporal Price Discrimination. *Amer. Econ.*, Spring 1985, *29*(1), pp. 84.

Feldman, Mark and Gilles, Christian. An Expository Note on Individual Risk without Aggregate Uncertainty. *J. Econ. Theory*, February 1985, *35*(1), pp. 26–32.

Fellingham, John C.; Newman, D. Paul and Suh, Yoon S. Contracts without Memory in Multiperiod Agency Models. *J. Econ. Theory*, December 1985, *37*(2), pp. 340–55.

Ferri, Giovanni and Jafarey, Saqib. Banking Crises and Welfare Implications of Foreign Lending under Informationally Limited Spatial Horizons. *Econ. Notes*, 1985, (3), pp. 121–33.

Fishburn, Peter C. Nontransitive Preference Theory and the Preference Reversal Phenomenon. *Rivista Int. Sci. Econ. Com.*, January 1985, *32*(1), pp. 39–50.

Florescu, Gabriela. Multicriterial Decision Making under Risk Modelled on the Basis of the Fuzzy Set Theory. *Econ. Computat. Cybern. Stud. Res.*, 1985, *20*(1), pp. 69–72.

Ford, J. L. Shackle's Theory of Decision Making under Uncertainty: Synopsis and Brief Appraisal. *J. Econ. Stud.*, 1985, *12*(1/2), pp. 59–69.

Fraser, R. W. Commodity Taxes under Uncertainty. *J. Public Econ.*, October 1985, *28*(1), pp. 127–34.

Freixas, Xavier; Guesnerie, Roger and Tirole, Jean. Planning under Incomplete Information and the Ratchet Effect. *Rev. Econ. Stud.*, April 1985, *52*(2), pp. 173–91.

French, George. Interest Rate, Demand and Input Price Uncertainty and the Value of Firms. *J. Econ. Dynam. Control*, December 1985, *9*(4), pp. 457–76.

Fudenberg, Drew; Levine, David K. and Tirole, Jean. Infinite-Horizon Models of Bargaining with One-Sided Incomplete Information. In *Roth, A. E., ed.*, 1985, pp. 73–98.

Fudenberg, Drew and Tirole, Jean. Preemption and Rent Equilization in the Adoption of New Technology. *Rev. Econ. Stud.*, July 1985, *52*(3), pp. 383–401.

Gale, Douglas and Hellwig, Martin F. Incentive-Compatible Debt Contracts: The One-Period Problem. *Rev. Econ. Stud.*, October 1985, *52*(4), pp. 647–63.

Gatignon, Hubert and Robertson, Thomas S. A Propositional Inventory for New Diffusion Research. *J. Cons. Res.*, March 1985, *11*(4), pp. 849–67.

Gibbard, Allan and Harper, William L. Counterfactuals and Two Kinds of Expected Utility. In *Campbell, R. and Sowden, L., eds.*, 1985, pp. 133–58.

Gilad, B.; Kaish, S. and Loeb, Peter D. A Theory of Surprise and Business Failure. *J. Behav. Econ.*, Winter 1985, *14*, pp. 35–55.

Glick, Reuven and Wihlborg, Clas. Price Determination in a Competitive Industry with Costly Information and a Production Lag. *Rand J. Econ.*, Spring 1985, *16*(1), pp. 127–40.

Gottfries, Nils. Multiple Perfect Foresight Equilibriums and Convergence of Learning Processes. *J. Money, Credit, Banking*, February 1985, *17*(1), pp. 111–17.

Gould, John P. and Verrecchia, Robert E. The Information Content of Specialist Pricing. *J. Polit. Econ.*, February 1985, *93*(1), pp. 66–83.

Grinblatt, Mark S. and Ross, Stephen A. Market Power in a Securities Market with Endogenous Information. *Quart. J. Econ.*, November 1985, *100*(4), pp. 1143–67.

Hahn, Frank. Uncertainty and the Cobweb. In *Hahn, F.*, 1985, pp. 210–28.

Hänchen, Thomas and von Ungern-Sternberg, Thomas. Information Costs, Intermediation and Equilibrium Price. *Economica*, November 1985, *52*(208), pp. 407–19.

Harris, Milton and Townsend, Robert M. Allocation Mechanisms, Asymmetric Information and the 'Revelation Principle.' In *Feiwel, G. R., ed. (II)*, 1985, pp. 379–94.

Heiner, Ronald A. Origin of Predictable Behavior: Further Modeling and Applications. *Amer. Econ. Rev.*, May 1985, 75(2), pp. 391–96.

Heiner, Ronald A. Predictable Behavior: Reply [The Origin of Predictable Behavior]. *Amer. Econ. Rev.*, June 1985, 75(3), pp. 579–85.

Helms, L. Jay. Expected Consumer's Surplus and the Welfare Effects of Price Stabilization. *Int. Econ. Rev.*, October 1985, 26(3), pp. 603–17.

Hey, John D. A Dynamic Model of the Competitive Firm with a Forward Market. *J. Econ. Stud.*, 1985, 12(3), pp. 21–35.

Hey, John D. Relative Risk Aversion in Comparative Statics: Comment. *Amer. Econ. Rev.*, March 1985, 75(1), pp. 284–85.

Hey, John D. The Possibility of Possibility. *J. Econ. Stud.*, 1985, 12(1/2), pp. 70–88.

Hogarth, Robin M. and Kunreuther, Howard. Ambiguity and Insurance Decisions. *Amer. Econ. Rev.*, May 1985, 75(2), pp. 386–90.
[G: U.S.]

Holmström, Bengt R. The Provision of Services in a Market Economy. In *Inman, R. P., ed.*, 1985, pp. 183–213.

Honda, Yuzo. Downside Risk and the Competitive Firm. *Metroecon.*, June 1985, 37(2), pp. 231–40.

Horgan, Terence. Counterfactuals and Newcomb's Problem. In *Campbell, R. and Sowden, L., eds.*, 1985, pp. 159–82.

Horgan, Terence. Newcomb's Problem: A Stalemate. In *Campbell, R. and Sowden, L., eds.*, 1985, pp. 223–34.

Hrnčíř, Miroslav. Central Regulation and Parametricity of Prices. *Czech. Econ. Pap.*, 1985, 23, pp. 7–38.

Huang, Chi-fu. Information Structure and Equilibrium Asset Prices. *J. Econ. Theory*, February 1985, 35(1), pp. 33–71.

Huang, Chi-fu. Information Structures and Viable Price Systems. *J. Math. Econ.*, 1985, 14(3), pp. 215–40.

Hurwicz, Leonid. Information and Incentives in Designing Non-wasteful Resource Allocation Systems. In *Feiwel, G. R., ed. (II)*, 1985, pp. 125–68.

Ireland, Norman J. Product Diversity and Monopolistic Competition under Uncertainty. *J. Ind. Econ.*, June 1985, 33(4), pp. 501–13.

Jackson, Frank and Pargetter, Robert. Where the Tickle Defense Goes Wrong. In *Campbell, R. and Sowden, L., eds.*, 1985, pp. 214–19.

Janko, Wolfgang. Searching for the Best Offer when the Distribution of Offers Is Truly Unknown. In *[Menges, G.]*, 1985, pp. 113–32.

Johnsen, Thore H. and Donaldson, John B. The Structure of Intertemporal Preferences under Uncertainty and Time Consistent Plans. *Econometrica*, November 1985, 53(6), pp. 1451–58.

Jordan, J. S. Learning Rational Expectations: The Finite State Case. *J. Econ. Theory*, August 1985, 36(2), pp. 257–76.

Kahn, Charles M. and Scheinkman, José A. Optimal Employment Contracts with Bankruptcy Constraints. *J. Econ. Theory*, April 1985, 35(2), pp. 343–65.

Karni, Edi. Increasing Risk with State-Dependent Preferences. *J. Econ. Theory*, February 1985, 35(1), pp. 172–77.

Katz, Eliakim. Relative Risk Aversion in Comparative Statics: Reply. *Amer. Econ. Rev.*, March 1985, 75(1), pp. 286–87.

Kim, Jae-Cheol. The Market for "Lemons" Reconsidered: A Model of the Used Car Market with Asymmetric Information. *Amer. Econ. Rev.*, September 1985, 75(4), pp. 836–43.

Kirzner, Israel M. Uncertainty, Discovery, and Human Action: A Study of the Entrepreneurial Profile in the Misesian System. In *Kirzner, I. M.*, 1985, pp. 40–67.

Klir, George J. The Many Faces of Complexity. In *Aida, S., et al.*, 1985, pp. 81–98.

Knez, Peter; Smith, Vernon L. and Williams, Arlington W. Individual Rationality, Market Rationality, and Value Estimation. *Amer. Econ. Rev.*, May 1985, 75(2), pp. 397–402.

Kumar, K. Ravi and Satterthwaite, Mark A. Monopolistic Competition, Aggregation of Competitive Information, and the Amount of Product Differentiation. *J. Econ. Theory*, October 1985, 37(1), pp. 32–54.

Kunreuther, Howard and Pauly, Mark V. Market Equilibrium with Private Knowledge: An Insurance Example. *J. Public Econ.*, April 1985, 26(3), pp. 269–88.

Kunreuther, Howard; Sanderson, Warren and Vetschera, Rudolf. A Behavioral Model of the Adoption of Protective Activities. *J. Econ. Behav. Organ.*, March 1985, 6(1), pp. 1–15.
[G: U.S.]

Kyle, Albert S. Continuous Auctions and Insider Trading. *Econometrica*, November 1985, 53(6), pp. 1315–35.

Laffond, Gilbert and Lesourne, Jacques. Market Dynamics with Search Processes and Information Costs. *Écon. Appl.*, 1985, 38(3/4), pp. 739–65.

Laffont, Jean-Jacques. On the Welfare Analysis of Rational Expectations Equilibria with Asymmetric Information. *Econometrica*, January 1985, 53(1), pp. 1–29.

Laitner, John P. Stationary Equilibrium Transition Rules for an Overlapping Generations Model with Uncertainty. *J. Econ. Theory*, February 1985, 35(1), pp. 83–108.

Lambert, David K. and McCarl, Bruce A. Risk Modeling Using Direct Solution of Nonlinear Approximations of the Utility Function. *Amer. J. Agr. Econ.*, November 1985, 67(4), pp. 846–52.

Landsberger, Michael and Meilijson, Isaac. Intertemporal Price Discrimination and Sales Strategy under Incomplete Information. *Rand J. Econ.*, Autumn 1985, 16(3), pp. 424–30.

Lawson, Tony. Uncertainty and Economic Analysis. *Econ. J.*, December 1985, 95(380), pp. 909–27.

Le Moigne, Jean-Louis. The Intelligence of Complexity. In *Aida, S., et al.*, 1985, pp. 35–61.

Leonard, Herman B. and Zeckhauser, Richard J. Financial Risk and the Burden of Contracts.

Amer. Econ. Rev., May 1985, *75*(2), pp. 375–80.

Lewis, Barry L. and Bell, Jan. Decisions Involving Sequential Events: Replications and Extensions. *J. Acc. Res.*, Spring 1985, *23*(1), pp. 228–39. [G: U.S.]

Li, Lode. Cournot Oligopoly with Information Sharing. *Rand J. Econ.*, Winter 1985, *16*(4), pp. 521–36.

Luhmann, Niklas. Complexity and Meaning. In *Aida, S., et al.*, 1985, pp. 99–104.

Machina, Mark J. Stochastic Choice Functions Generated from Deterministic Preferences over Lotteries. *Econ. J.*, September 1985, *95*(379), pp. 575–94.

Maskin, Eric S. and Riley, John G. Auction Theory with Private Values. *Amer. Econ. Rev.*, May 1985, *75*(2), pp. 150–55.

Masten, Scott E. and Crocker, Keith J. Efficient Adaptation in Long-term Contracts: Take-or-Pay Provisions for Natural Gas. *Amer. Econ. Rev.*, December 1985, *75*(5), pp. 1083–93. [G: U.S.]

Matthews, Steven and Postlewaite, Andrew. Quality Testing and Disclosure. *Rand J. Econ.*, Autumn 1985, *16*(3), pp. 328–40.

Mazón, Cristina. Un modelo de información imperfecta en el que se envían anuncios por correo. (With English summary.) *Revista Española Econ.*, 1985, *2*(1), pp. 35–48.

McCain, Roger A. Economic Planning for Market Economies: The Optimality of Planning in an Economy with Uncertainty and Asymmetrical Information. *Econ. Modelling*, October 1985, *2*(4), pp. 317–23.

McKelvey, Richard D. and Ordeshook, Peter C. Elections with Limited Information: A Fulfilled Expectations Model Using Contemporaneous Poll and Endorsement Data as Information Sources. *J. Econ. Theory*, June 1985, *36*(1), pp. 55–85.

Mendelson, Haim. Random Competitive Exchange: Price Distributions and Gain from Trade. *J. Econ. Theory*, December 1985, *37*(2), pp. 254–80.

Meyer, Jack and Ormiston, Michael B. Strong Increases in Risk and Their Comparative Statics. *Int. Econ. Rev.*, June 1985, *26*(2), pp. 425–37.

Miller, Ross M. and Plott, Charles R. Product Quality Signaling in Experimental Markets. *Econometrica*, July 1985, *53*(4), pp. 837–72.

Millon, Marcia H. and Thakor, Anjan V. Moral Hazard and Information Sharing: A Model of Financial Information Gathering Agencies. *J. Finance*, December 1985, *40*(5), pp. 1403–22.

Millsaps, Steven W. and Ott, Mack. Risk Aversion, Risk Sharing, and Joint Bidding: A Study of Outer Continental Shelf Petroleum Auctions. *Land Econ.*, November 1985, *61*(4), pp. 372–86. [G: U.S.]

Moore, John. Optimal Labour Contracts When Workers Have a Variety of Privately Observed Reservation Wages. *Rev. Econ. Stud.*, January 1985, *52*(1), pp. 37–67.

Morgan, Peter B. Distributions of the Duration and Value of Job Search with Learning. *Econometrica*, September 1985, *53*(5), pp. 1199–1232.

Morgan, Peter B. and Manning, Richard. Optimal Search. *Econometrica*, July 1985, *53*(4), pp. 923–44.

Morin, Edgar. On the Definition of Complexity. In *Aida, S., et al.*, 1985, pp. 62–68.

Moussa, Hassouna. An Alternative Solution to the Moral Hazard Problem and Some Sufficient Conditions for Its Absence. *Rech. Écon. Louvain*, 1985, *51*(2), pp. 181–94.

Moussa, Hassouna and Murota, Takeshi. Social Value of Public Information Re-examined. *J. Econ. Behav. Organ.*, September 1985, *6*(3), pp. 249–74.

Mushkat, Miron. Planning under Uncertainty in the Public Domain: A Critique of Conventional Approaches. *Rivista Int. Sci. Econ. Com.*, July–Aug. 1985, *32*(7–8), pp. 661–77.

Myerson, Roger B. Analysis of Two Bargaining Problems with Incomplete Information. In *Roth, A. E., ed.*, 1985, pp. 115–47.

Nielsen, Lars Tyge. Attractive Compounds of Unattractive Investments and Gambles. *Scand. J. Econ.*, 1985, *87*(3), pp. 463–73.

Nozick, Robert. Newcomb's Problem and Two Principles of Choice. In *Campbell, R. and Sowden, L., eds.*, 1985, pp. 107–33.

O'Hara, Maureen. Technology and Hedging Behavior: A Proof of Hicks' Conjecture. *Amer. Econ. Rev.*, December 1985, *75*(5), pp. 1186–90.

Orléan, André. Incertitude et paradoxe. (Uncertainty and Paradox. With English summary.) *Écon. Appl.*, 1985, *38*(1), pp. 133–53.

Palfrey, Thomas R. and Spatt, Chester S. Repeated Insurance Contracts and Learning. *Rand J. Econ.*, Autumn 1985, *16*(3), pp. 356–67.

Ploman, Edward W. The Science and Praxis of Complexity: Introduction. In *Aida, S., et al.*, 1985, pp. 7–22.

Postlewaite, Andrew. The Provision of Services in a Market Economy: Comment. In *Inman, R. P., ed.*, 1985, pp. 214–16.

Pribram, Karl H. Complexity and Causality. In *Aida, S., et al.*, 1985, pp. 119–32.

Prigogine, Ilya. New Perspectives on Complexity. In *Aida, S., et al.*, 1985, pp. 107–18.

Quinzii, Martine and Rochet, Jean-Charles. Multidimensional Signalling. *J. Math. Econ.*, 1985, *14*(3), pp. 261–84.

Ray, Dipankar. Can the Friedman–Savage Case Be Due to the Cost of Information? *Math. Soc. Sci.*, June 1985, *9*(3), pp. 275–85.

Ricci, Paolo F.; Crouch, Edmund C. and Cirillo, Mario C. Technological Risk Assessment: Measures and Methods. In *Ricci, P. F., ed.*, 1985, pp. 373–407.

Riley, John G. Competition with Hidden Knowledge. *J. Polit. Econ.*, October 1985, *93*(5), pp. 958–76.

Riordan, Michael H. Imperfect Information and Dynamic Conjectural Variations. *Rand J. Econ.*, Spring 1985, *16*(1), pp. 41–50.

Rob, Rafael. Equilibrium Price Distributions. *Rev. Econ. Stud.*, July 1985, *52*(3), pp. 487–504.

Roberts, Kevin. Cartel Behaviour and Adverse Selection. *J. Ind. Econ.*, June 1985, *33*(4), pp. 401–13.

Rochet, Jean-Charles. Bilateral Monopoly with Imperfect Information. *J. Econ. Theory*, August 1985, *36*(2), pp. 214–36.

Rochet, Jean-Charles. The Taxation Principle and Multi-time Hamilton–Jacobi Equations. *J. Math. Econ.*, 1985, *14*(2), pp. 113–28.

Rochet, Jean-Charles. Vers une tarification équitable de l'assurance? (Towards Equitable Insurance Tariffs. With English summary.) *L'Actual. Econ.*, December 1985, *61*(4), pp. 453–71.

Roe, Terry and Antonovitz, Frances. A Producer's Willingness to Pay for Information under Price Uncertainty: Theory and Application. *Southern Econ. J.*, October 1985, *52*(2), pp. 382–91. **[G: U.S.]**

Roemer, John E. Rationalizing Revolutionary Ideology. *Econometrica*, January 1985, *53*(1), pp. 85–108.

Rogerson, William P. The First-Order Approach to Principal–Agent Problems. *Econometrica*, November 1985, *53*(6), pp. 1357–67.

Rosen, Sherwin. Implicit Contracts: A Survey. *J. Econ. Lit.*, September 1985, *23*(3), pp. 1144–75.

Rousseau, J. M. Risque croissant et endettement. (Growing Risk and Indebtedness. With English summary.) *Écon. Soc.*, September 1985, *19*(9), pp. 53–79.

Rubinstein, Ariel. Choice of Conjectures in a Bargaining Game with Incomplete Information. In *Roth, A. E., ed.*, 1985, pp. 99–114.

Saari, Donald G. The Representation Problem and the Efficiency of the Price Mechanism. *J. Math. Econ.*, 1985, *14*(2), pp. 135–67.

Sakai, Yasuhiro. The Value of Information in a Simple Duopoly Model. *J. Econ. Theory*, June 1985, *36*(1), pp. 36–54.

Saloner, Garth. Old Boy Networks as Screening Mechanisms. *J. Lab. Econ.*, July 1985, *3*(3), pp. 255–67.

Sandler, Todd; Sterbenz, Frederic P. and Tschirhart, John. Uncertainty and Clubs. *Economica*, November 1985, *52*(208), pp. 467–77.

Scarsini, Marco. Stochastic Dominance and Regret. *Giorn. Econ.*, Mar.-Apr. 1985, *44*(3–4), pp. 209–12.

Scarsini, Marco. Stochastic Dominance with Pairwise Risk Aversion. *J. Math. Econ.*, 1985, *14*(2), pp. 187–201.

Schlesinger, Harris. Choosing a Deductible for Insurance Contracts: Best or Worst Insurance Policy? *J. Risk Ins.*, September 1985, *52*(3), pp. 522–27.

Schlesinger, Harris and Doherty, Neil A. Incomplete Markets for Insurance: An Overview. *J. Risk Ins.*, September 1985, *52*(3), pp. 402–23.

Schwartz, Alan and Wilde, Louis L. Product Quality and Imperfect Information. *Rev. Econ. Stud.*, April 1985, *52*(2), pp. 251–62.

Singh, Nirvikar. Monitoring and Hierarchies: The Marginal Value of Information in a Principal–Agent Model. *J. Polit. Econ.*, June 1985, *93*(3), pp. 599–609.

Smith, Michael L. and Witt, Robert C. An Economic Analysis of Retroactive Liability Insurance. *J. Risk Ins.*, September 1985, *52*(3), pp. 379–401. **[G: U.S.]**

Sobel, Jordan Howard. Utility Maximizers in Iterated Prisoner's Dilemmas. In *Campbell, R. and Sowden, L., eds.*, 1985, pp. 306–19.

Stahl, Dale O., II. Bankruptcies in Temporary Equilibrium Forward Markets with and without Institutional Restrictions. *Rev. Econ. Stud.*, July 1985, *52*(3), pp. 459–71.

Stiglitz, Joseph E. Information and Economic Analysis: A Perspective. *Econ. J.*, Supplement 1985, *95*, pp. 21–41.

Stoica, M. and Raţiu Suciu, Camelia. The Relation between Heuristics and the Fuzzy Sets Theory. *Econ. Computat. Cybern. Stud. Res.*, 1985, *20*(4), pp. 19–22.

Strand, Jon. Work Effort and Search Subsidies with Long-run Equilibrium Contracts. *Europ. Econ. Rev.*, December 1985, *29*(3), pp. 387–406.

Takeshima, Masao. Optimal Labour Contract under Asymmetric Information. *Keio Econ. Stud.*, 1985, *22*(1), pp. 65–85.

Uecker, Wilfred C.; Schepanski, Albert and Shin, Joon. Toward a Positive Theory of Information Evaluation: Relevant Tests of Competing Models in a Principal-Agency Setting. *Accounting Rev.*, July 1985, *60*(3), pp. 430–57.

Vasiliauskas, A. A. The Quantitative Evaluation of the Properties of Economic Information. *Matekon*, Fall 1985, *22*(1), pp. 68–90.

Veljanovski, Cento G. Organized Futures Contracting. *Int. Rev. Law Econ.*, June 1985, *5*(1), pp. 25–38.

Viscusi, W. Kip. Are Individuals Bayesian Decision Makers? *Amer. Econ. Rev.*, May 1985, *75*(2), pp. 381–85.

Viscusi, W. Kip. Environmental Policy Choice with an Uncertain Chance of Irreversibility. *J. Environ. Econ. Manage.*, March 1985, *12*(1), pp. 28–44.

Voge, Jean. Management of Complexity. In *Aida, S., et al.*, 1985, pp. 298–311.

Wilde, Keith D.; LeBaron, Allen D. and Israelsen, L. Dwight. Knowledge, Uncertainty, and Behavior. *Amer. Econ. Rev.*, May 1985, *75*(2), pp. 403–08.

Williams, Steven R. Necessary and Sufficient Conditions for the Existence of a Locally Stable Message Process. *J. Econ. Theory*, February 1985, *35*(1), pp. 127–54.

Wilson, Robert B. Incentive Efficiency of Double Auctions. *Econometrica*, September 1985, *53*(5), pp. 1101–15.

Wolfstetter, Elmar. Optimale Arbeitsverträge bei asymmetrischer Information: Ein Beitrag zur Theorie der Arbeitslosigkeit. (With English summary.) *Z. Wirtschaft. Sozialwissen.*, 1985, *105*(4), pp. 433–58.

Yu, Eden S. H. and Ingene, Charles A. Resource Allocation with Factor Price Differentials under Price Uncertainty. *Southern Econ. J.*, October 1985, *52*(2), pp. 460–70.

0262 Game Theory and Bargaining Theory

Aghion, Philippe. On the Generic Inefficiency of Differentiable Market Games. *J. Econ. Theory*, October 1985, *37*(1), pp. 126–46.

Aiyagari, S. Rao and Riezman, Raymond G. Embargoes and Supply Shocks in a Market with a Dominant Seller. In *Sargent, T. J., ed.*, 1985, pp. 14–40.

Aoki, Masahiko. Dynamics of Unemployment, Vacancies and Real Wages with Trade Unions: Comment. *Scand. J. Econ.*, 1985, *87*(2), pp. 404–07.

Arvan, Lanny. Some Examples of Dynamic Cournot Duopoly with Inventory. *Rand J. Econ.*, Winter 1985, *16*(4), pp. 569–78.

d'Aspremont, Claude and Jacquemin, Alexis. Measuring the Power to Monopolize: A Simple-Game-Theoretic Approach. *Europ. Econ. Rev.*, February 1985, *27*(1), pp. 57–74.

Aumann, Robert J. An Axiomatization of the Non-transferable Utility Value. *Econometrica*, May 1985, *53*(3), pp. 599–612.

Aumann, Robert J. On the Non-transferable Utility Value: A Comment on the Roth–Shafer Examples [Values for Games without Side Payments: Some Difficulties with Current Concepts] [On the Existence and Interpretation of Value Allocations]. *Econometrica*, May 1985, *53*(3), pp. 667–77.

Aumann, Robert J. Repeated Games. In *Feiwel, G. R., ed. (II)*, 1985, pp. 209–42.

Aumann, Robert J. What Is Game Theory Trying to Accomplish? In *Arrow, K. J. and Honkapohja, S., eds.*, 1985, pp. 28–76.

Aumann, Robert J. and Maschler, Michael. Game Theoretic Analysis of a Bancruptcy Problem from the Talmud. *J. Econ. Theory*, August 1985, *36*(2), pp. 195–213. **[G: Israel]**

Başar, Tamer; Haurie, Alain and Ricci, Gianni. On the Dominance of Capitalists' Leadership in a 'Feedback-Stackelberg' Solution of a Differential Game Model of Capitalism. *J. Econ. Dynam. Control*, September 1985, *9*(1), pp. 101–25.

Başar, Tamer; Haurie, Alain and Ricci, Gianni. Errata [On the Dominance of Capitalists Leadership in a 'Feedback-Stackelberg' Solution of a Differential Game Model of Capitalism]. *J. Econ. Dynam. Control*, December 1985, *9*(4), pp. 493.

Bennett, Elaine. Endogenous vs. Exogenous Coalition Formation. *Écon. Appl.*, 1985, *38*(3/4), pp. 611–35.

Benoit, Jean-Pierre and Krishna, Vijay. Finitely Repeated Games. *Econometrica*, July 1985, *53*(4), pp. 905–22.

Bergstrom, Theodore C. and Varian, Hal R. When Are Nash Equilibria Independent of the Distribution of Agents' Characteristics? *Rev. Econ. Stud.*, October 1985, *52*(4), pp. 715–18.

Bergstrom, Theodore C. and Varian, Hal R. When Do Market Games Have Transferable

Utility? *J. Econ. Theory*, April 1985, *35*(2), pp. 222–33.

Binmore, K. G. Bargaining and Coalitions. In *Roth, A. E., ed.*, 1985, pp. 269–304.

Binmore, K. G. Equilibria in Extensive Games. *Econ. J.*, Supplement 1985, *95*, pp. 51–59.

Binmore, K. G.; Shaked, A. and Sutton, J. Testing Noncooperative Bargaining Theory: A Preliminary Study. *Amer. Econ. Rev.*, December 1985, *75*(5), pp. 1178–80.

Braden, John B. Uncertainty and Open Access: Implications from the Repeated Prisoners' Dilemma Game. *Amer. J. Agr. Econ.*, May 1985, *67*(2), pp. 356–59.

Brock, William A. and Scheinkman, José A. Price Setting Supergames with Capacity Constraints. *Rev. Econ. Stud.*, July 1985, *52*(3), pp. 371–82.

Bull, Clive and Schotter, Andrew. The Garbage Game, Inflation, and Incomes Policy. In *Maital, S. and Lipnowski, I., eds.*, 1985, pp. 121–40.

Campbell, Richmond. Paradoxes of Rationality and Cooperation: Prisoner's Dilemma and Newcomb's Problem: Background for the Uninitiated. In *Campbell, R. and Sowden, L., eds.*, 1985, pp. 3–41.

Canzoneri, Matthew B. and Gray, Jo Anna. Monetary Policy Games and the Consequences of Non-cooperative Behavior. *Int. Econ. Rev.*, October 1985, *26*(3), pp. 547–64.

Chatterjee, Kalyan. Disagreement in Bargaining: Models with Incomplete Information. In *Roth, A. E., ed.*, 1985, pp. 9–26.

Corcoran, William J. and Karels, Gordon V. Rent-seeking Behavior in the Long-run. *Public Choice*, 1985, *46*(3), pp. 227–46.

Cramton, Peter C. Sequential Bargaining Mechanisms. In *Roth, A. E., ed.*, 1985, pp. 149–79.

Crawford, Vincent P. Learning Behavior and Mixed-Strategy Nash Equilibria. *J. Econ. Behav. Organ.*, March 1985, *6*(1), pp. 69–78.

Crawford, Vincent P. The Role of Arbitration and the Theory of Incentives. In *Roth, A. E., ed.*, 1985, pp. 363–90.

Crouch, Glen J. and Skowronski, Janislaw M. Identification of Stock and System Parameters in a Pareto Harvesting Game of Two Players. In *Batten, D. F. and Lesse, P. F., eds.*, 1985, pp. 105–16.

Davidson, Carl and Martin, Lawrence W. General Equilibrium Tax Incidence under Imperfect Competition: A Quantity-setting Supergame Analysis. *J. Polit. Econ.*, December 1985, *93*(6), pp. 1212–23.

De Bruyne, Guido. Union Militancy, External Shocks and the Accommodation Dilemma: Comment. *Scand. J. Econ.*, 1985, *87*(2), pp. 352–54.

Demange, Gabrielle and Gale, David. The Strategy Structure of Two-sided Matching Markets. *Econometrica*, July 1985, *53*(4), pp. 873–88.

Dow, Gregory K. Internal Bargaining and Strategic Innovation in the Theory of the Firm. *J. Econ. Behav. Organ.*, September 1985, *6*(3), pp. 301–20.

Driessen, T. S. H. and Tijs, Stef H. The Cost Gap Method and Other Cost Allocation Methods for Multipurpose Water Projects. *Water Resources Res.*, October 1985, *21*(10), pp. 1469–75.

Driffill, John. Macroeconomic Stabilization Policy and Trade Union Behaviour as a Repeated Game. *Scand. J. Econ.*, 1985, *87*(2), pp. 300–326.

Dumitrescu, T. Some Properties of the Equilibrium Points for *N*-Person Games. *Econ. Computat. Cybern. Stud. Res.*, 1985, *20*(2), pp. 15–19.

Dupey, Pradeep and Kaneko, Mamoru. Information Patterns and Nash Equilibria in Extensive Games—II. *Math. Soc. Sci.*, December 1985, *10*(3), pp. 247–62.

Einy, Ezra. The Desirability Relation of Simple Games. *Math. Soc. Sci.*, October 1985, *10*(2), pp. 155–68.

Emmons, David W. and Scafuri, Allen J. Value Allocations: An Exposition. In *Aliprantis, C. D.; Burkinshaw, O. and Rothman, N. J., eds.*, 1985, pp. 55–78.

Fandel, Günter. Decision Concepts for Organisations. In *Fandel, G. and Spronk, J., eds.*, 1985, pp. 153–70.

Fandel, Günter. Game and Bargaining Solutions for Group Decision Problems. In *Grauer, M.; Thompson, M. and Wierzbicki, A. P., eds.*, 1985, pp. 187–201.

Fandel, Günter. On the Applicability of Game-Theoretic Bargaining Methods to a Wage Bargaining Problem. In *Fandel, G. and Spronk, J., eds.*, 1985, pp. 317 36.
[G: W. Germany]

Fischer, Stanley. Macroeconomic Stabilization Policy and Trade Union Behaviour as a Repeated Game: Comment. *Scand. J. Econ.*, 1985, *87*(2), pp. 327–31.

Fraysse, Jean and Moreaux, Michel. Collusive Equilibria in Oligopolies with Finite Lives. *Europ. Econ. Rev.*, February 1985, *27*(1), pp. 45–55.

Friedman, James W. Cooperative Equilibria in Finite Horizon Noncooperative Supergames. *J. Econ. Theory*, April 1985, *35*(2), pp. 390–98.

Fudenberg, Drew; Levine, David K. and Tirole, Jean. Infinite-Horizon Models of Bargaining with One-Sided Incomplete Information. In *Roth, A. E., ed.*, 1985, pp. 73–98.

Gal-Or, Esther. First Mover and Second Mover Advantages. *Int. Econ. Rev.*, October 1985, *26*(3), pp. 649–53.

Gallini, Nancy T. and Winter, Ralph A. Licensing in the Theory of Innovation. *Rand J. Econ.*, Summer 1985, *16*(2), pp. 237–52.

Gardner, R. Rationing, Bargaining, and Voting in 2-Sided Markets? *Soc. Choice Welfare*, May 1985, *2*(1), pp. 39–48.

Gauthier, David. Bargaining and Justice. In *Paul, E. F.; Paul, J. and Miller, F. D., Jr., eds.*, 1985, pp. 29–47.

Graham, John L. Cross-cultural Marketing Negotiations: A Laboratory Experiment. *Marketing Sci.*, Spring 1985, *4*(2), pp. 130–46.

Güth, Werner. An Extensive Game Approach to Modelling the Nuclear Deterrence Debate. *Z. ges. Staatswiss. (JITE)*, December 1985, *141*(4), pp. 525–38.

Gylfason, Thorvaldur. Workers versus Government—Who Adjusts to Whom? Comment. *Scand. J. Econ.*, 1985, *87*(2), pp. 293–97.
[G: Norway; U.K.]

Hansen, Lars Peter; Epple, Dennis and Roberds, William. Linear-Quadratic Duopoly Models of Resource Depletion. In *Sargent, T. J., ed.*, 1985, pp. 101–42.

Harker, Patrick T. Investigating the Use of the Core as a Solution Concept in Spatial Price Equilibrium Games. In *Harker, P. T., ed.*, 1985, pp. 41–72.

Harris, Christopher J. A Characterisation of the Perfect Equilibria of Infinite Horizon Games. *J. Econ. Theory*, October 1985, *37*(1), pp. 99–125.

Harris, Christopher J. An Alternative Solution to Rubinstein's Model of Sequential Bargaining under Incomplete Information. *Econ. J.*, Supplement 1985, *95*, pp. 102–12.

Harris, Christopher J. Existence and Characterization of Perfect Equilibrium in Games of Perfect Information. *Econometrica*, May 1985, *53*(3), pp. 613–28.

Harris, Christopher J. and Vickers, John. Perfect Equilibrium in a Model of a Race. *Rev. Econ. Stud.*, April 1985, *52*(2), pp. 193–209.

Harrison, Glenn W. and McKee, Michael. Experimental Evaluation of the Coase Theorem. *J. Law Econ.*, October 1985, *28*(3), pp. 653–70.

Harstad, Ronald M. and Levin, Dan. A Class of Dominance Solvable Common-Value Auctions. *Rev. Econ. Stud.*, July 1985, *52*(3), pp. 525–28.

Hart, Sergiu. An Axiomatization of Harsanyi's Nontransferable Utility Solution. *Econometrica*, November 1985, *53*(6), pp. 1295–1313.

Hart, Sergiu. Axiomatic Approaches to Coalitional Bargaining. In *Roth, A. E., ed.*, 1985, pp. 305–19.

Hart, Sergiu. Nontransferable Utility Games and Markets: Some Examples and the Harsanyi Solution. *Econometrica*, November 1985, *53*(6), pp. 1445–50.

Hersoug, Tor. Workers versus Government—Who Adjusts to Whom? *Scand. J. Econ.*, 1985, *87*(2), pp. 270–92.
[G: Norway]

Isermann, Heinz. Interactive Group Decision Making by Coalitions. In *Grauer, M.; Thompson, M. and Wierzbicki, A. P., eds.*, 1985, pp. 202–11.

John, Kose and Nachman, David C. Risky Debt, Investment Incentives, and Reputation in a Sequential Equilibrium. *J. Finance*, July 1985, *40*(3), pp. 863–78.

Kalai, Ehud. Solutions to the Bargaining Problem. In *[Pazner, E.]*, 1985, pp. 77–105.

Kalai, Ehud and Samet, Dov. Monotonic Solutions to General Cooperative Games. *Econometrica*, March 1985, *53*(2), pp. 307–27.

Kalai, Ehud and Stanford, William. Conjectural Variations Strategies in Accelerated Cournot Games. *Int. J. Ind. Organ.*, June 1985, *3*(2), pp. 133–52.

Katz, Michael L. and Shapiro, Carl. On the Licensing of Innovations. *Rand J. Econ.*, Winter 1985, *16*(4), pp. 504–20.

Khan, M. Ali. On Extensions of the Cournot–Nash Theorem. In *Aliprantis, C. D.; Burkinshaw, O. and Rothman, N. J., eds.*, 1985, pp. 79–106.

Kleinberg, Norman L. and Weiss, Jeffrey H. Algebraic Structure of Games. *Math. Soc. Sci.*, February 1985, *9*(1), pp. 35–44.

Kruś, Lech. An Interactive Method for Decision Support in a Two-Person Game with an Example from Regional Planning. In *Grauer, M.; Thompson, M. and Wierzbicki, A. P., eds.*, 1985, pp. 336–43.

Kurz, Mordecai. Cooperative Oligopoly Equilibrium. *Europ. Econ. Rev.*, February 1985, *27*(1), pp. 3–24.

Laskar, Daniel. Foreign Exchange Intervention Policies in a Two Country World: Optimum and Non-cooperative Equilibrium. *Economia (Portugal)*, January 1985, *9*(1), pp. 105–58.

Lensberg, Terje. Bargaining and Fair Allocation. In *Young, H. P., ed.*, 1985, pp. 101–16.

Lewis, Alain A. Hyperfinite von Neumann Games. *Math. Soc. Sci.*, April 1985, *9*(2), pp. 189–94.

Lewis, Alain A. Loeb-measurable Solutions to *Finite Games. *Math. Soc. Sci.*, June 1985, *9*(3), pp. 197–247.

Lipnowski, Irwin and Maital, Shlomo. Hanging Together or Separately: A Game-Theoretic Approach to Macroeconomic Conflict. In *Maital, S. and Lipnowski, I., eds.*, 1985, pp. 39–94.

Lipton, Michael. The Prisoners' Dilemma and Coase's Theorem: A Case for Democracy in Less Developed Countries? In *Matthews, R. C. O., ed.*, 1985, pp. 49–109.

MacLeod, W. Bentley. A Theory of Conscious Parallelism. *Europ. Econ. Rev.*, February 1985, *27*(1), pp. 25–44.

MacLeod, W. Bentley. On Adjustment Costs and the Stability of Equilibria. *Rev. Econ. Stud.*, October 1985, *52*(4), pp. 575–91.

Maskin, Eric S. The Theory of Implementation in Nash Equilibrium: A Survey. In *[Pazner, E.]*, 1985, pp. 173–204.

McClennen, Edward F. Prisoner's Dilemma and Resolute Choice. In *Campbell, R. and Sowden, L., eds.*, 1985, pp. 94–104.

McLennan, Andrew. Justifiable Beliefs in Sequential Equilibrium. *Econometrica*, July 1985, *53*(4), pp. 889–904.

Mirman, Leonard J.; Tauman, Yair and Zang, Israel. On the Use of Game-Theoretic Concepts in Cost Accounting. In *Young, H. P., ed.*, 1985, pp. 55–77.

Mookherjee, Dilip. Counterintuitive Results in Simultaneous-Move Incomplete Information Games: Some Examples. *Int. Econ. Rev.*, October 1985, *26*(3), pp. 655–59.

Myerson, Roger B. Analysis of Two Bargaining Problems with Incomplete Information. In *Roth, A. E., ed.*, 1985, pp. 115–47.

Nozick, Robert. Interpersonal Utility Theory. *Soc. Choice Welfare*, December 1985, *2*(3), pp. 161–79.

Osborne, Martin J. The Role of Risk Aversion in a Simple Bargaining Model. In *Roth, A. E., ed.*, 1985, pp. 181–213.

Ostmann, Axel. Decisions by Players of Comparable Strength. *Z. Nationalökon.*, 1985, *45*(3), pp. 267–84.

Pacheco, Fernando. A Role for an International Institution: A One-Shot Game-Theoretic Approach. *Rech. Écon. Louvain*, 1985, *51*(3–4), pp. 241–54.

Peleg, Bezalel. An Axiomatization of the Core of Cooperative Games without Side Payment. *J. Math. Econ.*, 1985, *14*(2), pp. 203–14.

Peschel, Manfred. Macromodels and Multiobjective Decision Making. In *Grauer, M.; Thompson, M. and Wierzbicki, A. P., eds.*, 1985, pp. 222–28.

Peters, Michael. Immobility, Rationing and Price Competition. *Rev. Econ. Stud.*, October 1985, *52*(4), pp. 593–604.

Phelps, Edmund S. Dynamics of Unemployment, Vacancies and Real Wages with Trade Unions: Comment. *Scand. J. Econ.*, 1985, *87*(2), pp. 408–10.

Pissarides, Christopher A. Dynamics of Unemployment, Vacancies and Real Wages with Trade Unions. *Scand. J. Econ.*, 1985, *87*(2), pp. 386–403.

Pohjola, Matti. Macroeconomic Stabilization Policy and Trade Union Behaviour as a Repeated Game: Comment. *Scand. J. Econ.*, 1985, *87*(2), pp. 332–34.

Postlewaite, Andrew. Implementation via Nash Equilibria in Economic Environments. In *[Pazner, E.]*, 1985, pp. 205–28.

Radner, Roy. Repeated Principal–Agent Games with Discounting. *Econometrica*, September 1985, *53*(5), pp. 1173–98.

Rapoport, Amnon and Golan, Esther. Assessment of Political Power in the Israeli Knesset. *Amer. Polit. Sci. Rev.*, September 1985, *79*(3), pp. 673–92.

Rapoport, Anatol. Uses of Experimental Games. In *Grauer, M.; Thompson, M. and Wierzbicki, A. P., eds.*, 1985, pp. 147–61.

Rashid, Salim. Nonstandard Analysis and Infinite Economies: The Cournot–Nash Solution. In *Aliprantis, C. D.; Burkinshaw, O. and Rothman, N. J., eds.*, 1985, pp. 173–84.

Rees, Ray. Cheating in a Duopoly Supergame. *J. Ind. Econ.*, June 1985, *33*(4), pp. 387–400.

Reinganum, Jennifer F. and Stokey, Nancy L. Oligopoly Extraction of a Common Property Natural Resource: The Importance of the Period of Commitment in Dynamic Games. *Int. Econ. Rev.*, February 1985, *26*(1), pp. 161–73.

Repullo, Rafael. Implementation in Dominant Strategies under Complete and Incomplete Information. *Rev. Econ. Stud.*, April 1985, *52*(2), pp. 223–29.

Rosenthal, Robert W. An Approach to Some Non-cooperative Game Situations with Special Attention to Bargaining. In *Roth, A. E., ed.*, 1985, pp. 63–72.

Roth, Alvin E. A Note on Risk Aversion in a Perfect Equilibrium Model of Bargaining. *Econometrica*, January 1985, *53*(1), pp. 207–11.

Roth, Alvin E. Common and Conflicting Interests in Two-sided Matching Markets. *Europ. Econ. Rev.*, February 1985, *27*(1), pp. 75–96.
[G: U.S.]

Roth, Alvin E. Game-Theoretic Models of Bargaining: Introduction and Overview. In *Roth, A. E., ed.*, 1985, pp. 1–7.

Roth, Alvin E. The College Admissions Problem Is Not Equivalent to the Marriage Problem. *J. Econ. Theory*, August 1985, *36*(2), pp. 277–88.

Roth, Alvin E. Toward a Focal-Point Theory of Bargaining. In *Roth, A. E., ed.*, 1985, pp. 259–68.

Rothschild, R. Noncooperative Behaviour as a Credible Threat. *Bull. Econ. Res.*, September 1985, *37*(3), pp. 245–48.

Rubinstein, Ariel. Choice of Conjectures in a Bargaining Game with Incomplete Information. In *Roth, A. E., ed.*, 1985, pp. 99–114.

Rubinstein, Ariel and Wolinsky, Asher. Equilibrium in a Market with Sequential Bargaining. *Econometrica*, September 1985, *53*(5), pp. 1133–50.

Runge, Carlisle Ford. The Innovation of Rules and the Structure of Incentives in Open Access Resources. *Amer. J. Agr. Econ.*, May 1985, *67*(2), pp. 368–72.

Safra, Zvi. Existence of Equilibrium for Walrasian Endowment Games. *J. Econ. Theory*, December 1985, *37*(2), pp. 366–78.

Salonen, H. A Solution for Two-Person Bargaining Problems. *Soc. Choice Welfare*, September 1985, *2*(2), pp. 139–46.

Samet, Dov. An Axiomatization of the Egalitarian Solutions. *Math. Soc. Sci.*, April 1985, *9*(2), pp. 173–81.

Samuelson, William. A Comment on the Coase Theorem. In *Roth, A. E., ed.*, 1985, pp. 321–39.

Schofield, N. Anarchy, Altruism and Cooperation: A Review. *Soc. Choice Welfare*, December 1985, *2*(3), pp. 207–19.

Schulz, Norbert and Stahl, Konrad. On the Non-existence of Oligopolistic Equilibria in Differentiated Products Spaces. *Reg. Sci. Urban Econ.*, June 1985, *15*(2), pp. 229–43.

Scotchmer, Suzanne. Profit-maximizing Clubs. *J. Public Econ.*, June 1985, *27*(1), pp. 25–45.

Seitz, Steven Thomas. Fuzzy Modeling and Conflict Analysis. *Conflict Manage. Peace Sci.*, Fall 1985, *9*(1), pp. 53–67.

Selten, Reinhard. What Is Game Theory Trying to Accomplish? Comment. In *Arrow, K. J. and Honkapohja, S., eds.*, 1985, pp. 77–87.

Shubik, Martin. Plausible Outcomes for Games in Strategic Form. In *Grauer, M.; Thompson, M. and Wierzbicki, A. P., eds.*, 1985, pp. 167–86.

Shubik, Martin. The Many Approaches to the Study of Monopolistic Competition. *Europ. Econ. Rev.*, February 1985, *27*(1), pp. 97–114.

Shubik, Martin. What Is Game Theory Trying to Accomplish? Comment. In *Arrow, K. J. and Honkapohja, S., eds.*, 1985, pp. 88–99.

Skowronski, Janislaw M. Competitive Differential Game of Harvesting Uncertain Resources. In *Batten, D. F. and Lesse, P. F., eds.*, 1985, pp. 87–103.

Sobel, Joel. A Theory of Credibility. *Rev. Econ. Stud.*, October 1985, *52*(4), pp. 557–73.

Sobel, Joel. Disclosure of Evidence and Resolution of Disputes: Who Should Bear the Burden of Proof? In *Roth, A. E., ed.*, 1985, pp. 341–61.

Söderström, Hans Tson. Union Militancy, External Shocks and the Accommodation Dilemma. *Scand. J. Econ.*, 1985, *87*(2), pp. 335–51.

Spatt, Chester S. Risky Debt, Investment Incentives, and Reputation in a Sequential Equilibrium: Discussion. *J. Finance*, July 1985, *40*(3), pp. 878–80.

Srivastava, Sanjay. Pure Strategy Nash Equilibria with Continuous Objectives. *J. Econ. Theory*, June 1985, *36*(1), pp. 26–35.

Thépot, Jacques. Conditioned Reflexes in Non-cooperative Games. *Econ. Stud. Quart.*, August 1985, *36*(2), pp. 97–105.

Thomson, William. Axiomatic Theory of Bargaining with a Variable Population: A Survey of Recent Results. In *Roth, A. E., ed.*, 1985, pp. 233–58.

Tijs, Stef H. and Peters, Hans. Risk Sensitivity and Related Properties for Bargaining Solutions. In *Roth, A. E., ed.*, 1985, pp. 215–31.

Tullock, Gordon. Adam Smith and the Prisoners' Dilemma. *Quart. J. Econ.*, Supp. 1985, *100*, pp. 1073–81.

Vaubel, Roland. International Collusion or Competition for Macroeconomic Policy Coordination? A Restatement. *Rech. Écon. Louvain*, 1985, *51*(3–4), pp. 223–40.

Vickers, John. Strategic Competition among the Few—Some Recent Developments in the Economics of Industry. *Oxford Rev. Econ. Policy*, Autumn 1985, *1*(3), pp. 39–62.

Wassenberg, A. F. P. Organizational Instinct: On the Political Economy of Bargaining. In *Rinnooy Kan, A. H. G., ed.*, 1985, pp. 159–77.

Wierzbicki, Andrzej. Negotiation and Mediation in Conflicts: II. Plural Rationality and Interactive Decision Processes. In *Grauer, M.; Thompson, M. and Wierzbicki, A. P., eds.*, 1985, pp. 114–31.

Wilson, Robert B. Reputations in Games and Markets. In *Roth, A. E., ed.*, 1985, pp. 27–62.

027 Economics of Centrally Planned Economies

0270 General

Abouchar, Alan J. Western Project-Investment Theory and Soviet Investment Rules. *J. Com-*

par. Econ., December 1985, *9*(4), pp. 345–62. **[G: U.S.S.R.]**

Antal, László. About the Property Incentive (Interest in Property). *Acta Oecon.*, 1985, *34*(3/4), pp. 275–86. **[G: Hungary]**

Balassa, Bela. Economic Reform in China. In *Balassa, B.*, 1985, pp. 310–36. **[G: China]**

Blaga, I., et al. Modelling of Territorial Development within the General Cybernetic System of National Economy. *Econ. Computat. Cybern. Stud. Res.*, 1985, *20*(2), pp. 5–14. **[G: Romania]**

Dai, Yuanchen. An Investigation of Fiscal Subsidy. *Chinese Econ. Stud.*, Summer 1985, *18*(4), pp. 71–77. **[G: China]**

Fedorenko, N. F. Planning and Management: What Should They Be Like? *Prob. Econ.*, December 1985, *28*(8), pp. 42–59. **[G: U.S.S.R.]**

Flakierski, Henryk. Economic Reform & Income Distribution: A Case Study of Hungary and Poland. *Eastern Europ. Econ.*, Fall-Winter 1985-86, *24*(1–2), pp. iii–194.

Freixas, Xavier; Guesnerie, Roger and Tirole, Jean. Planning under Incomplete Information and the Ratchet Effect. *Rev. Econ. Stud.*, April 1985, *52*(2), pp. 173–91.

He, Xiaofeng. A Preliminary Inquiry into the Theory of Service Value. *Chinese Econ. Stud.*, Winter 1984-85, *18*(2), pp. 39–57.

Iasin, E. G. Problems of Coordinating Planning with the Economic Mechanism for Plan Implementation. *Matekon*, Winter 1985-86, *22*(2), pp. 30–58.

Ji, Xianju. A Discussion of the Idea that Both Interpretations of Socially Necessary Labor Time Should Be Considered in the Determination of Value. *Chinese Econ. Stud.*, Spring 1985, *18*(3), pp. 77–91.

Kanbur, S. M. R. Corrigendum [Increases in Risk with Kinked Payoff Functions]. *J. Econ. Theory*, April 1985, *35*(2), pp. 399.

Kronrod, Ia. Improving the Mechanism of Economic Management and the Law of Value. *Prob. Econ.*, February 1985, *27*(10), pp. 65–84. **[G: U.S.S.R.]**

Leontief, Wassily. The Decline and Rise of Soviet Economic Science. In *Leontief, W.*, 1985, pp. 223–36.

Novichkov, V. and Abdykulova, G. Some Problems in Determining the National Economy's Priorities. *Prob. Econ.*, September 1985, *28*(5), pp. 20–31. **[G: U.S.S.R.]**

Oldak, P. G. Balanced Natural Resource Utilization and Economic Growth. *Prob. Econ.*, July 1985, *28*(3), pp. 3–17. **[G: U.S.S.R.]**

Ovsienko, Iu. V., et al. On the Relationship between Labor Productivity, Household Income, and Prices. *Matekon*, Summer 1985, *21*(4), pp. 3–22.

Pěnkava, Jaromír. Current Tasks in Economic Research. *Czech. Econ. Digest.*, February 1985, (1), pp. 24–40. **[G: Czechoslovakia]**

Raţiu Suciu, I. and Raţiu Suciu, Camelia. A Complex Analysis on Estimating the Technical and Qualitative Standards of Industrial Products.

Econ. Computat. Cybern. Stud. Res., 1985, *20*(3), pp. 49–53. **[G: Romania]**

Rutgaizer, V. and Teliukov, A. Improving the Methodology of the National Economic Accounting of Services. *Prob. Econ.*, March 1985, *27*(11), pp. 3–22. **[G: U.S.S.R.]**

Winiecki, Jan. Central Planning and Export Orientation in Manufactures. Theoretical Considerations on the Impact of System-Specific Features on Specialisation. *Econ. Notes*, 1985, (2), pp. 132–53.

Wu, Junyang. Current Economic Conditions and Reform of the Price System. *Chinese Econ. Stud.*, Spring 1985, *18*(3), pp. 55–76. **[G: China]**

Zhao, Lukuan. The Problem of Reforming the Wage System in Our Country. *Chinese Econ. Stud.*, Spring 1985, *18*(3), pp. 35–54. **[G: China]**

Zong, Han. Reduce the Consumption of Materialized Labor. *Chinese Econ. Stud.*, Summer 1985, *18*(4), pp. 62–70. **[G: China]**

0271 Microeconomic Theory

Aage, Hans. The State and the Kolkhoznik. *Econ. Anal. Worker's Manage.*, 1985, *19*(2), pp. 131–46. **[G: U.S.S.R.]**

Afanas'ev, M. Iu. and Bures, I. Encouraging Accurate Information Disclosure in a Planning System. *Matekon*, Summer 1985, *21*(4), pp. 66–78.

Bennett, John. Planning under Market Socialism When Iteration Is Incomplete. *J. Compar. Econ.*, September 1985, *9*(3), pp. 252–66.

Berliner, Joseph S. Managerial Incentives and Decision Making: A Comparison of the United States and the Soviet Union. In *Bornstein, M., ed.*, 1985, pp. 311–35. **[G: U.S.S.R.; U.S.]**

Bhagwati, Jagdish N. What Do Commissars Do? In *Bhagwati, J. N. (II)*, 1985, pp. 210–15. **[G: China]**

Bonin, John P. Labor Management and Capital Maintenance: Investment Decisions in the Socialist Labor-Managed Firm. In *Jones, D. C. and Svejnar, J., eds.*, 1985, pp. 55–69.

Bulgaru, M. An Overall Simulation Model of the Enterprise Activity within the Educational Process. *Econ. Computat. Cybern. Stud. Res.*, 1985, *20*(1), pp. 23–32.

Csillag, István and Szalai, Erzsébet. Basic Elements of an Anti-monopoly Policy. *Acta Oecon.*, 1985, *34*(1–2), pp. 65–77.

Drèze, Jacques H. Labor Management and General Equilibrium. In *Jones, D. C. and Svejnar, J., eds.*, 1985, pp. 3–20.

Estrin, Saul. Self-managed and Capitalist Behavior in Alternative Market Structures. In *Jones, D. C. and Svejnar, J., eds.*, 1985, pp. 71–86.

Falus-Szikra, Katalin. Small Enterprises in Private Ownership in Hungary. *Acta Oecon.*, 1985, *34*(1–2), pp. 13–26. **[G: Hungary]**

Finsinger, Jörg and Vogelsang, Ingo. Strategic Management Behavior under Reward Structures in a Planned Economy [Reward Structures in a Planned Economy: The Problem of

Incentives and Efficient Allocation of Resources]. *Quart. J. Econ.*, February 1985, *100*(1), pp. 263–69.

Glushkov, N. Planned Pricing: Ways to Improve. *Prob. Econ.*, December 1985, *28*(8), pp. 70–89. **[G: U.S.S.R.]**

Gomulka, S. Kornai's Soft Budget Constraint and the Shortage Phenemenon: A Criticism and Restatement. *Econ. Planning*, 1985, *19*(1), pp. 1–11.

Gravelle, H. S. E. Reward Structures in a Planned Economy: Some Difficulties. *Quart. J. Econ.*, February 1985, *100*(1), pp. 271–78.

Gui, Benedetto. Limits to External Financing: A Model and an Application to Labor-Managed Firms. In *Jones, D. C. and Svejnar, J., eds.*, 1985, pp. 107–20.

Haller, Hans. Separation of Ownership and Labour: Welfare Considerations. *Z. Nationalökon.*, 1985, *45*(3), pp. 245–65.

Haruna, Shoji. A Unified Theory of the Behaviour of Profit-maximising, Labour-managed and Joint-Stock Firms Operating under Uncertainty: A Comment. *Econ. J.*, December 1985, *95*(380), pp. 1093–94.

Hey, John D. A Unified Theory of the Behaviour of Profit-maximising, Labour-managed and Joint-Stock Firms Operating under Uncertainty: A Rejoinder. *Econ. J.*, December 1985, *95*(380), pp. 1095.

Iasin, E. G. Social Ownership, Economic Incentives, and Cost Accounting. *Prob. Econ.*, November 1985, *28*(7), pp. 48–67.
[G: U.S.S.R.]

Jia, Kechong. A Further Discussion of the Objective Bases for the Principle of Setting Price According to Quality. *Chinese Econ. Stud.*, Winter 1984-85, *18*(2), pp. 58–72.

Jiang, Qiwei. The Basis for Socialist Production Price: A Reassessment. *Chinese Econ. Stud.*, Winter 1984-85, *18*(2), pp. 23–38.

Kornai, János. Gomulka on the Soft Budget Constraint: A Reply [Kornai's Soft Budget Constraint and the Shortage Phenomenon: A Criticism and Restatement]. *Econ. Planning*, 1985, *19*(2), pp. 49–55.

Kotulan, Antonín. Theoretical Aspects of Incentives Systems. *Czech. Econ. Pap.*, 1985, *23*, pp. 55–73.

Labus, Miroljub. Price Adjustment in the Labor-Managed Economy: Theory and Some Yugoslav Evidence. In *Jones, D. C. and Svejnar, J., eds.*, 1985, pp. 137–51. **[G: Yugoslavia]**

Lin, Wenyi and Jia, Lurang. The Law of Supply and Demand and Its Role in a Socialist Economy. *Chinese Econ. Stud.*, Winter 1984-85, *18*(2), pp. 3–22.

Martin, Robert E. Random Capital Service in Labor-managed and Profit-maximizing Firms. *J. Compar. Econ.*, September 1985, *9*(3), pp. 296–313.

Matlin, A. On the Question of Developing the Theory and Practice of Planned Price Formation. *Prob. Econ.*, February 1985, *27*(10), pp. 23–42. **[G: U.S.S.R]**

McCain, Roger A. The Economics of a Labor-Managed Enterprise in the Short Run: An "Implicit Contracts" Approach. In *Jones, D. C. and Svejnar, J., eds.*, 1985, pp. 41–53.

Mednitskii, V. G., et al. On the Efficiency of the Technology for Computer Solutions of Problems of the Optimal Development and Location of Branches and Multibranch Complexes. *Matekon*, Fall 1985, *22*(1), pp. 23–42.

Mednitskii, V. G., et al. On Formulating Problems for Optimizing the Development and Location of Output in Multiproduct Branches and Multibranch Complexes. *Matekon*, Spring 1985, *21*(3), pp. 81–102.

Miyazaki, Hajime and Neary, Hugh M. Output, Work Hours and Employment in the Short Run of a Labour-managed Firm. *Econ. J.*, December 1985, *95*(380), pp. 1035–48.

Mstislavskii, P. The Dynamics of Labor Productivity and Wages. *Prob. Econ.*, May 1985, *28*(1), pp. 38–55. **[G: U.S.S.R.]**

Mymrikova, L. Product Quality and Pricing. *Prob. Econ.*, July 1985, *28*(3), pp. 52–66.

Neary, Hugh M. The Labour-managed Firm in Monopolistic Competition. *Economica*, November 1985, *52*(208), pp. 435–47.

Popov, G. Kh. Total Cost Accounting in the Economy's Basic Link. *Prob. Econ.*, August 1985, *28*(4), pp. 3–18.

Putterman, Louis. On the Interdependence of Labor Supplies in Producers' Cooperatives. In *Jones, D. C. and Svejnar, J., eds.*, 1985, pp. 87–105.

Racoveanu, N. and Dan, S. Analysis of Dynamic Systems in the State-Control Extended Space. *Econ. Computat. Cybern. Stud. Res.*, 1985, *20*(4), pp. 47–51.

Sokolovskii, L. E. Evaluating Enterprise Performance on the Basis of Efficiency and Intensification of Production. *Matekon*, Fall 1985, *22*(1), pp. 43–67.

Stahl, Dale O., II and Alexeev, Michael. The Influence of Black Markets on a Queue-rationed Centrally Planned Economy. *J. Econ. Theory*, April 1985, *35*(2), pp. 234–50.

Šuvaković, Đorđe. Modeliranje raspodele u samoupravnoj privredi i jugoslovenski program stabilizacije. (The Rule of Distribution in a Self-managed Economy and the Yugoslav Programme of Stabilization. With English summary.) *Econ. Anal. Worker's Manage.*, 1985, *19*(2), pp. 181–94. **[G: Yugoslavia]**

Tam, Mo-Yin S. Reward Structures in a Planned Economy: Some Further Thoughts. *Quart. J. Econ.*, February 1985, *100*(1), pp. 279–89.

Tian, Jiyun. Implement the Reform of the Price System Vigorously and Reliably. *Chinese Econ. Stud.*, Summer 1985, *18*(4), pp. 87–100.

Trzeciakowski, Witold. Decentralization and Financial Equilibrium in a Centrally Planned Economy. In *[Levcik, F.]*, 1985, pp. 171–80.

Valovoi, D. Indicators of Socialist Management: An Economist's Reflection. *Prob. Econ.*, June 1985, *28*(2), pp. 3–24. **[G: U.S.S.R.]**

Vanek, Jaroslav. The Participatory Economy. In *Bornstein, M., ed.*, 1985, pp. 131–40.

Wang, Weizhong and Hong, Dalin. How Do We

Interpret "Value Is the Relations of Production Cost and Utility"? *Chinese Econ. Stud.*, Winter 1984-85, *18*(2), pp. 73–87.

Wyzan, Michael L. Soviet Agricultural Procurement Pricing: A Study in Perversity. *J. Compar. Econ.*, March 1985, *9*(1), pp. 24–45.
[G: U.S.S.R.]

Zalai, Ernő. Joint Production and Labour Values. *Acta Oecon.*, 1985, *35*(3–4), pp. 327–36.

0272 Macroeconomic Theory

Andreff, Wladimir and Lavigne, Marie. La contrainte extérieure dans les économies du C.A.E.M. (The "Foreign Constraint" in the Comecon. With English summary.) *Écon. Soc.*, April 1985, *19*(4), pp. 237–81.
[G: CMEA]

Bagrinovskii, K. A.; Rimashevskaia, N. M. and Sheviakov, A. Iu. A Simulation System of Models for Coordinating Output Levels and Living Standards. *Matekon*, Spring 1985, *21*(3), pp. 47–62.
[G: U.S.S.R.]

Biji, Elena; Tănăsoiu, O. and Tănăsoiu, D. Maximizing the Development Fund Efficiency: A Criterion for Accumulation Rate Optimization. *Econ. Computat. Cybern. Stud. Res.*, 1985, *20*(3), pp. 27–32.

Brus, Wlodzimierz and Laski, Kazimierz. Repressed Inflation and Second Economy under Central Planning. In *Gaertner, W. and Wenig, A., eds.*, 1985, pp. 377–88.

Chow, Gregory C. A Model of Chinese National Income Determination. *J. Polit. Econ.*, August 1985, *93*(4), pp. 782–92. [G: China]

Feltenstein, Andrew. Stabilization of the Balance of Payments in a Small, Planned Economy, with an Application to Ethiopia. *J. Devel. Econ.*, May–June 1985, *18*(1), pp. 171–91.
[G: Ethiopia]

Galasi, Péter and Kertesi, Gábor. Second Economy, Competition, Inflation. *Acta Oecon.*, 1985, *35*(3–4), pp. 269–93.

Hartu, C. Models of Economical Increase and Preparation of Labour Manpower. *Econ. Computat. Cybern. Stud. Res.*, 1985, *20*(4), pp. 71–77.

Hrnčíř, Miroslav. Central Regulation and Parametricity of Prices. *Czech. Econ. Pap.*, 1985, *23*, pp. 7–38.

Kapustin, E. Improving the Management of the National Economy. *Prob. Econ.*, September 1985, *28*(5), pp. 69–88.

Kornai, János. On the Explanatory Theory of Shortage. Comments [A Propos the Explanation of Shortage Phenomena: Volume of Demand and Structural Inelasticity]. *Acta Oecon.*, 1985, *34*(1–2), pp. 145–62.

Kornai, János and Simonovits, András. Investment, Efficiency, and Shortage: A Macrogrowth Model. *Matekon*, Winter 1985-86, *22*(2), pp. 3–29.

Krasovskii, V. Intensification of the Economy and the Capital Intensity of Production. *Prob. Econ.*, February 1985, *27*(10), pp. 3–22.
[G: U.S.S.R.]

Nove, Alec. Money Supply and Inflation in the Soviet Union. In *[Levcik, F.]*, 1985, pp. 149–56. [G: U.S.S.R.]

Oyrzanowski, Bronislaw. I sintomi dell'inflazione nei paesi ad economia dirigista. (Symptom of Inflation in Countries with Policy of State Intervention. With English summary.) *Bancaria*, December 1985, *41*(12), pp. 1249–55.

Podkaminer, Leon. Investment Cycles in Centrally Planned Economies: An Explanation Invoking Consumer Market Disequilibrium and Labour Shortage. *Acta Oecon.*, 1985, *35*(1–2), pp. 133–44.

Rybin, V. Credit and the Intensification of Production. *Prob. Econ.*, July 1985, *28*(3), pp. 32–51.

Soós, K. A. A Rejoinder [A Propos the Explanation of Shortage Phenomena: Volume of Demand and Structural Inelasticity]. *Acta Oecon.*, 1985, *34*(1–2), pp. 162–64.

Ţigănescu, E. and Oprescu, G. Cybernetic Simulation of Control Processes through Economic Increase Equalization. *Econ. Computat. Cybern. Stud. Res.*, 1985, *20*(4), pp. 3–12.

Trzeciakowski, Witold. Decentralization and Financial Equilibrium in a Centrally Planned Economy. In *[Levcik, F.]*, 1985, pp. 171–80.

Trzeciakowski, Witold. The System of Structural Adjustment in Trade Dependent Small Centrally Planned Economies. In *Jungenfelt, K. and Hague, D. [Sir], eds.*, 1985, pp. 187–208.
[G: CMEA]

Winiecki, Jan. *Portes Ante Portas:* A Critique of the Revisionist Interpretation of Inflation under Central Planning. *Comparative Econ. Stud.*, Summer 1985, *27*(2), pp. 25–51.
[G: E. Europe]

Winiecki, Jan. Inflation under Central Planning: Sources, Processes and Manifestations. *Konjunkturpolitik*, 1985, *31*(4/5), pp. 238–60.
[G: E. Europe]

Wolf, Thomas A. Economic Stabilization in Planned Economies: Toward an Analytical Framework. *Int. Monet. Fund Staff Pap.*, March 1985, *32*(1), pp. 78–131.

Wolf, Thomas A. Exchange Rate Systems and Adjustment in Planned Economies. *Int. Monet. Fund Staff Pap.*, June 1985, *32*(2), pp. 211–47. [G: U.S.S.R.; Poland; Hungary; E. Germany]

Zieba, Andrzej. Maximum Principle for Speculative Money Balances. In *Gaertner, W. and Wenig, A., eds.*, 1985, pp. 389–91.

030 HISTORY OF THOUGHT; METHODOLOGY

031 History of Economic Thought

0310 General

Albert, Hans. On Using Leibniz in Economics: Comment. In *Koslowski, P., ed.*, 1985, pp. 68–78.

Arrow, Kenneth J. Economic History: A Necessary Thought Not Sufficient Condition for an Economist: Maine and Texas. *Amer. Econ.*

Rev., May 1985, *75*(2), pp. 320–23.

Buchanan, James M. Political Economy and Social Philosophy. In *Koslowski, P., ed.*, 1985, pp. 19–32.

Forte, Francesco. Political Economy and Social Philosophy: Comment. In *Koslowski, P., ed.*, 1985, pp. 33–36.

Hazlett, Thomas. The Curious Evolution of Natural Monopoly Theory. In *Poole, R. W., Jr., ed.*, 1985, pp. 1–25.

Koslowski, Peter. Economy Principle, Maximizing, and the Co-ordination of Individuals in Economics and Philosophy. In *Koslowski, P., ed.*, 1985, pp. 39–67.

Koslowski, Peter. Philosophy and Economics: An Introduction. In *Koslowski, P., ed.*, 1985, pp. 1–16.

Küng, Emil. Beyond Economic Man: Humanistic Economics: Comment. In *Koslowski, P., ed.*, 1985, pp. 121–23.

Lutz, Mark A. Beyond Economic Man: Humanistic Economics. In *Koslowski, P., ed.*, 1985, pp. 91–120.

Macpherson, C. B. Liberalism as Trade-offs. In *Macpherson, C. B.*, 1985, pp. 44–54.

Solow, Robert M. Economic History and Economics. *Amer. Econ. Rev.*, May 1985, *75*(2), pp. 328–31.

0311 Ancient, Medieval

Campbell, William F. The Free Market for Goods and the Free Market for Ideas in the Platonic Dialogues. *Hist. Polit. Econ.*, Summer 1985, *17*(2), pp. 187–97.

Kern, William S. Aristotle and the Problem of Insatiable Desires: A Reply [Returning to the Aristotelian Paradigm: Daly and Schumacher']. *Hist. Polit. Econ.*, Fall 1985, *17*(3), pp. 393–94.

Pack, Spencer J. Aristotle and the Problem of Insatiable Desires: A Comment on Kern's Interpretation of Aristotle [Returning to the Aristotelian Paradigm: Daly and Schumacher']. *Hist. Polit. Econ.*, Fall 1985, *17*(3), pp. 391–93.

0312 Pre-Classical

De Gleria, Silvana. Prodotto netto ed energia netta (ovvero: dogma fisiocratico e dogma energetico). (With English summary.) *Econ. Polít.*, August 1985, *2*(2), pp. 187–213.

Dunn, John. From Applied Theology to Social Analysis: The Break between John Locke and the Scottish Enlightenment. In *Hont, I. and Ignatieff, M., eds.*, 1985, pp. 119–35.

Giacometti, Jacques. Physique et métaphysique dans l'ordre naturel: le tableau économique de F. Quesnay. (On the Physiocracy: Physics and Metaphysics in "l'ordre naturel" and "le tableau économique." With English summary.) *Écon. Soc.*, March 1985, *19*(3), pp. 173–96.

Hont, Istvan. The 'Rich Country–Poor Country' Debate in Scottish Classical Political Economy. In *Hont, I. and Ignatieff, M., eds.*, 1985, pp. 271–315.

Moore, James and Silverthorne, Michael. Gershom Carmichael and the Natural Jurisprudence Tradition in Eighteenth-century Scotland. In *Hont, I. and Ignatieff, M., eds.*, 1985, pp. 73–87.

Pocock, J. G. A. Cambridge Paradigms and Scotch Philosophers: A Study of the Relations between the Civic Humanist and the Civil Jurisprudential Interpretation of Eighteenth-century Social Thought. In *Hont, I. and Ignatieff, M., eds.*, 1985, pp. 235–52.

Vaggi, Gianni. A Physiocratic Model of Relative Prices and Income Distribution. *Econ. J.*, December 1985, *95*(380), pp. 928–47.

Vaggi, Gianni. The Role of Profits in Physiocratic Economics. *Hist. Polit. Econ.*, Fall 1985, *17*(3), pp. 367–84.

Venturi, Franco. Scottish Echoes in Eighteenth-century Italy. In *Hont, I. and Ignatieff, M., eds.*, 1985, pp. 345–62.

0313 Mercantilist

Endres, Anthony M. The Functions of Numerical Data in the Writings of Graunt, Petty, and Davenant. *Hist. Polit. Econ.*, Summer 1985, *17*(2), pp. 245–64.

0314 Classical

Blaug, Mark. What Ricardo Said and What Ricardo Meant. In *Caravale, G. A., ed.*, 1985, pp. 3–10.

Caravale, Giovanni A. Diminishing Returns and Accumulation in Ricardo. In *Caravale, G. A., ed.*, 1985, pp. 127–88.

Cartelier, Jean. Théorie de la valeur ou hétérodoxie monétaire: les termes d'un choix. (Value Theory and Monetary Heterodoxy: The Crucial Choice. With English summary.) *Écon. Appl.*, 1985, *38*(1), pp. 63–82.

Casarosa, Carlo. The 'New View' of the Ricardian Theory of Distribution and Economic Growth. In *Caravale, G. A., ed.*, 1985, pp. 45–58.

Caton, Hiram. The Preindustrial Economics of Adam Smith. *J. Econ. Hist.*, December 1985, *45*(4), pp. 833–53.

Cooter, Robert D. and Rappoport, Peter. Reply to I. M. D. Little's Comment [Were the Ordinalists Wrong about Welfare Economics?]. *J. Econ. Lit.*, September 1985, *23*(3), pp. 1189–91.

Costa, Giacomo. Time in Ricardian Models: Some Critical Observations and Some New Results. In *Caravale, G. A., ed.*, 1985, pp. 59–83.

Costabile, Lilia and Rowthorn, Bob. Malthus's Theory of Wages and Growth. *Econ. J.*, June 1985, *95*(378), pp. 418–37.

Dubœuf, Françoise. Adam Smith: mesure et socialité. (Adam Smith: Measure and Sociality. With English summary.) *Écon. Soc.*, March 1985, *19*(3), pp. 73–107.

Eltis, Walter. Ricardo on Machinery and Technological Unemployment. In *Caravale, G. A., ed.*, 1985, pp. 257–84.

Garegnani, Pierangelo. On Hollander's Interpretation of Ricardo's Early Theory of Profits. In *Caravale, G. A., ed.*, 1985, pp. 87–104.

Gilbert, Geoffrey N. The *Morning Chronicle*, Poor Laws, and Political Economy. *Hist. Polit. Econ.*, Winter 1985, *17*(4), pp. 507–21.

Glasner, David. A Reinterpretation of Classical Monetary Theory. *Southern Econ. J.*, July 1985, *52*(1), pp. 46–67.

Grampp, William D. Rights Theory in Classic Liberalism. *Rivista Int. Sci. Econ. Com.*, February 1985, *32*(2), pp. 141–52.

Hausman, Daniel M. Classical Wage Theory and the Causal Complications of Explaining Distribution. In *Pitt, J. C., ed.*, 1985, pp. 171–97.

Hicks, John. Sraffa and Ricardo: A Critical View. In *Caravale, G. A., ed.*, 1985, pp. 305–19.

Hollander, Samuel. On the Substantive Identity of the Ricardian and Neoclassical Conceptions of Economic Organization: The French Connection in British Classicism. In *Caravale, G. A., ed.*, 1985, pp. 13–44.

Hont, Istvan and Ignatieff, Michael. Needs and Justice in the *Wealth of Nations:* An introductory Essay. In *Hont, I. and Ignatieff, M., eds.*, 1985, pp. 1–44.

Jäggi, Stefan. Karl Marx und die Malthusianische Bevölkerungstheorie. (Karl Marx and the Malthusian Population Theory. With English summary.) *Schweiz. Z. Volkswirtsch. Statist.*, June 1985, *121*(2), pp. 95–113.

Kindleberger, Charles P. Was Adam Smith a Monetarist or a Keynesian? In *Kindleberger, C. P.*, 1985, pp. 11–24.

Lapidus, André. Sur la question de l'existence de l'ornithorynque en économie politique (Éloge raisonné d'une contribution à la zoologie économique). (With English summary.) *Revue Écon. Polit.*, Mar.–Apr. 1985, *95*(2), pp. 189–207.

Leontief, Wassily. Postulates: Keynes's *General Theory* and the Classicists. In *Leontief, W.*, 1985, pp. 93–103.

Leontief, Wassily. The Consistency of the Classical Theory of Money and Prices. In *Leontief, W.*, 1985, pp. 104–07.

Levine, David P. On the Analysis of Advanced Capitalist Economy. In *[Magdoff, H. and Sweezy, P.]*, 1985, pp. 205–22.

Little, Ian M. D. Were the Ordinalists Wrong about Welfare Economics? A Comment. *J. Econ. Lit.*, September 1985, *23*(3), pp. 1186–88.

Macpherson, C. B. The Economic Penetration of Political Theory: Some Hypotheses. In *Macpherson, C. B.*, 1985, pp. 101–19.

Mainwaring, Lynn. The Treatment of Capital in the "Classical" Theory of International Trade. *Metroecon.*, February 1985, *37*(1), pp. 63–77.

Meacci, Ferdinando. Ricardo's Chapter on Machinery and the Theory of Capital. In *Caravale, G. A., ed.*, 1985, pp. 285–302.

Meldolesi, L. Georg Simmel e la filosofia del denaro. (With English summary.) *Stud. Econ.*, 1985, *40*(27), pp. 123–39.

Perelman, Michael A. Marx, Malthus, and the Organic Composition of Capital. *Hist. Polit.*

Econ., Fall 1985, *17*(3), pp. 461–90.

Perryman, M. Ray. Evolutionary Aspects of Corporate Concentration and Its Implications for Economic Theory and Policy. *J. Econ. Issues*, June 1985, *19*(2), pp. 375–81.

Platteau, J. Ph. The Political Economy of John Stuart Mill, or, the Coexistence of Orthodoxy, Heresy and Prophecy. *Int. J. Soc. Econ.*, 1985, *12*(1), pp. 3–26.

Pokorný, Dušan. Karl Marx and General Equilibrium. *Hist. Polit. Econ.*, Spring 1985, *17*(1), pp. 109–32.

Porta, Pier Luigi. The Debate on Ricardo: Old Results in New Frameworks. In *Caravale, G. A., ed.*, 1985, pp. 217–38.

Ranson, Baldwin. Government Deficits and Economic Stability: Evaluating Alternative Theories. *Écon. Soc.*, August 1985, *19*(8), pp. 197–207.

Riha, Tomas. German Political Economy: The History of an Alternative Economics. *Int. J. Soc. Econ.*, 1985, *12*(3/4/5/), pp. 1–252. [G: Germany]

Robertson, John. The Scottish Enlightenment at the Limits of the Civic Tradition. In *Hont, I. and Ignatieff, M., eds.*, 1985, pp. 137–78.

Roncaglia, Alessandro. Hollander's Ricardo. In *Caravale, G. A., ed.*, 1985, pp. 105–23.

Rosselli, Annalisa. The Theory of the Natural Wage. In *Caravale, G. A., ed.*, 1985, pp. 239–54.

Schabas, Margaret. Some Reactions to Jevons' Mathematical Program: The Case of Cairnes and Mill. *Hist. Polit. Econ.*, Fall 1985, *17*(3), pp. 337–53.

Sherwood, John M. Engels, Marx, Malthus, and the Machine. *Amer. Hist. Rev.*, October 1985, *90*(4), pp. 837–65.

Skinner, Andrew S. Adam Smith: Some Functions and Limitations of Government. In *[Recktenwald, H. C.]*, 1985, pp. 3–11.

Skinner, Andrew S. Smith and Shackle: History and Epistemics. *J. Econ. Stud.*, 1985, *12*(1/2), pp. 13–20.

Tosato, Domenico. A Reconsideration of Sraffa's Interpretation of Ricardo on Value and Distribution. In *Caravale, G. A., ed.*, 1985, pp. 189–216.

de Vivo, Giancarlo. Robert Torrens and Ricardo's 'Corn-Ratio' Theory of Profits. *Cambridge J. Econ.*, March 1985, *9*(1), pp. 89–92.

Wilson, Thomas. Invisible Hands: Public and Private. In *[Recktenwald, H. C.]*, 1985, pp. 13–21.

Winch, Donald. Economic Liberalism as Ideology: The Appleby Version. *Econ. Hist. Rev.*, 2nd Ser., May 1985, *38*(2), pp. 287–97.

Young, Jeffrey T. Natural Price and the Impartial Spectator: A New Perspective on Adam Smith as a Social Economist. *Int. J. Soc. Econ.*, 1985, *12*(6/7), pp. 118–33.

0315 Austrian, Marshallian, Neoclassical

Arrow, Kenneth J. The Potentials and Limits of the Market in Resource Allocation. In *Feiwel*,

G. R., ed. (II), 1985, pp. 107–24.

Birch, Thomas D. Marshall and Keynes Revisited [J. M. Keynes as a Marshallian]. *J. Econ. Issues*, March 1985, *19*(1), pp. 194–200.

Blaug, Mark. Marginal Cost Pricing: No Empty Box. In *[Peacock, A.]*, 1985, pp. 15–30.

Butos, William N. Hayek and General Equilibrium Analysis. *Southern Econ. J.*, October 1985, *52*(2), pp. 332–43.

Cooter, Robert D. and Rappoport, Peter. Reply to I. M. D. Little's Comment [Were the Ordinalists Wrong about Welfare Economics?]. *J. Econ. Lit.*, September 1985, *23*(3), pp. 1189–91.

Dumez, Hervé. Walras, Marshall: Stratégies scientifiques comparées. (With English summary.) *Revue Écon. Polit.*, Mar.–Apr. 1985, *95*(2), pp. 168–73.

Ebeling, Richard M. Ludwig von Mises and the Gold Standard. In *Rockwell, L. H., Jr., ed.*, 1985, pp. 35–59.

Ekelund, Robert B., Jr. and Hébert, Robert F. Consumer Surplus: The First Hundred Years. *Hist. Polit. Econ.*, Fall 1985, *17*(3), pp. 419–54.

Garrison, Roger W. Intertemporal Coordination and the Invisible Hand: An Austrian Perspective on the Keynesian Vision. *Hist. Polit. Econ.*, Summer 1985, *17*(2), pp. 309–21.

Gleicher, David. The Ontology of Labor Values: Remarks on the *Science & Society* Value Symposium. *Sci. Soc.*, Winter 1985-1986, *49*(4), pp. 463–71.

Gunning, James Patrick. Causes of Unemployment: The Austrian Perspective. *Hist. Polit. Econ.*, Summer 1985, *17*(2), pp. 223–44.

Hollander, Samuel. On the Substantive Identity of the Ricardian and Neoclassical Conceptions of Economic Organization: The French Connection in British Classicism. In *Caravale, G. A., ed.*, 1985, pp. 13–44.

Jensen, Hans E. Marshall Revisited: A Reply [J. M. Keynes as a Marshallian]. *J. Econ. Issues*, December 1985, *19*(4), pp. 967–74.

Kirzner, Israel M. Uncertainty, Discovery, and Human Action: A Study of the Entrepreneurial Profile in the Misesian System. In *Kirzner, I. M.*, 1985, pp. 40–67.

Lallement, Jérôme. L'utilité mesurée comme une grandeur de la physique. (Alfred Marshall: Utility Measured as a Physical Magnitude. With English summary.) *Écon. Soc.*, March 1985, *19*(3), pp. 147–71.

Langlois, Richard N. Knowledge and Rationality in the Austrian School: An Analytical Survey. *Eastern Econ. J.*, Oct.-Dec. 1985, *11*(4), pp. 309–30.

Little, Ian M. D. Were the Ordinalists Wrong about Welfare Economics? A Comment. *J. Econ. Lit.*, September 1985, *23*(3), pp. 1186–88.

Meacci, Ferdinando. On Disjunctive and Conjunctive Principles in the Austrian Theory: A Note and an Extension. *Rivista Int. Sci. Econ. Com.*, December 1985, *32*(12), pp. 1187–97.

Paul, Ron. The Political and Economic Agenda for a Real Gold Standard. In *Rockwell, L. H., Jr., ed.*, 1985 , pp. 129–40.   [G: U.S.]

Roncaglia, Alessandro. Hollander's Ricardo. In *Caravale, G. A., ed.*, 1985, pp. 105–23.

Sennholz, Hans F. The Monetary Writings of Carl Menger. In *Rockwell, L. H., Jr., ed.*, 1985, pp. 19–34.   [G: Austria]

Tobin, James. Neoclassical Theory in America: J. B. Clark and Fisher. *Amer. Econ. Rev.*, December 1985, *75*(6), pp. 28–38.

Vallageas, Bernard. Les circuits dans les analyses de Marx, Boehm-Bawerk, Hayek et Keynes. (Circuits in the Analyses of Marx, Boehm-Bawerk, Hayek and Keynes. With English summary.) *Écon. Soc.*, August 1985, *19*(8), pp. 47–68.

0316 General Equilibrium until 1945

Baletić, Zvonimir. Isaac Gervaise, prvi teoretičar opće ekonomske ravnoteže. (Isaac Gervaise, the First Theoretician of the General Economic Equilibrium. With English summary.) *Econ. Anal. Worker's Manage.*, 1985, *19*(3), pp. 263–79.

Barrère, Christian. L'objet d'une théorie de la régulation. (The Purpose of a Regulation Theory. With English summary.) *Écon. Soc.*, January 1985, *19*(1), pp. 9–28.

Dumez, Hervé. Walras, Marshall: Stratégies scientifiques comparées. (With English summary.) *Revue Écon. Polit.*, Mar.–Apr. 1985, *95*(2), pp. 168–73.

Lotter, Françoise. Léon Walras: de la mesure observée à la mesure imaginée. (Léon Walras: From "Observed" to "Fictive" Measurement. With English summary.) *Écon. Soc.*, March 1985, *19*(3), pp. 109–45.

Riha, Tomas. German Political Economy: The History of an Alternative Economics. *Int. J. Soc. Econ.*, 1985, *12*(3/4/5/), pp. 1–252.
          [G: Germany]

0317 Socialist and Marxian until 1945

Arneson, Richard J. Marxism and Secular Faith. *Amer. Polit. Sci. Rev.*, September 1985, *79*(3), pp. 627–40.

Barrère, Christian. L'objet d'une théorie de la régulation. (The Purpose of a Regulation Theory. With English summary.) *Écon. Soc.*, January 1985, *19*(1), pp. 9–28.

Bettelheim, Charles. Reflections on Concepts of Class and Class Struggle in Marx's Work. In *[Magdoff, H. and Sweezy, P.]*, 1985, pp. 15–29.

Bowles, Samuel and Gintis, Herbert. The Labor Theory of Value and the Specificity of Marxian Economics. In *[Magdoff, H. and Sweezy, P.]*, 1985, pp. 31–44.

Cartelier, Jean. Théorie de la valeur ou hétérodoxie monétaire: les termes d'un choix. (Value Theory and Monetary Heterodoxy: The Crucial Choice. With English summary.) *Écon. Appl.*, 1985, *38*(1), pp. 63–82.

Chavance, Bernard. The Utopian Dialectic of

Capitalism and Communism in Marx. *Econ. Anal. Worker's Manage.*, 1985, *19*(3), pp. 249–62.

Drugman, B. A nouveau sur la question de la régulation. Economie politique, Marxisme et... crise: quelle alternative réelle? (Theory of Regulation Revisited. Political Economy, Marxism and Crisis: Is There a Real Alternative? With English summary.) *Écon. Soc.*, January 1985, *19*(1), pp. 29–64.

Fine, Ben. Banking Capital and the Theory of Interest. *Sci. Soc.*, Winter 1985-1986, *49*(4), pp. 387–413.

Frank, Andre Gunder. A Marx, Keynes, Schumpeter Centenary and the Editors of Monthly Review. In *[Magdoff, H. and Sweezy, P.]*, 1985, pp. 115–26.

Fremer, Miloslav. Some Aspects of the Economy of Socialism and Its Contradictions. *Czech. Econ. Digest.*, May 1985, (3), pp. 29–52.

Gleicher, David. The Ontology of Labor Values: Remarks on the *Science & Society* Value Symposium. *Sci. Soc.*, Winter 1985-1986, *49*(4), pp. 463–71.

Harris, Donald J. Value, Exchange and Capital. In *[Magdoff, H. and Sweezy, P.]*, 1985, pp. 151–83.

Harvey, Philip. The Value-creating Capacity of Skilled Labor in Marxian Economics. *Rev. Radical Polit. Econ.*, Spring and Summer 1985, *17*(1/2), pp. 83–102.

Henderson, James P. An English Communist, Mr. Bray [and] His Remarkable Work. *Hist. Polit. Econ.*, Spring 1985, *17*(1), pp. 73–95.

Janover, Louis and Rubel, Maximilien. Matériaux pur un lexique de Marx. (Material for a Marx Lexikon: Revolution II. With English summary.) *Écon. Soc.*, November 1985, *19*(11), pp. 55–95.

Kelly, Kevin D. Capitalism, Socialism, Barbarism: Marxist Conceptions of the Soviet Union. *Rev. Radical Polit. Econ.*, Winter 1985, *17*(4), pp. 51–71.

Kozlov, Nicholas N. Nikolai Ivanovich Bukharin: Reconsiderations on 'Neo-Narodnik *Litterateur.*' *Rev. Radical Polit. Econ.*, Winter 1985, *17*(4), pp. 28–50.

Leadbeater, David. The Consistency of Marx's Categories of Productive and Unproductive Labour. *Hist. Polit. Econ.*, Winter 1985, *17*(4), pp. 591–618.

Leontief, Wassily. The Significance of Marxian Economics for Present-Day Economic Theory. In *Leontief, W.*, 1985, pp. 72–83.

Levine, David P. On the Analysis of Advanced Capitalist Economy. In *[Magdoff, H. and Sweezy, P.]*, 1985, pp. 205–22.

Lippi, Marco. Ancora su valore e costa reale in Marx: risposta alle critiche di petri. (Value and Real Cost in Marx Once Again. With English summary.) *Rivista Int. Sci. Econ. Com.*, July-Aug. 1985, *32*(7–8), pp. 635–59.

Little, Daniel. The Scientific Standing of Marx's *Capital*. *Rev. Radical Polit. Econ.*, Winter 1985, *17*(4), pp. 72–94.

Lunghini, Giorgio. Marx sulle macchine: note di lettura. (Marx on Machinery. With English summary.) *Rivista Int. Sci. Econ. Com.*, June 1985, *32*(6), pp. 517–24.

Macpherson, C. B. Democracy, Utopian and Scientific. In *Macpherson, C. B.*, 1985, pp. 120–32.

Mandel, Ernest. Marx and Engels on Commodity Production and Bureaucracy. In *[Magdoff, H. and Sweezy, P.]*, 1985, pp. 223–58.

Mills, Charles W. Marxism and Naturalistic Mystification. *Sci. Soc.*, Winter 1985-1986, *49*(4), pp. 472–83.

Naples, Michele I. Dynamic Adjustment and Long-run Inflation in a Marxian Model. *J. Post Keynesian Econ.*, Fall 1985, *8*(1), pp. 97–112.

Perelman, Michael A. Marx, Malthus, and the Organic Composition of Capital. *Hist. Polit. Econ.*, Fall 1985, *17*(3), pp. 461–90.

Ranson, Baldwin. Government Deficits and Economic Stability: Evaluating Alternative Theories. *Écon. Soc.*, August 1985, *19*(8), pp. 197–207.

Resnick, Stephen A. and Wolff, Richard D. A Marxian Reconceptualization of Income and its Distribution. In *[Magdoff, H. and Sweezy, P.]*, 1985, pp. 319–44.

Révész, Gábor. The Origins and Development of the Model of Socialist Economy. In *[Levcik, F.]*, 1985, pp. 21–30.

Rubel, Maximilien. Marx Jubiläums Edition (MJE) 1883–1983. Pour une Édition du Jubilé 1883–1983. (For a Jubilee Edition 1883–1983 Prologue (Annexe: Letter from Friedrich Adler to M. R. With English summary.) *Écon. Soc.*, November 1985, *19*(11), pp. 7–54.

Steedman, Ian. Heterogeneous Labour, Money Wages, and Marx's Theory. *Hist. Polit. Econ.*, Winter 1985, *17*(4), pp. 551–74.

Szymanski, Al. Crisis and Vitalization in Marxist Theory. *Sci. Soc.*, Fall 1985, *49*(3), pp. 315–31.

Tabukasch, Michael. The Notion of Labour: Reflections on Marx and Habermas. In *Gustavsson, B.; Karlsson, J. C. and Raftegard, C.*, 1985, pp. 33–43.

0318 Historical and Institutional

Alchian, Armen. A Weberian Analysis of Economic Progress: The Case of Resource Exporting LDCs: Comment. *Z. ges. Staatswiss. (JITE)*, March 1985, *141*(1), pp. 184–86.

Backhaus, Juergen. Public Policy toward Corporate Structures: Two Chicago Approaches. *J. Econ. Issues*, June 1985, *19*(2), pp. 365–73.

Bromley, Daniel W. Resources and Economic Development: An Institutionalist Perspective. *J. Econ. Issues*, September 1985, *19*(3), pp. 779–96.

Bronfenbrenner, Martin. Early American Leaders—Institutional and Critical Traditions. *Amer. Econ. Rev.*, December 1985, *75*(6), pp. 13–27.

Brown, Doug. Institutionalism, Critical Theory, and the Administered Society. *J. Econ. Issues*, June 1985, *19*(2), pp. 559–66.

Cain, Peter J. Hobson, Wilshire, and the Capitalist Theory of Capitalist Imperialism. *Hist. Polit. Econ.*, Fall 1985, *17*(3), pp. 455–60.

Cain, Peter J. J. A. Hobson, Financial Capitalism and Imperialism in Late Victorian and Edwardian England. In *Porter, A. N. and Holland, R. F., eds.*, 1985, pp. 1–27.

Endres, Anthony M. Veblen and Commons on Goodwill: A Case of Theoretical Divergence. *Hist. Polit. Econ.*, Winter 1985, *17*(4), pp. 637–49.

Hamilton, David. The Veblen–Commons Award: Wendell Gordon. *J. Econ. Issues*, June 1985, *19*(2), pp. 301–04.

Hodgson, Geoffrey M. The Rationalist Conception of Action. *J. Econ. Issues*, December 1985, *19*(4), pp. 825–51.

Hollander, Samuel. On the Substantive Identity of the Ricardian and Neoclassical Conceptions of Economic Organization: The French Connection in British Classicism. In *Caravale, G. A., ed.*, 1985, pp. 13–44.

McFarland, Floyd B. Thorstein Veblen versus the Institutionalists. *Rev. Radical Polit. Econ.*, Winter 1985, *17*(4), pp. 95–105.

Parsons, Kenneth H. John R. Commons: His Relevance to Contemporary Economics. *J. Econ. Issues*, September 1985, *19*(3), pp. 755–78.

Ranson, Baldwin. Government Deficits and Economic Stability: Evaluating Alternative Theories. *Écon. Soc.*, August 1985, *19*(8), pp. 197–207.

Riha, Tomas. German Political Economy: The History of an Alternative Economics. *Int. J. Soc. Econ.*, 1985, *12*(3/4/5/), pp. 1–252.
[G: Germany]

Seyfert, Wolfgang. A Weberian Analysis of Economic Progress: The Case of Resource-Exporting LDC's. *Z. ges. Staatswiss. (JITE)*, March 1985, *141*(1), pp. 170–83.

Stevenson, Rodney. Corporate Power and the Scope of Economic Analysis. *J. Econ. Issues*, June 1985, *19*(2), pp. 333–41.

Tilman, Rick. The Utopian Vision of Edward Bellamy and Thorstein Veblen. *J. Econ. Issues*, December 1985, *19*(4), pp. 879–98.

Williamson, Oliver E. Reflections on the New Institutional Economics. *Z. ges. Staatswiss. (JITE)*, March 1985, *141*(1), pp. 187–95.

032 History of Economic Thought (continued)

0321 Other Schools since 1800

Arndt, H. W. Political Economy: A Reply. *Econ. Rec.*, December 1985, *61*(175), pp. 752.

Benestad, J. Brian. Henry George and the Catholic View of Morality and the Common Good, I: George's Overall Critique of Pope Leo XIII's Classic Encyclical, 'Rerum Novarum.' *Amer. J. Econ. Soc.*, July 1985, *44*(3), pp. 365–78.

Berndt, Ernst R. From Technocracy to Net Energy Analysis: Engineers, Economists, and Recurring Energy Theories of Value. In *Scott, A., ed.*, 1985, pp. 337–67. [G: U.S.]

de Boyer, Jérôme. Circulation du revenu et circulation du capital: la distinction monnaie crédit chez Thomas Tooke. (Currency and Capital: The Distinction Established by Thomas Tooke between Money and Credit. With English summary.) *Revue Écon.*, May 1985, *36*(3), pp. 555–77.

Brems, Hans. Den økonomiske teori og dens pionerer. (Economic Theory and Its Pioneers. With English summary.) *Nationaløkon. Tidsskr.*, 1985, *123*(3), pp. 365–76.

Brunner, Karl. Ideology and Analysis in Macroeconomics: Comment. In *Koslowski, P., ed.*, 1985, pp. 208–18.

Cameron, Trudy Ann. From Technocracy to Net Energy Analysis: Engineers, Economists, and Recurring Energy Theories of Value: Comment. In *Scott, A., ed.*, 1985, pp. 370–75.
[G: U.S.]

Giarini, Orio. The Consequences of Complexity in Economics: Vulnerability, Risk, and Rigidity Factors in Supply. In *Aida, S., et al.*, 1985, pp. 133–45.

Groenewegen, Peter D. Professor Arndt on Political Economy: A Comment. *Econ. Rec.*, December 1985, *61*(175), pp. 744–51.

Kindleberger, Charles P. Keynesianism vs. Monetarism in Eighteenth- and Nineteenth-Century France. In *Kindleberger, C. P.*, 1985, pp. 41–62. [G: France]

Leijonhufvud, Axel. Ideology and Analysis in Macroeconomics. In *Koslowski, P., ed.*, 1985, pp. 182–207.

Leontief, Wassily. Implicit Theorizing: A Methodological Criticism of the Neo Cambridge School. In *Leontief, W.*, 1985, pp. 58–71.

Lissner, Will. A New School of Economic Theorists: The 'New Classical Economists.' *Amer. J. Econ. Soc.*, April 1985, *44*(2), pp. 255–56.

Lutz, Mark A. Pragmatism, Instrumental Value Theory and Social Economics. *Rev. Soc. Econ.*, October 1985, *43*(2), pp. 140–72. [G: U.S.]

Maritain, Jacques. A Society without Money. *Rev. Soc. Econ.*, April 1985, *43*(1), pp. 73–83.

Mawatari, Shohken. The Uno School: A Marxian Approach in Japan. *Hist. Polit. Econ.*, Fall 1985, *17*(3), pp. 403–18.

Musgrave, Richard A. Public Finance and Distributive Justice. In *[Peacock, A.]*, 1985, pp. 1–14.

Niedercorn, John H. Two Biblical Conceptions of an Equitable and Efficient Economy. *Rev. Soc. Econ.*, October 1985, *43*(2), pp. 181–92.

Riha, Tomas. German Political Economy: The History of an Alternative Economics. *Int. J. Soc. Econ.*, 1985, *12*(3/4/5/), pp. 1–252.
[G: Germany]

Scott, Anthony D. From Technocracy to Net Energy Analysis: Engineers, Economists, and Recurring Energy Theories of Value: Comment. In *Scott, A., ed.*, 1985, pp. 367–70.
[G: U.S.]

0322 Individuals

Siven, Claes-Henric. The End of the Stockholm

School. *Scand. J. Econ.*, 1985, *87*(4), pp. 577–93.

Aristotle

Brandis, Royall. Distribution Theory: Scientific Analysis or Moral Philosophy? *J. Econ. Issues*, December 1985, *19*(4), pp. 867–78.

Kern, William S. Aristotle and the Problem of Insatiable Desires: A Reply [Returning to the Aristotelian Paradigm: Daly and Schumacher]. *Hist. Polit. Econ.*, Fall 1985, *17*(3), pp. 393–94.

Pack, Spencer J. Aristotle and the Problem of Insatiable Desires: A Comment on Kern's Interpretation of Aristotle [Returning to the Aristotelian Paradigm: Daly and Schumacher]. *Hist. Polit. Econ.*, Fall 1985, *17*(3), pp. 391–93.

Arrow, Kenneth J.

Arrow, Kenneth J. On the Use of Winds in Flight Planning. In *Arrow, K. J. (I)*, 1985, pp. 1–24.

Bagiotti, Tullio

Agnati, Achille. Gli Editoriali di Tullio Bagiotti. (Tullio Bagiotti's Editorials. With English summary.) *Rivista Int. Sci. Econ. Com.*, September 1985, *32*(9), pp. 801–33.

Cantarelli, Davide. Ricordo di Tullio Bagiotti. (Reminiscences of Tullio Bagiotti. With English summary.) *Rivista Int. Sci. Econ. Com.*, February 1985, *32*(2), pp. 101–05.

Bellamy, Edward

Bronfenbrenner, Martin. Early American Leaders—Institutional and Critical Traditions. *Amer. Econ. Rev.*, December 1985, *75*(6), pp. 13–27.

Tilman, Rick. The Utopian Vision of Edward Bellamy and Thorstein Veblen. *J. Econ. Issues*, December 1985, *19*(4), pp. 879–98.

Bernácer, German

Villacís González, José. La teoria macroeconómica de German Bernácer. (With English summary.) *Economia (Portugal)*, October 1985, *9*(3), pp. 431–46.

Bloomfield, Arthur

Ethier, Wilfred J. and Marston, Richard C. International Financial Markets and Capital Movements: Introduction. In *[Bloomfield, A. I.]*, 1985, pp. 1–6.

von Boehm-Bawerk, Eugene

Vallageas, Bernard. Les circuits dans les analyses de Marx, Boehm-Bawerk, Hayek et Keynes. (Circuits in the Analyses of Marx, Boehm-Bawerk, Hayek and Keynes. With English summary.) *Écon. Soc.*, August 1985, *19*(8), pp. 47–68.

de Boisguillebert, Pierre

Teboul, René. Le circuit comme représentation de l'espace économique (une relecture de l'oeuvre de Pierre de Boisguillebert). (With English summary.) *Revue Écon. Polit.*, Mar.–Apr. 1985, *95*(2), pp. 117–33.

Boulding, Kenneth E.

Boulding, Kenneth E. My Life Philosophy. *Amer. Econ.*, Fall 1985, *29*(2), pp. 5–14.

Bray, John F.

Henderson, James P. An English Communist, Mr. Bray [and] His Remarkable Work. *Hist. Polit. Econ.*, Spring 1985, *17*(1), pp. 73–95.

Brown, James A. C.

Stone, Richard. James Alan Calvert Brown: An Appreciation. *Oxford Bull. Econ. Statist.*, August 1985, *47*(3), pp. 191–97.

Bukharin, Nikolai Ivanovich

Kozlov, Nicholas N. Nikolai Ivanovich Bukharin: Reconsiderations on 'Neo-Narodnik *Litterateur.*' *Rev. Radical Polit. Econ.*, Winter 1985, *17*(4), pp. 28–50.

Carmichael, Gershom

Moore, James and Silverthorne, Michael. Gershom Carmichael and the Natural Jurisprudence Tradition in Eighteenth-century Scotland. In *Hont, I. and Ignatieff, M.*, eds., 1985, pp. 73–87.

Cayley, Edward Stillingfleet.

Dutton, H. I. and King, J. E. An Economic Exile: Edward Stillingfleet Cayley, 1802-1862. *Hist. Polit. Econ.*, Summer 1985, *17*(2), pp. 203–18.   [G: U.K.]

Chamberlin, Edward H.

Blitch, Charles P. The Genesis of Chamberlinian Monopolistic Competition Theory: Addendum [The Origin and Early Development of Monopolistic Competition Theory]. *Hist. Polit. Econ.*, Fall 1985, *17*(3), pp. 395–400.

Reinwald, Thomas P. The Genesis of Chamberlinian Monopolistic Competition Theory: Addendum—A Comment [The Origin and Early Development of Monopolistic Competition Theory]. *Hist. Polit. Econ.*, Fall 1985, *17*(3), pp. 400–402.

Chevalier, Michel

Kindleberger, Charles P. Michel Chevalier (1806–1879), the Economic de Tocqueville. In *Kindleberger, C. P.*, 1985, pp. 25–40.

Clark, John Bates

Brandis, Royall. Distribution Theory: Scientific Analysis or Moral Philosophy? *J. Econ. Issues*, December 1985, *19*(4), pp. 867–78.

Tobin, James. Neoclassical Theory in America: J. B. Clark and Fisher. *Amer. Econ. Rev.*, December 1985, *75*(6), pp. 28–38.

Clark, John M.

Shute, Laurence. J. M. Clark on Corporate Concentration and Control. *J. Econ. Issues*, June 1985, *19*(2), pp. 409–18.

Coddington, Alan

Snippe, Jan. On the Scope of Hydraulic Macroeconomics: Some Reflections on Alan Coddington's Keynesian Economics. *De Economist*, 1985, *133*(4), pp. 467–83.

Commons, John R.

Endres, Anthony M. Veblen and Commons on Goodwill: A Case of Theoretical Divergence. *Hist. Polit. Econ.*, Winter 1985, *17*(4), pp. 637–49.

Parsons, Kenneth H. John R. Commons: His Relevance to Contemporary Economics. *J.*

Econ. Issues, September 1985, *19*(3), pp. 755–78.

Shalev, Michael. Labor Relations and Class Conflict: A Critical Survey of the Contributions of John R. Commons. **In** *Lipsky, D. B., ed.*, 1985, pp. 319–63. **[G: U.S.]**

de Condillac, Etienne Bonnot

Klein, Daniel Bruce. Deductive Economic Methodology in the French Enlightenment: Condillac and Destutt de Tracy. *Hist. Polit. Econ.*, Spring 1985, *17*(1), pp. 51–71.

Crawford, John [Sir]

Arndt, H. W. Sir John Crawford. *Econ. Rec.*, June 1985, *61*(173), pp. 507–15.

Davis, David Brion

Haskell, Thomas L. Capitalism and the Orgins of the Humanitarian Sensibility, Part 1. *Amer. Hist. Rev.*, April 1985, *90*(2), pp. 339–61.

Del Mar, Alexander

Tavlas, George S. and Aschheim, Joseph. Alexander Del Mar, Irving Fischer, and Monetary Economics. *Can. J. Econ.*, May 1985, *18*(2), pp. 294–313.

Destutt de Tracy, A. L. C.

Klein, Daniel Bruce. Deductive Economic Methodology in the French Enlightenment: Condillac and Destutt de Tracy. *Hist. Polit. Econ.*, Spring 1985, *17*(1), pp. 51–71.

Dyos, H. J.

Mandelbaum, Seymour J. H. J. Dyos and British Urban History. *Econ. Hist. Rev., 2nd Ser.*, August 1985, *38*(3), pp. 437–47.

Eccles, Marriner S.

Israelsen, L. Dwight. Macroeconomic Analysis of Leading Interwar Authorities: Marriner S. Eccles, Chairman of the Federal Reserve Board. *Amer. Econ. Rev.*, May 1985, *75*(2), pp. 357–62. **[G: U.S.]**

Eckstein, Otto

Jorgenson, Dale W. Otto Eckstein. *Eastern Econ. J.*, Jan.-Mar. 1985, *11*(1), pp. 1–2.

Kasputys, Joseph E. Moving Econometrics from Theory to Application. *Eastern Econ. J.*, Jan.-Mar. 1985, *11*(1), pp. 16–27.

Edison, Thomas Alva

Rubin, Israel. Thomas Alva Edison's "Treatise on National Economic Policy and Business." *Bus. Hist. Rev.*, Autumn 1985, *59*(3), pp. 433–64. **[G: U.S.]**

Engels, Friedrich

Mandel, Ernest. Marx and Engels on Commodity Production and Bureaucracy. **In** *[Magdoff, H. and Sweezy, P.]*, 1985, pp. 223–58.

Sherwood, John M. Engels, Marx, Malthus, and the Machine. *Amer. Hist. Rev.*, October 1985, *90*(4), pp. 837–65.

Eucken, Walter

Karsten, Siegfried G. Eucken's 'Social Market Economy' and Its Test in Post-war West Germany: The Economist as Social Philosopher Developed Ideas that Parallelled Progressive Thought in America. *Amer. J. Econ. Soc.*, April 1985, *44*(2), pp. 169–83. **[G: W. Germany]**

Ferrara, Francesco

Caffè, Federico. Il neoliberismo contemporaneo e l'eredità intellettuale di Francesco Ferrara. (The New Laissez-Faire in Contemporary Economics and the Intellectual Heritage of Francesco Ferrara. With English summary.) *Rivista Int. Sci. Econ. Com.*, January 1985, *32*(1), pp. 51–62.

Fisher, Irving

Beranek, William; Humphrey, Thomas M. and Timberlake, Richard H., Jr. Fisher, Thornton, and the Analysis of the Inflation Premium: A Note. *J. Money, Credit, Banking*, August 1985, *17*(3), pp. 370–77.

Tobin, James. Neoclassical Theory in America: J. B. Clark and Fisher. *Amer. Econ. Rev.*, December 1985, *75*(6), pp. 28–38.

Foner, Philip S.

Dubofsky, Melvyn. Give Us That Old Time Labor History: Philip S. Foner and the American Worker: Essay Review. *Labor Hist.*, Winter 1985, *26*(1), pp. 118–37.

George, Henry

Andelson, Robert V. Henry George and Economic Intervention: A Critic Proposes That George's Strictures on Industrial Monopolies Be Revised. *Amer. J. Econ. Soc.*, January 1985, *44*(1), pp. 97–105.

Benestad, J. Brian. Henry George and the Catholic View of Morality and the Common Good, I: George's Overall Critique of Pope Leo XIII's Classic Encyclical, 'Rerum Novarum.' *Amer. J. Econ. Soc.*, July 1985, *44*(3), pp. 365–78.

Bolton, Roger. Three Mysteries about Henry George. **In** *Lewis, S. R., Jr., ed.*, 1985, pp. 7–24.

Bronfenbrenner, Martin. Early American Leaders—Institutional and Critical Traditions. *Amer. Econ. Rev.*, December 1985, *75*(6), pp. 13–27.

Clark, Paul. Free Trade and Economic Development: Insights from Henry George: Comments. **In** *Lewis, S. R., Jr., ed.*, 1985, pp. 93–95.

Harriss, C. Lowell. Free Trade and Economic Development: Insights from Henry George. **In** *Lewis, S. R., Jr., ed.*, 1985, pp. 83–91.

Harriss, C. Lowell. Lessons of Enduring Value: Henry George a Century Later: The American Economist and Social Philosopher Can Help Us Solve Some of Today's Problems. *Amer. J. Econ. Soc.*, October 1985, *44*(4), pp. 479–89.

Nuesse, C. Joseph. Henry George and 'Rerun Novarum': Evidence Is Scant that the American Economist Was a Target of Leo XIII's Classical Encyclical. *Amer. J. Econ. Soc.*, April 1985, *44*(2), pp. 241–54.

Rafalko, Robert J. Was George a Dreamer or a Realist? Steven Cord's Book, Back in Print, Answers Marx's Taunt, Updates George's Ideas. *Amer. J. Econ. Soc.*, October 1985, *44*(4), pp. 491–95.

Gervaise, Isaac

Baletić, Zvonimir. Isaac Gervaise, prvi teoretičar opće ekonomske ravnoteže. (Isaac Gervaise, the First Theoretician of the General Economic Equilibrium. With English summary.) *Econ. Anal. Worker's Manage.*, 1985, *19*(3), pp. 263–79.

Goodwin, Richard
Harcourt, G. C. A Twentieth-Century Eclectic: Richard Goodwin. *J. Post Keynesian Econ.*, Spring 1985, *7*(3), pp. 410–21.

Gordon, Wendell
Hamilton, David. The Veblen–Commons Award: Wendell Gordon. *J. Econ. Issues*, June 1985, *19*(2), pp. 301–04.

Gossen, Herman Heinrich
Georgescu-Roegen, Nicholas. Time and Value in Economics and in Gossen's System. *Rivista Int. Sci. Econ. Com.*, December 1985, *32*(12), pp. 1121–40.

Guillaumin, Gilbert-Urbain
Levan-Lemesle, Lucette. Guillaumin, éditeur d'économie politique 1801–1864. (With English summary.) *Revue Écon. Polit.*, Mar.–Apr. 1985, *95*(2), pp. 134–49.

Harrod, Roy F.
Asimakopulos, Athanasios. Harrod on Harrod: The Evolution of a 'Line of Steady Growth.' *Hist. Polit. Econ.*, Winter 1985, *17*(4), pp. 619–35.
Kregel, J. A. Harrod and Keynes: Increasing Returns, the Theory of Employment and Dynamic Economics. In *Harcourt, G. C., ed.*, 1985, pp. 66–88.

Hawtrey, R. G.
de Boyer, Jérôme. Note sur la Theorie Monetaire de R. G. Hawtrey. (With English summary.) *Stud. Econ.*, 1985, *40*(25), pp. 3–27.
Howson, Susan. Tabled Paper: Hawtrey and the Real World. In *Harcourt, G. C., ed.*, 1985, pp. 142–88.

von Hayek, Friedrich A.
Falkena, H. B. On Hayek's Philosophy of Limited Government and the Economic Order (Review Article). *S. Afr. J. Econ.*, December 1985, *53*(4), pp. 366–80.
Vallageas, Bernard. Les circuits dane les analyses de Marx, Boehm-Bawerk, Hayek et Keynes. (Circuits in the Analyses of Marx, Boehm-Bawerk, Hayek and Keynes. With English summary.) *Écon. Soc.*, August 1985, *19*(8), pp. 47–68.

Hegel, G. W. Friedrich
Nitsch, Thomas O. Hegel: A Neglected Link in the Smith–Marx Connection. *Atlantic Econ. J.*, March 1985, *13*(1), pp. 98.

Heidhues, Theodor
Schmitt, Günther. Theodor Heidhues' Contribution to the Analysis of Agriculture and International Relations. In *[Heidhues, T.]*, 1985, pp. 17–28.

Heilperin, Michael A.
Salerno, Joseph T. Gold and the International Monetary System: The Contribution of Michael A. Heilperin. In *Rockwell, L. H., Jr., ed.*, 1985, pp. 81–111.

Hicks, John
Casarosa, Carlo and Zamagni, Stefano. Sir John Hicks: il pensiero e l'opera. (With English summary.) *Stud. Econ.*, 1985, *40*(27), pp. 3–75.
Hamouda, Omar F. The Evolution of Hicks' Theory of Money. *Bull. Econ. Res.*, May 1985, *37*(2), pp. 131–51.
Mahloudji, Farhad. Hicks and the Keynesian Revolution. *Hist. Polit. Econ.*, Summer 1985, *17*(2), pp. 287–307.

Hilferding, Rudolf
Darity, William A., Jr. and Horn, Bobbie L. Rudolf Hilferding: The Dominion of Capitalism and the Dominion of Gold. *Amer. Econ. Rev.*, May 1985, *75*(2), pp. 363–68. **[G: Germany]**
Harvey, Philip. The Value-creating Capacity of Skilled Labor in Marxian Economics. *Rev. Radical Polit. Econ.*, Spring and Summer 1985, *17*(1/2), pp. 83–102.

Hobbes, Thomas
Macpherson, C. B. Hobbes's Political Economy. In *Macpherson, C. B.*, 1985, pp. 133–46.

Hobson, John A.
Cain, Peter J. Hobson, Wilshire, and the Capitalist Theory of Capitalist Imperialism. *Hist. Polit. Econ.*, Fall 1985, *17*(3), pp. 455–60.

Home, Henry [Lord Kames]
Lieberman, David. The Legal Needs of a Commercial Society: The Jurisprudence of Lord Kames. In *Hont, I. and Ignatieff, M., eds.*, 1985, pp. 203–34.

Hutt, W. H.
Reynolds, Morgan O. An Interview with W. H. Hutt. *J. Lab. Res.*, Summer 1985, *6*(3), pp. 307–22.

Hymer, Stephen H.
Dunning, John H. and Rugman, Alan M. The Influence of Hymer's Dissertation on the Theory of Foreign Direct Investment. *Amer. Econ. Rev.*, May 1985, *75*(2), pp. 228–32.
Lecraw, Donald J. Hymer and Public Policy in *LDCs. Amer. Econ. Rev.*, May 1985, *75*(2), pp. 239–44. **[G: LDCs]**

Innis, Harold
Parker, Ian. Harold Innis: Staples, Communications, and the Economics of Capacity, Overhead Costs, Rigidity, and Bias. In *[Spry, I. M.]*, 1985, pp. 73–93.

Jefferson, Thomas
Foshee, Andrew W. Jeffersonian Political Economy and the Classical Republican Tradition: Jefferson, Taylor, and the Agrarian Republic. *Hist. Polit. Econ.*, Winter 1985, *17*(4), pp. 523–50. **[G: U.S.]**

Johansen, Leif
Solow, Robert M. Leif Johansen's Contributions to the Theory of Production, Planning, and Multisectoral Growth. In *[Johansen, L.]*, 1985, pp. 1–9.

Kalecki, Michal
Basile, Liliana and Salvadori, Neri. Kalecki's Pricing Theory. *J. Post Keynesian Econ.*,

Winter 1984–85, 7(2), pp. 249–62.

Halevi, Joseph. Effective Demand, Capacity Utilization and the Sectoral Distribution of Investment. *Écon. Soc.*, August 1985, *19*(8), pp. 25–45.

Langer, Gary F. Kalecki and the Keynesians. *Econ. Forum*, Winter 1985-1986, *15*(2), pp. 21–34.

Lee, Frederic S. "Kalecki's Pricing Theory": Two Comments. *J. Post Keynesian Econ.*, Fall 1985, *8*(1), pp. 145–48.

Lianos, Theodore P. A Note on Three Theories of the Relative Share of Labor. *Greek Econ. Rev.*, April 1985, 7(1), pp. 82–84.

Sawyer, Malcolm C. The Economics of Michal Kalecki. *Eastern Europ. Econ.*, Spring-Summer 1985, *23*(3–4), pp. 1–319.

Sawyer, Malcolm C. Towards a Post-Kaleckian Macroeconomics. **In** *Arestis, P. and Skouras, T., eds.*, 1985, pp. 146–79.

Keynes, John Maynard

Anyadike-Danes, M. K. Dennis Robertson and Keynes's General Theory. **In** *Harcourt, G. C., ed.*, 1985, pp. 105–23.

Asimakopulos, Athanasios. "Long-Period Employment" in *The General Theory*. *J. Post Keynesian Econ.*, Winter 1984–85, 7(2), pp. 207–13.

Asimakopulos, Athanasios. Finance, Saving and Investment in Keynes's Economics: A Comment. *Cambridge J. Econ.*, December 1985, *9*(4), pp. 405–07.

Asimakopulos, Athanasios. The Role of Finance in Keynes's General Theory. *Econ. Notes*, 1985, (3), pp. 5–16.

Backhaus, Juergen. Keynesianism in Germany. **In** *Lawson, T. and Pesaran, H., eds.*, 1985, pp. 209–53.

Barrère, Alain. Economie réelle—Economie monétaire: alternative ou conciliation? (Real Economy—Monetary Economy: Option or Adjustment? With English summary.) *Écon. Appl.*, 1985, *38*(1), pp. 17–61.

Barrère, Alain. Les rapports entre les problématiques de Joan Robinson et de J.M. Keynes. (The Relationship between the Theoretical Issues in Joan Robinson and in J. M. Keynes. With English summary.) *Écon. Appl.*, 1985, *38*(2), pp. 389–423.

Behrens, Rolf. What Keynes Knew about Marx. *Stud. Econ.*, 1985, *40*(26), pp. 3–14.
[G: Marx, Karl; Keynes, John Maynard]

Benetti, Carlo. Economie monétaire et économie de troc: la question de l'unité de compte commune. (Barter Economy and Monetary Economy: The Problem of the Single Standard of Value. With English summary.) *Écon. Appl.*, 1985, *38*(1), pp. 85–109.

Bernstein, Peter L. Wall Street's View of Keynes and Keynes's View of Wall Street. **In** *Wattel, H. L., ed.*, 1985, pp. 22–29.

Birch, Thomas D. Marshall and Keynes Revisited [J. M. Keynes as a Marshallian]. *J. Econ. Issues*, March 1985, *19*(1), pp. 194–200.

Boland, Lawrence A. The Foundations of

Keynes' Methodology:*The General Theory*. **In** *Lawson, T. and Pesaran, H., eds.*, 1985, pp. 181–94.

Booth, Alan. The "Keynesian Revolution" and Economic Policy-making: A Reply. *Econ. Hist. Rev., 2nd Ser.*, February 1985, *38*(1), pp. 101–06.

Brandis, Royall. Marx *and* Keynes? Marx *or* Keynes? *J. Econ. Issues*, September 1985, *19*(3), pp. 643–59.

Brown-Collier, Elba K. Keynes' View of an Organic Universe: The Implications. *Rev. Soc. Econ.*, April 1985, *43*(1), pp. 14–23.

Caprara, Ugo. Opinioni e teorie di John Maynard Keynes nella interpretazione di un economista aziendale. (Opinions and Theories of John Maynard Keynes as Interpreted by a Professor of Business Economics. With English summary.) *Rivista Int. Sci. Econ. Com.*, February 1985, *32*(2), pp. 167–82.

Carabelli, Anna. Keynes on Cause, Chance and Possibility. **In** *Lawson, T. and Pesaran, H., eds.*, 1985, pp. 151–80.

Chandavarkar, Anand G. Keynes and Central Banking. *Indian Econ. Rev.*, July-Dec. 1985, *20*(2), pp. 283–97.

Chick, Victoria. Time and the Wage-Unit in the Method of *The General Theory*: History and Equilibrium. **In** *Lawson, T. and Pesaran, H., eds.*, 1985, pp. 195–208.

Dillard, Dudley. The Influence of Keynesian Thought on German Economic Policy. **In** *Wattel, H. L., ed.*, 1985, pp. 116–27.
[G: W. Germany]

Dow, Alexander and Dow, Sheila C. Animal Spirits and Rationality. **In** *Lawson, T. and Pesaran, H., eds.*, 1985, pp. 46–65.

Eatwell, John. Keynes, Keynesians, and British Economic Policy. **In** *Wattel, H. L., ed.*, 1985, pp. 61–76. [G: OECD]

Estrin, Saul and Holmes, Peter. Uncertainty, Efficiency, and Economic Planning in Keynesian Economics. *J. Post Keynesian Econ.*, Summer 1985, 7(4), pp. 463–73.

Farina, Francesco. Keynes' Theory of Interest and Modern Monetary Analysis. **In** *Arena, R., et al.*, 1985, pp. 101–21.

Favereau, Olivier. L'incertain dans la "révolution keynésienne": l'hypothèse Wittgenstein. (Uncertainty in the Keynesian Revolution: The Wittgenstein Hypothesis. With English summary.) *Écon. Soc.*, March 1985, *19*(3), pp. 29–72.

de Finetti, Bruno. Cambridge Probability Theorists. *Manchester Sch. Econ. Soc. Stud.*, December 1985, *53*(4), pp. 348–63.

Fodor, Giorgio. I pericoli della stabilità: Keynes e i suoi avversari prima della "teoria generale." (The Dangers of Stability: Keynes and His Opponents after the General Theory. With English summary.) *Polit. Econ.*, December 1985, *1*(3), pp. 429–60.
[G: U.S.]

Galbraith, John Kenneth. Keynes, Roosevelt, and the Complementary Revolutions. **In** *Wattel, H. L., ed.*, 1985, pp. 54–60.

Garrison, Roger W. Intertemporal Coordination and the Invisible Hand: An Austrian Perspective on the Keynesian Vision. *Hist. Polit. Econ.*, Summer 1985, *17*(2), pp. 309–21.

Glynn, Sean; Booth, Alan and Howells, Peter. NEH, NEH, NEH and the 'Keynesian Solution' [Unemployment in the 1930s: The Keynesian Solution Reconsidered]. *Australian Econ. Hist. Rev.*, September 1985, *25*(2), pp. 149–57.   [G: U.K.]

Graziani, Augusto. Le débat sur le "motif de financement" de J. M. Keynes. (The Debate on Keynes's Financing Motive." With English summary.) *Écon. Appl.*, 1985, *38*(1), pp. 159–75.

Grellet, Gérard. La monnaie est-elle à l'origine du chômage? (Is Money Generating Unemployment? With English summary.) *Écon. Appl.*, 1985, *38*(1), pp. 301–08.

Griffin, Robert A. A Communicative Study of the Dissenting Views of John Maynard Keynes and Thorstein Veblen on the Treaty of Versailles. *Revue Écon. Polit.*, Mar.–Apr. 1985, *95*(2), pp. 174–88.

Haberler, Gottfried. Mr. Keynes' Theory of the "Multiplier": A Methodological Criticism. **In** *Haberler, G.*, 1985, pp. 553–60.

Haberler, Gottfried. The General Theory after Ten Years and Sixteen Years Later. **In** *Haberler, G.*, 1985, pp. 581–602.

Hansson, Björn. Keynes's Notion of Equilibrium in the *General Theory*. *J. Post Keynesian Econ.*, Spring 1985, *7*(3), pp. 332–41.

Harcourt, G. C. and O'Shaughnessy, T. J. Keynes's Unemployment Equilibrium: Some Insights from Joan Robinson, Piero Sraffa and Richard Kahn. **In** *Harcourt, G. C.*, ed., 1985, pp. 3–41.

Hatton, T. J. Unemployment in the 1930s and the 'Keynesian Solution': Some Notes of Dissent. *Australian Econ. Hist. Rev.*, September 1985, *25*(2), pp. 129–48.
                              [G: U.K.]

Hession, Charles H. Lord Keynes Meets Adam Smith. *Challenge*, May/June 1985, *28*(2), pp. 59–63.   [G: U.S.]

Hicks, John. Keynes and the World Economy. **In** *Vicarelli, F.*, ed., 1985, pp. 21–27.

Hodgson, Geoffrey M. Persuasion, Expectations and the Limits to Keynes. **In** *Lawson, T. and Pesaran, H.*, eds., 1985, pp. 10–45.

Howson, Susan. Tabled Paper: Hawtrey and the Real World. **In** *Harcourt, G. C.*, ed., 1985, pp. 142–88.

Jensen, Hans E. Marshall Revisited: A Reply [J. M. Keynes as a Marshallian]. *J. Econ. Issues*, December 1985, *19*(4), pp. 967–74.

Jha, L. K. The Relevance of Keynes Today. **In** *Jha, L. K.*, 1985, pp. 217–25.

Kahn, Richard. The Cambridge 'Circus' (1). **In** *Harcourt, G. C.*, ed., 1985, pp. 42–51.

Klant, Johannes J. The Slippery Transition. **In** *Lawson, T. and Pesaran, H.*, eds., 1985, pp. 80–98.

Kregel, J. A. Harrod and Keynes: Increasing Returns, the Theory of Employment and Dynamic Economics. **In** *Harcourt, G. C.*, ed., 1985, pp. 66–88.

Larceneux, A. Keynes et Ricardo: une synthe est-elle possible? (Keynes and Ricardo: The Impossible Synthesis. With English summary.) *Écon. Soc.*, August 1985, *19*(8), pp. 7–23.

Lavoie, Marc. Inflation, chômage et la planification des récessions: La Théorie générale" de Keynes et après. (Inflation, Unemployment and Planned Recessions: Keynes' 'General Theory' and After. With English summary.) *L'Actual. Econ.*, June 1985, *61*(2), pp. 171–99.

Lavoie, Marc. La distinction entre l'incertitude keynésienne et le risque néoclassique. (The Distinction between Keynesian Uncertainty and Neo-Classical Risk. With English summary.) *Écon. Appl.*, 1985, *38*(2), pp. 493–518.

Lawson, Tony. Keynes, Prediction and Econometrics. **In** *Lawson, T. and Pesaran, H.*, eds., 1985, pp. 116–33.

Lawson, Tony and Pesaran, Hashem M. Methodological Issues in Keynes' Economics: An Introduction. **In** *Lawson, T. and Pesaran, H.*, eds., 1985, pp. 1–9.

Le Héron, Edwin. Circulation industrielle, circulation financière et taux d'intérêt. (Industrial Circulation, Financial Circulation and Interest Rates. With English summary.) *Écon. Appl.*, 1985, *38*(1), pp. 211–34.

Lekachman, Robert. The Radical Keynes. **In** *Wattel, H. L.*, ed., 1985, pp. 30–38.

Leontief, Wassily. Postulates: Keynes's *General Theory* and the Classicists. **In** *Leontief, W.*, 1985, pp. 93–103.

Leontief, Wassily. The Fundamental Assumption of Mr. Keynes's Monetary Theory of Unemployment. **In** *Leontief, W.*, 1985, pp. 87–92.

Littleboy, Bruce and Mehta, Ghanshyam. Keynes and Scientific Methodology: Whither and Whence. *Indian Econ. J.*, July-Sept. 1985, *33*(1), pp. 66–76.

Lunghini, Giorgio. Capitalist Equilibrium: From Soho to Bloomsbury. **In** *Vicarelli, F.*, ed., 1985, pp. 51–72.

Mahloudji, Farhad. Hicks and the Keynesian Revolution. *Hist. Polit. Econ.*, Summer 1985, *17*(2), pp. 287–307.

Ménard, Claude. Le keynésianisme: naissance d'une illusion. (Keynesianism: The Genesis of an Illusion. With English summary.) *Écon. Soc.*, March 1985, *19*(3), pp. 3–27.

Miller, Edward McCarthy. Keynesian Economics as a Translation Error: An Essay on Keynes' Financial Theory. *Hist. Polit. Econ.*, Summer 1985, *17*(2), pp. 265–85.

Minsky, Hyman P. The Legacy of Keynes. *J. Econ. Educ.*, Winter 1985, *16*(1), pp. 5–15.

Mondello, Gérard. Étude de la liaison monnaie-revenu demande effective: les théories de Thomas Tooke et J. M. Keynes. (A Study about the Links between Money-Income-Effective Demand: The Theories of T. Tooke and J. M. Keynes. With English summary.) *Revue Écon.*, May 1985, *36*(3), pp. 509–54.

Pesaran, Hashem M. and Smith, R. P. Keynes on Econometrics. In *Lawson, T. and Pesaran, H., eds.*, 1985, pp. 134–50. [G: U.K.]

Pheby, John. Are Popperian Criticisms of Keynes Justified? In *Lawson, T. and Pesaran, H., eds.*, 1985, pp. 99–115.

Poulon, Frédéric. Contrainte extérieure et capacité de transfert d'un pays à l'étranger: Keynes et les réparations allemandes. (Foreign Constraints and the Ability to Transfer Payments Abroad: Keynes and German Reparations. With English summary.) *Écon. Soc.*, April 1985, *19*(4), pp. 27–43.

Poulon, Frédéric. Réponses de la théorie du circuit à quelques questions relatives au temps, à l'équilibre macro-économique et au libre-échange. (The Theory of Circuits Answers Questions Concerning Concepts of Time, Macroeconomic Equilibrium and Free Trade. With English summary.) *Écon. Soc.*, August 1985, *19*(8), pp. 69–84.

Robinson, Austin [Sir]. The Cambridge 'Circus' (2). In *Harcourt, G. C., ed.*, 1985, pp. 52–57.

Robinson, Joan. Ideology and Logic. In *Vicarelli, F., ed.*, 1985, pp. 73–98.

Rogers, C. A Critique of Clower's Dual Decision Hypothesis. *S. Afr. J. Econ.*, June 1985, *53*(2), pp. 111–23.

Rollings, N. The "Keynesian Revolution" and Economic Policy-making: A Comment. *Econ. Hist. Rev., 2nd Ser.*, February 1985, *38*(1), pp. 95–100. [G: U.K.]

Salant, Walter S. *Keynes and the Modern World:* A Review Article. *J. Econ. Lit.*, September 1985, *23*(3), pp. 1176–85.

Sawyer, Malcolm C. Towards a Post-Kaleckian Macroeconomics. In *Arestis, P. and Skouras, T., eds.*, 1985, pp. 146–79.

Singer, Hans W. Relevance of Keynes for Developing Countries. In *Wattel, H. L., ed.*, 1985, pp. 128–44.

Smithin, John Nicholas. The Definition of Involuntary Unemployment in Keynes' *General Theory:* A Note. *Hist. Polit. Econ.*, Summer 1985, *17*(2), pp. 219–22.

Snippe, Jan. Finance, Saving and Investment in Keynes's Economics. *Cambridge J. Econ.*, September 1985, *9*(3), pp. 257–69.

Steindl, Josef. J. M. Keynes: Society and the Economist. In *Vicarelli, F., ed.*, 1985, pp. 99–125.

Sweezy, Paul M. Listen Keynesians!! In *Wattel, H. L., ed.*, 1985, pp. 39–47.

Sylos Labini, Paolo. The *General Theory:* Critical Reflections Suggested by Some Important Problems of Our Time. In *Vicarelli, F., ed.*, 1985, pp. 126–54.

Tarascio, Vincent J. Keynes, Population, and Equity Prices. *J. Post Keynesian Econ.*, Spring 1985, *7*(3), pp. 303–10. [G: U.S.]

Tobin, James. Keynes's Policies in Theory and Practice. In *Wattel, H. L., ed.*, 1985, pp. 13–21.

Ture, Norman B. Keynes's Influence on Public Policy: A Conservative's View. In *Wattel, H. L., ed.*, 1985, pp. 48–53.

Vallageas, Bernard. Les circuits dane les analyses de Marx, Boehm-Bawerk, Hayek et Keynes. (Circuits in the Analyses of Marx, Boehm-Bawerk, Hayek and Keynes. With English summary.) *Écon. Soc.*, August 1985, *19*(8), pp. 47–68.

Vercelli, Alessandro. Money and Production in Schumpeter and Keynes: Two Dichotomies. In *Arena, R., et al.*, 1985, pp. 31–45.

Vicarelli, Fausto. From Equilibrium to Probability: A Reinterpretation of the Method of the *General Theory*. In *Vicarelli, F., ed.*, 1985, pp. 155–77.

Vincens, Jean. Réel, nominal, monétaire: Keynes et les salaires relatifs. (Real, Nominal and Monetary: Keynes and Relative Wages. With English summary.) *Écon. Appl.*, 1985, *38*(1), pp. 237–64.

Walker, Donald A. Keynes as a Historian of Economic Thought: The Biographical Essays on Neoclassical Economists. *Hist. Polit. Econ.*, Summer 1985, *17*(2), pp. 159–86.

Wattel, Harold L. The Policy Consequences of John Maynard Keynes: Introduction. In *Wattel, H. L., ed.*, 1985, pp. 3–12.

Williamson, John. Keynes and the Postwar International Economic Order. In *Wattel, H. L., ed.*, 1985, pp. 145–56.

Wilson, T. Dennis Robertson and Keynes's General Theory: Comment. In *Harcourt, G. C., ed.*, 1985, pp. 124–28.

King, Gregory

Laslett, Peter. Gregory King, Robert Malthus and the Origins of English Social Realism. *Population Stud.*, November 1985, *39*(3), pp. 351–62.

Knight, Frank H.

Lavoie, Marc. La distinction entre l'incertitude keynésienne et le risque néoclassique. (The Distinction between Keynesian Uncertainty and Neo-Classical Risk. With English summary.) *Écon. Appl.*, 1985, *38*(2), pp. 493–518.

Lanzoni, Primo

Zanetto, Gabriele. Primo Lanzoni, ovvero l'economia come antitesi all'ambientalismo nel pensiero geografico ottocentesco. (Primo Lanzoni, Economics and Naturalism in Geographical Thought. With English summary.) *Ricerche Econ.*, Jan.-Mar. 1985, *39*(1), pp. 70–103.

Lardner, Dionysius

Shieh, Yeung-Nan and Goldberg, Ira. Lardner's Law of Squares. *Economica*, November 1985, *52*(208), pp. 509–12.

Lerner, Abba P.
Shepherd, A. Ross. A Comment on Lerner's "Extortion Tax" Plan [Lerner's Contribution to Economics]. *J. Econ. Lit.*, September 1985, 23(3), pp. 1192.

Levcik, Friedrich
Fink, Gerhard. Socialist Economy and Economic Policy: Foreword. In *[Levcik, F.]*, 1985, pp. 5–9.

Lewis, W. Arthur
Bhagwati, Jagdish N. W. Arthur Lewis: An Appreciation. In *Bhagwati, J. N. (II)*, 1985, pp. 277–91.

Loria, Achille
Pinto, James V. Loria and Location Theory. *Ricerche Econ.*, Apr.-June 1985, 39(2), pp. 221–32.

Magdoff, Harry
Edel, Kim and Edel, Matthew. Dialogue, Utopia and the Division of Labor: Reflections on Some Themes by Harry Magdoff. In *[Magdoff, H. and Sweezy, P.]*, 1985, pp. 83–98.

Hillard, Michael. Harry Magdoff and Paul Sweezy: Biographical Notes. In *[Magdoff, H. and Sweezy, P.]*, 1985, pp. 397–404.

Resnick, Stephen A. and Wolff, Richard D. Rethinking Marxism: Introduction: Solutions and Problems. In *[Magdoff, H. and Sweezy, P.]*, 1985, pp. ix–xxxiv.

Malthus, Thomas Robert
Costabile, Lilia and Rowthorn, Bob. Malthus's Theory of Wages and Growth. *Econ. J.*, June 1985, 95(378), pp. 418–37.

Jäggi, Stefan. Karl Marx und die Malthusianische Bevölkerungstheorie. (Karl Marx and the Malthusian Population Theory. With English summary.) *Schweiz. Z. Volkswirtsch. Statist.*, June 1985, 121(2), pp. 95–113.

Laslett, Peter. Gregory King, Robert Malthus and the Origins of English Social Realism. *Population Stud.*, November 1985, 39(3), pp. 351–62.

Maritain, Jacques
Doering, Bernard. The Economics of Jacques Maritain. *Rev. Soc. Econ.*, April 1985, 43(1), pp. 64–72.

Marshall, Alfred
Dooley, Peter C. Alfred Marshall: Fitting the Theory to the Facts. *Cambridge J. Econ.*, September 1985, 9(3), pp. 245–55.

Dumez, Hervé. Walras, Marshall: Stratégies scientifiques comparées. (With English summary.) *Revue Écon. Polit.*, Mar.-Apr. 1985, 95(2), pp. 168–73.

Lallement, Jérôme. L'utilité mesurée comme une grandeur de la physique. (Alfred Marshall: Utility Measured as a Physical Magnitude. With English summary.) *Écon. Soc.*, March 1985, 19(3), pp. 147–71.

Marx, Karl
Barrère, Christian. L'objet d'une théorie de la régulation. (The Purpose of a Regulation Theory. With English summary.) *Écon. Soc.*, January 1985, 19(1), pp. 9–28.

Behrens, Rolf. What Keynes Knew about Marx. *Stud. Econ.*, 1985, 40(26), pp. 3–14. [G: Marx, Karl; Keynes, John Maynard]

Bellofiore, Riccardo. Money and Development in Schumpeter. *Rev. Radical Polit. Econ.*, Spring and Summer 1985, 17(1/2), pp. 21–40.

Benetti, Carlo. Economie monétaire et économie de troc: la question de l'unité de compte commune. (Barter Economy and Monetary Economy: The Problem of the Single Standard of Value. With English summary.) *Écon. Appl.*, 1985, 38(1), pp. 85–109.

Bettelheim, Charles. Reflections on Concepts of Class and Class Struggle in Marx's Work. In *[Magdoff, H. and Sweezy, P.]*, 1985, pp. 15–29.

Bishop, Robert L. Competitive Value When Only Labor Is Scarce. *Quart. J. Econ.*, November 1985, 100(4), pp. 1257–92.

Brandis, Royall. Marx *and* Keynes? Marx *or* Keynes? *J. Econ. Issues*, September 1985, 19(3), pp. 643–59.

Chavance, Bernard. The Utopian Dialectic of Capitalism and Communism in Marx. *Econ. Anal. Worker's Manage.*, 1985, 19(3), pp. 249–62.

Crotty, James R. The Centrality of Money, Credit, and Financial Intermediation in Marx's Crisis Theory: An Interpretation of Marx's Methodology. In *[Magdoff, H. and Sweezy, P.]*, 1985, pp. 45–81.

De Vroey, Michel. La théorie du salaire de Marx: une critique hétérodoxe. (Marx's Theory of Wages: An Heterodox Criticism. With English summary.) *Revue Écon.*, May 1985, 36(3), pp. 451–80.

Deleplace, Ghislain. Sur quelques difficultés de la théorie de la monnaie-marchandise chez Ricardo et Marx. (Some Problems in the Theory of Commodity Money by Ricardo and Marx. With English summary.) *Écon. Appl.*, 1985, 38(1), pp. 111–31.

Frank, Andre Gunder. A Marx, Keynes, Schumpeter Centenary and the Editors of Monthly Review. In *[Magdoff, H. and Sweezy, P.]*, 1985, pp. 115–26.

Guibert, Bernard. Théorie naive des ensembles capitalistes. (A Naive Theory of the Capitalist Sets. With English summary.) *Revue Écon.*, May 1985, 36(3), pp. 481–508.

Henderson, James P. An English Communist, Mr. Bray [and] His Remarkable Work. *Hist. Polit. Econ.*, Spring 1985, 17(1), pp. 73–95.

Jäggi, Stefan. Karl Marx und die Malthusianische Bevölkerungstheorie. (Karl Marx and the Malthusian Population Theory. With English summary.) *Schweiz. Z. Volkswirtsch. Statist.*, June 1985, 121(2), pp. 95–113.

Janover, Louis and Rubel, Maximilien. Matériaux pur un lexique de Marx. (Material for a Marx Lexikon: Revolution II. With English summary.) *Écon. Soc.*, November 1985, 19(11), pp. 55–95.

Ji, Xianju. A Discussion of the Idea that Both Interpretations of Socially Necessary Labor Time Should Be Considered in the Determination of Value. *Chinese Econ. Stud.*, Spring 1985, *18*(3), pp. 77–91.

Lapidus, André. Sur la question de l'existence de l'ornithorynque en économie politique (Éloge raisonné d'une contribution à la zoologie économique). (With English summary.) *Revue Écon. Polit.*, Mar.–Apr. 1985, *95*(2), pp. 189–207.

Leadbeater, David. The Consistency of Marx's Categories of Productive and Unproductive Labour. *Hist. Polit. Econ.*, Winter 1985, *17*(4), pp. 591–618.

Lebowitz, Michael A. The Theoretical Status of Monopoly Capital. In *[Magdoff, H. and Sweezy, P.]*, 1985, pp. 185–203.

Levine, David P. On the Analysis of Advanced Capitalist Economy. In *[Magdoff, H. and Sweezy, P.]*, 1985, pp. 205–22.

Lippi, Marco. Ancora su valore e costa reale in Marx: risposta alle critiche di petri. (Value and Real Cost in Marx Once Again. With English summary.) *Rivista Int. Sci. Econ. Com.*, July-Aug. 1985, *32*(7–8), pp. 635–59.

Little, Daniel. The Scientific Standing of Marx's *Capital. Rev. Radical Polit. Econ.*, Winter 1985, *17*(4), pp. 72–94.

Lunghini, Giorgio. Capitalist Equilibrium: From Soho to Bloomsbury. In *Vicarelli, F., ed.*, 1985, pp. 51–72.

Lyall, A. B. An Error in Marx's *Capital* II: Fixed Capital in Kind. *Hist. Polit. Econ.*, Winter 1985, *17*(4), pp. 651–55.

Mandel, Ernest. Marx and Engels on Commodity Production and Bureaucracy. In *[Magdoff, H. and Sweezy, P.]*, 1985, pp. 223–58.

Pokorný, Dušan. Karl Marx and General Equilibrium. *Hist. Polit. Econ.*, Spring 1985, *17*(1), pp. 109–32.

Roche, John. Marx's Theory of Money: A Reinterpretation. *Rev. Radical Polit. Econ.*, Spring and Summer 1985, *17*(1/2), pp. 201–11.

Rubel, Maximilien. Marx Jubiläums Edition (MJE) 1883–1983. Pour une Édition du Jubilé 1883–1983. (For a Jubilee Edition 1883–1983 Prologue (Annexe: Letter from Friedrich Adler to M. R. With English summary.) *Écon. Soc.*, November 1985, *19*(11), pp. 7–54.

Russell, James W. Method, Analysis, and Politics in Max Weber: Disentangling Marxian Affinities and Differences. *Hist. Polit. Econ.*, Winter 1985, *17*(4), pp. 575–90.

Szymanski, Al. Crisis and Vitalization in Marxist Theory. *Sci. Soc.*, Fall 1985, *49*(3), pp. 315–31.

Vallageas, Bernard. Les circuits dans les analyses de Marx, Boehm-Bawerk, Hayek et Keynes. (Circuits in the Analyses of Marx, Boehm-Bawerk, Hayek and Keynes. With English summary.) *Écon. Soc.*, August 1985, *19*(8), pp. 47–68.

Wallerstein, Immanuel. Marx and Underdevelopment. In *[Magdoff, H. and Sweezy, P.]*, 1985, pp. 379–95.

McCulloch, James Ramsey

Thweatt, William O. De Vivo's Neglected Evidence: A Reply [The Author of the Article on Owen in the October 1819 *Edinburgh Review:* Some Neglected Evidence]. *Hist. Polit. Econ.*, Summer 1985, *17*(2), pp. 201–02.

de Vivo, Giancarlo. The Author of the Article on Owen in the October 1819 *Edinburgh Review:* Some Neglected Evidence [Mr. Owen's Plans for Relieving the National Distress]. *Hist. Polit. Econ.*, Summer 1985, *17*(2), pp. 199–201.

Menger, Carl

Butos, William N. Menger: A Suggested Interpretation. *Atlantic Econ. J.*, July 1985, *13*(2), pp. 21–30.

Mill, John Stuart

Brandis, Royall. Distribution Theory: Scientific Analysis or Moral Philosophy? *J. Econ. Issues*, December 1985, *19*(4), pp. 867–78.

Davis, Elynor G. Mill, Socialism and the English Romantics: An Interpretation. *Economica*, August 1985, *52*(207), pp. 345–58.

Ekelund, Robert B., Jr. Mill's Recantation Once Again: Reply. *Oxford Econ. Pap.*, March 1985, *37*(1), pp. 152–53.

Negishi, Takashi. Mill's Recantation of the Wages Fund: Comment. *Oxford Econ. Pap.*, March 1985, *37*(1), pp. 148–51.

Platteau, J. Ph. The Political Economy of John Stuart Mill, or, the Coexistence of Orthodoxy, Heresy and Prophecy. *Int. J. Soc. Econ.*, 1985, *12*(1), pp. 3–26.

Smith, Vardaman R. John Stuart Mill's Famous Distinction between Production and Distribution. *Econ. Philos.*, October 1985, *1*(2), pp. 267–84.

Millar, John

Ignatieff, Michael. John Millar and Individualism. In *Hont, I. and Ignatieff, M., eds.*, 1985, pp. 317–43.

Minsky, Hyman P.

Minsky, Hyman P. Beginnings. *Banca Naz. Lavoro Quart. Rev.*, September 1985, (154), pp. 211–21.

von Mises, Ludwig

Kirzner, Israel M. Uncertainty, Discovery, and Human Action: A Study of the Entrepreneurial Profile in the Misesian System. In *Kirzner, I. M.*, 1985, pp. 40–67.

Orwell, George

Roback, Jennifer. The Economic Thought of George Orwell. *Amer. Econ. Rev.*, May 1985, *75*(2), pp. 127–32.

Pigou, Arthur C.

Haberler, Gottfried. The Pigou Effect Once More. In *Haberler, G.*, 1985, pp. 573–80.

Polanyi, Karl

Mayhew, Anne; Neale, Walter C. and Tandy, David W. Markets in the Ancient Near East: A Challenge to Silver's Argument and

Use of Evidence [Karl Polanyi and Markets in the Ancient Near East: The Challenge of the Evidence]. *J. Econ. Hist.*, March 1985, *45*(1), pp. 127–34.

[G: Middle East]

Silver, Morris. Markets in the Ancient Near East: A Challenge to Silver's Argument and Use of Evidence: Karl Polanyi and Markets in the Ancient Near East: Reply. *J. Econ. Hist.*, March 1985, *45*(1), pp. 135–37.

Quesnay, François

Giacometti, Jacques. Physique et métaphysique dans l'ordre naturel: le tableau économique de F. Quesnay. (On the Physiocracy: Physics and Metaphysics in "l'ordre naturel" and le "tableau économique." With English summary.) *Écon. Soc.*, March 1985, *19*(3), pp. 173–96.

Ricardo, David

Adams, Jack E. David Ricardo's Theory of Value: A Revisit. *Atlantic Econ. J.*, July 1985, *13*(2), pp. 69–72.

Ahiakpor, James C. W. Ricardo on Money: The Operational Significance of the Nonneutrality of Money in the Short Run. *Hist. Polit. Econ.*, Spring 1985, *17*(1), pp. 17–30.

Bishop, Robert L. Competitive Value When Only Labor Is Scarce. *Quart. J. Econ.*, November 1985, *100*(4), pp. 1257–92.

Blaug, Mark. What Ricardo Said and What Ricardo Meant. In *Caravale, G. A., ed.*, 1985, pp. 3–10.

Caravale, Giovanni A. Diminishing Returns and Accumulation in Ricardo. In *Caravale, G. A., ed.*, 1985, pp. 127–88.

Casarosa, Carlo. The 'New View' of the Ricardian Theory of Distribution and Economic Growth. In *Caravale, G. A., ed.*, 1985, pp. 45–58.

Costa, Giacomo. Time in Ricardian Models: Some Critical Observations and Some New Results. In *Caravale, G. A., ed.*, 1985, pp. 59–83.

Deleplace, Ghislain. Sur quelques difficultés de la théorie de la monnaie-marchandise chez Ricardo et Marx. (Some Problems in the Theory of Commodity Money by Ricardo and Marx. With English summary.) *Écon. Appl.*, 1985, *38*(1), pp. 111–31.

Eltis, Walter. Ricardo on Machinery and Technological Unemployment. In *Caravale, G. A., ed.*, 1985, pp. 257–84.

Garegnani, Pierangelo. On Hollander's Interpretation of Ricardo's Early Theory of Profits. In *Caravale, G. A., ed.*, 1985, pp. 87–104.

Heertje, A.; Weatherall, D. and Polak, R. W. An Unpublished Letter of David Ricardo to Francis Finch, 24 February 1823. *Econ. J.*, December 1985, *95*(380), pp. 1091–92.

Hicks, John. Sraffa and Ricardo: A Critical View. In *Caravale, G. A., ed.*, 1985, pp. 305–19.

Larceneux, A. Keynes et Ricardo: une synthe est-elle possible? (Keynes and Ricardo: The Impossible Synthesis. With English summary.) *Écon. Soc.*, August 1985, *19*(8), pp. 7–23.

Meacci, Ferdinando. Ricardo's Chapter on Machinery and the Theory of Capital. In *Caravale, G. A., ed.*, 1985, pp. 285–302.

Porta, Pier Luigi. The Debate on Ricardo: Old Results in New Frameworks. In *Caravale, G. A., ed.*, 1985, pp. 217–38.

Roncaglia, Alessandro. Hollander's Ricardo. In *Caravale, G. A., ed.*, 1985, pp. 105–23.

Rosselli, Annalisa. The Theory of the Natural Wage. In *Caravale, G. A., ed.*, 1985, pp. 239–54.

Sylos Labini, Paolo. Valore e distribuzione in un'economia robotizzata. (With English summary.) *Econ. Polít.*, December 1985, *2*(3), pp. 359–63.

Tosato, Domenico. A Reconsideration of Sraffa's Interpretation of Ricardo on Value and Distribution. In *Caravale, G. A., ed.*, 1985, pp. 189–216.

de Vivo, Giancarlo. Robert Torrens and Ricardo's 'Corn-Ratio' Theory of Profits. *Cambridge J. Econ.*, March 1985, *9*(1), pp. 89–92.

Robbins, Lionel

Baumol, William J. Obituary: Lionel Robbins. *Economica*, February 1985, *52*(205), pp. 5–7.

Meade, James E. Obituary: Lionel Robbins. *Economica*, February 1985, *52*(205), pp. 3–5.

Robertson, Dennis H.

Anyadike-Danes, M. K. Dennis Robertson and Keynes's General Theory. In *Harcourt, G. C., ed.*, 1985, pp. 105–23.

Costabile, Lilia. Credit Creation, Capital Formation and Abstinence in the Approach of D. H. Robertson. In *Arena, R., et al.*, 1985, pp. 265–86.

Wilson, T. Dennis Robertson and Keynes's General Theory: Comment. In *Harcourt, G. C., ed.*, 1985, pp. 124–28.

Robinson, Joan

Barrère, Alain. Les rapports entre les problématiques de Joan Robinson et de J.M. Keynes. (The Relationship between the Theoretical Issues in Joan Robinson and in J. M. Keynes. With English summary.) *Écon. Appl.*, 1985, *38*(2), pp. 389–423.

Kregel, J. A. Post-Keynesian Distribution Theory in Relation to Growth and Technical Progress. *Écon. Appl.*, 1985, *38*(2), pp. 375–88.

Weiller, Jean. Effets "normaux" ou "pervers"? Comment interpréter le "théorème des élasticités critiques" lorsque s'aggravent les déséquilibres. (Normal of "Perverse" Effects? On Interpreting the "Theorem of Critical Elasticities" When Disequilibria Grow. With English summary.) *Écon. Appl.*, 1985, *38*(2), pp. 471–92.

Weintraub, E. Roy. Joan Robinson's Critique of Equilibrium: An Appraisal. *Amer. Econ. Rev.*, May 1985, *75*(2), pp. 146–49.

Say, Jean-Baptiste

Martellaro, Joseph A. From Say's Law to Supply-Side Economics. *Rivista Int. Sci. Econ. Com.*, September 1985, *32*(9), pp. 887–903. [G: U.S.]

Polkinghorn, Bette. A Communication: An Unpublished Letter of J. B. Say. *Eastern Econ. J.*, April-June 1985, *11*(2), pp. 167–70.

Schumpeter, Joseph A.

Barrère, Alain. Economie réelle—Economie monétaire: alternative ou conciliation? (Real Economy—Monetary Economy: Option or Adjustment? With English summary.) *Écon. Appl.*, 1985, *38*(1), pp. 17–61.

Bellofiore, Riccardo. Money and Development in Schumpeter. *Rev. Radical Polit. Econ.*, Spring and Summer 1985, *17*(1/2), pp. 21–40.

Coe, Richard D. and Wilber, Charles K. Schumpeter Revisited: An Overview. In *Coe, R. D. and Wilber, C. K., eds.*, 1985, pp. 1–59.

Elliott, John E. Schumpeter's Theory of Economic Development and Social Change: Exposition and Assessment. *Int. J. Soc. Econ.*, 1985, *12*(6/7), pp. 6–33.

Haberler, Gottfried. Critical Notes on Schumpeter's Theory of Money—The Doctrine of the "Objective" Exchange Value of Money. In *Haberler, G.*, 1985, pp. 531–52.

Haberler, Gottfried. Schumpeter's Theory of Interest. In *Haberler, G.*, 1985, pp. 561–72.

Jensen, Hans E. J. A. Schumpeter on Economic Sociology. *Eastern Econ. J.*, July-Sept. 1985, *11*(3), pp. 257–66.

Marco, Luc V. A. Entrepreneur et innovation: les sources françaises de Joseph Schumpeter. (The Entrepreneur and Innovation: The French Heritage of Joseph Schumpeter. With English summary.) *Écon. Soc.*, October 1985, *19*(10), pp. 89–106.

Samuels, Warren J. A Critique of *Capitalism, Socialism, and Democracy*. In *Coe, R. D. and Wilber, C. K., eds.*, 1985, pp. 60–119.

Vercelli, Alessandro. Money and Production in Schumpeter and Keynes: Two Dichotomies. In *Arena, R., et al.*, 1985, pp. 31–45.

Zijlstra, Jelle. Introduction to 'Schumpeter's Vision.' In *Zijlstra, J.*, 1985, pp. 203–06.

Shackle, George L. S.

Ford, J. L. G. L. S. Shackle: A Brief Bio-bibliographical Portrait. *J. Econ. Stud.*, 1985, *12*(1/2), pp. 3–12.

Skinner, Andrew S. Smith and Shackle: History and Epistemics. *J. Econ. Stud.*, 1985, *12*(1/2), pp. 13–20.

Simmel, Georg

Meldolesi, L. Georg Simmel e la filosofia del denaro. (With English summary.) *Stud. Econ.*, 1985, *40*(27), pp. 123–39.

Simon, Herbert A.

Simon, Herbert A. My Life Philosophy. *Amer. Econ.*, Spring 1985, *29*(1), pp. 15–20.

Smith, Adam

Anderson, Gary M.; Shughart, William F., II and Tollison, Robert D. Adam Smith in the Customhouse. *J. Polit. Econ.*, August 1985, *93*(4), pp. 740–59.

Bishop, Robert L. Competitive Value When Only Labor Is Scarce. *Quart. J. Econ.*, November 1985, *100*(4), pp. 1257–92.

Caton, Hiram. The Preindustrial Economics of Adam Smith. *J. Econ. Hist.*, December 1985, *45*(4), pp. 833–53.

Cross, Melvin L. Are the Bishops Taking Us Back to Adam Smith? *Can. Public Policy*, December 1985, *11*(4), pp. 745–48.

Dubœuf, Françoise. Adam Smith: mesure et socialité. (Adam Smith: Measure and Sociality. With English summary.) *Écon. Soc.*, March 1985, *19*(3), pp. 73–107.

Hession, Charles H. Lord Keynes Meets Adam Smith. *Challenge*, May/June 1985, *28*(2), pp. 59–63. [G: U.S.]

Kindleberger, Charles P. Was Adam Smith a Monetarist or a Keynesian? In *Kindleberger, C. P.*, 1985, pp. 11–24.

Phillipson, Nicholas. Adam Smith as Civic Moralist. In *Hont, I. and Ignatieff, M., eds.*, 1985, pp. 179–202.

Winch, Donald. Adam Smith's 'Enduring Particular Result': A Political and Cosmopolitan Perspective. In *Hont, I. and Ignatieff, M., eds.*, 1985, pp. 253–69.

Young, Jeffrey T. Natural Price and the Impartial Spectator: A New Perspective on Adam Smith as a Social Economist. *Int. J. Soc. Econ.*, 1985, *12*(6/7), pp. 118–33.

Spry, Irene M.

Batts, John Stuart. "Down North" in 1935: A Diary of Irene M. Spry (née Biss). In *[Spry, I. M.]*, 1985, pp. 269–80.

Sraffa, Piero

Addi, Lahouari. Le statut de la rente chez Sraffa: contribution a un débat recent. (Sraffa's Status of Rent: Contribution to a Recent Debate. With English summary.) *Revue Écon.*, May 1985, *36*(3), pp. 579–601.

Baldone, Salvatore. Durable Capital Inputs: Conditions for Prices Ratios to Be Invariant to Profit-Rate Changes: A Comment. *Z. Nationalökon.*, 1985, *45*(4), pp. 409–20.

Garegnani, Pierangelo. On Hollander's Interpretation of Ricardo's Early Theory of Profits. In *Caravale, G. A., ed.*, 1985, pp. 87–104.

Hicks, John. Sraffa and Ricardo: A Critical View. In *Caravale, G. A., ed.*, 1985, pp. 305–19.

Levine, A. Lawrence. Sraffa's *Production of Commodities by Means of Commodities*, Returns to Scale, Relevance, and Other Matters: A Note. *J. Post Keynesian Econ.*, Spring 1985, *7*(3), pp. 342–49.

Pasinetti, Luigi. In memoria di Piero Sraffa: economista italiano a Cambridge. (With English summary.) *Econ. Polit.*, December 1985, *2*(3), pp. 315–32.

Pasinetti, Luigi. Piero Sraffa (1898–1983):

breve saggio bio-bibliografico. (With English summary.) *Econ. Polit.*, December 1985, *2*(3), pp. 333–41.

Salvadori, Neri. Was Sraffa Making No Assumption on Returns? *Metroecon.*, June 1985, *37*(2), pp. 175–86.

Stone, Richard

Johansen, Leif. Richard Stone's Contributions to Economics. *Scand. J. Econ.*, 1985, *87*(1), pp. 4–32.

Stone, Richard. Bibliography of Richard Stone's Works, 1936–1984. *Scand. J. Econ.*, 1985, *87*(1), pp. 33–43.

Surrey, Stanley S.

Lubick, Donald and Brannon, Gerard. Stanley S. Surrey and the Quality of Tax Policy Argument. *Nat. Tax J.*, September 1985, *38*(3), pp. 251–59.   [G: U.S.]

Oldman, Oliver. Stanley Surrey and the Developing Countries. *Nat. Tax J.*, September 1985, *38*(3), pp. 281–83. [G: LDCs; U.S.]

Tillinghast, David R. The Contributions of Stanley S. Surrey to the International Aspects of Taxation. *Nat. Tax J.*, September 1985, *38*(3), pp. 267–71.   [G: U.S.]

Sweezy, Paul

Edwards, Richard. Sweezy and the Proletariat. In *[Magdoff, H. and Sweezy, P.]*, 1985, pp. 99–114.

Hillard, Michael. Harry Magdoff and Paul Sweezy: Biographical Notes. In *[Magdoff, H. and Sweezy, P.]*, 1985, pp. 397–404.

Resnick, Stephen A. and Wolff, Richard D. Rethinking Marxism: Introduction: Solutions and Problems. In *[Magdoff, H. and Sweezy, P.]*, 1985, pp. ix–xxxiv.

Taimiyah, Ibn

Islahi, Abdul Azim. Ibn Taimiyah's Concept of Market Mechanism. *J. Res. Islamic Econ.*, Winter 1985, *2*(2), pp. 55–66.

Takahashi, Korekiyo

Nanto, Dick K. and Takagi, Shinji. Korekiyo Takahashi and Japan's Recovery from the Great Depression. *Amer. Econ. Rev.*, May 1985, *75*(2), pp. 369–74.   [G: Japan]

Tawney, R. H.

Martin, David A. R. H. Tawney's Normative Economic History of Capitalism. *Rev. Soc. Econ.*, April 1985, *43*(1), pp. 84–102.

Taylor, John

Foshee, Andrew W. Jeffersonian Political Economy and the Classical Republican Tradition: Jefferson, Taylor, and the Agrarian Republic. *Hist. Polit. Econ.*, Winter 1985, *17*(4), pp. 523–50.   [G: U.S.]

Thornton, Henry

Beranek, William; Humphrey, Thomas M. and Timberlake, Richard H., Jr. Fisher, Thornton, and the Analysis of the Inflation Premium: A Note. *J. Money, Credit, Banking*, August 1985, *17*(3), pp. 370–77.

Tinbergen, Jan

Pesaran, M. Hashem and Smith, R. P. Keynes on Econometrics. In *Lawson, T. and Pesaran, H., eds.*, 1985, pp. 134–50.
          [G: U.K.]

Tintner, Gerhard

Kadekodi, Gopal K. Gerhard Tintner: 1907–1983. *J. Quant. Econ.*, January 1985, *1*(1), pp. 161–63.

Matzner, Egon. In Memoriam Gerhard Tintner. *Amer. Econ.*, Fall 1985, *29*(2), pp. 3–4.

de Tocqueville, Alexis.

Wade, L. L. Tocqueville and Public Choice. *Public Choice*, 1985, *47*(3), pp. 491–508.
          [G: U.S.]

Tooke, Thomas

de Boyer, Jérôme. Circulation du revenu et circulation du capital: la distinction monnaie crédit chez Thomas Tooke. (Currency and Capital: The Distinction Established by Thomas Tooke between Money and Credit. With English summary.) *Revue Écon.*, May 1985, *36*(3), pp. 555–77.

Mondello, Gérard. Étude de la liaison monnaie-revenu demande effective: les théories de Thomas Tooke et J. M. Keynes. (A Study about the Links between Money-Income-Effective Demand: The Theories of T. Tooke and J. M. Keynes. With English summary.) *Revue Écon.*, May 1985, *36*(3), pp. 509–54.

Torrens, Robert

Thweatt, William O. De Vivo's Neglected Evidence: A Reply [The Author of the Article on Owen in the October 1819 *Edinburgh Review*: Some Neglected Evidence]. *Hist. Polit. Econ.*, Summer 1985, *17*(2), pp. 201–02.

de Vivo, Giancarlo. Robert Torrens and Ricardo's 'Corn-Ratio' Theory of Profits. *Cambridge J. Econ.*, March 1985, *9*(1), pp. 89–92.

de Vivo, Giancarlo. The Author of the Article on Owen in the October 1819 *Edinburgh Review*: Some Neglected Evidence [Mr. Owen's Plans for Relieving the National Distress]. *Hist. Polit. Econ.*, Summer 1985, *17*(2), pp. 199–201.

Turgot, Anne Robert Jacques

Crabbe, Philippe J. Turgot's *Brief on Mines and Quaries:* An Early Economic Analysis of Mineral Land Tenure. *Natural Res. J.*, April 1985, *25*(2), pp. 267–73.
          [G: France]

Uno, Kozo

Mawatari, Shohken. The Uno School: A Marxian Approach in Japan. *Hist. Polit. Econ.*, Fall 1985, *17*(3), pp. 403–18.

Veblen, Thorstein

Biddle, Jeff E. Veblen, Twain, and the Connecticut Yankee: A Note. *Hist. Polit. Econ.*, Spring 1985, *17*(1), pp. 97–107.

Endres, Anthony M. Veblen and Commons on Goodwill: A Case of Theoretical Divergence. *Hist. Polit. Econ.*, Winter 1985, *17*(4), pp. 637–49.

Griffin, Robert A. A Communicative Study of the Dissenting Views of John Maynard Keynes and Thorstein Veblen on the Treaty of Versailles. *Revue Écon. Polit.*, Mar.–Apr.

1985, 95(2), pp. 174–88.

McFarland, Floyd B. Thorstein Veblen versus the Institutionalists. *Rev. Radical Polit. Econ.*, Winter 1985, 17(4), pp. 95–105.

Tilman, Rick. The Utopian Vision of Edward Bellamy and Thorstein Veblen. *J. Econ. Issues*, December 1985, 19(4), pp. 879–98.

Tilman, Rick and Fontana, Andrea. Italian Debate and Dialogue on Thorstein Veblen: The Evolution of Appreciation for His Contributions Despite the Apathy of the Intelligentsia. *Amer. J. Econ. Soc.*, January 1985, 44(1), pp. 81–95.

Walras, Léon

Benetti, Carlo. Economie monétaire et économie de troc: la question de l'unité de compte commune. (Barter Economy and Monetary Economy: The Problem of the Single Standard of Value. With English summary.) *Écon. Appl.*, 1985, 38(1), pp. 85–109.

van Daal, J.; Henderiks, R. E. D. and Vorst, A. C. F. On Walras' Model of General Economic Equilibrium. *Z. Nationalökon.*, 1985, 45(3), pp. 219–44.

Dumez, Hervé. Walras, Marshall: Stratégies scientifiques comparées. (With English summary.) *Revue Écon. Polit.*, Mar.–Apr. 1985, 95(2), pp. 168–73.

Hart, Anna Jane McCreery; Holland, Thomas E. and Verbeeck, Rosalie. The Translation of Leon Walras's Correspondence with American Economists. *Atlantic Econ. J.*, July 1985, 13(2), pp. 83.

Lotter, Françoise. Léon Walras: de la mesure observée à la mesure imaginée. (Léon Walras: From "Observed" to "Fictive" Measurement. With English summary.) *Écon. Soc.*, March 1985, 19(3), pp. 109–45.

Weber, Max

Alchian, Armen. A Weberian Analysis of Economic Progress: The Case of Resource Exporting LDCs: Comment. *Z. ges. Staatswiss. (JITE)*, March 1985, 141(1), pp. 184–86.

Russell, James W. Method, Analysis, and Politics in Max Weber: Disentangling Marxian Affinities and Differences. *Hist. Polit. Econ.*, Winter 1985, 17(4), pp. 575–90.

Seyfert, Wolfgang. A Weberian Analysis of Economic Progress: The Case of Resource-Exporting LDC's. *Z. ges. Staatswiss. (JITE)*, March 1985, 141(1), pp. 170–83.

Weintraub, Sidney

Appelbaum, Eileen. Employment and the Distribution of Earned Income. *J. Post Keynesian Econ.*, Summer 1985, 7(4), pp. 594–602.

Bond, Patrick. A Student's Appreciation of Sidney Weintraub. *J. Post Keynesian Econ.*, Summer 1985, 7(4), pp. 530–32.

Davidson, Paul. Sidney Weintraub—An Economist of the Real World. *J. Post Keynesian Econ.*, Summer 1985, 7(4), pp. 533–39.

Galbraith, John Kenneth. A Tribute to Sidney Weintraub: Eulogy. *J. Post Keynesian Econ.*, Summer 1985, 7(4), pp. 508–09.

Hoaas, David J. The Personal and Professional Papers of Sidney Weintraub. *J. Post Keynesian Econ.*, Summer 1985, 7(4), pp. 603–06.

Kregel, J. A. Sidney Weintraub's Macrofoundations of Microeconomics and the Theory of Distribution. *J. Post Keynesian Econ.*, Summer 1985, 7(4), pp. 540–58.

Lianos, Theodore P. A Note on Three Theories of the Relative Share of Labor. *Greek Econ. Rev.*, April 1985, 7(1), pp. 82–84.

Rothschild, Kurt W. Some Notes on Weintraub's Eclectic Theory of Income Shares. *J. Post Keynesian Econ.*, Summer 1985, 7(4), pp. 575–93.   [G: Austria]

Sylos Labini, Paolo. Weintraub on the Price Level and Macroeconomics. *J. Post Keynesian Econ.*, Summer 1985, 7(4), pp. 559–74.

Weintraub, Sidney. A Jevonian Seditionist: A Mutiny to Enhance the Economic Bounty? *J. Post Keynesian Econ.*, Summer 1985, 7(4), pp. 510–29.

Wicksell, Knut

Coleman, William Oliver. Wicksell on Technical Change and Real Wages. *Hist. Polit. Econ.*, Fall 1985, 17(3), pp. 355–66.

Zijlstra, Jelle

Goedhart, C. Zijlstra's Concerto Grosso: *Fourteen Annual Reports: Themes and Variations (1967–1980).* In *Zijlstra, J.*, 1985, pp. 3–31.

0329 Other Special Topics

Adams, Jack E. David Ricardo's Theory of Value: A Revisit. *Atlantic Econ. J.*, July 1985, 13(2), pp. 69–72.

Asimakopulos, Athanasios. Finance, Saving and Investment in Keynes's Economics: A Comment. *Cambridge J. Econ.*, December 1985, 9(4), pp. 405–07.

Asimakopulos, Athanasios. Harrod on Harrod: The Evolution of a 'Line of Steady Growth.' *Hist. Polit. Econ.*, Winter 1985, 17(4), pp. 619–35.

Backhaus, Juergen. Keynesianism in Germany. In *Lawson, T. and Pesaran, H., eds.*, 1985, pp. 209–53.

Barrère, Alain. Les rapports entre les problématiques de Joan Robinson et de J.M. Keynes. (The Relationship between the Theoretical Issues in Joan Robinson and in J. M. Keynes. With English summary.) *Écon. Appl.*, 1985, 38(2), pp. 389–423.

Bellofiore, Riccardo. Money and Development in Schumpeter. *Rev. Radical Polit. Econ.*, Spring and Summer 1985, 17(1/2), pp. 21–40.

de Boyer, Jérôme. Note sur la Theorie Monetaire de R. G. Hawtrey. (With English summary.) *Stud. Econ.*, 1985, 40(25), pp. 3–27.

Brandis, Royall. Distribution Theory: Scientific Analysis or Moral Philosophy? *J. Econ. Issues*, December 1985, 19(4), pp. 867–78.

Brems, Hans. Den økonomiske teori og dens pionerer. (Economic Theory and Its Pioneers.

With English summary.) *Nationaløkon. Tidsskr.*, 1985, *123*(3), pp. 365–76.

Breton, Yves. Les économistes libéraux français de la période 1840–1914, précurseurs des théoriciens actuels du marche politique et de la bureaucratie? (With English summary.) *Revue Écon. Polit.*, Mar.–Apr. 1985, *95*(2), pp. 150–67. **[G: France]**

Burchardt, Michael. Die Banking–Currency-Kontroverse—Beitrag Nr. X. (The Banking-Currency Controversy—Essay No. X. With English summary.) *Kredit Kapital*, 1985, *18*(4), pp. 457–77.

Butos, William N. Menger: A Suggested Interpretation. *Atlantic Econ. J.*, July 1985, *13*(2), pp. 21–30.

Chick, Victoria. Time and the Wage-Unit in the Method of *The General Theory*: History and Equilibrium. In *Lawson, T. and Pesaran, H., eds.*, 1985, pp. 195–208.

Coleman, William Oliver. Wicksell on Technical Change and Real Wages. *Hist. Polit. Econ.*, Fall 1985, *17*(3), pp. 355–66.

Coomans, Gery. Régulation et fonctionnalisme. (Regulation and Functionalism. With English summary.) *Écon. Soc.*, January 1985, *19*(1), pp. 65–89.

Cooter, Robert D. and Rappoport, Peter. Reply to I. M. D. Little's Comment [Were the Ordinalists Wrong about Welfare Economics?]. *J. Econ. Lit.*, September 1985, *23*(3), pp. 1189–91.

Costabile, Lilia and Rowthorn, Bob. Malthus's Theory of Wages and Growth. *Econ. J.*, June 1985, *95*(378), pp. 418–37.

Dooley, Peter C. Giffen's Hint? *Australian Econ. Pap.*, June 1985, *24*(44), pp. 201–05.

Ekelund, Robert B., Jr. and Hébert, Robert F. Consumer Surplus: The First Hundred Years. *Hist. Polit. Econ.*, Fall 1985, *17*(3), pp. 419–54.

Elliott, John E. Schumpeter's Theory of Economic Development and Social Change: Exposition and Assessment. *Int. J. Soc. Econ.*, 1985, *12*(6/7), pp. 6–33.

Endres, Anthony M. Veblen and Commons on Goodwill: A Case of Theoretical Divergence. *Hist. Polit. Econ.*, Winter 1985, *17*(4), pp. 637–49.

Feiwel, George R. Quo Vadis Macroeconomics? Issues, Tensions and Challenges. In *Feiwel, G. R., ed. (I)*, 1985, pp. 1–100.

Foshee, Andrew W. Jeffersonian Political Economy and the Classical Republican Tradition: Jefferson, Taylor, and the Agrarian Republic. *Hist. Polit. Econ.*, Winter 1985, *17*(4), pp. 523–50. **[G: U.S.]**

Frank, Andre Gunder. A Marx, Keynes, Schumpeter Centenary and the Editors of Monthly Review. In *[Magdoff, H. and Sweezy, P.]*, 1985, pp. 115–26.

Fusfeld, Daniel R. Keynes and the Keynesian Cross: A Note. *Hist. Polit. Econ.*, Fall 1985, *17*(3), pp. 385–89.

Georgescu-Roegen, Nicholas. Time and Value in Economics and in Gossen's System. *Rivista Int.*

Sci. Econ. Com., December 1985, *32*(12), pp. 1121–40.

Gilbert, Geoffrey N. The *Morning Chronicle*, Poor Laws, and Political Economy. *Hist. Polit. Econ.*, Winter 1985, *17*(4), pp. 507–21.

Grampp, William D. Rights Theory in Classic Liberalism. *Rivista Int. Sci. Econ. Com.*, February 1985, *32*(2), pp. 141–52.

Guibert, Bernard. Théorie naive des ensembles capitalistes. (A Naive Theory of the Capitalist Sets. With English summary.) *Revue Écon.*, May 1985, *36*(3), pp. 481–508.

Gunning, James Patrick. Causes of Unemployment: The Austrian Perspective. *Hist. Polit. Econ.*, Summer 1985, *17*(2), pp. 223–44.

Haskell, Thomas L. Capitalism and the Origins of the Humanitarian Sensibility, Part 2. *Amer. Hist. Rev.*, June 1985, *90*(3), pp. 547–66.

Henderson, James P. The Whewell Group of Mathematical Economists. *Manchester Sch. Econ. Soc. Stud.*, December 1985, *53*(4), pp. 404–31.

Hudson, Michael A. German Economists and the Depression of 1929-1933. *Hist. Polit. Econ.*, Spring 1985, *17*(1), pp. 35–50. **[G: Germany]**

Humphrey, Thomas M. The Early History of the Phillips Curve. *Fed. Res. Bank Richmond Econ. Rev.*, Sept./Oct. 1985, *71*(5), pp. 17–24.

Jäggi, Stefan. Karl Marx und die Malthusianische Bevölkerungstheorie. (Karl Marx and the Malthusian Population Theory. With English summary.) *Schweiz. Z. Volkswirtsch. Statist.*, June 1985, *121*(2), pp. 95–113.

Jensen, Hans E. J. A. Schumpeter on Economic Sociology. *Eastern Econ. J.*, July-Sept. 1985, *11*(3), pp. 257–66.

Kahn, Richard. The Cambridge 'Circus' (1). In *Harcourt, G. C., ed.*, 1985, pp. 42–51.

Kompas, Thomas Frank. Traditional Notions of Equilibrium Reconsidered. *Eastern Econ. J.*, Oct.-Dec. 1985, *11*(4), pp. 361–72.

Kregel, J. A. Post-Keynesian Distribution Theory in Relation to Growth and Technical Progress. *Écon. Appl.*, 1985, *38*(2), pp. 375–88.

Larceneux, A. Keynes et Ricardo: une synthe est-elle possible? (Keynes and Ricardo: The Impossible Synthesis. With English summary.) *Écon. Soc.*, August 1985, *19*(8), pp. 7–23.

Lavoie, Marc. La distinction entre l'incertitude keynésienne et le risque néoclassique. (The Distinction between Keynesian Uncertainty and Neo-Classical Risk. With English summary.) *Écon. Appl.*, 1985, *38*(2), pp. 493–518.

Leadbeater, David. The Consistency of Marx's Categories of Productive and Unproductive Labour. *Hist. Polit. Econ.*, Winter 1985, *17*(4), pp. 591–618.

Lippi, Marco. Ancora su valore e costa reale in Marx: risposta alle critiche di petri. (Value and Real Cost in Marx Once Again. With English summary.) *Rivista Int. Sci. Econ. Com.*, July-Aug. 1985, *32*(7–8), pp. 635–59.

Lipsey, Richard G. What Have We Learned about Inflation in the Past 300 Years. *Atlantic Econ. J.*, March 1985, *13*(1), pp. 5–18.

Little, Ian M. D. Were the Ordinalists Wrong about Welfare Economics? A Comment. *J. Econ. Lit.*, September 1985, *23*(3), pp. 1186–88.

Marco, Luc V. A. Entrepreneur et innovation: les sources françaises de Joseph Schumpeter. (The Entrepreneur and Innovation: The French Heritage of Joseph Schumpeter. With English summary.) *Écon. Soc.*, October 1985, *19*(10), pp. 89–106.

Martellaro, Joseph A. From Say's Law to Supply-Side Economics. *Rivista Int. Sci. Econ. Com.*, September 1985, *32*(9), pp. 887–903. [G: U.S.]

Morris, Jacob. Value Relations and Divisions within the Working Class: A Comment. *Sci. Soc.*, Summer 1985, *49*(2), pp. 214–20.

Musgrave, Richard A. A Brief History of Fiscal Doctrine. In *Auerbach, A. J. and Feldstein, M.*, eds., 1985, pp. 1–59.

Negishi, Takashi. Non-Walrasian Foundations of Macroeconomics. In *Feiwel, G. R.*, ed. *(I)*, 1985, pp. 169–83.

Pastré, Olivier. Organisation du travail et croissance économique: un vieux débat anglo-saxon. (Division of Labour and Economic Growth: An Old Debate. With English summary.) *Revue Écon.*, March 1985, *36*(2), pp. 383–409. [G: OECD]

Pellanda, Anna. Riflessioni sul risparmio desunte da tre scandenze secolari: 1734, 1836, 1936. (Reflections on Savings from Three Centennial Dates: 1734, 1836, 1936. With English summary.) *Rivista Int. Sci. Econ. Com.*, April 1985, *32*(4), pp. 375–88.

Poulon, Frédéric. Réponses de la théorie du circuit à quelques questions relatives au temps, à l'équilibre macro-économique et au libre-échange. (The Theory of Circuits Answers Questions Concerning Concepts of Time, Macroeconomic Equilibrium and Free Trade. With English summary.) *Écon. Soc.*, August 1985, *19*(8), pp. 69–84.

Riha, Tomas. German Political Economy: The History of an Alternative Economics. *Int. J. Soc. Econ.*, 1985, *12*(3/4/5/), pp. 1–252. [G: Germany]

Robinson, Austin [Sir]. The Cambridge 'Circus' (2). In *Harcourt, G. C.*, ed., 1985, pp. 52–57.

Schabas, Margaret. Some Reactions to Jevons' Mathematical Program: The Case of Cairnes and Mill. *Hist. Polit. Econ.*, Fall 1985, *17*(3), pp. 337–53.

Segal, Harvey H. Money Markets against Governments: Two Centuries of a Spectacular Game. *Contemp. Policy Issues*, Fall 1985, *3*(5), pp. 35–41. [G: U.S.; Europe]

Sherman, Howard J. Monopoly Capital vs. the Fundamentalists. In *[Magdoff, H. and Sweezy, P.]*, 1985, pp. 359–77.

Smith, Vardaman R. John Stuart Mill's Famous Distinction between Production and Distribution. *Econ. Philos.*, October 1985, *1*(2), pp. 267–84.

Snippe, Jan. Finance, Saving and Investment in Keynes's Economics. *Cambridge J. Econ.*, September 1985, *9*(3), pp. 257–69.

Snippe, Jan. Loanable Funds Theory versus Liquidity Preference Theory. *De Economist*, 1985, *133*(2), pp. 129–50.

Steedman, Ian. Heterogeneous Labour, Money Wages, and Marx's Theory. *Hist. Polit. Econ.*, Winter 1985, *17*(4), pp. 551–74.

Vallageas, Bernard. Les circuits dans les analyses de Marx, Boehm-Bawerk, Hayek et Keynes. (Circuits in the Analyses of Marx, Boehm-Bawerk, Hayek and Keynes. With English summary.) *Écon. Soc.*, August 1985, *19*(8), pp. 47–68.

Villacís González, José. La teoria macroeconómica de German Bernácer. (With English summary.) *Economia (Portugal)*, October 1985, *9*(3), pp. 431–46.

Weintraub, E. Roy. Joan Robinson's Critique of Equilibrium: An Appraisal. *Amer. Econ. Rev.*, May 1985, *75*(2), pp. 146–49.

Whitwell, Greg. The Social Philosophy of the F and E Economists. *Australian Econ. Hist. Rev.*, March 1985, *25*(1), pp. 1–19. [G: Australia]

Winch, Donald. Economic Liberalism as Ideology: The Appleby Version. *Econ. Hist. Rev.*, 2nd Ser., May 1985, *38*(2), pp. 287–97.

036 Economic Methodology

0360 Economic Methodology

Arndt, H. W. Political Economy: A Reply. *Econ. Rec.*, December 1985, *61*(175), pp. 752.

Backhaus, Juergen. Keynesianism in Germany. In *Lawson, T. and Pesaran, H.*, eds., 1985, pp. 209–53.

Batemarco, Robert. Positive Economics and Praxeology: The Clash of Prediction and Explanation. *Atlantic Econ. J.*, July 1985, *13*(2), pp. 31–37.

Baum, Sandra R. Moral Philosophy, Cognitive Psychology and Economic Theory. *Eastern Econ. J.*, Oct.-Dec. 1985, *11*(4), pp. 422–36.

Baumol, William J. On Method in U.S. Economics a Century Earlier. *Amer. Econ. Rev.*, December 1985, *75*(6), pp. 1–12. [G: U.S.]

Bausor, Randall. Conceptual Evolution in Economics: The Case of Rational Expectations. *Eastern Econ. J.*, Oct.-Dec. 1985, *11*(4), pp. 297–308.

Bernstein, Michael A. The Methodological Resolution of the Cambridge Controversies: A Comment. *J. Post Keynesian Econ.*, Summer 1985, *7*(4), pp. 607–11.

Blandy, Richard. Soft Science. *Econ. Rec.*, December 1985, *61*(175), pp. 693–706.

Blaug, Mark. Karl Popper and Economic Methodology: A New Look: Comment. *Econ. Philos.*, October 1985, *1*(2), pp. 286–88.

Boland, Lawrence A. Reflections on Blaug's *Methodology of Economics*: Suggestions for a Revised Edition. *Eastern Econ. J.*, Oct.-Dec. 1985, *11*(4), pp. 450–54.

Boland, Lawrence A. The Foundations of Keynes'

Methodology:*The General Theory*. In *Lawson, T. and Pesaran, H., eds.*, 1985, pp. 181–94.

Brown-Collier, Elba K. Methodology and the Practice of Economics: A Critique of Patinkin's Interpretation of Keynes. *Eastern Econ. J.*, Oct.-Dec. 1985, *11*(4), pp. 373–83.

Caldwell, Bruce J. Some Reflections on *Beyond Positivism* [Review of Bruce Caldwell's *Beyond Positivism: Economic Methodology in the Twentieth Century*]. *J. Econ. Issues*, March 1985, *19*(1), pp. 187–94.

Caplovitz, David. Concepts, Indices and Contexts. In *Smith, R. B., ed.*, 1985, pp. 193–240. [G: U.S.]

Carabelli, Anna. Keynes on Cause, Chance and Possibility. In *Lawson, T. and Pesaran, H., eds.*, 1985, pp. 151–80.

Chakravarty, Sukhamoy. Methodology and Economics. *J. Quant. Econ.*, January 1985, *1*(1), pp. 1–9.

Chick, Victoria. Time and the Wage-Unit in the Method of *The General Theory*: History and Equilibrium. In *Lawson, T. and Pesaran, H., eds.*, 1985, pp. 195–208.

Cohen, Avi J. Issues in the Cambridge Controversies [The Methodological Resolution of the Cambridge Controversies]. *J. Post Keynesian Econ.*, Summer 1985, *7*(4), pp. 612–15.

Cross, Melvin L. Are the Bishops Taking Us Back to Adam Smith? *Can. Public Policy*, December 1985, *11*(4), pp. 745–48.

Demaria, Giovanni. Il problema della datità in economia. (The Problem of Economic and Extraeconomic Assumptions. With English summary.) *Rivista Int. Sci. Econ. Com.*, January 1985, *32*(1), pp. 5–38.

Dumez, Hervé. Walras, Marshall: Stratégies scientifiques comparées. (With English summary.) *Revue Écon. Polit.*, Mar.–Apr. 1985, *95*(2), pp. 168–73.

Earl, Peter E. and Kay, Neil M. How Economists Can Accept Shackle's Critique on Economic Doctrines without Arguing Themselves out of Their Jobs. *J. Econ. Stud.*, 1985, *12*(1/2), pp. 34–48.

Eichner, Alfred S. Post-Keynesian Theory and Empirical Research. In *Eichner, A. S.*, 1985, pp. 176–99.

Eichner, Alfred S. The New Paradigm and Macrodynamic Modeling. In *Eichner, A. S.*, 1985, pp. 151–75.

Fritz, Richard G. and Fritz, Judy M. Linguistic Structure and Economic Method. *J. Econ. Issues*, March 1985, *19*(1), pp. 75–101.

Gnanadoss, B. The Concept of Field in Economic Analysis. *Indian Econ. J.*, Apr.-June 1985, *32*(4), pp. 75–79.

Gowdy, John M. Evolutionary Theory and Economic Theory: Some Methodological Issues. *Rev. Soc. Econ.*, December 1985, *43*(3), pp. 316–24.

Groenewegen, Peter D. Professor Arndt on Political Economy: A Comment. *Econ. Rec.*, December 1985, *61*(175), pp. 744–51.

Hands, Douglas W. Karl Popper and Economic Methodology: A New Look. *Econ. Philos.*, April 1985, *1*(1), pp. 83–99.

Hands, Douglas W. Second Thoughts on Lakatos. *Hist. Polit. Econ.*, Spring 1985, *17*(1), pp. 1–16.

Hands, Douglas W. The Structuralist View of Economic Theories: A Review Essay: The Case of General Equilibrium in Particular. *Econ. Philos.*, October 1985, *1*(2), pp. 303–35.

Hartwell, R. Max. Economic History and Philosophy. In *Koslowski, P., ed.*, 1985, pp. 80–87.

Henderson, James P. The Whewell Group of Mathematical Economists. *Manchester Sch. Econ. Soc. Stud.*, December 1985, *53*(4), pp. 404–31.

Hirsch, Abraham. Review of Bruce Caldwell's *Beyond Positivism: Economic Methodology in the Twentieth Century*. *J. Econ. Issues*, March 1985, *19*(1), pp. 175–85.

Hirschman, Albert O. Against Parsimony: Three Easy Ways of Complicating Some Categories of Economic Discourse. *Econ. Philos.*, April 1985, *1*(1), pp. 7–21.

Hollis, Martin. The Emperor's Newest Clothes [The Rhetoric of Economics]. *Econ. Philos.*, April 1985, *1*(1), pp. 128–33.

Hutchison, Terence W. Philosophy and Economic Policy. In *Koslowski, P., ed.*, 1985, pp. 161–73.

Katzner, Donald W. Alternatives to Equilibrium Analysis. *Eastern Econ. J.*, Oct.-Dec. 1985, *11*(4), pp. 404–21.

Khan, Shahrukh Rafi. Islamic Economics: A Note on Methodology. *J. Res. Islamic Econ.*, Winter 1985, *2*(2), pp. 83–85.

Klant, Johannes J. The Slippery Transition. In *Lawson, T. and Pesaran, H., eds.*, 1985, pp. 80–98.

Klein, Daniel Bruce. Deductive Economic Methodology in the French Enlightenment: Condillac and Destutt de Tracy. *Hist. Polit. Econ.*, Spring 1985, *17*(1), pp. 51–71.

Koopmans, Tjalling C. Economics among the Sciences. In *Koopmans, T. C.*, 1985, pp. 237–49.

Laudan, Larry. Kuhn's Critique of Methodology. In *Pitt, J. C., ed.*, 1985, pp. 283–99.

Lawson, Tony. Keynes, Prediction and Econometrics. In *Lawson, T. and Pesaran, H., eds.*, 1985, pp. 116–33.

Lawson, Tony. Uncertainty and Economic Analysis. *Econ. J.*, December 1985, *95*(380), pp. 909–27.

Lawson, Tony and Pesaran, Hashem M. Methodological Issues in Keynes' Economics: An Introduction. In *Lawson, T. and Pesaran, H., eds.*, 1985, pp. 1–9.

Leontief, Wassily. Implicit Theorizing: A Methodological Criticism of the Neo-Cambridge School. In *Leontief, W.*, 1985, pp. 58–71.

Leontief, Wassily. Note on the Pluralistic Interpretation of History and the Problem of Interdisciplinary Co-operation. In *Leontief, W.*, 1985, pp. 3–11.

Leontief, Wassily. The Problem of Quality and Quantity in Economics. In *Leontief, W.*, 1985, pp. 45–57.

Leontief, Wassily. The Significance of Marxian Economics for Present-Day Economic Theory. In *Leontief, W.*, 1985, pp. 72–83.

Levy, David M. The Impossibility of a Complete Methodological Individualist: Reduction When Knowledge Is Imperfect. *Econ. Philos.*, April 1985, *1*(1), pp. 101–08.

Liebhafsky, H. H. and Liebhafsky, E. E. The Instrumentalisms of Dewey and Friedman: Comment. *J. Econ. Issues,* December 1985, *19*(4), pp. 974–83.

Littleboy, Bruce and Mehta, Ghanshyam. Keynes and Scientific Methodology: Whither and Whence. *Indian Econ. J.*, July-Sept. 1985, *33*(1), pp. 66–76.

Loasby, Brian J. Profit, Expectations and Coherence in Economic Systems. *J. Econ. Stud.*, 1985, *12*(1/2), pp. 21–33.

Lombardi, S. At the Roots of the Crisis in Economic Theory. *Econ. Int.*, Aug./Nov. 1985, *38*(3/4), pp. 323–50.

McCloskey, Donald N. A Conversation with Donald N. McCloskey about Rhetoric. *Eastern Econ. J.*, Oct.-Dec. 1985, *11*(4), pp. 293–96.

McCloskey, Donald N. Sartorial Epistemology in Tatters: A Reply [The Rhetoric of Economics]. *Econ. Philos.*, April 1985, *1*(1), pp. 134–37.

Morris, Derek J. The Economic System in the UK: Introduction. In *Morris, D., ed.*, 1985, pp. 3–26.

Mules, T. J. Where There's Smoke There's Fire—An Apology and a Statement. *Rev. Marketing Agr. Econ.*, April 1985, *53*(1), pp. 29–31.

Paqué, Karl-Heinz. How Far Is Vienna from Chicago? An Essay on the Methodology of Two Schools of Dogmatic Liberalism. *Kyklos*, 1985, *38*(3), pp. 412–34.

Pesaran, Hashem M. and Smith, R. P. Keynes on Econometrics. In *Lawson, T. and Pesaran, H., eds.*, 1985, pp. 134–50. [G: U.K.]

Pheby, John. Are Popperian Criticisms of Keynes Justified? In *Lawson, T. and Pesaran, H., eds.*, 1985, pp. 99–115.

Powell, Roy A.; Jensen, Rodney C. and West, Guy R. Responsibility and Objectivity in Economic Research. *Rev. Marketing Agr. Econ.*, April 1985, *53*(1), pp. 32–33.

Rubin, Paul H. Some Notes on Methodology in Law and Economics. In *Zerbe, R. O., Jr., ed.*, 1985, pp. 29–39.

Russell, James W. Method, Analysis, and Politics in Max Weber: Disentangling Marxian Affinities and Differences. *Hist. Polit. Econ.*, Winter 1985, *17*(4), pp. 575–90.

Salvati, Michele. Diversità e mutamento: osservazioni inconcludenti sul modello degli economisti. (With English summary.) *Econ. Polit.*, August 1985, *2*(2), pp. 249–92.

Scaperlanda, Anthony. Is Neo-Humanistic Economics the New Paradigm for Social Economists? *Rev. Soc. Econ.*, October 1985, *43*(2), pp. 173–80.

Schabas, Margaret. Some Reactions to Jevons' Mathematical Program: The Case of Cairnes and Mill. *Hist. Polit. Econ.*, Fall 1985, *17*(3), pp. 337–53.

Skinner, Andrew S. Smith and Shackle: History and Epistemics. *J. Econ. Stud.*, 1985, *12*(1/2), pp. 13–20.

Smith, Daniel Scott. Notes on the Measurement of Values. *J. Econ. Hist.*, June 1985, *45*(2), pp. 213–18.

Stanley, T. D. Positive Economics and Its Instrumental Defence. *Economica*, August 1985, *52*(207), pp. 305–19.

Vickers, Douglas. On Relational Structures and Non-equilibrium in Economic Theory. *Eastern Econ. J.*, Oct.-Dec. 1985, *11*(4), pp. 384–403.

Wagener, Hans-Jürgen. Structural Change and International Economic Comparisons. In *[Levcik, F.]*, 1985, pp. 83–95.

Weintraub, E. Roy. Appraising General Equilibrium Analysis. *Econ. Philos.*, April 1985, *1*(1), pp. 23–37.

Weintraub, E. Roy. Joan Robinson's Critique of Equilibrium: An Appraisal. *Amer. Econ. Rev.*, May 1985, *75*(2), pp. 146–49.

Wible, James R. An Epistemic Critique of Rational Expectations and the Neoclassical Macroeconomic Research Program. *J. Post Keynesian Econ.*, Winter 1984–85, *7*(2), pp. 269–81.

Wible, James R. Institutionaal Economics, Positive Eocnomics, Pragmatism, and Recent Philosphy of Science: Reply [The Instrumentalisms of Dewey and Friedman]. *J. Econ. Issues,* December 1985, *19*(4), pp. 984–95.

Wiseman, Jack. Philosophy and Economic Policy: Comment. In *Koslowski, P., ed.*, 1985, pp. 174–81.

Worrall, John. Scientific Discovery and Theory-Confirmation. In *Pitt, J. C., ed.*, 1985, pp. 301–31.

040 Economic History

041 Economic History: General

0410 General

Arrow, Kenneth J. Economic History: A Necessary Thought Not Sufficient Condition for an Economist: Maine and Texas. *Amer. Econ. Rev.*, May 1985, *75*(2), pp. 320–23.

Bruland, Kristine. Say's Law and the Single-Factor Explanation of British Industrialization: A Comment [The Cause of the Industrial Revolution: A Brief 'Single-Factor' Argument]. *J. Europ. Econ. Hist.*, Spring 1985, *14*(1), pp. 187–91. [G: U.K.]

Claydon, Tim; Partridge, Michael and Ville, Simon. List of Publications on the Economic and Social History of Great Britain in Ireland. *Econ. Hist. Rev., 2nd Ser.*, November 1985, *38*(4), pp. 597–636. [G: U.K.]

Haberler, Gottfried. Integration and Growth of the World Economy in Historical Perspective. In *Haberler, G.*, 1985, pp. 473–94.

Hilton, R. H. The Brenner Debate: Introduction. In *Aston, T. H. and Philpin, C. H. E., eds.*, 1985, pp. 1–9.

Kindleberger, Charles P. Losing Information:

The More We Study the Gold Standard the Less We Know about It. *Weltwirtsch. Arch.*, 1985, *121*(2), pp. 382–86.

Leinfellner, Werner. A Cyclic Model of Innovations. *Rivista Int. Sci. Econ. Com.*, September 1985, *32*(9), pp. 849–63.

Leontief, Wassily. When Should History Be Written Backwards? In *Leontief, W.*, 1985, pp. 12–21.

Lindenlaub, Dieter. What Can the Businessman Learn from History, Especially Business History? In *Engels, W. and Pohl, H., eds.*, 1985, pp. 25–53.

Martin, David A. R. H. Tawney's Normative Economic History of Capitalism. *Rev. Soc. Econ.*, April 1985, *43*(1), pp. 84–102.

Mundy, John Hine. Slavery, Marxism, and Liberty. *J. Europ. Econ. Hist.*, Sept.-Dec. 1985, *14*(3), pp. 585–99. **[G: Global]**

Solow, Robert M. Economic History and Economics. *Amer. Econ. Rev.*, May 1985, *75*(2), pp. 328–31.

Swanson, Dorothy. Annual Bibliography on American Labor History, 1984: Periodicals, Dissertations, and Research in Progress. *Labor Hist.*, Fall 1985, *26*(4), pp. 546–68. **[G: U.S.]**

0411 Development of the Discipline

Brody, David. The Old Labor History and the New: In Search of an American Working Class: Reply. In *Leab, D. J., ed.*, 1985, pp. 26–27. **[G: U.S.]**

Brody, David. The Old Labor History and the New: In Search of an American Working Class. In *Leab, D. J., ed.*, 1985, pp. 1–16. **[G: U.S.]**

Dubofsky, Melvyn. Give Us That Old Time Labor History: Philip S. Foner and the American Worker: Essay Review. *Labor Hist.*, Winter 1985, *26*(1), pp. 118–37.

Hartwell, R. Max. Economic History and Philosophy. In *Koslowski, P., ed.*, 1985, pp. 80–87.

Heller, Henry. The Transition Debate in Historical Perspective [Feudalism and Historical Materialism: A Critique and a Synthesis] [Modes of Production and Theories of Transition]. *Sci. Soc.*, Summer 1985, *49*(2), pp. 208–13.

Hoffman, John. The Dialectic of Abstraction and Concentration in Historical Materialism [Feudalism and Historical Materialism: A Critique and Synthesis] [Modes of Production and Theories of Transition]. *Sci. Soc.*, Winter 1985-1986, *49*(4), pp. 451–62.

James, John A. New Developments in the Application of General Equilibrium Models to Economic History. In *Piggott, J. and Whalley, J., eds.*, 1985, pp. 441–65.

Morris, James O. The Old Labor History and the New: In Search of an American Working Class: Comment. In *Leab, D. J., ed.*, 1985, pp. 17–26. **[G: U.S.]**

North, Douglass C. Transaction Costs in History. *J. Europ. Econ. Hist.*, Sept.-Dec. 1985, *14*(3), pp. 557–76.

Perrings, Charles. The Natural Economy Re-

visited. *Econ. Develop. Cult. Change*, July 1985, *33*(4), pp. 829–50.

Riha, Tomas. German Political Economy: The History of an Alternative Economics. *Int. J. Soc. Econ.*, 1985, *12*(3/4/5/), pp. 1–252. **[G: Germany]**

Smith, Daniel Scott. Notes on the Measurement of Values. *J. Econ. Hist.*, June 1985, *45*(2), pp. 213–18.

Wilson, R. G. and Hadwin, J. F. Economic and Social History at Advanced Level. *Econ. Hist. Rev., 2nd Ser.*, November 1985, *38*(4), pp. 548–68.

0412 Comparative Intercountry or Intertemporal Economic History

Alhadeff, Peter. Public Finance and the Economy in Argentina, Australia and Canada during the Depression of the 1930s. In *Platt, D. C. M. and di Tella, G., eds.*, 1985, pp. 161–78. **[G: Argentina; Australia; Canada]**

Amin, Samir. Modes of Production, History, and Unequal Development [Feudalism and Historical Materialism: A Critique and a Synthesis] [Modes of Production and Theories of Transition]. *Sci. Soc.*, Summer 1985, *49*(2), pp. 194–207.

Armstrong, Warwick. The Social Origins of Industrial Growth: Canada, Argentina and Australia, 1870–1930. In *Platt, D. C. M. and di Tella, G., eds.*, 1985, pp. 76–94. **[G: Argentina; Australia; Canada]**

Ashtor, Eliyahu. Banking Instruments between the Muslim East and the Christian West. In *Marx, A. V., ed.*, 1985, pp. 27–39.

Buiter, Willem H. International Policy Coordination in Historical Perspective: A View from the Interwar Years: Comment. In *Buiter, W. H. and Marston, R. C., eds.*, 1985, pp. 178–81.

Croot, Patricia and Parker, David. Agrarian Class Structure and the Development of Capitalism: France and England Compared. In *Aston, T. H. and Philpin, C. H. E., eds.*, 1985, pp. 79–90.

Eichengreen, Barry. International Policy Coordination in Historical Perspective: A View from the Interwar Years. In *Buiter, W. H. and Marston, R. C., eds.*, 1985, pp. 139–78.

Fogarty, John. Staples, Super-Staples and the Limits of Staple Theory: The Experiences of Argentina, Australia and Canada Compared. In *Platt, D. C. M. and di Tella, G., eds.*, 1985, pp. 19–36. **[G: Argentina; Australia; Canada]**

Fraginals, Manuel Moreno. Plantations in the Caribbean: Cuba, Puerto Rico, and the Dominican Republic in the Late Nineteenth Century. In *Moreno Franginals, M.; Moya Pons, F. and Engerman, S. L., eds.*, 1985, pp. 3–21. **[G: Caribbean]**

Gray, Jo Anna. International Policy Coordination in Historical Perspective: A View from the Interwar Years: Comment. In *Buiter, W. H. and Marston, R. C., eds.*, 1985, pp. 181–83.

Haberler, Gottfried. The Great Depression of the 1930s—Can It Happen Again? In *Haberler, G.*, 1985, pp. 405–27.

Haberler, Gottfried. The World Economy, Macroeconomic Theory and Policy—Sixty Years of Profound Change. In *Haberler, G.,* 1985, pp. 429–50.

Haberler, Gottfried. The World Economy, Money, and the Great Depression 1919–1939. In *Haberler, G.,* 1985, pp. 363–403. [G: U.S.; Japan; France; Germany]

Heller, Henry. The Transition Debate in Historical Perspective [Feudalism and Historical Materialism: A Critique and a Synthesis] [Modes of Production and Theories of Transition]. *Sci. Soc.,* Summer 1985, *49*(2), pp. 208–13.

Holt, James. Trade Unionism in the British and U.S. Steel Industries, 1880–1914: A Comparative Study. In *Leab, D. J., ed.,* 1985, pp. 166–96. [G: U.K.; U.S.]

Jones, Charles. The Fiscal Motive for Monetary and Banking Legislation in Argentina, Australia and Canada before 1914. In *Platt, D. C. M. and di Tella, G., eds.,* 1985, pp. 123–38. [G: Argentina; Australia; Canada]

Jones, E. L. Disasters and Economic Differentiation across Eurasia: A Reply [Natural Disaster and Historic Response]. *J. Econ. Hist.,* September 1985, *45*(3), pp. 675–82. [G: Europe]

Jones, F. Stuart. Britain and the Economic Development of Tropical Africa, Asia and South America in the Age of Imperialism (Review Article). *S. Afr. J. Econ.,* September 1985, *53*(3), pp. 264–86. [G: U.K.; LDCs]

Kindleberger, Charles P. Financial Institutions and Economic Development: A Comparison of Great Britain and France in the Eighteenth and Nineteenth Centuries. In *Kindleberger, C. P.,* 1985, pp. 65–85. [G: U.K.; France]

Kindleberger, Charles P. Historical Perspective on Today's Third-World Debt Problem. In *Kindleberger, C. P.,* 1985, pp. 190–209.

Kindleberger, Charles P. Historical Perspective on Today's Third-World Debt Problem. *Écon. Soc.,* September 1985, *19*(9), pp. 109–34. [G: LDCs]

Kindleberger, Charles P. International Monetary Reform in the Nineteenth Century. In *Kindleberger, C. P.,* 1985, pp. 213–25.

Kindleberger, Charles P. International Propagation of Financial Crises: The Experience of 1888–93. In *Kindleberger, C. P.,* 1985, pp. 226–39. [G: Selected Countries]

Kogane, Yoshihiro. Economic Growth before and after the Oil Crisis and the Possibility of Deindustrialization. In *Didsbury, H. F., Jr., ed.,* 1985, pp. 267–95. [G: Japan; W. Europe; U.S.]

Mokyr, Joel. Demand vs. Supply in the Industrial Revolution. In *Mokyr, J., ed.,* 1985, pp. 97–118. [G: U.K.]

Platt, Stephen. Suicidal Behaviour and Unemployment: A Literature Review. In *Westcott, G.; Svensson, P.-G. and Zollner, H. F. K., eds.,* 1985, pp. 87–132. [G: Global]

Pryor, Frederic L. Climatic Fluctuations as a Cause of the Differential Economic Growth of the Orient and Occident: A Comment [Natural Disaster and Historic Response]. *J. Econ.*

Hist., September 1985, *45*(3), pp. 667–73. [G: Europe]

Pugno, Maurizio. Are Long Waves Relevant in Economic Life? A Note. *Econ. Notes,* 1985, (2), pp. 68–77. [G: Global]

Rom, Michael. Export Controls: An Institutional and Historical Perspective. In *Weinblatt, J., ed.,* 1985, pp. 197–219.

Samsonowicz, Henryk and Maczak, Antoni. Feudalism and Capitalism: A Balance of Changes in East-central Europe. In *Mączak, A.; Samsonowicz, H. and Burke, P., eds.,* 1985, pp. 6–23. [G: E. Europe]

Saxonhouse, Gary R. Technology Choice in Cotton Textile Manufacturing. In *Ohkawa, K. and Ranis, G., eds.,* 1985, pp. 212–35. [G: Selected Countries]

Sayers, Richard. From Note Issue to Central Banking, 1800–1930. In *Marx, A. V., ed.,* 1985, pp. 339–44.

Tatsuki, Mariko. NYK and the Commercial Diplomacy of the Far Eastern Freight Conference, 1896–1956: Comment. In *Yui, T. and Nakagawa, K., eds.,* 1985, pp. 306–09. [G: Selected Countries]

di Tella, Guido. Rents, Quasi-rents, Normal Profits and Growth: Argentina and the Areas of Recent Settlement. In *Platt, D. C. M. and di Tella, G., eds.,* 1985, pp. 37–52. [G: Argentina; Selected OECD]

Twomey, Michael J. Economic Fluctuations in Argentina, Australia and Canada during the Depression of the 1930s. In *Platt, D. C. M. and di Tella, G., eds.,* 1985, pp. 179–93. [G: Argentina; Australia; Canada]

Weir, Margaret and Skocpol, Theda. State Structures and the Possibilities for "Keynesian" Responses to the Great Depression in Sweden, Britain, and the United States. In *Evans, P. B.; Rueschemeyer, D. and Skocpol, T., eds.,* 1985, pp. 107–63. [G: U.K.; U.S.; Sweden]

Wray, William D. NYK and the Commercial Diplomacy of the Far Eastern Freight Conference, 1896–1956: Response. In *Yui, T. and Nakagawa, K., eds.,* 1985, pp. 310–11. [G: Selected Countries]

Wray, William D. NYK and the Commercial Diplomacy of the Far Eastern Freight Conference, 1896–1956. In *Yui, T. and Nakagawa, K., eds.,* 1985, pp. 279–305. [G: Selected Countries]

Yasuba, Yasukichi and Dhiravegin, Likhit. Initial Conditions, Institutional Changes, Policy, and Their Consequences: Siam and Japan, 1850–1914. In *Ohkawa, K. and Ranis, G., eds.,* 1985, pp. 19–34. [G: Thailand; Japan]

042 Economic History: United States and Canada

0420 General

Allais, Maurice. A New Empirical Approach of the Hereditary and Relativistic Theory of the Demand for Money: The Rate of Increase of

Global Expenditure and the Velocity of Circulation of Money. *Rivista Int. Sci. Econ. Com.*, Oct.-Nov. 1985, *32*(10–11), pp. 905–48. [G: U.S.; W. Germany]

Bartoshesky, Florence. Business Records at the Harvard Business School: Archival Essay. *Bus. Hist. Rev.*, Autumn 1985, *59*(3), pp. 475–83. [G: U.S.]

Batra, R. N. The Future of the Debt Situation in the LDCs. In *Kaushik, S. K., ed.*, 1985, pp. 47–57. [G: U.S.]

Bernholz, Peter; Gärtner, Manfred and Heri, Erwin W. Historical Experiences with Flexible Exchange Rates: A Simulation of Common Qualitative Characteristics. *J. Int. Econ.*, August 1985, *19*(1/2), pp. 21–45. [G: Europe; U.S.]

de Cecco, Marcello. The International Debt Program in the Interwar Period. *Banca Naz. Lavoro Quart. Rev.*, March 1985, (152), pp. 45–64. [G: OECD]

Chida, Tomohei. The United States Merchant Marine in Foreign Trade, 1800–1939: Comment. In *Yui, T. and Nakagawa, K., eds.*, 1985, pp. 119–21. [G: U.S.]

Conde, Roberto Cortés. Some Notes on the Industrial Development of Argentina and Canada in the 1920s. In *Platt, D. C. M. and di Tella, G., eds.*, 1985, pp. 149–60. [G: Argentina; Canada]

Davidson, Lawrence S. and Fratianni, Michele. Economic Growth in the 1970s and Beyond. *Econ. Notes*, 1985, (3), pp. 17–34. [G: U.S.]

Flannery, Mark J. An Economic Evaluation of Bank Securities Activities before 1933. In *Walter, I., ed.*, 1985, pp. 67–87. [G: U.S.]

Foster, Mark S. Giant of the West: Henry J. Kaiser and Regional Industrialization, 1930–1950. *Bus. Hist. Rev.*, Spring 1985, *59*(1), pp. 1–23. [G: U.S.]

Fremling, Gertrud M. Did the United States Transmit the Great Depression to the Rest of the World? *Amer. Econ. Rev.*, December 1985, *75*(5), pp. 1181–85. [G: U.S.]

Glazer, Nathan. Clamor at the Gates: The New American Immigration: Introduction. In *Glazer, N., ed.*, 1985, pp. 3–13. [G: U.S.]

Hafer, R. W. The Stability of the Short-run Money Demand Function, 1920–1939. *Exploration Econ. Hist.*, July 1985, *22*(3), pp. 271–95. [G: U.S.]

Haskell, Thomas L. Capitalism and the Orgins of the Humanitarian Sensibility, Part 1. *Amer. Hist. Rev.*, April 1985, *90*(2), pp. 339–61.

Haskell, Thomas L. Capitalism and the Origins of the Humanitarian Sensibility, Part 2. *Amer. Hist. Rev.*, June 1985, *90*(3), pp. 547–66.

Jaenen, Cornelius J. The Role of Presents in French–Amerindian Trade. In *[Spry, I. M.]*, 1985, pp. 231–50. [G: Canada]

Kahn, James A. Another Look at Free Banking in the United States [New Evidence on the Free Banking Era]. *Amer. Econ. Rev.*, September 1985, *75*(4), pp. 881–85. [G: U.S.]

Kindleberger, Charles P. Banking and Industry between the Two Wars: An International Comparison. In *Kindleberger, C. P.*, 1985, pp. 293–313. [G: U.S.; Europe]

Kindleberger, Charles P. The Cyclical Pattern of Long-term Lending. In *Kindleberger, C. P.*, 1985, pp. 141–54. [G: Europe; U.S.]

Leontief, Wassily. Machines and Man. In *Leontief, W.*, 1985, pp. 187–99. [G: U.S.]

Lindert, Peter H. and Williamson, Jeffrey G. Growth, Equality, and History. *Exploration Econ. Hist.*, October 1985, *22*(4), pp. 341–77. [G: W. Europe; U.S.]

Lipartito, Kenneth. A Comparative Analysis of the Early History of the Southern and Northern Telephone Systems. In *Atack, J., ed.*, 1985, pp. 159–76. [G: U.S.]

Marchak, Patricia. The State and Transnational Corporations in Canada. In *Stauffer, R. B., ed.*, 1985, pp. 45–90. [G: Canada]

Neu, Irene D. My Nineteenth-Century Network: Erastus Corning, Benjamin Ingham, Edmond Forstall. In *Atack, J., ed.*, 1985, pp. 1–14. [G: U.S.]

Officer, Lawrence H. Integration in the American Foreign-Exchange Market, 1791–1900. *J. Econ. Hist.*, September 1985, *45*(3), pp. 557–85. [G: U.S.; U.K.]

Platt, D. C. M. The Financing of City Expansion: Buenos Aires and Montreal Compared, 1880–1914. In *Platt, D. C. M. and di Tella, G., eds.*, 1985, pp. 139–48. [G: Argentina; Canada]

Rockoff, Hugh. New Evidence on Free Banking in the United States [New Evidence on the Free Banking Era]. *Amer. Econ. Rev.*, September 1985, *75*(4), pp. 886–89. [G: U.S.]

Rush, Mark. Unexpected Monetary Disturbances during the Gold Standard Era. *J. Monet. Econ.*, May 1985, *15*(3), pp. 309–21. [G: U.S.]

Safford, Jeffrey J. The United States Merchant Marine in Foreign Trade, 1800–1939. In *Yui, T. and Nakagawa, K., eds.*, 1985, pp. 91–118. [G: U.S.]

Safford, Jeffrey J. The United States Merchant Marine in Foreign Trade, 1800–1939: Response. In *Yui, T. and Nakagawa, K., eds.*, 1985, pp. 121–22. [G: U.S.]

Schaefer, Donald and Schmitz, Mark D. The Parker–Gallman Sample and Wealth Distributions for the Antebellum South: A Comment [Notes on the Wealth Distribution of Farm Households in the United States, 1860: A New Look at Two Manuscript Census Samples]. *Exploration Econ. Hist.*, April 1985, *22*(2), pp. 220–26. [G: U.S.]

Scott, Anthony D. The State and Property: Water Rights in Western Canada. In *[Spry, I. M.]*, 1985, pp. 157–88. [G: Canada]

Solberg, Carl E. Land Tenure and Land Settlement: Policy and Patterns in the Canadian Prairies and the Argentine Pampas, 1880–1930. In *Platt, D. C. M. and di Tella, G., eds.*, 1985, pp. 53–75. [G: Argentina; Canada]

Sylos Labini, Paolo. The *General Theory*: Critical Reflections Suggested by Some Important

Problems of Our Time. In *Vicarelli, F., ed.*, 1985, pp. 126–54.

Thies, Clifford F. Interest Rates and Expected Inflation, 1831–1914: A Rational Expectations Approach. *Southern Econ. J.*, April 1985, *51*(4), pp. 1107–20. **[G: U.S.]**

Weiman, David F. The Economic Emancipation of the Non-slaveholding Class: Upcountry Farmers in the Georgia Cotton Economy. *J. Econ. Hist.*, March 1985, *45*(1), pp. 71–93. **[G: U.S.]**

Whatley, Warren C. A History of Mechanization in the Cotton South: The Institutional Hypothesis. *Quart. J. Econ.*, November 1985, *100*(4), pp. 1191–1215. **[G: U.S.]**

Yang, Donghyu. The Parker–Gallman Sample and Wealth Distributions for the Antebellum South: A Reply [Notes on the Wealth Distribution of Farm Households in the United States, 1860: A New Look at Two Manuscript Census Samples]. *Exploration Econ. Hist.*, April 1985, *22*(2), pp. 227–32. **[G: U.S.]**

0421 History of Product Prices and Markets

Adelman, Morris A. and Stangle, Bruce E. Profitability and Market Share. In *[McGowan, J. J.]*, 1985, pp. 101–13. **[G: U.S.]**

Albers, Patricia C. Autonomy and Dependency in the Lives of Dakota Women: A Study in Historical Change. *Rev. Radical Polit. Econ.*, Fall 1985, *17*(3), pp. 109–34. **[G: U.S.]**

Armstrong, Robert. The Quebec Asbestos Industry: Technological Change, 1878–1929. In *[Spry, I. M.]*, 1985, pp. 189 210. **[G: Canada]**

Atack, Jeremy. Industrial Structure and the Emergence of the Modern Industrial Corporation. *Exploration Econ. Hist.*, January 1985, *22*(1), pp. 29–52. **[G: U.S.]**

Baack, Bennett D. and Ray, Edward John. The Political Economy of the Origins of the Military-Industrial Complex in the United States. *J. Econ. Hist.*, June 1985, *45*(2), pp. 369–75. **[G: U.S.]**

Belk, Russell W. and Pollay, Richard W. Images of Ourselves: The Good Life in Twentieth Century Advertising. *J. Cons. Res.*, March 1985, *11*(4), pp. 887–97. **[G: U.S.]**

Belongia, Michael T. and Gilbert, R. Alton. The Farm Credit Crisis: Will It Hurt the Whole Economy? *Fed. Res. Bank St. Louis Rev.*, December 1985, *67*(10), pp. 5–15. **[G: U.S.]**

Beveridge, Andrew A. Local Lending Practice: Borrowers in a Small Northeastern Industrial City, 1832–1915. *J. Econ. Hist.*, June 1985, *45*(2), pp. 393–403. **[G: U.S.]**

Clark, William and Turner, Charlie G. International Trade and the Evolution of the American Capital Market, 1888–1911. *J. Econ. Hist.*, June 1985, *45*(2), pp. 405–10. **[G: U.S.]**

Coclanis, Peter A. Bitter Harvest: The South Carolina Low Country in Historic Perspective. *J. Econ. Hist.*, June 1985, *45*(2), pp. 251–59. **[G: U.S.]**

David, Paul A. Clio and the Economics of QWERTY. *Amer. Econ. Rev.*, May 1985, *75*(2), pp. 332–37. **[G: U.S.; U.K.]**

Dotsey, Michael. The Use of Electronic Funds Transfers to Capture the Effects of Cash Management Practices on the Demand for Demand Deposits: A Note. *J. Finance*, December 1985, *40*(5), pp. 1493–1503. **[G: U.S.]**

Dow, Alexander. Prometheus in Canada: The Expansion of Metal Mining, 1900–1950. In *[Spry, I. M.]*, 1985, pp. 211–28. **[G: Canada]**

Edison, Hali J. Purchasing Power Parity: A Quantitative Reassessment of the 1920s Experience. *J. Int. Money Finance*, September 1985, *4*(3), pp. 361–72. **[G: U.K.; U.S.; France]**

Eichengreen, Barry and Sachs, Jeffrey. Exchange Rates and Economic Recovery in the 1930s. *J. Econ. Hist.*, December 1985, *45*(4), pp. 925–46. **[G: U.S.; W. Europe]**

Ferleger, Louis. Capital Goods and Southern Economic Development. *J. Econ. Hist.*, June 1985, *45*(2), pp. 411–17. **[G: U.S.]**

Ford, Lacy K. Self-Sufficiency, Cotton, and Economic Development in the South Carolina Upcountry, 1800–1860. *J. Econ. Hist.*, June 1985, *45*(2), pp. 261–67. **[G: U.S.]**

Glenn, Evelyn Nakano. Racial Ethnic Women's Labor: The Intersection of Race, Gender and Class Oppression. *Rev. Radical Polit. Econ.*, Fall 1985, *17*(3), pp. 86–108. **[G: U.S.]**

Gorton, Gary. Clearinghouses and the Origin of Central Banking in the United States. *J. Econ. Hist.*, June 1985, *45*(2), pp. 277–83. **[G: U.S.]**

Hattwick, Richard E. Gustavus Franklin Swift. *J. Behav. Econ.*, Summer 1985, *14*(2), pp. 131–53. **[G: U.S.]**

Hutchinson, William K. Import Substitution, Structural Change, and Regional Economic Growth in the United States: The Northeast, 1870–1910. *J. Econ. Hist.*, June 1985, *45*(2), pp. 319–25. **[G: U.S.]**

Inwood, Kris. Productivity Growth in Obsolescence: Charcoal Iron Revisited. *J. Econ. Hist.*, June 1985, *45*(2), pp. 293–98. **[G: Canada]**

Jones, Geoffrey. The Gramophone Company: An Anglo-American Multinational, 1898–1931. *Bus. Hist. Rev.*, Spring 1985, *59*(1), pp. 76–100. **[G: U.K.; U.S.]**

Kornblith, Gary J. The Craftsman as Industrialist: Jonas Chickering and the Transformation of American Piano Making. *Bus. Hist. Rev.*, Autumn 1985, *59*(3), pp. 349–68. **[G: U.S.]**

Lazonick, William and Brush, Thomas. The "Horndal Effect" in Early U.S. Manufacturing. *Exploration Econ. Hist.*, January 1985, *22*(1), pp. 53–96. **[G: U.S.]**

Lucia, Joseph L. The Failure of the Bank of United States: A Reappraisal. *Exploration Econ. Hist.*, October 1985, *22*(4), pp. 402–16. **[G: U.S.]**

MacDonald, Ronald. The Norman Conquest of 86 and the Asset Approach to the Exchange Rate. *J. Int. Money Finance*, September 1985, *4*(3), pp. 373–87. **[G: U.K.; U.S.]**

MacMurray, Robert R. Technological Change in a Society in Transition: Work in Progress on a Unified Reference Work in Early American Patent History. *J. Econ. Hist.*, June 1985, 45(2), pp. 299–303. **[G: U.S.]**

Marx, Thomas G. The Development of the Franchise Distribution System in the U.S. Automobile Industry. *Bus. Hist. Rev.*, Autumn 1985, 59(3), pp. 465–74. **[G: U.S.]**

Neal, Larry. Integration of International Capital Markets: Quantitative Evidence from the Eighteenth to Twentieth Centuries. *J. Econ. Hist.*, June 1985, 45(2), pp. 219–26. **[G: U.S.; Netherlands; U.K.; France]**

Olmstead, Alan L. and Rhode, Paul. Rationing without Government: The West Coast Gas Famine of 1920. *Amer. Econ. Rev.*, December 1985, 75(5), pp. 1044–55. **[G: U.S.]**

Osband, Kent. The Boll Weevil versus "King Cotton." *J. Econ. Hist.*, September 1985, 45(3), pp. 627–43. **[G: U.S.]**

Peck, Anne E. The Economic Role of Traditional Commodity Futures Markets. In *Peck, A. E., ed. (II)*, 1985, pp. 1–81. **[G: Canada; U.S.; Argentina; Australia]**

Phillips, William H. Southern Textile Mill Villages on the Eve of World War II: The Courtenay Mill of South Carolina. *J. Econ. Hist.*, June 1985, 45(2), pp. 269–75. **[G: U.S.]**

Porter, Robert H. On the Incidence and Duration of Price Wars. In *Geroski, P. A.; Phlips, L. and Ulph, A., eds.*, 1985, pp. 47–58.
[G: U.S.]

Porter, Robert H. On the Incidence and Duration of Price Wars. *J. Ind. Econ.*, June 1985, 33(4), pp. 415–26. **[G: U.S.]**

Price, James E. The Remarkable Career of the Inflationary Gap. *J. Post Keynesian Econ.*, Fall 1985, 8(1), pp. 113–20. **[G: U.S.]**

Ray, Arthur J. Buying and Selling Hudson's Bay Company Furs in the Eighteenth Century. In *[Spry, I. M.]*, 1985, pp. 95–115.
[G: Canada]

Rothenberg, Winifred B. The Emergence of a Capital Market in Rural Massachusetts, 1730–1838. *J. Econ. Hist.*, December 1985, 45(4), pp. 781–808. **[G: U.S.]**

Schapiro, Morton Owen. A General Dynamic Model of 19th Century U.S. Population Change. *Econ. Modelling*, October 1985, 2(4), pp. 347–56. **[G: U.S.]**

Seftel, Howard. Government Regulation and the Rise of the California Fruit Industry: The Entrepreneurial Attack on Fruit Pests, 1880–1920. *Bus. Hist. Rev.*, Autumn 1985, 59(3), pp. 369–402. **[G: U.S.]**

Smiley, Gene. Banking Structure and the National Capital Market, 1869–1914: A Comment. *J. Econ. Hist.*, September 1985, 45(3), pp. 653–59. **[G: U.S.]**

Smith, Bruce D. American Colonial Monetary Regimes: The Failure of the Quantity Theory and Some Evidence in Favour of an Alternative View. *Can. J. Econ.*, August 1985, 18(3), pp. 531–65. **[G: U.S.]**

Smith, Bruce D. Some Colonial Evidence on Two Theories of Money: Maryland and the Carolinas. *J. Polit. Econ.*, December 1985, 93(6), pp. 1178–1211. **[G: U.S.]**

Sushka, Marie Elizabeth and Barrett, W. Brian. Banking Structure and the National Capital Market, 1869–1914: A Reply. *J. Econ. Hist.*, September 1985, 45(3), pp. 661–65.
[G: U.S.]

Temin, Peter and Peters, Geoffrey. Is History Stranger than Theory? The Origin of Telephone Separations. *Amer. Econ. Rev.*, May 1985, 75(2), pp. 324–27. **[G: U.S.]**

Thirtle, Colin G. Technological Change and the Productivity Slowdown in Field Crops: United States, 1939–78. *Southern J. Agr. Econ.*, December 1985, 17(2), pp. 33–42. **[G: U.S.]**

White, Eugene Nelson. The Merger Movement in Banking, 1919–1933. *J. Econ. Hist.*, June 1985, 45(2), pp. 285–91. **[G: U.S.]**

Wicker, Elmus. Colonial Monetary Standards Contrasted: Evidence from the Seven Years' War. *J. Econ. Hist.*, December 1985, 45(4), pp. 869–84. **[G: U.S.]**

Yamawaki, Hideki. Dominant Firm Pricing and Fringe Expansion: The Case of the U.S. Iron and Steel Industry, 1907–1930. *Rev. Econ. Statist.*, August 1985, 67(3), pp. 429–37.
[G: U.S.]

0422 History of Factor Prices and Markets

Adams, John W. and Kaskoff, Alice Bee. Wealth and Migration in Massachusetts and Maine: 1771–1798. *J. Econ. Hist.*, June 1985, 45(2), pp. 363–68. **[G: U.S.]**

Alston, Lee J. and Ferrie, Joseph P. Labor Costs, Paternalism, and Loyalty in Southern Agriculture: A Constraint on the Growth of the Welfare State. *J. Econ. Hist.*, March 1985, 45(1), pp. 95–117. **[G: U.S.]**

Anderton, Douglas L. and Bean, Lee L. Birth Spacing and Fertility Limitation: A Behavioral Analysis of a Nineteenth Century Frontier Population. *Demography*, May 1985, 22(2), pp. 169–83. **[G: U.S.]**

Bernstein, Irving. The Historical Significance of the CIO. In *Dennis, B. D., ed.*, 1985, pp. 654–58. **[G: U.S.]**

Blumin, Stuart M. The Hypothesis of Middle-Class Formation in Nineteenth-Century America: A Critique and Some Proposals. *Amer. Hist. Rev.*, April 1985, 90(2), pp. 299–338.
[G: U.S.]

Brody, David. The Old Labor History and the New: In Search of an American Working Class. In *Leab, D. J., ed.*, 1985, pp. 1–16.
[G: U.S.]

Brody, David. The Old Labor History and the New: In Search of an American Working Class: Reply. In *Leab, D. J., ed.*, 1985, pp. 26–27.
[G: U.S.]

Brown, Clair. An Institutional Model of Wives' Work Decisions. *Ind. Relat.*, Spring 1985, 24(2), pp. 182–204. **[G: U.S.]**

Brundage, David. The Producing Classes and the Saloon: Denver in the 1880s. *Labor Hist.*, Winter 1985, 26(1), pp. 29–52. **[G: U.S.]**

Carosso, Vincent P. American Private Banks in International Banking and Industrial Finance, 1870–1914. In *Atack, J., ed.*, 1985, pp. 19–26. [G: U.S.]

Carter, Michael J. and Carter, Susan B. Internal Labor Markets in Retailing: The Early Years. *Ind. Lab. Relat. Rev.*, July 1985, *38*(4), pp. 586–98. [G: U.S.]

Cohen, Isaac. Workers' Control in the Cotton Industry: A Comparative Study of British and American Mule Spinning. *Labor Hist.*, Winter 1985, *26*(1), pp. 53–85. [G: U.S.; U.K.]

Cohn, Raymond L. Deaths of Slaves in the Middle Passage. *J. Econ. Hist.*, September 1985, *45*(3), pp. 685–92. [G: U.K.; France; Portugal; U.S.; Netherlands]

Cornfield, Daniel B. Economic Segmentation and Expression of Labor Unrest: Striking versus Quitting in the Manufacturing Sector. *Soc. Sci. Quart.*, June 1985, *66*(2), pp. 247–65. [G: U.S.]

Cutcher-Gershenfeld, Joel. Reconceiving the Web of Labor–Management Relations. In *Dennis, B. D., ed.*, 1985, pp. 637–45. [G: U.S.]

Dubofsky, Melvyn. Give Us That Old Time Labor History: Philip S. Foner and the American Worker: Essay Review. *Labor Hist.*, Winter 1985, *26*(1), pp. 118–37.

Dubofsky, Melvyn. The Origins of Western Working-Class Radicalism, 1890–1905. In *Leab, D. J., ed.*, 1985, pp. 230–53. [G: U.S.]

Ebner, Michael H. The Passaic Strike of 1912 and the Two I.W.W.s. In *Leab, D. J., ed.*, 1985, pp. 254–68. [G: U.S.]

Egolf, Jeremy R. The Limits of Shop Floor Struggle: Workers vs. the Bedaux System at Willapa Harbor Lumber Mills, 1933–35. *Labor Hist.*, Spring 1985, *26*(2), pp. 195–229. [G: U.S.]

Field, Alexander James. On the Unimportance of Machinery. *Exploration Econ. Hist.*, October 1985, *22*(4), pp. 378–401. [G: U.S.; U.K.]

Fine, Sidney. Frank Murphy, the Thornhill Decision, and Picketing as Free Speech. In *Leab, D. J., ed.*, 1985, pp. 361–82. [G: U.S.]

Fishback, Price V. Discrimination on Nonwage Margins: Safety in the West Virginia Coal Industry, 1906–1925. *Econ. Inquiry*, October 1985, *23*(4), pp. 651–69. [G: U.S.]

Foster, James C. *The Western Dilemma:* Miners, Silicosis, and Compensation. *Labor Hist.*, Spring 1985, *26*(2), pp. 268–87. [G: U.S.]

Freeman, Joshua. Delivering the Goods: Industrial Unionism during World War II. In *Leab, D. J., ed.*, 1985, pp. 383–406. [G: U.S.]

Gabin, Nancy. Women Workers and the UAW in the Post-World War II Period: 1945–1954. In *Leab, D. J., ed.*, 1985, pp. 407–32. [G: U.S.]

Gaspari, K. Celeste and Woolf, Arthur G. Income, Public Works, and Mortality in Early Twentieth-Century American Cities. *J. Econ. Hist.*, June 1985, *45*(2), pp. 355–61. [G: U.S.]

Gitelman, H. M. Adolph Strasser and the Origins

of Pure and Simple Unionism. In *Leab, D. J., ed.*, 1985, pp. 153–65. [G: U.S.]

Gómez, Plácido. The History and Adjudication of the Common Lands of Spanish and Mexican Land Grants. *Natural Res. J.*, October 1985, *25*(4), pp. 1039–80. [G: Mexico; U.S.]

Grubb, Farley. The Incidence of Servitude in Trans-Atlantic Migration, 1771–1804. *Exploration Econ. Hist.*, July 1985, *22*(3), pp. 316–39.

Grubb, Farley. The Market for Indentured Immigrants: Evidence on the Efficiency of Forward-Labor Contracting in Philadelphia, 1745–1773. *J. Econ. Hist.*, December 1985, *45*(4), pp. 855–68. [G: U.S.]

Gutman, Herbert G. Trouble on the Railroads in 1873–1874: Prelude to the 1877 Crisis? In *Leab, D. J., ed.*, 1985, pp. 132–52. [G: U.S.]

Haines, Michael R. Inequality and Childhood Mortality: A Comparison of England and Wales, 1911, and the United States, 1900. *J. Econ. Hist.*, December 1985, *45*(4), pp. 885–912. [G: U.K.; U.S.]

Harris, Howell. The Snares of Liberalism? Politicians, Bureaucrats, and the Shaping of Federal Labour Relations Policy in the United States, ca. 1915–47. In *Tolliday, S. and Zeitlin, J., eds.*, 1985, pp. 148–91. [G: U.S.]

Henretta, James A. The Study of Social Mobility: Ideological Assumptions and Conceptual Bias. In *Leab, D. J., ed.*, 1985, pp. 28–41. [G: U.S.]

Huertas, Thomas F. The Rise of the Modern Business Enterprise: The Case of Citibank. In *Atack, J., ed.*, 1985, pp. 143–57. [G: U.S.]

Hunter, Gregory S. The Development of Bankers: Career Patterns and Corporate Form at the Manhattan Company, 1799–1842. In *Atack, J., ed.*, 1985, pp. 59–77. [G: U.S.]

James, John A. and Skinner, Jonathan S. The Resolution of the Labor-Scarcity Paradox. *J. Econ. Hist.*, September 1985, *45*(3), pp. 513–40. [G: U.S.; U.K.]

Kessler-Harris, Alice. Organizing the Unorganizable: Three Jewish Women and Their Union. In *Leab, D. J., ed.*, 1985, pp. 269–87. [G: U.S.]

Leab, Daniel J. "United We Eat": The Creation and Organization of the Unemployed Councils in 1930. In *Leab, D. J., ed.*, 1985, pp. 317–32. [G: U.S.]

Lebergott, Stanley. The Demand for Land: The United States, 1820–1860. *J. Econ. Hist.*, June 1985, *45*(2), pp. 181–212. [G: U.S.]

Martin, Charles H. The International Labor Defense and Black America. *Labor Hist.*, Spring 1985, *26*(2), pp. 165–94. [G: U.S.]

Mitchell, Daniel J. B. Wage Flexibility in the United States: Lessons from the Past. *Amer. Econ. Rev.*, May 1985, *75*(2), pp. 36–40. [G: U.S.]

Mitchell, Daniel J. B. Wage Flexibility: Then and Now. *Ind. Relat.*, Spring 1985, *24*(2), pp. 266–79. [G: U.S.]

Montgomery, David. Workers' Control of Machine Production in the Nineteenth Century.

In *Leab, D. J., ed.*, 1985, pp. 107–31.
[G: U.S.]

Morris, James O. The Old Labor History and the New: In Search of an American Working Class: Comment. In *Leab, D. J., ed.*, 1985, pp. 17–26. [G: U.S.]

Nash, Gary B. The Failure of Female Factory Labor in Colonial Boston. In *Leab, D. J., ed.*, 1985, pp. 42–65. [G: U.S.]

Nelson, Daniel. Origins of the Sit-Down Era: Worker Militancy and Innovation in the Rubber Industry, 1934–1938. In *Leab, D. J., ed.*, 1985, pp. 333–60. [G: U.S.]

Newman, Dale. Work and Community Life in a Southern Textile Town. In *Leab, D. J., ed.*, 1985, pp. 433–54. [G: U.S.]

Nugent, Angela. Organizing Trade Unions to Combat Disease: The Workers' Health Bureau, 1921–1928. *Labor Hist.*, Summer 1985, *26*(3), pp. 423–46. [G: U.S.]

Pessen, Edward. *Should* Labor Have Supported Jackson?; Or Questions the Quantitative Studies Do Not Answer. In *Leab, D. J., ed.*, 1985, pp. 96–106. [G: U.S.]

Peters, B. Guy. The United States: Absolute Change and Relative Stability. In *Rose, R.*, 1985, pp. 228–61. [G: U.S.]

Philips, Peter. A Note on the Apparent Constancy of the Racial Wage Gap in New Jersey Manufacturing, 1902 to 1979. *Rev. Black Polit. Econ.*, Spring 1985, *13*(4), pp. 71–76. [G: U.S.]

Piott, Steven L. The Chicago Teamsters' Strike of 1902: A Community Confronts the Beef Trust. *Labor Hist.*, Spring 1985, *26*(2), pp. 250–67. [G: U.S.]

Santos, Michael W. Community and Communism: The 1928 New Bedford Textile Strike. *Labor Hist.*, Spring 1985, *26*(2), pp. 230–49. [G: U.S.]

Schneider, Dorothee. The New York Cigarmakers Strike of 1877. *Labor Hist.*, Summer 1985, *26*(3), pp. 325–52. [G: U.S.]

Schweikart, Larry. Antebellum Southern Bankers: Origins and Mobility. In *Atack, J., ed.*, 1985, pp. 79–103. [G: U.S.]

Seccareccia, Mario S. Immigration and Business Cycles: Pauper Migration to Canada, 1815–1874. In *[Spry, I. M.]*, 1985, pp. 117–38. [G: Canada]

Shammas, Carole. Black Women's Work and the Evolution of Plantation Society in Virginia. *Labor Hist.*, Winter 1985, *26*(1), pp. 5–28. [G: U.S.]

Smith, James P. and Ward, Michael P. Time-Series Growth in the Female Labor Force. *J. Lab. Econ.*, Part 2 January 1985, *3*(1), pp. S59–90. [G: U.S.]

Stepina, Lee P. and Kircher, Kraig. Environmental Influences on the Development of U.S. Labor–Management Relations. In *Damjanovic, M. and Voich, D., Jr., eds.*, 1985, pp. 64–94. [G: U.S.]

Stevens, Errol Wayne. Labor and Socialism in an Indiana Mill Town, 1905–1921. *Labor Hist.*, Summer 1985, *26*(3), pp. 353–83. [G: U.S.]

Stott, Richard. British Immigrants and the American "Work Ethic" in the Mid-Nineteenth Century. *Labor Hist.*, Winter 1985, *26*(1), pp. 86–102. [G: U.S.; U.K.]

Stricker, Frank. Affluence for Whom?—Another Look at Prosperity and the Working Classes in the 1920s. In *Leab, D. J., ed.*, 1985, pp. 288–316. [G: U.S.]

Suits, Daniel B. U.S. Farm Migration: An Application of the Harris–Todaro Model. *Econ. Develop. Cult. Change*, July 1985, *33*(4), pp. 815–28. [G: U.S.]

Swanson, Dorothy. Annual Bibliography on American Labor History, 1983: Periodicals, Dissertations, and Research in Progress. *Labor Hist.*, Winter 1985, *26*(1), pp. 103–17.

Sylla, Richard. Early American Banking: The Significance of the Corporate Form. In *Atack, J., ed.*, 1985, pp. 105–23. [G: U.S.; U.K.]

Thies, Clifford F. New Estimates of the Term Structure of Interest Rates: 1920–1939. *J. Finan. Res.*, Winter 1985, *8*(4), pp. 297–306. [G: U.S.]

Wilkins, Mira. Foreign Banks and Foreign Investment in the United States. In *Atack, J., ed.*, 1985, pp. 27–34. [G: U.S.]

Worthman, Paul B. Black Workers and Labor Unions in Birmingham, Alabama, 1897–1904. In *Leab, D. J., ed.*, 1985, pp. 197–229. [G: U.S.]

Young, Alfred. The Mechanics and the Jeffersonians: New York, 1789–1801. In *Leab, D. J., ed.*, 1985, pp. 66–95. [G: U.S.]

Zieger, Robert H. Toward the History of the CIO: A Bibliographical Report. *Labor Hist.*, Fall 1985, *26*(4), pp. 485–516. [G: U.S.]

0423 History of Public Economic Policy (all levels)

Aalders, Gerard and Wiebes, Cees. Stockholms Enskilda Bank, German Bosch and IG Farben. A Short History of Cloaking. *Scand. Econ. Hist. Rev.*, 1985, *33*(1), pp. 25–50. [G: U.S.; Sweden]

Anderson, Elijah. The Social Context of Youth Employment Programs. In *Betsey, C. L.; Hollister, R. G., Jr. and Papageorgiou, M. R., eds.*, 1985, pp. 348–66. [G: U.S.]

Armstrong, Christopher and Nelles, H. V. The State and the Provision of Electricity in Canada and Australia, 1880–1965. In *Platt, D. C. M. and di Tella, G., eds.*, 1985, pp. 207–30. [G: Australia; Canada]

Baack, Bennett D. and Ray, Edward John. Special Interests and the Adoption of the Income Tax in the United States. *J. Econ. Hist.*, September 1985, *45*(3), pp. 607–25. [G: U.S.]

Baack, Bennett D. and Ray, Edward John. The Political Economy of the Origins of the Military-Industrial Complex in the United States. *J. Econ. Hist.*, June 1985, *45*(2), pp. 369–75. [G: U.S.]

Berkowitz, Edward D. and Berkowitz, Monroe. Challenges to Workers' Compensation: An Historical Analysis. In *Worrall, J. D. and Appel, D., eds.*, 1985, pp. 158–79. [G: U.S.]

Binder, John J. Measuring the Effects of Regulation with Stock Price Data. *Rand J. Econ.*, Summer 1985, *16*(2), pp. 167–83. [G: U.S.]

Bittlingmayer, George. Did Antitrust Policy Cause the Great Merger Wave? *J. Law Econ.*, April 1985, *28*(1), pp. 77–118. [G: U.S.]

Borcherding, Thomas E. The Causes of Government Expenditure Growth: A Survey of the U.S. Evidence. *J. Public Econ.*, December 1985, *28*(3), pp. 359–82. [G: U.S.]

Bryce, R. B. The Canadian Economy in the 1930s: Unemployment Relief under Bennett and Mackenzie King. In *[Spry, I. M.]*, 1985, pp. 7–26. [G: Canada]

Burbridge, John B. and Harrison, Alan. A Historical Decomposition of the Great Depression to Determine the Role of Money. *J. Monet. Econ.*, July 1985, *16*(1), pp. 45–54. [G: U.S.]

Carosso, Vincent P. Legislative History of the Glass-Steagall Act: An Economic Evaluation of Bank Securities Activities before 1933: Comment. In *Walter, I., ed.*, 1985, pp. 89–91. [G: U.S.]

Cartwright, Phillip A. and Kamerschen, David R. Variations in Antitrust Enforcement Activity. *Rev. Ind. Organ.*, 1985, *2*(1), pp. 0–31. [G: U.S.]

Cuzán, Alfred G. and Heggen, Richard J. Expenditures and Votes: In Search of Downward-sloping Curves in the United States and Great Britain. *Public Choice*, 1985, *45*(1), pp. 19–34. [G: U.S.]

Dowd, Kevin and Sayeed, Adil. Federal–Provincial Fiscal Relations: Some Background. In *Courchene, T. J.; Conklin, D. W. and Cook, G. C. A., eds. Vol. 2*, 1985, pp. 253–75. [G: Canada]

Drake, Louis S. Reconstruction of a Bimetallic Price Level. *Exploration Econ. Hist.*, April 1985, *22*(2), pp. 194–219. [G: U.S.]

Drummond, Ian M. Marketing Boards in the White Dominions, with Special Reference to Australia and Canada. In *Platt, D. C. M. and di Tella, G., eds.*, 1985, pp. 194–206. [G: Australia; Canada; New Zealand]

England, Richard W. Public School Finance in the United States: Historical Trends and Contending Interpretations. *Rev. Radical Polit. Econ.*, Spring and Summer 1985, *17*(1/2), pp. 129–55. [G: U.S.]

Galbraith, John Kenneth. Keynes, Roosevelt, and the Complementary Revolutions. In *Wattel, H. L., ed.*, 1985, pp. 54–60.

Gallarotti, Giulio M. Toward a Business-Cycle Model of Tariffs. *Int. Organ.*, Winter 1985, *39*(1), pp. 155–87. [G: U.S.; U.K.; Germany]

Gaspari, K. Celeste and Woolf, Arthur G. Income, Public Works, and Mortality in Early Twentieth-Century American Cities. *J. Econ. Hist.*, June 1985, *45*(2), pp. 355–61. [G: U.S.]

Gorton, Gary. Clearinghouses and the Origin of Central Banking in the United States. *J. Econ. Hist.*, June 1985, *45*(2), pp. 277–83. [G: U.S.]

Hannon, Joan Underhill. Poor Relief Policy in Antebellum New York State: The Rise and Decline of the Poorhouse. *Exploration Econ. Hist.*, July 1985, *22*(3), pp. 233–56. [G: U.S.]

Hartmann, Charles J. and Renas, Stephen M. Anglo-American Privacy Law: An Economic Analysis. *Int. Rev. Law Econ.*, December 1985, *5*(2), pp. 133–52. [G: U.S.; U.K.]

Hetzel, Robert L. The Rules versus Discretion Debate over Monetary Policy in the 1920s. *Fed. Res. Bank Richmond Econ. Rev.*, Nov./Dec. 1985, *71*(6), pp. 3–14. [G: U.S.]

Higgs, Robert. Crisis, Bigger Government, and Ideological Change: Two Hypotheses on the Ratchet Phenomenon. *Exploration Econ. Hist.*, January 1985, *22*(1), pp. 1–28. [G: U.S.]

Hovenkamp, Herbert. Antitrust Policy after Chicago. *Mich. Law Rev.*, November 1985, *84*(2), pp. 213–84. [G: U.S.]

Hutchinson, William K. Import Substitution, Structural Change, and Regional Economic Growth in the United States: The Northeast, 1870–1910. *J. Econ. Hist.*, June 1985, *45*(2), pp. 319–25. [G: U.S.]

Johnson, Eldon L. Some Development Lessons from the Early Land-Grant Colleges. *J. Devel. Areas*, January 1985, *19*(2), pp. 139–48. [G: LDCs; U.S.]

Keeley, Michael C. The Regulation of Bank Entry. *Fed. Res. Bank San Francisco Econ. Rev.*, Summer 1985, (3), pp. 5–13. [G: U.S.]

Kelly, Edward J., III. Legislative History of the Glass-Steagall Act. In *Walter, I., ed.*, 1985, pp. 41–65. [G: U.S.]

Kindleberger, Charles P. Keynesianism vs. Monetarism in the 1930s Depression and Recovery. In *Kindleberger, C. P.*, 1985, pp. 287–92. [G: U.S.]

Mayer, Thomas and Chatterji, Monojit. Political Shocks and Investment: Some Evidence from the 1930s. *J. Econ. Hist.*, December 1985, *45*(4), pp. 913–24. [G: U.S.]

Metzer, Jacob. How New Was the New Era? The Public Sector in the 1920s. *J. Econ. Hist.*, March 1985, *45*(1), pp. 119–26. [G: U.S.]

North, Douglass C. The Growth of Government in the United States: An Economic Historian's Perspective. *J. Public Econ.*, December 1985, *28*(3), pp. 383–99. [G: U.S.]

Oberg, Barbara. New York State and the "Specie Crisis" of 1837. In *Atack, J., ed.*, 1985, pp. 37–52. [G: U.S.]

Ornstein, Norman J. The Politics of the Deficit. In *Cagan, P. and Somensatto, E., eds.*, 1985, pp. 311–33. [G: U.S.]

Perkins, Edwin J. Lost Opportunities for Compromise in the Bank War: A Reassessment of Jackson's Veto Message. In *Atack, J., ed.*, 1985, pp. 53–56. [G: U.S.]

Phillips, Paul. Staples, Surplus, and Exchange: The Commercial-Industrial Question in the National Policy Period. In *[Spry, I. M.]*, 1985, pp. 27–43. [G: Canada]

du Pont, Peter. Kamikaze Economics. *Policy Rev.*, Fall 1985, (34), pp. 12–16. [G: U.S.]

Price, Daniel N. Unemployment Insurance, Then and Now, 1935–1985. *Soc. Sec. Bull.*, October 1985, *48*(10), pp. 22–32.   [G: U.S.]

Reno, Virginia P. and Grad, Susan. Economic Security, 1935–85. *Soc. Sec. Bull.*, December 1985, *48*(12), pp. 5–20.

Richards, John. The Staple Debates. In *[Spry, I. M.]*, 1985, pp. 45–72.   [G: Canada]

Rockoff, Hugh. The Origins of the Federal Budget. *J. Econ. Hist.*, June 1985, *45*(2), pp. 377–82.   [G: U.S.]

Rolnick, Arthur J. and Weber, Warren E. Banking Instability and Regulation in the U.S. Free Banking Era. *Fed. Res. Bank Minn. Rev.*, Summer 1985, *9*(3), pp. 2–9.   [G: U.S.]

Rosenberg, Emily S. Foundations of United States International Financial Power: Gold Standard Diplomacy, 1900–1905. *Bus. Hist. Rev.*, Summer 1985, *59*(2), pp. 169–202.   [G: U.S.]

Rubin, Israel. Thomas Alva Edison's "Treatise on National Economic Policy and Business." *Bus. Hist. Rev.*, Autumn 1985, *59*(3), pp. 433–64.   [G: U.S.]

Seftel, Howard. Government Regulation and the Rise of the California Fruit Industry: The Entrepreneurial Attack on Fruit Pests, 1880–1920. *Bus. Hist. Rev.*, Autumn 1985, *59*(3), pp. 369–402.   [G: U.S.]

Segal, Harvey H. Money Markets against Governments: Two Centuries of a Spectacular Game. *Contemp. Policy Issues*, Fall 1985, *3*(5), pp. 35–41.   [G: U.S.; Europe]

Shughart, William F., II and Tollison, Robert D. Corporate Chartering: An Exploration in the Economics of Legal Change. *Econ. Inquiry*, October 1985, *23*(4), pp. 585–99.   [G: U.S.]

Smith, Bruce D. Some Colonial Evidence on Two Theories of Money: Maryland and the Carolinas. *J. Polit. Econ.*, December 1985, *93*(6), pp. 1178–1211.   [G: U.S.]

Solomon, Robert. The United States as a Debtor in the 19th Century. *Écon. Soc.*, September 1985, *19*(9), pp. 33–52.   [G: U.S.]

Taggart, Robert A., Jr. Effects of Regulation on Utility Financing: Theory and Evidence. *J. Ind. Econ.*, March 1985, *33*(3), pp. 257–76.   [G: U.S.]

Toma, Mark. A Duopoly Theory of Government Money Production: The 1930s and 1940s. *J. Monet. Econ.*, May 1985, *15*(3), pp. 363–82.

Tucker, Edwin W. The Judicial Leap into the Glass-Steagall Thicket. In *Atack, J., ed.*, 1985, pp. 179–96.   [G: U.S.]

Weir, Margaret and Skocpol, Theda. State Structures and the Possibilities for "Keynesian" Responses to the Great Depression in Sweden, Britain, and the United States. In *Evans, P. B.; Rueschemeyer, D. and Skocpol, T., eds.*, 1985, pp. 107–63.   [G: U.K.; U.S.; Sweden]

White, Eugene Nelson. Voting for Costly Regulation: Evidence from Banking Referenda in Illinois, 1924. *Southern Econ. J.*, April 1985, *51*(4), pp. 1084–98.   [G: U.S.]

Wicker, Elmus. Colonial Monetary Standards Contrasted: Evidence from the Seven Years' War. *J. Econ. Hist.*, December 1985, *45*(4), pp. 869–84.   [G: U.S.]

Wood, Donna J. The Strategic Use of Public Policy: Business Support for the 1906 Food and Drug Act. *Bus. Hist. Rev.*, Autumn 1985, *59*(3), pp. 403–32.   [G: U.S.]

Yamashita, Robert C. and Park, Peter. The Politics of Race: The Open Door, Ozawa and the Case of the Japanese in America. *Rev. Radical Polit. Econ.*, Fall 1985, *17*(3), pp. 135–56.   [G: U.S.]

043 Economic History: Ancient and Medieval (until 1453)

0430 General

Amin, Samir. Modes of Production, History, and Unequal Development [Feudalism and Historical Materialism: A Critique and a Synthesis] [Modes of Production and Theories of Transition]. *Sci. Soc.*, Summer 1985, *49*(2), pp. 194–207.

Baumol, William J. Rebirth of a Fallen Leader: Italy and the Long Period Data. *Atlantic Econ. J.*, September 1985, *13*(3), pp. 12–26.   [G: Italy]

Bogucka, Maria. The Towns of East-central Europe from the Fourteenth to the Seventeenth Century. In *Mączak, A.; Samsonowicz, H. and Burke, P., eds.*, 1985, pp. 97–108.   [G: E. Europe]

Fügedi, Eric. The Demographic Landscape of East-central Europe. In *Mączak, A.; Samsonowicz, H. and Burke, P., eds.*, 1985, pp. 47–58.   [G: E. Europe]

Hallam, H. E. Age at First Marriage and Age at Death in the Lincolnshire Fenland, 1252–1478. *Population Stud.*, March 1985, *39*(1), pp. 55–69.   [G: U.K.]

Hoffman, John. The Dialectic of Abstraction and Concentration in Historical Materialism [Feudalism and Historical Materialism: A Critique and Synthesis] [Modes of Production and Theories of Transition]. *Sci. Soc.*, Winter 1985-1986, *49*(4), pp. 451–62.

Mákkai, Laszlo. Economic Landscapes: Historical Hungary from the Fourteenth to the Seventeenth Century. In *Mączak, A.; Samsonowicz, H. and Burke, P., eds.*, 1985, pp. 24–35.   [G: Hungary]

Malowist, Marian. Comments on the Circulation of Capital in East-central Europe. In *Mączak, A.; Samsonowicz, H. and Burke, P., eds.*, 1985, pp. 109–27.   [G: E. Europe]

Mayhew, Anne; Neale, Walter C. and Tandy, David W. Markets in the Ancient Near East: A Challenge to Silver's Argument and Use of Evidence [Karl Polanyi and Markets in the Ancient Near East: The Challenge of the Evidence]. *J. Econ. Hist.*, March 1985, *45*(1), pp. 127–34.   [G: Middle East]

Nightingale, Pamela. The Evolution of Weight-Standards and the Creation of New Monetary and Commercial Links in Northern Europe from the Tenth Century to the Twelfth Century. *Econ. Hist. Rev.*, *2nd Ser.*, May 1985, *38*(2), pp. 192–209. **[G: Europe]**

Silver, Morris. Markets in the Ancient Near East: A Challenge to Silver's Argument and Use of Evidence: Karl Polanyi and Markets in the Ancient Near East: Reply. *J. Econ. Hist.*, March 1985, *45*(1), pp. 135–37.

Wyrobisz, Andrzej. Economic Landscapes: Poland from the Fourteenth to the Seventeenth Century. In *Mączak, A.; Samsonowicz, H. and Burke, P., eds.*, 1985, pp. 36–46.

[G: Poland]

0431 History of Product Prices and Markets

Ashtor, Eliyahu. Investments in Levant Trade in the Period of the Crusades. *J. Europ. Econ. Hist.*, Sept.-Dec. 1985, *14*(3), pp. 427–41.

[G: Europe; Egypt]

Ashtor, Eliyahu. Recent Research on Levantine Trade: Review Article. *J. Europ. Econ. Hist.*, Fall 1985, *14*(2), pp. 361–85. **[G: Europe; Asia]**

Biddick, Kathleen. Medieval English Peasants and Market Involvement. *J. Econ. Hist.*, December 1985, *45*(4), pp. 823–31. **[G: U.K.]**

Blomquist, Thomas W. The Early History of European Banking: Merchants, Bankers and Lombards of Thirteenth-Century Lucca in the County of Champagne. *J. Europ. Econ. Hist.*, Sept.-Dec. 1985, *14*(3), pp. 521–36.

[G: Italy]

Carpi, Daniel. The Account Book of a Jewish Moneylender in Montepulciano (1409–1410). *J. Europ. Econ. Hist.*, Sept.-Dec. 1985, *14*(3), pp. 501–13. **[G: Italy]**

Goldsmith, R. W. Errata [An Estimate of the Size and Structure of the National Product of the Early Roman Empire]. *Rev. Income Wealth*, March 1985, *31*(1), pp. 101.

Goldthwaite, Richard A. Local Banking in Renaissance Florence. *J. Europ. Econ. Hist.*, Spring 1985, *14*(1), pp. 5–55. **[G: Italy]**

0432 History of Factor Prices and Markets

Baum, Hans-Peter. Annuities in Late Medieval Hanse Towns. *Bus. Hist. Rev.*, Spring 1985, *59*(1), pp. 24–48. **[G: Germany]**

Fryde, Edmund. Medieval London as a Financial Centre: Some Early Dealings in Royal Tallies of Assignment. In *Marx, A. V., ed.*, 1985, pp. 41–48. **[G: U.K.]**

McDonald, John W. and Snooks, G. D. The Determinants of Manorial Income in Domesday England: Evidence from Essex. *J. Econ. Hist.*, September 1985, *45*(3), pp. 541–56.

[G: U.K.]

Miskimin, Harry A. The Enforcement of Gresham's Law. In *Marx, A. V., ed.*, 1985, pp. 147–61. **[G: U.K.; France]**

Poos, L. R. The Rural Population of Essex in the Later Middle Ages. *Econ. Hist. Rev.*, *2nd Ser.*, November 1985, *38*(4), pp. 515–30.

[G: U.K.]

Svanidze, Adelaida. Promissory Notes and Their Regulations in Sweden during the XIII/XV Centuries. In *Marx, A. V., ed.*, 1985, pp. 49–51. **[G: Sweden]**

0433 History of Public Economic Policy (all levels)

Aumann, Robert J. and Maschler, Michael. Game Theoretic Analysis of a Bancruptcy Problem from the Talmud. *J. Econ. Theory*, August 1985, *36*(2), pp. 195–213. **[G: Israel]**

Biddick, Kathleen. Medieval English Peasants and Market Involvement. *J. Econ. Hist.*, December 1985, *45*(4), pp. 823–31. **[G: U.K.]**

de Cecco, Marcello. Monetary Theory and Roman History. *J. Econ. Hist.*, December 1985, *45*(4), pp. 809–22. **[G: Italy]**

Curtin, Philip D. Medical Knowledge and Urban Planning in Tropical Africa. *Amer. Hist. Rev.*, June 1985, *90*(3), pp. 594–613.

[G: Tropical Africa]

McDonald, John W. and Snooks, G. D. Were the Tax Assessments of Domesday England Artificial? *Econ. Hist. Rev.*, *2nd Ser.*, August 1985, *38*(3), pp. 352–72. **[G: U.K.]**

Miskimin, Harry A. The Enforcement of Gresham's Law. In *Marx, A. V., ed.*, 1985, pp. 147–61. **[G: U.K.; France]**

Nightingale, Pamela. The Evolution of Weight-Standards and the Creation of New Monetary and Commercial Links in Northern Europe from the Tenth Century to the Twelfth Century. *Econ. Hist. Rev.*, *2nd Ser.*, May 1985, *38*(2), pp. 192–209. **[G: Europe]**

044 Economic History: Europe

0440 General

Allais, Maurice. A New Empirical Approach of the Hereditary and Relativistic Theory of the Demand for Money: The Rate of Increase of Global Expenditure and the Velocity of Circulation of Money. *Rivista Int. Sci. Econ. Com.*, Oct.-Nov. 1985, *32*(10–11), pp. 905–48.

[G: U.S.; W. Germany]

Anderson, Barbara A. and Silver, Brian D. Demographic Consequences of World War II on the Non-Russian Nationalities of the USSR. In *Linz, S. J., ed.*, 1985, pp. 207–42.

[G: U.S.S.R.]

Barnett, C. Long-term Industrial Performance in the UK: The Role of Education and Research, 1850–1939. In *Morris, D., ed.*, 1985, pp. 668–89. **[G: OECD]**

Baumol, William J. Rebirth of a Fallen Leader: Italy and the Long Period Data. *Atlantic Econ. J.*, September 1985, *13*(3), pp. 12–26.

[G: Italy]

Bernholz, Peter. A Financial History of Western Europe: A Review. *Weltwirtsch. Arch.*, 1985, *121*(4), pp. 779–85. **[G: Europe]**

Bernholz, Peter; Gärtner, Manfred and Heri, Erwin W. Historical Experiences with Flexible Exchange Rates: A Simulation of Common Qualitative Characteristics. *J. Int. Econ.*, August 1985, *19*(1/2), pp. 21–45.   [G: Europe; U.S.]

Bogucka, Maria. The Towns of East-central Europe from the Fourteenth to the Seventeenth Century. In *Mączak, A.; Samsonowicz, H. and Burke, P.*, eds., 1985, pp. 97–108.
[G: E. Europe]

Bois, Guy. Against the Neo-Malthusian Orthodoxy. In *Aston, T. H. and Philpin, C. H. E.*, eds., 1985, pp. 107–18.

Brenner, Robert. Agrarian Class Structure and Economic Development in Pre-industrial Europe. In *Aston, T. H. and Philpin, C. H. E.*, eds., 1985, pp. 10–63.

Brenner, Robert. The Agrarian Roots of European Capitalism. In *Aston, T. H. and Philpin, C. H. E.*, eds., 1985, pp. 213–327.

Bruland, Kristine. Say's Law and the Single-Factor Explanation of British Industrialization: A Comment [The Cause of the Industrial Revolution: A Brief 'Single-Factor' Argument]. *J. Europ. Econ. Hist.*, Spring 1985, *14*(1), pp. 187–91.   [G: U.K.]

Brüninghaus, Beate. A Review of the New Literature on Business History. In *Engels, W. and Pohl, H.*, eds., 1985, pp. 129–50.

Bubis, Edward and Ruble, Blair A. The Impact of World War II on Leningrad. In *Linz, S. J.*, ed., 1985, pp. 189–206.   [G: U.S.S.R.]

Cameron, Rondo. A New View of European Industrialization. *Econ. Hist. Rev., 2nd Ser.*, February 1985, *38*(1), pp. 1–23. [G: Europe]

Capie, Forrest H. and Rodrik-Bali, Ghila. The Money Adjustment Process in the United Kingdom, 1870-1914. *Economica*, February 1985, *52*(205), pp. 117–22.   [G: U.K.]

Cassis, Y. Bankers in English Society in the Late Nineteenth Century. *Econ. Hist. Rev., 2nd Ser.*, May 1985, *38*(2), pp. 210–29.
[G: U.K.]

de Cecco, Marcello. The International Debt Program in the Interwar Period. *Banca Naz. Lavoro Quart. Rev.*, March 1985, (152), pp. 45–64.   [G: OECD]

Clarkson, L. A. An Economic History of Ulster 1820–1939: Population Change and Urbanisation, 1821–1911. In *Kennedy, L. and Ollerenshaw, P.*, eds., 1985, pp. 137–57. [G: U.K.]

Clendenning, P. H. The Economic Awakening of Russia in the Eighteenth Century. *J. Europ. Econ. Hist.*, Sept.-Dec. 1985, *14*(3), pp. 443–71.   [G: U.S.S.R.]

Cooper, J. P. In Search of Agrarian Capitalism. In *Aston, T. H. and Philpin, C. H. E.*, eds., 1985, pp. 138–91.

Crafts, N. F. R. Entrepreneurship and a Probabilistic View of the British Industrial Revolution: Reply. In *Mokyr, J.*, ed., 1985, pp. 135–36.
[G: U.K.; France]

Crafts, N. F. R. Industrial Revolution in England and France: Some Thoughts on the Question "Why Was England First?" In *Mokyr, J.*, ed., 1985, pp. 119–31.   [G: France; U.K.]

Croot, Patricia and Parker, David. Agrarian Class Structure and the Development of Capitalism: France and England Compared. In *Aston,*

T. H. and Philpin, C. H. E., eds., 1985, pp. 79–90.

Davies, Peter N. British Shipping and World Trade: Rise and Decline, 1820–1939: Response. In *Yui, T. and Nakagawa, K.*, eds., 1985, pp. 88–89.   [G: U.K.]

Davies, Peter N. British Shipping and World Trade: Rise and Decline, 1820–1939. In *Yui, T. and Nakagawa, K.*, eds., 1985, pp. 39–85.
[G: U.K.]

Davies, S. J. Classes and Police in Manchester 1829–1880. In *Kidd, A. J. and Roberts, K. W.*, 1985, pp. 26–47.   [G: U.K.]

Doyle, Michael W. Metropole, Periphery, and System: Empire on the Niger and the Nile. In *Evans, P.; Rueschemeyer, D. and Stephens, E. H.*, eds., 1985, pp. 151–91.   [G: Egypt; W. Africa; U.K.]

Dyson, Tim and Murphy, Mike. The Onset of Fertility Transition. *Population Devel. Rev.*, September 1985, *11*(3), pp. 399–440.
[G: LDCs; MDCs]

Fishlow, Albert. Lessons from the Past: Capital Markets during the 19th Century and the Interwar Period. *Int. Organ.*, Summer 1985, *39*(3), pp. 383–439.   [G: W. Europe; U.S.]

Fügedi, Eric. The Demographic Landscape of East-central Europe. In *Mączak, A.; Samsonowicz, H. and Burke, P.*, eds., 1985, pp. 47–58.   [G: E. Europe]

Galloway, P. R. Annual Variations in Deaths by Age, Deaths by Cause, Prices, and Weather in London 1670 to 1830. *Population Stud.*, November 1985, *39*(3), pp. 487–505. [G: U.K.]

Giner, Salvador. Political Economy, Legitimation and the State in Southern Europe. In *Hudson, R. and Lewis, J.*, eds., 1985, pp. 309–50.
[G: S. Europe]

Glynn, Sean; Booth, Alan and Howells, Peter. NEH, NEH, NEH and the 'Keynesian Solution' [Unemployment in the 1930s: The Keynesian Solution Reconsidered]. *Australian Econ. Hist. Rev.*, September 1985, *25*(2), pp. 149–57.   [G: U.K.]

Goto, Shin. British Shipping and World Trade: Rise and Decline, 1820–1939: Comment. In *Yui, T. and Nakagawa, K.*, eds., 1985, pp. 86–88.   [G: U.K.]

Guillerme, Jacques. "Invention" et "innovation" dans l'art du projet. ("Invention" and "Innovation" in Architectural Projects. With English summary.) *Écon. Soc.*, October 1985, *19*(10), pp. 71–87.   [G: France]

Harrison, Alan. The Distribution of Personal Wealth in Britain. In *Atkinson, G. B. J.*, ed., 1985, pp. 123–31.   [G: U.K.]

Hatton, T. J. Unemployment in the 1930s and the 'Keynesian Solution': Some Notes of Dissent. *Australian Econ. Hist. Rev.*, September 1985, *25*(2), pp. 129–48.   [G: U.K.]

Haynes, Stephen E.; Phillips, Llad and Votey, Harold L., Jr. An Econometric Test of Structural Change in the Demographic Transition. *Scand. J. Econ.*, 1985, *87*(3), pp. 554–67.
[G: Finland; Norway; Sweden; U.K.]

Hentschel, Volker. Breaks and Continuity in the

Economy and Social Structures between the Weimar Republic and the Third Reich. In *Engels, W. and Pohl, H., eds.*, 1985, pp. 95–128.
[G: Germany]

Hilton, R. H. A Crisis of Feudalism. In *Aston, T. H. and Philpin, C. H. E., eds.*, 1985, pp. 119–37.

Hornby, Ove. The Danish Shipping Industry, 1866–1939: Structure and Strategy. In *Yui, T. and Nakagawa, K., eds.*, 1985, pp. 157–81.
[G: Denmark]

Hornby, Ove. The Danish Shipping Industry, 1866–1939: Structure and Strategy: Response. In *Yui, T. and Nakagawa, K., eds.*, 1985, pp. 184.
[G: Denmark]

Hunter, Holland. Successful Spatial Management. In *Linz, S. J., ed.*, 1985, pp. 47–58.
[G: U.S.S.R.]

Inglehart, Ronald. Aggregate Stability and Individual-Level Flux in Mass Belief Systems: The Level of Analysis Paradox. *Amer. Polit. Sci. Rev.*, March 1985, 79(1), pp. 97–116.
[G: OECD]

Jackson, R. V. Growth and Deceleration in English Agriculture, 1660–1790. *Econ. Hist. Rev.*, 2nd Ser., August 1985, 38(3), pp. 333–51.
[G: U.K.]

Johnson, D. S. The Northern Ireland Economy, 1914–39. In *Kennedy, L. and Ollerenshaw, P., eds.*, 1985, pp. 184–223. **[G: U.K.]**

Jones, Peter. The Scottish Professoriate and the Polite Academy, 1720–46. In *Hont, I. and Ignatieff, M., eds.*, 1985, pp. 89–117.
[G: U.K.]

Kajimoto, Motonobu. Shipping Business in Germany in the Nineteenth and Twentieth Centuries: Comment. In *Yui, T. and Nakagawa, K., eds.*, 1985, pp. 214–16. **[G: Germany]**

Kennedy, Líam. An Economic History of Ulster 1820–1939: The Rural Economy, 1820–1914. In *Kennedy, L. and Ollerenshaw, P., eds.*, 1985, pp. 1–61. **[G: U.K.]**

Kidd, Alan J. 'Outcast Manchester': Voluntary Charity, Poor Relief and the Casual Poor 1860–1905. In *Kidd, A. J. and Roberts, K. W.*, 1985, pp. 48–73. **[G: U.K.]**

Kielstra, Nico. The Rural Languedoc: Periphery to "Relictual Space." In *Hudson, R. and Lewis, J., eds.*, 1985, pp. 246–62. **[G: France]**

Kindleberger, Charles P. Banking and Industry between the Two Wars: An International Comparison. In *Kindleberger, C. P.*, 1985, pp. 293–313. **[G: U.S.; Europe]**

Kindleberger, Charles P. British Financial Reconstruction, 1815–22 and 1918–25. In *Kindleberger, C. P.*, 1985, pp. 105–18. **[G: U.K.]**

Kindleberger, Charles P. Financial Institutions and Economic Development: A Comparison of Great Britain and France in the Eighteenth and Nineteenth Centuries. In *Kindleberger, C. P.*, 1985, pp. 65–85. **[G: U.K.; France]**

Kindleberger, Charles P. The Cyclical Pattern of Long-term Lending. In *Kindleberger, C. P.*, 1985, pp. 141–54. **[G: Europe; U.S.]**

Kindleberger, Charles P. The Financial After-

math of War. In *Kindleberger, C. P.*, 1985, pp. 168–89.

Kindleberger, Charles P. The Functioning of Financial Centers: Britain in the Nineteenth Century, the United States since 1945. In *[Bloomfield, A. I.]*, 1985, pp. 7–18.
[G: U.K.; U.S.]

Klima, Arnost. Agrarian Class Structure and Economic Development in Pre-industrial Bohemia. In *Aston, T. H. and Philpin, C. H. E., eds.*, 1985, pp. 192–212.

Komlos, John. The End of the Old Order in Rural Austria. *J. Europ. Econ. Hist.*, Sept.-Dec. 1985, 14(3), pp. 515–20. **[G: Austria]**

Kussmaul, Ann. Agrarian Change in Seventeenth-Century England: The Economic Historian as Paleontologist. *J. Econ. Hist.*, March 1985, 45(1), pp. 1–30. **[G: U.K.]**

Le Roy Ladurie, Emmanuel. Agrarian Class Structure and Economic Development in Pre-industrial Europe: A Reply. In *Aston, T. H. and Philpin, C. H. E., eds.*, 1985, pp. 101–06.

Leontief, Wassily. Capital Reconstruction and Postwar Development of Income and Consumption. In *Linz, S. J., ed.*, 1985, pp. 38–46. **[G: U.S.S.R.]**

Levan-Lemesle, Lucette. Innovations et institutions: Le Conservatoire des Arts et Métiers et la Faculté de Droit de Paris. (Innovations and Institutions: The Conservatory of Arts and Trades and the Law School of Paris. With English summary.) *Écon. Soc.*, October 1985, 19(10), pp. 107–19. **[G: France]**

Lindblad, Jan Thomas. Structural Change in the Dutch Trade with the Baltic in the Eighteenth Century. *Scand. Econ. Hist. Rev.*, 1985, 33(3), pp. 193–207. **[G: Netherlands; Baltic Countries]**

Lindert, Peter H. and Williamson, Jeffrey G. Growth, Equality, and History. *Exploration Econ. Hist.*, October 1985, 22(4), pp. 341–77.
[G: W. Europe; U.S.]

Linz, Susan J. Foreign Aid and Soviet Postwar Recovery. *J. Econ. Hist.*, December 1985, 45(4), pp. 947–54. **[G: U.S.S.R.]**

Linz, Susan J. World War II and Soviet Economic Growth, 1940–1953. In *Linz, S. J., ed.*, 1985, pp. 11–38. **[G: U.S.S.R.]**

Locke, Robert R. Business Education in Germany: Past Systems and Current Practice. *Bus. Hist. Rev.*, Summer 1985, 59(2), pp. 232–53.
[G: W. Germany]

Lundberg, Erik. The Rise and Fall of the Swedish Model. *J. Econ. Lit.*, March 1985, 23(1), pp. 1–36. **[G: Sweden]**

Mákkai, Laszlo. Economic Landscapes: Historical Hungary from the Fourteenth to the Seventeenth Century. In *Mączak, A.; Samsonowicz, H. and Burke, P., eds.*, 1985, pp. 24–35.
[G: Hungary]

Marx, Karl. Chroniques litté raires. (Literary Chronicles [1850]. With English summary.) *Écon. Soc.*, November 1985, 19(11), pp. 97–112. **[G: France]**

Matthews, Kent. Private Sector Expenditure in

the Inter-war Period: An Integrated Portfolio Approach. *Manchester Sch. Econ. Soc. Stud.*, March 1985, *53*(1), pp. 23–44. [G: U.K.]

McCloskey, Donald N. The Industrial Revolution 1780–1860: A Survey. In *Mokyr, J., ed.*, 1985, pp. 53–74. [G: U.K.]

McCutcheon, W. A. An Economic History of Ulster 1820–1939: Transport, 1820–1914. In *Kennedy, L. and Ollerenshaw, P., eds.*, 1985, pp. 109–36. [G: U.K.]

McDonald, John W. and Snooks, G. D. Statistical Analysis of Domesday Book (1086). *J. Roy. Statist. Soc.*, 1985, *148*(2), pp. 147–60. [G: U.K.]

McKenna, J. A. and Rodger, Richard G. Control by Coercion: Employers' Associations and the Establishment of Industrial Order in the Building Industry of England and Wales, 1860–1914. *Bus. Hist. Rev.*, Summer 1985, *59*(2), pp. 203–31. [G: U.K.]

McMichael, Philip. Britain's Hegemony in the Nineteenth-Century World-Economy. In *Evans, P.; Rueschemeyer, D. and Stephens, E. H., eds.*, 1985, pp. 117–50. [G: U.K.]

Mercer, A. J. Smallpox and Epidemiological–Demographic Change in Europe: The Role of Vaccination. *Population Stud.*, July 1985, *39*(2), pp. 287–307. [G: OECD]

Mokyr, Joel. Demand vs. Supply in the Industrial Revolution. In *Mokyr, J., ed.*, 1985, pp. 97–118. [G: U.K.]

Mokyr, Joel. The Industrial Revolution and the New Economic History. In *Mokyr, J., ed.*, 1985, pp. 1–51. [G: U.K.]

Monzani, Pierre. Innovation et nouveautés au XVIIIᵉ siècle. (Innovation and Novelties in the 18th Century. With English summary.) *Écon. Soc.*, October 1985, *19*(10), pp. 57–70. [G: France]

Neal, Larry. The Rise of a Financial Press: London and Amsterdam, 1681–1796. In *Atack, J., ed.*, 1985, pp. 139–41. [G: U.K.; Netherlands]

Newman, Karin. Hamburg in the European Economy, 1660–1750. *J. Europ. Econ. Hist.*, Spring 1985, *14*(1), pp. 57–93. [G: Germany]

Officer, Lawrence H. Integration in the American Foreign-Exchange Market, 1791–1900. *J. Econ. Hist.*, September 1985, *45*(3), pp. 557–85. [G: U.S.; U.K.]

Olsen, Randall J. Gold, Foreign Capital and the Industrialization of Russia. *J. Europ. Econ. Hist.*, Spring 1985, *14*(1), pp. 143–54. [G: U.S.S.R.]

Othick, John. The Economic History of Ulster: A Perspective. In *Kennedy, L. and Ollerenshaw, P., eds.*, 1985, pp. 224–40. [G: U.K.]

Pollard, Sidney. Industrialization and the European Economy. In *Mokyr, J., ed.*, 1985, pp. 165–76. [G: Europe]

Postan, M. M. and Hatcher, John. Population and Class Relations in Feudal Society. In *Aston, T. H. and Philpin, C. H. E., eds.*, 1985, pp. 64–78.

Ratcliffe, Barrie M. The Business Elite and the Development of Paris: Intervention in Ports

and Entrepôts, 1814–1834. *J. Europ. Econ. Hist.*, Spring 1985, *14*(1), pp. 95–142. [G: France]

Rostow, W. W. No Random Walk: A Comment on "Why Was England First?" In *Mokyr, J., ed.*, 1985, pp. 132–34. [G: France; U.K.]

Rudoph, Richard L. Agricultural Structure and Proto-Industrialization in Russia: Economic Development with Unfree Labor. *J. Econ. Hist.*, March 1985, *45*(1), pp. 47–69. [G: U.S.S.R.]

Samsonowicz, Henryk and Maczak, Antoni. Feudalism and Capitalism: A Balance of Changes in East-central Europe. In *Mączak, A.; Samsonowicz, H. and Burke, P., eds.*, 1985, pp. 6–23. [G: E. Europe]

Samura, Terutoshi. Proto-factories and Proto-industrialization. (In Japanese. With English summary.) *Osaka Econ. Pap.*, March 1985, *34*(4), pp. 1–15. [G: Europe]

Scholl, Lars U. Shipping Business in Germany in the Nineteenth and Twentieth Centuries. In *Yui, T. and Nakagawa, K., eds.*, 1985, pp. 185–213. [G: Germany]

Smout, T. C. Where Had the Scottish Economy Got to by the Third Quarter of the Eighteenth Century? In *Hont, I. and Ignatieff, M., eds.*, 1985, pp. 45–72. [G: U.K.]

Solow, Barbara L. Caribbean Slavery and British Growth: The Eric Williams Hypothesis. *J. Devel. Econ.*, January–February 1985, *17*(1–2), pp. 99–115. [G: U.K.]

Swenarton, Mark and Taylor, Sandra. The Scale and Nature of the Growth of Owner-Occupation in Britain between the Wars. *Econ. Hist. Rev., 2nd Ser.*, August 1985, *38*(3), pp. 373–92. [G: U.K.]

Tomita, Masahiro. The Danish Shipping Industry, 1866–1939: Structure and Strategy: Comment. In *Yui, T. and Nakagawa, K., eds.*, 1985, pp. 182–83. [G: Denmark]

Trussell, James and Wilson, C. Sterility in a Population with Natural Fertility. *Population Stud.*, July 1985, *39*(2), pp. 269–86. [G: U.K.]

von Tunzelmann, G. N. The Standard of Living Debate and Optimal Economic Growth. In *Mokyr, J., ed.*, 1985, pp. 207–26. [G: U.K.]

Turdeanu, Lucian and Marcu, Nicolae. Romania's Wealth Estimations before the Second World War. *Rev. Income Wealth*, March 1985, *31*(1), pp. 97–100. [G: Romania]

Vachel, Jan. Czechoslovakia's Economic and Social Development. *Czech. Econ. Digest.*, November 1985, (7), pp. 3–29. [G: Czechoslovakia]

Wenig, Alois. Übervölkerung—eine Kriegsursache? Einige Anmerkungen zur Bevölkerungslehre von Thomas Robert Malthus. (Overpopulation—A Cause for War? With English summary.) *Kyklos*, 1985, *38*(3), pp. 365–91. [G: Europe]

West, Edwin G. Literacy and the Industrial Revolution. In *Mokyr, J., ed.*, 1985, pp. 227–40. [G: U.K.]

Willcox, Walter. Walter Willcox on the Expansion

of Europe and Its Influence on Population. *Population Devel. Rev.*, September 1985, *11*(3), pp. 515–27. **[G: Europe]**

Worswick, G. D. N. Correction [Two Great Recessions]. *Scot. J. Polit. Econ.*, February 1985, *32*(1), pp. 111. **[G: U.S.; U.K.]**

Wunder, Heide. Peasant Organization and Class Conflict in Eastern and Western Germany. In *Aston, T. H. and Philpin, C. H. E., eds.*, 1985, pp. 91–100. **[G: W. Germany]**

Wyrobisz, Andrzej. Economic Landscapes: Poland from the Fourteenth to the Seventeenth Century. In *Mączak, A.; Samsonowicz, H. and Burke, P., eds.*, 1985, pp. 36–46. **[G: Poland]**

Zurawicka, Janina. Charity in Warsaw in the Second Half of the XIXth Century. *J. Europ. Econ. Hist.*, Fall 1985, *14*(2), pp. 319–30. **[G: Poland]**

Zytkowicz, Leonid. Trends of Agrarian Economy in Poland, Bohemia and Hungary from the Middle of the Fifteenth to the Middle of the Seventeenth Century. In *Mączak, A.; Samsonowicz, H. and Burke, P., eds.*, 1985, pp. 59–83. **[G: Poland; Hungary; Bohemia]**

0441 History of Product Prices and Markets

Ahvenainen, Jorma. The Competitive Position of the Finnish Sawmill Industry in the 1920s and 1930s. *Scand. Econ. Hist. Rev.*, 1985, *33*(3), pp. 173–92. **[G: Finland]**

Anderson, B. L. and Richardson, David. Market Structure and the Profits of the British African Slave Trade in the Late Eighteenth Century: A Rejoinder Rebutted. *J. Econ. Hist.*, September 1985, *45*(3), pp. 705–07. **[G: U.K.]**

Basberg, Bjørn L. Technological Transformation in the Norwegian Whaling Industry in the Interwar Period. *Scand. Econ. Hist. Rev.*, 1985, *33*(2), pp. 83–107. **[G: Norway]**

Bongaerts, Jan C. Financing Railways in the German States 1840–1860. A Preliminary View. *J. Europ. Econ. Hist.*, Fall 1985, *14*(2), pp. 331–45. **[G: Germany]**

Borscheid, Peter. The Establishment of the Life Insurance Business in Germany in the Nineteenth Century. In *Engels, W. and Pohl, H., eds.*, 1985, pp. 55–74. **[G: Germany]**

Cain, Louis P. William Dean's Theory of Urban Growth: Chicago's Commerce and Industry, 1854–1871. *J. Econ. Hist.*, June 1985, *45*(2), pp. 241–49. **[G: U.S]**

Chapman, S. D. British-based Investment Groups before 1914. *Econ. Hist. Rev.*, 2nd Ser., May 1985, *38*(2), pp. 230–51. **[G: U.K.]**

Crabbe, Philippe J. Turgot's *Brief on Mines and Quaries:* An Early Economic Analysis of Mineral Land Tenure. *Natural Res. J.*, April 1985, *25*(2), pp. 267–73. **[G: France]**

Darity, William A., Jr. The Numbers Game and the Profitability of the British Trade in Slaves. *J. Econ. Hist.*, September 1985, *45*(3), pp. 693–703. **[G: U.K.]**

David, Paul A. Clio and the Economics of QWERTY. *Amer. Econ. Rev.*, May 1985, *75*(2), pp. 332–37. **[G: U.S.; U.K.]**

Davies, Alun C. Rural Clockmaking in Eighteenth-Century Wales: Samuel Roberts of Llanfair Caereinion, 1755–1774. *Bus. Hist. Rev.*, Spring 1985, *59*(1), pp. 49–75. **[G: U.K.]**

Desaigues, Brigitte. Le rang de la France a-t-il changé (1860–1970)? Évolution de la position internationale de la France. (With English summary.) *Revue Écon. Polit.*, Sept.-Oct. 1985, *95*(5), pp. 531–43. **[G: France]**

Drescher, Seymour. British Slavers: A Comment [Market Structure and the Profits of the British African Slave Trade in the Late Eighteenth Century]. *J. Econ. Hist.*, September 1985, *45*(3), pp. 704. **[G: U.K.]**

Dwyer, Gerald P., Jr. Money, Income, and Prices in the United Kingdom: 1870–1913. *Econ. Inquiry*, July 1985, *23*(3), pp. 415–35. **[G: U.S.]**

Edison, Hali J. Purchasing Power Parity: A Quantitative Reassessment of the 1920s Experience. *J. Int. Money Finance*, September 1985, *4*(3), pp. 361–72. **[G: U.K.; U.S.; France]**

Eichengreen, Barry and Sachs, Jeffrey. Exchange Rates and Economic Recovery in the 1930s. *J. Econ. Hist.*, December 1985, *45*(4), pp. 925–46. **[G: U.S.; W. Europe]**

Foreman-Peck, James S. Seedcorn or Chaff? New Firm Formation and the Performance of the Interwar Economy. *Econ. Hist. Rev.*, 2nd Ser., August 1985, *38*(3), pp. 402–22. **[G: U.K.]**

Foreman-Peck, James S. and Waterson, Michael. The Comparative Efficiency of Public and Private Enterprise in Britain: Electricity Generation between the World Wars. *Econ. J.*, Supplement 1985, *95*, pp. 83–95. **[G: U.K.]**

Glassman, Debra and Redish, Angela. New Estimates of the Money Stock in France, 1493–1680. *J. Econ. Hist.*, March 1985, *45*(1), pp. 31–46. **[G: France]**

Goldthwaite, Richard A. Local Banking in Renaissance Florence. *J. Europ. Econ. Hist.*, Spring 1985, *14*(1), pp. 5–55. **[G: Italy]**

Harrison, Mark. Primary Accumulation in the Soviet Transition. In *Saith, A., ed.*, 1985, pp. 81–103. **[G: U.S.S.R.]**

Harrison, Mark. Primary Accumulation in the Soviet Transition. *J. Devel. Stud.*, October 1985, *22*(1), pp. 81–103. **[G: U.S.S.R.]**

Hassan, J. A. The Growth and Impact of the British Water Industry in the Nineteenth Century. *Econ. Hist. Rev.*, 2nd Ser., November 1985, *38*(4), pp. 531–47. **[G: U.K.]**

Inikori, J. E. Market Structure and Profits: A Further Rejoinder [Measuring the Atlantic Slave Trade: An Assessment of Curtin and Anstey]. *J. Econ. Hist.*, September 1985, *45*(3), pp. 708–11. **[G: U.K.]**

Jones, Geoffrey. The Gramophone Company: An Anglo-American Multinational, 1898–1931. *Bus. Hist. Rev.*, Spring 1985, *59*(1), pp. 76–100. **[G: U.K.; U.S.]**

Kindleberger, Charles P. A Structural View of

the German Inflation. In *Kindleberger, C. P.*, 1985, pp. 247–66.   [G: Germany]

Kiss, István N. Agricultural and Livestock Production: Wine and Oxen. The Case of Hungary. In *Mączak, A.; Samsonowicz, H. and Burke, P., eds.*, 1985, pp. 84–96.   [G: Hungary]

Lyons, John S. Vertical Integration in the British Cotton Industry, 1825–1850: A Revision. *J. Econ. Hist.*, June 1985, *45*(2), pp. 419–25.
                                    [G: U.K.]

Mantelli, Roberto. Industrialization in Southern Italy before and after Unification. *J. Europ. Econ. Hist.*, Sept.-Dec. 1985, *14*(3), pp. 577–83.   [G: Italy]

Margairaz, Dominique. L'office du blé, une innovation socialiste en régime capitaliste. (The Wheat Office: A Socialist Innovation within a Capitalist Regime. With English summary.) *Écon. Soc.*, October 1985, *19*(10), pp. 37–55.
                                   [G: France]

Marseille, Jacques. The Phases of French Colonial Imperialism: Towards a New Periodization. In *Porter, A. N. and Holland, R. F., eds.*, 1985, pp. 127–41.   [G: U.K.; France; Germany; Selected Countries]

Meier, Henri B. History of the Swiss Equity Market. In *Meier, H. B., ed.*, 1985, pp. 1–7.
                             [G: Switzerland]

Michie, R. C. The London Stock Exchange and the British Securities Market, 1850–1914. *Econ. Hist. Rev., 2nd Ser.*, February 1985, *38*(1), pp. 61–82.   [G: U.K.]

Modigliani, Franco and Jappelli, Tullio. Politica fiscale e risparmio in Italia: l'esperienza dell'ultimo secolo. (Fiscal Policy and Saving in Italy: The Experience of the Last Century. With English summary.) *Giorn. Econ.*, Sept.-Oct. 1985, *44*(9–10), pp. 475–518.

Mundle, Sudipto. The Agrarian Barrier to Industrial Growth. In *Saith, A., ed.*, 1985, pp. 49–80.   [G: W. Europe; Japan; India]

Mundle, Sudipto. The Agrarian Barrier to Industrial Growth. *J. Devel. Stud.*, October 1985, *22*(1), pp. 49–80.   [G: W. Europe; Japan; India]

Murota, Takeshi. Heat Economy of the Water Planet Earth: Part II/Revision and Some New Results. *Hitotsubashi J. Econ.*, December 1985, *26*(2), pp. 181–85.   [G: U.K.; Japan]

Myllyntaus, Timo. Initial Electrification in Three Main Branches of Finnish Industry, 1882–1920. *Scand. Econ. Hist. Rev.*, 1985, *33*(2), pp. 122–43.   [G: Finland]

Nove, Alec. Soviet Peasantry in World War II. In *Linz, S. J., ed.*, 1985, pp. 77–90.
                                  [G: U.S.S.R.]

Ollerenshaw, Philip. An Economic History of Ulster 1820–1939: Industry, 1820–1914. In *Kennedy, L. and Ollerenshaw, P., eds.*, 1985, pp. 62–108.   [G: U.K.]

Pryor, Frederic L. Climatic Fluctuations as a Cause of the Differential Economic Growth of the Orient and Occident [Natural Disaster and Historic Response]: A Rejoinder. *J. Econ. Hist.*, September 1985, *45*(3), pp. 683.
                                   [G: Europe]

Schachter, Stanley, et al. Was the South Sea Bubble a Random Walk? *J. Econ. Behav. Organ.*, December 1985, *6*(4), pp. 323–29. [G: U.K.]

Sullivan, Richard J. The Timing and Pattern of Technological Development in English Agriculture, 1611–1850. *J. Econ. Hist.*, June 1985, *45*(2), pp. 305–14.   [G: U.K.]

Thomas, Brinley. Food Supply in the United Kingdom during the Industrial Revolution. In *Mokyr, J., ed.*, 1985, pp. 137–50.   [G: U.K.]

Topolski, Jerzy. A Model of East-central European Continental Commerce in the Sixteenth and the First Half of the Seventeenth Century. In *Mączak, A.; Samsonowicz, H. and Burke, P., eds.*, 1985, pp. 128–39.   [G: E. Europe]

Urdank, Albion M. Economic Decline in the English Industrial Revolution: The Gloucester Wool Trade, 1800–1840. *J. Econ. Hist.*, June 1985, *45*(2), pp. 427–33.   [G: U.K.]

Vergani, Raffaello. Technology and Organization of Labour in the Venetian Copper Industry (16th–18th Centuries.) *J. Europ. Econ. Hist.*, Spring 1985, *14*(1), pp. 173–86.   [G: Italy]

Wicken, Olav. Learning, Inventions and Innovations: Productivity Increase and New Technology in an Industrial Firm. *Scand. Econ. Hist. Rev.*, 1985, *33*(2), pp. 144–72.   [G: Sweden]

Woodward, Donald. "Swords into Ploughshares": Recycling in Pre-industrial England. *Econ. Hist. Rev., 2nd Ser.*, May 1985, *38*(2), pp. 175–91.   [G: U.K.]

Zalin, Giovanni. L'irrigazione dell'alto agro e il recupero fondiario e agricolo dell'antica "companea" veronese. The Irrigation of Alto Agro and the Reclamation of the Land and Agriculture of Veronese Campanea. With English summary.) *Rivista Int. Sci. Econ. Com.*, December 1985, *32*(12), pp. 1141–53. [G: Italy]

0442 History of Factor Prices and Markets

Ananich, B. V. The Russian State Bank and Export of Capital (1894–1914). In *Marx, A. V., ed.*, 1985, pp. 329–33.   [G: U.S.S.R.]

Arndt, H. W. and Drake, P. J. Bank Loans or Bonds: Some Lessons of Historical Experience. *Banca Naz. Lavoro Quart. Rev.*, December 1985, (155), pp. 373–92.   [G: U.K.]

Bagchi, Amiya Kumar. Anglo-Indian Banking in British India: From the Paper Pound to the Gold Standard. In *Porter, A. N. and Holland, R. F., eds.*, 1985, pp. 93–108.

Buchanan, R. A. Institutional Proliferation in the British Engineering Profession, 1847–1914. *Econ. Hist. Rev., 2nd Ser.*, February 1985, *38*(1), pp. 42–60.   [G: U.K.]

Cassis, Y. The Banking Community of London, 1890–1914: A Survey. In *Porter, A. N. and Holland, R. F., eds.*, 1985, pp. 109–26.
                                    [G: U.K.]

Cesarini, Francesco. Il ruolo del mercato mobiliare nel primo trentennio del secolo. (The Role of the Stock Market during the Early Thirty Years of This Century. With English summary.) *Bancaria*, February 1985, *41*(2), pp. 181–86.   [G: Italy]

Cohen, Isaac. Workers' Control in the Cotton Industry: A Comparative Study of British and American Mule Spinning. *Labor Hist.*, Winter 1985, *26*(1), pp. 53–85.   [G: U.S.; U.K.]

Cohn, Raymond L. Deaths of Slaves in the Middle Passage. *J. Econ. Hist.*, September 1985, *45*(3), pp. 685–92.   [G: U.K.; France; Portugal; U.S.; Netherlands]

Confalonieri, Antonio. Il credito all'industria in Italia prima del 1914. (Industrial Credit in Italy Prior to 1914. With English summary.) *Bancaria*, February 1985, *41*(2), pp. 146–53.   [G: Italy]

Crafts, N. F. R. English Workers' Real Wages during the Industrial Revolution: Some Remaining Problems. *J. Econ. Hist.*, March 1985, *45*(1), pp. 139–44.   [G: U.K.]

Crafts, N. F. R. Income Elasticities of Demand and the Release of Labor by Agriculture during the British Industrial Revolution: A Further Appraisal. In *Mokyr, J., ed.*, 1985, pp. 151–63.   [G: U.K.]

Davis, Lance and Huttenback, Robert A. The Export of British Finance, 1865–1914. In *Porter, A. N. and Holland, R. F., eds.*, 1985, pp. 28–76.   [G: U.K.; Selected Countries]

Domar, Evsey D. and Machina, Mark J. The Profitability of Serfdom: A Reply [On the Profitability of Russian Serfdom]. *J. Econ. Hist.*, December 1985, *45*(4), pp. 960–62.

Field, Alexander James. On the Unimportance of Machinery. *Exploration Econ. Hist.*, October 1985, *22*(4), pp. 378–401.   [G: U.S.; U.K.]

Friedlander, Dov, et al. Socio-economic Characteristics and Life Expectancies in Nineteenth-Century England: A District Analysis. *Population Stud.*, March 1985, *39*(1), pp. 137–51.   [G: U.K.]

Fujimoto, Masakazu. Very Private Enterprise: Ownership and Finance in British Shipping, 1825–1940: Comment. In *Yui, T. and Nakagawa, K., eds.*, 1985, pp. 249–52. [G: U.K.]

Garside, W. R. and Hatton, T. J. Keynesian Policy and British Unemployment in the 1930s [Unemployment in Interwar Britain: A Case for Re-learning the Lessons of the 1930s?]. *Econ. Hist. Rev., 2nd Ser.*, February 1985, *38*(1), pp. 83–88.   [G: U.K.]

Glynn, Sean and Booth, Alan. Building Counterfactual Pyramids [Keynesian Policy and British Unemployment in the 1930s] [Unemployment in Interwar Britain: A Case for Re-learning the Lessons of the 1930s?]. *Econ. Hist. Rev., 2nd Ser.*, February 1985, *38*(1), pp. 89–94.   [G: U.K.]

Greasley, David. Wage Rates and Work Intensity in the South Wales Coalfield, 1874–1914. *Economica*, August 1985, *52*(207), pp. 383–89.   [G: U.K.]

Green, Edwin. Shipbuilding Finance of the *Shasen* Shipping Firms: 1920's–1930's: Comment. In *Yui, T. and Nakagawa, K., eds.*, 1985, pp. 273–77.   [G: Japan]

Green, Edwin. Very Private Enterprise: Ownership and Finance in British Shipping, 1825–1940. In *Yui, T. and Nakagawa, K., eds.*, 1985, pp. 219–48.   [G: U.K.]

Haines, Michael R. Inequality and Childhood Mortality: A Comparison of England and Wales, 1911, and the United States, 1900. *J. Econ. Hist.*, December 1985, *45*(4), pp. 885–912.   [G: U.K.; U.S.]

Hannah, Leslie. Why Employer-based Pension Plans? The Case of Britain. *J. Econ. Hist.*, June 1985, *45*(2), pp. 347–54.   [G: U.K.]

Hansen, Bent. Wage Differentials in Italy and Egypt. The Incentive to Migrate before World War I. *J. Europ. Econ. Hist.*, Fall 1985, *14*(2), pp. 347–60.   [G: Italy; Egypt]

Hartog, Joop and Theeuwes, Jules. The Emergence of the Working Wife in Holland. *J. Lab. Econ.*, Part 2 January 1985, *3*(1), pp. S235–55.   [G: Holland]

Hatton, T. J. The British Labor Market in the 1920s: A Test of the Search–Turnover Approach. *Exploration Econ. Hist.*, July 1985, *22*(3), pp. 257–70.   [G: U.K.]

Hausman, William J. British Coal: A Review Article. *J. Econ. Hist.*, September 1985, *45*(3), pp. 712–15.   [G: U.K.]

Hernandez Iglesias, Feliciano and Riboud, Michelle. Trends in Labor Force Participation of Spanish Women: An Interpretive Essay. *J. Lab. Econ.*, Part 2 January 1985, *3*(1), pp. S201–17.   [G: Spain]

Hirsch, Barry T. and Hausman, William J. Labour Productivity in the South Wales Coal Industry: Reply. *Economica*, August 1985, *52*(207), pp. 391–94.   [G: U.K.]

Hogan, Dennis P. and Kertzer, David I. Migration Patterns during Italian Urbanization, 1865–1921. *Demography*, August 1985, *22*(3), pp. 309–25.   [G: Italy]

Jackson, Marvin R. Comparing the Balkan Demographic Experience, 1860 to 1970. *J. Europ. Econ. Hist.*, Fall 1985, *14*(2), pp. 223–72.   [G: Bulgaria; Yugoslavia; Hungary; Greece; Romania]

James, John A. and Skinner, Jonathan S. The Resolution of the Labor-Scarcity Paradox. *J. Econ. Hist.*, September 1985, *45*(3), pp. 513–40.   [G: U.S.; U.K.]

Jones, M. E. F. Regional Employment Multipliers, Regional Policy, and Structural Change in Interwar Britain. *Exploration Econ. Hist.*, October 1985, *22*(4), pp. 417–39. [G: U.K.]

Kidd, Alan J. City, Class and Culture: Introduction: The Middle Class in Nineteenth-Century Manchester. In *Kidd, A. J. and Roberts, K. W.*, 1985, pp. 1–24.   [G: U.K.]

Kindleberger, Charles P. Integration of Financial Markets: The British and French Experience. In *Kindleberger, C. P.*, 1985, pp. 86–104.

Kindleberger, Charles P. Sweden in 1850 as an 'Impoverished Sophisticate': Comment. In *Kindleberger, C. P.*, 1985, pp. 240–43.   [G: Sweden]

Kleber, Wolfgang. Labor Force Change in Germany since 1882: A Life Cycle Perspective. *Exploration Econ. Hist.*, January 1985, *22*(1), pp. 97–126.   [G: W. Germany]

Klein, P. W. Banking and Economic Modernisation in the Netherlands during the Second Part of the 19th Century. In *Marx, A. V., ed.*, 1985, pp. 131–39. **[G: Netherlands]**

Komlos, John. Stature and Nutrition in the Habsburg Monarchy: The Standard of Living and Economic Development in the Eighteenth Century. *Amer. Hist. Rev.*, December 1985, *90*(5), pp. 1149–61. **[G: Europe]**

Lee, Ronald D. Inverse Projection and Back Projection: A Critical Appraisal, and Comparative Results for England, 1539 to 1871. *Population Stud.*, July 1985, *39*(2), pp. 233–48. **[G: U.K.]**

Lindert, Peter H. and Williamson, Jeffrey G. English Workers' Living Standards during the Industrial Revolution: A New Look. In *Mokyr, J., ed.*, 1985, pp. 177–205. **[G: U.K.]**

Lindert, Peter H. and Williamson, Jeffrey G. English Workers' Real Wages: Reply. *J. Econ. Hist.*, March 1985, *45*(1), pp. 145–53. **[G: U.K.]**

MacDonald, Ronald. The Norman Conquest of 86 and the Asset Approach to the Exchange Rate. *J. Int. Money Finance*, September 1985, *4*(3), pp. 373–87. **[G: U.K.; U.S.]**

Malowist, Marian. Comments on the Circulation of Capital in East-central Europe. In *Mączak, A.; Samsonowicz, H. and Burke, P., eds.*, 1985, pp. 109–27. **[G: E. Europe]**

Marseille, Jacques. The Phases of French Colonial Imperialism: Towards a New Periodization. In *Porter, A. N. and Holland, R. F., eds.*, 1985, pp. 127–41. **[G: U.K.; France; Germany; Selected Countries]**

Mathias, Peter. Credit Needs and Credit Supplies for Eighteenth Century Enterprise. In *Marx, A. V., ed.*, 1985, pp. 103–17. **[G: U.K.]**

Neal, Larry. Integration of International Capital Markets: Quantitative Evidence from the Eighteenth to Twentieth Centuries. *J. Econ. Hist.*, June 1985, *45*(2), pp. 219–26. **[G: U.S.; Netherlands; U.K.; France]**

Nicholas, Stephen. British Economic Performance and Total Factor Productivity Growth, 1870–1940. *Econ. Hist. Rev.*, *2nd Ser.*, November 1985, *38*(4), pp. 576–82. **[G: U.K.]**

Ofer, Gur and Vinokur, Aaron. Work and Family Roles of Soviet Women: Historical Trends and Cross-Section Analysis. *J. Lab. Econ.*, Part 2 January 1985, *3*(1), pp. S328–54. **[G: U.S.S.R.]**

Page, Edward. From *l'État* to Big Government. In *Rose, R.*, 1985, pp. 97–125. **[G: France]**

Pamuk, Elsie R. Social Class Inequality in Mortality from 1921 to 1972 in England and Wales. *Population Stud.*, March 1985, *39*(1), pp. 17–31. **[G: U.K.]**

Patterson, Henry. An Economic History of Ulster 1820–1939: Industrial Labour and the Labour Movement, 1820–1914. In *Kennedy, L. and Ollerenshaw, P., eds.*, 1985, pp. 158–83. **[G: U.K.]**

Perrot, Jean-Claude. Aléas d'une innovation: les banques foncières au XVIIIᵉ siècle. (The Hazards of Innovation: Land Banks in the 18th Century. With English summary.) *Écon. Soc.*, October 1985, *19*(10), pp. 5–36. **[G: France; U.K.]**

Pignatelli, Andrea Cendali. Italy: The Development of a Late Developing State. In *Rose, R.*, 1985, pp. 163–201. **[G: Italy]**

Platt, D. C. M. Canada and Argentina: The First Preference of the British Investor, 1904–14. In *Porter, A. N. and Holland, R. F., eds.*, 1985, pp. 77–92. **[G: Canada; Argentina; U.K.]**

Pohl, Hans. Forms and Phases of Industry Finance up to the Second World War. In *Engels, W. and Pohl, H., eds.*, 1985, pp. 75–94. **[G: Germany]**

Pollard, Sidney. Capital Exports, 1870–1914: Harmful or Beneficial? *Econ. Hist. Rev.*, *2nd Ser.*, November 1985, *38*(4), pp. 489–514. **[G: U.K.]**

Pressnell, L. S. Banks and Their Predecessors in the Economy of Eighteenth Century England. In *Marx, A. V., ed.*, 1985, pp. 277–81. **[G: U.K.]**

Quataert, Jean H. The Shaping of Women's Work in Manufacturing: Guilds, Households, and the State in Central Europe, 1648–1870. *Amer. Hist. Rev.*, December 1985, *90*(5), pp. 1122–48. **[G: Germany]**

Salais, Robert. La formation du chomage comme catégorie: le moment des années 1930. (The Forming of Unemployment as a Category during the Thirties. With English summary.) *Revue Écon.*, March 1985, *36*(2), pp. 321–65. **[G: France]**

Schultz, T. Paul. Changing World Prices, Women's Wages, and the Fertility Transition: Sweden, 1860–1910. *J. Polit. Econ.*, December 1985, *93*(6), pp. 1126–54. **[G: Sweden]**

Schwarz, L. D. The Standard of Living in the Long Run: London, 1700–1860. *Econ. Hist. Rev.*, *2nd Ser.*, February 1985, *38*(1), pp. 24–41. **[G: U.K.]**

Söderberg, Johan. Regional Economic Disparity and Dynamics, 1840–1914: A Comparison between France, Great Britain, Prussia, and Sweden. *J. Europ. Econ. Hist.*, Fall 1985, *14*(2), pp. 273–96. **[G: France; U.K.; Sweden; Prussia]**

Soltow, Lee. The Swedish Census of Wealth at the Beginning of the 19th Century. *Scand. Econ. Hist. Rev.*, 1985, *33*(1), pp. 1–24. **[G: Sweden]**

Stokes, Raymond G. The Oil Industry in Nazi Germany, 1936–1945. *Bus. Hist. Rev.*, Summer 1985, *59*(2), pp. 254–77. **[G: Germany]**

Stott, Richard. British Immigrants and the American "Work Ethic" in the Mid-Nineteenth Century. *Labor Hist.*, Winter 1985, *26*(1), pp. 86–102. **[G: U.S.; U.K.]**

Sugiyama, Kazuo. Shipbuilding Finance of the *Shasen* Shipping Firms: 1920's–1930's. In *Yui, T. and Nakagawa, K., eds.*, 1985, pp. 255–72. **[G: Japan]**

Taylor, William X. Productivity and Educational Values. In *Worswick, G. D. N., ed.*, 1985, pp. 101–12. **[G: U.K.]**

Thomas, Mark. Accounting for Growth, 1870–

1940: Stephen Nicholas and Total Factor Productivity Measurements. *Econ. Hist. Rev., 2nd Ser.,* November 1985, *38*(4), pp. 569–75. [G: U.K.]

Toumanoff, Peter G. The Profitability of Serfdom: A Comment [On the Profitability of Russian Serfdom]. *J. Econ. Hist.,* December 1985, *45*(4), pp. 955–59.

Vergani, Raffaello. Technology and Organization of Labour in the Venetian Copper Industry (16th–18th Centuries.) *J. Europ. Econ. Hist.,* Spring 1985, *14*(1), pp. 173–86. [G: Italy]

Williamson, Jeffrey G. The Historical Content of the Classical Labor Surplus Model. *Population Devel. Rev.,* June 1985, *11*(2), pp. 171–91. [G: U.K.]

Wingren, Gustaf. Everyday Life in Europe and the Effect of the 'Protestant Work Ethic.' In *Gustavsson, B.; Karlsson, J. C. and Raftegard, C.,* 1985, pp. 139–47.

Woods, Robert. The Effects of Population Redistribution on the Level of Mortality in Nineteenth-Century England and Wales. *J. Econ. Hist.,* September 1985, *45*(3), pp. 645–51. [G: U.K.]

0443 History of Public Economic Policy (all levels)

Aalders, Gerard and Wiebes, Cees. Stockholms Enskilda Bank, German Bosch and IG Farben. A Short History of Cloaking. *Scand. Econ. Hist. Rev.,* 1985, *33*(1), pp. 25–50. [G: U.S.; Sweden]

Ananich, B. V. The Russian State Bank and Export of Capital (1894–1914). In *Marx, A. V., ed.,* 1985, pp. 329–33. [G: U.S.S.R.]

Anderson, Gary M. and Tollison, Robert D. Ideology, Interest Groups, and the Repeal of the Corn Laws. *Z. ges. Staatswiss. (JITE),* June 1985, *141*(2), pp. 197–212. [G: U.K.]

Anderson, R. D. School Attendance in Nineteenth-Century Scotland: A Reply [Education and the State in Nineteenth-Century Scotland]. *Econ. Hist. Rev., 2nd Ser.,* May 1985, *38*(2), pp. 282–86. [G: Scotland]

Baratta, Paolo. Il credito industriale dal dibattito del 1911 alla constituzione dell'ICIPU. (Industrial Credit from the 1911 Debate to the Establishment of I.C.I.P.U. With English summary.) *Bancaria,* February 1985, *41*(2), pp. 174–80. [G: Italy]

Bartrip, Peter. Success or Failure? The Prosecution of the Early Factory Acts [The Successful Prosecution of the Factory Acts, 1833–55]. *Econ. Hist. Rev., 2nd Ser.,* August 1985, *38*(3), pp. 423–27. [G: U.K.]

Biscaini, Anna Maria; Gnes, Paolo and Roselli, Alessandro. Origini e sviluppo del Consorzio per Sovvenzioni su Valori Industriali durante il Governatorato Stringher. (Origins and Development of the *Consorzio per Sovvenzioni su Valori Industriali* during the Stringher Governorship. With English summary.) *Bancaria,* February 1985, *41*(2), pp. 154–73. [G: Italy]

Bongaerts, Jan C. Financing Railways in the German States 1840–1860. A Preliminary View. *J. Europ. Econ. Hist.,* Fall 1985, *14*(2), pp. 331–45. [G: Germany]

Booth, Alan. Economists and Points Rationing in the Second World War. *J. Europ. Econ. Hist.,* Fall 1985, *14*(2), pp. 297–317. [G: U.K.]

Booth, Alan. The "Keynesian Revolution" and Economic Policy-making: A Reply. *Econ. Hist. Rev., 2nd Ser.,* February 1985, *38*(1), pp. 101–06.

Boyer, George R. An Economic Model of the English Poor Law circa 1780–1834. *Exploration Econ. Hist.,* April 1985, *22*(2), pp. 129–67. [G: U.K.]

Brenner, Gabrielle A. Why Did Inheritance Laws Change? *Int. Rev. Law Econ.,* June 1985, *5*(1), pp. 91–106. [G: U.K.]

Conquest, Richard. The State and Commercial Expansion: England in the Years 1642–1688. *J. Europ. Econ. Hist.,* Spring 1985, *14*(1), pp. 155–72. [G: U.K.]

Cova, Alberto. Monete e circolazione monetaria in Lombardia a metà settecento in una memoria di Gabriele Verri. (Moneys and Monetary Circulation on Lombardy in the Middle of the XVIII Century: A Report by G. Verri. With English summary.) *Rivista Int. Sci. Econ. Com.,* June 1985, *32*(6), pp. 571–83. [G: Italy]

Curtin, Philip D. Medical Knowledge and Urban Planning in Tropical Africa. *Amer. Hist. Rev.,* June 1985, *90*(3), pp. 594–613. [G: Tropical Africa]

Cuzán, Alfred G. and Heggen, Richard J. Expenditures and Votes: In Search of Downward-sloping Curves in the United States and Great Britain. *Public Choice,* 1985, *45*(1), pp. 19–34. [G: U.S.]

Deakin, Nicholas. 'Vanishing Utopias': Planning and Participation in Twentieth Century Britain. *Reg. Stud.,* August 1985, *19*(4), pp. 291–300. [G: U.K.]

Dutton, H. I. and King, J. E. An Economic Exile: Edward Stillingfleet Cayley, 1802-1862. *Hist. Polit. Econ.,* Summer 1985, *17*(2), pp. 203–18. [G: U.K.]

Eichengreen, Barry; Watson, Mark W. and Grossman, Richard S. Bank Rate Policy under the Interwar Gold Standard: A Dynamic Probit Model. *Econ. J.,* September 1985, *95*(379), pp. 725–45. [G: U.K.]

Falter, Jürgen W., et al. Hat Arbeitslosigkeit tatsächlich den Aufstieg des Nationalsozialismus bewirkt? Eine Überprüfung der Analyse von Frey und Weck. (Did Unemployment Really Cause the Rise of National Socialism? With English summary.) *Jahr. Nationalökon. Statist.,* March 1985, *200*(2), pp. 121–36. [G: Germany]

Foreman-Peck, James S. and Waterson, Michael. The Comparative Efficiency of Public and Private Enterprise in Britain: Electricity Generation between the World Wars. *Econ. J.,* Supplement 1985, *95*, pp. 83–95. [G: U.K.]

Fratianni, Michele and Spinelli, Franco. Currency Competition, Fiscal Policy and the Money Supply Process in Italy from Unification to World War I. *J. Europ. Econ. Hist.*, Sept.-Dec. 1985, *14*(3), pp. 473–99. [G: Italy]

Gallarotti, Giulio M. Toward a Business-Cycle Model of Tariffs. *Int. Organ.*, Winter 1985, *39*(1), pp. 155–87. [G: U.S.; U.K.; Germany]

Garside, W. R. The Failure of the 'Radical Alternative': Public Works, Deficit Finance and British Interwar Unemployment. *J. Europ. Econ. Hist.*, Sept.-Dec. 1985, *14*(3), pp. 537–55. [G: U.K.]

Gedeon, Shirley J. The Theory of Endogenous Money as the Basis for Banking Reform. *Rivista Int. Sci. Econ. Com.*, Oct.-Nov. 1985, *32*(10–11), pp. 1011–30. [G: U.K.]

Gorton, Gary. Banking Theory and Free Banking History: A Review Essay. *J. Monet. Econ.*, September 1985, *16*(2), pp. 267–76.
  [G: U.K.]

Hartmann, Charles J. and Renas, Stephen M. Anglo-American Privacy Law: An Economic Analysis. *Int. Rev. Law Econ.*, December 1985, *5*(2), pp. 133–52. [G: U.S.; U.K.]

Jahnsson, Yrjö. Suomessa vallitsevan rahapulan syistä ja keinoista sen poistamiseksi. (On the Causes and Cures for Finland's Monetary Crisis. With English summary.) *Kansant. Aikak.*, 1985, *81*(1), pp. 5–19. [G: Finland]

Jones, M. E. F. The Regional Impact of an Overvalued Pound in the 1920s. *Econ. Hist. Rev.*, 2nd Ser., August 1985, *38*(3), pp. 393–401.
  [G: U.K.]

Keyder, Caglar. State and Industry in France, 1750–1914. *Amer. Econ. Rev.*, May 1985, 75(2), pp. 308–14. [G: France]

Kindleberger, Charles P. Keynesianism vs. Monetarism in Eighteenth- and Nineteenth-Century France. In *Kindleberger, C. P.*, 1985, pp. 41–62. [G: France]

Kindleberger, Charles P. The International Monetary Politics of a Near-Great Power: Two French Episodes, 1926–1936 and 1960–1970. In *Kindleberger, C. P.*, 1985, pp. 119–28.
  [G: France]

LaHaye, Laura. Inflation and Currency Reform. *J. Polit. Econ.*, June 1985, *93*(3), pp. 537–60.
  [G: Germany; Greece; Poland]

Lampert, Heinz. Die Wirtschafts- und Sozialpolitik im Dritten Reich. (Economic and Social Policy in the "Third Reich." With English summary.) *Jahr. Nationalökon. Statist.*, March 1985, *200*(2), pp. 101–20. [G: Germany]

Laureyssens, Julienne M. Growth of Central Banking: The Société Générale des Pays-Bas and the Impact of the Function of General State Cashier on Belgium's Monetary System (1822–1830) In *Atack, J., ed.*, 1985, pp. 125–38. [G: Netherlands; Belgium]

Marchese, Carla. Market and Non-market Alternatives in the Public Supply of Public Services: Some Empirical Evidence. In *Forte, F. and Peacock, A., eds.*, 1985, pp. 212–26.
  [G: OECD]

Marloie, Marcel. La stratégie alimentaire de la France au XIXe siècle: quelles leçons pour aujourd'hui? (The French Food Strategy in the 19th Century: What Lessons at Now? With

English summary.) *Écon. Soc.*, July 1985, *19*(7), pp. 179–205. [G: France]

Mason, D. M. School Attendance in Nineteenth-Century Scotland [Education and the State in Nineteenth-Century Scotland]. *Econ. Hist. Rev.*, 2nd Ser., May 1985, *38*(2), pp. 276–81.
  [G: Scotland]

Nardinelli, Clark. The Successful Prosecution of the Factory Acts: A Suggested Explanation. *Econ. Hist. Rev.*, 2nd Ser., August 1985, *38*(3), pp. 428–30. [G: U.K.]

Owen, Thomas C. The Russian Industrial Society and Tsarist Economic Policy, 1867–1905. *J. Econ. Hist.*, September 1985, *45*(3), pp. 587–606. [G: Russia]

Padoa-Schioppa, Tommaso. Bonaldo Stringher e la formazione della Banca d'Italia. (Bonaldo Stringer and the Shaping of the Bank of Italy. With English summary.) *Bancaria*, February 1985, *41*(2), pp. 141–45. [G: Italy]

Peacock, A. E. Factory Act Prosecutions: A Hidden Consensus? [The Successful Prosecution of the Factory Acts, 1833–55]. *Econ. Hist. Rev.*, 2nd Ser., August 1985, *38*(3), pp. 431–36. [G: U.K.]

Perkins, J. A. Rehearsal for Protectionism: Australian Wool Exports and German Agriculture, 1830–80. *Australian Econ. Hist. Rev.*, March 1985, *25*(1), pp. 20–38. [G: Australia; Germany]

Rasler, Karen A. and Thompson, William R. War Making and State Making: Governmental Expenditures, Tax Revenues, and Global Wars. *Amer. Polit. Sci. Rev.*, June 1985, 79(2), pp. 491–507. [G: U.S.; U.K.; France; Japan]

Reid, Alastair. Dilution, Trade Unionism and the State in Britain during the First World War. In *Tolliday, S. and Zeitlin, J., eds.*, 1985, pp. 46–74. [G: U.K.]

Rollings, N. The "Keynesian Revolution" and Economic Policy-making: A Comment. *Econ. Hist. Rev.*, 2nd Ser., February 1985, *38*(1), pp. 95–100. [G: U.K.]

Schiemann, Jürgen. Abwertung, Devisenbewirtschaftung und Handelsprotektionismus. Das Kardinalproblem der Währungspolitik eines Schuldnerlandes vor 50 Jahren während der Weltwirtschaftskrise und heute. (Devaluation, Exchange Control and Trade Protectionism: The Cardinal Problem of a Debtor Nation's Monetary Policy 50 Years Ago during the Great Depression and Today. With English summary.) *Konjunkturpolitik*, 1985, *31*(3), pp. 151–87. [G: W. Germany]

Segal, Harvey H. Money Markets against Governments: Two Centuries of a Spectacular Game. *Contemp. Policy Issues*, Fall 1985, *3*(5), pp. 35–41. [G: U.S.; Europe]

Selwyn, Percy. Costs and Benefits of a Modest Proposal. *World Devel.*, May 1985, *13*(5), pp. 653–58. [G: Ireland]

Sennholz, Hans F. The Monetary Writings of Carl Menger. In *Rockwell, L. H., Jr., ed.*, 1985, pp. 19–34. [G: Austria]

Sigurjonsson, Birgir Bjørn. National Sovereignty and Economic Policy. The Case of Iceland.

Scand. Econ. Hist. Rev., 1985, *33*(1), pp. 51–65.   **[G: Iceland]**

Verbík, Antonín. Nationalization. *Czech. Econ. Digest.*, December 1985, (8), pp. 29–38.   **[G: Czechoslovakia]**

Webb, Steven B. Government Debt and Inflationary Expectations as Determinants of the Money Supply in Germany, 1919–23. *J. Money, Credit, Banking*, Part 1, Nov. 1985, *17*(4), pp. 479–92.   **[G: Germany]**

Weir, Margaret and Skocpol, Theda. State Structures and the Possibilities for "Keynesian" Responses to the Great Depression in Sweden, Britain, and the United States. In *Evans, P. B.; Rueschemeyer, D. and Skocpol, T., eds.*, 1985, pp. 107–63.   **[G: U.K.; U.S.; Sweden]**

Whiteside, Noel. Public Policy and Port Labour Reform: The Dock Decasualisation Issue, 1910–50. In *Tolliday, S. and Zeitlin, J., eds.*, 1985, pp. 75–107.   **[G: U.K.]**

045 Economic History: Asia

0450 General

Alschuler, Lawrence R. The State and TNCs in the Development of the Semi-periphery: The Case of South Korea. In *Stauffer, R. B., ed.*, 1985, pp. 133–83.   **[G: S. Korea]**

Barlow, Colin. Indonesian and Malayan Agricultural Development, 1870–1940. *Bull. Indonesian Econ. Stud.*, April 1985, *21*(1), pp. 81–111.   **[G: Indonesia; Malaysia]**

Bhaduri, Amit. Class Relations and Commercialization in Indian Agriculture: A Study in the Post-independence Agrarian Reforms of Uttar Pradesh. In *Raj, K. N., et al., eds.*, 1985, pp. 306–18.   **[G: India]**

Davies, Peter N. Japanese Shipping in the Nineteeth and Twentieth Centuries: Strategy and Organization: Comment. In *Yui, T. and Nakagawa, K., eds.*, 1985, pp. 34–37.   **[G: Japan; Selected OECD]**

Dopfer, Kurt. Reconciling Economic Theory and Economic History: The Rise of Japan. *J. Econ. Issues*, March 1985, *19*(1), pp. 21–73.   **[G: Japan]**

Fei, John C. H.; Ohkawa, Kazushi and Ranis, Gustav. Economic Development in Historical Perspective: Japan, Korea, and Taiwan. In *Ohkawa, K. and Ranis, G., eds.*, 1985, pp. 35–64.   **[G: Japan; S. Korea; Taiwan]**

Hondai, Susumu. Changes in Intersectoral Terms of Trade and Their Effects on Labor Transfer. In *Ohkawa, K. and Ranis, G., eds.*, 1985, pp. 249–65.   **[G: Japan; Taiwan]**

Lindblad, Jan Thomas. Economic Change in Southeast Kalimantan 1880–1940. *Bull. Indonesian Econ. Stud.*, December 1985, *21*(3), pp. 69–103.   **[G: Indonesia]**

Metzer, Jacob and Kaplan, Oded. Jointly but Severally: Arab–Jewish Dualism and Economic Growth in Mandatory Palestine. *J. Econ. Hist.*, June 1985, *45*(2), pp. 327–45.   **[G: Israel]**

Nafziger, E. Wayne. Japanese Development Model. In *Didsbury, H. F., Jr., ed.*, 1985, pp. 111–34.   **[G: Japan]**

Nakagawa, Keiichiro. Japanese Shipping in the Nineteenth and Twentieth Centuries: Strategy and Organization. In *Yui, T. and Nakagawa, K., eds.*, 1985, pp. 1–33.   **[G: Japan; Selected OECD]**

Neelakantan, S. Bernier on Property Rights: A Note. *Hist. Polit. Econ.*, Spring 1985, *17*(1), pp. 31–34.   **[G: Turkey; India]**

Patrick, Hugh. Services in the Japanese Economy: Comment. In *Inman, R. P., ed.*, 1985, pp. 84–88.   **[G: Japan; OECD]**

Ranis, Gustav and Saxonhouse, Gary R. Determinants of Technology Choice: The Indian and Japanese Cotton Industries. In *Ohkawa, K. and Ranis, G., eds.*, 1985, pp. 135–54.   **[G: India; Japan]**

Saxonhouse, Gary R. Services in the Japanese Economy. In *Inman, R. P., ed.*, 1985, pp. 53–83.   **[G: Japan; OECD]**

Sen, Chiranjib. Commercialization, Class Relations and Agricultural Performance in Uttar Pradesh: A Note on Bhaduri's Hypothesis. In *Raj, K. N., et al., eds.*, 1985, pp. 319–30.   **[G: India]**

Yasuba, Yasukichi and Dhiravegin, Likhit. Initial Conditions, Institutional Changes, Policy, and Their Consequences: Siam and Japan, 1850–1914. In *Ohkawa, K. and Ranis, G., eds.*, 1985, pp. 19–34.   **[G: Thailand; Japan]**

Yonekawa, Shin-Ichi. Recent Writing on Japanese Economic and Social History. *Econ. Hist. Rev.*, 2nd Ser., February 1985, *38*(1), pp. 107–23.   **[G: Japan]**

Yui, Tsunehiko. Business History of Shipping: Introduction. In *Yui, T. and Nakagawa, K., eds.*, 1985, pp. ix–xxix.   **[G: Japan]**

0451 History of Product Prices and Markets

Bhattacharya, Neeladri. Agricultural Labour and Production: Central and South–East Punjab, 1870–1940. In *Raj, K. N., et al., eds.*, 1985, pp. 105–62.   **[G: India]**

Brandt, Loren. Chinese Agriculture and the International Economy, 1870–1930s: A Reassessment. *Exploration Econ. Hist.*, April 1985, *22*(2), pp. 168–93.   **[G: China]**

Hayami, Yujiro and Kikuchi, Masao. Agricultural Technology and Income Distribution: Two Indonesian Villages Viewed from the Japanese Experience. In *Ohkawa, K. and Ranis, G., eds.*, 1985, pp. 91–109. **[G: Indonesia; Japan]**

Hirashima, S. Poverty as a Generation's Problem: A Note on the Japanese Experience. In *Mellor, J. W. and Desai, G. M., eds.*, 1985, pp. 149–60.   **[G: Japan]**

Kikuchi, Masao and Hayami, Yujiro. Agricultural Growth against a Land-Resource Constraint: Japan, Taiwan, Korea, and the Philippines. In *Ohkawa, K. and Ranis, G., eds.*, 1985, pp. 67–90.   **[G: Japan; Taiwan; S. Korea; Philippines]**

Konoike, Nobuo, et al. The History of the Kōnoike Family—A Round-Table Talk. (In Japanese. With English summary.) *Osaka Econ. Pap.*, March 1985, *34*(4), pp. 155–85.   **[G: Japan]**

Mackie, J. A. C. The Changing Political Economy of an Export Crop: The Case of Jember's Tobacco Industry. *Bull. Indonesian Econ. Stud.,* April 1985, *21*(1), pp. 112–39. [G: Indonesia]

Mukherjee, Mridula. Commercialization and Agrarian Change in Pre-independence Punjab. In *Raj, K. N., et al., eds.,* 1985, pp. 51–104. [G: India]

Murota, Takeshi. Heat Economy of the Water Planet Earth: Part II/Revision and Some New Results. *Hitotsubashi J. Econ.,* December 1985, *26*(2), pp. 181–85. [G: U.K.; Japan]

Saxonhouse, Gary R. and Ranis, Gustav. Technology Choice and the Quality Dimension in the Japanese Cotton Textile Industry. In *Ohkawa, K. and Ranis, G., eds.,* 1985, pp. 155–76. [G: Japan]

Sumi, Kazuo and Hanayama, Ken. Existing Institutional Arrangements and Implications for Management of Tokyo Bay. *Natural Res. J.,* January 1985, *25*(1), pp. 167–93. [G: Japan]

Toniolo, Gianni. Intermediazione finanziaria e sviluppo economico in Giappone: nota sul periodo 1952–1972. (Financial Intermediation and Economic Growth in Japan: 1952–72. With English summary.) *Polit. Econ.,* August 1985, *1*(2), pp. 259–78. [G: Japan]

0452 History of Factor Prices and Markets

Bagchi, Amiya Kumar. Anglo-Indian Banking in British India: From the Paper Pound to the Gold Standard. In *Porter, A. N. and Holland, R. F., eds.,* 1985, pp. 93–108.

Bhattacharya, Neeladri. Agricultural Labour and Production: Central and South–East Punjab, 1870–1940. In *Raj, K. N., et al., eds.,* 1985, pp. 105–62. [G: India]

Chaudhuri, Pradipta. The Impact of Forced Commerce on the Pattern of Emigration from Orissa, 1901–21. In *Raj, K. N., et al., eds.,* 1985, pp. 184–209. [G: India]

Guha, Sumit. Some Aspects of Rural Economy in the Deccan 1820–1940. In *Raj, K. N., et al., eds.,* 1985, pp. 210–46. [G: India]

Mody, Ashoka; Mundle, Sudipto and Raj, K. N. Resource Flows from Agriculture: Japan and India. In *Ohkawa, K. and Ranis, G., eds.,* 1985, pp. 266–93. [G: Japan; India]

Reddy, M. Atchi. The Commercialization of Agriculture in Nellore District 1850–1916: Effects on Wages, Employment and Tenancy. In *Raj, K. N., et al., eds.,* 1985, pp. 163–83. [G: India]

Saxonhouse, Gary R. and Kiyokawa, Yukihiko. Supply and Demand for Quality Workers in Cotton Spinning in Japan and India. In *Ohkawa, K. and Ranis, G., eds.,* 1985, pp. 177–211. [G: Japan; India]

Teranishi, Juro. Government Credit to the Banking System: Rural Banks in Nineteenth Century Japan and the Postwar Philippines. In *Ohkawa, K. and Ranis, G., eds.,* 1985, pp. 294–310. [G: Japan; Philippines]

Youry, Rozaliev. Banks and Monopoly Capital in Asian Countries. In *Marx, A. V., ed.,* 1985, pp. 335–36. [G: Asia]

0453 History of Public Economic Policy (all levels)

Bayly, C. A. State and Economy in India over Seven Hundred Years. *Econ. Hist. Rev., 2nd Ser.,* November 1985, *38*(4), pp. 583–96. [G: India]

Fonkam, Azu'u. Insurance Law and Practice in Cameroon. *J. World Trade Law,* March:April 1985, *19*(2), pp. 136–46. [G: Cameroon]

Kobayashi, Masaaki. Maritime Policy in Japan: 1868–1937: Comment. In *Yui, T. and Nakagawa, K., eds.,* 1985, pp. 153–56. [G: Japan]

McPherson, Natalie. India and Japan: Laissez-Faire and Economic Development from 1850 to 1939. *Can. J. Devel. Stud.,* 1985, *6*(2), pp. 289–308. [G: India; Japan]

Miwa, Ryoichi. Maritime Policy in Japan: 1868–1937. In *Yui, T. and Nakagawa, K., eds.,* 1985, pp. 123–52. [G: Japan]

Nanto, Dick K. and Takagi, Shinji. Korekiyo Takahashi and Japan's Recovery from the Great Depression. *Amer. Econ. Rev.,* May 1985, *75*(2), pp. 369–74. [G: Japan]

Padhi, Sakti. Property in Land, Land Market and Tenancy Relations in the Colonial Period: A Review of Theoretical Categories and Study of a Zamindari District. In *Raj, K. N., et al., eds.,* 1985, pp. 1–50. [G: India]

Rasler, Karen A. and Thompson, William R. War Making and State Making: Governmental Expenditures, Tax Revenues, and Global Wars. *Amer. Polit. Sci. Rev.,* June 1985, *79*(2), pp. 491–507. [G: U.S.; U.K.; France; Japan]

Teranishi, Juro. Government Credit to the Banking System: Rural Banks in Nineteenth Century Japan and the Postwar Philippines. In *Ohkawa, K. and Ranis, G., eds.,* 1985, pp. 294–310. [G: Japan; Philippines]

046 Economic History: Africa

0460 General

Austen, Ralph A. African Economies in Historical Perspective: Review Article. *Bus. Hist. Rev.,* Spring 1985, *59*(1), pp. 101–13. [G: Sub-Saharan Africa]

Clarence-Smith, Gervase. Business Empires in Angola under Salazar, 1930–1961. *African Econ. Hist.,* 1985, *14*, pp. 1–13. [G: Angola]

Doyle, Michael W. Metropole, Periphery, and System: Empire on the Niger and the Nile. In *Evans, P.; Rueschemeyer, D. and Stephens, E. H., eds.,* 1985, pp. 151–91. [G: Egypt; W. Africa; U.K.]

Hansen, Bent. Egypt Decolonialized: Review Article. *J. Econ. Hist.,* September 1985, *45*(3), pp. 716–18. [G: Egypt]

0461 History of Product Prices and Markets

Isaacman, Allen. Chiefs, Rural Differentiation and Peasant Protest: The Mozambican Forced Cotton Regime 1938–1961. *African Econ. Hist.,* 1985, *14*, pp. 15–56. [G: Mozambique]

0462 History of Factor Prices and Markets

Booth, Alan R. Homestead, State, and Migrant Labor in Colonial Swaziland. *African Econ.*

Hist., 1985, *14*, pp. 107–45. **[G: Swaziland]**

Christelow, Alan. Slavery in Kano, 1913–1914: Evidence from the Judicial Records. *African Econ. Hist.*, 1985, *14*, pp. 57–74.
[G: Nigeria]

Hansen, Bent. Wage Differentials in Italy and Egypt. The Incentive to Migrate before World War I. *J. Europ. Econ. Hist.*, Fall 1985, *14*(2), pp. 347–60. **[G: Italy; Egypt]**

Kindleberger, Charles P. The 1929 World Depression in Latin America—From the Outside. In *Kindleberger, C. P.*, 1985, pp. 274–86.
[G: Latin America]

Oroge, E. Adeniyi. Iwofa: An Historical Survey of the Yoruba Institution of Indenture. *African Econ. Hist.*, 1985, *14*, pp. 75–106.
[G: Nigeria]

Ranney, Susan I. The Labour Market in a Dual Economy: Another Look at Colonial Rhodesia. *J. Devel. Stud.*, July 1985, *21*(4), pp. 505–24.
[G: Zimbabwe]

0463 History of Public Economic Policy (all levels)

Abedian, I. and Standish, B. Poor Whites and the Role of the State: The Evidence. *S. Afr. J. Econ.*, June 1985, *53*(2), pp. 141–65.
[G: S. Africa]

047 Economic History: Latin America and Caribbean

0470 General

Abel, Christopher. Politics and the Economy of the Dominican Republic, 1890–1930. In *Abel, C. and Lewis, C. M., eds.*, 1985, pp. 339–66. **[G: Dominican Republic]**

Abel, Christopher and Lewis, Colin M. The Classical Age of Imperialism: Introduction. In *Abel, C. and Lewis, C. M., eds.*, 1985, pp. 175–83. **[G: Latin America]**

Abel, Christopher and Lewis, Colin M. The Era of Disputed Hegemony: Introduction. In *Abel, C. and Lewis, C. M., eds.*, 1985, pp. 269–87. **[G: Latin America]**

Abreu, Marcelo de Paiva. Anglo–Brazilian Economic Relations and the Consolidation of American Pre-eminence in Brazil, 1930–1945. In *Abel, C. and Lewis, C. M., eds.*, 1985, pp. 379–93. **[G: Brazil; U.K.; U.S.]**

Abreu, Marcelo de Paiva. Errata [La Argentina y Brasil en los años treinta. Efectos de la política económica internacional británica y estadounidense]. *Desarrollo Econ.*, April–June 1985, *25*(97), p. 114. **[G: Argentina; Brazil; U.S.; U.K.]**

Abreu, Marcelo de Paiva. La Argentina y Brasil en los años treinta. Efectos de la política económica internacional británica y estadounidense. (With English summary.) *Desarrollo Econ.*, January-March 1985, *24*(96), pp. 543–59.
[G: Argentina; Brazil; U.S.; U.K.]

Conde, Roberto Cortés. Some Notes on the Industrial Development of Argentina and Canada in the 1920s. In *Platt, D. C. M. and di Tella,*

G., eds., 1985, pp. 149–60. **[G: Argentina; Canada]**

Díaz-Alejandro, Carlos F. Argentina, Australia and Brazil before 1929. In *Platt, D. C. M. and di Tella, G., eds.*, 1985, pp. 95–109.
[G: Argentina; Australia; Brazil]

Finch, M. H. J. British Imperialism in Uruguay: The Public Utility Companies and the *Batllista* State, 1900–1930. In *Abel, C. and Lewis, C. M., eds.*, 1985, pp. 250–66. **[G: U.K.; Uruguay]**

Knight, Alan. The Political Economy of Revolutionary Mexico, 1900–1940. In *Abel, C. and Lewis, C. M., eds.*, 1985, pp. 288–317.
[G: Mexico]

Korn, Francis and de la Torre, Lidia. La vivienda en Buenos Aires 1887–1914. (With English summary.) *Desarrollo Econ.*, July-Sept. 1985, *25*(98), pp. 245–58. **[G: Argentina]**

Lewis, Colin M. Railways and Industrialization: Argentina and Brazil, 1870–1929. In *Abel, C. and Lewis, C. M., eds.*, 1985, pp. 199–230.
[G: Argentina; Brazil]

Lundahl, Mats. Government and Inefficiency in the Haitian Economy: The Nineteenth Century Legacy. In *Connolly, M. B. and McDermott, J., eds.*, 1985, pp. 175–218. **[G: Haiti]**

McFarlane, Anthony. The Transition from Colonialism in Colombia, 1819–1875. In *Abel, C. and Lewis, C. M., eds.*, 1985, pp. 101–24.
[G: Colombia]

Nelles, H. V. Latin American Business History since 1965: A View from North of the Border. *Bus. Hist. Rev.*, Winter 1985, *59*(4), pp. 543–62. **[G: Latin America]**

O'Brien, Philip J. Dependency Revisited. In *Abel, C. and Lewis, C. M., eds.*, 1985, pp. 40–69. **[G: Latin America]**

O'Brien, Thomas F. Dependency Revisited: A Review Essay. *Bus. Hist. Rev.*, Winter 1985, *59*(4), pp. 663–69. **[G: Latin America]**

Palma, Gabriel. External Disequilibrium and Internal Industrialization: Chile, 1914–1935. In *Abel, C. and Lewis, C. M., eds.*, 1985, pp. 318–38. **[G: Chile]**

Pérez, Louis A., Jr. Vagrants, Beggars, and Bandits: Social Origins of Cuban Separatism, 1878–1895. *Amer. Hist. Rev.*, December 1985, *90*(5), pp. 1092–1121. **[G: Cuba]**

Platt, D. C. M. Dependency and the Historian: Further Objections. In *Abel, C. and Lewis, C. M., eds.*, 1985, pp. 29–39.
[G: Latin America]

Platt, D. C. M. The Financing of City Expansion: Buenos Aires and Montreal Compared, 1880–1914. In *Platt, D. C. M. and di Tella, G., eds.*, 1985, pp. 139–48. **[G: Argentina; Canada]**

Reber, Vera Blinn. Archival Sources for Latin American Business History. *Bus. Hist. Rev.*, Winter 1985, *59*(4), pp. 670–79.
[G: Latin America]

Solberg, Carl E. Land Tenure and Land Settlement: Policy and Patterns in the Canadian Prairies and the Argentine Pampas, 1880–1930. In

Platt, D. C. M. and di Tella, G., eds., 1985, pp. 53–75. **[G: Argentina; Canada]**

Thomson, Guy P. C. Protectionism and Industrialization in Mexico, 1821–1854: The Case of Puebla. In *Abel, C. and Lewis, C. M., eds.,* 1985, pp. 125–46. **[G: Mexico]**

0471 History of Product Prices and Markets

Albert, Bill. External Forces and the Transformation of Peruvian Coastal Agriculture, 1880–1930. In *Abel, C. and Lewis, C. M., eds.,* 1985, pp. 231–49. **[G: Peru]**

Brown, Jonathan C. Why Foreign Oil Companies Shifted Their Production from Mexico to Venezuela during the 1920s. *Amer. Hist. Rev.*, April 1985, 90(2), pp. 362–85. **[G: Mexico; Venezuela]**

Godey, Ricardo A. Technical and Economic Efficiency of Peasant Miners in Bolivia. *Econ. Develop. Cult. Change*, October 1985, 34(1), pp. 103–20. **[G: Bolivia]**

Jones, Charles. The State and Business Practice in Argentina 1862–1914. In *Abel, C. and Lewis, C. M., eds.,* 1985, pp. 184–98. **[G: Argentina; U.K.]**

Lundahl, Mats. Agricultural Stagnation in Chile, 1930–55: A Result of Factor Market Imperfections? In *Lundahl, M., ed.,* 1985, pp. 105–30. **[G: Chile]**

Randall, Robert W. British Company and Mexican Community: The English at Real del Monte, 1824–1849. *Bus. Hist. Rev.*, Winter 1985, 59(4), pp. 622–44. **[G: Mexico]**

Scott, Christopher D. The Decline of an Export Industry, or the Growth of Peruvian Sugar Consumption in the Long Run. *J. Devel. Stud.*, January 1985, 21(2), pp. 253–81. **[G: Peru]**

de Secada, C. Alexander G. Arms, Guano, and Shipping: The W. R. Grace Interests in Peru, 1865–1885. *Bus. Hist. Rev.*, Winter 1985, 59(4), pp. 597–621. **[G: Peru]**

Wasserman, Mark. Enrique C. Creel: Business and Politics in Mexico, 1880–1930. *Bus. Hist. Rev.*, Winter 1985, 59(4), pp. 645–62. **[G: Mexico]**

Whigham, Thomas L. Agriculture and the Upper Plata: The Tobacco Trade, 1780–1865. *Bus. Hist. Rev.*, Winter 1985, 59(4), pp. 563–96. **[G: Argentina; Paraguay]**

0472 History of Factor Prices and Markets

Allman, James. Conjugal Unions in Rural and Urban Haiti. *Soc. Econ. Stud.*, March 1985, 34(1), pp. 27–57. **[G: Haiti]**

Beckles, Hilary and Downes, Andrew. An Economic Formalization of the Origins of Black Slavery in the British West Indies, 1624–1645. *Soc. Econ. Stud.*, June 1985, 34(2), pp. 1–25. **[G: Barbados]**

Galenson, David W. Errata [Population Turnover in the British West Indies in the Late Seventeenth Century]. *J. Econ. Hist.*, September 1985, 45(3), pp. 719. **[G: Barbados]**

Galenson, David W. Population Turnover in the English West Indies in the Late Seventeenth Century: A Comparative Perspective. *J. Econ. Hist.*, June 1985, 45(2), pp. 227–35. **[G: Barbados]**

Gómez, Plácido. The History and Adjudication of the Common Lands of Spanish and Mexican Land Grants. *Natural Res. J.*, October 1985, 25(4), pp. 1039–80. **[G: Mexico; U.S.]**

Grubb, Farley. The Incidence of Servitude in Trans-Atlantic Migration, 1771–1804. *Exploration Econ. Hist.*, July 1985, 22(3), pp. 316–39.

Horowitz, Joel. Los trabajadores ferroviarios en la Argentina (1920–1943). La formación de una elite obrera. (With English summary.) *Desarrollo Econ.*, Oct.-Dec. 1985, 25(99), pp. 421–46. **[G: Argentina]**

Sabato, Hilda. La formación del mercado de trabajo en Buenos Aires, 1850–1880. (With English summary.) *Desarrollo Econ.*, January-March 1985, 24(96), pp. 561–92. **[G: Argentina]**

0473 History of Public Economic Policy (all levels)

Alhadeff, Peter. Dependency, Historiography and Objections to the Roca Pact. In *Abel, C. and Lewis, C. M., eds.,* 1985, pp. 367–78. **[G: Argentina]**

Biggs, Gonzalo. Legal Aspects of the Latin American Public Debt: Relations with the Commercial Banks. *Cepal Rev.*, April 1985, (25), pp. 163–87. **[G: Latin America]**

Kaufman, Robert R. Democratic and Authoritarian Responses to the Debt Issue: Argentina, Brazil, Mexico. *Int. Organ.*, Summer 1985, 39(3), pp. 472–503. **[G: Argentina; Brazil; Mexico]**

Ortega, Luis. Economic Policy and Growth in Chile from Independence to the War of the Pacific. In *Abel, C. and Lewis, C. M., eds.,* 1985, pp. 147–71. **[G: Chile]**

Whigham, Thomas L. Agriculture and the Upper Plata: The Tobacco Trade, 1780–1865. *Bus. Hist. Rev.*, Winter 1985, 59(4), pp. 563–96. **[G: Argentina; Paraguay]**

048 Economic History: Oceania

0480 General

Díaz-Alejandro, Carlos F. Argentina, Australia and Brazil before 1929. In *Platt, D. C. M. and di Tella, G., eds.,* 1985, pp. 95–109. **[G: Argentina; Australia; Brazil]**

Jonson, P. D. and Stevens, G. R. The Australian Economy in the 1930s and the 1980s: Some Facts. In *Argy, V. E. and Neville, J. W., eds.,* 1985, pp. 281–304. **[G: Australia]**

Lewis, Donald E. The Sources of Changes in the Occupational Segregation of Australian Women. *Econ. Rec.*, December 1985, 61(175), pp. 719–36. **[G: Australia]**

Marshall, Woodville K. Peasant Development in

the West Indies since 1838. In *Gomes, P. I.*, *ed.*, 1985, pp. 1–14. [G: Caribbean]

Mintz, Sidney W. Epilogue: The Divided Aftermaths of Freedom. In *Moreno Franginals, M.; Moya Pons, F. and Engerman, S. L.*, *eds.*, 1985, pp. 270–78.

Pemberton, Carlisle. Economic Behaviour of Peasants in Tobago. In *Gomes, P. I.*, *ed.*, 1985, pp. 76–102. [G: Trinidad and Tobago]

Segrera, Francisco López. Cuba: Dependence, Plantation Economy, and Social Classes, 1762–1902. In *Moreno Franginals, M.; Moya Pons, F. and Engerman, S. L.*, *eds.*, 1985, pp. 77–93. [G: Cuba]

Sleeman, Michael. The Agri-business Bourgeoisie of Barbados and Martinique. In *Gomes, P. I.*, *ed.*, 1985, pp. 15–33. [G: Caribbean]

0481 History of Product Prices and Markets

Abelson, Peter W. House and Land Prices in Sydney: 1925 to 1970. *Urban Stud.*, December 1985, 22(6), pp. 521–34. [G: Australia]

Acosta, Yvonne and Casimir, Jean. Social Origins of the Counter-plantation System in St. Lucia. In *Gomes, P. I.*, *ed.*, 1985, pp. 34–59. [G: St. Lucia]

del Castillo, José. The Formation of the Dominican Sugar Industry: From Competition to Monopoly, from National Semiproletariat to Foreign Proletariat. In *Moreno Franginals, M.; Moya Pons, F. and Engerman, S. L.*, *eds.*, 1985, pp. 215–34. [G: Dominican Republic]

Davies, Mel. Blainey Revisited: Mineral Discovery and the Business Cycle in South Australia. *Australian Econ. Hist. Rev.*, September 1985, 25(2), pp. 112–28. [G: Australia]

García, Fe Iglesias. The Development of Capitalism in Cuban Sugar Production, 1860–1900. In *Moreno Franginals, M.; Moya Pons, F. and Engerman, S. L.*, *eds.*, 1985, pp. 54–75. [G: Cuba]

Perkins, J. A. Rehearsal for Protectionism: Australian Wool Exports and German Agriculture, 1830–80. *Australian Econ. Hist. Rev.*, March 1985, 25(1), pp. 20–38. [G: Australia; Germany]

0482 History of Factor Prices and Markets

Bryan, Patrick E. The Question of Labor in the Sugar Industry of the Dominican Republic in the Late Nineteenth and Early Twentieth Centuries. In *Moreno Franginals, M.; Moya Pons, F. and Engerman, S. L.*, *eds.*, 1985, pp. 235–51. [G: Dominican Republic]

Curet, José. About Slavery and the Order of Things: Puerto Rico, 1845–1873. In *Moreno Franginals, M.; Moya Pons, F. and Engerman, S. L.*, *eds.*, 1985, pp. 117–140. [G: Puerto Rico]

Forster, Colin. An Economic Consequence of Mr Justice Higgins. *Australian Econ. Hist. Rev.*, September 1985, 25(2), pp. 95–111. [G: Australia]

Forster, Colin. Unemployment and Minimum Wages in Australia, 1900–1930. *J. Econ. Hist.*, June 1985, 45(2), pp. 383–88. [G: Australia]

Klein, Herbert S. and Engerman, Stanley L. The Transition from Slave to Free Labor: Notes on a Comparative Economic Model. In *Moreno Franginals, M.; Moya Pons, F. and Engerman, S. L.*, *eds.*, 1985, pp. 255–69. [G: Caribbean; Brazil; U.S.]

Knight, Franklin W. Jamaican Migrants and the Cuban Sugar Industry, 1900–1934. In *Moreno Franginals, M.; Moya Pons, F. and Engerman, S. L.*, *eds.*, 1985, pp. 94–114. [G: Jamaica; Cuba]

Mattei, Andrés A. Ramos. Technical Innovations and Social Change in the Sugar Industry of Puerto Rico, 1870–1880. In *Moreno Franginals, M.; Moya Pons, F. and Engerman, S. L.*, *eds.*, 1985, pp. 158–78. [G: Puerto Rico]

Nistal-Moret, Benjamín. Problems in the Social Structure of Slavery in Puerto Rico during the Process of Abolition, 1872. In *Moreno Franginals, M.; Moya Pons, F. and Engerman, S. L.*, *eds.*, 1985, pp. 141–57. [G: Puerto Rico]

Pons, Frank Moya. The Land Question in Haiti and Santo Domingo: The Sociopolitical Context of the Transition from Slavery to Free Labor, 1801–1843. In *Moreno Franginals, M.; Moya Pons, F. and Engerman, S. L.*, *eds.*, 1985, pp. 181–214. [G: Haiti; Dominican Republic]

Scott, Rebecca J. Explaining Abolition: Contradiction, Adaptation, and Challenge in Cuban Slave Society, 1860–1886. In *Moreno Franginals, M.; Moya Pons, F. and Engerman, S. L.*, *eds.*, 1985, pp. 25–53. [G: Cuba]

0483 History of Public Economic Policy (all levels)

Armstrong, Christopher and Nelles, H. V. The State and the Provision of Electricity in Canada and Australia, 1880–1965. In *Platt, D. C. M. and di Tella, G.*, *eds.*, 1985, pp. 207–30. [G: Australia; Canada]

Cain, Neville and Glynn, Sean. Imperial Relations under Strain: The British–Australian Debt Contretemps of 1933. *Australian Econ. Hist. Rev.*, March 1985, 25(1), pp. 39–58. [G: Australia]

Drummond, Ian M. Marketing Boards in the White Dominions, with Special Reference to Australia and Canada. In *Platt, D. C. M. and di Tella, G.*, *eds.*, 1985, pp. 194–206. [G: Australia; Canada; New Zealand]

Forster, Colin. Unemployment and Minimum Wages in Australia, 1900–1930. *J. Econ. Hist.*, June 1985, 45(2), pp. 383–88. [G: Australia]

Jackson, R. V. Short-run Interaction of Public and Private Sectors in Australia, 1861–90. *Australian Econ. Hist. Rev.*, March 1985, 25(1), pp. 59–75. [G: Australia]

Pons, Frank Moya. The Land Question in Haiti and Santo Domingo: The Sociopolitical Context of the Transition from Slavery to Free Labor, 1801–1843. In *Moreno Franginals, M.; Moya*

Pons, F. and Engerman, S. L., eds., 1985, pp. 181–214.   [G: Haiti; Dominican Republic]

Reece, Barry F. Simons' Account of Australian Taxation of Imputed Rental Income. *Australian Tax Forum*, Winter 1985, *2*(2), pp. 239–42.
[G: Australia]

Sinclair, W. A. The Australian Policy Tradition–Protection All Around. In *Scutt, J. A., ed.*, 1985, pp. 28–36.   [G: Australia]

Whitwell, Greg. The Social Philosophy of the F and E Economists. *Australian Econ. Hist. Rev.*, March 1985, *25*(1), pp. 1–19.
[G: Australia]

050 ECONOMIC SYSTEMS

0500 General

Amin, Samir. Modes of Production, History, and Unequal Development [Feudalism and Historical Materialism: A Critique and a Synthesis] [Modes of Production and Theories of Transition]. *Sci. Soc.*, Summer 1985, *49*(2), pp. 194–207.

Balassa, Bela. Prices, Incentives and Economic Growth. In *Balassa, B.*, 1985, pp. 3–23.
[G: Global]

Brunner, Karl. The Poverty of Nations. *Bus. Econ.*, January 1985, *20*(1), pp. 5–11.

Demaria, Giovanni. I rapporti tra endogeneità ed extraendogeneità. (With English summary.) *Econ. Polít.*, December 1985, *2*(3), pp. 343–58.

Evans, Peter B.; Rueschemeyer, Dietrich and Stephens, Evelyne Huber. States versus Markets in the World-System: Introduction. In *Evans, P.; Rueschemeyer, D. and Stephens, E. H., eds.*, 1985, pp. 11–30.

Hoffman, John. The Dialectic of Abstraction and Concentration in Historical Materialism [Feudalism and Historical Materialism: A Critique and Synthesis] [Modes of Production and Theories of Transition]. *Sci. Soc.*, Winter 1985-1986, *49*(4), pp. 451–62.

Hofstede, Geert. National Cultures and Organizational Cultures. *Liiketaloudellinen Aikak.*, 1985, *34*(1), pp. 3–19.
[G: Selected Countries]

Perrings, Charles. The Natural Economy Revisited. *Econ. Develop. Cult. Change*, July 1985, *33*(4), pp. 829–50.

Sah, Raaj Kumar and Stiglitz, Joseph E. Human Fallibility and Economic Organization. *Amer. Econ. Rev.*, May 1985, *75*(2), pp. 292–97.

Sylos Labini, Paolo. Valore e distribuzione in un'economia robotizzata. (With English summary.) *Econ. Polít.*, December 1985, *2*(3), pp. 359–63.

Watts, Michael. Economic Policy and the Lives of Contemplation, Civic Humanism, Collectivism and Individualism. *Int. J. Soc. Econ.*, 1985, *12*(6/7), pp. 54–67.

Zeleny, Milan. Spontaneous Social Orders. In *Aida, S., et al.*, 1985, pp. 312–28.

051 Capitalist Economic Systems: Market Economies

0510 Capitalist Economic Systems: Market Economies

Abel, Christopher and Lewis, Colin M. Latin America, Economic Imperialism and the State: Introduction. In *Abel, C. and Lewis, C. M., eds.*, 1985, pp. 1–25.   [G: Latin America]

Abel, Christopher and Lewis, Colin M. The Classical Age of Imperialism: Introduction. In *Abel, C. and Lewis, C. M., eds.*, 1985, pp. 175–83.
[G: Latin America]

Abel, Richard L. Risk as an Arena of Struggle. *Mich. Law Rev.*, February 1985, *83*(4), pp. 772–812.   [G: U.S.; U.K.]

Abel-Smith, Brian. The Major Problems of the Welfare State: Defining the Issues. In *Eisenstadt, S. N. and Ahimeir, O., eds.*, 1985, pp. 31–43.   [G: U.S.; W. Europe]

Abolafia, Mitchel Y. Self-regulation as Market Maintenance: An Organization Perspective. In *Noll, R. G., ed.*, 1985, pp. 312–43. [G: U.S.]

Adachi, Kyoichiro. Ideology, Present State and Problems of Yamagishikai. In *Bergmann, T. and Ogura, T. B., eds.*, 1985, pp. 113–30.
[G: Japan]

Adeyemo, Remi. A New Dimension in the Participatory Role of Self-managed Co-operative Unions in Development Projects. *Econ. Anal. Worker's Manage.*, 1985, *19*(3), pp. 317–25.
[G: Nigeria]

Alexander, Kenneth O. Worker Ownership and Participation in the Context of Social Change: Progress Is Slow and Difficult, But It Need Not Wait upon Massive Redistribution of Wealth. *Amer. J. Econ. Soc.*, July 1985, *44*(3), pp. 337–47.   [G: U.S.]

Amin, Samir. The Crisis, the Third World, and North–South, East–West Relations. In *[Magdoff, H. and Sweezy, P.]*, 1985, pp. 1–8.

Andelson, Robert V. Henry George and Economic Intervention: A Critic Proposes That George's Strictures on Industrial Monopolies Be Revised. *Amer. J. Econ. Soc.*, January 1985, *44*(1), pp. 97–105.

Andreatta, Benjamino. Public Intervention for Redistributive Ends. The Social Services Sector. *Ann. Pub. Co-op. Econ.*, January–June 1985, *56*(1–2), pp. 25–39.

Aranson, Peter H. Judicial Control of the Political Branches: Public Purpose and Public Law. *Cato J.*, Winter 1985, *4*(3), pp. 719–82.
[G: U.S.]

Arif, Muhammad. Toward a Definition of Islamic Economics: Some Scientific Considerations. *J. Res. Islamic Econ.*, Winter 1985, *2*(2), pp. 87–103.

Arneson, Richard J. Marxism and Secular Faith. *Amer. Polit. Sci. Rev.*, September 1985, *79*(3), pp. 627–40.

Ault, David E. and Rutman, Gilbert L. Freedom and Regulation: An Anthropological Critique of Free Market Ideology: Comment. In *Zerbe, R. O., Jr., ed.*, 1985, pp. 149–56.

Backhaus, Juergen. Public Policy toward Corporate Structures: Two Chicago Approaches. *J. Econ. Issues,* June 1985, *19*(2), pp. 365–73.

Balducci, Renato. Economia di partecipazione e accumulazione. (Share Economy and Accumulation. With English summary.) *Giorn. Econ.,* Nov.-Dec. 1985, *44*(11–12), pp. 639–50.

Bar-Yosef, Rivka. Welfare and Integration in Israel. In *Eisenstadt, S. N. and Ahimeir, O., eds.,* 1985, pp. 247–61. **[G: Israel]**

Baron, Harold M. Racism Transformed: The Implications of the 1960s. *Rev. Radical Polit. Econ.,* Fall 1985, *17*(3), pp. 10–33. **[G: U.S.]**

Barrère, Christian. L'objet d'une théorie de la régulation. (The Purpose of a Regulation Theory. With English summary.) *Écon. Soc.,* January 1985, *19*(1), pp. 9–28.

Barry, Norman P. In Defense of the Invisible Hand. *Cato J.,* Spring/Summer 1985, *5*(1), pp. 133–48.

Bartlett, Bruce. America's New Ideology: "Industrial Policy": With Neo-Keynesianism Joining Supply-Side Economics in History's Dust-bin, It's Splitting Economists. *Amer. J. Econ. Soc.,* January 1985, *44*(1), pp. 1–7. **[G: U.S.]**

Bartlett, Bruce. The Entrepreneurial Imperative. In *Boaz, D. and Crane, E. H., eds.,* 1985, pp. 75–90. **[G: U.S.]**

Başar, Tamer; Haurie, Alain and Ricci, Gianni. On the Dominance of Capitalists' Leadership in a 'Feedback-Stackelberg' Solution of a Differential Game Model of Capitalism. *J. Econ. Dynam. Control,* September 1985, *9*(1), pp. 101–25.

Başar, Tamer; Haurie, Alain and Ricci, Gianni. Errata [On the Dominance of Capitalists Leadership in a 'Feedback-Stackelberg' Solution of a Differential Game Model of Capitalism]. *J. Econ. Dynam. Control,* December 1985, *9*(4), pp. 493.

Baslé, M. Profitabilité, accumulation-répartition, et régulation d'ensemble: propositions de synthèse et premie application au cas de la France. (Profitability, Accumulation-Repartition, and Global Regulation. Some Propositions for Synthetic Analysis and a First Application in the French Case. With English summary.) *Écon. Soc.,* January 1985 cf, *19*(1), pp. 131–76. **[G: France]**

Bavly, Dan. Some Forms of Resistance to the Welfare State. In *Eisenstadt, S. N. and Ahimeir, O., eds.,* 1985, pp. 302–05. **[G: Israel]**

Bellofiore, Riccardo. Money and Development in Schumpeter. *Rev. Radical Polit. Econ.,* Spring and Summer 1985, *17*(1/2), pp. 21–40.

Ben-Hur, Raphaella Bilski. The Real Crises: Unattainable Goals and Moral Vagueness. In *Eisenstadt, S. N. and Ahimeir, O., eds.,* 1985, pp. 74–87. **[G: OECD]**

Benjamin, Roger and Duvall, Raymond. The Capitalist State in Context. In *Benjamin, R. and Elkin, S. L., eds.,* 1985, pp. 19–57.

Bennett, John C. Morality of the Market: Religious and Economic Perspectives: Overview. In *Block, W.; Brennan, G. and Elzinga, K., eds.,* 1985, pp. 547–66.

Bergsten, Gordon S. On the Role of Social Norms in a Market Economy. *Public Choice,* 1985, *45*(2), pp. 113–37.

de Bernis, Gévard. Sur quelques concepts nécessaires à la théorie de la régulation. (On Some Concepts Necessary for Regulation Theory. With English summary.) *Écon. Soc.,* January 1985, *19*(1), pp. 103–27.

Berns, Walter. Religion, Ethics and Politics in the 1980s: Comment. In *Block, W.; Brennan, G. and Elzinga, K., eds.,* 1985, pp. 524–31.

Bhaduri, Amit and Steindl, Josef. The Rise of Monetarism as a Social Doctrine. In *Arestis, P. and Skouras, T., eds.,* 1985, pp. 56–78. **[G: Selected Countries]**

Bhagwati, Jagdish N. Raul Prebisch: I [The Latin American Periphery in the Global System of Capitalism]. In *Bhagwati, J. N. (II),* 1985, pp. 292–96.

Bilmes, Jack. Freedom and Regulation: An Anthropological Critique of Free Market Ideology. In *Zerbe, R. O., Jr., ed.,* 1985, pp. 123–47.

Bilmes, Jack. Freedom and Regulation: An Anthropological Critique of Free Market Ideology: Rejoinder. In *Zerbe, R. O., Jr., ed.,* 1985, pp. 157–59.

Block, James E. The Shibboleth of Productivity: The Exhaustion of Industrial-Age Strategies in Post-industrial Society. *Rev. Radical Polit. Econ.,* Spring and Summer 1985, *17*(1/2), pp. 157–85.

Blomqvist, Kai. Cooperative Enterprise and New Relationships between Capital and Labour. *Ann. Pub. Co-op. Econ.,* January–June 1985, *56*(1–2), pp. 93–110.

Booth, Douglas E. The Problems of Corporate Bureaucracy and the Producer Cooperative as an Alternative. *Rev. Soc. Econ.,* December 1985, *43*(3), pp. 298–315. **[G: U.S.]**

Boston, Thomas D. Racial Inequality and Class Stratification: A Contribution to a Critique of Black Conservatism. *Rev. Radical Polit. Econ.,* Fall 1985, *17*(3), pp. 46–71. **[G: U.S.]**

Boulding, Kenneth E. Markets and Majorities, Morals and Madness: An Essay on Religion and Institutional Choice: Comment. In *Block, W.; Brennan, G. and Elzinga, K., eds.,* 1985, pp. 251–61. **[G: U.S.]**

Boulding, Kenneth E. Puzzles over Distribution. *Challenge,* Nov./Dec. 1985, *28*(5), pp. 4–10. **[G: U.S.]**

Bowles, Samuel. The Production Process in a Competitive Economy: Walrasian, Neo-Hobbesian, and Marxian Models. *Amer. Econ. Rev.,* March 1985, *75*(1), pp. 16–36.

Braybrooke, David. Contemporary Marxism on the Autonomy, Efficacy, and Legitimacy of the Capitalist State. In *Benjamin, R. and Elkin, S. L., eds.,* 1985, pp. 59–86.

Brennan, Geoffrey. Markets and Majorities, Morals and Madness: An Essay on Religion and Institutional Choice. In *Block, W.; Brennan, G. and Elzinga, K., eds.,* 1985, pp. 233–48.

Brenner, Robert. The Agrarian Roots of European Capitalism. In *Aston, T. H. and Philpin, C. H. E., eds.*, 1985, pp. 213–327.

Bricall, Josep M. Sur la demande effective et la crise. (On Effective Demand and Crisis. With English summary.) *Écon. Soc.*, August 1985, *19*(8), pp. 99–116.

Brittan, Samuel. Back to Full Employment: The Economic Aspect. *Nat. Westminster Bank Quart. Rev.*, May 1985, pp. 41–51.
[G: U.K.]

Browett, John. The Newly Industrializing Countries and Radical Theories of Development. *World Devel.*, July 1985, *13*(7), pp. 789–803.
[G: S. Korea; Taiwan; Hong Kong; Singapore]

Brown, Doug. Institutionalism, Critical Theory, and the Administered Society. *J. Econ. Issues*, June 1985, *19*(2), pp. 559–66.

Cain, Peter J. J. A. Hobson, Financial Capitalism and Imperialism in Late Victorian and Edwardian England. In *Porter, A. N. and Holland, R. F., eds.*, 1985, pp. 1–27.

Canto, Victor A. Property Rights, Land Reform, and Economic Well-being. *Cato J.*, Spring/Summer 1985, *5*(1), pp. 51–66. [G: Mexico; Chile; Jamaica; El Salvador]

Cawson, Alan. Corporatism and Local Politics. In *Grant, W., ed.*, 1985, pp. 126–47.
[G: U.K.]

Cecil, Andrew R. Economic Freedom: The Rights and Responsibilities of the Entrepreneur in Our Mixed Economy. In *Taitte, W. L., ed.*, 1985, pp. 147–200.

Chavance, Bernard. The Utopian Dialectic of Capitalism and Communism in Marx. *Econ. Anal. Worker's Manage.*, 1985, *19*(3), pp. 249–62.

Chernomas, Bob. A Malthusian Basis for Post-Keynesian Stagflation Theory and Policy: A Marxist Analysis. *Rev. Radical Polit. Econ.*, Spring and Summer 1985, *17*(1/2), pp. 230–40.

Chyba, Antonín. Global Problems of Mankind and the Present-Day World. *Czech. Econ. Digest.*, August 1985, (5), pp. 59–74. [G: Global]

Ciriacy-Wantrup, S. V. "Common Property" as a Concept in Natural Resources Policy. In *Ciriacy-Wantrup, S. V.*, 1985, pp. 25–37.
[G: U.S.]

Coe, Richard D. and Wilber, Charles K. Schumpeter Revisited: An Overview. In *Coe, R. D. and Wilber, C. K., eds.*, 1985, pp. 1–59.

Coleman, Jules L. Market Contractarianism and the Unanimity Rule. In *Paul, E. F.; Paul, J. and Miller, F. D., Jr., eds.*, 1985, pp. 69–114.

Coomans, Gery. Régulation et fonctionnalisme. (Regulation and Functionalism. With English summary.) *Écon. Soc.*, January 1985, *19*(1), pp. 65–89.

Coppe, A. "Long Waves" and Secular Expansion. *Tijdschrift Econ. Manage.*, 1985, *30*(3–4), pp. 397–414.

Cornell, Lasse; Karlsson, Jan Ch. and Lindqvist, Ulla. Missing Concepts of Work. In *Gustavsson, B.; Karlsson, J. C. and Raftegard, C.*, 1985, pp. 15–25.

Cowling, Keith. Economic Obstacles to Democracy. In *Matthews, R. C. O., ed.*, 1985, pp. 235–53.

Croot, Patricia and Parker, David. Agrarian Class Structure and the Development of Capitalism: France and England Compared. In *Aston, T. H. and Philpin, C. H. E., eds.*, 1985, pp. 79–90.

Crotty, James R. and Stormes, James R. The Bishops on the U.S. Economy. *Challenge*, March/April 1985, *28*(1), pp. 36–41.

Crouch, Colin. Corporatism in Industrial Relations: A Formal Model. In *Grant, W., ed.*, 1985, pp. 63–88.

Culyer, A. J. On Being Right or Wrong about the Welfare State. In *Bean, P.; Ferris, J. and Whynes, D., eds.*, 1985, pp. 122–41.
[G: U.K.]

Cypher, James M. Critical Analyses of Military Spending and Capitalism. *Eastern Econ. J.*, July-Sept. 1985, *11*(3), pp. 273–82. [G: U.S.]

Darity, William A., Jr. and Horn, Bobbie L. Rudolf Hilferding: The Dominion of Capitalism and the Dominion of Gold. *Amer. Econ. Rev.*, May 1985, *75*(2), pp. 363–68. [G: Germany]

Davidson, Paul. Can Effective Demand and the Movement toward Further Income Equality Be Maintained in the Face of Robotics? An Introduction. *J. Post Keynesian Econ.*, Spring 1985, *7*(3), pp. 422–25.

Defourney, Jacques; Estrin, Saul and Jones, Derek C. The Effects of Workers' Participation on Enterprise Performance: Empirical Evidence from French Cooperatives. *Int. J. Ind. Organ.*, June 1985, *3*(2), pp. 197–217.
[G: France]

Dorn, James A. Economic Liberties and the Judiciary. *Cato J.*, Winter 1985, *4*(3), pp. 661–87.

Drago, Robert. New Use of an Old Technology: The Growth of Worker Participation. *J. Post Keynesian Econ.*, Winter 1984–85, *7*(2), pp. 153–67.

Drugman, B. A nouveau sur la question de la régulation. Economie politique, Marxisme et… crise: quelle alternative réelle? (Theory of Regulation Revisited. Political Economy, Marxism and Crisis: Is There a Real Alternative? With English summary.) *Écon. Soc.*, January 1985, *19*(1), pp. 29–64.

Dugger, William M. The Continued Evolution of Corporate Power. *Rev. Soc. Econ.*, April 1985, *43*(1), pp. 1–13. [G: U.S.]

Dugger, William M. The Shortcomings of Concentration Ratios in the Conglomerate Age: New Sources and Uses of Corporate Power. *J. Econ. Issues*, June 1985, *19*(2), pp. 343–53.
[G: U.S.]

Eckel, Catherine C. and Vining, Aidan R. Elements of a Theory of Mixed Enterprise. *Scot. J. Polit. Econ.*, February 1985, *32*(1), pp. 82–94.

Edwards, Richard. Sweezy and the Proletariat. In *[Magdoff, H. and Sweezy, P.]*, 1985, pp. 99–114.

Eichner, Alfred S. Micro Foundations of the Corporate Economy. In *Eichner, A. S.*, 1985, pp. 28–74.

Eichner, Alfred S. Reflections on Social Democracy. In *Eichner, A. S.*, 1985, pp. 200–218.

Eichner, Alfred S. The Megacorp as a Social Innovation. In *Eichner, A. S.*, 1985, pp. 10–27.

Eisenstadt, S. N. The Welfare State and the Transformation of the Modern Social Order. In *Eisenstadt, S. N. and Ahimeir, O., eds.*, 1985, pp. 309–13.

Eisenstadt, S. N. The Welfare State: And Its Aftermath: Introduction. In *Eisenstadt, S. N. and Ahimeir, O., eds.*, 1985, pp. 1–7.

Eldridge, John. Industrial Democracy at Enterprise Level: Problems and Prospects. In *Matthews, R. C. O., ed.*, 1985, pp. 204–18.

Elkin, Stephen L. Between Liberalism and Capitalism: An Introduction to the Democratic State. In *Benjamin, R. and Elkin, S. L., eds.*, 1985, pp. 1–17.

Elwert, Bert. The Entrepreneurial Enigma. *Eastern Econ. J.*, July-Sept. 1985, *11*(3), pp. 267–72. **[G: U.S.]**

Elzinga, Kenneth G. Religion, Culture, and Technology: Comment. In *Block, W.; Brennan, G. and Elzinga, K., eds.*, 1985, pp. 322–29.

Epstein, Richard A. Judicial Review: Reckoning on Two Kinds of Error. *Cato J.*, Winter 1985, *4*(3), pp. 711–18. **[G: U.S.]**

Estrin, Saul. The Role of Producer Co-operatives in Employment Creation. *Econ. Anal. Worker's Manage.*, 1985, *19*(4), pp. 345–84. **[G: OECD]**

Etzioni, Amitai. Encapsulated Competition. *J. Post Keynesian Econ.*, Spring 1985, 7(3), pp. 287–302.

Etzioni, Amitai. On Solving Social Problems—Inducements or Coercion? *Challenge*, July/August 1985, *28*(3), pp. 35–40.

Falkena, H. B. On Hayek's Philosophy of Limited Government and the Economic Order (Review Article). *S. Afr. J. Econ.*, December 1985, *53*(4), pp. 366–80.

Fausto, Domenicantonio and Leccisotti, Mario. The Crisis of the "Welfare State." *Giorn. Econ.*, Jan.-Feb. 1985, *44*(1–2), pp. 5–16.

Ferris, John. Citizenship and the Crisis of the Welfare State. In *Bean, P.; Ferris, J. and Whynes, D., eds.*, 1985, pp. 46–73. **[G: U.K.]**

Flora, Peter. On the History and Current Problems of the Welfare State. In *Eisenstadt, S. N. and Ahimeir, O., eds.*, 1985, pp. 11–30. **[G: U.S.; W. Europe]**

Forrest, David. Privatisation. In *Atkinson, G. B. J., ed.*, 1985, pp. 101–21. **[G: U.K.]**

Foster, John Bellamy. Sources of Instability in the U.S. Political Economy and Empire. *Sci. Soc.*, Summer 1985, *49*(2), pp. 167–93. **[G: U.S.]**

Frankel, S. Herbert. Capitalism and the Jews: Comment. In *Block, W.; Brennan, G. and Elzinga, K., eds.*, 1985, pp. 429–42.

Friedman, David. Religion, Culture, and Technology: Comment. In *Block, W.; Brennan, G. and Elzinga, K., eds.*, 1985, pp. 313–21.

Friedman, Milton. Capitalism and the Jews. In *Block, W.; Brennan, G. and Elzinga, K., eds.*, 1985, pp. 401–18.

Friedman, Milton. Capitalism and the Jews: Reply. In *Block, W.; Brennan, G. and Elzinga, K., eds.*, 1985, pp. 443–46.

Furniss, Norman. Political Futures. In *Benjamin, R. and Elkin, S. L., eds.*, 1985, pp. 213–36.

Furubotn, Eirik G. Codetermination, Productivity Gains, and the Economics of the Firm. *Oxford Econ. Pap.*, March 1985, *37*(1), pp. 22–39.

George, Donald A. R. Collective Capital Formation: Implications of the Scandinavian Debate. *Econ. Anal. Worker's Manage.*, 1985, *19*(3), pp. 281–93. **[G: OECD]**

Ghose, Ajit Kumar. Transforming Feudal Agriculture: Agrarian Change in Ethiopia since 1974. In *Saith, A., ed.*, 1985, pp. 127–49. **[G: Ethiopia]**

Ghose, Ajit Kumar. Transforming Feudal Agriculture: Agrarian Change in Ethiopia since 1974. *J. Devel. Stud.*, October 1985, *22*(1), pp. 127–49. **[G: Ethiopia]**

Gibbard, Allan. What's Morally Special about Free Exchange. In *Paul, E. F.; Paul, J. and Miller, F. D., Jr., eds.*, 1985, pp. 20–28.

Giner, Salvador. Political Economy, Legitimation and the State in Southern Europe. In *Hudson, R. and Lewis, J., eds.*, 1985, pp. 309–50. **[G: S. Europe]**

Gleizal, J.-J. Critique du droit et théorie de la régulation. (Critique of Law and the Theory of Regulation. With English summary.) *Écon. Soc.*, January 1985, *19*(1), pp. 91–101.

Goldstein, Jonathan P. The Cyclical Profit Squeeze: A Marxian Microfoundation. *Rev. Radical Polit. Econ.*, Spring and Summer 1985, *17*(1/2), pp. 103–28.

Goldthorpe, John H. The End of Convergence: Corporatist and Dualist Tendencies in Modern Western Societies. In *Roberts, B.; Finnegan, R. and Gallie, D., eds.*, 1985, pp. 124–53.

Goodin, Robert E. Vulnerabilities and Responsibilities: An Ethical Defense of the Welfare State. *Amer. Polit. Sci. Rev.*, September 1985, *79*(3), pp. 775–87.

Gorin, Zeev. Socialist Societies and World System Theory: A Critical Survey. *Sci. Soc.*, Fall 1985, *49*(3), pp. 332–66.

Grant, Wyn. The Political Economy of Corporatism: Introduction. In *Grant, W., ed.*, 1985, pp. 1–31.

Griffin, Keith and Gurley, John. Radical Analyses of Imperialism, the Third World, and the Transition to Socialism: A Survey Article. *J. Econ. Lit.*, September 1985, *23*(3), pp. 1089–1143. **[G: Global]**

Gurdon, Michael A. Equity Participation by Employees: The Growing Debate in West Germany. *Ind. Relat.*, Winter 1985, *24*(1), pp. 113–29. **[G: W. Germany]**

Harris, Ralph. Can Democracy be Tamed? In *Matthews, R. C. O., ed.*, 1985, pp. 219–34.

Haskell, Thomas L. Capitalism and the Orgins of the Humanitarian Sensibility, Part 1. *Amer.*

Hist. Rev., April 1985, *90*(2), pp. 339–61.

Haskell, Thomas L. Capitalism and the Origins of the Humanitarian Sensibility, Part 2. *Amer. Hist. Rev.*, June 1985, *90*(3), pp. 547–66.

Hayek, Friedrich A. The Price System as a Mechanism for Using Knowledge. In *Bornstein, M., ed.*, 1985, pp. 29–40.

Heinsohn, Gunnar and Steiger, Otto. Technical Progress and Monetary Production: An Explanation. *Écon. Soc.*, August 1985, *19*(8), pp. 85–98.

Heller, Henry. The Transition Debate in Historical Perspective [Feudalism and Historical Materialism: A Critique and a Synthesis] [Modes of Production and Theories of Transition]. *Sci. Soc.*, Summer 1985, *49*(2), pp. 208–13.

Higgs, Robert. Crisis, Bigger Government, and Ideological Change: Two Hypotheses on the Ratchet Phenomenon. *Exploration Econ. Hist.*, January 1985, *22*(1), pp. 1–28. [G: U.S.]

Hintzen, Percy C. Ethnicity, Class, and International Capitalist Penetration in Guyana and Trinidad. *Soc. Econ. Stud.*, September 1985, *34*(3), pp. 107–63. [G: Trinidad and Tobago; Guyana]

Hogan, Michael J. American Marshall Planners and the Search for a European Neocapitalism. *Amer. Hist. Rev.*, February 1985, *90*(1), pp. 44–72. [G: EEC; U.S.]

Holland, David and Carvalho, Joe. The Changing Mode of Production in American Agriculture: Emerging Conflicts in Agriculture's Role in the Reproduction of Advanced Capitalism. *Rev. Radical Polit. Econ.*, Winter 1985, *17*(4), pp. 1–27. [G: U.S.]

Horn, Walter. Libertarianism and Private Property in Land: Compensatory Payments by Landholders Are Required by Both Utility and Justice. *Amer. J. Econ. Soc.*, January 1985, *44*(1), pp. 67–80.

Janover, Louis and Rubel, Maximilien. Matériaux pur un lexique de Marx. (Material for a Marx Lexikon: Revolution II. With English summary.) *Écon. Soc.*, November 1985, *19*(11), pp. 55–95.

Johansen, Lars Nørby and Kolberg, Jon Eivind. Welfare State Regression in Scandinavia? The Development of the Scandinavian Welfare States from 1970 to 1980. In *Eisenstadt, S. N. and Ahimeir, O., eds.*, 1985, pp. 143–76. [G: Scandinavia]

Jones, Derek C. and Svejnar, Jan. Advances in the Economic Analysis of Participatory and Labor-Managed Firms: Introduction. In *Jones, D. C. and Svejnar, J., eds.*, 1985, pp. xi–xiv.

Jones, Derek C. and Svejnar, Jan. Participation, Profit Sharing, Worker Ownership and Efficiency in Italian Producer Cooperative. *Economica*, November 1985, *52*(208), pp. 449–65. [G: Italy]

Kamerschen, David R. Wealth and Poverty: The Questionable and the Reasonable: A Review. *J. Behav. Econ.*, Summer 1985, *14*(2), pp. 77–94. [G: U.S.]

Karsten, Siegfried G. Eucken's 'Social Market Economy' and Its Test in Post-war West Germany: The Economist as Social Philosopher Developed Ideas that Parallelled Progressive Thought in America. *Amer. J. Econ. Soc.*, April 1985, *44*(2), pp. 169–83. [G: W. Germany]

Kaufmann, Franz-Xaver. Major Problems and Dimensions of the Welfare State. In *Eisenstadt, S. N. and Ahimeir, O., eds.*, 1985, pp. 44–56. [G: U.S.; W. Europe]

Khan, Muhammad Akram. Islamic Economics: Nature and Need. In *Khan, M. A.*, 1985, pp. 1–41.

Khan, Muhammad Akram. Islamic Economics: The State of the Art. In *Khan, M. A.*, 1985, pp. 42–71.

Khan, Muhammad Akram. Teaching Islamic Economics at University Level. In *Khan, M. A.*, 1985, pp. 72–91.

Khan, Shahrukh Rafi. Islamic Economics: A Note on Methodology. *J. Res. Islamic Econ.*, Winter 1985, *2*(2), pp. 83–85.

King, Roger. Corporatism and the Local Economy. In *Grant, W., ed.*, 1985, pp. 202–28. [G: U.K.]

Kirman, Alan P. Organisation et communication dans les marchés. (Organization and Communication in Markets. With English summary.) *Écon. Appl.*, 1985, *38*(3/4), pp. 597–609.

Kirzner, Israel M. Entrepreneurship and the Future of Capitalism. In *Kirzner, I. M.*, 1985, pp. 150–68.

Kirzner, Israel M. Entrepreneurship, Economics, and Economists. In *Kirzner, I. M.*, 1985, pp. 1–14.

Kirzner, Israel M. Taxes and Discovery: An Entrepreneurial Perspective. In *Kirzner, I. M.*, 1985, pp. 93–118.

Kirzner, Israel M. The Entrepreneurial Process. In *Kirzner, I. M.*, 1985, pp. 68–92.

Kirzner, Israel M. The Perils of Regulation: A Market-Process Approach. In *Kirzner, I. M.*, 1985, pp. 119–49.

Kirzner, Israel M. The Primacy of Entrepreneurial Discovery. In *Kirzner, I. M.*, 1985, pp. 15–39.

Kirzner, Israel M. Uncertainty, Discovery, and Human Action: A Study of the Entrepreneurial Profile in the Misesian System. In *Kirzner, I. M.*, 1985, pp. 40–67.

Lal, Deepak. Nationalism, Socialism and Planning: Influential Ideas in the South. *World Devel.*, June 1985, *13*(6), pp. 749–59. [G: LDCs]

Lash, Scott. The End of Neo-corporatism? The Breakdown of Centralised Bargaining in Sweden. *Brit. J. Ind. Relat.*, July 1985, *23*(2), pp. 215–39. [G: Sweden]

Laurinkari, Juhani and Laakkonen, Vesa. Probleme des genossenschaftswesens in Finnland in den 80er jahren. (Problems of the Co-operative Movement in Finland during the 1980's. With English summary.) *Ann. Pub. Co-op. Econ.*, Oct.-Dec. 1985, *56*(4), pp. 513–25. [G: Finland]

Lavoie, Don. Rebuilding America: A Blueprint for the New Economy: Review Article. *Com-*

parative *Econ. Stud.*, Fall 1985, *27*(3), pp. 99–113. **[G: U.S.]**

Lavoie, Marc. La thèse de la monnaie endogène face à la non-validation des crédits. (The Hypothesis of Endogeneous Money and the Non-validation of Credit. With English summary.) *Écon. Soc.*, August 1985, *19*(8), pp. 169–95.

Lebowitz, Michael A. The Theoretical Status of Monopoly Capital. In *[Magdoff, H. and Sweezy, P.]*, 1985, pp. 185–203.

Lekachman, Robert. SuperStock: A Conservative Alternative to the Welfare State. *J. Post Keynesian Econ.*, Spring 1985, *7*(3), pp. 440–42. **[G: U.S.]**

Lesourne, Jacques. Le marché et l'auto-organisation. (Market and Self-Organization. With English summary.) *Écon. Appl.*, 1985, *38*(3/4), pp. 663–701.

Levin, William R. The False Promise of Worker Capitalism: Congress and the Leveraged Employee Stock Ownership Plan. *Yale Law J.*, November 1985, *95*(1), pp. 148–73. **[G: U.S.]**

Levine, Aaron. Capitalism and the Jews: Comment. In *Block, W.; Brennan, G. and Elzinga, K.*, eds., 1985, pp. 419–29.

Levine, David P. On the Analysis of Advanced Capitalist Economy. In *[Magdoff, H. and Sweezy, P.]*, 1985, pp. 205–22.

Lichtenstein, Peter M. Neoclassical and Marxian Theories of Capitalist Organizations: Prospects for a Post-Keynesian Challenge. *Econ. Forum*, Winter 1985-1986, *15*(2), pp. 35–50.

Lim, Chee Peng. A Survey of Bumiputra RNA Entrepreneurs in Peninsular Malaysia. In *Mukhopadhyay, S. and Chee, P. L.*, eds. *(II)*, 1985, pp. 305–55. **[G: Malaysia]**

Lippit, Victor D. The Concept of the Surplus in Economic Development. *Rev. Radical Polit. Econ.*, Spring and Summer 1985, *17*(1/2), pp. 1–19. **[G: LDCs]**

Lubinsky, R. Policy, Power and Order—The Persistence of Economic Problems in Capitalist States (Review Note). *S. Afr. J. Econ.*, September 1985, *53*(3), pp. 297–301.

Lunghini, Giorgio. Marx sulle macchine: note di lettura. (Marx on Machinery. With English summary.) *Rivista Int. Sci. Econ. Com.*, June 1985, *32*(6), pp. 517–24.

Macarov, David. Planning for a Probability: The Almost-Workless World. *Int. Lab. Rev.*, Nov.-Dec. 1985, *124*(6), pp. 629–42.

Macpherson, C. B. Democracy, Utopian and Scientific. In *Macpherson, C. B.*, 1985, pp. 120–32.

Macpherson, C. B. Do We Need a Theory of the State? In *Macpherson, C. B.*, 1985, pp. 55–75.

Macpherson, C. B. Liberalism as Trade-offs. In *Macpherson, C. B.*, 1985, pp. 44–54.

Macpherson, C. B. The Prospects of Economic and Industrial Democracy. In *Macpherson, C. B.*, 1985, pp. 35–43.

Marco, Luc V. A. Entrepreneur et innovation: les sources françaises de Joseph Schumpeter. (The Entrepreneur and Innovation: The French Heritage of Joseph Schumpeter. With English summary.) *Écon. Soc.*, October 1985, *19*(10), pp. 89–106.

Margairaz, Dominique. L'office du blé, une innovation socialiste en régime capitaliste. (The Wheat Office: A Socialist Innovation within a Capitalist Regime. With English summary.) *Écon. Soc.*, October 1985, *19*(10), pp. 37–55. **[G: France]**

Marin, Bernd. Austria—The Paradigm Case of Liberal Corporatism? In *Grant, W.*, ed., 1985, pp. 89–125. **[G: Austria]**

Martin, David A. R. H. Tawney's Normative Economic History of Capitalism. *Rev. Soc. Econ.*, April 1985, *43*(1), pp. 84–102.

Marx, Karl. Chroniques litté raires. (Literary Chronicles [1850]. With English summary.) *Écon. Soc.*, November 1985, *19*(11), pp. 97–112. **[G: France]**

Matthews, Robin C. O. Competition in Economy and Polity. In *Matthews, R. C. O.*, ed., 1985, pp. 1–19.

Mayhew, Anne. Dangers in Using the Idea of Property Rights: Modern Property Rights Theory and the Neo-classical Trap. *J. Econ. Issues*, December 1985, *19*(4), pp. 959–66.

Maynard, Alan. Welfare: Who Pays? In *Bean, P.; Ferris, J. and Whynes, D.*, eds., 1985, pp. 142–61. **[G: U.K.]**

van Meerhaeghe, Marcel A. G. Right and Left—Ideology and Welfare State. *Rivista Int. Sci. Econ. Com.*, March 1985, *32*(3), pp. 263–70.

Meiselman, David I. Markets and Majorities, Morals and Madness: An Essay on Religion and Institutional Choice: Comment. In *Block, W.; Brennan, G. and Elzinga, K.*, eds., 1985, pp. 248–51.

Melody, William H. The Information Society: Implications for Economic Institutions and Market Theory. *J. Econ. Issues*, June 1985, *19*(2), pp. 523–39.

Miliband, Ralph. State Power and Capitalist Democracy. In *[Magdoff, H. and Sweezy, P.]*, 1985, pp. 259–71.

Miller, Edythe S. Controlling Power in the Social Economy: The Regulatory Approach. *Rev. Soc. Econ.*, October 1985, *43*(2), pp. 129–39.

Miller, S. M. Anglo–American Exceptionalism or Is the Welfare State in Danger? In *Eisenstadt, S. N. and Ahimeir, O.*, eds., 1985, pp. 224–28. **[G: U.K.; U.S.]**

Minsky, Hyman P. The Financial Instability Hypothesis: A Restatement. In *Arestis, P. and Skouras, T.*, eds., 1985, pp. 24–55.

Mishan, Ezra J. Religion, Culture, and Technology: Reply. In *Block, W.; Brennan, G. and Elzinga, K.*, eds., 1985, pp. 330–40.

Mishan, Ezra J. Religion, Culture, and Technology. In *Block, W.; Brennan, G. and Elzinga, K.*, eds., 1985, pp. 279–312.

Morehouse, Ward. Beyond SuperStock: The Three-tiered Plan for Universal Capital Ownership. *J. Post Keynesian Econ.*, Spring 1985, *7*(3), pp. 435–39. **[G: U.S.]**

Morris, Jacob. Value Relations and Divisions within the Working Class: A Comment. *Sci.*

Soc., Summer 1985, *49*(2), pp. 214–20.

Moseley, Fred. The Rate of Surplus Value in the Postwar U.S. Economy: A Critique of Weisskopf's Estimates. *Cambridge J. Econ.*, March 1985, *9*(1), pp. 57–79. [G: U.S.]

Neale, Walter C. Property in Land as Cultural Imperialism: Or, Why Ethnocentric Ideas Won't Work in India and Africa. *J. Econ. Issues*, December 1985, *19*(4), pp. 951–58. [G: India; Africa]

Neu, Irene D. My Nineteenth-Century Network: Erastus Corning, Benjamin Ingham, Edmond Forstall. In *Atack, J., ed.*, 1985, pp. 1–14. [G: U.S.]

Niedercorn, John H. and Lichman, Barbara. The Brotherhood Ideal in Western Civilisation. *Int. J. Soc. Econ.*, 1985, *12*(6/7), pp. 80–89.

Noll, Roger G. Self-Regulation as Market Maintenance: Comment. In *Noll, R. G., ed.*, 1985, pp. 343–47. [G: U.S.]

Norman, Edward R. Religion, Ethics and Politics in the 1980s. In *Block, W.; Brennan, G. and Elzinga, K., eds.*, 1985, pp. 511–23.

Novak, Michael. Morality of the Market: Religious and Economic Perspectives: Overview. In *Block, W.; Brennan, G. and Elzinga, K., eds.*, 1985, pp. 567–87. [G: U.S.]

O'Connor, James. Capital, Crisis, Class Struggle. In *[Magdoff, H. and Sweezy, P.]*, 1985, pp. 273–93.

O'Connor, Robert. Workers Co-operatives—Their Employment Potential. *Ann. Pub. Co-op. Econ.*, Oct.-Dec. 1985, *56*(4), pp. 539–51. [G: Europe]

Offe, Claus. Disorganized Capitalism: Introduction. In *Offe, C.*, 1985, pp. 1–9.

Optiz, Edmund A. *The Christian Century* on Religion and Society: Reply. In *Block, W.; Brennan, G. and Elzinga, K., eds.*, 1985, pp. 150–56.

Optiz, Edmund A. *The Christian Century* on Religion and Society. In *Block, W.; Brennan, G. and Elzinga, K., eds.*, 1985, pp. 119–42.

Pastré, Olivier. Organisation du travail et croissance économique: un vieux débat anglo-saxon. (Division of Labour and Economic Growth: An Old Debate. With English summary.) *Revue Écon.*, March 1985, *36*(2), pp. 383–409. [G: OECD]

Patel, S. J. Economic Crisis and the Transition from Capitalism. *Econ. Int.*, Aug./Nov. 1985, *38*(3/4), pp. 368–93. [G: Global]

Paul, Ellen Frankel. Public Use: A Vanishing Limitation on Governmental Takings. *Cato J.*, Winter 1985, *4*(3), pp. 835–51.

Perryman, M. Ray. Evolutionary Aspects of Corporate Concentration and Its Implications for Economic Theory and Policy. *J. Econ. Issues*, June 1985, *19*(2), pp. 375–81.

Peterson, Wallace C. The U.S. "Welfare State" and the Conservative Counterrevolution. *J. Econ. Issues*, September 1985, *19*(3), pp. 601–41. [G: U.S.]

Phillips, Paul. Staples, Surplus, and Exchange: The Commercial-Industrial Question in the National Policy Period. In *[Spry, I. M.]*, 1985, pp. 27–43. [G: Canada]

Pilon, Roger. Legislative Activism, Judicial Activism, and the Decline of Private Sovereignty. *Cato J.*, Winter 1985, *4*(3), pp. 813–33. [G: U.S.]

Plant, Raymond. The Very Idea of a Welfare State. In *Bean, P.; Ferris, J. and Whynes, D., eds.*, 1985, pp. 3–30. [G: U.K.]

Prebisch, Raúl. The Latin American Periphery in the Global Crisis of Capitalism. *Cepal Rev.*, August 1985, (26), pp. 63–88. [G: Latin America]

Pryor, Frederic L. The Islamic Economic System—Review Article. *J. Compar. Econ.*, June 1985, *9*(2), pp. 197–223.

Putterman, Louis. On the Interdependence of Labor Supplies in Producers' Cooperatives. In *Jones, D. C. and Svejnar, J., eds.*, 1985, pp. 87–105.

Putterman, Louis and DiGiorgio, Marie. Choice and Efficiency in a Model of Democratic Semicollective Agriculture. *Oxford Econ. Pap.*, March 1985, *37*(1), pp. 1–21.

Reynolds, R. Larry. Institutionally Determined Property Claims. *J. Econ. Issues*, December 1985, *19*(4), pp. 941–49.

Roback, Jennifer. The Economic Thought of George Orwell. *Amer. Econ. Rev.*, May 1985, *75*(2), pp. 127–32.

Rocard, Michel. Management of a National Economy during the 1980s. *Ann. Pub. Co-op. Econ.*, January–June 1985, *56*(1–2), pp. 11–23.

Rosner, M. Theories of Cooperative Degeneration and the Experience of the Kibbutz. *Ann. Pub. Co-op. Econ.*, Oct.-Dec. 1985, *56*(4), pp. 527–38. [G: Israel]

Rosner, M. and Shur, S. The Integration of Agriculture and Industry in Cooperative Villages: The Experience of the Kibbutz. In *Bergmann, T. and Ogura, T. B., eds.*, 1985, pp. 59–70. [G: Israel]

Rowthorn, Bob and Harris, Donald J. The Organic Composition of Capital and Capitalist Development. In *[Magdoff, H. and Sweezy, P.]*, 1985, pp. 345–57.

Roxborough, Ian. State, Multinationals and the Working Class in Brazil and Mexico. In *Abel, C. and Lewis, C. M., eds.*, 1985, pp. 430–50. [G: Brazil; Mexico]

Rüegg, Walter. Social Rights or Social Responsibilities? The Case of Switzerland. In *Eisenstadt, S. N. and Ahimeir, O., eds.*, 1985, pp. 183–99. [G: Switzerland]

Rumler, Miroslav. On the Causes of the Contemporary Prolonged Crisis in the Economy of Advanced Capitalist Countries (An Outline of the Politic–Economic Conception). *Czech. Econ. Pap.*, 1985, 23, pp. 111–36.

Salais, Robert. La formation du chomage comme catégorie: le moment des années 1930. (The Forming of Unemployment as a Category during the Thirties. With English summary.) *Revue Écon.*, March 1985, *36*(2), pp. 321–65. [G: France]

Samuels, Warren J. A Critique of *Capitalism,*

Socialism, and Democracy. In Coe, R. D. and Wilber, C. K., eds., 1985, pp. 60–119.

Samuelson, Paul A. Succumbing to Keynesianism. *Challenge,* January/February 1985, 27(6), pp. 4–11. [G: U.S.]

Sargent, Jane A. Corporatism and the European Community. In Grant, W., ed., 1985, pp. 229–53. [G: EEC]

Saxena, S. K. The International Cooperative Collaboration. *Ann. Pub. Co-op. Econ.,* January–June 1985, 56(1–2), pp. 155–63. [G: Global]

Scalia, Antonin. Economic Affairs as Human Affairs. *Cato J.,* Winter 1985, 4(3), pp. 703–10. [G: U.S.]

Schmitter, Philippe C. Neo-corporatism and the State. In Grant, W., ed., 1985, pp. 32–62.

Scitovsky, Tibor. Pricetakers' Plenty: A Neglected Benefit of Capitalism. *Kyklos,* 1985, 38(4), pp. 517–36.

Seal, W. B. On the Nature of the Firm and Trades Unions: A Critique of the Property Rights Literature. *Brit. Rev. Econ. Issues,* Spring 1985, 7(16), pp. 47–61.

Seldon, Arthur. The Idea of the Welfare State and Its Consequences. In Eisenstadt, S. N. and Ahimeir, O., eds., 1985, pp. 59–73. [G: U.K.]

Sen, Amartya. The Moral Standing of the Market. In Paul, E. F.; Paul, J. and Miller, F. D., Jr., eds., 1985, pp. 1–19.

Shackleton, J. R. Is Workers' Self-management the Answer? In Bornstein, M., ed., 1985, pp. 141–52.

Sharma, R. A. Industrial Entrepreneurship in India, 1961–1963. *Indian Econ. J.,* Oct.-Nov. 1985, 33(2), pp. 79–92. [G: India]

Shiratori, Rei. The Experience of the Welfare State in Japan and Its Problems. In Eisenstadt, S. N. and Ahimeir, O., eds., 1985, pp. 200–223. [G: Japan]

Shute, Laurence. J. M. Clark on Corporate Concentration and Control. *J. Econ. Issues,* June 1985, 19(2), pp. 409–18.

Siegan, Bernard H. Economic Liberties and the Constitution: Protection at the State Level. *Cato J.,* Winter 1985, 4(3), pp. 689–702. [G: U.S.]

Simmie, James. Corporatism and Planning. In Grant, W., ed., 1985, pp. 174–201. [G: U.K.]

Skouras, Thanos. The Political Economy of Rapid Industrialisation. In Arestis, P. and Skouras, T., eds., 1985, pp. 180–212.

Sleeman, Michael. The Agri-business Bourgeoisie of Barbados and Martinique. In Gomes, P. I., ed., 1985, pp. 15–33. [G: Caribbean]

Smith, Stephen C. Political Behavior as an Economic Externality: Econometric Evidence on the Relationship between Ownership and Decision Making Participation in U.S. Firms and Participation in Community Affairs. In Jones, D. C. and Svejnar, J., eds., 1985, pp. 123–36. [G: U.S.]

Sockell, Donna. Attitudes, Behavior, and Employee Ownership: Some Preliminary Data.

Ind. Relat., Winter 1985, 24(1), pp. 130–38. [G: U.S.]

Soukup, Václav. Economic Aggression of Imperialism against the Countries of the Socialist Community. *Czech. Econ. Digest.,* August 1985, (5), pp. 75–94. [G: CMEA; OECD]

Speiser, Stuart M. Broadened Capital Ownership—The Solution to Major Domestic and International Problems. *J. Post Keynesian Econ.,* Spring 1985, 7(3), pp. 426–34. [G: U.S.]

Sperry, Charles W. What Makes Mondragon Work? *Rev. Soc. Econ.,* December 1985, 43(3), pp. 345–56. [G: Spain]

Stauffer, Robert B. States and TNCs in the Capitalist World-Economy: Overview of Theory and Practice. In Stauffer, R. B., ed., 1985, pp. 1–43.

Steindl, Josef. Structural Problems in the Crisis. *Banca Naz. Lavoro Quart. Rev.,* September 1985, (154), pp. 223–32. [G: OECD]

Stevenson, Rodney. Corporate Power and the Scope of Economic Analysis. *J. Econ. Issues,* June 1985, 19(2), pp. 333–41.

Sufrin, Sidney C. Philosophical Foundations. An Essay in Economic Pragmatism. *Rivista Int. Sci. Econ. Com.,* June 1985, 32(6), pp. 525–49.

Sweeney, G. P. Innovation is Entrepreneur-Led. In Sweeney, G., ed., 1985, pp. 80–113. [G: OECD]

Sylos Labini, Paolo. XVth International CIRIEC Congress. *Ann. Pub. Co-op. Econ.,* January–June 1985, 56(1–2), pp. 165–75. [G: Global]

Teulade, René. The Role of Mutual Benefit Societies and Insurance Funds in Today's Economic and Social Policy. *Ann. Pub. Co-op. Econ.,* January–June 1985, 56(1–2), pp. 81–91. [G: France]

Thomas, Henk. The Dynamics of Social Ownership: Some Considerations in the Perspective of the Mondragon Experience. *Econ. Anal. Worker's Manage.,* 1985, 19(2), pp. 147–60. [G: Spain]

Tieber, Herbert. Public Enterprise and Employment Policy. *Ann. Pub. Co-op. Econ.,* January–June 1985, 56(1–2), pp. 63–70. [G: Austria]

Vanek, Jaroslav. The Participatory Economy. In Bornstein, M., ed., 1985, pp. 131–40.

Vedel-Petersen, Jacob. The Experience of the Danish Welfare State. In Eisenstadt, S. N. and Ahimeir, O., eds., 1985, pp. 229–36. [G: Denmark]

Walker, Richard A. Is There a Service Economy? The Changing Capitalist Division of Labor. *Sci. Soc.,* Spring 1985, 49(1), pp. 42–83.

Wall, James M. *The Christian Century* on Religion and Society: Comment. In Block, W.; Brennan, G. and Elzinga, K., eds., 1985, pp. 143–50.

Weeks, John. Epochs of Capitalism and the Progressiveness of Capital's Expansion. *Sci. Soc.,* Winter 1985-1986, 49(4), pp. 414–36.

Weisskopf, Thomas E. The Rate of Surplus Value in the Postwar U.S. Economy: A Response to Moseley's Critique. *Cambridge J. Econ.,*

March 1985, *9*(1), pp. 81–84.   [G: U.S.]

Weisskopf, Thomas E.; Bowles, Samuel and Gordon, David M. Two Views of Capitalist Stagnation: Underconsumption and Challenges to Capitalist Control. *Sci. Soc.*, Fall 1985, *49*(3), pp. 259–86.   [G: U.S.]

Weitzman, Martin L. Profit Sharing as Macroeconomic Policy. *Amer. Econ. Rev.*, May 1985, *75*(2), pp. 41–45.

Whynes, David. Markets and Neo-liberal Political Economy. In *Bean, P.; Ferris, J. and Whynes, D., eds.*, 1985, pp. 99–121.   [G: U.K.]

Willoughby, John. The Internationalization of Capital and the Future of Macroeconomic Policy. *Sci. Soc.*, Fall 1985, *49*(3), pp. 287–314.

Witt, Ulrich. Coordination of Individual Economic Activities as an Evolving Process of Self-Organization. *Écon. Appl.*, 1985, *38*(3/4), pp. 569–95.

Wootton, Barbara. The Moral Basis of the Welfare State. In *Bean, P.; Ferris, J. and Whynes, D., eds.*, 1985, pp. 31–45.   [G: U.K.]

Yeager, Leland B. Rights, Contract, and Utility in Policy Espousal. *Cato J.*, Spring/Summer 1985, *5*(1), pp. 259–94.

Yg, Chimezie A. B. Osigweh. International Business and the Growth Model. *J. Econ. Devel.*, December 1985, *10*(2), pp. 123–42.

052 Socialist and Communist Economic Systems

0520 Socialist and Communist Economic Systems

Abalkin, L. Developed Socialism and the Formation of Modern Economic Thought. *Prob. Econ.*, October 1985, *28*(6), pp. 3–22.

Abouchar, Alan J. Western Project-Investment Theory and Soviet Investment Rules. *J. Compar. Econ.*, December 1985, *9*(4), pp. 345–62.   [G: U.S.S.R.]

Anderson, Gary M. and Tollison, Robert D. Life in the Gulag: A Property Rights Perspective. *Cato J.*, Spring/Summer 1985, *5*(1), pp. 295–304.   [G: U.S.S.R]

Antal, László. About the Property Incentive (Interest in Property). *Acta Oecon.*, 1985, *34*(3/4), pp. 275–86.   [G: Hungary]

Austin, James; Fox, Jonathan and Kruger, Walter. The Role of the Revolutionary State in the Nicaraguan Food System. *World Devel.*, January 1985, *13*(1), pp. 15–40.
      [G: Nicaragua]

Bagrinovskii, K. A.; Rimashevskaia, N. M. and Sheviakov, A. Iu. A Simulation System of Models for Coordinating Output Levels and Living Standards. *Matekon*, Spring 1985, *21*(3), pp. 47–62.   [G: U.S.S.R.]

Balassa, Bela. Economic Reform in China. In *Balassa, B.*, 1985, pp. 310–36.   [G: China]

Balassa, Bela. Reforming the New Economic Mechanism in Hungary. In *Balassa, B.*, 1985, pp. 282–309.   [G: Hungary]

Balassa, Bela. The Hungarian Economic Reform, 1968–81. In *Balassa, B.*, 1985, pp. 261–81.
      [G: Hungary]

Bársony, Jenö and Síklaky, István. Some Reflections on Socialist Entrepreneurship. *Acta Oecon.*, 1985, *34*(1–2), pp. 51–64.
      [G: Hungary]

Bauer, Tamás. Reform Policy in the Complexity of Economic Policy. *Acta Oecon.*, 1985, *34*(3/4), pp. 263–73.   [G: Hungary]

Bergson, Abram. A Visit to China's Economic Reforms. *Comparative Econ. Stud.*, Summer 1985, *27*(2), pp. 71–82.   [G: China]

Bhagwati, Jagdish N. What Do Commissars Do? In *Bhagwati, J. N. (II)*, 1985, pp. 210–15.
      [G: China]

Bhagwati, Jagdish N. and Desai, Padma. Socialism and Indian Economic Policy. In *Bhagwati, J. N. (II)*, 1985, pp. 59–72.   [G: India]

Bislev, Claus. Planning in a Worker-Managed Economy. *Econ. Anal. Worker's Manage.*, 1985, *19*(4), pp. 385–94.   [G: Yugoslavia]

Blecher, Marc. The Structure and Contradictions of Productive Relations in Socialist Agrarian 'Reform': A Framework for Analysis and the Chinese Case. *J. Devel. Stud.*, October 1985, *22*(1), pp. 104–26.   [G: China]

Blecher, Marc. The Structure and Contradictions of Productive Relations in Socialist Agrarian 'Reform': A Framework for Analysis and the Chinese Case. In *Saith, A., ed.*, 1985, pp. 104–26.   [G: China]

Bognár, József. Evolution of Conception about Economic Policy and Control in Hungary in the Past Decades. *Acta Oecon.*, 1985, *34*(3/4), pp. 205–17.   [G: Hungary]

Bonin, John P. Labor Management and Capital Maintenance: Investment Decisions in the Socialist Labor-Managed Firm. In *Jones, D. C. and Svejnar, J., eds.*, 1985, pp. 55–69.

Bornstein, Morris. The Soviet Centrally Planned Economy. In *Bornstein, M., ed.*, 1985, pp. 188–219.   [G: U.S.S.R.]

Boyd, Michael L. The Effect of Policy on System Performance: The Case of Yugoslav Agriculture. *Comparative Econ. Stud.*, Summer 1985, *27*(2), pp. 1–23.   [G: Yugoslavia]

van Brabant, Jozef M. The Relationship between World and Socialist Trade Price—Some Empirical Evidence. *J. Compar. Econ.*, September 1985, *9*(3), pp. 233–51.   [G: CMEA]

Brezinski, Horst. The Second Economy in the Soviet Union and Its Implications for Economic Policy. In *Gaertner, W. and Wenig, A., eds.*, 1985, pp. 362–76.   [G: U.S.S.R.]

Brown, Alan A. and Neuberger, Egon. Basic Features of a Centrally Planned Economy. In *Bornstein, M., ed.*, 1985, pp. 177–87.

Brus, Wlodzimierz and Laski, Kazimierz. Repressed Inflation and Second Economy under Central Planning. In *Gaertner, W. and Wenig, A., eds.*, 1985, pp. 377–88.

Bunce, Valerie. The Empire Strikes Back: The Evolution of the Eastern Bloc from a Soviet Asset to a Soviet Liability. *Int. Organ.*, Winter 1985, *39*(1), pp. 1–46.   [G: U.S.S.R.]

Byrd, William. The Shanghai Market for the Means of Production: A Case Study of Reform in China's Material Supply System. *Compara-*

tive Econ. Stud., Winter 1985, *27*(4), pp. 1–29. **[G: China]**

Chang, Tse-Chung. The Main Aspects of China's Economic Reform. *Econ. Anal. Worker's Manage.*, 1985, *19*(3), pp. 307–15. **[G: China]**

Chyba, Antonín. Global Problems of Mankind and the Present-Day World. *Czech. Econ. Digest.*, August 1985, (5), pp. 59–74. **[G: Global]**

Csikós-Nagy, Béla. The Role of the Law of Value in Socialist Economy. In *[Levcik, F.]*, 1985, pp. 39–49.

Danilin, V. I., et al. Measuring Enterprise Efficiency in the Soviet Union: A Stochastic Frontier Analysis. *Economica*, May 1985, *52*(206), pp. 225–33. **[G: U.S.S.R.]**

Darity, William A., Jr. and Horn, Bobbie L. Rudolf Hilferding: The Dominion of Capitalism and the Dominion of Gold. *Amer. Econ. Rev.*, May 1985, *75*(2), pp. 363–68. **[G: Germany]**

Drach, Marcel. Le cycle de la relation État-entreprises en R.D.A. 1963–1983. *Écon. Soc.*, May 1985, *19*(5), pp. 117–53. **[G: E. Germany]**

Eckstein, Susan. State and Market Dynamics in Castro's Cuba. In *Evans, P.; Rueschemeyer, D. and Stephens, E. H., eds.*, 1985, pp. 217–45. **[G: Cuba]**

Falus-Szikra, Katalin. Small Enterprises in Private Ownership in Hungary. *Acta Oecon.*, 1985, *34*(1–2), pp. 13–26. **[G: Hungary]**

Fang, Shen. On the Issue of Utilizing Foreign Capital. *Chinese Econ. Stud.*, Summer 1985, *18*(4), pp. 101–06. **[G: China]**

Fedorenko, N. F. Planning and Management: What Should They Be Like? *Prob. Econ.*, December 1985, *28*(8), pp. 42–59. **[G: U.S.S.R.]**

FitzGerald, E. V. K. Agrarian Reform as a Model of Accumulation: The Case of Nicaragua since 1979. In *Saith, A., ed.*, 1985, pp. 208–26. **[G: Nicaragua]**

FitzGerald, E. V. K. Agrarian Reform as a Model of Accumluation: The Case of Nicaragua since 1979. *J. Devel. Stud.*, October 1985, *22*(1), pp. 208–26. **[G: Nicaragua]**

FitzGerald, E. V. K. The Problem of Balance in the Peripheral Socialist Economy: A Conceptual Note. *World Devel.*, January 1985, *13*(1), pp. 5–14.

Flakierski, Henryk. Economic Reform & Income Distribution: A Case Study of Hungary and Poland. *Eastern Europ. Econ.*, Fall-Winter 1985-86, *24*(1–2), pp. iii–194.

Fremer, Miloslav. Some Aspects of the Economy of Socialism and Its Contradictions. *Czech. Econ. Digest.*, May 1985, (3), pp. 29–52.

Galasi, Péter. Peculiarities and Limits of the Second Economy in Socialism (the Hungarian Case). In *Gaertner, W. and Wenig, A., eds.*, 1985, pp. 353–61. **[G: Hungary]**

Glushkov, N. Planned Pricing: Ways to Improve. *Prob. Econ.*, December 1985, *28*(8), pp. 70–89. **[G: U.S.S.R.]**

Goldman, Marshall I. Gorbachev and Economic Reform. *Foreign Aff.*, Fall 1985, *64*(1), pp. 56–73. **[G: U.S.S.R.]**

Gorin, Zeev. Socialist Societies and World System

Theory: A Critical Survey. *Sci. Soc.*, Fall 1985, *49*(3), pp. 332–66.

Griffin, Keith and Gurley, John. Radical Analyses of Imperialism, the Third World, and the Transition to Socialism: A Survey Article. *J. Econ. Lit.*, September 1985, *23*(3), pp. 1089–1143. **[G: Global]**

Grossman, Gregory. The "Second Economy" of the U.S.S.R. In *Bornstein, M., ed.*, 1985, pp. 220–41. **[G: U.S.S.R.]**

Gvishiani, D. Planned Improvements in the System for Managing the National Economy. *Prob. Econ.*, April 1985, *27*(12), pp. 63–81. **[G: U.S.S.R.]**

Harrison, Mark. Primary Accumulation in the Soviet Transition. In *Saith, A., ed.*, 1985, pp. 81–103. **[G: U.S.S.R.]**

Harrison, Mark. Primary Accumulation in the Soviet Transition. *J. Devel. Stud.*, October 1985, *22*(1), pp. 81–103. **[G: U.S.S.R.]**

Hartford, Kathleen. Hungarian Agriculture: A Model for the Socialist World? *World Devel.*, January 1985, *13*(1), pp. 123–50. **[G: Hungary]**

He, Jianzhang. Expansion of the Enterprise's Decision-making Power and Change in the Ownership Relation. *Chinese Econ. Stud.*, Fall 1985, *19*(1), pp. 10–16. **[G: China]**

Hough, Jerry F. Debates about the Postwar World. In *Linz, S. J., ed.*, 1985, pp. 253–81. **[G: U.S.S.R.]**

Iakovleva, E. Overcoming Social and Economic Differences in Labor. *Prob. Econ.*, December 1985, *28*(8), pp. 3–20. **[G: U.S.S.R.]**

Iasin, E. G. Social Ownership, Economic Incentives, and Cost Accounting. *Prob. Econ.*, November 1985, *28*(7), pp. 48–67. **[G: U.S.S.R.]**

Ivanchenko, V. Improving the Organization of Management. *Prob. Econ.*, July 1985, *28*(3), pp. 67–80. **[G: U.S.S.R.]**

Jones, Derek C. The Cooperative Sector and Dualism in Command Economies: Theory and Evidence for the Case of Poland. In *Jones, D. C. and Svejnar, J., eds.*, 1985, pp. 195–218. **[G: Poland]**

Jones, Derek C. The Economic Performance of Producer Co-operatives within Command Economies: Evidence for the Case of Poland. *Cambridge J. Econ.*, June 1985, *9*(2), pp. 111–26. **[G: Poland]**

Kapustin, E. Improving the Management of the National Economy. *Prob. Econ.*, September 1985, *28*(5), pp. 69–88.

Kelly, Kevin D. Capitalism, Socialism, Barbarism: Marxist Conceptions of the Soviet Union. *Rev. Radical Polit. Econ.*, Winter 1985, *17*(4), pp. 51–71.

Khavina, S. Bourgeois Economists on Scientific and Technical Progress under Socialism. *Prob. Econ.*, January 1985, *27*(9), pp. 42–61. **[G: U.S.S.R.]**

Klimentov, G. A. What Is Impeding the Potential of Collective Labor? *Prob. Econ.*, May 1985, *28*(1), pp. 24–37. **[G: U.S.S.R.]**

Kornai, János. Hungary's Reform: Halfway to the

Market. *Challenge*, May/June 1985, *28*(2), pp. 22–31. [G: Hungary]

Kornai, János. On the Explanatory Theory of Shortage. Comments [A Propos the Explanation of Shortage Phenomena: Volume of Demand and Structural Inelasticity]. *Acta Oecon.*, 1985, *34*(1–2), pp. 145–62.

Köves, András. The Import Restriction Squeeze and Import Maximizing Ambitions: Some Connections of East–West vs. Intra-CMEA Trade. *Acta Oecon.*, 1985, *34*(1–2), pp. 99–112. [G: CMEA]

Kuiper, Willem G. The Structure and Developments of Socialist Tax Law from a Western Point of View. *Bull. Int. Fiscal Doc.*, November 1985, *39*(11), pp. 483–88. [G: W. Europe]

Kulcsár, Kálmán. Public Finance and Social Policy—Explanation of Trends and Developments: The Case of Socialist Economies. In *Terny, G. and Culyer, A. J.*, eds., 1985, pp. 59–65.

Labus, Miroljub. Price Adjustment in the Labor-Managed Economy: Theory and Some Yugoslav Evidence. In *Jones, D. C. and Svejnar, J.*, eds., 1985, pp. 137–51. [G: Yugoslavia]

Lal, Deepak. Nationalism, Socialism and Planning: Influential Ideas in the South. *World Devel.*, June 1985, *13*(6), pp. 749–59. [G: LDCs]

Landorová, Anděla. Improvement of the Monetary System of the CMEA Countries. *Czech. Econ. Digest.*, May 1985, (3), pp. 53–78.

Lange, Oskar. On the Economic Theory of Socialism. In *Bornstein, M.*, ed., 1985, pp. 118–26.

Lange, Oskar. The Computer and the Market. In *Bornstein, M.*, ed., 1985, pp. 127–30.

Li, Honglin. Socialism and Opening Up to the Outside World. *Chinese Econ. Stud.*, Fall 1985, *19*(1), pp. 26–39. [G: China]

Lin, Zili. Socialism and the Commodity Economy. *Chinese Econ. Stud.*, Fall 1985, *19*(1), pp. 65–80. [G: China]

Mandel, Ernest. Marx and Engels on Commodity Production and Bureaucracy. In *[Magdoff, H. and Sweezy, P.]*, 1985, pp. 223–58.

Maritain, Jacques. A Society without Money. *Rev. Soc. Econ.*, April 1985, *43*(1), pp. 73–83.

Markovic, Ljubisav. Planning Systems: The Yugoslav Experience. In *Damjanovic, M. and Voich, D., Jr.*, eds., 1985, pp. 124–41. [G: Yugoslavia]

Matlin, A. On the Question of Developing the Theory and Practice of Planned Price Formation. *Prob. Econ.*, February 1985, *27*(10), pp. 23–42. [G: U.S.S.R]

van Meerhaeghe, Marcel A. G. Right and Left—Ideology and Welfare State. *Rivista Int. Sci. Econ. Com.*, March 1985, *32*(3), pp. 263–70.

von Mises, Ludwig. Economic Calculation in Socialism. In *Bornstein, M.*, ed., 1985, pp. 111–17.

Mujzel, Jan. Technocratic vs. Democratic Elements in the Polish Economic Reform. In *[Levcik, F.]*, 1985, pp. 51–59. [G: Poland]

Munslow, Barry. Prospects for the Socialist Transition of Agriculture in Zimbabwe. *World Devel.*, January 1985, *13*(1), pp. 41–58. [G: Zimbabwe]

Nagy, Tamás. Die ungarische Wirtschaftsreform und ihre Weiterentwicklung. (Development of the Hungarian Economic Reform. With English summary.) *Konjunkturpolitik*, 1985, *31*(6), pp. 361–79. [G: Hungary]

Novichkov, V. and Abdykulova, G. Some Problems in Determining the National Economy's Priorities. *Prob. Econ.*, September 1985, *28*(5), pp. 20–31. [G: U.S.S.R.]

Nyers, Resző. National Economic Objectives and the Reform Process in Hungary in the Eighties. *Acta Oecon.*, 1985, *35*(1–2), pp. 1–16. [G: Hungary]

Patel, S. J. Economic Crisis and the Transition from Capitalism. *Econ. Int.*, Aug./Nov. 1985, *38*(3/4), pp. 368–93. [G: Global]

Perry, Elizabeth J. and Wong, Christine. The Political Economy of Reform in Post-Mao China: Causes, Content, and Consequences. In *Perry, E. J. and Wong, C.*, eds., 1985 1985, pp. 1–27.

Petschnig, Mária. Causes of Difficulties in Changing the Normal State of the Hungarian Economy. *Acta Oecon.*, 1985, *35*(3–4), pp. 235–50. [G: Hungary]

Podunavac, Milan. Culture-Based Value Systems in Yugoslavia. In *Damjanovic, M. and Voich, D., Jr.*, eds., 1985, pp. 39–63. [G: Yugoslavia]

Pollitt, Brian H. Towards the Socialist Transformation of Cuban Agriculture 1959–1982. In *Gomes, P. I.*, ed., 1985, pp. 154–72. [G: Cuba]

Prybyla, Jan S. Economic Problems of Communism: A Case Study of China. In *Bornstein, M.*, ed., 1985, pp. 263–81. [G: China]

Putterman, Louis. Extrinsic versus Intrinsic Problems of Agricultural Cooperation: Anti-incentivism in Tanzania and China. *J. Devel. Stud.*, January 1985, *21*(2), pp. 175–204. [G: Tanzania; China]

Ranis, Gustav. China's Open Door Is Open for Good. *Challenge*, Nov./Dec. 1985, *28*(5), pp. 59–60. [G: China]

Ratkovic, Radoslav. Fundamentals of the Yugoslav Political Socialist Self-Management System. In *Damjanovic, M. and Voich, D., Jr.*, eds., 1985, pp. 10–20. [G: Yugoslavia]

Révész, Gábor. The Origins and Development of the Model of Socialist Economy. In *[Levcik, F.]*, 1985, pp. 21–30.

Roback, Jennifer. The Economic Thought of George Orwell. *Amer. Econ. Rev.*, May 1985, *75*(2), pp. 127–32.

Rogulska, Barbara. Le régulation indirecte ou les nouvelles relations Centre-entreprises en Pologne. (Indirect Regulation or New Relations between the Center and the Enterprises in Poland. With English summary.) *Écon. Soc.*, May 1985, *19*(5), pp. 69–115. [G: Poland]

Sacks, Stephen R. The Yugoslav Firm. In *Born-*

stein, M., ed., 1985, pp. 153–73.
[G: Yugoslavia]

Saith, Ashwani. Primitive Accumulation, Agrarian Reform and Socialist Transitions: An Argument. *J. Devel. Stud.*, October 1985, *22*(1), pp. 1–48. [G: U.S.S.R.; LDCs; China]

Saith, Ashwani. Primitive Accumulation, Agrarian Reform and Socialist Transitions: An Argument. In *Saith, A., ed.*, 1985, pp. 1–48.
[G: U.S.S.R.; LDCs; China]

Sawyer, Malcolm C. The Economics of Michal Kalecki. *Eastern Europ. Econ.*, Spring-Summer 1985, *23*(3–4), pp. 1–319.

Seldon, Mark. State, Market, and Sectoral Inequality in Contemporary China. In *Evans, P.; Rueschemeyer, D. and Stephens, E. H., eds.*, 1985, pp. 275–91. [G: China]

Shinohara, Miyohei. The Future of Chinese Economic Growth and the Role of Hong Kong. In *Shishido, T. and Sato, R., eds.*, 1985, pp. 127–46. [G: China; Hong Kong]

Skouras, Thanos. The Political Economy of Rapid Industrialisation. In *Arestis, P. and Skouras, T., eds.*, 1985, pp. 180–212.

Smekhov, B. M. The Logic of Planning. *Prob. Econ.*, November 1985, *28*(7), pp. 3–17.
[G: U.S.S.R.]

Soós, K. A. A Rejoinder [A Propos the Explanation of Shortage Phenomena: Volume of Demand and Structural Inelasticity]. *Acta Oecon.*, 1985, *34*(1–2), pp. 162–64.

Soukup, Václav. Economic Aggression of Imperialism against the Countries of the Socialist Community. *Czech. Econ. Digest.*, August 1985, (5), pp. 75–94. [G: CMEA; OECD]

Stanovcic, Vojislav. Basic Dilemmas and Tendencies in the System of Organization and Process of Management. In *Damjanovic, M. and Voich, D., Jr., eds.*, 1985, pp. 196–225.
[G: Yugoslavia]

Tian, Jiyun. Implement the Reform of the Price System Vigorously and Reliably. *Chinese Econ. Stud.*, Summer 1985, *18*(4), pp. 87–100.

Torkanovskii, E. State Economic Management and the Initiative of Work Collectives. *Prob. Econ.*, April 1985, *27*(12), pp. 49–62.

Trescott, Paul B. Incentives versus Equality: What Does China's Recent Experience Show? *World Devel.*, February 1985, *13*(2), pp. 205–17. [G: China]

Trzeciakowski, Witold. Decentralization and Financial Equilibrium in a Centrally Planned Economy. In *[Levcik, F.]*, 1985, pp. 171–80.

Ulybin, K. A. Scarcity and the Interaction of Partners. *Prob. Econ.*, December 1985, *28*(8), pp. 60–69. [G: U.S.S.R.]

Valovoi, D. Indicators of Socialist Management: An Economist's Reflection. *Prob. Econ.*, June 1985, *28*(2), pp. 3–24. [G: U.S.S.R.]

Verbík, Antonín. Nationalization. *Czech. Econ. Digest.*, December 1985, (8), pp. 29–38.
[G: Czechoslovakia]

Walder, Andrew G. China Turns to Industry Reform. *Challenge*, March/April 1985, *28*(1), pp. 42–47. [G: China]

Wolf, Thomas A. Exchange Rate Systems and Ad-

justment in Planned Economies. *Int. Monet. Fund Staff Pap.*, June 1985, *32*(2), pp. 211–47. [G: U.S.S.R.; Poland; Hungary; E. Germany]

Wu, Junyang. Current Economic Conditions and Reform of the Price System. *Chinese Econ. Stud.*, Spring 1985, *18*(3), pp. 55–76.
[G: China]

Wuyts, Marc. Money, Planning and Rural Transformation in Mozambique. In *Saith, A., ed.*, 1985, pp. 180–207. [G: Mozambique]

Wuyts, Marc. Money, Planning and Rural Transformation in Mozambique. *J. Devel. Stud.*, October 1985, *22*(1), pp. 180–207.
[G: Mozambique]

Yuan, Zhen. On the Question of Understanding the Improvement in the Method of Bonus Distribution. *Chinese Econ. Stud.*, Summer 1985, *18*(4), pp. 78–86. [G: China]

Zhao, Lukuan. The Problem of Reforming the Wage System in Our Country. *Chinese Econ. Stud.*, Spring 1985, *18*(3), pp. 35–54.
[G: China]

053 Comparative Economic Systems

0530 Comparative Economic Systems

Armour, Philip K. and Coughlin, Richard M. Social Control and Social Security: Theory and Research on Capitalist and Communist Nations. *Soc. Sci. Quart.*, December 1985, *66*(4), pp. 770–88. [G: CMEA; OECD]

Berliner, Joseph S. Managerial Incentives and Decision Making: A Comparison of the United States and the Soviet Union. In *Bornstein, M, ed.*, 1985, pp. 311–35. [G: U.S.S.R.; U.S.]

Blecher, Marc. Inequality and Socialism in Rural China: A Conceptual Note. *World Devel.*, January 1985, *13*(1), pp. 115–21. [G: China]

Bornstein, Morris. The Comparison of Economic Systems: An Integration. In *Bornstein, M., ed.*, 1985, pp. 3–17.

Bornstein, Morris. Unemployment in Capitalist Regulated Market Economies and in Socialist Centrally Planned Economies. In *Bornstein, M., ed.*, 1985, pp. 337–44.

Brada, Josef C. and Méndez, José A. Economic Integration among Developed, Developing and Centrally Planned Economies: A Comparative Analysis. *Rev. Econ. Statist.*, November 1985, *67*(4), pp. 549–56. [G: Global]

Browning, Martin J. The Trend Level of Imports by CMEA Countries. *J. Compar. Econ.*, December 1985, *9*(4), pp. 363–70. [G: CMEA]

Buck, Trevor. The Convergence of Economic Systems and the M-Form. *J. Econ. Behav. Organ.*, June 1985, *6*(2), pp. 123–37.
[G: U.S.S.R.; W. Germany]

Burkett, John P. Systemic Influences on the Physical Quality of Life: A Bayesian Analysis of Cross-sectional Data. *J. Compar. Econ.*, June 1985, *9*(2), pp. 145–63.

Cheng, Chu-yuan. Economic Development on Both Sides of the Taiwan Straits: New Trends for Convergence. *Hong Kong Econ. Pap.*, 1985, (16), pp. 54–73. [G: Taiwan; China]

Chishti, Salim U. Relative Stability of Interest-Free Economy. *J. Res. Islamic Econ.*, Summer 1985, *3*(1), pp. 3–12.

Csillag, István and Szalai, Erzsébet. Basic Elements of an Anti-monopoly Policy. *Acta Oecon.*, 1985, *34*(1–2), pp. 65–77.

Ehrlich, Éva. The Size Structure of Manufacturing Establishments and Enterprises: An International Comparison. *J. Compar. Econ.*, September 1985, *9*(3), pp. 267–95. [G: Europe; U.S.; Japan]

Gutiérrez, Alvaro Castro. Alternative Strategies to the Social Security Crisis: Socialist, Market and Mixed Approaches: Comment. In *Mesa-Lago, C.*, ed., 1985, pp. 362–65. [G: Chile; Costa Rica; Cuba]

Hasan, Zubair. Determination of Profit and Loss Sharing Ratios in Interest-Free Business Finance. *J. Res. Islamic Econ.*, Summer 1985, *3*(1), pp. 13–29.

Holzman, Franklyn D. A Comparative View of Foreign Trade Behavior: Market versus Centrally Planned Economies. In *Bornstein, M.*, ed., 1985, pp. 367–86.

Koopmans, Tjalling C. and Montias, John Michael. On the Description and Comparison of Economic Systems. In *Koopmans, T. C.*, 1985, pp. 29–80.

Leonard, William N. The State in a Mixed Economy. *Eastern Econ. J.*, July-Sept. 1985, *11*(3), pp. 190–99. [G: OECD; CMEA]

Mesa-Lago, Carmelo. Alternative Strategies to the Social Security Crisis: Socialist, Market and Mixed Approaches. In *Mesa-Lago, C.*, ed., 1985, pp. 311–61. [G: Chile; Costa Rica; Cuba]

Mitchell, William F. and Watts, Martin. Efficiency under Capitalist Production: A Critique and Reformulation. *Rev. Radical Polit. Econ.*, Spring and Summer 1985, *17*(1/2), pp. 212–20.

Schmiegelow, Michèle. Cutting across Doctrines: Positive Adjustment in Japan. *Int. Organ.*, Spring 1985, *39*(2), pp. 261–96. [G: Japan]

Seton, Francis. Corrigendum [A Quasi-competitive Price Basis for Intersystem Comparisons of Economic Structure and Performance]. *J. Compar. Econ.*, March 1985, *9*(1), pp. 123. [G: Kenya; U.S.S.R.; Japan; U.K.; U.S.]

Wiles, Peter. The Success of Capitalism and the Spread of Socialism. In *[Levcik, F.]*, 1985, pp. 263–71.

100 Economic Growth; Development; Planning; Fluctuations

110 ECONOMIC GROWTH; DEVELOPMENT; PLANNING THEORY AND POLICY

111 Economic Growth Theory and Models

1110 Growth Theories

Allsopp, C. J. The Economic System in the UK: Economic Growth. In *Morris, D.*, ed., 1985, pp. 627–67. [G: U.K.]

Anthony, Peter Dean. Basic Commodities, Growth and Labor Absorption. *Eastern Econ. J.*, July-Sept. 1985, *11*(3), pp. 248–56.

Arrow, Kenneth J. Applications of Control Theory to Economic Growth. In *Arrow, K. J. (I)*, 1985, pp. 261–96.

Arrow, Kenneth J. Classificatory Notes on the Production and Transmission of Technological Knowledge. In *Arrow, K. J. (I)*, 1985, pp. 297–306.

Arrow, Kenneth J. Economic Development: The Present State of the Art. In *Arrow, K. J. (II)*, 1985, pp. 183–207.

Becker, Robert A. Comparative Dynamics in Aggregate Models of Optimal Capital Accumulation. *Quart. J. Econ.*, November 1985, *100*(4), pp. 1235–56.

Bhaduri, Amit. L'accumulation du capital: temps logique et temps historique. (Capital Accumulation: Logical and Historical Time. With English summary.) *Écon. Appl.*, 1985, *38*(2), pp. 453–69.

Ciriacy-Wantrup, S. V. Natural Resources in Economic Growth: The Role of Institutions and Policies. In *Ciriacy-Wantrup, S. V.*, 1985, pp. 293–304. [G: India]

Coelho, Philip R. P. An Examination into the Causes of Economic Growth: Status as an Economic Good. In *Zerbe, R. O., Jr.*, ed., 1985, pp. 89–116.

Corden, W. Max. The Effects of Trade on the Rate of Growth. In *Corden, W. M.*, 1985, pp. 198–224.

Donders, J. H. M. The Golden Rule of Accumulation and the Open Economy. *De Economist*, 1985, *133*(4), pp. 545–57.

Falkinger, Josef. Optimales Wachstum bei Sättigung und Wachstumsaversion. (Optimal Growth in the Face of Satiation and Growth-Aversion. With English summary.) *Kyklos*, 1985, *38*(2), pp. 200–215.

Fazi, Elido and Salvadori, Neri. The Existence of a Two-Class Economy in a General Cambridge Model of Growth and Distribution. *Cambridge J. Econ.*, June 1985, *9*(2), pp. 155–64.

Findlay, Ronald F. Primary Exports, Manufacturing and Development. In *Lundahl, M.*, ed., 1985, pp. 218–33.

Franke, Reiner. On the Upper- and Lower-Bounds of Workers' Propensity to Save in a Two-Class Pasinetti Economy. *Australian Econ. Pap.*, December 1985, *24*(45), pp. 271–77.

Ghosh, Dipak. A Disequilibrium Interpretation of Kaldor's Technical Progress Function. *Bull. Econ. Res.*, January 1985, *37*(1), pp. 69–73.

Harris, Donald J. The Theory of Economic Growth: From Steady States to Uneven Development. In *Feiwel, G. R.*, ed. *(I)*, 1985, pp. 378–94.

Koopmans, Tjalling C. Concepts of Optimality and Their Uses. In *Koopmans, T. C.*, 1985, pp. 191–208.

Kormendi, Roger C. and Meguire, Philip G. Macroeconomic Determinants of Growth:

Cross-Country Evidence. *J. Monet. Econ.*, September 1985, *16*(2), pp. 141–63.

Laitner, John P. Stationary Equilibrium Transition Rules for an Overlapping Generations Model with Uncertainty. *J. Econ. Theory*, February 1985, *35*(1), pp. 83–108.

Leontief, Wassily. Theoretical Note on Time-Preference, Productivity of Capital, Stagnation, and Economic Growth. In *Leontief, W.*, 1985, pp. 175–84.

Manning, Richard. Optimal Human and Physical Capital Accumulation in a Fixed-Coefficients Economy. *Australian Econ. Pap.*, December 1985, *24*(45), pp. 258–70.

Mückl, Wolfgang J. Langfristige Grenzen der öffentlichen Kreditaufnahme. (Long-run Limits to Public Borrowing. With English summary.) *Jahr. Nationalökon. Statist.*, November 1985, *200*(6), pp. 565–81.

Nikaido, Hukukane. Dynamics of Growth and Capital Mobility in Marx's Scheme of Reproduction. *Z. Nationalökon.*, 1985, *45*(3), pp. 197–218.

Nuñez Miñana, Horacio. Distribución del ingreso y crecimiento económico: una propuesta de integracion de diferentes tradiciones. (Income Distribution and Economic Growth: An Integrated Proposal of Different Traditions. With English summary.) *Económica (La Plata)*, May-Dec. 1985, *31*(2–3), pp. 171–221.

Peschel, Manfred. Macromodels and Multiobjective Decision Making. In *Grauer, M.; Thompson, M. and Wierzbicki, A. P., eds.*, 1985, pp. 222–28.

Sato, Ryuzo. The Invariance Principle and Income– Wealth Conservation Laws: Application of Lie Groups and Related Transformations. *J. Econometrics*, Oct./Nov. 1985, *30*(1/2), pp. 365–89.

Steedman, Ian. On the 'Impossibility' of Hicks-Neutral Technical Change. *Econ. J.*, September 1985, *95*(379), pp. 746–58.

Taylor, Lance. A Stagnationist Model of Economic Growth. *Cambridge J. Econ.*, December 1985, *9*(4), pp. 383–403.

Zerbe, Richard O., Jr. Is the Attempt to Gain Status a Zero-Sum Game? In *Zerbe, R. O., Jr., ed.*, 1985, pp. 117–121.

1112 One and Two Sector Growth Models and Related Topics

Aiyagari, S. Rao. Observational Equivalence of the Overlapping Generations and the Discounted Dynamic Programming Frameworks for One-Sector Growth. *J. Econ. Theory*, April 1985, *35*(2), pp. 201–21.

Arrow, Kenneth J. Some Tests of the International Comparisons of Factor Efficiency with the CES Production Function: Reply. In *Arrow, K. J. (I)*, 1985, pp. 236–40.
[G: Selected Countries]

Arrow, Kenneth J. and Kurz, Mordecai. Optimal Growth with Irreversible Investment in a Ramsey Model. In *Arrow, K. J. (I)*, 1985, pp. 401–17.

Arrow, Kenneth J., et al. Capital–Labor Substitution and Economic Efficiency. In *Arrow, K. J. (I)*, 1985, pp. 50–103.
[G: Selected Countries]

Asimakopulos, Athanasios. Harrod on Harrod: The Evolution of a 'Line of Steady Growth.' *Hist. Polit. Econ.*, Winter 1985, *17*(4), pp. 619–35.

Bergan, Roar and Offerdal, Erik. Using the Oil Revenues: A Long Run Perspective. In *Bjerkholt, O. and Offerdal, E., eds.*, 1985, pp. 249–82.
[G: Norway]

Bhagwati, Jagdish N. Reflections on Unemployment Models in Development Theory. In *Bhagwati, J. N. (II)*, 1985, pp. 237–49.

Boyd, Chris. Industrial Investment in the European Community: Comment. In *Weiserbs, D., ed.*, 1985, pp. 21–23.
[G: EEC]

Carlberg, Michael. External versus Internal Public Debt—A Theoretical Analysis of the Long-run Burden. *Z. Nationalökon.*, 1985, *45*(2), pp. 141–54.

Chappell, David. On Optimal Economic Growth with Intertemporally Dependent Preferences. *Indian Econ. J.*, Apr.-June 1985, *32*(4), pp. 29–38.

Chisari, Omar O. Growth, Inflation and Rules of Active and Passive Mark-up Factor. *Econ. Notes*, 1985, (2), pp. 57–67.

Fazzari, Steven M. Keynes, Harrod, and the Rational Expectations Revolution. *J. Post Keynesian Econ.*, Fall 1985, *8*(1), pp. 66–80.

Furubotn, Eirik G. Long Swings of Economic Development, Social Time Preference and Institution Change: Comment. *Z. ges. Staatswiss. (JITE)*, March 1985, *141*(1), pp. 36–40.

George, Donald A. R. Wage-Earners' Investment Funds in the Long Run. *Econ. Anal. Worker's Manage.*, 1985, *19*(1), pp. 13–28.

Gerard, M. and Vanden Berghe, C. Econometric Analysis of Sectoral Investment in Belgium (1956–1982). In *Weiserbs, D., ed.*, 1985, pp. 81–110.
[G: Belgium]

Ginsburgh, Victor; Hénin, Pierre-Yves and Michel, Philippe. A Dual Decision Approach to Disequilibrium Growth. *Oxford Econ. Pap.*, September 1985, *37*(3), pp. 353–61.

Hahn, Frank. Equilibrium Dynamics with Heterogeneous Capital Goods. In *Hahn, F.*, 1985, pp. 243–60.

Hahn, Frank. On Two-Sector Growth Models. In *Hahn, F.*, 1985, pp. 231–42.

Hahn, Frank. The Stability of Growth Equilibrium. In *Hahn, F.*, 1985, pp. 278–300.

Imagawa, Takeshi. Export as an Additional Variable in the Income Determining Function of H-D Type Growth Model. *Devel. Econ.*, June 1985, *23*(2), pp. 105–20.
[G: LDCs]

Koopmans, Tjalling C. Some Observations on 'Optimal' Economic Growth and Exhaustible Resources. In *Koopmans, T. C.*, 1985, pp. 163–79.

Kornai, János and Simonovits, András. Investment, Efficiency, and Shortage: A Macrogrowth Model. *Matekon*, Winter 1985-86, *22*(2), pp. 3–29.

Krüger, Michael. A Reconsideration of the Stability Properties of Goodwin's Model of the Growth Cycle. *Econ. Notes,* 1985, (2), pp. 22–37.

Kümmel, Reiner and Strassl, W. Changing Energy Prices, Information Technology, and Industrial Growth. In *van Gool, W. and Bruggink, J. J. C., eds.,* 1985, pp. 175–94. [G: W. Germany; U.S.]

McDonald, Ian M. Market Power and Unemployment. *Int. J. Ind. Organ.,* March 1985, *3*(1), pp. 21–35.

Nakao, Takeo. The Effects of Demonopolization on Economic Growth. *Can. J. Econ.,* August 1985, *18*(3), pp. 622–35.

Neumann, Manfred. Long Swings in Economic Development, Social Time Preference and Institutional Change. *Z. ges. Staatswiss. (JITE),* March 1985, *141*(1), pp. 21–35. [G: U.S.]

van der Ploeg, Frederick. Classical Growth Cycles. *Metroecon.,* June 1985, *37*(2), pp. 221–30.

Reid, Gavin C. Keynes versus the Classics: Fluctuations and Growth. *Scot. J. Polit. Econ.,* November 1985, *32*(3), pp. 315–27.

Ritschl, Albrecht. On the Stability of the Steady State When Population Is Decreasing. *Z. Nationalökon.,* 1985, *45*(2), pp. 161–70.

Sato, Yoshikazu. Marx–Goodwin Growth Cycles in a Two-Sector Economy. *Z. Nationalökon.,* 1985, *45*(1), pp. 21–34.

Targetti, Ferdinando. Growth and the Terms of Trade: A Kaldorian Two Sector Model. *Metroecon.,* February 1985, *37*(1), pp. 79–96.

Tirole, Jean. Asset Bubbles and Overlapping Generations. *Econometrica,* November 1985, *53*(6), pp. 1499–1528.

Weiserbs, Daniel. Industrial Investment in the European Community. In *Weiserbs, D., ed.,* 1985, pp. 7–20. [G: EEC]

Westaway, A. J. Econometric Analysis of Sectoral Investment in Belgium (1956–1982): Comment. In *Weiserbs, D., ed.,* 1985, pp. 111–13. [G: Belgium]

Wildasin, David E. On the Analysis of Labor and Capital Income Taxation in a Growing Economy with Government Saving. *Public Finance,* 1985, *40*(1), pp. 114–32.

1113 Multisector Growth Models and Related Topics

Beals, Richard and Koopmans, Tjalling C. Maximizing Stationary Utility in a Constant Technology. In *Koopmans, T. C.,* 1985, pp. 13–27.

Benhabib, Jess and Nishimura, Kazuo. Competitive Equilibrium Cycles. *J. Econ. Theory,* April 1985, *35*(2), pp. 284–306.

Bergman, Lars. Extensions and Applications of the MSG-Model: A Brief Survey. In *[Johansen, L.],* 1985, pp. 127–61.

Biji, Elena; Tănăsoiu, O. and Tănăsoiu, D. Maximizing the Development Fund Efficiency: A Criterion for Accumulation Rate Optimization. *Econ. Computat. Cybern. Stud. Res.,* 1985, *20*(3), pp. 27–32.

Coles, Jeffrey Link. Equilibrium Turnpike Theory with Constant Returns to Scale and Possible Heterogeneous Discount Factors. *Int. Econ. Rev.,* October 1985, *26*(3), pp. 671–79.

DasGupta, Swapan. A Local Analysis of Stability and Regularity of Stationary States in Discrete Symmetric Optimal Capital Accumulation Models. *J. Econ. Theory,* August 1985, *36*(2), pp. 302–18.

Feinstein, C. D. and Oren, Shmuel S. A 'Funnel' Turnpike Theorem for Optimal Growth Problems with Discounting. *J. Econ. Dynam. Control,* September 1985, *9*(1), pp. 25–39.

Gaines, Robert E. and Peterson, James K. The Existence of Optimal Consumption Policies in Optimal Economic Growth Models with Nonconvex Technologies. *J. Econ. Theory,* October 1985, *37*(1), pp. 76–98.

Ghosh, Dipak and Mizuno, Yasumasa. Causes of Growth in the Japanese Economy from a Kaldorian Point of View. *Pakistan Econ. Soc. Rev.,* Winter 1985, *23*(2), pp. 151–63. [G: Japan]

Hahn, Frank. On the Disequilibrium Behaviour of a Multi-sectoral Growth Model. In *Hahn, F.,* 1985, pp. 301–21.

Hahn, Frank. On Some Equilibrium Paths. In *Hahn, F.,* 1985, pp. 322–37.

Hahn, Frank. On Warranted Growth Paths. In *Hahn, F.,* 1985, pp. 261–77.

Hansen, Terje and Koopmans, Tjalling C. On the Definition and Computation of a Capital Stock Invariant under Optimization. In *Koopmans, T. C.,* 1985, pp. 125–61.

Kaganovich, Mikhail. Efficiency of Sliding Plans in a Linear Model with Time-Dependent Technology. *Rev. Econ. Stud.,* October 1985, *52*(4), pp. 691–702.

Miernyk, William H. Bioeconomics: A Realistic Appraisal of Future Prospects. In *Didsbury, H. F., Jr., ed.,* 1985, pp. 334–52.

Pekkala, Ahti. Vuoden 1986 tulo- ja menoarvio. (The Budget for 1986. With English summary.) *Kansant. Aikak.,* 1985, *81*(4), pp. 375–80. [G: Finland]

Persson, Håkan. A Version of the MSG-Model with Putty–Clay and Vintage Technology. In *[Johansen, L.],* 1985, pp. 163–85.

Rubinov, A. M. Dynamics of Neumann-type Economic Macrosystems. In *Aubin, J.-P.; Saari, D. and Sigmund, K., eds.,* 1985, pp. 127–36.

Solow, Robert M. Leif Johansen's Contributions to the Theory of Production, Planning, and Multisectoral Growth. In *[Johansen, L.],* 1985, pp. 1–9.

Szyld, Daniel B. Conditions for the Existence of a Balanced Growth Solution for the Leontief Dynamic Input–Output Model. *Econometrica,* November 1985, *53*(6), pp. 1411–19.

Wolff, Reiner. Efficient Growth of an Agglomerating Regional Economy. *Reg. Sci. Urban Econ.,* November 1985, *15*(4), pp. 555–72.

Yano, Makoto. Competitive Equilibria on Turnpikes in a McKenzie Economy, II: An Asymptotic Turnpike Theorem. *Int. Econ. Rev.,* October 1985, *26*(3), pp. 661–69.

1114 Monetary Growth Models

Abel, Andrew B. Dynamic Behavior of Capital Accumulation in a Cash-in-Advance Model. *J. Monet. Econ.*, July 1985, *16*(1), pp. 55–71.

Cohen, Daniel. Inflation, Wealth and Interest Rates in an Intertemporal Optimizing Model. *J. Monet. Econ.*, July 1985, *16*(1), pp. 73–85.

Djondang, Paul. Financement extérieur et dynamique macroéconomique des pays en développement. (With English summary.) *Revue Écon. Polit.*, July-August 1985, *95*(4), pp. 442–68.

Hong, Kyttack. Macroeconomic Dynamics in a Financially Repressed Economy. *J. Econ. Devel.*, July 1985, *10*(1), pp. 169–94.
[G: LDCs]

Ihori, Toshihiro and Kurosaka, Yoshio. Fiscal Policies, Government's Deficits and Capital Formation. *Econ. Stud. Quart.*, August 1985, *36*(2), pp. 106–20.

Kapur, Basant K. Money in Development: Comment. *Southern Econ. J.*, April 1985, *51*(4), pp. 1230–39.

Kapur, Basant K. The Role of Financial Institutions in Economic Development—A Theoretical Analysis. In *Gutowski, A.; Arnaudo, A. A. and Scharrer, H.-E., eds.*, 1985, pp. 83–97.

Krelle, Wilhelm. On the Stability of Growth Models with Money. *Rivista Int. Sci. Econ. Com.*, March 1985, *32*(3), pp. 233–52.

Kumar, Ramesh S. Money in Development: Reply. *Southern Econ. J.*, April 1985, *51*(4), pp. 1240–44.

Neary, J. Peter. Real and Monetary Aspects of the 'Dutch Disease.' In *Jungenfelt, K. and Hague, D. [Sir], eds.*, 1985, pp. 353–80.

112 Economic Development Models and Theories

1120 Economic Development Models and Theories

Abel, Christopher and Lewis, Colin M. Latin America, Economic Imperialism and the State: Introduction. In *Abel, C. and Lewis, C. M., eds.*, 1985, pp. 1–25. [G: Latin America]

Afxentiou, P. C. Fiscal Structure, Tax Effort and Economic Development. *Econ. Int.*, Aug./Nov. 1985, *38*(3/4), pp. 286–302.

Agarwala, Ramgopal. Planning in Developing Countries. *Finance Develop.*, March 1985, *22*(1), pp. 13–16. [G: LDCs]

Agbonyitor, Alberto D. K. Recurrent Expenditure Commitment, External Imbalance, Devaluation and Inflation in the Developing Economies. *J. Econ. Devel.*, December 1985, *10*(2), pp. 87–99. [G: LDCs]

Ahiakpor, James C. W. The Success and Failure of Dependency Theory: The Experience of Ghana. *Int. Organ.*, Summer 1985, *39*(3), pp. 535–52. [G: Ghana]

Ahmed, Osman Sheikh and Field, Alfred J., Jr. Potential Effects of Income-Redistribution Policies on the Final Pattern of Income Distribution: The Case of Kenya. *J. Devel. Areas*, October 1985, *20*(1), pp. 1–21. [G: Kenya]

Ahsan, Syed M. and Ali, Ali A. G. Income Taxation, Migration, and Work Incentives in a Dual Economy Model. *Devel. Econ.*, March 1985, *23*(1), pp. 16–39.

Alam, M. Shahid. Some Notes on Work Ethos and Economic Development. *World Devel.*, February 1985, *13*(2), pp. 251–54.
[G: LDCs]

Alchian, Armen. A Weberian Analysis of Economic Progress: The Case of Resource Exporting LDCs: Comment. *Z. ges. Staatswiss. (JITE)*, March 1985, *141*(1), pp. 184–86.

de Almeida Vasconcelos, Pedro. Le travail informel urbain: Une évaluation de la littérature. (With English summary.) *Can. J. Devel. Stud.*, 1985, *6*(1), pp. 87–124. [G: Latin America]

Amin, Samir. The Crisis, the Third World, and North–South, East–West Relations. In *[Magdoff, H. and Sweezy, P.]*, 1985, pp. 1–8.

Anand, Sudhir and Kanbur, S. M. R. Poverty under the Kuznets Process. *Econ. J.*, Supplement 1985, *95*, pp. 42–50.

Andrews, Margaret S. Agricultural Terms of Trade and Distributional Perversities in a Neo-Ricardian Model. *J. Devel. Econ.*, January–February 1985, *17*(1–2), pp. 117–29.

Andrews, Margaret S. Profit, Rent, and the Terms of Trade: A Rejoinder [Agricultural Terms of Trade and Distributional Perversities in a Neo-Ricardian Model]. *J. Devel. Econ.*, January–February 1985, *17*(1–2), pp. 141–49.

Anthony, Peter Dean. Basic Commodities, Growth and Labor Absorption. *Eastern Econ. J.*, July-Sept. 1985, *11*(3), pp. 248–56.

Arndt, H. W. The Origins of Structuralism. *World Devel.*, February 1985, *13*(2), pp. 151–59.
[G: LDCs]

Arrow, Kenneth J. Economic Development: The Present State of the Art. In *Arrow, K. J. (II)*, 1985, pp. 183–207.

Bakalis, Steve and Hazari, Bharat R. Unemployment, Capital Underutilization and Welfare in a Small Open Economy. *Greek Econ. Rev.*, December 1985, *7*(3), pp. 226–41.

Balassa, Bela. Adjustment Policies in Developing Economies: A Reassessment. In *Balassa, B.*, 1985, pp. 89–101. [G: LDCs]

Balassa, Bela. Disequilibrium Analysis in Developing Economies: An Overview. In *Balassa, B.*, 1985, pp. 24–43. [G: LDCs]

Balassa, Bela. Exports, Policy Choices, and Economic Growth in Developing Countries after the 1973 Oil Shock. *J. Devel. Econ.*, May–June 1985, *18*(1), pp. 23–35. [G: LDCs]

Balassa, Bela. Structural Adjustment Policies in Developing Economies. In *Balassa, B.*, 1985, pp. 63–88. [G: LDCs]

Balassa, Bela. The Cambridge Group and the Developing Countries. *World Econ.*, September 1985, *8*(3), pp. 201–18.
[G: Mexico; Tanzania; LDCs]

Bandyopadhyay, R. Finance and Development: An Integrative Framework. In *Bandyopa-*

dhyay, R. and Khankhoje, D. P., eds., 1985, pp. 21–40.

Baum, Warren C. and Tolbert, Stokes M. Investing in Development: Lessons of World Bank Experience. *Finance Develop.*, December 1985, 22(4), pp. 25–30. **[G: LDCs]**

Berg-Schlosser, Dirk. Leistungen und Fehlleistungen politischer Systeme der Dritten Welt als Kriterium der Entwicklungspolitik. (The Performance of Third World Political Systems as a Criterion for Development Aid. With English summary.) *Konjunkturpolitik*, 1985, 31(1/2), pp. 79–114. **[G: LDCs]**

Bhagwati, Jagdish N. Development Economics: What Have We Learnt? In *Bhagwati, J. N. (II)*, 1985, pp. 13–31.

Bhagwati, Jagdish N. Developmental Strategy: Import Substitution versus Export Promotion. In *Bhagwati, J. N. (I)*, 1985, pp. 65–67.

Bhagwati, Jagdish N. Economic Structure: Regularities and Explanations. In *Bhagwati, J. N. (II)*, 1985, pp. 73–78.

Bhagwati, Jagdish N. Export Promotion as a Developmental Strategy. In *Shishido, T. and Sato, R., eds.*, 1985, pp. 59–68. **[G: LDCs]**

Bhagwati, Jagdish N. Food Aid, Agricultural Production and Welfare. In *Bhagwati, J. N. (I)*, 1985, pp. 285–97.

Bhagwati, Jagdish N. Foreign Trade Regimes. In *Bhagwati, J. N. (I)*, 1985, pp. 123–37.

Bhagwati, Jagdish N. Gunnar Myrdal [Need for Reforms in Underdeveloped Countries]. In *Bhagwati, J. N. (II)*, 1985, pp. 306–12.

Bhagwati, Jagdish N. Raul Prebisch: I [The Latin American Periphery in the Global System of Capitalism]. In *Bhagwati, J. N. (II)*, 1985, pp. 292–96.

Bhagwati, Jagdish N. Raul Prebisch: II [Five States in My Thinking on Development]. In *Bhagwati, J. N. (II)*, 1985, pp. 297–305.

Bhagwati, Jagdish N. The Nature of Balance of Payments Difficulties in Developing Countries. In *Bhagwati, J. N. (I)*, 1985, pp. 138–43.

Bhagwati, Jagdish N. W. Arthur Lewis: An Appreciation. In *Bhagwati, J. N. (II)*, 1985, pp. 277–91.

Bhagwati, Jagdish N. Wealth and Poverty: Introduction. In *Bhagwati, J. N. (II)*, 1985, pp. 1–9.

Bhagwati, Jagdish N. What We Need to Know. In *Bhagwati, J. N. (I)*, 1985, pp. 80–87.

Bhagwati, Jagdish N. Why Does the Share of Manufacturing in GNP Rise with Development? [Transitional Growth and World Industrialisation]. In *Bhagwati, J. N. (II)*, 1985, pp. 79–81. **[G: LDCs; MDCs]**

Bhagwati, Jagdish N. and Krueger, Anne O. Exchange Control, Liberalization and Economic Development. In *Bhagwati, J. N. (I)*, 1985, pp. 68–79.

Bhagwati, Jagdish N. and Sihag, Balabir S. Dual Markets, Rationing and Queues. In *Bhagwati, J. N. (II)*, 1985, pp. 205–09.

Bhagwati, Jagdish N. and Srinivasan, T. N. The Ranking of Policy Interventions under Factor Market Imperfections: The Case of Sector-Specific Sticky Wages and Unemployment. In *Bhagwati, J. N. (II)*, 1985, pp. 250–67.

Bhagwati, Jagdish N. and Srinivasan, T. N. Trade Policy and Development. In *Bhagwati, J. N. (I)*, 1985, pp. 88–122.

Bhalla, A. S. and Fluitman, A. G. Science and Technology Indicators and Socio-economic Development. *World Devel.*, February 1985, 13(2), pp. 177–90.

Bhattacharyya, Bharati. The Role of Family Decision in Internal Migration: The Case of India. *J. Devel. Econ.*, May–June 1985, 18(1), pp. 51–66. **[G: India]**

Blair, Harry W. Reorienting Development Administration: Review Article. *J. Devel. Stud.*, April 1985, 21(3), pp. 449–57.

Blau, David M. Self-Employment and Self-Selection in Developing Country Labor Markets. *Southern Econ. J.*, October 1985, 52(2), pp. 351–63. **[G: Malaysia]**

Blomqvist, Ake G. An Analytical Approach to Interest Rate Determination in Developing Countries: Comments. *Pakistan Devel. Rev.*, Autumn-Winter 1985, 24(3/4), pp. 494–95. **[G: Pakistan]**

Blomqvist, Ake G. On Some Neglected Topics in Development Economics: Comments. *Pakistan Devel. Rev.*, Autumn-Winter 1985, 24(3/4), pp. 260–63.

Blumenthal, Tuvia and Lee, Chung H. Development Strategies of Japan and the Republic of Korea: A Comparative Study. *Devel. Econ.*, September 1985, 23(3), pp. 221–35. **[G: Japan; S. Korea]**

Bois, Guy. Against the Neo-Malthusian Orthodoxy. In *Aston, T. H. and Philpin, C. H. E., eds.*, 1985, pp. 107–18.

Booth, David. Marxism and Development Sociology: Interpreting the Impasse. *World Devel.*, July 1985, 13(7), pp. 761–87. **[G: LDCs]**

Borpujari, Jitendra G. Savings Generation and Financial Programming in a Basic Need Constrained Developing Economy. In *Gutowski, A.; Arnaudo, A. A. and Scharrer, H.-E., eds.*, 1985, pp. 59–82. **[G: India]**

Brenner, Robert. Agrarian Class Structure and Economic Development in Pre-industrial Europe. In *Aston, T. H. and Philpin, C. H. E., eds.*, 1985, pp. 10–63.

Brenner, Robert. The Agrarian Roots of European Capitalism. In *Aston, T. H. and Philpin, C. H. E., eds.*, 1985, pp. 213–327.

Brochart, Françoise. Exportation et croissance économique: Application aux pays africains de la zone franc. (With English summary.) *Revue Écon. Polit.*, July-August 1985, 95(4), pp. 469–83. **[G: Africa]**

Bromley, Daniel W. Resources and Economic Development: An Institutionalist Perspective. *J. Econ. Issues*, September 1985, 19(3), pp. 779–96.

Browett, John. The Newly Industrializing Countries and Radical Theories of Development.

World Devel., July 1985, *13*(7), pp. 789–803.
[G: S. Korea; Taiwan; Hong Kong; Singapore]

Bruton, Henry J. The Search for a Development Economics. *World Devel.*, Oct./Nov. 1985, *13*(10/11), pp. 1099–1124.

Cernea, Michael M. Sociological Knowledge for Development Projects. In *Cernea, M. M., ed.*, 1985, pp. 3–21. [G: LDCs]

Chichilnisky, Graciela and Heal, Geoffrey M. Trade and Development in the 1980s. In *Bapna, A., ed.*, 1985, pp. 195–239.
[G: LDCs; MDCs]

Choudhry, Nanda K. and Datta, Arun K. Changing Perspectives on the Role of Multinationals in Economic Development: Some Evidence from India. *Can. J. Devel. Stud.*, 1985, *6*(1), pp. 77–85. [G: India]

Chu, David K. Y. and Wong, Kwan-Yiu. Modernization and the Lessons of the Special Economic Zones. In *Wong, K. and Chu, D. K. Y., eds.*, 1985, pp. 208–17.

Clausen, A. W. Population Growth and Economic and Social Development. *J. Econ. Educ.*, Summer 1985, *16*(3), pp. 165–76.

Cline, William R. Reply [Can the East Asian Model of Development Be Generalized?]. *World Devel.*, April 1985, *13*(4), pp. 547–48.

Cohen, John M.; Grindle, Merilee S. and Walker, S. Tjip. Foreign Aid and Conditions Precedent: Political and Bureaucratic Dimensions. *World Devel.*, December 1985, *13*(12), pp. 1211–30.

Cohen, Suleiman I. The Controversial Debate on Development Economics: An Opinion. *Pakistan Devel. Rev.*, Spring 1985, *24*(1), pp. 61–76.

Cole, William E. and Sanders, Richard D. Internal Migration and Urban Employment in the Third World. *Amer. Econ. Rev.*, June 1985, *75*(3), pp. 481–94. [G: Mexico; India; Colombia; Nigeria]

Connolly, Michael. On the Optimal Currency Peg for Developing Countries [A Survey of the Literature on the Optimal Peg]. *J. Devel. Econ.*, August 1985, *18*(2–3), pp. 555–59.
[G: LDCs]

Cooper, J. P. In Search of Agrarian Capitalism. In *Aston, T. H. and Philpin, C. H. E., eds.*, 1985, pp. 138–91.

Corden, W. Max and Findlay, Ronald F. Urban Unemployment, Intersectoral Capital Mobility and Development Policy. In *Corden, W. M.*, 1985, pp. 73–93.

Crnković-Pozaić, Sanja. The Relationship between the Level of Development and the Rate of Growth: Some Empirical Evidence. *Econ. Anal. Worker's Manage.*, 1985, *19*(1), pp. 29–63. [G: LDCs; MDCs]

Croot, Patricia and Parker, David. Agrarian Class Structure and the Development of Capitalism: France and England Compared. In *Aston, T. H. and Philpin, C. H. E., eds.*, 1985, pp. 79–90.

Cundiff, Edward W. and Hilger, Marye Tharp. The Consumption Function and the Role of

Marketing in Global Economic Development. In *Kaynak, E., ed. (I)*, 1985, pp. 121–32.
[G: LDCs]

Curry, Robert L., Jr. Mineral-based Growth and Development-generated Socioeconomic Problems in Botswana: Rural Inequality, Water Scarcity, Food Insecurity, and Foreign Dependence Challenge New Governing Class. *Amer. J. Econ. Soc.*, July 1985, *44*(3), pp. 319–36.
[G: Botswana]

Dietz, James L. Export-Enclave Economies, International Corporations, and Development. *J. Econ. Issues*, June 1985, *19*(2), pp. 512–22.

Dinwiddy, Caroline and Teal, Francis. Shadow Prices and Cost-Benefit Rules for Non-traded Commodities in a Second Best Economy. *Oxford Econ. Pap.*, December 1985, *37*(4), pp. 683–90.

Djondang, Paul. Financement extérieur et dynamique macroéconomique des pays en développement. (With English summary.) *Revue Écon. Polit.*, July-August 1985, *95*(4), pp. 442–68.

Dolman, Antony J. Paradise Lost? The Past Performance and Future Prospects of Small Island Developing Countries. In *Dommen, E. and Hein, P., eds.*, 1985, pp. 40–69.

Donaldson, Thomas. The Feasibility of Welfare Rights in Less Developed Countries: Comment: Trading Justice for Bread. In *Kipnis, K. and Meyers, D. T., eds.*, 1985, pp. 226–28.
[G: LDCs]

Dopfer, Kurt. Reconciling Economic Theory and Economic History: The Rise of Japan. *J. Econ. Issues*, March 1985, *19*(1), pp. 21–73.
[G: Japan]

Dowling, J. Malcolm, Jr.; Ali, Ifzal and Soo, David. Income Distribution, Poverty and Economic Growth in Developing Asian Countries. *Singapore Econ. Rev.*, April 1985, *30*(1), pp. 1–13. [G: Asia]

Elliott, John E. Schumpeter's Theory of Economic Development and Social Change: Exposition and Assessment. *Int. J. Soc. Econ.*, 1985, *12*(6/7), pp. 6–33.

Emmerij, Louis. National and International Strategies for Development. In *Bapna, A., ed.*, 1985, pp. 181–88. [G: LDCs; MDCs]

Eskridge, William N., Jr. Santa Claus and Sigmund Freud: Structural Contexts of the International Debt Problem. In *Eskridge, W. N., Jr., ed.*, 1985, pp. 27–101.

Esser, Klaus. Modification of the Industrialization Model in Latin America. *Cepal Rev.*, August 1985, (26), pp. 101–13. [G: Latin America]

Fairbairn, Te'o Ian and Kakazu, Hiroshi. Trade and Diversification in Small Island Economies with Particular Emphasis on the South Pacific. *Singapore Econ. Rev.*, October 1985, *30*(2), pp. 17–35. [G: Asia; Oceania]

FitzGerald, E. V. K. The Problem of Balance in the Peripheral Socialist Economy: A Conceptual Note. *World Devel.*, January 1985, *13*(1), pp. 5–14.

Fløystad, Gunnar. Free Trade versus Protection: Static and Dynamic Aspects. *Pakistan Devel.*

Rev., Spring 1985, *24*(1), pp. 39–50.
[G: LDCs]

Foggin, Peter M. Canadian Geographers and International Development Studies. *Can. J. Devel. Stud.*, 1985, *6*(2), pp. 313–22.
[G: Canada]

Foltýn, Jaroslav. Some Differentiation Trends in the Developing Countries and Their Significance for the Application of a Typologic Approach in Economic Research. *Czech. Econ. Pap.*, 1985, *23*, pp. 137–49. [G: LDCs]

Fransman, Martin. Conceptualising Technical Change in the Third World in the 1980s: An Interpretive Survey. *J. Devel. Stud.*, July 1985, *21*(4), pp. 572–652. [G: LDCs]

Freeman, Katherine B. Reflections on Need Achievement and International Differences in Income Growth: 1950–1960. *Econ. Develop. Cult. Change*, July 1985, *33*(4), pp. 865–77.

Froomkin, Joseph. Can Government Finance Play a Central Role in Economic Development? Review Article. *Econ. Develop. Cult. Change*, July 1985, *33*(4), pp. 879–86.
[G: LDCs]

Furubotn, Eirik G. Long Swings of Economic Development, Social Time Preference and Institution Change: Comment. *Z. ges. Staatswiss. (JITE)*, March 1985, *141*(1), pp. 36–40.

Gang, Ira N. and Gangapadhyay, Shubhashis. A Note on Optimal Policies in Dual Economies. *Quart. J. Econ.*, Supp. 1985, *100*, pp. 1067–71.

Garavello, Oscar. La svalutazione nei P.V.S. con estese rigidità dell'offerta: un'analisi settoriale. (Devaluation and Stagflation in L.D.C.s: The Role of Supply Rigidity. With English summary.) *Rivista Int. Sci. Econ. Com.*, May 1985, *32*(5), pp. 427–52. [G: LDCs]

Ghosh, Dipak. A Lewisian Model of Dual Economy with Rural–Urban Migration. *Scot. J. Polit. Econ.*, February 1985, *32*(1), pp. 95–106.

Gibson, Bill. A Structuralist Macromodel for Postrevolutionary Nicaragua. *Cambridge J. Econ.*, December 1985, *9*(4), pp. 347–69.
[G: Nicaragua]

Gibson, Bill and McLeon, Darryl. Profit, Rent, and the Terms of Trade: A Reply [Terms of Trade Policy in a Model with Non-produced Means of Production] [Agricultural Terms of Trade and Distributional Perversities in a Neo-Ricardian Model]. *J. Devel. Econ.*, January–February 1985, *17*(1–2), pp. 131–39.

Gorin, Zeev. Socialist Societies and World System Theory: A Critical Survey. *Sci. Soc.*, Fall 1985, *49*(3), pp. 332–66.

Grabowski, Richard and Sivan, David. The Price of Food, Labor Scarcity and the Real Wage: Egypt, 1950 to 1974. *Pakistan J. Appl. Econ.*, Winter 1985, *4*(2), pp. 93–99. [G: Egypt]

Griffin, Keith and Gurley, John. Radical Analyses of Imperialism, the Third World, and the Transition to Socialism: A Survey Article. *J. Econ. Lit.*, September 1985, *23*(3), pp. 1089–1143.
[G: Global]

Griffith-Jones, Stephany. World Prices and Development: Introduction. In *Griffith-Jones, S.*

and Harvey, C., eds., 1985, pp. 1–12.

Griffith-Jones, Stephany and Harvey, Charles. World Prices and Development: Conclusions. In *Griffith-Jones, S. and Harvey, C., eds.*, 1985, pp. 311–49. [G: Selected LDCs]

Grossman, Gene M. The Optimal Tariff for a Small Country under International Uncertainty: A Comment. *Oxford Econ. Pap.*, March 1985, *37*(1), pp. 154–58.

Gupta, Kanhaya L. Foreign Capital, Income Inequality, Demographic Pressures, Savings and Growth in Developing Countries: A Cross Country Analysis. *J. Econ. Devel.*, July 1985, *10*(1), pp. 63–88. [G: LDCs]

Hagen, Everett E. More on the Employment Effects of Innovation: More than a Response [Technological Disemployment and Economic Growth]. *J. Devel. Econ.*, January–February 1985, *17*(1–2), pp. 163–73.

Hall, P. H. and Heffernan, Shelagh A. More on the Employment Effects of Innovation [Technological Disemployment and Economic Growth]. *J. Devel. Econ.*, January–February 1985, *17*(1–2), pp. 151–62.

Hazari, Bharat R. and Bakalis, Steve. An Analysis of Capital Underutilization in Less Developed Countries—A Trade Theoretic Approach. *Devel. Econ.*, March 1985, *23*(1), pp. 3–15.

Hein, Philippe L. The Study of Microstates. In *Dommen, E. and Hein, P., eds.*, 1985, pp. 16–29. [G: Selected Countries]

Hilton, R. H. A Crisis of Feudalism. In *Aston, T. H. and Philpin, C. H. E., eds.*, 1985, pp. 119–37.

Hilton, R. H. The Brenner Debate: Introduction. In *Aston, T. H. and Philpin, C. H. E., eds.*, 1985, pp. 1–9.

Hoffman, Kurt. Microelectronics, International Competition and Development Strategies: The Unavoidable Issues—Editor's Introduction. *World Devel.*, March 1985, *13*(3), pp. 263–72.

Imagawa, Takeshi. Export as an Additional Variable in the Income Determining Function of H–D Type Growth Model. *Devel. Econ.*, June 1985, *23*(2), pp. 105–20. [G: LDCs]

Imam, M. Hasan and Whalley, John. Incidence Analysis of a Sector-specific Minimum Wage in a Two-Sector Harris–Todaro Model. *Quart. J. Econ.*, February 1985, *100*(1), pp. 207–24.
[G: Mexico]

Itagaki, Takao. Optimal Tariffs for a Large and a Small Country under Uncertain Terms of Trade. *Oxford Econ. Pap.*, June 1985, *37*(2), pp. 292–97.

Ize, Alain and Salas, Javier. Prices and Output in the Mexican Economy: Empirical Testing of Alternative Hypotheses. *J. Devel. Econ.*, April 1985, *17*(3), pp. 175–99. [G: Mexico]

Jabara, Cathy L. and Thompson, Robert L. The Optimal Tariff for a Small Country under International Price Uncertainty: A Reply. *Oxford Econ. Pap.*, March 1985, *37*(1), pp. 159.

James, Jeffrey. The Role of Appropriate Technology in a Redistributive Development Strategy. In *James, J. and Watanabe, S., eds.*, 1985, pp. 116–33.

James, Jeffrey and Gutkind, Efraim. Attitude Change Revisited: Cognitive Dissonance Theory and Development Policy. *World Devel.*, Oct./Nov. 1985, *13*(10/11), pp. 1139–49.

de Janvry, Alain. Social Disarticulation in Latin American History. In *Kim, K. S. and Ruccio, D. F., eds.*, 1985, pp. 32–73. [G: Argentina; Brazil; Chile]

Jao, Y. C. Financial Deepening and Economic Growth: Theory, Evidence and Policy. *Greek Econ. Rev.*, December 1985, *7*(3), pp. 187–225. [G: LDCs]

Jha, L. K. Demand Problem in Indian Economy. In *Jha, L. K.*, 1985, pp. 60–69. [G: India]

Jha, L. K. Development without Inflation. In *Jha, L. K.*, 1985, pp. 110–19. [G: India]

Jha, L. K. Political Economy of Underdevelopment. In *Jha, L. K.*, 1985, pp. 167–78. [G: India]

Jha, L. K. Technology and Development. In *Jha, L. K.*, 1985, pp. 1–22. [G: India]

Jones, F. Stuart. Britain and the Economic Development of Tropical Africa, Asia and South America in the Age of Imperialism (Review Article). *S. Afr. J. Econ.*, September 1985, *53*(3), pp. 264–86. [G: U.K.; LDCs]

Jorge, Antonio. Development Strategies, Trade and External Debt in Latin America. In *Jorge, A.; Salazar-Carrillo, J. and Diaz-Pou, F., eds.*, 1985, pp. 1–14. [G: Latin America]

Jung, Woo S. and Marshall, Peyton J. Exports, Growth, and Causality in Developing Countries. *J. Devel. Econ.*, May–June 1985, *18*(1), pp. 1–12. [G: LDCs]

Kader, Ahmad A. Development Patterns among Countries Reexamined. *Devel. Econ.*, September 1985, *23*(3), pp. 199–220. [G: LDCs; MDCs]

de Kadt, Emanuel. Of Markets, Might and Mullahs: A Case for Equity, Pluralism and Tolerance in Development [The Meaning of Development]. *World Devel.*, April 1985, *13*(4), pp. 549–56.

Kannappan, Subbiah. Urban Employment and the Labor Market in Developing Nations. *Econ. Develop. Cult. Change*, July 1985, *33*(4), pp. 699–730. [G: LDCs]

Kapur, Basant K. Money in Development: Comment. *Southern Econ. J.*, April 1985, *51*(4), pp. 1230–39.

Kavoussi, Rostam M. International Trade and Economic Development: The Recent Experience of Developing Countries. *J. Devel. Areas*, April 1985, *19*(3), pp. 379–92. [G: LDCs]

Kelley, Allen C. Population and Development: Controversy and Reconciliation. *J. Econ. Educ.*, Summer 1985, *16*(3), pp. 177–88.

Khan, M. Ali. On Some Neglected Topics in Development Economics. *Pakistan Devel. Rev.*, Autumn-Winter 1985, *24*(3/4), pp. 237–59.

Khan, M. Ali and Chaudhuri, T. Datta. Development Policies in LDC's with Several Ethnic Groups—A Theoretical Analysis. *Z. Nationalökon.*, 1985, *45*(1), pp. 1–19. [G: LDCs]

Khan, Mohsin S. An Analytical Approach to Interest Rate Determination in Developing Countries. *Pakistan Devel. Rev.*, Autumn-Winter 1985, *24*(3/4), pp. 481–93. [G: LDCs]

Kim, Kwan S. and Ruccio, David F. Debt and Development in Latin America: Introduction. In *Kim, K. S. and Ruccio, D. F., eds.*, 1985, pp. 1–5.

Klein, Saul A. The Role of Marketing in Economic Development. *Quart. J. Bus. Econ.*, Autumn 1985, *24*(4), pp. 54–69.

Klima, Arnost. Agrarian Class Structure and Economic Development in Pre-industrial Bohemia. In *Aston, T. H. and Philpin, C. H. E., eds.*, 1985, pp. 192–212.

Kondonassis, Alex J. Some Internal Problems of Social Sciences: The Economics of Less Developed Countries. *Soc. Sci. Quart.*, March 1985, *66*(1), pp. 172–77. [G: LDCs]

Krause, Lawrence B. Foreign Trade and Investment: Economic Growth in the Newly Industrializing Asian Countries: Introduction. In *Galenson, W., ed.*, 1985, pp. 3–41. [G: Hong Kong; Singapore; S. Korea; Taiwan]

Krueger, Anne O. Import Substitution versus Export Promotion. *Finance Develop.*, June 1985, *22*(2), pp. 20–23. [G: Brazil; Hong Kong; S. Korea; Singapore; Taiwan]

Kumar, Ramesh S. Money in Development: Reply. *Southern Econ. J.*, April 1985, *51*(4), pp. 1240–44.

Lal, Deepak. Nationalism, Socialism and Planning: Influential Ideas in the South. *World Devel.*, June 1985, *13*(6), pp. 749–59. [G: LDCs]

Lal, Deepak. The Misconceptions of "Development Economics." *Finance Develop.*, June 1985, *22*(2), pp. 10–13.

Landau, Daniel L. Explaining Differences in Per Capita Income between Countries: A Hypothesis and Test for 1950 and 1970. *Exploration Econ. Hist.*, July 1985, *22*(3), pp. 296–315.

Le Guay, François. The International Crisis and Latin American Development: Objectives and Instruments. *Cepal Rev.*, August 1985, (26), pp. 127–37. [G: Latin America]

Le Roy Ladurie, Emmanuel. Agrarian Class Structure and Economic Development in Pre-industrial Europe: A Reply. In *Aston, T. H. and Philpin, C. H. E., eds.*, 1985, pp. 101–06.

Lecraw, Donald J. Hymer and Public Policy in LDCs. *Amer. Econ. Rev.*, May 1985, *75*(2), pp. 239–44. [G: LDCs]

Leff, Nathaniel H. Optimal Investment Choice for Developing Countries: Rational Theory and Rational Decision-making. *J. Devel. Econ.*, August 1985, *18*(2–3), pp. 335–60. [G: LDCs]

Lim, Joseph. The Distributive Implications of Export-Led Industrialization in a Developing Economy. *Philippine Econ. J.*, 1985, *24*(4), pp. 223–33.

Lin, Tzong-Biau and Mok, Victor. Trade, Foreign Investment, and Development in Hong Kong. In *Galenson, W., ed.*, 1985, pp. 219–56. [G: Hong Kong]

Linder, Staffan Burenstam. Pacific Protagonist—Implications of the Rising Role of the Pacific.

Amer. Econ. Rev., May 1985, 75(2), pp. 279–84. [G: U.S.; E. Asia]

Lindert, Peter H. and Williamson, Jeffrey G. Growth, Equality, and History. *Exploration Econ. Hist.*, October 1985, 22(4), pp. 341–77. [G: W. Europe; U.S.]

Lippit, Victor D. The Concept of the Surplus in Economic Development. *Rev. Radical Polit. Econ.*, Spring and Summer 1985, 17(1/2), pp. 1–19. [G: LDCs]

Lipton, Michael. The Prisoners' Dilemma and Coase's Theorem: A Case for Democracy in Less Developed Countries? In *Matthews, R. C. O., ed.*, 1985, pp. 49–109.

Lysy, Frank J. Graciela Chichilnisky's Model of North–South Trade. *J. Devel. Econ.*, August 1985, 18(2–3), pp. 503–39.

Malaska, Pentti. Outline of a Policy for the Future. In *Aida, S., et al.*, 1985, pp. 338–54.

Marquez, Jaime. Foreign Exchange Constraints and Growth Possibilities in the LDCs. *J. Devel. Econ.*, Sept.-Oct. 1985, 19(1/2), pp. 39–57. [G: LDCs]

Mba, Harold C. and Qayum, Abdul. Development of an Absolute Scale for Measurement of Socioeconomic Development. *Econ. Int.*, May 1985, 38(2), pp. 197–213. [G: Global]

McPherson, Natalie. India and Japan: Laissez-Faire and Economic Development from 1850 to 1939. *Can. J. Devel. Stud.*, 1985, 6(2), pp. 289–308. [G: India; Japan]

Meier, Gerald M. The New Export Pessimism. In *Shishido, T. and Sato, R., eds.*, 1985, pp. 19–32. [G: LDCs]

Moore, Mick. On 'The Political Economy of Stabilization.' *World Devel.*, September 1985, 13(9), pp. 1087–91. [G: Ghana; Kenya; Sri Lanka; Jamaica; Zambia]

Mundle, Sudipto. The Agrarian Barrier to Industrial Growth. In *Saith, A., ed.*, 1985, pp. 49–80. [G: W. Europe; Japan; India]

Mundle, Sudipto. The Agrarian Barrier to Industrial Growth. *J. Devel. Stud.*, October 1985, 22(1), pp. 49–80. [G: W. Europe; Japan; India]

Myrdal, Gunnar. The Need for Reforms in Underdeveloped Countries. In *Bapna, A., ed.*, 1985, pp. 151–71. [G: LDCs]

Nafziger, E. Wayne. Japanese Development Model. In *Didsbury, H. F., Jr., ed.*, 1985, pp. 111–34. [G: Japan]

Naqvi, Syed Nawab Haider. The Importance of Being Defunct. *Pakistan Devel. Rev.*, Autumn-Winter 1985, 24(3/4), pp. 211–34. [G: Pakistan; India]

Naqvi, Syed Nawab Haider and Qadir, Asghar. Incrementalism and Structural Change: A Technical Note. *Pakistan Devel. Rev.*, Summer 1985, 24(2), pp. 87–102.

Nelson, Joan. On the Political Economy of Stabilization: Reply. *World Devel.*, September 1985, 13(9), pp. 1093–94. [G: Ghana; Kenya; Sri Lanka; Jamaica; Zambia]

Nerlove, Marc; Razin, Assaf and Sadka, Efraim. The 'Old Age Security Hypothesis' Reconsid-ered. *J. Devel. Econ.*, August 1985, 18(2–3), pp. 243–52. [G: LDCs]

Neumann, Manfred. Long Swings in Economic Development, Social Time Preference and Institutional Change. *Z. ges. Staatswiss. (JITE)*, March 1985, 141(1), pp. 21–35. [G: U.S.]

Nickel, James W. The Feasibility of Welfare Rights in Less Developed Countries. In *Kipnis, K. and Meyers, D. T., eds.*, 1985, pp. 217–25. [G: LDCs]

Nixson, Fred. Development Economics. In *Atkinson, G. B. J., ed.*, 1985, pp. 155–79. [G: LDCs]

O'Brien, Philip J. Dependency Revisited. In *Abel, C. and Lewis, C. M., eds.*, 1985, pp. 40–69. [G: Latin America]

O'Brien, Thomas F. Dependency Revisited: A Review Essay. *Bus. Hist. Rev.*, Winter 1985, 59(4), pp. 663–69. [G: Latin America]

O'Malley, Eoin. The Problem of Late Industrialisation and the Experience of the Republic of Ireland. *Cambridge J. Econ.*, June 1985, 9(2), pp. 141–54. [G: Ireland]

Ohkawa, Kazushi. Investment Criteria in Development Planning. In *Shishido, T. and Sato, R., eds.*, 1985, pp. 71–80. [G: Japan; LDCs]

Okita, Saburo. Economic Development in the Third World and International Economic Co-operation. In *Bapna, A., ed.*, 1985, pp. 81–91. [G: LDCs; MDCs]

Park, Se-Hark. Investment Planning and the Macroeconomic Constraints in Developing Countries: The Case of the Syrian Arab Republic. *World Devel.*, July 1985, 13(7), pp. 837–53. [G: Syria]

Pasha, Hafiz A. and Bengali, Kaiser. Impact of Fiscal Incentives on Industrialisation in Backward Areas: A Case Study of Hub Chowki in Baluchistan. *Pakistan J. Appl. Econ.*, Summer 1985, 4(1), pp. 1–16. [G: Pakistan]

Perez, Carlota. Microelectronics, Long Waves and World Structural Change: New Perspectives for Developing Countries. *World Devel.*, March 1985, 13(3), pp. 441–63.

Perinbam, Lewis. North and South: Toward a New Interdependence of Nations. In *Bapna, A., ed.*, 1985, pp. 93–116. [G: MDCs; LDCs]

Pfeffermann, Guy P. Overvalued Exchange Rates and Development. *Finance Develop.*, March 1985, 22(1), pp. 17–19. [G: LDCs]

Platt, D. C. M. Dependency and the Historian: Further Objections. In *Abel, C. and Lewis, C. M., eds.*, 1985, pp. 29–39. [G: Latin America]

Postan, M. M. and Hatcher, John. Population and Class Relations in Feudal Society. In *Aston, T. H. and Philpin, C. H. E., eds.*, 1985, pp. 64–78.

Pourgerami, Abbas. Exports Growth and Economic Development: A Comparative Logit Analysis. *J. Econ. Devel.*, July 1985, 10(1), pp. 117–28. [G: LDCs]

Prebisch, Raúl. Power Relations and Market Laws. In *Kim, K. S. and Ruccio, D. F., eds.*, 1985, pp. 9–31.

Prebisch, Raúl. The Latin American Periphery

in the Global Crisis of Capitalism. *Cepal Rev.*, August 1985, (26), pp. 63–88.
[G: Latin America]

Quan, Nguyen T. and Koo, Anthony Y. C. Concentration of Land Holdings: An Empirical Exploration of Kuznets' Conjecture. *J. Devel. Econ.*, May–June 1985, *18*(1), pp. 101–17.

Ram, Rati. Conventional and 'Real' GDP per Capita in Cross-Country Studies of Production Structure. *J. Devel. Econ.*, August 1985, *18*(2–3), pp. 463–77. [G: LDCs]

Ram, Rati. Exports and Economic Growth: Some Additional Evidence. *Econ. Develop. Cult. Change*, January 1985, *33*(2), pp. 415–25.
[G: LDCs]

Rama, Germán W. and Faletto, Enzo. Dependent Societies and Crisis in Latin America: The Challenges of Social and Political Transformation. *Cepal Rev.*, April 1985, (25), pp. 129–47. [G: Latin America]

Ranis, Gustav. Can the East Asian Model of Development Be Generalized? A Comment. *World Devel.*, April 1985, *13*(4), pp. 543–45.

Ranney, Susan I. The Labour Market in a Dual Economy: Another Look at Colonial Rhodesia. *J. Devel. Stud.*, July 1985, *21*(4), pp. 505–24.
[G: Zimbabwe]

Richter, Peter. Monetaristische Wirtschaftspolitik im südlichen Lateinamerika. Die Fälle Chile, Argentinien und Uruguay. (Monetarist Policies in Latin America—The Cases of Chile, Argentina, and Uruguay. With English summary.) *Konjunkturpolitik*, 1985, *31*(1/2), pp. 126–49. [G: Chile; Argentina; Uruguay]

Sachs, Jeffrey. External Debt and Macroeconomic Performance in Latin America and East Asia. *Brookings Pap. Econ. Act.*, 1985, (2), pp. 523–64. [G: Latin America; E. Asia]

Sah, Raaj Kumar and Stiglitz, Joseph E. The Social Cost of Labor and Project Evaluation: A General Approach. *J. Public Econ.*, November 1985, *28*(2), pp. 135–63.

Sahota, Gian Singh. Financial Analysis of a Development Project. *Indian J. Quant. Econ.*, 1985, *1*(1), pp. 1–31. [G: Nepal]

Saith, Ashwani. Primitive Accumulation, Agrarian Reform and Socialist Transitions: An Argument. In *Saith, A., ed.*, 1985, pp. 1–48.
[G: U.S.S.R.; LDCs; China]

Saith, Ashwani. Primitive Accumulation, Agrarian Reform and Socialist Transitions: An Argument. *J. Devel. Stud.*, October 1985, *22*(1), pp. 1–48. [G: U.S.S.R.; LDCs; China]

Samli, A. Coskun. Technology Transfer to Third World Countries and Economic Development. In *Samli, A. C., ed.*, 1985, pp. 17–26.

Santarelli, Enrico. A proposito di una nuova raccolta di scritti schumperiani. (With English summary.) *Stud. Econ.*, 1985, *40*(26), pp. 135–47.

Sapsford, D. The Statistical Debate on the Net Barter Terms of Trade between Primary Commodities and Manufactures: A Comment and Some Additional Evidence. *Econ. J.*, September 1985, *95*(379), pp. 781–88. [G: U.K.]

Sawyer, Malcolm C. The Economics of Michal Kalecki. *Eastern Europ. Econ.*, Spring-Summer 1985, *23*(3–4), pp. 1–319.

Schneider, Robert R. Food Subsidies: A Multiple Price Model. *Int. Monet. Fund Staff Pap.*, June 1985, *32*(2), pp. 289–316. [G: LDCs]

Scitovsky, Tibor. Economic Development in Taiwan and South Korea: 1965-81. *Food Res. Inst. Stud.*, 1985, *19*(3), pp. 214–64.
[G: S. Korea; Taiwan]

Seyfert, Wolfgang. A Weberian Analysis of Economic Progress: The Case of Resource-Exporting LDC's. *Z. ges. Staatswiss. (JITE)*, March 1985, *141*(1), pp. 170–83.

Sicat, Gerardo P. National Economic Management and Technocracy in Developing Countries. In *Shishido, T. and Sato, R., eds.*, 1985, pp. 81–94. [G: LDCs]

Simonato, Rogelio E. El Argumento de la Industria Incipiente y las Políticas de Industrialización Selectivas. (Incipient Industry and Selective Industrialization Policies. With English summary.) *Económica (La Plata)*, Jan.-Apr. 1985, *31*(1), pp. 99–127. [G: Argentina]

Singer, Hans W. Relevance of Keynes for Developing Countries. In *Wattel, H. L., ed.*, 1985, pp. 128–44.

Singh, Ram D. State Intervention, Foreign Economic Aid, Savings and Growth in LDCs: Some Recent Evidence. *Kyklos*, 1985, *38*(2), pp. 216–32. [G: LDCs]

Sirgy, M. Joseph. Achievement Motivation, Technology Transfer, and National Development: A System Model. In *Samli, A. C., ed.*, 1985, pp. 193–216.

Skouras, Thanos. The Political Economy of Rapid Industrialisation. In *Arestis, P. and Skouras, T., eds.*, 1985, pp. 180–212.

Soete, Luc. International Diffusion of Technology, Industrial Development and Technological Leapfrogging. *World Devel.*, March 1985, *13*(3), pp. 409–22.

Spraos, John. The Statistical Debate on the Net Barter Terms of Trade: A Response. *Econ. J.*, September 1985, *95*(379), pp. 789. [G: U.K.]

Standaert, Stan. The Foreign Exchange Constraint, Suppression of the Trade Deficit, and the Shadow Price of Foreign Exchange in a Fix-Price Economy. *J. Devel. Econ.*, May–June 1985, *18*(1), pp. 37–50.

Stewart, Frances. Macro Policies for Appropriate Technology: An Introductory Classification. In *James, J. and Watanabe, S., eds.*, 1985, pp. 19–46.

Stewart, Frances. The Fragile Foundations of the Neoclassical Approach to Development: Commentary. *J. Devel. Stud.*, January 1985, *21*(2), pp. 282–92.

Streeten, Paul. A Problem to Every Solution. *Finance Develop.*, June 1985, *22*(2), pp. 14–16.

Streeten, Paul. Development Economics: The Intellectual Divisions. *Eastern Econ. J.*, July-Sept. 1985, *11*(3), pp. 235–47.

Suits, Daniel B. U.S. Farm Migration: An Application of the Harris–Todaro Model. *Econ. Develop. Cult. Change*, July 1985, *33*(4), pp. 815–28. [G: U.S.]

Sundararajan, V. Debt–Equity Ratios of Firms and Interest Rate Policy: Macroeconomic Effects of High Leverage in Developing Countries. *Int. Monet. Fund Staff Pap.*, September 1985, *32*(3), pp. 430–74.

Thirlwall, A. P. and Bergevin, J. Trends, Cycles and Asymmetries in the Terms of Trade of Primary Commodities from Developed and Less Developed Countries. *World Devel.*, July 1985, *13*(7), pp. 805–17.

Thorp, Rosemary. The New Order: Introduction. In *Abel, C. and Lewis, C. M., eds.*, 1985, pp. 397–404. [G: Latin America]

Tisdell, Clement A. Externalities and Coasian Considerations in Project Evaluation: Aspects of Social CBA in LDCs. *Indian J. Quant. Econ.*, 1985, *1*(1), pp. 33–43.

Toye, John. *Dirigisme* and Development Economics. *Cambridge J. Econ.*, March 1985, *9*(1), pp. 1–14.

Tsiang, S. C. and Wu, Rong-I. Foreign Trade and Investment as Boosters for Take-off: The Experiences of the Four Asian Newly Industrializing Countries. In *Galenson, W., ed.*, 1985, pp. 301–32. [G: Hong Kong; Singapore; S. Korea; Taiwan]

Uppal, J. S. Economic Theory and the Asian Developing Economies: The Question of Relevance. *Indian J. Quant. Econ.*, 1985, *1*(2), pp. 109–18. [G: Asia]

Van Wijnbergen, Sweder. Macro-economic Effects of Changes in Bank Interest Rates: Simulation Results for South Korea. *J. Devel. Econ.*, August 1985, *18*(2–3), pp. 541–54. [G: S. Korea]

Vavouras, Ioannis S. The Accounting Prices of the Factors of Production: An Estimation of Their Parameters in the Case of Greece. *Bull. Econ. Res.*, May 1985, *37*(2), pp. 97–114. [G: Greece]

Vitta, Paul B. New Technologies and Their Implications for Developing Countries: Outlines of Possible Policy Responses. *Can. J. Devel. Stud.*, 1985, *6*(2), pp. 241–55. [G: LDCs]

Warr, Peter G. Sub-optimal Saving and the Shadow Price of Labor: The Public Good Argument. *J. Devel. Econ.*, April 1985, *17*(3), pp. 239–57.

Watanabe, Toshio. Economic Development in Korea: Lessons and Challenge. In *Shishido, T. and Sato, R., eds.*, 1985, pp. 95–111. [G: S. Korea]

Wignaraja, Ponna. Towards a New Praxis of Rural Development. *Ann. Pub. Co-op. Econ.*, January–June 1985, *56*(1–2), pp. 121–43. [G: LDCs]

Williamson, John. External Debt and Macroeconomic Performance in Latin America and East Asia: Comment. *Brookings Pap. Econ. Act.*, 1985, (2), pp. 565–70. [G: Latin America; E. Asia]

Williamson, John. On the Optimal Currency Peg for Developing Countries: Reply [A Survey of the Literature on the Optimal Peg]. *J. Devel. Econ.*, August 1985, *18*(2–3), pp. 561–62. [G: LDCs]

Wu, Jinglian. Developmental Guidelines in the Early Stages of the Battle for Economic Reform and Some Questions of Macroscopic Control. *Chinese Econ. Stud.*, Fall 1985, *19*(1), pp. 40–52. [G: China]

Wunder, Heide. Peasant Organization and Class Conflict in Eastern and Western Germany. In *Aston, T. H. and Philpin, C. H. E., eds.*, 1985, pp. 91–100. [G: W. Germany]

Yg, Chimezie A. B. Osigweh. International Business and the Growth Model. *J. Econ. Devel.*, December 1985, *10*(2), pp. 123–42.

Zee, Howell H. A General Equilibrium Model of Export Earnings Instability in Developing Economies. *Oxford Econ. Pap.*, December 1985, *37*(4), pp. 621–42.

Zylberberg, André. Migration Equilibrium with Price Rigidity: The Harris and Todaro Model Revisited. *J. Econ. Theory*, December 1985, *37*(2), pp. 281–309.

113 Economic Planning Theory and Policy

1130 General

Abouchar, Alan J. Western Project-Investment Theory and Soviet Investment Rules. *J. Compar. Econ.*, December 1985, *9*(4), pp. 345–62. [G: U.S.S.R.]

Agarwala, Ramgopal. Planning in Developing Countries. *Finance Develop.*, March 1985, *22*(1), pp. 13–16. [G: LDCs]

Arrow, Kenneth J. and Kurz, Mordecai. Optimal Public Investment Policy and Controllability with Fixed Private Savings Ratio. In *Arrow, K. J. (I)*, 1985, pp. 332–72.

Bautina, N. The Economic Mechanism of CMEA Member Nations (General Trends of Development). *Prob. Econ.*, January 1985, *27*(9), pp. 23–41. [G: CMEA]

Bhagwati, Jagdish N. Indian Economic Policy and Performance: A Framework for a Progressive Society. In *Bhagwati, J. N. (II)*, 1985, pp. 32–58. [G: India]

Bhagwati, Jagdish N. W. Arthur Lewis: An Appreciation. In *Bhagwati, J. N. (II)*, 1985, pp. 277–91.

Bhagwati, Jagdish N. and Desai, Padma. Socialism and Indian Economic Policy. In *Bhagwati, J. N. (II)*, 1985, pp. 59–72. [G: India]

Brown, Alan A. and Neuberger, Egon. Basic Features of a Centrally Planned Economy. In *Bornstein, M., ed.*, 1985, pp. 177–87.

Deakin, Nicholas. 'Vanishing Utopias': Planning and Participation in Twentieth Century Britain. *Reg. Stud.*, August 1985, *19*(4), pp. 291–300. [G: U.K.]

Dinwiddy, Caroline and Teal, Francis. Shadow Prices and Cost-Benefit Rules for Non-traded Commodities in a Second Best Economy. *Oxford Econ. Pap.*, December 1985, *37*(4), pp. 683–90.

Duchêne, Gérard. Vers une réforme de la planification des services en URSS? (Towards a Reform in Planning for Services in U.S.S.R. With English summary.) *Écon. Soc.*, May 1985, *19*(5), pp. 15–42. [G: U.S.S.R.]

Flakierski, Henryk. Economic Reform & Income Distribution: A Case Study of Hungary and Poland. *Eastern Europ. Econ.*, Fall-Winter 1985-86, *24*(1–2), pp. iii–194.

Gvishiani, D. Key Reserves in Managing the National Economy. *Prob. Econ.*, January 1985, *27*(9), pp. 3–22. **[G: U.S.S.R.]**

Gvishiani, D. Planned Improvements in the System for Managing the National Economy. *Prob. Econ.*, April 1985, *27*(12), pp. 63–81. **[G: U.S.S.R.]**

Khachaturov, T. Economic Methods of Managing Socialist Social Production. *Prob. Econ.*, March 1985, *27*(11), pp. 39–58. **[G: U.S.S.R.]**

Lal, Deepak. Nationalism, Socialism and Planning: Influential Ideas in the South. *World Devel.*, June 1985, *13*(6), pp. 749–59. **[G: LDCs]**

Leontief, Wassily. Modern Techniques for Economic Planning and Projection. In *Leontief, W.*, 1985, pp. 237–47.

Leontief, Wassily. National Economic Planning: Methods and Problems. In *Leontief, W.*, 1985, pp. 398–406.

Markovic, Ljubisav. Planning Systems: The Yugoslav Experience. In *Damjanovic, M. and Voich, D., Jr., eds.*, 1985, pp. 124–41. **[G: Yugoslavia]**

Novichkov, V. and Abdykulova, G. Some Problems in Determining the National Economy's Priorities. *Prob. Econ.*, September 1985, *28*(5), pp. 20–31. **[G: U.S.S.R.]**

Nyers, Reszö. National Economic Objectives and the Reform Process in Hungary in the Eighties. *Acta Oecon.*, 1985, *35*(1–2), pp. 1–16. **[G: Hungary]**

Prigozhin, A. Managerial Innovations and Economic Experiments. *Prob. Econ.*, February 1985, *27*(10), pp. 43–64. **[G: U.S.S.R.]**

Rugumyamheto, J. A. Manpower Forecasting in the United Republic of Tanzania. In *Youdi, R. V. and Hinchliffe, K., eds.*, 1985, pp. 229–46. **[G: Tanzania]**

Sicat, Gerardo P. National Economic Management and Technocracy in Developing Countries. In *Shishido, T. and Sato, R., eds.*, 1985, pp. 81–94. **[G: LDCs]**

Somogyi, Giovanni. Planning the Advanced Market Economies: The Italian Case. *Atlantic Econ. J.*, September 1985, *13*(3), pp. 27–32. **[G: Italy]**

Verma, M. C. Review of Skilled-Manpower Forecasts in India. In *Youdi, R. V. and Hinchliffe, K., eds.*, 1985, pp. 194–210. **[G: India]**

Wu, Jinglian. Developmental Guidelines in the Early Stages of the Battle for Economic Reform and Some Questions of Macroscopic Control. *Chinese Econ. Stud.*, Fall 1985, *19*(1), pp. 40–52. **[G: China]**

Yu, Guanyuan. Theoretical Basis for Reform of the Planning System. *Chinese Econ. Stud.*, Fall 1985, *19*(1), pp. 3–9. **[G: China]**

Zimmer, Terese S. Regional Input into Centralized Economic Planning: The Case of Soviet Central Asia. *Policy Sci.*, September 1985, *18*(2), pp. 111–26. **[G: U.S.S.R.]**

1132 Economic Planning Theory

Afanas'ev, M. Iu. and Bures, I. Encouraging Accurate Information Disclosure in a Planning System. *Matekon*, Summer 1985, *21*(4), pp. 66–78.

Aslaksen, Iulie and Bjerkholt, Olav. Certainty Equivalence Procedures in Decision-Making under Uncertainty: An Empirical Application. In *[Johansen, L.]*, 1985, pp. 289–329. **[G: Norway]**

Aslaksen, Iulie and Bjerkholt, Olav. Certainty Equivalence Procedures in the Macroeconomic Planning of an Oil Economy. In *Bjerkholt, O. and Offerdal, E., eds.*, 1985, pp. 283–318. **[G: Norway]**

Báger, Gustav H. The Plural Rationality and Interest of National Planners: Experiences in Hungary. In *Grauer, M.; Thompson, M. and Wierzbicki, A. P., eds.*, 1985, pp. 37–54. **[G: Hungary]**

Bennett, John. Planning under Market Socialism When Iteration Is Incomplete. *J. Compar. Econ.*, September 1985, *9*(3), pp. 252–66.

Csikós-Nagy, Béla. The Role of the Law of Value in Socialist Economy. In *[Levcik, F.]*, 1985, pp. 39–49.

Finsinger, Jörg and Vogelsang, Ingo. Strategic Management Behavior under Reward Structures in a Planned Economy [Reward Structures in a Planned Economy: The Problem of Incentives and Efficient Allocation of Resources]. *Quart. J. Econ.*, February 1985, *100*(1), pp. 263–69.

FitzGerald, E. V. K. The Problem of Balance in the Peripheral Socialist Economy: A Conceptual Note. *World Devel.*, January 1985, *13*(1), pp. 5–14.

Freixas, Xavier; Guesnerie, Roger and Tirole, Jean. Planning under Incomplete Information and the Ratchet Effect. *Rev. Econ. Stud.*, April 1985, *52*(2), pp. 173–91.

Gravelle, H. S. E. Reward Structures in a Planned Economy: Some Difficulties. *Quart. J. Econ.*, February 1985, *100*(1), pp. 271–78.

Iasin, E. G. Problems of Coordinating Planning with the Economic Mechanism for Plan Implementation. *Matekon*, Winter 1985-86, *22*(2), pp. 30–58.

Kaganovich, Mikhail. Efficiency of Sliding Plans in a Linear Model with Time-Dependent Technology. *Rev. Econ. Stud.*, October 1985, *52*(4), pp. 691–702.

Klusoň, Václav. Innovations and Planned Management. *Czech. Econ. Pap.*, 1985, 23, pp. 39–54.

Kotulan, Antonín. Theoretical Aspects of Incentives Systems. *Czech. Econ. Pap.*, 1985, 23, pp. 55–73.

Laffont, Jean-Jacques. Incitations dans les procédures de planification. (Incentives in Planning Procedures. With English summary.) *Ann. INSEE*, Apr.-June 1985, (58), pp. 3–37.

Laffont, Jean-Jacques and Rochet, Jean-Charles. Price-Quantity Duality in Planning Procedures. *Soc. Choice Welfare*, December 1985, 2(4), pp. 311–22.

Le Guay, François. The International Crisis and Latin American Development: Objectives and Instruments. *Cepal Rev.*, August 1985, (26), pp. 127–37. **[G: Latin America]**

McCain, Roger A. Economic Planning for Market Economies: The Optimality of Planning in an Economy with Uncertainty and Asymmetrical Information. *Econ. Modelling*, October 1985, 2(4), pp. 317–23.

Ohkawa, Kazushi. Investment Criteria in Development Planning. In *Shishido, T. and Sato, R., eds.*, 1985, pp. 71–80. **[G: Japan; LDCs]**

Révész, Gábor. The Origins and Development of the Model of Socialist Economy. In *[Levcik, F.]*, 1985, pp. 21–30.

Seddighi, H. R. A General Equilibrium Framework for Optimal Planning in an Oil-producing Economy. *Energy Econ.*, July 1985, 7(3), pp. 179–90.

Tam, Mo-Yin S. Reward Structures in a Planned Economy: Some Further Thoughts. *Quart. J. Econ.*, February 1985, 100(1), pp. 279–89.

Tompkinson, P. and Philpott, B. P. Uncertainty in the Terms of Trade and the Optimal Structure of a Small Open Economy. *Econ. Planning*, 1985, 19(1), pp. 12–18.

Trzeciakowski, Witold. Decentralization and Financial Equilibrium in a Centrally Planned Economy. In *[Levcik, F.]*, 1985, pp. 171–80.

1136 Economic Planning Policy

Adam, Jan. The State of the Hungarian Reform. In *[Levcik, F.]*, 1985, pp. 75–82. **[G: Hungary]**

Balassa, Bela. Reforming the New Economic Mechanism in Hungary. In *Balassa, B.*, 1985, pp. 282–309. **[G: Hungary]**

Balassa, Bela. The Hungarian Economic Reform, 1968–81. In *Balassa, B.*, 1985, pp. 261–81. **[G: Hungary]**

Baum, Warren C. and Tolbert, Stokes M. Investing in Development: Lessons of World Bank Experience. *Finance Develop.*, December 1985, 22(4), pp. 25–30. **[G: LDCs]**

Bislev, Claus. Planning in a Worker-Managed Economy. *Econ. Anal. Worker's Manage.*, 1985, 19(4), pp. 385–94. **[G: Yugoslavia]**

Bognár, József. Evolution of Conception about Economic Policy and Control in Hungary in the Past Decades. *Acta Oecon.*, 1985, 34(3/4), pp. 205–17. **[G: Hungary]**

Bornstein, Morris. The Soviet Industrial Price Revision. In *[Levcik, F.]*, 1985, pp. 157–70. **[G: U.S.S.R.]**

Bose, Ashish and Narain, Vir. Population. In *Mongia, J. N., ed.*, 1985, pp. 1–24. **[G: India]**

Canlas, Dante B. Comments on the Updated Philippine Development Plan, 1984–1987. *Philippine Econ. J.*, 1985, 24(1), pp. 8–12. **[G: Philippines]**

Cave, Martin. Decentralised Planning in Britain: Comment. *Econ. Planning*, 1985, 19(3), pp. 141–44. **[G: U.K.]**

Černý, Miroslav. Economic Cooperation and Coordination of National Economic Plans between Czechoslovakia and the Soviet Union after 1985. *Czech. Econ. Digest.*, February 1985, (1), pp. 41–49. **[G: Czechoslovakia; U.S.S.R.]**

Cohen, Suleiman I.; Havinga, Ivo C. and Saleem, Mohammad. A Simple Inter-Industry Model of Pakistan, with an Application to Pakistan's Sixth Five-Year Plan. *Pakistan Devel. Rev.*, Autumn-Winter 1985, 24(3/4), pp. 531–45. **[G: Pakistan]**

Comeliau, Christian. North–South Relations and Ninth French Plan. *Indian J. Quant. Econ.*, 1985, 1(2), pp. 89–98. **[G: France; LDCs]**

Cowling, Keith. Planning the British Economy: Some Comments. *Econ. Planning*, 1985, 19(3), pp. 145–49. **[G: U.K.]**

Dubhashi, P. R. Public Administration and Plan Implementation. In *Mongia, J. N., ed.*, 1985, pp. 617–40. **[G: India]**

Estrin, Saul. Decentralized Economic Planning: Some Issues [Britain in the 1980s: The Case for Decentralized Economic Planning]. *Econ. Planning*, 1985, 19(3), pp. 150–56. **[G: U.S.]**

Euzeby, Chantal. La protection sociale et le IXe Plan (1984–1988). (With English summary.) *Revue Écon. Polit.*, Sept.-Oct. 1985, 95(5), pp. 695–704. **[G: EEC]**

Fedorenko, N. F. Planning and Management: What Should They Be Like? *Prob. Econ.*, December 1985, 28(8), pp. 42–59. **[G: U.S.S.R.]**

Fine, Ben. Britain in the 1980s: The Case against 'Planning.' *Econ. Planning*, 1985, 19(3), pp. 157–60. **[G: U.K.]**

Gupta, Sanjeev. Poverty. In *Mongia, J. N., ed.*, 1985, pp. 495–516. **[G: India]**

Hanson, Philip. Gorbachev's Economic Strategy: A Comment. *Soviet Econ.*, Oct.-Dec. 1985, 1(4), pp. 306–12. **[G: U.S.S.R.]**

Hare, Paul. Britain in the 1980s: The Case for Decentralized Economic Planning. *Econ. Planning*, 1985, 19(3), pp. 127–40. **[G: U.K.]**

Havasi, Ferenc. The Economic Situation of Hungary and the Tasks to Be Faced. *Acta Oecon.*, 1985, 34(3/4), pp. 193–204. **[G: Hungary]**

Hayward, Jack. French Planning: Decline or Renewal?: Comment. In *Machin, H. and Wright, V., eds.*, 1985, pp. 113–16. **[G: France]**

Hentschel, Volker. Breaks and Continuity in the Economy and Social Structures between the Weimar Republic and the Third Reich. In *Engels, W. and Pohl, H., eds.*, 1985, pp. 95–128. **[G: Germany]**

Hewett, Ed A. Gorbachev's Economic Strategy: A Preliminary Assessment. *Soviet Econ.*, Oct.-Dec. 1985, 1(4), pp. 285–305. **[G: U.S.S.R.]**

Hoós, János. Alternatives of Growth and Priorities in the 7th Five-Year Plan of Hungary (1986–1990). *Acta Oecon.*, 1985, 35(1–2), pp. 17–28. **[G: Hungary]**

Hough, J. R. Economic Planning in France. In

Bornstein, M., ed., 1985, pp. 76–94. [G: France]

Hughes Hallett, A. J. Wage Policy, Competitiveness and Risk Management: The Internal Conflicts of Dutch Economic Policy. *Weltwirtsch. Arch.*, 1985, *121*(4), pp. 703–21. [G: Netherlands]

Hussain, Athar. Conditions for Collaborative Planning [Britain in the 1980s: The Case for Decentralized Economic Planning]. *Econ. Planning*, 1985, *19*(3), pp. 161–65. [G: U.K.]

Ivanchenko, V. Improving the Organization of Management. *Prob. Econ.*, July 1985, *28*(3), pp. 67–80. [G: U.S.S.R.]

Jha, L. K. India's Economic Strategies for the Nineties. In *Mongia, J. N., ed.*, 1985 , pp. 641–67. [G: India]

Kadir, Abdul. Electric Power in Indonesia's Fourth Five-Year Development Plan. *J. Energy Devel.*, Spring 1985, *10*(2), pp. 239–47. [G: Indonesia]

Khosla, S. L. Energy. In *Mongia, J. N., ed.*, 1985, pp. 417–51. [G: India]

Kiss, Otto; Mencl, Karel and Ulman, Václav. Social Consumption and Social Development Planning. *Czech. Econ. Digest.*, August 1985, (5), pp. 27–44. [G: Czechoslovakia]

Kornai, János. Hungary's Reform: Halfway to the Market. *Challenge*, May/June 1985, *28*(2), pp. 22–31. [G: Hungary]

Lér, Leopold. Financial Policy for the Years to Come. *Czech. Econ. Digest.*, February 1985, (1), pp. 3–23. [G: Czechoslovakia]

Lér, Leopold. Forty Years of Building up a Socialist Financial System in the Czechoslovak Socialist Republic. *Czech. Econ. Digest.*, September 1985, (6), pp. 33–57. [G: Czechoslovakia]

Littlechild, S. C. Economic Planning and Information [Britain in the 1980s: The Case for Decentralized Economic Planning]. *Econ. Planning*, 1985, *19*(3), pp. 166–69. [G: U.K.]

Mangahas, Mahar. Comments on the Updated Philippine Development Plan, 1984–1987. *Philippine Econ. J.*, 1985, *24*(1), pp. 13–23. [G: Philippines]

Mongia, J. N. Deficit Financing. In *Mongia, J. N., ed.*, 1985, pp. 201–37. [G: India]

Mujzel, Jan. Technocratic vs. Democratic Elements in the Polish Economic Reform. In *[Levcik, F.]*, 1985, pp. 51–59. [G: Poland]

Nagy, Tamás. Die ungarische Wirtschaftsreform und ihre Weiterentwicklung. (Development of the Hungarian Economic Reform. With English summary.) *Konjunkturpolitik*, 1985, *31*(6), pp. 361–79. [G: Hungary]

Neuburger, Henry. Economics of Planning [Britain in the 1980s: The Case for Decentralized Economic Planning]. *Econ. Planning*, 1985, *19*(3), pp. 170–73. [G: U.K.]

Nove, Alec. Paul Hare's Case for Decentralized Economic Planning. *Econ. Planning*, 1985, *19*(3), pp. 174–78. [G: U.K.]

Ozenda, Michel and Strauss-Kahn, Dominique. French Planning: Decline or Renewal? In *Ma-*

chin, H. and Wright, V., eds., 1985, pp. 101–13. [G: France]

Pěnkava, Jaromír. Current Tasks in Economic Research. *Czech. Econ. Digest.*, February 1985, (1), pp. 24–40. [G: Czechoslovakia]

Perry, Elizabeth J. and Wong, Christine. The Political Economy of Reform in Post-Mao China: Causes, Content, and Consequences. In *Perry, E. J. and Wong, C., eds.*, 1985 1985, pp. 1–27.

Potáč, Svatopluk. State Plan of Economic and Social Development for 1985. *Czech. Econ. Digest.*, March 1985, (2), pp. 35–76. [G: Czechoslovakia]

Potáč, Svatopluk. Victorious Road towards Building an Advanced Socialist Society. *Czech. Econ. Digest.*, September 1985, (6), pp. 3–23. [G: Czechoslovakia]

Prybyla, Jan S. Economic Problems of Communism: A Case Study of China. In *Bornstein, M., ed.*, 1985, pp. 263–81. [G: China]

Rasul, Ghulam. A Simpe Inter-Industry Model of Pakistan, with an Application to Pakistan's Sixth Five-Year Plan: Comments. *Pakistan Devel. Rev.*, Autumn-Winter 1985, *24*(3/4), pp. 546–50. [G: Pakistan]

Richet, Xavier. Planification macro-économique indicative et modélisation en Hongrie. (Macroeconomic Planning and Modelling in Hungary. With English summary.) *Écon. Soc.*, May 1985, *19*(5), pp. 43–68. [G: Hungary]

Schreiner, Per and Larsen, Knut Arild. On the Introduction and Application of the MSG-Model in the Norwegian Planning System. In *[Johansen, L.]*, 1985, pp. 241–69.

Sicat, Gerardo P. A Historical and Current Perspective of Philippine Economic Problems. *Philippine Econ. J.*, 1985, *24*(1), pp. 24–63. [G: Philippines]

Smekhov, B. M. The Logic of Planning. *Prob. Econ.*, November 1985, *28*(7), pp. 3–17. [G: U.S.S.R.]

Soulage, Bernard. Industrial Priorities in the Current French Plan. In *Zukin, S., ed.*, 1985, pp. 165–78. [G: France]

Štrougal, Lubomír. Every Effort for the Fulfilment of the 7th Five-Year Plan. *Czech. Econ. Digest.*, June 1985, (4), pp. 3–23. [G: Czechoslovakia]

Tikidzhiev, R. Balancing the Reproduction of Fixed Capital with Labor Resources. *Prob. Econ.*, March 1985, *27*(11), pp. 75–90. [G: U.S.S.R]

Ulybin, K. A. Scarcity and the Interaction of Partners. *Prob. Econ.*, December 1985, *28*(8), pp. 60–69. [G: U.S.S.R.]

Valdepeñas, Vicete B., Jr. The Updated Philippine Development Plan, 1984–1987. *Philippine Econ. J.*, 1985, *24*(1), pp. 1–7. [G: Philippines]

Vitin, A. Capital Investment Effectiveness in Planning. *Prob. Econ.*, October 1985, *28*(6), pp. 23–39. [G: U.S.S.R.]

Wuyts, Marc. Money, Planning and Rural Transformation in Mozambique. In *Saith, A., ed.*, 1985, pp. 180–207. [G: Mozambique]

Wuyts, Marc. Money, Planning and Rural Transformation in Mozambique. *J. Devel. Stud.*, October 1985, *22*(1), pp. 180–207.
[G: Mozambique]

Zhao, Ziyang. Report on the Sixth Five-Year Plan for National Economic and Social Development. *Chinese Econ. Stud.*, Summer 1985, *18*(4), pp. 3–61.
[G: China]

114 Economics of War, Defense, and Disarmament

1140 Economics of War, Defense, and Disarmament

Anderson, Barbara A. and Silver, Brian D. Demographic Consequences of World War II on the Non-Russian Nationalities of the USSR. In *Linz, S. J., ed.,* 1985, pp. 207–42.
[G: U.S.S.R.]

Anderton, Charles H. A Selected Bibliography of Arms Race Models and Related Subjects. *Conflict Manage. Peace Sci.*, Spring 1985, *8*(2), pp. 99–122.

Baack, Bennett D. and Ray, Edward John. The Political Economy of the Origins of the Military-Industrial Complex in the United States. *J. Econ. Hist.*, June 1985, *45*(2), pp. 369–75.
[G: U.S.]

Barrett, John and Ross, Douglas. The Air-launched Cruise Missile and Canadian Arms Control Policy. *Can. Public Policy*, December 1985, *11*(4), pp. 711–30. [G: Canada]

Blank, Rebecca M. and Rothschild, Emma. The Effect of United States Defence Spending on Employment and Output. *Int. Lab. Rev.*, Nov.-Dec. 1985, *124*(6), pp. 677–97.
[G: U.S.]

Bobrow, Davis B. and Hill, Stephen R. The Determinants of Military Budgets: The Japanese Case. *Conflict Manage. Peace Sci.*, Fall 1985, *9*(1), pp. 1–18. [G: Japan]

Booth, Alan. Economists and Points Rationing in the Second World War. *J. Europ. Econ. Hist.*, Fall 1985, *14*(2), pp. 297–317. [G: U.K.]

Bradford, James C. Canadian Defence Trade with the United States. In *Fretz, D.; Stern, R. and Whalley, J., eds.,* 1985, pp. 474–77.
[G: Canada; U.S.]

Brito, Dagobert L. and Intriligator, Michael D. Conflict, War, and Redistribution. *Amer. Polit. Sci. Rev.*, December 1985, *79*(4), pp. 943–57.

Brown, Charles. Military Enlistments: What Can We Learn from Geographic Variation? *Amer. Econ. Rev.*, March 1985, *75*(1), pp. 228–34.
[G: U.S.]

Bubis, Edward and Ruble, Blair A. The Impact of World War II on Leningrad. In *Linz, S. J., ed.,* 1985, pp. 189–206. [G: U.S.S.R.]

Bueno de Mesquita, Bruce. The War Trap Revisited: A Revised Expected Utility Model. *Amer. Polit. Sci. Rev.*, March 1985, *79*(1), pp. 156–77. [G: Global]

Carlson, Keith M. Controlling Federal Outlays: Trends and Proposals. *Fed. Res. Bank St. Louis Rev.*, June/July 1985, *67*(6), pp. 5–11.
[G: U.S.]

Carswell, Robert and Davis, Richard J. American Hostages in Iran: The Conduct of a Crisis: Crafting the Financial Settlement. In *Kreisberg, P. H., ed.,* 1985, pp. 201–34. [G: U.S.; Iran]

Carswell, Robert and Davis, Richard J. American Hostages in Iran: The Conduct of a Crisis: The Economic and Financial Pressures: Freeze and Sanctions. In *Kreisberg, P. H., ed.,* 1985, pp. 173–200. [G: U.S.; Iran]

de Cecco, Marcello. The International Debt Program in the Interwar Period. *Banca Naz. Lavoro Quart. Rev.*, March 1985, (152), pp. 45–64. [G: OECD]

Cooper, Julian M. Western Technology and the Soviet Defense Industry. In *Parrott, B., ed.,* 1985, pp. 169–202. [G: U.S.S.R.]

Cooper, Orah and Fogarty, Carol. Soviet Economic and Military Aid to the Less Developed Countries, 1954–78. *Soviet E. Europ. Foreign Trade*, Summer–Fall 1985, *21*(1–2–3), pp. 54–73. [G: LDCs; U.S.S.R.]

Cypher, James M. Critical Analyses of Military Spending and Capitalism. *Eastern Econ. J.*, July-Sept. 1985, *11*(3), pp. 273–82. [G: U.S.]

Dale, Charles and Gilroy, Curtis. Enlistments in the All-Volunteer Force: Note. *Amer. Econ. Rev.*, June 1985, *75*(3), pp. 547–51.
[G: U.S.]

Dale, Charles and Gilroy, Curtis. The Outlook for Army Recruiting. *Eastern Econ. J.*, April-June 1985, *11*(2), pp. 107–22. [G: U.S.]

Deger, Saadet. Does Defence Expenditure Mobilise Resources in LDCs? *J. Econ. Stud.*, 1985, *12*(4), pp. 15–29. [G: LDCs]

Deger, Saadet. Human Resources, Government Education Expenditure, and the Military Burden in Less Developed Countries. *J. Devel. Areas*, October 1985, *20*(1), pp. 37–48.
[G: LDCs]

Deger, Saadet. Soviet Arms Sales to Developing Countries: The Economic Forces. In *Cassen, R., ed.,* 1985, pp. 159–76. [G: LDCs; U.S.S.R.]

Deger, Saadet and Sen, Somnath. Technology Transfer and Arms Production in Developing Countries. *Industry Devel.*, 1985, (15), pp. 1–18. [G: LDCs]

DeSouza, Patrick J. Regulating Fraud in Military Procurement: A Legal Process Model. *Yale Law J.*, December 1985, *95*(2), pp. 390–413.
[G: U.S.]

Efremov, Aleksandr. The Effects of Disarmament on Employment in the USSR. *Int. Lab. Rev.*, July-Aug. 1985, *124*(4), pp. 423–34.

Engelhardt, Klaus. Conversion of Military Research and Development: Realism or Wishful Thinking? *Int. Lab. Rev.*, March-April 1985, *124*(2), pp. 181–92.

Fitzpatrick, Sheila. Postwar Soviet Society: The "Return to Normalcy," 1945–1953. In *Linz, S. J., ed.,* 1985, pp. 129–56. [G: U.S.S.R.]

Fredland, J. Eric and Little, Roger D. Socioeconomic Status of World War II Veterans by Race: An Empirical Test of the Bridging Hypothesis. *Soc. Sci. Quart.*, September 1985, *66*(3), pp. 533–51. **[G: U.S.]**

Goodman, Gary A. and Saunders, Robert M. U.S. Federal Regulation of Foreign Involvement in Aviation, Government Procurement, and National Security. *J. World Trade Law*, January:February 1985, *19*(1), pp. 54–61. **[G: U.S.]**

Greenwood, David. Public Expenditure Policy, 1985–86: Defence. In *Cockle, P., ed.*, 1985, pp. 101–19. **[G: U.K.]**

Güth, Werner. An Extensive Game Approach to Modelling the Nuclear Deterrence Debate. *Z. ges. Staatswiss. (JITE)*, December 1985, *141*(4), pp. 525–38.

Hoffman, John E., Jr. American Hostages in Iran: The Conduct of a Crisis: The Bankers' Channel. In *Kreisberg, P. H., ed.*, 1985, pp. 235–80. **[G: U.S.; Iran]**

Holloway, David. Causes of the Slowdown in Soviet Defense: Comments. *Soviet Econ.*, Jan.-Mar. 1985, *1*(1), pp. 37–41. **[G: U.S.S.R.]**

Horne, David K. Modeling Army Enlistment Supply for the All-Volunteer Force. *Mon. Lab. Rev.*, August 1985, *108*(8), pp. 35–39. **[G: U.S.]**

Hunter, Holland. Successful Spatial Management. In *Linz, S. J., ed.*, 1985, pp. 47–58. **[G: U.S.S.R.]**

Intriligator, Michael D. and Brito, Dagobert L. Wolfson on Economic Warfare. *Conflict Manage. Peace Sci.*, Spring 1985, *8*(2), pp. 21–25.

Isard, Walter and Anderton, Charles H. Arms Race Models: A Survey and Synthesis. *Conflict Manage. Peace Sci.*, Spring 1985, *8*(2), pp. 27–98.

Kaufman, Richard F. Causes of the Slowdown in Soviet Defense. *Soviet Econ.*, Jan.-Mar. 1985, *1*(1), pp. 9–31. **[G: U.S.S.R.]**

Kindleberger, Charles P. The Financial Aftermath of War. In *Kindleberger, C. P.*, 1985, pp. 168–89.

Lakhani, Hyder; Thomas, Shelley and Gilroy, Curtis. Army European Tour Extension: A Multivariate Approach. *J. Behav. Econ.*, Summer 1985, *14*(2), pp. 15–41. **[G: U.S.]**

Leontief, Wassily. Capital Reconstruction and Postwar Development of Income and Consumption. In *Linz, S. J., ed.*, 1985, pp. 38–46. **[G: U.S.S.R.]**

Liew, L. H. The Impact of Defence Spending on the Australian Economy. *Australian Econ. Pap.*, December 1985, *24*(45), pp. 326–36. **[G: Australia]**

Linz, Susan J. Introduction: War and Progress in the USSR. In *Linz, S. J., ed.*, 1985, pp. 1–7. **[G: U.S.S.R.]**

Linz, Susan J. World War II and Soviet Economic Growth, 1940–1953. In *Linz, S. J., ed.*, 1985, pp. 11–38. **[G: U.S.S.R.]**

Luckham, Robin. Soviet Arms and African Militarization. In *Cassen, R., ed.*, 1985, pp. 89–113. **[G: Africa; U.S.S.R.]**

Lynk, Edward and Hartley, Keith. Input Demands and Elasticities in U.K. Defence Indus-

tries. *Int. J. Ind. Organ.*, March 1985, *3*(1), pp. 71–83. **[G: U.K.]**

Lyon, Peter. The Soviet Union and South Asia in the 1980s. In *Cassen, R., ed.*, 1985, pp. 32–45. **[G: S. Asia; U.S.S.R.]**

Markusen, Ann R. Defense Spending as Industrial Policy. In *Zukin, S., ed.*, 1985, pp. 70–84. **[G: U.S.]**

Mehrotra, Santosh. The Political Economy of Indo–Soviet Relations. In *Cassen, R., ed.*, 1985, pp. 220–40. **[G: India; U.S.S.R.]**

Millar, James R. Conclusion: Impact and Aftermath of World War II. In *Linz, S. J., ed.*, 1985, pp. 283–91. **[G: U.S.S.R.]**

Murdoch, J. C. and Sandler, Todd. Australian Demand for Military Expenditures: 1961–1979. *Australian Econ. Pap.*, June 1985, *24*(44), pp. 142–53. **[G: Australia]**

Niksch, Larry A. Japanese Defense Policy: Issues for the United States. In *Nanto, D. K., ed.*, 1985, pp. 200–14. **[G: Japan; U.S.]**

Nötzold, Jürgen. Economic Relations—Interdependence or Marginal Factor?: Technology Transfer. In *Rode, R. and Jacobsen, H.-D., eds.*, 1985, pp. 50–62. **[G: U.S.S.R.]**

Perry, Yoram. The Military-Industrial Complex. In *Levinson, P. and Landau, P., eds.*, 1985, pp. 47–53. **[G: Israel]**

Przeworski, Adam and Wallerstein, Michael. Comment on Katz, Mahler, & Franz [The Impact of Taxes on Growth and Distribution in Developed Capitalist Countries: A Cross-National Study]. *Amer. Polit. Sci. Rev.*, June 1985, *79*(2), pp. 508–10. **[G: Selected OECD]**

Rasler, Karen A. and Thompson, William R. War Making and State Making: Governmental Expenditures, Tax Revenues, and Global Wars. *Amer. Polit. Sci. Rev.*, June 1985, *79*(2), pp. 491–507. **[G: U.S.; U.K.; France; Japan]**

Ravenal, Earl C. The Price and Perils of NATO. In *Boaz, D. and Crane, E. H., eds.*, 1985, pp. 111–43. **[G: U.S.]**

Riddell, Tom. Concentration and Inefficiency in the Defense Sector: Policy Options. *J. Econ. Issues*, June 1985, *19*(2), pp. 451–61. **[G: U.S.]**

Rüegg, Walter. Social Rights or Social Responsibilities? The Case of Switzerland. In *Eisenstadt, S. N. and Ahimeir, O., eds.*, 1985, pp. 183–99. **[G: Switzerland]**

Scheetz, Thomas. Gastos militares en Chile, Perú y la Argentina. (With English summary.) *Desarrollo Econ.*, Oct.-Dec. 1985, *25*(99), pp. 315–27.

de Secada, C. Alexander G. Arms, Guano, and Shipping: The W. R. Grace Interests in Peru, 1865–1885. *Bus. Hist. Rev.*, Winter 1985, *59*(4), pp. 597–621. **[G: Peru]**

Smith, Alan H. Soviet Trade Relations with the Third World. In *Cassen, R., ed.*, 1985, pp. 140–58. **[G: LDCs; U.S.S.R.]**

Steinberg, Gerald M. Comparing Technological Risks in Large Scale National Projects. *Policy Sci.*, March 1985, *18*(1), pp. 79–93. **[G: U.S.]**

Steinbruner, John D. Causes of the Slowdown in Soviet Defense: Comments. *Soviet Econ.*, Jan.-Mar. 1985, *1*(1), pp. 32–36.
[G: U.S.S.R.]

Steinbruner, John D. Security Policy. In *Chubb, J. E. and Peterson, P. E., eds.*, 1985, pp. 343–64.
[G: U.S.]

Thompson, Fred. Managing Defense Expenditures. In *Harriss, C. L., ed.*, 1985, pp. 72–84.
[G: U.S.]

Treddenick, John M. The Arms Race and Military Keynesianism. *Can. Public Policy*, March 1985, *11*(1), pp. 77–92.
[G: Canada]

Udis, Bernard. The High Technology Arms Race: The Western European Case. *Conflict Manage. Peace Sci.*, Fall 1985, *9*(1), pp. 19–31.
[G: W. Europe; U.S.]

Wenig, Alois. Übervölkerung—eine Kriegsursache? Einige Anmerkungen zur Bevölkerungslehre von Thomas Robert Malthus. (Overpopulation—A Cause for War? With English summary.) *Kyklos*, 1985, *38*(3), pp. 365–91.
[G: Europe]

Wolfson, Murray. Notes on Economic Warfare. *Conflict Manage. Peace Sci.*, Spring 1985, *8*(2), pp. 1–19.

120 COUNTRY STUDIES

121 Economic Studies of Developing Countries

1210 General

Alam, M. Shahid. Some Notes on Work Ethos and Economic Development. *World Devel.*, February 1985, *13*(2), pp. 251–54.
[G: LDCs]

Arellano, José-Pablo. Meeting Basic Needs: The Trade-off between the Quality and Coverage of the Programs. *J. Devel. Econ.*, May–June 1985, *18*(1), pp. 87–99.
[G: Chile]

Balassa, Bela. Adjustment Policies in Developing Economies: A Reassessment. In *Balassa, B.*, 1985, pp. 89–101.
[G: LDCs]

Balassa, Bela. Disequilibrium Analysis in Developing Economies: An Overview. In *Balassa, B.*, 1985, pp. 24–43.
[G: LDCs]

Balassa, Bela. Exports, Policy Choices, and Economic Growth in Developing Countries after the 1973 Oil Shock. *J. Devel. Econ.*, May–June 1985, *18*(1), pp. 23–35.
[G: LDCs]

Berg-Schlosser, Dirk. Leistungen und Fehlleistungen politischer Systeme der Dritten Welt als Kriterium der Entwicklungspolitik. (The Performance of Third World Political Systems as a Criterion for Development Aid. With English summary.) *Konjunkturpolitik*, 1985, *31*(1/2), pp. 79–114.
[G: LDCs]

Bhagwati, Jagdish N. and Wibulswasdi, Chaiyawat. A Statistical Analysis of Shifts in the Import Structure in LDCs. In *Bhagwati, J. N. (II)*, 1985, pp. 142–56.
[G: LDCs]

Bruton, Henry J. The Search for a Development Economics. *World Devel.*, Oct./Nov. 1985, *13*(10/11), pp. 1099–1124.

Cartwright, Phillip A.; DeLorme, Charles D.,

Jr. and Wood, Norman J. The By-Product Theory of Revolution: Some Empirical Evidence. *Public Choice*, 1985, *46*(3), pp. 265–74.
[G: Asia; Africa]

Deger, Saadet. Does Defence Expenditure Mobilise Resources in LDCs? *J. Econ. Stud.*, 1985, *12*(4), pp. 15–29.
[G: LDCs]

Drucker, Peter F. Multinationals and Developing Countries: Myths and Realities. In *Adams, J., ed.*, 1985, pp. 451–63.

Ewing, A. F. International Capital and Economic Development. *J. World Trade Law*, Sept.:Oct. 1985, *19*(5), pp. 537–42.
[G: Global]

Gupta, Kanhaya L. Foreign Capital, Income Inequality, Demographic Pressures, Savings and Growth in Developing Countries: A Cross Country Analysis. *J. Econ. Devel.*, July 1985, *10*(1), pp. 63–88.
[G: LDCs]

Hagen, Everett E. More on the Employment Effects of Innovation: More than a Response [Technological Disemployment and Economic Growth]. *J. Devel. Econ.*, January–February 1985, *17*(1–2), pp. 163–73.

Hall, P. H. and Heffernan, Shelagh A. More on the Employment Effects of Innovation [Technological Disemployment and Economic Growth]. *J. Devel. Econ.*, January–February 1985, *17*(1–2), pp. 151–62.

Johnson, Eldon L. Some Development Lessons from the Early Land-Grant Colleges. *J. Devel. Areas*, January 1985, *19*(2), pp. 139–48.
[G: LDCs; U.S.]

Jung, Woo S. and Marshall, Peyton J. Exports, Growth, and Causality in Developing Countries. *J. Devel. Econ.*, May–June 1985, *18*(1), pp. 1–12.
[G: LDCs]

Kader, Ahmad A. Development Patterns among Countries Reexamined. *Devel. Econ.*, September 1985, *23*(3), pp. 199–220.
[G: LDCs; MDCs]

Khan, Ghulam Ishaq. Adjustment and Growth: A Cooperative Approach. *Finance Develop.*, June 1985, *22*(2), pp. 6–7.
[G: LDCs]

Kirkpatrick, Colin H. and Onis, Ziya. Industrialisation as a Structural Determinant of Inflation Performance in IMF Stabilisation Programmes in Less Developed Countries. *J. Devel. Stud.*, April 1985, *21*(3), pp. 347–61.
[G: LDCs]

Mizoguchi, Toshiyuki. Economic Development Policy and Income Distribution: The Experience in East and Southeast Asia. *Devel. Econ.*, December 1985, *23*(4), pp. 307–24. [G: Asia]

Ondráček, Mojmír. Economic Policy of the Reagan Administration towards the Developing Countries. *Czech. Econ. Digest.*, February 1985, (1), pp. 63–89.
[G: U.S.; LDCs]

Ram, Rati. The Role of Real Income Level and Income Distribution in Fulfillment of Basic Needs. *World Devel.*, May 1985, *13*(5), pp. 589–94.
[G: LDCs]

UNCTAD Secretariat. Examination of the Particular Needs and Problems of Island Developing Countries. In *Dommen, E. and Hein, P., eds.*, 1985, pp. 119–51. [G: Selected Countries]

Wignaraja, Ponna. Towards a New Praxis of Rural Development. *Ann. Pub. Co-op. Econ.*, Janu-

ary–June 1985, *56*(1–2), pp. 121–43.
[G: LDCs]

Zaidi, Iqbal Mehdi. Saving, Investment, Fiscal Deficits, and the External Indebtedness of Developing Countries. *World Devel.*, May 1985, *13*(5), pp. 573–88. [G: LDCs]

1211 Comparative Country Studies

Balassa, Bela. Adjusting to External Shocks: The Newly-industrializing Developing Economies in 1974–1976 and 1979–1981. *Weltwirtsch. Arch.*, 1985, *121*(1), pp. 116–41.
[G: Selected LDCs]

Fields, Gary S. Industrialization and Employment in Hong Kong, Singapore, and Taiwan. In *Galenson, W., ed.*, 1985, pp. 333–75.
[G: Hong Kong; Singapore; S. Korea; Taiwan]

Foltýn, Jaroslav. Some Differentiation Trends in the Developing Countries and Their Significance for the Application of a Typologic Approach in Economic Research. *Czech. Econ. Pap.*, 1985, *23*, pp. 137–49. [G: LDCs]

Gupta, Sanjeev. Export Growth and Economic Growth Revisited. *Indian Econ. J.*, Jan.-Mar. 1985, *32*(3), pp. 52–59. [G: Israel; S. Korea]

Jones, F. Stuart. Britain and the Economic Development of Tropical Africa, Asia and South America in the Age of Imperialism (Review Article). *S. Afr. J. Econ.*, September 1985, *53*(3), pp. 264–86. [G: U.K.; LDCs]

Newlyn, W. T. Measuring Tax Effort in Developing Countries. *J. Devel. Stud.*, April 1985, *21*(3), pp. 390–405. [G: Selected LDCs]

Ranis, Gustav and Orrock, Louise. Latin American and East Asian NICs: Development Strategies Compared. In *Duran, E., ed.*, 1985, pp. 48–66. [G: Selected LDCs]

Sachs, Jeffrey. External Debt and Macroeconomic Performance in Latin America and East Asia. *Brookings Pap. Econ. Act.*, 1985, (2), pp. 523–64. [G: Latin America; E. Asia]

Scitovsky, Tibor. Economic Development in Taiwan and South Korea: 1965-81. *Food Res. Inst. Stud.*, 1985, *19*(3), pp. 214–64.
[G: S. Korea; Taiwan]

Tsiang, S. C. and Wu, Rong-I. Foreign Trade and Investment as Boosters for Take-off: The Experiences of the Four Asian Newly Industrializing Countries. In *Galenson, W., ed.*, 1985, pp. 301–32. [G: Hong Kong; Singapore; S. Korea; Taiwan]

Williamson, John. External Debt and Macroeconomic Performance in Latin America and East Asia: Comment. *Brookings Pap. Econ. Act.*, 1985, (2), pp. 565–70. [G: Latin America; E. Asia]

1213 European Countries

Balassa, Bela. Medium-term Economic Policies for Portugal. In *Balassa, B.*, 1985, pp. 185–207. [G: Portugal]

Barquero, Antonio Vazquez and Hebbert, Michael. Spain: Economy and State in Transition.

In *Hudson, R. and Lewis, J., eds.*, 1985, pp. 284–308. [G: Spain]

Green, Reginald Herbold. The Republic of Ireland: The Impact of Imported Inflation. In *Griffith-Jones, S. and Harvey, C., eds.*, 1985, pp. 145–68. [G: Ireland]

Hudson, Ray and Lewis, Jim. Recent Economic, Social and Political Changes in Southern Europe. In *Hudson, R. and Lewis, J., eds.*, 1985, pp. 1–53. [G: S. Europe]

Paricio, Joaquina and Quesada, Javier. Wages and Employment in the Spanish Economy: Behavior and Trends during the Crisis. *Z. Wirtschaft. Sozialwissen.*, 1985, *105*(2/3), pp. 341–56. [G: Spain]

de Pitta e Cunha, Paulo. The Portuguese Economic System and Accession to the European Community. *Economia (Portugal)*, May 1985, *9*(2), pp. 277–300. [G: Portugal]

1214 Asian Countries

Alschuler, Lawrence R. The State and TNCs in the Development of the Semi-periphery: The Case of South Korea. In *Stauffer, R. B., ed.*, 1985, pp. 133–83. [G: S. Korea]

Amsden, Alice H. The State and Taiwan's Economic Development. In *Evans, P. B.; Rueschemeyer, D. and Skocpol, T., eds.*, 1985, pp. 78–106. [G: Taiwan]

Androuais, Anne. Les investissements japonais en Asie du sud-est: compléments ou concurrents de l'industrie au Japon. (With English summary.) *Revue Écon. Polit.*, May–June 1985, *95*(3), pp. 320–45. [G: Japan; S. E. Asia]

Balassa, Bela. The Role of Foreign Trade in the Economic Development of Korea. In *Galenson, W., ed.*, 1985, pp. 141–75.
[G: S. Korea]

Basu, Sanjib. Nonalignment and Economic Development: Indian State Strategies, 1947–1962. In *Evans, P.; Rueschemeyer, D. and Stephens, E. H., eds.*, 1985, pp. 193–213. [G: India]

Bayly, C. A. State and Economy in India over Seven Hundred Years. *Econ. Hist. Rev.*, 2nd Ser., November 1985, *38*(4), pp. 583–96.
[G: India]

Bhagwati, Jagdish N. Indian Economic Policy and Performance: A Framework for a Progressive Society. In *Bhagwati, J. N. (II)*, 1985, pp. 32–58. [G: India]

Bhagwati, Jagdish N. and Desai, Padma. Socialism and Indian Economic Policy. In *Bhagwati, J. N. (II)*, 1985, pp. 59–72. [G: India]

Blair, Harry W. Participation, Public Policy, Political Economy and Development in Rural Bangladesh, 1958–85. *World Devel.*, December 1985, *13*(12), pp. 1231–47.
[G: Bangladesh]

Blau, David M. The Effects of Economic Development on Life Cycle Wage Rates and Labor Supply Behavior in Malaysia. *J. Devel. Econ.*, Sept.-Oct. 1985, *19*(1/2), pp. 163–85.
[G: Malaysia]

Browett, John. The Newly Industrializing Countries and Radical Theories of Development. *World Devel.*, July 1985, *13*(7), pp. 789–803. [G: S. Korea; Taiwan; Hong Kong; Singapore]

Chapman, Rod. Indonesia. In *Smith, M., et al.*, 1985, pp. 95–130. [G: Indonesia]

Cheng, Chu-yuan. Economic Development on Both Sides of the Taiwan Straits: New Trends for Convergence. *Hong Kong Econ. Pap.*, 1985, (16), pp. 54–73. [G: Taiwan; China]

Chia, Siow Yue. The Role of Foreign Trade and Investment in the Development of Singapore. In *Galenson, W., ed.*, 1985, pp. 259–97. [G: Singapore]

Chou, Tein-Chen. The Pattern and Strategy of Industrialization in Taiwan: Specialization and Offsetting Policy. *Devel. Econ.*, June 1985, *23*(2), pp. 138–57. [G: Taiwan]

Dick, Howard W. Survey of Recent Developments. *Bull. Indonesian Econ. Stud.*, December 1985, *21*(3), pp. 1–29. [G: Indonesia]

Dowling, J. Malcolm, Jr.; Ali, Ifzal and Soo, David. Income Distribution, Poverty and Economic Growth in Developing Asian Countries. *Singapore Econ. Rev.*, April 1985, *30*(1), pp. 1–13. [G: Asia]

Fairbairn, Te'o Ian and Kakazu, Hiroshi. Trade and Diversification in Small Island Economies with Particular Emphasis on the South Pacific. *Singapore Econ. Rev.*, October 1985, *30*(2), pp. 17–35. [G: Asia; Oceania]

Fei, John C. H.; Ohkawa, Kazushi and Ranis, Gustav. Economic Development in Historical Perspective: Japan, Korea, and Taiwan. In *Ohkawa, K. and Ranis, G., eds.*, 1985, pp. 35–64. [G: Japan; S. Korea; Taiwan]

Fforde, Adam. Economic Aspects of the Soviet-Vietnamese Relationship. In *Cassen, R., ed.*, 1985, pp. 192–219. [G: Vietnam; U.S.S.R.]

Glassburner, Bruce. Macroeconomics and the Agricultural Sector. *Bull. Indonesian Econ. Stud.*, August 1985, *21*(2), pp. 51–73. [G: Indonesia]

Islam, Syed Serajul. The Role of the State in the Economic Development of Bangladesh during the Mujib Regime (1972–1975). *J. Devel. Areas*, January 1985, *19*(2), pp. 185–208. [G: Bangladesh]

Jha, L. K. India's Economic Strategies for the Nineties. In *Mongia, J. N., ed.*, 1985 , pp. 641–67. [G: India]

Kaynak, Erdener. Comparative Study of Marketing and Management Systems in the Middle East. In *Kaynak, E., ed. (II)*, 1985, pp. 19–42. [G: N. Africa; Middle East]

Kim, In June. Imported Inflation and the Development of the Korean Economy. In *Griffith-Jones, S. and Harvey, C., eds.*, 1985, pp. 169–95. [G: S. Korea]

Krivine, David. The Economic Overview. In *Levinson, P. and Landau, P., eds.*, 1985, pp. 38–43. [G: Israel]

Krongkaew, Medhi. Agricultural Development, Rural Poverty, and Income Distribution in Thailand. *Devel. Econ.*, December 1985, *23*(4), pp. 325–46. [G: Thailand]

Kuo, Shirley W. Y. and Fei, John C. H. Causes and Roles of Export Expansion in the Republic of China. In *Galenson, W., ed.*, 1985, pp. 45–84. [G: Taiwan]

Kurukulasuriya, G. The Impact of Imported Inflation on National Development: Sri Lanka. In *Griffith-Jones, S. and Harvey, C., eds.*, 1985, pp. 75–92. [G: Sri Lanka]

Lal, Deepak. The Real Exchange Rate, Capital Inflows and Inflation: Sri Lanka 1970–1982. *Weltwirtsch. Arch.*, 1985, *121*(4), pp. 682–702. [G: Sri Lanka]

Large, Peter. Singapore. In *Smith, M., et al.*, 1985, pp. 67–93. [G: Singapore]

Lin, Tzong-Biau. Growth, Equity, and Income Distribution Policies in Hong Kong. *Devel. Econ.*, December 1985, *23*(4), pp. 391–413. [G: Hong Kong]

Lindblad, Jan Thomas. Economic Change in Southeast Kalimantan 1880–1940. *Bull. Indonesian Econ. Stud.*, December 1985, *21*(3), pp. 69–103. [G: Indonesia]

Malenbaum, Wilfred. Modern Economic Growth in India and China: Reply. *Econ. Develop. Cult. Change*, October 1985, *34*(1), pp. 161–66. [G: India; China]

McCawley, Peter. Survey of Recent Developments. *Bull. Indonesian Econ. Stud.*, April 1985, *21*(1), pp. 1–31. [G: Indonesia]

McLoughlin, Jane. South Korea. In *Smith, M., et al.*, 1985, pp. 39–64. [G: S. Korea]

Metzer, Jacob and Kaplan, Oded. Jointly but Severally: Arab–Jewish Dualism and Economic Growth in Mandatory Palestine. *J. Econ. Hist.*, June 1985, *45*(2), pp. 327–45. [G: Israel]

Mishalani, Philip. Jordan: The Case of Inevitable Imported Inflation in the 1970s. In *Griffith-Jones, S. and Harvey, C., eds.*, 1985, pp. 285–310. [G: Jordan]

Moulton, Edward C. South Asian Studies in Canada: A State of the Discipline Review. *Can. J. Devel. Stud.*, 1985, *6*(1), pp. 129–45. [G: Canada; Asia]

Naqvi, Syed Nawab Haider. The Importance of Being Defunct. *Pakistan Devel. Rev.*, Autumn-Winter 1985, *24*(3/4), pp. 211–34. [G: Pakistan; India]

Nasution, Anwar. Survey of Recent Developments. *Bull. Indonesian Econ. Stud.*, August 1985, *21*(2), pp. 1–23. [G: Indonesia]

Naya, Seiji. The Role of Small-Scale Industries in Employment and Exports of Asian Developing Countries. *Hitotsubashi J. Econ.*, December 1985, *26*(2), pp. 147–63. [G: Asian LDCs]

Park, Se-Hark. Investment Planning and the Macroeconomic Constraints in Developing Countries: The Case of the Syrian Arab Republic. *World Devel.*, July 1985, *13*(7), pp. 837–53. [G: Syria]

Perry, Elizabeth J. and Wong, Christine. The Political Economy of Reform in Post-Mao China: Causes, Content, and Consequences. In *Perry, E. J. and Wong, C., eds.*, 1985 1985, pp. 1–27.

Praedicta Ltd. Economic Developments in 1984. In *Levinson, P. and Landau, P., eds.*, 1985, pp. 6–28.   [G: Israel]

Roh, Jae Won. The Korean Development Model and Canada–Korea Trade Relations. *Can. J. Devel. Stud.*, 1985, 6(2), pp. 333–38.
                              [G: S. Korea; Canada]

Sadler, Peter. World Prices and Development: Kuwait. In *Griffith-Jones, S. and Harvey, C., eds.*, 1985, pp. 220–39.   [G: Kuwait]

Sethuraman, S. V. The Informal Sector in Indonesia: Policies and Prospects. *Int. Lab. Rev.*, Nov.-Dec. 1985, 124(6), pp. 719–35.
                              [G: Indonesia]

Sicat, Gerardo P. A Historical and Current Perspective of Philippine Economic Problems. *Philippine Econ. J.*, 1985, 24(1), pp. 24–63.
                              [G: Philippines]

Sundrum, R. M. Modern Economic Growth in India and China: Comment. *Econ. Develop. Cult. Change*, October 1985, 34(1), pp. 157–60.   [G: India; China]

Terasaki, Yasuhiro. Income Distribution and Development Policies in the Philippines. *Devel. Econ.*, December 1985, 23(4), pp. 368–90.
                              [G: Philippines]

Tobiesen, Per; Miranda, Armindo and Jerve, Alf Morten. The Contemporary Setting: An Overview. In *Jerve, A. M., ed.*, 1985, pp. 133–53.
                              [G: Pakistan]

Van Wijnbergen, Sweder. Macro-economic Effects of Changes in Bank Interest Rates: Simulation Results for South Korea. *J. Devel. Econ.*, August 1985, 18(2–3), pp. 541–54.
                              [G: S. Korea]

Watanabe, Toshio. Economic Development in Korea: Lessons and Challenge. In *Shishido, T. and Sato, R., eds.*, 1985, pp. 95–111.
                              [G: S. Korea]

1215 African Countries

Adams, Richard H., Jr. Development and Structural Change in Rural Egypt, 1952 to 1982. *World Devel.*, June 1985, 13(6), pp. 705–23.
                              [G: Egypt]

Ahiakpor, James C. W. The Success and Failure of Dependency Theory: The Experience of Ghana. *Int. Organ.*, Summer 1985, 39(3), pp. 535–52.   [G: Ghana]

Barker, Jonathan. Gaps in the Debates about Agriculture in Senegal, Tanzania and Mozambique. *World Devel.*, January 1985, 13(1), pp. 59–76. [G: Senegal; Tanzania; Mozambique]

Bhatia, Rattan J. Adjustment Efforts in Sub-Saharan Africa, 1980-84. *Finance Develop.*, September 1985, 22(3), pp. 19–22. [G: Sub-Saharan Africa]

Chambas, Gérard and Geourjon, Anne-Marie. Domestic Policies, Crisis and Adjustment in Senegal. In *Rose, T., ed.*, 1985, pp. 155–65.
                              [G: Senegal]

Curry, Robert L., Jr. Mineral-based Growth and Development-generated Socioeconomic Problems in Botswana: Rural Inequality, Water Scarcity, Food Insecurity, and Foreign Depen-

dence Challenge New Governing Class. *Amer. J. Econ. Soc.*, July 1985, 44(3), pp. 319–36.
                              [G: Botswana]

Curry, Robert L., Jr. Problems Produced by the Growth Pattern of Botswana's Mineral-based Economy: Inequities in Income, Assets and Land, Scarce Water, and Diminishing Food Crops Challenge Planners. *Amer. J. Econ. Soc.*, October 1985, 44(4), pp. 449–62.
                              [G: Botswana]

Green, Reginald Herbold and Kamori, D. J. M. Imported Inflation, Global Price Changes and Economic Crises in Tanzania, 1970–1982. In *Griffith-Jones, S. and Harvey, C., eds.*, 1985, pp. 52–74.   [G: Tanzania]

Hansen, Bent. Egypt Decolonialized: Review Article. *J. Econ. Hist.*, September 1985, 45(3), pp. 716–18.   [G: Egypt]

Kaynak, Erdener. Comparative Study of Marketing and Management Systems in the Middle East. In *Kaynak, E., ed. (II)*, 1985, pp. 19–42.   [G: N. Africa; Middle East]

Lundahl, Mats. Errata: Economic Effects of a Trade and Investment Boycott against South Africa. *Scand. J. Econ.*, 1985, 87(1), pp. 142.
                              [G: S. Africa]

Mackintosh, Maureen. Economic Tactics: Commercial Policy and the Socialization of African Agriculture. *World Devel.*, January 1985, 13(1), pp. 77–96.   [G: Africa]

Medani, A. I. Food and Stabilization in Developing Africa. *World Devel.*, June 1985, 13(6), pp. 685–90.   [G: Africa]

Meyer, W. N. The Present Economic Climate in South Africa. *J. Stud. Econ. Econometrics*, August 1985, (22), pp. 3–24.   [G: S. Africa]

Mishalani, Philip. Imported Inflation and Imported Growth: The Case of Tunisia's Studied Postponement. In *Griffith-Jones, S. and Harvey, C., eds.*, 1985, pp. 260–84. [G: Tunisia]

Munslow, Barry. Prospects for the Socialist Transition of Agriculture in Zimbabwe. *World Devel.*, January 1985, 13(1), pp. 41–58.
                              [G: Zimbabwe]

Okolo, Julius Emeka. Integrative and Cooperative Regionalism: The Economic Community of West Africa. *Int. Organ.*, Winter 1985, 39(1), pp. 121–53.   [G: W. Africa]

Robson, Peter. Performance and Priorities for Regional Integration with Special Reference to West Africa. In *Rose, T., ed.*, 1985, pp. 265–77.   [G: W. Africa]

Rossen, Stein. Aspects of Economic Integration Policies in Africa, with Special Reference to the Southern African Development Coordination Conference. In *Rose, T., ed.*, 1985, pp. 278–89.   [G: Sub-Saharan Africa]

Saith, Ashwani. The Distributional Dimensions of Revolutionary Transition: Ethiopia. In *Saith, A., ed.*, 1985, pp. 150–79.   [G: Ethiopia]

Saith, Ashwani. The Distributional Dimensions of Revolutionary Transition: Ethiopia. *J. Devel. Stud.*, October 1985, 22(1), pp. 150–79.
                              [G: Ethiopia]

Silver, M. S. United Republic of Tanzania: Overall Concentration, Regional Concentration, and the Growth of the Parastatal Sector in the Manufacturing Industry. *Industry Devel.*, 1985, (15), pp. 19–36. **[G: Tanzania]**

Snowdon, Brian. The Political Economy of the Ethiopian Famine. *Nat. Westminster Bank Quart. Rev.*, November 1985, pp. 41–55. **[G: Ethiopia]**

Wuyts, Marc. Money, Planning and Rural Transformation in Mozambique. *J. Devel. Stud.*, October 1985, *22*(1), pp. 180–207. **[G: Mozambique]**

Wuyts, Marc. Money, Planning and Rural Transformation in Mozambique. In *Saith, A., ed.*, 1985, pp. 180–207. **[G: Mozambique]**

Yeboah, Dickson A. Control Theory Application to Economic Policy Analysis in Ghana. *Appl. Econ.*, June 1985, *17*(3), pp. 395–419. **[G: Ghana]**

Zeineldin, Aly. The Egyptian Economy in 1999: An Input–Output Study. *Indian Econ. J.*, Oct.-Nov. 1985, *33*(2), pp. 34–44. **[G: Egypt]**

1216 Latin American and Caribbean Countries

Abreu, Marcelo de Paiva. Errata [La Argentina y Brasil en los años treinta. Efectos de la política económica internacional británica y estadounidense]. *Desarrollo Econ.*, April–June 1985, *25*(97), pp. 114. **[G: Argentina; Brazil; U.S.; U.K.]**

Abreu, Marcelo de Paiva. La Argentina y Brasil en los años treinta. Efectos de la política económica internacional británica y estadounidense. (With English summary.) *Desarrollo Econ.*, January-March 1985, *24*(96), pp. 543–59. **[G: Argentina; Brazil; U.S.; U.K.]**

Austin, James; Fox, Jonathan and Kruger, Walter. The Role of the Revolutionary State in the Nicaraguan Food System. *World Devel.*, January 1985, *13*(1), pp. 15–40. **[G: Nicaragua]**

Baker, George. The Size of the Oil Industry in Mexico's Economy. *J. Energy Devel.*, Spring 1985, *10*(2), pp. 213–30. **[G: Mexico]**

Balassa, Bela. Policy Experiments in Chile, 1973–83. In *Balassa, B.*, 1985, pp. 157–84. **[G: Chile]**

Balassa, Bela. Trade Policy in Mexico. In *Balassa, B.*, 1985, pp. 131–56. **[G: Mexico]**

Bandera, V. N. and Lucken, J. A. Simulation of a Debtor Country: The Example of Colombia. *J. Policy Modeling*, Fall 1985, 7(3), pp. 457–76. **[G: Colombia]**

Baxter, Marianne. The Role of Expectations in Stabilization Policy. *J. Monet. Econ.*, May 1985, *15*(3), pp. 343–62. **[G: Chile; Argentina]**

Bekerman, Marta. The Impact of the International Environment on Argentina. In *Griffith-Jones, S. and Harvey, C., eds.*, 1985, pp. 196–219. **[G: Argentina]**

Bekerman, Marta. The Impact of the International Environment on Brazil: From "Miracle" to Recession. In *Griffith-Jones, S. and Harvey, C., eds.*, 1985, pp. 113–44. **[G: Brazil]**

Blackburn, Lucy. The Current Economic Situa-

tion, Alternative Policy Choices and Future Perspectives. In *Hojman, D. E., ed.*, 1985, pp. 31–41. **[G: Chile]**

Brundenius, Claes and Zimbalist, Andrew. Cuban Economic Growth One More Time: A Response to "Imbroglios." [Recent Studies on Cuban Economic Growth: A Review]. *Comparative Econ. Stud.*, Fall 1985, *27*(3), pp. 115–31. **[G: Cuba]**

Brundenius, Claes and Zimbalist, Andrew. Cuban Growth: A Final Worth [Cuban Economic Growth One More Time: A Response to Imbroglios]. *Comparative Econ. Stud.*, Winter 1985, *27*(4), pp. 83–84. **[G: Cuba]**

Brundenius, Claes and Zimbalist, Andrew. Recent Studies on Cuban Economic Growth: A Review. *Comparative Econ. Stud.*, Spring 1985, *27*(1), pp. 21–45. **[G: Cuba]**

Bruno, Michael. The Reforms and Macroeconomic Adjustments: Introduction. *World Devel.*, August 1985, *13*(8), pp. 867–69. **[G: Argentina; Chile; Uruguay]**

Bulmer-Thomas, Victor. World Recession and Central American Depression: Lessons from the 1930s for the 1980s. In *Duran, E., ed.*, 1985, pp. 130–51. **[G: Central America]**

Condon, Timothy; Corbo, Vittorio and de Melo, Jaime. Productivity Growth, External Shocks, and Capital Inflows in Chile: A General Equilibrium Analysis. *J. Policy Modeling*, Fall 1985, 7(3), pp. 379–405. **[G: Chile]**

Congdon, Tim G. The Rise and Fall of the Chilean Economic Miracle. In *Duran, E., ed.*, 1985, pp. 98–119. **[G: Chile]**

Connolly, Michael and Hartpence, María. El ataque especulativo contra la tasa de cambio programada en Argentina: 1979–1981. (With English summary.) *Cuadernos Econ.*, December 1985, *22*(67), pp. 373–88. **[G: Argentina]**

Corbo, Vittorio. Reforms and Macroeconomic Adjustments in Chile during 1974–84. *World Devel.*, August 1985, *13*(8), pp. 893–916. **[G: Chile]**

Corbo, Vittorio and de Melo, Jaime. Liberalization with Stabilization in the Southern Cone of Latin America: Overview and Summary. *World Devel.*, August 1985, *13*(8), pp. 863–66. **[G: Argentina; Chile; Uruguay]**

Di Tella, Torcuato. The Political and Social Outlook for Latin America. *Cepal Rev.*, August 1985, (26), pp. 89–99. **[G: Latin America]**

Edwards, Sebastian. Stabilization with Liberalization: An Evaluation of Ten Years of Chile's Experiment with Free-Market Policies, 1973–1983. *Econ. Develop. Cult. Change*, January 1985, *33*(2), pp. 223–54. **[G: Chile]**

Estévez, Jaime. Crisis de pagos y proceso de ajuste en Brasil y México. (Payment Crisis and Adjustment Process in Brazil and Mexico. With English summary.) *Colección Estud. CIEPLAN*, September 1985, (17), pp. 33–67. **[G: Brazil; Mexico]**

Fendt, Roberto, Jr. and Salazar-Carrillo, Jorge. Brazil and the Future: Some Thoughts on the Eighties. In *Salazar-Carrillo, J. and Fendt, R., Jr., eds.*, 1985, pp. 12–24. **[G: Brazil]**

Fernandez, Roque B. The Expectations Management Approach to Stabilization in Argentina during 1976–82. *World Devel.*, August 1985, *13*(8), pp. 871–92.　　[G: Argentina]

Fischer, B.; Hiemenz, Ulrich and Trapp, P. Economic Development, Debt Crisis, and the Importance of Domestic Policies—The Case of Argentina. *Econ. Int.*, February 1985, *38*(1), pp. 21–48.　　[G: Argentina]

Fishlow, Albert. Brazil and the Future: Some Thoughts on the Eighties: Comments. In *Salazar-Carrillo, J. and Fendt, R., Jr., eds.*, 1985, pp. 34–37.　　[G: Brazil; U.S.]

Gálvez, Julio and Tybout, James R. Chile 1977–1981: impacto sobre las empresas chilenas de algunas reformas económicas e intentos de estabilización. (With English summary.) *Cuadernos Econ.*, April 1985, *22*(65), pp. 37–71.　　[G: Chile]

Garretón M., Manuel Antonio. Chile: en busca de la democracia perdida. (With English summary.) *Desarrollo Econ.*, Oct.-Dec. 1985, *25*(99), pp. 381–97.　　[G: Chile]

Gibson, Bill. A Structuralist Macromodel for Postrevolutionary Nicaragua. *Cambridge J. Econ.*, December 1985, *9*(4), pp. 347–69.　　[G: Nicaragua]

González, Norberto. Crisis and Development in Latin America and the Caribbean. *Cepal Rev.*, August 1985, (26), pp. 9–56.　　[G: Latin America]

Guillén Romo, Hector. Crise et austérité au Mexique. (Crisis and Austerity: The Case of Mexico. With English summary.) *Écon. Soc.*, August 1985, *19*(8), pp. 273–86.　　[G: Mexico]

Hanson, James A. and de Melo, Jaime. External Shocks, Financial Reforms, and Stabilization Attempts in Uruguay during 1974–83. *World Devel.*, August 1985, *13*(8), pp. 917–39.　　[G: Uruguay]

Harberger, Arnold C. Observations on the Chilean Economy, 1973–1983. *Econ. Develop. Cult. Change*, April 1985, *33*(3), pp. 451–62.　　[G: Chile]

Hausmann, Ricardo and Marquez, G. World Prices and National Development: The Case of Venezuela. In *Griffith-Jones, S. and Harvey, C., eds.*, 1985, pp. 240–59.　　[G: Venezuela]

Ibarra, David. Crisis, Adjustment and Economic Policy in Latin America. *Cepal Rev.*, August 1985, (26), pp. 147–54.　　[G: Latin America]

Iglesias, Enrique V. Statement Delivered at the Expert Meeting on Crisis and Development in Latin America and the Caribbean. *Cepal Rev.*, August 1985, (26), pp. 57–62.

Iglesias, Enrique V. The Latin American Economy during 1984: A Preliminary Overview. *Cepal Rev.*, April 1985, (25), pp. 7–44.　　[G: Latin America]

Imam, M. Hasan and Whalley, John. Incidence Analysis of a Sector-specific Minimum Wage in a Two-Sector Harris–Todaro Model. *Quart. J. Econ.*, February 1985, *100*(1), pp. 207–24.　　[G: Mexico]

Ize, Alain and Salas, Javier. Prices and Output in the Mexican Economy: Empirical Testing of Alternative Hypotheses. *J. Devel. Econ.*, April 1985, *17*(3), pp. 175–99.　　[G: Mexico]

de Janvry, Alain. Social Disarticulation in Latin American History. In *Kim, K. S. and Ruccio, D. F., eds.*, 1985, pp. 32–73.　　[G: Argentina; Brazil; Chile]

Knox, A. David. Resuming Growth in Latin America. *Finance Develop.*, September 1985, *22*(3), pp. 15–18.　　[G: Latin America]

Latortue, Paul R. The Taiwan Model and Economic Development of Haiti. In *Jorge, A.; Salazar-Carrillo, J. and Diaz-Pou, F., eds.*, 1985, pp. 145–55.　　[G: Haiti]

Le Guay, François. The International Crisis and Latin American Development: Objectives and Instruments. *Cepal Rev.*, August 1985, (26), pp. 127–37.　　[G: Latin America]

Lopez, Julio. The Post-war Latin American Economies: The End of the Long Boom. *Banca Naz. Lavoro Quart. Rev.*, September 1985, (154), pp. 233–60.　　[G: Latin America]

Mandle, Jay R. The Role of Agriculture in Self-Reliant Development. *Soc. Econ. Stud.*, June 1985, *34*(2), pp. 153–75.　　[G: Caribbean]

Mann, Arthur J. Economic Development, Income Distribution, and Real Income Levels: Puerto Rico, 1953–1977. *Econ. Develop. Cult. Change*, April 1985, *33*(3), pp. 485–502.　　[G: Puerto Rico]

Mares, David R. Explaining Choice of Development Strategies: Suggestions from Mexico, 1970–1982. *Int. Organ.*, Autumn 1985, *39*(4), pp. 667–97.　　[G: Mexico]

McCarthy, F. Desmond; Hanson, James A. and Kwon, Soonwon. Sources of Growth in Colombia, 1963–80. *J. Econ. Stud.*, 1985, *12*(4), pp. 3–14.　　[G: Colombia]

de Melo, Jaime; Pascale, Ricardo and Tybout, James R. Uruguay 1973–1981: interrelación entre shocks financieros y reales. (With English summary.) *Cuadernos Econ.*, April 1985, *22*(65), pp. 73–98.　　[G: Uruguay]

Mesa-Lago, Carmelo and Perez-Lopez, Jorge. Imbroglios on the Cuban Economy: A Reply. *Comparative Econ. Stud.*, Spring 1985, *27*(1), pp. 47–83.　　[G: Cuba]

Mesa-Lago, Carmelo and Perez-Lopez, Jorge. The Endless Cuban Economy Saga: A Terminal Rebuttal [Recent Studies on Cuban Economic Growth: A Review]. *Comparative Econ. Stud.*, Winter 1985, *27*(4), pp. 67–82.　　[G: Cuba]

Mosley, Paul. Achievements and Contradictions of the Peruvian Agrarian Reform: A Regional Perspective. *J. Devel. Stud.*, April 1985, *21*(3), pp. 440–48.　　[G: Peru]

Ortiz, Guillermo. Economic Expansion, Crisis and Adjustment in Mexico (1977–83). In *Connolly, M. B. and McDermott, J., eds.*, 1985, pp. 68–98.　　[G: Mexico]

Pérez, Louis A., Jr. Vagrants, Beggars, and Bandits: Social Origins of Cuban Separatism, 1878–1895. *Amer. Hist. Rev.*, December 1985, *90*(5), pp. 1092–1121.　　[G: Cuba]

Petrei, A. Humberto and Tybout, James R. Argentina 1976–1981: la importancia de variar los niveles de subsidios financieros. (With English summary.) *Cuadernos Econ.*, April 1985, 22(65), pp. 13–36.   **[G: Argentina]**

Pollard, H. J. The Erosion of Agriculture in an Oil Economy: The Case of Export Crop Production in Trinidad. *World Devel.*, July 1985, 13(7), pp. 819–35.   **[G: Trinidad]**

Pollard, Stephen K. and Graham, Douglas H. Price Policy and Agricultural Export Performance in Jamaica. *World Devel.*, September 1985, 13(9), pp. 1067–75.   **[G: Jamaica]**

Prebisch, Raúl. The Latin American Periphery in the Global Crisis of Capitalism. *Cepal Rev.*, August 1985, (26), pp. 63–88.
                         [G: Latin America]

Rama, Germán W. and Faletto, Enzo. Dependent Societies and Crisis in Latin America: The Challenges of Social and Political Transformation. *Cepal Rev.*, April 1985, (25), pp. 129–47.   **[G: Latin America]**

Ramos, Joseph. Stabilization and Adjustment Policies in the Southern Cone, 1974–1983. *Cepal Rev.*, April 1985, (25), pp. 85–109.
             [G: Argentina; Chile; Uruguay]

Reynolds, Clark W. Mexico and the United States: Studies in Economic Interaction: Fluctuations and Growth: Comments. In *Musgrave, P. B., ed.*, 1985, pp. 171– 75.
                          [G: Mexico; U.S.]

Sadoulet, Elisabeth. Investment Priorities and Income Distribution: The Case of Brazil in 1970. *J. Policy Modeling*, Fall 1985, 7(3), pp. 407–39.   **[G: Brazil]**

Schydlowsky, Daniel M. Mexico and the United States: Studies in Economic Interaction: Fluctuations and Growth: Comments. In *Musgrave, P. B., ed.*, 1985, pp. 177–82.
                          [G: Mexico; U.S.]

Street, James H. Development Planning and the International Debt Crisis in Latin America. *J. Econ. Issues*, June 1985, 19(2), pp. 397–408.
                         [G: Latin America]

Street, James H. Monetarism and Beyond: The Dilemma of the Southern Cone Countries: A Review Article. *J. Econ. Issues*, December 1985, 19(4), pp. 923–37.   **[G: Argentina; Chile; Uruguay]**

Taylor, Lance. The Crisis and Thereafter: Macroeconomic Policy Problems in Mexico. In *Musgrave, P. B., ed.*, 1985, pp. 147–70.
                          [G: Mexico]

Tokman, Victor E. The Process of Accumulation and the Weakness of the Protagonists. *Cepal Rev.*, August 1985, (26), pp. 115–26.
                         [G: Latin America]

Vincent, D. P. Exchange Rate Devaluation, Monetary Policy and Wages: A General Equilibrium Analysis for Chile. *Econ. Modelling*, January 1985, 2(1), pp. 17–32.   **[G: Chile]**

Zedillo Ponce de León, Ernesto. The Mexican External Debt: The Last Decade. In *Wionczek, M. S., ed.*, 1985, pp. 294–324.   **[G: Mexico]**

1217 Oceanic Countries

Fairbairn, Te'o Ian and Kakazu, Hiroshi. Trade and Diversification in Small Island Economies with Particular Emphasis on the South Pacific. *Singapore Econ. Rev.*, October 1985, 30(2), pp. 17–35.   **[G: Asia; Oceania]**

Howard, Michael. Export Processing Zones and Development Strategies in the South Pacific. In *Utrecht, E., ed.*, 1985, pp. 31–82.
                         [G: S. Pacific]

122 Economic Studies of Developed Countries

1220 General

Balassa, Bela. The Economic Consequences of Social Policies in the Industrial Countries. In *Balassa, B.*, 1985, pp. 44–59.   **[G: EEC; U.S.]**

Betbeze, Jean-Paul. 1982–1984 ou la rigueur en pratique. (With English summary.) *Revue Écon. Polit.*, Sept.-Oct. 1985, 95(5), pp. 714–24.   **[G: France; U.K.; U.S.; Japan; W. Germany]**

Bryant, J. Economics, Equilibrium and Thermodynamics. In *van Gool, W. and Bruggink, J. J. C., eds.*, 1985, pp. 197–221.   **[G: U.K.; OECD]**

Haberler, Gottfried. The World Economy, Money, and the Great Depression 1919–1939. In *Haberler, G.*, 1985, pp. 363–403.
             [G: U.S.; Japan; France; Germany]

1221 Comparative Country Studies

Barker, Kate, et al. Macroeconomic Policy in Germany and Britain. *Nat. Inst. Econ. Rev.*, November 1985, (114), pp. 69–89. **[G: U.K.; W. Germany]**

Bird, Richard M. Federal Finance in Comparative Perspective. In *Courchene, T. J.; Conklin, D. W. and Cook, G. C. A., eds. Vol. 1*, 1985, pp. 137–77.   **[G: Canada; Selected OECD]**

Bismut, Claude and Kröger, Jürgen. The Dilemmas of Economic Policy in France and Germany: Trade-offs between Inflation, Unemployment, and the Current Account. In *de Ménil, G. and Westphal, U., eds.*, 1985, pp. 303–47.   **[G: France; W. Germany]**

Costa, Antonio Maria. Multilateralism under Threat: Causes, Impact, and the Policy Debate on Government Intervention in Trade. *J. Policy Modeling*, Spring 1985, 7(1), pp. 181–217.
                          [G: OECD]

De Grauwe, Paul and Fratianni, Michele. Interdependence, Macro-economic Policies and All That. *World Econ.*, March 1985, 8(1), pp. 63–79.   **[G: OECD]**

Guglielmi, Jean-Louis. Conjoncture, structures économiques et monétarisme. (With English summary.) *Revue Écon. Polit.*, Sept.-Oct. 1985, 95(5), pp. 705–13.   **[G: OECD]**

Hibbs, Douglas A., Jr. Inflation, Political Support, and Macroeconomic Policy. In *Lindberg, L. N. and Maier, C. S., eds.*, 1985, pp. 175–95.   **[G: OECD]**

Hood, Neil and Young, Stephen. The United Kingdom and the Changing Economic World Order. In *Hochmuth, M. and Davidson, W.*, *eds.*, 1985, pp. 99–129. **[G: OECD; U.K.]**

Kindleberger, Charles P. Financial Institutions and Economic Development: A Comparison of Great Britain and France in the Eighteenth and Nineteenth Centuries. In *Kindleberger, C. P.*, 1985, pp. 65–85. **[G: U.K.; France]**

Leemans, Tom and Vuchelen, Jef. De economische ontwikkeling van Westerse landen: een beschrijving met cluster-algoritmen. (With English summary.) *Cah. Écon. Bruxelles*, 3rd Trimester 1985, (107), pp. 385–425. **[G: OECD]**

Patrick, Hugh. Services in the Japanese Economy: Comment. In *Inman, R. P., ed.*, 1985, pp. 84–88. **[G: Japan; OECD]**

Saxonhouse, Gary R. Services in the Japanese Economy. In *Inman, R. P., ed.*, 1985, pp. 53–83. **[G: Japan; OECD]**

Tabatoni, Pierre. The Market Economies Tack against the Wind: Coping with Economic Shocks: 1973–1983. In *Juris, H.; Thompson, M. and Daniels, W., eds.*, 1985, pp. 1–40. **[G: OECD]**

Tsurumi, Yoshi. Japan's Challenge to the United States: Industrial Policies and Corporate Strategies. In *Hochmuth, M. and Davidson, W., eds.*, 1985, pp. 39–79. **[G: U.S.; Japan]**

1223 European Countries

Andreatta, Nino and D'Adda, Carlo. Effetti reali o nominali della svalutazione? Una riflessione sull'esperienza italiana dopo il primo shock petrolifero. (Real and Nominal Effects of the Devaluation: the Italian Experience after the First Oil Shock. With English summary.) *Polit. Econ.*, April 1985, *1*(1), pp. 37–51. **[G: Italy]**

Baslé, M. Profitabilité, accumulation-répartition, et régulation d'ensemble: propositions de synthèse et premie application au cas de la France. (Profitability, Accumulation-Repartition, and Global Regulation. Some Propositions for Synthetic Analysis and a First Application in the French Case. With English summary.) *Écon. Soc.*, January 1985 cf, *19*(1), pp. 131–76. **[G: France]**

Beltensperger, Ernst. Disinflation—The Swiss Experience 1973-1983. *Z. Wirtschaft. Sozialwissen.*, 1985, *105*(2/3), pp. 271–93. **[G: Switzerland]**

Bjerkholt, Olav and Tveitereid, Sigurd. The Use of the MSG-Model in Preparing a "Perspective Analysis 1980–2000" for the Norwegian Economy. In *[Johansen, L.]*, 1985, pp. 271–87.

Boltho, Andrea. The European Economy. In *Morris, D., ed.*, 1985, pp. 503–25. **[G: EEC]**

Borner, Silvio, et al. Global Structural Change and International Competition among Industrial Firms: The Case of Switzerland. *Kyklos*, 1985, *38*(1), pp. 77–103. **[G: Switzerland]**

Branson, William H. Inflation, Employment and External Constraints: An Overview of the French Economy during the Seventies: Comments. In *Melitz, J. and Wyplosz, C., eds.*, 1985, pp. 43–47. **[G: France]**

Budd, Alan P. Macroeconomic Policy and the 1985 Budget. *Fisc. Stud.*, May 1985, *6*(2), pp. 10–22. **[G: U.K.]**

Cappelen, Adne; Offerdal, Erik and Strøm, Steinar. Oil Revenues and the Norwegian Economy in the Seventies. In *Bjerkholt, O. and Offerdal, E., eds.*, 1985, pp. 35–62. **[G: Norway]**

Christoffersen, Henrik. Vstforståelsen i dansk økonomisk politik. (The Growth Orientation in Danish Economic Policy. With English summary.) *Nationaløkon. Tidsskr.*, 1985, *123*(3), pp. 329–41. **[G: Denmark]**

Ciampi, Carlo Azeglio. I nodi da sciogliere per sospingere la ripresa. (The Obstacles to Be Overcome in Order to Enhance Recovery. With English summary.) *Bancaria*, March 1985, *41*(3), pp. 265–80. **[G: Italy]**

Cockerill, Anthony. The British Economy: Performance, Prospects and Policies. In *Meyer, F. V., ed.*, 1985, pp. 102–23. **[G: U.K.]**

Desaigues, Brigitte. Le rang de la France a-t-il changé (1860–1970)? Évolution de la position internationale de la France. (With English summary.) *Revue Écon. Polit.*, Sept.-Oct. 1985, *95*(5), pp. 531–43. **[G: France]**

Forssell, Osmo. Changes in the Structure of the Finnish Economy, 1970–1980. In *Smyshlyaev, A., ed.*, 1985, pp. 61–71. **[G: Finland]**

Gahlen, Bernhard. Trend und Zyklus—Aggregat und Struktur. (Trends and Cycles—Structure and the Aggregate. With English summary.) *Jahr. Nationalökon. Statist.*, September 1985, *200*(5), pp. 449–78. **[G: W. Germany]**

Goldman, Marshall I. Gorbachev and Economic Reform. *Foreign Aff.*, Fall 1985, *64*(1), pp. 56–73. **[G: U.S.S.R.]**

Grönberg, Rolf and Rahmeyer, Fritz. Preis- und Mengenanpassungen in den Konjunkturzyklen der Bundesrepublik Deutschland, 1963–1981. (Price and Quantity Adjustments in the Business Cycles of the Federal Republic of Germany, 1963–1981. With English summary.) *Jahr. Nationalökon. Statist.*, May 1985, *200*(3), pp. 239–61. **[G: W. Germany]**

Hentschel, Volker. Breaks and Continuity in the Economy and Social Structures between the Weimar Republic and the Third Reich. In *Engels, W. and Pohl, H., eds.*, 1985, pp. 95–128. **[G: Germany]**

Horn, Ernst-Jürgen. Positive and Defensive Strategies in Sectoral Adjustment. In *Jungenfelt, K. and Hague, D. [Sir], eds.*, 1985, pp. 533–70. **[G: W. Germany]**

Hudson, Ray and Lewis, Jim. Recent Economic, Social and Political Changes in Southern Europe. In *Hudson, R. and Lewis, J., eds.*, 1985, pp. 1–53. **[G: S. Europe]**

Kloten, Norbert; Ketterer, Karl-Heinz and Vollmer, Rainer. West Germany's Stabilization Performance. In *Lindberg, L. N. and Maier, C. S., eds.*, 1985, pp. 353–402. **[G: W. Germany]**

Kuipers, S. K., et al. A Putty–Clay Vintage Model for Sectors of Industry in The Netherlands. *De Economist*, 1985, *133*(2), pp. 151–75. **[G: Netherlands]**

Lesourne, Jacques. Social Values, Political Goals, and Economic Systems: The Issue of Employment in European Societies. In *Didsbury, H. F., Jr., ed.*, 1985, pp. 60–75.

Lindbeck, Assar. What Is Wrong with the West European Economies? *World Econ.*, June 1985, *8*(2), pp. 153–70.   [G: W. Europe]

Longva, Svein; Lorentsen, Lorents and Olsen, Øystein. The Multi-sectoral Growth Model MSG-4 Formal Structure and Empirical Characteristics. In *[Johansen, L.]*, 1985, pp. 187–240.   [G: Norway]

Lundberg, Erik. The Rise and Fall of the Swedish Model. *J. Econ. Lit.*, March 1985, *23*(1), pp. 1–36.   [G: Sweden]

Macharzina, Klaus. Development of the German Economy and National Economic Policy. In *Hochmuth, M. and Davidson, W., eds.*, 1985, pp. 81–97.   [G: OECD; W. Germany]

Martin, Andrew. Wages, Profits, and Investment in Sweden. In *Lindberg, L. N. and Maier, C. S., eds.*, 1985, pp. 403–66.   [G: Sweden]

Masera, Francesco. Moneta, spesa pubblica e occupazione nel quadro dell'esperienza italiana. (Money, Government Expenditure and Employment in the Italian Experience. With English summary.) *Bancaria*, December 1985, *41*(12), pp. 1226–42.   [G: Italy]

McCloskey, Donald N. The Industrial Revolution 1780–1860: A Survey. In *Mokyr, J., ed.*, 1985, pp. 53–74.   [G: U.K.]

Mokyr, Joel. The Industrial Revolution and the New Economic History. In *Mokyr, J., ed.*, 1985, pp. 1–51.   [G: U.K.]

Morris, Derek J. The UK in the 1980s: Theory, Policy, and Performance. In *Morris, D., ed.*, 1985, pp. 897–926.   [G: U.K.]

O'Malley, Eoin. The Problem of Late Industrialisation and the Experience of the Republic of Ireland. *Cambridge J. Econ.*, June 1985, *9*(2), pp. 141–54.   [G: Ireland]

Oudiz, Gilles and Sterdyniak, Henri. Inflation, Employment and External Constraints: An Overview of the French Economy during the Seventies. In *Melitz, J. and Wyplosz, C., eds.*, 1985, pp. 9–42.   [G: France]

Pekkarinen, Jukka and Sauramo, Pekka. Devaluations and Employment in the Economic Policy of the Nordic Countries—Some Reflections on the Finnish Experience. *Rech. Écon. Louvain*, 1985, *51*(3–4), pp. 343–62.   [G: Finland; Norway; Denmark; Sweden]

Romani, Claudine. Dinamiche dell'occupazione industriale nella crisi: un confronto tra Francia e Germania. (Dynamics of Industrial Employment in the Crisis: A Comparison France–Germany. With English summary.) *Econ. Lavoro*, Apr.-June 1985, *19*(2), pp. 35–48.   [G: France; W. Germany]

Sigurjonsson, Birgir Björn. National Sovereignty and Economic Policy. The Case of Iceland. *Scand. Econ. Hist. Rev.*, 1985, *33*(1), pp. 51–65.   [G: Iceland]

Söderström, Hans Tson. Exchange Rate Strategies and Real Adjustment after 1970. The Experience of the Smaller European Economies.

In *Peeters, T.; Praet, P. and Reding, P., eds.*, 1985, pp. 227–64.   [G: Europe]

Solow, Barbara L. Caribbean Slavery and British Growth: The Eric Williams Hypothesis. *J. Devel. Econ.*, January–February 1985, *17*(1–2), pp. 99–115.   [G: U.K.]

Woodham, Douglas M. How Fast Can Europe Grow? *Fed. Res. Bank New York Quart. Rev.*, Summer 1985, *10*(2), pp. 28–35.   [G: U.S.; W. Germany; U.K.]

Worswick, G. D. N. Correction [Two Great Recessions]. *Scot. J. Polit. Econ.*, February 1985, *32*(1), pp. 111.   [G: U.S.; U.K.]

van Zon, Andriaan H. A Simple Multisector Model with Six Sectors of Production: Estimation and Simulation Results for the 1950–1968 Period. *De Economist*, 1985, *133*(3), pp. 352–410.   [G: Netherlands]

1224 Asian Countries

Boltho, Andrea. Was Japan's Industrial Policy Successful? *Cambridge J. Econ.*, June 1985, *9*(2), pp. 187–201.   [G: Japan]

Boltho, Andrea and Hardie, C. J. M. The Japanese Economy. In *Morris, D., ed.*, 1985, pp. 527–48.   [G: Japan; OECD; U.S.S.R.]

Dopfer, Kurt. Reconciling Economic Theory and Economic History: The Rise of Japan. *J. Econ. Issues*, March 1985, *19*(1), pp. 21–73.   [G: Japan]

Fei, John C. H.; Ohkawa, Kazushi and Ranis, Gustav. Economic Development in Historical Perspective: Japan, Korea, and Taiwan. In *Ohkawa, K. and Ranis, G., eds.*, 1985, pp. 35–64.   [G: Japan; S. Korea; Taiwan]

Ohkawa, Kazushi and Ranis, Gustav. Japan and the Developing Countries: Introduction. In *Ohkawa, K. and Ranis, G., eds.*, 1985, pp. 1–16.   [G: Japan]

Patrick, Hugh and Rosovsky, Henry. The Japanese Economy in Transition. In *Shishido, T. and Sato, R., eds.*, 1985, pp. 159–70.   [G: Japan]

Sakamoto, Masahiro. Japan's Macroeconomic Performance and Its Effects on the Japanese–U.S. Economic Relationship. In *Nanto, D. K., ed.*, 1985, pp. 79–93.   [G: Japan; U.S.]

Schmiegelow, Michèle. Cutting across Doctrines: Positive Adjustment in Japan. *Int. Organ.*, Spring 1985, *39*(2), pp. 261–96.   [G: Japan]

Smith, Michael. Japan. In *Smith, M., et al.*, 1985, pp. 5–36.   [G: Japan]

Woronoff, Jon. Japan's Structural Shift from Exports to Domestic Demand. In *Nanto, D. K., ed.*, 1985, pp. 64–78.   [G: Japan]

Yamamura, Kozo. The Cost of Rapid Growth and Capitalist Democracy in Japan. In *Lindberg, L. N. and Maier, C. S., eds.*, 1985, pp. 467–508.   [G: Japan]

Yonekawa, Shin-Ichi. Recent Writing on Japanese Economic and Social History. *Econ. Hist. Rev.*, 2nd Ser., February 1985, *38*(1), pp. 107–23.   [G: Japan]

1227 Oceanic Countries

Dixon, Peter B. and McDonald, Daina. The Australian Economy in 1984–85 and 1985–86. *Australian Econ. Rev.*, 2nd Quarter 1985, (70), pp. 3–18. [G: Australia]

Groenewegen, Peter D. The Economy. In *Mathews, R., et al.*, 1985, pp. 1–28. [G: Australia]

Hughes, Barry. Brookings on the Australian Economy. *Econ. Rec.*, March 1985, *61*(172), pp. 405–14. [G: Australia]

Jonson, P. D. and Stevens, G. R. The Australian Economy in the 1930s and the 1980s: Some Facts. In *Argy, V. E. and Neville, J. W., eds.*, 1985, pp. 281–304. [G: Australia]

McDonald, Ian M. Macroeconomic Policy in Australia since the Sixties. *Australian Econ. Rev.*, 3rd Quarter, Spring 1985, (71), pp. 6–19. [G: Australia]

Sloan, Judith. The Australian Labour Market December 1985. *Australian Bull. Lab.*, December 1985, *12*(1), pp. 3–21. [G: Australia]

Walsh, Cliff. A View from the South on: 'The Australian Economy: A View from the North.' *Econ. Rec.*, March 1985, *61*(172), pp. 415–20. [G: Australia]

1228 North American Countries

Burbridge, John B. and Harrison, Alan. (Innovation) Accounting for the Impact of Fluctuations in U.S. Variables on the Canadian Economy. *Can. J. Econ.*, November 1985, *18*(4), pp. 784–98. [G: U.S.; Canada]

Daly, Michael J. and Rao, P. Someshwar. Some Myths and Realities Concerning Canada's Recent Productivity Slowdown, and Their Policy Implications. *Can. Public Policy*, June 1985, *11*(2), pp. 206–17. [G: Canada]

Due, John F. Federal and Foreign Trade Deficits and the Future of the U.S. Economy. *J. Econ. Educ.*, Summer 1985, *16*(3), pp. 194–202. [G: U.S.]

Feldstein, Martin. American Economic Policy and the World Economy. *Foreign Aff.*, Summer 1985, *63*(5), pp. 995–1008. [G: U.S.; OECD]

Foster, John Bellamy. Sources of Instability in the U.S. Political Economy and Empire. *Sci. Soc.*, Summer 1985, *49*(2), pp. 167–93. [G: U.S.]

Lipsey, Richard G. Canada and the United States: The Economic Dimension. In *Doran, C. F. and Sigler, J. H., eds.*, 1985, pp. 69–108. [G: Canada; U.S.]

Motley, Brian. Whither the Unemployment Rate? *Fed. Res. Bank San Francisco Econ. Rev.*, Spring 1985, (2), pp. 40–54. [G: U.S.]

Pierce, James L. Policy Making under Uncertainty: Some Lessons from the 1970s. In *[Weintraub, R. E.]*, 1985, pp. 55–75. [G: U.S.]

Sacchetti, Ugo. What Can Be Learned from the 1981–84 U.S. Experience. *Econ. Notes*, 1985, (3), pp. 49–88. [G: U.S.]

Volcker, Paul A. Economics in Policy and Practice: Opportunity out of Adversity. *Fed. Res. Bull.*, August 1985, *71*(8), pp. 601–06. [G: U.S.]

Wilson, Thomas A. Lessons of Recession. *Can. J. Econ.*, November 1985, *18*(4), pp. 693–722. [G: Canada]

123 Comparative Studies of Developing, Developed, and/or Centrally Planned Economies

1230 Comparative Studies of Developing, Developed, and/or Centrally Planned Economies

Abizadeh, Sohrab and Gray, John. Wagner's Law: A Pooled Time-Series, Cross-Section Comparison. *Nat. Tax J.*, June 1985, *38*(2), pp. 209–18.

Ali, M. Shaukat. Contribution of Education towards Labor Productivity: A Cross-Country Study. *Pakistan Econ. Soc. Rev.*, Summer 1985, *23*(1), pp. 41–54.

Bedrossian, A. and Hitiris, T. Trade Taxes as a Source of Government Revenue: A Re-estimation. *Scot. J. Polit. Econ.*, June 1985, *32*(2), pp. 199–204. [G: LDCs]

Bergson, Abram. Inventories: East and West. In *[Levcik, F.]*, 1985, pp. 239–43. [G: CMEA; OECD]

Bhagwati, Jagdish N. Why Are Services Cheaper in the Poor Countries? In *Bhagwati, J. N. (II)*, 1985, pp. 82–91.

Blumenthal, Tuvia and Lee, Chung H. Development Strategies of Japan and the Republic of Korea: A Comparative Study. *Devel. Econ.*, September 1985, *23*(3), pp. 221–35. [G: Japan; S. Korea]

Brewer, Thomas L. A Comparative Analysis of the Fiscal Policies of Industrial and Developing Countries—Policy Instability and Governmental-Regime Instability. *J. Compar. Econ.*, June 1985, *9*(2), pp. 191–96.

Burkett, John P. Systemic Influences on the Physical Quality of Life: A Bayesian Analysis of Cross-sectional Data. *J. Compar. Econ.*, June 1985, *9*(2), pp. 145–63.

Coutinho, Luciano. The Recent Performance and Future Challenges of Newly Industrializing Countries. In *Hochmuth, M. and Davidson, W., eds.*, 1985, pp. 131–62. [G: OECD; LDCs]

Crnković-Pozaić, Sanja. The Relationship between the Level of Development and the Rate of Growth: Some Empirical Evidence. *Econ. Anal. Worker's Manage.*, 1985, *19*(1), pp. 29–63. [G: LDCs; MDCs]

Dunning, John H. Multinational Enterprises, Economic Structure and International Competitiveness: Some Conclusions and Policy Implications. In *Dunning, J. H., ed.*, 1985, pp. 407–31. [G: Selected Countries]

Franz, Alfred. The Solution of Problems in International Comparisons of GDP through Price Adjustments. What to Learn from ECP 1980?

Statist. J., September 1985, *3*(3), pp. 307–19. [G: W. Europe]

Freeman, Katherine B. Reflections on Need Achievement and International Differences in Income Growth: 1950–1960. *Econ. Develop. Cult. Change*, July 1985, *33*(4), pp. 865–77.

Giannaros, Demetrios S. and Kolluri, Bharat R. Deficit Spending, Money, and Inflation: Some International Empirical Evidence. *J. Macroecon.*, Summer 1985, *7*(3), pp. 401–17. [G: OECD]

Giersch, Herbert. Perspectives on the World Economy. *Weltwirtsch. Arch.*, 1985, *121*(3), pp. 409–26. [G: Global]

Giersch, Herbert. Perspectives on the World Economy. *S. Afr. J. Econ.*, December 1985, *53*(4), pp. 333–50. [G: Global]

Goldstein, Joshua S. Basic Human Needs: The Plateau Curve. *World Devel.*, May 1985, *13*(5), pp. 595–609.

Greenaway, David. Trade Taxes as a Source of Government Revenue: A Comment on the Bedrossian-Hitiris Re-estimation. *Scot. J. Polit. Econ.*, June 1985, *32*(2), pp. 205–08.

Griffith-Jones, Stephany. Impact of World Prices on Development: The International Environment. In *Griffith-Jones, S. and Harvey, C., eds.*, 1985, pp. 13–51. [G: LDCs; MDCs]

Guinchard, Philippe. Prix relatifs et désindustrialisation. (Relative Prices and Deindustrialisation. With English summary.) *Revue Écon.*, March 1985, *36*(2), pp. 367–82. [G: Selected Countries]

Havrylyshyn, Oli and Civan, Engin. Intra-industry Trade among Developing Countries. *J. Devel. Econ.*, August 1985, *18*(2–3), pp. 253–71. [G: LDCs]

Himarios, Daniel. The Effects of Devaluation on the Trade Balance: A Critical View and Reexamination of Miles's 'New Results.' *J. Int. Money Finance*, December 1985, *4*(4), pp. 553–63.

Hondai, Susumu. Changes in Intersectoral Terms of Trade and Their Effects on Labor Transfer. In *Ohkawa, K. and Ranis, G., eds.*, 1985, pp. 249–65. [G: Japan; Taiwan]

Kawagoe, Toshihiko; Hayami, Yujiro and Ruttan, Vernon W. The Intercountry Agricultural Production Function and Productivity Differences among Countries. *J. Devel. Econ.*, Sept.-Oct. 1985, *19*(1/2), pp. 113–32. [G: Selected Countries]

Kovács, Ilona. International Comparison of Consumption Patterns by Cluster Analysis. *Acta Oecon.*, 1985, *35*(3–4), pp. 313–26. [G: OECD]

Lal, Deepak. Poor Countries and the Global Economy: Crisis and Adjustment. In *Bergsten, C. F., ed.*, 1985, pp. 65–76. [G: Global]

Landau, Daniel L. Explaining Differences in Per Capita Income between Countries: A Hypothesis and Test for 1950 and 1970. *Exploration Econ. Hist.*, July 1985, *22*(3), pp. 296–315.

de Larosière, Jacques. La croissance de la dette publique: causes, conséquences et remèdes. (The Growing Public Debt: Causes, Conse-

quences and Remedies. With English summary.) *Écon. Soc.*, September 1985, *19*(9), pp. 3–31. [G: OECD]

Larson, David. A Test of the Stability of the Relationship between the Physical Quality of Life Index and Gross National Product per Capita. *Indian Econ. J.*, Apr.-June 1985, *32*(4), pp. 1–7.

Leontief, Wassily. The Rates of Long-run Economic Growth and Capital Transfer from Developed to Underdeveloped Areas. In *Leontief, W.*, 1985, pp. 200–215. [G: LDCs; MDCs]

McGregor, Peter G. and Swales, J. K. Professor Thirlwall and Balance of Payments Constrained Growth. *Appl. Econ.*, February 1985, *17*(1), pp. 17–32. [G: OECD]

Michl, Thomas R. International Comparisons of Productivity Growth: Verdoorn's Law Revisited. *J. Post Keynesian Econ.*, Summer 1985, *7*(4), pp. 474–92. [G: OECD]

Mizoguchi, Toshiyuki. Economic Development Policy and Income Distribution: The Experience in East and Southeast Asia. *Devel. Econ.*, December 1985, *23*(4), pp. 307–24. [G: Asia]

Mundle, Sudipto. The Agrarian Barrier to Industrial Growth. *J. Devel. Stud.*, October 1985, *22*(1), pp. 49–80. [G: W. Europe; Japan; India]

Mundle, Sudipto. The Agrarian Barrier to Industrial Growth. In *Saith, A., ed.*, 1985, pp. 49–80. [G: W. Europe; Japan; India]

Nissan, Edward and Caveny, Regina. Quality of Life Indicators for Selected South American Nations. *Atlantic Econ. J.*, September 1985, *13*(3), pp. 93. [G: Latin America]

Park, Se-Hark. North–South Comparison of the Sources of Change in Manufacturing Value Added, 1975–80: A Decomposition Analysis. *J. Devel. Stud.*, January 1985, *21*(2), pp. 205–14. [G: Global]

Quan, Nguyen T. and Koo, Anthony Y. C. Concentration of Land Holdings: An Empirical Exploration of Kuznets' Conjecture. *J. Devel. Econ.*, May–June 1985, *18*(1), pp. 101–17.

Ram, Rati. Conventional and 'Real' GDP per Capita in Cross-Country Studies of Production Structure. *J. Devel. Econ.*, August 1985, *18*(2–3), pp. 463–77. [G: LDCs]

Ram, Rati. Level and Variability of Inflation: Time-Series and Cross-Section Evidence from 117 Countries. *Economica*, May 1985, *52*(206), pp. 209–23. [G: Global]

Román, Zoltán. Productivity Growth and Its Slowdown in the Hungarian Economy. *Acta Oecon.*, 1985, *35*(1–2), pp. 81–104. [G: Hungary]

Smith, Michael. Japan. In *Smith, M., et al.*, 1985, pp. 5–36. [G: Japan]

Taeho, Kim. Assessment of External Debt Servicing Capacity: An Alternative Methodology. *J. Econ. Devel.*, December 1985, *10*(2), pp. 35–52. [G: LDCs]

Teitel, Simón. Indicadores de ciencia y tecnología, tamaño de país y desarrollo económico: una comparación internacional. (With English summary.) *Desarrollo Econ.*, Oct.-Dec. 1985, 25(99), pp. 329–49.

Yoo, Jang H. Does Korea Trace Japan's Footsteps? A Macroeconomic Appraisal. *Kyklos,* 1985, 38(4), pp. 578–98.   [G: S. Korea; Japan]

124 Economic Studies of Centrally Planned Economies

1241 Comparative Country Studies

Dyba, Karel. Adjustment to International Disturbances: Czechoslovakia and Hungary. *Acta Oecon.*, 1985, 34(3/4), pp. 317–37.
[G: Czechoslovakia; Hungary]
Marinov, Georgi. Characteristics and Tendencies in the Economic Development of the Mongolian People's Republic, Cuba, and the People's Republic of Vietnam and Cooperation between Them and Bulgaria. *Soviet E. Europ. Foreign Trade,* Summer–Fall 1985, 21(1-2-3), pp. 191–203.   [G: Mongolia; Cuba; Vietnam; Bulgaria]
Whitesell, Robert S. The Influence of Central Planning on the Economic Slowdown in the Soviet Union and Eastern Europe: A Comparative Production Function Analysis. *Economica,* May 1985, 52(206), pp. 235 44.
[G: U.S.S.R.; E. Europe]

1243 European Countries

Aganbegian A. Important Positive Changes in the Country's Economic Life. *Prob. Econ.,* April 1985, 27(12), pp. 3–16.   [G: U.S.S.R.]
Andreff, Wladimir and Lavigne, Marie. La contrainte extérieure dans les économies du C.A.E.M. (The "Foreign Constraint" in the Comecon. With English summary.) *Écon. Soc.,* April 1985, 19(4), pp. 237–81.
[G: CMEA]
Balassa, Bela. Reforming the New Economic Mechanism in Hungary. In *Balassa, B.,* 1985, pp. 282–309.   [G: Hungary]
Balassa, Bela. The "New Growth Path" in Hungary. *Banca Naz. Lavoro Quart. Rev.,* December 1985, (155), pp. 347–72.   [G: Hungary]
Balassa, Bela. The Hungarian Economic Reform, 1968–81. In *Balassa, B.,* 1985, pp. 261–81.
[G: Hungary]
Bunce, Valerie. The Empire Strikes Back: The Evolution of the Eastern Bloc from a Soviet Asset to a Soviet Liability. *Int. Organ.,* Winter 1985, 39(1), pp. 1–46.   [G: U.S.S.R.]
Danilin, V. I., et al. Measuring Enterprise Efficiency in the Soviet Union: A Stochastic Frontier Analysis. *Economica,* May 1985, 52(206), pp. 225–33.   [G: U.S.S.R.]
Drach, Marcel. Le cycle de la relation État-entreprises en R.D.A. 1963–1983. *Écon. Soc.,* May 1985, 19(5), pp. 117–53.   [G: E. Germany]
Dyba, Karel and Vintrová, Ružena. Czechoslovak Economy in the 1980's. *Czech. Econ. Digest.,* December 1985, (8), pp. 3–28.
[G: Czechoslovakia]
Galasi, Péter and Sziráczki, György. State Regu-

lation, Enterprise Behaviour and the Labour Market in Hungary, 1968–83. *Cambridge J. Econ.,* September 1985, 9(3), pp. 203–19.
[G: Hungary]
Grossman, Gregory. The "Second Economy" of the U.S.S.R. In *Bornstein, M., ed.,* 1985, pp. 220–41.   [G: U.S.S.R.]
Halpern, László and Molnár, György. Income Formation, Accumulation and Price Trends in Hungary in the 1970s. *Acta Oecon.,* 1985, 35(1–2), pp. 105–32.   [G: Hungary]
Hanson, Philip. Gorbachev's Economic Strategy: A Comment. *Soviet Econ.,* Oct.-Dec. 1985, 1(4), pp. 306–12.   [G: U.S.S.R.]
Harrison, Mark. Primary Accumulation in the Soviet Transition. *J. Devel. Stud.,* October 1985, 22(1), pp. 81–103.   [G: U.S.S.R.]
Hartford, Kathleen. Hungarian Agriculture: A Model for the Socialist World? *World Devel.,* January 1985, 13(1), pp. 123–50.
[G: Hungary]
Havasi, Ferenc. The Economic Situation of Hungary and the Tasks to Be Faced. *Acta Oecon.,* 1985, 34(3/4), pp. 193–204.   [G: Hungary]
Hewett, Ed A. Gorbachev's Economic Strategy: A Preliminary Assessment. *Soviet Econ.,* Oct.-Dec. 1985, 1(4), pp. 285–305. [G: U.S.S.R.]
Hough, Jerry F. Debates about the Postwar World. In *Linz, S. J., ed.,* 1985, pp. 253–81.
[G: U.S.S.R.]
Jírava, Miroslav. Raising the Living Standard— The Aim and Prerequisite for Building an Advanced Socialist Society. *Czech. Econ. Digest.,* August 1985, (5), pp. 3–26.
[G: Czechoslovakia]
Jones, Derek C. The Cooperative Sector and Dualism in Command Economies: Theory and Evidence for the Case of Poland. In *Jones, D. C. and Svejnar, J., eds.,* 1985, pp. 195–218.   [G: Poland]
Kornai, János. Hungary's Reform: Halfway to the Market. *Challenge,* May/June 1985, 28(2), pp. 22–31.   [G: Hungary]
Leontief, Wassily. Capital Reconstruction and Postwar Development of Income and Consumption. In *Linz, S. J., ed.,* 1985, pp. 38–46.   [G: U.S.S.R.]
Linz, Susan J. World War II and Soviet Economic Growth, 1940–1953. In *Linz, S. J., ed.,* 1985, pp. 11–38.   [G: U.S.S.R.]
Loginov, V. National Income: Growth Factors. *Prob. Econ.,* November 1985, 28(7), pp. 18–32.   [G: U.S.S.R.]
Nagy, Tamás. Die ungarische Wirtschaftsreform und ihre Weiterentwicklung. (Development of the Hungarian Economic Reform. With English summary.) *Konjunkturpolitik,* 1985, 31(6), pp. 361–79.   [G: Hungary]
Nyers, Resző. National Economic Objectives and the Reform Process in Hungary in the Eighties. *Acta Oecon.,* 1985, 35(1–2), pp. 1–16.
[G: Hungary]
Petschnig, Mária. Causes of Difficulties in Changing the Normal State of the Hungarian Economy. *Acta Oecon.,* 1985, 35(3–4), pp. 235–50.
[G: Hungary]

Robinson, Sherman and Tyson, Laura D'Andrea.
Foreign Trade, Resource Allocation, and Structural Adjustment in Yugoslavia: 1976–1980. *J. Compar. Econ.*, March 1985, *9*(1), pp. 46–70.
[G: Yugoslavia]

Rogulska, Barbara. Le régulation indirecte ou les nouvelles relations Centre-entreprises en Pologne. (Indirect Regulation or New Relations between the Center and the Enterprises in Poland. With English summary.) *Écon. Soc.*, May 1985, *19*(5), pp. 69–115. [G: Poland]

Schroeder, Gertrude E. The Slowdown in Soviet Industry, 1976–1982. *Soviet Econ.*, Jan.-Mar. 1985, *1*(1), pp. 42–74. [G: U.S.S.R.]

Szakolczai, György; Bagdy, Gábor and Vindics, József. Dependence of the Hungarian Economic Performance on the World Economy. Facts and Economic Policy Inferences. *Acta Oecon.*, 1985, *35*(3–4), pp. 295–311.
[G: Hungary]

Tardos, Márton. Question Marks in Hungarian Fiscal and Monetary Policy (1979–1984). *Acta Oecon.*, 1985, *35*(1–2), pp. 29–52.
[G: Hungary]

Vachel, Jan. Czechoslovakia's Economic and Social Development. *Czech. Econ. Digest.*, November 1985, (7), pp. 3–29.
[G: Czechoslovakia]

Verbík, Antonín. Nationalization. *Czech. Econ. Digest.*, December 1985, (8), pp. 29–38.
[G: Czechoslovakia]

Winiecki, Jan. *Portes Ante Portas:* A Critique of the Revisionist Interpretation of Inflation under Central Planning. *Comparative Econ. Stud.*, Summer 1985, *27*(2), pp. 25–51.
[G: E. Europe]

1244 Asian Countries

Balassa, Bela. Economic Reform in China. In *Balassa, B.*, 1985, pp. 310–36. [G: China]

Bergson, Abram. A Visit to China's Economic Reforms. *Comparative Econ. Stud.*, Summer 1985, *27*(2), pp. 71–82. [G: China]

Blecher, Marc. Inequality and Socialism in Rural China: A Conceptual Note. *World Devel.*, January 1985, *13*(1), pp. 115–21. [G: China]

Byrd, William. The Shanghai Market for the Means of Production: A Case Study of Reform in China's Material Supply System. *Comparative Econ. Stud.*, Winter 1985, *27*(4), pp. 1–29. [G: China]

Cheng, Chu-yuan. Economic Development on Both Sides of the Taiwan Straits: New Trends for Convergence. *Hong Kong Econ. Pap.*, 1985, (16), pp. 54–73. [G: Taiwan; China]

De Wulf, Luc. Economic Reform in China. *Finance Develop.*, March 1985, *22*(1), pp. 8–11.
[G: China]

De Wulf, Luc. Financial Reform in China. *Finance Develop.*, December 1985, *22*(4), pp. 19–22. [G: China]

Deane, Hugh. Mao's Rural Strategies: What Went Wrong? *Sci. Soc.*, Spring 1985, *49*(1), pp. 101–07. [G: China]

Kaempfer, William H. and Min, Henry M., Jr.

The Role of Oil in China's Economic Development, Growth, and Internationalization. *J. Energy Devel.*, Autumn 1985, *11*(1), pp. 13–26.
[G: China]

Lyons, Thomas P. China's Cellular Economy: A Test of the Fragmentation Hypothesis. *J. Compar. Econ.*, June 1985, *9*(2), pp. 125–44.
[G: China]

Shinohara, Miyohei. The Future of Chinese Economic Growth and the Role of Hong Kong. In *Shishido, T. and Sato, R.*, eds., 1985, pp. 127–46. [G: China; Hong Kong]

Trescott, Paul B. Incentives versus Equality: What Does China's Recent Experience Show? *World Devel.*, February 1985, *13*(2), pp. 205–17. [G: China]

Ul'masov, A. and Sharifkhodzhaev, M. Formation and Development of the Socialist Economy in the Central Asian Republics. *Prob. Econ.*, October 1985, *28*(6), pp. 74–86.
[G: Central Asia]

Walder, Andrew G. China Turns to Industry Reform. *Challenge*, March/April 1985, *28*(1), pp. 42–47. [G: China]

White, Christine. Agricultural Planning, Pricing Policy and Co-operatives in Vietnam. *World Devel.*, January 1985, *13*(1), pp. 97–114.
[G: Vietnam]

World Bank. The Economic System of China. In *Bornstein, M.*, ed., 1985, pp. 242–62.
[G: China]

Wu, Jinglian; Li, Jiange and Ding, Ningning. Hold Down the Growth Rate of the National Economy within an Appropriate Range. *Chinese Econ. Stud.*, Fall 1985, *19*(1), pp. 53–64.
[G: China]

Wu, Junyang. Current Economic Conditions and Reform of the Price System. *Chinese Econ. Stud.*, Spring 1985, *18*(3), pp. 55–76.
[G: China]

1246 Latin American and Caribbean Countries

Eckstein, Susan. State and Market Dynamics in Castro's Cuba. In *Evans, P.; Rueschemeyer, D. and Stephens, E. H.*, eds., 1985, pp. 217–45. [G: Cuba]

130 ECONOMIC FLUCTUATIONS; FORECASTING; STABILIZATION; INFLATION

131 Economic Fluctuations

1310 General

Akerlof, George A. and Yellen, Janet L. A Near-rational Model of the Business Cycle, with Wage and Price Intertia. *Quart. J. Econ.*, Supp. 1985, *100*, pp. 823–38.

Azariadis, Costas. Weitzman's *The Share Economy: Conquering Stagflation. Rand J. Econ.*, Winter 1985, *16*(4), pp. 581–82.

Benhabib, Jess and Nishimura, Kazuo. Competitive Equilibrium Cycles. *J. Econ. Theory*, April 1985, *35*(2), pp. 284–306.

Boddy, Raford. Demand Distribution and Productivity Decline. *Econ. Forum,* Winter 1985-1986, *15*(2), pp. 15–20.

Boschen, John F. Employment and Output Effects of Observed and Unobserved Monetary Growth. *J. Money, Credit, Banking,* May 1985, *17*(2), pp. 153–63.   **[G: U.S.]**

Brandis, Royall. Marx *and* Keynes? Marx *or* Keynes? *J. Econ. Issues,* September 1985, *19*(3), pp. 643–59.

Buffie, Edward F. Price–Output Dynamics, Capital Inflows and Real Appreciation. *Oxford Econ. Pap.,* December 1985, *37*(4), pp. 529–51.

Butos, William N. Hayek and General Equilibrium Analysis. *Southern Econ. J.,* October 1985, *52*(2), pp. 332–43.

Cooley, Thomas F. Individual Forecasting and Aggregate Outcomes: A Review Essay. *J. Monet. Econ.,* March 1985, *15*(2), pp. 255–66.

Drazen, Allan. Cyclical Determinants of the Natural Level of Economic Activity. *Int. Econ. Rev.,* June 1985, *26*(2), pp. 387–97.

Eckalbar, John C. Inventory Fluctuations in a Disequilibrium Macro Model. *Econ. J.,* December 1985, *95*(380), pp. 976–91.

Ferri, Piero. Wage Dynamics and Instability Processes. *Econ. Notes,* 1985, (3), pp. 35–48.

Flood, Robert P. and Hodrick, Robert J. Optimal Price and Inventory Adjustment in an Open-Economy Model of the Business Cycle. *Quart. J. Econ.,* Supp. 1985, *100*(5), pp. 887–914.

Fodor, Giorgio. I pericoli della stabilità: Keynes e i suoi avversari prima della "teoria generale." (The Dangers of Stability: Keynes and His Opponents after the General Theory. With English summary.) *Polit. Econ.,* December 1985, *1*(3), pp. 429–60.   **[G: U.S.]**

Fremling, Gertrud M. Did the United States Transmit the Great Depression to the Rest of the World? *Amer. Econ. Rev.,* December 1985, *75*(5), pp. 1181–85.   **[G: U.S.]**

Furubotn, Eirik G. Long Swings of Economic Development, Social Time Preference and Institution Change: Comment. *Z. ges. Staatswiss. (JITE),* March 1985, *141*(1), pp. 36–40.

Gehrlein, William V. and McInish, Thomas H. Cyclical Variability of Bond Risk Premia: A Note. *J. Banking Finance,* March 1985, *9*(1), pp. 157–65.

Goldstein, Jonathan P. Pricing, Accumulation, and Crisis in Post Keynesian Theory. *J. Post Keynesian Econ.,* Fall 1985, *8*(1), pp. 121–34.

Grandmont, Jean-Michel. On Endogenous Competitive Business Cycles. *Econometrica,* September 1985, *53*(5), pp. 995–1045.

Hansen, Gary D. Indivisible Labor and the Business Cycle. *J. Monet. Econ.,* November 1985, *16*(3), pp. 309–27.

Hudson, Michael A. German Economists and the Depression of 1929-1933. *Hist. Polit. Econ.,* Spring 1985, *17*(1), pp. 35–50. **[G: Germany]**

Keech, William R. and Simon, Carl P. Electoral and Welfare Consequences of Political Manipulation of the Economy. *J. Econ. Behav. Organ.,* June 1985, *6*(2), pp. 177–202.

Kimbrough, Kent P. Futures Markets and Mone-

tary Policy. *J. Monet. Econ.,* January 1985, *15*(1), pp. 69–79.

Lächler, Ulrich. Fixed versus Flexible Exchange Rates in an Equilibrium Business Cycle Model. *J. Monet. Econ.,* July 1985, *16*(1), pp. 95–107.

Lempers, Fred. Medium Term Perspectives for the Dutch Economy. *Econ. Lavoro,* July-Sept. 1985, *19*(3), pp. 129–31.   **[G: Netherlands]**

Lempinen, Urho. Keynesiläinen kansantalous, rationaaliset taloudenpitäjät ja suhdannevaihtelut. (Rational Agents and the Keynesian Economy: Some Results in Business Cycle Theory. With English summary.) *Kansant. Aikak.,* 1985, *81*(2), pp. 150–59.

Levine, David K. A Simple Durable Goods Model. *Quart. J. Econ.,* August 1985, *100*(3), pp. 775–88.

Mankiw, N. Gregory. Small Menu Costs and Large Business Cycles: A Macroeconomic Model. *Quart. J. Econ.,* May 1985, *100*(2), pp. 529–38.

Mankiw, N. Gregory; Rotemberg, Julio J. and Summers, Lawrence H. Intertemporal Substitution in Macroeconomics. *Quart. J. Econ.,* February 1985, *100*(1), pp. 225–51.
[G: U.S.]

Mitchell, Mark L.; Wallace, Myles S. and Warner, John T. Real Wages over the Business Cycle: Some Further Evidence. *Southern Econ. J.,* April 1985, *51*(4), pp. 1162–73.
[G: U.S.]

Montgomery, Edward and Shaw, Kathryn. Long-term Contracts, Expectations and Wage Inertia. *J. Monet. Econ.,* September 1985, *16*(2), pp. 209–26.

Mott, Tracy. Kalecki's Principle of Increasing Risk and the Relation among Mark-up Pricing, Investment Fluctuations, and Liquidity Preference. *Econ. Forum,* Winter 1985-1986, *15*(2), pp. 65–76.

Myatt, Anthony. The Adverse Supply-Side Effects of High Interest Rates and Procyclical Real Wage Movements. *J. Macroecon.,* Spring 1985, *7*(2), pp. 237–46.

Nanto, Dick K. and Takagi, Shinji. Korekiyo Takahashi and Japan's Recovery from the Great Depression. *Amer. Econ. Rev.,* May 1985, *75*(2), pp. 369–74.   **[G: Japan]**

Neumann, Manfred. Long Swings in Economic Development, Social Time Preference and Institutional Change. *Z. ges. Staatswiss. (JITE),* March 1985, *141*(1), pp. 21–35.   **[G: U.S.]**

O'Brien, Anthony. The Cyclical Sensitivity of Wages [The Changing Cyclical Behavior of Wages and Prices: 1890–1976] [Cross-Country and Cross-Temporal Differences in Inflation Responsiveness]. *Amer. Econ. Rev.,* December 1985, *75*(5), pp. 1124–32.   **[G: U.S.]**

Pekkala, Ahti. Vuoden 1986 tulo- ja menoarvio. (The Budget for 1986. With English summary.) *Kansant. Aikak.,* 1985, *81*(4), pp. 375–80.
[G: Finland]

Perry, Motty and Solon, Gary R. Wage Bargaining, Labor Turnover, and the Business Cycle: A Model with Asymmetric Information. *J. Lab. Econ.,* October 1985, *3*(4), pp. 421–33.

van der Ploeg, Frederick. Classical Growth Cycles. *Metroecon.*, June 1985, *37*(2), pp. 221–30.

Podkaminer, Leon. Investment Cycles in Centrally Planned Economies: An Explanation Invoking Consumer Market Disequilibrium and Labour Shortage. *Acta Oecon.*, 1985, *35*(1–2), pp. 133–44.

Rasche, Robert H. What Would Nominal GNP Targeting Do to the Business Cycle? A Comment. *Carnegie-Rochester Conf. Ser. Public Policy*, Spring 1985, *22*, pp. 85–87.

Reid, Gavin C. Keynes versus the Classics: Fluctuations and Growth. *Scot. J. Polit. Econ.*, November 1985, *32*(3), pp. 315–27.

Rumler, Miroslav. On the Causes of the Contemporary Prolonged Crisis in the Economy of Advanced Capitalist Countries (An Outline of the Politic–Economic Conception). *Czech. Econ. Pap.*, 1985, *23*, pp. 111–36.

Samson, Lucie. A Study of the Impact of Sectoral Shifts on Aggregate Unemployment in Canada. *Can. J. Econ.*, August 1985, *18*(3), pp. 518–30. [G: Canada]

Sato, Yoshikazu. Marx–Goodwin Growth Cycles in a Two-Sector Economy. *Z. Nationalökon.*, 1985, *45*(1), pp. 21–34.

Schouten, D. B. J. Business Cycle and Wage Policy. *De Economist*, 1985, *133*(3), pp. 265–84. [G: Netherlands]

Seidmann, Daniel J. Target Buffer Stocks. *Europ. Econ. Rev.*, March 1985, *27*(2), pp. 165–82.

Spear, Stephen E. Rational Expectations in the Overlapping Generations Model. *J. Econ. Theory*, April 1985, *35*(2), pp. 251–75.

Sweezy, Paul M. Listen Keynesians!! In *Wattel, H. L., ed.*, 1985, pp. 39–47.

Taylor, John B. What Would Nominal GNP Targetting Do to the Business Cycle? *Carnegie-Rochester Conf. Ser. Public Policy*, Spring 1985, *22*, pp. 61–84.

Taylor, Lance and O'Connell, Stephen A. A Minsky Crisis. *Quart. J. Econ.*, Supp. 1985, *100*, pp. 871–85.

Thayer, Frederick C. The Crisis of Industrial Overcapacity: Avoiding Another Great Depression. In *Didsbury, H. F., Jr., ed.*, 1985, pp. 353–90. [G: U.S.]

Tichy, Gunther. Die endogene Innovation als Triebkraft in Schumpeters Konjunkturtheorie. (Endogeneous Innovations—The Driving Force in Schumpeter's Theory of Business Cycles. With English summary.) *Ifo-Studien*, 1985, *31*(1), pp. 1–27.

Tsujimura, Kotaro. Theory and Measurement of Acute Polypoly and Polyopsony: Inflationary Expectation and Market Paralysis at the First Oil Crisis in Japan. (In Japanese. With English summary.) *Econ. Stud. Quart.*, April 1985, *36*(1), pp. 1–14. [G: Japan]

Ueshima, Yasuhiro. Business Fluctuations and Employment Adjustments. (In Japanese. With English summary.) *Econ. Stud. Quart.*, December 1985, *36*(3), pp. 231–46.

Vandenbroucke, Frank. Conflicts in International Economic Policy and the World Recession: A Theoretical Analysis. *Cambridge J. Econ.*, March 1985, *9*(1), pp. 15–42.

Witte, Willard E. and Bhandari, Jagdeep S. Monetary Disturbances, Inventory Fluctuations and the Level of Sales: A Theoretical and Empirical Analysis. *Southern Econ. J.*, April 1985, *51*(4), pp. 1151–61. [G: U.S.]

Zarnowitz, Victor. Recent Work on Business Cycles in Historical Perspective: A Review of Theories and Evidence. *J. Econ. Lit.*, June 1985, *23*(2), pp. 523–80. [G: U.S.]

1312 Economic Fluctuations: Theory

Bricall, Josep M. Sur la demande effective et la crise. (On Effective Demand and Crisis. With English summary.) *Écon. Soc.*, August 1985, *19*(8), pp. 99–116.

Chisari, Omar O. Growth, Inflation and Rules of Active and Passive Mark-up Factor. *Econ. Notes*, 1985, (2), pp. 57–67.

Chishti, Salim U. Relative Stability of Interest-Free Economy. *J. Res. Islamic Econ.*, Summer 1985, *3*(1), pp. 3–12.

Collins, William H.; Collins, Carol B. and Gulati, Unmesh C. A Mathematical Model for Desired Capital– Catastrophe Theory. *Indian Econ. J.*, Apr.-June 1985, *32*(4), pp. 62–74.

Crotty, James R. The Centrality of Money, Credit, and Financial Intermediation in Marx's Crisis Theory: An Interpretation of Marx's Methodology. In *[Magdoff, H. and Sweezy, P.]*, 1985, pp. 45–81.

Day, Richard H. and Shafer, Wayne. Keynesian Chaos. *J. Macroecon.*, Summer 1985, *7*(3), pp. 277–95.

Dodd, Digby M. Towards Recovery? Convalescence or Rebirth. In *Meyer, F. V., ed.*, 1985, pp. 163–82.

Drobny, Andres and Klonis, Dimitris C. Equilibrium and Disequilibrium Macro Models: A Note on Price Inertia. *Greek Econ. Rev.*, December 1985, *7*(3), pp. 268–77.

Goldstein, Jonathan P. The Cyclical Profit Squeeze: A Marxian Microfoundation. *Rev. Radical Polit. Econ.*, Spring and Summer 1985, *17*(1/2), pp. 103–28.

Haberler, Gottfried. Notes on Rational and Irrational Expectations. In *Haberler, G.*, 1985, pp. 603–17.

Halevi, Joseph. Effective Demand, Capacity Utilization and the Sectoral Distribution of Investment. *Écon. Soc.*, August 1985, *19*(8), pp. 25–45.

Hobbs, G. D. Long Waves of Economic Activity. In *Morris, D., ed.*, 1985, pp. 718–43. [G: U.K.; Selected Countries]

Krüger, Michael. A Reconsideration of the Stability Properties of Goodwin's Model of the Growth Cycle. *Econ. Notes*, 1985, (2), pp. 22–37.

Meyer, F. V. The Economic Downturn of the Early 1980s. In *Meyer, F. V., ed.*, 1985, pp. 1–27. [G: U.K.]

Rowthorn, Bob and Harris, Donald J. The Organic Composition of Capital and Capitalist

Development. In *[Magdoff, H. and Sweezy, P.]*, 1985, pp. 345–57.

Saari, Donald G. Price Dynamics, Social Choice, Voting Methods, Probability and Chaos. In *Aliprantis, C. D.; Burkinshaw, O. and Rothman, N. J., eds.*, 1985, pp. 1–24.

1313 Economic Fluctuations: Studies

Alhadeff, Peter. Public Finance and the Economy in Argentina, Australia and Canada during the Depression of the 1930s. In *Platt, D. C. M. and di Tella, G., eds.*, 1985, pp. 161–78.
[G: Argentina; Australia; Canada]

Amacher, Ryan, et al. The Behavior of Regulatory Activity over the Business Cycle: An Empirical Test. *Econ. Inquiry*, January 1985, *23*(1), pp. 7–19. [G: U.S.]

Ball, James [Sir]. Demand Management and Economic Recovery: The United Kingdom Case. *Nat. Westminster Bank Quart. Rev.*, August 1985, pp. 2–17. [G: U.K.]

Barry, Brian. Does Democracy Cause Inflation? Political Ideas of Some Economists. In *Lindberg, L. N. and Maier, C. S., eds.*, 1985, pp. 280–317. [G: OECD]

Batra, R. N. The Future of the Debt Situation in the LDCs. In *Kaushik, S. K., ed.*, 1985, pp. 47–57. [G: U.S.]

Bils, Mark J. Real Wages over the Business Cycle: Evidence from Panel Data. *J. Polit. Econ.*, August 1985, *93*(4), pp. 666–89. [G: U.S.]

Bulmer-Thomas, Victor. World Recession and Central American Depression: Lessons from the 1930s for the 1980s. In *Duran, E., ed.*, 1985, pp. 130–51. [G: Central America]

Burgan, John U. Cyclical Behavior of High Tech Industries. *Mon. Lab. Rev.*, May 1985, *108*(5), pp. 9–15. [G: U.S.]

Burrows, P. F. Financial Markets at the Lower Turning Points of the Economic Cycle. In *Meyer, F. V., ed.*, 1985, pp. 28–62.
[G: U.S.; U.K.]

Buswell, R. J.; Easterbrook, R. P. and Morphet, C. S. Geography, Regions and Research and Development Activity: The Case of the United Kingdom. In *Thwaites, A. T. and Oakey, R. P., eds.*, 1985, pp. 36–66. [G: U.K.]

Carlson, Keith M. Monthly Economic Indicators: A Closer Look at the Coincident Index. *Fed. Res. Bank St. Louis Rev.*, November 1985, *67*(9), pp. 20–30. [G: U.S.]

Cartwright, Phillip A. and DeLorme, Charles D., Jr. The Unemployment–Inflation–Voter Utility Relationship in the Political Business Cycle: Some Evidence. *Southern Econ. J.*, January 1985, *51*(3), pp. 898–905. [G: U.S.]

de Cecco, Marcello. Italian Monetary Policy in the 1980s. *Z. Wirtschaft. Sozialwissen.*, 1985, *105*(2/3), pp. 311–26. [G: Italy]

Coates, J. H. UK Manufacturing Industry: Recession, Depression and Prospects for the Future. In *Meyer, F. V., ed.*, 1985, pp. 83–101.
[G: U.K.]

Cockerill, Anthony. The British Economy: Performance, Prospects and Policies. In *Meyer,*

F. V., ed., 1985, pp. 102–23. [G: U.K.]

Connaughton, John E. and Madsen, Ronald A. State and Regional Impact of the 1981–82 Recession. *Growth Change*, July 1985, *16*(3), pp. 1–10. [G: U.S.]

Contador, Claudio R. Inflation and Recession: Fate or Political Choice in Brazil Today? In *Salazar-Carrillo, J. and Fendt, R., Jr., eds.*, 1985, pp. 149–66. [G: Brazil]

Coppe, A. "Long Waves" and Secular Expansion. *Tijdschrift Econ. Manage.*, 1985, *30*(3–4), pp. 397–414.

Davidson, Lawrence S. and Fratianni, Michele. Economic Growth in the 1970s and Beyond. *Econ. Notes*, 1985, (3), pp. 17–34. [G: U.S.]

Davies, Mel. Blainey Revisited: Mineral Discovery and the Business Cycle in South Australia. *Australian Econ. Hist. Rev.*, September 1985, *25*(2), pp. 112–28. [G: Australia]

Dooley, David and Catalano, Ralph. Does Economic Change Increase Mental Disorder?: A Synthesis of Recent Research. In *Westcott, G.; Svensson, P.-G. and Zollner, H. F. K., eds.*, 1985, pp. 57–86.

Englander, A. Steven. Commodity Prices in the Current Recovery. *Fed. Res. Bank New York Quart. Rev.*, Spring 1985, *10*(1), pp. 11–19.
[G: Global]

Ersenkal, Caryl; Wallace, Myles S. and Warner, John T. Chairman Reappointments, Presidential Elections and Policy Actions of the Federal Reserve. *Policy Sci.*, November 1985, *18*(3), pp. 211–25. [G: U.S.]

Evans, Paul. Money, Output and Goodhart's Law: The U.S. Experience. *Rev. Econ. Statist.*, February 1985, *67*(1), pp. 1–8. [G: U.S.]

Fair, Ray C. Excess Labor and the Business Cycle. *Amer. Econ. Rev.*, March 1985, *75*(1), pp. 239–45. [G: U.S.]

Fay, Jon A. and Medoff, James L. Labor and Output over the Business Cycle: Some Direct Evidence. *Amer. Econ. Rev.*, September 1985, *75*(4), pp. 638–55. [G: U.S.]

Feito, José Luis. The World Monetary System, the International Business Cycle, and the External Debt Crisis. In *Wionczek, M. S., ed.*, 1985, pp. 193–227. [G: LDCs]

Feldstein, Martin. American Economic Policy and the World Economy. *Foreign Aff.*, Summer 1985, *63*(5), pp. 995–1008. [G: U.S.; OECD]

Franz, Wolfgang. Challenges to the German Economy 1973–1983. Supply Shocks, Investment Slowdown, Inflation Variability and the Underutilization of Labor. *Z. Wirtschaft. Sozialwissen.*, 1985, *105*(2/3), pp. 407–30.
[G: W. Germany]

Froyen, Richard T. and Waud, Roger N. Demand Variability, Supply Shocks and the Output–Inflation Tradeoff. *Rev. Econ. Statist.*, February 1985, *67*(1), pp. 9–15. [G: U.S.]

Gahlen, Bernhard. Trend und Zyklus—Aggregat und Struktur. (Trends and Cycles—Structure and the Aggregate. With English summary.) *Jahr. Nationalökon. Statist.*, September 1985, *200*(5), pp. 449–78. [G: W. Germany]

Gallarotti, Giulio M. Toward a Business-Cycle Model of Tariffs. *Int. Organ.*, Winter 1985, 39(1), pp. 155–87. [G: U.S.; U.K.; Germany]

García-Alba, Pasqual and Puche, Jaime Serra. Economic Fluctuations in Mexico and the United States. In *Musgrave, P. B., ed.*, 1985, pp. 123–45. [G: Mexico; U.S.]

Genberg, Hans and Swoboda, Alexander K. Internal and External Factors in the Swiss Business Cycle: 1964–1981. *Aussenwirtschaft*, September 1985, 40(3), pp. 275–95. [G: Switzerland]

Haberler, Gottfried. The Great Depression of the 1930s—Can It Happen Again? In *Haberler, G.*, 1985, pp. 405–27.

Haberler, Gottfried. The International Monetary System in the World Recession. In *Haberler, G.*, 1985, pp. 229–63. [G: OECD]

Haberler, Gottfried. The Problem of Stagflation. In *Haberler, G.*, 1985, pp. 349–62. [G: U.S.]

Haberler, Gottfried. The World Economy, Money, and the Great Depression 1919–1939. In *Haberler, G.*, 1985, pp. 363–403. [G: U.S.; Japan; France; Germany]

Hamilton, James D. Historical Causes of Postwar Oil Shocks and Recessions. *Energy J.*, January 1985, 6(1), pp. 97–116. [G: U.S.]

Harvey, A. C. Trends and Cycles in Macroeconomic Time Series. *J. Bus. Econ. Statist.*, July 1985, 3(3), pp. 216–27. [G: U.S.]

Hashemzadeh, Nozar and Long, Burl F. Cyclical Aspects of Black Unemployment: An Empirical Analysis. *Rev. Reg. Stud.*, Winter 1985, 15(1), pp. 7–19. [G: U.S.]

Hill, John K. and Smith, Scott L. The Political Timing of Errors in Inflation Forecasts. *Public Choice*, 1985, 46(2), pp. 215–20. [G: U.S.]

Hobbs, G. D. Long Waves of Economic Activity. In *Morris, D., ed.*, 1985, pp. 718–43. [G: U.K.; Selected Countries]

Huth, William L. A Quantitative Look at the System of Economic Indicators. *J. Macroecon.*, Spring 1985, 7(2), pp. 195–210. [G: U.S.]

Jackson, John D. and Smyth, David J. Specifying Differential Cyclical Response in Economic Time Series: Capacity Utilization and Demand for Imports. *Econ. Modelling*, April 1985, 2(2), pp. 149–61. [G: U.S.]

Jahnsson, Yrjö. Suomessa vallitsevan rahapulan syistä ja keinoista sen poistamiseksi. (On the Causes and Cures for Finland's Monetary Crisis. With English summary.) *Kansant. Aikak.*, 1985, 81(1), pp. 5–19. [G: Finland]

John, Jürgen. Economic Instability and Health: Infant Mortality and Suicide Reconsidered. In *Westcott, G.; Svensson, P.-G. and Zollner, H. F. K., eds.*, 1985, pp. 181–204. [G: W. Germany]

Jordan, Bill. Unemployment and the Recovery: The Future of Labour Utilisation. In *Meyer, F. V., ed.*, 1985, pp. 183–212. [G: OECD; U.K.]

Kindleberger, Charles P. Keynesianism vs. Monetarism in the 1930s Depression and Recovery. In *Kindleberger, C. P.*, 1985, pp. 287–92. [G: U.S.]

Kindleberger, Charles P. The 1929 World Depression in Latin America—From the Outside. In *Kindleberger, C. P.*, 1985, pp. 274–86. [G: Latin America]

Koganc, Yoshihiro. Economic Growth before and after the Oil Crisis and the Possibility of Deindustrialization. In *Didsbury, H. F., Jr., ed.*, 1985, pp. 267–95. [G: Japan; W. Europe; U.S.]

Larkins, Daniel and Gill, Gurmukh S. Interest Rates and Aggregate Inventory Investment. *Surv. Curr. Bus.*, June 1985, 65(6), pp. 17–20. [G: U.S.]

Lempert, Leonard H. Financial Markets and the Business Cycle. *Bus. Econ.*, April 1985, 20(2), pp. 31–36. [G: U.S.]

Liebling, Herman I. The Myth of the Keynesian Recovery. *J. Macroecon.*, Spring 1985, 7(2), pp. 257–60. [G: U.S.]

Maier, Charles S. Inflation and Stagnation as Politics and History. In *Lindberg, L. N. and Maier, C. S., eds.*, 1985, pp. 3–24. [G: OECD]

Matthews, Kent. Private Sector Expenditure in the Inter-war Period: An Integrated Portfolio Approach. *Manchester Sch. Econ. Soc. Stud.*, March 1985, 53(1), pp. 23–44. [G: U.K.]

McClain, David. Stabilizing Oil and Farm Prices Holds the Key. *Challenge*, Sept./Oct. 1985, 28(4), pp. 23–26. [G: U.S.]

Meier, Peter. Erklärung konjunktureller Schwankungsintensitäten im Querschnitt von Produktionssektoren—eine empirische Analyse für die Schwiez. (The Intensity of Cyclical Fluctuations in Different Industries—An Empirical Analysis for Switzerland. With English summary.) *Schweiz. Z. Volkswirtsch. Statist.*, June 1985, 121(2), pp. 115–38. [G: Switzerland]

Meyer, F. V. Prospects for Recovery in the British Economy: Towards a Conclusion. In *Meyer, F. V., ed.*, 1985, pp. 213–32. [G: U.K.]

Meyer, F. V. The Economic Downturn of the Early 1980s. In *Meyer, F. V., ed.*, 1985, pp. 1–27. [G: U.K.]

Morley, Samuel A. Inflation and Recession: Fate or Political Choice in Brazil Today: Comments. In *Salazar-Carrillo, J. and Fendt, R., Jr., eds.*, 1985, pp. 167–69. [G: Brazil]

Nelson, Charles R. Macroeconomic Time-Series, Business Cycles, and Macroeconomic Policies: A Comment. *Carnegie-Rochester Conf. Ser. Public Policy*, Spring 1985, 22, pp. 55–59. [G: U.S.; U.K.; France; W. Germany; Switzerland]

Oberhauser, Alois. Das Schuldenparadox. (Paradoxical Effects of the Public Debt. With English summary.) *Jahr. Nationalökon. Statist.*, July 1985, 200(4), pp. 333–48. [G: W. Germany]

Palash, Carl J. and Radecki, Lawrence J. Using Monetary and Financial Variables to Predict Cyclical Downturns. *Fed. Res. Bank New York Quart. Rev.*, Summer 1985, 10(2), pp. 36–45. [G: U.S.]

Patel, S. J. Economic Crisis and the Transition

from Capitalism. *Econ. Int.*, Aug./Nov. 1985, *38*(3/4), pp. 368–93. [G: Global]

Pugno, Maurizio. Are Long Waves Relevant in Economic Life? A Note. *Econ. Notes*, 1985, (2), pp. 68–77. [G: Global]

Ratti, Ronald A. A Descriptive Analysis of Economic Indicators. *Fed. Res. Bank St. Louis Rev.*, January 1985, *67*(1), pp. 14–24. [G: U.S.]

Reagan, Patricia and Sheehan, Dennis P. The Stylized Facts about the Behavior of Manufacturers' Inventories and Backorders over the Business Cycle: 1959–1980. *J. Monet. Econ.*, March 1985, *15*(2), pp. 217–46. [G: U.S.]

Reynolds, Clark W. Mexico and the United States: Studies in Economic Interaction: Fluctuations and Growth: Comments. In *Musgrave, P. B., ed.*, 1985, pp. 171–75. [G: Mexico; U.S.]

Richards, Gordon. Business Cycles, Macroeconomic Policy, and U.S. Industrial Performance. In *Yochelson, J. N., ed.*, 1985, pp. 77–117. [G: U.S.]

Ross, Howard N. and Krausz, Joshua. Cyclical Price Behaviour and Concentration: A Time Series Analysis. *Oxford Bull. Econ. Statist.*, August 1985, *47*(3), pp. 231–47. [G: U.S.]

Schor, Juliet B. Changes in the Cyclical Pattern of Rural Wages: Evidence from Nine Countries, 1955–80. *Econ. J.*, June 1985, *95*(378), pp. 452–68. [G: OECD]

Schydlowsky, Daniel M. Mexico and the United States: Studies in Economic Interaction: Fluctuations and Growth: Comments. In *Musgrave, P. B., ed.*, 1985, pp. 177–82. [G: Mexico; U.S.]

Shughart, William F., II and Tollison, Robert D. Legislation and Political Business Cycles. *Kyklos*, 1985, *38*(1), pp. 43–59. [G: U.S.]

Sterman, John D. A Behavioral Model of the Economic Long Wave. *J. Econ. Behav. Organ.*, March 1985, *6*(1), pp. 17–53. [G: U.S.]

Stokes, Graham. Epidemiological Studies of the Psychological Response to Economic Instability in England: A Summary. In *Westcott, G.; Svensson, P.-G. and Zollner, H. F. K., eds.*, 1985, pp. 133–42. [G: U.K.]

Strigel, Werner H. Das Geschäftsklima als Konjunkturindikator—eine Retrospektive. (The Business Climate as Leading Indicator. With English summary.) *Ifo-Studien*, 1985, *31*(1), pp. 29–68. [G: OECD]

Stulz, René M. and Wasserfallen, Walter. Macroeconomic Time-Series, Business Cycles, and Macroeconomic Policies. *Carnegie-Rochester Conf. Ser. Public Policy*, Spring 1985, *22*, pp. 9–53. [G: U.S.; U.K.; France; W. Germany; Switzerland]

Tarascio, Vincent J. Keynes, Population, and Equity Prices. *J. Post Keynesian Econ.*, Spring 1985, *7*(3), pp. 303–10. [G: U.S.]

Tokman, Victor E. Wages and Employment in International Recessions: Recent Latin American Experience. In *Kim, K. S. and Ruccio, D. F., eds.*, 1985, pp. 74–95. [G: Latin America]

Twomey, Michael J. Economic Fluctuations in Argentina, Australia and Canada during the Depression of the 1930s. In *Platt, D. C. M. and di Tella, G., eds.*, 1985, pp. 179–93. [G: Argentina; Australia; Canada]

Watkins, Stephen. Recession and Health—A Literature Review. In *Westcott, G.; Svensson, P.-G. and Zollner, H. F. K., eds.*, 1985, pp. 27–56. [G: U.S.; U.K.]

Watkins, Stephen J. Recession and Health—The Policy Implications. In *Westcott, G.; Svensson, P.-G. and Zollner, H. F. K., eds.*, 1985, pp. 347–56.

Weir, Margaret and Skocpol, Theda. State Structures and the Possibilities for "Keynesian" Responses to the Great Depression in Sweden, Britain, and the United States. In *Evans, P. B.; Rueschemeyer, D. and Skocpol, T., eds.*, 1985, pp. 107–63. [G: U.K.; U.S.; Sweden]

Wilson, Thomas A. Lessons of Recession. *Can. J. Econ.*, November 1985, *18*(4), pp. 693–722. [G: Canada]

Worswick, G. D. N. Correction [Two Great Recessions]. *Scot. J. Polit. Econ.*, February 1985, *32*(1), pp. 111. [G: U.S.; U.K.]

Zuscovitch, Ehud. La dynamique du développement des technologies: Éléments d'un cadre conceptuel. (The Economic Dynamics of Technologies Development. With English summary.) *Revue Écon.*, September 1985, *36*(5), pp. 897–915.

132 Forecasting; Econometric Models

1320 General

Ashley, William C. and Hall, Lynne. Nonextrapolative Strategy. In *Mendell, J. S., ed.*, 1985, pp. 61–75.

Ballard, Charles L. and Goulder, Larry H. Consumption Taxes, Foresight, and Welfare: A Computable General Equilibrium Analysis. In *Piggott, J. and Whalley, J., eds.*, 1985, pp. 253–82. [G: U.S.]

Boucher, Wayne I. Scenarios and Scenario Writing. In *Mendell, J. S., ed.*, 1985, pp. 47–59.

Bovenberg, A. Lans. Dynamic General Equilibrium Tax Models with Adjustment Costs. In *Manne, A. S., ed.*, 1985, pp. 40–55.

Broadie, Mark N. An Introduction to the Octahedral Algorithm for the Computation of Economic Equilibria. In *Manne, A. S., ed.*, 1985, pp. 121–43.

Chisholm, Anthony H. and Tyers, Rodney. Agricultural Protection and Market Insulation Policies: Applications of a Dynamic Multisectoral Model. In *Piggott, J. and Whalley, J., eds.*, 1985, pp. 189–220. [G: Selected Countries]

Christ, Carl F. Early Progress in Estimating Quantitative Economic Relationships in America. *Amer. Econ. Rev.*, December 1985, *75*(6), pp. 39–52. [G: U.S.]

Cline, William R. Long-term Forecasts in International Economics. *Amer. Econ. Rev.*, May 1985, *75*(2), pp. 120–26. [G: Global]

Cohen, Jacob and Husted, Steven. An Integrated

Accounting Matrix for Canada and the United States. *Amer. Econ. Rev.*, May 1985, *75*(2), pp. 211–16.   [G: Canada; U.S.]

Condon, Timothy; Robinson, Sherman and Urata, Shujiro. Coping with a Foreign Exchange Crisis: A General Equilibrium Model of Alternative Adjustment Mechanisms. In *Manne, A. S., ed.*, 1985, pp. 75–94.
                                      [G: Turkey]

Dagum, Camilo. Structural Stability, Structural Change and Economic Forecasting. In *[Rossier, Edouard]*, 1985, pp. 153–71.

Diewert, W. E. The Measurement of Waste and Welfare in Applied General Equilibrium Models. In *Piggott, J. and Whalley, J., eds.*, 1985, pp. 42–103.

Frenkel, Jacob A. Fiscal Policy and the Exchange Rate in the Big Seven: Transmission of U.S. Government Spending Shocks: Comment. *Europ. Econ. Rev.*, June-July 1985, *28*(1–2), pp. 43–47.   [G: OECD; U.S.]

Geweke, John. Macroeconometric Modeling and the Theory of the Representative Agent. *Amer. Econ. Rev.*, May 1985, *75*(2), pp. 206–10.

Ginsburgh, Victor and van der Heyden, Ludo. General Equilibrium with Wage Rigidities: An Application to Belgium. In *Manne, A. S., ed.*, 1985, pp. 23–39.   [G: Belgium]

Harrison, Glenn W. and Kimbell, Larry J. Economic Interdependence in the Pacific Basin: A General Equilbrium Approach. In *Piggott, J. and Whalley, J., eds.*, 1985, pp. 143–74.
                          [G: Selected Countries]

Heady, Christopher J. and Mitra, Pradeep K. A Computational Approach to Optimum Public Policies. In *Manne, A. S., ed.*, 1985, pp. 95–120.

Hendry, David F. Monetary Economic Myth and Econometric Reality. *Oxford Rev. Econ. Policy*, Spring 1985, *1*(1), pp. 72–84.

James, John A. New Developments in the Application of General Equilibrium Models to Economic History. In *Piggott, J. and Whalley, J., eds.*, 1985, pp. 441–65.

Jones, Rich; Whalley, John and Wigle, Randall. Regional Impacts of Tariffs in Canada: Preliminary Results from a Small Dimensional Numerical General Equilibrium Model. In *Piggott, J. and Whalley, J., eds.*, 1985, pp. 175–88.
                                      [G: Canada]

Jorgenson, Dale W. and Slesnick, Daniel T. General Equilibrium Analysis of Economic Policy. In *Piggott, J. and Whalley, J., eds.*, 1985, pp. 293–370.   [G: U.S.]

Kasputys, Joseph E. Moving Econometrics from Theory to Application. *Eastern Econ. J.*, Jan.-Mar. 1985, *11*(1), pp. 16–27.

Koehn, Hank E. The Futures Research Division of the Security Pacific Bank. In *Mendell, J. S., ed.*, 1985, pp. 109–13.   [G: U.S.]

Leontief, Wassily. Structure of the World Economy: Outline of a Simple Input–Output Formulation. In *Leontief, W.*, 1985, pp. 381–97.
                                      [G: Global]

Lin, Tzong-Biau. Can Econometric Forecasting Models Survive the Challenges? *Singapore Econ. Rev.*, October 1985, *30*(2), pp. 57–67.

Llewellyn, John and Richardson, Pete. Representing Recent Policy Concerns in OECD's Macroeconomic Model. *OECD Econ. Stud.*, Autumn 1985, (5), pp. 169–80.   [G: OECD]

Manne, Alan S. On the Formulation and Solution of Economic Equilibrium Models. In *Manne, A. S., ed.*, 1985, pp. 1–22.

Masson, Paul and Blundell-Wignall, Adrian. Fiscal Policy and the Exchange Rate in the Big Seven: Transmission of U.S. Government Spending Shocks. *Europ. Econ. Rev.*, June-July 1985, *28*(1–2), pp. 11–42.   [G: OECD; U.S.]

Mathiesen, Lars. Computation of Economic Equilibria by a Sequence of Linear Complementarity Problems. In *Manne, A. S., ed.*, 1985, pp. 144–62.

McNees, Stephen K. Which Forecast Should You Use? *New Eng. Econ. Rev.*, July/August 1985, pp. 36–42.   [G: U.S.]

Meagher, G. A., et al. Special Purpose Versions of a General Purpose Multisectoral Model: Tax Issues and the Australian Wine Industry. In *Piggott, J. and Whalley, J., eds.*, 1985, pp. 283–92.   [G: Australia]

de Ménil, Georges and Westphal, Uwe. Aims and Methods of an International Macroeconomic Comparison. In *de Ménil, G. and Westphal, U., eds.*, 1985, pp. 1–17.   [G: France; W. Germany]

Nguyen, Trien T. General Equilbrium with Price Rigidities. In *Piggott, J. and Whalley, J., eds.*, 1985, pp. 396–410.

Pagan, Adrian R. and Shannon, John H. Sensitivity Analysis for Linearized Computable General Equilibrium Models. In *Piggott, J. and Whalley, J., eds.*, 1985, pp. 104–18.

Phillips, Robert L. Computing Solutions to Generalized Equilibrium Models by Successive Under-Relaxation. In *Manne, A. S., ed.*, 1985, pp. 192–209.

Piggott, John R. New Developments in Applied General Equilibrium Analysis: Introduction. In *Piggott, J. and Whalley, J., eds.*, 1985, pp. 1–24.

Preckel, Paul V. Alternative Algorithms for Computing Economic Equilibria. In *Manne, A. S., ed.*, 1985, pp. 163–72.

Spencer, John E. The European Economic Community: General Equilibrium Computations and the Economic Implications of Membership. In *Piggott, J. and Whalley, J., eds.*, 1985, pp. 119–42.   [G: EEC]

Stein, Herbert. Are Economists Getting a Bum Rap? *Southern Econ. J.*, April 1985, *51*(4), pp. 975–82.   [G: U.S.]

Stone, John C. Sequential Optimization and Complementarity Techniques for Computing Economic Equilibria. In *Manne, A. S., ed.*, 1985, pp. 173–91.

Surrey, M. J. C. Modelling the Economy. In *Morris, D., ed.*, 1985, pp. 444–71. [G: U.K.]

Visco, Ignazio. Fiscal Policy and the Exchange Rate in the Big Seven: Transmission of U.S. Government Spending Shocks: Comment. *Eu-*

rop. Econ. Rev., June-July 1985, *28*(1–2), pp. 49–52. **[G: OECD; U.S.]**

Whalley, John. Hidden Challenges in Recent Applied General Equilibrium Exercises. In *Piggott, J. and Whalley, J., eds.*, 1985, pp. 25–41.

1322 General Forecasts and Models

Alogoskoufis, George S. Macroeconomic Policy and Aggregate Fluctuations in a Semi-industrialized Open Economy: Greece 1951–1980. *Europ. Econ. Rev.*, October 1985, *29*(1), pp. 35–61. **[G: Greece]**

Andrews, M. J., et al. Models of the UK Economy and the Real Wage–Employment Debate. *Nat. Inst. Econ. Rev.*, May 1985, (112), pp. 41–52. **[G: U.K.]**

Artus, Patrick. Fiscal and Monetary Policies under a Flexible Exchange-Rate System: Comments. In *Melitz, J. and Wyplosz, C., eds.*, 1985, pp. 335–37. **[G: France]**

Artus, Patrick; Avouyi-Dovi, Sanvi and Laroque, Guy. Estimation d'une maquette macroéconomique trimestrielle avec rationnements quantitatifs. (Estimation of a Small Quarterly Model with Quantity Rationing. With English summary.) *Ann. INSEE*, Jan.-Mar. 1985, (57), pp. 3–25.

Ashley, Richard A. On the Optimal Use of Suboptimal Forecasts of Explanatory Variables. *J. Bus. Econ. Statist.*, April 1985, *3*(2), pp. 129–31. **[G: U.S.]**

Aslaksen, Iulie and Bjerkholt, Olav. Certainty Equivalence Procedures in Decision-Making under Uncertainty: An Empirical Application. In *[Johansen, L.]*, 1985, pp. 289–329. **[G: Norway]**

Backus, David; Blanco, Herminio and Levine, David K. The Financial Sector in the Planning of Economic Development. In *Gutowski, A.; Arnaudo, A. A. and Scharrer, H.-E., eds.*, 1985, pp. 42–58.

Bagrinovskii, K. A.; Rimashevskaia, N. M. and Sheviakov, A. Iu. A Simulation System of Models for Coordinating Output Levels and Living Standards. *Matekon*, Spring 1985, *21*(3), pp. 47–62. **[G: U.S.S.R.]**

Bandera, V. N. and Lucken, J. A. Simulation of a Debtor Country: The Example of Colombia. *J. Policy Modeling*, Fall 1985, *7*(3), pp. 457–76. **[G: Colombia]**

Bean, Charles R. Macroeconomic Policy Co-ordination: Theory and Evidence. *Rech. Écon. Louvain*, 1985, *51*(3–4), pp. 267–83. **[G: OECD]**

Becker, Robin, et al. Optimal Policy under Model Uncertainty. In *Currie, D., ed.*, 1985, pp. 69–85. **[G: U.K.]**

Bental, Benjamin; Ben-Zion, Uri and Wenig, Alois. Macroeconomic Policy and the Shadow Economy. In *Gaertner, W. and Wenig, A., eds.*, 1985, pp. 179–93.

Berger, Allen N. and Krane, Spencer D. The Information Efficiency of Econometric Model Forecasts. *Rev. Econ. Statist.*, February 1985, *67*(1), pp. 128–34. **[G: U.S.]**

Bergman, Lars. Extensions and Applications of the MSG-Model: A Brief Survey. In *[Johansen, L.]*, 1985, pp. 127–61.

Bjerkholt, Olav and Tveitereid, Sigurd. The Use of the MSG-Model in Preparing a "Perspective Analysis 1980–2000" for the Norwegian Economy. In *[Johansen, L.]*, 1985, pp. 271–87.

Blaga, I., et al. Modelling of Territorial Development within the General Cybernetic System of National Economy. *Econ. Computat. Cybern. Stud. Res.*, 1985, *20*(2), pp. 5–14. **[G: Romania]**

Boamah, Daniel O. Wage Formation, Employment and Output in Barbados. *Soc. Econ. Stud.*, December 1985, *34*(4), pp. 199–218. **[G: Barbados]**

Brandsma, Andries S. and Pijpers, J. R. Coordinated Strategies for Economic Cooperation between Europe and the United States. *Weltwirtsch. Arch.*, 1985, *121*(4), pp. 661–81. **[G: U.S.; EEC]**

Brayton, Flint and Mauskopf, Eileen. The Federal Reserve Board MPS Quarterly Econometric Model of the U.S. Economy. *Econ. Modelling*, July 1985, *2*(3), pp. 170–292. **[G: U.S.]**

Brinner, Roger E. Reflections on Reflections: Comments [Thoughts on Public Expenditures] [The International Agenda] [Reflections on Macroeconomic Modelling; Confessions of a DRI Addict]. *Eastern Econ. J.*, Jan.-Mar. 1985, *11*(1), pp. 84–87.

Broer, D. P. and Siebrand, J. C. A Macroeconomic Disequilibrium Model of Product Market and Labour Market for the Netherlands. *Appl. Econ.*, August 1985, *17*(4), pp. 633–46. **[G: Netherlands]**

den Butter, Frank A. G. FREIA and KOMPAS, the Central Planning Bureau's New Generation of Macro-economic Policy Models: A Review Article. *De Economist*, 1985, *133*(1), pp. 43–63. **[G: Netherlands]**

Challen, D. W. Wages, Unemployment and Inflation. In *Argy, V. E. and Neville, J. W., eds.*, 1985, pp. 346–69. **[G: Australia]**

Chiarella, Carl. Analysis of the Effects of Time Lags and Nonlinearities in a Macroeconomic Model Incorporating the Government Budget Constraint. In *Batten, D. F. and Lesse, P. F., eds.*, 1985, pp. 131–52.

Chow, Gregory C. A Model of Chinese National Income Determination. *J. Polit. Econ.*, August 1985, *93*(4), pp. 782–92. **[G: China]**

Christiano, Lawrence J. A Method for Estimating the Timing Interval in a Linear Econometric Model, with an Application to Taylor's Model of Staggered Contracts. *J. Econ. Dynam. Control*, December 1985, *9*(4), pp. 363–404. **[G: U.S.]**

Cockle, Paul. Public Expenditure Policy, 1985–86: The Economic Environment. In *Cockle, P., ed.*, 1985, pp. 35–55. **[G: U.K.]**

Cohen, Darrel and Clark, Peter B. Effects of Fiscal Policy on the U.S. Economy: Empirical Estimates of Crowding Out. *J. Policy Modeling*, Winter 1985, *7*(4), pp. 573–93. **[G: U.S.]**

Cooper, Russel J.; McLaren, Keith R. and Pow-

ell, Alan A. Short-run Macroeconomic Closure in Applied General Equilbrium Modelling: Experience from ORANI and Agenda for Further Research. In *Piggott, J. and Whalley, J., eds.,* 1985, pp. 411–40. **[G: Australia]**

Cordova, Miguel L. Policy Planning Simulation for World Regional Development and Equity. *Econ. Planning,* 1985, *19*(2), pp. 92–117. **[G: Global]**

Cronin, M. R. The Orani Model in Short Run Mode: Theory versus Observation. *Australian Econ. Pap.,* June 1985, *24*(44), pp. 24–36. **[G: Australia]**

Dawson, Alistair. Comment upon a New-Classical Model of the Postwar UK. *Appl. Econ.,* April 1985, *17*(2), pp. 257–61. **[G: U.K.]**

Deardorff, Alan V. and Stern, Robert M. The Effects of Exchange-Rate Changes on Domestic Prices, Trade and Employment in the U.S., European Community and Japan. In *Jungenfelt, K. and Hague, D. [Sir], eds.,* 1985, pp. 282–306. **[G: OECD]**

DeRosa, Dean A. and Smeal, Gary. The International Transmission of Economic Activity. In *Arndt, S. W.; Sweeney, R. J. and Willett, T. D., eds.,* 1985, pp. 202–09. **[G: OECD]**

Dixon, Peter B. The Solution Procedure for the ORANI Model Explained by a Simple Example. In *Batten, D. F. and Lesse, P. F., eds.,* 1985, pp. 119–29. **[G: Australia]**

Dungan, Peter and Younger, Arthur. New Technology and Unemployment: A Simulation of Macroeconomic Impacts and Responses in Canada. *J. Policy Modeling,* Winter 1985, 7(4), pp. 595–619. **[G: Canada]**

Eriksen, Tore and Qvigstad, Jan Fredrik. The Use of Macroeconomic Models in Economic Policy Making: The Norwegian Experience. *Econ. Modelling,* January 1985, 2(1), pp. 59–66. **[G: Norway]**

Ewis, Nabil A. and Fisher, Douglas. A Short-term Macroeconometric Model of Egypt, 1950–79. *Indian Econ. J.,* July-Sept. 1985, *33*(1), pp. 42–65. **[G: Egypt]**

Favero, Carlo. Antilopi o cicogne? Un'analisi critica delle verifiche empiriche della teoria della neutralità della politica economica. (Antelopes or Storks? A Critical Analysis of the Empirical Tests of the Economic Policy Neutrality Theory. With English summary.) *Giorn. Econ.,* July-Aug. 1985, *44*(7–8), pp. 427–44. **[G: Italy]**

Filatov, Victor S. and Mattione, Richard P. Latin America's Recovery from Debt Problems: An Assessment of Model-based Projections. *J. Policy Modeling,* Fall 1985, 7(3), pp. 491–524. **[G: Brazil; Chile; Mexico]**

Foders, Federico and Kim, Chungsoo. Impact of Deep-Sea Mining on the World Metal Markets: Manganese. In *Donges, J. B., ed.,* 1985, pp. 204–52. **[G: Selected Countries]**

Gibson, Bill. A Structuralist Macromodel for Post-revolutionary Nicaragua. *Cambridge J. Econ.,* December 1985, 9(4), pp. 347–69. **[G: Nicaragua]**

Ginsburgh, Victor, et al. Macroeconomic Policy

in the Presence of an Irregular Sector. In *Gaertner, W. and Wenig, A., eds.,* 1985, pp. 194–217.

Gregory, Allan W. and Raynauld, Jacques. An Econometric Model of Canadian Monetary Policy over the 1970s. *J. Money, Credit, Banking,* February 1985, *17*(1), pp. 43–58. **[G: Canada]**

Hall, S. G. and Henry, S. G. B. Rational Expectations in an Econometric Model: NIESR Model 8. *Nat. Inst. Econ. Rev.,* November 1985, (114), pp. 58–68. **[G: U.K.]**

Hall, S. G.; Henry, S. G. B. and Johns, C. B. Forecasting with a Rational Expectations Model of the UK: A Comment. *Oxford Bull. Econ. Statist.,* November 1985, *47*(4), pp. 337–45. **[G: U.K.]**

Handa, Jagdish and Okiyama, Yukio. Inflation in a Large, Open Economy: The Scandinavian Model and the Japanese Economy. *Hitotsubashi J. Econ.,* June 1985, *26*(1), pp. 83–97. **[G: Japan]**

Heilemann, Ullrich. Zur Prognosepraxis ökonometrischer Modelle. (With English summary.) *Z. Wirtschaft. Sozialwissen.,* 1985, *105*(6), pp. 683–708. **[G: W. Germany]**

Hojman, David E. A Quarterly Econometric Model of Chile, 1974–1979, and an Application to the Analysis of the Fixed Exchange Rate Policy between 1979 and 1982. In *Hojman, D. E., ed.,* 1985, pp. 125–51. **[G: Chile]**

Hörngren, Lars. A Comparison of the Dynamic Properties of Five Nordic Macroeconometric Models—A Critical Note. *Scand. J. Econ.,* 1985, *87*(3), pp. 568–74. **[G: Sweden; Finland; Norway]**

Huth, William L. Intertemporal Relationships between Industrialized Economies. *Europ. Econ. Rev.,* August 1985, *28*(3), pp. 363–76. **[G: W. Europe; U.S.; Japan; Canada]**

Ishii, Naoko; McKibbin, Warwick and Sachs, Jeffrey. The Economic Policy Mix, Policy Cooperation, and Protectionism: Some Aspects of Macroeconomic Interdependence among the United States, Japan, and Other OECD Countries. *J. Policy Modeling,* Winter 1985, 7(4), pp. 533–72. **[G: OECD]**

Klein, Lawrence R. Did Mainstream Econometric Models Fail to Anticipate the Inflationary Surge? In *Feiwel, G. R., ed. (I),* 1985, pp. 289–96. **[G: U.S.]**

Klein, Lawrence R. New Developments in Project LINK. *Amer. Econ. Rev.,* May 1985, 75(2), pp. 223–27. **[G: Global]**

Klein, Lawrence R.; Bollino, Carlo Andrea and Fardoust, Shah. International Interactions of Industrial Policy: Simulations of the World Economy, 1982–1990. In *Adams, F. G., ed.,* 1985, pp. 15–30. **[G: OECD]**

Klein, Lawrence R.; Doud, Arthur and Sojo, E. Simplification of Large Scale Macroeconometric Models. *Eastern Econ. J.,* Jan.-Mar. 1985, *11*(1), pp. 28–40. **[G: U.S.]**

Knoester, Anthonie. The Forward Shifting of Taxes: A Comment [Stagnation and the Inverted Haavelmo Effect: Some International

Evidence]: Reply. *De Economist*, 1985, *133*(3), pp. 417–20.

Koefoed, O. The Forward Shifting of Taxes: A Comment [Stagnation and the Inverted Haavelmo Effect: Some International Evidence]. *De Economist*, 1985, *133*(3), pp. 415–17.

Kohn, Meir and Manchester, Joyce. International Evidence on Misspecification of the Standard Money Demand Equation. *J. Monet. Econ.*, July 1985, *16*(1), pp. 87–94.   **[G: OECD]**

Kooiman, Peter and Kloek, Teun. An Empirical Two Market Disequilibrium Model for Dutch Manufacturing. *Europ. Econ. Rev.*, December 1985, *29*(3), pp. 323–54.   **[G: Netherlands]**

Krishnamurty, K. Inflation and Growth: A Model for India. In *Krishnamurty, K. and Pandit, V.*, 1985, pp. 16–111.   **[G: India]**

Krishnamurty, K. and Pandit, V. Macroeconometric Modelling of the Indian Economy: An Overview. In *Krishnamurty, K. and Pandit, V.*, 1985, pp. 1–15.   **[G: India]**

Laffargue, Jean-Pierre. An Internal Evaluation Method of Multinational Models. *Economia (Portugal)*, January 1985, *9*(1), pp. 73–104.

Laffargue, Jean-Pierre. Fiscal and Monetary Policies under a Flexible Exchange-Rate System. In *Melitz, J. and Wyplosz, C., eds.*, 1985, pp. 309–34.   **[G: France]**

Lahiri, Ashok Kumar and Roy, Prannoy. Rainfall and Supply–Response: A Study of Rice in India. *J. Devel. Econ.*, August 1985, *18*(2–3), pp. 315–34.   **[G: India]**

Lambelet, Jean-Christian. Should Systems Like LINK Be Used for Long-Range Forecasts and Simulations? *Econ. Modelling*, April 1985, *2*(2), pp. 83–92.   **[G: Global]**

Leventakis, John A. Stabilization Policies in the Greek Economy: Will They Work? *J. Policy Modeling*, Fall 1985, *7*(3), pp. 441–55.   **[G: Greece]**

Litterman, Robert B. How Monetary Policy in 1985 Affects the Outlook. *Fed. Res. Bank Minn. Rev.*, Fall 1985, *9*(4), pp. 2–13.   **[G: U.S.]**

Longva, Svein; Lorentsen, Lorents and Olsen, Øystein. The Multi-sectoral Growth Model MSG-4 Formal Structure and Empirical Characteristics. In *[Johansen, L.]*, 1985, pp. 187–240.   **[G: Norway]**

Looney, Robert E. Pre-revolutionary Iranian Economic Policy Making: An Optimal Control Based Assessment. *Econ. Modelling*, October 1985, *2*(4), pp. 357–68.   **[G: Iran]**

Lybeck, Johan A. A Comparison of the Dynamic Properties of Five Nordic Macroeconomic Models—A Critical Note. Reply. *Scand. J. Econ.*, 1985, *87*(3), pp. 575.   **[G: Sweden; Finland; Norway]**

Manne, Alan S. and Preckel, Paul V. A Three-Region Intertemporal Model of Energy, International Trade and Capital Flows. In *Manne, A. S., ed.*, 1985, pp. 56–74.   **[G: OECD; OPEC; LDCs]**

Marshall, Rob. Public Expenditure Policy, 1985–86: Alternative Scenarios. In *Cockle, P., ed.*, 1985, pp. 57–75.   **[G: U.K.]**

Marwaha, S. and Peel, D. A. Behaviour of the Liverpool Model with Weight Given to Alternative Public Forecasts. *Econ. Modelling*, January 1985, *2*(1), pp. 33–38.   **[G: U.K.]**

Matlin, I. S.; Akhundova, T. A. and Kurkina, O. M. A Study of the Relationship between Balance in the Goods Market, Capital-Intensity, and Labor Productivity Based on a Dynamic Input–Output Model. *Matekon*, Spring 1985, *21*(3), pp. 63–80.   **[G: U.S.S.R.]**

Matthews, Kent. Forecasting with a Rational Expectations Model of the UK. *Oxford Bull. Econ. Statist.*, November 1985, *47*(4), pp. 311–36.   **[G: U.K.]**

Mercenier, Jean and Waelbroeck, Jean. The Impact of Protection on Developing Countries: A General Equilibrium Analysis. In *Jungenfelt, K. and Hague, D. [Sir], eds.*, 1985, pp. 219–39.   **[G: LDCs]**

Miller, Marcus. Fiscal and Monetary Policies under a Flexible Exchange-Rate System: Comments. In *Melitz, J. and Wyplosz, C., eds.*, 1985, pp. 339–42.   **[G: France]**

Motamen, Homa. The Wealth Effect of North Sea Oil. In *Bjerkholt, O. and Offerdal, E., eds.*, 1985, pp. 231–47.   **[G: U.K.]**

von Natzmer, Wulfheinrich. Econometric Policy Evaluation and Expectations. *Econ. Modelling*, January 1985, *2*(1), pp. 52–58.

Nelson, Charles R. Macroeconomic Time-Series, Business Cycles, and Macroeconomic Policies: A Comment. *Carnegie-Rochester Conf. Ser. Public Policy*, Spring 1985, *22*, pp. 55–59.   **[G: U.S.; U.K.; France; W. Germany; Switzerland]**

Neri, Fabio. On the Forecasting Performance of Some Small Macroeconomic Models. *Rivista Int. Sci. Econ. Com.*, Oct.-Nov. 1985, *32*(10–11), pp. 1097–1113.

Netzer, Dick. 1985 Projections of the New York Metropolitan Region Study. *Amer. Econ. Rev.*, May 1985, *75*(2), pp. 114–19.   **[G: U.S.]**

Neumann, Manfred J. M. and Buscher, Herbert S. Wirtschaftsprognosen im Vergleich: Eine Untersuchung anhand von Rationalitätstests. (Forecasts of the German Economy: An Evaluation Based on Rational Expectations. With English summary.) *Ifo-Studien*, 1985, *31*(3), pp. 183–201.   **[G: W. Germany]**

Olofin, S., et al. An Operational Econometric Model of the Nigerian Economy. *Empirical Econ.*, 1985, *10*(4), pp. 231–62.   **[G: Nigeria]**

Oudiz, Gilles. European Policy Coordination: An Evaluation. *Rech. Écon. Louvain*, 1985, *51*(3–4), pp. 301–39.   **[G: EEC]**

Palash, Carl J. and Radecki, Lawrence J. Using Monetary and Financial Variables to Predict Cyclical Downturns. *Fed. Res. Bank New York Quart. Rev.*, Summer 1985, *10*(2), pp. 36–45.   **[G: U.S.]**

Pandit, V. Macroeconomic Adjustments in a Developing Economy: A Medium Term Model of Outputs and Prices in India. In *Krishnamurty, K. and Pandit, V.*, 1985, pp. 112–51.   **[G: India]**

Pandit, V. Macroeconomic Structure and Policy

in a Less Developed Economy. *J. Quant. Econ.*, January 1985, *1*(1), pp. 49–79.
[G: India]

Park, Se-Hark. Investment Planning and the Macroeconomic Constraints in Developing Countries: The Case of the Syrian Arab Republic. *World Devel.*, July 1985, *13*(7), pp. 837–53. [G: Syria]

Parmenter, B. R. and Meagher, G. A. Policy Analysis Using a Computable General Equilibrium Model: A Review of Experience at the IMPACT Project. *Australian Econ. Rev.*, 1st Quarter 1985, (69), pp. 3–15. [G: Australia]

Personick, Valerie A. A Second Look at Industry Output and Employment Trends through 1995. *Mon. Lab. Rev.*, November 1985, *108*(11), pp. 26–41. [G: U.S.]

Persson, Håkan. A Version of the MSG-Model with Putty–Clay and Vintage Technology. In *[Johansen, L.]*, 1985, pp. 163–85.

Pikkarainen, Pentti; Tarkka, Juha and William, Alpo. Korkojen kokonaistaloudellisista vaikutuksista BOF3-mallissa. (On the Macroeconomic Effects of Interest Rates in the BOF3 Model. With English summary.) *Kansant. Aikak.*, 1985, *81*(2), pp. 160–70.
[G: Finland]

Powell, Alan A. Short-run Applications of Orani: An Impact Project Perspective. *Australian Econ. Pap.*, June 1985, *24*(44), pp. 37–53.
[G: Australia]

Rausser, Gordon C. Macroeconomics and U.S. Agricultural Policy. In *Gardner, B. L., ed.*, 1985, pp. 207–52. [G: U.S.]

Richet, Xavier. Planification macro-économique indicative et modélisation en Hongrie. (Macroeconomic Planning and Modelling in Hungary. With English summary.) *Écon. Soc.*, May 1985, *19*(5), pp. 43–68. [G: Hungary]

Robinson, Sherman and Tyson, Laura D'Andrea. Foreign Trade, Resource Allocation, and Structural Adjustment in Yugoslavia: 1976–1980. *J. Compar. Econ.*, March 1985, *9*(1), pp. 46–70.
[G: Yugoslavia]

Rossiter, Rosemary. A Modified Procedure for Simulation of Macroeconometric Models. *Econ. Modelling*, October 1985, *2*(4), pp. 324–30. [G: U.S.]

Sadoulet, Elisabeth. Investment Priorities and Income Distribution: The Case of Brazil in 1970. *J. Policy Modeling*, Fall 1985, *7*(3), pp. 407–39. [G: Brazil]

Sandblom, Carl-Louis and Banasik, John. Economic Policy with Bounded Controls. *Econ. Modelling*, April 1985, *2*(2), pp. 135–48.
[G: Canada]

Schreiner, Per and Larsen, Knut Arild. On the Introduction and Application of the MSG-Model in the Norwegian Planning System. In *[Johansen, L.]*, 1985, pp. 241–69.

Smit, B. W. and Meyer, B. S. The BER Quarterly Econometric Model of the South African Economy. *J. Stud. Econ. Econometrics*, November 1985, (23), pp. 99–140. [G: S. Africa]

Solow, Robert M. Reflections on Macroeconomic Modelling; Confessions of a DRI Addict. *East-*

ern Econ. J., Jan.-Mar. 1985, *11*(1), pp. 79–83.

Stockton, David J. and Glassman, James E. The Theory and Econometrics of Reduced-Form Nominal Income and Price Equations. *Southern Econ. J.*, July 1985, *52*(1), pp. 103–21.

Stulz, René M. and Wasserfallen, Walter. Macroeconomic Time-Series, Business Cycles, and Macroeconomic Policies. *Carnegie-Rochester Conf. Ser. Public Policy*, Spring 1985, *22*, pp. 9–53. [G: U.S.; U.K.; France; W. Germany; Switzerland]

Su, Betty W. The Economic Outlook to 1995: New Assumptions and Projections. *Mon. Lab. Rev.*, November 1985, *108*(11), pp. 3–16.
[G: U.S.]

Sujan, I. and Oleksa, M. A Quarterly Econometric Model for Short-term Analysis of the Czech Economy. *Matekon*, Spring 1985, *21*(3), pp. 31–46. [G: Czechoslovakia]

Szakolczai, György; Bagdy, Gábor and Vindics, József. Dependence of the Hungarian Economic Performance on the World Economy. Facts and Economic Policy Inferences. *Acta Oecon.*, 1985, *35*(3–4), pp. 295–311.
[G: Hungary]

Tarkka, Juha. Monetary Policy in the BOF3 Quarterly Model of the Finnish Economy. *Econ. Modelling*, October 1985, *2*(4), pp. 298–306. [G: Finland]

Tyers, Rodney. International Impacts of Protection: Model Structure and Results for EC Agricultural Policy. *J. Policy Modeling*, Summer 1985, *7*(2), pp. 219–51. [G: EEC]

Varshavskii, A. E. Models for Forecasting the Influence of Scientific and Technical Progress on Economic Growth. *Matekon*, Winter 1985-86, *22*(2), pp. 59–85. [G: U.S.S.R.]

Venieris, Yiannis P. and Gupta, Dipak K. Macro Interactions in a Social System: A Case Study of Great Britain. *Southern Econ. J.*, January 1985, *51*(3), pp. 681–96. [G: U.K.]

Vincent, D. P. Exchange Rate Devaluation, Monetary Policy and Wages: A General Equilibrium Analysis for Chile. *Econ. Modelling*, January 1985, *2*(1), pp. 17–32. [G: Chile]

Wagenhals, Gerhard. Impact of Deep-Sea Mining on the World Metal Markets: Copper. In *Donges, J. B., ed.*, 1985, pp. 113–203.
[G: Selected Countries]

Walker, John. The UK Economy: Analysis and Prospects. *Oxford Rev. Econ. Policy*, Autumn 1985, *1*(3), pp. 25–38. [G: U.K.]

Webb, Roy H. Forecasts 1985. *Fed. Res. Bank Richmond Econ. Rev.*, Jan./Feb. 1985, *71*(1), pp. 23–26. [G: U.S.]

Whalley, John and Wigle, Randall. Price and Quantity Rigidities in Adjustment to Trade Policy Changes: Alternative Formulations and Initial Calculations. In *Jungenfelt, K. and Hague, D. [Sir], eds.*, 1985, pp. 246–71. [G: Global]

Wrightsman, Dwayne. Forecasting with Velocity. *Challenge*, July/August 1985, *28*(3), pp. 58–60.
[G: U.S.; Canada]

Yeboah, Dickson A. Control Theory Application to Economic Policy Analysis in Ghana. *Appl.*

Econ., June 1985, *17*(3), pp. 395–419.
[G: Ghana]

van Zon, Andriaan H. A Simple Multisector Model with Six Sectors of Production: Estimation and Simulation Results for the 1950–1968 Period. *De Economist*, 1985, *133*(3), pp. 352–410. [G: Netherlands]

1323 Specific Forecasts and Models

Achio, Françoise. Forecasts of Skilled-Manpower Needs in the Ivory Coast: An Evaluation of Methods and Results. In *Youdi, R. V. and Hinchliffe, K., eds.*, 1985, pp. 211–28.
[G: Ivory Coast]

Adams, F. Gerard and Santarelli, Roberto. Econometric Modeling of Industries on the Microcomputer: A Model of the Italian Metal–Mechanical Industry. *Bus. Econ.*, April 1985, *20*(2), pp. 43–49. [G: Italy]

Anderson, James E. and Kraus, Marvin. An Econometric Model of Regulated Airline Flight Rivalry. In *Keeler, T. E., ed.*, 1985, pp. 1–26. [G: U.S.]

Arrow, Kenneth J. The Economic Cost to Western Europe of Restricted Availability of Oil Imports: A Linear Programming Computation. In *Arrow, K. J. (II)*, 1985, pp. 1–8.

Artus, Patrick and Muet, Pierre-Alain. Investment, Output and Labor Constraints, and Financial Constraints: The Estimation of a Model with Several Regimes. In *Weiserbs, D., ed.*, 1985, pp. 25–44. [G: France]

Artus, Patrick and Nasse, Philippe. Exchange Rates, Prices, Wages, and the Current Account in France. In *de Ménil, G. and Westphal, U., eds.*, 1985, pp. 147–80. [G: France]

Artus, Patrick, et al. Tax Incentives, Monetary Policy, and Investment in France and Germany. In *de Ménil, G. and Westphal, U., eds.*, 1985, pp. 105–41. [G: France; W. Germany]

Baker, Stephen A. and Van Tassel, Roger C. Forecasting the Price of Gold: A Fundamentalist Approach. *Atlantic Econ. J.*, December 1985, *13*(4), pp. 43–51. [G: Global]

Beenstock, Michael; Dalziel, Alan and Warburton, Peter J. Aggregate Investment and Output in the U.K. In *Weiserbs, D., ed.*, 1985, pp. 117–36. [G: U.K.]

Behring, Karin and Goldrian, Georg. The IFO Housing Market Model. In *Stahl, K., ed.*, 1985, pp. 119–43. [G: W. Germany]

Berkovec, James. New Car Sales and Used Car Stocks: A Model of the Automobile Market. *Rand J. Econ.*, Summer 1985, *16*(2), pp. 195–214. [G: U.S.]

Berndt, Ernst R. and Botero, German. Energy Demand in the Transportation Sector of Mexico. *J. Devel. Econ.*, April 1985, *17*(3), pp. 219–38. [G: Mexico]

Bingen, Georges and Dewatripont, Mathias. Vérification empirique de la théorie du consommateur: quelques testes emboîtés et non emboîtés. (With English summary.) *Cah. Écon. Bruxelles*, 1st Trimester 1985, (105), pp. 3–40. [G: Belgium]

Bismut, Claude and Kröger, Jürgen. The Dilemmas of Economic Policy in France and Germany: Trade-offs between Inflation, Unemployment, and the Current Account. In *de Ménil, G. and Westphal, U., eds.*, 1985, pp. 303–47. [G: France; W. Germany]

Blendon, Robert J. Public Choices for the 1990s: An Uncertain Look into America's Future. In *Ginzberg, E., ed.*, 1985, pp. 5–27. [G: U.S.]

Blinder, Alan S. and Deaton, Angus. The Time Series Consumption Function Revisited. *Brookings Pap. Econ. Act.*, 1985, (2), pp. 465–511. [G: U.S.]

Borooah, Vani K. and Sharpe, D. R. Household Income, Consumption and Savings in the United Kingdom, 1966–82. *Scot. J. Polit. Econ.*, November 1985, *32*(3), pp. 234–56.
[G: U.K.]

Boyd, Chris. Industrial Investment in the European Community: Comment. In *Weiserbs, D., ed.*, 1985, pp. 21–23. [G: EEC]

Carlson, Keith M. Monthly Economic Indicators: A Closer Look at the Coincident Index. *Fed. Res. Bank St. Louis Rev.*, November 1985, *67*(9), pp. 20–30. [G: U.S.]

Cartucho Pereira, Paulo. A procura energia no Plano Energético Nacional—Apreci̇ção crítica. (With English summary.) *Economia (Portugal)*, May 1985, *9*(2), pp. 301–15. [G: Portugal]

Caskey, John P. Modeling the Formation of Price Expectations: A Bayesian Approach. *Amer. Econ. Rev.*, September 1985, *75*(4), pp. 768–76. [G: U.S.]

Cassel, Eric and Mendelsohn, Robert. The Choice of Functional Forms for Hedonic Price Equations: Comment. *J. Urban Econ.*, September 1985, *18*(2), pp. 135–42. [G: U.S.]

Chalmers, James A. Synfuels Development in the USA: Case Studies of National Environmental Feasibility and Local Socioeconomic Impacts: The Cumulative Impacts Task Force Experience in Colorado. In *Lakshmanan, T. R. and Johansson, B., eds.*, 1985, pp. 100–110.
[G: U.S.]

Chambers, Robert G. Macroeconomics and U.S. Agricultural Policy: Commentary. In *Gardner, B. L., ed.*, 1985, pp. 253–56. [G: U.S.]

Cheffert, Jean-Marie; Deschamps, Robert and Reding, Paul. Export Price Setting for Selected Sectors of the Belgian Economy. In *Peeters, T.; Praet, P. and Reding, P., eds.*, 1985, pp. 201–24. [G: Belgium]

Chipman, John S. Relative Prices, Capital Movements, and Sectoral Technical Change: Theory and an Empirical Test. In *Jungenfelt, K. and Hague, D. [Sir], eds.*, 1985, pp. 395–454.
[G: W. Germany; Sweden]

Ciriacy-Wantrup, S. V. Conceptual Problems in Projecting the Demand for Land and Water. In *Ciriacy-Wantrup, S. V.*, 1985, pp. 149–75.
[G: U.S.]

Coates, Joseph F. Scenarios Part Two: Alternative Futures. In *Mendell, J. S., ed.*, 1985, pp. 21–46. [G: U.S.]

Davies, Gavyn and Piachaud, David. Public Expenditure on the Social Services: The Eco-

nomic and Political Constraints. In *Klein, R. and O'Higgins, M., ed.*, 1985, pp. 92–110.
[G: U.K.]

Debeauvais, Michel and Psacharopoulos, George. Forecasting the Needs for Qualified Manpower: Towards an Evaluation. In *Youdi, R. V. and Hinchliffe, K., eds.*, 1985, pp. 11–31.
[G: Selected LDCs]

Denton, Frank T. and Spencer, Byron G. Prospective Changes in Population and Their Implications for Government Expenditures. In *Courchene, T. J.; Conklin, D. W. and Cook, G. C. A., eds. Vol. 1*, 1985, pp. 44–95.
[G: Canada]

Dixon, Peter B.; Parmenter, B. R. and Rimmer, Russell J. The Sensitivity of ORANI Projections of the Short-run Effects of Increases in Protection to Variations in the Values Adopted for Export Demand Elasticities. In *Jungenfelt, K. and Hague, D. [Sir], eds.*, 1985, pp. 317–46.
[G: Australia; Selected Countries]

Donnelly, William A. Electricity Demand Modelling. In *Batten, D. F. and Lesse, P. F., eds.*, 1985, pp. 179–95.
[G: Australia]

Dougherty, C. R. S. Manpower Forecasting and Manpower-Development Planning in the United Kingdom. In *Youdi, R. V. and Hinchliffe, K., eds.*, 1985, pp. 75–98.
[G: U.K.]

Elam, Emmett W. and Holder, Shelby H. An Evaluation of the *Rice Outlook and Situation* Price Forecasts. *Southern J. Agr. Econ.*, December 1985, *17*(2), pp. 155–61.
[G: U.S.]

Epperson, James E. and Fletcher, Stanley M. Tandem Forecasting of Price and Probability—The Case of Watermelon. *Can. J. Agr. Econ.*, November 1985, *33*(3), pp. 375–85.
[G: U.S.]

Faini, Riccardo and Schiantarelli, Fabio. A Unified Framework for Firms' Decisions Theoretical Analysis and Empirical Application to Italy 1970–1980. In *Weiserbs, D., ed.*, 1985, pp. 51–74.
[G: Italy]

Falk, James E. and McCormick, Garth P. Computational Aspects of the International Coal Trade Model. In *Harker, P. T., ed.*, 1985, pp. 73–117.

Feroldi, Mathieu. Monetary Mechanisms and Exchange Rates in France. In *de Ménil, G. and Westphal, U., eds.*, 1985, pp. 227–62.
[G: France]

Fisher, Lawrence and Kamin, Jules H. Forecasting Systematic Risk: Estimates of "Raw" Beta That Take Account of the Tendency of Beta To Change and Heteroskedasticity of Risidual Returns. *J. Finan. Quant. Anal.*, June 1985, *20*(2), pp. 127–49.
[G: U.S.]

Førsund, Finn R. and Jansen, Eilev S. The Interplay between Sectoral Models Based on Micro Data and Models for the National Economy. In *[Johansen, L.]*, 1985, pp. 109–25.

Fullerton, Howard N., Jr. Erratum [The 1995 Labor Force: BLS' Latest Projections]. *Mon. Lab. Rev.*, December 1985, *108*(12), pp. 33.
[G: U.S.]

Fullerton, Howard N., Jr. The 1995 Labor Force:

BLS' Latest Projections. *Mon. Lab. Rev.*, November 1985, *108*(11), pp. 17–25.
[G: U.S.]

Gallow, Michael; Griffiths, Geoffrey and Affleck-Graves, John F. Earnings Forecasting on the JSE: An Empirical Study of Some Statistical Models. *J. Stud. Econ. Econometrics*, August 1985, (22), pp. 25–46.
[G: S. Africa]

Garner, C. Alan. Forecast Dispersion as a Measure of Economic Uncertainty. *Quart. Rev. Econ. Bus.*, Spring 1985, *25*(1), pp. 58–73.
[G: U.S.]

Gelauff, George M. M.; Wennekers, Sander R. M. and de Jong, André H. M. A Putty-Clay Model with Three Factors of Production and Partly Endogenous Technical Progress. *De Economist*, 1985, *133*(3), pp. 327–51.
[G: Netherlands]

Gerard, M. and Vanden Berghe, C. Econometric Analysis of Sectoral Investment in Belgium (1956–1982). In *Weiserbs, D., ed.*, 1985, pp. 81–110.
[G: Belgium]

Givoly, Dan. The Formation of Earnings Expectations. *Accounting Rev.*, July 1985, *60*(3), pp. 372–86.
[G: U.S.]

Green, Christopher J. An Empirical Note on the Fiscal Accommodation of an Oil Price Increase. *Appl. Econ.*, February 1985, *17*(1), pp. 107–15.
[G: U.K.]

Gregory, Allan W. Testing Nested Functional Forms of Money Demand for Canada. *J. Quant. Econ.*, July 1985, *1*(2), pp. 211–30.
[G: Canada]

Hafer, R. W. Money Demand Predictability: Comment. *J. Money, Credit, Banking*, Pt. 2, Nov. 1985, *17*(4), pp. 642–46. [G: U.S.]

Hafer, R. W. and Hein, Scott E. On the Accuracy of Time-Series, Interest Rate, and Survey Forecasts of Inflation. *J. Bus.*, October 1985, *58*(4), pp. 377–98. [G: U.S.]

Hall, Robert E. The Time Series Consumption Function Revisited: Comment. *Brookings Pap. Econ. Act.*, 1985, (2), pp. 512–13. [G: U.S.]

Heijke, Johannes A. M., et al. A Model of the Dutch Labour Market (AMO-K). *De Economist*, 1985, *133*(4), pp. 484–526.
[G: Netherlands]

Helliwell, John F., et al. Energy and the National Economy: An Overview of the MACE Model. In *Scott, A., ed.*, 1985, pp. 17–85.
[G: Canada]

Hight, Joseph E. Review of Manpower Forecasts and Changes in Occupational Structure in the United States of America. In *Youdi, R. V. and Hinchliffe, K., eds.*, 1985, pp. 99–115.
[G: U.S.]

Holt, Matthew T. and Brandt, Jon A. Combining Price Forecasting with Hedging of Hogs: An Evaluation Using Alternative Measures of Risk. *J. Futures Markets*, Fall 1985, *5*(3), pp. 297–309.
[G: U.S.]

Huang, Kuo S. Monthly Demand Relationships of U.S. Meat Commodities. *Agr. Econ. Res.*, Summer 1985, *37*(3), pp. 23–29. [G: U.S.]

Hubbard, R. Glenn. The Time Series Consumption Function Revisited: Comment. *Brookings*

Pap. Econ. Act., 1985, (2), pp. 514–19.
[G: U.S.]

Hubbard, R. Glenn and Weiner, Robert J. Modeling Oil Price Fluctuations and International Stockpile Coordination. *J. Policy Modeling*, Summer 1985, 7(2), pp. 339–59. [G: OECD]

Huth, William L. A Quantitative Look at the System of Economic Indicators. *J. Macroecon.*, Spring 1985, 7(2), pp. 195–210. [G: U.S.]

Hvidding, James M. Models of Inflation Expectations Formation: A Comment. *J. Money, Credit, Banking*, Part 1, Nov. 1985, 17(4), pp. 534–38. [G: U.S.]

Hwa, Erh-Cheng. A Model of Price and Quantity Adjustments in Primary Commodity Markets. *J. Policy Modeling*, Summer 1985, 7(2), pp. 305–38. [G: Global]

Ilzkovitz, Fabienne. Les déterminants des investissements des entreprises en Belgique. (With English summary.) *Cah. Écon. Bruxelles*, 4th Trimester 1985, (108), pp. 487–545.
[G: Belgium]

Imam, M. Hasan. The Welfare Cost of Interest Rate Ceilings in Developing Countries: A General Equilibrium Approach. In *Piggott, J. and Whalley, J.*, eds., 1985, pp. 371–95.
[G: India]

Ingham, A. Aggregate Investment and Output in the U.K.: Comment. In *Weiserbs, D.*, ed., 1985, pp. 137–43. [G: U.K.]

James, David. Environmental Economics, Industrial Process Models, and Regional-Residuals Management Models. In *Kneese, A. V. and Sweeney, J. L.*, eds. Vol. 1, 1985, pp. 271–321.

Kader, Ahmad A. The Stock Market as a Leading Indicator of Economic Activity. *Atlantic Econ. J.*, March 1985, 13(1), pp. 100.

Kain, John F. and Apgar, William C., Jr. The Harvard Urban Development Simulation Model. In *Stahl, K.*, ed., 1985, pp. 27–71.
[G: U.S.]

Karamouzis, Nicholas. An Evaluation of M1 Forecasting Errors by the Federal Reserve Staff in the 1970s: A Note. *J. Money, Credit, Banking*, Part 1, Nov. 1985, 17(4), pp. 512–16.
[G: U.S.]

Keating, Giles. The Financial Sector of the London Business School Model. In *Currie, D.*, ed., 1985, pp. 86–126. [G: U.K.]

Keen, Howard, Jr. Summary Measures of Economic Policy and Credit Conditions as Early Warning Forecasting Tools. *Bus. Econ.*, October 1985, 20(4), pp. 38–43. [G: U.S.]

Klein, Lawrence R. Energy and the National Economy: An Overview of the MACE Model: Comment. In *Scott, A.*, ed., 1985, pp. 85–89.
[G: Canada]

Kopcke, Richard W. The Determinants of Investment Spending. *New Eng. Econ. Rev.*, July/August 1985, pp. 19–35. [G: U.S.]

Kouri, Pentti J. K.; Braga de Macedo, Jorge and Viscio, Albert J. A Vintage Model of Supply Applied to French Manufacturing. *Economia (Portugal)*, January 1985, 9(1), pp. 159–93.
[G: France]

Krelle, Wilhelm and Sarrazin, Hermann. Simultaneous Determination of Capital Flows, the Exchange Rate and Interest Rates in the Bonn Forecasting Model 11. In *[Menges, G.]*, 1985, pp. 146–61. [G: W. Germany]

Kröger, Jürgen and Pauly, Peter. Exchange Rates, Prices, Wages, and the Current Account in Germany. In *de Ménil, G. and Westphal, U.*, eds., 1985, pp. 181–218.
[G: W. Germany]

Laidler, David. Money Demand Predictability: Comment. *J. Money, Credit, Banking*, Pt. 2, Nov. 1985, 17(4), pp. 647–53. [G: U.S.]

Lakshmanan, T. R. National and Regional Models for Economic Assessment of Energy Projects. In *Lakshmanan, T. R. and Johansson, B.*, eds., 1985, pp. 187–214.

Lakshmanan, T. R. and Johansson, B. Consequences of Energy Developments: An Approach to Assessment and Management. In *Lakshmanan, T. R. and Johansson, B.*, eds., 1985, pp. 1–24.

Lakshmanan, T. R. and Johansson, B. Energy Decisions and Models: Review and Prospects. In *Lakshmanan, T. R. and Johansson, B.*, eds., 1985, pp. 305–17. [G: U.S.; Canada; U.S.S.R.; Sweden]

Longworth, David. A Model of the Canadian Exchange Rate: A Test of the 1970s: Comment. *J. Policy Modeling*, Winter 1985, 7(4), pp. 673–79. [G: Canada]

van Loo, Peter D. Portfolio Selection and Interest Rate Setting by the Dutch Banking System. In *Currie, D.*, ed., 1985, pp. 127–58.
[G: Netherlands]

Lorentsen, Lorents and Roland, Kjell. Modelling the Crude Oil Market. Oil Prices in the Long Term. In *Bjerkholt, O. and Offerdal, E.*, eds., 1985, pp. 81–101.

Lundqvist, Lars. Tar Sands Development in Canada: A Case Study of Environmental Monitoring: On Canadian Energy Impact Assessments. In *Lakshmanan, T. R. and Johansson, B.*, eds., 1985, pp. 62–71. [G: Canada]

Makowski, Marek and Sosnowski, Janusz. A Decision Support System for Planning and Controlling Agricultural Production with a Decentralized Management Structure. In *Grauer, M.; Thompson, M. and Wierzbicki, A. P.*, eds., 1985, pp. 296–305.

Marwah, Kanta. A Prototype Model of the Foreign Exchange Market of Canada: Forecasting Capital Flows and Exchange Rates. *Econ. Modelling*, April 1985, 2(2), pp. 93–124.
[G: Canada]

Marwah, Kanta and Bodkin, Ronald G. A Model of the Canadian Global Exchange Rate: A Test of the 1970s: Countercomment. *J. Policy Modeling*, Winter 1985, 7(4), pp. 681–83.
[G: Canada]

Meagher, G. A., et al. ORANI-WINE: Tax Issues and the Australian Wine Industry. *Rev. Marketing Agr. Econ.*, August 1985, 53(2), pp. 47–62. [G: Australia]

de Melo, Jaime and Robinson, Sherman. Product Differentiation and Trade Dependence of the

Domestic Price System in Computable General Equilibrium Trade Models. In *Peeters, T.; Praet, P. and Reding, P., eds.*, 1985, pp. 91–107.

Mendell, Jay S. Forecasting Through Understanding Changes in Human Consciousness: Applications to Health Care Public Relations. In *Mendell, J. S., ed.*, 1985, pp. 91–98.
[G: U.S.]

de Ménil, Georges and Sastre, José. Transfer Policies, Income, and Employment in France. In *de Ménil, G. and Westphal, U., eds.*, 1985, pp. 23–58. [G: France]

de Ménil, Georges and Westphal, Uwe. The Transmission of International Disturbances to the French and German Economies, 1972–1980. In *de Ménil, G. and Westphal, U., eds.*, 1985, pp. 349–79. [G: France; W. Germany]

Miller, Tom W. and Stone, Bernell K. Daily Cash Forecasting and Seasonal Resolution: Alternative Models and Techniques for Using the Distribution Approach. *J. Finan. Quant. Anal.*, September 1985, *20*(3), pp. 335–51.

Montel, Jean-Jacques. Essai de modélisation économétrique du marché pharmaceutique. Modèle de part de marché. (Pharmaceutical Market. Econometric Modelisation Test Market Share Model. With English summary.) *Écon. Soc.*, December 1985, *19*(12), pp. 33–69. [G: France]

Moody, Carlisle E.; Valentine, Patrick L. and Kruvant, William J. The GAO Natural Gas Supply Model. *Energy Econ.*, January 1985, *7*(1), pp. 49–57. [G: U.S.]

Morgan, James N. Comparing Static and Dynamic Estimates of Behavioral Responses to Changes in Family Composition or Income. *J. Cons. Res.*, June 1985, *12*(1), pp. 83–89.
[G: U.S.]

Muet, Pierre-Alain. A Unified Framework for Firm's Decisions: Theoretical Analysis and Empirical Application to Italy 1970–1981: Comment. In *Weiserbs, D., ed.*, 1985, pp. 75–79. [G: Italy]

Musgrove, A. R. de L. and Stocks, K. J. Electricity and Gas Supply in South-eastern Australia, 1980–2020. *Energy Econ.*, January 1985, *7*(1), pp. 37–48. [G: Australia]

Muth, John F. Properties of Some Short-run Business Forecasts. *Eastern Econ. J.*, July-Sept. 1985, *11*(3), pp. 200–210. [G: U.S.]

Nelson, Charles R. and Peck, Stephen C. The NERC Fan: A Retrospective Analysis of the NERC Summary Forecasts. *J. Bus. Econ. Statist.*, July 1985, *3*(3), pp. 179–87.
[G: U.S.]

Neutmann, Wolf-Dieter and Sander, Uwe. Transfer Policies, Income, and Employment in Germany. In *de Ménil, G. and Westphal, U., eds.*, 1985, pp. 59–96. [G: W. Germany]

O'Higgins, Michael and Patterson, Alan. The Prospects for Public Expenditure: A Disaggregate Analysis. In *Klein, R. and O'Higgins, M., ed.*, 1985, pp. 111–30. [G: U.K.]

Öller, Lars-Erik. Mallin muisti—sovellutus Suomen bruttokansantuotteen suhdannevaih-

teluun. (Model Memory—An Application to Changes in General Business Activity in Finland. With English summary.) *Kansant. Aikak.*, 1985, *81*(3), pp. 304–13.
[G: Finland]

Parikh, Ashok; Booth, Anne and Sundrum, R. M. An Econometric Model of the Monetary Sector in Indonesia. *J. Devel. Stud.*, April 1985, *21*(3), pp. 406–21. [G: Indonesia]

Paris, Quirino and Easter, Christopher D. A Programming Model with Stochastic Technology and Prices: The Case of Australian Agriculture. *Amer. J. Agr. Econ.*, February 1985, *67*(1), pp. 120–29. [G: Australia]

Paul, Jean-Jacques. Basic Concepts and Methods Used in Forecasting Skilled-Manpower Requirements in France. In *Youdi, R. V. and Hinchliffe, K., eds.*, 1985, pp. 35–56.
[G: France]

Pell, C. M., et al. Uncertainty in Transportation Planning and Forecasting. In *Jansen, G. R. M.; Nijkamp, P. and Ruijgrok, C. J., eds.*, 1985, pp. 237–51.

Penman, Stephen H. A Comparison of the Information Content of Insider Trading and Management Earnings Forecasts. *J. Finan. Quant. Anal.*, March 1985, *20*(1), pp. 1–17.
[G: U.S.]

Pepper, M. P. G. Multivariate Box–Jenkins Analysis: A Case Study in UK Energy Demand Forecasting. *Energy Econ.*, July 1985, *7*(3), pp. 168–78. [G: U.K.]

Plasmans, Joseph. Investment, Output and Labor Constraints, and Financial Constraints: The Estimation of a Model with Several Regimes: Comment. In *Weiserbs, D., ed.*, 1985, pp. 45–49. [G: France]

Rafati, Reza. Impact of Deep-Sea Mining on the World Metal Markets: Cobalt. In *Donges, J. B., ed.*, 1985, pp. 62–112.
[G: Selected Countries]

Rafati, Reza. Impact of Deep-Sea Mining on the World Metal Markets: Nickel. In *Donges, J. B., ed.*, 1985, pp. 253–334.
[G: Selected Countries]

Roley, V. Vance. Money Demand Predictability. *J. Money, Credit, Banking*, Pt. 2, Nov. 1985, *17*(4), pp. 611–41. [G: U.S.]

Rose, Andrew K. An Alternative Approach to the American Demand for Money. *J. Money, Credit, Banking*, Part 1, Nov. 1985, *17*(4), pp. 439–55. [G: U.S.]

Saggar, R. K. and Mongia, J. N. Transport. In *Mongia, J. N., ed.*, 1985, pp. 453–94.
[G: India]

Saleh, Mamdouh. Retrospective Evaluation of Forecasting Methods for Qualified-Manpower Needs for Egypt. In *Youdi, R. V. and Hinchliffe, K., eds.*, 1985, pp. 175–93.
[G: Egypt]

Schulze-Ghattas, Marianne and Westphal, Uwe. Monetary Mechanisms, Government Deficits, and External Constraints in Germany. In *de Ménil, G. and Westphal, U., eds.*, 1985, pp. 263–97. [G: W. Germany]

Silvestri, George T. and Lukasiewicz, John M.

Occupational Employment Projections: The 1984–95 Outlook. *Mon. Lab. Rev.*, November 1985, *108*(11), pp. 42–57. **[G: U.S.]**

Slesser, M. The Use of Dynamic Energy Analysis in Energy Planning. **In** *van Gool, W. and Bruggink, J. J. C., eds.*, 1985, pp. 239–46. **[G: U.K.]**

Smith, Edward G.; Richardson, James W. and Knutson, Ronald D. Impact of Alternative Farm Programs on Different Size Cotton Farms in the Texas Southern High Plains: A Simulation Approach. *Western J. Agr. Econ.*, December 1985, *10*(2), pp. 365–74. **[G: U.S.]**

Smith, V. Kerry and Hill, Lawrence J. Validating Allocation Functions in Energy Models: An Experimental Methodology. *Energy J.*, October 1985, *6*(4), pp. 29–47.

Smyshlyaev, Anatoli. An Econometric Model of the Soviet Iron and Steel Industry. **In** *Smyshlyaev, A., ed.*, 1985, pp. 197–209. **[G: U.S.S.R.]**

Smyth, David J. and Ash, J. C. K. Some Evidence on the Variability of Multiperiod Forecasts. *Atlantic Econ. J.*, December 1985, *13*(4), pp. 84. **[G: U.S.]**

Steinherr, Alfred. Investment or Employment Subsidies for Rapid Employment Creation in the European Economic Community? **In** *Weiserbs, D., ed.*, 1985, pp. 145–80. **[G: OECD]**

Teräsvirta, Timo. Metalliteollisuustuotannon volyymin ennustaminen suhdannebarometrin avulla. (Forecasting the Output of the Metal and Engineering Industries Using the Finnish Business Survey. With English summary.) *Kansant. Aikak.*, 1985, *81*(3), pp. 288–97. **[G: Finland]**

Tessaring, Manfred. An Evaluation of Labour-Market and Educational Forecasts in the Federal Republic of Germany. **In** *Youdi, R. V. and Hinchliffe, K., eds.*, 1985, pp. 57–74.

Van Wijnbergen, Sweder. Macro-economic Effects of Changes in Bank Interest Rates: Simulation Results for South Korea. *J. Devel. Econ.*, August 1985, *18*(2–3), pp. 541–54. **[G: S. Korea]**

Waelbroeck, Jean. The Determinants of World Trade and Growth. **In** *Peeters, T.; Praet, P. and Reding, P., eds.*, 1985, pp. 55–89. **[G: Global]**

Warburton, Peter J. Investment or Employment Subsidies for Rapid Employment Creation in the EEC: Comment. **In** *Weiserbs, D., ed.*, 1985, pp. 181–82. **[G: OECD]**

Webb, Roy H. Toward More Accurate Macroeconomic Forecasts from Vector Autoregressions. *Fed. Res. Bank Richmond Econ. Rev.*, July/Aug. 1985, *71*(4), pp. 3–11.

Wegener, Michael. The Dortmund Housing Market Model: A Monte Carlo Simulation of a Regional Housing Market. **In** *Stahl, K., ed.*, 1985, pp. 144–91. **[G: W. Germany]**

Weiserbs, Daniel. Industrial Investment in the European Community. **In** *Weiserbs, D., ed.*, 1985, pp. 7–20. **[G: EEC]**

Westaway, A. J. Econometric Analysis of Sectoral

Investment in Belgium (1956–1982): Comment. **In** *Weiserbs, D., ed.*, 1985, pp. 111–13. **[G: Belgium]**

Wiesmeth, Hans. Fixprice Equilibria in a Rental Housing Market. **In** *Stahl, K., ed.*, 1985, pp. 72–118.

Williams, Ted. Synfuels Development in the USA: Case Studies of National Environmental Feasibility and Local Socioeconomic Impacts: The U.S. Synfuels Acceleration Program: An Environmental and Regional Impact Analysis. **In** *Lakshmanan, T. R. and Johansson, B., eds.*, 1985, pp. 77–99. **[G: U.S.]**

Wisley, T. O. and Johnson, Stanley R. An Evaluation of Alternative Investment Hypotheses Using Non-nested Tests. *Southern Econ. J.*, October 1985, *52*(2), pp. 422–30. **[G: U.S.]**

Wlodarczyk, W. Cezary. Health Status, Health Service and Socio Economic Development of Provinces in Poland. **In** *Westcott, G.; Svensson, P.-G. and Zollner, H. F. K., eds.*, 1985, pp. 299–324. **[G: Poland]**

Wren-Lewis, Simon. The Quantification of Survey Data on Expectations. *Nat. Inst. Econ. Rev.*, August 1985, (113), pp. 39–49. **[G: U.K.]**

Zarnowitz, Victor. Rational Expectations and Macroeconomic Forecasts. *J. Bus. Econ. Statist.*, October 1985, *3*(4), pp. 293–311. **[G: U.S.]**

1324 Forecasting and Econometric Models: Theory and Methodology

Alho, Juha M. and Spencer, Bruce D. Uncertain Population Forecasting. *J. Amer. Statist. Assoc.*, June 1985, *80*(390), pp. 306–14. **[G: U.S.]**

Amirkhalkhali, S.; Rao, U. L. G. and Amirkhalkhali, S. An Empirical Study of Selection and Estimation of Statistical Growth Models. *Empirical Econ.*, 1985, *10*(3), pp. 201–08. **[G: OECD]**

Ashley, Richard A. On the Optimal Use of Suboptimal Forecasts of Explanatory Variables. *J. Bus. Econ. Statist.*, April 1985, *3*(2), pp. 129–31. **[G: U.S.]**

Baumol, William J. and Quandt, Richard E. Chaos Models and Their Implications for Forecasting. *Eastern Econ. J.*, Jan.-Mar. 1985, *11*(1), pp. 3–15.

Cooley, Thomas F. and LeRoy, Stephen F. Atheoretical Macroeconometrics: A Critique. *J. Monet. Econ.*, November 1985, *16*(3), pp. 283–308.

Darian, Jean C. Family Resources and Buyer Behavior. **In** *Brown, R. C., ed.*, 1985, pp. 257–67.

DeGroot, M. H. and Eriksson, E. A. Probability Forecasting, Stochastic Dominance, and the Lorenz Curve. **In** *Bernardo, J. M., et al., eds.*, 1985, pp. 99–110.

Hertel, Thomas W. Partial vs. General Equilibrium Analysis and Choice of Functional Form: Implications for Policy Modeling. *J. Policy Modeling*, Summer 1985, *7*(2), pp. 281–303. **[G: U.S.]**

Jäger, Albert. A Note on the Informational Efficiency of Austrian Economic Forecasts. *Empirica*, 1985, *12*(2), pp. 247–60. [G: Austria]

Judge, Guy. Turning-point Errors and Directional Errors in Forecasting: A Note. *J. Macroecon.*, Spring 1985, *7*(2), pp. 261–63.

Kelly, Christopher M. A Cautionary Note on the Interpretation of Long-run Equilibrium Solutions in Conventional Macro Models [Economic Modelling of the Aggregate Time Series Relationship between Consumers' Expenditure and Income in the United Kingdom] [Serial Correlation as a Convenient Simplification, Not a Nuisance]. *Econ. J.*, December 1985, *95*(380), pp. 1078–86.

Klein, Lawrence R.; Doud, Arthur and Sojo, E. Simplification of Large Scale Macroeconometric Models. *Eastern Econ. J.*, Jan.-Mar. 1985, *11*(1), pp. 28–40. [G: U.S.]

Krishnamurty, K. and Pandit, V. Macroeconometric Modelling of the Indian Economy: An Overview. In *Krishnamurty, K. and Pandit, V.*, 1985, pp. 1–15. [G: India]

Lakshmanan, T. R. National and Regional Models for Economic Assessment of Energy Projects. In *Lakshmanan, T. R. and Johansson, B., eds.*, 1985, pp. 187–214.

Mariano, Roberto S. and Brown, Bryan W. Stochastic Prediction in Dynamic Nonlinear Econometric Systems. *Ann. INSEE*, July-Dec. 1985, (59/60), pp. 267–78.

Maybee, John S. Functional Models. In *[Rossier, Edouard]*, 1985, pp. 195–216.

Neftci, Salih N. A Note on the Use of Local Maxima to Predict Turning Points in Related Series. *J. Amer. Statist. Assoc.*, September 1985, *80*(391), pp. 553–57. [G: U.S.]

Nelson, Charles R. and Peck, Stephen C. The NERC Fan: A Retrospective Analysis of the NERC Summary Forecasts. *J. Bus. Econ. Statist.*, July 1985, *3*(3), pp. 179–87. [G: U.S.]

Nickell, Stephen. Error Correction, Partial Adjustment and All That: An Expository Note. *Oxford Bull. Econ. Statist.*, May 1985, *47*(2), pp. 119–29.

Öller, Lars-Erik. Mallin muisti—sovellutus Suomen bruttokansantuotteen suhdannevaihteluun. (Model Memory—An Application to Changes in General Business Activity in Finland. With English summary.) *Kansant. Aikak.*, 1985, *81*(3), pp. 304–13. [G: Finland]

Ratick, Samuel J. Assessing the Environmental Consequences of Large-scale Energy Projects. In *Lakshmanan, T. R. and Johansson, B., eds.*, 1985, pp. 233–55. [G: U.S.; U.S.S.R.; Sweden]

Royer, Daniel and Ritschard, Gilbert. Portée et limites des méthodes qualitatives d'analyse structurale. With English summary.) *Revue Écon. Polit.*, Nov.-Dec. 1985, *95*(6), pp. 777–94.

Schott, Francis H. The Virtues of Eclecticism in Forecasting 1985 (or Any Other Year!). *Bus.*

Econ., January 1985, *20*(1), pp. 17–20. [G: U.S.]

Solow, Robert M. Reflections on Macroeconomic Modelling; Confessions of a DRI Addict. *Eastern Econ. J.*, Jan.-Mar. 1985, *11*(1), pp. 79–83.

Tryfos, Peter and Blackmore, Russell. Forecasting Records. *J. Amer. Statist. Assoc.*, March 1985, *80*(389), pp. 46–50.

Vishwakarma, Keshav P. The State Space Software SARAS Forecasts Better than the Box–Jenkins Method. In *Batten, D. F. and Lesse, P. F., eds.*, 1985, pp. 163–78. [G: Australia]

Webb, Roy H. Toward More Accurate Macroeconomic Forecasts from Vector Autoregressions. *Fed. Res. Bank Richmond Econ. Rev.*, July/Aug. 1985, *71*(4), pp. 3–11.

Winkler, Othmar W. Statistical Flaws in Econometricians' Perception of Economic Reality. In *Brown, R. C., ed.*, 1985, pp. 295–354.

Wren-Lewis, Simon. Expectations in Keynesian Econometric Models. In *Lawson, T. and Pesaran, H., eds.*, 1985, pp. 66–79.

133 General Outlook and Stabilization Theories and Policies

1330 General Outlook and General Economic Policy Discussions

Adam, M. C. and Ginsburgh, Victor. The Effects of Irregular Markets on Macroeconomic Policy: Some Estimates for Belgium. *Europ. Econ. Rev.*, October 1985, *29*(1), pp. 15–33. [G: Belgium]

Allsopp, C. J. International Macroeconomic Policy. In *Morris, D., ed.*, 1985, pp. 581–623. [G: OECD]

Applegate, Charles and Fennell, Susan. Cooperating for Growth and Adjustment. *Finance Develop.*, December 1985, *22*(4), pp. 50–53.

Argy, Victor E. and Nevile, J. W. Inflation and Unemployment: Introduction. In *Argy, V. E. and Neville, J. W., eds.*, 1985, pp. 1–7. [G: OECD]

Balassa, Bela. Prices, Incentives and Economic Growth. In *Balassa, B.*, 1985, pp. 3–23. [G: Global]

Bauer, Tamás. Reform Policy in the Complexity of Economic Policy. *Acta Oecon.*, 1985, *34*(3/4), pp. 263–73. [G: Hungary]

Bergsten, C. Fred. The Second Debt Crisis Is Coming. *Challenge*, May/June 1985, *28*(2), pp. 14–21. [G: U.S.]

Berry, John M. Interstate Banking: Economic Implications of the Reagan Reelection. In *Federal Reserve Bank of Atlanta (II)*, 1985, pp. 229–36. [G: U.S.]

Betbeze, Jean-Paul. 1982–1984 ou la rigueur en pratique. (With English summary.) *Revue Écon. Polit.*, Sept.-Oct. 1985, *95*(5), pp. 714–24. [G: France; U.K.; U.S.; Japan; W. Germany]

Bird, Graham. Managing the World Economy: Old Order, New Order or Disorder?: Review Article. In *Saith, A., ed.*, 1985, pp. 243–50. [G: Global]

Bird, Graham. Managing the World Economy: Old Order, New Order or Disorder? *J. Devel. Stud.*, October 1985, *22*(1), pp. 243–50.
[G: Global]

Black, Philip and Dollery, Brian. Selective Intervention and the South African Economy. *J. Stud. Econ. Econometrics*, August 1985, (22), pp. 47–67.
[G: S. Africa]

Blackburn, Lucy. The Current Economic Situation, Alternative Policy Choices and Future Perspectives. In *Hojman, D. E., ed.*, 1985, pp. 31–41.
[G: Chile]

Bognár, József. Global Problems in an Interdependent World. In *Didsbury, H. F., Jr., ed.*, 1985, pp. 16–32.

Boltho, Andrea. The European Economy. In *Morris, D., ed.*, 1985, pp. 503–25. [G: EEC]

Boltho, Andrea and Hardie, C. J. M. The Japanese Economy. In *Morris, D., ed.*, 1985, pp. 527–48.
[G: Japan; OECD; U.S.S.R.]

Bond, Daniel and Klein, Lawrence R. The Global Environment and Its Impact on Soviet and East European Economies. In *Saunders, C. T., ed.*, 1985, pp. 19–41. [G: OECD; CMEA]

Borchardt, Knut. Can Societies Learn from Economic Crises? In *Engels, W. and Pohl, H., eds.*, 1985, pp. 13–24.

Brera, Paolo. Social Partnership and Economic Growth. Austria and Sweden after the Oil Shocks. *Ricerche Econ.*, Apr.-June 1985, *39*(2), pp. 201–20. [G: Austria; Sweden]

Brinner, Roger E. Reflections on Reflections: Comments [Thoughts on Public Expenditures] [The International Agenda] [Reflections on Macroeconomic Modelling; Confessions of a DRI Addict]. *Eastern Econ. J.*, Jan.-Mar. 1985, *11*(1), pp. 84–87.

Brittan, Samuel. Back to Full Employment: The Economic Aspect. *Nat. Westminster Bank Quart. Rev.*, May 1985, pp. 41–51.
[G: U.K.]

Britton, Andrew J. C. Disinflation in the United Kingdom 1979–1983. *Z. Wirtschaft. Sozialwissen.*, 1985, *105*(2/3), pp. 295–309. [G: U.K.]

Bronfenbrenner, Martin. Japan Faces Affluence. *Australian Econ. Pap.*, December 1985, *24*(45), pp. 227–41. [G: Japan]

Brunner, Karl. The Limits of Economic Policy. *Schweiz. Z. Volkswirtsch. Statist.*, September 1985, *121*(3), pp. 213–36.

Budd, Alan P. Macroeconomic Policy and the 1985 Budget. *Fisc. Stud.*, May 1985, *6*(2), pp. 10–22. [G: U.K.]

Bulmer-Thomas, Victor. World Recession and Central American Depression: Lessons from the 1930s for the 1980s. In *Duran, E., ed.*, 1985, pp. 130–51. [G: Central America]

Burns, Arthur F. An Economist's Perspective over 60 Years. *Challenge*, January/February 1985, *27*(6), pp. 17–25. [G: U.S.]

den Butter, Frank A. G. FREIA and KOMPAS, the Central Planning Bureau's New Generation of Macro-economic Policy Models: A Review Article. *De Economist*, 1985, *133*(1), pp. 43–63. [G: Netherlands]

Canlas, Dante B. Comments on the Updated Phil-

ippine Development Plan, 1984–1987. *Philippine Econ. J.*, 1985, *24*(1), pp. 8–12.
[G: Philippines]

Chimerine, Lawrence. A Supply-Side Miracle? *J. Bus. Econ. Statist.*, April 1985, *3*(2), pp. 101–03. [G: U.S.]

Chouraqui, Jean-Claude. Les Déficits Publics dans les Pays de l'OCDE: Causes, Conséquences et Remèdes. (Public Sector Deficits in OECD Countries: Causes, Consequences, and Policy Reactions. With English summary.) *Aussenwirtschaft*, May 1985, *40*(1/2), pp. 15–52. [G: OECD]

Chouraqui, Jean-Claude and Montador, B. Fiscal Policy in the Small OECD Countries since the Early Seventies. *Schweiz. Z. Volkswirtsch. Statist.*, September 1985, *121*(3), pp. 259–83.
[G: OECD]

Ciampi, Carlo Azeglio. Spesa pubblica e costo del lavoro, fattori condizionanti della politica monetaria. (Public Expenditure and Cost of Labour, as Factors Conditioning Monetary Policy. With English summary.) *Bancaria*, April 1985, *41*(4), pp. 402–05. [G: Italy]

Clark, Peter B. Inflation and Unemployment in the United States: Recent Experience and Policies. In *Argy, V. E. and Neville, J. W., eds.*, 1985, pp. 221–48. [G: U.S.]

da Conceição Tavares, María. The Revival of American Hegemony. *Cepal Rev.*, August 1985, (26), pp. 139–46. [G: U.S.; Latin America]

Congdon, Tim G. Does Mr. Lawson Really Believe in the Medium-term Financial Strategy? *Fisc. Stud.*, May 1985, *6*(2), pp. 7–9.
[G: U.K.]

Corbo, Vittorio. Reforms and Macroeconomic Adjustments in Chile during 1974–84. *World Devel.*, August 1985, *13*(8), pp. 893–916.
[G: Chile]

Corden, W. Max. Tell Us Where the New Jobs Will Come From. *World Econ.*, June 1985, *8*(2), pp. 183–88.

Corrigan, E. Gerald. A Look at the Economy and Some Banking Issues. *Fed. Res. Bank New York Quart. Rev.*, Spring 1985, *10*(1), pp. 1–6. [G: U.S.]

Costa, Antonio Maria. Multilateralism under Threat: Causes, Impact, and the Policy Debate on Government Intervention in Trade. *J. Policy Modeling*, Spring 1985, *7*(1), pp. 181–217.
[G: OECD]

Czamanski, Stan. The Brazilian Economy in the Eighties: Long-run Perspectives. In *Salazar-Carrillo, J. and Fendt, R., Jr., eds.*, 1985, pp. 187–89. [G: Brazil]

De Grauwe, Paul and Fratianni, Michele. Interdependence, Macro-economic Policies and All That. *World Econ.*, March 1985, *8*(1), pp. 63–79. [G: OECD]

Deakin, Nicholas. 'Vanishing Utopias': Planning and Participation in Twentieth Century Britain. *Reg. Stud.*, August 1985, *19*(4), pp. 291–300. [G: U.K.]

Di Tella, Torcuato. The Political and Social Outlook for Latin America. *Cepal Rev.*, August 1985, (26), pp. 89–99. [G: Latin America]

Dick, Howard W. Survey of Recent Developments. *Bull. Indonesian Econ. Stud.*, December 1985, *21*(3), pp. 1–29. [G: Indonesia]

Didsbury, Howard F., Jr. The Global Economy: Today, Tomorrow, and the Transition: Introduction. In *Didsbury, H. F., Jr., ed.*, 1985, pp. vii–xii.

Dixon, Peter B. and McDonald, Daina. The Australian Economy in 1984–85 and 1985–86. *Australian Econ. Rev.*, 2nd Quarter 1985, (70), pp. 3–18. [G: Australia]

Due, John F. Federal and Foreign Trade Deficits and the Future of the U.S. Economy. *J. Econ. Educ.*, Summer 1985, *16*(3), pp. 194–202. [G: U.S.]

Dyba, Karel and Vintrová, Ružena. Czechoslovak Economy in the 1980's. *Czech. Econ. Digest.*, December 1985, (8), pp. 3–28. [G: Czechoslovakia]

Edwards, Sebastian. Stabilization with Liberalization: An Evaluation of Ten Years of Chile's Experiment with Free-Market Policies, 1973–1983. *Econ. Develop. Cult. Change*, January 1985, *33*(2), pp. 223–54. [G: Chile]

Eichner, Alfred S. Reflections on Social Democracy. In *Eichner, A. S.*, 1985, pp. 200–218.

Etzioni, Amitai. Making Policy for Complex Systems: A Medical Model for Economics. *J. Policy Anal. Manage.*, Spring 1985, *4*(3), pp. 383–95.

Etzioni, Amitai. On Solving Social Problems—Inducements or Coercion? *Challenge*, July/August 1985, *28*(3), pp. 35–40.

Euzeby, Chantal. La protection sociale et le IXᵉ Plan (1984–1988). (With English summary.) *Revue Écon. Polit.*, Sept.-Oct. 1985, *95*(5), pp. 695–704. [G: EEC]

Faber, Mike and Green, Reginald Herbold. Sub-Saharan Africa's Economic Malaise: Some Questions and Answers. In *Rose, T., ed.*, 1985, pp. 14–25.

Feldstein, Martin. American Economic Policy and the World Economy. *Foreign Aff.*, Summer 1985, *63*(5), pp. 995–1008. [G: U.S.; OECD]

Feldstein, Martin. Global Economic Imbalances: The View from North America. In *Bergsten, C. F., ed.*, 1985, pp. 5–10. [G: U.S.]

Feldstein, Martin. International Trade, Budget Deficits, and the Interest Rate. *J. Econ. Educ.*, Summer 1985, *16*(3), pp. 189–93. [G: U.S.]

Fendt, Roberto, Jr. and Salazar-Carrillo, Jorge. Brazil and the Future: Some Thoughts on the Eighties. In *Salazar-Carrillo, J. and Fendt, R., Jr., eds.*, 1985, pp. 12–24. [G: Brazil]

Fernandez, Roque B. The Expectations Management Approach to Stabilization in Argentina during 1976–82. *World Devel.*, August 1985, *13*(8), pp. 871–92. [G: Argentina]

Fishlow, Albert. Brazil and the Future: Some Thoughts on the Eighties: Comments. In *Salazar-Carrillo, J. and Fendt, R., Jr., eds.*, 1985, pp. 34–37. [G: Brazil; U.S.]

Friedman, Benjamin M. Recent Perspectives in and on Macroeconomics. In *Feiwel, G. R., ed. (I)*, 1985, pp. 270–86. [G: U.S.]

Gandhi, Indira. Peace and Development. In *Bapna, A., ed.*, 1985, pp. 7–13. [G: Global]

Garretón M., Manuel Antonio. Chile: en busca de la democracia perdida. (With English summary.) *Desarrollo Econ.*, Oct.-Dec. 1985, *25*(99), pp. 381–97. [G: Chile]

Garten, Jeffrey E. Gunboat Economics. *Foreign Aff.*, 1985, *63*(3), pp. 538–59. [G: Global]

Giersch, Herbert. Perspectives on the World Economy. *Weltwirtsch. Arch.*, 1985, *121*(3), pp. 409–26. [G: Global]

Giersch, Herbert. Perspectives on the World Economy. *S. Afr. J. Econ.*, December 1985, *53*(4), pp. 333–50. [G: Global]

Gollas, Manuel. The Mexican Economy at the Crossroads. In *Jorge, A.; Salazar-Carrillo, J. and Diaz-Pou, F., eds.*, 1985, pp. 79–86. [G: Mexico]

González, Norberto. Crisis and Development in Latin America and the Caribbean. *Cepal Rev.*, August 1985, (26), pp. 9–56. [G: Latin America]

Gordon, Wendell. Economists Should Tell It Like It Is: Remarks upon Receipt of the Veblen–Commons Award. *J. Econ. Issues*, June 1985, *19*(2), pp. 305–09. [G: U.S.]

Goria, Giovanni. Situazione economica e problemi del credito: banche d'affari, sportelli e tassi. (Merchant Banks, Bank Branches and Interest Rates in the Framework of Economic Policy. With English summary.) *Bancaria*, April 1985, *41*(4), pp. 406–10. [G: Italy]

Green, Reginald Herbold. Reflections on the State of Knowledge and Ways Forward. In *Rose, T., ed.*, 1985, pp. 292–313. [G: Sub-Saharan Africa]

Haberler, Gottfried. Integration and Growth of the World Economy in Historical Perspective. In *Haberler, G.*, 1985, pp. 473–94.

Haberler, Gottfried. The World Economy, Macroeconomic Theory and Policy—Sixty Years of Profound Change. In *Haberler, G.*, 1985, pp. 429–50.

Hamada, Koichi. Lessons from the Macroeconomic Performance of the Japanese Economy. In *Argy, V. E. and Neville, J. W., eds.*, 1985, pp. 181–99. [G: Japan]

Hansen, Jørgen Drud. Statsgaeld og økonomisk politik. (Public Deficits and the Targets of Economic Policy. With English summary.) *Nationaløkon. Tidsskr.*, 1985, *123*(1), pp. 32–49.

Hanson, James A. and de Melo, Jaime. External Shocks, Financial Reforms, and Stabilization Attempts in Uruguay during 1974–83. *World Devel.*, August 1985, *13*(8), pp. 917–39. [G: Uruguay]

Hawke, R. J. L. Economic Policy Challenges for Sustained Growth. *Econ. Rec.*, June 1985, *61*(173), pp. 501–06. [G: Australia]

Heinemann, H. Erich. Commentary on Prospects for Money and the Economy. In *Shadow Open Market Committee.*, 1985, pp. 55–62. [G: U.S.; LDCs]

Henderson, Hazel. Post-economic Policies for Post-industrial Societies. In *Didsbury, H. F., Jr., ed.*, 1985, pp. 317–33.

Hession, Charles H. Lord Keynes Meets Adam Smith. *Challenge*, May/June 1985, *28*(2), pp. 59–63. [G: U.S.]

Hibbs, Douglas A., Jr. Inflation, Political Support, and Macroeconomic Policy. In *Lindberg, L. N. and Maier, C. S., eds.*, 1985, pp. 175–95. [G: OECD]

Hill, John K. and Smith, Scott L. The Political Timing of Errors in Inflation Forecasts. *Public Choice*, 1985, *46*(2), pp. 215–20. [G: U.S.]

Hinshaw, Randall. Global Economic Priorities: Prologue. In *Hinshaw, R., ed.*, 1985, pp. 15–21.

Holland, A. Steven. Rational Expectations and the Effects of Monetary Policy: A Guide for the Uninitiated. *Fed. Res. Bank St. Louis Rev.*, May 1985, *67*(5), pp. 5–11.

Houthakker, Hendrik S. The International Agenda. *Eastern Econ. J.*, Jan.-Mar. 1985, *11*(1), pp. 71–78. [G: Global]

Hughes, Barry. Brookings on the Australian Economy. *Econ. Rec.*, March 1985, *61*(172), pp. 405–14. [G: Australia]

Hughes, Helen. Australia and the World Environment—The Dynamics of International Competition and Wealth Creation. In *Scutt, J. A., ed.*, 1985, pp. 1–17. [G: Australia; Global]

Ibarra, David. Crisis, Adjustment and Economic Policy in Latin America. *Cepal Rev.*, August 1985, (26), pp. 147–54. [G: Latin America]

Iglesias, Enrique V. Statement Delivered at the Expert Meeting on Crisis and Development in Latin America and the Caribbean. *Cepal Rev.*, August 1985, (26), pp. 57–62.

Iglesias, Enrique V. The Latin American Economy during 1984: A Preliminary Overview. *Cepal Rev.*, April 1985, (25), pp. 7–44. [G: Latin America]

Jacob, Charles E. Reaganomics: The Revolution in American Political Economy. *Law Contemp. Probl.*, Autumn 1985, *48*(4), pp. 7–30. [G: U.S.]

Jha, L. K. Growth, Inflation and Other Issues: The Need for Rethinking. In *Jha, L. K.*, 1985, pp. 203–08. [G: India]

Jha, L. K. India's Economic Strategies for the Nineties. In *Mongia, J. N., ed.*, 1985 , pp. 641–67. [G: India]

Jha, L. K. Inflation, Unemployment, and Growth. In *Jha, L. K.*, 1985, pp. 120–29. [G: India]

Jonson, P. D. and Stevens, G. R. The Australian Economy in the 1930s and the 1980s: Some Facts. In *Argy, V. E. and Neville, J. W., eds.*, 1985, pp. 281–304. [G: Australia]

Jordon, Jerry L. Economic Outlook. In *Shadow Open Market Committee.*, 1985, pp. 9–18. [G: U.S.]

Kaufman, Robert R. Democratic and Authoritarian Responses to the Debt Issue: Argentina, Brazil, Mexico. *Int. Organ.*, Summer 1985, *39*(3), pp. 472–503. [G: Argentina; Brazil; Mexico]

Kay, John A. The Economy and the 1985 Budget: Introduction. *Fisc. Stud.*, May 1985, *6*(2), pp. 1–5. [G: U.K.]

Kindleberger, Charles P. The Dollar Yesterday, Today, and Tomorrow. *Banca Naz. Lavoro Quart. Rev.*, December 1985, (155), pp. 295–308.

Kindleberger, Charles P. 1929: Ten Lessons for Today. In *Kindleberger, C. P.*, 1985, pp. 314–19.

Korpinen, Pekka. Vart tog konjunkturerna vägen? (Have Cyclical Fluctuation Vanished? With English summary.) *Ekon. Samfundets Tidskr.*, 1985, *38*(4), pp. 191–94. [G: Finland; OECD]

Krivine, David. The Economic Overview. In *Levinson, P. and Landau, P., eds.*, 1985, pp. 38–43. [G: Israel]

Lamfalussy, Alexandre. Monetary Policy in Our Times: Concluding Comments. In *Ando, A., et al., eds.*, 1985, pp. 319–23. [G: Global]

de Larosière, Jacques. Princìpi, limiti e condizioni dell politiche per lo sviluppo. (Principles, Limits and Conditions of Development Policies. With English summary.) *Bancaria*, November 1985, *41*(11), pp. 1154–61.

Le Guay, François. The International Crisis and Latin American Development: Objectives and Instruments. *Cepal Rev.*, August 1985, (26), pp. 127–37. [G: Latin America]

Lecraw, Donald J. Hymer and Public Policy in LDCs. *Amer. Econ. Rev.*, May 1985, *75*(2), pp. 239–44. [G: LDCs]

Lér, Leopold. Financial Policy for the Years to Come. *Czech. Econ. Digest.*, February 1985, (1), pp. 3–23. [G: Czechoslovakia]

Lindbeck, Assar. What Is Wrong with the West European Economies? *World Econ.*, June 1985, *8*(2), pp. 153–70. [G: W. Europe]

Lipsey, Richard G. Canada and the United States: The Economic Dimension. In *Doran, C. F. and Sigler, J. H., eds.*, 1985, pp. 69–108. [G: Canada; U.S.]

Löwenthal, Paul. The Irrelevance of Aggregative Policies against Inflation under Conditions of Resource Misallocation. *Z. Wirtschaft. Sozialwissen.*, 1985, *105*(2/3), pp. 155–67. [G: OECD]

Lukaszewicz, Aleksander. Comments [The Global Environment and Its Impact on Soviet and East European Economies] [The Impact of Energy on East–West Trade: Retrospect and Prospects]. In *Saunders, C. T., ed.*, 1985, pp. 135–36. [G: OECD; CMEA; U.S.S.R.]

Lundberg, Erik. The Rise and Fall of the Swedish Model. *J. Econ. Lit.*, March 1985, *23*(1), pp. 1–36. [G: Sweden]

Machin, Howard and Wright, Vincent. Economic Policy under the Mitterrand Presidency, 1981–1984: An Introduction. In *Machin, H. and Wright, V., eds.*, 1985, pp. 1–43. [G: France]

Maier, Charles S. Inflation and Stagnation as Politics and History. In *Lindberg, L. N. and Maier, C. S., eds.*, 1985, pp. 3–24. [G: OECD]

Maier, Charles S. and Lindberg, Leon N. Alternatives for Future Crises. In *Lindberg, L. N. and Maier, C. S., eds.*, 1985, pp. 567–88.

Maldonado Lince, Guillermo. Latin America and Integration: Options in the Crisis. *Cepal Rev.*, December 1985, (27), pp. 55–68.
[G: Latin America]

Malinvaud, Edmond. European Development and the World Economy. In *Bergsten, C. F., ed.*, 1985, pp. 15–30. [G: W. Europe]

Mangahas, Mahar. Comments on the Updated Philippine Development Plan, 1984–1987. *Philippine Econ. J.*, 1985, *24*(1), pp. 13–23.
[G: Philippines]

Marris, Stephen N. The Decline and Fall of the Dollar: Some Policy Issues. *Brookings Pap. Econ. Act.*, 1985, (1), pp. 237–44.
[G: OECD]

Martellaro, Joseph A. From Say's Law to Supply-Side Economics. *Rivista Int. Sci. Econ. Com.*, September 1985, *32*(9), pp. 887–903.
[G: U.S.]

Martin, Preston. Innovation, Productivity, and Economic Policy. In *Federal Reserve Bank of Atlanta (I)*, 1985, pp. 41–46. [G: U.S.]

Maximova, Margarita. Comments [The Global Environment and Its Impact on Soviet and East European Economies] [Current Problems and Prospects of the World Economy in the Light of East–West Economic Relations]. In *Saunders, C. T., ed.*, 1985, pp. 127–30.
[G: OECD; CMEA]

Mayer, Colin. The Assessment: Recent Developments in Industrial Economics and Their Implications for Policy. *Oxford Rev. Econ. Policy*, Autumn 1985, *1*(3), pp. 1–24. [G: U.K.]

Mayes, David G. The Domestic Economy. In *Morris, D., ed.*, 1985, pp. 112–74. [G: U.K.]

McDonald, Daina and Parmenter, B. R. The Australian Economy: Current Situation and Outlook to 1986–87. *Australian Econ. Rev.*, 4th Quarter 1985, (72), pp. 3–20.
[G: Australia]

McDonald, Ian M. Macroeconomic Policy in Australia since the Sixties. *Australian Econ. Rev.*, 3rd Quarter, Spring 1985, (71), pp. 6–19.
[G: Australia]

McMillan, Melville L. Western Transition: The Economic Future of the West: Introduction. *Can. Public Policy*, Supplement July 1985, *11*(3), pp. 268–82. [G: Canada]

Meade, James E. Global Economic Priorities: Targets and Weapons for Economic Stabilization. In *Hinshaw, R., ed.*, 1985, pp. 203–25.

Meier, Alfred and Mettler, Daniel. Auf der Suche nach einem neuen Paradigma der Wirtschaftspolitik. (Toward a New Paradigm of Economic Policy. With English summary.) *Kyklos*, 1985, *38*(2), pp. 171–99.

Meyer, F. V. Prospects for Recovery in the British Economy: Towards a Conclusion. In *Meyer, F. V., ed.*, 1985, pp. 213–32. [G: U.K.]

Meyer, F. V. The Economic Downturn of the Early 1980s. In *Meyer, F. V., ed.*, 1985, pp. 1–27. [G: U.K.]

Meyer, W. N. The Present Economic Climate in South Africa. *J. Stud. Econ. Econometrics*, August 1985, (22), pp. 3–24. [G: S. Africa]

Morris, Derek J. The UK in the 1980s: Theory, Policy, and Performance. In *Morris, D., ed.*, 1985, pp. 897–926. [G: U.K.]

Nanto, Dick K. and Takagi, Shinji. Korekiyo Takahashi and Japan's Recovery from the Great Depression. *Amer. Econ. Rev.*, May 1985, *75*(2), pp. 369–74. [G: Japan]

Nasution, Anwar. Survey of Recent Developments. *Bull. Indonesian Econ. Stud.*, August 1985, *21*(2), pp. 1–23. [G: Indonesia]

Navarrete, Jorge Eduardo. Foreign Policy and International Financial Negotiations: The External Debt and the Cartagena Consensus. *Cepal Rev.*, December 1985, (27), pp. 7–25.
[G: Latin America]

Neuburger, Henry. Why Is Unemployment So High? *Nat. Westminster Bank Quart. Rev.*, May 1985, pp. 12–20. [G: W. Europe; U.S.]

Ondráček, Mojmír. Economic Policy of the Reagan Administration towards the Developing Countries. *Czech. Econ. Digest.*, February 1985, (1), pp. 63–89. [G: U.S.; LDCs]

Ortner, Robert. The Economic Environment. In *Konecci, E. B. and Kuhn, R. L., eds.*, 1985, pp. 59–67. [G: U.S.]

Palme, Olof. From Crisis to Prosperity. In *Bapna, A., ed.*, 1985, pp. 15–21. [G: Global]

Parravicini, Giannino. Il sistema bancario fra vincoli ed evoluzione. (The Italian Banking System between Constraints and Evolution. With English summary.) *Bancaria*, April 1985, *41*(4), pp. 393–401. [G: Italy]

Patrick, Hugh and Rosovsky, Henry. The Japanese Economy in Transition. In *Shishido, T. and Sato, R., eds.*, 1985, pp. 159–70.
[G: Japan]

Perez de Cuellar, Javier. An Urgent Need for Global Economic Recovery. In *Bapna, A., ed.*, 1985, pp. 1–5. [G: Global]

Peterson, Wallace C. and Estenson, Paul S. The Recovery: Supply-Side or Keynesian? *J. Post Keynesian Econ.*, Summer 1985, *7*(4), pp. 447–62. [G: U.S.]

Petrei, A. Humberto and Tybout, James R. Microeconomic Adjustments in Argentina during 1976–81: The Importance of Changing Levels of Financial Subsidies. *World Devel.*, August 1985, *13*(8), pp. 949–67. [G: Argentina]

Pinker, Robert. Social Welfare and the Thatcher Administration. In *Bean, P.; Ferris, J. and Whynes, D., eds.*, 1985, pp. 183–205.
[G: U.K.]

Pissulla, Petra. Western Policies: International Organizations. In *Rode, R. and Jacobsen, H.-D., eds.*, 1985, pp. 226–42. [G: CMEA]

Praedicta Ltd. Economic Developments in 1984. In *Levinson, P. and Landau, P., eds.*, 1985, pp. 6–28. [G: Israel]

Prebisch, Raúl. The External Debt of the Latin American Countries. *Cepal Rev.*, December 1985, (27), pp. 53–54. [G: Latin America]

Ranis, Gustav. China's Open Door Is Open for Good. *Challenge*, Nov./Dec. 1985, *28*(5), pp. 59–60. [G: China]

Robbins, Lionel. Global Economic Priorities: Reflections on the Dialogue. In *Hinshaw, R., ed.*, 1985, pp. 169–78.

Rocard, Michel. Management of a National Economy during the 1980s. *Ann. Pub. Co-op. Econ.*, January–June 1985, 56(1–2), pp. 11–23.

Rogers, William D. The United States and Latin America. *Foreign Aff.*, 1985, 63(3), pp. 560–80. **[G: Latin American; U.S.]**

Rostow, W. W. The World Economy since 1945: A Stylized Historical Analysis. *Econ. Hist. Rev.*, 2nd Ser., May 1985, 38(2), pp. 252–75. **[G: Global]**

Rozen, Marvin E. The Market Is No Miracle Worker. *Challenge*, Sept./Oct. 1985, 28(4), pp. 47–50. **[G: U.S.]**

Sacchetti, Ugo. What Can Be Learned from the 1981–84 U.S. Experience. *Econ. Notes*, 1985, (3), pp. 49–88. **[G: U.S.]**

Sadie, J. L. Reflections on Economic Policy in South Africa. *J. Stud. Econ. Econometrics*, March 1985, (21), pp. 9–40. **[G: S. Africa]**

Saulnier, Raymond J. The President's Economic Report: A Critique. *J. Portfol. Manage.*, Summer 1985, 11(4), pp. 61–62. **[G: U.S.]**

Saunders, Christopher T. Comments [The Global Environment and Its Impact on Soviet and East European Economies] [Current Problems and Prospects of the World Economy in the Light of East–West Economic Relations]. In *Saunders, C. T., ed.*, 1985, pp. 125–27. **[G: OECD; CMEA]**

Scarfe, Brian L. Prospects and Policies for Western Canadian Growth. *Can. Public Policy*, Supplement July 1985, 11(3), pp. 361–64. **[G: Canada]**

Schott, Francis H. The Virtues of Eclecticism in Forecasting 1985 (or Any Other Year!). *Bus. Econ.*, January 1985, 20(1), pp. 17–20. **[G: U.S.]**

Sengupta, Arjun. Recovery, Interdependence, and the Developing Economies. *Finance Develop.*, September 1985, 22(3), pp. 11–14. **[G: Global]**

Shaw, Timothy M. and Luke, David F. The Lagos Plan of Action and Africa's Future Economic Relations. *Can. J. Devel. Stud.*, 1985, 6(1), pp. 173–78. **[G: Africa]**

Sheehan, Richard G. Money, Anticipated Changes, and Policy Effectiveness. *Amer. Econ. Rev.*, June 1985, 75(3), pp. 524–29. **[G: U.S.]**

Shultz, George P. Economic Cooperation in the Pacific Basin. *J. Econ. Devel.*, December 1985, 10(2), pp. 7–17. **[G: Asia]**

Sicat, Gerardo P. A Historical and Current Perspective of Philippine Economic Problems. *Philippine Econ. J.*, 1985, 24(1), pp. 24–63. **[G: Philippines]**

Siebke, Jürgen. The Prospects for a Sustained Upswing. The 1984/85 Report of the German Council of Economic Experts. *Z. ges. Staatswiss. (JITE)*, June 1985, 141(2), pp. 336–44. **[G: W. Germany]**

Söderström, Hans Tson. Exchange Rate Strategies and Real Adjustment after 1970. The Ex-

perience of the Smaller European Economies. In *Peeters, T.; Praet, P. and Reding, P., eds.*, 1985, pp. 227–64. **[G: Europe]**

Steindl, Josef. Structural Problems in the Crisis. *Banca Naz. Lavoro Quart. Rev.*, September 1985, (154), pp. 223–32. **[G: OECD]**

Stephen, David. The Political Setting: 'Business as Usual' or a New Departure? In *Duran, E., ed.*, 1985, pp. 1–13.

Street, James H. Monetarism and Beyond: The Dilemma of the Southern Cone Countries: A Review Article. *J. Econ. Issues*, December 1985, 19(4), pp. 923–37. **[G: Argentina; Chile; Uruguay]**

Strigel, Werner H. Das Geschäftsklima als Konjunkturindikator—eine Retrospektive. (The Business Climate as Leading Indicator. With English summary.) *Ifo-Studien*, 1985, 31(1), pp. 29–68. **[G: OECD]**

Štrougal, Lubomír. Every Effort for the Fulfilment of the 7th Five-Year Plan. *Czech. Econ. Digest.*, June 1985, (4), pp. 3–23. **[G: Czechoslovakia]**

Su, Betty W. The Economic Outlook to 1995: New Assumptions and Projections. *Mon. Lab. Rev.*, November 1985, 108(11), pp. 3–16. **[G: U.S.]**

Summers, Anne. Poor Nation—Or Not? In *Scutt, J. A., ed.*, 1985, pp. 115–28. **[G: Australia]**

Sussman, Zvi. The Israel Economic and Business Review: 1985: Introduction. In *Levinson, P. and Landau, P., eds.*, 1985, pp. xi–xii. **[G: Israel]**

Swan, Neil M. and Slater, David W. Reflections on Western Transition. *Can. Public Policy*, Supplement July 1985, 11(3), pp. 365–70. **[G: Canada]**

Sylos Labini, Paolo. XVth International CIRIEC Congress. *Ann. Pub. Co-op. Econ.*, January–June 1985, 56(1–2), pp. 165–75. **[G: Global]**

Tardos, Márton. Question Marks in Hungarian Fiscal and Monetary Policy (1979–1984). *Acta Oecon.*, 1985, 35(1–2), pp. 29–52. **[G: Hungary]**

Throop, Adrian W. Current Fiscal Policy: Is It Stimulating Investment or Consumption? *Fed. Res. Bank San Francisco Econ. Rev.*, Winter 1985, (1), pp. 19–44. **[G: U.S.]**

Thurow, Lester C. Healing with a Thousand Bandages. *Challenge*, Nov./Dec. 1985, 28(5), pp. 22–31. **[G: U.S.]**

Tinbergen, Jan. How Do We Manage the Global Society? In *Didsbury, H. F., Jr., ed.*, 1985, pp. 3–15.

Tinbergen, Jan. Restructuring Our Societies: International Coordination Policies. In *Tinbergen, J.*, 1985, pp. 192–202.

Tobin, James. The Fiscal Revolution: Disturbing Prospects. *Challenge*, January/February 1985, 27(6), pp. 12–16. **[G: U.S.]**

Tumlir, Jan. Who Benefits from Discrimination? *Schweiz. Z. Volkswirtsch. Statist.*, September 1985, 121(3), pp. 249–58.

Valdepeñas, Vicete B., Jr. The Updated Philippine Development Plan, 1984–1987. *Philippine Econ. J.*, 1985, 24(1), pp. 1–7. **[G: Philippines]**

Vincent, D. P. Exchange Rate Devaluation, Monetary Policy and Wages: A General Equilibrium Analysis for Chile. *Econ. Modelling*, January 1985, *2*(1), pp. 17–32. [G: Chile]

Volcker, Paul A. Economics in Policy and Practice: Opportunity out of Adversity. *Fed. Res. Bull.*, August 1985, *71*(8), pp. 601–06. [G: U.S.]

Volcker, Paul A. Statement to the U.S. Congress Joint Economic Committee, February 5, 1985. *Fed. Res. Bull.*, April 1985, *71*(4), pp. 204–09. [G: U.S.]

Volcker, Paul A. Statement to the U.S. House Committee on the Budget, March 6, 1985. *Fed. Res. Bull.*, May 1985, *71*(5), pp. 304–06. [G: U.S.]

Volcker, Paul A. Statement to the U.S. House Subcommittee on Domestic Monetary Policy of the Committee on Banking, Finance and Urban Affairs, July 17, 1985. *Fed. Res. Bull.*, September 1985, *71*(9), pp. 690–97. [G: U.S.]

Volcker, Paul A. Statement to the U.S. Senate Committee on the Budget, February 8, 1985. *Fed. Res. Bull.*, April 1985, *71*(4), pp. 209–10. [G: U.S.]

Walker, John. The UK Economy: Analysis and Prospects. *Oxford Rev. Econ. Policy*, Autumn 1985, *1*(3), pp. 25–38. [G: U.K.]

Walker, John and Davies, Glenn. The UK Economy: Analysis and Prospects. *Oxford Rev. Econ. Policy*, Spring 1985, *1*(1), pp. 21–34. [G: U.K.]

Walker, John and Davies, Glenn. The UK Economy: Analysis and Prospects. *Oxford Rev. Econ. Policy*, Summer 1985, *1*(2), pp. 20–33. [G: U.K.]

Walsh, Cliff. A View from the South on: 'The Australian Economy: A View from the North.' *Econ. Rec.*, March 1985, *61*(172), pp. 415–20. [G: Australia]

Weitzman, Martin L. Profit Sharing as Macroeconomic Policy. *Amer. Econ. Rev.*, May 1985, *75*(2), pp. 41–45.

Willett, Thomas D. and Bremer, Marc. International Aspects of Macroeconomic Policy: An Overview. In *Arndt, S. W.; Sweeney, R. J. and Willett, T. D., eds.*, 1985, pp. 193–201. [G: U.S.]

Willoughby, John. The Internationalization of Capital and the Future of Macroeconomic Policy. *Sci. Soc.*, Fall 1985, *49*(3), pp. 287–314.

Wu, Jinglian. Developmental Guidelines in the Early Stages of the Battle for Economic Reform and Some Questions of Macroscopic Control. *Chinese Econ. Stud.*, Fall 1985, *19*(1), pp. 40–52. [G: China]

Wu, Junyang. Current Economic Conditions and Reform of the Price System. *Chinese Econ. Stud.*, Spring 1985, *18*(3), pp. 55–76. [G: China]

Yochelson, John N. Outlook for U.S. Economic Diplomacy: Europe and the Pacific Basin. In *Yochelson, J. N., ed.*, 1985, pp. 15–25. [G: U.S.]

Yoshitomi, Masaru. Japan's View of Current External Imbalances. In *Bergsten, C. F., ed.*, 1985, pp. 35–47. [G: Japan]

Zijlstra, Jelle. The Netherlands Economy after the Presentation of the Budget. In *Zijlstra, J.*, 1985, pp. 153–61. [G: Netherlands]

Zijlstra, Jelle. The Netherlands Economy in 1976—A Stock Taking. In *Zijlstra, J.*, 1985, pp. 125–35. [G: Netherlands]

Zijlstra, Jelle. The Netherlands Economy in 1977. In *Zijlstra, J.*, 1985, pp. 137–51. [G: Netherlands]

Zong, Han. Reduce the Consumption of Materialized Labor. *Chinese Econ. Stud.*, Summer 1985, *18*(4), pp. 62–70. [G: China]

1331 Stabilization Theories and Policies

Akiyama, Shigeru and Kawai, Masahiro. Welfare Implications of Commodity Price Stabilization with Partially Flexible Production, Private Storage and Buffer-Stock Costs. *Weltwirtsch. Arch.*, 1985, *121*(2), pp. 261–79.

Alhadeff, Peter. Public Finance and the Economy in Argentina, Australia and Canada during the Depression of the 1930s. In *Platt, D. C. M. and di Tella, G., eds.*, 1985, pp. 161–78. [G: Argentina; Australia; Canada]

Allsopp, C. J. and Mayes, David G. Demand Management in Practice. In *Morris, D., ed.*, 1985, pp. 398–443. [G: U.K.]

Allsopp, C. J. and Mayes, David G. Demand Management Policy: Theory and Measurement. In *Morris, D., ed.*, 1985, pp. 366–97. [G: U.K.]

Alogoskoufis, George S. Macroeconomic Policy and Aggregate Fluctuations in a Semi-industrialized Open Economy: Greece 1951–1980. *Europ. Econ. Rev.*, October 1985, *29*(1), pp. 35–61. [G: Greece]

Andersen, Torben M. Arbejdstidsforkortelse som konjunkturpolitisk instrument. (Shortening of Working Hours as an Instrument in Stabilization Policy. With English summary.) *Nationaløkon. Tidsskr.*, 1985, *123*(2), pp. 145–59. [G: Netherlands]

Ando, Albert. Coordination of Monetary and Fiscal Policies. In *Ando, A., et al., eds.*, 1985, pp. 253–89. [G: U.S.]

Ando, Albert and Kennickell, Arthur B. Some Results on Analytic Optimal Control Solution of a Simple Rational Expectations Model. *J. Econ. Dynam. Control*, September 1985, *9*(1), pp. 55–61.

Andreatta, Nino and D'Adda, Carlo. Effetti reali o nominali della svalutazione? Una riflessione sull'esperienza italiana dopo il primo shock petrolifero. (Real and Nominal Effects of the Devaluation: the Italian Experience after the First Oil Shock. With English summary.) *Polit. Econ.*, April 1985, *1*(1), pp. 37–51. [G: Italy]

Argy, Victor E. The Design of Monetary and Fiscal Policy: Monetarism and Supply-Side Economics. In *Argy, V. E. and Neville, J. W., eds.*, 1985, pp. 60–77.

Artis, Michael J. Policy Cooperation and the EMS Experience: Comment. In *Buiter, W. H. and*

Marston, R. C., eds., 1985, pp. 355–59.
[G: OECD]

Artus, Patrick. L'indexation des salaires: une optique de stabilisation macro-économique. (Price Indexation of Wages: A Stabilization Approach. With English summary.) *Revue Écon.*, March 1985, *36*(2), pp. 291–320. [G: France; W. Germany; U.K.]

Artus, Patrick, et al. Tax Incentives, Monetary Policy, and Investment in France and Germany. In *de Ménil, G. and Westphal, U., eds.*, 1985, pp. 105–41. [G: France; W. Germany]

Backus, David and Driffill, John. Policy Credibility and Unemployment in the U.K. In *Currie, D., ed.*, 1985, pp. 3–16. [G: U.K.]

Backus, David and Driffill, John. Rational Expectations and Policy Credibility Following a Change in Regime. *Rev. Econ. Stud.*, April 1985, *52*(2), pp. 211–21.

Balassa, Bela. Adjusting to External Shocks: The Newly-industrializing Developing Economies in 1974–1976 and 1979–1981. *Weltwirtsch. Arch.*, 1985, *121*(1), pp. 116–41.
[G: Selected LDCs]

Balassa, Bela. Adjustment Policies in Developing Economies: A Reassessment. In *Balassa, B.*, 1985, pp. 89–101. [G: LDCs]

Balassa, Bela. Economic Policies in France: Retrospect and Prospects. In *Balassa, B.*, 1985, pp. 339–62. [G: France]

Balassa, Bela. French Economic Policies under the Socialist Government: Year III. In *Balassa, B.*, 1985, pp. 384–99. [G: France]

Balassa, Bela. Korea in the 1980s: Policies and Prospects. In *Balassa, B.*, 1985, pp. 236–57.
[G: S. Korea; Singapore; Taiwan; Hong Kong]

Balassa, Bela. Medium-term Economic Policies for Portugal. In *Balassa, B.*, 1985, pp. 185–207. [G: Portugal]

Balassa, Bela. Outward Orientation and Exchange Rate Policy in Developing Countries: The Turkish Experience. In *Balassa, B.*, 1985, pp. 208–35. [G: Turkey]

Balassa, Bela. Structural Adjustment Policies in Developing Economies. In *Bapna, A., ed.*, 1985, pp. 251–77. [G: LDCs]

Balassa, Bela. Structural Adjustment Policies in Developing Economies. In *Balassa, B.*, 1985, pp. 63–88. [G: LDCs]

Balassa, Bela. The First Year of Socialist Government in France. In *Balassa, B.*, 1985, pp. 363–83. [G: France]

Ball, James [Sir]. Demand Management and Economic Recovery: The United Kingdom Case. *Nat. Westminster Bank Quart. Rev.*, August 1985, pp. 2–17. [G: U.K.]

Bandera, V. N. and Lucken, J. A. Simulation of a Debtor Country: The Example of Colombia. *J. Policy Modeling*, Fall 1985, 7(3), pp. 457–76. [G: Colombia]

Barker, Kate, et al. Macroeconomic Policy in Germany and Britain. *Nat. Inst. Econ. Rev.*, November 1985, (114), pp. 69–89. [G: U.K.; W. Germany]

Bartmann, Hermann and John, Klaus-Dieter. Entscheidungen, Erwartungen und Kontrakte bei Unsicherheit. Eine postkeynesianische Sicht. (Decisions, Expectations and Contracts under Uncertainty: A Post-Keynesian View. With English summary.) *Jahr. Nationalökon. Statist.*, May 1985, *200*(3), pp. 217–28.

Basevi, Giorgio. The Effects of Economic Structure and Policy Choices on Macroeconomic Outcomes in Ten Industrial Countries: Comments. In *Melitz, J. and Wyplosz, C., eds.*, 1985, pp. 301–02. [G: Selected OECD]

Baxter, Marianne. The Role of Expectations in Stabilization Policy. *J. Monet. Econ.*, May 1985, *15*(3), pp. 343–62. [G: Chile; Argentina]

Bean, Charles R. Macroeconomic Policy Co-ordination: Theory and Evidence. *Rech. Écon. Louvain*, 1985, *51*(3–4), pp. 267–83.
[G: OECD]

Becker, Robin, et al. Optimal Policy under Model Uncertainty. In *Currie, D., ed.*, 1985, pp. 69–85. [G: U.K.]

Begg, David K. H. Macroeconomic Policy Design in an Interdependent World: Comment. In *Buiter, W. H. and Marston, R. C., eds.*, 1985, pp. 268–71.

Benavie, Arthur. Monetary-Fiscal Policy under Rational Expectations in a Lucas–Rapping Macromodel. *Atlantic Econ. J.*, December 1985, *13*(4), pp. 1–9.

Benavie, Arthur and Froyen, Richard T. Optimal Monetary-Fiscal Stabilizers under an Indexed versus Nonindexed Tax Structure. *J. Econ. Bus.*, August 1985, *37*(3), pp. 197–208.

Bhandari, Jagdeep S. Informational Regimes, Economic Disturbances, and Exchange Rate Management. In *Bhandari, J. S., ed.*, 1985, pp. 126–53.

Bhatia, Rattan J. Adjustment Efforts in Sub-Saharan Africa, 1980–84. *Finance Develop.*, September 1985, *22*(3), pp. 19–22. [G: Sub-Saharan Africa]

Black, Stanley W. The Effect of Alternative Intervention Policies on the Variability of Exchange Rates: The Harrod Effect. In *Bhandari, J. S., ed.*, 1985, pp. 72–82.

Black, Stanley W. The Effects of Economic Structure and Policy Choices on Macroeconomic Outcomes in Ten Industrial Countries. In *Melitz, J. and Wyplosz, C., eds.*, 1985, pp. 279–300. [G: Selected OECD]

Black, Stanley W. The Effects of Economic Structure and Policy Choices on Macroeconomic Outcomes in Ten Industrial Countries: Reply to Basevi. In *Melitz, J. and Wyplosz, C., eds.*, 1985, pp. 307. [G: Selected OECD]

Boyer, Robert. The Influence of Keynes on French Economic Policy: Past and Present. In *Wattel, H. L., ed.*, 1985, pp. 77–115.
[G: France]

Braga de Macedo, Jorge. International Policy Coordination in Dynamic Macroeconomic Models: Comment. In *Buiter, W. H. and Marston, R. C., eds.*, 1985, pp. 319–26.

Brandsma, Andries S. and Pijpers, J. R. Coordinated Strategies for Economic Cooperation be-

tween Europe and the United States. *Weltwirtsch. Arch.*, 1985, *121*(4), pp. 661–81.
[G: U.S.; EEC]

Branson, William H. Inflation, Employment and External Constraints: An Overview of the French Economy during the Seventies: Comments. In *Melitz, J. and Wyplosz, C., eds.*, 1985, pp. 43–47. [G: France]

Britton, Andrew J. C. The Budget and Its Critics. *Fisc. Stud.*, May 1985, *6*(2), pp. 23–30.
[G: U.K.]

Brunner, Karl. The Limits of Economic Policy. *Schweiz. Z. Volkswirtsch. Statist.*, September 1985, *121*(3), pp. 213–36.

Bruno, Michael. The Reforms and Macroeconomic Adjustments: Introduction. *World Devel.*, August 1985, *13*(8), pp. 867–69.
[G: Argentina; Chile; Uruguay]

Bryant, Ralph C. Policy Coordination and Dynamic Games: Comment. In *Buiter, W. H. and Marston, R. C., eds.*, 1985, pp. 213–19.

Budd, Alan P. Macroeconomic Policy and the 1985 Budget. In *Kay, J., ed.*, 1985, pp. 10–22. [G: U.K.]

Buiter, Willem H. International Policy Coordination in Historical Perspective: A View from the Interwar Years: Comment. In *Buiter, W. H. and Marston, R. C., eds.*, 1985, pp. 178–81.

Buiter, Willem H. and Eaton, Jonathan. Policy Decentralization and Exchange Rate Management in Interdependent Economies. In *Bhandari, J. S., ed.*, 1985, pp. 31–54.

Buiter, Willem H. and Marston, Richard C. International Economic Policy Coordination: Introduction. In *Buiter, W. H. and Marston, R. C., eds.*, 1985, pp. 1–7.

Buiter, Willem H. and Miller, Marcus. Costs and Benefits of an Anti-inflationary Policy: Questions and Issues. In *Argy, V. E. and Neville, J. W., eds.*, 1985, pp. 11–38.

Burns, Michael E. and Mitchell, William F. Real Wages, Unemployment and Economic Policy in Australia. *Australian Econ. Pap.*, June 1985, *24*(44), pp. 1–23. [G: Australia]

Calmfors, Lars. The Roles of Stabilization Policy and Wage Setting for Macroeconomic Stability—The Experiences of Economies with Centralized Bargaining. *Kyklos*, 1985, *38*(3), pp. 329–47. [G: W. Europe]

Canzoneri, Matthew B. and Underwood, John M. Wage Contracting, Exchange Rate Volatility, and Exchange Intervention Policy. In *Bhandari, J. S., ed.*, 1985, pp. 247–71.

Cebula, Richard J. Crowding Out and Fiscal Policy in the United States: A Note on the Recent Experience. *Public Finance*, 1985, *40*(1), pp. 133–36. [G: U.S.]

Challen, D. W. Wages, Unemployment and Inflation. In *Argy, V. E. and Neville, J. W., eds.*, 1985, pp. 346–69. [G: Australia]

Chernomas, Bob. A Malthusian Basis for Post-Keynesian Stagflation Theory and Policy: A Marxist Analysis. *Rev. Radical Polit. Econ.*, Spring and Summer 1985, *17*(1/2), pp. 230–40.

Chopra, Ajai. The Speed of Adjustment of the Inflation Rate in Developing Countries: A Study of Inertia. *Int. Monet. Fund Staff Pap.*, December 1985, *32*(4), pp. 693–733.
[G: LDCs]

Chouraqui, Jean-Claude and Price, Robert. Fiscal and Monetary Strategy in OECD Countries: A Review of Recent Experiences. In *Argy, V. E. and Neville, J. W., eds.*, 1985, pp. 105–33. [G: OECD]

Colander, David C. Coopolization and Incomes Policy. *Eastern Econ. J.*, July-Sept. 1985, *11*(3), pp. 221–28.

Congdon, Tim G. The Rise and Fall of the Chilean Economic Miracle. In *Duran, E., ed.*, 1985, pp. 98–119. [G: Chile]

Corbo, Vittorio and de Melo, Jaime. Liberalization with Stabilization in the Southern Cone of Latin America: Overview and Summary. *World Devel.*, August 1985, *13*(8), pp. 863–66. [G: Argentina; Chile; Uruguay]

Corden, W. Max. Macroeconomic Policy Interaction under Flexible Exchange Rates: A Two-Country Model. *Economica*, February 1985, *52*(205), pp. 9–23.

Corden, W. Max. On Transmission and Coordination under Flexible Exchange Rates. In *Buiter, W. H. and Marston, R. C., eds.*, 1985, pp. 8–24.

Corden, W. Max. Relationships between Macroeconomic and Industrial Policies. In *Corden, W. M.*, 1985, pp. 288–301.

Currie, David. Macroeconomic Policy Design and Control Theory—A Failed Partnership? *Econ. J.*, June 1985, *95*(378), pp. 285–306.
[G: U.K.]

Currie, David and Levine, Paul. Macroeconomic Policy Design in an Interdependent World. In *Buiter, W. H. and Marston, R. C., eds.*, 1985, pp. 228–68.

Currie, David and Levine, Paul. Simple Macropolicy Rules for the Open Economy. *Econ. J.*, Supplement 1985, *95*, pp. 60–70.

Cvjetičanin, Daniel. Primena kriterijuma namenske raspodele iz dugoročnog programa ekonomske stabilizacije—empirijska analiza. (Empirical Analysis of the Rule for Income Distribution Proposed by the Yugoslav Economic Stabilization Programme. With English summary.) *Econ. Anal. Worker's Manage.*, 1985, *19*(2), pp. 223–35. [G: Yugoslavia]

Daly, Michael J. and Rao, P. Someshwar. Some Myths and Realities Concerning Canada's Recent Productivity Slowdown, and Their Policy Implications. *Can. Public Policy*, June 1985, *11*(2), pp. 206–17. [G: Canada]

Darrat, Ali F. 'Efficient' Market Testing of the Expectations-adjusted Supply Function Hypothesis for Italy. *Appl. Econ.*, December 1985, *17*(6), pp. 1065–70. [G: Italy]

Darrat, Ali F. Does Anticipated Fiscal Policy Matter? The Italian Evidence. *Public Finance Quart.*, July 1985, *13*(3), pp. 339–52.
[G: Italy]

Dauhajre, Andrés S. Dominican Republic: Eighteen Years of Economic Policy. In *Jorge, A.; Salazar-Carrillo, J. and Diaz-Pou, F., eds.*, 1985, pp. 129–43. [G: Dominican Republic]

Dauhajre, Andrés S. Dominican Republic: 18 Years of Economic Policy: 1966–1983. In *Salazar-Carrillo, J. and de Alonso, I. T., eds.,* 1985, pp. 1–25. **[G: Dominican Republic]**

Davis, Richard G. Policies to Overcome Stagflation: Comments. In *Ando, A., et al., eds.,* 1985, pp. 295–98. **[G: U.S.]**

De Bruyne, Guido. Union Militancy, External Shocks and the Accommodation Dilemma: Comment. *Scand. J. Econ.,* 1985, 87(2), pp. 352–54.

Díaz, Francisco Gil. Mexico and the United States: Studies in Economic Interaction: Changing Strategies. In *Musgrave, P. B., ed.,* 1985, pp. 249–57. **[G: Mexico; U.S.]**

Dillard, Dudley. The Influence of Keynesian Thought on German Economic Policy. In *Wattel, H. L., ed.,* 1985, pp. 116–27. **[G: W. Germany]**

Dornbusch, Rudiger. The French Economy: Theory and Policy: Introduction. In *Melitz, J. and Wyplosz, C., eds.,* 1985, pp. 1–7. **[G: France]**

Doroodian, Khosrow. The Effectiveness of IMF Conditionality in Non-oil Developing Countries: An Empirical Verification. *J. Econ. Devel.,* December 1985, 10(2), pp. 53–65. **[G: LDCs]**

Driffill, John. Macroeconomic Stabilization Policy and Trade Union Behaviour as a Repeated Game. *Scand. J. Econ.,* 1985, 87(2), pp. 300–326.

Driskill, Robert and McCafferty, Stephen. Exchange Market Intervention under Rational Expectations with Imperfect Capital Substitutability. In *Bhandari, J. S., ed.,* 1985, pp. 83–95.

Driskill, Robert and Sheffrin, Steven M. The "Patman Effect" and Stabilization Policy. *Quart. J. Econ.,* February 1985, 100(1), pp. 149–63.

Eatwell, John. Keynes, Keynesians, and British Economic Policy. In *Wattel, H. L., ed.,* 1985, pp. 61–76. **[G: OECD]**

Eichengreen, Barry. International Policy Coordination in Historical Perspective: A View from the Interwar Years. In *Buiter, W. H. and Marston, R. C., eds.,* 1985, pp. 139–78.

Eichner, Alfred S. Stagflation: Explaining the Inexplicable. In *Eichner, A. S.,* 1985, pp. 113–50. **[G: U.S.]**

Emerson, Michael. The Effects of American Policies—A New Classical Interpretation: Comment. In *Buiter, W. H. and Marston, R. C., eds.,* 1985, pp. 131–34. **[G: U.S.; OECD]**

Eriksen, Tore and Qvigstad, Jan Fredrik. The Use of Macroeconomic Models in Economic Policy Making: The Norwegian Experience. *Econ. Modelling,* January 1985, 2(1), pp. 59–66. **[G: Norway]**

Evans, Paul. Money, Output and Goodhart's Law: The U.S. Experience. *Rev. Econ. Statist.,* February 1985, 67(1), pp. 1–8. **[G: U.S.]**

Felmingham, Bruce S. A Second Best Strategy for the Recovery of Full Employment in the Open Economy. *J. Macroecon.,* Fall 1985, 7(4), pp. 469–91.

Fender, John. Counterinflationary Policy in a Unionised Economy with Nonsynchronised Wage Setting: Comment. *Scand. J. Econ.,* 1985, 87(2), pp. 379–81.

Fischer, B.; Hiemenz, Ulrich and Trapp, P. Economic Development, Debt Crisis, and the Importance of Domestic Policies—The Case of Argentina. *Econ. Int.,* February 1985, 38(1), pp. 21–48. **[G: Argentina]**

Fischer, Stanley. Macroeconomic Stabilization Policy and Trade Union Behaviour as a Repeated Game: Comment. *Scand. J. Econ.,* 1985, 87(2), pp. 327–31.

Fischer, Stanley. The Dollar and the Policy Mix: 1985: Comment. *Brookings Pap. Econ. Act.,* 1985, (1), pp. 186–90. **[G: U.S.]**

Fitoussi, Jean-Paul. Apprenticeship for Governing: An Assessment of French Socialism in Power: Comment. In *Machin, H. and Wright, V., eds.,* 1985, pp. 63–69. **[G: France]**

FitzGerald, E. V. K. Stabilization and Economic Justice: The Case of Nicaragua. In *Kim, K. S. and Ruccio, D. F., eds.,* 1985, pp. 191–204. **[G: Nicaragua]**

Flood, Robert P. and Hodrick, Robert J. Central Bank Intervention in a Rational Open Economy: A Model with Asymmetric Information. In *Bhandari, J. S., ed.,* 1985, pp. 154–85.

von Furstenberg, George M. Adjustment with IMF Lending. *J. Int. Money Finance,* June 1985, 4(2), pp. 209–22. **[G: LDCs]**

Galbraith, James K. Using the Presidency to Fight Inflation. *Challenge,* March/April 1985, 28(1), pp. 19–26. **[G: U.S.]**

Galbraith, John Kenneth. Keynes, Roosevelt, and the Complementary Revolutions. In *Wattel, H. L., ed.,* 1985, pp. 54–60.

Gapinski, James H. Capital Malleability, Macro Performance, and Policy Effectiveness. *Southern Econ. J.,* July 1985, 52(1), pp. 150–66.

Graham, Andrew W. M. The Economic System in the UK: Objectives and Instruments. In *Morris, D., ed.,* 1985, pp. 251–71. **[G: U.K.]**

Gray, Jo Anna. International Policy Coordination in Historical Perspective: A View from the Interwar Years: Comment. In *Buiter, W. H. and Marston, R. C., eds.,* 1985, pp. 181–83.

Gregory, R. G. and Smith, Ralph E. Unemployment, Inflation and Job Creation Policies in Australia. In *Argy, V. E. and Neville, J. W., eds.,* 1985, pp. 325–45. **[G: Australia]**

Gylfason, Thorvaldur. Counterinflationary Policy in a Unionised Economy with Nonsynchronised Wage Setting: Comment. *Scand. J. Econ.,* 1985, 87(2), pp. 382–85.

Hamada, Koichi. Macroeconomic Policy Design in an Interdependent World: Comment. In *Buiter, W. H. and Marston, R. C., eds.,* 1985, pp. 271–73.

Henderson, Dale W. On Transmission and Coordination under Flexible Exchange Rates: Comment. In *Buiter, W. H. and Marston, R. C., eds.,* 1985, pp. 24–32.

Hewson, J. R. and Nevile, J. W. Monetary and Fiscal Policy in Australia. In *Argy, V. E. and Neville, J. W., eds.,* 1985, pp. 305–24. **[G: Australia]**

Holmes, Peter. Economic Management and the International Environment, 1981–1983: Comment. In *Machin, H. and Wright, V., eds.*, 1985, pp. 96–100. **[G: France]**

Hough, J. R. Economic Planning in France. In *Bornstein, M., ed.*, 1985, pp. 76–94.
[G: France]

Hudson, Michael A. German Economists and the Depression of 1929-1933. *Hist. Polit. Econ.*, Spring 1985, *17*(1), pp. 35–50. **[G: Germany]**

Illing, G. The Need for Policy Coordination under Alternative Types of Macroeconomic Theory. *Rech. Écon. Louvain*, 1985, *51*(3–4), pp. 255–63.

Ishii, Naoko; McKibbin, Warwick and Sachs, Jeffrey. The Economic Policy Mix, Policy Cooperation, and Protectionism: Some Aspects of Macroeconomic Interdependence among the United States, Japan, and Other OECD Countries. *J. Policy Modeling*, Winter 1985, *7*(4), pp. 533–72. **[G: OECD]**

Jackman, Richard. Counterinflationary Policy in a Unionised Economy with Nonsynchronised Wage Setting. *Scand. J. Econ.*, 1985, *87*(2), pp. 357–78.

Jespersen, Jesper. Har vi afskåret os fra mulige den for at føre økonomisk politik? (Are We in a Position to Pursue an Active Economic Policy?. With English summary.) *Nationaløkon. Tidsskr.*, 1985, *123*(3), pp. 342–52.
[G: Denmark]

Jha, L. K. Demand Problem in Indian Economy. In *Jha, L. K.*, 1985, pp. 60–69. **[G: India]**

Jha, L. K. Fighting Inflation with Growth. In *Jha, L. K.*, 1985, pp. 104–09. **[G: India]**

Jha, L. K. How to Check Inflation without Stopping Growth? In *Jha, L. K.*, 1985, pp. 85–90.
[G: India]

Jha, L. K. Supply-Side Economics. In *Jha, L. K.*, 1985, pp. 130–39.

Jones-Hendrickson, S. B. Rational Expectations, Causality and Integrative Fiscal–Monetary Policy in the Caribbean. *Soc. Econ. Stud.*, December 1985, *34*(4), pp. 111–38.
[G: Caribbean]

Jorgenson, Dale W. and Slesnick, Daniel T. General Equilibrium Analysis of Economic Policy. In *Piggott, J. and Whalley, J., eds.*, 1985, pp. 293–370. **[G: U.S.]**

Kaldor, Nicholas. How Monetarism Failed. *Challenge*, May/June 1985, *28*(2), pp. 4–13.
[G: U.S.; U.K.]

Karlsson, Erik L. "Reaganomics" and Credibility: Comments. In *Ando, A., et al., eds.*, 1985, pp. 299–301. **[G: Sweden]**

Karp, Larry S. Higher Moments in the Linear-Quadratic-Gaussian Problem. *J. Econ. Dynam. Control*, September 1985, *9*(1), pp. 41–54.

Kawai, Masahiro. Exchange Rates, the Current Account and Monetary–Fiscal Policies in the Short Run and in the Long Run. *Oxford Econ. Pap.*, September 1985, *37*(3), pp. 391–425.

Kindleberger, Charles P. British Financial Reconstruction, 1815–22 and 1918–25. In *Kindleberger, C. P.*, 1985, pp. 105–18. **[G: U.K.]**

Kindleberger, Charles P. Keynesianism vs. Monetarism in Eighteenth- and Nineteenth-Century France. In *Kindleberger, C. P.*, 1985, pp. 41–62. **[G: France]**

Kindleberger, Charles P. Keynesianism vs. Monetarism in the 1930s Depression and Recovery. In *Kindleberger, C. P.*, 1985, pp. 287–92.
[G: U.S.]

Kindleberger, Charles P. The International Monetary Politics of a Near-Great Power: Two French Episodes, 1926–1936 and 1960–1970. In *Kindleberger, C. P.*, 1985, pp. 119–28.
[G: France]

Kirchgässner, Gebhard. Ist "rationale" Wirtschaftspolitik möglich? Zu den Auswirkungen der Theorie rationaler Erwartungen und der ökonomischen Theorie der Politik auf die Theorie der Wirtschaftspolitik. (Is There a Real Possibility for "Rational" Economic Policy making? With English Summary.) *Konjunkturpolitik*, 1985, *31*(4/5), pp. 209–37.

Kitromilides, Y. The Formation of Economic Policy: A Question for Economists? In *Arestis, P. and Skouras, T., eds.*, 1985, pp. 7–23.

Kloten, Norbert; Ketterer, Karl-Heinz and Vollmer, Rainer. West Germany's Stabilization Performance. In *Lindberg, L. N. and Maier, C. S., eds.*, 1985, pp. 353–402.
[G: W. Germany]

Kregel, J. A. Budget Deficits, Stabilisation Policy and Liquidity Preference: Keynes's Post-War Policy Proposals. In *Vicarelli, F., ed.*, 1985, pp. 28–50. **[G: OECD]**

Lai, Ching-chong and Chen, Chau-Nan. Flexible Exchange Rates, Tight Money Effects, and Macroeconomic Policy: Reply. *J. Post Keynesian Econ.*, Fall 1985, *8*(1), pp. 154–58.

Lavoie, Marc. Inflation, chômage et la planification des récessions: La "Théorie générale" de Keynes et après. (Inflation, Unemployment and Planned Recessions: Keynes' 'General Theory' and After. With English summary.) *L'Actual. Econ.*, June 1985, *61*(2), pp. 171–99.

Lempinen, Urho. Keynesiläinen kansantalous, rationaaliset taloudenpitäjät ja suhdannevaihtelut. (Rational Agents and the Keynesian Economy: Some Results in Business Cycle Theory. With English summary.) *Kansant. Aikak.*, 1985, *81*(2), pp. 150–59.

Leventakis, John A. Stabilization Policies in the Greek Economy: Will They Work? *J. Policy Modeling*, Fall 1985, *7*(3), pp. 441–55.
[G: Greece]

Levine, Paul and Currie, David. Optimal Feedback Rules in an Open Economy Macromodel with Rational Expectations. *Europ. Econ. Rev.*, March 1985, *27*(2), pp. 141–63.

Lindblom, Seppo. Tillväxtinriktad ekonomisk politik—med långsamma steg. (Growth-dominated Economic Policy—With Slow Progress. With English summary.) *Ekon. Samfundets Tidskr.*, 1985, *38*(2), pp. 69–78. **[G: Finland]**

Lombard, J. A. The Evolution of the Theory of Economic Policy. *S. Afr. J. Econ.*, December 1985, *53*(4), pp. 315–32. **[G: S. Africa]**

Looney, Robert E. Pre-revolutionary Iranian Economic Policy Making: An Optimal Control Based Assessment. *Econ. Modelling*, October 1985, *2*(4), pp. 357–68. **[G: Iran]**

Lundberg, Erik. The Rise and Fall of the Swedish Economic Model. In *Bornstein, M., ed.*, 1985, pp. 48–60. **[G: Sweden]**

Maier-Rigaud, Gerhard. Durch statisches Denken zur stationären Wirtschaft. (Through Static Economics to a Stationary Economy. With English summary.) *Konjunkturpolitik*, 1985, *31*(1/2), pp. 1–33. **[G: W. Germany]**

Mansfield, Charles Y. Tax Effort and Measures of Fiscal Stabilization Performance. *Bull. Int. Fiscal Doc.*, February 1985, *39*(2), pp. 77–85.

Marini, Giancarlo. Built-in Flexibility of Taxation, Public Spending Rules and Stabilisation Policy. *Econ. Notes*, 1985, (2), pp. 5–21.

Marston, Richard C. The Effects of American Policies—A New Classical Interpretation: Comment. In *Buiter, W. H. and Marston, R. C., eds.*, 1985, pp. 134–38. **[G: U.S.; OECD]**

Marston, Richard C. and Turnovsky, Stephen J. Imported Materials Prices, Wage Policy, and Macro-economic Stabilization. *Can. J. Econ.*, May 1985, *18*(2), pp. 273–84.

Marston, Richard C. and Turnovsky, Stephen J. Macroeconomic Stabilization through Taxation and Indexation: The Use of Firm-Specific Information. *J. Monet. Econ.*, November 1985, *16*(3), pp. 375–95.

Martin, John P. The Effects of Economic Structure and Policy Choices on Macroeconomic Outcomes in Ten Industrial Countries: Comments. In *Melitz, J. and Wyplosz, C., eds.*, 1985, pp. 303–05. **[G: Selected OECD]**

Maussner, Alfred. Ineffektivität der Wirtschaftspolitik bei "rationalen Erwartungen"? Ein Kommentar mit anderen Argumenten für eine unzureichend begründete These. (Ineffectiveness of Economic Policy under "Rational Expectations"? A Commentary with Different Arguments for an Insufficient Founded Thesis. With English summary.) *Kredit Kapital*, 1985, *18*(2), pp. 217–29.

McClam, W. D. and Andersen, P. S. Adjustment Performance of Small, Open Economies: Some International Comparisons. In *Argy, V. E. and Neville, J. W., eds.*, 1985, pp. 249–77. **[G: Austria; Canada; Belgium; Sweden]**

McCormick, Janice. Apprenticeship for Governing: An Assessment of French Socialism in Power. In *Machin, H. and Wright, V., eds.*, 1985, pp. 44–63. **[G: France]**

Ménard, Claude. Le keynésianisme: naissance d'une illusion. (Keynesianism: The Genesis of an Illusion. With English summary.) *Écon. Soc.*, March 1985, *19*(3), pp. 3–27.

de Ménil, Georges. On Transmission and Coordination under Flexible Exchange Rates: Comment. In *Buiter, W. H. and Marston, R. C., eds.*, 1985, pp. 32–36.

de Ménil, Georges and Westphal, Uwe. Aims and Methods of an International Macroeconomic Comparison. In *de Ménil, G. and Westphal,*

U., eds., 1985, pp. 1–17. **[G: France; W. Germany]**

Miller, Jeffrey B. and Schneider, Jerrold E. American Politics and Changing Macroeconomic Institutions. In *Maital, S. and Lipnowski, I., eds.*, 1985, pp. 207–39. **[G: U.S.]**

Miller, Marcus. Monetary Stabilization Policy in an Open Economy. *Scot. J. Polit. Econ.*, November 1985, *32*(3), pp. 220–33.

Miller, Marcus and Salmon, Mark. Dynamic Games and the Time Inconsistency of Optimal Policy in Open Economies. *Econ. J.*, Supplement 1985, *95*, pp. 124–37.

Miller, Marcus and Salmon, Mark. Policy Coordination and Dynamic Games. In *Buiter, W. H. and Marston, R. C., eds.*, 1985, pp. 184–213.

Miller, Preston J. and Wallace, Neil. International Coordination of Macroeconomic Policies: A Welfare Analysis. *Fed. Res. Bank Minn. Rev.*, Spring 1985, *9*(2), pp. 14–32.

Minford, Patrick. Demand Management–An Obituary: Review Article. *J. Econ. Stud.*, 1985, *12*(3), pp. 61–65. **[G: U.K.]**

Minford, Patrick. The Effects of American Policies—A New Classical Interpretation. In *Buiter, W. H. and Marston, R. C., eds.*, 1985, pp. 84–130. **[G: OECD; U.S.]**

Mohr, P. J. Monetary Policy and Inflation in South Africa: Reflections on the Final Report of the De Kock Commission. *J. Stud. Econ. Econometrics*, November 1985, (23), pp. 3–27. **[G: S. Africa]**

Moore, Michael J. Demand Management with Rationing. *Econ. J.*, March 1985, *95*(377), pp. 73–86.

Moore, Mick. On 'The Political Economy of Stabilization.' *World Devel.*, September 1985, *13*(9), pp. 1087–91. **[G: Ghana; Kenya; Sri Lanka; Jamaica; Zambia]**

Muet, Pierre-Alain. Economic Management and the International Environment, 1981–1983. In *Machin, H. and Wright, V., eds.*, 1985, pp. 70–96. **[G: France]**

Mussa, Michael L. Official Intervention and Exchange Rate Dynamics. In *Bhandari, J. S., ed.*, 1985, pp. 1–30.

Myatt, Anthony. Exchange Rates, Tight Money, and Macroeconomic Policy: A Comment. *J. Post Keynesian Econ.*, Fall 1985, *8*(1), pp. 151–53.

von Natzmer, Wulfheinrich. Econometric Policy Evaluation and Expectations. *Econ. Modelling*, January 1985, *2*(1), pp. 52–58.

Neck, Reinhard. On the Effects of Disinflationary Policies on Unemployment and Inflation: A Simulation Study with Keynesian and Monetarist Models for Austria. *Z. Wirtschaft. Sozialwissen.*, 1985, *105*(2/3), pp. 357–86. **[G: Austria]**

Nelson, Joan. On the Political Economy of Stabilization: Reply. *World Devel.*, September 1985, *13*(9), pp. 1093–94. **[G: Ghana; Kenya; Sri Lanka; Jamaica; Zambia]**

Nguyen, Duc-Tho. Money Financing and the Dynamic Effects of Fiscal and Monetary Policies in a Theoretical Simulation Model. *Manchester Sch. Econ. Soc. Stud.*, December 1985, *53*(4), pp. 432–56.

Nickerson, David. A Theorem on Policy Neutrality. *Europ. Econ. Rev.*, August 1985, *28*(3), pp. 331–45.

Nicolini, Jose Luis. The Degree of Monopoly, the Macroeconomic Balance and the International Current Account: The Adjustment to the Oil Shocks. *Cambridge J. Econ.*, June 1985, *9*(2), pp. 127–40.

Nicolini, Jose Luis. Erratum [The Degree of Monopoly, the Macroeconomic Balance and the International Current Account: The Adjustment to the Oil Shocks]. *Cambridge J. Econ.*, December 1985, *9*(4), pp. 411.

Obstfeld, Maurice. The Dollar and the Policy Mix: 1985: Comment. *Brookings Pap. Econ. Act.*, 1985, (1), pp. 190–95. **[G: U.S.]**

Onofri, Paolo and Salituro, Bruno. Inflazione e politiche di stabilizzazione in Italia: 1960–1984. (Inflation and Stabilization Policies in Italy: 1960–1984. With English summary.) *Polit. Econ.*, August 1985, *1*(2), pp. 167–96.
[G: Italy]

Ostry, Sylvia. Policies to Overcome Stagflation: Comments. In *Ando, A., et al., eds.*, 1985, pp. 291–94. **[G: U.S.]**

Oudiz, Gilles. European Policy Coordination: An Evaluation. *Rech. Écon. Louvain*, 1985, *51*(3–4), pp. 301–39. **[G: EEC]**

Oudiz, Gilles and Sachs, Jeffrey. International Policy Coordination in Dynamic Macroeconomic Models. In *Buiter, W. H. and Marston, R. C., eds.*, 1985, pp. 274–319.

Oudiz, Gilles and Sterdyniak, Henri. Inflation, Employment and External Constraints: An Overview of the French Economy during the Seventies. In *Melitz, J. and Wyplosz, C., eds.*, 1985, pp. 9–42. **[G: France]**

Pacheco, Fernando. A Role for an International Institution: A One-Shot Game-Theoretic Approach. *Rech. Écon. Louvain*, 1985, *51*(3–4), pp. 241–54.

Padoa-Schioppa, Tommaso. Policy Cooperation and the EMS Experience. In *Buiter, W. H. and Marston, R. C., eds.*, 1985, pp. 331–55.
[G: OECD]

Pandit, V. Macroeconomic Structure and Policy in a Less Developed Economy. *J. Quant. Econ.*, January 1985, *1*(1), pp. 49–79.
[G: India]

Payer, Cheryl. The Politics of Intervention: The Italian Crisis of 1976. In *[Magdoff, H. and Sweezy, P.]*, 1985, pp. 295–318. **[G: Italy]**

Peacock, Alan. Macro-economic Controls of Spending as a Device for Improving Efficiency in Government. In *Forte, F. and Peacock, A., eds.*, 1985, pp. 143–56. **[G: U.K.; U.S.; Italy]**

Peston, Maurice. The Efficacy of Macroeconomic Policy. In *[Peacock, A.]*, 1985, pp. 125–48.

Petit, Maria Luisa. Path Controllability of Dynamic Economic Systems. *Econ. Notes*, 1985, (1), pp. 26–42.

Phelps, Edmund S. Union Militancy, External Shocks and the Accommodation Dilemma:

Comment. *Scand. J. Econ.*, 1985, *87*(2), pp. 355–56.

Philip, George. Mexico: Learning to Live with the Crisis. In *Duran, E., ed.*, 1985, pp. 81–97. **[G: Mexico]**

Pierce, James L. Policy Making under Uncertainty: Some Lessons from the 1970s. In *[Weintraub, R. E.]*, 1985, pp. 55–75. **[G: U.S.]**

Plaut, Steven E. The Likud Years: 1977–83. In *Levinson, P. and Landau, P., eds.*, 1985, pp. 31–37. **[G: Israel]**

Pohjola, Matti. Macroeconomic Stabilization Policy and Trade Union Behaviour as a Repeated Game: Comment. *Scand. J. Econ.*, 1985, *87*(2), pp. 332–34.

Praedicta Ltd. The July 1985 Austerity Programme: Pro and Con. In *Levinson, P. and Landau, P., eds.*, 1985, pp. 3–5. **[G: Israel]**

Ramos, Joseph. Stabilization and Adjustment Policies in the Southern Cone, 1974–1983. *Cepal Rev.*, April 1985, (25), pp. 85–109.
[G: Argentina; Chile; Uruguay]

Rao, V. K. R. V. Indira Gandhi—A Tribute. In *Mongia, J. N., ed.*, 1985, pp. xxv–xxxiii.
[G: India]

Rasche, Robert H. Interest Rate Volatility and Alternative Monetary Control Procedures. *Fed. Res. Bank San Francisco Econ. Rev.*, Summer 1985, (3), pp. 46–63. **[G: U.S.]**

Reynolds, Clark W. Mexico and the United States: Studies in Economic Interaction: Fluctuations and Growth: Comments. In *Musgrave, P. B., ed.*, 1985, pp. 171–75.
[G: Mexico; U.S.]

Rogoff, Kenneth S. International Policy Coordination in Dynamic Macroeconomic Models: Comment. In *Buiter, W. H. and Marston, R. C., eds.*, 1985, pp. 327–30.

Sachs, Jeffrey. The Dollar and the Policy Mix: 1985. *Brookings Pap. Econ. Act.*, 1985, (1), pp. 117–85. **[G: U.S.]**

Salvati, Michele. "Effetti reali o nominali della svalutazione?": un commento all'articolo di Andreatta e D'Adda. (Real and Nominal Effects of the Devaluation: the Italian Experience after the First Oil Shock: a Comment. With English summary.) *Polit. Econ.*, August 1985, *1*(2), pp. 279–89. **[G: Italy]**

Salvemini, Maria Teresa. Costituzionalismo monetario e fiscale. (Monetary and Fiscal Constitutionalism. With English summary.) *Polit. Econ.*, April 1985, *1*(1), pp. 123–36.
[G: U.S.; Italy]

Sandblom, Carl-Louis and Banasik, John. Economic Policy with Bounded Controls. *Econ. Modelling*, April 1985, *2*(2), pp. 135–48.
[G: Canada]

Sargent, Thomas J. "Reaganomics" and Credibility. In *Ando, A., et al., eds.*, 1985, pp. 235–52. **[G: U.S.]**

Scherf, Wolfgang. Budgetmultiplikatoren. Eine Analyse der fiskalischen Wirkungen konjunkturbedingter und antizyklischer Defizite. (Budgetary Multiplier Effects of Cyclically Conditioned and Anticyclical Deficits. With English summary.) *Jahr. Nationalökon. Statist.*, July

1985, *200*(4), pp. 349–63. [G: W. Germany]

Schydlowsky, Daniel M. Mexico and the United States: Studies in Economic Interaction: Fluctuations and Growth: Comments. In *Musgrave, P. B., ed.*, 1985, pp. 177–82. [G: Mexico; U.S.]

Seidel, Hans. Die Stabilisierungsfunktion der Budgetpolitik: Gestern—Heute—Morgen. (With English summary.) *Empirica*, 1985, *12*(1), pp. 87–107. [G: Austria]

Shafer, Jeffrey R. Policy Cooperation and the EMS Experience: Comment. In *Buiter, W. H. and Marston, R. C., eds.*, 1985, pp. 359–65. [G: OECD]

Sharples, Adam. The Budget and the Government's Economic Strategy. *Fisc. Stud.*, May 1985, *6*(2), pp. 31–39. [G: U.K.]

Söderström, Hans Tson. Union Militancy, External Shocks and the Accommodation Dilemma. *Scand. J. Econ.*, 1985, *87*(2), pp. 335–51.

Sorensen, Peter Birch. Det monetaristiske syn på stabiliseringspolitikken. (A Macro-economic Model of Explaining Monetarist Assumptions in Stabilization Policy. With English summary.) *Nationaløkon. Tidsskr.*, 1985, *123*(1), pp. 64–76.

Sorsa, Pertti. Ar konjunkturpolitikens tid förbi—finländska ock utländska erfarenheter. (Is Stabilization Policy a Thing of the Past? Finnish and Foreign Experience. With English summary.) *Ekon. Samfundets Tidskr.*, 1985, 38(2), pp. 81–87. [G: Finland]

Spaventa, Luigi. "Effetti reali o nominali della svalutazione?": un commento all'articolo di Andreatta e D'Adda. (Real and Nominal Effects of the Devaluation in the Italian Experience after the First Oil Shock: A Comment. With English summary.) *Polit. Econ.*, August 1985, *1*(2), pp. 291–300. [G: Italy]

Steinherr, Alfred. Policy Coordination in the European Economic Community. *Rech. Écon. Louvain*, 1985, *51*(3–4), pp. 285–99. [G: EEC]

Suzuki, Yoshio. Monetary Policy in Our Times: Comments. In *Ando, A., et al., eds.*, 1985, pp. 303–06. [G: OECD]

Sylos Labini, Paolo. Weintraub on the Price Level and Macroeconomics. *J. Post Keynesian Econ.*, Summer 1985, *7*(4), pp. 559–74.

Taylor, Lance. The Crisis and Thereafter: Macroeconomic Policy Problems in Mexico. In *Musgrave, P. B., ed.*, 1985, pp. 147–70. [G: Mexico]

Tobin, James. Keynes's Policies in Theory and Practice. In *Wattel, H. L., ed.*, 1985, pp. 13–21.

Trejos, Rafael A. External Debt and the Economic Development of Costa Rica. In *Jorge, A.; Salazar-Carrillo, J. and Diaz-Pou, F., eds.*, 1985, pp. 87–92. [G: Costa Rica]

Ture, Norman B. Keynes's Influence on Public Policy: A Conservative's View. In *Wattel, H. L., ed.*, 1985, pp. 48–53.

Turnovsky, Stephen J. Optimal Exchange Market Intervention: Two Alternative Classes of Rules. In *Bhandari, J. S., ed.*, 1985, pp. 55–72.

Turnovsky, Stephen J. Policy Coordination and Dynamic Games: Comment. In *Buiter, W. H. and Marston, R. C., eds.*, 1985, pp. 220–27.

Vaubel, Roland. International Collusion or Competition for Macroeconomic Policy Coordination? A Restatement. *Rech. Écon. Louvain*, 1985, *51*(3–4), pp. 223–40.

Wahlroos, Björn. Ekonomisk politik och internationell konkurrenskraft på lång sikt. (Economic Policy and International Competitiveness in the Long Run. With English summary.) *Ekon. Samfundets Tidskr.*, 1985, *38*(3), pp. 145–55. [G: Finland]

Wahlroos, Björn. En modern konjunkturpolitik. (Modern Stabilization Policy. With English summary.) *Ekon. Samfundets Tidskr.*, 1985, *38*(2), pp. 89–95. [G: Finland]

Wan, Henry Y., Jr. The New Classical Economics—A Game-theoretic Critique. In *Feiwel, G. R., ed. (I)*, 1985, pp. 235–57.

Weigel, Wolfgang. Austrian Economic Policy: A Comment. *Empirica*, 1985, *12*(1), pp. 109–10. [G: Austria]

Whitehead, Laurence. Whatever Became of the 'Southern Cone Model'? In *Hojman, D. E., ed.*, 1985, pp. 9–30. [G: Argentina; Chile]

Williamson, John. Short-run Economic Policy in Brazil. In *Salazar-Carrillo, J. and Fendt, R., Jr., eds.*, 1985, pp. 183–86. [G: Brazil]

Willms, Manfred and Karsten, Ingo. Government Policies towards Inflation and Unemployment in West Germany. In *Argy, V. E. and Neville, J. W., eds.*, 1985, pp. 153–80. [G: W. Germany]

Wilson, Thomas A. Lessons of Recession. *Can. J. Econ.*, November 1985, *18*(4), pp. 693–722. [G: Canada]

Wojcikewych, Raymond. An Empirical Investigation of the Interrelationship between Monetary and Fiscal Policy Using Some Alternative Policy Measures. *Quart. J. Bus. Econ.*, Winter 1985, *24*(1), pp. 101–14. [G: U.S.]

Wolf, Thomas A. Economic Stabilization in Planned Economies: Toward an Analytical Framework. *Int. Monet. Fund Staff Pap.*, March 1985, *32*(1), pp. 78–131.

Wörgötter, Andreas. Supply Shocks, Stagflation and Wage Restraint. *Econ. Notes*, 1985, (2), pp. 38–56.

Woronoff, Jon. Japan's Structural Shift from Exports to Domestic Demand. In *Nanto, D. K., ed.*, 1985, pp. 64–78. [G: Japan]

Worswick, David. Jobs for All? *Econ. J.*, March 1985, *95*(377), pp. 1–14.

Yeboah, Dickson A. Control Theory Application to Economic Policy Analysis in Ghana. *Appl. Econ.*, June 1985, *17*(3), pp. 395–419. [G: Ghana]

1332 Wage and Price Controls

Abbott, John R. White. Energy Futures. In *Roberts, G., ed.*, 1985, pp. 80–83. [G: Global]

Aizenman, Joshua. Openness, Relative Prices, and Macro-policies. *J. Int. Money Finance*, March 1985, *4*(1), pp. 5–17.

Aizenman, Joshua and Frenkel, Jacob A. On the Tradeoff between Wage Indexation and Foreign Exchange Intervention. *Weltwirtsch. Arch.*, 1985, *121*(1), pp. 1–17.

Aizenman, Joshua and Frenkel, Jacob A. Optimal Wage Indexation, Foreign Exchange Intervention, and Monetary Policy. *Amer. Econ. Rev.*, June 1985, *75*(3), pp. 402–23.

Bental, Benjamin. Welfare Analysis of Income Distributions: A Neoclassical Approach. In *Maital, S. and Lipnowski, I., eds.*, 1985, pp. 153–61.

Braun, Anne Romanis. Some Conclusions from Incomes Policy Experience in Industrial Countries. In *Argy, V. E. and Neville, J. W., eds.*, 1985, pp. 134–52. [G: OECD]

Brunner, Lawrence P.; Beladi, Hamid and Zuberi, Habib A. Inflation and Indexation: An Empirical Approach. *Southern Econ. J.*, July 1985, *52*(1), pp. 250–64. [G: U.S.]

Bull, Clive and Schotter, Andrew. The Garbage Game, Inflation, and Incomes Policy. In *Maital, S. and Lipnowski, I., eds.*, 1985, pp. 121–40.

Butler, Tom. Gold. In *Roberts, G., ed.*, 1985, pp. 84–89. [G: Global]

Calmfors, Lars and Horn, Henrik. Classical Unemployment, Accommodation Policies and Adjustment of Real Wages. *Scand. J. Econ.*, 1985, *87*(2), pp. 234–61.

Carliner, Geoffrey and McKee, Michael J. Designing a Tax Incentive Scheme: The Case of a Wage TIP. *J. Policy Anal. Manage.*, Summer 1985, *4*(4), pp. 501–15. [G: U.S.]

Christofides, Louis N. The Impact of Controls on Wage Contract Duration. *Econ. J.*, March 1985, *95*(377), pp. 161–68. [G: Canada]

Christofides, Louis N. and Wilton, David A. Wage Determination in the Aftermath of Controls. *Economica*, February 1985, *52*(205), pp. 51–64. [G: Canada]

Clark, Gordon L. The Spatial Division of Labor and Wage and Price Controls of the Nixon Administration. *Econ. Geogr.*, April 1985, *61*(2), pp. 113–28. [G: U.S.]

Colander, David C. Coopolization and Incomes Policy. *Eastern Econ. J.*, July-Sept. 1985, *11*(3), pp. 221–28.

Colander, David C. Why an Incomes Policy Makes an Economy More Efficient. In *Maital, S. and Lipnowski, I., eds.*, 1985, pp. 97–119.

Davidson, Paul. Incomes Policy as a Social Institution. In *Maital, S. and Lipnowski, I., eds.*, 1985, pp. 141–51.

Dawkins, Peter and Blandy, Richard. Labour Costs and the Future of the Accord. *Australian Econ. Rev.*, 2nd Quarter 1985, (70), pp. 37–50. [G: Australia]

Dixit, Avinash K. and Newbery, David M. G. Setting the Price of Oil in a Distorted Economy. *Econ. J.*, Supplement 1985, 95, pp. 71–82. [G: Turkey]

Dolenc, Vladimir. Optimal Price Policy of Buffer Stocks. *Z. ges. Staatswiss. (JITE)*, September 1985, *141*(3), pp. 401–12.

Economou, George E. More Efficient Economic

Policies of Disinflation: The Case of Greece. *Rech. Écon. Louvain*, 1985, *51*(3–4), pp. 363–80. [G: Greece]

Evans, Robert, Jr. Lessons from Japan's Incomes Policy. *Challenge*, January/February 1985, *27*(6), pp. 33–39. [G: Japan]

Gemmill, Gordon. Forward Contracts or International Buffer Stocks? A Study of Their Relative Efficiencies in Stabilising Commodity Export Earnings. *Econ. J.*, June 1985, *95*(378), pp. 400–417. [G: Selected LDCs]

Gilbert, Christopher L. Futures Trading and the Welfare Evaluation of Commodity Price Stabilisation. *Econ. J.*, September 1985, *95*(379), pp. 637–61. [G: LDCs]

Ginsburgh, Victor and van der Heyden, Ludo. General Equilibrium with Wage Rigidities: An Application to Belgium. In *Manne, A. S., ed.*, 1985, pp. 23–39. [G: Belgium]

Granziol, Markus J. Direct Price Controls as a Source of Instability in the Interest Rate/Inflation Rate Relationship. *J. Banking Finance*, June 1985, *9*(2), pp. 275–88. [G: U.S.; Canada; France]

Guillén Romo, Hector. Crise et austérité au Mexique. (Crisis and Austerity: The Case of Mexico. With English summary.) *Écon. Soc.*, August 1985, *19*(8), pp. 273–86. [G: Mexico]

Haberler, Gottfried. Incomes Policies and Inflation: An Analysis of Basic Principles. In *Haberler, G.*, 1985, pp. 267–310.

Hagens, John B. and Russell, R. Robert. Testing for the Effectiveness of Wage–Price Controls: An Application to the Carter Program. *Amer. Econ. Rev.*, March 1985, *75*(1), pp. 191–207. [G: U.S.]

Helms, L. Jay. Errors in the Numerical Assessment of the Benefits of Price Stabilization. *Amer. J. Agr. Econ.*, February 1985, *67*(1), pp. 93–100.

Hughes Hallett, A. J. Wage Policy, Competitiveness and Risk Management: The Internal Conflicts of Dutch Economic Policy. *Weltwirtsch. Arch.*, 1985, *121*(4), pp. 703–21. [G: Netherlands]

Isaac, J. E. Continuity and Change in Australian Wages Policy: Comment. *Australian Econ. Rev.*, 3rd Quarter, Spring 1985, (71), pp. 68–69. [G: Australia]

Johnson, Ronald N. Retail Price Controls in the Dairy Industry: A Political Coalition Argument. *J. Law Econ.*, April 1985, *28*(1), pp. 55–75.

Jonung, Lars. Classical Unemployment, Accommodation Policies and Adjustment of Real Wages: Comment. *Scand. J. Econ.*, 1985, *87*(2), pp. 262–66.

Layard, Richard. Classical Unemployment, Accommodation Policies and Adjustment of Real Wages: Comment. *Scand. J. Econ.*, 1985, *87*(2), pp. 267–69.

Lipnowski, Irwin and Maital, Shlomo. Hanging Together or Separately: A Game-Theoretic Approach to Macroeconomic Conflict. In *Maital, S. and Lipnowski, I., eds.*, 1985, pp. 39–94.

Lipnowski, Irwin and Maital, Shlomo. Tax-Based

Incomes Policy as the Game of "Chicken." In *Maital, S. and Lipnowski, I., eds.*, 1985, pp. 165–71.

Macedo, Roberto. Remarks on Brazilian Inflation and Wage Policy. In *Salazar-Carrillo, J. and Fendt, R., Jr., eds.*, 1985, pp. 170–76.
[G: Brazil]

Maital, Shlomo and Lipnowski, Irwin. Social Institutions in the Non-zero-sum Society. In *Maital, S. and Lipnowski, I., eds.*, 1985, pp. 1–13.
[G: U.S.]

Maital, Shlomo and Meltz, Noah M. Labor and Management Attitudes toward a New Social Contract: A Comparison of Canada and the United States. In *Maital, S. and Lipnowski, I., eds.*, 1985, pp. 193–206.
[G: U.S.; Canada]

Maki, Dennis R. A Note on Money Wages, Prices, Controls, and Trade Unions in Canada. *Appl. Econ.*, February 1985, *17*(1), pp. 165–72.
[G: Canada]

Marty, Alvin L. Karni on Optimal Wage Indexation: A Correction. *J. Polit. Econ.*, August 1985, *93*(4), pp. 824–25.

McNelis, Paul D. Política de indización e inestabilidad inflacionaria en el Cono Sur. (With English summary.) *Cuadernos Econ.*, April 1985, *22*(65), pp. 99–116.
[G: Argentina; Brazil; Chile; Uruguay; Peru]

Miller, Jeffrey B. and Schneider, Jerrold E. American Politics and Changing Macroeconomic Institutions. In *Maital, S. and Lipnowski, I., eds.*, 1985, pp. 207–39.
[G: U.S.]

Mohr, P. J. Monetary Policy and Inflation in South Africa: Reflections on the Final Report of the De Kock Commission. *J. Stud. Econ. Econometrics*, November 1985, (23), pp. 3–27.
[G: S. Africa]

Ojha, P. D. Inflation Control and Price Regulation. In *Mongia, J. N., ed.*, 1985, pp. 239–89.
[G: India]

Plaut, Steven E. The Reverse Incomes Policy: An Institutional Cure for Inflation. In *Maital, S. and Lipnowski, I., eds.*, 1985, pp. 173–90.

Rizzi, Dino. A Tax-based Incomes Policy Involving Payroll Taxation: Theoretical and Empirical Analyses. *Rivista Int. Sci. Econ. Com.*, July-Aug. 1985, *32*(7–8), pp. 679–700. [G: Italy]

Roberts, Gerald. Silver. In *Roberts, G., ed.*, 1985, pp. 121–24. [G: Global]

Robinson, D. The Economic System in the UK: Government and Pay. In *Morris, D., ed.*, 1985, pp. 333–65. [G: U.K.]

Rosner, Peter, et al. Lohnzurückhaltung bei fixen und flexiblen Wechselkursen. (Wage Restraint under Fixed and Variable Exchange Rates. With English summary.) *Kredit Kapital*, 1985, *18*(3), pp. 299–319.

Scherer, Peter. Continuity and Change in Australian Wages Policy. *Australian Econ. Rev.*, 3rd Quarter, Spring 1985, (71), pp. 53–67.
[G: Australia]

Schouten, D. B. J. Business Cycle and Wage Policy. *De Economist*, 1985, *133*(3), pp. 265–84.
[G: Netherlands]

Van Kooten, G. C. and Schmitz, Andrew. Commodity Price Stabilization: The Price Uncertainty Case. *Can. J. Econ.*, May 1985, *18*(2), pp. 426–34. [G: Canada]

Wörgötter, Andreas. Output Effects of Incomes Policies in Open Economies. *Z. Wirtschaft. Sozialwissen.*, 1985, *105*(2/3), pp. 387–406.
[G: Austria]

Yohe, Gary W. Improving Tax-based Incomes Policies: The Lessons of the Environmental Literature. *Public Finance Quart.*, April 1985, *13*(2), pp. 183–205.

134 Inflation and Deflation

1340 General

Agbonyitor, Alberto D. K. Recurrent Expenditure Commitment, External Imbalance, Devaluation and Inflation in the Developing Economies. *J. Econ. Devel.*, December 1985, *10*(2), pp. 87–99. [G: LDCs]

Arak, Marcelle and Kreicher, Lawrence. The Real Rate of Interest: Inferences from the New U.K. Indexed Gilts. *Int. Econ. Rev.*, June 1985, *26*(2), pp. 399–408. [G: U.K.]

Artis, Michael J. and Lewis, M. K. Inflation in the United Kingdom. In *Argy, V. E. and Neville, J. W., eds.*, 1985, pp. 200–220.
[G: U.K.]

Artus, Patrick and Nasse, Philippe. Exchange Rates, Prices, Wages, and the Current Account in France. In *de Ménil, G. and Westphal, U., eds.*, 1985, pp. 147–80. [G: France]

Bismut, Claude and Kröger, Jürgen. The Dilemmas of Economic Policy in France and Germany: Trade-offs between Inflation, Unemployment, and the Current Account. In *de Ménil, G. and Westphal, U., eds.*, 1985, pp. 303–47. [G: France; W. Germany]

Bodie, Zvi; Kane, Alex and McDonald, Robert L. Inflation and the Role of Bonds in Investor Portfolios. In *Friedman, B. M., ed.*, 1985, pp. 167–94. [G: U.S.]

de Boissieu, Christian. Eléments d'une analyse de la rigidité à la baisse des taux d'intérêt. (Elements for an Analysis of Downward Stickiness in Interest Rates. With English summary.) *Écon. Appl.*, 1985, *38*(1), pp. 193–209.
[G: U.S.]

Booth, G. Geoffrey; Duggan, James E. and Koveos, Peter E. Deviations from Purchasing Power Parity, Relative Inflation, and Exchange Rates: The Recent Experience. *Financial Rev.*, May 1985, *20*(2), pp. 195–218. [G: OECD]

Brunner, Lawrence P.; Beladi, Hamid and Zuberi, Habib A. Inflation and Indexation: An Empirical Approach. *Southern Econ. J.*, July 1985, *52*(1), pp. 250–64. [G: U.S.]

Cameron, David R. Does Government Cause Inflation? Taxes, Spending, and Deficits. In *Lindberg, L. N. and Maier, C. S., eds.*, 1985, pp. 224–79. [G: OECD]

Campolongo, Alberto. La lira in settant'anni. (The Lira through Seventy Years of Vicissitude. With English summary.) *Bancaria*, March 1985, *41*(3), pp. 285–87. [G: Italy]

Canavese, Alfredo J. and Montuschi, Luisa. Inflation and the Financing of Alternative Development Strategies. In *Gutowski, A.; Arnaudo, A. A. and Scharrer, H.-E., eds.*, 1985, pp. 115–36. [G: Argentina]

Carline, Derek. Trade Unions and Wages. In *Carline, D., et al.*, 1985, pp. 186–232. [G: U.K.; U.S.]

Challen, D. W. Wages, Unemployment and Inflation. In *Argy, V. E. and Neville, J. W., eds.*, 1985, pp. 346–69. [G: Australia]

Chang, Rosita P.; Lord, Blair M. and Rhee, S. Ghon. Inflation-caused Wealth-transfer: A Case of the Insurance Industry. *J. Risk Ins.*, December 1985, 52(4), pp. 627–43. [G: U.S.]

Chisari, Omar O. Growth, Inflation and Rules of Active and Passive Mark-up Factor. *Econ. Notes*, 1985, (2), pp. 57–67.

Clark, Peter B. Inflation and Unemployment in the United States: Recent Experience and Policies. In *Argy, V. E. and Neville, J. W., eds.*, 1985, pp. 221–48. [G: U.S.]

Common, Michael S. Testing for Rational Expectations with Qualitative Survey Data. *Manchester Sch. Econ. Soc. Stud.*, June 1985, 53(2), pp. 138–48.

Contador, Claudio R. Inflation and Recession: Fate or Political Choice in Brazil Today? In *Salazar-Carrillo, J. and Fendt, R., Jr., eds.*, 1985, pp. 149–66. [G: Brazil]

Cosimano, Thomas F. Erratic Monetary Policy and Price Variability. *J. Macroecon.*, Summer 1985, 7(3), pp. 313–31.

Crouch, Colin. Conditions for Trade Union Wage Restraint. In *Lindberg, L. N. and Maier, C. S., eds.*, 1985, pp. 105–39. [G: OECD]

Danziger, Sheldon. Inflation Vulnerability, Income, and Wealth of the Elderly, 1969–1979: Comment. In *David, M. and Smeeding, T., eds.*, 1985, pp. 172–77. [G: U.S.]

Day, Theodore E. Expected Inflation and the Real Rate of Interest. *J. Banking Finance*, December 1985, 9(4), pp. 491–98.

Eckstein, Otto. Disinflation. In *Feiwel, G. R., ed. (I)*, 1985, pp. 297–323.
[G: Selected Countries]

Engle, Charles. Reliability of Policy Announcements and the Effects of Monetary Policy. *Europ. Econ. Rev.*, November 1985, 29(2), pp. 137–55.

Fullerton, Don; Lyon, Andrew B. and Rosen, Richard J. Uncertainty, Welfare Cost and the "Adaptability" of U.S. Corporate Taxes. In *Førsund, F. R. and Honkapohja, S., eds.*, 1985, pp. 131–45. [G: U.S.]

Green, Reginald Herbold. The Republic of Ireland: The Impact of Imported Inflation. In *Griffith-Jones, S. and Harvey, C., eds.*, 1985, pp. 145–68. [G: Ireland]

Green, Reginald Herbold and Kamori, D. J. M. Imported Inflation, Global Price Changes and Economic Crises in Tanzania, 1970–1982. In *Griffith-Jones, S. and Harvey, C., eds.*, 1985, pp. 52–74. [G: Tanzania]

Gregory, R. G. and Smith, Ralph E. Unemploy-

ment, Inflation and Job Creation Policies in Australia. In *Argy, V. E. and Neville, J. W., eds.*, 1985, pp. 325–45. [G: Australia]

Griffith-Jones, Stephany and Harvey, Charles. World Prices and Development: Conclusions. In *Griffith-Jones, S. and Harvey, C., eds.*, 1985, pp. 311–49. [G: Selected LDCs]

Gruber, Martin J. Inflation and the Role of Bonds in Investor Portfolios: Comment. In *Friedman, B. M., ed.*, 1985, pp. 194–96. [G: U.S.]

Haberler, Gottfried. International Aspects of U.S. Inflation. In *Haberler, G.*, 1985, pp. 311–34. [G: U.S.]

Haberler, Gottfried. Oil, Inflation, Recession and the International Monetary System. In *Haberler, G.*, 1985, pp. 335–47.

Haberler, Gottfried. The Problem of Stagflation. In *Haberler, G.*, 1985, pp. 349–62. [G: U.S.]

Hagens, John B. and Russell, R. Robert. Testing for the Effectiveness of Wage–Price Controls: An Application to the Carter Program. *Amer. Econ. Rev.*, March 1985, 75(1), pp. 191–207. [G: U.S.]

Hamada, Koichi. Lessons from the Macroeconomic Performance of the Japanese Economy. In *Argy, V. E. and Neville, J. W., eds.*, 1985, pp. 181–99. [G: Japan]

Haque, M. Badrul. Monetary Policy and Its Effects on Inflation. *Revue Écon.*, November 1985, 36(6), pp. 1271–99.

Harvey, Charles. World Prices and Development: Malawi. In *Griffith-Jones, S. and Harvey, C., eds.*, 1985, pp. 93–112. [G: Malawi]

Hausmann, Ricardo and Marquez, G. World Prices and National Development: The Case of Venezuela. In *Griffith-Jones, S. and Harvey, C., eds.*, 1985, pp. 240–59. [G: Venezuela]

Hibbs, Douglas A., Jr. Inflation, Political Support, and Macroeconomic Policy. In *Lindberg, L. N. and Maier, C. S., eds.*, 1985, pp. 175–95. [G: OECD]

Hinshaw, Randall. Inflation, Exchange Rates, and Domestic Policy: A Restatement. In *[Bloomfield, A. I.]*, 1985, pp. 57–67.

Hiraki, Takato. Testing the Proxy Effect Hypothesis of Inflation on Stock Returns for the Japanese Market. *Quart. J. Bus. Econ.*, Spring 1985, 24(2), pp. 73–87. [G: Japan]

Hirschman, Albert O. Reflections on the Latin American Experience. In *Lindberg, L. N. and Maier, C. S., eds.*, 1985, pp. 53–77.
[G: Latin America]

Hochman, Shalom and Palmon, Oded. The Impact of Inflation on the Aggregate Debt-Asset Ratio. *J. Finance*, September 1985, 40(4), pp. 1115–25.

Hurd, Michael D. and Shoven, John B. Inflation Vulnerability, Income, and Wealth of the Elderly, 1969–1979. In *David, M. and Smeeding, T., eds.*, 1985, pp. 125–72. [G: U.S.]

James, Christopher; Koreisha, Sergio and Partch, M. Megan. A VARMA Analysis of the Causal Relations among Stock Returns, Real Output, and Nominal Interest Rates. *J. Finance*, December 1985, 40(5), pp. 1375–84. [G: U.S.]

Jeanneney, Sylviane Guillaumont. La stabilisation des prix relatifs, objectif de la politique monétaire. (The Stabilising of Relative Prices, Goal of Monetary Policy. With English summary.) *Écon. Appl.*, 1985, *38*(1), pp. 309–23.

Jha, L. K. Demand Problem in Indian Economy. In *Jha, L. K.*, 1985, pp. 60–69. [G: India]

Jha, L. K. Development without Inflation. In *Jha, L. K.*, 1985, pp. 110–19. [G: India]

Jha, L. K. Fighting Inflation with Growth. In *Jha, L. K.*, 1985, pp. 104–09. [G: India]

Jha, L. K. How to Check Inflation without Stopping Growth? In *Jha, L. K.*, 1985, pp. 85–90. [G: India]

Jha, L. K. Inflation, Unemployment, and Growth. In *Jha, L. K.*, 1985, pp. 120–29. [G: India]

Jha, L. K. Inflation: A Non-monetary Approach. In *Jha, L. K.*, 1985, pp. 91–103. [G: India]

Jha, L. K. Strategy against Inflation. In *Jha, L. K.*, 1985, pp. 70–84. [G: India]

Jianakoplos, Nancy Ammon. Inflation and the Accumulation of Wealth by Older Households, 1966–1976. In *Hendershott, P. H., ed.*, 1985, pp. 151–80. [G: U.S.]

Keohane, Robert O. The International Politics of Inflation. In *Lindberg, L. N. and Maier, C. S., eds.*, 1985, pp. 78–104. [G: OECD]

Kim, In June. Imported Inflation and the Development of the Korean Economy. In *Griffith-Jones, S. and Harvey, C., eds.*, 1985, pp. 169–95. [G: S. Korea]

Kindleberger, Charles P. A Structural View of the German Inflation. In *Kindleberger, C. P.*, 1985, pp. 247–66. [G: Germany]

Klein, Lawrence R. Did Mainstream Econometric Models Fail to Anticipate the Inflationary Surge? In *Feiwel, G. R., ed. (I)*, 1985, pp. 289–96. [G: U.S.]

Klein, Rudolf. Public Expenditure in an Inflationary World. In *Lindberg, L. N. and Maier, C. S., eds.*, 1985, pp. 196–223. [G: OECD]

Koskela, Erkki and Virén, Matti. On the Role of Inflation in Consumption Function. *Weltwirtsch. Arch.*, 1985, *121*(2), pp. 252–60. [G: U.K.]

Krishnamurty, K. Inflation and Growth: A Model for India. In *Krishnamurty, K. and Pandit, V.*, 1985, pp. 16–111. [G: India]

Kröger, Jürgen and Pauly, Peter. Exchange Rates, Prices, Wages, and the Current Account in Germany. In *de Ménil, G. and Westphal, U., eds.*, 1985, pp. 181–218. [G: W. Germany]

Kurukulasuriya, G. The Impact of Imported Inflation on National Development: Sri Lanka. In *Griffith-Jones, S. and Harvey, C., eds.*, 1985, pp. 75–92. [G: Sri Lanka]

Landskroner, Yoram and Ruthenberg, David. Optimal Bank Behavior under Uncertain Inflation. *J. Finance*, September 1985, *40*(4), pp. 1159–71.

Macedo, Roberto. Remarks on Brazilian Inflation and Wage Policy. In *Salazar-Carrillo, J. and Fendt, R., Jr., eds.*, 1985, pp. 170–76. [G: Brazil]

Maier, Charles S. Inflation and Stagnation as Politics and History. In *Lindberg, L. N. and Maier, C. S., eds.*, 1985, pp. 3–24. [G: OECD]

Maier, Charles S. and Lindberg, Leon N. Alternatives for Future Crises. In *Lindberg, L. N. and Maier, C. S., eds.*, 1985, pp. 567–88.

Mandelker, Gershon and Tandon, Kishore. Common Stock Returns, Real Activity, Money, and Inflation: Some International Evidence. *J. Int. Money Finance*, June 1985, *4*(2), pp. 267–86. [G: Selected OECD]

Marston, Richard C. and Turnovsky, Stephen J. Macroeconomic Stabilization through Taxation and Indexation: The Use of Firm-Specific Information. *J. Monet. Econ.*, November 1985, *16*(3), pp. 375–95.

McClam, W. D. and Andersen, P. S. Adjustment Performance of Small, Open Economies: Some International Comparisons. In *Argy, V. E. and Neville, J. W., eds.*, 1985, pp. 249–77. [G: Austria; Canada; Belgium; Sweden]

McClure, J. Harold, Jr. Dollar Appreciation and the Reagan Disinflation. In *Arndt, S. W.; Sweeney, R. J. and Willett, T. D., eds.*, 1985, pp. 267–72. [G: U.S.]

de Ménil, Georges and Westphal, Uwe. The Transmission of International Disturbances to the French and German Economies, 1972–1980. In *de Ménil, G. and Westphal, U., eds.*, 1985, pp. 349–79. [G: France; W. Germany]

Mishalani, Philip. Imported Inflation and Imported Growth: The Case of Tunisia's Studied Postponement. In *Griffith-Jones, S. and Harvey, C., eds.*, 1985, pp. 260–84. [G: Tunisia]

Mishalani, Philip. Jordan: The Case of Inevitable Imported Inflation in the 1970s. In *Griffith-Jones, S. and Harvey, C., eds.*, 1985, pp. 285–310. [G: Jordan]

Mohr, P. J. Monetary Policy and Inflation in South Africa: Reflections on the Final Report of the De Kock Commission. *J. Stud. Econ. Econometrics*, November 1985, (23), pp. 3–27. [G: S. Africa]

Morley, Samuel A. Inflation and Recession: Fate or Political Choice in Brazil Today: Comments. In *Salazar-Carrillo, J. and Fendt, R., Jr., eds.*, 1985, pp. 167–69. [G: Brazil]

Myers, Stewart C.; Kolbe, A. Lawrence and Tye, William B. Inflation and Rate of Return Regulation. In *Keeler, T. E., ed.*, 1985, pp. 83–119. [G: U.S.]

Newlyn, W. T. The Role of the Public Sector in the Mobilisation and Allocation of Financial Resources. In *Gutowski, A.; Arnaudo, A. A. and Scharrer, H.-E., eds.*, 1985, pp. 98–114. [G: Selected LDCs]

Nove, Alec. Money Supply and Inflation in the Soviet Union. In *[Levcik, F.]*, 1985, pp. 149–56. [G: U.S.S.R.]

Ojha, P. D. Inflation Control and Price Regulation. In *Mongia, J. N., ed.*, 1985, pp. 239–89. [G: India]

Plaut, Steven E. The Likud Years: 1977–83. In *Levinson, P. and Landau, P., eds.*, 1985, pp. 31–37. [G: Israel]

Portes, Richard. The Control of Inflation: Lessons

from East European Experience. In *Bornstein, M., ed.*, 1985, pp. 346–65.   [G: E. Europe]

Sadler, Peter. World Prices and Development: Kuwait. In *Griffith-Jones, S. and Harvey, C., eds.*, 1985, pp. 220–39.   [G: Kuwait]

Salvati, Michele. The Italian Inflation. In *Lindberg, L. N. and Maier, C. S., eds.*, 1985, pp. 509–63.   [G: Italy; U.K.; France; W. Germany]

Sharkansky, Ira. Who Gets What amidst High Inflation: Winners and Losers in the Israeli Budget, 1978–84. *Public Budg. Finance*, Winter 1985, 5(4), pp. 64–74.   [G: Israel]

Sjaastad, Larry A. Exchange Rate Regimes and the Real Rate of Interest. In *Kim, K. S. and Ruccio, D. F., eds.*, 1985, pp. 163–87.   [G: Chile; Uruguay]

Taylor, Lance. A Stagnationist Model of Economic Growth. *Cambridge J. Econ.*, December 1985, 9(4), pp. 383–403.

Valentine, T. J. Indexed Securities. In *Argy, V. E. and Neville, J. W., eds.*, 1985, pp. 370–84.   [G: Australia]

Virts, John R. and Wilson, George W. The Determinants of Rising Health Care Costs: Some Empirical Assessments. In *Meyer, J. A., ed.*, 1985, pp. 67–95.   [G: U.S.]

Willett, Thomas D.; Khan, Waseem and Der Hovanessian, Aïda. Interest Rate Changes, Inflationary Expectations and Exchange Rate Overshooting: The Dollar–DM Rate. In *Arndt, S. W.; Sweeney, R. J. and Willett, T. D., eds.*, 1985, pp. 49–71.   [G: U.S.; W. Germany]

Willms, Manfred and Karsten, Ingo. Government Policies towards Inflation and Unemployment in West Germany. In *Argy, V. E. and Neville, J. W., eds.*, 1985, pp. 153–80.   [G: W. Germany]

Woolley, John T. Central Banks and Inflation. In *Lindberg, L. N. and Maier, C. S., eds.*, 1985, pp. 318–48.   [G: OECD]

Zweifel, Peter. Individual Choice in Social Health Insurance: A Curb on Inflation in the Health Care Sector? Evidence from Switzerland. In *Terny, G. and Culyer, A. J., eds.*, 1985, pp. 303–18.   [G: Switzerland]

Zysman, John. Inflation and the Politics of Supply. In *Lindberg, L. N. and Maier, C. S., eds.*, 1985, pp. 140–71.   [G: W. Germany; U.K.; France; Japan; U.S.]

1342 Inflation Theories; Studies Illustrating Inflation Theories

Abraham, Katharine G. Shifting Norms in Wage Determination: Comment. *Brookings Pap. Econ. Act.*, 1985, (2), pp. 600–605. [G: U.S.]

Ahking, Francis W. and Miller, Stephen M. The Relationship between Government Deficits, Money Growth, and Inflation. *J. Macroecon.*, Fall 1985, 7(4), pp. 447–67.   [G: U.S.]

Aizenman, Joshua and Frenkel, Jacob A. On the Tradeoff between Wage Indexation and Foreign Exchange Intervention. *Weltwirtsch. Arch.*, 1985, 121(1), pp. 1–17.

Aizenman, Joshua and Frenkel, Jacob A. Optimal Wage Indexation, Foreign Exchange Intervention, and Monetary Policy. *Amer. Econ. Rev.*, June 1985, 75(3), pp. 402–23.

Ambler, Steven and McKinnon, Ronald I. U.S. Monetary Policy and the Exchange Rate: Comment [A Critical Appraisal of McKinnon's World Money Supply Hypothesis]. *Amer. Econ. Rev.*, June 1985, 75(3), pp. 557–59.   [G: U.S.]

Arndt, H. W. The Origins of Structuralism. *World Devel.*, February 1985, 13(2), pp. 151–59.   [G: LDCs]

Artus, Jacques R. and Young, John H. Fixed and Flexible Exchange Rates: A Renewal of the Debate. In *Adams, J., ed.*, 1985, pp. 250–85.

Artus, Patrick. L'indexation des salaires: une-optique de stabilisation macro-économique. (Price Indexation of Wages: A Stabilization Approach. With English summary.) *Revue Écon.*, March 1985, 36(2), pp. 291–320. [G: France; W. Germany; U.K.]

Artus, Patrick. La politique monétaire en économie ouverte avec imparfaite mobilité des capitaux et réaction des autorités sur le marché des changes. (Monetary Policy in an Open Economy with Imperfect Capital Mobility and Central Bank Reaction on the Foreign Exchange Market. With English summary.) *Finance*, June 1985, 6(1), pp. 71–101.

Atkinson, Paul and Chouraqui, Jean-Claude. The Origins of High Real Interest Rates. *OECD Econ. Stud.*, Autumn 1985, (5), pp. 7–55.   [G: OECD]

Backus, David and Driffill, John. Inflation and Reputation. *Amer. Econ. Rev.*, June 1985, 75(3), pp. 530–38.

Backus, David and Driffill, John. Policy Credibility and Unemployment in the U.K. In *Currie, D., ed.*, 1985, pp. 3–16.   [G: U.K.]

Baglioni, Angelo. Alle origini dell'accondiscendenza monetaria verso l'inflazione. (At the Origins of Monetary Accommodation toward Inflation. With English summary.) *Giorn. Econ.*, Sept.-Oct. 1985, 44(9–10), pp. 545–65.

Barry, Brian. Does Democracy Cause Inflation? Political Ideas of Some Economists. In *Lindberg, L. N. and Maier, C. S., eds.*, 1985, pp. 280–317.   [G: OECD]

Baxter, Marianne. The Role of Expectations in Stabilization Policy. *J. Monet. Econ.*, May 1985, 15(3), pp. 343–62.   [G: Chile; Argentina]

Beleza, Luís Miguel and Cartaxo, Rui. Inflation and the Current Account in Portugal. *Economia (Portugal)*, January 1985, 9(1), pp. 195–205.   [G: Portugal]

Belongia, Michael T. The Impact of Inflation on the Real Income of U.S. Farmers: Discussion. *Amer. J. Agr. Econ.*, May 1985, 67(2), pp. 398–99.   [G: U.S.]

Beltensperger, Ernst. Disinflation—The Swiss Experience 1973-1983. *Z. Wirtschaft. Sozialwissen.*, 1985, 105(2/3), pp. 271–93.   [G: Switzerland]

Benderly, Jason and Zwick, Burton. Inflation, Real Balances, Output, and Real Stock Returns

[Stock Returns, Real Activity, Inflation, and Money]. *Amer. Econ. Rev.*, December 1985, *75*(5), pp. 1115–23. [G: U.S.]

Benderly, Jason and Zwick, Burton. Money, Unemployment and Inflation. *Rev. Econ. Statist.*, February 1985, *67*(1), pp. 139–43. [G: U.S.]

Bental, Benjamin. Welfare Analysis of Income Distributions: A Neoclassical Approach. In *Maital, S. and Lipnowski, I., eds.*, 1985, pp. 153–61.

Beranek, William; Humphrey, Thomas M. and Timberlake, Richard H., Jr. Fisher, Thornton, and the Analysis of the Inflation Premium: A Note. *J. Money, Credit, Banking*, August 1985, *17*(3), pp. 370–77.

Blad, Michael and Kirman, Alan P. L'évolution à long terme d'un modéle d'équilibre avec rationnement. (With English summary.) *Revue Écon. Polit.*, Nov.-Dec. 1985, *95*(6), pp. 795–808.

Bomberger, William A. and Makinen, Gail E. Inflation Uncertainty and the Demand for Money in Hyperinflation. *Atlantic Econ. J.*, July 1985, *13*(2), pp. 12–20. [G: Europe]

de Bouissieu, Christian. Some Monetary and Financial Aspects of the Disinflation Process. *Z. Wirtschaft. Sozialwissen.*, 1985, *105*(2/3), pp. 133–53. [G: OECD]

Bredahl, Maury E. The Effects of Inflation on the Welfare and Performance of Agriculture: Discussion [The Impact of Inflation on the Real Income of U.S. Farmers]. *Amer. J. Agr. Econ.*, May 1985, *67*(2), pp. 400–401. [G: U.S.]

Brinner, Roger E. and Kline, Kenneth J. A New Market Realism: Wage Moderation. *Challenge*, Sept./Oct. 1985, *28*(4), pp. 27–29. [G: U.S.]

Britton, Andrew J. C. Disinflation in the United Kingdom 1979–1983. *Z. Wirtschaft. Sozialwissen.*, 1985, *105*(2/3), pp. 295–309. [G: U.K.]

Brocato, Joe. Persistence under Alternative Forms of the Lucas Supply Function: Implications for the Lucas–Sargent Price Confusion Hypothesis and Barro-Type Money Models. *Quart. Rev. Econ. Bus.*, Spring 1985, *25*(1), pp. 28–39. [G: U.S.]

Brus, Wlodzimierz and Laski, Kazimierz. Repressed Inflation and Second Economy under Central Planning. In *Gaertner, W. and Wenig, A., eds.*, 1985, pp. 377–88.

Buehler, John E. The Specific Role of Interest in Financial and Economic Analysis under Inflation: Discussion. *Amer. J. Agr. Econ.*, May 1985, *67*(2), pp. 396–97.

Buiter, Willem H. and Miller, Marcus. Costs and Benefits of an Anti-inflationary Policy: Questions and Issues. In *Argy, V. E. and Neville, J. W., eds.*, 1985, pp. 11–38.

Camion, Caty and Levasseur, Michel. Analyse financière des entreprises, systèmes fiscaux et inflation anticipée: La valeur économique des nombres comptables. (Financial Analysis of Firms, Taxation Systems and Anticipated Inflation. The Economic Value of Accounting Numbers. With English summary.) *Écon. Soc.*, December 1985, *19*(12), pp. 129–43.

Carmichael, Benoît. Anticipated Inflation and the Stock Market. *Can. J. Econ.*, May 1985, *18*(2), pp. 285–93.

Carmichael, Jeffrey; Fahrer, Jerome and Hawkins, John. Some Macroeconomic Implications of Wage Indexation: A Survey. In *Argy, V. E. and Neville, J. W., eds.*, 1985, pp. 78–102.

Caskey, John P. Modeling the Formation of Price Expectations: A Bayesian Approach. *Amer. Econ. Rev.*, September 1985, *75*(4), pp. 768–76. [G: U.S.]

Cecchetti, Stephen G. Staggered Contracts and the Frequency of Price Adjustment. *Quart. J. Econ.*, Supp. 1985, *100*, pp. 935–59. [G: U.S.]

Chamley, Christophe. On a Simple Rule for the Optimal Inflation Rate in Second Best Taxation. *J. Public Econ.*, February 1985, *26*(1), pp. 35–50.

Chernomas, Bob. A Malthusian Basis for Post-Keynesian Stagflation Theory and Policy: A Marxist Analysis. *Rev. Radical Polit. Econ.*, Spring and Summer 1985, *17*(1/2), pp. 230–40.

Chopra, Ajai. The Speed of Adjustment of the Inflation Rate in Developing Countries: A Study of Inertia. *Int. Monet. Fund Staff Pap.*, December 1985, *32*(4), pp. 693–733. [G: LDCs]

Chouraqui, Jean-Claude. Les Déficits Publics dans les Pays de l'OCDE: Causes, Conséquences et Remèdes. (Public Sector Deficits in OECD Countries: Causes, Consequences, and Policy Reactions. With English summary.) *Aussenwirtschaft*, May 1985, *40*(1/2), pp. 15–52. [G: OECD]

Clem, Andrew G. Commodity Price Volatility: Trends during 1975–84. *Mon. Lab. Rev.*, June 1985, *108*(6), pp. 17–21.

Clements, R. T. Savings in New Zealand during Inflationary Times: Measurement, Determinants, and Implications. *J. Bus. Econ. Statist.*, July 1985, *3*(3), pp. 188–208. [G: New Zealand]

Coe, David T. Nominal Wages, the Nairu and Wage Flexibility. *OECD Econ. Stud.*, Autumn 1985, (5), pp. 87–126. [G: OECD]

Coe, David T. and Gagliardi, Francesco. La crescita dei salari nominali: la curva di Phillips in dieci paesi OCSE. (The Nominal Wage Growth: The Phillips Curve in Ten OECD Countries. With English summary.) *Econ. Lavoro*, Oct.-Dec. 1985, *19*(4), pp. 15–34. [G: OECD]

Cohen, Morris. The Inflation Dragon Remains under Control. *Bus. Econ.*, April 1985, *20*(2), pp. 5–11. [G: U.S.]

Corbo, Vittorio. International Prices, Wages and Inflation in an Open Economy: A Chilean Model. *Rev. Econ. Statist.*, November 1985, *67*(4), pp. 564–73. [G: Chile]

Cox, W. Michael. Inflation and Permanent Government Debt. *Fed. Res. Bank Dallas Econ. Rev.*, May 1985, pp. 13–26. [G: U.S.]

Creedy, John and Gemmell, Norman. The Indexation of Taxes and Transfers in Britain. *Man-*

chester Sch. Econ. Soc. Stud., December 1985, *53*(4), pp. 364–84. [G: U.K.]

Daly, Donald J. Inflation, Inflation Accounting and Its Effect, Canadian Manufacturing, 1966–82. *Rev. Income Wealth*, December 1985, *31*(4), pp. 355–74. [G: Canada]

Darrat, Ali F. 'Efficient' Market Testing of the Expectations-adjusted Supply Function Hypothesis for Italy. *Appl. Econ.*, December 1985, *17*(6), pp. 1065–70. [G: Italy]

Darrat, Ali F. Are Budget Deficits and Wage Costs Prime Determinants of Inflation? Another Look at the Evidence from the United States and the United Kingdom. *J. Post Keynesian Econ.*, Winter 1984–85, *7*(2), pp. 177–92. [G: U.S.; U.K.]

Darrat, Ali F. Inflation and Federal Budget Deficits: Some Empirical Results. *Public Finance Quart.*, April 1985, *13*(2), pp. 206–15.

Darrat, Ali F. Inflation in Saudi Arabia: An Econometric Investigation. *J. Econ. Stud.*, 1985, *12*(4), pp. 41–51. [G: Saudi Arabia]

Darrat, Ali F. Inflationary Expectations and Interest Rates à la Patinkin's General Equilibrium Model. *Amer. Econ.*, Fall 1985, *29*(2), pp. 55–56.

Darrat, Ali F. Inflationary Surprises and Real Economic Activity in Germany: Some Tests Based on 'Efficient Market' Expectations. *Kredit Kapital*, 1985, *18*(2), pp. 230–39. [G: W. Germany]

Darrat, Ali F. The Monetary Explanation of Inflation: The Experience of Three Major OPEC Economies. *J. Econ. Bus.*, August 1985, *37*(3), pp. 209–21. [G: Libya; Nigeria; Saudi Arabia]

Darrat, Ali F. Unanticipated Inflation and Real Output: The Canadian Evidence. *Can. J. Econ.*, February 1985, *18*(1), pp. 146–55. [G: Canada]

Davidson, Lawrence S. and Hafer, R. W. Relative Price Variability: Evidence from Supply and Demand Events. *J. Monet. Econ.*, May 1985, *15*(3), pp. 333–41. [G: U.S.]

Dawkins, Peter and Wooden, Mark. Labour Utilization and Wage Inflation in Australia: An Empirical Examination. *Econ. Rec.*, June 1985, *61*(173), pp. 516–21. [G: Australia]

Domínguez Martínez, José M. and Sánchez Maldonado, José. La política de dirección de la demanda y la inestabilidad de la curva de Phillips: Una visión de conjunto. (With English summary.) *Revista Española Econ.*, 1985, *2*(2), pp. 203–67.

Downes, Andrew. Inflation in Barbados: An Econometric Investigation. *Econ. Develop. Cult. Change*, April 1985, *33*(3), pp. 521–32. [G: Barbados]

Drazen, Allan. Tight Money and Inflation: Further Results. *J. Monet. Econ.*, January 1985, *15*(1), pp. 113–20.

Dreizzen, Julio. Fragilidad financiera y sistemas de crédito indexado. (With English summary.) *Desarrollo Econ.*, April–June 1985, *25*(97), pp. 3–24.

Driskill, Robert and Sheffrin, Steven M. The "Patman Effect" and Stabilization Policy.

Quart. J. Econ., February 1985, *100*(1), pp. 149–63.

Duggan, James E. and Clem, Andrew G. Input Prices and Cost Inflation in Three Manufacturing Industries. *Mon. Lab. Rev.*, May 1985, *108*(5), pp. 16–21. [G: U.S.]

Dwyer, Gerald P., Jr. Money, Deficits, and Inflation: A Comment. *Carnegie-Rochester Conf. Ser. Public Policy*, Spring 1985, *22*, pp. 197–205. [G: U.S.]

Dye, Richard F. Payroll Tax Effects on Wage Growth. *Eastern Econ. J.*, April-June 1985, *11*(2), pp. 89–100. [G: U.S.]

Ebrill, Liam P. Nominal Indexation of Taxes, Wages, and Bonds. *Finance Develop.*, September 1985, *22*(3), pp. 42–44.

Economou, George E. More Efficient Economic Policies of Disinflation: The Case of Greece. *Rech. Écon. Louvain*, 1985, *51*(3–4), pp. 363–80. [G: Greece]

Eden, Benjamin. Indexation and Related Issues: A Review Essay. *J. Monet. Econ.*, September 1985, *16*(2), pp. 259–66.

Edwards, J. S. S. and Keen, M. J. Inflation and Non-neutralities in the Taxation of Corporate Source Income. *Oxford Econ. Pap.*, December 1985, *37*(4), pp. 552–75.

Eichner, Alfred S. Stagflation: Explaining the Inexplicable. In *Eichner, A. S.*, 1985, pp. 113–50. [G: U.S.]

Evans, George. Bottlenecks and the Phillips Curve: A Disaggregated Keynesian Model of Inflation, Output, and Unemployment. *Econ. J.*, June 1985, *95*(378), pp. 345–57.

Fender, John. Counterinflationary Policy in a Unionised Economy with Nonsynchronised Wage Setting: Comment. *Scand. J. Econ.*, 1985, *87*(2), pp. 379–81.

Ferri, Piero. Wage Dynamics and Instability Processes. *Econ. Notes*, 1985, (3), pp. 35–48.

Fethke, Gary. The Conformity of Wage-Indexation Models with "Stylized Facts." *Amer. Econ. Rev.*, September 1985, *75*(4), pp. 856–61. [G: Canada; W. Germany; Japan; U.K.; U.S.]

Fischer, Stanley. Contracts, Credibility and Disinflation. In *Argy, V. E. and Neville, J. W.*, eds., 1985, pp. 39–59. [G: U.S.]

Fischer, Stanley. The Dollar and the Policy Mix: 1985: Comment. *Brookings Pap. Econ. Act.*, 1985, (1), pp. 186–90. [G: U.S.]

Fischer, Stanley. The Problem of Disinflation. *Z. Wirtschaft. Sozialwissen.*, 1985, *105*(2/3), pp. 123–31. [G: U.S.]

Foster, John Bellamy. Monopoly Capital Theory and Stagflation: A Comment [Monopoly, Inflation and Economic Crisis]. *Rev. Radical Polit. Econ.*, Spring and Summer 1985, *17*(1/2), pp. 221–25.

Franz, Wolfgang. Challenges to the German Economy 1973–1983. Supply Shocks, Investment Slowdown, Inflation Variability and the Underutilization of Labor. *Z. Wirtschaft. Sozialwissen.*, 1985, *105*(2/3), pp. 407–30. [G: W. Germany]

Franz, Wolfgang. Nicht-neutrale Effekte der Inflation auf die Preisstruktur: Theoretische

Überlegungen und empirische Resultate. (Non-neutral Effects of Inflation on Relative Price Variability: Theoretical Considerations and Empirical Results. With English summary.) *Jahr. Nationalökon. Statist.*, January 1985, *200*(1), pp. 41–55. [G: W. Germany]

Fratianni, Michele and Nabli, Mustapha. Inflation and Output with Rational Expectations in Open Economies. *Weltwirtsch. Arch.*, 1985, *121*(1), pp. 33–52. [G: Belgium; France; W. Germany; Italy; Netherlands]

Froyen, Richard T. and Waud, Roger N. Demand Variability, Supply Shocks and the Output–Inflation Tradeoff. *Rev. Econ. Statist.*, February 1985, *67*(1), pp. 9–15. [G: U.S.]

Fry, Vanessa C. and Pashardes, Panos. Distributional Aspects of Inflation: Who Has Suffered Most? *Fisc. Stud.*, November 1985, *6*(4), pp. 21–29. [G: U.K.]

Fuggetta, Massimo. L'inflazione in una economia di puro credito: commento. *Stud. Econ.*, 1985, *40*(26), pp. 127–32.

Gahlen, Bernhard. Trend und Zyklus—Aggregat und Struktur. (Trends and Cycles—Structure and the Aggregate. With English summary.) *Jahr. Nationalökon. Statist.*, September 1985, *200*(5), pp. 449–78. [G: W. Germany]

Galasi, Péter and Kertesi, Gábor. Second Economy, Competition, Inflation. *Acta Oecon.*, 1985, *35*(3–4), pp. 269–93.

Galbraith, James K. Using the Presidency to Fight Inflation. *Challenge*, March/April 1985, *28*(1), pp. 19–26. [G: U.S.]

Giannaros, Demetrios S. and Kolluri, Bharat R. Deficit Spending, Money, and Inflation: Some International Empirical Evidence. *J. Macroecon.*, Summer 1985, *7*(3), pp. 401–17. [G: OECD]

Gitlow, Abraham L. Economics Seen Darkly in a Political Mirror. *Rivista Int. Sci. Econ. Com.*, January 1985, *32*(1), pp. 87–98. [G: U.S.; LDCs]

Goldstein, Henry N. and Haynes, Stephen E. U.S. Monetary Policy and the Exchange Rate: Reply [A Critical Appraisal of McKinnon's World Money Supply Hypothesis]. *Amer. Econ. Rev.*, June 1985, *75*(3), pp. 560–61. [G: U.S.]

Gordon, Robert J. Understanding Inflation in the 1980s. *Brookings Pap. Econ. Act.*, 1985, (1), pp. 263–99. [G: U.S.]

Gottlieb, Daniel; Melnick, Rafi and Piterman, Sylvia. Inflationary Expectations in Israel: A Multiple Indicators Approach. *J. Bus. Econ. Statist.*, April 1985, *3*(2), pp. 112–17. [G: Israel]

Graham, Andrew W. M. Inflation and Unemployment. In *Morris, D., ed.*, 1985, pp. 217–48. [G: U.K.]

Granziol, Markus J. Direct Price Controls as a Source of Instability in the Interest Rate/Inflation Rate Relationship. *J. Banking Finance*, June 1985, *9*(2), pp. 275–88. [G: U.S.; Canada; France]

Graziani, Augusto. L'inflazione in una economia di puro credito: Replica. *Stud. Econ.*, 1985, *40*(26), pp. 133–34.

Grönberg, Rolf and Rahmeyer, Fritz. Preis- und Mengenanpassungen in den Konjunkturzyklen der Bundesrepublik Deutschland, 1963–1981. (Price and Quantity Adjustments in the Business Cycles of the Federal Republic of Germany, 1963–1981. With English summary.) *Jahr. Nationalökon. Statist.*, May 1985, *200*(3), pp. 239–61. [G: W. Germany]

Gustafson, Elizabeth F. and Hadley, Lawrence H. An Empirical Analysis of the Distributional Effects of Inflation on Wage Income by Occupation: 1969–1977. *Quart. J. Bus. Econ.*, Autumn 1985, *24*(4), pp. 29–43. [G: U.S.]

Gylfason, Thorvaldur. Counterinflationary Policy in a Unionised Economy with Nonsynchronised Wage Setting: Comment. *Scand. J. Econ.*, 1985, *87*(2), pp. 382–85.

Haberler, Gottfried. Incomes Policies and Inflation: An Analysis of Basic Principles. In *Haberler, G.*, 1985, pp. 267–310.

Hafer, R. W. and Hein, Scott E. On the Accuracy of Time-Series, Interest Rate, and Survey Forecasts of Inflation. *J. Bus.*, October 1985, *58*(4), pp. 377–98. [G: U.S.]

Hall, Robert E. Understanding Inflation in the 1980s: Comment. *Brookings Pap. Econ. Act.*, 1985, (1), pp. 300–301. [G: U.S.]

Hall, S. G.; Henry, S. G. B. and Johns, C. B. Forecasting with a Rational Expectations Model of the UK: A Comment. *Oxford Bull. Econ. Statist.*, November 1985, *47*(4), pp. 337–45. [G: U.K.]

Hamilton, James D. Uncovering Financial Market Expectations of Inflation. *J. Polit. Econ.*, December 1985, *93*(6), pp. 1224–41. [G: U.S.]

Hamilton, James D. and Whiteman, Charles H. The Observable Implications of Self-fulfilling Expectations. *J. Monet. Econ.*, November 1985, *16*(3), pp. 353–73.

Handa, Jagdish and Okiyama, Yukio. Inflation in a Large, Open Economy: The Scandinavian Model and the Japanese Economy. *Hitotsubashi J. Econ.*, June 1985, *26*(1), pp. 83–97. [G: Japan]

Hanson, James A. Inflation and Imported Input Prices in Some Inflationary Latin American Economies. *J. Devel. Econ.*, August 1985, *18*(2–3), pp. 395–410. [G: Argentina; Brazil; Chile; Colomiba; Uruguay]

Hasunuz, Zaman. Indexation—An Islamic Evaluation. *J. Res. Islamic Econ.*, Winter 1985, *2*(2), pp. 31–53.

Haynes, Stephen E. and Stone, Joe A. A Neglected Method of Separating Demand and Supply in Time Series Regression. *J. Bus. Econ. Statist.*, July 1985, *3*(3), pp. 238–43. [G: U.S.]

Herbst, Anthony F. Hedging against Price Index Inflation with Futures Contracts. *J. Futures Markets*, Winter 1985, *5*(4), pp. 489–504. [G: U.S.]

Hill, John K. and Smith, Scott L. The Political Timing of Errors in Inflation Forecasts. *Public Choice*, 1985, *46*(2), pp. 215–20. [G: U.S.]

Hirsch, Albert A. An Analysis of Disinflation:

1980–83. *Bus. Econ.*, January 1985, *20*(1), pp. 21–27. [G: U.S.]

Hoffman, Dennis L. and Schlagenhauf, Don E. Real Interest Rates, Anticipated Inflation, and Unanticipated Money: A Multi-country Study. *Rev. Econ. Statist.*, May 1985, *67*(2), pp. 284–96. [G: U.K.; W. Germany; Canada; U.S.]

Holder, Carlos and Worrell, DeLisle. A Model of Price Formation for Small Economies: Three Caribbean Examples. *J. Devel. Econ.*, August 1985, *18*(2–3), pp. 411–28. [G: Barbados; Jamaica; Trinidad and Tobago]

Honig, Solomon. Comparisons between Estimated and Simulated Phillips Curve: A Computer–Student Interaction. In *Brown, R. C., ed.*, 1985, pp. 361–74.

Howell, Craig and Thomas, William. Inflation Remained Low during 1984. *Mon. Lab. Rev.*, April 1985, *108*(4), pp. 3–9. [G: U.S.]

Hudson, John. Inflation and Unemployment Aversion. *Econ. J.*, Supplement 1985, *95*, pp. 148–50. [G: U.K.]

Humphrey, Thomas M. The Early History of the Phillips Curve. *Fed. Res. Bank Richmond Econ. Rev.*, Sept./Oct. 1985, *71*(5), pp. 17–24.

Humphrey, Thomas M. The Evolution and Policy Implications of Phillips Curve Analysis. *Fed. Res. Bank Richmond Econ. Rev.*, Mar./Apr. 1985, *71*(2), pp. 3–22.

Hvidding, James M. Models of Inflation Expectations Formation: A Comment. *J. Money, Credit, Banking*, Part 1, Nov. 1985, *17*(4), pp. 534–38. [G: U.S.]

Hvidding, James M. On the Rationality of Household Inflation Expectations. *Quart. J. Bus. Econ.*, Summer 1985, *24*(3), pp. 41–66. [G: U.S.]

Hylleberg, Svend and Paldam, Martin. Price and Wages in the OECD Area 1913–1980—A Study of the Time Series Evidence. *Z. Wirtschaft. Sozialwissen.*, 1985, *105*(2/3), pp. 193–221. [G: OECD]

Ihori, Toshihiro. On the Welfare Cost of Permanent Inflation. *J. Money, Credit, Banking*, May 1985, *17*(2), pp. 220–31.

Ihori, Toshihiro and Kurosaka, Yoshio. Fiscal Policies, Government's Deficits and Capital Formation. *Econ. Stud. Quart.*, August 1985, *36*(2), pp. 106–20.

Ilmakunnas, Pekka and Tsurumi, Hiroki. Testing the Lucas Hypothesis on Output–Inflation Trade-offs. *J. Bus. Econ. Statist.*, January 1985, *3*(1), pp. 43–53. [G: U.S.]

Ingberg, Mikael. Teemailtapäivä: verotus rakenne- ja suhdannepolitiikan välineenä. Näkökohtia veropaineinflaatiosta. (Some Remarks on Tax-induced Inflation. With English summary.) *Kansant. Aikak.*, 1985, *81*(1), pp. 25–39. [G: Finland]

Issing, Otmar. Disinflation: West European Experiences: An Introduction. *Z. Wirtschaft. Sozialwissen.*, 1985, *105*(2/3), pp. 117–22. [G: U.S.; W. Europe]

Ize, Alain and Salas, Javier. Prices and Output in the Mexican Economy: Empirical Testing of Alternative Hypotheses. *J. Devel. Econ.*, April 1985, *17*(3), pp. 175–99. [G: Mexico]

Jackman, Richard. Counterinflationary Policy in a Unionised Economy with Nonsynchronised Wage Setting. *Scand. J. Econ.*, 1985, *87*(2), pp. 357–78.

Jaffe, Jeffrey F. Inflation, the Interest Rate, and the Required Return on Equity. *J. Finan. Quant. Anal.*, March 1985, *20*(1), pp. 29–44.

Jung, Woo S. Output–Inflation Tradeoffs in Industrial and Developing Countries. *J. Macroecon.*, Winter 1985, *7*(1), pp. 101–13. [G: LDCs; MDCs]

Katsimbris, George M. The Relationship between the Inflation Rate, Its Variability, and Output Growth Variability: Disaggregated International Evidence. *J. Money, Credit, Banking*, May 1985, *17*(2), pp. 179–88. [G: OECD]

Kim, Moon K. and Young, Allan E. Inflation, the Value of the Firm, and Firm Size. *Quart. Rev. Econ. Bus.*, Summer 1985, *25*(2), pp. 81–90. [G: U.S.]

King, Robert G. and Plosser, Charles I. Money, Deficits, and Inflation. *Carnegie-Rochester Conf. Ser. Public Policy*, Spring 1985, *22*, pp. 147–95. [G: U.S.]

Kirkpatrick, Colin H. and Onis, Ziya. Industrialisation as a Structural Determinant of Inflation Performance in IMF Stabilisation Programmes in Less Developed Countries. *J. Devel. Stud.*, April 1985, *21*(3), pp. 347–61. [G: LDCs]

Kotz, David M. Reply to John Bellamy Foster, "Monopoly Capital Theory and Stagflation: A Comment." *Rev. Radical Polit. Econ.*, Spring and Summer 1985, *17*(1/2), pp. 226–29. [G: U.S.]

Kovačič, Zlatko. Inflacija i lični dohoci—analiza uzročnosti. (Inflation and Personal Incomes—Causality Analysis. With English summary.) *Econ. Anal. Worker's Manage.*, 1985, *19*(2), pp. 161–79. [G: Yugoslavia]

Krelle, Wilhelm. On the Stability of Growth Models with Money. *Rivista Int. Sci. Econ. Com.*, March 1985, *32*(3), pp. 233–52.

Krugman, Paul R.; Persson, Torsten and Svensson, Lars E. O. Inflation, Interest Rates, and Welfare. *Quart. J. Econ.*, August 1985, *100*(3), pp. 677–95.

Kugler, Peter. Autoregressive Modelling of Consumption, Income, Inflation, and Interest Rate Data: A Multicountry Study. *Empirical Econ.*, 1985, *10*(1), pp. 37–50. [G: U.S.; U.K.; W. Germany; France]

van der Laan, Paul and van Tuinen, Henk K. Interest, Distribution of Value Added and Inflation: Inflation-induced Difficulties in the Interpretation of Dutch National Accounts. *Rev. Income Wealth*, September 1985, *31*(3), pp. 255–83. [G: Netherlands]

LaHaye, Laura. Inflation and Currency Reform. *J. Polit. Econ.*, June 1985, *93*(3), pp. 537–60. [G: Germany; Greece; Poland]

Lavoie, Marc. Inflation, chômage et la planification des récessions: La "Théorie générale" de Keynes et après. (Inflation, Unemployment and Planned Recessions: Keynes' 'General

Theory' and After. With English summary.) *L'Actual. Econ.*, June 1985, *61*(2), pp. 171–99.

Lavoie, Marc. La thèse de la monnaie endogène face à la non-validation des crédits. (The Hypothesis of Endogeneous Money and the Nonvalidation of Credit. With English summary.) *Écon. Soc.*, August 1985, *19*(8), pp. 169–95.

Lenti, Libero. Lo zoccolo duro dell'inflazione. (The Hard Core of Inflation. With English summary.) *Rivista Int. Sci. Econ. Com.*, March 1985, *32*(3), pp. 201–06. **[G: Italy]**

Leventakis, John A. Inflation and the Formation of Expectations: Some Empirical Results. *Kredit Kapital*, 1985, *18*(4), pp. 515–26.
[G: Greece]

Liebermann, Yehoshua and Zilberfarb, Ben-Zion. Price Adjustment Strategy under Conditions of High Inflation: An Empirical Examination. *J. Econ. Bus.*, August 1985, *37*(3), pp. 253–65. **[G: Israel]**

Lim, Joseph. The Monetarist Models of Inflation: The Case of the Philippines. *Philippine Rev. Econ. Bus.*, Sept./Dec. 1985, *22*(3/4), pp. 155–75. **[G: Philippines]**

Lindberg, Leon N. Models of the Inflation–Disinflation Process. In *Lindberg, L. N. and Maier, C. S.*, eds., 1985, pp. 25–50. **[G: OECD]**

Lindblom, Seppo. Tillväxtinriktad ekonomisk politik—med långsamma steg. (Growth-dominated Economic Policy—With Slow Progress. With English summary.) *Ekon. Samfundets Tidskr.*, 1985, *38*(2), pp. 69–78. **[G: Finland]**

Lipsey, Richard G. What Have We Learned about Inflation in the Past 300 Years. *Atlantic Econ. J.*, March 1985, *13*(1), pp. 5–18.

Litterman, Robert B. and Weiss, Laurence M. Money, Real Interest Rates, and Output: A Reinterpretation of Postwar U.S. Data. *Econometrica*, January 1985, *53*(1), pp. 129–56.
[G: U.S.]

Looney, Robert E. Structural Origins of Mexican Inflation, 1951–1980. *Soc. Econ. Stud.*, September 1985, *34*(3), pp. 165–98. **[G: Mexico]**

Looney, Robert E. The Inflationary Process in Prerevolutionary Iran. *J. Devel. Areas*, April 1985, *19*(3), pp. 329–50. **[G: Iran]**

Loranger, Jean-Guy. Lien entre capital fictif, markup flexible et inflation. (Interrelations between Fictitious Capital, Flexible Markup and Inflation. With English summary.) *Écon. Soc.*, August 1985, *19*(8), pp. 145–68. **[G: Canada]**

Los, Cornelis A. Measurement Problems of Inflation Disaggregation. *J. Bus. Econ. Statist.*, July 1985, *3*(3), pp. 244–53. **[G: U.S.]**

Löwenthal, Paul. The Irrelevance of Aggregative Policies against Inflation under Conditions of Resource Misallocation. *Z. Wirtschaft. Sozialwissen.*, 1985, *105*(2/3), pp. 155–67.
[G: OECD]

Lützel, Heinrich. Inflation Accounting for the Federal Republic of Germany—Results Using Different Deflator Price Indices. *Rev. Income Wealth*, September 1985, *31*(3), pp. 207–21.
[G: W. Germany]

Machak, Joseph A.; Spivey, W. Allen and Wrobleski, William J. A Framework for Time Varying Parameter Regression Modeling. *J. Bus. Econ. Statist.*, April 1985, *3*(2), pp. 104–11.
[G: U.S.]

Maital, Shlomo and Meltz, Noah M. Labor and Management Attitudes toward a New Social Contract: A Comparison of Canada and the United States. In *Maital, S. and Lipnowski, I.*, eds., 1985, pp. 193–206. **[G: U.S.; Canada]**

Maki, Dennis R. A Note on Money Wages, Prices, Controls, and Trade Unions in Canada. *Appl. Econ.*, February 1985, *17*(1), pp. 165–72.
[G: Canada]

Marston, Richard C. and Turnovsky, Stephen J. Imported Materials Prices, Wage Policy, and Macro-economic Stabilization. *Can. J. Econ.*, May 1985, *18*(2), pp. 273–84.

Martin, Leonard W. 'Stagflation': A Condition Created by Accelerated Demand–Pull Inflation (Comment). *Amer. J. Econ. Soc.*, October 1985, *44*(4), pp. 497–501.

Matthews, Kent. Forecasting with a Rational Expectations Model of the UK. *Oxford Bull. Econ. Statist.*, November 1985, *47*(4), pp. 311–36. **[G: U.K.]**

McClain, David. Stabilizing Oil and Farm Prices Holds the Key. *Challenge*, Sept./Oct. 1985, *28*(4), pp. 23–26. **[G: U.S.]**

McElhattan, Rose. Inflation, Supply Shocks and the Stable-Inflation Rate of Capacity Utilization. *Fed. Res. Bank San Francisco Econ. Rev.*, Winter 1985, (1), pp. 45–63. **[G: U.S.]**

McKinney, George W., Jr. Inflation under Control? Don't Count on It! *Bus. Econ.*, July 1985, *20*(3), pp. 5–10. **[G: U.S.]**

McNelis, Paul D. Política de indización e inestabilidad inflacionaria en el Cono Sur. (With English summary.) *Cuadernos Econ.*, April 1985, *22*(65), pp. 99–116. **[G: Argentina; Brazil; Chile; Uruguay; Peru]**

Medani, A. I. Food and Stabilization in Developing Africa. *World Devel.*, June 1985, *13*(6), pp. 685–90. **[G: Africa]**

Mehra, Yash. Inflationary Expectations, Money Growth, and the Vanishing Liquidity Effect of Money on Interest: A Further Investigation. *Fed. Res. Bank Richmond Econ. Rev.*, Mar./Apr. 1985, *71*(2), pp. 23–35. **[G: U.S.]**

Mitchell, Daniel J. B. Shifting Norms in Wage Determination. *Brookings Pap. Econ. Act.*, 1985, (2), pp. 575–99. **[G: U.S.]**

Mohabbat, Khan A. and Arshanapalli, Gangadhar. Unemployment, Inflation and Compensation Growth—A Case Study of Italy, 1970–1980. *Econ. Int.*, May 1985, *38*(2), pp. 214–21. **[G: Italy]**

Naples, Michele I. Dynamic Adjustment and Long-run Inflation in a Marxian Model. *J. Post Keynesian Econ.*, Fall 1985, *8*(1), pp. 97–112.

Neck, Reinhard. On the Effects of Disinflationary Policies on Unemployment and Inflation: A Simulation Study with Keynesian and Monetarist Models for Austria. *Z. Wirtschaft. Sozial-*

wissen., 1985, *105*(2/3), pp. 357–86.

[G: Austria]

Neumann, Manfred J. M. and von Hagen, Jürgen. Inflation and Relative Price Risk. *Z. Wirtschaft. Sozialwissen.*, 1985, *105*(2/3), pp. 169–92.

[G: W. Germany]

O'Brien, Anthony. The Cyclical Sensitivity of Wages [The Changing Cyclical Behavior of Wages and Prices: 1890–1976] [Cross-Country and Cross-Temporal Differences in Inflation Responsiveness]. *Amer. Econ. Rev.*, December 1985, *75*(5), pp. 1124–32. [G: U.S.]

Obstfeld, Maurice. The Capital Inflows Problem Revisited: A Stylized Model of Southern Cone Disinflation. *Rev. Econ. Stud.*, October 1985, *52*(4), pp. 605–25.

Obstfeld, Maurice. The Dollar and the Policy Mix: 1985: Comment. *Brookings Pap. Econ. Act.*, 1985, (1), pp. 190–95. [G: U.S.]

Oyrzanowski, Bronislaw. I sintomi dell'inflazione nei paesi ad economia dirigista. (Symptom of Inflation in Countries with Policy of State Intervention. With English summary.) *Bancaria*, December 1985, *41*(12), pp. 1249–55.

Pagano, Marco. Relative Price Variability and Inflation: The Italian Evidence. *Europ. Econ. Rev.*, November 1985, *29*(2), pp. 193–223.

[G: Italy; U.S.; W. Germany]

Paricio, Joaquina and Quesada, Javier. Wages and Employment in the Spanish Economy: Behavior and Trends during the Crisis. *Z. Wirtschaft. Sozialwissen.*, 1985, *105*(2/3), pp. 341–56. [G: Spain]

Persico, Pasquale. Inflazione e prezzi relativi: un'interpretazione fisheriana della correlazione tra variabilitaà del tasso d'inflazione e variabilitaà dei prezzi relativi. (With English summary.) *Stud. Econ.*, 1985, *40*(26), pp. 117–26.

[G: Italy]

Pesaran, M. Hashem. Formation of Inflation Expectations in British Manufacturing Industries. *Econ. J.*, December 1985, *95*(380), pp. 948–75. [G: U.K.]

Pierce, James L. Policy Making under Uncertainty: Some Lessons from the 1970s. In *[Weintraub, R. E.]*, 1985, pp. 55–75. [G: U.S.]

Pigott, Charles and Reinhart, Vincent. The Strong Dollar and U.S. Inflation. *Fed. Res. Bank New York Quart. Rev.*, Autumn 1985, *10*(3), pp. 23–29. [G: U.S.]

Pigott, Charles; Rutledge, John and Willett, Thomas D. Estimating the Inflationary Effects of Exchange Rate Changes. In *Arndt, S. W.; Sweeney, R. J. and Willett, T. D.*, eds., 1985, pp. 245–65. [G: U.S.]

Pitchford, J. D. The Insulation Capacity of a Flexible Exchange Rate System in the Context of External Inflation. *Scand. J. Econ.*, 1985, *87*(1), pp. 44–65.

Plaut, Steven E. Interest vs. Maturity Indexation. *Quart. Rev. Econ. Bus.*, Winter 1985, *25*(4), pp. 95–106.

Plaut, Steven E. The Reverse Incomes Policy: An Institutional Cure for Inflation. In *Maital, S. and Lipnowski, I.*, eds., 1985, pp. 173–90.

Prat, Georges. Une mesure des anticipations d'in-flation à court terme des ménages en France 1964–1985. With English summary.) *Revue Écon. Polit.*, Nov.-Dec. 1985, *95*(6), pp. 749–76. [G: France]

Price, James E. The Remarkable Career of the Inflationary Gap. *J. Post Keynesian Econ.*, Fall 1985, *8*(1), pp. 113–20. [G: U.S.]

Puumanen, Kari. Inflationsmålet bör skärpas. (The Objective of the Inflation Rate Should Be Tightened. With English summary.) *Ekon. Samfundets Tidskr.*, 1985, *38*(4), pp. 195–98.

[G: Finland; OECD]

Rahmeyer, Fritz. Marktstruktur und industrielle Preisentwicklung. (Market Structure and Industrial Price Development. With English summary.) *Ifo-Studien*, 1985, *31*(4), pp. 295–330. [G: W. Germany]

Ram, Rati. Level and Variability of Inflation: Time-Series and Cross-Section Evidence from 117 Countries. *Economica*, May 1985, *52*(206), pp. 209–23. [G: Global]

Ramos, Joseph. Stabilization and Adjustment Policies in the Southern Cone, 1974–1983. *Cepal Rev.*, April 1985, (25), pp. 85–109.

[G: Argentina; Chile; Uruguay]

Rana, Pradumna B. and Dowling, J. Malcolm, Jr. Inflationary Effects of Small but Continuous Changes in Effective Exchange Rates: Nine Asian LDCs. *Rev. Econ. Statist.*, August 1985, *67*(3), pp. 496–500. [G: Asian LDCs]

Ratti, Ronald A. Sectoral Employment Variability and Unexpected Inflation. *Rev. Econ. Statist.*, May 1985, *67*(2), pp. 278–83. [G: U.S.]

Ratti, Ronald A. The Effects of Inflation Surprises and Uncertainty on Real Wages. *Rev. Econ. Statist.*, May 1985, *67*(2), pp. 309–14.

[G: U.S.]

Ring, Raymond J., Jr. Variability of Inflation and Income across Income Classes. *Soc. Sci. Quart.*, March 1985, *66*(1), pp. 203–09.

[G: U.S.]

Rogoff, Kenneth S. The Optimal Degree of Commitment to an Intermediate Monetary Target. *Quart. J. Econ.*, November 1985, *100*(4), pp. 1169–89.

Roley, V. Vance and Walsh, Carl E. Monetary Policy Regimes, Expected Inflation, and the Response of Interest Rates to Money Announcements. *Quart. J. Econ.*, Supp. 1985, *100*, pp. 1011–39. [G: U.S.]

Rymes, T. K. Inflation, Nonoptimal Monetary Arrangements and the Banking Imputation in the National Accounts. *Rev. Income Wealth*, March 1985, *31*(1), pp. 85–96.

Sachs, Jeffrey. The Dollar and the Policy Mix: 1985. *Brookings Pap. Econ. Act.*, 1985, (1), pp. 117–85. [G: U.S.]

Saikkonen, Pentti and Taräsvirta, Timo. Modelling the Dynamic Relationship between Wages and Prices in Finland. *Scand. J. Econ.*, 1985, *87*(1), pp. 102–19. [G: Finland]

Sawyer, Malcolm C. On the Nature of the Phillips Curve. *Brit. Rev. Econ. Issues*, Spring 1985, *7*(16), pp. 63–86.

Schmidt-Sørensen, Jan Beyer and Søndergaard, Jørgen. Beskæftigelsesvirkninger af en arbejdstidsforkortelse. (Employment Consequences of a Shortening of Working Hours. With English summary.) *Nationaløkon. Tidsskr.*, 1985, *123*(2), pp. 160–75.

Shamsuddin, A. F. M.; Holmes, Richard A. and Alam, Shamsul A. K. M. Univariate Arima and Bivariate Transfer Function Models for Inflation: Some Malaysian Evidence. *Philippine Econ. J.*, 1985, *24*(4), pp. 263–87.
[G: Malaysia]

Shashua, Leon and Goldschmidt, Yaaqov. The Specific Role of Interest in Financial and Economic Analysis under Inflation: Real, Nominal, or a Combination of Both. *Amer. J. Agr. Econ.*, May 1985, *67*(2), pp. 377–83.

Sheehey, Edmund J. and Kreinin, Mordechai E. Inflation Dispersion and Central Bank Accommodation of Supply Shocks. *Weltwirtsch. Arch.*, 1985, *121*(3), pp. 448–59. [G: OECD]

Sinai, Allen. The Dollar and Inflation. *Eastern Econ. J.*, July-Sept. 1985, *11*(3), pp. 211–20.
[G: U.S.]

Sinai, Allen. The Soaring Dollar Did It. *Challenge*, Sept./Oct. 1985, *28*(4), pp. 18–22.
[G: U.S.]

Smith, Bruce D. Government Expenditures, Deficits, and Inflation: On the Impossibility of a Balanced Budget. *Quart. J. Econ.*, August 1985, *100*(3), pp. 715–45.

Sorensen, Peter Birch. Det monetaristiske syn på stabiliseringspolitikken. (A Macro-economic Model of Explaining Monetarist Assumptions in Stabilization Policy. With English summary.) *Nationaløkon. Tidsskr.*, 1985, *123*(1), pp. 64–76.

Sorsa, Pertti. Är konjunkturpolitikens tid förbi—finländska ock utländska erfarenheter. (Is Stabilization Policy a Thing of the Past? Finnish and Foreign Experience. With English summary.) *Ekon. Samfundets Tidskr.*, 1985, *38*(2), pp. 81–87. [G: Finland]

Starleaf, Dennis R.; Meyers, William H. and Womack, Abner W. The Impact of Inflation on the Real Income of U.S. Farmers. *Amer. J. Agr. Econ.*, May 1985, *67*(2), pp. 384–89.
[G: U.S.]

Stiassny, Alfred. The Austrian Phillips Curve Reconsidered. *Empirica*, 1985, *12*(1), pp. 43–65.
[G: Austria]

Stockman, Alan C. Effects of Inflation on the Pattern of International Trade. *Can. J. Econ.*, August 1985, *18*(3), pp. 587–601.

Tarafás, Imre. The Possibility and Conditions of Anti-Inflationary Economic Policy in Hungary. *Acta Oecon.*, 1985, *34*(3/4), pp. 287–97.
[G: Hungary]

Tarling, Roger and Wilkinson, Frank. Mark-up Pricing, Inflation and Distributional Shares: A Note. *Cambridge J. Econ.*, June 1985, *9*(2), pp. 179–85.

Tronzano, Marco. Intersectoral Inflation Propagation and Macroeconomic Hypotheses: Recent Contributions and Further Outlook. *Rivista Polit. Econ.*, Suppl. Dec. 1985, 76, pp. 175–217.

Tryon, Ralph. The International Transmission of Inflation: A Review Essay. *J. Monet. Econ.*, November 1985, *16*(3), pp. 397–403.

Tsujimura, Kotaro. Theory and Measurement of Acute Polypoly and Polyopsony: Inflationary Expectation and Market Paralysis at the First Oil Crisis in Japan. (In Japanese. With English summary.) *Econ. Stud. Quart.*, April 1985, *36*(1), pp. 1–14. [G: Japan]

Uthoff B., Andras and Pollack E., Molly. Dinámica de salarios y precios en Costa Rica 1976–1983. (With English summary.) *Cuadernos Econ.*, December 1985, *22*(67), pp. 443–73.
[G: Costa Rica]

Vizeu, Maria Clementina. Inflação tradicional num modelo de desequilíbrio. (With English summary.) *Economia (Portugal)*, October 1985, *9*(3), pp. 467–84.

Wadhwani, Sushil B. Wage Inflation in the United Kingdom. *Economica*, May 1985, *52*(206), pp. 195–207. [G: U.K.]

Wahlroos, Björn. Money and Prices in a Small Economy. *Scand. J. Econ.*, 1985, *87*(4), pp. 605–24. [G: Finland]

Wasserfallen, Walter. Forecasting, Rational Expectations and the Phillips-Curve: An Empirical Investigation. *J. Monet. Econ.*, January 1985, *15*(1), pp. 7–27. [G: Switzerland]

Wasserfallen, Walter. Trends, Random Walks and the Expectations-Augmented Phillips-Curve—A Summary. *Rech. Écon. Louvain*, 1985, *51*(3–4), pp. 387–88.

Webb, Steven B. Government Debt and Inflationary Expectations as Determinants of the Money Supply in Germany, 1919–23. *J. Money, Credit, Banking*, Part 1, Nov. 1985, *17*(4), pp. 479–92. [G: Germany]

Weinblatt, J. and Rodrik-Farhi, Miriam. Monetary Effects of Export Restrictions on World Commodity Markets. In *Weinblatt, J., ed.*, 1985, pp. 143–60. [G: LDCs; MDCs]

Wheaton, William C. Life-Cycle Theory, Inflation, and the Demand for Housing. *J. Urban Econ.*, September 1985, *18*(2), pp. 161–79.

Winiecki, Jan. *Portes Ante Portas:* A Critique of the Revisionist Interpretation of Inflation under Central Planning. *Comparative Econ. Stud.*, Summer 1985, *27*(2), pp. 25–51.
[G: E. Europe]

Winiecki, Jan. Inflation under Central Planning: Sources, Processes and Manifestations. *Konjunkturpolitik*, 1985, *31*(4/5), pp. 238–60.
[G: E. Europe]

Wren-Lewis, Simon. Private Sector Earnings and Excess Demand from 1966 to 1980. *Oxford Bull. Econ. Statist.*, February 1985, *47*(1), pp. 1–18. [G: U.K.]

Young, Kan H. The Relative Effects of Demand and Supply on Output Growth and Price Change. *Rev. Econ. Statist.*, May 1985, *67*(2), pp. 314–18. [G: U.S.]

Zarnowitz, Victor. Rational Expectations and Macroeconomic Forecasts. *J. Bus. Econ. Statist.*, October 1985, *3*(4), pp. 293–311.
[G: U.S.]

Zenger, Christoph. Zinssätze und Inflation in der Schweiz: Ein alternativer Test des Fisher-Effektes. (Interest Rates and Inflation in Switzerland: An Alternative Test of the Fisher-Effect. With English summary.) *Schweiz. Z. Volkswirtsch. Statist.*, December 1985, *121*(4), pp. 353–74. [G: Switzerland]

Zijlstra, Jelle. Inflation and Its Impact on Society. In *Zijlstra, J.*, 1985, pp. 173–83.

Zonzilos, Nicholas G. The Demand for Money during a Period of Inflationary Expectations. Some FIML Based Estimates for Greece. *Empirical Econ.*, 1985, *10*(1), pp. 27–35. [G: Greece]

200 Quantitative Economic Methods and Data

210 ECONOMETRIC, STATISTICAL, AND MATHEMATICAL METHODS AND MODELS

211 Econometric and Statistical Methods and Models

2110 General

Andersen, Per Kragh. Statistical Models for Longitudinal Labor Market Data Based on Counting Processes. In *Heckman, J. J. and Singer, B.*, eds., 1985, pp. 294–307.

Anderson-Courtney, Linda D. *Journal of Econometrics* Subject Index Volumes 21–30, 1983–1985. *J. Econometrics*, December 1985, *30*(3), pp. 475–543.

Apps, Patricia. The Relative Deprivation Curve and Its Applications: Comment. *J. Bus. Econ. Statist.*, April 1985, *3*(2), pp. 169–71. [G: Australia]

Arrow, Kenneth J. The Combination of Time-Series and Cross-Section Data in Interindustry Flow Analysis. In *Arrow, K. J. (II)*, 1985, pp. 174–82.

Assenmacher, Walter. Eine wissenschaftstheoretische Begründung der Linearhypothese in angewandten ökonometrischen Modellen. (A Theory of Science Approach to the Linear Hypothesis in Applied Econometric Models. With English summary.) *Jahr. Nationalökon. Statist.*, January 1985, *200*(1), pp. 56–70.

Atwood, Joseph A. Demonstration of the Use of Lower Partial Moments to Improve Safety-First Probability Limits. *Amer. J. Agr. Econ.*, November 1985, *67*(4), pp. 787–93.

Bauwens, Luc and Richard, Jean-Francois. A 1–1 Poly *t* Random Variable Generator with Application to Monte Carlo Integration. *J. Econometrics*, July/August 1985, *29*(1/2), pp. 19–46.

Beach, Charles M. and Richmond, James. Joint Confidence Intervals for Income Shares and Lorenz Curves. *Int. Econ. Rev.*, June 1985, *26*(2), pp. 439–50. [G: Canada]

Berger, James O. In Defense of the Likelihood Principle: Axiomatics and Coherency. In *Bernardo, J. M., et al.*, eds., 1985, pp. 33–56.

Boland, Lawrence A. The Foundations of Econometrics—Are There Any? Comment. *Econo-metric Rev.*, 1985, *4*(1), pp. 63–67.

Chakravarty, Sukhamoy. Methodology and Economics. *J. Quant. Econ.*, January 1985, *1*(1), pp. 1–9.

Csiszár, I. An Extended Maximum Entropy Principle and a Bayesian Justification. In *Bernardo, J. M., et al.*, eds., 1985, pp. 83–93.

Dastoor, Naorayex K. A Classical Approach to Cox's Test for Non-nested Hypotheses. *J. Econometrics*, March 1985, *27*(3), pp. 363–70.

DeGroot, M. H. and Eriksson, E. A. Probability Forecasting, Stochastic Dominance, and the Lorenz Curve. In *Bernardo, J. M., et al.*, eds., 1985, pp. 99–110.

van Dijk, Herman K. and Kloek, Teun. Experiments with Some Alternatives for Simple Importance Sampling in Monte Carlo Integration. In *Bernardo, J. M., et al.*, eds., 1985, pp. 511–26.

van Dijk, Herman K.; Kloek, Teun and Boender, C. Guus. Posterior Moments Computed by Mixed Integration. *J. Econometrics*, July/August 1985, *29*(1/2), pp. 3–18.

Draper, Norman R. Corrections: The Box–Weitz Criterion versus R^2. *J. Roy. Statist. Soc.*, 1985, *148*(4), pp. 357.

Drèze, Jacques H. Econometrics in the General Economics Curriculum: Teachers in a Quandry? *Tijdschrift Econ. Manage.*, 1985, *30*(3–4), pp. 445–52. [G: Belgium]

Fiebig, Denzil G. Evaluating Estimators without Moments. *Rev. Econ. Statist.*, August 1985, *67*(3), pp. 529–34.

de Finetti, Bruno. Cambridge Probability Theorists. *Manchester Sch. Econ. Soc. Stud.*, December 1985, *53*(4), pp. 348–63.

Frydman, Halina and Singer, Burton. Assessing Qualitative Features of Longitudinal Data. In *Heckman, J. J. and Singer, B.*, eds., 1985, pp. 308–24.

Garthwaite, Paul H. and Dickey, James M. Double- and Single-Bisection Methods for Subjective Probability Assessment in a Location-Scale Family. *J. Econometrics*, July/August 1985, *29*(1/2), pp. 149–63.

Gastwirth, Joseph L. Measurement of Economic Distance between Blacks and Whites: Comment. *J. Bus. Econ. Statist.*, October 1985, *3*(4), pp. 405–07.

Geisser, Seymour. Interval Prediction for Pareto and Exponential Observables. *J. Econometrics*, July/August 1985, *29*(1/2), pp. 173–85.

Glymour, Clark. Interpreting Leamer [Let's Take the Con Out of Econometrics]. *Econ. Philos.*, October 1985, *1*(2), pp. 290–94. [G: U.S.]

Good, I. J. The Foundations of Econometrics—Are There Any? Comment. *Econometric Rev.*, 1985, *4*(1), pp. 69–74.

Gourieroux, Christian; Monfort, Alain and Trognon, Alain. Moindres carrés asymptotiques. (Asymptotic Least Squares. With English summary.) *Ann. INSEE*, Apr.-June 1985, (58), pp. 91–122.

Griliches, Zvi. Data and Econometricians—The Uneasy Alliance. *Amer. Econ. Rev.*, May 1985, *75*(2), pp. 196–200.

Huang, Kuo S. Monthly Demand Relationships of U.S. Meat Commodities. *Agr. Econ. Res.*, Summer 1985, *37*(3), pp. 23–29. [G: U.S.]

Iverson, G. and Falmagne, J.-C. Statistical Issues in Measurement. *Math. Soc. Sci.*, October 1985, *10*(2), pp. 131–53.

Johnstone, Iain M. and Velleman, Paul F. Efficient Scores, Variance Decompositions, and Monte Carlo Swindles. *J. Amer. Statist. Assoc.*, December 1985, *80*(392), pp. 851–62.

Judd, Kenneth L. The Law of Large Numbers with a Continuum of IID Random Variables. *J. Econ. Theory*, February 1985, *35*(1), pp. 19–25.

Kakwani, Nanak. The Relative Deprivation Curve and Its Applications: Reply. *J. Bus. Econ. Statist.*, April 1985, *3*(2), pp. 171–73.
[G: Australia]

Kiefer, Nicholas M. Specification Diagnostics Based on Laguerre Alteratives for Econometric Models of Duration. *J. Econometrics*, April 1985, *28*(1), pp. 135–54. [G: U.S.]

Lancaster, Tony. Generalised Residuals and Heterogeneous Duration Models: With Applications to the Weibull Model. *J. Econometrics*, April 1985, *28*(1), pp. 155–69.

Lax, David A. Robust Estimators of Scale: Finite-Sample Performance in Long-tailed Symmetric Distributions. *J. Amer. Statist. Assoc.*, September 1985, *80*(391), pp. 736–41.

Leamer, Edward E. Self-Interpretation [Let's Take the Con Out of Econometrics]. *Econ. Philos.*, October 1985, *1*(2), pp. 295–302.
[G: U.S.]

Leamer, Edward E. Sensitivity Analyses Would Help. *Amer. Econ. Rev.*, June 1985, *75*(3), pp. 308–13.

Loh, Wei-Yin. A New Method for Testing Separate Families of Hypotheses. *J. Amer. Statist. Assoc.*, June 1985, *80*(390), pp. 362–68.

McAleer, Michael; Pagan, Adrian R. and Volker, Paul A. What Will Take the Con out of Econometrics? *Amer. Econ. Rev.*, June 1985, *75*(3), pp. 293–307. [G: U.S.]

McCloskey, Donald N. The Loss Function Has Been Mislaid: The Rhetoric of Significance Tests. *Amer. Econ. Rev.*, May 1985, *75*(2), pp. 201–05.

Montinaro, Mario. Sull'accostamento tra le distribuzioni di X^2 e ψ^2 in presenza di frequenze teoriche inferiori ai limiti convenzionali. (On the Problem of Fit between X^2 e ψ^2 Distributions When Expected Frequencies Are Less Than Conventional Limits. With English summary.) *Statistica*, Jan.–Mar. 1985, *45*(1), pp. 105–14.

Newey, Whitney K. Generalized Method of Moments Specification Testing. *J. Econometrics*, September 1985, *29*(3), pp. 229–56.

Pesaran, M. Hashem. The Foundations of Econometrics—Are There Any? Comment. *Econometric Rev.*, 1985, *4*(1), pp. 75–80.

Phillips, Peter C. B. A Theorem on the Tail Behaviour of Probability Distributions with an Application to the Stable Family. *Can. J. Econ.*, February 1985, *18*(1), pp. 58–65.

Rutsch, Martin. Exploration and Inference. In *[Menges, G.]*, 1985, pp. 192–206.

Savage, I. Richard. Hard–Soft Problems. *J. Amer. Statist. Assoc.*, March 1985, *80*(389), pp. 1–7. [G: U.S.]

Seidenfeld, Teddy. The Foundations of Econometrics—Are There Any? Coherence, "Improper" Priors, and Finite Additivity. *Econometric Rev.*, 1985, *4*(1), pp. 81–91.

Shalit, Haim. Calculating the Gini Index of Inequality for Individual Data. *Oxford Bull. Econ. Statist.*, May 1985, *47*(2), pp. 185–89.

Shvyrkov, Vladislav V. Fundamental Problem of Statistical Science. In *Brown, R. C., ed.*, 1985, pp. 193–200.

Smiley, T. J. The Foundations of Econometrics—Are There Any? Comment. *Econometric Rev.*, 1985, *4*(1), pp. 93–99.

Smith, Robert B. A Handbook of Social Science Methods: Introduction: Linking Quality and Quantity. In *Smith, R. B., ed.*, 1985, pp. 1–51.

Smith, Robert B. Aspects of the Perspective and Method. In *Smith, R. B., ed.*, 1985, pp. 59–96.

Spencer, Bruce D. Optimal Data Quality. *J. Amer. Statist. Assoc.*, September 1985, *80*(391), pp. 564–73.

Sprott, D. A. and Viveros, R. The Estimation of Ratios and Related Quantities. In *[Menges, G.]*, 1985, pp. 242–51.

Ştefănescu, S. A Method of Generating the Autocorrelated Uniformly Distributed Random Numbers. *Econ. Computat. Cybern. Stud. Res.*, 1985, *20*(3), pp. 43–47.

Swamy, P. A. V. B.; Conway, Roger K. and von zur Muehlen, P. The Foundations of Econometrics—Are There Any? *Econometric Rev.*, 1985, *4*(1), pp. 1–61.

Swamy, P. A. V. B.; Conway, Roger K. and von zur Muehlen, P. The Foundations of Econometrics—Are There Any? Reply. *Econometric Rev.*, 1985, *4*(1), pp. 101–19.

Swierzbinski, Joseph. Statistical Methods Applicable to Selected Problems in Fisheries Biology and Economics. *Marine Resource Econ.*, 1985, *1*(3), pp. 209–33.

Tamminen, Rauno. Kato ja korrelaatio. (Incomplete Samples and the Correlation Coefficient. With English summary.) *Liiketaloudellinen Aikak.*, 1985, *34*(2), pp. 199–212.

Tauchen, George. Diagnostic Testing and Evaluation of Maximum Likelihood Models. *J. Econometrics*, Oct./Nov. 1985, *30*(1/2), pp. 415–43.

Thisayakorn, Nopharatna. Perspectives on Statistics for Qualifying Research. In *Brown, R. C., ed.*, 1985, pp. 413–23.

Thornton, Robert J. and Innes, Jon T. On Simpson's Paradox in Economic Statistics. *Oxford Bull. Econ. Statist.*, November 1985, *47*(4), pp. 387–94.

Vinod, H. D. Measurement of Economic Distance between Blacks and Whites: Reply. *J. Bus. Econ. Statist.*, October 1985, *3*(4), pp. 408–09.

Vinod, H. D. Measurement of Economic Distance

between Blacks and Whites. *J. Bus. Econ. Statist.*, January 1985, *3*(1), pp. 78–88.

Waldman, Donald M. Computation in Duration Models with Heterogeneity. *J. Econometrics*, April 1985, *28*(1), pp. 127–34. **[G: U.S.]**

Winkler, Othmar W. Statistical Flaws in Econometricians' Perception of Economic Reality. In *Brown, R. C., ed.*, 1985, pp. 295–354.

2112 Inferential Problems in Simultaneous Equation Systems

Attfield, Clifford L. F. Homogeneity and Endogeneity in Systems of Demand Equations. *J. Econometrics*, February 1985, *27*(2), pp. 197–209. **[G: U.K.]**

Bianchi, Carlo, et al. Asymptotic Properties of Dynamic Multipliers in Nonlinear Econometric Models. *Econ. Notes*, 1985, (2), pp. 97–117.

Binkley, James K. A Consideration in Estimating "Almost Nonsimultaneous" Market Models. *Amer. J. Agr. Econ.*, May 1985, *67*(2), pp. 320–24.

Bloom, David E. and Killingsworth, Mark R. Correcting for Truncation Bias Caused by a Latent Truncation Variable. *J. Econometrics*, January 1985, *27*(1), pp. 131–35.

Bollino, Carlo Andrea. La condizione di additività nella stima di sistemi di equazioni simultanee. (The Additivity Constraint in the Estimation of Simultaneous Equation Systems. With English summary.) *Giorn. Econ.*, Jan.-Feb. 1985, *44*(1–2), pp. 65–80.

Brown, Bryan W. The Identification Problem in Simultaneous Equation Models with Identities. *Int. Econ. Rev.*, February 1985, *26*(1), pp. 45–66.

Brown, G. F.; Ramage, J. G. and Srivastava, V. K. The *R*-Class Estimators of Disturbance Variance in Simultaneous Equation Models. *J. Quant. Econ.*, July 1985, *1*(2), pp. 231–51.

Cameron, Trudy Ann. Consistent Multinominal and Nested Logit Point Estimates: A Practical Note. *Oxford Bull. Econ. Statist.*, February 1985, *47*(1), pp. 83–89.

Chang, Y. C. A Note on the Covariance Matrix of the Maximum Likelihood Estimator in Constrained Multivariate Linear Regression. *J. Econometrics*, May 1985, *28*(2), pp. 247–52.

Chesher, Andrew. Score Tests for Zero Covariances in Recursive Linear Models for Grouped or Censored Data. *J. Econometrics*, June 1985, *28*(3), pp. 291–305.

Chow, Gregory C. and Reny, Philip J. On Two Methods for Solving and Estimating Linear Simultaneous Equations under Rational Expectations. *J. Econ. Dynam. Control*, September 1985, *9*(1), pp. 63–75.

Conniffe, Denis. Estimating Regression Equations with Common Explanatory Variables but Unequal Numbers of Observations. *J. Econometrics*, February 1985, *27*(2), pp. 179–96.

Crockett, Patrick W. Asymptotic Distribution of the Hildreth–Houck Estimator. *J. Amer. Statist. Assoc.*, March 1985, *80*(389), pp. 202–04.

Domowitz, Ian. New Directions in Non-linear Estimation with Dependent Observations. *Can. J. Econ.*, February 1985, *18*(1), pp. 1–27.

Giannini, Carlo. Problemi aperti nell'analisi econometrica dinamica. (Some Open Issues in Dynamic Econometric Analysis. With English summary.) *Giorn. Econ.*, Jan.-Feb. 1985, *44*(1–2), pp. 29–43.

Hansen, Lars Peter. A Method for Calculating Bounds on the Asymptotic Covariance Matrices of Generalized Method of Moments Estimators. *J. Econometrics*, Oct./Nov. 1985, *30*(1/2), pp. 203–38.

Haynes, Stephen E. and Stone, Joe A. A Neglected Method of Separating Demand and Supply in Time Series Regression. *J. Bus. Econ. Statist.*, July 1985, *3*(3), pp. 238–43. **[G: U.S.]**

Heckman, James J. and MaCurdy, Thomas E. A Simultaneous Equations Linear Probability Model. *Can. J. Econ.*, February 1985, *18*(1), pp. 28–37.

Heckman, James J. and Robb, Richard, Jr. Alternative Methods for Evaluating the Impact of Interventions: An Overview. *J. Econometrics*, Oct./Nov. 1985, *30*(1/2), pp. 239–67.

Ilmakunnas, Pekka. Bayesian Estimation of Cost Functions with Stochastic or Exact Constraints on Parameters. *Int. Econ. Rev.*, February 1985, *26*(1), pp. 111–34. **[G: U.S.]**

Kiviet, Jan F. Model Selection Test Procedures in a Single Linear Equation of a Dynamic Simultaneous System and Their Defects in Small Samples. *J. Econometrics*, June 1985, *28*(3), pp. 327–62.

Knight, John L. The Moments of OLS and 2SLS When the Disturbances Are Non-normal. *J. Econometrics*, January 1985, *27*(1), pp. 39–60.

Krasker, William S. and Welsch, Roy E. Resistant Estimation for Simultaneous-Equations Models Using Weighted Instrumental Variables. *Econometrica*, November 1985, *53*(6), pp. 1475–88.

Little, Roderick J. A. A Note about Models for Selectivity Bias. *Econometrica*, November 1985, *53*(6), pp. 1469–74.

Lubrano, Michel. Bayesian Analysis of Switching Regression Models. *J. Econometrics*, July/August 1985, *29*(1/2), pp. 69–95. **[G: U.S.; Italy]**

Lubrano, Michel. Some Aspects of Prior Elicitation Problems in Disequilibrium Models. *J. Econometrics*, July/August 1985, *29*(1/2), pp. 165–72. **[G: U.S.]**

Magdalinos, Michael A. Selecting the Best Instrumental Variables Estimator. *Rev. Econ. Stud.*, July 1985, *52*(3), pp. 473–85.

Mariano, Roberto S. and Brown, Bryan W. Stochastic Prediction in Dynamic Nonlinear Econometric Systems. *Ann. INSEE*, July-Dec. 1985, (59/60), pp. 267–78.

Matsuyama, Keisuke. On Mathematical Structures of Econometric Models. *Econ. Computat. Cybern. Stud. Res.*, 1985, *20*(2), pp. 57–74.

Mendelsohn, Robert. Identifying Structural

Equations with Single Market Data. *Rev. Econ. Statist.*, August 1985, *67*(3), pp. 525–29.

Meng, Chun-Lo and Schmidt, Peter. On the Cost of Partial Observability in the Bivariate Probit Model. *Int. Econ. Rev.*, February 1985, *26*(1), pp. 71–85.

Murphy, Kevin M. and Topel, Robert H. Estimation and Inference in Two-Step Econometric Models. *J. Bus. Econ. Statist.*, October 1985, *3*(4), pp. 370–79.

Nakamura, Alice and Nakamura, Masao. On the Performance of Tests by Wu and by Hausman for Detecting the Ordinary Least Squares Bias Problem. *J. Econometrics*, September 1985, *29*(3), pp. 213–27.

Narula, Subhash, C. and Wellington, John F. Regression Quantiles: An Example of Bicriteria Optimization. In *Haimes, Y. Y. and Chankong, V., eds.*, 1985, pp. 549–57.

Phillips, Peter C. B. The Exact Distribution of the SUR Estimator. *Econometrica*, July 1985, *53*(4), pp. 745–56.

Phillips, Peter C. B. The Exact Distribution of Exogenous Variable Coefficient Estimators: Corrigendum. *J. Econometrics*, May 1985, *28*(2), pp. 269.

Phillips, Peter C. B. The Exact Distribution of LIML: II. *Int. Econ. Rev.*, February 1985, *26*(1), pp. 21–36.

Pole, A. M. and Smith, A. F. M. A Bayesian Analysis of Some Threshold Switching Models. *J. Econometrics*, July/August 1985, *29*(1/2), pp. 97–119.

Poli, Irene. A Bayesian Non-parametric Estimate for Multivariate Regression. *J. Econometrics*, May 1985, *28*(2), pp. 171–82.   [G: Italy]

Prucha, Ingmar R. Maximum Likelihood and Instrumental Variable Estimation in Simultaneous Equation Systems with Error Components. *Int. Econ. Rev.*, June 1985, *26*(2), pp. 491–506.

Sahay, Surottam N. The Bias of the Forecast from Partially Restricted Reduced Form When There Are Three Endogenous Variables in the Structural Equations. *J. Quant. Econ.*, January 1985, *1*(1), pp. 135–49.

Smith, Richard J. Some Tests for Misspecification in Bivariate Limited Dependent Variable Models. *Ann. INSEE*, July-Dec. 1985, (59/60), pp. 97–123.

Sneessens, Henri R. Two Alternative Stochastic Specification and Estimation Methods for Quantity Rationing Models: A Monte-Carlo Comparison. *Europ. Econ. Rev.*, October 1985, *29*(1), pp. 111–36.

Takeuchi, Kei and Morimune, Kimio. Third-Order Efficiency of the Extended Maximum Likelihood Estimators in a Simultaneous Equation System. *Econometrica*, January 1985, *53*(1), pp. 177–200.

Turkington, Darrell A. A Note on Two-Stage Least Squares, Three-Stage Least Squares, and Maximum Likelihood Estimation in an Expectations Model. *Int. Econ. Rev.*, June 1985, *26*(2), pp. 507–10.

Upcher, M. R. The Problem of Aggregation over Time in Disequilibrium Models. *J. Quant. Econ.*, January 1985, *1*(1), pp. 11–25.

Wewel, Max Christoph. Parameter- und Prognoseschätzung in einem ökonometrischen Simultanmodell. Eine Monte-Carlo-Untersuchung. (On the Estimation and Forecasting in an Interdependent Econometric System: A Monte-Carlo-Research. With English summary.) *Jahr. Nationalökon. Statist.*, July 1985, *200*(4), pp. 401–19.

Wong, George Y. and Mason, William M. The Hierarchical Logistic Regression Model for Multilevel Analysis. *J. Amer. Statist. Assoc.*, September 1985, *80*(391), pp. 513–24.   [G: LDCs]

Zellner, Arnold. Bayesian Econometrics. *Econometrica*, March 1985, *53*(2), pp. 253–69.

2113 Distributed Lags and Serially Correlated Disturbance Terms; Inferential Problems in Single Equation Models

Ali, Mukhtar M. and Silver, J. Lew. Tests for Equality between Sets of Coefficients in Two Linear Regressions under Heteroscedasticity. *J. Amer. Statist. Assoc.*, September 1985, *80*(391), pp. 730–35.

Amemiya, Yasuo. Instrumental Variable Estimator for the Nonlinear Errors-in-Variables Model. *J. Econometrics*, June 1985, *28*(3), pp. 273–89.

Baksalary, Jerzy K. and Pordzik, Paweł R. A Note on Using Linear Restrictions in a Gauss–Markov Model. *Statistica*, April-June 1985, *45*(2), pp. 209–12.

Binotti, Annetta M. Il test di D. Currie sulle caratteristiche dinamiche di lungo periodo dei modelli autoregressivi a ritardi distribuiti. (The D. Currie's Test on the Long Run Dynamic Properties of the Autoregressive-distributed Lag Models. With English summary.) *Statistica*, April-June 1985, *45*(2), pp. 237–49.

Blommestein, H. J. Elimination of Circular Routes in Spatial Dynamic Regression Equations. *Reg. Sci. Urban Econ.*, February 1985, *15*(1), pp. 121–30.

Bloom, David E. and Killingsworth, Mark R. Correcting for Truncation Bias Caused by a Latent Truncation Variable. *J. Econometrics*, January 1985, *27*(1), pp. 131–35.

Bodkin, Ronald G. and Raj, Baldev. An Alternative Estimator of the Variance of the Disturbance Term in Extraneous and Mixed Estimation. *Int. Econ. Rev.*, February 1985, *26*(1), pp. 67–69.

Breiman, Leo and Friedman, Jerome H. Estimating Optimal Transformations for Multiple Regression and Correlation: Rejoinder. *J. Amer. Statist. Assoc.*, September 1985, *80*(391), pp. 614–19.

Breiman, Leo and Friedman, Jerome H. Estimating Optimal Transformations for Multiple Regression and Correlation. *J. Amer. Statist. Assoc.*, September 1985, *80*(391), pp. 580–98.

Buja, Andreas and Kass, Robert E. Some Observations on ACE Methodology: Comment [Estimating Optimal Transformations for Multiple Regression and Correlation]. *J. Amer. Statist. Assoc.*, September 1985, *80*(391), pp. 602–07.

Cameron, Trudy Ann. Consistent Multinominal and Nested Logit Point Estimates: A Practical Note. *Oxford Bull. Econ. Statist.*, February 1985, *47*(1), pp. 83–89.

Carroll, Raymond J.; Gallo, Paul and Gleser, Leon Jay. Comparison of Least Squares and Errors-in-Variables Regression, with Special Reference to Randomized Analysis of Covariance. *J. Amer. Statist. Assoc.*, December 1985, *80*(392), pp. 929–32.

Carter, R. A. L. Double *k*-Class Shrinkage Estimators in Multiple Regression. *J. Quant. Econ.*, January 1985, *1*(1), pp. 27–47.

Casella, George. Condition Numbers and Minimax Ridge Regression Estimators. *J. Amer. Statist. Assoc.*, September 1985, *80*(391), pp. 753–58.

Chalfant, James A. and Gallant, A. Ronald. Estimating Substitution Elasticities with the Fourier Cost Function: Some Monte Carlo Results. *J. Econometrics*, May 1985, *28*(2), pp. 205–22.

Chamberlain, Gary. Heterogeneity, Omitted Variable Bias, and Duration Dependence. In *Heckman, J. J. and Singer, B., eds.*, 1985, pp. 3–38.

Chesher, Andrew. Score Tests for Zero Covariances in Recursive Linear Models for Grouped or Censored Data. *J. Econometrics*, June 1985, *28*(3), pp. 291–305.

Chesher, Andrew; Lancaster, Tony and Irish, Margaret. On Detecting the Failure of Distributional Assumptions. *Ann. INSEE*, July-Dec. 1985, (59/60), pp. 7–45.

Conniffe, Denis. Estimating Regression Equations with Common Explanatory Variables but Unequal Numbers of Observations. *J. Econometrics*, February 1985, *27*(2), pp. 179–96.

Consigliere, Isabella. Testing for Heteroscedasticity with Ordinary Least Squres Residuals. *Giorn. Econ.*, Jan.-Feb. 1985, *44*(1–2), pp. 55–64.

Corker, Robert J. and Begg, David K. H. Rational Dummy Variables in an Intertemporal Optimisation Framework. *Oxford Bull. Econ. Statist.*, February 1985, *47*(1), pp. 71–78. [G: U.K.]

Cosslett, Stephen R. and Lee, Lung-Fei. Serial Correlation in Latent Discrete Variable Models. *J. Econometrics*, January 1985, *27*(1), pp. 79–97. [G: U.S.]

Coulson, N. Edward and Robins, Russell P. A Comment on the Testing of Functional Form in First Difference Models. *Rev. Econ. Statist.*, November 1985, *67*(4), pp. 710–12.

Crockett, Patrick W. Asymptotic Distribution of the Hildreth–Houck Estimator. *J. Amer. Statist. Assoc.*, March 1985, *80*(389), pp. 202–04.

Cushing, Matthew J. and McGarvey, Mary G. Identification by Disaggregation. *Amer. Econ. Rev.*, December 1985, *75*(5), pp. 1165–67.

Dastoor, Naorayex K. and McAleer, Michael. Testing Separate Models with Stochastic Regressors. *Econ. Modelling*, October 1985, *2*(4), pp. 331–38.

Davidson, Russell; Godfrey, Leslie and MacKinnon, James G. A Simplified Version of the Differencing Test. *Int. Econ. Rev.*, October 1985, *26*(3), pp. 639–47.

Davidson, Russell and MacKinnon, James G. Heteroskedasticity-Robust Tests in Regressions Directions. *Ann. INSEE*, July-Dec. 1985, (59/60), pp. 183–218.

Davidson, Russell and MacKinnon, James G. Testing Linear and Loglinear Regressions against Box–Cox Alternatives. *Can. J. Econ.*, August 1985, *18*(3), pp. 499–517.

Davidson, Russell and MacKinnon, James G. The Interpretation of Test Statistics. *Can. J. Econ.*, February 1985, *18*(1), pp. 38–57.

Denton, Frank T. Data Mining as an Industry. *Rev. Econ. Statist.*, February 1985, *67*(1), pp. 124–27.

Deprins, D. and Simar, L. A Note on the Asymptotic Relative Efficiency of M.L.E. in a Linear Model with Gamma Disturbances. *J. Econometrics*, March 1985, *27*(3), pp. 383–86.

Domowitz, Ian. New Directions in Non-linear Estimation with Dependent Observations. *Can. J. Econ.*, February 1985, *18*(1), pp. 1–27.

Drygas, Hilmar. Estimation without Invariance and Hsu's Theorem in Variance Component Models. In *[Menges, G.]*, 1985, pp. 56–69.

Dufour, Jean-Marie and Dagenais, Marcel G. Durbin–Watson Tests for Serial Correlation in Regressions with Missing Observations. *J. Econometrics*, March 1985, *27*(3), pp. 371–81.

Dufour, Jean-Marie; Gaudry, Marc J. I. and Hafer, R. W. Corrigendum [A Warning on the Use of the Cochrane–Orcutt Procedure Based on a Money Demand Equation]. *Empirical Econ.*, 1985, *10*(4), pp. 275. [G: U.S.]

Engle, Robert F.; Hendry, David F. and Trumble, David. Small-Sample Properties of ARCH Estimators and Tests. *Can. J. Econ.*, February 1985, *18*(1), pp. 66–93.

Epstein, Larry G. and Yatchew, Adonis John. Non-parametric Hypothesis Testing Procedures and Applications to Demand Analysis. *J. Econometrics*, Oct./Nov. 1985, *30*(1/2), pp. 149–69.

Erlat, Haluk. Testing for Structural Change at More than One Switch Point: Inadequate Degrees of Freedom and Dummy Variables. *Oxford Bull. Econ. Statist.*, August 1985, *47*(3), pp. 293–302.

Evans, Merran Anderson. The Invariance of Tests of Disturbance Specification to Multicollinearity. *Bull. Econ. Res.*, September 1985, *37*(3), pp. 195–99.

Evans, Merran Anderson and King, Maxwell L. A Point Optimal Test for Heteroscedastic Disturbances. *J. Econometrics*, February 1985, *27*(2), pp. 163–78.

Florens, Jean-Pierre and Mouchart, Michel. A Linear Theory for Noncausality. *Econometrica*, January 1985, *53*(1), pp. 157–75.

Førsund, Finn R. Frontier Production Functions: Comment. *Econometric Rev.*, 1985-86, *4*(2), pp. 329–34.

Fowlkes, E. B. and Kettenring, J. R. The ACE Method of Optimal Transformations: Comment [Estimating Optimal Transformations for Multiple Regression and Correlation]. *J. Amer. Statist. Assoc.*, September 1985, *80*(391), pp. 607–13.

Gallant, A. Ronald. Identification et convergence en régression semi-non-paramétrique. (Identification and Consistency in Semi-Non-Parametric Regression. With English summary.) *Ann. INSEE*, July-Dec. 1985, (59/60), pp. 239–65.

Giaccotto, Carmelo and Ali, Mukhtar M. Optimal Distribution-Free Tests and Further Evidence of Heteroscedasticity in the Market Model: A Reply. *J. Finance*, June 1985, *40*(2), pp. 607. [G: U.S.]

Giles, David E. A. A Note on Regression Estimation with Extraneous Information. *J. Quant. Econ.*, January 1985, *1*(1), pp. 151–59.

Gourieroux, Christian, et al. Résidus généralisés résidus simulés et leur utilisation dans les modèles non linéaires. (Generalized Residuals, Simulated Residuals and Their Applications in Non Linear Models. With English summary.) *Ann. INSEE*, July-Dec. 1985, (59/60), pp. 71–96.

Greene, William H. Frontier Production Functions: Comment. *Econometric Rev.*, 1985-86, *4*(2), pp. 335–38.

Gregory, Allan W. and Veall, Michael R. A Lagrange Multiplier Test of the Restrictions for a Simple Rational Expectations Model. *Can. J. Econ.*, February 1985, *18*(1), pp. 94–105. [G: Canada]

Gregory, Allan W. and Veall, Michael R. Formulating Wald Tests of Nonlinear Restrictions. *Econometrica*, November 1985, *53*(6), pp. 1465–68.

Guilkey, David K. and Price, J. Michael. Erratum [On Comparing Restricted Least Squares Estimators]. *J. Econometrics*, February 1985, *27*(2), pp. 271.

Harrison, Michael J. and Keogh, Gary. A Lagrange Multiplier Interpretation of Disturbance Estimators with an Application to Testing for Nonlinearity. *J. Econometrics*, February 1985, *27*(2), pp. 259–69.

Hatanaka, Michio and Tanaka, Katsuto. The Identification Problem in Regression Models with Time-varying Parameters in Random Walk. *Econ. Stud. Quart.*, August 1985, *36*(2), pp. 133–47.

Heckman, James A. and Singer, Burton. Erratum [Econometric Duration Analysis]. *J. Econometrics*, January 1985, *27*(1), pp. 137–38.

Heckman, James J. and Robb, Richard, Jr. Alternative Methods for Evaluating the Impact of Interventions. In *Heckman, J. J. and Singer, B., eds.*, 1985, pp. 156–245.

Heckman, James J. and Robb, Richard, Jr. Alternative Methods for Evaluating the Impact of Interventions: An Overview. *J. Econometrics*, Oct./Nov. 1985, *30*(1/2), pp. 239–67.

Hinck, Harriet. A Comparison of Logit Regression with Discriminant Analysis for (Discrete) Models of Qualitative Choice in Economics Research. In *Brown, R. C., ed.*, 1985, pp. 109–16.

Honda, Yuzo. Testing the Error Components Model with Non-normal Disturbances. *Rev. Econ. Stud.*, October 1985, *52*(4), pp. 681–90.

Hsiao, Cheng. Benefits and Limitations of Panel Data: Reply. *Econometric Rev.*, 1985, *4*(1), pp. 187–89.

Hsiao, Cheng. Benefits and Limitations of Panel Data. *Econometric Rev.*, 1985, *4*(1), pp. 121–74.

Hsieh, David A.; Manski, Charles F. and McFadden, Daniel. Estimation of Response Probabilities from Augmented Retrospective Observations. *J. Amer. Statist. Assoc.*, September 1985, *80*(391), pp. 651–62.

Im, Eric Iksoon. A Comment on Stochastic Parameter Variation. *Atlantic Econ. J.*, December 1985, *13*(4), pp. 85.

Jakubson, George and Kiefer, Nicholas M. Benefits and Limitations of Panel Data: Comment. *Econometric Rev.*, 1985, *4*(1), pp. 175–78.

Jeong, Ki-Jun. A New Approximation of the Critical Point of the Durbin–Watson Test for Serial Correlation. *Econometrica*, March 1985, *53*(2), pp. 477–82.

Kadiyala, Krishna. Misspecification: Excluding and Including Variables Simultaneously. *Australian Econ. Pap.*, June 1985, *24*(44), pp. 206–09.

Kang, Suk. A Note on the Equivalence of Specification Tests in the Two-Factor Multivariate Variance Components Model. *J. Econometrics*, May 1985, *28*(2), pp. 193–203.

Kariya, Takeaki. A Nonlinear Version of the Gauss–Markov Theorem. *J. Amer. Statist. Assoc.*, June 1985, *80*(390), pp. 476–77.

Keener, Robert W. and Waldman, Donald M. Maximum Likelihood Regression of Rank-censored Data. *J. Amer. Statist. Assoc.*, June 1985, *80*(390), pp. 385–92. [G: U.S.]

King, Maxwell L. A Point Optimal Test for Autoregressive Disturbances. *J. Econometrics*, January 1985, *27*(1), pp. 21–37.

Knottnerus, Paul. A Test Strategy for Discriminating between Autocorrelation and Misspecification in Regression Analysis: A Critical Note. *Rev. Econ. Statist.*, February 1985, *67*(1), pp. 175–77.

Kobayashi, Masahito. Comparison of Efficiencies of Several Estimators for Linear Regressions with Autocorrelated Errors. *J. Amer. Statist. Assoc.*, December 1985, *80*(392), pp. 951–53.

Kohler, Wilhelm K. The Impact of Measurement Errors on OLS Estimates of Import Demand Parameters. *Jahr. Nationalökon. Statist.*, March 1985, *200*(2), pp. 173–85.

Kooiman, Peter; van Dijk, Herman K. and Thurik, A. Roy. Likelihood Diagnostics and Bayesian Analysis of a Micro-Economic Disequilibrium Model for Retail Services. *J.*

Econometrics, July/August 1985, *29*(1/2), pp. 121–48.   [G: Netherlands]

Krämer, Walter. The Power of the Durbin–Watson Test for Regressions without an Intercept. *J. Econometrics*, June 1985, *28*(3), pp. 363–70.

Krämer, Walter, et al. Diagnostic Checking in Practice. *Rev. Econ. Statist.*, February 1985, *67*(1), pp. 118–23.

Lancaster, J. F. and Quade, Dana. A Nonparametric Test for Linear Regression Based on Combining Kendall's Tau with the Sign Test. *J. Amer. Statist. Assoc.*, June 1985, *80*(390), pp. 393–97.

Lancaster, Tony and Chesher, Andrew. Residuals, Tests and Plots with a Job Matching Illustration. *Ann. INSEE*, July-Dec. 1985, (59/60), pp. 47–70.

Lee, Lung-Fei and Maddala, G. S. The Common Structure of Tests for Selectivity Bias, Serial Correlation, Heteroscedaticity, and Non-normality in the Tobit Model. *Int. Econ. Rev.*, February 1985, *26*(1), pp. 1–20.

Lehmann, Bruce and Warga, Arthur D. Optimal Distribution-Free Tests and Further Evidence of Heteroscedasticity in the Market Model: A Comment. *J. Finance*, June 1985, *40*(2), pp. 603–05.   [G: U.S.]

Levine, David K. The Sensitivity of MLE to Measure Error. *J. Econometrics*, May 1985, *28*(2), pp. 223–30.

Little, Roderick J. A. A Note about Models for Selectivity Bias. *Econometrica*, November 1985, *53*(6), pp. 1469–74.

Lubrano, Michel. Bayesian Analysis of Switching Regression Models. *J. Econometrics*, July/August 1985, *29*(1/2), pp. 69–95.   [G: U.S.; Italy]

MacDonald, Glenn M. and Robinson, Chris. Cautionary Tails about Arbitrary Deletion of Observations; or, Throwing the Variance Out with the Bathwater. *J. Lab. Econ.*, April 1985, *3*(2), pp. 124–52.   [G: U.S.]

MacDonald, Glenn M. and MacKinnon, James G. Convenient Methods for Estimation of Linear Regression Models with MA(1) Errors. *Can. J. Econ.*, February 1985, *18*(1), pp. 106–16.

Machak, Joseph A.; Spivey, W. Allen and Wrobleski, William J. A Framework for Time Varying Parameter Regression Modeling. *J. Bus. Econ. Statist.*, April 1985, *3*(2), pp. 104–11.   [G: U.S.]

MacKinnon, James G. and White, Halbert. Some Heteroskedasticity-consistent Covariance Matrix Estimators with Improved Finite Sample Properties. *J. Econometrics*, September 1985, *29*(3), pp. 305–25.

Magee, Lonnie J. Efficiency of Iterative Estimators in the Regression Model with AR(1) Disturbances. *J. Econometrics*, September 1985, *29*(3), pp. 275–87.

Mankiw, N. Gregory and Shapiro, Matthew D. Trends, Random Walks, and Tests of the Permanent Income Hypothesis. *J. Monet. Econ.*, September 1985, *16*(2), pp. 165–74.

Manski, Charles F. Semiparametric Analysis of Discrete Response: Asymptotic Properties of the Maximum Score Estimator. *J. Econometrics*, March 1985, *27*(3), pp. 313–33.

Masson, Edwina A. The Value of Imperfect Sample Separation Information in Mixtures of Normal Distributions. *J. Econometrics*, September 1985, *29*(3), pp. 341–50.

McCulloch, J. Huston. On Heteros*edasticity. *Econometrica*, March 1985, *53*(2), pp. 403.

Mendelsohn, Robert. Identifying Structural Equations with Single Market Data. *Rev. Econ. Statist.*, August 1985, *67*(3), pp. 525–29.

Meng, Chun-Lo and Schmidt, Peter. On the Cost of Partial Observability in the Bivariate Probit Model. *Int. Econ. Rev.*, February 1985, *26*(1), pp. 71–85.

Mittelhammer, Ronald C. Quadratic Risk Domination of Restricted Least Squares Estimators via Stein-ruled Auxiliary Constraints. *J. Econometrics*, September 1985, *29*(3), pp. 289–303.

Nakamura, Alice and Nakamura, Masao. On the Performance of Tests by Wu and by Hausman for Detecting the Ordinary Least Squares Bias Problem. *J. Econometrics*, September 1985, *29*(3), pp. 213–27.

Nankervis, J. C. and Savin, N. E. Testing the Autoregressive Parameter with the *t* Statistic. *J. Econometrics*, February 1985, *27*(2), pp. 143–61.

Newey, Whitney K. Generalized Method of Moments Specification Testing. *J. Econometrics*, September 1985, *29*(3), pp. 229–56.

Newey, Whitney K. Maximum Likelihood Specification Testing and Conditional Moment Tests. *Econometrica*, September 1985, *53*(5), pp. 1047–70.

Newey, Whitney K. Semiparametric Estimation of Limited Dependent Variable Models with Endogenous Explanatory Variables. *Ann. INSEE*, July-Dec. 1985, (59/60), pp. 219–37.

Nickell, Stephen. Benefits and Limitations of Panel Data: Comment. *Econometric Rev.*, 1985, *4*(1), pp. 179–82.

Ohtani, Kazuhiro. Small Sample Properties of the Generalized Ridge Regression Predictor under Specification Error. *Econ. Stud. Quart.*, April 1985, *36*(1), pp. 53–60.

Ohtani, Kazuhiro and Katayama, Sei-ichi. An Alternative Gradual Switching Regression Model and Its Application. *Econ. Stud. Quart.*, August 1985, *36*(2), pp. 148–53.   [G: Japan]

Ohtani, Kazuhiro and Toyoda, Toshihisa. Small Sample Properties of Tests of Equality between Sets of Coefficients in Two Linear Regressions under Heteroscedasticity. *Int. Econ. Rev.*, February 1985, *26*(1), pp. 37–44.

Olsen, Randall J. Frontier Production Functions: Comment. *Econometric Rev.*, 1985-86, *4*(2), pp. 339–43.

Pantula, Sastry G. and Fuller, Wayne A. Mean Estimation Bias in Least Squares Estimation of Autoregressive Processes. *J. Econometrics*, January 1985, *27*(1), pp. 99–121.

Pearce, Douglas K. and Reiter, Sara A. Regression Strategies When Multicollinearity Is a Problem: A Methodological Note. *J. Acc. Res.*, Spring 1985, *23*(1), pp. 405–07.

Pesaran, M. Hashem; Smith, R. P. and Yeo, J. S. Testing for Structural Stability and Predictive Failure: A Review. *Manchester Sch. Econ. Soc. Stud.*, September 1985, *53*(3), pp. 280–95.

Pfeffermann, D. and Holmes, D. J. Robustness Considerations in the Choice of a Method of Inference for Regression Analysis of Survey Data. *J. Roy. Statist. Soc.*, 1985, *148*(3), pp. 268–78.

Pole, A. M. and Smith, A. F. M. A Bayesian Analysis of Some Threshold Switching Models. *J. Econometrics*, July/August 1985, *29*(1/2), pp. 97–119.

Powell, James L. and Stoker, Thomas M. The Estimation of Complete Aggregation Structures. *J. Econometrics*, Oct./Nov. 1985, *30*(1/2), pp. 317–44.

Pregibon, Daryl and Vardi, Yehuda. Estimating Optimal Transformations for Multiple Regression and Correlation: Comment. *J. Amer. Statist. Assoc.*, September 1985, *80*(391), pp. 598–601.

Robinson, P. M.; Bera, Anil K. and Jarque, Carlos M. Tests for Serial Dependence in Limited Dependent Variable Models. *Int. Econ. Rev.*, October 1985, *26*(3), pp. 629–38.

Ronchetti, E. Robust Estimators for Regression Models. In *Brown, R. C., ed.*, 1985, pp. 147–52.

Ruppert, David. On the Bounded-Influence Regression Estimator of Krasker and Welsch. *J. Amer. Statist. Assoc.*, March 1985, *80*(389), pp. 205–08.

Salon, Gary. Benefits and Limitations of Panel Data: Comment. *Econometric Rev.*, 1985, *4*(1), pp. 183–86.

Samarov, Alexander M. Bounded-Influence Regression via Local Minimax Mean Squared Error. *J. Amer. Statist. Assoc.*, December 1985, *80*(392), pp. 1032–40.

Sarkar, Nityananda. Consistency and Asymptotic Normality of the *ML* Estimator of Limited Dependent Variable Models with Heteroscedasticity. *J. Quant. Econ.*, July 1985, *1*(2), pp. 253–63.

Schmidt, Peter. Frontier Production Functions: Reply. *Econometric Rev.*, 1985-86, *4*(2), pp. 353–55.

Schmidt, Peter. Frontier Production Functions. *Econometric Rev.*, 1985-86, *4*(2), pp. 289–328.

Schneeweiss, Hans. Estimating Linear Relations with Errors in the Variables: The Merging of Two Approaches. In *[Menges, G.]*, 1985, pp. 207–21.

Sevestre, Patrick and Trognon, Alain. A Note on Autoregressive Error Components Models. *J. Econometrics*, May 1985, *28*(2), pp. 231–45.

Sharma, Subhash C. The Effects of Autocorrelation among Errors on the Consistency Property of OLS Variance Estimator. *J. Econometrics*, March 1985, *27*(3), pp. 335–61.

Sheehan, Dennis P. Second-Order Properties of Estimators of Serial Correlation from Regression Residuals. *J. Econometrics*, March 1985, *27*(3), pp. 299–311.

Shvyrkov, Vladislav V. and Lee, Kenneth R. Multicollinearity and Multiinterdependence Tests. In *Brown, R. C., ed.*, 1985, pp. 211–24.

Small, Kenneth A. and Hsiao, Cheng. Multinomial Logit Specification Tests. *Int. Econ. Rev.*, October 1985, *26*(3), pp. 619–27.

Smith, Richard J. Some Tests for Misspecification in Bivariate Limited Dependent Variable Models. *Ann. INSEE*, July-Dec. 1985, (59/60), pp. 97–123.

Sneessens, Henri R. Two Alternative Stochastic Specification and Estimation Methods for Quantity Rationing Models: A Monte-Carlo Comparison. *Europ. Econ. Rev.*, October 1985, *29*(1), pp. 111–36.

Spircu, Liliana. Criteria for Estimating the Regression Model Parameters. *Econ. Computat. Cybern. Stud. Res.*, 1985, *20*(3), pp. 61–64.

Stine, Robert A. Bootstrap Prediction Intervals for Regression. *J. Amer. Statist. Assoc.*, December 1985, *80*(392), pp. 1026–31.

Stoker, Thomas M. Aggregation, Structural Change, and Cross-Section Estimation. *J. Amer. Statist. Assoc.*, September 1985, *80*(391), pp. 720–29.

Storer, Barry E. and Crowley, John. A Diagnostic for Cox Regression and General Conditional Likelihoods. *J. Amer. Statist. Assoc.*, March 1985, *80*(389), pp. 139–47.

Swann, G. M. P. Uncertainty in Regression Estimates: The Relative Importance of Sampling and Non-sampling Uncertainty. *Oxford Bull. Econ. Statist.*, August 1985, *47*(3), pp. 303–10.

Sweeting, Trevor J. Consistent Prior Distributions for Transformed Models. In *Bernardo, J. M., et al., eds.*, 1985, pp. 755–62.

Terza, Joseph V. Reduced-Form Trinomial Probit: A Quantal Response Model without a Priori Restrictions. *J. Bus. Econ. Statist.*, January 1985, *3*(1), pp. 54–59.

Thélot, Claude. Lois logistiques à deux dimensions. (Logistic Distributions in Two Dimensions. With English summary.) *Ann. INSEE*, Apr.-June 1985, (58), pp. 123–50.

Thursby, Jerry G. A Test Strategy for Discriminating between Autocorrelation and Misspecification in Regression Analysis: Reply. *Rev. Econ. Statist.*, February 1985, *67*(1), pp. 177–78.

Thursby, Jerry G. The Relationship among the Specification Tests of Hausman, Ramsey, and Chow. *J. Amer. Statist. Assoc.*, December 1985, *80*(392), pp. 926–28.

Trivedi, Pravin K. Distributed Lags, Aggregation, and Compounding: Some Econometric Implications. *Rev. Econ. Stud.*, January 1985, *52*(1), pp. 19–35.

Tsay, Ruey S. Model Identification in Dynamic Regression (Distributed Lag) Models. *J. Bus. Econ. Statist.*, July 1985, *3*(3), pp. 228–37.

Tse, Y. K. Some Modified Versions of Durbin's

h-Statistic. *Rev. Econ. Statist.*, August 1985, 67(3), pp. 534–38.

Tsurumi, Hiroki and Sheflin, Neil. Some Tests for the Constancy of Regressions under Heteroscedasticity. *J. Econometrics*, February 1985, 27(2), pp. 221–34.

Ullah, Aman. Specification Analysis of Econometric Models. *J. Quant. Econ.*, July 1985, 1(2), pp. 187–209.

Wansbeek, Tom and Kapteyn, Arie. Estimation in a Linear Model with Serially Correlated Errors When Observations Are Missing. *Int. Econ. Rev.*, June 1985, 26(2), pp. 469–90.

Watson, Mark W. and Engle, Robert F. Testing for Regression Coefficient Stability with a Stationary AR(1) Alternative. *Rev. Econ. Statist.*, May 1985, 67(2), pp. 341–46.

White, Halbert. Tests de spécification dans les modèles dynamiques. (Specification Testing in Dynamic Models. With English summary.) *Ann. INSEE*, July-Dec. 1985, (59/60), pp. 125–81.

Williams, Donald R. A Comment on the Appropriateness of Fixed Effects Assumptions. *Quart. J. Bus. Econ.*, Winter 1985, 24(1), pp. 93–100.

Yatchew, Adonis John. Frontier Production Functions: Comment. *Econometric Rev.*, 1985-86, 4(2), pp. 345–52.

Yatchew, Adonis John and Griliches, Zvi. Specification Error in Probit Models. *Rev. Econ. Statist.*, February 1985, 67(1), pp. 134–39.

Zellner, Arnold and Moulton, Brent R. Bayesian Regression Diagnostics with Applications to International Consumption and Income Data. *J. Econometrics*, July/August 1985, 29(1/2), pp. 187–211.   **[G: LDCs; MDCs]**

2114 Multivariate Analysis, Statistical Information Theory, and Other Special Inferential Problems; Queuing Theory; Markov Chains

Amsler, Christine E. and Schmidt, Peter. A Monte Carlo Investigation of the Accuracy of Multivariate CAPM Tests. *J. Finan. Econ.*, September 1985, 14(3), pp. 359–75.

Basford, K. E. and McLachlan, G. J. Estimation of Allocation Rates in a Cluster Analysis Context. *J. Amer. Statist. Assoc.*, June 1985, 80(390), pp. 286–93.

Benasseni, Jacques. Reconstitution de l'opérateur de variance associé à un échantillon à partir d'un autre échantillon. (Reconstitution of the Variance Operator of One Sample Based on Another Sample. With English summary.) *Ann. INSEE*, Apr.-June 1985, (58), pp. 151–69.

Berliner, L. Mark. A Decision Theoretic Structure for Robust Bayesian Analysis with Applications to the Estimation of a Multivariate Normal Mean. In *Bernardo, J. M., et al., eds.*, 1985, pp. 619–28.

Bernardo, J. M. and Bermúdez, J. D. The Choice of Variables in Probabilistic Classification. In *Bernardo, J. M., et al., eds.*, 1985, pp. 67–77.

Burke, Peter J. and Knoke, David. A User's Guide to Log-Linear Models. In *Smith, R. B., ed.*, 1985, pp. 297–335.   **[G: U.S.]**

Cameron, Trudy Ann. Consistent Multinominal and Nested Logit Point Estimates: A Practical Note. *Oxford Bull. Econ. Statist.*, February 1985, 47(1), pp. 83–89.

Clayton, David and Cuzick, Jack. Multivariate Generalizations of the Proportional Hazards Model. *J. Roy. Statist. Soc.*, 1985, 148(2), pp. 82–108.

Conlisk, John. Comparative Statics for Markov Chains. *J. Econ. Dynam. Control*, October 1985, 9(2), pp. 139–51.

D'Ambra, Luigi. Alcune estensioni dell'analisi in componenti principali per lo studio di sistemi evolutivi. Uno studio sul commercio internzionale dell'elettronica. (Some Extensions of the Principal Component Analysis for the Study of Developing Systems. A Study Concerning the Electronic International Commerce. With English summary.) *Ricerche Econ.*, Apr.-June 1985, 39(2), pp. 233–60.   **[G: OECD; LDCs]**

Giovagnoli, A. and Verdinelli, I. Optimal Block Designs under a Hierarchical Linear Model. In *Bernardo, J. M., et al., eds.*, 1985, pp. 655–61.

Gupta, A. K. and Govindarajulu, Z. On Minimum Distance Classification Rules for c Multivariate Populations. *Statistica*, Jan.–Mar. 1985, 45(1), pp. 101–04.

Hassin, Refael. On the Optimality of First Come Last Served Queues. *Econometrica*, January 1985, 53(1), pp. 201–02.

Kalbfleisch, J. D. and Lawless, J. F. The Analysis of Panel Data under a Markov Assumption. *J. Amer. Statist. Assoc.*, December 1985, 80(392), pp. 863–71.

Lindley, Dennis V. Reconciliation of Discrete Probability Distributions. In *Bernardo, J. M., et al., eds.*, 1985, pp. 375–87.

Marsden, Peter V. D Systems and Effect Parameters: Some Complementarities. In *Smith, R. B., ed.*, 1985, pp. 367–89.   **[G: U.S.]**

Poli, Irene. Bayesian Estimation of k-Dimensional Distribution Functions via Neutral to the Right Priors. In *Bernardo, J. M., et al., eds.*, 1985, pp. 733–39.

Press, S. James. Multivariate Group Assessment of Probabilities of Nuclear War. In *Bernardo, J. M., et al., eds.*, 1985, pp. 425–55.

Raveh, Adi. A Note on Factor Analysis and Arbitrage Pricing Theory. *J. Banking Finance*, June 1985, 9(2), pp. 317–21.

Roll, Richard. A Note on the Geometry of Shanken's CSR T^2 Test for Mean/Variance Efficiency. *J. Finan. Econ.*, September 1985, 14(3), pp. 349–57.

Shanken, Jay. Multivariate Tests of the Zero-Beta CAPM. *J. Finan. Econ.*, September 1985, 14(3), pp. 327–48.

Staroverov, O. V. Surveys and Aggregation in Markov Models. *Matekon*, Summer 1985, 21(4), pp. 79–103.   **[G: U.S.S.R.]**

Swanson, Peggy E. and Edgar, S. Michael. An Alternative Approach to the Selection of "Representative" Variables. *J. Econ. Bus.*, February 1985, *37*(1), pp. 69–79.　　　　[G: U.S.]

2115 Bayesian Statistics and Bayesian Econometrics

Agnew, Carson E. Multiple Probability Assessments by Dependent Experts. *J. Amer. Statist. Assoc.*, June 1985, *80*(390), pp. 243–47.

Aitchison, J. Practical Bayesian Problems in Simplex Sample Spaces. In *Bernardo, J. M., et al., eds.*, 1985, pp. 15–26.

Albert, James H. Bayesian Estimation Methods for Incomplete Two-Way Contingency Tables Using Prior Beliefs of Association. In *Bernardo, J. M., et al., eds.*, 1985, pp. 589–602.

Amaral-Turkman, M. A. and Dunsmore, I. R. Measures of Information in the Predictive Distribution. In *Bernardo, J. M., et al., eds.*, 1985, pp. 603–12.

Ameen, J. R. M. and Harrison, P. Jeff. Normal Discount Bayesian Models. In *Bernardo, J. M., et al., eds.*, 1985, pp. 271–94.

Armero, C. Bayesian Analysis of M/M/1/∞ /FIFO Queues. In *Bernardo, J. M., et al., eds.*, 1985, pp. 613–17.　　　　[G: Spain]

Bauwens, Luc and Richard, Jean-Francois. A 1–1 Poly *t* Random Variable Generator with Application to Monte Carlo Integration. *J. Econometrics*, July/August 1985, *29*(1/2), pp. 19–46.

Berliner, L. Mark. A Decision Theoretic Structure for Robust Bayesian Analysis with Applications to the Estimation of a Multivariate Normal Mean. In *Bernardo, J. M., et al., eds.*, 1985, pp. 619–28.

Bernardo, J. M. and Bermúdez, J. D. The Choice of Variables in Probabilistic Classification. In *Bernardo, J. M., et al., eds.*, 1985, pp. 67–77.

Carlin, J. B.; Dempster, A. P. and Jonas, A. B. On Models and Methods for Bayesian Time Series Analysis. *J. Econometrics*, Oct./Nov. 1985, *30*(1/2), pp. 67–90.

Consonni, G. and Dawid, A. P. Invariant Normal Bayesian Linear Models and Experimental Designs. In *Bernardo, J. M., et al., eds.*, 1985, pp. 629–43.

Csiszár, I. An Extended Maximum Entropy Principle and a Bayesian Justification. In *Bernardo, J. M., et al., eds.*, 1985, pp. 83–93.

Davis, William W. Dynamic Generalized Linear Models and Bayesian Forecasting: Comment. *J. Amer. Statist. Assoc.*, March 1985, *80*(389), pp. 84–85.

Dawid, A. P. The Impossibility of Inductive Inference [Self-calibrating Priors Do Not Exist]. *J. Amer. Statist. Assoc.*, June 1985, *80*(390), pp. 340–41.

Dempster, A. P. Probability, Evidence, and Judgment. In *Bernardo, J. M., et al., eds.*, 1985, pp. 119–26.

Dempster, A. P. and Carlin, J. B. Dynamic Generalized Linear Models and Bayesian Forecasting: Comment. *J. Amer. Statist. Assoc.*, March 1985, *80*(389), pp. 85–88.

Diaconis, Persi and Ylvisaker, Donald. Quantify-

ing Prior Opinion. In *Bernardo, J. M., et al., eds.*, 1985, pp. 133–49.

Dickey, James M. and Chen, Chong-Hong. Direct Subjective-Probability Modelling Using Ellipsoidal Distributions. In *Bernardo, J. M., et al., eds.*, 1985, pp. 157–76.

van Dijk, Herman K. and Kloek, Teun. Experiments with Some Alternatives for Simple Importance Sampling in Monte Carlo Integration. In *Bernardo, J. M., et al., eds.*, 1985, pp. 511–26.

van Dijk, Herman K.; Kloek, Teun and Boender, C. Guus. Posterior Moments Computed by Mixed Integration. *J. Econometrics*, July/August 1985, *29*(1/2), pp. 3–18.

Ferrandiz, J. R. Bayesian Inference on Mahalanobis Distance: An Alternative Approach to Bayesian Model Testing. In *Bernardo, J. M., et al., eds.*, 1985, pp. 645–53.

Fienberg, Stephen E. and Tsay, Ruey S. Dynamic Generalized Linear Models and Bayesian Forecasting: Comment. *J. Amer. Statist. Assoc.*, March 1985, *80*(389), pp. 89–90.

Freedman, D. A. Some Subjective Bayesian Considerations in the Selection of Models: Comments on Hill's Model Selection Paper. *Econometric Rev.*, 1985-86, *4*(2), pp. 247–51.

French, Simon. Group Consensus Probability Distributions: A Critical Survey. In *Bernardo, J. M., et al., eds.*, 1985, pp. 183–97.

Gallant, A. Ronald. Identification et convergence en régression semi-non-paramétrique. (Identification and Consistency in Semi-Non-Parametric Regression. With English summary.) *Ann. INSEE*, July-Dec. 1985, (59/60), pp. 239–65.

Gallant, A. Ronald and Monahan, John F. Explicitly Infinite-Dimensional Bayesian Analysis of Production Technologies. *J. Econometrics*, Oct./Nov. 1985, *30*(1/2), pp. 171–201.　　　[G: U.S.]

Geisser, Seymour. Interval Prediction for Pareto and Exponential Observables. *J. Econometrics*, July/August 1985, *29*(1/2), pp. 173–85.

Geisser, Seymour. On the Prediction of Observables: A Selective Update. In *Bernardo, J. M., et al., eds.*, 1985, pp. 203–25.

Giovagnoli, A. and Verdinelli, I. Optimal Block Designs under a Hierarchical Linear Model. In *Bernardo, J. M., et al., eds.*, 1985, pp. 655–61.

Goldstein, Michael. Temporal Coherence. In *Bernardo, J. M., et al., eds.*, 1985, pp. 231–45.

Good, I. J. Weight of Evidence: A Brief Survey. In *Bernardo, J. M., et al., eds.*, 1985, pp. 249–64.

Guttman, I. and Pena, D. Dynamic Generalized Linear Models and Bayesian Forecasting: Comment: Robust Filtering. *J. Amer. Statist. Assoc.*, March 1985, *80*(389), pp. 91–92.

Hill, Bruce M. Some Subjective Bayesian Considerations in the Selection of Models. *Econometric Rev.*, 1985-86, *4*(2), pp. 191–246.

Hill, Bruce M. Some Subjective Bayesian Considerations in the Selection of Models: Reply. *Econometric Rev.*, 1985-86, *4*(2), pp. 277–88.

Hinkley, David. Comparison of Alternative Functional Forms in Production: Discussion. *J. Econometrics*, Oct./Nov. 1985, *30*(1/2), pp. 363–64.

Ilmakunnas, Pekka. Bayesian Estimation of Cost Functions with Stochastic or Exact Constraints on Parameters. *Int. Econ. Rev.*, February 1985, *26*(1), pp. 111–34. [G: U.S.]

Jaynes, E. T. Highly Informative Priors. In *Bernardo, J. M., et al., eds.*, 1985, pp. 329–52.

Jewell, W. S. Bayesian Estimation of Undetected Errors. In *Bernardo, J. M., et al., eds.*, 1985, pp. 663–71.

Kadane, Joseph B. Is Victimization Chronic? A Bayesian Analysis of Multinomial Missing Data. *J. Econometrics*, July/August 1985, *29*(1/2), pp. 47–67. [G: U.S.]

Kadane, Joseph B. and Wasilkowski, G. W. Average Case ϵ-Complexity in Computer Science—A Bayesian View. In *Bernardo, J. M., et al., eds.*, 1985, pp. 361–72.

Kokolakis, G. E. A Bayesian Criterion for the Selection of Binary Features in Classification Problems. In *Bernardo, J. M., et al., eds.*, 1985, pp. 673–79.

Kooiman, Peter; van Dijk, Herman K. and Thurik, A. Roy. Likelihood Diagnostics and Bayesian Analysis of a Micro-Economic Disequilibrium Model for Retail Services. *J. Econometrics*, July/August 1985, *29*(1/2), pp. 121–48. [G: Netherlands]

Lane, David A. Some Subjective Bayesian Considerations in the Selection of Models: Comments. *Econometric Rev.*, 1985-86, *4*(2), pp. 253–58.

Leamer, Edward E. Some Subjective Bayesian Considerations in the Selection of Models: Comment. *Econometric Rev.*, 1985-86, *4*(2), pp. 259–67.

Lindley, Dennis V. Reconciliation of Discrete Probability Distributions. In *Bernardo, J. M., et al., eds.*, 1985, pp. 375–87.

Los, Cornelis A. Dynamic Generalized Linear Models and Bayesian Forecasting: Comment. *J. Amer. Statist. Assoc.*, March 1985, *80*(389), pp. 92–93.

Lubrano, Michel. Bayesian Analysis of Switching Regression Models. *J. Econometrics*, July/August 1985, *29*(1/2), pp. 69–95. [G: U.S.; Italy]

Lubrano, Michel. Some Aspects of Prior Elicitation Problems in Disequilibrium Models. *J. Econometrics*, July/August 1985, *29*(1/2), pp. 165–72. [G: U.S.]

Meyer, Michael M. Dynamic Generalized Linear Models and Bayesian Forecasting: Comment. *J. Amer. Statist. Assoc.*, March 1985, *80*(389), pp. 94–95.

O'Hagan, A. Shoulders in Hierarchical Models. In *Bernardo, J. M., et al., eds.*, 1985, pp. 697–710.

Oakes, David. Self-calibrating Priors Do Not Exist. *J. Amer. Statist. Assoc.*, June 1985, *80*(390), p. 339.

Oman, Samuel D. Specifying a Prior Distribution in Structured Regression Problems. *J. Amer. Statist. Assoc.*, March 1985, *80*(389), pp. 190–95.

Pettit, L. I. and Smith, A. F. M. Outliers and Influential Observations in Linear Models. In *Bernardo, J. M., et al., eds.*, 1985, pp. 473–90.

Poirier, D. J. Bayesian Hypothesis Testing in Linear Models with Continuously Induced Conjugate Priors across Hypotheses. In *Bernardo, J. M., et al., eds.*, 1985, pp. 711–22.

Pole, A. M. and Smith, A. F. M. A Bayesian Analysis of Some Threshold Switching Models. *J. Econometrics*, July/August 1985, *29*(1/2), pp. 97–119.

Poli, Irene. A Bayesian Non-parametric Estimate for Multivariate Regression. *J. Econometrics*, May 1985, *28*(2), pp. 171–82. [G: Italy]

Poli, Irene. Bayesian Estimation of k-Dimensional Distribution Functions via Neutral to the Right Priors. In *Bernardo, J. M., et al., eds.*, 1985, pp. 733–39.

Pratt, John W. and Schlaifer, Robert. Repetitive Assessment of Judgmental Probability Distributions: A Case Study. In *Bernardo, J. M., et al., eds.*, 1985, pp. 393–418.

Press, S. James. Multivariate Group Assessment of Probabilities of Nuclear War. In *Bernardo, J. M., et al., eds.*, 1985, pp. 425–55.

Rossi, Peter E. Comparison of Alternative Functional Forms in Production. *J. Econometrics*, Oct./Nov. 1985, *30*(1/2), pp. 345–61. [G: U.S.]

Rubin, D. B. The Use of Propensity Scores in Applied Bayesian Inference. In *Bernardo, J. M., et al., eds.*, 1985, pp. 463–71.

Rust, Roland T. and Schmittlein, David C. A Bayesian Cross-validated Likelihood Method for Comparing Alternative Specifications of Quantitative Models. *Marketing Sci.*, Winter 1985, *4*(1), pp. 20–40.

Schervish, Mark J. Self-calibrating Priors Do Not Exist: Comment. *J. Amer. Statist. Assoc.*, June 1985, *80*(390), pp. 341–42.

Sims, Christopher A. Some Subjective Bayesian Considerations in the Selection of Models: Comment. *Econometric Rev.*, 1985-86, *4*(2), pp. 269–75.

Spiegelhalter, D. J. Exact Bayesian Inference on the Parameters of a Cauchy Distribution with Vague Prior Information. In *Bernardo, J. M., et al., eds.*, 1985, pp. 743–49.

Stewart, Leland. Multiparameter Bayesian Inference Using Monte Carlo Integration—Some Techniques for Bivariate Analysis. In *Bernardo, J. M., et al., eds.*, 1985, pp. 495–505.

Sugden, R. A. A Bayesian View of Ignorable Designs in Survey Sampling Inference. In *Bernardo, J. M., et al., eds.*, 1985, pp. 751–53.

Sweeting, Trevor J. Consistent Prior Distributions for Transformed Models. In *Bernardo, J. M., et al., eds.*, 1985, pp. 755–62.

West, Mike. Generalized Linear Models: Scale Parameters, Outlier Accommodation and Prior Distributions. In *Bernardo, J. M., et al., eds.*, 1985, pp. 531–53.

West, Mike; Harrison, P. Jeff and Migon, Helio

S. Dynamic Generalized Linear Models and Bayesian Forecasting: Rejoinder. *J. Amer. Statist. Assoc.*, March 1985, *80*(389), pp. 96–97.

West, Mike; Harrison, P. Jeff and Migon, Helio S. Dynamic Generalized Linear Models and Bayesian Forecasting. *J. Amer. Statist. Assoc.*, March 1985, *80*(389), pp. 73–83.

Winkler, Robert L. Dynamic Generalized Linear Models and Bayesian Forecasting: Comment: Bayesian Model Building and Forecasting. *J. Amer. Statist. Assoc.*, March 1985, *80*(389), pp. 95.

Winkler, Robert L. Information Loss in Noisy and Dependent Processes. In *Bernardo, J. M., et al., eds.*, 1985, pp. 559–68.

Zellner, Arnold. Bayesian Econometrics. *Econometrica*, March 1985, *53*(2), pp. 253–69.

Zellner, Arnold. Bayesian Statistics in Econometrics. In *Bernardo, J. M., et al., eds.*, 1985, pp. 571–81.

Zellner, Arnold and Moulton, Brent R. Bayesian Regression Diagnostics with Applications to International Consumption and Income Data. *J. Econometrics*, July/August 1985, *29*(1/2), pp. 187–211. [G: LDCs; MDCs]

2116 Time Series and Spectral Analysis

Abraham, Bovas. Seasonal Time Series and Transfer Function Modeling. *J. Bus. Econ. Statist.*, October 1985, *3*(4), pp. 356–61.

Ameen, J. R. M. and Harrison, P. Jeff. Normal Discount Bayesian Models. In *Bernardo, J. M., et al., eds.*, 1985, pp. 271–94.

Bell, William R. and Hillmer, Steven C. Reply [Issues Involved with the Seasonal Adjustment of Economic Time Series]. *J. Bus. Econ. Statist.*, January 1985, *3*(1), pp. 95–97.

Binotti, Annetta M. Il test di D. Currie sulle caratteristiche dinamiche di lungo periodo dei modelli autoregressivi a ritardi distribuiti. (The D. Currie's Test on the Long Run Dynamic Properties of the Autoregressive-distributed Lag Models. With English summary.) *Statistica*, April-June 1985, *45*(2), pp. 237–49.

Brorsen, B. Wade; Chavas, Jean-Paul and Grant, Warren R. A Dynamic Analysis of Prices in the U.S. Rice Marketing Channel. *J. Bus. Econ. Statist.*, October 1985, *3*(4), pp. 362–69. [G: U.S.]

Burridge, Peter and Wallis, Kenneth F. Calculating the Variance of Seasonally Adjusted Series. *J. Amer. Statist. Assoc.*, September 1985, *80*(391), pp. 541–52. [G: U.S.]

den Butter, Frank A. G.; Coenen, R. L. and van de Gevel, F. J. J. S. The Use of ARIMA Models in Seasonal Adjustment—A Comparative Study of Census X-11, X-11 ARIMA and Burman's Signal Extraction Method. *Empirical Econ.*, 1985, *10*(4), pp. 209–30. [G: Netherlands]

Carlin, J. B.; Dempster, A. P. and Jonas, A. B. On Models and Methods for Bayesian Time Series Analysis. *J. Econometrics*, Oct./Nov. 1985, *30*(1/2), pp. 67–90.

Chow, Gregory C. and Reny, Philip J. On Two Methods for Solving and Estimating Linear Simultaneous Equations under Rational Expectations. *J. Econ. Dynam. Control*, September 1985, *9*(1), pp. 63–75.

Cooley, Thomas F. and LeRoy, Stephen F. Atheoretical Macroeconometrics: A Critique. *J. Monet. Econ.*, November 1985, *16*(3), pp. 283–308.

Craven, Bruce D. Iterative Fitting of a Time Series Model. In *Batten, D. F. and Lesse, P. F., eds.*, 1985, pp. 155–62.

Davis, William W. Dynamic Generalized Linear Models and Bayesian Forecasting: Comment. *J. Amer. Statist. Assoc.*, March 1985, *80*(389), pp. 84–85.

Dempster, A. P. and Carlin, J. B. Dynamic Generalized Linear Models and Bayesian Forecasting: Comment. *J. Amer. Statist. Assoc.*, March 1985, *80*(389), pp. 85–88.

Dufour, Jean-Marie and Roy, Roch. Some Robust Exact Results on Sample Autocorrelations and Tests of Randomness. *J. Econometrics*, September 1985, *29*(3), pp. 257–73.

Eichenbaum, Martin S. Vector Autoregressions for Causal Inference? Comment. *Carnegie-Rochester Conf. Ser. Public Policy*, Spring 1985, *22*, pp. 305–18.

Engle, Robert F.; Hendry, David F. and Trumble, David. Small-Sample Properties of ARCH Estimators and Tests. *Can. J. Econ.*, February 1985, *18*(1), pp. 66–93.

Espasa, Antoni. El comportamiento de series económicas: movimientos atípicos y relaciones a corto y largo plazo. (With English summary.) *Revista Española Econ.*, 1985, *2*(2), pp. 365–87.

Fienberg, Stephen E. and Tsay, Ruey S. Dynamic Generalized Linear Models and Bayesian Forecasting: Comment. *J. Amer. Statist. Assoc.*, March 1985, *80*(389), pp. 89–90.

Florens, Jean-Pierre and Mouchart, Michel. A Linear Theory for Noncausality. *Econometrica*, January 1985, *53*(1), pp. 157–75.

Giannini, Carlo. Problemi aperti nell'analisi econometrica dinamica. (Some Open Issues in Dynamic Econometric Analysis. With English summary.) *Giorn. Econ.*, Jan.-Feb. 1985, *44*(1–2), pp. 29–43.

Guttman, I. and Pena, D. Dynamic Generalized Linear Models and Bayesian Forecasting: Comment: Robust Filtering. *J. Amer. Statist. Assoc.*, March 1985, *80*(389), pp. 91–92.

Hansen, Lars Peter. A Method for Calculating Bounds on the Asymptotic Covariance Matrices of Generalized Method of Moments Estimators. *J. Econometrics*, Oct./Nov. 1985, *30*(1/2), pp. 203–38.

Harvey, A. C. Trends and Cycles in Macroeconomic Time Series. *J. Bus. Econ. Statist.*, July 1985, *3*(3), pp. 216–27. [G: U.S.]

Harville, David A. Decomposition of Prediction Error. *J. Amer. Statist. Assoc.*, March 1985, *80*(389), pp. 132–38.

Hatanaka, Michio and Tanaka, Katsuto. The Identification Problem in Regression Models with Time-varying Parameters in Random Walk. *Econ. Stud. Quart.*, August 1985, *36*(2), pp. 133–47.

Hausman, Jerry A. and Watson, Mark W. Errors in Variables and Seasonal Adjustment Procedures. *J. Amer. Statist. Assoc.*, September 1985, *80*(391), pp. 531–40.   [G: U.S.]

Hillmer, Steven C. Measures of Variability for Model-based Seasonal Adjustment Procedures. *J. Bus. Econ. Statist.*, January 1985, *3*(1), pp. 60–68.

Hinich, Melvin J. and Patterson, Douglas M. Identification of the Coefficients in a Non-linear Time Series of the Quadratic Type. *J. Econometrics*, Oct./Nov. 1985, *30*(1/2), pp. 269–88.   [G: U.S.]

Hinich, Melvin J. and Patterson, Douglas M. On Non-linear Serial Dependencies in Stock Returns: Reply [Evidence of Nonlinearity in Daily Stock Returns]. *J. Econometrics*, Oct./Nov. 1985, *30*(1/2), pp. 297–99.   [G: U.S.]

Hsiao, Cheng. Benefits and Limitations of Panel Data: Reply. *Econometric Rev.*, 1985, *4*(1), pp. 187–89.

Hsiao, Cheng. Benefits and Limitations of Panel Data. *Econometric Rev.*, 1985, *4*(1), pp. 121–74.

Jakubson, George and Kiefer, Nicholas M. Benefits and Limitations of Panel Data: Comment. *Econometric Rev.*, 1985, *4*(1), pp. 175–78.

Kang, Heejoon. The Effects of Detrending in Granger Causality Tests. *J. Bus. Econ. Statist.*, October 1985, *3*(4), pp. 344–49.   [G: U.S.]

Kunitomo, Naoto and Yamamoto, Taku. Properties of Predictors in Misspecified Autoregressive Time Series Models. *J. Amer. Statist. Assoc.*, December 1985, *80*(392), pp. 941–50.

Leamer, Edward E. Vector Autoregressions for Causal Inference? *Carnegie-Rochester Conf. Ser. Public Policy*, Spring 1985, *22*, pp. 255–303.

Leiner, Bernd. Prediction with Arima Filters. In *[Menges, G.]*, 1985, pp. 177–91.

Los, Cornelis A. Dynamic Generalized Linear Models and Bayesian Forecasting: Comment. *J. Amer. Statist. Assoc.*, March 1985, *80*(389), pp. 92–93.

MacDonald, Glenn M. and MacKinnon, James G. Convenient Methods for Estimation of Linear Regression Models with MA(1) Errors. *Can. J. Econ.*, February 1985, *18*(1), pp. 106–16.

Machak, Joseph A.; Spivey, W. Allen and Wrobleski, William J. A Framework for Time Varying Parameter Regression Modeling. *J. Bus. Econ. Statist.*, April 1985, *3*(2), pp. 104–11.   [G: U.S.]

Magee, Lonnie J. Efficiency of Iterative Estimators in the Regression Model with AR(1) Disturbances. *J. Econometrics*, September 1985, *29*(3), pp. 275–87.

Maravall, Agustin. On Structural Time Series Models and the Characterization of Components. *J. Bus. Econ. Statist.*, October 1985, *3*(4), pp. 350–55.

Marsh, Terry A. On Non-linear Serial Dependen-

cies in Stock Returns [Evidence of Nonlinearity in Daily Stock Returns]. *J. Econometrics*, Oct./Nov. 1985, *30*(1/2), pp. 289–96.   [G: U.S.]

Meyer, Michael M. Dynamic Generalized Linear Models and Bayesian Forecasting: Comment. *J. Amer. Statist. Assoc.*, March 1985, *80*(389), pp. 94–95.

Mihai, V. Causality in Cybernetic-Economic Systems: A Statistical Approach. *Econ. Computat. Cybern. Stud. Res.*, 1985, *20*(4), pp. 61–64.

Nankervis, J. C. and Savin, N. E. Testing the Autoregressive Parameter with the *t* Statistic. *J. Econometrics*, February 1985, *27*(2), pp. 143–61.

Neftci, Salih N. A Note on the Use of Local Maxima to Predict Turning Points in Related Series. *J. Amer. Statist. Assoc.*, September 1985, *80*(391), pp. 553–57.   [G: U.S.]

Nickell, Stephen. Benefits and Limitations of Panel Data: Comment. *Econometric Rev.*, 1985, *4*(1), pp. 179–82.

Nickelsburg, Gerald. Small-Sample Properties of Dimensionality Statistics for Fitting VAR Models to Aggregate Economic Data: A Monte Carlo Study. *J. Econometrics*, May 1985, *28*(2), pp. 183–92.

Nowak, Eugen. Global Identification of the Dynamic Shock-Error Model. *J. Econometrics*, February 1985, *27*(2), pp. 211–19.

Pantula, Sastry G. and Fuller, Wayne A. Mean Estimation Bias in Least Squares Estimation of Autoregressive Processes. *J. Econometrics*, January 1985, *27*(1), pp. 99–121.

Pierce, David A. Topics in Seasonal and Trend Estimation. *Revista Española Econ.*, 1985, *2*(1), pp. 89–112.

Polasek, Wolfgang. Hierarchical Models for Seasonal Time Series. In *Bernardo, J. M., et al., eds.*, 1985, pp. 723–31.   [G: Austria]

Roberts, David L. and Nord, Stephen. Causality Tests and Functional Form Sensitivity. *Appl. Econ.*, February 1985, *17*(1), pp. 135–41.   [G: U.S.]

Rowley, J. C. Robin and Jain, Renuka. Sims on Causality: An Illustration of Soft Econometrics. In *Brown, R. C., ed.*, 1985, pp. 275–94.

Said, Said E. and Dickey, David A. Hypothesis Testing in ARIMA (*p*, 1, *q*) Models. *J. Amer. Statist. Assoc.*, June 1985, *80*(390), pp. 369–74.

Salon, Gary. Benefits and Limitations of Panel Data: Comment. *Econometric Rev.*, 1985, *4*(1), pp. 183–86.

Sevestre, Patrick and Trognon, Alain. A Note on Autoregressive Error Components Models. *J. Econometrics*, May 1985, *28*(2), pp. 231–45.

Sharma, Subhash C. The Effects of Autocorrelation among Errors on the Consistency Property of OLS Variance Estimator. *J. Econometrics*, March 1985, *27*(3), pp. 335–61.

Sheehan, Dennis P. Second-Order Properties of Estimators of Serial Correlation from Regression Residuals. *J. Econometrics*, March 1985, *27*(3), pp. 299–311.

Shvyrkov, Vladislav V.; Carroll, John and Rosen-

baum, Richard. A New Approach to a Random Walk Model. In *Brown, R. C., ed.*, 1985, pp. 201–09.

Sims, Christopher A. Comment on "Issues Involved with the Seasonal Adjustment of Economic Time Series." *J. Bus. Econ. Statist.*, January 1985, *3*(1), pp. 92–94.

Steece, Bert M. and Wood, Steven. A Test for the Equivalence of *k* ARMA Models. *Empirical Econ.*, 1985, *10*(1), pp. 1–11. [G: U.S.]

Teich, Isaac and Gommershtadt, Zeev. Some Aspects Concerning the Short-term Forecasting of Complex Economic Phenomena. *Statist. J.*, September 1985, *3*(3), pp. 321–25.

Thornton, Daniel L. and Batten, Dallas S. Lag-Length Selection and Tests of Granger Causality between Money and Income. *J. Money, Credit, Banking*, May 1985, *17*(2), pp. 164–78.

Thury, Gerhard. Seasonal Adjustment by Signal Extraction. *Empirica*, 1985, *12*(2), pp. 191–207. [G: Austria]

Tryfos, Peter and Blackmore, Russell. Forecasting Records. *J. Amer. Statist. Assoc.*, March 1985, *80*(389), pp. 46–50.

Tsay, Ruey S. Model Identification in Dynamic Regression (Distributed Lag) Models. *J. Bus. Econ. Statist.*, July 1985, *3*(3), pp. 228–37.

Vishwakarma, Keshav P. The State Space Software SARAS Forecasts Better than the Box-Jenkins Method. In *Batten, D. F. and Lesse, P. F., eds.*, 1985, pp. 163–78. [G: Australia]

Watson, Mark W. and Engle, Robert F. Testing for Regression Coefficient Stability with a Stationary AR(1) Alternative. *Rev. Econ. Statist.*, May 1985, *67*(2), pp. 341–46.

Webb, Robert Ivory. The Behavior of Speculative Prices and the Consistency of Economic Models. *J. Econometrics*, January 1985, *27*(1), pp. 123–30.

West, Mike; Harrison, P. Jeff and Migon, Helio S. Dynamic Generalized Linear Models and Bayesian Forecasting. *J. Amer. Statist. Assoc.*, March 1985, *80*(389), pp. 73–83.

West, Mike; Harrison, P. Jeff and Migon, Helio S. Dynamic Generalized Linear Models and Bayesian Forecasting: Rejoinder. *J. Amer. Statist. Assoc.*, March 1985, *80*(389), pp. 96–97.

Whiteman, Charles H. Spectral Utility, Wiener–Hopf Techniques, and Rational Expectations. *J. Econ. Dynam. Control*, October 1985, *9*(2), pp. 225–40.

Winkler, Robert L. Dynamic Generalized Linear Models and Bayesian Forecasting: Comment: Bayesian Model Building and Forecasting. *J. Amer. Statist. Assoc.*, March 1985, *80*(389), pp. 95.

Yakowitz, Sidney J. Nonparametric Density Estimation, Prediction, and Regression for Markov Sequences. *J. Amer. Statist. Assoc.*, March 1985, *80*(389), pp. 215–21.

Zellner, Arnold. Bayesian Econometrics. *Econometrica*, March 1985, *53*(2), pp. 253–69.

2117 Survey Methods; Sampling Methods

Biemer, Paul P. and Stokes, S. Lynne. Optimal Design of Interviewer Variance Experiments in Complex Surveys. *J. Amer. Statist. Assoc.*, March 1985, *80*(389), pp. 158–66. [G: U.S.]

Black, Robert W. Instead of the 1986 Census: The Potential Contribution of Enhanced Electoral Registers. *J. Roy. Statist. Soc.*, 1985, *148*(4), pp. 287–306. [G: U.K.]

David, Martin. The Design and Development of SIPP: Introduction. *J. Econ. Soc. Meas.*, December 1985, *13*(3–4), pp. 215–24. [G: U.S.]

Deaton, Angus. Panel Data from Time Series of Cross-Sections. *J. Econometrics*, Oct./Nov. 1985, *30*(1/2), pp. 109–26.

Finley, David R. Counterexamples to Proposed Dollar-Unit Sampling Algorithm [On Sampling Plan Selection with Dollar-Unit Sampling]. *J. Acc. Res.*, Spring 1985, *23*(1), pp. 402–04.

Glock, Charles Y. The Logic of Survey Analysis. In *Smith, R. B., ed.*, 1985, pp. 241–86. [G: U.S.]

Herberger, L. and Bretz, M. The Use of Population Censuses as Multi-subject Data Bases in the Federal Republic of Germany. *Statist. J.*, March 1985, *3*(1), pp. 115–33. [G: W. Germany]

Hoem, Jan M. Weighting, Misclassification, and Other Issues in the Analysis of Survey Samples of Life Histories. In *Heckman, J. J. and Singer, B., eds.*, 1985, pp. 249–93.

Hsieh, David A.; Manski, Charles F. and McFadden, Daniel. Estimation of Response Probabilities from Augmented Retrospective Observations. *J. Amer. Statist. Assoc.*, September 1985, *80*(391), pp. 651–62.

Hyman, Herbert H. Strategies in Comparative Survey Research. In *Smith, R. B., ed.*, 1985, pp. 97–153.

Jewell, W. S. Bayesian Estimation of Undetected Errors. In *Bernardo, J. M., et al., eds.*, 1985, pp. 663–71.

Kalton, Graham and Lepkowski, James. Following Rules in SIPP. *J. Econ. Soc. Meas.*, December 1985, *13*(3–4), pp. 319–29. [G: U.S.]

Kott, Phillip S. A Note on Model-based Stratification [Model-based Stratification in Inventory Cost Estimation]. *J. Bus. Econ. Statist.*, July 1985, *3*(3), pp. 284–86. [G: U.S.]

Nasatir, David. The Survey Research Process. In *Smith, R. B., ed.*, 1985, pp. 154–92.

Pfeffermann, D. and Holmes, D. J. Robustness Considerations in the Choice of a Method of Inference for Regression Analysis of Survey Data. *J. Roy. Statist. Soc.*, 1985, *148*(3), pp. 268–78.

Smeeding, Timothy M. The Scientific Potential of SIPP: Its Content and Methods Regarding Fringe Benefits, Noncash Income, and Value of Government Services. *J. Econ. Soc. Meas.*, December 1985, *13*(3–4), pp. 287–94. [G: U.S.]

Stenger, Horst. On a Concept of Asymptotical Risk in Survey Sampling. In *[Menges, G.]*, 1985, pp. 252–66.

Strecker, Heinrich and Wiegert, Rolf. Estimation of the Response Variance in Surveys. In *[Menges, G.]*, 1985, pp. 267–88.
[G: Belgium]

Stuart, O. D. J. Are Business and Consumer Surveys Still of Value? *J. Stud. Econ. Economet-rics*, November 1985, (23), pp. 29–50.

Sugden, R. A. A Bayesian View of Ignorable Designs in Survey Sampling Inference. In *Bernardo, J. M., et al., eds.*, 1985, pp. 751–53.

Winkler, Robert L. Information Loss in Noisy and Dependent Processes. In *Bernardo, J. M., et al., eds.*, 1985, pp. 559–68.

Wright, Roger L. Reply [Model-based Stratification in Inventory Cost Estimation]. *J. Bus. Econ. Statist.*, July 1985, *3*(3), pp. 286–88.
[G: U.S.]

2118 Theory of Index Numbers and Aggregation

Bamberg, Günter and Spremann, Klaus. Least-Squares Index Numbers. In *[Menges, G.]*, 1985, pp. 27–37.

Baumberger, Jörg and Keel, Alex. Der ökonomische Gehalt von Wechselkursindices: Arithmetische und geometrische Indices. (The Economic Meaning of Effective Exchange Rate Indices: Arithmetic and Geometric Indices. With English summary.) *Schweiz. Z. Volkswirtsch. Statist.*, June 1985, *121*(2), pp. 169–89.
[G: Switzerland]

Baye, Michael R. Price Dispersion and Functional Price Indices. *Econometrica*, January 1985, *53*(1), pp. 213–23.

Blankmeyer, Eric. Least-Squares Index Numbers of Prices and Quantities. *Atlantic Econ. J.*, March 1985, *13*(1), pp. 101.

Coles, Jeffrey Link and Harte-Chen, Paul. Real Wage Indices. *J. Lab. Econ.*, July 1985, *3*(3), pp. 317–36.
[G: U.S.]

De Bartolo, Gilbert and Holzman, Franklyn D. The Effects of Aggregation on the Difference between Laspeyres and Paasche Indices. *J. Compar. Econ.*, March 1985, *9*(1), pp. 71–79.

Frosini, Benito V. Comparing Inequality Measures. *Statistica*, July-Sept. 1985, *45*(3), pp. 299–317.
[G: Italy]

Heien, Dale and Dunn, James. The True Cost-of-Living Index with Changing Preferences. *J. Bus. Econ. Statist.*, October 1985, *3*(4), pp. 332–43.
[G: U.S.]

Kott, Phillip S. Corrections [A Superpopulation Theory Approach to the Design of Price Index Estimators with Small Sampling Biases]. *J. Bus. Econ. Statist.*, January 1985, *3*(1), pp. 100.
[G: U.S.]

Leontief, Wassily. Composite Commodities and the Problem of Index Numbers. In *Leontief, W.*, 1985, pp. 126–50.

Powell, James L. and Stoker, Thomas M. The Estimation of Complete Aggregation Structures. *J. Econometrics*, Oct./Nov. 1985, *30*(1/2), pp. 317–44.

Ratti, Ronald A. A Descriptive Analysis of Economic Indicators. *Fed. Res. Bank St. Louis Rev.*, January 1985, *67*(1), pp. 14–24.
[G: U.S.]

Upcher, M. R. The Problem of Aggregation over Time in Disequilibrium Models. *J. Quant. Econ.*, January 1985, *1*(1), pp. 11–25.

2119 Experimental Design; Social Experiments

Belton, Valerie and Gear, Tony. A Series of Experiments into the Use of Pairwise Comparison Techniques to Evaluate Criteria Weights. In *Haimes, Y. Y. and Chankong, V., eds.*, 1985, pp. 375–87.

Conlisk, John. Technical Problems in Social Experimentation: Cost versus Ease of Analysis: Comment. In *Hausman, J. A. and Wise, D. A., eds.*, 1985, pp. 208–14.

Hausman, Jerry A. and Wise, David A. Technical Problems in Social Experimentation: Cost versus Ease of Analysis. In *Hausman, J. A. and Wise, D. A., eds.*, 1985, pp. 187–208.
[G: U.S.]

Kadane, Joseph B. Toward Evaluating the Cost-Effectiveness of Medical and Social Experiments: Comment. In *Hausman, J. A. and Wise, D. A., eds.*, 1985, pp. 246–47.
[G: U.S.]

McFadden, Daniel. Technical Problems in Social Experimentation: Cost versus Ease of Analysis: Comment. In *Hausman, J. A. and Wise, D. A., eds.*, 1985, pp. 214–18.

Mosteller, Frederick and Weinstein, Milton C. Toward Evaluating the Cost-Effectiveness of Medical and Social Experiments. In *Hausman, J. A. and Wise, D. A., eds.*, 1985, pp. 221–46.
[G: U.S.]

Mundel, David S. The Use of Information in the Policy Process: Are Social-Policy Experiments Worthwhile? In *Hausman, J. A. and Wise, D. A., eds.*, 1985, pp. 251–56.

212 Construction, Analysis, and Use of Econometric Models

2120 Construction, Analysis, and Use of Econometric Models

Andersen, Per Kragh. Statistical Models for Longitudinal Labor Market Data Based on Counting Processes. In *Heckman, J. J. and Singer, B., eds.*, 1985, pp. 294–307.

Ando, Albert and Kennickell, Arthur B. Some Results on Analytic Optimal Control Solution of a Simple Rational Expectations Model. *J. Econ. Dynam. Control*, September 1985, *9*(1), pp. 55–61.

Arrow, Kenneth J. Applications of Control Theory to Economic Growth. In *Arrow, K. J. (I)*, 1985, pp. 261–96.

Artus, Patrick. Inventory Investment, Investment and Employment with Uncertain Demand. *Empirical Econ.*, 1985, *10*(3), pp. 177–200.
[G: France]

Aslaksen, Iulie and Bjerkholt, Olav. Certainty Equivalence Procedures in Decision-Making under Uncertainty: An Empirical Application. In *[Johansen, L.]*, 1985, pp. 289–329.
[G: Norway]

Assenmacher, Walter. Eine wissenschaftstheoretische Begründung der Linearhypothese in angewandten ökonometrischen Modellen. (A Theory of Science Approach to the Linear Hypothesis in Applied Econometric Models. With English summary.) *Jahr. Nationalökon. Statist.*, January 1985, *200*(1), pp. 56–70.

Attfield, Clifford L. F. Homogeneity and Endogeneity in Systems of Demand Equations. *J. Econometrics*, February 1985, *27*(2), pp. 197–209. [G: U.K.]

Attfield, Clifford L. F. and Browning, Martin J. A Differential Demand System, Rational Expectations and the Life Cycle Hypothesis. *Econometrica*, January 1985, *53*(1), pp. 31–48. [G: U.K.]

Aurikko, Esko. Testing Disequilibrium Adjustment Models for Finnish Exports of Goods. *Oxford Bull. Econ. Statist.*, February 1985, *47*(1), pp. 33–50. [G: Finland]

Barnett, William A. The Minflex-Laurent Translog Flexible Functional Form. *J. Econometrics*, Oct./Nov. 1985, *30*(1/2), pp. 33–44.

Barnett, William A. and Lee, Yul W. The Global Properties of the Miniflex Laurent, Generalized Leontief, and Translog Flexible Functional Forms. *Econometrica*, November 1985, *53*(6), pp. 1421–37.

Barnett, William A.; Lee, Yul W. and Wolfe, Michael D. The Three-Dimensional Global Properties of the Minflex Laurent, Generalized Leontief, and Translog Flexible Functional Forms. *J. Econometrics*, Oct./Nov. 1985, *30*(1/2), pp. 3–31.

Basmann, R. L., et al. On Deviations between Neoclassical and GFT-Based True Cost-of-Living Indexes Derived from the Same Demand Function System. *J. Econometrics*, Oct./Nov. 1985, *30*(1/2), pp. 45–66.

Baumol, William J. and Quandt, Richard E. Chaos Models and Their Implications for Forecasting. *Eastern Econ. J.*, Jan.-Mar. 1985, *11*(1), pp. 3–15.

Becker, Robin, et al. Optimal Policy under Model Uncertainty. In *Currie, D., ed.*, 1985, pp. 69–85. [G: U.K.]

Benabou, Roland. Le modèle d'optimisation dynamique de la consommation et de l'offre de travail: un test sur données françaises. (The Model of Dynamic Optimisation on Consumption and Labour Supply: A Test on French Data. With English summary.) *Ann. INSEE*, Jan.-Mar. 1985, (57), pp. 75–97. [G: France]

Bennett, R. J. and Haining, R. P. Spatial Structure and Spatial Interaction: Modelling Approaches to the Statistical Analysis of Geographical Data. *J. Roy. Statist. Soc.*, 1985, *148*(1), pp. 1–27. [G: U.S.; U.K.]

Berger, Allen N. and Krane, Spencer D. The Information Efficiency of Econometric Model Forecasts. *Rev. Econ. Statist.*, February 1985, *67*(1), pp. 128–34. [G: U.S.]

Bergman, Lars. Extensions and Applications of the MSG-Model: A Brief Survey. In *[Johansen, L.]*, 1985, pp. 127–61.

Bianchi, Carlo, et al. Asymptotic Properties of Dynamic Multipliers in Nonlinear Economet-

ric Models. *Econ. Notes*, 1985, (2), pp. 97–117.

Blanchard, Olivier J. Methods of Solution for Dynamic Rational Expectations Models: A Survey. In *Manne, A. S., ed.*, 1985, pp. 210–25.

Blatt, John M. Modelling and Optimal Control of Random Walk Processes in Economics. In *Batten, D. F. and Lesse, P. F., eds.*, 1985, pp. 37–45.

Blinder, Alan S. and Deaton, Angus. The Time Series Consumption Function Revisited. *Brookings Pap. Econ. Act.*, 1985, (2), pp. 465–511. [G: U.S.]

Bolton, Roger. Regional Econometric Models. *J. Reg. Sci.*, November 1985, *25*(4), pp. 495–520. [G: U.S.]

Brenner, David. On the Formation of Statistical Models. In *[Menges, G.]*, 1985, pp. 52–55.

Broer, D. P. and Siebrand, J. C. A Macroeconomic Disequilibrium Model of Product Market and Labour Market for the Netherlands. *Appl. Econ.*, August 1985, *17*(4), pp. 633–46. [G: Netherlands]

Broze, Laurence and Szafarz, Ariane. Solutions des modèles linéaires à anticipations rationnelles. (Solutions of Dynamic Linear Rational Expectations Models. With English summary.) *Ann. INSEE*, Jan.-Mar. 1985, (57), pp. 99–118.

Burdett, Kenneth; Kiefer, Nicholas M. and Sharma, Sunil. Layoffs and Duration Dependence in a Model of Turnover. *J. Econometrics*, April 1985, *28*(1), pp. 51–69. [G: U.S.]

Caskey, John P. Modeling the Formation of Price Expectations: A Bayesian Approach. *Amer. Econ. Rev.*, September 1985, *75*(4), pp. 768–76. [G: U.S.]

Chalfant, James A. and Gallant, A. Ronald. Estimating Substitution Elasticities with the Fourier Cost Function: Some Monte Carlo Results. *J. Econometrics*, May 1985, *28*(2), pp. 205–22.

Chamberlain, Gary. Heterogeneity, Omitted Variable Bias, and Duration Dependence. In *Heckman, J. J. and Singer, B., eds.*, 1985, pp. 3–38.

Chambers, Robert G.; Just, Richard E. and Moffitt, L. Joe. Estimation in Markets with Unobserved Price Barriers: An Application to the California Retail Milk Market. *Appl. Econ.*, December 1985, *17*(6), pp. 991–1002. [G: U.S.]

Charnes, A., et al. Foundations of Data Envelopment Analysis for Pareto–Koopmans Efficient Empirical Production Functions. *J. Econometrics*, Oct./Nov. 1985, *30*(1/2), pp. 91–107.

Chesher, Andrew. Score Tests for Zero Covariances in Recursive Linear Models for Grouped or Censored Data. *J. Econometrics*, June 1985, *28*(3), pp. 291–305.

Chiarella, Carl. Analysis of the Effects of Time Lags and Nonlinearities in a Macroeconomic Model Incorporating the Government Budget Constraint. In *Batten, D. F. and Lesse, P. F., eds.*, 1985, pp. 131–52.

Chow, Gregory C. and Reny, Philip J. On Two Methods for Solving and Estimating Linear

Simultaneous Equations under Rational Expectations. *J. Econ. Dynam. Control,* September 1985, 9(1), pp. 63–75.

Christ, Carl F. Early Progress in Estimating Quantitative Economic Relationships in America. *Amer. Econ. Rev.,* December 1985, 75(6), pp. 39–52. [G: U.S.]

Christiano, Lawrence J. A Method for Estimating the Timing Interval in a Linear Econometric Model, with an Application to Taylor's Model of Staggered Contracts. *J. Econ. Dynam. Control,* December 1985, 9(4), pp. 363–404. [G: U.S.]

Common, Michael S. Testing for Rational Expectations with Qualitative Survey Data. *Manchester Sch. Econ. Soc. Stud.,* June 1985, 53(2), pp. 138–48.

Congdon, Peter. Heterogeneity and Timing Effects in Occupational Mobility: A General Model. *Oxford Bull. Econ. Statist.,* November 1985, 47(4), pp. 347–69. [G: Ireland]

Cooley, Thomas F. and LeRoy, Stephen F. Atheoretical Macroeconometrics: A Critique. *J. Monet. Econ.,* November 1985, 16(3), pp. 283–308.

Cooper, Russel J.; McLaren, Keith R. and Powell, Alan A. Short-run Macroeconomic Closure in Applied General Equilbrium Modelling: Experience from ORANI and Agenda for Further Research. In *Piggott, J. and Whalley, J., eds.,* 1985, pp. 411–40. [G: Australia]

Corker, Robert J. and Begg, David K. H. Rational Dummy Variables in an Intertemporal Optimisation Framework. *Oxford Bull. Econ. Statist.,* February 1985, 47(1), pp. 71–78. [G: U.K.]

Cosslett, Stephen R. and Lee, Lung-Fei. Serial Correlation in Latent Discrete Variable Models. *J. Econometrics,* January 1985, 27(1), pp. 79–97. [G: U.S.]

Currie, David. Structural Instability in a Rational Expectations Model of a Small Open Economy with a J-Curve. *Economica,* February 1985, 52(205), pp. 25–36.

Cuttance, Peter. A General Structural Equation Modeling Framework for the Social and Behavioral Sciences. In *Smith, R. B., ed.,* 1985, pp. 408–63.

Dar, Atul and DasGupta, Swapan. The Estimation of Production Functions: The CRES and CDE Approaches Applied to U.S. Manufacturing Data—A Comparative Study. *Appl. Econ.,* June 1985, 17(3), pp. 437–49. [G: U.S.]

Davidson, James E. H. Econometric Modelling of the Sterling Effective Exchange Rate. *Rev. Econ. Stud.,* April 1985, 52(2), pp. 231–50. [G: U.K.]

Deaton, Angus. Panel Data from Time Series of Cross-Sections. *J. Econometrics,* Oct./Nov. 1985, 30(1/2), pp. 109–26.

DeGroot, M. H. and Eriksson, E. A. Probability Forecasting, Stochastic Dominance, and the Lorenz Curve. In *Bernardo, J. M., et al., eds.,* 1985, pp. 99–110.

Diewert, W. E. and Parkan, C. Tests for the Consistency of Consumer Data. *J. Econometrics,* Oct./Nov. 1985, 30(1/2), pp. 127–47.

Eckalbar, John C. On the Use and Misuse of the Instantaneous Speed of Adjustment Assumption. *Econ. Modelling,* January 1985, 2(1), pp. 3–7.

Engle, Robert F.; Lilien, David M. and Watson, Mark. A Dynamic Model of Housing Price Determination. *J. Econometrics,* June 1985, 28(3), pp. 307–26. [G: U.S.]

Epstein, Larry G. and Yatchew, Adonis John. Non-parametric Hypothesis Testing Procedures and Applications to Demand Analysis. *J. Econometrics,* Oct./Nov. 1985, 30(1/2), pp. 149–69.

Epstein, Larry G. and Yatchew, Adonis John. The Empirical Determination of Technology and Expectations: A Simplified Procedure. *J. Econometrics,* February 1985, 27(2), pp. 235–58. [G: U.S.]

Evans, George. Expectational Stability and the Multiple Equilibria Problem in Linear Rational Expectations Models. *Quart. J. Econ.,* November 1985, 100(4), pp. 1217–33.

Evers, Gerard H. M. and van der Veen, Anne. A Simultaneous Non-linear Model for Labour Migration and Commuting. *Reg. Stud.,* June 1985, 19(3), pp. 217–29. [G: Netherlands]

Färe, Rolf; Jansson, Leif and Lovell, C. A. Knox. Modelling Scale Economies with Ray-Homothetic Production Functions. *Rev. Econ. Statist.,* November 1985, 67(4), pp. 624–29. [G: U.S.]

Fischer, Manfred M. and Nijkamp, Peter. Categorical Data and Choice Analysis in a Spatial Context. In *Hutchinson, B. G.; Nijkamp, P. and Batty, M., eds.,* 1985, pp. 1–30.

Førsund, Finn R. Frontier Production Functions: Comment. *Econometric Rev.,* 1985-86, 4(2), pp. 329–34.

Førsund, Finn R. and Jansen, Eilev S. The Interplay between Sectoral Models Based on Micro Data and Models for the National Economy. In *[Johansen, L.],* 1985, pp. 109–25.

Fourgeaud, C.; Gourieroux, Christian and Pradel, J. Rational Expectations Models and Bounded Memory. *Econometrica,* July 1985, 53(4), pp. 977–85.

Fraser, D. A. S. Statistical Modelling. In *[Menges, G.],* 1985, pp. 89–100.

Freedman, D. A. Some Subjective Bayesian Considerations in the Selection of Models: Comments on Hill's Model Selection Paper. *Econometric Rev.,* 1985-86, 4(2), pp. 247–51.

Frydman, Halina and Singer, Burton. Assessing Qualitative Features of Longitudinal Data. In *Heckman, J. J. and Singer, B., eds.,* 1985, pp. 308–24.

Galeazzi, Giorgio. International Differences in Comparative Price Levels and Exchange Rates: An Analysis by Production Sectors in a Varying Parameter Model. *Rivista Polit. Econ.,* Suppl. Dec. 1985, 76, pp. 3–40.

Gallant, A. Ronald and Monahan, John F. Explicitly Infinite-Dimensional Bayesian Analysis of Production Technologies. *J. Econometrics,* Oct./Nov. 1985, 30(1/2), pp. 171–201. [G: U.S.]

Garner, C. Alan. Forecast Dispersion as a Mea-

sure of Economic Uncertainty. *Quart. Rev. Econ. Bus.*, Spring 1985, *25*(1), pp. 58–73.
[G: U.S.]

Geisser, Seymour. On the Prediction of Observables: A Selective Update. In *Bernardo, J. M., et al., eds.*, 1985, pp. 203–25.

George, Donald A. R. and Oxley, Leslie T. Structural Stability and Model Design. *Econ. Modelling*, October 1985, *2*(4), pp. 307–16.

George, Edward I. and Wecker, William E. Estimating Damages in a Class Action Litigation. *J. Bus. Econ. Statist.*, April 1985, *3*(2), pp. 132–39.

Geweke, John. Macroeconometric Modeling and the Theory of the Representative Agent. *Amer. Econ. Rev.*, May 1985, *75*(2), pp. 206–10.

Giannini, Carlo. Problemi aperti nell'analisi econometrica dinamica. (Some Open Issues in Dynamic Econometric Analysis. With English summary.) *Giorn. Econ.*, Jan.-Feb. 1985, *44*(1–2), pp. 29–43.

Glymour, Clark. Interpreting Leamer [Let's Take the Con Out of Econometrics]. *Econ. Philos.*, October 1985, *1*(2), pp. 290–94. [G: U.S.]

Greene, William H. Frontier Production Functions: Comment. *Econometric Rev.*, 1985-86, *4*(2), pp. 335–38.

Gregory, Allan W. and Veall, Michael R. A Lagrange Multiplier Test of the Restrictions for a Simple Rational Expectations Model. *Can. J. Econ.*, February 1985, *18*(1), pp. 94–105.
[G: Canada]

Griffin, James M. and Egan, Bruce L. Demand System Estimation in the Presence of Multiblock Tariffs: A Telecommunications Example. *Rev. Econ. Statist.*, August 1985, *67*(3), pp. 520–24. [G: U.S.]

Hall, Robert E. The Time Series Consumption Function Revisited: Comment. *Brookings Pap. Econ. Act.*, 1985, (2), pp. 512–13. [G: U.S.]

Hall, S. G. On the Solution of Large Economic Models with Consistent Expectations. *Bull. Econ. Res.*, May 1985, *37*(2), pp. 157–61.

Hall, S. G. and Henry, S. G. B. Rational Expectations in an Econometric Model: NIESR Model 8. *Nat. Inst. Econ. Rev.*, November 1985, (114), pp. 58–68. [G: U.K.]

Hamilton, James D. and Whiteman, Charles H. The Observable Implications of Self-fulfilling Expectations. *J. Monet. Econ.*, November 1985, *16*(3), pp. 353–73.

Harris, Britton. Urban Simulation Models in Regional Science. *J. Reg. Sci.*, November 1985, *25*(4), pp. 545–67.

Harris, R. I. D. Interrelated Demand for Factors of Production in the U.K. Engineering Industry, 1968–81. *Econ. J.*, December 1985, *95*(380), pp. 1049–68. [G: U.K.]

Hausman, Jerry A. The Econometrics of Nonlinear Budget Sets. *Econometrica*, November 1985, *53*(6), pp. 1255–82. [G: U.S.]

Haynes, Stephen E. and Stone, Joe A. A Neglected Method of Separating Demand and Supply in Time Series Regression. *J. Bus. Econ. Statist.*, July 1985, *3*(3), pp. 238–43.
[G: U.S.]

Heckman, James J. and Robb, Richard, Jr. Alter-native Methods for Evaluating the Impact of Interventions: An Overview. *J. Econometrics*, Oct./Nov. 1985, *30*(1/2), pp. 239–67.

Heckman, James J. and Robb, Richard, Jr. Alternative Methods for Evaluating the Impact of Interventions. In *Heckman, J. J. and Singer, B., eds.*, 1985, pp. 156–245.

Heckman, James J. and Sedlacek, Guilherme. Heterogeneity, Aggregation, and Market Wage Functions: An Empirical Model of Self-selection in the Labor Market. *J. Polit. Econ.*, December 1985, *93*(6), pp. 1077–1125.
[G: U.S.]

Heckman, James J. and Singer, Burton. Social Science Duration Analysis. In *Heckman, J. J. and Singer, B., eds.*, 1985, pp. 39–110.
[G: U.S.]

Hertel, Thomas W. Partial vs. General Equilibrium Analysis and Choice of Functional Form: Implications for Policy Modeling. *J. Policy Modeling*, Summer 1985, *7*(2), pp. 281–303.
[G: U.S.]

Hill, Bruce M. Some Subjective Bayesian Considerations in the Selection of Models: Reply. *Econometric Rev.*, 1985-86, *4*(2), pp. 277–88.

Hill, Bruce M. Some Subjective Bayesian Considerations in the Selection of Models. *Econometric Rev.*, 1985-86, *4*(2), pp. 191–246.

Hinich, Melvin J. and Patterson, Douglas M. Identification of the Coefficients in a Non-linear Time Series of the Quadratic Type. *J. Econometrics*, Oct./Nov. 1985, *30*(1/2), pp. 269–88. [G: U.S.]

Hinkley, David. Comparison of Alternative Functional Forms in Production: Discussion. *J. Econometrics*, Oct./Nov. 1985, *30*(1/2), pp. 363–64.

Hsiao, Cheng and Mountain, Dean C. Estimating the Short-run Income Elasticity of Demand for Electricity by Using Cross-sectional Categorized Data. *J. Amer. Statist. Assoc.*, June 1985, *80*(390), pp. 259–65. [G: Canada]

Hsiao, Frank S. T. and Hsiao, Mei-Chu Wang. Elasticities, Ratios, and Energy Modelling. *Energy Econ.*, July 1985, *7*(3), pp. 153–58.
[G: U.K.]

Hubbard, R. Glenn. The Time Series Consumption Function Revisited: Comment. *Brookings Pap. Econ. Act.*, 1985, (2), pp. 514–19.
[G: U.S.]

Ilmakunnas, Pekka. Bayesian Estimation of Cost Functions with Stochastic or Exact Constraints on Parameters. *Int. Econ. Rev.*, February 1985, *26*(1), pp. 111–34. [G: U.S.]

Jackson, John D. and Smyth, David J. Specifying Differential Cyclical Response in Economic Time Series: Capacity Utilization and Demand for Imports. *Econ. Modelling*, April 1985, *2*(2), pp. 149–61. [G: U.S.]

James, David. Environmental Economics, Industrial Process Models, and Regional-Residuals Management Models. In *Kneese, A. V. and Sweeney, J. L., eds. Vol. 1*, 1985, pp. 271–324.

Jorgenson, Dale W. and Slesnick, Daniel T. Efficiency versus Equity in Natural Gas Price Regulation. *J. Econometrics*, Oct./Nov. 1985, *30*(1/2), pp. 301–16. **[G: U.S.]**

Karadeloglou, Pavlos. Détermination simultanée des prix et volumes dans le processus productif: Une étude empirique. (The Simultaneous Determination of Prices and Quantities in the Production Process: An Empirical Study. With English summary.) *Ann. INSEE*, Apr.-June 1985, (58), pp. 69–89. **[G: France]**

Keener, Robert W. and Waldman, Donald M. Maximum Likelihood Regression of Rank-censored Data. *J. Amer. Statist. Assoc.*, June 1985, *80*(390), pp. 385–92. **[G: U.S.]**

Keller, W. J. and van Driel, J. Differential Consumer Demand Systems. *Europ. Econ. Rev.*, April 1985, *27*(3), pp. 375–90. **[G: Netherlands]**

Kelly, Christopher M. A Cautionary Note on the Interpretation of Long-run Equilibrium Solutions in Conventional Macro Models [Economic Modelling of the Aggregate Time Series Relationship between Consumers' Expenditure and Income in the United Kingdom] [Serial Correlation as a Convenient Simplification, Not a Nuisance]. *Econ. J.*, December 1985, *95*(380), pp. 1078–86.

Kennan, John. The Duration of Contract Strikes in U.S. Manufacturing. *J. Econometrics*, April 1985, *28*(1), pp. 5–28. **[G: U.S.]**

Kiefer, Nicholas M. Specification Diagnostics Based on Laguerre Alteratives for Econometric Models of Duration. *J. Econometrics*, April 1985, *28*(1), pp. 135–54. **[G: U.S.]**

Knoke, David. A Path Analysis Primer. In *Smith, R. B.*, ed., 1985, pp. 390–407.

Kollintzas, Tryphon. The Symmetric Linear Rational Expectations Model. *Econometrica*, July 1985, *53*(4), pp. 963–76.

Kooiman, Peter; van Dijk, Herman K. and Thurik, A. Roy. Likelihood Diagnostics and Bayesian Analysis of a Micro-Economic Disequilibrium Model for Retail Services. *J. Econometrics*, July/August 1985, *29*(1/2), pp. 121–48. **[G: Netherlands]**

Kooiman, Peter and Kloek, Teun. An Empirical Two Market Disequilibrium Model for Dutch Manufacturing. *Europ. Econ. Rev.*, December 1985, *29*(3), pp. 323–54. **[G: Netherlands]**

Krämer, Walter, et al. Diagnostic Checking in Practice. *Rev. Econ. Statist.*, February 1985, *67*(1), pp. 118–23.

Kulatilaka, Nalin. Tests on the Validity of Static Equilibrium Models. *J. Econometrics*, May 1985, *28*(2), pp. 253–68. **[G: U.S.]**

Laffargue, Jean-Pierre. An Internal Evaluation Method of Multinational Models. *Economia (Portugal)*, January 1985, *9*(1), pp. 73–104.

Laffargue, Jean-Pierre. Une méthode d'évaluation interne des modèles multinationaux. (An Internal Evaluation Procedure of Multinational Models. With English summary.) *Ann. INSEE*, Jan.-Mar. 1985, (57), pp. 119–44.

Lancaster, Tony. Generalised Residuals and Heterogeneous Duration Models: With Applications to the Weibull Model. *J. Econometrics*, April 1985, *28*(1), pp. 155–69.

Lancaster, Tony. Simultaneous Equations Models in Applied Search Theory. *J. Econometrics*, April 1985, *28*(1), pp. 113–26. **[G: U.K.]**

Lancaster, Tony and Chesher, Andrew. Residuals, Tests and Plots with a Job Matching Illustration. *Ann. INSEE*, July-Dec. 1985, (59/60), pp. 47–70.

Lane, David A. Some Subjective Bayesian Considerations in the Selection of Models: Comments. *Econometric Rev.*, 1985-86, *4*(2), pp. 253–58.

Lawson, Tony. Keynes, Prediction and Econometrics. In *Lawson, T. and Pesaran, H., eds.*, 1985, pp. 116–33.

Leamer, Edward E. Self-Interpretation [Let's Take the Con Out of Econometrics]. *Econ. Philos.*, October 1985, *1*(2), pp. 295–302. **[G: U.S.]**

Leamer, Edward E. Sensitivity Analyses Would Help. *Amer. Econ. Rev.*, June 1985, *75*(3), pp. 308–13.

Leamer, Edward E. Some Subjective Bayesian Considerations in the Selection of Models: Comment. *Econometric Rev.*, 1985-86, *4*(2), pp. 259–67.

Leitmann, George. Feedback and Adaptive Control for Uncertain Dynamical Systems. In *Batten, D. F. and Lesse, P. F., eds.*, 1985, pp. 15–35.

Lerman, Steven R. Random Utility Models of Spatial Choice. In *Hutchinson, B. G.; Nijkamp, P. and Batty, M., eds.*, 1985, pp. 200–217.

Levine, David K. The Sensitivity of MLE to Measure Error. *J. Econometrics*, May 1985, *28*(2), pp. 223–30.

Lippi, Marco. Sulla dinamica delle relazioni tra variabili aggregate. (On the Dynamics of Aggregate Variables in Econometrics. With English summary.) *Polit. Econ.*, August 1985, *1*(2), pp. 141–66.

Litterman, Robert B. and Weiss, Laurence M. Money, Real Interest Rates, and Output: A Reinterpretation of Postwar U.S. Data. *Econometrica*, January 1985, *53*(1), pp. 129–56. **[G: U.S.]**

Little, Roderick J. A. A Note about Models for Selectivity Bias. *Econometrica*, November 1985, *53*(6), pp. 1469–74.

Lubrano, Michel. Some Aspects of Prior Elicitation Problems in Disequilibrium Models. *J. Econometrics*, July/August 1985, *29*(1/2), pp. 165–72. **[G: U.S.]**

Luoma, Martti. Malli taloustieteellisessä tutkimuksessa. (The Model in Economic and Business Research. With English summary.) *Liiketaloudellinen Aikak.*, 1985, *34*(3), pp. 292–97.

MacDonald, Glenn M. and Robinson, Chris. Cautionary Tails about Arbitrary Deletion of Observations; or, Throwing the Variance Out with the Bathwater. *J. Lab. Econ.*, April 1985, *3*(2), pp. 124–52. **[G: U.S.]**

Machak, Joseph A.; Spivey, W. Allen and Wrobleski, William J. A Framework for Time Varying Parameter Regression Modeling. *J. Bus.*

Econ. Statist., April 1985, *3*(2), pp. 104–11. [G: U.S.]

MaCurdy, Thomas E. Interpreting Empirical Models of Labor Supply in an Intertemporal Framework with Uncertainty. In *Heckman, J. J. and Singer, B., eds.*, 1985, pp. 111–55. [G: U.S.]

Mănescu, Manea. The Oil Industry—A Complex Cybernetics System. *Econ. Computat. Cybern. Stud. Res.*, 1985, *20*(3), pp. 3–20.

Mankiw, N. Gregory. Consumer Durables and the Real Interest Rate. *Rev. Econ. Statist.*, August 1985, *67*(3), pp. 353–62. [G: U.S.]

Manne, Alan S. On the Formulation and Solution of Economic Equilibrium Models. In *Manne, A. S., ed.*, 1985, pp. 1–22.

Mariano, Roberto S. and Brown, Bryan W. Stochastic Prediction in Dynamic Nonlinear Econometric Systems. *Ann. INSEE*, July-Dec. 1985, (59/60), pp. 267–78.

McAleer, Michael; Pagan, Adrian R. and Volker, Paul A. What Will Take the Con out of Econometrics? *Amer. Econ. Rev.*, June 1985, *75*(3), pp. 293–307. [G: U.S.]

McCaffrey, David P., et al. Modeling Complexity: Using Dynamic Simulation to Link Regression and Case Studies. *J. Policy Anal. Manage.*, Winter 1985, *4*(2), pp. 196–216.

Mihai, V. Causality in Cybernetic-Economic Systems: A Statistical Approach. *Econ. Computat. Cybern. Stud. Res.*, 1985, *20*(4), pp. 61–64.

Montgomery, Edward. An Ordered Probit Analysis of Saving Behavior. *Quart. Rev. Econ. Bus.*, Autumn 1985, *25*(3), pp. 22–35. [G: U.S.]

Moore, Elvin J. On System-theoretic Methods and Econometric Modeling. *Int. Econ. Rev.*, February 1985, *26*(1), pp. 87–110.

Murphy, Kevin M. and Topel, Robert H. Estimation and Inference in Two-Step Econometric Models. *J. Bus. Econ. Statist.*, October 1985, *3*(4), pp. 370–79.

Nakamura, Alice and Nakamura, Masao. Dynamic Models of the Labor Force Behavior of Married Women Which Can Be Estimated Using Limited Amounts of Past Information. *J. Econometrics*, March 1985, *27*(3), pp. 273–98. [G: U.S.]

Nakamura, Shinichiro. A Test of Restrictions in a Dynamic Singular Demand System: An Application to the Import of Intermediate Goods in West Germany. *Z. Nationalökon.*, 1985, *45*(3), pp. 313–30. [G: W. Germany]

Nickell, Stephen. Error Correction, Partial Adjustment and All That: An Expository Note. *Oxford Bull. Econ. Statist.*, May 1985, *47*(2), pp. 119–29.

Ohsfeldt, Robert L. and Smith, Barton A. Estimating the Demand for Heterogeneous Goods. *Rev. Econ. Statist.*, February 1985, *67*(1), pp. 165–71.

Ohtani, Kazuhiro and Katayama, Sei-ichi. An Alternative Gradual Switching Regression Model and Its Application. *Econ. Stud. Quart.*, August 1985, *36*(2), pp. 148–53. [G: Japan]

Olsen, Randall J. Frontier Production Functions:

Comment. *Econometric Rev.*, 1985-86, *4*(2), pp. 339–43.

Ondrich, Jan I. The Initial Conditions Problem in Work History Data. *Rev. Econ. Statist.*, August 1985, *67*(3), pp. 441–21. [G: U.S.]

Pagan, Adrian R. Time Series Behaviour and Dynamic Specification. *Oxford Bull. Econ. Statist.*, August 1985, *47*(3), pp. 199–211.

Panas, E. E. An Empirical Examination of Alternative Error Specification in a Production Function: The Case of Greece. *Rivista Int. Sci. Econ. Com.*, July-Aug. 1985, *32*(7–8), pp. 751–64. [G: Greece]

Parke, Darrel W. and Zagardo, Janice. Stochastic Coefficient Regression Estimates of the Sources of Shifts into MMDA Deposits Using Cross-Section Data. *J. Econometrics*, September 1985, *29*(3), pp. 327–40. [G: U.S.]

Parmenter, B. R. and Meagher, G. A. Policy Analysis Using a Computable General Equilibrium Model: A Review of Experience at the IMPACT Project. *Australian Econ. Rev.*, 1st Quarter 1985, (69), pp. 3–15. [G: Australia]

Patterson, Kerry D. Income Adjustments and the Role of Consumers' Durables in Some Leading Consumption Functions. *Econ. J.*, June 1985, *95*(378), pp. 469–79. [G: U.K.]

Persson, Håkan. A Version of the MSG-Model with Putty–Clay and Vintage Technology. In *[Johansen, L.]*, 1985, pp. 163–85.

Pesaran, M. Hashem and Smith, R. P. Evaluation of Macroeconometric Models. *Econ. Modelling*, April 1985, *2*(2), pp. 125–34.

Pesaran, M. Hashem and Smith, R. P. Keynes on Econometrics. In *Lawson, T. and Pesaran, H., eds.*, 1985, pp. 134–50. [G: U.K.]

Pesaran, M. Hashem; Smith, R. P. and Yeo, J. S. Testing for Structural Stability and Predictive Failure: A Review. *Manchester Sch. Econ. Soc. Stud.*, September 1985, *53*(3), pp. 280–95.

Petit, Maria Luisa. Path Controllability of Dynamic Economic Systems. *Econ. Notes*, 1985, (1), pp. 26–42.

Powell, James L. and Stoker, Thomas M. The Estimation of Complete Aggregation Structures. *J. Econometrics*, Oct./Nov. 1985, *30*(1/2), pp. 317–44.

Quandt, Richard E. Concepts and Structures in Disequilibrium Models. *Rivista Int. Sci. Econ. Com.*, March 1985, *32*(3), pp. 207–32.

Ray, Ranjan. Specification and Time Series Estimation of Dynamic Gorman Polar Form Demand Systems. *Europ. Econ. Rev.*, April 1985, *27*(3), pp. 357–74. [G: U.K.]

Rose, Andrew K. An Alternative Approach to the American Demand for Money. *J. Money, Credit, Banking*, Part 1, Nov. 1985, *17*(4), pp. 439–55. [G: U.S.]

Rossi, Peter E. Comparison of Alternative Functional Forms in Production. *J. Econometrics*, Oct./Nov. 1985, *30*(1/2), pp. 345–61. [G: U.S.]

Royer, Daniel and Ritschard, Gilbert. Portée et limites des méthodes qualitatives d'analyse structurale. With English summary.) *Revue*

Écon. Polit., Nov.-Dec. 1985, *95*(6), pp. 777–94.

Rust, Roland T. and Schmittlein, David C. A Bayesian Cross-validated Likelihood Method for Comparing Alternative Specifications of Quantitative Models. *Marketing Sci.*, Winter 1985, *4*(1), pp. 20–40.

Sahay, Surottam N. The Bias of the Forecast from Partially Restricted Reduced Form When There Are Three Endogenous Variables in the Structural Equations. *J. Quant. Econ.*, January 1985, *1*(1), pp. 135–49.

Samuelson, Larry and Moussavian, Mohammed H. Sufficient Conditions in Optimal Control Theory with Unbounded Objectives. *Int. Econ. Rev.*, February 1985, *26*(1), pp. 271–75.

Sato, Ryuzo. The Invariance Principle and Income–Wealth Conservation Laws: Application of Lie Groups and Related Transformations. *J. Econometrics*, Oct./Nov. 1985, *30*(1/2), pp. 365–89.

Schmidt, Peter. Frontier Production Functions: Reply. *Econometric Rev.*, 1985-86, *4*(2), pp. 353–55.

Schmidt, Peter. Frontier Production Functions. *Econometric Rev.*, 1985-86, *4*(2), pp. 289–328.

Seddighi, H. R. A General Equilibrium Framework for Optimal Planning in an Oil-producing Economy. *Energy Econ.*, July 1985, *7*(3), pp. 179–90.

Segerson, Kathleen and Mount, Timothy D. A Non-homothetic Two-Stage Decision Model Using AIDS. *Rev. Econ. Statist.*, November 1985, *67*(4), pp. 630–39. [G: U.S.]

Shonkwiler, J. Scott and Maddala, G. S. Modeling Expectations of Bounded Prices: An Application to the Market for Corn. *Rev. Econ. Statist.*, November 1985, *67*(4), pp. 697–702. [G: U.S.]

Sickles, Robin C. A Nonlinear Multivariate Error Components Analysis of Technology and Specific Factor Productivity Growth with an Application to the U.S. Airlines. *J. Econometrics*, January 1985, *27*(1), pp. 61–78. [G: U.S.]

Sims, Christopher A. Some Subjective Bayesian Considerations in the Selection of Models: Comment. *Econometric Rev.*, 1985-86, *4*(2), pp. 269–75.

Singleton, Kenneth J. Testing Specifications of Economic Agents' Intertemporal Optimum Problems in the Presence of Alternative Models. *J. Econometrics*, Oct./Nov. 1985, *30*(1/2), pp. 391–413. [G: U.S.]

Small, Kenneth A. and Hsiao, Cheng. Multinomial Logit Specification Tests. *Int. Econ. Rev.*, October 1985, *26*(3), pp. 619–27.

Smith, Richard J. Some Tests for Misspecification in Bivariate Limited Dependent Variable Models. *Ann. INSEE*, July-Dec. 1985, (59/60), pp. 97–123.

Sneessens, Henri R. Two Alternative Stochastic Specification and Estimation Methods for Quantity Rationing Models: A Monte-Carlo Comparison. *Europ. Econ. Rev.*, October 1985, *29*(1), pp. 111–36.

Spencer, Peter D. Bounded Shooting: A Method for Solving Large Non-Linear Econometric Models under the Assumption of Consistent Expectations. *Oxford Bull. Econ. Statist.*, February 1985, *47*(1), pp. 79–82.

Stockton, David J. and Glassman, James E. The Theory and Econometrics of Reduced-Form Nominal Income and Price Equations. *Southern Econ. J.*, July 1985, *52*(1), pp. 103–21.

Stoker, Thomas M. Aggregation, Structural Change, and Cross-Section Estimation. *J. Amer. Statist. Assoc.*, September 1985, *80*(391), pp. 720–29.

Tauchen, George. Diagnostic Testing and Evaluation of Maximum Likelihood Models. *J. Econometrics*, Oct./Nov. 1985, *30*(1/2), pp. 415–43.

Țigănescu, E. and Oprescu, G. Cybernetic Simulation of Control Processes through Economic Increase Equalization. *Econ. Computat. Cybern. Stud. Res.*, 1985, *20*(4), pp. 3–12.

Trivedi, Pravin K. Distributed Lags, Aggregation, and Compounding: Some Econometric Implications. *Rev. Econ. Stud.*, January 1985, *52*(1), pp. 19–35.

Ullah, Aman. Specification Analysis of Econometric Models. *J. Quant. Econ.*, July 1985, *1*(2), pp. 187–209.

Upcher, M. R. The Problem of Aggregation over Time in Disequilibrium Models. *J. Quant. Econ.*, January 1985, *1*(1), pp. 11–25.

Varian, Hal R. Non-parametric Analysis of Optimizing Behavior with Measurement Error. *J. Econometrics*, Oct./Nov. 1985, *30*(1/2), pp. 445–58. [G: U.S.]

Waldman, Donald M. Computation in Duration Models with Heterogeneity. *J. Econometrics*, April 1985, *28*(1), pp. 127–34. [G: U.S.]

Webb, Robert Ivory. The Behavior of Speculative Prices and the Consistency of Economic Models. *J. Econometrics*, January 1985, *27*(1), pp. 123–30.

Weber, James S. and Sen, Ashish K. On the Sensitivity of Gravity Model Forecasts. *J. Reg. Sci.*, August 1985, *25*(3), pp. 317–36.

Weber, James S. and Sen, Ashish K. On the Sensitivity of Maximum Likelihood Estimates of Gravity Model Parameters. In *Hutchinson, B. G.; Nijkamp, P. and Batty, M., eds.*, 1985, pp. 148–61.

White, Halbert. Tests de spécification dans les modèles dynamiques. (Specification Testing in Dynamic Models. With English summary.) *Ann. INSEE*, July-Dec. 1985, (59/60), pp. 125–81.

Wohltmann, Hans-Werner. On the Controllability of Continuous-Time Macroeconomic Models. *Z. Nationalökon.*, 1985, *45*(1), pp. 47–66.

Wolff, Reiner. On a Family of Utility Functions as a Basis of Separable Demand. *Z. Nationalökon.*, 1985, *45*(2), pp. 171–77.

Wren-Lewis, Simon. Expectations in Keynesian Econometric Models. In *Lawson, T. and Pesaran, H., eds.*, 1985, pp. 66–79.

Yatchew, Adonis John. Frontier Production Functions: Comment. *Econometric Rev.*, 1985-86, *4*(2), pp. 345–52.

Yatchew, Adonis John. Labor Supply in the Presence of Taxes: An Alternative Specification. *Rev. Econ. Statist.*, February 1985, *67*(1), pp. 27–33. [G: U.S.]

Yatchew, Adonis John and Griliches, Zvi. Specification Error in Probit Models. *Rev. Econ. Statist.*, February 1985, *67*(1), pp. 134–39.

213 Mathematical Methods and Models

2130 General

Aubin, Jean-Pierre and Frankowska, Halina. Heavy Viable Trajectories of Controlled Systems. In *Aubin, J.-P.; Saari, D. and Sigmund, K., eds.*, 1985, pp. 148–67.

Barnett, William A. and Lee, Yul W. The Global Properties of the Miniflex Laurent, Generalized Leontief, and Translog Flexible Functional Forms. *Econometrica*, November 1985, *53*(6), pp. 1421–37.

Batten, David F. New Mathematical Advances in Economic Dynamics: Introduction. In *Batten, D. F. and Lesse, P. F., eds.*, 1985, pp. 1–12.

Bridges, Douglas S. Representing Interval Orders by a Single Real-valued Function. *J. Econ. Theory*, June 1985, *36*(1), pp. 149–55.

Chi, Wan Fu. In Defense of the First Derivative Test. *Atlantic Econ. J.*, December 1985, *13*(4), pp. 75–77.

Cowell, Frank A. Measures of Distributional Change: An Axiomatic Approach. *Rev. Econ. Stud.*, January 1985, *52*(1), pp. 135–51.

Debreu, Gerard and Koopmans, Tjalling C. Additively Decomposed Quasiconvex Functions. In *Koopmans, T. C.*, 1985, pp. 273–310.

Demyanov, V. F.; Lemaréchal, C. and Zowe, J. Attempts to Approximate a Set-Valued Mapping. In *Demyanov, V. F. and Pallaschke, D., eds.*, 1985, pp. 3–7.

Feldman, Mark and Gilles, Christian. An Expository Note on Individual Risk without Aggregate Uncertainty. *J. Econ. Theory*, February 1985, *35*(1), pp. 26–32.

Fischer, Edwin O. Katastrophentheorie und ihre Anwendung in der Wirtschaftswissenschaft. (Catastrophe Theory and Its Applications in Economics. With English summary.) *Jahr. Nationalökon. Statist.*, January 1985, *200*(1), pp. 3–26.

Goodwin, Richard. A Personal Perspective on Mathematical Economics. *Banca Naz. Lavoro Quart. Rev.*, March 1985, (152), pp. 3–13.

Judd, Kenneth L. The Law of Large Numbers with a Continuum of IID Random Variables. *J. Econ. Theory*, February 1985, *35*(1), pp. 19–25.

Leontief, Wassily. Introduction to a Theory of the Internal Structure of Functional Relationships. In *Leontief, W.*, 1985, pp. 151–65.

Lewis, Alain A. The Minimum Degree of Recursively Representable Choice Functions. *Math. Soc. Sci.*, October 1985, *10*(2), pp. 179–88.

Maybee, John S. Functional Models. In *[Rossier, Edouard]*, 1985, pp. 195–216.

Popovici, Al. A. Automatic Evaluation of Emergency Minimal Modes in the Fault-Tree. *Econ. Computat. Cybern. Stud. Res.*, 1985, *20*(3), pp. 55–60.

Rochet, Jean-Charles. The Taxation Principle and Multi-time Hamilton–Jacobi Equations. *J. Math. Econ.*, 1985, *14*(2), pp. 113–28.

Rubinov, A. M. Upper-Semicontinuously Directionally Differentiable Functions. In *Demyanov, V. F. and Pallaschke, D., eds.*, 1985, pp. 74–86.

Saari, Donald G. Random Behavior in Numerical Analysis, Decision Theory, and Macrosystems: Some Impossibility Theorems. In *Aubin, J.-P.; Saari, D. and Sigmund, K., eds.*, 1985, pp. 115–26.

Scitovski, Rudolf and Kosanović, Slavica. Rate of Change in Economic Research. *Econ. Anal. Worker's Manage.*, 1985, *19*(1), pp. 65–73.

Segal, Uzi. On the Separability of the Quasi Concave Closure of an Additively Separable Function. *J. Math. Econ.*, 1985, *14*(2), pp. 129–34.

Sonnenschein, Hugo. The Role of Mathematics in Economic Theory. *Revista Española Econ.*, 1985, *2*(2), pp. 307–20.

2132 Optimization Techniques

Balder, E. J. Seminormal Functions in Optimization Theory. In *Demyanov, V. F. and Pallaschke, D., eds.*, 1985, pp. 165–69.

Bayrhamer, Walter. Some Remarks on Quasirandom Optimization. In *Demyanov, V. F. and Pallaschke, D., eds.*, 1985, pp. 305–09.

Beals, Richard and Koopmans, Tjalling C. Maximizing Stationary Utility in a Constant Technology. In *Koopmans, T. C.*, 1985, pp. 13–27.

Blatt, John M. Modelling and Optimal Control of Random Walk Processes in Economics. In *Batten, D. F. and Lesse, P. F., eds.*, 1985, pp. 37–45.

Breslawski, Steven and Zionts, Stanley. An Interactive Multiple Criteria Linear Programming Package. In *Haimes, Y. Y. and Chankong, V., eds.*, 1985, pp. 282–86.

Chankong, V., et al. Multiple Criteria Optimization: A State of the Art Review. In *Haimes, Y. Y. and Chankong, V., eds.*, 1985, pp. 36–90.

Ciurea, E. Two Classes of Maximal Dynamic Flows. *Econ. Computat. Cybern. Stud. Res.*, 1985, *20*(1), pp. 73–79.

Dixon, L. C. W.; Hersom, S. E. and Maany, Z. Optimal Satellite Trajectories: A Source of Difficult Nonsmooth Optimization Problems. In *Demyanov, V. F. and Pallaschke, D., eds.*, 1985, pp. 310–17.

Dontchev, A. L. Continuity and Asymptotic Behaviour of the Marginal Function in Optimal Control. In *Anderson, E. J. and Philpott, A. B., eds.*, 1985, pp. 185–93.

Elster, K.-H. and Thierfelder, J. The General Concept of Cone Approximations in Nondifferentiable Optimization. In *Demyanov, V. F. and Pallaschke, D., eds.*, 1985, pp. 170–89.

Evtushenko, Y. and Potapov, M. A Nondifferentiable Approach to Multicriteria Optimization. In *Demyanov, V. F. and Pallaschke, D., eds.*, 1985, pp. 97–102.

Fabian, Cs. Economic Pre-optimizing Algorithms for Integer Programming. *Econ. Computat. Cybern. Stud. Res.*, 1985, 20(1), pp. 33–42.

Gal, Tomas and Wolf, Hartmut. Solving Stochastic Linear Programs via Goal Programming. In *Haimes, Y. Y. and Chankong, V., eds.*, 1985, pp. 126–43.

Haneveld, W. K. Klein. Some Linear Programs in Probabilities and Their Duals. In *Ponstein, J., ed.*, 1985, pp. 95–141.

Hansen, Terje and Koopmans, Tjalling C. On the Definition and Computation of a Capital Stock Invariant under Optimization. In *Koopmans, T. C.*, 1985, pp. 125–61.

Hazen, Gordon B. Partial Preference Information and First Order Differential Optimality: An Illustration. In *Haimes, Y. Y. and Chankong, V., eds.*, 1985, pp. 153–57.

Hiriart-Urruty, J.-B. Generalized Differentiability, Duality and Optimization for Problems Dealing with Differences of Convex Functions. In *Ponstein, J., ed.*, 1985, pp. 37–70.

Hiriart-Urruty, J.-B. Mathematical Faits Divers. In *Ponstein, J., ed.*, 1985, pp. 1–9.

Hiriart-Urruty, J.-B. Miscellanies on Nonsmooth Analysis and Optimization. In *Demyanov, V. F. and Pallaschke, D., eds.*, 1985, pp. 8–24.

Jongen, H. Th. and Zwier, G. On Regular Semiinfinite Optimization. In *Anderson, E. J. and Philpott, A. B., eds.*, 1985, pp. 53–64.

Karp, Larry S. Higher Moments in the Linear-Quadratic-Gaussian Problem. *J. Econ. Dynam. Control*, September 1985, 9(1), pp. 41–54.

Kiwiel, K. C. Descent Methods for Nonsmooth Convex Constrained Minimization. In *Demyanov, V. F. and Pallaschke, D., eds.*, 1985, pp. 203–14.

Klatte, Diethard and Kummer, Bernd. Stability Properties of Infima and Optimal Solutions of Parametric Optimization Problems. In *Demyanov, V. F. and Pallaschke, D., eds.*, 1985, pp. 215–29.

Kollintzas, Tryphon. The Symmetric Linear Rational Expectations Model. *Econometrica*, July 1985, 53(4), pp. 963–76.

Komiya, H. Minimum Norm Problems in Normed Vector Lattices. In *Anderson, E. J. and Philpott, A. B., eds.*, 1985, pp. 219–25.

Korhonen, Pekka J. and Laakso, Jukka. On Developing A Visual Interactive Multiple Criteria Method—An Outline. In *Haimes, Y. Y. and Chankong, V., eds.*, 1985, pp. 272–81.

Leitmann, George. Feedback and Adaptive Control for Uncertain Dynamical Systems. In *Batten, D. F. and Lesse, P. F., eds.*, 1985, pp. 15–35.

Lemaire, B. Application of a Subdifferential of a Convex Composite Functional to Optimal Control in Variational Inequalities. In *Demyanov, V. F. and Pallaschke, D., eds.*, 1985, pp. 103–17.

Lewandowski, A.; Rogowski, T. and Kręglewski, T. A Trajectory-Oriented Extension of DIDASS and Its Applications. In *Grauer, M.; Thompson, M. and Wierzbicki, A. P., eds.*, 1985, pp. 261–68.

Lommatzsch, K. and Van Thoai, Nguyen. On Methods for Solving Optimization Problems without Using Derivatives. In *Demyanov, V. F. and Pallaschke, D., eds.*, 1985, pp. 230–36.

Majchrzak, Janusz. DISCRET—A Package for Multicriteria Optimization and Decision Problems with Discrete Alternatives. In *Grauer, M.; Thompson, M. and Wierzbicki, A. P., eds.*, 1985, pp. 319–24.

Mifflin, Robert. The Solution of a Nested Nonsmooth Optimization Problem. In *Demyanov, V. F. and Pallaschke, D., eds.*, 1985, pp. 34–40.

Nakayama, Hirotaka J. Duality Theory in Vector Optimization: An Overview. In *Haimes, Y. Y. and Chankong, V., eds.*, 1985, pp. 109–25.

Outrata, J. V. and Schindler, Z. On Some Nondifferentiable Problems in Optimal Control. In *Demyanov, V. F. and Pallaschke, D., eds.*, 1985, pp. 118–28.

Paizerova, F. A. An Accelerated Method for Minimizing a Convex Function of Two Variables. In *Demyanov, V. F. and Pallaschke, D., eds.*, 1985, pp. 237–51.

Pallaschke, D. and Recht, P. On the Steepest-Descent Method for a Class of Quasi-differentiable Optimization Problems. In *Demyanov, V. F. and Pallaschke, D., eds.*, 1985, pp. 252–63.

Papageorgiou, Nikolaos S. Stochastic Nonsmooth Analysis and Optimization in Banach Spaces. In *Anderson, E. J. and Philpott, A. B., eds.*, 1985, pp. 226–42.

Ray, Subhash C. Methods in Estimating the Input Coefficients for Linear Programming Models. *Amer. J. Agr. Econ.*, August 1985, 67(3), pp. 660–65.

Reiland, Thomas W. and Chou, J. H. Nonsmooth Analysis and Optimization for a Class of Nonconvex Mappings. In *Anderson, E. J. and Philpott, A. B., eds.*, 1985, pp. 204–18.

Rockafellar, R. Tyrrell. Lipschitzian Stability in Optimization: The Role of Nonsmooth Analysis. In *Demyanov, V. F. and Pallaschke, D., eds.*, 1985, pp. 55–73.

Rolewicz, S. On Sufficient Conditions for Optimality of Lipschitz Functions and Their Applications to Vector Optimization. In *Demyanov, V. F. and Pallaschke, D., eds.*, 1985, pp. 129–38.

Rubinov, A. M. Dynamics of Neumann-type Economic Macrosystems. In *Aubin, J.-P.; Saari, D. and Sigmund, K., eds.*, 1985, pp. 127–36.

Rubio, J. E. Nonlinear Optimal Control Problems as Infinite-Dimensional Linear Programming Problems. In *Anderson, E. J. and Philpott, A. B., eds.*, 1985, pp. 172–84.

Samuelson, Larry and Moussavian, Mohammed H. Sufficient Conditions in Optimal Control Theory with Unbounded Objectives. *Int.*

Econ. Rev., February 1985, *26*(1), pp. 271–75.

Silverman, Joe; Steuer, Ralph E. and Whisman, Alan W. Computer Graphics at the Multicriterion Computer/User Interface. In *Haimes, Y. Y. and Chankong, V., eds.*, 1985, pp. 201–13.

Sonnevend, G. A Modified Ellipsoid Method for the Minimization of Convex Functions with Superlinear Convergence (or Finite Termination) for Well-Conditioned C^3 Smooth (or Piecewise Linear) Functions. In *Demyanov, V. F. and Pallaschke, D., eds.*, 1985, pp. 264–77.

Tanino, Tetsuzo. Some Basic Theoretical Results in Multiobjective Optimization. In *Haimes, Y. Y. and Chankong, V., eds.*, 1985, pp. 144–52.

Tiba, Dan. Optimal Control of Hyperbolic Variational Inequalities. In *Demyanov, V. F. and Pallaschke, D., eds.*, 1985, pp. 139–49.

Toman, Michael A. Optimal Control with an Unbounded Horizon. *J. Econ. Dynam. Control*, November 1985, *9*(3), pp. 291–316.

Tomiyama, Ken. Two-Stage Optimal Control Problems and Optimality Conditions. *J. Econ. Dynam. Control*, November 1985, *9*(3), pp. 317–37.

Treiman, Jay S. A New Approach to Clarke's Gradients in Infinite Dimensions. In *Demyanov, V. F. and Pallaschke, D., eds.*, 1985, pp. 87–93.

Vályi, István. On Duality Theory Related to Approximate Solutions of Vector-Valued Optimization Problems. In *Demyanov, V. F. and Pallaschke, D., eds.*, 1985, pp. 150–62.

Watson, G. A. Lagrangian Methods for Semi infinite Programming Problems. In *Anderson, E. J. and Philpott, A. B., eds.*, 1985, pp. 90–107.

Wohltmann, Hans-Werner. On the Controllability of Continuous-Time Macroeconomic Models. *Z. Nationalökon.*, 1985, *45*(1), pp. 47–66.

2133 Existence and Stability Conditions of Equilibrium

Eaves, B. Curtis. Finite Solution of Pure Trade Markets with Cobb-Douglas Utilities. In *Manne, A. S., ed.*, 1985, pp. 226–39.

Evans, George. Expectational Stability and the Multiple Equilibria Problem in Linear Rational Expectations Models. *Quart. J. Econ.*, November 1985, *100*(4), pp. 1217–33.

Fujimoto, Takao. Stability of Nonlinear Homogeneous Difference Equations [Equilibrium, Stability, and Growth]. *J. Econ. Theory*, February 1985, *35*(1), pp. 186–90.

Giavazzi, Francesco and Wyplosz, Charles. The Zero Root Problem: A Note on the Dynamic Determination of the Stationary Equilibrium in Linear Models. *Rev. Econ. Stud.*, April 1985, *52*(2), pp. 353–57.

Jordan, J. S. Learning Rational Expectations: The Finite State Case. *J. Econ. Theory*, August 1985, *36*(2), pp. 257–76.

Kehoe, Timothy J. A Numerical Investigation of Multiplicity of Equilibria. In *Manne, A. S.,*
ed., 1985 , pp. 240–58.

Kehoe, Timothy J. Multiplicity of Equilibria and Comparative Statics. *Quart. J. Econ.*, February 1985, *100*(1), pp. 119–47.

Kehoe, Timothy J. and Whalley, John. Uniqueness of Equilibrium in Large-Scale Numerical General Equilibrium Models. *J. Public Econ.*, November 1985, *28*(2), pp. 247–54.

Manne, Alan S. On the Formulation and Solution of Economic Equilibrium Models. In *Manne, A. S., ed.*, 1985, pp. 1–22.

Toman, Michael A. Optimal Control with an Unbounded Horizon. *J. Econ. Dynam. Control*, November 1985, *9*(3), pp. 291–316.

Williams, Steven R. Necessary and Sufficient Conditions for the Existence of a Locally Stable Message Process. *J. Econ. Theory*, February 1985, *35*(1), pp. 127–54.

2134 Computational Techniques

Anderson, E. J. A New Primal Algorithm for Semi-infinite Linear Programming. In *Anderson, E. J. and Philpott, A. B., eds.*, 1985, pp. 108–22.

Blanchard, Olivier J. Methods of Solution for Dynamic Rational Expectations Models: A Survey. In *Manne, A. S., ed.*, 1985, pp. 210–25.

Broadie, Mark N. An Introduction to the Octahedral Algorithm for the Computation of Economic Equilibria. In *Manne, A. S., ed.*, 1985, pp. 121–43.

Eaves, B. Curtis. Finite Solution of Pure Trade Markets with Cobb-Douglas Utilities. In *Manne, A. S., ed.*, 1985, pp. 226–39.

Gaudioso, Manlio. An Algorithm for Convex NDO Based on Properties of the Contour Lines of Convex Quadratic Functions. In *Demyanov, V. F. and Pallaschke, D., eds.*, 1985, pp. 190–96.

Goldstein, A. A. A Note on the Complexity of an Algorithm for Tchebycheff Approximation. In *Demyanov, V. F. and Pallaschke, D., eds.*, 1985, pp. 197–202.

Hanscom, M. A.; Nguyen, V. H. and Strodiot, J. J. A Reduced Subgradient Algorithm for Network Flow Problems with Convex Nondifferentiable Costs. In *Demyanov, V. F. and Pallaschke, D., eds.*, 1985, pp. 318–22.

Heady, Christopher J. and Mitra, Pradeep K. A Computational Approach to Optimum Public Policies. In *Manne, A. S., ed.*, 1985, pp. 95–120.

Jones, Philip C.; Saigal, Romesh and Schneider, Michael. Demand Homotopies for Computing Nonlinear and Multi-commodity Spatial Equilibria. In *Harker, P. T., ed.*, 1985, pp. 118–35.

Karwan, Mark H., et al. An Improved Interactive Multicriteria Integer Programming Algorithm. In *Haimes, Y. Y. and Chankong, V., eds.*, 1985, pp. 261–71.

Kehoe, Timothy J. A Numerical Investigation of Multiplicity of Equilibria. In *Manne, A. S., ed.*, 1985 , pp. 240–58.

Khilnani, Arvind and Tse, Edison. A Fixed Point

Algorithm with Economic Applications. *J. Econ. Dynam. Control*, October 1985, *9*(2), pp. 127–37.

Kiwiel, K. C. Descent Methods for Nonsmooth Convex Constrained Minimization. In *Demyanov, V. F. and Pallaschke, D., eds.*, 1985, pp. 203–14.

Korhonen, Pekka J. and Laakso, Jukka. On Developing A Visual Interactive Multiple Criteria Method—An Outline. In *Haimes, Y. Y. and Chankong, V., eds.*, 1985, pp. 272–81.

van der Laan, Gerard. The Computation of General Equilibrium in Economies with a Block Diagonal Pattern. *Econometrica*, May 1985, *53*(3), pp. 658–65.

Lemaréchal, C. and Strodiot, J. J. Bundle Methods, Cutting-Plane Algorithms and σ-Newton Directions. In *Demyanov, V. F. and Pallaschke, D., eds.*, 1985, pp. 25–33.

Lewis, A. S. Extreme Points and Purification Algorithms in General Linear Programming. In *Anderson, E. J. and Philpott, A. B., eds.*, 1985, pp. 123–35.

Mathiesen, Lars. Computation of Economic Equilibria by a Sequence of Linear Complementarity Problems. In *Manne, A. S., ed.*, 1985, pp. 144–62.

Nakayama, Hirotaka J. On the Components in Interactive Multiobjective Programming Methods. In *Grauer, M.; Thompson, M. and Wierzbicki, A. P., eds.*, 1985, pp. 234–47.

O'Leary, Daniel E. The Use of Conjoint Analysis in the Determination of Goal Programming Weights for a Decision Support System. In *Haimes, Y. Y. and Chankong, V., eds.*, 1985, pp. 287–99.

Önal, Hayri. Competitive Equilibrium Computations under Separated Demand Functions. *METU*, 1985, *12*(3/4), pp. 333–42.
[G: Turkey]

Pang, Jong-Shi and Lin, Yuh-Yang. A Dual Conjugate Gradient Method for the Single-Commodity Spatial Price Equilibrium Problem. In *Harker, P. T., ed.*, 1985, pp. 136–57.

Phillips, Robert L. Computing Solutions to Generalized Equilibrium Models by Successive Under-Relaxation. In *Manne, A. S., ed.*, 1985, pp. 192–209.

Preckel, Paul V. Alternative Algorithms for Computing Economic Equilibria. In *Manne, A. S., ed.*, 1985, pp. 163–72.

Stone, John C. Sequential Optimization and Complementarity Techniques for Computing Economic Equilibria. In *Manne, A. S., ed.*, 1985, pp. 173–91.

Van Thuong, Nguyen and Tuy, Hoang. A Finite Algorithm for Solving Linear Programs with an Additional Reverse Convex Constraint. In *Demyanov, V. F. and Pallaschke, D., eds.*, 1985, pp. 291–302.

Whalley, John and White, Philip M. A Decomposition Algorithm for General Equilibrium Computation with Application to International Trade Models: A Correction. *Econometrica*, May 1985, *53*(3), pp. 679.

Wiegard, Wolfgang. Die Algorithmen von Scarf und Merrill zur numerischen Berechnung allgemeiner Gleichgewichte. Eine Einführung mit Beispielen aus der Steuerpolitik. (With English summary.) *Z. Wirtschaft. Sozialwissen.*, 1985, *105*(6), pp. 709–41.

2135 Construction, Analysis, and Use of Mathematical Programming Models

Anderson, E. J. A New Primal Algorithm for Semi-infinite Linear Programming. In *Anderson, E. J. and Philpott, A. B., eds.*, 1985, pp. 108–22.

Batten, David F. Conflict, Inertia, and Adaptive Learning in Urban Systems Modelling. In *Hutchinson, B. G.; Nijkamp, P. and Batty, M., eds.*, 1985, pp. 87–114.

Batterham, R. L. A Note on Maximizing Utility in Quadratic Programming Models for Farm Planning. *Rev. Marketing Agr. Econ.*, April 1985, *53*(1), pp. 25–28.

Bector, C. R. and Bhatia, B. L. Generalized Duality for Nonlinear Programming in Complex Space. *Econ. Computat. Cybern. Stud. Res.*, 1985, *20*(2), pp. 75–80.

Boucher, Jacqueline and Smeers, Yves. Programmation mathématique et modélisation énergétique. (Mathematical Programming and Energy Modelling. With English summary.) *L'Actual. Econ.*, March 1985, *61*(1), pp. 24–50.

Breslawski, Steven and Zionts, Stanley. An Interactive Multiple Criteria Linear Programming Package. In *Haimes, Y. Y. and Chankong, V., eds.*, 1985, pp. 282–86.

Büttler, Hans-Jürg. A Combined Linear/Nonlinear Programming Model of Employment, Transportation, and Housing in an Urban Economy. In *Hutchinson, B. G.; Nijkamp, P. and Batty, M., eds.*, 1985, pp. 32–49.

Chetty, V. K. Fenchel's Duality Theorem and the Dual in Nonlinear Programming. *J. Quant. Econ.*, July 1985, *1*(2), pp. 273–84.

Drynan, Ross G. A Generalised Maximin Approach to Imprecise Objective Function Coefficients in Linear Programs. *Australian J. Agr. Econ.*, August 1985, *29*(2), pp. 142–48.

Fabian, Cs. Economic Pre-optimizing Algorithms for Integer Programming. *Econ. Computat. Cybern. Stud. Res.*, 1985, *20*(1), pp. 33–42.

Gal, Tomas and Wolf, Hartmut. Solving Stochastic Linear Programs via Goal Programming. In *Haimes, Y. Y. and Chankong, V., eds.*, 1985, pp. 126–43.

Gonzalez, Juan J.; Reeves, Gary R. and Franz, Lori S. An Interactive Procedure for Solving Multiple Objective Integer Linear Programming Problems. In *Haimes, Y. Y. and Chankong, V., eds.*, 1985, pp. 250–60.

Górecki, H., et al. Decision Support Based on the Skeleton Method—The HG Package. In *Grauer, M.; Thompson, M. and Wierzbicki, A. P., eds.*, 1985, pp. 269–80.

Grauer, Manfred; Messner, Sabine and Strubegger, Manfred. An Integrated Programming Package for Multiple-Criteria Decision Analysis. In *Grauer, M.; Thompson, M. and Wierzbicki, A. P.*, *eds.*, 1985, pp. 248–60.

[G: Selected Countries]

Haneveld, W. K. Klein. Some Linear Programs in Probabilities and Their Duals. In *Ponstein, J.*, *ed.*, 1985, pp. 95–141.

Isermann, Heinz. Mathematics of the Multiple Objective Programming Problem—A Tutorial. In *Fandel, G. and Spronk, J.*, *eds.*, 1985, pp. 129–52.

Kantorovich, L. V. and Romanovskii, I. V. Column Generation in the Simplex Method. *Matekon*, Fall 1985, 22(1), pp. 3–22.

Karney, D. F. Symmetric Duality: A Prelude. In *Anderson, E. J. and Philpott, A. B.*, *eds.*, 1985, pp. 29–36.

Karwan, Mark H., et al. An Improved Interactive Multicriteria Integer Programming Algorithm. In *Haimes, Y. Y. and Chankong, V.*, *eds.*, 1985, pp. 261–71.

Lachica-Sosa, Mary Ann Celeste. The Linear Programming Approach in the Derivation of a Food Price Index. *Philippine Econ. J.*, 1985, 24(2–3), pp. 181–99.   [G: Philippines]

Lewis, A. S. Extreme Points and Purification Algorithms in General Linear Programming. In *Anderson, E. J. and Philpott, A. B.*, *eds.*, 1985, pp. 123–35.

Mednitskii, V. G., et al. On the Efficiency of the Technology for Computer Solutions of Problems of the Optimal Development and Location of Branches and Multibranch Complexes. *Matekon*, Fall 1985, 22(1), pp. 23–42.

Mednitskii, V. G., et al. On Formulating Problems for Optimizing the Development and Location of Output in Multiproduct Branches and Multibranch Complexes. *Matekon*, Spring 1985, 21(3), pp. 81–102.

Miller, Ronald E. Multiple Optimal Solutions in Linear Programming Models: A Further Comment. *Amer. J. Agr. Econ.*, February 1985, 67(1), p. 153.

Nash, Peter. Algebraic Fundamentals of Linear Programming. In *Anderson, E. J. and Philpott, A. B.*, *eds.*, 1985, pp. 37–52.

Neumann, Michael M. The Theorem of Gale for Infinite Networks and Applications. In *Anderson, E. J. and Philpott, A. B.*, *eds.*, 1985, pp. 154–71.

van de Panne, C. and Rahnama, F. The First Algorithm for Linear Programming: An Analysis of Kantorovich's Method. *Econ. Planning*, 1985, 19(2), pp. 76–91.

Paris, Quirino. A Primer on Karmarkar's Algorithm for Linear Programming. *METU*, 1985, 12(1/2), pp. 131–55.

Paris, Quirino. Multiple Optimal Solutions in Linear Programming Models: A Further Reply. *Amer. J. Agr. Econ.*, February 1985, 67(1), pp. 154–55.

Paris, Quirino. Sector Models with Explicit Expectations and Adjustments. *Statistica*, Oct.-Dec. 1985, 45(4), pp. 465–78.

Penot, Jean-Paul. Variations on the Theme of Nonsmooth Analysis: Another Subdifferential.

In *Demyanov, V. F. and Pallaschke, D.*, *eds.*, 1985, pp. 41–54.

Philpott, A. B. Network Programming in Continuous Time with Node Storage. In *Anderson, E. J. and Philpott, A. B.*, *eds.*, 1985, pp. 136–53.

Pomerol, J. Ch. Openness, Closedness and Duality in Banach Spaces with Applications to Continuous Linear Programming. In *Anderson, E. J. and Philpott, A. B.*, *eds.*, 1985, pp. 1–15.

Ponstein, J. From Convex to Mixed Programming. In *Ponstein, J.*, *ed.*, 1985, pp. 71–94.

Rockafellar, R. Tyrrell. Monotropic Programming: A Generalization of Linear Programming and Network Programming. In *Ponstein, J.*, *ed.*, 1985, pp. 10–36.

Rubio, J. E. Nonlinear Optimal Control Problems as Infinite-Dimensional Linear Programming Problems. In *Anderson, E. J. and Philpott, A. B.*, *eds.*, 1985, pp. 172–84.

Sharpe, Ron. An Optimum Economic/Energy Land-Use Transportation Model. In *Hutchinson, B. G.; Nijkamp, P. and Batty, M.*, *eds.*, 1985, pp. 50–66.

Ştefănescu, Maria Viorica. Fundamental Algorithms for Hierarchical Classification. *Econ. Computat. Cybern. Stud. Res.*, 1985, 20(2), pp. 37–48.

Strongin, Roman G. Numerical Methods for Multiextremal Nonlinear Programming Problems with Nonconvex Constraints. In *Demyanov, V. F. and Pallaschke, D.*, *eds.*, 1985, pp. 278–83.

Tarasov, V. N. and Popova, N. K. A Modification of the Cutting-Plane Method with Accelerated Convergence. In *Demyanov, V. F. and Pallaschke, D.*, *eds.*, 1985, pp. 284–90.

Watson, G. A. Lagrangian Methods for Semi-infinite Programming Problems. In *Anderson, E. J. and Philpott, A. B.*, *eds.*, 1985, pp. 90–107.

Wendell, Richard E. Goal Programming Sensitivity Analysis: The Tolerance Approach. In *Haimes, Y. Y. and Chankong, V.*, *eds.*, 1985, pp. 300–07.

Zeleny, Milan. Multicriterion Design of High-Productivity Systems: Extensions and Applications. In *Haimes, Y. Y. and Chankong, V.*, *eds.*, 1985, pp. 308–21.

Zionts, Stanley. Multiple Criteria Mathematical Programming: An Overview and Several Approaches. In *Fandel, G. and Spronk, J.*, *eds.*, 1985, pp. 85–128.

214 Computer Programs

2140 Computer Programs

Anderson, Kim B. and Ikerd, John E. Whole Farm Risk-rating Microcomputer Model. *Southern J. Agr. Econ.*, July 1985, 17(1), pp. 183–87.

Bischoff, Eberhard. Two Empirical Tests with Approaches to Multiple-Criteria Decision Making. In *Grauer, M.; Thompson, M. and*

Wierzbicki, A. P., eds., 1985, pp. 344–47.

Diaconescu, G. and Velicanu, M. The SA-V Organized Data Base—A Relational Approach. *Econ. Computat. Cybern. Stud. Res.*, 1985, 20(3), pp. 93–97.

Dumitrescu, Vl., et al. CP/M—An Operating System for Microcomputers (II). *Econ. Computat. Cybern. Stud. Res.*, 1985, 20(2), pp. 49–56.

Dumitrescu, Vl., et al. CP/M—An Operating System for Microcomputers. *Econ. Computat. Cybern. Stud. Res.*, 1985, 20(1), pp. 57–68.

Dumitrescu, Vl., et al. CP/M—An Operating System for Microcomputers (III). *Econ. Computat. Cybern. Stud. Res.*, 1985, 20(3), pp. 83–91.

Dumitrescu, Vl., et al. CP/M—An Operating System for Microcomputers (IV). *Econ. Computat. Cybern. Stud. Res.*, 1985, 20(4), pp. 83–92.

Fichefet, Jean. Computer Selection and Multicriteria Decision Aid. In *Fandel, G. and Spronk, J., eds.*, 1985, pp. 337–46.

Fichefet, Jean. Data Structures and Complexity of Algorithms for Discrete MCDM Methods. In *Fandel, G. and Spronk, J., eds.*, 1985, pp. 197–226.

Górecki, H., et al. Decision Support Based on the Skeleton Method—The HG Package. In *Grauer, M.; Thompson, M. and Wierzbicki, A. P., eds.*, 1985, pp. 269–80.

Grauer, Manfred; Messner, Sabine and Strubegger, Manfred. An Integrated Programming Package for Multiple-Criteria Decision Analysis. In *Grauer, M.; Thompson, M. and Wierzbicki, A. P., eds.*, 1985, pp. 248–60.
[G: Selected Countries]

Jelassi, Mohamed Tawfik; Jarke, Matthias and Checroun, Alain. Data Base Approach for Multicriteria Decision Support Systems (MCDSS). In *Fandel, G. and Spronk, J., eds.*, 1985, pp. 227–44.

Lewandowski, A.; Rogowski, T. and Kręglewski, T. A Trajectory-Oriented Extension of DIDASS and Its Applications. In *Grauer, M.; Thompson, M. and Wierzbicki, A. P., eds.*, 1985, pp. 261–68.

Majchrzak, Janusz. DISCRET—A Package for Multicriteria Optimization and Decision Problems with Discrete Alternatives. In *Grauer, M.; Thompson, M. and Wierzbicki, A. P., eds.*, 1985, pp. 319–24.

Nakayama, Hirotaka J. On the Components in Interactive Multiobjective Programming Methods. In *Grauer, M.; Thompson, M. and Wierzbicki, A. P., eds.*, 1985, pp. 234–47.

de la Viña, Lynda Y. Econometrics Software for Microcomputers. *J. Bus. Econ. Statist.*, January 1985, 3(1), pp. 89–91.

Vishwakarma, Keshav P. The State Space Software SARAS Forecasts Better than the Box–Jenkins Method. In *Batten, D. F. and Lesse, P. F., eds.*, 1985, pp. 163–78. [G: Australia]

Zebrowski, M.; Dobrowolski, G. and Ryś, T. An Experimental Session with the HG Package. In *Grauer, M.; Thompson, M. and Wierzbicki, A. P., eds.*, 1985, pp. 329–35.

215 Experimental Economic Methods

2150 Experimental Economic Methods

Ang, James S. and Schwarz, Thomas. Risk Aversion and Information Structure: An Experimental Study of Price Variability in the Securities Markets. *J. Finance*, July 1985, 40(3), pp. 825–44.

Batsell, Richard R. and Polking, John C. A New Class of Market Share Models. *Marketing Sci.*, Summer 1985, 4(3), pp. 177–98. [G: U.S.]

Battalio, Raymond C.; Kagel, John H. and MacDonald, Don N. Animals' Choices over Uncertain Outcomes: Some Initial Experimental Results. *Amer. Econ. Rev.*, September 1985, 75(4), pp. 597–613.

Bischoff, Eberhard. Two Empirical Tests with Approaches to Multiple-Criteria Decision Making. In *Grauer, M.; Thompson, M. and Wierzbicki, A. P., eds.*, 1985, pp. 344–47.

Cohen, Kalman J. Risk Aversion and Information Structure: An Experimental Study of Price Variability in the Securities Markets: Discussion. *J. Finance*, July 1985, 40(3), pp. 845–46.

DeJong, Douglas V.; Forsythe, Robert and Lundholm, Russell J. Ripoffs, Lemons, and Reputation Formation in Agency Relationships: A Laboratory Market Study. *J. Finance*, July 1985, 40(3), pp. 809–20.

DeJong, Douglas V., et al. A Laboratory Investigation of the Moral Hazard Problem in an Agency Relationship. *J. Acc. Res.*, Supp. 1985, 23, pp. 81–120. [G: U.S.]

Friedman, Daniel. Experimental Economics: Comment. *Amer. Econ. Rev.*, March 1985, 75(1), pp. 264.

Graham, John L. Cross-cultural Marketing Negotiations: A Laboratory Experiment. *Marketing Sci.*, Spring 1985, 4(2), pp. 130–46.

Harrison, Glenn W. and McKee, Michael. Experimental Evaluation of the Coase Theorem. *J. Law Econ.*, October 1985, 28(3), pp. 653–70.

Harrison, Glenn W. and McKee, Michael. Monopoly Behavior, Decentralized Regulation, and Contestable Markets: An Experimental Evaluation. *Rand J. Econ.*, Spring 1985, 16(1), pp. 51–69.

Heiner, Ronald A. Experimental Economics: Comment. *Amer. Econ. Rev.*, March 1985, 75(1), pp. 260–63.

Holt, Charles A. An Experimental Test of the Consistent-Conjectures Hypothesis. *Amer. Econ. Rev.*, June 1985, 75(3), pp. 314–25.

Isaac, R. Mark and Smith, Vernon L. In Search of Predatory Pricing. *J. Polit. Econ.*, April 1985, 93(2), pp. 320–45.

Miller, Ross M. and Plott, Charles R. Product Quality Signaling in Experimental Markets. *Econometrica*, July 1985, 53(4), pp. 837–72.

Rapoport, Amnon. Provision of Public Goods and the MCS Experimental Paradigm. *Amer. Polit. Sci. Rev.*, March 1985, 79(1), pp. 148–55.

Rapoport, Anatol. Uses of Experimental Games. In *Grauer, M.; Thompson, M. and Wierzbicki, A. P., eds.*, 1985, pp. 147–61.

Samples, Karl C. A Note on the Existence of Starting Point Bias in Iterative Bidding Games. *Western J. Agr. Econ.*, July 1985, *10*(1), pp. 32–40. [G: U.S.]

Smith, Vernon L. Experimental Economics: Reply. *Amer. Econ. Rev.*, March 1985, *75*(1), pp. 264–72.

Spriggs, John and Sigurdson, Dale. Seller Cooperation in an Oligopoly–Monopsony Market: An Analysis Involving Experimental Economics. *Can. J. Agr. Econ.*, November 1985, *33*(3), pp. 359–73. [G: Global]

Uecker, Wilfred C.; Schepanski, Albert and Shin, Joon. Toward a Positive Theory of Information Evaluation: Relevant Tests of Competing Models in a Principal-Agency Setting. *Accounting Rev.*, July 1985, *60*(3), pp. 430–57.

Waller, William S. and Chow, Chee W. The Self-selection and Effort Effects Standard-based Employment Contracts: A Framework and Some Empirical Evidence. *Accounting Rev.*, July 1985, *60*(3), pp. 458–76.

Young, S. Mark. A Laboratory Investigation of the Moral Hazard Problem in an Agency Relationship: Discussion. *J. Acc. Res.*, Supp. 1985, *23*, pp. 121–23.

220 ECONOMIC AND SOCIAL STATISTICAL DATA AND ANALYSIS

2200 General

Boruch, Robert F. Definitions, Products, and Distinctions in Data Sharing. In *Fienberg, S. E.; Martin, M. E. and Straf, M. L., eds.*, 1985, pp. 89–122.

Boruch, Robert F. and Cordray, David S. Professional Codes and Guidelines in Data Sharing. In *Fienberg, S. E.; Martin, M. E. and Straf, M. L., eds.*, 1985, pp. 199–225.

Bulgaru, M., et al. The Concept of a Data Bank for Economic Scientific Research in Education. *Econ. Computat. Cybern. Stud. Res.*, 1985, *20*(4), pp. 33–42. [G: Romania]

Bulgaru, M., et al. Trends and Perspectives in the Field of Data Banks. *Econ. Computat. Cybern. Stud. Res.*, 1985, *20*(3), pp. 75–81.

Butz, William P. Goals for Statistical Uses of Administrative Records: The Next 10 Years: Comment: The Future of Administrative Records in the Census Bureau's Demographic Activity. *J. Bus. Econ. Statist.*, October 1985, *3*(4), pp. 393–95. [G: U.S.]

Carroll, John J. Goals for Statistical Uses of Administrative Records: The Next 10 Years: Comment: Uses of Administrative Records: A Social Security Point of View. *J. Bus. Econ. Statist.*, October 1985, *3*(4), pp. 396–97. [G: U.S.]

Cecil, Joe Shelby and Griffin, Eugene. The Role of Legal Policies in Data Sharing. In *Fienberg, S. E.; Martin, M. E. and Straf, M. L., eds.*, 1985, pp. 148–98.

Charlton, Martin; Openshaw, Stan and Wymer, Colin. Some New Classifications of Census Enumeration Districts in Britain: A Poor Man's ACORN. *J. Econ. Soc. Meas.*, April 1985, *13*(1), pp. 69–96. [G: U.K.]

Clubb, Jerome M., et al. Sharing Research Data in the Social Sciences. In *Fienberg, S. E.; Martin, M. E. and Straf, M. L., eds.*, 1985, pp. 39–88.

David, Martin. The Design and Development of SIPP: Introduction. *J. Econ. Soc. Meas.*, December 1985, *13*(3–4), pp. 215–24. [G: U.S.]

David, Martin; Robbin, Alice and Rockwell, Richard C. Second SSRC Syposium on the Scientific and Research Potential of SIPP—June 28–29, 1985: Summary and Recommendations. *J. Econ. Soc. Meas.*, December 1985, *13*(3–4), pp. 385–92. [G: U.S.]

David, Martin, et al. Summary of the SIPP Conference and Recommendations of the Conferees. *J. Econ. Soc. Meas.*, December 1985, *13*(3–4), pp. 377–83. [G: U.S.]

Denham, Chris. The 1981 Census in Retrospect. *J. Econ. Soc. Meas.*, April 1985, *13*(1), pp. 5–17. [G: U.K.]

Dumas, Cécile. Unfamiliar Sources of Data from Statistics Canada. In *Economic Council of Canada.*, 1985, pp. 149–55. [G: Canada]

Duncan, Greg J. and Hill, Martha S. Conceptions of Longitudinal Households: Fertile or Futile? *J. Econ. Soc. Meas.*, December 1985, *13*(3–4), pp. 361–75.

Griliches, Zvi. Data and Econometricians—The Uneasy Alliance. *Amer. Econ. Rev.*, May 1985, *75*(2), pp. 196–200.

Günlük-Şenesen, Gülay. Richard Stone'un sosyal hesaplar sistemi. (The Social Accounting System of Richard Stone. With English summary.) *METU*, 1985, *12*(1/2), pp. 173–83.

Haber, Sheldon E. A Perspective on Linking SIPP to Administrative and Statistical Records. *J. Econ. Soc. Meas.*, December 1985, *13*(3–4), pp. 331–40.

Hedrick, Terry Elizabeth. Justifications for and Obstacles to Data Sharing. In *Fienberg, S. E.; Martin, M. E. and Straf, M. L., eds.*, 1985, pp. 123–47.

Jabine, Thomas B. Goals for Statistical Uses of Administrative Records: The Next 10 Years: Reply. *J. Bus. Econ. Statist.*, October 1985, *3*(4), pp. 402–04. [G: U.S.]

Jabine, Thomas B. and Scheuren, Fritz. Goals for Statistical Uses of Administrative Records: The Next 10 Years. *J. Bus. Econ. Statist.*, October 1985, *3*(4), pp. 380–91. [G: U.S.]

Kalton, Graham and Lepkowski, James. Following Rules in SIPP. *J. Econ. Soc. Meas.*, December 1985, *13*(3–4), pp. 319–29. [G: U.S.]

Leontief, Wassily. Capital Reconstruction and Postwar Development of Income and Consumption. In *Linz, S. J., ed.*, 1985, pp. 38–46. [G: U.S.S.R.]

Leontief, Wassily. The Balance of the Economy of the USSR: A Methodological Analysis of the Work of the Central Statistical Administration.

In *Leontief, W.*, 1985, pp. 251–57.
[G: U.S.S.R.]

Masters, R. J. The Scottish Experience in 1981: A Guide to the Future? *J. Econ. Soc. Meas.*, April 1985, *13*(1), pp. 19–28. [G: U.K.]

McDonald, John W. and Snooks, G. D. Statistical Analysis of Domesday Book (1086). *J. Roy. Statist. Soc.*, 1985, *148*(2), pp. 147–60.
[G: U.K.]

McMillen, David Byron and Herriot, Roger. Toward a Longitudinal Definition of Households. *J. Econ. Soc. Meas.*, December 1985, *13*(3–4), pp. 349–60.

Miller, Ed. ADP Strategic Planning in a National Statistical Agency—An Overview. *Statist. J.*, December 1985, *3*(4), pp. 339–46.

Neumann, Klaus and Rauch, Lars. Results of the Statistical Computing Project—An Example of Successful International Cooperation. *Statist. J.*, December 1985, *3*(4), pp. 375–79.
[G: Europe]

Norwood, Janet L. Goals for Statistical Uses of Administrative Records: The Next 10 Years: Comment: Administrative Statistics: A BLS Perspective. *J. Bus. Econ. Statist.*, October 1985, *3*(4), pp. 398–400. [G: U.S.]

Pyatt, Graham. Commodity Balances and National Accounts: A SAM Perspective. *Rev. Income Wealth*, June 1985, *31*(2), pp. 155–69.

Rhind, David. Successors to the Census of Population. *J. Econ. Soc. Meas.*, April 1985, *13*(1), pp. 29–38. [G: U.K.]

Round, Jeffrey I. Decomposing Multipliers for Economic Systems Involving Regional and World Trade. *Econ. J.*, June 1985, *95*(378), pp. 383–99. [G: Malaysia]

Saunders, Christopher T. The Integration of Economic and Social Statistics—General Issues. *Statist. J.*, May 1985, *3*(2), pp. 137–51.

Savage, I. Richard. Hard–Soft Problems. *J. Amer. Statist. Assoc.*, March 1985, *80*(389), pp. 1–7. [G: U.S.]

Smith, James D. A Little SIPP: Old Wine in New Bottles—Let's Recask It. *J. Econ. Soc. Meas.*, December 1985, *13*(3–4), pp. 341–47.

Stone, Richard. Bibliography of Richard Stone's Works, 1936–1984. *Scand. J. Econ.*, 1985, *87*(1), pp. 33–43.

Wahlström, Staffan and Wallberg, Klas. Coordination of Statistics on Households and Families: The Case of Sweden. *Statist. J.*, March 1985, *3*(1), pp. 69–84.

Waite, Charles A. Goals for Statistical Uses of Administrative Records: The Next 10 Years: Comment: The Future of Administrative Records in the Economic Programs of the Census Bureau. *J. Bus. Econ. Statist.*, October 1985, *3*(4), pp. 400–401. [G: U.S.]

221 National Income Accounting

2210 National Income Accounting Theory and Procedures

Arkhipoff, Oleg. Un, deux, trois, beaucoup ou comment l'imprécision vient aux comptables.

(One, Two, Three, Many—Or How Imprecision Comes to Accountants. With English summary.) *Écon. Soc.*, June 1985, *19*(6), pp. 185–99.

Arya, P. L. Rejoinder [Measuring Economic Growth]. *Rev. Income Wealth*, December 1985, *31*(4), pp. 415–16.

Arya, P. L. Reply [Measuring Economic Growth—A Critique of the Views of Fell and Greenfield]. *Rev. Income Wealth*, December 1985, *31*(4), pp. 423–24. [G: Canada]

Balassa, Bela. Policy Experiments in Chile, 1973–83. In *Balassa, B.*, 1985, pp. 157–84.
[G: Chile]

Chawla, R. K. and Oja, G. Measuring Economic Growth—Critique of Arya's Application of Fell and Greenfield's Method. *Rev. Income Wealth*, December 1985, *31*(4), pp. 417–22.
[G: Canada]

David, Martin. The Distribution of Income in the United States: Implications for the Design of the SIPP Panel. *J. Econ. Soc. Meas.*, December 1985, *13*(3–4), pp. 305–17. [G: U.S.]

Duchêne, Gérard. Vers une réforme de la planification des services en URSS? (Towards a Reform in Planning for Services in U.S.S.R. With English summary.) *Écon. Soc.*, May 1985, *19*(5), pp. 15–42. [G: U.S.S.R.]

Eisner, Robert. The Total Incomes System of Accounts. *Surv. Curr. Bus.*, January 1985, *65*(1), pp. 24–48. [G: U.S.]

Fell, H. A. and Greenfield, C. C. Measuring Economic Growth: A Reply. *Rev. Income Wealth*, December 1985, *31*(4), pp. 413–14.

Fellows, James A. The Economic and Accounting Definitions of Income: Proposals for Reform, a Note. *Amer. Econ.*, Fall 1985, *29*(2), pp. 57–62.

Franz, Alfred. The Solution of Problems in International Comparisons of GDP through Price Adjustments. What to Learn from ECP 1980? *Statist. J.*, September 1985, *3*(3), pp. 307–19.
[G: W. Europe]

He, Xiaofeng. A Preliminary Inquiry into the Theory of Service Value. *Chinese Econ. Stud.*, Winter 1984-85, *18*(2), pp. 39–57.

Herbel, Norbert and Bald, Christiane. New Calculation of the Production and Productivity Indexes in the Federal Republic of Germany. *Statist. J.*, May 1985, *3*(2), pp. 185–209.
[G: W. Germany]

Johansen, Leif. Richard Stone's Contributions to Economics. *Scand. J. Econ.*, 1985, *87*(1), pp. 4–32.

Landefeld, J. Steven and Hines, James R. National Accounting for Non-renewable Natural Resources in the Mining Industries. *Rev. Income Wealth*, March 1985, *31*(1), pp. 1–20.
[G: U.S.]

Leontief, Wassily. An Alternative to Aggregation in Input–Output Analysis and National Accounts. In *Leontief, W.*, 1985, pp. 283–97.
[G: U.S.]

Lippit, Victor D. The Concept of the Surplus in Economic Development. *Rev. Radical Polit.*

Econ., Spring and Summer 1985, *17*(1/2), pp. 1–19. [G: LDCs]

Meller, Patricio and Arrau, Patricio. Revision metodologica y cuantificacion de los cuentas nacionales chilenas. (A Methodological Analysis and Quantification of the Chilean National Accounts. With English summary.) *Colección Estud. CIEPLAN*, 1985, (18), pp. 95–184. [G: Chile]

Mouyelo-Katoula, Michel and Munnsad, Kantilal. A Note on Methodologies Used in a Comparison of Purchasing Power Parities and Real Economic Aggregates in Fifteen African Countries. *Statist. J.*, September 1985, *3*(3), pp. 289–305. [G: Africa]

Nevalainen, Kari. The Use of Industrial Statistics to Estimate the Generation of Recycled and Waste Residuals in Finland. *Statist. J.*, May 1985, *3*(2), pp. 161–74. [G: Finland]

Okishio, Nobuo and Nakatani, Takeshi. A Measurement of the Rate of Surplus Value in Japan; the 1980 Case. *Kobe Univ. Econ.*, 1985, (31), pp. 1–13. [G: Japan]

Parker, Robert P. and Fox, Douglas R. An Advance Overview of the Comprehensive Revision of the National Income and Product Accounts. *Surv. Curr. Bus.*, October 1985, *65*(10), pp. 19–28. [G: U.S.]

Pfähler, Wilhelm. Relative Concentration Curve: Functional Form and Measures of Non-proportionality. *Bull. Econ. Res.*, September 1985, *37*(3), pp. 201–11.

van der Ploeg, Frederick. Econometrics and Inconsistencies in the National Accounts. *Econ. Modelling*, January 1985, *2*(1), pp. 8–16. [G: U.K.]

Pyatt, Graham. Commodity Balances and National Accounts: A SAM Perspective. *Rev. Income Wealth*, June 1985, *31*(2), pp. 155–69.

Roman, Jean-Claude. Treatment of Subsidies in National Accounts. *Rev. Income Wealth*, March 1985, *31*(1), pp. 39–61. [G: OECD]

Rutgaizer, V. and Teliukov, A. Improving the Methodology of the National Economic Accounting of Services. *Prob. Econ.*, March 1985, *27*(11), pp. 3–22. [G: U.S.S.R.]

Rymes, T. K. Inflation, Nonoptimal Monetary Arrangements and the Banking Imputation in the National Accounts. *Rev. Income Wealth*, March 1985, *31*(1), pp. 85–96.

Schettkat, Ronald. The Size of Household Production: Methodological Problems and Estimates for the Federal Republic of Germany in the Period 1964 to 1980. *Rev. Income Wealth*, September 1985, *31*(3), pp. 309–21. [G: W. Germany]

Tinbergen, Jan. The Measurement of Social Welfare. In *Tinbergen, J.*, 1985, pp. 113–22.

Weale, Martin. Testing Linear Hypotheses on National Account Data. *Rev. Econ. Statist.*, November 1985, *67*(4), pp. 685–89. [G: U.S.]

Young, Allan H. and Tice, Helen Stone. An Introduction to National Economic Accounting. *Surv. Curr. Bus.*, March 1985, *65*(3), pp. 59–74, 76. [G: U.S.]

2212 National Income Accounts

Adam, M. C. and Ginsburgh, Victor. The Effects of Irregular Markets on Macroeconomic Policy: Some Estimates for Belgium. *Europ. Econ. Rev.*, October 1985, *29*(1), pp. 15–33. [G: Belgium]

Aganbegian A. Important Positive Changes in the Country's Economic Life. *Prob. Econ.*, April 1985, *27*(12), pp. 3–16. [G: U.S.S.R.]

Al-Sadik, A. T. National Accounting and Income Illusion of Petroleum Exports: The Case of the Arab Gulf Co-operation Council Members (AGCC) In *Niblock, T. and Lawless, R., eds.*, 1985, pp. 86–115. [G: OPEC]

Alm, James. The Welfare Cost of the Underground Economy. *Econ. Inquiry*, April 1985, *23*(2), pp. 243–63. [G: U.S.]

Arellano, José-Pablo. Políticas para promover el ahorro en América Latina. (Saving Policies in Latin America. With English summary.) *Colección Estud. CIEPLAN*, September 1985, (17), pp. 127–51. [G: Latin America]

Artus, Patrick, et al. Tax Incentives, Monetary Policy, and Investment in France and Germany. In *de Ménil, G. and Westphal, U., eds.*, 1985, pp. 105–41. [G: France; W. Germany]

Bailey, Will J. Capital Markets and the Climate for Investment. In *Scutt, J. A., ed.*, 1985, pp. 93–102. [G: Australia]

Baumol, William J. Measurement of Output and Productivity in the Service Sector: Comment. In *Inman, R. P., ed.*, 1985, pp. 124–26. [G: U.S.]

Baumol, William J. Rebirth of a Fallen Leader: Italy and the Long Period Data. *Atlantic Econ. J.*, September 1985, *13*(3), pp. 12–26. [G: Italy]

Behrman, Jere R. Services in the International Economy: Comment. In *Inman, R. P., ed.*, 1985, pp. 49–52. [G: Selected Countries]

Belongia, Michael T. The Impact of Inflation on the Real Income of U.S. Farmers: Discussion. *Amer. J. Agr. Econ.*, May 1985, *67*(2), pp. 398–99. [G: U.S.]

Benjamini, Yael and Maital, Shlomo. Optimal Tax Evasion and Optimal Tax Evasion Policy: Behavioral Aspects. In *Gaertner, W. and Wenig, A., eds.*, 1985, pp. 245–64. [G: Israel]

Biswas, Rajiv; Johns, Christopher and Savage, David. The Measurement of Fiscal Stance. *Nat. Inst. Econ. Rev.*, August 1985, (113), pp. 50–64. [G: U.K.]

Blades, Derek W. Crime: What Should Be Recorded in the National Accounts; and What Difference Would It Make? In *Gaertner, W. and Wenig, A., eds.*, 1985, pp. 45–58. [G: U.S.]

Blejer, Mario I. and Khan, Mohsin S. Public Investment and Crowding Out in the Caribbean Basin Countries. In *Connolly, M. B. and McDermott, J., eds.*, 1985, pp. 219–36. [G: Caribbean]

Borooah, Vani K. and Sharpe, D. R. Household Income, Consumption and Savings in the United Kingdom, 1966–82. *Scot. J. Polit.*

Econ., November 1985, *32*(3), pp. 234–56.
[G: U.K.]

Boulding, Kenneth E. Puzzles over Distribution. *Challenge*, Nov./Dec. 1985, *28*(5), pp. 4–10.
[G: U.S.]

van Brabant, Jozef M. Yugoslavia's Foreign Trade Statistics: A Methodological Inquiry. *Comparative Econ. Stud.*, Winter 1985, *27*(4), pp. 31–51.
[G: Yugoslavia]

Brezinski, Horst. The Second Economy in the Soviet Union and Its Implications for Economic Policy. In *Gaertner, W. and Wenig, A., eds.*, 1985, pp. 362–76.
[G: U.S.S.R.]

Broesterhuizen, G. A. A. M. The Unobserved Economy and the National Accounts in the Netherlands: A Sensitivity Analysis. In *Gaertner, W. and Wenig, A., eds.*, 1985, pp. 105–26.
[G: Netherlands]

Cagan, Phillip. Financing the Deficit, Interest Rates, and Monetary Policy. In *Cagan, P. and Somensatto, E., eds.*, 1985, pp. 195–221.
[G: U.S.]

Cameron, David R. Public Expenditure and Economic Performance in International Perspective. In *Klein, R. and O'Higgins, M., ed.*, 1985, pp. 8–21.
[G: OECD]

Chadeau, Ann. Measuring Household Activities: Some International Comparisons. *Rev. Income Wealth*, September 1985, *31*(3), pp. 237–53.
[G: U.S.; Canada; France; Finland]

Chan-Lee, James H. and Sutch, Helen. Profits and Rates of Return. *OECD Econ. Stud.*, Autumn 1985, (5), pp. 127–67.
[G: OECD]

Chow, Gregory C. A Model of Chinese National Income Determination. *J. Polit. Econ.*, August 1985, *93*(4), pp. 782–92.
[G: China]

Cocheba, Donald J.; Gilmer, Robert W. and Mack, Richard S. Data Refinement Recommendations and Their Impact on a Study of the Tennessee Valley: Measuring Changes in Service Sector Activity. *Growth Change*, October 1985, *16*(4), pp. 20–42.
[G: U.S.]

Drechsler, László and Horváth, Piroska. Some Problems of the Measurement of Total Consumption in Hungary. *Rev. Income Wealth*, June 1985, *31*(2), pp. 171–87.
[G: Hungary]

Eisner, Robert. The Total Incomes System of Accounts. *Surv. Curr. Bus.*, January 1985, *65*(1), pp. 24–48.
[G: U.S.]

Elias, Victor J. La productividad del sector público en la Argentina. (The Productivity of the Public Sector in Argentina. With English summary.) *Económica (La Plata)*, May-Dec. 1985, *31*(2–3), pp. 133–45.

Feige, Edgar L. The Meaning of the "Underground Economy" and the Full Compliance Deficit. In *Gaertner, W. and Wenig, A., eds.*, 1985, pp. 19–36.
[G: U.S.]

Ferrari, Camillo. Il risparmio per l'oggi e per il domani: problemi di formazione, di remunerazione, di investimento. (Saving for Today and for Tomorrow: The Formation, Remuneration and Investment of Savings. With English summary.) *Bancaria*, January 1985, *41*(1), pp. 32–44.
[G: Italy]

Forssell, Osmo. Changes in the Structure of the

Finnish Economy, 1970–1980. In *Smyshlyaev, A., ed.*, 1985, pp. 61–71.
[G: Finland]

Franz, Alfred. Estimates of the Hidden Economy in Austria on the Basis of Official Statistics. *Rev. Income Wealth*, December 1985, *31*(4), pp. 325–36.
[G: Austria]

Galasi, Péter. Peculiarities and Limits of the Second Economy in Socialism (the Hungarian Case). In *Gaertner, W. and Wenig, A., eds.*, 1985, pp. 353–61.
[G: Hungary]

García-Alba, Pasqual and Puche, Jaime Serra. Economic Fluctuations in Mexico and the United States. In *Musgrave, P. B., ed.*, 1985, pp. 123–45.
[G: Mexico; U.S.]

Glatzer, Wolfgang and Berger, Regina. Household Composition, Social Networks and Household Production. In *Gaertner, W. and Wenig, A., eds.*, 1985, pp. 330–51.
[G: W. Germany]

Glennon, Dennis. An Examination of the Stability of the Gross Private Saving Rate. *Quart. J. Bus. Econ.*, Autumn 1985, *24*(4), pp. 44–53.
[G: U.S.]

Goldsmith, R. W. Errata [An Estimate of the Size and Structure of the National Product of the Early Roman Empire]. *Rev. Income Wealth*, March 1985, *31*(1), pp. 101.

Gutmann, Peter M. The Subterranean Economy, Redux. In *Gaertner, W. and Wenig, A., eds.*, 1985, pp. 2–18.
[G: U.S.]

Herbel, Norbert and Bald, Christiane. New Calculation of the Production and Productivity Indexes in the Federal Republic of Germany. *Statist. J.*, May 1985, *3*(2), pp. 185–209.
[G: W. Germany]

Higgiston, James. Domestic Barter. In *Fisher, B. S. and Harte, K. M., eds.*, 1985, pp. 156–67.
[G: U.S.]

Hulten, Charles R. Measurement of Output and Productivity in the Service Sector: Comment. In *Inman, R. P., ed.*, 1985, pp. 127–30.
[G: U.S.]

Iglesias, Enrique V. The Latin American Economy during 1984: A Preliminary Overview. *Cepal Rev.*, April 1985, (25), pp. 7–44.
[G: Latin America]

Isachsen, Arne Jon and Strøm, Steinar. The Size and Growth of the Hidden Economy in Norway. *Rev. Income Wealth*, March 1985, *31*(1), pp. 21–38.
[G: Norway]

Jackson, R. V. Short-run Interaction of Public and Private Sectors in Australia, 1861–90. *Australian Econ. Hist. Rev.*, March 1985, *25*(1), pp. 59–75.
[G: Australia]

Johnson, Kenneth P. and Friedenberg, Howard L. Regional and State Projections of Income, Employment, and Population to the Year 2000. *Surv. Curr. Bus.*, May 1985, *65*(5), pp. 39–63.
[G: U.S.]

Kang, Heejoon. The Effects of Detrending in Granger Causality Tests. *J. Bus. Econ. Statist.*, October 1985, *3*(4), pp. 344–49.
[G: U.S.]

Kendrick, John W. Measurement of Output and Productivity in the Service Sector. In *Inman, R. P., ed.*, 1985, pp. 111–23.
[G: U.S.]

Kopcke, Richard W. Investment Spending and

the Federal Taxation of Business Income. *New Eng. Econ. Rev.*, Sept./Oct. 1985, pp. 9–34. [G: U.S.]

Kopcke, Richard W. The Determinants of Investment Spending. *New Eng. Econ. Rev.*, July/August 1985, pp. 19–35. [G: U.S.]

Kravis, Irving B. Services in World Transactions. In *Inman, R. P., ed.*, 1985, pp. 135–60. [G: Selected Countries]

van der Laan, Paul and van Tuinen, Henk K. Interest, Distribution of Value Added and Inflation: Inflation-induced Difficulties in the Interpretation of Dutch National Accounts. *Rev. Income Wealth*, September 1985, *31*(3), pp. 255–83. [G: Netherlands]

Landau, Daniel L. Explaining Differences in Per Capita Income between Countries: A Hypothesis and Test for 1950 and 1970. *Exploration Econ. Hist.*, July 1985, *22*(3), pp. 296–315.

Landau, Daniel L. Government Expenditure and Economic Growth in the Developed Countries: 1952–76. *Public Choice*, 1985, *47*(3), pp. 459–77. [G: W. Europe; U.S.; Canada; Japan]

de Leeuw, Frank. An Indirect Technique for Measuring the Underground Economy. *Surv. Curr. Bus.*, April 1985, *65*(4), pp. 64–72. [G: U.S.]

Leveson, Irving. Services in the U.S. Economy. In *Inman, R. P., ed.*, 1985, pp. 89–102. [G: U.S.]

Lim, G. C. GDP Growth Rates Calculated from Quarterly National Accounts: Discrepancies and Revisions. *Australian Econ. Rev.*, 4th Quarter 1985, (72), pp. 21–27. [G: Australia]

Loginov, V. National Income: Growth Factors. *Prob. Econ.*, November 1985, *28*(7), pp. 18–32. [G: U.S.S.R.]

Lützel, Heinrich. Inflation Accounting for the Federal Republic of Germany—Results Using Different Deflator Price Indices. *Rev. Income Wealth*, September 1985, *31*(3), pp. 207–21. [G: W. Germany]

Lynch, Gerald J. Currency, Marginal Tax Rates, and the Underground Economy. *J. Econ. Bus.*, February 1985, *37*(1), pp. 59–67. [G: U.S.]

Makin, John H. The Effect of Government Deficits on Capital Formation. In *Cagan, P. and Somensatto, E., eds.*, 1985, pp. 163–94. [G: U.S.]

Mann, Duncan. Services in the U.S. Economy: Comment. In *Inman, R. P., ed.*, 1985, pp. 103–04. [G: U.S.]

Mayes, David G. The Domestic Economy. In *Morris, D., ed.*, 1985, pp. 112–74. [G: U.K.]

McLoughlin, Jane. South Korea. In *Smith, M., et al.*, 1985, pp. 39–64. [G: S. Korea]

Meller, Patricio and Arrau, Patricio. Revision metodologica y cuantificacion de los cuentas nacionales chilenas. (A Methodological Analysis and Quantification of the Chilean National Accounts. With English summary.) *Colección Estud. CIEPLAN*, 1985, (18), pp. 95–184. [G: Chile]

Mogensen, Gunnar Viby. Forskning i sort økonomi—en oversigt. (The Hidden Economy—

A Survey Article. With English summary.) *Nationaløkon. Tidsskr.*, 1985, *123*(1), pp. 1–19. [G: Denmark]

Najjar, Annette and Marcelle, Hazel. Estimating a National Savings Series for Trinidad and Tobago: 1970–1983. *Soc. Econ. Stud.*, December 1985, *34*(4), pp. 165–97. [G: Trinidad and Tobago]

Norwood, Janet L. Measurement of Output and Productivity in the Service Sector: Comment. In *Inman, R. P., ed.*, 1985, pp. 131–33. [G: U.S.]

O'Higgins, Michael. The Relationship between the Formal and Hidden Economies: An Exploratory Analysis for Four Countries. In *Gaertner, W. and Wenig, A., eds.*, 1985, pp. 127–43. [G: Canada; U.S.; U.K.; W. Germany]

Park, Thae S. Personal Income and Adjusted Gross Income, 1981–83. *Surv. Curr. Bus.*, April 1985, *65*(4), pp. 32–40. [G: U.S.]

Peterson, Milo O. Gross Product by Industry, 1984. *Surv. Curr. Bus.*, April 1985, *65*(4), pp. 20. [G: U.S.]

Plihon, D. and Zagamé, Paul. L'investissement et l'épargne. Tendances et perspectives à moyen terme. (With English summary.) *Revue Écon. Polit.*, Sept.-Oct. 1985, *95*(5), pp. 596–610. [G: France]

Ram, Rati. The Role of Real Income Level and Income Distribution in Fulfillment of Basic Needs. *World Devel.*, May 1985, *13*(5), pp. 589–94. [G: LDCs]

Raman, C. S. Testing the Constancy of the Capital-Output Ratio under Structural Change. *Indian Econ. J.*, Oct.-Nov. 1985, *33*(2), pp. 10–16. [G: India]

Rose, Richard. Getting By in Three Economies: The Resources of the Official, Unofficial and Domestic Economies. In *Lane, J.-E., ed.*, 1985, pp. 103–41. [G: OECD]

Schettkat, Ronald. The Size of Household Production: Methodological Problems and Estimates for the Federal Republic of Germany in the Period 1964 to 1980. *Rev. Income Wealth*, September 1985, *31*(3), pp. 309–21. [G: W. Germany]

Seskin, Eugene P. Plant and Equipment Expenditures, First and Second Quarters and Second Half of 1985. *Surv. Curr. Bus.*, April 1985, *65*(4), pp. 21–25. [G: U.S.]

Seskin, Eugene P. and Sullivan, David F. Plant and Equipment Expenditures, of the Four Quarters of 1985. *Surv. Curr. Bus.*, September 1985, *65*(9), pp. 19–21. [G: U.S.]

Seskin, Eugene P. and Sullivan, David F. Plant and Equipment Expenditures: Quarters of 1985; First and Second Quarters of 1986; Year 1986. *Surv. Curr. Bus.*, December 1985, *65*(12), pp. 34–36. [G: U.S.]

Seskin, Eugene P. and Sullivan, David F. Plant and Equipment Expenditures, the Four Quarters of 1985. *Surv. Curr. Bus.*, June 1985, *65*(6), pp. 21–24. [G: U.S.]

Seskin, Eugene P. and Sullivan, David F. Revised Estimates of New Plant and Equipment Expenditures in the United States, 1947–83. *Surv. Curr. Bus.*, February 1985, 65(2), pp. 16–47.   [G: U.S.]

Shiratori, Rei. The Experience of the Welfare State in Japan and Its Problems. In *Eisenstadt, S. N. and Ahimeir, O., eds.*, 1985, pp. 200–223.   [G: Japan]

Skolka, Jiri. The Parallel Economy in Austria. In *Gaertner, W. and Wenig, A., eds.*, 1985, pp. 60–75.   [G: Austria]

Smith, James D. Market Motives in the Informal Economy. In *Gaertner, W. and Wenig, A., eds.*, 1985, pp. 161–77.   [G: U.S.]

Stark-Veltel, Gerd and Westphal, Uwe. Schzung des Produktionspotentials mit einem Putty-Clay-Ansatz. (A Putty-Clay Approach to the Estimation of Potential Output. With English summary.) *Ifo-Studien*, 1985, 31(4), pp. 269–93.   [G: W. Germany]

Starleaf, Dennis R.; Meyers, William H. and Womack, Abner W. The Impact of Inflation on the Real Income of U.S. Farmers. *Amer. J. Agr. Econ.*, May 1985, 67(2), pp. 384–89.   [G: U.S.]

Stauffer, Thomas R. Accounting for "Wasting Assets": Measurements of Income and Dependency in Oil-Rentier States. *J. Energy Devel.*, Autumn 1985, 11(1), pp. 69–93.   [G: OPEC]

Summers, Robert. Services in the International Economy. In *Inman, R. P., ed.*, 1985, pp. 27–48.   [G: Selected Countries]

Sumner, Michael. A Note on Replacement Investment. *Oxford Bull. Econ. Statist.*, November 1985, 47(4), pp. 395–400.   [G: U.K.]

Talafha, Hussain. The Effects of Workers' Remittances on the Jordanian Economy. *METU*, 1985, 12(1/2), pp. 119–30.   [G: Jordan]

Tatom, John A. Two Views of the Effects of Government Budget Deficits in the 1980s. *Fed. Res. Bank St. Louis Rev.*, October 1985, 67(8), pp. 5–16.   [G: U.S.]

Tiwari, S. G. Government Services in Relation to Total Consumption of the Population in Asian and Pacific Countries, with Special Reference to India. *Rev. Income Wealth*, June 1985, 31(2), pp. 189–200.   [G: India]

Tokman, Victor E. The Process of Accumulation and the Weakness of the Protagonists. *Cepal Rev.*, August 1985, (26), pp. 115–26.   [G: Latin America]

Trengove, Chris D. Measuring the Hidden Economy. *Australian Tax Forum*, Autumn 1985, 2(1), pp. 85–95.   [G: U.S.]

Walsh, Carl E. Revisions in the "Flash" Estimates of GNP Growth: Measurement Error or Forecast Error? *Fed. Res. Bank San Francisco Econ. Rev.*, Fall 1985, (4), pp. 5–13.   [G: U.S.]

Weale, Martin. Testing Linear Hypotheses on National Account Data. *Rev. Econ. Statist.*, November 1985, 67(4), pp. 685–89.   [G: U.S.]

Weck-Hannemann, Hannelore and Frey, Bruno S. Measuring the Shadow Economy: The Case of Switzerland. In *Gaertner, W. and Wenig, A., eds.*, 1985, pp. 76–104. [G: Switzerland]

Yaşer, Betty S. and Rajan, T. R. Thiaga. Share of Government in Gross National Product: Cross-Section and Time-Series Analysis, 1950–1982. *METU*, 1985, 12(1/2), pp. 107–18.   [G: LDCs; MDCs]

Yu, Eden S. H. and Choi, Jai-Young. The Causal Relationship between Energy and GNP: An International Comparison. *J. Energy Devel.*, Spring 1985, 10(2), pp. 249–72.   [G: U.S.; U.K.; Poland; S. Korea; Philippines]

2213 Income Distribution

Aaron, Henry J. The Distributional Impact of Social Security: Comment. In *Wise, D. A., ed.*, 1985, pp. 215–21.   [G: U.S.]

Adiseshiah, Malcolm S. Wages and Incomes. In *Mongia, J. N., ed.*, 1985, pp. 349–84.   [G: India; Selected Countries]

Ahmed, Osman Sheikh and Field, Alfred J., Jr. Potential Effects of Income-Redistribution Policies on the Final Pattern of Income Distribution: The Case of Kenya. *J. Devel. Areas*, October 1985, 20(1), pp. 1–21.   [G: Kenya]

Alchin, Terry. Prota: A New Measure of the Progressivity of Personal Income Taxation. *Australian Econ. Pap.*, June 1985, 24(44), pp. 185–200.   [G: Australia]

Ali, M. Shaukat. From Functional to Personal Distribution: A Decomposition Analysis of Inequality Trend in Pakistan. *Indian J. Quant. Econ.*, 1985, 1(2), pp. 99–108. [G: Pakistan]

Apps, Patricia. The Relative Deprivation Curve and Its Applications: Comment. *J. Bus. Econ. Statist.*, April 1985, 3(2), pp. 169–71.   [G: Australia]

Basu, Kaushik. Poverty Measurement: A Decomposition of the Normalization Axion [Cardinal Utility, Utilitarianism and a Class of Invariance Axioms in Welfare Analysis] [Poverty: An Ordinal Approach to Measurement]. *Econometrica*, November 1985, 53(6), pp. 1439–43.

Beach, Charles M. and Richmond, James. Joint Confidence Intervals for Income Shares and Lorenz Curves. *Int. Econ. Rev.*, June 1985, 26(2), pp. 439–50.   [G: Canada]

Behrman, Jere R.; Wolfe, Barbara L. and Blau, David M. Human Capital and Earnings Distribution in a Developing Country: The Case of Prerevolutionary Nicaragua. *Econ. Develop. Cult. Change*, October 1985, 34(1), pp. 1–29.   [G: Nicaragua]

Berrebi, Z. M. and Silber, Jacques. Income Inequality Indices and Deprivation: A Generalization [Relative Deprivation and the Gini Coefficient]. *Quart. J. Econ.*, August 1985, 100(3), pp. 807–10.

Berrebi, Z. M. and Silber, Jacques. The Gini Coefficient and Negative Income: A Comment. *Oxford Econ. Pap.*, September 1985, 37(3), pp. 525–26.

Berry, Albert. On Trends in the Gap between Rich and Poor in Less Developed Countries: Why We Know So Little. *Rev. Income Wealth*, December 1985, 31(4), pp. 337–54.   [G: Philippines; Sri Lanka; Colombia]

Bhagwati, Jagdish N. Education, Class Structure and Income Equality. In *Bhagwati, J. N. (II)*, 1985, pp. 170–204. [G: India]

Bourguignon, François and Morrisson, Christian. Une analyse de décomposition de l'inégalite des revenus individuels en France. (A Decomposition Analysis of Income Inequality in France. With English summary.) *Revue Écon.*, July 1985, *36*(4), pp. 741–77. [G: France]

Burkhauser, Richard V.; Butler, J. S. and Wilkinson, James T. Estimating Changes in Well-Being across Life: A Realized vs. Comprehensive Income Approach. In *David, M. and Smeeding, T., eds.*, 1985, pp. 69–87. [G: U.S.]

Cheema, Aftab Ahmad and Malik, Muhammad Hussain. Changes in Consumption Patterns and Employment under Alternative Income Distributions in Pakistan. *Pakistan Devel. Rev.*, Spring 1985, *24*(1), pp. 1–22. [G: Pakistan]

Chen, Chau-Nan; Tsuar, Tien-Wang and Rhai, Tong-Shieng. The Gini Coefficient and Negative Income: Reply. *Oxford Econ. Pap.*, September 1985, *37*(3), pp. 527–28.

Civardi, Marisa Bottiroli. La distribuzione personale dei redditi: analisi delle diseguaglianze entor e tra le regioni. (Personal Income Distribution: An Analysis of Internal and Interregional Inequalities. With English summary.) *Ricerche Econ.*, July-Sept. 1985, *39*(3), pp. 337–56. [G: Italy]

Cowell, Frank A. Multilevel Decomposition of Theil's Index of Inequality [Decomposing Theil's Index of Inequality into Between and Within Components: A Note]. *Rev. Income Wealth*, June 1985, *31*(2), pp. 201–05. [G: Israel]

Cox, Donald and Raines, Fredric. Interfamily Transfers and Income Redistribution. In *David, M. and Smeeding, T., eds.*, 1985, pp. 393–421. [G: U.S.]

Cvjetičanin, Daniel. Primena kriterijuma namenske raspodele iz dugoročnog programa ekonomske stabilizacije—empirijska analiza. (Empirical Analysis of the Rule for Income Distribution Proposed by the Yugoslav Economic Stabilization Programme. With English summary.) *Econ. Anal. Worker's Manage.*, 1985, *19*(2), pp. 223–35. [G: Yugoslavia]

Daly, Herman E. Marx and Malthus in Northeast Brazil: A Note on the World's Largest Class Difference in Fertility and Its Recent Trends. *Population Stud.*, July 1985, *39*(2), pp. 329–38. [G: Brazil]

Danziger, Sheldon and Smolensky, Eugene. Abrupt Changes in Social Policy: The Redistributive Effects of Reagan's Budget and Tax Cuts. In *Terny, G. and Culyer, A. J., eds.*, 1985, pp. 209–23. [G: U.S.]

Dooley, Martin and Gottschalk, Peter. The Increasing Proportion of Men with Low Earnings in the United States. *Demography*, February 1985, *22*(1), pp. 25–34. [G: U.S.]

Dowling, J. Malcolm, Jr.; Ali, Ifzal and Soo, David. Income Distribution, Poverty and Economic Growth in Developing Asian Countries. *Singapore Econ. Rev.*, April 1985, *30*(1), pp. 1–13. [G: Asia]

Duncan, Greg J. and Hoffman, Saul D. Economic Consequences of Marital Instability. In *David, M. and Smeeding, T., eds.*, 1985, pp. 427–67. [G: U.S.]

Fields, Gary S. Industrialization and Employment in Hong Kong, Singapore, and Taiwan. In *Galenson, W., ed.*, 1985, pp. 333–75. [G: Hong Kong; Singapore; S. Korea; Taiwan]

Flakierski, Henryk. Economic Reform & Income Distribution: A Case Study of Hungary and Poland. *Eastern Europ. Econ.*, Fall-Winter 1985-86, *24*(1–2), pp. iii–194.

Formby, John P. and Smith, W. James. Income Inequality across Nations and over Time: Comment. *Southern Econ. J.*, October 1985, *52*(2), pp. 562–63. [G: LDCs; OECD]

Frosini, Benito V. Comparing Inequality Measures. *Statistica*, July-Sept. 1985, *45*(3), pp. 299–317. [G: Italy]

Gastwirth, Joseph L. Measurement of Economic Distance between Blacks and Whites: Comment. *J. Bus. Econ. Statist.*, October 1985, *3*(4), pp. 405–07.

Gottschalk, Peter and Danziger, Sheldon. A Framework for Evaluating the Effects of Economic Growth and Transfers on Poverty. *Amer. Econ. Rev.*, March 1985, *75*(1), pp. 153–61. [G: U.S.]

Gramlich, Edward M. A Comparison of Measures of Horizontal Inequity: Comment. In *David, M. and Smeeding, T., eds.*, 1985, pp. 264–68. [G: U.S.]

Green, Gordon. Estimating After-Tax Income Using Survey and Administrative Data. *Statist. J.*, March 1985, *3*(1), pp. 85–113. [G: U.S.]

Grubb, David B. Ability and Power over Production in the Distribution of Earnings. *Rev. Econ. Statist.*, May 1985, *67*(2), pp. 188–94. [G: W. Europe; U.S.; Australia]

Grüske, Karl-Dieter. Redistributive Effects of the Integrated Financial and Social Budgets in West Germany. In *Terny, G. and Culyer, A. J., eds.*, 1985, pp. 239–57. [G: W. Germany]

Gupta, Gir S. and Singh, Ram D. Income Inequality across Nations and over Time: Reply. *Southern Econ. J.*, October 1985, *52*(2), pp. 564–65. [G: LDCs; OECD]

Haveman, Robert H. and Wolfe, Barbara L. Income, Inequality, and Uncertainty: Differences between the Disabled and Nondisabled. In *David, M. and Smeeding, T., eds.*, 1985, pp. 293–319. [G: U.S.]

Hurd, Michael D. and Shoven, John B. The Distributional Impact of Social Security. In *Wise, D. A., ed.*, 1985, pp. 193–215. [G: U.S.]

Ikemoto, Yukio. Income Distribution in Malaysia: 1957–80. *Devel. Econ.*, December 1985, *23*(4), pp. 347–67. [G: Malaysia]

Kakwani, Nanak. The Relative Deprivation Curve and Its Applications: Reply. *J. Bus. Econ.*

Statist., April 1985, *3*(2), pp. 171–73.
[G: Australia]

Kapteyn, Arie; van de Geer, Sara and van de Stadt, Huib. The Impact of Changes in Income and Family Composition on Subjective Measures of Well-Being. In *David, M. and Smeeding, T., eds.*, 1985, pp. 35–64.
[G: Netherlands]

Kazi, Shahnaz and Sathar, Zeba A. Differences in Household Characteristics by Income Distribution in Pakistan. *Pakistan Devel. Rev.*, Autumn-Winter 1985, *24*(3/4), pp. 657–67.
[G: Pakistan]

Kemal, A. R. Changes in Poverty and Income Inequality in Pakistan during the 1970s: Comments. *Pakistan Devel. Rev.*, Autumn-Winter 1985, *24*(3/4), pp. 420–22.
[G: Pakistan]

Keuning, Steven J. Segmented Development and the Way Profits Go: The Case of Indonesia. *Rev. Income Wealth*, December 1985, *31*(4), pp. 375–95.
[G: Indonesia]

Kovačič, Zlatko. Inflacija i lični dohoci—analiza uzročnosti. (Inflation and Personal Incomes—Causality Analysis. With English summary.) *Econ. Anal. Worker's Manage.*, 1985, *19*(2), pp. 161–79.
[G: Yugoslavia]

Krongkaew, Medhi. Agricultural Development, Rural Poverty, and Income Distribution in Thailand. *Devel. Econ.*, December 1985, *23*(4), pp. 325–46.
[G: Thailand]

Krotki, Karol J. Differences in Household Characteristics by Income Distribution in Pakistan: Comments. *Pakistan Devel. Rev.*, Autumn-Winter 1985, *24*(3/4), pp. 668–69.
[G: Pakistan]

de Kruijk, Hans and van Leeuwen, Myrna. Changes in Poverty and Income Inequality in Pakistan during the 1970s. *Pakistan Devel. Rev.*, Autumn-Winter 1985, *24*(3/4), pp. 407–19.
[G: Pakistan]

Lerman, Robert I. and Yitzhaki, Shlomo. Income Inequality Effects by Income Source: A New Approach and Applications to the United States. *Rev. Econ. Statist.*, February 1985, *67*(1), pp. 151–56.
[G: U.S.]

Levy, Frank. Happiness, Affluence, and Altruism in the Postwar Period. In *David, M. and Smeeding, T., eds.*, 1985, pp. 7–29.
[G: U.S.]

Lillard, Lee A. Estimating Changes in Well-Being across Life: A Realized vs. Comprehensive Income Approach: Comment. In *David, M. and Smeeding, T., eds.*, 1985, pp. 88–90.
[G: U.S.]

Lin, Tzong-Biau. Growth, Equity, and Income Distribution Policies in Hong Kong. *Devel. Econ.*, December 1985, *23*(4), pp. 391–413.
[G: Hong Kong]

Lorence, Jon. Establishment Size and Metropolitan Earnings Inequality: An Examination of Lydall's Managerial Hierarchy Hypothesis. *Soc. Sci. Quart.*, December 1985, *66*(4), pp. 886–902.
[G: U.S.]

Lundborg, Per. The Distribution of Income in Brazil and Its Dependence on International and Domestic Agricultural Policies. In *Lun-*

dahl, M., ed., 1985, pp. 131–51. [G: Brazil]

Mann, Arthur J. Economic Development, Income Distribution, and Real Income Levels: Puerto Rico, 1953–1977. *Econ. Develop. Cult. Change*, April 1985, *33*(3), pp. 485–502.
[G: Puerto Rico]

McGreevey, William Paul. The Impact of Social Security on Income Distribution: Comment. In *Mesa-Lago, C., ed.*, 1985, pp. 209–15.
[G: Brazil]

Menchik, Paul L. Interfamily Transfers and Income Redistribution: Comment. In *David, M. and Smeeding, T., eds.*, 1985, pp. 421–25.
[G: U.S.]

Mizoguchi, Toshiyuki. Economic Development Policy and Income Distribution: The Experience in East and Southeast Asia. *Devel. Econ.*, December 1985, *23*(4), pp. 307–24. [G: Asia]

Murphy, D. C. Calculation of Gini and Theil Inequality Coefficients for Irish Household Incomes in 1973 and 1980. *Econ. Soc. Rev.*, April 1985, *16*(3), pp. 225–49. [G: Ireland]

Musgrove, Philip. The Impact of Social Security on Income Distribution. In *Mesa-Lago, C., ed.*, 1985, pp. 185–208. [G: Latin America]

O'Higgins, Michael. Welfare, Redistribution, and Inequality—Disillusion, Illusion, and Reality. In *Bean, P.; Ferris, J. and Whynes, D., eds.*, 1985, pp. 162–79. [G: U.K.]

Paul, Satya. On the Measurement of Inequality: A Note. *Indian Econ. J.*, Apr.-June 1985, *32*(4), pp. 58–61.

Persky, Joseph J. and Tam, Mo-Yin S. The Optimal Convergence of Regional Incomes. *J. Reg. Sci.*, August 1985, *25*(3), pp. 337–51.

Plotnick, Robert D. A Comparison of Measures of Horizontal Inequity. In *David, M. and Smeeding, T., eds.*, 1985, pp. 239–63.
[G: U.S.]

Plotnick, Robert D. and Winters, Richard F. A Politico-economic Theory of Income Redistribution. *Amer. Polit. Sci. Rev.*, June 1985, *79*(2), pp. 458–73. [G: U.S.]

Pomanskii, A. B. An Analysis of the Incentive Model and the Log-Normal Distribution of Income. *Matekon*, Winter 1985-86, *22*(2), pp. 86–104.

Porter, Philip K. and Slottje, Daniel J. A Comprehensive Analysis of Inequality in the Size Distribution of Income for the United States, 1952–1981. *Southern Econ. J.*, October 1985, *52*(2), pp. 412–21. [G: U.S.]

Przeworski, Adam and Wallerstein, Michael. Comment on Katz, Mahler, & Franz [The Impact of Taxes on Growth and Distribution in Developed Capitalist Countries: A Cross-National Study]. *Amer. Polit. Sci. Rev.*, June 1985, *79*(2), pp. 508–10.
[G: Selected OECD]

Quan, Nguyen T. and Koo, Anthony Y. C. Concentration of Land Holdings: An Empirical Exploration of Kuznets' Conjecture. *J. Devel. Econ.*, May–June 1985, *18*(1), pp. 101–17.

Radner, Daniel B. Family Income, Age, and Size of Unit: Selected International Comparisons.

Rev. Income Wealth, June 1985, *31*(2), pp. 103–26. **[G: U.S.; Canada; Norway; Israel]**

Rainwater, Lee. Happiness, Affluence, and Altruism in the Postwar Period: Comment. **In** *David, M. and Smeeding, T., eds.*, 1985, pp. 29–33. **[G: U.S.]**

Ray, Ranjan. Prices, Children and Inequality: Further Evidence for the United Kingdom, 1965–82. *Econ. J.*, December 1985, *95*(380), pp. 1069–77. **[G: U.K.]**

Ring, Raymond J., Jr. Variability of Inflation and Income across Income Classes. *Soc. Sci. Quart.*, March 1985, *66*(1), pp. 203–09. **[G: U.S.]**

Robinson, Ray; O'Sullivan, Tony and Le Grand, Julian. Inequality and Housing. *Urban Stud.*, June 1985, *22*(3), pp. 249–56. **[G: U.K.]**

Sadoulet, Elisabeth. Investment Priorities and Income Distribution: The Case of Brazil in 1970. *J. Policy Modeling*, Fall 1985, *7*(3), pp. 407–39. **[G: Brazil]**

Sawhill, Isabel V. Economic Consequences of Marital Instability: Comment. **In** *David, M. and Smeeding, T., eds.*, 1985, pp. 467–70. **[G: U.S.]**

Schaefer, Donald and Schmitz, Mark D. The Parker–Gallman Sample and Wealth Distributions for the Antebellum South: A Comment [Notes on the Wealth Distribution of Farm Households in the United States, 1860: A New Look at Two Manuscript Census Samples]. *Exploration Econ. Hist.*, April 1985, *22*(2), pp. 220–26. **[G: U.S.]**

Shalit, Haim. Calculating the Gini Index of Inequality for Individual Data. *Oxford Bull. Econ. Statist.*, May 1985, *47*(2), pp. 185–89.

Sigit, Hananto. Income Distribution and Household Characteristics. *Bull. Indonesian Econ. Stud.*, December 1985, *21*(3), pp. 51–68. **[G: Indonesia]**

Sinclair, Peter. The Economic System in the UK: Public Finance. **In** *Morris, D., ed.*, 1985, pp. 272–94. **[G: U.K.]**

Terasaki, Yasuhiro. Income Distribution and Development Policies in the Philippines. *Devel. Econ.*, December 1985, *23*(4), pp. 368–90. **[G: Philippines]**

Tinbergen, Jan. Theories of Income Distribution in Developed Countries. **In** *Feiwel, G. R., ed. (I)*, 1985, pp. 335–65. **[G: U.S.]**

Tinbergen, Jan. Two Approaches to Quantify the Concept of Equitable Income Distribution. **In** *Tinbergen, J.*, 1985, pp. 101–10.

Trescott, Paul B. Incentives versus Equality: What Does China's Recent Experience Show? *World Devel.*, February 1985, *13*(2), pp. 205–17. **[G: China]**

Usher, Dan. Income, Inequality, and Uncertainty: Differences between the Disabled and Nondisabled: Comment. **In** *David, M. and Smeeding, T., eds.*, 1985, pp. 319–21. **[G: U.S.]**

Verbon, Harry A. A. Measuring the Redistributive Impact of Public Pensions. *De Economist*, 1985, *133*(1), pp. 87–98. **[G: Netherlands]**

Vinod, H. D. Measurement of Economic Distance between Blacks and Whites: Reply. *J. Bus. Econ. Statist.*, October 1985, *3*(4), pp. 408–09.

Vinod, H. D. Measurement of Economic Distance between Blacks and Whites. *J. Bus. Econ. Statist.*, January 1985, *3*(1), pp. 78–88.

Watts, Harold W. The Impact of Changes in Income and Family Composition on Subjective Measures of Well-Being: Comment. **In** *David, M. and Smeeding, T., eds.*, 1985, pp. 64–67. **[G: Netherlands]**

Yang, Donghyu. The Parker–Gallman Sample and Wealth Distributions for the Antebellum South: A Reply [Notes on the Wealth Distribution of Farm Households in the United States, 1860: A New Look at Two Manuscript Census Samples]. *Exploration Econ. Hist.*, April 1985, *22*(2), pp. 227–32. **[G: U.S.]**

Yoneda, Kimimaru. A Note on Income Distribution in Indonesia. *Devel. Econ.*, December 1985, *23*(4), pp. 414–22. **[G: Indonesia]**

222 Input–Output

2220 Input–Output

Arrow, Kenneth J. The Combination of Time-Series and Cross-Section Data in Interindustry Flow Analysis. **In** *Arrow, K. J. (II)*, 1985, pp. 174–82.

Ayeni, Bola. Interdependence Relations in Interaction Data: An Analysis of the Structure of the Nigerian Economy. **In** *Hutchinson, B. G.; Nijkamp, P. and Batty, M., eds.*, 1985, pp. 180–98. **[G: Nigeria]**

Barker, Terry S. Endogenising Input–Output Coefficients by Means of Industrial Submodels. **In** *Smyshlyaev, A., ed.*, 1985, pp. 183–92. **[G: U.K.]**

Barnabani, Marco and Grassini, Maurizio. On Modeling Foreign Trade in an Input–Output Model of an Open Economy. **In** *Smyshlyaev, A., ed.*, 1985, pp. 95–104. **[G: OECD]**

Caravani, Paolo and De Luca, Alessandro. Aggregazione settoriale: una applicazione al modello sraffiano di produzione semplice. (Sectoral Aggregation: An Application to the Sraffian Model of Simple Production. With English summary.) *Ricerche Econ.*, July-Sept. 1985, *39*(3), pp. 293–317.

Ciaschini, Maurizio. An Attempt to Evaluate the Impact of Changes in Interindustry Interactions. **In** *Smyshlyaev, A., ed.*, 1985, pp. 249–59. **[G: Italy]**

Cohen, Suleiman I.; Havinga, Ivo C. and Saleem, Mohammad. A Simple Inter-Industry Model of Pakistan, with an Application to Pakistan's Sixth Five-Year Plan. *Pakistan Devel. Rev.*, Autumn-Winter 1985, *24*(3/4), pp. 531–45. **[G: Pakistan]**

Czyzewski, B.; Tomaszewicz, Andrzej and Tomaszewicz, Lucija. Proposals for the Linkage of CMEA-Country Models. **In** *Smyshlyaev, A., ed.*, 1985, pp. 29–42. **[G: CMEA]**

Daniel, S., et al. A Structural Analysis of the Jamaican Economy 1974. *Soc. Econ. Stud.*, September 1985, *34*(3), pp. 1–69. **[G: Jamaica]**

Deardorff, Alan V. and Stern, Robert M. Input–Output Technologies and the Effects of Tariff Reductions. *J. Policy Modeling*, Summer 1985, *7*(2), pp. 253–79. **[G: U.S.; EEC; Japan; Brazil]**

Dietzenbacher, Erik and Steenge, Albert E. Seton's Eigenprices: Comparisons between Post-War Holland and Hungary. In *Smyshlyaev, A., ed.*, 1985, pp. 237–48. **[G: Hungary; Netherlands]**

Duchin, F. and Szyld, Daniel B. A Dynamic Input–Output Model with Assured Positive Output. *Metroecon.*, October 1985, 37(3), pp. 269–82. **[G: U.S.]**

Dupont, Pierre. Substitutions énergie-travail dans le modèle de prix de Statistique Canada. (Energy-Labour Substitutions in the Price Model of Statistic Canada [Using Exogenous Elasticities to Induce Factor Substitution Input–Output Price Models]. With English summary.) *L'Actual. Econ.*, March 1985, *61*(1), pp. 112–26. **[G: Canada]**

Feldman, Stanley J. and Palmer, Karen. Structural Change in the United States: Changing Input–Output Coefficients. *Bus. Econ.*, January 1985, *20*(1), pp. 38–54. **[G: U.S.]**

Forssell, Osmo. Changes in the Structure of the Finnish Economy, 1970–1980. In *Smyshlyaev, A., ed.*, 1985, pp. 61–71. **[G: Finland]**

Førsund, Finn R. Input–Output Models, National Economic Models, and the Environment. In *Kneese, A. V. and Sweeney, J. L., eds. Vol. 1*, 1985, pp. 325–41. **[G: Norway]**

Freeman, Daniel; Alperovich, Gershon and Weksler, Itzhak. Inter-regional Input–Output Model—The Israeli Case. *Appl. Econ.*, June 1985, *17*(3), pp. 381–93. **[G: Israel]**

Fujimoto, Takao; Herrero, Carmen and Villar, Antonio. A Sensitivity Analysis in a Nonlinear Leontief Model. *Z. Nationalökon.*, 1985, *45*(1), pp. 67–71.

Gardini, Attilio. Structural Form, Interdependence and Statistical Estimation in the Input–Output Model. *Ricerche Econ.*, Jan.-Mar. 1985, *39*(1), pp. 29–39.

Garhart, Robert, Jr. The Role of Error Structure in Simulations on Regional Input–Output Analysis. *J. Reg. Sci.*, August 1985, *25*(3), pp. 353–66.

Ghosh, Atish R. A Characterization of the 'Heuristic Solution' of the Optimal Ordering Problem of an Input–Output Matrix as a Nash Point with Some Further Observations on the Ordering Problem as a Game. *Econ. Planning*, 1985, *19*(2), pp. 118–25.

Ghosh, Atish R. The Equivalence of the Optimal Ordering with the Maximum Row–Column Correlation Coefficient in an Input–Output Table. *Econ. Planning*, 1985, *19*(1), pp. 19–23.

Grassini, Laura. On the Endogenous Determination of Import Coefficients in an Input–Output Model: Theoretical and Practical Problems. In *Smyshlyaev, A., ed.*, 1985, pp. 163–72. **[G: Italy]**

Grassini, Maurizio and Richter, Josef. Austrian-Italian Interdependence: Some Linking Experiments. In *Smyshlyaev, A., ed.*, 1985, pp. 19–28. **[G: Austria; Italy]**

Guccioni, Antonio. Aggregation and Disaggregation of Input–Output Models: Some Final Remarks. *Ricerche Econ.*, Apr.-June 1985, *39*(2), pp. 261–64.

Habib, Ahsanul; Stahl, Charles and Alauddin, Mohammad. Inter-industry Analysis of Employment Linkages in Bangladesh. *Econ. Planning*, 1985, *19*(1), pp. 24–38. **[G: Bangladesh]**

Henry, Mark S. and Schluter, Gerald. Measuring Backward and Forward Linkages in the U.S. Food and Fiber System. *Agr. Econ. Res.*, Fall 1985, *37*(4), pp. 33–39. **[G: U.S.]**

Holub, Hans-Werner and Schnabl, H. Qualitative Input–Output Analysis and Structural Information. *Econ. Modelling*, January 1985, *2*(1), pp. 67–73.

Holub, Hans-Werner; Schnabl, H. and Tappeiner, G. Qualitative Input–Output Analysis with Variable Filter. *Z. ges. Staatswiss. (JITE)*, June 1985, *141*(2), pp. 282–300.

Jakobsen, Arvid Stentoft. Changes in Factor Input Coefficients and the Leontief Paradox. In *Smyshlyaev, A., ed.*, 1985, pp. 105–17. **[G: Denmark]**

Johansen, Leif. Richard Stone's Contributions to Economics. *Scand. J. Econ.*, 1985, *87*(1), pp. 4–32.

Kubo, Yuji. A Cross-country Comparison of Interindustry Linkages and the Role of Imported Intermediate Inputs. *World Devel.*, December 1985, *13*(12), pp. 1287–98. **[G: Selected Countries]**

Kuehn, John A.; Procter, Michael H. and Braschler, Curtis H. Comparisons of Multipliers from Input–Output and Economic Base Models. *Land Econ.*, May 1985, *61*(2), pp. 129–35. **[G: U.S.]**

Lager, Christian and Schöpp, Wolfgang. Estimation of Input–Output Coefficients Using Neoclassical Production Theory. In *Smyshlyaev, A., ed.*, 1985, pp. 151–61. **[G: Canada]**

Lahiri, Sajal. Nonlinear Generalizations of the Hawkins–Simon Conditions: Some Comparisons. *Math. Soc. Sci.*, June 1985, *9*(3), pp. 293–97.

Leontief, Wassily. An Alternative to Aggregation in Input–Output Analysis and National Accounts. In *Leontief, W.*, 1985, pp. 283–97. **[G: U.S.]**

Leontief, Wassily. Environmental Repercussions and the Economic Structure: An Input–Output Approach. In *Leontief, W.*, 1985, pp. 326–46. **[G: U.S.]**

Leontief, Wassily. Structure of the World Economy: Outline of a Simple Input–Output Formulation. In *Leontief, W.*, 1985, pp. 381–97. **[G: Global]**

Leontief, Wassily. The Dynamic Inverse. In *Leontief, W.*, 1985, pp. 298–325. **[G: U.S.]**

Leontief, Wassily. Why Economics Needs Input–Output Analysis. *Challenge*, March/April 1985, *28*(1), pp. 27–35.

Levy, Santiago. A Mark-Up Pricing Model for Price Simulations. *J. Devel. Econ.*, December 1985, *19*(3), pp. 299–320. [G: Mexico]

Matlin, I. S.; Akhundova, T. A. and Kurkina, O. M. A Study of the Relationship between Balance in the Goods Market, Capital-Intensity, and Labor Productivity Based on a Dynamic Input–Output Model. *Matekon*, Spring 1985, *21*(3), pp. 63–80. [G: U.S.S.R.]

Milana, C. Direct and Indirect Requirements for Gross Output in Input–Output Analysis. *Metroecon.*, October 1985, *37*(3), pp. 283–92. [G: Italy]

Montuschi, Luisa. Los Sectores Claves para el Trabajo Asalariado en la Economía Argentina 1963–1970. (The Key Sectors for the Labor Force in the Argentine Economy. With English summary.) *Económica (La Plata)*, Jan.-Apr. 1985, *31*(1), pp. 81–98. [G: Argentina]

Nishimiya, Ryoichi. Input–Output Techniques in the Japanese Econometric Model. In *Smyshlyaev, A., ed.*, 1985, pp. 173–81. [G: Japan]

Olsen, J. Asger. Adaptation of Detailed Input–Output Information: Restructuring and Aggregation. *Rev. Income Wealth*, December 1985, *31*(4), pp. 397–411. [G: Denmark]

Pieplow, Rolf. Some Experience in the Planning of Input Coefficients. In *Smyshlyaev, A., ed.*, 1985, pp. 118–27. [G: E. Germany]

Pigozzi, Bruce Wm. and Hinojosa, Rene C. Regional Input–Output Inverse Coefficients Adjusted from National Tables. *Growth Change*, January 1985, *16*(1), pp. 8–12. [G: U.S.]

Porter, Dwight A. The Inforum-IIASA Family of Input–Output Models: A Brief Historical Review, Progress in 1984, and Future Prospects for Growth. In *Smyshlyaev, A., ed.*, 1985, pp. 43–50.

Primero, Elidoro P. Effects of Changing Industrial Structures and Changing Levels and Composition of the Final Demand Bill on the Input Factor Requirements of the Economy: An Application of Input–Output Analysis. *Philippine Econ. J.*, 1985, *24*(2–3), pp. 200–221. [G: Philippines]

Raffaelli, Cristina. On Modeling Structural Changes in Sectoral Wage Distribution in a Modern Input–Output Model. In *Smyshlyaev, A., ed.*, 1985, pp. 79–94. [G: Italy]

Rasul, Ghulam. A Simpe Inter-Industry Model of Pakistan, with an Application to Pakistan's Sixth Five-Year Plan: Comments. *Pakistan Devel. Rev.*, Autumn-Winter 1985, *24*(3/4), pp. 546–50. [G: Pakistan]

Rasul, Ghulam. Analysis of Inter-Industry Relations in Pakistan for 1975–76: Comments. *Pakistan Devel. Rev.*, Autumn-Winter 1985, *24*(3/4), pp. 528–30. [G: Pakistan]

Rettig, Rudi. Changes in Input Coefficients in the German Economy. In *Smyshlyaev, A., ed.*, 1985, pp. 141–50. [G: W. Germany]

Richardson, Harry W. Input–Output and Economic Base Multipliers: Looking Backward and Forward. *J. Reg. Sci.*, November 1985, *25*(4), pp. 607–61.

Schintke, Joachim and Stäglin, Reiner. Stability

of Import Input Coefficients. In *Smyshlyaev, A., ed.*, 1985, pp. 129–39. [G: W. Germany]

Silverstein, Gerald. New Structures and Equipment by Using Industries, 1977. *Surv. Curr. Bus.*, November 1985, *65*(11), pp. 26–35. [G: U.S.]

Stahmer, Carsten. Transformation Matrices in Input–Output Compilation. In *Smyshlyaev, A., ed.*, 1985, pp. 225–36. [G: W. Germany]

Syed, Aftab Ali. Analysis of Inter-Industry Relations in Pakistan for 1975–76. *Pakistan Devel. Rev.*, Autumn-Winter 1985, *24*(3/4), pp. 513–27. [G: Pakistan]

Szyld, Daniel B. Conditions for the Existence of a Balanced Growth Solution for the Leontief Dynamic Input–Output Model. *Econometrica*, November 1985, *53*(6), pp. 1411–19.

Tahon, Hilda and Vanwynsberghe, Dirk. Structural Change in the Belgian Economy. In *Smyshlyaev, A., ed.*, 1985, pp. 193–96. [G: Belgium]

Tronzano, Marco. Intersectoral Inflation Propagation and Macroeconomic Hypotheses: Recent Contributions and Further Outlook. *Rivista Polit. Econ.*, Suppl. Dec. 1985, *76*, pp. 175–217.

Villar, Antonio and Herrero, Carmen. Un modelo *input–output* no lineal. (With English summary.) *Revista Española Econ.*, 1985, *2*(2), pp. 333–45.

Wohltmann, Hans-Werner. Zur Steuerbarkeit volkswirtschaftlicher Input–Output-Modelle. (Controllability of Economic Input–Output Models. With English summary.) *Jahr. Nationalökon. Statist.*, November 1985, *200*(6), pp. 602–21.

Wolff, Edward N. Industrial Composition, Interindustry Effects, and the U.S. Productivity Slowdown. *Rev. Econ. Statist.*, May 1985, *67*(2), pp. 268–77. [G: U.S.]

Yuskavage, Robert E. Employment and Employee Compensation in the 1977 Input–Output Accounts. *Surv. Curr. Bus.*, November 1985, *65*(11), pp. 11–25. [G: U.S.]

Zeineldin, Aly. The Egyptian Economy in 1999: An Input–Output Study. *Indian Econ. J.*, Oct.-Nov. 1985, *33*(2), pp. 34–44. [G: Egypt]

223 Financial Accounts

2230 Financial Accounts; Financial Statistics; Empirical Analyses of Capital Adequacy

Ahmed, Masood. An Analysis of Flow-of-Funds Accounts for Pakistan Economy 1980–81. *Pakistan Econ. Soc. Rev.*, Summer 1985, *23*(1), pp. 56–63. [G: Pakistan]

Backus, David; Blanco, Herminio and Levine, David K. The Financial Sector in the Planning of Economic Development. In *Gutowski, A.; Arnaudo, A. A. and Scharrer, H.-E., eds.*, 1985, pp. 42–58.

Balassa, Bela. French Economic Policies under the Socialist Government: Year III. In *Balassa, B.*, 1985, pp. 384–99. [G: France]

Bhagwati, Jagdish N. Savings and the Foreign

Trade Regime. In *Bhagwati, J. N. (I)*, 1985, pp. 277–84. [G: India]

Bhagwati, Jagdish N. Substitution between Foreign Capital and Domestic Saving. In *Bhagwati, J. N. (I)*, 1985, pp. 269–76.

Boquist, John A. and Long, Michael S. Capital Equilibrium for the Energy Industry, 1977-2000. *Econ. Notes*, 1985, (1), pp. 104–47. [G: U.S.]

Bosworth, Derek and Westaway, A. J. The Theory and Measurement of Capital Utilisation and Its Role in Modelling Investment. In *Weiserbs, D., ed.*, 1985, pp. 291–317. [G: U.K.]

Cable, John R. The Bank–Industry Relationship in West Germany: Performance and Policy Aspects. In *Schwalbach, J., ed.*, 1985, pp. 17–40. [G: W. Germany]

Canavese, Alfredo J. and Montuschi, Luisa. Inflation and the Financing of Alternative Development Strategies. In *Gutowski, A.; Arnaudo, A. A. and Scharrer, H.-E., eds.*, 1985, pp. 115–36. [G: Argentina]

Ciccolo, John H., Jr. and Baum, Christopher F. Changes in the Balance Sheet of the U.S. Manufacturing Sector, 1926–1977. In *Friedman, B. M., ed.*, 1985, pp. 81–109. [G: U.S.]

Cohen, Jacob and Husted, Steven. An Integrated Accounting Matrix for Canada and the United States. *Amer. Econ. Rev.*, May 1985, 75(2), pp. 211–16. [G: Canada; U.S.]

Cook, Timothy Q. and Rowe, Timothy D. Are NOWs Being Used as Savings Accounts? *Fed. Res. Bank Richmond Econ. Rev.*, May/June 1985, 71(3), pp. 3–13. [G: U.S.]

Dow, Sheila C. Microfoundations: A Diversity of Treatments. *Eastern Econ. J.*, Oct.-Dec. 1985, 11(4), pp. 342–60.

Ferrari, Camillo. Il risparmio per l'oggi e per il domani: problemi di formazione, di remunerazione, di investimento. (Saving for Today and for Tomorrow: The Formation, Remuneration and Investment of Savings. With English summary.) *Bancaria*, January 1985, 41(1), pp. 32–44. [G: Italy]

Hendriks, Marc. Flow of Funds: Consistency and Completeness. *Bus. Econ.*, October 1985, 20(4), pp. 35–37. [G: U.S.]

Leontief, Wassily. The Rates of Long-run Economic Growth and Capital Transfer from Developed to Underdeveloped Areas. In *Leontief, W.*, 1985, pp. 200–215. [G: LDCs; MDCs]

Lintner, John. Secular Patterns in the Financing of Corporations: Comment. In *Friedman, B. M., ed.*, 1985, pp. 75–80. [G: U.S.]

Mayer, Colin and Meadowcroft, Shirley A. Equity Rates of Return in the UK—Evidence from Panel Data. In *Weiserbs, D., ed.*, 1985, pp. 351–86. [G: U.K.]

Modigliani, Franco. Changes in the Balance Sheet, 1926–1977: Comment. In *Friedman, B. M., ed.*, 1985, pp. 109–15. [G: U.S.]

Naughton, Barry. False Starts and Second Wind: Financial Reforms in China's Industrial System. In *Perry, E. J. and Wong, C., eds.*, 1985, pp. 223–52. [G: China]

Nepal Rastra Bank. The Role of Central Banks in Development Finance. In *Bandyopadhyay, R. and Khankhoje, D. P., eds.*, 1985, pp. 185–201. [G: Nepal]

Newlyn, W. T. The Role of the Public Sector in the Mobilisation and Allocation of Financial Resources. In *Gutowski, A.; Arnaudo, A. A. and Scharrer, H.-E., eds.*, 1985, pp. 98–114. [G: Selected LDCs]

Noguchi, Yukio. Tax Structure and Saving–Investment Balance. *Hitotsubashi J. Econ.*, June 1985, 26(1), pp. 45–58. [G: U.S.; Japan]

Plihon, D. and Zagamé, Paul. L'investissement et l'épargne. Tendances et perspectives à moyen terme. (With English summary.) *Revue Écon. Polit.*, Sept.-Oct. 1985, 95(5), pp. 596–610. [G: France]

Stewart, Douglas B. and Venieris, Yiannis P. Sociopolitical Instability and the Behavior of Savings in Less-Developed Countries. *Rev. Econ. Statist.*, November 1985, 67(4), pp. 557–63. [G: LDCs]

Taggart, Robert A., Jr. Secular Patterns in the Financing of U.S. Corporations. In *Friedman, B. M., ed.*, 1985, pp. 13–75. [G: U.S.]

Takigawa, Yoshio. Money Finance, Bond Finance and "Yw cho (Postal Savings) Finance." *Kobe Univ. Econ.*, 1985, (31), pp. 53–68. [G: Japan]

Triffin, Robert. The International Accounts of the United States and Their Impact upon the Rest of the World. *Banca Naz. Lavoro Quart. Rev.*, March 1985, (152), pp. 15–30. [G: U.S.; EEC]

Ulph, A. Equity Rates of Return in the U.K.; Evidence from Panel Data: Comment. In *Weiserbs, D., ed.*, 1985, pp. 387–89. [G: U.K.]

Vitin, A. Capital Investment Effectiveness in Planning. *Prob. Econ.*, October 1985, 28(6), pp. 23–39. [G: U.S.S.R.]

Zhuravlev, S. N. A Model for Forecasting Prices and Financial Proportions. *Matekon*, Summer 1985, 21(4), pp. 23–43.

224 National Wealth and Balance Sheets

2240 National Wealth and Balance Sheets

Aaron, Henry J. The Distributional Impact of Social Security: Comment. In *Wise, D. A., ed.*, 1985, pp. 215–21. [G: U.S.]

Adams, John W. and Kaskoff, Alice Bee. Wealth and Migration in Massachusetts and Maine: 1771–1798. *J. Econ. Hist.*, June 1985, 45(2), pp. 363–68. [G: U.S.]

Apps, Patricia. The Relative Deprivation Curve and Its Applications: Comment. *J. Bus. Econ. Statist.*, April 1985, 3(2), pp. 169–71. [G: Australia]

Berry, Albert. On Trends in the Gap between Rich and Poor in Less Developed Countries: Why We Know So Little. *Rev. Income Wealth*, December 1985, 31(4), pp. 337–54. [G: Philippines; Sri Lanka; Colombia]

Bourque, Philip J. The Infrastructure Gap. *Growth Change*, January 1985, 16(1), pp. 17–23. [G: U.S.]

Burbridge, John B. and Robb, A. Leslie. Evidence on Wealth-Age Profiles in Canadian Cross-Section Data. *Can. J. Econ.*, November 1985, *18*(4), pp. 854–75. [G: Canada]

Canterbery, E. Ray and Nosari, E. Joe. The Forbes Four Hundred: The Determinants of Super-wealth. *Southern Econ. J.*, April 1985, *51*(4), pp. 1173–83. [G: U.S.]

Cartwright, William S. and Friedland, Robert T. The President's Commission on Pension Policy Household Survey 1979: Net Wealth Distributions by Type and Age for the United States. *Rev. Income Wealth*, September 1985, *31*(3), pp. 285–308. [G: U.S.]

Cox, Donald and Raines, Fredric. Interfamily Transfers and Income Redistribution. In *David, M. and Smeeding, T., eds.*, 1985, pp. 393–421. [G: U.S.]

Danziger, Sheldon. Inflation Vulnerability, Income, and Wealth of the Elderly, 1969–1979: Comment. In *David, M. and Smeeding, T., eds.*, 1985, pp. 172–77. [G: U.S.]

David, Martin and Menchik, Paul L. The Effect of Social Security on Lifetime Wealth Accumulation and Bequests. *Economica*, November 1985, *52*(208), pp. 421–34. [G: U.S.]

Dixon, Robert. Indices of the Average Age of Structures and Equipment in Australia 1955/56—1982/83. *Econ. Rec.*, June 1985, *61*(173), pp. 564–66. [G: Australia]

Dixon, Robert. Movements in the Average Age of the Capital Stock. *Oxford Econ. Pap.*, March 1985, *37*(1), pp. 93–99. [G: U.K.]

Farley, Pamela J. and Wilensky, Gail R. Household Wealth and Health Insurance as Protection against Medical Risks. In *David, M. and Smeeding, T., eds.*, 1985, pp. 323–54. [G: U.S.]

Field, Alexander James. On the Unimportance of Machinery. *Exploration Econ. Hist.*, October 1985, *22*(4), pp. 378–401. [G: U.S.; U.K.]

Friedman, Benjamin M. Corporate Capital Structures in the United States: An Introduction and Overview. In *Friedman, B. M., ed.*, 1985, pp. 1–11. [G: U.S.]

George, Donald A. R. Collective Capital Formation: Implications of the Scandinavian Debate. *Econ. Anal. Worker's Manage.*, 1985, *19*(3), pp. 281–93. [G: OECD]

Gorman, John A., et al. Fixed Private Capital in the United States (Revised Estimates, 1925–81) (Estimates by Industry, 1947–81). *Surv. Curr. Bus.*, July 1985, *65*(7), pp. 36–59. [G: U.S.]

Gramlich, Edward M. A Comparison of Measures of Horizontal Inequity: Comment. In *David, M. and Smeeding, T., eds.*, 1985, pp. 264–68. [G: U.S.]

Groenewegen, Peter D. Options for the Taxation of Wealth. *Australian Tax Forum*, Spring 1985, *2*(3), pp. 305–26. [G: Australia]

Harrison, Alan. The Distribution of Personal Wealth in Britain. In *Atkinson, G. B. J., ed.*, 1985, pp. 123–31. [G: U.K.]

Hendershott, Patric H. and Peek, Joe. Real Household Capital Gains and Wealth Accumulation. In *Hendershott, P. H., ed.*, 1985, pp. 41–61. [G: U.S.]

Hurd, Michael D. and Shoven, John B. Inflation Vulnerability, Income, and Wealth of the Elderly, 1969–1979. In *David, M. and Smeeding, T., eds.*, 1985, pp. 125–72. [G: U.S.]

Hurd, Michael D. and Shoven, John B. The Distributional Impact of Social Security. In *Wise, D. A., ed.*, 1985, pp. 193–215. [G: U.S.]

Jenkins, Stephen P. The Implications of 'Stochastic' Demographic Assumptions for Models of the Distribution of Inherited Wealth. *Bull. Econ. Res.*, September 1985, *37*(3), pp. 231–44.

Jianakoplos, Nancy Ammon. Inflation and the Accumulation of Wealth by Older Households, 1966–1976. In *Hendershott, P. H., ed.*, 1985, pp. 151–80. [G: U.S.]

Kakwani, Nanak. The Relative Deprivation Curve and Its Applications: Reply. *J. Bus. Econ. Statist.*, April 1985, *3*(2), pp. 171–73. [G: Australia]

Kane, Edward J. Microeconomic Evidence on the Composition of Household Savings in Recent Years. In *Hendershott, P. H., ed.*, 1985, pp. 101–49. [G: U.S.]

Kregel, J. A. Budget Deficits, Stabilisation Policy and Liquidity Preference: Keynes's Post-War Policy Proposals. In *Vicarelli, F., ed.*, 1985, pp. 28–50. [G: OECD]

Kushlin, V. I. The Development of the Production Apparatus and Investment Processes. *Prob. Econ.*, November 1985, *28*(7), pp. 33–47. [G: U.S.S.R.]

Lennings, Manfred. Structural Problems of German Industry in International Comparison. In *Engels, W. and Pohl, H., eds.*, 1985, pp. 1–12. [G: Selected Countries]

Lock, J. D. Measuring the Value of the Capital Stock by Direct Observation. *Rev. Income Wealth*, June 1985, *31*(2), pp. 127–38. [G: Netherlands]

Lopes, Antonio. Scelte di portafoglio delle famiglie, finanziamento del tesoro ed aspettative inflazionistiche in Italia (1979–1983). (With English summary.) *Stud. Econ.*, 1985, *40*(25), pp. 29–70. [G: Italy]

Lützel, Heinrich. Inflation Accounting for the Federal Republic of Germany—Results Using Different Deflator Price Indices. *Rev. Income Wealth*, September 1985, *31*(3), pp. 207–21. [G: W. Germany]

Menchik, Paul L. Interfamily Transfers and Income Redistribution: Comment. In *David, M. and Smeeding, T., eds.*, 1985, pp. 421–25. [G: U.S.]

Merrifield, David E. Imputed Rental Prices and Capital Stock Estimates for Equipment and Structures in the U.S. Lumber and Plywood Industries. *Appl. Econ.*, April 1985, *17*(2), pp. 243–56. [G: U.S.]

Newhouse, Joseph P. Household Wealth and Health Insurance as Protection against Medical Risks: Comment. In *David, M. and Smeeding, T., eds.*, 1985, pp. 354–58. [G: U.S.]

Plotnick, Robert D. A Comparison of Measures of Horizontal Inequity. In *David, M. and Smeeding, T., eds.*, 1985, pp. 239–63.
[G: U.S.]

Quinn, Joseph F. Retirement Income Rights as a Component of Wealth in the United States. *Rev. Income Wealth*, September 1985, *31*(3), pp. 223–36.
[G: U.S.]

Rothenberg, Winifred B. The Emergence of a Capital Market in Rural Massachusetts, 1730–1838. *J. Econ. Hist.*, December 1985, *45*(4), pp. 781–808.
[G: U.S.]

Smith, James D. Wealth, Realized Income, and the Measure of Well-Being: Comment. In *David, M. and Smeeding, T., eds.*, 1985, pp. 117–24.
[G: U.S.]

Soltow, Lee. The Swedish Census of Wealth at the Beginning of the 19th Century. *Scand. Econ. Hist. Rev.*, 1985, *33*(1), pp. 1–24.
[G: Sweden]

Steuerle, C. Eugene. Wealth, Realized Income, and the Measure of Well-Being. In *David, M. and Smeeding, T., eds.*, 1985, pp. 91–117.
[G: U.S.]

Turdeanu, Lucian and Marcu, Nicolae. Romania's Wealth Estimations before the Second World War. *Rev. Income Wealth*, March 1985, *31*(1), pp. 97–100.
[G: Romania]

225 Social Indicators: Data and Analysis

2250 Social Indicators: Data and Analysis

Burkett, John P. Systemic Influences on the Physical Quality of Life: A Bayesian Analysis of Cross-sectional Data. *J. Compar. Econ.*, June 1985, *9*(2), pp. 145–63.

Clark, Terry Nichols. Fiscal Strain: How Different Are Snow Belt and Sun Belt Cities? In *Peterson, P. E., ed.*, 1985, pp. 253–80.
[G: U.S.]

Gershuny, J. I. and Miles, I. D. Towards a New Social Economics. In *Roberts, B.; Finnegan, R. and Gallie, D., eds.*, 1985, pp. 24–47.
[G: U.K.]

Jacob, Herbert. Policy Responses to Crime. In *Peterson, P. E., ed.*, 1985, pp. 225–52.
[G: U.S.]

Larson, David. A Test of the Stability of the Relationship between the Physical Quality of Life Index and Gross National Product per Capita. *Indian Econ. J.*, Apr.-June 1985, *32*(4), pp. 1–7.

Nissan, Edward and Caveny, Regina. Quality of Life Indicators for Selected South American Nations. *Atlantic Econ. J.*, September 1985, *13*(3), pp. 93.
[G: Latin America]

Ram, Rati. The Role of Real Income Level and Income Distribution in Fulfillment of Basic Needs. *World Devel.*, May 1985, *13*(5), pp. 589–94.
[G: LDCs]

Sørensen, Rune J. Economic Relations between City and Suburban Governments. In *Lane, J.-E., ed.*, 1985, pp. 83–99.
[G: Sweden]

Van Moeseke, Paul. Socio-economic Interface and Social Income. *Math. Soc. Sci.*, June 1985, *9*(3), pp. 263–73.

Wilson, William Julius. The Urban Underclass in Advanced Industrial Society. In *Peterson, P. E., ed.*, 1985, pp. 129–60.
[G: U.S.]

226 Productivity and Growth: Theory and Data

2260 Productivity and Growth: Theory and Data

Adamowicz, Wiktor L. and Manning, Travis W. The Measurement of Growth Rates from Time Series. *Can. J. Agr. Econ.*, July 1985, *33*(2), pp. 231–42.
[G: Canada]

Adams, Roy J. Industrial Relations and the Economic Crisis: Canada Moves Toward Europe. In *Juris, H.; Thompson, M. and Daniels, W., eds.*, 1985, pp. 115–49.
[G: OECD]

Aganbegian A. Important Positive Changes in the Country's Economic Life. *Prob. Econ.*, April 1985, *27*(12), pp. 3–16.
[G: U.S.S.R.]

Allen, Steven G. Why Construction Industry Productivity Is Declining. *Rev. Econ. Statist.*, November 1985, *67*(4), pp. 661–69.
[G: U.S.]

Allsopp, C. J. The Economic System in the UK: Economic Growth. In *Morris, D., ed.*, 1985, pp. 627–67.
[G: U.K.]

Amirkhalkhali, S.; Rao, U. L. G. and Amirkhalkhali, S. An Empirical Study of Selection and Estimation of Statistical Growth Models. *Empirical Econ.*, 1985, *10*(3), pp. 201–08.
[G: OECD]

Armstrong, Warwick. The Social Origins of Industrial Growth: Canada, Argentina and Australia, 1870–1930. In *Platt, D. C. M. and di Tella, G., eds.*, 1985, pp. 76–94.
[G: Argentina; Australia; Canada]

Arrow, Kenneth J. Knowledge, Productivity, and Practice. In *Arrow, K. J. (I)*, 1985, pp. 191–99.

Arrow, Kenneth J. Some Tests of the International Comparisons of Factor Efficiency with the CES Production Function: Reply. In *Arrow, K. J. (I)*, 1985, pp. 236–40.
[G: Selected Countries]

Arrow, Kenneth J. The Economic Implications of Learning by Doing. In *Arrow, K. J. (I)*, 1985, pp. 157–80.

Arrow, Kenneth J., et al. Capital–Labor Substitution and Economic Efficiency. In *Arrow, K. J. (I)*, 1985, pp. 50–103.
[G: Selected Countries]

Baily, Martin Neil and Chakrabarti, Alok K. Innovation and Productivity in U.S. Industry. *Brookings Pap. Econ. Act.*, 1985, (2), pp. 609–32.
[G: U.S.]

Ball, V. Eldon. Output, Input, and Productivity Measurement in U.S. Agriculture, 1948-79. *Amer. J. Agr. Econ.*, August 1985, *67*(3), pp. 475–86.
[G: U.S.]

Barnett, C. Long-term Industrial Performance in the UK: The Role of Education and Research, 1850–1939. In *Morris, D., ed.*, 1985, pp. 668–89.
[G: OECD]

Baumol, William J. Rebirth of a Fallen Leader:

Italy and the Long Period Data. *Atlantic Econ. J.*, September 1985, *13*(3), pp. 12–26.
[G: Italy]

Baumol, William J.; Blackman, Sue Anne Batey and Wolff, Edward N. Unbalanced Growth Revisited: Asymptotic Stagnancy and New Evidence. *Amer. Econ. Rev.*, September 1985, *75*(4), pp. 806–17. [G: U.S.]

Bergson, Abram. Gorbachev Calls for Intensive Growth. *Challenge*, Nov./Dec. 1985, *28*(5), pp. 11–14. [G: U.S.S.R.]

Bhagwati, Jagdish N. Development Economics: What Have We Learnt? In *Bhagwati, J. N. (II)*, 1985, pp. 13–31.

Block, James E. The Shibboleth of Productivity: The Exhaustion of Industrial-Age Strategies in Post-industrial Society. *Rev. Radical Polit. Econ.*, Spring and Summer 1985, *17*(1/2), pp. 157–85.

Boddy, Raford. A Specious Solution to the "Problem" of Procyclical Productivity. *J. Polit. Econ.*, August 1985, *93*(4), pp. 816–23.
[G: U.S.]

Bowles, Samuel; Gordon, David M. and Weisskopf, Thomas E. In Defense of the "Social Model." *Challenge*, May/June 1985, *28*(2), pp. 57–59. [G: U.S.]

Brada, Josef C. and Hoffman, Dennis L. The Productivity Differential between Soviet and Western Capital and the Benefits of Technology Imports to the Soviet Economy. *Quart. Rev. Econ. Bus.*, Spring 1985, *25*(1), pp. 6–18. [G: U.S.S.R.]

Branson, William H. International Comparison of the Sources of Productivity Slowdown, 1973-1982: Comment. *Europ. Econ. Rev.*, June-July 1985, *28*(1–2), pp. 193–95. [G: OECD]

Bruland, Kristine. Say's Law and the Single-Factor Explanation of British Industrialization: A Comment [The Cause of the Industrial Revolution: A Brief 'Single-Factor' Argument]. *J. Europ. Econ. Hist.*, Spring 1985, *14*(1), pp. 187–91. [G: U.K.]

Brundenius, Claes and Zimbalist, Andrew. Cuban Economic Growth One More Time: A Response to "Imbroglios." [Recent Studies on Cuban Economic Growth: A Review]. *Comparative Econ. Stud.*, Fall 1985, *27*(3), pp. 115–31. [G: Cuba]

Brundenius, Claes and Zimbalist, Andrew. Cuban Growth: A Final Worth [Cuban Economic Growth One More Time: A Response to Imbroglios]. *Comparative Econ. Stud.*, Winter 1985, *27*(4), pp. 83–84. [G: Cuba]

Brundenius, Claes and Zimbalist, Andrew. Recent Studies on Cuban Economic Growth: A Review. *Comparative Econ. Stud.*, Spring 1985, *27*(1), pp. 21–45. [G: Cuba]

Bryant, J. Economics, Equilibrium and Thermodynamics. In *van Gool, W. and Bruggink, J. J. C., eds.*, 1985, pp. 197–221. [G: U.K.; OECD]

Cameron, David R. Public Expenditure and Economic Performance in International Perspective. In *Klein, R. and O'Higgins, M., ed.*, 1985, pp. 8–21. [G: OECD]

Cazes, Bernard. France. In *Hochmuth, M. and Davidson, W., eds.*, 1985, pp. 163–88.
[G: France]

Christainsen, G. B. and Tietenberg, T. H. Distributional and Macroeconomic Aspects of Environmental Policy. In *Kneese, A. V. and Sweeney, J. L., eds. Vol. 1*, 1985, pp. 345–93.
[G: U.S.]

Christoffersen, Henrik. Vstforståelsen i dansk økonomisk politik. (The Growth Orientation in Danish Economic Policy. With English summary.) *Nationaløkon. Tidsskr.*, 1985, *123*(3), pp. 329–41. [G: Denmark]

Cockerill, Anthony. The British Economy: Performance, Prospects and Policies. In *Meyer, F. V., ed.*, 1985, pp. 102–23. [G: U.K.]

Condon, Timothy; Corbo, Vittorio and de Melo, Jaime. Productivity Growth, External Shocks, and Capital Inflows in Chile: A General Equilibrium Analysis. *J. Policy Modeling*, Fall 1985, *7*(3), pp. 379–405. [G: Chile]

Coutinho, Luciano. The Recent Performance and Future Challenges of Newly Industrializing Countries. In *Hochmuth, M. and Davidson, W., eds.*, 1985, pp. 131–62. [G: OECD; LDCs]

Daly, Donald J. Technology Transfer and Canada's Competitive Performance. In *Stern, R. M., ed.*, 1985, pp. 304–33. [G: Canada]

Daly, Michael J. and Rao, P. Someshwar. Some Myths and Realities Concerning Canada's Recent Productivity Slowdown, and Their Policy Implications. *Can. Public Policy*, June 1985, *11*(2), pp. 206–17. [G: Canada]

Davidson, Lawrence S. and Fratianni, Michele. Economic Growth in the 1970s and Beyond. *Econ. Notes*, 1985, (3), pp. 17–34. [G: U.S.]

Desai, Padma. Total Factor Productivity in Postwar Soviet Industry and Its Branches. *J. Compar. Econ.*, March 1985, *9*(1), pp. 1–23.
[G: U.S.S.R.]

Díaz-Alejandro, Carlos F. Argentina, Australia and Brazil before 1929. In *Platt, D. C. M. and di Tella, G., eds.*, 1985, pp. 95–109.
[G: Argentina; Australia; Brazil]

Dowling, J. Malcolm, Jr.; Ali, Ifzal and Soo, David. Income Distribution, Poverty and Economic Growth in Developing Asian Countries. *Singapore Econ. Rev.*, April 1985, *30*(1), pp. 1–13. [G: Asia]

Eatwell, John. Keynes, Keynesians, and British Economic Policy. In *Wattel, H. L., ed.*, 1985, pp. 61–76. [G: OECD]

Elias, Victor J. La productividad del sector público en la Argentina. (The Productivity of the Public Sector in Argentina. With English summary.) *Económica (La Plata)*, May-Dec. 1985, *31*(2–3), pp. 133–45.

Faini, Riccardo. International Comparison of the Sources of Productivity Slowdown, 1973-1982: Comment. *Europ. Econ. Rev.*, June-July 1985, *28*(1–2), pp. 197–200. [G: OECD]

Fei, John C. H.; Ohkawa, Kazushi and Ranis, Gustav. Economic Development in Historical Perspective: Japan, Korea, and Taiwan. In *Oh-*

kawa, K. and Ranis, G., eds., 1985, pp. 35–64.   [G: Japan; S. Korea; Taiwan]

Feiwel, George R. Some Observations on the Engine and Fuel of Economic Growth. In *Feiwel, G. R.,* ed. *(I),* 1985, pp. 395–428.

Forssell, Osmo. Changes in the Structure of the Finnish Economy, 1970–1980. In *Smyshlyaev, A.,* ed., 1985, pp. 61–71.   [G: Finland]

Foss, Murray F. Changing Utilization of Fixed Capital: An Element in Long-term Growth. *Mon. Lab. Rev.,* May 1985, *108*(5), pp. 3–8.   [G: U.S.]

Friedman, Benjamin M. Saving, Investment, and Government Deficits in the 1980s. In *Scott, B. R. and Lodge, G. C.,* eds., 1985, pp. 395–428.   [G: U.S.; OECD]

Gann, Pamela B. Neutral Taxation of Capital Income: An Achievable Goal? *Law Contemp. Probl.,* Autumn 1985, *48*(4), pp. 77–149.
                                                 [G: U.S.]

Ghosh, Dipak and Mizuno, Yasumasa. Causes of Growth in the Japanese Economy from a Kaldorian Point of View. *Pakistan Econ. Soc. Rev.,* Winter 1985, *23*(2), pp. 151–63.   [G: Japan]

Helliwell, John F.; Sturm, Peter H. and Salou, Gérard. International Comparison of the Sources of Productivity Slowdown, 1973-1982. *Europ. Econ. Rev.,* June-July 1985, *28*(1–2), pp. 157–91.   [G: OECD]

Herbel, Norbert and Bald, Christiane. New Calculation of the Production and Productivity Indexes in the Federal Republic of Germany. *Statist. J.,* May 1985, *3*(2), pp. 185–209.
                                        [G: W. Germany]

Hochmuth, Milton. From Challenger to Challenged. In *Hochmuth, M. and Davidson, W.,* eds., 1985, pp. 1–16.   [G: U.S.]

Hochmuth, Milton. Revitalizing American Industry: Analysis and Summary. In *Hochmuth, M. and Davidson, W.,* eds., 1985, pp. 375–95.
                                   [G: Selected Countries]

Hondai, Susumu. Changes in Intersectoral Terms of Trade and Their Effects on Labor Transfer. In *Ohkawa, K. and Ranis, G.,* eds., 1985, pp. 249–65.   [G: Japan; Taiwan]

Hood, Neil and Young, Stephen. The United Kingdom and the Changing Economic World Order. In *Hochmuth, M. and Davidson, W.,* eds., 1985, pp. 99–129.   [G: OECD; U.K.]

Horn, Ernst-Jürgen. Positive and Defensive Strategies in Sectoral Adjustment. In *Jungenfelt, K. and Hague, D. [Sir],* eds., 1985, pp. 533–70.   [G: W. Germany]

Hughes, Helen. Australia and the World Environment—The Dynamics of International Competition and Wealth Creation. In *Scutt, J. A.,* ed., 1985, pp. 1–17.   [G: Australia; Global]

Jerome, Robert T., Jr. Estimates of Sources of Growth in Bulgaria, Greece, and Yugoslavia, 1950–1980. *Comparative Econ. Stud.,* Fall 1985, 27(3), pp. 31–82. [G: Bulgaria; Greece; Yugoslavia]

Jordan, Bill. Unemployment and the Recovery: The Future of Labour Utilisation. In *Meyer, F. V.,* ed., 1985, pp. 183–212.   [G: OECD; U.K.]

Jorgenson, Dale W. The Great Transition: Energy and Economic Change. In *Shishido, T. and Sato, R.,* eds., 1985, pp. 260–86. [G: OECD]

Junge, Georg. The Impact of Swiss Taxation on Economic Growth. *Schweiz. Z. Volkswirtsch. Statist.,* March 1985, *121*(1), pp. 23–34.
                                      [G: Switzerland]

Katsimbris, George M. The Relationship between the Inflation Rate, Its Variability, and Output Growth Variability: Disaggregated International Evidence. *J. Money, Credit, Banking,* May 1985, *17*(2), pp. 179–88.   [G: OECD]

Kloten, Norbert; Ketterer, Karl-Heinz and Vollmer, Rainer. West Germany's Stabilization Performance. In *Lindberg, L. N. and Maier, C. S.,* eds., 1985, pp. 353–402.
                                        [G: W. Germany]

Kogane, Yoshihiro. Economic Growth before and after the Oil Crisis and the Possibility of Deindustrialization. In *Didsbury, H. F., Jr.,* ed., 1985, pp. 267–95.   [G: Japan; W. Europe; U.S.]

Kolm, Serge-Christophe. Must One Be Buddhist to Grow? An Analysis of the Cultural Basis of Japanese Productivity. In *Koslowski, P.,* ed., 1985, pp. 221–42.

Kormendi, Roger C. and Meguire, Philip G. Macroeconomic Determinants of Growth: Cross-Country Evidence. *J. Monet. Econ.,* September 1985, *16*(2), pp. 141–63.

Kouri, Pentti J. K.; Braga de Macedo, Jorge and Viscio, Albert J. Profitability, Employment and Structural Adjustment in France. In *Melitz, J. and Wyplosz, C.,* eds., 1985, pp. 85–112.   [G: France]

Krupp, Helmar. Public Promotion of Innovation—Disappointments and Hopes. In *Sweeney, G.,* ed., 1985, pp. 48–79.   [G: OECD]

Kümmel, Reiner, et al. Technical Progress and Energy Dependent Production Functions. *Z. Nationalökon.,* 1985, *45*(3), pp. 285–311.
                                     [G: U.S.; W. Germany]

Landau, Daniel L. Government Expenditure and Economic Growth in the Developed Countries: 1952–76. *Public Choice,* 1985, *47*(3), pp. 459–77.   [G: W. Europe; U.S.; Canada; Japan]

Leemans, Tom and Vuchelen, Jef. De economische ontwikkeling van Westerse landen: een beschrijving met cluster-algoritmen. (With English summary.) *Cah. Écon. Bruxelles,* 3rd Trimester 1985, (107), pp. 385–425.
                                                 [G: OECD]

Leijonhufvud, Axel. Buddhist Values and Japanese Growth: Comment. In *Koslowski, P.,* ed., 1985, pp. 243–47.

Leontief, Wassily. Machines and Man. In *Leontief, W.,* 1985, pp. 187–99.   [G: U.S.]

Leontief, Wassily. The Rates of Long-run Economic Growth and Capital Transfer from Developed to Underdeveloped Areas. In *Leontief, W.,* 1985, pp. 200–215.   [G: LDCs; MDCs]

Leslie, Derek. Productivity Growth in UK Manufacturing and Production Industries, 1948–68. *Appl. Econ.,* February 1985, *17*(1), pp. 1–16.
                                                 [G: U.K.]

Lesourne, Jacques. Social Values, Political Goals, and Economic Systems: The Issue of Employment in European Societies. In *Didsbury, H. F., Jr., ed.*, 1985, pp. 60–75.

Levin, Richard C. Innovation and Productivity in U.S. Industry: Comment. *Brookings Pap. Econ. Act.*, 1985, (2), pp. 633–37. [**G: U.S.**]

Lim, G. C. GDP Growth Rates Calculated from Quarterly National Accounts: Discrepancies and Revisions. *Australian Econ. Rev.*, 4th Quarter 1985, (72), pp. 21–27. [**G: Australia**]

Lindert, Peter H. and Williamson, Jeffrey G. Growth, Equality, and History. *Exploration Econ. Hist.*, October 1985, 22(4), pp. 341–77. [**G: W. Europe; U.S.**]

Linz, Susan J. World War II and Soviet Economic Growth, 1940–1953. In *Linz, S. J., ed.*, 1985, pp. 11–38. [**G: U.S.S.R.**]

Loginov, V. National Income: Growth Factors. *Prob. Econ.*, November 1985, 28(7), pp. 18–32. [**G: U.S.S.R.**]

Macarov, David. The Prospect of Work in the Western Context. In *Didsbury, H. F., Jr., ed.*, 1985, pp. 76–108.

Maier, Charles S. Inflation and Stagnation as Politics and History. In *Lindberg, L. N. and Maier, C. S., eds.*, 1985, pp. 3–24. [**G: OECD**]

Mairesse, Jacques. Profitability, Employment and Structural Adjustment in France: Comments. In *Melitz, J. and Wyplosz, C., eds.*, 1985, pp. 114–16. [**G: France**]

Malaska, Pentti. Outline of a Policy for the Future. In *Aida, S., et al.*, 1985, pp. 338–54.

Malenbaum, Wilfred. Modern Economic Growth in India and China: Reply. *Econ. Develop. Cult. Change*, October 1985, 34(1), pp. 161–66. [**G: India; China**]

Martin, Preston. Innovation, Productivity, and Economic Policy. In *Federal Reserve Bank of Atlanta (I)*, 1985, pp. 41–46. [**G: U.S.**]

McCarthy, F. Desmond; Hanson, James A. and Kwon, Soonwon. Sources of Growth in Colombia, 1963–80. *J. Econ. Stud.*, 1985, 12(4), pp. 3–14. [**G: Colombia**]

McCloskey, Donald N. The Industrial Revolution 1780–1860: A Survey. In *Mokyr, J., ed.*, 1985, pp. 53–74. [**G: U.K.**]

McCombie, J. S. L. Economic Growth, the Harrod Foreign Trade Multiplier and the Hicks Super-multiplier. *Appl. Econ.*, February 1985, 17(1), pp. 55–72. [**G: OECD**]

McGregor, Peter G. and Swales, J. K. Professor Thirlwall and Balance of Payments Constrained Growth. *Appl. Econ.*, February 1985, 17(1), pp. 17–32. [**G: OECD**]

McLoughlin, Jane. South Korea. In *Smith, M., et al.*, 1985, pp. 39–64. [**G: S. Korea**]

McMillion, Charles W. The Global Economy Requires Greater U.S. Productivity. In *Didsbury, H. F., Jr., ed.*, 1985, pp. 251–64. [**G: U.S.**]

Mesa-Lago, Carmelo and Perez-Lopez, Jorge. Imbroglios on the Cuban Economy: A Reply. *Comparative Econ. Stud.*, Spring 1985, 27(1), pp. 47–83. [**G: Cuba**]

Mesa-Lago, Carmelo and Perez-Lopez, Jorge. The Endless Cuban Economy Saga: A Terminal Rebuttal [Recent Studies on Cuban Economic Growth: A Review]. *Comparative Econ. Stud.*, Winter 1985, 27(4), pp. 67–82. [**G: Cuba**]

Michl, Thomas R. International Comparisons of Productivity Growth: Verdoorn's Law Revisited. *J. Post Keynesian Econ.*, Summer 1985, 7(4), pp. 474–92. [**G: OECD**]

Miernyk, William H. Bioeconomics: A Realistic Appraisal of Future Prospects. In *Didsbury, H. F., Jr., ed.*, 1985, pp. 334–52.

Miller, Edward McCarthy. On the Importance of the Embodiment of Technology Effect: A Comment on Denison's Growth Accounting Methodology. *J. Macroecon.*, Winter 1985, 7(1), pp. 85–99.

Moroz, Andrew R. Technology Transfer and Canada's Competitive Performance: Comments. In *Stern, R. M., ed.*, 1985, pp. 339–44. [**G: Canada**]

Moseley, Fred. Can the "Social Model" of Productivity Stand Scrutiny? *Challenge*, May/June 1985, 28(2), pp. 55–57. [**G: U.S.**]

Motley, Brian. Whither the Unemployment Rate? *Fed. Res. Bank San Francisco Econ. Rev.*, Spring 1985, (2), pp. 40–54. [**G: U.S.**]

Nicholas, Stephen. British Economic Performance and Total Factor Productivity Growth, 1870–1940. *Econ. Hist. Rev., 2nd Ser.*, November 1985, 38(4), pp. 576–82. [**G: U.K.**]

Pastré, Olivier. Organisation du travail et croissance économique: un vieux débat anglo-saxon. (Division of Labour and Economic Growth: An Old Debate. With English summary.) *Revue Écon.*, March 1985, 36(2), pp. 383–409. [**G: OECD**]

Patrick, Hugh. Services in the Japanese Economy: Comment. In *Inman, R. P., ed.*, 1985, pp. 84–88. [**G: Japan; OECD**]

Pollard, Sidney. Capital Exports, 1870–1914: Harmful or Beneficial? *Econ. Hist. Rev., 2nd Ser.*, November 1985, 38(4), pp. 489–514. [**G: U.K.**]

Porter, Michael G. The Labour of Liberalisation. In *Scutt, J. A., ed.*, 1985, pp. 37–61. [**G: Australia**]

Przeworski, Adam and Wallerstein, Michael. Comment on Katz, Mahler, & Franz [The Impact of Taxes on Growth and Distribution in Developed Capitalist Countries: A Cross-National Study]. *Amer. Polit. Sci. Rev.*, June 1985, 79(2), pp. 508–10. [**G: Selected OECD**]

Pugno, Maurizio. Are Long Waves Relevant in Economic Life? A Note. *Econ. Notes*, 1985, (2), pp. 68–77. [**G: Global**]

Ram, Rati. Conventional and 'Real' GDP per Capita in Cross-Country Studies of Production Structure. *J. Devel. Econ.*, August 1985, 18(2–3), pp. 463–77. [**G: LDCs**]

Richards, Gordon. Business Cycles, Macroeconomic Policy, and U.S. Industrial Performance. In *Yochelson, J. N., ed.*, 1985, pp. 77–117. [**G: U.S.**]

Richardson, Harry W. Regional Policy in a 'Slowth' Economy. In *Richardson, H. W. and*

Turek, J. H., eds., 1985, pp. 243–63.
[G: U.S.]

Román, Zoltán. Productivity Growth and Its Slowdown in the Hungarian Economy. *Acta Oecon.*, 1985, *35*(1–2), pp. 81–104.
[G: Hungary]

Rostow, W. W. The World Economy since 1945: A Stylized Historical Analysis. *Econ. Hist. Rev.*, *2nd Ser.*, May 1985, *38*(2), pp. 252–75.
[G: Global]

Rothschild, Kurt W. Exports, Growth, and Catching-up: Some Remarks and Crude Calculations. *Weltwirtsch. Arch.*, 1985, *121*(2), pp. 304–14.
[G: OECD]

Saxena, A. N. Productivity. In *Mongia, J. N., ed.*, 1985, pp. 385–416.
[G: India]

Saxonhouse, Gary R. Services in the Japanese Economy. In *Inman, R. P., ed.*, 1985, pp. 53–83.
[G: Japan; OECD]

Saxonhouse, Gary R. Technology Transfer and Canada's Competitive Performance: Comments. In *Stern, R. M., ed.*, 1985, pp. 334–38.
[G: Canada]

Schroeder, Gertrude E. The Slowdown in Soviet Industry, 1976–1982. *Soviet Econ.*, Jan.-Mar. 1985, *1*(1), pp. 42–74.
[G: U.S.S.R.]

Scott, Bruce R. National Strategies: Key to International Competition. In *Scott, B. R. and Lodge, G. C., eds.*, 1985, pp. 71–143.
[G: U.S.]

Scott, Bruce R. U.S. Competitiveness: Concepts, Performance, and Implications. In *Scott, B. R. and Lodge, G. C., eds.*, 1985, pp. 13–70.
[G: U.S.]

Shaldina, G. E. The Intensification of Natural Resource Utilization and the Reproduction of Resources. *Prob. Econ.*, June 1985, *28*(2), pp. 80–92.
[G: U.S.S.R.]

Sickles, Robin C. A Nonlinear Multivariate Error Components Analysis of Technology and Specific Factor Productivity Growth with an Application to the U.S. Airlines. *J. Econometrics*, January 1985, *27*(1), pp. 61–78.
[G: U.S.]

Simon, Herbert A. Japan's Emerging Multinationals: Foreward. In *Takamiya, S. and Thurley, K., eds.*, 1985, pp. 3–12.

Smith, Michael. Japan. In *Smith, M., et al.*, 1985, pp. 5–36.
[G: Japan]

Soete, Luc and Patel, Pari. Recherche-développement importations de technologie et croissance Économique: Une tentative de comparaison internationale. (R-D, International Technology Imports and Economic Growth: An International Comparison. With English summary.) *Revue Écon.*, September 1985, *36*(5), pp. 975–1000.
[G: OECD]

Solow, Robert M. and Temin, Peter. The Inputs for Growth. In *Mokyr, J., ed.*, 1985, pp. 75–96.

Soulage, Bernard. Industrial Priorities in the Current French Plan. In *Zukin, S., ed.*, 1985, pp. 165–78.
[G: France]

Stevens, Benjamin H. Regional Cost Equalization and the Potential for Manufacturing Recovery in the Industrial North. In *Richardson, H. W.*

and Turek, J. H., eds., 1985, pp. 85–103.
[G: U.S.]

Sundrum, R. M. Modern Economic Growth in India and China: Comment. *Econ. Develop. Cult. Change*, October 1985, *34*(1), pp. 157–60.
[G: India; China]

Sunkel, Osvaldo. Past, Present and Future of the International Economic Crisis. In *Gauhar, A., ed.*, 1985, pp. 1–41. [G: Selected Countries]

Tabatoni, Pierre. The Market Economies Tack against the Wind: Coping with Economic Shocks: 1973–1983. In *Juris, H.; Thompson, M. and Daniels, W., eds.*, 1985, pp. 1–40.
[G: OECD]

di Tella, Guido. Rents, Quasi-rents, Normal Profits and Growth: Argentina and the Areas of Recent Settlement. In *Platt, D. C. M. and di Tella, G., eds.*, 1985, pp. 37–52.
[G: Argentina; Selected OECD]

Thomas, Mark. Accounting for Growth, 1870–1940: Stephen Nicholas and Total Factor Productivity Measurements. *Econ. Hist. Rev.*, *2nd Ser.*, November 1985, *38*(4), pp. 569–75.
[G: U.K.]

Thurow, Lester C. Healing with a Thousand Bandages. *Challenge*, Nov./Dec. 1985, *28*(5), pp. 22–31.
[G: U.S.]

Todd, Douglas. Factor Productivity Growth in Four EEC Countries, 1960–1981. *Cah. Écon. Bruxelles*, 3rd Trimester 1985, (107), pp. 279–325. [G: Italy; France; W. Germany; U.K.]

Tsurumi, Yoshi. Japan's Challenge to the United States: Industrial Policies and Corporate Strategies. In *Hochmuth, M. and Davidson, W., eds.*, 1985, pp. 39–79. [G: U.S.; Japan]

von Tunzelmann, G. N. The Standard of Living Debate and Optimal Economic Growth. In *Mokyr, J., ed.*, 1985, pp. 207–26. [G: U.K.]

Vernon, Raymond. The Analytical Challenge. In *Hochmuth, M. and Davidson, W., eds.*, 1985, pp. 17–37.
[G: U.S.]

Whitesell, Robert S. The Influence of Central Planning on the Economic Slowdown in the Soviet Union and Eastern Europe: A Comparative Production Function Analysis. *Economica*, May 1985, *52*(206), pp. 235–44.
[G: U.S.S.R.; E. Europe]

Wolff, Edward N. Industrial Composition, Interindustry Effects, and the U.S. Productivity Slowdown. *Rev. Econ. Statist.*, May 1985, *67*(2), pp. 268–77.
[G: U.S.]

Woodham, Douglas M. How Fast Can Europe Grow? *Fed. Res. Bank New York Quart. Rev.*, Summer 1985, *10*(2), pp. 28–35. [G: U.S.; W. Germany; U.K.]

Wu, Jinglian; Li, Jiange and Ding, Ningning. Hold Down the Growth Rate of the National Economy within an Appropriate Range. *Chinese Econ. Stud.*, Fall 1985, *19*(1), pp. 53–64.
[G: China]

Yamamura, Kozo. The Cost of Rapid Growth and Capitalist Democracy in Japan. In *Lindberg, L. N. and Maier, C. S., eds.*, 1985, pp. 467–508.
[G: Japan]

Young, Kan H. The Relative Effects of Demand and Supply on Output Growth and Price

Change. *Rev. Econ. Statist.*, May 1985, 67(2), pp. 314–18. **[G: U.S.]**

Zysman, John. Inflation and the Politics of Supply. In *Lindberg, L. N. and Maier, C. S., eds.*, 1985, pp. 140–71. **[G: W. Germany; U.K.; France; Japan; U.S.]**

227 Prices

2270 Prices

Abelson, Peter W. and Markandya, A. The Interpretation of Capitalized Hedonic Prices in a Dynamic Environment. *J. Environ. Econ. Manage.*, September 1985, 12(3), pp. 195–206.

Askanas, Benedykt and Laski, Kazimierz. Consumer Prices and Private Consumption in Poland and Austria. *J. Compar. Econ.*, June 1985, 9(2), pp. 164–77. **[G: Poland; Austria]**

Balbinot, Pierangelo. Indicizzazione dei redditi e formazione dei prezzi nel settore commerciale: una verifica econometrica (Income Indexation and Price Formation in the Trade Sector. An Econometric Test. With English summary.) *Econ. Lavoro*, Oct.-Dec. 1985, 19(4), pp. 3–13. **[G: Italy]**

Barnett, Colin J. An Application of the Hedonic Price Model to the Perth Residential Land Market. *Econ. Rec.*, March 1985, 61(172), pp. 476–81. **[G: Australia]**

Baye, Michael R. Price Dispersion and Functional Price Indices. *Econometrica*, January 1985, 53(1), pp. 213–23.

Belongia, Michael T. The Impact of Inflation on the Real Income of U.S. Farmers: Discussion. *Amer. J. Agr. Econ.*, May 1985, 67(2), pp. 398–99. **[G: U.S.]**

Bemelmans-Spork, Mieke and Sikkel, Dirk. Observation of Prices with Hand-held Computers. *Statist. J.*, May 1985, 3(2), pp. 153–60. **[G: Netherlands]**

Bhagwati, Jagdish N. Why Are Services Cheaper in the Poor Countries? In *Bhagwati, J. N. (II)*, 1985, pp. 82–91.

Blang, Hans-Georg and Schöler, Klaus. Zur Rationalität der Preiserwartungen deutscher Unternehmen. (On Rational Price Expectations of German Firms. With English summary.) *Ifo-Studien*, 1985, 31(3), pp. 239–58. **[G: W. Germany]**

Bordes, Christian; Driscoll, Michael J. and MacDonald, Garry. Le contenu en information des agrégats monétaires français. (The Information Content of French Monetary Aggregates. With English summary.) *Revue Écon.*, November 1985, 36(6), pp. 1169–1205. **[G: France]**

Bornstein, Morris. The Soviet Industrial Price Revision. In *[Levcik, F.]*, 1985, pp. 157–70. **[G: U.S.S.R.]**

Boskin, Michael J. and Hurd, Michael D. Indexing Social Security Benefits: A Separate Price Index for the Elderly? *Public Finance Quart.*, October 1985, 13(4), pp. 436–49. **[G: U.S.]**

Bourgel, Guy; Brignier, Jean-Marie and Certhoux, Gilles. Perception et réalité des prix. (Price Perception and Price Reality. With English summary.) *Écon. Soc.*, December 1985, 19(12), pp. 73–104. **[G: France]**

Boyd, Milton S. and Brorsen, B. Wade. Dynamic Relationship of Weekly Prices in the United States Beef and Pork Marketing Channels. *Can. J. Agr. Econ.*, November 1985, 33(3), pp. 331–42. **[G: U.S.]**

van Brabant, Jozef M. Yugoslavia's Foreign Trade Statistics: A Methodological Inquiry. *Comparative Econ. Stud.*, Winter 1985, 27(4), pp. 31–51. **[G: Yugoslavia]**

Bredahl, Maury E. The Effects of Inflation on the Welfare and Performance of Agriculture: Discussion [The Impact of Inflation on the Real Income of U.S. Farmers]. *Amer. J. Agr. Econ.*, May 1985, 67(2), pp. 400–401. **[G: U.S.]**

Brorsen, B. Wade; Chavas, Jean-Paul and Grant, Warren R. A Dynamic Analysis of Prices in the U.S. Rice Marketing Channel. *J. Bus. Econ. Statist.*, October 1985, 3(4), pp. 362–69. **[G: U.S.]**

Brorsen, B. Wade; Grant, Warren R. and Chavas, Jean-Paul. Dynamic Relationships and Efficiency of Rice Byproduct Prices. *Agr. Econ. Res.*, Spring 1985, 37(2), pp. 15–26. **[G: U.S.]**

Buck, Andrew J. An Empirical Note on the Foundations of Rational Expectations. *J. Post Keynesian Econ.*, Spring 1985, 7(3), pp. 311–23. **[G: W. Germany]**

Campolongo, Alberto. La lira in settant'anni. (The Lira through Seventy Years of Vicissitude. With English summary.) *Bancaria*, March 1985, 41(3), pp. 285–87. **[G: Italy]**

Caskey, John P. Modeling the Formation of Price Expectations: A Bayesian Approach. *Amer. Econ. Rev.*, September 1985, 75(4), pp. 768–76. **[G: U.S.]**

Cassel, Eric and Mendelsohn, Robert. The Choice of Functional Forms for Hedonic Price Equations: Comment. *J. Urban Econ.*, September 1985, 18(2), pp. 135–42. **[G: U.S.]**

Cecchetti, Stephen G. Staggered Contracts and the Frequency of Price Adjustment. *Quart. J. Econ.*, Supp. 1985, 100, pp. 935–59. **[G: U.S.]**

Clem, Andrew G. Commodity Price Volatility: Trends during 1975–84. *Mon. Lab. Rev.*, June 1985, 108(6), pp. 17–21.

Cliffe, Mark. Commodity Prices and World Economic Recovery. In *Meyer, F. V., ed.*, 1985, pp. 144–62. **[G: OECD]**

Colman, David. Imperfect Transmission of Policy Prices. *Europ. Rev. Agr. Econ.*, 1985, 12(3), pp. 171–86. **[G: U.K.]**

Crafts, N. F. R. English Workers' Real Wages during the Industrial Revolution: Some Remaining Problems. *J. Econ. Hist.*, March 1985, 45(1), pp. 139–44. **[G: U.K.]**

Davidson, Lawrence S. and Hafer, R. W. Relative Price Variability: Evidence from Supply and Demand Events. *J. Monet. Econ.*, May 1985, 15(3), pp. 333–41. **[G: U.S.]**

Downes, Andrew. Inflation in Barbados: An Econometric Investigation. *Econ. Develop.*

Cult. Change, April 1985, *33*(3), pp. 521–32.
[G: Barbados]

Drake, Louis S. Reconstruction of a Bimetallic Price Level. *Exploration Econ. Hist.*, April 1985, *22*(2), pp. 194–219. [G: U.S.]

Driscoll, Michael J.; Ford, J. L. and Mullineux, A. W. The Elasticity of Prices with Respect to Monetary Components: Some Estimates for the UK, 1948–1979. *Appl. Econ.*, February 1985, *17*(1), pp. 95–106. [G: U.K.]

Duggan, James E. and Clem, Andrew G. Input Prices and Cost Inflation in Three Manufacturing Industries. *Mon. Lab. Rev.*, May 1985, *108*(5), pp. 16–21. [G: U.S.]

Dwyer, Gerald P., Jr. Money, Income, and Prices in the United Kingdom: 1870–1913. *Econ. Inquiry*, July 1985, *23*(3), pp. 415–35. [G: U.S.]

Eckstein, Otto. Disinflation. In *Feiwel, G. R., ed. (I)*, 1985, pp. 297–323. [G: Selected Countries]

Englander, A. Steven. Commodity Prices in the Current Recovery. *Fed. Res. Bank New York Quart. Rev.*, Spring 1985, *10*(1), pp. 11–19. [G: Global]

Epperson, James E. and Fletcher, Stanley M. Tandem Forecasting of Price and Probability— The Case of Watermelon. *Can. J. Agr. Econ.*, November 1985, *33*(3), pp. 375–85. [G: U.S.]

Fieleke, Norman S. Dollar Appreciation and U.S. Import Prices. *New Eng. Econ. Rev.*, Nov./ Dec. 1985, pp. 49–54. [G: U.S.]

Flowers, Marilyn R. Owner-occupied Housing, the CPI, and Indexing. *Public Finance Quart.*, January 1985, *13*(1), pp. 74–80.

Frankel, Jeffrey A. and Hardouvelis, Gikas A. Commodity Prices, Money Surprises and Fed Credibility. *J. Money, Credit, Banking*, Part 1, Nov. 1985, *17*(4), pp. 425–38. [G: U.S.]

Frantzen, Dirk J. Some Empirical Evidence on the Behaviour of Export and Domestic Prices in Belgian Manufacturing Industry. *Rech. Écon. Louvain*, 1985, *51*(1), pp. 29–49. [G: Belgium]

Frantzen, Dirk J. The Influence of Short-term Demand on the Mark-up in Belgian Manufacturing Industry. *Tijdschrift Econ. Manage.*, 1985, *30*(2), pp. 199–219. [G: Belgium]

Frantzen, Dirk J. The Pricing of Manufactures in an Open Economy: A Study of Belgium. *Cambridge J. Econ.*, December 1985, *9*(4), pp. 371–82. [G: Belgium]

Franz, Alfred. The Solution of Problems in International Comparisons of GDP through Price Adjustments. What to Learn from ECP 1980? *Statist. J.*, September 1985, *3*(3), pp. 307–19. [G: W. Europe]

Franz, Wolfgang. Nicht-neutrale Effekte der Inflation auf die Preisstruktur: Theoretische Überlegungen und empirische Resultate. (Non-neutral Effects of Inflation on Relative Price Variability: Theoretical Considerations and Empirical Results. With English summary.) *Jahr. Nationalökon. Statist.*, January 1985, *200*(1), pp. 41–55. [G: W. Germany]

Fry, Vanessa C. and Pashardes, Panos. Distributional Aspects of Inflation: Who Has Suffered Most? *Fisc. Stud.*, November 1985, *6*(4), pp. 21–29. [G: U.K.]

Gahlen, Bernhard. Trend und Zyklus—Aggregat und Struktur. (Trends and Cycles—Structure and the Aggregate. With English summary.) *Jahr. Nationalökon. Statist.*, September 1985, *200*(5), pp. 449–78. [G: W. Germany]

Galeazzi, Giorgio. International Differences in Comparative Price Levels and Exchange Rates: An Analysis by Production Sectors in a Varying Parameter Model. *Rivista Polit. Econ.*, Suppl. Dec. 1985, *76*, pp. 3–40.

Griffith-Jones, Stephany. Impact of World Prices on Development: The International Environment. In *Griffith-Jones, S. and Harvey, C., eds.*, 1985, pp. 13–51. [G: LDCs; MDCs]

Guinchard, Philippe. Prix relatifs et désindustrialisation. (Relative Prices and Deindustrialisation. With English summary.) *Revue Écon.*, March 1985, *36*(2), pp. 367–82. [G: Selected Countries]

Havlik, Peter. A Comparison of Purchasing Power Parity and Consumption Levels in Austria and Czechoslovakia. *J. Compar. Econ.*, June 1985, *9*(2), pp. 178–90. [G: Austria; Czechoslovakia]

Hawdon, David. Survey of Oil Price Expectations 22/23 March 1984. In *Hawdon, D., ed.*, 1985, pp. 106–12. [G: OPEC]

Holder, Carlos and Worrell, DeLisle. A Model of Price Formation for Small Economies: Three Caribbean Examples. *J. Devel. Econ.*, August 1985, *18*(2–3), pp. 411–28. [G: Barbados; Jamaica; Trinidad and Tobago]

Howell, Craig and Thomas, William. Inflation Remained Low during 1984. *Mon. Lab. Rev.*, April 1985, *108*(4), pp. 3–9. [G: U.S.]

Hvidding, James M. Models of Inflation Expectations Formation: A Comment. *J. Money, Credit, Banking*, Part 1, Nov. 1985, *17*(4), pp. 534–38. [G: U.S.]

Hvidding, James M. On the Rationality of Household Inflation Expectations. *Quart. J. Bus. Econ.*, Summer 1985, *24*(3), pp. 41–66. [G: U.S.]

Hylleberg, Svend and Paldam, Martin. Price and Wages in the OECD Area 1913–1980—A Study of the Time Series Evidence. *Z. Wirtschaft. Sozialwissen.*, 1985, *105*(2/3), pp. 193–221. [G: OECD]

Kott, Phillip S. Corrections [A Superpopulation Theory Approach to the Design of Price Index Estimators with Small Sampling Biases]. *J. Bus. Econ. Statist.*, January 1985, *3*(1), pp. 100. [G: U.S.]

Kumar, Rajendra; Sharma, R. C. and Phillip, P. J. Determinants of Industrial Production and Prices in India. *Indian Econ. J.*, Oct.-Nov. 1985, *33*(2), pp. 1–9. [G: India]

Lachica-Sosa, Mary Ann Celeste. The Linear Programming Approach in the Derivation of a Food Price Index. *Philippine Econ. J.*, 1985, *24*(2–3), pp. 181–99. [G: Philippines]

Lakonishok, Josef and Ofer, Aharon R. The Information Content of General Price Level Earnings: A Reply. *Accounting Rev.*, October 1985, *60*(4), pp. 711–13. **[G: U.S.]**

Leontief, Wassily. Composite Commodities and the Problem of Index Numbers. In *Leontief, W.*, 1985, pp. 126–50.

Levy, Santiago. A Mark-Up Pricing Model for Price Simulations. *J. Devel. Econ.*, December 1985, *19*(3), pp. 299–320. **[G: Mexico]**

Liebermann, Yehoshua and Zilberfarb, Ben-Zion. Price Adjustment Strategy under Conditions of High Inflation: An Empirical Examination. *J. Econ. Bus.*, August 1985, *37*(3), pp. 253–65. **[G: Israel]**

Lindberg, Leon N. Models of the Inflation–Disinflation Process. In *Lindberg, L. N. and Maier, C. S., eds.*, 1985, pp. 25–50. **[G: OECD]**

Lindert, Peter H. and Williamson, Jeffrey G. English Workers' Real Wages: Reply. *J. Econ. Hist.*, March 1985, *45*(1), pp. 145–53. **[G: U.K.]**

Lloyd, P. J. and Sandilands, R. J. Terms of Trade Indices in the Presence of Re-export Trade. *Econ. Rec.*, September 1985, *61*(174), pp. 667–73. **[G: Singapore]**

Looney, Robert E. The Inflationary Process in Prerevolutionary Iran. *J. Devel. Areas*, April 1985, *19*(3), pp. 329–50. **[G: Iran]**

Marcoot, John L. Revision of Consumer Price Index Is Now Under Way. *Mon. Lab. Rev.*, April 1985, *108*(4), pp. 27–38. **[G: U.S.]**

McClain, David. Stabilizing Oil and Farm Prices Holds the Key. *Challenge*, Sept./Oct. 1985, *28*(4), pp. 23–26. **[G: U.S.]**

McGarvey, Mary G. U.S. Evidence on Linear Feedback from Money Growth Shocks to Relative Price Changes, 1954 to 1979. *Rev. Econ. Statist.*, November 1985, *67*(4), pp. 675–80. **[G: U.S.]**

de Melo, Jaime and Robinson, Sherman. Product Differentiation and Trade Dependence of the Domestic Price System in Computable General Equilibrium Trade Models. In *Peeters, T.; Praet, P. and Reding, P., eds.*, 1985, pp. 91–107.

Mongia, J. N. Deficit Financing. In *Mongia, J. N., ed.*, 1985, pp. 201–37. **[G: India]**

Morciano, Michele. Il ruolo delle aspettative e della domanda nella formazione dei prezzi al consumo. (Effects of Expectations and Demand on Retail Prices. With English summary.) *Ricerche Econ.*, Jan.-Mar. 1985, *39*(1), pp. 40–69. **[G: Italy]**

Mouyelo-Katoula, Michel and Munnsad, Kantilal. A Note on Methodologies Used in a Comparison of Purchasing Power Parities and Real Economic Aggregates in Fifteen African Countries. *Statist. J.*, September 1985, *3*(3), pp. 289–305. **[G: Africa]**

Mueller, Michael J. and Gorin, Daniel R. Informative Trends in Natural Resource Commodity Prices: A Comment. *J. Environ. Econ. Manage.*, March 1985, *12*(1), pp. 89–95. **[G: U.S.]**

Murty, G. V. S. N. Prices and Inequalities in a Developing Economy: The Case of India. *J.*

Devel. Stud., July 1985, *21*(4), pp. 533–47. **[G: India]**

Neumann, Manfred J. M. and von Hagen, Jürgen. Inflation and Relative Price Risk. *Z. Wirtschaft. Sozialwissen.*, 1985, *105*(2/3), pp. 169–92. **[G: W. Germany]**

Ojha, P. D. Inflation Control and Price Regulation. In *Mongia, J. N., ed.*, 1985, pp. 239–89. **[G: India]**

Oyrzanowski, Bronislaw. I sintomi dell'inflazione nei paesi ad economia dirigista. (Symptom of Inflation in Countries with Policy of State Intervention. With English summary.) *Bancaria*, December 1985, *41*(12), pp. 1249–55.

Pagano, Marco. Relative Price Variability and Inflation: The Italian Evidence. *Europ. Econ. Rev.*, November 1985, *29*(2), pp. 193–223. **[G: Italy; U.S.; W. Germany]**

Parikh, Ashok. The Behaviour of Export Price Deflators in Selected Asian Developing Countries. *Singapore Econ. Rev.*, October 1985, *30*(2), pp. 68–90. **[G: Asia]**

Pellegrini, Luca. The Distributive Trades in the Italian Economy: Some Remarks on the Decade 1970–80. *Rev. Econ. Cond. Italy*, May-Aug. 1985, (2), pp. 191–220. **[G: Italy]**

Persico, Pasquale. Inflazione e prezzi relativi: un'interpretazione fisheriana della correlazione tra variabilitaà del tasso d'inflazione e variabilitaà dei prezzi relativi. (With English summary.) *Stud. Econ.*, 1985, *40*(26), pp. 117–26. **[G: Italy]**

Pesando, James E. and Turnbull, Stuart M. The Time Path of Homeowner's Equity under Different Mortgage Instruments: A Simulation Study. *Housing Finance Rev.*, January 1985, *4*(1), pp. 483–504. **[G: Canada]**

Pigott, Charles and Sweeney, Richard J. Testing the Exchange Rate Implications of Two Popular Monetary Models. In *Arndt, S. W.; Sweeney, R. J. and Willett, T. D., eds.*, 1985, pp. 91–106. **[G: U.S.; Switzerland]**

Prat, Georges. Une mesure des anticipations d'inflation à court terme des ménages en France 1964–1985. With English summary.) *Revue Écon. Polit.*, Nov.-Dec. 1985, *95*(6), pp. 749–76. **[G: France]**

Ray, Ranjan. Prices, Children and Inequality: Further Evidence for the United Kingdom, 1965–82. *Econ. J.*, December 1985, *95*(380), pp. 1069–77. **[G: U.K.]**

Ross, Howard N. and Krausz, Joshua. Cyclical Price Behaviour and Concentration: A Time Series Analysis. *Oxford Bull. Econ. Statist.*, August 1985, *47*(3), pp. 231–47. **[G: U.S.]**

Salvati, Michele. The Italian Inflation. In *Lindberg, L. N. and Maier, C. S., eds.*, 1985, pp. 509–63. **[G: Italy; U.K.; France; W. Germany]**

Samuelson, Bruce A. and Murdoch, Brock. The Information Content of General Price Level Adjusted Earnings: A Comment. *Accounting Rev.*, October 1985, *60*(4), pp. 706–10. **[G: U.S.]**

Schwenk, Albert E. Introducing New Weights for the Employment Cost Index. *Mon. Lab. Rev.*,

June 1985, *108*(6), pp. 22–27.   [G: U.S.]

Slade, Margaret E. Noninformative Trends in Natural Resource Commodity Prices: U-shaped Price Paths Exonerated: Reply [Trends in Natural-Resource Commodity Prices: An Analysis of the Time Domain]. *J. Environ. Econ. Manage.*, June 1985, *12*(2), pp. 181–92.   [G: U.S.]

Szarek, Patricia and Costello, Brian. Prices of U.S. Imports and Exports Declined in 1984. *Mon. Lab. Rev.*, April 1985, *108*(4), pp. 10–26.   [G: U.S.]

Tarafás, Imre and Szabó, Judit. Hungary's Exchange Rate Policy in the 1980s. *Acta Oecon.*, 1985, *35*(1–2), pp. 53–79.   [G: Hungary]

Taylor, Stephen J. The Behaviour of Futures Prices over Time. *Appl. Econ.*, August 1985, *17*(4), pp. 713–34.   [G: U.S.; U.K.; W. Germany; Switzerland; Australia]

Thirlwall, A. P. and Bergevin, J. Trends, Cycles and Asymmetries in the Terms of Trade of Primary Commodities from Developed and Less Developed Countries. *World Devel.*, July 1985, *13*(7), pp. 805–17.

Tian, Jiyun. Implement the Reform of the Price System Vigorously and Reliably. *Chinese Econ. Stud.*, Summer 1985, *18*(4), pp. 87–100.

Wren-Lewis, Simon. The Quantification of Survey Data on Expectations. *Nat. Inst. Econ. Rev.*, August 1985, (113), pp. 39–49.   [G: U.K.]

Young, Kan H. The Relative Effects of Demand and Supply on Output Growth and Price Change. *Rev. Econ. Statist.*, May 1985, *67*(2), pp. 314–18.   [G: U.S.]

Yuravlivker, David E. Precios relativos effectivos versus de equilibiro: el impacto de la política cambiaria. (With English summary.) *Cuadernos Econ.*, April 1985, *22*(65), pp. 145–52.   [G: Argentina; Chile; Uruguay]

Zhuravlev, S. N. A Model for Forecasting Prices and Financial Proportions. *Matekon*, Summer 1985, *21*(4), pp. 23–43.

228 Regional Statistics

2280 Regional Statistics

Cocheba, Donald J.; Gilmer, Robert W. and Mack, Richard S. Data Refinement Recommendations and Their Impact on a Study of the Tennessee Valley: Measuring Changes in Service Sector Activity. *Growth Change*, October 1985, *16*(4), pp. 20–42.   [G: U.S.]

Drugge, Sten E. Nonneutral Technical Change and Regional Wage Differentials: A Comment. *J. Reg. Sci.*, February 1985, *25*(1), pp. 135–36.   [G: U.S.]

Garnick, Daniel H. Patterns of Growth in Metropolitan and Nonmetropolitan Areas: An Update. *Surv. Curr. Bus.*, May 1985, *65*(5), pp. 33–38.   [G: U.S.]

Johnson, Kenneth P. and Friedenberg, Howard L. Regional and State Projections of Income, Employment, and Population to the Year 2000. *Surv. Curr. Bus.*, May 1985, *65*(5), pp. 39–63.   [G: U.S.]

Kuehn, John A. and Bender, Lloyd D. Nonmetropolitan Economic Bases and Their Policy Implications. *Growth Change*, January 1985, *16*(1), pp. 24–29.   [G: U.S.]

Levin, David J. State and Local Government Fiscal Position in 1984. *Surv. Curr. Bus.*, January 1985, *65*(1), pp. 19–23.   [G: U.S.]

Sternlieb, George and Hughes, James W. The National Economy and the Northeast: A Context for Discussion. In *Richardson, H. W. and Turek, J. H., eds.*, 1985, pp. 66–84.   [G: U.S.]

Turek, Joseph H. The Northeast in a National Context: Background Trends in Population, Income, and Employment. In *Richardson, H. W. and Turek, J. H., eds.*, 1985, pp. 28–65.   [G: U.S.]

Yadav, Hanuman Singh. Real Income and Income Potential Surface in India. *Indian Econ. J.*, Apr.-June 1985, *32*(4), pp. 8–16.   [G: India]

229 Microdata and Database Analysis

2290 Microdata and Database Analysis

Goode, Frank M. The Use of Microdata to Measure Employment Changes in Small Communities. *J. Econ. Soc. Meas.*, July 1985, *13*(2), pp. 187–97.   [G: U.S.]

MacDonald, James M. Dun & Bradstreet Business Microdata: Research Applications, and the Detection and Correction of Errors. *J. Econ. Soc. Meas.*, July 1985, *13*(2), pp. 173–85.   [G: U.S.]

Wahlström, Staffan and Wallberg, Klas. Coordination of Statistics on Households and Families: The Case of Sweden. *Statist. J.*, March 1985, *3*(1), pp. 69–84.

300 Domestic Monetary and Fiscal Theory and Institutions

310 DOMESTIC MONETARY AND FINANCIAL THEORY AND INSTITUTIONS

3100 General

Amsler, Christine E. A Survey of Ten Money and Banking Textbooks. *J. Econ. Educ.*, Fall 1985, *16*(4), pp. 313–18.

Anderson, Dennis and Khambata, Farida. Financing Small-Scale Industry and Agriculture in Developing Countries: The Merits and Limitations of "Commercial" Policies. *Econ. Develop. Cult. Change*, January 1985, *33*(2), pp. 349–71.   [G: LDCs]

Bandyopadhyay, R. Finance and Development: An Integrative Framework. In *Bandyopadhyay, R. and Khankhoje, D. P., eds.*, 1985, pp. 21–40.

Capriglione, Francesco and Mezzacapo, Vincenzo. Evoluzione del sistema finanziario italiano e attività di "merchant banking"—II. (Evolution of the Italian Financial System and Merchant Banking Services—II. With English summary.) *Bancaria*, April 1985, *41*(4), pp. 419–37.   [G: Italy]

Díaz-Alejandro, Carlos F. Good-bye Financial Repression, Hello Financial Crash. *J. Devel. Econ.*, Sept.-Oct. 1985, *19*(1/2), pp. 1–24.
[G: Chile; Argentina; Uruguay]

Edwards, Sebastian and Khan, Mohsin S. Interest Rate Determination in Developing Countries: A Conceptual Framework. *Int. Monet. Fund Staff Pap.*, September 1985, *32*(3), pp. 377–403.   [G: Colombia; Singapore]

Germany, J. David and Morton, John E. Financial Innovation and Deregulation in Foreign Industrial Countries. *Fed. Res. Bull.*, October 1985, *71*(10), pp. 745–53.   [G: OECD]

Hall, Maximilian J. B. Financial Deregulation in Australia. *Nat. Westminster Bank Quart. Rev.*, August 1985, pp. 18–29.   [G: Australia]

Higgins, Robert C. Introduction to Japanese Finance: Markets, Institutions, and Firms. *J. Finan. Quant. Anal.*, June 1985, *20*(2), pp. 169–72.   [G: Japan]

Kindleberger, Charles P. Financial Institutions and Economic Development: A Comparison of Great Britain and France in the Eighteenth and Nineteenth Centuries. In *Kindleberger, C. P.*, 1985, pp. 65–85.   [G: U.K.; France]

Kindleberger, Charles P. The Functioning of Financial Centers: Britain in the Nineteenth Century, the United States since 1945. In *[Bloomfield, A. I.]*, 1985, pp. 7–18.
[G: U.K.; U.S.]

Landorová, Anděla. Improvement of the Monetary System of the CMEA Countries. *Czech. Econ. Digest.*, May 1985, (3), pp. 53–78.

Lér, Leopold. Forty Years of Building up a Socialist Financial System in the Czechoslovak Socialist Republic. *Czech. Econ. Digest.*, September 1985, (6), pp. 33–57.
[G: Czechoslovakia]

Melitz, Jacques. The French Financial System: Mechanism and Questions of Reform. In *Melitz, J. and Wyplosz, C., eds.*, 1985, pp. 361–86.   [G: France]

Millon, Marcia H. and Thakor, Anjan V. Moral Hazard and Information Sharing: A Model of Financial Information Gathering Agencies. *J. Finance*, December 1985, *40*(5), pp. 1403–22.

Moore, Craig L.; Karaska, Gerald J. and Hill, Joanne M. The Impact of the Banking System on Regional Analyses. *Reg. Stud.*, February 1985, *19*(1), pp. 29–35.   [G: U.S.]

Nepal Rastra Bank. The Role of Central Banks in Development Finance. In *Bandyopadhyay, R. and Khankhoje, D. P., eds.*, 1985, pp. 185–201.   [G: Nepal]

Roehl, Tom. Data Sources for Research in Japanese Finance. *J. Finan. Quant. Anal.*, June 1985, *20*(2), pp. 273–76.   [G: Japan]

Sarmiento, Eduardo. The Imperfections of the Capital Market. *Cepal Rev.*, December 1985, (27), pp. 97–116.   [G: Colombia]

Shapiro, Eli. The Financial System, Financial Regulation, and Financial Innovation. In *Shishido, T. and Sato, R., eds.*, 1985, pp. 287–98.   [G: U.S.]

Toniolo, Gianni. Intermediazione finanziaria e sviluppo economico in Giappone: nota sul periodo 1952–1972. (Financial Intermediation and Economic Growth in Japan: 1952–72. With English summary.) *Polit. Econ.*, August 1985, *1*(2), pp. 259–78.   [G: Japan]

Vaciaga, Giacomo. Financial Innovation and Monetary Policy: Italy *versus* the United States. *Banca Naz. Lavoro Quart. Rev.*, December 1985, (155), pp. 309–26.   [G: Italy; U.S.]

Van Horne, James C. Of Financial Innovations and Excesses. *J. Finance*, July 1985, *40*(3), pp. 621–31.   [G: U.S.]

Wellons, Philip A. Competitiveness in the World Economy: The Role of the U.S. Financial System. In *Scott, B. R. and Lodge, G. C., eds.*, 1985, pp. 357–94.   [G: U.S.; OECD]

311 Domestic Monetary and Financial Theory and Policy

3110 Domestic Monetary Theory and Policy

Ambler, Steven and McKinnon, Ronald I. U.S. Monetary Policy and the Exchange Rate: Comment [A Critical Appraisal of McKinnon's World Money Supply Hypothesis]. *Amer. Econ. Rev.*, June 1985, *75*(3), pp. 557–59.
[G: U.S.]

Atkinson, Paul and Chouraqui, Jean-Claude. The Origins of High Real Interest Rates. *OECD Econ. Stud.*, Autumn 1985, (5), pp. 7–55.
[G: OECD]

Axilrod, Stephen H. On Consequences and Criticisms of Monetary Targeting: Comment. *J. Money, Credit, Banking*, Pt. 2, Nov. 1985, *17*(4), pp. 598–602.   [G: U.S.]

Bergstrand, Jeffrey H. Exchange Rate Variation and Monetary Policy. *New Eng. Econ. Rev.*, May/June 1985, pp. 5–18.   [G: U.S.]

Bernholz, Peter. A Financial History of Western Europe: A Review. *Weltwirtsch. Arch.*, 1985, *121*(4), pp. 779–85.   [G: Europe]

Bohanon, Cecil E.; Lynch, Gerald J. and Van Cott, T. Norman. A Supply and Demand Exposition of the Operation of a Gold Standard in a Closed Economy. *J. Econ. Educ.*, Winter 1985, *16*(1), pp. 16–26.

Bouchal, Milan. Trends in Private Cash Holdings. *Czech. Econ. Digest.*, June 1985, (4), pp. 85–95.   [G: Czechoslovakia]

de Boyer, Jérôme. Circulation du revenu et circulation du capital: la distinction monnaie crédit chez Thomas Tooke. (Currency and Capital: The Distinction Established by Thomas Tooke between Money and Credit. With English summary.) *Revue Écon.*, May 1985, *36*(3), pp. 555–77.

Brunner, Karl. Monetary Policy and Monetary Order. In *[Weintraub, R. E.]*, 1985, pp. 4–21.

Cagan, Phillip and Dewald, William G. Monetary Policy in a Changing Financial Environment: Introduction. *J. Money, Credit, Banking*, Pt. 2, Nov. 1985, *17*(4), pp. 565–69.   [G: U.S.]

Cencini, Alvaro. La teoria quantica della produzione. (With English summary.) *Econ. Polít.*, August 1985, *2*(2), pp. 215–43.

Chandavarkar, Anand G. Keynes and Central Banking. *Indian Econ. Rev.*, July-Dec. 1985, *20*(2), pp. 283–97.

Cooper, Kathleen M. Will High Real Interest Rates Persist? *Bus. Econ.*, April 1985, *20*(2), pp. 12–18.   [G: U.S.]

Crawford, Peter. Interest Rate Outlook: Focus on Credit Supply. *Bus. Econ.*, July 1985, *20*(3), pp. 34–39.   [G: U.S.]

Crotty, James R. The Centrality of Money, Credit, and Financial Intermediation in Marx's Crisis Theory: An Interpretation of Marx's Methodology. In *[Magdoff, H. and Sweezy, P.]*, 1985, pp. 45–81.

Eichenbaum, Martin S. and Wallace, Neil. A Shred of Evidence on Public Acceptance of Privately Issued Currency. *Fed. Res. Bank Minn. Rev.*, Winter 1985, *9*(1), pp. 2–4.
[G: Canada]

Fernandez, Roque B. The Expectations Management Approach to Stabilization in Argentina during 1976–82. *World Devel.*, August 1985, *13*(8), pp. 871–92.   [G: Argentina]

Feroldi, Mathieu. Monetary Mechanisms and Exchange Rates in France. In *de Ménil, G. and Westphal, U., eds.*, 1985, pp. 227–62.
[G: France]

Forrest, George. A Positive Role for Credit in the Economic Recovery. In *Meyer, F. V., ed.*, 1985, pp. 63–82.   [G: U.K.]

Fratianni, Michele and Spinelli, Franco. Currency Competition, Fiscal Policy and the Money Supply Process in Italy from Unification to World War I. *J. Europ. Econ. Hist.*, Sept.-Dec. 1985, *14*(3), pp. 473–99.   [G: Italy]

Friedman, Benjamin M. Portfolio Choice and the Debt-to-Income Relationship. *Amer. Econ. Rev.*, May 1985, *75*(2), pp. 338–43.
[G: U.S.]

Friedman, Milton. Monetarism in Rhetoric and in Practice. In *Ando, A., et al., eds.*, 1985, pp. 15–28.   [G: U.S.]

Friedman, Milton. The Case for Overhauling the Federal Reserve. *Challenge*, July/August 1985, *28*(3), pp. 4–12.   [G: U.S.]

Fujita, Seiichi. A Critical Note on "Dollar Standard." *Kobe Univ. Econ.*, 1985, (31), pp. 69–91.   [G: U.S.]

Gedeon, Shirley J. Money and Banking in Yugoslavia: A Socialist Dilemma. *Rev. Radical Polit. Econ.*, Spring and Summer 1985, *17*(1/2), pp. 41–58.   [G: Yugoslavia]

Glassman, Debra and Redish, Angela. New Estimates of the Money Stock in France, 1493–1680. *J. Econ. Hist.*, March 1985, *45*(1), pp. 31–46.   [G: France]

Goldin, Ephraim. Statistical Analysis of Coins Lost in Circulation. *J. Bus. Econ. Statist.*, January 1985, *3*(1), pp. 36–42.   [G: Israel]

Goldstein, Henry N. and Haynes, Stephen E. U.S. Monetary Policy and the Exchange Rate: Reply [A Critical Appraisal of McKinnon's World Money Supply Hypothesis]. *Amer. Econ. Rev.*, June 1985, *75*(3), pp. 560–61.
[G: U.S.]

Goodhart, Charles A. E. Alternative Monetary Regimes. *Hong Kong Econ. Pap.*, 1985, (16), pp. 1–13.   [G: OECD]

Gorton, Gary. Banking Theory and Free Banking History: A Review Essay. *J. Monet. Econ.*, September 1985, *16*(2), pp. 267–76.
[G: U.K.]

Gregory, Allan W. and Raynauld, Jacques. An Econometric Model of Canadian Monetary Policy over the 1970s. *J. Money, Credit, Banking*, February 1985, *17*(1), pp. 43–58.
[G: Canada]

Hahn, Frank. On Transaction Costs, Inessential Sequence Economies and Money. In *Hahn, F.*, 1985, pp. 105–27.

Hamermesh, Daniel S. and Johannes, James M. Food Stamps as Money: The Macroeconomics of a Transfer Program. *J. Polit. Econ.*, February 1985, *93*(1), pp. 205–13.   [G: U.S.]

Hotson, John H. Professor Friedman's Goals Applauded, His Means Questioned. *Challenge*, Sept./Oct. 1985, *28*(4), pp. 59–61.   [G: U.S.]

Hsu, John C. Exchange Rate Management without a Central Bank: The Hong Kong Experience. *Hong Kong Econ. Pap.*, 1985, (16), pp. 14–26.   [G: Hong Kong]

Jones, Charles. The Fiscal Motive for Monetary and Banking Legislation in Argentina, Australia and Canada before 1914. In *Platt, D. C. M. and di Tella, G., eds.*, 1985, pp. 123–38.
[G: Argentina; Australia; Canada]

Kearney, Colm. Money and Monetary Control. In *Atkinson, G. B. J., ed.*, 1985, pp. 63–80.
[G: U.K.]

Kindleberger, Charles P. British Financial Reconstruction, 1815–22 and 1918–25. In *Kindleberger, C. P.*, 1985, pp. 105–18.   [G: U.K.]

Kindleberger, Charles P. The International Causes and Consequences of the Great Crash. In *Kindleberger, C. P.*, 1985, pp. 267–73.
[G: U.S.]

Kirchgässner, Gebhard. Die Schweiz im internationalen Zinszusammenhang. Eine zeitreihenanalytische Untersuchung für die Zeit von 1974 bis 1983. (Switzerland and the International Interest Rate Linkage: A Time Series Analysis for the Period from 1974 to 1983. With English summary.) *Schweiz. Z. Volkswirtsch. Statist.*, December 1985, *121*(4), pp. 329–51.
[G: Switzerland]

Kopcke, Richard W. Bank Funding Strategy and the Money Stock. *New Eng. Econ. Rev.*, January/February 1985, pp. 5–14.   [G: U.S.]

Kyriazis, Nicholas K. The Drachma's Adhesion to the European Monetary System. Possible Effects. *Kredit Kapital*, 1985, *18*(4), pp. 504–14.   [G: Greece]

Lamfalussy, Alexandre. Monetary Policy in Our Times: Concluding Comments. In *Ando, A., et al., eds.*, 1985, pp. 319–23.   [G: Global]

Lamfalussy, Alexandre. The Changing Environment of Central Bank Policy. *Amer. Econ. Rev.*, May 1985, *75*(2), pp. 409–13.

Mark, Nelson C. Some Evidence on the International Inequality of Real Interest Rates. *J. Int. Money Finance*, June 1985, *4*(2), pp. 189–208. [G: Selected OECD]

Masera, Francesco. Moneta, spesa pubblica e occupazione nel quadro dell'esperienza italiana. (Money, Government Expenditure and Employment in the Italian Experience. With English summary.) *Bancaria*, December 1985, *41*(12), pp. 1226–42. [G: Italy]

McCallum, Bennett T. On Consequences and Criticisms of Monetary Targeting. *J. Money, Credit, Banking*, Pt. 2, Nov. 1985, *17*(4), pp. 570–97. [G: U.S.]

Meigs, A. James. The Politics and Economics of Monetary Policy: Introduction. *Contemp. Policy Issues*, Fall 1985, *3*(5), pp. 33–34. [G: U.S.]

O'Driscoll, Gerald P., Jr. Money in a Deregulated Financial System. *Fed. Res. Bank Dallas Econ. Rev.*, May 1985, pp. 1–12. [G: U.S.]

O'Leary, James J. The Outlook for the Money and Capital Markets and for Interest Rates in 1985. *Bus. Econ.*, April 1985, *20*(2), pp. 24–30. [G: U.S.]

Olsen, Erling. Finansiel Know-How. (Financial Know-How. With English summary.) *Nationaløkon. Tidsskr.*, 1985, *123*(3), pp. 377–88.

Phelps, Edmund S. The Real Interest Rate Quiz. *Atlantic Econ. J.*, March 1985, *13*(1), pp. 1–4. [G: U.S.]

Pollin, Robert. Stability and Instability in the Debt–Income Relationship. *Amer. Econ. Rev.*, May 1985, *75*(2), pp. 344–50. [G: U.S.]

Poole, William. On Consequences and Criticisms of Monetary Targeting: Comment. *J. Money, Credit, Banking*, Pt. 2, Nov. 1985, *17*(4), pp. 602–05. [G: U.S.]

Schulze-Ghattas, Marianne and Westphal, Uwe. Monetary Mechanisms, Government Deficits, and External Constraints in Germany. In *de Ménil, G. and Westphal, U., eds.*, 1985, pp. 263–97. [G: W. Germany]

Segal, Harvey H. Money Markets against Governments: Two Centuries of a Spectacular Game. *Contemp. Policy Issues*, Fall 1985, *3*(5), pp. 35–41. [G: U.S.; Europe]

Street, James H. Monetarism and Beyond: The Dilemma of the Southern Cone Countries: A Review Article. *J. Econ. Issues*, December 1985, *19*(4), pp. 923–37. [G: Argentina; Chile; Uruguay]

Tatom, John A. Interest Rate Variability and Economic Performance: Further Evidence [The Effects on Output of Money Growth and Interest Rate Volatility in the United States]. *J. Polit. Econ.*, October 1985, *93*(5), pp. 1008–18. [G: U.S.]

Timme, Stephen G. and Eisemann, Peter C. The Impact of Same Day Settlement on the Variability of the Federal Funds Rate. *Quart. J. Bus. Econ.*, Winter 1985, *24*(1), pp. 61–74. [G: U.S.]

Tobin, James. On Consequences and Criticisms of Monetary Targeting, or *Monetary Targeting:*

Dead at Last? Comment. *J. Money, Credit, Banking*, Pt. 2, Nov. 1985, *17*(4), pp. 605–09. [G: U.S.]

Tryon, Ralph. The International Transmission of Inflation: A Review Essay. *J. Monet. Econ.*, November 1985, *16*(3), pp. 397–403.

Vaciago, Giacomo. Monetary Policy with Credit Targets: The Italian Experience. *Greek Econ. Rev.*, April 1985, *7*(1), pp. 1–33. [G: Italy]

Vercelli, Alessandro. Money and Production in Schumpeter and Keynes: Two Dichotomies. In *Arena, R., et al.*, 1985, pp. 31–45.

Wicker, Elmus. Colonial Monetary Standards Contrasted: Evidence from the Seven Years' War. *J. Econ. Hist.*, December 1985, *45*(4), pp. 869–84. [G: U.S.]

Zenger, Christoph. Zinssätze und Inflation in der Schweiz: Ein alternativer Test des Fisher-Effektes. (Interest Rates and Inflation in Switzerland: An Alternative Test of the Fisher-Effect. With English summary.) *Schweiz. Z. Volkswirtsch. Statist.*, December 1985, *121*(4), pp. 353–74. [G: Switzerland]

Zijlstra, Jelle. Monetary Theory and Monetary Policy: A Central Banker's View. In *Zijlstra, J.*, 1985, pp. 185–202.

3112 Monetary Theory; Empirical Studies Illustrating Theory

Abel, Andrew B. Dynamic Behavior of Capital Accumulation in a Cash-in-Advance Model. *J. Monet. Econ.*, July 1985, *16*(1), pp. 55–71.

Agbonyitor, Alberto D. K. Recurrent Expenditure Commitment, External Imbalance, Devaluation and Inflation in the Developing Economies. *J. Econ. Devel.*, December 1985, *10*(2), pp. 87–99. [G: LDCs]

Ahiakpor, James C. W. Ricardo on Money: The Operational Significance of the Non-neutrality of Money in the Short Run. *Hist. Polit. Econ.*, Spring 1985, *17*(1), pp. 17–30.

Ahking, Francis W. and Miller, Stephen M. The Relationship between Government Deficits, Money Growth, and Inflation. *J. Macroecon.*, Fall 1985, *7*(4), pp. 447–67. [G: U.S.]

Ahn, Chul Won and Jung, Woo S. The Choice of a Monetary Instrument in a Small Open Economy: The Case of Korea. *J. Int. Money Finance*, December 1985, *4*(4), pp. 469–84. [G: S. Korea]

Aiyagari, S. Rao. Deficits, Interest Rates, and the Tax Distribution. *Fed. Res. Bank Minn. Rev.*, Winter 1985, *9*(1), pp. 5–14.

Aiyagari, S. Rao and Gertler, Mark. The Backing of Government Bonds and Monetarism. *J. Monet. Econ.*, July 1985, *16*(1), pp. 19–44.

Aizenman, Joshua. Adjustment to Monetary Policy and Devaluation under Two-Tier and Fixed Exchange Rate Regimes. *J. Devel. Econ.*, May–June 1985, *18*(1), pp. 153–69.

Aizenman, Joshua. Openness, Relative Prices, and Macro-policies. *J. Int. Money Finance*, March 1985, *4*(1), pp. 5–17.

Aizenman, Joshua and Frenkel, Jacob A. Optimal Wage Indexation, Foreign Exchange Intervention, and Monetary Policy. *Amer. Econ. Rev.*, June 1985, *75*(3), pp. 402–23.

Akerlof, George A. and Yellen, Janet L. A Near-rational Model of the Business Cycle, with Wage and Price Intertia. *Quart. J. Econ.*, Supp. 1985, *100*, pp. 823–38.

Allais, Maurice. A New Empirical Approach of the Hereditary and Relativistic Theory of the Demand for Money: The Rate of Increase of Global Expenditure and the Velocity of Circulation of Money. *Rivista Int. Sci. Econ. Com.*, Oct.-Nov. 1985, *32*(10–11), pp. 905–48.
[G: U.S.; W. Germany]

Alogoskoufis, George S. Macroeconomic Policy and Aggregate Fluctuations in a Semi-industrialized Open Economy: Greece 1951–1980. *Europ. Econ. Rev.*, October 1985, *29*(1), pp. 35–61. [G: Greece]

Amsler, Christine E. What Determines Expected Real Interest Rates? *Quart. Rev. Econ. Bus.*, Winter 1985, *25*(4), pp. 59–67. [G: U.S.]

Andersen, Torben M. Uncoordinated Prices and Monetary Policy. *Revue Écon.*, November 1985, *36*(6), pp. 1247–70.

Ando, Albert. Coordination of Monetary and Fiscal Policies. In *Ando, A., et al., eds.,* 1985, pp. 253–89. [G: U.S.]

Angeloni, Ignazio and Galli, Giampaolo. The Interaction of Credit and Foreign Exchange Markets in a Stylized Model of the Italian Financial Sector. *Greek Econ. Rev.*, April 1985, *7*(1), pp. 53–70.

Aoki, Masanao. Monetary Reaction Functions in a Small Open Economy. *J. Econ. Dynam. Control,* September 1985, *9*(1), pp. 1–24.

Arak, Marcelle and Kreicher, Lawrence. The Real Rate of Interest: Inferences from the New U.K. Indexed Gilts. *Int. Econ. Rev.*, June 1985, *26*(2), pp. 399–408. [G: U.K.]

Argy, Victor E. The Design of Monetary and Fiscal Policy: Monetarism and Supply-Side Economics. In *Argy, V. E. and Neville, J. W., eds.,* 1985, pp. 60–77.

Argy, Victor E. and Murray, G. L. Effects of Sterilising a Balance of Payments Surplus on Domestic Yields—A Formal Analysis. *J. Int. Money Finance,* June 1985, *4*(2), pp. 223–36.

Arize, Augustine and Lott, Elizabeth J. A Reexamination of the Demand for Money in Nigeria. *Atlantic Econ. J.,* March 1985, *13*(1), pp. 27–35. [G: Nigeria]

Artis, Michael J. and Karakitsos, E. Monetary and Exchange Rate Targets in an Optimal Control Setting. In *Bhandari, J. S., ed.,* 1985, pp. 212–46.

Artus, Patrick. La politique monétaire en économie ouverte avec imparfaite mobilité des capitaux et réaction des autorités sur le marché des changes. (Monetary Policy in an Open Economy with Imperfect Capital Mobility and Central Bank Reaction on the Foreign Exchange Market. With English summary.) *Finance,* June 1985, *6*(1), pp. 71–101.

Artus, Patrick. Rationnement de crédit et réactions des entreprises. (Credit Rationing and

Firms' Reactions. With English summary.) *Revue Écon.*, November 1985, *36*(6), pp. 1207–46. [G: France]

Asimakopulos, Athanasios. Finance, Saving and Investment in Keynes's Economics: A Comment. *Cambridge J. Econ.,* December 1985, *9*(4), pp. 405–07.

Asimakopulos, Athanasios. The Role of Finance in Keynes's General Theory. *Econ. Notes,* 1985, (3), pp. 5–16.

d'Autume, Antoine and Michel, Philippe. Épargne, investissement et monnaie dans une perspective intertemporelle. (Saving, Investment, and Money in an Intertemporal Setting. With English summary.) *Revue Écon.*, March 1985, *36*(2), pp. 243–90.

Axilrod, Stephen H. Domestic Aspects of Monetary Policy: Comments. In *Ando, A., et al., eds.,* 1985, pp. 123–26. [G: Japan; U.S.]

Backus, David and Driffill, John. Policy Credibility and Unemployment in the U.K. In *Currie, D., ed.,* 1985, pp. 3–16. [G: U.K.]

Baglioni, Angelo. Alle origini dell'accondiscendenza monetaria verso l'inflazione. (At the Origins of Monetary Accommodation toward Inflation. With English summary.) *Giorn. Econ.,* Sept.-Oct. 1985, *44*(9–10), pp. 545–65.

Bain, A. D. and McGregor, Peter G. Buffer-Stock Monetarism and the Theory of Financial Buffers. *Manchester Sch. Econ. Soc. Stud.,* December 1985, *53*(4), pp. 385–403.

Balducci, Renato. É efficiente decentrare le decisioni di politica economica? (Are Decentralized Policies Efficient? With English summary.) *Polit. Econ.,* December 1985, *1*(3), pp. 399–428.

Baltensperger, Ernst and Devinney, Timothy M. Credit Rationing Theory: A Survey and Synthesis. *Z. ges. Staatswiss. (JITE),* December 1985, *141*(4), pp. 475–502.

Barrère, Alain. Economie réelle—Economie monétaire: alternative ou conciliation? (Real Economy—Monetary Economy: Option or Adjustment? With English summary.) *Écon. Appl.,* 1985, *38*(1), pp. 17–61.

Barrère, Christian. Prix réels et prix monétaires. (Real Prices and Monetary Prices. With English summary.) *Écon. Appl.,* 1985, *38*(1), pp. 265–97.

Barro, Robert J. Bank Deregulation, Accounting Systems of Exchange, and the Unit of Account: A Critical Review: A Comment. *Carnegie-Rochester Conf. Ser. Public Policy,* Autumn 1985, *23*, pp. 47–53.

Barro, Robert J. Federal Deficits, Interest Rates, and Monetary Policy: Comment. *J. Money, Credit, Banking,* Pt. 2, Nov. 1985, *17*(4), pp. 682–85. [G: U.S.]

Barth, James R.; Iden, George and Russek, Frank S. Federal Borrowing and Short Term Interest Rates: Comment. *Southern Econ. J.,* October 1985, *52*(2), pp. 554–59.

Bartmann, Hermann and John, Klaus-Dieter. Entscheidungen, Erwartungen und Kontrakte bei Unsicherheit. Eine postkeynesianische Sicht. (Decisions, Expectations and Contracts under Uncertainty: A Post-Keynesian View.

With English summary.) *Jahr. Nationalökon. Statist.*, May 1985, *200*(3), pp. 217–28.

Batten, Dallas S. and Hafer, R. W. Money, Income, and Currency Substitution: Evidence from Three Countries. *Fed. Res. Bank St. Louis Rev.*, May 1985, *67*(5), pp. 27–35.
[G: U.S.; W. Germany; Japan]

Batten, Dallas S. and Thornton, Daniel L. Are Weighted Monetary Aggregates Better than Simple-Sum M1? *Fed. Res. Bank St. Louis Rev.*, June/July 1985, *67*(6), pp. 29–40.
[G: U.S.]

Batten, Dallas S. and Thornton, Daniel L. The Andersen–Jordan Equation Revisited. *J. Macroecon.*, Summer 1985, *7*(3), pp. 419–32.
[G: U.S.]

Béguelin, Jean-Pierre and Schiltknecht, Kurt. Monetarism—A View from a Central Bank. In *Feiwel, G. R., ed. (I)*, 1985, pp. 324–32.

Bellofiore, Riccardo. Money and Development in Schumpeter. *Rev. Radical Polit. Econ.*, Spring and Summer 1985, *17*(1/2), pp. 21–40.

Benavie, Arthur. Monetary-Fiscal Policy under Rational Expectations in a Lucas–Rapping Macromodel. *Atlantic Econ. J.*, December 1985, *13*(4), pp. 1–9.

Benavie, Arthur and Froyen, Richard T. Optimal Monetary-Fiscal Stabilizers under an Indexed versus Nonindexed Tax Structure. *J. Econ. Bus.*, August 1985, *37*(3), pp. 197–208.

Benderly, Jason and Zwick, Burton. Inflation, Real Balances, Output, and Real Stock Returns [Stock Returns, Real Activity, Inflation, and Money]. *Amer. Econ. Rev.*, December 1985, *75*(5), pp. 1115–23. [G: U.S.]

Benetti, Carlo. Economie monétaire et économie de troc: la question de l'unité de compte commune. (Barter Economy and Monetary Economy: The Problem of the Single Standard of Value. With English summary.) *Écon. Appl.*, 1985, *38*(1), pp. 85–109.

Beranek, William; Humphrey, Thomas M. and Timberlake, Richard H., Jr. Fisher, Thornton, and the Analysis of the Inflation Premium: A Note. *J. Money, Credit, Banking*, August 1985, *17*(3), pp. 370–77.

Bester, Helmut. Screening vs. Rationing in Credit Markets with Imperfect Information. *Amer. Econ. Rev.*, September 1985, *75*(4), pp. 850–55.

Bester, Helmut. The Level of Investment in Credit Markets with Imperfect Information. *Z. ges. Staatswiss. (JITE)*, December 1985, *141*(4), pp. 503–15.

Bhaduri, Amit and Steindl, Josef. The Rise of Monetarism as a Social Doctrine. In *Arestis, P. and Skouras, T., eds.*, 1985, pp. 56–78.
[G: Selected Countries]

Bhattacharya, B. B. and Sharma, P. D. Relationship between Money and Price in India: Some Evidence from Bivariate Causality Tests. *J. Quant. Econ.*, July 1985, *1*(2), pp. 285–98.
[G: India]

Bini Smaghi, L. Dinamica dei tassi di cambio e interventi. (The Dynamics of Exchange Rates and Interventions. With English summary.)

Giorn. Econ., Nov.-Dec. 1985, *44*(11–12), pp. 619–38.

Blinder, Alan S. Federal Deficits, Interest Rates, and Monetary Policy: Comment. *J. Money, Credit, Banking*, Pt. 2, Nov. 1985, *17*(4), pp. 685–89.

Blomqvist, Ake G. An Analytical Approach to Interest Rate Determination in Developing Countries: Comments. *Pakistan Devel. Rev.*, Autumn-Winter 1985, *24*(3/4), pp. 494–95.
[G: Pakistan]

Boatler, Robert W. Determinants of Treasury Bill Auction Spreads: An Update with Evidence of Market Learning to Cope with Instability. *Quart. J. Bus. Econ.*, Winter 1985, *24*(1), pp. 36–42. [G: U.S.]

Boediono. Demand for Money in Indonesia, 1975–1984. *Bull. Indonesian Econ. Stud.*, August 1985, *21*(2), pp. 74–94.

de Boissieu, Christian. Eléments d'une analyse de la rigidité à la baisse des taux d'intérêt. (Elements for an Analysis of Downward Stickiness in Interest Rates. With English summary.) *Écon. Appl.*, 1985, *38*(1), pp. 193–209.
[G: U.S.]

Bomberger, William A. and Makinen, Gail E. Inflation Uncertainty and the Demand for Money in Hyperinflation. *Atlantic Econ. J.*, July 1985, *13*(2), pp. 12–20. [G: Europe]

Bootle, Roger P. The Economic System in the UK: Monetary Policy. In *Morris, D., ed.*, 1985, pp. 295–332. [G: U.K.]

Bordo, Michael David and Ellson, Richard Wayne. A Model of the Classical Gold Standard with Depletion. *J. Monet. Econ.*, July 1985, *16*(1), pp. 109–20.

Boschen, John F. Employment and Output Effects of Observed and Unobserved Monetary Growth. *J. Money, Credit, Banking*, May 1985, *17*(2), pp. 153–63. [G: U.S.]

de Bouissieu, Christian. Some Monetary and Financial Aspects of the Disinflation Process. *Z. Wirtschaft. Sozialwissen.*, 1985, *105*(2/3), pp. 133–53. [G: OECD]

de Boyer, Jérôme. Note sur la Theorie Monetaire de R. G. Hawtrey. (With English summary.) *Stud. Econ.*, 1985, *40*(25), pp. 3–27.

Bricall, Josep M. Sur la demande effective et la crise. (On Effective Demand and Crisis. With English summary.) *Écon. Soc.*, August 1985, *19*(8), pp. 99–116.

Brissimis, Sophocles N. and Leventakis, John A. Specification Tests of the Money Demand Function in an Open Economy. *Rev. Econ. Statist.*, August 1985, *67*(3), pp. 482–89.
[G: Greece]

Brocato, Joe. Persistence under Alternative Forms of the Lucas Supply Function: Implications for the Lucas–Sargent Price Confusion Hypothesis and Barro-Type Money Models. *Quart. Rev. Econ. Bus.*, Spring 1985, *25*(1), pp. 28–39. [G: U.S.]

Brunner, Karl and Meltzer, Allan H. The "New Monetary Economics," Fiscal Issues, and Unemployment. *Carnegie-Rochester Conf. Ser. Public Policy*, Autumn 1985, *23*, pp. 1–11.

Brunner, Karl and Meltzer, Allan H. Understanding Monetary Regimes. *Carnegie-Rochester Conf. Ser. Public Policy*, Spring 1985, *22*, pp. 1–7.

Bryant, John. A Clower Constraint Model of Unbacked Money. *J. Banking Finance*, June 1985, *9*(2), pp. 289–95.

Bryant, John. Analyzing Deficit Finance in a Regime of Unbacked Government Paper. *Fed. Res. Bank Dallas Econ. Rev.*, January 1985, pp. 17–27.

Bryant, John. Monetarist Objectives versus Monetarist Prescriptions. *Fed. Res. Bank Dallas Econ. Rev.*, November 1985, pp. 13–19.

Buiter, Willem H. and Eaton, Jonathan. Policy Decentralization and Exchange Rate Management in Interdependent Economies. In *Bhandari, J. S., ed.*, 1985, pp. 31–54.

Burbridge, John B. and Harrison, Alan. A Historical Decomposition of the Great Depression to Determine the Role of Money. *J. Monet. Econ.*, July 1985, *16*(1), pp. 45–54. [G: U.S.]

Burchardt, Michael. Die Banking–Currency-Kontroverse—Beitrag Nr. X. (The Banking–Currency Controversy—Essay No. X. With English summary.) *Kredit Kapital*, 1985, *18*(4), pp. 457–77.

Calvo, Guillermo A. Currency Substitution and the Real Exchange Rate: The Utility Maximization Approach. *J. Int. Money Finance*, June 1985, *4*(2), pp. 175–88.

Calvo, Guillermo A. Macroeconomic Implications of the Government Budget: Some Basic Considerations. *J. Monet. Econ.*, January 1985, *15*(1), pp. 95–112.

Canto, Victor A. Monetary Policy, 'Dollarization,' and Parallel Market Exchange Rates: The Case of the Dominican Republic. *J. Int. Money Finance*, December 1985, *4*(4), pp. 507–21. [G: Dominican Republic]

Canto, Victor A.; Findlay, M. C. and Reinganum, Marc R. Inflation, Money, and Stock Prices: An Alternative Interpretation. *Financial Rev.*, February 1985, *20*(1), pp. 95–101. [G: U.S.]

Canzoneri, Matthew B. Monetary Policy Games and the Role of Private Information. *Amer. Econ. Rev.*, December 1985, *75*(5), pp. 1056–70.

Canzoneri, Matthew B. and Gray, Jo Anna. Monetary Policy Games and the Consequences of Non-cooperative Behavior. *Int. Econ. Rev.*, October 1985, *26*(3), pp. 547–64.

Capie, Forrest H. and Rodrik-Bali, Ghila. The Money Adjustment Process in the United Kingdom, 1870-1914. *Economica*, February 1985, *52*(205), pp. 117–22. [G: U.K.]

Capitelli, René. Eine empirische Untersuchung über den Zusammenhang von kurz-, mittel- und langfristigen schweizerischen Zinssätzen. (Some Empirical Evidence on the Relationship between Short, Medium, and Long-term Swiss Interest Rates. With English summary.) *Schweiz. Z. Volkswirtsch. Statist.*, March 1985, *121*(1), pp. 1–22. [G: Switzerland]

Caranza, Cesare. International Aspects of Monetary Policy: Comments. In *Ando, A., et al., eds.*, 1985, pp. 223–24.

Carlozzi, Nicholas and Taylor, John B. International Capital Mobility and the Coordination of Monetary Rules. In *Bhandari, J. S., ed.*, 1985, pp. 186–211.

Carmichael, Jeffrey and Stebbing, Peter W. Fisher's Paradox: Reply [Fisher's Paradox and the Theory of Interest]. *Amer. Econ. Rev.*, June 1985, *75*(3), pp. 569–70.

Carr, Jack; Darby, Michael R. and Thornton, Daniel L. Monetary Anticipations and the Demand for Money: Reply [The Role of Money Supply Shocks in the Short Run Demand for Money]. *J. Monet. Econ.*, September 1985, *16*(2), pp. 251–57.

Cartelier, Jean. Théorie de la valeur ou hétérodoxie monétaire: les termes d'un choix. (Value Theory and Monetary Heterodoxy: The Crucial Choice. With English summary.) *Écon. Appl.*, 1985, *38*(1), pp. 63–82.

Cebula, Richard J. Money Multipliers and the Slopes of IS and LM: Comment. *Southern Econ. J.*, January 1985, *51*(3), pp. 906–08.

Cebula, Richard J. New Evidence on Financial Crowding Out. *Public Choice*, 1985, *46*(3), pp. 305–09. [G: U.S.]

Cencini, Alvaro. Moneta e produzione. (With English summary.) *Stud. Econ.*, 1985, *40*(25), pp. 105–29.

Cencini, Alvaro. Moneta e produzione: Replica. (With English summary.) *Stud. Econ.*, 1985, *40*(25), pp. 143–49.

Cerro, Ana María. Determinantes de la Tasa de interés: La Paradoja de Gibson y la Teoría de Fisher. (Interest Rate Determinants: The Gibson Paradox and Fisher's Theory. With English summary.) *Económica (La Plata)*, Jan.-Apr. 1985, *31*(1), pp. 21–56. [G: Argentina; Brazil; U.S.]

Chan, Yuk-Shee and Kanatas, George. Asymmetric Valuations and the Role of Collateral in Loan Agreements. *J. Money, Credit, Banking*, February 1985, *17*(1), pp. 84–95.

Chappell, Henry W., Jr. and Keech, William R. The Political Viability of Rule-based Monetary Policy. *Public Choice*, 1985, *46*(2), pp. 125–40. [G: U.S.]

Chevallier, François and Pollin, Jean-Paul. La transmission internationale des chocs monétaires en changes flexibles. (The International Transmission of Monetary Shocks into Flexible Changes. With English summary.) *Revue Écon.*, November 1985, *36*(6), pp. 1301–44.

Chick, Victoria. Keynesians, Monetarists and Keynes: The End of the Debate—or a Beginning? In *Arestis, P. and Skouras, T., eds.*, 1985, pp. 79–98.

Chotigeat, T. Sequential Auctions in Informal Credit and Savings Societies: Asian Auctions. *J. Econ. Devel.*, December 1985, *10*(2), pp. 67–85. [G: S. Asia]

Claassen, Emil-Maria and Wyplosz, Charles. Capital Controls: Some Principles and the French Experience. In *Melitz, J. and Wyplosz, C., eds.*, 1985, pp. 237–67. [G: France]

Clark, Larry R. Another Look at the Secondary Reserve Requirement as an Instrument of Monetary Policy. *Quart. Rev. Econ. Bus.*, Spring 1985, *25*(1), pp. 96–109. [G: Canada]

Clark, Simon J. The Effects of Government Expenditure on the Term Structure of Interest Rates: A Comment. *J. Money, Credit, Banking*, August 1985, *17*(3), pp. 397–400.

Cohen, Daniel. Inflation, Wealth and Interest Rates in an Intertemporal Optimizing Model. *J. Monet. Econ.*, July 1985, *16*(1), pp. 73–85.

Cooley, Thomas F. *Individual Forecasting and Aggregate Outcomes:* A Review Essay. *J. Monet. Econ.*, March 1985, *15*(2), pp. 255–66.

Cornell, Bradford. The Money Supply Announcements Puzzle: Reply. *Amer. Econ. Rev.*, June 1985, *75*(3), pp. 565–66.

Cornell, Bradford and Shapiro, Alan C. Interest Rates and Exchange Rates: Some New Empirical Results. *J. Int. Money Finance*, December 1985, *4*(4), pp. 431–42. [G: U.S.]

Cosimano, Thomas F. Erratic Monetary Policy and Price Variability. *J. Macroecon.*, Summer 1985, *7*(3), pp. 313–31.

Costabile, Lilia. Credit Creation, Capital Formation and Abstinence in the Approach of D. H. Robertson. In *Arena, R., et al.*, 1985, pp. 265–86.

Currie, David. Macroeconomic Policy Design and Control Theory—A Failed Partnership? *Econ. J.*, June 1985, *95*(378), pp. 285–306. [G: U.K.]

Dadkhah, Kamran M. and Mookerjee, Rajen. Evolution of the Currency Deposit Ratio in the Process of Economic Development. *Indian Econ. J.*, July-Sept. 1985, *33*(1), pp. 1–12. [G: India; Iran]

Daniel, Betty C. Monetary Autonomy and Exchange Rate Dynamics under Currency Substitution. *J. Int. Econ.*, August 1985, *19*(1/2), pp. 119–39.

Daniel, Betty C. Optimal Foreign Exchange-Rate Policy for a Small Open Economy. *J. Int. Money Finance*, December 1985, *4*(4), pp. 523–36.

Darby, Michael R. Monetary Policy in the Large Open Economy. In *Ando, A., et al., eds.*, 1985, pp. 143–67. [G: OECD]

Darrat, Ali F. Anticipated versus Unanticipated Monetary Policy and Real Output in West Germany. *Amer. Econ.*, Spring 1985, *29*(1), pp. 73–77. [G: W. Germany]

Darrat, Ali F. Anticipated Money and Real Output in Italy: Some Tests of a Rational Expectations Approach. *J. Post Keynesian Econ.*, Fall 1985, *8*(1), pp. 81–90. [G: Italy]

Darrat, Ali F. Does Anticipated Monetary Policy Matter? The Canadian Evidence. *Atlantic Econ. J.*, March 1985, *13*(1), pp. 19–26. [G: Canada]

Darrat, Ali F. Inflationary Expectations and Interest Rates à'la Patinkin's General Equilibrium Model. *Amer. Econ.*, Fall 1985, *29*(2), pp. 55–56.

Darrat, Ali F. Inflationary Surprises and Real Economic Activity in Germany: Some Tests Based on 'Efficient Market' Expectations. *Kredit Kapital*, 1985, *18*(2), pp. 230–39. [G: W. Germany]

Darrat, Ali F. Money Demand in Saudi Arabia: An Exchange of Views: The Money Demand Relationship in Saudi Arabia: An Empirical Investigation: Reply. *J. Econ. Stud.*, 1985, *12*(5), pp. 65–67. [G: Saudi Arabia]

Darrat, Ali F. Money Demand in Saudi Arabia: An Exchange of Views: The Money Demand Relationship in Saudi Arabia: An Empirical Investigation: Rejoinder. *J. Econ. Stud.*, 1985, *12*(5), pp. 71. [G: Saudi Arabia]

Darrat, Ali F. The Demand for Money in a Developing Economy: The Case of Kenya. *World Devel.*, Oct./Nov. 1985, *13*(10/11), pp. 1163–70. [G: Kenya]

Darrat, Ali F. The Demand for Money in Brazil: Some Further Results. *J. Devel. Econ.*, August 1985, *18*(2–3), pp. 485–91. [G: Cardosa; Brazil]

Darrat, Ali F. The Monetarist versus the New Classical Economics and the Money Unemployment Linkage: Some European Evidence. *Quart. J. Bus. Econ.*, Summer 1985, *24*(3), pp. 78–91. [G: U.K.; Italy; W. Germany]

Darrat, Ali F. The Monetary Explanation of Inflation: The Experience of Three Major OPEC Economies. *J. Econ. Bus.*, August 1985, *37*(3), pp. 209–21. [G: Libya; Nigeria; Saudi Arabia]

Davidson, Lawrence S. and Hafer, R. W. Relative Price Variability: Evidence from Supply and Demand Events. *J. Monet. Econ.*, May 1985, *15*(3), pp. 333–41. [G: U.S.]

Davis, Richard G. Policies to Overcome Stagflation: Comments. In *Ando, A., et al., eds.*, 1985, pp. 295–98. [G: U.S.]

Dawson, Alistair. Comment upon a New-Classical Model of the Postwar UK. *Appl. Econ.*, April 1985, *17*(2), pp. 257–61. [G: U.K.]

Day, Theodore E. Expected Inflation and the Real Rate of Interest. *J. Banking Finance*, December 1985, *9*(4), pp. 491–98.

De Grauwe, Paul. Capital Controls: Some Principles and the French Experience: Comments. In *Melitz, J. and Wyplosz, C., eds.*, 1985, pp. 269–73. [G: France]

Delbono, Flavio. Equazioni fondamentali e teoria quantitativa nel "Treatise on Money" di J. M. Keynes: Una nota. (With English summary.) *Stud. Econ.*, 1985, *40*(26), pp. 65–85.

Delbono, Flavio. On the Determination of Effective Demands in Benassy's Model. *Econ. Notes*, 1985, (3), pp. 115–20.

Deleplace, Ghislain. Sur quelques difficultés de la théorie de la monnaie-marchandise chez Ricardo et Marx. (Some Problems in the Theory of Commodity Money by Ricardo and Marx. With English summary.) *Écon. Appl.*, 1985, *38*(1), pp. 111–31.

Do, Toan Q. and Chateau, John Peter B. A Geometrical Exposition of the Credit Setting Strategies of the Banking Firm under Loan Rate Uncertainty. *Finance*, June 1985, *6*(1), pp. 103–19.

Dotsey, Michael. Is There an Operational Interest Rate Rule? *Amer. Econ. Rev.*, June 1985, 75(3), pp. 552–56.

Doukas, John. The Rationality of Money Supply Expectations and the Canadian-U.S. Exchange Rate Response to Money Supply Announcements. *Financial Rev.*, May 1985, 20(2), pp. 180–94. **[G: U.S.]**

Drazen, Allan. Tight Money and Inflation: Further Results. *J. Monet. Econ.*, January 1985, 15(1), pp. 113–20.

Dreizzen, Julio. Fragilidad financiera y sistemas de crédito indexado. (With English summary.) *Desarrollo Econ.*, April–June 1985, 25(97), pp. 3–24.

Driscoll, Michael J.; Ford, J. L. and Mullineux, A. W. The Elasticity of Prices with Respect to Monetary Components: Some Estimates for the UK, 1948–1979. *Appl. Econ.*, February 1985, 17(1), pp. 95–106. **[G: U.K.]**

Driscoll, Michael J.; Mullineux, A. W. and Sen, Somnath. Testing the Rational Expectations and Structural Neutrality Hypotheses: Some Further Results for the U.K. *Empirical Econ.*, 1985, 10(1), pp. 51–58. **[G: U.K.]**

Driscoll, Michael J., et al. Monetary Aggregates, Their Information Content, and Their Aggregation Error: Some Preliminary Findings for Austria, 1965–1980. *Empirical Econ.*, 1985, 10(1), pp. 13–25. **[G: Austria]**

Driskill, Robert and Sheffrin, Steven M. The "Patman Effect" and Stabilization Policy. *Quart. J. Econ.*, February 1985, 100(1), pp. 149–63.

Dudler, Hermann-Josef. The Conduct of Domestic Monetary Policy: Comments. In *Ando, A., et al., eds.*, 1985, pp. 127–29. **[G: U.S.]**

Dufour, Jean-Marie; Gaudry, Marc J. I. and Hafer, R. W. Corrigendum [A Warning on the Use of the Cochrane–Orcutt Procedure Based on a Money Demand Equation]. *Empirical Econ.*, 1985, 10(4), pp. 275. **[G: U.S.]**

Dutkowsky, Donald and Foote, William. Switching, Aggregation, and the Demand for Borrowed Reserves. *Rev. Econ. Statist.*, May 1985, 67(2), pp. 331–35. **[G: U.S.]**

Dwyer, Gerald P., Jr. Federal Deficits, Interest Rates, and Monetary Policy. *J. Money, Credit, Banking*, Pt. 2, Nov. 1985, 17(4), pp. 655–81. **[G: U.S.]**

Dwyer, Gerald P., Jr. Money, Deficits, and Inflation: A Comment. *Carnegie-Rochester Conf. Ser. Public Policy*, Spring 1985, 22, pp. 197–205. **[G: U.S.]**

Dwyer, Gerald P., Jr. Money, Income, and Prices in the United Kingdom: 1870–1913. *Econ. Inquiry*, July 1985, 23(3), pp. 415–35. **[G: U.S.]**

Eaton, Jonathan. Optimal and Time Consistent Exchange-Rate Management in an Overlapping-Generations Economy. *J. Int. Money Finance*, March 1985, 4(1), pp. 83–100.

Edwards, J. R. Effective Demand Failure: Critique of an Anti-monetary Theory. *S. Afr. J. Econ.*, June 1985, 53(2), pp. 124–40.

Edwards, Sebastian. Money, the Rate of Devaluation, and Interest Rates in a Semiopen Economy: Colombia, 1968–82. *J. Money, Credit, Banking*, February 1985, 17(1), pp. 59–68. **[G: Colombia]**

Edwards, Sebastian and Khan, Mohsin S. Interest Rate Determination in Developing Countries: A Conceptual Framework. *Int. Monet. Fund Staff Pap.*, September 1985, 32(3), pp. 377–403. **[G: Colombia; Singapore]**

Edwards, Sebastian and Khan, Mohsin S. Interest Rates in Developing Countries. *Finance Develop.*, June 1985, 22(2), pp. 28–31. **[G: LDCs]**

Eichenbaum, Martin S. Vector Autoregressions for Causal Inference? Comment. *Carnegie-Rochester Conf. Ser. Public Policy*, Spring 1985, 22, pp. 305–18.

Eichner, Alfred S. The Demand Curve for Money Further Considered. In *Eichner, A. S.*, 1985, pp. 98–112. **[G: U.S.]**

Engels, Wolfram. The Competitive Creation of Money: State-defined Currency and Free Issue of Banknotes. *Z. Wirtschaft. Sozialwissen.*, 1985, 105(5), pp. 589–601.

Engle, Charles. Reliability of Policy Announcements and the Effects of Monetary Policy. *Europ. Econ. Rev.*, November 1985, 29(2), pp. 137–55.

Esposito, Gaetano Fausto. Moneta e monetarismo. (With English summary.) *Stud. Econ.*, 1985, 40(26), pp. 149–59.

Evans, Paul. Do Large Deficits Produce High Interest Rates? *Amer. Econ. Rev.*, March 1985, 75(1), pp. 68–87. **[G: U.S.]**

Evans, Paul. Money, Output and Goodhart's Law: The U.S. Experience. *Rev. Econ. Statist.*, February 1985, 67(1), pp. 1–8. **[G: U.S.]**

Ewis, Nabil A. and Fisher, Douglas. Toward a Consistent Estimate of the Demand for Monies: An Application of the Fourier Flexible Form. *J. Macroecon.*, Spring 1985, 7(2), pp. 151–74. **[G: U.S.]**

Fackler, James S. An Empirical Analysis of the Markets for Goods, Money, and Credit. *J. Money, Credit, Banking*, February 1985, 17(1), pp. 28–42. **[G: U.S.]**

Fadil, Farah. Money Demand in Saudi Arabia: An Exchange of Views: Saudi Arabia's Money Demand Function: A Further Comment. *J. Econ. Stud.*, 1985, 12(5), pp. 67–70. **[G: Saudi Arabia]**

Fadil, Farah. Money Demand in Saudi Arabia: An Exchange of Views: GNP as a Variable for the Demand for Money in Small Oil Economies: A Comment. *J. Econ. Stud.*, 1985, 12(5), pp. 62–64. **[G: Saudi Arabia]**

Falk, Barry and Orazem, Peter F. The Money Supply Announcements Puzzle: Comment. *Amer. Econ. Rev.*, June 1985, 75(3), pp. 562–64.

Falls, Gregory A. and Hill, James Richard. Monetary Policy and Causality. *Atlantic Econ. J.*, December 1985, 13(4), pp. 10–18. **[G: U.S.]**

Fama, Eugene F. What's Different about Banks? *J. Monet. Econ.*, January 1985, 15(1), pp. 29–39. **[G: U.S.]**

Farina, Francesco. Keynes' Theory of Interest

and Modern Monetary Analysis. In *Arena, R., et al.*, 1985, pp. 101–21.

Ferguson, J. David and Hart, William R. The Implications of Spillover for the Design of Monetary Policy: An Empirical Analysis of Income and Price Determination in Nonclearing Markets. *Amer. Econ. Rev.*, December 1985, 75(5), pp. 1133–42. **[G: U.S.]**

Ferrante, Vittorio E. La teoria di Keynes del deporto normale e l'assunzione di preferenza per la liquidità. (With English summary.) *Econ. Polit.*, April 1985, 2(1), pp. 81–94.

Fethke, Gary. The Conformity of Wage-Indexation Models with "Stylized Facts." *Amer. Econ. Rev.*, September 1985, 75(4), pp. 856–61. **[G: Canada; W. Germany; Japan; U.K.; U.S.]**

Fine, Ben. Banking Capital and the Theory of Interest. *Sci. Soc.*, Winter 1985-1986, 49(4), pp. 387–413.

Fischer, Stanley. Contracts, Credibility and Disinflation. In *Argy, V. E. and Neville, J. W., eds.*, 1985, pp. 39–59. **[G: U.S.]**

Fischer, Stanley. Supply Shocks, Wage Stickiness, and Accommodation. *J. Money, Credit, Banking*, February 1985, 17(1), pp. 1–15.

Flood, Robert P. and Hodrick, Robert J. Central Bank Intervention in a Rational Open Economy: A Model with Asymmetric Information. In *Bhandari, J. S., ed.*, 1985, pp. 154–85.

Frankel, Jeffrey A. The Dazzling Dollar. *Brookings Pap. Econ. Act.*, 1985, (1), pp. 199–217. **[G: U.S.]**

Frankel, Jeffrey A. and Hardouvelis, Gikas A. Commodity Prices, Money Surprises and Fed Credibility. *J. Money, Credit, Banking*, Part 1, Nov. 1985, 17(4), pp. 425–38. **[G: U.S.]**

Freeman, Scott. Transactions Costs and the Optimal Quantity of Money. *J. Polit. Econ.*, February 1985, 93(1), pp. 146–57.

Frenkel, Jeffrey A. Monetary Targets, Real Exchange Rates and Macroeconomic Stability. *Europ. Econ. Rev.*, June-July 1985, 28(1–2), pp. 151–52. **[G: Spain]**

Fuggetta, Massimo. L'inflazione in una economia di puro credito: commento. *Stud. Econ.*, 1985, 40(26), pp. 127–32.

Fukiharu, Toshitaka. Static Macroeconomics from the Neoclassical Viewpoint. *Kobe Univ. Econ.*, 1985, (31), pp. 33–52.

Gahvari, Firouz. A Note on Inflation, Taxation, and Interest Rates [The Financial and Tax Effects of Monetary Policy on Interest Rates]. *Southern Econ. J.*, January 1985, 51(3), pp. 874–79.

Galli, Giampaolo. International Coordination in the Design of Macroeconomic Policies: Comment. *Europ. Econ. Rev.*, June-July 1985, 28(1–2), pp. 83–87. **[G: OECD]**

Gedeon, Shirley J. A Comment on and Extension of Lavoie's "The Endogenous Flow of Credit and the Post Keynesian Theory of Money." *J. Econ. Issues*, September 1985, 19(3), pp. 837–43.

Gerlach, Stefan and Nadal de Simone, Francisco. A Money Demand Equation for Brazil: Com-

ments and Additional Evidence. *J. Devel. Econ.*, August 1985, 18(2–3), pp. 493–501. **[G: Brazil]**

Ghosh, Dilip K. and Elyasiani, Elyas. Money Multipliers and the Slopes of IS-LM: Comment. *Southern Econ. J.*, January 1985, 51(3), pp. 909–15.

Ghosh, Madhusudan. Transaction Costs, Mean-Variance Approach and Liquidity Trap. *Indian Econ. J.*, July-Sept. 1985, 33(1), pp. 85–91.

Giannola, A. Some Notes on Income Distribution, Activity Levels and the Structure of Interest Rates in a Pure Credit Economy. In *Arena, R., et al.*, 1985, pp. 179–90.

Giavazzi, Francesco and Giovannini, Alberto. Tassi di cambio manovrati e politica monetaria. (Monetary Policy in a System of Managed Exchange Rates. With English summary.) *Giorn. Econ.*, Mar.-Apr. 1985, 44(3–4), pp. 117–33.

Giovannini, Alberto. Saving and the Real Interest Rate in LDCs. *J. Devel. Econ.*, August 1985, 18(2–3), pp. 197–217. **[G: LDCs]**

Girton, Lance and Nattress, Dayle. Monetary Innovations and Interest Rates. *J. Money, Credit, Banking*, August 1985, 17(3), pp. 289–97. **[G: U.S.]**

Glasner, David. A Reinterpretation of Classical Monetary Theory. *Southern Econ. J.*, July 1985, 52(1), pp. 46–67.

Goedhart, C. Zijlstra's Concerto Grosso: *Fourteen Annual Reports: Themes and Variations (1967–1980).* In *Zijlstra, J.*, 1985, pp. 3–31.

Goldberg, Michael A. The Relevance of Margin Regulations: A Note. *J. Money, Credit, Banking*, Part 1, Nov. 1985, 17(4), pp. 521–27.

Goodfriend, Marvin. *Monetary Theory and Practice, The U.K. Experience:* Book Review. *J. Monet. Econ.*, May 1985, 15(3), pp. 383–88. **[G: U.K.]**

Goodfriend, Marvin. Reinterpreting Money Demand Regressions: Errata. *Carnegie-Rochester Conf. Ser. Public Policy*, Autumn 1985, 23, pp. 211–12.

Goodfriend, Marvin. Reinterpreting Money Demand Regressions. *Carnegie-Rochester Conf. Ser. Public Policy*, Spring 1985, 22, pp. 207–41.

Goodhart, Charles A. E. Monetary Policy in Postwar Japan: Comments. In *Ando, A., et al., eds.*, 1985, pp. 131–33. **[G: Japan]**

Goodhart, Charles A. E. and Smith, Richard G. The Impact of News on Financial Markets in the United Kingdom: A Note. *J. Money, Credit, Banking*, Part 1, Nov. 1985, 17(4), pp. 507–11. **[G: U.K.]**

Gordon, Robert J. The Conduct of Domestic Monetary Policy. In *Ando, A., et al., eds.*, 1985, pp. 45–81. **[G: U.S.]**

Gorres, Peter Anselm. Die Ausschüttung der Notenbankgewinne an den Bund—weder "free lunch" noch unsittlicher Griff in die Ladenkasse. (On the Distribution of Central Bank Profits to the Federal Government: Free Lunch or Act of Piracy. With English summary.) *Jahr. Nationalökon. Statist.*, July 1985, 200(4), pp. 381–400. **[G: W. Germany]**

Gorton, Gary. Bank Suspension of Convertibility. *J. Monet. Econ.*, March 1985, *15*(2), pp. 177–93.

Gottlieb, Daniel; Melnick, Rafi and Piterman, Sylvia. Inflationary Expectations in Israel: A Multiple Indicators Approach. *J. Bus. Econ. Statist.*, April 1985, *3*(2), pp. 112–17.
[G: Israel]

Grandmont, Jean-Michel. On Endogenous Competitive Business Cycles. *Econometrica*, September 1985, *53*(5), pp. 995–1045.

Granziol, Markus J. Direct Price Controls as a Source of Instability in the Interest Rate/Inflation Rate Relationship. *J. Banking Finance*, June 1985, *9*(2), pp. 275–88. [G: U.S.; Canada; France]

Graziani, Augusto. L'inflazione in una economia di puro credito: Replica. *Stud. Econ.*, 1985, *40*(26), pp. 133–34.

Graziani, Augusto. Le débat sur le "motif de financement" de J. M. Keynes. (The Debate on Keynes's Financing Motive." With English summary.) *Écon. Appl.*, 1985, *38*(1), pp. 159–75.

Graziani, Augusto. Moneta e produzione: Commento. (With English summary.) *Stud. Econ.*, 1985, *40*(25), pp. 131–42.

Graziani, Augusto. Monnaie, intérêt dépense publique. (Money, Interest and Government Spending. With English summary.) *Écon. Soc.*, August 1985, *19*(8), pp. 209–27.

Gregory, Allan W. Testing Nested Functional Forms of Money Demand for Canada. *J. Quant. Econ.*, July 1985, *1*(2), pp. 211–30.
[G: Canada]

Gregory, Allan W. and Veall, Michael R. A Lagrange Multiplier Test of the Restrictions for a Simple Rational Expectations Model. *Can. J. Econ.*, February 1985, *18*(1), pp. 94–105.
[G: Canada]

Grellet, Gérard. La monnaie est-elle à l'origine du chômage? (Is Money Generating Unemployment? With English summary.) *Écon. Appl.*, 1985, *38*(1), pp. 301–08.

Guido, Vinicio. Sull'esistenza dell'equilibrio temporaneo in economie monetarie con produzione. (With English summary.) *Econ. Polít.*, December 1985, *2*(3), pp. 403–20.

Guiso, Luigi. Crowding-out and Rational Expectations. *Giorn. Econ.*, May-June 1985, *44*(5–6), pp. 239–57.

Gupta, Kanhaya L. Money and the Bias of Technical Progress. *Appl. Econ.*, February 1985, *17*(1), pp. 87–93. [G: India]

Haavisto, Esko and Tarkka, Juha. Pankkiluottojen korkoporrastus keskikorkosäännöstelyn vallitessa. (Setting the Interest Rates on Bank Loans When the Average Lending Rate Is Regulated. With English summary.) *Liiketaloudellinen Aikak.*, 1985, *34*(3), pp. 272–83.

Haberler, Gottfried. Critical Notes on Schumpeter's Theory of Money—The Doctrine of the "Objective" Exchange Value of Money. In *Haberler, G.*, 1985, pp. 531–52.

Haberler, Gottfried. Schumpeter's Theory of Interest. In *Haberler, G.*, 1985, pp. 561–72.

Hafer, R. W. Choosing between M1 and Debt as an Intermediate Target for Monetary Control. *Carnegie-Rochester Conf. Ser. Public Policy*, Spring 1985, *22*, pp. 89–132. [G: U.S.]

Hafer, R. W. Monetary Stabilization Policy: Evidence from Money Demand Forecasts. *Fed. Res. Bank St. Louis Rev.*, May 1985, *67*(5), pp. 21–16. [G: U.S.]

Hafer, R. W. Money Demand Predictability: Comment. *J. Money, Credit, Banking*, Pt. 2, Nov. 1985, *17*(4), pp. 642–46. [G: U.S.]

Hafer, R. W. The Stability of the Short-run Money Demand Function, 1920–1939. *Exploration Econ. Hist.*, July 1985, *22*(3), pp. 271–95. [G: U.S.]

Hahn, Frank. Money and General Equilibrium. In *Hahn, F.*, 1985, pp. 31–45.

Hahn, Frank. Some Keynesian Reflections on Monetarism. In *Vicarelli, F., ed.*, 1985, pp. 1–20.

Hahn, Frank. The General Equilibrium Theory of Money: A Comment. In *Hahn, F.*, 1985, pp. 46–55.

Hahn, Frank. The Rate of Interest and General Equilibrium Analysis. In *Hahn, F.*, 1985, pp. 56–74.

Hamada, Koichi. Lessons from the Macroeconomic Performance of the Japanese Economy. In *Argy, V. E. and Neville, J. W., eds.*, 1985, pp. 181–99. [G: Japan]

Hamada, Koichi and Hayashi, Fumio. Monetary Policy in Postwar Japan. In *Ando, A., et al., eds.*, 1985, pp. 83–121. [G: Japan]

Hamouda, Omar F. The Evolution of Hicks' Theory of Money. *Bull. Econ. Res.*, May 1985, *37*(2), pp. 131–51.

Hancock, Diana. Bank Profitability, Interest Rates, and Monetary Policy. *J. Money, Credit, Banking*, May 1985, *17*(2), pp. 189–202.
[G: U.S.]

Hancock, Diana. The Financial Firm: Production with Monetary and Nonmonetary Goods. *J. Polit. Econ.*, October 1985, *93*(5), pp. 859–80.
[G: U.S.]

Handler, Heinz. Capital Mobility versus Sterilization Policy: A Time Series Approach for Austria. *Empirica*, 1985, *12*(2), pp. 163–90.
[G: Austria]

Haque, M. Badrul. Monetary Policy and Its Effects on Inflation. *Revue Écon.*, November 1985, *36*(6), pp. 1271–99.

Hardouvelis, Gikas A. Exchange Rates, Interest Rates, and Money-Stock Announcements: A Theoretical Exposition. *J. Int. Money Finance*, December 1985, *4*(4), pp. 443–54. [G: U.S.]

Hartman, Richard. Uncertainty in Future Government Spending and Investment. *Quart. J. Econ.*, November 1985, *100*(4), pp. 1339–47.

Hegji, Charles E. The Behavior of Market Interest Rates When Information Is Incomplete. *Atlantic Econ. J.*, December 1985, *13*(4), pp. 19–25.

Hein, Scott E. The Response of Short-term Interest Rates to Weekly Money Announcements: A Comment. *J. Money, Credit, Banking*, May 1985, *17*(2), pp. 264–71. [G: U.S.]

Heinsohn, Gunnar and Steiger, Otto. Technical Progress and Monetary Production: An Explanation. *Écon. Soc.*, August 1985, *19*(8), pp. 85–98.

Hellwig, Martin F. What Do We Know about Currency Competition? *Z. Wirtschaft. Sozialwissen.*, 1985, *105*(5), pp. 565–88.

Hendry, David F. Monetary Economic Myth and Econometric Reality. *Oxford Rev. Econ. Policy*, Spring 1985, *1*(1), pp. 72–84.

Heri, Erwin W. The Short-run Demand for Money in Germany: Some Caveats for Empirical Work. *Weltwirtsch. Arch.*, 1985, *121*(3), pp. 524–40. [G: W. Germany]

Heyman, Matthew D. The Controllability of the Money Supply. *Amer. Econ.*, Fall 1985, *29*(2), pp. 42–48. [G: U.S.]

Hillier, Brian. Rational Expectations, the Government Budget Constraint, and the Optimal Money Supply. *J. Macroecon.*, Winter 1985, *7*(1), pp. 39–50.

Ho, Thomas S. Y. and Saunders, Anthony. A Micro Model of the Federal Funds Market. *J. Finance*, July 1985, *40*(3), pp. 977–88.

Hoelscher, Gregory P. Federal Borrowing and Short Term Interest Rates: Reply. *Southern Econ. J.*, October 1985, *52*(2), pp. 560–61.

Hoffman, Dennis L. and Schlagenhauf, Don E. Real Interest Rates, Anticipated Inflation, and Unanticipated Money: A Multi-country Study. *Rev. Econ. Statist.*, May 1985, *67*(2), pp. 284–96. [G: U.K.; W. Germany; Canada; U.S.]

Holland, A. Steven. Rational Expectations and the Effects of Monetary Policy: A Guide for the Uninitiated. *Fed. Res. Bank St. Louis Rev.*, May 1985, *67*(5), pp. 5–11.

Hong, Kyttack. Macroeconomic Dynamics in a Financially Repressed Economy. *J. Econ. Devel.*, July 1985, *10*(1), pp. 169–94. [G: LDCs]

Honohan, Patrick. Fisher's Paradox: Comment [Fisher's Paradox and the Theory of Interest]. *Amer. Econ. Rev.*, June 1985, *75*(3), pp. 567–68.

Hörngren, Lars. Regulatory Monetary Policy and Uncontrolled Financial Intermediaries. *J. Money, Credit, Banking*, May 1985, *17*(2), pp. 203–19.

Hosek, William R. and Zahn, Frank. An Alternative Approach to the Estimation of the Real Rate of Interest. *J. Macroecon.*, Spring 1985, *7*(2), pp. 211–22. [G: U.S.]

Husted, Steven and Kitchen, John. Some Evidence on the International Transmission of U.S. Money Supply Announcement Effects. *J. Money, Credit, Banking*, Part 1, Nov. 1985, *17*(4), pp. 456–66. [G: U.S.; Canada; W. Germany]

Hwang, Hae-shin. Test of the Adjustment Process and Linear Homogeneity in a Stock Adjustment Model of Money Demand. *Rev. Econ. Statist.*, November 1985, *67*(4), pp. 689–92. [G: U.S.]

Hwang, Hae-shin. The Term Structure of Interest Rates in Money Demand: A Reevaluation: A

Note. *J. Money, Credit, Banking*, August 1985, *17*(3), pp. 391–96. [G: U.S.]

Imam, M. Hasan. The Welfare Cost of Interest Rate Ceilings in Developing Countries: A General Equilibrium Approach. In *Piggott, J. and Whalley, J., eds.*, 1985, pp. 371–95. [G: India]

Issing, Otmar. Optimale Währung und Zins. (With English summary.) *Z. Wirtschaft. Sozialwissen.*, 1985, *105*(5), pp. 603–08.

James, Christopher; Koreisha, Sergio and Partch, M. Megan. A VARMA Analysis of the Causal Relations among Stock Returns, Real Output, and Nominal Interest Rates. *J. Finance*, December 1985, *40*(5), pp. 1375–84. [G: U.S.]

Jander, Sigurd; Menkhoff, Lukas and Palm, Adalbert. Situationskonsistente Erwartungsstruktur und Geldpolitik in der Bundesrepublik. (Situation-Consistent Expectation Structure and Monetary Policy in the Federal Republic. With English summary.) *Kredit Kapital*, 1985, *18*(2), pp. 151–72. [G: W. Germany]

Jansen, Dennis W. Real Balances in an Ad Hoc Keynesian Model and Policy Ineffectiveness: A Note. *J. Money, Credit, Banking*, August 1985, *17*(3), pp. 378–86.

Jao, Y. C. Financial Deepening and Economic Growth: Theory, Evidence and Policy. *Greek Econ. Rev.*, December 1985, *7*(3), pp. 187–225. [G: LDCs]

Jeanneney, Sylviane Guillaumont. La stabilisation des prix relatifs, objectif de la politique monétaire. (The Stabilising of Relative Prices, Goal of Monetary Policy. With English summary.) *Écon. Appl.*, 1985, *38*(1), pp. 309–23.

Johannes, James M. and Nasseh, Ali Reza. Income or Wealth in Money Demand: An Application of Non-nested Hypothesis Tests. *Southern Econ. J.*, April 1985, *51*(4), pp. 1099–1106. [G: U.S.]

Joines, Douglas H. International Currency Substitution and the Income Velocity of Money. *J. Int. Money Finance*, September 1985, *4*(3), pp. 303–16. [G: Selected OECD]

Jones-Hendrickson, S. B. Rational Expectations, Causality and Integrative Fiscal–Monetary Policy in the Caribbean. *Soc. Econ. Stud.*, December 1985, *34*(4), pp. 111–38. [G: Caribbean]

Jones, J. D. Money, Economic Activity, and Causality (A Look at the Empirical Evidence for Canada, 1957–1983). *Econ. Int.*, May 1985, *38*(2), pp. 167–78. [G: Canada]

Jüttner, D. Johannes; Tuckwell, Roger H. and Luedecke, Bernd P. Are Expectations of Short-term Interest Rates Rational? *Australian Econ. Pap.*, December 1985, *24*(45), pp. 356–69. [G: U.S.; Australia]

Kaldor, Nicholas. How Monetarism Failed. *Challenge*, May/June 1985, *28*(2), pp. 4–13. [G: U.S.; U.K.]

Kamas, Linda. External Disturbances and the Independence of Monetary Policy under the Crawling Peg in Colombia. *J. Int. Econ.*, No-

vember 1985, *19*(3/4), pp. 313–27.
[G: Colombia]

Kamath, Shyam J. An Investigation of the Demand for and Supply of Money in India, 1951–1976. *Weltwirtsch. Arch.*, 1985, *121*(3), pp. 501–23. [G: India]

Kamath, Shyam J. Monetary Aggregates, Income and Causality in a Developing Economy. *J. Econ. Stud.*, 1985, *12*(3), pp. 36–53.
[G: India]

Kano, Masao. Money, Financial Assets and Pasinetti's Theory of Profit. (In Japanese. With English summary.) *Econ. Stud. Quart.*, August 1985, *36*(2), pp. 169–77.

Kapur, Basant K. A Theoretical Model of 'Singapore-Type' Financial and Foreign-Exchange Systems. *Singapore Econ. Rev.*, October 1985, *30*(2), pp. 91–102. [G: LDCs]

Kapur, Basant K. Money in Development: Comment. *Southern Econ. J.*, April 1985, *51*(4), pp. 1230–39.

Karacaoglu, Girol. Liquidity Preference, Loanable Funds, and Exchange-Rate and Interest-Rate Dynamics. *J. Macroecon.*, Winter 1985, *7*(1), pp. 69–83.

Karlsson, Erik L. "Reaganomics" and Credibility: Comments. In *Ando, A., et al., eds.*, 1985, pp. 299–301. [G: Sweden]

Kearney, Colm. The Demand for Money and the Term Structure of Interest Rates in Ireland, 1971–1981. *Econ. Soc. Rev.*, January 1985, *16*(2), pp. 157–66. [G: Ireland]

Kearney, Colm and MacDonald, Ronald. Public Sector Borrowing, the Money Supply and Interest Rates. *Oxford Bull. Econ. Statist.*, August 1985, *47*(3), pp. 249–73. [G: U.K.]

Kent, Richard J. The Demand for the Services of Money. *Appl. Econ.*, October 1985, *17*(5), pp. 817–26. [G: U.S.]

Kerr, Peter M. Turnover Statistics and Federal Government Balances in Money Supply Targets. *Southern Econ. J.*, October 1985, *52*(2), pp. 344–50. [G: U.S.]

Khan, Mohsin S. An Analytical Approach to Interest Rate Determination in Developing Countries. *Pakistan Devel. Rev.*, Autumn-Winter 1985, *24*(3/4), pp. 481–93. [G: LDCs]

Kimbrough, Kent P. Futures Markets and Monetary Policy. *J. Monet. Econ.*, January 1985, *15*(1), pp. 69–79.

King, Robert G. On Monetary Reform. In *[Weintraub, R. E.]*, 1985, pp. 40–54. [G: U.S.]

King, Robert G. and Plosser, Charles I. Money, Deficits, and Inflation. *Carnegie-Rochester Conf. Ser. Public Policy*, Spring 1985, 22, pp. 147–95. [G: U.S.]

Knoester, Anthonie and van Sinderen, Jarig. Money, the Balance of Payments and Economic Policy. *Appl. Econ.*, April 1985, *17*(2), pp. 215–40. [G: W. Germany; Japan; Netherlands; U.K.; U.S.]

Kohn, Meir and Manchester, Joyce. International Evidence on Misspecification of the Standard Money Demand Equation. *J. Monet. Econ.*, July 1985, *16*(1), pp. 87–94. [G: OECD]

Kregel, J. A. Constraints on the Expansion of Out-

put and Employment: Real or Monetary? *J. Post Keynesian Econ.*, Winter 1984–85, *7*(2), pp. 139–52.

Kregel, J. A. Hamlet without the Prince: Cambridge Macroeconomics without Money. *Amer. Econ. Rev.*, May 1985, *75*(2), pp. 133–39.

Krelle, Wilhelm. On the Stability of Growth Models with Money. *Rivista Int. Sci. Econ. Com.*, March 1985, *32*(3), pp. 233–52.

Krishna Rao, Ch. A. and Ratnam, C. The IS–LM Curves Revisited with the Aid of Geometry of International Trade: A Comment. *Indian Econ. J.*, Jan.-Mar. 1985, *32*(3), pp. 90–91.

Krugman, Paul R.; Persson, Torsten and Svensson, Lars E. O. Inflation, Interest Rates, and Welfare. *Quart. J. Econ.*, August 1985, *100*(3), pp. 677–95.

Kuipers, S. K. Interest Rate, Savings Shortage and Liquidity Shortage: Theoretical Considerations in the Light of the Discussions about the High Rate of Interest during the Depression of the Early 1980's. *De Economist*, 1985, *133*(3), pp. 306–26.

Kulkarni, Kishore G. Capital Flows as an Offset to Monetary Policy: The Netherlands Evidence. *Indian Econ. J.*, July-Sept. 1985, *33*(1), pp. 127–29. [G: Netherlands]

Kumar, Ramesh S. Money in Development: Reply. *Southern Econ. J.*, April 1985, *51*(4), pp. 1240–44.

LaHaye, Laura. Inflation and Currency Reform. *J. Polit. Econ.*, June 1985, *93*(3), pp. 537–60.
[G: Germany; Greece; Poland]

Lai, Ching-chong and Chang, Wen-ya. Monetary Policy under Alternative Exchange Rates: A Reconsideration. *Indian Econ. J.*, Jan.-Mar. 1985, *32*(3), pp. 24–26.

Laidler, David. Expectations and Adjustment in the Monetary Sector Revisited: A Comment. *Carnegie-Rochester Conf. Ser. Public Policy*, Spring 1985, 22, pp. 243–54.

Laidler, David. Money Demand Predictability: Comment. *J. Money, Credit, Banking*, Pt. 2, Nov. 1985, *17*(4), pp. 647–53. [G: U.S.]

Lambert, Marie-Henriette. Monetary Policy in Postwar Japan: Comments. In *Ando, A., et al., eds.*, 1985, pp. 135–37. [G: Japan]

Lane, Timothy D. The Rationale for Money-Supply Targets: A Survey. *Manchester Sch. Econ. Soc. Stud.*, June 1985, *53*(2), pp. 179–207.

Lang, Harald. Expectations and the Neutrality of Money: A Comment. *J. Econ. Theory*, August 1985, *36*(2), pp. 392–93.

Langfeldt, Enno. Is a Growing Unobserved Sector Undermining Monetary Policy in the Federal Republic of Germany? In *Gaertner, W. and Wenig, A., eds.*, 1985, pp. 301–14.
[G: W. Germany]

Langohr, Herwig and Santomero, Anthony M. Commercial Bank Refinancing and Economic Stability: An Analysis of European Features. *J. Banking Finance*, December 1985, *9*(4), pp. 535–52. [G: EEC]

Larceneux, A. Keynes et Ricardo: une synthe est-elle possible? (Keynes and Ricardo: The Impossible Synthesis. With English summary.) *Écon. Soc.*, August 1985, *19*(8), pp. 7–23.

Lavoie, Marc. La thèse de la monnaie endogène face à la non-validation des crédits. (The Hypothesis of Endogeneous Money and the Non-validation of Credit. With English summary.) *Écon. Soc.*, August 1985, *19*(8), pp. 169–95.

Layton, Allan P. A Causal Caveat in the Australian Money/Income Relation. *Appl. Econ.*, April 1985, *17*(2), pp. 263–69. **[G: Australia]**

Le Héron, Edwin. Circulation industrielle, circulation financière et taux d'intérêt. (Industrial Circulation, Financial Circulation and Interest Rates. With English summary.) *Écon. Appl.*, 1985, *38*(1), pp. 211–34.

Leahey, Cary and Robins, Russell P. Alternative Specifications of the Demand for Money and their Implications for Forecasting and Policy Analysis with Large Macroeconomic Models. *J. Policy Modeling*, Summer 1985, *7*(2), pp. 361–73. **[G: U.S.]**

Leamer, Edward E. Vector Autoregressions for Causal Inference? *Carnegie-Rochester Conf. Ser. Public Policy*, Spring 1985, *22*, pp. 255–303.

Lee, S. Y. and Li, W. K. The Lead-Lag Relationship of Money, Income, and Prices in Malaysia. *Singapore Econ. Rev.*, April 1985, *30*(1), pp. 68–76. **[G: Malaysia]**

de Leeuw, Frank and Holloway, Thomas M. The Measurement and Significance of the Cyclically Adjusted Federal Budget and Debt. *J. Money, Credit, Banking*, May 1985, *17*(2), pp. 232–42. **[G: U.S.]**

Léonard, Jacques. Minsky entre Keynes et Hayek: Une autre lecture de la crise. (Minsky between Keynes and Hayek: A New Interpretation of the Crisis. With English summary.) *Écon. Soc.*, August 1985, *19*(8), pp. 117–44.

Leutwiler, Fritz. Staatsverschuldung und Geldpolitik. (National Indebtedness and Monetary Policy. With English summary.) *Aussenwirtschaft*, May 1985, *40*(1/2), pp. 157–68. **[G: U.S.]**

Levine, Paul and Currie, David. Optimal Feedback Rules in an Open Economy Macromodel with Rational Expectations. *Europ. Econ. Rev.*, March 1985, *27*(2), pp. 141–63.

Lim, Joseph. The Monetarist Models of Inflation: The Case of the Philippines. *Philippine Rev. Econ. Bus.*, Sept./Dec. 1985, *22*(3/4), pp. 155–75. **[G: Philippines]**

Lipsey, Richard G. What Have We Learned about Inflation in the Past 300 Years. *Atlantic Econ. J.*, March 1985, *13*(1), pp. 5–18.

Litterman, Robert B. and Weiss, Laurence M. Money, Real Interest Rates, and Output: A Reinterpretation of Postwar U.S. Data. *Econometrica*, January 1985, *53*(1), pp. 129–56. **[G: U.S.]**

Loeys, Jan G. Changing Interest Rate Responses to Money Announcements: 1977–1983. *J. Monet. Econ.*, May 1985, *15*(3), pp. 323–32. **[G: U.S.]**

Lombra, Raymond E. and Kaufman, Herbert M. The Money Supply Process: Reply [The Money

Supply Process: Identification, Stability, and Estimation]. *Southern Econ. J.*, October 1985, *52*(2), pp. 527–31. **[G: U.S.]**

Loranger, Jean-Guy. Lien entre capital fictif, markup flexible et inflation. (Interrelations between Fictitious Capital, Flexible Markup and Inflation. With English summary.) *Écon. Soc.*, August 1985, *19*(8), pp. 145–68. **[G: Canada]**

Lothian, James R. Equilibrium Relationships between Money and Other Economic Variables. *Amer. Econ. Rev.*, September 1985, *75*(4), pp. 828–35. **[G: OECD]**

Lynch, Gerald J. Currency, Marginal Tax Rates, and the Underground Economy. *J. Econ. Bus.*, February 1985, *37*(1), pp. 59–67. **[G: U.S.]**

Malissen, Walthère and Khelifa, Aïssa. Préférence pour le financement interne et contrainte d'endettement. (Preference for Internal Financing and the Indebtedness Constraint. With English summary.) *Écon. Appl.*, 1985, *38*(1), pp. 177–90. **[G: France; W. Germany]**

Marini, Giancarlo. Intertemporal Substitution and the Role of Monetary Policy. *Econ. J.*, March 1985, *95*(377), pp. 87–100.

Mark, Nelson C. A Note on International Real Interest Rate Differentials. *Rev. Econ. Statist.*, November 1985, *67*(4), pp. 681–84. **[G: U.S.; Canada; W. Europe]**

Mason, Paul M. An Assessment of Tobin's Interpretation of Keynes' Liquidity Preference Theory. *Amer. Econ.*, Fall 1985, *29*(2), pp. 49–54.

Masson, P. R. The Sustainability of Fiscal Deficits. *Int. Monet. Fund Staff Pap.*, December 1985, *32*(4), pp. 577–605.

Maussner, Alfred. Ineffektivität der Wirtschaftspolitik bei "rationalen Erwartungen"? Ein Kommentar mit anderen Argumenten für eine unzureichend begründete These. (Ineffectiveness of Economic Policy under "Rational Expectations"? A Commentary with Different Arguments for an Insufficient Founded Thesis. With English summary.) *Kredit Kapital*, 1985, *18*(2), pp. 217–29.

McAleer, Michael; Pagan, Adrian R. and Volker, Paul A. What Will Take the Con out of Econometrics? *Amer. Econ. Rev.*, June 1985, *75*(3), pp. 293–307. **[G: U.S.]**

McAuliffe, Robert E. The Rational Expectations Hypothesis and Economic Analysis. *Eastern Econ. J.*, Oct.-Dec. 1985, *11*(4), pp. 331–41.

McCallum, Bennett T. Bank Deregulation, Accounting Systems of Exchange, and the Unit of Account: A Critical Review. *Carnegie-Rochester Conf. Ser. Public Policy*, Autumn 1985, *23*, pp. 13–45.

McClean, A. W. A. A Further Comment on Conventional Money Multiplier. *Soc. Econ. Stud.*, September 1985, *34*(3), pp. 259–64. **[G: Jamaica]**

McDermott, John. Interest Rates and the Banking System with Imperfect Capital Markets and Mobility. In *Connolly, M. B. and McDermott, J., eds.*, 1985, pp. 165–72.

McGarvey, Mary G. U.S. Evidence on Linear Feedback from Money Growth Shocks to Relative Price Changes, 1954 to 1979. *Rev. Econ. Statist.*, November 1985, *67*(4), pp. 675–80. [G: U.S.]

McGee, Robert T. and Stasiak, Richard T. Does Anticipated Monetary Policy Matter? Another Look. *J. Money, Credit, Banking,* February 1985, *17*(1), pp. 16–27. [G: U.S.]

McGibany, James M. and Nourzad, Farrokh. Income Taxes and the Income Velocity of Money: An Empirical Analysis. *J. Macroecon.,* Fall 1985, *7*(4), pp. 523–35. [G: U.S.]

McGregor, Peter G. Professor Shackle and the Liquidity Preference Theory of Interest Rates. *J. Econ. Stud.*, 1985, *12*(1/2), pp. 89–106.

McKinnon, Ronald I. How to Manage a Repressed Economy. In *Gutowski, A.; Arnaudo, A. A. and Scharrer, H.-E., eds.,* 1985, pp. 182–209. [G: Chile; Argentina]

McMillan, W. Douglas. Money, Government Debt, *q*, and Investment. *J. Macroecon.,* Winter 1985, *7*(1), pp. 19–37.

Mehra, Yash. Inflationary Expectations, Money Growth, and the Vanishing Liquidity Effect of Money on Interest: A Further Investigation. *Fed. Res. Bank Richmond Econ. Rev.,* Mar./Apr. 1985, *71*(2), pp. 23–35. [G: U.S.]

Meldolesi, L. Georg Simmel e la filosofia del denaro. (With English summary.) *Stud. Econ.,* 1985, *40*(27), pp. 123–39.

Meltzer, Allan H. Monetary Reform in an Uncertain Environment. In *[Weintraub, R. E.],* 1985, pp. 22–39.

Meyer, Paul A. Money Multipliers and the Slopes of IS-LM: Reply. *Southern Econ. J.,* January 1985, *51*(3), pp. 916–20.

Milbourne, Ross. Distinguishing between Australian Demand for Money Models. *Australian Econ. Pap.,* June 1985, *24*(44), pp. 154–68. [G: Australia]

Miller, Marcus. Monetary Stabilization Policy in an Open Economy. *Scot. J. Polit. Econ.,* November 1985, *32*(3), pp. 220–33.

Miller, Preston J. and Wallace, Neil. International Coordination of Macroeconomic Policies: A Welfare Analysis. *Fed. Res. Bank Minn. Rev.,* Spring 1985, *9*(2), pp. 14–32.

Minsky, Hyman P. An Introduction to Post-Keynesian Economics. *Econ. Forum,* Winter 1985-1986, *15*(2), pp. 1–13.

Minsky, Hyman P. The Financial Instability Hypothesis: A Restatement. In *Arestis, P. and Skouras, T., eds.,* 1985, pp. 24–55.

Misra, G. D. Demand for Money in India: An Empirical Evaluation. *Indian Econ. J.,* July-Sept. 1985, *33*(1), pp. 77–84. [G: India]

Mitchell, Douglas W. Expected Inflation and Interest Rates in a Multi-asset Model: A Note. *J. Finance,* June 1985, *40*(2), pp. 595–99.

Mondello, Gérard. Étude de la liaison monnaie-revenu demande effective: les théories de Thomas Tooke et J. M. Keynes. (A Study about the Links between Money-Income-Effective Demand: The Theories of T. Tooke and J. M. Keynes. With English summary.) *Revue Écon.,* May 1985, *36*(3), pp. 509–54.

Moore, Michael J. Demand Management with

Rationing. *Econ. J.*, March 1985, *95*(377), pp. 73–86.

Mott, Tracy. Kalecki's Principle of Increasing Risk and the Relation among Mark-up Pricing, Investment Fluctuations, and Liquidity Preference. *Econ. Forum,* Winter 1985-1986, *15*(2), pp. 65–76.

Nachane, D. M. and Nadkarni, R. M. Empirical Testing of Certain Monetarist Propositions via Causality Theory: The Indian Case. *Indian Econ. J.*, July-Sept. 1985, *33*(1), pp. 13–41. [G: India]

Neldner, Manfred. Die volkswirtschaftliche Produktivität des Geldes. Theoretische Überlegungen und einige empirische Ergebnisse für die Bundesrepublik Deutschland. (The Productivity of Money: Theoretical Remarks and Empirical Findings for West Germany. With English summary.) *Jahr. Nationalökon. Statist.,* July 1985, *200*(4), pp. 364–80. [G: W. Germany]

Nellor, David C. L. Tax Policy, Regulated Interest Rates, and Saving. *World Devel.,* June 1985, *13*(6), pp. 725–36. [G: LDCs]

Nelson, Charles R. Macroeconomic Time-Series, Business Cycles, and Macroeconomic Policies: A Comment. *Carnegie-Rochester Conf. Ser. Public Policy,* Spring 1985, *22*, pp. 55–59. [G: U.S.; U.K.; France; W. Germany; Switzerland]

Nguyen, Duc-Tho. Money Financing and the Dynamic Effects of Fiscal and Monetary Policies in a Theoretical Simulation Model. *Manchester Sch. Econ. Soc. Stud.,* December 1985, *53*(4), pp. 432–56.

Nickelsburg, Gerald. Monetary Policy and Commodity Money Equilibria. *J. Monet. Econ.,* January 1985, *15*(1), pp. 81–94.

Nickerson, David. A Theorem on Policy Neutrality. *Europ. Econ. Rev.,* August 1985, *28*(3), pp. 331–45.

Nickerson, David. Optimal Monetary Policy with a Flexible Price-setting Rule. *Kredit Kapital,* 1985, *18*(3), pp. 289–98.

Nicola, Pier Carlo. Sulla introduzione di una moneta nell'equilibrio generale. (With English summary.) *Econ. Polit.,* April 1985, *2*(1), pp. 11–30.

Niggle, Christopher. Increasing Private Indebtedness and Speculation, Credit Crunches and Monetary Policy. *Econ. Forum,* Winter 1985-1986, *15*(2), pp. 77–93. [G: U.S.]

Nordhaus, William. International Coordination in the Design of Macroeconomic Policies: Comment. *Europ. Econ. Rev.,* June-July 1985, *28*(1–2), pp. 89–92. [G: OECD]

Norton, William E. Monetary Policy in Postwar Japan: Comments. In *Ando, A., et al., eds.,* 1985, pp. 139–40.

Nove, Alec. Money Supply and Inflation in the Soviet Union. In *[Levcik, F.],* 1985, pp. 149–56. [G: U.S.S.R.]

Obstfeld, Maurice. Capital Controls: Some Principles and the French Experience: Comments. In *Melitz, J. and Wyplosz, C., eds.,* 1985, pp. 275–77. [G: France]

Orléan, André. Incertitude et paradoxe. (Uncertainty and Paradox. With English summary.) *Écon. Appl.*, 1985, *38*(1), pp. 133–53.

Osano, Hiroshi and Tsutsui, Yoshiro. Implicit Contracts in the Japanese Bank Loan Market. *J. Finan. Quant. Anal.*, June 1985, *20*(2), pp. 211–29. **[G: Japan]**

Osborne, Dale K. What Is Money Today? *Fed. Res. Bank Dallas Econ. Rev.*, January 1985, pp. 1–15. **[G: U.S.]**

Ostry, Sylvia. Policies to Overcome Stagflation: Comments. In *Ando, A., et al., eds.*, 1985, pp. 291–94. **[G: U.S.]**

Otani, Kiyoshi. Rational Expectations and Nonneutrality of Money. *Weltwirtsch. Arch.*, 1985, *121*(2), pp. 203–16.

Parguez, Alain. La monnaie, les déficits et la crise: dans le circuit dynamique l'effect d'éviction est un mythe. (Money, Deficits and Crisis: In the Dynamic Circuit of Money, Crowding-out Effects Are Just a Myth. With English summary.) *Écon. Soc.*, August 1985, *19*(8), pp. 229–51.

Parikh, Ashok; Booth, Anne and Sundrum, R. M. An Econometric Model of the Monetary Sector in Indonesia. *J. Devel. Stud.*, April 1985, *21*(3), pp. 406–21. **[G: Indonesia]**

Peel, D. A. Global Capital Markets and the Impact of Changes in the Money Stock on Real Activity. *J. Macroecon.*, Fall 1985, *7*(4), pp. 577–82.

Peled, Dan. Stochastic Inflation and Government Provision of Indexed Bonds. *J. Monet. Econ.*, May 1985, *15*(3), pp. 291–308.

Penati, Alessandro. Monetary Targets, Real Exchange Rates and Macroeconomic Stability. *Europ. Econ. Rev.*, June-July 1985, *28*(1–2), pp. 129–50. **[G: Spain]**

Peréz, José. Monetary Targets, Real Exchange Rates and Macroeconomic Stability: Comment. *Europ. Econ. Rev.*, June-July 1985, *28*(1–2), pp. 153–55. **[G: Spain]**

Pesek, Boris P. A Curse on Several Houses. *Amer. Econ. Rev.*, March 1985, *75*(1), pp. 259.

Phaneuf, Louis. Rigidités de prix contractuelles, anticipations rationnelles et cycle économique. (Contractual Price Rigidities, Rational Expectations and the Business Cycle. With English summary.) *L'Actual. Econ.*, June 1985, *61*(2), pp. 252–73.

Pikkarainen, Pentti; Tarkka, Juha and William, Alpo. Korkojen kokonaistaloudellisista vaikutuksista BOF3-mallissa. (On the Macroeconomic Effects of Interest Rates in the BOF3 Model. With English summary.) *Kansant. Aikak.*, 1985, *81*(2), pp. 160–70. **[G: Finland]**

Pinho, Manuel A. and Villa, Pierre. Règles monétaires et dynamique du taux de change dans économique de crédit. (With English summary.) *Economia (Portugal)*, January 1985, *9*(1), pp. 29–72.

Pippenger, John. Stock Flow versus Efficient Commodity Markets: A Test of Alternative Theories. *Econ. Notes*, 1985, (2), pp. 167–70. **[G: U.S.; Switzerland]**

Placone, Dennis; Ulbrich, Holley and Wallace, Myles S. The Crowding Out Debate: It's Over When It's Over and It Isn't Over Yet. *J. Post Keynesian Econ.*, Fall 1985, *8*(1), pp. 91–96. **[G: U.S.]**

Plaut, Steven E. Interest vs. Maturity Indexation. *Quart. Rev. Econ. Bus.*, Winter 1985, *25*(4), pp. 95–106.

Plaut, Steven E. The Theory of Collateral. *J. Banking Finance*, September 1985, *9*(3), pp. 401–19.

Poole, William. The Money Markets. In *Shadow Open Market Committee.*, 1985, pp. 19–23.

Porter, Richard D. Choosing between M1 and Debt as an Intermediate Target for Monetary Control: A Comment. *Carnegie-Rochester Conf. Ser. Public Policy*, Spring 1985, *22*, pp. 133–46. **[G: U.S.]**

Potiowsky, Thomas P.; Koot, Ronald S. and Smith, W. James. Factor Analysis and the Empirical Definition of Money. *Quart. J. Bus. Econ.*, Spring 1985, *24*(2), pp. 104–19. **[G: U.S.]**

Radcliffe, Christopher; Warga, Arthur D. and Willett, Thomas D. International Influences on U.S. National Income: Currency Substitution, Exchange Rate Changes, and Commodity Shocks. In *Arndt, S. W.; Sweeney, R. J. and Willett, T. D., eds.*, 1985, pp. 213–26. **[G: U.S.]**

Radecki, Lawrence J. and Wenninger, John. Recent Instability in M1's Velocity. *Fed. Res. Bank New York Quart. Rev.*, Autumn 1985, *10*(3), pp. 16–22. **[G: U.S.]**

Ramirez-Rojas, C. L. Currency Substitution in Argentina, Mexico, and Uruguay. *Int. Monet. Fund Staff Pap.*, December 1985, *32*(4), pp. 629–67. **[G: Argentina; Mexico; Uruguay]**

Rankin, Neil. Debt Neutrality in Disequilibrium. In *Currie, D., ed.*, 1985, pp. 17–40.

Rapping, Leonard A. and Pulley, Lawrence B. Speculation, Deregulation, and the Interest Rates. *Amer. Econ. Rev.*, May 1985, *75*(2), pp. 108–13. **[G: U.S.]**

Rasche, Robert H. Interest Rate Volatility and Alternative Monetary Control Procedures. *Fed. Res. Bank San Francisco Econ. Rev.*, Summer 1985, (3), pp. 46–63. **[G: U.S.]**

Rasche, Robert H. Update to the September, 1985 Shadow Open Market Committee Report: The Behavior of the Monetary Aggregates in August, 1985 or: "The Grinch that Stole Christmas." In *Shadow Open Market Committee.*, 1985, pp. 49–53. **[G: U.S.]**

Rasche, Robert H. What Would Nominal GNP Targeting Do to the Business Cycle? A Comment. *Carnegie-Rochester Conf. Ser. Public Policy*, Spring 1985, *22*, pp. 85–87.

Rasche, Robert H. Where Is the Mystery in the Behavior of the Monetary Aggregates? In *Shadow Open Market Committee.*, 1985, pp. 35–47. **[G: U.S.]**

Reid, Bradford G. Government Debt, National Income and Causality. *Appl. Econ.*, April 1985, *17*(2), pp. 321–30. **[G: U.S.]**

Renas, Stephen M. What Role Do Lagged Values of Target Variables Play in Monetary Policy?

Econ. Notes, 1985, (1), pp. 177–83.
[G: U.S.]

Resler, D. H., et al. Detecting and Estimating Changing Economic Relationships: The Case of Discount Window Borrowings. *Appl. Econ.*, June 1985, *17*(3), pp. 509–27. [G: U.S.]

Rich, Georg. International Aspects of Monetary Policy: Comments. In *Ando, A., et al., eds.*, 1985, pp. 225–27. [G: OECD]

Richter, Peter. Monetaristische Wirtschaftspolitik im südlichen Lateinamerika. Die Fälle Chile, Argentinien und Uruguay. (Monetarist Policies in Latin America—The Cases of Chile, Argentina, and Uruguay. With English summary.) *Konjunkturpolitik*, 1985, *31*(1/2), pp. 126–49. [G: Chile; Argentina; Uruguay]

Rinaldi, Roberto. Interrelationships between the Floating Exchange Rate, Money and Price. A Test of Causality Applied to the Italian Experience: Some Comments. *Econ. Notes*, 1985, (2), pp. 154–66. [G: Italy]

Roberts, David L. and Nord, Stephen. Causality Tests and Functional Form Sensitivity. *Appl. Econ.*, February 1985, *17*(1), pp. 135–41. [G: U.S.]

Roche, John. Marx's Theory of Money: A Re-interpretation. *Rev. Radical Polit. Econ.*, Spring and Summer 1985, *17*(1/2), pp. 201–11.

Rogers, C. The Monetary Control System of the South African Reserve Bank: Monetarist or Post Keynesian? *S. Afr. J. Econ.*, September 1985, *53*(3), pp. 241–47. [G: S. Africa]

Rogoff, Kenneth S. Can International Monetary Policy Cooperation Be Counterproductive? *J. Int. Econ.*, May 1985, *18*(3/4), pp. 199–217.

Rogoff, Kenneth S. The Optimal Degree of Commitment to an Intermediate Monetary Target. *Quart. J. Econ.*, November 1985, *100*(4), pp. 1169–89.

Rohde, Armin. Anmerkungen zur gegenwärtigen Feinsteuerungsstrategie der Deutschen Bundesbank. (Observations on the Current Fine-Control Strategy of the German Bundesbank. With English summary.) *Kredit Kapital*, 1985, *18*(3), pp. 418–27. [G: W. Germany]

Roley, V. Vance. Money Demand Predictability. *J. Money, Credit, Banking*, Pt. 2, Nov. 1985, *17*(4), pp. 611–41. [G: U.S.]

Roley, V. Vance. Reply [The Response of Short-term Interest Rates to Weekly Money Announcements: A Note]. *J. Money, Credit, Banking*, May 1985, *17*(2), pp. 271–73.
[G: U.S.]

Roley, V. Vance and Walsh, Carl E. Monetary Policy Regimes, Expected Inflation, and the Response of Interest Rates to Money Announcements. *Quart. J. Econ.*, Supp. 1985, *100*, pp. 1011–39. [G: U.S.]

Romer, David. Financial Intermediation, Reserve Requirements, and Inside Money: A General Equilibrium Analysis. *J. Monet. Econ.*, September 1985, *16*(2), pp. 175–94.

Rose, Andrew K. An Alternative Approach to the American Demand for Money. *J. Money, Credit, Banking*, Part 1, Nov. 1985, *17*(4), pp. 439–55. [G: U.S.]

Rose, Hugh. A Policy Rule for 'Say's Law' in a Theory of Temporary Equilibrium. *J. Macroecon.*, Winter 1985, *7*(1), pp. 1–17.

Rotemberg, Julio J. Money and the Terms of Trade. *J. Int. Econ.*, August 1985, *19*(1/2), pp. 141–60.

Roth, Timothy P. Tax Rates, Income Flows, and Money Demand. *Quart. Rev. Econ. Bus.*, Spring 1985, *25*(1), pp. 74–84. [G: U.S.]

Rousseas, Stephen. A Markup Theory of Bank Loan Rates. *J. Post Keynesian Econ.*, Fall 1985, *8*(1), pp. 135–44. [G: U.S.]

Rush, Mark. Unexpected Monetary Disturbances during the Gold Standard Era. *J. Monet. Econ.*, May 1985, *15*(3), pp. 309–21.
[G: U.S.]

Santarelli, Enrico. A proposito di una nuova raccolta di scritti schumperiani. (With English summary.) *Stud. Econ.*, 1985, *40*(26), pp. 135–47.

Sargent, Thomas J. "Reaganomics" and Credibility. In *Ando, A., et al., eds.*, 1985, pp. 235–52. [G: U.S.]

Sargent, Thomas J. and Wallace, Neil. Interest on Reserves. *J. Monet. Econ.*, May 1985, *15*(3), pp. 279–90.

Sargent, Thomas J. and Wallace, Neil. Some Unpleasant Monetarist Arithmetic. *Fed. Res. Bank Minn. Rev.*, Winter 1985, *9*(1), pp. 15–31. [G: U.S.]

Scarth, William M. A Note on Non-uniqueness in Rational Expectations Models. *J. Monet. Econ.*, March 1985, *15*(2), pp. 247–54.

Schneider, Rolf. Wertpapieremission, Wertpapiererwerb und Zinsbildung am Rentenmarkt. (Security Issuing, Security Purchasing and Interest Rate Formation on the Bond Market. With English summary.) *Kredit Kapital*, 1985, *18*(3), pp. 372–401. [G: U.S.; W. Germany]

Schuh, Norbert. A Test for the Policy Ineffectiveness Theory for Austria. *Empirica*, 1985, *12*(1), pp. 67–85. [G: Austria]

Sealey, C. W., Jr. and Heinkel, Robert. Asymmetric Information and a Theory of Compensating Balances. *J. Banking Finance*, June 1985, *9*(2), pp. 193–205.

Seccareccia, Mario S. The Role of Saving and Financial Acquisition in the Process of Capital Formation under Policies of Austerity: The Case of Canada. *Écon. Soc.*, August 1985, *19*(8), pp. 253–71. [G: Canada]

Sennholz, Hans F. The Monetary Writings of Carl Menger. In *Rockwell, L. H., Jr., ed.*, 1985, pp. 19–34. [G: Austria]

Sharpe, Ian G. Interest Parity, Monetary Policy and the Volatility of Australian Short-term Interest Rates: 1978–1982. *Econ. Rec.*, March 1985, *61*(172), pp. 436–44. [G: Australia]

Shea, Gary S. Interest Rate Term Structure Estimation with Exponential Splines: A Note. *J. Finance*, March 1985, *40*(1), pp. 319–25.

Sheehan, Richard G. Money, Anticipated Changes, and Policy Effectiveness. *Amer. Econ. Rev.*, June 1985, *75*(3), pp. 524–29.
[G: U.S.]

Sheehan, Richard G. Weekly Money Announcements: New Information and Its Effects. *Fed. Res. Bank St. Louis Rev.*, Aug./Sept. 1985, 67(7), pp. 25–34. **[G: U.S.]**

Sheffrin, Steven M. Accommodation, Supply Shocks, and Sluggish Real Wages. *J. Macroecon.*, Summer 1985, 7(3), pp. 333–46.

Shinkai, Yoichi. Monetary Policy in Our Times: Summing Up. In *Ando, A., et al., eds.*, 1985, pp. 309–18.

Siegel, Jeremy J. Money Supply Announcements and Interest Rates: Does Monetary Policy Matter? *J. Monet. Econ.*, March 1985, 15(2), pp. 163–76.

Simos, Evangelos O. and Triantis, John E. Human and Non-human Capital and the Velocity of Money. *Rivista Int. Sci. Econ. Com.*, Oct.-Nov. 1985, 32(10–11), pp. 1003–10.
[G: U.S.]

Sims, Grant E. and Takayama, Akira. On the Demand for and Supply of Money: An Empirical Study. *Keio Econ. Stud.*, 1985, 22(1), pp. 1–26. **[G: U.S.]**

Smith, Bruce D. American Colonial Monetary Regimes: The Failure of the Quantity Theory and Some Evidence in Favour of an Alternative View. *Can. J. Econ.*, August 1985, 18(3), pp. 531–65. **[G: U.S.]**

Smith, Bruce D. Some Colonial Evidence on Two Theories of Money: Maryland and the Carolinas. *J. Polit. Econ.*, December 1985, 93(6), pp. 1178–1211. **[G: U.S.]**

Smith, Gregor W. Inflationary Expectations and the Demand for Money: The Greek Experience: Another Comment. *Kredit Kapital*, 1985, 18(4), pp. 527–28. **[G: Greece]**

Smith, Richard G. and Goodhart, Charles A. E. The Relationship between Exchange Rate Movements and Monetary Surprises: Results for the United Kingdom and the United States Compared and Contrasted: Erratum. *Manchester Sch. Econ. Soc. Stud.*, September 1985, 53(3), pp. 315. **[G: U.S.; U.K.]**

Smith, Richard G. and Goodhart, Charles A. E. The Relationship between Exchange Rate Movements and Monetary Surprises: Results for the United Kingdom and the United States Compared and Contrasted. *Manchester Sch. Econ. Soc. Stud.*, March 1985, 53(1), pp. 2–22. **[G: U.S.; U.K.]**

Snippe, Jan. Finance, Saving and Investment in Keynes's Economics. *Cambridge J. Econ.*, September 1985, 9(3), pp. 257–69.

Snippe, Jan. Loanable Funds Theory versus Liquidity Preference Theory. *De Economist*, 1985, 133(2), pp. 129–50.

Snippe, Jan. On the Integration of Spending and Portfolio Decisions and the Coordination Problem in Macroeconomic Analysis. *Metroecon.*, October 1985, 37(3), pp. 293–305.

Sorensen, Peter Birch. Det monetaristiske syn på stabiliseringspolitikken. (A Macro-economic Model of Explaining Monetarist Assumptions in Stabilization Policy. With English summary.) *Nationaløkon. Tidsskr.*, 1985, 123(1), pp. 64–76.

Spencer, David E. Money Demand and the Price Level. *Rev. Econ. Statist.*, August 1985, 67(3), pp. 490–96. **[G: U.S.]**

Spindt, Paul A. A Micro Model of the Federal Funds Market: Discussion. *J. Finance*, July 1985, 40(3), pp. 988–90.

Spindt, Paul A. Money Is What Money Does: Monetary Aggregation and the Equation of Exchange. *J. Polit. Econ.*, February 1985, 93(1), pp. 175–204. **[G: U.S.]**

Spinelli, Franco. Should the Hypothesis of a Well Defined and Stable World Demand for M1 Be Reinstated? *Kredit Kapital*, 1985, 18(2), pp. 193–203. **[G: Global]**

Sprenkle, Case M. On the Precautionary Demand for Assets. *J. Banking Finance*, December 1985, 9(4), pp. 499–515.

Steindl, Frank G. On Inflation, Income Taxes, Tax Rules, and the Rate of Interest: A General Equilibrium Analysis. *Southern Econ. J.*, January 1985, 51(3), pp. 868–73.

Steindl, Frank G. The Money Supply Process: Comment [The Money Supply Process: Identification, Stability, and Estimation]. *Southern Econ. J.*, October 1985, 52(2), pp. 523–26. **[G: U.S.]**

Stockton, David J. and Glassman, James E. The Theory and Econometrics of Reduced-Form Nominal Income and Price Equations. *Southern Econ. J.*, July 1985, 52(1), pp. 103–21.

Stulz, René M. and Wasserfallen, Walter. Macroeconomic Time-Series, Business Cycles, and Macroeconomic Policies. *Carnegie-Rochester Conf. Ser. Public Policy*, Spring 1985, 22, pp. 9–53. **[G: U.S.; U.K.; France; W. Germany; Switzerland]**

Sundararajan, V. Debt–Equity Ratios of Firms and Interest Rate Policy: Macroeconomic Effects of High Leverage in Developing Countries. *Int. Monet. Fund Staff Pap.*, September 1985, 32(3), pp. 430–74.

Suzuki, Yoshio. Monetary Policy in Our Times: Comments. In *Ando, A., et al., eds.*, 1985, pp. 303–06. **[G: OECD]**

Svensson, Lars E. O. Money and Asset Prices in a Cash-in-Advance Economy. *J. Polit. Econ.*, October 1985, 93(5), pp. 919–44.

Sweeney, Richard J. Short-run Money Demand Functions: Estimated Speeds of Adjustment and Serial Correlation. *J. Macroecon.*, Spring 1985, 7(2), pp. 247–56. **[G: U.S.]**

Swofford, James L. and Whitney, Gerald A. Nominal Costs and the Demand for Real Transactions Balances. *Econ. Inquiry*, October 1985, 23(4), pp. 725–40. **[G: U.S.]**

Tabellini, Guido. Accomodative Monetary Policy and Central Bank Reputation. *Giorn. Econ.*, July-Aug. 1985, 44(7–8), pp. 389–425.

Tabellini, Guido. The Specification of Asset Equilibrium in Models of the Open Economy. *Giorn. Econ.*, Jan.-Feb. 1985, 44(1–2), pp. 17–27.

Takigawa, Yoshio. Money Finance, Bond Finance and "Yw cho (Postal Savings) Finance." *Kobe Univ. Econ.*, 1985, (31), pp. 53–68.
[G: Japan]

Talele, Chaitram J. An Examination of Friedman's "Optimum Quantity of Money." *Indian Econ. J.*, July-Sept. 1985, *33*(1), pp. 140–51.

Tanzi, Vito. Fiscal Deficits and Interest Rates in the United States: An Empirical Analysis, 1960–84. *Int. Monet. Fund Staff Pap.*, December 1985, *32*(4), pp. 551–76.   [G: U.S.]

Tanzi, Vito. Monetary Policy and Control of Public Expenditure. In *Forte, F. and Peacock, A., eds.*, 1985, pp. 157–68.   [G: OECD]

Taub, Bart. Equilibrium Traits of Durable Commodity Money. *J. Banking Finance*, March 1985, *9*(1), pp. 5–34.

Taub, Bart. Private Fiat Money with Many Suppliers. *J. Monet. Econ.*, September 1985, *16*(2), pp. 195–208.

Taurand, Francis. Une approche néo-Robertsonienne simple des fondements microéconomiques de la théorie monétaire. (A Simple Neo-Robertsonian Approach to the Microfoundations of Monetary Theory. With English summary.) *L'Actual. Econ.*, December 1985, *61*(4), pp. 472–88.

Tavlas, George S. and Aschheim, Joseph. Alexander Del Mar, Irving Fischer, and Monetary Economics. *Can. J. Econ.*, May 1985, *18*(2), pp. 294–313.

Taylor, John B. International Coordination in the Design of Macroeconomic Policy Rules. *Europ. Econ. Rev.*, June-July 1985, *28*(1–2), pp. 53–81.   [G: OECD]

Taylor, John B. What Would Nominal GNP Targetting Do to the Business Cycle? *Carnegie-Rochester Conf. Ser. Public Policy*, Spring 1985, *22*, pp. 61–84.

Taylor, Lance. A Stagnationist Model of Economic Growth. *Cambridge J. Econ.*, December 1985, *9*(4), pp. 383–403.

Taylor, Lance and O'Connell, Stephen A. A Minsky Crisis. *Quart. J. Econ.*, Supp. 1985, *100*, pp. 871–85.

Thies, Clifford F. Interest Rates and Expected Inflation, 1831–1914: A Rational Expectations Approach. *Southern Econ. J.*, April 1985, *51*(4), pp. 1107–20.   [G: U.S.]

Thies, Clifford F. New Estimates of the Term Structure of Interest Rates: 1920–1939. *J. Finan. Res.*, Winter 1985, *8*(4), pp. 297–306.   [G: U.S.]

Thomas, Lee R. Portfolio Theory and Currency Substitution. *J. Money, Credit, Banking*, August 1985, *17*(3), pp. 347–57.

Thornton, Daniel L. Money Demand Dynamics: Some New Evidence. *Fed. Res. Bank St. Louis Rev.*, March 1985, *67*(3), pp. 14–23.   [G: U.S.]

Thornton, Daniel L. The Appropriate Interest Race and Scale Variable in Money Demand: Results from Non-nested Tests. *Appl. Econ.*, August 1985, *17*(4), pp. 735–44.   [G: U.S.]

Thornton, Daniel L. and Batten, Dallas S. Lag-Length Selection and Tests of Granger Causality between Money and Income. *J. Money, Credit, Banking*, May 1985, *17*(2), pp. 164–78.

Thornton, John. The Role of Rediscount Quotas: A Note. *J. Money, Credit, Banking*, August

1985, *17*(3), pp. 387–90.   [G: W. Germany]

Tobin, James. La teoria macreconomica in discussione. (Macreconomics under Debate. With English summary.) *Bancaria*, January 1985, *41*(1), pp. 13–31.

Toma, Mark. A Duopoly Theory of Government Money Production: The 1930s and 1940s. *J. Monet. Econ.*, May 1985, *15*(3), pp. 363–82.

Trehan, Bharat. The Information Content of Credit Aggregates. *Fed. Res. Bank San Francisco Econ. Rev.*, Spring 1985, (2), pp. 28–39.   [G: U.S.]

Turnovsky, Stephen J. Optimal Exchange Market Intervention: Two Alternative Classes of Rules. In *Bhandari, J. S., ed.*, 1985, pp. 55–72.

Uddin, Mohammad Sohrab. Monetary Approach to Balance of Payments: Evidence from Less Developed Countries. *Indian Econ. J.*, July-Sept. 1985, *33*(1), pp. 92–104.   [G: India; Pakistan; Thailand]

Vaciaga, Giacomo. Financial Innovation and Monetary Policy: Italy *versus* the United States. *Banca Naz. Lavoro Quart. Rev.*, December 1985, (155), pp. 309–26.   [G: Italy; U.S.]

Vaciago, Giacomo. A Note on Credit Aggregates as Targets or Indicators of Monetary Policy. *Banca Naz. Lavoro Quart. Rev.*, June 1985, (153), pp. 155–71.   [G: U.S.]

Vallageas, Bernard. Les circuits dans les analyses de Marx, Boehm-Bawerk, Hayek et Keynes. (Circuits in the Analyses of Marx, Boehm-Bawerk, Hayek and Keynes. With English summary.) *Écon. Soc.*, August 1985, *19*(8), pp. 47–68.

Van Wijnbergen, Sweder. Macro-economic Effects of Changes in Bank Interest Rates: Simulation Results for South Korea. *J. Devel. Econ.*, August 1985, *18*(2–3), pp. 541–54.   [G: S. Korea]

VanHoose, David D. Bank Competition and Optimal Monetary Policies under Alternative Reserve Accounting Schemes. *J. Macroecon.*, Fall 1985, *7*(4), pp. 537–52.

VanHoose, David D. Bank Market Structure and Monetary Control. *J. Money, Credit, Banking*, August 1985, *17*(3), pp. 298–311.

Vaubel, Roland. Competing Currencies: The Case for Free Entry. *Z. Wirtschaft. Sozialwissen.*, 1985, *105*(5), pp. 547–64.

Vihriälä, Vesa. The Monetary Autonomy of Finland: What Can the Time Series Analysis Tell Us? *Empirical Econ.*, 1985, *10*(4), pp. 263–74.   [G: Finland]

Vizeu, Maria Clementina. Inflação tradicional num modelo de desequilíbrio. (With English summary.) *Economia (Portugal)*, October 1985, *9*(3), pp. 467–84.

Wahlroos, Björn. Money and Prices in a Small Economy. *Scand. J. Econ.*, 1985, *87*(4), pp. 605–24.   [G: Finland]

Waldo, Douglas G. Bank Runs, the Deposit–Currency Ratio, and the Interest Rate. *J. Monet. Econ.*, May 1985, *15*(3), pp. 269–77.

Waldo, Douglas G. Open Market Operations in an Overlapping Generations Model. *J. Polit.*

Econ., December 1985, *93*(6), pp. 1242–57.

Wasserfallen, Walter. Forecasting, Rational Expectations and the Phillips-Curve: An Empirical Investigation. *J. Monet. Econ.*, January 1985, *15*(1), pp. 7–27. **[G: Switzerland]**

Wellink, Nout and Halberstadt, Victor. Monetary Policy and Control of Public Expenditure with Special Reference to the Netherlands. In *Forte, F. and Peacock, A., eds.*, 1985, pp. 169–91. **[G: OECD; Netherlands]**

White, Lawrence H. Free Banking and the Gold Standard. In *Rockwell, L. H., Jr., ed.*, 1985, pp. 113–28.

Whittaker, J. The Demand for Money in South Africa: A Comment. *S. Afr. J. Econ.*, June 1985, *53*(2), pp. 184–96. **[G: S. Africa]**

van Wijk, H. H. International Aspects of Monetary Policy: Comments. In *Ando, A., et al., eds.*, 1985, pp. 229–32. **[G: Netherlands; OECD]**

Willett, Thomas D.; Khan, Waseem and Der Hovanessian, Aïda. Interest Rate Changes, Inflationary Expectations and Exchange Rate Overshooting: The Dollar–DM Rate. In *Arndt, S. W.; Sweeney, R. J. and Willett, T. D., eds.*, 1985, pp. 49–71. **[G: U.S.; W. Germany]**

Worrell, DeLisle. Monetary Mechanisms in Open Economies: A Model for the Caribbean. In *Connolly, M. B. and McDermott, J., eds.*, 1985, pp. 119–34. **[G: Barbados; Jamaica; Trinidad and Tobago]**

Worrell, Keith. Preliminary Estimates of the Demand for Money Function in Jamaica 1962–1979. *Soc. Econ. Stud.*, September 1985, *34*(3), pp. 265–81. **[G: Jamaica]**

Wrightsman, Dwayne. Forecasting with Velocity. *Challenge*, July/August 1985, *28*(3), pp. 58–60. **[G: U.S.; Canada]**

Zieba, Andrzej. Maximum Principle for Speculative Money Balances. In *Gaertner, W. and Wenig, A., eds.*, 1985, pp. 389–91.

Ziegelschmidt, Helmut. The Demand for Money in Austria: Is It Stable? *Empirica*, 1985, *12*(1), pp. 3–24. **[G: Austria]**

Zinn, Karl Georg. Wachstum, Zeitallokation und die Grenzen der Geldvermögenspräferenz. (Growth, Allocation of Time, and the Limits to the Preference for Money Capital-Accumulation. With English summary.) *Konjunkturpolitik*, 1985, *31*(1/2), pp. 34–51.

Zonzilos, Nicholas G. The Demand for Money during a Period of Inflationary Expectations. Some FIML Based Estimates for Greece. *Empirical Econ.*, 1985, *10*(1), pp. 27–35. **[G: Greece]**

3116 Monetary Policy, Including All Central Banking Topics

Al-Timimi, W. The Evolution of the Saudi Arabian Monetary System. *Banca Naz. Lavoro Quart. Rev.*, March 1985, (152), pp. 77–83. **[G: Saudi Arabia]**

Allison, Theodore E. Statement to the U.S. House Subcommittee on Financial Institutions Supervision, Regulation and Insurance of the Committee on Banking, Finance and Urban Affairs, April 4, 1985. *Fed. Res. Bull.*, June 1985, *71*(6), pp. 422–23. **[G: U.S.]**

Allsopp, C. The Assessment: Monetary and Fiscal Policy in the 1980s. *Oxford Rev. Econ. Policy*, Spring 1985, *1*(1), pp. 1–20. **[G: U.K.]**

Arcelli, Mario. Public Deficit and Monetary Course Change in Italy since 1981. *Z. Wirtschaft. Sozialwissen.*, 1985, *105*(2/3), pp. 327–39. **[G: Italy]**

Argy, Victor E. Effects of Changes in Banking and Exchange Control Legislation in the United Kingdom on the Significance of the Money Aggregates as Indicators, 1971–81. *Banca Naz. Lavoro Quart. Rev.*, March 1985, (152), pp. 31–44. **[G: U.K.]**

Argy, Victor E. The West German Experience with Monetary and Exchange Rate Management, 1973–1981. *Rivista Int. Sci. Econ. Com.*, Oct.-Nov. 1985, *32*(10–11), pp. 1047–70. **[G: W. Germany]**

Auerbach, Robert D. Politics and the Federal Reserve. *Contemp. Policy Issues*, Fall 1985, *3*(5), pp. 43–58. **[G: U.S.]**

Axilrod, Stephen H. Domestic Aspects of Monetary Policy: Comments. In *Ando, A., et al., eds.*, 1985, pp. 123–26. **[G: Japan; U.S.]**

Axilrod, Stephen H. U.S. Monetary Policy in Recent Years: An Overview. *Fed. Res. Bull.*, January 1985, *71*(1), pp. 14–24. **[G: U.S.]**

Backus, David; Blanco, Herminio and Levine, David K. The Financial Sector in the Planning of Economic Development. In *Gutowski, A.; Arnaudo, A. A. and Scharrer, H.-E., eds.*, 1985, pp. 42–58.

Baratta, Paolo. Il credito industriale dal dibattito del 1911 alla constituzione dell'ICIPU. (Industrial Credit from the 1911 Debate to the Establishment of I.C.I.P.U. With English summary.) *Bancaria*, February 1985, *41*(2), pp. 174–80. **[G: Italy]**

Bartels, Andrew H. Volcker's Revolution at the Fed. *Challenge*, Sept./Oct. 1985, *28*(4), pp. 35–42. **[G: U.S.]**

Batra, R. N. The Future of the Debt Situation in the LDCs. In *Kaushik, S. K., ed.*, 1985, pp. 47–57. **[G: U.S.]**

Batten, Dallas S. and Ott, Mack. The Interrelationship of Monetary Policies under Floating Exchange Rates: A Note. *J. Money, Credit, Banking*, February 1985, *17*(1), pp. 103–10. **[G: OECD]**

Batten, Dallas S. and Thornton, Daniel L. Are Weighted Monetary Aggregates Better than Simple-Sum M1? *Fed. Res. Bank St. Louis Rev.*, June/July 1985, *67*(6), pp. 29–40. **[G: U.S.]**

Batten, Dallas S. and Thornton, Daniel L. The Discount Rate, Interest Rates and Foreign Exchange Rates: An Analysis with Daily Data. *Fed. Res. Bank St. Louis Rev.*, February 1985, *67*(2), pp. 22–30. **[G: U.K.; Canada; France; Germany; Japan]**

Beltensperger, Ernst. Disinflation—The Swiss Experience 1973-1983. *Z. Wirtschaft. Sozial-*

wissen., 1985, *105*(2/3), pp. 271–93.
[G: Switzerland]

Bergstrand, Jeffrey H. Money, Interest Rates, and Foreign Exchange Rates as Indicators for Monetary Policy. *New Eng. Econ. Rev.*, Nov./ Dec. 1985, pp. 3–13. [G: N. America; France; W. Germany; Switzerland; U.K.]

Bhatnagar, R. G. Integrated Structural, Institutional and Procedural Innovations Formulated by State Bank of India for Increasing Rural Lendings. In *Bandyopadhyay, R. and Khankhoje, D. P., eds.*, 1985, pp. 171–79.
[G: India]

Biscaini, Anna Maria; Gnes, Paolo and Roselli, Alessandro. Origini e sviluppo del Consorzio per Sovvenzioni su Valori Industriali durante il Governatorato Stringher. (Origins and Development of the *Consorzio per Sovvenzioni su Valori Industriali* during the Stringher Governorship. With English summary.) *Bancaria*, February 1985, *41*(2), pp. 154–73. [G: Italy]

Black, Philip and Dollery, Brian. Selective Intervention and the South African Economy. *J. Stud. Econ. Econometrics*, August 1985, (22), pp. 47–67. [G: S. Africa]

Bomhoff, Eduard J. Monetary Targeting in West Germany, Holland, and Switzerland. *Contemp. Policy Issues*, Fall 1985, *3*(5), pp. 85–98. [G: W. Germany; Netherlands; Switzerland]

Bootle, Roger P. The Economic System in the UK: Monetary Policy. In *Morris, D., ed.*, 1985, pp. 295–332. [G: U.K.]

Bordes, Christian; Driscoll, Michael J. and MacDonald, Garry. Le contenu en information des agrégats monétaires français. (The Information Content of French Monetary Aggregates. With English summary.) *Revue Écon.*, November 1985, *36*(6), pp. 1169–1205.
[G: France]

Bowring, Philip. Prudential Supervision of Financial Institutions in Hong Kong. *Hong Kong Econ. Pap.*, 1985, (16), pp. 97–111.
[G: Hong Kong]

Buckley, Robert M. and Gross, David J. Selective Credit Policies and the Mortgage Market: Cross-sectional Evidence. *J. Money, Credit, Banking*, August 1985, *17*(3), pp. 358–70.
[G: U.S.]

Budd, Alan P.; Dicks, Geoffrey and Keating, Giles. Government Borrowing and Financial Markets. *Nat. Inst. Econ. Rev.*, August 1985, (113), pp. 89–97. [G: U.K.]

Cagan, Phillip. Financing the Deficit, Interest Rates, and Monetary Policy. In *Cagan, P. and Somensatto, E., eds.*, 1985, pp. 195–221.
[G: U.S.]

Carli, Guido. The Internationalization of Financial and Credit Systems. *Rev. Econ. Cond. Italy*, Sept.-Dec. 1985, (3), pp. 341–51.
[G: Global]

Carosso, Vincent P. Legislative History of the Glass-Steagall Act: An Economic Evaluation of Bank Securities Activities before 1933: Comment. In *Walter, I., ed.*, 1985, pp. 89–91.
[G: U.S.]

Cassese, Sabino. Major Banks and New Legislative Structures. *Rev. Econ. Cond. Italy*, Sept.-Dec. 1985, (3), pp. 383–91. [G: U.S.; U.K.; Italy; W. Germany]

de Cecco, Marcello. Italian Monetary Policy in the 1980s. *Z. Wirtschaft. Sozialwissen.*, 1985, *105*(2/3), pp. 311–26. [G: Italy]

Chan, Yuk-Shee and Mak, King-Tim. Depositors' Welfare, Deposit Insurance, and Deregulation. *J. Finance*, July 1985, *40*(3), pp. 959–74.
[G: U.S.]

Chase, Samuel. Bank Regulation and Monetary Policy: Comment. *J. Money, Credit, Banking*, Pt. 2, Nov. 1985, *17*(4), pp. 718–21.
[G: U.S.]

Chouraqui, Jean-Claude and Price, Robert. Fiscal and Monetary Strategy in OECD Countries: A Review of Recent Experiences. In *Argy, V. E. and Neville, J. W., eds.*, 1985, pp. 105–33. [G: OECD]

Claassen, Emil-Maria. The Lender-of-Last-Resort Function in the Context of National and International Financial Crises. *Weltwirtsch. Arch.*, 1985, *121*(2), pp. 217–37.

Clark, Larry R. Another Look at the Secondary Reserve Requirement as an Instrument of Monetary Policy. *Quart. Rev. Econ. Bus.*, Spring 1985, *25*(1), pp. 96–109. [G: Canada]

Clark, Peter B. Inflation and Unemployment in the United States: Recent Experience and Policies. In *Argy, V. E. and Neville, J. W., eds.*, 1985, pp. 221–48. [G: U.S.]

Connolly, Michael and Hartpence, María. El ataque especulativo contra la tasa de cambio programada en Argentina: 1979–1981. (With English summary.) *Cuadernos Econ.*, December 1985, *22*(67), pp. 373–88. [G: Argentina]

Corrigan, E. Gerald. Bank Supervision in a Changing Financial Environment. *Fed. Res. Bank New York Quart. Rev.*, Winter 1985-86, *10*(4), pp. 1–5. [G: U.S.]

Corrigan, E. Gerald. Statement to the U.S. House Subcommittee on Commerce, Consumer, and Monetary Affairs of the Committee on Government Operations, May 15, 1985. *Fed. Res. Bull.*, July 1985, *71*(7), pp. 524–28.
[G: U.S.]

Corrigan, E. Gerald. Statement to the U.S. Senate Subcommittee on Securities of the Committee on Banking, Housing, and Urban Affairs, May 9, 1985. *Fed. Res. Bull.*, July 1985, *71*(7), pp. 520–24. [G: U.S.]

Cosentino, Antonello. L'autonomia dell'Istituto di emissione nel finanziare il fabbisogno del Tesaro. (The Autonomy of the Bank of Italy in Financing Treasury Needs–II. With English summary.) *Bancaria*, December 1985, *41*(12), pp. 1216–25. [G: Italy]

Cosentino, Antonello. L'autonomia dell'Istituto di emissione nel finanziare il fabbisogno del Tesoro. (The Autonomy of the Bank of Italy in Financing Treasury Needs–I. With English summary.) *Bancaria*, November 1985, *41*(11), pp. 1125–36. [G: Italy]

Cottarelli, Carlo; Cotula, Franco and Pittaluga, Giovanni. Differenziazione dei tassi sui depositi: effetti sulla politica monetaria e sulla gestione delle banche. (Differentiation of Rates on Deposits: Effects on the Monetary Policy on the Management of Banks. With English summary.) *Bancaria,* May 1985, *41*(5), pp. 524–38. [G: Italy]

Cova, Alberto. Monete e circolazione monetaria in Lombardia a metà settecento in una memoria di Gabriele Verri. (Moneys and Monetary Circulation on Lombardy in the Middle of the XVIII Century: A Report by G. Verri. With English summary.) *Rivista Int. Sci. Econ. Com.,* June 1985, *32*(6), pp. 571–83. [G: Italy]

Cross, Sam Y. Treasury and Federal Reserve Foreign Exchange Operations. *Fed. Res. Bank New York Quart. Rev.,* Winter 1985-86, *10*(4), pp. 45–48. [G: U.S.]

Cross, Sam Y. Treasury and Federal Reserve Foreign Exchange Operations. *Fed. Res. Bank New York Quart. Rev.,* Autumn 1985, *10*(3), pp. 50–64. [G: U.S.]

Cross, Sam Y. Treasury and Federal Reserve Foreign Exchange Operations. *Fed. Res. Bull.,* November 1985, *71*(11), pp. 850–61. [G: U.S.; OECD; Mexico; Argentina]

Cross, Sam Y. Treasury and Federal Reserve Foreign Exchange Operations. *Fed. Res. Bull.,* May 1985, *71*(5), pp. 287–99. [G: U.S.]

Cross, Sam Y. and Alford, Richard F. Treasury and Federal Reserve Foreign Exchange Operations: Interim Report. *Fed. Res. Bull.,* February 1985, *71*(2), pp. 82–84. [G: U.S.]

Cross, Sam Y. and Alford, Richard F. Treasury and Federal Reserve Foreign Exchange Operations: Interim Report. *Fed. Res. Bull.,* August 1985, *71*(8), pp. 607–08. [G: U.S.]

Cumming, Christine M. Federal Deposit Insurance and Deposits at Foreign Branches of U.S. Banks. *Fed. Res. Bank New York Quart. Rev.,* Autumn 1985, *10*(3), pp. 30–38. [G: U.S.]

Davis, Kevin. Australian Monetary Policy: Recent Experience and Some Current Issues. *Australian Econ. Rev.,* 4th Quarter 1985, (72), pp. 37–50. [G: Australia]

De Mattia, Renato. The Forces at Work in the Evolution of Payment Systems in the 1980s. *J. Bank Res.,* Winter 1985, *15*(4), pp. 211–21. [G: Italy]

DeLorme, Charles D., Jr.; Elliott, Donald A. and Kamerschen, David R. The St. Louis Federal Reserve Bank, 1960–1985. *Econ. Notes,* 1985, (3), pp. 134–64. [G: U.S.]

Dudler, Hermann-Josef. The Conduct of Domestic Monetary Policy: Comments. In *Ando, A., et al., eds.,* 1985, pp. 127–29. [G: U.S.]

Dyl, Edward A. and Hoffmeister, J. Ronald. Efficiency and Volatility in the Federal Funds Market. *J. Bank Res.,* Winter 1985, *15*(4), pp. 234–39. [G: U.S.]

Eichengreen, Barry; Watson, Mark W. and Grossman, Richard S. Bank Rate Policy under the Interwar Gold Standard: A Dynamic Probit Model. *Econ. J.,* September 1985, *95*(379), pp. 725–45. [G: U.K.]

Ersenkal, Caryl; Wallace, Myles S. and Warner,

John T. Chairman Reappointments, Presidential Elections and Policy Actions of the Federal Reserve. *Policy Sci.,* November 1985, *18*(3), pp. 211–25. [G: U.S.]

Falls, Gregory A. and Hill, James Richard. Monetary Policy and Causality. *Atlantic Econ. J.,* December 1985, *13*(4), pp. 10–18. [G: U.S.]

Fand, David. Paul Volcker's Legacy. *Policy Rev.,* Fall 1985, (34), pp. 58–63. [G: U.S.]

Fazio, Antonio. L'automazione in Banca d'Italia e i riflessi sul sistema bancario. (Automation in the Bank of Italy and Reflexive Effects on the Banking System. With English summary.) *Bancaria,* January 1985, *41*(1), pp. 63–67. [G: Italy]

Feldstein, Martin. International Trade, Budget Deficits, and the Interest Rate. *J. Econ. Educ.,* Summer 1985, *16*(3), pp. 189–93. [G: U.S.]

Francis, Carlene Y. The Offshore Banking Sector in the Bahamas. *Soc. Econ. Stud.,* December 1985, *34*(4), pp. 91–110. [G: Bahamas]

Friedman, Stephen J. On the Expansion of Banking Powers: Comment. In *Walter, I., ed.,* 1985, pp. 35–40. [G: U.S.]

Füllenkemper, Horst and Rehm, Hannes. Internationale Finanzmärkte unter Innovations- und Liberalisierungsdruck. (International Financial Markets under Innovation and Liberalization Pressure. With English summary.) *Kredit Kapital,* 1985, *18*(4), pp. 553–85. [G: W. Germany]

Gedeon, Shirley J. The Theory of Endogenous Money as the Basis for Banking Reform. *Rivista Int. Sci. Econ. Com.,* Oct.-Nov. 1985, *32*(10–11), pp. 1011–30. [G: U.K.]

Gelsomino, Cosìmo. Mercato monetario e controllo della liquidità in Inghilterra. (Monetary Market and Control of Liquidity in the U.K. With English summary.) *Bancaria,* May 1985, *41*(5), pp. 554–63. [G: U.K.]

Gennari, Fiorella. La disciplina valutaria si evolve senza toccare la gestione delle valute. Rimangono comunque fermi i principi fondamentali del nostro ordinamento. (Foreign Exchange Control Evolves Out of the Management of Currency. With English summary.) *Bancaria,* June 1985, *41*(6), pp. 685–89. [G: Italy]

Giannaros, Demetrios S. and Kolluri, Bharat R. Deficit Spending, Money, and Inflation: Some International Empirical Evidence. *J. Macroecon.,* Summer 1985, *7*(3), pp. 401–17. [G: OECD]

Gidlow, R. M. Forward Exchange Policy in South Africa: Guidelines for Reform. *S. Afr. J. Econ.,* September 1985, *53*(3), pp. 226–40. [G: S. Africa]

Gidlow, R. M. The Modified Role of Discount Houses and Accommodation Policies of the Reserve Bank. *S. Afr. J. Econ.,* March 1985, *53*(1), pp. 67–81. [G: S. Africa]

Gilbert, R. Alton. New Seasonal Factors for the Adjusted Monetary Base. *Fed. Res. Bank St. Louis Rev.,* December 1985, *67*(10), pp. 29–33. [G: U.S.]

Gilbert, R. Alton. Operating Procedures for Conducting Monetary Policy. *Fed. Res. Bank St.*

Louis Rev., February 1985, *67*(2), pp. 13–21. [G: U.S.]

Gilbert, R. Alton. Recent Changes in Handling Bank Failures and Their Effects on the Banking Industry. *Fed. Res. Bank St. Louis Rev.*, June/July 1985, *67*(6), pp. 21–28. [G: U.S.]

Gilbert, R. Alton; Stone, Courtenay C. and Trebing, Michael E. The New Bank Capital Adequacy Standards. *Fed. Res. Bank St. Louis Rev.*, May 1985, *67*(5), pp. 12–20. [G: U.S.]

Godano, Giuseppe. Aumenta ovunque nel mondo la complessità del compito del banchiere. (Bankers' Tasks Are Becoming More Complex All over the World. With English summary.) *Bancaria*, December 1985, *41*(12), pp. 1209–15. [G: OECD]

Goldfaden, Lynn C. and Hurst, Gerald P. Regulatory Responses to Changes in the Consumer Financial Services Industry. *Fed. Res. Bull.*, February 1985, *71*(2), pp. 75–81. [G: U.S.]

Goodfriend, Marvin. *Monetary Theory and Practice, The U.K. Experience:* Book Review. *J. Monet. Econ.*, May 1985, *15*(3), pp. 383–88. [G: U.K.]

Goodhart, Charles A. E. Monetary Policy in Postwar Japan: Comments. In *Ando, A., et al., eds.*, 1985, pp. 131–33. [G: Japan]

Gordon, Robert J. The Conduct of Domestic Monetary Policy. In *Ando, A., et al., eds.*, 1985, pp. 45–81. [G: U.S.]

Gorton, Gary. Clearinghouses and the Origin of Central Banking in the United States. *J. Econ. Hist.*, June 1985, *45*(2), pp. 277–83. [G: U.S.]

Hafer, R. W. The FOMC in 1983–1984: Setting Policy in an Uncertain World. *Fed. Res. Bank St. Louis Rev.*, April 1985, *67*(4), pp. 15–37. [G: U.S.]

Hall, Maximilian J. B. Financial Deregulation and Monetary Policy in Australia. *Banca Naz. Lavoro Quart. Rev.*, September 1985, (154), pp. 261–77. [G: Australia]

Hall, Maximilian J. B. The Reform of Banking Supervision in Hong Kong. *Hong Kong Econ. Pap.*, 1985, (16), pp. 74–96. [G: Hong Kong]

Hamada, Koichi and Hayashi, Fumio. Monetary Policy in Postwar Japan. In *Ando, A., et al., eds.*, 1985, pp. 83–121. [G: Japan]

Heinkel, Robert. Depositors' Welfare, Deposit Insurance, and Deregulation: Discussion. *J. Finance*, July 1985, *40*(3), pp. 975. [G: U.S.]

Hetzel, Robert L. A Mandate of Price Stability for the Federal Reserve System. *Contemp. Policy Issues*, Fall 1985, *3*(5), pp. 59–67. [G: U.S.]

Hetzel, Robert L. The Rules versus Discretion Debate over Monetary Policy in the 1920s. *Fed. Res. Bank Richmond Econ. Rev.*, Nov./Dec. 1985, *71*(6), pp. 3–14. [G: U.S.]

Hewson, J. R. and Nevile, J. W. Monetary and Fiscal Policy in Australia. In *Argy, V. E. and Neville, J. W., eds.*, 1985, pp. 305–24. [G: Australia]

Hooper, Peter. International Repercussions of the U.S. Budget Deficit. *Aussenwirtschaft*, May 1985, *40*(1/2), pp. 117–55. [G: U.S.; OECD]

Horn, Karen N. Statement to the U.S. House Subcommittee on Commerce, Consumer, and Monetary Affairs of the Committee on Government Operations, April 3, 1985. *Fed. Res. Bull.*, June 1985, *71*(6), pp. 415–18. [G: U.S.]

Horne, Jocelyn and Monadjemi, Mehdi. Debt, Credit and Monetary Targeting in Australia. *Econ. Rec.*, June 1985, *61*(173), pp. 522–34. [G: Australia]

Hoskins, W. Lee. Foreign Experiences with Monetary Targeting: A Practitioner's Perspective. *Contemp. Policy Issues*, Fall 1985, *3*(5), pp. 71–83. [G: W. Europe; U.S.; Japan; Canada]

Hotson, John H. Ending the Debt-Money System. *Challenge*, March/April 1985, *28*(1), pp. 48–50. [G: U.S.]

Humphrey, David Burras. Resource Use in Federal Reserve Check and ACH Operations after Pricing. *J. Bank Res.*, Spring 1985, *16*(1), pp. 45–53. [G: U.S.]

Isaac, Alan G. Currency Substitution: Intuition and Implications. *Atlantic Econ. J.*, December 1985, *13*(4), pp. 87–88.

Israelsen, L. Dwight. Macroeconomic Analysis of Leading Interwar Authorities: Marriner S. Eccles, Chairman of the Federal Reserve Board. *Amer. Econ. Rev.*, May 1985, *75*(2), pp. 357–62. [G: U.S.]

Jahnsson, Yrjö. Suomessa vallitsevan rahapulan syistä ja keinoista sen poistamiseksi. (On the Causes and Cures for Finland's Monetary Crisis. With English summary.) *Kansant. Aikak.*, 1985, *81*(1), pp. 5–19. [G: Finland]

Joines, Douglas H. Deficits and Money Growth in the United States, 1872–1983. *J. Monet. Econ.*, November 1985, *16*(3), pp. 329–51. [G: U.S.]

Jordan, Jerry L. Experiences with Monetary Targeting: Introduction. *Contemp. Policy Issues*, Fall 1985, *3*(5), pp. 69–70. [G: U.S.; Europe]

Jordon, Jerry L. Economic Outlook. In *Shadow Open Market Committee.*, 1985, pp. 9–18. [G: U.S.]

Kaldor, Nicholas. How Monetarism Failed. *Challenge*, May/June 1985, *28*(2), pp. 4–13. [G: U.S.; U.K.]

Karafiath, Imre. A Stochastic Model of the Competitive Banking Firm with Lagged and Contemporaneous Reserve Accounting. *J. Money, Credit, Banking*, May 1985, *17*(2), pp. 253–57. [G: U.S.]

Karafiath, Imre. Will a Risk-averse Competitive Bank Prefer Contemporaneous Reserve Accounting? *Financial Rev.*, February 1985, *20*(1), pp. 111–15.

Karamouzis, Nicholas. An Evaluation of M1 Forecasting Errors by the Federal Reserve Staff in the 1970s: A Note. *J. Money, Credit, Banking*, Part 1, Nov. 1985, *17*(4), pp. 512–16. [G: U.S.]

Keeley, Michael C. and Zimmerman, Gary C. Competition for Money Market Deposit Accounts. *Fed. Res. Bank San Francisco Econ. Rev.*, Spring 1985, (2), pp. 5–27. [G: U.S.]

Keen, Howard, Jr. Summary Measures of Economic Policy and Credit Conditions as Early Warning Forecasting Tools. *Bus. Econ.*, October 1985, *20*(4), pp. 38–43. [G: U.S.]

Kelly, Edward J., III. Legislative History of the Glass-Steagall Act. In *Walter, I., ed.*, 1985, pp. 41–65. [G: U.S.]

Kerr, Peter M. Turnover Statistics and Federal Government Balances in Money Supply Targets. *Southern Econ. J.*, October 1985, *52*(2), pp. 344–50. [G: U.S.]

Keyder, Nur. The Money Stock Determination in Turkey 1970–1984. *METU*, 1985, *12*(1/2), pp. 1–26. [G: Turkey]

King, Robert G. On Monetary Reform. In *[Weintraub, R. E.]*, 1985, pp. 40–54. [G: U.S.]

Kullberg, Rolf. Kansantaloudellisen yhdistyksen kokouksissa pidettyjä esitelmiä. Rahapolitiikka murroksessa. (Finnish Monetary Policy in Transition. With English summary.) *Kansant. Aikak.*, 1985, *81*(1), pp. 73–80. [G: Finland]

Kuprianov, Anatoli. The Monetary Control Act and the Role of the Federal Reserve in the Interbank Clearing Market. *Fed. Res. Bank Richmond Econ. Rev.*, July/Aug. 1985, *71*(4), pp. 23–35. [G: U.S.]

Laidler, David. Monetary Policy in Britain: Successes and Shortcomings. *Oxford Rev. Econ. Policy*, Spring 1985, *1*(1), pp. 35–43. [G: U.K.]

Lambert, Marie-Henriette. Monetary Policy in Postwar Japan: Comments. In *Ando, A., et al., eds.*, 1985, pp. 135–37. [G: Japan]

Laney, Leroy O. An International Comparison of Experiences with Monetary Targeting: A Reaction Function Approach. *Contemp. Policy Issues*, Fall 1985, *3*(5), pp. 99–112. [G: W. Europe; U.S.; Japan; Canada]

Laureyssens, Julienne M. Growth of Central Banking: The Société Générale des Pays-Bas and the Impact of the Function of General State Cashier on Belgium's Monetary System (1822–1830) In *Atack, J., ed.*, 1985, pp. 125–38. [G: Netherlands; Belgium]

Lér, Leopold. Financial Policy for the Years to Come. *Czech. Econ. Digest.*, February 1985, (1), pp. 3–23. [G: Czechoslovakia]

Lever, Harold. The Dollar and the World Economy: The Case for Concerted Management. *Lloyds Bank Rev.*, July 1985, (157), pp. 1–12. [G: Global]

Lichtenstein, Cynthia C. U.S. Response to the International Debt Crisis: The International Lending Supervision Act of 1983 and the Regulations Issued under the Act. In *Eskridge, W. N., Jr., ed.*, 1985, pp. 177–206. [G: U.S.]

Litan, Robert E. Evaluating and Controlling the Risks of Financial Product Deregulation. *Yale J. Regul.*, Fall 1985, *3*(1), pp. 1–52. [G: U.S.]

Litterman, Robert B. How Monetary Policy in 1985 Affects the Outlook. *Fed. Res. Bank Minn. Rev.*, Fall 1985, *9*(4), pp. 2–13. [G: U.S.]

Maccarone, Salvatore. La compensazione nei rapporti bancari in conto corrente. (Compensation in Banks' Current Account. With English summary.) *Bancaria*, November 1985, *41*(11), pp. 1147–53. [G: Italy]

Mahoney, Patrick I. and White, Alice P. The Thrift Industry in Transition. *Fed. Res. Bull.*, March 1985, *71*(3), pp. 137–56. [G: U.S.]

Maier, Gerhard. Geldmengenkontrolle in weltoffener Wirtschaft: Die aussenwirtschaftliche Unabhängigkeit der Deutschen Bundesbank. (Monetary Control in an Open Economy: The External Independence of the Deutsche Bundesbank. With English Summary.) *Aussenwirtschaft*, September 1985, *40*(3), pp. 255–73. [G: W. Germany]

Martin, Preston. Statement to the U.S. House Subcommittee on Financial Institutions Supervision, Regulation and Insurance of the Committee on Banking, Finance and Urban Affairs, October 10, 1985. *Fed. Res. Bull.*, December 1985, *71*(12), pp. 937–41. [G: U.S.]

Martin, Preston. Statement to the U.S. House Subcommittee on Economic Stabilization of the Committee on Banking, Finance and Urban Affairs, July 18, 1985. *Fed. Res. Bull.*, September 1985, *71*(9), pp. 697–701. [G: U.S.]

Martin, Preston. Statement to the U.S. House Subcommittee on Commerce, Consumer, and Monetary Affairs of the Committee on Government Operations, April 3, 1985. *Fed. Res. Bull.*, June 1985, *71*(6), pp. 412–15. [G: U.S.]

Martin, Preston. Statement to the U.S. Senate Subcommittee on Securities of the Committee on Banking, Housing, and Urban Affairs, April 4, 1985. *Fed. Res. Bull.*, June 1985, *71*(6), pp. 418–22. [G: U.S.]

Melitz, Jacques. The French Financial System: Mechanism and Questions of Reform. In *Melitz, J. and Wyplosz, C., eds.*, 1985, pp. 361–86. [G: France]

Merrick, John J., Jr. and Saunders, Anthony. Bank Regulation and Monetary Policy. *J. Money, Credit, Banking*, Pt. 2, Nov. 1985, *17*(4), pp. 691–717. [G: U.S.]

Miller, Jeffrey B. and Schneider, Jerrold E. American Politics and Changing Macroeconomic Institutions. In *Maital, S. and Lipnowski, I., eds.*, 1985, pp. 207–39. [G: U.S.]

Minsky, Hyman P. Money and the Lender of Last Resort. *Challenge*, March/April 1985, *28*(1), pp. 12–18. [G: U.S.]

Miskimin, Harry A. The Enforcement of Gresham's Law. In *Marx, A. V., ed.*, 1985, pp. 147–61. [G: U.K.; France]

Mongia, J. N. Deficit Financing. In *Mongia, J. N., ed.*, 1985, pp. 201–37. [G: India]

Morris, Frank E. Rules Plus Discretion in Monetary Policy—An Appraisal of Our Experience since October 1979. *New Eng. Econ. Rev.*, Sept./Oct. 1985, pp. 3–8. [G: U.S.]

Mounts, Wm. Stewart, Jr.; Sowell, Clifford and Lindley, James T. Rent-seeking over Time: The Continuity of Capture. *Public Choice*, 1985, *46*(1), pp. 87–94. [G: U.S.]

Mullineux, A. W. Do We Need the Bank of England? *Lloyds Bank Rev.*, July 1985, (157), pp. 13–24. [G: U.K.]

Musalem, Alberto Roque. El enfoque monetario de balanza de pagos y la presión en el mercado de cambio en Argentina. (With English summary.) *Cuadernos Econ.*, December 1985, 22(67), pp. 389–98. [G: Argentina]

Nepal Rastra Bank. The Role of Central Banks in Development Finance. In *Bandyopadhyay, R. and Khankhoje, D. P., eds.*, 1985, pp. 185–201. [G: Nepal]

Norton, William E. Monetary Policy in Postwar Japan: Comments. In *Ando, A., et al., eds.*, 1985, pp. 139–40.

O'Sullivan, Patrick H. P. International Banking Facilities and the Eurodollar Market: Comment. In *Savona, P. and Sutija, G., eds.*, 1985, pp. 206–09. [G: U.S.; U.K.]

Obstfeld, Maurice. The Dollar and the Policy Mix: 1985: Comment. *Brookings Pap. Econ. Act.*, 1985, (1), pp. 190–95. [G: U.S.]

Padoa-Schioppa, Tommaso. Bonaldo Stringher e la formazione della Banca d'Italia. (Bonaldo Stringer and the Shaping of the Bank of Italy. With English summary.) *Bancaria*, February 1985, 41(2), pp. 141–45. [G: Italy]

Partee, J. Charles. Statement to the U.S. House Subcommittee on Telecommunications, Consumer Protection, and Finance of the Committee on Energy and Commerce, April 2, 1985. *Fed. Res. Bull.*, June 1985, 71(6), pp. 409–12. [G: U.S.]

Peel, D. A. and Pope, P. F. Federal Reserve Money-Supply Announcements and the Behaviour of UK Interest Rates. *J. Econ. Stud.*, 1985, 12(3), pp. 54–60. [G: U.K.; U.S.]

Pierce, James L. On the Expansion of Banking Powers. In *Walter, I., ed.*, 1985, pp. 13–34. [G: U.S.]

Pierce, James L. Policy Making under Uncertainty: Some Lessons from the 1970s. In *[Weintraub, R. E.]*, 1985, pp. 55–75. [G: U.S.]

Plaut, Steven E. The Likud Years: 1977–83. In *Levinson, P. and Landau, P., eds.*, 1985, pp. 31–37. [G: Israel]

Podolski, T. M. Control of a Monetary Quantity: Constraint or Contumacy. *Brit. Rev. Econ. Issues*, Autumn 1985, 7(17), pp. 1–37. [G: U.K.]

Pollin, Jean-Paul. Les agrégats de monnaie et de crédit: leur utilisation dans la conduite de la politique monétaire française. (The Use of Money and Credit Aggregates in Defining the Objectives of French Monetary Policy. With English summary.) *Écon. Appl.*, 1985, 38(1), pp. 325–55. [G: France]

Pontolillo, Vincenzo. Il fattore concorrenza negli interventi dell'autorità sul sistema creditizio. (Competition and Intervention of Supervisory Authorities on the Credit System. With English summary.) *Bancaria*, June 1985, 41(6), pp. 639–54. [G: Italy]

Porter, R. Roderick. International Banking Facilities and the Eurodollar Market: Comment. In *Savona, P. and Sutija, G., eds.*, 1985, pp. 209–10. [G: U.S.; U.K.]

Pozdena, Randall J. and Hotti, Kristin L. Developments in British Banking: Lessons for Regulation and Supervision. *Fed. Res. Bank San Francisco Econ. Rev.*, Fall 1985, (4), pp. 14–25. [G: U.K.]

Pyle, David H. Bank Regulation and Monetary Policy: Comment. *J. Money, Credit, Banking*, Pt. 2, Nov. 1985, 17(4), pp. 722–24. [G: U.S.]

Reichert, Alan K.; Strauss, William and Merris, Randall C. An Economic Analysis of Short-run Fluctuations in Federal Reserve Wire Transfer Volume. *J. Bank Res.*, Winter 1985, 15(4), pp. 222–28. [G: U.S.]

Resler, D. H., et al. Detecting and Estimating Changing Economic Relationships: The Case of Discount Window Borrowings. *Appl. Econ.*, June 1985, 17(3), pp. 509–27. [G: U.S.]

Rich, Georg and Béguelin, Jean-Pierre. Swiss Monetary Policy in the 1970s and 1980s. In *[Weintraub, R. E.]*, 1985, pp. 76–111. [G: Switzerland]

Rohde, Armin. Anmerkungen zur gegenwärtigen Feinsteuerungsstrategie der Deutschen Bundesbank. (Observations on the Current Fine-Control Strategy of the German Bundesbank. With English summary.) *Kredit Kapital*, 1985, 18(3), pp. 418–27. [G: W. Germany]

Rolnick, Arthur J. and Weber, Warren E. Banking Instability and Regulation in the U.S. Free Banking Era. *Fed. Res. Bank Minn. Rev.*, Summer 1985, 9(3), pp. 2–9. [G: U.S.]

Rossi, Enzo and Stolfa, Fabio. Recent Developments in the Instruments for the Control of Bank Liquidity. *Rev. Econ. Cond. Italy*, May–Aug. 1985, (2), pp. 273–86. [G: Italy]

Ruggeri, Giovanni. Notes on the Control of the Public Deficit in the Medium Term. *Rev. Econ. Cond. Italy*, January–April 1985, (1), pp. 37–74. [G: Italy]

Salvemini, Maria Teresa. Costituzionalismo monetario e fiscale. (Monetary and Fiscal Constitutionalism. With English summary.) *Polit. Econ.*, April 1985, 1(1), pp. 123–36. [G: U.S.; Italy]

Santoni, G. J. The Monetary Control Act, Reserve Taxes and the Stock Prices of Commercial Banks. *Fed. Res. Bank St. Louis Rev.*, June/July 1985, 67(6), pp. 12–20. [G: U.S.]

Saulnier, Raymond J. The President's Economic Report: A Critique. *J. Portfol. Manage.*, Summer 1985, 11(4), pp. 61–62. [G: U.S.]

Sayers, Richard. From Note Issue to Central Banking, 1800–1930. In *Marx, A. V., ed.*, 1985, pp. 339–44.

Schiemann, Jürgen. Abwertung, Devisenbewirtschaftung und Handelsprotektionismus. Das Kardinalproblem der Währungspolitik eines Schuldnerlandes vor 50 Jahren während der Weltwirtschaftskrise und heute. (Devaluation, Exchange Control and Trade Protectionism: The Cardinal Problem of a Debtor Nation's Monetary Policy 50 Years Ago during the Great Depression and Today. With English summary.) *Konjunkturpolitik*, 1985, 31(3), pp. 151–87. [G: W. Germany]

Schnabel, Jacques A. Monetary Instability and Share-Market Risk: Canadian Evidence. *Managerial Dec. Econ.*, September 1985, 6(3), pp. 180–82. [G: Canada]

Seger, Martha R. Statement to the U.S. Subcommittee on Consumer Affairs and Coinage of the Committee on Banking, Finance and Urban Affairs, October 29, 1985. *Fed. Res. Bull.*, December 1985, 71(12), pp. 944–48. [G: U.S.]

Shafer, Jeffrey R. International Banking Facilities and the Eurodollar Market: Comment. In *Savona, P. and Sutija, G., eds.*, 1985, pp. 210–15. [G: U.S.; U.K.]

Sheehan, Richard G. The Federal Reserve Reaction Function: Does Debt Growth Influence Monetary Policy? *Fed. Res. Bank St. Louis Rev.*, March 1985, 67(3), pp. 24–33.

Sheehey, Edmund J. and Kreinin, Mordechai E. Inflation Dispersion and Central Bank Accommodation of Supply Shocks. *Weltwirtsch. Arch.*, 1985, 121(3), pp. 448–59. [G: OECD]

Short, Eugenie D. FDIC Settlement Practices and the Size of Failed Banks. *Fed. Res. Bank Dallas Econ. Rev.*, March 1985, pp. 12–20. [G: U.S.]

Sjaastad, Larry A. Exchange Rate Regimes and the Real Rate of Interest. In *Kim, K. S. and Ruccio, D. F., eds.*, 1985, pp. 163–87. [G: Chile; Uruguay]

Smirlock, Michael J. and Yawitz, Jess Barry. Asset Returns, Discount Rate Changes, and Market Efficiency. *J. Finance*, September 1985, 40(4), pp. 1141–58. [G: U.S.]

Soda, Antonio Pasquale. Efficienza ed omogeneità dei controlli sulle nuove forme di intermediazione finanziaria. (Efficiency and Homogeneity of Controls on New Forms of Financial Intermediation. With English summary.) *Bancaria*, June 1985, 41(6), pp. 655–64. [G: Italy]

Spaventa, Luigi. Adjustment Plans, Fiscal Policy and Monetary Policy. *Rev. Econ. Cond. Italy*, January–April 1985, (1), pp. 9–35. [G: Italy]

Spencer, Peter D. Official Intervention in the Foreign Exchange Market. *J. Polit. Econ.*, October 1985, 93(5), pp. 1019–24.

Sternlight, Peter D.; McCurdy, Christopher J. and Meulendyke, Ann-Marie. Monetary Policy and Open Market Operations in 1984. *Fed. Res. Bank New York Quart. Rev.*, Spring 1985, 10(1), pp. 36–56. [G: U.S.]

Sutija, George. International Banking Facilities and the Eurodollar Market: Comment. In *Savona, P. and Sutija, G., eds.*, 1985, pp. 215–17. [G: U.S.; U.K.]

Tarafás, Imre. The Possibility and Conditions of Anti-Inflationary Economic Policy in Hungary. *Acta Oecon.*, 1985, 34(3/4), pp. 287–97. [G: Hungary]

Tardos, Márton. Question Marks in Hungarian Fiscal and Monetary Policy (1979–1984). *Acta Oecon.*, 1985, 35(1–2), pp. 29–52. [G: Hungary]

Tarkka, Juha. Monetary Policy in the BOF3 Quarterly Model of the Finnish Economy. *Econ. Modelling*, October 1985, 2(4), pp. 298–306. [G: Finland]

Taylor, William. Statement to the U.S. House Subcommittee on Commerce, Consumer, and Monetary Affairs of the Committee on Government Operations, May 15, 1985. *Fed. Res. Bull.*, July 1985, 71(7), pp. 528–32. [G: U.S.]

Teal, Francis and Giwa, Y. M. Domestic Credit and the Balance of Payments in Ghana: A Comment. *J. Devel. Stud.*, July 1985, 21(4), pp. 548–61. [G: Ghana]

Terrell, Henry S. and Mills, Rodney H., Jr. International Banking Facilities and the Eurodollar Market. In *Savona, P. and Sutija, G., eds.*, 1985, pp. 183–206. [G: U.S.; U.K.]

Thottathil, Pelis. A Note on Eurodollar Borrowing by U.S. Banks: Derivation of Reg D Equation. *J. Bank Res.*, Spring 1985, 16(1), pp. 40–44. [G: U.S.]

Timberlake, Richard H., Jr. Legislative Construction of the Monetary Control Act of 1980. *Amer. Econ. Rev.*, May 1985, 75(2), pp. 97–102. [G: U.S.]

Tobin, James. Monetary Policy in an Uncertain World. In *Ando, A., et al., eds.*, 1985, pp. 29–42.

Toma, Eugenia Froedge and Toma, Mark. Research Activities and Budget Allocations among Federal Reserve Banks. *Public Choice*, 1985, 45(2), pp. 175–91. [G: U.S.]

Toma, Mark. A Duopoly Theory of Government Money Production: The 1930s and 1940s. *J. Monet. Econ.*, May 1985, 15(3), pp. 363–82.

Vaciago, Giacomo. A Note on Credit Aggregates as Targets or Indicators of Monetary Policy. *Banca Naz. Lavoro Quart. Rev.*, June 1985, (153), pp. 155–71. [G: U.S.]

Vaciago, Giacomo. Evoluzione e prospettive del sistema bancario americano. (Recent Developments and Trends in the U.S. Banking System. With English summary.) *Bancaria*, January 1985, 41(1), pp. 45–53. [G: U.S.]

Vihriälä, Vesa. Alueellisesta rahapolitiikasta. (On Regional Monetary Policy. With English summary.) *Kansant. Aikak.*, 1985, 81(3), pp. 255–65. [G: Finland]

Volcker, Paul A. Statement to the Subcommittee on Economic Goals and Intergovernmental Policy of the Joint Economic Committee, June 27, 1985. *Fed. Res. Bull.*, August 1985, 71(8), pp. 624–28. [G: U.S.]

Volcker, Paul A. Statement to the U.S. House Subcommittee on Domestic Monetary Policy of the Committee on Banking, Finance and Urban Affairs, July 9, 1985. *Fed. Res. Bull.*, September 1985, 71(9), pp. 687–89. [G: U.S.]

Volcker, Paul A. Statement to the U.S. House Subcommittee on Domestic Monetary Policy of the Committee on Banking, Finance and Urban Affairs, July 17, 1985. *Fed. Res. Bull.*, September 1985, 71(9), pp. 690–97. [G: U.S.]

Volcker, Paul A. Statement to the U.S. House Subcommittee on Telecommunications, Consumer Protection, and Finance of the Committee on Energy and Commerce, June 26, 1985.

Fed. Res. Bull., August 1985, *71*(8), pp. 621–23.   [G: U.S.]

Volcker, Paul A. Statement to the U.S. House Subcommittee on Commerce, Consumer, and Monetary Affairs, of the Committee on Government Operations, March 27, 1985. *Fed. Res. Bull.*, May 1985, *71*(5), pp. 312–21.
[G: U.S.]

Volcker, Paul A. Statement to the U.S. Senate Committee on Banking, Housing, and Urban Affairs, September 11, 1985. *Fed. Res. Bull.*, November 1985, *71*(11), pp. 866–73.
[G: U.S.]

Volcker, Paul A. Statement to the U.S. Senate Committee on Banking, Housing, and Urban Affairs, February 20, 1985. *Fed. Res. Bull.*, April 1985, *71*(4), pp. 211–20.   [G: U.S.]

Wallich, Henry C. U.S. Monetary Policy in an Interdependent World. In *[Bloomfield, A. I.]*, 1985, pp. 33–44.

Walter, Ingo. Deregulating Wall Street: Summary and Implications for Policy. In *Walter, I., ed.*, 1985, pp. 293–302.

Wanatabe, Atsushi. International Banking Facilities and the Eurodollar Market: Comment. In *Savona, P. and Sutija, G., eds.*, 1985 , pp. 217–19.   [G: U.S.; Japan]

Webb, Steven B. Government Debt and Inflationary Expectations as Determinants of the Money Supply in Germany, 1919–23. *J. Money, Credit, Banking*, Part 1, Nov. 1985, *17*(4), pp. 479–92.   [G: Germany]

Weigel, Wolfgang. Austrian Economic Policy: A Comment. *Empirica*, 1985, *12*(1), pp. 109–10.
[G: Austria]

Wellink, Nout and Halberstadt, Victor. Monetary Policy and Control of Public Expenditure with Special Reference to the Netherlands. In *Forte, F. and Peacock, A., eds.*, 1985, pp. 169–91.   [G: OECD; Netherlands]

Wenninger, John and Radecki, Lawrence J. The Monetary Aggregates in 1985. *Fed. Res. Bank New York Quart. Rev.*, Winter 1985-86, *10*(4), pp. 6–10.   [G: U.S.]

Willms, Manfred and Karsten, Ingo. Government Policies towards Inflation and Unemployment in West Germany. In *Argy, V. E. and Neville, J. W., eds.*, 1985, pp. 153–80.
[G: W. Germany]

Wilson, Thomas A. and MacGregor, Mary E. The 1985 Federal Budget: Macroeconomic and Fiscal Effects. *Can. Public Policy*, September 1985, *11*(3), pp. 602–16.   [G: Canada]

Wojcikewych, Raymond. An Empirical Investigation of the Interrelationship between Monetary and Fiscal Policy Using Some Alternative Policy Measures. *Quart. J. Bus. Econ.*, Winter 1985, *24*(1), pp. 101–14.   [G: U.S.]

Woolley, John T. Central Banks and Inflation. In *Lindberg, L. N. and Maier, C. S., eds.*, 1985, pp. 318–48.   [G: OECD]

Yeager, Leland B. Deregulation and Monetary Reform. *Amer. Econ. Rev.*, May 1985, *75*(2), pp. 103–07.   [G: U.S.]

Yuravlivker, David E. Crawling Peg and the Real Exchange Rate: Some Evidence from the Southern Cone. *J. Devel. Econ.*, August 1985, *18*(2–3), pp. 381–93.   [G: Argentina; Chile; Brazil; Uruguay]

Zijlstra, Jelle. Central Banking with the Benefit of Hindsight. In *Zijlstra, J.*, 1985, pp. 207–21.

312 Commercial Banking

3120 Commercial Banking

Aharony, Joseph; Saunders, Anthony and Swary, Itzhak. The Effects of the International Banking Act on Domestic Bank Profitability and Risk. *J. Money, Credit, Banking*, Part 1, Nov. 1985, *17*(4), pp. 493–506.   [G: U.S.]

Al-Timimi, W. The Evolution of the Saudi Arabian Monetary System. *Banca Naz. Lavoro Quart. Rev.*, March 1985, (152), pp. 77–83.
[G: Saudi Arabia]

Alexander, Donald L. An Empirical Test of the Mutual Forebearance Hypothesis: The Case of Bank Holding Companies. *Southern Econ. J.*, July 1985, *52*(1), pp. 122–40.   [G: U.S.]

Aliber, Robert Z. Eurodollars: An Economic Analysis. In *Savona, P. and Sutija, G., eds.*, 1985, pp. 77–98.

Angeloni, Ignazio. The Dynamic Behavior of Business Loans and the Prime Rate: A Comment. *J. Banking Finance*, December 1985, *9*(4), pp. 577–80.   [G: U.S.]

Argy, Victor E. Effects of Changes in Banking and Exchange Control Legislation in the United Kingdom on the Significance of the Money Aggregates as Indicators, 1971–81. *Banca Naz. Lavoro Quart. Rev.*, March 1985, (152), pp. 31–44.   [G: U.K.]

Arnould, Richard J. Agency Costs in Banking Firms: An Analysis of Expense Preference Behavior. *J. Econ. Bus.*, May 1985, *37*(2), pp. 103–12.   [G: U.S.]

Ashtor, Eliyahu. Banking Instruments between the Muslim East and the Christian West. In *Marx, A. V., ed.*, 1985, pp. 27–39.

Atkinson, Lloyd C. The Canadian Treatment of Foreign Banks: A Case Study in the Workings of the National Treatment Approach: Comments. In *Stern, R. M., ed.*, 1985, pp. 253–55.   [G: Canada; U.S.]

Bagchi, Amiya Kumar. Anglo-Indian Banking in British India: From the Paper Pound to the Gold Standard. In *Porter, A. N. and Holland, R. F., eds.*, 1985, pp. 93–108.

Barata, José Martins. A Global Model of Bank Profitability: A Non-competitive Market Case with Restrictive Monetary Policy. *Econ. Notes*, 1985, (2), pp. 78–96.   [G: Portugal]

Barkley, David L. and Helander, Peter E. Commercial Bank Loans and Non-metropolitan Economic Activity: A Question of Causality. *Rev. Reg. Stud.*, Winter 1985, *15*(1), pp. 26–32.   [G: U.S.]

Barth, James R. and Pelzman, Joseph. International Debt: Conflict and Resolution. In *Adams, J., ed.*, 1985, pp. 358–91.   [G: U.S.; Global]

Beatty, Randolph P.; Reim, John F. and Schapperle, Robert F. The Effect of Barriers to Entry on Bank Shareholder Wealth: Implications for Interstate Banking. *J. Bank Res.*, Spring 1985, *16*(1), pp. 8–15. [G: U.S.]

Bedingfield, James P.; Reckers, Philip M. J. and Stagliano, A. J. Distributions of Financial Ratios in the Commercial Banking Industry. *J. Finan. Res.*, Spring 1985, *8*(1), pp. 77–81. [G: U.S.]

Beebe, Jack. Bank Stock Performance since the 1970s. *Fed. Res. Bank San Francisco Econ. Rev.*, Winter 1985, (1), pp. 5–18. [G: U.S.]

Belongia, Michael T. and Santoni, G. J. Cash Flow or Present Value: What's Lurking behind That Hedge? *Fed. Res. Bank St. Louis Rev.*, January 1985, *67*(1), pp. 5–13. [G: U.S.]

Bennett, Robert A. The State of Banking. In *Kaushik, S. K., ed.*, 1985 , pp. 121–24. [G: U.S.]

Benston, George J. Large Bank–Small Bank Competition: What Does Experience Tell Us about Competition? In *Federal Reserve Bank of Atlanta (II)*, 1985, pp. 139–45. [G: U.S.]

Bergés, Angel; Fanjul, Oscar and Maravall, Fernando. Impacto bursátil de cambios en la regulación bancaria. (With English summary.) *Revista Española Econ.*, 1985, *2*(1), pp. 49–71. [G: Spain]

Bester, Helmut. Screening vs. Rationing in Credit Markets with Imperfect Information. *Amer. Econ. Rev.*, September 1985, *75*(4), pp. 850–55.

Bhatnagar, R. G. Regional Rural Banks. In *Bandyopadhyay, R. and Khankhoje, D. P., eds.*, 1985, pp. 181–84. [G: India]

Bhatnagar, R. G. Regional Rural Banks: A Critical Review. In *Bandyopadhyay, R. and Khankhoje, D. P., eds.*, 1985, pp. 147–51. [G: India]

Billingsley, Randall S. and Thompson, G. Rodney. Determinants of Stock Repurchases by Bank Holding Companies. *J. Bank Res.*, Autumn 1985, *16*(3), pp. 128–35. [G: U.S.]

Black, Fischer. The Future for Financial Services. In *Inman, R. P., ed.*, 1985, pp. 223–30.

Black, Harold A. and Schweitzer, Robert L. A Canonical Analysis of Mortgage Lending Terms: Testing for Lending Discrimination at a Commerical Bank. *Urban Stud.*, February 1985, *22*(1), pp. 13–19. [G: U.S.]

Blomquist, Thomas W. The Early History of European Banking: Merchants, Bankers and Lombards of Thirteenth-Century Lucca in the County of Champagne. *J. Europ. Econ. Hist.*, Sept.-Dec. 1985, *14*(3), pp. 521–36. [G: Italy]

Boisi, James O. Communications Advances and the Payments System. In *Kaushik, S. K., ed.*, 1985, pp. 93–98.

Booth, James R. and Officer, Dennis T. Expectations, Interest Rates, and Commercial Bank Stocks. *J. Finan. Res.*, Spring 1985, *8*(1), pp. 51–58. [G: U.S.]

Booth, James R.; Officer, Dennis T. and Henderson, Glenn V., Jr. Commercial Bank Stocks, Interest Rates, and Systematic Risk. *J. Econ. Bus.*, December 1985, *37*(4), pp. 303–10. [G: U.S.]

Bourne, Compton. Banking in Boom and Bust Economies: Lessons from Trinidad and Tobago, and Jamaica. *Soc. Econ. Stud.*, December 1985, *34*(4), pp. 139–63. [G: Trinidad and Tobago; Jamaica]

Bowring, Philip. Prudential Supervision of Financial Institutions in Hong Kong. *Hong Kong Econ. Pap.*, 1985, (16), pp. 97–111. [G: Hong Kong]

Brady, Thomas F. Changes in Loan Pricing and Business Lending at Commercial Banks. *Fed. Res. Bull.*, January 1985, *71*(1), pp. 1–13. [G: U.S.]

Broaddus, Alfred. Financial Innovation in the United States—Background, Current Status and Prospects. *Fed. Res. Bank Richmond Econ. Rev.*, Jan./Feb. 1985, *71*(1), pp. 2–22. [G: U.S.]

Bronsteen, Peter. Product Market Definition in Commercial Bank Merger Cases. *Antitrust Bull.*, Fall 1985, *30*(3), pp. 677–94. [G: U.S.]

Burke, Jon R. Interstate Strategies—Smaller Banks: Strategies for Potential Acquirees. In *Federal Reserve Bank of Atlanta (II)*, 1985, pp. 85–91. [G: U.S.]

Cable, John R. Capital Market Information and Industrial Performance: The Role of West German Banks. *Econ. J.*, March 1985, *95*(377), pp. 118–32. [G: W. Germany]

Cable, John R. The Bank–Industry Relationship in West Germany: Performance and Policy Aspects. In *Schwalbach, J., ed.*, 1985, pp. 17–40. [G: W. Germany]

Calabresi, Gian Franco. Automazione, efficienza e costi nell'azienda bancaria e nel mercato. (Automation, Performance and Costs in Banks and in the Market. With English summary.) *Bancaria*, January 1985, *41*(1), pp. 54–62. [G: Italy]

Cantoni, Giampiero. Le carte di credito: profili economici, tecnologici, giuridici. (Credit Cards: Economic, Technological and Legal Aspects. With English summary.) *Bancaria*, September 1985, *41*(9), pp. 955–61. [G: Italy]

Caprara, Ugo. Gli indicatori per la valutazione dell'affidabilità creditizia. (The Indicators for Assessing Credit Reliability. With English summary.) *Bancaria*, October 1985, *41*(10), pp. 1070–76. [G: Italy]

Carli, Guido. The Internationalization of Financial and Credit Systems. *Rev. Econ. Cond. Italy*, Sept.-Dec. 1985, (3), pp. 341–51. [G: Global]

Carosso, Vincent P. American Private Banks in International Banking and Industrial Finance, 1870–1914. In *Atack, J., ed.*, 1985, pp. 19–26. [G: U.S.]

Carosso, Vincent P. Legislative History of the Glass-Steagall Act: An Economic Evaluation of Bank Securities Activities before 1933: Comment. In *Walter, I., ed.*, 1985, pp. 89–91. [G: U.S.]

Cassese, Sabino. É ancora attuale la legge banca-

ria del 1936? (Is the Italian Banking Law of 1936 Still Vital? With English summary.) *Bancaria*, March 1985, *41*(3), pp. 281–84.
[G: Italy]

Cassese, Sabino. Major Banks and New Legislative Structures. *Rev. Econ. Cond. Italy*, Sept.-Dec. 1985, (3), pp. 383–91. [G: U.S.; U.K.; Italy; W. Germany]

Cassis, Y. Bankers in English Society in the Late Nineteenth Century. *Econ. Hist. Rev., 2nd Ser.*, May 1985, *38*(2), pp. 210–29.
[G: U.K.]

Cassis, Y. The Banking Community of London, 1890–1914: A Survey. In *Porter, A. N. and Holland, R. F., eds.*, 1985, pp. 109–26.
[G: U.K.]

Cates, David C. Prices Paid for Banks. In *Federal Reserve Bank of Atlanta (II)*, 1985, pp. 99–107.
[G: U.S.]

Ceccatelli, Ercole. The Role of the Major Banks in Italy: Problems and Prospects. *Rev. Econ. Cond. Italy*, Sept.-Dec. 1985, (3), pp. 363–82.
[G: Italy]

Chan, Yuk-Shee and Kanatas, George. Asymmetric Valuations and the Role of Collateral in Loan Agreements. *J. Money, Credit, Banking*, February 1985, *17*(1), pp. 84–95.

Chan, Yuk-Shee and Mak, King-Tim. Depositors' Welfare, Deposit Insurance, and Deregulation. *J. Finance*, July 1985, *40*(3), pp. 959–74.
[G: U.S.]

Chandavarkar, Anand G. The Financial Pull of Urban Areas in LDCs. *Finance Develop.*, June 1985, *22*(2), pp. 24–27. [G: Thailand; India]

Chant, John F. The Canadian Treatment of Foreign Banks: A Case Study in the Workings of the National Treatment Approach. In *Stern, R. M., ed.*, 1985, pp. 215–44. [G: Canada; U.S.]

Chase, Samuel. Bank Regulation and Monetary Policy: Comment. *J. Money, Credit, Banking*, Pt. 2, Nov. 1985, *17*(4), pp. 718–21.
[G: U.S.]

Chateau, John Peter D. Liability Management of Financial Intermediaries in a Dynamic and Uncertain Perspective. *Europ. Econ. Rev.*, March 1985, *27*(2), pp. 183–200.

Churchill, Neil C. and Lewis, Virginia L. Profitability of Small-Business Lending. *J. Bank Res.*, Summer 1985, *16*(2), pp. 63–71.
[G: U.S.]

Cingano, Francesco. La banca negli anni '90: evoluzione tecnoligica e professionalità. (The Bank in the Nineties: Technological Evolution and Professionalism. With English summary.) *Bancaria*, April 1985, *41*(4), pp. 411–18.
[G: Italy]

Claassen, Emil-Maria. The Lender-of-Last-Resort Function in the Context of National and International Financial Crises. *Weltwirtsch. Arch.*, 1985, *121*(2), pp. 217–37.

Clair, Robert T. A Comparative Analysis of Mature Hispanic-owned Banks. *Fed. Res. Bank Dallas Econ. Rev.*, March 1985, pp. 1–11.
[G: U.S.]

Coates, Joseph F. Scenarios Part Two: Alternative

Futures. In *Mendell, J. S., ed.*, 1985, pp. 21–46.
[G: U.S.]

Cole, John A., et al. Black Banks: A Survey and Analysis of the Literature. *Rev. Black Polit. Econ.*, Summer 1985, *14*(1), pp. 29–50.
[G: U.S.]

Collins, John T. Congressional Update and Outlook on Interstate Banking. In *Federal Reserve Bank of Atlanta (II)*, 1985, pp. 17–24.
[G: U.S.]

Cook, Timothy Q. and Rowe, Timothy D. Are NOWs Being Used as Savings Accounts? *Fed. Res. Bank Richmond Econ. Rev.*, May/June 1985, *71*(3), pp. 3–13. [G: U.S.]

Corrigan, E. Gerald. A Look at the Economy and Some Banking Issues. *Fed. Res. Bank New York Quart. Rev.*, Spring 1985, *10*(1), pp. 1–6. [G: U.S.]

Corrigan, E. Gerald. Bank Supervision in a Changing Financial Environment. *Fed. Res. Bank New York Quart. Rev.*, Winter 1985-86, *10*(4), pp. 1–5. [G: U.S.]

Cottarelli, Carlo; Cotula, Franco and Pittaluga, Giovanni. Differenziazione dei tassi sui depositi: effetti sulla politica monetaria e sulla gestione delle banche. (Differentiation of Rates on Deposits: Effects on the Monetary Policy on the Management of Banks. With English summary.) *Bancaria*, May 1985, *41*(5), pp. 524–38. [G: Italy]

Cumming, Christine M. Federal Deposit Insurance and Deposits at Foreign Branches of U.S. Banks. *Fed. Res. Bank New York Quart. Rev.*, Autumn 1985, *10*(3), pp. 30–38. [G: U.S.]

Cuthbertson, Keith. Sterling Bank Lending to UK Industrial and Commercial Companies. *Oxford Bull. Econ. Statist.*, May 1985, *47*(2), pp. 91–118. [G: U.K.]

Danforth, John T. Interstate Strategies—Large Banks: An Overview of Acquirers' Strategic Choices. In *Federal Reserve Bank of Atlanta (II)*, 1985, pp. 37–41. [G: U.S.]

Danker, Deborah J. and McLaughlin, Mary M. Profitability of Insured Commercial Banks in 1984. *Fed. Res. Bull.*, November 1985, *71*(11), pp. 836–49. [G: U.S.]

Daskin, Alan J. Aggregate Concentration and Geographic Diversification in U.S. Commercial Banking, 1970–1982. *J. Econ. Bus.*, August 1985, *37*(3), pp. 237–51. [G: U.S.]

Daskin, Alan J. Dynamics of Canadian Deposit-taking Institutions: Comment. *J. Ind. Econ.*, March 1985, *33*(3), pp. 353–58. [G: Canada]

Daskin, Alan J. Horizontal Merger Guidelines and the Line of Commerce in Banking: An Algebraic and Graphical Approach. *Antitrust Bull.*, Fall 1985, *30*(3), pp. 651–76. [G: U.S.]

De Mattia, Renato. The Forces at Work in the Evolution of Payment Systems in the 1980s. *J. Bank Res.*, Winter 1985, *15*(4), pp. 211–21.
[G: Italy]

Dermine, Jean. The Measurement of Interest-Rate Risk by Financial Intermediaries. *J. Bank Res.*, Summer 1985, *16*(2), pp. 86–90.

Desai, Anand S. and Stover, Roger D. Bank Holding Company Acquisitions, Stockholder

Returns, and Regulatory Uncertainty. *J. Finan. Res.*, Summer 1985, 8(2), pp. 145–56.
[G: U.S.]

Díaz-Alejandro, Carlos F. Good-bye Financial Repression, Hello Financial Crash. *J. Devel. Econ.*, Sept.-Oct. 1985, 19(1/2), pp. 1–24.
[G: Chile; Argentina; Uruguay]

Dini, Lamberto. The Italian Case: Balance Sheet Trends. *Rev. Econ. Cond. Italy*, Sept.-Dec. 1985, (3), pp. 329–40.
[G: Italy]

Do, Toan Q. and Chateau, John Peter B. A Geometrical Exposition of the Credit Setting Strategies of the Banking Firm under Loan Rate Uncertainty. *Finance*, June 1985, 6(1), pp. 103–19.

Dotsey, Michael. The Use of Electronic Funds Transfers to Capture the Effects of Cash Management Practices on the Demand for Demand Deposits: A Note. *J. Finance*, December 1985, 40(5), pp. 1493–1503.
[G: U.S.]

Duncan, F. H. Intermarket Bank Expansions: Implications for Interstate Banking. *J. Bank Res.*, Spring 1985, 16(1), pp. 16–21.
[G: U.S.]

Dutkowsky, Donald and Foote, William. Switching, Aggregation, and the Demand for Borrowed Reserves. *Rev. Econ. Statist.*, May 1985, 67(2), pp. 331–35.
[G: U.S.]

Dye, Thomas R. Strategic Ownership Positions in U.S. Industry and Banking. *Amer. J. Econ. Soc.*, January 1985, 44(1), pp. 9–22.
[G: U.S.]

Dyl, Edward A. and Hoffmeister, J. Ronald. Efficiency and Volatility in the Federal Funds Market. *J. Bank Res.*, Winter 1985, 15(4), pp. 234–39.
[G: U.S.]

Eickhoff, Gerald E. Going Interstate by Franchises or Networks. In *Federal Reserve Bank of Atlanta (II)*, 1985, pp. 93–98.
[G: U.S.]

Eisenbeis, Robert A. Interstate Banking's Impact upon Financial System Risk. In *Federal Reserve Bank of Atlanta (II)*, 1985, pp. 177–86.
[G: U.S.]

Fabra, Paul. Banking Policy under the Socialists. In *Machin, H. and Wright, V., eds.*, 1985, pp. 173–83.
[G: France]

Fama, Eugene F. What's Different about Banks? *J. Monet. Econ.*, January 1985, 15(1), pp. 29–39.
[G: U.S.]

Fant, Julian E., Jr. Large Bank–Small Bank Competition: Small Banks' Strengths and Weaknesses. In *Federal Reserve Bank of Atlanta (II)*, 1985, pp. 147–54.
[G: U.S.]

Fazio, Antonio. L'automazione in Banca d'Italia e i riflessi sul sistema bancario. (Automation in the Bank of Italy and Reflexive Effects on the Banking System. With English summary.) *Bancaria*, January 1985, 41(1), pp. 63–67.
[G: Italy]

Felgran, Steven D. Banks as Insurance Agencies: Legal Constraints and Competitive Advances. *New Eng. Econ. Rev.*, Sept./Oct. 1985, pp. 34–49.
[G: U.S.]

Felgran, Steven D. From ATM to POS Networks: Branching, Access, and Pricing. *New Eng. Econ. Rev.*, May/June 1985, pp. 44–61.
[G: U.S.]

Ferri, Giovanni and Jafarey, Saqib. Banking Crises and Welfare Implications of Foreign Lending under Informationally Limited Spatial Horizons. *Econ. Notes*, 1985, (3), pp. 121–33.

Flannery, Mark J. An Economic Evaluation of Bank Securities Activities before 1933. In *Walter, I., ed.*, 1985, pp. 67–87.
[G: U.S.]

Flannery, Mark J. The Future for Financial Services: Comment. In *Inman, R. P., ed.*, 1985, pp. 234–38.

Flood, Eugene. Currency Risk and Country Risk in International Banking: Discussion. *J. Finance*, July 1985, 40(3), pp. 892–93.

Folkerts-Landau, David. The Changing Role of International Bank Lending in Development Finance. *Int. Monet. Fund Staff Pap.*, June 1985, 32(2), pp. 317–63.
[G: LDCs]

Francis, Carlene Y. The Offshore Banking Sector in the Bahamas. *Soc. Econ. Stud.*, December 1985, 34(4), pp. 91–110.
[G: Bahamas]

Fraser, Donald R. and Groth, John C. Listing and the Liquidity of Bank Stocks. *J. Bank Res.*, Autumn 1985, 16(3), pp. 136–44.
[G: U.S.]

Fraser, Donald R. and Richards, R. Malcolm. The Penn Square Bank Failure and the Inefficient Market. *J. Portfol. Manage.*, Spring 1985, 11(3), pp. 34–36.
[G: U.S.]

Fraser, Donald R.; Richards, R. Malcolm and Fosberg, Richard II. A Note on Deposit Rate Deregulation, Super Nows, and Bank Security Returns. *J. Banking Finance*, December 1985, 9(4), pp. 585–95.
[G: U.S.]

Frieder, Larry A. Florida's Interstate Banking Debate. In *Federal Reserve Bank of Atlanta (II)*, 1985, pp. 187–210.
[G: U.S.]

Friedman, Stephen J. On the Expansion of Banking Powers: Comment. In *Walter, I., ed.*, 1985, pp. 35–40.
[G: U.S.]

Friend, Irwin. The Future for Financial Services: Comment. In *Inman, R. P., ed.*, 1985, pp. 231–33.

Füllenkemper, Horst and Rehm, Hannes. Internationale Finanzmärkte unter Innovations- und Liberalisierungsdruck. (International Financial Markets under Innovation and Liberalization Pressure. With English summary.) *Kredit Kapital*, 1985, 18(4), pp. 553–85.
[G: W. Germany]

Furash, Edward E. Preparing for Interstate Banking. In *Federal Reserve Bank of Atlanta (II)*, 1985, pp. 75–84.
[G: U.S.]

Gavin, Bridig. A GATT for International Banking? *J. World Trade Law*, March:April 1985, 19(2), pp. 121–35.
[G: OECD; Asia]

Gedeon, Shirley J. Money and Banking in Yugoslavia: A Socialist Dilemma. *Rev. Radical Polit. Econ.*, Spring and Summer 1985, 17(1/2), pp. 41–58.
[G: Yugoslavia]

Gedeon, Shirley J. The Theory of Endogenous Money as the Basis for Banking Reform. *Rivista Int. Sci. Econ. Com.*, Oct.-Nov. 1985, 32(10–11), pp. 1011–30.
[G: U.K.]

Ghantus, Elias T. Developing a Worldwide Arab Banking System. In *Czinkota, M. R. and Marciel, S., eds.*, 1985, pp. 129–37.
[G: OPEC]

Gianini, Felice. L'automazione nel rapporto fra

banca e impresa. Lineamenti per una strategia di sistema. (Automation in Banking Services for Businesses. With English summary.) *Bancaria*, January 1985, *41*(1), pp. 68–72. [G: Italy]

Giddy, Ian H. Is Equity Underwriting Risky for Commercial Bank Affiliates? In *Walter, I., ed.*, 1985, pp. 145–69. [G: U.S.]

Gidlow, R. M. The Modified Role of Discount Houses and Accommodation Policies of the Reserve Bank. *S. Afr. J. Econ.*, March 1985, *53*(1), pp. 67–81. [G: S. Africa]

Gilbert, R. Alton. Recent Changes in Handling Bank Failures and Their Effects on the Banking Industry. *Fed. Res. Bank St. Louis Rev.*, June/July 1985, *67*(6), pp. 21–28. [G: U.S.]

Gilbert, R. Alton and Ott, Mack. Why the Big Rise in Business Loans at Banks Last Year? *Fed. Res. Bank St. Louis Rev.*, March 1985, *67*(3), pp. 5–13. [G: U.S.]

Gilbert, R. Alton; Stone, Courtenay C. and Trebing, Michael E. The New Bank Capital Adequacy Standards. *Fed. Res. Bank St. Louis Rev.*, May 1985, *67*(5), pp. 12–20. [G: U.S.]

Gladen, Werner. Kundenstruktureffekte von Gebühren im Privatgiroverkehr der Kreditinstitute. (Clientele Structure Effects of Charges in the Private Giro Business of the Banks. With English summary.) *Kredit Kapital*, 1985, *18*(3), pp. 402–17.

Glascock, John L. and Davidson, Wallace N., III. The Effect of Bond Deratings on Bank Stock Returns. *J. Bank Res.*, Autumn 1985, *16*(3), pp. 120–27. [G: U.S.]

Godano, Giuseppe. Aumenta ovunque nel mondo la complessità del compito del banchiere. (Bankers' Tasks Are Becoming More Complex All over the World. With English summary.) *Bancaria*, December 1985, *41*(12), pp. 1209–15. [G: OECD]

Goldberg, Michael A. and Lloyd-Davies, Peter R. Standby Letters of Credit: Are Banks Overextending Themselves? *J. Bank Res.*, Spring 1985, *16*(1), pp. 28–39. [G: U.S.]

Goldfaden, Lynn C. and Hurst, Gerald P. Regulatory Responses to Changes in the Consumer Financial Services Industry. *Fed. Res. Bull.*, February 1985, *71*(2), pp. 75–81. [G: U.S.]

Goldthwaite, Richard A. Local Banking in Renaissance Florence. *J. Europ. Econ. Hist.*, Spring 1985, *14*(1), pp. 5–55. [G: Italy]

Gorton, Gary. Bank Suspension of Convertibility. *J. Monet. Econ.*, March 1985, *15*(2), pp. 177–93.

Gorton, Gary. Banking Theory and Free Banking History: A Review Essay. *J. Monet. Econ.*, September 1985, *16*(2), pp. 267–76. [G: U.K.]

Gorton, Gary. Clearinghouses and the Origin of Central Banking in the United States. *J. Econ. Hist.*, June 1985, *45*(2), pp. 277–83. [G: U.S.]

Graddy, Duane B. and Hall, Gary. Unionization and Productivity in Commercial Banking. *J. Lab. Res.*, Summer 1985, *6*(3), pp. 249–62. [G: U.S.]

Gradi, Florio. Realtà, equivoci ed errori lungo la strada verso la riduzione dei tassi. (Facts, Misunderstandings and Errors along the Road towards Reducing Bank Rates. With English summary.) *Bancaria*, September 1985, *41*(9), pp. 948–54. [G: Italy]

Greenbaum, Stuart I. and Venezia, Itzhak. Partial Exercise of Loan Commitments under Adaptive Pricing. *J. Finan. Res.*, Winter 1985, *8*(4), pp. 251–63.

Gupta, Kanhaya L. Portfolio Behaviour of Selected Financial Institutions in Canada. *Appl. Econ.*, April 1985, *17*(2), pp. 341–58. [G: Canada]

Haavisto, Esko and Tarkka, Juha. Pankkiluottojen korkoporrastus keskikorkosäännöstelyn vallitessa. (Setting the Interest Rates on Bank Loans When the Average Lending Rate Is Regulated. With English summary.) *Liiketaloudellinen Aikak.*, 1985, *34*(3), pp. 272–83.

Hall, Maximilian J. B. Financial Deregulation and Monetary Policy in Australia. *Banca Naz. Lavoro Quart. Rev.*, September 1985, (154), pp. 261–77. [G: Australia]

Hall, Maximilian J. B. The Reform of Banking Supervision in Hong Kong. *Hong Kong Econ. Pap.*, 1985, (16), pp. 74–96. [G: Hong Kong]

Hancock, Diana. Bank Profitability, Interest Rates, and Monetary Policy. *J. Money, Credit, Banking*, May 1985, *17*(2), pp. 189–202. [G: U.S.]

Hancock, Diana. The Financial Firm: Production with Monetary and Nonmonetary Goods. *J. Polit. Econ.*, October 1985, *93*(5), pp. 859–80. [G: U.S.]

Hawke, John D., Jr. Interstate Banking in Congress, the States, and the Courts: Implications of Recent Court Decisions. In *Federal Reserve Bank of Atlanta (II)*, 1985, pp. 3–10. [G: U.S.]

Heebner, A. Gilbert. Deregulation in Commercial Banking: A Reply. *Bus. Econ.*, October 1985, *20*(4), pp. 59. [G: U.S.]

Heebner, A. Gilbert. Deregulation in Commercial Banking. *Bus. Econ.*, July 1985, *20*(3), pp. 15–20. [G: U.S.]

Heinkel, Robert. Depositors' Welfare, Deposit Insurance, and Deregulation: Discussion. *J. Finance*, July 1985, *40*(3), pp. 975. [G: U.S.]

Hoffman, John E., Jr. American Hostages in Iran: The Conduct of a Crisis: The Bankers' Channel. In *Kreisberg, P. H., ed.*, 1985, pp. 235–80. [G: U.S.; Iran]

Hooks, Donald L. and Martell, Terrence F. Multibank Holding Company Activity and Local Market Structure: Some Implications for Intra- and Interstate Banking. *J. Econ. Bus.*, December 1985, *37*(4), pp. 327–41. [G: U.S.]

Hörngren, Lars. Regulatory Monetary Policy and Uncontrolled Financial Intermediaries. *J. Money, Credit, Banking*, May 1985, *17*(2), pp. 203–19.

Horvitz, Paul M. The Combination of Banking and Insurance: Implications for Regulation. *Growth Change*, October 1985, *16*(4), pp. 10–19. [G: U.S.]

Huertas, Thomas F. An Analysis of the Competitive Effects of Allowing Commercial Bank Affiliates to Underwrite Corporate Securities: Comment. In *Walter, I., ed.*, 1985, pp. 141–43. [G: U.S.]

Huertas, Thomas F. The Rise of the Modern Business Enterprise: The Case of Citibank. In *Atack, J., ed.*, 1985, pp. 143–57. [G: U.S.]

Hultman, Charles W. International Banking and U.S. Commercial Policy. *J. World Trade Law*, May:June 1985, *19*(3), pp. 219–28. [G: OECD; U.S.]

Hunter, Gregory S. The Development of Bankers: Career Patterns and Corporate Form at the Manhattan Company, 1799–1842. In *Atack, J., ed.*, 1985, pp. 59–77. [G: U.S.]

Jacobsen, Thomas H. Innovation through Experimentation. In *Federal Reserve Bank of Atlanta (1)*, 1985, pp. 81–87. [G: U.S.]

Jones, Charles. The Fiscal Motive for Monetary and Banking Legislation in Argentina, Australia and Canada before 1914. In *Platt, D. C. M. and di Tella, G., eds.*, 1985, pp. 123–38. [G: Argentina; Australia; Canada]

Jones, Charles. The State and Business Practice in Argentina 1862–1914. In *Abel, C. and Lewis, C. M., eds.*, 1985, pp. 184–98. [G: Argentina; U.K.]

Kahn, James A. Another Look at Free Banking in the United States [New Evidence on the Free Banking Era]. *Amer. Econ. Rev.*, September 1985, *75*(4), pp. 881–85. [G: U.S.]

Karafiath, Imre. A Stochastic Model of the Competitive Banking Firm with Lagged and Contemporaneous Reserve Accounting. *J. Money, Credit, Banking*, May 1985, *17*(2), pp. 253–57. [G: U.S.]

Karafiath, Imre. Will a Risk-averse Competitive Bank Prefer Contemporaneous Reserve Accounting? *Financial Rev.*, February 1985, *20*(1), pp. 111–15.

Keating, Giles. The Financial Sector of the London Business School Model. In *Currie, D., ed.*, 1985, pp. 86–126. [G: U.K.]

Keeley, Michael C. The Regulation of Bank Entry. *Fed. Res. Bank San Francisco Econ. Rev.*, Summer 1985, (3), pp. 5–13. [G: U.S.]

Keeley, Michael C. and Zimmerman, Gary C. Competition for Money Market Deposit Accounts. *Fed. Res. Bank San Francisco Econ. Rev.*, Spring 1985, (2), pp. 5–27. [G: U.S.]

Keeley, Michael C. and Zimmerman, Gary C. Determining Geographic Markets for Deposit Competition in Banking. *Fed. Res. Bank San Francisco Econ. Rev.*, Summer 1985, (3), pp. 25–45. [G: U.S.]

Kelly, Edward J., III. Conflicts of Interest: A Legal View. In *Walter, I., ed.*, 1985, pp. 231–54. [G: U.S.]

Kelly, Edward J., III. Legislative History of the Glass-Steagall Act. In *Walter, I., ed.*, 1985, pp. 41–65. [G: U.S.]

Kim, Moshe. Scale Economies in Banking: A Methodological Note. *J. Money, Credit, Banking*, February 1985, *17*(1), pp. 96–102. [G: U.S.]

Kindleberger, Charles P. Banking and Industry between the Two Wars: An International Comparison. In *Kindleberger, C. P.*, 1985, pp. 293–313. [G: U.S.; Europe]

Kindleberger, Charles P. Sweden in 1850 as an 'Impoverished Sophisticate': Comment. In *Kindleberger, C. P.*, 1985, pp. 240–43. [G: Sweden]

Klein, P. W. Banking and Economic Modernisation in the Netherlands during the Second Part of the 19th Century. In *Marx, A. V., ed.*, 1985, pp. 131–39. [G: Netherlands]

Kling, John L. The Dynamic Behavior of Business Loans and the Prime Rate. *J. Banking Finance*, September 1985, *9*(3), pp. 421–42. [G: U.S.]

Kling, John L. The Dynamic Behavior of Business Loans and the Prime Rate: Reply. *J. Banking Finance*, December 1985, *9*(4), pp. 581–84. [G: U.S.]

Koehn, Hank E. The Futures Research Division of the Security Pacific Bank. In *Mendell, J. S., ed.*, 1985, pp. 109–13. [G: U.S.]

Kolari, James W. and Di Clemente, John. A Case Study of Geographic Deregulation: The New Illinois Bank Holding Company Act. *J. Bank Res.*, Autumn 1985, *16*(3), pp. 150–57. [G: U.S.]

Kopcke, Richard W. Bank Funding Strategy and the Money Stock. *New Eng. Econ. Rev.*, January/February 1985, pp. 5–14. [G: U.S.]

Koppenhaver, G. D. A Note on Managing Deposit Flows with Cash and Futures Market Decisions. *J. Banking Finance*, June 1985, *9*(2), pp. 323–31.

Koppenhaver, G. D. Bank Funding Risks, Risk Aversion, and the Choice of Futures Hedging Instrument. *J. Finance*, March 1985, *40*(1), pp. 241–55. [G: U.S.]

Koppenhaver, G. D. Variable-Rate Loan Commitments, Deposit Withdrawal Risk, and Anticipatory Hedging. *J. Futures Markets*, Fall 1985, *5*(3), pp. 317–30. [G: U.S.]

Korobow, Leon and Budzeika, George. Financial Limits on Interstate Bank Expansion. *Fed. Res. Bank New York Quart. Rev.*, Summer 1985, *10*(2), pp. 13–27. [G: U.S.]

Korobow, Leon and Stuhr, David. Performance Measurement of Early Warning Models: Comments on West and Other Weakness/Failure Prediction Models. *J. Banking Finance*, June 1985, *9*(2), pp. 267–73. [G: U.S.]

Kuprianov, Anatoli. The Monetary Control Act and the Role of the Federal Reserve in the Interbank Clearing Market. *Fed. Res. Bank Richmond Econ. Rev.*, July/Aug. 1985, *71*(4), pp. 23–35. [G: U.S.]

Lam, Chun H. and Chen, Andrew H. Joint Effects of Interest Rate Deregulation and Capital Requirements on Optimal Bank Portfolio Adjustments. *J. Finance*, June 1985, *40*(2), pp. 563–75.

Landau, Pinhas. Banking in 1984—The Year After. In *Levinson, P. and Landau, P., eds.*, 1985, pp. 129–33. [G: Israel]

Landskroner, Yoram and Ruthenberg, David. Optimal Bank Behavior under Uncertain Inflation. *J. Finance*, September 1985, *40*(4), pp. 1159–71.

Langenfeld, James and McKenzie, Joseph A. Financial Deregulation and Geographic Market Delineation: An Application of the Justice Guidelines to Banking. *Antitrust Bull.*, Fall 1985, *30*(3), pp. 695–712.   [G: U.S.]

Langohr, Herwig and Santomero, Anthony M. Commercial Bank Refinancing and Economic Stability: An Analysis of European Features. *J. Banking Finance*, December 1985, *9*(4), pp. 535–52.   [G: EEC]

Langohr, Herwig and Santomero, Anthony M. The Extent of Equity Investment by European Banks: A Note. *J. Money, Credit, Banking*, May 1985, *17*(2), pp. 243–52.   [G: EEC]

Lassila, Jaakko. Bankerna och industripolitiken. (Banks and Industrial Policy. With English summary.) *Ekon. Samfundets Tidskr.*, 1985, *38*(4), pp. 179–86.   [G: Finland]

Lee, B. E. Determinants of the Commercial Loan Rate Revisited. *Quart. J. Bus. Econ.*, Autumn 1985, *24*(4), pp. 85–95.   [G: U.S.]

van Leeuwen, Peter H. The Prediction of Business Failure at Rabobank. *J. Bank Res.*, Summer 1985, *16*(2), pp. 91–98.

Levich, Richard M. A View from the International Capital Markets. In *Walter, I., ed.*, 1985, pp. 255–92.   [G: OECD]

Litan, Robert E. Evaluating and Controlling the Risks of Financial Product Deregulation. *Yale J. Regul.*, Fall 1985, *3*(1), pp. 1–52.
[G: U.S.]

Loevinger, Lee. Antitrust, Banking, and Competition. *Antitrust Bull.*, Fall 1985, *30*(3), pp. 583–615.   [G: U.S.]

Long, Perrin H., Jr. Nonbanks' Interstate Banking Performance. In *Federal Reserve Bank of Atlanta (II)*, 1985, pp. 129–33.   [G: U.S.]

van Loo, Peter D. Portfolio Selection and Interest Rate Setting by the Dutch Banking System. In *Currie, D., ed.*, 1985, pp. 127–58.
[G: Netherlands]

Lucia, Joseph L. The Failure of the Bank of United States: A Reappraisal. *Exploration Econ. Hist.*, October 1985, *22*(4), pp. 402–16.
[G: U.S.]

Maccarone, Salvatore. La compensazione nei rapporti bancari in conto corrente. (Compensation in Banks' Current Account. With English summary.) *Bancaria*, November 1985, *41*(11), pp. 1147–53.   [G: Italy]

Madeo, Silvia A. and Pincus, Morton. Stock Market Behavior and Tax Rule Changes: The Case of the Disallowance of Certain Interest Deductions Claimed by Banks. *Accounting Rev.*, July 1985, *60*(3), pp. 407–29.   [G: U.S.]

Maineri, Bruno. Alla ricerca di un metodo per calcolare la produttività nelle aziende di credito. E' il mercato ad imporre l'adozione di nuovi strumenti manageriali. La sperimentazione del Sistema BAI nella realtà italiana. (A System for Measuring Productivity of Banks. With English summary.) *Bancaria*, June 1985, *41*(6), pp. 629–38.   [G: Italy]

Manghetti, Gianni. The Banking System: A Composite World. A Photograph and Some Proposals. *Rev. Econ. Cond. Italy*, May-Aug. 1985, (2), pp. 223–41.   [G: Italy]

Marchetti, Piergaetano. La pubblicità nella concorrenza fra emittenti sul mercato del risparmio. (Advertising in the Competition among Issues on the Savings Market. With English summary.) *Bancaria*, May 1985, *41*(5), pp. 515–23.   [G: Italy]

Martin, Preston. Statement to the U.S. House Subcommittee on Telecommunications, Consumer Protection, and Finance of the Committee on Energy and Commerce, May 2, 1985. *Fed. Res. Bull.*, July 1985, *71*(7), pp. 508–13.
[G: U.S.]

Martin, Preston. Statement to the U.S. House Subcommittee on Financial Institutions Supervision, Regulation and Insurance of the Committee on Banking, Finance and Urban Affairs, October 10, 1985. *Fed. Res. Bull.*, December 1985, *71*(12), pp. 937–41.   [G: U.S.]

Martin, Preston. Statement to the U.S. House Subcommittee on Telecommunications, Consumer Protection, and Finance of the Committee on Energy and Commerce, April 23, 1985. *Fed. Res. Bull.*, June 1985, *71*(6), pp. 428–30.   [G: U.S.]

Mathias, Peter. Credit Needs and Credit Supplies for Eighteenth Century Enterprise. In *Marx, A. V., ed.*, 1985, pp. 103–17.   [G: U.K.]

McColl, Hugh L., Jr. A Rationale for Regional Interstate Banking. In *Federal Reserve Bank of Atlanta (II)*, 1985, pp. 61–66.   [G: U.S.]

McCulloch, J. Huston. Interest-Risk Sensitive Deposit Insurance Premia: Stable ACH Estimates. *J. Banking Finance*, March 1985, *9*(1), pp. 137–56.   [G: U.S.]

McDermott, John. Interest Rates and the Banking System with Imperfect Capital Markets and Mobility. In *Connolly, M. B. and McDermott, J., eds.*, 1985, pp. 165–72.

McShane, R. W. and Sharpe, Ian G. A Time Series/Cross Section Analysis of the Determinants of Australian Trading Bank Loan/Deposit Interest Margins: 1962–1981. *J. Banking Finance*, March 1985, *9*(1), pp. 115–36.
[G: Australia]

Mengle, David L. Daylight Overdrafts and Payments System Risks. *Fed. Res. Bank Richmond Econ. Rev.*, May/June 1985, *71*(3), pp. 14–27.
[G: U.S.]

Mengle, David L. and Walter, John R. A Review of Bank Performance in the Fifth District, 1984. *Fed. Res. Bank Richmond Econ. Rev.*, July/Aug. 1985, *71*(4), pp. 12–22.   [G: U.S.]

Merrick, John J., Jr. and Saunders, Anthony. Bank Regulation and Monetary Policy. *J. Money, Credit, Banking*, Pt. 2, Nov. 1985, *17*(4), pp. 691–717.   [G: U.S.]

Merris, Randall C. Explicit Interest and Demand Deposit Service Charges: A Note. *J. Money, Credit, Banking*, Part 1, Nov. 1985, *17*(4), pp. 528–33.

Moore, Basil J. and Threadgold, Andrew R. Corporate Bank Borrowing in the UK, 1965-1981.

Economica, February 1985, *52*(205), pp. 65–78. **[G: U.K.]**

Mote, Larry R. and Baer, Herbert, Jr. Foreign Experience with Nationwide Banking. In *Federal Reserve Bank of Atlanta (II),* 1985, pp. 211–22. **[G: U.S.; Selected OECD]**

Mujumdar, N. A. Structural Transformation in the Deployment of Credit: Some Implications. In *Bandyopadhyay, R. and Khankhoje, D. P., eds.,* 1985, pp. 41–54. **[G: India]**

Mullineux, A. W. Do We Need the Bank of England? *Lloyds Bank Rev.,* July 1985, (157), pp. 13–24. **[G: U.K.]**

Myers, Forest E. and Van Walleghem, Joe. Management Transferability in Rural Banks. *J. Bank Res.,* Winter 1985, *15*(4), pp. 229–33. **[G: U.S.]**

Nars, Kari. Finlands banksektor i korseld. (The Finnish Banking Sector in Crossfire. With English summary.) *Ekon. Samfundets Tidskr.,* 1985, *38*(1), pp. 13–22. **[G: Finland]**

Narube, Savenaca and Whiteside, Barry T. Financial Institutions and Markets in Fiji. In *Skully, M. T., ed.,* 1985, pp. 94–159. **[G: Fiji]**

Nelson, Richard W. Branching, Scale Economies, and Banking Costs. *J. Banking Finance,* June 1985, *9*(2), pp. 177–91. **[G: U.S.]**

Nelson, Richard W. Large Bank–Small Bank Competition: Large Banks' Strengths and Weaknesses. In *Federal Reserve Bank of Atlanta (II),* 1985, pp. 155–63. **[G: U.S.]**

Neu, C. R. The Canadian Treatment of Foreign Banks: A Case Study in the Workings of the National Treatment Approach: Comments. In *Stern, R. M., ed.,* 1985, pp. 245–52. **[G: Canada; U.S.]**

Nicholl, Peter and King, Maree F. Financial Institutions and Markets in New Zealand. In *Skully, M. T., ed.,* 1985, pp. 160–244. **[G: New Zealand]**

Nunnenkamp, Peter. Bank Lending to Developing Countries and Possible Solutions to International Debt Problems. *Kyklos,* 1985, *38*(4), pp. 555–77. **[G: LCDs; MDCs]**

O'Driscoll, Gerald P., Jr. Money in a Deregulated Financial System. *Fed. Res. Bank Dallas Econ. Rev.,* May 1985, pp. 1–12. **[G: U.S.]**

O'Sullivan, Patrick H. P. International Banking Facilities and the Eurodollar Market: Comment. In *Savona, P. and Sutija, G., eds.,* 1985, pp. 206–09. **[G: U.S.; U.K.]**

Oberg, Barbara. New York State and the "Specie Crisis" of 1837. In *Atack, J., ed.,* 1985, pp. 37–52. **[G: U.S.]**

Ollerenshaw, Philip. An Economic History of Ulster 1820–1939: Industry, 1820–1914. In *Kennedy, L. and Ollerenshaw, P., eds.,* 1985, pp. 62–108. **[G: U.K.]**

Oppenheimer, Peter M. Eurodollars: An Economic Analysis: Comment. In *Savona, P. and Sutija, G., eds.,* 1985, pp. 98–106.

Osano, Hiroshi and Tsutsui, Yoshiro. Implicit Contracts in the Japanese Bank Loan Market. *J. Finan. Quant. Anal.,* June 1985, *20*(2), pp. 211–29. **[G: Japan]**

Parke, Darrel W. and Zagardo, Janice. Stochastic Coefficient Regression Estimates of the Sources of Shifts into MMDA Deposits Using Cross-Section Data. *J. Econometrics,* September 1985, *29*(3), pp. 327–40. **[G: U.S.]**

Parravicini, Giannino. Il sistema bancario fra vincoli ed evoluzione. (The Italian Banking System between Constraints and Evolution. With English summary.) *Bancaria,* April 1985, *41*(4), pp. 393–401. **[G: Italy]**

Partee, J. Charles. Statement to the Subcommittee on Agriculture and Transportation of the Joint Economic Committee, June 19, 1985. *Fed. Res. Bull.,* August 1985, *71*(8), pp. 614–18. **[G: U.S.]**

Partee, J. Charles. Statement to the U.S. House Subcommittee on Financial Institutions Supervision, Regulation and Insurance, of the Committee on Banking, Finance and Urban Affairs, September 11, 1985. *Fed. Res. Bull.,* November 1985, *71*(11), pp. 874–77. **[G: U.S.]**

Partee, J. Charles. Statement to the U.S. House Subcommittee on Telecommunications, Consumer Protection, and Finance of the Committee on Energy and Commerce, April 2, 1985. *Fed. Res. Bull.,* June 1985, *71*(6), pp. 409–12. **[G: U.S.]**

Partee, J. Charles. Statement to the U.S. Senate Subcommittee on Financial Institutions of the Committee on Banking, Housing, and Urban Affairs, April 26, 1985. *Fed. Res. Bull.,* June 1985, *71*(6), pp. 435–39. **[G: U.S.]**

Patil, R. K. and Patel, K. V. Rural Development: Organisation and Management Issues. In *Bandyopadhyay, R. and Khankhoje, D. P., eds.,* 1985, pp. 77–98. **[G: India]**

Patrick, Hugh and Moreno, Honorata A. Philippine Private Domestic Commercial Banking, 1946–80, in the Light of Japanese Experience. In *Ohkawa, K. and Ranis, G., eds.,* 1985, pp. 311–65.

Perkins, Edwin J. Lost Opportunities for Compromise in the Bank War: A Reassessment of Jackson's Veto Message. In *Atack, J., ed.,* 1985, pp. 53–56. **[G: U.S.]**

Perrot, Jean-Claude. Aléas d'une innovation: les banques foncières au XVIIIe siècle. (The Hazards of Innovation: Land Banks in the 18th Century. With English summary.) *Écon. Soc.,* October 1985, *19*(10), pp. 5–36. **[G: France; U.K.]**

Petrochilos, George A. Foreign Banks in Greece. *Nat. Westminster Bank Quart. Rev.,* February 1985, pp. 57–69. **[G: Greece]**

Philip, Alan Butt. Banking Policy under the Socialists: Comment. In *Machin, H. and Wright, V., eds.,* 1985, pp. 183–86. **[G: France]**

Phillips, Bruce D. The Effect of Industry Deregulation on the Small Business Sector. *Bus. Econ.,* January 1985, *20*(1), pp. 28–37. **[G: U.S.]**

Pierce, James L. On the Expansion of Banking Powers. In *Walter, I., ed.,* 1985, pp. 13–34. **[G: U.S.]**

Pontolillo, Vincenzo. Il fattore concorrenza negli interventi dell'autorità sul sistema creditizio.

(Competition and Intervention of Supervisory Authorities on the Credit System. With English summary.) *Bancaria*, June 1985, *41*(6), pp. 639–54. [G: Italy]

Porter, R. Roderick. International Banking Facilities and the Eurodollar Market: Comment. In *Savona, P. and Sutija, G., eds.*, 1985, pp. 209–10. [G: U.S.; U.K.]

Pozdena, Randall J. and Hotti, Kristin L. Developments in British Banking: Lessons for Regulation and Supervision. *Fed. Res. Bank San Francisco Econ. Rev.*, Fall 1985, (4), pp. 14–25. [G: U.K.]

Pressnell, L. S. Banks and Their Predecessors in the Economy of Eighteenth Century England. In *Marx, A. V., ed.*, 1985, pp. 277–81. [G: U.K.]

Pugel, Thomas A. and White, Lawrence J. An Analysis of the Competitive Effects of Allowing Commercial Bank Affiliates to Underwrite Corporate Securities. In *Walter, I., ed.*, 1985, pp. 93–139. [G: U.S.]

Pyle, David H. Bank Regulation and Monetary Policy: Comment. *J. Money, Credit, Banking*, Pt. 2, Nov. 1985, *17*(4), pp. 722–24. [G: U.S.]

Resler, D. H., et al. Detecting and Estimating Changing Economic Relationships: The Case of Discount Window Borrowings. *Appl. Econ.*, June 1985, *17*(3), pp. 509–27. [G: U.S.]

Revell, Jack R. Payment Systems over the Next Decade. *J. Bank Res.*, Winter 1985, *15*(4), pp. 200–210.

Revell, Jack R. The Structures of the Credit Systems: Concentration and Fragmentation. *Rev. Econ. Cond. Italy*, Sept.-Dec. 1985, (3), pp. 393–411. [G: OECD]

Rhoades, Stephen A. Interstate Banking: Impacts on the Banking System and the Public: Concentration in Local and National Markets. In *Federal Reserve Bank of Atlanta (II)*, 1985, pp. 171–76. [G: U.S.]

Rhoades, Stephen A. Market Performance and the Nature of a Competitive Fringe. *J. Econ. Bus.*, May 1985, *37*(2), pp. 141–57. [G: U.S.]

Rhoades, Stephen A. Market Share as a Source of Market Power: Implications and Some Evidence. *J. Econ. Bus.*, December 1985, *37*(4), pp. 343–63. [G: U.S.]

Rhoades, Stephen A. Mergers of the 20 Largest Banks and Industrials, All Bank Mergers (1960–1983), and Some Related Issues. *Antitrust Bull.*, Fall 1985, *30*(3), pp. 617–49. [G: U.S.]

Rhoades, Stephen A. and Heggestad, Arnold A. Multimarket Interdependence and Performance in Banking: Two Tests. *Antitrust Bull.*, Winter 1985, *30*(4), pp. 975–95. [G: U.S.]

Richard, Robert A. States' Interstate Banking Initiatives. In *Federal Reserve Bank of Atlanta (II)*, 1985, pp. 11–16. [G: U.S.]

Rockoff, Hugh. New Evidence on Free Banking in the United States [New Evidence on the Free Banking Era]. *Amer. Econ. Rev.*, September 1985, *75*(4), pp. 886–89.

Rogers, Ronald C.; Murphy, Neil B. and Owers,

James E. Financial Innovation, Balance Sheets Cosmetics and Market Response: The Case of Equity-for-Debt Exchanges in Banking. *J. Bank Res.*, Autumn 1985, *16*(3), pp. 145–49. [G: U.S.]

Rolfes, Bernd. Ansätze zur Steuerung von Zinsänderungsrisiken. (Approaches to Control of the Risk of Interest Rate Changes. With English summary.) *Kredit Kapital*, 1985, *18*(4), pp. 529–52.

Rolnick, Arthur J. and Weber, Warren E. Banking Instability and Regulation in the U.S. Free Banking Era. *Fed. Res. Bank Minn. Rev.*, Summer 1985, *9*(3), pp. 2–9. [G: U.S.]

Rose, John T. Interstate Banking, Potential Competition, and the Attractiveness of Banking Markets for New Entry. *Antitrust Bull.*, Fall 1985, *30*(3), pp. 729–43. [G: U.S.]

Rose, Peter S. and Kolari, James W. Early Warning Systems as a Monitoring Device for Bank Condition. *Quart. J. Bus. Econ.*, Winter 1985, *24*(1), pp. 43–60.

Rose, Peter S.; Kolari, James W. and Riener, Kenneth W. A National Survey Study of Bank Services and Prices Arrayed by Size and Structure. *J. Bank Res.*, Summer 1985, *16*(2), pp. 72–85. [G: U.S.]

Rousseas, Stephen. A Markup Theory of Bank Loan Rates. *J. Post Keynesian Econ.*, Fall 1985, *8*(1), pp. 135–44. [G: U.S.]

Rymes, T. K. Inflation, Nonoptimal Monetary Arrangements and the Banking Imputation in the National Accounts. *Rev. Income Wealth*, March 1985, *31*(1), pp. 85–96.

Santoni, G. J. The Monetary Control Act, Reserve Taxes and the Stock Prices of Commercial Banks. *Fed. Res. Bank St. Louis Rev.*, June/July 1985, *67*(6), pp. 12–20. [G: U.S.]

Saunders, Anthony. Bank Safety and Soundness and the Risks of Corporate Securities Activities. In *Walter, I., ed.*, 1985, pp. 171–206. [G: U.S.]

Saunders, Anthony. Conflicts of Interest: An Economic View. In *Walter, I., ed.*, 1985, pp. 207–30. [G: U.S.]

Savona, Paolo. Eurodollars: An Economic Analysis: Comment. In *Savona, P. and Sutija, G., eds.*, 1985, pp. 106–10.

Scamacci, Paolo. Il recepimento delle direttive comunitarie nell'ordinamento bancario italiano. (The Incorporation of EC Community Directives into the Italian Banking Law. With English summary.) *Bancaria*, May 1985, *41*(5), pp. 564–68. [G: EEC; Italy]

Schweikart, Larry. Antebellum Southern Bankers: Origins and Mobility. In *Atack, J., ed.*, 1985, pp. 79–103. [G: U.S.]

Scott, Jonathan A.; Hempel, George H. and Peavy, John W., III. The Effect of Stock-for-Debt Swaps on Bank Holding Companies. *J. Banking Finance*, June 1985, *9*(2), pp. 233–51. [G: U.S.]

Sealey, C. W., Jr. Portfolio Separation for Stockholder Owned Depository Financial Intermediaries. *J. Banking Finance*, December 1985, *9*(4), pp. 477–90.

Sealey, C. W., Jr. and Heinkel, Robert. Asymmetric Information and a Theory of Compensating Balances. *J. Banking Finance*, June 1985, *9*(2), pp. 193–205.

Shafer, Jeffrey R. International Banking Facilities and the Eurodollar Market: Comment. In *Savona, P. and Sutija, G., eds.*, 1985, pp. 210–15. [G: U.S.; U.K.]

Shaffer, Sherrill. Competition, Economies of Scale, and Diversity of Firm Sizes. *Appl. Econ.*, June 1985, *17*(3), pp. 467–76. [G: U.S.]

Shah, A. C. Evolving Role of Banks in Rural Credit. In *Bandyopadhyay, R. and Khankhoje, D. P., eds.*, 1985, pp. 109–23. [G: India]

Shah, A. C. Innovations of Structural, Institutional and Procedural Concepts in Rural Finance Introduced by Bank of Baroda. In *Bandyopadhyay, R. and Khankhoje, D. P., eds.*, 1985, pp. 161–70. [G: India]

Shapiro, Alan C. Currency Risk and Country Risk in International Banking. *J. Finance*, July 1985, *40*(3), pp. 881–91.

Sherman, H. David and Gold, Franklin. Bank Branch Operating Efficiency: Evaluation with Data Envelopment Analysis. *J. Banking Finance*, June 1985, *9*(2), pp. 297–315.

Shirilla, Robert M. Deregulation in Commercial Banking: A Comment. *Bus. Econ.*, October 1985, *20*(4), pp. 58. [G: U.S.]

Short, Eugenie D. FDIC Settlement Practices and the Size of Failed Banks. *Fed. Res. Bank Dallas Econ. Rev.*, March 1985, pp. 12–20. [G: U.S.]

Singh, Sampat P. Redesigning System for Bank Lending to Industry. In *Bandyopadhyay, R. and Khankhoje, D. P., eds.*, 1985, pp. 63–75. [G: India]

Skully, Michael T. Financial Institutions and Markets in Papua New Guinea. In *Skully, M. T., ed.*, 1985, pp. 245–339. [G: Papua New Guinea]

Skully, Michael T. Financial Institutions and Markets in Australia. In *Skully, M. T., ed.*, 1985, pp. 1–93. [G: Australia]

Smiley, Gene. Banking Structure and the National Capital Market, 1869–1914: A Comment. *J. Econ. Hist.*, September 1985, *45*(3), pp. 653–59. [G: U.S.]

Smirlock, Michael J. Evidence on the (Non) Relationship between Concentration and Profitability in Banking. *J. Money, Credit, Banking*, February 1985, *17*(1), pp. 69–83.

Solomon, Elinor H. The Dynamics of Banking Antitrust: The New Technology, the Product Realignment. *Antitrust Bull.*, Fall 1985, *30*(3), pp. 537–81. [G: U.S.]

Spiegel, John W. SunTrust: A Case Study in Interstate Strategy. In *Federal Reserve Bank of Atlanta (I)*, 1985, pp. 49–53. [G: U.S.]

Spronk, Jaap and Zambruno, Giovanni. Interactive Multiple Goal Programming for Bank Portfolio Selection. In *Fandel, G. and Spronk, J., eds.*, 1985, pp. 289–306.

Stewart, Frances. The International Debt Situation and North–South Relations. *World Devel.*,

February 1985, *13*(2), pp. 191–204. [G: Global]

Strobel, Frederick R. The U.S. Banking and Corporate Structure: Some Implications for Industrial Policy. *J. Econ. Issues*, June 1985, *19*(2), pp. 541–49. [G: U.S.]

Sushka, Marie Elizabeth and Barrett, W. Brian. Banking Structure and the National Capital Market, 1869–1914: A Reply. *J. Econ. Hist.*, September 1985, *45*(3), pp. 661–65. [G: U.S.]

Sutija, George. International Banking Facilities and the Eurodollar Market: Comment. In *Savona, P. and Sutija, G., eds.*, 1985, pp. 215–17. [G: U.S.; U.K.]

Sylla, Richard. Early American Banking: The Significance of the Corporate Form. In *Atack, J., ed.*, 1985, pp. 105–23. [G: U.S.; U.K.]

Syron, Richard F. Interstate Banking Strategies in New England. In *Federal Reserve Bank of Atlanta (II)*, 1985, pp. 43–48. [G: U.S.]

Tacci, Marcello. L'automazione della banca. Quali le attese e quali i ritorni? (Automation in Banking: Expectations and Returns. With English summary.) *Bancaria*, January 1985, *41*(1), pp. 73–80. [G: Italy]

Talamona, Mario. Considerazioni in tema di gestione economica delle aziende di credito. (Some Considerations on the Efficiency in the Management of Banks. With English summary.) *Rivista Int. Sci. Econ. Com.*, Oct.-Nov. 1985, *32*(10–11), pp. 949–64. [G: Italy]

Tartaglia, Elio. Non sempre equilibrate le deroghe al principio del segreto banario. (Derogations of the Principle of Banking Secrecy Are Not Always Balanced. With English summary.) *Bancaria*, October 1985, *41*(10), pp. 1059–62. [G: Italy]

Taylor, William. Statement to the U.S. House Subcommittee on Financial Institutions Supervision, Regulation and Insurance, of the Committee on Banking, Finance and Urban Affairs, September 11, 1985. *Fed. Res. Bull.*, November 1985, *71*(11), pp. 877–81. [G: U.S.]

Taylor, William. Statement to the U.S. House Subcommittee on Commerce, Consumer, and Monetary Affairs of the Committee on Government Operations, May 15, 1985. *Fed. Res. Bull.*, July 1985, *71*(7), pp. 528–32. [G: U.S.]

Teas, R. Kenneth and Dellva, W. L. Conjoint Measurement of Consumers' Preferences for Multiattribute Financial Services. *J. Bank Res.*, Summer 1985, *16*(2), pp. 99–112.

Tedeschi, Adelmo. Le sofferenze nel nostro sistema creditizio: un'indagine di lungo periodo. (Bad Debts in the Italian Credit System: A Structural Survey—Part I. With English summary.) *Bancaria*, May 1985, *41*(5), pp. 539–53. [G: Italy]

Tedeschi, Adelmo. Le sofferenze nel nostro sistema creditizio: un'indagine di lungo periodo. (Bad Debts in the Italian Credit System: A Structural Survey—Part II. With English summary.) *Bancaria*, June 1985, *41*(6), pp. 670–78. [G: Italy]

Telgen, Jan. MCDM Problems in Rabobank Nederland. In *Fandel, G. and Spronk, J., eds.*, 1985, pp. 307–16. [G: Netherlands]

Terrell, Henry S. and Mills, Rodney H., Jr. International Banking Facilities and the Eurodollar Market. In *Savona, P. and Sutija, G., eds.*, 1985, pp. 183–206. [G: U.S.; U.K.]

Thingalaya, N. K.; Khankhoje, D. P. and Godse, V. T. Systems and Procedures in Rural Banking: Some Operational Aspects. In *Bandyopadhyay, R. and Khankhoje, D. P., eds.*, 1985, pp. 99–108. [G: India]

Thornton, John. The Role of Rediscount Quotas: A Note. *J. Money, Credit, Banking*, August 1985, *17*(3), pp. 387–90. [G: W. Germany]

Thottathil, Pelis. A Note on Eurodollar Borrowing by U.S. Banks: Derivation of Reg D Equation. *J. Bank Res.*, Spring 1985, *16*(1), pp. 40–44. [G: U.S.]

Thurow, Lester C. The Politics of Deregulation; Evolution of the Major Banks and the Financial Intermediaries in the U.S.A. *Rev. Econ. Cond. Italy*, Sept.-Dec. 1985, (3), pp. 353–62. [G: U.S.]

Timberlake, Richard H., Jr. Legislative Construction of the Monetary Control Act of 1980. *Amer. Econ. Rev.*, May 1985, *75*(2), pp. 97–102. [G: U.S.]

Tonnel-Martinache, Mariette. La délocalisation de l'activité financière bancaire. (With English summary.) *Revue Écon. Polit.*, May–June 1985, *95*(3), pp. 346–76. [G: OECD]

Tucker, Edwin W. The Judicial Leap into the Glass-Steagall Thicket. In *Atack, J., ed.*, 1985, pp. 179–96. [G: U.S.]

Ugolini, Ernesto. Struttura e costi dell'attività bancaria nel mercato mobiliare e gestione accentrata dei titoli. (Structure and Costs of Banking in the Securities Market and the Centralized Management of Securities. With English summary.) *Bancaria*, April 1985, *41*(4), pp. 438–45. [G: Italy]

Vaciago, Giacomo. Evoluzione e prospettive del sistema bancario americano. (Recent Developments and Trends in the U.S. Banking System. With English summary.) *Bancaria*, January 1985, *41*(1), pp. 45–53. [G: U.S.]

VanHoose, David D. Bank Market Structure and Monetary Control. *J. Money, Credit, Banking*, August 1985, *17*(3), pp. 298–311.

Volcker, Paul A. Statement to the U.S. House Subcommittee on Commerce, Consumer, and Monetary Affairs, of the Committee on Government Operations, March 27, 1985. *Fed. Res. Bull.*, May 1985, *71*(5), pp. 312–21. [G: U.S.]

Volcker, Paul A. Statement to the U.S. House Subcommittee on Financial Institutions Supervision, Regulation and Insurance of the Committee on Banking, Finance and Urban Affairs, April 24, 1985. *Fed. Res. Bull.*, June 1985, *71*(6), pp. 430–35. [G: U.S.]

Volcker, Paul A. Statement to the U.S. House Subcommittee on Financial Institutions Supervision, Regulation and Insurance of the Committee on Banking, Finance and Urban Affairs,

April 17, 1985. *Fed. Res. Bull.*, June 1985, *71*(6), pp. 424–27. [G: U.S.]

Volcker, Paul A. Statement to the U.S. Senate Committee on Banking, Housing, and Urban Affairs, September 11, 1985. *Fed. Res. Bull.*, November 1985, *71*(11), pp. 866–73. [G: U.S.]

Volcker, Paul A. Statement to the U.S. Senate Committee on Banking, Housing, and Urban Affairs, May 8, 1985. *Fed. Res. Bull.*, July 1985, *71*(7), pp. 517–20. [G: U.S.]

Waldo, Douglas G. Bank Runs, the Deposit–Currency Ratio, and the Interest Rate. *J. Monet. Econ.*, May 1985, *15*(3), pp. 269–77.

Wall, Larry. Why Are Some Banks More Profitable Than Others? *J. Bank Res.*, Winter 1985, *15*(4), pp. 240–56. [G: U.S.]

Wallich, Henry C. Whither American Banking Reform? *Challenge*, Sept./Oct. 1985, *28*(4), pp. 43–46. [G: U.S.]

Walter, Ingo. Deregulating Wall Street: Introduction and Overview. In *Walter, I., ed.*, 1985, pp. 1–12. [G: U.S.]

Walter, Ingo. Deregulating Wall Street: Summary and Implications for Policy. In *Walter, I., ed.*, 1985, pp. 293–302.

Wanatabe, Atsushi. International Banking Facilities and the Eurodollar Market: Comment. In *Savona, P. and Sutija, G., eds.*, 1985 , pp. 217–19. [G: U.S.; Japan]

Watkins, Thomas G. Probable Future Competition in Banking. *Antitrust Bull.*, Fall 1985, *30*(3), pp. 713–27. [G: U.S.]

Watkins, Thomas G.; Spong, Kenneth R. and Eichholz, Mark J. Potential Competition and the Factors Influencing Banking Concentration. *Rev. Ind. Organ.*, 1985, *2*(2), pp. 94–105. [G: U.S.]

Welch, Patrick J. and Naes, Jude L., Jr. The Merger Guidelines, Concentration and Excess Capacity in Local Commercial Banking Markets. *J. Bank Res.*, Autumn 1985, *16*(3), pp. 158–60. [G: U.S.]

Wellons, Philip A. International Debt: The Behavior of Banks in a Politicized Environment. *Int. Organ.*, Summer 1985, *39*(3), pp. 441–71. [G: OECD; LDCs]

Wells, Joel R., Jr. Customer and Employee Feedback. In *Federal Reserve Bank of Atlanta (I)*, 1985, pp. 31–34. [G: U.S.]

West, Robert Craig. A Factor-Analytic Approach to Bank Condition. *J. Banking Finance*, June 1985, *9*(2), pp. 253–66. [G: U.S.]

White, Eugene Nelson. The Merger Movement in Banking, 1919–1933. *J. Econ. Hist.*, June 1985, *45*(2), pp. 285–91. [G: U.S.]

White, Eugene Nelson. Voting for Costly Regulation: Evidence from Banking Referenda in Illinois, 1924. *Southern Econ. J.*, April 1985, *51*(4), pp. 1084–98. [G: U.S.]

White, Lawrence H. Free Banking and the Gold Standard. In *Rockwell, L. H., Jr., ed.*, 1985, pp. 113–28.

Whitehead, David D., III. Interstate Operations by Banks. In *Federal Reserve Bank of Atlanta (II)*, 1985, pp. 113–28. [G: U.S.]

Wilbur, William L.; Miller, George L. and Brown, William J. A Pooled Time-Series–Cross Section Analysis of Returns on Alternative Sources of Bank Capital. *Appl. Econ.*, December 1985, *17*(6), pp. 1023–41. [G: U.S.]

Wolfson, Martin H. Financial Developments of Bank Holding Companies in 1984. *Fed. Res. Bull.*, December 1985, *71*(12), pp. 924–32. [G: U.S.]

Yeager, Leland B. Deregulation and Monetary Reform. *Amer. Econ. Rev.*, May 1985, *75*(2), pp. 103–07. [G: U.S.]

313 Capital Markets

3130 General

Amoako-Adu, Ben; Marmer, Harry and Yagil, Joseph. The Efficiency of Certain Speculative Markets and Gambler Behavior. *J. Econ. Bus.*, December 1985, *37*(4), pp. 365–78. [G: U.S.]

Bench, Robert R. Deregulation—A Worldwide Phenomenon? In *Kaushik, S. K., ed.*, 1985, pp. 85–91.

Bernstein, Peter L. Wall Street's View of Keynes and Keynes's View of Wall Street. In *Wattel, H. L., ed.*, 1985, pp. 22–29.

Black, Fischer. The Future for Financial Services. In *Inman, R. P., ed.*, 1985, pp. 223–30.

Booth, James R. and Smith, Richard L. The Application of Errors-in-Variables Methodology to Capital Market Research: Evidence on the Small-Firm Effect. *J. Finan. Quant. Anal.*, December 1985, *20*(4), pp. 501–15. [G: U.S.]

Buttler, Günter and Heinlein, Werner. Untersuchungen zuer empirischen Evidenz ökonomischer Spekulationstheorien. (Empirical Evidence of Economic Theories of Speculation. With English summary.) *Jahr. Nationalökon. Statist.*, September 1985, *200*(5), pp. 486–507.

Denton, Frank T. The Effect of Professional Advice on the Stability of a Speculative Market. *J. Polit. Econ.*, October 1985, *93*(5), pp. 977–93.

Easterbrook, Frank H. Insider Trading as an Agency Problem. In *Pratt, J. W. and Zeckhauser, R. J., eds.*, 1985, pp. 81–100.

Flannery, Mark J. The Future for Financial Services: Comment. In *Inman, R. P., ed.*, 1985, pp. 234–38.

Friend, Irwin. Effects of Taxation on Financial Markets. In *Pechman, J. A., ed. (II)*, 1985, pp. 87–106. [G: U.S.]

Friend, Irwin. The Future for Financial Services: Comment. In *Inman, R. P., ed.*, 1985, pp. 231–33.

Garth, Bryant G.; Nagel, Ilene H. and Plager, Sheldon J. Empirical Research and the Shareholder Derivative Suit: Toward a Better-informed Debate. *Law Contemp. Probl.*, Summer 1985, *48*(3), pp. 137–59. [G: U.S.]

Giaccotto, Carmelo and Ali, Mukhtar M. Optimal Distribution-Free Tests and Further Evidence of Heteroscedasticity in the Market Model: A Reply. *J. Finance*, June 1985, *40*(2), pp. 607. [G: U.S.]

Ginglinger, Édith. Le prix d'émission des actions nouvelles: une application de la théorie des options aux agumentations de capital. (The Pricing of Equity Issues: An Application of Option Theory. With English summary.) *Finance*, June 1985, *6*(1), pp. 23–40. [G: France]

Jao, Y. C. Financial Deepening and Economic Growth: Theory, Evidence and Policy. *Greek Econ. Rev.*, December 1985, *7*(3), pp. 187–225. [G: LDCs]

Kader, Ahmad A. The Stock Market as a Leading Indicator of Economic Activity. *Atlantic Econ. J.*, March 1985, *13*(1), pp. 100.

Kahl, Kandice H.; Rutz, Roger D. and Sinquefield, Jeanne C. The Economics of Performance Margins in Futures Markets. *J. Futures Markets*, Spring 1985, *5*(1), pp. 103–12.

Keating, Giles. The Financial Sector of the London Business School Model. In *Currie, D., ed.*, 1985, pp. 86–126. [G: U.K.]

Kindleberger, Charles P. Integration of Financial Markets: The British and French Experience. In *Kindleberger, C. P.*, 1985, pp. 86–104.

Kindleberger, Charles P. The International Causes and Consequences of the Great Crash. In *Kindleberger, C. P.*, 1985, pp. 267–73. [G: U.S.]

Kochman, Ladd Michael. Questioning the Less-than-Perfect Correlation Rule for Combining Stocks. *Atlantic Econ. J.*, July 1985, *13*(2), pp. 85.

Lakonishok, Josef and Ofer, Aharon R. The Information Content of General Price Level Earnings: A Reply. *Accounting Rev.*, October 1985, *60*(4), pp. 711–13. [G: U.S.]

Lehmann, Bruce and Warga, Arthur D. Optimal Distribution-Free Tests and Further Evidence of Heteroscedasticity in the Market Model: A Comment. *J. Finance*, June 1985, *40*(2), pp. 603–05. [G: U.S.]

Mikkelsen, Richard. Brancheglidning på kapitalmarkedet. (Drift among Financial Institutions in the Danish Capital Market. With English summary.) *Nationaløkon. Tidsskr.*, 1985, *123*(1), pp. 20–31. [G: Denmark]

Moor, Roy E. Economics of Financial Markets. *Bus. Econ.*, April 1985, *20*(2), pp. 37–42.

Pfleiderer, Paul. Finance Anthropology. *J. Portfol. Manage.*, Fall 1985, *12*(1), pp. 52–53.

Samuelson, Bruce A. and Murdoch, Brock. The Information Content of General Price Level Adjusted Earnings: A Comment. *Accounting Rev.*, October 1985, *60*(4), pp. 706–10. [G: U.S.]

Summers, Lawrence H. On Economics and Finance. *J. Finance*, July 1985, *40*(3), pp. 633–35.

Thies, Clifford F. New Estimates of the Term Structure of Interest Rates: 1920–1939. *J. Finan. Res.*, Winter 1985, *8*(4), pp. 297–306. [G: U.S.]

Thompson, Rex. Conditioning the Return-generating Process of Firm-specific Events: A Discussion of Event Study Methods. *J. Finan. Quant. Anal.*, June 1985, *20*(2), pp. 151–68.

Webb, Robert Ivory. The Behavior of Speculative

Prices and the Consistency of Economic Models. *J. Econometrics*, January 1985, *27*(1), pp. 123–30.

3131 Capital Markets: Theory, Including Portfolio Selection, and Empirical Studies Illustrating Theory

Admati, Anat R. A Noisy Rational Expectations Equilibrium for Multi-asset Securities Markets. *Econometrica*, May 1985, *53*(3), pp. 629–57.

Admati, Anat R. and Pfleiderer, Paul. Interpreting the Factor Risk Premia in the Arbitrage Pricing Theory [The Arbitrage Theory of Capital Asset Pricing]. *J. Econ. Theory*, February 1985, *35*(1), pp. 191–95.

Admati, Anat R. and Ross, Stephen A. Measuring Investment Performance in a Rational Expectations Equilibrium Model. *J. Bus.*, January 1985, *58*(1), pp. 1–26.

Alexander, Gordon J. and Resnick, Bruce G. More on Estimation Risk and Simple Rules for Optimal Portfolio Selection. *J. Finance*, March 1985, *40*(1), pp. 125–33.

Alexander, Gordon J. and Resnick, Bruce G. Using Linear and Goal Programming to Immunize Bond Portfolios. *J. Banking Finance*, March 1985, *9*(1), pp. 35–54. [G: U.S.]

Amershi, Amin H. A Complete Analysis of Full Pareto Efficiency in Financial Markets for Arbitrary Preferences. *J. Finance*, September 1985, *40*(4), pp. 1235–43.

Amsler, Christine E. and Schmidt, Peter. A Monte Carlo Investigation of the Accuracy of Multivariate CAPM Tests. *J. Finan. Econ.*, September 1985, *14*(3), pp. 359–75.

Andersen, Torben M. Recent Developments in the Theory of Efficient Capital Markets. *Kredit Kapital*, 1985, *18*(3), pp. 347–71.

Ang, James S. and Schwarz, Thomas. Risk Aversion and Information Structure: An Experimental Study of Price Variability in the Securities Markets. *J. Finance*, July 1985, *40*(3), pp. 825–44.

Anthony, Robert N. How to Measure Fixed-Income Performance *Correctly*. *J. Portfol. Manage.*, Winter 1985, *11*(2), pp. 61–65. [G: U.S.]

Argy, Victor E. and Murray, G. L. Effects of Sterilising a Balance of Payments Surplus on Domestic Yields—A Formal Analysis. *J. Int. Money Finance*, June 1985, *4*(2), pp. 223–36.

Arndt, Sven W. and Pigott, Charles. Exchange Rate Models: Evolution and Policy Implications. In *Arndt, S. W.; Sweeney, R. J. and Willett, T. D., eds.*, 1985, pp. 19–48. [G: U.S.]

Arrow, Kenneth J. Comment on Duesenberry's "Portfolio Approach to the Demand for Money and Other Assets." In *Arrow, K. J. (II)*, 1985, pp. 9–14.

Bahmani-Oskooee, Mohsen and Das, Satya P. Transaction Costs and the Interest Parity Theorem. *J. Polit. Econ.*, August 1985, *93*(4), pp. 793–99. [G: U.S.; U.K.; W. Germany]

Balasko, Yves. Preferences, Price Expectations and Speculation. In *[Rossier, Edouard]*, 1985, pp. 1–16.

Ball, Clifford A. and Torous, Walter N. On Jumps in Common Stock Prices and Their Impact on Call Option Pricing. *J. Finance*, March 1985, *40*(1), pp. 155–73. [G: U.S.]

Banks, Jeffrey S. Price-conveyed Information versus Observed Insider Behavior: A Note on Rational Expectations Convergence [Efficiency of Experimental Security Markets with Insider Information: An Application of Rational-Expectations Models]. *J. Polit. Econ.*, August 1985, *93*(4), pp. 807–15.

Barnes, Tom. Markowitz Allocation—Fixed Income Securities. *J. Finan. Res.*, Fall 1985, *8*(3), pp. 181–91. [G: U.S.; Canada]

Barone-Adesi, Giovanni. Arbitrage Equilibrium with Skewed Asset Returns. *J. Finan. Quant. Anal.*, September 1985, *20*(3), pp. 299–313. [G: U.S.]

Barry, Christopher B. and Brown, Stephen J. Differential Information and Security Market Equilibrium. *J. Finan. Quant. Anal.*, December 1985, *20*(4), pp. 407–22.

Bawa, Vijay S., et al. On Determination of Stochastic Dominance Optimal Sets. *J. Finance*, June 1985, *40*(2), pp. 417–31.

Beckers, Stan and Sercu, Piet. Foreign Exchange Pricing under Free Floating versus Admissible Band Regimes. *J. Int. Money Finance*, September 1985, *4*(3), pp. 317–29.

Belongia, Michael T. and Santoni, G. J. Cash Flow or Present Value: What's Lurking behind That Hedge? *Fed. Res. Bank St. Louis Rev.*, January 1985, *67*(1), pp. 5–13. [G: U.S.]

Benderly, Jason and Zwick, Burton. Inflation, Real Balances, Output, and Real Stock Returns [Stock Returns, Real Activity, Inflation, and Money]. *Amer. Econ. Rev.*, December 1985, *75*(5), pp. 1115–23. [G: U.S.]

Benninga, Simon Z. and Blume, Marshall E. On the Optimality of Portfolio Insurance. *J. Finance*, December 1985, *40*(5), pp. 1341–52.

Benson, Earl; Sprecher, C. Ronald and Willman, Elliott S. Cyclical Variation in Corporate Bond Yield Spreads: New Evidence. *Quart. J. Bus. Econ.*, Summer 1985, *24*(3), pp. 3–18. [G: U.S.]

Berck, Peter and Cecchetti, Stephen G. Portfolio Diversification, Futures Markets, and Uncertain Consumption Prices. *Amer. J. Agr. Econ.*, August 1985, *67*(3), pp. 497–507.

Bergman, Yaacov Z. Time Preference and Capital Asset Pricing Models. *J. Finan. Econ.*, March 1985, *14*(1), pp. 145–59.

Best, Michael J. and Grauer, Robert R. Capital Asset Pricing Compatible with Observed Market Value Weights. *J. Finance*, March 1985, *40*(1), pp. 85–103. [G: U.S.]

Bhattacharya, Sudipto and Pfleiderer, Paul. Delegated Portfolio Management. *J. Econ. Theory*, June 1985, *36*(1), pp. 1–25.

Black, Fischer. Contingent Claims Valuation of Corporate Liabilities: Theory and Empirical

Tests: Comment. In *Friedman, B. M., ed.*, 1985, pp. 262–63. [G: U.S.]

Bodie, Zvi; Kane, Alex and McDonald, Robert L. Inflation and the Role of Bonds in Investor Portfolios. In *Friedman, B. M., ed.*, 1985, pp. 167–94. [G: U.S.]

Bond, Gary E. and Thompson, Stanley R. Risk Aversion and the Recommended Hedging Ratio. *Amer. J. Agr. Econ.*, November 1985, 67(4), pp. 870–72.

Bookstaber, Richard. The Use of Options in Performance Structuring. *J. Portfol. Manage.*, Summer 1985, 11(4), pp. 36–50.

Bray, Davide. Fondi comuni d'investimento: un'applicazione della teoria della selezione di portafoglio. (The Management of Unit Trusts: An Application of the Portfolio Selection Theory. With English summary.) *Bancaria*, May 1985, 41(5), pp. 569–81. [G: Italy]

Bray, Margaret. Rational Expectations, Information and Asset Markets: An Introduction. *Oxford Econ. Pap.*, June 1985, 37(2), pp. 161–95.

Brennan, Michael J. and Schwartz, Eduado S. On the Geometric Mean Index: A Note. *J. Finan. Quant. Anal.*, March 1985, 20(1), pp. 119–22.

Brenner, Menachem; Courtadon, Georges and Subrahmanyam, Marti G. Options on the Spot and Options on Futures. *J. Finance*, December 1985, 40(5), pp. 1303–17. [G: U.S.; W. Germany]

Bresnahan, Timothy F. and Suslow, Valerie Y. Inventories as an Asset: The Volatility of Copper Prices. *Int. Econ. Rev.*, June 1985, 26(2), pp. 409–24. [G: U.K.]

Brick, Ivan E. and Ravid, S. Abraham. On the Relevance of Debt Maturity Structure. *J. Finance*, December 1985, 40(5), pp. 1423–37. [G: U.S.]

Brick, Ivan E. and Wallingford, Buckner A. The Relative Tax Benefits of Alternative Call Features in Corporate Debt. *J. Finan. Quant. Anal.*, March 1985, 20(1), pp. 95–105.

Brown, David P. and Gibbons, Michael R. A Simple Econometric Approach for Utility-based Asset Pricing Models. *J. Finance*, June 1985, 40(2), pp. 359–81.

Brown, Keith C.; Lockwood, Larry J. and Lummer, Scott L. An Examination of Event Dependency and Structural Change in Security Pricing Models. *J. Finan. Quant. Anal.*, September 1985, 20(3), pp. 315–34. [G: U.S.]

Brown, Stewart L. A Reformulation of the Portfolio Model of Hedging. *Amer. J. Agr. Econ.*, August 1985, 67(3), pp. 508–12. [G: U.S.]

Brownschidle, Terry. A Generalized Stochastic Dominance Approach to Analyze Financial Decisions. In *Brown, R. C., ed.*, 1985, pp. 3–14. [G: U.S.]

Caks, John, et al. A Simple Formula for Duration. *J. Finan. Res.*, Fall 1985, 8(3), pp. 245–49.

Campbell, Robert B. and Turnovsky, Stephen J. An Analysis of the Stabilizing and Welfare Effects of Intervention in Spot and Futures

Markets. *J. Public Econ.*, November 1985, 28(2), pp. 165–209.

Campbell, Tim S. and Kracaw, William A. The Market for Managerial Labor Services and Capital Market Equilibrium. *J. Finan. Quant. Anal.*, September 1985, 20(3), pp. 277–97.

Canto, Victor A.; Findlay, M. C. and Reinganum, Marc R. Inflation, Money, and Stock Prices: An Alternative Interpretation. *Financial Rev.*, February 1985, 20(1), pp. 95–101. [G: U.S.]

Carmichael, Benoît. Anticipated Inflation and the Stock Market. *Can. J. Econ.*, May 1985, 18(2), pp. 285–93.

Carmichael, Jeffrey and Stebbing, Peter W. Fisher's Paradox: Reply [Fisher's Paradox and the Theory of Interest]. *Amer. Econ. Rev.*, June 1985, 75(3), pp. 569–70.

Chance, Don M. A Semi-strong Form Test of the Efficiency of the Treasury Bond Futures Market. *J. Futures Markets*, Fall 1985, 5(3), pp. 385–405. [G: U.S.]

Chang, Eric C. and Lewellen, Wilbur G. An Arbitrage Pricing Approach to Evaluating Mutual Fund Performance. *J. Finan. Res.*, Spring 1985, 8(1), pp. 15–30. [G: U.S.]

Chen, Nai-fu and Johnson, Herb. Hedging Options. *J. Finan. Econ.*, June 1985, 14(2), pp. 317–21.

Chen, Son-Nan and Moore, William T. Uncertain Inflation and Optimal Portfolio Selection: A Simplified Approach. *Financial Rev.*, November 1985, 20(4), pp. 343–56.

Clayton, Ronnie J. and Navratil, Frank J. The Management of Interest Rate Risk: Comment. *J. Portfol. Manage.*, Summer 1985, 11(4), pp. 64–66.

Cloninger, Dale O. An Analysis of the Effect of Illegal Corporate Activity on Share Value. *J. Behav. Econ.*, Summer 1985, 14(2), pp. 1–13.

Cohen, Kalman J. Risk Aversion and Information Structure: An Experimental Study of Price Variability in the Securities Markets: Discussion. *J. Finance*, July 1985, 40(3), pp. 845–46.

Constantinides, George M. The Disposition to Sell Winners Too Early and Ride Losers Too Long: Theory and Evidence: Discussion. *J. Finance*, July 1985, 40(3), pp. 791–92. [G: U.S.]

Cooper, S. Kerry; Groth, John C. and Avera, William E. Liquidity, Exchange Listing, and Common Stock Performance. *J. Econ. Bus.*, February 1985, 37(1), pp. 19–33. [G: U.S.]

Cornell, Bradford. The Money Supply Announcements Puzzle: Reply. *Amer. Econ. Rev.*, June 1985, 75(3), pp. 565–66.

Courtadon, Georges. Une synthèse des modèles d'évaluation d'options sur obligations. (A Survey of Debt Option Valuation Models. With English summary.) *Finance*, December 1985, 6(2), pp. 161–86.

Cox, John C.; Ingersoll, Jonathan E., Jr. and Ross, Stephen A. A Theory of the Term Structure of Interest Rates. *Econometrica*, March 1985, 53(2), pp. 385–407.

Cox, John C.; Ingersoll, Jonathan E., Jr. and

Ross, Stephen A. An Intertemporal General Equilibrium Model of Asset Prices. *Econometrica*, March 1985, 53(2), pp. 363–84.

Damodaran, Aswath. Economic Events, Information Structure, and the Return-generating Process. *J. Finan. Quant. Anal.*, December 1985, 20(4), pp. 423–34.

DeJong, Douglas V. and Collins, Daniel W. Explanations for the Instability of Equity Beta: Risk-Free Rate Changes and Leverage Effects. *J. Finan. Quant. Anal.*, March 1985, 20(1), pp. 73–94. [G: U.S.]

Dhrymes, Phoebus J. On the Empirical Relevance of APT: Comment. *J. Portfol. Manage.*, Summer 1985, 11(4), pp. 70–71. [G: U.S.]

Dhrymes, Phoebus J., et al. An Empirical Examination of the Implications of Arbitrage Pricing Theory. *J. Banking Finance*, March 1985, 9(1), pp. 73–99. [G: U.S.]

Dhrymes, Phoebus J., et al. New Tests of the APT and Their Implications. *J. Finance*, July 1985, 40(3), pp. 659–74. [G: U.S.]

Diamond, Douglas W. Optimal Release of Information by Firms. *J. Finance*, September 1985, 40(4), pp. 1071–94.

Dornbusch, Rudiger and Pechman, Clarice. The Bid–Ask Spread in the Black Market for Dollars in Brazil: A Note. *J. Money, Credit, Banking*, Part 1, Nov. 1985, 17(4), pp. 517–20. [G: Brazil]

Dowen, Richard J. A Note: Hedging Market Risk for Capital Investment Projects. *J. Futures Markets*, Winter 1985, 5(4), pp. 621–24.

Dubofsky, David A. The Effects of Maturing Debt on Equity Risk. *Quart. Rev. Econ. Bus.*, Autumn 1985, 25(3), pp. 36–47. [G: U.S.]

Dybvig, Philip H. Acknowledgment: Kinks on the Mean-Variance Frontier. *J. Finance*, March 1985, 40(1), pp. 345.

Dybvig, Philip H. and Ross, Stephen A. Differential Information and Performance Measurement Using a Security Market Line. *J. Finance*, June 1985, 40(2), pp. 383–99.

Dybvig, Philip H. and Ross, Stephen A. The Analytics of Performance Measurement Using a Security Market Line. *J. Finance*, June 1985, 40(2), pp. 401–16.

Dybvig, Philip H. and Ross, Stephen A. Yes, the APT Is Testable. *J. Finance*, September 1985, 40(4), pp. 1173–88.

Eaker, Mark R. and Grant, Dwight. Optimal Hedging of Uncertain and Long-term Foreign Exchange Exposure. *J. Banking Finance*, June 1985, 9(2), pp. 221–31.

Eddy, Albert and Seifert, Bruce. Inflation, the Fisher Hypothesis, and Long Term Bonds. *Financial Rev.*, February 1985, 20(1), pp. 21–35. [G: U.S.; Germany]

Eichengreen, Barry. The Franc and the French Financial Sector: Comments. In *Melitz, J. and Wyplosz, C., eds.*, 1985, pp. 175–79. [G: France]

Errunza, Vihang R. and Losq, Etienne. International Asset Pricing under Mild Segmentation: Theory and Test. *J. Finance*, March 1985, 40(1), pp. 105–24. [G: U.S.; LDCs]

Eun, Cheol S. A Model of International Asset Pricing under Imperfect Commodity Arbitrage. *J. Econ. Dynam. Control*, November 1985, 9(3), pp. 273–89.

Falk, Barry and Orazem, Peter F. The Money Supply Announcements Puzzle: Comment. *Amer. Econ. Rev.*, June 1985, 75(3), pp. 562–64.

Feroldi, Mathieu and Melitz, Jacques. The Franc and the French Financial Sector. In *Melitz, J. and Wyplosz, C., eds.*, 1985, pp. 149–74. [G: France]

Ferrante, Vittorio E. La teoria di Keynes del deporto normale e l'assunzione di preferenza per la liquidità. (With English summary.) *Econ. Polit.*, April 1985, 2(1), pp. 81–94.

Figlewski, Stephen. Hedging with Stock Index Futures: Theory and Application in a New Market. *J. Futures Markets*, Summer 1985, 5(2), pp. 183–99. [G: U.S.]

Frankel, Jeffrey A. Portfolio Shares as 'Beta Breakers.' *J. Portfol. Manage.*, Summer 1985, 11(4), pp. 18–23. [G: U.S.]

Frankfurter, George M. and Booth, G. Geoffrey. Further Evidence of the Role of Nonsystematic Risk in Efficent Portfolios. *Quart. Rev. Econ. Bus.*, Summer 1985, 25(2), pp. 38–48. [G: U.S.]

Garman, Mark B. The Duration of Option Portfolios. *J. Finan. Econ.*, June 1985, 14(2), pp. 309–15.

Garman, Mark B. Towards a Semigroup Pricing Theory. *J. Finance*, July 1985, 40(3), pp. 847–61.

Gehrlein, William V. and McInish, Thomas H. Cyclical Variability of Bond Risk Premia: A Note. *J. Banking Finance*, March 1985, 9(1), pp. 157–65.

Geske, Robert and Shastri, Kuldeep. The Early Exercise of American Puts. *J. Banking Finance*, June 1985, 9(2), pp. 207–19. [G: U.S.]

Geske, Robert and Shastri, Kuldeep. Valuation by Approximation: A Comparison of Alternative Option Valuation Techniques. *J. Finan. Quant. Anal.*, March 1985, 20(1), pp. 45–71.

Gibbons, Michael R. and Ferson, Wayne. Testing Asset Pricing Models with Changing Expectations and an Unobservable Market Portfolio. *J. Finan. Econ.*, June 1985, 14(2), pp. 217–36. [G: U.S.]

Gilbert, Christopher L. Futures Trading and the Welfare Evaluation of Commodity Price Stabilisation. *Econ. J.*, September 1985, 95(379), pp. 637–61. [G: LDCs]

Gilberto, Michael. Interest Rate Sensitivity in the Common Stocks of Financial Intermediaries: A Methodological Note. *J. Finan. Quant. Anal.*, March 1985, 20(1), pp. 123–26.

Giles, David E. A.; Goss, Barry A. and Chin, Olive P. L. Intertemporal Allocation in the Corn and Soybean Markets with Rational Expectations. *Amer. J. Agr. Econ.*, November 1985, 67(4), pp. 749–60. [G: U.S.]

Glosten, Lawrence R. and Milgrom, Paul R. Bid, Ask, and Transaction Prices in a Specialist Market with Heterogeneously Informed Traders.

J. Finan. Econ., March 1985, *14*(1), pp. 71–100.

Goldberg, Michael A. The Relevance of Margin Regulations: A Note. *J. Money, Credit, Banking*, Part 1, Nov. 1985, *17*(4), pp. 521–27.

Goodhart, Charles A. E. and Smith, Richard G. The Impact of News on Financial Markets in the United Kingdom: A Note. *J. Money, Credit, Banking*, Part 1, Nov. 1985, *17*(4), pp. 507–11. [G: U.K.]

Goodman, David A. and Peavy, John W., III. The Risk Universal Nature of the P/E Effect. *J. Portfol. Manage.*, Summer 1985, *11*(4), pp. 14–16.

Goodman, Laurie S. Put-Call Parity with Coupon Instruments. *J. Portfol. Manage.*, Winter 1985, *11*(2), pp. 59–60. [G: U.S.]

Gordon, Roger H. Taxation of Corporate Capital Income: Tax Revenues versus Tax Distortions. *Quart. J. Econ.*, February 1985, *100*(1), pp. 1–27.

Gottlieb, Gary and Kalay, Avner. Implications of the Discreteness of Observed Stock Prices. *J. Finance*, March 1985, *40*(1), pp. 135–53. [G: U.S.]

Green, Richard C. and Srivastava, Sanjay. Risk Aversion and Arbitrage. *J. Finance*, March 1985, *40*(1), pp. 257–68.

Grinblatt, Mark S. and Ross, Stephen A. Market Power in a Securities Market with Endogenous Information. *Quart. J. Econ.*, November 1985, *100*(4), pp. 1143–67.

Grinblatt, Mark S. and Titman, Sheridan. Approximate Factor Structures: Interpretations and Implications for Empirical Tests. *J. Finance*, December 1985, *40*(5), pp. 1367–73.

Gruber, Martin J. Inflation and the Role of Bonds in Investor Portfolios: Comment. In *Friedman, B. M., ed.*, 1985, pp. 194–96. [G: U.S.]

Gultekin, N. Bulent and Rogalski, Richard J. Government Bond Returns, Measurement of Interest Rate Risk, and the Arbitrage Pricing Theory. *J. Finance*, March 1985, *40*(1), pp. 43–61. [G: U.S.]

Hadaway, Beverly. Discretionary Managerial Behaviour Effects of Savings and Loan Conversions: Competitive Implications for the Industry in a Deregulated Environment. *Appl. Econ.*, June 1985, *17*(3), pp. 451–66. [G: U.S.]

Hakansson, Nils H.; Beja, Avraham and Kale, Jivendra. On the Feasibility of Automated Market Making by a Programmed Specialist. *J. Finance*, March 1985, *40*(1), pp. 1–20. [G: U.S.]

Harris, Milton and Raviv, Artur. A Sequential Signalling Model of Convertible Debt Call Policy. *J. Finance*, December 1985, *40*(5), pp. 1263–81.

Hasager, Leif and Møller, Michael. Rentestruktur og implicitte forewardrenter. (The Term Structure of Interest and the Implicit Forward Interest Rate. With English summary.) *Nationaløkon. Tidsskr.*, 1985, *123*(3), pp. 399–407.

Hassett, Matt; Sears, R. Stephen and Trennepohl, Gary L. Asset Preference, Skewness, and

the Measurement of Expected Utility. *J. Econ. Bus.*, February 1985, *37*(1), pp. 35–47. [G: U.S.]

Hauschild, Karsten and Winkelmann, Michael. Kapitalmarkteffizienz und Point and Figure Analyse. (Capital Market Efficiency and Point and Figure Analysis. With English summary.) *Kredit Kapital*, 1985, *18*(2), pp. 240–64. [G: W. Germany]

Hauser, Robert J. and Neff, David. Pricing Options on Agricultural Futures: Departures from Traditional Theory. *J. Futures Markets*, Winter 1985, *5*(4), pp. 539–77. [G: U.S.]

Ho, Thomas S. Y.; Schwartz, Robert A. and Whitcomb, David K. The Trading Decision and Market Clearing under Transaction Price Uncertainty. *J. Finance*, March 1985, *40*(1), pp. 21–42.

Hoffman, Dennis L. and Schlagenhauf, Don E. The Impact of News and Alternative Theories of Exchange Rate Determination. *J. Money, Credit, Banking*, August 1985, *17*(3), pp. 328–46. [G: France; Japan; W. Germany; U.K.]

Hollenbeck, Frank. Treating Spot Speculation as Equivalent to a Combined Arbitrage–Speculative Transaction: A Comment. *Rivista Int. Sci. Econ. Com.*, July-Aug. 1985, *32*(7–8), pp. 701–04.

Honohan, Patrick. Fisher's Paradox: Comment [Fisher's Paradox and the Theory of Interest]. *Amer. Econ. Rev.*, June 1985, *75*(3), pp. 567–68.

Horvath, Philip A. A Pedagogic Note on Intraperiod Compounding and Discounting. *Financial Rev.*, February 1985, *20*(1), pp. 116–18.

Horvath, Philip A. and Scott, Robert C. An Expected Utility Explanation of Plunging and Dumping Behavior. *Financial Rev.*, May 1985, *20*(2), pp. 219–28.

Huang, Chi-fu. Information Structure and Equilibrium Asset Prices. *J. Econ. Theory*, February 1985, *35*(1), pp. 33–71.

Huang, Chi-fu. Information Structures and Viable Price Systems. *J. Math. Econ.*, 1985, *14*(3), pp. 215–40.

Huang, Chi-fu. Towards a Semigroup Pricing Theory: Discussion. *J. Finance*, July 1985, *40*(3), pp. 861–62.

Huang, Chi-fu and Litzenberger, Robert H. On the Necessary Condition for Linear Sharing and Separation: A Note. *J. Finan. Quant. Anal.*, September 1985, *20*(3), pp. 381–84.

Jaffe, Jeffrey F. Inflation, the Interest Rate, and the Required Return on Equity. *J. Finan. Quant. Anal.*, March 1985, *20*(1), pp. 29–44.

Jagannathan, Ravi. An Investigation of Commodity Futures Prices Using the Consumption-based Intertemporal Capital Asset Pricing Model. *J. Finance*, March 1985, *40*(1), pp. 175–91. [G: U.S.]

Jagannathan, Ravi. Errata [Call Options and the Risk of Underlying Securities]. *J. Finan. Econ.*, June 1985, *14*(2), pp. 323.

James, Christopher; Koreisha, Sergio and Partch, M. Megan. A VARMA Analysis of the Causal Relations among Stock Returns, Real

Output, and Nominal Interest Rates. *J. Finance*, December 1985, *40*(5), pp. 1375–84. [G: U.S.]

John, Kose and Williams, Joseph T. Dividends, Dilution, and Taxes: A Signalling Equilibrium. *J. Finance*, September 1985, *40*(4), pp. 1053–70.

Jonas, Stan. Trading Bond Spreads in the Delivery Month: Comment. *J. Futures Markets*, Fall 1985, *5*(3), pp. 451–52.

Jones, E. Philip; Mason, Scott P. and Rosenfeld, Eric. Contingent Claims Valuation of Corporate Liabilities: Theory and Empirical Tests. In *Friedman, B. M., ed.*, 1985, pp. 239–61. [G: U.S.]

Jordan, Bradford D. and Pettway, Richard H. The Pricing of Short-term Debt and the Miller Hypothesis: A Note [Debt and Taxes]. *J. Finance*, June 1985, *40*(2), pp. 589–94.

Kanbur, S. M. R. Corrigendum [Increases in Risk with Kinked Payoff Functions]. *J. Econ. Theory*, April 1985, *35*(2), pp. 399.

Karson, Marvin J. and Cheng, David C. Estimation of Multiperiod Expected Rates of Return When Investment Relatives Are Lognormally Distributed. *J. Bus. Econ. Statist.*, April 1985, *3*(2), pp. 140–48. [G: U.S.]

Kawaller, Ira. Hedging with Stock Index Futures: Theory and Application in a New Market: A Comment. *J. Futures Markets*, Fall 1985, *5*(3), pp. 447–49. [G: U.S.]

Khoury, Nabil T. and Martel, Jean-Marc. Optimal Futures Hedging in the Presence of Asymmetric Information. *J. Futures Markets*, Winter 1985, *5*(4), pp. 595–605.

Kim, Moon K. and Booth, G. Geoffrey. Yield Structure of Taxable vs. Nontaxable Bonds. *J. Finan. Res.*, Summer 1985, *8*(2), pp. 95–105.

Kolodny, Richard and Suhler, Diane Rizzuto. Changes in Capital Structure, New Equity Issues, and Scale Effects. *J. Finan. Res.*, Summer 1985, *8*(2), pp. 127–36. [G: U.S.]

Koppenhaver, G. D. Bank Funding Risks, Risk Aversion, and the Choice of Futures Hedging Instrument. *J. Finance*, March 1985, *40*(1), pp. 241–55. [G: U.S.]

Koppenhaver, G. D. Variable-Rate Loan Commitments, Deposit Withdrawal Risk, and Anticipatory Hedging. *J. Futures Markets*, Fall 1985, *5*(3), pp. 317–30. [G: U.S.]

Kwon, Young K. Derivation of the Capital Asset Pricing Model without Normality or Quadratic Preference: A Note. *J. Finance*, December 1985, *40*(5), pp. 1505–09.

de La Bruslerie, Hubert. Une étude empirique de l'efficience des marchés euro-obligataires. (An Empirical Survey about Efficiency of Eurobond Markets. With English summary.) *Écon. Soc.*, June 1985, *19*(6), pp. 77–101. [G: France]

Lam, Chun H. and Chen, Andrew H. Joint Effects of Interest Rate Deregulation and Capital Requirements on Optimal Bank Portfolio Adjustments. *J. Finance*, June 1985, *40*(2), pp. 563–75.

Lazimy, Rafael. Equilibrium in a Market with

Divisible and Indivisible Risky Assets. *Keio Econ. Stud.*, 1985, *22*(1), pp. 27–45.

Leland, Hayne E. Option Pricing and Replication with Transactions Costs. *J. Finance*, December 1985, *40*(5), pp. 1283–1301.

Levy, Haim. Upper and Lower Bounds of Put and Call Option Value: Stochastic Dominance Approach. *J. Finance*, September 1985, *40*(4), pp. 1197–1217.

Levy, Haim and Lerman, Zvi. Testing P/E Ratios Filters with Stochastic Dominance. *J. Portfol. Manage.*, Winter 1985, *11*(2), pp. 31–40. [G: U.S.]

van Loo, Peter D. Portfolio Selection and Interest Rate Setting by the Dutch Banking System. In *Currie, D., ed.*, 1985, pp. 127–58. [G: Netherlands]

Maberly, Edwin D. Testing Futures Market Efficiency—A Restatement. *J. Futures Markets*, Fall 1985, *5*(3), pp. 425–32. [G: U.S.]

Macey, Jonathan R. and McChesney, Fred S. A Theoretical Analysis of Corporate Greenmail. *Yale Law J.*, November 1985, *95*(1), pp. 13–61. [G: U.S.]

Makowski, Louis and Pepall, Lynne. Easy Proofs of Unanimity and Optimality without Spanning: A Pedagogical Note. *J. Finance*, September 1985, *40*(4), pp. 1245–50.

Mankiw, N. Gregory; Romer, David and Shapiro, Matthew D. An Unbiased Reexamination of Stock Market Volatility. *J. Finance*, July 1985, *40*(3), pp. 677–87. [G: U.S.]

Mark, Nelson C. On Time Varying Risk Premia in the Foreign Exchange Market: An Econometric Analysis. *J. Monet. Econ.*, July 1985, *16*(1), pp. 3–18.

Marston, Richard C. The Franc and the French Financial Sector: Comments. In *Melitz, J. and Wyplosz, C., eds.*, 1985, pp. 181–83. [G: France]

Martin, Linda J. Uncertain? How Do *You* Spell Relief? *J. Portfol. Manage.*, Spring 1985, *11*(3), pp. 5–8.

McCulloch, J. Huston. Interest-Risk Sensitive Deposit Insurance Premia: Stable ACH Estimates. *J. Banking Finance*, March 1985, *9*(1), pp. 137–56. [G: U.S.]

McDonald, Robert L. and Siegel, Daniel R. Investment and the Valuation of Firms When There Is an Option to Shut Down. *Int. Econ. Rev.*, June 1985, *26*(2), pp. 331–49.

McEnally, Richard W. Time Diversification: Surest Route to Lower Risk? *J. Portfol. Manage.*, Summer 1985, *11*(4), pp. 24–26. [G: U.S.]

McShane, R. W. and Sharpe, Ian G. A Time Series/Cross Section Analysis of the Determinants of Australian Trading Bank Loan/Deposit Interest Margins: 1962–1981. *J. Banking Finance*, March 1985, *9*(1), pp. 115–36. [G: Australia]

Mehra, Rajnish and Prescott, Edward C. The Equity Premium: A Puzzle. *J. Monet. Econ.*, March 1985, *15*(2), pp. 145–61.

Mendelson, Haim. Random Competitive Exchange: Price Distributions and Gain from

Trade. *J. Econ. Theory*, December 1985, 37(2), pp. 254–80.

Moore, William T. and Sartoris, William L. Dividends and Taxes: Another Look at the Electric Utility Industry. *Financial Rev.*, February 1985, 20(1), pp. 1–20. [G: U.S.]

Moray, Myriam. Impact de la fiscalité sur la composition optimale d'un portefeuille d'obligations d'Etat belge. (With English summary.) *Cah. Écon. Bruxelles*, 1st Trimester 1985, (105), pp. 91–118. [G: Belgium]

Morris, Victor F. Central Value in Review. *J. Portfol. Manage.*, Fall 1985, 12(1), pp. 44–49.

Nairay, Alain. Recoverability of Uzawa Utility Functionals under Asset Price Lognormality. *J. Econ. Dynam. Control*, October 1985, 9(2), pp. 241–50.

Nelson, Ray D. and Collins, Robert A. A Measure of Hedging's Performance. *J. Futures Markets*, Spring 1985, 5(1), pp. 45–55. [G: U.S.]

Neusser, Klaus. Portfolio Selection by Austrian Insurance Companies. *Empirica*, 1985, 12(1), pp. 25–41. [G: Austria]

Park, Sang Yong and Williams, Joseph T. Taxes, Capital Structure, and Bondholder Clienteles. *J. Bus.*, April 1985, 58(2), pp. 203–24.

Parsons, John E. and Raviv, Artur. Underpricing of Seasoned Issues. *J. Finan. Econ.*, September 1985, 14(3), pp. 377–97.

Peters, Ed. The Growing Efficiency of Index Futures Markets. *J. Portfol. Manage.*, Summer 1985, 11(4), pp. 52–56. [G: U.S.]

Pfeifer, Phillip E. Market Timing and Risk Reduction. *J. Finan. Quant. Anal.*, December 1985, 20(4), pp. 451–59.

Pitts, Mark. The Management of Interest Rate Risk: Comment. *J. Portfol. Manage.*, Summer 1985, 11(4), pp. 67–69.

Pitts, Mark. The Pricing of Options on Debt Securities. *J. Portfol. Manage.*, Winter 1985, 11(2), pp. 41–50. [G: U.S.]

Plaut, Steven E. Interest vs. Maturity Indexation. *Quart. Rev. Econ. Bus.*, Winter 1985, 25(4), pp. 95–106.

Pulley, Lawrence B. Mean-Variance versus Direct Utility Maximization: A Comment. *J. Finance*, June 1985, 40(2), pp. 601–02.

[G: U.S.]

Ramaswamy, Krishna and Sundaresan, Suresh M. The Valuation of Options on Futures Contracts. *J. Finance*, December 1985, 40(5), pp. 1319–40.

Raveh, Adi. A Note on Factor Analysis and Arbitrage Pricing Theory. *J. Banking Finance*, June 1985, 9(2), pp. 317–21.

Ritchken, Peter H. Enhancing Mean-Variance Analysis with Options. *J. Portfol. Manage.*, Spring 1985, 11(3), pp. 67–71.

Ritchken, Peter H. On Option Pricing Bounds. *J. Finance*, September 1985, 40(4), pp. 1219–33.

Roll, Richard. A Note on the Geometry of Shanken's CSR T^2 Test for Mean/Variance Efficiency. *J. Finan. Econ.*, September 1985, 14(3), pp. 349–57.

Ross, Stephen A. On the Empirical Relevance

of APT: Reply. *J. Portfol. Manage.*, Summer 1985, 11(4), pp. 72–73. [G: U.S.]

Rossini, Gianpaolo. A Note on the Cost of Diversification and the Optimal Number of Activities. *Giorn. Econ.*, May-June 1985, 44(5–6), pp. 285–99.

Sarig, Oded H. On Mergers, Divestments, and Options: A Note. *J. Finan. Quant. Anal.*, September 1985, 20(3), pp. 385–89.

Sarig, Oded H. and Scott, James. The Puzzle of Financial Leverage Clienteles. *J. Finance*, December 1985, 40(5), pp. 1459–67. [G: U.S.]

Schnabel, Jacques A. Determinants of Yield Differentials: Canadian Evidence. *Atlantic Econ. J.*, September 1985, 13(3), pp. 94.

[G: Canada]

Schulman, Evan. Central Value in Review: A Comment. *J. Portfol. Manage.*, Fall 1985, 12(1), pp. 50–51.

Scott, Louis O. The Present Value Model of Stock Prices: Regression Tests and Monte Carlo Results. *Rev. Econ. Statist.*, November 1985, 67(4), pp. 599–605. [G: U.S.]

Sealey, C. W., Jr. Portfolio Separation for Stockholder Owned Depository Financial Intermediaries. *J. Banking Finance*, December 1985, 9(4), pp. 477–90.

Sears, R. Stephen and Wei, K. C. John. Asset Pricing, Higher Moments, and the Market Risk Premium: A Note. *J. Finance*, September 1985, 40(4), pp. 1251–53.

Sell, Friedrich L. and Schmidt, Felix. Risikominderung durch Terminkontraktmärkte. Empirische Evidenz für sogenannte "Kernrohstoffe." (With English summary.) *Z. Wirtschaft. Sozialwissen.*, 1985, 105(4), pp. 481–505.

[G: U.K.]

Sengupta, Jati K. and Sfeir, Raymond E. Tests of Efficiency of Limited Diversification Portfolios. *Appl. Econ.*, December 1985, 17(6), pp. 933–45. [G: U.S.]

Shanken, Jay. Multi-Beta CAPM or Equilibrium-APT? A Reply [An Empirical Investigation of the Arbitrage Pricing Theory] [The Arbitrage Pricing Theory: Is It Testable?]. *J. Finance*, September 1985, 40(4), pp. 1189–96.

Shanken, Jay. Multivariate Tests of the Zero-Beta CAPM. *J. Finan. Econ.*, September 1985, 14(3), pp. 327–48.

Sharp, Peter A. Determinants of Forward Exchange Risk Premia in Efficient Markets. In *Arndt, S. W.; Sweeney, R. J. and Willett, T. D., eds.*, 1985, pp. 167–80.

Shea, Gary S. Interest Rate Term Structure Estimation with Exponential Splines: A Note. *J. Finance*, March 1985, 40(1), pp. 319–25.

Shefrin, Hersh and Statman, Meir. The Disposition to Sell Winners Too Early and Ride Losers Too Long: Theory and Evidence. *J. Finance*, July 1985, 40(3), pp. 777–90. [G: U.S.]

Shiller, Robert. An Unbiased Reexamination of Stock Market Volatility: Discussion. *J. Finance*, July 1985, 40(3), pp. 688–89.

[G: U.S.]

Shvyrkov, Vladislav V.; Carroll, John and Rosenbaum, Richard. A New Approach to a Random

Walk Model. In *Brown, R. C., ed.*, 1985, pp. 201–09.

Smirlock, Michael J. and Starks, Laura. A Further Examination of Stock Price Changes and Transaction Volume. *J. Finan. Res.*, Fall 1985, *8*(3), pp. 217–25. **[G: U.S.]**

Sorensen, Eric H. In Defense of Technical Analysis: Discussion. *J. Finance*, July 1985, *40*(3), pp. 773–75.

Sprenkle, Case M. On the Precautionary Demand for Assets. *J. Banking Finance*, December 1985, *9*(4), pp. 499–515.

Spronk, Jaap and Zambruno, Giovanni. Interactive Multiple Goal Programming for Bank Portfolio Selection. In *Fandel, G. and Spronk, J., eds.*, 1985, pp. 289–306.

Stahl, Dale O., II. Bankruptcies in Temporary Equilibrium Forward Markets with and without Institutional Restrictions. *Rev. Econ. Stud.*, July 1985, *52*(3), pp. 459–71.

Stahl, Dale O., II. Relaxing the Sure-Solvency Conditions in Temporary Equilibrium Models. *J. Econ. Theory*, October 1985, *37*(1), pp. 1–18.

Stein, Jerome L. Exchange Rate Management with Rational Expectations but Diverse Precisions. In *Bhandari, J. S., ed.*, 1985, pp. 96–125.

Stein, Jerome L. Futures Markets and Capital Formation. In *Peck, A. E., ed. (II)*, 1985, pp. 115–204. **[G: U.S.]**

Stiglitz, Joseph E. Credit Markets and the Control of Capital. *J. Money, Credit, Banking*, May 1985, *17*(2), pp. 133–52.

Stoll, Hans R. and Whaley, Robert E. The New Option Markets. In *Peck, A. E., ed. (II)*, 1985, pp. 205–89. **[G: U.S.]**

Stulz, René M. and Johnson, Herb. An Analysis of Secured Debt. *J. Finan. Econ.*, December 1985, *14*(4), pp. 501–21.

Summers, Lawrence H. The Asset Price Approach to the Analysis of Capital Income Taxation. In *Feiwel, G. R., ed. (I)*, 1985, pp. 429–43.

Svensson, Lars E. O. Money and Asset Prices in a Cash-in-Advance Economy. *J. Polit. Econ.*, October 1985, *93*(5), pp. 919–44.

Talmor, Eli. Personal Tax Considerations in Portfolio Construction: Tilting the Optimal Portfolio Selection. *Quart. Rev. Econ. Bus.*, Autumn 1985, *25*(3), pp. 55–71.

Talmor, Eli; Haugen, Robert A. and Barnea, Amir. The Value of the Tax Subsidy on Risky Debt. *J. Bus.*, April 1985, *58*(2), pp. 191–202.

Tirole, Jean. Asset Bubbles and Overlapping Generations. *Econometrica*, November 1985, *53*(6), pp. 1499–1528.

Titman, Sheridan. The Effect of Forward Markets on the Debt-Equity Mix of Investor Portfolios and the Optimal Capital Structure of Firms. *J. Finan. Quant. Anal.*, March 1985, *20*(1), pp. 19–27.

Toevs, Alden L. Interest Rate Risk and Uncertain Lives. *J. Portfol. Manage.*, Spring 1985, *11*(3), pp. 45–56.

Torous, Walter N. Differential Taxation and the Equilibrium Structure of Interest Rates. *J. Banking Finance*, September 1985, *9*(3), pp. 363–85.

Treynor, Jack L. and Ferguson, Robert. In Defense of Technical Analysis. *J. Finance*, July 1985, *40*(3), pp. 757–73.

Turnovsky, Stephen J. and Campbell, Robert B. The Stabilizing and Welfare Properties of Futures Markets: A Simulation Approach. *Int. Econ. Rev.*, June 1985, *26*(2), pp. 277–303.

Varian, Hal R. Divergence of Opinion in Complete Markets: A Note. *J. Finance*, March 1985, *40*(1), pp. 309–17.

Veljanovski, Cento G. Organized Futures Contracting. *Int. Rev. Law Econ.*, June 1985, *5*(1), pp. 25–38.

Walsh, Carl E. A Rational Expectations Model of Term Premia with Some Implications for Empirical Asset Demand Equations. *J. Finance*, March 1985, *40*(1), pp. 63–83. **[G: U.S.]**

Werner, Jan. Equilibrium in Economies with Incomplete Financial Markets. *J. Econ. Theory*, June 1985, *36*(1), pp. 110–19.

Wilson, Earl R. and Howard, Thomas P. Information for Municipal Bond Investment Decisions: Synthesis of Prior Research, an Extension and Policy Implications. In *Chan, J. L., ed.*, 1985, pp. 213–63. **[G: U.S.]**

Wolfson, Mark A. Empirical Evidence of Incentive Problems and Their Mitigation in Oil and Gas Tax Shelter Programs. In *Pratt, J. W. and Zeckhauser, R. J., eds.*, 1985, pp. 101–25. **[G: U.S.]**

Yaari, Uzi and Fabozzi, Frank J. Why IRA and Keogh Plans Should Avoid Growth Stocks. *J. Finan. Res.*, Fall 1985, *8*(3), pp. 203–15. **[G: U.S.]**

Yawitz, Jess Barry; Maloney, Kevin J. and Ederington, Louis H. Taxes, Default Risk, and Yield Spreads. *J. Finance*, September 1985, *40*(4), pp. 1127–40. **[G: U.S.]**

Yawitz, Jess Barry and Marshall, William J. The Use of Futures in Immunized Portfolios. *J. Portfol. Manage.*, Winter 1985, *11*(2), pp. 51–58. **[G: U.S.]**

van Zijl, Tony. Beta Loss, Beta Quotient: Comment. *J. Portfol. Manage.*, Summer 1985, *11*(4), pp. 75–78.

3132 Capital Markets: Empirical Studies, Including Regulation

Ajinkya, Bipin B. and Gift, Michael J. Dispersion of Financial Analysts' Earnings Forecasts and the (Option Model) Implied Standard Deviations of Stock Returns. *J. Finance*, December 1985, *40*(5), pp. 1353–65.

Ambachtsheer, Keith P. "Pensions in the American Economy": A Review Article. *J. Portfol. Manage.*, Spring 1985, *11*(3), pp. 77–78. **[G: U.S.]**

Anderson, Ronald W. Some Determinants of the Volatility of Futures Prices. *J. Futures Markets*, Fall 1985, *5*(3), pp. 331–48. **[G: U.S.]**

Ang, James S. and Peterson, David R. Return,

Risk, and Yield: Evidence from Ex Ante Data. *J. Finance*, June 1985, *40*(2), pp. 537–48. [G: U.S.]

Ang, James S.; Peterson, David R. and Peterson, Pamela P. Marginal Tax Rates: Evidence from Nontaxable Corporate Bonds: A Note. *J. Finance*, March 1985, *40*(1), pp. 327–32. [G: U.S.]

Ang, James S.; Peterson, Pamela P. and Peterson, David R. Investigations into the Determinants of Risk: A New Look. *Quart. J. Bus. Econ.*, Winter 1985, *24*(1), pp. 3–20. [G: U.S.]

Apostolou, Nicholas G.; Giroux, Gary A. and Welker, Robert B. The Information Content of Municipal Spending Rate Data. *J. Acc. Res.*, Autumn 1985, *23*(2), pp. 853–58. [G: U.S.]

Arak, Marcelle. Profit Opportunities with Old OIDs. *J. Portfol. Manage.*, Spring 1985, *11*(3), pp. 63–66. [G: U.S.]

Arak, Marcelle and Kreicher, Lawrence. The Real Rate of Interest: Inferences from the New U.K. Indexed Gilts. *Int. Econ. Rev.*, June 1985, *26*(2), pp. 399–408. [G: U.K.]

Arbel, Avner. Erratum [Generic Stocks: An Old Product in a New Package]. *J. Portfol. Manage.*, Fall 1985, *12*(1), pp. 43. [G: U.S.]

Arbel, Avner. Generic Stocks: An Old Product in a New Package. *J. Portfol. Manage.*, Summer 1985, *11*(4), pp. 4–13. [G: U.S.]

Ariovich, G. The Economics of Diamond Price Movements. *Managerial Dec. Econ.*, December 1985, *6*(4), pp. 234–40. [G: Global]

Arnott, Robert D. The Use and Misuse of Consensus Earnings. *J. Portfol. Manage.*, Spring 1985, *11*(3), pp. 18–27. [G: U.S.]

Atiase, Rowland Kwame. Predisclosure Information, Firm Capitalization, and Security Price Behavior around Earnings Announcements. *J. Acc. Res.*, Spring 1985, *23*(1), pp. 21–36. [G: U.S.]

Bailey, DeeVon and Brorsen, B. Wade. Hedging Carcass Beef to Reduce the Short-term Price Risk of Meat Packers. *Western J. Agr. Econ.*, December 1985, *10*(2), pp. 330–37. [G: U.S.]

Baillie, Richard T. and McMahon, Patrick C. Some Joint Tests of Market Efficiency: The Case of the Forward Premium. *J. Macroecon.*, Spring 1985, *7*(2), pp. 137–50. [G: U.K.; W. Germany; Italy]

Baker, Stephen A. and Van Tassel, Roger C. Forecasting the Price of Gold: A Fundamentalist Approach. *Atlantic Econ. J.*, December 1985, *13*(4), pp. 43–51. [G: Global]

Ball, Clifford A.; Torous, Walter N. and Tschoegl, Adrian E. An Empirical Investigation of the EOE Gold Options Market. *J. Banking Finance*, March 1985, *9*(1), pp. 101–13. [G: Netherlands]

Ball, Clifford A.; Torous, Walter N. and Tschoegl, Adrian E. The Degree of Price Resolution: The Case of the Gold Market. *J. Futures Markets*, Spring 1985, *5*(1), pp. 29–43. [G: U.K.]

Banks, Doyle W. Information Uncertainty and Trading Volume. *Financial Rev.*, February 1985, *20*(1), pp. 83–94. [G: U.S.]

Barr, G. D. I. and Affleck-Graves, John F. Gold Shares or Gold Bullion—Which Is the Better Investment? *Managerial Dec. Econ.*, December 1985, *6*(4), pp. 241–45. [G: S. Africa; U.S.]

Baum, Hans-Peter. Annuities in Late Medieval Hanse Towns. *Bus. Hist. Rev.*, Spring 1985, *59*(1), pp. 24–48. [G: Germany]

Bauman, W. Scott and Komarynsky, Jaroslaw. Controlling Risk in Internationally Diversified Portfolios. *Rivista Int. Sci. Econ. Com.*, Oct.-Nov. 1985, *32*(10–11), pp. 1071–95. [G: W. Europe; U.S.; Canada; Japan]

Baxter, Jennefer; Conine, Thomas E., Jr. and Tamarkin, Maurry. On Commodity Market Risk Premiums: Additional Evidence. *J. Futures Markets*, Spring 1985, *5*(1), pp. 121–25. [G: U.S.]

Beebe, Jack. Bank Stock Performance since the 1970s. *Fed. Res. Bank San Francisco Econ. Rev.*, Winter 1985, (1), pp. 5–18. [G: U.S.]

Benninga, Simon Z. and Smirlock, Michael J. An Empirical Analysis of the Delivery Option, Marking to Market, and the Pricing of Treasury Bond Futures. *J. Futures Markets*, Fall 1985, *5*(3), pp. 361–74. [G: U.S.]

Benston, George J. The Self-serving Management Hypothesis: Some Evidence. *J. Acc. Econ.*, April 1985, *7*(1–3), pp. 67–84. [G: U.S.]

Benz, Urs W. The Foreign Investor and the Swiss Equity Market: Legal and Fiscal Aspects. In *Meier, H. B., ed.*, 1985, pp. 107–18. [G: Switzerland]

Beranek, William and Clayton, Ronnie J. Risk Differences and Financial Reporting. *J. Finan. Res.*, Winter 1985, *8*(4), pp. 327–34. [G: U.S.]

Bernstein, Peter L. Does the Stock Market Overreact? Discussion. *J. Finance*, July 1985, *40*(3), pp. 806–08. [G: U.S.]

Berry, Thomas D. and Gehr, Adam K., Jr. FNMA Mortgage Purchase Commitments as Put Options: An Empirical Examination. *Amer. Real Estate Urban Econ. Assoc. J.*, Spring 1985, *13*(1), pp. 93–105. [G: U.S.]

Bhagat, Sanjai; Brickley, James A. and Lease, Ronald C. Incentive Effects of Stock Purchase Plans. *J. Finan. Econ.*, June 1985, *14*(2), pp. 195–215. [G: U.S.]

Bhagat, Sanjai; Marr, M. Wayne and Thompson, G. Rodney. The Rule 415 Experiment: Equity Markets. *J. Finance*, December 1985, *40*(5), pp. 1385–1401. [G: U.S.]

Bigman, David and Goldfarb, David. Efficiency and Efficient Trading Rules for Food and Feed Grains in the World Commodity Markets: The Israeli Experience. *J. Futures Markets*, Spring 1985, *5*(1), pp. 1–10. [G: Israel]

Billingsley, Randall S. and Chance, Don M. Options Market Efficiency and the Box Spread Strategy. *Financial Rev.*, November 1985, *20*(4), pp. 287–301. [G: U.S.]

Billingsley, Randall S. and Thompson, G. Rodney. Determinants of Stock Repurchases by

Bank Holding Companies. *J. Bank Res.*, Autumn 1985, *16*(3), pp. 128–35.   [G: U.S.]

Binder, John J. Measuring the Effects of Regulation with Stock Price Data. *Rand J. Econ.*, Summer 1985, *16*(2), pp. 167–83.   [G: U.S.]

Bird, Peter J. W. N. Dependency and Efficiency in the London Terminal Markets. *J. Futures Markets*, Fall 1985, *5*(3), pp. 433–46.
[G: U.K.]

Bird, Peter J. W. N. The Weak Form Efficiency of the London Metal Exchange. *Appl. Econ.*, August 1985, *17*(4), pp. 571–87.   [G: U.K.]

Bito, Christian. Evaluation des obligations renouvelables du Trésor. (The Pricing of ORT. With English summary.) *Finance*, December 1985, *6*(2), pp. 231–48.   [G: France]

Bloch, Howard R. and Lareau, Thomas J. Should We Invest in "Socially Irresponsible" Firms? *J. Portfol. Manage.*, Summer 1985, *11*(4), pp. 27–31.   [G: U.S.]

Bond, Gary E.; Thompson, Stanley R. and Geldard, Jane M. Basis Risk and Hedging Strategies for Australian Wheat Exports. *Australian J. Agr. Econ.*, December 1985, *29*(3), pp. 199–209.   [G: Australia]

Booth, James R. and Officer, Dennis T. Expectations, Interest Rates, and Commercial Bank Stocks. *J. Finan. Res.*, Spring 1985, *8*(1), pp. 51–58.   [G: U.S.]

Booth, James R.; Officer, Dennis T. and Henderson, Glenn V., Jr. Commercial Bank Stocks, Interest Rates, and Systematic Risk. *J. Econ. Bus.*, December 1985, *37*(4), pp. 303–10.
[G: U.S.]

Booth, James R.; Tehranian, Hassan and Trennepohl, Gary L. Efficiency Analysis and Option Portfolio Selection. *J. Finan. Quant. Anal.*, December 1985, *20*(4), pp. 435–50.
[G: U.S.]

Boyle, Phelim P. Prices Instead of Yields to Model the Term Structure. *Finance*, December 1985, *6*(2), pp. 217–29.   [G: U.S.]

Branch, Ben and Chang, Kyungchun. Tax-Loss Trading, Is the Game Over or Have the Rules Changed? *Financial Rev.*, February 1985, *20*(1), pp. 55–69.   [G: U.S.]

Brandt, Jon A. Forecasting and Hedging: An Illustration of Risk Reduction in the Hog Industry. *Amer. J. Agr. Econ.*, February 1985, *67*(1), pp. 24–31.   [G: U.S.]

Brickley, James A.; Bhagat, Sanjai and Lease, Ronald C. The Impact of Long-range Managerial Compensation Plans on Shareholder Wealth. *J. Acc. Econ.*, April 1985, *7*(1–3), pp. 115–29.   [G: U.S.]

Brickley, James A. and Schallheim, James S. Lifting the Lid on Closed-End Investment Companies: A Case of Abnormal Returns. *J. Finan. Quant. Anal.*, March 1985, *20*(1), pp. 107–17.
[G: U.S.]

Brinson, Gary P. and Fachler, Nimrod. Measuring Non-U.S. Equity Portfolio Performance. *J. Portfol. Manage.*, Spring 1985, *11*(3), pp. 73–76.   [G: OECD]

Brown, Stephen J. and Warner, Jerold B. Using Daily Stock Returns: The Case of Event Studies. *J. Finan. Econ.*, March 1985, *14*(1), pp. 3–31.   [G: U.S.]

Brown, Stephen J. and Weinstein, Mark I. Derived Factors in Event Studies. *J. Finan. Econ.*, September 1985, *14*(3), pp. 491–95.

Burrows, P. F. Financial Markets at the Lower Turning Points of the Economic Cycle. In *Meyer, F. V., ed.*, 1985, pp. 28–62.
[G: U.S.; U.K.]

Bütler, Theo. The Swiss Equity Market: Types of Securities Traded. In *Meier, H. B., ed.*, 1985, pp. 44–61.   [G: Switzerland]

Byers, J. David and Peel, D. A. Some Further Evidence on the Predictability of UK Asset Prices [Efficient Capital Markets: A Review of Theory and Empirical Work]. *Bull. Econ. Res.*, September 1985, *37*(3), pp. 249–57.
[G: U.K.]

Cable, John R. Capital Market Information and Industrial Performance: The Role of West German Banks. *Econ. J.*, March 1985, *95*(377), pp. 118–32.   [G: W. Germany]

Calley, Nicholas O.; Chambers, Donald R. and Woolridge, J. Randall. A Note on Standardized Unexpected Earnings: The Case of the Electric Utility Industry. *Financial Rev.*, February 1985, *20*(1), pp. 102–10.   [G: U.S.]

Canarella, Giorgio and Pollard, Stephen K. Efficiency of Commodity Futures: A Vector Autoregression Analysis. *J. Futures Markets*, Spring 1985, *5*(1), pp. 57–76.   [G: U.S.]

Cantoni, Renato. Le Borse estere nel 1984. (Foreign Stock Exchanges in 1984. With English summary.) *Bancaria*, February 1985, *41*(2), pp. 187–99.   [G: OECD; Hong Kong; Australia]

Cantoni, Renato. Le Borse italiane nel 1984. (The Italian Stock Market in 1984. With English summary.) *Bancaria*, January 1985, *41*(1), pp. 81–90.   [G: Italy]

Capitelli, René. Eine empirische Untersuchung über den Zusammenhang von kurz-, mittel- und langfristigen schweizerischen Zinssätzen. (Some Empirical Evidence on the Relationship between Short, Medium, and Long-term Swiss Interest Rates. With English summary.) *Schweiz. Z. Volkswirtsch. Statist.*, March 1985, *121*(1), pp. 1–22.   [G: Switzerland]

Carosso, Vincent P. Legislative History of the Glass-Steagall Act: An Economic Evaluation of Bank Securities Activities before 1933: Comment. In *Walter, I., ed.*, 1985, pp. 89–91.
[G: U.S.]

Carter, Colin A. Hedging Opportunities for Canadian Grains. *Can. J. Agr. Econ.*, March 1985, *33*(1), pp. 37–45.   [G: Canada]

Carter, Colin A. and Loyns, R. M. A. Hedging Feedlot Cattle: A Canadian Perspective. *Amer. J. Agr. Econ.*, February 1985, *67*(1), pp. 32–39.   [G: U.S.; Canada]

Cesarini, Francesco. Il ruolo del mercato mobiliare nel primo trentennio del secolo. (The Role of the Stock Market during the Early Thirty Years of This Century. With English summary.) *Bancaria*, February 1985, *41*(2), pp. 181–86. **[G: Italy]**

Chan, K. C.; Chen, Nai-fu and Hsieh, David A. An Exploratory Investigation of the Firm Size Effect. *J. Finan. Econ.*, September 1985, *14*(3), pp. 451–71. **[G: U.S.]**

Chance, Don M. and Ferris, Stephen P. The CBOE Call Option Index: A Historical Record. *J. Portfol. Manage.*, Fall 1985, *12*(1), pp. 75–83. **[G: U.S.]**

Chandy, P. R.; Davidson, Wallace N., III and Garrison, Sharon. Bad News = Good News! Who Can Tell? *J. Portfol. Manage.*, Fall 1985, *12*(1), pp. 24–27. **[G: U.S.]**

Chang, Eric C. Returns to Speculators and the Theory of Normal Backwardation. *J. Finance*, March 1985, *40*(1), pp. 193–208. **[G: U.S.]**

Chang, Eric C. and Stevenson, Richard A. The Timing Performance of Small Traders. *J. Futures Markets*, Winter 1985, *5*(4), pp. 517–27. **[G: U.S.]**

Chapra, M. Umer. The Role of the Stock Exchange in an Islamic Economy: Comments. *J. Res. Islamic Econ.*, Summer 1985, *3*(1), pp. 75–81.

Chen, Andrew H. and Sanger, Gary C. An Analysis of the Impact of Regulatory Change: The Case of Natural Gas Deregulation. *Financial Rev.*, February 1985, *20*(1), pp. 36–54. **[G: U.S.]**

Choi, Jin W. and Longstaff, Francis A. Pricing Options on Agricultural Futures: An Application of the Constant Elasticity of Variance Option Pricing Model. *J. Futures Markets*, Summer 1985, *5*(2), pp. 247–58. **[G: U.S.]**

Christensen, Peter Ove; Nielsen, Jørgen Aase and Sørensen, Bjarne G. Skatteklienteller på det danske obligationsmarked. (Optimal Bond Investments and the Tax Bracket of the Investor. With English summary.) *Nationaløkon. Tidsskr.*, 1985, *123*(3), pp. 389–98. **[G: Denmark]**

Clark, William and Turner, Charlie G. International Trade and the Evolution of the American Capital Market, 1888–1911. *J. Econ. Hist.*, June 1985, *45*(2), pp. 405–10. **[G: U.S.]**

Clifton, Eric V. The Currency Futures Market and Interbank Foreign Exchange Trading. *J. Futures Markets*, Fall 1985, *5*(3), pp. 375–84. **[G: U.S.; Canada]**

Clubley, Sally. The Gasoil Market. In *Roberts, G., ed.*, 1985, pp. 35–37. **[G: U.K.; U.S.]**

Cluff, George S. and Farnham, Paul G. A Problem of Discrete Choice: Moody's Municipal Bond Ratings. *J. Econ. Bus.*, December 1985, *37*(4), pp. 277–302. **[G: U.S.]**

Coffee, John C., Jr. The Unfaithful Champion: The Plaintiff as Monitor in Shareholder Litigation. *Law Contemp. Probl.*, Summer 1985, *48*(3), pp. 5–81. **[G: U.S.]**

Conn, Robert L. A Re-examination of Merger Studies That Use the Capital Asset Pricing Model Methodology. *Cambridge J. Econ.*, March 1985, *9*(1), pp. 43–56.

Cornell, Bradford. Taxes and the Pricing of Stock Index Futures: Empirical Results. *J. Futures*

Markets, Spring 1985, *5*(1), pp. 89–101. **[G: U.S.]**

Cornell, Bradford. The Weekly Pattern in Stock Returns: Cash versus Futures: A Note. *J. Finance*, June 1985, *40*(2), pp. 583–88. **[G: U.S.]**

Corrigan, E. Gerald. Statement to the U.S. House Subcommittee on Commerce, Consumer, and Monetary Affairs of the Committee on Government Operations, May 15, 1985. *Fed. Res. Bull.*, July 1985, *71*(7), pp. 524–28. **[G: U.S.]**

Corrigan, E. Gerald. Statement to the U.S. House Subcommittee on Domestic Monetary Policy of the Committee on Banking, Finance and Urban Affairs, April 1, 1985. *Fed. Res. Bull.*, June 1985, *71*(6), pp. 405–09. **[G: U.S.]**

Corrigan, E. Gerald. Statement to the U.S. Senate Subcommittee on Securities of the Committee on Banking, Housing, and Urban Affairs, May 9, 1985. *Fed. Res. Bull.*, July 1985, *71*(7), pp. 520–24. **[G: U.S.]**

Cox, Clifford T. Further Evidence on the Representativeness of Management Earnings Forecasts. *Accounting Rev.*, October 1985, *60*(4), pp. 692–701. **[G: U.S.]**

Cox, W. Michael. The Behavior of Treasury Securities: Monthly, 1942–1984. *J. Monet. Econ.*, September 1985, *16*(2), pp. 227–50. **[G: U.S.]**

Crawford, Peter. Interest Rate Outlook: Focus on Credit Supply. *Bus. Econ.*, July 1985, *20*(3), pp. 34–39. **[G: U.S.]**

Davidson, Wallace N., III and Glascock, John L. The Announcement Effects of Preferred Stock Re-ratings. *J. Finan. Res.*, Winter 1985, *8*(4), pp. 317–25. **[G: U.S.]**

Dawson, Steve. A Somber Fifteenth Euroconvertible Bond Reunion. *J. Portfol. Manage.*, Winter 1985, *11*(2), pp. 85–87. **[G: U.S.]**

De Bondt, Werner F. M. and Thaler, Richard. Does the Stock Market Overreact? *J. Finance*, July 1985, *40*(3), pp. 793–805. **[G: U.S.]**

Desai, Anand S. and Stover, Roger D. Bank Holding Company Acquisitions, Stockholder Returns, and Regulatory Uncertainty. *J. Finan. Res.*, Summer 1985, *8*(2), pp. 145–56. **[G: U.S.]**

Dhrymes, Phoebus J. On the Empirical Relevance of APT: Comment. *J. Portfol. Manage.*, Summer 1985, *11*(4), pp. 70–71. **[G: U.S.]**

Dietrich, J. Richard and Deitrick, James W. Bond Exchanges in the Airline Industry: Analyzing Public Disclosures. *Accounting Rev.*, January 1985, *60*(1), pp. 109–26. **[G: U.S.]**

Domowitz, Ian and Hakkio, Craig S. Conditional Variance and the Risk Premium in the Foreign Exchange Market. *J. Int. Econ.*, August 1985, *19*(1/2), pp. 47–66. **[G: U.K.; France; W. Germany; Japan; Switzerland]**

Draper, Dennis W. The Small Public Trader in Futures Markets. In *Peck, A. E., ed. (I)*, 1985, pp. 211–69. **[G: U.S.]**

Dubler, Heini P. Listing of Shares on Swiss Stock

Exchanges. In *Meier, H. B., ed.,* 1985, pp. 93–106. [G: Switzerland]

Dubler, Heini P. The Swiss Equity Market: New Issue Procedures. In *Meier, H. B., ed.,* 1985, pp. 62–70. [G: Switzerland]

Dubofsky, David A. Capital Market Credit Rationing and Stock Risk. *Southern Econ. J.,* July 1985, *52*(1), pp. 191–202. [G: U.S.]

Dyl, Edward A. and Martin, Stanley A., Jr. Weekend Effects on Stock Returns: A Comment. *J. Finance,* March 1985, *40*(1), pp. 347–49. [G: U.S.]

Eades, Kenneth M.; Hess, Patrick J. and Kim, E. Han. Market Rationality and Dividend Announcements. *J. Finan. Econ.,* December 1985, *14*(4), pp. 581–604. [G: U.S.]

Easton, Peter D. Accounting Earnings and Security Valuation: Empirical Evidence of the Fundamental Links. *J. Acc. Res.,* Supp. 1985, *23,* pp. 54–77. [G: U.S.]

Eckbo, B. Espen. Mergers and the Market Concentration Doctrine: Evidence from the Capital Market. *J. Bus.,* July 1985, *58*(3), pp. 325–49. [G: U.S.]

Ederington, Louis H. Classification Models and Bond Ratings. *Financial Rev.,* November 1985, *20*(4), pp. 237–62. [G: U.S.]

Edwards, Sebastian. Money, the Rate of Devaluation, and Interest Rates in a Semiopen Economy: Colombia, 1968–82. *J. Money, Credit, Banking,* February 1985, *17*(1), pp. 59–68. [G: Colombia]

Elliott, John A. and Swieringa, Robert J. Aetna, the SEC and Tax Benefits of Loss Carryforwards. *Accounting Rev.,* July 1985, *60*(3), pp. 531–46. [G: U.S.]

Ellis, J. C. Fundamental Supply and Demand Factors in the Grain Futures Markets. In *Roberts, G., ed.,* 1985, pp. 38–44. [G: U.S.; EEC]

Errunza, Vihang R. and Losq, Etienne. The Behavior of Stock Prices on LDC Markets. *J. Banking Finance,* December 1985, *9*(4), pp. 561–75. [G: Selected LDCs]

Evnine, Jeremy and Rudd, Andrew. Index Options: The Early Evidence. *J. Finance,* July 1985, *40*(3), pp. 743–56. [G: U.S.]

Farrelly, Gail E.; Ferris, Kenneth R. and Reichenstein, William R. Perceived Risk, Market Risk, and Accounting Determined Risk Measures. *Accounting Rev.,* April 1985, *60*(2), pp. 278–88. [G: U.S.]

Feldman, Robert A. Foreign Currency Options. *Finance Develop.,* December 1985, *22*(4), pp. 38–41.

Ferri, Michael G.; Goldstein, Steven J. and Oberhelman, H. Dennis. The Performance of the When-issued Market for T-Bills. *J. Portfol. Manage.,* Spring 1985, *11*(3), pp. 57–61. [G: U.S.]

Fieleke, Norman S. The Foreign Currency Futures Market: Some Reflections on Competitiveness and Growth. *J. Futures Markets,* Winter 1985, *5*(4), pp. 625–31. [G: U.S.; Canada; W. Germany; Japan; U.K.]

Fisher, Lawrence and Kamin, Jules H. Forecast-

ing Systematic Risk: Estimates of "Raw" Beta That Take Account of the Tendency of Beta To Change and Heteroskedasticity of Risidual Returns. *J. Finan. Quant. Anal.,* June 1985, *20*(2), pp. 127–49. [G: U.S.]

Flannery, Mark J. An Economic Evaluation of Bank Securities Activities before 1933. In *Walter, I., ed.,* 1985, pp. 67–87. [G: U.S.]

Fogler, H. Russell; Granito, Michael R. and Smith, Laurence R. A Theoretical Analysis of Real Estate Returns. *J. Finance,* July 1985, *40*(3), pp. 711–19. [G: U.S.]

Fong, H. Gifford and Fabozzi, Frank J. How to Enhance Bond Returns with Naive Strategies. *J. Portfol. Manage.,* Summer 1985, *11*(4), pp. 57–60. [G: U.S.]

Fontaine, P. Un test du modèle international d'arbitrage et de l'intégration finacière. (A Test of the International Arbitrage Model and of Financial Integration. With English summary.) *Finance,* June 1985, *6*(1), pp. 121–41.

Frankel, Jeffrey A. Portfolio Crowding-out, Empirically Estimated. *Quart. J. Econ.,* Supp. 1985, *100,* pp. 1041–65. [G: U.S.]

Frankel, Jeffrey A. The Dazzling Dollar. *Brookings Pap. Econ. Act.,* 1985, (1), pp. 199–217. [G: U.S.]

Fraser, Donald R. and Groth, John C. Listing and the Liquidity of Bank Stocks. *J. Bank Res.,* Autumn 1985, *16*(3), pp. 136–44. [G: U.S.]

Fraser, Donald R. and Richards, R. Malcolm. The Penn Square Bank Failure and the Inefficient Market. *J. Portfol. Manage.,* Spring 1985, *11*(3), pp. 34–36. [G: U.S.]

Fraser, Donald R.; Richards, R. Malcolm and Fosberg, Richard H. A Note on Deposit Rate Deregulation, Super Nows, and Bank Security Returns. *J. Banking Finance,* December 1985, *9*(4), pp. 585–95. [G: U.S.]

Frefel, Jean-Pierre. The Swiss Equity Market: Share Trading Procedures and Cost. In *Meier, H. B., ed.,* 1985, pp. 71–92. [G: Switzerland]

French, Dan W. and Henderson, Glenn V., Jr. How Well Does Performance Evaluation Perform? *J. Portfol. Manage.,* Winter 1985, *11*(2), pp. 15–18. [G: U.S.]

Friedman, Benjamin M. Portfolio Choice and the Debt-to-Income Relationship. *Amer. Econ. Rev.,* May 1985, *75*(2), pp. 338–43. [G: U.S.]

Friedman, Benjamin M. The Effect of Large Government Deficits on Interest Rates and Equity Returns. *Oxford Rev. Econ. Policy,* Spring 1985, *1*(1), pp. 58–71.

Friedman, Benjamin M. The Substitutability of Debt and Equity Securities. In *Friedman, B. M., ed.,* 1985, pp. 197–233. [G: U.S.]

Friedman, Stephen J. On the Expansion of Banking Powers: Comment. In *Walter, I., ed.,* 1985, pp. 35–40. [G: U.S.]

Fung, William K. H.; Schwartz, Robert A. and Whitcomb, David K. Adjusting for the Intervalling Effect Bias in Beta: A Test Using Paris Bourse Data. *J. Banking Finance,* September 1985, *9*(3), pp. 443–60. [G: France]

Gallais-Hamonno, Georges. A Markowitz Approach to Regulation: The Case of French Open Mutual Funds. In *Currie, D., ed.*, 1985, pp. 159–70. [G: France]

Galli, Alexander F. Influences on the Swiss Equity Market. In *Meier, H. B., ed.*, 1985, pp. 8–27. [G: Switzerland]

Gallow, Michael; Griffiths, Geoffrey and Affleck-Graves, John F. Earnings Forecasting on the JSE: An Empirical Study of Some Statistical Models. *J. Stud. Econ. Econometrics*, August 1985, (22), pp. 25–46. [G: S. Africa]

Gau, George W. Public Information and Abnormal Returns in Real Estate Investment. *Amer. Real Estate Urban Econ. Assoc. J.*, Spring 1985, 13(1), pp. 15–31. [G: Canada]

Gendreau, Brian C. Carrying Costs and Treasury Bill Futures. *J. Portfol. Manage.*, Fall 1985, 12(1), pp. 58–64. [G: U.S.]

Giannaros, Demetrios S. Forecasting the Long-term Real Treasury Bill Rate. *Atlantic Econ. J.*, December 1985, 13(4), pp. 83. [G: U.S.]

Giddy, Ian H. Is Equity Underwriting Risky for Commercial Bank Affiliates? In *Walter, I., ed.*, 1985, pp. 145–69. [G: U.S.]

Givoly, Dan and Palmon, Dan. Insider Trading and the Exploitation of Inside Information: Some Empirical Evidence. *J. Bus.*, January 1985, 58(1), pp. 69–87. [G: U.S.]

Gjølberg, Ole. Is the Spot Market for Oil Products Efficient? Some Rotterdam Evidence. *Energy Econ.*, October 1985, 7(4), pp. 231–36. [G: Netherlands]

Glascock, John L. and Davidson, Wallace N., III. The Effect of Bond Deratings on Bank Stock Returns. *J. Bank Res.*, Autumn 1985, 16(3), pp. 120–27. [G: U.S.]

Goh, L. Y. and Allen, D. E. Errata [A Note on Put–Call Parity and the Market Efficiency of the London Traded Options Market]. *Managerial Dec. Econ.*, June 1985, 6(2), pp. 129. [G: U.K.]

Goodman, Laurie S.; Ross, Susan and Schmidt, Frederick. Are Foreign Currency Options Overvalued? The Early Experience of the Philadelphia Stock Exchange. *J. Futures Markets*, Fall 1985, 5(3), pp. 349–59. [G: U.S.]

Gupta, Kanhaya L. Portfolio Behaviour of Selected Financial Institutions in Canada. *Appl. Econ.*, April 1985, 17(2), pp. 341–58. [G: Canada]

Halpern, Paul J. and Turnbull, Stuart M. Empirical Tests of Boundary Conditions for Toronto Stock Exchange Options. *J. Finance*, June 1985, 40(2), pp. 481–500. [G: Canada]

Hamilton, James D. Uncovering Financial Market Expectations of Inflation. *J. Polit. Econ.*, December 1985, 93(6), pp. 1224–41. [G: U.S.]

Hamilton, James D. and Whiteman, Charles H. The Observable Implications of Self-fulfilling Expectations. *J. Monet. Econ.*, November 1985, 16(3), pp. 353–73.

Harris, William G. Inflation Risk as a Determinant of the Discount Rate in Tort Settlements:

Reply. *J. Risk Ins.*, September 1985, 52(3), pp. 533–36. [G: U.S.]

Haugen, Robert A.; Ortiz, Edgar and Arjona, Enrique. Market Efficiency: Mexico versus the U.S. *J. Portfol. Manage.*, Fall 1985, 12(1), pp. 28–32. [G: Mexico; U.S.]

Hawawini, Gabriel A.; Michel, Pierre A. and Corhay, Albert. New Evidence on Beta Stationarity and Forecast for Belgian Common Stocks. *J. Banking Finance*, December 1985, 9(4), pp. 553–60. [G: Belgium]

Hayward, Brian. The Grain Trader and Market Outlook Usefulness. *Can. J. Agr. Econ.*, August 1985, 32, pp. 77–85.

Hegde, Shantaram P. and Branch, Ben. An Empirical Analysis of Arbitrage Opportunities in the Treasury Bill Futures Market. *J. Futures Markets*, Fall 1985, 5(3), pp. 407–24. [G: U.S.]

Hegde, Shantaram P. and Nunn, Kenneth P., Jr. A Multivariate Analysis of the Cross-hedging Performance of T-Bond and GNMA Futures Markets. *Financial Rev.*, May 1985, 20(2), pp. 143–63. [G: U.S.]

Hegde, Shantaram P. and Nunn, Kenneth P., Jr. Interest Rate Volatility, Trading Volume, and the Hedging Performance of T-Bond and GNMA Futures—A Note. *J. Futures Markets*, Summer 1985, 5(2), pp. 273–86. [G: U.S.]

Helms, Billy P. and Martell, Terrence F. An Examination of the Distribution of Futures Price Changes. *J. Futures Markets*, Summer 1985, 5(2), pp. 259–72. [G: U.S.]

Hendershott, Patric H. and Huang, Roger D. Debt and Equity Yields, 1926–1980. In *Friedman, B. M., ed.*, 1985, pp. 117–63. [G: U.S.]

Herbst, Anthony F. Hedging against Price Index Inflation with Futures Contracts. *J. Futures Markets*, Winter 1985, 5(4), pp. 489–504. [G: U.S.]

Hess, James. The Use of Collateral to Enforce Debt: Profit Maximization. *Econ. Inquiry*, April 1985, 23(2), pp. 349–56.

Hewson, Margot. Computerized Futures Trading. In *Roberts, G., ed.*, 1985, pp. 25–27. [G: Global]

Hindley, Brian. Commodity Markets in Their Policy Context. In *Yamey, B. S.; Sandor, R. L. and Hindley, B.*, 1985, pp. 1–13.

Hinich, Melvin J. and Patterson, Douglas M. Evidence of Nonlinearity in Daily Stock Returns. *J. Bus. Econ. Statist.*, January 1985, 3(1), pp. 69–77. [G: U.S.]

Hinich, Melvin J. and Patterson, Douglas M. Identification of the Coefficients in a Non-linear Time Series of the Quadratic Type. *J. Econometrics*, Oct./Nov. 1985, 30(1/2), pp. 269–88. [G: U.S.]

Hinich, Melvin J. and Patterson, Douglas M. On Non-linear Serial Dependencies in Stock Returns: Reply [Evidence of Nonlinearity in Daily Stock Returns]. *J. Econometrics*, Oct./Nov. 1985, 30(1/2), pp. 297–99. [G: U.S.]

Hiraki, Takato. Testing the Proxy Effect Hypothesis of Inflation on Stock Returns for the Japanese Market. *Quart. J. Bus. Econ.*, Spring

1985, *24*(2), pp. 73–87. [G: Japan]

Hoggarth, Glenn and Ormerod, Paul. The Demand for Long-term Government Securities in the UK by the Non-bank Private Sector. In *Currie, D., ed.*, 1985, pp. 171–91.
[G: U.K.]

Holderness, Clifford G. and Sheehan, Dennis P. Raiders or Saviors? The Evidence on Six Controversial Investors. *J. Finan. Econ.*, December 1985, *14*(4), pp. 555–79. [G: U.S.]

Holt, Matthew T. and Brandt, Jon A. Combining Price Forecasting with Hedging of Hogs: An Evaluation Using Alternative Measures of Risk. *J. Futures Markets*, Fall 1985, *5*(3), pp. 297–309. [G: U.S.]

Hood, Donald C.; Andreassen, Paul and Schachter, Stanley. Random and Non-random Walks on the New York Stock Exchange. *J. Econ. Behav. Organ.*, December 1985, *6*(4), pp. 331–38. [G: U.S.]

Hopwood, William S. and McKeown, James C. The Incremental Information Content of Interim Expenses over Interim Sales. *J. Acc. Res.*, Spring 1985, *23*(1), pp. 161–74.
[G: U.S.]

Hubbard, R. Glenn. Personal Taxation, Pension Wealth, and Portfolio Composition. *Rev. Econ. Statist.*, February 1985, *67*(1), pp. 53–60.
[G: U.S.]

Huberman, Gur and Schwert, G. William. Information Aggregation, Inflation, and the Pricing of Indexed Bonds. *J. Polit. Econ.*, February 1985, *93*(1), pp. 92–114. [G: Israel]

Huertas, Thomas F. An Analysis of the Competitive Effects of Allowing Commercial Bank Affiliates to Underwrite Corporate Securities: Comment. In *Walter, I., ed.*, 1985, pp. 141–43. [G: U.S.]

Hwa, Erh-Cheng. A Model of Price and Quantity Adjustments in Primary Commodity Markets. *J. Policy Modeling*, Summer 1985, *7*(2), pp. 305–38. [G: Global]

Ibbotson, Roger G.; Siegel, Laurence B. and Love, Kathryn S. World Wealth: Market Values and Returns. *J. Portfol. Manage.*, Fall 1985, *12*(1), pp. 4–23. [G: OECD]

Ingram, Robert W. A Descriptive Analysis of Municipal Bond Price Data for Use in Accounting Research. *J. Acc. Res.*, Autumn 1985, *23*(2), pp. 595–618. [G: U.S.]

Irwin, Scott H. and Brorsen, B. Wade. Public Futures Funds. *J. Futures Markets*, Summer 1985, *5*(2), pp. 149–71. [G: U.S.]

Ivanovitch, Michael S. Recent Interest Rate Developments in Major World Financial Markets. *Bus. Econ.*, October 1985, *20*(4), pp. 30–34.
[G: U.S.; W. Europe]

Jackson, John D. and Skomp, Stephen E. On the Relative Performance of Registered versus Non-registered Mutual Funds. *Southern Econ. J.*, October 1985, *52*(2), pp. 392–401.
[G: U.S.]

Jaffe, Jeffrey F. and Westerfield, Randolph. Patterns in Japanese Common Stock Returns: Day of the Week and Turn of the Year Effects. *J.*

Finan. Quant. Anal., June 1985, *20*(2), pp. 261–72. [G: Japan]

Jaffe, Jeffrey F. and Westerfield, Randolph. The Week-End Effect in Common Stock Returns: The International Evidence. *J. Finance*, June 1985, *40*(2), pp. 433–54. [G: U.S.; U.K.; Japan; Australia; Canada]

Jain, Prem C. The Effect of Voluntary Sell-off Announcements on Shareholder Wealth. *J. Finance*, March 1985, *40*(1), pp. 209–24.
[G: U.S.]

Jarrell, Gregg A. and Peltzman, Sam. The Impact of Product Recalls on the Wealth of Sellers. *J. Polit. Econ.*, June 1985, *93*(3), pp. 512–36.
[G: U.S.]

Jennings, Robert and Starks, Laura. Information Content and the Speed of Stock Price Adjustment. *J. Acc. Res.*, Spring 1985, *23*(1), pp. 336–50. [G: U.S.]

Jensen, Michael C. Capital Structure Change and Decreases in Stockholders' Wealth: A Cross-Sectional Study of Convertible Security Calls: Comment. In *Friedman, B. M., ed.*, 1985, pp. 296–300. [G: U.S.]

Jianakoplos, Nancy Ammon. Inflation and the Accumulation of Wealth by Older Households, 1966–1976. In *Hendershott, P. H., ed.*, 1985, pp. 151–80. [G: U.S.]

Johnson, Philip McBride. Federal Regulation in Securities and Futures Markets. In *Peck, A. E., ed. (II)*, 1985, pp. 291–325. [G: U.S.]

Johnson, W. Bruce. Valuation Implications of SFAS No. 33 Data for Electric Utility Investors: Discussion. *J. Acc. Res.*, Supp. 1985, *23*, pp. 48–53. [G: U.S.]

Johnson, W. Bruce, et al. An Analysis of the Stock Price Reaction to Sudden Executive Deaths: Implications for the Managerial Labor Market. *J. Acc. Econ.*, April 1985, *7*(1–3), pp. 151–74.
[G: U.S.]

Jones, Charles P.; Rendleman, Richard J., Jr. and Latané, Henry A. Earnings Announcements: Pre-and-Post Responses. *J. Portfol. Manage.*, Spring 1985, *11*(3), pp. 28–32.
[G: U.S.]

Jones, Robert A. Conversion Factor Risk in Treasury Bond Futures: Comment. *J. Futures Markets*, Spring 1985, *5*(1), pp. 115–19.
[G: U.S.]

Jorion, Philippe. International Portfolio Diversification with Estimation Risk. *J. Bus.*, July 1985, *58*(3), pp. 259–78. [G: OECD]

Junkus, Joan C. and Lee, Cheng F. Use of Three Stock Index Futures in Hedging Decisions. *J. Futures Markets*, Summer 1985, *5*(2), pp. 201–22. [G: U.S.]

Jüttner, D. Johannes; Tuckwell, Roger H. and Luedecke, Bernd P. Are Expectations of Short-term Interest Rates Rational? *Australian Econ. Pap.*, December 1985, *24*(45), pp. 356–69.
[G: U.S.; Australia]

Kahl, Kandice H. Effects of the Economic Recovery Tax Act of 1981 on Futures Market Volume. *J. Futures Markets*, Summer 1985, *5*(2), pp. 239–46. [G: U.S.]

Kalay, Avner and Loewenstein, Uri. Predictable

Events and Excess Returns: The Case of Dividend Announcements. *J. Finan. Econ.*, September 1985, *14*(3), pp. 423–49. [G: U.S.]

Kalotay, Andrew J. The After-Tax Duration of Original Issue Discount Bonds. *J. Portfol. Manage.*, Winter 1985, *11*(2), pp. 70–72. [G: U.S.]

Kanemasu, Hiromitsu; Litzenberger, Robert H. and Rolfo, Jacques. Pricing U.S. Treasury Securities with Tax Effects Using the Likelihood Function. *Finance*, December 1985, *6*(2), pp. 187–216. [G: U.S.]

Kaplan, Howard M. Farmland as a Portfolio Investment. *J. Portfol. Manage.*, Winter 1985, *11*(2), pp. 73–78. [G: U.S.]

Kato, Kiyoshi and Schallheim, James S. Seasonal and Size Anomalies in the Japanese Stock Market. *J. Finan. Quant. Anal.*, June 1985, *20*(2), pp. 243–60. [G: Japan]

Keim, Donald B. Dividend Yields and Stock Returns: Implications of Abnormal January Returns. *J. Finan. Econ.*, September 1985, *14*(3), pp. 473–89. [G: U.S.]

Kelly, Edward J., III. Conflicts of Interest: A Legal View. In *Walter, I., ed.*, 1985, pp. 231–54. [G: U.S.]

Kindleberger, Charles P. Key Currencies and Financial Centres. In *Kindleberger, C. P.*, 1985, pp. 155–67. [G: OECD]

King, John R. What Future for Capital Gains Tax? In *Kay, J., ed.*, 1985, pp. 71–77. [G: U.K.]

Klemkosky, Robert C. and Conroy, Robert M. Competition and the Cost of Liquidity to Investors. *J. Econ. Bus.*, August 1985, *37*(3), pp. 183–95. [G: U.S.]

Klemkosky, Robert C. and Lasser, Dennis J. An Efficiency Analysis of the T-Bond Futures Market. *J. Futures Markets*, Winter 1985, *5*(4), pp. 607–20. [G: U.S.]

Kling, John L. Oil Price Shocks and Stock Market Behavior. *J. Portfol. Manage.*, Fall 1985, *12*(1), pp. 34–39. [G: U.S.]

Kolari, James W. and Apilado, Vincent P. The Cyclical Effect of Default Risk on Industrial Bond Yields. *J. Econ. Bus.*, December 1985, *37*(4), pp. 311–25. [G: U.S.]

Kolari, James W. and Di Clemente, John. A Case Study of Geographic Deregulation: The New Illinois Bank Holding Company Act. *J. Bank Res.*, Autumn 1985, *16*(3), pp. 150–57. [G: U.S.]

Kolb, Robert W. and Gay, Gerald D. A Pricing Anomaly in Treasury Bill Futures. *J. Finan. Res.*, Summer 1985, *8*(2), pp. 157–67. [G: U.S.]

Korajczyk, Robert A. The Pricing of Forward Contracts for Foreign Exchange. *J. Polit. Econ.*, April 1985, *93*(2), pp. 346–68. [G: U.S.; W. Europe; Canada]

Kraus, Alan. New Tests of the APT and Their Implications: Discussion. *J. Finance*, July 1985, *40*(3), pp. 674–75.

Krausz, Joshua. Option Parameter Analysis and Market Efficiency Tests: A Simultaneous Solution Approach. *Appl. Econ.*, October 1985, *17*(5), pp. 885–96. [G: U.S.]

Krinsky, Itzhak. Mean–Variance Utility Functions, Flexible Functional Forms, and the Investment Behavior of Canadian Life Insurers. *J. Risk Ins.*, June 1985, *52*(2), pp. 241–68. [G: Canada]

Kripke, Homer. Manne's Insider Trading Thesis and Other Failures of Conservative Economics [Insider Trading and Property Rights in New Information]. *Cato J.*, Winter 1985, *4*(3), pp. 945–57.

Kross, William. The Size Effect Is Primarily a Price Effect. *J. Finan. Res.*, Fall 1985, *8*(3), pp. 169–79. [G: U.S.]

Kunimura, Michio and Iihara, Yoshio. Valuation of Underwriting Agreements for Raising Capital in the Japanese Capital Market. *J. Finan. Quant. Anal.*, June 1985, *20*(2), pp. 231–41. [G: Japan]

de La Bruslerie, Hubert. Test d'une stratégie d'arbitrage systématique sur le marché euro-obligataire. (A Test of a Systematic Arbitrage Strategy on the Eurobond Market. With English summary.) *Finance*, December 1985, *6*(2), pp. 249–74. [G: W. Europe]

Lakonishok, Josef and Levi, Maurice. Weekend Effects on Stock Returns: A Reply. *J. Finance*, March 1985, *40*(1), pp. 351–52. [G: U.S.]

Lambert, Richard A. and Larcker, David F. Golden Parachutes, Executive Decision-making and Shareholder Wealth. *J. Acc. Econ.*, April 1985, *7*(1–3), pp. 179–203. [G: U.S.]

Landes, William J.; Stoffels, John D. and Seifert, James A. An Empirical Test of a Duration-based Hedge: The Case of Corporate Bonds. *J. Futures Markets*, Summer 1985, *5*(2), pp. 173–82. [G: U.S.]

Langohr, Herwig and Santomero, Anthony M. The Extent of Equity Investment by European Banks: A Note. *J. Money, Credit, Banking*, May 1985, *17*(2), pp. 243–52. [G: EEC]

Lee, Cheng F. and Wu, Chunchi. The Impacts of Kurtosis on Risk Stationarity: Some Empirical Evidence. *Financial Rev.*, November 1985, *20*(4), pp. 263–69. [G: U.S.]

Lee, Chi-Wen Jevons. Market Model Stationarity and Timing of Structural Change. *Financial Rev.*, November 1985, *20*(4), pp. 329–42. [G: U.S.]

Lee, Moon H. and Bishara, Halim. Securities Regulation and Market Efficiency. *Int. Rev. Law Econ.*, December 1985, *5*(2), pp. 247–54. [G: Canada]

Lempert, Leonard H. Financial Markets and the Business Cycle. *Bus. Econ.*, April 1985, *20*(2), pp. 31–36. [G: U.S.]

Levich, Richard M. A View from the International Capital Markets. In *Walter, I., ed.*, 1985, pp. 255–92. [G: OECD]

Lewellen, Wilbur G.; Loderer, Claudio and Rosenfeld, Ahron. Merger Decisions and Executive Stock Ownership in Acquiring Firms. *J. Acc. Econ.*, April 1985, *7*(1–3), pp. 209–31. [G: U.S.]

Liljeblom, Eva. Economic Exposure on the Helsinki Stock Exchange and a Test for Market

Efficiency. *Liiketaloudellinen Aikak.*, 1985, 34(2), pp. 147–65. **[G: Finland]**

Lowinger, Thomas C.; Wihlborg, Clas and Willman, Elliott S. OPEC in World Financial Markets: Oil Prices and Interest Rates. *J. Int. Money Finance*, June 1985, 4(2), pp. 253–66. **[G: OECD; OPEC]**

Ma, Christopher K. Spreading between the Gold and Silver Markets: Is There a Parity? *J. Futures Markets*, Winter 1985, 5(4), pp. 579–94. **[G: U.K.]**

MacBeth, James D. Index Options: The Early Evidence: Discussion. *J. Finance*, July 1985, 40(3), pp. 756. **[G: U.S.]**

Madeo, Silvia A. and Pincus, Morton. Stock Market Behavior and Tax Rule Changes: The Case of the Disallowance of Certain Interest Deductions Claimed by Banks. *Accounting Rev.*, July 1985, 60(3), pp. 407–29. **[G: U.S.]**

Madura, Jeff and Reiff, Wallace. A Hedge Strategy for International Portfolios. *J. Portfol. Manage.*, Fall 1985, 12(1), pp. 70–74.

Magliolo, Joseph, III. Accounting Earnings and Security Valuation: Empirical Evidence of the Fundamental Links: Discussion. *J. Acc. Res.*, Supp. 1985, 23, pp. 78–80.

Malatesta, Paul H. and Thompson, Rex. Partially Anticipated Events: A Model of Stock Price Reactions with an Application to Corporate Acquisitions. *J. Finan. Econ.*, June 1985, 14(2), pp. 237–50. **[G: U.S.]**

Mandelker, Gershon and Tandon, Kishore. Common Stock Returns, Real Activity, Money, and Inflation: Some International Evidence. *J. Int. Money Finance*, June 1985, 4(2), pp. 267–86. **[G: Selected OECD]**

Manne, Henry G. Insider Trading and Property Rights in New Information. *Cato J.*, Winter 1985, 4(3), pp. 933–43.

Mark, Nelson C. Some Evidence on the International Inequality of Real Interest Rates. *J. Int. Money Finance*, June 1985, 4(2), pp. 189–208. **[G: Selected OECD]**

Marks, Barry R. and Raman, Krishnamurthy K. The Importance of Pension Data for Municipal and State Creditor Decisions: Replication and Extensions. *J. Acc. Res.*, Autumn 1985, 23(2), pp. 878–86. **[G: U.S.]**

Marr, M. Wayne and Thompson, G. Rodney. Primary Market Pricing of Convertible Preferred Stock. *Quart. Rev. Econ. Bus.*, Summer 1985, 25(2), pp. 73–80. **[G: U.S.]**

Marsh, Terry A. On Non-linear Serial Dependencies in Stock Returns [Evidence of Nonlinearity in Daily Stock Returns]. *J. Econometrics*, Oct./Nov. 1985, 30(1/2), pp. 289–96. **[G: U.S.]**

Martin, Preston. Statement to the U.S. House Subcommittee on Domestic Monetary Policy of the Committee on Banking, Finance, and Urban Affairs, May 3, 1985. *Fed. Res. Bull.*, July 1985, 71(7), pp. 514–17. **[G: U.S.]**

Martin, Preston. Statement to the U.S. House Subcommittee on Telecommunications, Consumer Protection, and Finance of the Committee on Energy and Commerce, May 2, 1985.

Fed. Res. Bull., July 1985, 71(7), pp. 508–13. **[G: U.S.]**

Maru, Junko and Takahashi, Toshiharu. Recent Developments of Interdealer Brokerage in the Japanese Secondary Bond Markets. *J. Finan. Quant. Anal.*, June 1985, 20(2), pp. 193–210. **[G: Japan]**

Matthews, Kent. Private Sector Expenditure in the Inter-war Period: An Integrated Portfolio Approach. *Manchester Sch. Econ. Soc. Stud.*, March 1985, 53(1), pp. 23–44. **[G: U.K.]**

Mayer, Colin and Meadowcroft, Shirley A. Selling Public Assets: Techniques and Financial Implications. *Fisc. Stud.*, November 1985, 6(4), pp. 42–56. **[G: U.K.]**

McConnell, John J. and Muscarella, Chris J. Corporate Capital Expenditure Decisions and the Market Value of the Firm. *J. Finan. Econ.*, September 1985, 14(3), pp. 399–422. **[G: U.S.]**

McConnell, John J. and Nantell, Timothy J. Corporate Combinations and Common Stock Returns: The Case of Joint Ventures. *J. Finance*, June 1985, 40(2), pp. 519–36. **[G: U.S.]**

McDonald, Bill. Making Sense out of Unstable Alphas and Betas. *J. Portfol. Manage.*, Winter 1985, 11(2), pp. 19–22. **[G: U.S.]**

McInish, Thomas H. and Wood, Robert A. A New Approach to Controlling for Thin Trading. *J. Finan. Res.*, Spring 1985, 8(1), pp. 69–75. **[G: U.S.]**

McInish, Thomas H. and Wood, Robert A. Intraday and Overnight Returns and Day-of-the-Week Effects. *J. Finan. Res.*, Summer 1985, 8(2), pp. 119–26. **[G: U.S.]**

Meier, Henri B. History of the Swiss Equity Market. In *Meier, H. B., ed.*, 1985, pp. 1–7. **[G: Switzerland]**

Michie, R. C. The London Stock Exchange and the British Securities Market, 1850–1914. *Econ. Hist. Rev., 2nd Ser.*, February 1985, 38(1), pp. 61–82. **[G: U.K.]**

Mikkelson, Wayne H. Capital Structure Change and Decreases in Stockholders' Wealth: A Cross-Sectional Study of Convertible Security Calls. In *Friedman, B. M., ed.*, 1985, pp. 265–96. **[G: U.S.]**

Mikkelson, Wayne H. and Partch, M. Megan. Stock Price Effects and Costs of Secondary Distributions. *J. Finan. Econ.*, June 1985, 14(2), pp. 165–94. **[G: U.S.]**

Mikkelson, Wayne H. and Ruback, Richard S. An Empirical Analysis of the Interfirm Equity Investment Process. *J. Finan. Econ.*, December 1985, 14(4), pp. 523–53. **[G: U.S.]**

Miller, Stephen E. Simple and Multiple Cross-hedging of Millfeeds. *J. Futures Markets*, Spring 1985, 5(1), pp. 21–28. **[G: U.S.]**

Mills, Terence C. and Stephenson, Michael J. An Empirical Analysis of the UK Treasury Bill Market. *Appl. Econ.*, August 1985, 17(4), pp. 689–703. **[G: U.K.]**

Milonas, Nicholaos T.; Koveos, Peter E. and Booth, G. Geoffrey. Memory in Commodity Futures Contracts: A Comment. *J. Futures*

Markets, Spring 1985, *5*(1), pp. 113–14.
[G: U.S.]

Moray, Myriam. Impact de la fiscalité sur la composition optimale d'un portefeuille d'obligations d'Etat belge. (With English summary.) *Cah. Écon. Bruxelles*, 1st Trimester 1985, (105), pp. 91–118. [G: Belgium]

Moriarty, Eugene J. and Tosini, Paula A. Futures Trading and the Price Volatility of GNMA Certificates—Further Evidence. *J. Futures Markets*, Winter 1985, *5*(4), pp. 633–41.
[G: U.S.]

Murphy, J. E. and Osborne, M. F. M. Predicting the Volatility of Interest Rates. *J. Portfol. Manage.*, Winter 1985, *11*(2), pp. 66–69.
[G: U.S.]

Murphy, Kevin J. Corporate Performance and Managerial Remuneration: An Empirical Analysis. *J. Acc. Econ.*, April 1985, *7*(1–3), pp. 11–42. [G: U.S.]

Murray, Dennis. Further Evidence on the Liquidity Effects of Stock Splits and Stock Dividends. *J. Finan. Res.*, Spring 1985, *8*(1), pp. 59–67. [G: U.S.]

Narube, Savenaca and Whiteside, Barry T. Financial Institutions and Markets in Fiji. In *Skully, M. T., ed.*, 1985, pp. 94–159.
[G: Fiji]

Neal, Larry. Integration of International Capital Markets: Quantitative Evidence from the Eighteenth to Twentieth Centuries. *J. Econ. Hist.*, June 1985, *45*(2), pp. 219–26. [G: U.S.; Netherlands; U.K.; France]

Neal, Larry. The Rise of a Financial Press: London and Amsterdam, 1681–1796. In *Atack, J., ed.*, 1985, pp. 139–41. [G: U.K.; Netherlands]

Nelson, Ray D. Forward and Futures Contracts as Preharvest Commodity Marketing Instruments. *Amer. J. Agr. Econ.*, February 1985, *67*(1), pp. 15–23. [G: U.S.]

Newman, A. C. An Introduction to Options. In *Roberts, G., ed.*, 1985, pp. 32–34.

Nicholl, Peter and King, Maree F. Financial Institutions and Markets in New Zealand. In *Skully, M. T., ed.*, 1985, pp. 160–244.
[G: New Zealand]

O'Leary, James J. The Outlook for the Money and Capital Markets and for Interest Rates in 1985. *Bus. Econ.*, April 1985, *20*(2), pp. 24–30. [G: U.S.]

Oellermann, Charles M. and Farris, Paul L. Futures or Cash: Which Market Leads Live Beef Cattle Prices? *J. Futures Markets*, Winter 1985, *5*(4), pp. 529–38. [G: U.S.]

Ohlson, James A. and Penman, Stephen H. Volatility Increases Subsequent to Stock Splits: An Empirical Aberration. *J. Finan. Econ.*, June 1985, *14*(2), pp. 251–66. [G: U.S.]

Olsen, Chris. Valuation Implications of SFAS No. 33 Data for Electric Utility Investors. *J. Acc. Res.*, Supp. 1985, *23*, pp. 28–47. [G: U.S.]

Ott, Mack and Santoni, G. J. Mergers and Takeovers—The Value of Pradators' Information. *Fed. Res. Bank St. Louis Rev.*, December 1985, *67*(10), pp. 16–28. [G: U.S.]

Owen, P. Dorian. Systems Testing of Wealth-Aggregation Restrictions in an Integrated Model of Expenditure and Asset Behaviour. *Appl. Econ.*, December 1985, *17*(6), pp. 1099–1115.
[G: U.K.]

Owens, Robert W. and Willinger, G. Lee. Investment Potential of an Individual Retirement Account. *J. Bank Res.*, Autumn 1985, *16*(3), pp. 161–68. [G: U.S.]

Pakes, Ariel. On Patents, R&D, and the Stock Market Rate of Return. *J. Polit. Econ.*, April 1985, *93*(2), pp. 390–409. [G: U.S.]

Pari, Robert A. and Chen, Son-Nan. Estimation Risk and Optimal Portfolios. *J. Portfol. Manage.*, Fall 1985, *12*(1), pp. 40–43. [G: U.S.]

Park, Hun Y. Reexamination of Normal Backwardation Hypothesis in Futures Markets. *J. Futures Markets*, Winter 1985, *5*(4), pp. 505–15. [G: U.S.; U.K.; France; Japan; Switzerland]

Park, Hun Y. and Chen, Andrew H. Differences between Futures and Forward Prices: A Further Investigation of the Marking-to-Market Effects. *J. Futures Markets*, Spring 1985, *5*(1), pp. 77–88. [G: U.S.; U.K.; W. Germany; Japan; Switzerland]

Park, Hun Y. and Sears, R. Stephen. Changing Volatility and the Pricing of Options on Stock Index Futures. *J. Finan. Res.*, Winter 1985, *8*(4), pp. 265–74. [G: U.S.]

Park, Hun Y. and Sears, R. Stephen. Estimating Stock Index Futures Volatility through the Prices of Their Options. *J. Futures Markets*, Summer 1985, *5*(2), pp. 223–37. [G: U.S.]

Parkinson, J. M. Thin Capital Markets. A Case Study of the Kuwaiti Stock Market. A Further Note. *Appl. Econ.*, December 1985, *17*(6), pp. 955–58. [G: Kuwait]

Paul, Allen B. The Role of Cash Settlement in Futures Contract Specification. In *Peck, A. E., ed. (I)*, 1985, pp. 271–328. [G: U.S.]

Pearce, Douglas K. and Roley, V. Vance. Stock Prices and Economic News. *J. Bus.*, January 1985, *58*(1), pp. 49–67. [G: U.S.]

Peavy, John W., III and Scott, Jonathan A. The Effect of Stock for Debt Swaps on Security Returns. *Financial Rev.*, November 1985, *20*(4), pp. 303–27. [G: U.S.]

Peck, Anne E. Commentary [Toward a Market Orientation: The Dilemma Facing Farm Policy in the 1980s] [Automatic Adjustment Rules in Commodity Programs]. In *Gardner, B. L., ed.*, 1985, pp. 382–85. [G: U.S.]

Peck, Anne E. The Economic Role of Traditional Commodity Futures Markets. In *Peck, A. E., ed. (II)*, 1985, pp. 1–81. [G: Canada; U.S.; Argentina; Australia]

Penman, Stephen H. A Comparison of the Information Content of Insider Trading and Management Earnings Forecasts. *J. Finan. Quant. Anal.*, March 1985, *20*(1), pp. 1–17.
[G: U.S.]

Perry, Larry G. The Effect of Bond Rating Agencies on Bond Rating Models. *J. Finan. Res.*, Winter 1985, *8*(4), pp. 307–15. [G: U.S.]

Perry, Philip R. Portfolio Serial Correlation and

Nonsynchronous Trading. *J. Finan. Quant. Anal.*, December 1985, *20*(4), pp. 517–23. [G: U.S.]

Peters, Ed. The Growing Efficiency of Index Futures Markets. *J. Portfol. Manage.*, Summer 1985, *11*(4), pp. 52–56. [G: U.S.]

Pettengill, Glenn N. Persistent Seasonal Return Patterns. *Financial Rev.*, November 1985, *20*(4), pp. 271–86. [G: U.S.]

Petzel, Todd E. Toward a Market Orientation: The Dilemma Facing Farm Policy in the 1980s. In *Gardner, B. L., ed.*, 1985, pp. 350–54. [G: U.S.]

Pierce, James L. On the Expansion of Banking Powers. In *Walter, I., ed.*, 1985, pp. 13–34. [G: U.S.]

Plato, Gerald. Valuing American Options on Commodity Futures Contracts. *Agr. Econ. Res.*, Spring 1985, *37*(2), pp. 1–14. [G: U.S.; Europe]

Pluhar, Darwin M.; Shafer, Carl E. and Sporleder, Thomas L. The Systematic Downward Bias in Live Cattle Futures: A Further Evaluation. *J. Futures Markets*, Spring 1985, *5*(1), pp. 11–20. [G: U.S.]

Praetz, Peter. A Note on "Quarterly Returns to Investment in Ordinary Shares, 1919–1970": Two Tests of Market Efficiency. *Economica*, August 1985, *52*(207), pp. 379–81. [G: U.K.; U.S.]

Proctor, Allen J. and Rappaport, Julie N. Federal Tax Reform and the Regional Character of the Municipal Bond Market. *Fed. Res. Bank New York Quart. Rev.*, Autumn 1985, *10*(3), pp. 6–15. [G: U.S.]

Pugel, Thomas A. and White, Lawrence J. An Analysis of the Competitive Effects of Allowing Commercial Bank Affiliates to Underwrite Corporate Securities. In *Walter, I., ed.*, 1985, pp. 93–139. [G: U.S.]

Purcell, Wayne D. and Hudson, Michael A. The Economic Roles and Implications of Trade in Livestock Futures. In *Peck, A. E., ed. (I)*, 1985, pp. 329–76. [G: U.S.]

Quattropani, Pier-Luigi. The Organisation of Swiss Stock Exchanges. In *Meier, H. B., ed.*, 1985, pp. 28–43. [G: Switzerland]

Randall, Alan J. Commentary [Toward a Market Orientation: The Dilemma Facing Farm Policy in the 1980s] [Automatic Adjustment Rules in Commodity Programs]. In *Gardner, B. L., ed.*, 1985, pp. 378–81. [G: U.S.]

Raviv, Artur. Management Compensation and the Managerial Labor Market: An Overview. *J. Acc. Econ.*, April 1985, *7*(1–3), pp. 239–45.

Redhead, Keith. Hedging with Financial Futures. *Nat. Westminster Bank Quart. Rev.*, February 1985, pp. 42–56. [G: U.K.]

Reilly, Frank K. and Gustavson, Sandra G. Investing in Options on Stocks Announcing Splits. *Financial Rev.*, May 1985, *20*(2), pp. 121–42. [G: U.S.]

Renshaw, Edward F. A Risk Premium Model for Market Timing. *J. Portfol. Manage.*, Summer 1985, *11*(4), pp. 33–35. [G: U.S.]

Ricks, William E. and Hughes, John S. Market

Reactions to a Non-discretionary Accounting Change: The Case of Long-term Investments. *Accounting Rev.*, January 1985, *60*(1), pp. 33–52. [G: U.S.]

Rogers, Ronald C.; Murphy, Neil B. and Owers, James E. Financial Innovation, Balance Sheets Cosmetics and Market Response: The Case of Equity-for-Debt Exchanges in Banking. *J. Bank Res.*, Autumn 1985, *16*(3), pp. 145–49. [G: U.S.]

Rogers, Ronald C. and Owers, James E. The Investment Performance of Real Estate Limited Partnerships. *Amer. Real Estate Urban Econ. Assoc. J.*, Summer 1985, *13*(2), pp. 153–66. [G: U.S.]

Rosen, Sherwin. Golden Parachutes, Executive Decision-making, and Shareholder Wealth: Commentary. *J. Acc. Econ.*, April 1985, *7*(1–3), pp. 205–08. [G: U.S.]

Rosenberg, Barr. Prediction of Common Stock Betas. *J. Portfol. Manage.*, Winter 1985, *11*(2), pp. 5–14. [G: U.S.]

Rosenberg, Barr; Reid, Kenneth and Lanstein, Ronald. Persuasive Evidence of Market Inefficiency. *J. Portfol. Manage.*, Spring 1985, *11*(3), pp. 9–16. [G: U.S.]

Ross, Stephen A. On the Empirical Relevance of APT: Reply. *J. Portfol. Manage.*, Summer 1985, *11*(4), pp. 72–73. [G: U.S.]

Rothenberg, Winifred B. The Emergence of a Capital Market in Rural Massachusetts, 1730–1838. *J. Econ. Hist.*, December 1985, *45*(4), pp. 781–808. [G: U.S.]

Rubinstein, Mark. Nonparametric Tests of Alternative Option Pricing Models Using All Reported Trades and Quotes on the 30 Most Active CBOE Option Classes from August 23, 1976 through August 31, 1978. *J. Finance*, June 1985, *40*(2), pp. 455–80. [G: U.S.]

Ryals, Stanley D. Secular and Cyclical Trends in Price–Earnings Ratios. *Bus. Econ.*, April 1985, *20*(2), pp. 19–23. [G: U.S.]

Sandor, Richard L. Creation of a Plywood Futures Contract. In *Yamey, B. S.; Sandor, R. L. and Hindley, B.*, 1985, pp. 39–64. [G: U.S.]

Santoni, G. J. The Monetary Control Act, Reserve Taxes and the Stock Prices of Commercial Banks. *Fed. Res. Bank St. Louis Rev.*, June/July 1985, *67*(6), pp. 12–20. [G: U.S.]

Saunders, Anthony. Bank Safety and Soundness and the Risks of Corporate Securities Activities. In *Walter, I., ed.*, 1985, pp. 171–206. [G: U.S.]

Saunders, Anthony. Conflicts of Interest: An Economic View. In *Walter, I., ed.*, 1985, pp. 207–30. [G: U.S.]

Schachter, Stanley, et al. Some Causes and Consequences of Dependence and Independence in the Stock Market. *J. Econ. Behav. Organ.*, December 1985, *6*(4), pp. 339–57. [G: U.S.]

Schachter, Stanley, et al. Was the South Sea Bubble a Random Walk? *J. Econ. Behav. Organ.*, December 1985, *6*(4), pp. 323–29. [G: U.K.]

Schipper, Katherine and Thompson, Rex. The

Impact of Merger-related Regulations Using Exact Distributions of Test Statistics [The Impact of Merger-related Regulations on the Shareholders of Acquiring Firms]. *J. Acc. Res.*, Spring 1985, *23*(1), pp. 408–15. [G: U.S.]

Schnabel, Jacques A. Monetary Instability and Share-Market Risk: Canadian Evidence. *Managerial Dec. Econ.*, September 1985, *6*(3), pp. 180–82. [G: Canada]

Schneider, Rolf. Wertpapieremission, Wertpapiererwerb und Zinsbildung am Rentenmarkt. (Security Issuing, Security Purchasing and Interest Rate Formation on the Bond Market. With English summary.) *Kredit Kapital*, 1985, *18*(3), pp. 372–401. [G: U.S.; W. Germany]

Schott, Francis H. and Oliver, R. Wayne. Changing Institutional Investment Strategy at Life Insurance and Thrift Institutions. *Bus. Econ.*, April 1985, *20*(2), pp. 50–54. [G: U.S.]

Schultz, Joseph J., Jr.; Gustavson, Sandra G. and Reilly, Frank K. Factors Influencing the New York Stock Exchange Specialists' Price-Setting Behavior: An Experiment. *J. Finan. Res.*, Summer 1985, *8*(2), pp. 137–44. [G: U.S.]

Schultz, Paul. Personal Income Taxes and the January Effect: Small Firm Stock Returns before the War Revenue Act of 1917: A Note. *J. Finance*, March 1985, *40*(1), pp. 333–43. [G: U.S.]

Schwert, G. William. A Discussion of CEO Deaths and the Reaction of Stock Prices. *J. Acc. Econ.*, April 1985, *7*(1–3), pp. 175–78. [G: U.S.]

Scott, Jonathan A.; Hempel, George H. and Peavy, John W., III. The Effect of Stock-for-Debt Swaps on Bank Holding Companies. *J. Banking Finance*, June 1985, *9*(2), pp. 233–51. [G: U.S.]

Seeger, Charles M. The Development of Congressional Concern about Financial Futures Markets. In *Peck, A. E., ed. (I)*, 1985, pp. 1–47. [G: U.S.]

Shaked, Israel. International Equity Markets and the Investment Horizon. *J. Portfol. Manage.*, Winter 1985, *11*(2), pp. 80–84. [G: OECD]

Shaked, Israel. Measuring Prospective Probabilities of Insolvency: An Application to the Life Insurance Industry. *J. Risk Ins.*, March 1985, *52*(1), pp. 59–80. [G: U.S.]

Shastri, Kuldeep and Tandon, Kishore. Arbitrage Tests of the Efficiency of the Foreign Currency Options Market. *J. Int. Money Finance*, December 1985, *4*(4), pp. 455–68. [G: U.S.]

Shilling, James D.; Benjamin, John D. and Sirmans, C. F. Contracts as Options: Some Evidence from Condominium Developments. *Amer. Real Estate Urban Econ. Assoc. J.*, Summer 1985, *13*(2), pp. 143–52. [G: U.S.]

Silber, William L. The Economic Role of Financial Futures. In *Peck, A. E., ed. (II)*, 1985, pp. 83–114. [G: U.S.]

Simpson, W. Gary and Ireland, Timothy C. The Impact of Financial Futures on the Cash Market for Treasury Bills. *J. Finan. Quant. Anal.*, September 1985, *20*(3), pp. 371–79. [G: U.S.]

Skully, Michael T. Financial Institutions and Markets in Papua New Guinea. In *Skully, M. T., ed.*, 1985, pp. 245–339. [G: Papua New Guinea]

Skully, Michael T. Financial Institutions and Markets in Australia. In *Skully, M. T., ed.*, 1985, pp. 1–93. [G: Australia]

Smidt, Seymour. Trading Floor Practices on Futures and Securities Exchanges: Economics, Regulation, and Policy Issues. In *Peck, A. E., ed. (I)*, 1985, pp. 49–142. [G: U.S.]

Smirlock, Michael J. Seasonality and Bond Market Returns. *J. Portfol. Manage.*, Spring 1985, *11*(3), pp. 42–44. [G: U.S.]

Smirlock, Michael J. and Yawitz, Jess Barry. Asset Returns, Discount Rate Changes, and Market Efficiency. *J. Finance*, September 1985, *40*(4), pp. 1141–58. [G: U.S.]

Smith, Gary. The Substitutability of Debt and Equity Securities: Comment. In *Friedman, B. M., ed.*, 1985, pp. 233–38. [G: U.S.]

Smith, Richard L. and Booth, James R. The Risk Structure of Interest Rates and Interdependent Borrowing Costs: The Impact of Major Defaults. *J. Finan. Res.*, Summer 1985, *8*(2), pp. 83–94. [G: U.S.]

Soldofsky, Robert M. Return Premiums on Utility Common Stocks. *Quart. Rev. Econ. Bus.*, Summer 1985, *25*(2), pp. 60–72. [G: U.S.]

Solt, Michael E. and Miller, Norman G. Managerial Incentives: Implications for the Financial Performance of Real Estate Investment Trusts. *Amer. Real Estate Urban Econ. Assoc. J.*, Winter 1985, *13*(4), pp. 404–23. [G: U.S.]

Statman, Meir. A Theoretical Analysis of Real Estate Returns: Discussion. *J. Finance*, July 1985, *40*(3), pp. 719–21. [G: U.S.]

Stein, Jerome L. Futures Markets and Capital Formation. In *Peck, A. E., ed. (II)*, 1985, pp. 115–204. [G: U.S.]

Stickel, Scott E. The Effect of Value Line Investment Survey Rank Changes on Common Stock Prices. *J. Finan. Econ.*, March 1985, *14*(1), pp. 121–43. [G: U.S.]

Stigler, George J. and Sherwin, Robert A. The Extent of the Market. *J. Law Econ.*, October 1985, *28*(3), pp. 555–85. [G: U.S.]

Stock, Duane. Price Volatility of Municipal Discount Bonds. *J. Finan. Res.*, Spring 1985, *8*(1), pp. 1–13. [G: U.S.]

Stoll, Hans R. and Whaley, Robert E. The New Option Markets. In *Peck, A. E., ed. (II)*, 1985, pp. 205–89. [G: U.S.]

Strohmaier, Jay S. and Dahl, Reynold P. Price Relationships between Wheat Futures Markets: Implications for Hedging. *Food Res. Inst. Stud.*, 1985, *19*(3), pp. 265–92. [G: U.S.]

Sudarsanam, P. S. and Taffler, R. J. Industrial Classification in UK Capital Markets: A Test of Economic Homogeneity. *Appl. Econ.*, April 1985, *17*(2), pp. 291–308. [G: U.K.]

Swanson, Peggy E. and Edgar, S. Michael. An Alternative Approach to the Selection of "Representative" Variables. *J. Econ. Bus.*, February 1985, *37*(1), pp. 69–79. [G: U.S.]

Sweeney, Richard J. Stabilizing or Destabilizing

Speculation? Evidence from the Foreign Exchange Markets. In *Arndt, S. W.; Sweeney, R. J. and Willett, T. D., eds.*, 1985, pp. 107–23. [G: OECD]

Tanzi, Vito. The Deficit Experience in Industrial Countries. In *Cagan, P. and Somensatto, E., eds.*, 1985, pp. 81–119. [G: OECD]

Tarascio, Vincent J. Keynes, Population, and Equity Prices. *J. Post Keynesian Econ.*, Spring 1985, 7(3), pp. 303–10. [G: U.S.]

Tauchen, George. An Investigation of Transactions Data for NYSE Stocks: Discussion. *J. Finance*, July 1985, 40(3), pp. 739–41. [G: U.S.]

Taylor, Stephen J. The Behaviour of Futures Prices over Time. *Appl. Econ.*, August 1985, 17(4), pp. 713–34. [G: U.S.; U.K.; W. Germany; Switzerland; Australia]

Taylor, William. Statement to the U.S. House Subcommittee on Commerce, Consumer, and Monetary Affairs of the Committee on Government Operations, May 15, 1985. *Fed. Res. Bull.*, July 1985, 71(7), pp. 528–32. [G: U.S.]

Tehranian, Hassan and Waegelein, James F. Market Reaction to Short-term Executive Compensation Plan Adoption. *J. Acc. Econ.*, April 1985, 7(1–3), pp. 131–44. [G: U.S.]

Terry, Nicholas G. The 'Big Bang' at the Stock Exchange. *Lloyds Bank Rev.*, April 1985, (156), pp. 16–30. [G: U.K.]

Thatcher, Janet Solverson. The Choice of Call Provision Terms: Evidence of the Existence of Agency Costs of Debt. *J. Finance*, June 1985, 40(2), pp. 549–61. [G: U.S.]

Thomas, Lee R., III. A Winning Strategy for Currency-Futures Speculation. *J. Portfol. Manage.*, Fall 1985, 12(1), pp. 65–69. [G: U.S.]

Thompson, R. S. Risk Reduction and International Diversification: An Analysis of Large UK Multinational Companies [Internationally Diversified Portfolios: Welfare Gains and Capital Flows] [International Diversification of Investment Portfolios]. *Appl. Econ.*, June 1985, 17(3), pp. 529–41. [G: U.K.]

Toder, Eric and Neubig, Thomas S. Revenue Cost Estimates of Tax Expenditures: The Case of Tax-Exempt Bonds. *Nat. Tax J.*, September 1985, 38(3), pp. 395–414. [G: U.S.]

Tomek, William G. Margins on Futures Contracts: Their Economic Roles and Regulation. In *Peck, A. E., ed. (I)*, 1985, pp. 143–209. [G: U.S.]

Tucker, Alan L. Empirical Tests of the Efficiency of the Currency Option Market. *J. Finan. Res.*, Winter 1985, 8(4), pp. 275–85. [G: U.S.]

Ugolini, Ernesto. Struttura e costi dell'attività bancaria nel mercato mobiliare e gestione accentrata dei titoli. (Structure and Costs of Banking in the Securities Market and the Centralized Management of Securities. With English summary.) *Bancaria*, April 1985, 41(4), pp. 438–45. [G: Italy]

Valentine, T. J. Indexed Securities. In *Argy, V. E. and Neville, J. W., eds.*, 1985, pp. 370–84. [G: Australia]

Vernon, Jack. Inflation Risk as Determinant of the Discount Rate in Tort Settlements: Comment. *J. Risk Ins.*, September 1985, 52(3), pp. 528–32. [G: U.S.]

Volcker, Paul A. Statement to the U.S. House Subcommittee on Telecommunications, Consumer Protection, and Finance of the Committee on Energy and Commerce, June 26, 1985. *Fed. Res. Bull.*, August 1985, 71(8), pp. 621–23. [G: U.S.]

Volcker, Paul A. Statement to the U.S. House Subcommittee on Domestic Monetary Policy of the Committee on Banking, Finance and Urban Affairs, July 9, 1985. *Fed. Res. Bull.*, September 1985, 71(9), pp. 687–89. [G: U.S.]

Walkling, Ralph A. Predicting Tender Offer Success: A Logistic Analysis. *J. Finan. Quant. Anal.*, December 1985, 20(4), pp. 461–78. [G: U.S.]

Walter, Ingo. Deregulating Wall Street: Summary and Implications for Policy. In *Walter, I., ed.*, 1985, pp. 293–302.

Wansley, James W. and Clauretie, Terrence M. The Impact of CreditWatch Placement on Equity Returns and Bond Prices. *J. Finan. Res.*, Spring 1985, 8(1), pp. 31–42. [G: U.S.]

Warner, Jerold B. Stock Market Reaction to Management Incentive Plan Adoption: An Overview. *J. Acc. Econ.*, April 1985, 7(1–3), pp. 145–49. [G: U.S.]

Wasserfallen, Walter and Zimmermann, Heinz. The Behavior of Intra-daily Exchange Rates. *J. Banking Finance*, March 1985, 9(1), pp. 55–72. [G: Switzerland]

Weinstein, Mark I. The Equity Component of Corporate Bonds. *J. Portfol. Manage.*, Spring 1985, 11(3), pp. 37–41. [G: U.S.]

Whitford, David T. and Reilly, Frank K. What Makes Stock Prices Move? *J. Portfol. Manage.*, Winter 1985, 11(2), pp. 23–30. [G: U.S.]

Wood, Robert A. and McInish, Thomas H. Bias from Nonsynchronous Trading in Tests of the Levhari–Levy Hypothesis. *Rev. Econ. Statist.*, May 1985, 67(2), pp. 346–51. [G: U.S.]

Wood, Robert A.; McInish, Thomas H. and Ord, J. Keith. An Investigation of Transactions Data for NYSE Stocks. *J. Finance*, July 1985, 40(3), pp. 723–39. [G: U.S.]

Yamey, Basil S. Scope for Futures Trading and Conditions for Success. In *Yamey, B. S.; Sandor, R. L. and Hindley, B.*, 1985, pp. 14–38.

Yawitz, Jess Barry. Debt and Equity Yields, 1926–1980: Comment. In *Friedman, B. M., ed.*, 1985, pp. 163–65. [G: U.S.]

Zaima, Janis K. and Hearth, Douglas. The Wealth Effects of Voluntary Selloffs: Implications for Divesting and Acquiring Firms. *J. Finan. Res.*, Fall 1985, 8(3), pp. 227–36. [G: U.S.]

Ziebart, David A. Control of Beta Reliability in Studies of Abnormal Return Magnitudes: A Methodological Note. *J. Acc. Res.*, Autumn 1985, 23(2), pp. 920–26. [G: U.S.]

Zimmermann, Heinz. Eine Illustration zur Verteilung spekulativer Preise. (The Distribution of Speculative Prices: An Illustration. With English summary.) *Jahr. Nationalökon. Statist.*, July 1985, *200*(4), pp. 420–27.

314 Financial Intermediaries

3140 Financial Intermediaries

Ambachtsheer, Keith P. "Pensions in the American Economy": A Review Article. *J. Portfol. Manage.*, Spring 1985, *11*(3), pp. 77–78.
[G: U.S.]

Armandi, Barry R. and Mills, Edgar W., Jr. Bureaucratic and Personalized Strategies for Efficiency and Organization: An Investigation of Structures and Efficiency in a Set of 104 Profit-seeking Firms. *Amer. J. Econ. Soc.*, July 1985, *44*(3), pp. 261–77.
[G: U.S.]

Babcock, Guilford C. The Integration of Insurance and Taxes in Corporate Pension Strategy: Discussion. *J. Finance*, July 1985, *40*(3), pp. 955–57.
[G: U.S.]

Barth, James R., et al. Insolvency and Risk-taking in the Thrift Industry: Implications for the Future. *Contemp. Policy Issues*, Fall 1985, *3*(5), pp. 1–32.
[G: U.S.]

Belongia, Michael T. and Santoni, G. J. Cash Flow or Present Value: What's Lurking behind That Hedge? *Fed. Res. Bank St. Louis Rev.*, January 1985, *67*(1), pp. 5–13.
[G: U.S.]

Bhatnagar, R. G. Regional Rural Banks. In *Bandyopadhyay, R. and Khankhoje, D. P., eds.*, 1985, pp. 181–84.
[G: India]

Bicksler, James L. The Integration of Insurance and Taxes in Corporate Pension Strategy. *J. Finance*, July 1985, *40*(3), pp. 943–55.
[G: U.S.]

Black, Fischer. The Future for Financial Services. In *Inman, R. P., ed.*, 1985, pp. 223–30.

Black, Harold A. and Schweitzer, Robert L. Black-controlled Credit Unions: A Comparative Analysis. *J. Finan. Res.*, Fall 1985, *8*(3), pp. 193–202.

Broaddus, Alfred. Financial Innovation in the United States—Background, Current Status and Prospects. *Fed. Res. Bank Richmond Econ. Rev.*, Jan./Feb. 1985, *71*(1), pp. 2–22.
[G: U.S.]

Buckley, Robert M. and Gross, David J. Selective Credit Policies and the Mortgage Market: Cross-sectional Evidence. *J. Money, Credit, Banking*, August 1985, *17*(3), pp. 358–70.
[G: U.S.]

Cable, John R. and Turner, Paul. Asymmetric Information and Credit Rationing: Another View of Industrial Bank Lending and Britain's Economic Problem. In *Currie, D., ed.*, 1985, pp. 207–20.

Capriglione, Francesco and Mezzacapo, Vincenzo. Evoluzione del sistema finanziario italiano e attività di "merchant banking." (Evolution of the Italian Financial System and Merchant Banking Services—I. With English summary.) *Bancaria*, March 1985, *41*(3), pp. 288–304.
[G: Italy]

Carboni, Gaetano. Il "merchant banking" nella realtà inglese. (Merchant Banking in the U.K.—I. With English summary.) *Bancaria*, March 1985, *41*(3), pp. 320–27.
[G: U.K.; W. Germany; France; U.S.]

Cassis, Y. The Banking Community of London, 1890–1914: A Survey. In *Porter, A. N. and Holland, R. F., eds.*, 1985, pp. 109–26.
[G: U.K.]

Castaldi, Giovanni. Gli istituti per il finanziamento a medio termine alle piccolo e media imprese: aspetti istituzionali. (Institutes for Medium Term Financing of Small and Medium Enterprises: Institutional Aspects. With English summary.) *Bancaria*, October 1985, *41*(10), pp. 1047–58.
[G: Italy]

Chan, Yuk-Shee and Kanatas, George. Asymmetric Valuations and the Role of Collateral in Loan Agreements. *J. Money, Credit, Banking*, February 1985, *17*(1), pp. 84–95.

Chase, Samuel. Bank Regulation and Monetary Policy: Comment. *J. Money, Credit, Banking*, Pt. 2, Nov. 1985, *17*(4), pp. 718–21.
[G: U.S.]

Chateau, John Peter D. Liability Management of Financial Intermediaries in a Dynamic and Uncertain Perspective. *Europ. Econ. Rev.*, March 1985, *27*(2), pp. 183–200.

Chotigeat, T. Sequential Auctions in Informal Credit and Savings Societies: Asian Auctions. *J. Econ. Devel.*, December 1985, *10*(2), pp. 67–85.
[G: S. Asia]

Cingano, Francesco. La banca negli anni '90: evoluzione tecnoligica e professionalità. (The Bank in the Nineties: Technological Evolution and Professionalism. With English summary.) *Bancaria*, April 1985, *41*(4), pp. 411–18.
[G: Italy]

Coates, Joseph F. Scenarios Part Two: Alternative Futures. In *Mendell, J. S., ed.*, 1985, pp. 21–46.
[G: U.S.]

Crotty, James R. The Centrality of Money, Credit, and Financial Intermediation in Marx's Crisis Theory: An Interpretation of Marx's Methodology. In *[Magdoff, H. and Sweezy, P.]*, 1985, pp. 45–81.

Daskin, Alan J. Dynamics of Canadian Deposit-taking Institutions: Comment. *J. Ind. Econ.*, March 1985, *33*(3), pp. 353–58. [G: Canada]

Daskin, Alan J. Horizontal Merger Guidelines and the Line of Commerce in Banking: An Algebraic and Graphical Approach. *Antitrust Bull.*, Fall 1985, *30*(3), pp. 651–76. [G: U.S.]

Dermine, Jean. The Measurement of Interest-Rate Risk by Financial Intermediaries. *J. Bank Res.*, Summer 1985, *16*(2), pp. 86–90.

Dunham, Constance R. Mutual-to-Stock Conversion by Thrifts: Implications for Soundness. *New Eng. Econ. Rev.*, January/February 1985, pp. 31–45.
[G: U.S.]

Dunham, Constance R. Recent Developments in Thrift Commercial Lending. *New Eng. Econ. Rev.*, Nov./Dec. 1985, pp. 41–48.

Dye, Thomas R. Strategic Ownership Positions in U.S. Industry and Banking. *Amer. J. Econ. Soc.*, January 1985, *44*(1), pp. 9–22.
[G: U.S.]

Flannery, Mark J. The Future for Financial Services: Comment. In *Inman, R. P., ed.,* 1985, pp. 234–38.

Friedman, Stephen J. On the Expansion of Banking Powers: Comment. In *Walter, I., ed.,* 1985, pp. 35–40. [G: U.S.]

Friend, Irwin. The Future for Financial Services: Comment. In *Inman, R. P., ed.,* 1985, pp. 231–33.

Furlong, Frederick T. Savings and Loan Asset Composition and the Mortgage Market. *Fed. Res. Bank San Francisco Econ. Rev.,* Summer 1985, (3), pp. 14–24. [G: U.S.]

Gaetano, Carboni. Il "merchant banking" nella realtà inglese. (Merchant Banking in the U.K.—II. With English summary.) *Bancaria,* April 1985, *41*(4), pp. 446–52. [G: U.K.]

Gasper, Louis C. Selling ARMs in Secondary Markets: Panel Presentation. In *Federal Home Loan Bank of San Francisco.,* 1985, pp. 180–83. [G: U.S.]

Gidlow, R. M. The Modified Role of Discount Houses and Accommodation Policies of the Reserve Bank. *S. Afr. J. Econ.,* March 1985, *53*(1), pp. 67–81. [G: S. Africa]

Goria, Giovanni. Situazione economica e problemi del credito: banche d'affari, sportelli e tassi. (Merchant Banks, Bank Branches and Interest Rates in the Framework of Economic Policy. With English summary.) *Bancaria,* April 1985, *41*(4), pp. 406–10. [G: Italy]

Gray, Edwin J. Remarks from the Chairman: Bank Board Priorities. In *Federal Home Loan Bank of San Francisco.,* 1985, pp. 56–65. [G: U.S.]

Hadaway, Beverly. Discretionary Managerial Behaviour Effects of Savings and Loan Conversions: Competitive Implications for the Industry in a Deregulated Environment. *Appl. Econ.,* June 1985, *17*(3), pp. 451–66. [G: U.S.]

Hall, Maximilian J. B. Financial Deregulation and Monetary Policy in Australia. *Banca Naz. Lavoro Quart. Rev.,* September 1985, (154), pp. 261–77. [G: Australia]

Hammond, Elizabeth M. and Kay, John A. Insurance Regulation in the United Kingdom and the Federal Republic of Germany. In *Currie, D., ed.,* 1985, pp. 192–206. [G: U.K.; W. Germany]

Hancock, Diana. The Financial Firm: Production with Monetary and Nonmonetary Goods. *J. Polit. Econ.,* October 1985, *93*(5), pp. 859–80. [G: U.S.]

Heaton, Gary G. and Dunham, Constance R. The Growing Competitiveness of Credit Unions. *New Eng. Econ. Rev.,* May/June 1985, pp. 19–34. [G: U.S.]

Hendershott, Patric H. Pricing Adjustable-Rate Mortgages. In *Federal Home Loan Bank of San Francisco.,* 1985, pp. 98–119. [G: U.S.]

Horn, Karen N. Statement to the U.S. House Subcommittee on Commerce, Consumer, and Monetary Affairs of the Committee on Government Operations, April 3, 1985. *Fed. Res.*

Bull., June 1985, *71*(6), pp. 415–18. [G: U.S.]

Horvitz, Paul M. The Combination of Banking and Insurance: Implications for Regulation. *Growth Change,* October 1985, *16*(4), pp. 10–19. [G: U.S.]

Johnson, Linda L. The Effectiveness of Savings and Loan Political Action Committees. *Public Choice,* 1985, *46*(3), pp. 289–304. [G: U.S.]

Kanvinde, D. J. Lead Bank Scheme: A Critical Review. In *Bandyopadhyay, R. and Khankhoje, D. P., eds.,* 1985, pp. 125–45. [G: India]

Kaufman, George C. Integrating Asset/Liability Management to Finance Mortgage Portfolios. In *Federal Home Loan Bank of San Francisco.,* 1985, pp. 158–77. [G: U.S.]

Keating, Giles. The Financial Sector of the London Business School Model. In *Currie, D., ed.,* 1985, pp. 86–126. [G: U.K.]

Keeley, Michael C. and Zimmerman, Gary C. Competition for Money Market Deposit Accounts. *Fed. Res. Bank San Francisco Econ. Rev.,* Spring 1985, (2), pp. 5–27. [G: U.S.]

Kopcke, Richard W. The Federal Income Taxation of Life Insurance Companies. *New Eng. Econ. Rev.,* March/April 1985, pp. 5–19. [G: U.S.]

Krinsky, Itzhak. Mean–Variance Utility Functions, Flexible Functional Forms, and the Investment Behavior of Canadian Life Insurers. *J. Risk Ins.,* June 1985, *52*(2), pp. 241–68. [G: Canada]

Lea, Michael J. An Empirical Analysis of the Value of ARM Features. *Housing Finance Rev.,* January 1985, *4*(1), pp. 467–81. [G: U.S.]

Lea, Michael J. Rational ARM Pricing and Design. In *Federal Home Loan Bank of San Francisco.,* 1985, pp. 120–31. [G: U.S.]

Lee, Cheng F. and Lynge, Morgan J., Jr. Return, Risk and Cost of Equity for Stock S&L Firms: Theory and Empirical Results. *Amer. Real Estate Urban Econ. Assoc. J.,* Summer 1985, *13*(2), pp. 167–80. [G: U.S.]

Litan, Robert E. Evaluating and Controlling the Risks of Financial Product Deregulation. *Yale J. Regul.,* Fall 1985, *3*(1), pp. 1–52. [G: U.S.]

Long, Perrin H., Jr. Nonbanks' Interstate Banking Performance. In *Federal Reserve Bank of Atlanta (II),* 1985, pp. 129–33. [G: U.S.]

Mahoney, Patrick I. and White, Alice P. The Thrift Industry in Transition. *Fed. Res. Bull.,* March 1985, *71*(3), pp. 137–56. [G: U.S.]

Mamalakis, Markos J. Financial Services and the Debt Problem in Latin America. In *Jorge, A.; Salazar-Carrillo, J. and Diaz-Pou, F., eds.,* 1985, pp. 29–37. [G: Latin America]

Marchetti, Piergaetano. La pubblicità nella concorrenza fra emittenti sul mercato del risparmio. (Advertising in the Competition among Issues on the Savings Market. With English summary.) *Bancaria,* May 1985, *41*(5), pp. 515–23. [G: Italy]

Marcus, Alan J. Spinoff/Terminations and the Value of Pension Insurance. *J. Finance,* July 1985, *40*(3), pp. 911–24.   [G: U.S.]

Martin, Preston. Statement to the U.S. House Subcommittee on Commerce, Consumer, and Monetary Affairs of the Committee on Government Operations, April 3, 1985. *Fed. Res. Bull.,* June 1985, *71*(6), pp. 412–15.
[G: U.S.]

Martin, Preston. Statement to the U.S. House Subcommittee on Financial Institutions Supervision, Regulation and Insurance of the Committee on Banking, Finance and Urban Affairs, October 10, 1985. *Fed. Res. Bull.,* December 1985, *71*(12), pp. 937–41.   [G: U.S.]

McCulloch, J. Huston. Interest-Risk Sensitive Deposit Insurance Premia: Stable ACH Estimates. *J. Banking Finance,* March 1985, *9*(1), pp. 137–56.   [G: U.S.]

Merrick, John J., Jr. and Saunders, Anthony. Bank Regulation and Monetary Policy. *J. Money, Credit, Banking,* Pt. 2, Nov. 1985, *17*(4), pp. 691–717.   [G: U.S.]

Merville, Larry. Spinoff/Terminations and the Value of Pension Insurance: Discussion. *J. Finance,* July 1985, *40*(3), pp. 924–26.
[G: U.S.]

Mikkelsen, Richard. Brancheglidning på kapitalmarkedet. (Drift among Financial Institutions in the Danish Capital Market. With English summary.) *Nationaløkon. Tidsskr.,* 1985, *123*(1), pp. 20–31.   [C: Denmark]

Moran, Michael J. The Federally Sponsored Credit Agencies: An Overview. *Fed. Res. Bull.,* June 1985, *71*(6), pp. 373–88.
[G: U.S.]

Narube, Savenaca and Whiteside, Barry T. Financial Institutions and Markets in Fiji. In *Skully, M. T., ed.,* 1985, pp. 94–159.
[G: Fiji]

Nepal Rastra Bank. Priority Sector Credit: Objectives, Policies and Programmes. In *Bandyopadhyay, R. and Khankhoje, D. P., eds.,* 1985, pp. 203–13.   [G: Nepal]

Nicholl, Peter and King, Maree F. Financial Institutions and Markets in New Zealand. In *Skully, M. T., ed.,* 1985, pp. 160–244.
[G: New Zealand]

Partee, J. Charles. Statement to the U.S. House Subcommittee on Financial Institutions Supervision, Regulation and Insurance, of the Committee on Banking, Finance and Urban Affairs, September 11, 1985. *Fed. Res. Bull.,* November 1985, *71*(11), pp. 874–77.   [G: U.S.]

Partee, J. Charles. Statement to the U.S. House Subcommittee on Telecommunications, Consumer Protection, and Finance of the Committee on Energy and Commerce, April 2, 1985. *Fed. Res. Bull.,* June 1985, *71*(6), pp. 409–12.   [G: U.S.]

Patil, R. K. and Patel, K. V. Rural Development: Organisation and Management Issues. In *Bandyopadhyay, R. and Khankhoje, D. P., eds.,* 1985, pp. 77–98.   [G: India]

Patrick, Hugh and Moreno, Honorata A. Philip-pine Private Domestic Commercial Banking, 1946–80, in the Light of Japanese Experience. In *Ohkawa, K. and Ranis, G., eds.,* 1985, pp. 311–65.

Pauchard, A. Analysis of the Shares of Leading Companies in Switzerland. In *Meier, H. B., ed.,* 1985, pp. 135–77.   [G: Switzerland]

Pierce, James L. On the Expansion of Banking Powers. In *Walter, I., ed.,* 1985, pp. 13–34.
[G: U.S.]

Pitelis, Christos N. The Effects of Life Assurance and Pension Funds on Other Savings: The Postwar UK Experience. *Bull. Econ. Res.,* September 1985, *37*(3), pp. 213–29.
[G: U.K.]

Pontolillo, Vincenzo. Il fattore concorrenza negli interventi dell'autorità sul sistema creditizio. (Competition and Intervention of Supervisory Authorities on the Credit System. With English summary.) *Bancaria,* June 1985, *41*(6), pp. 639–54.   [G: Italy]

Pozdena, Randall J. and Hotti, Kristin L. Developments in British Banking: Lessons for Regulation and Supervision. *Fed. Res. Bank San Francisco Econ. Rev.,* Fall 1985, (4), pp. 14–25.   [G: U.K.]

Pratt, Richard T. Current Issues in the Thrift/ Mortgage Relationship. In *Federal Home Loan Bank of San Francisco.,* 1985, pp. 4–10.
[G: U.S.]

Pyle, David H. Bank Regulation and Monetary Policy: Comment. *J. Money, Credit, Banking,* Pt. 2, Nov. 1985, *17*(4), pp. 722–24.
[G: U.S.]

Ruta, Guido. Gli statuti delle Casse di Risparmio e l'immissione di capitale privato. (The Articles of Association of Savings Banks and the Introduction of Private Capital. With English summary.) *Bancaria,* October 1985, *41*(10), pp. 1063–69.   [G: Italy]

Schaeffers, Hans. Design of Computer Support for Multicriteria and Multiperson Decisions in Regional Water Resources Planning. In *Fandel, G. and Spronk, J., eds.,* 1985, pp. 245–66.

Schott, Francis H. and Oliver, R. Wayne. Changing Institutional Investment Strategy at Life Insurance and Thrift Institutions. *Bus. Econ.,* April 1985, *20*(2), pp. 50–54.   [G: U.S.]

Sealey, C. W., Jr. Portfolio Separation for Stockholder Owned Depository Financial Intermediaries. *J. Banking Finance,* December 1985, *9*(4), pp. 477–90.

Shapiro, Arnold F. Contributions to the Evolution of Pension Cost Analysis. *J. Risk Ins.,* March 1985, *52*(1), pp. 81–99.

Shirilla, Robert M. Deregulation and Thrift Strategies: A Comment. *Bus. Econ.,* October 1985, *20*(4), pp. 59–60.   [G: U.S.]

Short, Eugenie D. FDIC Settlement Practices and the Size of Failed Banks. *Fed. Res. Bank Dallas Econ. Rev.,* March 1985, pp. 12–20.
[G: U.S.]

Skully, Michael T. Financial Institutions and Markets in Papua New Guinea. In *Skully, M. T.,*

ed., 1985, pp. 245–339.
[G: Papua New Guinea]

Skully, Michael T. Financial Institutions and Markets in Australia. In *Skully, M. T., ed.*, 1985, pp. 1–93. [G: Australia]

Taylor, William. Statement to the U.S. House Subcommittee on Financial Institutions Supervision, Regulation and Insurance, of the Committee on Banking, Finance and Urban Affairs, September 11, 1985. *Fed. Res. Bull.*, November 1985, *71*(11), pp. 877–81. [G: U.S.]

Tedeschi, Adelmo. Le sofferenze nel nostro sistema creditizio: un'indagine di lungo periodo. (Bad Debts in the Italian Credit System: A Structural Survey—Part I. With English summary.) *Bancaria*, May 1985, *41*(5), pp. 539–53. [G: Italy]

Tedeschi, Adelmo. Le sofferenze nel nostro sistema creditizio: un'indagine di lungo periodo. (Bad Debts in the Italian Credit System: A Structural Survey—Part II. With English summary.) *Bancaria*, June 1985, *41*(6), pp. 670–78. [G: Italy]

Thingalaya, N. K. Rural Financing: Syndicate Bank's Experience. In *Bandyopadhyay, R. and Khankhoje, D. P., eds.*, 1985, pp. 153–59. [G: India]

Tuccillo, John A. Deregulation and Thrift Strategies. *Bus. Econ.*, July 1985, *20*(3), pp. 21–26. [G: U.S.]

Tuccillo, John A. Deregulation and Thrift Strategies: A Reply. *Bus. Econ.*, October 1985, *20*(4), pp. 60. [G: U.S.]

Volcker, Paul A. Statement to the U.S. House Subcommittee on Commerce, Consumer, and Monetary Affairs, of the Committee on Government Operations, March 27, 1985. *Fed. Res. Bull.*, May 1985, *71*(5), pp. 312–21. [G: U.S.]

Volcker, Paul A. Statement to the U.S. Senate Committee on Banking, Housing, and Urban Affairs, September 11, 1985. *Fed. Res. Bull.*, November 1985, *71*(11), pp. 866–73. [G: U.S.]

Waldman, Michael. Constructive Use of Fixed-Rate Mortgages for Thrift Portfolios. In *Federal Home Loan Bank of San Francisco.*, 1985, pp. 134–56. [G: U.S.]

Walter, Ingo. Deregulating Wall Street: Introduction and Overview. In *Walter, I., ed.*, 1985, pp. 1–12. [G: U.S.]

Wolfe, Harold T., Sr. Eighteen Years of Variable-Rate Portfolio Lending: Panel Presentation. In *Federal Home Loan Bank of San Francisco.*, 1985, pp. 48–55. [G: U.S.]

Wolfson, Martin H. Financial Developments of Bank Holding Companies in 1984. *Fed. Res. Bull.*, December 1985, *71*(12), pp. 924–32. [G: U.S.]

Wolken, John D. and Navratil, Frank J. The Choice of Regulatory Regime: A Logit Analysis of Credit Union Chartering. *Quart. Rev. Econ. Bus.*, Spring 1985, *25*(1), pp. 40–57. [G: U.S.]

315 Credit to Business, Consumer, etc. (including mortgages)

3150 General

Baltensperger, Ernst and Devinney, Timothy M. Credit Rationing Theory: A Survey and Synthesis. *Z. ges. Staatswiss. (JITE)*, December 1985, *141*(4), pp. 475–502.

Bester, Helmut. Screening vs. Rationing in Credit Markets with Imperfect Information. *Amer. Econ. Rev.*, September 1985, *75*(4), pp. 850–55.

Beveridge, Andrew A. Local Lending Practice: Borrowers in a Small Northeastern Industrial City, 1832–1915. *J. Econ. Hist.*, June 1985, *45*(2), pp. 393–403. [G: U.S.]

Chan, Yuk-Shee and Kanatas, George. Asymmetric Valuations and the Role of Collateral in Loan Agreements. *J. Money, Credit, Banking*, February 1985, *17*(1), pp. 84–95.

Chandavarkar, Anand G. The Financial Pull of Urban Areas in LDCs. *Finance Develop.*, June 1985, *22*(2), pp. 24–27. [G: Thailand; India]

Corrigan, E. Gerald. Public and Private Debt Accumulation: A Perspective. *Fed. Res. Bank New York Quart. Rev.*, Autumn 1985, *10*(3), pp. 1–5. [G: U.S.]

Crawford, Peter. Interest Rate Outlook: Focus on Credit Supply. *Bus. Econ.*, July 1985, *20*(3), pp. 34–39. [G: U.S.]

Dubofsky, David A. Capital Market Credit Rationing and Stock Risk. *Southern Econ. J.*, July 1985, *52*(1), pp. 191–202. [G: U.S.]

Füllenkemper, Horst and Rehm, Hannes. Internationale Finanzmärkte unter Innovations- und Liberalisierungsdruck. (International Financial Markets under Innovation and Liberalization Pressure. With English summary.) *Kredit Kapital*, 1985, *18*(4), pp. 553–85. [G: W. Germany]

Greenbaum, Stuart I. and Venezia, Itzhak. Partial Exercise of Loan Commitments under Adaptive Pricing. *J. Finan. Res.*, Winter 1985, *8*(4), pp. 251–63.

Martin, Preston. Statement to the U.S. House Subcommittee on Telecommunications, Consumer Protection, and Finance of the Committee on Energy and Commerce, April 23, 1985. *Fed. Res. Bull.*, June 1985, *71*(6), pp. 428–30. [G: U.S.]

Martin, Preston. Statement to the U.S. Senate Subcommittee on Securities of the Committee on Banking, Housing, and Urban Affairs, April 4, 1985. *Fed. Res. Bull.*, June 1985, *71*(6), pp. 418–22. [G: U.S.]

McKinley, Sue; Pany, Kurt and Reckers, Philip M. J. An Examination of the Influence of CPA Firm Type, Size, and MAS Provision on Loan Officer Decisions and Perceptions. *J. Acc. Res.*, Autumn 1985, *23*(2), pp. 887–96. [G: U.S.]

Moran, Michael J. The Federally Sponsored Credit Agencies: An Overview. *Fed. Res. Bull.*, June 1985, *71*(6), pp. 373–88. [G: U.S.]

Narube, Savenaca and Whiteside, Barry T. Financial Institutions and Markets in Fiji. In *Skully, M. T., ed.*, 1985, pp. 94–159.
[G: Fiji]

Nicholl, Peter and King, Maree F. Financial Institutions and Markets in New Zealand. In *Skully, M. T., ed.*, 1985, pp. 160–244.
[G: New Zealand]

O'Leary, James J. The Outlook for the Money and Capital Markets and for Interest Rates in 1985. *Bus. Econ.*, April 1985, *20*(2), pp. 24–30.
[G: U.S.]

Osano, Hiroshi and Tsutsui, Yoshiro. Implicit Contracts in the Japanese Bank Loan Market. *J. Finan. Quant. Anal.*, June 1985, *20*(2), pp. 211–29.
[G: Japan]

Plaut, Steven E. The Theory of Collateral. *J. Banking Finance*, September 1985, *9*(3), pp. 401–19.

Skully, Michael T. Financial Institutions and Markets in Papua New Guinea. In *Skully, M. T., ed.*, 1985, pp. 245–339.
[G: Papua New Guinea]

Skully, Michael T. Financial Institutions and Markets in Australia. In *Skully, M. T., ed.*, 1985, pp. 1–93.
[G: Australia]

Smith, Dolores S. Revision of the Board's Equal Credit Regulation: An Overview. *Fed. Res. Bull.*, December 1985, *71*(12), pp. 913–23.
[G: U.S.]

Teal, Francis and Giwa, Y. M. Domestic Credit and the Balance of Payments in Ghana: A Comment. *J. Devel. Stud.*, July 1985, *21*(4), pp. 548–61.
[G: Ghana]

Tedeschi, Adelmo. Le sofferenze nel nostro sistema creditizio: un'indagine di lungo periodo. (Bad Debts in the Italian Credit System: A Structural Survey—Part I. With English summary.) *Bancaria*, May 1985, *41*(5), pp. 539–53.
[G: Italy]

Tedeschi, Adelmo. Le sofferenze nel nostro sistema creditizio: un'indagine di lungo periodo. (Bad debts in the Italian Credit System: A Structural Survey—Part II. With English summary.) *Bancaria*, June 1985, *41*(6), pp. 670–78.
[G: Italy]

Trehan, Bharat. The Information Content of Credit Aggregates. *Fed. Res. Bank San Francisco Econ. Rev.*, Spring 1985, (2), pp. 28–39.
[G: U.S.]

Wojnilower, Albert M. Private Credit Demand, Supply, and Crunches—How Different Are the 1980's? *Amer. Econ. Rev.*, May 1985, *75*(2), pp. 351–56.
[G: U.S.]

3151 Consumer Finance

Cantoni, Giampiero. Le carte di credito: profili economici, tecnologici, giuridici. (Credit Cards: Economic, Technological and Legal Aspects. With English summary.) *Bancaria*, September 1985, *41*(9), pp. 955–61.
[G: Italy]

El-Sheikh, S. Consumption and Credit in a Less Developed Country: An Econometric Analysis of Egypt. *Empirical Econ.*, 1985, *10*(3), pp. 143–61.
[G: Egypt]

Goldfaden, Lynn C. and Hurst, Gerald P. Regulatory Responses to Changes in the Consumer Financial Services Industry. *Fed. Res. Bull.*, February 1985, *71*(2), pp. 75–81.
[G: U.S.]

Goodman, John L., Jr. and Luckett, Charles A. Adjustable-Rate Financing in Mortgage and Consumer Credit Markets. *Fed. Res. Bull.*, November 1985, *71*(11), pp. 823–35.
[G: U.S.]

Heaton, Gary G. and Dunham, Constance R. The Growing Competitiveness of Credit Unions. *New Eng. Econ. Rev.*, May/June 1985, pp. 19–34.
[G: U.S.]

Luckett, Charles A. and August, James D. The Growth of Consumer Debt. *Fed. Res. Bull.*, June 1985, *71*(6), pp. 389–402.
[G: U.S.]

Seger, Martha R. Statement to the U.S. Subcommittee on Consumer Affairs and Coinage of the Committee on Banking, Finance and Urban Affairs, October 29, 1985. *Fed. Res. Bull.*, December 1985, *71*(12), pp. 944–48.
[G: U.S.]

Tapscott, Tracy R. Consumer Installment Credit, 1980–85. *Surv. Curr. Bus.*, August 1985, *65*(8), pp. 12–16.
[G: U.S.]

3152 Mortgage Market

Agarwal, Vinod B. and Philips, Richard A. The Effects of Assumption Financing across Housing Price Categories. *Amer. Real Estate Urban Econ. Assoc. J.*, Spring 1985, *13*(1), pp. 48–57.
[G: U.S.]

Alm, James; Follain, James R. and Beeman, Mary Anne. Tax Expenditures and Other Programs to Stimulate Housing: Do We Need More? *J. Urban Econ.*, September 1985, *18*(2), pp. 180–95.
[G: U.S.]

Berry, Thomas D. and Gehr, Adam K., Jr. FNMA Mortgage Purchase Commitments as Put Options: An Empirical Examination. *Amer. Real Estate Urban Econ. Assoc. J.*, Spring 1985, *13*(1), pp. 93–105.
[G: U.S.]

Black, Harold A. and Schweitzer, Robert L. A Canonical Analysis of Mortgage Lending Terms: Testing for Lending Discrimination at a Commerical Bank. *Urban Stud.*, February 1985, *22*(1), pp. 13–19.
[G: U.S.]

Brennan, Michael J. and Schwartz, Eduardo S. Determinants of GNMA Mortgage Prices. *Amer. Real Estate Urban Econ. Assoc. J.*, Fall 1985, *13*(3), pp. 209–28.
[G: U.S.]

Brooks, Edwin B., Jr. Solving the Mortgage Menu Problem: Panel Presentation. In *Federal Home Loan Bank of San Francisco.*, 1985, pp. 38–41.
[G: U.S.]

Brueckner, Jan K. A Simple Model of Mortgage Insurance. *Amer. Real Estate Urban Econ. Assoc. J.*, Summer 1985, *13*(2), pp. 129–42.

Buckley, Robert M. and Gross, David J. Selective Credit Policies and the Mortgage Market: Cross-sectional Evidence. *J. Money, Credit, Banking*, August 1985, *17*(3), pp. 358–70.
[G: U.S.]

Buser, Stephen A.; Hendershott, Patric H. and Sanders, Anthony B. Pricing Life-of-Loan Rate Caps on Default-Free Adjustable-Rate Mortgages. *Amer. Real Estate Urban Econ. Assoc. J.*, Fall 1985, *13*(3), pp. 248–60. [G: U.S.]

Corkett, C. Earl. Minimizing Mortgage Loan Default Risks: Panel Presentation. In *Federal Home Loan Bank of San Francisco.*, 1985, pp. 70–77. [G: U.S.]

Doling, John; Karn, Valerie and Stafford, Bruce. How Far Can Privatization Go? Owner-Occupation and Mortgage Default. *Nat. Westminster Bank Quart. Rev.*, August 1985, pp. 42–52. [G: U.K.]

Dunn, Kenneth B. and Spatt, Chester S. An Analysis of Mortgage Contracting: Prepayment Penalties and the Due-on-Sale Clause. *J. Finance*, March 1985, *40*(1), pp. 293–308.

Durning, Dan and Quigley, John M. On the Distributional Implications of Mortgage Revenue Bonds and Creative Finance. *Nat. Tax J.*, December 1985, *38*(4), pp. 513–23. [G: U.S.]

Epley, Donald R.; Cronan, Timothy P. and Perry, Larry G. A Research Note on Discrimination in Mortgage Lending. *Amer. Real Estate Urban Econ. Assoc. J.*, Winter 1985, *13*(4), pp. 446–51.

Epperson, James E., et al. Pricing Default Risk in Mortgages. *Amer. Real Estate Urban Econ. Assoc. J.*, Fall 1985, *13*(3), pp. 261–72.

Evans, Richard D.; Maris, Brian A. and Weinstein, Robert I. Expected Loss and Mortgage Default Risk. *Quart. J. Bus. Econ.*, Winter 1985, *24*(1), pp. 75–92. [G: U.S.]

Foster, Chester and Van Order, Robert. FHA Terminations: A Prelude to Rational Mortgage Pricing. *Amer. Real Estate Urban Econ. Assoc. J.*, Fall 1985, *13*(3), pp. 273–91. [G: U.S.]

Furlong, Frederick T. Savings and Loan Asset Composition and the Mortgage Market. *Fed. Res. Bank San Francisco Econ. Rev.*, Summer 1985, (3), pp. 14–24. [G: U.S.]

Gasper, Louis C. Selling ARMs in Secondary Markets: Panel Presentation. In *Federal Home Loan Bank of San Francisco.*, 1985, pp. 180–83. [G: U.S.]

Goldberg, Michael A. Urban Programs: Transportation and Housing: Commentary. In *Quigley, J. M. and Rubinfeld, D. L., eds.*, 1985, pp. 285–93. [G: Canada; U.S.]

Goodman, John L., Jr. and Luckett, Charles A. Adjustable-Rate Financing in Mortgage and Consumer Credit Markets. *Fed. Res. Bull.*, November 1985, *71*(11), pp. 823–35. [G: U.S.]

Gray, Edwin J. Remarks from the Chairman: Bank Board Priorities. In *Federal Home Loan Bank of San Francisco.*, 1985, pp. 56–65. [G: U.S.]

Guttentag, Jack M. Revisiting the ARM Menu Problem: The Role of Regulation, Disclosure, and Innovation. In *Federal Home Loan Bank of San Francisco.*, 1985, pp. 12–27. [G: U.S.]

Guttentag, Jack M. and Hurst, E. Gerald, Jr. Truth-in-Lending as Applied to Mortgages: What Should Be Disclosed, and When? *Housing Finance Rev.*, January 1985, *4*(1), pp. 551–68. [G: U.S.]

Hall, Arden R. Valuing the Mortgage Borrower's Prepayment Option. *Amer. Real Estate Urban Econ. Assoc. J.*, Fall 1985, *13*(3), pp. 229–47. [G: U.S.]

Harris, John M., Jr. and Page, Daniel E. Rate Level Indexed Mortgages: An Evaluation. *Amer. Real Estate Urban Econ. Assoc. J.*, Summer 1985, *13*(2), pp. 195–207. [G: U.S.]

Hendershott, Patric H. Pricing Adjustable-Rate Mortgages. In *Federal Home Loan Bank of San Francisco.*, 1985, pp. 98–119. [G: U.S.]

Hendershott, Patric H. and Shilling, James D. Valuing ARM Rate Caps: Implications of 1970–84 Interest Rate Behavior. *Amer. Real Estate Urban Econ. Assoc. J.*, Fall 1985, *13*(3), pp. 317–32. [G: U.S.]

Kau, James B., et al. Rational Pricing of Adjustable Rate Mortgages. *Amer. Real Estate Urban Econ. Assoc. J.*, Summer 1985, *13*(2), pp. 117–28.

Kaufman, George C. Integrating Asset/Liability Management to Finance Mortgage Portfolios. In *Federal Home Loan Bank of San Francisco.*, 1985, pp. 158–77. [G: U.S.]

Kendall, Leon T. Mastering Mortgage Loan Portfolio Risks in Deregulated Markets: Panel Presentation. In *Federal Home Loan Bank of San Francisco.*, 1985, pp. 78–82. [G: U.S.]

Kugler, Peter. Ungleichgewichtsökonometrie für den schweizerischen Hypothekarzinssatz. (Disequilibrium Econometrics for the Swiss Mortgage Interest Rate. With English summary.) *Schweiz. Z. Volkswirtsch. Statist.*, March 1985, *121*(1), pp. 35–44. [G: Switzerland]

Lea, Michael J. An Empirical Analysis of the Value of ARM Features. *Housing Finance Rev.*, January 1985, *4*(1), pp. 467–81. [G: U.S.]

Lea, Michael J. Rational ARM Pricing and Design. In *Federal Home Loan Bank of San Francisco.*, 1985, pp. 120–31. [G: U.S.]

Leahy, Peter J. Are Racial Factors Important for the Allocation of Mortgage Money? A Quasi-experimental Approach to an Aspect of Discrimination. *Amer. J. Econ. Soc.*, April 1985, *44*(2), pp. 185–96. [G: U.S.]

Linneman, Peter and Voith, Richard. Would Mortgage Borrowers Benefit from the Provision of APR Schedules? [Truth-in-Lending as Applied to Mortgages: What Should Be Disclosed, and When?]. *Housing Finance Rev.*, January 1985, *4*(1), pp. 569–76. [G: U.S.]

Maisel, Sherman. The Agenda for Metropolitan Housing Policies. In *Quigley, J. M. and Rubinfeld, D. L., eds.*, 1985, pp. 224–52. [G: U.S.]

Manchester, Joyce. Evidence on Possible Default under Three Mortgage Contracts. *Housing Finance Rev.*, January 1985, *4*(1), pp. 517–36. [G: U.S.]

Mayer, Neil S. The Impacts of Lending, Race, and Ownership on Rental Housing Rehabilitation. *J. Urban Econ.*, May 1985, *17*(3), pp. 349–74. [G: U.S.]

Meador, Mark. The Effects of Federally Sponsored Credit on Housing Markets: Some Evidence from Multivariate Exogeneity Tests. *Housing Finance Rev.*, January 1985, *4*(1), pp. 505–15. [G: U.S.]

Montgomery, James F. Solving the Mortgage Menu Problem: Panel Presentation. In *Federal Home Loan Bank of San Francisco.*, 1985, pp. 30–36. [G: U.S.]

Muth, Richard F. Urban Programs: Transportation and Housing: Commentary. In *Quigley, J. M. and Rubinfeld, D. L., eds.*, 1985, pp. 297–303. [G: U.S.]

Navratil, Frank J. The Estimation of Mortgage Prepayment Rates. *J. Finan. Res.*, Summer 1985, *8*(2), pp. 107–17. [G: U.S.]

Nothaft, Frank E. Survey of Home-Seller Finance, 1983. *Fed. Res. Bull.*, October 1985, *71*(10), pp. 767–75. [G: U.S.]

Ostas, James R. Reduced Form Coefficients, Structural Coefficients, and Mortgage Redlining. *Amer. Real Estate Urban Econ. Assoc. J.*, Spring 1985, *13*(1), pp. 76–92.

Palash, Carl J. and Stoddard, Robert B. ARMs: Their Financing Rate and Impact on Housing. *Fed. Res. Bank New York Quart. Rev.*, Autumn 1985, *10*(3), pp. 39–49. [G: U.S.]

Pesando, James E. and Turnbull, Stuart M. Mortgage Rate Insurance and the Canadian Mortgage Market: Some Further Reflections. *Can. Public Policy*, March 1985, *11*(1), pp. 115–17. [G: Canada]

Pesando, James E. and Turnbull, Stuart M. The Time Path of Homeowner's Equity under Different Mortgage Instruments: A Simulation Study. *Housing Finance Rev.*, January 1985, *4*(1), pp. 483–504. [G: Canada]

Plaut, Steven E. Tenure Decisions, Mortgage Interest, and the Spatial Distribution of Household Demand: A Theoretical Analysis. *Reg. Sci. Urban Econ.*, February 1985, *15*(1), pp. 65–76.

Pratt, Richard T. Current Issues in the Thrift/Mortgage Relationship. In *Federal Home Loan Bank of San Francisco.*, 1985, pp. 4–10. [G: U.S.]

Rodeno, Raymond A. Mortgage Insurance Risk: Implications for Mortgage Design and Pricing: Panel Presentation. In *Federal Home Loan Bank of San Francisco.*, 1985, pp. 84–88. [G: U.S.]

Schwab, Robert M. Renovation and Mobility: An Application of the Theory of Rationing. *Southern Econ. J.*, July 1985, *52*(1), pp. 203–15.

Shanahan, Edmond M. Special Mortgage Menu Problems in Illinois: Panel Presentation. In *Federal Home Loan Bank of San Francisco.*, 1985, pp. 42–46. [G: U.S.]

Shear, William B. and Yezer, Anthony M. J. Discrimination in Urban Housing Finance: An Empirical Study across Cities. *Land Econ.*, August 1985, *61*(3), pp. 292–302. [G: U.S.]

Simpson, William A. Conforming Adjustable Mortgage Loans: Panel Presentation. In *Federal Home Loan Bank of San Francisco.*, 1985, pp. 90–96. [G: U.S.]

Smilow, Michael A. ARMs Development—The Third Stage: Panel Presentation. In *Federal Home Loan Bank of San Francisco.*, 1985, pp. 184–89. [G: U.S.]

Stansell, Stanley R. and Mitchell, A. Cameron.

The Impact of Credit Rationing on the Real Sector: A Study of the Effect of Mortgage Rates and Terms on Housing Starts. *Appl. Econ.*, October 1985, *17*(5), pp. 781–800. [G: U.S.]

Stutzer, Michael J. and Roberds, William. Adjustable Rate Mortgages: Increasing Efficiency More than Housing Activity. *Fed. Res. Bank Minn. Rev.*, Summer 1985, *9*(3), pp. 10–20. [G: U.S.]

Thom, Rodney. The Relationship between Housing Starts and Mortgage Availability. *Rev. Econ. Statist.*, November 1985, *67*(4), pp. 693–96. [G: U.S.]

Thygerson, Kenneth J. Selling ARMs in Secondary Markets: Summary of Issues Presented: Panel Presentation. In *Federal Home Loan Bank of San Francisco.*, 1985, pp. 190–94. [G: U.S.]

Vandell, Kerry D. and Thibodeau, Thomas. Estimation of Mortgage Defaults Using Disaggregate Loan History Data. *Amer. Real Estate Urban Econ. Assoc. J.*, Fall 1985, *13*(3), pp. 292–316. [G: U.S.]

Waldman, Michael. Constructive Use of Fixed-Rate Mortgages for Thrift Portfolios. In *Federal Home Loan Bank of San Francisco.*, 1985, pp. 134–56. [G: U.S.]

Wolfe, Harold T., Sr. Eighteen Years of Variable-Rate Portfolio Lending: Panel Presentation. In *Federal Home Loan Bank of San Francisco.*, 1985, pp. 48–55. [G: U.S.]

You, Jong Keun and Falk, Laurence H. Estimation of the Countercyclical Effect of Mortgage Interest Subsidies. In *Brown, R. C., ed.*, 1985, pp. 231–48. [G: U.S.]

3153 Business Credit

Alexander, Donald L. An Empirical Test of the Mutual Forebearance Hypothesis: The Case of Bank Holding Companies. *Southern Econ. J.*, July 1985, *52*(1), pp. 122–40. [G: U.S.]

Angeloni, Ignazio. The Dynamic Behavior of Business Loans and the Prime Rate: A Comment. *J. Banking Finance*, December 1985, *9*(4), pp. 577–80. [G: U.S.]

Artus, Patrick. Rationnement de crédit et réactions des entreprises. (Credit Rationing and Firms' Reactions. With English summary.) *Revue Écon.*, November 1985, *36*(6), pp. 1207–46. [G: France]

Baratta, Paolo. Il credito industriale dal dibattito del 1911 alla constituzione dell'ICIPU. (Industrial Credit from the 1911 Debate to the Establishment of I.C.I.P.U. With English summary.) *Bancaria*, February 1985, *41*(2), pp. 174–80. [G: Italy]

Belongia, Michael T. and Carraro, Kenneth C. The Status of Farm Lenders: An Assessment of Eighth District and National Trends. *Fed. Res. Bank St. Louis Rev.*, October 1985, *67*(8), pp. 17–27. [G: U.S.]

Besley, Scott and Osteryoung, Jerome S. Survey of Current Practices in Establishing Trade-Credit Limits. *Financial Rev.*, February 1985, *20*(1), pp. 70–82.

Bester, Helmut. The Level of Investment in

Credit Markets with Imperfect Information. *Z. ges. Staatswiss. (JITE)*, December 1985, *141*(4), pp. 503–15.

Biscaini, Anna Maria; Gnes, Paolo and Roselli, Alessandro. Origini e sviluppo del Consorzio per Sovvenzioni su Valori Industriali durante il Governatorato Stringher. (Origins and Development of the *Consorzio per Sovvenzioni su Valori Industriali* during the Stringher Governorship. With English summary.) *Bancaria*, February 1985, *41*(2), pp. 154–73.
[G: Italy]

Brady, Thomas F. Changes in Loan Pricing and Business Lending at Commercial Banks. *Fed. Res. Bull.*, January 1985, *71*(1), pp. 1–13.
[G: U.S.]

Cable, John R. and Turner, Paul. Asymmetric Information and Credit Rationing: Another View of Industrial Bank Lending and Britain's Economic Problem. In *Currie, D., ed.*, 1985, pp. 207–20.

Capriglione, Francesco and Mezzacapo, Vincenzo. Evoluzione del sistema finanziario italiano e attività di "merchant banking." (Evolution of the Italian Financial System and Merchant Banking Services—I. With English summary.) *Bancaria*, March 1985, *41*(3), pp. 288–304.
[G: Italy]

Chitnis, S. M. Innovative Term Lending. In *Bandyopadhyay, R. and Khankhoje, D. P., eds.*, 1985, pp. 55–62.
[G: India]

Churchill, Neil C. and Lewis, Virginia L. Profitability of Small-Business Lending. *J. Bank Res.*, Summer 1985, *16*(2), pp. 63–71.
[G: U.S.]

Confalonieri, Antonio. Il credito all'industria in Italia prima del 1914. (Industrial Credit in Italy Prior to 1914. With English summary.) *Bancaria*, February 1985, *41*(2), pp. 146–53.
[G: Italy]

Cornell, Bradford and Sand, Ole Christian. The Value of Base Rate Options in the Eurocredit Market. *J. Bank Res.*, Spring 1985, *16*(1), pp. 22–27.
[G: U.S.]

Cuthbertson, Keith. Sterling Bank Lending to UK Industrial and Commercial Companies. *Oxford Bull. Econ. Statist.*, May 1985, *47*(2), pp. 91–118.
[G: U.K.]

Do, Toan Q. and Chateau, John Peter B. A Geometrical Exposition of the Credit Setting Strategies of the Banking Firm under Loan Rate Uncertainty. *Finance*, June 1985, *6*(1), pp. 103–19.

Dunham, Constance R. Recent Developments in Thrift Commercial Lending. *New Eng. Econ. Rev.*, Nov./Dec. 1985, pp. 41–48.

Forrest, George. A Positive Role for Credit in the Economic Recovery. In *Meyer, F. V., ed.*, 1985, pp. 63–82.
[G: U.K.]

Frydman, Halina; Altman, Edward I. and Kao, Duen-Li. Introducing Recursive Partitioning for Financial Classification: The Case of Financial Distress. *J. Finance*, March 1985, *40*(1), pp. 269–91.
[G: U.S.]

Gianini, Felice. L'automazione nel rapporto fra banca e impresa. Lineamenti per una strategia di sistema. (Automation in Banking Services for Businesses. With English summary.) *Bancaria*, January 1985, *41*(1), pp. 68–72.
[G: Italy]

Gilbert, R. Alton and Ott, Mack. Why the Big Rise in Business Loans at Banks Last Year? *Fed. Res. Bank St. Louis Rev.*, March 1985, *67*(3), pp. 5–13.
[G: U.S.]

Goldberg, Michael A. and Lloyd-Davies, Peter R. Standby Letters of Credit: Are Banks Overextending Themselves? *J. Bank Res.*, Spring 1985, *16*(1), pp. 28–39.
[G: U.S.]

Gradi, Florio. Realtà, equivoci ed errori lungo la strada verso la riduzione dei tassi. (Facts, Misunderstandings and Errors along the Road towards Reducing Bank Rates. With English summary.) *Bancaria*, September 1985, *41*(9), pp. 948–54.
[G: Italy]

Kling, John L. The Dynamic Behavior of Business Loans and the Prime Rate: Reply. *J. Banking Finance*, December 1985, *9*(4), pp. 581–84.
[G: U.S.]

Kling, John L. The Dynamic Behavior of Business Loans and the Prime Rate. *J. Banking Finance*, September 1985, *9*(3), pp. 421–42.
[G: U.S.]

Martin, Preston. Statement to the U.S. House Subcommittee on Domestic Monetary Policy of the Committee on Banking, Finance, and Urban Affairs, May 3, 1985. *Fed. Res. Bull.*, July 1985, *71*(7), pp. 514–17.
[G: U.S.]

Mathias, Peter. Credit Needs and Credit Supplies for Eighteenth Century Enterprise. In *Marx, A. V., ed.*, 1985, pp. 103–17.
[G: U.K.]

Moore, Basil J. and Threadgold, Andrew R. Corporate Bank Borrowing in the UK, 1965-1981. *Economica*, February 1985, *52*(205), pp. 65–78.
[G: U.K.]

Mujumdar, N. A. Structural Transformation in the Deployment of Credit: Some Implications. In *Bandyopadhyay, R. and Khankhoje, D. P., eds.*, 1985, pp. 41–54.
[G: India]

Nepal Rastra Bank. Priority Sector Credit: Objectives, Policies and Programmes. In *Bandyopadhyay, R. and Khankhoje, D. P., eds.*, 1985, pp. 203–13.
[G: Nepal]

Rice, Emmett J. Statement to the U.S. House Subcommittee on General Oversight and the Economy of the Committee on Small Business, June 25, 1985. *Fed. Res. Bull.*, August 1985, *71*(8), pp. 618–20.
[G: U.S.]

Shaffer, Ron E. and Pulver, Glen C. Regional Variations in Capital Structure of New Small Businesses: The Wisconsin Case. In *Storey, D. J., ed.*, 1985, pp. 166–92.
[G: U.S.]

Singh, Manmohan. Finance and Development: Inaugural Address. In *Bandyopadhyay, R. and Khankhoje, D. P., eds.*, 1985, pp. ix–xiii.
[G: LDCs]

Singh, Sampat P. Redesigning System for Bank Lending to Industry. In *Bandyopadhyay, R. and Khankhoje, D. P., eds.*, 1985, pp. 63–75.
[G: India]

Wellons, Philip A. Competitiveness in the World Economy: The Role of the U.S. Financial System. In *Scott, B. R. and Lodge, G. C., eds.*, 1985, pp. 357–94.
[G: U.S.; OECD]

320 Fiscal Theory and Policy; Public Finance

3200 General

Bird, Richard M. Federal Finance in Comparative Perspective. In *Courchene, T. J.; Conklin, D. W. and Cook, G. C. A., eds. Vol. 1*, 1985, pp. 137–77. **[G: Canada; Selected OECD]**

Buchanan, James M. The Moral Dimension of Debt Financing. *Econ. Inquiry*, January 1985, *23*(1), pp. 1–6.

Cima, Lawrence R. and Cotter, Patrick S. The Coherence of the Concept of Limited Government. *J. Policy Anal. Manage.*, Winter 1985, *4*(2), pp. 266–69.

Cockle, Paul. Public Expenditure Policy, 1985–86: The Economic Environment. In *Cockle, P., ed.*, 1985, pp. 35–55. **[G: U.K.]**

Collinge, Robert A. Toward 'Privatization' of Public Sector Output: Decentralized Contracting for Public and Private Goods. *J. Public Econ.*, August 1985, *27*(3), pp. 371–87.

Crain, W. Mark, et al. Legislator Specialization and the Size of Government. *Public Choice*, 1985, *46*(3), pp. 311–15. **[G: U.S.]**

Fausto, Domenicantonio and Leccisotti, Mario. The Crisis of the Welfare State." *Giorn. Econ.*, Jan.-Feb. 1985, *44*(1–2), pp. 5–16.

Fisher, Ronald C. Taxes and Expenditures in the U.S.: Public Opinion Surveys and Incidence Analysis Compared. *Econ. Inquiry*, July 1985, *23*(3), pp. 525–50. **[G: U.S.]**

Forte, Francesco. Control of Public-Spending Growth and Majority Rule. In *Forte, F. and Peacock, A., eds.*, 1985, pp. 132–42.

Forte, Francesco and Peacock, Alan. Public Expenditure and Government Growth: Introduction: The Political Economy of Public-Sector Growth and Its Control. In *Forte, F. and Peacock, A., eds.*, 1985, pp. 1–10.

Frey, Bruno S. Are There Natural Limits to the Growth of Government? In *Forte, F. and Peacock, A., eds.*, 1985, pp. 101–18.

Hansen, Susan B. Citizen Preferences and Participatory Roles: Comment. In *Clark, T. N., ed.*, 1985, pp. 263–67. **[G: U.S.]**

Higgs, Robert. Crisis, Bigger Government, and Ideological Change: Two Hypotheses on the Ratchet Phenomenon. *Exploration Econ. Hist.*, January 1985, *22*(1), pp. 1–28. **[G: U.S.]**

Horvat, Branko. Efficiency of the Public Sector. *Econ. Anal. Worker's Manage.*, 1985, *19*(2), pp. 195–203.

Jackson, Peter M. Fiscal Containment and Local Government Finance in the U.K. In *Gramlich, E. M. and Ysander, B.-C., eds.*, 1985, pp. 175–228. **[G: U.K.]**

Jha, L. K. Improving Profitability of the Public Sector. In *Jha, L. K.*, 1985, pp. 179–86. **[G: India]**

Jha, L. K. Investment Pattern and National Objectives. In *Jha, L. K.*, 1985, pp. 241–50. **[G: India]**

Jha, L. K. Techniques of Economic Management.

In *Jha, L. K.*, 1985, pp. 45–52. **[G: India]**

Klein, Philip A. Economic Activity and the Public Sector: Is Small Beautiful? *J. Econ. Issues*, June 1985, *19*(2), pp. 419–28. **[G: U.S.]**

Knoke, David. Citizen Preferences and Participatory Roles: Comments. In *Clark, T. N., ed.*, 1985, pp. 259–62. **[G: U.S.]**

Lane, Jan-Erik. State and Market: The Politics of the Public and the Private: Introduction: Public Policy or Markets? The Demarcation Problem. In *Lane, J.-E., ed.*, 1985, pp. 3–52.

Leonard, William N. The State in a Mixed Economy. *Eastern Econ. J.*, July-Sept. 1985, *11*(3), pp. 190–99. **[G: OECD; CMEA]**

Lombard, J. A. The Evolution of the Theory of Economic Policy. *S. Afr. J. Econ.*, December 1985, *53*(4), pp. 315–32. **[G: S. Africa]**

Lundahl, Mats. Government and Inefficiency in the Haitian Economy: The Nineteenth Century Legacy. In *Connolly, M. B. and McDermott, J., eds.*, 1985, pp. 175–218. **[G: Haiti]**

Margolis, Julius. The United States Federal System: Commentary. In *Quigley, J. M. and Rubinfeld, D. L., eds.*, 1985, pp. 80–86. **[G: U.S.]**

Marshall, Rob. Public Expenditure Policy, 1985–86: Alternative Scenarios. In *Cockle, P., ed.*, 1985, pp. 57–75. **[G: U.K.]**

Martelli, Paolo. Legislative Choice and Public-Spending Growth. In *Forte, F. and Peacock, A., eds.*, 1985, pp. 37–51.

Mueller, Dennis C. and Murrell, Peter. Interest Groups and the Political Economy of Government Size. In *Forte, F. and Peacock, A., eds.*, 1985, pp. 13–36. **[G: OECD]**

Musgrave, Richard A. A Brief History of Fiscal Doctrine. In *Auerbach, A. J. and Feldstein, M., eds.*, 1985, pp. 1–59.

Musgrave, Richard A. Perspectives on and Limits to Public Finance for the Financing of Social Policy in Market Economies. In *Terny, G. and Culyer, A. J., eds.*, 1985, pp. 261–70.

Myhrman, Johan. Reflections on the Growth of Government: Introduction. *J. Public Econ.*, December 1985, *28*(3), pp. 275–85.

Oates, Wallace E. The Public Sector in Economics: An Analytical Chameleon. In *[Recktenwald, H. C.]*, 1985, pp. 45–58.

Paul, Samuel. Privatization and the Public Sector. *Finance Develop.*, December 1985, *22*(4), pp. 42–45. **[G: LDCs]**

Rizzo, Ilde. Regional Disparities and Decentralization as Determinants of Public-Sector Expenditure Growth in Italy (1960–81). In *Forte, F. and Peacock, A., eds.*, 1985, pp. 65–82. **[G: Italy]**

Robert, Michel. 'Challenges and Choices': Implications for Fiscal Federalism. In *Courchene, T. J.; Conklin, D. W. and Cook, G. C. A., eds. Vol. 1*, 1985, pp. 22–28. **[G: Canada]**

Roxborough, Ian. State, Multinationals and the Working Class in Brazil and Mexico. In *Abel, C. and Lewis, C. M., eds.*, 1985, pp. 430–50. **[G: Brazil; Mexico]**

Saunders, Peter and Klau, Friedrich. The Role of the Public Sector: Causes and Consequences

of the Growth of Government. *OECD Econ. Stud.*, Spring 1985, (4), pp. 5–239.
[G: OECD]

Schmidt, Kurt. Is There a Natural Limit to Public-Spending Growth? Or, the Spirit of the Age as a Determinant of the Development of Public Spending. In *Forte, F. and Peacock, A., eds.*, 1985, pp. 119–31. [G: W. Germany]

Simeon, Richard. Federalism in the 1980s. In *Courchene, T. J.; Conklin, D. W. and Cook, G. C. A., eds. Vol. 1*, 1985, pp. 29–43.
[G: Canada]

Skinner, Andrew S. Adam Smith: Some Functions and Limitations of Government. In *[Recktenwald, H. C.]*, 1985, pp. 3–11.

Wildavsky, Aaron. Budgets as Social Orders. In *Clark, T. N., ed.*, 1985, pp. 183–97.

Wildavsky, Aaron. Equality, Spending Limits, and the Growth of Government. In *Harriss, C. L., ed.*, 1985, pp. 59–71. [G: U.S.]

Wildavsky, Aaron. The Logic of Public Sector Growth. In *Lane, J.-E., ed.*, 1985, pp. 231–70.

321 Fiscal Theory and Policy

3210 Fiscal Theory and Policy

Aaron, Henry J. Social Science Analysis and the Formulation of Public Policy: Illustrations of What the President "Knows" and How He Comes to "Know" It: Comment. In *Hausman, J. A. and Wise, D. A., eds.*, 1985, pp. 272–77.

Arrow, Kenneth J. Criteria for Social Investment. In *Arrow, K. J. (I)*, 1985, pp. 200–214.

Arrow, Kenneth J. Discounting and Public Investment Criteria. In *Arrow, K. J. (I)*, 1985, pp. 215–35.

Arrow, Kenneth J. The Social Discount Rate. In *Arrow, K. J. (I)*, 1985, pp. 382–400.

Arrow, Kenneth J. and Kurz, Mordecai. Optimal Public Investment Policy and Controllability with Fixed Private Savings Ratio. In *Arrow, K. J. (I)*, 1985, pp. 332–72.

Baldwin, G. B. The Appraisal of Rural Water Supplies: Reply [Why Present Value Calculations Should Not Be Used in Choosing Rural Water Supply Technology]. *World Devel.*, Oct./Nov. 1985, *13*(10/11), pp. 1179–80. [G: LDCs]

Bartlett, Bruce. Supply-Side Economics: Theory and Evidence. *Nat. Westminster Bank Quart. Rev.*, February 1985, pp. 18–29. [G: U.S.]

Baum, Warren C. and Tolbert, Stokes M. Investing in Development: Lessons of World Bank Experience. *Finance Develop.*, December 1985, *22*(4), pp. 25–30. [G: LDCs]

Berlage, L. and Renard, R. The Discount Rate in Cost–Benefit Analysis and the Choice of a Numeraire. *Oxford Econ. Pap.*, December 1985, *37*(4), pp. 691–99.

Bhagwati, Jagdish N. and Sihag, Balabir S. Dual Markets, Rationing and Queues. In *Bhagwati, J. N. (II)*, 1985, pp. 205–09.

Blankart, Charles. Market and Non-market Alternatives in the Supply of Public Goods: General Issues. In *Forte, F. and Peacock, A., eds.*, 1985, pp. 192–202.

Blejer, Mario I. and Khan, Mohsin S. Public Investment and Crowding Out in the Caribbean Basin Countries. In *Connolly, M. B. and McDermott, J., eds.*, 1985, pp. 219–36.
[G: Caribbean]

Bohanon, Cecil E. Externalities: A Note on Avoiding Confusion. *J. Econ. Educ.*, Fall 1985, *16*(4), pp. 305–07.

Bureau, Donomique. Cohérence entre choix des projets et politique de régulation macroéconomique. (Coherent Choices of Projects and Policy of Macroeconomic Regulation. With English summary.) *Ann. INSEE*, Jan.-Mar. 1985, (57), pp. 51–73.

Ciriacy-Wantrup, S. V. Benefit–Cost Analysis and Public Resource Development. In *Ciriacy-Wantrup, S. V.*, 1985, pp. 135–47.

Cordes, Joseph J. and Weisbrod, Burton A. When Government Programs Create Inequities: A Guide to Compensation Policies. *J. Policy Anal. Manage.*, Winter 1985, *4*(2), pp. 178–95. [G: U.S.]

Currie, David. The Conduct of Fiscal Policy. *Nat. Inst. Econ. Rev.*, August 1985, (113), pp. 81–88. [G: U.K.]

Dinwiddy, Caroline and Teal, Francis. Shadow Prices and Cost-Benefit Rules for Non-traded Commodities in a Second Best Economy. *Oxford Econ. Pap.*, December 1985, *37*(4), pp. 683–90.

Fullerton, Don. Which Effective Tax Rate? A Reply. *Nat. Tax J.*, March 1985, *38*(1), pp. 109–10. [G: U.S.]

Gellerson, Mark. The Economics of Small Hydro Power. *Pakistan Econ. Soc. Rev.*, Summer 1985, *23*(1), pp. 25–39. [G: Pakistan]

Glejser, H. and Kirschen, E. S. Le taux d'actualisation. (With English summary.) *Cah. Écon. Bruxelles*, 3rd Trimester 1985, (107), pp. 351–83. [G: Belgium]

Gravelle, Jane G. "Which Effective Tax Rate?" A Comment and Extension. *Nat. Tax J.*, March 1985, *38*(1), pp. 103–08. [G: U.S.]

Hamlin, Alan P. Federalism, Horizontal Equity, and the Optimal Grant. *Public Finance Quart.*, April 1985, *13*(2), pp. 115–31.

Hanson, Gregory D. Financial Analysis of a Proposed Large-Scale Ethanol Cogeneration Project. *Southern J. Agr. Econ.*, December 1985, *17*(2), pp. 67–76. [G: U.S.]

Hörngren, Lars. A Comparison of the Dynamic Properties of Five Nordic Macroeconometric Models—A Critical Note. *Scand. J. Econ.*, 1985, *87*(3), pp. 568–74. [G: Sweden; Finland; Norway]

Jenkins, Glenn P. and Kuo, Chun-Yan. On Measuring the Social Opportunity Cost of Foreign Exchange. *Can. J. Econ.*, May 1985, *18*(2), pp. 400–415. [G: Canada]

Knoester, Anthonie. The Forward Shifting of Taxes: A Comment [Stagnation and the Inverted Haavelmo Effect: Some International Evidence]: Reply. *De Economist*, 1985, *133*(3), pp. 417–20.

Koefoed, O. The Forward Shifting of Taxes: A Comment [Stagnation and the Inverted Haavelmo Effect: Some International Evidence]. *De Economist*, 1985, *133*(3), pp. 415–17.

Kula, Erhun. The Social Time Preference Rate for Portugal. *Economia (Portugal)*, October 1985, *9*(3), pp. 447–66. [G: Portugal]

Leff, Nathaniel H. Optimal Investment Choice for Developing Countries: Rational Theory and Rational Decision-making. *J. Devel. Econ.*, August 1985, *18*(2–3), pp. 335–60. [G: LDCs]

Leff, Nathaniel H. The Use of Policy-Science Tools in Public-Sector Decision Making: Social Benefit–Cost Analysis in the World Bank. *Kyklos*, 1985, *38*(1), pp. 60–76. [G: LDCs]

Lybeck, Johan A. A Comparison of the Dynamic Properties of Five Nordic Macroeconomic Models—A Critical Note. Reply. *Scand. J. Econ.*, 1985, *87*(3), p. 575. [G: Sweden; Finland; Norway]

Lynn, Laurence E., Jr. Social Science Analysis and the Formulation of Public Policy: Illustrations of What the President "Knows" and How He Comes to "Know" It: Comment. In *Hausman, J. A. and Wise, D. A., eds.*, 1985, pp. 277–78.

Marchand, Maurice; Mintz, Jack and Pestieau, Pierre. Public Production and Shadow Pricing in a Model of Disequilibrium in Labour and Capital Markets. *J. Econ. Theory*, August 1985, *36*(2), pp. 237–56.

Marchese, Carla. Market and Non-market Alternatives in the Public Supply of Public Services: Some Empirical Evidence. In *Forte, F. and Peacock, A., eds.*, 1985, pp. 212–26. [G: OECD]

McNeill, Desmond. The Appraisal of Rural Water Supplies [Why Present Value Calculations Should Not Be Used in Choosing Rural Water Supply Technology]. *World Devel.*, Oct./Nov. 1985, *13*(10/11), pp. 1175–78. [G: LDCs]

McNeill, Desmond. The Appraisal of Rural Water Supplies: Rejoinder [Why Present Value Calculations Should Not Be Used in Choosing Rural Water Supply Technology]. *World Devel.*, Oct./Nov. 1985, *13*(10/11), p. 1181. [G: LDCs]

Mundel, David S. The Use of Information in the Policy Process: Are Social-Policy Experiments Worthwhile? In *Hausman, J. A. and Wise, D. A., eds.*, 1985, pp. 251–56.

Nioche, Jean-Pierre and Poinsard, Robert. Public Policy Evaluation in France. *J. Policy Anal. Manage.*, Fall 1985, *5*(1), pp. 58–72. [G: France]

Oates, Wallace E. Searching for Leviathan: An Empirical Study. *Amer. Econ. Rev.*, September 1985, *75*(4), pp. 748–57.

Ohkawa, Kazushi. Investment Criteria in Development Planning. In *Shishido, T. and Sato, R., eds.*, 1985, pp. 71–80. [G: Japan; LDCs]

Price, Colin and Nair, C. T. S. Social Discounting and the Distribution of Project Benefits. *J. Devel. Stud.*, July 1985, *21*(4), pp. 525–32.

Prince, Raymond and Rosser, J. Barkley, Jr. Some Implications of Delayed Environmental Costs for Benefit Cost Analysis: A Study of Reswitching in the Western Coal Lands. *Growth Change*, April 1985, *16*(2), pp. 18–25. [G: U.S.]

Qureshi, Muzaffar Mahmood. Project Appraisal in Pakistan: A Review: Comments. *Pakistan Devel. Rev.*, Autumn-Winter 1985, *24*(3/4), pp. 699–701. [G: Pakistan]

Ranson, Baldwin. Government Deficits and Economic Stability: Evaluating Alternative Theories. *Écon. Soc.*, August 1985, *19*(8), pp. 197–207.

Sahibzada, Shamim A. and Mahmood, Mir Annice. Project Appraisal in Pakistan: A Review. *Pakistan Devel. Rev.*, Autumn-Winter 1985, *24*(3/4), pp. 687–98. [G: Pakistan]

Selan, Valerio. La determinazione del così detto "livello di intermediazione pubblica." The Determinations of the So-called Public Level of Intermediation." With English summary.) *Bancaria*, September 1985, *41*(9), pp. 969–77.

Selwyn, Percy. Costs and Benefits of a Modest Proposal. *World Devel.*, May 1985, *13*(5), pp. 653–58. [G: Ireland]

Staiger, Robert W. and Richardson, Barbara C. A Discounting Framework for Regulatory Impact Analysis. *Policy Sci.*, March 1985, *18*(1), pp. 33–54.

Steinberg, Gerald M. Comparing Technological Risks in Large Scale National Projects. *Policy Sci.*, March 1985, *18*(1), pp. 79–93. [G: U.S.]

Stewart, D. F. Options for Cement Production in Papua New Guinea: A Study in Choice of Technology. *World Devel.*, May 1985, *13*(5), pp. 639–51. [G: Papua New Guinea]

Stromsdorfer, Ernst W. Social Science Analysis and the Formulation of Public Policy: Illustrations of What the President "Knows" and How He Comes to "Know" It. In *Hausman, J. A. and Wise, D. A., eds.*, 1985, pp. 257–72.

Tinbergen, Jan. On Collective and Part-Collective Goods. In *Tinbergen, J.*, 1985, pp. 43–55.

Tisdell, Clement A. Externalities and Coasian Considerations in Project Evaluation: Aspects of Social CBA in LDCs. *Indian J. Quant. Econ.*, 1985, *1*(1), pp. 33–43.

Tsuneki, Atsushi. On the Choice of Large Projects: A Generalization. *Can. J. Econ.*, August 1985, *18*(3), pp. 660–64.

Tuckman, Howard P. Alternative Approaches to Correcting Public Sector Inefficiency. *Amer. J. Econ. Soc.*, January 1985, *44*(1), pp. 55–65.

Vavouras, Ioannis S. The Accounting Prices of the Factors of Production: An Estimation of Their Parameters in the Case of Greece. *Bull. Econ. Res.*, May 1985, *37*(2), pp. 97–114. [G: Greece]

Weber, Shlomo and Zamir, Shmuel. Proportional Taxation: Nonexistence of Stable Structures in an Economy with a Public Good [Second Best Taxation as a Game]. *J. Econ. Theory*, February 1985, *35*(1), pp. 178–85.

Wright, R. W. The Social Discount Rate: Jenkins

vs. Lind. *Can. Public Policy*, September 1985, *11*(3), pp. 629–30. **[G: Canada]**

3212 Fiscal Theory; Empirical Studies Illustrating Fiscal Theory

Adolph, Brigitte and Wolfstetter, Elmar. Pareto-Verbessernde Fiskalpolitik im allgemeinen Gleichgewicht bei rationalen Erwartungen. (With English summary.) *Z. Wirtschaft. Sozialwissen.*, 1985, *105*(1), pp. 51–63.

Ahking, Francis W. and Miller, Stephen M. The Relationship between Government Deficits, Money Growth, and Inflation. *J. Macroecon.*, Fall 1985, *7*(4), pp. 447–67. **[G: U.S.]**

Aiyagari, S. Rao. Deficits, Interest Rates, and the Tax Distribution. *Fed. Res. Bank Minn. Rev.*, Winter 1985, *9*(1), pp. 5–14.

Aiyagari, S. Rao and Gertler, Mark. The Backing of Government Bonds and Monetarism. *J. Monet. Econ.*, July 1985, *16*(1), pp. 19–44.

Allen, Franklin. Achieving the First Best in Small Economies. *J. Public Econ.*, July 1985, *27*(2), pp. 255–60.

Alpine, R. L. W. A Pedagogical Note on Bond Financing of Government Expenditure. *J. Econ. Stud.*, 1985, *12*(4), pp. 58–61.

Ando, Albert. Coordination of Monetary and Fiscal Policies. In *Ando, A., et al., eds.*, 1985, pp. 253–89. **[G: U.S.]**

Arestis, P. Is There Any Crowding-out of Private Expenditure by Fiscal Actions? In *Arestis, P. and Skouras, T., eds.*, 1985, pp. 99–124.

Argy, Victor E. Targeting the Budget Deficit in the Face of a Downward Expenditure Shock. *Aussenwirtschaft*, May 1985, *40*(1/2), pp. 83–102. **[G: Australia; U.K.]**

Argy, Victor E. The Design of Monetary and Fiscal Policy: Monetarism and Supply-Side Economics. In *Argy, V. E. and Neville, J. W., eds.*, 1985, pp. 60–77.

Arrow, Kenneth J. and Lind, Robert C. Uncertainty and the Evaluation of Public Investment Decisions: Reply. In *Arrow, K. J. (I)*, 1985, pp. 440–42.

Arrow, Kenneth J. and Lind, Robert C. Uncertainty and the Evaluation of Public Investment Decisions. In *Arrow, K. J. (I)*, 1985, pp. 418–39.

Aschauer, David Alan. Fiscal Policy and Aggregate Demand. *Amer. Econ. Rev.*, March 1985, *75*(1), pp. 117–27. **[G: U.S.]**

Aschauer, David Alan and Greenwood, Jeremy. Macroeconomic Effects of Fiscal Policy. *Carnegie-Rochester Conf. Ser. Public Policy*, Autumn 1985, *23*, pp. 91–138.

Aschinger, Gerhard. Probleme der Staatsverschuldung. (Problems of Government Indebtedness. With English summary.) *Jahr. Nationalökon. Statist.*, November 1985, *200*(6), pp. 582–601.

Auerbach, Alan J. The Theory of Excess Burden and Optimal Taxation. In *Auerbach, A. J. and Feldstein, M., eds.*, 1985, pp. 61–127.

Balasko, Yves and Shell, Karl. On Taxation and Competitive Equilibria. In *[Rossier,*

Edouard], 1985, pp. 69–83.

Balducci, Renato. É efficiente decentrare le decisioni di politica economica? (Are Decentralized Policies Efficient? With English summary.) *Polit. Econ.*, December 1985, *1*(3), pp. 399–428.

Ballard, Charles L. and Goulder, Larry H. Consumption Taxes, Foresight, and Welfare: A Computable General Equilibrium Analysis. In *Piggott, J. and Whalley, J., eds.*, 1985, pp. 253–82. **[G: U.S.]**

Ballard, Charles L.; Shoven, John B. and Whalley, John. General Equilibrium Computations of the Marginal Welfare Costs of Taxes in the United States. *Amer. Econ. Rev.*, March 1985, *75*(1), pp. 128–38. **[G: U.S.]**

Baltensperger, Ernst. Staatsverschuldung, Geldpolitik und Währungsstabilität. (Public Debt, Monetary Policy, and Currency Stability. With English summary.) *Aussenwirtschaft*, May 1985, *40*(1/2), pp. 71–81.

Barro, Robert J. Federal Deficits, Interest Rates, and Monetary Policy: Comment. *J. Money, Credit, Banking*, Pt. 2, Nov. 1985, *17*(4), pp. 682–85. **[G: U.S.]**

Barry, Frank G. Fiscal Policy in a Small Open Economy with Unemployment and Capital Accumulation. *Scand. J. Econ.*, 1985, *87*(3), pp. 474–86.

Becker, Gary S. Public Policies, Pressure Groups, and Dead Weight Costs. *J. Public Econ.*, December 1985, *28*(3), pp. 329–47.

Becker, Robert A. Capital Income Taxation and Perfect Foresight. *J. Public Econ.*, March 1985, *26*(2), pp. 147–67.

Benavie, Arthur. Monetary-Fiscal Policy under Rational Expectations in a Lucas–Rapping Macromodel. *Atlantic Econ. J.*, December 1985, *13*(4), pp. 1–9.

Benavie, Arthur and Froyen, Richard T. Optimal Monetary-Fiscal Stabilizers under an Indexed versus Nonindexed Tax Structure. *J. Econ. Bus.*, August 1985, *37*(3), pp. 197–208.

Benjamini, Yael and Maital, Shlomo. Optimal Tax Evasion and Optimal Tax Evasion Policy: Behavioral Aspects. In *Gaertner, W. and Wenig, A., eds.*, 1985, pp. 245–64. **[G: Israel]**

Bergström, Villy and Södersten, Jan. Do Tax Allowances Stimulate Investment? In *Førsund, F. R. and Honkapohja, S., eds.*, 1985, pp. 146–70. **[G: Sweden]**

Biørn, Erik. Inflation, Depreciation and the Neutrality of the Corporate Income Tax. In *Førsund, F. R. and Honkapohja, S., eds.*, 1985, pp. 116–30. **[G: Norway]**

Bird, Richard M. and Brean, Donald J. S. Canada/U.S. Tax Relations: Issues and Perspectives. In *Fretz, D.; Stern, R. and Whalley, J., eds.*, 1985, pp. 391–425. **[G: Canada; U.S.]**

Blanchard, Olivier J. Debt, Deficits, and Finite Horizons. *J. Polit. Econ.*, April 1985, *93*(2), pp. 223–47.

Blanchard, Olivier J.; Dornbusch, Rudiger and Buiter, Willem H. Debito pubblico e politiche fiscali responsabili. (Debt and Financial Responsibility. With English summary.) *Polit.*

Econ., December 1985, *1*(3), pp. 305–40.
[G: EEC]

Blanchard, Olivier J. and Sachs, Jeffrey. Anticipations, Recessions and Policy; An Intertemporal Disequilibrium Model. In *Melitz, J. and Wyplosz, C., eds.*, 1985, pp. 117–44.

Blinder, Alan S. Federal Deficits, Interest Rates, and Monetary Policy: Comment. *J. Money, Credit, Banking*, Pt. 2, Nov. 1985, *17*(4), pp. 685–89.

Blinder, Alan S. and Rosen, Harvey S. Notches. *Amer. Econ. Rev.*, September 1985, *75*(4), pp. 736–47.

Blomquist, N. Sören. Labour Supply in a Two-Period Model: The Effect of a Nonlinear Progressive Income Tax. *Rev. Econ. Stud.*, July 1985, *52*(3), pp. 515–24.

Blomquist, N. Sören. The Wage Rate Tax—An Alternative to the Income Tax? In *Førsund, F. R. and Honkapohja, S., eds.*, 1985, pp. 171–87.

Boadway, Robin W.; Bruce, Neil and Mintz, Jack. The Role and Design of the Corporate Income Tax. In *Førsund, F. R. and Honkapohja, S., eds.*, 1985, pp. 188–201.

Bös, Dieter. Income Taxation, Public Sector Pricing and Redistribution. In *Førsund, F. R. and Honkapohja, S., eds.*, 1985, pp. 68–85.

Bös, Dieter. Public Sector Pricing. In *Auerbach, A. J. and Feldstein, M., eds.*, 1985, pp. 129–211.

Bös, Dieter and Tillmann, Georg. An 'Envy Tax': Theoretical Principles and Applications to the German Surcharge on the Rich. *Public Finance*, 1985, *40*(1), pp. 35–63.

Boskin, Michael J. and Kotlikoff, Laurence J. Public Debt and United States Saving: A New Test of the Neutrality Hypothesis. *Carnegie-Rochester Conf. Ser. Public Policy*, Autumn 1985, *23*, pp. 55–86. [G: U.S.]

Bovenberg, A. Lans. Dynamic General Equilibrium Tax Models with Adjustment Costs. In *Manne, A. S., ed.*, 1985, pp. 40–55.

Brander, James A. and Spencer, Barbara J. Ramsey Optimal Two Part Tariffs: The Case of Many Heterogeneous Groups. *Public Finance*, 1985, *40*(3), pp. 335–46.

Breeden, Charles H. and Hunter, William J. Tax Revenue and Tax Structure. *Public Finance Quart.*, April 1985, *13*(2), pp. 216–24. [G: U.S.]

Brennan, Goeffrey and Walsh, Cliff. Private Markets in (Excludable) Public Goods: A Reexamination [Private Markets in Public Goods (or Qualities)]. *Quart. J. Econ.*, August 1985, *100*(3), pp. 811–19.

Browning, Edgar K. Tax Incidence, Indirect Taxes, and Transfers. *Nat. Tax J.*, December 1985, *38*(4), pp. 525–33.

Browning, Edgar K. The Marginal Social Security Tax on Labor. *Public Finance Quart.*, July 1985, *13*(3), pp. 227–51. [G: U.S.]

Brunner, Karl and Meltzer, Allan H. The "New Monetary Economics," Fiscal Issues, and Unemployment. *Carnegie-Rochester Conf. Ser. Public Policy*, Autumn 1985, *23*, pp. 1–11.

Bryant, John. Analyzing Deficit Finance in a Regime of Unbacked Government Paper. *Fed. Res. Bank Dallas Econ. Rev.*, January 1985, pp. 17–27.

Buchanan, James M. The Ethical Limits of Taxation. In *Førsund, F. R. and Honkapohja, S., eds.*, 1985, pp. 4–16.

Byrnes, Patrica; Grosskopf, Shawna and Hayes, Kathy J. How 'Exact' are Exact Measures of Welfare Loss? *Appl. Econ.*, December 1985, *17*(6), pp. 1071–81. [G: U.S.]

Caesar, Rolf. Crowding out in der Bundesrepublik Deutschland: Eine empirische Bestandsaufnahme. (Crowding Out in the Federal Republic of Germany: An Empirical Stock-taking. With English summary.) *Kredit Kapital*, 1985, *18*(2), pp. 265–76. [G: W. Germany]

Calvo, Guillermo A. Macroeconomic Implications of the Government Budget: Some Basic Considerations. *J. Monet. Econ.*, January 1985, *15*(1), pp. 95–112.

Calvo, Guillermo A. The Inefficiency of Unemployment: The Supervision Perspective. *Quart. J. Econ.*, May 1985, *100*(2), pp. 373–87.

Caniglia, Alan S. Do Recipients Necessarily Prefer Cash Grants to Excise Subsidies? *Public Finance Quart.*, October 1985, *13*(4), pp. 422–35.

Canzoneri, Matthew B. Fiscal Expenditures and International Economic Interdependence: Comment. In *Buiter, W. H. and Marston, R. C., eds.*, 1985, pp. 73–75.

Carlberg, Michael. External versus Internal Public Debt—A Theoretical Analysis of the Long-run Burden. *Z. Nationalökon.*, 1985, *45*(2), pp. 141–54.

Cavaco-Silva, Anibal A. Forced Loans: Tax Element, Equity and Effects on Consumption. In *[Peacock, A.]*, 1985, pp. 51–66.

Cebula, Richard J. The 'Crowding Out' Effect of Fiscal Policy: Correction [An Empirical Analysis of the Crowding Out" Effect of Fiscal Policy in the United States and Canada]. *Kyklos*, 1985, *38*(3), pp. 435–37.

Chakravarty, Satya R. Normative Indices for the Measurement of Horizontal Inequity. *J. Quant. Econ.*, January 1985, *1*(1), pp. 81–89.

Chamley, Christophe. Efficient Tax Reform in a Dynamic Model of General Equilibrium. *Quart. J. Econ.*, May 1985, *100*(2), pp. 335–56.

Chamley, Christophe. Efficient Taxation in a Stylized Model of Intertemporal General Equilibrium. *Int. Econ. Rev.*, June 1985, *26*(2), pp. 451–68.

Chamley, Christophe. On a Simple Rule for the Optimal Inflation Rate in Second Best Taxation. *J. Public Econ.*, February 1985, *26*(1), pp. 35–50.

Chaney, Paul K. and Thakor, Anjan V. Incentive Effects of Benevolent Intervention: The Case of Government Loan Guarantees. *J. Public Econ.*, March 1985, *26*(2), pp. 169–89. [G: U.S.]

Chang, Ching-huei. A General Disequilibrium

Model of Tax Incidence. *J. Public Econ.*, February 1985, *26*(1), pp. 123–33.

Chari, V. V. Macroeconomic Effects of Fiscal Policy: A Comment. *Carnegie-Rochester Conf. Ser. Public Policy*, Autumn 1985, *23*, pp. 139–41.

Chiesa, Gabriella. La politica ottimale del debito pubblico e del debito estero. Le implicazioni sulla risposta ottimale alla riduzione del prezzo del petrolio. (Government and Foreign Debt Policy: The Optimal Use of the Oil-Bill Reduction. With English summary.) *Giorn. Econ.*, Sept.-Oct. 1985, *44*(9–10), pp. 519–44.

Christiansen, Vidar. The Choice of Excise Taxes When Savings and Labour Decisions Are Distorted. *J. Public Econ.*, October 1985, *28*(1), pp. 95–110.

Clark, Simon J. The Effects of Government Expenditure on the Term Structure of Interest Rates: A Comment. *J. Money, Credit, Banking*, August 1985, *17*(3), pp. 397–400.

Conrad, Robert F. and Gillis, Malcolm. Progress and Poverty in Developing Countries: Rents and Resource Taxation. In *Lewis, S. R., Jr., ed.*, 1985, pp. 25–47.

Constantinides, George M. Debt and Taxes and Uncertainty: Discussion. *J. Finance*, July 1985, *40*(3), pp. 657–58.

Cordes, Joseph J. and Galper, Harvey. Tax Shelter Activity: Lessons from Twenty Years of Evidence. *Nat. Tax J.*, September 1985, *38*(3), pp. 305–24. [G: U.S.]

Cornes, Richard and Sandler, Todd. Externalities, Expectations, and Pigouvian Taxes. *J. Environ. Econ. Manage.*, March 1985, *12*(1), pp. 1–13.

Cornes, Richard and Sandler, Todd. On the Consistency of Conjectures with Public Goods. *J. Public Econ.*, June 1985, *27*(1), pp. 125–29.

Cornes, Richard and Sandler, Todd. The Simple Analytics of Pure Public Good Provision. *Economica*, February 1985, *52*(205), pp. 103–16.

Cowell, Frank A. Public Policy and Tax Evasion: Some Problems. In *Gaertner, W. and Wenig, A., eds.*, 1985, pp. 273–84.

Cowell, Frank A. Tax Evasion with Labour Income. *J. Public Econ.*, February 1985, *26*(1), pp. 19–34.

Cowell, Frank A. The Economic Analysis of Tax Evasion. *Bull. Econ. Res.*, September 1985, *37*(3), pp. 163–93.

Cowen, Tyler. Public Goods Definitions and Their Institutional Context: A Critique of Public Goods Theory. *Rev. Soc. Econ.*, April 1985, *43*(1), pp. 53–63.

Cox, W. Michael. Inflation and Permanent Government Debt. *Fed. Res. Bank Dallas Econ. Rev.*, May 1985, pp. 13–26. [G: U.S.]

Creedy, John and Gemmell, Norman. The Indexation of Taxes and Transfers in Britain. *Manchester Sch. Econ. Soc. Stud.*, December 1985, *53*(4), pp. 364–84. [G: U.K.]

Cremer, Helmuth; de Kerchove, Anne-Marie and Thisse, Jacques-François. An Economic Theory of Public Facilities in Space. *Math. Soc. Sci.*, June 1985, *9*(3), pp. 249–62.

Crémer, Jacques and Riordan, Michael H. A Sequential Solution to the Public Goods Problem. *Econometrica*, January 1985, *53*(1), pp. 77–84.

Crocker, Keith J. and Snow, Arthur. A Simple Tax Structure for Competitive Equilibrium and Redistribution in Insurance Markets with Asymmetric Information. *Southern Econ. J.*, April 1985, *51*(4), pp. 1142–50.

Cuddington, John T.; Johansson, Per-Olov and Ohlsson, Henry. Optimal Policy Rules and Regime Switching in Disequilibrium Models. *J. Public Econ.*, July 1985, *27*(2), pp. 247–54.

Currie, David. Macroeconomic Policy Design and Control Theory—A Failed Partnership? *Econ. J.*, June 1985, *95*(378), pp. 285–306. [G: U.K.]

Danthine, Jean-Pierre and Donaldson, John B. A Note on the Effects of Capital Income Taxation on the Dynamics of a Competitive Economy. *J. Public Econ.*, November 1985, *28*(2), pp. 255–65.

Darrat, Ali F. Does Anticipated Fiscal Policy Matter? The Italian Evidence. *Public Finance Quart.*, July 1985, *13*(3), pp. 339–52. [G: Italy]

Darrat, Ali F. The Impact of Fiscal Policy under Rational Expectations: Some Tests. *J. Macroecon.*, Fall 1985, *7*(4), pp. 553–65. [G: Canada]

Davidson, Carl and Martin, Lawrence W. General Equilibrium Tax Incidence under Imperfect Competition: A Quantity-setting Supergame Analysis. *J. Polit. Econ.*, December 1985, *93*(6), pp. 1212–23.

Davis, Evan H. and Kay, John A. Extending the VAT Base: Problems and Possibilities. *Fisc. Stud.*, February 1985, *6*(1), pp. 1–16. [G: U.K.]

Davis, Richard G. Policies to Overcome Stagflation: Comments. In *Ando, A., et al., eds.*, 1985, pp. 295–98. [G: U.S.]

De Gijsel, Peter. A Microeconomic Analysis of Black Labour Demand and Supply. In *Gaertner, W. and Wenig, A., eds.*, 1985, pp. 218–26.

Denzau, Arthur T. and Mackay, Robert J. Tax Systems and Tax Shares. *Public Choice*, 1985, *45*(1), pp. 35–47.

Diewert, W. E. The Measurement of Waste and Welfare in Applied General Equilibrium Models. In *Piggott, J. and Whalley, J., eds.*, 1985, pp. 42–103.

DiLorenzo, Thomas J. The Rhetoric and Reality of Tax Reform [Normative and Positive Foundations of Tax Reform]. *Cato J.*, Fall 1985, *5*(2), pp. 401–06.

Dixit, Avinash K. Tax Policy in Open Economies. In *Auerbach, A. J. and Feldstein, M., eds.*, 1985, pp. 313–74.

Dobbs, Ian M. Shadow Prices, Consistency and the Value of Life. *J. Public Econ.*, July 1985, *27*(2), pp. 177–93.

Dotsey, Michael. Controversy over the Federal Budget Deficit: A Theoretical Perspective. *Fed. Res. Bank Richmond Econ. Rev.*, Sept./Oct. 1985, *71*(5), pp. 3–16.

Dotsey, Michael. The Use of Electronic Funds Transfers to Capture the Effects of Cash Management Practices on the Demand for Demand Deposits: A Note. *J. Finance,* December 1985, *40*(5), pp. 1493–1503. [G: U.S.]

Dragun, Andrew K. Property Rights and Pigovian Taxes. *J. Econ. Issues,* March 1985, *19*(1), pp. 111–22.

Drèze, Jacques H. Second-best Analysis with Markets in Disequilibrium: Public Sector Pricing in a Keynesian Regime. *Europ. Econ. Rev.,* December 1985, *29*(3), pp. 263–301.

Dwyer, Gerald P., Jr. Federal Deficits, Interest Rates, and Monetary Policy. *J. Money, Credit, Banking,* Pt. 2, Nov. 1985, *17*(4), pp. 655–81. [G: U.S.]

Easley, David; Kiefer, Nicholas M. and Possen, Uri. An Equilibrium Analysis of Optimal Unemployment Insurance and Taxation. *Quart. J. Econ.,* Supp. 1985, *100*, pp. 989–1010.

Eckart, Wolfgang and Schulz, Norbert. Distributional Equity and Two-part Tariffs. *Z. ges. Staatswiss. (JITE),* June 1985, *141*(2), pp. 301–11.

Eden, Benjamin. Indexation and Related Issues: A Review Essay. *J. Monet. Econ.,* September 1985, *16*(2), pp. 259–66.

Edwards, J. S. S. and Keen, M. J. Taxes, Investment and *Q. Rev. Econ. Stud.,* October 1985, *52*(4), pp. 665–79.

Englund, Peter. Taxation of Capital Gains on Owner-occupied Homes: Accrual vs Realization. *Europ. Econ. Rev.,* April 1985, *27*(3), pp. 311–34.

Feldstein, Martin. Debt and Taxes in the Theory of Public Finance. *J. Public Econ.,* November 1985, *28*(2), pp. 233–45.

Fernández-Diaz, Andrés. Consequences of Budgetary Restraint for Social Policy. In *Terny, G. and Culyer, A. J., eds.,* 1985, pp. 171–82.

Fløystad, Gunnar. On Tariffs and Optimal Taxation Policy in Developing Countries. *Pakistan Devel. Rev.,* Autumn-Winter 1985, *24*(3/4), pp. 443–50. [G: LDCs]

Fox, Lawrence A. Canada/U.S. Tax Relations: Issues and Perspectives: Comments. In *Fretz, D.; Stern, R. and Whalley, J., eds.,* 1985, pp. 426–33. [G: Canada; U.S.]

Frankel, Jeffrey A. Portfolio Crowding-out, Empirically Estimated. *Quart. J. Econ.,* Supp. 1985, *100*, pp. 1041–65. [G: U.S.]

Fraser, R. W. Commodity Taxes under Uncertainty. *J. Public Econ.,* October 1985, *28*(1), pp. 127–34.

Fraser, R. W. Severance Taxes, Uncertainty, and Natural Resources: The Effect of Investment of the Choice of Tax Base. *Public Finance,* 1985, *40*(2), pp. 172–81.

Frenkel, Jacob A. Fiscal Policy and the Exchange Rate in the Big Seven: Transmission of U.S. Government Spending Shocks: Comment. *Europ. Econ. Rev.,* June-July 1985, *28*(1–2), pp. 43–47. [G: OECD; U.S.]

Frenkel, Jacob A. and Razin, Assaf. Fiscal Expenditures and International Economic Interdependence. In *Buiter, W. H. and Marston,*

R. C., eds., 1985, pp. 37–73.

Frenkel, Jacob A. and Razin, Assaf. Government Spending, Debt, and International Economic Interdependence. *Econ. J.,* September 1985, *95*(379), pp. 619–36.

Froomkin, Joseph. Can Government Finance Play a Central Role in Economic Development? Review Article. *Econ. Develop. Cult. Change,* July 1985, *33*(4), pp. 879–86. [G: LDCs]

Fullerton, Don; Lyon, Andrew B. and Rosen, Richard J. Uncertainty, Welfare Cost and the "Adaptability" of U.S. Corporate Taxes. In *Førsund, F. R. and Honkapohja, S., eds.,* 1985, pp. 131–45. [G: U.S.]

Gahvari, Firouz. A Note on Inflation, Taxation, and Interest Rates [The Financial and Tax Effects of Monetary Policy on Interest Rates]. *Southern Econ. J.,* January 1985, *51*(3), pp. 874–79.

Gahvari, Firouz. Taxation of Housing, Capital Accumulation, and Welfare: A Study in Dynamic Tax Reform. *Public Finance Quart.,* April 1985, *13*(2), pp. 132–60. [G: U.S.]

Galli, Giampaolo. International Coordination in the Design of Macroeconomic Policies: Comment. *Europ. Econ. Rev.,* June-July 1985, *28*(1–2), pp. 83–87. [G: OECD]

Gamponia, Villamor and Mendelsohn, Robert. The Taxation of Exhaustible Resources. *Quart. J. Econ.,* February 1985, *100*(1), pp. 165–81. [G: U.S.]

Gazioğlu, Şaziye. Treasury Bill Financing and the Government Budget Constraint. *Public Finance,* 1985, *40*(2), pp. 182–89.

Genovese, Frank C. Land Value Taxation in Developing Countries: The Case of Jamaica: Comments. In *Lewis, S. R., Jr., ed.,* 1985, pp. 79–81. [G: Jamaica]

Giavazzi, Francesco and Sheen, Jeffrey. Fiscal Policy and the Real Exchange Rate. In *Currie, D., ed.,* 1985, pp. 41–58.

Glazer, Amihai. Using Corrective Taxes to Remedy Consumer Misperceptions. *J. Public Econ.,* October 1985, *28*(1), pp. 85–94.

Goodman, John C. and Porter, Philip K. Majority Voting and Pareto Optimality. *Public Choice,* 1985, *46*(2), pp. 173–86.

Gordon, Roger H. Taxation of Corporate Capital Income: Tax Revenues versus Tax Distortions. *Quart. J. Econ.,* February 1985, *100*(1), pp. 1–27.

Gottlieb, Daniel. Tax Evasion and the Prisoner's Dilemma. *Math. Soc. Sci.,* August 1985, *10*(1), pp. 81–89.

Gramlich, Edward M. Government Services. In *Inman, R. P., ed.,* 1985, pp. 273–89. [G: U.S.]

Greenwood, Jeremy and Kimbrough, Kent P. Capital Controls and Fiscal Policy in the World Economy. *Can. J. Econ.,* November 1985, *18*(4), pp. 743–65.

Grewal, Bhajan and Mathews, Russell L. Federalism, Locational Surplus and the Redistributive Role of Subnational Governments. In

Terny, G. and Culyer, A. J., eds., 1985, pp. 355–70.

Grieson, Ronald E. and Musgrave, Richard A. Wealth Utility and Tax Neutrality. *Public Finance*, 1985, *40*(2), pp. 168–17.

Grinols, Earl L. Public Investment and Social Risk-sharing. *Europ. Econ. Rev.*, December 1985, *29*(3), pp. 303–21.

Guiso, Luigi. Crowding-out and Rational Expectations. *Giorn. Econ.*, May-June 1985, *44*(5–6), pp. 239–57.

Halperin, Robert and Tzur, Joseph. The Effects of Nontaxable Employee Benefits on Employer Profits and Employee Work Effort. *Nat. Tax J.*, March 1985, *38*(1), pp. 65–79.

Hamilton, Bob and Whalley, John. Tax Treatment of Housing in a Dynamic Sequenced General Equilibrium Model. *J. Public Econ.*, July 1985, *27*(2), pp. 157–75. [G: Canada]

Hansen, Jørgen Drud. Statsgaeld og økonomisk politik. (Public Deficits and the Targets of Economic Policy. With English summary.) *Nationaløkon. Tidsskr.*, 1985, *123*(1), pp. 32–49.

Hansson, Ingemar. Marginal Cost of Public Funds for Different Tax Instruments and Government Expenditures. In *Førsund, F. R. and Honkapohja, S., eds.*, 1985, pp. 17–32.
[G: Sweden]

Hansson, Ingemar. Tax Evasion and Government Policy. In *Gaertner, W. and Wenig, A., eds.*, 1985, pp. 285–300.

Hansson, Ingemar and Stuart, Charles. Progressive Taxation as Social Insurance and as a Median-Voter Outcome: An Empirical Assessment. *Scand. J. Econ.*, 1985, *87*(3), pp. 487–99. [G: Sweden]

Hansson, Ingemar and Stuart, Charles. Tax Revenue and the Marginal Cost of Public Funds in Sweden. *J. Public Econ.*, August 1985, *27*(3), pp. 331–53. [G: Sweden]

Hartman, David G. The Economics of Incremental Incentive Programs: The Example of Employment Subsidies. *Public Finance Quart.*, October 1985, *13*(4), pp. 375–95.

Hausman, Jerry A. Taxes and Labor Supply. In *Auerbach, A. J. and Feldstein, M., eds.*, 1985, pp. 213–63. [G: U.S.]

Head, John G. and Brennan, Geoffrey. Free Provision, Tax Limits and Fiscal Reform. In *[Recktenwald, H. C.]*, 1985, pp. 193–207.

Heady, Christopher J. and Mitra, Pradeep K. A Computational Approach to Optimum Public Policies. In *Manne, A. S., ed.*, 1985, pp. 95–120.

Heaps, Terry. The Taxation of Nonreplenishable Natural Resources Revisited. *J. Environ. Econ. Manage.*, March 1985, *12*(1), pp. 14–27.

Heaps, Terry and Helliwell, John F. The Taxation of Natural Resources. In *Auerbach, A. J. and Feldstein, M., eds.*, 1985, pp. 421–72.

Henderson, J. Vernon. Property Tax Incidence with a Public Sector. *J. Polit. Econ.*, August 1985, *93*(4), pp. 648–65.

Henderson, J. Vernon. The Tiebout Model: Bring Back the Entrepreneurs. *J. Polit. Econ.*, April 1985, *93*(2), pp. 248–64.

Hettich, Walter and Winer, Stanley. Blueprints and Pathways: The Shifting Foundations of Tax Reform. *Nat. Tax J.*, December 1985, *38*(4), pp. 423–45. [G: U.S.; Canada]

Hillier, Brian. Rational Expectations, the Government Budget Constraint, and the Optimal Money Supply. *J. Macroecon.*, Winter 1985, *7*(1), pp. 39–50.

Holcombe, Randall G. and Caudill, Steven B. Tax Shares and Government Spending in a Median Voter Model. *Public Choice*, 1985, *46*(2), pp. 197–205.

Holland, Daniel M. Land Value Taxation in Developing Countries: The Case of Jamaica. In *Lewis, S. R., Jr., ed.*, 1985, pp. 53–78.
[G: Jamaica]

Honkapohja, Seppo and Kanniainen, Vesa. Adjustment Costs, Optimal Capacity Utilization, and the Corporation Tax. *Oxford Econ. Pap.*, September 1985, *37*(3), pp. 486–99.

Hubbard, R. Glenn. Social Security, Liquidity Constraints, and Pre-retirement Consumption. *Southern Econ. J.*, October 1985, *52*(2), pp. 471–83.

Ihori, Toshihiro and Kurosaka, Yoshio. Fiscal Policies, Government's Deficits and Capital Formation. *Econ. Stud. Quart.*, August 1985, *36*(2), pp. 106–20.

Imam, M. Hasan and Whalley, John. Incidence Analysis of a Sector-specific Minimum Wage in a Two-Sector Harris–Todaro Model. *Quart. J. Econ.*, February 1985, *100*(1), pp. 207–24.
[G: Mexico]

Inman, Robert P. Government Services: Comment. In *Inman, R. P., ed.*, 1985, pp. 290–94. [G: U.S.]

Ippolito, Richard A. Income Tax Policy and Lifetime Labor Supply. *J. Public Econ.*, April 1985, *26*(3), pp. 327–47. [G: U.S.]

Isaac, R. Mark; McCue, Kenneth F. and Plott, Charles R. Public Goods Provision in an Experimental Environment. *J. Public Econ.*, February 1985, *26*(1), pp. 51–74.

Isachsen, Arne Jon; Samuelson, Sven Ove and Strøm, Steinar. The Behavior of Tax Evaders. In *Gaertner, W. and Wenig, A., eds.*, 1985, pp. 227–44. [G: Norway]

Jha, L. K. Supply-Side Economics. In *Jha, L. K.*, 1985, pp. 130–39.

Jones-Hendrickson, S. B. Rational Expectations, Causality and Integrative Fiscal–Monetary Policy in the Caribbean. *Soc. Econ. Stud.*, December 1985, *34*(4), pp. 111–38.
[G: Caribbean]

Jorgenson, Dale W. and Slesnick, Daniel T. General Equilibrium Analysis of Economic Policy. In *Piggott, J. and Whalley, J., eds.*, 1985, pp. 293–370. [G: U.S.]

Judd, Kenneth L. Redistributive Taxation in a Simple Perfect Foresight Model. *J. Public Econ.*, October 1985, *28*(1), pp. 59–83.

Judd, Kenneth L. Short-run Analysis of Fiscal Policy in a Simple Perfect Foresight Model. *J. Polit. Econ.*, April 1985, *93*(2), pp. 298–319.

Karlsson, Erik L. "Reaganomics" and Credibility:

Comments. In *Ando, A., et al., eds.*, 1985, pp. 299–301. **[G: Sweden]**

Karwani, Nanak. Applications of Concentration Curves to Optimal Negative Income Taxation. *J. Quant. Econ.*, July 1985, *1*(2), pp. 165–86.

Katz, Avery and Mankiw, N. Gregory. How Should Fringe Benefits Be Taxed? *Nat. Tax J.*, March 1985, *38*(1), pp. 37–46. **[G: U.S.]**

Katz, Michael L. and Rosen, Harvey S. Tax Analysis in an Oligopoly Model. *Public Finance Quart.*, January 1985, *13*(1), pp. 3–19.

Kayaalp, Orhan. Public-Choice Elements of the Italian Theory of Public Goods. *Public Finance*, 1985, *40*(3), pp. 395–410. **[G: Italy]**

Keenan, Donald C. and Rubin, Paul H. The Limits of the Equity–Efficiency Tradeoff. *Public Choice*, 1985, *47*(3), pp. 425–36.

Kehoe, Timothy J. The Comparative Statics Properties of Tax Models. *Can. J. Econ.*, May 1985, *18*(2), pp. 314–34.

Khan, M. Ali and Vohra, Rajiv. On the Existence of Lindahl Equilibria in Economies with a Measure Space of Non-transitive Consumers. *J. Econ. Theory*, August 1985, *36*(2), pp. 319–32.

Khan, Mohsin S. On Tariffs and Optimal Taxation Policy in Developing Countries: Comments. *Pakistan Devel. Rev.*, Autumn-Winter 1985, *24*(3/4), pp. 451–52. **[G: LDCs]**

Kiesling, Herbert J. Violations of Scientific Impartiality in Tax Analysis. *Public Finance*, 1985, *40*(2), pp. 157–67.

Killingsworth, Mark R. Substitution and Output Effects on Labor Demand: Theory and Policy Applications. *J. Human Res.*, Winter 1985, *20*(1), pp. 142–52. **[G: U.S.]**

Kimbrough, Kent P. An Examination of the Effects of Government Purchases in an Open Economy. *J. Int. Money Finance*, March 1985, *4*(1), pp. 113–33.

Koenig, Evan F. Indirect Methods for Regulating Externalities under Uncertainty. *Quart. J. Econ.*, May 1985, *100*(2), pp. 479–93.

Kohn, Robert E. and Aucamp, Donald C. Lower Level Inefficiencies as Second Best Correctives. *Public Finance*, 1985, *40*(2), pp. 220–29. **[G: U.S.]**

Kollintzas, Tryphon and Rowley, J. C. Robin. Nonstatic Expectations, Nonexponential Decay, and the Post Tax Rental Cost of Capital. *Public Finance*, 1985, *40*(3), pp. 411–40.

Kollintzas, Tryphon and Thorn, Richard S. The Generalized User Cost of Capital. *Public Finance Quart.*, October 1985, *13*(4), pp. 355–74.

Kouri, Pentti. Anticipations, Recessions and Policy; An Intertemporal Disequilibrium Model: Comments. In *Melitz, J. and Wyplosz, C., eds.*, 1985, pp. 147–48.

Krzyzaniak, Marian. The Dynamic Incidence of the Long-term Government Debt in a Neoclassical World. *Public Finance*, 1985, *40*(3), pp. 307–34.

Laffont, Jean-Jacques. Incitations dans les procédures de planification. (Incentives in Planning Procedures. With English summary.) *Ann.*

INSEE, Apr.-June 1985, (58), pp. 3–37.

Lal, Deepak and van Wijnbergen, Sweder. Government Deficits, the Real Interest Rate and LDC Debt: On Global Crowding Out. *Europ. Econ. Rev.*, November 1985, *29*(2), pp. 157–91. **[G: Global]**

Lambert, Peter J. On the Redistributive Effect of Taxes and Benefits. *Scot. J. Polit. Econ.*, February 1985, *32*(1), pp. 39–54. **[G: U.K.; U.S.]**

Lavoie, Marc. The Post Keynesian Theory of Endogenous Money: A Reply [The Endogenous Flow of Credit and the Post Keynesian Theory of Money]. *J. Econ. Issues*, September 1985, *19*(3), pp. 843–48.

Le Grand, Julian. On Measuring the Distributional Impact of Public Expenditure. In *Terny, G. and Culyer, A. J., eds.*, 1985, pp. 197–208.

Le Pen, Claude. Emplois publics et distribution des revenus. (Public Employment and Distribution of Income. With English summary.) *Revue Écon.*, July 1985, *36*(4), pp. 715–39. **[G: France]**

Lee, Dwight R. Rent-seeking and Its Implications for Pollution Taxation. *Southern Econ. J.*, January 1985, *51*(3), pp. 731–44.

de Leeuw, Frank and Holloway, Thomas M. The Measurement and Significance of the Cyclically Adjusted Federal Budget and Debt. *J. Money, Credit, Banking*, May 1985, *17*(2), pp. 232–42. **[G: U.S.]**

Lehment, Harmen. Crowding-out in der Bundesrepublik: Wechselkurseffekte, Zinseffekte und empirischer Befund. (Crowding-out in the Federal Republic of Germany: Exchange Rate Effects, Interest Effects, and Empirical Findings. With English summary.) *Aussenwirtschaft*, May 1985, *40*(1/2), pp. 53–70. **[G: W. Germany]**

Levin, Dan. Taxation within Cournot Oligopoly. *J. Public Econ.*, August 1985, *27*(3), pp. 281–90.

Lewis, Stephen R., Jr. Progress and Poverty in Developing Countries: Rents and Resource Taxation: Comments. In *Lewis, S. R., Jr., ed.*, 1985, pp. 49–51.

Lindbeck, Assar. Redistribution Policy and the Expansion of the Public Sector. *J. Public Econ.*, December 1985, *28*(3), pp. 309–28.

Liu, Pak-Wai. Lorenz Domination and Global Tax Progressivity. *Can. J. Econ.*, May 1985, *18*(2), pp. 395–99.

Manning, Richard; Markusen, James R. and McMillan, John. Paying for Public Inputs. *Amer. Econ. Rev.*, March 1985, *75*(1), pp. 235–38.

Marfán, Manuel. El conflicto entre la recaudación de impuestos y la inversión privada: elementos teóricos para una reforma tributaria. (The Trade-off between Tax Revenues and Private Investment: Theoretical Elements for a Tax Reform. With English summary.) *Colección Estud. CIEPLAN*, 1985, (18), pp. 63–93.

Marini, Giancarlo. Built-in Flexibility of Taxation, Public Spending Rules and Stabilisation Policy. *Econ. Notes*, 1985, (2), pp. 5–21.

Marston, Richard C. and Turnovsky, Stephen J. Macroeconomic Stabilization through Taxation and Indexation: The Use of Firm-Specific Information. *J. Monet. Econ.*, November 1985, *16*(3), pp. 375–95.

Martinich, Joseph S. and Hurter, Arthur P., Jr. Price Uncertainty, Factor Substitution, and the Locational Bias of Business Taxes. *J. Reg. Sci.*, May 1985, *25*(2), pp. 175–90.

Maskin, Eric S. and Riley, John G. Input versus Output Incentive Schemes. *J. Public Econ.*, October 1985, *28*(1), pp. 1–23.

Masson, P. R. The Sustainability of Fiscal Deficits. *Int. Monet. Fund Staff Pap.*, December 1985, *32*(4), pp. 577–605.

Masson, Paul and Blundell-Wignall, Adrian. Fiscal Policy and the Exchange Rate in the Big Seven: Transmission of U.S. Government Spending Shocks. *Europ. Econ. Rev.*, June–July 1985, *28*(1–2), pp. 11–42. **[G: OECD; U.S.]**

Maussner, Alfred. Ineffektivität der Wirtschaftspolitik bei "rationalen Erwartungen"? Ein Kommentar mit anderen Argumenten für eine unzureichend begründete These. (Ineffectiveness of Economic Policy under "Rational Expectations"? A Commentary with Different Arguments for an Insufficient Founded Thesis. With English summary.) *Kredit Kapital*, 1985, *18*(2), pp. 217–29.

McGuire, Martin C. and Groth, Carl H., Jr. A Method for Identifying the Public Good Allocation Process within a Group. *Quart. J. Econ.*, Supp. 1985, *100*, pp. 915–34.

McMillan, W. Douglas. Money, Government Debt, q, and Investment. *J. Macroecon.*, Winter 1985, *7*(1), pp. 19–37.

Meltzer, Allan H. and Richard, Scott F. A Positive Theory of In-Kind Transfers and the Negative Income Tax. *Public Choice*, 1985, *47*(1), pp. 231–65.

Mieszkowski, Peter and Zodrow, George R. The Incidence of a Partial State Corporate Income Tax. *Nat. Tax J.*, December 1985, *38*(4), pp. 489–96. **[G: U.S.]**

Miller, Edward McCarthy. Keynesian Economics as a Translation Error: An Essay on Keynes' Financial Theory. *Hist. Polit. Econ.*, Summer 1985, *17*(2), pp. 265–85.

Mincer, Jacob. The Effect of Immigrants on Natives' Incomes through the Use of Capital: Discussion. *J. Devel. Econ.*, January–February 1985, *17*(1–2), pp. 95–97. **[G: U.S.]**

Mirman, Leonard J. and Spulber, Daniel F. Fishery Regulation with Harvest Uncertainty. *Int. Econ. Rev.*, October 1985, *26*(3), pp. 731–46.

Modigliani, Franco; Jappelli, Tullio and Pagona, Marco. The Impact of Fiscal Policy and Inflation on National Saving: The Italian Case. *Banca Naz. Lavoro Quart. Rev.*, June 1985, (153), pp. 91–126. **[G: Italy]**

Moore, Michael J. Demand Management with Rationing. *Econ. J.*, March 1985, *95*(377), pp. 73–86.

Morey, Edward R. Characteristics, Consumer Surplus, and New Activities: A Proposed Ski Area. *J. Public Econ.*, March 1985, *26*(2), pp. 221–36. **[G: U.S.]**

Mückl, Wolfgang J. Langfristige Grenzen der öffentlichen Kreditaufnahme. (Long-run Limits to Public Borrowing. With English summary.) *Jahr. Nationalökon. Statist.*, November 1985, *200*(6), pp. 565–81.

Musgrave, Richard A. Death and Taxes. In *[Recktenwald, H. C.]*, 1985, pp. 149–55.

Musgrave, Richard A. Excess Bias and the Nature of Budget Growth. *J. Public Econ.*, December 1985, *28*(3), pp. 287–308.

Musgrave, Richard A. Public Finance and Distributive Justice. In *[Peacock, A.]*, 1985, pp. 1–14.

Naqib, Fadle and Stollery, Kenneth R. The Effects of Alternative Public Pension Financing on Capital Formation: Consumption versus Payroll Taxes. *Economica*, May 1985, *52*(206), pp. 257–61.

Negishi, Takashi. Advertising and the Social Imbalance between Private and Public Goods. *Rivista Int. Sci. Econ. Com.*, January 1985, *32*(1), pp. 64–70.

Nellor, David C. L. Tax Policy, Regulated Interest Rates, and Saving. *World Devel.*, June 1985, *13*(6), pp. 725–36. **[G: LDCs]**

Nellor, David C. L. Taxpayer Anticipation, Changing Tax Rates, and the Choice of Tax Base. *Public Finance*, 1985, *40*(2), pp. 247–62. **[G: U.S.]**

Nguyen, Duc-Tho. Money Financing and the Dynamic Effects of Fiscal and Monetary Policies in a Theoretical Simulation Model. *Manchester Sch. Econ. Soc. Stud.*, December 1985, *53*(4), pp. 432–56.

Nordhaus, William. International Coordination in the Design of Macroeconomic Policies: Comment. *Europ. Econ. Rev.*, June–July 1985, *28*(1–2), pp. 89–92. **[G: OECD]**

Osband, Kent and Reichelstein, Stefan. Information-eliciting Compensation Schemes. *J. Public Econ.*, June 1985, *27*(1), pp. 107–15.

Ostry, Sylvia. Policies to Overcome Stagflation: Comments. In *Ando, A., et al., eds.*, 1985, pp. 291–94. **[G: U.S.]**

Otani, Kiyoshi. Effects of Fiscal Policy on Consumption in a Neoclassical Intertemporal Optimization Model. *Econ. Stud. Quart.*, December 1985, *36*(3), pp. 193–208.

Paladini, Ruggero. Il ruolo dell'imposta ordinaria sul patrimonio nell'imposizione diretta: una rassegna critica. (The Role of the Ordinary Wealth Tax: A Survey. With English summary.) *Polit. Econ.*, December 1985, *1*(3), pp. 341–97.

Pallada, Fred W. M. The Terms of Trade between the Public and Private Sector. *De Economist*, 1985, *133*(2), pp. 176–98. **[G: Netherlands]**

Parguez, Alain. La monnaie, les déficits et la crise: dans le circuit dynamique l'effet d'éviction est un mythe. (Money, Deficits and Crisis: In the Dynamic Circuit of Money, Crowding-out Effects Are Just a Myth. With English summary.) *Écon. Soc.*, August 1985, *19*(8), pp. 229–51.

Peled, Dan. Stochastic Inflation and Government Provision of Indexed Bonds. *J. Monet. Econ.*, May 1985, *15*(3), pp. 291–308.

Persson, Mats and Wissén, Pehr. Redistributional Aspects of Tax Evasion. In *Førsund, F. R. and Honkapohja, S., eds.*, 1985, pp. 33–51.

Persson, Torsten. Deficits and Intergenerational Welfare in Open Economies. *J. Int. Econ.*, August 1985, *19*(1/2), pp. 67–84.

Peters, Wolfgang. Can Inefficient Public Production Promote Welfare? *Z. Nationalökon.*, 1985, *45*(4), pp. 395–407.

Pines, David; Sadka, Efraim and Sheshinski, Eytan. The Normative and Positive Aspects of the Taxation of Imputed Rent on Owner-occupied Housing. *J. Public Econ.*, June 1985, *27*(1), pp. 1–23.

Pissarides, Christopher A. Taxes, Subsidies, and Equilibrium Unemployment. *Rev. Econ. Stud.*, January 1985, *52*(1), pp. 121–33.

Pohjola, Matti. Built-in Flexibility of Progressive Taxation and the Dynamics of Income: Stability, Cycles, or Chaos? *Public Finance*, 1985, *40*(2), pp. 263–73.

Prest, Alan R. Implicit Taxes. In *[Recktenwald, H. C.]*, 1985, pp. 157–70.

Purvis, Douglas D. Public Sector Deficits, International Capital Movements, and the Domestic Economy: The Medium-term Is the Message. *Can. J. Econ.*, November 1985, *18*(4), pp. 723–42.

Rankin, Neil. Debt Neutrality in Disequilibrium. In *Currie, D., ed.*, 1985, pp. 17–40.

Rau, Nicholas. Simplifying the Theory of the Government Budget Restraint. *Oxford Econ. Pap.*, June 1985, *37*(2), pp. 210–29.

Reece, William S. and Zieschang, Kimberly D. Consistent Estimation of the Impact of Tax Deductibility on the Level of Charitable Contributions. *Econometrica*, March 1985, *53*(2), pp. 271–93. **[G: U.S.]**

Reid, Bradford G. Government Debt, National Income and Causality. *Appl. Econ.*, April 1985, *17*(2), pp. 321–30. **[G: U.S.]**

Reinganum, Jennifer F. and Wilde, Louis L. Income Tax Compliance in a Principal–Agent Framework. *J. Public Econ.*, February 1985, *26*(1), pp. 1–18.

Rhodes, George F., Jr. and Sampath, Rajan K. On Optimal Investment in and Pricing of Public Intermediate Goods. *Atlantic Econ. J.*, December 1985, *13*(4), pp. 63–67.

Riew, John. Equal Sacrifice Principle and Intertemporal Equity. *Public Finance*, 1985, *40*(2), pp. 274–79.

Roberts, Russell D. A Taxonomy of Public Provision: Reply. *Public Choice*, 1985, *47*(1), pp. 311–12.

Roberts, Russell D. A Taxonomy of Public Provision. *Public Choice*, 1985, *47*(1), pp. 267–303.

Roberts, Russell D. Recipient Preferences and the Design of Government Transfer Programs. *J. Law Econ.*, April 1985, *28*(1), pp. 27–54. **[G: U.S.]**

Robinson, P. William. Capacity Constraints, Real Wages and the Role of the Public Sector in Creating Jobs. *Fisc. Stud.*, May 1985, *6*(2), pp. 40–50. **[G: U.K.]**

Rochet, Jean-Charles. The Taxation Principle and Multi-time Hamilton–Jacobi Equations. *J. Math. Econ.*, 1985, *14*(2), pp. 113–28.

Röell, Ailsa A. A Note on the Marginal Tax Rate in a Finite Economy. *J. Public Econ.*, November 1985, *28*(2), pp. 267–72.

Rosen, Harvey S. Housing Subsidies: Effects on Housing Decisions, Efficiency, and Equity. In *Auerbach, A. J. and Feldstein, M., eds.*, 1985, pp. 375–420. **[G: OECD]**

Roskamp, Karl W. and Scafuri, Allen J. Distributional Constraints on Optimal Commodity Taxes. In *[Recktenwald, H. C.]*, 1985, pp. 171–75.

Ross, Stephen A. Debt and Taxes and Uncertainty. *J. Finance*, July 1985, *40*(3), pp. 637–57.

Sah, Raaj Kumar and Stiglitz, Joseph E. The Social Cost of Labor and Project Evaluation: A General Approach. *J. Public Econ.*, November 1985, *28*(2), pp. 135–63.

Sandmo, Agnar. The Effects of Taxation on Savings and Risk Taking. In *Auerbach, A. J. and Feldstein, M., eds.*, 1985, pp. 265–311.

Sarantis, Nicholas. Fiscal Policies and Consumer Behaviour in Western Europe. *Kyklos*, 1985, *38*(2), pp. 233–48. **[G: W. Europe]**

Sargent, Thomas J. "Reaganomics" and Credibility. In *Ando, A., et al., eds.*, 1985, pp. 235–52. **[G: U.S.]**

Sargent, Thomas J. and Wallace, Neil. Some Unpleasant Monetarist Arithmetic. *Fed. Res. Bank Minn. Rev.*, Winter 1985, *9*(1), pp. 15–31. **[G: U.S.]**

Sato, Ryuzo and Rizzo, John. Measuring the Burden of Property and Income Taxation. In *[Recktenwald, H. C.]*, 1985, pp. 309–17.

Schenone, Osvaldo H. La regla "Gravar en Función Inversa a la Elasticidad" y la tributación optima. (With English summary.) *Cuadernos Econ.*, April 1985, *22*(65), pp. 117–22.

Scherf, Wolfgang. Budgetmultiplikatoren. Eine Analyse der fiskalischen Wirkungen konjunkturbedingter und antizyklischer Defizite. (Budgetary Multiplier Effects of Cyclically Conditioned and Anticyclical Deficits. With English summary.) *Jahr. Nationalökon. Statist.*, July 1985, *200*(4), pp. 349–63. **[G: W. Germany]**

Schoettle, Ferdinand P. A Three-Sector Model for Real Property Tax Incidence. *J. Public Econ.*, August 1985, *27*(3), pp. 355–70. **[G: U.S.]**

Schwab, Robert M. Pay-as-You-Go versus Advance-funded Public Pension Systems under Imperfect Capital Markets. *Public Finance Quart.*, July 1985, *13*(3), pp. 269–91.

Seater, John J. Does Government Debt Matter? A Review. *J. Monet. Econ.*, July 1985, *16*(1), pp. 121–31.

Seley, John E. and Wolpert, Julian. The Savings/Harm Tableau for Social Impact Assessment of Retrenchment Policies. *Econ. Geogr.*, April 1985, *61*(2), pp. 158–71.

Shinkai, Yoichi. Monetary Policy in Our Times:

Summing Up. In *Ando, A., et al., eds.*, 1985, pp. 309–18.

Simon, Julian L. and Heins, A. James. The Effect of Immigrants on Natives' Incomes through the Use of Capital. *J. Devel. Econ.*, January–February 1985, *17*(1–2), pp. 75–93.   [G: U.S.]

Slemrod, Joel B. A General Equilibrium Model of Taxation that Uses Micro-unit Data: With an Application to the Impact of Instituting a Flat-Rate Income Tax. In *Piggott, J. and Whalley, J., eds.*, 1985, pp. 221–52.   [G: U.S.]

Smith, Bruce D. Government Expenditures, Deficits, and Inflation: On the Impossibility of a Balanced Budget. *Quart. J. Econ.*, August 1985, *100*(3), pp. 715–45.

Soldatos, Gerasimos T. The Impact of the Reagan Tax Cuts on the International Economy. *Indian Econ. J.*, Oct.-Nov. 1985, *33*(2), pp. 116–22.

Spulber, Daniel F. Effluent Regulation and Long-run Optimality. *J. Environ. Econ. Manage.*, June 1985, *12*(2), pp. 103–16.

Steindl, Frank G. On Inflation, Income Taxes, Tax Rules, and the Rate of Interest: A General Equilibrium Analysis. *Southern Econ. J.*, January 1985, *51*(3), pp. 868–73.

Steinherr, Alfred. Investment or Employment Subsidies for Rapid Employment Creation in the European Economic Community? In *Weiserbs, D., ed.*, 1985, pp. 145–80.   [G: OECD]

Stiglitz, Joseph E. The General Theory of Tax Avoidance. *Nat. Tax J.*, September 1985, *38*(3), pp. 325–37.   [G: U.S.]

Sugden, Robert. Consistent Conjectures and Voluntary Contributions to Public Goods: Why the Conventional Theory Does Not Work. *J. Public Econ.*, June 1985, *27*(1), pp. 117–24.

Sullivan, Arthur M. The General-Equilibrium Effects of the Residential Property Tax: Incidence and Excess Burden. *J. Urban Econ.*, September 1985, *18*(2), pp. 235–50.

Summers, Lawrence H. The Asset Price Approach to the Analysis of Capital Income Taxation. In *Feiwel, G. R., ed. (I)*, 1985, pp. 429–43.

Suzuki, Yoshio. Monetary Policy in Our Times: Comments. In *Ando, A., et al., eds.*, 1985, pp. 303–06.   [G: OECD]

Swint, J. Michael; Stone, Gerald W., Jr. and Byrns, Ralph T. The Revenue Adequacy of Site Value Taxation in a Ricardian System of Economic Growth. *Amer. J. Econ. Soc.*, January 1985, *44*(1), pp. 107–19.

Tanzi, Vito and Iden, George. The Impact of Taxes on Wages: Reply. *Econ. Notes*, 1985, (2), pp. 175–78.   [G: U.S.]

Tatom, John A. Two Views of the Effects of Government Budget Deficits in the 1980s. *Fed. Res. Bank St. Louis Rev.*, October 1985, *67*(8), pp. 5–16.   [G: U.S.]

Taylor, John B. International Coordination in the Design of Macroeconomic Policy Rules. *Europ. Econ. Rev.*, June-July 1985, *28*(1–2), pp. 53–81.   [G: OECD]

Tobin, James. La teoria macreconomica in discussione. (Macreconomics under Debate. With English summary.) *Bancaria*, January 1985, *41*(1), pp. 13–31.

Tramontana, Antonino. The Wealth Effect of the Public Debt: A Macroeconomic Approach. *Econ. Notes*, 1985, (1), pp. 71–103.

Tridimas, George. Economic Theory and the Allocation of Public Expenditures in Greece. *Greek Econ. Rev.*, April 1985, *7*(1), pp. 34–52.   [G: Greece]

Tsuneki, Atsushi. On the Neutrality of Local Public Bond in a Spatial Economy. *Econ. Stud. Quart.*, April 1985, *36*(1), pp. 46–52.

Tuomala, Matti. Optimal Degree of Progressivity under Income Uncertainty. In *Førsund, F. R. and Honkapohja, S., eds.*, 1985, pp. 86–95.

Tuomala, Matti. Simplified Formulae for Optimal Linear Income Taxation. *Scand. J. Econ.*, 1985, *87*(4), pp. 668–72.

Turnbull, Geoffrey K. On the Interpretation of Reduced Form Public Demand Parameter Estimates. *Nat. Tax J.*, December 1985, *38*(4), pp. 567–69.

Usategui Díaz de Otalora, José M. Congestión desigual y eficiencia. (With English summary.) *Revista Española Econ.*, 1985, *2*(1), pp. 73–87.

Usher, Dan. A Taxonomy of Public Provision: Comment. *Public Choice*, 1985, *47*(1), pp. 305–10.

Vaghari, Jila. Tax Discounting Review of Recent Literature. *Indian Econ. J.*, July-Sept. 1985, *33*(1), pp. 130–39.   [G: U.S.]

Verbon, Harry A. A. On the Independence of Financing Methods and Redistributive Aspects of Pensions Plans. *Public Finance*, 1985, *40*(2), pp. 280–90.

Viñals, José. Gasto público, estructura impositiva y actividad macroeconómica en una economía abierta. (With English summary.) *Revista Española Econ.*, 1985, *2*(1), pp. 113–33.

Vines, David. Fiscal Expenditures and International Economic Interdependence: Comment. In *Buiter, W. H. and Marston, R. C., eds.*, 1985, pp. 75–83.

Visco, Ignazio. Fiscal Policy and the Exchange Rate in the Big Seven: Transmission of U.S. Government Spending Shocks: Comment. *Europ. Econ. Rev.*, June-July 1985, *28*(1–2), pp. 49–52.   [G: OECD; U.S.]

Wagner, Richard E. Normative and Positive Foundations of Tax Reform. *Cato J.*, Fall 1985, *5*(2), pp. 385–99.

Wallace, Myles S. Fiscal Expansion and Falling Interest Rates? Another Case against Crowding Out. *Econ. Notes*, 1985, (1), pp. 162–68.

Warburton, Peter J. Investment or Employment Subsidies for Rapid Employment Creation in the EEC: Comment. In *Weiserbs, D., ed.*, 1985, pp. 181–82.   [G: OECD]

Warr, Peter G. Sub-optimal Saving and the Shadow Price of Labor: The Public Good Argument. *J. Devel. Econ.*, April 1985, *17*(3), pp. 239–57.

Waterson, Michael. On Progressive Taxation and Risk-taking. *Oxford Econ. Pap.*, September 1985, *37*(3), pp. 510–19.

Waud, Roger N. Politics, Deficits, and the Laffer Curve. *Public Choice*, 1985, *47*(3), pp. 509–17.

Weiss, Jeffrey H. Can Donations Reduce a Donor's Welfare? *Public Choice*, 1985, *47*(2), pp. 337–47.

Weymark, John A. Majority-Rule Directions of Income Tax Reform and Second-Best Optimality. In *Førsund, F. R. and Honkapohja, S., eds.*, 1985, pp. 96–115.

Wijkander, Hans. Correcting Externalities through Taxes On/Subsidies to Related Goods. *J. Public Econ.*, October 1985, *28*(1), pp. 111–25.

Wijnbergen, Sweder. Optimal Taxation of Imported Energy under Price Uncertainty. *Oxford Econ. Pap.*, March 1985, *37*(1), pp. 83–92.

van Wijnbergen, Sweder. Taxation of International Capital Flows, the Intertemporal Terms of Trade and the Real Price of Oil. *Oxford Econ. Pap.*, September 1985, *37*(3), pp. 382–90.

Wildasin, David E. On the Analysis of Labor and Capital Income Taxation in a Growing Economy with Government Saving. *Public Finance*, 1985, *40*(1), pp. 114–32.

Wilson, John D. Optimal Property Taxation in the Presence of Interregional Capital Mobility. *J. Urban Econ.*, July 1985, *18*(1), pp. 73–89.

Wiltshaw, Desmond G. Jobs and Local Authority Subsidies. *Urban Stud.*, October 1985, *22*(5), pp. 433–37. [G: U.K.]

Wittman, Donald. Pigovian Taxes Which Work in the Small-Number Case. *J. Environ. Econ. Manage.*, June 1985, *12*(2), pp. 144–54.

Wolfson, Dirk J. Criteria in Engineering Social Justice. In *Terny, G. and Culyer, A. J., eds.*, 1985, pp. 185–96.

Yamada, Masatoshi. More on Production Efficiency in the Optimal Tax Economy. *Econ. Stud. Quart.*, April 1985, *36*(1), pp. 87–90.

Zee, Howell H. An Efficient Method of Calculating the Impact of Finite Tax Changes in an Intertemporal Framework. *Atlantic Econ. J.*, December 1985, *13*(4), pp. 26–33.

Zodrow, George R. Optimal Tax Reform in the Presence of Adjustment Costs. *J. Public Econ.*, July 1985, *27*(2), pp. 211–30.

Zodrow, George R. Partial Tax Reform: An Optimal Taxation Perspective. *Can. J. Econ.*, May 1985, *18*(2), pp. 335–46.

3216 Fiscal Policy

Aaron, Henry J. The United States Federal System: Commentary. In *Quigley, J. M. and Rubinfeld, D. L., eds.*, 1985, pp. 70–74. [G: U.S.]

Aitkin, Don. Taxation and Policy Change: A Median Voter Model for Australia 1968–69 to 1981–82: Comment. *Australian Econ. Rev.*, 3rd Quarter, Spring 1985, (71), pp. 34–35. [G: Australia]

Alhadeff, Peter. Public Finance and the Economy in Argentina, Australia and Canada during the Depression of the 1930s. In *Platt, D. C. M. and di Tella, G., eds.*, 1985, pp. 161–78. [G: Argentina; Australia; Canada]

Allsopp, C. The Assessment: Monetary and Fiscal Policy in the 1980s. *Oxford Rev. Econ. Policy*, Spring 1985, *1*(1), pp. 1–20. [G: U.K.]

Auerbach, Alan J. The Corporation Income Tax. In *Pechman, J. A., ed. (II)*, 1985, pp. 59–86. [G: U.S.]

Barth, James R.; Iden, George and Russek, Frank S. Federal Borrowing and Short Term Interest Rates: Comment. *Southern Econ. J.*, October 1985, *52*(2), pp. 554–59.

Break, George F. The United States Federal System: Commentary. In *Quigley, J. M. and Rubinfeld, D. L., eds.*, 1985, pp. 75–79. [G: U.S.]

Break, George F. The Value-Added Tax. In *Pechman, J. A., ed. (II)*, 1985, pp. 128–57. [G: U.S.]

Brennan, Geoffrey. Taxation and Policy Change: A Median Voter Model for Australia 1968–69 to 1981–82. *Australian Econ. Rev.*, 3rd Quarter, Spring 1985, (71), pp. 20–33. [G: Australia]

Brewer, Thomas L. A Comparative Analysis of the Fiscal Policies of Industrial and Developing Countries—Policy Instability and Governmental-Regime Instability. *J. Compar. Econ.*, June 1985, *9*(2), pp. 191–96.

Budd, Alan P.; Dicks, Geoffrey and Keating, Giles. Government Borrowing and Financial Markets. *Nat. Inst. Econ. Rev.*, August 1985, (113), pp. 89–97. [G: U.K.]

Byatt, Ian. Market and Non-market Alternatives in the Public Supply of Public Services: British Experience with Privatization. In *Forte, F. and Peacock, A., eds.*, 1985, pp. 203–11. [G: U.K.]

Caesar, Rolf. Crowding out in der Bundesrepublik Deutschland: Eine empirische Bestandsaufnahme. (Crowding Out in the Federal Republic of Germany: An Empirical Stock-taking. With English summary.) *Kredit Kapital*, 1985, *18*(2), pp. 265–76. [G: W. Germany]

Chouraqui, Jean-Claude and Montador, B. Fiscal Policy in the Small OECD Countries since the Early Seventies. *Schweiz. Z. Volkswirtsch. Statist.*, September 1985, *121*(3), pp. 259–83. [G: OECD]

Cockle, Paul. Public Expenditure Policy, 1985–86: Overview. In *Cockle, P., ed.*, 1985, pp. 1–33. [G: U.K.]

Cohen, Darrel and Clark, Peter B. Effects of Fiscal Policy on the U.S. Economy: Empirical Estimates of Crowding Out. *J. Policy Modeling*, Winter 1985, *7*(4), pp. 573–93. [G: U.S.]

Danziger, Sheldon and Smolensky, Eugene. Abrupt Changes in Social Policy: The Redistributive Effects of Reagan's Budget and Tax Cuts. In *Terny, G. and Culyer, A. J., eds.*, 1985, pp. 209–23. [G: U.S.]

Faustini, Gino. A Medium-term Perspective for Budget Policy. *Rev. Econ. Cond. Italy*, January–April 1985, (1), pp. 99–118. [G: W. Europe]

Garside, W. R. The Failure of the 'Radical Alternative': Public Works, Deficit Finance and British Interwar Unemployment. *J. Europ. Econ. Hist.*, Sept.-Dec. 1985, *14*(3), pp. 537–55. [G: U.K.]

Gillis, Malcolm. Micro and Macroeconomics of Tax Reform: Indonesia. *J. Devel. Econ.*, December 1985, *19*(3), pp. 221–54. [G: Indonesia]

Graetz, Michael J. The Estate Tax—Whither or Wither? In *Pechman, J. A., ed. (II)*, 1985, pp. 158–83. [G: U.S.]

Haberler, Gottfried. International Issues Raised by Criticisms of the U.S. Budget Deficits. In *Cagan, P. and Somensatto, E., eds.*, 1985, pp. 121–45. [G: U.S.; OECD; LDCs]

Harberger, Arnold C. Tax Policy in a Small, Open, Developing Economy. In *Connolly, M. B. and McDermott, J., eds.*, 1985, pp. 1–11.

Hewson, J. R. and Nevile, J. W. Monetary and Fiscal Policy in Australia. In *Argy, V. E. and Neville, J. W., eds.*, 1985, pp. 305–24. [G: Australia]

Hoelscher, Gregory P. Federal Borrowing and Short Term Interest Rates: Reply. *Southern Econ. J.*, October 1985, *52*(2), pp. 560–61.

Hooper, Peter. International Repercussions of the U.S. Budget Deficit. *Aussenwirtschaft*, May 1985, *40*(1/2), pp. 117–55. [G: U.S.; OECD]

Ingberg, Mikael. Offentliga transfereringar och konjunkturpolitiken. (Public Transfers and Stabilization Policy. With English summary.) *Ekon. Samfundets Tidskr.*, 1985, *38*(2), pp. 97–112. [G: Finland]

Inman, Robert P. Fiscal Allocations in a Federalist Economy: Understanding the "New" Federalism. In *Quigley, J. M. and Rubinfeld, D. L., eds.*, 1985, pp. 3–33. [G: U.S.]

Jacob, Charles E. Reaganomics: The Revolution in American Political Economy. *Law Contemp. Probl.*, Autumn 1985, *48*(4), pp. 7–30. [G: U.S.]

Joines, Douglas H. Deficits and Money Growth in the United States, 1872–1983. *J. Monet. Econ.*, November 1985, *16*(3), pp. 329–51. [G: U.S.]

Jones, Leroy P. Public Enterprise for Whom? Perverse Distributional Consequences of Public Operational Decisions. *Econ. Develop. Cult. Change*, January 1985, *33*(2), pp. 333–47. [G: LDCs]

Keen, Howard, Jr. Summary Measures of Economic Policy and Credit Conditions as Early Warning Forecasting Tools. *Bus. Econ.*, October 1985, *20*(4), pp. 38–43. [G: U.S.]

Lee, Sang Man. The Controllability of the Monetary Base: The Central Bank's Reaction Function in Korea. *J. Econ. Devel.*, December 1985, *10*(2), pp. 171–91. [G: S. Korea]

Lermer, George and Stanbury, W. T. Measuring the Cost of Redistributing Income by Means of Direct Regulation. *Can. J. Econ.*, February 1985, *18*(1), pp. 190–207. [G: Canada]

Lubick, Donald and Brannon, Gerard. Stanley S. Surrey and the Quality of Tax Policy Argu-

ment. *Nat. Tax J.*, September 1985, *38*(3), pp. 251–59. [G: U.S.]

Margolis, Julius. The United States Federal System: Commentary. In *Quigley, J. M. and Rubinfeld, D. L., eds.*, 1985, pp. 80–86. [G: U.S.]

Miller, Marcus. Measuring the Stance of Fiscal Policy. *Oxford Rev. Econ. Policy*, Spring 1985, *1*(1), pp. 44–57.

Modigliani, Franco and Jappelli, Tullio. Politica fiscale e risparmio in Italia: l'esperienza dell'ultimo secolo. (Fiscal Policy and Saving in Italy: The Experience of the Last Century. With English summary.) *Giorn. Econ.*, Sept.-Oct. 1985, *44*(9–10), pp. 475–518.

Musgrave, Richard A. Perspectives on and Limits to Public Finance for the Financing of Social Policy in Market Economies. In *Terny, G. and Culyer, A. J., eds.*, 1985, pp. 261–70.

Newlyn, W. T. The Role of the Public Sector in the Mobilisation and Allocation of Financial Resources. In *Gutowski, A.; Arnaudo, A. A. and Scharrer, H.-E., eds.*, 1985, pp. 98–114. [G: Selected LDCs]

Obstfeld, Maurice. The Dollar and the Policy Mix: 1985: Comment. *Brookings Pap. Econ. Act.*, 1985, (1), pp. 190–95. [G: U.S.]

Odling-Smee, John and Riley, Chris. Approaches to the PSBR. *Nat. Inst. Econ. Rev.*, August 1985, (113), pp. 65–80. [G: U.K.]

Ortega, Luis. Economic Policy and Growth in Chile from Independence to the War of the Pacific. In *Abel, C. and Lewis, C. M., eds.*, 1985, pp. 147–71. [G: Chile]

Peacock, Alan. Macro-economic Controls of Spending as a Device for Improving Efficiency in Government. In *Forte, F. and Peacock, A., eds.*, 1985, pp. 143–56. [G: U.K.; U.S.; Italy]

Pechman, Joseph A. The Promise of Tax Reform: Introduction. In *Pechman, J. A., ed. (II)*, 1985, pp. 1–7. [G: U.S.]

Penketh, Keith. Whither Fiscal Policy?—The United Kingdom from the Perspective of the European Economic Community. *Brit. Rev. Econ. Issues*, Autumn 1985, *7*(17), pp. 87–113. [G: U.K.; EEC]

Peterson, Paul E. The New Politics of Deficits. In *Chubb, J. E. and Peterson, P. E., eds.*, 1985, pp. 365–97. [G: U.S.]

Placone, Dennis; Ulbrich, Holley and Wallace, Myles S. The Crowding Out Debate: It's Over When It's Over and It Isn't Over Yet. *J. Post Keynesian Econ.*, Fall 1985, *8*(1), pp. 91–96. [G: U.S.]

Prud'homme, Rémy. Federalisme Fiscal et Politiques Sociales. (With English summary). In *Terny, G. and Culyer, A. J., eds.*, 1985, pp. 339–53. [G: OECD]

Quigley, John M. and Rubinfeld, Daniel L. Domestic Priorities in Our Federal System. In *Quigley, J. M. and Rubinfeld, D. L., eds.*, 1985, pp. 381–95. [G: U.S.]

Salvemini, Maria Teresa. Costituzionalismo monetario e fiscale. (Monetary and Fiscal Constitutionalism. With English summary.) *Polit.*

Econ., April 1985, *1*(1), pp. 123–36.
[G: U.S.; Italy]

Seidel, Hans. Die Stabilisierungsfunktion der Budgetpolitik: Gestern—Heute—Morgen. (With English summary.) *Empirica*, 1985, *12*(1), pp. 87–107. [G: Austria]

Spaventa, Luigi. Adjustment Plans, Fiscal Policy and Monetary Policy. *Rev. Econ. Cond. Italy*, January–April 1985, (1), pp. 9–35. [G: Italy]

Steuerle, C. Eugene. The Prospects for Tax Reform. *Nat. Tax J.*, September 1985, *38*(3), pp. 291–94. [G: U.S.]

Stiglitz, Joseph E. The Consumption-Expenditure Tax. In *Pechman, J. A., ed. (II)*, 1985, pp. 107–27. [G: U.S.]

Sunley, Emil M. Alternatives for Tax Restructuring and Increased Revenue. In *Pechman, J. A., ed. (II)*, 1985, pp. 184–200. [G: U.S.]

Tardos, Márton. Question Marks in Hungarian Fiscal and Monetary Policy (1979–1984). *Acta Oecon.*, 1985, *35*(1–2), pp. 29–52.
[G: Hungary]

Thirsk, Wayne R. Should Taxes Be Included in Trade Agreements? In *Conklin, D. W. and Courchene, T. J., eds.*, 1985, pp. 138–52.
[G: Canada]

Throop, Adrian W. Current Fiscal Policy: Is It Stimulating Investment or Consumption? *Fed. Res. Bank San Francisco Econ. Rev.*, Winter 1985, (1), pp. 19–44. [G: U.S.]

Tobin, James. The Fiscal Revolution: Disturbing Prospects. *Challenge*, January/February 1985, *27*(6), pp. 12–16. [G: U.S.]

Tuomala, Matti. Optimal Degree of Progressivity under Income Uncertainty. In *Førsund, F. R. and Honkapohja, S., eds.*, 1985, pp. 86–95.

Walters, Alan. Deficits in the United Kingdom. In *Cagan, P. and Somensatto, E., eds.*, 1985, pp. 147–62. [G: U.K.]

Warren, Alvin C., Jr. The Individual Income Tax. In *Pechman, J. A., ed. (II)*, 1985, pp. 37–58.

Weigel, Wolfgang. Austrian Economic Policy: A Comment. *Empirica*, 1985, *12*(1), pp. 109–10.
[G: Austria]

Willms, Manfred and Karsten, Ingo. Government Policies towards Inflation and Unemployment in West Germany. In *Argy, V. E. and Neville, J. W., eds.*, 1985, pp. 153–80.
[G: W. Germany]

Wilson, Thomas A. and MacGregor, Mary E. The 1985 Federal Budget: Macroeconomic and Fiscal Effects. *Can. Public Policy*, September 1985, *11*(3), pp. 602–16. [G: Canada]

Witte, John F. Democratic Procedures and Tax Policy. In *Pechman, J. A., ed. (I)*, 1985, pp. 134–52. [G: U.S.]

Wojcikewych, Raymond. An Empirical Investigation of the Interrelationship between Monetary and Fiscal Policy Using Some Alternative Policy Measures. *Quart. J. Bus. Econ.*, Winter 1985, *24*(1), pp. 101–14. [G: U.S.]

Wolfe, Barbara L., et al. The Contribution of Income Transfers to Lagging Economic Performance: The United States and the Netherlands

in the 1970s. In *Terny, G. and Culyer, A. J., eds.*, 1985, pp. 109–21. [G: U.S.; Netherlands]

Ysander, Bengt-Christer and Nordström, Tomas. Local Authorities, Economic Stability and the Efficiency of Fiscal Policy. In *Gramlich, E. M. and Ysander, B.-C., eds.*, 1985, pp. 347–98.
[G: Sweden]

322 National Government Expenditures and Budgeting

3220 General

Afxentiou, P. C. Fiscal Structure, Tax Effort and Economic Development. *Econ. Int.*, Aug./Nov. 1985, *38*(3/4), pp. 286–302.

Asher, Mukul G. Fiscal System and Economic Development: The ASEAN Case. *Bull. Int. Fiscal Doc.*, May 1985, *39*(5), pp. 195–208.
[G: S.E. Asia]

Bingman, Charles F. The President as Manager of the Federal Government. In *Harriss, C. L., ed.*, 1985, pp. 146–61. [G: U.S.]

Boskin, Michael J., et al. New Estimates of the Value of Federal Mineral Rights and Land. *Amer. Econ. Rev.*, December 1985, *75*(5), pp. 923–36. [G: U.S.]

Bowsher, Charles A. Governmental Financial Management at the Crossroads: The Choice Is between Reactive and Proactive Financial Management. *Public Budg. Finance*, Summer 1985, *5*(2), pp. 9–29. [G: U.S.]

Brinner, Roger E. Reflections on Reflections: Comments [Thoughts on Public Expenditures] [The International Agenda] [Reflections on Macroeconomic Modelling; Confessions of a DRI Addict]. *Eastern Econ. J.*, Jan.-Mar. 1985, *11*(1), pp. 84–87.

Brown, Richard E. and Copeland, Ronald M. Current Issues and Developments in Governmental Accounting and Auditing: Impact on Public Policy. *Public Budg. Finance*, Summer 1985, *5*(2), pp. 3–8. [G: U.S.]

Buchanan, James M. The Moral Dimension of Debt Financing. *Econ. Inquiry*, January 1985, *23*(1), pp. 1–6.

Cameron, David R. Does Government Cause Inflation? Taxes, Spending, and Deficits. In *Lindberg, L. N. and Maier, C. S., eds.*, 1985, pp. 224–79. [G: OECD]

Chiarella, Carl. Analysis of the Effects of Time Lags and Nonlinearities in a Macroeconomic Model Incorporating the Government Budget Constraint. In *Batten, D. F. and Lesse, P. F., eds.*, 1985, pp. 131–52.

Dempsey, Charles L. The Inspector General Concept: Where It's Been, Where It's Going. *Public Budg. Finance*, Summer 1985, *5*(2), pp. 39–51. [G: U.S.]

Elias, Victor J. La productividad del sector público en la Argentina. (The Productivity of the Public Sector in Argentina. With English summary.) *Económica (La Plata)*, May-Dec. 1985, *31*(2–3), pp. 133–45.

Faustini, Gino. A Medium-term Perspective for Budget Policy. *Rev. Econ. Cond. Italy,* January–April 1985, (1), pp. 99–118.
[G: W. Europe]

Filosa, Vincenzo. Stato creditore-stato debitore: per una rilettura dell'art. 53 della Costituzione. (The State as a Creditor and as a Debtor: A New Interpretation of the Constitution Article 53. With English summary.) *Rivista Int. Sci. Econ. Com.,* December 1985, *32*(12), pp. 1199–1216.
[G: Italy]

Fisher, Louis. Ten Years of the Budget Act: Still Searching for Controls. *Public Budg. Finance,* Autumn 1985, *5*(3), pp. 3–28.
[G: U.S.]

Forte, Francesco. Competitive Democracy and Fiscal Constitution. *Atlantic Econ. J.,* September 1985, *13*(3), pp. 1–11.

Greene, Kenneth V. Fiscal Decentralization: Evidence on the Role of Income and Other Determinants. *Public Finance,* 1985, *40*(2), pp. 291–98.
[G: U.S.]

Mathews, Russell L. Public Finance. In *Mathews, R., et al.,* 1985, pp. 71–94.
[G: Australia]

Mayer, Colin and Meadowcroft, Shirley A. Selling Public Assets: Techniques and Financial Implications. *Fisc. Stud.,* November 1985, *6*(4), pp. 42–56.
[G: U.K.]

Murrell, Peter. The Size of Public Employment: An Empirical Study. *J. Compar. Econ.,* December 1985, *9*(4), pp. 424–37.
[G: OECD]

Musgrave, Richard A. Excess Bias and the Nature of Budget Growth. *J. Public Econ.,* December 1985, *28*(3), pp. 287–308.

Neuthinger, Egon. The Fiscal Policy Concept of the Federal Government. *Econ. Lavoro,* July-Sept. 1985, *19*(3), pp. 133–35.
[G: W. Germany]

Pedone, Antonio. Regole costituzionali in materia di finanza pubblica. (Constitutional Rules in Budgetary Policy. With English summary.) *Polit. Econ.,* April 1985, *1*(1), pp. 111–22.
[G: Italy]

Penketh, Keith. Whither Fiscal Policy?—The United Kingdom from the Perspective of the European Economic Community. *Brit. Rev. Econ. Issues,* Autumn 1985, *7*(17), pp. 87–113.
[G: U.K.; EEC]

Peterson, Wallace C. The U.S. "Welfare State" and the Conservative Counterrevolution. *J. Econ. Issues,* September 1985, *19*(3), pp. 601–41.
[G: U.S.]

Phaup, Marvin. Accounting for Federal Credit: A Better Way. *Public Budg. Finance,* Autumn 1985, *5*(3), pp. 29–39.
[G: U.S.]

Rasler, Karen A. and Thompson, William R. War Making and State Making: Governmental Expenditures, Tax Revenues, and Global Wars. *Amer. Polit. Sci. Rev.,* June 1985, *79*(2), pp. 491–507.
[G: U.S.; U.K.; France; Japan]

Rivlin, Alice M. Thoughts on Public Expenditures. *Eastern Econ. J.,* Jan.-Mar. 1985, *11*(1), pp. 64–70.
[G: U.S.]

Stockfisch, J. A. Value-added Taxes and the Size of Government: Some Evidence. *Nat. Tax J.,* December 1985, *38*(4), pp. 547–52.
[G: OECD]

Thimmaiah, G. Fiscal Management. In *Mongia, J. N., ed.,* 1985, pp. 153–99.
[G: India]

3221 National Government Expenditures

Abizadeh, Sohrab and Gray, John. Wagner's Law: A Pooled Time-Series, Cross-Section Comparison. *Nat. Tax J.,* June 1985, *38*(2), pp. 209–18.

Beck, Morris. Public Expenditure, Relative Prices, and Resource Allocation. *Public Finance,* 1985, *40*(1), pp. 17–34.
[G: U.S.]

Birch, Stephen and Maynard, Alan. Public Expenditure Policy, 1985–86: Health and Personal Social Services. In *Cockle, P., ed.,* 1985, pp. 223–42.
[G: U.K.]

Bootle, Roger P. Public Expenditure Policy, 1985–86: Privatisation. In *Cockle, P., ed.,* 1985, pp. 77–99.
[G: U.K.]

Borcherding, Thomas E. The Causes of Government Expenditure Growth: A Survey of the U.S. Evidence. *J. Public Econ.,* December 1985, *28*(3), pp. 359–82.
[G: U.S.]

Borooah, Vani K. The Interaction between Economic Policy and Political Performance. In *Matthews, R. C. O., ed.,* 1985, pp. 20–48.
[G: U.K.]

Bottiroli Civardi, Marisa and Fraschini, Angela. Indices of Allocation of Expenditure in the Public Works Sector. *Ann. Pub. Co-op. Econ.,* Oct.-Dec. 1985, *56*(4), pp. 463–83.
[G: Italy]

Bradshaw, Jonathan. A Defence of Social Security. In *Bean, P.; Ferris, J. and Whynes, D., eds.,* 1985, pp. 227–56.
[G: U.K.]

Cameron, David R. Public Expenditure and Economic Performance in International Perspective. In *Klein, R. and O'Higgins, M., ed.,* 1985, pp. 8–21.
[G: OECD]

Carlson, Keith M. Controlling Federal Outlays: Trends and Proposals. *Fed. Res. Bank St. Louis Rev.,* June/July 1985, *67*(6), pp. 5–11.
[G: U.S.]

Chouraqui, Jean-Claude and Price, Robert. Fiscal and Monetary Strategy in OECD Countries: A Review of Recent Experiences. In *Argy, V. E. and Neville, J. W., eds.,* 1985, pp. 105–33.
[G: OECD]

Cockle, Paul. Public Expenditure Policy, 1985–86: Overview. In *Cockle, P., ed.,* 1985, pp. 1–33.
[G: U.K.]

Collings, John. Public Expenditure Policy, 1985–86: Transport. In *Cockle, P., ed.,* 1985, pp. 243–50.
[G: U.K.]

Cuzán, Alfred G. and Heggen, Richard J. Expenditures and Votes: In Search of Downward-sloping Curves in the United States and Great Britain. *Public Choice,* 1985, *45*(1), pp. 19–34.
[G: U.S.]

Davies, Gavyn and Piachaud, David. Public Expenditure on the Social Services: The Economic and Political Constraints. In *Klein, R. and O'Higgins, M., ed.,* 1985, pp. 92–110.
[G: U.K.]

Denton, Frank T. and Spencer, Byron G. Prospective Changes in Population and Their Implications for Government Expenditures. In

Courchene, T. J.; Conklin, D. W. and Cook, G. C. A., eds. Vol. 1, 1985, pp. 44–95. [G: Canada]

Disney, Richard. Public Expenditure Policy, 1985–86: Social Security. In Cockle, P., ed., 1985, pp. 121–51. [G: U.K.]

Feldman, Allan M. A Model of Majority Voting and Growth in Government Expenditure. Public Choice, 1985, 46(1), pp. 3–17. [G: U.S.]

Ferris, James M. Interrelationships among Public Spending Preferences: A Micro Analysis. Public Choice, 1985, 45(2), pp. 139–53. [G: U.S.]

Frederiksen, John. Offentlig ungiftspolitik. (Political Decisions of Public Expenditures. With English summary.) Nationaløkon. Tidsskr., 1985, 123(3), pp. 319–28.

Gemmell, Norman. The Incidence of Government Expenditure and Redistribution in the United Kingdom. Economica, August 1985, 52(207), pp. 335–44. [G: U.K.]

Gillion, Colin and Hemming, Richard. Social Expenditure in the United Kingdom in a Comparative Context: Trends, Explanations and Projections. In Klein, R. and O'Higgins, M., ed., 1985, pp. 22–36. [G: U.K.; OECD]

Gramlich, Edward M. Government Services. In Inman, R. P., ed., 1985, pp. 273–89. [G: U.S.]

Greenwood, David. Public Expenditure Policy, 1985–86: Defence. In Cockle, P., ed., 1985, pp. 101–19. [G: U.K.]

Hanke, Steve H. Privatization: Theory, Evidence, and Implementation. In Harriss, C. L., ed., 1985, pp. 101–13. [G: U.S.]

Hansson, Ingemar. Marginal Cost of Public Funds for Different Tax Instruments and Government Expenditures. In Førsund, F. R. and Honkapohja, S., eds., 1985, pp. 17–32. [G: Sweden]

Harriss, C. Lowell. Blueprints for Cost Control: Recommendations of the Grace Commission. In Harriss, C. L., ed., 1985, pp. 1–26. [G: U.S.]

Harriss, C. Lowell. Government Spending: A Private Sector Effort for Cost Control (Grace Commission). Rivista Int. Sci. Econ. Com., June 1985, 32(6), pp. 507–16. [G: U.S.]

Harriss, C. Lowell. Organization and Operation of the Grace Commission. In Harriss, C. L., ed., 1985, pp. 27–37. [G: U.S.]

Hewitt, Daniel. Demand for National Public Goods: Estimates from Surveys. Econ. Inquiry, July 1985, 23(3), pp. 487–506. [G: U.S.]

Houttuin, G. Demand Oriented Instruments in Innovation Policy: Government Procurement and Regulation. In Sweeney, G., ed., 1985, pp. 152–66. [G: OECD]

Inman, Robert P. Government Services: Comment. In Inman, R. P., ed., 1985, pp. 290–94. [G: U.S.]

Johansen, Lars Nørby and Kolberg, Jon Eivind. Welfare State Regression in Scandinavia? The Development of the Scandinavian Welfare States from 1970 to 1980. In Eisenstadt,

S. N. and Ahimeir, O., eds., 1985, pp. 143–76. [G: Scandinavia]

Kay, John A. and Llewellyn Smith, Chris H. Science Policy and Public Spending. Fisc. Stud., August 1985, 6(3), pp. 14–23.

Klein, Rudolf. Public Expenditure in an Inflationary World. In Lindberg, L. N. and Maier, C. S., eds., 1985, pp. 196–223. [G: OECD]

Landau, Daniel L. Government Expenditure and Economic Growth in the Developed Countries: 1952–76. Public Choice, 1985, 47(3), pp. 459–77. [G: W. Europe; U.S.; Canada; Japan]

Landymore, P. J. A. Education and Industry Since the War. In Morris, D., ed., 1985, pp. 690–717. [G: U.K.; EEC]

Mace, John. Public Expenditure Policy, 1985–86: Education and Science. In Cockle, P., ed., 1985, pp. 203–22. [G: U.K.]

Martelli, Paolo. Legislative Choice and Public-Spending Growth. In Forte, F. and Peacock, A., eds., 1985, pp. 37–51.

Mathews, Russell L. Programs and Policies. In Mathews, R., et al., 1985, pp. 108–58. [G: Australia]

Metzer, Jacob. How New Was the New Era? The Public Sector in the 1920s. J. Econ. Hist., March 1985, 45(1), pp. 119–26. [G: U.S.]

North, Douglass C. The Growth of Government in the United States: An Economic Historian's Perspective. J. Public Econ., December 1985, 28(3), pp. 383–99. [G: U.S.]

O'Higgins, Michael and Patterson, Alan. The Prospects for Public Expenditure: A Disaggregate Analysis. In Klein, R. and O'Higgins, M., ed., 1985, pp. 111–30. [G: U.K.]

Peacock, Alan. Macro-economic Controls of Spending as a Device for Improving Efficiency in Government. In Forte, F. and Peacock, A., eds., 1985, pp. 143–56. [G: U.K.; U.S.; Italy]

Quigley, John M. and Rubinfeld, Daniel L. Domestic Priorities in Our Federal System. In Quigley, J. M. and Rubinfeld, D. L., eds., 1985, pp. 381–95. [G: U.S.]

Ravenal, Earl C. The Price and Perils of NATO. In Boaz, D. and Crane, E. H., eds., 1985, pp. 111–43. [G: U.S.]

Reid, Bradford G. Aggregate Consumption and Deficit Financing: An Attempt to Separate Permanent from Transitory Effects. Econ. Inquiry, July 1985, 23(3), pp. 475–86. [G: U.S.]

Richardson, Harry W. and Turek, Joseph H. The Scope and Limits of Federal Intervention. In Richardson, H. W. and Turek, J. H., eds., 1985, pp. 211–42. [G: U.S.]

Rizzo, Ilde. Regional Disparities and Decentralization as Determinants of Public-Sector Expenditure Growth in Italy (1960–81). In Forte, F. and Peacock, A., eds., 1985, pp. 65–82. [G: Italy]

Scheetz, Thomas. Gastos militares en Chile, Perú y la Argentina. (With English summary.) Desarrollo Econ., Oct.-Dec. 1985, 25(99), pp. 315–27.

Schiff, Jerald. Does Government Spending Crowd Out Charitable Contributions? Nat. Tax

J., December 1985, *38*(4), pp. 535–46.
[G: U.S.]

Schleck, Robert W. Reforming Federal Pension Programs. In *Harriss, C. L., ed.*, 1985, pp. 85–100. [G: U.S.]

Schmidt, Kurt. Is There a Natural Limit to Public-Spending Growth? Or, the Spirit of the Age as a Determinant of the Development of Public Spending. In *Forte, F. and Peacock, A., eds.*, 1985, pp. 119–31. [G: W. Germany]

Sinclair, Peter. The Economic System in the UK: Public Finance. In *Morris, D., ed.*, 1985, pp. 272–94. [G: U.K.]

Tanzi, Vito. Monetary Policy and Control of Public Expenditure. In *Forte, F. and Peacock, A., eds.*, 1985, pp. 157–68. [G: OECD]

Taylor-Gooby, Peter. The Politics of Welfare: Public Attitudes and Behaviour. In *Klein, R. and O'Higgins, M., ed.*, 1985, pp. 72–91.
[G: U.K.]

Thompson, Fred. Managing Defense Expenditures. In *Harriss, C. L., ed.*, 1985, pp. 72–84. [G: U.S.]

Tiwari, S. G. Government Services in Relation to Total Consumption of the Population in Asian and Pacific Countries, with Special Reference to India. *Rev. Income Wealth*, June 1985, *31*(2), pp. 189–200. [G: India]

Treddenick, John M. The Arms Race and Military Keynesianism. *Can. Public Policy*, March 1985, *11*(1), pp. 77–92. [G: Canada]

Tridimas, George. Budget Deficits and the Growth of Public Expenditure in South Africa. *S. Afr. J. Econ.*, December 1985, *53*(4), pp. 393–401. [G: S. Africa]

Tridimas, George. Economic Theory and the Allocation of Public Expenditures in Greece. *Greek Econ. Rev.*, April 1985, *7*(1), pp. 34–52. [G: Greece]

Ullman, Al. Federal Spending and the Budget Crisis. In *Harriss, C. L., ed.*, 1985, pp. 38–46. [G: U.S.]

Valdés, Alberto. Subsidios alimentarios en países en desarrollo: estimaciones de sus costos y efectos distributivos. (With English summary.) *Cuadernos Econ.*, August 1985, *22*(66), pp. 329–36. [G: LDCs]

Weaver, R. Kent. Controlling Entitlements. In *Chubb, J. E. and Peterson, P. E., eds.*, 1985, pp. 307–41. [G: U.S.]

Weidenbaum, Murray L. The Budget Dilemma and Its Solution. In *Harriss, C. L., ed.*, 1985, pp. 47–58. [G: U.S.]

Wellink, Nout and Halberstadt, Victor. Monetary Policy and Control of Public Expenditure with Special Reference to the Netherlands. In *Forte, F. and Peacock, A., eds.*, 1985, pp. 169–91. [G: OECD; Netherlands]

Wildavsky, Aaron. A Cultural Theory of Expenditure Growth and (Un)balanced Budgets. *J. Public Econ.*, December 1985, *28*(3), pp. 349–57.

Wilson, Robert Andrew. Public Expenditure Policy, 1985–86: Employment. In *Cockle, P., ed.*, 1985, pp. 153–85. [G: U.K.]

Yaşer, Betty S. and Rajan, T. R. Thiaga. Share of Government in Gross National Product: Cross-Section and Time-Series Analysis, 1950–1982. *METU*, 1985, *12*(1/2), pp. 107–18.
[G: LDCs; MDCs]

Zandano, Gianni. Collective Choice, Social Welfare and Economic Growth. In *Forte, F. and Peacock, A., eds.*, 1985, pp. 83–98.
[G: OECD]

Zinam, Oleg. A Note on Tax Elasticity of Government Expenditures: Italian Experience. *Atlantic Econ. J.*, July 1985, *13*(2), pp. 84.
[G: Italy]

Zycher, Benjamin. Institutional and Mechanical Control of Federal Spending. In *Harriss, C. L., ed.*, 1985, pp. 137–45. [G: U.S.]

3226 National Government Budgeting and Deficits

Argy, Victor E. Targeting the Budget Deficit in the Face of a Downward Expenditure Shock. *Aussenwirtschaft*, May 1985, *40*(1/2), pp. 83–102. [G: Australia; U.K.]

Arnold, Roger A. and Wyrick, Thomas L. Continuing the Debate on NABR: Reply [Budgetary Referenda: An Efficient Alternative to Representative Democracy]. *Cato J.*, Spring/Summer 1985, *5*(1), pp. 345–50. [G: U.S.]

Aschheim, Joseph; Bailey, Martin J. and Tavlas, George S. Dollar Appreciation, Deficit Stimulation, and the New Protectionism. *J. Policy Modeling*, Spring 1985, *7*(1), pp. 107–21.
[G: U.S.]

Balassa, Bela. The Problem of the Debt in Developing Countries. In *Balassa, B.*, 1985, pp. 102–27. [G: LDCs]

Beeman, William J.; Dreyer, Jacob S. and Van de Water, Paul N. Dimensions of the Deficit Problem. In *Cagan, P. and Somensatto, E., eds.*, 1985, pp. 33–58. [G: U.S.]

Behn, Robert D. Cutback Budgeting. *J. Policy Anal. Manage.*, Winter 1985, *4*(2), pp. 155–77. [G: U.S.]

Belongia, Michael T. and Stone, Courtenay C. Would Lower Federal Deficits Increase U.S. Farm Exports? *Fed. Res. Bank St. Louis Rev.*, November 1985, *67*(9), pp. 5–19. [G: U.S.]

Bickley, James M. The Federal Financing Bank: Assessments of Its Effectiveness and Budgetary Status. *Public Budg. Finance*, Winter 1985, *5*(4), pp. 51–63. [G: U.S.]

Biswas, Rajiv; Johns, Christopher and Savage, David. The Measurement of Fiscal Stance. *Nat. Inst. Econ. Rev.*, August 1985, (113), pp. 50–64. [G: U.K.]

Blanchard, Olivier J.; Dornbusch, Rudiger and Buiter, Willem H. Debito pubblico e politiche fiscali responsabili. (Debt and Financial Responsibility. With English summary.) *Polit. Econ.*, December 1985, *1*(3), pp. 305–40.
[G: EEC]

Bobrow, Davis B. and Hill, Stephen R. The Determinants of Military Budgets: The Japanese Case. *Conflict Manage. Peace Sci.*, Fall 1985, *9*(1), pp. 1–18. [G: Japan]

Bolnick, Bruce R. The National Budget Referendum: Proceed with Caution [Budgetary Referenda: An Efficient Alternative to Representative Democracy]. *Cato J.*, Spring/Summer 1985, *5*(1), pp. 337–43.　　　[G: U.S.]

Break, George F. The Tax Expenditure Budget— The Need for a Fuller Accounting. *Nat. Tax J.*, September 1985, *38*(3), pp. 261–65.
　　　[G: U.S.]

Brewer, Thomas L. A Comparative Analysis of the Fiscal Policies of Industrial and Developing Countries—Policy Instability and Governmental-Regime Instability. *J. Compar. Econ.*, June 1985, *9*(2), pp. 191–96.

Britton, Andrew J. C. The Budget and its Critics. In *Kay, J., ed.*, 1985, pp. 23–30.

Britton, Andrew J. C. The Budget and Its Critics. *Fisc. Stud.*, May 1985, *6*(2), pp. 23–30.
　　　[G: U.K.]

Browning, Edgar K. and Browning, Jacquelene M. Tax Reform and Deficit Reduction. In *Cagan, P. and Somensatto, E., eds.*, 1985, pp. 281–310.　　　[G: U.S.]

Budd, Alan P. Macroeconomic Policy and the 1985 Budget. *Fisc. Stud.*, May 1985, *6*(2), pp. 10–22.　　　[G: U.K.]

Budd, Alan P. Macroeconomic Policy and the 1985 Budget. In *Kay, J., ed.*, 1985, pp. 10–22.　　　[G: U.K.]

Butler, Stuart. Privatization: A Strategy to Cut the Budget. *Cato J.*, Spring/Summer 1985, *5*(1), pp. 325–35.　　　[G: U.S.]

Cagan, Phillip. Financing the Deficit, Interest Rates, and Monetary Policy. In *Cagan, P. and Somensatto, E., eds.*, 1985, pp. 195–221.
　　　[G: U.S.]

Cagan, Phillip. The Economy in Deficit: Introduction. In *Cagan, P. and Somensatto, E., eds.*, 1985, pp. 1–4.　　　[G: U.S.]

Caiden, Naomi J. Comparing Budget Systems: Budgeting in ASEAN Countries. *Public Budg. Finance*, Winter 1985, *5*(4), pp. 23–38.
　　　[G: ASEAN]

Carlson, Keith M. Controlling Federal Outlays: Trends and Proposals. *Fed. Res. Bank St. Louis Rev.*, June/July 1985, *67*(6), pp. 5–11.
　　　[G: U.S.]

Cebula, Richard J. New Evidence on Financial Crowding Out. *Public Choice*, 1985, *46*(3), pp. 305–09.　　　[G: U.S.]

Chouraqui, Jean-Claude. Les Déficits Publics dans les Pays de l'OCDE: Causes, Conséquences et Remèdes. (Public Sector Deficits in OECD Countries: Causes, Consequences, and Policy Reactions. With English summary.) *Aussenwirtschaft*, May 1985, *40*(1/2), pp. 15–52.　　　[G: OECD]

Chouraqui, Jean-Claude and Montador, B. Fiscal Policy in the Small OECD Countries since the Early Seventies. *Schweiz. Z. Volkswirtsch. Statist.*, September 1985, *121*(3), pp. 259–83.
　　　[G: OECD]

Congdon, Tim G. Does Mr. Lawson Really Believe in the Medium-term Financial Strategy? *Fisc. Stud.*, May 1985, *6*(2), pp. 7–9.
　　　[G: U.K.]

Congdon, Tim G. Does Mr. Lawson Really Believe in the Medium-term Financial Strategy? In *Kay, J., ed.*, 1985, pp. 6–9.　　　[G: U.K.]

Darrat, Ali F. Inflation and Federal Budget Deficits: Some Empirical Results. *Public Finance Quart.*, April 1985, *13*(2), pp. 206–15.

Davidson, James Dale. The Balanced Budget Amendment: A Truly Marginal Reform. In *Boaz, D. and Crane, E. H., eds.*, 1985, pp. 13–28.　　　[G: U.S.]

Davies, Gavyn and Piachaud, David. Public Expenditure on the Social Services: The Economic and Political Constraints. In *Klein, R. and O'Higgins, M., ed.*, 1985, pp. 92–110.
　　　[G: U.K.]

Dewald, William G. CBO and OMB Projections, Adjusted for Inflation, Show Federal Budget Deficit under Control. *Fed. Res. Bank Richmond Econ. Rev.*, Nov./Dec. 1985, *71*(6), pp. 14–22.　　　[G: U.S.]

Due, John F. Federal and Foreign Trade Deficits and the Future of the U.S. Economy. *J. Econ. Educ.*, Summer 1985, *16*(3), pp. 194–202.
　　　[G: U.S.]

Emerson, Michael. The Effects of American Policies—A New Classical Interpretation: Comment. In *Buiter, W. H. and Marston, R. C., eds.*, 1985, pp. 131–34.　　　[G: U.S.; OECD]

Evans, Paul. Do Large Deficits Produce High Interest Rates? *Amer. Econ. Rev.*, March 1985, *75*(1), pp. 68–87.　　　[G: U.S.]

Ezejelue, A. C. Analysis of Some Tax Issues in the 1985 Federal Government Budget. *Bull. Int. Fiscal Doc.*, July 1985, *39*(7), pp. 307–14.　　　[G: Nigeria]

Feldstein, Martin. Global Economic Imbalances: The View from North America. In *Bergsten, C. F., ed.*, 1985, pp. 5–10.　　　[G: U.S.]

Feldstein, Martin. International Trade, Budget Deficits, and the Interest Rate. *J. Econ. Educ.*, Summer 1985, *16*(3), pp. 189–93.　　　[G: U.S.]

Frank, M. Considérations critiques sur l'inventaire des dépenses fiscales établi en 1984 par le Conseil Supérieur des Finances. (With English summary.) *Cah. Écon. Bruxelles*, 2nd Trimester 1985, (106), pp. 59–91. [G: Belgium]

Friedman, Benjamin M. Saving, Investment, and Government Deficits in the 1980s. In *Scott, B. R. and Lodge, G. C., eds.*, 1985, pp. 395–428.　　　[G: U.S.; OECD]

Giannaros, Demetrios S. Forecasting the Long-term Real Treasury Bill Rate. *Atlantic Econ. J.*, December 1985, *13*(4), pp. 83. [G: U.S.]

Giannaros, Demetrios S. and Kolluri, Bharat R. Deficit Spending, Money, and Inflation: Some International Empirical Evidence. *J. Macroecon.*, Summer 1985, *7*(3), pp. 401–17.
　　　[G: OECD]

Gittins, Ross. The Federal Budget: How Much Difference Do Elections Make? Comment. *Australian Econ. Rev.*, 3rd Quarter, Spring 1985, (71), pp. 51–52.　　　[G: Australia]

Gruen, Fred H. The Federal Budget: How Much Difference Do Elections Make? *Australian Econ. Rev.*, 3rd Quarter, Spring 1985, (71), pp. 36–49.　　　[G: Australia]

Grüske, Karl-Dieter. Redistributive Effects of the

Integrated Financial and Social Budgets in West Germany. In *Terny, G. and Culyer, A. J., eds.,* 1985, pp. 239–57.
[G: W. Germany]

Gunasekaran, S. The 1985–86 Budgetary Measures. *Bull. Int. Fiscal Doc.,* June 1985, *39*(6), pp. 271–74. [G: India]

Haberler, Gottfried. International Issues Raised by Criticisms of the U.S. Budget Deficits. In *Cagan, P. and Somensatto, E., eds.,* 1985, pp. 121–45. [G: U.S.; OECD; LDCs]

Harriss, C. Lowell. Blueprints for Cost Control: Recommendations of the Grace Commission. In *Harriss, C. L., ed.,* 1985, pp. 1–26.
[G: U.S.]

Harriss, C. Lowell. Government Spending: A Private Sector Effort for Cost Control (Grace Commission). *Rivista Int. Sci. Econ. Com.,* June 1985, *32*(6), pp. 507–16. [G: U.S.]

Harriss, C. Lowell. Organization and Operation of the Grace Commission. In *Harriss, C. L., ed.,* 1985, pp. 27–37. [G: U.S.]

Heller, Peter S. Analyzing and Adjusting Government Expenditure in LDCs. *Finance Develop.,* June 1985, *22*(2), pp. 2–5. [G: LDCs]

Heller, Walter W. Tax Reform, Tax Revenue, and the Deficit. *Eastern Econ. J.,* Jan.-Mar. 1985, *11*(1), pp. 51–63. [G: U.S.]

Holloway, Thomas M. and Wakefield, Joseph C. Sources of Change in the Federal Government Deficit, 1970–86. *Surv. Curr. Bus.,* May 1985, *65*(5), pp. 25–32. [G: U.S.]

Hooper, Peter. International Repercussions of the U.S. Budget Deficit. *Aussenwirtschaft,* May 1985, *40*(1/2), pp. 117–55. [G: U.S.; OECD]

Hutchison, Michael M. and Throop, Adrian W. U.S. Budget Deficits and the Real Value of the Dollar. *Fed. Res. Bank San Francisco Econ. Rev.,* Fall 1985, (4), pp. 26–43.
[G: U.S.]

Jap, K. S. An Outline of the 1985 Budget Tax Proposals. *Bull. Int. Fiscal Doc.,* March 1985, *39*(3), pp. 128–30. [G: Malaysia]

Johnson, Ronald N. U.S. Forest Service Policy and Its Budget. In *Deacon, R. T. and Johnson, M. B., eds.,* 1985, pp. 103–33. [G: U.S.]

Joines, Douglas H. Deficits and Money Growth in the United States, 1872–1983. *J. Monet. Econ.,* November 1985, *16*(3), pp. 329–51.
[G: U.S.]

Jonsson, Ernst. Budget-making with the Aid of an Equation Relating to Cost-determining Factors. *Public Finance,* 1985, *40*(2), pp. 210–19.
[G: Sweden]

Kamlet, Mark S. and Mowery, David C. The First Decade of the Congressional Budget Act: Legislative Imitation and Adaptation in Budgeting. *Policy Sci.,* December 1985, *18*(4), pp. 313–34. [G: U.S.]

Kay, John A. The Economy and the 1985 Budget: Introduction. In *Kay, J., ed.,* 1985, pp. 1–5.
[G: U.K.]

Kay, John A. The Economy and the 1985 Budget: Introduction. *Fisc. Stud.,* May 1985, *6*(2), pp. 1–5. [G: U.K.]

Keech, William R. A Theoretical Analysis of the

Case for a Balanced Budget Amendment. *Policy Sci.,* September 1985, *18*(2), pp. 157–68.
[G: U.S.]

Keith, Robert and Davis, Edward. Congress and Continuing Appropriations: New Variations on an Old Theme. *Public Budg. Finance,* Spring 1985, *5*(1), pp. 97–100. [G: U.S.]

Kemp, David. The Federal Budget: How Much Difference Do Elections Make? Comment. *Australian Econ. Rev.,* 3rd Quarter, Spring 1985, (71), pp. 50. [G: Australia]

Kudlow, Lawrence A. On the Deficit: Amateurs vs. Experts. *Challenge,* January/February 1985, *27*(6), pp. 48–49. [G: U.S.]

Laband, David N. Federal Budget Cuts: Rejoinder [Federal Budget Cuts: Bureaucrats Trim the Meat, Not the Fat]. *Public Choice,* 1985, *45*(2), pp. 221–22.

Lal, Deepak and van Wijnbergen, Sweder. Government Deficits, the Real Interest Rate and LDC Debt: On Global Crowding Out. *Europ. Econ. Rev.,* November 1985, *29*(2), pp. 157–91. [G: Global]

Lambro, Donald. The Republic Pork Barrel: Why It's So Hard to Cut the Budget. *Policy Rev.,* Summer 1985, (33), pp. 54–56. [G: U.S.]

Lanthier, Allan R. 1985–86 Federal Budget; Business Purpose and Advance Rulings; Treaty Developments. *Bull. Int. Fiscal Doc.,* October 1985, *39*(10), pp. 452–55. [G: Canada]

Lecerf, Michel. The Cameroon 1984/1985 Budget. *Bull. Int. Fiscal Doc.,* March 1985, *39*(3), pp. 127. [G: Cameroon]

de Leeuw, Frank and Holloway, Thomas M. The Measurement and Significance of the Cyclically Adjusted Federal Budget and Debt. *J. Money, Credit, Banking,* May 1985, *17*(2), pp. 232–42. [G: U.S.]

Leutwiler, Fritz. Staatsverschuldung und Geldpolitik. (National Indebtedness and Monetary Policy. With English summary.) *Aussenwirtschaft,* May 1985, *40*(1/2), pp. 157–68.
[G: U.S.]

Levy, Mickey D. Recent Budget Policy and Economic Impact. In *Shadow Open Market Committee.,* 1985, pp. 25–33. [G: U.S.]

Low, Linda. The Financing Process in the Public Sector in Singapore: Tax and Non-tax Revenue. *Bull. Int. Fiscal Doc.,* April 1985, *39*(4), pp. 148–65. [G: Singapore]

Makin, John H. The Effect of Government Deficits on Capital Formation. In *Cagan, P. and Somensatto, E., eds.,* 1985, pp. 163–94.
[G: U.S.]

Mansfield, Charles Y. Tax Effort and Measures of Fiscal Stabilization Performance. *Bull. Int. Fiscal Doc.,* February 1985, *39*(2), pp. 77–85.

Marlow, Michael L. Federal Budget Cuts: Bureaucrats Trim the Meat, Not the Fat: Comment. *Public Choice,* 1985, *45*(2), pp. 215–19.

Marston, Richard C. The Effects of American Policies—A New Classical Interpretation: Comment. In *Buiter, W. H. and Marston, R. C., eds.,* 1985, pp. 134–38. [G: U.S.; OECD]

Miller, Marcus. Measuring the Stance of Fiscal

Policy. *Oxford Rev. Econ. Policy*, Spring 1985, *1*(1), pp. 44–57.

Mills, Gregory B. The President's Budget for Fiscal Year 1986. *Public Budg. Finance*, Summer 1985, *5*(2), pp. 89–107. [G: U.S.]

Minford, Patrick. The Effects of American Policies—A New Classical Interpretation. In *Buiter, W. H. and Marston, R. C., eds.*, 1985, pp. 84–130. [G: OECD; U.S.]

Modigliani, Franco; Jappelli, Tullio and Pagona, Marco. The Impact of Fiscal Policy and Inflation on National Saving: The Italian Case. *Banca Naz. Lavoro Quart. Rev.*, June 1985, (153), pp. 91–126. [G: Italy]

Mongia, J. N. Deficit Financing. In *Mongia, J. N., ed.*, 1985, pp. 201–37. [G: India]

Munnell, Alicia H. Social Security and the Budget. *New Eng. Econ. Rev.*, July/August 1985, pp. 5–18. [G: U.S.]

Oberhauser, Alois. Das Schuldenparadox. (Paradoxical Effects of the Public Debt. With English summary.) *Jahr. Nationalökon. Statist.*, July 1985, *200*(4), pp. 333–48.
[G: W. Germany]

Odling-Smee, John and Riley, Chris. Approaches to the PSBR. *Nat. Inst. Econ. Rev.*, August 1985, (113), pp. 65–80. [G: U.K.]

Ohkawa, Masazo. The Role of Political Parties and Executive Bureaucrats in Governmental Budget-Making—The Case of Japan. In *[Recktenwald, H. C.]*, 1985, pp. 123–34.
[G: Japan]

Ornstein, Norman J. The Politics of the Deficit. In *Cagan, P. and Somensatto, E., eds.*, 1985, pp. 311–33. [G: U.S.]

Peterson, Paul E. The New Politics of Deficits. In *Chubb, J. E. and Peterson, P. E., eds.*, 1985, pp. 365–97. [G: U.S.]

Praedicta Ltd. The July 1985 Austerity Programme: Pro and Con. In *Levinson, P. and Landau, P., eds.*, 1985, pp. 3–5. [G: Israel]

Reynolds, Clark W. Mexico and the United States: Studies in Economic Interaction: Fluctuations and Growth: Comments. In *Musgrave, P. B., ed.*, 1985, pp. 171– 75.
[G: Mexico; U.S.]

Rockoff, Hugh. The Origins of the Federal Budget. *J. Econ. Hist.*, June 1985, *45*(2), pp. 377–82. [G: U.S.]

Ruggeri, Giovanni. Notes on the Control of the Public Deficit in the Medium Term. *Rev. Econ. Cond. Italy*, January–April 1985, (1), pp. 37–74. [G: Italy]

Sakamoto, Masahiro. Japan's Macroeconomic Performance and Its Effects on the Japanese–U.S. Economic Relationship. In *Nanto, D. K., ed.*, 1985, pp. 79–93. [G: Japan; U.S.]

Sarantis, Nicholas. Government Deficits and Personal Expenditure in the E.E.C. *Rivista Int. Sci. Econ. Com.*, July-Aug. 1985, *32*(7–8), pp. 723–34. [G: EEC]

Schmidt, Ronald H. and Dunstan, Roger H. Effects of Reducing the Deficit with an Oil Import Tariff. *Fed. Res. Bank Dallas Econ. Rev.*, September 1985, pp. 15–24.

Schröder, Jürgen. Government Deficits and Current Account. *Aussenwirtschaft*, May 1985, *40*(1/2), pp. 103–15.

Schydlowsky, Daniel M. Mexico and the United States: Studies in Economic Interaction: Fluctuations and Growth: Comments. In *Musgrave, P. B., ed.*, 1985, pp. 177–82.
[G: Mexico; U.S.]

Sharkansky, Ira. Who Gets What amidst High Inflation: Winners and Losers in the Israeli Budget, 1978–84. *Public Budg. Finance*, Winter 1985, *5*(4), pp. 64–74. [G: Israel]

Sharples, Adam. The Budget and the Government's Economic Strategy. *Fisc. Stud.*, May 1985, *6*(2), pp. 31–39. [G: U.K.]

Sharples, Adam. The Budget and the Government's Economic Strategy. In *Kay, J., ed.*, 1985, pp. 31–39. [G: U.K.]

Shepsle, Kenneth A. and Weingast, Barry R. Policy Consequences of Government by Congressional Subcommittees. In *Harriss, C. L., ed.*, 1985, pp. 114–31. [G: U.S.]

Somensatto, Eduardo. Budget Deficits, Exchange Rates, International Capital Flows, and Trade. In *Cagan, P. and Somensatto, E., eds.*, 1985, pp. 223–79. [G: U.S.; OECD]

Suits, Daniel B. and Fisher, Ronald C. A Balanced Budget Constitutional Amendment: Economic Complexities and Uncertainties. *Nat. Tax J.*, December 1985, *38*(4), pp. 467–77. [G: U.S.]

Tanzi, Vito. Fiscal Deficits and Interest Rates in the United States: An Empirical Analysis, 1960–84. *Int. Monet. Fund Staff Pap.*, December 1985, *32*(4), pp. 551–76. [G: U.S.]

Tanzi, Vito. Fiscal Management and External Debt Problems. In *Mehran, H., ed.*, 1985, pp. 65–87. [G: Selected LDCs]

Tanzi, Vito. The Deficit Experience in Industrial Countries. *Finance Develop.*, December 1985, *22*(4), pp. 15–18. [G: OECD]

Tanzi, Vito. The Deficit Experience in Industrial Countries. In *Cagan, P. and Somensatto, E., eds.*, 1985, pp. 81–119. [G: OECD]

Tatom, John A. Two Views of the Effects of Government Budget Deficits in the 1980s. *Fed. Res. Bank St. Louis Rev.*, October 1985, *67*(8), pp. 5–16. [G: U.S.]

Taylor, Lance. The Crisis and Thereafter: Macroeconomic Policy Problems in Mexico. In *Musgrave, P. B., ed.*, 1985, pp. 147–70.
[G: Mexico]

Tridimas, George. Budget Deficits and the Growth of Public Expenditure in South Africa. *S. Afr. J. Econ.*, December 1985, *53*(4), pp. 393–401. [G: S. Africa]

Ullman, Al. Federal Spending and the Budget Crisis. In *Harriss, C. L., ed.*, 1985, pp. 38–46. [G: U.S.]

Valentine, T. J. Indexed Securities. In *Argy, V. E. and Neville, J. W., eds.*, 1985, pp. 370–84. [G: Australia]

Van de Water, Paul N. and Ruffing, Kathy A. Federal Deficits, Debt, and Interest Costs. *Public Budg. Finance*, Spring 1985, *5*(1), pp. 54–66. [G: U.S.]

Wakefield, Joseph C. Federal Budget Developments. *Surv. Curr. Bus.*, April 1985, *65*(4), pp. 26–27, 35. [G: U.S.]

Wakefield, Joseph C. Federal Budget Developments. *Surv. Curr. Bus.*, September 1985, *65*(9), pp. 16–18. [G: U.S.]

Wakefield, Joseph C. and Ziemer, Richard C. Federal Fiscal Programs. *Surv. Curr. Bus.*, February 1985, *65*(2), pp. 10–15. [G: U.S.]

Walters, Alan. Deficits in the United Kingdom. In *Cagan, P. and Somensatto, E., eds.*, 1985, pp. 147–62. [G: U.K.]

Waud, Roger N. Politics, Deficits, and the Laffer Curve. *Public Choice*, 1985, *47*(3), pp. 509–17.

Weicher, John C. Accounting for the Deficit. In *Cagan, P. and Somensatto, E., eds.*, 1985, pp. 5–31. [G: U.S.]

Weicher, John C. The State and Local Government Sector and the Federal Deficit. In *Cagan, P. and Somensatto, E., eds.*, 1985, pp. 59–79. [G: U.S.]

Weidenbaum, Murray L. The Budget Dilemma and Its Solution. In *Harriss, C. L., ed.*, 1985, pp. 47–58. [G: U.S.]

Willett, Thomas D. The Deficit and the Dollar. In *Arndt, S. W.; Sweeney, R. J. and Willett, T. D., eds.*, 1985, pp. 273–82.

Wilson, Thomas A. and MacGregor, Mary E. The 1985 Federal Budget: Macroeconomic and Fiscal Effects. *Can. Public Policy*, September 1985, *11*(3), pp. 602–16. [G: Canada]

Zycher, Benjamin. Institutional and Mechanical Control of Federal Spending. In *Harriss, C. L., ed.*, 1985, pp. 137–45. [G: U.S.]

3228 National Government Debt Management

Aschinger, Gerhard. Probleme der Staatsverschuldung. (Problems of Government Indebtedness. With English summary.) *Jahr. Nationalökon. Statist.*, November 1985, *200*(6), pp. 582–601.

Baltensperger, Ernst. Staatsverschuldung, Geldpolitik und Währungsstabilität. (Public Debt, Monetary Policy, and Currency Stability. With English summary.) *Aussenwirtschaft*, May 1985, *40*(1/2), pp. 71–81.

Bianchi, Bruno. Stati Uniti e Italia: due esperienze nelle gestione del debito pubblico. (United States and Italy: Two Experiences in Public Debt Management. With English summary.) *Bancaria*, September 1985, *41*(9), pp. 933–42. [G: U.S.; Italy]

Bickley, James M. The Federal Financing Bank: Assessments of Its Effectiveness and Budgetary Status. *Public Budg. Finance*, Winter 1985, *5*(4), pp. 51–63. [G: U.S.]

Biswas, Rajiv; Johns, Christopher and Savage, David. The Measurement of Fiscal Stance. *Nat. Inst. Econ. Rev.*, August 1985, (113), pp. 50–64. [G: U.K.]

Boskin, Michael J. and Kotlikoff, Laurence J. Public Debt and United States Saving: A New Test of the Neutrality Hypothesis. *Carnegie-Rochester Conf. Ser. Public Policy*, Autumn 1985, *23*, pp. 55–86. [G: U.S.]

Cavaco-Silva, Anibal A. Forced Loans: Tax Element, Equity and Effects on Consumption. In *[Peacock, A.]*, 1985, pp. 51–66.

Cebula, Richard J. Crowding Out and Fiscal Policy in the United States: A Note on the Recent Experience. *Public Finance*, 1985, *40*(1), pp. 133–36. [G: U.S.]

Corrigan, E. Gerald. Public and Private Debt Accumulation: A Perspective. *Fed. Res. Bank New York Quart. Rev.*, Autumn 1985, *10*(3), pp. 1–5. [G: U.S.]

Corrigan, E. Gerald. Statement to the U.S. House Subcommittee on Commerce, Consumer, and Monetary Affairs of the Committee on Government Operations, May 15, 1985. *Fed. Res. Bull.*, July 1985, *71*(7), pp. 524–28. [G: U.S.]

Corrigan, E. Gerald. Statement to the U.S. House Subcommittee on Domestic Monetary Policy of the Committee on Banking, Finance and Urban Affairs, April 1, 1985. *Fed. Res. Bull.*, June 1985, *71*(6), pp. 405–09. [G: U.S.]

Corrigan, E. Gerald. Statement to the U.S. Senate Subcommittee on Securities of the Committee on Banking, Housing, and Urban Affairs, May 9, 1985. *Fed. Res. Bull.*, July 1985, *71*(7), pp. 520–24. [G: U.S.]

Cosentino, Antonello. L'autonomia dell'Istituto di emissione nel finanziare il fabbisogno del Tesaro. (The Autonomy of the Bank of Italy in Financing Treasury Needs–II. With English summary.) *Bancaria*, December 1985, *41*(12), pp. 1216–25. [G: Italy]

Cosentino, Antonello. L'autonomia dell'Istituto di emissione nel finanziare il fabbisogno del Tesoro. (The Autonomy of the Bank of Italy in Financing Treasury Needs–I. With English summary.) *Bancaria*, November 1985, *41*(11), pp. 1125–36. [G: Italy]

Cox, W. Michael. Inflation and Permanent Government Debt. *Fed. Res. Bank Dallas Econ. Rev.*, May 1985, pp. 13–26. [G: U.S.]

Cox, W. Michael. The Behavior of Treasury Securities: Monthly, 1942–1984. *J. Monet. Econ.*, September 1985, *16*(2), pp. 227–50. [G: U.S.]

Dietsch, Michel. Les imperfections des marchés financiers et l'effet d'éviction directe de la dette publique: Le cas de la France. (Imperfect Financial Markets and the Crowding Out Effect of Public Debt: The French Case. With English summary.) *Écon. Soc.*, September 1985, *19*(9), pp. 81–108. [G: France]

Dwyer, Gerald P., Jr. Money, Deficits, and Inflation: A Comment. *Carnegie-Rochester Conf. Ser. Public Policy*, Spring 1985, *22*, pp. 197–205. [G: U.S.]

Frankel, Jeffrey A. Portfolio Crowding-out, Empirically Estimated. *Quart. J. Econ.*, Supp. 1985, *100*, pp. 1041–65. [G: U.S.]

Friedman, Benjamin M. The Effect of Large Government Deficits on Interest Rates and Equity Returns. *Oxford Rev. Econ. Policy*, Spring 1985, *1*(1), pp. 58–71.

Kearney, Colm and MacDonald, Ronald. Public

Sector Borrowing, the Money Supply and Interest Rates. *Oxford Bull. Econ. Statist.*, August 1985, 47(3), pp. 249–73. **[G: U.K.]**

King, Robert G. and Plosser, Charles I. Money, Deficits, and Inflation. *Carnegie-Rochester Conf. Ser. Public Policy*, Spring 1985, 22, pp. 147–95. **[G: U.S.]**

Krzyzaniak, Marian. The Dynamic Incidence of the Long-term Government Debt in a Neoclassical World. *Public Finance*, 1985, 40(3), pp. 307–34.

de Larosière, Jacques. La croissance de la dette publique: causes, conséquences et remèdes. (The Growing Public Debt: Causes, Consequences and Remedies. With English summary.) *Écon. Soc.*, September 1985, 19(9), pp. 3–31. **[G: OECD]**

de Leeuw, Frank and Holloway, Thomas M. The Measurement and Significance of the Cyclically Adjusted Federal Budget and Debt. *J. Money, Credit, Banking*, May 1985, 17(2), pp. 232–42. **[G: U.S.]**

Low, Linda. The Financing Process in the Public Sector in Singapore: Tax and Non-tax Revenue. *Bull. Int. Fiscal Doc.*, April 1985, 39(4), pp. 148–65. **[G: Singapore]**

Miller, Marcus. Measuring the Stance of Fiscal Policy. *Oxford Rev. Econ. Policy*, Spring 1985, 1(1), pp. 44–57.

Odling-Smee, John and Riley, Chris. Approaches to the PSBR. *Nat. Inst. Econ. Rev.*, August 1985, (113), pp. 65–80. **[G: U.K.]**

Pollin, Robert. Stability and Instability in the Debt–Income Relationship. *Amer. Econ. Rev.*, May 1985, 75(2), pp. 344–50. **[G: U.S.]**

Reid, Bradford G. Government Debt, National Income and Causality. *Appl. Econ.*, April 1985, 17(2), pp. 321–30. **[G: U.S.]**

Romer, Paul M. Public Debt Policies and United States Saving: A Comment. *Carnegie-Rochester Conf. Ser. Public Policy*, Autumn 1985, 23, pp. 87–89. **[G: U.S.]**

Ruggeri, Giovanni. Notes on the Control of the Public Deficit in the Medium Term. *Rev. Econ. Cond. Italy*, January–April 1985, (1), pp. 37–74. **[G: Italy]**

Seater, John J. Does Government Debt Matter? A Review. *J. Monet. Econ.*, July 1985, 16(1), pp. 121–31.

Sheehan, Richard G. The Federal Reserve Reaction Function: Does Debt Growth Influence Monetary Policy? *Fed. Res. Bank St. Louis Rev.*, March 1985, 67(3), pp. 24–33.

Spaventa, Luigi. Adjustment Plans, Fiscal Policy and Monetary Policy. *Rev. Econ. Cond. Italy*, January–April 1985, (1), pp. 9–35. **[G: Italy]**

Tanzi, Vito. Fiscal Deficits and Interest Rates in the United States: An Empirical Analysis, 1960–84. *Int. Monet. Fund Staff Pap.*, December 1985, 32(4), pp. 551–76. **[G: U.S.]**

Tanzi, Vito. Fiscal Management and External Debt Problems. In *Mehran, H., ed.*, 1985, pp. 65–87. **[G: Selected LDCs]**

Tanzi, Vito. Monetary Policy and Control of Public Expenditure. In *Forte, F. and Peacock, A., eds.*, 1985, pp. 157–68. **[G: OECD]**

Valiani, Rolando. What Solutions Are There to Italy's Public Debt? *Rev. Econ. Cond. Italy*, January–April 1985, (1), pp. 75–95. **[G: Italy]**

Van de Water, Paul N. and Ruffing, Kathy A. Federal Deficits, Debt, and Interest Costs. *Public Budg. Finance*, Spring 1985, 5(1), pp. 54–66. **[G: U.S.]**

Webb, Steven B. Government Debt and Inflationary Expectations as Determinants of the Money Supply in Germany, 1919–23. *J. Money, Credit, Banking*, Part 1, Nov. 1985, 17(4), pp. 479–92. **[G: Germany]**

Wellink, Nout and Halberstadt, Victor. Monetary Policy and Control of Public Expenditure with Special Reference to the Netherlands. In *Forte, F. and Peacock, A., eds.*, 1985, pp. 169–91. **[G: OECD; Netherlands]**

323 National Taxation, Revenue, and Subsidies

3230 National Taxation, Revenue, and Subsidies

Aaron, Henry J. The United States Federal System: Commentary. In *Quigley, J. M. and Rubinfeld, D. L., eds.*, 1985, pp. 70–74. **[G: U.S.]**

Aaron, Henry J. and Galper, Harvey. A Cash Flow Tax System. In *Pechman, J. A., ed. (I)*, 1985, pp. 113–19. **[G: U.S.]**

Abizadeh, Sohrab and Yousefi, Mahmood. International Trade Taxes and Economic Development: An Empirical Analysis. *Rivista Int. Sci. Econ. Com.*, July-Aug. 1985, 32(7–8), pp. 735–49. **[G: Selected LDCs]**

Abrams, Burton A. and Schmitz, Mark D. The Crowding-out Effect of Governmental Transfers: A Rejoinder. *Nat. Tax J.*, December 1985, 38(4), pp. 575–76. **[G: U.S.]**

Adamache, Killard W. and Sloan, Frank A. Fringe Benefits: To Tax or Not to Tax? *Nat. Tax J.*, March 1985, 38(1), pp. 47–64. **[G: U.S.]**

Adams, F. Gerard and Duggal, Vijaya G. General versus Industry-Specific Industrial Policies: Quantifying the National and Sectoral Impacts. In *Adams, F. G., ed.*, 1985, pp. 31–47. **[G: U.S.]**

Afxentiou, P. C. Fiscal Structure, Tax Effort and Economic Development. *Econ. Int.*, Aug./Nov. 1985, 38(3/4), pp. 286–302.

Aidinoff, M. Bernard. Furniss v Dawson: The U.S. Experience. *Fisc. Stud.*, November 1985, 6(4), pp. 66–76. **[G: U.S.]**

Aitkin, Don. Taxation and Policy Change: A Median Voter Model for Australia 1968–69 to 1981–82: Comment. *Australian Econ. Rev.*, 3rd Quarter, Spring 1985, (71), pp. 34–35. **[G: Australia]**

Alam, Kazi F. The Influence of Tax Incentives on the Investment Decisions in U.K. Manufacturing. *METU*, 1985, 12(3/4), pp. 301–16. **[G: U.K.]**

Alam, Kazi F. and Stafford, L. W. T. Tax Incentives and Investment Policy: A Survey Report on the United Kingdom Manufacturing Industry. *Managerial Dec. Econ.*, March 1985, 6(1), pp. 27–32. **[G: U.K.]**

Alchin, Terry. Prota: A New Measure of the Progressivity of Personal Income Taxation. *Australian Econ. Pap.*, June 1985, *24*(44), pp. 185–200.   **[G: Australia]**

Ali, M. Shaukat. Who Bears the Burden of Federal Taxes in Pakistan? Comments. *Pakistan Devel. Rev.*, Autumn-Winter 1985, *24*(3/4), pp. 508–09.   **[G: Pakistan]**

Allen, Franklin. Achieving the First Best in Small Economies. *J. Public Econ.*, July 1985, *27*(2), pp. 255–60.

Allén, Tuovi. Vähennykset tuloverotuksessa—tulonsiirtopolitiikan jatke? (Deductions in Personal Income Taxation—Substitutes for Government Transfer Programmes? With English summary.) *Kansant. Aikak.*, 1985, *81*(1), pp. 65–72.

Alm, James. The Welfare Cost of the Underground Economy. *Econ. Inquiry*, April 1985, *23*(2), pp. 243–63.   **[G: U.S.]**

Alm, James; Follain, James R. and Beeman, Mary Anne. Tax Expenditures and Other Programs to Stimulate Housing: Do We Need More? *J. Urban Econ.*, September 1985, *18*(2), pp. 180–95.   **[G: U.S.]**

de Almeida Sampaio, Carlos. L'établissement et la perception des impôts à charge des non-résidents: Portugal. (The Assessment and Collection of Tax from Non-residents: Portugal. With English summary.) In *International Fiscal Association (I)*, 1985, pp. 563–72. **[G: Portugal]**

Alvarez, J. The Assessment and Collection of Tax from Non-residents: Colombia. In *International Fiscal Association (I)*, 1985, pp. 335–49.   **[G: Colombia]**

Amerkhail, Valerie; Lucke, Robert and Marcuss, Rosemary D. Revenue Estimation and Comprehensive Tax Reform. *Nat. Tax J.*, September 1985, *38*(3), pp. 373–94.   **[G: U.S.]**

Anandalingam, G. Government Policy and Industrial Investment in Cogeneration in the USA. *Energy Econ.*, April 1985, *7*(2), pp. 117–26.   **[G: U.S.]**

Anderson, Kenneth E. A Horizontal Equity Analysis of the Minimum Tax Provisions: An Empirical Study. *Accounting Rev.*, July 1985, *60*(3), pp. 357–71.   **[G: U.S.]**

Ang, James S.; Peterson, David R. and Peterson, Pamela P. Marginal Tax Rates: Evidence from Nontaxable Corporate Bonds: A Note. *J. Finance*, March 1985, *40*(1), pp. 327–32.   **[G: U.S.]**

Aoki, Torao. A Survey of the Japanese Tax System. *Bull. Int. Fiscal Doc.*, October 1985, *39*(10), pp. 435–45.   **[G: Japan]**

Asher, Mukul G. Fiscal System and Economic Development: The ASEAN Case. *Bull. Int. Fiscal Doc.*, May 1985, *39*(5), pp. 195–208.   **[G: S.E. Asia]**

Atkinson, Glen W. Reforming or Transforming the Federal Tax System: (A Review Essay). *Amer. J. Econ. Soc.*, July 1985, *44*(3), pp. 379–83.   **[G: U.S.]**

Auerbach, Alan J. The Corporation Income Tax. In *Pechman, J. A., ed. (II)*, 1985, pp. 59–86.   **[G: U.S.]**

Auerbach, Alan J. The Theory of Excess Burden and Optimal Taxation. In *Auerbach, A. J. and Feldstein, M., eds.*, 1985, pp. 61–127.

Baack, Bennett D. and Ray, Edward John. Special Interests and the Adoption of the Income Tax in the United States. *J. Econ. Hist.*, September 1985, *45*(3), pp. 607–25.   **[G: U.S.]**

Babcock, Guilford C. The Integration of Insurance and Taxes in Corporate Pension Strategy: Discussion. *J. Finance*, July 1985, *40*(3), pp. 955–57.   **[G: U.S.]**

Bale, Gordon. The Treasury's Proposals for Tax Reform: A Canadian Perspective. *Law Contemp. Probl.*, Autumn 1985, *48*(4), pp. 151–95.   **[G: U.S.; Canada]**

Ballard, Charles L. and Goulder, Larry H. Consumption Taxes, Foresight, and Welfare: A Computable General Equilibrium Analysis. In *Piggott, J. and Whalley, J., eds.*, 1985, pp. 253–82.   **[G: U.S.]**

Ballard, Charles L.; Shoven, John B. and Whalley, John. General Equilibrium Computations of the Marginal Welfare Costs of Taxes in the United States. *Amer. Econ. Rev.*, March 1985, *75*(1), pp. 128–38.   **[G: U.S.]**

Ballard, Charles L.; Shoven, John B. and Whalley, John. The Total Welfare Cost of the United States Tax System: A General Equilibrium Approach. *Nat. Tax J.*, June 1985, *38*(2), pp. 125–40.   **[G: U.S.]**

Banting, Keith G. Federalism and Income Security: Themes and Variations. In *Courchene, T. J.; Conklin, D. W. and Cook, G. C. A., eds. Vol. 1*, 1985, pp. 253–76.   **[G: Canada]**

Barichello, Richard R. and Glenday, Graham. The Tax Expenditure of Agricultural Marketing Quota Deductibility. *Can. J. Agr. Econ.*, November 1985, *33*(3), pp. 263–84.
[G: Canada]

Bartlett, Bruce. Tax Americana: What Goes Up Doesn't Always Come Down. *Policy Rev.*, Spring 1985, (32), pp. 54–55.   **[G: U.S.]**

Bartlett, Bruce. The Entrepreneurial Imperative. In *Boaz, D. and Crane, E. H., eds.*, 1985, pp. 75–90.   **[G: U.S.]**

Batte, Marvin T. and Sonka, Steven T. Before- and After-Tax Size Economies: An Example for Cash Grain Production in Illinois. *Amer. J. Agr. Econ.*, August 1985, *67*(3), pp. 600–608.   **[G: U.S.]**

Batten, Dallas S. and Ott, Mack. The President's Proposed Corporate Tax Reforms: A Move toward Tax Neutrality. *Fed. Res. Bank St. Louis Rev.*, Aug./Sept. 1985, *67*(7), pp. 5–17.
[G: U.S.]

Becker, Gary S. Public Policies, Pressure Groups, and Dead Weight Costs. *J. Public Econ.*, December 1985, *28*(3), pp. 329–47.

Becker, Robert A. Capital Income Taxation and Perfect Foresight. *J. Public Econ.*, March 1985, *26*(2), pp. 147–67.

Bedrossian, A. and Hitiris, T. Trade Taxes as a Source of Government Revenue: A Re-estimation. *Scot. J. Polit. Econ.*, June 1985, *32*(2), pp. 199–204. [G: LDCs]

Bergström, Villy and Södersten, Jan. Do Tax Allowances Stimulate Investment? In *Førsund, F. R. and Honkapohja, S., eds.*, 1985, pp. 146–70. [G: Sweden]

Berliant, Marcus and Strauss, Robert P. The Horizontal and Vertical Equity Characteristics of the Federal Individual Income Tax, 1966–1977. In *David, M. and Smeeding, T., eds.*, 1985, pp. 179–211. [G: U.S.]

Bhagwati, Jagdish N. Taxation and International Migration: Recent Policy Issues. In *Bhagwati, J. N. (I)*, 1985, pp. 347–61. [G: U.S.; LDCs]

Bhagwati, Jagdish N. The Brain Drain: International Resource Flow Accounting, Compensation, Taxation and Related Policy Proposals. In *Bhagwati, J. N. (I)*, 1985, pp. 303–46. [G: Selected LDCs; U.S.; Canada]

Bhagwati, Jagdish N. and Srinivasan, T. N. The Ranking of Policy Interventions under Factor Market Imperfections: The Case of Sector-Specific Sticky Wages and Unemployment. In *Bhagwati, J. N. (II)*, 1985, pp. 250–67.

Bicksler, James L. The Integration of Insurance and Taxes in Corporate Pension Strategy. *J. Finance*, July 1985, *40*(3), pp. 943–55. [G: U.S.]

Biddle, Gary C. and Martin, R. Kipp. Inflation, Taxes, and Optimal Inventory Policies. *J. Acc. Res.*, Spring 1985, *23*(1), pp. 57–83.

Bierlaagh, Hubert M. M. The Assessment and Collection of Tax from Non-residents: Netherlands. In *International Fiscal Association (I)*, 1985, pp. 547–61. [G: Netherlands]

Bingham, Tayler H.; Anderson, Donald W. and Cooley, Philip C. Distributional Implications of the Highway Revenue Act. *Public Finance Quart.*, January 1985, *13*(1), pp. 99–112. [G: U.S.]

Biørn, Erik. Inflation, Depreciation and the Neutrality of the Corporate Income Tax. In *Førsund, F. R. and Honkapohja, S., eds.*, 1985, pp. 116–30. [G: Norway]

Birch, Melissa H. and Due, John F. The Retail Sales Tax (Impuesto a las Ventas). *Bull. Int. Fiscal Doc.*, March 1985, *39*(3), pp. 103–07. [G: Paraguay]

Bird, Richard M. and Brean, Donald J. S. Canada/U.S. Tax Relations: Issues and Perspectives. In *Fretz, D.; Stern, R. and Whalley, J., eds.*, 1985, pp. 391–425. [G: Canada; U.S.]

Bird, Richard M.; Bucovetsky, Meyer W. and Yatchew, Adonis John. Tax Incentives for Film Production: The Canadian Experience. *Public Finance Quart.*, October 1985, *13*(4), pp. 396–421. [G: Canada]

Bito, Christian. Evaluation des obligations renouvelables du Trésor. (The Pricing of ORT. With English summary.) *Finance*, December 1985, *6*(2), pp. 231–48. [G: France]

Blomquist, N. Sören. Labour Supply in a Two-Period Model: The Effect of a Nonlinear Progressive Income Tax. *Rev. Econ. Stud.*, July 1985, *52*(3), pp. 515–24.

Blum, Walter. A Handy Summary of the Capital Gains Arguments. *Australian Tax Forum*, Autumn 1985, *2*(1), pp. 97–125.

Boidman, Nathan. Some Current Issues with Treaty Tax-sparing Provisions. *Bull. Int. Fiscal Doc.*, Aug./Sept. 1985, *39*(8/9), pp. 387–91. [G: Canada]

Boily, Nicole. Daycare and Public Policy: Comments. In *Economic Council of Canada.*, 1985, pp. 16–18. [G: Canada]

Bolus, Claude and Lagae, Jean-Pierre. L'établissement et la perception des impôts à charge des non-résidents: Belgique. (The Assessment and Collection of Tax from Non-residents: Belgium. With English summary.) In *International Fiscal Association (I)*, 1985, pp. 275–98. [G: Belgium]

Borooah, Vani K. The Interaction between Economic Policy and Political Performance. In *Matthews, R. C. O., ed.*, 1985, pp. 20–48. [G: U.K.]

Boskin, Michael J.; Robinson, Marc S. and Ferron, Mark J. Economic Aspects of the Taxation of Decontrolled Natural Gas. *Nat. Tax J.*, June 1985, *38*(2), pp. 179–90. [G: U.S.]

Bossons, John. Inflation, Indexation and the Capital Gains Tax. *Australian Tax Forum*, Spring 1985, *2*(3), pp. 249–72. [G: Australia]

Bosworth, Barry P. Taxes and the Investment Recovery. *Brookings Pap. Econ. Act.*, 1985, (1), pp. 1–38. [G: U.S.]

Bovenberg, A. Lans. Dynamic General Equilibrium Tax Models with Adjustment Costs. In *Manne, A. S., ed.*, 1985, pp. 40–55.

Boxer, Alan. Tax Reform Revisited. *Australian Tax Forum*, Summer 1985, *2*(4), pp. 363–83. [G: Australia]

Boyd, Roy and Daniels, Barbara J. Capital Gains Treatment of Timber Income: Incidence and Welfare Implications. *Land Econ.*, November 1985, *61*(4), pp. 354–62. [G: U.S.]

Bozeman, Barry and Link, Albert N. Public Support for Private R and D: The Case of the Research Tax Credit. *J. Policy Anal. Manage.*, Spring 1985, *4*(3), pp. 370–82. [G: U.S.]

Bradley, Bill. The Fair Tax. In *Pechman, J. A., ed. (I)*, 1985, pp. 80–102. [G: U.S.]

Break, George F. The Tax Expenditure Budget— The Need for a Fuller Accounting. *Nat. Tax J.*, September 1985, *38*(3), pp. 261–65. [G: U.S.]

Break, George F. The United States Federal System: Commentary. In *Quigley, J. M. and Rubinfeld, D. L., eds.*, 1985, pp. 75–79. [G: U.S.]

Break, George F. The Value-Added Tax. In *Pechman, J. A., ed. (II)*, 1985, pp. 128–57. [G: U.S.]

Breeden, Charles H. and Hunter, William J. Tax Revenue and Tax Structure. *Public Finance Quart.*, April 1985, *13*(2), pp. 216–24. [G: U.S.]

Brennan, Geoffrey. Taxation and Policy Change: A Median Voter Model for Australia 1968–69 to 1981–82. *Australian Econ. Rev.*, 3rd Quar-

ter, Spring 1985, (71), pp. 20–33.
[G: Australia]

Brick, Ivan E. and Ravid, S. Abraham. On the Relevance of Debt Maturity Structure. *J. Finance,* December 1985, *40*(5), pp. 1423–37.
[G: U.S.]

Brick, Ivan E. and Wallingford, Buckner A. The Relative Tax Benefits of Alternative Call Features in Corporate Debt. *J. Finan. Quant. Anal.,* March 1985, *20*(1), pp. 95–105.

Briggs, Norma. Individual Income Taxation and Social Benefits of Sweden, the United Kingdom and the U.S.A.—A Study of Their Interrelationships and Their Effects on Lower-Income Couples and Single Heads of Household. (With English summary.) *Bull. Int. Fiscal Doc.,* June 1985, *39*(6), pp. 243–61, 282. [G: U.S.; U.K.; Sweden]

Britton, John N. H. Research and Development in the Canadian Economy: Sectoral, Ownership, Locational, and Policy Issues. In *Thwaites, A. T. and Oakey, R. P., eds.,* 1985, pp. 67–114. [G: Canada]

Briys, Eric P. and Eeckhoudt, Louis. Relative Risk Aversion in Comparative Statics: Comment. *Amer. Econ. Rev.,* March 1985, *75*(1), pp. 281–83.

van den Broek, Peter. Tax Summit. *Bull. Int. Fiscal Doc.,* November 1985, *39*(11), pp. 489–90. [G: Australia]

Browning, Edgar K. A Critical Appraisal of Hausman's Welfare Cost Estimates. *J. Polit. Econ.,* October 1985, *93*(5), pp. 1025–34. [G: U.S.]

Browning, Edgar K. Tax Incidence, Indirect Taxes, and Transfers. *Nat. Tax J.,* December 1985, *38*(4), pp. 525–33.

Browning, Edgar K. The Marginal Social Security Tax on Labor. *Public Finance Quart.,* July 1985, *13*(3), pp. 227–51. [G: U.S.]

Browning, Edgar K. and Browning, Jacquelene M. Tax Reform and Deficit Reduction. In *Cagan, P. and Somensatto, E., eds.,* 1985, pp. 281–310. [G: U.S.]

Browning, Edgar K. and Browning, Jacquelene M. Why Not a True Flat Rate Tax? *Cato J.,* Fall 1985, *5*(2), pp. 629–50. [G: U.S.]

Brownlee, Helen. Poverty Traps. *Australian Tax Forum,* Winter 1985, *2*(2), pp. 161–72.
[G: Australia]

Brownlee, Helen. The Dependent Spouse Rebate. *Australian Tax Forum,* Summer 1985, *2*(4), pp. 427–38. [G: Australia]

Brownstone, David; Englund, Peter and Persson, Mats. Effects of the Swedish 1983–85 Tax Reform on the Demand for Owner-occupied Housing: A Microsimulation Approach. *Scand. J. Econ.,* 1985, *87*(4), pp. 625–46.
[G: Sweden]

Brunner, Johann K. and Petersen, Hans-Georg. Marginal Tax Burden: A Case Study of Austria and the Federal Republic of Germany. *Empirica,* 1985, *12*(2), pp. 209–26. [G: Austria; W. Germany]

Burgat, Paul and Jeanrenaud, Claude. Consequences d'une perequation tarifaire spatiale du point de vue du bien-etre et de la redistribu-

tion des revenus. (Consequences of Interregional Cross Subsidization with Regard to Welfare and Redistribution. With English summary.) *Public Finance,* 1985, *40*(1), pp. 64–81.

Burkhauser, Richard V. and Turner, John A. Is the Social Security Payroll Tax a Tax? *Public Finance Quart.,* July 1985, *13*(3), pp. 253–67.
[G: U.S.]

Burtless, Gary. Are Targeted Wage Subsidies Harmful? Evidence from a Wage Voucher Experiment. *Ind. Lab. Relat. Rev.,* October 1985, *39*(1), pp. 105–14. [G: U.S.]

Caballero, M. A. G. Income Tax on Gifts. *Bull. Int. Fiscal Doc.,* April 1985, *39*(4), pp. 171.
[G: Mexico]

Caballero, M. A. G. Taxation of Gifts and Inheritances: A Practical Approach. *Bull. Int. Fiscal Doc.,* February 1985, *39*(2), pp. 55–76.
[G: Latin America]

Cairns, Robert D. Reform of Exhaustible Resource Taxation. *Can. Public Policy,* December 1985, *11*(4), pp. 649–58.

Cameron, David R. Does Government Cause Inflation? Taxes, Spending, and Deficits. In *Lindberg, L. N. and Maier, C. S., eds.,* 1985, 224–79. [G: OECD]

Camion, Caty and Levasseur, Michel. Analyse financière des entreprises, systèmes fiscaux et inflation anticipée: La valeur économique des nombres comptables. (Financial Analysis of Firms, Taxation Systems and Anticipated Inflation. The Economic Value of Accounting Numbers. With English summary.) *Écon. Soc.,* December 1985, *19*(12), pp. 129–43.

Campbell, Harry F. and Lindner, R. K. A Model of Mineral Exploration and Resource Taxation. *Econ. J.,* March 1985, *95*(377), pp. 146–60.

Campbell, Harry F. and Lindner, R. K. Mineral Exploration and the Neutrality of Rent Royalties. *Econ. Rec.,* March 1985, *61*(172), pp. 445–49.

Caniglia, Alan S. Do Recipients Necessarily Prefer Cash Grants to Excise Subsidies? *Public Finance Quart.,* October 1985, *13*(4), pp. 422–35.

Canterbery, E. Ray; Cook, Eric W. and Schmitt, Bernard A. The Flat Tax, Negative Tax, and VAT: Gaining Progressivity and Revenue. *Cato J.,* Fall 1985, *5*(2), pp. 521–36. [G: U.S.]

Carliner, Geoffrey and McKee, Michael J. Designing a Tax Incentive Scheme: The Case of a Wage TIP. *J. Policy Anal. Manage.,* Summer 1985, *4*(4), pp. 501–15. [G: U.S.]

Carpenter, Edwin H. and Durham, Cathy. Again, Federal Tax Credits Are Found Effective: A Reply. *Energy J.,* July 1985, *6*(3), pp. 127–28. [G: U.S.]

Castan, Ron. Self-policing by Advisers in Taxation. *Australian Tax Forum,* Autumn 1985, *2*(1), pp. 79–83.

Chamley, Christophe. Efficient Tax Reform in a Dynamic Model of General Equilibrium. *Quart. J. Econ.,* May 1985, *100*(2), pp. 335–56.

Chamley, Christophe. Efficient Taxation in a Stylized Model of Intertemporal General Equilibrium. *Int. Econ. Rev.*, June 1985, *26*(2), pp. 451–68.

Chamley, Christophe. On a Simple Rule for the Optimal Inflation Rate in Second Best Taxation. *J. Public Econ.*, February 1985, *26*(1), pp. 35–50.

Chandra, Subodh. The Assessment and Collection of Tax from Non-residents: India. In *International Fiscal Association (I)*, 1985, pp. 445–63. [G: India]

Chang, Ching-huei. A General Disequilibrium Model of Tax Incidence. *J. Public Econ.*, February 1985, *26*(1), pp. 123–33.

Chapoton, John E. Uniform Tax Structures. In *Pechman, J. A., ed. (I)*, 1985, pp. 58–79. [G: U.S.]

Chernick, Howard and Reschovsky, Andrew. The Taxation of Social Security. *Nat. Tax J.*, June 1985, *38*(2), pp. 141–52. [G: U.S.]

Chevalier, J. P. L'établissement et la perception des impôts à charge des non-résidents: France. (The Assessment and Collection of Tax from Non-residents: France. With English summary.) In *International Fiscal Association (I)*, 1985, pp. 397–411. [G: France]

Chimerine, Lawrence. A Supply-Side Miracle? *J. Bus. Econ. Statist.*, April 1985, *3*(2), pp. 101–03. [G: U.S.]

Chiorazzi, Michael. Tax Reform during President Reagan's First Four Years: A Selective Bibliography. *Law Contemp. Probl.*, Autumn 1985, *48*(4), pp. 301–09. [G: U.S.]

Chown, John and Dewhurst, John. Capital Gains Tax and Corporation Tax: The UK Experience. *Australian Tax Forum*, Spring 1985, *2*(3), pp. 295–303. [G: U.K.]

Christiansen, Vidar. The Choice of Excise Taxes When Savings and Labour Decisions Are Distorted. *J. Public Econ.*, October 1985, *28*(1), pp. 95–110.

Chul, Song Lee. International Double Taxation of Inheritances and Gifts: Republic of Korea. In *International Fiscal Association (II)*, 1985, pp. 513–17. [G: S. Korea]

Ciriacy-Wantrup, S. V. Social Objectives of Conservation of Natural Resources with Particular Reference to Taxation of Forests. In *Ciriacy-Wantrup, S. V.*, 1985, pp. 269–76. [G: U.S.]

Clark, Graham. The Assessment and Collection of Tax from Non-residents: Singapore. In *International Fiscal Association (I)*, 1985, pp. 595–605. [G: Singapore]

Cloete, S. A. A Note on State Assistance to Marginal Gold Mines. *S. Afr. J. Econ.*, December 1985, *53*(4), pp. 424–28. [G: S. Africa]

Clotfelter, Charles T. Charitable Giving and Tax Legislation in the Reagan Era. *Law Contemp. Probl.*, Autumn 1985, *48*(4), pp. 197–212. [G: U.S.]

Cohen, Darrel and Clark, Peter B. Effects of Fiscal Policy on the U.S. Economy: Empirical Estimates of Crowding Out. *J. Policy Modeling*, Winter 1985, *7*(4), pp. 573–93. [G: U.S.]

Collins, David J. Designing a Tax System for Papua New Guinea. *Australian Tax Forum*,

Spring 1985, *2*(3), pp. 327–47.

Collins, M. H. The Policy and Practice of the United Kingdom in the Tax Treatment of Transfer Pricing. *Bull. Int. Fiscal Doc.*, Aug./Sept. 1985, *39*(8/9), pp. 354–62. [G: U.K.]

Conklin, David W. Subsidy Pacts. In *Fretz, D.; Stern, R. and Whalley, J., eds.*, 1985, pp. 434–59.

Conrad, Klaus. The Use of Standards and Prices for Environment Protection and Their Impact on Costs. *Z. ges. Staatswiss. (JITE)*, September 1985, *141*(3), pp. 390–400.

Conrad, Robert F. and Gillis, Malcolm. Progress and Poverty in Developing Countries: Rents and Resource Taxation. In *Lewis, S. R., Jr., ed.*, 1985, pp. 25–47.

Constantinides, George M. Debt and Taxes and Uncertainty: Discussion. *J. Finance*, July 1985, *40*(3), pp. 657–58.

Cook, Eric W. Revenue and Distributional Impacts of the Hall–Rabushka Flat Tax Proposal [The Route to a Progressive Flat Tax]. *Cato J.*, Fall 1985, *5*(2), pp. 477–80. [G: U.S.]

Cord, Steven. How Much Revenue Would a Full Land Value Tax Yield? In the United States in 1981, Census and Federal Reserve Data Indicate It Would Nearly Equal All Taxes. *Amer. J. Econ. Soc.*, July 1985, *44*(3), pp. 279–93. [G: U.S.]

Cordes, Joseph J. and Galper, Harvey. Tax Shelter Activity: Lessons from Twenty Years of Evidence. *Nat. Tax J.*, September 1985, *38*(3), pp. 305–24. [G: U.S.]

Corker, Robert J. and Begg, David K. H. Rational Dummy Variables in an Intertemporal Optimisation Framework. *Oxford Bull. Econ. Statist.*, February 1985, *47*(1), pp. 71–78. [G: U.K.]

Cornes, Richard and Sandler, Todd. Externalities, Expectations, and Pigouvian Taxes. *J. Environ. Econ. Manage.*, March 1985, *12*(1), pp. 1–13.

Cowell, Frank A. Tax Evasion with Labour Income. *J. Public Econ.*, February 1985, *26*(1), pp. 19–34.

Cowell, Frank A. The Economic Analysis of Tax Evasion. *Bull. Econ. Res.*, September 1985, *37*(3), pp. 163–93.

Crane, Steven E. and Nourzad, Farrokh. Time Value of Money and Income Tax Evasion under Risk-averse Behavior: Theoretical Analysis and Empirical Evidence. *Public Finance*, 1985, *40*(3), pp. 481–94. [G: U.S.]

Creedy, John and Gemmell, Norman. The Indexation of Taxes and Transfers in Britain. *Manchester Sch. Econ. Soc. Stud.*, December 1985, *53*(4), pp. 364–84. [G: U.K.]

Crocker, Keith J. and Snow, Arthur. A Simple Tax Structure for Competitive Equilibrium and Redistribution in Insurance Markets with Asymmetric Information. *Southern Econ. J.*, April 1985, *51*(4), pp. 1142–50.

Cullity, Maurice C. International Double Taxation of Inheritances and Gifts: Canada. In *International Fiscal Association (II)*, 1985, pp. 293–96. [G: Canada]

Danthine, Jean-Pierre and Donaldson, John B. A Note on the Effects of Capital Income Taxation on the Dynamics of a Competitive Economy. *J. Public Econ.*, November 1985, *28*(2), pp. 255–65.

Danziger, Sheldon and Smolensky, Eugene. Abrupt Changes in Social Policy: The Redistributive Effects of Reagan's Budget and Tax Cuts. In *Terny, G. and Culyer, A. J., eds.*, 1985, pp. 209–23. [G: U.S.]

Davey, Bernadette P. Gift and Inheritance Taxes in the African Continent. *Bull. Int. Fiscal Doc.*, March 1985, *39*(3), pp. 123–26. [G: Africa]

Davidson, Carl and Martin, Lawrence W. General Equilibrium Tax Incidence under Imperfect Competition: A Quantity-setting Supergame Analysis. *J. Polit. Econ.*, December 1985, *93*(6), pp. 1212–23.

Davis, Evan H. and Dilnot, Andrew W. The Restructuring of National Insurance Contributions in the 1985 Budget. *Fisc. Stud.*, May 1985, *6*(2), pp. 51–60. [G: U.K.]

Davis, Evan H. and Dilnot, Andrew W. The Restructuring of National Insurance Contributions in the 1985 Budget. In *Kay, J., ed.*, 1985, pp. 51–60. [G: U.S.]

Davis, Evan H. and Kay, John A. Extending the VAT Base: Problems and Possibilities. *Fisc. Stud.*, February 1985, *6*(1), pp. 1–16. [G: U.K.]

Debatin, Helmut. The Role of Tax Treaties as an Instrument of Economic Cooperation between "Capitalist" and "Socialist" Countries. *Bull. Int. Fiscal Doc.*, Aug./Sept. 1985, *39*(8/9), pp. 393–99.

Deblauwe, R. La double imposition internationale des successions et donations: Belgique. (International Double Taxation of Inheritances and Gifts: Belgium. With English summary.) In *International Fiscal Association (II)*, 1985, pp. 269–91. [G: Belgium]

Denzau, Arthur T. and Mackay, Robert J. Tax Systems and Tax Shares. *Public Choice*, 1985, *45*(1), pp. 35–47.

Deutsch, Antal. Review of "Building Better Pensions for Canadians." *Can. Public Policy*, September 1985, *11*(3), pp. 617–22. [G: Canada]

Dilger, Robert Jay. Eliminating the Deductibility of State and Local Taxes: Impacts on States and Cities. *Public Budg. Finance*, Winter 1985, *5*(4), pp. 75–90. [G: U.S.]

Dilnot, Andrew W.; Kay, John A. and Morris, Nick. The UK Tax System, Structure and Progressivity, 1948–1982. In *Førsund, F. R. and Honkapohja, S., eds.*, 1985, pp. 52–67. [G: U.K.]

DiLorenzo, Thomas J. The Rhetoric and Reality of Tax Reform [Normative and Positive Foundations of Tax Reform]. *Cato J.*, Fall 1985, *5*(2), pp. 401–06.

Dixit, Avinash K. Tax Policy in Open Economies. In *Auerbach, A. J. and Feldstein, M., eds.*, 1985, pp. 313–74.

Dixon, Daryl. Tax Avoidance and Withholding Tax. *Australian Tax Forum*, Autumn 1985, *2*(1), pp. 33–52. [G: Australia]

Dixon, Daryl. Taxation of the Income from Capital—Potential Income as the Tax Base. *Australian Tax Forum*, Winter 1985, *2*(2), pp. 173–90. [G: Australia]

Dixon, Daryl and Foster, Chris. The Age Composition of Australian Taxpayers. *Australian Tax Forum*, Summer 1985, *2*(4), pp. 439–50. [G: Australia]

Dorn, James A. The Principles and Politics of Tax Reform: Introduction. *Cato J.*, Fall 1985, *5*(2), pp. 361–83. [G: U.S.]

Doye, Damona G. and Boehlje, Michael D. A Flat Rate Tax: Impacts on Representative Hog and Grain Farms. *Western J. Agr. Econ.*, December 1985, *10*(2), pp. 147–61. [G: U.S.]

Dragun, Andrew K. Property Rights and Pigovian Taxes. *J. Econ. Issues*, March 1985, *19*(1), pp. 111–22.

Driessen, Patrick A. The Crowding-out Effect of Governmental Transfers on Private Charitable Contributions: Comment. *Nat. Tax J.*, December 1985, *38*(4), pp. 571–73. [G: U.S.]

Dukes, A. Taxation Policy for 1985–86. *Bull. Int. Fiscal Doc.*, March 1985, *39*(3), pp. 134–37. [G: Ireland]

Dunn, Patricia. Foreign Sales Corporations (FSC): A Survey of Selected Locations. *Bull. Int. Fiscal Doc.*, March 1985, *39*(3), pp. 117–22. [G: U.S.; Caribbean; W. Europe]

Dunn, Patricia. U.S.A.: FIRPTA and Tax Treaties. *Bull. Int. Fiscal Doc.*, December 1985, *39*(12), pp. 550–53. [G: U.S.; Canada]

Durinck, E. and Fabry, J. Een evaluatietechniek voor financiële leasing in België. (With English summary.) *Cah. Écon. Bruxelles*, 1st Trimester 1985, (105), pp. 41–57. [G: Belgium]

Dworin, Lowell and Kennedy, Michael. The Taxation of International Oil Production. *Nat. Tax J.*, March 1985, *38*(1), pp. 81–95. [G: U.S.]

Dye, Richard F. Influencing Retirement Behavior: Untangling the Effects of Income Taxation of Social Security Benefits. *J. Policy Anal. Manage.*, Fall 1985, *5*(1), pp. 150–54. [G: U.S.]

Dye, Richard F. Payroll Tax Effects on Wage Growth. *Eastern Econ. J.*, April-June 1985, *11*(2), pp. 89–100. [G: U.S.]

Dye, Thomas R. Impact of Federal Tax Reform on State–Local Finances. *Cato J.*, Fall 1985, *5*(2), pp. 597–608. [G: U.S.]

Easley, David; Kiefer, Nicholas M. and Possen, Uri. An Equilibrium Analysis of Optimal Unemployment Insurance and Taxation. *Quart. J. Econ.*, Supp. 1985, *100*, pp. 989–1010.

Edwards, J. S. S. and Keen, M. J. Inflation and Non-neutralities in the Taxation of Corporate Source Income. *Oxford Econ. Pap.*, December 1985, *37*(4), pp. 552–75.

Edwards, J. S. S. and Keen, M. J. Taxes, Investment and *Q. Rev. Econ. Stud.*, October 1985, *52*(4), pp. 665–79.

Edwards, P. S. A. International Double Taxation of Inheritances and Gifts: Hong Kong. In *International Fiscal Association (II)*, 1985, pp. 397–412. [G: Hong Kong]

Egger, John B. The FLANVAT as Tax Reform [The Flat Tax, Negative Tax, and VAT: Gaining

Progressivity and Revenue]. *Cato J.*, Fall 1985, 5(2), pp. 537–42. **[G: U.S.]**

Eilbott, Peter. The Revenue Effects of a Lower Capital Gains Tax. *Nat. Tax J.*, December 1985, 38(4), pp. 553–59. **[G: U.S.]**

Elliott, John A. and **Swieringa, Robert J.** Aetna, the SEC and Tax Benefits of Loss Carryforwards. *Accounting Rev.*, July 1985, 60(3), pp. 531–46. **[G: U.S.]**

Emerson, Craig. Mining Taxation in Malaysia. *Singapore Econ. Rev.*, April 1985, 30(1), pp. 34–55. **[G: Malaysia]**

Emmanuel, A. B. C. Advantages Offered to Foreign Investment. *Bull. Int. Fiscal Doc.*, March 1985, 39(3), pp. 113–16. **[G: Zambia]**

Englund, Peter. Taxation of Capital Gains on Owner-occupied Homes: Accrual vs Realization. *Europ. Econ. Rev.*, April 1985, 27(3), pp. 311–34.

Ezejelue, A. C. Analysis of Some Tax Issues in the 1985 Federal Government Budget. *Bull. Int. Fiscal Doc.*, July 1985, 39(7), pp. 307–14. **[G: Nigeria]**

Ezejelue, A. C. Nigeria: Crucial Amendments to Income Tax Laws. *Bull. Int. Fiscal Doc.*, December 1985, 39(12), pp. 533–38.
[G: Nigeria]

Faustini, Gino. A Medium-term Perspective for Budget Policy. *Rev. Econ. Cond. Italy*, January–April 1985, (1), pp. 99–118.
[G: W. Europe]

Fayle, Richard D. Controlling Abusive Tax Shelters. *Australian Tax Forum*, Autumn 1985, 2(1), pp. 53–69. **[G: Australia]**

Feige, Edgar L. The Meaning of the "Underground Economy" and the Full Compliance Deficit. In *Gaertner, W. and Wenig, A., eds.*, 1985, pp. 19–36. **[G: U.S.]**

Fellingham, John C. and **Wolfson, Mark A.** Taxes and Risk Sharing. *Accounting Rev.*, January 1985, 60(1), pp. 10–17.

Ferrara, Peter J. The National Commission's Failure to Achieve Real Reform: Comment. In *Ferrara, P. J., ed.*, 1985, pp. 49–58.
[G: U.S.]

Filosa, Vincenzo. Stato creditore–stato debitore: per una rilettura dell'art. 53 della Costituzione. (The State as a Creditor and as a Debtor: A New Interpretation of the Constitution Article 53. With English summary.) *Rivista Int. Sci. Econ. Com.*, December 1985, 32(12), pp. 1199–1216. **[G: Italy]**

Fisher, Peter S. Corporate Tax Incentives: The American Version of Industrial Policy. *J. Econ. Issues*, March 1985, 19(1), pp. 1–19.
[G: U.S.]

Fisher, Ronald C. Taxes and Expenditures in the U.S.: Public Opinion Surveys and Incidence Analysis Compared. *Econ. Inquiry*, July 1985, 23(3), pp. 525–50. **[G: U.S.]**

Flåm, Sjur D. and **Stensland, Gunnar.** Exploration and Taxation: Some Normative Issues. *Energy Econ.*, October 1985, 7(4), pp. 237–40.
[G: Norway]

Flowers, Marilyn R. Public Choice and the Flat

Tax. *Cato J.*, Fall 1985, 5(2), pp. 625–28.
[G: U.S.]

Fox, Lawrence A. Canada/U.S. Tax Relations: Issues and Perspectives: Comments. In *Fretz, D.; Stern, R. and Whalley, J., eds.*, 1985, 426–33. **[G: Canada; U.S.]**

Frank, M. Considérations critiques sur l'inventaire des dépenses fiscales établi en 1984 par le Conseil Supérieur des Finances. (With English summary.) *Cah. Écon. Bruxelles*, 2nd Trimester 1985, (106), pp. 59–91. **[G: Belgium]**

Fraser, R. W. Commodity Taxes under Uncertainty. *J. Public Econ.*, October 1985, 28(1), pp. 127–34.

Fraser, R. W. Severance Taxes, Uncertainty, and Natural Resources: The Effect of Investment of the Choice of Tax Base. *Public Finance*, 1985, 40(2), pp. 172–81.

Friend, Irwin. Effects of Taxation on Financial Markets. In *Pechman, J. A., ed. (II)*, 1985, pp. 87–106. **[G: U.S.]**

Fullerton, Don. Which Effective Tax Rate? A Reply. *Nat. Tax J.*, March 1985, 38(1), pp. 109–10. **[G: U.S.]**

Fullerton, Don and **Henderson, Yolanda Kodrzycki.** Long-run Effects of the Accelerated Cost Recovery System. *Rev. Econ. Statist.*, August 1985, 67(3), pp. 363–72. **[G: U.S.]**

Gadó, Ottó. Perspectives on and Limits to Public Finance for the Financing of Social Policy Goals in Socialist Economies (The Example of Hungary). In *Terny, G. and Culyer, A. J., eds.*, 1985, pp. 271–77. **[G: Hungary]**

Gallagher, James R. Irish Tax Proposals. *Australian Tax Forum*, Spring 1985, 2(3), pp. 285–93. **[G: Ireland]**

Galper, Harvey. The Tax Proposals of the U.S. Treasury Department. *Australian Tax Forum*, Winter 1985, 2(2), pp. 191–222. **[G: U.S.]**

Galvin, Charles O. Tax Legislation in the Reagan Era—Movement to or from a Consumption Base? *Law Contemp. Probl.*, Autumn 1985, 48(4), pp. 31–55.

Gammie, Malcomb J. The Implications of *Furniss v Dawson. Fisc. Stud.*, August 1985, 6(3), pp. 51–65. **[G: U.K.]**

Gamponia, Villamor and **Mendelsohn, Robert.** The Taxation of Exhaustible Resources. *Quart. J. Econ.*, February 1985, 100(1), pp. 165–81.
[G: U.S.]

Gann, Pamela B. Neutral Taxation of Capital Income: An Achievable Goal? *Law Contemp. Probl.*, Autumn 1985, 48(4), pp. 77–149.
[G: U.S.]

Geeroms, Hans J. A. and **Wilmots, Hendrik.** An Empirical Model of Tax Evasion and Tax Avoidance. *Public Finance*, 1985, 40(2), pp. 190–209.
[G: Belgium]

Gemmell, Norman. Tax Revenue Shares and Income Growth: A Note. *Public Finance*, 1985, 40(1), pp. 137–45. **[G: U.K.]**

Gemmell, Norman. The Incidence of Government Expenditure and Redistribution in the United Kingdom. *Economica*, August 1985, 52(207), pp. 335–44. **[G: U.K.]**

Genovese, Frank C. Land Value Taxation in Developing Countries: The Case of Jamaica: Comments. In *Lewis, S. R., Jr., ed.*, 1985, pp. 79–81. [G: Jamaica]

Gensheimer, Cynthia Francis. Reform of the Individual Income Tax: Effects on Tax Preferences for Medical Care. In *Meyer, J. A., ed.*, 1985, pp. 53–66. [G: U.S.]

Georgakopoulos, Theodore A. Indirect Taxes and Industrial Exports in Greece: The Case of Cement. *Greek Econ. Rev.*, December 1985, 7(3), pp. 255–67. [G: Greece]

Gephardt, Richard. The Economics and Politics of Tax Reform. *Cato J.*, Fall 1985, 5(2), pp. 455–64. [G: U.S.]

Gestrin, Henrik. Skattepolitiken och handelns utsikter. (Tax Policy and Trade Prospects. With English summary.) *Ekon. Samfundets Tidskr.*, 1985, 38(4), pp. 199–202. [G: Finland]

Gillioz, Pierre. La double imposition internationale des successions et donations: Suisse. (International Double Taxation of Inheritances and Gifts: Switzerland. With English summary.) In *International Fiscal Association (II)*, 1985, pp. 547–61. [G: Switzerland]

Gillis, Malcolm. Micro and Macroeconomics of Tax Reform: Indonesia. *J. Devel. Econ.*, December 1985, 19(3), pp. 221–54. [G: Indonesia]

del Giudice, Michele. L'établissement et la perception des impôts à charge des non-résidents: Italie. (The Assessment and Collection of Tax from Non-residents: Italy. With English summary.) In *International Fiscal Association (I)*, 1985, pp. 465–76. [G: Italy]

Glazer, Amihai. Using Corrective Taxes to Remedy Consumer Misperceptions. *J. Public Econ.*, October 1985, 28(1), pp. 85–94.

Gofran, K. A. Bangladesh: Some Highlights of the 1985–86 National Budget. *Bull. Int. Fiscal Doc.*, December 1985, 39(12), pp. 547–50. [G: Bangladesh]

Goldberg, Sanford H.; Stapper, Erik J. and Carlson, George N. International Double Taxation of Inheritances and Gifts: United States. In *International Fiscal Association (II)*, 1985, pp. 337–47. [G: U.S.]

Goldman, Richard L.; Karp, Joel J. and Monahan, John M. The Assessment and Collection of Tax from Non-residents: United States. In *International Fiscal Association (I)*, 1985, pp. 365–84. [G: U.S.]

Goode, Richard. Overview of the U.S. Tax System. In *Pechman, J. A., ed. (II)*, 1985, pp. 8–36. [G: U.S.]

Goodman, Wolfe D. International Double Taxation of Inheritances and Gifts: General Report. In *International Fiscal Association (II)*, 1985, pp. 15–61. [G: OECD]

Gordon, Roger H. Taxation of Corporate Capital Income: Tax Revenues versus Tax Distortions. *Quart. J. Econ.*, February 1985, 100(1), pp. 1–27.

Gottlieb, Daniel. Tax Evasion and the Prisoner's Dilemma. *Math. Soc. Sci.*, August 1985, 10(1), pp. 81–89.

Govind, Har. India: The Doctrine of "Merger"

in Appellate Procedures Concerning Direct Taxes. *Bull. Int. Fiscal Doc.*, December 1985, 39(12), pp. 539–46. [G: India]

Graetz, Michael J. Reform of Australian Business Taxation. *Australian Tax Forum*, Summer 1985, 2(4), pp. 385–414. [G: Australia]

Graetz, Michael J. The Estate Tax—Whither or Wither? In *Pechman, J. A., ed. (II)*, 1985, pp. 158–83. [G: U.S.]

Graetz, Michael J. and Wilde, Louis L. The Economics of Tax Compliance: Fact and Fantasy. *Nat. Tax J.*, September 1985, 38(3), pp. 355–63. [G: U.S.]

Graham, John F. Funding of Universities of Canada. In *Courchene, T. J.; Conklin, D. W. and Cook, G. C. A., eds. Vol. 1*, 1985, pp. 323–34. [G: Canada]

Gramlich, Edward M. Reforming U.S. Federal Fiscal Arrangements. In *Quigley, J. M. and Rubinfeld, D. L., eds.*, 1985, pp. 34–69. [G: U.S.]

Gramlich, Edward M. The Deductibility of State and Local Taxes. *Nat. Tax J.*, December 1985, 38(4), pp. 447–65. [G: U.S.]

Gravelle, Jane G. "Which Effective Tax Rate?" A Comment and Extension. *Nat. Tax J.*, March 1985, 38(1), pp. 103–08. [G: U.S.]

Green, Christopher J. An Empirical Note on the Fiscal Accommodation of an Oil Price Increase. *Appl. Econ.*, February 1985, 17(1), pp. 107–15. [G: U.K.]

Green, Edwin. Shipbuilding Finance of the *Shasen* Shipping Firms: 1920's–1930's: Comment. In *Yui, T. and Nakagawa, K., eds.*, 1985, pp. 273–77. [G: Japan]

Green, Richard A. and Harley, Geoffrey J. The Assessment and Collection of Tax from Non-residents: New Zealand. In *International Fiscal Association (I)*, 1985, pp. 509–25. [G: New Zealand]

Green, Richard C. and Talmor, Eli. The Structure and Incentive Effects of Corporate Tax Liabilities. *J. Finance*, September 1985, 40(4), pp. 1095–114.

Greenaway, David. Trade Taxes as a Source of Government Revenue: A Comment on the Bedrossian-Hitiris Re-estimation. *Scot. J. Polit. Econ.*, June 1985, 32(2), pp. 205–08.

Grieson, Ronald E. and Musgrave, Richard A. Wealth Utility and Tax Neutrality. *Public Finance*, 1985, 40(2), pp. 168–17.

Griliches, Zvi. Income-Maintenance Policy and Work Effort: Learning from Experiments and Labor-Market Studies: Comment. In *Hausman, J. A. and Wise, D. A., eds.*, 1985, pp. 137–38.

Groenewegen, Peter D. Options for the Taxation of Wealth. *Australian Tax Forum*, Spring 1985, 2(3), pp. 305–26. [G: Australia]

Gwartney, James and Long, James E. Is the Flat Tax a Radical Idea? *Cato J.*, Fall 1985, 5(2), pp. 407–32. [G: U.S.]

Hahn, Frank. On Optimum Taxation. In *Hahn, F.*, 1985, pp. 364–76.

Hall, Robert E. and Rabushka, Alvin. A Simple Income Tax with Low Marginal Rates. In *Pech-*

man, J. A., ed. (I), 1985, pp. 120–33.
[G: U.S.]

Hall, Robert E. and Rabushka, Alvin. The Route to a Progressive Flat Tax. *Cato J.*, Fall 1985, 5(2), pp. 465–76. [G: U.S.]

Halperin, Robert and Tzur, Joseph. The Effects of Nontaxable Employee Benefits on Employer Profits and Employee Work Effort. *Nat. Tax J.*, March 1985, 38(1), pp. 65–79.

Hamaekers, H. M. A. L. The OECD Report on the Allocation of Central Management and Service Costs. *Bull. Int. Fiscal Doc.*, December 1985, 39(12), pp. 530–33. [G: OECD]

Hamilton, Bob and Whalley, John. Tax Treatment of Housing in a Dynamic Sequenced General Equilibrium Model. *J. Public Econ.*, July 1985, 27(2), pp. 157–75. [G: Canada]

Hammond, Elizabeth M. and Morris, C. Nick. Matrimonial Property Law, Independent Taxation and Pensions: A Search for Consistency. *Fisc. Stud.*, November 1985, 6(4), pp. 57–65. [G: U.K.]

Hann, Danny. Political and Bureaucratic Pressures on U.K. Oil Taxation Policy. *Scot. J. Polit. Econ.*, November 1985, 32(3), pp. 278–95. [G: U.K.]

Hansen, Susan B. Tax Reform: Sound Economics or Power Politics? [Impact of Federal Tax Reform on State–Local Finances]. *Cato J.*, Fall 1985, 5(2), pp. 609–12. [G: U.S.]

Hanson, Gregory D. and Eidman, Vernon R. Agricultural Income Tax Expenditure—A Microeconomic Analysis. *Amer. J. Agr. Econ.*, May 1985, 67(2), pp. 271–78. [G: U.S.]

Hansson, Ingemar. Marginal Cost of Public Funds for Different Tax Instruments and Government Expenditures. In *Førsund, F. R. and Honkapohja, S., eds.*, 1985, pp. 17–32. [G: Sweden]

Hansson, Ingemar and Stuart, Charles. Progressive Taxation as Social Insurance and as a Median-Voter Outcome: An Empirical Assessment. *Scand. J. Econ.*, 1985, 87(3), pp. 487–99. [G: Sweden]

Hansson, Ingemar and Stuart, Charles. Tax Revenue and the Marginal Cost of Public Funds in Sweden. *J. Public Econ.*, August 1985, 27(3), pp. 331–53. [G: Sweden]

Harberger, Arnold C. Tax Policy in a Small, Open, Developing Economy. In *Connolly, M. B. and McDermott, J., eds.*, 1985, pp. 1–11.

Harboe, Einar. International Double Taxation of Inheritances and Gifts: Norway. In *International Fiscal Association (II)*, 1985, pp. 453–57. [G: Norway]

Harding, Ann. Tax Reform, Equity, and Social Security. *Australian Tax Forum*, Winter 1985, 2(2), pp. 223–38. [G: Australia]

Harriss, C. Lowell. Taxation, Incentives and Disincentives, and Human Motivation: Social Effects Are a Prime Consideration in Any Reform of the Tax Structure. *Amer. J. Econ. Soc.*, April 1985, 44(2), pp. 129–36. [G: U.S.]

Harte, Kathleen M. Legal Implications of Barter and Countertrade Transactions. In *Fisher,*

B. S. and Harte, K. M., eds., 1985, pp. 217–53. [G: U.S.; EEC]

Hartman, David G. Tax Policy and Foreign Direct Investment. *J. Public Econ.*, February 1985, 26(1), pp. 107–21. [G: U.S.]

Hartman, David G. The Economics of Incremental Incentive Programs: The Example of Employment Subsidies. *Public Finance Quart.*, October 1985, 13(4), pp. 375–95.

Hassler, Paul B. Die Steuerveranlagung und -erhebung bei Nichtansässigen: Österreich. (The Assessment and Collection of Tax from Non-residents: Austria. With English summary.) In *International Fiscal Association (I)*, 1985, pp. 249–74. [G: Austria]

Hattersley, Roy. A New Exchange Control Scheme. *Fisc. Stud.*, August 1985, 6(3), pp. 9–13. [G: U.K.]

Hausman, Jerry A. Taxes and Labor Supply. In *Auerbach, A. J. and Feldstein, M., eds.*, 1985, pp. 213–63. [G: U.S.]

Hawkins, Gregory D. Determinants of Corporate Leasing Policy: Discussion. *J. Finance*, July 1985, 40(3), pp. 909–10.

Head, John G. Towards the Tax Summit. *Australian Tax Forum*, Winter 1985, 2(2), pp. 129–45. [G: Australia]

Heady, Christopher J. and Mitra, Pradeep K. A Computational Approach to Optimum Public Policies. In *Manne, A. S., ed.*, 1985, pp. 95–120.

Heaps, Terry. The Taxation of Nonreplenishable Natural Resources Revisited. *J. Environ. Econ. Manage.*, March 1985, 12(1), pp. 14–27.

Heaps, Terry and Helliwell, John F. The Taxation of Natural Resources. In *Auerbach, A. J. and Feldstein, M., eds.*, 1985, pp. 421–72.

Heaver, Trevor D. The Effects of Fiscal Policies on the Development of International Shipping. *Logist. Transp. Rev.*, March 1985, 21(1), pp. 77–91. [G: Canada]

Helbich, Franz. Internationale Doppelbesteuerung bei Erbschaften und Schenkungen: Österreich. (International Double Taxation of Inheritances and Gifts: Austria. With English summary.) In *International Fiscal Association (II)*, 1985, pp. 253–67. [G: Austria]

Heller, Walter W. Tax Reform, Tax Revenue, and the Deficit. *Eastern Econ. J.*, Jan.-Mar. 1985, 11(1), pp. 51–63. [G: U.S.]

Henderson, J. Vernon. Property Tax Incidence with a Public Sector. *J. Polit. Econ.*, August 1985, 93(4), pp. 648–65.

Henrich, Amy L. Preferential Treatment of Charities under the Unemployment Insurance Laws. *Yale Law J.*, May 1985, 94(6), pp. 1472–92. [G: U.S.]

Herbert, Jule R., Jr. An Agenda for Tax Reform. In *Boaz, D. and Crane, E. H., eds.*, 1985, pp. 29–49. [G: U.S.]

Hettich, Walter and Winer, Stanley. Blueprints and Pathways: The Shifting Foundations of Tax Reform. *Nat. Tax J.*, December 1985, 38(4), pp. 423–45. [G: U.S.; Canada]

Hewitt, Daniel. Demand for National Public Goods: Estimates from Surveys. *Econ. In-*

quiry, July 1985, *23*(3), pp. 487–506.
[G: U.S.]

Hey, John D. Relative Risk Aversion in Comparative Statics: Comment. *Amer. Econ. Rev.*, March 1985, *75*(1), pp. 284–85.

Hochman, Shalom and Palmon, Oded. The Impact of Inflation on the Aggregate Debt-Asset Ratio. *J. Finance*, September 1985, *40*(4), pp. 1115–25.

Holcombe, Randall G. New Evidence for Flat Tax Reform [Federal Tax Reform: Lessons from the States]. *Cato J.*, Fall 1985, *5*(2), pp. 591–96.
[G: U.S.]

Holland, Daniel M. Land Value Taxation in Developing Countries: The Case of Jamaica. In *Lewis, S. R., Jr., ed.*, 1985, pp. 53–78.
[G: Jamaica]

Honkapohja, Seppo and Kanniainen, Vesa. Adjustment Costs, Optimal Capacity Utilization, and the Corporation Tax. *Oxford Econ. Pap.*, September 1985, *37*(3), pp. 486–99.

Honkavaara, Lauri. Yritysverotuksen kehittämislinjakomitean ehdotukset. (The Recommendations of the Finnish Committee on the Development of Business Taxation. With English summary.) *Kansant. Aikak.*, 1985, *81*(1), pp. 56–64.
[G: Finland]

Hood, Christopher C. British Tax Structure Development as Administrative Adaption. *Policy Sci.*, March 1985, *18*(1), pp. 3–31. [G: U.K.]

Horsley, David B. The Assessment and Collection of Tax from Non-residents: Canada. In *International Fiscal Association (I)*, 1985, pp. 315–34.
[G: Canada]

Howard, Theodore E. Estate Planning for Nonindustrial Forest Owners. *Land Econ.*, November 1985, *61*(4), pp. 363–71. [G: U.S.]

Howell, H. Wayne. State Securities Regulation of Tax Shelters. *Nat. Tax J.*, September 1985, *38*(3), pp. 339–43. [G: U.S.]

Hubbard, R. Glenn. Personal Taxation, Pension Wealth, and Portfolio Composition. *Rev. Econ. Statist.*, February 1985, *67*(1), pp. 53–60.
[G: U.S.]

Huggett, Donald R. Search and Seizure: A Gallimaufry of Events Relating to the Powers of the Fisc. *Bull. Int. Fiscal Doc.*, October 1985, *39*(10), pp. 456–60. [G: U.S.; Canada]

Hughes, Edward and McFetridge, Donald G. A Theoretical Analysis of Incremental Investment Incentives with an Application to the Case of Industrial R and D. *J. Public Econ.*, August 1985, *27*(3), pp. 311–29.

Hunt, Janet C.; Hill, C. R. and Kiker, B. F. The Effect of Taxation on Labour Supply: The Case of Moonlighting. *Appl. Econ.*, October 1985, *17*(5), pp. 897–905. [G: U.S.]

Ingberg, Mikael. Teemailtapäivä: verotus rakenne- ja suhdannepolitiikan välineenä. Näkökohtia veropaineinflaatiosta. (Some Remarks on Tax-induced Inflation. With English summary.) *Kansant. Aikak.*, 1985, *81*(1), pp. 25–39.
[G: Finland]

Ippolito, Richard A. Income Tax Policy and Lifetime Labor Supply. *J. Public Econ.*, April 1985, *26*(3), pp. 327–47. [G: U.S.]

Isachsen, Arne Jon; Samuelson, Sven Ove and Strøm, Steinar. The Behavior of Tax Evaders. In *Gaertner, W. and Wenig, A., eds.*, 1985, pp. 227–44.
[G: Norway]

Jackson, Ira. Bringing Tax Administration Out of the Bureaucratic Closet. *J. Policy Anal. Manage.*, Fall 1985, *5*(1), pp. 139–43. [G: U.S.]

Jacob, Charles E. Reaganomics: The Revolution in American Political Economy. *Law Contemp. Probl.*, Autumn 1985, *48*(4), pp. 7–30.
[G: U.S.]

Jap, K. S. An Outline of the 1985 Budget Tax Proposals. *Bull. Int. Fiscal Doc.*, March 1985, *39*(3), pp. 128–30. [G: Malaysia]

Jehle, Eugen. Taxation in the People's Republic of China: Tax Laws—Tax Incentives—Tax Treaties: A Brief Introduction. *Bull. Int. Fiscal Doc.*, Aug./Sept. 1985, *39*(8/9), pp. 405–27.
[G: Republic of China]

Jha, L. K. Reform of the Tax Structure. In *Jha, L. K.*, 1985, pp. 226–40. [G: India]

Jobin, Jacques and Dufour, Jean-Marie. Mesure et incidence des dépenses fiscales au Québec. (Measurement and Incidence of Tax Expenditures in Quebec. With English summary.) *L'Actual. Econ.*, March 1985, *61*(1), pp. 93–111. [G: Canada]

John, Kose and Williams, Joseph T. Dividends, Dilution, and Taxes: A Signalling Equilibrium. *J. Finance*, September 1985, *40*(4), pp. 1053–70.

Johnson, Manuel H. President Reagan's Modified Flat Tax: Analysis and Comparison. *Cato J.*, Fall 1985, *5*(2), pp. 499–520. [G: U.S.]

Jones, J. F. Avery. International Double Taxation of Inheritances and Gifts: United Kingdom. In *International Fiscal Association (II)*, 1985, pp. 519–35. [G: U.K.]

Jones, Melinda. The Politics of Tax Reform. *Australian Tax Forum*, Winter 1985, *2*(2), pp. 147–60. [G: Australia]

Jordan, Bradford D. and Pettway, Richard H. The Pricing of Short-term Debt and the Miller Hypothesis: A Note [Debt and Taxes]. *J. Finance*, June 1985, *40*(2), pp. 589–94.

Judd, Kenneth L. Redistributive Taxation in a Simple Perfect Foresight Model. *J. Public Econ.*, October 1985, *28*(1), pp. 59–83.

Junge, Georg. The Impact of Swiss Taxation on Economic Growth. *Schweiz. Z. Volkswirtsch. Statist.*, March 1985, *121*(1), pp. 23–34.
[G: Switzerland]

Kahl, Kandice H. Effects of the Economic Recovery Tax Act of 1981 on Futures Market Volume. *J. Futures Markets*, Summer 1985, *5*(2), pp. 239–46. [G: U.S.]

Kalinijabo, Charles. Summary of Income Tax Assessment. *Bull. Int. Fiscal Doc.*, May 1985, *39*(5), pp. 209–16. [G: Rwanda]

Kaneko, Hiroshi. The Assessment and Collection of Tax from Non-residents: Japan. In *International Fiscal Association (I)*, 1985, pp. 477–91.
[G: Japan]

Kanemasu, Hiromitsu; Litzenberger, Robert H. and Rolfo, Jacques. Pricing U.S. Treasury Securities with Tax Effects Using the Likelihood

Function. *Finance*, December 1985, *6*(2), pp. 187–216. [G: U.S.]

Kantowicz, Edward R. The Limits of Incrementalism: Carter's Efforts at Tax Reform. *J. Policy Anal. Manage.*, Winter 1985, *4*(2), pp. 217–33. [G: U.S.]

Kaplan, Steven E. and Reckers, Philip M. J. A Study of Tax Evasion Judgments. *Nat. Tax J.*, March 1985, *38*(1), pp. 97–102. [G: U.S.]

Karwani, Nanak. Applications of Concentration Curves to Optimal Negative Income Taxation. *J. Quant. Econ.*, July 1985, *1*(2), pp. 165–86.

Katz, Avery and Mankiw, N. Gregory. How Should Fringe Benefits Be Taxed? *Nat. Tax J.*, March 1985, *38*(1), pp. 37–46. [G: U.S.]

Katz, Eliakim. Relative Risk Aversion in Comparative Statics: Reply. *Amer. Econ. Rev.*, March 1985, *75*(1), pp. 286–87.

Katz, Michael L. and Rosen, Harvey S. Tax Analysis in an Oligopoly Model. *Public Finance Quart.*, January 1985, *13*(1), pp. 3–19.

Kauffman, Jean and Schmitt, Alex. L'établissement et la perception des impôts à charge des non-résidents: Luxembourg. (The Assessment and Collection of Tax from Non-residents: Luxemburg. With English summary.) In *International Fiscal Association (I)*, 1985, pp. 493–507. [G: Luxemburg]

Kay, John A. Changes in Tax Progressivity, 1951-85. *Fisc. Stud.*, May 1985, *6*(2), pp. 61–66. [G: U.K.]

Kay, John A. Changes in Tax Progressivity, 1951–85. In *Kay, J., ed.*, 1985, pp. 61–66. [G: U.K.]

Kay, John A. Transferable Tax Allowances. *Fisc. Stud.*, May 1985, *6*(2), pp. 67–70 [G: U.K.]

Kay, John A. Transferable Tax Allowances. In *Kay, J., ed.*, 1985, pp. 67–70. [G: U.K.]

Keating, Paul. Australia: Reform of the Taxation System. *Bull. Int. Fiscal Doc.*, December 1985, *39*(12), pp. 554–60.

Keating, Paul J. Interest Withholding Tax. *Bull. Int. Fiscal Doc.*, February 1985, *39*(2), pp. 89. [G: Australia]

Kehoe, Timothy J. and Whalley, John. Uniqueness of Equilibrium in Large-Scale Numerical General Equilibrium Models. *J. Public Econ.*, November 1985, *28*(2), pp. 247–54.

Kelley, Patrick L. Belgian Coordination Centers Prove Success. *Bull. Int. Fiscal Doc.*, July 1985, *39*(7), pp. 295–300. [G: Belgium]

Kelly, Tony. Reciprocal Exemption: A Regime to Treasure. *Bull. Int. Fiscal Doc.*, June 1985, *39*(6), pp. 267–70.

Kemp, Jack. A Fair, Simple, and Pro-growth Tax Reform. *Cato J.*, Fall 1985, *5*(2), pp. 481–98. [G: U.S.]

Kemp, Jack. The Fair and Simple Tax (FAST). In *Pechman, J. A., ed. (I)*, 1985, pp. 103–12. [G: U.S.]

van Kempen, Jan M. The Business Purpose Test: The Dutch Approach. *Fisc. Stud.*, August 1985, *6*(3), pp. 66–76. [G: Netherlands]

Kiesling, Herbert J. Violations of Scientific Impartiality in Tax Analysis. *Public Finance*, 1985, *40*(2), pp. 157–67.

Kim, Moon K. and Booth, G. Geoffrey. Yield Structure of Taxable vs. Nontaxable Bonds. *J. Finan. Res.*, Summer 1985, *8*(2), pp. 95–105.

Kim, Woo Taik. The Assessment and Collection of Tax from Non-residents: Republic of Korea. In *International Fiscal Association (I)*, 1985, pp. 573–79. [G: S. Korea]

Kindleberger, Charles P. Multinational Enterprise: Unit or Agglomeration? In *Shishido, T. and Sato, R., eds.*, 1985, pp. 33–45. [G: Global]

King, John R. What Future for Capital Gains Tax? *Fisc. Stud.*, May 1985, *6*(2), pp. 71–77. [G: U.K.]

King, John R. What Future for Capital Gains Tax? In *Kay, J., ed.*, 1985, pp. 71–77. [G: U.K.]

Kirzner, Israel M. Taxes and Discovery: An Entrepreneurial Perspective. In *Kirzner, I. M.*, 1985, pp. 93–118.

Kneebone, Susan. Estoppel as the Basis of Judicial Review: R v Inland Revenue Commissioners ex parte Preston [1985] 2 WLR 836. *Australian Tax Forum*, Spring 1985, *2*(3), pp. 349–62. [G: U.K.]

Knoester, Anthonie. The Forward Shifting of Taxes: A Comment [Stagnation and the Inverted Haavelmo Effect: Some International Evidence]: Reply. *De Economist*, 1985, *133*(3), pp. 417–20.

Kobayashi, Masaaki. Maritime Policy in Japan: 1868–1937: Comment. In *Yui, T. and Nakagawa, K., eds.*, 1985, pp. 153–56. [G: Japan]

Koefoed, O. The Forward Shifting of Taxes: A Comment [Stagnation and the Inverted Haavelmo Effect: Some International Evidence]. *De Economist*, 1985, *133*(3), pp. 415–17.

Kollintzas, Tryphon and Rowley, J. C. Robin. Nonstatic Expectations, Nonexponential Decay, and the Post Tax Rental Cost of Capital. *Public Finance*, 1985, *40*(3), pp. 411–40.

Kopcke, Richard W. Investment Spending and the Federal Taxation of Business Income. *New Eng. Econ. Rev.*, Sept./Oct. 1985, pp. 9–34. [G: U.S.]

Kopcke, Richard W. The Federal Income Taxation of Life Insurance Companies. *New Eng. Econ. Rev.*, March/April 1985, pp. 5–19. [G: U.S.]

Krashinsky, Michael. Daycare and Public Policy. In *Economic Council of Canada.*, 1985, pp. 9–16. [G: Canada]

Krause, Michael. Die Steuerveranlagung und -erhebung bei Nichtansässigen: Deutschland. (The Assessment and Collection of Tax from Non-residents: Germany. With English summary.) In *International Fiscal Association (I)*, 1985, pp. 197–211. [G: W. Germany]

Kremer, Claude and Elvinger, Jacques. La double imposition internationale des successions et donations: Luxembourg. (International Double Taxation of Inheritances and Gifts: Luxemburg. With English summary.) In *International Fiscal Association (II)*, 1985, pp. 441–51. [G: Luxemburg]

Krupp, Helmar. Public Promotion of Innovation—Disappointments and Hopes. In *Swee-*

ney, G., ed., 1985, pp. 48–79.   [G: OECD]

Kuiper, Willem G. Selected Problems of International Tax Law: Meeting of the German Tax Law Association. *Bull. Int. Fiscal Doc.*, January 1985, *39*(1), pp. 15–18.
[G: W. Germany]

Kuiper, Willem G. The Structure and Developments of Socialist Tax Law from a Western Point of View. *Bull. Int. Fiscal Doc.*, November 1985, *39*(11), pp. 483–88.[G: W. Europe]

van de Laar, Aart. Interest Groups and Development. In *Jerve, A. M., ed.*, 1985, pp. 155–66.   [G: Pakistan]

Lambert, Peter J. On the Redistributive Effect of Taxes and Benefits. *Scot. J. Polit. Econ.*, February 1985, *32*(1), pp. 39–54.   [G: U.K.; U.S.]

Lampreave, José L. International Double Taxation of Inheritances and Gifts: Spain. In *International Fiscal Association (II)*, 1985, pp. 321–35.   [G: Spain]

Lave, Charles A. The Private Challenge to Public Transportation—An Overview. In *Lave, C. A., ed.*, 1985, pp. 1–29.   [G: U.S.]

Lawson, Nigel. Tax Reform in the United Kingdom. *Bull. Int. Fiscal Doc.*, Aug./Sept. 1985, *39*(8/9), pp. 349–53.   [G: U.K.]

Lecerf, Michel. The Cameroon 1984/1985 Budget. *Bull. Int. Fiscal Doc.*, March 1985, *39*(3), pp. 127.   [G: Cameroon]

Lee, Dwight R. Are Politicians Interested in Honest Tax Reform? [Is the Flat Tax a Radical Idea?]. *Cato J.*, Fall 1985, *5*(2), pp. 433–36.   [G: U.S.]

Lermer, George and Stanbury, W. T. Measuring the Cost of Redistributing Income by Means of Direct Regulation. *Can. J. Econ.*, February 1985, *18*(1), pp. 190–207.   [G: Canada]

Lethaus, Hans J. Internationale Doppelbesteuerung bei Erbschaften und Schenkungen: Deutschland. (International Double Taxation of Inheritances and Gifts: Germany. With English summary.) In *International Fiscal Association (II)*, 1985, pp. 227–45.   [G: Germany]

Leuthold, Jane H. Labor Supply with an Endogenous Tax Rate. *Public Finance*, 1985, *40*(1), pp. 82–92.   [G: U.S.]

Leuthold, Jane H. Work Incentives and the Two-Earner Deduction. *Public Finance Quart.*, January 1985, *13*(1), pp. 63–73.   [G: U.S.]

Levačić, Rosalind. Supply Side Economics. In *Atkinson, G. B. J., ed.*, 1985, pp. 133–53.
[G: U.K.]

Levin, Dan. Taxation within Cournot Oligopoly. *J. Public Econ.*, August 1985, *27*(3), pp. 281–90.

Levy, Mickey D. Recent Budget Policy and Economic Impact. In *Shadow Open Market Committee.*, 1985, pp. 25–33.   [G: U.S.]

Lewis, Stephen R., Jr. Progress and Poverty in Developing Countries: Rents and Resource Taxation: Comments. In *Lewis, S. R., Jr., ed.*, 1985, pp. 49–51.

Liu, Pak-Wai. Lorenz Domination and Global Tax Progressivity. *Can. J. Econ.*, May 1985, *18*(2), pp. 395–99.

Low, Linda. The Financing Process in the Public Sector in Singapore: Tax and Non-tax Revenue. *Bull. Int. Fiscal Doc.*, April 1985, *39*(4), pp. 148–65.   [G: Singapore]

Lowenberg-DeBoer, J. and Boehlje, Michael D. The Estate Tax Provision of the 1981 Economic Recovery Tax Act: Which Farmers Benefit? *Southern J. Agr. Econ.*, December 1985, *17*(2), pp. 77–86.   [G: U.S.]

Lubick, Donald and Brannon, Gerard. Stanley S. Surrey and the Quality of Tax Policy Argument. *Nat. Tax J.*, September 1985, *38*(3), pp. 251–59.   [G: U.S.]

Lynch, Gerald J. Currency, Marginal Tax Rates, and the Underground Economy. *J. Econ. Bus.*, February 1985, *37*(1), pp. 59–67.   [G: U.S.]

Madeo, Silvia A. and Pincus, Morton. Stock Market Behavior and Tax Rule Changes: The Case of the Disallowance of Certain Interest Deductions Claimed by Banks. *Accounting Rev.*, July 1985, *60*(3), pp. 407–29.   [G: U.S.]

Magnani, Livio. Solo un piccolo colpo di freno all'azione dell "fiscal-drag." Un raffronto tra l'incidenza dell'IRPEF prevista dalla proposta del ministro Visentini e quella iniziale stabilita nel 1973 dalla riforma tributaria. (Only a Slight Brake on the Fiscal-Drag Action. With English summary.) *Bancaria*, September 1985, *41*(9), pp. 943–47.   [G: Italy]

Maisel, Sherman. The Agenda for Metropolitan Housing Policies. In *Quigley, J. M. and Rubinfeld, D. L., eds.*, 1985, pp. 224–52.
[G: U.S.]

Malecki, Edward J. Public Sector Research and Development and Regional Economic Performance in the United States. In *Thwaites, A. T. and Oakey, R. P., eds.*, 1985, pp. 115–31.   [G: U.S.]

Malik, Muhammad Hussain and Najam-us-Saqib. Who Bears the Burden of Federal Taxes in Pakistan? *Pakistan Devel. Rev.*, Autumn-Winter 1985, *24*(3/4), pp. 497–507. [G: Pakistan]

Mansfield, Charles Y. Tax Effort and Measures of Fiscal Stabilization Performance. *Bull. Int. Fiscal Doc.*, February 1985, *39*(2), pp. 77–85.

Mansfield, Edwin and Switzer, Lorne. How Effective Are Canada's Direct Tax Incentives for R and D? *Can. Public Policy*, June 1985, *11*(2), pp. 241–46.   [G: Canada]

Mantell, Edmund H. On the Economics and the Politics of Environmental Protection: Policy Conflicts Can Be Mitigated by Selective Enforcement and Tax-financed Subsidies. *Amer. J. Econ. Soc.*, October 1985, *44*(4), pp. 435–47.

Marfán, Manuel. El conflicto entre la recaudación de impuestos y la inversión privada: elementos teóricos para una reforma tributaria. (The Trade-off between Tax Revenues and Private Investment: Theoretical Elements for a Tax Reform. With English summary.) *Colección Estud. CIEPLAN*, 1985, (18), pp. 63–93.

Margolis, Julius. The United States Federal System: Commentary. In *Quigley, J. M. and Ru-*

binfeld, D. L., eds., 1985, pp. 80–86.
[G: U.S.]

Martinich, Joseph S. and Hurter, Arthur P., Jr. Price Uncertainty, Factor Substitution, and the Locational Bias of Business Taxes. *J. Reg. Sci.*, May 1985, 25(2), pp. 175–90.

Marzorati, Osvaldo J. International Double Taxation of Inheritances and Gifts: Argentina. In *International Fiscal Association (II)*, 1985, pp. 247–52. [G: Argentina]

Maskin, Eric S. and Riley, John G. Input versus Output Incentive Schemes. *J. Public Econ.*, October 1985, 28(1), pp. 1–23.

Mason, Greg. The Manitoba Basic Annual Income Data Base. *Can. Public Policy*, March 1985, 11(1), pp. 113–14. [G: Canada]

Mathews, Russell L. Federal–State Fiscal Arrangements in Australia. In *Drysdale, P. and Shibata, H., eds.*, 1985, pp. 43–66.
[G: Australia]

Mathews, Russell L. Public Finance. In *Mathews, R., et al.*, 1985, pp. 71–94. [G: Australia]

Mathews, Russell L. Some Reflections on the 1985 Tax Reforms (With Special Reference to Business Taxation). *Australian Tax Forum*, Summer 1985, 2(4), pp. 415–25.
[G: Australia]

Matteuzzi, Massimo. Vecchi e nuovi problemi nella tassazione delle società di capitali con redditi esenti. (Old and New Problems in Taxation of Joint-Stock Companies with Exempt Income. With English summary.) *Bancaria*, March 1985, 41(3), pp. 305–19. [G: Italy]

Mayr, Siegfried. International Double Taxation of Inheritances and Gifts: Italy. In *International Fiscal Association (II)*, 1985, pp. 413–22. [G: Italy]

McCaleb, Thomas S. Public Choice Perspectives on the Flat Tax Follies. *Cato J.*, Fall 1985, 5(2), pp. 613–24. [G: U.S.]

McDaniel, Paul R. Identification of the "Tax" in "Effective Tax Rates," "Tax Reform" and "Tax Equity." *Nat. Tax J.*, September 1985, 38(3), pp. 273–79. [G: U.S.]

McDonald, John W. and Snooks, G. D. Were the Tax Assessments of Domesday England Artificial? *Econ. Hist. Rev., 2nd Ser.*, August 1985, 38(3), pp. 352–72. [G: U.K.]

McGibany, James M. and Nourzad, Farrokh. Income Taxes and the Income Velocity of Money: An Empirical Analysis. *J. Macroecon.*, Fall 1985, 7(4), pp. 523–35. [G: U.S.]

McGuinness, Norman W. Comments on the Difficulties in Regulating Transfer Prices. In *Rugman, A. M. and Eden, L., eds.*, 1985, pp. 309–15.

McHugh, Richard. The Potential for Private Cost-increasing Technological Innovation under a Tax-based, Economic Incentive Pollution Control Policy. *Land Econ.*, February 1985, 61(1), pp. 58–64.

McIntyre, Robert S. and Tipps, Dean C. Exploding the Investment-Incentive Myth. *Challenge*, May/June 1985, 28(2), pp. 47–52.
[G: U.S.]

McMillion, Charles W. The Global Economy Re-

quires Greater U.S. Productivity. In *Didsbury, H. F., Jr., ed.*, 1985, pp. 251–64. [G: U.S.]

McRae, Robert N. Petroleum Taxation: A Comparison Between Canada and the U.S. In *Bjerkholt, O. and Offerdal, E., eds.*, 1985, pp. 177–99. [G: Canada; U.S.]

Meagher, G. A., et al. Special Purpose Versions of a General Purpose Multisectoral Model: Tax Issues and the Australian Wine Industry. In *Piggott, J. and Whalley, J., eds.*, 1985, pp. 283–92. [G: Australia]

Mendelson, Michael. Rationalization of Income Security in Canada. In *Courchene, T. J.; Conklin, D. W. and Cook, G. C. A., eds. Vol. 1*, 1985, pp. 229–52.

de Ménil, Georges and Sastre, José. Transfer Policies, Income, and Employment in France. In *de Ménil, G. and Westphal, U., eds.*, 1985, pp. 23–58. [G: France]

Metzer, Jacob. How New Was the New Era? The Public Sector in the 1920s. *J. Econ. Hist.*, March 1985, 45(1), pp. 119–26. [G: U.S.]

Miles, James A. and Ezzell, John R. Reformulating Tax Shield Valuation: A Note. *J. Finance*, December 1985, 40(5), pp. 1485–92.

Miller, Barbara D. and Wozny, James A. Land Tenure Patterns in Bangladesh: Implications for the Revenue and Distributional Effects of Changes in Land Taxation. *J. Devel. Areas*, July 1985, 19(4), pp. 459–81.
[G: Bangladesh]

Miller, Victor J. Recent Changes in Federal Grants and State Budgets. In *Lewin, M. E., ed.*, 1985, pp. 44–64. [G: U.S.]

Milliron, Valerie C. A Behavioral Study of the Meaning and Influence of Tax Complexity. *J. Acc. Res.*, Autumn 1985, 23(2), pp. 794–816.
[G: U.S.]

Minarik, Joseph J. Semantics of the Flat Rate Tax and Tax Reform. *Cato J.*, Fall 1985, 5(2), pp. 437–48. [G: U.S.]

Minarik, Joseph J. Tax Reform at the Crossroads. *Challenge*, March/April 1985, 28(1), pp. 4–11.
[G: U.S.]

Miwa, Ryoichi. Maritime Policy in Japan: 1868–1937. In *Yui, T. and Nakagawa, K., eds.*, 1985, pp. 123–52. [G: Japan]

Moray, Myriam. Impact de la fiscalité sur la composition optimale d'un portefeuille d'obligations d'Etat belge. (With English summary.) *Cah. Écon. Bruxelles*, 1st Trimester 1985, (105), pp. 91–118. [G: Belgium]

Moscholios, Nicholas. The Assessment and Collection of Tax from Non-residents: Greece. In *International Fiscal Association (I)*, 1985, pp. 413–32. [G: Greece]

Mumy, Gene E. The Role of Taxes and Social Security in Determining the Structure of Wages and Pensions. *J. Polit. Econ.*, June 1985, 93(3), pp. 574–85. [G: U.S.]

Mumy, Gene E. and Manson, William D. The Relative Importance of Tax and Agency Incentives to Offer Pensions: A Test Using the Impact of ERISA. *Public Finance Quart.*, October 1985, 13(4), pp. 464–85. [G: U.S.]

Murby, D. J. Dual Resident Companies—Uses

and Abuses. *Bull. Int. Fiscal Doc.*, Aug./Sept. 1985, *39*(8/9), pp. 373–78. **[G: U.K.]**

Musgrave, Richard A. Death and Taxes. In *[Recktenwald, H. C.]*, 1985, pp. 149–55.

Muth, Richard F. Urban Programs: Transportation and Housing: Commentary. In *Quigley, J. M. and Rubinfeld, D. L., eds.*, 1985, pp. 297–303. **[G: U.S.]**

Mutti, John H. and Grubert, Harry. The Taxation of Capital Income in an Open Economy: The Importance of Resident–Nonresident Tax Treatment. *J. Public Econ.*, August 1985, *27*(3), pp. 291–309. **[G: U.S.]**

Naqib, Fadle and Stollery, Kenneth R. The Effects of Alternative Public Pension Financing on Capital Formation: Consumption versus Payroll Taxes. *Economica*, May 1985, *52*(206), pp. 257–61.

Nellor, David C. L. Taxpayer Anticipation, Changing Tax Rates, and the Choice of Tax Base. *Public Finance*, 1985, *40*(2), pp. 247–62. **[G: U.S.]**

Neutmann, Wolf-Dieter and Sander, Uwe. Transfer Policies, Income, and Employment in Germany. In *de Ménil, G. and Westphal, U., eds.*, 1985, pp. 59–96.
[G: W. Germany]

Newlyn, W. T. Measuring Tax Effort in Developing Countries. *J. Devel. Stud.*, April 1985, *21*(3), pp. 390–405. **[G: Selected LDCs]**

Nielsen, Thøger. International Double Taxation of Inheritances and Gifts: Denmark. In *International Fiscal Association (II)*, 1985, pp. 305–319. **[G: Denmark]**

Noguchi, Yukio. Tax Structure and Saving–Investment Balance. *Hitotsubashi J. Econ.*, June 1985, *26*(1), pp. 45–58. **[G: U.S.; Japan]**

Norman, Neville. The Economics of Tax Ploision and Corporate Tax Integration. *Australian Tax Forum*, Autumn 1985, *2*(1), pp. 71–77.

Norris, Keith. Taxes, Transfers, and the Social Wage in Australia 1975–84. *Australian Bull. Lab.*, September 1985, *11*(4), pp. 212–35.
[G: Australia]

Oates, Wallace E. Searching for Leviathan: An Empirical Study. *Amer. Econ. Rev.*, September 1985, *75*(4), pp. 748–57.

Oldman, Oliver. Stanley Surrey and the Developing Countries. *Nat. Tax J.*, September 1985, *38*(3), pp. 281–83. **[G: LDCs; U.S.]**

Orrock, D. C. Tax Reform. *Bull. Int. Fiscal Doc.*, November 1985, *39*(11), pp. 490–93.
[G: Australia]

Orrock, D. C. The Assessment and Collection of Tax from Non-residents: Australia. In *International Fiscal Association (I)*, 1985, pp. 233–47. **[G: Australia]**

Ortiz Amaya, Bernardo and Gonzalez Parada, Hernan Alberto. La double imposition internationale des successions et donations: Colombie. (International Double Taxation of Inheritances and Gifts: Colombia. With English summary.) In *International Fiscal Association (II)*, 1985, pp. 297–303. **[G: Colombia]**

Otsuka, Masatami. International Double Taxation of Inheritances and Gifts: Japan. In *International Fiscal Association (II)*, 1985, pp. 423–40. **[G: Japan]**

Owens, Jeffrey and Roberti, Paolo. The Financing of Social Security Systems: International Comparisons: Trends and Policy Issues. In *Terny, G. and Culyer, A. J., eds.*, 1985, pp. 3–20. **[G: OECD]**

Owers, James E. and Rogers, Ronald C. The Windfall of Safe Harbor Leasing: Evidence from Capital Markets. *Nat. Tax J.*, December 1985, *38*(4), pp. 561–65. **[G: U.S.]**

Pagan, Jill C. U.K. Taxation and Currency Fluctuations. *Bull. Int. Fiscal Doc.*, Aug./Sept. 1985, *39*(8/9), pp. 379–86. **[G: U.K.]**

Paladini, Ruggero. Il ruolo dell'imposta ordinaria sul patrimonio nell'imposizione diretta: una rassegna critica. (The Role of the Ordinary Wealth Tax: A Survey. With English summary.) *Polit. Econ.*, December 1985, *1*(3), pp. 341–97.

Papps, Ivy E. Controlling and Monitoring Pollution: A Comment on "The Criminal Waste Discharger." *Scot. J. Polit. Econ.*, June 1985, *32*(2), pp. 171–80.

Parikh, Parimal M. Taxes on Capital. *Bull. Int. Fiscal Doc.*, October 1985, *39*(10), pp. 445–46. **[G: India]**

Park, Sang Yong and Williams, Joseph T. Taxes, Capital Structure, and Bondholder Clienteles. *J. Bus.*, April 1985, *58*(2), pp. 203–24.

Park, Thae S. Federal Personal Income Taxes: Liabilities and Payments, 1981–83. *Surv. Curr. Bus.*, May 1985, *65*(5), pp. 24.
[G: U.S.]

Paroutsas, Athanasios D. International Double Taxation of Inheritances and Gifts: Greece. In *International Fiscal Association (II)*, 1985, pp. 379–95. **[G: Greece]**

Pechman, Joseph A. A Citizen's Guide to the New Tax Reforms: Introduction. In *Pechman, J. A., ed. (I)*, 1985, pp. 1–20. **[G: U.S.]**

Pechman, Joseph A. The Promise of Tax Reform: Introduction. In *Pechman, J. A., ed. (II)*, 1985, pp. 1–7. **[G: U.S.]**

Perkins, Frances. Financing and Charging for Infrastructure. In *Drysdale, P. and Shibata, H., eds.*, 1985, pp. 151–76. **[G: Australia]**

Petersen, H. Craig. Solar versus Conservation Tax Credits. *Energy J.*, July 1985, *6*(3), pp. 129–35. **[G: U.S.]**

Peterson, Pamela P. Lingering Questions about Tax Reform [Why Not a True Flat Rate Tax?]. *Cato J.*, Fall 1985, *5*(2), pp. 651–56.

Peterson, Pamela P.; Peterson, David R. and Ang, James S. Direct Evidence on the Marginal Rate of Taxation on Dividend Income. *J. Finan. Econ.*, June 1985, *14*(2), pp. 267–82. **[G: U.S.]**

Peterson, Wallace C. The U.S. "Welfare State" and the Conservative Counterrevolution. *J. Econ. Issues*, September 1985, *19*(3), pp. 601–41. **[G: U.S.]**

Petrei, A. Humberto and Tybout, James R. Argentina 1976–1981: la importancia de variar los niveles de subsidios financieros. (With English summary.) *Cuadernos Econ.*, April 1985,

22(65), pp. 13–36.   [G: Argentina]

Phelps, Charles E. Taxing Health Insurance: How Much Is Enough? *Contemp. Policy Issues,* Winter 1984-85, *3*(2), pp. 47–54.   [G: U.S.]

Phillips, J. S. and Collins, M. H. The Assessment and Collection of Tax from Non-residents: General Report. In *International Fiscal Association (I),* 1985, pp. 15–55.

Phypers, Dean. A Businessman's View of Tax Reform. *Nat. Tax J.,* September 1985, *38*(3), pp. 285–90.   [G: U.S.]

Pines, David; Sadka, Efraim and Sheshinski, Eytan. The Normative and Positive Aspects of the Taxation of Imputed Rent on Owner-occupied Housing. *J. Public Econ.,* June 1985, *27*(1), pp. 1–23.

Plasschaert, Sylvain R. F. The Treatment of Spouses' Incomes in Schedular and Global Models of Income Taxation. *Bull. Int. Fiscal Doc.,* July 1985, *39*(7), pp. 301–06.

Plasschaert, Sylvain R. F. Transfer Pricing Problems in Developing Countries. In *Rugman, A. M. and Eden, L.,* eds., 1985, pp. 247–66.   [G: Selected LDCs]

Pohjola, Matti. Built-in Flexibility of Progressive Taxation and the Dynamics of Income: Stability, Cycles, or Chaos? *Public Finance,* 1985, *40*(2), pp. 263–73.

Porter, Michael G.; Cox, Jim and Bascand, Geoffrey. Tax Reform Proposal from Centre of Policy Studies. *Australian Tax Forum,* Spring 1985, *2*(3), pp. 273–84.   [G: Australia]

Prebble, John. International Double Taxation of Inheritances and Gifts: New Zealand. In *International Fiscal Association (II),* 1985, pp. 459–70.   [G: New Zealand]

Prest, Alan R. Implicit Taxes. In *[Recktenwald, H. C.],* 1985, pp. 157–70.

Proctor, Allen J. and Rappaport, Julie N. Federal Tax Reform and the Regional Character of the Municipal Bond Market. *Fed. Res. Bank New York Quart. Rev.,* Autumn 1985, *10*(3), pp. 6–15.   [G: U.S.]

Przeworski, Adam and Wallerstein, Michael. Comment on Katz, Mahler, & Franz [The Impact of Taxes on Growth and Distribution in Developed Capitalist Countries: A Cross-National Study]. *Amer. Polit. Sci. Rev.,* June 1985, *79*(2), pp. 508–10.
[G: Selected OECD]

Rao, M. B. Collaboration Agreements—Some Issues. *Bull. Int. Fiscal Doc.,* Aug./Sept. 1985, *39*(8/9), pp. 400–404.   [G: India; U.S.]

Raynauld, André. Government Export Subsidies. In *Conklin, D. W. and Courchene, T. J.,* eds., 1985, pp. 250–62.   [G: Canada]

Reece, Barry F. Simons' Account of Australian Taxation of Imputed Rental Income. *Australian Tax Forum,* Winter 1985, *2*(2), pp. 239–42.
[G: Australia]

Reece, William S. and Zieschang, Kimberly D. Consistent Estimation of the Impact of Tax Deductibility on the Level of Charitable Contributions. *Econometrica,* March 1985, *53*(2), pp. 271–93.   [G: U.S.]

Reinganum, Jennifer F. and Wilde, Louis L. In-

come Tax Compliance in a Principal–Agent Framework. *J. Public Econ.,* February 1985, *26*(1), pp. 1–18.

Reynolds, Alan. Some International Comparisons of Supply-Side Tax Policy. *Cato J.,* Fall 1985, *5*(2), pp. 543–69.   [G: OECD; LDCs]

Richardson, Harry W. and Turek, Joseph H. The Scope and Limits of Federal Intervention. In *Richardson, H. W. and Turek, J. H.,* eds., 1985, pp. 211–42.   [G: U.S.]

Richardson, Ivor L. M. Appellate Court Responsibilities and Tax Avoidance. *Australian Tax Forum,* Autumn 1985, *2*(1), pp. 3–20.
[G: New Zealand]

Riener, Kenneth D. A Pedagogic Note on the Cost of Capital with Personal Taxes and Risky Debt. *Financial Rev.,* May 1985, *20*(2), pp. 229–35.

Riethmuller, Max. Tax Shelters—As Seen by the Commissioner. *Australian Tax Forum,* Autumn 1985, *2*(1), pp. 21–32.   [G: Australia]

Riew, John. Equal Sacrifice Principle and Intertemporal Equity. *Public Finance,* 1985, *40*(2), pp. 274–79.

Rizzi, Dino. A Tax-based Incomes Policy Involving Payroll Taxation: Theoretical and Empirical Analyses. *Rivista Int. Sci. Econ. Com.,* July-Aug. 1985, *32*(7–8), pp. 679–700.   [G: Italy]

Roberts, Russell D. Recipient Preferences and the Design of Government Transfer Programs. *J. Law Econ.,* April 1985, *28*(1), pp. 27–54.
[G: U.S.]

Roberts, Shelagh. Income Taxation and Equal Treatment for Men and Women. *Bull. Int. Fiscal Doc.,* November 1985, *39*(11), pp. 501–07.
[G: EEC]

Robertson, A. Haeworth. The National Commission's Failure to Achieve Real Reform. In *Ferrara, P. J.,* ed., 1985, pp. 37–48.   [G: U.S.]

Robinson, P. William. Capacity Constraints, Real Wages and the Role of the Public Sector in Creating Jobs. In *Kay, J.,* ed., 1985, pp. 40–50.   [G: U.K.]

del Roccili, John A. and Luce, Priscilla. Regionalized Analysis of Industrial Policy. In *Adams, F. G.,* ed., 1985, pp. 49–65.   [G: U.S.]

Rock, Steven M. The Impact of Deductibility on the Incidence of a General Sales Tax: Reply. *Nat. Tax J.,* December 1985, *38*(4), pp. 579.
[G: U.S.]

Rockoff, Hugh. The Origins of the Federal Budget. *J. Econ. Hist.,* June 1985, *45*(2), pp. 377–82.   [G: U.S.]

Röell, Ailsa A. A Note on the Marginal Tax Rate in a Finite Economy. *J. Public Econ.,* November 1985, *28*(2), pp. 267–72.

Rogulska, Barbara. Le régulation indirecte ou les nouvelles relations Centre-entreprises en Pologne. (Indirect Regulation or New Relations between the Center and the Enterprises in Poland. With English summary.) *Écon. Soc.,* May 1985, *19*(5), pp. 69–115.   [G: Poland]

Rose, Richard. Getting By in Three Economies: The Resources of the Official, Unofficial and Domestic Economies. In *Lane, J.-E.,* ed., 1985, pp. 103–41.   [G: OECD]

Rosen, Harvey S. Housing Subsidies: Effects on Housing Decisions, Efficiency, and Equity. In *Auerbach, A. J. and Feldstein, M., eds.*, 1985, pp. 375–420. **[G: OECD]**

Rosen, Sherwin. Income-Maintenance Policy and Work Effort: Learning from Experiments and Labor-Market Studies: Comment. In *Hausman, J. A. and Wise, D. A., eds.*, 1985, pp. 134–37. **[G: U.S.]**

Roskamp, Karl W. and Scafuri, Allen J. Distributional Constraints on Optimal Commodity Taxes. In *[Recktenwald, H. C.]*, 1985, pp. 171–75.

Ross, Stephen A. Debt and Taxes and Uncertainty. *J. Finance*, July 1985, *40*(3), pp. 637–57.

Roth, Timothy P. Tax Rates, Income Flows, and Money Demand. *Quart. Rev. Econ. Bus.*, Spring 1985, *25*(1), pp. 74–84. **[G: U.S.]**

Rowlatt, Don. The Social-Security System in the 1990s: Comments. In *Courchene, T. J.; Conklin, D. W. and Cook, G. C. A., eds. Vol. 1,* 1985, pp. 277–83. **[G: Canada]**

Saarinen, Ola. International Double Taxation of Inheritances and Gifts: Finland. In *International Fiscal Association (II)*, 1985, pp. 349–63. **[G: Finland]**

Sabine, Basil. The Assessment and Collection of Tax from Non-residents: United Kingdom. In *International Fiscal Association (I)*, 1985, pp. 581–93. **[G: U.K.]**

Sadowski, Dieter and Schittenhelm, Rainer. Tax Subsidies and the Intra-organizational Trading of Fringe Benefits: An Economic Model Building Approach. In *Niehaus, R. J., ed.*, 1985, pp. 121–44. **[G: W. Germany]**

Sammartino, Frank J. and Kasten, Richard A. The Distributional Consequences of Taxing Social Security Benefits: Current Law and Alternative Schemes. *J. Post Keynesian Econ.*, Fall 1985, *8*(1), pp. 28–46. **[G: U.S.]**

Sandmo, Agnar. The Effects of Taxation on Savings and Risk Taking. In *Auerbach, A. J. and Feldstein, M., eds.*, 1985, pp. 265–311.

Sarantis, Nicholas. Government Deficits and Personal Expenditure in the E.E.C. *Rivista Int. Sci. Econ. Com.*, July-Aug. 1985, *32*(7–8), pp. 723–34. **[G: EEC]**

Sarig, Oded H. and Scott, James. The Puzzle of Financial Leverage Clienteles. *J. Finance*, December 1985, *40*(5), pp. 1459–67. **[G: U.S.]**

Sato, Ryuzo and Rizzo, John. Measuring the Burden of Property and Income Taxation. In *[Recktenwald, H. C.]*, 1985, pp. 309–17.

Scalone, Enrique Luis. The Assessment and Collection of Tax from Non-residents: Argentina. In *International Fiscal Association (I)*, 1985, pp. 213–32. **[G: Argentina]**

Schenone, Osvaldo H. La regla "Gravar en Función Inversa a la Elasticidad" y la tributación optima. (With English summary.) *Cuadernos Econ.*, April 1985, *22*(65), pp. 117–22.

Schindler, Guenter and Henderson, David. Intercorporate Transfer Pricing: The Role of the Functionally Determined Profit Split Ex-

plored. *Bull. Int. Fiscal Doc.*, March 1985, *39*(3), pp. 108–12. **[G: U.S.]**

Schmalbeck, Richard L. Tax Legislation in the Reagan Era: Foreward. *Law Contemp. Probl.*, Autumn 1985, *48*(4), pp. 1–6. **[G: U.S.]**

Schmidt, Ronald H. and Dunstan, Roger H. Effects of Reducing the Deficit with an Oil Import Tariff. *Fed. Res. Bank Dallas Econ. Rev.*, September 1985, pp. 15–24.

Schneider, Robert R. Food Subsidies: A Multiple Price Model. *Int. Monet. Fund Staff Pap.*, June 1985, *32*(2), pp. 289–316. **[G: LDCs]**

Schorr, Alvin L. The Refundable Tax Credit: A Cubist Policy Analysis. *Policy Sci.*, December 1985, *18*(4), pp. 335–55. **[G: U.S.]**

Schwab, Robert M. Regional Effects of Investment Incentives. *J. Urban Econ.*, September 1985, *18*(2), pp. 125–34. **[G: U.S.]**

Schwab, Robert M. The Benefits of In-Kind Government Programs. *J. Public Econ.*, July 1985, *27*(2), pp. 195–210. **[G: U.S.]**

Schwartz, J. Brad. Student Financial Aid and the College Enrollment Decision: The Effects of Public and Private Grants and Interest Subsidies. *Econ. Educ. Rev.*, 1985, *4*(2), pp. 129–44.

Seater, John J. On the Construction of Marginal Federal Personal and Social Security Tax Rates in the U.S. *J. Monet. Econ.*, January 1985, *15*(1), pp. 121–35.

Seitz, R. Lorne. Government Support for Canadian Exporters. In *Conklin, D. W. and Courchene, T. J., eds.*, 1985, pp. 227–49. **[G: Canada]**

Sekiguchi, Sueo and Horiuchi, Toshihiro. Myth and Reality of Japan's Industrial Policies. *World Econ.*, December 1985, *8*(4), pp. 373–91. **[G: Japan]**

Shabman, Leonard A. and Capps, Oral, Jr. Benefit Taxation for Environmental Improvement: A Case Example from Virginia's Soft Crab Fishery. *Land Econ.*, November 1985, *61*(4), pp. 398–408. **[G: U.S.]**

Shome, Parthasarathi. Is the Corporate Tax Shifted? Empirical Evidence from ASEAN. *Public Finance Quart.*, January 1985, *13*(1), pp. 21–46. **[G: ASEAN]**

Short, Cameron and McNeill, Roger. Tractor Costs and Canadian Tax Policy. *Can. J. Agr. Econ.*, November 1985, *33*(3), pp. 343–58. **[G: Canada]**

Shorten, Sarah J. The Funding of Postsecondary Education: Proposals of the Canadian Association of University Teachers. In *Courchene, T. J.; Conklin, D. W. and Cook, G. C. A., eds. Vol. 1,* 1985, pp. 335–39. **[G: Canada]**

Shoup, Carl S. International Arbitration of Transfer Pricing Disputes under Income Taxation. In *Rugman, A. M. and Eden, L., eds.*, 1985, pp. 291–309.

Shoven, John B. Taxes and the Investment Recovery: Comment. *Brookings Pap. Econ. Act.*, 1985, (1), pp. 39–41. **[G: U.S.]**

Sinclair, Peter. The Economic System in the UK: Public Finance. In *Morris, D., ed.*, 1985, pp. 272–94. **[G: U.K.]**

Skaar, Arvid Aage. The Assessment and Collection of Tax from Non-residents: Norway. In *International Fiscal Association (I)*, 1985, pp. 527–45. **[G: Norway]**

Skinner, Jonathan S. and Slemrod, Joel B. An Economic Perspective on Tax Evasion. *Nat. Tax J.*, September 1985, *38*(3), pp. 345–53. **[G: U.S.]**

Slemrod, Joel B. A General Equilibrium Model of Taxation that Uses Micro-unit Data: With an Application to the Impact of Instituting a Flat-Rate Income Tax. In *Piggott, J. and Whalley, J., eds.*, 1985, pp. 221–52. **[G: U.S.]**

Slemrod, Joel B. An Empirical Test for Tax Evasion. *Rev. Econ. Statist.*, May 1985, *67*(2), pp. 232–38. **[G: U.S.]**

Smith, Clifford W., Jr. and Wakeman, L. MacDonald. Determinants of Corporate Leasing Policy. *J. Finance*, July 1985, *40*(3), pp. 895–908.

Smith, Donald J. A Comment on IRAs and Keoghs. *Nat. Tax J.*, March 1985, *38*(1), pp. 111–12. **[G: U.S.]**

Smith, James D. Wealth, Realized Income, and the Measure of Well-Being: Comment. In *David, M. and Smeeding, T., eds.*, 1985, pp. 117–24. **[G: U.S.]**

Sneum, Jonna. The Assessment and Collection of Tax from Non-residents: Denmark. In *International Fiscal Association (I)*, 1985, pp. 351–63. **[G: Denmark]**

Söderholm, Rainer. The Assessment and Collection of Tax from Non-residents: Finland. In *International Fiscal Association (I)*, 1985, pp. 385–95. **[G: Finland]**

Soldatos, Gerasimos T. The Impact of the Reagan Tax Cuts on the International Economy. *Indian Econ. J.*, Oct.-Nov. 1985, *33*(2), pp. 116–22.

Solon, Gary R. Work Incentive Effects of Taxing Unemployment Benefits. *Econometrica*, March 1985, *53*(2), pp. 295–306. **[G: U.S.]**

Solow, John L. General Equilibrium Incidence of Energy Taxation. *Southern Econ. J.*, April 1985, *51*(4), pp. 1018–30. **[G: U.S.]**

Soos, Piroska E. Basic Principles Affecting the Income Taxation of Foreign Persons. *Bull. Int. Fiscal Doc.*, January 1985, *39*(1), pp. 19–28. **[G: U.S.]**

Sørensen, Christen. Real indkomstbeskatning. (Taxation of Real Income. With English summary.) *Nationaløkon. Tidsskr.*, 1985, *123*(2), pp. 220–38. **[G: Iceland; Norway; Sweden]**

Spicer, Michael W. and Hero, Rodney E. Tax Evasion and Heuristics: A Research Note. *J. Public Econ.*, March 1985, *26*(2), pp. 263–67. **[G: U.S.]**

Spiro, Erwin. The 1985 Income Tax Changes. *Bull. Int. Fiscal Doc.*, May 1985, *39*(5), pp. 227–29. **[G: S. Africa]**

Sproule, Robert A. Tax Evasion and Labor Supply under Imperfect Information about Individual Parameters of the Tax System. *Public Finance*, 1985, *40*(3), pp. 441–56.

Srinivasan, T. N. The Horizontal and Vertical Equity Characteristics of the Federal Individual Income Tax, 1966–1977: Comment. In *Da-*

vid, M. and Smeeding, T., eds., 1985, pp. 212–14. **[G: U.S.]**

Stafford, Frank P. Income-Maintenance Policy and Work Effort: Learning from Experiments and Labor-Market Studies. In *Hausman, J. A. and Wise, D. A., eds.*, 1985, pp. 95–134. **[G: U.S.]**

Steinherr, Alfred. Investment or Employment Subsidies for Rapid Employment Creation in the European Economic Community? In *Weiserbs, D., ed.*, 1985, pp. 145–80. **[G: OECD]**

Stelcner, Morton and Breslaw, Jon. Income Taxes and the Labor Supply of Married Women in Quebec. *Southern Econ. J.*, April 1985, *51*(4), pp. 1053–72. **[G: Canada]**

Steuerle, C. Eugene. The Prospects for Tax Reform. *Nat. Tax J.*, September 1985, *38*(3), pp. 291–94. **[G: U.S.]**

Steuerle, C. Eugene. Wealth, Realized Income, and the Measure of Well-Being. In *David, M. and Smeeding, T., eds.*, 1985, pp. 91–117. **[G: U.S.]**

Stiglitz, Joseph E. The Consumption-Expenditure Tax. In *Pechman, J. A., ed. (II)*, 1985, pp. 107–27. **[G: U.S.]**

Stiglitz, Joseph E. The General Theory of Tax Avoidance. *Nat. Tax J.*, September 1985, *38*(3), pp. 325–37. **[G: U.S.]**

Stockfisch, J. A. Value-added Taxes and the Size of Government: Some Evidence. *Nat. Tax J.*, December 1985, *38*(4), pp. 547–52. **[G: OECD]**

Stolerman, J. P. The Assessment and Collection of Tax from Non-residents: Hong Kong. In *International Fiscal Association (I)*, 1985, pp. 433–44. **[G: Hong Kong]**

Stroup, Richard L. The Progressive Rate—Progressive Revenue Myth [Semantics of the Flat Rate Tax and Tax Reform]. *Cato J.*, Fall 1985, *5*(2), pp. 449–53. **[G: U.S.]**

Stutzer, Michael J. The Statewide Economic Impact of Small-Issue Industrial Revenue Bonds. *Fed. Res. Bank Minn. Rev.*, Spring 1985, *9*(2), pp. 2–13. **[G: U.S.]**

Sugiyama, Kazuo. Shipbuilding Finance of the Shasen Shipping Firms: 1920's–1930's. In *Yui, T. and Nakagawa, K., eds.*, 1985, pp. 255–72. **[G: Japan]**

Suits, Daniel B. and Fisher, Ronald C. A Balanced Budget Constitutional Amendment: Economic Complexities and Uncertainties. *Nat. Tax J.*, December 1985, *38*(4), pp. 467–77. **[G: U.S.]**

Summers, Lawrence H. Taxes and the Investment Recovery: Comment. *Brookings Pap. Econ. Act.*, 1985, (1), pp. 42–44. **[G: U.S.]**

Sumner, Michael. The Effect of an Anticipated Tax Change on Investment in Britain. *J. Public Econ.*, March 1985, *26*(2), pp. 237–47. **[G: U.K.]**

Sundqvist, Kent. The Assessment and Collection of Tax from Non-residents: Sweden. In *International Fiscal Association (I)*, 1985, pp. 607–23. **[G: Sweden]**

Sunley, Emil M. Alternatives for Tax Restructuring and Increased Revenue. In *Pechman,*

J. A., ed. (II), 1985, pp. 184–200. [G: U.S.]

Sury, M. M. Buoyancy and Elasticity of Union Excise Revenue in India: 1950–51 to 1980–81. *Margin*, October 1985, *18*(1), pp. 40–68.
[G: India]

Talmor, Eli. Personal Tax Considerations in Portfolio Construction: Tilting the Optimal Portfolio Selection. *Quart. Rev. Econ. Bus.*, Autumn 1985, *25*(3), pp. 55–71.

Talmor, Eli; Haugen, Robert A. and Barnea, Amir. The Value of the Tax Subsidy on Risky Debt. *J. Bus.*, April 1985, *58*(2), pp. 191–202.

Tanzi, Vito and Iden, George. The Impact of Taxes on Wages: Reply. *Econ. Notes*, 1985, (2), pp. 175–78. [G: U.S.]

Tatom, John A. Federal Income Tax Reform in 1985: Indexation. *Fed. Res. Bank St. Louis Rev.*, February 1985, *67*(2), pp. 5–12.
[G: U.S.]

Taverne, Dick. United Kingdom: The Search for Fiscal Neutrality in the Tax Treatment of Savings. *Bull. Int. Fiscal Doc.*, October 1985, *39*(10), pp. 447–51. [G: U.K.]

Taylor, M. E. C. The Taxation of Oil Companies. *Bull. Int. Fiscal Doc.*, April 1985, *39*(4), pp. 167–70. [G: Kenya]

Taylor, Willard B. Tax Policy and Changes to Subchapter C. *Law Contemp. Probl.*, Autumn 1985, *48*(4), pp. 57–75. [G: U.S.]

Teixeira Pinto, Luiz Fernando. The Assessment and Collection of Tax from Non-residents: Brazil. In *International Fiscal Association (I)*, 1985, pp. 299–313. [G: Brazil]

Terki, N. Joint Venture Enterprises. *Bull. Int. Fiscal Doc.*, January 1985, *39*(1), pp. 35–38.
[G: Algeria]

van Thiel, Servaas. Economic Cooperation in Central Africa: Some Tax Aspects. *Bull. Int. Fiscal Doc.*, February 1985, *39*(2), pp. 86–87.
[G: Central Africa]

Thimmaiah, G. Eighth Finance Commission Report: An Evaluation. *Margin*, January 1985, *17*(2), pp. 30–46. [G: India]

Thimmaiah, G. Fiscal Management. In *Mongia, J. N., ed.*, 1985, pp. 153–99. [G: India]

Thomassen, Henry. Tax Reform: The View from the States. *Nat. Tax J.*, September 1985, *38*(3), pp. 295–304. [G: U.S.]

Thomson, Norm. The South Australian Bushfire Cost to Government. In *Healey, D. T.; Jarrett, F. G. and McKay, J. M., eds.*, 1985, pp. 28–40. [G: Australia]

Tillinghast, David R. The Contributions of Stanley S. Surrey to the International Aspects of Taxation. *Nat. Tax J.*, September 1985, *38*(3), pp. 267–71. [G: U.S.]

Tinbergen, Jan. Some Remarks on the Optimal Tax System. In *Tinbergen, J.*, 1985, pp. 158–67.

Toder, Eric and Neubig, Thomas S. Revenue Cost Estimates of Tax Expenditures: The Case of Tax-Exempt Bonds. *Nat. Tax J.*, September 1985, *38*(3), pp. 395–414. [G: U.S.]

Tokman, Victor E. The Impact of Social Security

on Employment: Comment. In *Mesa-Lago, C., ed.*, 1985, pp. 279–84. [G: Colombia; Mexico; Venezuela]

Torous, Walter N. Differential Taxation and the Equilibrium Structure of Interest Rates. *J. Banking Finance*, September 1985, *9*(3), pp. 363–85.

Tramontana, Antonino. Ipostesi di riforma dell'Ilor per recuperarne il carattere locale. (Suggestions for Reforming Ilor in Order to Recover Its Local Character. With English summary.) *Bancaria*, November 1985, *41*(11), pp. 1137–46. [G: Italy]

Trengove, Chris D. Measuring the Hidden Economy. *Australian Tax Forum*, Autumn 1985, *2*(1), pp. 85–95. [G: U.S.]

Truog, Roman. Die Steuerveranlagung und -erhebung bei Nichtansässigen: Schweiz. (The Assessment and Collection of Tax from Non-residents: Switzerland. With English summary.) In *International Fiscal Association (I)*, 1985, pp. 625–38. [G: Switzerland]

Tuomala, Matti. Simplified Formulae for Optimal Linear Income Taxation. *Scand. J. Econ.*, 1985, *87*(4), pp. 668–72.

Tuomala, Matti. Verotuksen painopiste kotitalouksien verotuksessa. (Issues in the Taxation of Households. With English summary.) *Kansant. Aikak.*, 1985, *81*(1), pp. 42–52.
[G: Finland]

Vaghari, Jila. Tax Discounting Review of Recent Literature. *Indian Econ. J.*, July-Sept. 1985, *33*(1), pp. 130–39. [G: U.S.]

Valdés, Alberto. Subsidios alimentarios en países en desarrollo: estimaciones de sus costos y efectos distributivos. (With English summary.) *Cuadernos Econ.*, August 1985, *22*(66), pp. 329–36. [G: LDCs]

VanBeek, James R. A Note on the Impact of Deductibility on the Incidence of a General Sales Tax. *Nat. Tax J.*, December 1985, *38*(4), pp. 577–78. [G: U.S.]

Vann, Richard J. International Implications of Imputation. *Australian Tax Forum*, Summer 1985, *2*(4), pp. 451–99. [G: Australia]

Vasche, Jon David. Are Taxes on Lotteries Too High? *J. Policy Anal. Manage.*, Winter 1985, *4*(2), pp. 269–71. [G: U.S.]

Vedder, Richard. Federal Tax Reform: Lessons from the States. *Cato J.*, Fall 1985, *5*(2), pp. 571–90. [G: U.S.]

de Vin, Willem E. International Double Taxation of Inheritances and Gifts: Netherlands. In *International Fiscal Association (II)*, 1985, pp. 471–91. [G: Netherlands]

Viñals, José. Gasto público, estructura impositiva y actividad macroeconómica en una economía abierta. (With English summary.) *Revista Española Econ.*, 1985, *2*(1), pp. 113–33.

Vogel, Klaus. Taxation of Foreign Income—Principles and Practice. *Bull. Int. Fiscal Doc.*, January 1985, *39*(1), pp. 4–14.
[G: W. Germany]

Wachs, M. The Politicization of Transit Subsidy Policy in America. In *Jansen, G. R. M.;*

Nijkamp, P. and Ruijgrok, C. J., eds., 1985, pp. 353–66. [G: U.S.]

Wagner, Richard E. Normative and Positive Foundations of Tax Reform. *Cato J.*, Fall 1985, 5(2), pp. 385–99.

Waller, Erik. International Double Taxation of Inheritances and Gifts: Sweden. In *International Fiscal Association (II)*, 1985, pp. 537–45. [G: Sweden]

Warburton, Peter J. Investment or Employment Subsidies for Rapid Employment Creation in the EEC: Comment. In *Weiserbs, D., ed.*, 1985, pp. 181–82. [G: OECD]

Warren, Alvin C., Jr. The Individual Income Tax. In *Pechman, J. A., ed. (II)*, 1985, pp. 37–58.

Waterson, Michael. On Progressive Taxation and Risk-taking. *Oxford Econ. Pap.*, September 1985, 37(3), pp. 510–19.

Watson, Harry. Tax Evasion and Labor Markets. *J. Public Econ.*, July 1985, 27(2), pp. 231–46.

Waud, Roger N. Politics, Deficits, and the Laffer Curve. *Public Choice*, 1985, 47(3), pp. 509–17.

Weaver, R. Kent. Controlling Entitlements. In *Chubb, J. E. and Peterson, P. E., eds.*, 1985, pp. 307–41. [G: U.S.]

Welham, P. J. Reform of Tax Reliefs for Owner-Occupation. *J. Econ. Stud.*, 1985, 12(4), pp. 30–40. [G: U.K.]

West, Edwin G. The Real Costs of Tuition Tax Credits. *Public Choice*, 1985, 46(1), pp. 61–70. [G: U.S.]

Westworth, Chris N. Accounting Standards—A Framework for Tax Assessment. *Australian Tax Forum*, Spring 1985, 2(3), pp. 243–47.

Wheeler, Joanna C. U.K. Tax Congress, 1984. *Bull. Int. Fiscal Doc.*, February 1985, 39(2), pp. 91–92. [G: U.K.]

Whyte, William Foote. New Approaches to Industrial Development and Community Development. In *Woodworth, W.; Meek, C. and Whyte, W. F., eds.*, 1985, pp. 15–27. [G: U.S.]

Wijkander, Hans. Correcting Externalities through Taxes On/Subsidies to Related Goods. *J. Public Econ.*, October 1985, 28(1), pp. 111–25.

Wijnbergen, Sweder. Optimal Taxation of Imported Energy under Price Uncertainty. *Oxford Econ. Pap.*, March 1985, 37(1), pp. 83–92.

Wildasin, David E. Income Taxes and Urban Spatial Structure. *J. Urban Econ.*, November 1985, 18(3), pp. 313–33.

Wildasin, David E. On the Analysis of Labor and Capital Income Taxation in a Growing Economy with Government Saving. *Public Finance*, 1985, 40(1), pp. 114–32.

Willcocks, A. J. In Defence of the National Health Service. In *Bean, P.; Ferris, J. and Whynes, D., eds.*, 1985, pp. 257–71. [G: U.K.]

Willett, Ken. Mining Taxation Issues in the Australian Federal System. In *Drysdale, P. and Shibata, H., eds.*, 1985, pp. 105–26. [G: Australia]

Wilson, Richard R. The Impact of Social Security on Employment. In *Mesa-Lago, C., ed.*, 1985, pp. 245–78. [G: Colombia; Mexico; Venezuela]

Witte, Ann D. and Woodbury, Diane F. The Effect of Tax Laws and Tax Administration on Tax Compliance: The Case of the U.S. Individual Income Tax. *Nat. Tax J.*, March 1985, 38(1), pp. 1–13. [G: U.S.]

Witte, John F. Democratic Procedures and Tax Policy. In *Pechman, J. A., ed. (I)*, 1985, pp. 134–52. [G: U.S.]

Wolfson, Mark A. Empirical Evidence of Incentive Problems and Their Mitigation in Oil and Gas Tax Shelter Programs. In *Pratt, J. W. and Zeckhauser, R. J., eds.*, 1985, pp. 101–25. [G: U.S.]

Yaari, Uzi and Fabozzi, Frank J. Why IRA and Keogh Plans Should Avoid Growth Stocks. *J. Finan. Res.*, Fall 1985, 8(3), pp. 203–15. [G: U.S.]

Yaşer, Betty S. and Rajan, T. R. Thiaga. Share of Government in Gross National Product: Cross-Section and Time-Series Analysis, 1950–1982. *METU*, 1985, 12(1/2), pp. 107–18. [G: LDCs; MDCs]

Yatchew, Adonis John. Labor Supply in the Presence of Taxes: An Alternative Specification. *Rev. Econ. Statist.*, February 1985, 67(1), pp. 27–33. [G: U.S.]

Yawitz, Jess Barry; Maloney, Kevin J. and Ederington, Louis H. Taxes, Default Risk, and Yield Spreads. *J. Finance*, September 1985, 40(4), pp. 1127–40. [G: U.S.]

You, Jong Keun and Falk, Laurence H. Estimation of the Countercyclical Effect of Mortgage Interest Subsidies. In *Brown, R. C., ed.*, 1985, pp. 231–48. [G: U.S.]

Zee, Howell H. An Efficient Method of Calculating the Impact of Finite Tax Changes in an Intertemporal Framework. *Atlantic Econ. J.*, December 1985, 13(4), pp. 26–33.

Ziemer, Richard C. Impact of Recent Tax Law Changes. *Surv. Curr. Bus.*, April 1985, 65(4), pp. 28–31.

Zinam, Oleg. A Note on Tax Elasticity of Government Expenditures: Italian Experience. *Atlantic Econ. J.*, July 1985, 13(2), pp. 84. [G: Italy]

Zodrow, George R. Optimal Tax Reform in the Presence of Adjustment Costs. *J. Public Econ.*, July 1985, 27(2), pp. 211–30.

Zodrow, George R. Partial Tax Reform: An Optimal Taxation Perspective. *Can. J. Econ.*, May 1985, 18(2), pp. 335–46.

324 State and Local Government Finance

3240 General

Agarwal, Vinod B. and Morgan, W. Douglas. The Interindustry Effects of Tax and Expenditure Limitations: The California Case. *Growth Change*, April 1985, 16(2), pp. 3–11. [G: U.S.]

Arrow, Kenneth J. The Effect of the Price System and Market on Urban Economic Development.

In *Arrow, K. J. (II)*, 1985, pp. 56–62.

Bahl, Roy. Fiscal Problems of Cities in the Northeast. In *Richardson, H. W. and Turek, J. H., eds.*, 1985, pp. 150–63. [G: U.S.]

Barnett, Richard R. An Analysis of Local Government Response to Grants-in-Aid: A Case of User Charges. *Bull. Econ. Res.*, May 1985, 37(2), pp. 123–30.

Beck, Morris. Public Expenditure, Relative Prices, and Resource Allocation. *Public Finance*, 1985, 40(1), pp. 17–34. [G: U.S.]

Bowsher, Charles A. Governmental Financial Management at the Crossroads: The Choice Is between Reactive and Proactive Financial Management. *Public Budg. Finance*, Summer 1985, 5(2), pp. 9–29. [G: U.S.]

Brosio, Giorgio. Fiscal Autonomy of Non-central Government and the Problem of Public-Spending Growth. In *Forte, F. and Peacock, A., eds.*, 1985, pp. 52–64.

Brown, Richard E. On the State of State Auditing: Analysis; Reflections. *Public Budg. Finance*, Summer 1985, 5(2), pp. 75–88.

Butt, Henry A. Value for Money Auditing in Local Administration. *Public Budg. Finance*, Summer 1985, 5(2), pp. 63–74.

Chaudry-Shah, Anwar M. Empirical Approaches to Efficiency and Equity Issues in Local Public Finance. In *Brown, R. C., ed.*, 1985, pp. 39–57.

Chicoine, David L. and Walzer, Norman. Governmental Structure, Service Quality, and Citizens' Perceptions. *Public Finance*, 1985, 40(3), pp. 463–80. [G: U.S.]

Clark, Terry Nichols. Choose Austerity Strategies that Work for You. In *Clark, T. N., ed.*, 1985, pp. 71–88. [G: U.S.]

Clark, Terry Nichols. Fiscal Strain: How Different Are Snow Belt and Sun Belt Cities? In *Peterson, P. E., ed.*, 1985, pp. 253–80. [G: U.S.]

Clark, Terry Nichols. The Fiscal Austerity and Urban Innovation Project. In *Clark, T. N., ed.*, 1985, pp. 357–63. [G: U.S.]

Clarke, Susan E. and Rich, Michael J. Making Money Work: The New Urban Policy Arena. In *Clark, T. N., ed.*, 1985, pp. 101–15. [G: U.S.]

Cornwell, Elmer E. Comments [Constitutional Change and Agenda Control] [Demographic Factors Affecting Constitutional Decisions: The Case of Municipal Charters]. *Public Choice*, 1985, 47(1), pp. 219–29. [G: U.S.]

Danziger, James N. Leaders, Perceptions and Policy under Austerity. In *Clark, T. N., ed.*, 1985, pp. 89–93. [G: Denmark; U.S.]

Deno, Kevin T. and Mehay, Stephen L. Institutional Constraints on Local Jurisdiction Formation. *Public Finance Quart.*, October 1985, 13(4), pp. 450–63. [G: U.S.]

Derycke, Pierre-Henri. Les enjeux financiers de la dé centralisation. (With English summary.) *Revue Écon. Polit.*, Sept.-Oct. 1985, 95(5), pp. 673–83. [G: France]

Dowd, Kevin and Sayeed, Adil. Federal–Provincial Fiscal Relations: Some Background. In *Courchene, T. J.; Conklin, D. W. and Cook, G. C. A., eds. Vol. 2*, 1985, pp. 253–75. [G: Canada]

Dye, Thomas R. Impact of Federal Tax Reform on State–Local Finances. *Cato J.*, Fall 1985, 5(2), pp. 597–608. [G: U.S.]

Eberts, Paul R. Fiscal Austerity and Its Consequences in Local Governments. In *Clark, T. N., ed.*, 1985, pp. 365–86. [G: U.S.]

England, Richard W. Public School Finance in the United States: Historical Trends and Contending Interpretations. *Rev. Radical Polit. Econ.*, Spring and Summer 1985, 17(1/2), pp. 129–55. [G: U.S.]

Farnham, Paul G. and Bryant, Stephen N. Form of Local Government: Structural Policies of Citizen Choice. *Soc. Sci. Quart.*, June 1985, 66(2), pp. 386–400. [G: U.S.]

Gonzalez, Rodolfo A. and Mehay, Stephen L. Bureaucracy and the Divisibility of Local Public Output. *Public Choice*, 1985, 45(1), pp. 89–101. [G: U.S.]

Gramlich, Edward M. and Ysander, Bengt-Christer. Control of Local Government: Introduction. In *Gramlich, E. M. and Ysander, B.-C., eds.*, 1985, pp. 9–25.

Gurr, Ted Robert and King, Desmond S. The Post-industrial City in Transition from Private to Public. In *Lane, J.-E., ed.*, 1985, pp. 271–93.

Hansen, Susan B. Tax Reform: Sound Economics or Power Politics? [Impact of Federal Tax Reform on State–Local Finances]. *Cato J.*, Fall 1985, 5(2), pp. 609–12. [G: U.S.]

Henderson, J. Vernon. The Tiebout Model: Bring Back the Entrepreneurs. *J. Polit. Econ.*, April 1985, 93(2), pp. 248–64.

Hill, Richard Child and Negrey, Cynthia. The Politics of Industrial Policy in Michigan. In *Zukin, S., ed.*, 1985, pp. 119–38. [G: U.S.]

Hymans, Saul H. Median Voter Models and the Growth of Government Services. In *Gramlich, E. M. and Ysander, B.-C., eds.*, 1985, pp. 75–89. [G: U.S.]

Jackson, Peter M. Fiscal Containment and Local Government Finance in the U.K. In *Gramlich, E. M. and Ysander, B.-C., eds.*, 1985, pp. 175–228. [G: U.K.]

Johnson, Michael S. Metropolitan Dependence on Intergovenmental Aid. *Soc. Sci. Quart.*, September 1985, 66(3), pp. 713–23. [G: U.S.]

Jones, Geoffrey and Stewart, J. D. The Future of Local Government. *Reg. Stud.*, April 1985, 19(2), pp. 165–73. [G: U.K.]

Keating, Michael. Local Authorities and Economic Policy: Comment. In *Machin, H. and Wright, V., eds.*, 1985, pp. 200–204. [G: France]

Konukiewitz, Manfred and Wollmann, Hellmut. Urban Innovation: A Response to Deficiencies of the Intervention and Welfare State? In *Clark, T. N., ed.*, 1985, pp. 327–39. [G: W. Germany]

Leeds, Michael A. Property Values and Pension Underfunding in the Local Public Sector. *J. Urban Econ.*, July 1985, *18*(1), pp. 34–46.
[G: U.S.]

Lyons, William. Commentary: Urban Politics and Fiscal Strain. In *Clark, T. N., ed.*, 1985, pp. 95–98. [G: Denmark; U.S.]

Marks, Barry R. and Raman, Krishnamurthy K. The Importance of Pension Data for Municipal and State Creditor Decisions: Replication and Extensions. *J. Acc. Res.*, Autumn 1985, *23*(2), pp. 878–86. [G: U.S.]

Martinez-Vazquez, Jorge and Seaman, Bruce A. Private Schooling and the Tiebout Hypothesis. *Public Finance Quart.*, July 1985, *13*(3), pp. 293–318.

Maser, Steven M. Demographic Factors Affecting Constitutional Decisions: The Case of Municipal Charters. *Public Choice*, 1985, *47*(1), pp. 121–62. [G: U.S.]

Mathews, Russell L. Intergovernmental Relations. In *Mathews, R., et al.*, 1985, pp. 159–92. [G: Australia]

Mathews, Russell L. Public Finance. In *Mathews, R., et al.*, 1985, pp. 71–94. [G: Australia]

Mathis, Edward J. and Zech, Charles E. The Community Demand for Police Officers: Relative to the Maximum Base Salary, Citizen Wants Tend to Be Elastic. *Amer. J. Econ. Soc.*, October 1985, *44*(4), pp. 401–10. [G: U.S.]

Melck, Antony. On Subsidizing Education with Block Grants. *Econ. Educ. Rev.*, 1985, *4*(3), pp. 253–59. [G: U.S.]

Mény, Yves. Local Authorities and Economic Policy. In *Machin, H. and Wright, V., eds.*, 1985, pp. 187–99. [G: France]

Miller, Gary J. Progressive Reform as Induced Institutional Preferences [Demographic Factors Affecting Constitutional Decisions: The Case of Municipal Charters]. *Public Choice*, 1985, *47*(1), pp. 163–81. [G: U.S.]

Murray, Richard. Central Control of the Local Government Sector in Sweden. In *Gramlich, E. M. and Ysander, B.-C., eds.*, 1985, pp. 295–345. [G: Sweden]

Perkins, Frances. Financing and Charging for Infrastructure. In *Drysdale, P. and Shibata, H., eds.*, 1985, pp. 151–76. [G: Australia]

Peterson, George E. Pricing and Privatization of Public Services. In *Gramlich, E. M. and Ysander, B.-C., eds.*, 1985, pp. 137–72. [G: U.S.]

Picur, Ronald D. Cost Accounting Services to Governments: An Agency Theory Perspective. In *Clark, T. N., ed.*, 1985, pp. 117–33.
[G: U.S.]

Pines, David. Profit Maximizing Developers and the Optimal Provision of Local Public Good in a Closed System of a Few Cities. *Revue Écon.*, January 1985, *36*(1), pp. 45–62.

Platt, D. C. M. The Financing of City Expansion: Buenos Aires and Montreal Compared, 1880–1914. In *Platt, D. C. M. and di Tella, G., eds.*, 1985, pp. 139–48. [G: Argentina; Canada]

Polivka, Larry and Osterholt, B. Jack. The Gov-

ernor as Manager: Agency Autonomy and Accountability. *Public Budg. Finance*, Winter 1985, *5*(4), pp. 91–104. [G: U.S.]

Rizzo, Ilde. Regional Disparities and Decentralization as Determinants of Public-Sector Expenditure Growth in Italy (1960–81). In *Forte, F. and Peacock, A., eds.*, 1985, pp. 65–82.
[G: Italy]

Romano, Roberta. Law as a Product: Some Pieces of the Incorporation Puzzle. *J. Law, Econ., Organ.*, Fall 1985, *1*(2), pp. 225–83.
[G: U.S.]

Santerre, Rexford E. Spatial Differences in the Demands for Local Public Goods. *Land Econ.*, May 1985, *61*(2), pp. 119–28. [G: U.S.]

Saunders, Peter. Corporatism and Urban Service Provision. In *Grant, W., ed.*, 1985, pp. 148–73. [G: Australia; U.K.]

Schoettle, Ferdinand P. A Three-Sector Model for Real Property Tax Incidence. *J. Public Econ.*, August 1985, *27*(3), pp. 355–70.
[G: U.S.]

Schwab, Robert M. Pay-as-You-Go versus Advance-funded Public Pension Systems under Imperfect Capital Markets. *Public Finance Quart.*, July 1985, *13*(3), pp. 269–91.

Slack, Enid and Crocker, Douglas. The Impact of Federal–Provincial Transfers on Provincial Revenues and Expenditures: A Review. In *Courchene, T. J.; Conklin, D. W. and Cook, G. C. A., eds. Vol. 2*, 1985, pp. 311–43.
[G: Canada]

Stine, William F. Estimating the Responsiveness of Local Revenue to Intergovernmental Aid. *Nat. Tax J.*, June 1985, *38*(2), pp. 227–34.
[G: U.S.]

Thimmaiah, G. Eighth Finance Commission Report: An Evaluation. *Margin*, January 1985, *17*(2), pp. 30–46. [G: India]

Turk, Herman and Zucker, Lynne G. Structural Bases of Minority Effects on Majority-supported Change. *Soc. Sci. Quart.*, June 1985, *66*(2), pp. 365–85. [G: U.S.]

Vavouras, Ioannis S. Local Government and the Social Sector: An Evaluation of the Recent Institutional Arrangements in Greece. *Ann. Pub. Co-op. Econ.*, Oct.-Dec. 1985, *56*(4), pp. 497–512. [G: Greece]

Wallace, Wanda A. Accounting Policies and the Measurement of Urban Fiscal Strain. In *Chan, J. L., ed.*, 1985, pp. 181–212. [G: U.S.]

Weicher, John C. The State and Local Government Sector and the Federal Deficit. In *Cagan, P. and Somensatto, E., eds.*, 1985, pp. 59–79.
[G: U.S.]

Wetzel, James N. Transferable Property Rights to Education. *Land Econ.*, May 1985, *61*(2), pp. 213–16.

Whalley, Diane. Hedonic Price Functions and Progressive Neighborhood Improvement: A Theoretical Exploration. *Math. Soc. Sci.*, December 1985, *10*(3), pp. 275–79.

Zorn, Peter M. Capitalization, Population Movement, and the Local Public Sector: A Probabilistic Analysis. *J. Urban Econ.*, March 1985, *17*(2), pp. 189–207.   [G: U.S.]

3241 State and Local Government Expenditures and Budgeting

Andersen, Bent Rold. Det kommunale selvstyre i lyset af Københavnerundersøgelsen. (Local Self-government and Metropolitan Public Expenditures in Denmark. With English summary.) *Nationaløkon. Tidsskr.*, 1985, *123*(3), pp. 353–64.   [G: Denmark]

Ansari, M. M. Flow of Financial Resources and Inter-state Disparities: Implications for a Federal Set-up. *Indian Econ. J.*, July-Sept. 1985, *33*(1), pp. 105–26.   [G: India]

Bennett, R. J. Central City–City Region Fiscal Disparities in Austria: Estimates for 1979. *Urban Stud.*, February 1985, *22*(1), pp. 69–81.   [G: Austria]

Benson, Charles S. State Government Contributions to the Public Schools. In *Augenblick, J., ed.*, 1985, pp. 11–23.   [G: U.S.]

Blank, Rebecca M. The Impact of State Economic Differentials on Household Welfare and Labor Force Behavior. *J. Public Econ.*, October 1985, *28*(1), pp. 25–58.   [G: U.S.]

Borcherding, Thomas E. The Causes of Government Expenditure Growth: A Survey of the U.S. Evidence. *J. Public Econ.*, December 1985, *28*(3), pp. 359–82.   [G: U.S.]

Bottiroli Civardi, Marisa and Fraschini, Angela. Indices of Allocation of Expenditure in the Public Works Sector. *Ann. Pub. Co-op. Econ.*, Oct.-Dec. 1985, *56*(4), pp. 463–83. [G: Italy]

Bourque, Philip J. The Infrastructure Gap. *Growth Change*, January 1985, *16*(1), pp. 17–23.   [G: U.S.]

Brecher, Charles. Management Strategies and Budgetary Politics. *Public Budg. Finance*, Autumn 1985, *5*(3), pp. 58–75.   [G: U.S.]

Citrin, Jack and Green, Donald Philip. Policy and Opinion in California after Proposition 13. *Nat. Tax J.*, March 1985, *38*(1), pp. 15–35.   [G: U.S.]

Conte, Michael A. Do Wealth Neutralizing Matching Grants Neutralize the Effects of Wealth? *Rev. Econ. Statist.*, August 1985, *67*(3), pp. 508–14.   [G: U.S.]

Danziger, James N. Leaders, Perceptions and Policy under Austerity. In *Clark, T. N., ed.*, 1985, pp. 89–93.   [G: Denmark; U.S.]

Denton, Frank T. and Spencer, Byron G. Prospective Changes in Population and Their Implications for Government Expenditures. In *Courchene, T. J.; Conklin, D. W. and Cook, G. C. A., eds. Vol. 1*, 1985, pp. 44–95.   [G: Canada]

Ferris, James M. Interrelationships among Public Spending Preferences: A Micro Analysis. *Public Choice*, 1985, *45*(2), pp. 139–53.   [G: U.S.]

Gold, Steven D. State Aid for Local Schools: Trends and Prospects. In *Augenblick, J., ed.*, 1985, pp. 24–34.   [G: U.S.]

Gramlich, Edward M. Excessive Government

Spending in the U.S.: Facts and Theories. In *Gramlich, E. M. and Ysander, B.-C., eds.*, 1985, pp. 29–73.   [G: U.S.]

Grosskopf, Shawna; Hayes, Kathy J. and Kennedy, Thomas E. Supply and Demand Effects of Underfunding of Pensions on Public Employee Wages. *Southern Econ. J.*, January 1985, *51*(3), pp. 745–53.   [G: U.S.]

Hadley, Garland R. Interstate Migration, Income and Public School Expenditures: An Update of an Experiment. *Public Choice*, 1985, *46*(2), pp. 207–14.   [G: U.S.]

Hayes, Kathy. Congestion Measures for Local Public Goods in Metropolitan and Nonmetropolitan Cities. *Growth Change*, October 1985, *16*(4), pp. 1–9.   [G: U.S.]

Hepworth, Noel P. Control of Local Authority Expenditure—The Use of Cash Limits. In *Gramlich, E. M. and Ysander, B.-C., eds.*, 1985, pp. 229–92.   [G: U.K.]

Kemp, Roger L. Services: Choosing among Policy Options: Comments. In *Clark, T. N., ed.*, 1985, pp. 175–78.   [G: U.S.]

Lankford, Ralph Hamilton. Preferences of Citizens for Public Expenditures on Elementary and Secondary Education. *J. Econometrics*, January 1985, *27*(1), pp. 1–20.   [G: U.S.]

Lauth, Thomas P. Performance Evaluation in the Georgia Budgetary Process. *Public Budg. Finance*, Spring 1985, *5*(1), pp. 67–82.   [G: U.S.]

Levin, David J. State and Local Government Fiscal Position in 1984. *Surv. Curr. Bus.*, January 1985, *65*(1), pp. 19–23.   [G: U.S.]

Loehman, Edna and Emerson, Robert D. A Simultaneous Equation Model of Local Government Expenditure Decisions. *Land Econ.*, November 1985, *61*(4), pp. 419–32.   [G: U.S.]

Lyons, William. Commentary: Urban Politics and Fiscal Strain. In *Clark, T. N., ed.*, 1985, pp. 95–98.   [G: Denmark; U.S.]

Megdal, Sharon Bernstein. A Note on "Estimating School District Expenditure Functions under Conditions of Closed-End Matching Aid": Closed-End Matching Aid in the Context of a Two-Part Tariff. *J. Urban Econ.*, January 1985, *17*(1), pp. 19–29.   [G: U.S.]

Mehay, Stephen L. and Gonzalez, Rodolfo A. Economic Incentives under Contract Supply of Local Government Services. *Public Choice*, 1985, *46*(1), pp. 79–86.   [G: U.S.]

Miller, Victor J. Recent Changes in Federal Grants and State Budgets. In *Lewin, M. E., ed.*, 1985, pp. 44–64.   [G: U.S.]

Mouritzen, Poul Erik. Local Resource Allocation: Partisan Politics or Sector Politics. In *Clark, T. N., ed.*, 1985, pp. 3–17.   [G: Denmark]

Oates, Wallace E. Fiscal Limitations: An Assessment of the U.S. Experience. In *Gramlich, E. M. and Ysander, B.-C., eds.*, 1985, pp. 91–136.   [G: U.S.]

Pascal, Anthony, et al. Financing Local Government in Tough Times: A Summary of Research Findings and a Proposal for Reform. In *Clark, T. N., ed.*, 1985, pp. 135–60.   [G: U.S.]

Reed, Sarah A. The Impact of Budgetary Roles

upon Perspectives. *Public Budg. Finance,* Spring 1985, *5*(1), pp. 83–96.　　[G: U.S.]

Rose-Ackerman, Susan and Evenson, Robert E. The Political Economy of Agricultural Research and Extension: Grants, Votes, and Reapportionment. *Amer. J. Agr. Econ.,* February 1985, *67*(1), pp. 1–14.　　[G: U.S.]

Seley, John E. and Wolpert, Julian. The Savings/Harm Tableau for Social Impact Assessment of Retrenchment Policies. *Econ. Geogr.,* April 1985, *61*(2), pp. 158–71.

Skovsgaard, Carl-Johan. Budget-Making and Fiscal Austerity: A Case Study of Danish Local Government. In *Clark, T. N., ed.,* 1985, pp. 19–37.　　[G: Denmark]

Southwick, Lawrence, Jr. and Butler, Richard J. Fire Department Demand and Supply in Large Cities. *Appl. Econ.,* December 1985, *17*(6), pp. 1043–64.　　[G: U.S.]

Suits, Daniel B. and Fisher, Ronald C. A Balanced Budget Constitutional Amendment: Economic Complexities and Uncertainties. *Nat. Tax J.,* December 1985, *38*(4), pp. 467–77.　　[G: U.S.]

Travers, Tony. Public Expenditure Policy, 1985–86: Local Government. In *Cockle, P., ed.,* 1985, pp. 187–202.　　[G: U.K.]

Walzer, Norman. Fiscal Austerity in Mid-size Cities: Preliminary Findings. In *Clark, T. N., ed.,* 1985, pp. 161–73.　　[G: U.S.]

Ysander, Bengt-Christer and Nordström, Tomas. Local Authorities, Economic Stability and the Efficiency of Fiscal Policy. In *Gramlich, E. M. and Ysander, B.-C., eds.,* 1985, pp. 347–98.
　　[G: Sweden]

3242 State and Local Government Taxation, Subsidies, and Revenue

Ahmad, Nuzhat. Biases in Tax Assessment of Residential Properties in Karachi. *Pakistan J. Appl. Econ.,* Winter 1985, *4*(2), pp. 53–67.
　　[G: Pakistan]

Allen, Douglas W. Evidence of 'Tax' Farming: Tests Using Differential Land Assessments for BC Farms. *Can. Public Policy,* December 1985, *11*(4), pp. 659–64.　　[G: Canada]

Bennett, R. J. Central City–City Region Fiscal Disparities in Austria: Estimates for 1979. *Urban Stud.,* February 1985, *22*(1), pp. 69–81.
　　[G: Austria]

Botha, D. J. J. The Differential Impact of a Change in the Rating System. *S. Afr. J. Econ.,* September 1985, *53*(3), pp. 258–63.
　　[G: S. Africa]

Boucher, Michel. Le régime d'épargne-actions du Québec: mal réellement nécessaire? (With English summary.) *Can. Public Policy,* June 1985, *11*(2), pp. 196–205.　　[G: Canada]

Boyd, Roy and Daniels, Barbara J. Capital Gains Treatment of Timber Income: Incidence and Welfare Implications. *Land Econ.,* November 1985, *61*(4), pp. 354–62.　　[G: U.S.]

Bradbury, Katharine L. and Ladd, Helen F. Changes in the Revenue-raising Capacity of U.S. Cities, 1970–1982. *New Eng. Econ. Rev.,*

March/April 1985, pp. 20–37.　　[G: U.S.]

Chicoine, David L. and Hendricks, A. Donald. Evidence on Farm Use Value Assessment, Tax Shifts, and State School Aid. *Amer. J. Agr. Econ.,* May 1985, *67*(2), pp. 266–70.
　　[G: U.S.]

Chun, Dong Hoon and Linneman, Peter. An Empirical Analysis of the Determinants of Intrajurisdictional Property Tax Payment Inequities. *J. Urban Econ.,* July 1985, *18*(1), pp. 90–102.　　[G: U.S.]

Citrin, Jack and Green, Donald Philip. Policy and Opinion in California after Proposition 13. *Nat. Tax J.,* March 1985, *38*(1), pp. 15–35.
　　[G: U.S.]

Copithorne, Lawrence; MacFadyen, Alan and Bell, Bruce. Revenue Sharing and the Efficient Valuation of Natural Resources. *Can. Public Policy,* Supplement July 1985, *11*(3), pp. 465–78.　　[G: Canada]

Cord, Steven. How Much Revenue Would a Full Land Value Tax Yield? In the United States in 1981, Census and Federal Reserve Data Indicate It Would Nearly Equal All Taxes. *Amer. J. Econ. Soc.,* July 1985, *44*(3), pp. 279–93.
　　[G: U.S.]

Courchene, Thomas J. Equalization Payments in the 1990s. In *Courchene, T. J.; Conklin, D. W. and Cook, G. C. A., eds. Vol. 2,* 1985, pp. 73–92.　　[G: Canada]

Cullity, Maurice C. International Double Taxation of Inheritances and Gifts: Canada. In *International Fiscal Association (II),* 1985, pp. 293–96.　　[G: Canada]

DeBoer, Larry. Administrative Costs of State Lotteries. *Nat. Tax J.,* December 1985, *38*(4), pp. 479–87.　　[G: U.S.]

Dilger, Robert Jay. Eliminating the Deductibility of State and Local Taxes: Impacts on States and Cities. *Public Budg. Finance,* Winter 1985, *5*(4), pp. 75–90.　　[G: U.S.]

Due, John F. Trends in State Sales Tax Audit Selection since 1960. *Nat. Tax J.,* June 1985, *38*(2), pp. 235–40.

Durning, Dan and Quigley, John M. On the Distributional Implications of Mortgage Revenue Bonds and Creative Finance. *Nat. Tax J.,* December 1985, *38*(4), pp. 513–23.　　[G: U.S.]

Feehan, James P. Provincial Government Taxation of Clothing and Footwear: Revenue and Equity Aspects. *Can. Public Policy,* March 1985, *11*(1), pp. 26–39.　　[G: Canada]

Fisher, Vickie L. Recent Innovations in State Tax Compliance Programs. *Nat. Tax J.,* September 1985, *38*(3), pp. 565–71.　　[G: U.S.]

Fraker, Thomas; Moffitt, Robert and Wolf, Douglas. Effective Tax Rates and Guarantees in the AFDC Program, 1967–1982. *J. Human Res.,* Spring 1985, *20*(2), pp. 251–63.
　　[G: U.S.]

Freedman, D. A. The Mean versus the Median: A Case Study in 4-R Act Litigation. *J. Bus. Econ. Statist.,* January 1985, *3*(1), pp. 1–13.
　　[G: U.S.]

Fujii, Edwin T.; Khaled, Mohammed and Mak, James. The Exportability of Hotel Occupancy and Other Tourist Taxes. *Nat. Tax J.*, June 1985, *38*(2), pp. 169–77. [G: U.S.]

Gerking, Shelby and Dickie, Mark. Systematic Assessment Error and Intrajurisdiction Property Tax Capitalization: Comment. *Southern Econ. J.*, January 1985, *51*(3), pp. 886–90. [G: U.S.]

Goldberg, Kalman and Scott, Robert C. City Sales and Property Tax Restructuring: Household and Business Incidence Effects. *Public Budg. Finance*, Autumn 1985, *5*(3), pp. 89–98. [G: U.S.]

Goode, Richard. Overview of the U.S. Tax System. In *Pechman, J. A., ed. (II)*, 1985, pp. 8–36. [G: U.S.]

Gramlich, Edward M. The Deductibility of State and Local Taxes. *Nat. Tax J.*, December 1985, *38*(4), pp. 447–65. [G: U.S.]

Haley, A. J. A Five Year Update of Central City/Suburban Municipal Recreation Operating Expenditures. *J. Cult. Econ.*, December 1985, *9*(2), pp. 91–93. [G: U.S.]

Hansen, Susan B. Citizen Preferences and Participatory Roles: Comment. In *Clark, T. N., ed.*, 1985, pp. 263–67. [G: U.S.]

Harris, Stuart. State and Federal Objectives and Policies for the Use and Development of Resources. In *Drysdale, P. and Shibata, H., eds.*, 1985, pp. 67–89. [G: Australia]

Hayes, Kathy J. and Grosskopf, Shawna. Measuring the Welfare Loss of Pension Mandates: A Methodology and Example. *Public Finance Quart.*, January 1985, *13*(1), pp. 47–62. [G: U.S.]

Helms, L. Jay. The Effect of State and Local Taxes on Economic Growth: A Time Series–Cross Section Approach. *Rev. Econ. Statist.*, November 1985, *67*(4), pp. 574–82. [G: U.S.]

Henderson, J. Vernon. Property Tax Incidence with a Public Sector. *J. Polit. Econ.*, August 1985, *93*(4), pp. 648–65.

Hertel, Thomas W. and Mount, Timothy D. The Pricing of Natural Resources in a Regional Economy. *Land Econ.*, August 1985, *61*(3), pp. 229–43. [G: U.S.]

Jobin, Jacques and Dufour, Jean-Marie. Mesure et incidence des dépenses fiscales au Québec. (Measurement and Incidence of Tax Expenditures in Quebec. With English summary.) *L'Actual. Econ.*, March 1985, *61*(1), pp. 93–111. [G: Canada]

Joulfaian, David. Revenue Estimation and Progressivity: The Case of the Massachusetts Income Tax. *Nat. Tax J.*, September 1985, *38*(3), pp. 415–19. [G: U.S.]

Kanemoto, Yoshitsugu. Housing as an Asset and the Effects of Property Taxation on the Residential Development Process. *J. Urban Econ.*, March 1985, *17*(2), pp. 145–66.

Kemp, Roger L. Services: Choosing among Policy Options: Comments. In *Clark, T. N., ed.*, 1985, pp. 175–78. [G: U.S.]

Knoke, David. Citizen Preferences and Participatory Roles: Comments. In *Clark, T. N., ed.*, 1985, pp. 259–62. [G: U.S.]

Kolstad, Charles D. and Wolak, Frank A., Jr.

Strategy and Market Structure in Western Coal Taxation. *Rev. Econ. Statist.*, May 1985, *67*(2), pp. 239–49. [G: U.S.]

Ladd, Helen F. and Wilson, Julie Boatright. Proposition 2½: Explaining the Vote. In *Clark, T. N., ed.*, 1985, pp. 199–243. [G: U.S.]

Lankford, Ralph Hamilton. Efficiency and Equity in the Provision of Public Education. *Rev. Econ. Statist.*, February 1985, *67*(1), pp. 70–80. [G: U.S.]

Levin, David J. State and Local Government Fiscal Position in 1984. *Surv. Curr. Bus.*, January 1985, *65*(1), pp. 19–23. [G: U.S.]

Lin, Chuan. Labor Mobility and the Incidence of the Residential Property Tax: A Comment. *J. Urban Econ.*, July 1985, *18*(1), pp. 28–33.

Liu, Ben-chieh. Mathis and Zech's 'Empirical Test' of Land Value and Taxation: A Critique of a Commendable but Unsuccessful Effort to Measure the Effects of a Basic Levy. *Amer. J. Econ. Soc.*, April 1985, *44*(2), pp. 137–43. [G: U.S.]

Lowery, David. Public Opinion, Fiscal Illusion, and Tax Revolution: The Political Demise of the Property Tax. *Public Budg. Finance*, Autumn 1985, *5*(3), pp. 76–88.

Marlin, Matthew R. Industrial Revenue Bonds: Evolution of a Subsidy. *Growth Change*, January 1985, *16*(1), pp. 30–35. [G: U.S.]

Mathis, Edward J. and Zech, Charles E. It Raises Interesting Questions, But Its Logic Is Not Compelling: A Reply [The Economic Effects of Land Value Taxation: An Empirical Test]. *Amer. J. Econ. Soc.*, July 1985, *44*(3), pp. 351–53. [G: U.S.]

McGinley, Ron. Equalization Payments in the 1990s: Comments. In *Courchene, T. J.; Conklin, D. W. and Cook, G. C. A., eds. Vol. 2*, 1985, pp. 93–97. [G: Canada]

McGuire, Therese J. Are Local Property Taxes Important in the Intrametropolitan Location Decisions of Firms? An Empirical Analysis of the Minneapolis–St. Paul Metropolitan Area. *J. Urban Econ.*, September 1985, *18*(2), pp. 226–34. [G: U.S.]

Mieszkowski, Peter and Zodrow, George R. The Incidence of a Partial State Corporate Income Tax. *Nat. Tax J.*, December 1985, *38*(4), pp. 489–96. [G: U.S.]

Moore, Michael L.; Steece, Bert M. and Swenson, Charles W. Some Empirical Evidence on Taxpayer Rationality. *Accounting Rev.*, January 1985, *60*(1), pp. 18–32. [G: U.S.]

Morgan, William E. and Mutti, John H. The Exportation of State and Local Taxes in a Multilateral Framework: The Case of Business Type Taxes. *Nat. Tax J.*, June 1985, *38*(2), pp. 191–208. [G: U.S.]

Oates, Wallace E. Searching for Leviathan: An Empirical Study. *Amer. Econ. Rev.*, September 1985, *75*(4), pp. 748–57.

Pascal, Anthony, et al. Financing Local Government in Tough Times: A Summary of Research Findings and a Proposal for Reform. In *Clark, T. N., ed.*, 1985, pp. 135–60. [G: U.S.]

Pelissero, John P. Welfare and Education Aid to

Cities: An Analysis of State Responsiveness to Needs. *Soc. Sci. Quart.*, June 1985, *66*(2), pp. 444–52. [G: U.S.]

Pescatrice, Donn R. An Intertrack Wagering Experiment. *Eastern Econ. J.*, April-June 1985, *11*(2), pp. 157–60. [G: U.S.]

Phares, Donald. State and Local Tax Burdens across the Fifty States. *Growth Change*, April 1985, *16*(2), pp. 34–42. [G: U.S.]

Pickrell, Don H. Rising Deficits and the Uses of Transit Subsidies in the United States. *J. Transp. Econ. Policy*, September 1985, *19*(3), pp. 281–98. [G: U.S.]

Pratt, Michael D. and Hoffer, George E. The Responsiveness of Heavy Vehicle Registrations to Interstate Tax Differentials. *Atlantic Econ. J.*, September 1985, *13*(3), pp. 95–96. [G: U.S.]

Ranck, Edward L. On the Incidence of Ad Valorem Severance Taxes. *Nat. Tax J.*, June 1985, *38*(2), pp. 241–45.

Reeb, Donald J. and Howe, Edward T. State and Local Taxation of Electric Utilities: A Study of the Record. In *Crew, M. A.*, ed., 1985, pp. 59–74. [G: U.S.]

Reeb, Donald J. and Tomson, Louis R. Challenges to the Ideal Property Tax: Proposals of Administrative Measures for Property Tax Reform. *Amer. J. Econ. Soc.*, October 1985, *44*(4), pp. 463–78. [G: U.S.]

Roin, Kathleen Leslie. Due Process Limits on State Estate Taxation: An Analogy to the State Corporate Income Tax. *Yale Law J.*, April 1985, *94*(5), pp. 1229–51. [G: U.S.]

Sayeed, Adil. The Canada Assistance Plan: Some Background. In *Courchene, T. J.; Conklin, D. W. and Cook, G. C. A.*, eds. *Vol. 2*, 1985, pp. 276–310. [G: Canada]

Shabman, Leonard A. and Capps, Oral, Jr. Benefit Taxation for Environmental Improvement: A Case Example from Virginia's Soft Crab Fishery. *Land Econ.*, November 1985, *61*(4), pp. 398–408. [G: U.S.]

Solomon, D. The Site Value Tax: An Evaluation. *S. Afr. J. Econ.*, September 1985, *53*(3), pp. 248–57. [G: S. Africa]

Stephenson, Susan C. and Hewett, Roger S. Strategies for States in Fiscal Competition. *Nat. Tax J.*, June 1985, *38*(2), pp. 219–26. [G: U.S.]

Stokes, Charles J. Do Urban Tax Rates Converge? They Do in Cities Alike in Population, Settlement Density and Dependence on Non-property Tax Revenues. *Amer. J. Econ. Soc.*, January 1985, *44*(1), pp. 29–38. [G: U.S.]

Stutzer, Michael J. The Statewide Economic Impact of Small-Issue Industrial Revenue Bonds. *Fed. Res. Bank Minn. Rev.*, Spring 1985, *9*(2), pp. 2–13. [G: U.S.]

Sullivan, Arthur M. The General-Equilibrium Effects of the Residential Property Tax: Incidence and Excess Burden. *J. Urban Econ.*, September 1985, *18*(2), pp. 235–50.

Tanzer, Ellen P. The Effect on Housing Quality of Reducing the Structure Tax Rate. *J. Urban Econ.*, May 1985, *17*(3), pp. 305–18. [G: U.S.]

Thomassen, Henry. Tax Reform: The View from the States. *Nat. Tax J.*, September 1985, *38*(3), pp. 295–304. [G: U.S.]

Tramontana, Antonino. Ipostesi di riforma dell'Ilor per recuperarne il carattere locale. (Suggestions for Reforming Ilor in Order to Recover Its Local Character. With English summary.) *Bancaria*, November 1985, *41*(11), pp. 1137–46. [G: Italy]

Walzer, Norman. Fiscal Austerity in Mid-size Cities: Preliminary Findings. In *Clark, T. N.*, ed., 1985, pp. 161–73. [G: U.S.]

Wasylenko, Michael and McGuire, Therese J. Jobs and Taxes: The Effect of Business Climate on States' Employment Growth Rates. *Nat. Tax J.*, December 1985, *38*(4), pp. 497–511. [G: U.S.]

Willett, Ken. Mining Taxation Issues in the Australian Federal System. In *Drysdale, P. and Shibata, H.*, eds., 1985, pp. 105–26. [G: Australia]

Williams, K. G. and Fraser, R. W. State Taxation of the Iron Ore Industry in Western Australia. *Australian Econ. Rev.*, 1st Quarter 1985, (69), pp. 30–36. [G: Australia]

Willis, K. G. Estimating the Benefits of Job Creation from Local Investment Subsidies. *Urban Stud.*, April 1985, *22*(2), pp. 163–77. [G: U.K.]

Wilson, John D. Optimal Property Taxation in the Presence of Interregional Capital Mobility. *J. Urban Econ.*, July 1985, *18*(1), pp. 73–89.

Wiltshaw, Desmond G. Jobs and Local Authority Subsidies. *Urban Stud.*, October 1985, *22*(5), pp. 433–37. [G: U.K.]

Wolkoff, Michael J. Chasing a Dream: The Use of Tax Abatements to Spur Urban Economic Development. *Urban Stud.*, August 1985, *22*(4), pp. 305–15. [G: U.S.]

Ysander, Bengt-Christer and Nordström, Tomas. Local Authorities, Economic Stability and the Efficiency of Fiscal Policy. In *Gramlich, E. M. and Ysander, B.-C.*, eds., 1985, pp. 347–98. [G: Sweden]

3243 State and Local Government Borrowing

Cluff, George S. and Farnham, Paul G. A Problem of Discrete Choice: Moody's Municipal Bond Ratings. *J. Econ. Bus.*, December 1985, *37*(4), pp. 277–302. [G: U.S.]

Farnham, Paul G. Re-examining Local Debt Limits: A Disaggregated Analysis. *Southern Econ. J.*, April 1985, *51*(4), pp. 1186–1201. [G: U.S.]

Proctor, Allen J. and Rappaport, Julie N. Federal Tax Reform and the Regional Character of the Municipal Bond Market. *Fed. Res. Bank New York Quart. Rev.*, Autumn 1985, *10*(3), pp. 6–15. [G: U.S.]

Smith, Richard L. and Booth, James R. The Risk Structure of Interest Rates and Interdependent Borrowing Costs: The Impact of Major Defaults. *J. Finan. Res.*, Summer 1985, *8*(2), pp. 83–94. [G: U.S.]

Stutzer, Michael J. The Statewide Economic Impact of Small-Issue Industrial Revenue Bonds. *Fed. Res. Bank Minn. Rev.*, Spring 1985, *9*(2), pp. 2–13.   [G: U.S.]

Taylor, William L. Section 1983 in State Court: A Remedy for Unconstitutional State Taxation. *Yale Law J.*, December 1985, *95*(2), pp. 414–35.   [G: U.S.]

Tsuneki, Atsushi. On the Neutrality of Local Public Bond in a Spatial Economy. *Econ. Stud. Quart.*, April 1985, *36*(1), pp. 46–52.

325 Intergovernmental Financial Relationships

3250 Intergovernmental Financial Relationships

Aaron, Henry J. The United States Federal System: Commentary. In *Quigley, J. M. and Rubinfeld, D. L., eds.*, 1985, pp. 70–74.
[G: U.S.]

Ansari, M. M. Flow of Financial Resources and Inter-state Disparities: Implications for a Federal Set-up. *Indian Econ. J.*, July-Sept. 1985, *33*(1), pp. 105–26.   [G: India]

Barnett, Richard R. An Analysis of Local Government Response to Grants-in-Aid: A Case of User Charges. *Bull. Econ. Res.*, May 1985, *37*(2), pp. 123–30.

Bird, Richard M. Federal Finance in Comparative Perspective. In *Courchene, T. J.; Conklin, D. W. and Cook, G. C. A., eds. Vol. 1*, 1985, pp. 137–77.   [G: Canada; Selected OECD]

Break, George F. The United States Federal System: Commentary. In *Quigley, J. M. and Rubinfeld, D. L., eds.*, 1985, pp. 75–79.
[G: U.S.]

Brosio, Giorgio. Fiscal Autonomy of Non-central Government and the Problem of Public-Spending Growth. In *Forte, F. and Peacock, A., eds.*, 1985, pp. 52–64.

Chaudry-Shah, Anwar M. Provincial Transportation Grants to Alberta Cities: Structure, Evaluation and a Proposal for an Alternate Design. In *Brown, R. C., ed.*, 1985, pp. 59–107.
[G: Canada]

Chubb, John E. Federalism and the Bias for Centralization. In *Chubb, J. E. and Peterson, P. E., eds.*, 1985, pp. 273–306.   [G: U.S.]

Chubb, John E. The Political Economy of Federalism. *Amer. Polit. Sci. Rev.*, December 1985, *79*(4), pp. 994–1015.

Cohn, Elchanan. Implementation of Federal Chapter 2 Block Grants to Education in South Carolina. *Econ. Educ. Rev.*, 1985, *4*(3), pp. 215–25.   [G: U.S.]

Courchene, Thomas J. Equalization Payments in the 1990s. In *Courchene, T. J.; Conklin, D. W. and Cook, G. C. A., eds. Vol. 2*, 1985, pp. 73–92.   [G: Canada]

Courchene, Thomas J. The Fiscal Arrangements: Focus on 1987. In *Courchene, T. J.; Conklin, D. W. and Cook, G. C. A., eds. Vol. 1*, 1985, pp. 3–21.   [G: Canada]

Cumming, Peter A. Federal–Provincial Fiscal Arrangements and the Search for Fiscal Equity through Reformulation of the Equalization Program. In *Courchene, T. J.; Conklin, D. W. and Cook, G. C. A., eds. Vol. 1*, 1985, pp. 96–124.   [G: Canada]

Dobell, Rodney. The Consultation Process: Prospects for 1987 and Beyond. In *Courchene, T. J.; Conklin, D. W. and Cook, G. C. A., eds. Vol. 2*, 1985, pp. 144–61.   [G: Canada]

Dowd, Kevin and Sayeed, Adil. Federal–Provincial Fiscal Relations: Some Background. In *Courchene, T. J.; Conklin, D. W. and Cook, G. C. A., eds. Vol. 2*, 1985, pp. 253–75.
[G: Canada]

Drysdale, Peter. Federalism and Resource Development: The Australian Case: Summary and Comment. In *Drysdale, P. and Shibata, H., eds.*, 1985, pp. 218–41.   [G: Australia]

Drysdale, Peter and Shibata, Hirofumi. Federalism and Resource Development: The Australian Case: Perspectives. In *Drysdale, P. and Shibata, H., eds.*, 1985, pp. 15–24.
[G: Australia]

Egbert, Robert L.; Kluender, Mary M. and Roach, James L. Rural Elementary School Districts in Nebraska: Their Application for ECIA Funds as Related to Demographic and Economic Issues. *Econ. Educ. Rev.*, 1985, *4*(3), pp. 189–95.   [G: U.S.]

Elmore, Richard F. Implementation of Chapter 2 in Washington State. *Econ. Educ. Rev.*, 1985, *4*(3), pp. 245–52.   [G: U.S.]

Evans, Andrew. Equalising Grants for Public Transport Subsidy. *J. Transp. Econ. Policy*, May 1985, *19*(2), pp. 105–38.   [G: U.K.]

Eyler, Janet. Implementation of Chapter 2 in Tennessee. *Econ. Educ. Rev.*, 1985, *4*(3), pp. 227–35.   [G: U.S.]

Goldberg, Michael A. Urban Programs: Transportation and Housing: Commentary. In *Quigley, J. M. and Rubinfeld, D. L., eds.*, 1985, pp. 285–93.   [G: Canada; U.S.]

Gomez-Ibañez, Jose A. The Federal Role in Urban Transportation. In *Quigley, J. M. and Rubinfeld, D. L., eds.*, 1985, pp. 183–223.
[G: U.S.]

Gramlich, Edward M. Reforming U.S. Federal Fiscal Arrangements. In *Quigley, J. M. and Rubinfeld, D. L., eds.*, 1985, pp. 34–69.
[G: U.S.]

Grewal, Bhajan and Mathews, Russell L. Federalism, Locational Surplus and the Redistributive Role of Subnational Governments. In *Terny, G. and Culyer, A. J., eds.*, 1985, pp. 355–70.

Grundmann, Herman F. Adult Assistance Programs under the Social Security Act. *Soc. Sec. Bull.*, October 1985, *48*(10), pp. 10–21.
[G: U.S.]

Hamlin, Alan P. Federalism, Horizontal Equity, and the Optimal Grant. *Public Finance Quart.*, April 1985, *13*(2), pp. 115–31.

Hepworth, Noel P. Control of Local Authority Expenditure—The Use of Cash Limits. In *Gramlich, E. M. and Ysander, B.-C., eds.*, 1985, pp. 229–92.   [G: U.K.]

Inman, Robert P. Fiscal Allocations in a Federalist Economy: Understanding the "New" Federalism. In *Quigley, J. M. and Rubinfeld, D. L., eds.*, 1985, pp. 3–33. **[G: U.S.]**

Jobin, Jacques and Dufour, Jean-Marie. Mesure et incidence des dépenses fiscales au Québec. (Measurement and Incidence of Tax Expenditures in Quebec. With English summary.) *L'Actual. Econ.*, March 1985, *61*(1), pp. 93–111. **[G: Canada]**

Johnson, A. W. Federal–Provincial Fiscal Relations: An Historical Perspective. In *Courchene, T. J.; Conklin, D. W. and Cook, G. C. A., eds. Vol. 2*, 1985, pp. 107–43. **[G: Canada]**

Johnson, Michael S. Metropolitan Dependence on Intergovenmental Aid. *Soc. Sci. Quart.*, September 1985, *66*(3), pp. 713–23. **[G: U.S.]**

Katzman, Martin T. Implementation of Chapter 2 of ECIA in Texas. *Econ. Educ. Rev.*, 1985, *4*(3), pp. 237–43. **[G: U.S.]**

Kearney, C. Philip. Michigan's Experience with Federal Education Block Grant. *Econ. Educ. Rev.*, 1985, *4*(3), pp. 181–88. **[G: U.S.]**

Keating, Michael. Local Authorities and Economic Policy: Comment. In *Machin, H. and Wright, V., eds.*, 1985, pp. 200–204. **[G: France]**

Keeler, Theodore E. Urban Programs: Transportation and Housing: Commentary. In *Quigley, J. M. and Rubinfeld, D. L., eds.*, 1985, pp. 294–96. **[G: U.S.]**

Kirlin, John J. Toward a Differentiated Theory of Federalism: Education and Housing Policy in the 1980s: Comment. In *Clark, T. N., ed.*, 1985, pp. 349–52. **[G: U.S.]**

Kuriloff, Peter J. The Distributive and Education Consequences of Chapter 2 Block Grants in Pennsylvania. *Econ. Educ. Rev.*, 1985, *4*(3), pp. 197–214. **[G: U.S.]**

Lee, Dwight R. Reverse Revenue Sharing: A Modest Proposal. *Public Choice*, 1985, *45*(3), pp. 279–89.

Lemelin, Claude. A Federal View of Consultation. In *Courchene, T. J.; Conklin, D. W. and Cook, G. C. A., eds. Vol. 2*, 1985, pp. 183–88. **[G: Canada]**

Levin, Henry M. Are Block Grants the Answaer to the Federal Role in Education? *Econ. Educ. Rev.*, 1985, *4*(3), pp. 261–69. **[G: U.S.]**

Macleod, John D. S. The Mining Industry in the Federal System. In *Drysdale, P. and Shibata, H., eds.*, 1985, pp. 127–39. **[G: Australia]**

Madden, J. R.; Challen, D. W. and Hagger, A. J. The Grants Commission's Relativities Proposals: Effects on the State Economies—A Reply. *Australian Econ. Pap.*, June 1985, *24*(44), pp. 218–21. **[G: Australia]**

Margolis, Julius. The United States Federal System: Commentary. In *Quigley, J. M. and Rubinfeld, D. L., eds.*, 1985, pp. 80–86. **[G: U.S.]**

Mathews, Russell L. Federal–State Fiscal Arrangements in Australia. In *Drysdale, P. and Shibata, H., eds.*, 1985, pp. 43–66. **[G: Australia]**

Mathews, Russell L. Intergovernmental Relations. In *Mathews, R., et al.*, 1985, pp. 159–92. **[G: Australia]**

Mathews, Russell L. The Grants Commission's Relativities Proposals: A Comment. *Australian Econ. Pap.*, June 1985, *24*(44), pp. 214–17. **[G: Australia]**

McGinley, Ron. Equalization Payments in the 1990s: Comments. In *Courchene, T. J.; Conklin, D. W. and Cook, G. C. A., eds. Vol. 2*, 1985, pp. 93–97. **[G: Canada]**

Melck, Antony. On Subsidizing Education with Block Grants. *Econ. Educ. Rev.*, 1985, *4*(3), pp. 253–59. **[G: U.S.]**

Mény, Yves. Local Authorities and Economic Policy. In *Machin, H. and Wright, V., eds.*, 1985, pp. 187–99. **[G: France]**

Miller, Victor J. Recent Changes in Federal Grants and State Budgets. In *Lewin, M. E., ed.*, 1985, pp. 44–64. **[G: U.S.]**

Munnell, Alicia H. Social Security and the Budget. *New Eng. Econ. Rev.*, July/August 1985, pp. 5–18. **[G: U.S.]**

Murray, Richard. Central Control of the Local Government Sector in Sweden. In *Gramlich, E. M. and Ysander, B.-C., eds.*, 1985, pp. 295–345. **[G: Sweden]**

Nagel, Stuart S. Optimally Allocating Federal Money to Cities. *Public Budg. Finance*, Winter 1985, *5*(4), pp. 39–50. **[G: U.S.]**

Nathan, Richard P. Reagan and the Cities: How to Meet the Challenge. *Challenge*, Sept./Oct. 1985, *28*(4), pp. 4–8. **[G: U.S.]**

Pelissero, John P. Welfare and Education Aid to Cities: An Analysis of State Responsiveness to Needs. *Soc. Sci. Quart.*, June 1985, *66*(2), pp. 444–52. **[G: U.S.]**

Perkins, Frances. Financing and Charging for Infrastructure. In *Drysdale, P. and Shibata, H., eds.*, 1985, pp. 151–76. **[G: Australia]**

Peterson, Paul E. and Wong, Kenneth K. Toward a Differentiated Theory of Federalism: Education and Housing Policy in the 1980s. In *Clark, T. N., ed.*, 1985, pp. 301–24. **[G: U.S.]**

Picur, Ronald D. Cost Accounting Services to Governments: An Agency Theory Perspective. In *Clark, T. N., ed.*, 1985, pp. 117–33. **[G: U.S.]**

Pooley, F. G. H. State and Federal Attitudes to Foreign Investment and Its Regulation. In *Drysdale, P. and Shibata, H., eds.*, 1985, pp. 140–50. **[G: Australia]**

Quigley, John M. and Rubinfeld, Daniel L. Domestic Priorities in Our Federal System. In *Quigley, J. M. and Rubinfeld, D. L., eds.*, 1985, pp. 381–95. **[G: U.S.]**

Richardson, Harry W. and Turek, Joseph H. The Scope and Limits of Federal Intervention. In *Richardson, H. W. and Turek, J. H., eds.*, 1985, pp. 211–42. **[G: U.S.]**

Romanow, Roy J. Fiscal Arrangements: A Western Perspective. In *Courchene, T. J.; Conklin, D. W. and Cook, G. C. A., eds. Vol. 1*, 1985, pp. 181–97. **[G: Canada]**

Rose-Ackerman, Susan and Evenson, Robert E. The Political Economy of Agricultural Research and Extension: Grants, Votes, and Reapportionment. *Amer. J. Agr. Econ.*, February 1985, 67(1), pp. 1–14. **[G: U.S.]**

Rose, James. Implementation of Federal ECIA Block Grants to Education in Colorado. *Econ. Educ. Rev.*, 1985, 4(3), pp. 171–79.
[G: U.S.]

Ross, Jo Anne B. Fifty Years of Service to Children and Their Families. *Soc. Sec. Bull.*, October 1985, 48(10), pp. 5–9. **[G: U.S.]**

Rothenberg, Jerome. Regional Issues: Commentary. In *Quigley, J. M. and Rubinfeld, D. L., eds.*, 1985, pp. 373–77. **[G: U.S.]**

Ryan, Claude. Federal Transfer Payments: A Quebec Perspective. In *Courchene, T. J.; Conklin, D. W. and Cook, G. C. A., eds. Vol. 1*, 1985, pp. 198–220. **[G: Canada]**

Santoni, G. J. Local Area Labor Statistics—A Phantom Army of the Unemployed? *Fed. Res. Bank St. Louis Rev.*, April 1985, 67(4), pp. 5–14. **[G: U.S.]**

Sayeed, Adil. The Canada Assistance Plan: Some Background. In *Courchene, T. J.; Conklin, D. W. and Cook, G. C. A., eds. Vol. 2*, 1985, pp. 276–310. **[G: Canada]**

Scott, G. W. S. Health Care in the 1990s: Comments. In *Courchene, T. J.; Conklin, D. W. and Cook, G. C. A., eds. Vol. 2*, 1985, pp. 58–65. **[G: Canada]**

Slack, Enid and Crocker, Douglas. The Impact of Federal–Provincial Transfers on Provincial Revenues and Expenditures: A Review. In *Courchene, T. J.; Conklin, D. W. and Cook, G. C. A., eds. Vol. 2*, 1985, pp. 311–43.
[G: Canada]

Sørensen, Rune J. Economic Relations between City and Suburban Governments. In *Lane, J.-E., ed.*, 1985, pp. 83–99. **[G: Sweden]**

Stanfield, Robert L. Federal Transfer Payments: Centralization or Decentralization? In *Courchene, T. J.; Conklin, D. W. and Cook, G. C. A., eds. Vol. 1*, 1985, pp. 221–26.
[G: Canada]

Stein, Robert M. Implementation of Federal Policy: An Extension of the "Differentiated Theory of Federalism." In *Clark, T. N., ed.*, 1985, pp. 341–48. **[G: U.S.]**

Stine, William F. Estimating the Responsiveness of Local Revenue to Intergovernmental Aid. *Nat. Tax J.*, June 1985, 38(2), pp. 227–34.
[G: U.S.]

Stutzer, Michael J. The Statewide Economic Impact of Small-Issue Industrial Revenue Bonds. *Fed. Res. Bank Minn. Rev.*, Spring 1985, 9(2), pp. 2–13. **[G: U.S.]**

Thimmaiah, G. Eighth Finance Commission Report: An Evaluation. *Margin*, January 1985, 17(2), pp. 30–46. **[G: India]**

Thimmaiah, G. Fiscal Management. In *Mongia, J. N., ed.*, 1985, pp. 153–99. **[G: India]**

Thomassen, Henry. Tax Reform: The View from the States. *Nat. Tax J.*, September 1985, 38(3), pp. 295–304. **[G: U.S.]**

Trebilcock, Michael J. The Politics of Positive Sum. In *Courchene, T. J.; Conklin, D. W. and Cook, G. C. A., eds. Vol. 2*, 1985, pp. 235–50. **[G: Canada]**

Waelti, John J. Cost Sharing for Federal Water Projects: Trends and Implications. *Water Resources Res.*, February 1985, 21(2), pp. 153–58. **[G: U.S.]**

Warhurst, John and O'Loghlin, Gillian. Federal–State Issues in External Economic Relations. In *Drysdale, P. and Shibata, H., eds.*, 1985, pp. 190–202. **[G: Australia]**

Watson, William G. Health Care and Federalism. In *Courchene, T. J.; Conklin, D. W. and Cook, G. C. A., eds. Vol. 2*, 1985, pp. 40–57.
[G: Canada]

Webber, Melvin M. Urban Programs: Transportation and Housing: Commentary. In *Quigley, J. M. and Rubinfeld, D. L., eds.*, 1985, pp. 304–07. **[G: U.S.]**

Wedeman, Sara Capen; Passman, Vicki Fay and Day, James Merideth. Education Block Grants: Introduction to the Debate. *Econ. Educ. Rev.*, 1985, 4(3), pp. 163–70.
[G: U.S.]

Weicher, John C. The State and Local Government Sector and the Federal Deficit. In *Cagan, P. and Somensatto, E., eds.*, 1985, pp. 59–79.
[G: U.S.]

West, Edwin G. Public Aid to Ontario's Independent Schools. *Can. Public Policy*, December 1985, 11(4), pp. 701–10. **[G: Canada]**

Whyte, William Foote. New Approaches to Industrial Development and Community Development. In *Woodworth, W.; Meek, C. and Whyte, W. F., eds.*, 1985, pp. 15–27.
[G: U.S.]

Willett, Ken. Mining Taxation Issues in the Australian Federal System. In *Drysdale, P. and Shibata, H., eds.*, 1985, pp. 105–26.
[G: Australia]

400 International Economics

4000 General

Bapna, Ashok. One World One Future: New International Strategies for Development: Introduction. In *Bapna, A., ed.*, 1985, pp. xv–xxxvi.
[G: Global]

Bhagwati, Jagdish N. Rethinking Global Negotiations. In *Bhagwati, J. N. (I)*, 1985, pp. 39–48.

Bhagwati, Jagdish N. Retrospect and Prospect in North–South Negotiations. In *Bhagwati, J. N. (I)*, 1985, pp. 49–64.

Bhagwati, Jagdish N. The New International Economic Order. In *Bhagwati, J. N. (I)*, 1985, pp. 13–38.

Bird, Graham. Managing the World Economy: Old Order, New Order or Disorder?: Review Article. In *Saith, A., ed.*, 1985, pp. 243–50.
[G: Global]

Bird, Graham. Managing the World Economy: Old Order, New Order or Disorder? *J. Devel. Stud.*, October 1985, 22(1), pp. 243–50.
[G: Global]

Bognár, József. Global Problems in an Interdependent World. In *Didsbury, H. F., Jr., ed.,* 1985, pp. 16–32.

Charles, Koilpillai J. Transnational Corporations and North–South Relations. In *Utrecht, E., ed.,* 1985, pp. 17–30.   [G: LDCs; MDCs]

Coate, Roger A. The International Seabed Authority: Progressive Development or Creative Camouflage? In *Jordan, R. S., ed.,* 1985, pp. 99–131.

Didsbury, Howard F., Jr. The Global Economy: Today, Tomorrow, and the Transition: Introduction. In *Didsbury, H. F., Jr., ed.,* 1985, pp. vii–xii.

Eichner, Alfred S. Reflections on Social Democracy. In *Eichner, A. S.,* 1985, pp. 200–218.

Emmerij, Louis. National and International Strategies for Development. In *Bapna, A., ed.,* 1985, pp. 181–88.   [G: LDCs; MDCs]

Evans, Peter B. Transnational Linkages and the Economic Role of the State: An Analysis of Developing and Industrialized Nations in the Post-World War II Period. In *Evans, P. B.; Rueschemeyer, D. and Skocpol, T., eds.,* 1985, pp. 192–226.

Gandhi, Indira. Peace and Development. In *Bapna, A., ed.,* 1985, pp. 7–13. [G: Global]

Giersch, Herbert. Perspectives on the World Economy. *S. Afr. J. Econ.,* December 1985, 53(4), pp. 333–50.   [G: Global]

Giersch, Herbert. Perspectives on the World Economy. *Weltwirtsch. Arch.,* 1985, 121(3), pp. 409–26.   [G: Global]

Gross, Bertram and Singh, Kusum. Global Unemployment: Challenge to Futurists. In *Didsbury, H. F., Jr., ed.,* 1985, pp. 35–59.

Grubel, Herbert G. The Case against the New International Economic Order. In *Adams, J., ed.,* 1985, pp. 524–45.

Heath, Edward. General Policies for International Development and Cooperation. *Ann. Pub. Co-op. Econ.,* January–June 1985, 56(1–2), pp. 111–19.

Helleiner, Gerald K. South–South Economic Cooperation in the 1980s. In *Bapna, A., ed.,* 1985, pp. 279–91.   [G: LDCs]

Hinshaw, Randall. Global Economic Priorities: Prologue. In *Hinshaw, R., ed.,* 1985, pp. 15–21.

Holub, Alois. What Hinders Development Should Stimulate It. *Czech. Econ. Digest.,* March 1985, (2), pp. 77–86.   [G: Global]

Jha, L. K. New Parameters in the North–South Dialogue. In *Jha, L. K.,* 1985, pp. 148–58.   [G: Global]

Jha, L. K. The Inter-dependent World. In *Jha, L. K.,* 1985, pp. 140–47.   [G: Global]

Jha, L. K. The North–South Issues and the United Nations: The Need for a New Approach. In *Bapna, A., ed.,* 1985, pp. 131–36.   [G: Global]

Krueger, Anne O. Importance of General Policies to Promote Economic Growth. *World Econ.,* June 1985, 8(2), pp. 93–108.   [G: Global]

Lamfalussy, Alexandre. Monetary Policy in Our Times: Concluding Comments. In *Ando, A.,*

et al., eds., 1985, pp. 319–23.   [G: Global]

Lawson, Colin W. The Soviet Union in North–South Negotiations: Revealing Preferences. In *Cassen, R., ed.,* 1985, pp. 177–91.   [G: U.S.S.R.; LDCs; MDCs]

Linder, Staffan Burenstam. Pacific Protagonist—Implications of the Rising Role of the Pacific. *Amer. Econ. Rev.,* May 1985, 75(2), pp. 279–84.   [G: U.S.; E. Asia]

Marshall, Peter. Reflections on North–South Relations and the Commonwealth. *J. World Trade Law,* May:June 1985, 19(3), pp. 191–98.   [G: British Commonwealth]

McCulloch, Rachel. U.S. Relations with Developing Countries: Conflict and Opportunity. In *Adams, J., ed.,* 1985, pp. 478–87.   [G: U.S.; LDCs]

McNamara, Robert S. Economic Interdependence and Global Poverty: The Challenge of Our Time. In *Bapna, A., ed.,* 1985, pp. 33–48.   [G: Global]

Meade, James E. Global Economic Priorities: Targets and Weapons for Economic Stabilization. In *Hinshaw, R., ed.,* 1985, pp. 203–25.

Okita, Saburo. Economic Development in the Third World and International Economic Cooperation. In *Bapna, A., ed.,* 1985, pp. 81–91.   [G: LDCs; MDCs]

Palme, Olof. From Crisis to Prosperity. In *Bapna, A., ed.,* 1985, pp. 15–21.   [G: Global]

Perez de Cuellar, Javier. An Urgent Need for Global Economic Recovery. In *Bapna, A., ed.,* 1985, pp. 1–5.   [G: Global]

Perinbam, Lewis. North and South: Toward a New Interdependence of Nations. In *Bapna, A., ed.,* 1985, pp. 93–116. [G: MDCs; LDCs]

Perlman, Mark. A Coming Inflection in American Economic Policy? In *[Recktenwald, H. C.],* 1985, pp. 135–45.   [G: U.S.]

Pissulla, Petra. Western Policies: International Organizations. In *Rode, R. and Jacobsen, H.-D., eds.,* 1985, pp. 226–42.   [G: CMEA]

Robbins, Lionel. Global Economic Priorities: Reflections on the Dialogue. In *Hinshaw, R., ed.,* 1985, pp. 169–78.

Rosenstein-Rodan, Paul N. The New International Economic Order: Relations between the Haves and Have-nots (North–South) In *Bapna, A., ed.,* 1985, pp. 241–50. [G: LDCs; MDCs]

Rostow, W. W. Is There Need for Economic Leadership? Japanese or U.S.? *Amer. Econ. Rev.,* May 1985, 75(2), pp. 285–91.   [G: Japan; U.S.]

Salda, Anne C. M. The International Monetary Fund, 1984: A Selected Bibliography. *Int. Monet. Fund Staff Pap.,* Suppl. Dec. 1985, 32, pp. 749–87.

Shultz, George P. New Realities and New Ways of Thinking. *Foreign Aff.,* Spring 1985, 63(4), pp. 706–21.

Singer, Hans W. Further Thoughts on North–South Negotiations: A Review of Bhagwati and Ruggie [Power, Passions and Purpose. Prospects for North–South Negotiations]. *World Devel.,* February 1985, 13(2), pp. 255–59.   [G: Global]

Singh, Manmohan. Toward a New International Economic Order. In *Bapna, A., ed.*, 1985, pp. 293–307.

Snidal, Duncan. The Limits of Hegemonic Stability Theory. *Int. Organ.*, Autumn 1985, *39*(4), pp. 579–614.

Soedjatmoko. The Science and Praxis of Complexity: Opening Statement. In *Aida, S., et al.*, 1985, pp. 1–6.

Steele, D. B. The Case for Global Economic Management and UN System Reform. *Int. Organ.*, Summer 1985, *39*(3), pp. 561–78. [G: Global]

Streeten, Paul. Approaches to a New International Economic Order. In *Adams, J., ed.*, 1985, pp. 495–524.

Sylos Labini, Paolo. XVth International CIRIEC Congress. *Ann. Pub. Co-op. Econ.*, January–June 1985, *56*(1–2), pp. 165–75. [G: Global]

Taylor, Kenneth B. The Economic Impact of the Emerging Global Information Economy on Lesser Developed Nations. In *Didsbury, H. F., Jr., ed.*, 1985, pp. 147–63. [G: LDCs]

Thorp, Rosemary. The New Order: Introduction. In *Abel, C. and Lewis, C. M., eds.*, 1985, pp. 397–404. [G: Latin America]

Tinbergen, Jan. How Do We Manage the Global Society? In *Didsbury, H. F., Jr., ed.*, 1985, pp. 3–15.

Tooze, Roger. International Political Economy. In *Smith, S., ed.*, 1985, pp. 108–25.

Tsanacas, Demetri. The Transborder Data Flow in the New World Information Order: Privacy or Control. *Rev. Soc. Econ.*, December 1985, *43*(3), pp. 357–70. [G: U.S.]

Weiller, Jean. Circuits des capitaux, balances extérieurers et flux majeurs d'investissement. (Capital Circuits, Foreign Balances and Major Flows of Investment. With English summary.) *Écon. Soc.*, April 1985, *19*(4), pp. 7–18.

Weiss, Thomas G. Alternatives for Multilateral Development Diplomacy: Some Suggestions. *World Devel.*, December 1985, *13*(12), pp. 1187–1209.

Weiss, Thomas G. UNCTAD: What Next? *J. World Trade Law*, May:June 1985, *19*(3), pp. 251–68. [G: Global]

Williamson, John. International Agencies and the Peacock Critique. In *[Peacock, A.]*, 1985, pp. 167–75.

Willoughby, John. The Internationalization of Capital and the Future of Macroeconomic Policy. *Sci. Soc.*, Fall 1985, *49*(3), pp. 287–314.

Zijlstra, Jelle. Reflections on International Economic and Monetary Problems. In *Zijlstra, J.*, 1985, pp. 75–87.

410 INTERNATIONAL TRADE THEORY

411 International Trade Theory

4110 General

Caves, Richard E. International Trade and Industrial Organization: Problems, Solved and Unsolved. *Europ. Econ. Rev.*, August 1985, *28*(3), pp. 377–95.

Corden, W. Max. International Trade Theory and the Multinational Enterprise. In *Corden, W. M.*, 1985, pp. 157–77.

Corden, W. Max. The Enclave Approach. In *Corden, W. M.*, 1985, pp. 178–83.

Dinwiddy, Caroline and Teal, Francis. Shadow Prices and Cost-Benefit Rules for Non-traded Commodities in a Second Best Economy. *Oxford Econ. Pap.*, December 1985, *37*(4), pp. 683–90.

Grossman, Gene M. and Shapiro, Carl. Normative Issues Raised by International Trade in Technology Services. In *Stern, R. M., ed.*, 1985, pp. 83–113. [G: OECD]

McCulloch, Rachel. Normative Issues Raised by International Trade in Technology Services: Comments. In *Stern, R. M., ed.*, 1985, pp. 114–18. [G: OECD]

Rugman, Alan M. Normative Issues Raised by International Trade in Technology Services: Comments. In *Stern, R. M., ed.*, 1985, pp. 119–25. [G: OECD]

Secchi, Carlo. L'internazionalizzazione dei servizi e la teoria del commercio internazionale. (The Internationalization of Services and the Theory of International Trade. With English summary.) *Rivista Int. Sci. Econ. Com.*, April 1985, *32*(4), pp. 359–74. [G: Global]

Shepherd, A. Ross. A Comment on Lerner's 'Extortion Tax" Plan [Lerner's Contribution to Economics]. *J. Econ. Lit.*, September 1985, *23*(3), pp. 1192.

4112 Theory of International Trade

Adams, Charles and Greenwood, Jeremy. Dual Exchange Rate Systems and Capital Controls: An Investigation. *J. Int. Econ.*, February 1985, *18*(1/2), pp. 43–63.

Arndt, Sven W.; Thursby, Marie and Willett, Thomas D. Flexible Exchange Rates and International Trade: An Overview. In *Arndt, S. W.; Sweeney, R. J. and Willett, T. D., eds.*, 1985, pp. 127–35.

Ashiquzzaman, Shah M. and Ghosh, Atish R. Profits, Tariffs, and Intra-industry Trade. *Indian Econ. J.*, Oct.-Nov. 1985, *33*(2), pp. 106–15.

Balassa, Bela and Bauwens, Luc. Comparative Advantage in Manufactured Goods in a Multicountry, Multi-industry, and Multi-factor Model. In *Peeters, T.; Praet, P. and Reding, P., eds.*, 1985, pp. 31–52. [G: Selected Countries]

Ballance, Robert; Forstner, Helmut and Murray, Tracy. On Measuring Comparative Advantage: A Note on Bowen's Indices. *Weltwirtsch. Arch.*, 1985, *121*(2), pp. 346–50.

Bental, Benjamin. Is Capital Mobility Always Desirable? A Welfare Analysis of Portfolio Autarky in a Growing Economy. *Int. Econ. Rev.*, February 1985, *26*(1), pp. 203–12.

Bergstrand, Jeffrey H. The Gravity Equation in International Trade: Some Microeconomic Foundations and Empirical Evidence. *Rev. Econ. Statist.*, August 1985, *67*(3), pp. 474–81. [G: OECD]

Betancourt, Roger; Clague, Christopher K. and Panagariya, Arvind. Capital Utilization and Factor Specificity. *Rev. Econ. Stud.*, April 1985, *52*(2), pp. 311–29.　　[G: U.S.; U.K.]

Bhagwati, Jagdish N. Structural Adjustment and International Factor Mobility: Some Issues. In *Jungenfelt, K. and Hague, D. [Sir], eds.*, 1985, pp. 127–49.

Bhagwati, Jagdish N. and Brecher, Richard A. Extending Free Trade to Include International Investment: A Welfare-Theoretic Analysis. In *Bhagwati, J. N. (I)*, 1985, pp. 383–88.

Bhagwati, Jagdish N.; Brecher, Richard A. and Hatta, Tatsuo. The Generalized Theory of Transfers and Welfare: Exogenous (Policy-imposed) and Endogenous (Transfer-induced) Distortions. *Quart. J. Econ.*, August 1985, *100*(3), pp. 697–714.

Bhagwati, Jagdish N.; Brecher, Richard A. and Hatta, Tatsuo. The Generalized Theory of Transfers and Welfare: Bilateral Transfers in a Multilateral World. In *Bhagwati, J. N. (II)*, 1985, pp. 216–28.

Bigman, David. International Trade and Trade Creation under Instability. *Europ. Econ. Rev.*, August 1985, *28*(3), pp. 309–30.

Binh, Tran Nam. A Neo-Ricardian Trade Model with Overlapping Generations. *Econ. Rec.*, December 1985, *61*(175), pp. 707–18.

Brander, James A. and Spencer, Barbara J. Export Subsidies and International Market Share and Rivalry. *J. Int. Econ.*, February 1985, *18*(1/2), pp. 83–100.

Brewer, Anthony. Trade with Fixed Real Wages and Mobile Capital. *J. Int. Econ.*, February 1985, *18*(1/2), pp. 177–86.

Butlin, M. W. Imported Inputs in an Optimising Model of a Small Open Economy. *J. Int. Econ.*, February 1985, *18*(1/2), pp. 101–21.

Casas, François R. and Choi, Eun Kwan. Some Paradoxes of Transport Costs in International Trade. *Southern Econ. J.*, April 1985, *51*(4), pp. 983–97.

Cassing, James H. and Warr, Peter G. The Distributional Impact of a Resource Boom. *J. Int. Econ.*, May 1985, *18*(3/4), pp. 301–19.

Chacholiades, Miltiades. Circulating Capital in the Theory of International Trade. *Southern Econ. J.*, July 1985, *52*(1), pp. 1–22.

Choi, Jai-Young and Yu, Eden S. H. Technical Progress, Terms of Trade and Welfare under Variable Returns to Scale. *Economica*, August 1985, *52*(207), pp. 365–77.

Clague, Christopher K. A Model of Real National Price Levels. *Southern Econ. J.*, April 1985, *51*(4), pp. 998–1017.

Collier, Paul. Commodity Aggregation in Customs Unions [3 by 3 Theory of Customs Unions]. *Oxford Econ. Pap.*, December 1985, *37*(4), pp. 677–82.

Collins, Susan M. Technical Progress in a Three-Country Ricardian Model with a Continuum of Goods. *J. Int. Econ.*, August 1985, *19*(1/2), pp. 171–79.

Corden, W. Max. Booming Sector and Dutch Disease Economics: Survey and Consolidation. In *Corden, W. M.*, 1985, pp. 246–68.

Corden, W. Max. Economic Expansion and International Trade: A Geometric Approach. In *Corden, W. M.*, 1985, pp. 187–97.

Corden, W. Max. The Effects of Trade on the Rate of Growth. In *Corden, W. M.*, 1985, pp. 198–224.

Corden, W. Max and Neary, J. Peter. Booming Sector and De-industrialization in a Small Open Economy. In *Corden, W. M.*, 1985, pp. 225–45.

Dalal, A. J. Using a GNP Function to Obtain Comparative Statics for the Production Sector. *Econ. Int.*, Aug./Nov. 1985, *38*(3/4), pp. 303–08.

Deardorff, Alan V. Comparative Advantage and International Trade and Investment in Services. In *Stern, R. M., ed.*, 1985, pp. 39–71.

Deardorff, Alan V. Major Recent Developments in International Trade Theory. In *Peeters, T.; Praet, P. and Reding, P., eds.*, 1985, pp. 3–27.

Dornbusch, Rudiger. Intergenerational and International Trade. *J. Int. Econ.*, February 1985, *18*(1/2), pp. 123–39.

Ethier, Wilfred J. International Trade and Labor Migration. *Amer. Econ. Rev.*, September 1985, *75*(4), pp. 691–707.

Feenstra, Robert C. Anticipated Devaluations, Currency Flight, and Direct Trade Controls in a Monetary Economy. *Amer. Econ. Rev.*, June 1985, *75*(3), pp. 386–401.

Flam, Harry. A Heckscher–Ohlin Analysis of the Law of Declining International Trade. *Can. J. Econ.*, August 1985, *18*(3), pp. 602–15.

Ford, J. L. The Ricardian–Ohlin Explanation of Trade: A Comment on a General Theorem Which Is Not General: Comment. *Oxford Econ. Pap.*, March 1985, *37*(1), pp. 134–37.

Forstner, Helmut. A Note on the General Validity of the Heckscher–Ohlin Theorem. *Amer. Econ. Rev.*, September 1985, *75*(4), pp. 844–49.

Fukushima, Takashi. On Negative Shadow Factor Prices in the Presence of Factor Market Distortion. *J. Int. Econ.*, May 1985, *18*(3/4), pp. 365–71.

Fukushima, Takashi. Price–Output Response Is Always Normal Despite Factor Market Distortions. *Econ. Stud. Quart.*, December 1985, *36*(3), pp. 247–51.

Gaparetto, Marialuisa Manfredini. Il commercio intra-industriale e la teoria dinamizzata dei costi comparati. (Intra-industrial Trade and the Dynamic Theory of Comparative Costs. With English summary.) *Rivista Int. Sci. Econ. Com.*, September 1985, *32*(9), pp. 865–85.

Gehrels, Franz. Allocations, Outputs and Rentals in General Equilibrium with a Limiting Factor. *Rivista Int. Sci. Econ. Com.*, April 1985, *32*(4), pp. 323–41.

Giovannetti, Giorgia. The International Transmission of Price Level and Output Disturbances between Raw Material Producer Countries and Industrial Countries: A Theoretical Analysis. *Econ. Notes*, 1985, (1), pp. 148–61.

Gray, H. Peter. Domestic Efficiency, International Efficiency and Gains from Trade. *Weltwirtsch. Arch.*, 1985, *121*(3), pp. 460–70.

Gray, H. Peter. Multinationals Corporations and Global Welfare: An Extension of Kojima and Ozawa. *Hitotsubashi J. Econ.*, December 1985, *26*(2), pp. 125–33.

Greenaway, David. Models of Trade in Differentiated Goods and Commercial Policy. In *Greenaway, D., ed.*, 1985, pp. 81–97.

Gremmen, Hans J. Testing the Factor Price Equalization Theorem in the EC: An Alternative Approach. *J. Common Market Stud.*, March 1985, *23*(3), pp. 277–86. [G: EEC]

Grinols, Earl L. International Trade and Incomplete Markets. *Economica*, May 1985, *52*(206), pp. 245–55.

Grinols, Earl L. Trade, Distortions, and Welfare under Uncertainty. *Oxford Econ. Pap.*, September 1985, *37*(3), pp. 362–74.

Grossman, Gene M. and Razin, Assaf. The Pattern of Trade in a Ricardian Model with Country-Specific Uncertainty. *Int. Econ. Rev.*, February 1985, *26*(1), pp. 193–202.

Haberler, Gottfried. A Survey of International Trade Theory. In *Haberler, G.*, 1985, pp. 55–108.

Haberler, Gottfried. Currency Depreciation and the Terms of Trade. In *Haberler, G.*, 1985, pp. 167–74.

Haberler, Gottfried. Some Problems in the Pure Theory of International Trade. In *Haberler, G.*, 1985, pp. 37–54.

Haberler, Gottfried. Survey of Circumstances Affecting the Location of Production and International Trade as Analysed in the Theoretical Literature. In *Haberler, G.*, 1985, pp. 109–29.

Haberler, Gottfried. The Theory of Comparative Costs and Its Use in the Defense of Free Trade. In *Haberler, G.*, 1985, pp. 3–19.

Haberler, Gottfried. Transfer and Price Movements. In *Haberler, G.*, 1985, pp. 133–42.

Harford, Jon D. and Park, Keehwan. Resource Allocation under Production Uncertainty: Closed Economy vs. Open Economy. *Atlantic Econ. J.*, July 1985, *13*(2), pp. 38–43.

Heinemann, Hans-Joachim. Zum Zusammenwirken von Direktinvestitionen und Technologietransfer. (On Direct Investment Combined with Technology Transfer. With English summary.) *Ifo-Studien*, 1985, *31*(2), pp. 93–107.

Helpman, Elhanan. International Trade in Differentiated Middle Products. In *Jungenfelt, K. and Hague, D. [Sir], eds.*, 1985, pp. 3–23.

Helpman, Elhanan. Multinational Corporations and Trade Structure. *Rev. Econ. Stud.*, July 1985, *52*(3), pp. 443–57.

Hillman, Arye L. and Long, Ngo Van. Monopolistic Recycling of Oil Revenue and Intertemporal Bias in Oil Depletion and Trade. *Quart. J. Econ.*, August 1985, *100*(3), pp. 597–624.

Inoue, Tadashi. Theories of International Trade with Transport Costs. *Econ. Stud. Quart.*, April 1985, *36*(1), pp. 23–34.

Inoue, Tadashi. Theories of International Trade with Nontraded Goods. *Econ. Stud. Quart.*, August 1985, *36*(2), pp. 121–32.

Jakobsen, Arvid Stentoft. Changes in Factor Input Coefficients and the Leontief Paradox. In *Smyshlyaev, A., ed.*, 1985, pp. 105–17. [G: Denmark]

Jones, Ronald W. A Theorem on Income Distribution in a Small Open Economy. *J. Int. Econ.*, February 1985, *18*(1/2), pp. 171–76.

Jones, Ronald W. Comparative Advantage and International Trade and Investment in Services: Comments. In *Stern, R. M., ed.*, 1985, pp. 72–76.

Jones, Ronald W. and Coelho, Isaias. International Factor Movements and the Ramaswami Argument. *Economica*, August 1985, *52*(207), pp. 359–64.

Jones, Ronald W. and Marjit, Sugata. A Simple Production Model with Stolper-Samuelson Properties. *Int. Econ. Rev.*, October 1985, *26*(3), pp. 565–67.

Kemp, Murray C. and Kojima, Shoichi. The Welfare Economics of Foreign Aid. In *Feiwel, G. R., ed. (II)*, 1985, pp. 470–83.

Kemp, Murray C. and Kojima, Shoichi. Tied Aid and the Paradoxes of Donor-Enrichment and Recipient-Impoverishment. *Int. Econ. Rev.*, October 1985, *26*(3), pp. 721–29.

Khanna, Ashok. A Note on the Dynamic Aspects of the Heckscher–Ohlin Model: Some Empirical Evidence. *World Devel.*, Oct./Nov. 1985, *13*(10/11), pp. 1171–74. [G: S. Korea]

Kierzkowski, Henryk. Models of International Trade in Differentiated Goods. In *Greenaway, D., ed.*, 1985, pp. 7–24.

Koenig, Evan F. Indirect Methods for Regulating Externalities under Uncertainty. *Quart. J. Econ.*, May 1985, *100*(2), pp. 479–93.

Kojima, Kiyoshi and Ozawa, Terutomo. Toward a Theory of Industrial Restructuring and Dynamic Comparative Advantage. *Hitotsubashi J. Econ.*, December 1985, *26*(2), pp. 135–45.

Krugman, Paul R. A 'Technology Gap' Model of International Trade. In *Jungenfelt, K. and Hague, D. [Sir], eds.*, 1985, pp. 35–49.

Krugman, Paul R. New Theories of Trade among Industrial Countries. In *Adams, J., ed.*, 1985, pp. 17–23.

van der Laan, Gerard. The Computation of General Equilibrium in Economies with a Block Diagonal Pattern. *Econometrica*, May 1985, *53*(3), pp. 658–65.

Lane, Julia. An Empirical Estimate of the Effects of Labor-Market Distortions on the Factor Content of U.S. Trade. *J. Int. Econ.*, February 1985, *18*(1/2), pp. 187–93. [G: U.S.]

Leontief, Wassily. An International Comparison of Factor Costs and Factor Use: A Review Article. In *Leontief, W.*, 1985, pp. 359–72.

Leontief, Wassily. Explanatory Power of the Comparative Cost Theory of International Trade and Its Limits. In *Leontief, W.*, 1985, pp. 373–80. [G: U.S.]

Leontief, Wassily. The Use of Indifference Curves in the Analysis of Foreign Trade. In *Leontief, W.*, 1985, pp. 116–25.

Lloyd, P. J. The Ricardian and Heckscher–Ohlin

Explanations of Trade: A Comment on a General Theorem Which Is Not General [The Ricardian–Ohlin Explanations of Trade: A General Proof of an Equivalence Theorem and Its Empirical Implications]. *Oxford Econ. Pap.*, March 1985, 37(1), pp. 138–41.

Lundahl, Mats. International Migration, Remittances and Real Incomes: Effects on the Source Country. *Scand. J. Econ.*, 1985, 87(4), pp. 647–57.

Mainwaring, Lynn. The Treatment of Capital in the "Classical" Theory of International Trade. *Metroecon.*, February 1985, 37(1), pp. 63–77.

Majumdar, Mukul and Mitra, Tapan. A Result on the Transfer Problem in International Trade Theory. *J. Int. Econ.*, August 1985, 19(1/2), pp. 161–70.

Maneschi, Andrea. The Shadow Pricing of Factors in a Multicommodity Specific-Factors Model. *Can. J. Econ.*, November 1985, 18(4), pp. 843–53.

Markusen, James R. and Svensson, Lars E. O. Trade in Goods and Factors with International Differences in Technology. *Int. Econ. Rev.*, February 1985, 26(1), pp. 175–92.

Maskus, Keith E. A Test of the Heckscher–Ohlin–Vanek Theorem: The Leontief Commonplace. *J. Int. Econ.*, November 1985, 19(3/4), pp. 201–12.   [G: U.S.]

Matusz, Steven J. The Heckscher-Ohlin-Samuelson Model with Implicit Contracts. *Quart. J. Econ.*, November 1985, 100(4), pp. 1313–29.

McDermott, John. The Rybczynski Theorem: Short-run Adjustment. *Southern Econ. J.*, July 1985, 52(1), pp. 241–49.

Melvin, James R. Comparative Advantage and International Trade and Investment in Services: Comments. In *Stern, R. M., ed.*, 1985, pp. 77–82.

Melvin, James R. Domestic Taste Differences, Transportation Costs, and International Trade. *J. Int. Econ.*, February 1985, 18(1/2), pp. 65–82.

Melvin, James R. Unemployment, International Trade, and Welfare in a Fixed-Coefficient Model. *Manchester Sch. Econ. Soc. Stud.*, June 1985, 53(2), pp. 149–55.

Méndez, José A. A Note on the Neoclassical Ambiguity and the Specific Factor Production Model under Variable Returns to Scale. *J. Int. Econ.*, May 1985, 18(3/4), pp. 357–63.

Moussavian, Mohammed H. Growth Rates with an Exhaustible Resource and Home Goods. *J. Int. Econ.*, May 1985, 18(3/4), pp. 281–99.

Mutti, John H. and Grubert, Harry. The Taxation of Capital Income in an Open Economy: The Importance of Resident–Nonresident Tax Treatment. *J. Public Econ.*, August 1985, 27(3), pp. 291–309.   [G: U.S.]

Neary, J. Peter. International Factor Mobility, Minimum Wage Rates, and Factor-Price Equalization: A Synthesis. *Quart. J. Econ.*, August 1985, 100(3), pp. 551–70.

Neary, J. Peter. The Observational Equivalence of the Ricardian and Heckscher–Ohlin Explanations of Trade Patterns [The Ricardian and Heckscher–Ohlin Explanations of Trade: A General Proof of an Equivalence Theorem and Its Empirical Implications]. *Oxford Econ. Pap.*, March 1985, 37(1), pp. 142–47.

Neary, J. Peter. Theory and Policy of Adjustment in an Open Economy. In *Greenaway, D., ed.*, 1985, pp. 43–61.

Neary, J. Peter. Two-by-Two International Trade Theory with Many Goods and Factors. *Econometrica*, September 1985, 53(5), pp. 1233–47.

Okamoto, Hisayuki. Production Possibilities and International Trade with Public Intermediate Good: A Generalization. *Econ. Stud. Quart.*, April 1985, 36(1), pp. 35–45.

Persson, Torsten. Deficits and Intergenerational Welfare in Open Economies. *J. Int. Econ.*, August 1985, 19(1/2), pp. 67–84.

Persson, Torsten and Svensson, Lars E. O. Current Account Dynamics and the Terms of Trade: Harberger–Laursen–Metzler Two Generations Later. *J. Polit. Econ.*, February 1985, 93(1), pp. 43–65.

Petri, Peter A. International Trade Based on the Ability to Adjust. In *Jungenfelt, K. and Hague, D. [Sir], eds.*, 1985, pp. 62–79.

Preusse, Heinz Gert. Inter- and Intra-industrial Division of Labour and the Gains from Trade. *Aussenwirtschaft*, December 1985, 40(4), pp. 389–405.

Roland, Gérard. Contrainte extérieure et dynamique internationale de la valeur. (Foreign Constraint and the International Dynamics of Value. With English summary.) *Écon. Soc.*, April 1985, 19(4), pp. 161–73.

Rossini, Gianpaolo. Price Uncertainty and International Specialization. *Econ. Notes*, 1985, (3), pp. 89–100.

Ruffin, Roy J. Taxing International Capital Movements in a Growing World. *J. Int. Econ.*, May 1985, 18(3/4), pp. 261–79.

Sarkar, Abhirup. A Model of Trade in Intermediate Goods. *J. Int. Econ.*, August 1985, 19(1/2), pp. 85–98.

Serra, Pablo J. Comercio y bienestar en un modelo con traslapo de generaciones. (With English summary.) *Cuadernos Econ.*, December 1985, 22(67), pp. 399–418.

Sibert, Anne C. Capital Accumulation and Foreign Investment Taxation. *Rev. Econ. Stud.*, April 1985, 52(2), pp. 331–45.

Siebert, Horst. Spatial Aspects of Environmental Economics. In *Kneese, A. V. and Sweeney, J. L., eds. Vol. 1*, 1985, pp. 125–64.

Sihag, Balabir S. and Snoonian, Paul E. Ricardo–Pasinetti Model of International Trade. *Indian Econ. J.*, Jan.-Mar. 1985, 32(3), pp. 42–51.

Steedman, Ian and Metcalfe, J. S. Capital Goods and the Pure Theory of Trade. In *Greenaway, D., ed.*, 1985, pp. 25–42.

Stockman, Alan C. Effects of Inflation on the Pattern of International Trade. *Can. J. Econ.*, August 1985, 18(3), pp. 587–601.

Svensson, Lars E. O. Currency Prices, Terms of Trade, and Interest Rates: A General Equilibrium Asset-pricing Cash-in-Advance Approach.

J. Int. Econ., February 1985, *18*(1/2), pp. 17–41.

Tharakan, P. K. M. Empirical Analyses of the Commodity Composition of Trade. In *Greenaway, D., ed.*, 1985, pp. 63–79.

Thompson, Henry. Complementarity in a Simple General Equilibrium Production Model. *Can. J. Econ.*, August 1985, *18*(3), pp. 616–21.

Thompson, Henry. International Capital Mobility in a Specific Factor Model [International Factor Movements, Commodity Trade and Commercial Policy in a Specific Factor Model]. *Atlantic Econ. J.*, July 1985, *13*(2), pp. 76–79.

Tompkinson, P. Optimal Distortions for a Small Country Facing Random Prices. *Oxford Econ. Pap.*, September 1985, *37*(3), pp. 520–224.

Tompkinson, P. and Philpott, B. P. Uncertainty in the Terms of Trade and the Optimal Structure of a Small Open Economy. *Econ. Planning*, 1985, *19*(1), pp. 12–18.

Tremblay, Rodrigue. A Quebec Perspective on Canadian Trade Options. In *Conklin, D. W. and Courchene, T. J., eds.*, 1985, pp. 57–76. [G: Canada]

Van Bemmelen, Michael. On the Choice between International Capital and Labor Mobility. *Europ. Econ. Rev.*, December 1985, *29*(3), pp. 355–79.

Venables, Anthony J. Trade and Trade Policy with Imperfect Competition: The Case of Identical Products and Free Entry. *J. Int. Econ.*, August 1985, *19*(1/2), pp. 1–19.

Wang, Leonard F. S. Factor Market Distortions, the Transfer Problem, and Welfare. *Keio Econ. Stud.*, 1985, *22*(1), pp. 57–64.

Whalley, John and White, Philip M. A Decomposition Algorithm for General Equilibrium Computation with Application to International Trade Models: A Correction. *Econometrica*, May 1985, *53*(3), pp. 679.

Wooton, Ian. Labour Migration in a Model of North–South Trade. *Econ. Modelling*, October 1985, *2*(4), pp. 339–46.

Yeh, Yeong-Her. Export Subsidies, Factor Inflows, and Income Distribution [Factor Endowments and Relative Commodity Prices]. *Atlantic Econ. J.*, July 1985, *13*(2), pp. 73–75.

Zweifel, Peter. Wettbewerbsfähigkeit im internationalen Handel: Konzeptionelle Klärung. (Competitiveness in International Trade: A Conceptual Clarification. With English summary.) *Aussenwirtschaft*, December 1985, *40*(4), pp. 407–26.

4113 Theory of Protection

Aiyagari, S. Rao and Riezman, Raymond G. Embargoes and Supply Shocks in a Market with a Dominant Seller. In *Sargent, T. J., ed.*, 1985, pp. 14–40.

Aizenman, Joshua. Tariff Liberalization Policy and Financial Restrictions. *J. Int. Econ.*, November 1985, *19*(3/4), pp. 241–55.

Anderson, James E. The Relative Inefficiency of Quotas: The Cheese Case. *Amer. Econ. Rev.*, March 1985, *75*(1), pp. 178–90. [G: U.S.]

Balassa, Bela. Disequilibrium Analysis in Developing Economies: An Overview. In *Balassa, B.*, 1985, pp. 24–43. [G: LDCs]

Blejer, Mario I. and Hillman, Arye L. On the Dynamic Non-equivalence of Tariffs and Quotas in the Monetary Model of the Balance of Payments: Reply. *J. Int. Econ.*, May 1985, *18*(3/4), pp. 381–82.

Brander, James A. and Spencer, Barbara J. Export Subsidies and International Market Share and Rivalry. *J. Int. Econ.*, February 1985, *18*(1/2), pp. 83–100.

Buffie, Edward F. Quantitative Restrictions and the Welfare Effects of Capital Inflows. *J. Int. Econ.*, November 1985, *19*(3/4), pp. 291–303.

Casas, François R. Tariff Protection and Taxation of Foreign Capital: The Welfare Implications for a Small Country. *J. Int. Econ.*, August 1985, *19*(1/2), pp. 181–88.

Casas, François R. and Choi, Eun Kwan. The Metzler Paradox and the Non-equivalence of Tariffs and Quotas: Further Results. *J. Econ. Stud.*, 1985, *12*(5), pp. 53–57.

Cassing, James H. and Hillman, Arye L. Political Influence Motives and the Choice between Tariffs and Quotas. *J. Int. Econ.*, November 1985, *19*(3/4), pp. 279–90.

Chen, Tain-Jy. Alternative Policies for Foreign Investment in the Presence of Tariff Distortions. *Australian Econ. Pap.*, December 1985, *24*(45), pp. 394–403.

Condon, Timothy; Robinson, Sherman and Urata, Shujiro. Coping with a Foreign Exchange Crisis: A General Equilibrium Model of Alternative Adjustment Mechanisms. In *Manne, A. S., ed.*, 1985, pp. 75–94. [G: Turkey]

Cooper, J. H. Sanctions and Economic Theory. *S. Afr. J. Econ.*, September 1985, *53*(3), pp. 287–96.

Corden, W. Max. Effective Protection Revisited. In *Corden, W. M.*, 1985, pp. 141–53.

Corden, W. Max. Effective Protective Rates in the General Equilibrium Model: A Geometric Note. In *Corden, W. M.*, 1985, pp. 118–24.

Corden, W. Max. Exchange Rate Protection. In *Corden, W. M.*, 1985, pp. 271–87. [G: U.K.]

Corden, W. Max. Monopoly, Tariffs and Subsidies. In *Corden, W. M.*, 1985, pp. 46–57.

Corden, W. Max. Protection and the Real Exchange Rate. In *Corden, W. M.*, 1985, pp. 302–10.

Corden, W. Max. Real Wage Rigidity, Devaluation and Import Restrictions. In *Corden, W. M.*, 1985, pp. 311–26.

Corden, W. Max. Relationships between Macroeconomic and Industrial Policies. In *Corden, W. M.*, 1985, pp. 288–301.

Corden, W. Max. Tariffs, Subsidies and the Terms of Trade. In *Corden, W. M.*, 1985, pp. 29–45.

Corden, W. Max. Tell Us Where the New Jobs Will Come From. *World Econ.*, June 1985, *8*(2), pp. 183–88.

Corden, W. Max. The Structure of a Tariff System and the Effective Protective Rate. In *Corden,*

W. M., 1985, pp. 97–117.

Corden, W. Max. The Substitution Problem in the Theory of Effective Protection. In *Corden, W. M.*, 1985, pp. 125–40.

Corden, W. Max and Gruen, Fred H. A Tariff That Worsens the Terms of Trade. In *Corden, W. M.*, 1985, pp. 69–72.

Criel, G. The Infant Industry Argument for Protection: A Reevaluation. *De Economist*, 1985, *133*(2), pp. 199–217.

Daniel, Betty C.; Fried, Harold O. and Tower, Edward. On the Dynamic Non-equivalence of Tariffs and Quotas in the Monetary Model of the Balance of Payments: Comment. *J. Int. Econ.*, May 1985, *18*(3/4), pp. 373–79.

Dei, Fumio. Voluntary Export Restraints and Foreign Investment. *J. Int. Econ.*, November 1985, *19*(3/4), pp. 305–12.

Diewert, W. E. A Dynamic Approach to the Measurement of Waste in an Open Economy. *J. Int. Econ.*, November 1985, *19*(3/4), pp. 213–40.

Dixit, Avinash K. Tax Policy in Open Economies. In *Auerbach, A. J. and Feldstein, M., eds.*, 1985, pp. 313–74.

Dixit, Avinash K. and Kyle, Albert S. The Use of Protection and Subsidies for Entry Promotion and Deterrence. *Amer. Econ. Rev.*, March 1985, *75*(1), pp. 139–52.

Dixon, Peter B.; Parmenter, B. R. and Rimmer, Russell J. The Sensitivity of ORANI Projections of the Short-run Effects of Increases in Protection to Variations in the Values Adopted for Export Demand Elasticities. In *Jungenfelt, K. and Hague, D. [Sir], eds.*, 1985, pp. 317–46.   [G: Australia; Selected Countries]

Donnenfeld, S. and Weber, S. Lobbying for Tariffs and the Cost of Protection. *Rech. Écon. Louvain*, 1985, *51*(1), pp. 21–27.

Donnenfeld, S.; Weber, Shlomo and Ben-Zion, Uri. Import Controls under Imperfect Information. *J. Int. Econ.*, November 1985, *19*(3/4), pp. 341–54.

Eaton, Jonathan and Grossman, Gene M. Tariffs as Insurance: Optimal Commercial Policy When Domestic Markets Are Incomplete. *Can. J. Econ.*, May 1985, *18*(2), pp. 258–72.

Eckstein, Zvi and Eichenbaum, Martin S. Oil Supply Disruptions and the Optimal Tariff in a Dynamic Stochastic Equilibrium Model. In *Sargent, T. J., ed.*, 1985, pp. 41–69.

Fløystad, Gunnar. Free Trade versus Protection: Static and Dynamic Aspects. *Pakistan Devel. Rev.*, Spring 1985, *24*(1), pp. 39–50.   [G: LDCs]

Fløystad, Gunnar. On Tariffs and Optimal Taxation Policy in Developing Countries. *Pakistan Devel. Rev.*, Autumn-Winter 1985, *24*(3/4), pp. 443–50.   [G: LDCs]

Frey, Bruno S. The Political Economy of Protection. In *Greenaway, D., ed.*, 1985, pp. 139–57.   [G: OECD]

Fried, Harold O. and Tower, Edward. On Using a Single Tariff to Exploit Market Power on Many Traded Goods. *Econ. Int.*, Aug./Nov.

1985, *38*(3/4), pp. 318–22.

Greenaway, David. Models of Trade in Differentiated Goods and Commercial Policy. In *Greenaway, D., ed.*, 1985, pp. 81–97.

Grinols, Earl L. Trade, Distortions, and Welfare under Uncertainty. *Oxford Econ. Pap.*, September 1985, *37*(3), pp. 362–74.

Grossman, Gene M. The Optimal Tariff for a Small Country under International Uncertainty: A Comment. *Oxford Econ. Pap.*, March 1985, *37*(1), pp. 154–58.

Hamilton, Carl. Economic Aspects of Voluntary Export Restraints. In *Greenaway, D., ed.*, 1985, pp. 99–117.   [G: Selected Countries]

Harris, Richard. Why Voluntary Export Restraints Are 'Voluntary.' *Can. J. Econ.*, November 1985, *18*(4), pp. 799–809.

Hartigan, James C. What Can We Learn from the Effective Rate of Protection? *Weltwirtsch. Arch.*, 1985, *121*(1), pp. 53–60.   [G: U.S.]

Hesse, Helmut. Export Restrictions as a Means of Avoiding "Critical Shortages." In *[Heidhues, T.]*, 1985, pp. 195–213.

Hillman, Arye L. and Templeman, Joseph. On the Use of Trade Policy Measures by a Small Country to Counter Foreign Monopoly Power. *Oxford Econ. Pap.*, June 1985, *37*(2), pp. 346–52.

Ilmakunnas, Pekka. Identification and Estimation of the Degree of Oligopoly Power in Industries Facing Domestic and Import Competition. In *Schwalbach, J., ed.*, 1985, pp. 287–308.   [G: W. Germany]

Itagaki, Takao. Optimal Tariffs for a Large and a Small Country under Uncertain Terms of Trade. *Oxford Econ. Pap.*, June 1985, *37*(2), pp. 292–97.

Jabara, Cathy L. and Thompson, Robert L. The Optimal Tariff for a Small Country under International Price Uncertainty: A Reply. *Oxford Econ. Pap.*, March 1985, *37*(1), pp. 159.

Jones, Ronald W. Income Effects and Paradoxes in the Theory of International Trade. *Econ. J.*, June 1985, *95*(378), pp. 330–44.

Karp, Larry S. Higher Moments in the Linear-Quadratic-Gaussian Problem. *J. Econ. Dynam. Control*, September 1985, *9*(1), pp. 41–54.

Keppler, Horst. Commodity Export Taxes as a Means of Promoting Internal Processing Industries—A General Equilibrium Model. In *Weinblatt, J., ed.*, 1985, pp. 51–70.

Keppler, Horst. Free Access to Supplies versus Restrictive Supply Policies: The Ability of LDCs to Control Commodity Markets. In *Weinblatt, J., ed.*, 1985, pp. 71–115.   [G: Selected LDCs]

Khan, Mohsin S. On Tariffs and Optimal Taxation Policy in Developing Countries: Comments. *Pakistan Devel. Rev.*, Autumn-Winter 1985, *24*(3/4), pp. 451–52.   [G: LDCs]

Kiguel, Miguel A. and Wooton, Ian. Tariff Policy and Equilibrium Growth in the World Economy. *J. Devel. Econ.*, Sept.-Oct. 1985, *19*(1/2), pp. 187–98.

Kimbrough, Kent P. Tariffs, Quotas and Welfare in a Monetary Economy. *J. Int. Econ.*, November 1985, *19*(3/4), pp. 257–77.

Kirschke, Dieter. Trade Uncertainty in a Price Fixing Protective System. *Z. ges. Staatswiss. (JITE)*, June 1985, *141*(2), pp. 269–81.

Krueger, Anne O. How to Liberalize a Small, Open Economy. In *Connolly, M. B. and McDermott, J., eds.*, 1985, pp. 12–23.

Kumcu, M. Ercan. The Theory of Commercial Policy in a Monetary Economy with Sticky Wages. *J. Int. Econ.*, February 1985, *18*(1/2), pp. 159–70.

McKenzie, George. A Problem in Measuring the Cost of Protection. *Manchester Sch. Econ. Soc. Stud.*, March 1985, *53*(1), pp. 45–54.

Melvin, James R. Domestic Taste Differences, Transportation Costs, and International Trade. *J. Int. Econ.*, February 1985, *18*(1/2), pp. 65–82.

Melvin, James R. The Regional Economic Consequences of Tariffs and Domestic Transportation Costs. *Can. J. Econ.*, May 1985, *18*(2), pp. 237–57.

Mercenier, Jean and Waelbroeck, Jean. The Impact of Protection on Developing Countries: A General Equilibrium Analysis. In *Jungenfelt, K. and Hague, D. [Sir], eds.*, 1985, pp. 219–39. **[G: LDCs]**

Orden, David. When Are Export Subsidies Rational? A Comment. *Agr. Econ. Res.*, Winter 1985, *37*(1), pp. 14–16.

Parai, Amar K. and Mohanty, Bidhu B. Optimal Policy to Achieve Debt Repayment of the LDCs. *J. Devel. Econ.*, August 1985, *18*(2–3), pp. 479–83. **[G: LDCs]**

Prebisch, Raúl. Power Relations and Market Laws. In *Kim, K. S. and Ruccio, D. F., eds.*, 1985, pp. 9–31.

Samuelson, Paul A. Analytics of Free-Trade or Protectionist Response by America to Japan's Growth Spurt. In *Shishido, T. and Sato, R., eds.*, 1985, pp. 3–18. **[G: Japan; U.S.]**

Van Bemmelen, Michael. On the Choice between International Capital and Labor Mobility. *Europ. Econ. Rev.*, December 1985, *29*(3), pp. 355–79.

Venables, Anthony J. Trade and Trade Policy with Imperfect Competition: The Case of Identical Products and Free Entry. *J. Int. Econ.*, August 1985, *19*(1/2), pp. 1–19.

Webb, Michael A. Optimal Commercial Policy with Imperfect Foreign Supply. *Atlantic Econ. J.*, December 1985, *13*(4), pp. 39–42.

Weinblatt, J. and Nathanson, R. Export Restrictions as a Means of Redistributing World Income: An Appraisal. In *Weinblatt, J., ed.*, 1985, pp. 116–27.

Weinblatt, J. and Nathanson, R. The Effects of Export Restrictions on Economic Growth in LDCs. In *Weinblatt, J., ed.*, 1985, pp. 181–96. **[G: Selected LDCs]**

Whalley, John and Wigle, Randall. Price and Quantity Rigidities in Adjustment to Trade Policy Changes: Alternative Formulations and Initial Calculations. In *Jungenfelt, K. and Hague, D. [Sir], eds.*, 1985, pp. 246–71. **[G: Global]**

van Wijnbergen, Sweder. Taxation of International Capital Flows, the Intertemporal Terms of Trade and the Real Price of Oil. *Oxford Econ. Pap.*, September 1985, *37*(3), pp. 382–90.

Yarbrough, Beth V. and Yarbrough, Robert M. Free Trade, Hegemony, and the Theory of Agency. *Kyklos*, 1985, *38*(3), pp. 348–64.

Yeh, Yeong-Her. Export Subsidies, Factor Inflows, and Income Distribution [Factor Endowments and Relative Commodity Prices]. *Atlantic Econ. J.*, July 1985, *13*(2), pp. 73–75.

Yvars, Bernard. Protection et mobilité internationale du capital dans une économie ou ce facteur est spécifique. (Protection and International Capital Mobility in an Economy Where This Factor Is Specific. With English summary.) *Revue Écon.*, July 1985, *36*(4), pp. 687–714.

4114 Theory of International Trade and Economic Development

Aliber, Robert Z. External Financing and the Level of Development: A Conceptual Approach. In *Gutowski, A.; Arnaudo, A. A. and Scharrer, H.-E., eds.*, 1985, pp. 234–48.

Bakalis, Steve and Hazari, Bharat R. Unemployment, Capital Underutilization and Welfare in a Small Open Economy. *Greek Econ. Rev.*, December 1985, *7*(3), pp. 226–41.

Bender, Dieter. Wechselkursbindung in Entwicklungsländern: Eine optimale Anpassungsstrategie an flexible Wechselkurse? (Basket Pegging in Developing Countries. With English summary.) *Kredit Kapital*, 1985, *18*(3), pp. 320–46. **[G: LDCs]**

Bhagwati, Jagdish N. Developmental Strategy: Import Substitution versus Export Promotion. In *Bhagwati, J. N. (I)*, 1985, pp. 65–67.

Bhagwati, Jagdish N. Foreign Trade Regimes. In *Bhagwati, J. N. (I)*, 1985, pp. 123–37.

Bhagwati, Jagdish N. What We Need to Know. In *Bhagwati, J. N. (I)*, 1985, pp. 80–87.

Bhagwati, Jagdish N. and Cheh, John. LDC Exports: A Cross-Sectional Analysis. In *Bhagwati, J. N. (II)*, 1985, pp. 157–66. **[G: LDCs]**

Bhagwati, Jagdish N. and Krueger, Anne O. Exchange Control, Liberalization and Economic Development. In *Bhagwati, J. N. (I)*, 1985, pp. 68–79.

Bhagwati, Jagdish N. and Srinivasan, T. N. Trade Policy and Development. In *Bhagwati, J. N. (I)*, 1985, pp. 88–122.

Bhagwati, Jagdish N. and Wibulswasdi, Chaiyawat. A Statistical Analysis of Shifts in the Import Structure in LDCs. In *Bhagwati, J. N. (II)*, 1985, pp. 142–56. **[G: LDCs]**

Brochart, Françoise. Exportation et croissance économique: Application aux pays africains de la zone franc. (With English summary.) *Revue Écon. Polit.*, July-August 1985, *95*(4), pp. 469–83. **[G: Africa]**

Burgstaller, André. North–South Trade and Capital Flows in a Ricardian Model of Accumulation. *J. Int. Econ.*, May 1985, *18*(3/4), pp. 241–60.

Canavese, Alfredo J. and Montuschi, Luisa. Inflation and the Financing of Alternative Development Strategies. In *Gutowski, A.; Arnaudo, A. A. and Scharrer, H.-E., eds.*, 1985, pp. 115–36. **[G: Argentina]**

Chu, David K. Y. The Politico-economic Background to the Development of the Special Economic Zones. In *Wong, K. and Chu, D. K. Y., eds.*, 1985, pp. 25–39. **[G: China]**

Chu, David K. Y. and Wong, Kwan-Yiu. Modernization and the Lessons of the Special Economic Zones. In *Wong, K. and Chu, D. K. Y., eds.*, 1985, pp. 208–17.

Clark, Paul. Free Trade and Economic Development: Insights from Henry George: Comments. In *Lewis, S. R., Jr., ed.*, 1985, pp. 93–95.

Cooper, J. H. Sanctions and Economic Theory. *S. Afr. J. Econ.*, September 1985, 53(3), pp. 287–96.

Criel, G. The Infant Industry Argument for Protection: A Reevaluation. *De Economist*, 1985, 133(2), pp. 199–217.

Díaz-Alejandro, Carlos F. International Markets for LDCs—The Old and the New. In *Adams, J., ed.*, 1985, pp. 487–95.

Dietz, James L. Export-Enclave Economies, International Corporations, and Development. *J. Econ. Issues*, June 1985, 19(2), pp. 512–22.

Findlay, Ronald F. Primary Exports, Manufacturing and Development. In *Lundahl, M., ed.*, 1985, pp. 218–33.

Fogarty, John. Staples, Super-Staples and the Limits of Staple Theory: The Experiences of Argentina, Australia and Canada Compared. In *Platt, D. C. M. and di Tella, G., eds.*, 1985, pp. 19–36. **[G: Argentina; Australia; Canada]**

Gupta, Sanjeev. Export Growth and Economic Growth Revisited. *Indian Econ. J.*, Jan.-Mar. 1985, 32(3), pp. 52–59. **[G: Israel; S. Korea]**

Gutowski, Armin. Foreign Indebtedness and Economic Growth: Is There a Limit to Foreign Financing? In *Gutowski, A.; Arnaudo, A. A. and Scharrer, H.-E., eds.*, 1985, pp. 249–67.

Haberler, Gottfried. International Trade and Economic Development. In *Haberler, G.*, 1985, pp. 495–527.

Haberler, Gottfried. Terms of Trade and Economic Development. In *Haberler, G.*, 1985, pp. 453–72.

Hazari, Bharat R. and Bakalis, Steve. An Analysis of Capital Underutilization in Less Developed Countries—A Trade Theoretic Approach. *Devel. Econ.*, March 1985, 23(1), pp. 3–15.

Howard, Michael. Export Processing Zones and Development Strategies in the South Pacific. In *Utrecht, E., ed.*, 1985, pp. 31–82. **[G: S. Pacific]**

Jorge, Antonio. Development Strategies, Trade and External Debt in Latin America. In *Jorge, A.; Salazar-Carrillo, J. and Diaz-Pou, F., eds.*, 1985, pp. 1–14. **[G: Latin America]**

Jorge, Antonio and Salazar-Carrillo, Jorge. Development Strategies, Trade and External Debt in Latin America: An Overview. In *Salazar-Carrillo, J. and de Alonso, I. T., eds.*, 1985, pp. 1–34. **[G: Latin America]**

Kemp, Murray C. and Kojima, Shoichi. Tied Aid and the Paradoxes of Donor-Enrichment and Recipient-Impoverishment. *Int. Econ. Rev.*, October 1985, 26(3), pp. 721–29.

Keppler, Horst. Commodity Export Taxes as a Means of Promoting Internal Processing Industries—A General Equilibrium Model. In *Weinblatt, J., ed.*, 1985, pp. 51–70.

Keppler, Horst. Free Access to Supplies versus Restrictive Supply Policies: The Ability of LDCs to Control Commodity Markets. In *Weinblatt, J., ed.*, 1985, pp. 71–115. **[G: Selected LDCs]**

Lauridsen, Laurids S. Export-Oriented Industrialization in Latin America, South and East Asia. In *Utrecht, E., ed.*, 1985, pp. 83–136. **Econom[G: Latin America; E. Asia; S. Asia]**

Lim, Joseph. The Distributive Implications of Export-Led Industrialization in a Developing Economy. *Philippine Econ. J.*, 1985, 24(4), pp. 223–33.

Lysy, Frank J. Graciela Chichilnisky's Model of North–South Trade. *J. Devel. Econ.*, August 1985, 18(2–3), pp. 503–39.

Montuschi, Luisa. Un indicador para medir el efectivo alcance de la sustitución de importaciones. (An Indicator to Measure the Actual Extent of Import Substitution. With English summary.) *Económica (La Plata)*, May-Dec. 1985, 31(2–3), pp. 229–34.

Pourgerami, Abbas. Exports Growth and Economic Development: A Comparative Logit Analysis. *J. Econ. Devel.*, July 1985, 10(1), pp. 117–28. **[G: LDCs]**

Prebisch, Raúl. Power Relations and Market Laws. In *Kim, K. S. and Ruccio, D. F., eds.*, 1985, pp. 9–31.

Ram, Rati. Exports and Economic Growth: Some Additional Evidence. *Econ. Develop. Cult. Change*, January 1985, 33(2), pp. 415–25. **[G: LDCs]**

Ranis, Gustav and Orrock, Louise. Latin American and East Asian NICs: Development Strategies Compared. In *Duran, E., ed.*, 1985, pp. 48–66. **[G: Selected LDCs]**

Roemer, Michael. Dutch Disease in Developing Countries: Swallowing Bitter Medicine. In *Lundahl, M., ed.*, 1985, pp. 234–52. **[G: LDCs]**

Sapsford, D. The Statistical Debate on the Net Barter Terms of Trade between Primary Commodities and Manufactures: A Comment and Some Additional Evidence. *Econ. J.*, September 1985, 95(379), pp. 781–88. **[G: U.K.]**

Simonsen, Mario Henrique. Indebted Developing-Country Prospects and Macroeconomic Policies in the OECD. In *Bergsten, C. F., ed.*, 1985, pp. 51–64.

Spraos, John. The Statistical Debate on the Net Barter Terms of Trade: A Response. *Econ. J.*, September 1985, 95(379), pp. 789. **[G: U.K.]**

Tabaczyński, Eugeniusz. Problems of Export-Oriented Restructuring of Polish Industry. In *[Levcik, F.]*, 1985, pp. 117–21.

Utrecht, Ernst. Gains and Losses in 25 Years of Export-Oriented Industrialization in South and

Southeast Asia. In *Utrecht, E., ed.*, 1985, pp. 137–58. **[G: S. Asia; S.E. Asia]**

Weinblatt, J. and Nathanson, R. Export Restrictions as a Means of Redistributing World Income: An Appraisal. In *Weinblatt, J., ed.*, 1985, pp. 116–27.

Weinblatt, J. and Nathanson, R. The Effects of Export Restrictions on Economic Growth in LDCs. In *Weinblatt, J., ed.*, 1985, pp. 181–96. **[G: Selected LDCs]**

Weinblatt, J. and Schrager, Nora. Exports from LDCs: Impacts on Economic Growth. In *Weinblatt, J., ed.*, 1985, pp. 161–80. **[G: LDCs]**

Wong, Kwan-Yiu and Chu, David K. Y. Export Processing Zones and Special Economic Zones as Locomotives of Export-Led Economic Growth. In *Wong, K. and Chu, D. K. Y., eds.*, 1985, pp. 1–24. **[G: Asia]**

420 TRADE RELATIONS; COMMERCIAL POLICY; INTERNATIONAL ECONOMIC INTEGRATION

4200 General

Al-Hoss, Salim. The Political Element in U.S.–Arab Economic Relations. In *Czinkota, M. R. and Marciel, S., eds.*, 1985, pp. 298–303. **[G: U.S.; Middle East]**

Balassa, Bela. U.S. Direct Foreign Investment and Trade: Theories, Trends and Public Policy Issues: Comment. In *Erdilek, A., ed.*, 1985, pp. 151–54. **[G: U.S.]**

Bhagwati, Jagdish N. Rethinking Global Negotiations. In *Bhagwati, J. N. (I)*, 1985, pp. 39–48.

Bhagwati, Jagdish N. Whither the Global Negotiations? In *Bapna, A., ed.*, 1985, pp. 189–94.

Bogomolov, Oleg. Current Problems and Prospects of the World Economy in the Light of East–West Economic Relations. In *Saunders, C. T., ed.*, 1985, pp. 43–59.

Chaikin, Sol C. Trade, Investment, and Deindustrialization: Myth and Reality. In *Moran, T. H., ed.*, 1985, pp. 159–72. **[G: U.S.]**

Chichilnisky, Graciela and Heal, Geoffrey M. Trade and Development in the 1980s. In *Bapna, A., ed.*, 1985, pp. 195–239. **[G: LDCs; MDCs]**

Cline, William R. Changing Stresses on the World Economy. *World Econ.*, June 1985, 8(2), pp. 135–52. **[G: Global]**

Coutinho, Luciano. The Recent Performance and Future Challenges of Newly Industrializing Countries. In *Hochmuth, M. and Davidson, W., eds.*, 1985, pp. 131–62. **[G: OECD; LDCs]**

Czinkota, Michael R. Current Problems and Future Prospects of U.S.–Arab Economic Relations. In *Czinkota, M. R. and Marciel, S., eds.*, 1985, pp. 304–08. **[G: U.S.; Middle East]**

Evans, Peter B.; Rueschemeyer, Dietrich and Stephens, Evelyne Huber. States versus Markets in the World-System: Introduction. In *Evans, P.; Rueschemeyer, D. and Stephens, E. H., eds.*, 1985, pp. 11–30.

Grossman, Gene M. U.S. Direct Foreign Invest-

ment and Trade: Theories, Trends and Public Policy Issues: Comment. In *Erdilek, A., ed.*, 1985, pp. 155–59. **[G: U.S.]**

Hathaway, Dale E. Food Issues in North–South Relations. In *[Heidhues, T.]*, 1985, pp. 289–301.

Hay, D. A. International Trade and Development. In *Morris, D., ed.*, 1985, pp. 475–502. **[G: U.K.]**

Hochmuth, Milton. Revitalizing American Industry: Analysis and Summary. In *Hochmuth, M. and Davidson, W., eds.*, 1985, pp. 375–95. **[G: Selected Countries]**

Howard, Michael. Export Processing Zones and Development Strategies in the South Pacific. In *Utrecht, E., ed.*, 1985, pp. 31–82. **[G: S. Pacific]**

Jha, L. K. Export Strategy for the 80s. In *Jha, L. K.*, 1985, pp. 209–16. **[G: India]**

Jha, L. K. The Role of Developing Countries in Promoting World Employment. In *Jha, L. K.*, 1985, pp. 159–66. **[G: Global]**

Jordan, Robert S. Conclusions: The Global Interest or the National Interest: Must They Lead to Conflict or Can They Lead to Cooperation? In *Jordan, R. S., ed.*, 1985, pp. 151–66.

Jungenfelt, Karl. Structural Adjustment in Developed Open Economies: Introduction. In *Jungenfelt, K. and Hague, D. [Sir], eds.*, 1985, pp. xiii–xxvi.

Kessler, Richard J. No Fuel for Development: United States Policy toward Managing International Energy Resources. In *Jordan, R. S., ed.*, 1985, pp. 21–42.

Kindleberger, Charles P. The Importance of Free Trade for Developing Countries. *Indian J. Quant. Econ.*, 1985, 1(1), pp. 45–60. **[G: Latin America]**

Knirsch, Peter. Economic Relations—Interdependence or Marginal Factor?: Summary of Economic Relations. In *Rode, R. and Jacobsen, H.-D., eds.*, 1985, pp. 86–98. **[G: CMEA]**

Kornyshev, V. Commercial and Economic Relations between the USSR and Argentina Are in Full Swing. *Soviet E. Europ. Foreign Trade*, Summer–Fall 1985, 21(1–2–3), pp. 247–52. **[G: U.S.S.R.; Argentina]**

Krueger, Anne O. Importance of General Policies to Promote Economic Growth. *World Econ.*, June 1985, 8(2), pp. 93–108. **[G: Global]**

Maldonado Lince, Guillermo. Latin America and Integration: Options in the Crisis. *Cepal Rev.*, December 1985, (27), pp. 55–68. **[G: Latin America]**

Maximova, Margarita. Comments [The Global Environment and Its Impact on Soviet and East European Economies] [Current Problems and Prospects of the World Economy in the Light of East–West Economic Relations]. In *Saunders, C. T., ed.*, 1985, pp. 127–30. **[G: OECD; CMEA]**

McCulloch, Rachel. U.S. Direct Foreign Investment and Trade: Theories, Trends and Public Policy Issues. In *Erdilek, A., ed.*, 1985, pp. 129–51. **[G: U.S.]**

McFarlane, Anthony. The Transition from Colo-

nialism in Colombia, 1819–1875. In *Abel, C. and Lewis, C. M., eds.*, 1985, pp. 101–24.
[G: Colombia]
Ranis, Gustav. Adjustment in East Asia: Lessons for Latin America. In *Jorge, A.; Salazar-Carrillo, J. and Diaz-Pou, F., eds.*, 1985, pp. 43–56. [G: East Asia]
Rode, Reinhard. East–West Trade and Détente. In *Rode, R. and Jacobsen, H.-D., eds.*, 1985, pp. 3–15.
Saunders, Christopher T. Comments [The Global Environment and Its Impact on Soviet and East European Economies] [Current Problems and Prospects of the World Economy in the Light of East–West Economic Relations]. In *Saunders, C. T., ed.*, 1985, pp. 125–27.
[G: OECD; CMEA]
Schott, Jeffrey J. The GATT Ministerial: A Postmortem. In *Adams, J., ed.*, 1985, pp. 84–92.
[G: U.S.; EEC; LDCs]
Waldmann, Raymond J. U.S.–Arab Economic Relations: A U.S. Perspective. In *Czinkota, M. R. and Marciel, S., eds.*, 1985, pp. 17–22. [G: U.S.; OPEC]
Wolff von Amerongen, Otto. Economic Relations with the Soviet Union: Foreword. In *Stent, A. E., ed.*, 1985, pp. xi–xiv. [G: OECD; CMEA]

421 Trade Relations

4210 Trade Relations

Abbott, Alden F. Foreign Competition and Relevant Market Definition under the Department of Justice's Merger Guidelines. *Antitrust Bull.*, Summer 1985, *30*(2), pp. 299–336.
Adedeji, Adebayo. Special Measures for the Least Developed and Other Low-Income Countries. In *Preeg, E. H., ed.*, 1985, pp. 135–63.
[G: Sub-Saharan Africa]
Afanasjew, Michail. East–West Cooperation in Energy. In *Saunders, C. T., ed.*, 1985, pp. 201–16. [G: U.S.S.R.; OECD]
Agarwal, Suraj Mal. Electronics in India: Past Strategies and Future Possibilities. *World Devel.*, March 1985, *13*(3), pp. 273–92.
[G: India]
Ahmad, Jaleel. Prospects of Trade Liberalization between the Developed and the Developing Countries. *World Devel.*, September 1985, *13*(9), pp. 1077–86. [G: OECD; LDCs]
Aho, C. Michael and Bayard, Thomas O. The 1980s: Twilight of the Open Trading System? In *Adams, J., ed.*, 1985, pp. 92–119.
[G: Global]
Ahumada, Hildegart A. An Encompassing Test of Two Models of the Balance of Trade for Argentina. *Oxford Bull. Econ. Statist.*, February 1985, *47*(1), pp. 51–70. [G: Argentina]
Ajanant, Juanjai. Economic Relations between Thailand and South Asia. In *Wadhva, C. D. and Asher, M. G., eds.*, 1985, pp. 185–222.
[G: Thailand; S. Asia]
Akder, Halis. Reflections on Turkish Agriculture and Common Agricultural Policy. *METU,*

1985, *12*(3/4), pp. 343–51. [G: Turkey; EEC]
Al-Dabbagh, Abdullah Taher. The Influence of Oil Revenues on U.S.–Arab Trade: Possible Changes in Arab Imports. In *Czinkota, M. R. and Marciel, S., eds.*, 1985, pp. 269–97.
[G: U.S.; Middle East]
Al-Imadi, Mohammed. Inter-Arab Aid and Its Impact on Trade and Interdependence. In *Czinkota, M. R. and Marciel, S., eds.*, 1985, pp. 203–35. [G: OPEC; LDCs]
Al-Sadik, A. T. National Accounting and Income Illusion of Petroleum Exports: The Case of the Arab Gulf Co-operation Council Members (AGCC) In *Niblock, T. and Lawless, R., eds.*, 1985, pp. 86–115. [G: OPEC]
Alam, Syed N. Canada–India Trade: A Market Share Analysis. *Indian Econ. J.*, Oct.-Nov. 1985, *33*(2), pp. 45–56. [G: India; Canada]
Alézard, Gérald. Transnational Activity and Domestic Recovery. In *Zukin, S., ed.*, 1985, pp. 239–45. [G: France]
Altmann, Franz-Lothar. East–West Relations in Energy, Agriculture and Technology: Comments. In *Saunders, C. T., ed.*, 1985, pp. 242–46. [G: U.S.S.R.; OECD]
Altmann, Franz-Lothar. Eastern Policies: Eastern Europe (CMEA 6) In *Rode, R. and Jacobsen, H.-D., eds.*, 1985, pp. 266–80.
[G: CMEA; OECD; LDCs]
Amsden, Alice H. The Division of Labour Is Limited by the Rate of Growth of the Market: The Taiwan Machine Tool Industry in the 1970s. *Cambridge J. Econ.*, September 1985, *9*(3), pp. 271–84. [G: Taiwan]
Anderson, David L. Market Power and the Saskatchewan Potash Industry. *Can. Public Policy*, Supplement July 1985, *11*(3), pp. 321–28.
[G: Canada]
Anderson, Kym and Garnaut, Ross. Australia's Trade Growth with Developing Countries. *Devel. Econ.*, June 1985, *23*(2), pp. 121–37.
[G: Australia; LDCs]
Androuais, Anne. Les investissements japonais en Asie du sud-est: compléments ou concurrents de l'industrie au Japon. (With English summary.) *Revue Écon. Polit.*, May–June 1985, *95*(3), pp. 320–45. [G: Japan; S. E. Asia]
Anwar, Sajid. Export Functions for Pakistan: A Simultaneous Equations Approach. *Pakistan J. Appl. Econ.*, Summer 1985, *4*(1), pp. 29–34.
[G: Pakistan]
Ariff, Mohamed. Malaysia–South Asia Economic Relations. In *Wadhva, C. D. and Asher, M. G., eds.*, 1985, pp. 66–114. [G: Malaysia; S. Asia]
Arize, Augustine and Afifi, Rasoul. A Simultaneous Equations Model of Demand for Imports in Twenty-Seven African Countries: Evidence of Structural Change. *Indian Econ. J.*, Oct.-Nov. 1985, *33*(2), pp. 93–105. [G: Africa]
Arnaud-Ameller, Paule. Investissements directs et flux commerciaux compléments ou substituts? Le cas français 1968–1978. (With English summary.) *Revue Écon. Polit.*, May–June 1985, *95*(3), pp. 299–319. [G: France]
Artto, Eero. Kansainvälinen kilpailukyky yritys-

ja toimialatasolla—V. (International Competitiveness at Enterprise and Industry Level—V. With English summary.) *Liiketaloudellinen Aikak.*, 1985, *34*(1), pp. 32–73.   [G: Finland; W. Germany; Canada; U.S.; Sweden]

Asher, Mukul G. Economic Relations between Singapore and South Asia. In *Wadhva, C. D. and Asher, M. G., eds.*, 1985, pp. 138–84.
[G: Singapore; S. Asia]

Asher, Mukul G. and Wadhva, Charan D. ASEAN–South Asia Economic Relations: An Overview. In *Wadhva, C. D. and Asher, M. G., eds.*, 1985, pp. 1–26.   [G: ASEAN; S. Asia]

Ashiquzzaman, Shah M. and Ghosh, Atish R. Profits, Tariffs, and Intra-industry Trade. *Indian Econ. J.*, Oct.-Nov. 1985, *33*(2), pp. 106–15.

Atkinson, Thomas R. Canada/U.S. Automotive Trade and Trade-policy Issues: Comments. In *Fretz, D.; Stern, R. and Whalley, J., eds.*, 1985, pp. 333–37.   [G: Canada; U.S.]

Aurikko, Esko. A Dynamic Disaggregated Model of Finnish Imports of Goods. *Empirical Econ.*, 1985, *10*(2), pp. 103–20.   [G: Finland]

Aurikko, Esko. Testing Disequilibrium Adjustment Models for Finnish Exports of Goods. *Oxford Bull. Econ. Statist.*, February 1985, *47*(1), pp. 33–50.   [G: Finland]

Avramovič, Dragoslav. Collapse of Intra-Latin American Trade 1980–83: Causes and Prospects. In *Gauhar, A., ed.*, 1985, pp. 133–38.
[G: Latin America]

Aw, Bee Yan and Roberts, Mark J. The Role of Imports from the Newly-industrializing Countries in U.S. Production. *Rev. Econ. Statist.*, February 1985, *67*(1), pp. 108–17.   [G: U.S.; LDCs]

Bach, Christopher L. U.S. International Transactions, Fourth Quarter and Year 1984. *Surv. Curr. Bus.*, March 1985, *65*(3), pp. 29–58.
[G: U.S.]

Bahmani-Oskooee, Mohsen. Devaluation and the J-Curve: Some Evidence from LDCs. *Rev. Econ. Statist.*, August 1985, *67*(3), pp. 500–504.   [G: Greece; India; Korea; Thailand]

Balassa, Bela. Adjustment Policies in Developing Economies: A Reassessment. In *Balassa, B.*, 1985, pp. 89–101.   [G: LDCs]

Balassa, Bela. Exports, Policy Choices, and Economic Growth in Developing Countries after the 1973 Oil Shock. *J. Devel. Econ.*, May–June 1985, *18*(1), pp. 23–35.   [G: LDCs]

Balassa, Bela. Industrial Protection in the Developed Countries. In *Balassa, B.*, 1985, pp. 427–47.   [G: EEC; U.S.; Japan]

Balassa, Bela. The "New Growth Path" in Hungary. *Banca Naz. Lavoro Quart. Rev.*, December 1985, (155), pp. 347–72.   [G: Hungary]

Balassa, Bela. The Cambridge Group and the Developing Countries. *World Econ.*, September 1985, *8*(3), pp. 201–18.   [G: Mexico; Tanzania; LDCs]

Balassa, Bela. The Role of Foreign Trade in the Economic Development of Korea. In *Galen-*

son, W., ed., 1985, pp. 141–75.
[G: S. Korea]

Balassa, Bela. Trade and Trade Relations between Developed and Developing Countries in the Decade Ahead. In *Balassa, B.*, 1985, pp. 448–68.   [G: LDCs; OECD]

Balassa, Bela. Trade Policy in Mexico. In *Balassa, B.*, 1985, pp. 131–56.   [G: Mexico]

Balassa, Bela. Trends in International Trade in Manufactured Goods and Structural Change in the Industrial Countries. In *Balassa, B.*, 1985, pp. 403–26.   [G: Global]

Balassa, Bela and Bauwens, Luc. Comparative Advantage in Manufactured Goods in a Multi-country, Multi-industry, and Multi-factor Model. In *Peeters, T.; Praet, P. and Reding, P., eds.*, 1985, pp. 31–52.
[G: Selected Countries]

Baldinelli, Elvio. Latin America—The Hour for Unity. In *Gauhar, A., ed.*, 1985, pp. 194–209.
[G: Latin America]

Baldwin, Robert E. and Parker, Stephen A. The Sectoral Adjustment Implications of Current U.S. Trends in Trade Competitiveness. In *Jungenfelt, K. and Hague, D. [Sir], eds.*, 1985, pp. 466–77.   [G: U.S.]

Barker, Terry S. Endogenising Input–Output Coefficients by Means of Industrial Submodels. In *Smyshlyaev, A., ed.*, 1985, pp. 183–92.
[G: U.K.]

Barnabani, Marco and Grassini, Maurizio. On Modeling Foreign Trade in an Input–Output Model of an Open Economy. In *Smyshlyaev, A., ed.*, 1985, pp. 95–104.   [G: Italy; OECD]

Barth, James R. and Pelzman, Joseph. International Debt: Conflict and Resolution. In *Adams, J., ed.*, 1985, pp. 358–91.   [G: U.S.; GLobal]

Barthel-Rosa, Paulo. Developing-Country Trade Policies and the International Economic System: Comment. In *Preeg, E. H., ed.*, 1985, pp. 61–62.   [G: Selected LDCs]

Bautista, Romeo M. Does Increasing Agricultural Exports Raise Income Instability? An Empirical Note. *Philippine Rev. Econ. Bus.*, Sept./Dec. 1985, *22*(3/4), pp. 247–58.
[G: Philippines]

Beer, Barbo. Informatics in International Trade: Harmonization of Standards for Telecommunicated Messages. *J. World Trade Law*, Nov.:Dec. 1985, *19*(6), pp. 570–78.
[G: Global]

Bekerman, Marta. The Impact of the International Environment on Argentina. In *Griffith-Jones, S. and Harvey, C., eds.*, 1985, pp. 196–219.   [G: Argentina]

Bekerman, Marta. The Impact of the International Environment on Brazil: From "Miracle" to Recession. In *Griffith-Jones, S. and Harvey, C., eds.*, 1985, pp. 113–44.   [G: Brazil]

Bellon, Bertrand. Strengths and Weaknesses of French Industry. In *Zukin, S., ed.*, 1985, pp. 141–51.   [G: France]

Belongia, Michael T. and Stone, Courtenay C. Would Lower Federal Deficits Increase U.S. Farm Exports? *Fed. Res. Bank St. Louis Rev.*,

November 1985, *67*(9), pp. 5–19.   [G: U.S.]

Benz, Steven F. Trade Liberalization and the Global Service Economy. *J. World Trade Law*, March:April 1985, *19*(2), pp. 95–120.
[G: OECD]

Bergsten, C. Fred. The U.S.–Japan Trade Imbroglio. *Challenge*, July/August 1985, *28*(3), pp. 13–17.   [G: U.S.; Japan]

Bergstrand, Jeffrey H. The Gravity Equation in International Trade: Some Microeconomic Foundations and Empirical Evidence. *Rev. Econ. Statist.*, August 1985, *67*(3), pp. 474–81.   [G: OECD]

de Bernis, Gévard. Observations sur la "contrainte extérieure." (Comments of "Foreign Constraints." With English summary.) *Écon. Soc.*, April 1985, *19*(4), pp. 191–229.
[G: France]

Bertsch, Gary K. American Politics and Trade with the USSR. In *Parrott, B., ed.*, 1985, pp. 243–82.   [G: U.S.S.R.; U.S.]

Betancourt, Roger; Clague, Christopher K. and Panagariya, Arvind. Capital Utilization and Factor Specificity. *Rev. Econ. Stud.*, April 1985, *52*(2), pp. 311–29.   [G: U.S.; U.K.]

Bethkenhagen, Jochen. Economic Relations—Interdependence or Marginal Factor?: Trade. In *Rode, R. and Jacobsen, H.-D., eds.*, 1985, pp 17–35.   [G: CMEA; OECD]

Bethkenhagen, Jochen. Soviet–West German Economic Relations: The West German Perspective. In *Stent, A. E., ed.*, 1985, pp. 69–89.   [G: W. Germany; U.S.S.R.; E. Germany; CMEA]

Bethkenhagen, Jochen. The Impact of Energy on East–West Trade: Retrospect and Prospects. In *Saunders, C. T., ed.*, 1985, pp. 179–99.
[G: U.S.S.R.; OECD; CMEA]

Bhaduri, Amit. Financial Reconstruction for North–South and South–South Trade. *Industry Devel.*, 1985, (14), pp. 37–45.   [G: Global]

Bhagwati, Jagdish N. Export Promotion as a Developmental Strategy. In *Shishido, T. and Sato, R., eds.*, 1985, pp. 59–68.   [G: LDCs]

Bhagwati, Jagdish N. Indian Balance of Payments Policy and Exchange Auctions. In *Bhagwati, J. N. (I)*, 1985, pp. 144–62.   [G: India]

Bhagwati, Jagdish N. and Bharadwaj, Ranganath N. Human Capital and the Pattern of Foreign Trade: The Indian Case. In *Bhagwati, J. N. (II)*, 1985, pp. 104–34.   [G: India]

Bhagwati, Jagdish N. and Cheh, John. LDC Exports: A Cross-Sectional Analysis. In *Bhagwati, J. N. (II)*, 1985, pp. 157–66.   [G: LDCs]

Bhagwati, Jagdish N.; Krueger, Anne O. and Wibulswasdi, Chaiyawat. Capital Flight from LDCs: A Statistical Analysis. In *Bhagwati, J. N. (II)*, 1985, pp. 135–41.   [G: LDCs]

Bhagwati, Jagdish N. and Wibulswasdi, Chaiyawat. A Statistical Analysis of Shifts in the Import Structure in LDCs. In *Bhagwati, J. N. (II)*, 1985, pp. 142–56.   [G: LDCs]

Birenbaum, David E. and Rosenblatt, Samuel. Trade Trends and Trade Issues in the Pacific Basin. *Philippine Econ. J.*, 1985, *24*(4), pp. 288–301.   [G: Pacific Basin; U.S.]

Bitar, Sergio. Crisis financiera e industrialización de América Latina. (With English summary.) *Desarrollo Econ.*, July-Sept. 1985, *25*(98), pp. 217–43.   [G: Latin America]

Bitar, Sergio. Industrialización y crisis económica externa en América Latina. (Industrialization and External Economic Crisis in Latin America. With English summary.) *Colección Estud. CIEPLAN*, September 1985, (17), pp. 101–25.
[G: Latin America]

Bogatyi, N. and Ol'shanyi, A. O. Economic and Trade Cooperation between the CMEA Countries and India. *Soviet E. Europ. Foreign Trade*, Summer–Fall 1985, *21*(1–2–3), pp. 233–46.   [G: CMEA; India]

Böhm, Arnošt. Economic Cooperation with Non-Socialist Countries. *Czech. Econ. Digest.*, June 1985, (4), pp. 72–84.   [G: Czechoslovakia]

Bolyard, Joan E. International Travel and Passenger Fares, 1984. *Surv. Curr. Bus.*, May 1985, *65*(5), pp. 14–17.   [G: U.S.]

Bolz, Klaus. Economic Relations—Interdependence or Marginal Factor?: Industrial Cooperation. In *Rode, R. and Jacobsen, H.-D., eds.*, 1985, pp. 63–72.   [G: CMEA; W. Europe; U.S.]

Bond, Daniel and Klein, Lawrence R. The Global Environment and Its Impact on Soviet and East European Economies. In *Saunders, C. T., ed.*, 1985, pp. 19–41.   [G: OECD; CMEA]

Bond, Gary E.; Thompson, Stanley R. and Geldard, Jane M. Basis Risk and Hedging Strategies for Australian Wheat Exports. *Australian J. Agr. Econ.*, December 1985, *29*(3), pp. 199–209.   [G: Australia]

Bond, Marian E. Export Demand and Supply for Groups of Non-oil Developing Countries. *Int. Monet. Fund Staff Pap.*, March 1985, *32*(1), pp. 56–77.   [G: LDCs]

Borner, Silvio, et al. Global Structural Change and International Competition among Industrial Firms: The Case of Switzerland. *Kyklos*, 1985, *38*(1), pp. 77–103.   [G: Switzerland]

Borrus, Michael and Zysman, John. Japan's Industrial Policy and Its Pattern of Trade. In *Nanto, D. K., ed.*, 1985, pp. 13–22.
[G: Japan]

Botifoll, Luis. The Caribbean Basin Initiative: A Brief Comment. In *Jorge, A.; Salazar-Carrillo, J. and Diaz-Pou, F., eds.*, 1985, pp. 157–59.
[G: U.S.; Caribbean]

Boucher, Jacqueline and Smeers, Yves. Gas Trade in the European Community during the 1970s. *Energy Econ.*, April 1985, *7*(2), pp. 102–16.   [G: EEC]

Bower, Joseph L. Restructuring Petrochemicals: A Comparative Study of Business and Government Strategy to Deal with a Declining Sector of the Economy. In *Scott, B. R. and Lodge, G. C., eds.*, 1985, pp. 263–300.   [G: U.S.; OECD]

van Brabant, Jozef M. The Relationship between World and Socialist Trade Price—Some Empirical Evidence. *J. Compar. Econ.*, September 1985, *9*(3), pp. 233–51.   [G: CMEA]

van Brabant, Jozef M. Yugoslavia's Foreign Trade

Statistics: A Methodological Inquiry. *Comparative Econ. Stud.*, Winter 1985, *27*(4), pp. 31–51. [G: Yugoslavia]

Brada, Josef C. Soviet–Western Trade and Technology Transfer: An Economic Overview. In *Parrott, B., ed.*, 1985, pp. 3–34. [G: U.S.S.R.; OECD]

Brada, Josef C. and Méndez, José A. Economic Integration among Developed, Developing and Centrally Planned Economies: A Comparative Analysis. *Rev. Econ. Statist.*, November 1985, *67*(4), pp. 549–56. [G: Global]

Bradford, James C. Canadian Defence Trade with the United States. In *Fretz, D.; Stern, R. and Whalley, J., eds.*, 1985, pp. 474–77. [G: Canada; U.S.]

Brandt, Loren. Chinese Agriculture and the International Economy, 1870–1930s: A Reassessment. *Exploration Econ. Hist.*, April 1985, *22*(2), pp. 168–93. [G: China]

Branson, William H. Policy and Performance Links between LDC Debtors and Industrial Nations: Comment. *Brookings Pap. Econ. Act.*, 1985, (2), pp. 357–61. [G: LDCs; OECD]

Brochart, Françoise. Exportation et croissance économique: Application aux pays africains de la zone franc. (With English summary.) *Revue Écon. Polit.*, July-August 1985, *95*(4), pp. 469–83. [G: Africa]

Broll, Udo and Gilroy, B. Michael. International Division of Labour and Intra-Trade. *Econ. Int.*, May 1985, *38*(2), pp. 161–66. [G: W. Europe]

Brooks, Harvey. Technology as a Factor in U.S. Competitiveness. In *Scott, B. R. and Lodge, G. C., eds.*, 1985, pp. 328–56. [G: U.S.; OECD]

Browne, Lynn E. Autos—Another Steel? *New Eng. Econ. Rev.*, Nov./Dec. 1985, pp. 14–29. [G: U.S.]

Browne, Lynn E. Steel—An Industry Beset on All Sides. *New Eng. Econ. Rev.*, May/June 1985, pp. 35–43. [G: U.S.]

Browning, Martin J. The Trend Level of Imports by CMEA Countries. *J. Compar. Econ.*, December 1985, *9*(4), pp. 363–70. [G: CMEA]

Buchholz, Horst E. International Relationships in the World Beef Trade: Comment. In *[Heidhues, T.]*, 1985, pp. 189–91. [G: Selected Countries]

Bunce, Valerie. The Empire Strikes Back: The Evolution of the Eastern Bloc from a Soviet Asset to a Soviet Liability. *Int. Organ.*, Winter 1985, *39*(1), pp. 1–46. [G: U.S.S.R.]

Callier, Andres Passicot. The Chilean Economy and the International Crisis. In *Jorge, A.; Salazar-Carrillo, J. and Diaz-Pou, F., eds.*, 1985, pp. 181–89. [G: Chile]

Carré, Denis. Les modalités de la concurrence internationale et les performances des secteurs industriels français. (The International Competition and the Performance of French Industries. With English summary.) *L'Actual. Econ.*, March 1985, *61*(1), pp. 51–72. [G: France]

Carter, Colin A. High Technology in Agriculture and International Trade. *Can. J. Agr. Econ.*, August 1985, *32*, pp. 24–35. [G: Canada]

Carter, Colin A. International Trade Opportunities for Canadian Agriculture. *Can. J. Agr. Econ.*, July 1985, *32*, pp. 1–17. [G: Canada]

Carvalho, Jose L. Commercial Policy in Brazil: An Overview. In *Salazar-Carrillo, J. and Fendt, R., Jr., eds.*, 1985, pp. 81–120. [G: Brazil]

Casas, François R. and Choi, Eun Kwan. The Leontief Paradox: Continued or Resolved? *J. Polit. Econ.*, June 1985, *93*(3), pp. 610–15. [G: U.S.]

Cassels, John. Manufacturing, Trade and the Far-sighted Manager in Britain. *World Econ.*, December 1985, *8*(4), pp. 409–11. [G: U.K.]

Cazes, Bernard. France. In *Hochmuth, M. and Davidson, W., eds.*, 1985, pp. 163–88. [G: France]

Černohubý, Milan. Relations between Czechoslovakia and the European Economic Community. *Czech. Econ. Digest.*, February 1985, (1), pp. 50–62. [G: EEC; Czechoslovakia]

Chan, Patrick K. L. and Wong, Jim H. Y. The Effect of Exchange Rate Variability on Hong Kong's Exports. *Hong Kong Econ. Pap.*, 1985, (16), pp. 27–39. [G: Hong Kong]

Chan, Paul and Lloyd, P. J. Analysis of Export–Import Instability in Peninsular Malaysia, 1960–80. *Singapore Econ. Rev.*, October 1985, *30*(2), pp. 1–16. [G: Malaysia]

Charette, Michael F. Determinants of Export Instability in the Primary Commodity Trade of LDC's. *J. Devel. Econ.*, May–June 1985, *18*(1), pp. 13–21. [G: LDCs]

Chase, Ernest F. Prospective Changes in U.S. Merchandise Exports to Arab Countries. In *Czinkota, M. R. and Marciel, S., eds.*, 1985, pp. 255–62. [G: U.S.; OPEC]

Cheffert, Jean-Marie; Deschamps, Robert and Reding, Paul. Export Price Setting for Selected Sectors of the Belgian Economy. In *Peeters, T.; Praet, P. and Reding, P., eds.*, 1985, pp. 201–24. [G: Belgium]

Chia, Siow Yue. The Role of Foreign Trade and Investment in the Development of Singapore. In *Galenson, W., ed.*, 1985, pp. 259–97. [G: Singapore]

Chida, Tomohei. The United States Merchant Marine in Foreign Trade, 1800–1939: Comment. In *Yui, T. and Nakagawa, K., eds.*, 1985, pp. 119–21. [G: U.S.]

Chisholm, Michael. De-industrialization and British Regional Policy. *Reg. Stud.*, August 1985, *19*(4), pp. 301–13. [G: U.K.]

Chou, Tein-Chen. The Pattern and Strategy of Industrialization in Taiwan: Specialization and Offsetting Policy. *Devel. Econ.*, June 1985, *23*(2), pp. 138–57. [G: Taiwan]

Christelow, Dorothy. Japan's Intangible Barriers to Trade in Manufactures. *Fed. Res. Bank New York Quart. Rev.*, Winter 1985-86, *10*(4), pp. 11–18. [G: Japan]

Chudnovsky, Daniel. La difusión de tecnologías de punta en la Argentina: el caso de las máquinas herramientas con control numérico, el CAD/CAM y los robots. (With English summary.) *Desarrollo Econ.*, January-March 1985, *24*(96), pp. 483–515.   [G: Argentina]

Citrin, Daniel. Exchange Rate Changes and Exports of Selected Japanese Industries. *Int. Monet. Fund Staff Pap.*, September 1985, *32*(3), pp. 404–29.   [G: Japan]

Clark, Don P. Protection and Developing Country Exports: The Case of Vegetable Oils. *J. Econ. Stud.*, 1985, *12*(5), pp. 3–18.
          [G: LDCs]

Clark, William and Turner, Charlie G. International Trade and the Evolution of the American Capital Market, 1888–1911. *J. Econ. Hist.*, June 1985, *45*(2), pp. 405–10.   [G: U.S.]

Cleveland, Douglas. It's Time to Retire the Import Penetration Ratio. *Challenge*, Sept./Oct. 1985, *28*(4), pp. 50–53.   [G: U.S.]

Clifton, Eric V. Real Exchange Rates, Import Penetration, and Protectionism in Industrial Countries. *Int. Monet. Fund Staff Pap.*, September 1985, *32*(3), pp. 513–36.   [G: U.S.; U.K.; W. Germany]

Cline, William R. Long-term Forecasts in International Economics. *Amer. Econ. Rev.*, May 1985, *75*(2), pp. 120–26.   [G: Global]

Cline, William R. Policy and Performance Links between LDC Debtors and Industrial Nations: Comment. *Brookings Pap. Econ. Act.*, 1985, (2), pp. 361–66.   [G: LDCs; OECD]

Cline, William R. Reply [Can the East Asian Model of Development Be Generalized?]. *World Devel.*, April 1985, *13*(4), pp. 547–48.

Cloete, S. A. The Structure of the International Supply of Coal—A Qualitative View. *J. Stud. Econ. Econometrics*, March 1985, (21), pp. 67–102.

Coker, Christopher. Eastern Europe and the Middle East: The Forgotten Dimension of Soviet Policy. In *Cassen, R., ed.*, 1985, pp. 46–67.   [G: CMEA; Middle East]

de Combret, François. A European View of the Internationalization of Industry. In *Zukin, S., ed.*, 1985, pp. 90–95.

da Conceiçáo Tavares, María. The Revival of American Hegemony. *Cepal Rev.*, August 1985, (26), pp. 139–46.   [G: U.S.; Latin America]

Cordova, Miguel L. Policy Planning Simulation for World Regional Development and Equity. *Econ. Planning*, 1985, *19*(2), pp. 92–117.
          [G: Global]

Coughlin, Cletus C. and Watkins, Thomas G. The Impact of International Intra-firm Trade on Domestic Concentration Ratios. *Rev. Ind. Organ.*, 1985, *2*(3), pp. 232–49.   [G: U.S.]

Crane, Keith and Kohler, Daniel F. Removing Export-Credit Subsidies to the Soviet Bloc: Who Gets Hurt and by How Much. *J. Compar. Econ.*, December 1985, *9*(4), pp. 371–90.
          [G: CMEA]

Crawford, John C. Attitudes toward Latin American Products. In *Kaynak, E., ed. (I)*, 1985, pp. 149–54.   [G: Latin America; U.S.]

Crockett, Andrew. Exchange Rates and Trade:

Is There a Problem for Policy? In *Peeters, T.; Praet, P. and Reding, P., eds.*, 1985, pp. 267–97.   [G: OECD]

Cruz, Robert D. Forecasting the Economic Interaction between Latin America and Miami. In *Jorge, A.; Salazar-Carrillo, J. and Diaz-Pou, F., eds.*, 1985, pp. 165–80.   [G: U.S.; Latin America]

Culem, Claudy and Chau, Nguyen T. M. Les performances relatives à l'exportation de produits manufacturés de l'EUBL au cours de la période 1970–1980. (With English summary.) *Cah. Écon. Bruxelles*, 2nd Trimester 1985, (106), pp. 126–57.   [G: EEC]

Cuthbertson, Keith. The Behaviour of UK Imports of Manufactured Goods. *Nat. Inst. Econ. Rev.*, August 1985, (113), pp. 31–38.
          [G: U.K.]

Czepurko, Aleksander. Projections of East–West Trade—Past Experience and Future Uses. In *[Levcik, F.]*, 1985, pp. 191–202.   [G: CMEA; OECD]

Czyzewski, B.; Tomaszewicz, Andrzej and Tomaszewicz, Lucija. Proposals for the Linkage of CMEA-Country Models. In *Smyshlyaev, A., ed.*, 1985, pp. 29–42.   [G: CMEA]

D'Ambra, Luigi. Alcune estensioni dell'analisi in componenti principali per lo studio di sistemi evolutivi. Uno studio sul commercio internzionale dell'elettronica. (Some Extensions of the Principal Component Analysis for the Study of Developing Systems. A Study Concerning the Electronic International Commerce. With English summary.) *Ricerche Econ.*, Apr.-June 1985, *39*(2), pp. 233–60.   [G: OECD; LDCs]

Daly, Donald J. Microeconomic Performance: Interrelations between Trade and Industrial Policies. In *Conklin, D. W. and Courchene, T. J., eds.*, 1985, pp. 156–87.   [G: OECD; Canada]

Daniel, Philip. Minerals in Sub-Saharan Africa—Problems and Prospects. In *Rose, T., ed.*, 1985, pp. 145–48.   [G: Sub-Saharan Africa]

Darr, Todd and Gribbons, Gerry. How U.S. Exports Are Faring in the World Wheat Market. *Mon. Lab. Rev.*, October 1985, *108*(10), pp. 10–24.   [G: U.S.]

Das, Dilip K. The New U.S. Customs Regulation and China. *J. World Trade Law*, May:June 1985, *19*(3), pp. 287–89.   [G: China; U.S.]

Davidson, William. The Information Technology Sector. In *Hochmuth, M. and Davidson, W., eds.*, 1985, pp. 293–332.   [G: OECD]

Davies, Peter N. British Shipping and World Trade: Rise and Decline, 1820–1939: Response. In *Yui, T. and Nakagawa, K., eds.*, 1985, pp. 88–89.   [G: U.K.]

Davies, Peter N. British Shipping and World Trade: Rise and Decline, 1820–1939. In *Yui, T. and Nakagawa, K., eds.*, 1985, pp. 39–85.
          [G: U.K.]

Deardorff, Alan V. and Stern, Robert M. Input–Output Technologies and the Effects of Tariff Reductions. *J. Policy Modeling*, Summer 1985, *7*(2), pp. 253–79.   [G: U.S.; EEC; Japan; Brazil]

Deger, Saadet. Soviet Arms Sales to Developing Countries: The Economic Forces. In *Cassen, R., ed.,* 1985, pp. 159–76.   [G: LDCs; U.S.S.R.]

Deger, Saadet and Sen, Somnath. Technology Transfer and Arms Production in Developing Countries. *Industry Devel.,* 1985, (15), pp. 1–18.   [G: LDCs]

DeRosa, Dean A. Equilibrium Exchange Rate Adjustments to Exongenous Changes in International Capital Flows. In *Arndt, S. W.; Sweeney, R. J. and Willett, T. D., eds.,* 1985, pp. 14–17.   [G: OECD]

DeRosa, Dean A. and Smeal, Gary. The International Transmission of Economic Activity. In *Arndt, S. W.; Sweeney, R. J. and Willett, T. D., eds.,* 1985, pp. 202–09.   [G: OECD]

Desaigues, Brigitte. Le rang de la France a-t-il changé (1860–1970)? Évolution de la position internationale de la France. (With English summary.) *Revue Écon. Polit.,* Sept.-Oct. 1985, *95*(5), pp. 531–43.   [G: France]

Díaz-Alejandro, Carlos F. International Markets for LDCs—The Old and the New. In *Adams, J., ed.,* 1985, pp. 487–95.

Dilullo, Anthony J. U.S. International Transactions, Third Quarter 1985. *Surv. Curr. Bus.,* December 1985, *65*(12), pp. 58–88.   [G: U.S.]

Djojohadikusumo, Sumitro. Common Interests of Industrial and Developing Countries. *World Econ.,* December 1985, *8*(4), pp. 325–37.   [G: Global]

Dlouhý, Vladimír and Dyba, Karel. Modelling Czechoslovak Foreign Trade Flows with Non-Socialist Countries (Equilibrium and Some Disequilibrium Estimation). *Czech. Econ. Pap.,* 1985, *23*, pp. 91–110.   [G: Czechoslovakia]

Dobozi, István. Factors Affecting Hungary's Economic Relations with the Third World up to 2000. *Soviet E. Europ. Foreign Trade,* Summer–Fall 1985, *21*(1–2–3), pp. 253–79.   [G: LDCs]

Dobozi, István. Prospects for East–South Economic Interaction in the Changing International Environment. *Soviet E. Europ. Foreign Trade,* Summer–Fall 1985, *21*(1–2–3), pp. 27–53.   [G: CMEA; LDCs]

von Doellinger, Carlos. Exports and Foreign Debt in Brazil: Forecasting the Eighties. In *Salazar-Carrillo, J. and Fendt, R., Jr., eds.,* 1985, pp. 59–76.   [G: Brazil]

Dommen, E. C. and Hein, Philippe L. Foreign Trade in Goods and Services: The Dominant Activity of Small Island Economies. In *Dommen, E. and Hein, P., eds.,* 1985, pp. 152–84.   [G: Selected Countries]

Donges, Jürgen B. and Schatz, Klaus-Werner. The Iberian Countries Facing EC Membership: Starting Conditions for Their Industry. *Weltwirtsch. Arch.,* 1985, *121*(4), pp. 756–78.   [G: Spain; Portugal]

Dornbusch, Rudiger. Policy and Performance Links between LDC Debtors and Industrial Nations. *Brookings Pap. Econ. Act.,* 1985, (2),

pp. 303–56.   [G: LDCs; OECD]

Doroodian, Khosrow and Koshal, Rajinder K. An Explanation to the U.S. Trade Deficit with Canada. *Atlantic Econ. J.,* December 1985, *13*(4), pp. 86.   [G: U.S.; Canada]

Doyle, Michael W. Metropole, Periphery, and System: Empire on the Niger and the Nile. In *Evans, P.; Rueschemeyer, D. and Stephens, E. H., eds.,* 1985, pp. 151–91.   [G: Egypt; W. Africa; U.K.]

Doz, Yves. Automobiles: Shifts in International Competitiveness. In *Hochmuth, M. and Davidson, W., eds.,* 1985, pp. 189–212.   [G: Japan; U.S.]

Draper, Niek A. G. Exports of the Manufacturing Industry, an Econometric Analysis of the Significance of Capacity. *De Economist,* 1985, *133*(3), pp. 285–305.   [G: Netherlands]

Driver, Ciaran; Kilpatrick, Andrew and Naisbitt, Barry. The Employment Effects of Changes in the Structure of UK Trade. *J. Econ. Stud.,* 1985, *12*(5), pp. 19–38.   [G: U.K.]

Drysdale, Peter. Building the Foundations of a Pacific Economic Community. In *Shishido, T. and Sato, R., eds.,* 1985, pp. 46–58.   [G: E. Asia]

Dunning, John H. Multinational Enterprises and Industrial Restructuring in the UK. *Lloyds Bank Rev.,* October 1985, (158), pp. 1–19.   [G: U.K.]

Dunning, John H. and Norman, George. Intra-industry Production as a Form of International Economic Involvement: An Exploratory Analysis. In *Erdilek, A., ed.,* 1985, pp. 9–29.

Duvvury, Nata. Tobacco Trading and Forms of Market Organization: A Case Study of Guntur District. In *Raj, K. N., et al., eds.,* 1985, pp. 273–305.   [G: India]

Eisenbrand, Lynn. Why Is Counter-Trade Thriving? *Industry Devel.,* 1985, (15), pp. 37–54.

El-Kuwaiz, Abdullah. Dynamics of Trade in Refined Petroleum Products between the Gulf Cooperation Council and Western Europe. *J. Energy Devel.,* Autumn 1985, *11*(1), pp. 5–11.   [G: W. Europe; Middle East]

Erber, Fabio Stefano. The Development of the 'Electonics Complex' and Government Policies in Brazil. *World Devel.,* March 1985, *13*(3), pp. 293–309.   [G: Brazil]

Erdilek, Asim and Rapoport, Alan. Conceptual and Measurement Problems in International Technology Transfer: A Critical Analysis. In *Samli, A. C., ed.,* 1985, pp. 249–61.

Ernst, Dieter. Automation and the Worldwide Restructuring of the Electronics Industry: Strategic Implications for Developing Countries. *World Devel.,* March 1985, *13*(3), pp. 333–52.   [G: LDCs]

Eskelinen, Heikki. International Integration and Regional Economic Development: The Finnish Experience. *J. Common Market Stud.,* March 1985, *23*(3), pp. 229–55.   [G: EEC; Finland]

Evan-Zohar, Chaim. The Diamond Industry. In *Levinson, P. and Landau, P., eds.,* 1985, pp. 90–93.   [G: Israel]

Fairbairn, Te'o Ian and Kakazu, Hiroshi. Trade

and Diversification in Small Island Economies with Particular Emphasis on the South Pacific. *Singapore Econ. Rev.*, October 1985, *30*(2), pp. 17–35. **[G: Asia; Oceania]**

Fakiolas, T. Basic Causes of Soviet Industry's Low International Competitiveness. *J. Econ. Stud.*, 1985, *12*(5), pp. 39–52. **[G: U.S.S.R.]**

Falk, James E. and McCormick, Garth P. Computational Aspects of the International Coal Trade Model. In *Harker, P. T., ed.*, 1985, pp. 73–117.

Fase, Martin M. G. The Statistical Properties of Glejser's Measure of Intra-industry Trade Specialisation. *J. Int. Econ.*, November 1985, *19*(3/4), pp. 375–82.

Faucher, Jean-Jacques and Schneider, Hartmut. Agricultural Crisis: Structural Constraints, Prices and Other Policy Issues. In *Rose, T., ed.*, 1985, pp. 50–65. **[G: Sub-Saharan Africa]**

Feenstra, Robert C. Automobile Prices and Protection: The U.S.–Japan Trade Restraint. *J. Policy Modeling*, Spring 1985, *7*(1), pp. 49–68. **[G: U.S.; Japan]**

Fekrat, M. Ali. U.S.–Arab Trade and Arab Economic Development. In *Czinkota, M. R. and Marciel, S., eds.*, 1985, pp. 40–55. **[G: U.S.; OPEC]**

Fforde, Adam. Economic Aspects of the Soviet–Vietnamese Relationship. In *Cassen, R., ed.*, 1985, pp. 192–219. **[G: Vietnam; U.S.S.R.]**

Ffrench-Davis, Ricardo and De Gregorio, José. La renegociación de la deuda externa de Chile en 1985: antecedentes y comentarios. (The Rescheduling of Chile's Foreign Debt in 1985: Background and Comments. With English summary.) *Colección Estud. CIEPLAN*, September 1985, (17), pp. 9–32. **[G: Chile]**

Fieleke, Norman S. Dollar Appreciation and U.S. Import Prices. *New Eng. Econ. Rev.*, Nov./Dec. 1985, pp. 49–54. **[G: U.S.]**

Fieleke, Norman S. The Foreign Trade Deficit and American Industry. *New Eng. Econ. Rev.*, July/August 1985, pp. 43–52. **[G: U.S.]**

Finan, William F. and LaMond, Annette M. Sustaining U.S. Competitiveness in Microelectronics: The Challenge to U.S. Policy. In *Scott, B. R. and Lodge, G. C., eds.*, 1985, pp. 144–75. **[G: Japan; U.S.]**

Finger, J. Michael. Trade and the Structure of American Industry. In *Adams, J., ed.*, 1985, pp. 8–16. **[G: U.S.]**

Fishlow, Albert. Revisiting the Great Debt Crisis of 1982. In *Kim, K. S. and Ruccio, D. F., eds.*, 1985, pp. 99–132. **[G: LDCs]**

Fleming, E. M. and Piaggott, R. R. Analysis of Export Earnings Instability in the South Pacific Region. *Singapore Econ. Rev.*, April 1985, *30*(1), pp. 14–33. **[G: Papua New Guinea; Tonga; Solomon Islands; W. Samoa]**

Foders, Federico and Kim, Chungsoo. Impact of Deep-Sea Mining on the World Metal Markets: Manganese. In *Donges, J. B., ed.*, 1985, pp. 204–52. **[G: Selected Countries]**

Fogarty, John. Staples, Super-Staples and the Limits of Staple Theory: The Experiences of Argentina, Australia and Canada Compared. In *Platt, D. C. M. and di Tella, G., eds.*, 1985, pp. 19–36. **[G: Argentina; Australia; Canada]**

Ford, J. L. The Ricardian–Ohlin Explanation of Trade: A Comment on a General Theorem Which Is Not General: Comment. *Oxford Econ. Pap.*, March 1985, *37*(1), pp. 134–37.

Frantzen, Dirk J. Some Empirical Evidence on the Behaviour of Export and Domestic Prices in Belgian Manufacturing Industry. *Rech. Écon. Louvain*, 1985, *51*(1), pp. 29–49. **[G: Belgium]**

Fritsch-Bournazel, Renata. Western Policies: France. In *Rode, R. and Jacobsen, H.-D., eds.*, 1985, pp. 128–40. **[G: France; CMEA]**

Gasiorowski, Mark J. The Structure of Third World Economic Interdependence. *Int. Organ.*, Spring 1985, *39*(2), pp. 331–42. **[G: LDCs]**

Georgakopoulos, Theodore A. Indirect Taxes and Industrial Exports in Greece: The Case of Cement. *Greek Econ. Rev.*, December 1985, *7*(3), pp. 255–67. **[G: Greece]**

Gerami, Shahin. Export Alliances as a Device of Dependence Control: A Comparative Analysis. *Soc. Sci. Quart.*, March 1985, *66*(1), pp. 105–19. **[G: LDCs]**

Gilless, James Keith and Buongiorno, Joseph. Simulation of Future Trade in Wood Pulp between Canada and the United States. *Ann. Reg. Sci.*, July 1985, *19*(2), pp. 47–60. **[G: U.S.; Canada]**

Gillis, K. G., et al. The Prospects for Export of Primal Beef Cuts to California. *Can. J. Agr. Econ.*, July 1985, *33*(2), pp. 171–94. **[G: Canada; U.S.]**

Glenn, Marcia. International Trade Opportunities for Canadian Agriculture: Rapporteur's Report. *Can. J. Agr. Econ.*, July 1985, *32*, pp. 18–23. **[G: Canada]**

Godfrey, Martin. Trade and Exchange Rate Policy: A Further Contribution to the Debate. In *Rose, T., ed.*, 1985, pp. 168–79. **[G: Sub-Saharan Africa]**

Goldar, B. N. and Bharadwaj, Ranganath N. Determinants of Iron and Steel Exports. *Devel. Econ.*, March 1985, *23*(1), pp. 40–52. **[G: Selected Countries]**

Goodman, S. E. Technology Transfer and the Development of the Soviet Computer Industry. In *Parrott, B., ed.*, 1985, pp. 117–40. **[G: U.S.S.R.]**

Gormely, Patrick J. Impact of EEC Enlargement on Ireland's Trade in Manufactured Goods. *Econ. Soc. Rev.*, October 1985, *17*(1), pp. 1–10. **[G: Ireland; Greece; EEC; Portugal]**

Goto, Shin. British Shipping and World Trade: Rise and Decline, 1820–1939: Comment. In *Yui, T. and Nakagawa, K., eds.*, 1985, pp. 86–88. **[G: U.K.]**

Gotur, Padma. Effects of Exchange Rate Volatility on Trade: Some Further Evidence. *Int. Monet. Fund Staff Pap.*, September 1985, *32*(3), pp. 475–512. **[G: U.S.; U.K.; W. Germany; Japan; France]**

Gould, B. W. and Kulshreshtha, S. N. An Input–

Output Analysis of the Impacts of Increased Export Demand for Saskatchewan Products. *Can. J. Agr. Econ.*, July 1985, *33*(2), pp. 127–49. [G: Canada]

Grassini, Laura. On the Endogenous Determination of Import Coefficients in an Input–Output Model: Theoretical and Practical Problems. In *Smyshlyaev, A., ed.*, 1985, pp. 163–72. [G: Italy]

Grassini, Maurizio and Richter, Josef. Austrian–Italian Interdependence: Some Linking Experiments. In *Smyshlyaev, A., ed.*, 1985, pp. 19–28. [G: Austria; Italy]

Gray, H. Peter. Trade Policy in the 1980s: A Review Article. *Weltwirtsch. Arch.*, 1985, *121*(1), pp. 142–50. [G: Global]

Green, Reginald Herbold. The Republic of Ireland: The Impact of Imported Inflation. In *Griffith-Jones, S. and Harvey, C., eds.*, 1985, pp. 145–68. [G: Ireland]

Greenaway, David and Milner, Chris. Categorical Aggregation and International Trade: A Reply. *Econ. J.*, June 1985, *95*(378), pp. 486–87.

Griffith-Jones, Stephany. Impact of World Prices on Development: The International Environment. In *Griffith-Jones, S. and Harvey, C., eds.*, 1985, pp. 13–51. [G: LDCs; MDCs]

Griffith-Jones, Stephany and Harvey, Charles. World Prices and Development: Conclusions. In *Griffith-Jones, S. and Harvey, C., eds.*, 1985, pp. 311–49. [G: Selected LDCs]

Grigorova, Ekaterina. International Specialization and Cooperation in Production among the CMEA Countries in Foreign Trade with Machinery and Equipment. *Soviet E. Europ. Foreign Trade*, Winter 1985-86, *21*(4), pp. 90–103. [G: CMEA]

Grossman, Gene M. and Shapiro, Carl. Normative Issues Raised by International Trade in Technology Services. In *Stern, R. M., ed.*, 1985, pp. 83–113. [G: OECD]

Grozdanova, Sasha. Trade and Economic Relations between Bulgaria and the Arab Countries. *Soviet E. Europ. Foreign Trade*, Summer–Fall 1985, *21*(1–2–3), pp. 120–28. [G: Bulgaria; Middle East]

Grunwald, Joseph. Mexico and the United States: Studies in Economic Interaction: Trade and Industry: Comments. In *Musgrave, P. B., ed.*, 1985, pp. 113–19. [G: Mexico]

Guma, X. P. The Rand Monetary Area Agreement. *S. Afr. J. Econ.*, June 1985, *53*(2), pp. 166–83. [G: S. Africa; Swaziland; Lesotho; Botswana]

Haberler, Gottfried. Integration and Growth of the World Economy in Historical Perspective. In *Haberler, G.*, 1985, pp. 473–94.

Hakogi, Masumi. Trade Restrictions and Trade Promotion: Comments. In *Saunders, C. T., ed.*, 1985, pp. 309–12. [G: CMEA; OECD]

Hale, David D. Japanese–American Economic Relations and the World Expansion. *Challenge*, Nov./Dec. 1985, *28*(5), pp. 54–57. [G: U.S.; Japan]

Halliday, Fred. The Soviet Union and South Yemen: Relations with a 'State of Socialist Ori-

entation.' In *Cassen, R., ed.*, 1985, pp. 241–54. [G: U.S.S.R.; S. Yemen]

Hamilton, Carl. Voluntary Export Restraints and Trade Diversion. *J. Common Market Stud.*, June 1985, *23*(4), pp. 345–55. [G: Global]

Hamilton, Robert W. and Whalley, John. Geographically Discriminatory Trade Arrangements. *Rev. Econ. Statist.*, August 1985, *67*(3), pp. 446–55. [G: Global]

Handa, Jagdish and Okiyama, Yukio. Inflation in a Large, Open Economy: The Scandinavian Model and the Japanese Economy. *Hitotsubashi J. Econ.*, June 1985, *26*(1), pp. 83–97. [G: Japan]

Hanson, James A. Inflation and Imported Input Prices in Some Inflationary Latin American Economies. *J. Devel. Econ.*, August 1985, *18*(2–3), pp. 395–410. [G: Argentina; Brazil; Chile; Colomiba; Uruguay]

Hanson, Philip. Soviet Assimilation of Western Technology. In *Parrott, B., ed.*, 1985, pp. 63–81. [G: U.S.S.R.]

Hardt, John P. and Gold, Donna L. Agricultural Trade: U.S.A. and U.S.S.R. In *Saunders, C. T., ed.*, 1985, pp. 217–30. [G: U.S.; U.S.S.R.]

Harris, Richard G. Canada/U.S. Trade and Investment Frictions: The U.S. View: Comments. In *Fretz, D.; Stern, R. and Whalley, J., eds.*, 1985, pp. 64–68. [G: Canada; U.S.]

Harrison, Glenn W. and Kimbell, Larry J. Economic Interdependence in the Pacific Basin: A General Equilbrium Approach. In *Piggott, J. and Whalley, J., eds.*, 1985, pp. 143–74. [G: Selected Countries]

Harte, Kathleen M. Legal Implications of Barter and Countertrade Transactions. In *Fisher, B. S. and Harte, K. M., eds.*, 1985, pp. 217–53. [G: U.S.; EEC]

Hartland-Thunberg, Penelope. Structural Adjustment: Challenges and Opportunities in U.S.–Arab Trade. In *Czinkota, M. R. and Marciel, S., eds.*, 1985, pp. 239–54. [G: U.S.; OPEC]

Harvey, Charles. World Prices and Development: Malawi. In *Griffith-Jones, S. and Harvey, C., eds.*, 1985, pp. 93–112. [G: Malawi]

Hatzichronoglou, Thomas. Mutuations technologiques et compétitivité de l'industrie franç aise: dix constatations. (With English summary.) *Revue Écon. Polit.*, Sept.-Oct. 1985, *95*(5), pp. 578–95. [G: OECD]

Hausmann, Ricardo and Marquez, G. World Prices and National Development: The Case of Venezuela. In *Griffith-Jones, S. and Harvey, C., eds.*, 1985, pp. 240–59. [G: Venezuela]

Havlik, Peter. The Scope and Structure of Czechoslovak Foreign Trade: Effects of Applying Realistic Exchange Rates. *Comparative Econ. Stud.*, Spring 1985, *27*(1), pp. 1–19. [G: Czechoslovakia]

Havrylyshyn, Oli. The Direction of Developing Country Trade: Empirical Evidence of Differences between South–South and South–North Trade. *J. Devel. Econ.*, December 1985, *19*(3), pp. 255–81. [G: LDCs]

Havrylyshyn, Oli and Civan, Engin. Intra-industry Trade among Developing Countries. *J. Devel. Econ.*, August 1985, *18*(2–3), pp. 253–71.   [G: LDCs]

Haynes, Stephen E. and Stone, Joe A. A Neglected Method of Separating Demand and Supply in Time Series Regression. *J. Bus. Econ. Statist.*, July 1985, *3*(3), pp. 238–43.   [G: U.S.]

Hayuth, Yehuda. Freight Modal-Split Analysis of Air and Sea Transportation. *Logist. Transp. Rev.*, December 1985, *21*(4), pp. 389–402.   [G: Israel]

Helmar, Michael D. and Yanagida, John F. Effects of Restrictions on Softwood Lumber and Plywood Trade in the Pacific Basin: Application of the Spatial Temporal Forest Products (STFP) Model. *J. Econ. Devel.*, December 1985, *10*(2), pp. 143–59. [G: U.S.; Canada; Japan]

Henley, John S. and Nyaw, Mee-Kau. A Reappraisal of the Capital Goods Sector in Hong Kong: The Case for Free Trade. *World Devel.*, June 1985, *13*(6), pp. 737–48.
[G: Hong Kong]

Herander, Mark G. The Relative Impact of US Specific Tariffs on Manufactured Imports from Developing and Developed Countries. *Quart. Rev. Econ. Bus.*, Summer 1985, *25*(2), pp. 91–108.   [G: U.S.]

Hill, Roger. Canada/U.S. Trade and Investment Frictions: The U.S. View: Comments. In *Fretz, D.; Stern, R. and Whalley, J., eds.*, 1985, pp. 69–71.   [G: Canada; U.S.]

Hirsch, Seev and Bijaoui, Ilan. R&D Intensity and Export Performance: A Micro View. *Weltwirtsch. Arch.*, 1985, *121*(2), pp. 238–51.
[G: Israel]

Hoffman, Kurt. Clothing, Chips and Competitive Advantage: The Impact of Microelectronics on Trade and Production in the Garment Industry. *World Devel.*, March 1985, *13*(3), pp. 371–92.   [G: LDCs]

Holder, Carlos and Worrell, DeLisle. A Model of Price Formation for Small Economies: Three Caribbean Examples. *J. Devel. Econ.*, August 1985, *18*(2–3), pp. 411–28.   [G: Barbados; Jamaica; Trinidad and Tobago]

Holliday, George D. Western Technology Transfer to the Soviet Automotive Industry. In *Parrott, B., ed.*, 1985, pp. 82–116.
[G: U.S.S.R.; OECD; Czechoslovakia; Hungary]

Holzman, Franklyn D. A Comparative View of Foreign Trade Behavior: Market versus Centrally Planned Economies. In *Bornstein, M., ed.*, 1985, pp. 367–86.

Horesh, Edward and Joekes, Susan. The Impact of Primary Exports on the Ghanaian Economy: Linkages and Leakages from Mining and Cocoa 1956–69. In *Lundahl, M., ed.*, 1985, pp. 181–205.   [G: Ghana]

Horn, Ernst-Jürgen. Positive and Defensive Strategies in Sectoral Adjustment. In *Jungenfelt, K. and Hague, D. [Sir], eds.*, 1985, pp. 533–70.   [G: W. Germany]

Hornby, Ove. The Danish Shipping Industry,

1866–1939: Structure and Strategy. In *Yui, T. and Nakagawa, K., eds.*, 1985, pp. 157–81.
[G: Denmark]

Hornby, Ove. The Danish Shipping Industry, 1866–1939: Structure and Strategy: Response. In *Yui, T. and Nakagawa, K., eds.*, 1985, pp. 184.   [G: Denmark]

Houthakker, Hendrik S. The International Agenda. *Eastern Econ. J.*, Jan.-Mar. 1985, *11*(1), pp. 71–78.   [G: Global]

Huszagh, Sandra M. and Greene, Mark R. How Exporters View Credit Risk and FCIA Insurance—The Georgia Experience. *J. Risk Ins.*, March 1985, *52*(1), pp. 117–32.   [G: U.S.]

Hutchinson, William K. Import Substitution, Structural Change, and Regional Economic Growth in the United States: The Northeast, 1870–1910. *J. Econ. Hist.*, June 1985, *45*(2), pp. 319–25.   [G: U.S.]

Ilmakunnas, Pekka. Identification and Estimation of the Degree of Oligopoly Power in Industries Facing Domestic and Import Competition. In *Schwalbach, J., ed.*, 1985, pp. 287–308.
[G: W. Germany]

Imagawa, Takeshi. Export as an Additional Variable in the Income Determining Function of H–D Type Growth Model. *Devel. Econ.*, June 1985, *23*(2), pp. 105–20.   [G: LDCs]

Inotai, András. East–West Relations in Energy, Agriculture and Technology: Comments. In *Saunders, C. T., ed.*, 1985, pp. 246–51.
[G: CMEA]

Iqbal, B. A. and Farooqi, S. U. Taiwan's Trade: Problem of Plenty. *J. World Trade Law*, Nov.:Dec. 1985, *19*(6), pp. 673–74.
[G: Taiwan]

Jackson, John D. and Smyth, David J. Specifying Differential Cyclical Response in Economic Time Series: Capacity Utilization and Demand for Imports. *Econ. Modelling*, April 1985, *2*(2), pp. 149–61.   [G: U.S.]

Jackson, Marvin R. The Economics and the Political Economics of East–South Relations in the 1980s: An Overview and Review of the Literature. *Soviet E. Europ. Foreign Trade*, Summer–Fall 1985, *21*(1–2–3), pp. 3–26.
[G: CMEA; Selected Countries]

Jacobsen, Hanns-Dieter. Western Policies: The Special Case of Inter-German Relations. In *Rode, R. and Jacobsen, H.-D., eds.*, 1985, pp. 120–27.   [G: W. Germany; E. Germany]

Jacobsson, Staffan. Technical Change and Industrial Policy: The Case of Computer Numerically Controlled Lathes in Argentina, Korea and Taiwan. *World Devel.*, March 1985, *13*(3), pp. 353–70.   [G: Argentina; Korea; Taiwan; OECD]

Jaenen, Cornelius J. The Role of Presents in French–Amerindian Trade. In *[Spry, I. M.]*, 1985, pp. 231–50.   [G: Canada]

Jakobsen, Arvid Stentoft. Changes in Factor Input Coefficients and the Leontief Paradox. In *Smyshlyaev, A., ed.*, 1985, pp. 105–17.
[G: Denmark]

Jenkins, Rhys O. Internationalization of Capital and the Semi-industrialized Countries: The

Case of the Motor Industry. *Rev. Radical Polit. Econ.*, Spring and Summer 1985, *17*(1/2), pp. 59–81. **[G: LDCs]**

Jenkins, Rhys O. Latin America and the New International Division of Labour: A Critique of Some Recent Views. In *Abel, C. and Lewis, C. M., eds.*, 1985, pp. 415–29.
[G: Latin America]

Jones, Daniel T. and Womack, James P. Developing Countries and the Future of the Automobile Industry. *World Devel.*, March 1985, *13*(3), pp. 393–407. **[G: Global]**

Jopp, Mathias. Western Policies: The European Community. In *Rode, R. and Jacobsen, H.-D., eds.*, 1985, pp. 166–83. **[G: EEC; CMEA]**

Jorge, Antonio and Salazar-Carrillo, Jorge. Development Strategies, Trade and External Debt in Latin America: An Overview. In *Salazar-Carrillo, J. and de Alonso, I. T., eds.*, 1985, pp. 1–34. **[G: Latin America]**

Jung, Woo S. and Marshall, Peyton J. Exports, Growth, and Causality in Developing Countries. *J. Devel. Econ.*, May–June 1985, *18*(1), pp. 1–12. **[G: LDCs]**

Jung, Zdeněk. Trade Normalization—An Insoluble Problem. *Czech. Econ. Digest.*, September 1985, (6), pp. 87–95. **[G: U.S.; Czechoslovakia]**

Kádár, Béla. Hungarian Industrial Development in the Light of World Economic Changes. *Acta Oecon.*, 1985, *34*(3/4), pp. 241–62.
[G: Hungary]

Kaempfer, William H. and Min, Henry M., Jr. The Role of Oil in China's Economic Development, Growth, and Internationalization. *J. Energy Devel.*, Autumn 1985, *11*(1), pp. 13–26. **[G: China]**

Kajimoto, Motonobu. Shipping Business in Germany in the Nineteenth and Twentieth Centuries: Comment. In *Yui, T. and Nakagawa, K., eds.*, 1985, pp. 214–16. **[G: Germany]**

Kalirajan, K. P. Economic Relations between Indonesia and South Asia. In *Wadhva, C. D. and Asher, M. G., eds.*, 1985, pp. 29–65.
[G: Indonesia; S. Asia]

Kalirajan, K. P. Trade among Developing Countries: The Case of South Asian Regional Cooperation. *J. Econ. Devel.*, July 1985, *10*(1), pp. 153–67. **[G: Bangladesh; India; Pakistan; Sri Lanka]**

Kalmbach, Peter and Kurz, Heinz D. Internationale Wettbewerbsfähigkeit und Technologieintensität—Eine Anwendung des Subsystem-Ansatzes. (International Competitiveness and the Technological Intensity of Production: An Application of the Sub-system Approach. With English summary.) *Ifo-Studien*, 1985, *31*(2), pp. 149–68. **[G: W. Germany]**

Kaser, Michael. Energy Trade within COMECON. In *[Levcik, F.]*, 1985, pp. 215–30.
[G: COMECON; CMEA]

Katz, Eliakim; Rosenberg, J. and Zilberfarb, Ben-Zion. The Demand for Liquid Assets and Involvement in Exports; Some Empirical Re-

sults. *Empirical Econ.*, 1985, *10*(2), pp. 125–29. **[G: Israel]**

Kavoussi, Rostam M. International Trade and Economic Development: The Recent Experience of Developing Countries. *J. Devel. Areas*, April 1985, *19*(3), pp. 379–92. **[G: LDCs]**

Kaynak, Erdener. Correlates of Export Performance in Resource-Based Industries. In *Kaynak, E., ed. (I)*, 1985, pp. 197–210.
[G: Canada]

Kaynak, Erdener. Future Directions for Marketing and Management in the Middle East. In *Kaynak, E., ed. (II)*, 1985, pp. 233–43.
[G: Middle East]

Kaynak, Erdener and Gürol, Metin N. An Export Marketing Model for Developing Middle Eastern Countries: What Lessons Countries of the Region Learn from Each Other. In *Kaynak, E., ed. (II)*, 1985, pp. 199–216. **[G: Turkey; Japan]**

Keesing, Donald B. Linking up to Distant Markets: South to North Exports of Manufactured Consumer Goods. In *Adams, J., ed.*, 1985, pp. 23–30.

Kellman, Mitchell. The Crumbling Embargo? Evidence of OECD Cohesiveness from the Composition of Manufactured Exports to the USSR. *Comparative Econ. Stud.*, Summer 1985, *27*(2), pp. 53–70. **[G: OECD; U.S.S.R.]**

Keppler, Horst. Free Access to Supplies versus Restrictive Supply Policies: The Ability of LDCs to Control Commodity Markets. In *Weinblatt, J., ed.*, 1985, pp. 71–115.
[G: Selected LDCs]

Kerr, William A. The Changing Economics of the Western Livestock Industry. *Can. Public Policy*, Supplement July 1985, *11*(3), pp. 294–300.
[G: Canada]

Kerr, William A. The Livestock Industry and Canadian Economic Development. *Can. J. Agr. Econ.*, July 1985, *32*, pp. 64–104.
[G: Canada]

Khanna, Ashok. A Note on the Dynamic Aspects of the Heckscher–Ohlin Model: Some Empirical Evidence. *World Devel.*, Oct./Nov. 1985, *13*(10/11), pp. 1171–74. **[G: S. Korea]**

Kim, In June. Imported Inflation and the Development of the Korean Economy. In *Griffith-Jones, S. and Harvey, C., eds.*, 1985, pp. 169–95. **[G: S. Korea]**

Klein, Lawrence R. World Trade Growth and Industrial Policy. In *Peeters, T.; Praet, P. and Reding, P., eds.*, 1985, pp. 111–30. **[G: U.S.; OECD]**

Kline, John M. Multinational Corporations in Euro–American Trade: Crucial Linking Mechanisms in an Evolving Trade Structure. In *Moran, T. H., ed.*, 1985, pp. 199–218.
[G: Europe; U.S.]

Koester, Ulrich. Agricultural Market Intervention and International Trade. *Europ. Rev. Agr. Econ.*, 1985, *12*(1/2), pp. 87–99. **[G: EEC; U.S.]**

Kohler, Wilhelm K. The Impact of Measurement Errors on OLS Estimates of Import Demand Parameters. *Jahr. Nationalökon. Statist.*,

March 1985, *200*(2), pp. 173–85.

Kohli, Ulrich. U.S. Imports by Origin: A System Approach. *Weltwirtsch. Arch.*, 1985, *121*(4), pp. 741–55.   [G: U.S.]

Kojima, Kiyoshi. Japanese and American Direct Investment in Asia: A Comparative Analysis. *Hitotsubashi J. Econ.*, June 1985, *26*(1), pp. 1–35.   [G: U.S.; Japan; S.E. Asia]

Koo, Bohn-Young. Multinational Enterprises, Economic Structure and International Competitiveness: Korea. In *Dunning, J. H., ed.,* 1985, pp. 281–307.   [G: S. Korea]

Koschik, David N. Structuring Barter and Countertrade Transactions. In *Fisher, B. S. and Harte, K. M., eds.,* 1985, pp. 37–82.

Kosenko, Rustan and Samli, A. Coskun. China's Four Modernizations Program and Technology Transfer. In *Samli, A. C., ed.,* 1985, pp. 107–31.   [G: China]

Köves, András. The Import Restriction Squeeze and Import Maximizing Ambitions: Some Connections of East–West vs. Intra-CMEA Trade. *Acta Oecon.*, 1985, *34*(1–2), pp. 99–112.   [G: CMEA]

Kozolaev, A. Cooperation of the CMEA Countries with Syria. *Soviet E. Europ. Foreign Trade*, Summer–Fall 1985, *21*(1–2–3), pp. 129–34.   [G: CMEA; Syria]

Krapp, Thea. The Limitation Convention for International Sale of Goods. *J. World Trade Law*, July:Aug. 1985, *19*(4), pp. 343–72.   [G: Global]

Krause, Lawrence B. Foreign Trade and Investment: Economic Growth in the Newly Industrializing Asian Countries: Introduction. In *Galenson, W., ed.,* 1985, pp. 3–41.   [G: Hong Kong; Singapore; S. Korea; Taiwan]

Kravis, Irving B. Global Dimensions and Determinants of International Trade and Investment in Services: Comments. In *Stern, R. M., ed.,* 1985, pp. 169–75.   [G: U.S.; Canada; Japan; EEC]

Kravis, Irving B. Services in World Transactions. In *Inman, R. P., ed.,* 1985, pp. 135–60.   [G: Selected Countries]

Kreinin, Mordechai E. United States Trade and Possible Restrictions in High-Technology Products. *J. Policy Modeling*, Spring 1985, *7*(1), pp. 69–105.   [G: U.S.; Japan; EEC; Canada]

Kreinin, Mordechai E. Wage Competitiveness in the U.S. Auto and Steel Industries. In *Adams, J., ed.,* 1985, pp. 174–88.   [G: U.S.]

Krueger, Anne O. and Michalopoulos, Constantine. Developing-Country Trade Policies and the International Economic System. In *Preeg, E. H., ed.,* 1985, pp. 39–57.   [G: Selected LDCs]

Krueger, Russell C. U.S. International Transactions, Second Quarter 1985. *Surv. Curr. Bus.*, September 1985, *65*(9), pp. 28–52. [G: U.S.]

Krueger, Russell C. U.S. International Transactions, First Quarter 1985. *Surv. Curr. Bus.*, June 1985, *65*(6), pp. 34–73.   [G: U.S.]

Krüger, Hans-Peter. Comments [East–West Economic Relations: Expectations a Decade Ago and the Outcome] [East–West Economic Relations in the 1970s and 1980s]. In *Saunders, C. T., ed.,* 1985, pp. 131–34.   [G: OMEA; OECD]

Krugman, Paul R. Intra-industry Production as a Form of International Economic Involvement: An Exploratory Analysis: Comment. In *Erdilek, A., ed.,* 1985, pp. 33–37.

Kubo, Yuji. A Cross-country Comparison of Inter-industry Linkages and the Role of Imported Intermediate Inputs. *World Devel.*, December 1985, *13*(12), pp. 1287–98.   [G: Selected Countries]

Kumar, Manmohan S. International Trade and Industrial Concentration. *Oxford Econ. Pap.*, March 1985, *37*(1), pp. 125–33.   [G: U.K.]

Kuo, Shirley W. Y. and Fei, John C. H. Causes and Roles of Export Expansion in the Republic of China. In *Galenson, W., ed.,* 1985, pp. 45–84.   [G: Taiwan]

Kurukulasuriya, G. The Impact of Imported Inflation on National Development: Sri Lanka. In *Griffith-Jones, S. and Harvey, C., eds.,* 1985, pp. 75–92.   [G: Sri Lanka]

Lächler, Ulrich. The Elasticity of Substitution between Imported and Domestically Produced Goods in Germany. *Weltwirtsch. Arch.*, 1985, *121*(1), pp. 74–96.   [G: W. Germany]

Lafay, Gérard. Spécialisation française: des handicaps structurels. (With English summary.) *Revue Écon. Polit.*, Sept.-Oct. 1985, *95*(5), pp. 627–39.   [G: France; U.K.; U.S.; W. Germany; Japan]

Lahera, Eugenio. The Transnational Corporations and Latin America's International Trade. *Cepal Rev.*, April 1985, (25), pp. 45–65.   [G: Latin America]

Lal, Deepak. Poor Countries and the Global Economy: Crisis and Adjustment. In *Bergsten, C. F., ed.,* 1985, pp. 65–76.   [G: Global]

Lall, Sanjaya. Trade in Technology by a Slowly Industrializing Country: India. In *Rosenberg, N. and Frischtak, C., eds.,* 1985, pp. 45–76.   [G: India]

Lande, Steve and VanGrasstek, Craig. Trade with the Developing Countries: The Reagan Record and Prospects. In *Sewell, J. W.; Feinberg, R. E. and Kallab, V., eds.,* 1985, pp. 73–94.   [G: U.S.; LDCs]

Lane, Julia. An Empirical Estimate of the Effects of Labor-Market Distortions on the Factor Content of U.S. Trade. *J. Int. Econ.*, February 1985, *18*(1/2), pp. 187–93.   [G: U.S.]

Langhammer, Rolf J. and Hiemenz, Ulrich. Declining Competitiveness of EC Suppliers in ASEAN Markets: Singular Case or Symptom? *J. Common Market Stud.*, December 1985, *24*(2), pp. 105–19.   [G: EEC; ASEAN]

Lányi, Kamilla. Hungarian Agriculture: Export Surplus or Superfluous Growth? (Contribution to the Development Strategy of Hungarian Agriculture). *Acta Oecon.*, 1985, *34*(3/4), pp. 299–315.   [G: Hungary]

Lauridsen, Laurids S. Export-Oriented Industrialization in Latin America, South and East

Asia. In *Utrecht, E., ed.*, 1985, pp. 83–136.
[G: Latin America; E. Asia; S. Asia]

Lecraw, Donald J. Some Evidence on Transfer Pricing by Multinational Corporations. In *Rugman, A. M. and Eden, L., eds.*, 1985, pp. 223–40. [G: OECD; LDCs]

Leela, P. Analysis of Fast Growing Exports of India. *Indian Econ. J.*, Jan.-Mar. 1985, *32*(3), pp. 82–89. [G: India]

Leela, P. Export Performance of India: A Disaggregate Analysis. *Margin*, July 1985, *17*(4), pp. 71–79. [G: India]

Lele, Uma. Terms of Trade, Agricultural Growth, and Rural Poverty in Africa. In *Mellor, J. W. and Desai, G. M., eds.*, 1985, pp. 161–80.
[G: Sub-Saharan Africa]

Leontief, Wassily. Explanatory Power of the Comparative Cost Theory of International Trade and Its Limits. In *Leontief, W.*, 1985, pp. 373–80. [G: U.S.]

Levcik, Friedrich and Stankovsky, Jan. East–West Economic Relations in the 1970s and 1980s. In *Saunders, C. T., ed.*, 1985, pp. 77–124. [G: CMEA; OECD]

Levy, Santiago. Mexico and the United States: Studies in Economic Interaction: Trade and Industry: Comments. In *Musgrave, P. B., ed.*, 1985, pp. 109–12. [G: Mexico]

Lewis, John P. Special Measures for the Least Developed and Other Low-Income Countries: Comment. In *Preeg, E. H., ed.*, 1985, pp. 164–66. [G: Sub-Saharan Africa]

Li, Honglin. Socialism and Opening Up to the Outside World. *Chinese Econ. Stud.*, Fall 1985, *19*(1), pp. 26–39. [G: China]

Lim, Chee Peng and Ling, Sieh Mei. Malaysia–Australia Trade. In *Lim, D., ed.*, 1985, pp. 23–38. [G: Malaysia; Australia]

Lim, Chee Peng and Ling, Sieh Mei. Malaysian Import Demand Analysis. In *Lim, D., ed.*, 1985, pp. 150–63. [G: Malaysia; Australia]

Lim, Chee Peng and Ling, Sieh Mei. Malaysian Import Survey Analysis. In *Lim, D., ed.*, 1985, pp. 222–30. [G: Malaysia; Australia]

Lim, David. Australia–SEAN Trade. In *Lim, D., ed.*, 1985, pp. 2–13. [G: Australia; Selected Countries]

Lim, David. Australian Import Survey Analysis. In *Lim, D., ed.*, 1985, pp. 202–10.
[G: Australia; ASEAN]

Lim, David. ASEAN–Australia Trade in Manufactures: Introduction. In *Lim, D., ed.*, 1985, pp. ix–xii.

Lim, David. ASEAN–Australia Trade in Manufactures: Concluding Remarks. In *Lim, D., ed.*, 1985, pp. 256–61. [G: Australia; ASEAN]

Lim, Hank. Singapore–Australia Trade. In *Lim, D., ed.*, 1985, pp. 46–53. [G: ASEAN]

Lim, Hank. Singaporean Import Demand Analysis. In *Lim, D., ed.*, 1985, pp. 179–90.
[G: Singapore]

Lim, Hank. Singaporean Import Survey Analysis. In *Lim, D., ed.*, 1985, pp. 241–46.
[G: Singapore; Australia]

Lin, Tzong-Biau and Mok, Victor. Trade, Foreign Investment, and Development in Hong Kong.

In *Galenson, W., ed.*, 1985, pp. 219–56.
[G: Hong Kong]

Lindblad, Jan Thomas. Economic Change in Southeast Kalimantan 1880–1940. *Bull. Indonesian Econ. Stud.*, December 1985, *21*(3), pp. 69–103. [G: Indonesia]

Lindblad, Jan Thomas. Structural Change in the Dutch Trade with the Baltic in the Eighteenth Century. *Scand. Econ. Hist. Rev.*, 1985, *33*(3), pp. 193–207. [G: Netherlands; Baltic Countries]

Linder, Staffan Burenstam. Pacific Protagonist—Implications of the Rising Role of the Pacific. *Amer. Econ. Rev.*, May 1985, *75*(2), pp. 279–84. [G: U.S.; E. Asia]

Lipner, J. Kenneth. Past and Present Trade Activity in Miami. In *Jorge, A.; Salazar-Carrillo, J. and Diaz-Pou, F., eds.*, 1985, pp. 161–64.
[G: U.S.; Latin America]

Lippert, Alice A. Trip Expenditure Comparisons from 1972–73 to 1980–81. *Mon. Lab. Rev.*, July 1985, *108*(7), pp. 46–48. [G: U.S.]

Lipsey, Robert E. and Kravis, Irving B. The Competitive Position of U.S. Manufacturing Firms. *Banca Naz. Lavoro Quart. Rev.*, June 1985, (153), pp. 127–54. [G: U.S.]

Lloyd, P. J. The Ricardian and Heckscher–Ohlin Explanations of Trade: A Comment on a General Theorem Which Is Not General [The Ricardian–Ohlin Explanations of Trade: A General Proof of an Equivalence Theorem and Its Empirical Implications]. *Oxford Econ. Pap.*, March 1985, *37*(1), pp. 138–41.

Lloyd, P. J. and Sandilands, R. J. Terms of Trade Indices in the Presence of Re-export Trade. *Econ. Rec.*, September 1985, *61*(174), pp. 667–73. [G: Singapore]

Lopez, Julio. The Post-war Latin American Economies: The End of the Long Boom. *Banca Naz. Lavoro Quart. Rev.*, September 1985, (154), pp. 233–60. [G: Latin America]

Lorentsen, Lorents and Roland, Kjell. Norway's Export of Natural Gas to the European Gas Market. Policy Issues and Model Tools. In *Bjerkholt, O. and Offerdal, E., eds.*, 1985, pp. 103–22. [G: Norway; W. Europe]

Love, James. Export Instability: An Alternative Analysis of Causes. *J. Devel. Stud.*, January 1985, *21*(2), pp. 244–52. [G: LDCs]

Loyns, R. M. A. The Livestock Industry and Canadian Economic Development: Rapporteur's Report. *Can. J. Agr. Econ.*, July 1985, *32*, pp. 105–10. [G: Canada]

Lubrano, Michel. Bayesian Analysis of Switching Regression Models. *J. Econometrics*, July/August 1985, *29*(1/2), pp. 69–95. [G: U.S.; Italy]

Lukaszewicz, Aleksander. Comments [The Global Environment and Its Impact on Soviet and East European Economies] [The Impact of Energy on East–West Trade: Retrospect and Prospects]. In *Saunders, C. T., ed.*, 1985, pp. 135–36. [G: OECD; CMEA; U.S.S.R.]

Lukaszewicz, Aleksander. Trade Restrictions and Trade Promotion: Comments. In *Saunders,*

C. T., ed., 1985, pp. 312–14. **[G: CMEA; OECD]**

Lundahl, Mats. Errata: Economic Effects of a Trade and Investment Boycott against South Africa. *Scand. J. Econ.*, 1985, *87*(1), pp. 142. **[G: S. Africa]**

Lynn, Leonard H. Technology Transfer to Japan: What We Know, What We Need to Know, and What We Know that May Not Be So. In *Rosenberg, N. and Frischtak, C., eds.*, 1985, pp. 255–76. **[G: Japan]**

Lyon, Peter. The Soviet Union and South Asia in the 1980s. In *Cassen, R., ed.*, 1985, pp. 32–45. **[G: S. Asia; U.S.S.R.]**

Lysy, Frank J. Graciela Chichilnisky's Model of North–South Trade. *J. Devel. Econ.*, August 1985, *18*(2–3), pp. 503–39.

Machowski, Heinrich. Soviet–West German Economic Relations: The Soviet Perspective. In *Stent, A. E., ed.*, 1985, pp. 49–67. **[G: U.S.S.R.; W. Germany]**

Mackie, J. A. C. The Changing Political Economy of an Export Crop: The Case of Jember's Tobacco Industry. *Bull. Indonesian Econ. Stud.*, April 1985, *21*(1), pp. 112–39. **[G: Indonesia]**

MacPhee, Craig R. Evaluation of the Trade Effects of the Generalized System of Preferences. In *United Nations Conference on Trade and Development.*, 1985, pp. 57–86. **[G: OECD]**

Mahmood, Muhammad. An Integrated Model of Production, Consumption and Export of Jute in Bangladesh. *Singapore Econ. Rev.*, April 1985, *30*(1), pp. 56–67. **[G: Bangladesh]**

Mainardi, Stefano. Verso una misurazione dinamica del commercio intra-industriale. (Towards a Dynamic Measurement of Intra-industry Trade. With English summary.) *Giorn. Econ.*, Jan.-Feb. 1985, *44*(1–2), pp. 81–92.

Makhoul, Robert B. The Outlook for U.S.–Arab Trade in Services: The Insurance Industry. In *Czinkota, M. R. and Marciel, S., eds.*, 1985, pp. 263–68. **[G: U.S.; OPEC]**

Malish, Anton F. Soviet Trade in Agricultural Commodities and Technology. In *Parrott, B., ed.*, 1985, pp. 203–40. **[G: U.S.S.R.; U.S.]**

Mann, Catherine L. U.S. International Transactions in 1984. *Fed. Res. Bull.*, May 1985, *71*(5), pp. 277–86. **[G: U.S.]**

Marinov, Georgi. Characteristics and Tendencies in the Economic Development of the Mongolian People's Republic, Cuba, and the People's Republic of Vietnam and Cooperation between Them and Bulgaria. *Soviet E. Europ. Foreign Trade*, Summer–Fall 1985, *21*(1–2–3), pp. 191–203. **[G: Mongolia; Cuba; Vietnam; Bulgaria]**

Marquez, Jaime. Foreign Exchange Constraints and Growth Possibilities in the LDCs. *J. Devel. Econ.*, Sept.-Oct. 1985, *19*(1/2), pp. 39–57. **[G: LDCs]**

Marseille, Jacques. The Phases of French Colonial Imperialism: Towards a New Periodization. In *Porter, A. N. and Holland, R. F., eds.*, 1985, pp. 127–41. **[G: U.K.; France; Germany; Selected Countries]**

Marshall, Peter. Reflections on North–South Relations and the Commonwealth. *J. World Trade Law*, May:June 1985, *19*(3), pp. 191–98. **[G: British Commonwealth]**

Marwah, Kanta. The Indian Trade Structure and the Optimality of Indo–U.S. Bilateral Trade Flows. *J. Quant. Econ.*, January 1985, *1*(1), pp. 91–123. **[G: India; U.S.]**

Maskus, Keith E. A Test of the Heckscher–Ohlin–Vanek Theorem: The Leontief Commonplace. *J. Int. Econ.*, November 1985, *19*(3/4), pp. 201–12. **[G: U.S.]**

Maximova, Margarita. Comments [The Global Environment and Its Impact on Soviet and East European Economies] [Current Problems and Prospects of the World Economy in the Light of East–West Economic Relations]. In *Saunders, C. T., ed.*, 1985, pp. 127–30. **[G: OECD; CMEA]**

McCulloch, Rachel. Normative Issues Raised by International Trade in Technology Services: Comments. In *Stern, R. M., ed.*, 1985, pp. 114–18. **[G: OECD]**

McCulloch, Rachel. U.S. Relations with Developing Countries: Conflict and Opportunity. In *Adams, J., ed.*, 1985, pp. 478–87. **[G: U.S.; LDCs]**

McDonald, Donogh C. Trade Data Discrepancies and the Incentive to Smuggle: An Empirical Analysis. *Int. Monet. Fund Staff Pap.*, December 1985, *32*(4), pp. 668–92. **[G: LDCs]**

McFarland, Henry. Transportation Costs for U.S. Imports from Developed and Developing Countries. *J. Devel. Stud.*, July 1985, *21*(4), pp. 562–71. **[G: LDCs; MDCs; U.S.]**

McVey, Thomas B. Overview of the Commercial Practice of Countertrade. In *Fisher, B. S. and Harte, K. M., eds.*, 1985, pp. 9–36. **[G: Global]**

Medani, A. I. Food and Stabilization in Developing Africa. *World Devel.*, June 1985, *13*(6), pp. 685–90. **[G: Africa]**

Mehrotra, Santosh. The Political Economy of Indo–Soviet Relations. In *Cassen, R., ed.*, 1985, pp. 220–40. **[G: India; U.S.S.R.]**

Meier, Gerald M. The New Export Pessimism. In *Shishido, T. and Sato, R., eds.*, 1985, pp. 19–32. **[G: LDCs]**

de Melo, Jaime and Robinson, Sherman. Product Differentiation and Trade Dependence of the Domestic Price System in Computable General Equilibrium Trade Models. In *Peeters, T.; Praet, P. and Reding, P., eds.*, 1985, pp. 91–107.

de Ménil, Georges and Westphal, Uwe. The Transmission of International Disturbances to the French and German Economies, 1972–1980. In *de Ménil, G. and Westphal, U., eds.*, 1985, pp. 349–79. **[G: France; W. Germany]**

Merrill, Stephen A. The United States and the New Technological Competition. In *Yochelson, J. N., ed.*, 1985, pp. 45–76. **[G: U.S.]**

Michaely, Michael. The Demand for Protection against Exports of Newly Industrializing Countries. *J. Policy Modeling*, Spring 1985, *7*(1), pp. 123–32. **[G: Brazil; Korea; Mexico; Hong Kong; Singapore]**

Mieszkowski, Peter. The Differential Effect of the Foreign Trade Deficit on Regions in the United States. In *Quigley, J. M. and Rubinfeld, D. L., eds.*, 1985, pp. 346–63. [G: U.S.]

Millar, James R. The Impact of Trade and Trade Denial on the U.S. Economy. In *Parrott, B., ed.*, 1985, pp. 324–50. [G: U.S.S.R.; U.S.]

Miller, Nikki and Whitehead, Laurence. The Soviet Interest in Latin America: An Economic Perspective. In *Cassen, R., ed.*, 1985, pp. 114–39. [G: Latin America; U.S.S.R.]

Miranda, Casimiro V., Jr. Philippines Import Demand Analysis. In *Lim, D., ed.*, 1985, pp. 164–78. [G: Philippines; Australia; Japan; U.S.]

Miranda, Casimiro V., Jr. Philippines Import Survey Analysis. In *Lim, D., ed.*, 1985, pp. 231–40. [G: Philippines; Selected Countries]

Miranda, Casimiro V., Jr. Philippines–Australia Trade. In *Lim, D., ed.*, 1985, pp. 39–45. [G: Philippines; Australia]

Mishalani, Philip. Imported Inflation and Imported Growth: The Case of Tunisia's Studied Postponement. In *Griffith-Jones, S. and Harvey, C., eds.*, 1985, pp. 260–84. [G: Tunisia]

Mishalani, Philip. Jordan: The Case of Inevitable Imported Inflation in the 1970s. In *Griffith-Jones, S. and Harvey, C., eds.*, 1985, pp. 285–310. [G: Jordan]

Mody, Ashoka; Mundle, Sudipto and Raj, K. N. Resource Flows from Agriculture: Japan and India. In *Ohkawa, K. and Ranis, G., eds.*, 1985, pp. 266–93. [G: Japan; India]

Monke, Eric A. and Taylor, Lester D. International Trade Constraints and Commodity Market Models: An Application to the Cotton Market. *Rev. Econ. Statist.*, February 1985, *67*(1), pp. 98–107. [G: Global]

Montuschi, Luisa. Un indicador para medir el efectivo alcance de la sustitución de importaciones. (An Indicator to Measure the Actual Extent of Import Substitution. With English summary.) *Económica (La Plata)*, May-Dec. 1985, *31*(2–3), pp. 229–34.

Moroz, Andrew R. Canada/U.S. Automotive Trade and Trade-policy Issues. In *Fretz, D.; Stern, R. and Whalley, J., eds.*, 1985, pp. 278–332. [G: Canada; U.S.]

Mueller, Hans. The Changing U.S. Position in the International Steel Market: Output, Trade, and Performance. In *Hochmuth, M. and Davidson, W., eds.*, 1985, pp. 213–62. [G: U.S.; Global]

Mukherjee, Neela. Terms of Trade for India's Invisibles. *Indian Econ. J.*, Jan.-Mar. 1985, *32*(3), pp. 27–35. [G: India]

Müller, Friedemann. Economic Relations—Interdependence or Marginal Factor?: Energy. In *Rode, R. and Jacobsen, H.-D., eds.*, 1985, pp. 73–85. [G: U.S.S.R.]

Müller, Jürgen and Owen, Nicholas. The Effect of Trade on Plant Size. In *Schwalbach, J., ed.*, 1985, pp. 41–60. [G: W. Germany]

Mun, Kin-chok. Export Pricing of China's Industrial Goods: Problems and Suggested Solu-

tions. In *Kaynak, E., ed. (I)*, 1985, pp. 95–107. [G: China]

Mutti, John H. and Grubert, Harry. The Taxation of Capital Income in an Open Economy: The Importance of Resident–Nonresident Tax Treatment. *J. Public Econ.*, August 1985, *27*(3), pp. 291–309. [G: U.S.]

Nagy, András. Changes in the Structure and Intensity of East–West Trade. *Acta Oecon.*, 1985, *35*(3–4), pp. 359–75. [G: CMEA]

Nagy, András. International Trade Alternatives for 1990. In *Jungenfelt, K. and Hague, D. [Sir], eds.*, 1985, pp. 91–114. [G: Global]

Nakamura, Shinichiro. A Test of Restrictions in a Dynamic Singular Demand System: An Application to the Import of Intermediate Goods in West Germany. *Z. Nationalökon.*, 1985, *45*(3), pp. 313–30. [G: W. Germany]

Nanto, Dick K. Dimensions and Perceptions of the Trade Problem with Japan. In *Nanto, D. K., ed.*, 1985, pp. 23–40. [G: Japan; U.S.]

Nathanson, R. and Weinblatt, J. The General Effect of Export Restrictions on Commodity Markets. In *Weinblatt, J., ed.*, 1985, pp. 10–50. [G: LDCs; MDCs]

Navrozov, P. and Plotnikov, E. Soviet–Vietnamese Friendship—A Factor of Peace and Construction. *Soviet E. Europ. Foreign Trade*, Summer–Fall 1985, *21*(1–2–3), pp. 204–21. [G: U.S.S.R.; Vietnam]

Naya, Seiji. The Role of Small-Scale Industries in Employment and Exports of Asian Developing Countries. *Hitotsubashi J. Econ.*, December 1985, *26*(2), pp. 147–63. [G: Asian LDCs]

Neary, J. Peter. The Observational Equivalence of the Ricardian and Heckscher–Ohlin Explanations of Trade Patterns [The Ricardian and Heckscher–Ohlin Explanations of Trade: A General Proof of an Equivalence Theorem and Its Empirical Implications]. *Oxford Econ. Pap.*, March 1985, *37*(1), pp. 142–47.

Nehmer, Stanley and Love, Mark W. Textiles and Apparel: A Negotiated Approach to International Competition. In *Scott, B. R. and Lodge, G. C., eds.*, 1985, pp. 230–62. [G: U.S.]

Neumann, Manfred; Böbel, Ingo and Haid, Alfred. Domestic Concentration, Foreign Trade, and Economic Performance. *Int. J. Ind. Organ.*, March 1985, *3*(1), pp. 1–19. [G: W. Germany]

Newman, Karin. Hamburg in the European Economy, 1660–1750. *J. Europ. Econ. Hist.*, Spring 1985, *14*(1), pp. 57–93. [G: Germany]

Nogués, Julio J. Distortions, Factor Proportions and Efficiency Losses: Argentina in the Latin American Scenario. *Weltwirtsch. Arch.*, 1985, *121*(2), pp. 280–303. [G: Argentina]

Nolutshungu, Sam C. Soviet–African Relations: Promise and Limitations. In *Cassen, R., ed.*, 1985, pp. 68–88. [G: Africa; U.S.S.R.]

Nugent, Jeffrey. The Potential for South–South Trade in Capital Goods Industries. *Industry Devel.*, 1985, (14), pp. 99–141. [G: Global]

Nyers, J. and Szatmári, T. The Exploitation of

Licences and Economic Policy in Hungary. *Acta Oecon.*, 1985, *35*(3–4), pp. 377–91.
[G: Hungary]

Nyhus, Douglas. A Multi-country, Multi-industry Historical View of International Trade Competitiveness. In *Smyshlyaev, A., ed.*, 1985, pp. 7–18. [G: OECD]

Oblath, Gábor and Pete, Péter. Trade with the Soviet Union: The Finnish Case. *Acta Oecon.*, 1985, *35*(1–2), pp. 165–94. [G: U.S.S.R.; Finland]

Ocampo, José Antonio. Financial Aspects of Intraregional Trade in Latin America. In *Gauhar, A., ed.*, 1985, pp. 112–32.
[G: Latin America]

Ojala, Eric M. International Relationships in the World Beef Trade. In *[Heidhues, T.]*, 1985, pp. 172–88. [G: Selected Countries]

Oleson, B. T. Linkage of Agricultural Policy and Long Term Prospects in the International Grain Trade. *Can. J. Agr. Econ.*, August 1985, *32*, pp. 186–206.

Orléan, André. Spécialisation et taux de change: une vue d'ensemble. (International Specialization and Exchange Rates: A General View. With English summary.) *Écon. Soc.*, April 1985, *19*(4), pp. 67–94. [G: OECD]

Ostry, Bernard. Canada/U.S. Automotive Trade and Trade-policy Issues: Comments. In *Fretz, D.; Stern, R. and Whalley, J., eds.*, 1985, pp. 338–40. [G: Canada; U.S.]

Ozawa, Terutomo. Macroeconomic Factors Affecting Japan's Technology Inflows and Outflows: The Postwar Experience. In *Rosenberg, N. and Frischtak, C., eds.*, 1985, pp. 222–54.
[G: Japan]

Paliwoda, Stanley J. and Liebrenz, Marilyn L. Technology Transfer to Eastern Europe. In *Samli, A. C., ed.*, 1985, pp. 55–85.
[G: E. Europe]

Panchmukhi, V. R. Foreign Trade and Balance of Payment. In *Mongia, J. N., ed.*, 1985, pp. 291–314. [G: India]

Parikh, Ashok. The Behaviour of Export Price Deflators in Selected Asian Developing Countries. *Singapore Econ. Rev.*, October 1985, *30*(2), pp. 68–90. [G: Asia]

Parrott, Bruce. Soviet Foreign Policy, Internal Politics, and Trade with the West. In *Parrott, B., ed.*, 1985, pp. 35–60. [G: U.S.S.R.]

Pavitt, Keith. Technology Transfer among the Industrially Advanced Countries: An Overview. In *Rosenberg, N. and Frischtak, C., eds.*, 1985, pp. 3–23. [G: OECD]

Pearson, Charles and Ellyne, Mark. Surges of Imports: Perceptions versus Evidence. *World Econ.*, September 1985, *8*(3), pp. 299–315.
[G: OECD]

Pemberton, Carlisle. Economic Behaviour of Peasants in Tobago. In *Gomes, P. I., ed.*, 1985, pp. 76–102. [G: Trinidad and Tobago]

Perkins, J. A. Rehearsal for Protectionism: Australian Wool Exports and German Agriculture, 1830–80. *Australian Econ. Hist. Rev.*, March 1985, *25*(1), pp. 20–38. [G: Australia; Germany]

Petit, Michel. Agricultural Market Intervention and International Trade: Opening of the Discussion. *Europ. Rev. Agr. Econ.*, 1985, *12*(1/2), pp. 100–101. [G: EEC]

Petoussis, Emmanuel. The Aggregate Import Equation: Price Homogeneity and Monetary Effects. *Empirical Econ.*, 1985, *10*(2), pp. 91–101. [G: U.K.; U.S.]

Pigott, Charles and Reinhart, Vincent. The Strong Dollar and U.S. Inflation. *Fed. Res. Bank New York Quart. Rev.*, Autumn 1985, *10*(3), pp. 23–29. [G: U.S.]

Polasek, Wolfgang. Hierarchical Models for Seasonal Time Series. In *Bernardo, J. M., et al., eds.*, 1985, pp. 723–31. [G: Austria]

Pollard, H. J. The Erosion of Agriculture in an Oil Economy: The Case of Export Crop Production in Trinidad. *World Devel.*, July 1985, *13*(7), pp. 819–35. [G: Trinidad]

Pollard, Stephen K. and Graham, Douglas H. Price Policy and Agricultural Export Performance in Jamaica. *World Devel.*, September 1985, *13*(9), pp. 1067–75. [G: Jamaica]

Pomfret, Richard. Categorical Aggregation and International Trade: A Comment. *Econ. J.*, June 1985, *95*(378), pp. 483–85.

Pomfret, Richard. The Trade Diversion Due to EC Enlargement: A Comment on Sawyer's Estimate [The Effects of the Second Enlargement of the EC on U.S. Exports to Europe]. *Weltwirtsch. Arch.*, 1985, *121*(3), pp. 560–61.
[G: EEC; U.S.]

Portney, Paul R. Regional Issues: Commentary. In *Quigley, J. M. and Rubinfeld, D. L., eds.*, 1985, pp. 364–68. [G: U.S.]

Pourgerami, Abbas. Exports Growth and Economic Development: A Comparative Logit Analysis. *J. Econ. Devel.*, July 1985, *10*(1), pp. 117–28. [G: LDCs]

Ram, Rati. Exports and Economic Growth: Some Additional Evidence. *Econ. Develop. Cult. Change*, January 1985, *33*(2), pp. 415–25.
[G: LDCs]

Ramamurti, Ravi. High Technology Exports by State Enterprises in LDCs: The Brazilian Aircraft Industry. *Devel. Econ.*, September 1985, *23*(3), pp. 254–80. [G: Brazil]

Ranis, Gustav. Can the East Asian Model of Development Be Generalized? A Comment. *World Devel.*, April 1985, *13*(4), pp. 543–45.

Ranis, Gustav and Schive, Chi. Direct Foreign Investment in Taiwan's Development. In *Galenson, W., ed.*, 1985, pp. 85–137.
[G: Taiwan]

Reich, Robert B. Beyond Free Trade. In *Adams, J., ed.*, 1985, pp. 188–217. [G: U.S.]

Reza, Sadrel. Bangladesh–ASEAN Trade Relations. In *Wadhva, C. D. and Asher, M. G., eds.*, 1985, pp. 225–52. [G: S. Asia; Bangladesh]

Rice, Gillian and Mahmoud, Essam. The Prospects for Export Marketing to Egypt. In *Kaynak, E., ed. (II)*, 1985, pp. 217–29.
[G: Egypt]

Richards, Gordon. Business Cycles, Macroeconomic Policy, and U.S. Industrial Performance. In *Yochelson, J. N., ed.*, 1985, pp. 77–117. [G: U.S.]

Richter, Sándor. Trade with the Soviet Union: The Case of Austria. *Acta Oecon.*, 1985, *34*(3/4), pp. 339–59. [G: U.S.S.R.; Austria]

Riordan, E. B. Estimation of a Bilateral Trade Model for a Food Processing Service: Obstacles to Trade in Deboned Beef. *Irish J. Agr. Econ. Rural Soc.*, 1984-1985, *10*(2), pp. 145–64. [G: Ireland; U.K.]

Rode, Reinhard. Western Policies: The United States. In *Rode, R. and Jacobsen, H.-D., eds.*, 1985, pp. 184–99. [G: U.S.; U.S.S.R.; CMEA]

Roemer, Michael. Dutch Disease in Developing Countries: Swallowing Bitter Medicine. In *Lundahl, M., ed.*, 1985, pp. 234–52. [G: LDCs]

Roepstorff, Torben M. Industrial Development in Indonesia: Performance and Prospects. *Bull. Indonesian Econ. Stud.*, April 1985, *21*(1), pp. 32–61. [G: Indonesia]

Roessler, Frieder. Countertrade and the GATT Legal System. *J. World Trade Law*, Nov.:Dec. 1985, *19*(6), pp. 604–14. [G: Global]

Roh, Jae Won. The Korean Development Model and Canada–Korea Trade Relations. *Can. J. Devel. Stud.*, 1985, *6*(2), pp. 333–38. [G: S. Korea; Canada]

Rosenthal, Gert. The Lessons of Economic Integration in Latin America: The Case of Central America. In *Gauhar, A., ed.*, 1985, pp. 139–58. [G: Central America]

Rossini, Gianpaolo. Price Uncertainty and International Specialization. *Econ. Notes*, 1985, (3), pp. 89–100.

Rostow, W. W. Is There Need for Economic Leadership? Japanese or U.S.? *Amer. Econ. Rev.*, May 1985, *75*(2), pp. 285–91. [G: Japan; U.S.]

Rostow, W. W. The World Economy since 1945: A Stylized Historical Analysis. *Econ. Hist. Rev.*, 2nd Ser., May 1985, *38*(2), pp. 252–75. [G: Global]

Rothschild, Kurt W. Exports, Growth, and Catching-up: Some Remarks and Crude Calculations. *Weltwirtsch. Arch.*, 1985, *121*(2), pp. 304–14. [G: OECD]

Rousslang, Donald J. and Suomela, John W. The Trade Effects of a U.S. Import Surcharge. *J. World Trade Law*, Sept.:Oct. 1985, *19*(5), pp. 441–50. [G: U.S.; Japan]

Rugman, Alan M. Normative Issues Raised by International Trade in Technology Services: Comments. In *Stern, R. M., ed.*, 1985, pp. 119–25. [G: OECD]

Rutledge, Ian and Wright, Phil. Coal Worldwide: The International Context of the British Miners' Strike. *Cambridge J. Econ.*, December 1985, *9*(4), pp. 303–26. [G: U.K.]

Rye, Ajit Singh. Philippine–South Asia Economic Relations. In *Wadhva, C. D. and Asher, M. G., eds.*, 1985, pp. 115–37. [G: Philippines; S. Asia]

Sadler, Peter. World Prices and Development: Kuwait. In *Griffith-Jones, S. and Harvey, C.,*

eds., 1985, pp. 220–39. [G: Kuwait]

Safarian, A. E. The Relationship between Trade Agreements and International Direct Investment. In *Conklin, D. W. and Courchene, T. J., eds.*, 1985, pp. 206–19. [G: Canada]

Safford, Jeffrey J. The United States Merchant Marine in Foreign Trade, 1800–1939. In *Yui, T. and Nakagawa, K., eds.*, 1985, pp. 91–118. [G: U.S.]

Safford, Jeffrey J. The United States Merchant Marine in Foreign Trade, 1800–1939: Response. In *Yui, T. and Nakagawa, K., eds.*, 1985, pp. 121–22. [G: U.S.]

Sakurai, Makoto. A Japanese Perspective on Resource Trade with Australia. In *Drysdale, P. and Shibata, H., eds.*, 1985, pp. 177–89. [G: Australia; Japan]

Salazar-Carrillo, Jorge. Review of the External Debt and World Trade Panorama. In *Jorge, A.; Salazar-Carrillo, J. and Diaz-Pou, F., eds.*, 1985, pp. 15–21. [G: LDCs]

Salazar-Carrillo, Jorge and Fendt, Roberto, Jr. Some Additional Thoughts on Brazilian Trade, Prices and Exchange Rates. In *Salazar-Carrillo, J. and Fendt, R., Jr., eds.*, 1985, pp. 25–33. [G: Brazil; U.S.]

Salter, Malcolm S.; Webber, Alan M. and Dyer, Davis. U.S. Competitiveness in Global Industries: Lessons from the Auto Industry. In *Scott, B. R. and Lodge, G. C., eds.*, 1985, pp. 185–229. [G: U.S.; Selected OECD]

Samii, Massood V. OPEC in an Interdependent Global Economy. *J. Energy Devel.*, Autumn 1985, *11*(1), pp. 95–103. [G: OPEC]

Sampson, Gary P. and Snape, Richard H. Identifying the Issues in Trade in Services. *World Econ.*, June 1985, *8*(2), pp. 171–82.

Sapir, André. North–South Issues in Trade in Services. *World Econ.*, March 1985, *8*(1), pp. 27–42. [G: Global]

Sapsford, D. The Statistical Debate on the Net Barter Terms of Trade between Primary Commodities and Manufactures: A Comment and Some Additional Evidence. *Econ. J.*, September 1985, *95*(379), pp. 781–88. [G: U.K.]

Sarkar, Prabirjit. An Econometric Study of Trade Flows: A Case Study of ESCAP Countries. *Indian Econ. J.*, Jan.-Mar. 1985, *32*(3), pp. 15–23. [G: Asia]

Sarmad, Khwaja and Mahmood, Riaz. Price and Income Elasticities of Consumer Goods Imports of Pakistan. *Pakistan Devel. Rev.*, Autumn-Winter 1985, *24*(3/4), pp. 453–60. [G: Pakistan]

Saunders, Christopher T. Comments [The Global Environment and Its Impact on Soviet and East European Economies] [Current Problems and Prospects of the World Economy in the Light of East–West Economic Relations]. In *Saunders, C. T., ed.*, 1985, pp. 125–27. [G: OECD; CMEA]

Saunders, Christopher T. East–West Trade and Finance in the World Economy: A New Look for the 1980s: Introduction. In *Saunders, C. T., ed.*, 1985, pp. 1–18.

Sawyer, W. Charles. The Effects of the Second

Enlargement of the EC on U.S. Exports to Europe: Reply. *Weltwirtsch. Arch.*, 1985, *121*(3), pp. 562–63. **[G: EEC; U.S.]**

Sazanami, Yoko and Matsumura, Atsuko. Income and Price Elasticities in U.S.–Japan Bilateral Trade. *Keio Econ. Stud.*, 1985, *22*(1), pp. 47–56. **[G: U.S.; Japan]**

Scheetz, Thomas. Gastos militares en Chile, Perú y la Argentina. (With English summary.) *Desarrollo Econ.*, Oct.-Dec. 1985, *25*(99), pp. 315–27.

Schiavone, Giuseppe. Western Policies: Italy. In *Rode, R. and Jacobsen, H.-D., eds.*, 1985, pp. 157–65. **[G: CMEA; Italy]**

Schintke, Joachim and Stäglin, Reiner. Stability of Import Input Coefficients. In *Smyshlyaev, A., ed.*, 1985, pp. 129–39. **[G: W. Germany]**

Scholl, Lars U. Shipping Business in Germany in the Nineteenth and Twentieth Centuries. In *Yui, T. and Nakagawa, K., eds.*, 1985, pp. 185–213. **[G: Germany]**

Schwenk, Millicent H. North–South Barter Trade. In *Fisher, B. S. and Harte, K. M., eds.*, 1985, pp. 94–119. **[G: Indonesia; Malysia; Selected LDCs]**

Scott, Bruce R. National Strategies: Key to International Competition. In *Scott, B. R. and Lodge, G. C., eds.*, 1985, pp. 71–143. **[G: U.S.]**

Scott, Bruce R. U.S. Competitiveness: Concepts, Performance, and Implications. In *Scott, B. R. and Lodge, G. C., eds.*, 1985, pp. 13–70. **[G: U.S.]**

Scott, Christopher D. The Decline of an Export Industry, or the Growth of Peruvian Sugar Consumption in the Long Run. *J. Devel. Stud.*, January 1985, *21*(2), pp. 253–81. **[G: Peru]**

Scott, Norman. From Non-conventional to New Instruments of Trade Promotion? In *Saunders, C. T., ed.*, 1985, pp. 265–86. **[G: CMEA; OECD]**

de Secada, C. Alexander G. Arms, Guano, and Shipping: The W. R. Grace Interests in Peru, 1865–1885. *Bus. Hist. Rev.*, Winter 1985, *59*(4), pp. 597–621. **[G: Peru]**

Secchi, Carlo. L'internazionalizzazione dei servizi e la teoria del commercio internazionale. (The Internationalization of Services and the Theory of International Trade. With English summary.) *Rivista Int. Sci. Econ. Com.*, April 1985, *32*(4), pp. 359–74. **[G: Global]**

Shihab-Eldin, Adnan. U.S.–Arab Trade and Economic Relations: An Arab Perspective. In *Czinkota, M. R. and Marciel, S., eds.*, 1985, pp. 3–16. **[G: U.S.; OPEC]**

Shilling, A. Gary. U.S. Imports: Sailing through a Narrow Passage. *Bus. Econ.*, October 1985, *20*(4), pp. 18–23. **[G: U.S.; U.K.; W. Germany; Japan]**

Shimada, Haruo. International Trade and Labour Market Adjustment: The Case of Japan. *Econ. Lavoro*, July-Sept. 1985, *19*(3), pp. 3–30. **[G: Japan]**

Shultz, George P. Economic Cooperation in the Pacific Basin. *J. Econ. Devel.*, December 1985, *10*(2), pp. 7–17. **[G: Asia]**

Sigit, Hananto and Asra, Abuzar. Indonesia–Australia Trade. In *Lim, D., ed.*, 1985, pp. 14–22. **[G: Indonesia; Australia]**

Sigit, Hananto and Asra, Abuzar. Indonesian Import Demand Analysis. In *Lim, D., ed.*, 1985, pp. 132–49. **[G: Indonesia; Australia]**

Sigit, Hananto and Asra, Abuzar. Indonesian Import Survey Analysis. In *Lim, D., ed.*, 1985, pp. 211–21. **[G: Indonesia; Selected Countries]**

Silvapulla, Paramosathy and Phillips, Prue. Australian Import Demand Analysis. In *Lim, D., ed.*, 1985, pp. 108–31. **[G: Australia; Selected Countries]**

Simonazzi, Annamaria. Crediti all'esportazione e concorrenza internazionale. (Export Credit and International Competition. With English summary.) *Polit. Econ.*, August 1985, *1*(2), pp. 229–58. **[G: Global]**

Simões, Vitor Corado. Multinational Enterprises, Economic Structure and International Competitiveness: Portugal. In *Dunning, J. H., ed.*, 1985, pp. 337–78. **[G: Portugal]**

Sjaastad, Larry A. Commercial Policy in Brazil: An Overview: Comments. In *Salazar-Carrillo, J. and Fendt, R., Jr., eds.*, 1985, pp. 121–23. **[G: Brazil]**

Smith, Alan H. Soviet Trade Relations with the Third World. In *Cassen, R., ed.*, 1985, pp. 140–58. **[G: LDCs; U.S.S.R.]**

Smith, Ben. Resource Markets and Resource Trade Issues. In *Drysdale, P. and Shibata, H., eds.*, 1985, pp. 203–17. **[G: Australia]**

Soldaczuk, Józef. East–West Economic Relations: Expectations a Decade Ago and the Outcome. In *Saunders, C. T., ed.*, 1985, pp. 61–75. **[G: CMEA; OECD]**

Somensatto, Eduardo. Budget Deficits, Exchange Rates, International Capital Flows, and Trade. In *Cagan, P. and Somensatto, E., eds.*, 1985, pp. 223–79. **[G: U.S.; OECD]**

Soukup, Václav. Economic Aggression of Imperialism against the Countries of the Socialist Community. *Czech. Econ. Digest.*, August 1985, (5), pp. 75–94. **[G: CMEA; OECD]**

Spraos, John. The Statistical Debate on the Net Barter Terms of Trade: A Response. *Econ. J.*, September 1985, *95*(379), pp. 789. **[G: U.K.]**

Steinherr, Alfred. Competitiveness and Exchange Rates: Policy Issues for Europe. In *Peeters, T.; Praet, P. and Reding, P., eds.*, 1985, pp. 163–89. **[G: U.K.; Belgium; W. Germany]**

Stent, Angela E. Western Policies: The Federal Republic of Germany. In *Rode, R. and Jacobsen, H.-D., eds.*, 1985, pp. 99–119. **[G: W. Germany; CMEA]**

Stern, Robert M. Canada–U.S. Trade and Investment Frictions: The U.S. View. In *Fretz, D.; Stern, R. and Whalley, J., eds.*, 1985, pp. 32–63. **[G: Canada; U.S.]**

Stern, Robert M. Global Dimensions and Determinants of International Trade and Investment in Services. In *Stern, R. M., ed.*, 1985, pp. 126–68. **[G: U.S.; Canada; Japan; EEC]**

Strange, Susan. Protectionism and World Politics.

Int. Organ., Spring 1985, *39*(2), pp. 233–59. [G: Global]

Streeten, Paul. Developing-Country Trade Policies and the International Economic System: Comment. In *Preeg, E. H., ed.*, 1985, pp. 58–60. [G: Selected LDCs]

Sureshwaran, S. Sri Lanka–ASEAN Economic Relations. In *Wadhva, C. D. and Asher, M. G., eds.*, 1985, pp. 341–74. [G: Sri Lanka; ASEAN]

Syed, Aftab Ali. Price and Income Elasticities of Consumer Goods Imports of Pakistan: Comments. *Pakistan Devel. Rev.*, Autumn-Winter 1985, *24*(3/4), pp. 461–62.

Szakolczai, György; Bagdy, Gábor and Vindics, József. Dependence of the Hungarian Economic Performance on the World Economy. Facts and Economic Policy Inferences. *Acta Oecon.*, 1985, *35*(3–4), pp. 295–311. [G: Hungary]

Szarek, Patricia and Costello, Brian. Prices of U.S. Imports and Exports Declined in 1984. *Mon. Lab. Rev.*, April 1985, *108*(4), pp. 10–26. [G: U.S.]

Szeskin, A. and Sternlicht, R. Analysis of Agricultural Developments. In *Levinson, P. and Landau, P., eds.*, 1985, pp. 115–23. [G: Israel]

Tambunlertchai, Somsak. Thai Import Survey Analysis. In *Lim, D., ed.*, 1985, pp. 247–54. [G: Thailand; Selected Countries]

Tambunlertchai, Somsak. Thailand Import Demand Analysis. In *Lim, D., ed.*, 1985, pp. 191–99. [G: Australia; Thailand]

Tambunlertchai, Somsak. Thailand–Australia Trade. In *Lim, D., ed.*, 1985, pp. 54–59. [G: Thailand; Australia; ASEAN]

Tarafás, Imre and Szabó, Judit. Hungary's Exchange Rate Policy in the 1980s. *Acta Oecon.*, 1985, *35*(1–2), pp. 53–79. [G: Hungary]

Tharakan, P. K. M. Empirical Analyses of the Commodity Composition of Trade. In *Greenaway, D., ed.*, 1985, pp. 63–79.

Theriot, Lawrence H. and Matheson, JeNelle. Soviet Economic Relations with the Non-European CMEA: Cuba, Vietnam, and Mongolia. *Soviet E. Europ. Foreign Trade,* Summer–Fall 1985, *21*(1–2–3), pp. 144–90. [G: Cuba; Mongolia; Vietnam; U.S.S.R.]

Thirlwall, A. P. and Bergevin, J. Trends, Cycles and Asymmetries in the Terms of Trade of Primary Commodities from Developed and Less Developed Countries. *World Devel.*, July 1985, *13*(7), pp. 805–17.

Thurow, Lester C. Exports and the Japanese Economy. In *Nanto, D. K., ed.*, 1985, pp. 1–12. [G: Japan; U.S.]

Thurow, Lester C. Healing with a Thousand Bandages. *Challenge*, Nov./Dec. 1985, *28*(5), pp. 22–31. [G: U.S.]

Thursby, Marie C. and Thursby, Jerry G. The Uncertainty Effects of Floating Exchange Rates: Empirical Evidence on International Trade Flows. In *Arndt, S. W.; Sweeney, R. J. and Willett, T. D., eds.*, 1985, pp. 153–65. [G: Selected Countries]

Tironi B., Ernesto. A Reappraisal of the Role of

Primary Exports in Latin America. In *Abel, C. and Lewis, C. M., eds.*, 1985, pp. 472–81. [G: Latin America]

Tiwari, R. S. Constant–Market-Share Analysis of Export Growth: The Indian Case. *Pakistan J. Appl. Econ.*, Winter 1985, *4*(2), pp. 101–18. [G: India]

Tomita, Masahiro. The Danish Shipping Industry, 1866–1939: Structure and Strategy: Comment. In *Yui, T. and Nakagawa, K., eds.*, 1985, pp. 182–83. [G: Denmark]

Tremblay, Rodrigue. A Quebec Perspective on Canadian Trade Options. In *Conklin, D. W. and Courchene, T. J., eds.*, 1985, pp. 57–76. [G: Canada]

Tschoegl, Adrian E. Modern Barter. *Lloyds Bank Rev.*, October 1985, (158), pp. 32–40.

Tsiang, S. C. and Wu, Rong-I. Foreign Trade and Investment as Boosters for Take-off: The Experiences of the Four Asian Newly Industrializing Countries. In *Galenson, W., ed.*, 1985, pp. 301–32. [G: Hong Kong; Singapore; S. Korea; Taiwan]

Tucker, Stuart K. Hard Bargaining Ahead: U.S. Trade Policy and Developing Countries: Statistical Annexes. In *Preeg, E. H., ed.*, 1985, pp. 185–207. [G: Global; U.S.; LDCs]

Tyers, Rodney and Phillips, Prue. Australia, ASEAN and Pacific Basin Merchandise Trade: Factor Composition and Performance in the 1970s. In *Lim, D., ed.*, 1985, pp. 78–106. [G: Australia; ASEAN; Pacific Basin]

Tyers, Rodney; Phillips, Prue and Lim, David. ASEAN–Australia Trade in Manufactures: A Constant Market Share Analysis, 1970–79. In *Lim, D., ed.*, 1985, pp. 62–77. [G: ASEAN; Australia]

Tyler, William G. Exports and Foreign Debt in Brazil: Forecasting the Eighties: Comments. In *Salazar-Carrillo, J. and Fendt, R., Jr., eds.*, 1985, pp. 77–80. [G: Brazil]

Udis, Bernard. The High Technology Arms Race: The Western European Case. *Conflict Manage. Peace Sci.*, Fall 1985, *9*(1), pp. 19–31. [G: W. Europe; U.S.]

Ukawa, Hidetoshi. Japan's Perspective on Trade. *Challenge*, July/August 1985, *28*(3), pp. 18–26. [G: Japan; U.S.]

Unakul, Snoh and Akrasanee, Narongchai. Structural Adjustment in Thai–Japanese Economic Relations. In *Shishido, T. and Sato, R., eds.*, 1985, pp. 112–26. [G: Japan; Thailand]

Utrecht, Ernst. Gains and Losses in 25 Years of Export-Oriented Industrialization in South and Southeast Asia. In *Utrecht, E., ed.*, 1985, pp. 137–58. [G: S. Asia; S.E. Asia]

Vaince, Z. A. Assessment of Trade Effects of the EEC–GSP Scheme on Pakistan and Projections. *Pakistan Econ. Soc. Rev.*, Winter 1985, *23*(2), pp. 113–34. [G: EEC; Pakistan]

Valcamonici, Roberto. Processi di ristrutturazione, internazionalizzazione dell'economia italiana e vincolo esterno: 1970–1984. (Production Structure, Internationalization and the External Constraint in the Italian Economy: 1970–1984. With English summary.) *Polit. Econ.*,

August 1985, *1*(2), pp. 197–227.   [G: Italy]

Vanden Abeele, Michel. International Trade and Exchange Rates: Concluding Remarks. In *Peeters, T.; Praet, P. and Reding, P.*, eds., 1985, pp. 413–18.

Vandenbroucke, Frank. Conflicts in International Economic Policy and the World Recession: A Theoretical Analysis. *Cambridge J. Econ.*, March 1985, *9*(1), pp. 15–42.

Vaňous, Jan. Soviet and East European Trade and Financial Relations with the Middle East. *Soviet E. Europ. Foreign Trade*, Summer–Fall 1985, *21*(1–2–3), pp. 86–119.   [G: CMEA; Middle East]

Vellas, François. Les critéres de la hiérchie é conomique internationale el l'hypothése du pays intermédiaire. (With English summary.) *Revue Écon. Polit.*, Sept.-Oct. 1985, *95*(5), pp. 544–55.   [G: France]

Vernon, Raymond. Intra-industry Production as a Form of International Economic Involvement: An Exploratory Analysis: Comment. In *Erdilek, A.*, ed., 1985, pp. 29–33.

Vernon, Raymond. Technology's Effects on International Trade: A Look Ahead. In *Vernon, R.*, 1985, pp. 29–47.   [G: OECD]

Vernon, Raymond. The Fragile Foundations of East–West Trade. In *Vernon, R.*, 1985, pp. 199–212.

Vernon, Raymond. The Product Cycle Hypothesis in a New International Environment. In *Adams, J.*, ed., 1985, pp. 408–22.

Vernon, Raymond and Levy, Brian. State-Owned Enterprises in the World Economy: The Case of Iron Ore. In *Vernon, R.*, 1985, pp. 113–31.   [G: Selected Countries]

Viatte, Gérard. Agricultural Market Intervention and International Trade: Comment. *Europ. Rev. Agr. Econ.*, 1985, *12*(1/2), pp. 101–03.   [G: EEC]

Vogt, Donna U. Barter of Agriculture Commodities among Developing Countries. In *Fisher, B. S. and Harte, K. M.*, eds., 1985, pp. 120–55.   [G: LDCs]

Vogt, Donna U. U.S. Government International Barter. In *Fisher, B. S. and Harte, K. M.*, eds., 1985, pp. 168–214.   [G: U.S.; Jamaica; Selected Countries]

Vogt, Gerhart and Nowak, Heinrick. Countertrade—As Practiced in Eastern Europe. In *Fisher, B. S. and Harte, K. M.*, eds., 1985, pp. 85–93.   [G: E. Europe]

Volcker, Paul A. Statement to the U.S. Senate Foreign Relations Committee, February 27, 1985. *Fed. Res. Bull.*, April 1985, *71*(4), pp. 221–24.   [G: U.S.]

Volk, Raija. Suomen ja Neuvostoliiton kaupan bilateraalisuuden vaikutuksista Suomen talouden kasvuun ja stabiilisuuteen. (Effects of Bilateral Trade between Finland and the Soviet Union on the Growth and Stability of the Finnish Economy. With English summary.) *Kansant. Aikak.*, 1985, *81*(4), pp. 395–403.   [G: Finland; U.S.S.R.]

Wadhva, Charan D. India–ASEAN Economic Relations. In *Wadhva, C. D. and Asher, M. G.*, eds., 1985, pp. 269–320.   [G: India; ASEAN]

Wadhva, Charan D. and Pradhan, Radhe S. Nepal–ASEAN Economic Relations. In *Wadhva, C. D. and Asher, M. G.*, eds., 1985, pp. 321–40.   [G: Nepal; S. Asia]

Waelbroeck, Jean. The Determinants of World Trade and Growth. In *Peeters, T.; Praet, P. and Reding, P.*, eds., 1985, pp. 55–89.   [G: Global]

Wagenhals, Gerhard. Impact of Deep-Sea Mining on the World Metal Markets: Copper. In *Donges, J. B.*, ed., 1985, pp. 113–203.   [G: Selected Countries]

Wallich, Henry C. Statement to the U.S. House Subcommittee on International Economic Policy and Trade of the Committee on Foreign Affairs, March 22, 1985. *Fed. Res. Bull.*, May 1985, *71*(5), pp. 308–12.   [G: U.S.]

Wallich, Henry C. U.S. Monetary Policy in an Interdependent World. In *[Bloomfield, A. I.]*, 1985, pp. 33–44.

Walsh, B. M. Production of and International Trade in Alcoholic Drinks: Possible Public Health Implications. In *Grant, M.*, ed., 1985, pp. 23–44.   [G: Global]

Walsh, James I. The Effect on Third Countries of Mandated Countertrade. *J. World Trade Law*, Nov.:Dec. 1985, *19*(6), pp. 592–603.

Wang, Jikuan. International Trade Engineering Is an Emerging Science. *Chinese Econ. Stud.*, Fall 1985, *19*(1), pp. 81–88.   [G: China]

Wassermann, Ursula. China's Expanding Trade. *J. World Trade Law*, Sept.:Oct. 1985, *19*(5), pp. 542–46.   [G: China]

Watkins, G. C. and Waverman, Leonard. Canadian Natural Gas Export Pricing Behaviour. *Can. Public Policy*, Supplement July 1985, *11*(3), pp. 415–26.   [G: Canada]

Weinblatt, J. and Nathanson, R. The Effects of Export Restrictions on Economic Growth in LDCs. In *Weinblatt, J.*, ed., 1985, pp. 181–96.   [G: Selected LDCs]

Weinblatt, J. and Schrager, Nora. Exports from LDCs: Impacts on Economic Growth. In *Weinblatt, J.*, ed., 1985, pp. 161–80.   [G: LDCs]

Weintraub, Sidney. Trade and Structural Change. In *Musgrave, P. B.*, ed., 1985, pp. 79–107.   [G: Mexico; U.S.]

Wescott, Robert F. Industrial Policy and Optimization in the Coal Industry. In *Adams, F. G.*, ed., 1985, pp. 181–209.   [G: U.S.]

Westphal, Larry E.; Kim, Linsu and Dahlman, Carl J. Reflections on the Republic of Korea's Acquisition of Technological Capability. In *Rosenberg, N. and Frischtak, C.*, eds., 1985, pp. 167–221.   [G: S. Korea]

Wethington, Olin. East–West Trade: A Commerce Department Perspective. In *Stent, A. E.*, ed., 1985, pp. 125–29.   [G: U.S.]

Whigham, Thomas L. Agriculture and the Upper Plata: The Tobacco Trade, 1780–1865. *Bus. Hist. Rev.*, Winter 1985, *59*(4), pp. 563–96.   [G: Argentina; Paraguay]

Willett, Thomas D. and Bremer, Marc. International Aspects of Macroeconomic Policy: An Overview. In *Arndt, S. W.; Sweeney, R. J.*

and Willett, T. D., eds., 1985, pp. 193–201.
[G: U.S.]

Williams, Marion. An Analysis of Regional Trade and Payments Arrangements in CARICOM 1971–1983. *Soc. Econ. Stud.*, December 1985, *34*(4), pp. 3–33. [G: Caribbean]

Winiecki, Jan. Central Planning and Export Orientation in Manufactures. Theoretical Considerations on the Impact of System-Specific Features on Specialisation. *Econ. Notes*, 1985, (2), pp. 132–53.

Winters, L. Alan. Separability and the Modelling of International Economic Integration: U.K. Exports to Five Industrial Countries. *Europ. Econ. Rev.*, April 1985, *27*(3), pp. 335–53.
[G: EEC; U.S.; Japan]

Wolf, Thomas A. An Empirical Analysis of Soviet Economic Relations with Developing Countries. *Soviet Econ.*, July-Sept. 1985, *1*(3), pp. 232–60. [G: U.S.S.R.; LDCs; CMEA]

Wolf, Thomas A. Estimating "Foregone Gains" in Soviet–East European Trade: A Methodological Note. *Comparative Econ. Stud.*, Fall 1985, *27*(3), pp. 83–98. [G: CMEA]

Wonnacott, Ronald J. Global Dimensions and Determinants of International Trade and Investment in Services: Comments. In *Stern, R. M., ed.*, 1985, pp. 176–80. [G: U.S.; Canada; Japan; EEC]

Woolcock, Stephen. Western Policies: Great Britain. In *Rode, R. and Jacobsen, H.-D., eds.*, 1985, pp. 141–56. [G: U.K.; CMEA]

Woronoff, Jon. Japan's Structural Shift from Exports to Domestic Demand. In *Nanto, D. K., ed.*, 1985, pp. 64–78. [G: Japan]

Yamawaki, Hideki. International Trade and Foreign Direct Investment in West German Manufacturing Industries. In *Schwalbach, J., ed.*, 1985, pp. 247–86. [G: W. Germany]

Yamazawa, Ippei and Kohama, Hirohisa. Trading Companies and the Expansion of Foreign Trade: Japan, Korea, and Thailand. In *Ohkawa, K. and Ranis, G., eds.*, 1985, pp. 426–46. [G: Japan; S. Korea; Thailand]

Yamazawa, Ippei and Tambunlertchai, Somsak. Manufactured Exports and Developing Countries: The Thai Textile Industry and the Japanese Experience. In *Ohkawa, K. and Ranis, G., eds.*, 1985, pp. 369–88. [G: Thailand; Japan]

Yannopoulos, George N. EC External Commercial Policies and East–West Trade in Europe. *J. Common Market Stud.*, September 1985, *24*(1), pp. 21–38. [G: EEC; CMEA]

Yeats, Alexander J. On the Appropriate Interpretation of the Revealed Comparative Advantage Index: Implications of a Methodology Based on Industry Sector Analysis. *Weltwirtsch. Arch.*, 1985, *121*(1), pp. 61–73.
[G: Selected Countries]

422 Commercial Policy

4220 Commercial Policy

Abizadeh, Sohrab and Yousefi, Mahmood. International Trade Taxes and Economic Develop-

ment: An Empirical Analysis. *Rivista Int. Sci. Econ. Com.*, July-Aug. 1985, *32*(7–8), pp. 735–49. [G: Selected LDCs]

Abreu, Marcelo de Paiva. Errata [La Argentina y Brasil en los años treinta. Efectos de la política económica internacional británica y estadounidense]. *Desarrollo Econ.*, April–June 1985, *25*(97), pp. 114. [G: Argentina; Brazil; U.S.; U.K.]

Abreu, Marcelo de Paiva. La Argentina y Brasil en los años treinta. Efectos de la política económica internacional británica y estadounidense. (With English summary.) *Desarrollo Econ.*, January-March 1985, *24*(96), pp. 543–59.
[G: Argentina; Brazil; U.S.; U.K.]

Adams, Charles and Greenwood, Jeremy. Dual Exchange Rate Systems and Capital Controls: An Investigation. *J. Int. Econ.*, February 1985, *18*(1/2), pp. 43–63.

Adams, F. Gerard; Klein, Lawrence R. and Duggal, Vijaya G. The Effects of Foreign Export-Promotion Policies on the United States: Macro Model Simulations. In *Adams, F. G., ed.*, 1985, pp. 67–84. [G: U.S.]

Adedeji, Adebayo. Special Measures for the Least Developed and Other Low-Income Countries. In *Preeg, E. H., ed.*, 1985, pp. 135–63.
[G: Sub-Saharan Africa]

Adelman, Morris A. An Unstable World Oil Market. *Energy J.*, January 1985, *6*(1), pp. 17–22.

Adler-Karlsson, Gunnar. Political and Economic Consequences: The Efficiency of Embargoes and Sanctions. In *Rode, R. and Jacobsen, H.-D., eds.*, 1985, pp. 281–93. [G: U.S.; U.S.S.R.]

Agege, Charles O. Dumping of Dangerous American Products Overseas: Should Congress Sit and Watch? *J. World Trade Law*, July:Aug. 1985, *19*(4), pp. 403–10. [G: LDCs; U.S.]

Ahearn, Raymond J. Market Access in Japan: The U.S. Experience. In *Nanto, D. K., ed.*, 1985, pp. 41–63. [G: Japan; U.S.]

Ahmad, Jaleel. Prospects of Trade Liberalization between the Developed and the Developing Countries. *World Devel.*, September 1985, *13*(9), pp. 1077–86. [G: OECD; LDCs]

Aho, C. Michael. U.S. Labor-Market Adjustment and Import Restrictions. In *Preeg, E. H., ed.*, 1985, pp. 87–112. [G: U.S.]

Aho, C. Michael and Bayard, Thomas O. The 1980s: Twilight of the Open Trading System? In *Adams, J., ed.*, 1985, pp. 92–119.
[G: Global]

Aislabie, Colin J. Subsidies as an Alternative to the Australian Tariff. *Appl. Econ.*, August 1985, *17*(4), pp. 589–601. [G: Australia]

Aizenman, Joshua. Tariff Liberalization Policy and Financial Restrictions. *J. Int. Econ.*, November 1985, *19*(3/4), pp. 241–55.

Aktan, Okan H. and Baysan, Tercan. Türk ekonomisinin dünya ekonomisine entegrasyonu: liberasyon, karşilaştirmali üstünlük ve optimum politikalar. (Integration of the Turkish Economy into the World Economy: Trade Liberalization, Comparataive Advantage and Optimum Policies. With English summary.)

METU, 1985, *12*(1/2), pp. 49–106.
[G: Turkey]

Altmann, Franz-Lothar. East–West Relations in Energy, Agriculture and Technology: Comments. In *Saunders, C. T., ed.*, 1985, pp. 242–46. [G: U.S.S.R.; OECD]

Altmann, Franz-Lothar. Eastern Policies: Eastern Europe (CMEA 6) In *Rode, R. and Jacobsen, H.-D., eds.*, 1985, pp. 266–80.
[G: CMEA; OECD; LDCs]

Anderson, David L. Market Power and the Saskatchewan Potash Industry. *Can. Public Policy*, Supplement July 1985, *11*(3), pp. 321–28.
[G: Canada]

Anderson, James E. The Relative Inefficiency of Quotas: The Cheese Case. *Amer. Econ. Rev.*, March 1985, *75*(1), pp. 178–90. [G: U.S.]

Anderson, Kym and Garnaut, Ross. Australia's Trade Growth with Developing Countries. *Devel. Econ.*, June 1985, *23*(2), pp. 121–37.
[G: Australia; LDCs]

Anderson, W. J. and Gellner, J. A. Canadian Agricultural Policy in the Export Sector. *Can. J. Agr. Econ.*, August 1985, *32*, pp. 170–85.
[G: Canada]

Appleyard, Dennis R.; Field, Alfred J., Jr. and Tower, Edward. Further Analysis of the Effects of Offshore Assembly Provisions on the U.S. Tariff Structures. *J. Econ. Stud.*, 1985, *12*(4), pp. 62–65. [G: U.S.]

Armstrong, Harvey W. The Reform of the European Community Regional Policy. *J. Common Market Stud.*, June 1985, *23*(4), pp. 319–43.
[G: EEC]

Arndt, Sven W. U.S. Labor-Market Adjustment and Import Restrictions: Comment. In *Preeg, E. H., ed.*, 1985, pp. 113–15. [G: U.S.]

Aronson, Jonathan D. and Krugman, Paul R. The Linkage between International Trade and Financial Policy. In *Yochelson, J. N., ed.*, 1985, pp. 27–44. [G: U.S.]

Arronte, Ricardo Carrillo. The NICs in a New Trade Round: Comment. In *Preeg, E. H., ed.*, 1985, pp. 85–86. [G: LDCs]

Aschheim, Joseph; Bailey, Martin J. and Tavlas, George S. Dollar Appreciation, Deficit Stimulation, and the New Protectionism. *J. Policy Modeling*, Spring 1985, *7*(1), pp. 107–21.
[G: U.S.]

Atkinson, Thomas R. Canada/U.S. Automotive Trade and Trade-policy Issues: Comments. In *Fretz, D.; Stern, R. and Whalley, J., eds.*, 1985, pp. 333–37. [G: Canada; U.S.]

Aw, Bee Yan and Roberts, Mark J. The Role of Imports from the Newly-industrializing Countries in U.S. Production. *Rev. Econ. Statist.*, February 1985, *67*(1), pp. 108–17. [G: U.S.; LDCs]

Baker, Greg and Mori, Hiroshi. Strawmen in Trade Protectionism: The Case of Citrus Import Quotas. *Western J. Agr. Econ.*, December 1985, *10*(2), pp. 338–43. [G: Japan; U.S.]

Balassa, Bela. Disequilibrium Analysis in Developing Economies: An Overview. In *Balassa, B.*, 1985, pp. 24–43. [G: LDCs]

Balassa, Bela. Industrial Protection in the Devel-

oped Countries. In *Balassa, B.*, 1985, pp. 427–47. [G: EEC; U.S.; Japan]

Balassa, Bela. Prices, Incentives and Economic Growth. In *Balassa, B.*, 1985, pp. 3–23.
[G: Global]

Balassa, Bela. Structural Adjustment Policies in Developing Economies. In *Bapna, A., ed.*, 1985, pp. 251–77. [G: LDCs]

Balassa, Bela. The Cambridge Group and the Developing Countries. *World Econ.*, September 1985, *8*(3), pp. 201–18. [G: Mexico; Tanzania; LDCs]

Balassa, Bela. The Role of Foreign Trade in the Economic Development of Korea. In *Galenson, W., ed.*, 1985, pp. 141–75.
[G: S. Korea]

Balassa, Bela. Trade and Trade Relations between Developed and Developing Countries in the Decade Ahead. In *Balassa, B.*, 1985, pp. 448–68. [G: LDCs; OECD]

Balassa, Bela. Trade Policy in Mexico. In *Balassa, B.*, 1985, pp. 131–56. [G: Mexico]

Balasubramanyam, V. N. and Rothschild, R. Free Port Zones in the United Kingdom. *Lloyds Bank Rev.*, October 1985, (158), pp. 20–31. [G: U.K.]

Baldwin, Robert E. Canada/U.S. Economic Relations: A Canadian View: Comments. In *Fretz, D.; Stern, R. and Whalley, J., eds.*, 1985, pp. 98–105. [G: Canada; U.S.]

Baldwin, Robert E. Ineffectiveness of Protection in Promoting Social Goals. *World Econ.*, June 1985, *8*(2), pp. 109–18. [G: U.S.]

Baldwin, Robert E. Negotiating about Trade and Investment in Services: Comments. In *Stern, R. M., ed.*, 1985, pp. 195–99.

Banks, Gary. Constrained Markets, 'Surplus' Commodities and International Barter. *Kyklos*, 1985, *38*(2), pp. 249–67. [G: Global]

Barber, William J. Recreating the Science and Art of Political Economy: Lessons from the Energy Crisis. In *Schorr, P., ed.*, 1985, pp. 73–87. [G: U.S.]

Barthel-Rosa, Paulo. Developing-Country Trade Policies and the International Economic System: Comment. In *Preeg, E. H., ed.*, 1985, pp. 61–62. [G: Selected LDCs]

Bates, Robert H. and Lien, Dau-Hsiang Donald. On the Operations of the International Coffee Agreement. *Int. Organ.*, Summer 1985, *39*(3), pp. 553–59. [G: U.S.; Europe; Brazil; Colombia; Kenya]

Bautista, Romeo M. Effects of Trade and Exchange Rate Policies on Export Production Incentives in Philippine Agriculture. *Philippine Econ. J.*, 1985, *24*(2–3), pp. 87–115.
[G: Philippines]

Bedrossian, A. and Hitiris, T. Trade Taxes as a Source of Government Revenue: A Re-estimation. *Scot. J. Polit. Econ.*, June 1985, *32*(2), pp. 199–204. [G: LDCs]

Beigie, Carl E. and Stewart, James K. An Ontario Perspective on Canadian Trade Options. In *Conklin, D. W. and Courchene, T. J., eds.*, 1985, pp. 77–94. [G: Canada]

Benson, Sumner. United States Policy on Strategic Trade with the Soviet Bloc. In *Stent, A. E., ed.*, 1985, pp. 99–123. **[G: OECD; CMEA; U.S.]**

Benz, Steven F. Trade Liberalization and the Global Service Economy. *J. World Trade Law*, March:April 1985, *19*(2), pp. 95–120. **[G: OECD]**

Bergsten, C. Fred. The U.S.–Japan Trade Imbroglio. *Challenge*, July/August 1985, *28*(3), pp. 13–17. **[G: U.S.; Japan]**

Bergström, Clas; Loury, Glenn C. and Persson, Mats. Embargo Threats and the Management of Emergency Reserves. *J. Polit. Econ.*, February 1985, *93*(1), pp. 26–42.

Bertsch, Gary K. American Politics and Trade with the USSR. In *Parrott, B., ed.*, 1985, pp. 243–82. **[G: U.S.S.R.; U.S.]**

Bhagwati, Jagdish N. Export Promotion as a Developmental Strategy. In *Shishido, T. and Sato, R., eds.*, 1985, pp. 59–68. **[G: LDCs]**

Bhagwati, Jagdish N. Indian Balance of Payments Policy and Exchange Auctions. In *Bhagwati, J. N. (I)*, 1985, pp. 144–62. **[G: India]**

Bhagwati, Jagdish N. Protectionism: Old Wine in New Bottles. *J. Policy Modeling*, Spring 1985, *7*(1), pp. 23–33. **[G: Global]**

Bhagwati, Jagdish N. Splintering and Disembodiment of Services and Developing Nations. In *Bhagwati, J. N. (II)*, 1985, pp. 92–103. **[G: LDCs; U.S.; U.K.]**

Bhagwati, Jagdish N. and Srinivasan, T. N. Trade Policy and Development. In *Bhagwati, J. N. (I)*, 1985, pp. 88–122.

Bird, Graham. Managing the World Economy: Old Order, New Order or Disorder? *J. Devel. Stud.*, October 1985, *22*(1), pp. 243–50. **[G: Global]**

Bird, Graham. Managing the World Economy: Old Order, New Order or Disorder?: Review Article. In *Saith, A., ed.*, 1985, pp. 243–50. **[G: Global]**

Bird, Richard M. and Brean, Donald J. S. Canada/U.S. Tax Relations: Issues and Perspectives. In *Fretz, D.; Stern, R. and Whalley, J., eds.*, 1985, pp. 391–425. **[G: Canada; U.S.]**

Birenbaum, David E. and Rosenblatt, Samuel. Trade Trends and Trade Issues in the Pacific Basin. *Philippine Econ. J.*, 1985, *24*(4), pp. 288–301. **[G: Pacific Basin; U.S.]**

Blackwell, Michael. Lomé III: The Search for Greater Effectiveness. *Finance Develop.*, September 1985, *22*(3), pp. 31–34. **[G: Selected Countries]**

Bolz, Klaus. Economic Relations—Interdependence or Marginal Factor?: Industrial Cooperation. In *Rode, R. and Jacobsen, H.-D., eds.*, 1985, pp. 63–72. **[G: CMEA; W. Europe; U.S.]**

Bond, Eric W. and Guisinger, Stephen E. Investment Incentives as Tariff Substitutes: A Comprehensive Measure of Protection. *Rev. Econ. Statist.*, February 1985, *67*(1), pp. 91–97. **[G: U.K.]**

Boyer, Kenneth D. Canada/U.S. Transportation Issues. In *Fretz, D.; Stern, R. and Whalley,*

J., eds., 1985, pp. 341–78. **[G: Canada; U.S.]**

Brander, James A. and Spencer, Barbara J. Export Subsidies and International Market Share and Rivalry. *J. Int. Econ.*, February 1985, *18*(1/2), pp. 83–100.

Brock, Michael. Canada/U.S. Transportation Issues: Comments. In *Fretz, D.; Stern, R. and Whalley, J., eds.*, 1985, pp. 385–90. **[G: Canada; U.S.]**

Brock, William E. U.S. Trade Policy toward Developing Countries. In *Preeg, E. H., ed.*, 1985, pp. 35–38. **[G: U.S.; LDCs]**

Buess, Thomas. Perspektiven für eine engere Zusammenarbeit zwischen der Europäischen Gemeinschaft und den EFTA-Mitgliedstaaten. (Perspectives for Closer Cooperation between the European Community and the EFTA-Member Countries. With English summary.) *Aussenwirtschaft*, December 1985, *40*(4), pp. 341–87. **[G: EEC]**

Burgess, David F. Canada/U.S. Energy Issues: A Canadian Perspective. In *Fretz, D.; Stern, R. and Whalley, J., eds.*, 1985, pp. 213–51. **[G: Canada; U.S.]**

Bykov, Alexandr. East–West Technology Transfers: Now and in the Future. In *Saunders, C. T., ed.*, 1985, pp. 231–42. **[G: U.S.; CMEA]**

Cameron, Laurie A. and Berg, Gerald C. The U.S. Countervailing Duty Law and the Principle of General Availability. *J. World Trade Law*, Sept.:Oct. 1985, *19*(5), pp. 497–507. **[G: U.S.]**

Carbaugh, Robert and Wassink, Darwin. Joint Ventures, Voluntary Export Quotas, and Domestic Content Requirements. *Quart. J. Bus. Econ.*, Spring 1985, *24*(2), pp. 21–36. **[G: U.S.]**

Cartwright, Alton S. Options for Canada/U.S. Trade: A Business View. In *Conklin, D. W. and Courchene, T. J., eds.*, 1985, pp. 35–43. **[G: Canada; U.S.]**

Carvalho, Jose L. Commercial Policy in Brazil: An Overview. In *Salazar-Carrillo, J. and Fendt, R., Jr., eds.*, 1985, pp. 81–120. **[G: Brazil]**

Černohubý, Milan. Relations between Czechoslovakia and the European Economic Community. *Czech. Econ. Digest.*, February 1985, (1), pp. 50–62. **[G: EEC; Czechoslovakia]**

Chan, Kenneth S. The International Negotiation Game: Some Evidence from the Tokyo Round. *Rev. Econ. Statist.*, August 1985, *67*(3), pp. 456–64. **[G: Global]**

Chia, Siow Yue. The Role of Foreign Trade and Investment in the Development of Singapore. In *Galenson, W., ed.*, 1985, pp. 259–97. **[G: Singapore]**

Chisholm, Anthony H. and Tyers, Rodney. Agricultural Protection and Market Insulation Policies: Applications of a Dynamic Multisectoral Model. In *Piggott, J. and Whalley, J., eds.*, 1985, pp. 189–220. **[G: Selected Countries]**

Christelow, Dorothy. Japan's Intangible Barriers to Trade in Manufactures. *Fed. Res. Bank New*

York Quart. Rev., Winter 1985-86, *10*(4), pp. 11–18. **[G: Japan]**

Chu, David K. Y. The Politico-economic Background to the Development of the Special Economic Zones. In *Wong, K. and Chu, D. K. Y., eds.*, 1985, pp. 25–39. **[G: China]**

Chudson, Walter A. The Regulation of Transfer Prices by Developing Countries: Second-Best Policies? In *Rugman, A. M. and Eden, L., eds.*, 1985, pp. 267–90.

Clark, Don P. Protection and Developing Country Exports: The Case of Vegetable Oils. *J. Econ. Stud.*, 1985, *12*(5), pp. 3–18.

[G: LDCs]

Clark, M. G. Nontariff Measures: Perceptions and Reality. In *Conklin, D. W. and Courchene, T. J., eds.*, 1985, pp. 265–87. **[G: Canada; U.S.]**

Clausen, A. W. Corrective Initiatives in International Trade and Finance. In *Bapna, A., ed.*, 1985, pp. 23–31. **[G: Global]**

de Clercq, Willy. International Monetary Problems and Trade. In *Peeters, T.; Praet, P. and Reding, P., eds.*, 1985, pp. 397–403.

Clifton, Eric V. Real Exchange Rates, Import Penetration, and Protectionism in Industrial Countries. *Int. Monet. Fund Staff Pap.*, September 1985, *32*(3), pp. 513–36. **[G: U.S.; U.K.; W. Germany]**

Cline, William R. Canada/U.S. Trade Policy Issues: Do We Need a New Institution?: Institutional Arrangements for Managing the Canada/U.S. Economic Relationship: Comments. In *Fretz, D.; Stern, R. and Whalley, J., eds.*, 1985, pp. 152–57. **[G: Canada; U.S.]**

Conklin, David W. Options for New International Agreements: An Overview. In *Conklin, D. W. and Courchene, T. J., eds.*, 1985, pp. 3–15. **[G: Canada]**

Conklin, David W. Subsidy Pacts. In *Fretz, D.; Stern, R. and Whalley, J., eds.*, 1985, pp. 434–59.

Conquest, Richard. The State and Commercial Expansion: England in the Years 1642–1688. *J. Europ. Econ. Hist.*, Spring 1985, *14*(1), pp. 155–72. **[G: U.K.]**

Cooper, J. H. Sanctions and Economic Theory. *S. Afr. J. Econ.*, September 1985, *53*(3), pp. 287–96.

Cooper, Richard N. The Future of the International Trading System. In *Conklin, D. W. and Courchene, T. J., eds.*, 1985, pp. 407–22.

[G: Canada]

Cooper, Russel J.; McLaren, Keith R. and Powell, Alan A. Short-run Macroeconomic Closure in Applied General Equilbrium Modelling: Experience from ORANI and Agenda for Further Research. In *Piggott, J. and Whalley, J., eds.*, 1985, pp. 411–40. **[G: Australia]**

Corbet, Hugh. Agricultural Priorities after the Tokyo Round Negotiations. In *[Heidhues, T.]*, 1985, pp. 235–47.

Corden, W. Max. Protection, the Exchange Rate, and Macroeconomic Policy. *Finance Develop.*, June 1985, *22*(2), pp. 17–19. **[G: U.S.]**

Corden, W. Max. Tell Us Where the New Jobs Will Come From. *World Econ.*, June 1985, *8*(2), pp. 183–88.

Corden, W. Max. The Structure of a Tariff System and the Effective Protective Rate. In *Corden, W. M.*, 1985, pp. 97–117.

Costa, Antonio Maria. Multilateralism under Threat: Causes, Impact, and the Policy Debate on Government Intervention in Trade. *J. Policy Modeling*, Spring 1985, *7*(1), pp. 181–217.

[G: OECD]

Coughlin, Cletus C. Domestic Content Legislation: House Voting and the Economic Theory of Regulation. *Econ. Inquiry*, July 1985, *23*(3), pp. 437–48. **[G: U.S.]**

Cowhey, Peter F. and Aronson, Jonathan D. Trade in Communications and Data Processing. In *Stern, R. M., ed.*, 1985, pp. 256–90. **[G: Canada; U.S.]**

Cox, David and Harris, Richard. Trade Liberalization and Industrial Organization: Some Estimates for Canada. *J. Polit. Econ.*, February 1985, *93*(1), pp. 115–45. **[G: Canada]**

Crandall, Robert W. What Have Auto-Import Quotas Wrought? *Challenge*, January/February 1985, *27*(6), pp. 40–47. **[G: U.S.]**

Cresson, Edith. French Attitude to a New GATT Round. *World Econ.*, September 1985, *8*(3), pp. 317–19. **[G: France]**

Crispo, John. The Case for Free Trade with the United States. In *Conklin, D. W. and Courchene, T. J., eds.*, 1985, pp. 308–17. **[G: Canada; U.S.]**

Cronin, M. R. Protection and Employment in the Motor Car Sector: A Further Comment. *Australian Econ. Pap.*, June 1985, *24*(44), pp. 225.

Crutchfield, Stephen R. The Impact of Groundfish Imports on the United States Fishing Industry: An Empirical Analysis. *Can. J. Agr. Econ.*, July 1985, *33*(2), pp. 195–207.

[G: U.S.]

Cuddy, John D. A. Commodity Trade. In *Preeg, E. H., ed.*, 1985, pp. 117–33. **[G: LDCs; U.S.]**

Curtis, John M. Institutional Arrangements for Managing the Canada/U.S. Economic Relationship. In *Fretz, D.; Stern, R. and Whalley, J., eds.*, 1985, pp. 126–51. **[G: Canada; U.S.]**

Dajani, Burhan. Trends in U.S.–Arab Economic Relations. In *Czinkota, M. R. and Marciel, S., eds.*, 1985, pp. 23–39. **[G: U.S.; OPEC]**

Daly, Donald J. Microeconomic Performance: Interrelations between Trade and Industrial Policies. In *Conklin, D. W. and Courchene, T. J., eds.*, 1985, pp. 156–87. **[G: OECD; Canada]**

Das, Dilip K. Dismantling the Multifibre Arrangement? *J. World Trade Law*, January: February 1985, *19*(1), pp. 67–80. **[G: Global]**

Das, Dilip K. Management of U.S. Trade in Technology. *J. World Trade Law*, January:February 1985, *19*(1), pp. 80–82. **[G: U.S.]**

Das, Dilip K. The New U.S. Customs Regulation and China. *J. World Trade Law*, May:June 1985, *19*(3), pp. 287–89. **[G: China; U.S.]**

Deardorff, Alan V. and Stern, Robert M. Input–

Output Technologies and the Effects of Tariff Reductions. *J. Policy Modeling,* Summer 1985, 7(2), pp. 253–79.   [G: U.S.; EEC; Japan; Brazil]

Deardorff, Alan V. and Stern, Robert M. The Structure of Tariff Protection: Effects of Foreign Tariffs and Existing NTBs. *Rev. Econ. Statist.,* November 1985, 67(4), pp. 539–48.
[G: Global]

Denis, Jean-Emile and Poirier, René. The North American Chemical Industry in the Tokyo Round: Participation of Canadian and American Firms in the GATT Negotiation Process. *J. World Trade Law,* July:Aug. 1985, 19(4), pp. 315–42.   [G: Canada; U.S.]

Dixit, Avinash K. Tax Policy in Open Economies. In *Auerbach, A. J. and Feldstein, M., eds.,* 1985, pp. 313–74.

Dixit, Avinash K. and Kyle, Albert S. The Use of Protection and Subsidies for Entry Promotion and Deterrence. *Amer. Econ. Rev.,* March 1985, 75(1), pp. 139–52.

Dixit, Avinash K. and Newbery, David M. G. Setting the Price of Oil in a Distorted Economy. *Econ. J.,* Supplement 1985, 95, pp. 71–82.   [G: Turkey]

Dixon, Peter B.; Parmenter, B. R. and Rimmer, Russell J. The Sensitivity of ORANI Projections of the Short-run Effects of Increases in Protection to Variations in the Values Adopted for Export Demand Elasticities. In *Jungenfelt, K. and Hague, D. [Sir], eds.,* 1985, pp. 317–46.   [G: Australia; Selected Countries]

Djojohadikusumo, Sumitro. Common Interests of Industrial and Developing Countries. *World Econ.,* December 1985, 8(4), pp. 325–37.
[G: Global]

Donges, Jürgen B. International Agricultural Policy: A Role for National Food Programmes?: Comment. In *[Heidhues, T.],* 1985, pp. 286–88.

Drobnick, Richard L. The United States as the World's Largest Debtor: Implications for the International Trade Environment. In *Didsbury, H. F., Jr., ed.,* 1985, pp. 175–90.
[G: U.S.]

Dutton, H. I. and King, J. E. An Economic Exile: Edward Stillingfleet Cayley, 1802-1862. *Hist. Polit. Econ.,* Summer 1985, 17(2), pp. 203–18.   [G: U.K.]

Eaton, Jonathan and Grossman, Gene M. Tariffs as Insurance: Optimal Commercial Policy When Domestic Markets Are Incomplete. *Can. J. Econ.,* May 1985, 18(2), pp. 258–72.

Ewing, A. F. Why Freer Trade in Services Is in the Interest of Developing Countries. *J. World Trade Law,* March:April 1985, 19(2), pp. 147–69.   [G: Global]

Feenstra, Robert C. Automobile Prices and Protection: The U.S.–Japan Trade Restraint. *J. Policy Modeling,* Spring 1985, 7(1), pp. 49–68.   [G: U.S.; Japan]

Feigenbaum, Susan; Ortiz, Henry and Willett, Thomas D. Protectionist Pressures and Aggregate Economic Conditions: Comment [Pressures for Protectionism: An Empirical Analysis]. *Econ. Inquiry,* January 1985, 23(1), pp. 175–82.   [G: U.S.]

Feigenbaum, Susan and Willett, Thomas D. Domestic versus International Influences on Protectionist Pressures in the United States. In *Arndt, S. W.; Sweeney, R. J. and Willett, T. D., eds.,* 1985, pp. 181–90.   [G: U.S.]

Feketekuty, Geza. Negotiating about Trade and Investment in Services: Comments. In *Stern, R. M., ed.,* 1985, pp. 200–202.

Feketekuty, Geza. Negotiating Strategies for Liberalizing Trade and Investment in Services. In *Stern, R. M., ed.,* 1985, pp. 203–14.

Feldstein, Martin. Is Industrial Policy the Answer? In *Adams, J., ed.,* 1985, pp. 217–26.
[G: U.S.]

Findlay, Christopher C. The Persistence and Pervasiveness of the Regulation of International Trade in Civil Aviation Services. *Singapore Econ. Rev.,* April 1985, 30(1), pp. 77–89.

Finger, J. Michael. Incorporating the Gains from Trade into Policy. In *Adams, J., ed.,* 1985, pp. 163–74.   [G: U.S.; Global]

Forsyth, P. J. Trade and Industry Policy. *Australian Econ. Rev.,* 3rd Quarter, Spring 1985, (71), pp. 70–81.   [G: Australia]

Fox, Lawrence A. Canada/U.S. Tax Relations: Issues and Perspectives: Comments. In *Fretz, D.; Stern, R. and Whalley, J., eds.,* 1985, pp. 426–33.   [G: Canada; U.S.]

Fretz, Deborah; Stern, Robert M. and Whalley, John. Canada/United States Trade and Investment Issues: Introduction and Overview. In *Fretz, D.; Stern, R. and Whalley, J., eds.,* 1985, pp. 3–20.   [G: Canada; U.S.]

Frey, Bruno S. The Political Economy of Protection. In *Greenaway, D., ed.,* 1985, pp. 139–57.   [G: OECD]

Fritsch-Bournazel, Renata. Western Policies: France. In *Rode, R. and Jacobsen, H.-D., eds.,* 1985, pp. 128–40.   [G: France; CMEA]

Gadbaw, R. Michael. The Implications of Countertrade under the General Agreement on Tariffs and Trade. In *Fisher, B. S. and Harte, K. M., eds.,* 1985, pp. 254–66.   [G: Global]

Gallarotti, Giulio M. Toward a Business-Cycle Model of Tariffs. *Int. Organ.,* Winter 1985, 39(1), pp. 155–87. [G: U.S.; U.K.; Germany]

Gardner, Bruce. Export Subsidies Are Still Irrational. *Agr. Econ. Res.,* Winter 1985, 37(1), pp. 17–19.   [G: U.S.]

Garten, Jeffrey E. Gunboat Economics. *Foreign Aff.,* 1985, 63(3), pp. 538–59.   [G: Global]

Gemmill, Gordon. Forward Contracts or International Buffer Stocks? A Study of Their Relative Efficiencies in Stabilising Commodity Export Earnings. *Econ. J.,* June 1985, 95(378), pp. 400–417.   [G: Selected LDCs]

Gemmill, Gordon. Optimal Hedging on Futures Markets for Commodity-exporting Nations. *Europ. Econ. Rev.,* March 1985, 27(2), pp. 243–61.   [G: LDCs]

Gerami, Shahin. Export Alliances as a Device of Dependence Control: A Comparative Analysis.

Soc. Sci. Quart., March 1985, *66*(1), pp. 105–19.   **[G: LDCs]**

Gibbs, Murray. Continuing the International Debate on Services. *J. World Trade Law*, May-:June 1985, *19*(3), pp. 199–218.   **[G: Global]**

Godek, Paul E. Industry Structure and Redistribution through Trade Restrictions. *J. Law Econ.*, October 1985, *28*(3), pp. 687–703.   **[G: U.S.]**

Goldman, Marshall I. and Vernon, Raymond. U.S. Economic Policies toward the Soviet Union [Economic Relations]. In *Vernon, R.*, 1985, pp. 177–97.   **[G: U.S.; U.S.S.R.]**

Gray, H. Peter. Trade Policy in the 1980s: A Review Article. *Weltwirtsch. Arch.*, 1985, *121*(1), pp. 142–50.   **[G: Global]**

Greenaway, David. Trade Taxes as a Source of Government Revenue: A Comment on the Bedrossian-Hitiris Re-estimation. *Scot. J. Polit. Econ.*, June 1985, *32*(2), pp. 205–08.

Grey, Rodney de C. Canada/U.S. Trade Policy Issues: Do We Need a New Institution? In *Fretz, D.; Stern, R. and Whalley, J., eds.*, 1985, pp. 113–25.   **[G: Canada; U.S.]**

Grey, Rodney de C. Negotiating about Trade and Investment in Services. In *Stern, R. M., ed.*, 1985, pp. 181–94.

Grunwald, Joseph. Mexico and the United States: Studies in Economic Interaction: Trade and Industry: Comments. In *Musgrave, P. B., ed.*, 1985, pp. 113–19.   **[G: Mexico]**

Guillaumont, Patrick. External Factors and Economic Policy in Sub-Saharan Africa. In *Rose, T., ed.*, 1985, pp. 37–47.   **[G: Sub-Saharan Africa]**

Haberler, Gottfried. International Trade and Economic Development. In *Haberler, G.*, 1985, pp. 495–527.

Haen, Hartwig; de Johnson, Glenn L. and Tangermann, Stefan. Agriculture & International Relations: Analysis and Policy: Introduction. In *[Heidhues, T.]*, 1985, pp. 1–16.

Hakogi, Masumi. Trade Restrictions and Trade Promotion: Comments. In *Saunders, C. T., ed.*, 1985, pp. 309–12.   **[G: CMEA; OECD]**

Hamilton, Carl. Economic Aspects of Voluntary Export Restraints. In *Greenaway, D., ed.*, 1985, pp. 99–117.   **[G: Selected Countries]**

Hamilton, Carl. Follies of Policies for Textile Imports in Western Europe. *World Econ.*, September 1985, *8*(3), pp. 219–34.   **[G: W. Europe]**

Hamilton, Carl. Voluntary Export Restraints and Trade Diversion. *J. Common Market Stud.*, June 1985, *23*(4), pp. 345–55.   **[G: Global]**

Hamilton, Robert W. and Whalley, John. Geographically Discriminatory Trade Arrangements. *Rev. Econ. Statist.*, August 1985, *67*(3), pp. 446–55.   **[G: Global]**

Handerson, Harold. Canada/U.S. Transportation Issues: Comments. In *Fretz, D.; Stern, R. and Whalley, J., eds.*, 1985, pp. 379–84.   **[G: Canada; U.S.]**

Hardt, John P. The Future of Inter-German Political and Economic Relations. In *Stent, A. E., ed.*, 1985, pp. 147–67.   **[G: W. Germany; E. Germany]**

Hardt, John P. and Gold, Donna L. Agricultural Trade: U.S.A. and U.S.S.R. In *Saunders, C. T., ed.*, 1985, pp. 217–30.   **[G: U.S.; U.S.S.R.]**

Harling, Kenneth F. and Thompson, Robert L. Government Intervention in Poultry Industries: A Cross-Country Comparison. *Amer. J. Agr. Econ.*, May 1985, *67*(2), pp. 243–50.   **[G: Canada; W. Germany; U.K.]**

Harris, Richard. Why Voluntary Export Restraints Are 'Voluntary.' *Can. J. Econ.*, November 1985, *18*(4), pp. 799–809.

Harris, Richard G. Jobs and Free Trade. In *Conklin, D. W. and Courchene, T. J., eds.*, 1985, pp. 188–203.   **[G: Canada]**

Harrison, Glenn W. and Kimbell, Larry J. Economic Interdependence in the Pacific Basin: A General Equilbrium Approach. In *Piggott, J. and Whalley, J., eds.*, 1985, pp. 143–74.   **[G: Selected Countries]**

Harte, Kathleen M. Legal Implications of Barter and Countertrade Transactions. In *Fisher, B. S. and Harte, K. M., eds.*, 1985, pp. 217–53.   **[G: U.S.; EEC]**

Hartigan, James C. What Can We Learn from the Effective Rate of Protection? *Weltwirtsch. Arch.*, 1985, *121*(1), pp. 53–60.   **[G: U.S.]**

Helliwell, John F. Trade and Macroeconomic Policies. In *Conklin, D. W. and Courchene, T. J., eds.*, 1985, pp. 115–37.   **[G: OECD; Canada]**

Herander, Mark G. The Relative Impact of US Specific Tariffs on Manufactured Imports from Developing and Developed Countries. *Quart. Rev. Econ. Bus.*, Summer 1985, *25*(2), pp. 91–108.   **[G: U.S.]**

Hesp, Paul and van der Laan, Laurens. Marketing Boards in Tropical Africa: A Survey. In *Arhin, K.; Hesp, P. and van der Laan, L., eds.*, 1985, pp. 1–36.   **[G: Africa]**

Hesse, Helmut. Export Restrictions as a Means of Avoiding "Critical Shortages." In *[Heidhues, T.]*, 1985, pp. 195–213.

Hesse, Helmut. The Economics of Export Restrictions: Free Access to Commodity Markets and the NIEO: Summary of Findings and Main Conclusions. In *Weinblatt, J., ed.*, 1985, pp. 258–61.   **[G: Global]**

Hewett, Ed A. Basic Issues in U.S.–Soviet Economic Relations. In *Stent, A. E., ed.*, 1985, pp. 91–98.   **[G: U.S.; U.S.S.R.]**

Hill, Roger. An Ontario Perspective on Trade Issues between Canada and the United States. In *Fretz, D.; Stern, R. and Whalley, J., eds.*, 1985, pp. 478–94.   **[G: Canada; U.S.]**

Hillman, Arye L. and Long, Ngo Van. Monopolistic Recycling of Oil Revenue and Intertemporal Bias in Oil Depletion and Trade. *Quart. J. Econ.*, August 1985, *100*(3), pp. 597–624.

Hillman, Jimmye S. Evolution of American Agricultural Trade Policy and European Interaction. In *[Heidhues, T.]*, 1985, pp. 155–69.   **[G: U.S.]**

Holub, Alois. What Hinders Development Should

Stimulate It. *Czech. Econ. Digest.*, March 1985, (2), pp. 77–86. **[G: Global]**

Holzman, Franklyn D. A Comparative View of Foreign Trade Behavior: Market versus Centrally Planned Economies. **In** *Bornstein, M., ed.*, 1985, pp. 367–86.

Hufbauer, Gary Clyde and Schott, Jeffrey J. The Role of Bilateral Investment Talks. **In** *Conklin, D. W. and Courchene, T. J., eds.*, 1985, pp. 343–49. **[G: Canada; U.S.]**

Hufbauer, Gary Clyde and Schott, Jeffrey J. The Soviet–European Gas Pipeline: A Case of Failed Sanction. **In** *Moran, T. H., ed.*, 1985, pp. 219–45. **[G: U.S.; U.S.S.R.]**

Hultman, Charles W. International Banking and U.S. Commercial Policy. *J. World Trade Law*, May:June 1985, *19*(3), pp. 219–28. **[G: OECD; U.S.]**

Huszagh, Sandra M. and Greene, Mark R. How Exporters View Credit Risk and FCIA Insurance—The Georgia Experience. *J. Risk Ins.*, March 1985, *52*(1), pp. 117–32. **[G: U.S.]**

Hutchinson, William K. Import Substitution, Structural Change, and Regional Economic Growth in the United States: The Northeast, 1870–1910. *J. Econ. Hist.*, June 1985, *45*(2), pp. 319–25. **[G: U.S.]**

Inotai, András. East–West Relations in Energy, Agriculture and Technology: Comments. **In** *Saunders, C. T., ed.*, 1985, pp. 246–51. **[G: CMEA]**

Jackson, John H. Canada/U.S. Trade Policy Issues: Do We Need a New Institution?: Institutional Arrangements for Managing the Canada/U.S. Economic Relationship: Comments. **In** *Fretz, D.; Stern, R. and Whalley, J., eds.*, 1985, pp. 158–64. **[G: Canada; U.S.]**

Jackson, John H. Mechanics for the Ratification, Enforcement, and Abrogation of International Agreements in U.S. Law. **In** *Conklin, D. W. and Courchene, T. J., eds.*, 1985, pp. 350–61. **[G: Canada; U.S.]**

Jacobsen, Hanns-Dieter. The Fragile U.S.–West German Consensus. **In** *Stent, A. E., ed.*, 1985, pp. 131–46. **[G: OECD; CMEA; U.S.; W. Germany]**

Jacobsen, Hanns-Dieter. Western Policies: U.S. Export Control and Export Administration Legislation. **In** *Rode, R. and Jacobsen, H.-D., eds.*, 1985, pp. 213–25. **[G: CMEA; U.S.]**

Jacobsen, Hanns-Dieter. Western Policies: The Special Case of Inter-German Relations. **In** *Rode, R. and Jacobsen, H.-D., eds.*, 1985, pp. 120–27. **[G: W. Germany; E. Germany]**

Jacobsen, Hanns-Dieter and Rode, Reinhard. Political and Economic Consequences: Economic Relations as a Prop for Détente? **In** *Rode, R. and Jacobsen, H.-D., eds.*, 1985, pp. 294–98. **[G: U.S.; W. Europe; CMEA]**

Jenkins, Rhys O. Latin America and the New International Division of Labour: A Critique of Some Recent Views. **In** *Abel, C. and Lewis, C. M., eds.*, 1985, pp. 415–29. **[G: Latin America]**

Jones, Kent. Trade in Steel: Another Turn in the Protectionist Spiral. *World Econ.*, December 1985, *8*(4), pp. 393–408. **[G: EEC; U.S.]**

Jones, Rich; Whalley, John and Wigle, Randall. Regional Impacts of Tariffs in Canada: Preliminary Results from a Small Dimensional Numerical General Equilibrium Model. **In** *Piggott, J. and Whalley, J., eds.*, 1985, pp. 175–88. **[G: Canada]**

Jopp, Mathias. Western Policies: The European Community. **In** *Rode, R. and Jacobsen, H.-D., eds.*, 1985, pp. 166–83. **[G: EEC; CMEA]**

Josling, Timothy E. International Agricultural Policy: A Role for National Food Programmes? **In** *[Heidhues, T.]*, 1985, pp. 273–85.

Joson, S. S. The GATT Agreement on Government Procurement: Canada and Australia. *Australian Econ. Pap.*, June 1985, *24*(44), pp. 76–94. **[G: Australia; Canada]**

Jung, Zdeněk. Trade Normalization—An Insoluble Problem. *Czech. Econ. Digest.*, September 1985, (6), pp. 87–95. **[G: U.S.; Czechoslovakia]**

Kalirajan, K. P. Trade among Developing Countries: The Case of South Asian Regional Cooperation. *J. Econ. Devel.*, July 1985, *10*(1), pp. 153–67. **[G: Bangladesh; India; Pakistan; Sri Lanka]**

Kellman, Mitchell. The Crumbling Embargo? Evidence of OECD Cohesiveness from the Composition of Manufactured Exports to the USSR. *Comparative Econ. Stud.*, Summer 1985, *27*(2), pp. 53–70. **[G: OECD; U.S.S.R.]**

Keppler, Horst. Free Access to Supplies versus Restrictive Supply Policies: The Ability of LDCs to Control Commodity Markets. **In** *Weinblatt, J., ed.*, 1985, pp. 71–115. **[G: Selected LDCs]**

Khan, Mohsin S. and Zahler, Roberto. Trade and Financial Liberalization Given External Shocks and Inconsistent Domestic Policies. *Int. Monet. Fund Staff Pap.*, March 1985, *32*(1), pp. 22–55. **[G: LDCs]**

Kihwan, Kim. An Agenda for U.S. Trade Policy toward Developing Countries: Comment. **In** *Preeg, E. H., ed.*, 1985, pp. 21–22. **[G: LDCs]**

Kim, Kwan S. Industrial Development in Mexico: Problems, Policy Issues, and Perspectives. **In** *Kim, K. S. and Ruccio, D. F., eds.*, 1985, pp. 205–26. **[G: Mexico]**

Kirkpatrick, Colin H. Improving Food Security in Developing Countries: A Role for the IMF. *Banca Naz. Lavoro Quart. Rev.*, June 1985, (153), pp. 174–85. **[G: LDCs]**

Kirschke, Dieter. Trade Uncertainty in a Price Fixing Protective System. *Z. ges. Staatswiss. (JITE)*, June 1985, *141*(2), pp. 269–81.

Klein, Lawrence R. Empirical Aspects of Protectionism: LINK Results. *J. Policy Modeling*, Spring 1985, *7*(1), pp. 35–47. **[G: Global]**

Klein, Lawrence R. World Trade Growth and Industrial Policy. **In** *Peeters, T.; Praet, P. and Reding, P., eds.*, 1985, pp. 111–30. **[G: U.S.; OECD]**

Kollist, Ingrid and Searing, Marjory E. Government Policy toward High-Tech Industry. **In**

Zukin, S., ed., 1985, pp. 107–18.   [G: U.S.]

Kostecki, M. M. and Tymowski, M. J. Customs Duties versus Other Important Charges in the Developing Countries. *J. World Trade Law*, May:June 1985, *19*(3), pp. 269–86.
[G: LDCs]

Kreinin, Mordechai E. United States Trade and Possible Restrictions in High-Technology Products. *J. Policy Modeling*, Spring 1985, *7*(1), pp. 69–105.   [G: U.S.; Japan; EEC; Canada]

Krueger, Anne O. Import Substitution versus Export Promotion. *Finance Develop.*, June 1985, *22*(2), pp. 20–23.   [G: Brazil; Hong Kong; S. Korea; Singapore; Taiwan]

Krueger, Anne O. and Michalopoulos, Constantine. Developing-Country Trade Policies and the International Economic System. In *Preeg, E. H., ed.*, 1985, pp. 39–57.
[G: Selected LDCs]

Kuo, Shirley W. Y. and Fei, John C. H. Causes and Roles of Export Expansion in the Republic of China. In *Galenson, W., ed.*, 1985, pp. 45–84.   [G: Taiwan]

de Lacharrière, Guy Ladreit. Case for a Tribunal to Assist in Settling Trade Disputes. *World Econ.*, December 1985, *8*(4), pp. 339–52.
[G: Global]

Lachaux, Claude. Trade Restrictions: Economic Necessity or Political Weapon? A Western View. In *Saunders, C. T., ed.*, 1985, pp. 287–97.   [G: U.S.; U.S.S.R.]

Lande, Steve and VanGrasstek, Craig. Trade with the Developing Countries: The Reagan Record and Prospects. In *Sewell, J. W.; Feinberg, R. E. and Kallab, V., eds.*, 1985, pp. 73–94.   [G: U.S.; LDCs]

de Larosière, Jacques. Interrelationships between Protectionism and the Debt Crisis. *Aussenwirtschaft*, September 1985, *40*(3), pp. 219–28.   [G: Global]

Lavigne, Marie. East–West Trade and Finance in the World Economy: A New Look for the 1980s: General Evaluations. In *Saunders, C. T., ed.*, 1985, pp. 317–20.

Lavigne, Marie. Intra-CMEA Integration and Foreign Economic Relations of the CMEA Countries. In *[Levcik, F.]*, 1985, pp. 231–37.
[G: CMEA]

Lecraw, Donald J. Hymer and Public Policy in LDCs. *Amer. Econ. Rev.*, May 1985, *75*(2), pp. 239–44.   [G: LDCs]

Leela, P. Analysis of Fast Growing Exports of India. *Indian Econ. J.*, Jan.-Mar. 1985, *32*(3), pp. 82–89.   [G: India]

Levcik, Friedrich and Fink, Gerhard. East–West Trade and Finance in the World Economy: A New Look for the 1980s: General Evaluations. In *Saunders, C. T., ed.*, 1985, pp. 322–23.

Levy, Santiago. Mexico and the United States: Studies in Economic Interaction: Trade and Industry: Comments. In *Musgrave, P. B., ed.*, 1985, pp. 109–12.   [G: Mexico]

Lewis, John P. Special Measures for the Least Developed and Other Low-Income Countries:

Comment. In *Preeg, E. H., ed.*, 1985, pp. 164–66.   [G: Sub-Saharan Africa]

Lipsey, Richard G. Canada and the United States: The Economic Dimension. In *Doran, C. F. and Sigler, J. H., eds.*, 1985, pp. 69–108.
[G: Canada; U.S.]

Lipsey, Richard G. Rapporteur's Comments: Which Way for Canada at the Crossroads? In *Conklin, D. W. and Courchene, T. J., eds.*, 1985, pp. 434–51.   [G: Canada]

Lloyd, P. J. The Australian Textile and Clothing Industry Group: Untoward Effects of Government Intervention. In *Jungenfelt, K. and Hague, D. [Sir], eds.*, 1985, pp. 485–522.
[G: Australia]

Lodge, George C. and Crum, William C. U.S. Competitiveness in the World Economy: The Pursuit of Remedies. In *Scott, B. R. and Lodge, G. C., eds.*, 1985, pp. 479–502.
[G: U.S.]

Logan, Robert G. Trade in Communications and Data Processing: Comments. In *Stern, R. M., ed.*, 1985, pp. 299–303.   [G: Canada; U.S.]

Lukaszewicz, Aleksander. Trade Restrictions and Trade Promotion: Comments. In *Saunders, C. T., ed.*, 1985, pp. 312–14.   [G: CMEA; OECD]

Lundahl, Mats. Errata: Economic Effects of a Trade and Investment Boycott against South Africa. *Scand. J. Econ.*, 1985, *87*(1), pp. 142.
[G: S. Africa]

Machowski, Heinrich. Eastern Policies: The Soviet Union. In *Rode, R. and Jacobsen, H.-D., eds.*, 1985, pp. 251–65.   [G: U.S.S.R.; CMEA]

MacPhee, Craig R. Evaluation of the Trade Effects of the Generalized System of Preferences. In *United Nations Conference on Trade and Development.*, 1985, pp. 57–86.   [G: OECD]

Malmgren, Harald B. Negotiating International Rules for Trade in Services. *World Econ.*, March 1985, *8*(1), pp. 11–26.   [G: Global]

Malmgren, Harald B. Trade Policy and Trade Negotiations in the 1980s. In *Yochelson, J. N., ed.*, 1985, pp. 1–13.

Marshall, Peter. Reflections on North–South Relations and the Commonwealth. *J. World Trade Law*, May:June 1985, *19*(3), pp. 191–98.   [G: British Commonwealth]

Martin, David Dale. The Iron and Steel Industry: Transnational Control without TNCs? In *Newfarmer, R. S., ed.*, 1985, pp. 151–92.
[G: Selected Countries]

Mateev, Evgeni. Trade Restrictions: Economic Necessity or Political Weapon? An Eastern View. In *Saunders, C. T., ed.*, 1985, pp. 299–308.   [G: EEC; CMEA]

McCulloch, Rachel. Unexpected Real Consequences of Floating Exchange Rates. In *Adams, J., ed.*, 1985, pp. 286–306. [G: OECD]

McGuinness, Norman W. Comments on the Difficulties in Regulating Transfer Prices. In *Rugman, A. M. and Eden, L., eds.*, 1985, pp. 309–15.

McKenzie, George. A Problem in Measuring the Cost of Protection. *Manchester Sch. Econ. Soc.*

Stud., March 1985, *53*(1), pp. 45–54.

McLachlan, D. L. Discriminatory Public Procurement, Economic Integration and the Role of Bureaucracy. *J. Common Market Stud.*, June 1985, *23*(4), pp. 357–72.   [G: U.S.; Canada; EEC; Japan]

McNiven, James. Canadian Trade Options from a Regional Perspective. In *Conklin, D. W. and Courchene, T. J., eds.*, 1985, pp. 47–56.   [G: Canada; U.S.]

McVey, Thomas B. Policy Issues in Countertrade. In *Fisher, B. S. and Harte, K. M., eds.*, 1985, pp. 267–79.   [G: U.S.]

Meier, Gerald M. The New Export Pessimism. In *Shishido, T. and Sato, R., eds.*, 1985, pp. 19–32.   [G: LDCs]

Mercenier, Jean and Waelbroeck, Jean. The Impact of Protection on Developing Countries: A General Equilibrium Analysis. In *Jungenfelt, K. and Hague, D. [Sir], eds.*, 1985, pp. 219–39.   [G: LDCs]

Merkin, William S. Canada/U.S. Economic Relations: A Canadian View: Comments. In *Fretz, D.; Stern, R. and Whalley, J., eds.*, 1985, pp. 106–12.   [G: Canada; U.S.]

Michaely, Michael. The Demand for Protection against Exports of Newly Industrializing Countries. *J. Policy Modeling*, Spring 1985, *7*(1), pp. 123–32.   [G: Brazil; Korea; Mexico; Hong Kong; Singapore]

Mieli, Renato. East–West Trade and Finance in the World Economy: A New Look for the 1980s: General Evaluations. In *Saunders, C. T., ed.*, 1985, pp. 320–22.

Millar, James R. The Impact of Trade and Trade Denial on the U.S. Economy. In *Parrott, B., ed.*, 1985, pp. 324–50.   [G: U.S.S.R.; U.S.]

Milner, Chris. Empirical Analyses of the Costs of Protection. In *Greenaway, D., ed.*, 1985, pp. 119–37.   [G: Global]

Monke, Eric A. International Agriculture and Trade Policies: Implications for the United States: Commentary. In *Gardner, B. L., ed.*, 1985, pp. 79–82.   [G: U.S.; Global]

Monke, Eric A. and Taylor, Lester D. International Trade Constraints and Commodity Market Models: An Application to the Cotton Market. *Rev. Econ. Statist.*, February 1985, *67*(1), pp. 98–107.   [G: Global]

Moroz, Andrew R. Canada/U.S. Automotive Trade and Trade-policy Issues. In *Fretz, D.; Stern, R. and Whalley, J., eds.*, 1985, pp. 278–332.   [G: Canada; U.S.]

Mwase, Ngila. The African Preferential Trade Area: Towards a Sub-regional Economic Community in Eastern and Southern Africa. *J. World Trade Law*, Nov.:Dec. 1985, *19*(6), pp. 622–36.   [G: Africa]

Nanto, Dick K. Dimensions and Perceptions of the Trade Problem with Japan. In *Nanto, D. K., ed.*, 1985, pp. 23–40. [G: Japan; U.S.]

Nathanson, R. and Weinblatt, J. The General Effect of Export Restrictions on Commodity Markets. In *Weinblatt, J., ed.*, 1985, pp. 10–50.   [G: LDCs; MDCs]

Nau, Henry R. The NICs in a New Trade Round.

In *Preeg, E. H., ed.*, 1985, pp. 63–84.   [G: LDCs]

Nehmer, Stanley and Love, Mark W. Textiles and Apparel: A Negotiated Approach to International Competition. In *Scott, B. R. and Lodge, G. C., eds.*, 1985, pp. 230–62.   [G: U.S.]

Ng, Yen-Tak and Chu, David K. Y. The Geographical Endowment of China's Special Economic Zones. In *Wong, K. and Chu, D. K. Y., eds.*, 1985, pp. 40–56.   [G: China]

Nicolaides, P. Preferences for Developing Countries: A Critique. *J. World Trade Law*, July:Aug. 1985, *19*(4), pp. 373–86.   [G: LDCs]

Nogués, Julio J. Agriculture and Developing Countries in the GATT. *World Econ.*, June 1985, *8*(2), pp. 119–33.   [G: EEC]

Nogués, Julio J. Distortions, Factor Proportions and Efficiency Losses: Argentina in the Latin American Scenario. *Weltwirtsch. Arch.*, 1985, *121*(2), pp. 280–303.   [G: Argentina]

Nykryn, Jaroslav. Combining Import Deals with Export Activities. In *Saunders, C. T., ed.*, 1985, pp. 253–64.

Oblath, Gábor and Pete, Péter. Trade with the Soviet Union: The Finnish Case. *Acta Oecon.*, 1985, *35*(1–2), pp. 165–94.   [G: U.S.S.R.; Finland]

Oleson, B. T. Linkage of Agricultural Policy and Long Term Prospects in the International Grain Trade. *Can. J. Agr. Econ.*, August 1985, *32*, pp. 186–206.

Ondráček, Mojmír. Economic Policy of the Reagan Administration towards the Developing Countries. *Czech. Econ. Digest.*, February 1985, (1), pp. 63–89.   [G: U.S.; LDCs]

Orden, David. When Are Export Subsidies Rational? A Comment. *Agr. Econ. Res.*, Winter 1985, *37*(1), pp. 14–16.

Ortega, Luis. Economic Policy and Growth in Chile from Independence to the War of the Pacific. In *Abel, C. and Lewis, C. M., eds.*, 1985, pp. 147–71.   [G: Chile]

Ostry, Bernard. Canada/U.S. Automotive Trade and Trade-policy Issues: Comments. In *Fretz, D.; Stern, R. and Whalley, J., eds.*, 1985, pp. 338–40.   [G: Canada; U.S.]

Ostry, Sylvia. The World Trading Environment and Canadian Trade Policy. In *Conklin, D. W. and Courchene, T. J., eds.*, 1985, pp. 16–24.   [G: Canada]

Oswald, Rudy. Statement on U.S. Aims at the World Trade Ministers' Meeting: A Labor View. In *Adams, J., ed.*, 1985, pp. 78–84.   [G: U.S.]

Paarlberg, Philip L. When Are Export Subsidies Rational? A Reply. *Agr. Econ. Res.*, Winter 1985, *37*(1), pp. 20–22.   [G: U.S.]

Parks, Richard W. and Cox, Judith. The Economic Implications of Log Export Restrictions: Analysis of Existing and Proposed Legislation. In *Deacon, R. T. and Johnson, M. B., eds.*, 1985, pp. 247–73.   [G: Japan; U.S.]

Parrott, Bruce. Soviet Foreign Policy, Internal Politics, and Trade with the West. In *Parrott,*

B., ed., 1985, pp. 35–60.   **[G: U.S.S.R.]**

Parrott, Bruce. Trade, Technology, and Soviet-American Relations: Conclusion. **In** *Parrott, B., ed.*, 1985, pp. 351–62.   **[G: U.S.S.R.; U.S.]**

Parry, Thomas G. Protection and Employment in the Motor Car Sector: A Note. *Australian Econ. Pap.*, June 1985, *24*(44), pp. 222–24.

Pasurka, Carl A., Jr. Environmental Control Costs and U.S. Effective Rates of Protection. *Public Finance Quart.*, April 1985, *13*(2), pp. 161–82.   **[G: U.S.; OECD]**

Pearson, Charles and Ellyne, Mark. Surges of Imports: Perceptions versus Evidence. *World Econ.*, September 1985, *8*(3), pp. 299–315.   **[G: OECD]**

Perkins, J. A. Rehearsal for Protectionism: Australian Wool Exports and German Agriculture, 1830–80. *Australian Econ. Hist. Rev.*, March 1985, *25*(1), pp. 20–38.   **[G: Australia; Germany]**

Petit, Michel. Conflits entre stratégies agro-alimentaires: la confrontation entre les États-Unis et la Communauté Européenne. (Conflicts between Agri-Food Strategies: The Confrontation between the United States and the European Community. With English summary.) *Écon. Soc.*, July 1985, *19*(7), pp. 208–28.   **[G: U.S.; EEC]**

Pickford, Michael. A New Test for Manufacturing Industry Efficiency: An Analysis of the Results of Import License Tendering in New Zealand. *Int. J. Ind. Organ.*, June 1985, *3*(2), pp. 153–77.   **[G: New Zealand]**

Pilkey, Clifford G. Free Trade or Fair Trade: A Question of Who Profits. **In** *Conklin, D. W. and Courchene, T. J., eds.*, 1985, pp. 25–34.   **[G: Canada]**

Pomfret, Richard. Discrimination in International Trade: Extent, Motivation and Implications. *Econ. Int.*, February 1985, *38*(1), pp. 49–65.   **[G: OECD]**

Pomfret, Richard. The Trade Diversion Due to EC Enlargement: A Comment on Sawyer's Estimate [The Effects of the Second Enlargement of the EC on U.S. Exports to Europe]. *Weltwirtsch. Arch.*, 1985, *121*(3), pp. 560–61.   **[G: EEC; U.S.]**

du Pont, Peter. Kamikaze Economics. *Policy Rev.*, Fall 1985, (34), pp. 12–16.   **[G: U.S.]**

Porter, Michael G. The Labour of Liberalisation. **In** *Scutt, J. A., ed.*, 1985, pp. 37–61.   **[G: Australia]**

Preeg, Ernest H. An Agenda for U.S. Trade Policy toward Developing Countries. **In** *Preeg, E. H., ed.*, 1985, pp. 1–20. **[G: U.S.; LDCs]**

Pugel, Thomas A. and Walter, Ingo. U.S. Corporate Interests and the Political Economy of Trade Policy. *Rev. Econ. Statist.*, August 1985, *67*(3), pp. 465–73.   **[G: U.S.]**

Quirin, Brendan E. Issues in Canada/U.S. Energy Trade and Investment: A U.S. Perspective. **In** *Fretz, D.; Stern, R. and Whalley, J., eds.*, 1985, pp. 256–77.   **[G: Canada; U.S.]**

Raynauld, André. Government Export Subsidies. **In** *Conklin, D. W. and Courchene, T. J., eds.*, 1985, pp. 250–62.   **[G: Canada]**

Razavi, Hossein. Oil Production Policy and Economic Development in Mexico. *Energy J.*, April 1985, *6*(2), pp. 61–71.   **[G: Mexico]**

Reich, Robert B. Beyond Free Trade. **In** *Adams, J., ed.*, 1985, pp. 188–217.   **[G: U.S.]**

Reisman, Simon S. Trade Policy Options in Perspective. **In** *Conklin, D. W. and Courchene, T. J., eds.*, 1985, pp. 385–400. **[G: Canada]**

Reynolds, Clark W. Mexico and the United States: Studies in Economic Interaction: Fluctuations and Growth: Comments. **In** *Musgrave, P. B., ed.*, 1985, pp. 171– 75.   **[G: Mexico; U.S.]**

Roarty, Michael J. The EEC Common Agricultural Policy and Its Effects on Less-developed Countries. *Nat. Westminster Bank Quart. Rev.*, February 1985, pp. 2–17.   **[G: EEC; LDCs]**

Roberts, Roland K. and Martin, William J. The Effects of Alternative Beef Import Quota Regimes on the Beef Industries of the Aggregate United States and Hawaii. *Western J. Agr. Econ.*, December 1985, *10*(2), pp. 230–44.   **[G: U.S.]**

Robinson, Kenneth L. The Use of Agricultural Export Restrictions as an Instrument of Foreign Policy. **In** *[Heidhues, T.]*, 1985, pp. 214–28.   **[G: Selected Countries]**

Rode, Reinhard. Summary of Western Policies. **In** *Rode, R. and Jacobsen, H.-D., eds.*, 1985, pp. 243–50.   **[G: CMEA]**

Rode, Reinhard. Western Policies: The United States. **In** *Rode, R. and Jacobsen, H.-D., eds.*, 1985, pp. 184–99   **[G: U.S.; U.S.S.R.; CMEA]**

Roe, Terry and Senauer, Benjamin. Simulating Alternative Foodgrain Price and Trade Policies: An Application for the Dominican Republic. *J. Policy Modeling*, Winter 1985, *7*(4), pp. 635–48.   **[G: Dominican Republic]**

Roessler, Freider. The Provisional Application of the GATT: Note on the Report of the GATT Panel on the "Manufacturing Clause" in the U.S. Copyright Legislature. *J. World Trade Law*, May:June 1985, *19*(3), pp. 289–95.   **[G: U.S.]**

Roessler, Frieder. Countertrade and the GATT Legal System. *J. World Trade Law*, Nov.:Dec. 1985, *19*(6), pp. 604–14.   **[G: Global]**

Roessler, Frieder. The Scope, Limits and Function of the GATT Legal System. *World Econ.*, September 1985, *8*(3), pp. 287–98.   **[G: Global]**

Rom, Michael. Export Controls: An Institutional and Historical Perspective. **In** *Weinblatt, J., ed.*, 1985, pp. 197–219.

Rom, Michael. The Analysis of the GATT Provision. **In** *Weinblatt, J., ed.*, 1985, pp. 220–57.

Rotstein, Abraham. The Peaceable Kingdom of Free Trade. **In** *Conklin, D. W. and Courchene, T. J., eds.*, 1985, pp. 318–28.   **[G: Canada; U.S.]**

Rousslang, Donald J. and Suomela, John W. The Trade Effects of a U.S. Import Surcharge. *J.*

World Trade Law, Sept.:Oct. 1985, *19*(5), pp. 441–50. **[G: U.S.; Japan]**

Salvatore, Dominick. The New Protectionism and the Threat to World Welfare: Editor's Introduction. *J. Policy Modeling*, Spring 1985, *7*(1), pp. 1–22. **[G: U.S.; LDCs]**

Samuelson, Paul A. Analytics of Free-Trade or Protectionist Response by America to Japan's Growth Spurt. In *Shishido, T. and Sato, R., eds.*, 1985, pp. 3–18. **[G: Japan; U.S.]**

Sapir, André. North–South Issues in Trade in Services. *World Econ.*, March 1985, *8*(1), pp. 27–42. **[G: Global]**

Sarna, A. J. The Impact of a Canada–U.S. Free Trade Area. *J. Common Market Stud.*, June 1985, *23*(4), pp. 299–318. **[G: U.S.; Canada]**

Sawyer, W. Charles. The Effects of the Second Enlargement of the EC on U.S. Exports to Europe: Reply. *Weltwirtsch. Arch.*, 1985, *121*(3), pp. 562–63. **[G: EEC; U.S.]**

Scarfe, Brian L. A Western Perspective on Canadian Trade Options. In *Conklin, D. W. and Courchene, T. J., eds.*, 1985, pp. 95–103. **[G: Canada]**

Schiavone, Giuseppe. Western Policies: Italy. In *Rode, R. and Jacobsen, H.-D., eds.*, 1985, pp. 157–65. **[G: CMEA; Italy]**

Schmidt, Janet K. Some Issues in the Multilateral Management of Food Resources. In *Jordan, R. S., ed.*, 1985, pp. 65–95. **[G: U.S.]**

Schmidt, Ronald H. and Dunstan, Roger H. Effects of Reducing the Deficit with an Oil Import Tariff. *Fed. Res. Bank Dallas Econ. Rev.*, September 1985, pp. 15–24.

Schott, Jeffrey J. The GATT Ministerial: A Postmortem. In *Adams, J., ed.*, 1985, pp. 84–92. **[G: U.S.; EEC; LDCs]**

Schuh, G. Edward. International Agriculture and Trade Policies: Implications for the United States. In *Gardner, B. L., ed.*, 1985, pp. 56–78. **[G: U.S.; Global]**

Schultz, Siegfried. Neuer Protektionismus: Formen und Folgen im industriellen Bereich. (The New Protectionism—Its Forms and Consequences in the Industrial Sector. With English summary.) *Konjunkturpolitik*, 1985, *31*(3), pp. 188–207. **[G: OECD]**

Schydlowsky, Daniel M. Mexico and the United States: Studies in Economic Interaction: Fluctuations and Growth: Comments. In *Musgrave, P. B., ed.*, 1985, pp. 177–82. **[G: Mexico; U.S.]**

Scott, Norman. From Non-conventional to New Instruments of Trade Promotion? In *Saunders, C. T., ed.*, 1985, pp. 265–86. **[G: CMEA; OECD]**

Seitz, R. Lorne. Government Support for Canadian Exporters. In *Conklin, D. W. and Courchene, T. J., eds.*, 1985, pp. 227–49. **[G: Canada]**

Shihab-Eldin, Adnan. U.S.–Arab Trade and Economic Relations: An Arab Perspective. In *Czinkota, M. R. and Marciel, S., eds.*, 1985, pp. 3–16. **[G: U.S.; OPEC]**

Shoup, Carl S. International Arbitration of Transfer Pricing Disputes under Income Taxation.

In *Rugman, A. M. and Eden, L., eds.*, 1985, pp. 291–309.

Simonato, Rogelio E. El Argumento de la Industria Incipiente y las Políticas de Industrialización Selectivas. (Incipient Industry and Selective Industrialization Policies. With English summary.) *Económica (La Plata)*, Jan.-Apr. 1985, *31*(1), pp. 99–127. **[G: Argentina]**

Simonazzi, Annamaria. Crediti all'esportazione e concorrenza internazionale. (Export Credit and International Competition. With English summary.) *Polit. Econ.*, August 1985, *1*(2), pp. 229–58. **[G: Global]**

Sinclair, W. A. The Australian Policy Tradition–Protection All Around. In *Scutt, J. A., ed.*, 1985, pp. 28–36. **[G: Australia]**

Sit, Victor F. S. The Special Economic Zones of China: A New Type of Export Processing Zone? *Devel. Econ.*, March 1985, *23*(1), pp. 69–87. **[G: China]**

Sjaastad, Larry A. Commercial Policy in Brazil: An Overview: Comments. In *Salazar-Carrillo, J. and Fendt, R., Jr., eds.*, 1985, pp. 121–23. **[G: Brazil]**

Smith, Alan H. Soviet Trade Relations with the Third World. In *Cassen, R., ed.*, 1985, pp. 140–58. **[G: LDCs; U.S.S.R.]**

Smith, Arthur. The Role of Government in Export Promotion. In *Conklin, D. W. and Courchene, T. J., eds.*, 1985, pp. 222–26. **[G: Canada]**

Smith, Ian. UNCTAD: Failure of the UN Sugar Conference. *J. World Trade Law*, May:June 1985, *19*(3), pp. 296–301. **[G: Global]**

Smith, Murray G. and Steger, Debra P. Canada's Constitutional Quandary: The Federal/Provincial Dimension in International Economic Agreements. In *Conklin, D. W. and Courchene, T. J., eds.*, 1985, pp. 362–79. **[G: Canada]**

Snape, Richard H. Trade and Industry Policy: Comment. *Australian Econ. Rev.*, 3rd Quarter, Spring 1985, (71), pp. 82. **[G: Australia]**

Soukup, Václav. Economic Aggression of Imperialism against the Countries of the Socialist Community. *Czech. Econ. Digest.*, August 1985, (5), pp. 75–94. **[G: CMEA; OECD]**

Spero, Joan Edelman. U.S. Trade Policy and International Service Transactions: Comment. In *Inman, R. P., ed.*, 1985, pp. 179–81. **[G: U.S.]**

Spinelli, Franco. Protectionism and Real Wage Rigidity: A Discussion of the Macroeconomic Literature. *J. Policy Modeling*, Spring 1985, *7*(1), pp. 157–80. **[G: U.K.]**

Stainer, Robin. Commodity Agreements. In *Roberts, G., ed.*, 1985, pp. 17–24. **[G: Global]**

Stalson, Helena. U.S. Trade Policy and International Service Transactions. In *Inman, R. P., ed.*, 1985, pp. 161–78. **[G: U.S.]**

Steele, D. B. The Case for Global Economic Management and UN System Reform. *Int. Organ.*, Summer 1985, *39*(3), pp. 561–78. **[G: Global]**

Stegemann, Klaus. Anti-dumping Policy and the Consumer. *J. World Trade Law*, Sept.:Oct. 1985, *19*(5), pp. 466–84. **[G: U.S.; Canada]**

Stent, Angela E. Western Policies: The Federal Republic of Germany. In *Rode, R. and Jacobsen, H.-D., eds.*, 1985, pp. 99–119.
[G: W. Germany; CMEA]

Stent, Angela E. East–West Economic Relations and the Western Alliance. In *Parrott, B., ed.*, 1985, pp. 283–323. [G: OECD; U.S.S.R.]

Strange, Susan. Protectionism and World Politics. *Int. Organ.*, Spring 1985, *39*(2), pp. 233–59.
[G: Global]

Streeten, Paul. Developing-Country Trade Policies and the International Economic System: Comment. In *Preeg, E. H., ed.*, 1985, pp. 58–60. [G: Selected LDCs]

Sureshwaran, S. Sri Lanka–ASEAN Economic Relations. In *Wadhva, C. D. and Asher, M. G., eds.*, 1985, pp. 341–74.
[G: Sri Lanka; ASEAN]

Tabaczyński, Eugeniusz. Problems of Export-Oriented Restructuring of Polish Industry. In *[Levcik, F.]*, 1985, pp. 117–21.

Takacs, Wendy E. More on Protectionist Pressure and Aggregate Economic Conditions: A Reply [Pressures for Protectionism: An Empirical Analysis]. *Econ. Inquiry*, January 1985, *23*(1), pp. 183–84. [G: U.S.]

Taylor, Lance. The Crisis and Thereafter: Macroeconomic Policy Problems in Mexico. In *Musgrave, P. B., ed.*, 1985, pp. 147–70.
[G: Mexico]

Theriot, Lawrence H. and Matheson, JeNelle. Soviet Economic Relations with the Non-European CMEA: Cuba, Vietnam, and Mongolia. *Soviet E. Europ. Foreign Trade*, Summer–Fall 1985, *21*(1–2–3), pp. 144–90. [G: Cuba; Mongolia; Vietnam; U.S.S.R.]

Thirsk, Wayne R. Should Taxes Be Included in Trade Agreements? In *Conklin, D. W. and Courchene, T. J., eds.*, 1985, pp. 138–52.
[G: Canada]

Thomson, Guy P. C. Protectionism and Industrialization in Mexico, 1821–1854: The Case of Puebla. In *Abel, C. and Lewis, C. M., eds.*, 1985, pp. 125–46. [G: Mexico]

Thurow, Lester C. Exports and the Japanese Economy. In *Nanto, D. K., ed.*, 1985, pp. 1–12. [G: Japan; U.S.]

Tinbergen, Jan. International Trade, Protectionism, and the Third World. In *Bapna, A., ed.*, 1985, pp. 173–79. [G: LDCs]

Tolonen, Yrjänä. Neuvostoliiton-kaupan vaikutuksista Suomen vientiteollisuuden rakenteeseen. (Effects of Soviet Trade on the Structure of Finnish Export Industries. With English summary.) *Kansant. Aikak.*, 1985, *81*(3), pp. 298–303. [G: Finland; U.S.S.R.]

Tongzon, Jose L. and Felmingham, Bruce S. The Australian System of Tariff Preferences: ASEAN Experience. *Philippine Rev. Econ. Bus.*, Mar./June 1985, *22*(1/2), pp. 1–21.
[G: Australia; ASEAN]

Tracy, Michael. Evolution of American Agricultural Trade Policy and European Interaction: Comment. In *[Heidhues, T.]*, 1985, pp. 170–71. [G: U.S.]

Tremblay, Rodrigue. A Quebec Perspective on Canadian Trade Options. In *Conklin, D. W. and Courchene, T. J., eds.*, 1985, pp. 57–76.
[G: Canada]

Trimble, Phillip R. International Trade and the "Rule of Law." *Mich. Law Rev.*, February 1985, *83*(4), pp. 1016–32. [G: Global]

Tumlir, Jan. Who Benefits from Discrimination? *Schweiz. Z. Volkswirtsch. Statist.*, September 1985, *121*(3), pp. 249–58.

Tussie, Diana. El GATT y el comercio Norte-Sur: el caso del sector textil. (With English summary.) *Desarrollo Econ.*, April–June 1985, *25*(97), pp. 85–106. [G: Global]

Tyers, Rodney and Anderson, Kym. Price, Trade and Welfare Effects of Agricultural Protection: The Case of East Asia. *Rev. Marketing Agr. Econ.*, December 1985, *53*(3), pp. 113–40.
[G: Japan; S. Korea; Taiwan]

Tyler, William G. Effective Incentives for Domestic Market Sales and Exports: View of Anti-export Biases and Commercial Policy in Brazil, 1980–81. *J. Devel. Econ.*, August 1985, *18*(2–3), pp. 219–42. [G: Brazil]

Ukawa, Hidetoshi. Japan's Perspective on Trade. *Challenge*, July/August 1985, *28*(3), pp. 18–26.
[G: Japan; U.S.]

von Urff, Winfried. The Use of Agricultural Export Restrictions as an Instrument of Foreign Policy: Comment. In *[Heidhues, T.]*, 1985, pp. 229–31.

Vaince, Z. A. Assessment of Trade Effects of the EEC-GSP Scheme on Pakistan and Projections. *Pakistan Econ. Soc. Rev.*, Winter 1985, *23*(2), pp. 113–34. [G: EEC; Pakistan]

Van den Panhuyzen, W. Japan's Industrial Policy: From Promotion to Protection. *Tijdschrift Econ. Manage.*, 1985, *30*(1), pp. 45–74.
[G: Japan]

Vanden Abeele, Michel. International Trade and Exchange Rates: Concluding Remarks. In *Peeters, T.; Praet, P. and Reding, P., eds.*, 1985, pp. 413–18.

Vernardakis, Nikos. Capital Utilization, Its Determinants and Export Subsidies. *Greek Econ. Rev.*, August 1985, *7*(2), pp. 125–43.
[G: Greece]

Vernon, Raymond. Old Rules and New Players: GATT in the World Trading System. In *Vernon, R.*, 1985, pp. 3–28.

Vernon, Raymond. Soviet Commodity Power in International Economic Relations. In *Vernon, R.*, 1985, pp. 167–75. [G: U.S.S.R.]

Viatte, Gérard. Agricultural Trade Policy Issues in the 1980s: Comment. In *[Heidhues, T.]*, 1985, pp. 266–69.

Wallich, Henry C. Statement to the U.S. House Subcommittee on International Economic Policy and Trade of the Committee on Foreign Affairs, March 22, 1985. *Fed. Res. Bull.*, May 1985, *71*(5), pp. 308–12. [G: U.S.]

Walsh, James I. The Effect on Third Countries of Mandated Countertrade. *J. World Trade Law*, Nov.-Dec. 1985, *19*(6), pp. 592–603.

Warhurst, John and O'Loghlin, Gillian. Federal–State Issues in External Economic Relations.

In *Drysdale, P. and Shibata, H., eds.*, 1985, pp. 190–202. [G: Australia]

Warley, Thorald K. Agricultural Trade Policy Issues in the 1980s. In *[Heidhues, T.]*, 1985, pp. 248–65.

Warren, Jake. Canada/United States Trade and Investment Issues: Keynote Address. In *Fretz, D.; Stern, R. and Whalley, J., eds.*, 1985, pp. 21–31. [G: Canada; U.S.]

Waverman, Leonard. Trade in Communications and Data Processing: Comments. In *Stern, R. M., ed.*, 1985, pp. 291–98. [G: Canada; U.S.]

Weidenbaum, Murray L. Freeing Trade. In *Boaz, D. and Crane, E. H., eds.*, 1985, pp. 91–110. [G: U.S.]

Weigel, Wolfgang. Austrian Economic Policy: A Comment. *Empirica*, 1985, *12*(1), pp. 109–10. [G: Austria]

Weinblatt, J. and Nathanson, R. Restrictions of Exports from LDCs and Their Impact on World Economy. In *Weinblatt, J., ed.*, 1985, pp. 128–42. [G: LDCs; MDCs]

Weinblatt, J. and Nathanson, R. The Effects of Export Restrictions on Economic Growth in LDCs. In *Weinblatt, J., ed.*, 1985, pp. 181–96. [G: Selected LDCs]

Weinblatt, J. and Rodrik-Farhi, Miriam. Monetary Effects of Export Restrictions on World Commodity Markets. In *Weinblatt, J., ed.*, 1985, pp. 143–60. [G: LDCs; MDCs]

Weinstein, Michael M. Job Impact Statements: A Lesson from the 1930s. *Challenge*, Sept./Oct. 1985, *28*(4), pp. 55–58. [G: U.S.]

Weintraub, Sidney. Selective Trade Liberalization and Restriction. In *Preeg, E. H., ed.*, 1985, pp. 167–84.

Weintraub, Sidney. Trade and Structural Change. In *Musgrave, P. B., ed.*, 1985, pp. 79–107. [G: Mexico; U.S.]

Wendt, E. Allan. Oil Products Prospects for an Open Trading Regime. *J. Energy Devel.*, Autumn 1985, *11*(1), pp. 1–4. [G: OECD]

Wetter, Theresa. Trade Policy Developments in the Steel Sector. *J. World Trade Law*, Sept.:Oct. 1985, *19*(5), pp. 485–96. [G: EEC; U.S.; Japan]

Whalley, John. Canada/U.S. Energy Issues: A Canadian Perspective: Comments. In *Fretz, D.; Stern, R. and Whalley, J., eds.*, 1985, pp. 252–55. [G: Canada; U.S.]

Whalley, John and Wigle, Randall. Price and Quantity Rigidities in Adjustment to Trade Policy Changes: Alternative Formulations and Initial Calculations. In *Jungenfelt, K. and Hague, D. [Sir], eds.*, 1985, pp. 246–71. [G: Global]

Wijnbergen, Sweder. Optimal Taxation of Imported Energy under Price Uncertainty. *Oxford Econ. Pap.*, March 1985, *37*(1), pp. 83–92.

Wilkinson, B. W. Canada/U.S. Free Trade and Canadian Economic, Cultural, and Political Sovereignty. In *Conklin, D. W. and Courchene, T. J., eds.*, 1985, pp. 291–307. [G: Canada; U.S.]

Wolf, Martin. How to Unravel the Multi-fibre Arrangement. *World Econ.*, September 1985, *8*(3), pp. 235–48. [G: Global]

Wolff, Alan Wm. International Competitiveness of American Industry: The Role of U.S. Trade Policy. In *Scott, B. R. and Lodge, G. C., eds.*, 1985, pp. 301–27. [G: U.S.]

Wong, Kwan-Yiu and Chu, David K. Y. Export Processing Zones and Special Economic Zones as Locomotives of Export-Led Economic Growth. In *Wong, K. and Chu, D. K. Y., eds.*, 1985, pp. 1–24. [G: Asia]

Wonnacott, Ronald J. Bilateral Trade Liberalization with the United States and Multilateral Liberalization in the GATT: Selected Observations. In *Conklin, D. W. and Courchene, T. J., eds.*, 1985, pp. 335–40. [G: Canada; U.S.]

Wonnacott, Ronald J. Canada/U.S. Economic Relations: A Canadian View. In *Fretz, D.; Stern, R. and Whalley, J., eds.*, 1985, pp. 72–97. [G: Canada; U.S.]

Woolcock, Stephen. Western Policies: Great Britain. In *Rode, R. and Jacobsen, H.-D., eds.*, 1985, pp. 141–56. [G: U.K.; CMEA]

Yannopoulos, George N. EC External Commercial Policies and East–West Trade in Europe. *J. Common Market Stud.*, September 1985, *24*(1), pp. 21–38. [G: EEC; CMEA]

Yannopoulos, George N. The European Community's Common External Commercial Policy: Internal Contradictions and Institutional Weaknesses. *J. World Trade Law*, Sept.:Oct. 1985, *19*(5), pp. 451–65. [G: EEC]

Yarbrough, Beth V. and Yarbrough, Robert M. Free Trade, Hegemony, and the Theory of Agency. *Kyklos*, 1985, *38*(3), pp. 348–64.

Yochelson, John N. Outlook for U.S. Economic Diplomacy: Europe and the Pacific Basin. In *Yochelson, J. N., ed.*, 1985, pp. 15–25. [G: U.S.]

423 Economic Integration

4230 General

Aktan, Okan H. The Second Enlargement of the European Communities: Probable Effects on the Members and the New Entrants. *Europ. Econ. Rev.*, August 1985, *28*(3), pp. 279–308. [G: EEC]

Bautina, N. The Economic Mechanism of CMEA Member Nations (General Trends of Development). *Prob. Econ.*, January 1985, *27*(9), pp. 23–41. [G: CMEA]

Gauhar, Altaf. Regional Integration: The Latin American Experience: Introduction. In *Gauhar, A., ed.*, 1985, pp. vii–xvii. [G: Latin America]

4232 Theory of Economic Integration

Collier, Paul. Commodity Aggregation in Customs Unions [3 by 3 Theory of Customs Unions]. *Oxford Econ. Pap.*, December 1985, *37*(4), pp. 677–82.

Corden, W. Max. Economies of Scale and Customs Union Theory. In *Corden, W. M.*, 1985, pp. 58–68.

El-Agraa, Ali M. International Economic Integration. In *Greenaway, D., ed.*, 1985, pp. 183–206. [G: Global]

Neven, Damien J. and Phlips, Louis. Discriminating Oligopolists and Common Markets. *J. Ind. Econ.*, December 1985, *34*(2), pp. 133–49.

Patterson, Seymour. Trade Creation and Trade Diversion and Transport Costs. *Atlantic Econ. J.*, December 1985, *13*(4), pp. 34–38.

Riezman, Raymond G. Customs Unions and the Core. *J. Int. Econ.*, November 1985, *19*(3/4), pp. 355–65.

Yu, Eden S. H. Toward a Theory of Customs Unions with Foreign Investment. *Econ. Int.*, May 1985, *38*(2), pp. 222–35.

4233 Economic Integration: Policy and Empirical Studies

Ajanant, Juanjai. Economic Relations between Thailand and South Asia. In *Wadhva, C. D. and Asher, M. G., eds.*, 1985, pp. 185–222. [G: Thailand; S. Asia]

Altmann, Franz-Lothar. Eastern Policies: Eastern Europe (CMEA 6) In *Rode, R. and Jacobsen, H.-D., eds.*, 1985, pp. 266–80. [G: CMEA; OECD; LDCs]

Ariff, Mohamed. Malaysia–South Asia Economic Relations. In *Wadhva, C. D. and Asher, M. G., eds.*, 1985, pp. 66–114. [G: Malaysia; S. Asia]

Armstrong, Harvey W. The Reform of the European Community Regional Policy. *J. Common Market Stud.*, June 1985, *23*(4), pp. 319–43. [G: EEC]

Asher, Mukul G. Economic Relations between Singapore and South Asia. In *Wadhva, C. D. and Asher, M. G., eds.*, 1985, pp. 138–84. [G: Singapore; S. Asia]

Asher, Mukul G. and Wadhva, Charan D. ASEAN–South Asia Economic Relations: An Overview. In *Wadhva, C. D. and Asher, M. G., eds.*, 1985, pp. 1–26. [G: ASEAN; S. Asia]

Avramović, Dragoslav. Collapse of Intra-Latin American Trade 1980–83: Causes and Prospects. In *Gauhar, A., ed.*, 1985, pp. 133–38. [G: Latin America]

Baibakov, Nikolai. Cooperation of the Member Nations of the CMEA in Planning Activity at the Contemporary Stage. *Soviet E. Europ. Foreign Trade*, Winter 1985-86, *21*(4), pp. 6–15. [G: CMEA]

Baldinelli, Elvio. Latin America—The Hour for Unity. In *Gauhar, A., ed.*, 1985, pp. 194–209. [G: Latin America]

Bennett, Karl M. A Note on Exchange Rate Policy and Caribbean Integration. *Soc. Econ. Stud.*, December 1985, *34*(4), pp. 35–43. [G: Caribbean]

Bergmann, Denis. Une stratégie exportatrice pour l'agriculture de la CEE. (An Export Strategy for the E.E.C. Farming. With English summary.) *Écon. Soc.*, July 1985, *19*(7), pp. 229–42. [G: EEC]

Bethkenhagen, Jochen. Economic Relations—Interdependence or Marginal Factor?: Trade. In *Rode, R. and Jacobsen, H.-D., eds.*, 1985, pp. 17–35. [G: CMEA; OECD]

Bourguignon-Wittke, R., et al. Five Years of the Directly Elected European Parliament: Performance and Prospects. *J. Common Market Stud.*, September 1985, *24*(1), pp. 39–59. [G: EEC]

van Brabant, Jozef M. The Relationship between World and Socialist Trade Price—Some Empirical Evidence. *J. Compar. Econ.*, September 1985, *9*(3), pp. 233–51. [G: CMEA]

Brada, Josef C. Soviet Subsidization of Eastern Europe: The Primacy of Economics over Politics? *J. Compar. Econ.*, March 1985, *9*(1), pp. 80–92. [G: CMEA]

Brada, Josef C. and Méndez, José A. Economic Integration among Developed, Developing and Centrally Planned Economies: A Comparative Analysis. *Rev. Econ. Statist.*, November 1985, *67*(4), pp. 549–56. [G: Global]

Browning, Martin J. The Trend Level of Imports by CMEA Countries. *J. Compar. Econ.*, December 1985, *9*(4), pp. 363–70. [G: CMEA]

Buess, Thomas. Perspektiven für eine engere Zusammenarbeit zwischen der Europäischen Gemeinschaft und den EFTA-Mitgliedstaaten. (Perspectives for Closer Cooperation between the European Community and the EFTA-Member Countries. With English summary.) *Aussenwirtschaft*, December 1985, *40*(4), pp. 341–87. [G: EEC]

Bulmer, Simon. The European Council's First Decade: Between Interdependence and Domestic Politics. *J. Common Market Stud.*, December 1985, *24*(2), pp. 89–104. [G: EEC]

Bunce, Valerie. The Empire Strikes Back: The Evolution of the Eastern Bloc from a Soviet Asset to a Soviet Liability. *Int. Organ.*, Winter 1985, *39*(1), pp. 1–46. [G: U.S.S.R.]

Burnside, Alec. Enforcement of EEC Competition Law by Interim Measures: The *Ford* Case. *J. World Trade Law*, January:February 1985, *19*(1), pp. 34–53. [G: EEC]

Černý, Miroslav. Economic Cooperation and Coordination of National Economic Plans between Czechoslovakia and the Soviet Union after 1985. *Czech. Econ. Digest.*, February 1985, (1), pp. 41–49. [G: Czechoslovakia; U.S.S.R.]

Černohubý, Milan. Relations between Czechoslovakia and the European Economic Community. *Czech. Econ. Digest.*, February 1985, (1), pp. 50–62. [G: EEC; Czechoslovakia]

Cherviakov, Igor' and Nikht, Lotar. The Most Important Factor for Accelerating Scientific and Technical Progress. *Soviet E. Europ. Foreign Trade*, Winter 1985-86, *21*(4), pp. 29–36. [G: CMEA]

Cioffi, Antonio, et al. An Evaluation of the Effects of the EC Quota System on the Italian Dairy Market. *Europ. Rev. Agr. Econ.*, 1985, *12*(4), pp. 389–400. [G: Italy]

Corado, Cristina and de Melo, Jaime. A Simulation Model to Estimate the Effects of Portugal's Entry into the Common Market. *Economia (Portugal)*, October 1985, 9(3), pp. 403–30.
[G: Portugal; EEC]

Csáki, Csaba. An Outlook of Food Supply and Demand in the CMEA Countries: Results of the IIASA/FAP Model System. *Acta Oecon.*, 1985, 35(1–2), pp. 145–64. [G: CMEA]

Culem, Claudy and Chau, Nguyen T. M. Les performances relatives à l'exportation de produits manufacturés de l'EUBL au cours de la période 1970–1980. (With English summary.) *Cah. Écon. Bruxelles*, 2nd Trimester 1985, (106), pp. 126–57. [G: EEC]

Czepurko, Aleksander. Projections of East–West Trade—Past Experience and Future Uses. In *[Levcik, F.]*, 1985, pp. 191–202. [G: CMEA; OECD]

Czyzewski, B.; Tomaszewicz, Andrzej and Tomaszewicz, Lucija. Proposals for the Linkage of CMEA-Country Models. In *Smyshlyaev, A., ed.*, 1985, pp. 29–42. [G: CMEA]

Debonneuil, Xavier and Galy, Michel. Can Exchange Rate Predictability Be Achieved without Monetary Convergence?—Evidence from the EMS: Comment. *Europ. Econ. Rev.*, June-July 1985, 28(1–2), pp. 117–20.
[G: W. Europe]

Demas, William G. and Scotland, Jasper. Experiences in Regional Integration and Cooperation: The Case of the Caribbean Community and Common Market (CARICOM). In *Gauhar, A., ed.*, 1985, pp. 159–70. [G: CARICOM]

Donges, Jürgen B. and Schatz, Klaus-Werner. The Iberian Countries Facing EC Membership: Starting Conditions for Their Industry. *Weltwirtsch. Arch.*, 1985, 121(4), pp. 756–78.
[G: Spain; Portugal]

Drysdale, Peter. Building the Foundations of a Pacific Economic Community. In *Shishido, T. and Sato, R., eds.*, 1985, pp. 46–58.
[G: E. Asia]

El-Agraa, Ali M. International Economic Integration. In *Greenaway, D., ed.*, 1985, pp. 183–206. [G: Global]

El-Agraa, Ali M. On 'Measuring the Economic Consequences of British Membership of the European Economic Community.' *Appl. Econ.*, August 1985, 17(4), pp. 709–11.
[G: U.K.]

Eskelinen, Heikki. International Integration and Regional Economic Development: The Finnish Experience. *J. Common Market Stud.*, March 1985, 23(3), pp. 229–55. [G: EEC; Finland]

Fennell, Rosemary. A Reconsideration of the Objectives of the Common Agricultural Policy. *J. Common Market Stud.*, March 1985, 23(3), pp. 257–76. [G: EEC]

Flemming, J. S. Can Exchange Rate Predictability Be Achieved without Monetary Convergence?—Evidence from the EMS: Comment. *Europ. Econ. Rev.*, June-July 1985, 28(1–2), pp. 121–22. [G: W. Europe]

Forte, Francesco. The Theory of Social Contract

and the EEC. In *[Peacock, A.]*, 1985, pp. 149–66.

Fritsch-Bournazel, Renata. Western Policies: France. In *Rode, R. and Jacobsen, H.-D., eds.*, 1985, pp. 128–40. [G: France; CMEA]

Garvey, Tom. The Role of the European Community. In *Wells, N., ed.*, 1985, pp. 76–90.
[G: EEC]

Gormely, Patrick J. Impact of EEC Enlargement on Ireland's Trade in Manufactured Goods. *Econ. Soc. Rev.*, October 1985, 17(1), pp. 1–10. [G: Ireland; Greece; EEC; Portugal]

Grant, Rudolph W. and Paul, Una M. Perceptions of Caribbean Regional Integration: A Comparative Study of the Perceptions of Caribbean Teacher Trainees. *Soc. Econ. Stud.*, March 1985, 34(1), pp. 1–26. [G: Guyana]

Grigorova, Ekaterina. International Specialization and Cooperation in Production among the CMEA Countries in Foreign Trade with Machinery and Equipment. *Soviet E. Europ. Foreign Trade*, Winter 1985-86, 21(4), pp. 90–103.
[G: CMEA]

Harrison, Glenn W. and Kimbell, Larry J. Economic Interdependence in the Pacific Basin: A General Equilbrium Approach. In *Piggott, J. and Whalley, J., eds.*, 1985, pp. 143–74.
[G: Selected Countries]

Harrop, Jeffrey. Crisis in the Machine Tool Industry: A Policy Dilemma for the European Community. *J. Common Market Stud.*, September 1985, 24(1), pp. 61–75. [G: EEC]

Harvey, D. R. and Thomson, Kenneth J. Costs, Benefits and the Future of the Common Agricultural Policy. *J. Common Market Stud.*, September 1985, 24(1), pp. 1–20. [G: EEC]

Hogan, Michael J. American Marshall Planners and the Search for a European Neocapitalism. *Amer. Hist. Rev.*, February 1985, 90(1), pp. 44–72. [G: EEC; U.S.]

Holub, Alois. What Hinders Development Should Stimulate It. *Czech. Econ. Digest.*, March 1985, (2), pp. 77–86. [G: Global]

Holzman, Franklyn D. Comecon: A "Trade-destroying" Customs Union? *J. Compar. Econ.*, December 1985, 9(4), pp. 410–23.
[G: CMEA]

Joefield-Napier, Wallace. External Public Debt and Public Finance in OECS Member Countries and Belize: 1977–1982. *Soc. Econ. Stud.*, December 1985, 34(4), pp. 59–89.
[G: Caribbean]

Jopp, Mathias. Western Policies: The European Community. In *Rode, R. and Jacobsen, H.-D., eds.*, 1985, pp. 166–83. [G: EEC; CMEA]

Kalirajan, K. P. Economic Relations between Indonesia and South Asia. In *Wadhva, C. D. and Asher, M. G., eds.*, 1985, pp. 29–65.
[G: Indonesia; S. Asia]

Kalirajan, K. P. Trade among Developing Countries: The Case of South Asian Regional Cooperation. *J. Econ. Devel.*, July 1985, 10(1), pp. 153–67. [G: Bangladesh; India; Pakistan; Sri Lanka]

Kitamura, Hiroshi. Japan and Asian–Pacific Economic Integration. In *Didsbury, H. F., Jr.*, ed., 1985, pp. 193–210. [G: ASEAN]

Köves, András. The Import Restriction Squeeze and Import Maximizing Ambitions: Some Connections of East–West vs. Intra-CMEA Trade. *Acta Oecon.*, 1985, *34*(1–2), pp. 99–112. [G: CMEA]

Langeheine, Bernd and Weinstock, Ulrich. Graduated Integration: A Modest Path towards Progress. *J. Common Market Stud.*, March 1985, *23*(3), pp. 185–97. [G: EEC]

Langhammer, Rolf J. and Hiemenz, Ulrich. Declining Competitiveness of EC Suppliers in ASEAN Markets: Singular Case or Symptom? *J. Common Market Stud.*, December 1985, *24*(2), pp. 105–19. [G: EEC; ASEAN]

Lavigne, Marie. Intra-CMEA Integration and Foreign Economic Relations of the CMEA Countries. In *[Levcik, F.]*, 1985, pp. 231–37. [G: CMEA]

Machowski, Heinrich. Eastern Policies: The Soviet Union. In *Rode, R. and Jacobsen, H.-D.*, eds., 1985, pp. 251–65. [G: U.S.S.R.; CMEA]

Malinvaud, Edmond. European Development and the World Economy. In *Bergsten, C. F.*, ed., 1985, pp. 15–30. [G: W. Europe]

McLachlan, D. L. Discriminatory Public Procurement, Economic Integration and the Role of Bureaucracy. *J. Common Market Stud.*, June 1985, *23*(4), pp. 357–72. [G: U.S.; Canada; EEC; Japan]

Melvin, Michael. Currency Substitution and Western European Monetary Unification. *Economica*, February 1985, *52*(205), pp. 79–91. [G: EEC]

Mertens, Yves and Ginsburgh, Victor. Product Differentiation and Price Discrimination in the European Community: The Case of Automobiles. *J. Ind. Econ.*, December 1985, *34*(2), pp. 151–66. [G: Belgium; France; W. Germany; Italy; U.K.]

Micossi, Stefano. The Intervention and Financing Mechanisms of the EMS and the Role of the ECU. *Banca Naz. Lavoro Quart. Rev.*, December 1985, (155), pp. 327–45.

Montes, Iván Lavados. The Role of the University in Integration. In *Gauhar, A.*, ed., 1985, pp. 234–47. [G: Latin America]

Mwase, Ngila. The African Preferential Trade Area: Towards a Sub-regional Economic Community in Eastern and Southern Africa. *J. World Trade Law*, Nov.:Dec. 1985, *19*(6), pp. 622–36. [G: Africa]

Nagy, András. Changes in the Structure and Intensity of East–West Trade. *Acta Oecon.*, 1985, *35*(3–4), pp. 359–75. [G: CMEA]

Neuman, Henri. Institutional and Financial Aspects of Public Enterprise International Cooperation. *Ann. Pub. Co-op. Econ.*, January–June 1985, *56*(1–2), pp. 145–54. [G: EEC]

Nicoll, William. Paths to European Unity. *J. Common Market Stud.*, March 1985, *23*(3), pp. 199–206. [G: EEC]

Ocampo, José Antonio. Financial Aspects of Intraregional Trade in Latin America. In *Gauhar, A.*, ed., 1985, pp. 112–32. [G: Latin America]

Okolo, Julius Emeka. Integrative and Cooperative Regionalism: The Economic Community of West Africa. *Int. Organ.*, Winter 1985, *39*(1), pp. 121–53. [G: W. Africa]

Orlando, Luigi. Anche le imprese sono responsabili dei ritardi dell'integrazione europea. (Companies Too Are Responsible for Delays toward European Integration. With English summary.) *Bancaria*, October 1985, *41*(10), pp. 1036–40. [G: EEC]

Oudiz, Gilles. European Policy Coordination: An Evaluation. *Rech. Écon. Louvain*, 1985, *51*(3–4), pp. 301–39. [G: EEC]

Paliwoda, Stanley J. and Liebrenz, Marilyn L. Technology Transfer within Eastern Europe. In *Samli, A. C.*, ed., 1985, pp. 87–106. [G: CMEA]

Parravicini, Giannino. Una moneta più del mercato che del principe: lo scudo. (The Market Starts Using the Money Created by EEC. With English summary.) *Bancaria*, October 1985, *41*(10), pp. 1029–35. [G: EEC]

Penaherrera, Germanico Salgado. The Andean Pact: Problems and Perspectives. In *Gauhar, A.*, ed., 1985, pp. 171–93. [G: ANDEAN]

Perova, V. CMEA-Member Countries' Cooperation in Constructing Industrial Projects. *Soviet E. Europ. Foreign Trade*, Winter 1985-86, *21*(4), pp. 79–89. [G: CMEA]

Petit, Michel. Conflits entre stratégies agro-alimentaires: la confrontation entre les États-Unis et la Communauté Européenne. (Conflicts between Agri-Food Strategies: The Confrontation between the United States and the European Community. With English summary.) *Écon. Soc.*, July 1985, *19*(7), pp. 208–28. [G: U.S.; EEC]

de Pitta e Cunha, Paulo. The Portuguese Economic System and Accession to the European Community. *Economia (Portugal)*, May 1985, *9*(2), pp. 277–300. [G: Portugal]

Pomfret, Richard. Measuring the Economic Consequences of British Membership of the European Economic Community. *Appl. Econ.*, August 1985, *17*(4), pp. 705–07. [G: U.K.]

Raines, J. Patrick. Common Market Competition Policy: The EC–IBM Settlement. *J. Common Market Stud.*, December 1985, *24*(2), pp. 137–47. [G: EEC]

Reza, Sadrel. Bangladesh–ASEAN Trade Relations. In *Wadhva, C. D. and Asher, M. G.*, eds., 1985, pp. 225–52. [G: S. Asia; Bangladesh]

Ritson, Christopher. Implications of Non-monetary Objectives in the Agricultural Policy of the European Community: Comment. In *[Heidhues, T.]*, 1985, pp. 150–51. [G: EEC]

Roarty, Michael J. The EEC Common Agricultural Policy and Its Effects on Less-developed Countries. *Nat. Westminster Bank Quart. Rev.*, February 1985, pp. 2–17. [G: EEC; LDCs]

Robson, Peter. Performance and Priorities for Regional Integration with Special Reference to

West Africa. In *Rose, T., ed.*, 1985, pp. 265–77. [G: W. Africa]

Rode, Reinhard. Summary of Western Policies. In *Rode, R. and Jacobsen, H.-D., eds.*, 1985, pp. 243–50. [G: CMEA]

Rode, Reinhard. Western Policies: The United States. In *Rode, R. and Jacobsen, H.-D., eds.*, 1985, pp. 184–99. [G: U.S.; U.S.S.R.; CMEA]

Rogoff, Kenneth S. Can Exchange Rate Predictability Be Achieved without Monetary Convergence? Evidence from the EMS. *Europ. Econ. Rev.*, June-July 1985, 28(1–2), pp. 93–115. [G: W. Europe]

Rosenthal, Gert. The Lessons of Economic Integration in Latin America: The Case of Central America. In *Gauhar, A., ed.*, 1985, pp. 139–58. [G: Central America]

Rossen, Stein. Aspects of Economic Integration Policies in Africa, with Special Reference to the Southern African Development Coordination Conference. In *Rose, T., ed.*, 1985, pp. 278–89. [G: Sub-Saharan Africa]

Rye, Ajit Singh. Philippine–South Asia Economic Relations. In *Wadhva, C. D. and Asher, M. G., eds.*, 1985, pp. 115–37. [G: Philippines; S. Asia]

Sargent, Jane A. Corporatism and the European Community. In *Grant, W., ed.*, 1985, pp. 229–53. [G: EEC]

Sarna, A. J. The Impact of a Canada–U.S. Free Trade Area. *J. Common Market Stud.*, June 1985, 23(4), pp. 299–318. [G: U.S.; Canada]

Scamacci, Paolo. Il recepimento delle direttive comunitarie nell'ordinamento bancario italiano. (The Incorporation of EC Community Directives into the Italian Banking Law. With English summary.) *Bancaria*, May 1985, 41(5), pp. 564–68. [G: EEC; Italy]

Schiavone, Giuseppe. Western Policies: Italy. In *Rode, R. and Jacobsen, H.-D., eds.*, 1985, pp. 157–65. [G: CMEA; Italy]

Siddiqi, Hafiz G. A. Bangladesh–ASEAN Investment Relations. In *Wadhva, C. D. and Asher, M. G., eds.*, 1985, pp. 253–68. [G: Bangladesh; ASEAN]

Somavía, Juan. Political Cooperation, Border Disputes and Democracy. In *Gauhar, A., ed.*, 1985, pp. 98–111. [G: Latin America]

Spencer, John E. The European Economic Community: General Equilibrium Computations and the Economic Implications of Membership. In *Piggott, J. and Whalley, J., eds.*, 1985, pp. 119–42. [G: EEC]

Steinherr, Alfred. Policy Coordination in the European Economic Community. *Rech. Écon. Louvain*, 1985, 51(3–4), pp. 285–99. [G: EEC]

Stent, Angela E. Western Policies: The Federal Republic of Germany. In *Rode, R. and Jacobsen, H.-D., eds.*, 1985, pp. 99–119. [G: W. Germany; CMEA]

Sureshwaran, S. Sri Lanka–ASEAN Economic Relations. In *Wadhva, C. D. and Asher, M. G., eds.*, 1985, pp. 341–74. [G: Sri Lanka; ASEAN]

van Thiel, Servaas. Economic Cooperation in Central Africa: Some Tax Aspects. *Bull. Int. Fiscal Doc.*, February 1985, 39(2), pp. 86–87. [G: Central Africa]

Tomassini, Luciano. The Disintegration of the Integration Process: Towards New Forms of Regional Cooperation. In *Gauhar, A., ed.*, 1985, pp. 210–33. [G: Latin America]

Tsoukalis, Loukas and Strauss, Robert. Crisis and Adjustment in European Steel: Beyond Laisse-Faire. *J. Common Market Stud.*, March 1985, 23(3), pp. 207–28. [G: EEC]

Usher, J. A. The Scope of Community Competence—Its Recognition and Enforcement. *J. Common Market Stud.*, December 1985, 24(2), pp. 121–36. [G: EEC]

Venit, James S. EEC Patent Licensing Revisited: The Commission's Patent License Regulation. *Antitrust Bull.*, Summer 1985, 30(2), pp. 457–526.

Vernon, Raymond. The Fragile Foundations of East–West Trade. In *Vernon, R.*, 1985, pp. 199–212.

Wadhva, Charan D. India–ASEAN Economic Relations. In *Wadhva, C. D. and Asher, M. G., eds.*, 1985, pp. 269–320. [G: India; ASEAN]

Wadhva, Charan D. and Pradhan, Radhe S. Nepal–ASEAN Economic Relations. In *Wadhva, C. D. and Asher, M. G., eds.*, 1985, pp. 321–40. [G: Nepal; S. Asia]

Weinschenck, Günther. Implications of Nonmonetary Objectives in the Agricultural Policy of the European Community. In *[Heidhues, T.]*, 1985, pp. 135–49. [G: EEC]

Weintraub, Sidney. A U.S.–Israel Free-Trade Area. *Challenge*, July/August 1985, 28(3), pp. 47–50. [G: U.S.; Israel]

Williams, Marion. An Analysis of Regional Trade and Payments Arrangements in CARICOM 1971–1983. *Soc. Econ. Stud.*, December 1985, 34(4), pp. 3–33. [G: Caribbean]

Winters, L. Alan. Separability and the Modelling of International Economic Integration: U.K. Exports to Five Industrial Countries. *Europ. Econ. Rev.*, April 1985, 27(3), pp. 335–53. [G: EEC; U.S.; Japan]

Wolf, Thomas A. Estimating "Foregone Gains" in Soviet–East European Trade: A Methodological Note. *Comparative Econ. Stud.*, Fall 1985, 27(3), pp. 83–98. [G: CMEA]

Woolcock, Stephen. Western Policies: Great Britain. In *Rode, R. and Jacobsen, H.-D., eds.*, 1985, pp. 141–56. [G: U.K.; CMEA]

Yannopoulos, George N. EC External Commercial Policies and East–West Trade in Europe. *J. Common Market Stud.*, September 1985, 24(1), pp. 21–38. [G: EEC; CMEA]

Yannopoulos, George N. The European Community's Common External Commercial Policy: Internal Contradictions and Institutional Weaknesses. *J. World Trade Law*, Sept.:Oct. 1985, 19(5), pp. 451–65. [G: EEC]

Zorrilla, Jorge Torres and Gana, Eduardo. Trade and Equilibrium among the ALADI Countries. *Cepal Rev.*, December 1985, (27), pp. 69–77. [G: Latin America]

430 INTERNATIONAL FINANCE

4300 General

Brandsma, Andries S. and Pijpers, J. R. Coordinated Strategies for Economic Cooperation between Europe and the United States. *Weltwirtsch. Arch.*, 1985, *121*(4), pp. 661–81. [G: U.S.; EEC]

Clausen, A. W. Corrective Initiatives in International Trade and Finance. In *Bapna, A., ed.*, 1985, pp. 23–31. [G: Global]

Cline, William R. Changing Stresses on the World Economy. *World Econ.*, June 1985, *8*(2), pp. 135–52. [G: Global]

Jolly, Richard. Structural Change within the North. In *Bapna, A., ed.*, 1985, pp. 71–79. [G: LDCs; MDCs]

de Larosière, Jacques. Policy Options for Developed and Developing Economies. In *Bapna, A., ed.*, 1985, pp. 59–69. [G: LDCs; MDCs]

Wallich, Henry C. U.S. Monetary Policy in an Interdependent World. In *[Bloomfield, A. I.]*, 1985, pp. 33–44.

431 Open Economy Macroeconomics; Exchange Rates

4310 General

Artus, Jacques R. and Young, John H. Fixed and Flexible Exchange Rates: A Renewal of the Debate. In *Adams, J., ed.*, 1985, pp. 250–85.

Balassa, Bela. Korea in the 1980s: Policies and Prospects. In *Balassa, B.*, 1985, pp. 236–57. [G: S. Korea; Singapore; Taiwan; Hong Kong]

de Bernis, Gévard. Observations sur la "contrainte extérieure." (Comments of "Foreign Constraints." With English summary.) *Écon. Soc.*, April 1985, *19*(4), pp. 191–229. [G: France]

Branson, William H. Inflation, Employment and External Constraints: An Overview of the French Economy during the Seventies: Comments. In *Melitz, J. and Wyplosz, C., eds.*, 1985, pp. 43–47. [G: France]

Bruno, Michael. The Reforms and Macroeconomic Adjustments: Introduction. *World Devel.*, August 1985, *13*(8), pp. 867–69. [G: Argentina; Chile; Uruguay]

Buiter, Willem H. and Marston, Richard C. International Economic Policy Coordination: Introduction. In *Buiter, W. H. and Marston, R. C., eds.*, 1985, pp. 1–7.

Cline, William R. Long-term Forecasts in International Economics. *Amer. Econ. Rev.*, May 1985, *75*(2), pp. 120–26. [G: Global]

Fernandez, Roque B. The Expectations Management Approach to Stabilization in Argentina during 1976–82. *World Devel.*, August 1985, *13*(8), pp. 871–92. [G: Argentina]

Goodhart, Charles A. E. Alternative Monetary Regimes. *Hong Kong Econ. Pap.*, 1985, (16), pp. 1–13. [G: OECD]

Griffith-Jones, Stephany. Impact of World Prices on Development: The International Environment. In *Griffith-Jones, S. and Harvey, C., eds.*, 1985, pp. 13–51. [G: LDCs; MDCs]

Griffith-Jones, Stephany. World Prices and Development: Introduction. In *Griffith-Jones, S. and Harvey, C., eds.*, 1985, pp. 1–12.

Griffith-Jones, Stephany and Harvey, Charles. World Prices and Development: Conclusions. In *Griffith-Jones, S. and Harvey, C., eds.*, 1985, pp. 311–49. [G: Selected LDCs]

Hattersley, Roy. A New Exchange Control Scheme. *Fisc. Stud.*, August 1985, *6*(3), pp. 9–13. [G: U.K.]

Iglesias, Enrique V. Crisis, Development and Options. In *Gauhar, A., ed.*, 1985, pp. 42–68. [G: Latin America]

Kemp, Donald S. Balance-of-Payments Concepts—What Do They Really Mean? In *Adams, J., ed.*, 1985, pp. 232–50.

Krugman, Paul R. U.S. Macro-Economic Policy and the Developing Countries. In *Sewell, J. W.; Feinberg, R. E. and Kallab, V., eds.*, 1985, pp. 31–49. [G: U.S.; LDCs]

Kyriazis, Nicholas K. The Drachma's Adhesion to the European Monetary System. Possible Effects. *Kredit Kapital*, 1985, *18*(4), pp. 504–14. [G: Greece]

Lal, Deepak and van Wijnbergen, Sweder. Government Deficits, the Real Interest Rate and LDC Debt: On Global Crowding Out. *Europ. Econ. Rev.*, November 1985, *29*(2), pp. 157–91. [G: Global]

McCombie, J. S. L. Economic Growth, the Harrod Foreign Trade Multiplier and the Hicks Super-multiplier. *Appl. Econ.*, February 1985, *17*(1), pp. 55–72. [G: OECD]

Oudiz, Gilles and Sterdyniak, Henri. Inflation, Employment and External Constraints: An Overview of the French Economy during the Seventies. In *Melitz, J. and Wyplosz, C., eds.*, 1985, pp. 9–42. [G: France]

Rhomberg, Rudolf R. Balance of Payments Financing and Reserve Creation. *Int. Monet. Fund Staff Pap.*, March 1985, *32*(1), pp. 1–21.

Schüller, Alfred and Hamel, Hannelore. On the Membership of Socialist Countries in the International Monetary Fund. *Acta Oecon.*, 1985, *34*(1–2), pp. 113–30.

Shepherd, A. Ross. A Comment on Lerner's "Extortion Tax" Plan [Lerner's Contribution to Economics]. *J. Econ. Lit.*, September 1985, *23*(3), pp. 1192.

4312 Open Economy Macroeconomic Theory: Balance of Payments and Adjustment Mechanisms

Agbonyitor, Alberto D. K. Recurrent Expenditure Commitment, External Imbalance, Devaluation and Inflation in the Developing Economies. *J. Econ. Devel.*, December 1985, *10*(2), pp. 87–99. [G: LDCs]

Aizenman, Joshua. Adjustment to Monetary Policy and Devaluation under Two-Tier and Fixed Exchange Rate Regimes. *J. Devel. Econ.*, May–June 1985, *18*(1), pp. 153–69.

Aizenman, Joshua. Openness, Relative Prices, and Macro-policies. *J. Int. Money Finance*, March 1985, *4*(1), pp. 5–17.

Aizenman, Joshua. Tariff Liberalization Policy and Financial Restrictions. *J. Int. Econ.*, November 1985, *19*(3/4), pp. 241–55.

Aizenman, Joshua. Wage Flexibility and Openness. *Quart. J. Econ.*, May 1985, *100*(2), pp. 539–50.

Aizenman, Joshua and Frenkel, Jacob A. On the Tradeoff between Wage Indexation and Foreign Exchange Intervention. *Weltwirtsch. Arch.*, 1985, *121*(1), pp. 1–17.

Alogoskoufis, George S. Macroeconomic Policy and Aggregate Fluctuations in a Semi-industrialized Open Economy: Greece 1951–1980. *Europ. Econ. Rev.*, October 1985, *29*(1), pp. 35–61. [G: Greece]

Amano, Akihiro. Alternative Approaches to Exchange-Rate Determination and Some Implications of the Structural Balance-of-Payments Approach for International Macroeconomic Interdependence. In *Ando, A., et al., eds.*, 1985, pp. 169–216. [G: Selected Countries; Japan]

Ambler, Steven and McKinnon, Ronald I. U.S. Monetary Policy and the Exchange Rate: Comment [A Critical Appraisal of McKinnon's World Money Supply Hypothesis]. *Amer. Econ. Rev.*, June 1985, *75*(3), pp. 557–59. [G: U.S.]

Ancot, J.-P.; Paelinck, J. H. P. and Viaene, Jean-Marie. A Dynamic Exchange-Rate Model. In *Peeters, T.; Praet, P. and Reding, P., eds.*, 1985, pp. 347–75. [G: U.S.; W. Germany; Netherlands]

Andersen, Torben M. Arbejdstidsforkortelse som konjunkturpolitisk instrument. (Shortening of Working Hours as an Instrument in Stabilization Policy. With English summary.) *Nationaløkon. Tidsskr.*, 1985, *123*(2), pp. 145–59. [G: Netherlands]

Angeloni, Ignazio and Galli, Giampaolo. The Interaction of Credit and Foreign Exchange Markets in a Stylized Model of the Italian Financial Sector. *Greek Econ. Rev.*, April 1985, *7*(1), pp. 53–70.

Aoki, Masanao. Misadjustment to Anticipated Shocks: An Example of Exchange-Rate Response. *J. Int. Money Finance*, September 1985, *4*(3), pp. 415–20.

Aoki, Masanao. Monetary Reaction Functions in a Small Open Economy. *J. Econ. Dynam. Control*, September 1985, *9*(1), pp. 1–24.

Argy, Victor E. Flexible Exchange Rates—Twelve Years After—Are There Alternatives? *Australian Econ. Rev.*, 2nd Quarter 1985, (70), pp. 27–36.

Argy, Victor E. and Murray, G. L. Effects of Sterilising a Balance of Payments Surplus on Domestic Yields—A Formal Analysis. *J. Int. Money Finance*, June 1985, *4*(2), pp. 223–36.

Artis, Michael J. and Karakitsos, E. Monetary and Exchange Rate Targets in an Optimal Control Setting. In *Bhandari, J. S., ed.*, 1985, pp. 212–46.

Artus, Patrick. Fiscal and Monetary Policies under a Flexible Exchange-Rate System: Comments. In *Melitz, J. and Wyplosz, C., eds.*, 1985, pp. 335–37. [G: France]

Artus, Patrick. L'indexation des salaires: une optique de stabilisation macro-économique. (Price Indexation of Wages: A Stabilization Approach. With English summary.) *Revue Écon.*, March 1985, *36*(2), pp. 291–320. [G: France; W. Germany; U.K.]

Artus, Patrick. La politique monétaire en économie ouverte avec imparfaite mobilité des capitaux et réaction des autorités sur le marché des changes. (Monetary Policy in an Open Economy with Imperfect Capital Mobility and Central Bank Reaction on the Foreign Exchange Market. With English summary.) *Finance*, June 1985, *6*(1), pp. 71–101.

Aschauer, David Alan and Greenwood, Jeremy. Macroeconomic Effects of Fiscal Policy. *Carnegie-Rochester Conf. Ser. Public Policy*, Autumn 1985, *23*, pp. 91–138.

Bahmani-Oskooee, Mohsen. Demand for International Reserves: Survey of Recent Empirical Studies. *Appl. Econ.*, April 1985, *17*(2), pp. 359–75.

Bakalis, Steve and Hazari, Bharat R. Unemployment, Capital Underutilization and Welfare in a Small Open Economy. *Greek Econ. Rev.*, December 1985, *7*(3), pp. 226–41.

Barro, Robert J. Federal Deficits, Interest Rates, and Monetary Policy: Comment. *J. Money, Credit, Banking*, Pt. 2, Nov. 1985, *17*(4), pp. 682–85. [G: U.S.]

Barry, Frank G. Fiscal Policy in a Small Open Economy with Unemployment and Capital Accumulation. *Scand. J. Econ.*, 1985, *87*(3), pp. 474–86.

Basevi, Giorgio and Cavazzuti, Filippo. Regole del gioco o discrezionalità amministrativa? Il caso della libertà di movimento di capitali in Italia. (Rules vs discretion: the Case of Capital Movements in the Italian Balance of Payments. With English summary.) *Polit. Econ.*, April 1985, *1*(1), pp. 53–70. [G: Italy]

Baumgarten, Klaus and Linsenbühler, Georg. An Integrated Portfolio Model of a Small Open Economy, or Fleming–Mundell Revisited. *Jahr. Nationalökon. Statist.*, May 1985, *200*(3), pp. 262–79.

Bean, Charles R. Macroeconomic Policy Co-ordination: Theory and Evidence. *Rech. Écon. Louvain*, 1985, *51*(3–4), pp. 267–83. [G: OECD]

Begg, David K. H. Macroeconomic Policy Design in an Interdependent World: Comment. In *Buiter, W. H. and Marston, R. C., eds.*, 1985, pp. 268–71.

Bender, Dieter. Wechselkursbindung in Entwicklungsländern: Eine optimale Anpassungsstrategie an flexible Wechselkurse? (Basket Pegging in Developing Countries. With English summary.) *Kredit Kapital*, 1985, *18*(3), pp. 320–46. [G: LDCs]

Bhagwati, Jagdish N. The Nature of Balance of Payments Difficulties in Developing Countries. In *Bhagwati, J. N. (I)*, 1985, pp. 138–43.

Bhagwati, Jagdish N.; Brecher, Richard A. and Hatta, Tatsuo. The Generalized Theory of Transfers and Welfare: Bilateral Transfers in a Multilateral World. In *Bhagwati, J. N. (II)*, 1985, pp. 216–28.

Bhandari, Jagdeep S. Experiments with the Optimal Currency Composite. *Southern Econ. J.*, January 1985, *51*(3), pp. 711–30.

Bhandari, Jagdeep S. Informational Regimes, Economic Disturbances, and Exchange Rate Management. In *Bhandari, J. S., ed.*, 1985, pp. 126–53.

Bhandari, Jagdeep S. Speculation and the Crawling Peg: Some Further Issues. *De Economist*, 1985, *133*(1), pp. 78–86.

Bhandari, Jagdeep S. The Flexible Exchange Basket: A Macroeconomic Analysis. *J. Int. Money Finance*, March 1985, *4*(1), pp. 19–41.

Bhandari, Jagdeep S. World Trade Ptterns, Economic Disturbances, and Exchange-Rate Management. *J. Int. Money Finance*, September 1985, *4*(3), pp. 331–60.

Bilson, John F. O. On the Franc: Comments. In *Melitz, J. and Wyplosz, C., eds.*, 1985, pp. 223–27. **[G: France]**

Birolo, Adriano. Equilibrio esterno, inflazione e crescita in un modello multisettoriale. (With English summary.) *Econ. Polít.*, August 1985, *2*(2), pp. 161–85.

Black, Stanley W. The Effect of Alternative Intervention Policies on the Variability of Exchange Rates: The Harrod Effect. In *Bhandari, J. S., ed.*, 1985, pp. 72–82.

Blejer, Mario I. and Hillman, Arye L. On the Dynamic Non-equivalence of Tariffs and Quotas in the Monetary Model of the Balance of Payments: Reply. *J. Int. Econ.*, May 1985, *18*(3/4), pp. 381–82.

Blinder, Alan S. Federal Deficits, Interest Rates, and Monetary Policy: Comment. *J. Money, Credit, Banking*, Pt. 2, Nov. 1985, *17*(4), pp. 685–89.

Blomqvist, Ake G. An Analytical Approach to Interest Rate Determination in Developing Countries: Comments. *Pakistan Devel. Rev.*, Autumn-Winter 1985, *24*(3/4), pp. 494–95. **[G: Pakistan]**

Bordo, Michael David and Ellson, Richard Wayne. A Model of the Classical Gold Standard with Depletion. *J. Monet. Econ.*, July 1985, *16*(1), pp. 109–20.

Braga de Macedo, Jorge. International Policy Coordination in Dynamic Macroeconomic Models: Comment. In *Buiter, W. H. and Marston, R. C., eds.*, 1985, pp. 319–26.

Braga de Macedo, Jorge. Macroeconomic Policy under Currency Inconvertibility. In *Connolly, M. B. and McDermott, J., eds.*, 1985, pp. 336–55.

Branson, William H. International Capital Movements. *Economia (Portugal)*, January 1985, *9*(1), pp. 3–28. **[G: Asia]**

Branson, William H. The Dynamic Interaction of Exchange Rates and Trade Flows. In *Peeters,*

T.; Praet, P. and Reding, P., eds., 1985, pp. 133–60.

de Brunhoft, Suzanne. Taux de change et monnaie internationale. (Exchange Rates and International Money. With English summary.) *Écon. Soc.*, April 1985, *19*(4), pp. 53–65.

Bryant, Ralph C. Policy Coordination and Dynamic Games: Comment. In *Buiter, W. H. and Marston, R. C., eds.*, 1985, pp. 213–19.

Buffie, Edward F. Price–Output Dynamics, Capital Inflows and Real Appreciation. *Oxford Econ. Pap.*, December 1985, *37*(4), pp. 529–51.

Buiter, Willem H. International Policy Coordination in Historical Perspective: A View from the Interwar Years: Comment. In *Buiter, W. H. and Marston, R. C., eds.*, 1985, pp. 178–81.

Buiter, Willem H. The Real Wage Gap and Employment: Comments. In *Melitz, J. and Wyplosz, C., eds.*, 1985, pp. 71–80. **[G: France; U.S.; EEC]**

Buiter, Willem H. and Eaton, Jonathan. Policy Decentralization and Exchange Rate Management in Interdependent Economies. In *Bhandari, J. S., ed.*, 1985, pp. 31–54.

Bureau, Donomique. Cohérence entre choix des projets et politique de régulation macroéconomique. (Coherent Choices of Projects and Policy of Macroeconomic Regulation. With English summary.) *Ann. INSEE*, Jan.-Mar. 1985, (57), pp. 51–73.

Butlin, M. W. Imported Inputs in an Optimising Model of a Small Open Economy. *J. Int. Econ.*, February 1985, *18*(1/2), pp. 101–21.

Büttler, Hans-Jürg. Real Effective Exchange Rates of Imports, Exports, and Trade Balance. *Schweiz. Z. Volkswirtsch. Statist.*, December 1985, *121*(4), pp. 375–90. **[G: Switzerland]**

Calvo, Guillermo A. Currency Substitution and the Real Exchange Rate: The Utility Maximization Approach. *J. Int. Money Finance*, June 1985, *4*(2), pp. 175–88.

Calvo, Guillermo A. Reserves and the Managed Float: A Search for the Essentials. *J. Int. Money Finance*, March 1985, *4*(1), pp. 43–60.

Canzoneri, Matthew B. Fiscal Expenditures and International Economic Interdependence: Comment. In *Buiter, W. H. and Marston, R. C., eds.*, 1985, pp. 73–75.

Canzoneri, Matthew B. and Gray, Jo Anna. Monetary Policy Games and the Consequences of Non-cooperative Behavior. *Int. Econ. Rev.*, October 1985, *26*(3), pp. 547–64.

Canzoneri, Matthew B. and Underwood, John M. Wage Contracting, Exchange Rate Volatility, and Exchange Intervention Policy. In *Bhandari, J. S., ed.*, 1985, pp. 247–71.

Cappelen, Adne; Offerdal, Erik and Strøm, Steinar. Oil Revenues and the Norwegian Economy in the Seventies. In *Bjerkholt, O. and Offerdal, E., eds.*, 1985, pp. 35–62. **[G: Norway]**

Caranza, Cesare. International Aspects of Monetary Policy: Comments. In *Ando, A., et al., eds.*, 1985, pp. 223–24.

Carlberg, Michael. External versus Internal Public Debt—A Theoretical Analysis of the Long-run Burden. Z. *Nationalökon.*, 1985, *45*(2), pp. 141–54.

Carlozzi, Nicholas and Taylor, John B. International Capital Mobility and the Coordination of Monetary Rules. In *Bhandari, J. S., ed.*, 1985, pp. 186–211.

Casas, François R. and Choi, Eun Kwan. The Leontief Paradox: Continued or Resolved? *J. Polit. Econ.*, June 1985, *93*(3), pp. 610–15.
[G: U.S.]

Chand, Sheetal K. and Onitsuka, Yusuke. Stocks, Flows, and Some Exchange Rate Dynamics for the Currency Substitution Model. *J. Int. Money Finance*, March 1985, *4*(1), pp. 61–82.

Chevallier, François and Pollin, Jean-Paul. La transmission internationale des chocs monétaires en changes flexibles. (The International Transmission of Monetary Shocks into Flexible Changes. With English summary.) *Revue Écon.*, November 1985, *36*(6), pp. 1301–44.

Chiesa, Gabriella. Oil Shock, Saving, Investment and Trade Balance: The Role of Short Run Rigidity versus Long Run Flexibility. An Intertemporal Approach. *Econ. Int.*, February 1985, *38*(1), pp. 1–20.

Chipman, John S. Relative Prices, Capital Movements, and Sectoral Technical Change: Theory and an Empirical Test. In *Jungenfelt, K. and Hague, D. [Sir], eds.*, 1985, pp. 395–454.
[G: W. Germany; Sweden]

Claassen, Emil-Maria and Wyplosz, Charles. Capital Controls: Some Principles and the French Experience. In *Melitz, J. and Wyplosz, C., eds.*, 1985, pp. 237–67. [G: France]

Coes, Donald V. Imperfect Capital Mobility, Risk, and Brazilian Foreign Borrowing. In *Salazar-Carrillo, J. and Fendt, R., Jr., eds.*, 1985, pp. 38–52. [G: Brazil]

Cooper, Richard N. Floating Exchange Rates: Experience and Prospects: Comment. *Brookings Pap. Econ. Act.*, 1985, (2), pp. 451–56.
[G: U.S.; Japan; W. Germany; France; U.K.]

Coppock, D. J. The Impact Effects of Devaluation in a Three Sector Monetary Model. *Brit. Rev. Econ. Issues*, Spring 1985, *7*(16), pp. 1–46.

Corden, W. Max. Booming Sector and Dutch Disease Economics: Survey and Consolidation. In *Corden, W. M.*, 1985, pp. 246–68.

Corden, W. Max. Exchange Rate Protection. In *Corden, W. M.*, 1985, pp. 271–87. [G: U.K.]

Corden, W. Max. Macroeconomic Policy Interaction under Flexible Exchange Rates: A Two-Country Model. *Economica*, February 1985, *52*(205), pp. 9–23.

Corden, W. Max. On Transmission and Coordination under Flexible Exchange Rates. In *Buiter, W. H. and Marston, R. C., eds.*, 1985, pp. 8–24.

Corden, W. Max. Protection and the Real Exchange Rate. In *Corden, W. M.*, 1985, pp. 302–10.

Corden, W. Max. Real Wage Rigidity, Devaluation and Import Restrictions. In *Corden, W. M.*, 1985, pp. 311–26.

Corden, W. Max and Neary, J. Peter. Booming

Sector and De-industrialization in a Small Open Economy. In *Corden, W. M.*, 1985, pp. 225–45.

Currie, David. Overlapping Wage Contracts and Exchange Rate Overshooting. *Greek Econ. Rev.*, April 1985, *7*(1), pp. 71–81.

Currie, David. Structural Instability in a Rational Expectations Model of a Small Open Economy with a J-Curve. *Economica*, February 1985, *52*(205), pp. 25–36.

Currie, David and Levine, Paul. Macroeconomic Policy Design in an Interdependent World. In *Buiter, W. H. and Marston, R. C., eds.*, 1985, pp. 228–68.

Currie, David and Levine, Paul. Simple Macropolicy Rules for the Open Economy. *Econ. J.*, Supplement 1985, *95*, pp. 60–70.

Daniel, Betty C. Monetary Autonomy and Exchange Rate Dynamics under Currency Substitution. *J. Int. Econ.*, August 1985, *19*(1/2), pp. 119–39.

Daniel, Betty C. Optimal Foreign Exchange-Rate Policy for a Small Open Economy. *J. Int. Money Finance*, December 1985, *4*(4), pp. 523–36.

Daniel, Betty C.; Fried, Harold O. and Tower, Edward. On the Dynamic Non-equivalence of Tariffs and Quotas in the Monetary Model of the Balance of Payments: Comment. *J. Int. Econ.*, May 1985, *18*(3/4), pp. 373–79.

Darby, Michael R. Monetary Policy in the Large Open Economy. In *Ando, A., et al., eds.*, 1985, pp. 143–67. [G: OECD]

De Grauwe, Paul. Capital Controls: Some Principles and the French Experience: Comments. In *Melitz, J. and Wyplosz, C., eds.*, 1985, pp. 269–73. [G: France]

Decaluwe, Bernard and Bhandari, Jagdeep S. Cloisonnements imparfaits double marché des changes et anticipations rationnelles. (Imperfect Segmentation, Dual Exchange Markets and Rational Expectations. With English summary.) *Revue Écon.*, November 1985, *36*(6), pp. 1345–71.

Decaluwe, Bernard and Bhandari, Jagdeep S. Le régime du double marché des changes sous les Tropiques: une analayse théorique. (A Model of a Dual Exchange-Rate System. With English summary.) *L'Actual. Econ.*, December 1985, *61*(4), pp. 428–52.

Donders, J. H. M. The Golden Rule of Accumulation and the Open Economy. *De Economist*, 1985, *133*(4), pp. 545–57.

Dornbusch, Rudiger. Imperfect Capital Mobility, Exchange Risk and Brazilian Foreign Borrowing: Comments. In *Salazar-Carrillo, J. and Fendt, R., Jr., eds.*, 1985, pp. 53–58.
[G: Brazil]

Dornbusch, Rudiger. Intergenerational and International Trade. *J. Int. Econ.*, February 1985, *18*(1/2), pp. 123–39.

Driskill, Robert and McCafferty, Stephen. Exchange Market Intervention under Rational Expectations with Imperfect Capital Substitutability. In *Bhandari, J. S., ed.*, 1985, pp. 83–95.

Driskill, Robert and McCafferty, Stephen. Exchange Rate Dynamics with Wealth Effects: Some Theoretical Ambiguities. *J. Int. Econ.*, November 1985, *19*(3/4), pp. 329–40.

Dwyer, Gerald P., Jr. Federal Deficits, Interest Rates, and Monetary Policy. *J. Money, Credit, Banking*, Pt. 2, Nov. 1985, *17*(4), pp. 655–81. [G: U.S.]

Eaton, Jonathan. Optimal and Time Consistent Exchange-Rate Management in an Overlapping-Generations Economy. *J. Int. Money Finance*, March 1985, *4*(1), pp. 83–100.

Edison, Hali J. The Rise and Fall of Sterling: Testing Alternative Models of Exchange Rate Determination. *Appl. Econ.*, December 1985, *17*(6), pp. 1003–21. [G: U.K.]

Eichengreen, Barry. International Policy Coordination in Historical Perspective: A View from the Interwar Years. In *Buiter, W. H. and Marston, R. C., eds.*, 1985, pp. 139–78.

Eichengreen, Barry. The Franc and the French Financial Sector: Comments. In *Melitz, J. and Wyplosz, C., eds.*, 1985, pp. 175–79. [G: France]

Emerson, Michael. The Effects of American Policies—A New Classical Interpretation: Comment. In *Buiter, W. H. and Marston, R. C., eds.*, 1985, pp. 131–34. [G: U.S.; OECD]

Engel, Charles M. and Flood, Robert P. Exchange Rate Dynamics, Sticky Prices and the Current Account. *J. Money, Credit, Banking*, August 1985, *17*(3), pp. 312–27.

Engle, Charles. Reliability of Policy Announcements and the Effects of Monetary Policy. *Europ. Econ. Rev.*, November 1985, *29*(2), pp. 137–55.

Eun, Cheol S. A Model of International Asset Pricing under Imperfect Commodity Arbitrage. *J. Econ. Dynam. Control*, November 1985, *9*(3), pp. 273–89.

Faini, Riccardo. Macroeconomic Adjustment under Foreign Investment: Comment. In *Weiserbs, D., ed.*, 1985, pp. 203–07. [G: Netherlands; Spain]

Feenstra, Robert C. Anticipated Devaluations, Currency Flight, and Direct Trade Controls in a Monetary Economy. *Amer. Econ. Rev.*, June 1985, *75*(3), pp. 386–401.

Feldstein, Martin. Global Economic Imbalances: The View from North America. In *Bergsten, C. F., ed.*, 1985, pp. 5–10. [G: U.S.]

Felmingham, Bruce S. A Second Best Strategy for the Recovery of Full Employment in the Open Economy. *J. Macroecon.*, Fall 1985, *7*(4), pp. 469–91.

Fender, John. Oil in a Dynamic Two Good Model. *Oxford Econ. Pap.*, June 1985, *37*(2), pp. 249–63.

Feroldi, Mathieu and Melitz, Jacques. The Franc and the French Financial Sector. In *Melitz, J. and Wyplosz, C., eds.*, 1985, pp. 149–74. [G: France]

Flood, Robert P. and Hodrick, Robert J. Central Bank Intervention in a Rational Open Economy: A Model with Asymmetric Information. In *Bhandari, J. S., ed.*, 1985, pp. 154–85.

Flood, Robert P. and Hodrick, Robert J. Optimal Price and Inventory Adjustment in an Open-Economy Model of the Business Cycle. *Quart. J. Econ.*, Supp. 1985, *100*, pp. 887–914.

Frankel, Jeffrey A. On the Franc. In *Melitz, J. and Wyplosz, C., eds.*, 1985, pp. 185–221. [G: France]

Fratianni, Michele and Nabli, Mustapha. Inflation and Output with Rational Expectations in Open Economies. *Weltwirtsch. Arch.*, 1985, *121*(1), pp. 33–52. [G: Belgium; France; W. Germany; Italy; Netherlands]

Freedman, Charles. Alternative Approaches to Exchange-Rate Determination and Some Implications of the Structural Balance-of-Payments Approach for International Macroeconomic Interdepedence: Comments. In *Ando, A., et al., eds.*, 1985, pp. 217–21. [G: Japan; Selected Countries]

Frenkel, Jacob A. Fiscal Policy and the Exchange Rate in the Big Seven: Transmission of U.S. Government Spending Shocks: Comment. *Europ. Econ. Rev.*, June-July 1985, *28*(1–2), pp. 43–47. [G: OECD; U.S.]

Frenkel, Jacob A. On the Franc: Comments. In *Melitz, J. and Wyplosz, C., eds.*, 1985, pp. 233–36. [G: France; Selected OECD]

Frenkel, Jacob A. and Razin, Assaf. Fiscal Expenditures and International Economic Interdependence. In *Buiter, W. H. and Marston, R. C., eds.*, 1985, pp. 37–73.

Frenkel, Jacob A. and Razin, Assaf. Government Spending, Debt, and International Economic Interdependence. *Econ. J.*, September 1985, *95*(379), pp. 619–36.

Frisch, Helmut. Real and Nominal Shocks in an Open Economy Model with Wage Contracts. *Giorn. Econ.*, July-Aug. 1985, *44*(7–8), pp. 347–73.

Fuhrmann, Wilfried. Zur Verbindung von Elastizitätsansatz und J-Kurve. (Elasticity Approach and the J-Curve. With English summary.) *Jahr. Nationalökon. Statist.*, May 1985, *200*(3), pp. 229–38.

Fujita, Seiichi. A Critical Note on "Dollar Standard." *Kobe Univ. Econ.*, 1985, (31), pp. 69–91. [G: U.S.]

von Furstenberg, George M. Adjustment with IMF Lending. *J. Int. Money Finance*, June 1985, *4*(2), pp. 209–22. [G: LDCs]

Galli, Giampaolo. International Coordination in the Design of Macroeconomic Policies: Comment. *Europ. Econ. Rev.*, June-July 1985, *28*(1–2), pp. 83–87. [G: OECD]

Garavello, Oscar. La svalutazione nei P.V.S. con estese rigidità dell'offerta: un'analisi settoriale. (Devaluation and Stagflation in L.D.C.s: The Role of Supply Rigidity. With English summary.) *Rivista Int. Sci. Econ. Com.*, May 1985, *32*(5), pp. 427–52. [G: LDCs]

Gardner, Grant W. Money, Prices, and the Current Account in a Dual Exchange Rate Regime. *J. Int. Econ.*, May 1985, *18*(3/4), pp. 321–38.

Giavazzi, Francesco and Giovannini, Alberto. Tassi di cambio manovrati e politica monetaria. (Monetary Policy in a System of Managed Exchange Rates. With English summary.) *Giorn. Econ.*, Mar.-Apr. 1985, *44*(3–4), pp. 117–33.

Giovannetti, Giorgia. The International Transmission of Price Level and Output Disturbances between Raw Material Producer Countries and Industrial Countries: A Theoretical Analysis. *Econ. Notes*, 1985, (1), pp. 148–61.

Glasner, David. A Reinterpretation of Classical Monetary Theory. *Southern Econ. J.*, July 1985, *52*(1), pp. 46–67.

Goldstein, Henry N. and Haynes, Stephen E. U.S. Monetary Policy and the Exchange Rate: Reply [A Critical Appraisal of McKinnon's World Money Supply Hypothesis]. *Amer. Econ. Rev.*, June 1985, *75*(3), pp. 560–61. [G: U.S.]

Gray, Jo Anna. International Policy Coordination in Historical Perspective: A View from the Interwar Years: Comment. In *Buiter, W. H. and Marston, R. C., eds.*, 1985, pp. 181–83.

Greenwood, Jeremy and Kimbrough, Kent P. Capital Controls and Fiscal Policy in the World Economy. *Can. J. Econ.*, November 1985, *18*(4), pp. 743–65.

Haberler, Gottfried. The Market for Foreign Exchange and the Stability of the Balance of Payments: A Theoretical Analysis. In *Haberler, G.*, 1985, pp. 143–65.

Hamada, Koichi. Macroeconomic Policy Design in an Interdependent World: Comment. In *Buiter, W. H. and Marston, R. C., eds.*, 1985, pp. 271–73.

Handler, Heinz. Capital Mobility versus Sterilization Policy: A Time Series Approach for Austria. *Empirica*, 1985, *12*(2), pp. 163–90. [G: Austria]

Harkness, Jon. Optimal Exchange Intervention for a Small Open Economy. *J. Int. Money Finance*, March 1985, *4*(1), pp. 101–12.

Harkness, Jon. OPEC, Rationality, and the Macroeconomy. *J. Macroecon.*, Fall 1985, *7*(4), pp. 567–76.

Heinemann, Hans-Joachim. Zum Zusammenwirken von Direktinvestitionen und Technologietransfer. (On Direct Investment Combined with Technology Transfer. With English summary.) *Ifo-Studien*, 1985, *31*(2), pp. 93–107.

Helpman, Elhanan and Razin, Assaf. Floating Exchange Rates with Liquidity Constraints in Financial Markets. *J. Int. Econ.*, August 1985, *19*(1/2), pp. 99–117.

Henderson, Dale W. On Transmission and Coordination under Flexible Exchange Rates: Comment. In *Buiter, W. H. and Marston, R. C., eds.*, 1985, pp. 24–32.

Henderson, Dale W. The Effects of Autonomous Capital Inflows: An Elaboration of Bloomfield's Analysis. In *[Bloomfield, A. I.]*, 1985, pp. 45–56.

Hinshaw, Randall. Inflation, Exchange Rates, and Domestic Policy: A Restatement. In *[Bloomfield, A. I.]*, 1985, pp. 57–67.

Isard, Peter and Stekler, Lois. U.S. International Capital Flows and the Dollar. *Brookings Pap. Econ. Act.*, 1985, (1), pp. 219–36. [G: U.S.]

Jenkins, Glenn P. and Kuo, Chun-Yan. On Mea-suring the Social Opportunity Cost of Foreign Exchange. *Can. J. Econ.*, May 1985, *18*(2), pp. 400–415. [G: Canada]

Joines, Douglas H. International Currency Substitution and the Income Velocity of Money. *J. Int. Money Finance*, September 1985, *4*(3), pp. 303–16. [G: Selected OECD]

Kapur, Basant K. A Theoretical Model of 'Singapore-Type' Financial and Foreign-Exchange Systems. *Singapore Econ. Rev.*, October 1985, *30*(2), pp. 91–102. [G: LDCs]

Karacaoglu, Girol. Liquidity Preference, Loanable Funds, and Exchange-Rate and Interest-Rate Dynamics. *J. Macroecon.*, Winter 1985, *7*(1), pp. 69–83.

Kawai, Masahiro. Exchange Rates, the Current Account and Monetary–Fiscal Policies in the Short Run and in the Long Run. *Oxford Econ. Pap.*, September 1985, *37*(3), pp. 391–425.

Kearney, Colm and MacDonald, Ronald. Asset Markets and the Exchange Rate: A Structural Model of the Sterling–Dollar Rate 1972–1982. *J. Econ. Stud.*, 1985, *12*(3), pp. 3–20. [G: U.S.; U.K.]

Kemp, Murray C. and Shimomura, Koji. Do Labour Unions Drive Out Capital? *Econ. J.*, December 1985, *95*(380), pp. 1087–90.

Kenen, Peter B. Forward Rates, Interest Rates, and Expectations under Alternative Exchange Rate Regimes. *Econ. Rec.*, September 1985, *61*(174), pp. 654–66.

Khan, Mohsin S. An Analytical Approach to Interest Rate Determination in Developing Countries. *Pakistan Devel. Rev.*, Autumn-Winter 1985, *24*(3/4), pp. 481–93. [G: LDCs]

Kim, Kyung-Soo. Currency Substitution in a Production Economy. *J. Int. Econ.*, February 1985, *18*(1/2), pp. 141–58.

Kimbrough, Kent P. An Examination of the Effects of Government Purchases in an Open Economy. *J. Int. Money Finance*, March 1985, *4*(1), pp. 113–33.

Kimbrough, Kent P. Rational Expectations, Market Shocks, and the Exchange Rate. *J. Macroecon.*, Summer 1985, *7*(3), pp. 297–312.

Kimbrough, Kent P. Tariffs, Quotas and Welfare in a Monetary Economy. *J. Int. Econ.*, November 1985, *19*(3/4), pp. 257–77.

Knoester, Anthonie and van Sinderen, Jarig. Money, the Balance of Payments and Economic Policy. *Appl. Econ.*, April 1985, *17*(2), pp. 215–40. [G: W. Germany; Japan; Netherlands; U.K.; U.S.]

Krelle, Wilhelm and Welsch, Heinz. Exchange Rate Determination for Interdependent Economies. *Z. Nationalökon.*, 1985, *45*(4), pp. 373–93. [G: OECD]

Krugman, Paul R. Floating Exchange Rates: Experience and Prospects: Comment. *Brookings Pap. Econ. Act.*, 1985, (2), pp. 456–59. [G: U.S.; Japan; W. Germany; France; U.K.]

Krugman, Paul R. The Real Wage Gap and Employment. In *Melitz, J. and Wyplosz, C., eds.*, 1985, pp. 51–69. [G: France; U.S.; EEC]

Kulkarni, Kishore G. Capital Flows as an Offset to Monetary Policy: The Netherlands Evidence. *Indian Econ. J.*, July-Sept. 1985, *33*(1), pp. 127–29. **[G: Netherlands]**

Kumcu, M. Ercan. The Theory of Commercial Policy in a Monetary Economy with Sticky Wages. *J. Int. Econ.*, February 1985, *18*(1/2), pp. 159–70.

Lächler, Ulrich. Fixed versus Flexible Exchange Rates in an Equilibrium Business Cycle Model. *J. Monet. Econ.*, July 1985, *16*(1), pp. 95–107.

Laffargue, Jean-Pierre. An Internal Evaluation Method of Multinational Models. *Economia (Portugal)*, January 1985, *9*(1), pp. 73–104.

Laffargue, Jean-Pierre. Fiscal and Monetary Policies under a Flexible Exchange-Rate System. In *Melitz, J. and Wyplosz, C., eds.*, 1985, pp. 309–34. **[G: France]**

Laffargue, Jean-Pierre. Une méthode d'évaluation interne des modèles multinationaux. (An Internal Evaluation Procedure of Multinational Models. With English summary.) *Ann. INSEE*, Jan.-Mar. 1985, (57), pp. 119–44.

Lafrance, Robert and Racette, Daniel. The Canadian–U.S. Dollar Exchange Rate: A Test of Alternative Models for the Seventies. *J. Int. Money Finance*, June 1985, *4*(2), pp. 237–52. **[G: U.S.; Canada]**

Lai, Ching-chong and Chang, Wen-ya. Monetary Policy under Alternative Exchange Rates: A Reconsideration. *Indian Econ. J.*, Jan.-Mar. 1985, *32*(3), pp. 24–26.

Lai, Ching-chong and Chen, Chau-Nan. Flexible Exchange Rates, Tight Money Effects, and Macroeconomic Policy: Reply. *J. Post Keynesian Econ.*, Fall 1985, *8*(1), pp. 154–58.

Lai, Ching-chong; Hsiao, Wen-tzong and Chang, Wen-ya. Managed Floating Exchange Rates, Intervention Policy and Macroeconomic Policies. *J. Econ. Stud.*, 1985, *12*(4), pp. 52–57.

Lempinen, Urho. Keynesiläinen kansantalous, rationaaliset taloudenpitäjät ja suhdannevaihtelut. (Rational Agents and the Keynesian Economy: Some Results in Business Cycle Theory. With English summary.) *Kansant. Aikak.*, 1985, *81*(2), pp. 150–59.

Levin, Jay H. Does Leaning against the Wind Improve Exchange-Rate Performance? *J. Int. Money Finance*, March 1985, *4*(1), pp. 135–49.

Levine, Paul and Currie, David. Optimal Feedback Rules in an Open Economy Macromodel with Rational Expectations. *Europ. Econ. Rev.*, March 1985, *27*(2), pp. 141–63.

MacDonald, Ronald. Buffer Stocks, Exchange Rates and Deviations from Purchasing Power Parity. *Empirical Econ.*, 1985, *10*(3), pp. 163–75.

Malinvaud, Edmond. The Real Wage Gap and Employment: Comments. In *Melitz, J. and Wyplosz, C., eds.*, 1985, pp. 81–83. **[G: France; U.S.; EEC]**

Manne, Alan S. and Preckel, Paul V. A Three-Region Intertemporal Model of Energy, International Trade and Capital Flows. In *Manne, A. S., ed.*, 1985, pp. 56–74. **[G: OECD; OPEC; LDCs]**

Mantel, Rolf R. and Martirena Mantel, Ana M.

Acerca de las ventajas comparadas de sistemas de "Crawling-Peg" activo y pasivo en la economía pequeña. (On the Comparative Advantage of an Active and a Passive "Crawling-Peg" Exchange Rate System for the Small Economy. With English summary.) *Económica (La Plata)*, May-Dec. 1985, *31*(2–3), pp. 147–70.

Marston, Richard C. The Effects of American Policies—A New Classical Interpretation: Comment. In *Buiter, W. H. and Marston, R. C., eds.*, 1985, pp. 134–38. **[G: U.S.; OECD]**

Marston, Richard C. The Franc and the French Financial Sector: Comments. In *Melitz, J. and Wyplosz, C., eds.*, 1985, pp. 181–83. **[G: France]**

Marston, Richard C. and Turnovsky, Stephen J. Imported Materials Prices, Wage Policy, and Macro-economic Stabilization. *Can. J. Econ.*, May 1985, *18*(2), pp. 273–84.

Masson, Paul and Blundell-Wignall, Adrian. Fiscal Policy and the Exchange Rate in the Big Seven: Transmission of U.S. Government Spending Shocks. *Europ. Econ. Rev.*, June-July 1985, *28*(1–2), pp. 11–42. **[G: OECD; U.S.]**

McDermott, John. Interest Rates and the Banking System with Imperfect Capital Markets and Mobility. In *Connolly, M. B. and McDermott, J., eds.*, 1985, pp. 165–72.

McKinnon, Ronald I. Two Concepts of International Currency Substitution. In *Connolly, M. B. and McDermott, J., eds.*, 1985, pp. 101–13.

Melitz, Jacques. The Welfare Case for the European Monetary System. *J. Int. Money Finance*, December 1985, *4*(4), pp. 485–506. **[G: Europe]**

de Ménil, Georges. On Transmission and Coordination under Flexible Exchange Rates: Comment. In *Buiter, W. H. and Marston, R. C., eds.*, 1985, pp. 32–36.

Mercenier, Jean and Praet, Peter. A Prototype Model for a Small Open Economy with Quantity Rationing and Endogenous Capital under Rational Expectations. In *Peeters, T.; Praet, P. and Reding, P., eds.*, 1985, pp. 377–93.

Miller, Marcus. Fiscal and Monetary Policies under a Flexible Exchange-Rate System: Comments. In *Melitz, J. and Wyplosz, C., eds.*, 1985, pp. 339–42. **[G: France]**

Miller, Marcus. Monetary Stabilization Policy in an Open Economy. *Scot. J. Polit. Econ.*, November 1985, *32*(3), pp. 220–33.

Miller, Marcus and Salmon, Mark. Dynamic Games and the Time Inconsistency of Optimal Policy in Open Economies. *Econ. J.*, Supplement 1985, *95*, pp. 124–37.

Miller, Marcus and Salmon, Mark. Policy Coordination and Dynamic Games. In *Buiter, W. H. and Marston, R. C., eds.*, 1985, pp. 184–213.

Miller, Preston J. and Wallace, Neil. International Coordination of Macroeconomic Policies: A Welfare Analysis. *Fed. Res. Bank Minn. Rev.*, Spring 1985, *9*(2), pp. 14–32.

Minford, Patrick. The Effects of American Policies—A New Classical Interpretation. In *Buiter, W. H. and Marston, R. C., eds.*, 1985, pp. 84–130. [G: OECD; U.S.]

Montiel, Peter. A Monetary Analysis of a Small Open Economy with a Keynesian Structure. *Int. Monet. Fund Staff Pap.*, June 1985, 32(2), pp. 179–210.

Moussavian, Mohammed H. Growth Rates with an Exhaustible Resource and Home Goods. *J. Int. Econ.*, May 1985, 18(3/4), pp. 281–99.

Mussa, Michael L. Official Intervention and Exchange Rate Dynamics. In *Bhandari, J. S., ed.*, 1985, pp. 1–30.

Myatt, Anthony. Exchange Rates, Tight Money, and Macroeconomic Policy: A Comment. *J. Post Keynesian Econ.*, Fall 1985, 8(1), pp. 151–53.

Neary, J. Peter. Real and Monetary Aspects of the 'Dutch Disease.' In *Jungenfelt, K. and Hague, D. [Sir], eds.*, 1985, pp. 353–80.

Newton, Scott. Britain, the Sterling Area and European Integration, 1945–50. In *Porter, A. N. and Holland, R. F., eds.*, 1985, pp. 163–82. [G: U.K.]

Nicolini, Jose Luis. The Degree of Monopoly, the Macroeconomic Balance and the International Current Account: The Adjustment to the Oil Shocks. *Cambridge J. Econ.*, June 1985, 9(2), pp. 127–40.

Nicolini, Jose Luis. Erratum [The Degree of Monopoly, the Macroeconomic Balance and the International Current Account: The Adjustment to the Oil Shocks]. *Cambridge J. Econ.*, December 1985, 9(4), pp. 411.

Nordhaus, William. International Coordination in the Design of Macroeconomic Policies: Comment. *Europ. Econ. Rev.*, June-July 1985, 28(1–2), pp. 89–92. [G: OECD]

Obstfeld, Maurice. Capital Controls: Some Principles and the French Experience: Comments. In *Melitz, J. and Wyplosz, C., eds.*, 1985, pp. 275–77. [G: France]

Obstfeld, Maurice. Floating Exchange Rates: Experience and Prospects. *Brookings Pap. Econ. Act.*, 1985, (2), pp. 369–450. [G: U.S.; Japan; W. Germany; France; U.K.]

Obstfeld, Maurice. The Capital Inflows Problem Revisited: A Stylized Model of Southern Cone Disinflation. *Rev. Econ. Stud.*, October 1985, 52(4), pp. 605–25.

Ohr, Renate. Wechselkurserwartungen und Stabilität des Devisenmarktes. (Exchange-Rate Expectations and Stability of the Exchange-Market. With English summary.) *Jahr. Nationalökon. Statist.*, May 1985, 200(3), pp. 298–309.

Ohyama, Michihiro. Foreign Price Disturbances and the Internal and External Adjustment of a Small Open Economy under Fixed and Flexible Exchange Rates. In *Jungenfelt, K. and Hague, D. [Sir], eds.*, 1985, pp. 158–78.

Oudiz, Gilles. European Policy Coordination: An Evaluation. *Rech. Écon. Louvain*, 1985, 51(3–4), pp. 301–39. [G: EEC]

Oudiz, Gilles and Sachs, Jeffrey. International Policy Coordination in Dynamic Macroeconomic Models. In *Buiter, W. H. and Marston, R. C., eds.*, 1985, pp. 274–319.

Owen, Robert F. A Two-Country Disequilibrium Model. *J. Int. Econ.*, May 1985, 18(3/4), pp. 339–55.

Pacheco, Fernando. A Role for an International Institution: A One-Shot Game-Theoretic Approach. *Rech. Écon. Louvain*, 1985, 51(3–4), pp. 241–54.

Papell, David H. Activist Monetary Policy, Imperfect Capital Mobility, and the Overshooting Hypothesis. *J. Int. Econ.*, May 1985, 18(3/4), pp. 219–40. [G: W. Germany; Japan]

Persson, Torsten. Deficits and Intergenerational Welfare in Open Economies. *J. Int. Econ.*, August 1985, 19(1/2), pp. 67–84.

Persson, Torsten and Svensson, Lars E. O. Current Account Dynamics and the Terms of Trade: Harberger–Laursen–Metzler Two Generations Later. *J. Polit. Econ.*, February 1985, 93(1), pp. 43–65.

Petoussis, Emmanuel. Short-run Data and Long-run Theories: Testing the Monetary Approach to the Balance of Payments. *Kredit Kapital*, 1985, 18(2), pp. 204–16.

Pikoulakis, Emmanuel. Exchange Rates and the Current Account Re-examined. *Greek Econ. Rev.*, August 1985, 7(2), pp. 89–107.

Pinho, Manuel A. and Villa, Pierre. Règles monétaires et dynamique du taux de change dans économique de crédit. (With English summary.) *Economia (Portugal)*, January 1985, 9(1), pp. 29–72.

Pitchford, J. D. The Insulation Capacity of a Flexible Exchange Rate System in the Context of External Inflation. *Scand. J. Econ.*, 1985, 87(1), pp. 44–65.

Purvis, Douglas D. Public Sector Deficits, International Capital Movements, and the Domestic Economy: The Medium-term Is the Message. *Can. J. Econ.*, November 1985, 18(4), pp. 723–42.

Rich, Georg. International Aspects of Monetary Policy: Comments. In *Ando, A., et al., eds.*, 1985, pp. 225–27. [G: OECD]

Rødseth, Asbjørn. Dynamics of Wages and Trade in a Fixed-Exchange-Rate Economy. *Scand. J. Econ.*, 1985, 87(1), pp. 120–36.

Rogoff, Kenneth S. Can International Monetary Policy Cooperation Be Counterproductive? *J. Int. Econ.*, May 1985, 18(3/4), pp. 199–217.

Rogoff, Kenneth S. International Policy Coordination in Dynamic Macroeconomic Models: Comment. In *Buiter, W. H. and Marston, R. C., eds.*, 1985, pp. 327–30.

Rosendre R., Francisco. Tipo de cambio y salarios reales: consideraciones sobre el caso chileno. (With English summary.) *Cuadernos Econ.*, December 1985, 22(67), pp. 343–55. [G: Chile]

Rosner, Peter, et al. Lohnzurückhaltung bei fixen und flexiblen Wechselkursen. (Wage Restraint under Fixed and Variable Exchange Rates.

With English summary.) *Kredit Kapital*, 1985, *18*(3), pp. 299–319.

Rotemberg, Julio J. Money and the Terms of Trade. *J. Int. Econ.*, August 1985, *19*(1/2), pp. 141–60.

Rothschild, Kurt W. Der Multiplikator in der offenen Wirtschaft. (The Multiplier in an Open Economy. With English summary.) *Jahr. Nationalökon. Statist.*, November 1985, *200*(6), pp. 637–43.

Schäfer, Wolf. Anmerkungen zur J-Kurve. (Observation on the J Curve. With English summary.) *Kredit Kapital*, 1985, *18*(4), pp. 490–503. [G: W. Germany]

Schröder, Jürgen. Government Deficits and Current Account. *Aussenwirtschaft*, May 1985, *40*(1/2), pp. 103–15.

Schröder, Jürgen. Two Concepts of International Currency Substitution: Comment. In *Connolly, M. B. and McDermott, J., eds.*, 1985, pp. 113–18.

Shinkai, Yoichi. Monetary Policy in Our Times: Summing Up. In *Ando, A., et al., eds.*, 1985, pp. 309–18.

Siebert, Horst. Wirtschaftliche Zwänge für offene Volkswirtschaften. (With English summary.) *Weltwirtsch. Arch.*, 1985, *121*(4), pp. 609–27.

Sjaastad, Larry A. Exchange Rate Regimes and the Real Rate of Interest. In *Connolly, M. B. and McDermott, J., eds.*, 1985, pp. 135–64. [G: Chile; Uruguay]

Soldatos, Gerasimos T. The Impact of the Reagan Tax Cuts on the International Economy. *Indian Econ. J.*, Oct.-Nov. 1985, *33*(2), pp. 116–22.

Solnik, Bruno. On the Franc: Comments. In *Melitz, J. and Wyplosz, C., eds.*, 1985, pp. 229–31. [G: France]

Spinelli, Franco. Protectionism and Real Wage Rigidity: A Discussion of the Macroeconomic Literature. *J. Policy Modeling*, Spring 1985, *7*(1), pp. 157–80. [G: U.K.]

Standaert, Stan. The Foreign Exchange Constraint, Suppression of the Trade Deficit, and the Shadow Price of Foreign Exchange in a Fix-Price Economy. *J. Devel. Econ.*, May–June 1985, *18*(1), pp. 37–50.

Stein, Jerome L. Exchange Rate Management with Rational Expectations but Diverse Precisions. In *Bhandari, J. S., ed.*, 1985, pp. 96–125.

Stockman, Alan C. Effects of Inflation on the Pattern of International Trade. *Can. J. Econ.*, August 1985, *18*(3), pp. 587–601.

Sundquist, Barbara. Monetary and Political Influences on Balances of Payments and Exchange Rates and Their Redistributive Effects. *Amer. Econ.*, Fall 1985, *29*(2), pp. 15–26.

Svensson, Lars E. O. Currency Prices, Terms of Trade, and Interest Rates: A General Equilibrium Asset-pricing Cash-in-Advance Approach. *J. Int. Econ.*, February 1985, *18*(1/2), pp. 17–41.

Sweeney, Richard J. Automatic Stabilization from Exchange Rate Regimes: A General Equilibrium Approach. In *Arndt, S. W.; Sweeney, R. J. and Willett, T. D., eds.*, 1985, pp. 227–44.

Tabellini, Guido. The Specification of Asset Equilibrium in Models of the Open Economy. *Giorn. Econ.*, Jan.-Feb. 1985, *44*(1–2), pp. 17–27.

Taylor, John B. International Coordination in the Design of Macroeconomic Policy Rules. *Europ. Econ. Rev.*, June-July 1985, *28*(1–2), pp. 53–81. [G: OECD]

Thomas, Lee R. Portfolio Theory and Currency Substitution. *J. Money, Credit, Banking*, August 1985, *17*(3), pp. 347–57.

Tomlinson, B. R. Indo-British Relations in the Post-Colonial Era: The Sterling Balances Negotiations, 1947–49. In *Porter, A. N. and Holland, R. F., eds.*, 1985, pp. 142–62. [G: U.K.; India]

Trzeciakowski, Witold. The System of Structural Adjustment in Trade Dependent Small Centrally Planned Economies. In *Jungenfelt, K. and Hague, D. [Sir], eds.*, 1985, pp. 187–208. [G: CMEA]

Turnovsky, Stephen J. Domestic and Foreign Disturbances in an Optimizing Model of Exchange-Rate Determination. *J. Int. Money Finance*, March 1985, *4*(1), pp. 151–71.

Turnovsky, Stephen J. Optimal Exchange Market Intervention: Two Alternative Classes of Rules. In *Bhandari, J. S., ed.*, 1985, pp. 55–72.

Turnovsky, Stephen J. Policy Coordination and Dynamic Games: Comment. In *Buiter, W. H. and Marston, R. C., eds.*, 1985, pp. 220–27.

Uddin, Mohammad Sohrab. Monetary Approach to Balance of Payments: Evidence from Less Developed Countries. *Indian Econ. J.*, July-Sept. 1985, *33*(1), pp. 92–104. [G: India; Pakistan; Thailand]

Van Wijnbergen, Sweder. Oil Price Shocks, Unemployment, Investment and the Current Account: An Intertemporal Disequilibrium Analysis. *Rev. Econ. Stud.*, October 1985, *52*(4), pp. 627–45.

Vandenbroucke, Frank. Conflicts in International Economic Policy and the World Recession: A Theoretical Analysis. *Cambridge J. Econ.*, March 1985, *9*(1), pp. 15–42.

Vaubel, Roland. International Collusion or Competition for Macroeconomic Policy Coordination? A Restatement. *Rech. Écon. Louvain*, 1985, *51*(3–4), pp. 223–40.

Viaene, Jean-Marie. Macroeconomic Adjustment under Foreign Investments. In *Weiserbs, D., ed.*, 1985, pp. 185–201. [G: Netherlands; Spain]

Viaene, Jean-Marie and de Vries, Casper. Welfare Implications of Foreign Exchange Intervention, Theory and Measurement. In *Peeters, T.; Praet, P. and Reding, P., eds.*, 1985, pp. 299–322. [G: U.S.; W. Germany]

Villanueva, Javier. Breve examen de las teorías relacionadas con la determinación de la tasa de cambio. (With English summary.) *Desarrollo Econ.*, Oct.-Dec. 1985, *25*(99), pp. 351–79.

Vines, David. Fiscal Expenditures and International Economic Interdependence: Comment. In *Buiter, W. H. and Marston, R. C., eds.,* 1985, pp. 75–83.

Visco, Ignazio. Fiscal Policy and the Exchange Rate in the Big Seven: Transmission of U.S. Government Spending Shocks: Comment. *Europ. Econ. Rev.,* June-July 1985, *28*(1–2), pp. 49–52. [G: OECD; U.S.]

Wang, Chun-Yan and Wang, Leonard F. S. Currency Devaluation and the Cooper Paradox in the Open-Economy Macro-Disequilibrium Model. *Weltwirtsch. Arch.,* 1985, *121*(4), pp. 628–37.

Weinblatt, J. and Nathanson, R. Restrictions of Exports from LDCs and Their Impact on World Economy. In *Weinblatt, J., ed.,* 1985, pp. 128–42. [G: LDCs; MDCs]

Weinblatt, J. and Rodrik-Farhi, Miriam. Monetary Effects of Export Restrictions on World Commodity Markets. In *Weinblatt, J., ed.,* 1985, pp. 143–60. [G: LDCs; MDCs]

Wickens, M. R. Rational Expectations and Exchange Rate Dynamics. In *Peeters, T.; Praet, P. and Reding, P., eds.,* 1985, pp. 325–46.

van Wijk, H. H. International Aspects of Monetary Policy: Comments. In *Ando, A., et al., eds.,* 1985, pp. 229–32. [G: Netherlands; OECD]

van Wijnbergen, Sweder. Oil Discoveries, Intertemporal Adjustment and Public Policy. In *Bjerkholt, O. and Offerdal, E., eds.,* 1985, pp. 3–33. [G: Norway]

van Wijnbergen, Sweder. Optimal Capital Accumulation and the Allocation of Investment between Traded and Nontraded Sectors in Oil-producing Countries. *Scand. J. Econ.,* 1985, *87*(1), pp. 89–101. [G: LDCs]

van Wijnbergen, Sweder. Taxation of International Capital Flows, the Intertemporal Terms of Trade and the Real Price of Oil. *Oxford Econ. Pap.,* September 1985, *37*(3), pp. 382–90.

Wolf, Thomas A. Economic Stabilization in Planned Economies: Toward an Analytical Framework. *Int. Monet. Fund Staff Pap.,* March 1985, *32*(1), pp. 78–131.

Wörgötter, Andreas. Output Effects of Incomes Policies in Open Economies. *Z. Wirtschaft. Sozialwissen.,* 1985, *105*(2/3), pp. 387–406. [G: Austria]

Worrell, DeLisle. Monetary Mechanisms in Open Economies: A Model for the Caribbean. In *Connolly, M. B. and McDermott, J., eds.,* 1985, pp. 119–34. [G: Barbados; Jamaica; Trinidad and Tobago]

Zee, Howell H. A General Equilibrium Model of Export Earnings Instability in Developing Economies. *Oxford Econ. Pap.,* December 1985, *37*(4), pp. 621–42.

Zenger, Christoph. Ertragsbilanz und Portfoliotheorie der Wechselkurse: Eine grafische Illustration. (Trade Balance and Portfolio Theory of Exchange Rates: A Graphic Illustration. With English summary.) *Kredit Kapital,* 1985, *18*(4), pp. 478–89.

4313 Open Economy Macroeconomic Studies: Balance of Payments and Adjustment Mechanisms

Ahn, Chul Won and Jung, Woo S. The Choice of a Monetary Instrument in a Small Open Economy: The Case of Korea. *J. Int. Money Finance,* December 1985, *4*(4), pp. 469–84. [G: S. Korea]

Ahumada, Hildegart A. An Encompassing Test of Two Models of the Balance of Trade for Argentina. *Oxford Bull. Econ. Statist.,* February 1985, *47*(1), pp. 51–70. [G: Argentina]

Andreatta, Nino and D'Adda, Carlo. Effetti reali o nominali della svalutazione? Una riflessione sull'esperienza italiana dopo il primo shock petrolifero. (Real and Nominal Effects of the Devaluation: the Italian Experience after the First Oil Shock. With English summary.) *Polit. Econ.,* April 1985, *1*(1), pp. 37–51. [G: Italy]

Andreff, Wladimir and Lavigne, Marie. La contrainte extérieure dans les économies du C.A.E.M. (The "Foreign Constraint" in the Comecon. With English summary.) *Écon. Soc.,* April 1985, *19*(4), pp. 237–81. [G: CMEA]

Asheghian, Parviz. The Impact of Devaluation on the Balance of Payments of the Less Developed Countries: A Monetary Approach. *J. Econ. Devel.,* July 1985, *10*(1), pp. 143–51. [G: LDCs]

Atkinson, Paul and Chouraqui, Jean-Claude. The Origins of High Real Interest Rates. *OECD Econ. Stud.,* Autumn 1985, (5), pp. 7–55. [G: OECD]

Bach, Christopher L. U.S. International Transactions, Fourth Quarter and Year 1984. *Surv. Curr. Bus.,* March 1985, *65*(3), pp. 29–58. [G: U.S.]

Bahmani-Oskooee, Mohsen. Demand for and Supply of International Reserves: A Simultaneous Approach. *J. Post Keynesian Econ.,* Summer 1985, *7*(4), pp. 493–503.

Balassa, Bela. Adjusting to External Shocks: The Newly-industrializing Developing Economies in 1974–1976 and 1979–1981. *Weltwirtsch. Arch.,* 1985, *121*(1), pp. 116–41. [G: Selected LDCs]

Balassa, Bela. Adjustment Policies in Developing Economies: A Reassessment. In *Balassa, B.,* 1985, pp. 89–101. [G: LDCs]

Balassa, Bela. Policy Experiments in Chile, 1973–83. In *Balassa, B.,* 1985, pp. 157–84. [G: Chile]

Balassa, Bela. Structural Adjustment Policies in Developing Economies. In *Balassa, B.,* 1985, pp. 63–88. [G: LDCs]

Balassa, Bela. Structural Adjustment Policies in Developing Economies. In *Bapna, A., ed.,* 1985, pp. 251–77. [G: LDCs]

Balassa, Bela. Trade Policy in Mexico. In *Balassa, B.,* 1985, pp. 131–56. [G: Mexico]

Bandera, V. N. and Lucken, J. A. Simulation of a Debtor Country: The Example of Colombia. *J. Policy Modeling,* Fall 1985, *7*(3), pp. 457–76. [G: Colombia]

Batista, Paulo Nogueira, Jr. Rescheduling Brazil's Foreign Debt: Recent Developments and Prospects. In *Wionczek, M. S., ed.*, 1985, pp. 277–93. **[G: Brazil]**

Batten, Dallas S. and Hafer, R. W. Money, Income, and Currency Substitution: Evidence from Three Countries. *Fed. Res. Bank St. Louis Rev.*, May 1985, 67(5), pp. 27–35. **[G: U.S.; W. Germany; Japan]**

Bekerman, Marta. The Impact of the International Environment on Argentina. In *Griffith-Jones, S. and Harvey, C., eds.*, 1985, pp. 196–219. **[G: Argentina]**

Bekerman, Marta. The Impact of the International Environment on Brazil: From "Miracle" to Recession. In *Griffith-Jones, S. and Harvey, C., eds.*, 1985, pp. 113–44. **[G: Brazil]**

Beleza, Luís Miguel and Cartaxo, Rui. Inflation and the Current Account in Portugal. *Economia (Portugal)*, January 1985, 9(1), pp. 195–205. **[G: Portugal]**

Bergsten, C. Fred. The Second Debt Crisis Is Coming. *Challenge*, May/June 1985, 28(2), pp. 14–21. **[G: U.S.]**

Bergsten, C. Fred. The U.S.–Japan Trade Imbroglio. *Challenge*, July/August 1985, 28(3), pp. 13–17. **[G: U.S.; Japan]**

Bhagwati, Jagdish N. Indian Balance of Payments Policy and Exchange Auctions. In *Bhagwati, J. N. (I)*, 1985, pp. 144–62. **[G: India]**

Bhagwati, Jagdish N.; Krueger, Anne O. and Wibulswasdi, Chaiyawat. Capital Flight from LDCs: A Statistical Analysis. In *Bhagwati, J. N. (II)*, 1985, pp. 135–41. **[G: LDCs]**

Blanc, Jacques. L'économie française face à l'apprentissage de la gestion de son endettement extérieur. (With English summary.) *Revue Écon. Polit.*, Sept.-Oct. 1985, 95(5), pp. 658–72. **[G: France]**

Blank, Barry W. and Sein, Lila. U.S. Banking Adjustments to Changes in Gulf Liquidity. In *Czinkota, M. R. and Marciel, S., eds.*, 1985, pp. 101–28. **[G: U.S.; OPEC]**

de Boissieu, Christian. Contrainte externe et arriérés de paiement intérieurs dans les pays en développement. (External Constraint and Domestic Arrears in Developing Countries. With English summary.) *Écon. Soc.*, September 1985, 19(9), pp. 135–45. **[G: LDCs]**

Bond, Daniel and Klein, Lawrence R. The Global Environment and Its Impact on Soviet and East European Economies. In *Saunders, C. T., ed.*, 1985, pp. 19–41. **[G: OECD; CMEA]**

Branson, William H. Policy and Performance Links between LDC Debtors and Industrial Nations: Comment. *Brookings Pap. Econ. Act.*, 1985, (2), pp. 357–61. **[G: LDCs; OECD]**

Burbridge, John B. and Harrison, Alan. (Innovation) Accounting for the Impact of Fluctuations in U.S. Variables on the Canadian Economy. *Can. J. Econ.*, November 1985, 18(4), pp. 784–98. **[G: U.S.; Canada]**

Callier, Andres Passicot. The Chilean Economy and the International Crisis. In *Jorge, A.; Sala-*

zar-Carrillo, J. and Diaz-Pou, F., eds., 1985, pp. 181–89. **[G: Chile]**

Chipman, John S. Relative Prices, Capital Movements, and Sectoral Technical Change: Theory and an Empirical Test. In *Jungenfelt, K. and Hague, D. [Sir], eds.*, 1985, pp. 395–454. **[G: W. Germany; Sweden]**

Cline, William R. Policy and Performance Links between LDC Debtors and Industrial Nations: Comment. *Brookings Pap. Econ. Act.*, 1985, (2), pp. 361–66. **[G: LDCs; OECD]**

Codrington, Harold. An Explanation of Short Term Capital Movements in Barbados. *Soc. Econ. Stud.*, December 1985, 34(4), pp. 45–57. **[G: Barbados]**

Cohen, Jacob and Husted, Steven. An Integrated Accounting Matrix for Canada and the United States. *Amer. Econ. Rev.*, May 1985, 75(2), pp. 211–16. **[G: Canada; U.S.]**

Colaço, Francis X. Capital Requirements in Economic Development: The Decade Ahead. In *Gutowski, A.; Arnaudo, A. A. and Scharrer, H.-E., eds.*, 1985, pp. 3–26. **[G: LDCs]**

Condon, Timothy; Corbo, Vittorio and de Melo, Jaime. Productivity Growth, External Shocks, and Capital Inflows in Chile: A General Equilibrium Analysis. *J. Policy Modeling*, Fall 1985, 7(3), pp. 379–405. **[G: Chile]**

Connolly, Michael. The Exchange Rate and Monetary and Fiscal Problems in Jamaica: 1961–82. In *Connolly, M. B. and McDermott, J., eds.*, 1985, pp. 237–50. **[G: Jamaica]**

Cooper, Richard N. Three Discussion Papers from the Symposium on Exchange Rates. *Brookings Pap. Econ. Act.*, 1985, (1), pp. 245–59. **[G: U.S.; Canada]**

Corbo, Vittorio. Reforms and Macroeconomic Adjustments in Chile during 1974–84. *World Devel.*, August 1985, 13(8), pp. 893–916. **[G: Chile]**

Crane, Keith. Poland's Mountain of Debt: Will It Dwindle? *Comparative Econ. Stud.*, Fall 1985, 27(3), pp. 1–29. **[G: Poland]**

Daniel, Philip. Minerals in Sub-Saharan Africa—Problems and Prospects. In *Rose, T., ed.*, 1985, pp. 145–48. **[G: Sub-Saharan Africa]**

DeRosa, Dean A. and Smeal, Gary. The International Transmission of Economic Activity. In *Arndt, S. W.; Sweeney, R. J. and Willett, T. D., eds.*, 1985, pp. 202–09. **[G: OECD]**

Diamond, Marcelo and Naszewski, Daniel. Argentina's Foreign Debt: Its Origin and Consequences. In *Wionczek, M. S., ed.*, 1985, pp. 231–76. **[G: Argentina]**

Díaz, Francisco Gil. Investment and Debt. In *Musgrave, P. B., ed.*, 1985, pp. 3–32. **[G: Mexico]**

Dilullo, Anthony J. U.S. International Transactions, Third Quarter 1985. *Surv. Curr. Bus.*, December 1985, 65(12), pp. 58–88. **[G: U.S.]**

Dlouhý, Vladimír and Dyba, Karel. Modelling Czechoslovak Foreign Trade Flows with Non-Socialist Countries (Equilibrium and Some Disequilibrium Estimation). *Czech. Econ.*

Pap., 1985, *23*, pp. 91–11[]G: Czechoslovakia]

von Doellinger, Carlos. Exports and Foreign Debt in Brazil: Forecasting the Eighties. In *Salazar-Carrillo, J. and Fendt, R., Jr., eds.*, 1985, pp. 59–76.   [G: Brazil]

Dornbusch, Rudiger. Policy and Performance Links between LDC Debtors and Industrial Nations. *Brookings Pap. Econ. Act.*, 1985, (2), pp. 303–56.   [G: LDCs; OECD]

Doroodian, Khosrow. Determinants of Current Account Balances of Non-oil Developing Countries in the 1970s: Comment. *Int. Monet. Fund Staff Pap.*, March 1985, *32*(1), pp. 160–64.
[G: LDCs]

Doroodian, Khosrow. The Effectiveness of IMF Conditionality in Non-oil Developing Countries: An Empirical Verification. *J. Econ. Devel.*, December 1985, *10*(2), pp. 53–65.
[G: LDCs]

Doroodian, Khosrow and Koshal, Rajindar K. An Explanation to the U.S. Trade Deficit with Canada. *Atlantic Econ. J.*, December 1985, *13*(4), pp. 86.   [G: U.S.; Canada]

Due, John F. Federal and Foreign Trade Deficits and the Future of the U.S. Economy. *J. Econ. Educ.*, Summer 1985, *16*(3), pp. 194–202.
[G: U.S.]

Dyba, Karel. Adjustment to International Disturbances: Czechoslovakia and Hungary. *Acta Oecon.*, 1985, *34*(3/4), pp. 317–37.
[G: Czechoslovakia; Hungary]

Edwards, Sebastian. Money, the Rate of Devaluation, and Interest Rates in a Semiopen Economy: Colombia, 1968–82. *J. Money, Credit, Banking*, February 1985, *17*(1), pp. 59–68.
[G: Colombia]

Edwards, Sebastian. On the Interest-rate Elasticity of the Demand for International Reserves: Some Evidence from Developing Countries. *J. Int. Money Finance*, June 1985, *4*(2), pp. 287–95.   [G: LDCs]

El-Beblawi, Hazem. Oil Surplus Funds: The Impact of the Mode of Placement. In *Gutowski, A.; Arnaudo, A. A. and Scharrer, H.-E., eds.*, 1985, pp. 210–33.   [G: LDCs; OPEC]

Estévez, Jaime. Crisis de pagos y proceso de ajuste en Brasil y México. (Payment Crisis and Adjustment Process in Brazil and Mexico. With English summary.) *Colección Estud. CIEPLAN*, September 1985, (17), pp. 33–67.
[G: Brazil; Mexico]

Feldstein, Martin. International Trade, Budget Deficits, and the Interest Rate. *J. Econ. Educ.*, Summer 1985, *16*(3), pp. 189–93.   [G: U.S.]

Feltenstein, Andrew. Stabilization of the Balance of Payments in a Small, Planned Economy, with an Application to Ethiopia. *J. Devel. Econ.*, May–June 1985, *18*(1), pp. 171–91.
[G: Ethiopia]

Ferrer, Aldo. Self-reliance for Self-determination: The Challenge of Latin American Foreign Debt. In *Gauhar, A., ed.*, 1985, pp. 88–97.
[G: Latin America]

Ffrench-Davis, Ricardo. The External Debt Crisis in Latin America: Trends and Outlook. In

Kim, K. S. and Ruccio, D. F., eds., 1985, pp. 133–62.   [G: LDCs]

Filatov, Victor S. and Mattione, Richard P. Latin America's Recovery from Debt Problems: An Assessment of Model-based Projections. *J. Policy Modeling*, Fall 1985, *7*(3), pp. 491–524.
[G: Brazil; Chile; Mexico]

Fishlow, Albert. Coping with the Creeping Crisis of Debt. In *Wionczek, M. S., ed.*, 1985, pp. 97–144.   [G: LDCs]

Fishlow, Albert. Mexico's Integration into the World Economy. In *Musgrave, P. B., ed.*, 1985, pp. 237–48.   [G: Mexico; U.S.]

Fishlow, Albert. Revisiting the Great Debt Crisis of 1982. In *Kim, K. S. and Ruccio, D. F., eds.*, 1985, pp. 99–132.   [G: LDCs]

FitzGerald, E. V. K. Stabilization and Economic Justice: The Case of Nicaragua. In *Kim, K. S. and Ruccio, D. F., eds.*, 1985, pp. 191–204.
[G: Nicaragua]

Flamm, Kenneth. Mexico and the United States: Studies in Economic Interaction: Finance: Comments. In *Musgrave, P. B., ed.*, 1985, pp. 71–76.   [G: Mexico]

Frenkel, Jeffrey A. Monetary Targets, Real Exchange Rates and Macroeconomic Stability. *Europ. Econ. Rev.*, June-July 1985, *28*(1–2), pp. 151–52.   [G: Spain]

Green, Reginald Herbold. The Republic of Ireland: The Impact of Imported Inflation. In *Griffith-Jones, S. and Harvey, C., eds.*, 1985, pp. 145–68.   [G: Ireland]

Green, Reginald Herbold and Kamori, D. J. M. Imported Inflation, Global Price Changes and Economic Crises in Tanzania, 1970–1982. In *Griffith-Jones, S. and Harvey, C., eds.*, 1985, pp. 52–74.   [G: Tanzania]

Guillaumont, Patrick. External Factors and Economic Policy in Sub-Saharan Africa. In *Rose, T., ed.*, 1985, pp. 37–47.   [G: Sub-Saharan Africa]

Guma, X. P. The Rand Monetary Area Agreement. *S. Afr. J. Econ.*, June 1985, *53*(2), pp. 166–83.   [G: S. Africa; Swaziland; Lesotho; Botswana]

Haberler, Gottfried. International Issues Raised by Criticisms of the U.S. Budget Deficits. In *Cagan, P. and Somensatto, E., eds.*, 1985, pp. 121–45.   [G: U.S.; OECD; LDCs]

Haberler, Gottfried and Willett, Thomas D. A Strategy for U.S. Balance of Payments Policy. In *Haberler, G.*, 1985, pp. 175–206.

Hanson, James A. and de Melo, Jaime. External Shocks, Financial Reforms, and Stabilization Attempts in Uruguay during 1974–83. *World Devel.*, August 1985, *13*(8), pp. 917–39.
[G: Uruguay]

Harberger, Arnold C. Observations on the Chilean Economy, 1973–1983. *Econ. Develop. Cult. Change*, April 1985, *33*(3), pp. 451–62.
[G: Chile]

Harvey, Charles. World Prices and Development: Malawi. In *Griffith-Jones, S. and Harvey, C., eds.*, 1985, pp. 93–112. [G: Malawi]

Hausmann, Ricardo and Marquez, G. World Prices and National Development: The Case of Venezuela. In *Griffith-Jones, S. and Harvey, C., eds.*, 1985, pp. 240–59. **[G: Venezuela]**

Helliwell, John F. Trade and Macroeconomic Policies. In *Conklin, D. W. and Courchene, T. J., eds.*, 1985, pp. 115–37. **[G: OECD; Canada]**

Himarios, Daniel. The Effects of Devaluation on the Trade Balance: A Critical View and Reexamination of Miles's 'New Results.' *J. Int. Money Finance*, December 1985, *4*(4), pp. 553–63.

Huguel, Catherine. La balance des paiements française. Des comptes extérieurs en net redressement. (With English summary.) *Revue Écon. Polit.*, Sept.-Oct. 1985, *95*(5), pp. 640–57. **[G: France]**

Ishii, Naoko; McKibbin, Warwick and Sachs, Jeffrey. The Economic Policy Mix, Policy Cooperation, and Protectionism: Some Aspects of Macroeconomic Interdependence among the United States, Japan, and Other OECD Countries. *J. Policy Modeling*, Winter 1985, *7*(4), pp. 533–72. **[G: OECD]**

Ivanovitch, Michael S. Recent Interest Rate Developments in Major World Financial Markets. *Bus. Econ.*, October 1985, *20*(4), pp. 30–34. **[G: U.S.; W. Europe]**

Jorge, Antonio and Salazar-Carrillo, Jorge. Development Strategies, Trade and External Debt in Latin America: An Overview. In *Salazar-Carrillo, J. and de Alonso, I. T., eds.*, 1985, pp. 1–34. **[G: Latin America]**

Kafka, Alexandre. Exchange-Rate Policy, International Capital Movements and the Financing of Development. In *Gutowski, A.; Arnaudo, A. A. and Scharrer, H.-E., eds.*, 1985, pp. 268–94. **[G: LDCs]**

Kamas, Linda. External Disturbances and the Independence of Monetary Policy under the Crawling Peg in Colombia. *J. Int. Econ.*, November 1985, *19*(3/4), pp. 313–27. **[G: Colombia]**

Kenneally, Martin and Finn, Mary. The Balance of Payments as a Monetary Phenomenon: A Review and Consideration of Irish Evidence 1960–1978. *Econ. Soc. Rev.*, October 1985, *17*(1), pp. 39–72. **[G: Ireland]**

Khan, Mohsin S. and Zahler, Roberto. Trade and Financial Liberalization Given External Shocks and Inconsistent Domestic Policies. *Int. Monet. Fund Staff Pap.*, March 1985, *32*(1), pp. 22–55. **[G: LDCs]**

Kim, In June. Imported Inflation and the Development of the Korean Economy. In *Griffith-Jones, S. and Harvey, C., eds.*, 1985, pp. 169–95. **[G: S. Korea]**

Kim, Inchul. Exchange Market Pressure in Korea: An Application of the Girton–Roper Monetary Model. *J. Money, Credit, Banking*, May 1985, *17*(2), pp. 258–63. **[G: Korea]**

Kneer, Josef. Zur Diskussion um die Auswirkungen der steigenden internationalen Zinssätze auf die Verschuldungsproblematik der Entwicklungsländer: Die amerikanische "Kompensationsthese." (The Impact of Increasing International Interest Rates on the Current Ac-

counts of Deeply Indebted Developing Countries: The American "Compensation Thesis." With English summary.) *Konjunkturpolitik*, 1985, *31*(1/2), pp. 115–25. **[G: Argentina; Brazil; Mexico; Venezuela; Chile]**

Knoester, Anthonie and van Sinderen, Jarig. Money, the Balance of Payments and Economic Policy. *Appl. Econ.*, April 1985, *17*(2), pp. 215–40. **[G: W. Germany; Japan; Netherlands; U.K.; U.S.]**

Köves, András. Some Questions of Energy Policy in East European Countries: Energy Supply and Foreign Economic Policy. *Acta Oecon.*, 1985, *35*(3–4), pp. 345–57. **[G: CMEA]**

Krueger, Russell C. U.S. International Transactions, Second Quarter 1985. *Surv. Curr. Bus.*, September 1985, *65*(9), pp. 28–52. **[G: U.S.]**

Krueger, Russell C. U.S. International Transactions, First Quarter 1985. *Surv. Curr. Bus.*, June 1985, *65*(6), pp. 34–73. **[G: U.S.]**

Kuczynski, Pedro-Pablo. Latin American Debt: Act Two. In *Wionczek, M. S., ed.*, 1985, pp. 145–69. **[G: Selected LDCs; Latin America]**

Kullberg, Rolf. Kansantaloudellisen yhdistyksen kokouksissa pidettyjä esitelmiä. Rahapolitiikka murroksessa. (Finnish Monetary Policy in Transition. With English summary.) *Kansant. Aikak.*, 1985, *81*(1), pp. 73–80. **[G: Finland]**

Kurukulasuriya, G. The Impact of Imported Inflation on National Development: Sri Lanka. In *Griffith-Jones, S. and Harvey, C., eds.*, 1985, pp. 75–92. **[G: Sri Lanka]**

Laidler, David. Monetary Policy in Britain: Successes and Shortcomings. *Oxford Rev. Econ. Policy*, Spring 1985, *1*(1), pp. 35–43. **[G: U.K.]**

Lal, Deepak. Poor Countries and the Global Economy: Crisis and Adjustment. In *Bergsten, C. F., ed.*, 1985, pp. 65–76. **[G: Global]**

Lal, Deepak. The Real Exchange Rate, Capital Inflows and Inflation: Sri Lanka 1970–1982. *Weltwirtsch. Arch.*, 1985, *121*(4), pp. 682–702. **[G: Sri Lanka]**

Landefeld, J. Steven and Young, Kan H. The Trade Deficit and the Value of the Dollar. *Bus. Econ.*, October 1985, *20*(4), pp. 11–17. **[G: U.S.]**

Lee, Sang Man. The Controllability of the Monetary Base: The Central Bank's Reaction Function in Korea. *J. Econ. Devel.*, December 1985, *10*(2), pp. 171–91. **[G: S. Korea]**

Lukaszewicz, Aleksander. Comments [The Global Environment and Its Impact on Soviet and East European Economies] [The Impact of Energy on East–West Trade: Retrospect and Prospects]. In *Saunders, C. T., ed.*, 1985, pp. 135–36. **[G: OECD; CMEA; U.S.S.R.]**

Mann, Catherine L. U.S. International Transactions in 1984. *Fed. Res. Bull.*, May 1985, *71*(5), pp. 277–86. **[G: U.S.]**

Marris, Stephen N. The Decline and Fall of the Dollar: Some Policy Issues. *Brookings Pap. Econ. Act.*, 1985, (1), pp. 237–44. **[G: OECD]**

Martin, Preston. Statement to the U.S. House

Subcommittee on Economic Stabilization of the Committee on Banking, Finance and Urban Affairs, July 18, 1985. *Fed. Res. Bull.*, September 1985, *71*(9), pp. 697–701. **[G: U.S.]**

Marwah, Kanta; Klein, Lawrence R. and Bodkin, Ronald G. Bilateral Capital Flows and the Exchange Rate: The Case of the U.S.A. vis-à-vis Canada, France, West Germany and the U.K. *Europ. Econ. Rev.*, October 1985, *29*(1), pp. 89–110. **[G: U.S.; Canada; France; U.K.; W. Germany]**

Maximova, Margarita. Comments [The Global Environment and Its Impact on Soviet and East European Economies] [Current Problems and Prospects of the World Economy in the Light of East–West Economic Relations]. In *Saunders, C. T.*, ed., 1985, pp. 127–30. **[G: OECD; CMEA]**

McClam, W. D. and Andersen, P. S. Adjustment Performance of Small, Open Economies: Some International Comparisons. In *Argy, V. E. and Neville, J. W.*, eds., 1985, pp. 249–77. **[G: Austria; Canada; Belgium; Sweden]**

McGregor, Peter G. and Swales, J. K. Professor Thirlwall and Balance of Payments Constrained Growth. *Appl. Econ.*, February 1985, *17*(1), pp. 17–32. **[G: OECD]**

Melvin, Michael. Currency Substitution and Western European Monetary Unification. *Economica*, February 1985, *52*(205), pp. 79–91. **[G: EEC]**

Mercenier, Jean and Waelbroeck, Jean. The Impact of Protection on Developing Countries: A General Equilibrium Analysis. In *Jungenfelt, K. and Hague, D. [Sir]*, eds., 1985, pp. 219–39. **[G: LDCs]**

Mieszkowski, Peter. The Differential Effect of the Foreign Trade Deficit on Regions in the United States. In *Quigley, J. M. and Rubinfeld, D. L.*, eds., 1985, pp. 346–63. **[G: U.S.]**

Mishalani, Philip. Imported Inflation and Imported Growth: The Case of Tunisia's Studied Postponement. In *Griffith-Jones, S. and Harvey, C.*, eds., 1985, pp. 260–84. **[G: Tunisia]**

Mishalani, Philip. Jordan: The Case of Inevitable Imported Inflation in the 1970s. In *Griffith-Jones, S. and Harvey, C.*, eds., 1985, pp. 285–310. **[G: Jordan]**

Musalem, Alberto Roque. El enfoque monetario de balanza de pagos y la presión en el mercado de cambio en Argentina. (With English summary.) *Cuadernos Econ.*, December 1985, *22*(67), pp. 389–98. **[G: Argentina]**

Ocampo, José Antonio. Financial Aspects of Intraregional Trade in Latin America. In *Gauhar, A.*, ed., 1985, pp. 112–32. **[G: Latin America]**

Ortiz, Guillermo. Economic Expansion, Crisis and Adjustment in Mexico (1977–83). In *Connolly, M. B. and McDermott, J.*, eds., 1985, pp. 68–98. **[G: Mexico]**

Panchmukhi, V. R. Foreign Trade and Balance of Payment. In *Mongia, J. N.*, ed., 1985, pp. 291–314. **[G: India]**

Payer, Cheryl. The Politics of Intervention: The Italian Crisis of 1976. In *[Magdoff, H. and*

Sweezy, P.], 1985, pp. 295–318. **[G: Italy]**

Penati, Alessandro. Monetary Targets, Real Exchange Rates and Macroeconomic Stability. *Europ. Econ. Rev.*, June-July 1985, *28*(1–2), pp. 129–50. **[G: Spain]**

Peréz, José. Monetary Targets, Real Exchange Rates and Macroeconomic Stability: Comment. *Europ. Econ. Rev.*, June-July 1985, *28*(1–2), pp. 153–55. **[G: Spain]**

Portney, Paul R. Regional Issues: Commentary. In *Quigley, J. M. and Rubinfeld, D. L.*, eds., 1985, pp. 364–68. **[G: U.S.]**

Radcliffe, Christopher; Warga, Arthur D. and Willett, Thomas D. International Influences on U.S. National Income: Currency Substitution, Exchange Rate Changes, and Commodity Shocks. In *Arndt, S. W.; Sweeney, R. J. and Willett, T. D.*, eds., 1985, pp. 213–26. **[G: U.S.]**

Ramos, Joseph. Stabilization and Adjustment Policies in the Southern Cone, 1974–1983. *Cepal Rev.*, April 1985, (25), pp. 85–109. **[G: Argentina; Chile; Uruguay]**

Ranis, Gustav. Adjustment in East Asia: Lessons for Latin America. In *Jorge, A.; Salazar-Carrillo, J. and Diaz-Pou, F.*, eds., 1985, pp. 43–56. **[G: East Asia]**

Robinson, Sherman and Tyson, Laura D'Andrea. Foreign Trade, Resource Allocation, and Structural Adjustment in Yugoslavia: 1976–1980. *J. Compar. Econ.*, March 1985, *9*(1), pp. 46–70. **[G: Yugoslavia]**

Rush, Mark. Unexpected Monetary Disturbances during the Gold Standard Era. *J. Monet. Econ.*, May 1985, *15*(3), pp. 309–21. **[G: U.S.]**

Rybczynski, T. M. The Role of International Financial Markets in the Financing of Development. In *Gutowski, A.; Arnaudo, A. A. and Scharrer, H.-E.*, eds., 1985, pp. 162–81. **[G: LDCs]**

Sadler, Peter. World Prices and Development: Kuwait. In *Griffith-Jones, S. and Harvey, C.*, eds., 1985, pp. 220–39. **[G: Kuwait]**

Sakamoto, Masahiro. Japan's Macroeconomic Performance and Its Effects on the Japanese–U.S. Economic Relationship. In *Nanto, D. K.*, ed., 1985, pp. 79–93. **[G: Japan; U.S.]**

Salvati, Michele. "Effetti reali o nominali della svalutazione?": un commento all'articolo di Andreatta e D'Adda. (Real and Nominal Effects of the Devaluation: the Italian Experience after the First Oil Shock: a Comment. With English summary.) *Polit. Econ.*, August 1985, *1*(2), pp. 279–89. **[G: Italy]**

Saunders, Christopher T. Comments [The Global Environment and Its Impact on Soviet and East European Economies] [Current Problems and Prospects of the World Economy in the Light of East–West Economic Relations]. In *Saunders, C. T.*, ed., 1985, pp. 125–27. **[G: OECD; CMEA]**

Schiemann, Jürgen. Abwertung, Devisenbewirtschaftung und Handelsprotektionismus. Das Kardinalproblem der Währungspolitik eines Schuldnerlandes vor 50 Jahren während der

Weltwirtschaftskrise und heute. (Devaluation, Exchange Control and Trade Protectionism: The Cardinal Problem of a Debtor Nation's Monetary Policy 50 Years Ago during the Great Depression and Today. With English summary.) *Konjunkturpolitik*, 1985, *31*(3), pp. 151–87. **[G: W. Germany]**

Scholl, Russell B. The International Investment Position of the United States in 1984. *Surv. Curr. Bus.*, June 1985, *65*(6), pp. 25–33. **[G: U.S.]**

Sharpe, Ian G. Interest Parity, Monetary Policy and the Volatility of Australian Short-term Interest Rates: 1978–1982. *Econ. Rec.*, March 1985, *61*(172), pp. 436–44. **[G: Australia]**

Shimada, Haruo. International Trade and Labour Market Adjustment: The Case of Japan. *Econ. Lavoro*, July-Sept. 1985, *19*(3), pp. 3–30. **[G: Japan]**

Sinclair, Peter. The Balance of Payments and the Exchange Rate. In *Morris, D., ed.*, 1985, pp. 175–216. **[G: U.K.]**

Solomon, Anthony M. Domestic and International Imbalances and the Question of Sustainability. *Aussenwirtschaft*, May 1985, *40*(1/2), pp. 169–76. **[G: U.S.; Europe; Japan; LDCs]**

Somensatto, Eduardo. Budget Deficits, Exchange Rates, International Capital Flows, and Trade. In *Cagan, P. and Somensatto, E., eds.*, 1985, pp. 223–79. **[G: U.S.; OECD]**

Spaventa, Luigi. "Effetti reali o nominali della svalutazione?": un commento all'articolo di Andreatta e D'Adda. (Real and Nominal Effects of the Devaluation in the Italian Experience after the First Oil Shock. A Comment. With English summary.) *Polit. Econ.*, August 1985, *1*(2), pp. 291–300. **[G: Italy]**

Straubhaar, Thomas. Der Zahlungsbilanzeffekt der Devisentransfers ausgewanderter Arbeitskräfte für ihre Herkunftsländer. (The Balance of Payments Effect for Their Home Country of Migrant Workers' Remittances. With English summary.) *Jahr. Nationalökon. Statist.*, May 1985, *200*(3), pp. 280–97. **[G: Greece; Spain; Portugal; Turkey]**

Talafha, Hussain. The Effects of Workers' Remittances on the Jordanian Economy. *METU*, 1985, *12*(1/2), pp. 119–30. **[G: Jordan]**

Teal, Francis and Giwa, Y. M. Domestic Credit and the Balance of Payments in Ghana: A Comment. *J. Devel. Stud.*, July 1985, *21*(4), pp. 548–61. **[G: Ghana]**

Trebat, Thomas J. Mexico's Foreign Financing. In *Musgrave, P. B., ed.*, 1985, pp. 33–70. **[G: Mexico]**

Triffin, Robert. The International Accounts of the United States and Their Impact upon the Rest of the World. *Banca Naz. Lavoro Quart. Rev.*, March 1985, (152), pp. 15–30. **[G: U.S.; EEC]**

Tryon, Ralph. The International Transmission of Inflation: A Review Essay. *J. Monet. Econ.*, November 1985, *16*(3), pp. 397–403.

Tyler, William G. Exports and Foreign Debt in Brazil: Forecasting the Eighties: Comments.

In *Salazar-Carrillo, J. and Fendt, R., Jr., eds.*, 1985, pp. 77–80. **[G: Brazil]**

Valcamonici, Roberto. Processi di ristrutturazione, internationalizzazione dell'economia italiana e vincolo esterno: 1970–1984. (Production Structure, Internationalization and the External Constraint in the Italian Economy: 1970–1984. With English summary.) *Polit. Econ.*, August 1985, *1*(2), pp. 197–227. **[G: Italy]**

Waelbroeck, Jean. The Determinants of World Trade and Growth. In *Peeters, T.; Praet, P. and Reding, P., eds.*, 1985, pp. 55–89. **[G: Global]**

Weiller, Jean. Circuits des capitaux, balances extérieurers et flux majeurs d'investissement. (Capital Circuits, Foreign Balances and Major Flows of Investment. With English summary.) *Écon. Soc.*, April 1985, *19*(4), pp. 7–18.

Wells, Graeme and Evans, Lewis. The Impact of Traded Goods Prices on the New Zealand Economy. *Econ. Rec.*, March 1985, *61*(172), pp. 421–35. **[G: New Zealand]**

Williamson, John. A Comparison of Macroeconomic Strategies in South America. In *Duran, E., ed.*, 1985, pp. 38–47. **[G: Columbia; Chile; Argentina]**

Yoshitomi, Masaru. Japan's View of Current External Imbalances. In *Bergsten, C. F., ed.*, 1985, pp. 35–47. **[G: Japan]**

Zaidi, Iqbal Mehdi. Saving, Investment, Fiscal Deficits, and the External Indebtedness of Developing Countries. *World Devel.*, May 1985, *13*(5), pp. 573–88. **[G: LDCs]**

4314 Exchange Rates and Markets: Theory and Studies

Abraham, Filip. Efficiency, Predictability, and News on the Foreign Exchange Markets: Floating Exchange Rates versus Adjustable E.M.S. Rates. *Weltwirtsch. Arch.*, 1985, *121*(1), pp. 18–32. **[G: U.S.; U.K.; W. Germany; France; Belgium]**

Adams, Charles and Greenwood, Jeremy. Dual Exchange Rate Systems and Capital Controls: An Investigation. *J. Int. Econ.*, February 1985, *18*(1/2), pp. 43–63.

Aizenman, Joshua and Frenkel, Jacob A. Optimal Wage Indexation, Foreign Exchange Intervention, and Monetary Policy. *Amer. Econ. Rev.*, June 1985, *75*(3), pp. 402–23.

Amano, Akihiro. Alternative Approaches to Exchange-Rate Determination and Some Implications of the Structural Balance-of-Payments Approach for International Macroeconomic Interdependence. In *Ando, A., et al., eds.*, 1985, pp. 169–216. **[G: Selected Countries; Japan]**

Ancot, J.-P.; Paelinck, J. H. P. and Viaene, Jean-Marie. A Dynamic Exchange-Rate Model. In *Peeters, T.; Praet, P. and Reding, P., eds.*, 1985, pp. 347–75. **[G: U.S.; W. Germany; Netherlands]**

Andreatta, Nino and D'Adda, Carlo. Effetti reali o nominali della svalutazione? Una riflessione sull'esperienza italiana dopo il primo shock petrolifero. (Real and Nominal Effects of the Devaluation: the Italian Experience after the First Oil Shock. With English summary.) *Polit. Econ.*, April 1985, *1*(1), pp. 37–51. [G: Italy]

Aoki, Masanao. Misadjustment to Anticipated Shocks: An Example of Exchange-Rate Response. *J. Int. Money Finance*, September 1985, *4*(3), pp. 415–20.

Argy, Victor E. Effects of Changes in Banking and Exchange Control Legislation in the United Kingdom on the Significance of the Money Aggregates as Indicators, 1971–81. *Banca Naz. Lavoro Quart. Rev.*, March 1985, (152), pp. 31–44. [G: U.K.]

Argy, Victor E. Targeting the Budget Deficit in the Face of a Downward Expenditure Shock. *Aussenwirtschaft*, May 1985, *40*(1/2), pp. 83–102. [G: Australia; U.K.]

Argy, Victor E. The West German Experience with Monetary and Exchange Rate Management, 1973–1981. *Rivista Int. Sci. Econ. Com.*, Oct.-Nov. 1985, *32*(10–11), pp. 1047–70. [G: W. Germany]

Arndt, Sven W. and Pigott, Charles. Exchange Rate Models: Evolution and Policy Implications. In *Arndt, S. W.; Sweeney, R. J. and Willett, T. D., eds.*, 1985, pp. 19–48. [G: U.S.]

Arndt, Sven W.; Sweeney, Richard J. and Willett, Thomas D. Exchange Rates, Trade, and the U.S. Economy: Introduction. In *Arndt, S. W.; Sweeney, R. J. and Willett, T. D., eds.*, 1985, pp. xvii–xxi.

Arndt, Sven W.; Thursby, Marie and Willett, Thomas D. Flexible Exchange Rates and International Trade: An Overview. In *Arndt, S. W.; Sweeney, R. J. and Willett, T. D., eds.*, 1985, pp. 127–35.

Aronson, Jonathan D. and Krugman, Paul R. The Linkage between International Trade and Financial Policy. In *Yochelson, J. N., ed.*, 1985, pp. 27–44. [G: U.S.]

Artis, Michael J. and Karakitsos, E. Monetary and Exchange Rate Targets in an Optimal Control Setting. In *Bhandari, J. S., ed.*, 1985, pp. 212–46.

Artus, Patrick and Nasse, Philippe. Exchange Rates, Prices, Wages, and the Current Account in France. In *de Ménil, G. and Westphal, U., eds.*, 1985, pp. 147–80. [G: France]

Aschheim, Joseph; Bailey, Martin J. and Tavlas, George S. Dollar Appreciation, Deficit Stimulation, and the New Protectionism. *J. Policy Modeling*, Spring 1985, *7*(1), pp. 107–21. [G: U.S.]

Bach, Christopher L. U.S. International Transactions, Fourth Quarter and Year 1984. *Surv. Curr. Bus.*, March 1985, *65*(3), pp. 29–58. [G: U.S.]

Bahmani-Oskooee, Mohsen. Demand for International Reserves: Survey of Recent Empirical Studies. *Appl. Econ.*, April 1985, *17*(2), pp. 359–75.

Bahmani-Oskooee, Mohsen. Devaluation and the J-Curve: Some Evidence from LDCs. *Rev. Econ. Statist.*, August 1985, *67*(3), pp. 500–504. [G: Greece; India; Korea; Thailand]

Bahmani-Oskooee, Mohsen and Das, Satya P. Transaction Costs and the Interest Parity Theorem. *J. Polit. Econ.*, August 1985, *93*(4), pp. 793–99. [G: U.S.; U.K.; W. Germany]

Baillie, Richard T. and McMahon, Patrick C. Some Joint Tests of Market Efficiency: The Case of the Forward Premium. *J. Macroecon.*, Spring 1985, *7*(2), pp. 137–50. [G: U.K.; W. Germany; Italy]

Balassa, Bela. Korea in the 1980s: Policies and Prospects. In *Balassa, B.*, 1985, pp. 236–57. [G: S. Korea; Singapore; Taiwan; Hong Kong]

Balassa, Bela. Outward Orientation and Exchange Rate Policy in Developing Countries: The Turkish Experience. In *Balassa, B.*, 1985, pp. 208–35. [G: Turkey]

Balassa, Bela. Trade Policy in Mexico. In *Balassa, B.*, 1985, pp. 131–56. [G: Mexico]

Baltensperger, Ernst. Staatsverschuldung, Geldpolitik und Währungsstabilität. (Public Debt, Monetary Policy, and Currency Stability. With English summary.) *Aussenwirtschaft*, May 1985, *40*(1/2), pp. 71–81.

Batista, Paulo Nogueira, Jr. Rescheduling Brazil's Foreign Debt: Recent Developments and Prospects. In *Wionczek, M. S., ed.*, 1985, pp. 277–93. [G: Brazil]

Batten, Dallas S. and Ott, Mack. The Interrelationship of Monetary Policies under Floating Exchange Rates: A Note. *J. Money, Credit, Banking*, February 1985, *17*(1), pp. 103–10. [G: OECD]

Batten, Dallas S. and Thornton, Daniel L. The Discount Rate, Interest Rates and Foreign Exchange Rates: An Analysis with Daily Data. *Fed. Res. Bank St. Louis Rev.*, February 1985, *67*(2), pp. 22–30. [G: U.K.; Canada; France; Germany; Japan]

Baumberger, Jörg and Keel, Alex. Der ökonomische Gehalt von Wechselkursindices: Arithmetische und geometrische Indices. (The Economic Meaning of Effective Exchange Rate Indices: Arithmetic and Geometric Indices. With English summary.) *Schweiz. Z. Volkswirtsch. Statist.*, June 1985, *121*(2), pp. 169–89. [G: Switzerland]

Bautista, Romeo M. Effects of Trade and Exchange Rate Policies on Export Production Incentives in Philippine Agriculture. *Philippine Econ. J.*, 1985, *24*(2–3), pp. 87–115. [G: Philippines]

Baxter, Marianne. The Role of Expectations in Stabilization Policy. *J. Monet. Econ.*, May 1985, *15*(3), pp. 343–62. [G: Chile; Argentina]

Beckers, Stan and Sercu, Piet. Foreign Exchange Pricing under Free Floating versus Admissible Band Regimes. *J. Int. Money Finance*, September 1985, *4*(3), pp. 317–29.

Beenstock, Michael. Foreward Exchange Rates and "Seigel's Paradox" [Risk, Interest Rates and Forward Exchange]. *Oxford Econ. Pap.*, June 1985, *37*(2), pp. 298–303. [G: U.K.; U.S.]

Belongia, Michael T. and Stone, Courtenay C.

Would Lower Federal Deficits Increase U.S. Farm Exports? *Fed. Res. Bank St. Louis Rev.*, November 1985, *67*(9), pp. 5–19. [G: U.S.]

Beltensperger, Ernst. Disinflation—The Swiss Experience 1973-1983. *Z. Wirtschaft. Sozialwissen.*, 1985, *105*(2/3), pp. 271–93. [G: Switzerland]

Bender, Dieter. Wechselkursbindung in Entwicklungsländern: Eine optimale Anpassungsstrategie an flexible Wechselkurse? (Basket Pegging in Developing Countries. With English summary.) *Kredit Kapital*, 1985, *18*(3), pp. 320–46. [G: LDCs]

Bennett, Karl M. A Note on Exchange Rate Policy and Caribbean Integration. *Soc. Econ. Stud.*, December 1985, *34*(4), pp. 35–43. [G: Caribbean]

Benninga, Simon Z.; Eldor, Rafael and Zilcha, Itzhak. Optimal International Hedging in Commodity and Currency Forward Markets. *J. Int. Money Finance*, December 1985, *4*(4), pp. 537–52.

Bergstrand, Jeffrey H. Exchange Rate Variation and Monetary Policy. *New Eng. Econ. Rev.*, May/June 1985, pp. 5–18. [G: U.S.]

Bergstrand, Jeffrey H. Money, Interest Rates, and Foreign Exchange Rates as Indicators for Monetary Policy. *New Eng. Econ. Rev.*, Nov./Dec. 1985, pp. 3–13. [G: N. America; France; W. Germany; Switzerland; U.K.]

Bernholz, Peter; Gärtner, Manfred and Heri, Erwin W. Historical Experiences with Flexible Exchange Rates: A Simulation of Common Qualitative Characteristics. *J. Int. Econ.*, August 1985, *19*(1/2), pp. 21–45. [G: Europe; U.S.]

Bhagwati, Jagdish N. The Case for Devaluation. In *Bhagwati, J. N. (I)*, 1985, pp. 163–68.

Bhagwati, Jagdish N. and Krueger, Anne O. Exchange Control, Liberalization and Economic Development. In *Bhagwati, J. N. (I)*, 1985, pp. 68–79.

Bhandari, Jagdeep S. Experiments with the Optimal Currency Composite. *Southern Econ. J.*, January 1985, *51*(3), pp. 711–30.

Bhandari, Jagdeep S. Informational Regimes, Economic Disturbances, and Exchange Rate Management. In *Bhandari, J. S., ed.*, 1985, pp. 126–53.

Bhandari, Jagdeep S. Speculation and the Crawling Peg: Some Further Issues. *De Economist*, 1985, *133*(1), pp. 78–86.

Bhandari, Jagdeep S. The Flexible Exchange Basket: A Macroeconomic Analysis. *J. Int. Money Finance*, March 1985, *4*(1), pp. 19–41.

Bhandari, Jagdeep S. and Decaluwe, Bernard. Stochastic Implications of Incomplete Separation between Commercial and Financial Exchange Markets. In *Connolly, M. B. and McDermott, J., eds.*, 1985, pp. 302–35.

Bilson, John F. O. Macroeconomic Stability and Flexible Exchange Rates. *Amer. Econ. Rev.*, May 1985, *75*(2), pp. 62–67. [G: U.S.]

Bilson, John F. O. On the Franc: Comments. In *Melitz, J. and Wyplosz, C., eds.*, 1985, pp. 223–27. [G: France]

Bini Smaghi, L. Dinamica dei tassi di cambio e interventi. (The Dynamics of Exchange Rates and Interventions. With English summary.) *Giorn. Econ.*, Nov.-Dec. 1985, *44*(11–12), pp. 619–38.

Bismut, Claude and Kröger, Jürgen. The Dilemmas of Economic Policy in France and Germany: Trade-offs between Inflation, Unemployment, and the Current Account. In *de Ménil, G. and Westphal, U., eds.*, 1985, pp. 303–47. [G: France; W. Germany]

Black, Stanley W. The Effect of Alternative Intervention Policies on the Variability of Exchange Rates: The Harrod Effect. In *Bhandari, J. S., ed.*, 1985, pp. 72–82.

Blundell-Wignall, Adrian and Masson, P. R. Exchange Rate Dynamics and Intervention Rules. *Int. Monet. Fund Staff Pap.*, March 1985, *32*(1), pp. 132–59. [G: W. Germany]

Bofinger, Peter. Stabilitätsgerechte Festkurssysteme. (Stability-Consonant Fixed Exchange Rate Systems. With English summary.) *Kredit Kapital*, 1985, *18*(2), pp. 173–92. [G: U.S.; Japan; W. Germany; OECD]

Booth, G. Geoffrey; Duggan, James E. and Koveos, Peter E. Deviations from Purchasing Power Parity, Relative Inflation, and Exchange Rates: The Recent Experience. *Financial Rev.*, May 1985, *20*(2), pp. 195–218. [G: OECD]

Braga de Macedo, Jorge. Macroeconomic Policy under Currency Inconvertibility. In *Connolly, M. B. and McDermott, J., eds.*, 1985, pp. 336–55.

Branson, William H. International Capital Movements. *Economia (Portugal)*, January 1985, *9*(1), pp. 3–28. [G: Asia]

Branson, William H. The Dynamic Interaction of Exchange Rates and Trade Flows. In *Peeters, T.; Praet, P. and Reding, P., eds.*, 1985, pp. 133–60.

Brissimis, Sophocles N. and Leventakis, John A. Estimation of the Monetary Model of Exchange-Rate Determination under Rational Expectations. *J. Econ. Dynam. Control*, December 1985, *9*(4), pp. 477–91. [G: W. Germany; U.S.]

Britton, Andrew J. C. Disinflation in the United Kingdom 1979–1983. *Z. Wirtschaft. Sozialwissen.*, 1985, *105*(2/3), pp. 295–309. [G: U.K.]

de Brunhoft, Suzanne. Taux de change et monnaie internationale. (Exchange Rates and International Money. With English summary.) *Écon. Soc.*, April 1985, *19*(4), pp. 53–65.

Buiter, Willem H. and Eaton, Jonathan. Policy Decentralization and Exchange Rate Management in Interdependent Economies. In *Bhandari, J. S., ed.*, 1985, pp. 31–54.

Burbridge, John B. and Harrison, Alan. (Innovation) Accounting for the Impact of Fluctuations in U.S. Variables on the Canadian Economy. *Can. J. Econ.*, November 1985, *18*(4), pp. 784–98. [G: U.S.; Canada]

Büttler, Hans-Jürg. Real Effective Exchange Rates of Imports, Exports, and Trade Balance. *Schweiz. Z. Volkswirtsch. Statist.*, December 1985, *121*(4), pp. 375–90. [G: Switzerland]

Callen, Jeffrey L.; Kwan, Clarence C. Y. and Yip, Patrick C. Y. Foreign-Exchange Rate Dynamics: An Empirical Study Using Maximum Entropy Spectral Analysis. *J. Bus. Econ. Statist.*, April 1985, *3*(2), pp. 149–55. [G: OECD]

Callier, Philippe. Exchange Rates, Purchasing Power Parity and Efficient Allocation of Physical Capital. In *Peeters, T.; Praet, P. and Reding, P., eds.*, 1985, pp. 191–99.

Calomiris, Charles W. A Retrospective on the Classical Gold Standard: Two Views. *J. Econ. Hist.*, December 1985, *45*(4), pp. 963–68.

Calvo, Guillermo A. Reserves and the Managed Float: A Search for the Essentials. *J. Int. Money Finance*, March 1985, *4*(1), pp. 43–60.

Camacho, Arnoldo R. and Gonzalez-Vega, Claudio. Foreign Exchange Speculation, Currency Substitution, and Domestic Deposit Mobilization: The Case of Costa Rica. In *Connolly, M. B. and McDermott, J., eds.*, 1985, pp. 251–83. [G: Costa Rica]

Canarella, Giorgio. Econometric Testing of the Efficiency Hypothesis in Foreign Exchange Markets. *Rivista Int. Sci. Econ. Com.*, Oct.-Nov. 1985, *32*(10–11), pp. 1031–46. [G: W. Europe]

Canto, Victor A. Monetary Policy, 'Dollarization,' and Parallel Market Exchange Rates: The Case of the Dominican Republic. *J. Int. Money Finance*, December 1985, *4*(4), pp. 507–21. [G: Dominican Republic]

Caranza, Cesare. International Aspects of Monetary Policy: Comments. In *Ando, A., et al., eds.*, 1985, pp. 223–24.

Cartapanis, André. Éléments pour une interprétation positive du change. (Essay in Positive Exchange Rate Economics. With English summary.) *Écon. Soc.*, April 1985, *19*(4), pp. 99–135. [G: OECD]

Cesarano, Filippo. On the Viability of Monetary Unions. *J. Int. Econ.*, November 1985, *19*(3/4), pp. 367–74.

Chambers, Robert G. Credit Constraints, Interest Rates, and Agricultural Prices [Exchange Rates and U.S. Agriculture]. *Amer. J. Agr. Econ.*, May 1985, *67*(2), pp. 390–95. [G: U.S.]

Chan, Patrick K. L. and Wong, Jim H. Y. The Effect of Exchange Rate Variability on Hong Kong's Exports. *Hong Kong Econ. Pap.*, 1985, (16), pp. 27–39. [G: Hong Kong]

Chand, Sheetal K. and Onitsuka, Yusuke. Stocks, Flows, and Some Exchange Rate Dynamics for the Currency Substitution Model. *J. Int. Money Finance*, March 1985, *4*(1), pp. 61–82.

Chiang, Thomas C. The Impact of Unexpected Macro-disturbances on Exchange Rates in Monetary Models. *Quart. Rev. Econ. Bus.*, Summer 1985, *25*(2), pp. 49–59. [G: U.K.; Italy; France; W. Germany]

Čičin-Šain, Ante. A "Foreign Exchange System" under Soft Budget Constraints. In *[Levcik, F.]*, 1985, pp. 181–90. [G: Yugoslavia]

Citrin, Daniel. Exchange Rate Changes and Exports of Selected Japanese Industries. *Int. Monet. Fund Staff Pap.*, September 1985, *32*(3), pp. 404–29. [G: Japan]

Clague, Christopher K. A Model of Real National Price Levels. *Southern Econ. J.*, April 1985, *51*(4), pp. 998–1017.

Clifton, Eric V. Real Exchange Rates, Import Penetration, and Protectionism in Industrial Countries. *Int. Monet. Fund Staff Pap.*, September 1985, *32*(3), pp. 513–36. [G: U.S.; U.K.; W. Germany]

Clifton, Eric V. The Currency Futures Market and Interbank Foreign Exchange Trading. *J. Futures Markets*, Fall 1985, *5*(3), pp. 375–84. [G: U.S.; Canada]

Condon, Timothy; Robinson, Sherman and Urata, Shujiro. Coping with a Foreign Exchange Crisis: A General Equilibrium Model of Alternative Adjustment Mechanisms. In *Manne, A. S., ed.*, 1985, pp. 75–94. [G: Turkey]

Connolly, Michael. On the Optimal Currency Peg for Developing Countries [A Survey of the Literature on the Optimal Peg]. *J. Devel. Econ.*, August 1985, *18*(2–3), pp. 555–59. [G: LDCs]

Connolly, Michael. The Exchange Rate and Monetary and Fiscal Problems in Jamaica: 1961–82. In *Connolly, M. B. and McDermott, J., eds.*, 1985, pp. 237–50. [G: Jamaica]

Connolly, Michael and Hartpence, María. El ataque especulativo contra la tasa de cambio programada en Argentina: 1979–1981. (With English summary.) *Cuadernos Econ.*, December 1985, *22*(67), pp. 373–88. [G: Argentina]

Cooper, Richard N. Exchange Rate Management under Uncertainty: Foreword. In *Bhandari, J. S., ed.*, 1985, pp. vii–xi.

Cooper, Richard N. Floating Exchange Rates: Experience and Prospects: Comment. *Brookings Pap. Econ. Act.*, 1985, (2), pp. 451–56. [G: U.S.; Japan; W. Germany; France; U.K.]

Cooper, Richard N. Three Discussion Papers from the Symposium on Exchange Rates. *Brookings Pap. Econ. Act.*, 1985, (1), pp. 245–59. [G: U.S.; Canada]

Coppock, D. J. The Impact Effects of Devaluation in a Three Sector Monetary Model. *Brit. Rev. Econ. Issues*, Spring 1985, *7*(16), pp. 1–46.

Corbo, Vittorio. International Prices, Wages and Inflation in an Open Economy: A Chilean Model. *Rev. Econ. Statist.*, November 1985, *67*(4), pp. 564–73. [G: Chile]

Corden, W. Max. Exchange Rate Protection. In *Corden, W. M.*, 1985, pp. 271–87. [G: U.K.]

Corden, W. Max. On Transmission and Coordination under Flexible Exchange Rates. In *Buiter, W. H. and Marston, R. C., eds.*, 1985, pp. 8–24.

Corden, W. Max. Protection and the Real Exchange Rate. In *Corden, W. M.*, 1985, pp. 302–10.

Corden, W. Max. Protection, the Exchange Rate, and Macroeconomic Policy. *Finance Develop.*, June 1985, *22*(2), pp. 17–19. [G: U.S.]

Corden, W. Max. Real Wage Rigidity, Devaluation and Import Restrictions. In *Corden, W. M.*, 1985, pp. 311–26.

Corden, W. Max. Relationships between Macroeconomic and Industrial Policies. In *Corden, W. M.*, 1985, pp. 288–301.

Cornell, Bradford and Shapiro, Alan C. Interest Rates and Exchange Rates: Some New Empirical Results. *J. Int. Money Finance*, December 1985, *4*(4), pp. 431–42. [G: U.S.]

Crockett, Andrew. Exchange Rates and Trade: Is There a Problem for Policy? In *Peeters, T.; Praet, P. and Reding, P., eds.*, 1985, pp. 267–97. [G: OECD]

Cross, Sam Y. Treasury and Federal Reserve Foreign Exchange Operations. *Fed. Res. Bull.*, May 1985, *71*(5), pp. 287–99. [G: U.S.]

Cross, Sam Y. Treasury and Federal Reserve Foreign Exchange Operations. *Fed. Res. Bull.*, November 1985, *71*(11), pp. 850–61. [G: U.S.; OECD; Mexico; Argentina]

Cross, Sam Y. Treasury and Federal Reserve Foreign Exchange Operations. *Fed. Res. Bank New York Quart. Rev.*, Winter 1985-86, *10*(4), pp. 45–48. [G: U.S.]

Cross, Sam Y. Treasury and Federal Reserve Foreign Exchange Operations. *Fed. Res. Bank New York Quart. Rev.*, Autumn 1985, *10*(3), pp. 50–64. [G: U.S.]

Cross, Sam Y. and Alford, Richard F. Treasury and Federal Reserve Foreign Exchange Operations: Interim Report. *Fed. Res. Bull.*, August 1985, *71*(8), pp. 607–08. [G: U.S.]

Cross, Sam Y. and Alford, Richard F. Treasury and Federal Reserve Foreign Exchange Operations: Interim Report. *Fed. Res. Bull.*, February 1985, *71*(2), pp. 82–84. [G: U.S.]

Currie, David. Overlapping Wage Contracts and Exchange Rate Overshooting. *Greek Econ. Rev.*, April 1985, *7*(1), pp. 71–81.

Curzio, Alberto Quadrio. Dal rifiuto del numerario aureo ai prezzi quasi-ufficiali dell'oro. (From the Rejection of the Gold-Numeraire to Quasi-official Gold Prices. With English summary.) *Rivista Int. Sci. Econ. Com.*, Oct.-Nov. 1985, *32*(10–11), pp. 965–87. [G: Global]

Cushman, David O. Real Exchange Rate Risk, Expectations, and the Level of Direct Investment. *Rev. Econ. Statist.*, May 1985, *67*(2), pp. 297–308. [G: U.S.; W. Europe; Japan; Canada]

Daniel, Betty C. Monetary Autonomy and Exchange Rate Dynamics under Currency Substitution. *J. Int. Econ.*, August 1985, *19*(1/2), pp. 119–39.

Daniel, Betty C. Optimal Foreign Exchange-Rate Policy for a Small Open Economy. *J. Int. Money Finance*, December 1985, *4*(4), pp. 523–36.

Davidson, James E. H. Econometric Modelling of the Sterling Effective Exchange Rate. *Rev. Econ. Stud.*, April 1985, *52*(2), pp. 231–50. [G: U.K.]

Davutyan, Nurhan and Pippenger, John. Purchasing Power Parity Did Not Collapse during

the 1970's. *Amer. Econ. Rev.*, December 1985, *75*(5), pp. 1151–58. [G: U.S.; W. Europe; Canada; Japan]

De Grauwe, Paul and Fratianni, Michele. Interdependence, Macro-economic Policies and All That. *World Econ.*, March 1985, *8*(1), pp. 63–79. [G: OECD]

Deardorff, Alan V. and Stern, Robert M. The Effects of Exchange-Rate Changes on Domestic Prices, Trade and Employment in the U.S., European Community and Japan. In *Jungenfelt, K. and Hague, D. [Sir], eds.*, 1985, pp. 282–306. [G: OECD]

Debonneuil, Xavier and Galy, Michel. Can Exchange Rate Predictability Be Achieved without Monetary Convergence?—Evidence from the EMS: Comment. *Europ. Econ. Rev.*, June-July 1985, *28*(1–2), pp. 117–20. [G: W. Europe]

Decaluwe, Bernard and Bhandari, Jagdeep S. Cloisonnements imparfaits double marché des changes et anticipations rationnelles. (Imperfect Segmentation, Dual Exchange Markets and Rational Expectations. With English summary.) *Revue Écon.*, November 1985, *36*(6), pp. 1345–71.

DeRosa, Dean A. Equilibrium Exchange Rate Adjustments to Exongenous Changes in International Capital Flows. In *Arndt, S. W.; Sweeney, R. J. and Willett, T. D., eds.*, 1985, pp. 14–17. [G: OECD]

Di Pierro, Alberto. Notes on U.S. Economic Policy and on the Level of the Dollar. *Econ. Scelte Pubbliche/J. Public Finance Public Choice*, 1985, (1), pp. 31–36. [G: U.S.; EEC]

Domowitz, Ian and Hakkio, Craig S. Conditional Variance and the Risk Premium in the Foreign Exchange Market. *J. Int. Econ.*, August 1985, *19*(1/2), pp. 47–66. [G: U.K.; France; W. Germany; Japan; Switzerland]

Donges, Jürgen B. and Schatz, Klaus-Werner. The Iberian Countries Facing EC Membership: Starting Conditions for Their Industry. *Weltwirtsch. Arch.*, 1985, *121*(4), pp. 756–78. [G: Spain; Portugal]

Dornbusch, Rudiger and Pechman, Clarice. The Bid–Ask Spread in the Black Market for Dollars in Brazil: A Note. *J. Money, Credit, Banking*, Part 1, Nov. 1985, *17*(4), pp. 517–20. [G: Brazil]

Doukas, John. The Rationality of Money Supply Expectations and the Canadian-U.S. Exchange Rate Response to Money Supply Announcements. *Financial Rev.*, May 1985, *20*(2), pp. 180–94. [G: U.S.]

Driskill, Robert and McCafferty, Stephen. Exchange Market Intervention under Rational Expectations with Imperfect Capital Substitutability. In *Bhandari, J. S., ed.*, 1985, pp. 83–95.

Driskill, Robert and McCafferty, Stephen. Exchange Rate Dynamics with Wealth Effects: Some Theoretical Ambiguities. *J. Int. Econ.*, November 1985, *19*(3/4), pp. 329–40.

Dubois, McClellan A. Japan: Foreign Exchange

Policy. In *Nanto, D. K., ed.*, 1985, pp. 94–101. **[G: Japan]**

Eaker, Mark R. and Grant, Dwight. Optimal Hedging of Uncertain and Long-term Foreign Exchange Exposure. *J. Banking Finance*, June 1985, *9*(2), pp. 221–31.

Eaton, Jonathan. Optimal and Time Consistent Exchange-Rate Management in an Overlapping-Generations Economy. *J. Int. Money Finance*, March 1985, *4*(1), pp. 83–100.

Edison, Hali J. Purchasing Power Parity: A Quantitative Reassessment of the 1920s Experience. *J. Int. Money Finance*, September 1985, *4*(3), pp. 361–72. **[G: U.K.; U.S.; France]**

Edison, Hali J. The Rise and Fall of Sterling: Testing Alternative Models of Exchange Rate Determination. *Appl. Econ.*, December 1985, *17*(6), pp. 1003–21. **[G: U.K.]**

Eichengreen, Barry. The Franc and the French Financial Sector: Comments. In *Melitz, J. and Wyplosz, C., eds.*, 1985, pp. 175–79.
[G: France]

Eichengreen, Barry and Sachs, Jeffrey. Exchange Rates and Economic Recovery in the 1930s. *J. Econ. Hist.*, December 1985, *45*(4), pp. 925–46. **[G: U.S.; W. Europe]**

Fatemi, Ali M. The Yen and the Dollar: Their Purchasing Power Parity in Efficient Markets. *Hitotsubashi J. Econ.*, June 1985, *26*(1), pp. 37–43. **[G: U.S.; Japan]**

Feenstra, Robert C. Anticipated Devaluations, Currency Flight, and Direct Trade Controls in a Monetary Economy. *Amer. Econ. Rev.*, June 1985, *75*(3), pp. 386–401.

Feldman, Robert A. Foreign Currency Options. *Finance Develop.*, December 1985, *22*(4), pp. 38–41.

Feldstein, Martin. International Trade, Budget Deficits, and the Interest Rate. *J. Econ. Educ.*, Summer 1985, *16*(3), pp. 189–93. **[G: U.S.]**

Feroldi, Mathieu. Monetary Mechanisms and Exchange Rates in France. In *de Ménil, G. and Westphal, U., eds.*, 1985, pp. 227–62.
[G: France]

Feroldi, Mathieu and Melitz, Jacques. The Franc and the French Financial Sector. In *Melitz, J. and Wyplosz, C., eds.*, 1985, pp. 149–74.
[G: France]

Fieleke, Norman S. Dollar Appreciation and U.S. Import Prices. *New Eng. Econ. Rev.*, Nov./Dec. 1985, pp. 49–54. **[G: U.S.]**

Fieleke, Norman S. The Foreign Currency Futures Market: Some Reflections on Competitiveness and Growth. *J. Futures Markets*, Winter 1985, *5*(4), pp. 625–31. **[G: U.S.; Canada; W. Germany; Japan; U.K.]**

Fieleke, Norman S. The Rise of the Foreign Currency Futures Market. *New Eng. Econ. Rev.*, March/April 1985, pp. 38–47. **[G: U.S.]**

Fischer, Stanley. The Dollar and the Policy Mix: 1985: Comment. *Brookings Pap. Econ. Act.*, 1985, (1), pp. 186–90. **[G: U.S.]**

Flemming, J. S. Can Exchange Rate Predictability Be Achieved without Monetary Convergence?—Evidence from the EMS: Comment.

Europ. Econ. Rev., June-July 1985, *28*(1–2), pp. 121–22. **[G: W. Europe]**

Flood, Robert P. and Hodrick, Robert J. Central Bank Intervention in a Rational Open Economy: A Model with Asymmetric Information. In *Bhandari, J. S., ed.*, 1985, pp. 154–85.

Fontaine, P. Un test du modèle international d'arbitrage et de l'intégration finacière. (A Test of the International Arbitrage Model and of Financial Integration. With English summary.) *Finance*, June 1985, *6*(1), pp. 121–41.

Fortune, J. Neill. Expected Purchasing Power Parity. *Weltwirtsch. Arch.*, 1985, *121*(1), pp. 97–104. **[G: U.S.; U.K.]**

Frankel, Jeffrey A. On the Franc. In *Melitz, J. and Wyplosz, C., eds.*, 1985, pp. 185–221.
[G: France]

Frankel, Jeffrey A. The Dazzling Dollar. *Brookings Pap. Econ. Act.*, 1985, (1), pp. 199–217.
[G: U.S.]

Franz, Alfred. The Solution of Problems in International Comparisons of GDP through Price Adjustments. What to Learn from ECP 1980? *Statist. J.*, September 1985, *3*(3), pp. 307–19.
[G: W. Europe]

Freedman, Charles. Alternative Approaches to Exchange-Rate Determination and Some Implications of the Structural Balance-of-Payments Approach for International Macroeconomic Interdepedence: Comments. In *Ando, A., et al., eds.*, 1985, pp. 217–21. **[G: Japan; Selected Countries]**

Frenkel, Jacob A. A Note on 'The Good Fix' and 'The Bad Fix.' Comment. *Europ. Econ. Rev.*, June-July 1985, *28*(1–2), pp. 125–27.

Frenkel, Jacob A. Fiscal Policy and the Exchange Rate in the Big Seven: Transmission of U.S. Government Spending Shocks: Comment. *Europ. Econ. Rev.*, June-July 1985, *28*(1–2), pp. 43–47. **[G: OECD; U.S.]**

Frenkel, Jacob A. On the Franc: Comments. In *Melitz, J. and Wyplosz, C., eds.*, 1985, pp. 233–36. **[G: France; Selected OECD]**

Galeazzi, Giorgio. International Differences in Comparative Price Levels and Exchange Rates: An Analysis by Production Sectors in a Varying Parameter Model. *Rivista Polit. Econ.*, Suppl. Dec. 1985, 76, pp. 3–40.

Gálvez, Julio and Tybout, James R. Chile 1977–1981: impacto sobre las empresas chilenas de algunas reformas económicas e intentos de estabilización. (With English summary.) *Cuadernos Econ.*, April 1985, *22*(65), pp. 37–71.
[G: Chile]

Garber, Peter M. The Collapse of Asset Price-Fixing Regimes. In *Connolly, M. B. and McDermott, J., eds.*, 1985, pp. 287–301.

Gardner, Grant W. Money, Prices, and the Current Account in a Dual Exchange Rate Regime. *J. Int. Econ.*, May 1985, *18*(3/4), pp. 321–38.

Genberg, Hans. Still More on Choosing . . . [On Choosing the Right Rules for Exchange-Rate Management]. *World Econ.*, March 1985, *8*(1), pp. 83–84.

Genberg, Hans and Swoboda, Alexander K. Internal and External Factors in the Swiss Busi-

ness Cycle: 1964–1981. *Aussenwirtschaft*, September 1985, *40*(3), pp. 275–95.
[G: Switzerland]

Gennari, Fiorella. La disciplina valutaria si evolve senza toccare la gestione delle valute. Rimangono comunque fermi i principi fondamentali del nostro ordinamento. (Foreign Exchange Control Evolves Out of the Management of Currency. With English summary.) *Bancaria*, June 1985, *41*(6), pp. 685–89.   [G: Italy]

Giavazzi, Francesco and Sheen, Jeffrey. Fiscal Policy and the Real Exchange Rate. In *Currie, D., ed.*, 1985, pp. 41–68.

Gidlow, R. M. Forward Exchange Policy in South Africa: Guidelines for Reform. *S. Afr. J. Econ.*, September 1985, *53*(3), pp. 226–40.
[G: S. Africa]

Giersch, Herbert. Real Exchange Rates and Economic Development. In *[Peacock, A.]*, 1985, pp. 176–92.

Godfrey, Martin. Trade and Exchange Rate Policy: A Further Contribution to the Debate. In *Rose, T., ed.*, 1985, pp. 168–79. [G: Sub-Saharan Africa]

Goodman, Laurie S.; Ross, Susan and Schmidt, Frederick. Are Foreign Currency Options Overvalued? The Early Experience of the Philadelphia Stock Exchange. *J. Futures Markets*, Fall 1985, *5*(3), pp. 349–59.   [G: U.S.]

Gotur, Padma. Effects of Exchange Rate Volatility on Trade: Some Further Evidence. *Int. Monet. Fund Staff Pap.*, September 1985, *32*(3), pp. 475–512.   [G: U.S.; U.K.; W. Germany; Japan; France]

Gramley, Lyle E. The Effects of Exchange Rate Changes on the U.S. Economy. *Bus. Econ.*, July 1985, *20*(3), pp. 40–44.   [G: U.S.]

Granziol, Markus J. On the Neglect of Foreign Exchange Risk Premiums. *Empirical Econ.*, 1985, *10*(1), pp. 59–64.   [G: W. Europe; U.S.]

Granziol, Markus J. and Denzler, Matthias. Zinssätze als Mittel zur Wechselkurs-Prognose? (Interest Rates as a Means of Forecasting the Exchange Rate. With English summary.) *Schweiz. Z. Volkswirtsch. Statist.*, June 1985, *121*(2), pp. 83–94.   [G: U.S.; W. Germany; U.K.; France]

Haberler, Gottfried. Currency Depreciation and the Terms of Trade. In *Haberler, G.*, 1985, pp. 167–74.

Haberler, Gottfried. International Aspects of U.S. Inflation. In *Haberler, G.*, 1985, pp. 311–34.   [G: U.S.]

Haberler, Gottfried. The International Monetary System in the World Recession. In *Haberler, G.*, 1985, pp. 229–63.   [G: OECD]

Haberler, Gottfried. The Market for Foreign Exchange and the Stability of the Balance of Payments: A Theoretical Analysis. In *Haberler, G.*, 1985, pp. 143–65.

Haberler, Gottfried and Willett, Thomas D. A Strategy for U.S. Balance of Payments Policy. In *Haberler, G.*, 1985, pp. 175–206.

Hakkio, Craig S. and Pearce, Douglas K. The Reaction of Exchange Rates to Economic News. *Econ. Inquiry*, October 1985, *23*(4), pp. 621–36.   [G: U.S.; W. Europe; Japan; Canada]

Hamaui, Rony. La scelta della valute di fatturazione nel commercio internazionale: una sintesi. (The Choice of Invoicing Currencies in International Trade: A Synthesis. With English summary.) *Giorn. Econ.*, May-June 1985, *44*(5–6), pp. 259–84.

Hardouvelis, Gikas A. Exchange Rates, Interest Rates, and Money-Stock Announcements: A Theoretical Exposition. *J. Int. Money Finance*, December 1985, *4*(4), pp. 443–54. [G: U.S.]

Harkness, Jon. Optimal Exchange Intervention for a Small Open Economy. *J. Int. Money Finance*, March 1985, *4*(1), pp. 101–12.

Harnack, Joachim. The Cyclical Behavior of Exchange Rates. In *Arndt, S. W.; Sweeney, R. J. and Willett, T. D., eds.*, 1985, pp. 210–12.   [G: OECD]

Harrell, Louis and Fischer, Dale. The 1982 Mexican Peso Devaluation and Border Area Employment. *Mon. Lab. Rev.*, October 1985, *108*(10), pp. 25–32.   [G: Mexico; U.S.]

Havlik, Peter. The Scope and Structure of Czechoslovak Foreign Trade: Effects of Applying Realistic Exchange Rates. *Comparative Econ. Stud.*, Spring 1985, *27*(1), pp. 1–19.
[G: Czechoslovakia]

Helliwell, John F. Trade and Macroeconomic Policies. In *Conklin, D. W. and Courchene, T. J., eds.*, 1985, pp. 115–37.   [G: OECD; Canada]

Helpman, Elhanan and Razin, Assaf. Floating Exchange Rates with Liquidity Constraints in Financial Markets. *J. Int. Econ.*, August 1985, *19*(1/2), pp. 99–117.

Henderson, Dale W. On Transmission and Coordination under Flexible Exchange Rates: Comment. In *Buiter, W. H. and Marston, R. C., eds.*, 1985, pp. 24–32.

Hinshaw, Randall. Inflation, Exchange Rates, and Domestic Policy: A Restatement. In *[Bloomfield, A. I.]*, 1985, pp. 57–67.

Hoffman, Dennis L. and Schlagenhauf, Don E. The Impact of News and Alternative Theories of Exchange Rate Determination. *J. Money, Credit, Banking*, August 1985, *17*(3), pp. 328–46. [G: France; Japan; W. Germany; U.K.]

Hojman, David E. A Quarterly Econometric Model of Chile, 1974–1979, and an Application to the Analysis of the Fixed Exchange Rate Policy between 1979 and 1982. In *Hojman, D. E., ed.*, 1985, pp. 125–51.   [G: Chile]

Holden, M. G. and Holden, P. Alternative Measures of Exchange Rates and Exchange Rate Policy in South Africa. *S. Afr. J. Econ.*, December 1985, *53*(4), pp. 351–65.
[G: S. Africa]

Hollenbeck, Frank. Treating Spot Speculation as Equivalent to a Combined Arbitrage–Speculative Transaction: A Comment. *Rivista Int. Sci. Econ. Com.*, July-Aug. 1985, *32*(7–8), pp. 701–04.

Holmes, Peter. Economic Management and the International Environment, 1981–1983: Comment. In *Machin, H. and Wright, V., eds.*, 1985, pp. 96–100.   [G: France]

Hooper, Peter. International Repercussions of the U.S. Budget Deficit. *Aussenwirtschaft*, May 1985, *40*(1/2), pp. 117–55. [G: U.S.; OECD]

Hörngren, Lars. A Comparison of the Dynamic Properties of Five Nordic Macroeconometric Models—A Critical Note. *Scand. J. Econ.*, 1985, *87*(3), pp. 568–74.   [G: Sweden; Finland; Norway]

Houthakker, Hendrik S. The International Agenda. *Eastern Econ. J.*, Jan.-Mar. 1985, *11*(1), pp. 71–78.   [G: Global]

Hsu, John C. Exchange Rate Management without a Central Bank: The Hong Kong Experience. *Hong Kong Econ. Pap.*, 1985, (16), pp. 14–26.   [G: Hong Kong]

Husted, Steven and Kitchen, John. Some Evidence on the International Transmission of U.S. Money Supply Announcement Effects. *J. Money, Credit, Banking*, Part 1, Nov. 1985, *17*(4), pp. 456–66.   [G: U.S.; Canada; W. Germany]

Hutchison, Michael M. and Throop, Adrian W. U.S. Budget Deficits and the Real Value of the Dollar. *Fed. Res. Bank San Francisco Econ. Rev.*, Fall 1985, (4), pp. 26–43.
                               [G: U.S.]

Isaac, Alan G. Currency Substitution: Intuition and Implications. *Atlantic Econ. J.*, December 1985, *13*(4), pp. 87–88.

James, Emile. Quasi tutte cadute le illusioni sui cambi fluttuanti. (The End of Many Hopes on Floating Exchange Rates. With English summary.) *Bancaria*, June 1985, *41*(6), pp. 665–69.   [G: OECD]

Jeanneney, Sylviane Guillaumont. Foreign Exchange Policy and Economic Performance: A Study of Senegal, Madagascar and Guinea. In *Rose, T., ed.*, 1985, pp. 180–98. [G: Senegal; Madagascar; Guinea]

Jenkins, Glenn P. and Kuo, Chun-Yan. On Measuring the Social Opportunity Cost of Foreign Exchange. *Can. J. Econ.*, May 1985, *18*(2), pp. 400–415.   [G: Canada]

Jones, M. E. F. The Regional Impact of an Overvalued Pound in the 1920s. *Econ. Hist. Rev.*, 2nd Ser., August 1985, *38*(3), pp. 393–401.
                               [G: U.K.]

Junge, Georg. Trends and Random Walks of Real Exchange Rates. *Weltwirtsch. Arch.*, 1985, *121*(3), pp. 427–37. [G: U.S.; U.K.; W. Germany; France; Switzerland]

Kafka, Alexandre. Exchange-Rate Policy, International Capital Movements and the Financing of Development. In *Gutowski, A.; Arnaudo, A. A. and Scharrer, H.-E., eds.*, 1985, pp. 268–94.   [G: LDCs]

Karacaoglu, Girol. Liquidity Preference, Loanable Funds, and Exchange-Rate and Interest-Rate Dynamics. *J. Macroecon.*, Winter 1985, *7*(1), pp. 69–83.

Kawai, Masahiro. Exchange Rates, the Current Account and Monetary–Fiscal Policies in the Short Run and in the Long Run. *Oxford Econ. Pap.*, September 1985, *37*(3), pp. 391–425.

Kearney, Colm and MacDonald, Ronald. Asset Markets and the Exchange Rate: A Structural Model of the Sterling–Dollar Rate 1972–1982. *J. Econ. Stud.*, 1985, *12*(3), pp. 3–20.
                               [G: U.S.; U.K.]

Kenen, Peter B. Forward Rates, Interest Rates, and Expectations under Alternative Exchange Rate Regimes. *Econ. Rec.*, September 1985, *61*(174), pp. 654–66.

Kim, Inchul. Exchange Market Pressure in Korea: An Application of the Girton–Roper Monetary Model. *J. Money, Credit, Banking*, May 1985, *17*(2), pp. 258–63.   [G: Korea]

Kim, Kyung-Soo. Currency Substitution in a Production Economy. *J. Int. Econ.*, February 1985, *18*(1/2), pp. 141–58.

Kimbrough, Kent P. Rational Expectations, Market Shocks, and the Exchange Rate. *J. Macroecon.*, Summer 1985, *7*(3), pp. 297–312.

Kindleberger, Charles P. International Monetary Reform in the Nineteenth Century. In *Kindleberger, C. P.*, 1985, pp. 213–25.

Kindleberger, Charles P. The Dollar Yesterday, Today, and Tomorrow. *Banca Naz. Lavoro Quart. Rev.*, December 1985, (155), pp. 295–308.

Kindleberger, Charles P. The International Monetary Politics of a Near-Great Power: Two French Episodes, 1926–1936 and 1960–1970. In *Kindleberger, C. P.*, 1985, pp. 119–28.
                               [G: France]

Korajczyk, Robert A. The Pricing of Forward Contracts for Foreign Exchange. *J. Polit. Econ.*, April 1985, *93*(2), pp. 346–68.
            [G: U.S.; W. Europe; Canada]

Krelle, Wilhelm and Sarrazin, Hermann. Simultaneous Determination of Capital Flows, the Exchange Rate and Interest Rates in the Bonn Forecasting Model 11. In *[Menges, G.]*, 1985, pp. 146–61.   [G: W. Germany]

Krelle, Wilhelm and Welsch, Heinz. Exchange Rate Determination for Interdependent Economies. *Z. Nationalökon.*, 1985, *45*(4), pp. 373–93.   [G: OECD]

Kröger, Jürgen and Pauly, Peter. Exchange Rates, Prices, Wages, and the Current Account in Germany. In *de Ménil, G. and Westphal, U., eds.*, 1985, pp. 181–218.
                               [G: W. Germany]

Krueger, Russell C. U.S. International Transactions, Second Quarter 1985. *Surv. Curr. Bus.*, September 1985, *65*(9), pp. 28–52. [G: U.S.]

Krueger, Russell C. U.S. International Transactions, First Quarter 1985. *Surv. Curr. Bus.*, June 1985, *65*(6), pp. 34–73.   [G: U.S.]

Krugman, Paul R. Floating Exchange Rates: Experience and Prospects: Comment. *Brookings Pap. Econ. Act.*, 1985, (2), pp. 456–59.
            [G: U.S.; Japan; W. Germany; France; U.K.]

Lafrance, Robert and Racette, Daniel. The Canadian–U.S. Dollar Exchange Rate: A Test of Alternative Models for the Seventies. *J. Int. Money Finance*, June 1985, *4*(2), pp. 237–52.
                               [G: U.S.; Canada]

Lai, Ching-chong and Chen, Chau-Nan. Flexible Exchange Rates, Tight Money Effects, and

Macroeconomic Policy: Reply. *J. Post Keynesian Econ.*, Fall 1985, *8*(1), pp. 154–58.

Lal, Deepak. The Real Exchange Rate, Capital Inflows and Inflation: Sri Lanka 1970–1982. *Weltwirtsch. Arch.*, 1985, *121*(4), pp. 682–702.
[G: Sri Lanka]

Landefeld, J. Steven and Young, Kan H. The Trade Deficit and the Value of the Dollar. *Bus. Econ.*, October 1985, *20*(4), pp. 11–17.
[G: U.S.]

Laskar, Daniel. Foreign Exchange Intervention Policies in a Two Country World: Optimum and Non-cooperative Equilibrium. *Economia (Portugal)*, January 1985, *9*(1), pp. 105–58.

Lehment, Harmen. Crowding-out in der Bundesrepublik: Wechselkurseffekte, Zinseffekte und empirischer Befund. (Crowding-out in the Federal Republic of Germany: Exchange Rate Effects, Interest Effects, and Empirical Findings. With English summary.) *Aussenwirtschaft*, May 1985, *40*(1/2), pp. 53–70.
[G: W. Germany]

Lever, Harold. The Dollar and the World Economy: The Case for Concerted Management. *Lloyds Bank Rev.*, July 1985, (157), pp. 1–12.
[G: Global]

Levin, Jay H. Does Leaning against the Wind Improve Exchange-Rate Performance? *J. Int. Money Finance*, March 1985, *4*(1), pp. 135–49.

Liljeblom, Eva. Economic Exposure on the Helsinki Stock Exchange and a Test for Market Efficiency. *Liiketaloudellinen Aikak.*, 1985, *34*(2), pp. 147–65.
[G: Finland]

Lim, G. C. and Parmenter, B. R. An Analysis of Recent Changes in the Australian Exchange Rate: Nominal and Real. *Australian Econ. Rev.*, 2nd Quarter 1985, (70), pp. 19–26.
[G: Australia]

Lizondo, José Saul. Unifying Multiple Exchange Rates. *Finance Develop.*, December 1985, *22*(4), pp. 23–24, 37.
[G: Selected Countries]

Longworth, David. A Model of the Canadian Exchange Rate: A Test of the 1970s: Comment. *J. Policy Modeling*, Winter 1985, *7*(4), pp. 673–79.
[G: Canada]

Lybeck, Johan A. A Comparison of the Dynamic Properties of Five Nordic Macroeconomic Models—A Critical Note. Reply. *Scand. J. Econ.*, 1985, *87*(3), pp. 575.
[G: Sweden; Finland; Norway]

MacDonald, Ronald. Are Deviations from Purchasing Power Parity Efficient? Some Further Answers. *Weltwirtsch. Arch.*, 1985, *121*(4), pp. 638–45.
[G: France; U.K.; U.S.]

MacDonald, Ronald. Buffer Stocks, Exchange Rates and Deviations from Purchasing Power Parity. *Empirical Econ.*, 1985, *10*(3), pp. 163–75.

MacDonald, Ronald. The Norman Conquest of 86 and the Asset Approach to the Exchange Rate. *J. Int. Money Finance*, September 1985, *4*(3), pp. 373–87.
[G: U.K.; U.S.]

Maier, Gerhard. Geldmengenkontrolle in weltoffener Wirtschaft: Die aussenwirtschaftliche

Unabhängigkeit der Deutschen Bundesbank. (Monetary Control in an Open Economy: The External Independence of the Deutsche Bundesbank. With English Summary.) *Aussenwirtschaft*, September 1985, *40*(3), pp. 255–73.
[G: W. Germany]

Mantel, Rolf R. and Martirena Mantel, Ana M. Acerca de las ventajas comparadas de sistemas de "Crawling-Peg" activo y pasivo en la economía pequeña. (On the Comparative Advantage of an Active and a Passive "Crawling-Peg" Exchange Rate System for the Small Economy. With English summary.) *Económica (La Plata)*, May-Dec. 1985, *31*(2–3), pp. 147–70.

Marin, Dalia. Structural Change through Exchange Rate Policy. *Weltwirtsch. Arch.*, 1985, *121*(3), pp. 471–91.
[G: Austria]

Mark, Nelson C. On Time Varying Risk Premia in the Foreign Exchange Market: An Econometric Analysis. *J. Monet. Econ.*, July 1985, *16*(1), pp. 3–18.

Mark, Nelson C. Some Evidence on the International Inequality of Real Interest Rates. *J. Int. Money Finance*, June 1985, *4*(2), pp. 189–208.
[G: Selected OECD]

Marris, Stephen N. The Decline and Fall of the Dollar: Some Policy Issues. *Brookings Pap. Econ. Act.*, 1985, (1), pp. 237–44.
[G: OECD]

Marston, Richard C. Financial Disturbances and the Effects of an Exchange Rate Union. In *Bhandari, J. S., ed.*, 1985, pp. 272–91.

Marston, Richard C. The Franc and the French Financial Sector: Comments. In *Melitz, J. and Wyplosz, C., eds.*, 1985, pp. 181–83.
[G: France]

Martin, Preston. Statement to the U.S. House Subcommittee on Economic Stabilization of the Committee on Banking, Finance and Urban Affairs, July 18, 1985. *Fed. Res. Bull.*, September 1985, *71*(9), pp. 697–701. [G: U.S.]

Marwah, Kanta. A Prototype Model of the Foreign Exchange Market of Canada: Forecasting Capital Flows and Exchange Rates. *Econ. Modelling*, April 1985, *2*(2), pp. 93–124.
[G: Canada]

Marwah, Kanta and Bodkin, Ronald G. A Model of the Canadian Global Exchange Rate: A Test of the 1970s: Countercomment. *J. Policy Modeling*, Winter 1985, *7*(4), pp. 681–83.
[G: Canada]

Marwah, Kanta; Klein, Lawrence R. and Bodkin, Ronald G. Bilateral Capital Flows and the Exchange Rate: The Case of the U.S.A. vis-à-vis Canada, France, West Germany and the U.K. *Europ. Econ. Rev.*, October 1985, *29*(1), pp. 89–110. [G: U.S.; Canada; France; U.K.; W. Germany]

Masson, Paul and Blundell-Wignall, Adrian. Fiscal Policy and the Exchange Rate in the Big Seven: Transmission of U.S. Government Spending Shocks. *Europ. Econ. Rev.*, June-July 1985, *28*(1–2), pp. 11–42. [G: OECD; U.S.]

McClure, J. Harold, Jr. Dollar Appreciation and the Reagan Disinflation. In *Arndt, S. W.;*

Sweeney, R. J. and Willett, T. D., eds., 1985, pp. 267–72. **[G: U.S.]**

McCulloch, Rachel. Unexpected Real Consequences of Floating Exchange Rates. In *Adams, J., ed.*, 1985, pp. 286–306. **[G: OECD]**

McDonald, Ronald. Do Deviations of the Real Effective Exchange Rate Follow a Random Walk? *Econ. Notes*, 1985, (1), pp. 63–70. **[G: U.S.; Canada; Japan; W. Europe]**

McKinnon, Ronald I. How to Manage a Repressed Economy. In *Gutowski, A.; Arnaudo, A. A. and Scharrer, H.-E., eds.*, 1985, pp. 182–209. **[G: Chile; Argentina]**

McKinnon, Ronald I. Two Concepts of International Currency Substitution. In *Connolly, M. B. and McDermott, J., eds.*, 1985, pp. 101–13.

de Melo, Jaime; Pascale, Ricardo and Tybout, James R. Uruguay 1973–1981: interrelación entre shocks financieros y reales. (With English summary.) *Cuadernos Econ.*, April 1985, 22(65), pp. 73–98. **[G: Uruguay]**

Melvin, Michael. The Choice of an Exchange Rate System and Macroeconomic Stability. *J. Money, Credit, Banking*, Part 1, Nov. 1985, 17(4), pp. 467–78. **[G: Selected Countries]**

de Ménil, Georges. On Transmission and Coordination under Flexible Exchange Rates: Comment. In *Buiter, W. H. and Marston, R. C., eds.*, 1985, pp. 32–36.

de Ménil, Georges and Westphal, Uwe. The Transmission of International Disturbances to the French and German Economies, 1972–1980. In *de Ménil, G. and Westphal, U., eds.*, 1985, pp. 349–79. **[G: France; W. Germany]**

Micossi, Stefano. The Intervention and Financing Mechanisms of the EMS and the Role of the ECU. *Banca Naz. Lavoro Quart. Rev.*, December 1985, (155), pp. 327–45.

Monke, Eric A. International Agriculture and Trade Policies: Implications for the United States: Commentary. In *Gardner, B. L., ed.*, 1985, pp. 79–82. **[G: U.S.; Global]**

Mouyelo-Katoula, Michel and Munnsad, Kantilal. A Note on Methodologies Used in a Comparison of Purchasing Power Parities and Real Economic Aggregates in Fifteen African Countries. *Statist. J.*, September 1985, 3(3), pp. 289–305. **[G: Africa]**

Muet, Pierre-Alain. Economic Management and the International Environment, 1981–1983. In *Machin, H. and Wright, V., eds.*, 1985, pp. 70–96. **[G: France]**

Mundell, Robert A. A Note on 'The Good Fix' and 'The Bad Fix.' *Europ. Econ. Rev.*, June-July 1985, 28(1–2), pp. 123–24.

Murphy, J. Carter. Reflections on the Exchange Rate System. *Amer. Econ. Rev.*, May 1985, 75(2), pp. 68–73.

Musalem, Alberto Roque. El enfoque monetario de balanza de pagos y la presión en el mercado de cambio en Argentina. (With English summary.) *Cuadernos Econ.*, December 1985, 22(67), pp. 389–98. **[G: Argentina]**

Mussa, Michael L. Official Intervention and Exchange Rate Dynamics. In *Bhandari, J. S., ed.*, 1985, pp. 1–30.

Myatt, Anthony. Exchange Rates, Tight Money, and Macroeconomic Policy: A Comment. *J. Post Keynesian Econ.*, Fall 1985, 8(1), pp. 151–53.

Ngiam, K. J. Exchange Rate Behavior with Currency Substitution. *Atlantic Econ. J.*, December 1985, 13(4), pp. 89. **[G: Canada]**

Nielsen, Søren Bo. Valutakursvirkninger af olieprisstigninger. (The Impact of Oil Price Increases on Exchange Rate. With English summary.) *Nationaløkon. Tidsskr.*, 1985, 123(1), pp. 50–63. **[G: U.S.; OPEC; U.K.; Japan]**

Nowak, Michael. Black Markets in Foreign Exchange. *Finance Develop.*, March 1985, 22(1), pp. 20–23.

Obstfeld, Maurice. Floating Exchange Rates: Experience and Prospects. *Brookings Pap. Econ. Act.*, 1985, (2), pp. 369–450. **[G: U.S.; Japan; W. Germany; France; U.K.]**

Obstfeld, Maurice. The Dollar and the Policy Mix: 1985: Comment. *Brookings Pap. Econ. Act.*, 1985, (1), pp. 190–95. **[G: U.S.]**

Officer, Lawrence H. Integration in the American Foreign-Exchange Market, 1791–1900. *J. Econ. Hist.*, September 1985, 45(3), pp. 557–85. **[G: U.S.; U.K.]**

Ohr, Renate. Wechselkurserwartungen und Stabilität des Devisenmarktes. (Exchange-Rate Expectations and Stability of the Exchange-Market. With English summary.) *Jahr. Nationalökon. Statist.*, May 1985, 200(3), pp. 298–309.

Oksanen, Heikki. The Basket-Peg System in Exchange Rate Policy: Some Implications and Applications. *Liiketaloudellinen Aikak.*, 1985, 34(2), pp. 166–76. **[G: Finland; Norway; Sweden]**

Orléan, André. Spécialisation et taux de change: une vue d'ensemble. (International Specialization and Exchange Rates: A General View. With English summary.) *Écon. Soc.*, April 1985, 19(4), pp. 67–94. **[G: OECD]**

Owen, Robert F. A Two-Country Disequilibrium Model. *J. Int. Econ.*, May 1985, 18(3/4), pp. 339–55.

Pagan, Jill C. U.K. Taxation and Currency Fluctuations. *Bull. Int. Fiscal Doc.*, Aug./Sept. 1985, 39(8/9), pp. 379–86. **[G: U.K.]**

Papell, David H. Activist Monetary Policy, Imperfect Capital Mobility, and the Overshooting Hypothesis. *J. Int. Econ.*, May 1985, 18(3/4), pp. 219–40. **[G: W. Germany; Japan]**

Park, Hun Y. and Chen, Andrew H. Differences between Futures and Forward Prices: A Further Investigation of the Marking-to-Market Effects. *J. Futures Markets*, Spring 1985, 5(1), pp. 77–88. **[G: U.S.; U.K.; W. Germany; Japan; Switzerland]**

Pekkarinen, Jukka. 1982 års devalveringar: Nordisk växelkurspolitik på villovä gar? (Devaluations in 1982: Has the Nordic Exchange Rate Policy Gone Astray? With English summary.) *Ekon. Samfundets Tidskr.*, 1985, 38(4), pp. 211–16. **[G: Sweden]**

Pekkarinen, Jukka and Sauramo, Pekka. Devaluations and Employment in the Economic Policy of the Nordic Countries—Some Reflections on the Finnish Experience. *Rech. Écon. Louvain*, 1985, *51*(3–4), pp. 343–62. **[G: Finland; Norway; Denmark; Sweden]**

Pekkarinen, Jukka and Suaramo, Pekka. Devalvaatiosykli: Mallit ja valuuttakurssipoliittinen keskustelu. (Devaluation Cycle: The Models and the Exchange Rate Policy Debate. With English summary.) *Kansant. Aikak.*, 1985, *81*(3), pp. 326–39.

Pfeffermann, Guy P. Overvalued Exchange Rates and Development. *Finance Develop.*, March 1985, *22*(1), pp. 17–19. **[G: LDCs]**

Pigott, Charles and Reinhart, Vincent. The Strong Dollar and U.S. Inflation. *Fed. Res. Bank New York Quart. Rev.*, Autumn 1985, *10*(3), pp. 23–29. **[G: U.S.]**

Pigott, Charles; Rutledge, John and Willett, Thomas D. Estimating the Inflationary Effects of Exchange Rate Changes. In *Arndt, S. W.; Sweeney, R. J. and Willett, T. D., eds.*, 1985, pp. 245–65. **[G: U.S.]**

Pigott, Charles and Sweeney, Richard J. Purchasing Power Parity and Exchange Rate Dynamics: Some Empirical Results. In *Arndt, S. W.; Sweeney, R. J. and Willett, T. D., eds.*, 1985, pp. 73–89. **[G: OECD]**

Pigott, Charles and Sweeney, Richard J. Testing the Exchange Rate Implications of Two Popular Monetary Models. In *Arndt, S. W.; Sweeney, R. J. and Willett, T. D., eds.*, 1985, pp. 91–106. **[G: U.S.; Switzerland]**

Pigott, Charles; Sweeney, Richard J. and Willett, Thomas D. On the Costs of Disequilibrium under Pegged and Flexible Exchange Rates. In *Arndt, S. W.; Sweeney, R. J. and Willett, T. D., eds.*, 1985, pp. 137–44.

Pikoulakis, Emmanuel. Exchange Rates and the Current Account Re-examined. *Greek Econ. Rev.*, August 1985, *7*(2), pp. 89–107.

Pinho, Manuel A. and Villa, Pierre. Règles monétaires et dynamique du taux de change dans économique de crédit. (With English summary.) *Economia (Portugal)*, January 1985, *9*(1), pp. 29–72.

Pippenger, John. Stock Flow versus Efficient Commodity Markets: A Test of Alternative Theories. *Econ. Notes*, 1985, (2), pp. 167–70. **[G: U.S.; Switzerland]**

Plane, Patrick. Are Sub-Saharan Currencies Overvalued? In *Rose, T., ed.*, 1985, pp. 199–210. **[G: Sub-Saharan Africa]**

Polasek, M. and Lewis, M. K. Australia's Transition from Crawling Peg to Floating Exchange Rate. *Banca Naz. Lavoro Quart. Rev.*, June 1985, (153), pp. 187–203. **[G: Australia]**

Pollack, Gerald A. The Dollar. *Bus. Econ.*, October 1985, *20*(4), pp. 5–10. **[G: U.S.]**

Radcliffe, Christopher; Warga, Arthur D. and Willett, Thomas D. International Influences on U.S. National Income: Currency Substitution, Exchange Rate Changes, and Commodity Shocks. In *Arndt, S. W.; Sweeney, R. J. and*

Willett, T. D., eds., 1985, pp. 213–26. **[G: U.S.]**

Ramirez-Rojas, C. L. Currency Substitution in Argentina, Mexico, and Uruguay. *Int. Monet. Fund Staff Pap.*, December 1985, *32*(4), pp. 629–67. **[G: Argentina; Mexico; Uruguay]**

Rana, Pradumna B. and Dowling, J. Malcolm, Jr. Inflationary Effects of Small but Continuous Changes in Effective Exchange Rates: Nine Asian LDCs. *Rev. Econ. Statist.*, August 1985, *67*(3), pp. 496–500. **[G: Asian LDCs]**

Reszat, Beate. Technische Ursachen kurzfristiger Wechselkursbewegungen. (Technical Causes of Short-term Exchange Rate Movements. With English summary.) *Kredit Kapital*, 1985, *18*(3), pp. 428–45. **[G: W. Germany]**

Rich, Georg. International Aspects of Monetary Policy: Comments. In *Ando, A., et al., eds.*, 1985, pp. 225–27. **[G: OECD]**

Rich, Georg and Béguelin, Jean-Pierre. Swiss Monetary Policy in the 1970s and 1980s. In *[Weintraub, R. E.]*, 1985, pp. 76–111. **[G: Switzerland]**

Richardson, David R. On Proposals for a Clearing Union. *J. Post Keynesian Econ.*, Fall 1985, *8*(1), pp. 14–27.

Rinaldi, Roberto. Interrelationships between the Floating Exchange Rate, Money and Price. A Test of Causality Applied to the Italian Experience: Some Comments. *Econ. Notes*, 1985, (2), pp. 154–66. **[G: Italy]**

Rogoff, Kenneth S. Can Exchange Rate Predictability Be Achieved without Monetary Convergence? Evidence from the EMS. *Europ. Econ. Rev.*, June-July 1985, *28*(1–2), pp. 93–115. **[G: W. Europe]**

Rosenberg, Emily S. Foundations of United States International Financial Power: Gold Standard Diplomacy, 1900–1905. *Bus. Hist. Rev.*, Summer 1985, *59*(2), pp. 169–202. **[G: U.S.]**

Rosendre R., Francisco. Tipo de cambio y salarios reales: consideraciones sobre el caso chileno. (With English summary.) *Cuadernos Econ.*, December 1985, *22*(67), pp. 343–55. **[G: Chile]**

Rotemberg, Julio J. Money and the Terms of Trade. *J. Int. Econ.*, August 1985, *19*(1/2), pp. 141–60.

Rush, Mark and Husted, Steven. Purchasing Power Parity in the Long Run. *Can. J. Econ.*, February 1985, *18*(1), pp. 137–45. **[G: U.S.; Japan; Europe]**

Sachs, Jeffrey. The Dollar and the Policy Mix: 1985. *Brookings Pap. Econ. Act.*, 1985, (1), pp. 117–85. **[G: U.S.]**

Salazar-Carrillo, Jorge and Fendt, Roberto, Jr. Some Additional Thoughts on Brazilian Trade, Prices and Exchange Rates. In *Salazar-Carrillo, J. and Fendt, R., Jr., eds.*, 1985, pp. 25–33. **[G: Brazil; U.S.]**

Salvati, Michele. "Effetti reali o nominali della svalutazione?": un commento all'articolo di Andreatta e D'Adda. (Real and Nominal Effects of the Devaluation: the Italian Experience after the First Oil Shock: a Comment. With English summary.) *Polit. Econ.*, August 1985, *1*(2), pp. 279–89.   [G: Italy]

Salvatore, Dominick. The New Protectionism and the Threat to World Welfare: Editor's Introduction. *J. Policy Modeling*, Spring 1985, *7*(1), pp. 1–22.   [G: U.S.; LDCs]

Schäfer, Wolf. Anmerkungen zur J-Kurve. (Observation on the J Curve. With English summary.) *Kredit Kapital*, 1985, *18*(4), pp. 490–503.   [G: W. Germany]

Schiemann, Jürgen. Abwertung, Devisenbewirtschaftung und Handelsprotektionismus. Das Kardinalproblem der Währungspolitik eines Schuldnerlandes vor 50 Jahren während der Weltwirtschaftskrise und heute. (Devaluation, Exchange Control and Trade Protectionism: The Cardinal Problem of a Debtor Nation's Monetary Policy 50 Years Ago during the Great Depression and Today. With English summary.) *Konjunkturpolitik*, 1985, *31*(3), pp. 151–87.   [G: W. Germany]

Schioppa, Ciro. The Purchasing Power Parity Theory in Some Recent Models of the Exchange Rate Determination and Inflation Transmission. *Stud. Econ.*, 1985, *40*(25), pp. 71–103.

Schröder, Jürgen. Two Concepts of International Currency Substitution: Comment. In *Connolly, M. B. and McDermott, J., eds.*, 1985, pp. 113–18.

Schuh, G. Edward. International Agriculture and Trade Policies: Implications for the United States. In *Gardner, B. L., ed.*, 1985, pp. 56–78.   [G: U.S.; Global]

Schulze-Ghattas, Marianne and Westphal, Uwe. Monetary Mechanisms, Government Deficits, and External Constraints in Germany. In *de Ménil, G. and Westphal, U., eds.*, 1985, pp. 263–97.   [G: W. Germany]

Sharp, Peter A. Determinants of Forward Exchange Risk Premia in Efficient Markets. In *Arndt, S. W.; Sweeney, R. J. and Willett, T. D., eds.*, 1985, pp. 167–80.

Shastri, Kuldeep and Tandon, Kishore. Arbitrage Tests of the Efficiency of the Foreign Currency Options Market. *J. Int. Money Finance*, December 1985, *4*(4), pp. 455–68.   [G: U.S.]

Sinai, Allen. The Dollar and Inflation. *Eastern Econ. J.*, July-Sept. 1985, *11*(3), pp. 211–20.   [G: U.S.]

Sinai, Allen. The Soaring Dollar Did It. *Challenge*, Sept./Oct. 1985, *28*(4), pp. 18–22.   [G: U.S.]

Sinclair, Peter. The Balance of Payments and the Exchange Rate. In *Morris, D., ed.*, 1985, pp. 175–216.   [G: U.K.]

Sjaastad, Larry A. Exchange Rate Regimes and the Real Rate of Interest. In *Kim, K. S. and Ruccio, D. F., eds.*, 1985, pp. 163–87.   [G: Chile; Uruguay]

Sjaastad, Larry A. Exchange Rate Regimes and the Real Rate of Interest. In *Connolly, M. B. and McDermott, J., eds.*, 1985, pp. 135–64.   [G: Chile; Uruguay]

Smaghi, Lorenzo Bini. Have Exchange Rates Varied Too Much with Respect to Market Funda-mentals? *Giorn. Econ.*, Jan.-Feb. 1985, *44*(1–2), pp. 45–54.   [G: OECD]

Smith, Richard G. and Goodhart, Charles A. E. The Relationship between Exchange Rate Movements and Monetary Surprises: Results for the United Kingdom and the United States Compared and Contrasted. *Manchester Sch. Econ. Soc. Stud.*, March 1985, *53*(1), pp. 2–22.   [G: U.S.; U.K.]

Smith, Richard G. and Goodhart, Charles A. E. The Relationship between Exchange Rate Movements and Monetary Surprises: Results for the United Kingdom and the United States Compared and Contrasted: Erratum. *Manchester Sch. Econ. Soc. Stud.*, September 1985, *53*(3), pp. 315.   [G: U.S.; U.K.]

Söderström, Hans Tson. Exchange Rate Strategies and Real Adjustment after 1970. The Experience of the Smaller European Economies. In *Peeters, T.; Praet, P. and Reding, P., eds.*, 1985, pp. 227–64.   [G: Europe]

Solnik, Bruno. On the Franc: Comments. In *Melitz, J. and Wyplosz, C., eds.*, 1985, pp. 229–31.   [G: France]

Solomon, Anthony M. Domestic and International Imbalances and the Question of Sustainability. *Aussenwirtschaft*, May 1985, *40*(1/2), pp. 169–76.   [G: U.S.; Europe; Japan; LDCs]

Somensatto, Eduardo. Budget Deficits, Exchange Rates, International Capital Flows, and Trade. In *Cagan, P. and Somensatto, E., eds.*, 1985, pp. 223–79.   [G: U.S.; OECD]

Spaventa, Luigi. "Effetti reali o nominali della svalutazione?": un commento all'articolo di Andreatta e D'Adda. (Real and Nominal Effects of the Devaluation in the Italian Experience after the First Oil Shock: A Comment. With English summary.) *Polit. Econ.*, August 1985, *1*(2), pp. 291–300.   [G: Italy]

Spencer, Peter D. Official Intervention in the Foreign Exchange Market. *J. Polit. Econ.*, October 1985, *93*(5), pp. 1019–24.

Spinelli, Franco. Should the Hypothesis of a Well Defined and Stable World Demand for M1 Be Reinstated? *Kredit Kapital*, 1985, *18*(2), pp. 193–203.   [G: Global]

Stein, Jerome L. Exchange Rate Management with Rational Expectations but Diverse Precisions. In *Bhandari, J. S., ed.*, 1985, pp. 96–125.

Steinherr, Alfred. Competitiveness and Exchange Rates: Policy Issues for Europe. In *Peeters, T.; Praet, P. and Reding, P., eds.*, 1985, pp. 163–89.   [G: U.K.; Belgium; W. Germany]

Sundquist, Barbara. Monetary and Political Influences on Balances of Payments and Exchange Rates and Their Redistributive Effects. *Amer. Econ.*, Fall 1985, *29*(2), pp. 15–26.

Sweeney, Richard J. Stabilizing or Destabilizing Speculation? Evidence from the Foreign Exchange Markets. In *Arndt, S. W.; Sweeney, R. J. and Willett, T. D., eds.*, 1985, pp. 107–23.   [G: OECD]

Tandon, Kishore and Simaan, Yusif. The Reaction of Effective Exchange Rates to Information about Inflation. *Financial Rev.*, May 1985, *20*(2), pp. 164–79. **[G: U.S.]**

Tarafás, Imre and Szabó, Judit. Hungary's Exchange Rate Policy in the 1980s. *Acta Oecon.*, 1985, *35*(1–2), pp. 53–79. **[G: Hungary]**

Tew, J. H. B. The International Monetary System. In *Morris, D., ed.*, 1985, pp. 549–80. **[G: Selected Countries]**

Thomas, Lee R., III. A Winning Strategy for Currency-Futures Speculation. *J. Portfol. Manage.*, Fall 1985, *12*(1), pp. 65–69.

Thursby, Marie C. and Thursby, Jerry G. The Uncertainty Effects of Floating Exchange Rates: Empirical Evidence on International Trade Flows. In *Arndt, S. W.; Sweeney, R. J. and Willett, T. D., eds.*, 1985, pp. 153–65. **[G: Selected Countries]**

Thygesen, Niels. New Approaches to Development Finance: A Critical Look at the Brandt Proposals. In *Gutowski, A.; Arnaudo, A. A. and Scharrer, H.-E., eds.*, 1985 , pp. 297–316. **[G: LDCs]**

Tucker, Alan L. Empirical Tests of the Efficiency of the Currency Option Market. *J. Finan. Res.*, Winter 1985, *8*(4), pp. 275–85. **[G: U.S.]**

Turnovsky, Stephen J. Domestic and Foreign Disturbances in an Optimizing Model of Exchange-Rate Determination. *J. Int. Money Finance*, March 1985, *4*(1), pp. 151–71.

Turnovsky, Stephen J. Optimal Exchange Market Intervention: Two Alternative Classes of Rules. In *Bhandari, J. S., ed.*, 1985, pp. 55–72.

Vanden Abeele, Michel. International Trade and Exchange Rates: Concluding Remarks. In *Peeters, T.; Praet, P. and Reding, P., eds.*, 1985, pp. 413–18.

Viaene, Jean-Marie and de Vries, Casper. Welfare Implications of Foreign Exchange Intervention, Theory and Measurement. In *Peeters, T.; Praet, P. and Reding, P., eds.*, 1985, pp. 299–322. **[G: U.S.; W. Germany]**

Villani, Marco. Productivity and Purchasing Power Parity. *Econ. Notes*, 1985, (3), pp. 101–14. **[G: W. Europe; U.S.; Canada; Japan]**

Villanueva, Javier. Breve examen de las teorías relacionadas con la determinación de la tasa de cambio. (With English summary.) *Desarrollo Econ.*, Oct.-Dec. 1985, *25*(99), pp. 351–79.

Vincent, D. P. Exchange Rate Devaluation, Monetary Policy and Wages: A General Equilibrium Analysis for Chile. *Econ. Modelling*, January 1985, *2*(1), pp. 17–32. **[G: Chile]**

Visco, Ignazio. Fiscal Policy and the Exchange Rate in the Big Seven: Transmission of U.S. Government Spending Shocks: Comment. *Europ. Econ. Rev.*, June-July 1985, *28*(1–2), pp. 49–52. **[G: OECD; U.S.]**

Wallich, Henry C. Statement to the U.S. House Subcommittee on International Economic Policy and Trade of the Committee on Foreign Affairs, March 22, 1985. *Fed. Res. Bull.*, May 1985, *71*(5), pp. 308–12. **[G: U.S.]**

Wang, Chun-Yan and Wang, Leonard F. S. Currency Devaluation and the Cooper Paradox in the Open-Economy Macro-Disequilibrium

Model. *Weltwirtsch. Arch.*, 1985, *121*(4), pp. 628–37.

Wasserfallen, Walter and Kyburz, Hans. The Behavior of Flexible Exchange Rates in the Short Run—A Systematic Investigation. *Weltwirtsch. Arch.*, 1985, *121*(4), pp. 646–60. **[G: Selected Countries]**

Wasserfallen, Walter and Zimmermann, Heinz. The Behavior of Intra-daily Exchange Rates. *J. Banking Finance*, March 1985, *9*(1), pp. 55–72. **[G: Switzerland]**

Wells, Graeme and Evans, Lewis. The Impact of Traded Goods Prices on the New Zealand Economy. *Econ. Rec.*, March 1985, *61*(172), pp. 421–35. **[G: New Zealand]**

Wickens, M. R. Rational Expectations and Exchange Rate Dynamics. In *Peeters, T.; Praet, P. and Reding, P., eds.*, 1985, pp. 325–46.

Wickham, Peter. The Choice of Exchange Rate Regime in Developing Countries: A Survey of the Literature. *Int. Monet. Fund Staff Pap.*, June 1985, *32*(2), pp. 248–88. **[G: LDCs]**

van Wijk, H. H. International Aspects of Monetary Policy: Comments. In *Ando, A., et al., eds.*, 1985, pp. 229–32. **[G: Netherlands; OECD]**

Willett, Thomas D. Modern Exchange Rate Analysis. In *Arndt, S. W.; Sweeney, R. J. and Willett, T. D., eds.*, 1985, pp. 3–13.

Willett, Thomas D. The Deficit and the Dollar. In *Arndt, S. W.; Sweeney, R. J. and Willett, T. D., eds.*, 1985, pp. 273–82.

Willett, Thomas D. and Flacco, Paul R. The Reallocation Effects of Exchange Rate Fluctuations under Uncertainty with Efficient Speculation. In *Arndt, S. W.; Sweeney, R. J. and Willett, T. D., eds.*, 1985, pp. 145–52.

Willett, Thomas D.; Khan, Waseem and Der Hovanessian, Aïda. Interest Rate Changes, Inflationary Expectations and Exchange Rate Overshooting: The Dollar–DM Rate. In *Arndt, S. W.; Sweeney, R. J. and Willett, T. D., eds.*, 1985, pp. 49–71. **[G: U.S.; W. Germany]**

Williamson, John. More on Choosing the Right Rules for Exchange-Rate Management [On Choosing the Right Rules for Exchange-Rate Management]. *World Econ.*, March 1985, *8*(1), pp. 81–83.

Williamson, John. On the Optimal Currency Peg for Developing Countries: Reply [A Survey of the Literature on the Optimal Peg]. *J. Devel. Econ.*, August 1985, *18*(2–3), pp. 561–62. **[G: LDCs]**

Wolf, Thomas A. Exchange Rate Systems and Adjustment in Planned Economies. *Int. Monet. Fund Staff Pap.*, June 1985, *32*(2), pp. 211–47. **[G: U.S.S.R.; Poland; Hungary; E. Germany]**

Woo, Wing T. The Monetary Approach to Exchange Rate Determination under Rational Expectations: The Dollar-Deutschmark Rate. *J. Int. Econ.*, February 1985, *18*(1/2), pp. 1–16. **[G: U.S.; W. Germany]**

Yuravlivker, David E. Crawling Peg and the Real Exchange Rate: Some Evidence from the

Southern Cone. *J. Devel. Econ.*, August 1985, *18*(2–3), pp. 381–93.   [G: **Argentina; Chile; Brazil; Uruguay**]

Yuravlivker, David E. Precios relativos effectivos versus de equilibiro: el impacto de la política cambiaria. (With English summary.) *Cuadernos Econ.*, April 1985, *22*(65), pp. 145–52.
[G: **Argentina; Chile; Uruguay**]

Zenger, Christoph. Ertragsbilanz und Portfoliotheorie der Wechselkurse: Eine grafische Illustration. (Trade Balance and Portfolio Theory of Exchange Rates: A Graphic Illustration. With English summary.) *Kredit Kapital*, 1985, *18*(4), pp. 478–89.

Zijlstra, Jelle. International Monetary Reform. In *Zijlstra, J.*, 1985, pp. 57–64.

432 International Monetary Arrangements

4320 International Monetary Arrangements

Aliber, Robert Z. Eurodollars: An Economic Analysis. In *Savona, P. and Sutija, G., eds.*, 1985, pp. 77–98.

Applegate, Charles and Fennell, Susan. Cooperating for Growth and Adjustment. *Finance Develop.*, December 1985, *22*(4), pp. 50–53.

Artis, Michael J. Policy Cooperation and the EMS Experience: Comment. In *Buiter, W. H. and Marston, R. C., eds.*, 1985, pp. 355–59.
[G: **OECD**]

Bácskai, Tamás. East–West Financial Problems and Their Solution in a World-Wide Context. In *Saunders, C. T., ed.*, 1985, pp. 137–46.
[G: **CMEA**]

Batten, Dallas S. and Ott, Mack. The Interrelationship of Monetary Policies under Floating Exchange Rates: A Note. *J. Money, Credit, Banking*, February 1985, *17*(1), pp. 103–10.
[G: **OECD**]

Bhaduri, Amit. Financial Reconstruction for North–South and South–South Trade. *Industry Devel.*, 1985, (14), pp. 37–45.   [G: **Global**]

Bhaduri, Amit and Steindl, Josef. The Rise of Monetarism as a Social Doctrine. In *Arestis, P. and Skouras, T., eds.*, 1985, pp. 56–78.
[G: **Selected Countries**]

Bienen, Henry S. and Gersovitz, Mark. Economic Stabilization, Conditionality, and Political Stability. *Int. Organ.*, Autumn 1985, *39*(4), pp. 728–54.   [G: **LDCs**]

Bilson, John F. O. Macroeconomic Stability and Flexible Exchange Rates. *Amer. Econ. Rev.*, May 1985, *75*(2), pp. 62–67.   [G: **U.S.**]

Bird, Graham and Oppenheim, Jeremy. A Critical Review of Proposals for Financial Co-operation among Developing Countries. *Banca Naz. Lavoro Quart. Rev.*, September 1985, (154), pp. 279–90.   [G: **LDCs**]

Bofinger, Peter. Stabilitätsgerechte Festkurssysteme. (Stability-Consonant Fixed Exchange Rate Systems. With English summary.) *Kredit Kapital*, 1985, *18*(2), pp. 173–92.   [G: **U.S.; Japan; W. Germany; OECD**]

Brinner, Roger E. Reflections on Reflections: Comments [Thoughts on Public Expenditures]

[The International Agenda] [Reflections on Macroeconomic Modelling; Confessions of a DRI Addict]. *Eastern Econ. J.*, Jan.-Mar. 1985, *11*(1), pp. 84–87.

Brunner, Karl. Monetary Policy and Monetary Order. In *[Weintraub, R. E.]*, 1985, pp. 4–21.

Buiter, Willem H. International Policy Coordination in Historical Perspective: A View from the Interwar Years: Comment. In *Buiter, W. H. and Marston, R. C., eds.*, 1985, pp. 178–81.

Byrne, William J. Evolution of the SDR, 1974–1981. In *Adams, J., ed.*, 1985, pp. 340–50.

Carli, Guido. Eurodollars: Policy Analysis. In *Savona, P. and Sutija, G., eds.*, 1985, pp. 139–61.   [G: **OECD**]

Cesarano, Filippo. On the Viability of Monetary Unions. *J. Int. Econ.*, November 1985, *19*(3/4), pp. 367–74.

Cheney, David M. The OECD Export Credits Agreement. *Finance Develop.*, September 1985, *22*(3), pp. 35–38.   [G: **OECD**]

Claassen, Emil-Maria. The Lender-of-Last-Resort Function in the Context of National and International Financial Crises. *Weltwirtsch. Arch.*, 1985, *121*(2), pp. 217–37.

de Clercq, Willy. International Monetary Problems and Trade. In *Peeters, T.; Praet, P. and Reding, P., eds.*, 1985, pp. 397–403.

Curzio, Alberto Quadrio. Dal rifiuto del numerario aureo ai prezzi quasi-ufficiali dell'oro. (From the Rejection of the Gold-Numeraire to Quasi-official Gold Prices. With English summary.) *Rivista Int. Sci. Econ. Com.*, Oct.-Nov. 1985, *32*(10–11), pp. 965–87.
[G: **Global**]

Debonneuil, Xavier and Galy, Michel. Can Exchange Rate Predictability Be Achieved without Monetary Convergence?—Evidence from the EMS: Comment. *Europ. Econ. Rev.*, June-July 1985, *28*(1–2), pp. 117–20.
[G: **W. Europe**]

Dell, Sidney. The Fifth Credit Tranche. *World Devel.*, February 1985, *13*(2), pp. 245–49.

Dillon, K. Burke and Lipton, David. External Debt and Economic Management: The Role of the International Monetary Fund. In *Mehran, H., ed.*, 1985, pp. 31–52.

Drake, Louis S. Reconstruction of a Bimetallic Price Level. *Exploration Econ. Hist.*, April 1985, *22*(2), pp. 194–219.   [G: **U.S.**]

Ebeling, Richard M. Ludwig von Mises and the Gold Standard. In *Rockwell, L. H., Jr., ed.*, 1985, pp. 35–59.

Eichengreen, Barry. International Policy Coordination in Historical Perspective: A View from the Interwar Years. In *Buiter, W. H. and Marston, R. C., eds.*, 1985, pp. 139–78.

Feito, José Luis. The World Monetary System, the International Business Cycle, and the External Debt Crisis. In *Wionczek, M. S., ed.*, 1985, pp. 193–227.   [G: **LDCs**]

Fiallo, Fabio R. A Two-Front Attack to Overcome the Payment Crisis of Developing Countries. *Cepal Rev.*, December 1985, (27), pp. 79–96.
[G: **LDCs**]

Flemming, J. S. Can Exchange Rate Predictability Be Achieved without Monetary Convergence?—Evidence from the EMS: Comment. *Europ. Econ. Rev.*, June-July 1985, *28*(1–2), pp. 121–22. **[G: W. Europe]**

Francis, Carlene Y. The Offshore Banking Sector in the Bahamas. *Soc. Econ. Stud.*, December 1985, *34*(4), pp. 91–110. **[G: Bahamas]**

Fujita, Seiichi. A Critical Note on "Dollar Standard." *Kobe Univ. Econ.*, 1985, (31), pp. 69–91. **[G: U.S.]**

Füllenkemper, Horst and Rehm, Hannes. Internationale Finanzmärkte unter Innovations- und Liberalisierungsdruck. (International Financial Markets under Innovation and Liberalization Pressure. With English summary.) *Kredit Kapital*, 1985, *18*(4), pp. 553–85. **[G: W. Germany]**

Furtado, Celso. Crisis and Change in the World Economy. In *Gauhar, A., ed.*, 1985, pp. 69–87.

Garrison, Roger W. The Costs of a Gold Standard. In *Rockwell, L. H., Jr., ed.*, 1985, pp. 61–79.

Gavin, Bridig. A GATT for International Banking? *J. World Trade Law*, March:April 1985, *19*(2), pp. 121–35. **[G: OECD; Asia]**

Giddy, Ian H. Eurocurrency Arbitrage. In *Savona, P. and Sutija, G., eds.*, 1985, pp. 123–36.

Goedhart, C. Zijlstra's Concerto Grosso: *Fourteen Annual Reports: Themes and Variations (1967–1980)*. In *Zijlstra, J.*, 1985, pp. 3–31.

Goodhart, Charles A. E. Alternative Monetary Regimes. *Hong Kong Econ. Pap.*, 1985, (16), pp. 1–13. **[G: OECD]**

Goodhart, Charles A. E. Eurodollars: Policy Analysis: Comment. In *Savona, P. and Sutija, G., eds.*, 1985, pp. 161–67. **[G: OECD]**

Gray, Jo Anna. International Policy Coordination in Historical Perspective: A View from the Interwar Years: Comment. In *Buiter, W. H. and Marston, R. C., eds.*, 1985, pp. 181–83.

Guma, X. P. The Rand Monetary Area Agreement. *S. Afr. J. Econ.*, June 1985, *53*(2), pp. 166–83. **[G: S. Africa; Swaziland; Lesotho; Botswana]**

Haberler, Gottfried. International Aspects of U.S. Inflation. In *Haberler, G.*, 1985, pp. 311–34. **[G: U.S.]**

Haberler, Gottfried. Oil, Inflation, Recession and the International Monetary System. In *Haberler, G.*, 1985, pp. 335–47.

Haberler, Gottfried. The International Monetary System in the World Recession. In *Haberler, G.*, 1985, pp. 229–63. **[G: OECD]**

Herrera, Felipe. Twenty-five Years of the Inter-American Development Bank. *Cepal Rev.*, December 1985, (27), pp. 143–51.

Herring, Richard J. The Interbank Market. In *Savona, P. and Sutija, G., eds.*, 1985, pp. 111–21.

Higonnet, René P. Eurobanks, Eurodollars and International Debt. In *Savona, P. and Sutija, G., eds.*, 1985, pp. 15–52. **[G: OECD]**

Houthakker, Hendrik S. The International

Agenda. *Eastern Econ. J.*, Jan.-Mar. 1985, *11*(1), pp. 71–78. **[G: Global]**

Jamal, Amir H. Development Means Structural Adjustment. In *Bapna, A., ed.*, 1985, pp. 49–57. **[G: Tanzania; LDCs]**

James, Emile. Quasi tutte cadute le illusioni sui cambi fluttuanti. (The End of Many Hopes on Floating Exchange Rates. With English summary.) *Bancaria*, June 1985, *41*(6), pp. 665–69. **[G: OECD]**

Johnson, G. G. Enhancing the Effectiveness of Surveillance. *Finance Develop.*, December 1985, *22*(4), pp. 2–6.

Kahler, Miles. Politics and International Debt: Explaining the Crisis. *Int. Organ.*, Summer 1985, *39*(3), pp. 357–82. **[G: Global]**

Kindleberger, Charles P. International Monetary Reform in the Nineteenth Century. In *Kindleberger, C. P.*, 1985, pp. 213–25.

Kindleberger, Charles P. Key Currencies and Financial Centres. In *Kindleberger, C. P.*, 1985, pp. 155–67. **[G: OECD]**

Kindleberger, Charles P. Losing Information: The More We Study the Gold Standard the Less We Know about It. *Weltwirtsch. Arch.*, 1985, *121*(2), pp. 382–86.

Kindleberger, Charles P. The Dollar Yesterday, Today, and Tomorrow. *Banca Naz. Lavoro Quart. Rev.*, December 1985, (155), pp. 295–308.

Kyriazis, Nicholas K. The Drachma's Adhesion to the European Monetary System. Possible Effects. *Kredit Kapital*, 1985, *18*(4), pp. 504–14. **[G: Greece]**

Lever, Harold. The Dollar and the World Economy: The Case for Concerted Management. *Lloyds Bank Rev.*, July 1985, (157), pp. 1–12. **[G: Global]**

Levich, Richard M. A View from the International Capital Markets. In *Walter, I., ed.*, 1985, pp. 255–92. **[G: OECD]**

Little, Jane Sneddon. Eurobanks, Eurodollars and International Debt: Comment. In *Savona, P. and Sutija, G., eds.*, 1985, pp. 52–58. **[G: OECD]**

Lüke, Rolf E. The Schacht and the Keynes Plan. *Banca Naz. Lavoro Quart. Rev.*, March 1985, (152), pp. 65–76. **[G: EEC]**

Marston, Richard C. Financial Disturbances and the Effects of an Exchange Rate Union. In *Bhandari, J. S., ed.*, 1985, pp. 272–91.

Masera, Rainer S. Eurobanks, Eurodollars and International Debt: Comment. In *Savona, P. and Sutija, G., eds.*, 1985, pp. 59–66.

Mayer, Helmut W. Eurobanks, Eurodollars and International Debt: Comment. In *Savona, P. and Sutija, G., eds.*, 1985, pp. 66–73. **[G: OECD]**

McCulloch, Rachel. Unexpected Real Consequences of Floating Exchange Rates. In *Adams, J., ed.*, 1985, pp. 286–306. **[G: OECD]**

Melitz, Jacques. The Welfare Case for the European Monetary System. *J. Int. Money Finance*, December 1985, *4*(4), pp. 485–506. **[G: Europe]**

Melvin, Michael. Currency Substitution and

Western European Monetary Unification. *Economica*, February 1985, 52(205), pp. 79–91. [G: EEC]

Melvin, Michael. The Choice of an Exchange Rate System and Macroeconomic Stability. *J. Money, Credit, Banking*, Part 1, Nov. 1985, 17(4), pp. 467–78. [G: Selected Countries]

Micossi, Stefano. The Intervention and Financing Mechanisms of the EMS and the Role of the ECU. *Banca Naz. Lavoro Quart. Rev.*, December 1985, (155), pp. 327–45.

Mullineux, A. W. Do We Need the Bank of England? *Lloyds Bank Rev.*, July 1985, (157), pp. 13–24. [G: U.K.]

Mushin, J. D. Flaws in Metghalchi's Test of E.M.S. Success. *Atlantic Econ. J.*, March 1985, 13(1), pp. 102. [G: EEC]

Narasimham, M. The International Financial and Monetary Systems and the Developing Countries. *Indian Econ. J.*, Jan.-Mar. 1985, 32(3), pp. 1–14. [G: LDCs]

Newton, Scott. Britain, the Sterling Area and European Integration, 1945–50. In *Porter, A. N. and Holland, R. F., eds.*, 1985, pp. 163–82. [G: U.K.]

Nicoll, William. Paths to European Unity. *J. Common Market Stud.*, March 1985, 23(3), pp. 199–206. [G: EEC]

Nightingale, Pamela. The Evolution of Weight-Standards and the Creation of New Monetary and Commercial Links in Northern Europe from the Tenth Century to the Twelfth Century. *Econ. Hist. Rev.*, 2nd Ser., May 1985, 38(2), pp. 192–209. [G: Europe]

O'Sullivan, Patrick H. P. International Banking Facilities and the Eurodollar Market: Comment. In *Savona, P. and Sutija, G., eds.*, 1985, pp. 206–09. [G: U.S.; U.K.]

Oppenheimer, Peter M. Eurodollars: An Economic Analysis: Comment. In *Savona, P. and Sutija, G., eds.*, 1985, pp. 98–106.

Orlando, Luigi. Anche le imprese sono responsabili dei ritardi dell'integrazione europea. (Companies Too Are Responsible for Delays toward European Integration. With English summary.) *Bancaria*, October 1985, 41(10), pp. 1036–40. [G: EEC]

Padoa-Schioppa, Tommaso. Policy Cooperation and the EMS Experience. In *Buiter, W. H. and Marston, R. C., eds.*, 1985, pp. 331–55. EMS: [G: OECD]

Parravicini, Giannino. Una moneta più del mercato che del principe: lo scudo. (The Market Starts Using the Money Created by EEC. With English summary.) *Bancaria*, October 1985, 41(10), pp. 1029–35. [G: EEC]

Paul, Ron. The Political and Economic Agenda for a Real Gold Standard. In *Rockwell, L. H., Jr., ed.*, 1985 , pp. 129–40. [G: U.S.]

Payer, Cheryl. The Politics of Intervention: The Italian Crisis of 1976. In *[Magdoff, H. and Sweezy, P.]*, 1985, pp. 295–318. [G: Italy]

Porter, R. Roderick. International Banking Facilities and the Eurodollar Market: Comment. In *Savona, P. and Sutija, G., eds.*, 1985, pp. 209–10. [G: U.S.; U.K.]

Rhomberg, Rudolf R. Balance of Payments Financing and Reserve Creation. *Int. Monet. Fund Staff Pap.*, March 1985, 32(1), pp. 1–21.

Richardson, David R. On Proposals for a Clearing Union. *J. Post Keynesian Econ.*, Fall 1985, 8(1), pp. 14–27.

Rogoff, Kenneth S. Can Exchange Rate Predictability Be Achieved without Monetary Convergence? Evidence from the EMS. *Europ. Econ. Rev.*, June-July 1985, 28(1–2), pp. 93–115. [G: W. Europe]

Rogoff, Kenneth S. Can International Monetary Policy Cooperation Be Counterproductive? *J. Int. Econ.*, May 1985, 18(3/4), pp. 199–217.

Rosenberg, Emily S. Foundations of United States International Financial Power: Gold Standard Diplomacy, 1900–1905. *Bus. Hist. Rev.*, Summer 1985, 59(2), pp. 169–202. [G: U.S.]

Rothbard, Murray N. The Case for a Genuine Gold Dollar. In *Rockwell, L. H., Jr., ed.*, 1985, pp. 1–17. [G: U.S.]

Rybczynski, T. M. The International Monetary System: Retrospect and Prospect. *Bus. Econ.*, October 1985, 20(4), pp. 24–29. [G: Global]

Sakamoto, Masahiro. Japan's Macroeconomic Performance and Its Effects on the Japanese–U.S. Economic Relationship. In *Nanto, D. K., ed.*, 1985, pp. 79–93. [G: Japan; U.S.]

Salerno, Joseph T. Gold and the International Monetary System: The Contribution of Michael A. Heilperin. In *Rockwell, L. H., Jr., ed.*, 1985, pp. 81–111.

Savona, Paolo. Eurodollars: An Economic Analysis: Comment. In *Savona, P. and Sutija, G., eds.*, 1985, pp. 106–10.

Savona, Paolo and Sutija, George. Eurodollars and International Banking: Introduction. In *Savona, P. and Sutija, G., eds.*, 1985, pp. 1–12.

Schüller, Alfred and Hamel, Hannelore. On the Membership of Socialist Countries in the International Monetary Fund. *Acta Oecon.*, 1985, 34(1–2), pp. 113–30.

Sennholz, Hans F. The Monetary Writings of Carl Menger. In *Rockwell, L. H., Jr., ed.*, 1985, pp. 19–34. [G: Austria]

Shafer, Jeffrey R. International Banking Facilities and the Eurodollar Market: Comment. In *Savona, P. and Sutija, G., eds.*, 1985, pp. 210–15. [G: U.S.; U.K.]

Shafer, Jeffrey R. Policy Cooperation and the EMS Experience: Comment. In *Buiter, W. H. and Marston, R. C., eds.*, 1985, pp. 359–65. [G: OECD]

Spinelli, Franco. Should the Hypothesis of a Well Defined and Stable World Demand for M1 Be Reinstated? *Kredit Kapital*, 1985, 18(2), pp. 193–203. [G: Global]

Steele, D. B. The Case for Global Economic Management and UN System Reform. *Int. Organ.*, Summer 1985, 39(3), pp. 561–78. [G: Global]

Steinherr, Alfred. Competitiveness and Exchange Rates: Policy Issues for Europe. In *Peeters,*

T.; Praet, P. and Reding, P., eds., 1985, pp. 163–89. **[G: U.K.; Belgium; W. Germany]**

Sunkel, Osvaldo. Past, Present and Future of the International Economic Crisis. In *Gauhar, A., ed.*, 1985, pp. 1–41. **[G: Selected Countries]**

Sutija, George. International Banking Facilities and the Eurodollar Market: Comment. In *Savona, P. and Sutija, G., eds.*, 1985, pp. 215–17. **[G: U.S.; U.K.]**

Swoboda, Alexander K. Eurodollars: Policy Analysis: Comment. In *Savona, P. and Sutija, G., eds.*, 1985, pp. 167–75. **[G: OECD]**

Terrell, Henry S. and Mills, Rodney H., Jr. International Banking Facilities and the Eurodollar Market. In *Savona, P. and Sutija, G., eds.*, 1985, pp. 183–206. **[G: U.S.; U.K.]**

Tew, J. H. B. The International Monetary System. In *Morris, D., ed.*, 1985, pp. 549–80. **[G: Selected Countries]**

Thompson, Mark and Slayton, Gregory W. An Essay on Credit Arrangements between the IMF and the Republic of the Philippines: 1970–1983. *Philippine Rev. Econ. Bus.*, Mar./June 1985, 22(1/2), pp. 59–81. **[G: Philippines]**

Thygesen, Niels. New Approaches to Development Finance: A Critical Look at the Brandt Proposals. In *Gutowski, A.; Arnaudo, A. A. and Scharrer, H.-E., eds.*, 1985 , pp. 297–316. **[G: LDCs]**

Tomlinson, B. R. Indo-British Relations in the Post-Colonial Era: The Sterling Balances Negotiations, 1947–49. In *Porter, A. N. and Holland, R. F., eds.*, 1985, pp. 142–62. **[G: U.K.; India]**

Triffin, Robert. Before and After the Bonn Summit Meeting. In *Peeters, T.; Praet, P. and Reding, P., eds.*, 1985, pp. 405–11. **[G: U.S.]**

Triffin, Robert. The International Accounts of the United States and Their Impact upon the Rest of the World. *Banca Naz. Lavoro Quart. Rev.*, March 1985, (152), pp. 15–30. **[G: U.S.; EEC]**

Ukawa, Hidetoshi. Japan's Perspective on Trade. *Challenge*, July/August 1985, 28(3), pp. 18–26. **[G: Japan; U.S.]**

Volcker, Paul A. Statement to the U.S. House Subcommittee on International Development Institutions and Finance of the Committee on Banking, Finance and Urban Affairs, July 30, 1985. *Fed. Res. Bull.*, September 1985, 71(9), pp. 701–05. **[G: LDCs]**

de Vries, Margaret Garritsen. The IMF: 40 Years of Challenge and Change. *Finance Develop.*, September 1985, 22(3), pp. 7–10.

Wanatabe, Atsushi. International Banking Facilities and the Eurodollar Market: Comment. In *Savona, P. and Sutija, G., eds.*, 1985 , pp. 217–19. **[G: U.S.; Japan]**

White, Lawrence H. Free Banking and the Gold Standard. In *Rockwell, L. H., Jr., ed.*, 1985, pp. 113–28.

Wickham, Peter. The Choice of Exchange Rate Regime in Developing Countries: A Survey of the Literature. *Int. Monet. Fund Staff Pap.*, June 1985, 32(2), pp. 248–88. **[G: LDCs]**

Williams, Marion. An Analysis of Regional Trade and Payments Arrangements in CARICOM 1971–1983. *Soc. Econ. Stud.*, December 1985, 34(4), pp. 3–33. **[G: Caribbean]**

Williams, Richard C. Eurodollars: Policy Analysis: Comment. In *Savona, P. and Sutija, G., eds.*, 1985, pp. 176–80. **[G: OECD]**

Williamson, John. Keynes and the Postwar International Economic Order. In *Wattel, H. L., ed.*, 1985, pp. 145–56.

Williamson, John. On the System in Bretton Woods. *Amer. Econ. Rev.*, May 1985, 75(2), pp. 74–79. **[G: Global]**

Williamson, John. On Seeking to Improve IMF Conditionality. In *Adams, J., ed.*, 1985, pp. 351–58.

Zijlstra, Jelle. International Monetary Reform. In *Zijlstra, J.*, 1985, pp. 57–64.

Zijlstra, Jelle. Reflections on International Economic and Monetary Problems. In *Zijlstra, J.*, 1985, pp. 75–87.

Zijlstra, Jelle. Some Aspects of International Monetary Reform. In *Zijlstra, J.*, 1985, pp. 47–55.

Zijlstra, Jelle. Speech at BIS Annual Meeting, 1981. In *Zijlstra, J.*, 1985, pp. 113–21.

Zijlstra, Jelle. Speech at BIS Annual Meeting, 1974. In *Zijlstra, J.*, 1985, pp. 89–97.

Zijlstra, Jelle. Statement at IMF Annual Meeting, 1969. In *Zijlstra, J.*, 1985, pp. 43–45.

Zijlstra, Jelle. Statement at IMF Annual Meeting, 1967. In *Zijlstra, J.*, 1985, pp. 35–38.

Zijlstra, Jelle. Statement at IMF Annual Meeting, 1968. In *Zijlstra, J.*, 1985, pp. 39–42.

Zijlstra, Jelle. Statement at Joint Annual Session of the IMF and World Bank, 1975. In *Zijlstra, J.*, 1985, pp. 99–103.

Zijlstra, Jelle. The Banking System and the EEC. In *Zijlstra, J.*, 1985, pp. 65–74. **[G: EEC]**

Zijlstra, Jelle. The World Economy and the Monetary System. In *Zijlstra, J.*, 1985, pp. 105–12.

Zis, George. Whither ECU? *Greek Econ. Rev.*, August 1985, 7(2), pp. 108–24. **[G: EEC]**

433 Private International Lending

4330 Private International Lending

Abreu, Marcelo de Paiva. Errata [La Argentina y Brasil en los años treinta. Efectos de la política económica internacional británica y estadounidense]. *Desarrollo Econ.*, April–June 1985, 25(97), pp. 114. **[G: Argentina; Brazil; U.S., U.K.]**

Abreu, Marcelo de Paiva. La Argentina y Brasil en los años treinta. Efectos de la política económica internacional británica y estadounidense. (With English summary.) *Desarrollo Econ.*, January-March 1985, 24(96), pp. 543–59. **[G: Argentina; Brazil; U.S.; U.K.]**

Arndt, H. W. and Drake, P. J. Bank Loans or Bonds: Some Lessons of Historical Experience. *Banca Naz. Lavoro Quart. Rev.*, December 1985, (155), pp. 373–92. **[G: U.K.]**

Avramović, Dragoslav. External Debt of Developing Countries in Late 1983. In *Wionczek,*

M. S., ed., 1985, pp. 6–35.   [G: LDCs]

Baer, Donald E. Economic Relations between Latin America and Miami. In *Jorge, A.; Salazar-Carrillo, J. and Diaz-Pou, F., eds.*, 1985, pp. 221–23.   [G: U.S.]

Baker, James A. Lineamenti di un piano contro la crisi dei paesi debitori. (Outline of a Plan against Debtor Countries' Crises summary.) *Bancaria*, November 1985, *41*(11), pp. 1162–67.   [G: Global]

Barth, James R. and Pelzman, Joseph. International Debt: Conflict and Resolution. In *Adams, J., ed.*, 1985, pp. 358–91.   [G: U.S.; GLobal]

Bergsten, C. Fred. The Second Debt Crisis Is Coming. *Challenge*, May/June 1985, *28*(2), pp. 14–21.   [G: U.S.]

Bhaduri, Amit and Steindl, Josef. The Rise of Monetarism as a Social Doctrine. In *Arestis, P. and Skouras, T., eds.*, 1985, pp. 56–78.   [G: Selected Countries]

Biggs, Gonzalo. Legal Aspects of the Latin American Public Debt: Relations with the Commercial Banks. *Cepal Rev.*, April 1985, (25), pp. 163–87.   [G: Latin America]

Blanc, Jacques. L'économie française face à l'apprentissage de la gestion de son endettement extérieur. (With English summary.) *Revue Écon. Polit.*, Sept.-Oct. 1985, *95*(5), pp. 658–72.   [G: France]

Blank, Barry W. and Sein, Lila. U.S. Banking Adjustments to Changes in Gulf Liquidity. In *Czinkota, M. R. and Marciel, S., eds.*, 1985, pp. 101–28.   [G: U.S.; OPEC]

de Boissieu, Christian. Contrainte externe et arriérés de paiement intérieurs dans les pays en développement. (External Constraint and Domestic Arrears in Developing Countries. With English summary.) *Écon. Soc.*, September 1985, *19*(9), pp. 135–45.   [G: LDCs]

Bourne, Compton. The International Debt Crisis and Development Strategies in the Caribbean. In *Salazar-Carrillo, J. and de Alonso, I. T., eds.*, 1985, pp. 1–35.   [G: Caribbean]

Brainard, Lawrence J. Current Illusions about the International Debt Crisis. *World Econ.*, March 1985, *8*(1), pp. 1–9.   [G: Global]

Branson, William H. Policy and Performance Links between LDC Debtors and Industrial Nations: Comment. *Brookings Pap. Econ. Act.*, 1985, (2), pp. 357–61.   [G: LDCs; OECD]

Brovedani, Bruno. Obstacles in the Way of a Resumption of Spontaneous International Bank Lending. In *Jorge, A.; Salazar-Carrillo, J. and Diaz-Pou, F., eds.*, 1985, pp. 23–28.   [G: LDCs]

Buira, Ariel. Capital Market Financing to Developing Countries. In *Wionczek, M. S., ed.*, 1985, pp. 170–92.   [G: LDCs]

Burton, F. N. and Inoue, H. The Influence of Country Risk Factors on Interest Rate Differentials on International Bank Lending to Sovereign Borrowers. *Appl. Econ.*, June 1985, *17*(3), pp. 491–507.

Caballero, Carlos. A Closer Look at Colombia's

Foreign Debt. In *Salazar-Carrillo, J. and de Alonso, I. T., eds.*, 1985, pp. 1–14.   [G: Latin America; Colombia]

Callier, Philippe. Further Results on Countries' Debt-servicing Performance: The Relevance of Structural Factors. *Weltwirtsch. Arch.*, 1985, *121*(1), pp. 105–15.   [G: LDCs]

Campbell, Bruce. Transnational Bank Lending, Debt and Balance of Payments Deficits in Third World Countries. *Can. J. Devel. Stud.*, 1985, *6*(1), pp. 45–64.   [G: LDCs]

Carli, Guido. The Internationalization of Financial and Credit Systems. *Rev. Econ. Cond. Italy*, Sept.-Dec. 1985, (3), pp. 341–51.   [G: Global]

Catan, Luis. The Future of Debtor Countries in Latin America. In *Kaushik, S. K., ed.*, 1985, pp. 17–31.

de Cecco, Marcello. The International Debt Program in the Interwar Period. *Banca Naz. Lavoro Quart. Rev.*, March 1985, (152), pp. 45–64.   [G: OECD]

Chacel, Julian M. Brazil's Foreign Debt: The National Debate. In *Duran, E., ed.*, 1985, pp. 69–80.   [G: Brazil]

Cline, William R. International Debt: From Crisis to Recovery? *Amer. Econ. Rev.*, May 1985, *75*(2), pp. 185–90.   [G: LDCs; OECD]

Cline, William R. Policy and Performance Links between LDC Debtors and Industrial Nations: Comment. *Brookings Pap. Econ. Act.*, 1985, (2), pp. 361–66.   [G: LDCs; OECD]

Coes, Donald V. Imperfect Capital Mobility, Risk, and Brazilian Foreign Borrowing. In *Salazar-Carrillo, J. and Fendt, R., Jr., eds.*, 1985, pp. 38–52.   [G: Brazil]

Cohen, Benjamin J. International Debt and Linkage Strategies: Some Foreign-Policy Implications for the United States. *Int. Organ.*, Autumn 1985, *39*(4), pp. 699–727.   [G: U.S.]

Colaço, Francis X. International Capital Flows and Economic Development. *Finance Develop.*, September 1985, *22*(3), pp. 2–6.   [G: Global]

Cornell, Bradford and Sand, Ole Christian. The Value of Base Rate Options in the Eurocredit Market. *J. Bank Res.*, Spring 1985, *16*(1), pp. 22–27.   [G: U.S.]

Devlin, Robert. External Debt and Crisis: The Decline of the Orthodox Strategy. *Cepal Rev.*, December 1985, (27), pp. 35–52.   [G: Latin America]

Devlin, Robert. Le deuda externa vs. el desarrollo económico: América Latina en la encrucijada. (The Foreing Debt vs. Economic Development: Latin America at a Crossroads. With English summary.) *Colección Estud. CIEPLAN*, September 1985, (17), pp. 69–100.   [G: Latin America]

Devlin, Robert and de la Piedra, Enrique. Pen and Its Private Bankers: Scenes from an Unhappy Marriage. In *Wionczek, M. S., ed.*, 1985, pp. 383–426.   [G: Peru]

Dornbusch, Rudiger. Imperfect Capital Mobility, Exchange Risk and Brazilian Foreign Borrowing: Comments. In *Salazar-Carrillo, J. and*

Fendt, R., Jr., eds., 1985, pp. 53–58.
[G: Brazil]

Dornbusch, Rudiger. Policy and Performance Links between LDC Debtors and Industrial Nations. *Brookings Pap. Econ. Act.*, 1985, (2), pp. 303–56. **[G: LDCs; OECD]**

Echevarria, Oscar A. Solutions to the Debt Issue: A Latin American Perspective. In *Jorge, A.; Salazar-Carrillo, J. and Diaz-Pou, F., eds.*, 1985, pp. 225–31. **[G: Latin America]**

Eskridge, William N., Jr. Santa Claus and Sigmund Freud: Structural Contexts of the International Debt Problem. In *Eskridge, W. N., Jr., ed.*, 1985, pp. 27–101.

Estévez, Jaime. Crisis de pagos y proceso de ajuste en Brasil y México. (Payment Crisis and Adjustment Process in Brazil and Mexico. With English summary.) *Colección Estud. CIEPLAN*, September 1985, (17), pp. 33–67. **[G: Brazil; Mexico]**

Feder, Gershon and Uy, Lily V. The Determinants of International Creditworthiness and Their Policy Implications. *J. Policy Modeling*, Spring 1985, 7(1), pp. 133–56. **[G: LDCs]**

Feinberg, Richard E. International Finance and Investment: A Surging Public Sector. In *Sewell, J. W.; Feinberg, R. E. and Kallab, V., eds.*, 1985, pp. 51–71. **[G: U.S.; LDCs]**

Feinberg, Richard E. LDC Debt and the Public-Sector Rescue. *Challenge*, July/August 1985, 28(3), pp. 27–34. **[G: LDCs; U.S.]**

Felix, David. How to Resolve Latin America's Debt Crisis. *Challenge*, Nov./Dec. 1985, 28(5), pp. 44–51. **[G: Latin America]**

Ferri, Giovanni and Jafarey, Saqib. Banking Crises and Welfare Implications of Foreign Lending under Informationally Limited Spatial Horizons. *Econ. Notes*, 1985, (3), pp. 121–33.

Ffrench-Davis, Ricardo. The External Debt Crisis in Latin America: Trends and Outlook. In *Kim, K. S. and Ruccio, D. F., eds.*, 1985, pp. 133–62. **[G: LDCs]**

Ffrench-Davis, Ricardo. The External Debt, Financial Liberalization and Crisis in Chile. In *Wionczek, M. S., ed.*, 1985, pp. 348–82. **[G: Chile]**

Ffrench-Davis, Ricardo and De Gregorio, José. La renegociación de la deuda externa de Chile en 1985: antecedentes y comentarios. (The Rescheduling of Chile's Foreign Debt in 1985: Background and Comments. With English summary.) *Colección Estud. CIEPLAN*, September 1985, (17), pp. 9–32. **[G: Chile]**

Fishlow, Albert. Lessons from the Past: Capital Markets during the 19th Century and the Interwar Period. *Int. Organ.*, Summer 1985, 39(3), pp. 383–439. **[G: W. Europe; U.S.]**

FitzGerald, E. V. K. Foreign Finance and Capital Accumulation in Latin America: A Critical Approach. In *Abel, C. and Lewis, C. M., eds.*, 1985, pp. 451–71. **[G: Latin America]**

Flamm, Kenneth. Mexico and the United States: Studies in Economic Interaction: Finance: Comments. In *Musgrave, P. B., ed.*, 1985, pp. 71–76. **[G: Mexico]**

Flood, Eugene. Currency Risk and Country Risk in International Banking: Discussion. *J. Finance*, July 1985, 40(3), pp. 892–93.

Folkerts-Landau, David. The Changing Role of International Bank Lending in Development Finance. *Int. Monet. Fund Staff Pap.*, June 1985, 32(2), pp. 317–63. **[G: LDCs]**

Foxley, Alejandro. El problema de la deuda externa visto desde américa latina. (The Problem of Foreign Debt from a Latin American Perspective. With English summary.) *Colección Estud. CIEPLAN*, 1985, (18), pp. 39–62. **[G: Latin America]**

Führer, Helmut. The Flow of Public and Private Financial Resources to Developing Countries: Recent Trends. In *Gutowski, A.; Arnaudo, A. A. and Scharrer, H.-E., eds.*, 1985, pp. 139–61. **[G: Selected LDCs]**

Furtado, Celso. Crisis and Change in the World Economy. In *Gauhar, A., ed.*, 1985, pp. 69–87.

Garten, Jeffrey E. Gunboat Economics. *Foreign Aff.*, 1985, 63(3), pp. 538–59. **[G: Global]**

Gavin, Bridig. A GATT for International Banking? *J. World Trade Law*, March:April 1985, 19(2), pp. 121–35. **[G: OECD; Asia]**

Ghantus, Elias T. Developing a Worldwide Arab Banking System. In *Czinkota, M. R. and Marciel, S., eds.*, 1985, pp. 129–37. **[G: OPEC]**

Gitlow, Abraham L. Economics Seen Darkly in a Political Mirror. *Rivista Int. Sci. Econ. Com.*, January 1985, 32(1), pp. 87–98. **[G: U.S.; LDCs]**

Godano, Giuseppe. Aumenta ovunque nel mondo la complessità del compito del banchiere. (Bankers' Tasks Are Becoming More Complex All over the World. With English summary.) *Bancaria*, December 1985, 41(12), pp. 1209–15. **[G: OECD]**

Goldsbrough, David. Foreign Direct Investment in Developing Countries. *Finance Develop.*, March 1985, 22(1), pp. 31–34. **[G: LDCs]**

Gomez-Samper, Henry. The Management of Venezuela's External Debt: Makings of a Management Epic. In *Salazar-Carrillo, J. and de Alonso, I. T., eds.*, 1985, pp. 1–15. **[G: Venezuela]**

Green, Donald W. The Global Impact of Debt Rescheduling. In *Saunders, C. T., ed.*, 1985, pp. 147–60. **[G: Selected Countries]**

Gurría Trevino, José Angel. Borrowing Strategies and Market Conditions: A Sovereign Borrower's Perspective of Negotiating Loans with Transnational Banks. In *Mehran, H., ed.*, 1985, pp. 112–25. **[G: LDCs]**

Guttentag, Jack M. and Herring, Richard J. Funding Risk in the International Interbank Market. In *[Bloomfield, A. I.]*, 1985, pp. 19–32.

Hakim, Jonathan. Latin America's Financial Crisis: Causes and Cures. In *Duran, E., ed.*, 1985, pp. 17–37. **[G: Latin America]**

Heath, Edward. General Policies for International Development and Cooperation. *Ann. Pub. Co-op. Econ.*, January–June 1985, 56(1–2), pp. 111–19.

Heffernan, Shelagh A. Country Risk Analysis:

The Demand and Supply of Sovereign Loans. *J. Int. Money Finance*, September 1985, *4*(3), pp. 389–413. [G: LDCs]

Heinemann, H. Erich. Commentary on Prospects for Money and the Economy. In *Shadow Open Market Committee.*, 1985, pp. 55–62. [G: U.S.; LDCs]

Higonnet, René P. Eurobanks, Eurodollars and International Debt. In *Savona, P. and Sutija, G., eds.*, 1985, pp. 15–52. [G: OECD]

Hoch, Standley H. LDC Debt and a Multinational Company. In *Kaushik, S. K., ed.*, 1985, pp. 33–40.

Hurlock, James. Debt Restructure Agreements: Perspective of Counsel for Borrowing Countries. In *Eskridge, W. N., Jr., ed.*, 1985, pp. 119–34. [G: LDCs]

Iglesias, Enrique V. External Debt Problems of Latin America. In *Wionczek, M. S., ed.*, 1985, pp. 73–96. [G: Latin America]

Jackson, Henry F. The African Crisis: Drought and Debt. *Foreign Aff.*, Summer 1985, *63*(5), pp. 1081–94. [G: Africa]

Joefield-Napier, Wallace. External Public Debt and Public Finance in OECS Member Countries and Belize: 1977–1982. *Soc. Econ. Stud.*, December 1985, *34*(4), pp. 59–89. [G: Caribbean]

Kaffman, Luis. External Debt and Renegotiation: Is Chile a Special Case? In *Hojman, D. E., ed.*, 1985, pp. 115–24. [G: Chile; Latin America]

Kahler, Miles. Politics and International Debt: Explaining the Crisis. *Int. Organ.*, Summer 1985, *39*(3), pp. 357–82. [G: Global]

Kaufman, Robert R. Democratic and Authoritarian Responses to the Debt Issue: Argentina, Brazil, Mexico. *Int. Organ.*, Summer 1985, *39*(3), pp. 472–503. [G: Argentina; Brazil; Mexico]

Kaushik, S. K. The Debt Crisis and Financial Stability: The Future: Introduction. In *Kaushik, S. K., ed.*, 1985, pp. 5–13.

Kindleberger, Charles P. Historical Perspective on Today's Third-World Debt Problem. *Écon. Soc.*, September 1985, *19*(9), pp. 109–34. [G: LDCs]

Kindleberger, Charles P. The Cyclical Pattern of Long-term Lending. In *Kindleberger, C. P.*, 1985, pp. 141–54. [G: Europe; U.S.]

Kloten, Norbert. International Indebtedness: Trends and Prospects. *Acta Oecon.*, 1985, *34*(1–2), pp. 131–43.

Kneer, Josef. Zur Diskussion um die Auswirkungen der steigenden internationalen Zinssätze auf die Verschuldungsproblematik der Entwicklungsländer: Die amerikanische "Kompensationsthese." (The Impact of Increasing International Interest Rates on the Current Accounts of Deeply Indebted Developing Countries: The American "Compensation Thesis." With English summary.) *Konjunkturpolitik*, 1985, *31*(1/2), pp. 115–25. [G: Argentina; Brazil; Mexico; Venezuela; Chile]

Lal, Deepak and van Wijnbergen, Sweder. Government Deficits, the Real Interest Rate and LDC Debt: On Global Crowding Out. *Europ. Econ. Rev.*, November 1985, *29*(2), pp. 157–91. [G: Global]

Lichtenstein, Cynthia C. U.S. Response to the International Debt Crisis: The International Lending Supervision Act of 1983 and the Regulations Issued under the Act. In *Eskridge, W. N., Jr., ed.*, 1985, pp. 177–206. [G: U.S.]

Little, Jane Sneddon. Eurobanks, Eurodollars and International Debt: Comment. In *Savona, P. and Sutija, G., eds.*, 1985, pp. 52–58. [G: OECD]

Masera, Rainer S. Eurobanks, Eurodollars and International Debt: Comment. In *Savona, P. and Sutija, G., eds.*, 1985, pp. 59–66. [G: OECD]

Mayer, Helmut W. Eurobanks, Eurodollars and International Debt: Comment. In *Savona, P. and Sutija, G., eds.*, 1985, pp. 66–73. [G: OECD]

Melvin, Michael and Schlagenhauf, Don E. A Country Risk Index: Econometric Formulation and an Application to Mexico. *Econ. Inquiry*, October 1985, *23*(4), pp. 601–19. [G: Mexico]

Mohammed, Azizali F. The Case by Case Approach to Debt Problems. *Finance Develop.*, March 1985, *22*(1), pp. 27–30. [G: Selected Countries]

Mudge, Alfred. Sovereign Debt Restructure: A Perspective of Counsel to Agent Banks, Bank Advisory Groups, and Servicing Banks. In *Eskridge, W. N., Jr., ed.*, 1985, pp. 105–18.

Mukherjee, Amitabha. Loan Commitment of Less Developed Countries: A Study in Retrospect. *Indian Econ. J.*, Jan.-Mar. 1985, *32*(3), pp. 60–81. [G: LDCs]

Navarrete, Jorge Eduardo. Foreign Policy and International Financial Negotiations: The External Debt and the Cartagena Consensus. *Cepal Rev.*, December 1985, (27), pp. 7–25. [G: Latin America]

Niehans, Jürg. International Debt with Unenforceable Claims. *Fed. Res. Bank San Francisco Econ. Rev.*, Winter 1985, (1), pp. 64–79. [G: LDCs]

Nunnenkamp, Peter. Bank Lending to Developing Countries and Possible Solutions to International Debt Problems. *Kyklos*, 1985, *38*(4), pp. 555–77. [G: LCDs; MDCs]

Quale, Andrew C., Jr. The International Debt Roller Coaster: Time for a New Approach. In *Eskridge, W. N., Jr., ed.*, 1985, pp. 153–76. [G: LDCs; MDCs]

Rączkowski, Stanisław. Debt Rescheduling: Benefits and Costs for Debtors and Creditors. In *Saunders, C. T., ed.*, 1985, pp. 161–75.

Rhodes, William R. Debt Restructuring and Creditors. In *Kaushik, S. K., ed.*, 1985, pp. 41–45.

Rogers, William D. The United States and Latin America. *Foreign Aff.*, 1985, *63*(3), pp. 560–80. [G: Latin American; U.S.]

Rousseau, J. M. Risque croissant et endettement. (Growing Risk and Indebtedness. With English summary.) *Écon. Soc.*, September 1985, *19*(9), pp. 53–79.

Sachs, Jeffrey. External Debt and Macroeconomic Performance in Latin America and East Asia. *Brookings Pap. Econ. Act.*, 1985, (2), pp. 523–64.   [G: Latin America; E. Asia]

Schirano, Louis G. A Dance along the Precipice: The Political and Economic Dimensions of the International Debt Problem: A Banker's View. In *Eskridge, W. N., Jr., ed.*, 1985, pp. 17–25.

Schröder, Klaus. Economic Relations—Interdependence or Marginal Factor?: Credit. In *Rode, R. and Jacobsen, H.-D., eds.*, 1985, pp. 36–49.   [G: CMEA]

Sengupta, Arjun. Recovery, Interdependence, and the Developing Economies. *Finance Develop.*, September 1985, *22*(3), pp. 11–14.   [G: Global]

Shapiro, Alan C. Currency Risk and Country Risk in International Banking. *J. Finance*, July 1985, *40*(3), pp. 881–91.

Shipley, Walter V. Economic Development and a Strong U.S. Banking Industry. In *Kaushik, S. K., ed.*, 1985, pp. 71–75.

Solomon, Robert. The United States as a Debtor in the 19th Century. *Écon. Soc.*, September 1985, *19*(9), pp. 33–52.   [G: U.S.]

Stewart, Frances. The International Debt Situation and North–South Relations. *World Devel.*, February 1985, *13*(2), pp. 191–204.   [G: Global]

Street, James H. Development Planning and the International Debt Crisis in Latin America. *J. Econ. Issues*, June 1985, *19*(2), pp. 397–408.   [G: Latin America]

Taeho, Kim. Assessment of External Debt Servicing Capacity: An Alternative Methodology. *J. Econ. Devel.*, December 1985, *10*(2), pp. 35–52.   [G: LDCs]

Thurow, Lester C. The Politics of Deregulation; Evolution of the Major Banks and the Financial Intermediaries in the U.S.A. *Rev. Econ. Cond. Italy*, Sept.-Dec. 1985, (3), pp. 353–62.   [G: U.S.]

Thygesen, Niels. New Approaches to Development Finance: A Critical Look at the Brandt Proposals. In *Gutowski, A.; Arnaudo, A. A. and Scharrer, H.-E., eds.*, 1985, pp. 297–316.   [G: LDCs]

Tonnel-Martinache, Mariette. La délocalisation de l'activité financière bancaire. (With English summary.) *Revue Écon. Polit.*, May–June 1985, *95*(3), pp. 346–76.   [G: OECD]

Trebat, Thomas J. Mexico's Foreign Financing. In *Musgrave, P. B., ed.*, 1985, pp. 33–70.   [G: Mexico]

Tutino, Franco. Oneri e vincoli imposti dalla forte crescita dell'indebitamento sull'estero. (Burdens and Restraints Imposed by the Strong Growth of Foreign Debt. With English summary.) *Bancaria*, September 1985, *41*(9), pp. 962–68.   [G: Italy]

Weinberg, Carl B. The Language and Techniques of Multiyear Restructuring of Sovereign Debt: Lessons from the Mexican Experience. *J. Pol-*

icy Modeling, Fall 1985, *7*(3), pp. 477–90.   [G: Mexico]

Wellons, Philip A. Business–Government Relations in International Bank Lending: The Debt Crisis. In *Eskridge, W. N., Jr., ed.*, 1985, pp. 135–50.   [G: France; Japan; U.K.; U.S.; W. Germany]

Wellons, Philip A. International Debt: The Behavior of Banks in a Politicized Environment. *Int. Organ.*, Summer 1985, *39*(3), pp. 441–71.   [G: OECD; LDCs]

Wiesner, Eduardo. Domestic and External Causes of the Latin American Debt Crisis. *Finance Develop.*, March 1985, *22*(1), pp. 24–26.   [G: Latin America]

Wiesner, Eduardo. Latin American Debt: Lessons and Pending Issues. *Amer. Econ. Rev.*, May 1985, *75*(2), pp. 191–95.   [G: Latin America]

Wilkins, Mira. Foreign Banks and Foreign Investment in the United States. In *Atack, J., ed.*, 1985, pp. 27–34.   [G: U.S.]

Williamson, John. External Debt and Macroeconomic Performance in Latin America and East Asia: Comment. *Brookings Pap. Econ. Act.*, 1985, (2), pp. 565–70.   [G: Latin America; E. Asia]

Zaidi, Iqbal Mehdi. Saving, Investment, Fiscal Deficits, and the External Indebtedness of Developing Countries. *World Devel.*, May 1985, *13*(5), pp. 573–88.   [G: LDCs]

440 INTERNATIONAL INVESTMENT AND FOREIGN AID

441 International Investment and Long-term Capital Movements

4410 General

Agarwal, J. P. Intra-LDCs Foreign Direct Investment: A Comparative Analysis of Third World Multinationals. *Devel. Econ.*, September 1985, *23*(3), pp. 236–53.   [G: LDCs]

Balassa, Bela. U.S. Direct Foreign Investment and Trade: Theories, Trends and Public Policy Issues: Comment. In *Erdilek, A., ed.*, 1985, pp. 151–54.   [G: U.S.]

Bale, Harvey E., Jr. National and International Data Problems and Solutions in the Empirical Analysis of Intra-industry Direct Foreign Investment: Comment. In *Erdilek, A., ed.*, 1985, pp. 189–92.   [G: Global; U.S.]

Branson, William H. International Capital Movements. *Economia (Portugal)*, January 1985, *9*(1), pp. 3–28.   [G: Asia]

Buckley, Peter J. Testing Theories of the Multinational Enterprise: A Review of the Evidence. In *Buckley, P. J. and Casson, M.*, 1985, pp. 192–211.   [G: LDCs; MDCs]

Buffie, Edward F. Quantitative Restrictions and the Welfare Effects of Capital Inflows. *J. Int. Econ.*, November 1985, *19*(3/4), pp. 291–303.

Burgstaller, André. North–South Trade and Capital Flows in a Ricardian Model of Accumulation. *J. Int. Econ.*, May 1985, *18*(3/4), pp. 241–60.

Calderón-Rossell, Jorge R. Towards the Theory of Foreign Direct Investment. *Oxford Econ. Pap.*, June 1985, *37*(2), pp. 282–91.

Davidson, Carl; Matusz, Steven J. and Kreinin, Mordechai E. Analysis of Performance Standards for Direct Foreign Investments. *Can. J. Econ.*, November 1985, *18*(4), pp. 876–90.

Dei, Fumio. Voluntary Export Restraints and Foreign Investment. *J. Int. Econ.*, November 1985, *19*(3/4), pp. 305–12.

Dunning, John H. and Rugman, Alan M. The Influence of Hymer's Dissertation on the Theory of Foreign Direct Investment. *Amer. Econ. Rev.*, May 1985, *75*(2), pp. 228–32.

Gray, H. Peter. Multinationals Corporations and Global Welfare: An Extension of Kojima and Ozawa. *Hitotsubashi J. Econ.*, December 1985, *26*(2), pp. 125–33.

Grossman, Gene M. U.S. Direct Foreign Investment and Trade: Theories, Trends and Public Policy Issues: Comment. In *Erdilek, A., ed.,* 1985, pp. 155–59. [G: U.S.]

Grossman, Gene M. and Razin, Assaf. Direct Foreign Investment and the Choice of Technique under Uncertainty. *Oxford Econ. Pap.*, December 1985, *37*(4), pp. 606–20.

Hawkins, Robert G. Antitrust Policy and Intra-industry Direct Foreign Investment: Cause and Effect: Comment. In *Erdilek, A., ed.,* 1985, pp. 123–25. [G: U.S.]

Heinemann, Hans-Joachim. Zum Zusammenwirken von Direktinvestitionen und Technologietransfer. (On Direct Investment Combined with Technology Transfer. With English summary.) *Ifo-Studien*, 1985, *31*(2), pp. 93–107.

Jha, L. K. Regulation of Foreign Investment. In *Jha, L. K.,* 1985, pp. 34–44.

Khan, Mohsin S. and Ul Haque, Nadeem. Foreign Borrowing and Capital Flight: A Formal Analysis. *Int. Monet. Fund Staff Pap.*, December 1985, *32*(4), pp. 606–28. [G: LDCs]

Kojima, Kiyoshi and Ozawa, Terutomo. Toward a Theory of Industrial Restructuring and Dynamic Comparative Advantage. *Hitotsubashi J. Econ.*, December 1985, *26*(2), pp. 135–45.

Kravis, Irving B. The Determinants of Intra-industry Direct Foreign Investment: Comment. In *Erdilek, A., ed.,* 1985, pp. 60–64.

Lipsey, Robert E. National and International Data Problems and Solutions in the Empirical Analysis of Intra-industry Direct Foreign Investment: Comment. In *Erdilek, A., ed.,* 1985, pp. 185–89. [G: Global; U.S.]

Marquez, Jaime. Foreign Exchange Constraints and Growth Possibilities in the LDCs. *J. Devel. Econ.*, Sept.-Oct. 1985, *19*(1/2), pp. 39–57. [G: LDCs]

McCulloch, Rachel. U.S. Direct Foreign Investment and Trade: Theories, Trends and Public Policy Issues. In *Erdilek, A., ed.,* 1985, pp. 129–51. [G: U.S.]

Moran, Theodore H. Multinational Corporations: The Political Economy of Foreign Direct Investment: Conclusions and Policy Implications. In *Moran, T. H., ed.,* 1985, pp. 263–77.

Moran, Theodore H. Multinational Corporations and the Developing Countries: An Analytical Overview. In *Moran, T. H., ed.,* 1985, pp. 3–24. [G: LDCs]

Nelson, Philip and Silvia, Louis. Antitrust Policy and Intra-industry Direct Foreign Investment: Cause and Effect. In *Erdilek, A., ed.,* 1985, pp. 97–123. [G: U.S.]

Newfarmer, Richard S. Profits, Progress and Poverty: Case Studies of International Industries in Latin America: An Introduction to the Issues. In *Newfarmer, R. S., ed.,* 1985, pp. 1–12.

Nye, William W. Antitrust Policy and Intra-industry Direct Foreign Investment: Cause and Effect: Comment. In *Erdilek, A., ed.,* 1985, pp. 125–28. [G: U.S.]

Parry, Thomas G. Internalisation as a General Theory of Foreign Direct Investment: A Critique. *Weltwirtsch. Arch.*, 1985, *121*(3), pp. 564–69.

Poulon, Frédéric. Contrainte extérieure et capacité de transfert d'un pays à l'étranger: Keynes et les réparations allemandes. (Foreign Constraints and the Ability to Transfer Payments Abroad: Keynes and German Reparations. With English summary.) *Écon. Soc.*, April 1985, *19*(4), pp. 27–43.

Rousslang, Donald J. The Determinants of Intra-industry Direct Foreign Investment: Comment. In *Erdilek, A., ed.,* 1985, pp. 64–66.

Ruffin, Roy J. Taxing International Capital Movements in a Growing World. *J. Int. Econ.*, May 1985, *18*(3/4), pp. 261–79.

Rugman, Alan M. Internalization Is Still a General Theory of Foreign Direct Investment [Internalization as a General Theory of Foreign Direct Investment: A Re-Appraisal of the Literature]. *Weltwirtsch. Arch.*, 1985, *121*(3), pp. 570–75.

Rugman, Alan M. The Determinants of Intra-industry Direct Foreign Investment. In *Erdilek, A., ed.,* 1985, pp. 38–59. [G: Global]

Sibert, Anne C. Capital Accumulation and Foreign Investment Taxation. *Rev. Econ. Stud.*, April 1985, *52*(2), pp. 331–45.

Vukmanic, Frank G.; Czinkota, Michael R. and Ricks, David A. National and International Data Problems and Solutions in the Empirical Analysis of Intra-industry Direct Foreign Investment. In *Erdilek, A., ed.,* 1985, pp. 160–84. [G: Global; U.S.]

Yu, Eden S. H. Toward a Theory of Customs Unions with Foreign Investment. *Econ. Int.*, May 1985, *38*(2), pp. 222–35.

Yvars, Bernard. Protection et mobilité internationale du capital dans une économie ou ce facteur est spécifique. (Protection and International Capital Mobility in an Economy Where This Factor Is Specific. With English summary.) *Revue Écon.*, July 1985, *36*(4), pp. 687–714.

4411 International Investment and Long-term Capital Movements: Theory

Aliber, Robert Z. External Financing and the Level of Development: A Conceptual Approach. In *Gutowski, A.; Arnaudo, A. A. and Scharrer, H.-E., eds.*, 1985, pp. 234–48.

Balasubramanyam, V. N. Foreign Direct Investment and the International Transfer of Technology. In *Greenaway, D., ed.*, 1985, pp. 159–81. [G: LDCs]

Bhagwati, Jagdish N. Substitution between Foreign Capital and Domestic Saving. In *Bhagwati, J. N. (I)*, 1985, pp. 269–76.

Bhagwati, Jagdish N. and Brecher, Richard A. Extending Free Trade to Include International Investment: A Welfare-Theoretic Analysis. In *Bhagwati, J. N. (I)*, 1985, pp. 383–88.

Buckley, Peter J. A Critical View of Theories of the Multinational Enterprise. In *Buckley, P. J. and Casson, M.*, 1985, pp. 1–19. [G: Japan]

Buckley, Peter J. and Casson, Mark. The Optimal Timing of a Foreign Direct Investment. In *Buckley, P. J. and Casson, M.*, 1985, pp. 98–112.

Callier, Philippe. Exchange Rates, Purchasing Power Parity and Efficient Allocation of Physical Capital. In *Peeters, T.; Praet, P. and Reding, P., eds.*, 1985, pp. 191–99.

Carlozzi, Nicholas and Taylor, John B. International Capital Mobility and the Coordination of Monetary Rules. In *Bhandari, J. S., ed.*, 1985, pp. 186–211.

Casson, Mark. Entrepreneurship and the Dynamics of Foreign Direct Investment. In *Buckley, P. J. and Casson, M.*, 1985, pp. 172–91.

Casson, Mark. The Theory of Foreign Direct Investment. In *Buckley, P. J. and Casson, M.*, 1985, pp. 113–43.

Chen, Tain-Jy. Alternative Policies for Foreign Investment in the Presence of Tariff Distortions. *Australian Econ. Pap.*, December 1985, 24(45), pp. 394–403.

Davis, Lance and Huttenback, Robert A. The Export of British Finance, 1865–1914. In *Porter, A. N. and Holland, R. F., eds.*, 1985, pp. 28–76. [G: U.K.; Selected Countries]

Dunning, John H. and Norman, George. Intra-industry Production as a Form of International Economic Involvement: An Exploratory Analysis. In *Erdilek, A., ed.*, 1985, pp. 9–29.

Faini, Riccardo. Macroeconomic Adjustment under Foreign Investment: Comment. In *Weiserbs, D., ed.*, 1985, pp. 203–07. [G: Netherlands; Spain]

Finan, William F. Intra-industry Direct Foreign Investment, Market Structure, Firm Rivalry and Technological Performance: Comment. In *Erdilek, A., ed.*, 1985, pp. 94–96. [G: U.S.]

Graham, Edward M. Intra-industry Direct Foreign Investment, Market Structure, Firm Rivalry and Technological Performance. In *Erdilek, A., ed.*, 1985, pp. 67–88. [G: U.S.]

Guisinger, Stephen E. Investment Incentives and Performance Requirements: A Comparative Study of Country Policies. In *Guisinger, S. E., et al.*, 1985, pp. 1–55. [G: Global]

Hennart, Jean-François. Intra-industry Direct Foreign Investment, Market Structure, Firm Rivalry and Technological Performance: Comment. In *Erdilek, A., ed.*, 1985, pp. 88–93. [G: U.S.]

Krugman, Paul R. Intra-industry Production as a Form of International Economic Involvement: An Exploratory Analysis: Comment. In *Erdilek, A., ed.*, 1985, pp. 33–37.

McKinnon, Ronald I. How to Manage a Repressed Economy. In *Gutowski, A.; Arnaudo, A. A. and Scharrer, H.-E., eds.*, 1985, pp. 182–209. [G: Chile; Argentina]

Owen, Robert F. and Auburtin, Pascal. A Comparative Study of the Inter-industry Determinants and Economic Performance of Foreign Direct Investments in France and Canada. In *Weiserbs, D., ed.*, 1985, pp. 209–50. [G: France; Canada]

Sleuwaegen, Leo. Comparative Study of the Inter-industry Determinants and Economic Performance of Foreign Direct Investments in France and Canada: Comments. In *Weiserbs, D., ed.*, 1985, pp. 251–55. [G: France; Canada]

Vernon, Raymond. Intra-industry Production as a Form of International Economic Involvement: An Exploratory Analysis: Comment. In *Erdilek, A., ed.*, 1985, pp. 29–33.

Viaene, Jean-Marie. Macroeconomic Adjustment under Foreign Investments. In *Weiserbs, D., ed.*, 1985, pp. 185–201. [G: Netherlands; Spain]

4412 International Investment and Long-term Capital Movements: Studies

Agarwal, J. P. Intra-LDCs Foreign Direct Investment: A Comparative Analysis of Third World Multinationals. *Devel. Econ.*, September 1985, 23(3), pp. 236–53. [G: LDCs]

Androuais, Anne. Les investissements japonais en Asie du sud-est: compléments ou concurrents de l'industrie au Japon. (With English summary.) *Revue Écon. Polit.*, May–June 1985, 95(3), pp. 320–45. [G: Japan; S. E. Asia]

Arnaud-Ameller, Paule. Investissements directs et flux commerciaux compléments ou substituts? Le cas français 1968–1978. (With English summary.) *Revue Écon. Polit.*, May–June 1985, 95(3), pp. 299–319. [G: France]

Artisien, Patrick F. R. and Buckley, Peter J. Western Investment and the New Law in Yugoslavia. *J. World Trade Law*, Sept.:Oct. 1985, 19(5), pp. 522–36. [G: Yugoslavia]

Baer, Werner. Foreign Investments in Brazil: Their Benefits and Costs. In *Salazar-Carrillo, J. and Fendt, R., Jr., eds.*, 1985, pp. 124–46. [G: Brazil]

Balasubramanyam, V. N. Foreign Direct Investment and the International Transfer of Technology. In *Greenaway, D., ed.*, 1985, pp. 159–81. [G: LDCs]

Bale, Harvey E., Jr. Investment Frictions and Opportunities in Bilateral Trade Relations. In *Fretz, D.; Stern, R. and Whalley, J., eds.,* 1985, pp. 165–97. **[G: Canada; U.S.]**

Basile, Antoine. Les nouvelles formes d'investissement (NFI). Définition, contraintes et perspectives. (With English summary.) *Revue Écon. Polit.,* May–June 1985, 95(3), pp. 275–98. **[G: Global]**

Bhagwati, Jagdish N. Savings and the Foreign Trade Regime. In *Bhagwati, J. N. (I),* 1985, pp. 277–84. **[G: India]**

Blank, Barry W. and Sein, Lila. U.S. Banking Adjustments to Changes in Gulf Liquidity. In *Czinkota, M. R. and Marciel, S., eds.,* 1985, pp. 101–28. **[G: U.S.; OPEC]**

Bond, Eric W. and Guisinger, Stephen E. Investment Incentives as Tariff Substitutes: A Comprehensive Measure of Protection. *Rev. Econ. Statist.,* February 1985, 67(1), pp. 91–97. **[G: U.K.]**

Cacnis, Demitrios G. The Translog Production Function and the Substitution of Factors of Production in England 1950–1976. *Greek Econ. Rev.,* August 1985, 7(2), pp. 161–78. **[G: U.K.]**

Carswell, Robert and Davis, Richard J. American Hostages in Iran: The Conduct of a Crisis: The Economic and Financial Pressures: Freeze and Sanctions. In *Kreisberg, P. H., ed.,* 1985, pp. 173–200. **[G: U.S.; Iran]**

Carswell, Robert and Davis, Richard J. American Hostages in Iran: The Conduct of a Crisis: Crafting the Financial Settlement. In *Kreisberg, P. H., ed.,* 1985, pp. 201–34. **[G: U.S.; Iran]**

Cazes, Bernard. France. In *Hochmuth, M. and Davidson, W., eds.,* 1985, pp. 163–88. **[G: France]**

Chia, Siow Yue. The Role of Foreign Trade and Investment in the Development of Singapore. In *Galenson, W., ed.,* 1985, pp. 259–97. **[G: Singapore]**

Colaço, Francis X. Capital Requirements in Economic Development: The Decade Ahead. In *Gutowski, A.; Arnaudo, A. A. and Scharrer, H.-E., eds.,* 1985, pp. 3–26. **[G: LDCs]**

Colaço, Francis X. International Capital Flows and Economic Development. *Finance Develop.,* September 1985, 22(3), pp. 2–6. **[G: Global]**

Contractor, Farok J. Licensing versus Foreign Direct Investment in U.S. Corporate Strategy: An Analysis of Aggregate U.S. Data. In *Rosenberg, N. and Frischtak, C., eds.,* 1985, pp. 277–320. **[G: U.S.]**

Cushman, David O. Real Exchange Rate Risk, Expectations, and the Level of Direct Investment. *Rev. Econ. Statist.,* May 1985, 67(2), pp. 297–308. **[G: U.S.; W. Europe; Japan; Canada]**

Davis, Lance and Huttenback, Robert A. The Export of British Finance, 1865–1914. In *Porter, A. N. and Holland, R. F., eds.,* 1985, pp. 28–76. **[G: U.K.; Selected Countries]**

Deardorff, Alan V. Investment Frictions and Op-portunities in Bilateral Trade Relations: Comments. In *Fretz, D.; Stern, R. and Whalley, J., eds.,* 1985, pp. 198–206. **[G: Canada; U.S.]**

Dunning, John H. Multinational Enterprises, Economic Structure and International Competitiveness: The United Kingdom. In *Dunning, J. H., ed.,* 1985, pp. 13–56. **[G: U.K.]**

Dunning, John H. Multinational Enterprises, Economic Structure and International Competitiveness: Some Conclusions and Policy Implications. In *Dunning, J. H., ed.,* 1985, pp. 407–31. **[G: Selected Countries]**

Encarnation, Dennis J. and Wells, Louis T., Jr. Sovereignty en garde: Negotiating with Foreign Investors. *Int. Organ.,* Winter 1985, 39(1), pp. 47–78. **[G: India; Singapore; Philippines; Indonesia]**

Ewing, A. F. International Capital and Economic Development. *J. World Trade Law,* Sept.:Oct. 1985, 19(5), pp. 537–42. **[G: Global]**

Feinberg, Richard E. International Finance and Investment: A Surging Public Sector. In *Sewell, J. W.; Feinberg, R. E. and Kallab, V., eds.,* 1985, pp. 51–71. **[G: U.S.; LDCs]**

Feinberg, Richard E. LDC Debt and the Public-Sector Rescue. *Challenge,* July/August 1985, 28(3), pp. 27–34. **[G: LDCs; U.S.]**

Fishlow, Albert. Lessons from the Past: Capital Markets during the 19th Century and the Interwar Period. *Int. Organ.,* Summer 1985, 39(3), pp. 383–439. **[G: W. Europe; U.S.]**

Fretz, Deborah; Stern, Robert M. and Whalley, John. Canada/United States Trade and Investment Issues: Introduction and Overview. In *Fretz, D.; Stern, R. and Whalley, J., eds.,* 1985, pp. 3–20. **[G: Canada; U.S.]**

Führer, Helmut. The Flow of Public and Private Financial Resources to Developing Countries: Recent Trends. In *Gutowski, A.; Arnaudo, A. A. and Scharrer, H.-E., eds.,* 1985, pp. 139–61. **[G: Selected LDCs]**

Gasiorowski, Mark J. The Structure of Third World Economic Interdependence. *Int. Organ.,* Spring 1985, 39(2), pp. 331–42. **[G: LDCs]**

Globerman, Steven. Multinational Enterprises, Economic Structure and International Competitiveness: Canada. In *Dunning, J. H., ed.,* 1985, pp. 187–215. **[G: Canada]**

Goldsbrough, David. Foreign Direct Investment in Developing Countries. *Finance Develop.,* March 1985, 22(1), pp. 31–34. **[G: LDCs]**

Gray, H. Peter and Walter, Ingo. Investment Incentives and Performance Requirements: The Petrochemical Industry. In *Guisinger, S. E., et al.,* 1985, pp. 237–312. **[G: Selected Countries]**

Guenther, Harry P. Arab Investment in the United States and U.S. Public Policy. In *Czinkota, M. R. and Marciel, S., eds.,* 1985, pp. 159–82. **[G: U.S.; OPEC]**

Guisinger, Stephen E. Investment Incentives and Performance Requirements: Summary and Conclusions. In *Guisinger, S. E., et al.,* 1985, pp. 313–20. **[G: Selected Countries]**

Guisinger, Stephen E. Investment Incentives and Performance Requirements: A Comparative Study of Country Policies. In *Guisinger, S. E., et al.*, 1985, pp. 1–55. [G: Global]

Gupta, Kanhaya L. Foreign Capital, Income Inequality, Demographic Pressures, Savings and Growth in Developing Countries: A Cross Country Analysis. *J. Econ. Devel.*, July 1985, *10*(1), pp. 63–88. [G: LDCs]

Hamlin, Alan P. Capital and Labour Movements in the European Community: Comment. In *Weiserbs, D., ed.*, 1985, pp. 285–87. [G: EEC]

Harris, Richard G. Canada/U.S. Trade and Investment Frictions: The U.S. View: Comments. In *Fretz, D.; Stern, R. and Whalley, J., eds.*, 1985, pp. 64–68. [G: Canada; U.S.]

Hartman, David G. Tax Policy and Foreign Direct Investment. *J. Public Econ.*, February 1985, *26*(1), pp. 107–21. [G: U.S.]

Hattersley, Roy. A New Exchange Control Scheme. *Fisc. Stud.*, August 1985, *6*(3), pp. 9–13. [G: U.K.]

Hill, Hal and Johns, Brian. The Role of Direct Foreign Investment in Developing East Asian Countries. *Weltwirtsch. Arch.*, 1985, *121*(2), pp. 355–81. [G: E. Asia; U.S.; Japan]

Hill, Roger. Canada/U.S. Trade and Investment Frictions: The U.S. View: Comments. In *Fretz, D.; Stern, R. and Whalley, J., eds.*, 1985, pp. 69–71. [G: Canada; U.S.]

Hood, Neil and Young, Stephen. Investment Incentives and Performance Requirements: The Automobile Industry. In *Guisinger, S. E., et al.*, 1985, pp. 96–167. [G: Selected Countries]

Howenstine, Ned G. U.S. Affiliates of Foreign Companies: Operations in 1983. *Surv. Curr. Bus.*, November 1985, *65*(11), pp. 36–50. [G: U.S.]

Hufbauer, Gary Clyde and Schott, Jeffrey J. The Role of Bilateral Investment Talks. In *Conklin, D. W. and Courchene, T. J., eds.*, 1985, pp. 343–49. [G: Canada; U.S.]

Isard, Peter and Stekler, Lois. U.S. International Capital Flows and the Dollar. *Brookings Pap. Econ. Act.*, 1985, (1), pp. 219–36. [G: U.S.]

Joseph, J. J. Foreign Investment and Profits in Developing Countries. In *Utrecht, E., ed.*, 1985, pp. 1–15. [G: U.S.]

Juhl, Paulgeorg. Multinational Enterprises, Economic Structure and International Competitiveness: The Federal Republic of Germany. In *Dunning, J. H., ed.*, 1985, pp. 127–54. [G: W. Germany]

Kaynak, Erdener. Transfer of Technology from Developed to Developing Countries: Some Insights from Turkey. In *Samli, A. C., ed.*, 1985, pp. 155–76. [G: OECD; LDCs]

Kindleberger, Charles P. International Propagation of Financial Crises: The Experience of 1888–93. In *Kindleberger, C. P.*, 1985, pp. 226–39. [G: Selected Countries]

Kindleberger, Charles P. The Cyclical Pattern of Long-term Lending. In *Kindleberger, C. P.*, 1985, pp. 141–54. [G: Europe; U.S.]

Kojima, Kiyoshi. Japanese and American Direct Investment in Asia: A Comparative Analysis. *Hitotsubashi J. Econ.*, June 1985, *26*(1), pp. 1–35. [G: U.S.; Japan; S.E. Asia]

Kojima, Kiyoshi. The Allocation of Japanese Direct Foreign Investment and Its Evolution in Asia. *Hitotsubashi J. Econ.*, December 1985, *26*(2), pp. 99–116. [G: Japan]

Koo, Bohn-Young. Multinational Enterprises, Economic Structure and International Competitiveness: Korea. In *Dunning, J. H., ed.*, 1985, pp. 281–307. [G: S. Korea]

Koo, Bohn-Young. The Role of Direct Foreign Investment in Korea's Recent Economic Growth. In *Galenson, W., ed.*, 1985, pp. 176–216. [G: S. Korea]

Koshiro, Kazutoshi. Foreign Direct Investment and Industrial Relations: Japanese Experience after the Oil Crisis. In *Takamiya, S. and Thurley, K., eds.*, 1985, pp. 205–27. [G: Japan; Selected Countries]

Kozlow, Ralph. Capital Expenditures by Majority-owned Foreign Affiliates of U.S. Companies, 1985 and 1986. *Surv. Curr. Bus.*, September 1985, *65*(9), pp. 22–27. [G: U.S.]

Kozlow, Ralph. Capital Expenditures by Majority-owned Foreign Affiliates of U.S. Companies, 1985. *Surv. Curr. Bus.*, March 1985, *65*(3), pp. 23–28. [G: U.S.]

Krause, Lawrence B. Foreign Trade and Investment: Economic Growth in the Newly Industrializing Asian Countries: Introduction. In *Galenson, W., ed.*, 1985, pp. 3–41. [G: Hong Kong; Singapore; S. Korea; Taiwan]

Lall, Sanjaya. Multinational Enterprises, Economic Structure and International Competitiveness: India. In *Dunning, J. H., ed.*, 1985, pp. 309–35. [G: India]

Lall, Sanjaya. Trade in Technology by a Slowly Industrializing Country: India. In *Rosenberg, N. and Frischtak, C., eds.*, 1985, pp. 45–76. [G: India]

Lecraw, Donald J. Multinational Enterprises, Economic Structure and International Competitiveness: Singapore. In *Dunning, J. H., ed.*, 1985, pp. 379–405. [G: Selected Countries; Singapore]

Leeds, Roger S. IFC's New Approach to Project Promotion. *Finance Develop.*, March 1985, *22*(1), pp. 5–7. [G: LDCs]

Leontief, Wassily. The Rates of Long-run Economic Growth and Capital Transfer from Developed to Underdeveloped Areas. In *Leontief, W.*, 1985, pp. 200–215. [G: LDCs; MDCs]

Levich, Richard M. A View from the International Capital Markets. In *Walter, I., ed.*, 1985, pp. 255–92. [G: OECD]

Lin, Tzong-Biau and Mok, Victor. Trade, Foreign Investment, and Development in Hong Kong. In *Galenson, W., ed.*, 1985, pp. 219–56. [G: Hong Kong]

Lindsey, Charles W. The Philippine State and Transnational Investment. In *Stauffer, R. B., ed.*, 1985, pp. 185–223. [G: Philippines]

Little, Jane Sneddon. Foreign Direct Investment

in New England. *New Eng. Econ. Rev.*, March/ April 1985, pp. 48–57. [G: U.S.]

Little, Jane Sneddon. Multinational Corporations and Foreign Investment: Current Trends and Issues. In *Adams, J., ed.*, 1985, pp. 397–407. [G: U.S.]

Logan, Robert G. Investment Frictions and Opportunities in Bilateral Trade Relations: Comments. In *Fretz, D.; Stern, R. and Whalley, J., eds.*, 1985, pp. 207–12. [G: Canada; U.S.]

Lundahl, Mats. Errata: Economic Effects of a Trade and Investment Boycott against South Africa. *Scand. J. Econ.*, 1985, 87(1), pp. 142. [G: S. Africa]

Macharzina, Klaus. Development of the German Economy and National Economic Policy. In *Hochmuth, M. and Davidson, W., eds.*, 1985, pp. 81–97. [G: OECD; W. Germany]

Makdisi, Samir A. Observations on Investment Behavior of the Arab Countries. In *Czinkota, M. R. and Marciel, S., eds.*, 1985, pp. 183–89. [G: OPEC]

Mason, R. Hal. Investment Incentives and Performance Requirements: The International Food Processing Industry. In *Guisinger, S. E., et al.*, 1985, pp. 56–95. [G: Selected Countries]

Mayes, David G. Capital and Labour Movements in the European Community. In *Weiserbs, D., ed.*, 1985, pp. 257–83. [G: EEC]

Michalet, Charles Albert and Chevallier, Thérèse. Multinational Enterprises, Economic Structure and International Competitiveness: France. In *Dunning, J. H., ed.*, 1985, pp. 91–125. [G: OECD; France]

Miller, Robert R. Investment Incentives and Performance Requirements: Computers. In *Guisinger, S. E., et al.*, 1985, pp. 168–236. [G: Selected Countries]

Mohl, Andrew and Sobol, Dorothy. Currency Diversification and LDC Debt. In *Eskridge, W. N., Jr., ed.*, 1985, pp. 231–33. [G: LDCs]

Mortimore, Michael. The Subsidiary Role of Direct Foreign Investment in Industrialization: The Colombian Manufacturing Sector. *Cepal Rev.*, April 1985, (25), pp. 67–84. [G: Colombia]

Mucchielli, Jean-Louis. Les firmes multinationales françaises et la hiérarchisation des nations. (With English summary.) *Revue Écon. Polit.*, Sept.-Oct. 1985, 95(5), pp. 611–26. [G: OECD]

Olsen, Randall J. Gold, Foreign Capital and the Industrialization of Russia. *J. Europ. Econ. Hist.*, Spring 1985, 14(1), pp. 143–54. [G: U.S.S.R.]

Oweiss, Ibrahim M. Impediments to Arab Investment in the United States. In *Czinkota, M. R. and Marciel, S., eds.*, 1985, pp. 138–58. [G: U.S.; OPEC]

Ozawa, Terutomo. Multinational Enterprises, Economic Structure and International Competitiveness: Japan. In *Dunning, J. H., ed.*, 1985, pp. 155–85. [G: Japan]

Parry, Thomas G. Foreign Direct Investment in

Papua New Guinea. *J. World Trade Law,* July:Aug. 1985, 19(4), pp. 411–22. [G: Papua New Guinea]

Petrochilos, George A. Foreign Banks in Greece. *Nat. Westminster Bank Quart. Rev.*, February 1985, pp. 57–69. [G: Greece]

Platt, D. C. M. Canada and Argentina: The First Preference of the British Investor, 1904–14. In *Porter, A. N. and Holland, R. F., eds.*, 1985, pp. 77–92. [G: Canada; Argentina; U.K.]

Pollard, Sidney. Capital Exports, 1870–1914: Harmful or Beneficial? *Econ. Hist. Rev.*, 2nd Ser., November 1985, 38(4), pp. 489–514. [G: U.K.]

Porquet, Nicole. Multinationalisation des firmes et avantages comparatifs des pays: une vue d'ensemble. (With English summary.) *Revue Écon. Polit.*, May–June 1985, 95(3), pp. 243–74.

Pugel, Thomas A. Multinational Enterprises, Economic Structure and International Competitiveness: The United States. In *Dunning, J. H., ed.*, 1985, pp. 57–90. [G: U.S.]

Ranis, Gustav and Schive, Chi. Direct Foreign Investment in Taiwan's Development. In *Galenson, W., ed.*, 1985, pp. 85–137. [G: Taiwan]

Rybczynski, T. M. The Role of International Financial Markets in the Financing of Development. In *Gutowski, A.; Arnaudo, A. A. and Scharrer, H.-E., eds.*, 1985, pp. 162–81. [G: LDCs]

Ryrie, William [Sir]. Development through the Private Sector. *Finance Develop.*, March 1985, 22(1), pp. 2–4. [G: LDCs]

Safarian, A. E. The Relationship between Trade Agreements and International Direct Investment. In *Conklin, D. W. and Courchene, T. J., eds.*, 1985, pp. 206–19. [G: Canada]

Sakurai, Makoto. A Japanese Perspective on Resource Trade with Australia. In *Drysdale, P. and Shibata, H., eds.*, 1985, pp. 177–89. [G: Australia; Japan]

Schneider, Friedrich and Frey, Bruno S. Economic and Political Determinants of Foreign Direct Investment. *World Devel.*, February 1985, 13(2), pp. 161–75. [G: LDCs]

Scholl, Russell B. The International Investment Position of the United States in 1984. *Surv. Curr. Bus.*, June 1985, 65(6), pp. 25–33. [G: U.S.]

Siddiqi, Hafiz G. A. Bangladesh–ASEAN Investment Relations. In *Wadhva, C. D. and Asher, M. G., eds.*, 1985, pp. 253–68. [G: Bangladesh; ASEAN]

Simões, Vitor Corado. Multinational Enterprises, Economic Structure and International Competitiveness: Portugal. In *Dunning, J. H., ed.*, 1985, pp. 337–78. [G: Portugal]

Sit, Victor F. S. The Special Economic Zones of China: A New Type of Export Processing Zone? *Devel. Econ.*, March 1985, 23(1), pp. 69–87. [G: China]

Sleuwaegen, Leo. Recent Trends in Foreign Direct Investment and Disinvestment in Belgium. *Tijdschrift Econ. Manage.*, 1985, *30*(1), pp. 7–44. **[G: Belgium; OECD]**

Stern, Robert M. Canada–U.S. Trade and Investment Frictions: The U.S. View. In *Fretz, D.; Stern, R. and Whalley, J., eds.*, 1985, pp. 32–63. **[G: Canada; U.S.]**

Swedenborg, Birgitta. Multinational Enterprises, Economic Structure and International Competitiveness: Sweden. In *Dunning, J. H., ed.*, 1985, pp. 217–48. **[G: Sweden]**

Torrisi, C. R. The Determinants of Direct Foreign Investment in a Small LDC. *J. Econ. Devel.*, July 1985, *10*(1), pp. 29–45.

Tsiang, S. C. and Wu, Rong-I. Foreign Trade and Investment as Boosters for Take-off: The Experiences of the Four Asian Newly Industrializing Countries. In *Galenson, W., ed.*, 1985, pp. 301–32. **[G: Hong Kong; Singapore; S. Korea; Taiwan]**

Unakul, Snoh and Akrasanee, Narongchai. Structural Adjustment in Thai–Japanese Economic Relations. In *Shishido, T. and Sato, R., eds.*, 1985, pp. 112–26. **[G: Japan; Thailand]**

Utrecht, Ernst. Gains and Losses in 25 Years of Export-Oriented Industrialization in South and Southeast Asia. In *Utrecht, E., ed.*, 1985, pp. 137–58. **[G: S. Asia; S.E. Asia]**

Van Den Bulcke, Daniel. Multinational Enterprises, Economic Structure and International Competitiveness: Belgium. In *Dunning, J. H., ed.*, 1985, pp. 249–80. **[G: Belgium]**

Vernon, Raymond. Organizational and Institutional Responses to International Risk. In *Vernon, R.*, 1985, pp. 63–85.

Vernon, Raymond. The Product Cycle Hypothesis in a New International Environment. In *Adams, J., ed.*, 1985, pp. 408–22.

Wadhva, Charan D. India–ASEAN Economic Relations. In *Wadhva, C. D. and Asher, M. G., eds.*, 1985, pp. 269–320. **[G: India; ASEAN]**

Weiller, Jean. Circuits des capitaux, balances extérieurers et flux majeurs d'investissement. (Capital Circuits, Foreign Balances and Major Flows of Investment. With English summary.) *Écon. Soc.*, April 1985, *19*(4), pp. 7–18.

Westphal, Larry E.; Kim, Linsu and Dahlman, Carl J. Reflections on the Republic of Korea's Acquisition of Technological Capability. In *Rosenberg, N. and Frischtak, C., eds.*, 1985, pp. 167–221. **[G: S. Korea]**

Whichard, Obie G. and Shea, Michael A. 1982 Benchmark Survey of U.S. Direct Investment Abroad. *Surv. Curr. Bus.*, December 1985, *65*(12), pp. 37–57. **[G: U.S.]**

White, John. External Development Finance and the Choice of Technology. In *James, J. and Watanabe, S., eds.*, 1985, pp. 183–216.

Wilkins, Mira. Foreign Banks and Foreign Investment in the United States. In *Atack, J., ed.*, 1985, pp. 27–34. **[G: U.S.]**

Wuffli, Peter A. Wandel der mexikanischen Politik gegenuber Auslandsinvestitionen? Die "irationale" Komponente der Mexikanisierungsstrategie. (Change in the Mexican Attitude towards Foreign Direct Investment? The "Irrational" Elements of Mexicanization Strat-

egy. With English summary.) *Aussenwirtschaft*, September 1985, *40*(3), pp. 229–54. **[G: Mexico]**

442 International Business and Multinational Enterprises

4420 International Business and Multinational Enterprises

Aalders, Gerard and Wiebes, Cees. Stockholms Enskilda Bank, German Bosch and IG Farben. A Short History of Cloaking. *Scand. Econ. Hist. Rev.*, 1985, *33*(1), pp. 25–50. **[G: U.S.; Sweden]**

Abreu, Marcelo de Paiva. Anglo–Brazilian Economic Relations and the Consolidation of American Pre-eminence in Brazil, 1930–1945. In *Abel, C. and Lewis, C. M., eds.*, 1985, pp. 379–93. **[G: Brazil; U.K.; U.S.]**

Agarwal, J. P. Intra-LDCs Foreign Direct Investment: A Comparative Analysis of Third World Multinationals. *Devel. Econ.*, September 1985, *23*(3), pp. 236–53. **[G: LDCs]**

Ahearn, Raymond J. Market Access in Japan: The U.S. Experience. In *Nanto, D. K., ed.*, 1985, pp. 41–63. **[G: Japan; U.S.]**

Ajami, Riad A. International Business and the Middle East: Recent Developments and Prospects. In *Kaynak, E., ed. (II)*, 1985, pp. 103–11. **[G: Arab Countries]**

Ajami, Riad A. The Arabian American Oil Company (ARAMCO) and Saudi Society: A Study in Interaction. In *Kaynak, E., ed. (II)*, 1985, pp. 127–36. **[G: Saudi Arabia]**

Aliber, Robert Z. Transfer Pricing: A Taxonomy of Impacts on Economic Welfare. In *Rugman, A. M. and Eden, L., eds.*, 1985, pp. 82–97.

Alschuler, Lawrence R. The State and TNCs in the Development of the Semi-periphery: The Case of South Korea. In *Stauffer, R. B., ed.*, 1985, pp. 133–83. **[G: S. Korea]**

Antonelli, Cristiano. The Diffusion of an Organizational Innovation: International Data Telecommunications and Multinational Industrial Firms. *Int. J. Ind. Organ.*, March 1985, *3*(1), pp. 109–18. **[G: OECD]**

Artisien, Patrick F. R. and Buckley, Peter J. Western Investment and the New Law in Yugoslavia. *J. World Trade Law*, Sept.:Oct. 1985, *19*(5), pp. 522–36. **[G: Yugoslavia]**

Asheghian, Parviz and Foote, William. In the Productivities of U.S. Multinationals in the Industrial Sector of the Canadian Economy. *Eastern Econ. J.*, April-June 1985, *11*(2), pp. 123–33. **[G: Canada]**

Ashiquzzaman, Shah M. and Ghosh, Atish R. Profits, Tariffs, and Intra-industry Trade. *Indian Econ. J.*, Oct.-Nov. 1985, *33*(2), pp. 106–15.

Atkinson, Lloyd C. The Canadian Treatment of Foreign Banks: A Case Study in the Workings of the National Treatment Approach: Comments. In *Stern, R. M., ed.*, 1985, pp. 253–55. **[G: Canada; U.S.]**

Atkinson, Thomas R. Canada/U.S. Automotive

Trade and Trade-policy Issues: Comments. In *Fretz, D.; Stern, R. and Whalley, J., eds.,* 1985, pp. 333–37. [G: Canada; U.S.]

Baer, Werner. Foreign Investments in Brazil: Their Benefits and Costs. In *Salazar-Carrillo, J. and Fendt, R., Jr., eds.,* 1985, pp. 124–46. [G: Brazil]

Balassa, Bela. U.S. Direct Foreign Investment and Trade: Theories, Trends and Public Policy Issues: Comment. In *Erdilek, A., ed.,* 1985, pp. 151–54. [G: U.S.]

Balasubramanyam, V. N. Foreign Direct Investment and the International Transfer of Technology. In *Greenaway, D., ed.,* 1985, pp. 159–81. [G: LDCs]

Baranson, Jack and Roark, Robin. Trends in North–South Transfer of High Technology. In *Rosenberg, N. and Frischtak, C., eds.,* 1985, pp. 24–42. [G: LDCs; MDCs]

Basile, Antoine. Les nouvelles formes d'investissement (NFI). Définition, contraintes et perspectives. (With English summary.) *Revue Écon. Polit.,* May–June 1985, *95*(3), pp. 275–98. [G: Global]

Becker, David G. Nonferrous Metals, Class Formation, and the State in Peru. In *Evans, P.; Rueschemeyer, D. and Stephens, E. H., eds.,* 1985, pp. 67–89. [G: Peru]

Beer, Barbo. Informatics in International Trade: Harmonization of Standards for Telecommunicated Messages. *J. World Trade Law,* Nov.:Dec. 1985, *19*(6), pp. 570–78. [G: Global]

Bennett, Douglas C. and Sharpe, Kenneth E. The World Automobile Industry and its Implications. In *Newfarmer, R. S., ed.,* 1985, pp. 193–226. [G: Latin America; Selected Countries]

Benvignati, Anita M. An Empirical Investigation of International Transfer Pricing by U.S. Manufacturing Firms. In *Rugman, A. M. and Eden, L., eds.,* 1985, pp. 193–211. [G: U.S.]

Borner, Silvio, et al. Global Structural Change and International Competition among Industrial Firms: The Case of Switzerland. *Kyklos,* 1985, *38*(1), pp. 77–103. [G: Switzerland]

Brada, Josef C. Soviet–Western Trade and Technology Transfer: An Economic Overview. In *Parrott, B., ed.,* 1985, pp. 3–34. [G: U.S.S.R.; OECD]

Bradbury, J. J. International Movements and Crises in Resource Oriented Companies: The case of INCO in the Nickel Sector. *Econ. Geogr.,* April 1985, *61*(2), pp. 129–43. [G: Canada; Guatemala; Indonesia]

Brean, Donald J. S. Financial Dimensions of Transfer Pricing. In *Rugman, A. M. and Eden, L., eds.,* 1985, pp. 149–64.

Broadman, Harry G. and Dunkerley, Joy. The Drilling Gap in Non-OPEC Developing Countries: The Role of Contractual and Fiscal Arrangements. *Natural Res. J.,* April 1985, *25*(2), pp. 415–28. [G: LDCs]

Brown, Jonathan C. Why Foreign Oil Companies Shifted Their Production from Mexico to Venezuela during the 1920s. *Amer. Hist. Rev.,* April 1985, *90*(2), pp. 362–85. [G: Mexico; Venezuela]

Bruton, Henry J. On the Production of a National Technology. In *James, J. and Watanabe, S., eds.,* 1985, pp. 81–115.

Buatsi, Seth N.; Pradhan, Suresh and Apasu, Yao. Human Resources, Managerial Perceptions, and the Global Marketing Behavior of Firms. In *Kaynak, E., ed. (I),* 1985, pp. 183–96. [G: U.K.]

Buckley, Peter J. A Critical View of Theories of the Multinational Enterprise. In *Buckley, P. J. and Casson, M.,* 1985, pp. 1–19. [G: Japan]

Buckley, Peter J. New Forms of International Industrial Co-operation. In *Buckley, P. J. and Casson, M.,* 1985, pp. 39–59. [G: LDCs; MDCs]

Buckley, Peter J. Testing Theories of the Multinational Enterprise: A Review of the Evidence. In *Buckley, P. J. and Casson, M.,* 1985, pp. 192–211. [G: LDCs; MDCs]

Buckley, Peter J. The Economic Analysis of the Multinational Enterprise: Reading versus Japan? *Hitotsubashi J. Econ.,* December 1985, *26*(2), pp. 117–24. [G: Japan]

Buckley, Peter J. and Casson, Mark. The Optimal Timing of a Foreign Direct Investment. In *Buckley, P. J. and Casson, M.,* 1985, pp. 98–112.

Cain, Peter J. Hobson, Wilshire, and the Capitalist Theory of Capitalist Imperialism. *Hist. Polit. Econ.,* Fall 1985, *17*(3), pp. 455–60.

Calderón-Rossell, Jorge R. Towards the Theory of Foreign Direct Investment. *Oxford Econ. Pap.,* June 1985, *37*(2), pp. 282–91.

Casson, Mark. Entrepreneurship and the Dynamics of Foreign Direct Investment. In *Buckley, P. J. and Casson, M.,* 1985, pp. 172–91.

Casson, Mark. Multinational Monopolies and International Cartels. In *Buckley, P. J. and Casson, M.,* 1985, pp. 60–97.

Casson, Mark. Multinationals and Intermediate Product Trade. In *Buckley, P. J. and Casson, M.,* 1985, pp. 144–71.

Casson, Mark. The Theory of Foreign Direct Investment. In *Buckley, P. J. and Casson, M.,* 1985, pp. 113–43.

Casson, Mark. Transaction Costs and the Theory of the Multinational Enterprise. In *Buckley, P. J. and Casson, M.,* 1985, pp. 20–38.

Caves, Richard E. Income Distribution and Labor Relations. In *Moran, T. H., ed.,* 1985, pp. 173–98. [G: U.S.]

Cavusgil, S. Tamer. Decision Making in Global Marketing. In *Kaynak, E., ed. (I),* 1985, pp. 173–82.

Cavusgil, S. Tamer. Mutinational Corporations and the Management of Technology Transfers. In *Samli, A. C., ed.,* 1985, pp. 217–29.

Chaikin, Sol C. Trade, Investment, and Deindustrialization: Myth and Reality. In *Moran, T. H., ed.,* 1985, pp. 159–72. [G: U.S.]

Chant, John F. The Canadian Treatment of Foreign Banks: A Case Study in the Workings of the National Treatment Approach. In *Stern,*

R. M., *ed.*, 1985, pp. 215–44. **[G: Canada; U.S.]**

Chapman, S. D. British-based Investment Groups before 1914. *Econ. Hist. Rev., 2nd Ser.*, May 1985, *38*(2), pp. 230–51. **[G: U.K.]**

Charles, Koilpillai J. Transnational Corporations and North–South Relations. In *Utrecht, E., ed.*, 1985, pp. 17–30. **[G: LDCs; MDCs]**

Choudhry, Nanda K. and Datta, Arun K. Changing Perspectives on the Role of Multinationals in Economic Development: Some Evidence from India. *Can. J. Devel. Stud.*, 1985, *6*(1), pp. 77–85. **[G: India]**

Chudson, Walter A. The Regulation of Transfer Prices by Developing Countries: Second-Best Policies? In *Rugman, A. M. and Eden, L., eds.*, 1985, pp. 267–90.

Cieślik, Jerzy. Food-processing Contracts with Developing Countries. *J. World Trade Law*, July:Aug. 1985, *19*(4), pp. 387–402. **[G: Selected LDCs]**

Clarence-Smith, Gervase. Business Empires in Angola under Salazar, 1930–1961. *African Econ. Hist.*, 1985, *14*, pp. 1–13. **[G: Angola]**

Contractor, Farok J. Licensing versus Foreign Direct Investment in U.S. Corporate Strategy: An Analysis of Aggregate U.S. Data. In *Rosenberg, N. and Frischtak, C., eds.*, 1985, pp. 277–320. **[G: U.S.]**

Coomans, Gery. Note sur la transnationalisation de l'économie belge. (Note on the Transnationalisation of the Belgian Economy. With English summary.) *Écon. Soc.*, April 1985, *19*(4), pp. 141–59. **[G: Belgium]**

Corden, W. Max. International Trade Theory and the Multinational Enterprise. In *Corden, W. M.*, 1985, pp. 157–77.

Corden, W. Max. The Enclave Approach. In *Corden, W. M.*, 1985, pp. 178–83.

Crawford, John C. Attitudes toward Latin American Products. In *Kaynak, E., ed. (I)*, 1985, pp. 149–54. **[G: Latin America; U.S.]**

Dhesi, Autar S. and Malhotra, Anju. Foreign Direct Investment in Manufacturing from an LDC: India. *Indian Econ. J.*, Jan.-Mar. 1985, *32*(3), pp. 36–41. **[G: India]**

Dietz, James L. Export-Enclave Economies, International Corporations, and Development. *J. Econ. Issues*, June 1985, *19*(2), pp. 512–22.

Diewert, W. E. Transfer Pricing and Economic Efficiency. In *Rugman, A. M. and Eden, L., eds.*, 1985, pp. 47–81.

Doyle, Michael W. Metropole, Periphery, and System: Empire on the Niger and the Nile. In *Evans, P.; Rueschemeyer, D. and Stephens, E. H., eds.*, 1985, pp. 151–91. **[G: Egypt; W. Africa; U.K.]**

Drucker, Peter F. Multinationals and Developing Countries: Myths and Realities. In *Adams, J., ed.*, 1985, pp. 451–63.

Dunning, John H. Multinational Enterprises, Economic Structure and International Competitiveness: Some Conclusions and Policy Implications. In *Dunning, J. H., ed.*, 1985, pp. 407–31. **[G: Selected Countries]**

Dunning, John H. Multinational Enterprises and Industrial Restructuring in the UK. *Lloyds Bank Rev.*, October 1985, (158), pp. 1–19. **[G: U.K.]**

Dunning, John H. Multinational Enterprises, Economic Structure and International Competitiveness: The United Kingdom. In *Dunning, J. H., ed.*, 1985, pp. 13–56. **[G: U.K.]**

Dunning, John H. Multinational Enterprises, Economic Structure and International Competitiveness: Introduction. In *Dunning, J. H., ed.*, 1985, pp. 1–11.

Dunning, John H. and Norman, George. Intra-industry Production as a Form of International Economic Involvement: An Exploratory Analysis. In *Erdilek, A., ed.*, 1985, pp. 9–29.

Eden, Lorraine. The Microeconomics of Transfer Pricing. In *Rugman, A. M. and Eden, L., eds.*, 1985, pp. 13–46.

El-Ansary, Adel I. Managerial Gap Analysis: A Frame of Reference for Improving International Business Relations with the Middle East. In *Kaynak, E., ed. (II)*, 1985, pp. 43–56. **[G: Middle East]**

El-Haddad, Awad B. An Analysis of the Current Status of Marketing in the Middle East. In *Kaynak, E., ed. (II)*, 1985, pp. 177–97. **[G: Middle East; Egypt]**

Emmanuel, A. B. C. Advantages Offered to Foreign Investment. *Bull. Int. Fiscal Doc.*, March 1985, *39*(3), pp. 113–16. **[G: Zambia]**

Encarnation, Dennis J. and Wells, Louis T., Jr. Sovereignty en garde: Negotiating with Foreign Investors. *Int. Organ.*, Winter 1985, *39*(1), pp. 47–78. **[G: India; Singapore; Philippines; Indonesia]**

Erdilek, Asim. International Technology Transfer in the Middle East. In *Kaynak, E., ed. (II)*, 1985, pp. 85–99. **[G: Middle East]**

Ernst, Dieter. Automation and the Worldwide Restructuring of the Electronics Industry: Strategic Implications for Developing Countries. *World Devel.*, March 1985, *13*(3), pp. 333–52. **[G: LDCs]**

Evans, Peter B. Transnational Linkages and the Economic Role of the State: An Analysis of Developing and Industrialized Nations in the Post-World War II Period. In *Evans, P. B.; Rueschemeyer, D. and Skocpol, T., eds.*, 1985, pp. 192–226.

Fang, Shen. On the Issue of Utilizing Foreign Capital. *Chinese Econ. Stud.*, Summer 1985, *18*(4), pp. 101–06. **[G: China]**

Finan, William F. Intra-industry Direct Foreign Investment, Market Structure, Firm Rivalry and Technological Performance: Comment. In *Erdilek, A., ed.*, 1985, pp. 94–96. **[G: U.S.]**

Finch, M. H. J. British Imperialism in Uruguay: The Public Utility Companies and the *Batllista* State, 1900–1930. In *Abel, C. and Lewis, C. M., eds.*, 1985, pp. 250–66. **[G: U.K.; Uruguay]**

Fox, William F., Jr. *Mitsubishi v. Soler* and Its Impact on International Commercial Arbitration. *J. World Trade Law*, Nov.:Dec. 1985, *19*(6), pp. 579–91. **[G: U.S.]**

Furtado, Celso. Crisis and Change in the World Economy. In *Gauhar, A., ed.,* 1985, pp. 69–87.

Gereffi, Gary. The Global Pharmaceutical Industry and its Impact in Latin America. In *Newfarmer, R. S., ed.,* 1985, pp. 259–97.
[G: Latin America]

Gereffi, Gary. The Renegotiation of Dependency and the Limits of State Autonomy in Mexico (1975–1982.) In *Moran, T. H., ed.,* 1985, pp. 83–106. [G: Mexico; Selected Countries]

Gereffi, Gary and Newfarmer, Richard S. International Oligopoly and Uneven Development: Some Lessons from Industrial Case Studies. In *Newfarmer, R. S., ed.,* 1985, pp. 385–444.

Geyikdagi, Yasar M. and Geyikdagi, Necla V. International Diversification and Investments in the Middle East. In *Kaynak, E., ed. (II),* 1985, pp. 77–84. [G: Selected Countries]

Ginzberg, Eli. Work and Workers: Transatlantic Comparisons. In *Ginzberg, E.,* 1985, pp. 465–74. [G: U.S.; W. Europe]

Globerman, Steven. Multinational Enterprises, Economic Structure and International Competitiveness: Canada. In *Dunning, J. H., ed.,* 1985, pp. 187–215. [G: Canada]

Goldberg, Walter H. Socialist Multinational Corporations in Socialist Countries. In *Takamiya, S. and Thurley, K., eds.,* 1985, pp. 79–92. [G: CMEA]

Goldsmith, Arthur. The Private Sector and Rural Development: Can Agribusiness Help the Small Farmer? *World Devel.,* Oct./Nov. 1985, *13*(10/11), pp. 1125–38. [G: LDCs]

Goodman, Gary A. and Saunders, Robert M. U.S. Federal Regulation of Foreign Involvement in Aviation, Government Procurement, and National Security. *J. World Trade Law,* January:February 1985, *19*(1), pp. 54–61. [G: U.S.]

Graham, Edward M. Intra-industry Direct Foreign Investment, Market Structure, Firm Rivalry and Technological Performance. In *Erdilek, A., ed.,* 1985, pp. 67–88. [G: U.S.]

Gray, H. Peter. Multinationals Corporations and Global Welfare: An Extension of Kojima and Ozawa. *Hitotsubashi J. Econ.,* December 1985, *26*(2), pp. 125–33.

Gray, H. Peter and Walter, Ingo. Investment Incentives and Performance Requirements: The Petrochemical Industry. In *Guisinger, S. E., et al.,* 1985, pp. 237–312. [G: Selected Countries]

Grieco, Joseph M. Between Dependency and Autonomy: India's Experience with the International Computer Industry. In *Moran, T. H., ed.,* 1985, pp. 55–81. [G: India]

Griffin, Keith and Gurley, John. Radical Analyses of Imperialism, the Third World, and the Transition to Socialism: A Survey Article. *J. Econ. Lit.,* September 1985, *23*(3), pp. 1089–1143. [G: Global]

Grossman, Gene M. U.S. Direct Foreign Investment and Trade: Theories, Trends and Public Policy Issues: Comment. In *Erdilek, A., ed.,* 1985, pp. 155–59. [G: U.S.]

Grossman, Gene M. and Shapiro, Carl. Normative Issues Raised by International Trade in Technology Services. In *Stern, R. M., ed.,* 1985, pp. 83–113. [G: OECD]

Grubert, Harry. Comments on Unresolved Issues in Transfer Pricing Models. In *Rugman, A. M. and Eden, L., eds.,* 1985, pp. 164–69.

Guisinger, Stephen E. Investment Incentives and Performance Requirements: A Comparative Study of Country Policies. In *Guisinger, S. E., et al.,* 1985, pp. 1–55. [G: Global]

Guisinger, Stephen E. Investment Incentives and Performance Requirements: Summary and Conclusions. In *Guisinger, S. E., et al.,* 1985, pp. 313–20. [G: Selected Countries]

Hamaui, Rony. La scelta della valute di fatturazione nel commercio internazionale: una sintesi. (The Choice of Invoicing Currencies in International Trade: A Synthesis. With English summary.) *Giorn. Econ.,* May-June 1985, *44*(5–6), pp. 259–84.

Hamlin, Alan P. Capital and Labour Movements in the European Community: Comment. In *Weiserbs, D., ed.,* 1985, pp. 285–87. [G: EEC]

Harris, Martha Caldwell. Japan's International Technology Transfers. In *Nanto, D. K., ed.,* 1985, pp. 114–42. [G: Japan; U.S.]

Helleiner, Gerald K. Comments on Efficiency, Equity and Transfer Pricing in LDCs. In *Rugman, A. M. and Eden, L., eds.,* 1985, pp. 240–44. [G: LDCs]

Helpman, Elhanan. Multinational Corporations and Trade Structure. *Rev. Econ. Stud.,* July 1985, *52*(3), pp. 443–57.

Hennart, Jean-François. Intra-industry Direct Foreign Investment, Market Structure, Firm Rivalry and Technological Performance: Comment. In *Erdilek, A., ed.,* 1985, pp. 88–93. [G: U.S.]

Hillman, Arye L. and Templeman, Joseph. On the Use of Trade Policy Measures by a Small Country to Counter Foreign Monopoly Power. *Oxford Econ. Pap.,* June 1985, *37*(2), pp. 346–52.

Hintzen, Percy C. Ethnicity, Class, and International Capitalist Penetration in Guyana and Trinidad. *Soc. Econ. Stud.,* September 1985, *34*(3), pp. 107–63. [G: Trinidad and Tobago; Guyana]

Hoch, Standley H. LDC Debt and a Multinational Company. In *Kaushik, S. K., ed.,* 1985, pp. 33–40.

Hood, Neil and Young, Stephen. Investment Incentives and Performance Requirements: The Automobile Industry. In *Guisinger, S. E., et al.,* 1985, pp. 96–167. [G: Selected Countries]

Howard, Michael. Export Processing Zones and Development Strategies in the South Pacific. In *Utrecht, E., ed.,* 1985, pp. 31–82. [G: S. Pacific]

Hufbauer, Gary Clyde and Schott, Jeffrey J. The Soviet–European Gas Pipeline: A Case of Failed Sanction. In *Moran, T. H., ed.,* 1985, pp. 219–45. [G: U.S.; U.S.S.R.]

Itagaki, Takao. The Equivalence of Tariffs and Quotas in the Multinational Enterprise. In *Rugman, A. M. and Eden, L., eds.*, 1985, pp. 117–31.

Janet, C.; Gorse, P. and Bouquery, J. M. Le rôle des grandes entreprises diversifiées du pétrole et de la chimie dans la production alimentaire. (Activities of Big Petrochemical and Chemical Diversified Firms in Food Production. With English summary.) *Écon. Soc.*, July 1985, 19(7), pp. 243–84.   [G: France; U.S.]

Jenkins, Rhys O. Internationalization of Capital and the Semi-industrialized Countries: The Case of the Motor Industry. *Rev. Radical Polit. Econ.*, Spring and Summer 1985, 17(1/2), pp. 59–81.   [G: LDCs]

Jenkins, Rhys O. Latin America and the New International Division of Labour: A Critique of Some Recent Views. In *Abel, C. and Lewis, C. M., eds.*, 1985, pp. 415–29.
[G: Latin America]

Jenkins, Rhys O. and West, Peter J. The International Tractor Industry and its Impact in Latin America. In *Newfarmer, R. S., ed.*, 1985, pp. 299–342.   [G: Latin America]

Jenner, Faith S. and Trevor, Malcolm H. Personnel Management in Four U.K. Electronics Plants. In *Takamiya, S. and Thurley, K., eds.*, 1985, pp. 113–48.   [G: U.K.; U.S.; Japan]

Jha, L. K. Multinationals as a Source of Technology for Developing Countries. In *Jha, L. K.*, 1985, pp. 23–33.   [G: Global]

Jha, L. K. Regulation of Foreign Investment. In *Jha, L. K.*, 1985, pp. 34–44.

Jones, Charles. The State and Business Practice in Argentina 1862–1014. In *Abel, C. and Lewis, C. M., eds.*, 1985, pp. 184–98.
[G: Argentina; U.K.]

Jones, Geoffrey. The Gramophone Company: An Anglo-American Multinational, 1898–1931. *Bus. Hist. Rev.*, Spring 1985, 59(1), pp. 76–100.   [G: U.K.; U.S.]

Jones, R. J. Barry. Transnational Corporations and the United Kingdom. In *Stauffer, R. B., ed.*, 1985, pp. 91–131.   [G: U.K.]

Joseph, J. J. Foreign Investment and Profits in Developing Countries. In *Utrecht, E., ed.*, 1985, pp. 1–15.   [G: U.S.]

Juhl, Paulgeorg. Multinational Enterprises, Economic Structure and International Competitiveness: The Federal Republic of Germany. In *Dunning, J. H., ed.*, 1985, pp. 127–54.
[G: W. Germany]

Kaplinsky, Raphael. Does De-industrialisation Beget Industrialisation which Begets Re-industrialisation?: Review Article. In *Saith, A., ed.*, 1985, pp. 227–42.   [G: Global]

Kaplinsky, Raphael. Does De-industrialisation Beget Industrialisation Which Begets Re-industrialisation? Review Article. *J. Devel. Stud.*, October 1985, 22(1), pp. 227–42.
[G: Global]

Kaynak, Erdener. Comparative Study of Marketing and Management Systems in the Middle East. In *Kaynak, E., ed. (II)*, 1985, pp. 19–42.   [G: N. Africa; Middle East]

Kaynak, Erdener. Correlates of Export Performance in Resource-Based Industries. In *Kaynak, E., ed. (I)*, 1985, pp. 197–210.
[G: Canada]

Kaynak, Erdener. Future Developments in Marketing around the World. In *Kaynak, E., ed. (I)*, 1985, pp. 233–48.   [G: Global]

Kaynak, Erdener. Global Spread of Supermarkets: Some Experiences from Turkey. In *Kaynak, E., ed. (I)*, 1985, pp. 77–93.
[G: Switzerland; Turkey]

Kaynak, Erdener. Globalization in International Markets. In *Kaynak, E., ed. (I)*, 1985, pp. 5–22.

Kaynak, Erdener. International Business in the Middle East. In *Kaynak, E., ed. (II)*, 1985, pp. 3–18.

Kaynak, Erdener. Transfer of Technology from Developed to Developing Countries: Some Insights from Turkey. In *Samli, A. C., ed.*, 1985, pp. 155–76.   [G: OECD; LDCs]

Kelley, Patrick L. Belgian Coordination Centers Prove Success. *Bull. Int. Fiscal Doc.*, July 1985, 39(7), pp. 295–300.   [G: Belgium]

Khera, Inder and Karns, David. Perceived Country Attractiveness: A Conjoint Measurement Approach. In *Kaynak, E., ed. (I)*, 1985, pp. 67–76.   [G: U.S.]

Kindleberger, Charles P. Multinational Enterprise: Unit or Agglomeration? In *Shishido, T. and Sato, R., eds.*, 1985, pp. 33–45.
[G: Global]

Kindleberger, Charles P. Multinational Ownership of Shipping Activities. *World Econ.*, September 1985, 8(3), pp. 249–65.

Kline, John M. Multinational Corporations in Euro–American Trade: Crucial Linking Mechanisms in an Evolving Trade Structure. In *Moran, T. H., ed.*, 1985, pp. 199–218.
[G: Europe; U.S.]

Kobayashi, Noritake. The Patterns of Management Style Developing in Japanese Multinationals in the 1980s. In *Takamiya, S. and Thurley, K., eds.*, 1985, pp. 229–64.   [G: Japan; U.S.; U.K.; W. Germany; France]

Kojima, Kiyoshi. Japanese and American Direct Investment in Asia: A Comparative Analysis. *Hitotsubashi J. Econ.*, June 1985, 26(1), pp. 1–35.   [G: U.S.; Japan; S.E. Asia]

Kojima, Kiyoshi. The Allocation of Japanese Direct Foreign Investment and Its Evolution in Asia. *Hitotsubashi J. Econ.*, December 1985, 26(2), pp. 99–116.   [G: Japan]

Kojima, Kiyoshi and Ozawa, Terutomo. Toward a Theory of Industrial Restructuring and Dynamic Comparative Advantage. *Hitotsubashi J. Econ.*, December 1985, 26(2), pp. 135–45.

Koo, Bohn-Young. Multinational Enterprises, Economic Structure and International Competitiveness: Korea. In *Dunning, J. H., ed.*, 1985, pp. 281–307.   [G: S. Korea]

Koo, Bohn-Young. The Role of Direct Foreign Investment in Korea's Recent Economic Growth. In *Galenson, W., ed.*, 1985, pp. 176–216.   [G: S. Korea]

Koshiro, Kazutoshi. Foreign Direct Investment

and Industrial Relations: Japanese Experience after the Oil Crisis. In *Takamiya, S. and Thurley, K., eds.*, 1985, pp. 205–27. **[G: Japan; Selected Countries]**

Kozlow, Ralph. Capital Expenditures by Majority-owned Foreign Affiliates of U.S. Companies, 1985 and 1986. *Surv. Curr. Bus.*, September 1985, 65(9), pp. 22–27. **[G: U.S.]**

Krapp, Thea. The Limitation Convention for International Sale of Goods. *J. World Trade Law*, July:Aug. 1985, 19(4), pp. 343–72.
[G: Global]

Kravis, Irving B. Global Dimensions and Determinants of International Trade and Investment in Services: Comments. In *Stern, R. M., ed.*, 1985, pp. 169–75. **[G: U.S.; Canada; Japan; EEC]**

Kravis, Irving B. Services in World Transactions. In *Inman, R. P., ed.*, 1985, pp. 135–60.
[G: Selected Countries]

Kravis, Irving B. The Determinants of Intra-industry Direct Foreign Investment: Comment. In *Erdilek, A., ed.*, 1985, pp. 60–64.

Krugman, Paul R. Intra-industry Production as a Form of International Economic Involvement: An Exploratory Analysis: Comment. In *Erdilek, A., ed.*, 1985, pp. 33–37.

Laffargue, Jean-Pierre. Une méthode d'évaluation interne des modèles multinationaux. (An Internal Evaluation Procedure of Multinational Models. With English summary.) *Ann. INSEE*, Jan.-Mar. 1985, (57), pp. 119–44.

Lahera, Eugenio. The Transnational Corporations and Latin America's International Trade. *Cepal Rev.*, April 1985, (25), pp. 45–65.
[G: Latin America]

Lall, Sanjaya. Appropriate Pharmaceutical Policies in Developing Countries. *Managerial Dec. Econ.*, December 1985, 6(4), pp. 226–33.
[G: LDCs]

Lall, Sanjaya. Multinational Enterprises, Economic Structure and International Competitiveness: India. In *Dunning, J. H., ed.*, 1985, pp. 309–35. **[G: India]**

Lall, Sanjaya. Pharmaceuticals and the Third World Poor. In *Wells, N., ed.*, 1985, pp. 91–97.

Landaburu, Eneko. Multinational Enterprises, Economic Structure and International Competitiveness: Foreword. In *Dunning, J. H., ed.*, 1985, pp. ix–xxiii.

Lauridsen, Laurids S. Export-Oriented Industrialization in Latin America, South and East Asia. In *Utrecht, E., ed.*, 1985, pp. 83–136.
[G: Latin America; E. Asia; S. Asia]

Lecraw, Donald J. Multinational Enterprises, Economic Structure and International Competitiveness: Singapore. In *Dunning, J. H., ed.*, 1985, pp. 379–405.
[G: Selected Countries; Singapore]

Lecraw, Donald J. Some Evidence on Transfer Pricing by Multinational Corporations. In *Rugman, A. M. and Eden, L., eds.*, 1985, pp. 223–40. **[G: OECD; LDCs]**

Liebrenz, Marilyn L. Global Franchising. In *Kay-*

nak, E., ed. (I), 1985, pp. 53–63.
[G: Global]

Lindsey, Charles W. The Philippine State and Transnational Investment. In *Stauffer, R. B., ed.*, 1985, pp. 185–223. **[G: Philippines]**

Lipsey, Robert E. and Kravis, Irving B. The Competitive Position of U.S. Manufacturing Firms. *Banca Naz. Lavoro Quart. Rev.*, June 1985, (153), pp. 127–54. **[G: U.S.]**

Little, Jane Sneddon. Multinational Corporations and Foreign Investment: Current Trends and Issues. In *Adams, J., ed.*, 1985, pp. 397–407.
[G: U.S.]

Magee, Stephen P. The Appropriability Theory of the Multinational Corporation. In *Adams, J., ed.*, 1985, pp. 436–50. **[G: Global]**

Marchak, Patricia. The State and Transnational Corporations in Canada. In *Stauffer, R. B., ed.*, 1985, pp. 45–90. **[G: Canada]**

Marseille, Jacques. The Phases of French Colonial Imperialism: Towards a New Periodization. In *Porter, A. N. and Holland, R. F., eds.*, 1985, pp. 127–41. **[G: U.K.; France; Germany; Selected Countries]**

Martin, David Dale. The Iron and Steel Industry: Transnational Control without TNCs? In *Newfarmer, R. S., ed.*, 1985, pp. 151–92.
[G: Selected Countries]

Mason, R. Hal. Investment Incentives and Performance Requirements: The International Food Processing Industry. In *Guisinger, S. E., et al.*, 1985, pp. 56–95.
[G: Selected Countries]

Mayes, David G. Capital and Labour Movements in the European Community. In *Weiserbs, D., ed.*, 1985, pp. 257–83. **[G: EEC]**

McCulloch, Rachel. Normative Issues Raised by International Trade in Technology Services: Comments. In *Stern, R. M., ed.*, 1985, pp. 114–18. **[G: OECD]**

McCulloch, Rachel. U.S. Direct Foreign Investment and Trade: Theories, Trends and Public Policy Issues. In *Erdilek, A., ed.*, 1985, pp. 129–51. **[G: U.S.]**

McGuinness, Norman W. Comments on the Difficulties in Regulating Transfer Prices. In *Rugman, A. M. and Eden, L., eds.*, 1985, pp. 309–15.

McLellan, Susan. Malaysia's New Economic Policy: The Role of the Transnational Corporations. *Can. J. Devel. Stud.*, 1985, 6(1), pp. 65–75. **[G: Malaysia]**

Melody, William H. The Information Society: Implications for Economic Institutions and Market Theory. *J. Econ. Issues*, June 1985, 19(2), pp. 523–39.

Michalet, Charles Albert and Chevallier, Thérèse. Multinational Enterprises, Economic Structure and International Competitiveness: France. In *Dunning, J. H., ed.*, 1985, pp. 91–125. **[G: OECD; France]**

Mihăiţă, N. V. Identification of Relations, Interactions and Potential for Informational Change. Mappings for Decisions in the Foreign Trade Field. *Econ. Computat. Cybern. Stud. Res.*, 1985, 20(1), pp. 43–56.

Mihăiţă, N. V. Illustration of the Interaction Potential in Marketing. *Econ. Computat. Cybern. Stud. Res.*, 1985, 20(2), pp. 31–36.

Miller, Robert R. Investment Incentives and Performance Requirements: Computers. In *Guisinger, S. E., et al.*, 1985, pp. 168–236.
[G: Selected Countries]

Miret, Pierre. Interactive Decision-Support System: New Aids for Human Resource Policy Analysis and Formulation. In *Niehaus, R. J., ed.*, 1985, pp. 77–91. [G: France]

Moran, Theodore H. International Political Risk Assessment, Corporate Planning, and Strategies to Offset Political Risk. In *Moran, T. H., ed.*, 1985, pp. 107–17. [G: LDCs]

Moran, Theodore H. Multinational Corporations and the Developing Countries: An Analytical Overview. In *Moran, T. H., ed.*, 1985, pp. 3–24. [G: LDCs]

Moran, Theodore H. Multinational Corporations and the Developed World: An Analytical Overview. In *Moran, T. H., ed.*, 1985, pp. 139–57.

Moran, Theodore H. Multinational Corporations: The Political Economy of Foreign Direct Investment: Conclusions and Policy Implications. In *Moran, T. H., ed.*, 1985, pp. 263–77.

Moroz, Andrew R. Canada/U.S. Automotive Trade and Trade-policy Issues. In *Fretz, D.; Stern, R. and Whalley, J., eds.*, 1985, pp. 278–332. [G: Canada; U.S.]

Mortimore, Michael. The Subsidiary Role of Direct Foreign Investment in Industrialization: The Colombian Manufacturing Sector. *Cepal Rev.*, April 1985, (25), pp. 67–84.
[G: Colombia]

Mucchielli, Jean-Louis. Les firmes multinationales françaises et la hiérarchisation des nations. (With English summary.) *Revue Écon. Polit.*, Sept.-Oct. 1985, 95(5), pp. 611–26.
[G: OECD]

Mun, Kin-chok. Export Pricing of China's Industrial Goods: Problems and Suggested Solutions. In *Kaynak, E., ed. (I)*, 1985, pp. 95–107. [G: China]

Murby, D. J. Dual Resident Companies—Uses and Abuses. *Bull. Int. Fiscal Doc.*, Aug./Sept. 1985, 39(8/9), pp. 373–78. [G: U.K.]

Murphy, Kathleen J. Toward a U.S. Technology Agenda: Insights from Third-World Macroprojects. In *Konecci, E. B. and Kuhn, R. L., eds.*, 1985, pp. 117–133. [G: U.S.; LDCs]

Mytelka, Lynn Krieger. Stimulating Effective Technology Transfer: The Case of Textiles in Africa. In *Rosenberg, N. and Frischtak, C., eds.*, 1985, pp. 77–126. [G: Ivory Coast; Kenya; Nigeria; Tanzania]

Natke, Paul A. A Comparison of Import Pricing by Foreign and Domestic Firms in Brazil. In *Rugman, A. M. and Eden, L., eds.*, 1985, pp. 212–22. [G: Brazil]

Negandhi, Anant R. Peanut Philanthropy: Contributions of the Multinationals to the Host Countries' Economies. In *Takamiya, S. and Thurley, K., eds.*, 1985, pp. 59–78.
[G: Selected Countries]

Neu, C. R. The Canadian Treatment of Foreign Banks: A Case Study in the Workings of the National Treatment Approach: Comments. In *Stern, R. M., ed.*, 1985, pp. 245–52.
[G: Canada; U.S.]

Newfarmer, Richard S. International Industrial Organization and Development: A Survey. In *Newfarmer, R. S., ed.*, 1985, pp. 13–61.

Newfarmer, Richard S. International Oligopoly in the Electrical Industry. In *Newfarmer, R. S., ed.*, 1985, pp. 113–49. [G: Brazil; Selected Countries]

Newfarmer, Richard S. Profits, Progress and Poverty: Case Studies of International Industries in Latin America: An Introduction to the Issues. In *Newfarmer, R. S., ed.*, 1985, pp. 1–12.

Nikolinakos, Marios. Transnationalization of Production, Location of Industry and the Deformation of Regional Development in Peripheral Countries: The Case of Greece. In *Hudson, R. and Lewis, J., eds.*, 1985, pp. 192–210.
[G: Greece]

O'Malley, Eoin. The Problem of Late Industrialisation and the Experience of the Republic of Ireland. *Cambridge J. Econ.*, June 1985, 9(2), pp. 141–54. [G: Ireland]

Ostry, Bernard. Canada/U.S. Automotive Trade and Trade-policy Issues: Comments. In *Fretz, D.; Stern, R. and Whalley, J., eds.*, 1985, pp. 338–40. [G: Canada; U.S.]

Otterbeck, Lars. Joint International Business Ventures: Their Motives and Their Management. In *Takamiya, S. and Thurley, K., eds.*, 1985, pp. 49–57.

Owen, Robert F. and Auburtin, Pascal. A Comparative Study of the Inter-industry Determinants and Economic Performance of Foreign Direct Investments in France and Canada. In *Weiserbs, D., ed.*, 1985, pp. 209–50.
[G: France; Canada]

Ozawa, Terutomo. Multinational Enterprises, Economic Structure and International Competitiveness: Japan. In *Dunning, J. H., ed.*, 1985, pp. 155–85. [G: Japan]

Ozawa, Terutomo. On New Trends in Internationalization: A Synthesis toward a General Model. *Econ. Notes*, 1985, (1), pp. 5–25.
[G: OECD]

Paliwoda, Stanley J. and Liebrenz, Marilyn L. Technology Transfer to Eastern Europe. In *Samli, A. C., ed.*, 1985, pp. 55–85.
[G: E. Europe]

Parry, Thomas G. Foreign Direct Investment in Papua New Guinea. *J. World Trade Law*, July:Aug. 1985, 19(4), pp. 411–22.
[G: Papua New Guinea]

Petit, Michel. U.S.–EEC Confrontation in the International Trade of Agricultural Products: Consequences for Third Parties. *Can. J. Agr. Econ.*, August 1985, 32, pp. 146–69.
[G: U.S.; EEC]

Pettigrew, Andrew M. Examining Change in the Long-term Context of Culture and Politics. In *Pennings, J. M., et al.*, 1985, pp. 269–318.
[G: U.K.]

Plasschaert, Sylvain R. F. Transfer Pricing Problems in Developing Countries. In *Rugman, A. M. and Eden, L., eds.*, 1985, pp. 247–66. [G: Selected LDCs]

Pooley, F. G. H. State and Federal Attitudes to Foreign Investment and Its Regulation. In *Drysdale, P. and Shibata, H., eds.*, 1985, pp. 140–50. [G: Australia]

Porquet, Nicole. Multinationalisation des firmes et avantages comparatifs des pays: une vue d'ensemble. (With English summary.) *Revue Écon. Polit.*, May–June 1985, *95*(3), pp. 243–74.

Pugel, Thomas A. Multinational Enterprises, Economic Structure and International Competitiveness: The United States. In *Dunning, J. H., ed.*, 1985, pp. 57–90. [G: U.S.]

Pugel, Thomas A. and Walter, Ingo. U.S. Corporate Interests and the Political Economy of Trade Policy. *Rev. Econ. Statist.*, August 1985, *67*(3), pp. 465–73. [G: U.S.]

Quirin, Brendan E. Issues in Canada/U.S. Energy Trade and Investment: A U.S. Perspective. In *Fretz, D.; Stern, R. and Whalley, J., eds.*, 1985, pp. 256–77. [G: Canada; U.S.]

Quirin, G. David. Fiscal Transfer Pricing: Accounting for Reality. In *Rugman, A. M. and Eden, L., eds.*, 1985, pp. 132–48.

Raines, J. Patrick. Common Market Competition Policy: The EC–IBM Settlement. *J. Common Market Stud.*, December 1985, *24*(2), pp. 137–47. [G: EEC]

Randall, Robert W. British Company and Mexican Community: The English at Real del Monte, 1824–1849. *Bus. Hist. Rev.*, Winter 1985, *59*(4), pp. 622–44. [G: Mexico]

Ranis, Gustav and Schive, Chi. Direct Foreign Investment in Taiwan's Development. In *Galenson, W., ed.*, 1985, pp. 85–137. [G: Taiwan]

Reitsperger, Wolf. Personnel Policy and Employee Satisfaction. In *Takamiya, S. and Thurley, K., eds.*, 1985, pp. 149–81. [G: U.S.; U.K.; Japan]

Rojot, Jacques. The 1984 Revision of the OECD Guidelines for Multinational Enterprises. *Brit. J. Ind. Relat.*, November 1985, *23*(3), pp. 379–97. [G: OECD; LDCs]

Rousslang, Donald J. The Determinants of Intra-industry Direct Foreign Investment: Comment. In *Erdilek, A., ed.*, 1985, pp. 64–66.

Roxborough, Ian. State, Multinationals and the Working Class in Brazil and Mexico. In *Abel, C. and Lewis, C. M., eds.*, 1985, pp. 430–50. [G: Brazil; Mexico]

Rugman, Alan M. Normative Issues Raised by International Trade in Technology Services: Comments. In *Stern, R. M., ed.*, 1985, pp. 119–25. [G: OECD]

Rugman, Alan M. The Behaviour of U.S. Subsidiaries in Canada: Implications for Trade and Investment. In *Fretz, D.; Stern, R. and Whalley, J., eds.*, 1985, pp. 460–73. [G: Canada; U.S.]

Rugman, Alan M. The Determinants of Intra-industry Direct Foreign Investment. In *Erdilek,*

A., ed., 1985, pp. 38–59. [G: Global]

Rugman, Alan M. Transfer Pricing in the Canadian Petroleum Industry. In *Rugman, A. M. and Eden, L., eds.*, 1985, pp. 173–92. [G: Selected Countries]

Rugman, Alan M. and Eden, Lorraine. Multinationals and Transfer Pricing: Introduction. In *Rugman, A. M. and Eden, L., eds.*, 1985, pp. 1–10.

Safarian, A. E. The Relationship between Trade Agreements and International Direct Investment. In *Conklin, D. W. and Courchene, T. J., eds.*, 1985, pp. 206–19. [G: Canada]

Samiee, Saeed. Global Retail Strategy and Productivity Planning: Some International Comparisons. In *Kaynak, E., ed. (I)*, 1985, pp. 23–36.

Samli, A. Coskun and Gimpl, Martin L. Transferring Technology to Generate Effective Entrepreneurs in Less Developed Countries. In *Samli, A. C., ed.*, 1985, pp. 231–47.

Samuelson, Larry. Transfer Pricing in Exhaustible Resource Markets. In *Rugman, A. M. and Eden, L., eds.*, 1985, pp. 98–116.

Schindler, Guenter and Henderson, David. Intercorporate Transfer Pricing: The Role of the Functionally Determined Profit Split Explored. *Bull. Int. Fiscal Doc.*, March 1985, *39*(3), pp. 108–12. [G: U.S.]

Schoenberger, Erica. Foreign Manufacturing Investment in the United States: Competitive Strategies and International Location. *Econ. Geogr.*, July 1985, *61*(3), pp. 241–59. [G: U.S.]

Scott, Christopher D. Transnational Corporations, Comparative Advantage and Food Security in Latin America. In *Abel, C. and Lewis, C. M., eds.*, 1985, pp. 482–99. [G: Latin America]

de Secada, C. Alexander G. Arms, Guano, and Shipping: The W. R. Grace Interests in Peru, 1865–1885. *Bus. Hist. Rev.*, Winter 1985, *59*(4), pp. 597–621. [G: Peru]

Seidman, Robert B. Foreign Private Investors and the Host Country. *J. World Trade Law*, Nov.:Dec. 1985, *19*(6), pp. 637–65. [G: LDCs]

Shafer, Michael. Capturing the Mineral Multinationals: Advantage or Disadvantage? In *Moran, T. H., ed.*, 1985, pp. 25–53. [G: Zaire; Zambia]

Sharp, Daniel A. French Industrial Policy in the Office Automation Industry: A View from a French/American Firm. In *Zukin, S., ed.*, 1985, pp. 195–202. [G: France; U.S.]

Shepherd, Philip L. Transnational Corporations and the International Cigarette Industry. In *Newfarmer, R. S., ed.*, 1985, pp. 63–112. [G: Selected Countries; U.S.]

Shinohara, Miyohei. The Future of Chinese Economic Growth and the Role of Hong Kong. In *Shishido, T. and Sato, R., eds.*, 1985, pp. 127–46. [G: China; Hong Kong]

Shoup, Carl S. International Arbitration of Transfer Pricing Disputes under Income Taxation.

In *Rugman, A. M. and Eden, L., eds.*, 1985, pp. 291–309.

Siddiqi, Hafiz G. A. Bangladesh–ASEAN Investment Relations. In *Wadhva, C. D. and Asher, M. G., eds.*, 1985, pp. 253–68.
[G: Bangladesh; ASEAN]

Simões, Vitor Corado. Multinational Enterprises, Economic Structure and International Competitiveness: Portugal. In *Dunning, J. H., ed.*, 1985, pp. 337–78. [G: Portugal]

Sit, Victor F. S. The Special Economic Zones of China: A New Type of Export Processing Zone? *Devel. Econ.*, March 1985, *23*(1), pp. 69–87.
[G: China]

Sleuwaegen, Leo. Comparative Study of the Inter-industry Determinants and Economic Performance of Foreign Direct Investments in France and Canada: Comments. In *Weiserbs, D., ed.*, 1985, pp. 251–55. [G: France; Canada]

Soos, Piroska E. Basic Principles Affecting the Income Taxation of Foreign Persons. *Bull. Int. Fiscal Doc.*, January 1985, *39*(1), pp. 19–28.
[G: U.S.]

Sorge, Arndt. History of the IIM-LSE Research Project on Japanese Multinationals. In *Takamiya, S. and Thurley, K., eds.*, 1985, pp. 95–99. [G: Japan]

Stankovsky, Jan. East–West Joint Ventures. In *[Levcik, F.]*, 1985, pp. 203–14. [G: CMEA]

Stauffer, Robert B. States and TNCs in the Capitalist World-Economy: Overview of Theory and Practice. In *Stauffer, R. B., ed.*, 1985, pp. 1–43.

Stephens, Evelyne Huber and Stephens, John D. Bauxite and Democratic Socialism in Jamaica. In *Evans, P.; Rueschemeyer, D. and Stephens, E. H., eds.*, 1985, pp. 33–66.
[G: Jamaica; Selected Countries]

Stern, Robert M. Global Dimensions and Determinants of International Trade and Investment in Services. In *Stern, R. M., ed.*, 1985, pp. 126–68. [G: U.S.; Canada; Japan; EEC]

Sunkel, Osvaldo. Past, Present and Future of the International Economic Crisis. In *Gauhar, A., ed.*, 1985, pp. 1–41. [G: Selected Countries]

Swedenborg, Birgitta. Multinational Enterprises, Economic Structure and International Competitiveness: Sweden. In *Dunning, J. H., ed.*, 1985, pp. 217–48. [G: Sweden]

Takamiya, Makoto. Conclusions and Policy Implications. In *Takamiya, S. and Thurley, K., eds.*, 1985, pp. 183–201. [G: U.K.; U.S.; Japan]

Takamiya, Makoto. Plan for the Research. In *Takamiya, S. and Thurley, K., eds.*, 1985, pp. 101–11.

Takamiya, Makoto. The Degree of Organizational Centralization in Multinational Corporations. In *Takamiya, S. and Thurley, K., eds.*, 1985, pp. 35–47.

Tanguay, A. Brian. Quebec's Asbestos Policy: A Preliminary Assessment. *Can. Public Policy*, June 1985, *11*(2), pp. 227–40. [G: Canada]

Teece, David J. Multinational Enterprise, Internal Governance, and Industrial Organization.

Amer. Econ. Rev., May 1985, *75*(2), pp. 233–38.

Terki, N. Joint Venture Enterprises. *Bull. Int. Fiscal Doc.*, January 1985, *39*(1), pp. 35–38.
[G: Algeria]

van Theil, Servaas. New Investment Code. *Bull. Int. Fiscal Doc.*, January 1985, *39*(1), pp. 33–34. [G: Cameroon]

van Theil, Servaas. U.N. Draft Code of Conduct on Transnational Corporations. *Bull. Int. Fiscal Doc.*, January 1985, *39*(1), pp. 29–33, 44.

Thompson, R. S. Risk Reduction and International Diversification: An Analysis of Large UK Multinational Companies [Internationally Diversified Portfolios: Welfare Gains and Capital Flows] [International Diversification of Investment Portfolios]. *Appl. Econ.*, June 1985, *17*(3), pp. 529–41. [G: U.K.]

Torrisi, C. R. The Determinants of Direct Foreign Investment in a Small LDC. *J. Econ. Devel.*, July 1985, *10*(1), pp. 29–45.

Tussie, Diana. El GATT y el comercio Norte-Sur: el caso del sector textil. (With English summary.) *Desarrollo Econ.*, April–June 1985, *25*(97), pp. 85–106. [G: Global]

Utrecht, Ernst. Gains and Losses in 25 Years of Export-Oriented Industrialization in South and Southeast Asia. In *Utrecht, E., ed.*, 1985, pp. 137–58. [G: S. Asia; S.E. Asia]

Van Den Bulcke, Daniel. Multinational Enterprises, Economic Structure and International Competitiveness: Belgium. In *Dunning, J. H., ed.*, 1985, pp. 249–80. [G: Belgium]

Vernon, Raymond. *Sovereignty at Bay:* Ten Years After. In *Moran, T. H., ed.*, 1985, pp. 247–59.

Vernon, Raymond. *Sovereignty at Bay:* Ten Years After. In *Vernon, R.*, 1985, pp. 51–62.

Vernon, Raymond. Codes on Transnationals: Ingredients for an Effective International Regime. In *Vernon, R.*, 1985, pp. 87–97.

Vernon, Raymond. Intra-industry Production as a Form of International Economic Involvement: An Exploratory Analysis: Comment. In *Erdilek, A., ed.*, 1985, pp. 29–33.

Vernon, Raymond. Organizational and Institutional Responses to International Risk. In *Vernon, R.*, 1985, pp. 63–85.

Vernon, Raymond. Sovereignty at Bay, Ten Years After. In *Adams, J., ed.*, 1985, pp. 423–35.
[G: Global]

Vernon, Raymond. Technology's Effects on International Trade: A Look Ahead. In *Vernon, R.*, 1985, pp. 29–47. [G: OECD]

Vernon, Raymond. The International Aspects of State-Owned Enterprises. In *Vernon, R.*, 1985, pp. 101–11.

Vernon, Raymond. The Product Cycle Hypothesis in a New International Environment. In *Adams, J., ed.*, 1985, pp. 408–22.

Vogel, Klaus. Taxation of Foreign Income—Principles and Practice. *Bull. Int. Fiscal Doc.*, January 1985, *39*(1), pp. 4–14.
[G: W. Germany]

Wadhva, Charan D. India–ASEAN Economic Re-

lations. In *Wadhva, C. D. and Asher, M. G.,
eds.*, 1985, pp. 269–320. **[G: India; ASEAN]**

Wälde, Thomas. Third World Mineral Development in Crisis: The Impact of the Worldwide Recession on Legal Instruments Governing Third World Mineral Development. *J. World Trade Law*, January:February 1985, *19*(1), pp. 3–33. **[G: LDCs]**

Warhurst, John and O'Loghlin, Gillian. Federal–State Issues in External Economic Relations. In *Drysdale, P. and Shibata, H., eds.*, 1985, pp. 190–202. **[G: Australia]**

Wellons, Philip A. International Debt: The Behavior of Banks in a Politicized Environment. *Int. Organ.*, Summer 1985, *39*(3), pp. 441–71. **[G: OECD; LDCs]**

Wells, Louis T., Jr. Small-scale Manufacturing as a Competitive Advantage. In *Moran, T. H., ed.*, 1985, pp. 119–36.
[G: Selected Countries]

West, Peter J. International Expansion and Concentration of Tire Industry and Implications for Latin America. In *Newfarmer, R. S., ed.*, 1985, pp. 227–58. **[G: U.S.; OECD]**

Whiting, Van R., Jr. Transnational Enterprise in the Food Processing Industry. In *Newfarmer, R. S., ed.*, 1985, pp. 343–83. **[G: Mexico]**

Williams, Steven D. and Brinker, William J. A Survey of Foreign Firms Recently Locating in Tennessee. *Growth Change*, July 1985, *16*(3), pp. 54–63. **[G: U.S.]**

Wonnacott, Ronald J. Global Dimensions and Determinants of International Trade and Investment in Services: Comments. In *Stern, R. M., ed.*, 1985, pp. 176–80. **[G: U.S.; Canada; Japan; EEC]**

Wuffli, Peter A. Wandel der mexikanischen Politik gegenuber Auslandsinvestitionen? Die "irationale" Komponente der Mexikanisierungsstrategie. (Change in the Mexican Attitude towards Foreign Direct Investment? The "Irrational" Elements of Mexicanization Strategy. With English summary.) *Aussenwirtschaft*, September 1985, *40*(3), pp. 229–54.
[G: Mexico]

Yamawaki, Hideki. International Trade and Foreign Direct Investment in West German Manufacturing Industries. In *Schwalbach, J., ed.*, 1985, pp. 247–86. **[G: W. Germany]**

Yamazaki, Ippei and Kohama, Hirohisa. Trading Companies and the Expansion of Foreign Trade: Japan, Korea, and Thailand. In *Ohkawa, K. and Ranis, G., eds.*, 1985 , pp. 426–46. **[G: Japan; S. Korea; Thailand]**

Yamazawa, Ippei and Tambunlertchai, Somsak. Manufactured Exports and Developing Countries: The Thai Textile Industry and the Japanese Experience. In *Ohkawa, K. and Ranis, G., eds.*, 1985, pp. 369–88. **[G: Thailand; Japan]**

Yaprak, Attila. Political Risk Assessment by Multinationals in the Middle East: Past Research, Current Methods, and a New Framework. In *Kaynak, E., ed. (II)*, 1985, pp. 57–76.

Yeh, Anthony G. O. Physical Planning. In *Wong, K. and Chu, D. K. Y., eds.*, 1985, pp. 108–30. **[G: China]**

443 International Lending and Aid (public)

4430 International Lending and Aid (public)

Ahmad, Ramly. Malaysia. In *Mehran, H., ed.*, 1985, pp. 235–37. **[G: Malaysia]**

Ainley, Michael. Supplementing the Fund's Lending Capacity. *Finance Develop.*, June 1985, *22*(2), pp. 41–45. **[G: Global]**

Al-Imadi, Mohammed. Inter-Arab Aid and Its Impact on Trade and Interdependence. In *Czinkota, M. R. and Marciel, S., eds.*, 1985, pp. 203–35. **[G: OPEC; LDCs]**

Al Khadat, Djafar. The Role of Foreign Financial Aid in the Financing of Capital Investments in the People's Republic of Yemen. *Soviet E. Europ. Foreign Trade*, Summer–Fall 1985, *21*(1–2–3), pp. 222–32. **[G: Yemen]**

Aliber, Robert Z. Adjustments to the External Debt Burden of the Developing Countries. In *Jorge, A.; Salazar-Carrillo, J. and Diaz-Pou, F., eds.*, 1985, pp. 213–220. **[G: LDCs]**

Ally, Asgar. Jamaica. In *Mehran, H., ed.*, 1985, pp. 230–32. **[G: Jamaica]**

Altshuler, Arkadiy B. East–West Financial Relations: Comments. In *Saunders, C. T., ed.*, 1985, pp. 177–78.

Amorim, Paulo. Portugal. In *Mehran, H., ed.*, 1985, pp. 251–64. **[G: Portugal]**

Aronson, Jonathan D. and Krugman, Paul R. The Linkage between International Trade and Financial Policy. In *Yochelson, J. N., ed.*, 1985, pp. 27–44. **[G: U.S.]**

Ask, Karin. The Position of Women and Women as a Target Group for Development Assistance. In *Jerve, A. M., ed.*, 1985, pp. 327–45.
[G: Pakistan; Norway]

Aubanel, Gérard. External Debt Accounting Issues. In *Mehran, H., ed.*, 1985, pp. 146–58.

Avramović, Dragoslav. External Debt of Developing Countries in Late 1983. In *Wionczek, M. S., ed.*, 1985, pp. 6–35. **[G: LDCs]**

Babiker, Mohamed Abdel-Allah. Sudan. In *Mehran, H., ed.*, 1985, pp. 273–80. **[G: Sudan]**

Bácskai, Tamás. East–West Financial Problems and Their Solution in a World-Wide Context. In *Saunders, C. T., ed.*, 1985, pp. 137–46.
[G: CMEA]

Baker, James A. Lineamenti di un piano contro la crisi dei paesi debitori. (Outline of a Plan against Debtor Countries' Crises summary.) *Bancaria*, November 1985, *41*(11), pp. 1162–67. **[G: Global]**

Balassa, Bela. The Problem of the Debt in Developing Countries. In *Balassa, B.*, 1985, pp. 102–27. **[G: LDCs]**

Barth, James R. and Pelzman, Joseph. International Debt: Conflict and Resolution. In *Adams, J., ed.*, 1985, pp. 358–91. **[G: U.S.; GLobal]**

Batista, Paulo Nogueira, Jr. Rescheduling Brazil's Foreign Debt: Recent Developments and Prospects. In *Wionczek, M. S., ed.*, 1985, pp. 277–93. **[G: Brazil]**

Batra, R. N. The Future of the Debt Situation in the LDCs. In *Kaushik, S. K., ed.*, 1985, pp. 47–57.   [G: U.S.]

Berg, Alan. Bank Interventions in Nutrition. In *Davis, T. J., ed.*, 1985, pp. 145–52.

Berg, Alan. Improving Nutrition: The Bank's Experience. *Finance Develop.*, June 1985, *22*(2), pp. 32–35.   [G: Brazil; Indonesia; Colombia; India]

Berg-Schlosser, Dirk. Leistungen und Fehlleistungen politischer Systeme der Dritten Welt als Kriterium der Entwicklungspolitik. (The Performance of Third World Political Systems as a Criterion for Development Aid. With English summary.) *Konjunkturpolitik*, 1985, *31*(1/2), pp. 79–114.   [G: LDCs]

Bernal, Richard L. The Vicious Circle of Foreign Indebtedness: The Case of Jamaica. In *Jorge, A.; Salazar-Carrillo, J. and Diaz-Pou, F., eds.*, 1985, pp. 111–28.   [G: Jamaica]

Bhagwati, Jagdish N. Alternative Estimates of the Real Cost of Aid. In *Bhagwati, J. N. (I)*, 1985, pp. 252–68.   [G: Portugal; OECD]

Bhagwati, Jagdish N. Food Aid, Agricultural Production and Welfare. In *Bhagwati, J. N. (I)*, 1985, pp. 285–97.

Bhagwati, Jagdish N. Foreign Assistance. In *Bhagwati, J. N. (I)*, 1985, pp. 169–72.

Bhagwati, Jagdish N. Substitution between Foreign Capital and Domestic Saving. In *Bhagwati, J. N. (I)*, 1985, pp. 269–76.

Bhagwati, Jagdish N. The Tying of Aid. In *Bhagwati, J. N. (I)*, 1985, pp. 204–51.   [G: OECD; Pakistan]

Bhagwati, Jagdish N.; Brecher, Richard A. and Hatta, Tatsuo. The Generalized Theory of Transfers and Welfare: Bilateral Transfers in a Multilateral World. In *Bhagwati, J. N. (II)*, 1985, pp. 216–28.

Bhatia, Rattan J. Adjustment Efforts in Sub-Saharan Africa, 1980-84. *Finance Develop.*, September 1985, *22*(3), pp. 19–22.   [G: Sub-Saharan Africa]

Bienen, Henry S. and Gersovitz, Mark. Economic Stabilization, Conditionality, and Political Stability. *Int. Organ.*, Autumn 1985, *39*(4), pp. 728–54.   [G: LDCs]

Biggs, Gonzalo. Legal Aspects of the Latin American Public Debt: Relations with the Commercial Banks. *Cepal Rev.*, April 1985, (25), pp. 163–87.   [G: Latin America]

Blackwell, Michael. Lomé III: The Search for Greater Effectiveness. *Finance Develop.*, September 1985, *22*(3), pp. 31–34.   [G: Selected Countries]

Blanc, Jacques. L'économie française face à l'apprentissage de la gestion de son endettement extérieur. (With English summary.) *Revue Écon. Polit.*, Sept.-Oct. 1985, *95*(5), pp. 658–72.   [G: France]

Blanchi, Claude. Senegal: Agricultural Policy Dialogue. In *Davis, T. J., ed.*, 1985, pp. 198–206.   [G: Senegal]

Blejer, Mario I. Remarks on Argentina and the Latin American Foreign Debt. In *Jorge, A.;* *Salazar-Carrillo, J. and Diaz-Pou, F., eds.*, 1985, pp. 205–07.   [G: Argentina]

de Boissieu, Christian. Contrainte externe et arriérés de paiement intérieurs dans les pays en développement. (External Constraint and Domestic Arrears in Developing Countries. With English summary.) *Écon. Soc.*, September 1985, *19*(9), pp. 135–45.   [G: LDCs]

Boros, Imre. Hungary. In *Mehran, H., ed.*, 1985, pp. 221–24.   [G: Hungary]

Bouaouaja, Mohamed. Tunisia. In *Mehran, H., ed.*, 1985, pp. 292–98.

Bourne, Compton. The Debt Crisis and Development Strategies in the Caribbean. In *Jorge, A.; Salazar-Carrillo, J. and Diaz-Pou, F., eds.*, 1985, pp. 97–110.   [G: Caribbean]

Bourne, Compton. The International Debt Crisis and Development Strategies in the Caribbean. In *Salazar-Carrillo, J. and de Alonso, I. T., eds.*, 1985, pp. 1–35.   [G: Caribbean]

Brada, Josef C. Soviet Subsidization of Eastern Europe: The Primacy of Economics over Politics? *J. Compar. Econ.*, March 1985, *9*(1), pp. 80–92.   [G: CMEA]

Brainard, Lawrence J. Current Illusions about the International Debt Crisis. *World Econ.*, March 1985, *8*(1), pp. 1–9.   [G: Global]

Branson, William H. Policy and Performance Links between LDC Debtors and Industrial Nations: Comment. *Brookings Pap. Econ. Act.*, 1985, (2), pp. 357–61.   [G: LDCs; OECD]

Brovedani, Bruno. Obstacles in the Way of a Resumption of Spontaneous International Bank Lending. In *Jorge, A.; Salazar-Carrillo, J. and Diaz-Pou, F., eds.*, 1985, pp. 23–28.   [G: LDCs]

Buira, Ariel. Capital Market Financing to Developing Countries. In *Wionczek, M. S., ed.*, 1985, pp. 170–92.   [G: LDCs]

Bunce, Valerie. The Empire Strikes Back: The Evolution of the Eastern Bloc from a Soviet Asset to a Soviet Liability. *Int. Organ.*, Winter 1985, *39*(1), pp. 1–46.   [G: U.S.S.R.]

Burcroff, Richard, II. Turkey: Agricultural Sector Adjustment Loan. In *Davis, T. J., ed.*, 1985, pp. 207–10.   [G: Turkey]

Caballero, Carlos. A Closer Look at Colombia's Foreign Debt. In *Salazar-Carrillo, J. and de Alonso, I. T., eds.*, 1985, pp. 1–14.   [G: Latin America; Colombia]

Caballero, Carlos. A Closer Look at Columbia's Foreign Debt. In *Jorge, A.; Salazar-Carrillo, J. and Diaz-Pou, F., eds.*, 1985, pp. 71–78.   [G: Colombia]

Cain, Neville and Glynn, Sean. Imperial Relations under Strain: The British–Australian Debt Contretemps of 1933. *Australian Econ. Hist. Rev.*, March 1985, *25*(1), pp. 39–58.   [G: Australia]

Callier, Andres Passicot. The Chilean Economy and the International Crisis. In *Jorge, A.; Salazar-Carrillo, J. and Diaz-Pou, F., eds.*, 1985, pp. 181–89.   [G: Chile]

Callier, Philippe. Further Results on Countries' Debt-servicing Performance: The Relevance of

Structural Factors. *Weltwirtsch. Arch.*, 1985, *121*(1), pp. 105–15. [G: LDCs]

Camacho, Arnoldo R. and Gonzalez-Vega, Claudio. Foreign Exchange Speculation, Currency Substitution, and Domestic Deposit Mobilization: The Case of Costa Rica. In *Connolly, M. B. and McDermott, J., eds.*, 1985, pp. 251–83. [G: Costa Rica]

Campbell, Bruce. Transnational Bank Lending, Debt and Balance of Payments Deficits in Third World Countries. *Can. J. Devel. Stud.*, 1985, *6*(1), pp. 45–64. [G: LDCs]

Carli, Guido. Eurodollars: Policy Analysis. In *Savona, P. and Sutija, G., eds.*, 1985, pp. 139–61. [G: OECD]

Catan, Luis. The Future of Debtor Countries in Latin America. In *Kaushik, S. K., ed.*, 1985, pp. 17–31. [G: LDCs]

Chacel, Julian M. Brazil's Foreign Debt: The National Debate. In *Duran, E., ed.*, 1985, pp. 69–80. [G: Brazil]

Chanmugam, C. Sri Lanka. In *Mehran, H., ed.*, 1985, pp. 266–72. [G: Sri Lanka]

Chaudhri, Makhdoom H. Pakistan. In *Mehran, H., ed.*, 1985, pp. 242–51. [G: Pakistan]

Cheney, David M. The OECD Export Credits Agreement. *Finance Develop.*, September 1985, *22*(3), pp. 35–38. [G: OECD]

Chichilnisky, Graciela and Heal, Geoffrey M. Trade and Development in the 1980s. In *Bapna, A., ed.*, 1985, pp. 195–239. [G: LDCs; MDCs]

Chitundu, David. Zambia. In *Mehran, H., ed.*, 1985, pp. 307–12. [G: Zambia]

Claassen, Emil-Maria. The Latin American Debt Problem and the Lender-of-Last-Resort Function. In *Connolly, M. B. and McDermott, J., eds.*, 1985, pp. 27–67. [G: Latin America]

Clarke, Giles T. R. Jakarta, Indonesia; Planning to Solve Urban Conflicts. In *Lea, J. P. and Courtney, J. M., eds.*, 1985, pp. 35–58. [G: Indonesia]

Clausen, A. W. Corrective Initiatives in International Trade and Finance. In *Bapna, A., ed.*, 1985, pp. 23–31. [G: Global]

Cline, William R. International Debt: From Crisis to Recovery? *Amer. Econ. Rev.*, May 1985, *75*(2), pp. 185–90. [G: LDCs; OECD]

Cline, William R. Policy and Performance Links between LDC Debtors and Industrial Nations: Comment. *Brookings Pap. Econ. Act.*, 1985, (2), pp. 361–66. [G: LDCs; OECD]

Cohen, Benjamin J. International Debt and Linkage Strategies: Some Foreign-Policy Implications for the United States. *Int. Organ.*, Autumn 1985, *39*(4), pp. 699–727. [G: U.S.]

Cohen, John M.; Grindle, Merilee S. and Walker, S. Tjip. Foreign Aid and Conditions Precedent: Political and Bureaucratic Dimensions. *World Devel.*, December 1985, *13*(12), pp. 1211–30.

Colaço, Francis X. Capital Requirements in Economic Development: The Decade Ahead. In *Gutowski, A.; Arnaudo, A. A. and Scharrer, H.-E., eds.*, 1985, pp. 3–26. [G: LDCs]

Colaço, Francis X. International Capital Flows

and Economic Development. *Finance Develop.*, September 1985, *22*(3), pp. 2–6. [G: Global]

Comeliau, Christian. North–South Relations and Ninth French Plan. *Indian J. Quant. Econ.*, 1985, *1*(2), pp. 89–98. [G: France; LDCs]

Cook, W. J. P. New Zealand. In *Mehran, H., ed.*, 1985, pp. 239–42. [G: New Zealand]

Cooper, Lauren. "Twinning" of Institutions. *Finance Develop.*, June 1985, *22*(2), pp. 38–41. [G: Ireland; Zambia]

Cooper, Orah and Fogarty, Carol. Soviet Economic and Military Aid to the Less Developed Countries, 1954–78. *Soviet E. Europ. Foreign Trade*, Summer–Fall 1985, *21*(1–2–3), pp. 54–73. [G: LDCs; U.S.S.R.]

Crane, Keith. Poland's Mountain of Debt: Will It Dwindle? *Comparative Econ. Stud.*, Fall 1985, *27*(3), pp. 1–29. [G: Poland]

Crane, Keith and Kohler, Daniel F. Removing Export-Credit Subsidies to the Soviet Bloc: Who Gets Hurt and by How Much. *J. Compar. Econ.*, December 1985, *9*(4), pp. 371–90. [G: CMEA]

Dajani, Burhan. Trends in U.S.–Arab Economic Relations. In *Czinkota, M. R. and Marciel, S., eds.*, 1985, pp. 23–39. [G: U.S.; OPEC]

Dalby Jensen, Flemming. Denmark. In *Mehran, H., ed.*, 1985, pp. 208–18. [G: Denmark]

Dauhajre, Andrés S. Dominican Republic: 18 Years of Economic Policy: 1966–1983. In *Salazar-Carrillo, J. and de Alonso, I. T., eds.*, 1985, pp. 1–25. [G: Dominican Republic]

Dawson, Anthony. In Defence of Food Aid: Some Answers to Its Critics. *Int. Lab. Rev.*, January–February 1985, *124*(1), pp. 17–30. [G: LDCs]

de la Dehesa, Guillermo. Institutional Structure for External Debt Management. In *Mehran, H., ed.*, 1985, pp. 88–98.

de la Dehesa, Guillermo. Spain. In *Mehran, H., ed.*, 1985, pp. 264–66. [G: Spain]

Dell, Sidney. The Fifth Credit Tranche. *World Devel.*, February 1985, *13*(2), pp. 245–49.

Devlin, Robert and de la Piedra, Enrique. Pen and Its Private Bankers: Scenes from an Unhappy Marriage. In *Wionczek, M. S., ed.*, 1985, pp. 383–426. [G: Peru]

Diamond, Marcelo and Naszewski, Daniel. Argentina's Foreign Debt: Its Origin and Consequences. In *Wionczek, M. S., ed.*, 1985, pp. 231–76. [G: Argentina]

Dillon, K. Burke and Lipton, David. External Debt and Economic Management: The Role of the International Monetary Fund. In *Mehran, H., ed.*, 1985, pp. 31–52.

Djojohadikusumo, Sumitro. Common Interests of Industrial and Developing Countries. *World Econ.*, December 1985, *8*(4), pp. 325–37. [G: Global]

Djondang, Paul. Financement extérieur et dynamique macroéconomique des pays en développement. (With English summary.) *Revue Écon. Polit.*, July-August 1985, *95*(4), pp. 442–68.

von Doellinger, Carlos. Exports and Foreign

Debt in Brazil: Forecasting the Eighties. In *Salazar-Carrillo, J. and Fendt, R., Jr., eds.*, 1985, pp. 59–76. **[G: Brazil]**

Dornbusch, Rudiger. Policy and Performance Links between LDC Debtors and Industrial Nations. *Brookings Pap. Econ. Act.*, 1985, (2), pp. 303–56. **[G: LDCs; OECD]**

Doroodian, Khosrow. Determinants of Current Account Balances of Non-oil Developing Countries in the 1970s: Comment. *Int. Monet. Fund Staff Pap.*, March 1985, 32(1), pp. 160–64. **[G: LDCs]**

Doroodian, Khosrow. The Effectiveness of IMF Conditionality in Non-oil Developing Countries: An Empirical Verification. *J. Econ. Devel.*, December 1985, 10(2), pp. 53–65. **[G: LDCs]**

Dowling, J. Malcolm, Jr. and Hiemenz, Ulrich. Biases in the Allocation of Foreign Aid: Some New Evidence. *World Devel.*, April 1985, 13(4), pp. 535–41. **[G: LDCs]**

Drobnick, Richard L. The United States as the World's Largest Debtor: Implications for the International Trade Environment. In *Didsbury, H. F., Jr., ed.*, 1985, pp. 175–90. **[G: U.S.]**

Dubey, Vinod. Policy Based Lending and the World Bank. In *Davis, T. J., ed.*, 1985, pp. 166–73.

Durán, Esperanza. Latin America and the World Recession: Conclusion. In *Duran, E., ed.*, 1985, pp. 152–56. **[G: Latin America]**

Echevarria, Oscar A. Solutions to the Debt Issue: A Latin American Perspective. In *Jorge, A.; Salazar-Carrillo, J. and Diaz-Pou, F., eds.*, 1985, pp. 225–31. **[G: Latin America]**

El-Beblawi, Hazem. Oil Surplus Funds: The Impact of the Mode of Placement. In *Gutowski, A.; Arnaudo, A. A. and Scharrer, H.-E., eds.*, 1985, pp. 210–33. **[G: LDCs; OPEC]**

Escovar Salom, Ramón. Venezuela: The Oil Boom and the Debt Crisis. In *Duran, E., ed.*, 1985, pp. 120–29. **[G: Venezuela]**

Eskridge, William N., Jr. Santa Claus and Sigmund Freud: Structural Contexts of the International Debt Problem. In *Eskridge, W. N., Jr., ed.*, 1985, pp. 27–101.

Estévez, Jaime. Crisis de pagos y proceso de ajuste en Brasil y México. (Payment Crisis and Adjustment Process in Brazil and Mexico. With English summary.) *Colección Estud. CIEPLAN*, September 1985, (17), pp. 33–67. **[G: Brazil; Mexico]**

Evans, Clifford W. Commercial Bank Debt Rescheduling. In *Mehran, H., ed.*, 1985, pp. 137–45.

Ewing, A. F. International Capital and Economic Development. *J. World Trade Law*, Sept.:Oct. 1985, 19(5), pp. 537–42. **[G: Global]**

Faouzi, Abdellatif. Morocco. In *Mehran, H., ed.*, 1985, pp. 237–39. **[G: Morocco]**

Feder, Gershon and Uy, Lily V. The Determinants of International Creditworthiness and Their Policy Implications. *J. Policy Modeling*, Spring 1985, 7(1), pp. 133–56. **[G: LDCs]**

Feinberg, Richard E. International Finance and

Investment: A Surging Public Sector. In *Sewell, J. W.; Feinberg, R. E. and Kallab, V., eds.*, 1985, pp. 51–71. **[G: U.S.; LDCs]**

Feinberg, Richard E. LDC Debt and the Public-Sector Rescue. *Challenge*, July/August 1985, 28(3), pp. 27–34. **[G: LDCs; U.S.]**

Feito, José Luis. The World Monetary System, the International Business Cycle, and the External Debt Crisis. In *Wionczek, M. S., ed.*, 1985, pp. 193–227. **[G: LDCs]**

Felix, David. How to Resolve Latin America's Debt Crisis. *Challenge*, Nov./Dec. 1985, 28(5), pp. 44–51. **[G: Latin America]**

Fendt, Roberto, Jr. The Brazilian Debt and its Renegotiation: A Hypothetical Exercise. In *Jorge, A.; Salazar-Carrillo, J. and Diaz-Pou, F., eds.*, 1985, pp. 209–12. **[G: Brazil]**

Fernandez, Roque B. External Debt and Development Strategy in Latin America: The Case of Argentina. In *Jorge, A.; Salazar-Carrillo, J. and Diaz-Pou, F., eds.*, 1985, pp. 201–03. **[G: Argentina]**

Ferrer, Aldo. Self-reliance for Self-determination: The Challenge of Latin American Foreign Debt. In *Gauhar, A., ed.*, 1985, pp. 88–97. **[G: Latin America]**

Fforde, Adam. Economic Aspects of the Soviet–Vietnamese Relationship. In *Cassen, R., ed.*, 1985, pp. 192–219. **[G: Vietnam; U.S.S.R.]**

Ffrench-Davis, Ricardo. The External Debt Crisis in Latin America: Trends and Outlook. In *Kim, K. S. and Ruccio, D. F., eds.*, 1985, pp. 133–62. **[G: LDCs]**

Ffrench-Davis, Ricardo. The External Debt, Financial Liberalization and Crisis in Chile. In *Wionczek, M. S., ed.*, 1985, pp. 348–82. **[G: Chile]**

Ffrench-Davis, Ricardo and De Gregorio, José. La renegociación de la deuda externa de Chile en 1985: antecedentes y comentarios. (The Rescheduling of Chile's Foreign Debt in 1985: Background and Comments. With English summary.) *Colección Estud. CIEPLAN*, September 1985, (17), pp. 9–32. **[G: Chile]**

Fiallo, Fabio R. A Two-Front Attack to Overcome the Payment Crisis of Developing Countries. *Cepal Rev.*, December 1985, (27), pp. 79–96. **[G: LDCs]**

Filatov, Victor S. and Mattione, Richard P. Latin America's Recovery from Debt Problems: An Assessment of Model-based Projections. *J. Policy Modeling*, Fall 1985, 7(3), pp. 491–524. **[G: Brazil; Chile; Mexico]**

Fink, Gerhard. East–West Financial Relations: Comments. In *Saunders, C. T., ed.*, 1985, pp. 175–77.

Fischer, B.; Hiemenz, Ulrich and Trapp, P. Economic Development, Debt Crisis, and the Importance of Domestic Policies—The Case of Argentina. *Econ. Int.*, February 1985, 38(1), pp. 21–48. **[G: Argentina]**

Fischer, Fritz. The Spring 1985 Meeting of the Development Committee. *Finance Develop.*, June 1985, 22(2), pp. 8–9. **[G: Global]**

Fishlow, Albert. Coping with the Creeping Crisis

of Debt. In *Wionczek, M. S., ed.*, 1985, pp. 97–144. [G: LDCs]

Fishlow, Albert. Lessons from the Past: Capital Markets during the 19th Century and the Interwar Period. *Int. Organ.*, Summer 1985, *39*(3), pp. 383–439. [G: W. Europe; U.S.]

Fishlow, Albert. Revisiting the Great Debt Crisis of 1982. In *Kim, K. S. and Ruccio, D. F., eds.*, 1985, pp. 99–132. [G: LDCs]

FitzGerald, E. V. K. Foreign Finance and Capital Accumulation in Latin America: A Critical Approach. In *Abel, C. and Lewis, C. M., eds.*, 1985, pp. 451–71. [G: Latin America]

Flamm, Kenneth. Mexico and the United States: Studies in Economic Interaction: Finance: Comments. In *Musgrave, P. B., ed.*, 1985, pp. 71–76. [G: Mexico]

Ford, W. Antoinette. The Outlook for U.S. Aid Policy in the Arab World. In *Czinkota, M. R. and Marciel, S., eds.*, 1985, pp. 195–202. [G: U.S.; OPEC]

Foxley, Alejandro. El problema de la deuda externa visto desde américa latina. (The Problem of Foreign Debt from a Latin American Perspective. With English summary.) *Colección Estud. CIEPLAN*, 1985, (18), pp. 39–62. [G: Latin America]

Frey, Bruno S., et al. A Formulation and Test of a Simple Model of World Bank Behavior. *Weltwirtsch. Arch.*, 1985, *121*(3), pp. 438–47.

Friedman, Irving S. Yes, There Will Be a Tomorrow. In *Kaushik, S. K., ed.*, 1985, pp. 99–106.

Froomkin, Joseph. Can Government Finance Play a Central Role in Economic Development? Review Article. *Econ. Develop. Cult. Change*, July 1985, *33*(4), pp. 879–86. [G: LDCs]

Führer, Helmut. The Flow of Public and Private Financial Resources to Developing Countries: Recent Trends. In *Gutowski, A.; Arnaudo, A. A. and Scharrer, H.-E., eds.*, 1985, pp. 139–61. [G: Selected LDCs]

von Furstenberg, George M. Adjustment with IMF Lending. *J. Int. Money Finance*, June 1985, *4*(2), pp. 209–22. [G: LDCs]

Gitlow, Abraham L. Economics Seen Darkly in a Political Mirror. *Rivista Int. Sci. Econ. Com.*, January 1985, *32*(1), pp. 87–98. [G: U.S.; LDCs]

Gomez-Samper, Henry. The Management of Venezuela's External Debt. In *Jorge, A.; Salazar-Carrillo, J. and Diaz-Pou, F., eds.*, 1985, pp. 57–63. [G: Venezuela]

Gomez-Samper, Henry. The Management of Venezuela's External Debt: Makings of a Management Epic. In *Salazar-Carrillo, J. and de Alonso, I. T., eds.*, 1985, pp. 1–15. [G: Venezuela]

González del Valle, Jorge. The Role of External Debt Problems in Central America. In *Wionczek, M. S., ed.*, 1985, pp. 427–36. [G: Costa Rica; El Salvador; Guatemala; Honduras; Nicaragua]

Goodhart, Charles A. E. Eurodollars: Policy Analysis: Comment. In *Savona, P. and Sutija, G., eds.*, 1985, pp. 161–67. [G: OECD]

Green, Donald W. The Global Impact of Debt Rescheduling. In *Saunders, C. T., ed.*, 1985, pp. 147–60. [G: Selected Countries]

Green, Reginald Herbold and Griffith-Jones, Stephany. External Debt: Sub-Saharan Africa's Emerging Iceberg. In *Rose, T., ed.*, 1985, pp. 211–30. [G: Sub-Saharan Africa]

Gutowski, Armin. Foreign Indebtedness and Economic Growth: Is There a Limit to Foreign Financing? In *Gutowski, A.; Arnaudo, A. A. and Scharrer, H.-E., eds.*, 1985, pp. 249–67.

Haggard, Stephan. The Politics of Adjustment: Lessons from the IMF's Extended Fund Facility. *Int. Organ.*, Summer 1985, *39*(3), pp. 505–34. [G: LDCs]

Hakim, Jonathan. Latin America's Financial Crisis: Causes and Cures. In *Duran, E., ed.*, 1985, pp. 17–37. [G: Latin America]

Halliday, Fred. The Soviet Union and South Yemen: Relations with a 'State of Socialist Orientation.' In *Cassen, R., ed.*, 1985, pp. 241–54. [G: U.S.S.R.; S. Yemen]

Haryono, Subaliono. Indonesia. In *Mehran, H., ed.*, 1985, pp. 224–30. [G: Indonesia]

Hassan, Mostafa F. Venezuela's External Debt and Public Policy. In *Salazar-Carrillo, J. and de Alonso, I. T., eds.*, 1985, pp. 1–11. [G: Venezuela]

Hassan, Mostafa F. Venezuela's External Debt and Public Policy. In *Jorge, A.; Salazar-Carrillo, J. and Diaz-Pou, F., eds.*, 1985, pp. 65–69. [G: Venezuela]

Healey, Denis. The Strategic Aspects of the Debt Problem. In *Kaushik, S. K., ed.*, 1985, pp. 107–14.

Heath, Edward. General Policies for International Development and Cooperation. *Ann. Pub. Co-op. Econ.*, January–June 1985, *56*(1–2), pp. 111–19.

Heffernan, Shelagh A. Country Risk Analysis: The Demand and Supply of Sovereign Loans. *J. Int. Money Finance*, September 1985, *4*(3), pp. 389–413. [G: LDCs]

Henward, Howard B., Jr. Metro Manila, Philippines: Conflicts and Illusions in Planning Urban Development. In *Lea, J. P. and Courtney, J. M., eds.*, 1985, pp. 19–33. [G: Philippines]

Higonnet, René P. Eurobanks, Eurodollars and International Debt. In *Savona, P. and Sutija, G., eds.*, 1985, pp. 15–52. [G: OECD]

Hogan, Michael J. American Marshall Planners and the Search for a European Neocapitalism. *Amer. Hist. Rev.*, February 1985, *90*(1), pp. 44–72. [G: EEC; U.S.]

Hope, Nicholas. Information for External Debt Management: The Debtor Reporting System of the World Bank. In *Mehran, H., ed.*, 1985, pp. 174–87.

Husain, S. Shahid. Proceedings of the Fifth Agriculture Sector Symposium: Population and Food: Closing Remarks. In *Davis, T. J., ed.*, 1985 , pp. 220–26.

Iglesias, Enrique V. Crisis, Development and Options. In *Gauhar, A., ed.*, 1985, pp. 42–68. [G: Latin America]

Iglesias, Enrique V. External Debt Problems of

Latin America. In *Wionczek, M. S., ed.*, 1985, pp. 73–96. [G: Latin America]

Jackson, Henry F. The African Crisis: Drought and Debt. *Foreign Aff.*, Summer 1985, 63(5), pp. 1081–94. [G: Africa]

Jackson, R. V. Short-run Interaction of Public and Private Sectors in Australia, 1861–90. *Australian Econ. Hist. Rev.*, March 1985, 25(1), pp. 59–75. [G: Australia]

Jamal, Amir H. Development Means Structural Adjustment. In *Bapna, A., ed.*, 1985, pp. 49–57. [G: Tanzania; LDCs]

Jerve, Alf Morten and Tobiesen, Per. The Role of Foreign Aid in the Development of Pakistan. In *Jerve, A. M., ed.*, 1985, pp. 213–21. [G: Pakistan]

Joefield-Napier, Wallace. External Public Debt and Public Finance in OECS Member Countries and Belize: 1977–1982. *Soc. Econ. Stud.*, December 1985, 34(4), pp. 59–89. [G: Caribbean]

Jolly, Richard. Structural Change within the North. In *Bapna, A., ed.*, 1985, pp. 71–79. [G: LDCs; MDCs]

Jorge, Antonio and Salazar-Carrillo, Jorge. Development Strategies, Trade and External Debt in Latin America: An Overview. In *Salazar-Carrillo, J. and de Alonso, I. T., eds.*, 1985, pp. 1–34. [G: Latin America]

Kaffman, Luis. External Debt and Renegotiation: Is Chile a Special Case? In *Hojman, D. E., ed.*, 1985, pp. 115–24. [G: Chile; Latin America]

Kafka, Alexandre. Exchange-Rate Policy, International Capital Movements and the Financing of Development. In *Gutowski, A.; Arnaudo, A. A. and Scharrer, H.-E., eds.*, 1985, pp. 268–94. [G: LDCs]

Kahler, Miles. Politics and International Debt: Explaining the Crisis. *Int. Organ.*, Summer 1985, 39(3), pp. 357–82. [G: Global]

Kalderen, Lars. Sweden. In *Mehran, H., ed.*, 1985, pp. 280–86. [G: Sweden]

Kalderen, Lars. Techniques of External Debt Management. In *Mehran, H., ed.*, 1985, pp. 99–111.

Kaufman, Robert R. Democratic and Authoritarian Responses to the Debt Issue: Argentina, Brazil, Mexico. *Int. Organ.*, Summer 1985, 39(3), pp. 472–503. [G: Argentina; Brazil; Mexico]

Kaushik, S. K. The Debt Crisis and Financial Stability: The Future: Introduction. In *Kaushik, S. K., ed.*, 1985, pp. 5–13.

Kemp, Murray C. and Kojima, Shoichi. The Welfare Economics of Foreign Aid. In *Feiwel, G. R., ed. (II)*, 1985, pp. 470–83.

Khan, Ghulam Ishaq. Adjustment and Growth: A Cooperative Approach. *Finance Develop.*, June 1985, 22(2), pp. 6–7. [G: LDCs]

Khan, Mohsin S. and Ul Haque, Nadeem. Foreign Borrowing and Capital Flight: A Formal Analysis. *Int. Monet. Fund Staff Pap.*, December 1985, 32(4), pp. 606–28. [G: LDCs]

Kindleberger, Charles P. Historical Perspective on Today's Third-World Debt Problem. *Écon.*

Soc., September 1985, 19(9), pp. 109–34. [G: LDCs]

Kindleberger, Charles P. Historical Perspective on Today's Third-World Debt Problem. In *Kindleberger, C. P.*, 1985, pp. 190–209.

Kirkpatrick, Colin H. and Onis, Ziya. Industrialisation as a Structural Determinant of Inflation Performance in IMF Stabilisation Programmes in Less Developed Countries. *J. Devel. Stud.*, April 1985, 21(3), pp. 347–61. [G: LDCs]

Kloten, Norbert. International Indebtedness: Trends and Prospects. *Acta Oecon.*, 1985, 34(1–2), pp. 131–43.

Kneer, Josef. Zur Diskussion um die Auswirkungen der steigenden internationalen Zinssätze auf die Verschuldungsproblematik der Entwicklungsländer: Die amerikanische "Kompensationsthese." (The Impact of Increasing International Interest Rates on the Current Accounts of Deeply Indebted Developing Countries: The American "Compensation Thesis." With English summary.) *Konjunkturpolitik*, 1985, 31(1/2), pp. 115–25. [G: Argentina; Brazil; Mexico; Venezuela; Chile]

Knox, A. David. Resuming Growth in Latin America. *Finance Develop.*, September 1985, 22(3), pp. 15–18. [G: Latin America]

Kozolaev, A. Cooperation of the CMEA Countries with Syria. *Soviet E. Europ. Foreign Trade*, Summer–Fall 1985, 21(1–2–3), pp. 129–34. [G: CMEA; Syria]

Kubarych, Roger M. The Financial Vulnerability of the LDCs: Six Factors. In *Eskridge, W. N., Jr., ed.*, 1985, pp. 3–15. [G: LDCs]

Kuczynski, Pedro-Pablo. Latin American Debt: Act Two. In *Wionczek, M. S., ed.*, 1985, pp. 145–69. [G: Selected LDCs; Latin America]

Kwon, Seung-Woo. The Republic of Korea. In *Mehran, H., ed.*, 1985, pp. 233–34. [G: S. Korea]

Lal, Deepak. Poor Countries and the Global Economy: Crisis and Adjustment. In *Bergsten, C. F., ed.*, 1985, pp. 65–76. [G: Global]

Landell-Mills, Joslin. The Role of Development Finance Corporations. *Finance Develop.*, March 1985, 22(1), pp. 43–45. [G: India; S. Korea]

de Larosière, Jacques. External Debt Management: Opening Remarks by the Managing Director of the Fund. In *Mehran, H., ed.*, 1985, pp. 25–30.

de Larosière, Jacques. Interrelationships between Protectionism and the Debt Crisis. *Aussenwirtschaft*, September 1985, 40(3), pp. 219–28. [G: Global]

de Larosière, Jacques. Policy Options for Developed and Developing Economies. In *Bapna, A., ed.*, 1985, pp. 59–69. [G: LDCs; MDCs]

de Larosière, Jacques. Princìpi, limiti e condizioni dell politiche per lo sviluppo. (Principles, Limits and Conditions of Development Policies. With English summary.) *Bancaria*, November 1985, 41(11), pp. 1154–61.

Lea, John P. and Courtney, John M. Conflict/Resolution and the Asian City: An Overview.

In *Lea, J. P. and Courtney, J. M., eds.*, 1985, pp. 3–15. [G: Asia]

Lecomte, Bernard. Aid Agency Practices and Self-Reliance Policies. In *Rose, T., ed.*, 1985, pp. 253–64.

Leeds, Roger S. IFC's New Approach to Project Promotion. *Finance Develop.*, March 1985, *22*(1), pp. 5–7. [G: LDCs]

Leff, Nathaniel H. The Use of Policy-Science Tools in Public-Sector Decision Making: Social Benefit–Cost Analysis in the World Bank. *Kyklos*, 1985, *38*(1), pp. 60–76. [G: LDCs]

Lembruger, Antonio Carlos. Brazil's Foreign Indebtedness—Determinants and Limits. In *Salazar-Carrillo, J. and Fendt, R., Jr., eds.*, 1985, pp. 179–82. [G: Brazil]

Lichtenstein, Cynthia C. U.S. Response to the International Debt Crisis: The International Lending Supervision Act of 1983 and the Regulations Issued under the Act. In *Eskridge, W. N., Jr., ed.*, 1985, pp. 177–206.
[G: U.S.]

Lindquist, Roger and Wibe, Soren. Remarks and Comments [The Real Cost of the External Debt for the Creditor and the Debtor]. *Cepal Rev.*, August 1985, (26), pp. 155.

Linz, Susan J. Foreign Aid and Soviet Postwar Recovery. *J. Econ. Hist.*, December 1985, *45*(4), pp. 947–54. [G: U.S.S.R.]

Little, Jane Sneddon. Eurobanks, Eurodollars and International Debt: Comment. In *Savona, P. and Sutija, G., eds.*, 1985, pp. 52–58.
[G: OECD]

Lyon, Peter. The Soviet Union and South Asia in the 1980s. In *Cassen, R., ed.*, 1985, pp. 32–45. [G: S. Asia; U.S.S.R.]

Macgregor, John. Philippines: Agricultural Sector/Inputs Project. In *Davis, T. J., ed.*, 1985, pp. 189–97. [G: Philippines]

Mamalakis, Markos J. Financial Services and the Debt Problem in Latin America. In *Jorge, A.; Salazar-Carrillo, J. and Diaz-Pou, F., eds.*, 1985, pp. 29–37. [G: Latin America]

Masera, Rainer S. Eurobanks, Eurodollars and International Debt: Comment. In *Savona, P. and Sutija, G., eds.*, 1985, pp. 59–66.

Masoni, Vittorio. Nongovernmental Organizations and Development. *Finance Develop.*, September 1985, *22*(3), pp. 38–41.

Massad, Carlos. A Reply [The Real Cost of the External Debt for the Creditor and the Debtor]. *Cepal Rev.*, August 1985, (26), pp. 155.

Mathonnat, Jacky. The Impact of External Factors and of Domestic Policies on External Debt. In *Rose, T., ed.*, 1985, pp. 231–40.
[G: Sub-Saharan Africa]

Mayer, Helmut W. Eurobanks, Eurodollars and International Debt: Comment. In *Savona, P. and Sutija, G., eds.*, 1985, pp. 66–73.
[G: OECD]

Mayobre, Eduardo. The Renegotiation of Venezuela's Foreign Debt During 1982 and 1983. In *Wionczek, M. S., ed.*, 1985, pp. 325–47.
[G: Venezuela]

McLaughlin, Peter A. Australia. In *Mehran, H.,*

ed., 1985, pp. 191–204. [G: Australia]

McNamara, Robert S. Economic Interdependence and Global Poverty: The Challenge of Our Time. In *Bapna, A., ed.*, 1985, pp. 33–48. [G: Global]

Mehran, Hassanali; Johnston, R. Barry and Landell-Mills, Joslin. External Debt Management: Introduction. In *Mehran, H., ed.*, 1985, pp. 3–21.

Mehrotra, Santosh. The Political Economy of Indo–Soviet Relations. In *Cassen, R., ed.*, 1985, pp. 220–40. [G: India; U.S.S.R.]

Menezes, Braz O. Calcutta, India: Conflict or Consistency? In *Lea, J. P. and Courtney, J. M., eds.*, 1985, pp. 61–78. [G: India]

Miller, Nikki and Whitehead, Laurence. The Soviet Interest in Latin America: An Economic Perspective. In *Cassen, R., ed.*, 1985, pp. 114–39. [G: Latin America; U.S.S.R.]

Mohammed, Azizali F. The Case by Case Approach to Debt Problems. *Finance Develop.*, March 1985, *22*(1), pp. 27–30.
[G: Selected Countries]

Mohl, Andrew and Sobol, Dorothy. Currency Diversification and LDC Debt. In *Eskridge, W. N., Jr., ed.*, 1985, pp. 231–33.
[G: LDCs]

Moncarz, Raul. The IMF, External Debt and Latin America in the Eighties. In *Jorge, A.; Salazar-Carrillo, J. and Diaz-Pou, F., eds.*, 1985, pp. 233–41. [G: Latin America]

Moore, Mick. On 'The Political Economy of Stabilization.' *World Devel.*, September 1985, *13*(9), pp. 1087–91. [G: Ghana; Kenya; Sri Lanka; Jamaica; Zambia]

Mosley, Paul. The Political Economy of Foreign Aid: A Model of the Market for a Public Good. *Econ. Develop. Cult. Change*, January 1985, *33*(2), pp. 373–93. [G: OECD]

Mosley, Paul. Towards a Predictive Model of Overseas Aid Expenditures. *Scot. J. Polit. Econ.*, February 1985, *32*(1), pp. 1–19.
[G: OECD]

Mukherjee, Amitabha. Loan Commitment of Less Developed Countries: A Study in Retrospect. *Indian Econ. J.*, Jan.-Mar. 1985, *32*(3), pp. 60–81. [G: LDCs]

Mulindwa, Ivan. Uganda. In *Mehran, H., ed.*, 1985, pp. 302–06. [G: Uganda]

Narasimham, M. The International Financial and Monetary Systems and the Developing Countries. *Indian Econ. J.*, Jan.-Mar. 1985, *32*(3), pp. 1–14. [G: LDCs]

Navarrete, Jorge Eduardo. Foreign Policy and International Financial Negotiations: The External Debt and the Cartagena Consensus. *Cepal Rev.*, December 1985, (27), pp. 7–25.
[G: Latin America]

Nelson, Joan. On the Political Economy of Stabilization: Reply. *World Devel.*, September 1985, *13*(9), pp. 1093–94. [G: Ghana; Kenya; Sri Lanka; Jamaica; Zambia]

Nolutshungu, Sam C. Soviet–African Relations: Promise and Limitations. In *Cassen, R., ed.*, 1985, pp. 68–88. [G: Africa; U.S.S.R.]

Nunnenkamp, Peter. Bank Lending to Developing Countries and Possible Solutions to International Debt Problems. *Kyklos*, 1985, *38*(4), pp. 555–77. **[G: LCDs; MDCs]**

O'Connor, John C. The Work of the International Monetary Fund in External Debt Statistics. In *Mehran, H., ed.*, 1985, pp. 159–73.

O'Donnell, Guillermo. External Debt: Why Don't Our Governments Do the Obvious? *Cepal Rev.*, December 1985, (27), pp. 27–33.

Oktem, Ayse. Turkey. In *Mehran, H., ed.*, 1985, pp. 299–302. **[G: Turkey]**

Ondráček, Mojmír. Economic Policy of the Reagan Administration towards the Developing Countries. *Czech. Econ. Digest.*, February 1985, (1), pp. 63–89. **[G: U.S.; LDCs]**

Oudiz, Gilles. Latin American Debt: A European Perspective. In *Jorge, A.; Salazar-Carrillo, J. and Diaz-Pou, F., eds.*, 1985, pp. 243–51. **[G: Latin America; W. Europe]**

Panchmukhi, V. R. Foreign Trade and Balance of Payment. In *Mongia, J. N., ed.*, 1985, pp. 291–314. **[G: India]**

Parai, Amar K. and Mohanty, Bidhu B. Optimal Policy to Achieve Debt Repayment of the LDCs. *J. Devel. Econ.*, August 1985, *18*(2–3), pp. 479–83. **[G: LDCs]**

Pasugswad, Suwan. Thailand. In *Mehran, H., ed.*, 1985, pp. 286–91. **[G: Thailand]**

Pazos, Felipe. Conference on the Debt Crisis and Development Strategies in Latin America. In *Salazar-Carrillo, J. and de Alonso, I. T., eds.*, 1985, pp. 1–9. **[G: Latin America]**

Pazos, Felipe. Development Policies, External Conditions and the Latin American Debt. In *Jorge, A.; Salazar-Carrillo, J. and Diaz-Pou, F., eds.*, 1985, pp. 39–42. **[G: Latin America]**

Pekonen, Kari. Finland. In *Mehran, H., ed.*, 1985, pp. 219–20. **[G: Finland]**

Pendse, Dattatraya R. Some Reflections on the Role of Donor Agencies in the Privatization Process. *Nat. Westminster Bank Quart. Rev.*, November 1985, pp. 2–18. **[G: LDCs]**

Pfeffermann, Guy P. World Bank Policies in Relation to the External Debt of Member Countries. In *Mehran, H., ed.*, 1985, pp. 53–64. **[G: LDCs]**

Philip, George. Mexico: Learning to Live with the Crisis. In *Duran, E., ed.*, 1985, pp. 81–97. **[G: Mexico]**

Pratt, Cranford. Canadian Policy towards the International Monetary Fund: An Attempt to Define a Position. *Can. J. Devel. Stud.*, 1985, *6*(1), pp. 9–26. **[G: Canada; LDCs]**

Prebisch, Raúl. The External Debt of the Latin American Countries. *Cepal Rev.*, December 1985, (27), pp. 53–54. **[G: Latin America]**

Quale, Andrew C., Jr. The International Debt Roller Coaster: Time for a New Approach. In *Eskridge, W. N., Jr., ed.*, 1985, pp. 153–76. **[G: LDCs; MDCs]**

Rączkowski, Stanisław. Debt Rescheduling: Benefits and Costs for Debtors and Creditors. In *Saunders, C. T., ed.*, 1985, pp. 161–75.

Rhodes, William R. Debt Restructuring and

Creditors. In *Kaushik, S. K., ed.*, 1985, pp. 41–45.

Roett, Riordan. The Foreign Debt Crisis and the Process of Redemocratization in Latin America. In *Eskridge, W. N., Jr., ed.*, 1985, pp. 207–30. **[G: Latin America]**

Rohlíček, Rudolf. Prospects and Certainty. *Czech. Econ. Digest.*, September 1985, (6), pp. 24–32. **[G: U.S.S.R.; Czechoslovakia]**

Rondinelli, Dennis A. Development Administration and American Foreign Assistance Policy: An Assessment of Theory and Practice in Aid. *Can. J. Devel. Stud.*, 1985, *6*(2), pp. 211–40. **[G: U.S.; LDCs]**

Rose, Tore. Aid Modalities: Sector Aid as an Instrument in Sub-Saharan Africa. In *Rose, T., ed.*, 1985, pp. 241–52. **[G: Sub-Saharan Africa]**

von Rosen, Rüdiger. Seoul: Neue Lösungsansätze für die Schuldenkrise. (Seoul: New Approaches to a Solution of the Debt Crisis. With English summary.) *Kredit Kapital*, 1985, *18*(4), pp. 586–97.

Rybczynski, T. M. The Role of International Financial Markets in the Financing of Development. In *Gutowski, A.; Arnaudo, A. A. and Scharrer, H.-E., eds.*, 1985, pp. 162–81. **[G: LDCs]**

Ryrie, William [Sir]. Development through the Private Sector. *Finance Develop.*, March 1985, *22*(1), pp. 2–4. **[G: LDCs]**

Sachs, Jeffrey. External Debt and Macroeconomic Performance in Latin America and East Asia. *Brookings Pap. Econ. Act.*, 1985, (2), pp. 523–64. **[G: Latin America; E. Asia]**

Saieh, Alvaro. On Latin America's Foreign Debt: Is There a Way Out? In *Jorge, A.; Salazar-Carrillo, J. and Diaz-Pou, F., eds.*, 1985, pp. 191–200. **[G: Latin America]**

Salazar-Carrillo, Jorge. Review of the External Debt and World Trade Panorama. In *Jorge, A.; Salazar-Carrillo, J. and Diaz-Pou, F., eds.*, 1985, pp. 15–21. **[G: LDCs]**

Schröder, Klaus. Economic Relations—Interdependence or Marginal Factor?: Credit. In *Rode, R. and Jacobsen, H.-D., eds.*, 1985, pp. 36–49. **[G: CMEA]**

Schultz, Theodore W. The Economics of Poverty in Low-income Countries. In *Bapna, A., ed.*, 1985, pp. 137–49. **[G: LDCs]**

Scoville, Orlin J. Relief and Rehabilitation in Kampuchea. *J. Devel. Areas*, October 1985, *20*(1), pp. 23–36. **[G: Kampuchea]**

Sewell, John W. and Contee, Christine E. U.S. Foreign Aid in the 1980s: Reordering Priorities. In *Sewell, J. W.; Feinberg, R. E. and Kallab, V., eds.*, 1985, pp. 95–118. **[G: U.S.; LDCs]**

Shivakumar, J. Sudan: Agricultural Rehabilitation Program Credits. In *Davis, T. J., ed.*, 1985, pp. 179–88. **[G: Sudan]**

Simonsen, Mario Henrique. Indebted Developing-Country Prospects and Macroeconomic Policies in the OECD. In *Bergsten, C. F., ed.*, 1985, pp. 51–64.

Singh, Ram D. State Intervention, Foreign Economic Aid, Savings and Growth in LDCs: Some Recent Evidence. *Kyklos*, 1985, *38*(2), pp. 216–32. **[G: LDCs]**

Somerville, Hernán. Chile. In *Mehran, H., ed.*, 1985, pp. 204–08. **[G: Chile]**

Stewart, Frances. The International Debt Situation and North–South Relations. *World Devel.*, February 1985, *13*(2), pp. 191–204.
[G: Global]

Street, James H. Development Planning and the International Debt Crisis in Latin America. *J. Econ. Issues*, June 1985, *19*(2), pp. 397–408.
[G: Latin America]

Sunkel, Osvaldo. Past, Present and Future of the International Economic Crisis. In *Gauhar, A., ed.*, 1985, pp. 1–41. **[G: Selected Countries]**

Swoboda, Alexander K. Eurodollars: Policy Analysis: Comment. In *Savona, P. and Sutija, G., eds.*, 1985, pp. 167–75. **[G: OECD]**

Taeho, Kim. Assessment of External Debt Servicing Capacity: An Alternative Methodology. *J. Econ. Devel.*, December 1985, *10*(2), pp. 35–52. **[G: LDCs]**

Tanzi, Vito. Fiscal Management and External Debt Problems. In *Mehran, H., ed.*, 1985, pp. 65–87. **[G: Selected LDCs]**

Taylor, Marvin. The Debt Problem in Central America. In *Jorge, A.; Salazar-Carrillo, J. and Diaz-Pou, F., eds.*, 1985, pp. 93–96.
[G: Central America]

Tew, J. H. B. The International Monetary System. In *Morris, D., ed.*, 1985, pp. 549–80.
[G: Selected Countries]

Theriot, Lawrence H. and Matheson, JeNelle. Soviet Economic Relations with the Non-European CMEA: Cuba, Vietnam, and Mongolia. *Soviet E. Europ. Foreign Trade*, Summer–Fall 1985, *21*(1–2–3), pp. 144–90. **[G: Cuba; Mongolia; Vietnam; U.S.S.R.]**

Thomas, Scott and Shane, Mathew. Insolvency and LDC Debt. *Challenge*, January/February 1985, *27*(6), pp. 52–55. **[G: LDCs]**

Thompson, Mark and Slayton, Gregory W. An Essay on Credit Arrangements between the IMF and the Republic of the Philippines: 1970–1983. *Philippine Rev. Econ. Bus.*, Mar./June 1985, *22*(1/2), pp. 59–81. **[G: Philippines]**

Tomassini, Luciano. The International Scene and the Latin American External Debt. In *Wionczek, M. S., ed.*, 1985, pp. 53–72.

Tomlinson, B. R. Indo-British Relations in the Post-Colonial Era: The Sterling Balances Negotiations, 1947–49. In *Porter, A. N. and Holland, R. F., eds.*, 1985, pp. 142–62.
[G: U.K.; India]

Trebat, Thomas J. Mexico's Foreign Financing. In *Musgrave, P. B., ed.*, 1985, pp. 33–70.
[G: Mexico]

Trejos, Rafael A. External Debt and the Economic Development of Costa Rica. In *Jorge, A.; Salazar-Carrillo, J. and Diaz-Pou, F., eds.*, 1985, pp. 87–92. **[G: Costa Rica]**

Trejos, Rafael A. External Debt and Economic Development of Costa Rica. In *Salazar-Carrillo, J. and de Alonso, I. T., eds.*, 1985, pp. 1–13. **[G: Costa Rica]**

Trichet, Jean-Claude. Official Debt Rescheduling. In *Mehran, H., ed.*, 1985, pp. 126–36.
[G: LDCs]

Trzeciakowski, Witold. The System of Structural Adjustment in Trade Dependent Small Centrally Planned Economies. In *Jungenfelt, K. and Hague, D. [Sir], eds.*, 1985, pp. 187–208.
[G: CMEA]

Tutino, Franco. Oneri e vincoli imposti dalla forte crescita dell'indebitamento sull'estero. (Burdens and Restraints Imposed by the Strong Growth of Foreign Debt. With English summary.) *Bancaria*, September 1985, *41*(9), pp. 962–68. **[G: Italy]**

Tyler, William G. Exports and Foreign Debt in Brazil: Forecasting the Eighties: Comments. In *Salazar-Carrillo, J. and Fendt, R., Jr., eds.*, 1985, pp. 77–80. **[G: Brazil]**

Unakul, Snoh and Akrasanee, Narongchai. Structural Adjustment in Thai–Japanese Economic Relations. In *Shishido, T. and Sato, R., eds.*, 1985, pp. 112–26. **[G: Japan; Thailand]**

UNCTAD Secretariat. Examination of the Particular Needs and Problems of Island Developing Countries. In *Dommen, E. and Hein, P., eds.*, 1985, pp. 119–51. **[G: Selected Countries]**

Urquidi, Víctor L. The World Crisis and the Outlook for Latin America. In *Wionczek, M. S., ed.*, 1985, pp. 36–52. **[G: Latin America]**

Volcker, Paul A. Statement to the U.S. House Subcommittee on International Development Institutions and Finance of the Committee on Banking, Finance and Urban Affairs, July 30, 1985. *Fed. Res. Bull.*, September 1985, *71*(9), pp. 701–05. **[G: LDCs]**

Weinberg, Carl B. The Language and Techniques of Multiyear Restructuring of Sovereign Debt: Lessons from the Mexican Experience. *J. Policy Modeling*, Fall 1985, *7*(3), pp. 477–90.
[G: Mexico]

White, John. External Development Finance and the Choice of Technology. In *James, J. and Watanabe, S., eds.*, 1985, pp. 183–216.

Wiesner, Eduardo. Domestic and External Causes of the Latin American Debt Crisis. *Finance Develop.*, March 1985, *22*(1), pp. 24–26. **[G: Latin America]**

Wiesner, Eduardo. Latin American Debt: Lessons and Pending Issues. In *Didsbury, H. F., Jr., ed.*, 1985, pp. 167–74. **[G: Argentina; Brazil; Mexico]**

Wiesner, Eduardo. Latin American Debt: Lessons and Pending Issues. *Amer. Econ. Rev.*, May 1985, *75*(2), pp. 191–95.
[G: Latin America]

Williams, Richard C. Eurodollars: Policy Analysis: Comment. In *Savona, P. and Sutija, G., eds.*, 1985, pp. 176–80. **[G: OECD]**

Williamson, John. External Debt and Macroeconomic Performance in Latin America and East Asia: Comment. *Brookings Pap. Econ. Act.*, 1985, (2), pp. 565–70. **[G: Latin America; E. Asia]**

Wionczek, Miguel S. Where Do We Go from Here? In *Wionczek, M. S., ed.*, 1985, pp. 437–59. **[G: LDCs]**

Yuravlivker, David E. The External Debt of Developing Countries—The Borrower's Perspectives. In *Jorge, A.; Salazar-Carrillo, J. and Diaz-Pou, F., eds.*, 1985, pp. 253–69.
[G: LDCs]

Zedillo Ponce de León, Ernesto. The Mexican External Debt: The Last Decade. In *Wionczek, M. S., ed.*, 1985, pp. 294–324. [G: Mexico]

500 Administration; Business Finance; Marketing; Accounting

510 ADMINISTRATION

511 Organization and Decision Theory

5110 Organization and Decision Theory

Andriole, Stephen. The Crisis Mangement Approach to Short-range Forecasting and Decision Making. In *Mendell, J. S., ed.*, 1985, pp. 153–57.

Anthony, William P. Authority and Organization Structure. In *Damjanovic, M. and Voich, D., Jr., eds.*, 1985, pp. 226–45.

Argyris, Chris. Dealing with Threat and Defensiveness. In *Pennings, J. M., et al.*, 1985, pp. 412–430.

Armandi, Barry R. and Mills, Edgar W., Jr. Bureaucratic and Personalized Strategies for Efficiency and Organization: An Investigation of Structures and Efficiency in a Set of 104 Profit-seeking Firms. *Amer. J. Econ. Soc.*, July 1985, 44(3), pp. 261–77. [G: U.S.]

Ashton, Alison Hubbard. Does Consensus Imply Accuracy in Accounting Studies of Decision Making? *Accounting Rev.*, April 1985, 60(2), pp. 173–85. [G: U.S.]

Baciu, Aurora; Pascu, Anca and Puşcaş, Elena. Fuzzy-Diameter Method for Multicriterial Analysis. *Econ. Computat. Cybern. Stud. Res.*, 1985, 20(3), pp. 65–67.

Beckmann, Martin J. Stationary State Equations for Personnel Flows in Hierarchical Organizations with Entry at Lowest Rank and Promotion from Within. In *[Menges, G.]*, 1985, pp. 38–45.

Belton, Valerie and Gear, Tony. A Series of Experiments into the Use of Pairwise Comparison Techniques to Evaluate Criteria Weights. In *Haimes, Y. Y. and Chankong, V., eds.*, 1985, pp. 375–87.

Booth, Douglas E. The Problems of Corporate Bureaucracy and the Producer Cooperative as an Alternative. *Rev. Soc. Econ.*, December 1985, 43(3), pp. 298–315. [G: U.S.]

Brownell, Peter. Budgetary Systems and the Control of Functionally Differentiated Organizational Activities. *J. Acc. Res.*, Autumn 1985, 23(2), pp. 502–12.

Brownschidle, Terry. A Generalized Stochastic Dominance Approach to Analyze Financial Decisions. In *Brown, R. C., ed.*, 1985, pp. 3–14. [G: U.S.]

Cable, John R. and Yasuki, Hirohiko. Internal Organisation, Business Groups and Corporate Performance: An Empirical Test of the Multidivisional Hypothesis in Japan. *Int. J. Ind. Organ.*, December 1985, 3(4), pp. 401–20.
[G: Japan; U.K.; U.S.; W. Germany]

Camerer, Colin. Thinking Economically about Strategy. In *Pennings, J. M., et al.*, 1985, pp. 64–75.

Campbell, Richmond. Paradoxes of Rationality and Cooperation: Prisoner's Dilemma and Newcomb's Problem: Background for the Uninitiated. In *Campbell, R. and Sowden, L., eds.*, 1985, pp. 3–41.

Cârlan, M. R. and Filip, Argentina. An Application of Fuzzy Decisions in Operating a Power Unit. *Econ. Computat. Cybern. Stud. Res.*, 1985, 20(3), pp. 69–74.

Cavusgil, S. Tamer. Decision Making in Global Marketing. In *Kaynak, E., ed. (I)*, 1985, pp. 173–82.

Charreaux, Gérard and Pitol-Belin, J.-P. La théorie contractuelle des organisations: une application au conseil d'administration. (The Contractual Theory of Organizations: Application to the Case of Boards of Directors. With English summary.) *Écon. Soc.*, June 1985, 19(6), pp. 149–81. [G: France]

Checkland, Peter. The Approach to Plural Rationality through Soft Systems Methodology. In *Grauer, M.; Thompson, M. and Wierzbicki, A. P., eds.*, 1985, pp. 8–21.

Choo, Eng Ung and Wedley, William C. Optimal Criterion Weights in Multicriteria Decision Making. In *Haimes, Y. Y. and Chankong, V., eds.*, 1985, pp. 345–57. [G: Canada]

Ciobanu, G., et al. Reduction of the Large Size Graphs with a View to Their Scheduling. *Econ. Computat. Cybern. Stud. Res.*, 1985, 20(3), pp. 39–42.

Colson, Gerard. Theories of Risk and MCDM. In *Fandel, G. and Spronk, J., eds.*, 1985, pp. 171–96.

Comanor, William S. and Miyao, Takahiro. The Organization and Relative Productivity of Japanese and American Industry. *Managerial Dec. Econ.*, June 1985, 6(2), pp. 88–92.
[G: Japan; U.S.]

Copp, David. Morality, Reason, and Management Science: The Rationale of Cost–Benefit Analysis. In *Paul, E. F.; Paul, J. and Miller, F. D., Jr., eds.*, 1985, pp. 128–51.

Cox, James D. and Munsinger, Harry L. Bias in the Boardroom: Psychological Foundations and Legal Implications of Corporate Cohesion. *Law Contemp. Probl.*, Summer 1985, 48(3), pp. 83–135. [G: U.S.]

Davis, Lawrence H. Is the Symmetry Argument Valid? In *Campbell, R. and Sowden, L., eds.*, 1985, pp. 255–63.

Davis, Lawrence H. Prisoners, Paradox, and Rationality. In *Campbell, R. and Sowden, L., eds.*, 1985, pp. 45–59.

Degot, Vincent. Gestion symbolique et manipulation. Le cas de la gestion de carrière des cadres. (Symbolic Management and Manipulation: A Case Study about the Management of Executives' Careers. With English summary.) *Écon. Soc.*, December 1985, 19(12), pp. 175–201.

Dreyfus, Stuart E. Beyond Rationality. In *Grauer, M.; Thompson, M. and Wierzbicki, A. P., eds.*, 1985, pp. 55–64.

Dugger, William M. Centralization, Diversification, and Administrative Burden in U.S. Enterprises. *J. Econ. Issues*, September 1985, *19*(3), pp. 687–701. [G: U.S.]

Dutton, John M. Toward a Broadly Applicable Strategic Framework. In *Pennings, J. M., et al.*, 1985, pp. 143–56. [G: U.K.]

Eells, Ellery. Causality, Decision, and Newcomb's Paradox. In *Campbell, R. and Sowden, L., eds.*, 1985, pp. 183–213.

Eichner, Alfred S. The Megacorp as a Social Innovation. In *Eichner, A. S.*, 1985, pp. 10–27.

Etzioni, Amitai. Guidance Rules and Rational Decision Making. *Soc. Sci. Quart.*, December 1985, *66*(4), pp. 753–69.

Fama, Eugene F. and Jensen, Michael C. Organizational Forms and Investment Decisions. *J. Finan. Econ.*, March 1985, *14*(1), pp. 101–19.

Fandel, Günter. Decision Concepts for Organisations. In *Fandel, G. and Spronk, J., eds.*, 1985, pp. 153–70.

Fandel, Günter and Spronk, Jaap. Multiple Criteria Decision Methods and Applications: Introduction: MCDM on Its Way to Maturity. In *Fandel, G. and Spronk, J., eds.*, 1985, pp. 1–8.

Fershtman, Chaim. Managerial Incentives as a Strategic Variable in Duopolistic Environment. *Int. J. Ind. Organ.*, June 1985, *3*(2), pp. 245–53.

Fichefet, Jean. Computer Selection and Multicriteria Decision Aid. In *Fandel, G. and Spronk, J., eds.*, 1985, pp. 337–46.

Fichefet, Jean. Data Structures and Complexity of Algorithms for Discrete MCDM Methods. In *Fandel, G. and Spronk, J., eds.*, 1985, pp. 197–226.

Florescu, Gabriela. Multicriterial Decision Making under Risk Modelled on the Basis of the Fuzzy Set Theory. *Econ. Computat. Cybern. Stud. Res.*, 1985, *20*(1), pp. 69–72.

Fortuin, L. and Lootsma, F. A. Future Directions in Operations Research. In *Rinnooy Kan, A. H. G., ed.*, 1985, pp. 55–80.

Frantz, Roger S. and Galloway, Fred. A Theory of Multidimensional Effort Decisions. *J. Behav. Econ.*, Winter 1985, *14*, pp. 69–82.

Gibbard, Allan and Harper, William L. Counterfactuals and Two Kinds of Expected Utility. In *Campbell, R. and Sowden, L., eds.*, 1985, pp. 133–58.

Gladstein, Deborah and Quinn, James Brian. Making Decisions and Producing Action: The Two Faces of Strategy. In *Pennings, J. M., et al.*, 1985, pp. 198–216.

Grauer, Manfred. Multiple Criteria Analysis in Energy Planning and Policy Assessment. In *Fandel, G. and Spronk, J., eds.*, 1985 , pp. 382–99.

Gvishiani, D. Key Reserves in Managing the National Economy. *Prob. Econ.*, January 1985, *27*(9), pp. 3–22. [G: U.S.S.R.]

Haimes, Yacov Y. and Leach, Mark R. Risk Assessment and Management in a Multiobjective Framework. In *Haimes, Y. Y. and Chankong, V., eds.*, 1985, pp. 23–35.

Hammond, Thomas H. and Horn, Jeffrey H. 'Putting One Over on the Boss': The Political Economy of Strategic Behavior in Organizations. *Public Choice*, 1985, *45*(1), pp. 49–71.

Harris, D. John and Williams, D. Glyn. The Use of Risk Analysis within British Rail. *Managerial Dec. Econ.*, December 1985, *6*(4), pp. 202–09. [G: U.K.]

Harris, Frederick H. deB. and Dennis, Richard L. Managerial Utility-maximizing Operating Decisions under Compound Demand Risk. *Managerial Dec. Econ.*, March 1985, *6*(1), pp. 19–26.

Hassin, Refael. On the Optimality of First Come Last Served Queues. *Econometrica*, January 1985, *53*(1), pp. 201–02.

Heller, Frank A. Some Problems in Multinational Research on Organizations. In *Takamiya, S. and Thurley, K., eds.*, 1985, pp. 21–33.

Hermon-Taylor, Richard J. Finding New Ways of Overcoming Resistance to Change. In *Pennings, J. M., et al.*, 1985, pp. 383–411.

Hickson, David J., et al. Comparing 150 Decision Processes. In *Pennings, J. M., et al.*, 1985, pp. 114–42. [G: U.K.]

Hill, Charles W. L. Internal Organization and Enterprise Performance: Some UK Evidence. *Managerial Dec. Econ.*, December 1985, *6*(4), pp. 210–16. [G: U.K.]

Hill, Charles W. L. Oliver Williamson and the M-Form Firm: A Critical Review. *J. Econ. Issues*, September 1985, *19*(3), pp. 731–51. [G: U.K.]

Hobbs, Benjamin F. Experiments in Multicriteria Decision Making and What We Can Learn from Them: An Example. In *Haimes, Y. Y. and Chankong, V., eds.*, 1985, pp. 400–23.

Horgan, Terence. Counterfactuals and Newcomb's Problem. In *Campbell, R. and Sowden, L., eds.*, 1985, pp. 159–82.

Horgan, Terence. Newcomb's Problem: A Stalemate. In *Campbell, R. and Sowden, L., eds.*, 1985, pp. 223–34.

Hulin, Charles L. and Roznowski, Mary. Organizational Technologies: Effects on Organizations' Characteristics and Individuals' Responses. In *Cummings, L. L. and Staw, B. M., eds.*, 1985, pp. 39–85.

Hyvärinen, Anssi. Organisaatiotutkimuksen monitieteisyys—ongelma vai rikkaus? (Multidisciplinarity of Organizational Research—A Problem or an Advantage. With English summary.) *Liiketaloudellinen Aikak.*, 1985, *34*(3), pp. 284–91.

Ichiishi, Tatsuro. Management versus Ownership, II. *Europ. Econ. Rev.*, March 1985, *27*(2), pp. 115–38.

Isermann, Heinz. An Analysis of the Decision Behavior of Individual Decision Makers in the Course of a Computer-Assisted Interactive Decision Process. In *Haimes, Y. Y. and Chankong, V., eds.*, 1985, pp. 236–49.

Isermann, Heinz. Mathematics of the Multiple

Objective Programming Problem—A Tutorial. In *Fandel, G. and Spronk, J., eds.*, 1985, pp. 129–52.

Jackson, Frank and Pargetter, Robert. Where the Tickle Defense Goes Wrong. In *Campbell, R. and Sowden, L., eds.*, 1985, pp. 214–19.

Jacquet-Lagrèze, Eric. Basic Concepts for Multicriteria Decision Support. In *Fandel, G. and Spronk, J., eds.*, 1985, pp. 11–26.

Jameux, Claude. Organisation du pouvoir et pouvoir de l'organisation. (Power's Organization and Organization's Power. With English summary.) *Écon. Soc.*, December 1985, *19*(12), pp. 147–72.

Janis, Irving L. Sources of Error in Strategic Decision Making. In *Pennings, J. M., et al.*, 1985, pp. 157–97.

Janssen, Ron; Nijkamp, Peter and Voogd, Henk. A Methodology for Multiple Criteria Environmental Plan Evaluation. In *Fandel, G. and Spronk, J., eds.*, 1985, pp. 347–60.

Jelassi, Mohamed Tawfik; Jarke, Matthias and Checroun, Alain. Data Base Approach for Multicriteria Decision Support Systems (MCDSS). In *Fandel, G. and Spronk, J., eds.*, 1985, pp. 227–44.

Jelassi, Mohamed Tawfik; Jarke, Matthias and Stohr, Edward A. Designing a Generalized Multiple Criteria Decision Support System. In *Haimes, Y. Y. and Chankong, V., eds.*, 1985, pp. 214–35.

Jüttler, Helmut. Interpretation and Representation of Decision Problems under Uncertainty as Fuzzy Decision Problems. *Econ. Computat. Cybern. Stud. Res.*, 1985, *20*(4), pp. 93–100.

Kersten, Grzegorz. An Interactive Procedure for Solving Group Decision Problems. In *Haimes, Y. Y. and Chankong, V., eds.*, 1985, pp. 331–44.

Kesner, Idalene F. and Dalton, Dan R. The Effect of Board Composition on CEO Succession and Organizational Performance. *Quart. J. Bus. Econ.*, Spring 1985, *24*(2), pp. 3–20. [G: U.S.]

Khachaturov, T. Economic Methods of Managing Socialist Social Production. *Prob. Econ.*, March 1985, *27*(11), pp. 39–58. [G: U.S.S.R.]

Koenig, Gérard. La vulnérabilité de l'entreprise. (Vulnerability of the Firm. With English summary.) *Écon. Soc.*, June 1985, *19*(6), pp. 5–42.

Kofler, Eduard. Fuzzy Weighting in Multiple-Objective Decision Making: The Contributions of Menges and Some New Developments. In *[Menges, G.]*, 1985, pp. 133–45.

Koopmans, Tjalling C. Note on a Social System Composed of Hierarchies with Overlapping Personnel. In *Koopmans, T. C.*, 1985, pp. 1–11.

Koopmans, Tjalling C. and Montias, John Michael. On the Description and Comparison of Economic Systems. In *Koopmans, T. C.*, 1985, pp. 29–80.

Korhonen, Pekka J. A Principle for Solving Qualitative Multiple-Criteria Problems. In *Grauer,*

M.; Thompson, M. and Wierzbicki, A. P., eds., 1985, pp. 281–95.

Krieger, Martin H. The Culture of Decision Making. In *Grauer, M.; Thompson, M. and Wierzbicki, A. P., eds.*, 1985, pp. 65–74.

Kronrod, Ia. Improving the Mechanism of Economic Management and the Law of Value. *Prob. Econ.*, February 1985, *27*(10), pp. 65–84. [G: U.S.S.R.]

Kubačka, Jozef. Optimal Size of Industrial Enterprises—An Important Factor of Intensification of the Reproduction Process. *Czech. Econ. Digest.*, September 1985, (6), pp. 72–86. [G: Czechoslovakia]

Kuhn, Robert Lawrence. Industrial Policy versus Creative Management: The Search for Economic Direction. In *Konecci, E. B. and Kuhn, R. L., eds.*, 1985, pp. 82–89. [G: U.S.]

Kuss, Uwe. C-Optimal Decisions with Optimality Properties for Finite Sample Size. In *[Menges, G.]*, 1985, pp. 162–76.

Laitinen, Erkki K. A Modular Resource Allocation Model of the Firm. *Liiketaloudellinen Aikak.*, 1985, *34*(4), pp. 366–82.

Laki, M. Central Economic Management and the Enterprise Crisis in Hungary. *Acta Oecon.*, 1985, *35*(1–2), pp. 195–211. [G: Hungary]

Lawrence, Paul R. In Defense of Planning as a Rational Approach to Change. In *Pennings, J. M., et al.*, 1985, pp. 373–82.

Levi, Isaac. Common Causes, Smoking, and Lung Cancer. In *Campbell, R. and Sowden, L., eds.*, 1985, pp. 234–47.

Lewis, Barry L. and Bell, Jan. Decisions Involving Sequential Events: Replications and Extensions. *J. Acc. Res.*, Spring 1985, *23*(1), pp. 228–39. [G: U.S.]

Lockett, Geoff; Hetherington, Barrie and Yallup, Peter. Subjective Estimation and Its Use in MCDM. In *Haimes, Y. Y. and Chankong, V., eds.*, 1985, pp. 358–74. [G: U.K.; U.S.; Australia; S. Africa; China]

Lorange, Peter. Strengthening Organizational Capacity to Execute Strategic Change. In *Pennings, J. M., et al.*, 1985, pp. 449–67.

Lord, Robert G. An Information Processing Approach to Social Perceptions, Leadership and Behavioral Measurement in Organizations. In *Cummings, L. L. and Staw, B. M., eds.*, 1985, pp. 87–128.

MacCrimmon, Kenneth R. Understanding Strategic Decisions: Three Systematic Approaches. In *Pennings, J. M., et al.*, 1985, pp. 76–98.

Malakooti, B. A Nonlinear Multi-attribute Utility Theory. In *Haimes, Y. Y. and Chankong, V., eds.*, 1985, pp. 190–200.

Mandell, Marvin B. Monitoring and Evaluating New Managerial Technologies. In *Samli, A. C., ed.*, 1985, pp. 263–83.

Marchesnay, Michel and Rudel, Sylvie. La gestion du risque dans la T.P.E. Faits et théories. (Management of Risks with Very Small Firms. Facts and Theory. With English summary.) *Écon. Soc.*, June 1985, *19*(6), pp. 43–74.

Marginson, Paul. The Multidivisional Firm and Control over the Work Process. *Int. J. Ind.*

Organ., March 1985, *3*(1), pp. 37–56.
[G: U.K.]

Meško, Ivan. Optimization of Business Processes by Mixed Integer Programming. *Econ. Anal. Worker's Manage.*, 1985, *19*(2), pp. 237–41.

Miller, Edward McCarthy. Decision-making under Uncertainty for Capital Budgeting and Hiring. *Managerial Dec. Econ.*, March 1985, *6*(1), pp. 11–18.

Mohr, Lawrence B. Forces Influencing Decision and Change Behaviors. In *Pennings, J. M., et al.*, 1985, pp. 249–68.

Mushkat, Miron. Planning under Uncertainty in the Public Domain: A Critique of Conventional Approaches. *Rivista Int. Sci. Econ. Com.*, July-Aug. 1985, *32*(7–8), pp. 661–77.

Nagel, Stuart S. Policy/Goal Percentaging as a Form of MCDM. In *Haimes, Y. Y. and Chankong, V., eds.*, 1985, pp. 558–62.

Newgren, Kenneth E. and Brechtel, Donald L. Environmental Scanning. In *Damjanovic, M. and Voich, D., Jr., eds.*, 1985, pp. 142–58.

Newman, William H. Formulating an Integrated View of Strategic Management. In *Pennings, J. M., et al.*, 1985, pp. 431–39.

Nica, V. and Fabian, Cs. Elaboration of Cooperation Programmes at a Group and Branch Level. *Econ. Computat. Cybern. Stud. Res.*, 1985, *20*(4), pp. 43–46.

Nicholas, Nick L. Methodological Issues Raised in the Measurement of Family Decision-Making Processes. In *Brown, R. C., ed.*, 1985, pp. 269–73.

Nijkamp, Peter and Voogd, Henk. An Informal Introduction to Multicriteria Evaluation. In *Fandel, G. and Spronk, J., eds.*, 1985, pp. 61–84.

Normann, Richard. Developing Capabilities for Organizational Learning. In *Pennings, J. M., et al.*, 1985, pp. 217–48.

Nozick, Robert. Newcomb's Problem and Two Principles of Choice. In *Campbell, R. and Sowden, L., eds.*, 1985, pp. 107–33.

Ostanello, Anna. Outranking Methods. In *Fandel, G. and Spronk, J., eds.*, 1985, pp. 41–60.

Otterbeck, Lars. Joint International Business Ventures: Their Motives and Their Management. In *Takamiya, S. and Thurley, K., eds.*, 1985, pp. 49–57.

Ozawa, Terutomo. On New Trends in Internationalization: A Synthesis toward a General Model. *Econ. Notes*, 1985, (1), pp. 5–25.
[G: OECD]

Ozernoy, Vladimir M. Generating Alternatives in Multiple Criteria Decision Making Problems: A Survey. In *Haimes, Y. Y. and Chankong, V., eds.*, 1985, pp. 322–30.

Pennings, Johannes M. Introduction: On the Nature and Theory of Strategic Decisions. In *Pennings, J. M., et al.*, 1985, pp. 1–34.

Pennings, Johannes M. Toward Convergence in Strategic Theory and Practice. In *Pennings, J. M., et al.*, 1985, pp. 468–94.

Peschel, Manfred. Macromodels and Multiobjective Decision Making. In *Grauer, M.; Thomp-

son, M. and Wierzbicki, A. P., eds.*, 1985, pp. 222–28.

Popovici, Al. A. Automatic Evaluation of Emergency Minimal Modes in the Fault-Tree. *Econ. Computat. Cybern. Stud. Res.*, 1985, *20*(3), pp. 55–60.

Puşcaş, Elena and Mihăilescu-Stoica, Gabriela. A Model of Multiobjective Technical and Material Supply. *Econ. Computat. Cybern. Stud. Res.*, 1985, *20*(4), pp. 65–69.

Racoveanu, N. and Dan, S. Analysis of Dynamic Systems in the State-Control Extended Space. *Econ. Computat. Cybern. Stud. Res.*, 1985, *20*(4), pp. 47–51.

Rousseau, Denise M. Issues of Level in Organizational Research: Multi-level and Cross-level Perspectives. In *Cummings, L. L. and Staw, B. M., eds.*, 1985, pp. 1–37.

Roy, Bernard and Bouyssou, Denis. An Example of Comparison of Two Decision-Aid Models. In *Fandel, G. and Spronk, J., eds.*, 1985, pp. 361–81.

Saaty, Thomas L. Axiomatization of the Analytic Hierarchy Process. In *Haimes, Y. Y. and Chankong, V., eds.*, 1985, pp. 91–108.

Sah, Raaj Kumar and Stiglitz, Joseph E. Human Fallibility and Economic Organization. *Amer. Econ. Rev.*, May 1985, *75*(2), pp. 292–97.

Schaeffers, Hans. Design of Computer Support for Multicriteria and Multiperson Decisions in Regional Water Resources Planning. In *Fandel, G. and Spronk, J., eds.*, 1985, pp. 245–66.

Simon, Herbert A. Japan's Emerging Multinationals: Foreward. In *Takamiya, S. and Thurley, K., eds.*, 1985, pp. 3–12.

Sobel, Jordan Howard. Not Every Prisoner's Dilemma Is a Newcomb Problem. In *Campbell, R. and Sowden, L., eds.*, 1985, pp. 263–74.

Sobel, Jordan Howard. Utility Maximizers in Iterated Prisoner's Dilemmas. In *Campbell, R. and Sowden, L., eds.*, 1985, pp. 306–19.

Sorge, Arndt. History of the IIM-LSE Research Project on Japanese Multinationals. In *Takamiya, S. and Thurley, K., eds.*, 1985, pp. 95–99.
[G: Japan]

Spronk, Jaap. Financial Planning with Conflicting Objectives. In *Fandel, G. and Spronk, J., eds.*, 1985, pp. 269–88.

Spronk, Jaap and Zambruno, Giovanni. Interactive Multiple Goal Programming for Bank Portfolio Selection. In *Fandel, G. and Spronk, J., eds.*, 1985, pp. 289–306.

Srivastava, Rajendra P. A Note on Internal Control Systems with Control Components in Series. *Accounting Rev.*, July 1985, *60*(3), pp. 504–07.

Stair, Ralph. Computerized Control and Information Systems. In *Damjanovic, M. and Voich, D., Jr., eds.*, 1985, pp. 325–42.

Starbuck, William H. Acting First and Thinking Later: Theory versus Reality in Strategic Change. In *Pennings, J. M., et al.*, 1985, pp. 336–72.

Stoica, M. and Raţiu Suciu, Camelia. The Relation between Heuristics and the Fuzzy Sets

Theory. *Econ. Computat. Cybern. Stud. Res.*, 1985, *20*(4), pp. 19–22.

Takamiya, Makoto. The Degree of Organizational Centralization in Multinational Corporations. In *Takamiya, S. and Thurley, K., eds.*, 1985, pp. 35–47.

Takeda, E.; Yu, P. L. and Cogger, K. O. A Comparative Study on Eigen Weight Vectors. In *Haimes, Y. Y. and Chankong, V., eds.*, 1985, pp. 388–99.

Teece, David J. Applying Concepts of Economic Analysis to Strategic Management. In *Pennings, J. M., et al.*, 1985, pp. 35–63.

Telgen, Jan. MCDM Problems in Rabobank Nederland. In *Fandel, G. and Spronk, J., eds.*, 1985, pp. 307–16.   [G: Netherlands]

Tietz, Reinhard. On the Structure, Stabilization and Accuracy of the Decision Process. In *Grauer, M.; Thompson, M. and Wierzbicki, A. P., eds.*, 1985, pp. 132–46.

Tushman, Michael L. and Romanelli, Elaine. Organizational Evolution: A Metamorphosis Model of Convergence and Reorientation. In *Cummings, L. L. and Staw, B. M., eds.*, 1985, pp. 171–222.   [G: U.S.]

Van de Ven, Andrew H. and Drazin, Robert. The Concept of Fit in Contingency Theory. In *Cummings, L. L. and Staw, B. M., eds.*, 1985, pp. 333–65.

Van de Ven, Andrew H. and Hudson, Roger. Increasing Organizational Attention to Strategic Choices. In *Pennings, J. M., et al.*, 1985, pp. 440–48.

Vickers, John. Delegation and the Theory of the Firm. *Econ. J.*, Supplement 1985, *95*, pp. 138–47.

Vincke, Philippe. Multiattribute Utility Theory as a Basic Approach. In *Fandel, G. and Spronk, J., eds.*, 1985, pp. 27–40.

Voge, Jean. Management of Complexity. In *Aida, S., et al.*, 1985, pp. 298–311.

Weiss, Howard M. and Ilgen, Daniel R. Routinized Behavior in Organizations. *J. Behav. Econ.*, Winter 1985, *14*, pp. 57–67.

White, Chelsea C., III. Use of Intuitive Preference in Directing Utility Assessment. In *Haimes, Y. Y. and Chankong, V., eds.*, 1985, pp. 162–69.

Wierzbicki, Andrzej. Negotiation and Mediation in Conflicts: II. Plural Rationality and Interactive Decision Processes. In *Grauer, M.; Thompson, M. and Wierzbicki, A. P., eds.*, 1985, pp. 114–31.

Winter, Sidney G. The Case for "Mechanistic" Decision Making. In *Pennings, J. M., et al.*, 1985, pp. 99–113.

Young, H. Peyton. Methods and Principles of Cost Allocation. In *Young, H. P., ed.*, 1985, pp. 3–29.   [G: U.K.; Sweden]

Young, William E. An Overview of Decision Making Processes in Business and Economics. In *Damjanovic, M. and Voich, D., Jr., eds.*, 1985, pp. 178–95.

Zammuto, Raymond F. and Cameron, Kim S. Environmental Decline and Organizational Response. In *Cummings, L. L. and Staw, B. M.,*

eds., 1985, pp. 223–62.

Zardet, Véronique. Des systèmes d'informations vivants: Étude des conditions d'efficacité 2B partir d'expérimentations. (Living Information Systems: A Study of the Conditions for Effective Implementation Based on Practical Experience. With English summary.) *Écon. Soc.*, June 1985, *19*(6), pp. 229–70.

Zionts, Stanley. Multiple Criteria Mathematical Programming: An Overview and Several Approaches. In *Fandel, G. and Spronk, J., eds.*, 1985, pp. 85–128.

512 Managerial Economics

5120 Managerial Economics

Abel, Andrew B. Inventories, Stock-Outs and Production Smoothing. *Rev. Econ. Stud.*, April 1985, *52*(2), pp. 283–93.

Aislabie, Colin J. The Joint Determination of 'Quality' and Price in Standardized Products: A Comparative Dynamic Analysis. *Managerial Dec. Econ.*, September 1985, *6*(3), pp. 141–46.

Aliber, Robert Z. Transfer Pricing: A Taxonomy of Impacts on Economic Welfare. In *Rugman, A. M. and Eden, L., eds.*, 1985, pp. 82–97.

Amoako-Adu, Ben; Marmer, Harry and Yagil, Joseph. The Efficiency of Certain Speculative Markets and Gambler Behavior. *J. Econ. Bus.*, December 1985, *37*(4), pp. 365–78.   [G: U.S.]

Armandi, Barry R. and Mills, Edgar W., Jr. Bureaucratic and Personalized Strategies for Efficiency and Organization: An Investigation of Structures and Efficiency in a Set of 104 Profit-seeking Firms. *Amer. J. Econ. Soc.*, July 1985, *44*(3), pp. 261–77.   [G: U.S.]

Arrow, Kenneth J.; Harris, Theodore E. and Marschak, Jacob. Optimal Inventory Policy. In *Arrow, K. J. (I)*, 1985, pp. 25–49.

Arrow, Kenneth J. and Nerlove, Marc. Optimal Advertising Policy under Dynamic Conditions. In *Arrow, K. J. (I)*, 1985, pp. 140–56.

Artto, Eero. Kansainvälinen kilpailukyky yritys- ja toimialatasolla—V. (International Competitiveness at Enterprise and Industry Level—V. With English summary.) *Liiketaloudellinen Aikak.*, 1985, *34*(1), pp. 32–73.   [G: Finland; W. Germany; Canada; U.S.; Sweden]

Artus, Patrick. Rationnement de crédit et réactions des entreprises. (Credit Rationing and Firms' Reactions. With English summary.) *Revue Écon.*, November 1985, *36*(6), pp. 1207–46.   [G: France]

Atack, Jeremy. Industrial Structure and the Emergence of the Modern Industrial Corporation. *Exploration Econ. Hist.*, January 1985, *22*(1), pp. 29–52.   [G: U.S.]

Awh, Robert Y. and Primeaux, Walter J., Jr. Managerial Discretion and Expense Preference Behavior. *Rev. Econ. Statist.*, May 1985, *67*(2), pp. 224–31.   [G: U.S.]

Basu, Amiya K., et al. Salesforce Compensation

Plans: An Agency Theoretic Perspective. *Marketing Sci.*, Fall 1985, *4*(4), pp. 267–91.

Baysinger, Barry D. and Butler, Henry N. Corporate Governance and the Board of Directors: Performance Effects of Changes in Board Composition. *J. Law, Econ., Organ.*, Spring 1985, *1*(1), pp. 101–24. **[G: U.S.]**

Beker, Víctor A. La inflexibilidad descendente de los precios y la teoría de la empresa. (Price Inflexibility and the Theory of the Firm. With English summary.) *Económica (La Plata)*, Jan.-Apr. 1985, *31*(1), pp. 3–19.

Benninga, Simon Z.; Eldor, Rafael and Zilcha, Itzhak. Optimal International Hedging in Commodity and Currency Forward Markets. *J. Int. Money Finance*, December 1985, *4*(4), pp. 537–52.

Benston, George J. The Self-serving Management Hypothesis: Some Evidence. *J. Acc. Econ.*, April 1985, *7*(1–3), pp. 67–84. **[G: U.S.]**

Benvignati, Anita M. An Empirical Investigation of International Transfer Pricing by U.S. Manufacturing Firms. In *Rugman, A. M. and Eden, L., eds.*, 1985, pp. 193–211. **[G: U.S.]**

Bhagat, Sanjai; Brickley, James A. and Lease, Ronald C. Incentive Effects of Stock Purchase Plans. *J. Finan. Econ.*, June 1985, *14*(2), pp. 195–215. **[G: U.S.]**

Biddle, Gary C. and Steinberg, Richard. Common Cost Allocation in the Firm. In *Young, H. P., ed.*, 1985, pp. 31–54.

Blang, Hans-Georg and Schöler, Klaus. Zur Rationalitä t der Preiserwartungen deutscher Unternehmen. (On Rational Price Expectations of German Firms. With English summary.) *Ifo-Studien*, 1985, *31*(3), pp. 239–58. **[G: W. Germany]**

Bradford, G. L. and Debertin, David L. Establishing Linkages between Economic Theory and Enterprise Budgeting for Teaching and Extension Programs. *Southern J. Agr. Econ.*, December 1985, *17*(2), pp. 221–30.

Brambilla, Francesco. Una semplice dimostrazione della legge di Zipf nelle attività produttive. (A Simple Demonstration of Zipf's Law in Productive Activities. With English summary.) *Rivista Int. Sci. Econ. Com.*, January 1985, *32*(1), pp. 84–86.

Brickley, James A.; Bhagat, Sanjai and Lease, Ronald C. The Impact of Long-range Managerial Compensation Plans on Shareholder Wealth. *J. Acc. Econ.*, April 1985, *7*(1–3), pp. 115–29. **[G: U.S.]**

Brown, Robert M. On Carrying Costs and the EOQ Model: A Pedagogical Note. *Financial Rev.*, November 1985, *20*(4), pp. 357–60.

Burlaud, Alain and Simon, Claude. L'évolution des systèmes coûts/contrôle: un phénomène culturel. (The Evolution of Cost-Control Systems: A Cultural Phenomenon. With English summary.) *Écon. Soc.*, December 1985, *19*(12), pp. 107–27.

Cameron, Samuel and Shipley, David D. A Discretionary Model of Industrial Buying. *Managerial Dec. Econ.*, June 1985, *6*(2), pp. 102–11. **[G: U.K.]**

Chapman, C. B. and Cooper, Dale F. A Programmed Equity-Redemption Approach to the Finance of Public Projects. *Managerial Dec. Econ.*, June 1985, *6*(2), pp. 112–18.

Charles, Anthony T. and Munro, Gordon R. Irreversible Investment and Optimal Fisheries Management: A Stochastic Analysis. *Marine Resource Econ.*, 1985, *1*(3), pp. 247–64.

Chen, K. C. and Scott, Louis O. Uncertain Inflation and the Input–Output Choices of Competitive Firms. *Quart. Rev. Econ. Bus.*, Autumn 1985, *25*(3), pp. 48–54.

Ciobanu, G., et al. Reduction of the Large Size Graphs with a View to Their Scheduling. *Econ. Computat. Cybern. Stud. Res.*, 1985, *20*(3), pp. 39–42.

Comanor, William S. and Miyao, Takahiro. The Organization and Relative Productivity of Japanese and American Industry. *Managerial Dec. Econ.*, June 1985, *6*(2), pp. 88–92. **[G: Japan; U.S.]**

Coughlan, Anne T. and Schmidt, Ronald M. Executive Compensation, Management Turnover, and Firm Performance: An Empirical Investigation. *J. Acc. Econ.*, April 1985, *7*(1–3), pp. 43–66. **[G: U.S.]**

Cox, Clifford T. Further Evidence on the Representativeness of Management Earnings Forecasts. *Accounting Rev.*, October 1985, *60*(4), pp. 692–701. **[G: U.S.]**

Cromley, Robert G. and Green, Milford B. Joint Venture Activity Patterns of U.S. Firms, 1972–1979. *Growth Change*, July 1985, *16*(3), pp. 40–53. **[G: U.S.]**

Czamanski, Daniel Z. and Fogel, Smadar. Industrial Location and the Divorce of Management and Ownership. *Ann. Reg. Sci.*, March 1985, *19*(1), pp. 77–86.

Dhebar, Anirudh and Oren, Shmuel S. Optimal Dynamic Pricing for Expanding Networks. *Marketing Sci.*, Fall 1985, *4*(4), pp. 336–51.

Diewert, W. E. Transfer Pricing and Economic Efficiency. In *Rugman, A. M. and Eden, L., eds.*, 1985, pp. 47–81.

Dye, Ronald A. Disclosure of Nonproprietary Information. *J. Acc. Res.*, Spring 1985, *23*(1), pp. 123–45.

Dye, Thomas R. Strategic Ownership Positions in U.S. Industry and Banking. *Amer. J. Econ. Soc.*, January 1985, *44*(1), pp. 9–22. **[G: U.S.]**

Eden, Lorraine. The Microeconomics of Transfer Pricing. In *Rugman, A. M. and Eden, L., eds.*, 1985, pp. 13–46.

El-Ansary, Adel I. Managerial Gap Analysis: A Frame of Reference for Improving International Business Relations with the Middle East. In *Kaynak, E., ed. (II)*, 1985, pp. 43–56. **[G: Middle East]**

Endres, Alfred. Tie-in Financing and Pragmatic Price Discrimination. *Metroecon.*, February 1985, *37*(1), pp. 119–33.

Fama, Eugene F. and Jensen, Michael C. Organizational Forms and Investment Decisions. *J. Finan. Econ.*, March 1985, *14*(1), pp. 101–19.

Felder, Joseph. Why Firms Change Hands. *J.*

Econ. Educ., Summer 1985, *16*(3), pp. 203–11.

Fellingham, John C. and Wolfson, Mark A. Taxes and Risk Sharing. *Accounting Rev.*, January 1985, *60*(1), pp. 10–17.

Flath, David and Knoeber, Charles R. Managerial Shareholding. *J. Ind. Econ.*, September 1985, *34*(1), pp. 93–99. [G: U.S.]

Formby, John P. and Millner, Edward L. The Convergence of Utility and Profit Maximization. *Southern Econ. J.*, April 1985, *51*(4), pp. 1174–85.

Fortuin, L. and Lootsma, F. A. Future Directions in Operations Research. In *Rinnooy Kan, A. H. G., ed.*, 1985, pp. 55–80.

Frantz, Roger S. Symposium on Decision Making in the Firm: An Introduction. *J. Behav. Econ.*, Winter 1985, *14*, pp. 1–4.

Frantz, Roger S. X-Efficiency Theory and Its Critics. *Quart. Rev. Econ. Bus.*, Winter 1985, *25*(4), pp. 38–58.

Frantz, Roger S. and Galloway, Fred. A Theory of Multidimensional Effort Decisions. *J. Behav. Econ.*, Winter 1985, *14*, pp. 69–82.

Furubotn, Eirik G. Codetermination, Productivity Gains, and the Economics of the Firm. *Oxford Econ. Pap.*, March 1985, *37*(1), pp. 22–39.

Gálvez, Julio and Tybout, James R. Microeconomic Adjustments in Chile during 1977–81: The Importance of Being a *Grupo*. *World Devel.*, August 1985, *13*(8), pp. 969–94. [G: Chile]

Gandhi, Devinder K.; Hausmann, Robert, Jr. and Saunders, Anthony. On Syndicate Sharing Rules for Unanimous Project Rankings. *J. Banking Finance*, December 1985, *9*(4), pp. 517–34.

Gilley, Otis W.; Karels, Gordon V. and Lyon, Randolph M. Joint Ventures and Offshore Oil Lease Sales. *Econ. Inquiry*, April 1985, *23*(2), pp. 321–39. [G: U.S.]

Goisis, Gianandrea. Domanda variabile, prezzi dei fattori e scelta degli assetti produttivi: alcuni recenti contributi. (Variability of Demand, Prices of Inputs and Choice of Technologies: Some Recent Contributions. With English summary.) *Rivista Int. Sci. Econ. Com.*, May 1985, *32*(5), pp. 467–80.

Goldberg, Victor P. Economic Aspects of Bankruptcy Law: Comment. *Z. ges. Staatswiss. (JITE)*, March 1985, *141*(1), pp. 99–103.

Gort, Michael; Grabowski, Henry and McGuckin, Robert. Organizational Capital and the Choice between Specialization and Diversification. *Managerial Dec. Econ.*, March 1985, *6*(1), pp. 2–10. [G: U.S.]

Gramm, Warren S. Behavioral Elements in the Theory of the Firm: An Historical Perspective. *J. Behav. Econ.*, Winter 1985, *14*, pp. 21–34.

Green, Paul E. and Krieger, Abba M. Models and Heuristics for Product Line Selection. *Marketing Sci.*, Winter 1985, *4*(1), pp. 1–19.

Gregory, S. A. Strategy and Design: A Micro Level View. In *Langdon, R. and Rothwell, R., eds.*, 1985, pp. 1–17.

Groves, Theodore. The Impossibility of Incentive-Compatible and Efficient Full Cost Allocation Schemes. In *Young, H. P., ed.*, 1985, pp. 95–100.

Grubert, Harry. Comments on Unresolved Issues in Transfer Pricing Models. In *Rugman, A. M. and Eden, L., eds.*, 1985, pp. 164–69.

Guerard, John B., Jr. and Buell, Stephen G. Multiple-Criteria Financial Planning Model of Public Utility Firms. In *Haimes, Y. Y. and Chankong, V., eds.*, 1985, pp. 475–81. [G: U.S.]

Hallagan, William S. and Joerding, Wayne. Polymorphism in Competitive Strategies: Trading Stamps. *J. Econ. Bus.*, February 1985, *37*(1), pp. 1–17.

Halperin, Robert and Tzur, Joseph. Monetary Compensation and Nontaxable Employee Benefits: An Analytical Perspective. *Accounting Rev.*, October 1985, *60*(4), pp. 670–80.

Harris, D. John and Williams, D. Glyn. The Use of Risk Analysis within British Rail. *Managerial Dec. Econ.*, December 1985, *6*(4), pp. 202–09. [G: U.K.]

Harris, Frederick H. deB. and Dennis, Richard L. Managerial Utility-maximizing Operating Decisions under Compound Demand Risk. *Managerial Dec. Econ.*, March 1985, *6*(1), pp. 19–26.

Hartmann, Arntraud and Nawab, Syed Ali. Evaluating Public Manufacturing Enterprises in Pakistan. *Finance Develop.*, September 1985, *22*(3), pp. 27–30. [G: Pakistan]

Hassin, Refael. On the Optimality of First Come Last Served Queues. *Econometrica*, January 1985, *53*(1), pp. 201–02.

Hax, Herbert. Economic Aspects of Bankruptcy Law. *Z. ges. Staatswiss. (JITE)*, March 1985, *141*(1), pp. 80–98.

Healy, Paul M. The Effect of Bonus Schemes on Accounting Decisions. *J. Acc. Econ.*, April 1985, *7*(1–3), pp. 85–107. [G: U.S.]

Hill, Charles W. L. Internal Organization and Enterprise Performance: Some UK Evidence. *Managerial Dec. Econ.*, December 1985, *6*(4), pp. 210–16. [G: U.K.]

Hirschey, Mark. Market Structure and Market Value. *J. Bus.*, January 1985, *58*(1), pp. 89–98. [G: U.S.]

Holderness, Clifford G. and Sheehan, Dennis P. Raiders or Saviors? The Evidence on Six Controversial Investors. *J. Finan. Econ.*, December 1985, *14*(4), pp. 555–79. [G: U.S.]

Holmström, Bengt R. and Weiss, Laurence M. Managerial Incentives, Investment, and Aggregate Implications: Scale Effects. *Rev. Econ. Stud.*, July 1985, *52*(3), pp. 403–25.

Honko, Jaakko. Liiketaloustieteen tutkimuksen ja opetuksen keskeisiä Kysymyksiä. (Key Questions in Managerial and Business Economics Research and Teaching. With English summary.) *Liiketaloudellinen Aikak.*, 1985, *34*(1), pp. 20–31. [G: Finland]

Horowitz, Ira. The Risk-averse Price-taking Firm: A Partial Synthesis. *Quart. J. Bus. Econ.*, Summer 1985, *24*(3), pp. 30–40.

Houston, Douglas A. and Howe, John S. An Economic Rationale for Couponing. *Quart. J. Bus. Econ.*, Spring 1985, *24*(2), pp. 37–50.

Jarrell, Gregg A. and Peltzman, Sam. The Impact of Product Recalls on the Wealth of Sellers. *J. Polit. Econ.*, June 1985, *93*(3), pp. 512–36. [G: U.S.]

Jensen, Michael C. and Zimmerman, Jerold L. Management Compensation and the Managerial Labor Market. *J. Acc. Econ.*, April 1985, *7*(1–3), pp. 3–9.

Jeuland, Abel P. and Narasimhan, Chakravarthi. Dealing—Temporary Price Cuts—by Seller as a Buyer Discrimination Mechanism. *J. Bus.*, July 1985, *58*(3), pp. 295–308.

Joskow, Paul L. Vertical Integration and Long-term Contracts: The Case of Coal-burning Electric Generating Plants. *J. Law, Econ., Organ.*, Spring 1985, *1*(1), pp. 33–80. [G: U.S.]

Kanodia, Chandra S. Stochastic Monitoring and Moral Hazard. *J. Acc. Res.*, Spring 1985, *23*(1), pp. 175–93.

Kaplan, Robert S. Evidence on the Effect of Bonus Schemes on Accounting Procedure and Accrual Decisions: Comments. *J. Acc. Econ.*, April 1985, *7*(1–3), pp. 109–13. [G: U.S.]

Koenig, Gérard. La vulnérabilité de l'entreprise. (Vulnerability of the Firm. With English summary.) *Écon. Soc.*, June 1985, *19*(6), pp. 5–42.

Kott, Phillip S. A Note on Model-based Stratification [Model-based Stratification in Inventory Cost Estimation]. *J. Bus. Econ. Statist.*, July 1985, *3*(3), pp. 284–86. [G: U.S.]

Laitinen, Erkki K. A Modular Resource Allocation Model of the Firm. *Liiketaloudellinen Aikak.*, 1985, *34*(4), pp. 366–82.

Laitinen, Erkki K. A Simulation Model of Alternative Pricing Strategies. *Liiketaloudellinen Aikak.*, 1985, *34*(3), pp. 244–71.

Laky, Teréz. Enterprise Business Work Partnership and Enterprise Interest. *Acta Oecon.*, 1985, *34*(1–2), pp. 27–49. [G: Hungary]

Lambert, Richard A. and Larcker, David F. Golden Parachutes, Executive Decision-making and Shareholder Wealth. *J. Acc. Econ.*, April 1985, *7*(1–3), pp. 179–203. [G: U.S.]

Lecraw, Donald J. Some Evidence on Transfer Pricing by Multinational Corporations. In *Rugman, A. M. and Eden, L., eds.*, 1985, pp. 223–40. [G: OECD; LDCs]

Lee, Cheng F. and Primeaux, Walter J., Jr. Relative Importance of Current vs. Permanent Income for Payment Decisions in the Electric Utility Industry. *J. Behav. Econ.*, Winter 1985, *14*, pp. 83–97. [G: U.S.]

Lee, Frederic S. "Full Costx" Prices, Classical Price Theory, and Long Period Method Analysis: A Critical Evaluation. *Metroecon.*, June 1985, *37*(2), pp. 199–219.

Leontief, Wassily. The Theory and Statistical Description of Concentration. In *Leontief, W.*, 1985, pp. 258–71.

Liebermann, Yehoshua and Zilberfarb, Ben-Zion. Price Adjustment Strategy under Conditions of High Inflation: An Empirical Examina-

tion. *J. Econ. Bus.*, August 1985, *37*(3), pp. 253–65. [G: Israel]

Maddigan, Ruth J. and Zaima, Janis K. The Profitability of Vertical Integration. *Managerial Dec. Econ.*, September 1985, *6*(3), pp. 178–79. [G: U.S.]

Maital, Shlomo and Roll, Yaakov. Solving for 'X': Theory & Measurement of Allocative and X-Efficiency at the Plant Level. *J. Behav. Econ.*, Winter 1985, *14*, pp. 99–116.

Marchesnay, Michel and Rudel, Sylvie. La gestion du risque dans la T.P.E. Faits et théories. (Management of Risks with Very Small Firms. Facts and Theory. With English summary.) *Écon. Soc.*, June 1985, *19*(6), pp. 43–74.

de Melo, Jaime; Pascale, Ricardo and Tybout, James R. Microeconomic Adjustments in Uruguay during 1973–81: The Interplay of Real and Financial Shocks. *World Devel.*, August 1985, *13*(8), pp. 995–1015. [G: Uruguay]

Mikkelson, Wayne H. and Ruback, Richard S. Takeovers and Managerial Compensation: A Discussion [Merger Decisions and Executive Stock Ownership in Acquiring Firms] [Agency Theory, Managerial Welfare, and Takeover Bid Resistance]. *J. Acc. Econ.*, April 1985, *7*(1–3), pp. 233–38.

Miller, Edward McCarthy. Decision-making under Uncertainty for Capital Budgeting and Hiring. *Managerial Dec. Econ.*, March 1985, *6*(1), pp. 11–18.

Mirman, Leonard J.; Tauman, Yair and Zang, Israel. On the Use of Game-Theoretic Concepts in Cost Accounting. In *Young, H. P., ed.*, 1985, pp. 55–77.

Murphy, Kevin J. Corporate Performance and Managerial Remuneration: An Empirical Analysis. *J. Acc. Econ.*, April 1985, *7*(1–3), pp. 11–42. [G: U.S.]

Muškardin, Virgilio. Suvremeni pristup financijskoj matematici. (Modern Approach to the Mathematics of Finance. With English summary.) *Econ. Anal. Worker's Manage.*, 1985, *19*(1), pp. 75–99.

Muth, John F. Properties of Some Short-run Business Forecasts. *Eastern Econ. J.*, July-Sept. 1985, *11*(3), pp. 200–210. [G: U.S.]

Nakamura, Alice and Nakamura, Masao. Rational Expectations and the Firm's Dividend Behavior. *Rev. Econ. Statist.*, November 1985, *67*(4), pp. 606–15. [G: U.S.; Japan]

Narayanan, M. P. Managerial Incentives for Short-term Results. *J. Finance*, December 1985, *40*(5), pp. 1469–84.

Narayanan, M. P. Observability and the Payback Criterion. *J. Bus.*, July 1985, *58*(3), pp. 309–23.

de Oliveira Marques, Manuel. The Formulation of a Strategy for Short-term Financial Decision-making: A Goal Programming Model with a Piecewise-linear Objective Function. *Economia (Portugal)*, May 1985, *9*(2), pp. 257–76.

Ozawa, Terutomo. On New Trends in Internationalization: A Synthesis toward a General Model. *Econ. Notes*, 1985, (1), pp. 5–25. [G: OECD]

Pasour, E. C., Jr. Opportunity Cost, Sunk Cost, and Entrepreneurial Choice. *Econ. Scelte Pubbliche/J. Public Finance Public Choice*, 1985, (1), pp. 19–30.

Petrei, A. Humberto and Tybout, James R. Microeconomic Adjustments in Argentina during 1976–81: The Importance of Changing Levels of Financial Subsidies. *World Devel.*, August 1985, *13*(8), pp. 949–67. [G: Argentina]

Plasschaert, Sylvain R. F. Transfer Pricing Problems in Developing Countries. In *Rugman, A. M. and Eden, L., eds.*, 1985, pp. 247–66. [G: Selected LDCs]

Prigozhin, A. Managerial Innovations and Economic Experiments. *Prob. Econ.*, February 1985, *27*(10), pp. 43–64. [G: U.S.S.R.]

Quirin, G. David. Fiscal Transfer Pricing: Accounting for Reality. In *Rugman, A. M. and Eden, L., eds.*, 1985, pp. 132–48.

Raviv, Artur. Management Compensation and the Managerial Labor Market: An Overview. *J. Acc. Econ.*, April 1985, *7*(1–3), pp. 239–45.

Rosen, Sherwin. Golden Parachutes, Executive Decision-making, and Shareholder Wealth: Commentary. *J. Acc. Econ.*, April 1985, *7*(1–3), pp. 205–08. [G: U.S.]

Roy, Bernard and Bouyssou, Denis. Comparison of a Multi-attribute Utility and an Outranking Model Applied to a Nuclear Power Plant Siting Example. In *Haimes, Y. Y. and Chankong, V., eds.*, 1985, pp. 482–94.

Rugman, Alan M. Transfer Pricing in the Canadian Petroleum Industry. In *Rugman, A. M. and Eden, L., eds.*, 1985, pp. 173–92. [G: Selected Countries]

Rugman, Alan M. and Eden, Lorraine. Multinationals and Transfer Pricing: Introduction. In *Rugman, A. M. and Eden, L., eds.*, 1985, pp. 1–10.

Salmi, Timo; Dahlstedt, Roy and Luoma, Martti. Improving Firm-level Growth Estimates by Eliminating Cycles. *Liiketaloudellinen Aikak.*, 1985, *34*(4), pp. 383–410. [G: Finland]

Samuelson, Larry. Transfer Pricing in Exhaustible Resource Markets. In *Rugman, A. M. and Eden, L., eds.*, 1985, pp. 98–116.

Scognamiglio, Angelo. Alcune riflessioni su una "teoria matematica del bilancio contabile." (With English summary.) *Stud. Econ.*, 1985, *40*(25), pp. 151–67.

Seal, W. B. On the Nature of the Firm and Trades Unions: A Critique of the Property Rights Literature. *Brit. Rev. Econ. Issues*, Spring 1985, *7*(16), pp. 47–61.

Shaffer, Sherrill. Counterproductive Risk Pooling. *Atlantic Econ. J.*, March 1985, *13*(1), pp. 99.

Shubik, Martin. The Cooperative Form, the Value, and the Allocation of Joint Costs and Benefits. In *Young, H. P., ed.*, 1985, pp. 79–94.

Spulber, Daniel F. Risk Sharing and Inventories. *J. Econ. Behav. Organ.*, March 1985, *6*(1), pp. 55–68.

Stuart, O. D. J. Are Business and Consumer Surveys Still of Value? *J. Stud. Econ. Economet-*rics, November 1985, (23), pp. 29–50.

Stymne, B. Reorganization of Work: Causes and Effects. In *Rinnooy Kan, A. H. G., ed.*, 1985, pp. 93–113.

Swanson, Edward P.; Shearon, Winston T. and Thomas, Lynn R. Predicting Current Cost Operating Profit Using Component Models Incorporating Analysts' Forecasts. *Accounting Rev.*, October 1985, *60*(4), pp. 681–91. [G: U.S.]

Taşnadi, Al. A Cybernetic Model of the Circulating Means Rotation in an Industrial Enterprise. *Econ. Computat. Cybern. Stud. Res.*, 1985, *20*(4), pp. 13–18. [G: Romania]

Troie, L. et al. Dynamic Model for Determining the Optimal Intervals between Two Successive Repairs. *Econ. Computat. Cybern. Stud. Res.*, 1985, *20*(4), pp. 23–28.

Tybout, James R. Microeconomic Adjustments during the Reforms: Introduction. *World Devel.*, August 1985, *13*(8), pp. 941–47.

von Ungern-Sternberg, Thomas and von Weizsäcker, Carl Christian. The Supply of Quality on a Market for "Experience Goods." In *Geroski, P. A.; Phlips, L. and Ulph, A., eds.*, 1985, pp. 163–72.

Vincke, Philippe. Multiattribute Utility Theory as a Basic Approach. In *Fandel, G. and Spronk, J., eds.*, 1985, pp. 27–40.

Virtanen, Kalervo. Suomalaisten tulosyksikköorganisaatioiden ohjausjärjestelmät. (Management Control Practices in Finnish Divisionalised Firms. With English summary.) *Liiketaloudellinen Aikak.*, 1985, *34*(1), pp. 74–97. [G: Finland]

Waller, William S. and Chow, Chee W. The Self-selection and Effort Effects Standard-based Employment Contracts: A Framework and Some Empirical Evidence. *Accounting Rev.*, July 1985, *60*(3), pp. 458–76.

Warner, Jerold B. Stock Market Reaction to Management Incentive Plan Adoption: An Overview. *J. Acc. Econ.*, April 1985, *7*(1–3), pp. 145–49. [G: U.S.]

Weinrich, John E. The Dynamics of Managing the Change Process: A Persistent Challenge. *Rivista Int. Sci. Econ. Com.*, June 1985, *32*(6), pp. 551–70.

Williams, Joseph T. Trading and Valuing Depreciable Assets. *J. Finan. Econ.*, June 1985, *14*(2), pp. 283–308.

Williamson, Oliver E. Assessing Contract. *J. Law, Econ., Organ.*, Spring 1985, *1*(1), pp. 177–208.

Woodward, Susan E. Limited Liability in the Theory of the Firm. *Z. ges. Staatswiss. (JITE)*, December 1985, *141*(4), pp. 601–11.

Wright, Roger L. Reply [Model-based Stratification in Inventory Cost Estimation]. *J. Bus. Econ. Statist.*, July 1985, *3*(3), pp. 286–88. [G: U.S.]

Young, H. Peyton. Methods and Principles of Cost Allocation. In *Young, H. P., ed.*, 1985, pp. 3–29. [G: U.K.; Sweden]

Young, H. Peyton. Producer Incentives in Cost Allocation. *Econometrica*, July 1985, *53*(4), pp. 757–65.

Ziegler, Charles A. Innovation and the Imitative

Entrepreneur. *J. Econ. Behav. Organ.*, June 1985, *6*(2), pp. 103–21. **[G: U.S.]**

513 Business and Public Administration

5130 General

Abdel-Khalik, A. Rashad. The Effect of LIFO-Switching and Firm Ownership on Executives' Pay. *J. Acc. Res.*, Autumn 1985, *23*(2), pp. 427–47. **[G: U.S.]**

Ajami, Riad A. The Arabian American Oil Company (ARAMCO) and Saudi Society: A Study in Interaction. In *Kaynak, E., ed. (II)*, 1985, pp. 127–36. **[G: Saudi Arabia]**

Ali, Abbas and Swiercz, Paul M. The Relationship between Managerial Decision Styles and Work Satisfaction in Saudi Arabia. In *Kaynak, E., ed. (II)*, 1985, pp. 137–49.
[G: Saudi Arabia]

Armandi, Barry R. and Mills, Edgar W., Jr. Bureaucratic and Personalized Strategies for Efficiency and Organization: An Investigation of Structures and Efficiency in a Set of 104 Profit-seeking Firms. *Amer. J. Econ. Soc.*, July 1985, *44*(3), pp. 261–77. **[G: U.S.]**

Baber, William R. Budget-based Compensation and Discretionary Spending. *Accounting Rev.*, January 1985, *60*(1), pp. 1–9.

Beckmann, Martin J. Stationary State Equations for Personnel Flows in Hierarchical Organizations with Entry at Lowest Rank and Promotion from Within. In *[Menges, G.]*, 1985, pp. 38–45.

Berliner, Joseph S. Managerial Incentives and Decision Making: A Comparison of the United States and the Soviet Union. In *Bornstein, M., ed.*, 1985, pp. 311–35. **[G: U.S.S.R.; U.S.]**

Charreaux, Gérard and Pitol-Belin, J.-P. La théorie contractuelle des organisations: une application au conseil d'administration. (The Contractual Theory of Organizations: Application to the Case of Boards of Directors. With English summary.) *Écon. Soc.*, June 1985, *19*(6), pp. 149–81. **[G: France]**

Cohen, Suleiman I. A Cost–Benefit Analysis of Industrial Training. *Econ. Educ. Rev.*, 1985, *4*(4), pp. 327–39. **[G: Malaysia]**

Damjanovic, Mijat and Voich, Dan, Jr. The Impact of Culture-Based Value Systems on Management Policies and Practices: Yugoslav and United States Issues and Viewpoints: Introduction and Overview. In *Damjanovic, M. and Voich, D., Jr., eds.*, 1985, pp. 1–9.
[G: Yugoslavia; U.S.]

Kaynak, Erdener. International Business in the Middle East. In *Kaynak, E., ed. (II)*, 1985, pp. 3–18.

Kolluri, Bharat R. and Piette, Michael J. The Determinants of the Salaries of Chief Academic Administrators. *Atlantic Econ. J.*, July 1985, *13*(2), pp. 61–68. **[G: U.S.]**

Lord, Robert G. An Information Processing Approach to Social Perceptions, Leadership and Behavioral Measurement in Organizations. In *Cummings, L. L. and Staw, B. M., eds.*, 1985, pp. 87–128.

Mallia, Linda Baylis. Human Resource Planning in a Decentralized Market Driven Environment. In *Niehaus, R. J., ed.*, 1985, pp. 67–76. **[G: U.S.]**

Matic, Milan. Leadership Motivation and Communication: The Yugoslav Experience. In *Damjanovic, M. and Voich, D., Jr., eds.*, 1985, pp. 246–78. **[G: Yugoslavia]**

Razzouk, Nabil Y. and Masters, Lance A. Cultural Marginality in the Arab World: Implications for Western Marketers. In *Kaynak, E., ed. (II)*, 1985, pp. 151–59.
[G: Arab Countries]

Sadowski, Dieter and Schittenhelm, Rainer. Tax Subsidies and the Intra-organizational Trading of Fringe Benefits: An Economic Model Building Approach. In *Niehaus, R. J., ed.*, 1985, pp. 121–44. **[G: W. Germany]**

Shrode, William A. and Voich, Dan, Jr. Impact of Socio-economic–Political Tenets on Organizations and Management. In *Damjanovic, M. and Voich, D., Jr., eds.*, 1985, pp. 21–38.

Young, S. Mark. Participative Budgeting: The Effects of Risk Aversion and Asymmetric Information on Budgetary Slack. *J. Acc. Res.*, Autumn 1985, *23*(2), pp. 829–42.

5131 Business Administration

Antle, Rick and Smith, Abbie. Measuring Executive Compensation: Methods and an Application. *J. Acc. Res.*, Spring 1985, *23*(1), pp. 296–325. **[G: U.S.]**

Arnould, Richard J. Agency Costs in Banking Firms: An Analysis of Expense Preference Behavior. *J. Econ. Bus.*, May 1985, *37*(2), pp. 103–12. **[G: U.S.]**

Asher, Shigeko M. and Inoue, Ken. Industrial Manpower Development in Japan. *Finance Develop.*, September 1985, *22*(3), pp. 23–26.
[G: Japan]

Bartlett, Robin L. and Miller, Timothy I. Executive Compensation: Female Executives and Networking. *Amer. Econ. Rev.*, May 1985, *75*(2), pp. 266–70. **[G: U.S.]**

Basu, Amiya K., et al. Salesforce Compensation Plans: An Agency Theoretic Perspective. *Marketing Sci.*, Fall 1985, *4*(4), pp. 267–91.

Baysinger, Barry D. and Butler, Henry N. Corporate Governance and the Board of Directors: Performance Effects of Changes in Board Composition. *J. Law, Econ., Organ.*, Spring 1985, *1*(1), pp. 101–24. **[G: U.S.]**

Benston, George J. The Self-serving Management Hypothesis: Some Evidence. *J. Acc. Econ.*, April 1985, *7*(1–3), pp. 67–84. **[G: U.S.]**

Bhagat, Sanjai; Brickley, James A. and Lease, Ronald C. Incentive Effects of Stock Purchase Plans. *J. Finan. Econ.*, June 1985, *14*(2), pp. 195–215. **[G: U.S.]**

Booth, Douglas E. The Problems of Corporate Bureaucracy and the Producer Cooperative as an Alternative. *Rev. Soc. Econ.*, December 1985, *43*(3), pp. 298–315. **[G: U.S.]**

Brickley, James A.; Bhagat, Sanjai and Lease, Ronald C. The Impact of Long-range Managerial Compensation Plans on Shareholder Wealth. *J. Acc. Econ.*, April 1985, 7(1–3), pp. 115–29. [G: U.S.]

Brockway, George P. Executive Salaries and Their Justification. *J. Post Keynesian Econ.*, Winter 1984–85, 7(2), pp. 168–76.

Coughlan, Anne T. and Schmidt, Ronald M. Executive Compensation, Management Turnover, and Firm Performance: An Empirical Investigation. *J. Acc. Econ.*, April 1985, 7(1–3), pp. 43–66. [G: U.S.]

DeAngelo, Harry and DeAngelo, Linda. Managerial Ownership of Voting Rights: A Study of Public Corporations with Dual Classes of Common Stock. *J. Finan. Econ.*, March 1985, 14(1), pp. 33–69.

Degot, Vincent. Gestion symbolique et manipulation. Le cas de la gestion de carrière des cadres. (Symbolic Management and Manipulation: A Case Study about the Management of Executives' Careers. With English summary.) *Écon. Soc.*, December 1985, 19(12), pp. 175–201.

Dunlevy, James A. Econometric Issues in the Analysis of Executive Compensation: A Comment [The Effects of Regulation on Executive Compensation]. *Rev. Econ. Statist.*, February 1985, 67(1), pp. 171–74. [G: U.S.]

Eickhoff, Gerald E. Leveraging a Consulting Operation. In *Federal Reserve Bank of Atlanta (I)*, 1985, pp. 35–40. [G: U.S.]

Flath, David and Knoeber, Charles R. Managerial Shareholding. *J. Ind. Econ.*, September 1985, 34(1), pp. 93–99. [G: U.S.]

Gomez-Mejia, Luis R.; McCann, Joseph E. and Page, Ronald C. The Structure of Managerial Behaviors and Rewards. *Ind. Relat.*, Winter 1985, 24(1), pp. 147–54. [G: U.S.]

Healy, Paul M. The Effect of Bonus Schemes on Accounting Decisions. *J. Acc. Econ.*, April 1985, 7(1–3), pp. 85–107. [G: U.S.]

Hoch, Róbert. The Maxi and Mini (Reflections on the Hungarian Debate on Large Firms). *Acta Oecon.*, 1985, 35(3–4), pp. 251–67. [G: Hungary]

Jacobsen, Thomas H. Innovation through Experimentation. In *Federal Reserve Bank of Atlanta (I)*, 1985, pp. 81–87. [G: U.S.]

Jenner, Faith S. and Trevor, Malcolm H. Personnel Management in Four U.K. Electronics Plants. In *Takamiya, S. and Thurley, K., eds.*, 1985, pp. 113–48. [G: U.K.; U.S.; Japan]

Jensen, Michael C. and Zimmerman, Jerold L. Management Compensation and the Managerial Labor Market. *J. Acc. Econ.*, April 1985, 7(1–3), pp. 3–9.

Johnsen, Kenneth C. Golden Parachutes and the Business Judgment Rule: Toward a Proper Standard of Review. *Yale Law J.*, March 1985, 94(4), pp. 909–28. [G: U.S.]

Johnson, W. Bruce, et al. An Analysis of the Stock Price Reaction to Sudden Executive Deaths: Implications for the Managerial Labor Market. *J. Acc. Econ.*, April 1985, 7(1–3), pp. 151–74. [G: U.S.]

Judd, L. Lynn; Taylor, Raymond E. and Powell, Garth A. The Personal Characteristics of the Small Business Retailer: Do They Affect Store Profits and Retail Strategies? *J. Behav. Econ.*, Summer 1985, 14(2), pp. 59–75. [G: U.S.]

Kaplan, Robert S. Evidence on the Effect of Bonus Schemes on Accounting Procedure and Accrual Decisions: Comments. *J. Acc. Econ.*, April 1985, 7(1–3), pp. 109–13. [G: U.S.]

Kesner, Idalene F. and Dalton, Dan R. The Effect of Board Composition on CEO Succession and Organizational Performance. *Quart. J. Bus. Econ.*, Spring 1985, 24(2), pp. 3–20. [G: U.S.]

Kobayashi, Noritake. The Patterns of Management Style Developing in Japanese Multinationals in the 1980s. In *Takamiya, S. and Thurley, K., eds.*, 1985, pp. 229–64. [G: Japan; U.S.; U.K.; W. Germany; France]

Lambert, Richard A. and Larcker, David F. Golden Parachutes, Executive Decision-making and Shareholder Wealth. *J. Acc. Econ.*, April 1985, 7(1–3), pp. 179–203. [G: U.S.]

McKinney, Fred. JTPA, Black Employment, and Occupational Change: Separating Out Cyclical Changes from Program Changes. *Rev. Black Polit. Econ.*, Summer 1985, 14(1), pp. 75–87. Swiercz [G: U.S.]

Mikkelson, Wayne H. and Ruback, Richard S. Takeovers and Managerial Compensation: A Discussion [Merger Decisions and Executive Stock Ownership in Acquiring Firms] [Agency Theory, Managerial Welfare, and Takeover Bid Resistance]. *J. Acc. Econ.*, April 1985, 7(1–3), pp. 233–38.

Miret, Pierre. Interactive Decision-Support System: New Aids for Human Resource Policy Analysis and Formulation. In *Niehaus, R. J., ed.*, 1985, pp. 77–91. [G: France]

Murphy, Kevin J. Corporate Performance and Managerial Remuneration: An Empirical Analysis. *J. Acc. Econ.*, April 1985, 7(1–3), pp. 11–42. [G: U.S.]

Myers, Forest E. and Van Walleghem, Joe. Management Transferability in Rural Banks. *J. Bank Res.*, Winter 1985, 15(4), pp. 229–33. [G: U.S.]

Narayanan, M. P. Managerial Incentives for Short-term Results. *J. Finance*, December 1985, 40(5), pp. 1469–84.

Raviv, Artur. Management Compensation and the Managerial Labor Market: An Overview. *J. Acc. Econ.*, April 1985, 7(1–3), pp. 239–45.

Reitsperger, Wolf. Personnel Policy and Employee Satisfaction. In *Takamiya, S. and Thurley, K., eds.*, 1985, pp. 149–81. [G: U.S.; U.K.; Japan]

Rosen, Sherwin. Golden Parachutes, Executive Decision-making, and Shareholder Wealth: Commentary. *J. Acc. Econ.*, April 1985, 7(1–3), pp. 205–08. [G: U.S.]

Schwert, G. William. A Discussion of CEO Deaths and the Reaction of Stock Prices. *J. Acc. Econ.*, April 1985, 7(1–3), pp. 175–78. [G: U.S.]

Sharma, R. A. Industrial Entrepreneurship in India, 1961–1963. *Indian Econ. J.*, Oct.-Nov. 1985, 33(2), pp. 79–92. [G: India]

Smiley, Robert. Management Compensation in Regulated Industries. In *Crew, M. A., ed.,* 1985, pp. 111–25. [G: U.S.]

Solt, Michael E. and Miller, Norman G. Managerial Incentives: Implications for the Financial Performance of Real Estate Investment Trusts. *Amer. Real Estate Urban Econ. Assoc. J.,* Winter 1985, *13*(4), pp. 404–23. [G: U.S.]

Takamiya, Makoto. Conclusions and Policy Implications. In *Takamiya, S. and Thurley, K., eds.,* 1985, pp. 183–201. [G: U.K.; U.S.; Japan]

Tehranian, Hassan and Waegelein, James F. Market Reaction to Short-term Executive Compensation Plan Adoption. *J. Acc. Econ.,* April 1985, 7(1–3), pp. 131–44. [G: U.S.]

Tinbergen, Jan. Determinants of Manager Incomes. In *Tinbergen, J.,* 1985, pp. 85–100. [G: OECD]

Tomita, Teruhiko. Japanese Management as Applied in the Philippines. *Philippine Rev. Econ. Bus.,* Mar./June 1985, 22(1/2), pp. 23–57. [G: Philippines]

Virtanen, Kalervo. Suomalaisten tulosyksikköorganisaatioiden ohjausjärjestelmät. (Management Control Practices in Finnish Divisionalised Firms. With English summary.) *Liiketaloudellinen Aikak.,* 1985, *34*(1), pp. 74–97. [G: Finland]

Warner, Jerold B. Stock Market Reaction to Management Incentive Plan Adoption: An Overview. *J. Acc. Econ.,* April 1985, 7(1–3), pp. 145–49. [G: U.S.]

Yücelt, Ugur. Managerial Practices in the Middle East. In *Kaynak, E., ed. (II),* 1985, pp. 113–26. [G: Turkey]

5132 Public Administration

Atwater, D. M.; Bres, E. S., III and Niehaus, Richard J. Human Resources Supply–Demand Policy Analysis Models. In *Niehaus, R. J., ed.,* 1985, pp. 92–120. [G: U.S.]

Dubhashi, P. R. Public Administration and Plan Implementation. In *Mongia, J. N., ed.,* 1985, pp. 617–40. [G: India]

Dunson, Bruce H. Pay, Experience, and Productivity: The Government-Sector Case. *J. Human Res.,* Winter 1985, 20(1), pp. 153–60. [G: U.S.]

Goldenberg, Edie N. The Grace Commission and Civil Service Reform: Seeking a Common Understanding. In *Levine, C. H., ed.,* 1985, pp. 69–94. [G: U.S.]

Hentschke, Guilbert C. Emerging Roles of School District Administrators: Implications for Planning, Budgeting, and Management. In *Augenblick, J., ed.,* 1985, pp. 59–70. [G: U.S.]

Hentschke, Guilbert C. Emerging Roles of School District Administrators: Implications for Planning, Budgeting, and Management. *Public Budg. Finance,* Spring 1985, 5(1), pp. 15–26. [G: U.S.]

Hussenot, P. Management in the Public Sector. In *Rinnooy Kan, A. H. G., ed.,* 1985, pp. 179–88.

Jonsson, Ernst. A Model of a Non–budget-maximizing Bureau. In *Lane, J.-E., ed.,* 1985, pp. 70–82. [G: Sweden]

Levine, Charles H. The Unfinished Agenda for Civil Service Reform *Implications of the Grace Commission Report:* Introduction. In *Levine, C. H., ed.,* 1985, pp. 1–14. [G: U.S.]

Lundquist, Lennart. From Order to Chaos: Recent Trends in the Study of Public Administration. In *Lane, J.-E., ed.,* 1985, pp. 201–30.

McGregor, Eugene B., Jr. The Grace Commission's Challenge to Public Personnel Administration. In *Levine, C. H., ed.,* 1985, pp. 43–59. [G: U.S.]

Murray, David J. Public Administration in the Microstates of the Pacific. In *Dommen, E. and Hein, P., eds.,* 1985, pp. 185–203.

Mushkat, Miron. Planning under Uncertainty in the Public Domain: A Critique of Conventional Approaches. *Rivista Int. Sci. Econ. Com.,* July-Aug. 1985, *32*(7–8), pp. 661–77.

Peters, B. Guy. Administrative Change and the Grace Commission. In *Levine, C. H., ed.,* 1985, pp. 19–39. [G: U.S.]

Pitkänen, Eero. Julkisyhteisöjen talous liiketaloustieteen, erityisesti laskentatoimen tutkimuskohteena. (Research on the Economics of Public Organizations in Business Economics, Especially in Accounting and Finance. With English summary.) *Liiketaloudellinen Aikak.,* 1985, *34*(1), pp. 98–107. [G: Finland]

Polivka, Larry and Osterholt, B. Jack. The Governor as Manager: Agency Autonomy and Accountability. *Public Budg. Finance,* Winter 1985, 5(4), pp. 91–104. [G: U.S.]

Reich, Robert B. Public Administration and Public Deliberation: An Interpretive Essay. *Yale Law J.,* June 1985, *94*(7), pp. 1617–41. [G: U.S.]

Rosen, Bernard. Civil Service Reform: Are the Constraints Impenetrable? In *Levine, C. H., ed.,* 1985, pp. 102–114. [G: U.S.]

Sicat, Gerardo P. National Economic Management and Technocracy in Developing Countries. In *Shishido, T. and Sato, R., eds.,* 1985, pp. 81–94. [G: LDCs]

Swire, Peter P. Incorporation of Independent Agencies into the Executive Branch. *Yale Law J.,* June 1985, *94*(7), pp. 1766–86. [G: U.S.]

Vernon, Raymond. Linking Managers with Ministers: Dilemmas of the State-Owned Enterprise. In *Vernon, R.,* 1985, pp. 149–64.

Wade, Robert. The Market for Public Office: Why the Indian State Is Not Better at Development. *World Devel.,* April 1985, *13*(4), pp. 467–97.

514 Goals and Objectives of Firms

5140 Goals and Objectives of Firms

Albert, Stuart and Whetten, David A. Organizational Identity. In *Cummings, L. L. and Staw, B. M., eds.,* 1985, pp. 263–95.

Argyris, Chris. Dealing with Threat and Defensiveness. In *Pennings, J. M., et al.,* 1985, pp. 412–430.

Arrow, Kenneth J. Social Responsibility and Economic Efficiency. In *Arrow, K. J. (II)*, 1985, pp. 130–42.

Ashley, William C. Strategic Issues Forecasting and Monitoring at Sears. In *Mendell, J. S., ed.*, 1985, pp. 125–32. [G: U.S.]

Awh, Robert Y. and Primeaux, Walter J., Jr. Managerial Discretion and Expense Preference Behavior. *Rev. Econ. Statist.*, May 1985, 67(2), pp. 224–31. [G: U.S.]

Backhaus, Juergen. Public Policy toward Corporate Structures: Two Chicago Approaches. *J. Econ. Issues*, June 1985, 19(2), pp. 365–73.

Bloch, Howard R. and Lareau, Thomas J. Should We Invest in "Socially Irresponsible" Firms? *J. Portfol. Manage.*, Summer 1985, 11(4), pp. 27–31. [G: U.S.]

Cain, James E. and Cain, A. Sue. An Economic Analysis of Accounting Decision Variables Used to Determine the Nature of Corporate Giving. *Quart. J. Bus. Econ.*, Autumn 1985, 24(4), pp. 15–28. [G: U.S.]

Cloninger, Dale O. An Analysis of the Effect of Illegal Corporate Activity on Share Value. *J. Behav. Econ.*, Summer 1985, 14(2), pp. 1–13.

Dugger, William M. The Continued Evolution of Corporate Power. *Rev. Soc. Econ.*, April 1985, 43(1), pp. 1–13. [G: U.S.]

Elliott, John A. Market Association Tests and FASB Statement No. 33 Disclosures: A Reexamination: Discussion. *J. Acc. Res.*, Supp. 1985, 23, pp. 24–27. [G: U.S.]

He, Jianzhang. Expansion of the Enterprise's Decision-making Power and Change in the Ownership Relation. *Chinese Econ. Stud.*, Fall 1985, 19(1), pp. 10–16. [G: China]

Hermon-Taylor, Richard J. Finding New Ways of Overcoming Resistance to Change. In *Pennings, J. M., et al.*, 1985, pp. 383–411.

Kanter, Rosabeth Moss. Providing the Corporate Environment to Foster Innovation. In *Federal Reserve Bank of Atlanta (I)*, 1985, pp. 111–22.

Laki, M. Central Economic Management and the Enterprise Crisis in Hungary. *Acta Oecon.*, 1985, 35(1–2), pp. 195–211. [G: Hungary]

Lorange, Peter. Strengthening Organizational Capacity to Execute Strategic Change. In *Pennings, J. M., et al.*, 1985, pp. 449–67.

Lupica, Lena. Environmental Scanning at AT&T. In *Mendell, J. S., ed.*, 1985, pp. 115–23. [G: U.S.]

MacCrimmon, Kenneth R. Understanding Strategic Decisions: Three Systematic Approaches. In *Pennings, J. M., et al.*, 1985, pp. 76–98.

McElroy, Katherine Maddox and Siegfried, John J. The Effect of Firm Size on Corporate Philanthropy. *Quart. Rev. Econ. Bus.*, Summer 1985, 25(2), pp. 18–26. [G: U.S.]

Newgren, Kenneth E. and Brechtel, Donald L. Environmental Scanning. In *Damjanovic, M. and Voich, D., Jr., eds.*, 1985, pp. 142–58.

Pennings, Johannes M. Introduction: On the Nature and Theory of Strategic Decisions. In *Pennings, J. M., et al.*, 1985, pp. 1–34.

Petschnig, Mária. Causes of Difficulties in Changing the Normal State of the Hungarian Econ-omy. *Acta Oecon.*, 1985, 35(3–4), pp. 235–50. [G: Hungary]

Renfro, William. Issues Management: The Changing Corporate Role. In *Mendell, J. S., ed.*, 1985, pp. 147–51.

Sarkis, Henry D., Jr. Let's Put the Futurist Back in the Executive Suite. In *Mendell, J. S., ed.*, 1985, pp. 99–107.

Shrode, William A. and Voich, Dan, Jr. Impact of Socio-economic–Political Tenets on Organizations and Management. In *Damjanovic, M. and Voich, D., Jr., eds.*, 1985, pp. 21–38.

Stevenson, Rodney. Corporate Power and the Scope of Economic Analysis. *J. Econ. Issues*, June 1985, 19(2), pp. 333–41.

Tetlock, Philip E. Accountability: The Neglected Social Context of Judgment and Choice. In *Cummings, L. L. and Staw, B. M., eds.*, 1985, pp. 297–332.

Valli, George and Dauman, Jan. Designing and Installing a System for Environmental Assessment and Forecasting. In *Mendell, J. S., ed.*, 1985, pp. 133–45.

Winter, Sidney G. The Case for "Mechanistic" Decision Making. In *Pennings, J. M., et al.*, 1985, pp. 99–113.

520 BUSINESS FINANCE AND INVESTMENT

5200 Business Finance and Investment

Boadway, Robin W.; Bruce, Neil and Mintz, Jack. The Role and Design of the Corporate Income Tax. In *Førsund, F. R. and Honkapohja, S., eds.*, 1985, pp. 188–201.

Brennan, Michael J. and Schwartz, Eduardo S. Evaluating Natural Resource Investments. *J. Bus.*, April 1985, 58(2), pp. 135–57. [G: U.S.]

Chen, K. C. and Scott, Louis O. Uncertain Inflation and the Input–Output Choices of Competitive Firms. *Quart. Rev. Econ. Bus.*, Autumn 1985, 25(3), pp. 48–54.

Fullerton, Don and Henderson, Yolanda Kodrzycki. Long-run Effects of the Accelerated Cost Recovery System. *Rev. Econ. Statist.*, August 1985, 67(3), pp. 363–72. [G: U.S.]

Haka, Susan F.; Gordon, Lawrence A. and Pinches, George E. Sophisticated Capital Budgeting Selection Techniques and Firm Performance. *Accounting Rev.*, October 1985, 60(4), pp. 651–69. [G: U.S.]

Miller, Edward McCarthy. Decision-making under Uncertainty for Capital Budgeting and Hiring. *Managerial Dec. Econ.*, March 1985, 6(1), pp. 11–18.

Morris, Derek J. The Behaviour of Firms. In *Morris, D., ed.*, 1985, pp. 53–85. [G: U.K.]

Spronk, Jaap. Financial Planning with Conflicting Objectives. In *Fandel, G. and Spronk, J., eds.*, 1985, pp. 269–88.

Thompson, Howard E. Estimating Return Deficiencies of Electric Utilities 1963–1981. In *Crew, M. A., ed.*, 1985, pp. 17–37. [G: U.S.]

Woodward, Susan E. Limited Liability in the

Theory of the Firm. *Z. ges. Staatswiss. (JITE)*, December 1985, *141*(4), pp. 601–11.

521 Business Finance

5210 Business Finance

Abel, Andrew B. A Stochastic Model of Investment, Marginal *q* and the Market Value of the Firm. *Int. Econ. Rev.*, June 1985, *26*(2), pp. 305–22.

Adelman, Morris A. and Stangle, Bruce E. Profitability and Market Share. In *[McGowan, J. J.]*, 1985, pp. 101–13. [G: U.S.]

Ang, James S. and Peterson, David R. Return, Risk, and Yield: Evidence from Ex Ante Data. *J. Finance*, June 1985, *40*(2), pp. 537–48. [G: U.S.]

Ang, James S.; Peterson, Pamela P. and Peterson, David R. Investigations into the Determinants of Risk: A New Look. *Quart. J. Bus. Econ.*, Winter 1985, *24*(1), pp. 3–20. [G: U.S.]

Appleyard, A. R. and Strong, N. C. Textbook Inconsistencies in Graphing Valuation Equations: A Note. *Financial Rev.*, November 1985, *20*(4), pp. 361–67.

Artus, Patrick. Rationnement de crédit et réactions des entreprises. (Credit Rationing and Firms' Reactions. With English summary.) *Revue Écon.*, November 1985, *36*(6), pp. 1207–46. [G: France]

Auerbach, Alan J. Real Determinants of Corporate Leverage. In *Friedman, B. M., ed.*, 1985, pp. 301–22. [G: U.S.]

Babcock, Guilford C. The Integration of Insurance and Taxes in Corporate Pension Strategy: Discussion. *J. Finance*, July 1985, *40*(3), pp. 955–57. [G: U.S.]

Ballantine, John W.; Cleveland, Frederick W. and Koeller, C. Timothy. Profit Differences and Corporate Power: Some Empirical Surprises. *J. Econ. Issues*, June 1985, *19*(2), pp. 355–64. [G: U.S.]

Bates, Timothy. Impact of Preferential Procurement Policies on Minority-owned Businesses. *Rev. Black Polit. Econ.*, Summer 1985, *14*(1), pp. 51–65. [G: U.S.]

Benninga, Simon Z.; Eldor, Rafael and Zilcha, Itzhak. Optimal International Hedging in Commodity and Currency Forward Markets. *J. Int. Money Finance*, December 1985, *4*(4), pp. 537–52.

Beranek, William and Clayton, Ronnie J. Risk Differences and Financial Reporting. *J. Finan. Res.*, Winter 1985, *8*(4), pp. 327–34. [G: U.S.]

Besley, Scott and Osteryoung, Jerome S. Survey of Current Practices in Establishing Trade-Credit Limits. *Financial Rev.*, February 1985, *20*(1), pp. 70–82.

Bicksler, James L. The Integration of Insurance and Taxes in Corporate Pension Strategy. *J. Finance*, July 1985, *40*(3), pp. 943–55. [G: U.S.]

Billingsley, Randall S., et al. Explaining Yield Savings on New Convertible Bond Issues. *Quart. J. Bus. Econ.*, Summer 1985, *24*(3), pp. 92–104. [G: U.S.]

Billingsley, Randall S. and Thompson, G. Rodney. Determinants of Stock Repurchases by Bank Holding Companies. *J. Bank Res.*, Autumn 1985, *16*(3), pp. 128–35. [G: U.S.]

Black, Fischer. Contingent Claims Valuation of Corporate Liabilities: Theory and Empirical Tests: Comment. In *Friedman, B. M., ed.*, 1985, pp. 262–63. [G: U.S.]

Booth, James R.; Officer, Dennis T. and Henderson, Glenn V., Jr. Commercial Bank Stocks, Interest Rates, and Systematic Risk. *J. Econ. Bus.*, December 1985, *37*(4), pp. 303–10. [G: U.S.]

Bosworth, Barry P. Taxes and the Investment Recovery. *Brookings Pap. Econ. Act.*, 1985, (1), pp. 1–38. [G: U.S.]

Brean, Donald J. S. Financial Dimensions of Transfer Pricing. In *Rugman, A. M. and Eden, L., eds.*, 1985, pp. 149–64.

Brick, Ivan E. and Ravid, S. Abraham. On the Relevance of Debt Maturity Structure. *J. Finance*, December 1985, *40*(5), pp. 1423–37. [G: U.S.]

Brick, Ivan E. and Wallingford, Buckner A. The Relative Tax Benefits of Alternative Call Features in Corporate Debt. *J. Finan. Quant. Anal.*, March 1985, *20*(1), pp. 95–105.

Brown, Robert M. On Carrying Costs and the EOQ Model: A Pedagogical Note. *Financial Rev.*, November 1985, *20*(4), pp. 357–60.

Buehler, John E. The Specific Role of Interest in Financial and Economic Analysis under Inflation: Discussion. *Amer. J. Agr. Econ.*, May 1985, *67*(2), pp. 396–97.

Cable, John R. and Yasuki, Hirohiko. Internal Organisation, Business Groups and Corporate Performance: An Empirical Test of the Multidivisional Hypothesis in Japan. *Int. J. Ind. Organ.*, December 1985, *3*(4), pp. 401–20.
[G: Japan; U.K.; U.S.; W. Germany]

Caprara, Ugo. Gli indicatori per la valutazione dell'affidabilità creditizia. (The Indicators for Assessing Credit Reliability. With English summary.) *Bancaria*, October 1985, *41*(10), pp. 1070–76. [G: Italy]

Casey, Cornelius and Bartczak, Norman. Using Operating Cash Flow Data to Predict Financial Distress: Some Extensions. *J. Acc. Res.*, Spring 1985, *23*(1), pp. 384–401. [G: U.S.]

Casler, Darwin J. and Hall, Thomas W. Firm-specific Asset Valuation Accuracy Using a Composite Price Index. *J. Acc. Res.*, Spring 1985, *23*(1), pp. 110–22.

Casson, Mark. The Theory of Foreign Direct Investment. In *Buckley, P. J. and Casson, M.*, 1985, pp. 113–43.

Chalos, Peter. Financial Distress: A Comparative Study of Individual, Model, and Committee Assessments. *J. Acc. Res.*, Autumn 1985, *23*(2), pp. 527–43. [G: U.S.]

Chan-Lee, James H. and Sutch, Helen. Profits and Rates of Return. *OECD Econ. Stud.*, Autumn 1985, (5), pp. 127–67. [G: OECD]

Chaney, Paul K. and Thakor, Anjan V. Incentive Effects of Benevolent Intervention: The Case of Government Loan Guarantees. *J. Public Econ.*, March 1985, *26*(2), pp. 169–89.
[G: U.S.]

Chapman, C. B. and Cooper, Dale F. A Programmed Equity-Redemption Approach to the Finance of Public Projects. *Managerial Dec. Econ.*, June 1985, *6*(2), pp. 112–18.

Ciccolo, John H., Jr. and Baum, Christopher F. Changes in the Balance Sheet of the U.S. Manufacturing Sector, 1926–1977. In *Friedman, B. M., ed.*, 1985, pp. 81–109.   [G: U.S.]

Connolly, Robert A. and Schwartz, Steven. The Intertemporal Behavior of Economic Profits. *Int. J. Ind. Organ.*, December 1985, *3*(4), pp. 379–400.   [G: U.S.]

Constantinides, George M. Debt and Taxes and Uncertainty: Discussion. *J. Finance*, July 1985, *40*(3), pp. 657–58.

Cornell, Bradford. Taxes and the Pricing of Stock Index Futures: Empirical Results. *J. Futures Markets*, Spring 1985, *5*(1), pp. 89–101.
[G: U.S.]

Cuthbertson, Keith. Sterling Bank Lending to UK Industrial and Commercial Companies. *Oxford Bull. Econ. Statist.*, May 1985, *47*(2), pp. 91–118.   [G: U.K.]

Daly, Donald J. Inflation, Inflation Accounting and Its Effect, Canadian Manufacturing, 1966–82. *Rev. Income Wealth*, December 1985, *31*(4), pp. 355–74.   [G: Canada]

DeAngelo, Harry and DeAngelo, Linda. Managerial Ownership of Voting Rights: A Study of Public Corporations with Dual Classes of Common Stock. *J. Finan. Econ.*, March 1985, *14*(1), pp. 33–69.

Dhaliwal, Dan S. The Agency Cost Rationale for Refunding Discounted Bonds. *J. Finan. Res.*, Spring 1985, *8*(1), pp. 43–50.   [G: U.S.]

Dotan, Amihud and Ravid, S. Abraham. On the Interaction of Real and Financial Decisions of the Firm under Uncertainty. *J. Finance*, June 1985, *40*(2), pp. 501–17.

Dubofsky, David A. The Effects of Maturing Debt on Equity Risk. *Quart. Rev. Econ. Bus.*, Autumn 1985, *25*(3), pp. 36–47.   [G: U.S.]

Dubois, Michel. Les déterminants de la structure financière: le cas des grandes entreprises françaises. (The Determinants of Financial Structure: The Case of Large French Firms. With English summary.) *Finance*, June 1985, *6*(1), pp. 41–70.   [G: France]

Durinck, E. and Fabry, J. Een evaluatietechniek voor financiële leasing in België. (With English summary.) *Cah. Écon. Bruxelles*, 1st Trimester 1985, (105), pp. 41–57.   [G: Belgium]

Eades, Kenneth M.; Hess, Patrick J. and Kim, E. Han. Market Rationality and Dividend Announcements. *J. Finan. Econ.*, December 1985, *14*(4), pp. 581–604.   [G: U.S.]

Easton, Peter D. Accounting Earnings and Security Valuation: Empirical Evidence of the Fundamental Links. *J. Acc. Res.*, Supp. 1985, *23*, pp. 54–77.   [G: U.S.]

Edwards, J. S. S. and Keen, M. J. Inflation and Non-neutralities in the Taxation of Corporate Source Income. *Oxford Econ. Pap.*, December 1985, *37*(4), pp. 552–75.

Eilbott, Peter. The Revenue Effects of a Lower Capital Gains Tax. *Nat. Tax J.*, December 1985, *38*(4), pp. 553–59.   [G: U.S.]

Felder, Joseph. Why Firms Change Hands. *J. Econ. Educ.*, Summer 1985, *16*(3), pp. 203–11.

Ferrão, João. Regional Variations in the Rate of Profit in Portuguese Industry. In *Hudson, R. and Lewis, J., eds.*, 1985, pp. 211–45.
[G: Portugal]

French, George. Interest Rate, Demand and Input Price Uncertainty and the Value of Firms. *J. Econ. Dynam. Control*, December 1985, *9*(4), pp. 457–76.

Friedman, Benjamin M. Corporate Capital Structures in the United States: An Introduction and Overview. In *Friedman, B. M., ed.*, 1985, pp. 1–11.   [G: U.S.]

Frydman, Halina; Altman, Edward I. and Kao, Duen-Li. Introducing Recursive Partitioning for Financial Classification: The Case of Financial Distress. *J. Finance*, March 1985, *40*(1), pp. 269–91.   [G: U.S.]

Gale, Douglas and Hellwig, Martin F. Incentive-Compatible Debt Contracts: The One-Period Problem. *Rev. Econ. Stud.*, October 1985, *52*(4), pp. 647–63.

Gálvez, Julio and Tybout, James R. Microeconomic Adjustments in Chile during 1977–81: The Importance of Being a *Grupo. World Devel.*, August 1985, *13*(8), pp. 969–94.
[G: Chile]

Gandhi, Devinder K.; Hausmann, Robert, Jr. and Saunders, Anthony. On Syndicate Sharing Rules for Unanimous Project Rankings. *J. Banking Finance*, December 1985, *9*(4), pp. 517–34.

Gentry, James A.; Newbold, Paul and Whitford, David T. Classifying Bankrupt Firms with Funds Flow Components. *J. Acc. Res.*, Spring 1985, *23*(1), pp. 146–60.

Geske, Robert and Shastri, Kuldeep. The Early Exercise of American Puts. *J. Banking Finance*, June 1985, *9*(2), pp. 207–19.   [G: U.S.]

Ginglinger, Édith. L'évaluation de la commission de garantie lors d'une émission d'actions nouvelles. (Assessment of the Stock Exchange Guarantee Commitee When Issuing New Shares. With English summary.) *Écon. Soc.*, June 1985, *19*(6), pp. 103–17.   [G: France]

Ginglinger, Édith. Le prix d'émission des actions nouvelles: une application de la théorie des options aux augmentations de capital. (The Pricing of Equity Issues: An Application of Option Theory. With English summary.) *Finance*, June 1985, *6*(1), pp. 23–40.   [G: France]

Gnes, Paolo. La Centrale dei Bilanci moltiplica le possibilità dell'analisi finanziaria. (The "Accounts Clearing House" Widens the Sphere of Financial Analysis. With English summary.) *Bancaria*, October 1985, *41*(10), pp. 1041–46.
[G: Italy]

Gordon, Roger H. Real Determinants of Corporate Leverage: Comment. In *Friedman, B. M.*, *ed.*, 1985, pp. 322–24. **[G: U.S.]**

Goria, Giovanni. Situazione economica e problemi del credito: banche d'affari, sportelli e tassi. (Merchant Banks, Bank Branches and Interest Rates in the Framework of Economic Policy. With English summary.) *Bancaria*, April 1985, *41*(4), pp. 406–10. **[G: Italy]**

Grubert, Harry. Comments on Unresolved Issues in Transfer Pricing Models. In *Rugman, A. M. and Eden, L., eds.*, 1985, pp. 164–69.

Guerard, John B., Jr. and Buell, Stephen G. Multiple-Criteria Financial Planning Model of Public Utility Firms. In *Haimes, Y. Y. and Chankong, V., eds.*, 1985, pp. 475–81.
[G: U.S.]

Gui, Benedetto. Limits to External Financing: A Model and an Application to Labor-Managed Firms. In *Jones, D. C. and Svejnar, J., eds.*, 1985, pp. 107–20.

Haavisto, Esko. Bankruptcy Risk and Capital Structure: Empirical Evidence on Firms in the U.S. *Liiketaloudellinen Aikak.*, 1985, *34*(4), pp. 329–37. **[G: U.S.]**

Harris, Milton and Raviv, Artur. A Sequential Signalling Model of Convertible Debt Call Policy. *J. Finance*, December 1985, *40*(5), pp. 1263–81.

Harris, Robert S. and Pringle, John J. Risk-adjusted Discount Rates—Extensions from the Average-Risk Case. *J. Finan. Res.*, Fall 1985, *8*(3), pp. 237–44.

Hasan, Zubair. Determination of Profit and Loss Sharing Ratios in Interest-Free Business Finance. *J. Res. Islamic Econ.*, Summer 1985, *3*(1), pp. 13–29.

Hasbrouck, Joel. The Characteristics of Takeover Targets: *q* and Other Measures. *J. Banking Finance*, September 1985, *9*(3), pp. 351–62.
[G: U.S.]

Hawkins, Gregory D. Determinants of Corporate Leasing Policy: Discussion. *J. Finance*, July 1985, *40*(3), pp. 909–10.

Hayashi, Fumio. Corporate Finance Side of the *Q* Theory of Investment. *J. Public Econ.*, August 1985, *27*(3), pp. 261–80.

Hess, James. The Use of Collateral to Enforce Debt: Profit Maximization. *Econ. Inquiry*, April 1985, *23*(2), pp. 349–56.

Hill, Charles W. L. Internal Organization and Enterprise Performance: Some UK Evidence. *Managerial Dec. Econ.*, December 1985, *6*(4), pp. 210–16. **[G: U.K.]**

Hirschey, Mark and Weygandt, Jerry J. Amortization Policy for Advertising and Research and Development Expenditures. *J. Acc. Res.*, Spring 1985, *23*(1), pp. 326–35. **[G: U.S.]**

Hochman, Shalom and Palmon, Oded. The Impact of Inflation on the Aggregate Debt-Asset Ratio. *J. Finance*, September 1985, *40*(4), pp. 1115–25.

Hodder, James E. and Tschoegal, Adrian E. Some Aspects of Japanese Corporate Finance. *J. Finan. Quant. Anal.*, June 1985, *20*(2), pp. 173–91. **[G: Japan]**

Hopwood, William S. and McKeown, James C. The Incremental Information Content of Interim Expenses over Interim Sales. *J. Acc. Res.*, Spring 1985, *23*(1), pp. 161–74.
[G: U.S.]

Huffman, Gregory W. Adjustment Costs and Capital Asset Pricing. *J. Finance*, July 1985, *40*(3), pp. 691–705.

Irsch, Norbert. Erträge, Eigenkapitalausstattung und Investitionsneigung. Thesen und empirische Belege. (Yields, Equity Capital Ratio, and Investment Propensity. With English summary.) *Konjunkturpolitik*, 1985, *31*(6), pp. 319–35. **[G: W. Germany]**

Jaffe, Jeffrey F. Inflation, the Interest Rate, and the Required Return on Equity. *J. Finan. Quant. Anal.*, March 1985, *20*(1), pp. 29–44.

Jahera, John S., Jr.; Hand, John and Lloyd, William P. An Empirical Inquiry into the Premiums for Controlling Interests. *Quart. J. Bus. Econ.*, Summer 1985, *24*(3), pp. 67–77.
[G: U.S.]

John, Kose and Nachman, David C. Risky Debt, Investment Incentives, and Reputation in a Sequential Equilibrium. *J. Finance*, July 1985, *40*(3), pp. 863–78.

John, Kose and Williams, Joseph T. Dividends, Dilution, and Taxes: A Signalling Equilibrium. *J. Finance*, September 1985, *40*(4), pp. 1053–70.

Jones, E. Philip; Mason, Scott P. and Rosenfeld, Eric. Contingent Claims Valuation of Corporate Liabilities: Theory and Empirical Tests. In *Friedman, B. M., ed.*, 1985, pp. 239–61.
[G: U.S.]

Jordan, Bradford D. and Pettway, Richard H. The Pricing of Short-term Debt and the Miller Hypothesis: A Note [Debt and Taxes]. *J. Finance*, June 1985, *40*(2), pp. 589–94.

Kalay, Avner and Loewenstein, Uri. Predictable Events and Excess Returns: The Case of Dividend Announcements. *J. Finan. Econ.*, September 1985, *14*(3), pp. 423–49. **[G: U.S.]**

Kane, Alex; Marcus, Alan J. and McDonald, Robert L. Debt Policy and the Rate of Return Premium to Leverage. *J. Finan. Quant. Anal.*, December 1985, *20*(4), pp. 479–99.

Katz, Eliakim; Rosenberg, J. and Zilberfarb, Ben-Zion. The Demand for Liquid Assets and Involvement in Exports; Some Empirical Results. *Empirical Econ.*, 1985, *10*(2), pp. 125–29. **[G: Israel]**

Keim, Donald B. Dividend Yields and Stock Returns: Implications of Abnormal January Returns. *J. Finan. Econ.*, September 1985, *14*(3), pp. 473–89. **[G: U.S.]**

Khoury, Nabil T. and Medina, Ephraïm. La structure du capital: une synthe des orientations théoriques et empiriques de la derniére décennie. (The Firm's Capital Structure in the Last Decade: A Synthesis. With English summary.) *L'Actual. Econ.*, September 1985, *61*(3), pp. 362–87.

Kilpatrick, Bob; Putnam, Karl and Schneider, Harold. Convertible Securities and Earnings per Share: A Competitive Ranking Algorithm.

Accounting Rev., July 1985, *60*(3), pp. 526–30.

Kim, Moon K. and Booth, G. Geoffrey. Yield Structure of Taxable vs. Nontaxable Bonds. *J. Finan. Res.*, Summer 1985, *8*(2), pp. 95–105.

Kim, Moon K. and Young, Allan E. Inflation, the Value of the Firm, and Firm Size. *Quart. Rev. Econ. Bus.*, Summer 1985, *25*(2), pp. 81–90. [G: U.S.]

Knight, Peter T. Financial Discipline and Structural Adjustment in Yugoslavia: Rehabilitation and Bankruptcy of Loss-making Enterprises. *Econ. Anal. Worker's Manage.*, 1985, *19*(1), pp. 101–26. [G: Yugoslavia]

Koenig, Gérard. La vulnérabilité de l'entreprise. (Vulnerability of the Firm. With English summary.) *Écon. Soc.*, June 1985, *19*(6), pp. 5–42.

Kolari, James W. and Apilado, Vincent P. The Cyclical Effect of Default Risk on Industrial Bond Yields. *J. Econ. Bus.*, December 1985, *37*(4), pp. 311–25. [G: U.S.]

Kollintzas, Tryphon and Thorn, Richard S. The Generalized User Cost of Capital. *Public Finance Quart.*, October 1985, *13*(4), pp. 355–74.

Kolodny, Richard and Suhler, Diane Rizzuto. Changes in Capital Structure, New Equity Issues, and Scale Effects. *J. Finan. Res.*, Summer 1985, *8*(2), pp. 127–36. [G: U.S.]

Kraus, Alan. New Tests of the APT and Their Implications: Discussion. *J. Finance*, July 1985, *40*(3), pp. 674–75.

Krouse, Clement G. Competition and Unanimity Revisited, Again. *Amer. Econ. Rev.*, December 1985, *75*(5), pp. 1109–14.

Kumar, P. Corporate Growth and Profitability in the Large Indian Companies. *Margin*, July 1985, *17*(4), pp. 32–36. [G: India]

Kunimura, Michio and Iihara, Yoshio. Valuation of Underwriting Agreements for Raising Capital in the Japanese Capital Market. *J. Finan. Quant. Anal.*, June 1985, *20*(2), pp. 231–41. [G: Japan]

Laitinen, Erkki K. The Effect of Asset Valuation and Inflation on Profitability Ratios. *Liiketaloudellinen Aikak.*, 1985, *34*(2), pp. 131–46.

Lee, Cheng F. and Lynge, Morgan J., Jr. Return, Risk and Cost of Equity for Stock S&L Firms: Theory and Empirical Results. *Amer. Real Estate Urban Econ. Assoc. J.*, Summer 1985, *13*(2), pp. 167–80. [G: U.S.]

Lee, Cheng F. and Primeaux, Walter J., Jr. Relative Importance of Current vs. Permanent Income for Payment Decisions in the Electric Utility Industry. *J. Behav. Econ.*, Winter 1985, *14*, pp. 83–97. [G: U.S.]

Lee, Chi-Wen Jevons. Stochastic Properties of Cross-sectional Financial Data. *J. Acc. Res.*, Spring 1985, *23*(1), pp. 213–27. [G: U.S.]

van Leeuwen, Peter H. The Prediction of Business Failure at Rabobank. *J. Bank Res.*, Summer 1985, *16*(2), pp. 91–98.

Lewellen, Wilbur G.; Loderer, Claudio and Rosenfeld, Ahron. Merger Decisions and Executive Stock Ownership in Acquiring Firms. *J.*

Acc. Econ., April 1985, *7*(1–3), pp. 209–31. [G: U.S.]

Lintner, John. Secular Patterns in the Financing of Corporations: Comment. In *Friedman, B. M., ed.*, 1985, pp. 75–80. [G: U.S.]

Lloyd, William P.; Jahera, John S., Jr. and Page, Daniel E. Agency Costs and Dividend Payout Ratios. *Quart. J. Bus. Econ.*, Summer 1985, *24*(3), pp. 19–29. [G: U.S.]

Long, Michael S. and Malitz, Ileen B. Investment Patterns and Financial Leverage. In *Friedman, B. M., ed.*, 1985, pp. 325–48. [G: U.S.]

Macey, Jonathan R. and McChesney, Fred S. A Theoretical Analysis of Corporate Greenmail. *Yale Law J.*, November 1985, *95*(1), pp. 13–61. [G: U.S.]

Maddigan, Ruth J. and Zaima, Janis K. The Profitability of Vertical Integration. *Managerial Dec. Econ.*, September 1985, *6*(3), pp. 178–79. [G: U.S.]

Magliolo, Joseph, III. Accounting Earnings and Security Valuation: Empirical Evidence of the Fundamental Links: Discussion. *J. Acc. Res.*, Supp. 1985, *23*, pp. 78–80.

Malatesta, Paul H. and Thompson, Rex. Partially Anticipated Events: A Model of Stock Price Reactions with an Application to Corporate Acquisitions. *J. Finan. Econ.*, June 1985, *14*(2), pp. 237–50. [G: U.S.]

Malécot, J.-F. Structure du capital et hypothèse de compensation: une point de vue critique. (Capital Structure and the Balancing of Fiscal Benefits and Costs of Default: A Critical Evaluation. With English summary.) *Finance*, June 1985, *6*(1), pp. 7–21. [G: France]

Malissen, Walthère and Khelifa, Aïssa. Préférence pour le financement interne et contrainte d'endettement. (Preference for Internal Financing and the Indebtedness Constraint. With English summary.) *Écon. Appl.*, 1985, *38*(1), pp. 177–90. [G: France; W. Germany]

Marr, M. Wayne and Thompson, G. Rodney. Primary Market Pricing of Convertible Preferred Stock. *Quart. Rev. Econ. Bus.*, Summer 1985, *25*(2), pp. 73–80. [G: U.S.]

Matteuzzi, Massimo. Vecchi e nuovi problemi nella tassazione delle società di capitali con redditi esenti. (Old and New Problems in Taxation of Joint-Stock Companies with Exempt Income. With English summary.) *Bancaria*, March 1985, *41*(3), pp. 305–19. [G: Italy]

McConnell, John J. and Muscarella, Chris J. Corporate Capital Expenditure Decisions and the Market Value of the Firm. *J. Finan. Econ.*, September 1985, *14*(3), pp. 399–422. [G: U.S.]

McMullen, B. Starr. Trunk Airline Financial Requirements and Economic Performance. In *Keeler, T. E., ed.*, 1985, pp. 121–47. [G: U.S.]

de Melo, Jaime; Pascale, Ricardo and Tybout, James R. Microeconomic Adjustments in Uruguay during 1973–81: The Interplay of Real and Financial Shocks. *World Devel.*, August 1985, *13*(8), pp. 995–1015. [G: Uruguay] de Melo, Jaime; Pascale, Ricardo and Tybout, James R. Uruguay 1973–1981: interrelación entre shocks financieros y reales. (With English summary.) *Cuadernos Econ.*, April 1985, 22(65), pp. 73–98. [G: Uruguay]

Mikkelson, Wayne H. and Ruback, Richard S. An Empirical Analysis of the Interfirm Equity Investment Process. *J. Finan. Econ.*, December 1985, 14(4), pp. 523–53. [G: U.S.]

Miles, James A. and Ezzell, John R. Reformulating Tax Shield Valuation: A Note. *J. Finance*, December 1985, 40(5), pp. 1485–92.

Miller, Merton H. and Rock, Kevin. Dividend Policy under Asymmetric Information. *J. Finance*, September 1985, 40(4), pp. 1031–51.

Miller, Tom W. and Stone, Bernell K. Daily Cash Forecasting and Seasonal Resolution: Alternative Models and Techniques for Using the Distribution Approach. *J. Finan. Quant. Anal.*, September 1985, 20(3), pp. 335–51.

Millsaps, Steven W. and Ott, Mack. Risk Aversion, Risk Sharing, and Joint Bidding: A Study of Outer Continental Shelf Petroleum Auctions. *Land Econ.*, November 1985, 61(4), pp. 372–86. [G: U.S.]

Modigliani, Franco. Changes in the Balance Sheet, 1926–1977: Comment. In *Friedman, B. M., ed.*, 1985, pp. 109–15. [G: U.S.]

Mueller, Dennis C. Mergers and the Long Run Profitability of Large Corporations. In *Schwalbach, J., ed.*, 1985, pp. 113–38. [G: U.S.]

Mulford, Charles W. The Importance of a Market Value Measurement of Debt in Leverage Ratios: Replication and Extensions. *J. Acc. Res.*, Autumn 1985, 23(2), pp. 897–906. [G: U.S.]

Murray, Dennis. Further Evidence on the Liquidity Effects of Stock Splits and Stock Dividends. *J. Finan. Res.*, Spring 1985, 8(1), pp. 59–67. [G: U.S.]

Muškardin, Virgilio. Suvremeni pristup financijskoj matematici. (Modern Approach to the Mathematics of Finance. With English summary.) *Econ. Anal. Worker's Manage.*, 1985, 19(1), pp. 75–99.

Myers, Stewart C. Investment Patterns and Financial Leverage: Comment. In *Friedman, B. M., ed.*, 1985, pp. 348–51. [G: U.S.]

Nakamura, Alice and Nakamura, Masao. Rational Expectations and the Firm's Dividend Behavior. *Rev. Econ. Statist.*, November 1985, 67(4), pp. 606–15. [G: U.S.; Japan]

Narayanan, M. P. Managerial Incentives for Short-term Results. *J. Finance*, December 1985, 40(5), pp. 1469–84.

Narayanan, M. P. Observability and the Payback Criterion. *J. Bus.*, July 1985, 58(3), pp. 309–23.

Nguyen, The-Hiep. Firm Size, Profitability, and Savings in Canada. *J. Econ. Bus.*, May 1985, 37(2), pp. 113–21. [G: Canada]

Nicodano, Giovanna. Decisioni d'investimento e di finanziamento dell'impresa: un'integrazione formale. (Investment and Financing Decisions of the Firm: A Formal Integration. With English summary.) *Ricerche Econ.*, July-Sept. 1985, 39(3), pp. 378–97.

Nicodano, Giovanna. Struttura finanziaria e deci-

sioni d'investimento: una verifica econometrica. (Financial Structure and Investment Decisions: An Econometric Model. With English summary.) *Giorn. Econ.*, Mar.-Apr. 1985, 44(3–4), pp. 179–207. [G: Italy]

Ohlson, James A. Ex Post Stockholder Unanimity: A Complete and Simplified Treatment. *J. Banking Finance*, September 1985, 9(3), pp. 387–99.

Oksanen, Heikki. Inflaation vaikutus yritysten kirjanpitoon, yritysverotukseen ja yritystutkimuksen tunnuslukuihin. (The Effect on Inflation of Accounting, Corporate Taxation, and Financial Ratios. With English summary.) *Liiketaloudellinen Aikak.*, 1985, 34(4), pp. 422–38.

de Oliveira Marques, Manuel. The Formulation of a Strategy for Short-term Financial Decisionmaking: A Goal Programming Model with a Piecewise-linear Objective Function. *Economia (Portugal)*, May 1985, 9(2), pp. 257–76.

Ott, Mack and Santoni, G. J. Mergers and Takeovers—The Value of Pradators' Information. *Fed. Res. Bank St. Louis Rev.*, December 1985, 67(10), pp. 16–28. [G: U.S.]

Otterbeck, Lars. Joint International Business Ventures: Their Motives and Their Management. In *Takamiya, S. and Thurley, K., eds.*, 1985, pp. 49–57.

Owers, James E. and Rogers, Ronald C. The Windfall of Safe Harbor Leasing: Evidence from Capital Markets. *Nat. Tax J.*, December 1985, 38(4), pp. 561–65. [G: U.S.]

Park, Sang Yong and Williams, Joseph T. Taxes, Capital Structure, and Bondholder Clienteles. *J. Bus.*, April 1985, 58(2), pp. 203–24.

Parsons, John E. and Raviv, Artur. Underpricing of Seasoned Issues. *J. Finan. Econ.*, September 1985, 14(3), pp. 377–97.

Peavy, John W., III and Scott, Jonathan A. The Effect of Stock for Debt Swaps on Security Returns. *Financial Rev.*, November 1985, 20(4), pp. 303–27. [G: U.S.]

Peterson, Pamela P.; Peterson, David R. and Ang, James S. Direct Evidence on the Marginal Rate of Taxation on Dividend Income. *J. Finan. Econ.*, June 1985, 14(2), pp. 267–82. [G: U.S.]

Petrei, A. Humberto and Tybout, James R. Microeconomic Adjustments in Argentina during 1976–81: The Importance of Changing Levels of Financial Subsidies. *World Devel.*, August 1985, 13(8), pp. 949–67. [G: Argentina]

Pettigrew, Andrew M. Examining Change in the Long-term Context of Culture and Politics. In *Pennings, J. M., et al.*, 1985, pp. 269–318. [G: U.K.]

Pfleiderer, Paul. Finance Anthropology. *J. Portfol. Manage.*, Fall 1985, 12(1), pp. 52–53.

Pohl, Hans. Forms and Phases of Industry Finance up to the Second World War. In *Engels, W. and Pohl, H., eds.*, 1985, pp. 75–94. [G: Germany]

Redhead, Keith. Hedging with Financial Futures. *Nat. Westminster Bank Quart. Rev.*, February 1985, pp. 42–56. [G: U.K.]

Rice, Emmett J. Statement to the U.S. House

Subcommittee on General Oversight and the Economy of the Committee on Small Business, June 25, 1985. *Fed. Res. Bull.*, August 1985, 71(8), pp. 618–20. [G: U.S.]

Ricks, William E. and Hughes, John S. Market Reactions to a Non-discretionary Accounting Change: The Case of Long-term Investments. *Accounting Rev.*, January 1985, 60(1), pp. 33–52. [G: U.S.]

Riener, Kenneth D. A Pedagogic Note on the Cost of Capital with Personal Taxes and Risky Debt. *Financial Rev.*, May 1985, 20(2), pp. 229–35.

Rogers, Ronald C.; Murphy, Neil B. and Owers, James E. Financial Innovation, Balance Sheets Cosmetics and Market Response: The Case of Equity-for-Debt Exchanges in Banking. *J. Bank Res.*, Autumn 1985, 16(3), pp. 145–49. [G: U.S.]

Rolfes, Bernd. Ansätze zur Steuerung von Zinsänderungsrisiken. (Approaches to Control of the Risk of Interest Rate Changes. With English summary.) *Kredit Kapital*, 1985, 18(4), pp. 529–52.

Ross, Stephen A. Debt and Taxes and Uncertainty. *J. Finance*, July 1985, 40(3), pp. 637–57.

Salamon, Gerald L. Accounting Rates of Return. *Amer. Econ. Rev.*, June 1985, 75(3), pp. 495–504. [G: U.S.]

Sarig, Oded H. and Scott, James. The Puzzle of Financial Leverage Clienteles. *J. Finance*, December 1985, 40(5), pp. 1459–67. [G: U.S.]

Sarmiento, Eduardo. The Imperfections of the Capital Market. *Cepal Rev.*, December 1985, (27), pp. 97–116. [G: Colombia]

Schachter, Barry. Open Interest and Consensus among Investors. *J. Acc. Res.*, Autumn 1985, 23(2), pp. 907–10.

Schallheim, James S. and McConnell, John J. A Model for the Determination of "Fair" Premiums on Lease Cancellation Insurance Policies. *J. Finance*, December 1985, 40(5), pp. 1439–57.

Scott, John T. Capital Structure and the Product Market Environment: Comment. In *Friedman, B. M., ed.*, 1985, pp. 378–82. [G: U.S.]

Scott, Louis O. The Present Value Model of Stock Prices: Regression Tests and Monte Carlo Results. *Rev. Econ. Statist.*, November 1985, 67(4), pp. 599–605. [G: U.S.]

Shaffer, Ron E. and Pulver, Glen C. Regional Variations in Capital Structure of New Small Businesses: The Wisconsin Case. In *Storey, D. J., ed.*, 1985, pp. 166–92. [G: U.S.]

Shaffer, Sherrill. Counterproductive Risk Pooling. *Atlantic Econ. J.*, March 1985, 13(1), pp. 99.

Shashua, Leon and Goldschmidt, Yaaqov. The Specific Role of Interest in Financial and Economic Analysis under Inflation: Real, Nominal, or a Combination of Both. *Amer. J. Agr. Econ.*, May 1985, 67(2), pp. 377–83.

Shoven, John B. Taxes and the Investment Recovery: Comment. *Brookings Pap. Econ. Act.*, 1985, (1), pp. 39–41. [G: U.S.]

Singleton, Kenneth J. Adjustment Costs and Capital Asset Pricing: Discussion. *J. Finance*, July 1985, 40(3), pp. 705–09.

Smith, Clifford W., Jr. and Stulz, René M. The Determinants of Firms' Hedging Policies. *J. Finan. Quant. Anal.*, December 1985, 20(4), pp. 391–405.

Smith, Clifford W., Jr. and Wakeman, L. Mac-Donald. Determinants of Corporate Leasing Policy. *J. Finance*, July 1985, 40(3), pp. 895–908.

Spatt, Chester S. Risky Debt, Investment Incentives, and Reputation in a Sequential Equilibrium: Discussion. *J. Finance*, July 1985, 40(3), pp. 878–80.

Spence, A. Michael. Capital Structure and the Corporation's Product Market Environment. In *Friedman, B. M., ed.*, 1985, pp. 353–77. [G: U.S.]

Stapleton, R. C. and Subrahmanyam, Marti G. Finance Research—The Next 10 Years. In *Rinnooy Kan, A. H. G., ed.*, 1985, pp. 45–54.

Stulz, René M. and Johnson, Herb. An Analysis of Secured Debt. *J. Finan. Econ.*, December 1985, 14(4), pp. 501–21.

Summers, Lawrence H. On Economics and Finance. *J. Finance*, July 1985, 40(3), pp. 633–35.

Summers, Lawrence H. Taxes and the Investment Recovery: Comment. *Brookings Pap. Econ. Act.*, 1985, (1), pp. 42–44. [G: U.S.]

Swieringa, Robert J. and Morse, Dale. Accounting for Hybrid Convertible Debentures. *Accounting Rev.*, January 1985, 60(1), pp. 127–33. [G: U.S.]

Taggart, Robert A., Jr. Effects of Regulation on Utility Financing: Theory and Evidence. *J. Ind. Econ.*, March 1985, 33(3), pp. 257–76. [G: U.S.]

Taggart, Robert A., Jr. Secular Patterns in the Financing of U.S. Corporations. In *Friedman, B. M., ed.*, 1985, pp. 13–75. [G: U.S.]

Talmor, Eli; Haugen, Robert A. and Barnea, Amir. The Value of the Tax Subsidy on Risky Debt. *J. Bus.*, April 1985, 58(2), pp. 191–202.

Thatcher, Janet Solverson. The Choice of Call Provision Terms: Evidence of the Existence of Agency Costs of Debt. *J. Finance*, June 1985, 40(2), pp. 549–61.

Thompson, Howard E. The Magnitude and Reliability of Equity Capital Cost Estimates: A Statistical Approach. *Managerial Dec. Econ.*, September 1985, 6(3), pp. 132–40. [G: U.S.]

Titman, Sheridan. The Effect of Forward Markets on the Debt-Equity Mix of Investor Portfolios and the Optimal Capital Structure of Firms. *J. Finan. Quant. Anal.*, March 1985, 20(1), pp. 19–27.

Tutino, Franco. Oneri e vincoli imposti dalla forte crescita dell'indebitamento sull'estero. (Burdens and Restraints Imposed by the Strong Growth of Foreign Debt. With English summary.) *Bancaria*, September 1985, 41(9), pp. 962–68. [G: Italy]

Tybout, James R. Microeconomic Adjustments during the Reforms: Introduction. *World*

Devel., August 1985, *13*(8), pp. 941–47.

Vickson, R. G. Simple Optimal Policy for Cash Management: The Average Balance Requirement Case. *J. Finan. Quant. Anal.*, September 1985, *20*(3), pp. 353–69.

Waagstein, Thorbjørn. Er industriens afkastningsgrad fejlvurderet? (Are Reported Profit Rates for the Danish Industry Misleading? With English summary.) *Nationaløkon. Tidsskr.*, 1985, *123*(1), pp. 94–103.
[G: Denmark]

Waymire, Gregory. Earnings Volatility and Voluntary Management Forecast Disclosure. *J. Acc. Res.*, Spring 1985, *23*(1), pp. 268–95.
[G: U.S.]

Weinstein, Mark I. The Equity Component of Corporate Bonds. *J. Portfol. Manage.*, Spring 1985, *11*(3), pp. 37–41. [G: U.S.]

Wolfson, Mark A. Tax, Incentive, and Risk-sharing Issues in the Allocation of Property Rights: The Generalized Lease-or-Buy Problem. *J. Bus.*, April 1985, *58*(2), pp. 159–71.

Yarrow, George K. Shareholder Protection, Compulsory Acquisition and the Efficiency of the Takeover Process. *J. Ind. Econ.*, September 1985, *34*(1), pp. 3–16. [G: U.K.]

Yawitz, Jess Barry. Debt and Equity Yields, 1926–1980: Comment. In *Friedman, B. M., ed.*, 1985, pp. 163–65. [G: U.S.]

522 Business Investment

5220 Business Investment

Abel, Andrew B. A Stochastic Model of Investment, Marginal *q* and the Market Value of the Firm. *Int. Econ. Rev.*, June 1985, *26*(2), pp. 305–22.

Alam, Kazi F. The Influence of Tax Incentives on the Investment Decisions in U.K. Manufacturing. *METU*, 1985, *12*(3/4), pp. 301–16.
[G: U.K.]

Alam, Kazi F. and Stafford, L. W. T. Tax Incentives and Investment Policy: A Survey Report on the United Kingdom Manufacturing Industry. *Managerial Dec. Econ.*, March 1985, *6*(1), pp. 27–32. [G: U.K.]

Amerkhail, Valerie; Lucke, Robert and Marcuss, Rosemary D. Revenue Estimation and Comprehensive Tax Reform. *Nat. Tax J.*, September 1985, *38*(3), pp. 373–94. [G: U.S.]

Andersson, Roland and Taylor, Lewis. The Investment Criteria of the Swedish Electricity Industry. *Energy Econ.*, January 1985, *7*(1), pp. 13–19. [G: Sweden]

Arrow, Kenneth J. Optimal Capital Policy, the Cost of Capital, and Myopic Decision Rules. In *Arrow, K. J. (I)*, 1985, pp. 181–90.

Arrow, Kenneth J. and Levhari, David. Uniqueness of the Internal Rate of Return with Variable Life of Investment. In *Arrow, K. J. (I)*, 1985, pp. 373–81.

Auerbach, Alan J. Real Determinants of Corporate Leverage. In *Friedman, B. M., ed.*, 1985, pp. 301–22. [G: U.S.]

Bergström, Villy and Södersten, Jan. Do Tax Al-

lowances Stimulate Investment? In *Førsund, F. R. and Honkapohja, S., eds.*, 1985, pp. 146–70. [G: Sweden]

Bester, Helmut. The Level of Investment in Credit Markets with Imperfect Information. *Z. ges. Staatswiss. (JITE)*, December 1985, *141*(4), pp. 503–15.

Biddle, Gary C. and Martin, R. Kipp. Inflation, Taxes, and Optimal Inventory Policies. *J. Acc. Res.*, Spring 1985, *23*(1), pp. 57–83.

Biørn, Erik. Inflation, Depreciation and the Neutrality of the Corporate Income Tax. In *Førsund, F. R. and Honkapohja, S., eds.*, 1985, pp. 116–30. [G: Norway]

Blejer, Mario I. and Khan, Mohsin S. Public Investment and Crowding Out in the Caribbean Basin Countries. In *Connolly, M. B. and McDermott, J., eds.*, 1985, pp. 219–36.
[G: Caribbean]

Bonin, John P. Labor Management and Capital Maintenance: Investment Decisions in the Socialist Labor-Managed Firm. In *Jones, D. C. and Svejnar, J., eds.*, 1985, pp. 55–69.

Bosworth, Barry P. Taxes and the Investment Recovery. *Brookings Pap. Econ. Act.*, 1985, (1), pp. 1–38. [G: U.S.]

Braga de Macedo, Jorge. Labor and Investment Demand at the Firm Level: A Comparison of French, German and U.S. Manufacturing, 1970-79: Comment. *Europ. Econ. Rev.*, June-July 1985, *28*(1–2), pp. 237–41. [G: France; U.S.; W. Germany]

Buehler, John E. The Specific Role of Interest in Financial and Economic Analysis under Inflation: Discussion. *Amer. J. Agr. Econ.*, May 1985, *67*(2), pp. 396–97.

Cardani, Angelo M. Labor and Investment Demand at the Firm Level: A Comparison of French, German and U.S. Manufacturing, 1970-79: Comment. *Europ. Econ. Rev.*, June-July 1985, *28*(1–2), pp. 233–36. [G: France; U.S.; W. Germany]

Chishti, Salim U. Relative Stability of Interest-Free Economy. *J. Res. Islamic Econ.*, Summer 1985, *3*(1), pp. 3–12.

Ciccolo, John H., Jr. and Baum, Christopher F. Changes in the Balance Sheet of the U.S. Manufacturing Sector, 1926–1977. In *Friedman, B. M., ed.*, 1985, pp. 81–109. [G: U.S.]

Dixon, Huw. Strategic Investment in an Industry with a Competitive Product Market. In *Geroski, P. A.; Phlips, L. and Ulph, A., eds.*, 1985, pp. 115–31.

Dotan, Amihud and Ravid, S. Abraham. On the Interaction of Real and Financial Decisions of the Firm under Uncertainty. *J. Finance*, June 1985, *40*(2), pp. 501–17.

Edwards, J. S. S. and Keen, M. J. Taxes, Investment and Q. *Rev. Econ. Stud.*, October 1985, *52*(4), pp. 665–79.

Epstein, Eugene. Innovation and Economic Growth. In *Federal Reserve Bank of Atlanta (I)*, 1985, pp. 89–95. [G: U.S.]

Faini, Riccardo and Schiantarelli, Fabio. Oligopolistic Models of Investment and Employment Decisions in a Regional Context: Theory and Empirical Evidence from a Putty–Clay Model. *Europ. Econ. Rev.*, March 1985, 27(2), pp. 221–42. **[G: Italy]**

Fama, Eugene F. and Jensen, Michael C. Organizational Forms and Investment Decisions. *J. Finan. Econ.*, March 1985, 14(1), pp. 101–19.

Fisher, Peter S. Corporate Tax Incentives: The American Version of Industrial Policy. *J. Econ. Issues*, March 1985, 19(1), pp. 1–19. **[G: U.S.]**

Fortune, J. Neill. Manufacturers' Aggregate Inventory Accumulation and Unfilled Orders. *J. Post Keynesian Econ.*, Spring 1985, 7(3), pp. 324–31. **[G: U.S.]**

Friedman, Benjamin M. Corporate Capital Structures in the United States: An Introduction and Overview. In *Friedman, B. M., ed.*, 1985, pp. 1–11. **[G: U.S.]**

Fritsch, Michael and Maas, Christof. Das Investitionsverhalten von Industriebetrieben. Ergebnisse aus einer Interviewstudie. (The Investment Behaviour of West German Industry—Results of an Interview Study. With English summary.) *Konjunkturpolitik*, 1985, 31(1/2), pp. 52–78. **[G: W. Germany]**

Fullerton, Don; Lyon, Andrew B. and Rosen, Richard J. Uncertainty, Welfare Cost and the "Adaptability" of U.S. Corporate Taxes. In *Førsund, F. R. and Honkapohja, S., eds.*, 1985, pp. 131–45. **[G: U.S.]**

Gandhi, Devinder K.; Hausmann, Robert, Jr. and Saunders, Anthony. On Syndicate Sharing Rules for Unanimous Project Rankings. *J. Banking Finance*, December 1985, 9(4), pp. 517–34.

Gann, Pamela B. Neutral Taxation of Capital Income: An Achievable Goal? *Law Contemp. Probl.*, Autumn 1985, 48(4), pp. 77–149. **[G: U.S.]**

Garofalo, Gasper A. and Malhotra, Devinder M. The Impact of Changes in Input Prices on Net Investment in U.S. Manufacturing. *Atlantic Econ. J.*, December 1985, 13(4), pp. 52–62. **[G: U.S.]**

Gordon, Roger H. Real Determinants of Corporate Leverage: Comment. In *Friedman, B. M., ed.*, 1985, pp. 322–24. **[G: U.S.]**

Gordon, Roger H. Taxation of Corporate Capital Income: Tax Revenues versus Tax Distortions. *Quart. J. Econ.*, February 1985, 100(1), pp. 1–27.

Green, Richard C. and Talmor, Eli. The Structure and Incentive Effects of Corporate Tax Liabilities. *J. Finance*, September 1985, 40(4), pp. 1095–114.

Harris, Robert S. and Pringle, John J. Risk-adjusted Discount Rates—Extensions from the Average-Risk Case. *J. Finan. Res.*, Fall 1985, 8(3), pp. 237–44.

Hawkins, Gregory D. Determinants of Corporate Leasing Policy: Discussion. *J. Finance*, July 1985, 40(3), pp. 909–10.

Hayashi, Fumio. Corporate Finance Side of the Q Theory of Investment. *J. Public Econ.*, August 1985, 27(3), pp. 261–80.

Holmström, Bengt R. and Weiss, Laurence M.

Managerial Incentives, Investment, and Aggregate Implications: Scale Effects. *Rev. Econ. Stud.*, July 1985, 52(3), pp. 403–25.

Hosek, William R. and Zahn, Frank. An Alternative Approach to the Estimation of the Real Rate of Interest. *J. Macroecon.*, Spring 1985, 7(2), pp. 211–22. **[G: U.S.]**

Houttuin, G. Venture Capitalism. In *Sweeney, G., ed.*, 1985, pp. 189–96. **[G: OECD]**

Huffman, Gregory W. Adjustment Costs and Capital Asset Pricing. *J. Finance*, July 1985, 40(3), pp. 691–705.

Hughes, Edward and McFetridge, Donald G. A Theoretical Analysis of Incremental Investment Incentives with an Application to the Case of Industrial R and D. *J. Public Econ.*, August 1985, 27(3), pp. 311–29.

Ilzkovitz, Fabienne. Les déterminants des investissements des entreprises en Belgique. (With English summary.) *Cah. Écon. Bruxelles*, 4th Trimester 1985, (108), pp. 487–545. **[G: Belgium]**

Irsch, Norbert. Erträge, Eigenkapitalausstattung und Investitionsneigung. Thesen und empirische Belege. (Yields, Equity Capital Ratio, and Investment Propensity. With English summary.) *Konjunkturpolitik*, 1985, 31(6), pp. 319–35. **[G: W. Germany]**

John, Kose and Nachman, David C. Risky Debt, Investment Incentives, and Reputation in a Sequential Equilibrium. *J. Finance*, July 1985, 40(3), pp. 863–78.

Khoury, Nabil T. and Medina, Ephraïm. La structure du capital: une synthe des orientations théoriques et empiriques de la derniére décennie. (The Firm's Capital Structure in the Last Decade: A Synthesis. With English summary.) *L'Actual. Econ.*, September 1985, 61(3), pp. 362–87.

Kollintzas, Tryphon and Rowley, J. C. Robin. Nonstatic Expectations, Nonexponential Decay, and the Post Tax Rental Cost of Capital. *Public Finance*, 1985, 40(3), pp. 411–40.

Kollintzas, Tryphon and Thorn, Richard S. The Generalized User Cost of Capital. *Public Finance Quart.*, October 1985, 13(4), pp. 355–74.

Kopcke, Richard W. Investment Spending and the Federal Taxation of Business Income. *New Eng. Econ. Rev.*, Sept./Oct. 1985, pp. 9–34. **[G: U.S.]**

Kozlow, Ralph. Capital Expenditures by Majority-owned Foreign Affiliates of U.S. Companies, 1985. *Surv. Curr. Bus.*, March 1985, 65(3), pp. 23–28. **[G: U.S.]**

Larkins, Daniel. Comment on Aggregate Inventory Behavior: Response to Uncertainty and Interest Rates. *J. Post Keynesian Econ.*, Fall 1985, 8(1), pp. 149–50.

Larkins, Daniel and Gill, Gurmukh S. Interest Rates and Aggregate Inventory Investment. *Surv. Curr. Bus.*, June 1985, 65(6), pp. 17–20. **[G: U.S.]**

Lawrence, Colin and Siow, Aloysius. Interest Rates and Investment Spending: Some Empirical Evidence for Postwar U.S. Producer Equipment, 1947—1980. *J. Bus.*, October 1985, 58(4), pp. 359–75. [G: U.S.]

LeBlanc, Michael and Hrubovcak, James. The Effects of Interest Rates on Agricultural Machinery Investment. *Agr. Econ. Res.*, Summer 1985, 37(3), pp. 12–22. [G: U.S.]

Lewellen, Wilbur G. and Emery, Douglas R. Security-Holder Cash Flows and the Valuation of Corporate Investment Projects. *Managerial Dec. Econ.*, June 1985, 6(2), pp. 80–87.

Long, Michael S. and Malitz, Ileen B. Investment Patterns and Financial Leverage. In *Friedman, B. M., ed.*, 1985, pp. 325–48. [G: U.S.]

Mairesse, Jacques and Dormont, Brigitte. Labor and Investment Demand at the Firm Level: A Comparison of French, German and U.S. Manufacturing, 1970-79. *Europ. Econ. Rev.*, June-July 1985, 28(1–2), pp. 201–31. [G: France; U.S.; W. Germany]

Marfán, Manuel. El conflicto entre la recaudación de impuestos y la inversión privada: elementos teóricos para una reforma tributaria. (The Trade-off between Tax Revenues and Private Investment: Theoretical Elements for a Tax Reform. With English summary.) *Colección Estud. CIEPLAN*, 1985, (18), pp. 63–93.

Mayer, Colin and Meadowcroft, Shirley A. Equity Rates of Return in the UK—Evidence from Panel Data. In *Weiserbs, D., ed.*, 1985, pp. 351–86. [G: U.K.]

Mayer, Thomas and Chatterji, Monojit. Political Shocks and Investment: Some Evidence from the 1930s. *J. Econ. Hist.*, December 1985, 45(4), pp. 913–24. [G: U.S.]

McConnell, John J. and Muscarella, Chris J. Corporate Capital Expenditure Decisions and the Market Value of the Firm. *J. Finan. Econ.*, September 1985, 14(3), pp. 399–422. [G: U.S.]

McDonald, Robert L. and Siegel, Daniel R. Investment and the Valuation of Firms When There Is an Option to Shut Down. *Int. Econ. Rev.*, June 1985, 26(2), pp. 331–49.

McIntyre, Robert S. and Tipps, Dean C. Exploding the Investment-Incentive Myth. *Challenge*, May/June 1985, 28(2), pp. 47–52. [G: U.S.]

McMillan, W. Douglas. Money, Government Debt, *q*, and Investment. *J. Macroecon.*, Winter 1985, 7(1), pp. 19–37.

Miller, Merton H. and Rock, Kevin. Dividend Policy under Asymmetric Information. *J. Finance*, September 1985, 40(4), pp. 1031–51.

Modigliani, Franco. Changes in the Balance Sheet, 1926–1977: Comment. In *Friedman, B. M., ed.*, 1985, pp. 109–15. [G: U.S.]

Moene, Karl Ove. Shopping for an Investment Good. *Int. Econ. Rev.*, June 1985, 26(2), pp. 351–63.

Myers, Stewart C. Investment Patterns and Financial Leverage: Comment. In *Friedman, B. M., ed.*, 1985, pp. 348–51. [G: U.S.]

Narayanan, M. P. Observability and the Payback Criterion. *J. Bus.*, July 1985, 58(3), pp. 309–23.

Nicodano, Giovanna. Struttura finanziaria e decisioni d'investimento: una verifica econometrica. (Financial Structure and Investment Decisions: An Econometric Model. With English summary.) *Giorn. Econ.*, Mar.-Apr. 1985, 44(3–4), pp. 179–207. [G: Italy]

Noguchi, Yukio. Tax Structure and Saving–Investment Balance. *Hitotsubashi J. Econ.*, June 1985, 26(1), pp. 45–58. [G: U.S.; Japan]

Paci, Raffaele. Accumulation Process and Investment Incentives in a Vintage Investment Model: The Case of Sardinia. *Rivista Int. Sci. Econ. Com.*, July-Aug. 1985, 32(7–8), pp. 765–94. [G: Italy]

Reagan, Patricia and Sheehan, Dennis P. The Stylized Facts about the Behavior of Manufacturers' Inventories and Backorders over the Business Cycle: 1959–1980. *J. Monet. Econ.*, March 1985, 15(2), pp. 217–46. [G: U.S.]

Riener, Kenneth D. A Pedagogic Note on the Cost of Capital with Personal Taxes and Risky Debt. *Financial Rev.*, May 1985, 20(2), pp. 229–35.

Rossana, Robert J. Delivery Lags and Buffer Stocks in the Theory of Investment by the Firm. *J. Econ. Dynam. Control*, October 1985, 9(2), pp. 153–93.

Sarkar, Swapna and Sarkar, Debjani. A Study of Investment in the Jute Manufacturing Industry. *Indian Econ. J.*, Oct.-Nov. 1985, 33(2), pp. 57–68. [G: India]

Schwalbach, Joachim. Multi-plant Operation Economies in the West German Beer and Cement Industries. In *Schwalbach, J., ed.*, 1985, pp. 167–95. [G: W. Germany]

Scott, John T. Capital Structure and the Product Market Environment: Comment. In *Friedman, B. M., ed.*, 1985, pp. 378–82. [G: U.S.]

Seskin, Eugene P. Plant and Equipment Expenditures, First and Second Quarters and Second Half of 1985. *Surv. Curr. Bus.*, April 1985, 65(4), pp. 21–25. [G: U.S.]

Seskin, Eugene P. and Sullivan, David F. Plant and Equipment Expenditures, of the Four Quarters of 1985. *Surv. Curr. Bus.*, September 1985, 65(9), pp. 19–21. [G: U.S.]

Seskin, Eugene P. and Sullivan, David F. Plant and Equipment Expenditures, the Four Quarters of 1985. *Surv. Curr. Bus.*, June 1985, 65(6), pp. 21–24. [G: U.S.]

Seskin, Eugene P. and Sullivan, David F. Revised Estimates of New Plant and Equipment Expenditures in the United States, 1947–83. *Surv. Curr. Bus.*, February 1985, 65(2), pp. 16–47. [G: U.S.]

Shashua, Leon and Goldschmidt, Yaaqov. The Specific Role of Interest in Financial and Economic Analysis under Inflation: Real, Nominal, or a Combination of Both. *Amer. J. Agr. Econ.*, May 1985, 67(2), pp. 377–83.

Sheets, Robert G.; Smith, Russell L. and Voytek, Kenneth P. Corporate Disinvestment and Metropolitan Manufacturing Job Loss. *Soc. Sci. Quart.*, March 1985, 66(1), pp. 218–26. [G: U.S.]

Short, Daniel G. A Comparison of Alternative Methods of Estimating Constant Dollar Depreciation. *Accounting Rev.*, July 1985, *60*(3), pp. 500–503.

Shoven, John B. Taxes and the Investment Recovery: Comment. *Brookings Pap. Econ. Act.*, 1985, (1), pp. 39–41. [G: U.S.]

Singleton, Kenneth J. Adjustment Costs and Capital Asset Pricing: Discussion. *J. Finance*, July 1985, *40*(3), pp. 705–09.

Smith, Clifford W., Jr. and Wakeman, L. MacDonald. Determinants of Corporate Leasing Policy. *J. Finance*, July 1985, *40*(3), pp. 895–908.

Spatt, Chester S. Risky Debt, Investment Incentives, and Reputation in a Sequential Equilibrium: Discussion. *J. Finance*, July 1985, *40*(3), pp. 878–80.

Spence, A. Michael. Capital Structure and the Corporation's Product Market Environment. In *Friedman, B. M., ed.*, 1985, pp. 353–77. [G: U.S.]

Spulber, Daniel F. Risk Sharing and Inventories. *J. Econ. Behav. Organ.*, March 1985, *6*(1), pp. 55–68.

Starck, Christian C. Vinsten och företagets investeringsefterfrägan. (The Profit and the Investment Behaviour of the Enterprise. With English summary.) *Ekon. Samfundets Tidskr.*, 1985, *38*(1), pp. 35–50. [G: OECD]

Summers, Lawrence H. Taxes and the Investment Recovery: Comment. *Brookings Pap. Econ. Act.*, 1985, (1), pp. 42–44. [G: U.S.]

Sumner, Michael. A Note on Replacement Investment. *Oxford Bull. Econ. Statist.*, November 1985, *47*(4), pp. 395–400. [G: U.K.]

Sumner, Michael. The Effect of an Anticipated Tax Change on Investment in Britain. *J. Public Econ.*, March 1985, *26*(2), pp. 237–47. [G: U.K.]

Tomiyama, Ken. Two-Stage Optimal Control Problems and Optimality Conditions. *J. Econ. Dynam. Control*, November 1985, *9*(3), pp. 317–37.

Ulph, A. Equity Rates of Return in the U.K.; Evidence from Panel Data: Comment. In *Weiserbs, D., ed.*, 1985, pp. 387–89. [G: U.K.]

Vanzetti, David and Quiggin, John. A Comparative Analysis of Agricultural Tractor Investment Models. *Australian J. Agr. Econ.*, August 1985, *29*(2), pp. 122–41. [G: Australia]

Verma, Anil. Relative Flow of Capital to Union and Nonunion Plants within a Firm. *Ind. Relat.*, Fall 1985, *24*(3), pp. 395–405. [G: U.S.]

Wescoe, Clarke. Factors in Pharmaceutical Investment. In *Wells, N., ed.*, 1985, pp. 210–17.

Williams, Joseph T. Trading and Valuing Depreciable Assets. *J. Finan. Econ.*, June 1985, *14*(2), pp. 283–308.

Wisley, T. O. and Johnson, Stanley R. An Evaluation of Alternative Investment Hypotheses Using Non-nested Tests. *Southern Econ. J.*, October 1985, *52*(2), pp. 422–30. [G: U.S.]

Wolfson, Mark A. Empirical Evidence of Incentive Problems and Their Mitigation in Oil and Gas Tax Shelter Programs. In *Pratt, J. W. and Zeckhauser, R. J., eds.*, 1985, pp. 101–25. [G: U.S.]

530 MARKETING AND ADVERTISING

531 Marketing and Advertising

5310 Marketing and Advertising

Ahmed, Momtaz Uddin. Institutional Framework Concerning Promotion of Rural Industries in Bangladesh: An Evaluation. In *Mukhopadhyay, S. and Chee, P. L., eds. (II)*, 1985, pp. 227–301. [G: Bangladesh]

Allen, Chris T. and Madden, Thomas J. A Closer Look at Classical Conditioning. *J. Cons. Res.*, December 1985, *12*(3), pp. 301–15. [G: U.S.]

Amine, Lyn S. and Cavusgil, S. Tamer. Consumer Market Environment in the Middle East. In *Kaynak, E., ed. (II)*, 1985, pp. 163–76. [G: Middle East]

Anderson, Erin M. The Salesperson as Outside Agent or Employee: A Transaction Cost Analysis. *Marketing Sci.*, Summer 1985, *4*(3), pp. 234–54. [G: U.S.]

Andreasen, Alan R. Consumer Responses to Dissatisfaction in Loose Monopolies. *J. Cons. Res.*, September 1985, *12*(2), pp. 135–41. [G: U.S.]

Arrow, Kenneth J. and Nerlove, Marc. Optimal Advertising Policy under Dynamic Conditions. In *Arrow, K. J. (I)*, 1985, pp. 140–56.

Basu, Amiya K., et al. Salesforce Compensation Plans: An Agency Theoretic Perspective. *Marketing Sci.*, Fall 1985, *4*(4), pp. 267–91.

Batsell, Richard R. and Polking, John C. A New Class of Market Share Models. *Marketing Sci.*, Summer 1985, *4*(3), pp. 177–98. [G: U.S.]

Bechtel, Gordon G. Generalizing the Rasch Model for Consumer Rating Scales. *Marketing Sci.*, Winter 1985, *4*(1), pp. 62–73. [G: U.S.]

Belk, Russell W. and Pollay, Richard W. Images of Ourselves: The Good Life in Twentieth Century Advertising. *J. Cons. Res.*, March 1985, *11*(4), pp. 887–97. [G: U.S.]

Bernheim, B. Douglas and Whinston, Michael D. Common Marketing Agency as a Device for Facilitating Collusion. *Rand J. Econ.*, Summer 1985, *16*(2), pp. 269–81.

Bierley, Calvin; McSweeney, Frances K. and Vannieuwkerk, Renee. Classical Conditioning of Preferences for Stimuli. *J. Cons. Res.*, December 1985, *12*(3), pp. 316–23. [G: U.S.]

Boddewyn, Jean J. Global Perspectives on Advertising Control. In *Kaynak, E., ed. (I)*, 1985, pp. 37–51. [G: Global]

Bourgel, Guy; Brignier, Jean-Marie and Certhoux, Gilles. Perception et réalité des prix. (Price Perception and Price Reality. With English summary.) *Écon. Soc.*, December 1985, *19*(12), pp. 73–104. [G: France]

Brown, Roy Chamberlain. Statistical Science Rationale for Micromarketing Decision Support

Systems. In *Brown, R. C., ed.*, 1985, pp. 251–55.

Brucks, Merrie. The Effects of Product Class Knowledge on Information Search Behavior. *J. Cons. Res.*, June 1985, *12*(1), pp. 1–16. [G: U.S.]

Buatsi, Seth N.; Pradhan, Suresh and Apasu, Yao. Human Resources, Managerial Perceptions, and the Global Marketing Behavior of Firms. In *Kaynak, E., ed. (I)*, 1985, pp. 183–96. [G: U.K.]

Buchanan, Bruce S. and Morrison, Donald G. Measuring Simple Preferences: An Approach to Blind, Forced Choice Product Testing. *Marketing Sci.*, Spring 1985, *4*(2), pp. 93–109.

Bultez, A. and Naert, P. Control of Advertising Expenditures Based on Aggregate Models of Carryover Effects. In *Rinnooy Kan, A. H. G., ed.*, 1985, pp. 31–44.

Cameron, Samuel and Shipley, David D. A Discretionary Model of Industrial Buying. *Managerial Dec. Econ.*, June 1985, *6*(2), pp. 102–11. [G: U.K.]

Carli, Carlo. Situazione della ricera scientifica sulla misura dell'efficacia della pubblicità. (The Situation of Scientific Research on the Measure of Advertising Effectiveness. With English summary.) *Rivista Int. Sci. Econ. Com.*, March 1985, *32*(3), pp. 271–94.

Carroll, Vincent P., et al. The Navy Enlistment Marketing Experiment. *Marketing Sci.*, Fall 1985, *4*(4), pp. 352–74. [G: U.S.]

Cavusgil, S. Tamer. Decision Making in Global Marketing. In *Kaynak, E., ed. (I)*, 1985, pp. 173–82.

Childers, Terry L.; Houston, Michael J. and Heckler, Susan E. Measurement of Individual Differences in Visual versus Verbal Information Processing. *J. Cons. Res.*, September 1985, *12*(2), pp. 125–34. [G: U.S.]

Cote, Joseph A.; McCullough, James and Reilly, Michael. Effects of Unexpected Situations on Behavior–Intention Differences: A Garbology Analysis. *J. Cons. Res.*, September 1985, *12*(2), pp. 188–94. [G: U.S.]

Coughlan, Anne T. Competition and Cooperation in Marketing Channel Choice: Theory and Application. *Marketing Sci.*, Spring 1985, *4*(2), pp. 110–29. [G: Global]

Cundiff, Edward W. and Hilger, Marye Tharp. The Consumption Function and the Role of Marketing in Global Economic Development. In *Kaynak, E., ed. (I)*, 1985, pp. 121–32. [G: LDCs]

Darling, John R. An Analysis of Finnish Consumer Attitudes toward the Products and Associated Marketing Practices of Various Selected Countries, 1975, 1980, and 1985. *Liiketaloudellinen Aikak.*, 1985, *34*(4), pp. 319–28. [G: Finland]

Dawson, John A. Structural Change in European Retailing: The Polarization of Operating Scale. In *Kaynak, E., ed. (I)*, 1985, pp. 211–29. [G: W. Europe]

Dhebar, Anirudh and Oren, Shmuel S. Optimal Dynamic Pricing for Expanding Networks. *Marketing Sci.*, Fall 1985, *4*(4), pp. 336–51.

Dillon, William R.; Frederick, Donald G. and Tangpanichdee, Vanchai. Decision Issues in Building Perceptual Product Spaces with Multi-attribute Rating Data. *J. Cons. Res.*, June 1985, *12*(1), pp. 47–63.

Dubinsky, Alan J. and Yammarino, Francis J. Job-related Responses of Insurance Agents: A Multi-firm Investigation. *J. Risk Ins.*, September 1985, *52*(3), pp. 501–17. [G: U.S.]

El-Ansary, Adel I. Managerial Gap Analysis: A Frame of Reference for Improving International Business Relations with the Middle East. In *Kaynak, E., ed. (II)*, 1985, pp. 43–56. [G: Middle East]

El-Haddad, Awad B. An Analysis of the Current Status of Marketing in the Middle East. In *Kaynak, E., ed. (II)*, 1985, pp. 177–97. [G: Middle East; Egypt]

Erickson, Gary M. and Johansson, Johny K. The Role of Price in Multi-attribute Product Evaluations. *J. Cons. Res.*, September 1985, *12*(2), pp. 195–99. [G: U.S.]

Friedman, Monroe. The Changing Language of a Consumer Society: Brand Name Usage in Popular American Novels in the Postwar Era. *J. Cons. Res.*, March 1985, *11*(4), pp. 927–38. [G: U.S.]

Gatignon, Hubert and Robertson, Thomas S. A Propositional Inventory for New Diffusion Research. *J. Cons. Res.*, March 1985, *11*(4), pp. 849–67.

Gerstner, Eitan. Sales: Demand-Supply Variation or Price Discrimination? *J. Econ. Bus.*, May 1985, *37*(2), pp. 171–82. [G: U.S.]

Gorn, Gerald J. and Florsheim, Renée. The Effects of Commercials for Adult Products on Children. *J. Cons. Res.*, March 1985, *11*(4), pp. 962–67. [G: U.S.]

Graeser, Paul. Rationality, Rent, and the Marginal Customer. *Atlantic Econ. J.*, December 1985, *13*(4), pp. 81.

Graham, John L. Cross-cultural Marketing Negotiations: A Laboratory Experiment. *Marketing Sci.*, Spring 1985, *4*(2), pp. 130–46.

Green, Paul E. and Krieger, Abba M. Models and Heuristics for Product Line Selection. *Marketing Sci.*, Winter 1985, *4*(1), pp. 1–19.

Grönroos, Christian. Konkurrenskraft genom kund-och servicebaserade strategier i marknadsföringen. (The Competitiveness of Customer-oriented and Service-oriented Strategies in Marketing. With English summary.) *Ekon. Samfundets Tidskr.*, 1985, *38*(3), pp. 131–43.

Grover, Rajiv and Dillon, William R. Probabilistic Model for Testing Hypothesized Hierarchical Market Structures. *Marketing Sci.*, Fall 1985, *4*(4), pp. 312–35.

Hallagan, William S. and Joerding, Wayne. Polymorphism in Competitive Strategies: Trading Stamps. *J. Econ. Bus.*, February 1985, *37*(1), pp. 1–17.

Happel, Stephen K. The Effect of Adverse Publicity on Sales: A Case Study. *Managerial Dec. Econ.*, December 1985, *6*(4), pp. 257–59. [G: U.S.]

Harris, Frederick H. deB. and Dennis, Richard L. Managerial Utility-maximizing Operating Decisions under Compound Demand Risk. *Managerial Dec. Econ.*, March 1985, *6*(1), pp. 19–26.

Helle, Reijo. Alueellinen portfolioanalyysi. (Portfolio Analysis as a Device for Spatial Marketing Strategy. With English summary.) *Liiketaloudellinen Aikak.*, 1985, *34*(2), pp. 191–98.

Hirschey, Mark and Weygandt, Jerry J. Amortization Policy for Advertising and Research and Development Expenditures. *J. Acc. Res.*, Spring 1985, *23*(1), pp. 326–35. [G: U.S.]

Hirschman, Elizabeth C. Primitive Aspects of Consumption in Modern American Society. *J. Cons. Res.*, September 1985, *12*(2), pp. 142–54. [G: U.S.]

Hirschman, Elizabeth C. and Pieros, Andrew, Jr. Relationships among Indicators of Success in Broadway Plays and Motion Pictures. *J. Cult. Econ.*, June 1985, *9*(1), pp. 35–63. [G: U.S.]

Holbrook, Morris B., et al. Nonisomorphism, Shadow Features and Imputed Preferences. *Marketing Sci.*, Summer 1985, *4*(3), pp. 215–33.

Holstius, Karin. Retail Marketing of Convenience Goods in Finland: Special Offers Combining Customer and Retailer Benefit. *Liiketaloudellinen Aikak.*, 1985, *34*(4), pp. 338–65. [G: Finland]

Holstius, Karin. Strategy and Market-Orientation in Producer Goods Companies. *Liiketaloudellinen Aikak.*, 1985, *34*(3), pp. 237–43.

Houston, Douglas A. and Howe, John S. An Economic Rationale for Couponing. *Quart. J. Bus. Econ.*, Spring 1985, *24*(2), pp. 37–50.

Hunt, Herbert G., III. Potential Determinants of Corporate Inventory Accounting Decisions. *J. Acc. Res.*, Autumn 1985, *23*(2), pp. 448–67. [G: U.S.]

van Iwaarden, M. J. Public Health Aspects of the Marketing of Alcoholic Drinks. In *Grant, M., ed.*, 1985, pp. 45–55. [G: Netherlands]

Jackson, Ralph W.; McDaniel, Stephen W. and Rao, C. P. Food Shopping and Preparation: Psychographic Differences of Working Wives and Housewives. *J. Cons. Res.*, June 1985, *12*(1), pp. 110–13. [G: U.S.]

Jeuland, Abel P. and Narasimhan, Chakravarthi. Dealing—Temporary Price Cuts—by Seller as a Buyer Discrimination Mechanism. *J. Bus.*, July 1985, *58*(3), pp. 295–308.

Johnson, Richard D. and Levin, Irwin P. More than Meets the Eye: The Effect of Missing Information on Purchase Evaluations. *J. Cons. Res.*, September 1985, *12*(2), pp. 169–77. [G: U.S.]

Johnson, Scott Lee; Sommer, Robert and Martino, Victor. Consumer Behavior at Bulk Food Bins. *J. Cons. Res.*, June 1985, *12*(1), pp. 114–17. [G: U.S.]

Kahle, Lynn R. and Homer, Pamela M. Physical Attractiveness of the Celebrity Endorser: A Social Adaptation Perspective. *J. Cons. Res.*, March 1985, *11*(4), pp. 954–61. [G: U.S.]

Kaserman, David L. and Mayo, John W. Advertising and the Residential Demand for Electricity. *J. Bus.*, October 1985, *58*(4), pp. 399–408. [G: U.S.]

Kaynak, Erdener. Comparative Study of Marketing and Management Systems in the Middle East. In *Kaynak, E., ed. (II)*, 1985, pp. 19–42. [G: N. Africa; Middle East]

Kaynak, Erdener. Correlates of Export Performance in Resource-Based Industries. In *Kaynak, E., ed. (I)*, 1985, pp. 197–210. [G: Canada]

Kaynak, Erdener. Future Developments in Marketing around the World. In *Kaynak, E., ed. (I)*, 1985, pp. 233–48. [G: Global]

Kaynak, Erdener. Future Directions for Marketing and Management in the Middle East. In *Kaynak, E., ed. (II)*, 1985, pp. 233–43. [G: Middle East]

Kaynak, Erdener. Global Spread of Supermarkets: Some Experiences from Turkey. In *Kaynak, E., ed. (I)*, 1985, pp. 77–93. [G: Switzerland; Turkey]

Kaynak, Erdener. Globalization in International Markets. In *Kaynak, E., ed. (I)*, 1985, pp. 5–22.

Kaynak, Erdener. International Business in the Middle East. In *Kaynak, E., ed. (II)*, 1985, pp. 3–18.

Kaynak, Erdener and Gürol, Metin N. An Export Marketing Model for Developing Middle Eastern Countries: What Lessons Countries of the Region Learn from Each Other. In *Kaynak, E., ed. (II)*, 1985, pp. 199–216. [G: Turkey; Japan]

Khera, Inder and Karns, David. Perceived Country Attractiveness: A Conjoint Measurement Approach. In *Kaynak, E., ed. (I)*, 1985, pp. 67–76. [G: U.S.]

Kirkpatrick, Jerry. Theory and History in Marketing: Reply. *Managerial Dec. Econ.*, September 1985, *6*(3), pp. 186–88.

Klein, Benjamin and Saft, Lester F. The Law and Economics of Franchise Tying Contracts. *J. Law Econ.*, May 1985, *28*(2), pp. 345–61. [G: U.S.]

Klein, Saul A. The Role of Marketing in Economic Development. *Quart. J. Bus. Econ.*, Autumn 1985, *24*(4), pp. 54–69.

Laitinen, Erkki K. A Simulation Model of Alternative Pricing Strategies. *Liiketaloudellinen Aikak.*, 1985, *34*(3), pp. 244–71.

Leffler, Keith. Toward a Reasonable Rule of Reason: Comments. *J. Law Econ.*, May 1985, *28*(2), pp. 381–86. [G: U.S.]

Leonard-Barton, Dorothy. Experts as Negative Opinion Leaders in the Diffusion of a Technological Innovation. *J. Cons. Res.*, March 1985, *11*(4), pp. 914–26. [G: U.S.]

Liebermann, Yehoshua. The Role of Economic Analysis in Media-planning. *Managerial Dec. Econ.*, March 1985, *6*(1), pp. 33–40. [G: Israel]

Liebrenz, Marilyn L. Global Franchising. In *Kaynak, E., ed. (I)*, 1985, pp. 53–63. [G: Global]

Liefeld, John and Heslop, Louise A. Reference Prices and Deception in Newspaper Advertising. *J. Cons. Res.*, March 1985, *11*(4), pp. 868–76. [G: U.S.]

Loken, Barbara and Hoverstad, Ronald. Relationships between Information Recall and Subsequent Attitudes: Some Exploratory Findings. *J. Cons. Res.*, September 1985, *12*(2), pp. 155–68. [G: U.S.]

Lynk, William J. The Price and Output of Beer Revisited [Interpreting Rising Concentration: The Case of Beer]. *J. Bus.*, October 1985, *58*(4), pp. 433–37. [G: U.S.]

Marchetti, Piergaetano. La pubblicità nella concorrenza fra emittenti sul mercato del risparmio. (Advertising in the Competition among Issues on the Savings Market. With English summary.) *Bancaria*, May 1985, *41*(5), pp. 515–23. [G: Italy]

Markovits, Richard S. The Functions, Allocative Efficiency, and Legality of Tie-ins: A Comment. *J. Law Econ.*, May 1985, *28*(2), pp. 387–404. [G: U.S.]

Marvel, Howard P. and McCafferty, Stephen. The Welfare Effects of Resale Price Maintenance. *J. Law Econ.*, May 1985, *28*(2), pp. 363–79. [G: U.S.]

Mathewson, G. Frank and Winter, Ralph A. The Economics of Franchise Contracts. *J. Law Econ.*, October 1985, *28*(3), pp. 503–26.

Meyer, Robert J. and Sathi, Arvind. A Multiattribute Model of Consumer Choice during Product Learning. *Marketing Sci.*, Winter 1985, *4*(1), pp. 41–61.

Migon, Helio S. and Harrison, P. Jeff. An Application of Non-linear Bayesian Forecasting to Television Advertising. In *Bernardo, J. M., et al., eds.*, 1985, pp. 681–96. [G: U.K.]

Mihăiţă, N. V. Identification of Relations, Interactions and Potential for Informational Change. Mappings for Decisions in the Foreign Trade Field. *Econ. Computat. Cybern. Stud. Res.*, 1985, *20*(1), pp. 43–56.

Mihăiţă, N. V. Illustration of the Interaction Potential in Marketing. *Econ. Computat. Cybern. Stud. Res.*, 1985, *20*(2), pp. 31–36.

Mitchell, Ivor. Correlates of Consumer Shopping Behaviour in the Cooperative Socialist Republic of Guyana. *Soc. Econ. Stud.*, June 1985, *34*(2), pp. 26–68. [G: Guyana]

Montel, Jean-Jacques. Essai de modélisation économétrique du marché pharmaceutique. Modèle de part de marché. (Pharmaceutical Market. Econometric Modelisation Test Market Share Model. With English summary.) *Écon. Soc.*, December 1985, *19*(12), pp. 33–69. [G: France]

Moore, Ellen M.; Bearden, William O. and Teel, Jesse E. Use of Labeling and Assertions of Dependency in Appeals for Consumer Support. *J. Cons. Res.*, June 1985, *12*(1), pp. 90–96. [G: U.S.]

Moschis, George P. The Role of Family Communication in Consumer Socialization of Children and Adolescents. *J. Cons. Res.*, March 1985, *11*(4), pp. 898–913.

Mun, Kin-chok. Export Pricing of China's Industrial Goods: Problems and Suggested Solutions. In *Kaynak, E., ed. (I)*, 1985, pp. 95–107. [G: China]

Nadel, Mark S. Comment: Multichannel Video Competition. In *Noam, E. M., ed.*, 1985, pp. 174–79. [G: U.S.]

Negishi, Takashi. Advertising and the Social Imbalance between Private and Public Goods. *Rivista Int. Sci. Econ. Com.*, January 1985, *32*(1), pp. 64–70.

Neslin, Scott A.; Henderson, Caroline and Quelch, John. Consumer Promotions and the Acceleration of Product Purchases. *Marketing Sci.*, Spring 1985, *4*(2), pp. 147–65. [G: U.S.]

Nichols, Len M. Advertising and Economic Welfare. *Amer. Econ. Rev.*, March 1985, *75*(1), pp. 213–18.

Nyström, Harry. Company Strategies for Designing and Marketing New Products in the Electrotechnical Industry. In *Langdon, R. and Rothwell, R., eds.*, 1985, pp. 18–26.

Obermiller, Carl. Varieties of Mere Exposure: The Effects of Processing Style and Repetition on Affective Response. *J. Cons. Res.*, June 1985, *12*(1), pp. 17–30.

Oliver, Richard L. and Bearden, William O. Crossover Effects in the Theory of Reasoned Action: A Moderating Influence Attempt. *J. Cons. Res.*, December 1985, *12*(3), pp. 324–40. [G: U.S.]

Oren, Shmuel S. and Rothkopf, Michael H. A Market Dynamics Model for New Industrial Products and Its Application: Erratum. *Marketing Sci.*, Winter 1985, *4*(1), pp. 90.

Ornstein, Stanley I. and Hanssens, Dominique M. Alcohol Control Laws and the Consumption of Distilled Spirits and Beer. *J. Cons. Res.*, September 1985, *12*(2), pp. 200–213. [G: U.S.]

Painton, Scott and Gentry, James W. Another Look at the Impact of Information Presentation Format. *J. Cons. Res.*, September 1985, *12*(2), pp. 240–44. [G: U.S.]

Paltschik, Mikael. Log-lineaariset mallit ja markkinointitutkimus. (Log- linear Models and Marketing Research. With English summary.) *Liiketaloudellinen Aikak.*, 1985, *34*(3), pp. 298–305.

Pasternack, Barry Alan. Optimal Pricing and Return Policies for Perishable Commodities. *Marketing Sci.*, Spring 1985, *4*(2), pp. 166–76.

Peterson, Robert A.; Albaum, Gerald and Beltramini, Richard F. A Meta-Analysis of Effect Sizes in Consumer Behavior Experiments. *J. Cons. Res.*, June 1985, *12*(1), pp. 97–103. [G: U.S.]

Radfar, Mehran. The Effect of Advertising on Total Consumption of Cigarettes in the U.K.: A Comment. *Europ. Econ. Rev.*, November 1985, *29*(2), pp. 225–31. [G: U.K.]

Rice, Gillian and Mahmoud, Essam. The Prospects for Export Marketing to Egypt. In *Kay-*

nak, E., ed. (II), 1985, pp. 217–29.

[G: Egypt]

Runde, J. H. Theory and History in Marketing: A Comment. *Managerial Dec. Econ.*, September 1985, *6*(3), pp. 183–85.

Runde, J. H. Theory and History in Marketing: Rejoinder. *Managerial Dec. Econ.*, September 1985, *6*(3), pp. 189–90.

Rust, Roland T. and Schmittlein, David C. A Bayesian Cross-validated Likelihood Method for Comparing Alternative Specifications of Quantitative Models. *Marketing Sci.*, Winter 1985, *4*(1), pp. 20–40.

Saegert, Joel; Hoover, Robert J. and Hilger, Marye Tharp. Characteristics of Mexican American Consumers. *J. Cons. Res.*, June 1985, *12*(1), pp. 104–09. [G: U.S.]

Samiee, Saeed. Global Retail Strategy and Productivity Planning: Some International Comparisons. In *Kaynak, E., ed. (I)*, 1985, pp. 23–36.

Sappington, David E. M. and Wernerfelt, Birger. To Brand or Not to Brand? A Theoretical and Empirical Question. *J. Bus.*, July 1985, *58*(3), pp. 279–93. [G: U.S.]

Schmittlein, David C.; Bemmaor, Albert C. and Morrison, Donald G. Why Does the NBD Model Work? Robustness in Representing Product Purchases, Brand Purchases and Imperfectly Recorded Purchases. *Marketing Sci.*, Summer 1985, *4*(3), pp. 255–66.

Schurr, Paul H. and Ozanne, Julie L. Influence on Exchange Processes: Buyers' Preconceptions of a Seller's Trustworthiness and Bargaining Toughness. *J. Cons. Res.*, March 1985, *11*(4), pp. 939–53.

Simon-Miller, Françoise. Marketing Policies and Strategies in West Africa. In *Kaynak, E., ed. (I)*, 1985, pp. 109–17. [G: W. Africa]

Sirgy, M. Joseph; Morris, Michael and Samli, A. Coskun. The Question of Value in Social Marketing: Use of a Quality-of-Life Theory to Achieve Long-term Life Satisfaction. *Amer. J. Econ. Soc.*, April 1985, *44*(2), pp. 215–28.

Smith, Ruth Ann and Houston, Michael J. A Psychometric Assessment of Measures of Scripts in Consumer Memory. *J. Cons. Res.*, September 1985, *12*(2), pp. 214–24. [G: U.S.]

Sujan, Mita. Consumer Knowledge: Effects on Evaluation Strategies Mediating Consumer Judgments. *J. Cons. Res.*, June 1985, *12*(1), pp. 31–46. [G: U.S.]

Swales, J. K. Advertising as an Intangible Asset: Profitability and Entry Barriers. A Comment. *Appl. Econ.*, August 1985, *17*(4), pp. 603–17. [G: U.K.]

Swasy, John L. and Munch, James M. Examining the Target of Receiver Elaborations: Rhetorical Question Effects on Source Processing and Persuasion. *J. Cons. Res.*, March 1985, *11*(4), pp. 877–86. [G: U.S.]

Teas, R. Kenneth and Dellva, W. L. Conjoint Measurement of Consumers' Preferences for Multiattribute Financial Services. *J. Bank Res.*, Summer 1985, *16*(2), pp. 99–112.

Thaler, Richard. Mental Accounting and Con-

sumer Choice. *Marketing Sci.*, Summer 1985, *4*(3), pp. 199–214.

Tremblay, Victor J. A Reappraisal of Interpreting Rising Concentration: The Case of Beer. *J. Bus.*, October 1985, *58*(4), pp. 419–31.

[G: U.S.]

Tremblay, Victor J. Strategic Groups and the Demand for Beer. *J. Ind. Econ.*, December 1985, *34*(2), pp. 183–98. [G: U.S.]

Wagle, John S. and Kaminski, Peter F. Territoriality: A Key to Strategic Retail Planning. *METU*, 1985, *12*(3/4), pp. 285–300.

Webber, Richard. The Use of Census-derived Classifications in the Marketing of Consumer Products in the United Kingdom. *J. Econ. Soc. Meas.*, April 1985, *13*(1), pp. 113–24.

[G: U.K.]

Webbink, Douglas W. Comment: Empirical Studies of Media Competition. In *Noam, E. M., ed.*, 1985, pp. 168–73. [G: U.S.]

Wernerfelt, Birger. Brand Loyalty and User Skills. *J. Econ. Behav. Organ.*, December 1985, *6*(4), pp. 381–85.

Winer, Russell S. A Price Vector Model of Demand for Consumer Durables: Preliminary Developments. *Marketing Sci.*, Winter 1985, *4*(1), pp. 74–90. [G: U.S.]

Wirth, Michael O. and Bloch, Harry. The Broadcasters: The Future Role of Local Stations and the Three Networks. In *Noam, E. M., ed.*, 1985, pp. 121–37. [G: U.S.]

Woods, Walter A.; Chéron, Emmanuel J. and Kim, Dong Man. Strategic Implications of Differences in Consumer Purposes for Purchasing in Three Global Markets. In *Kaynak, E., ed. (I)*, 1985, pp. 155–70. [G: Canada; S. Korea; U.S.]

Zaichkowsky, Judith Lynne. Measuring the Involvement Construct. *J. Cons. Res.*, December 1985, *12*(3), pp. 341–52. [G: U.S.]

540 ACCOUNTING

541 Accounting

5410 Accounting

Abdel-Khalik, A. Rashad. The Effect of LIFO-Switching and Firm Ownership on Executives' Pay. *J. Acc. Res.*, Autumn 1985, *23*(2), pp. 427–47. [G: U.S.]

Anderson, Matthew J. Some Evidence on the Effect of Verbalization on Process: A Methodological Note. *J. Acc. Res.*, Autumn 1985, *23*(2), pp. 843–52.

Apostolou, Nicholas G.; Giroux, Gary A. and Welker, Robert B. The Information Content of Municipal Spending Rate Data. *J. Acc. Res.*, Autumn 1985, *23*(2), pp. 853–58. [G: U.S.]

Arkhipoff, Oleg. Un, deux, trois, beaucoup ou comment l'imprécision vient aux comptables. (One, Two, Three, Many—Or How Imprecision Comes to Accountants. With English summary.) *Écon. Soc.*, June 1985, *19*(6), pp. 185–99.

Arrington, C. Edward; Bailey, Charles D. and

Hopwood, William S. An Attribution Analysis of Responsibility Assessment for Audit Performance. *J. Acc. Res.*, Spring 1985, *23*(1), pp. 1–20.

Ashton, Alison Hubbard. Does Consensus Imply Accuracy in Accounting Studies of Decision Making? *Accounting Rev.*, April 1985, *60*(2), pp. 173–85. [G: U.S.]

Atiase, Rowland Kwame. Predisclosure Information, Firm Capitalization, and Security Price Behavior around Earnings Announcements. *J. Acc. Res.*, Spring 1985, *23*(1), pp. 21–36. [G: U.S.]

Baber, William R. A Framework for Making a Class of Internal Accounting Control Decisions. *J. Acc. Res.*, Spring 1985, *23*(1), pp. 360–69.

Baber, William R. Budget-based Compensation and Discretionary Spending. *Accounting Rev.*, January 1985, *60*(1), pp. 1–9.

Bailey, Andrew D., Jr., et al. TICOM and the Analysis of Internal Controls. *Accounting Rev.*, April 1985, *60*(2), pp. 186–201.

Baiman, Stanley and Noel, James. Noncontrollable Costs and Responsibility Accounting. *J. Acc. Res.*, Autumn 1985, *23*(2), pp. 486–501.

Beck, Paul J. and Solomon, Ira. Sampling Risks and Audit Consequences under Alternative Testing Approaches. *Accounting Rev.*, October 1985, *60*(4), pp. 714–23.

Beck, Paul J.; Solomon, Ira and Tomassini, Lawrence A. Subjective Prior Probability Distributions and Audit Risk. *J. Acc. Res.*, Spring 1985, *23*(1), pp. 37–56.

Benston, George J. The Validity of Profits-Structure Studies with Particular Reference to the FTC's Line of Business Data. *Amer. Econ. Rev.*, March 1985, *75*(1), pp. 37–67. [G: U.S.]

Bernard, Victor L. Vertical Information Transfers: The Association between Retailers' Sales Announcements and Suppliers' Security Returns: Discussion. *J. Acc. Res.*, Supp. 1985, *23*, pp. 167–69. [G: U.S.]

Biddle, Gary C. and Martin, R. Kipp. Inflation, Taxes, and Optimal Inventory Policies. *J. Acc. Res.*, Spring 1985, *23*(1), pp. 57–83.

Biddle, Gary C. and Steinberg, Richard. Common Cost Allocation in the Firm. In *Young, H. P., ed.*, 1985, pp. 31–54.

Biggs, Stanley F. and Wild, John J. An Investigation of Auditor Judgment in Analytical Review. *Accounting Rev.*, October 1985, *60*(4), pp. 607–33.

Binder, John J. On the Use of the Multivariate Regression Model in Event Studies [Econometric Models for Testing a Class of Financial Models—An Application of the Nonlinear Multivariate Regression Model]. *J. Acc. Res.*, Spring 1985, *23*(1), pp. 370–83. [G: U.S.]

Boadway, Robin W.; Bruce, Neil and Mintz, Jack. The Role and Design of the Corporate Income Tax. In *Førsund, F. R. and Honkapohja, S., eds.*, 1985, pp. 188–201.

Bradford, G. L. and Debertin, David L. Establishing Linkages between Economic Theory and Enterprise Budgeting for Teaching and Extension Programs. *Southern J. Agr. Econ.*, December 1985, *17*(2), pp. 221–30.

Brown, Lawrence D. and Gardner, John C. Applying Citation Analysis to Evaluate the Research Contributions of Acounting Faculty and Doctoral Programs. *Accounting Rev.*, April 1985, *60*(2), pp. 262–77. [G: U.S.]

Brown, Lawrence D. and Gardner, John C. Using Citation Analysis to Assess the Impact of Journals and Articles on Contemporary Accounting Research (CAR). *J. Acc. Res.*, Spring 1985, *23*(1), pp. 84–109.

Brown, Richard E. Symposium on Current Issues and Developments in Governmental Accounting and Auditing: Their Imapct on Public Policy. *Public Budg. Finance*, Autumn 1985, *5*(3), pp. 116–22.

Brown, Richard E. and Copeland, Ronald M. Current Issues and Developments in Governmental Accounting and Auditing: Impact on Public Policy. *Public Budg. Finance*, Summer 1985, *5*(2), pp. 3–8. [G: U.S.]

Brownell, Peter. Budgetary Systems and the Control of Functionally Differentiated Organizational Activities. *J. Acc. Res.*, Autumn 1985, *23*(2), pp. 502–12.

Bublitz, Bruce; Frecka, Thomas J. and McKeown, James C. Market Association Tests and FASB Statement No. 33 Disclosures: A Reexamination. *J. Acc. Res.*, Supp. 1985, *23*, pp. 1–23. [G: U.S.]

Butler, Stephen A. Application of a Decision Aid in the Judgmental Evaluation of Substantive Test of Details Samples. *J. Acc. Res.*, Autumn 1985, *23*(2), pp. 513–26.

Camion, Caty and Levasseur, Michel. Analyse financière des entreprises, systèmes fiscaux et inflation anticipée: La valeur économique des nombres comptables. (Financial Analysis of Firms, Taxation Systems and Anticipated Inflation. The Economic Value of Accounting Numbers. With English summary.) *Écon. Soc.*, December 1985, *19*(12), pp. 129–43.

Casey, Cornelius and Bartczak, Norman. Using Operating Cash Flow Data to Predict Financial Distress: Some Extensions. *J. Acc. Res.*, Spring 1985, *23*(1), pp. 384–401. [G: U.S.]

Casler, Darwin J. and Hall, Thomas W. Firm-specific Asset Valuation Accuracy Using a Composite Price Index. *J. Acc. Res.*, Spring 1985, *23*(1), pp. 110–22.

Chalos, Peter. Financial Distress: A Comparative Study of Individual, Model, and Committee Assessments. *J. Acc. Res.*, Autumn 1985, *23*(2), pp. 527–43. [G: U.S.]

Chan, James L. The Birth of the Governmental Accounting Standards Board: How? Why? What Next? In *Chan, J. L., ed.*, 1985, pp. 3–32. [G: U.S.]

Clark, Ronald L. and Sweeney, Robert B. Admission to Accounting Programs: Using a Discriminant Model as a Classification Procedure. *Accounting Rev.*, July 1985, *60*(3), pp. 508–18.

Cox, Clifford T. Further Evidence on the Representativeness of Management Earnings Forecasts. *Accounting Rev.*, October 1985, *60*(4), pp. 692–701.   [G: U.S.]

Crum, William F. and Garner, Don E. 1983 Survey of Doctoral Programs in Accounting in the United States and Canada. *Accounting Rev.*, July 1985, *60*(3), pp. 519–25.

Curien, Nicolas. Cost Allocation and Pricing Policy: The Case of French Telecommunications. In *Young, H. P., ed.*, 1985, pp. 167–78.
[G: France]

DeJong, Douglas V.; Forsythe, Robert and Uecker, Wilfred C. The Methodology of Laboratory Markets and Its Implications for Agency Research in Acounting and Auditing. *J. Acc. Res.*, Autumn 1985, *23*(2), pp. 753–93.

Dietrich, J. Richard and Deitrick, James W. Bond Exchanges in the Airline Industry: Analyzing Public Disclosures. *Accounting Rev.*, January 1985, *60*(1), pp. 109–26.   [G: U.S.]

Drtina, Ralph E. and Largay, James A., III. Pitfalls in Calculating Cash Flow from Operations. *Accounting Rev.*, April 1985, *60*(2), pp. 314–26.

Dye, Ronald A. Disclosure of Nonproprietary Information. *J. Acc. Res.*, Spring 1985, *23*(1), pp. 123–45.

Dye, Ronald A. Strategic Accounting Choice and the Effect of Alternative Financial Reporting Requirements. *J. Acc. Res.*, Autumn 1985, *23*(2), pp. 544–74.

Easton, Peter D. Accounting Earnings and Security Valuation: Empirical Evidence of the Fundamental Links. *J. Acc. Res.*, Supp. 1985, *23*, pp. 54–77.   [G: U.S.]

Ekholm, Bo-Göran. Affärsstödjande redovisning. (Business-supporting Accountancy. With English summary.) *Ekon. Samfundets Tidskr.*, 1985, *38*(4), pp. 205–10.

Elliott, John A. and Swieringa, Robert J. Aetna, the SEC and Tax Benefits of Loss Carryforwards. *Accounting Rev.*, July 1985, *60*(3), pp. 531–46.   [G: U.S.]

Farrelly, Gail E.; Ferris, Kenneth R. and Reichenstein, William R. Perceived Risk, Market Risk, and Accounting Determined Risk Measures. *Accounting Rev.*, April 1985, *60*(2), pp. 278–88.   [G: U.S.]

Fellingham, John C. and Newman, D. Paul. Strategic Considerations in Auditing. *Accounting Rev.*, October 1985, *60*(4), pp. 634–50.

Fellingham, John C. and Wolfson, Mark A. Taxes and Risk Sharing. *Accounting Rev.*, January 1985, *60*(1), pp. 10–17.

Fellows, James A. The Economic and Accounting Definitions of Income: Proposals for Reform, a Note. *Amer. Econ.*, Fall 1985, *29*(2), pp. 57–62.

Finley, David R. Counterexamples to Proposed Dollar-Unit Sampling Algorithm [On Sampling Plan Selection with Dollar-Unit Sampling]. *J. Acc. Res.*, Spring 1985, *23*(1), pp. 402–04.

Fried, Dov and Livnat, Joshua. Alternative Interim Reporting Techniques within a Dynamic Framework: A Reply [Interim Statements: An Analytiacal Examination of Alternative Accounting Techniques]. *Accounting Rev.*, April

1985, *60*(2), pp. 295–97.

Fullerton, Don; Lyon, Andrew B. and Rosen, Richard J. Uncertainty, Welfare Cost and the "Adaptability" of U.S. Corporate Taxes. In *Førsund, F. R. and Honkapohja, S., eds.*, 1985, pp. 131–45.   [G: U.S.]

Gálvez, Julio and Tybout, James R. Microeconomic Adjustments in Chile during 1977–81: The Importance of Being a *Grupo*. *World Devel.*, August 1985, *13*(8), pp. 969–94.
[G: Chile]

Gentry, James A.; Newbold, Paul and Whitford, David T. Classifying Bankrupt Firms with Funds Flow Components. *J. Acc. Res.*, Spring 1985, *23*(1), pp. 146–60.

Givoly, Dan. The Formation of Earnings Expectations. *Accounting Rev.*, July 1985, *60*(3), pp. 372–86.   [G: U.S.]

Glezen, G. William and Millar, James A. An Empirical Investigation of Stockholder Reaction to Disclosure Required by ASR No. 250. *J. Acc. Res.*, Autumn 1985, *23*(2), pp. 859–70.
[G: U.S.]

Gnes, Paolo. La Centrale dei Bilanci moltiplica le possibilità dell'analisi finanziaria. (The "Accounts Clearing House" Widens the Sphere of Financial Analysis. With English summary.) *Bancaria*, October 1985, *41*(10), pp. 1041–46.
[G: Italy]

Grimlund, Richard A. A Proposal for Implementing the FASB's "Reasonably Possible" Disclosure Provision for Product Warranty Liabilities. *J. Acc. Res.*, Autumn 1985, *23*(2), pp 575–94.   [G: U.S.]

Groves, Theodore. The Impossibility of Incentive-Compatible and Efficient Full Cost Allocation Schemes. In *Young, H. P., ed.*, 1985, pp. 95–100.

Haka, Susan F.; Gordon, Lawrence A. and Pinches, George E. Sophisticated Capital Budgeting Selection Techniques and Firm Performance. *Accounting Rev.*, October 1985, *60*(4), pp. 651–69.   [G: U.S.]

Ham, Jane; Losell, Donna and Smieliauskas, Wally. An Empirical Study of Error Characteristics in Accounting Populations. *Accounting Rev.*, July 1985, *60*(3), pp. 387–406.

Harrell, Adrian; Caldwell, Charles and Doty, Edwin. Within-Person Expectancy Theory Predictions of Accounting Students' Motivation to Achieve Academic Success. *Accounting Rev.*, October 1985, *60*(4), pp. 724–35.
[G: U.S.]

Healy, Paul M. The Effect of Bonus Schemes on Accounting Decisions. *J. Acc. Econ.*, April 1985, *7*(1–3), pp. 85–107.   [G: U.S.]

Hirschey, Mark and Weygandt, Jerry J. Amortization Policy for Advertising and Research and Development Expenditures. *J. Acc. Res.*, Spring 1985, *23*(1), pp. 326–35.   [G: U.S.]

Hopwood, William S. and McKeown, James C. The Incremental Information Content of Interim Expenses over Interim Sales. *J. Acc. Res.*, Spring 1985, *23*(1), pp. 161–74.
[G: U.S.]

Hopwood, William S. and Newbold, Paul. Alternative Interim Reporting Techniques within a Dynamic Framework: Comments and Extensions [Interim Statements: An Analytical Examination of Alternative Accounting Techniques]. *Accounting Rev.*, April 1985, *60*(2), pp. 289–94.

Hunt, Herbert G., III. Potential Determinants of Corporate Inventory Accounting Decisions. *J. Acc. Res.*, Autumn 1985, *23*(2), pp. 448–67. [G: U.S.]

Ingram, Robert W. A Descriptive Analysis of Municipal Bond Price Data for Use in Accounting Research. *J. Acc. Res.*, Autumn 1985, *23*(2), pp. 595–618. [G: U.S.]

Jennings, Robert and Starks, Laura. Information Content and the Speed of Stock Price Adjustment. *J. Acc. Res.*, Spring 1985, *23*(1), pp. 336–50. [G: U.S.]

Johnson, Steven B. The Economic Function of Doctoral Programs in Accounting: Alternative Theories and Educational Implications. *Accounting Rev.*, October 1985, *60*(4), pp. 736–43.

Johnson, W. Bruce. Valuation Implications of SFAS No. 33 Data for Electric Utility Investors: Discussion. *J. Acc. Res.*, Supp. 1985, *23*, pp. 48–53. [G: U.S.]

Jorgensen, Jerry L. and Mano, Ronald M. Financial Statement Disclosure of Uninsured Risks. *J. Risk Ins.*, March 1985, *52*(1), pp. 133–43. [G: U.S.]

Kanodia, Chandra S. Stochastic Monitoring and Moral Hazard. *J. Acc. Res.*, Spring 1985, *23*(1), pp. 175–93.

Kaplan, Robert S. Evidence on the Effect of Bonus Schemes on Accounting Procedure and Accrual Decisions: Comments. *J. Acc. Econ.*, April 1985, *7*(1–3), pp. 109–13. [G: U.S.]

Kaplan, Steven E. The Effect of Combining Compliance and Substantive Tasks on Auditor Consensus. *J. Acc. Res.*, Autumn 1985, *23*(2), pp. 871–77.

Kaplan, Steven E. and Reckers, Philip M. J. An Examination of Auditor Performance Evaluation. *Accounting Rev.*, July 1985, *60*(3), pp. 477–87.

Kelly, Lauren. Corporate Management Lobbying on FAS No. 8: Some Further Evidence. *J. Acc. Res.*, Autumn 1985, *23*(2), pp. 619–32. [G: U.S.]

Kettunen, Pertti. Tuloslaskennan teorian kehittämisen perusvalinnat. (Alternative Avenues Open to the Development of Financial Accounting Theories. With English summary.) *Liiketaloudellinen Aikak.*, 1985, *34*(2), pp. 177–90.

Khan, Muhammad Akram. Role of the Auditor in an Islamic Economy. *J. Res. Islamic Econ.*, Summer 1985, *3*(1), pp. 31–42.

Kilpatrick, Bob; Putnam, Karl and Schneider, Harold. Convertible Securities and Earnings per Share: A Competitive Ranking Algorithm. *Accounting Rev.*, July 1985, *60*(3), pp. 526–30.

Knapp, Michael C. Audit Conflict: An Empirical Study of the Perceived Ability of Auditors to Resist Management Pressure. *Accounting Rev.*, April 1985, *60*(2), pp. 202–11. [G: U.S.]

Knechel, W. Robert. An Analysis of Alternative Error Assumptions in Modeling the Reliability of Accounting Systems. *J. Acc. Res.*, Spring 1985, *23*(1), pp. 194–212.

Kott, Phillip S. A Note on Model-based Stratification [Model-based Stratification in Inventory Cost Estimation]. *J. Bus. Econ. Statist.*, July 1985, *3*(3), pp. 284–86. [G: U.S.]

Lakonishok, Josef and Ofer, Aharon R. The Information Content of General Price Level Earnings: A Reply. *Accounting Rev.*, October 1985, *60*(4), pp. 711–13. [G: U.S.]

Lee, Chi-Wen Jevons. Stochastic Properties of Cross-sectional Financial Data. *J. Acc. Res.*, Spring 1985, *23*(1), pp. 213–27. [G: U.S.]

Lee, Chi-Wen Jevons and Hsieh, David A. Choice of Inventory Accounting Methods: Comparative Analyses Alternative Hypotheses. *J. Acc. Res.*, Autumn 1985, *23*(2), pp. 468–85. [G: U.S.]

van Leeuwen, Peter H. The Prediction of Business Failure at Rabobank. *J. Bank Res.*, Summer 1985, *16*(2), pp. 91–98.

Leonard, Herman B. Measuring and Reporting the Financial Condition of Public Organizations. In *Chan, J. L., ed.*, 1985, pp. 117–48. [G: U.S.]

Libby, Robert. Availability and the Generation of Hypotheses in Analytical Review. *J. Acc. Res.*, Autumn 1985, *23*(2), pp. 648–67. [G: U.S.]

Libby, Robert; Artman, James T. and Willingham, John J. Process Susceptibility, Control Risk, and Audit Planning. *Accounting Rev.*, April 1985, *60*(2), pp. 212–30.

Magliolo, Joseph, III. Accounting Earnings and Security Valuation: Empirical Evidence of the Fundamental Links: Discussion. *J. Acc. Res.*, Supp. 1985, *23*, pp. 78–80.

McKinley, Sue; Pany, Kurt and Reckers, Philip M. J. An Examination of the Influence of CPA Firm Type, Size, and MAS Provision on Loan Officer Decisions and Perceptions. *J. Acc. Res.*, Autumn 1985, *23*(2), pp. 887–96. [G: U.S.]

McNichols, Maureen. The Ex Ante Information Content of Accounting Information Systems: Discussion. *J. Acc. Res.*, Supp. 1985, *23*, pp. 140–43. [G: U.S.]

Mirman, Leonard J.; Tauman, Yair and Zang, Israel. On the Use of Game-Theoretic Concepts in Cost Accounting. In *Young, H. P., ed.*, 1985, pp. 55–77.

Mutchler, Jane F. A Multivariate Analysis of the Auditor's Going-Concern Opinion Decision. *J. Acc. Res.*, Autumn 1985, *23*(2), pp. 668–82. [G: U.S.]

Nakamura, Nobuichiro and Iyoda, Takatoshi. A Note of Study on the Accounting Institutions in France (2)—Concerning the New Provisions on Accounting of the "Code de commerce" and "Loi n° 66–537 du 24 juillet 1966 sur les sociétés commerciales." (In Japanese. With English summary.) *Osaka Econ. Pap.*, March 1985, *34*(4), pp. 46–80.   [G: France]

Neter, John; Johnson, Johnny R. and Leitch, Robert A. Characteristics of Dollar-Unit Taints and Error Rates in Accounts Receivable and Inventory. *Accounting Rev.*, July 1985, *60*(3), pp. 488–99.   [G: U.S.]

Nobes, Christopher W. International Variations in Perceptions of Accounting Journals. *Accounting Rev.*, October 1985, *60*(4), pp. 702–05.

Oksanen, Heikki. Inflaation vaikutus yritysten kirjanpitoon, yritysverotukseen ja yritystutkimuksen tunnuslukuihin. (The Effect on Inflation of Accounting, Corporate Taxation, and Financial Ratios. With English summary.) *Liiketaloudellinen Aikak.*, 1985, *34*(4), pp. 422–38.

Olsen, Chris. Valuation Implications of SFAS No. 33 Data for Electric Utility Investors. *J. Acc. Res.*, Supp. 1985, *23*, pp. 28–47.   [G: U.S.]

Olsen, Chris and Dietrich, J. Richard. Vertical Information Transfers: The Association between Retailers' Sales Announcements and Suppliers' Security Returns. *J. Acc. Res.*, Supp. 1985, *23*, pp. 144–66.   [G: U.S.]

Parry, Robert W., Jr. A Digest of Authoritative Pronouncements on Governmental Accounting and Reporting. In *Chan, J. L., ed.*, 1985, pp. 77–84.   [G: U.S.]

Patton, James M. The Governmental Financial Reporting Entity: Review and Analysis. In *Chan, J. L., ed.*, 1985, pp. 85–116.   [G: U.S.]

Pauchard, A. Corporate Financial Reporting in Switzerland and Accounting Principles. In *Meier, H. B., ed.*, 1985, pp. 119–33.   [G: Switzerland]

Penno, Mark. Informational Issues in the Financial Reporting Process. *J. Acc. Res.*, Spring 1985, *23*(1), pp. 240–55.

Picur, Ronald D. Cost Accounting Services to Governments: An Agency Theory Perspective. In *Clark, T. N., ed.*, 1985, pp. 117–33.   [G: U.S.]

Plumlee, R. David. The Standard of Objectivity for Internal Auditors: Memory and Bias Effects. *J. Acc. Res.*, Autumn 1985, *23*(2), pp. 683–99.   [G: U.S.]

Popov, G. Kh. Total Cost Accounting in the Economy's Basic Link. *Prob. Econ.*, August 1985, *28*(4), pp. 3–18.

Quirin, G. David. Fiscal Transfer Pricing: Accounting for Reality. In *Rugman, A. M. and Eden, L., eds.*, 1985, pp. 132–48.

Ransom, Charles R. The Ex Ante Information Content of Accounting Information Systems. *J. Acc. Res.*, Supp. 1985, *23*, pp. 124–39.   [G: U.S.]

Richardson, A. W. The Measurement of the Current Portion of Long-term Lease Obligations—Some Evidence from Practice [When Current Is Noncurrent and Vice Versa!]. *Accounting Rev.*, October 1985, *60*(4), pp. 744–52.   [G: U.S.]

Ricks, William E. and Hughes, John S. Market Reactions to a Non-discretionary Accounting

Change: The Case of Long-term Investments. *Accounting Rev.*, January 1985, *60*(1), pp. 33–52.   [G: U.S.]

Rogers, Richard L. and Menon, Krishnagopal. Accounting for Deferred-Payment Notes. *Accounting Rev.*, July 1985, *60*(3), pp. 547–57.

Salamon, Gerald L. Accounting Rates of Return. *Amer. Econ. Rev.*, June 1985, *75*(3), pp. 495–504.   [G: U.S.]

Samuelson, Bruce A. and Murdoch, Brock. The Information Content of General Price Level Adjusted Earnings: A Comment. *Accounting Rev.*, October 1985, *60*(4), pp. 706–10.   [G: U.S.]

Scapens, Robert W. and Sale, J. Timothy. An International Study of Accounting Practices in Divisionalized Companies and Their Associations with Organizational Variables. *Accounting Rev.*, April 1985, *60*(2), pp. 231–47.   [G: U.S.; U.K.]

Schneider, Arnold. The Reliance of External Auditors on the Internal Audit Function. *J. Acc. Res.*, Autumn 1985, *23*(2), pp. 911–19.   [G: U.S.]

Schreuder, H. Accounting Research and Practice. In *Rinnooy Kan, A. H. G., ed.*, 1985, pp. 1–30.

Schwartz, Kenneth B. and Menon, Krishnagopal. Auditor Switches by Failing Firms. *Accounting Rev.*, April 1985, *60*(2), pp. 248–61.   [G: U.S.]

Scognamiglio, Angelo. Alcune riflessioni su una "teoria matematica del bilancio contabile." (With English summary.) *Stud. Econ.*, 1985, *40*(25), pp. 151–67.

Selto, Frank H. and Clouse, Maclyn L. An Investigation of Managers' Adaptation to SFAS No. 2: Accounting for Research and Development Costs. *J. Acc. Res.*, Autumn 1985, *23*(2), pp. 700–717.   [G: U.S.]

Shalchi, Hossein and Smith, Charles H. Research on Accounting for Changing Prices: Theory, Evidence, and Implications. *Quart. Rev. Econ. Bus.*, Winter 1985, *25*(4), pp. 5–37.   [G: U.S.]

Sharp, Florence C. and Ingram, Robert W. Measuring the Periodic Performance of Government: Policy and Research Issues. In *Chan, J. L., ed.*, 1985, pp. 149–79.   [G: U.S.]

Short, Daniel G. A Comparison of Alternative Methods of Estimating Constant Dollar Depreciation. *Accounting Rev.*, July 1985, *60*(3), pp. 500–503.

Shubik, Martin. The Cooperative Form, the Value, and the Allocation of Joint Costs and Benefits. In *Young, H. P., ed.*, 1985, pp. 79–94.

Smieliauskas, Wally. Sensitivity Analysis of the Realized Risks of Auditing with Uncertainty Concerning Internal Control Evaluations. *J. Acc. Res.*, Autumn 1985, *23*(2), pp. 718–39.

Srivastava, Rajendra P. A Note on Internal Control Systems with Control Components in Series. *Accounting Rev.*, July 1985, *60*(3), pp. 504–07.

Staubus, George J. An Induced Theory of Accounting Measurement. *Accounting Rev.*, January 1985, *60*(1), pp. 53–75. [G: U.S.]

Strecker, Mary F. Selected Teaching and Learning Aids in the Area of Governmental and Nonprofit Accountability. *Public Budg. Finance,* Spring 1985, *5*(1), pp. 100–106. [G: U.S.]

Swanson, Edward P.; Shearon, Winston T. and Thomas, Lynn R. Predicting Current Cost Operating Profit Using Component Models Incorporating Analysts' Forecasts. *Accounting Rev.,* October 1985, *60*(4), pp. 681–91. [G: U.S.]

Swieringa, Robert J. and Morse, Dale. Accounting for Hybrid Convertible Debentures. *Accounting Rev.*, January 1985, *60*(1), pp. 127–33. [G: U.S.]

Toribe, Shinji and Touhara, Hideko. Segment Financial Disclosure and CAPM. (In Japanese. With English summary.) *Osaka Econ. Pap.,* March 1985, *34*(4), pp. 23–45. [G: U.S.]

Trotman, Ken T. The Review Process and the Accuracy of Auditor Judgments. *J. Acc. Res.,* Autumn 1985, *23*(2), pp. 740–52.
[G: Australia]

Trotman, Ken T. and Yetton, Philip W. The Effect of the Review Process on Auditor Judgments. *J. Acc. Res.,* Spring 1985, *23*(1), pp. 256–67.

Tsui, Kam-Wah; Matsumura, Ella Mae and Tsui, Kwok-Leung. Multinomial-Dirichlet Bounds for Dollar-Unit Sampling in Auditing. *Accounting Rev.,* January 1985, *60*(1), pp. 76–96.

Tybout, James R. Microeconomic Adjustments during the Reforms: Introduction. *World Devel.,* August 1985, *13*(8), pp. 941–47.

Uecker, Wilfred C.; Schepanski, Albert and Shin, Joon. Toward a Positive Theory of Information Evaluation: Relevant Tests of Competing Models in a Principal-Agency Setting. *Accounting Rev.,* July 1985, *60*(3), pp. 430–57.

Umapathy, Srinivasan. Teaching Behavioral Aspects of Performance Evaluation: An Experiential Approach. *Accounting Rev.,* January 1985, *60*(1), pp. 97–108. [G: U.S.]

Van Wymeersch, Charles. Le traitement comptable des logiciels informatiques. (With English summary.) *Cah. Écon. Bruxelles,* 2nd Trimester 1985, (106), pp. 217–45. [G: U.S.; EEC]

Wallace, Wanda A. Accounting Policies and the Measurement of Urban Fiscal Strain. In *Chan, J. L., ed.,* 1985, pp. 181–212. [G: U.S.]

Wallace, Wanda A. Objectives for the Governmental Accounting Standards Board. In *Chan, J. L., ed.,* 1985, pp. 33–76. [G: U.S.]

Waller, William S. Self-selection and the Probability of Quitting: A Contracting Approach to Employee Turnover in Public Accounting. *J. Acc. Res.,* Autumn 1985, *23*(2), pp. 817–28.

Waymire, Gregory. Earnings Volatility and Voluntary Management Forecast Disclosure. *J. Acc. Res.,* Spring 1985, *23*(1), pp. 268–95.
[G: U.S.]

Westworth, Chris N. Accounting Standards—A Framework for Tax Assessment. *Australian Tax Forum,* Spring 1985, *2*(3), pp. 243–47.

Williams, Paul F. A Descriptive Analysis of Authorship in *The Accounting Review. Account-*

ing Rev., April 1985, *60*(2), pp. 300–313.
[G: U.S.]

Willinger, G. Lee. A Contingent Claims Model for Pension Costs. *J. Acc. Res.,* Spring 1985, *23*(1), pp. 351–59.

Wright, Roger L. Reply [Model-based Stratification in Inventory Cost Estimation]. *J. Bus. Econ. Statist.,* July 1985, *3*(3), pp. 286–88.
[G: U.S.]

Young, H. Peyton. Producer Incentives in Cost Allocation. *Econometrica,* July 1985, *53*(4), pp. 757–65.

Young, S. Mark. Participative Budgeting: The Effects of Risk Aversion and Asymmetric Information on Budgetary Slack. *J. Acc. Res.,* Autumn 1985, *23*(2), pp. 829–42.

600 Industrial Organization; Technological Change; Industry Studies

610 INDUSTRIAL ORGANIZATION AND PUBLIC POLICY

611 Market Structure and Corporate Strategy

6110 Market Structure and Corporate Strategy

Abbott, Alden F. Foreign Competition and Relevant Market Definition under the Department of Justice's Merger Guidelines. *Antitrust Bull.,* Summer 1985, *30*(2), pp. 299–336.

Abolafia, Mitchel Y. Self-regulation as Market Maintenance: An Organization Perspective. In *Noll, R. G., ed.,* 1985, pp. 312–43. [G: U.S.]

Adelman, Morris A. and Stangle, Bruce E. Profitability and Market Share. In *[McGowan, J. J.],* 1985, pp. 101–13. [G: U.S.]

Afridi, Usman. Dynamics of Change in Pakistan's Large-Scale Manufacturing Sector. *Pakistan Devel. Rev.,* Autumn-Winter 1985, *24*(3/4), pp. 463–76. [G: Pakistan]

Agthe, Donald E. Revenue Effects from Changes in a Declining Block Pricing Structure: Comment. *Land Econ.,* February 1985, *61*(1), pp. 79–80. [G: U.S.]

Ahmed, Meekal Aziz. Dynamics of Change in Pakistan's Large-Scale Manufacturing Sector: Comments. *Pakistan Devel. Rev.,* Autumn-Winter 1985, *24*(3/4), pp. 477–78.

Aislabie, Colin J. The Joint Determination of 'Quality' and Price in Standardized Products: A Comparative Dynamic Analysis. *Managerial Dec. Econ.,* September 1985, *6*(3), pp. 141–46.

Alexander, Donald L. An Empirical Test of the Mutual Forebearance Hypothesis: The Case of Bank Holding Companies. *Southern Econ. J.,* July 1985, *52*(1), pp. 122–40. [G: U.S.]

Aliber, Robert Z. Transfer Pricing: A Taxonomy of Impacts on Economic Welfare. In *Rugman, A. M. and Eden, L., eds.,* 1985, pp. 82–97.

Amato, Louis and Wilder, Ronald P. The Effects of Firm Size on Profit Rates in U.S. Manufacturing. *Southern Econ. J.,* July 1985, *52*(1), pp. 181–90. [G: U.S.]

Amsden, Alice H. The Division of Labour Is Limited by the Rate of Growth of the Market: The Taiwan Machine Tool Industry in the 1970s. *Cambridge J. Econ.*, September 1985, 9(3), pp. 271–84. **[G: Taiwan]**

Andersen, Arthur T. Industrial Organization in Oil Markets since the Embargo. *Rev. Ind. Organ.*, 1985, 2(2), pp. 194–216. **[G: Global]**

Anderson, James E. and Kraus, Marvin. An Econometric Model of Regulated Airline Flight Rivalry. In *Keeler, T. E., ed.*, 1985, pp. 1–26. **[G: U.S.]**

Anderson, Simon. Product Choice with Economies of Scope. *Reg. Sci. Urban Econ.*, June 1985, 15(2), pp. 277–94.

Angelmar, Reinhard. Market Structure and Research Intensity in High-Technological-Opportunity Industries. *J. Ind. Econ.*, September 1985, 34(1), pp. 69–79. **[G: U.S.; Canada; EEC]**

Antal, László. About the Property Incentive (Interest in Property). *Acta Oecon.*, 1985, 34(3/4), pp. 275–86. **[G: Hungary]**

Appelbaum, Elie and Lim, Chin. Contestable Markets under Uncertainty. *Rand J. Econ.*, Spring 1985, 16(1), pp. 28–40.

d'Aspremont, Claude and Gabszewicz, Jean Jaskold. Quasi-monopolies. *Economica*, May 1985, 52(206), pp. 141–51.

d'Aspremont, Claude and Jacquemin, Alexis. Measuring the Power to Monopolize: A Simple-Game Theoretic Approach. *Europ. Econ. Rev.*, February 1985, 27(1), pp. 57–74.

Atack, Jeremy. Industrial Structure and the Emergence of the Modern Industrial Corporation. *Exploration Econ. Hist.*, January 1985, 22(1), pp. 29–52. **[G: U.S.]**

Awh, Robert Y. and Primeaux, Walter J., Jr. Managerial Discretion and Expense Preference Behavior. *Rev. Econ. Statist.*, May 1985, 67(2), pp. 224–31. **[G: U.S.]**

Baker, Jonathan B. and Bresnahan, Timothy F. The Gains from Merger or Collusion in Product-Differentiated Industries. In *Geroski, P. A.; Phlips, L. and Ulph, A., eds.*, 1985, pp. 59–76. **[G: U.S.]**

Baker, Jonathan B. and Bresnahan, Timothy F. The Gains from Merger or Collusion in Product-differentiated Industries. *J. Ind. Econ.*, June 1985, 33(4), pp. 427–44. **[G: U.S.]**

Baldwin, John R. and Górecki, Paul K. The Determinants of Small Plant Market Share in Canadian Manufacturing Industries in the 1970s. *Rev. Econ. Statist.*, February 1985, 67(1), pp. 156–61. **[G: Canada]**

Ballantine, John W.; Cleveland, Frederick W. and Koeller, C. Timothy. Profit Differences and Corporate Power: Some Empirical Surprises. *J. Econ. Issues*, June 1985, 19(2), pp. 355–64. **[G: U.S.]**

Barca, Fabrizio. Modifiche nella relazione fra scala produttiva ed efficienza economica e sviluppo della piccola impresa. (Changes in the Relations between Size and Economic Efficiency and Development of Small Company. With English summary.) *Econ. Lavoro*, Jan.-Mar. 1985, 19(1), pp. 61–79. **[G: Italy]**

Barca, Fabrizio. Tendenze nella struttura dimensionale dell'industria italiana: una verifica empirica del "modello di specializzazione flessibile.". (Changes in the Size of Structure of the Italian Industry: a Test of the "Flexible Specialization Model." With English summary.) *Polit. Econ.*, April 1985, 1(1), pp. 71–109. **[G: Italy]**

Barron, John M.; Loewenstein, Mark A. and Umbeck, John R. Predatory Pricing: The Case of the Retail Gasoline Market. *Contemp. Policy Issues*, Spring, Pt. 2, 1985, 3(3), pp. 131–39. **[G: U.S.]**

Bársony, Jenö and Síklaky, István. Some Reflections on Socialist Entrepreneurship. *Acta Oecon.*, 1985, 34(1–2), pp. 51–64. **[G: Hungary]**

Barzel, Yoram. Transaction Costs: Are They Just Costs? *Z. ges. Staatswiss. (JITE)*, March 1985, 141(1), pp. 4–16.

Bates, Timothy. Impact of Preferential Procurement Policies on Minority-owned Businesses. *Rev. Black Polit. Econ.*, Summer 1985, 14(1), pp. 51–65. **[G: U.S.]**

Batsell, Richard R. and Polking, John C. A New Class of Market Share Models. *Marketing Sci.*, Summer 1985, 4(3), pp. 177–98. **[G: U.S.]**

Bauer, Tamás. Reform Policy in the Complexity of Economic Policy. *Acta Oecon.*, 1985, 34(3/4), pp. 263–73. **[G: Hungary]**

Baumol, William J. Industry Structure Analysis and Public Policy. In *Feiwel, G. R., ed. (II)*, 1985, pp. 311–27.

Baumol, William J. and Ordover, Janusz A. Use of Antitrust to Subvert Competition. *J. Law Econ.*, May 1985, 28(2), pp. 247–65. **[G: OECD]**

Baysinger, Barry D. and Butler, Henry N. The Role of Corporate Law in the Theory of the Firm. *J. Law Econ.*, April 1985, 28(1), pp. 179–91. **[G: U.S.]**

Becker, Edmund R. and Sloan, Frank A. Hospital Ownership and Performance. *Econ. Inquiry*, January 1985, 23(1), pp. 21–36. **[G: U.S.]**

Behrens, Peter. The Firm as a Complex Institution. *Z. ges. Staatswiss. (JITE)*, March 1985, 141(1), pp. 62–75.

Bennett, Douglas C. and Sharpe, Kenneth E. The World Automobile Industry and its Implications. In *Newfarmer, R. S., ed.*, 1985, pp. 193–226. **[G: Latin America; Selected Countries]**

Benston, George J. The Validity of Profits-Structure Studies with Particular Reference to the FTC's Line of Business Data. *Amer. Econ. Rev.*, March 1985, 75(1), pp. 37–67. **[G: U.S.]**

Bernheim, B. Douglas and Whinston, Michael D. Common Marketing Agency as a Device for Facilitating Collusion. *Rand J. Econ.*, Summer 1985, 16(2), pp. 269–81.

Besen, Stanley M. and Johnson, Leland L. Regulation of Broadcast Station Ownership: Evidence and Theory. In *Noam, E. M., ed.*, 1985, pp. 364–89. **[G: U.S.]**

Bhattacharya, Gautam. Strategic Learning and Entry-Equilibrium. *J. Econ. Dynam. Control*, October 1985, *9*(2), pp. 195–223.

Bittlingmayer, George. Did Antitrust Policy Cause the Great Merger Wave? *J. Law Econ.*, April 1985, *28*(1), pp. 77–118.   [G: U.S.]

Blair, Roger D.; Cooper, Thomas E. and Kaserman, David L. A Note on Vertical Integration as Entry. *Int. J. Ind. Organ.*, June 1985, *3*(2), pp. 219–29.

Blair, Roger D. and Kaserman, David L. Unanswered Questions about Franchising: Reply. *Southern Econ. J.*, January 1985, *51*(3), pp. 933–36.

Bock, Betty. An Economist Appraises Vertical Restraints. *Antitrust Bull.*, Spring 1985, *30*(1), pp. 117–41.   [G: U.S.]

Borenstein, Severin. Price Discrimination in Free-Entry Markets. *Rand J. Econ.*, Autumn 1985, *16*(3), pp. 380–97.

Borner, Silvio, et al. Global Structural Change and International Competition among Industrial Firms: The Case of Switzerland. *Kyklos*, 1985, *38*(1), pp. 77–103.   [G: Switzerland]

Bowie, Nolan A. Comment: Antitrust, Concentration, and Competition. In *Noam, E. M., ed.*, 1985, pp. 397–402.   [G: U.S.]

Bowman, Edward H. Generalizing about Strategic Change: Methodological Pitfalls and Promising Solutions. In *Pennings, J. M., et al.*, 1985, pp. 319–35.

Boyer, Kenneth D. Is There a Principle for Defining Industries? Reply. *Southern Econ. J.*, October 1985, *52*(2), pp. 542–46.

Boyer, Marcel and Jacquemin, Alexis. Organizational and Industrial Actions for Efficiency and Market Power: An Integrated Approach. In *Schwalbach, J., ed.*, 1985, pp. 223–46.

Brambilla, Francesco. Una semplice dimostrazione della legge di Zipf nelle attività produttive. (A Simple Demonstration of Zipf's Law in Productive Activities. With English summary.) *Rivista Int. Sci. Econ. Com.*, January 1985, *32*(1), pp. 84–86.

Brander, James A. and Spencer, Barbara J. Tacit Collusion, Free Entry, and Welfare. *J. Ind. Econ.*, March 1985, *33*(3), pp. 277–94.

Bresnahan, Timothy F. Post-entry Competition in the Plain Paper Copier Market. *Amer. Econ. Rev.*, May 1985, *75*(2), pp. 15–19. [G: U.S.]

Bresnahan, Timothy F. and Reiss, Peter C. Dealer and Manufacturer Margins. *Rand J. Econ.*, Summer 1985, *16*(2), pp. 253–68.   [G: U.S.]

Brock, William A. and Evans, David S. The Economics of Regulatory Tiering. *Rand J. Econ.*, Autumn 1985, *16*(3), pp. 398–409.

Brotman, Stuart N. Comment: Analyzing the Critical, Unknown Factor. In *Noam, E. M., ed.*, 1985, pp. 180–86.   [G: U.S.]

Buck, Trevor. The Convergence of Economic Systems and the M-Form. *J. Econ. Behav. Organ.*, June 1985, *6*(2), pp. 123–37.
          [G: U.S.S.R.; W. Germany]

Bühner, Rolf. Internal Organization and Returns: An Empirical Analysis of Large Diversified German Corporations. In *Schwalbach, J., ed.*, 1985, pp. 197–222.   [G: W. Germany]

Bulow, Jeremy I.; Geanakoplos, John D. and Klemperer, Paul D. Multimarket Oligopoly: Strategic Substitutes and Complements. *J. Polit. Econ.*, June 1985, *93*(3), pp. 488–511.

Burns, Penny. Market Structure and Buyer Behaviour: Price Adjustment in a Multi-object Progressive Oral Auction. *J. Econ. Behav. Organ.*, September 1985, *6*(3), pp. 275–300.

Button, K. J. Potential Differences in the Degree of X-Inefficiency between Industrial Sectors in the United Kingdom. *Quart. Rev. Econ. Bus.*, Autumn 1985, *25*(3), pp. 85–95.   [G: U.K.]

Cable, John R. Capital Market Information and Industrial Performance: The Role of West German Banks. *Econ. J.*, March 1985, *95*(377), pp. 118–32.   [G: W. Germany]

Cable, John R. The Bank–Industry Relationship in West Germany: Performance and Policy Aspects. In *Schwalbach, J., ed.*, 1985, pp. 17–40.   [G: W. Germany]

Cable, John R. and Yasuki, Hirohiko. Internal Organisation, Business Groups and Corporate Performance: An Empirical Test of the Multidivisional Hypothesis in Japan. *Int. J. Ind. Organ.*, December 1985, *3*(4), pp. 401–20.
          [G: Japan; U.K.; U.S.; W. Germany]

Calvani, Terry and Langenfeld, James. An Overview of the Current Debate on Resale Price Maintenance. *Contemp. Policy Issues*, Spring, Pt. 1, 1985, *3*(3), pp. 1–8.   [G: U.S.]

Camerer, Colin. Thinking Economically about Strategy. In *Pennings, J. M., et al.*, 1985, pp. 64–75.

Carré, Denis. Les modalités de la concurrence internationale et les performances des secteurs industriels français. (The International Competition and the Performance of French Industries. With English summary.) *L'Actual. Econ.*, March 1985, *61*(1), pp. 51–72.
          [G: France]

Casson, Mark. Multinational Monopolies and International Cartels. In *Buckley, P. J. and Casson, M.*, 1985, pp. 60–97.

Casson, Mark. Multinationals and Intermediate Product Trade. In *Buckley, P. J. and Casson, M.*, 1985, pp. 144–71.

Castanias, Richard P. A Test of the OPEC Cartel Hypothesis: 1974–1983: Discussion. *J. Finance*, July 1985, *40*(3), pp. 1006–08.
          [G: OPEC]

Cave, Jonathan A. K. A Further Comment on Preemptive Patenting and the Persistence of Monopoly. *Amer. Econ. Rev.*, March 1985, *75*(1), pp. 256–58.

Caves, Douglas W., et al. The Effect of New Entry on Productivity Growth in the U.S. Airline Industry 1947–1981. *Logist. Transp. Rev.*, December 1985, *21*(4), pp. 299–335.   [G: U.S.]

Caves, Richard E. International Trade and Industrial Organization: Problems, Solved and Unsolved. *Europ. Econ. Rev.*, August 1985, *28*(3), pp. 377–95.

Caves, Richard E. and Williamson, Peter J. What

Is Product Differentiation, *Really? J. Ind. Econ.*, December 1985, *34*(2), pp. 113–32. [G: Australia]

Channon, D. F. Strategic Management: Key Concepts and Future Directions. In *Rinnooy Kan, A. H. G., ed.*, 1985, pp. 115–39. [G: U.S.; Japan]

Chappell, Henry W., Jr. and Addison, John T. Relative Prices, Concentration, and Money Growth: Reply. *Amer. Econ. Rev.*, March 1985, *75*(1), pp. 279–80. [G: U.S.]

Chappell, William F. and Cottle, Rex L. Sources of Concentration-related Profits. *Southern Econ. J.*, April 1985, *51*(4), pp. 1031–37. [G: U.S.]

Choi, Eun Kwan; Menezes, Carmen F. and Tressler, John H. A Theory of Price-fixing Rings. *Quart. J. Econ.*, May 1985, *100*(2), pp. 465–78.

Churchill, Neil C. and Lewis, Virginia L. Profitability of Small-Business Lending. *J. Bank Res.*, Summer 1985, *16*(2), pp. 63–71. [G: U.S.]

Clark, Robert C. Agency Costs versus Fiduciary Duties. In *Pratt, J. W. and Zeckhauser, R. J., eds.*, 1985, pp. 55–79.

Coate, Malcolm B. Techniques for Protecting against Collusion in Sealed Bid Markets. *Antitrust Bull.*, Winter 1985, *30*(4), pp. 897–913. [G: U.S.]

Cohen, Linda. Private Contracting versus Public Regulation as a Solution to the Natural Monopoly Problem: Comment. In *Poole, R. W., Jr., ed.*, 1985, pp. 115–19. [G: U.S.]

Comanor, William S. and Frech, H. E., III. The Competitive Effects of Vertical Agreements? *Amer. Econ. Rev.*, June 1985, *75*(3), pp. 539–46. [G: U.S.]

Comanor, William S. and Kirkwood, John B. Resale Price Maintenance and Antitrust Policy. *Contemp. Policy Issues*, Spring, Pt. 1, 1985, *3*(3), pp. 9–16. [G: U.S.]

Comanor, William S. and Miyao, Takahiro. The Organization and Relative Productivity of Japanese and American Industry. *Managerial Dec. Econ.*, June 1985, *6*(2), pp. 88–92. [G: Japan; U.S.]

de Combret, François. A European View of the Internationalization of Industry. In *Zukin, S., ed.*, 1985, pp. 90–95.

Conn, Robert L. A Re-examination of Merger Studies That Use the Capital Asset Pricing Model Methodology. *Cambridge J. Econ.*, March 1985, *9*(1), pp. 43–56.

Connolly, Robert A. and Schwartz, Steven. The Intertemporal Behavior of Economic Profits. *Int. J. Ind. Organ.*, December 1985, *3*(4), pp. 379–400. [G: U.S.]

Coughlan, Anne T. Competition and Cooperation in Marketing Channel Choice: Theory and Application. *Marketing Sci.*, Spring 1985, *4*(2), pp. 110–29. [G: Global]

Coughlin, Cletus C. and Watkins, Thomas G. The Impact of International Intra-firm Trade on Domestic Concentration Ratios. *Rev. Ind. Organ.*, 1985, *2*(3), pp. 232–49. [G: U.S.]

Cox, David and Harris, Richard. Trade Liberalization and Industrial Organization: Some Estimates for Canada. *J. Polit. Econ.*, February 1985, *93*(1), pp. 115–45. [G: Canada]

Coxon, P. J. and Jones, J. C. H. Positive Economics and Public Policy: Some Canadian Evidence on Policy Change and Antitrust. *Antitrust Bull.*, Summer 1985, *30*(2), pp. 365–99. [G: Canada]

Cramer, Curtis A. Horizontal Integration of the Natural Gas Pipeline Industry: An Exercise in Gas Pooling. *Rev. Ind. Organ.*, 1985, *2*(1), pp. 68–78. [G: U.S.]

Crampes, Claude and Moreaux, Michel. Intégration verticale et rendements décroissants. (Vertical Integration and Decreasing Returns. With English summary.) *Revue Écon.*, July 1985, *36*(4), pp. 669–85.

Craven, John. Peak-Load Pricing and Short-run Marginal Cost. *Econ. J.*, September 1985, *95*(379), pp. 778–80.

Crew, Michael A. and Kleindorfer, Paul R. Governance Costs of Rate-of-Return Regulation. *Z. ges. Staatswiss. (JITE)*, March 1985, *141*(1), pp. 104–23.

Cromley, Robert G. and Green, Milford B. Joint Venture Activity Patterns of U.S. Firms, 1972–1979. *Growth Change*, July 1985, *16*(3), pp. 40–53. [G: U.S.]

Culbertson, John D. Econometric Tests of the Market Structural Determinants of R&D Investment: Consistency of Absolute and Relative Firm Size Models. *J. Ind. Econ.*, September 1985, *34*(1), pp. 101–08. [G: U.S.]

Culbertson, John D. and Mueller, Williard E. The Influence of Market Structure on Technological Performance in the Food-manufacturing Industries. *Rev. Ind. Organ.*, 1985, *2*(1), pp. 40–54. [G: U.S.]

Daems, H. The Economics of Hierarchical Organization. *Tijdschrift Econ. Manage.*, 1985, *30*(3–4), pp. 339–48.

Dasgupta, Partha. Evolution of Market Structure in a Dominant Firm Model with Exhaustible Resources: Comment. In *Scott, A., ed.*, 1985, pp. 257–59.

Dasgupta, Sreemanta. Firm Size and Rate of Growth: An Empirical Analysis of Gibrat's Law. *Indian Econ. J.*, Oct.-Nov. 1985, *33*(2), pp. 69–78. [G: India]

Daskin, Alan J. Horizontal Merger Guidelines and the Line of Commerce in Banking: An Algebraic and Graphical Approach. *Antitrust Bull.*, Fall 1985, *30*(3), pp. 651–76. [G: U.S.]

De Bondt, R. R. Strategies with Potential Competition. In *Rinnooy Kan, A. H. G., ed.*, 1985, pp. 141–58.

DeBrock, Lawrence M. Market Structure, Innovation, and Optimal Patent Life. *J. Law Econ.*, April 1985, *28*(1), pp. 223–44.

DeBrock, Lawrence M. and Masson, Robert T. Sooner or Later? Inventive Rivalry and Welfare. *Int. J. Ind. Organ.*, December 1985, *3*(4), pp. 421–38.

Defourney, Jacques; Estrin, Saul and Jones, Derek C. The Effects of Workers' Participation on Enterprise Performance: Empirical Evidence from French Cooperatives. *Int. J. Ind. Organ.*, June 1985, *3*(2), pp. 197–217. [G: France]

Demsetz, Harold and Lehn, Kenneth. The Structure of Corporate Ownership: Causes and Consequences. *J. Polit. Econ.*, December 1985, *93*(6), pp. 1155–77. [G: U.S.]

Deneckere, Raymond and Davidson, Carl. Incentives to Form Coalitions with Bertrand Competition. *Rand J. Econ.*, Winter 1985, *16*(4), pp. 473–86.

Dhebar, Anirudh and Oren, Shmuel S. Optimal Dynamic Pricing for Expanding Networks. *Marketing Sci.*, Fall 1985, *4*(4), pp. 336–51.

DiLorenzo, Thomas J. The Origins of Antitrust: An Interest-Group Perspective. *Int. Rev. Law Econ.*, June 1985, *5*(1), pp. 73–90. [G: U.S.]

Dixon, Huw. Strategic Investment in an Industry with a Competitive Product Market. In *Geroski, P. A.; Phlips, L. and Ulph, A., eds.*, 1985, pp. 115–31.

Doi, Noriyuki. Diversification and R&D Activity in Japanese Manufacturing Firms. *Managerial Dec. Econ.*, September 1985, *6*(3), pp. 147–52. [G: Japan]

Domberger, Simon and Middleton, Julian. Franchising in Practice: The Case of Independent Television in the UK. *Fisc. Stud.*, February 1985, *6*(1), pp. 17–32. [G: U.K.]

Donsimoni, Marie-Paule. Stable Heterogeneous Cartels. *Int. J. Ind. Organ.*, December 1985, *3*(4), pp. 451–67.

Dow, Gregory K. Internal Bargaining and Strategic Innovation in the Theory of the Firm. *J. Econ. Behav. Organ.*, September 1985, *6*(3), pp. 301–20.

Dowd, Bryan and Feldman, Roger. Biased Selection in Twin Cities Health Plans. In *Scheffler, R. M. and Rossiter, L. F., eds.*, 1985, pp. 253–71. [G: U.S.]

Dubois, Michel. Les déterminants de la structure financière: le cas des grandes entreprises françaises. (The Determinants of Financial Structure: The Case of Large French Firms. With English summary.) *Finance*, June 1985, *6*(1), pp. 41–70. [G: France]

Dugger, William M. Centralization, Diversification, and Administrative Burden in U.S. Enterprises. *J. Econ. Issues*, September 1985, *19*(3), pp. 687–701. [G: U.S.]

Dugger, William M. The Shortcomings of Concentration Ratios in the Conglomerate Age: New Sources and Uses of Corporate Power. *J. Econ. Issues*, June 1985, *19*(2), pp. 343–53. [G: U.S.]

Dutton, John M. Toward a Broadly Applicable Strategic Framework. In *Pennings, J. M., et al.*, 1985, pp. 143–56. [G: U.K.]

Dye, Ronald A. Costly Contract Contingencies. *Int. Econ. Rev.*, February 1985, *26*(1), pp. 233–50.

Dye, Thomas R. Strategic Ownership Positions in U.S. Industry and Banking. *Amer. J. Econ. Soc.*, January 1985, *44*(1), pp. 9–22. [G: U.S.]

Easley, David; Masson, Robert T. and Reynolds, Robert J. Preying for Time. *J. Ind. Econ.*, June 1985, *33*(4), pp. 445–60.

Easley, David; Masson, Robert T. and Reynolds, Robert J. Preying for Time. In *Geroski, P. A.; Phlips, L. and Ulph, A., eds.*, 1985, pp. 77–92.

Eaton, B. Curtis and Wooders, Myrna Holtz. Sophisticated Entry in a Model of Spatial Competition. *Rand J. Econ.*, Summer 1985, *16*(2), pp. 282–97.

Eckbo, B. Espen. Mergers and the Market Concentration Doctrine: Evidence from the Capital Market. *J. Bus.*, July 1985, *58*(3), pp. 325–49. [G: U.S.]

Eckbo, B. Espen and Wier, Peggy. Antimerger Policy under the Hart–Scott–Rodino Act: A Reexamination of the Market Power Hypothesis. *J. Law Econ.*, April 1985, *28*(1), pp. 119–49. [G: U.S.]

Ehrlich, Éva. The Size Structure of Manufacturing Establishments and Enterprises: An International Comparison. *J. Compar. Econ.*, September 1985, *9*(3), pp. 267–95. [G: Europe; U.S.; Japan]

Eichner, Alfred S. Micro Foundations of the Corporate Economy. In *Eichner, A. S.*, 1985, pp. 28–74.

Eichner, Alfred S. The Megacorp as a Social Innovation. In *Eichner, A. S.*, 1985, pp. 10–27.

Eswaran, Mukesh and Lewis, Tracy R. Evolution of Market Structure in a Dominant Firm Model with Exhaustible Resources. In *Scott, A., ed.*, 1985, pp. 242–57.

Etzioni, Amitai. Encapsulated Competition. *J. Post Keynesian Econ.*, Spring 1985, *7*(3), pp. 287–302.

Faini, Riccardo. Incentivi e poccole e medie imprese nel mezzogiorno. (Incentives and Small Firms in the Mezzogiorno. With English summary.) *Ricerche Econ.*, July–Sept. 1985, *39*(3), pp. 318–36. [G: Italy]

Fairburn, James A. British Merger Policy. *Fisc. Stud.*, February 1985, *6*(1), pp. 70–81. [G: U.K.]

Falus-Szikra, Katalin. Small Enterprises in Private Ownership in Hungary. *Acta Oecon.*, 1985, *34*(1–2), pp. 13–26. [G: Hungary]

Farrell, Joseph and Saloner, Garth. Standardization, Compatability, and Innovation. *Rand J. Econ.*, Spring 1985, *16*(1), pp. 70–83.

Farrow, Scott. Flexible Manufacturing: Market Structure and Market Failure. *J. Policy Anal. Manage.*, Summer 1985, *4*(4), pp. 583–87.

Feinberg, Robert M. "Sales-at-Risk": A Test of the Mutual Forebearance Theory of Conglomerate Behavior. *J. Bus.*, April 1985, *58*(2), pp. 225–41. [G: U.S.]

Feinberg, Robert M. and Sherman, Roger. An Experimental Investigation of Mutual Forebearance by Conglomerate Firms. In *Schwalbach, J., ed.*, 1985, pp. 139–66.

Ferguson, Paul R. The Monopolies and Mergers Commission and Economic Theory. *Nat. Westminster Bank Quart. Rev.*, November 1985, pp. 30–40. [G: U.K.]

Fershtman, Chaim. Managerial Incentives as a Strategic Variable in Duopolistic Environment. *Int. J. Ind. Organ.*, June 1985, 3(2), pp. 245–53.

Finan, William F. Intra-industry Direct Foreign Investment, Market Structure, Firm Rivalry and Technological Performance: Comment. In *Erdilek, A., ed.*, 1985, pp. 94–96. [G: U.S.]

Finger, J. Michael. Trade and the Structure of American Industry. In *Adams, J., ed.*, 1985, pp. 8–16. [G: U.S.]

Fink, Richard H. General and Partial Equilibrium Theory in Bork's Antitrust Analysis. *Contemp. Policy Issues*, Winter 1984-85, 3(2), pp. 12–20.

Fisher, Franklin M. Can Exclusive Franchises Be Bad? In *[McGowan, J. J.]*, 1985, pp. 153–71.

Foote, William and Asheghian, Parviz. X-Inefficiency and Interfirm Comparison of U.S. and Canadian Manufacturing Firms in Canada. *Quart. J. Bus. Econ.*, Autumn 1985, 24(4), pp. 3–14. [G: U.S.; Canada]

Forsyth, David J. C. Government Policy, Market Structure and Choice of Technology in Egypt. In *James, J. and Watanabe, S., eds.*, 1985, pp. 137–82. [G: Egypt]

Foster, John Bellamy. Monopoly Capital Theory and Stagflation: A Comment [Monopoly, Inflation and Economic Crisis]. *Rev. Radical Polit. Econ.*, Spring and Summer 1985, 17(1/2), pp. 221–25. [G: U.S.]

Fournier, Gary M. Nonprice Competition and the Dissipation of Rents from Television Regulation. *Southern Econ. J.*, January 1985, 51(3), pp. 754–65. [G: U.S.]

Frantzen, Dirk J. Cost Shifting and Price Flexibility in the Small Open Economy: A Disaggregated Study for Belgian Manufacturing. *Appl. Econ.*, February 1985, 17(1), pp. 173–89. [G: Belgium]

Frantzen, Dirk J. The Influence of Short-term Demand on the Mark-up in Belgian Manufacturing Industry. *Tijdschrift Econ. Manage.*, 1985, 30(2), pp. 199–219. [G: Belgium]

Fratrik, Mark R. and Lafferty, Ronald N. Unanswered Questions about Franchising: Comment [Optimal Franchising]. *Southern Econ. J.*, January 1985, 51(3), pp. 927–32.

Frey, Bruno S. Transaction Costs: Are They Just Costs? Comment. *Z. ges. Staatswiss. (JITE)*, March 1985, 141(1), pp. 17–20.

Fuhr, Joseph P., Jr. A Measurement of the Welfare Loss in the Terminal Equipment Market. *Rev. Ind. Organ.*, 1985, 2(1), pp. 80–93. [G: U.S.]

Gal-Or, Esther. Differentiated Industries without Entry Barriers. *J. Econ. Theory*, December 1985, 37(2), pp. 310–39.

Galasi, Péter and Kertesi, Gábor. Second Economy, Competition, Inflation. *Acta Oecon.*, 1985, 35(3–4), pp. 269–93.

Gálvez, Julio and Tybout, James R. Microeconomic Adjustments in Chile during 1977–81: The Importance of Being a *Grupo. World*

Devel., August 1985, 13(8), pp. 969–94. [G: Chile]

George, Kenneth D. Monopoly and Merger Policy. *Fisc. Stud.*, February 1985, 6(1), pp. 34–48. [G: U.K.]

Gereffi, Gary and Newfarmer, Richard S. International Oligopoly and Uneven Development: Some Lessons from Industrial Case Studies. In *Newfarmer, R. S., ed.*, 1985, pp. 385–444.

Geroski, P. A.; Phlips, Louis and Ulph, A. Oligopoly, Competition and Welfare: Some Recent Developments. In *Geroski, P. A.; Phlips, L. and Ulph, A., eds.*, 1985, pp. 1–18.

Geroski, P. A.; Phlips, Louis and Ulph, A. Oligopoly, Competition and Welfare: Some Recent Developments. *J. Ind. Econ.*, June 1985, 33(4), pp. 369–86. [G: U.S.; U.K.]

Ghemawat, Pankaj and Nalebuff, Barry. Exit. *Rand J. Econ.*, Summer 1985, 16(2), pp. 184–94.

Ghemawat, Pankaj and Spence, A. Michael. Learning Curve Spillovers and Market Performance. *Quart. J. Econ.*, Supp. 1985, 100, pp. 839–52.

Gisser, Micha. Welfare Implications of Oligopoly in U.S. Food Manufacturing: Reply. *Amer. J. Agr. Econ.*, February 1985, 67(1), pp. 146. [G: U.S.]

Glazer, Amihai. The Advantages of Being First. *Amer. Econ. Rev.*, June 1985, 75(3), pp. 473–80. [G: U.S.]

Glick, Mark. Monopoly or Competition in the U.S. Economy? *Rev. Radical Polit. Econ.*, Winter 1985, 17(4), pp. 121–27. [G: U.S.]

Goldberg, Victor P. Economic Aspects of Bankruptcy Law: Comment. *Z. ges. Staatswiss. (JITE)*, March 1985, 141(1), pp. 99–103.

Goldberg, Victor P. Production Functions, Transactions Costs and the New Institutionalism. In *Feiwel, G. R., ed. (II)*, 1985, pp. 395–402.

Goldberg, Victor P. Relational Exchange, Contract Law, and the *Boomer* Problem. *Z. ges. Staatswiss. (JITE)*, December 1985, 141(4), pp. 570–75.

Gordon, Myron J. The Postwar Growth in Monopoly Power. *J. Post Keynesian Econ.*, Fall 1985, 8(1), pp. 3–13. [G: U.S.]

Gort, Michael; Grabowski, Henry and McGuckin, Robert. Organizational Capital and the Choice between Specialization and Diversification. *Managerial Dec. Econ.*, March 1985, 6(1), pp. 2–10. [G: U.S.]

Graham, Edward M. Intra-industry Direct Foreign Investment, Market Structure, Firm Rivalry and Technological Performance. In *Erdilek, A., ed.*, 1985, pp. 67–88. [G: U.S.]

Greenaway, David. Models of Trade in Differentiated Goods and Commercial Policy. In *Greenaway, D., ed.*, 1985, pp. 81–97.

Gregory, S. A. Strategy and Design: A Micro Level View. In *Langdon, R. and Rothwell, R., eds.*, 1985, pp. 1–17.

Griffin, James M. OPEC Behavior: A Test of Alternative Hypotheses. *Amer. Econ. Rev.*, December 1985, 75(5), pp. 954–63. [G: OPEC]

Grimm, Curtis M. Horizontal Competitive Effects

in Railroad Mergers. In *Keeler, T. E., ed.*, 1985, pp. 27–53. [G: U.S.]

Gruchy, Allan G. Corporate Concentration and the Restructuring of the American Economy. *J. Econ. Issues*, June 1985, *19*(2), pp. 429–39. [G: U.S.]

Guerard, John B., Jr. The Determinants and Profitability of Large Corporate Mergers, 1976–1979: Should Large Corporate Mergers Be Banned? In *Brown, R. C., ed.*, 1985, pp. 117–45. [G: U.S.]

Hallagan, William S. and Joerding, Wayne. Polymorphism in Competitive Strategies: Trading Stamps. *J. Econ. Bus.*, February 1985, *37*(1), pp. 1–17.

Hamilton, Robert T. Closure Rates in Scottish Manufacturing Industries. *Scot. J. Polit. Econ.*, November 1985, *32*(3), pp. 333–42. [G: U.K.]

Hamilton, Robert T. Interindustry Variation in Gross Entry Rates of 'Independent' and 'Dependent' Businesses. *Appl. Econ.*, April 1985, *17*(2), pp. 271–80. [G: U.K.]

Hänchen, Thomas and von Ungern-Sternberg, Thomas. Information Costs, Intermediation and Equilibrium Price. *Economica*, November 1985, *52*(208), pp. 407–19.

Hansmann, Henry. The Organization of Insurance Companies: Mutual versus Stock. *J. Law, Econ., Organ.*, Spring 1985, *1*(1), pp. 125–53. [G: U.S.]

Hardie, C. J. M. Competition Policy. In *Morris, D., ed.*, 1985, pp. 798–828. [G: U.K.]

Harpaz, Giora. Learning by a Dominant Firm. *Managerial Dec. Econ.*, March 1985, *6*(1), pp. 59–63.

Harris, Christopher J. and Vickers, John. Patent Races and the Persistence of Monopoly. In *Geroski, P. A.; Phlips, L. and Ulph, A., eds.*, 1985, pp. 93–113.

Harris, R. Scott. Planning, Flexibility, and Joint Specificity of Inputs: The Use of First-Refusal Rights. *Z. ges. Staatswiss. (JITE)*, December 1985, *141*(4), pp. 576–85.

Haruna, Shoji. A Unified Theory of the Behaviour of Profit-maximising, Labour-managed and Joint-Stock Firms Operating under Uncertainty: A Comment. *Econ. J.*, December 1985, *95*(380), pp. 1093–94.

Hasbrouck, Joel. The Characteristics of Takeover Targets: *q* and Other Measures. *J. Banking Finance*, September 1985, *9*(3), pp. 351–62. [G: U.S.]

Hax, Herbert. Economic Aspects of Bankruptcy Law. *Z. ges. Staatswiss. (JITE)*, March 1985, *141*(1), pp. 80–98.

Hay, George A. Competition Policy. *Oxford Rev. Econ. Policy*, Autumn 1985, *1*(3), pp. 63–79.

Hay, George A. and Reynolds, Robert J. Competition and Antitrust in the Petroleum Industry: An Application of the Merger Guidelines. In *[McGowan, J. J.]*, 1985, pp. 15–48. [G: U.S.]

Hazlett, Thomas. Private Contracting versus Public Regulation as a Solution to the Natural Monopoly Problem. In *Poole, R. W., Jr., ed.*, 1985, pp. 71–114. [G: U.S.]

Hazlett, Thomas. The Curious Evolution of Natural Monopoly Theory. In *Poole, R. W., Jr., ed.*, 1985, pp. 1–25.

Helwege, Ann and Hendricks, Ann. Contestability and Creative Destruction: Two Approaches to Monopoly. *Rev. Ind. Organ.*, 1985, *2*(3), pp. 218–30.

Helwege, Ann and Hendricks, Ann. Three Problems in Applying Contestability to Regulated Markets. *Rev. Ind. Organ.*, 1985, *2*(2), pp. 132–43. [G: U.S.]

Hennart, Jean-François. Intra-industry Direct Foreign Investment, Market Structure, Firm Rivalry and Technological Performance: Comment. In *Erdilek, A., ed.*, 1985, pp. 88–93. [G: U.S.]

Hey, John D. A Unified Theory of the Behaviour of Profit-maximising, Labour-managed and Joint-Stock Firms Operating under Uncertainty: A Rejoinder. *Econ. J.*, December 1985, *95*(380), pp. 1095.

Hickson, David J., et al. Comparing 150 Decision Processes. In *Pennings, J. M., et al.*, 1985, pp. 114–42. [G: U.K.]

Hill, Charles W. L. Diversified Growth and Competition: The Experience of Twelve Large UK Firms. *Appl. Econ.*, October 1985, *17*(5), pp. 827–47. [G: U.K.]

Hill, Charles W. L. Internal Organization and Enterprise Performance: Some UK Evidence. *Managerial Dec. Econ.*, December 1985, *6*(4), pp. 210–16. [G: U.K.]

Hill, Charles W. L. Oliver Williamson and the M-Form Firm: A Critical Review. *J. Econ. Issues*, September 1985, *19*(3), pp. 731–51. [G: U.K.]

Hill, James Richard. The Threat of Free Agency and Exploitation in Professional Baseball: 1976–1979. *Quart. Rev. Econ. Bus.*, Winter 1985, *25*(4), pp. 68–82. [G: U.S.]

Hirschey, Mark. Market Structure and Market Value. *J. Bus.*, January 1985, *58*(1), pp. 89–98. [G: U.S.]

Hoch, Róbert. The Maxi and Mini (Reflections on the Hungarian Debate on Large Firms). *Acta Oecon.*, 1985, *35*(3–4), pp. 251–67. [G: Hungary]

Holler, Manfred J. Kritische Anmerkungen zur Theorie der umstrittenen Märkte. (Critical Comments on the Theory of Contestable Markets. With English summary.) *Jahr. Nationalökon. Statist.*, September 1985, *200*(5), pp. 479–85.

Holler, Manfred J. The Theory of Contestable Markets: Comment [Contestable Markets: An Uprising in the Theory of Industry Structure]. *Bull. Econ. Res.*, January 1985, *37*(1), pp. 65–67.

Honeycutt, T. Crawford. Competition in Controlled and Uncontrolled Gasoline Markets. *Contemp. Policy Issues*, Spring, Pt. 2, 1985, *3*(3), pp. 105–18. [G: U.S.]

Hooks, Donald L. and Martell, Terrence F. Multibank Holding Company Activity and Local

Market Structure: Some Implications for Intra- and Interstate Banking. *J. Econ. Bus.*, December 1985, *37*(4), pp. 327–41.　　**[G: U.S.]**

Hoppes, R. Bradley. Pooled Regression and Co-variance Analysis of SMSA Selected Services: Earnings and Firm Size. *Reg. Sci. Persp.*, 1985, *15*(1), pp. 31–45.　　**[G: U.S.]**

Horowitz, Ira. On the Probability of Entry in Potential Competition Cases. *Managerial Dec. Econ.*, June 1985, *6*(2), pp. 119–24.
　　[G: U.S.]

Houston, Douglas A. Revenue Effects from Changes in a Declining Block Pricing Structure: Reply. *Land Econ.*, February 1985, *61*(1), pp. 81–82.　　**[G: U.S.]**

Huertas, Thomas F. An Analysis of the Competitive Effects of Allowing Commercial Bank Affiliates to Underwrite Corporate Securities: Comment. In *Walter, I., ed.*, 1985, pp. 141–43.　　**[G: U.S.]**

Ilmakunnas, Pekka. Identification and Estimation of the Degree of Oligopoly Power in Industries Facing Domestic and Import Competition. In *Schwalbach, J., ed.*, 1985, pp. 287–308.
　　[G: W. Germany]

Ireland, Norman J. Product Diversity and Monopolistic Competition under Uncertainty. In *Geroski, P. A.; Phlips, L. and Ulph, A., eds.*, 1985, pp. 133–45.

Isaac, R. Mark and Smith, Vernon L. In Search of Predatory Pricing. *J. Polit. Econ.*, April 1985, *93*(2), pp. 320–45.

Isaac, R. Mark and Walker, James M. Information and Conspiracy in Sealed Bid Auctions. *J. Econ. Behav. Organ.*, June 1985, *6*(2), pp. 139–59.

Ishikawa, Akihiro. Participation and the Effect of New Technology upon Work: The Case of Small- and Medium-scale Manufacturing Firms in Tokyo. *Econ. Anal. Worker's Manage.*, 1985, *19*(3), pp. 295–305.　　**[G: Japan]**

Jahera, John S., Jr.; Hand, John and Lloyd, William P. An Empirical Inquiry into the Premiums for Controlling Interests. *Quart. J. Bus. Econ.*, Summer 1985, *24*(3), pp. 67–77.
　　[G: U.S.]

Jarrell, Gregg A. The Wealth Effects of Litigation by Targets: Do Interests Diverge in a Merge? *J. Law Econ.*, April 1985, *28*(1), pp. 151–77.

Jensen, Michael C. and Zimmerman, Jerold L. Management Compensation and the Managerial Labor Market. *J. Acc. Econ.*, April 1985, *7*(1–3), pp. 3–9.

Jones, Derek C. and Svejnar, Jan. Participation, Profit Sharing, Worker Ownership and Efficiency in Italian Producer Cooperative. *Economica*, November 1985, *52*(208), pp. 449–65.
　　[G: Italy]

Joskow, Paul L. Long Term Vertical Relationships and the Study of Industrial Organization and Government Regulation. *Z. ges. Staatswiss. (JITE)*, December 1985, *141*(4), pp. 586–93.
　　[G: U.S.]

Joskow, Paul L. Vertical Integration and Long-term Contracts: The Case of Coal-burning Electric Generating Plants. *J. Law, Econ., Or-*

gan., Spring 1985, *1*(1), pp. 33–80. **[G: U.S.]**

Judd, Kenneth L. Credible Spatial Preemption. *Rand J. Econ.*, Summer 1985, *16*(2), pp. 153–66.

Judd, Kenneth L. and Petersen, Bruce C. Dynamic Limit Pricing: A Reformulation. *Rev. Ind. Organ.*, 1985, *2*(2), pp. 160–77.

Kantrow, Alan M. America's Industrial Renaissance. In *Federal Reserve Bank of Atlanta (I)*, 1985, pp. 97–110.　　**[G: U.S.]**

Karier, Thomas M. Unions and Monopoly Profits. *Rev. Econ. Statist.*, February 1985, *67*(1), pp. 34–42.　　**[G: U.S.]**

Katz, Michael L. and Shapiro, Carl. Network Externalities, Competition, and Compatibility. *Amer. Econ. Rev.*, June 1985, *75*(3), pp. 424–40.

Kaufer, Erich. The Transaction Costs of Rate-of-Return Regulation: Comment. *Z. ges. Staatswiss. (JITE)*, March 1985, *141*(1), pp. 124–26.

Kelton, Christina M. L. Earnings Behavior in Food and Tobacco Manufacturing. *Rev. Ind. Organ.*, 1985, *2*(3), pp. 266–91.　　**[G: U.S.]**

Kenney, Genevieve M. Welfare Implications of Oligopoly in U.S. Food Manufacturing: Comment. *Amer. J. Agr. Econ.*, February 1985, *67*(1), pp. 144–45.　　**[G: U.S.]**

Kierzkowski, Henryk. Models of International Trade in Differentiated Goods. In *Greenaway, D., ed.*, 1985, pp. 7–24.

Klein, Benjamin. Self-enforcing Contracts. *Z. ges. Staatswiss. (JITE)*, December 1985, *141*(4), pp. 594–600.

Klein, Christopher C. Is There a Principle for Defining Industries? Comment. *Southern Econ. J.*, October 1985, *52*(2), pp. 537–41.

Klein, Philip A. Economic Activity and the Public Sector: Is Small Beautiful? *J. Econ. Issues*, June 1985, *19*(2), pp. 419–28.　　**[G: U.S.]**

Kobrin, Paul. Joint Bidding, Collusion, and Bid Clustering in Competitive Auctions: Comment. *Southern Econ. J.*, April 1985, *51*(4), pp. 1216–18.

Kohn, Meir and Scott, John T. Scale Economies in Research and Development: A Reply. *J. Ind. Econ.*, March 1985, *33*(3), pp. 363.

Kotz, David M. Reply to John Bellamy Foster, "Monopoly Capital Theory and Stagflation: A Comment." *Rev. Radical Polit. Econ.*, Spring and Summer 1985, *17*(1/2), pp. 226–29.
　　[G: U.S.]

Kreps, David M. and Spence, A. Michael. Modelling the Role of History in Industrial Organization and Competition. In *Feiwel, G. R., ed. (II)*, 1985, pp. 340–78.

Kronman, Anthony T. Contract Law and the State of Nature. *J. Law, Econ., Organ.*, Spring 1985, *1*(1), pp. 5–32.

Krouse, Clement G. Competition and Unanimity Revisited, Again. *Amer. Econ. Rev.*, December 1985, *75*(5), pp. 1109–14.

Kubačka, Jozef. Optimal Size of Industrial Enterprises—An Important Factor of Intensification of the Reproduction Process. *Czech. Econ. Di-*

gest., September 1985, (6), pp. 72–86.
[G: Czechoslovakia]

Kuenne, Robert E. The Oligopolistic Industry under Rivalrous Consonance with Target-Rate-of-Return Objectives. In *Feiwel, G. R., ed. (II)*, 1985, pp. 281–308.

Kumar, Manmohan S. Growth, Acquisition Activity and Firm Size: Evidence from the United Kingdom. *J. Ind. Econ.*, March 1985, 33(3), pp. 327–38. [G: U.K.]

Kumar, Manmohan S. International Trade and Industrial Concentration. *Oxford Econ. Pap.*, March 1985, 37(1), pp. 125–33. [G: U.K.]

Kwoka, John E., Jr. The Herfindahl Index in Theory and Practice. *Antitrust Bull.*, Winter 1985, 30(4), pp. 915–47. [G: U.S.]

Laffont, Jean-Jacques and Moreaux, Michel. Large-Market Cournot Equilibria in Labour-managed Economies. *Economica*, May 1985, 52(206), pp. 153–65.

Lafuente Félez, Alberto; Salas Fumás, Vicente and Yagüe Guillén, María Jesús. Formación de capital tecnológico en la industria española. (With English summary.) *Revista Española Econ.*, 1985, 2(2), pp. 269–90. [G: Spain]

Laky, Teréz. Enterprise Business Work Partnership and Enterprise Interest. *Acta Oecon.*, 1985, 34(1–2), pp. 27–49. [G: Hungary]

Landis, Robin C. and Rolfe, Ronald S. Market Conduct under Section 2: When Is It Anticompetitive? In *[McGowan, J. J.]*, 1985, pp. 131–52. [G: U.S.]

Lean, David F.; Ogur, Jonathan D. and Rogers, Robert P. Does Collusion Pay . . . Does Antiturst Work? *Southern Econ. J.*, January 1985, 51(3), pp. 828–41. [G: U.S.]

Leffler, Keith. Toward a Reasonable Rule of Reason: Comments. *J. Law Econ.*, May 1985, 28(2), pp. 381–86. [G: U.S.]

Leontief, Wassily. The Theory and Statistical Description of Concentration. In *Leontief, W.*, 1985, pp. 258–71.

Levin, Harvey J. Comment: Antitrust, Concentration, and Competition. In *Noam, E. M., ed.*, 1985, pp. 390–96. [G: U.S.]

Levin, Richard C.; Cohen, Wesley M. and Mowery, David C. R&D Appropriability, Opportunity, and Market Structure: New Evidence on Some Schumpeterian Hypotheses. *Amer. Econ. Rev.*, May 1985, 75(2), pp. 20–24. [G: U.S.]

Levin, Sharon G.; Levin, Stanford L. and Meisel, John B. Intermarket Differences in the Early Diffusion of an Innovation. *Southern Econ. J.*, January 1985, 51(3), pp. 672–80. [G: U.S.]

Levy, David T. Specifying the Dynamics of Industry Concentration. *J. Ind. Econ.*, September 1985, 34(1), pp. 55–68. [G: U.S.]

Levy, David T. The Transactions Cost Approach to Vertical Integration: An Empirical Examination. *Rev. Econ. Statist.*, August 1985, 67(3), pp. 438–45. [G: U.S.]

Lewellen, Wilbur G.; Loderer, Claudio and Rosenfeld, Ahron. Merger Decisions and Executive Stock Ownership in Acquiring Firms. *J.*

Acc. Econ., April 1985, 7(1–3), pp. 209–31. [G: U.S.]

Libecap, Gary D. and Wiggins, Steven N. The Influence of Private Contractual Failure on Regulation: The Case of Oil Field Unitization. *J. Polit. Econ.*, August 1985, 93(4), pp. 690–714. [G: U.S.]

Lichty, Richard W.; Steinnes, Donald N. and Vose, David A. Strategic Planning of Economic Development Based on an Analysis of the Extent and Pattern of Importation. *Reg. Sci. Persp.*, 1985, 15(1), pp. 46–62. [G: U.S.]

Liebeler, Wesley J. Antitrust and Economic Efficiency: Comment. *J. Law Econ.*, May 1985, 28(2), pp. 335–43.

Lindenberg, Siegwart and de Vos, Henk. The Limits of Solidarity: Relational Contracting in Perspective and Some Criticism of Traditional Sociology. *Z. ges. Staatswiss. (JITE)*, December 1985, 141(4), pp. 558–69.

Lindenlaub, Dieter. What Can the Businessman Learn from History, Especially Business History? In *Engels, W. and Pohl, H., eds.*, 1985, pp. 25–53.

Livesey, Frank. Monopoly and Competition. In *Atkinson, G. B. J., ed.*, 1985, pp. 81–99. [G: U.K.]

Loderer, Claudio. A Test of the OPEC Cartel Hypothesis: 1974–1983. *J. Finance*, July 1985, 40(3), pp. 991–1006. [G: OPEC]

Louitri, Abdenbi. La validité empirique de la mesure catégorielle de diversification de Rumelt dans les groupes industriels français. (The Empirical Validity of Rumelt's Measure of Diversification in French Industrial Groups. With English summary.) *Écon. Soc.*, December 1985, 19(12), pp. 205–24. [G: France]

Lynk, William J. The Price and Output of Beer Revisited [Interpreting Rising Concentration: The Case of Beer]. *J. Bus.*, October 1985, 58(4), pp. 433–37. [G: U.S.]

MacDonald, James M. Market Exchange or Vertical Integration: An Empirical Analysis. *Rev. Econ. Statist.*, May 1985, 67(2), pp. 327–31. [G: U.S.]

MacDonald, James M. R and D and the Directions of Diversification. *Rev. Econ. Statist.*, November 1985, 67(4), pp. 583–90. [G: U.S.]

Macey, Jonathan R. and McChesney, Fred S. A Theoretical Analysis of Corporate Greenmail. *Yale Law J.*, November 1985, 95(1), pp. 13–61. [G: U.S.]

Macneil, Ian R. Reflections on Relational Contract. *Z. ges. Staatswiss. (JITE)*, December 1985, 141(4), pp. 541–46.

Maddigan, Ruth J. and Zaima, Janis K. The Profitability of Vertical Integration. *Managerial Dec. Econ.*, September 1985, 6(3), pp. 178–79. [G: U.S.]

Marginson, Paul. The Multidivisional Firm and Control over the Work Process. *Int. J. Ind. Organ.*, March 1985, 3(1), pp. 37–56. [G: U.K.]

Markovits, Richard S. The Functions, Allocative Efficiency, and Legality of Tie-ins: A Comment. *J. Law Econ.*, May 1985, *28*(2), pp. 387–404. **[G: U.S.]**

Martin, David Dale. The Iron and Steel Industry: Transnational Control without TNCs? In *Newfarmer, R. S.*, ed., 1985, pp. 151–92.
[G: Selected Countries]

Martin, Leonard W. 'Stagflation': A Condition Created by Accelerated Demand–Pull Inflation (Comment). *Amer. J. Econ. Soc.*, October 1985, *44*(4), pp. 497–501.

Martin, Preston. Statement to the U.S. House Subcommittee on Telecommunications, Consumer Protection, and Finance of the Committee on Energy and Commerce, April 23, 1985. *Fed. Res. Bull.*, June 1985, *71*(6), pp. 428–30. **[G: U.S.]**

Martin, Preston. Statement to the U.S. House Subcommittee on Domestic Monetary Policy of the Committee on Banking, Finance, and Urban Affairs, May 3, 1985. *Fed. Res. Bull.*, July 1985, *71*(7), pp. 514–17. **[G: U.S.]**

Martin, Preston. Statement to the U.S. Senate Subcommittee on Securities of the Committee on Banking, Housing, and Urban Affairs, April 4, 1985. *Fed. Res. Bull.*, June 1985, *71*(6), pp. 418–22. **[G: U.S.]**

Marvel, Howard P. How Fair Is Fair Trade? *Contemp. Policy Issues*, Spring, Pt. 1, 1985, *3*(3), pp. 23–35. **[G: U.S.]**

Marvel, Howard P. and McCafferty, Stephen. The Welfare Effects of Resale Price Maintenance. *J. Law Econ.*, May 1985, *28*(2), pp. 363–79. **[G: U.S.]**

Mas-Colell, Andreu. La libre entrada y la eficiencia económica. Un análisis de equilibrio parcial. (Free Entry and Economic Efficiency: A Partial Equilibrium Analysis. With English summary.) *Revista Española Econ.*, 1985, *2*(1), pp. 135–52.

Mas-Colell, Andreu. La libre entrada y la eficiencia económica: un análisis de equilibrio parcial. Corrección. (With English summary.) *Revista Española Econ.*, 1985, *2*(2), pp. 389.

Mason, Charles F. On Scale Economies and Exhaustible Resource Markets. *Rev. Ind. Organ.*, 1985, *2*(2), pp. 144–59.

Mathewson, G. Frank and Winter, Ralph A. The Economics of Franchise Contracts. *J. Law Econ.*, October 1985, *28*(3), pp. 503–26.

Mayer, Colin. The Assessment: Recent Developments in Industrial Economics and Their Implications for Policy. *Oxford Rev. Econ. Policy*, Autumn 1985, *1*(3), pp. 1–24. **[G: U.K.]**

McConnell, John J. and Nantell, Timothy J. Corporate Combinations and Common Stock Returns: The Case of Joint Ventures. *J. Finance*, June 1985, *40*(2), pp. 519–36. **[G: U.S.]**

McDonald, Ian M. Market Power and Unemployment. *Int. J. Ind. Organ.*, March 1985, *3*(1), pp. 21–35.

McGowan, John J. Mergers for Power or Progress? In *[McGowan, J. J.]*, 1985, pp. 1–13.
[G: U.S.]

McRae, James J. and Tapon, Francis. Some Empirical Evidence on Post-patent Barriers to Entry in the Canadian Pharmaceutical Industry.

J. Health Econ., March 1985, *4*(1), pp. 43–61. **[G: Canada]**

Meek, Christopher and Woodworth, Warner. Absentee Ownership, Industrial Decline, and Organizational Renewal. In *Woodworth, W.; Meek, C. and Whyte, W. F.*, eds., 1985, pp. 78–96. **[G: U.S.]**

Meier, Peter. Erklärung konjunktureller Schwankungsintensitäten im Querschnitt von Produktionssektoren—eine empirische Analyse für die Schwiez. (The Intensity of Cyclical Fluctuations in Different Industries—An Empirical Analysis for Switzerland. With English summary.) *Schweiz. Z. Volkswirtsch. Statist.*, June 1985, *121*(2), pp. 115–38. **[G: Switzerland]**

Mertens, Yves and Ginsburgh, Victor. Product Differentiation and Price Discrimination in the European Community: The Case of Automobiles. *J. Ind. Econ.*, December 1985, *34*(2), pp. 151–66. **[G: Belgium; France; W. Germany; Italy; U.K.]**

Michelini, Claudio and Pickford, Michael. Estimating the Herfindahl Index from Concentration Ratio Data. *J. Amer. Statist. Assoc.*, June 1985, *80*(390), pp. 301–05.
[G: New Zealand]

Mikkelson, Wayne H. and Ruback, Richard S. Takeovers and Managerial Compensation: A Discussion [Merger Decisions and Executive Stock Ownership in Acquiring Firms] [Agency Theory, Managerial Welfare, and Takeover Bid Resistance]. *J. Acc. Econ.*, April 1985, *7*(1–3), pp. 233–38.

Miller, James C., III. Use of Antitrust to Subvert Competition: Comment. *J. Law Econ.*, May 1985, *28*(2), pp. 267–70. **[G: OECD]**

Miller, James C., III and Pautler, Paul. Predation: The Changing View in Economics and the Law. *J. Law Econ.*, May 1985, *28*(2), pp. 495–502. **[G: U.S.]**

Mills, David E. and Schumann, Laurence. Industry Structure with Fluctuating Demand. *Amer. Econ. Rev.*, September 1985, *75*(4), pp. 758–67. **[G: U.S.]**

Mirman, Leonard J.; Tauman, Yair and Zang, Israel. Monopoly and Sustainable Prices as a Nash Equilibrium in Contestable Markets. In *Feiwel, G. R.*, ed. *(II)*, 1985, pp. 328–39.

Mirman, Leonard J.; Tauman, Yair and Zang, Israel. Supportability, Sustainability, and Subsidy-free Prices. *Rand J. Econ.*, Spring 1985, *16*(1), pp. 114–26.

Mote, Larry R. and Baer, Herbert, Jr. Foreign Experience with Nationwide Banking. In *Federal Reserve Bank of Atlanta (II)*, 1985, pp. 211–22. **[G: U.S.; Selected OECD]**

Mueller, Dennis C. Mergers and the Long Run Profitability of Large Corporations. In *Schwalbach, J.*, ed., 1985, pp. 113–38. **[G: U.S.]**

Mueller, Dennis C. Mergers and Market Share. *Rev. Econ. Statist.*, May 1985, *67*(2), pp. 259–67. **[G: U.S.]**

Mukhopadhyay, Arun K. Returns to Scale in R&D and the Schumpeterian Hypothesis: A Comment. *J. Ind. Econ.*, March 1985, *33*(3), pp. 359–61.

Mukhopadhyay, Arun K. Technological Progress and Change in Market Concentration in the U.S., 1963–77. *Southern Econ. J.*, July 1985, *52*(1), pp. 141–49. [G: U.S.]

Müller-Graff, Peter-Christian. Long-term Business Relations: Conflicts and the Law. *Z. ges. Staatswiss. (JITE)*, December 1985, *141*(4), pp. 547–57.

Müller, Jürgen and Owen, Nicholas. The Effect of Trade on Plant Size. In *Schwalbach, J., ed.*, 1985, pp. 41–60. [G: W. Germany]

Munkirs, John R. and Sturgeon, James I. Oligopolistic Cooperation: Conceptual and Empirical Evidence of Market Structure Evolution. *J. Econ. Issues*, December 1985, *19*(4), pp. 899–921. [G: U.S.]

Nadel, Mark S. Comment: Multichannel Video Competition. In *Noam, E. M., ed.*, 1985, pp. 174–79. [G: U.S.]

Natke, Paul A. A Comparison of Import Pricing by Foreign and Domestic Firms in Brazil. In *Rugman, A. M. and Eden, L., eds.*, 1985, pp. 212–22. [G: Brazil]

Neary, Hugh M. The Labour-managed Firm in Monopolistic Competition. *Economica*, November 1985, *52*(208), pp. 435–47.

Neumann, Manfred; Böbel, Ingo and Haid, Alfred. Domestic Concentration, Foreign Trade, and Economic Performance. *Int. J. Ind. Organ.*, March 1985, *3*(1), pp. 1–19. [G: W. Germany]

Neumann, Manfred and Haid, Alfred. Concentration and Economic Performance: A Cross-Section Analysis of West German Industries. In *Schwalbach, J., ed.*, 1985, pp. 61–84. [G: W. Germany]

Neven, Damien J. and Phlips, Louis. Discriminating Oligopolists and Common Markets. *J. Ind. Econ.*, December 1985, *34*(2), pp. 133–49.

Newfarmer, Richard S. International Industrial Organization and Development: A Survey. In *Newfarmer, R. S., ed.*, 1985, pp. 13–61.

Newfarmer, Richard S. International Oligopoly in the Electrical Industry. In *Newfarmer, R. S., ed.*, 1985, pp. 113–49. [G: Brazil; Selected Countries]

Newfarmer, Richard S. Profits, Progress and Poverty: Case Studies of International Industries in Latin America: An Introduction to the Issues. In *Newfarmer, R. S., ed.*, 1985, pp. 1–12.

Niccoli, Alberto. Efficiency of Microeconomic Income Distribution and Global Productivity Differentials. *Rivista Polit. Econ.*, Suppl. Dec. 1985, *76*, pp. 65–119. [G: Italy]

Nissan, Edward and Caveny, Regina. Relative Concentration of the Largest Firms [An Entropy Measure of Relative Concentration]. *Southern Econ. J.*, January 1985, *51*(3), pp. 880–81. [G: U.S.]

Noam, Eli M. Economies of Scale in Cable Television: A Multiproduct Analysis. In *Noam, E. M., ed.*, 1985, pp. 93–120. [G: U.S.]

Noll, Roger G. Self-Regulation as Market Mainte-

nance: Comment. In *Noll, R. G., ed.*, 1985, pp. 343–47. [G: U.S.]

North, Douglass C. Transaction Costs in History. *J. Europ. Econ. Hist.*, Sept.-Dec. 1985, *14*(3), pp. 557–76.

Ordover, Janusz A.; Sykes, A. O. and Willig, Robert D. Nonprice Anticompetitive Behavior by Dominant Firms toward the Producers of Complementary Products. In *[McGowan, J. J.]*, 1985, pp. 115–30. [G: U.S.]

Ornstein, Stanley I. Resale Price Maintenance and Cartels. *Antitrust Bull.*, Summer 1985, *30*(2), pp. 401–32. [G: U.S.]

Ott, Mack and Santoni, G. J. Mergers and Takeovers—The Value of Pradators' Information. *Fed. Res. Bank St. Louis Rev.*, December 1985, *67*(10), pp. 16–28. [G: U.S.]

Outreville, J. François and Proulx, Carol. Fusions et économies de dimension sur le marché des assurances générales au Québec. (Mergers and Economies of Scale in the Quebec Property-Liability Insurance Industry. With English summary.) *L'Actual. Econ.*, September 1985, *61*(3), pp. 350–61. [G: Canada]

Overstreet, Thomas R., Jr. and Fisher, Alan A. Resale Price Maintenance and Distributional Efficiency: Some Lessons from the Past. *Contemp. Policy Issues*, Spring, Pt. 1, 1985, *3*(3), pp. 43–58. [G: U.S.]

Palay, Thomas M. Avoiding Regulatory Constraints: Contracting Safeguards and the Role of Informal Agreements. *J. Law, Econ., Organ.*, Spring 1985, *1*(1), pp. 155–75. [G: U.S.]

Paroush, Jacob. Notes on Partnerships in the Services Sector. *J. Econ. Behav. Organ.*, March 1985, *6*(1), pp. 79–87.

Parris, Carl. Power and Privilege in Trinidad and Tabago. *Soc. Econ. Stud.*, June 1985, *34*(2), pp. 97–109. [G: Trinidad and Tabago]

Penrose, Edith. Downstream Implications of Structural Change. In *Hawdon, D., ed.*, 1985, pp. 80–91.

Perry, Martin K. and Groff, Robert H. Resale Price Maintenance and Forward Integration into a Monopolistically Competitive Industry. *Quart. J. Econ.*, November 1985, *100*(4), pp. 1293–1311.

Perry, Martin K. and Porter, Robert H. Oligopoly and the Incentive for Horizontal Merger. *Amer. Econ. Rev.*, March 1985, *75*(1), pp. 219–27.

Perryman, M. Ray. Evolutionary Aspects of Corporate Concentration and Its Implications for Economic Theory and Policy. *J. Econ. Issues*, June 1985, *19*(2), pp. 375–81.

Pettigrew, Andrew M. Examining Change in the Long-term Context of Culture and Politics. In *Pennings, J. M., et al.*, 1985, pp. 269–318. [G: U.K.]

Phillips, Almarin and Mahoney, Joseph. Unreasonable Rules and Rules of Reason: Economic Aspects of Vertical Price-fixing. *Antitrust Bull.*, Spring 1985, *30*(1), pp. 99–115. [G: U.S.]

Phillips, Bruce D. The Effect of Industry Deregulation on the Small Business Sector. *Bus.*

Econ., January 1985, *20*(1), pp. 28–37.
[G: U.S.]

Pickford, Michael. A New Test for Manufacturing Industry Efficiency: An Analysis of the Results of Import License Tendering in New Zealand. *Int. J. Ind. Organ.*, June 1985, *3*(2), pp. 153–77.
[G: New Zealand]

Pindyck, Robert S. The Measurement of Monopoly Power in Dynamic Markets. *J. Law Econ.*, April 1985, *28*(1), pp. 193–222.

Pöll, Günther. Introduction to the Sustainability Analysis of Contested Markets and the Multiproduct Firm: A Graphical Exposition. *Z. ges. Staatswiss. (JITE)*, September 1985, *141*(3), pp. 413–34.

Porter, Robert H. On the Incidence and Duration of Price Wars. *J. Ind. Econ.*, June 1985, *33*(4), pp. 415–26.
[G: U.S.]

Porter, Robert H. On the Incidence and Duration of Price Wars. In *Geroski, P. A.; Phlips, L. and Ulph, A.*, eds., 1985, pp. 47–58.
[G: U.S.]

Price, James R. and Mays, James W. Selection and the Competitive Standing of Health Plans in a Multiple-Choice, Multiple-Insurer Market. In *Scheffler, R. M. and Rossiter, L. F.*, eds., 1985, pp. 127–47.
[G: U.S.]

Primeaux, Walter J., Jr. Dismantling Competition in a Natural Monopoly. *Quart. Rev. Econ. Bus.*, Autumn 1985, *25*(3), pp. 6–21.
[G: U.S.]

Pugel, Thomas A. and White, Lawrence J. An Analysis of the Competitive Effects of Allowing Commercial Bank Affiliates to Underwrite Corporate Securities. In *Walter, I.*, ed., 1985, pp. 93–139.
[G: U.S.]

Raab, Raymond and Wong, Shee Q. Measuring the Interrelationships between Concentration and Price Cost Margins. *Rev. Ind. Organ.*, 1985, *2*(3), pp. 292–98.
[G: U.S.]

Rahmeyer, Fritz. Marktstruktur und industrielle Preisentwicklung. (Market Structure and Industrial Price Development. With English summary.) *Ifo-Studien*, 1985, *31*(4), pp. 295–330.
[G: W. Germany]

Raţiu Suciu, I. and Raţiu Suciu, Camelia. A Complex Analysis on Estimating the Technical and Qualitative Standards of Industrial Products. *Econ. Computat. Cybern. Stud. Res.*, 1985, *20*(3), pp. 49–53.
[G: Romania]

Raviv, Artur. Management Compensation and the Managerial Labor Market: An Overview. *J. Acc. Econ.*, April 1985, *7*(1–3), pp. 239–45.

Reekie, W. Duncan and Allen, D. E. Generic Substitution in the UK Pharmaceutical Industry: A Markovian Analysis. *Managerial Dec. Econ.*, June 1985, *6*(2), pp. 93–101.
[G: U.K.]

Rees, Ray. Cheating in a Duopoly Supergame. In *Geroski, P. A.; Phlips, L. and Ulph, A.*, eds., 1985, pp. 19–32.

Reich, Robert B. Bailout: A Comparative Study in Law and Industrial Structure. *Yale J. Regul.*, 1985, *2*(2), pp. 163–224.
[G: U.S.; U.K.; W. Germany; Japan]

Reinganum, Jennifer F. Innovation and Industry Evolution. *Quart. J. Econ.*, February 1985, *100*(1), pp. 81–99.

Revell, Jack R. The Structures of the Credit Systems: Concentration and Fragmentation. *Rev. Econ. Cond. Italy*, Sept.-Dec. 1985, (3), pp. 393–411.
[G: OECD]

Reynolds, Stanley S. Capacity, Output, and Sequential Entry: Comment. *Amer. Econ. Rev.*, September 1985, *75*(4), pp. 894–96.

Rhoades, Stephen A. Interstate Banking: Impacts on the Banking System and the Public: Concentration in Local and National Markets. In *Federal Reserve Bank of Atlanta (II)*, 1985, pp. 171–76.
[G: U.S.]

Rhoades, Stephen A. Market Performance and the Nature of a Competitive Fringe. *J. Econ. Bus.*, May 1985, *37*(2), pp. 141–57.
[G: U.S.]

Rhoades, Stephen A. Market Share as a Source of Market Power: Implications and Some Evidence. *J. Econ. Bus.*, December 1985, *37*(4), pp. 343–63.
[G: U.S.]

Rhoades, Stephen A. Mergers of the 20 Largest Banks and Industrials, All Bank Mergers (1960–1983), and Some Related Issues. *Antitrust Bull.*, Fall 1985, *30*(3), pp. 617–49.
[G: U.S.]

Rhoades, Stephen A. and Heggestad, Arnold A. Multimarket Interdependence and Performance in Banking: Two Tests. *Antitrust Bull.*, Winter 1985, *30*(4), pp. 975–95.
[G: U.S.]

Rice, Emmett J. Statement to the U.S. House Subcommittee on General Oversight and the Economy of the Committee on Small Business, June 25, 1985. *Fed. Res. Bull.*, August 1985, *71*(8), pp. 618–20.
[G: U.S.]

Richards, Daniel J. Relative Prices, Concentration, and Money Growth: Comment. *Amer. Econ. Rev.*, March 1985, *75*(1), pp. 273–78.
[G: U.S.]

Riddell, Tom. Concentration and Inefficiency in the Defense Sector: Policy Options. *J. Econ. Issues*, June 1985, *19*(2), pp. 451–61.
[G: U.S.]

Riordan, Michael H. and Williamson, Oliver E. Asset Specificity and Economic Organization. *Int. J. Ind. Organ.*, December 1985, *3*(4), pp. 365–78.

Roberts, Kevin. Cartel Behaviour and Adverse Selection. In *Geroski, P. A.; Phlips, L. and Ulph, A.*, eds., 1985, pp. 33–45.

Robinson, Marc S. Collusion and the Choice of Auction. *Rand J. Econ.*, Spring 1985, *16*(1), pp. 141–45.

Rodriguez, Alvaro. Entry and Price Dynamics in a Perfect Foresight Model. *J. Econ. Dynam. Control*, November 1985, *9*(3), pp. 251–71.

Román, Zoltán. The Conditions of Market Competition in the Hungarian Industry. *Acta Oecon.*, 1985, *34*(1–2), pp. 79–97.
[G: Hungary]

Romano, Richard E. and Berg, Sanford V. The Identification of Predatory Behavior in the Presence of Uncertainty. *Int. J. Ind. Organ.*, June 1985, *3*(2), pp. 231–43.

Romano, Roberta. Law as a Product: Some Pieces of the Incorporation Puzzle. *J. Law, Econ.*,

Organ., Fall 1985, *1*(2), pp. 225–83.
[G: U.S.]

Rose, John T. Interstate Banking, Potential Competition, and the Attractiveness of Banking Markets for New Entry. *Antitrust Bull.*, Fall 1985, *30*(3), pp. 729–43. [G: U.S.]

Ross, Howard N. and Krausz, Joshua. Cyclical Price Behaviour and Concentration: A Time Series Analysis. *Oxford Bull. Econ. Statist.*, August 1985, *47*(3), pp. 231–47. [G: U.S.]

Rothblum, Uriel G. and Winter, Sidney G. Asymptotic Behavior of Market Shares for a Stochastic Growth Model. *J. Econ. Theory*, August 1985, *36*(2), pp. 352–66.

Russell, Raymond. Employee Ownership and Internal Governance. *J. Econ. Behav. Organ.*, September 1985, *6*(3), pp. 217–41. [G: U.S.]

Sarig, Oded H. On Mergers, Divestments, and Options: A Note. *J. Finan. Quant. Anal.*, September 1985, *20*(3), pp. 385–89.

Sarmad, Khwaja. Evaluating the Operational Performance of Manufacturing Enterprises: An Evaluation Framework and Application to Pakistani Industry: Comments. *Pakistan Devel. Rev.*, Autumn-Winter 1985, *24*(3/4), pp. 718–19. [G: Pakistan]

Saunders, Ronald S. Learning by Doing and Dominant Firm Pricing Strategy. *Rev. Ind. Organ.*, 1985, *2*(1), pp. 32–39.

Saxonhouse, Gary R. and Ranis, Gustav. Technology Choice and the Quality Dimension in the Japanese Cotton Textile Industry. In *Ohkawa, K. and Ranis, G., eds.*, 1985, pp. 155–76. [G: Japan]

Scarpa, Carlo. Innovazioni, esternalità e barriere all'entrata in mercati altamente innovativi. (Innovations, Externalities and Barriers to Entry in Highly Innovative Markets. With English summary.) *Ricerche Econ.*, Apr.-June 1985, *39*(2), pp. 180–200.

Schaerr, Gene C. The *Cellophane* Fallacy and the Justice Department's Guidelines for Horizontal Mergers. *Yale Law J.*, January 1985, *94*(3), pp. 670–93. [G: U.S.]

Schäfer, Helmut. A European View of Competition and Control in a Multimedia Society. In *Noam, E. M., ed.*, 1985, pp. 405–15.
[G: W. Europe]

Scherer, F. M. Post-patent Barriers to Entry in the Pharmaceutical Industry. *J. Health Econ.*, March 1985, *4*(1), pp. 83–87. [G: OECD]

Schipper, Katherine and Thompson, Rex. The Impact of Merger-related Regulations Using Exact Distributions of Test Statistics [The Impact of Merger-related Regulations on the Shareholders of Acquiring Firms]. *J. Acc. Res.*, Spring 1985, *23*(1), pp. 408–15. [G: U.S.]

Schmalensee, Richard. Do Markets Differ Much? *Amer. Econ. Rev.*, June 1985, *75*(3), pp. 341–51. [G: U.S.]

Schmalensee, Richard. Econometric Diagnosis of Competitive Localization. *Int. J. Ind. Organ.*, 1985, *3*(1), pp. 57–70. [G: U.S.]

Scotchmer, Suzanne. Two-tier Pricing of Shared Facilities in a Free-Entry Equilibrium. *Rand J. Econ.*, Winter 1985, *16*(4), pp. 456–72.

Scott, D. R. and Reekie, W. Duncan. Competition in Atomistic and Oligopsonistic Markets: The South African Pharmaceutical Industry. *S. Afr. J. Econ.*, March 1985, *53*(1), pp. 39–54.
[G: S. Africa]

Scott, John T. Capital Structure and the Product Market Environment: Comment. In *Friedman, B. M., ed.*, 1985, pp. 378–82. [G: U.S.]

Scott, Kenneth E. The Firm as a Complex Institution: Comment. *Z. ges. Staatswiss. (JITE)*, March 1985, *141*(1), pp. 76–79.

Secchi, Carlo. On the Role of Small and Medium-Sized Enterprises in the Improvement of the Production Structure of Developing Countries. *Cepal Rev.*, December 1985, (27), pp. 131–41. [G: Italy]

Shaffer, Sherrill. Competition, Economies of Scale, and Diversity of Firm Sizes. *Appl. Econ.*, June 1985, *17*(3), pp. 467–76.
[G: U.S.]

Shaffer, Sherrill. Counterproductive Risk Pooling. *Atlantic Econ. J.*, March 1985, *13*(1), pp. 99.

Shaffer, Sherrill. Price Leadership without Collusion. *Australian Econ. Pap.*, June 1985, *24*(44), pp. 210–13.

Shaikh, Abdul Hafeez. Evaluating the Operational Performance of Manufacturing Enterprises: An Evaluation Framework and Application to Pakistani Industry. *Pakistan Devel. Rev.*, Autumn-Winter 1985, *24*(3/4), pp. 703–17. [G: Pakistan]

Sharir, Shmuel. A Note on the Measurement of Welfare Changes Due to a Merger. *Scot. J. Polit. Econ.*, February 1985, *32*(1), pp. 107–10.

Sharkey, William W. Economic and Game-Theoretic Issues Associated with Cost Allocation in a Telecommunications Network. In *Young, H. P., ed.*, 1985, pp. 155–65.

Sharp, Benjamin S. How Fair Is Fair Trade? Comment. *Contemp. Policy Issues*, Spring, Pt. 1, 1985, *3*(3), pp. 37–42. [G: U.S.]

Sharpe, Thomas. British Competition Policy in Perspective. *Oxford Rev. Econ. Policy*, Autumn 1985, *1*(3), pp. 80–94. [G: U.K.]

Shepherd, Philip L. Transnational Corporations and the International Cigarette Industry. In *Newfarmer, R. S., ed.*, 1985, pp. 63–112.
[G: Selected Countries; U.S.]

Shleifer, Andrei. A Theory of Yardstick Competition. *Rand J. Econ.*, Autumn 1985, *16*(3), pp. 319–27.

Shubik, Martin. The Many Approaches to the Study of Monopolistic Competition. *Europ. Econ. Rev.*, February 1985, *27*(1), pp. 97–114.

Shughart, William F., II and Tollison, Robert D. The Welfare Basis of the "Failing Company" Doctrine. *Antitrust Bull.*, Summer 1985, *30*(2), pp. 357–64.

Siegel, Daniel R. Estimating Potential Social Losses from Market Failure: Oil Exploration in Alberta. *Rand J. Econ.*, Winter 1985, *16*(4), pp. 537–52. [G: Canada]

Silhan, Peter A. and McKeown, James C. Further Evidence on the Usefulness of Simulated

Mergers. *J. Acc. Res.*, Spring 1985, *23*(1), pp. 416–26. [G: U.S.]

Silva, Francesco. Qualcosa di nuovo nelle teoria dell'impresa? (With English summary.) *Econ. Polit.*, April 1985, *2*(1), pp. 95–134.

Silver, M. S. On the Measurement of Changes in Aggregate Concentration, Market Concentration and Diversification. *J. Ind. Econ.*, March 1985, *33*(3), pp. 349–52.

Smirlock, Michael J. Evidence on the (Non) Relationship between Concentration and Profitability in Banking. *J. Money, Credit, Banking*, February 1985, *17*(1), pp. 69–83.

Smith, James L. Joint Bidding, Collusion, and Bid Clustering in Competitive Auctions: Reply. *Southern Econ. J.*, April 1985, *51*(4), pp. 1219–20.

Spence, A. Michael. Capital Structure and the Corporation's Product Market Environment. In *Friedman, B. M., ed.*, 1985, pp. 353–77. [G: U.S.]

Spiller, Pablo T. On Vertical Mergers. *J. Law, Econ., Organ.*, Fall 1985, *1*(2), pp. 285–312. [G: U.S.]

Spulber, Daniel F. Capacity, Output, and Sequential Entry: Reply. *Amer. Econ. Rev.*, September 1985, *75*(4), pp. 897–98.

Steiner, Robert L. The Nature of Vertical Restraints. *Antitrust Bull.*, Spring 1985, *30*(1), pp. 143–97. [G: U.S.]

Stevens, Paul. A Survey of Structural Change in the International Oil Industry 1945–1984. In *Hawdon, D., ed.*, 1985, pp. 18–51.

Stigler, George J. and Sherwin, Robert A. The Extent of the Market. *J. Law Econ.*, October 1985, *28*(3), pp. 555–85. [G: U.S.]

Storper, Michael. Oligopoly and the Product Cycle: Essentialism in Economic Geography. *Econ. Geogr.*, July 1985, *61*(3), pp. 260–82.

Stratton, Richard W. Monopoly, Monopsony, and Union Strength and Local Market Wage Differentials: Some Empirical Evidence on Their Impacts. *Amer. J. Econ. Soc.*, July 1985, *44*(3), pp. 305–18. [G: U.S.]

Strickland, Allyn D. Conglomerate Mergers, Mutual Forbearance Behavior and Price Competition. *Managerial Dec. Econ.*, September 1985, *6*(3), pp. 153–59. [G: U.S.]

Strobel, Frederick R. The U.S. Banking and Corporate Structure: Some Implications for Industrial Policy. *J. Econ. Issues*, June 1985, *19*(2), pp. 541–49. [G: U.S.]

Sullivan, Daniel. Testing Hypotheses about Firm Behavior in the Cigarette Industry. *J. Polit. Econ.*, June 1985, *93*(3), pp. 586–98. [G: U.S.]

Swales, J. K. Advertising as an Intangible Asset: Profitability and Entry Barriers. A Comment. *Appl. Econ.*, August 1985, *17*(4), pp. 603–17. [G: U.K.]

Takamiya, Makoto. The Degree of Organizational Centralization in Multinational Corporations. In *Takamiya, S. and Thurley, K., eds.*, 1985, pp. 35–47.

Teece, David J. Applying Concepts of Economic Analysis to Strategic Management. In *Pen-*

nings, J. M., et al., 1985, pp. 35–63.

Teece, David J. Multinational Enterprise, Internal Governance, and Industrial Organization. *Amer. Econ. Rev.*, May 1985, *75*(2), pp. 233–38.

Thorpe, Kenneth. The Impact of Competing Technologies on Cable Television. In *Noam, E. M., ed.*, 1985, pp. 138–67. [G: U.S.]

Tisdell, Clement A. Conceptual Issues in the Measurement of Economic and Productive Efficiencies. *S. Afr. J. Econ.*, March 1985, *53*(1), pp. 55–66.

Townsend, Alan and Peck, Francis. An Approach to the Analysis of Redundancies in the UK (Post-1976): Some Methodological Problems and Policy Implications. In *Massey, D. and Meegan, R., eds.*, 1985, pp. 64–87. [G: U.K.]

Tremblay, Victor J. A Reappraisal of Interpreting Rising Concentration: The Case of Beer. *J. Bus.*, October 1985, *58*(4), pp. 419–31. [G: U.S.]

Tremblay, Victor J. Strategic Groups and the Demand for Beer. *J. Ind. Econ.*, December 1985, *34*(2), pp. 183–98. [G: U.S.]

Tsujimura, Kotaro. Theory and Measurement of Acute Polypoly and Polyopsony: Inflationary Expectation and Market Paralysis at the First Oil Crisis in Japan. (In Japanese. With English summary.) *Econ. Stud. Quart.*, April 1985, *36*(1), pp. 1–14. [G: Japan]

Tucci, Gianrocco. Regulation and "Contestability" in Formulating an Air Transport Policy for the European Community. *Rivista Polit. Econ.*, Suppl. Dec. 1985, *76*, pp. 219–39. [C: EEC]

Tushman, Michael L. and Romanelli, Elaine. Organizational Evolution: A Metamorphosis Model of Convergence and Reorientation. In *Cummings, L. L. and Staw, B. M., eds.*, 1985, pp. 171–222. [G: U.S.]

Tye, William B. On the Application of the "Williamsonian Welfare Tradeoff" to Rail Mergers. *Logist. Transp. Rev.*, September 1985, *21*(3), pp. 239–48. [G: U.S.]

Tye, William B. The Applicability of the Theory of Contestable Markets to Rail/Water Carrier Mergers. *Logist. Transp. Rev.*, March 1985, *21*(1), pp. 57–76. [G: U.S.]

Uri, Noel D. and Rifkin, Edward J. Geographic Markets, Causality and Railroad Deregulation. *Rev. Econ. Statist.*, August 1985, *67*(3), pp. 422–28. [G: U.S.]

Veloce, William and Zellner, Arnold. Entry and Empirical Demand and Supply Analysis for Competitive Industries. *J. Econometrics,* Oct./ Nov. 1985, *30*(1/2), pp. 459–71. [G: Canada]

Vickers, John. Pre-emptive Patenting, Joint Ventures, and the Persistence of Oligopoly. *Int. J. Ind. Organ.*, September 1985, *3*(3), pp. 261–73.

Vickers, John. Strategic Competition among the Few—Some Recent Developments in the Economics of Industry. *Oxford Rev. Econ. Policy*, Autumn 1985, *1*(3), pp. 39–62.

Vickers, John. The Economics of Predatory Practices. *Fisc. Stud.*, August 1985, *6*(3), pp. 24–36.

Vogt, Roy. Corporate Power and the Development of New Competition Policies in Canada. *J. Econ. Issues*, June 1985, *19*(2), pp. 551–58. [G: Canada]

Wall, Anders. Industrins strukturomvandling via ägarförändringar. (The Structural Change in the Industrial Sector from Shifts in Ownership Positions. With English summary.) *Ekon. Samfundets Tidskr.*, 1985, *38*(1), pp. 7–12. [G: Sweden]

Walters, Stephen J. K. Reciprocity, Rebating, and Regulation. *Southern Econ. J.*, January 1985, *51*(3), pp. 766–75. [G: U.S.]

Wang Chiang, Judy S. and Friedlaender, Ann F. Truck Technology and Efficient Market Structure. *Rev. Econ. Statist.*, May 1985, *67*(2), pp. 250–58. [G: U.S.]

Warden, Gregory J. Is There a Principle for Defining Industries? Comment. *Southern Econ. J.*, October 1985, *52*(2), pp. 532–36.

Ware, Roger. Inventory Holding as a Strategic Weapon to Deter Entry. *Economica*, February 1985, *52*(205), pp. 93–101.

Waterman, David. Prerecorded Home Video and the Distribution of Theatrical Feature Films. In *Noam, E. M., ed.*, 1985, pp. 221–43. [G: U.S.]

Waterson, Michael. Lessons for Competition Policy from Industrial Economic Theory. *Fisc. Stud.*, February 1985, *6*(1), pp. 49–58.

Waterson, Michael and Stoneman, Paul L. Employment, Technological Diffusion and Oligopoly. *Int. J. Ind. Organ.*, September 1985, *3*(3), pp. 327–44.

Watkins, Thomas G.; Spong, Kenneth R. and Eichholz, Mark J. Potential Competition and the Factors Influencing Banking Concentration. *Rev. Ind. Organ.*, 1985, *2*(2), pp. 94–105. [G: U.S.]

Webbink, Douglas W. Comment: Empirical Studies of Media Competition. In *Noam, E. M., ed.*, 1985, pp. 168–73. [G: U.S.]

Weiss, Leonard W. Concentration and Price—A Possible Way Out of a Box. In *Schwalbach, J., ed.*, 1985, pp. 85–111. [G: OECD]

Welch, Patrick J. and Naes, Jude L., Jr. The Merger Guidelines, Concentration and Excess Capacity in Local Commercial Banking Markets. *J. Bank Res.*, Autumn 1985, *16*(3), pp. 158–60. [G: U.S.]

West, Peter J. International Expansion and Concentration of Tire Industry and Implications for Latin America. In *Newfarmer, R. S., ed.*, 1985, pp. 227–58. [G: U.S.; OECD]

Wheeler, James O. and Brown, Catherine L. The Metropolitan Corporate Hierarchy in the U.S. South, 1960–1980. *Econ. Geogr.*, January 1985, *61*(1), pp. 66–78. [G: U.S.]

White, Eugene Nelson. The Merger Movement in Banking, 1919–1933. *J. Econ. Hist.*, June 1985, *45*(2), pp. 285–91. [G: U.S.]

White, Lawrence J. Antitrust and Video Markets: The Merger of Showtime and the Movie Chan-

nel as a Case Study. In *Noam, E. M., ed.*, 1985, pp. 338–63. [G: U.S.]

White, Lawrence J. Resale Price Maintenance and the Problem of Marginal and Inframarginal Customers. *Contemp. Policy Issues*, Spring, Pt. 1, 1985, *3*(3), pp. 17–21. [G: U.S.]

Whyte, William Foote and Blasi, Joseph. The Potential of Employee Ownership. In *Woodworth, W.; Meek, C. and Whyte, W. F., eds.*, 1985, pp. 181–94. [G: U.S.]

Wiggins, Steven N. and Libecap, Gary D. Oil Field Unitization: Contractual Failure in the Presence of Imperfect Information. *Amer. Econ. Rev.*, June 1985, *75*(3), pp. 368–85. [G: U.S.]

Williamson, Oliver E. Assessing Contract. *J. Law, Econ., Organ.*, Spring 1985, *1*(1), pp. 177–208.

Williamson, Oliver E. Employee Ownership and Internal Governance: A Perspective. *J. Econ. Behav. Organ.*, September 1985, *6*(3), pp. 243–45.

Williamson, Oliver E. Reflections on the New Institutional Economics. *Z. ges. Staatswiss.* (*JITE*), March 1985, *141*(1), pp. 187–95.

Wirth, Michael O. and Bloch, Harry. The Broadcasters: The Future Role of Local Stations and the Three Networks. In *Noam, E. M., ed.*, 1985, pp. 121–37. [G: U.S.]

Yamawaki, Hideki. Dominant Firm Pricing and Fringe Expansion: The Case of the U.S. Iron and Steel Industry, 1907–1930. *Rev. Econ. Statist.*, August 1985, *67*(3), pp. 429–37. [G: U.S.]

Yamey, Basil S. Deconcentration as Antitrust Policy: The Rise and Fall of the Concentration Ratio. *Rivista Int. Sci. Econ. Com.*, February 1985, *32*(2), pp. 119–40.

Yarrow, George K. Shareholder Protection, Compulsory Acquisition and the Efficiency of the Takeover Process. *J. Ind. Econ.*, September 1985, *34*(1), pp. 3–16. [G: U.K.]

Yarrow, George K. Welfare Losses in Oligopoly and Monopolistic Competition. In *Geroski, P. A.; Phlips, L. and Ulph, A., eds.*, 1985, pp. 147–61.

Zardkoohi, Asghar. On the Political Participation of the Firm in the Electoral Process. *Southern Econ. J.*, January 1985, *51*(3), pp. 804–17. [G: U.S.]

Zigiotti, Ermanno. Incertezza probabilistica, rischi assicurabili e integrazione verticale. (Probabilistic Uncertainty, Insurable Risks, and Vertical Integration. With English summary.) *Giorn. Econ.*, May-June 1985, *44*(11–12), pp. 301–12.

612 Public Policy Toward Monopoly and Competition

6120 Public Policy Toward Monopoly and Competition

Abbott, Alden F. Foreign Competition and Relevant Market Definition under the Department of Justice's Merger Guidelines. *Antitrust Bull.*, Summer 1985, *30*(2), pp. 299–336.

Adelstein, Richard P. and Peretz, Steven I. The Competition of Technologies in Markets for Ideas: Copyright and Fair Use in Evolutionary Perspective. *Int. Rev. Law Econ.*, December 1985, 5(2), pp. 209–38. [G: U.S.]

Amacher, Ryan, et al. The Behavior of Regulatory Activity over the Business Cycle: An Empirical Test. *Econ. Inquiry*, January 1985, 23(1), pp. 7–19. [G: U.S.]

Anthony, Peter Dean. Regulation and Supply Externalities. *Atlantic Econ. J.*, July 1985, 13(2), pp. 86.

Armentano, D. T. Efficiency, Liberty, and Antitrust Policy [Public Choice and Antitrust]. *Cato J.*, Winter 1985, 4(3), pp. 925–32. [G: U.S.]

Ayres, Ian. Rationalizing Antitrust Cluster Markets. *Yale Law J.*, November 1985, 95(1), pp. 109–24. [G: U.S.]

Bannerman, R. M. Development of Trade Practices Law and Administration. *Australian Econ. Rev.*, 3rd Quarter, Spring 1985, (71), pp. 83–95. [G: Australia]

Baumol, William J. Industry Structure Analysis and Public Policy. In *Feiwel, G. R., ed. (II)*, 1985, pp. 311–27.

Baumol, William J. and Ordover, Janusz A. Use of Antitrust to Subvert Competition. *J. Law Econ.*, May 1985, 28(2), pp. 247–65. [G: OECD]

Bernard, Keith. Deregulation in Telecommunications: A Comment. *Bus. Econ.*, October 1985, 20(4), pp. 55–56. [G: U.S.]

Bittlingmayer, George. Did Antitrust Policy Cause the Great Merger Wave? *J. Law Econ.*, April 1985, 28(1), pp. 77–118. [G: U.S.]

Blair, Roger D. A Suggestion for Improved Antitrust Enforcement. *Antitrust Bull.*, Summer 1985, 30(2), pp. 433–56.

Blumenfeld, Sue D. Public Utilities: Antitrust Law and Deregulation: Comment. In *Poole, R. W., Jr., ed.*, 1985, pp. 67–70. [G: U.S.]

Bock, Betty. An Economist Appraises Vertical Restraints. *Antitrust Bull.*, Spring 1985, 30(1), pp. 117–41. [G: U.S.]

Bork, Robert H. Economics and Antitrust: Response. *Contemp. Policy Issues*, Winter 1984-85, 3(2), pp. 35–41. [G: U.S.]

Bowie, Nolan A. Comment: Antitrust, Concentration, and Competition. In *Noam, E. M., ed.*, 1985, pp. 397–402. [G: U.S.]

Boyer, Kenneth D. Is There a Principle for Defining Industries? Reply. *Southern Econ. J.*, October 1985, 52(2), pp. 542–46.

Brander, James A. and Spencer, Barbara J. Tacit Collusion, Free Entry, and Welfare. *J. Ind. Econ.*, March 1985, 33(3), pp. 277–94.

Breit, William and Elzinga, Kenneth G. Private Antitrust Enforcement: The New Learning. *J. Law Econ.*, May 1985, 28(2), pp. 405–43. [G: U.S.]

Brett, Barry J. *Monsanto:* Great Expectations Unfulfilled. *Antitrust Bull.*, Spring 1985, 30(1), pp. 39–65. [G: U.S.]

Bronsteen, Peter. Product Market Definition in Commercial Bank Merger Cases. *Antitrust Bull.*, Fall 1985, 30(3), pp. 677–94. [G: U.S.]

Calvani, Terry and Langenfeld, James. An Overview of the Current Debate on Resale Price Maintenance. *Contemp. Policy Issues*, Spring, Pt. 1, 1985, 3(3), pp. 1–8. [G: U.S.]

Cartwright, Phillip A. and Kamerschen, David R. Variations in Antitrust Enforcement Activity. *Rev. Ind. Organ.*, 1985, 2(1), pp. 0–31. [G: U.S.]

Cave, Jonathan A. K. A Further Comment on Preemptive Patenting and the Persistence of Monopoly. *Amer. Econ. Rev.*, March 1985, 75(1), pp. 256–58.

Christianson, Jon B. Current Strategies for Containing Health Care Expenditures: Increased Competition Over Prices and Premiums. In *Christianson, J. B. and Smith, K. R., eds.*, 1985, pp. 52–75. [G: U.S.]

Coate, Malcolm B. Techniques for Protecting against Collusion in Sealed Bid Markets. *Antitrust Bull.*, Winter 1985, 30(4), pp. 897–913. [G: U.S.]

Comanor, William S. and Kirkwood, John B. Resale Price Maintenance and Antitrust Policy. *Contemp. Policy Issues*, Spring, Pt. 1, 1985, 3(3), pp. 9–16. [G: U.S.]

Cotter, Francis P. Strategic Implications of the Changing Economy: Business/Industry Perspective. In *Konecci, E. B. and Kuhn, R. L., eds.*, 1985, pp. 68–73. [G: U.S.]

Coxon, P. J. and Jones, J. C. H. Positive Economics and Public Policy: Some Canadian Evidence on Policy Change and Antitrust. *Antitrust Bull.*, Summer 1985, 30(2), pp. 365–99. [G: Canada]

Crew, Michael A. and Kleindorfer, Paul R. Governance Structures for Natural Monopoly: A Comparative Institutional Assessment. *J. Behav. Econ.*, Winter 1985, 14, pp. 117–40.

Csillag, István and Szalai, Erzsébet. Basic Elements of an Anti-monopoly Policy. *Acta Oecon.*, 1985, 34(1–2), pp. 65–77.

Daskin, Alan J. Horizontal Merger Guidelines and the Line of Commerce in Banking: An Algebraic and Graphical Approach. *Antitrust Bull.*, Fall 1985, 30(3), pp. 651–76. [G: U.S.]

De Alessi, Louis. Property Rights and the Judiciary. *Cato J.*, Winter 1985, 4(3), pp. 805–11. [G: U.S.]

DeBrock, Lawrence M. Market Structure, Innovation, and Optimal Patent Life. *J. Law Econ.*, April 1985, 28(1), pp. 223–44.

Dewey, Donald. What Price Theory Can—and Cannot—Do for Antitrust. *Contemp. Policy Issues*, Winter 1984-85, 3(2), pp. 3–11. [G: U.S.]

DiLorenzo, Thomas J. The Origins of Antitrust: An Interest-Group Perspective. *Int. Rev. Law Econ.*, June 1985, 5(1), pp. 73–90. [G: U.S.]

Easley, David; Masson, Robert T. and Reynolds, Robert J. Preying for Time. In *Geroski, P. A.; Phlips, L. and Ulph, A., eds.*, 1985, pp. 77–92.

Easley, David; Masson, Robert T. and Reynolds, Robert J. Preying for Time. *J. Ind. Econ.*, June 1985, 33(4), pp. 445–60.

Easterbrook, Frank H. Detrebling Antitrust

Damages. *J. Law Econ.*, May 1985, *28*(2), pp. 445–67. **[G: U.S.]**

Eckbo, B. Espen and Wier, Peggy. Antimerger Policy under the Hart–Scott–Rodino Act: A Reexamination of the Market Power Hypothesis. *J. Law Econ.*, April 1985, *28*(1), pp. 119–49. **[G: U.S.]**

Elzinga, Kenneth G. Public Choice and Antitrust: A Comment. *Cato J.*, Winter 1985, *4*(3), pp. 917–23. **[G: U.S.]**

England, Catherine. Beyond the Status Quo: Policy Proposals for America: Antitrust. In *Boaz, D. and Crane, E. H.*, eds., 1985, pp. 165–81. **[G: U.S.]**

Fairburn, James A. British Merger Policy. *Fisc. Stud.*, February 1985, *6*(1), pp. 70–81. **[G: U.K.]**

Feinberg, Robert M. The Enforcement and Effects of European Competition Policy: Results of a Survey of Legal Opinion. *J. Common Market Stud.*, June 1985, *23*(4), pp. 373–84. **[G: EEC]**

Ferguson, Paul R. The Monopolies and Mergers Commission and Economic Theory. *Nat. Westminster Bank Quart. Rev.*, November 1985, pp. 30–40. **[G: U.K.]**

Fink, Richard H. General and Partial Equilibrium Theory in Bork's Antitrust Analysis. *Contemp. Policy Issues*, Winter 1984-85, *3*(2), pp. 12–20.

Fisher, Franklin M. The Financial Interest and Syndication Rules in Network Television: Regulatory Fantasy and Reality. In *[McGowan, J. J.]*, 1985, pp. 263–98. **[G: U.S.]**

Fisher, Franklin M. The Social Costs of Monopoly and Regulation: Posner Reconsidered. *J. Polit. Econ.*, April 1985, *93*(2), pp. 410–16. **[G: U.S.]**

Foote, William and Asheghian, Parviz. X-Inefficiency and Interfirm Comparison of U.S. and Canadian Manufacturing Firms in Canada. *Quart. J. Bus. Econ.*, Autumn 1985, *24*(4), pp. 3–14. **[G: U.S.; Canada]**

Forkosch, Morris D. Halt the New Satellite Giveaway. *Amer. J. Econ. Soc.*, April 1985, *44*(2), pp. 196–98. **[G: U.S.]**

Fox, William F., Jr. *Mitsubishi v. Soler* and Its Impact on International Commercial Arbitration. *J. World Trade Law*, Nov.:Dec. 1985, *19*(6), pp. 579–91. **[G: U.S.]**

Gallini, Nancy T. and Winter, Ralph A. Licensing in the Theory of Innovation. *Rand J. Econ.*, Summer 1985, *16*(2), pp. 237–52.

Gallo, Joseph C.; Craycraft, Joseph L. and Bush, Steven C. Guess Who Came to Dinner—An Empirical Study of Federal Antitrust Enforcement for the Period 1963–1984. *Rev. Ind. Organ.*, 1985, *2*(2), pp. 106–31. **[G: U.S.]**

George, Kenneth D. Monopoly and Merger Policy. *Fisc. Stud.*, February 1985, *6*(1), pp. 34–48. **[G: U.K.]**

Gordon, Ken. Technology Venturing: Private/Public Partnerships. In *Konecci, E. B. and Kuhn, R. L.*, eds., 1985, pp. 185–91. **[G: U.S.]**

Gruchy, Allan G. Corporate Concentration and the Restructuring of the American Economy. *J. Econ. Issues*, June 1985, *19*(2), pp. 429–39. **[G: U.S.]**

Hardie, C. J. M. Competition Policy. In *Morris, D.*, ed., 1985, pp. 798–828. **[G: U.K.]**

Harris, Christopher J. and Vickers, John. Patent Races and the Persistence of Monopoly. *J. Ind. Econ.*, June 1985, *33*(4), pp. 461–81.

Harris, Christopher J. and Vickers, John. Patent Races and the Persistence of Monopoly. In *Geroski, P. A.; Phlips, L. and Ulph, A.*, eds., 1985, pp. 93–113.

Harrison, Glenn W. and McKee, Michael. Monopoly Behavior, Decentralized Regulation, and Contestable Markets: An Experimental Evaluation. *Rand J. Econ.*, Spring 1985, *16*(1), pp. 51–69.

Harte, Kathleen M. Legal Implications of Barter and Countertrade Transactions. In *Fisher, B. S. and Harte, K. M.*, eds., 1985, pp. 217–53. **[G: U.S.; EEC]**

Hawkins, Robert G. Antitrust Policy and Intra-industry Direct Foreign Investment: Cause and Effect: Comment. In *Erdilek, A.*, ed., 1985, pp. 123–25. **[G: U.S.]**

Hay, George A. Anti-trust and Economic Theory: Some Observations from the U.S. Experience. *Fisc. Stud.*, February 1985, *6*(1), pp. 59–69. **[G: U.S.]**

Hay, George A. Competition Policy. *Oxford Rev. Econ. Policy*, Autumn 1985, *1*(3), pp. 63–79.

Hay, George A. Vertical Restraints. *Fisc. Stud.*, August 1985, *6*(3), pp. 37–50. **[G: U.S.]**

Hay, George A. and Reynolds, Robert J. Competition and Antitrust in the Petroleum Industry: An Application of the Merger Guidelines. In *[McGowan, J. J.]*, 1985, pp. 15–48. **[G: U.S.]**

Helwege, Ann and Hendricks, Ann. Contestability and Creative Destruction: Two Approaches to Monopoly. *Rev. Ind. Organ.*, 1985, *2*(3), pp. 218–30.

Helwege, Ann and Hendricks, Ann. Three Problems in Applying Contestability to Regulated Markets. *Rev. Ind. Organ.*, 1985, *2*(2), pp. 132–43. **[G: U.S.]**

High, Jack. Bork's Paradox: Static vs. Dynamic Efficiency in Antitrust Analysis. *Contemp. Policy Issues*, Winter 1984-85, *3*(2), pp. 21–34.

Honeycutt, T. Crawford. Competition in Controlled and Uncontrolled Gasoline Markets. *Contemp. Policy Issues*, Spring, Pt. 2, 1985, *3*(3), pp. 105–18. **[G: U.S.]**

Horowitz, Ira. On the Probability of Entry in Potential Competition Cases. *Managerial Dec. Econ.*, June 1985, *6*(2), pp. 119–24. **[G: U.S.]**

Horowitz, Ira. On Whether to Prosecute Suspected Price-Fixing Conspiracies: A Hypothesis-Testing Approach. *Rev. Ind. Organ.*, 1985, *2*(3), pp. 250–64.

Hovenkamp, Herbert. Antitrust Policy after Chicago. *Mich. Law Rev.*, November 1985, *84*(2), pp. 213–84. **[G: U.S.]**

Howard, Jeffrey H. Applying the Antitrust Laws to Local Governments: Congress Changes the

Approach. *Antitrust Bull.*, Winter 1985, *30*(4), pp. 745–90. **[G: U.S.]**

Johnson, William R. The Economics of Copying. *J. Polit. Econ.*, February 1985, *93*(1), pp. 158–74.

Joskow, Paul L. Mixing Regulatory and Antitrust Policies in the Electric Power Industry: The Price Squeeze and Retail Market Competition. In *[McGowan, J. J.]*, 1985, pp. 173–239. **[G: U.S.]**

Judd, Kenneth L. On the Performance of Patents. *Econometrica*, May 1985, *53*(3), pp. 567–85.

Katz, Michael L. and Shapiro, Carl. On the Licensing of Innovations. *Rand J. Econ.*, Winter 1985, *16*(4), pp. 504–20.

Kirim, Arman S. Reconsidering Patents and Economic Development: A Case Study of the Turkish Pharmaceutical Industry. *World Devel.*, February 1985, *13*(2), pp. 219–36. **[G: Turkey]**

Klein, Benjamin and Saft, Lester F. The Law and Economics of Franchise Tying Contracts. *J. Law Econ.*, May 1985, *28*(2), pp. 345–61. **[G: U.S.]**

Klein, Christopher C. Is There a Principle for Defining Industries? Comment. *Southern Econ. J.*, October 1985, *52*(2), pp. 537–41.

Kolasky, William J., Jr.; Proger, Phillip A. and Englert, Roy T., Jr. Anticompetitive Mergers: Prevention and Cure. In *[McGowan, J. J.]*, 1985, pp. 49–84. **[G: U.S.]**

Lande, Robert H. and Zerbe, Richard O., Jr. Reducing Unions' Monopoly Power: Costs and Benefits. *J. Law Econ.*, May 1985, *28*(2), pp. 297–310. **[G: U.S.]**

Landis, Robin C. and Rolfe, Ronald S. Market Conduct under Section 2: When Is It Anticompetitive? In *[McGowan, J. J.]*, 1985, pp. 131–52. **[G: U.S.]**

Langenfeld, James and McKenzie, Joseph A. Financial Deregulation and Geographic Market Delineation: An Application of the Justice Guidelines to Banking. *Antitrust Bull.*, Fall 1985, *30*(3), pp. 695–712. **[G: U.S.]**

Lean, David F.; Ogur, Jonathan D. and Rogers, Robert P. Does Collusion Pay . . . Does Antiturst Work? *Southern Econ. J.*, January 1985, *51*(3), pp. 828–41. **[G: U.S.]**

Leffler, Keith. Toward a Reasonable Rule of Reason: Comments. *J. Law Econ.*, May 1985, *28*(2), pp. 381–86. **[G: U.S.]**

Leontief, Wassily. On Assignment of Patent Rights on Inventions Made under Government Research Contracts. In *Leontief, W.*, 1985, pp. 216–22.

Levin, Harvey J. Comment: Antitrust, Concentration, and Competition. In *Noam, E. M., ed.*, 1985, pp. 390–96. **[G: U.S.]**

Liebeler, Wesley J. A Property Rights Approach to Judicial Decision Making. *Cato J.*, Winter 1985, *4*(3), pp. 783–804. **[G: U.S.]**

Liebeler, Wesley J. Antitrust and Economic Efficiency: Comment. *J. Law Econ.*, May 1985, *28*(2), pp. 335–43.

Livesey, Frank. Monopoly and Competition. In *Atkinson, G. B. J., ed.*, 1985, pp. 81–99. **[G: U.K.]**

Lockerby, Michael J. Franchise Termination Restrictions: A Guide for Practitioners and Policy Makers. *Antitrust Bull.*, Winter 1985, *30*(4), pp. 791–872. **[G: U.S.]**

Loevinger, Lee. Antitrust, Banking, and Competition. *Antitrust Bull.*, Fall 1985, *30*(3), pp. 583–615. **[G: U.S.]**

MacAvoy, Paul W. and Robinson, Kenneth. Losing by Judicial Policymaking: The First Year of the AT&T Divestiture. *Yale J. Regul.*, 1985, *2*(2), pp. 225–62. **[G: U.S.]**

Markovits, Richard S. The Functions, Allocative Efficiency, and Legality of Tie-ins: A Comment. *J. Law Econ.*, May 1985, *28*(2), pp. 387–404. **[G: U.S.]**

Marks, David H. and Jacobson, Jonathan M. Price-fixing: An Overview. *Antitrust Bull.*, Spring 1985, *30*(1), pp. 199–256. **[G: U.S.; U.K.]**

Marvel, Howard P. How Fair Is Fair Trade? *Contemp. Policy Issues*, Spring, Pt. 1, 1985, *3*(3), pp. 23–35. **[G: U.S.]**

Marvel, Howard P. and McCafferty, Stephen. The Welfare Effects of Resale Price Maintenance. *J. Law Econ.*, May 1985, *28*(2), pp. 363–79. **[G: U.S.]**

McGibbon, James R. Proof of a Vertical Conspiracy under *Monsanto*. *Antitrust Bull.*, Spring 1985, *30*(1), pp. 11–38. **[G: U.S.]**

McGowan, John J. Mergers for Power or Progress? In *[McGowan, J. J.]*, 1985, pp. 1–13. **[G: U.S.]**

McKie, James W. Market Definition and the SIC Approach. In *[McGowan, J. J.]*, 1985, pp. 85–100. **[G: U.S.]**

McRae, James J. and Tapon, Francis. Some Empirical Evidence on Post-patent Barriers to Entry in the Canadian Pharmaceutical Industry. *J. Health Econ.*, March 1985, *4*(1), pp. 43–61. **[G: Canada]**

Mellor, William H., III and Allen, Malcolm B., Jr. Public Utilities: Antitrust Law and Deregulation. In *Poole, R. W., Jr., ed.*, 1985, pp. 51–65. **[G: U.S.]**

Militzer, Kenneth H. and Wolf, Martin H. Deregulation in Telecommunications: A Reply. *Bus. Econ.*, October 1985, *20*(4), pp. 57–58. **[G: U.S.]**

Militzer, Kenneth H. and Wolf, Martin H. Deregulation in Telecommunications. *Bus. Econ.*, July 1985, *20*(3), pp. 27–33. **[G: U.S.]**

Miller, James C., III. The FTC and Voluntary Standards: Maximizing the Net Benefits of Self-Regulation. *Cato J.*, Winter 1985, *4*(3), pp. 897–903. **[G: U.S.]**

Miller, James C., III. Use of Antitrust to Subvert Competition: Comment. *J. Law Econ.*, May 1985, *28*(2), pp. 267–70. **[G: OECD]**

Miller, James C., III and Pautler, Paul. Predation: The Changing View in Economics and the Law. *J. Law Econ.*, May 1985, *28*(2), pp. 495–502. **[G: U.S.]**

Moore, Thomas Gale. Antitrust and Economic Efficiency: Introduction. *J. Law Econ.*, May

1985, 28(2), pp. 245–46.

Morash, Edward A. The Economic Relationship between Service Quality and Market Protection for Regulated Household-Goods Moving. *J. Econ. Bus.*, May 1985, 37(2), pp. 123–40. [G: U.S.]

Nelson, Philip and Silvia, Louis. Antitrust Policy and Intra-industry Direct Foreign Investment: Cause and Effect. In *Erdilek, A., ed.*, 1985, pp. 97–123. [G: U.S.]

Nissan, Edward and Caveny, Regina. Relative Concentration of the Largest Firms [An Entropy Measure of Relative Concentration]. *Southern Econ. J.*, January 1985, 51(3), pp. 880–81. [G: U.S.]

Nye, William W. Antitrust Policy and Intra-industry Direct Foreign Investment: Cause and Effect: Comment. In *Erdilek, A., ed.*, 1985, pp. 125–28. [G: U.S.]

O'Hare, Michael. Copyright: When Is Monopoly Efficient? *J. Policy Anal. Manage.*, Spring 1985, 4(3), pp. 407–18.

Ordover, Janusz A. and Willig, Robert D. Antitrust for High-Technology Industries: Assessing Research Joint Ventures and Mergers. *J. Law Econ.*, May 1985, 28(2), pp. 311–33.

Ornstein, Stanley I. Resale Price Maintenance and Cartels. *Antitrust Bull.*, Summer 1985, 30(2), pp. 401–32. [G: U.S.]

Overstreet, Thomas R., Jr. and Fisher, Alan A. Resale Price Maintenance and Distributional Efficiency: Some Lessons from the Past. *Contemp. Policy Issues*, Spring, Pt. 1, 1985, 3(3), pp. 43–58. [G: U.S.]

Pacey, Patricia L. The Courts and College Football: New Playing Rules off the Field? *Amer. J. Econ. Soc.*, April 1985, 44(2), pp. 145–54. [G: U.S.]

Palay, Thomas M. Avoiding Regulatory Constraints: Contracting Safeguards and the Role of Informal Agreements. *J. Law, Econ., Organ.*, Spring 1985, 1(1), pp. 155–75. [G: U.S.]

Perrakis, Stylianos and Silva-Echenique, Julio. The Profitability and Risk of Television Stations in Canada. *Appl. Econ.*, August 1985, 17(4), pp. 745–59. [G: Canada]

Peterson, Laura Bennett. Comment on Antitrust Remedies [Detrebling Antitrust Damages] [Private Antitrust Enforcement: The New Learning]. *J. Law Econ.*, May 1985, 28(2), pp. 483–88. [G: U.S.]

Phillips, Almarin and Mahoney, Joseph. Unreasonable Rules and Rules of Reason: Economic Aspects of Vertical Price-fixing. *Antitrust Bull.*, Spring 1985, 30(1), pp. 99–115. [G: U.S.]

Picot, Arnold. Intellectual Property Rights in Bio-Technology and Computer-Technology: Comment. *Z. ges. Staatswiss. (JITE)*, March 1985, 141(1), pp. 142–45.

Pittman, Russell. Tying without Exclusive Dealing. *Antitrust Bull.*, Summer 1985, 30(2), pp. 279–97.

Popofsky, M. Laurence and Bomse, Stephen V. From *Sylvania* to *Monsanto:* No Longer a "Free Ride." *Antitrust Bull.*, Spring 1985,

30(1), pp. 67–98. [G: U.S.]

Primeaux, Walter J., Jr. Dismantling Competition in a Natural Monopoly. *Quart. Rev. Econ. Bus.*, Autumn 1985, 25(3), pp. 6–21. [G: U.S.]

Ramseyer, J. Mark. The Costs of the Consensual Myth: Antitrust Enforcement and Institutional Barriers to Litigation in Japan. *Yale Law J.*, January 1985, 94(3), pp. 604–45. [G: Japan]

Reynolds, R. Larry. The Regulation of Regulation. *J. Econ. Issues*, March 1985, 19(1), pp. 103–10.

Romano, Richard E. and Berg, Sanford V. The Identification of Predatory Behavior in the Presence of Uncertainty. *Int. J. Ind. Organ.*, June 1985, 3(2), pp. 231–43.

Romano, Roberta. Law as a Product: Some Pieces of the Incorporation Puzzle. *J. Law, Econ., Organ.*, Fall 1985, 1(2), pp. 225–83. [G: U.S.]

Rose, John T. Interstate Banking, Potential Competition, and the Attractiveness of Banking Markets for New Entry. *Antitrust Bull.*, Fall 1985, 30(3), pp. 729–43. [G: U.S.]

Ross, Howard N. John Blair and Monopoly. *Antitrust Bull.*, Winter 1985, 30(4), pp. 997–1009. [G: U.S.]

Rubin, Israel. Thomas Alva Edison's "Treatise on National Economic Policy and Business." *Bus. Hist. Rev.*, Autumn 1985, 59(3), pp. 433–64. [G: U.S.]

Sagoff, Mark. Must Regulatory Reform Fail? *J. Policy Anal. Manage.*, Spring 1985, 4(3), pp. 433–36. [G: U.S.]

Sandage, John Byron. *Forum Non Conveniens* and the Extraterritorial Application of United States Antitrust Law. *Yale Law J.*, June 1985, 94(7), pp. 1693–1714. [G: U.S.]

Savage, Christopher W. Antitrust Considerations Relating to the Distribution of Intangible Information Services. *Antitrust Bull.*, Winter 1985, 30(4), pp. 873–96. [G: U.S.]

Schaerr, Gene C. The *Cellophane* Fallacy and the Justice Department's Guidelines for Horizontal Mergers. *Yale Law J.*, January 1985, 94(3), pp. 670–93. [G: U.S.]

Schankerman, Mark and Pakes, Ariel. Valeur et obsolescence des brevets: Une analyse des statistiques de renouvellement des brevets européens. (The Rate of Obsolescence and the Distribution of Patent Values: Some Evidence from European Patent Renewals. With English summary.) *Revue Écon.*, September 1985, 36(5), pp. 917–41. [G: W. Germany; U.K.; France; Netherlands; Switzerland]

Schmid, A. Allan. Intellectual Property Rights in Bio-Technology and Computer Technology. *Z. ges. Staatswiss. (JITE)*, March 1985, 141(1), pp. 127–41.

Shapiro, Carl. Patent Licensing and R&D Rivalry. *Amer. Econ. Rev.*, May 1985, 75(2), pp. 25–30.

Sharp, Benjamin S. How Fair Is Fair Trade? Comment. *Contemp. Policy Issues*, Spring, Pt. 1, 1985, 3(3), pp. 37–42. [G: U.S.]

Sharpe, Thomas. British Competition Policy in

Perspective. *Oxford Rev. Econ. Policy*, Autumn 1985, *1*(3), pp. 80–94. **[G: U.K.]**

Shaw, Richard and Simpson, Paul. The Monopolies Commission and the Process of Competition. *Fisc. Stud.*, February 1985, *6*(1), pp. 82–96. **[G: U.K.]**

Shepherd, Philip L. Transnational Corporations and the International Cigarette Industry. In *Newfarmer, R. S., ed.*, 1985, pp. 63–112.
[G: Selected Countries; U.S.]

Shughart, William F., II and Tollison, Robert D. Corporate Chartering: An Exploration in the Economics of Legal Change. *Econ. Inquiry*, October 1985, *23*(4), pp. 585–99.
[G: U.S.]

Shughart, William F., II and Tollison, Robert D. The Positive Economics of Antitrust Policy: A Survey Article. *Int. Rev. Law Econ.*, June 1985, *5*(1), pp. 39–57. **[G: U.S.]**

Shughart, William F., II and Tollison, Robert D. The Welfare Basis of the "Failing Company" Doctrine. *Antitrust Bull.*, Summer 1985, *30*(2), pp. 357–64.

Slawson, W. David. A New Concept of Competition: Reanalyzing Tie-in Doctrine after *Hyde*. *Antitrust Bull.*, Summer 1985, *30*(2), pp. 257–78.

Snyder, Edward A. Efficient Assignment of Rights to Sue for Antitrust Damages. *J. Law Econ.*, May 1985, *28*(2), pp. 469–82. **[G: U.S.]**

Solomon, Elinor H. The Dynamics of Banking Antitrust: The New Technology, the Product Realignment. *Antitrust Bull.*, Fall 1985, *30*(3), pp. 537–81. **[G: U.S.]**

Spiller, Pablo T. Comments on Easterbrook and Snyder [Detrebling Antitrust Damages] [Efficient Assignment of Rights to Sue for Antitrust Damages]. *J. Law Econ.*, May 1985, *28*(2), pp. 489–94. **[G: U.S.]**

Steiner, Robert L. The Nature of Vertical Restraints. *Antitrust Bull.*, Spring 1985, *30*(1), pp. 143–97. **[G: U.S.]**

Steuer, Richard M. *Monsanto* and the Mothball Fleet of Antitrust. *Antitrust Bull.*, Spring 1985, *30*(1), pp. 1–10. **[G: U.S.]**

Telser, Lester G. Cooperation, Competition, and Efficiency. *J. Law Econ.*, May 1985, *28*(2), pp. 271–95.

Tollison, Robert D. Public Choice and Antitrust. *Cato J.*, Winter 1985, *4*(3), pp. 905–16.
[G: U.S.]

Uri, Noel D.; Howell, John and Rifkin, Edward J. On Defining Geographic Markets. *Appl. Econ.*, December 1985, *17*(6), pp. 959–77.
[G: U.S.]

Veall, Michael R. On Product Standardization as Competition Policy. *Can. J. Econ.*, May 1985, *18*(2), pp. 416–25.

Venit, James S. EEC Patent Licensing Revisited: The Commission's Patent License Regulation. *Antitrust Bull.*, Summer 1985, *30*(2), pp. 457–526.

Vickers, John. Pre-emptive Patenting, Joint Ventures, and the Persistence of Oligopoly. *Int. J. Ind. Organ.*, September 1985, *3*(3), pp. 261–73.

Vietor, Richard H. K. and Davidson, Dekkers L. Economics and Politics of Deregulation: The Issue of Telephone Access Charges. *J. Policy Anal. Manage.*, Fall 1985, *5*(1), pp. 3–22.
[G: U.S.]

Vogt, Roy. Corporate Power and the Development of New Competition Policies in Canada. *J. Econ. Issues*, June 1985, *19*(2), pp. 551–58.
[G: Canada]

Walters, Stephen J. K. Reciprocity, Rebating, and Regulation. *Southern Econ. J.*, January 1985, *51*(3), pp. 766–75. **[G: U.S.]**

Warden, Gregory J. Is There a Principle for Defining Industries? Comment. *Southern Econ. J.*, October 1985, *52*(2), pp. 532–36.

Waterson, Michael. Lessons for Competition Policy from Industrial Economic Theory. *Fisc. Stud.*, February 1985, *6*(1), pp. 49–58.

Watkins, Thomas G. Probable Future Competition in Banking. *Antitrust Bull.*, Fall 1985, *30*(3), pp. 713–27. **[G: U.S.]**

Webb, L. Roy. Development of Trade Practices Law and Administration: Comment. *Australian Econ. Rev.*, 3rd Quarter, Spring 1985, (71), pp. 96–97. **[G: Australia]**

Welch, Patrick J. and Naes, Jude L., Jr. The Merger Guidelines, Concentration and Excess Capacity in Local Commercial Banking Markets. *J. Bank Res.*, Autumn 1985, *16*(3), pp. 158–60. **[G: U.S.]**

White, Lawrence J. Antitrust and Video Markets: The Merger of Showtime and the Movie Channel as a Case Study. In *Noam, E. M., ed.*, 1985, pp. 338–63. **[G: U.S.]**

White, Lawrence J. Resale Price Maintenance and the Problem of Marginal and Inframarginal Customers. *Contemp. Policy Issues*, Spring, Pt. 1, 1985, *3*(3), pp. 17–21. **[G: U.S.]**

Willard, Stephen Hopkins. A New Method of Calculating Copyright Liability for Cable Rebroadcasting of Distant Television Signals. *Yale Law J.*, May 1985, *94*(6), pp. 1512–28. **[G: U.S.]**

Yamey, Basil S. Deconcentration as Antitrust Policy: The Rise and Fall of the Concentration Ratio. *Rivista Int. Sci. Econ. Com.*, February 1985, *32*(2), pp. 119–40.

613 Regulation of Public Utilities

6130 Regulation of Public Utilities

Abel, Richard L. Risk as an Arena of Struggle. *Mich. Law Rev.*, February 1985, *83*(4), pp. 772–812. **[G: U.S.; U.K.]**

Aigner, Dennis J. The Residential Electricity Time-of-Use Pricing Experiments: What Have We Learned? In *Hausman, J. A. and Wise, D. A., eds.*, 1985, pp. 11–41. **[G: U.S.]**

Aigner, Dennis J. and Hirschberg, Joseph G. Commercial/Industrial Customer Response to Time-of-Use Electricity Prices: Some Experimental Results. *Rand J. Econ.*, Autumn 1985, *16*(3), pp. 341–55. **[G: U.S.]**

Andersson, Roland and Bohman, Mats. Short- and Long-run Marginal Cost Pricing: On Their Alleged Equivalence. *Energy Econ.*, October

1985, 7(4), pp. 279–88.

Anthony, Peter Dean. Regulation and Supply Externalities. *Atlantic Econ. J.*, July 1985, *13*(2), pp. 86.

Armstrong, Christopher and Nelles, H. V. The State and the Provision of Electricity in Canada and Australia, 1880–1965. In *Platt, D. C. M. and di Tella, G., eds.*, 1985, pp. 207–30. [G: Australia; Canada]

Bandow, Doug. The Terrible Ten: America's Worst Regulations. *Policy Rev.*, Spring 1985, (32), pp. 42–46. [G: U.S.]

Beilock, Richard. Is Regulation Necessary for Value-of-Service Pricing? *Rand J. Econ.*, Spring 1985, *16*(1), pp. 93–102. [G: U.S.]

Berry, William W. Total Deregulation of Electric Utilities: A Viable Policy Choice: Comment. In *Poole, R. W., Jr., ed.*, 1985, pp. 147–52. [G: U.S.]

Besanko, David. On the Use of Revenue Requirements Regulation under Imperfect Information. In *Crew, M. A., ed.*, 1985, pp. 39–58.

Blair, Roger D.; Kaserman, David L. and Pacey, Patricia L. A Note on Purchased Power Adjustment Clauses. *J. Bus.*, October 1985, *58*(4), pp. 409–17. [G: U.S.]

Bös, Dieter. Public Sector Pricing. In *Auerbach, A. J. and Feldstein, M., eds.*, 1985, pp. 129–211.

Braunstein, Yale M. and White, Lawrence J. Setting Technical Compatibility Standards: An Economic Analysis. *Antitrust Bull.*, Summer 1985, *30*(2), pp. 337–55.

Brown, Stephen P. A. Consumers May Not Benefit from Wellhead Price Controls on Natural Gas. *Fed. Res. Bank Dallas Econ. Rev.*, July 1985, pp. 1–11. [G: U.S.]

Bruggink, Thomas H. Monopoly Pricing as a Consumer Exaction in the Public Utility Sector: Monopoly Welfare Loss and Regulation in the Municipal Water Industry. *Amer. J. Econ. Soc.*, April 1985, *44*(2), pp. 229–39. [G: U.S.]

Bubnys, Edward L. and Primeaux, Walter J., Jr. Rate-Base Valuation Methods and Firm Efficiency. *Managerial Dec. Econ.*, September 1985, *6*(3), pp. 167–71. [G: U.S.]

Buell, Stephen G. and Guerard, John B., Jr. An Econometric Analysis of the Formal Regulatory Process. In *Brown, R. C., ed.*, 1985, pp. 15–38. [G: U.S.]

Burgat, Paul and Jeanrenaud, Claude. Consequences d'une perequation tarifaire spatiale du point de vue du bien-etre et de la redistribution des revenus. (Consequences of Interregional Cross Subsidization with Regard to Welfare and Redistribution. With English summary.) *Public Finance*, 1985, *40*(1), pp. 64–81.

Byatt, Ian. Market and Non-market Alternatives in the Public Supply of Public Services: British Experience with Privatization. In *Forte, F. and Peacock, A., eds.*, 1985, pp. 203–11. [G: U.K.]

Cairns, Robert D. Rent Seeking, Deregulation and Regulatory Reform. *Can. Public Policy*,

September 1985, *11*(3), pp. 591–601. [G: Canada]

Chen, Andrew H. and Sanger, Gary C. An Analysis of the Impact of Regulatory Change: The Case of Natural Gas Deregulation. *Financial Rev.*, February 1985, *20*(1), pp. 36–54. [G: U.S.]

Cohen, Linda. Private Contracting versus Public Regulation as a Solution to the Natural Monopoly Problem: Comment. In *Poole, R. W., Jr., ed.*, 1985, pp. 115–19. [G: U.S.]

Copeland, Basil L., Jr. and Severn, Alan K. Price Theory and Telecommunications Regulation: A Dissenting View. *Yale J. Regul.*, Fall 1985, *3*(1), pp. 53–85. [G: U.S.]

Cornell, Nina W. and Webbink, Douglas W. Public Utility Rate-of-Return Regulation: Can It Ever Protect Customers? In *Poole, R. W., Jr., ed.*, 1985, pp. 27–47. [G: U.S.]

Craven, John. Peak-Load Pricing and Short-run Marginal Cost. *Econ. J.*, September 1985, *95*(379), pp. 778–80.

Crew, Michael A. and Kleindorfer, Paul R. Governance Costs of Rate-of-Return Regulation. *Z. ges. Staatswiss. (JITE)*, March 1985, *141*(1), pp. 104–23.

Crew, Michael A. and Schlenger, Donald L. Opportunities for Regulation and Rate Design of Innovative Metering Technology in Water Utilities. In *Crew, M. A., ed.*, 1985, pp. 161–81. [G: U.S.]

Díaz, Francisco Gil. Investment and Debt. In *Musgrave, P. B., ed.*, 1985, pp. 3–32. [G: Mexico]

Eckart, Wolfgang and Schulz, Norbert. Distributional Equity and Two-part Tariffs. *Z. ges. Staatswiss. (JITE)*, June 1985, *141*(2), pp. 301–11.

Elkin, Stephen L. Regulation as a Political Question. *Policy Sci.*, March 1985, *18*(1), pp. 95–108.

Eppler, Dale. Fifth Circuit Expands 'Not Substantially Developed' Exception to FERC Jurisdiction under the Natural Gas Act of 1938. *Natural Res. J.*, July 1985, *25*(3), pp. 813–27. [G: U.S.]

Färe, Rolf; Grosskopf, Shawna and Logan, J. The Relative Performance of Publicly Owned and Privately Owned Electric Utilities. *J. Public Econ.*, February 1985, *26*(1), pp. 89–106. [G: U.S.]

Finch, M. H. J. British Imperialism in Uruguay: The Public Utility Companies and the *Batllista* State, 1900–1930. In *Abel, C. and Lewis, C. M., eds.*, 1985, pp. 250–66. [G: U.K.; Uruguay]

Fix, Michael and Eads, George C. The Prospects for Regulatory Reform: The Legacy of Reagan's First Term. *Yale J. Regul.*, 1985, *2*(2), pp. 293–318. [G: U.S.]

Foreman-Peck, James S. and Waterson, Michael. The Comparative Efficiency of Public and Private Enterprise in Britain: Electricity Generation between the World Wars. *Econ. J.*, Supplement 1985, *95*, pp. 83–95. [G: U.K.]

Frost, Robert L. Economists as Nationalised Sector Managers: Reforms of the Electrical Rate Structure in France, 1946–1969. *Cambridge J. Econ.*, September 1985, *9*(3), pp. 285–300. [G: France]

Gollop, Frank M. and Roberts, Mark J. Cost-minimizing Regulation of Sulfur Emissions: Regional Gains in Electric Power. *Rev. Econ. Statist.*, February 1985, *67*(1), pp. 81–90. [G: U.S.]

Guerard, John B., Jr. and Buell, Stephen G. Multiple-Criteria Financial Planning Model of Public Utility Firms. In *Haimes, Y. Y. and Chankong, V., eds.*, 1985, pp. 475–81. [G: U.S.]

Hammond, Elizabeth M.; Helm, Dieter R. and Thompson, David J. British Gas: Options for Privatisation. *Fisc. Stud.*, November 1985, *6*(4), pp. 1–20. [G: U.K.]

Hayashi, Paul M.; Sevier, Melanie and Trapani, John M. Pricing Efficiency under Rate-of-Return Regulation: Some Empirical Evidence for the Electric Utility Industry. *Southern Econ. J.*, January 1985, *51*(3), pp. 776–92. [G: U.S.]

Hazlett, Thomas. Private Contracting versus Public Regulation as a Solution to the Natural Monopoly Problem. In *Poole, R. W., Jr., ed.*, 1985, pp. 71–114. [G: U.S.]

Hazlett, Thomas. The Curious Evolution of Natural Monopoly Theory. In *Poole, R. W., Jr., ed.*, 1985, pp. 1–25.

Helliwell, John F., et al. Energy Deregulation and Uncertain World Oil Prices: What Are the Connections? *Can. Public Policy*, Supplement July 1985, *11*(3), pp. 479–91. [G: Canada]

Henderson, J. Stephen. Cost Estimation for Vertically Integrated Firms: The Case of Electricity. In *Crew, M. A., ed.*, 1985, pp. 75–94. [G: U.S.]

Hendrickson, Chris T. and McMichael, Francis Clay. Controlling Contradictions among Regulations: Note. *Amer. Econ. Rev.*, September 1985, *75*(4), pp. 876–77. [G: U.S.]

Herriott, Scott R. The Organizational Economics of Power Brokers and Centrally Dispatched Power Pools. *Land Econ.*, August 1985, *61*(3), pp. 308–13.

Hobbs, Benjamin F. and Schuler, Richard E. Evaluation of Electric Power Deregulation Using Network Models of Oligopolistic Spatial Markets. In *Harker, P. T., ed.*, 1985, pp. 208–54. [G: U.S.]

Jackson, Charles L. Cable and Public Utility Regulation. In *Poole, R. W., Jr., ed.*, 1985, pp. 153–71. [G: U.S.]

Jenkins, Glenn P. Public Utility Finance and Economic Waste. *Can. J. Econ.*, August 1985, *18*(3), pp. 484–98. [G: Canada]

Johnson, Leland L. Public Utility Rate-of-Return Regulation: Can It Ever Protect Customers?: Comment. In *Poole, R. W., Jr., ed.*, 1985, pp. 49–50. [G: U.S.]

Johnson, W. Bruce. Valuation Implications of SFAS No. 33 Data for Electric Utility Investors: Discussion. *J. Acc. Res.*, Supp. 1985, *23*, pp. 48–53. [G: U.S.]

Jones, Ian S. Distortions in Electricity Pricing in the UK: A Comment. *Oxford Bull. Econ. Statist.*, August 1985, *47*(3), pp. 275–85.

Jordan, W. John. Capacity Costs, Heterogeneous Users, and Peak-Load Pricing [Heterogeneous Users and the Peak-load Pricing model]. *Quart. J. Econ.*, November 1985, *100*(4), pp. 1335–37.

Jorgenson, Dale W. and Slesnick, Daniel T. Efficiency versus Equity in Natural Gas Price Regulation. *J. Econometrics*, Oct./Nov. 1985, *30*(1/2), pp. 301–16. [G: U.S.]

Joskow, Paul L. Mixing Regulatory and Antitrust Policies in the Electric Power Industry: The Price Squeeze and Retail Market Competition. In *[McGowan, J. J.]*, 1985, pp. 173–239. [G: U.S.]

Joskow, Paul L. The Residential Electricity Time-of-Use Pricing Experiments: What Have We Learned? Comment. In *Hausman, J. A. and Wise, D. A., eds.*, 1985, pp. 42–48. [G: U.S.]

Joskow, Paul L. and Rose, Nancy L. The Effects of Technological Change, Experience, and Environmental Regulation on the Construction Cost of Coal-burning Generating Units. *Rand J. Econ.*, Spring 1985, *16*(1), pp. 1–27. [G: U.S.]

Kaufer, Erich. The Transaction Costs of Rate-of-Return Regulation: Comment. *Z. ges. Staatswiss. (JITE)*, March 1985, *141*(1), pp. 124–26.

Knieps, Günther. Möglichkeiten des Wettbewerbs im schweizerischen Telekommunikationssektor. (The Role of Competition in the Swiss Telecommunications Sector. With English summary.) *Schweiz. Z. Volkswirtsch. Statist.*, December 1985, *121*(4), pp. 407–20. [G: Switzerland]

LeBlanc, Michael. The Effects of Natural Gas Decontrol on Fertilizer Demand, Production Costs, and Income in Agriculture. *Energy J.*, January 1985, *6*(1), pp. 117–35. [G: U.S.]

Libecap, Gary D. and Wiggins, Steven N. The Influence of Private Contractual Failure on Regulation: The Case of Oil Field Unitization. *J. Polit. Econ.*, August 1985, *93*(4), pp. 690–714. [G: U.S.]

Lipman, Barton L. Dynamic Behavior of a Firm Subject to Stochastic Regulatory Review: A Comment. *Int. Econ. Rev.*, June 1985, *26*(2), pp. 511–16.

Marchese, Carla. Market and Non-market Alternatives in the Public Supply of Public Services: Some Empirical Evidence. In *Forte, F. and Peacock, A., eds.*, 1985, pp. 212–26. [G: OECD]

McBain, Helen. Towards a Viable Water Utility in Jamaica. *Soc. Econ. Stud.*, March 1985, *34*(1), pp. 77–96. [G: Jamaica]

Mellor, William H., III and Allen, Malcolm B., Jr. Public Utilities: Antitrust Law and Deregulation. In *Poole, R. W., Jr., ed.*, 1985, pp. 51–65. [G: U.S.]

Miller, Edythe S. Controlling Power in the Social Economy: The Regulatory Approach. *Rev. Soc.*

Econ., October 1985, *43*(2), pp. 129–39.

Miller, James C., III. The FTC and Voluntary Standards: Maximizing the Net Benefits of Self-Regulation. *Cato J.*, Winter 1985, *4*(3), pp. 897–903. [G: U.S.]

Noll, Roger G. "Let Them Make Toll Calls": A State Regulator's Lament. *Amer. Econ. Rev.*, May 1985, *75*(2), pp. 52–56. [G: U.S.]

Norton, Seth W. Regulation and Systematic Risk: The Case of Electric Utilities. *J. Law Econ.*, October 1985, *28*(3), pp. 671–86. [G: U.S.]

Olmstead, Alan L. and Rhode, Paul. Rationing without Government: The West Coast Gas Famine of 1920. *Amer. Econ. Rev.*, December 1985, *75*(5), pp. 1044–55. [G: U.S.]

Olsen, Chris. Valuation Implications of SFAS No. 33 Data for Electric Utility Investors. *J. Acc. Res.*, Supp. 1985, *23*, pp. 28–47. [G: U.S.]

Oren, Shmuel S.; Smith, Stephen S. and Wilson, Robert B. Capacity Pricing. *Econometrica*, May 1985, *53*(3), pp. 545–66.

Phillips, Almarin. The Reintegration of Telecommunications: An Interim View. **In** *Crew, M. A., ed.*, 1985, pp. 5–16. [G: U.S.]

Phillips, Almarin and Roberts, Gary L. Borrowing from Peter to Pay Paul: More on Departures of Price from Marginal Cost. **In** *[McGowan, J. J.]*, 1985 report, pp. 299–307.

Phillips, Bruce D. The Effect of Industry Deregulation on the Small Business Sector. *Bus. Econ.*, January 1985, *20*(1), pp. 28–37. [G: U.S.]

Primeaux, Walter J., Jr. Dismantling Competition in a Natural Monopoly. *Quart. Rev. Econ. Bus.*, Autumn 1985, *25*(3), pp. 6–21. [G: U.S.]

Primeaux, Walter J., Jr. Total Deregulation of Electric Utilities: A Viable Policy Choice. **In** *Poole, R. W., Jr., ed.*, 1985, pp. 121–46. [G: U.S.]

Primeaux, Walter J., Jr. and Mann, Patrick C. Voter Power and Electricity Prices. *Public Choice*, 1985, *47*(3), pp. 519–25. [G: U.S.]

Renshaw, Edward F. A Note on Equity and Efficiency in the Pricing of Local Telephone Services. *Amer. Econ. Rev.*, June 1985, *75*(3), pp. 515–18. [G: U.S.]

Reynolds, R. Larry. The Regulation of Regulation. *J. Econ. Issues*, March 1985, *19*(1), pp. 103–10.

Richter, Wolfram F. and Weimann, Joachim. Ramsey Pricing the Telephone Services of the Deutsche Bundespost. *Z. ges. Staatswiss. (JITE)*, December 1985, *141*(4), pp. 516–24. [G: W. Germany]

Ross, Thomas W. Extracting Regulators' Implied Welfare Weights: Some Further Developments and Applications. *Quart. Rev. Econ. Bus.*, Autumn 1985, *25*(3), pp. 72–84. [G: U.S.]

Rozek, Richard P. Competition as a Complement to Regulation. *Energy J.*, July 1985, *6*(3), pp. 79–90. [G: U.S.]

Samuel, Peter. Telecommunications: After the Bell Break-up. **In** *Poole, R. W., Jr., ed.*, 1985, pp. 177–203. [G: U.S.]

Schefter, J. E. and David, E. L. Estimating Residential Water Demand under Multi-part Tariffs Using Aggregate Data. *Land Econ.*, August 1985, *61*(3), pp. 272–80. [G: U.S.]

Schwartz, David S. Idealism and Realism: An Institutionalist View of Corporate Power in the Regulated Utilities. *J. Econ. Issues*, June 1985, *19*(2), pp. 311–31. [G: U.S.]

Scott, Frank A., Jr. The Effect of a Fuel Adjustment Clause on a Regulated Firm's Selection of Inputs. *Energy J.*, April 1985, *6*(2), pp. 117–26.

Shaffer, Sherrill. Regulatory Inertia and Risk Reduction. *Rev. Ind. Organ.*, 1985, *2*(1), pp. 56–67.

Sherman, Roger. The Averch and Johnson Analysis of Public Utility Regulation Twenty Years Later. *Rev. Ind. Organ.*, 1985, *2*(2), pp. 178–93.

Shughart, William F., II and Tollison, Robert D. The Cyclical Character of Regulatory Activity. *Public Choice*, 1985, *45*(3), pp. 303–11. [G: U.S.]

Sibley, David S. Response to Lipman and Further Results [Dynamic Behavior of a Firm Subject to Stochastic Regulatory Review]. *Int. Econ. Rev.*, June 1985, *26*(2), pp. 517–20.

Slater, M. D. E. and Yarrow, George K. Distortions in Electricity Pricing in the UK: Reply, *Oxford Bull. Econ. Statist.*, August 1985 *47*(3), pp. 287–91.

Smiley, Robert. Management Compensation in Regulated Industries. **In** *Crew, M. A., ed.*, 1985, pp. 111–25. [G: U.S.]

Sohl, Jeffrey E. An Application of Quadratic Programming to the Deregulation of Natural Gas. **In** *Harker, P. T., ed.*, 1985, pp. 196–207. [G: U.S.]

de Sola Pool, Ithiel. Cable and Public Utility Regulation: Comment. **In** *Poole, R. W., Jr., ed.*, 1985, pp. 173–76. [G: U.S.]

Soldofsky, Robert M. Return Premiums on Utility Common Stocks. *Quart. Rev. Econ. Bus.*, Summer 1985, *25*(2), pp. 60–72. [G: U.S.]

Taggart, Robert A., Jr. Effects of Regulation on Utility Financing: Theory and Evidence. *J. Ind. Econ.*, March 1985, *33*(3), pp. 257–76. [G: U.S.]

Taylor, Lester D. The Residential Electricity Time-of-Use Pricing Experiments: What Have We Learned? Comment. **In** *Hausman, J. A. and Wise, D. A., eds.*, 1985, pp. 49–50. [G: U.S.]

Thayer, Frederick C. The Crisis of Industrial Overcapacity: Avoiding Another Great Depression. **In** *Didsbury, H. F., Jr., ed.*, 1985, pp. 353–90. [G: U.S.]

Thompson, Howard E. Estimating Return Deficiencies of Electric Utilities 1963–1981. **In** *Crew, M. A., ed.*, 1985, pp. 17–37. [G: U.S.]

Trebing, Harry M. The Impact of Diversification on Economic Regulation. *J. Econ. Issues*, June 1985, *19*(2), pp. 463–74. [G: U.S.]

Vickrey, William. The Fallacy of Using Long-run Cost for Peak-Load Pricing [Heterogeneous

Users and the Peak-load Pricing model]. *Quart. J. Econ.*, November 1985, *100*(4), pp. 1331–34.

Watkins, G. C. and Waverman, Leonard. Canadian Natural Gas Export Pricing Behaviour. *Can. Public Policy*, Supplement July 1985, *11*(3), pp. 415–26. [G: Canada]

Wiggins, Patrick K. Telecommunications: After the Bell Break-up: Comment. In *Poole, R. W., Jr., ed.*, 1985, pp. 205–13. [G: U.S.]

Woo, Chi-Keung. An Application of the Expenditure Function in Electricity Pricing: Optimal Residential Time-of-Use Rate Option. *Energy J.*, April 1985, *6*(2), pp. 89–99.

Zajac, Edward E. Perceived Economic Justice: The Example of Public Utility Regulation. In *Young, H. P., ed.*, 1985, pp. 119–53.

Zuker, R. C. and Pastor, M.-H. Financial Policies in the Canadian Electric Utility Sector: Origins, Practices, and Questions. *Can. Public Policy*, Supplement July 1985, *11*(3), pp. 427–37. [G: Canada]

614 Public Enterprises

6140 Public Enterprises

Adie, Douglas K. Abolishing the Postal Monopoly: A Comment [End the Postal Monopoly]. *Cato J.*, Fall 1985, *5*(2), pp. 657–61. [G: U.S.]

Ahrens, Karl. Public Enterprise between Growth and Stagnation. *Ann. Pub. Co-op. Econ.*, January–June 1985, *56*(1–2), pp. 51–61. [G: W. Germany]

Albon, Robert P. The Effects of Financial Targets on the Behaviour of Monopoly Public Enterprises. *Australian Econ. Pap.*, June 1985, *24*(44), pp. 54–65. [G: Australia]

Bachleitner, A., et al. Öffentliche unternehmen in österreich. (Public Enterprises in Austria. With English summary.) *Ann. Pub. Co-op. Econ.*, July–Sept. 1985, *56*(3), pp. 273–85. [G: Austria]

Barrington, T. J. Public Enterprise in Ireland. *Ann. Pub. Co-op. Econ.*, July–Sept. 1985, *56*(3), pp. 287–311. [G: Ireland]

Bellon, Bertrand. Strengths and Weaknesses of French Industry. In *Zukin, S., ed.*, 1985, pp. 141–51. [G: France]

Bertrand, Claude-Jean. Cable Television in France. In *Negrine, R. M., ed.*, 1985, pp. 134–63. [G: France]

Bootle, Roger P. Public Expenditure Policy, 1985–86: Privatisation. In *Cockle, P., ed.*, 1985, pp. 77–99. [G: U.K.]

Bös, Dieter. Public Sector Pricing. In *Auerbach, A. J. and Feldstein, M., eds.*, 1985, pp. 129–211.

Brander, James A. and Spencer, Barbara J. Ramsey Optimal Two Part Tariffs: The Case of Many Heterogeneous Groups. *Public Finance*, 1985, *40*(3), pp. 335–46.

Brech, M. J. Nationalized Industries. In *Morris, D., ed.*, 1985, pp. 771–97. [G: U.K.]

Bruton, Henry J. On the Production of a National Technology. In *James, J. and Watanabe, S.,*

eds., 1985, pp. 81–115.

Byatt, Ian. Market and Non-market Alternatives in the Public Supply of Public Services: British Experience with Privatization. In *Forte, F. and Peacock, A., eds.*, 1985, pp. 203–11. [G: U.K.]

Dacey, Robert J. Public Works and Their Impacts on Infrastructure and the National Economy. In *Konecci, E. B. and Kuhn, R. L., eds.*, 1985, pp. 134–41. [G: U.S.]

Dick, Howard W. Interisland Shipping: Progress, Problems and Prospects. *Bull. Indonesian Econ. Stud.*, August 1985, *21*(2), pp. 95–114. [G: Indonesia]

Dodson, D. Keith. The Roles of Private and Public Sectors in Large-scale Public Works. In *Konecci, E. B. and Kuhn, R. L., eds.*, 1985, pp. 192–98. [G: U.S.]

Durupty, Michel. La place du nouveau secteur public dans l'économie nationale. (The Place of the New Public Sector in the French National Economy. With English summary.) *Ann. Pub. Co-op. Econ.*, July–Sept. 1985, *56*(3), pp. 343–63. [G: France]

Eckel, Catherine C. and Vining, Aidan R. Elements of a Theory of Mixed Enterprise. *Scot. J. Polit. Econ.*, February 1985, *32*(1), pp. 82–94.

Egan, John J. Industry and Government in Space: Making the Long-term Commitment. In *Konecci, E. B. and Kuhn, R. L., eds.*, 1985, pp. 144–63. [G: U.S.]

Fabra, Paul. Banking Policy under the Socialists. In *Machin, H. and Wright, V., eds.*, 1985, pp. 173–83. [G: France]

Färe, Rolf; Grosskopf, Shawna and Logan, J. The Relative Performance of Publicly Owned and Privately Owned Electric Utilities. *J. Public Econ.*, February 1985, *26*(1), pp. 89–106. [G: U.S.]

Ferner, Anthony. Political Constraints and Management Strategies: The Case of Working Practices in British Rail. *Brit. J. Ind. Relat.*, March 1985, *23*(1), pp. 47–70. [G: U.K.]

Foreman-Peck, James S. and Waterson, Michael. The Comparative Efficiency of Public and Private Enterprise in Britain: Electricity Generation between the World Wars. *Econ. J.*, Supplement 1985, *95*, pp. 83–95. [G: U.K.]

Forrest, David. Privatisation. In *Atkinson, G. B. J., ed.*, 1985, pp. 101–21. [G: U.K.]

Frech, H. E., III. The Property Rights Theory of the Firm: Some Evidence from the U.S. Nursing Home Industry. *Z. ges. Staatswiss. (JITE)*, March 1985, *141*(1), pp. 146–66. [G: U.S.]

Freixas, Xavier and Laffont, Jean-Jacques. Average Cost Pricing versus Marginal Cost Pricing under Moral Hazard. *J. Public Econ.*, March 1985, *26*(2), pp. 135–46.

Frost, Robert L. Economists as Nationalised Sector Managers: Reforms of the Electrical Rate Structure in France, 1946–1969. *Cambridge J. Econ.*, September 1985, *9*(3), pp. 285–300. [G: France]

Gäfgen, Gérard. The Property Rights Theory of

the Firm: Some Evidence from the U.S. Nursing Home Industry: Comment. *Z. ges. Staatswiss. (JITE)*, March 1985, *141*(1), pp. 167–69.

Halevi, Joseph. Effective Demand, Capacity Utilization and the Sectoral Distribution of Investment. *Écon. Soc.*, August 1985, *19*(8), pp. 25–45.

Halpern, Dan. The Structure of Industry in Israel. In *Levinson, P. and Landau, P., eds.*, 1985, pp. 73–74. [G: Israel]

Hammond, Elizabeth M.; Helm, Dieter R. and Thompson, David J. British Gas: Options for Privatisation. *Fisc. Stud.*, November 1985, *6*(4), pp. 1–20. [G: U.K.]

Hanke, Steve H. Privatization: Theory, Evidence, and Implementation. In *Harriss, C. L., ed.*, 1985, pp. 101–13. [G: U.S.]

Hartmann, Arntraud and Nawab, Syed Ali. Evaluating Public Manufacturing Enterprises in Pakistan. *Finance Develop.*, September 1985, *22*(3), pp. 27–30. [G: Pakistan]

Himmelmann, Gerhard. Public Enterprises in the Federal Republic of Germany. *Ann. Pub. Co-op. Econ.*, July-Sept. 1985, *56*(3), pp. 365–91. [G: W. Germany]

Jha, L. K. Improving Profitability of the Public Sector. In *Jha, L. K.*, 1985, pp. 179–86. [G: India]

Jha, L. K. Investment Pattern and National Objectives. In *Jha, L. K.*, 1985, pp. 241–50. [G: India]

Jones, Leroy P. Public Enterprise for Whom? Perverse Distributional Consequences of Public Operational Decisions. *Econ. Develop. Cult. Change*, January 1985, *33*(2), pp. 333–47. [G: LDCs]

Kemp, Michael A. and Kirby, Ronald F. Government Policies Affecting Competition in Public Transportation. In *Lave, C. A., ed.*, 1985, pp. 277–98. [G: U.S.]

Laux, Jeanne Kirk. Social Democracy and State Capital: Potash in Saskatchewan. In *[Spry, I. M.]*, 1985, pp. 141–55. [G: Canada]

Marchese, Carla. Market and Non-market Alternatives in the Public Supply of Public Services: Some Empirical Evidence. In *Forte, F. and Peacock, A., eds.*, 1985, pp. 212–26. [G: OECD]

Matzner, Egon. Technological and Institutional Innovation. *Ann. Pub. Co-op. Econ.*, January–June 1985, *56*(1–2), pp. 71–80. [G: Austria]

Mayer, Colin and Meadowcroft, Shirley A. Selling Public Assets: Techniques and Financial Implications. *Fisc. Stud.*, November 1985, *6*(4), pp. 42–56. [G: U.K.]

Miller, James C., III. End the Postal Monopoly. *Cato J.*, Spring/Summer 1985, *5*(1), pp. 149–55. [G: U.S.]

Mujumdar, N. A. Structural Transformation in the Deployment of Credit: Some Implications. In *Bandyopadhyay, R. and Khankhoje, D. P., eds.*, 1985, pp. 41–54. [G: India]

Naughton, Barry. False Starts and Second Wind: Financial Reforms in China's Industrial System. In *Perry, E. J. and Wong, C., eds.*, 1985,

pp. 223–52. [G: China]

Neuman, Henri. Institutional and Financial Aspects of Public Enterprise International Cooperation. *Ann. Pub. Co-op. Econ.*, January–June 1985, *56*(1–2), pp. 145–54. [G: EEC]

Orski, C. Kenneth. The Private Challenge to Public Transportation. In *Lave, C. A., ed.*, 1985, pp. 311–31. [G: U.S.]

Parris, Henry. Public Enterprises in Great Britain. *Ann. Pub. Co-op. Econ.*, July-Sept. 1985, *56*(3), pp. 393–410. [G: U.K.]

Pendse, Dattatraya R. Some Reflections on the Role of Donor Agencies in the Privatization Process. *Nat. Westminster Bank Quart. Rev.*, November 1985, pp. 2–18. [G: LDCs]

Pestieau, Pierre. Belgian Public Enterprises. *Ann. Pub. Co-op. Econ.*, July-Sept. 1985, *56*(3), pp. 411–24. [G: Belgium]

Peston, Maurice H. The Nationalized Industries in Great Britain. In *Bornstein, M., ed.*, 1985, pp. 61–75. [G: U.K.]

Peters, Wolfgang. Can Inefficient Public Production Promote Welfare? *Z. Nationalökon.*, 1985, *45*(4), pp. 395–407.

Peterson, George E. Pricing and Privatization of Public Services. In *Gramlich, E. M. and Ysander, B.-C., eds.*, 1985, pp. 137–72. [G: U.S.]

Philip, Alan Butt. Banking Policy under the Socialists: Comment. In *Machin, H. and Wright, V., eds.*, 1985, pp. 183–86. [G: France]

Pirie, Madsen. Sale of the Century: Britain's Privatization Bonanza. *Policy Rev.*, Winter 1985, (31), pp. 79–80. [G: U.K.]

Pitkänen, Eero. Julkisyhteisöjen talous liiketaloustieteen, erityisesti laskentatoimen tutkimuskohteena. (Research on the Economics of Public Organizations in Business Economics, Especially in Accounting and Finance. With English summary.) *Liiketaloudellinen Aikak.*, 1985, *34*(1), pp. 98–107. [G: Finland]

Rajalakshmi, K. Production Function Analysis of Public Sector Transport Equipment Industry in India. *Indian Econ. J.*, Oct.-Nov. 1985, *33*(2), pp. 17–33. [G: India]

Ramamurti, Ravi. High Technology Exports by State Enterprises in LDCs: The Brazilian Aircraft Industry. *Devel. Econ.*, September 1985, *23*(3), pp. 254–80. [G: Brazil]

Romagnoli, Gian Cesare. Les entreprises a participation d'etat dans la politique de l'emploi. (The Role of Enterprises with State Share Holdings in Employment Policy. With English summary.) *Ann. Pub. Co-op. Econ.*, Oct.-Dec. 1985, *56*(4), pp. 485–95. [G: Italy]

de Ru, H. J. Public Enterprises in the Netherlands: A Tradition in Privatization. *Ann. Pub. Co-op. Econ.*, July-Sept. 1985, *56*(3), pp. 313–41. [G: Netherlands]

Rueschemeyer, Dietrich and Evans, Peter B. The State and Economic Transformation: Toward an Analysis of the Conditions Underlying Effective Intervention. In *Evans, P. B.; Rueschemeyer, D. and Skocpol, T., eds.*, 1985, pp. 44–77.

Santoro, Francesco. A New Government Plan for the Reform of the State Railways. *Rev. Econ.*

Cond. Italy, January–April 1985, (1), pp. 121–35. [G: Italy]

Sarmad, Khwaja. Evaluating the Operational Performance of Manufacturing Enterprises: An Evaluation Framework and Application to Pakistani Industry: Comments. *Pakistan Devel. Rev.*, Autumn-Winter 1985, *24*(3/4), pp. 718–19. [G: Pakistan]

Scott, Frank A., Jr. The Pricing Policy of the Postal Service: Economics Misapplied. *J. Policy Anal. Manage.*, Winter 1985, *4*(2), pp. 251–56. [G: U.S.]

Shaikh, Abdul Hafeez. Evaluating the Operational Performance of Manufacturing Enterprises: An Evaluation Framework and Application to Pakistani Industry. *Pakistan Devel. Rev.*, Autumn-Winter 1985, *24*(3/4), pp. 703–17. [G: Pakistan]

Sheehan, Michael F. Plant Closings and the Community: The Instrumental Value of Public Enterprise in Countering Corporate Flight. *Amer. J. Econ. Soc.*, October 1985, *44*(4), pp. 423–33. [G: U.S.]

Soskice, David. The Nationalizations: An Initial Assessment, 1981–1984: Comment. In *Machin, H. and Wright, V., eds.*, 1985, pp. 169–72. [G: France]

Starkie, David N. M. and Thompson, David J. The Airports Policy White Paper: Privatisation and Regulation. *Fisc. Stud.*, November 1985, *6*(4), pp. 30–41. [G: U.K.]

Stoffaës, Christian. The Nationalizations: An Initial Assessment, 1981–1984. In *Machin, H. and Wright, V., eds.*, 1985, pp. 144–69. [G: France]

Sunley, Emil M. Private/Public Venturing Activities and Opportunities. In *Konecci, E. B. and Kuhn, R. L., eds.*, 1985, pp. 171–84. [G: U.S.]

Tanguay, A. Brian. Quebec's Asbestos Policy: A Preliminary Assessment. *Can. Public Policy*, June 1985, *11*(2), pp. 227–40. [G: Canada]

Teeguarden, Dennis E. and Thomas, David. A Public Corporation Model for Federal Forest Land Management. *Natural Res. J.*, April 1985, *25*(2), pp. 373–87. [G: U.S.]

Tieber, Herbert. Public Enterprise and Employment Policy. *Ann. Pub. Co-op. Econ.*, January–June 1985, *56*(1–2), pp. 63–70. [G: Austria]

Trotter, S. D. The Price-discriminating Public Enterprise, with Special Reference to British Rail. *J. Transp. Econ. Policy*, January 1985, *19*(1), pp. 41–64. [G: U.K.]

Tye, William B. Measurement of Volume Variability for Mail Delivery Costs. *Logist. Transp. Rev.*, December 1985, *21*(4), pp. 337–52. [G: U.S.]

Tye, William B. The Pricing Policy of the Postal Service: Policymaking Misunderstood. *J. Policy Anal. Manage.*, Winter 1985, *4*(2), pp. 256–62. [G: U.S.]

Vernon, Raymond. Linking Managers with Ministers: Dilemmas of the State-Owned Enterprise. In *Vernon, R.*, 1985, pp. 149–64.

Vernon, Raymond. The International Aspects of State-Owned Enterprises. In *Vernon, R.*, 1985, pp. 101–11.

Vernon, Raymond. The State-Owned Enterprise and Industrial Policy. In *Shishido, T. and Sato, R., eds.*, 1985, pp. 215–24.

Vernon, Raymond. Uncertainty in the Resource Industries: The Special Role of State-Owned Enterprises. In *Vernon, R.*, 1985, pp. 133–48. [G: LDCs]

Vernon, Raymond and Levy, Brian. State-Owned Enterprises in the World Economy: The Case of Iron Ore. In *Vernon, R.*, 1985, pp. 113–31. [G: Selected Countries]

Young, H. Peyton. Methods and Principles of Cost Allocation. In *Young, H. P., ed.*, 1985, pp. 3–29. [G: U.K.; Sweden]

615 Economics of Transportation

6150 Economics of Transportation

Acker, Mary H. Assessing the Impact of Regulation of Trucking Firms. *Eastern Econ. J.*, April–June 1985, *11*(2), pp. 135–43. [G: U.S.]

Adler, Moshe. Street Parking: The Case for Communal Property. *Logist. Transp. Rev.*, December 1985, *21*(4), pp. 375–87.

Agarwal, Vinod B. and Talley, Wayne K. The Demand for International Air Passenger Service Provided by U.S. Air Carriers. *Int. J. Transport Econ.*, February 1985, *12*(1), pp. 63–70. [G: U.S.]

Anas, Alex. Modeling the Dynamic Evolution of Land Use in Response to Transportation Improvement Policies. In *Jansen, G. R. M.; Nijkamp, P. and Ruijgrok, C. J., eds.*, 1985, pp. 227–36. [G: U.S.]

Anas, Alex. The Combined Equilibrium of Travel Networks and Residential Location Markets. *Reg. Sci. Urban Econ.*, February 1985, *15*(1), pp. 1–21.

Anderson, James E. and Kraus, Marvin. An Econometric Model of Regulated Airline Flight Rivalry. In *Keeler, T. E., ed.*, 1985, pp. 1–26. [G: U.S.]

Arnott, Richard J. Quelques résultats relatifs a l'analyse économique. (Some Issues Related to the Economics of Now-Stationary State Traffic Flow. With English summary.) *Revue Écon.*, January 1985, *36*(1), pp. 11–43.

Baanders, A.; Kremer-Nass, J. and Ruijgrok, C. J. Income Decline and Travel Behaviour: Some Recent Dutch Findings and Research Orientations. In *Jansen, G. R. M.; Nijkamp, P. and Ruijgrok, C. J., eds.*, 1985, pp. 37–53. [G: Netherlands]

Bailey, Elizabeth E. Airline Deregulation in the United States: The Benefits Provided and the Lessons Learned. *Int. J. Transport Econ.*, June 1985, *12*(2), pp. 119–44. [G: U.S.]

Balinski, Michel L. and Sand, Francis M. Auctioning Landing Rights at Congested Airports. In *Young, H. P., ed.*, 1985, pp. 179–92.

Beckmann, Martin J. Spatial Price Policy and the Demand for Transportation. *J. Reg. Sci.*, August 1985, *25*(3), pp. 367–71.

Beilock, Richard. Are Truckers Forced to Speed? *Logist. Transp. Rev.*, September 1985, *21*(3), pp. 277–91. [G: U.S.]

Beilock, Richard. Is Regulation Necessary for Value-of-Service Pricing? *Rand J. Econ.*, Spring 1985, *16*(1), pp. 93–102. [G: U.S.]

van den Berg, L. and Klaassen, L. H. Economic Cycles, Spatial Cycles and Transportation Structures in Urban Areas. In *Jansen, G. R. M.; Nijkamp, P. and Ruijgrok, C. J., eds.*, 1985, pp. 259–73. [G: Netherlands]

Berndt, Ernst R. and Botero, German. Energy Demand in the Transportation Sector of Mexico. *J. Devel. Econ.*, April 1985, *17*(3), pp. 219–38. [G: Mexico]

Bingham, Tayler H.; Anderson, Donald W. and Cooley, Philip C. Distributional Implications of the Highway Revenue Act. *Public Finance Quart.*, January 1985, *13*(1), pp. 99–112. [G: U.S.]

Block, Richard N. and McLennan, Kenneth. Structural Economic Change and Industrial Relations in the United States' Manufacturing Sectors and Transportation since 1973. In *Juris, H.; Thompson, M. and Daniels, W., eds.*, 1985, pp. 337–82. [G: U.S.]

Bly, P. H. Effects of the Recession on Travel Expenditure and Travel Patterns. In *Jansen, G. R. M.; Nijkamp, P. and Ruijgrok, C. J., eds.*, 1985, pp. 15–36. [G: OECD]

Boger, Daniel C. Measuring Private and Social Costs in Inland Waterway Freight Transportation. In *Keeler, T. E., ed.*, 1985, pp. 149–212. [G: U.S.]

Bongaerts, Jan C. Financing Railways in the German States 1840–1860. A Preliminary View. *J. Europ. Econ. Hist.*, Fall 1985, *14*(2), pp. 331–45. [G: Germany]

Boyer, Kenneth D. Canada/U.S. Transportation Issues. In *Fretz, D.; Stern, R. and Whalley, J., eds.*, 1985, pp. 341–78. [G: Canada; U.S.]

Braeutigam, Ronald R. Efficient Pricing with Rivalry between a Railroad and a Pipeline. In *Daughety, A. F., ed.*, 1985, pp. 207–20.

Brilliant, Joshua. Aviation. In *Levinson, P. and Landau, P., eds.*, 1985, pp. 139–43. [G: Israel]

Brock, Michael. Canada/U.S. Transportation Issues: Comments. In *Fretz, D.; Stern, R. and Whalley, J., eds.*, 1985, pp. 385–90. [G: Canada; U.S.]

Brown, Anthony. The Regulatory Policy Cycle and the Airline Deregulation Movement. *Soc. Sci. Quart.*, September 1985, *66*(3), pp. 552–63. [G: U.S.]

Brueckner, Jan K. A Note on the Determinants of Metropolitan Airline Traffic. *Int. J. Transport Econ.*, June 1985, *12*(2), pp. 175–84. [G: U.S.]

Cafruny, Alan W. The Political Economy of International Shipping: Europe versus America. *Int. Organ.*, Winter 1985, *39*(1), pp. 79–119. [G: OECD]

Cain, Louis P. William Dean's Theory of Urban Growth: Chicago's Commerce and Industry,

1854–1871. *J. Econ. Hist.*, June 1985, *45*(2), pp. 241–49. [G: U.S.]

Call, Gregory D. and Keeler, Theodore E. Airline Deregulation, Fares, and Market Behavior: Some Empirical Evidence. In *Daughety, A. F., ed.*, 1985, pp. 221–47. [G: U.S.]

Cappelli, Peter. Competitive Pressures and Labor Relations in the Airline Industry. *Ind. Relat.*, Fall 1985, *24*(3), pp. 316–38. [G: U.S.]

Carey, Malachy and Else, Peter K. A Reformulation of the Theory of Optimal Congestion Taxes. *J. Transp. Econ. Policy*, January 1985, *19*(1), pp. 91–94.

Casas, François R. and Choi, Eun Kwan. Some Paradoxes of Transport Costs in International Trade. *Southern Econ. J.*, April 1985, *51*(4), pp. 983–97.

Caves, Douglas W., et al. Network Effects and the Measurement of Returns to Scale and Density for U.S. Railroads. In *Daughety, A. F., ed.*, 1985, pp. 97–120. [G: U.S.]

Caves, Douglas W., et al. The Effect of New Entry on Productivity Growth in the U.S. Airline Industry 1947–1981. *Logist. Transp. Rev.*, December 1985, *21*(4), pp. 299–335. [G: U.S.]

Cesario, Frank J. and Knetsch, Jack L. Economic Benefits of Developing and Improving Small Boat Harbors. *Water Resources Res.*, September 1985, *21*(9), pp. 1303–06.

Chida, Tomohei. The United States Merchant Marine in Foreign Trade, 1800–1939: Comment. In *Yui, T. and Nakagawa, K., eds.*, 1985, pp. 119–21. [G: U.S.]

Chu, David K. Y. Forecasting Future Transportation Demand and the Planned Road Network. In *Wong, K. and Chu, D. K. Y., eds.*, 1985, pp. 140–58. [G: China]

Claybrook, Joan and Bollier, David. The Hidden Benefits of Regulation: Disclosing the Auto Safety Payoff. *Yale J. Regul.*, Fall 1985, *3*(1), pp. 87–131. [G: U.S.]

le Clercq, F. Dynamics in Transportation Planning: An Overview. In *Jansen, G. R. M.; Nijkamp, P. and Ruijgrok, C. J., eds.*, 1985, pp. 1–8.

Collings, John. Public Expenditure Policy, 1985–86: Transport. In *Cockle, P., ed.*, 1985, pp. 243–50. [G: U.K.]

Cook, Cynthia C. Social Analysis in Rural Road Projects. In *Cernea, M. M., ed.*, 1985, pp. 297–321. [G: Selected LDCs]

Cordes, Joseph J. and Weisbrod, Burton A. When Government Programs Create Inequities: A Guide to Compensation Policies. *J. Policy Anal. Manage.*, Winter 1985, *4*(2), pp. 178–95. [G: U.S.]

Cory, Dennis C. Congestion Costs and Quality-adjusted User Fees: A Methodological Note. *Land Econ.*, November 1985, *61*(4), pp. 452–55.

Cosslett, Stephen R. and Lee, Lung-Fei. Serial Correlation in Latent Discrete Variable Models. *J. Econometrics*, January 1985, *27*(1), pp. 79–97. [G: U.S.]

Cowen, Janna L. and Felton, John Richard. Operating-Ratio Regulation and Truck-leasing

Practices. *Logist. Transp. Rev.*, June 1985, *21*(2), pp. 145–60. [G: U.S.]

Das, Chandrasekhar and Verma, Anil. A Heuristic Method for Finding the Optimal Location and Size of Facilities with Variable Demands. *Logist. Transp. Rev.*, June 1985, *21*(2), pp. 115–31.

Daughety, Andrew F. Analytical Transport Economics—Structure and Overview. In *Daughety, A. F., ed.*, 1985, pp. 3–25.

Daughety, Andrew F.; Nelson, Forrest D. and Vigdor, William R. An Econometric Analysis of the Cost and Production Structure of the Trucking Industry. In *Daughety, A. F., ed.*, 1985, pp. 65–95. [G: U.S.]

Davies, Peter N. British Shipping and World Trade: Rise and Decline, 1820–1939. In *Yui, T. and Nakagawa, K., eds.*, 1985, pp. 39–85. [G: U.K.]

Davies, Peter N. British Shipping and World Trade: Rise and Decline, 1820–1939: Response. In *Yui, T. and Nakagawa, K., eds.*, 1985, pp. 88–89. [G: U.K.]

Davies, Peter N. Japanese Shipping in the Nineteeth and Twentieth Centuries: Strategy and Organization: Comment. In *Yui, T. and Nakagawa, K., eds.*, 1985, pp. 34–37. [G: Japan; Selected OECD]

Derthick, Martha and Quirk, Paul J. Why the Regulators Chose to Deregulate. In *Noll, R. G., ed.*, 1985, pp. 200–231.

Dick, Howard W. Interisland Shipping: Progress, Problems and Prospects. *Bull. Indonesian Econ. Stud.*, August 1985, *21*(2), pp. 95–114. [G: Indonesia]

Dietrich, J. Richard and Deitrick, James W. Bond Exchanges in the Airline Industry: Analyzing Public Disclosures. *Accounting Rev.*, January 1985, *60*(1), pp. 109–26. [G: U.S.]

Docwra, George and Strong, Sam M. Road Fund Allocation: An Analysis of Decision Criteria. *Int. J. Transport Econ.*, October 1985, *12*(3), pp. 283–300. [G: Australia]

Else, Peter K. Optimal Pricing and Subsidies for Scheduled Transport Services. *J. Transp. Econ. Policy*, September 1985, *19*(3), pp. 263–79. [G: U.K.]

Evans, Andrew. Equalising Grants for Public Transport Subsidy. *J. Transp. Econ. Policy*, May 1985, *19*(2), pp. 105–38. [G: U.K.]

Feitelson, Eran. Transportation. In *Levinson, P. and Landau, P., eds.*, 1985, pp. 147–54. [G: Israel]

Ferguson, G. J. W. A. and Mogridge, M. J. H. Is Car Ownership and Use Stagnating? Fuel Consumption Models and their Implications. In *Jansen, G. R. M.; Nijkamp, P. and Ruijgrok, C. J., eds.*, 1985, pp. 55–74. [G: U.K.; U.S.]

Ferner, Anthony. Political Constraints and Management Strategies: The Case of Working Practices in British Rail. *Brit. J. Ind. Relat.*, March 1985, *23*(1), pp. 47–70. [G: U.K.]

Finch, Robert A. and Henry, Mark S. An Interindustry Approach to Financing Small Port Development and Maintenance. *Growth Change*, April 1985, *16*(2), pp. 26–33. [G: U.S.]

Findlay, Christopher C. Effects of Australian International Air Transport Regulation. *J. Ind. Econ.*, December 1985, *34*(2), pp. 199–216. [G: Australia]

Findlay, Christopher C. The Persistence and Pervasiveness of the Regulation of International Trade in Civil Aviation Services. *Singapore Econ. Rev.*, April 1985, *30*(1), pp. 77–89.

Folayan, Adekunle. Rural Accessibility Theory of Agricultural Productivity. *Int. J. Transport Econ.*, June 1985, *12*(2), pp. 165–74.

Freedman, D. A. The Mean versus the Median: A Case Study in 4-R Act Litigation. *J. Bus. Econ. Statist.*, January 1985, *3*(1), pp. 1–13. [G: U.S.]

Freeman, Kenneth D., et al. The Total Factor Productivity of the Canadian Class I Railways: 1956–1981. *Logist. Transp. Rev.*, September 1985, *21*(3), pp. 249–76. [G: Canada]

Frendreis, John P. and Waterman, Richard W. PAC Contributions and Legislative Behavior: Senate Voting on Trucking Deregulation. *Soc. Sci. Quart.*, June 1985, *66*(2), pp. 401–12. [G: U.S.]

Friedlaender, Ann F. and Bruce, Sharon Schur. Augmentation Effects and Technical Change in the Regulated Trucking Industry, 1974–1979. In *Daughety, A. F., ed.*, 1985, pp. 29–63. [G: U.S.]

Friesz, Terry L. and Harker, Patrick T. Freight Network Equilibrium: A Review of the State of the Art. In *Daughety, A. F., ed.*, 1985, pp. 161–206. [G: U.S.]

Friesz, Terry L.; Viton, Philip A. and Tobin, Roger L. Economic and Computational Aspects of Freight Network Equilibrium Models: A Synthesis. *J. Reg. Sci.*, February 1985, *25*(1), pp. 29–49.

Fujimoto, Masakazu. Very Private Enterprise: Ownership and Finance in British Shipping, 1825–1940: Comment. In *Yui, T. and Nakagawa, K., eds.*, 1985, pp. 249–52. [G: U.K.]

Garrod, Peter and Miklius, Walter. The Optimal Ship Size: A Comment. *J. Transp. Econ. Policy*, January 1985, *19*(1), pp. 83–90. [G: Israel]

Goedman, J.; van de Hoef, G. and Timmerman, F. Transportation and Urban Form. In *Jansen, G. R. M.; Nijkamp, P. and Ruijgrok, C. J., eds.*, 1985, pp. 275–93. [G: Netherlands]

Goldberg, Michael A. Urban Programs: Transportation and Housing: Commentary. In *Quigley, J. M. and Rubinfeld, D. L., eds.*, 1985, pp. 285–93. [G: Canada; U.S.]

Gomez-Ibañez, Jose A. The Federal Role in Urban Transportation. In *Quigley, J. M. and Rubinfeld, D. L., eds.*, 1985, pp. 183–223. [G: U.S.]

Gomez-Ibañez, Jose A. Transportation Policy as a Tool for Shaping Metropolitan Development. In *Keeler, T. E., ed.*, 1985, pp. 55–81. [G: U.S.]

Goodman, Gary A. and Saunders, Robert M. U.S. Federal Regulation of Foreign Involvement in Aviation, Government Procurement, and National Security. *J. World Trade Law,*

January:February 1985, *19*(1), pp. 54–61. [G: U.S.]

Goodwin, P. B. and Layzell, A. D. Longitudinal Analysis for Public Transport Policy Issues. In *Jansen, G. R. M.; Nijkamp, P. and Ruijgrok, C. J., eds.*, 1985, pp. 185–200. [G: U.K.]

Goto, Shin. British Shipping and World Trade: Rise and Decline, 1820–1939: Comment. In *Yui, T. and Nakagawa, K., eds.*, 1985, pp. 86–88. [G: U.K.]

Grandjean, Alain and Henry, Claude. Choix autoroutiers et calcul économique. (With English summary.) *Revue Écon. Polit.*, January–February 1985, *95*(1), pp. 1–26. [G: France]

Green, Edwin. Shipbuilding Finance of the *Shasen* Shipping Firms: 1920's–1930's: Comment. In *Yui, T. and Nakagawa, K., eds.*, 1985, pp. 273–77. [G: Japan]

Green, Edwin. Very Private Enterprise: Ownership and Finance in British Shipping, 1825–1940. In *Yui, T. and Nakagawa, K., eds.*, 1985, pp. 219–48. [G: U.K.]

Grimm, Curtis M. Horizontal Competitive Effects in Railroad Mergers. In *Keeler, T. E., ed.*, 1985, pp. 27–53. [G: U.S.]

Grzelakowski, Andrzej S. Natural Equilibrium as Optimum Condition of Port-Services Market. *Int. J. Transport Econ.*, October 1985, *12*(3), pp. 261–72.

Guria, Jagadish C. and Gollin, Anthony E. A. Influence of Income and Public Transit Accessibility on the Modal Choice Behaviour of the New Zealand Labour Force. *Int. J. Transport Econ.*, October 1985, *12*(3), pp. 301–13. [G: New Zealand]

Gutman, Herbert G. Trouble on the Railroads in 1873–1874: Prelude to the 1877 Crisis? In *Leab, D. J., ed.*, 1985, pp. 132–52. [G: U.S.]

Hall, P. Urban Transportation: Paradoxes for the 1980s. In *Jansen, G. R. M.; Nijkamp, P. and Ruijgrok, C. J., eds.*, 1985, pp. 367–75.

Hall, Randolph W. Heuristics for Selecting Facility Locations. *Logist. Transp. Rev.*, December 1985, *21*(4), pp. 353–73. [G: U.S.]

Henderson, Harold. Canada/U.S. Transportation Issues: Comments. In *Fretz, D.; Stern, R. and Whalley, J., eds.*, 1985, pp. 379–84. [G: Canada; U.S.]

Hanjoul, Pierre and Thisse, Jacques-François. Localisation de la firme sur un réseau. (The Location of a Firm on a Network. With English summary.) *Revue Écon.*, January 1985, *36*(1), pp. 63–101.

Harmatuck, Donald J. Short Run Motor Carrier Cost Functions for Five Large Common Carriers. *Logist. Transp. Rev.*, September 1985, *21*(3), pp. 217–37. [G: U.S.]

Harris, D. John and Williams, D. Glyn. The Use of Risk Analysis within British Rail. *Managerial Dec. Econ.*, December 1985, *6*(4), pp. 202–09. [G: U.K.]

Hau, Timothy Doe-Kwong. A Hicksian Approach to Cost–Benefit Analysis with Discrete-Choice Models. *Economica*, November 1985, *52*(208), pp. 479–90.

Hauser, Robert J.; Beaulieu, Jeffrey and Bau-

mel, C. Phillip. Impacts of Inland Waterway User Fees on Grain Transportation and Implied Barge Rate Elasticities. *Logist. Transp. Rev.*, March 1985, *21*(1), pp. 37–55. [G: U.S.]

Hayuth, Yehuda. Freight Modal-Split Analysis of Air and Sea Transportation. *Logist. Transp. Rev.*, December 1985, *21*(4), pp. 389–402. [G: Israel]

Heaver, Trevor D. The Effects of Fiscal Policies on the Development of International Shipping. *Logist. Transp. Rev.*, March 1985, *21*(1), pp. 77–91. [G: Canada]

Hensher, David A. Empirical Vehicle Choice and Usage Models in the Household Sector: A Review. *Int. J. Transport Econ.*, October 1985, *12*(3), pp. 231–59. [G: U.S.; Australia; Israel]

Hensher, David A. and Truong, Truong P. Valuation of Travel Time Savings: A Direct Experimental Approach. *J. Transp. Econ. Policy*, September 1985, *19*(3), pp. 237–61. [G: Australia]

Heston, Alan, et al. The Economics of Camel Transport in Pakistan. *Econ. Develop. Cult. Change*, October 1985, *34*(1), pp. 121–41. [G: Pakistan]

Higgins, Thomas J. Implementation Revisited: The Case of Federal Demonstrations. *J. Policy Anal. Manage.*, Spring 1985, *4*(3), pp. 436–40. [G: U.S.]

Holtgrefe, A. A. I. Stagnation and Public Transport in the Netherlands: Demand, Cost, Supply and Planning. In *Jansen, G. R. M.; Nijkamp, P. and Ruijgrok, C. J., eds.*, 1985, pp. 335–51. [G: Netherlands]

Hornby, Ove. The Danish Shipping Industry, 1866–1939: Structure and Strategy: Response. In *Yui, T. and Nakagawa, K., eds.*, 1985, pp. 184. [G: Denmark]

Hornby, Ove. The Danish Shipping Industry, 1866–1939: Structure and Strategy. In *Yui, T. and Nakagawa, K., eds.*, 1985, pp. 157–81. [G: Denmark]

Horowitz, Joel. Los trabajadores ferroviarios en la Argentina (1920–1943). La formación de una elite obrera. (With English summary.) *Desarrollo Econ.*, Oct.-Dec. 1985, *25*(99), pp. 421–46. [G: Argentina]

Horowitz, Joel. Random Utility Travel Demand Models. In *Jansen, G. R. M.; Nijkamp, P. and Ruijgrok, C. J., eds.*, 1985, pp. 141–55.

Hunter, Holland. Successful Spatial Management. In *Linz, S. J., ed.*, 1985, pp. 47–58. [G: U.S.S.R.]

Hunter, Holland, et al. Soviet Transport Trends, 1950–1990. *Soviet Econ.*, July-Sept. 1985, *1*(3), pp. 195–227. [G: U.S.S.R.]

James, George W. Airline Deregulation: Has It Worked? *Bus. Econ.*, July 1985, *20*(3), pp. 11–14. [G: U.S.]

Jansson, Jan Owen and Shneerson, Dan. Economies of Trade Density in Linear Shipping and Optimal Pricing. *J. Transp. Econ. Policy*, January 1985, *19*(1), pp. 7–22. [G: U.S.]

Jansson, Jan Owen and Shneerson, Dan. A Model of Scheduled Liner Freight Services: Balancing

Inventory Cost against Shipowners' Costs. *Logist. Transp. Rev.*, September 1985, *21*(3), pp. 195–215.

Johnson, Richard L. Networking and Market Entry in the Airline Industry: Some Early Evidence from Deregulation. *J. Transp. Econ. Policy*, September 1985, *19*(3), pp. 299–304. **[G: U.S.]**

Jones-Lee, M. W.; Hammerton, M. and Philips, P. R. The Value of Safety: Results of a National Sample Survey. *Econ. J.*, March 1985, *95*(377), pp. 49–72. **[G: U.K.]**

Kajimoto, Motonobu. Shipping Business in Germany in the Nineteenth and Twentieth Centuries: Comment. **In** *Yui, T. and Nakagawa, K.*, eds., 1985, pp. 214–16. **[G: Germany]**

Kanemoto, Yoshitsugu and Mera, Koichi. General Equilibrium Analysis of the Benefits of Large Transportation Improvements. *Reg. Sci. Urban Econ.*, August 1985, *15*(3), pp. 343–63.

Kappler, Frederick G. and Rutledge, Gary L. Expenditures for Abating Pollutant Emissions from Motor Vehicles, 1968–84. *Surv. Curr. Bus.*, July 1985, *65*(7), pp. 29–35. **[G: U.S.]**

Keeler, James P. Effects of Cost-based Regulation of Prices. *Int. J. Transport Econ.*, February 1985, *12*(1), pp. 51–61. **[G: U.S.]**

Keeler, Theodore E. Urban Programs: Transportation and Housing: Commentary. **In** *Quigley, J. M. and Rubinfeld, D. L.*, eds., 1985, pp. 294–96. **[G: U.S.]**

Kelly, Tony. Reciprocal Exemption: A Regime to Treasure. *Bull. Int. Fiscal Doc.*, June 1985, *39*(6), pp. 267–70.

Kim, Moshe. Total Factor Productivity in Bus Transport. *J. Transp. Econ. Policy*, May 1985, *19*(2), pp. 173–82. **[G: Israel]**

Kim, Tschangho John and Kim, Jong Gie. Issues in Building a National Transportation Development Model: Experience from a Korean Application. *Ann. Reg. Sci.*, March 1985, *19*(1), pp. 18–36. **[G: S. Korea]**

Kindleberger, Charles P. Multinational Ownership of Shipping Activities. *World Econ.*, September 1985, *8*(3), pp. 249–65.

Kirby, Michael G. and Albon, Robert P. Property Rights, Regulation and Efficiency: A Further Comment on Australia's Two-Airline Policy. *Econ. Rec.*, June 1985, *61*(173), pp. 535–39. **[G: Australia]**

Klaassen, L. H. The Accessibility of Rural Areas. *Int. J. Transport Econ.*, June 1985, *12*(2), pp. 157–63.

van Knippenberg, C. and Lameijer, I. Simulation Studies as a Tool for Determining Public Transport Services in Rural Areas. **In** *Jansen, G. R. M.; Nijkamp, P. and Ruijgrok, C. J.*, eds., 1985, pp. 323–33. **[G: Netherlands]**

Kobayashi, Masaaki. Maritime Policy in Japan: 1868–1937: Comment. **In** *Yui, T. and Nakagawa, K.*, eds., 1985, pp. 153–56. **[G: Japan]**

Koshal, Rajindar K. and Koshal, Manjulika. Energy Alternatives for Railways: Some Experience from Indian Railways. *Int. J. Transport Econ.*, June 1985, *12*(2), pp. 185–91. **[G: India]**

Kroes, E. P. and Sheldon, R. J. Stated Preference Techniques in Measuring Travel Elasticities. **In** *Jansen, G. R. M.; Nijkamp, P. and Ruijgrok, C. J.*, eds., 1985, pp. 201–10.

Kutter, E. New Targets for Transport Facilities Planning. **In** *Jansen, G. R. M.; Nijkamp, P. and Ruijgrok, C. J.*, eds., 1985, pp. 377–88. **[G: W. Germany]**

Kyle, Reuben, III and Phillips, Laurence T. Airline Deregulation: Did Economists Promise Too Much or Too Little? *Logist. Transp. Rev.*, March 1985, *21*(1), pp. 3–25. **[G: U.S.]**

Lave, Charles A. Speeding, Coordination, and the 55 MPH Limit. *Amer. Econ. Rev.*, December 1985, *75*(5), pp. 1159–64. **[G: U.S.]**

Lave, Charles A. The Private Challenge to Public Transportation—An Overview. **In** *Lave, C. A.*, ed., 1985, pp. 1–29. **[G: U.S.]**

Lee, Dwight R. Policing Cost, Evasion Cost, and the Optimal Speed Limit. *Southern Econ. J.*, July 1985, *52*(1), pp. 34–45.

Lehmacher, M. H. and Charcke, R. UNECE: Highlights in the Transport Sector. *J. World Trade Law*, Nov.:Dec. 1985, *19*(6), pp. 666–68. **[G: Europe]**

Lesourne, Jacques. Les infrastructures de transport et la localisation des agents économiques: quelques évidences. (Transportation Infrastructures and Agents' Location: An Analysis of a Few Simple Facts. With English summary.) *Revue Écon.*, January 1985, *36*(1), pp. 169–214.

Lewis, Colin M. Railways and Industrialization: Argentina and Brazil, 1870–1929. **In** *Abel, C. and Lewis, C. M.*, eds., 1985, pp. 199–230. **[G: Argentina; Brazil]**

Liew, Chong K. and Liew, Chung J. Measuring the Development Impact of a Transportation System: A Simplified Approach. *J. Reg. Sci.*, May 1985, *25*(2), pp. 241–58. **[G: U.S.]**

Loeb, Peter D. The Efficacy and Cost Effectiveness of Motor Vehicle Inspection Using Cross-Sectional Data—An Econometric Analysis. *Southern Econ. J.*, October 1985, *52*(2), pp. 500–509. **[G: U.S.]**

Lyons, Thomas P. China's Cellular Economy: A Test of the Fragmentation Hypothesis. *J. Compar. Econ.*, June 1985, *9*(2), pp. 125–44. **[G: China]**

Lyons, Thomas P. Transportation in Chinese Development, 1952–1982. *J. Devel. Areas*, April 1985, *19*(3), pp. 305–28. **[G: China]**

Main, Timothy. An Economic Evaluation of Child Restraints. *J. Transp. Econ. Policy*, January 1985, *19*(1), pp. 23–40. **[G: New Zealand]**

Mason, Charles F. and Train, Kenneth E. A Route Forecasting Method for the Portland Area. **In** *Keeler, T. E.*, ed., 1985, pp. 239–59. **[G: U.S.]**

McCarthy, Patrick S. An Econometric Analysis of Automobile Transactions. *Int. J. Transport Econ.*, February 1985, *12*(1), pp. 71–92. **[G: U.S.]**

McCutcheon, W. A. An Economic History of Ulster 1820–1939: Transport, 1820–1914. **In** *Ken-*

nedy, L. and Ollerenshaw, P., eds., 1985, pp. 109–36. **[G: U.K.]**

McDonald, Nicholas. Regulating Hours of Work in the Road Haulage Industry: The Case for Social Criteria. *Int. Lab. Rev.,* Sept.-Oct. 1985, *124*(5), pp. 577–92. **[G: EEC; U.S.]**

McFadden, Daniel; Winston, Clifford and Boersch-Supan, Axel. Joint Estimation of Freight Transportation Decisions under Non-random Sampling. In *Daughety, A. F., ed.,* 1985, pp. 137–57. **[G: U.S.]**

McFarland, Henry. Transportation Costs for U.S. Imports from Developed and Developing Countries. *J. Devel. Stud.,* July 1985, *21*(4), pp. 562–71. **[G: LDCs; MDCs; U.S.]**

McMullen, B. Starr. Commodity Specific Rate Differentials in a Competitive Trucking Industry. *Logist. Transp. Rev.,* June 1985, *21*(2), pp. 133–44. **[G: U.S.]**

McMullen, B. Starr. Trunk Airline Financial Requirements and Economic Performance. In *Keeler, T. E., ed.,* 1985, pp. 121–47 **[G: U.S.]**

Meyer, John R. and Tye, William B. The Regulatory Transition. *Amer. Econ. Rev.,* May 1985, *75*(2), pp. 46–51. **[G: U.S.]**

Meyer, M. D. Urban Transportation Planning in the United States: Current Trends and Future Directions. In *Jansen, G. R. M.; Nijkamp, P. and Ruijgrok, C. J., eds.,* 1985, pp. 313–22.

Miller, Ted R. A Cost–Benefit Analysis of the 55 MPH Speed Limit: Comment. *Southern Econ. J.,* October 1985, *52*(2), pp. 547–49. **[G: U.S.]**

Miwa, Ryoichi. Maritime Policy in Japan: 1868–1937. In *Yui, T. and Nakagawa, K., eds.,* 1985, pp. 123–52. **[G: Japan]**

Mogridge, M. J. H. Transport, Land Use and Energy Interaction. *Urban Stud.,* December 1985, *22*(6), pp. 481–92. **[G: France; U.K.]**

Mohring, Herbert. Profit Maximization, Cost Minimization, and Pricing for Congestion-prone Facilities. *Logist. Transp. Rev.,* March 1985, *21*(1), pp. 27–36.

Morash, Edward A. The Economic Relationship between Service Quality and Market Protection for Regulated Household-Goods Moving. *J. Econ. Bus.,* May 1985, *37*(2), pp. 123–40. **[G: U.S.]**

Morrison, Steven A. and Winston, Clifford. An Econometric Analysis of the Demand for Intercity Passenger Transportation. In *Keeler, T. E., ed.,* 1985, pp. 213–37. **[G: U.S.]**

Morrison, Steven A. and Winston, Clifford. Intercity Transportation Route Structures under Deregulation: Some Assessments Motivated by the Airline Experience. *Amer. Econ. Rev.,* May 1985, *75*(2), pp. 57–61. **[G: U.S.]**

Mowery, David C. and Rosenberg, Nathan. Government Policy, Technical Change, and Industrial Structure: The U.S. and Japanese Commercial Aircraft Industries, 1945–1983. In *Langdon, R. and Rothwell, R., eds.,* 1985, pp. 73–102. **[G: Japan]**

Nakagawa, Keiichiro. Japanese Shipping in the Nineteenth and Twentieth Centuries: Strategy and Organization. In *Yui, T. and Nakagawa, K., eds.,* 1985, pp. 1–33. **[G: Japan; Selected OECD]**

Nijkamp, Peter; Rima, A. and van Wissen, L. Spatial Mobility in Models for Structural Urban Dynamics. In *Jansen, G. R. M.; Nijkamp, P. and Ruijgrok, C. J., eds.,* 1985, pp. 121–40.

North, Robert. Soviet Transport Trends, 1950–1990: Comments. *Soviet Econ.,* July-Sept. 1985, *1*(3), pp. 228–31. **[G: U.S.S.R.]**

Nutley, S. D. Planning Options for the Improvement of Rural Accessibility: Use of the Time-Space Approach. *Reg. Stud.,* February 1985, *19*(1), pp. 37–50. **[G: U.K.]**

Orski, C. Kenneth. Redesigning Local Transportation Service. In *Lave, C. A., ed.,* 1985, pp. 255–75. **[G: U.S.]**

Pachauri, R. K.; Chen, Chia-Yon and Srivastava, Leena. Coal Transportation System Modeling—The Case of Taiwan: A Comment. *Energy J.,* July 1985, *6*(3), pp. 109–14. **[G: Taiwan]**

Pell, C. M., et al. Uncertainty in Transportation Planning and Forecasting. In *Jansen, G. R. M.; Nijkamp, P. and Ruijgrok, C. J., eds.,* 1985, pp. 237–51.

Phillips, Bruce D. The Effect of Industry Deregulation on the Small Business Sector. *Bus. Econ.,* January 1985, *20*(1), pp. 28–37. **[G: U.S.]**

Pickup, L. Women's Travel Needs in a Period of Rising Female Employment. In *Jansen, G. R. M.; Nijkamp, P. and Ruijgrok, C. J., eds.,* 1985, pp. 97–113. **[G: U.K.]**

Pines, David and Sadka, Efraim. Zoning, First-Best, Second-Best, and Third-Best Criteria for Allocating Land for Roads. *J. Urban Econ.,* March 1985, *17*(2), pp. 167–83.

Porter, Robert H. On the Incidence and Duration of Price Wars. *J. Ind. Econ.,* June 1985, *33*(4), pp. 415–26. **[G: U.S.]**

Porter, Robert H. On the Incidence and Duration of Price Wars. In *Geroski, P. A.; Phlips, L. and Ulph, A., eds.,* 1985, pp. 47–58. **[G: U.S.]**

Pratt, Michael D. and Hoffer, George E. The Responsiveness of Heavy Vehicle Registrations to Interstate Tax Differentials. *Atlantic Econ. J.,* September 1985, *13*(3), pp. 95–96. **[G: U.S.]**

Pustay, Michael W. A Comparison of Pre- and Post-reform Motor Carrier Service to Small Communities. *Growth Change,* January 1985, *16*(1), pp. 47–54. **[G: U.S.]**

Ratcliffe, Barrie M. The Business Elite and the Development of Paris: Intervention in Ports and Entrepôts, 1814–1834. *J. Europ. Econ. Hist.,* Spring 1985, *14*(1), pp. 95–142. **[G: France]**

Recker, W. W. and Kitamura, R. Activity-based Travel Analysis. In *Jansen, G. R. M.; Nijkamp, P. and Ruijgrok, C. J., eds.,* 1985, pp. 157–83. **[G: U.S.]**

Roberts, Roland K. Transportation Costs in Econometric Models of State Agricultural Sectors: The Case of Beef in Hawaii. *Western J.*

Agr. Econ., July 1985, *10*(1), pp. 93–109.
[G: U.S.]

Rose, Nancy L. The Incidence of Regulatory Rents in the Motor Carrier Industry. *Rand J. Econ.*, Autumn 1985, *16*(3), pp. 299–318.
[G: U.S.]

Rosenbloom, Sandra. The Growth of Non-traditional Families: A Challenge to Traditional Planning Approaches. In *Jansen, G. R. M.; Nijkamp, P. and Ruijgrok, C. J., eds.*, 1985, pp. 75–96.
[G: U.S.; Netherlands]

Rotemberg, Julio J. The Efficiency of Equilibrium Traffic Flows. *J. Public Econ.*, March 1985, *26*(2), pp. 191–205.

Safford, Jeffrey J. The United States Merchant Marine in Foreign Trade, 1800–1939. In *Yui, T. and Nakagawa, K., eds.*, 1985, pp. 91–118.
[G: U.S.]

Safford, Jeffrey J. The United States Merchant Marine in Foreign Trade, 1800–1939: Response. In *Yui, T. and Nakagawa, K., eds.*, 1985, pp. 121–22.
[G: U.S.]

Sagers, Matthew J. and Green, Milford B. The Freight Rate Structure of Soviet Railroads. *Econ. Geogr.*, October 1985, *61*(4), pp. 305–22.
[G: U.S.S.R.]

Saggar, R. K. and Mongia, J. N. Transport. In *Mongia, J. N., ed.*, 1985, pp. 453–94.
[G: India]

Salomon, Ilan. Telecommunications and Travel: Substitution or Modified Mobility? *J. Transp. Econ. Policy*, September 1985, *19*(3), pp. 219–35.
[G: U.S.; MDCs]

Santoro, Francesco. A New Government Plan for the Reform of the State Railways. *Rev. Econ. Cond. Italy*, January–April 1985, (1), pp. 121–35.
[G: Italy]

Sargious, Michel and Tam, Timmy. Modelling Rail and Truck Freight Rates in Canada. *Logist. Transp. Rev.*, June 1985, *21*(2), pp. 173–84.
[G: Canada]

Schofer, J. L. The Role of Planning in the Preservation of Transportation Infrastructure. In *Jansen, G. R. M.; Nijkamp, P. and Ruijgrok, C. J., eds.*, 1985, pp. 295–311.
[G: U.S.]

Scholl, Lars U. Shipping Business in Germany in the Nineteenth and Twentieth Centuries. In *Yui, T. and Nakagawa, K., eds.*, 1985, pp. 185–213.
[G: Germany]

Shepsle, Kenneth A. Why the Regulators Chose to Deregulate: Comment. In *Noll, R. G., ed.*, 1985, pp. 231–37.

Shughart, William F., II and Tollison, Robert D. The Cyclical Character of Regulatory Activity. *Public Choice*, 1985, *45*(3), pp. 303–11.
[G: U.S.]

Sickles, Robin C. A Nonlinear Multivariate Error Components Analysis of Technology and Specific Factor Productivity Growth with an Application to the U.S. Airlines. *J. Econometrics*, January 1985, *27*(1), pp. 61–78.
[G: U.S.]

Simpson, Anthony U. Implications of Efficiency Incentives on Use of Private Sector Contracting by the Public Transit Industry. In *Lave, C. A., ed.*, 1985, pp. 299–309.

Singell, Larry D. and McNown, Robert F. A

Cost–Benefit Analysis of the 55 MPH Speed Limit: Reply. *Southern Econ. J.*, October 1985, *52*(2), pp. 550–53.
[G: U.S.]

Small, Kenneth A. Transportation and Urban Change. In *Peterson, P. E., ed.*, 1985, pp. 197–223.
[G: U.S.]

Sommers, Paul M. Drinking Age and the 55 MPH Speed Limit. *Atlantic Econ. J.*, March 1985, *13*(1), pp. 43–48.
[G: U.S.]

Spady, Richard H. Using Indexed Quadratic Cost Functions to Model Network Technologies. In *Daughety, A. F., ed.*, 1985, pp. 121–35.

Starkie, David N. M. and Thompson, David J. The Airports Policy White Paper: Privatisation and Regulation. *Fisc. Stud.*, November 1985, *6*(4), pp. 30–41.
[G: U.K.]

Sugiyama, Kazuo. Shipbuilding Finance of the *Shasen* Shipping Firms: 1920's–1930's. In *Yui, T. and Nakagawa, K., eds.*, 1985, pp. 255–72.
[G: Japan]

Svidén, Ove. Automobile Usage in a Future Information Society. In *Langdon, R. and Rothwell, R., eds.*, 1985, pp. 27–43.
[G: Sweden]

Talley, Wayne K. and Pope, James A. Determinants of Liner Conference Rates under Containerization. *Int. J. Transport Econ.*, June 1985, *12*(2), pp. 145–55.
[G: U.S.]

Taplin, J. H. E. and Waters, W. G., II. Boiteux–Ramsey Pricing of Road and Rail under a Single Budget Constraint. *Australian Econ. Pap.*, December 1985, *24*(45), pp. 337–49.
[G: Australia]

Tatsuki, Mariko. NYK and the Commercial Diplomacy of the Far Eastern Freight Conference, 1896–1956: Comment. In *Yui, T. and Nakagawa, K., eds.*, 1985, pp. 306–09.
[G: Selected Countries]

Theologitis, J. M. Transportation Planning and Social Forces in a Changing World Environment. *Int. J. Transport Econ.*, February 1985, *12*(1), pp. 31–50.

Tomita, Masahiro. The Danish Shipping Industry, 1866–1939: Structure and Strategy: Comment. In *Yui, T. and Nakagawa, K., eds.*, 1985, pp. 182–83.
[G: Denmark]

Trotter, S. D. The Price-discriminating Public Enterprise, with Special Reference to British Rail. *J. Transp. Econ. Policy*, January 1985, *19*(1), pp. 41–64.
[G: U.K.]

Trozzo, Charles L. and Davis, H. Craig. The Economic Effects of Levying a Harbor User Charge on Waterborne Commerce. *Rev. Reg. Stud.*, Winter 1985, *15*(1), pp. 33–45.
[G: U.S.]

Truong, Truong P. and Hensher, David A. Measurement of Travel Time Values and Opportunity Cost from a Discrete-Choice Model. *Econ. J.*, June 1985, *95*(378), pp. 438–51.
[G: Australia]

Tucci, Gianrocco. Regulation and "Contestability" in Formulating an Air Transport Policy for the European Community. *Rivista Polit. Econ.*, Suppl. Dec. 1985, *76*, pp. 219–39.
[G: EEC]

Tye, William B. On the Application of the "Williamsonian Welfare Tradeoff" to Rail Mergers.

Logist. Transp. Rev., September 1985, *21*(3), pp. 239–48.   [G: U.S.]

Tye, William B. Problems of Applying Stand-alone Costs as an Indicator of Market Dominance and Rail Rate Reasonableness. *Int. J. Transport Econ.*, February 1985, *12*(1), pp. 7–30.   [G: U.S.]

Tye, William B. The Applicability of the Theory of Contestable Markets to Rail/Water Carrier Mergers. *Logist. Transp. Rev.*, March 1985, *21*(1), pp. 57–76.   [G: U.S.]

Tzeng, Gwo-Hshiung. Coal Transportation System Modeling: The Case of Taiwan. *Energy J.*, January 1985, *6*(1), pp. 145–56.
                    [G: Taiwan]

Uri, Noel D. and Rifkin, Edward J. Geographic Markets, Causality and Railroad Deregulation. *Rev. Econ. Statist.*, August 1985, *67*(3), pp. 422–28.   [G: U.S.]

Van Kooten, G. C. and Spriggs, John. Public Policy and the Prairie Branch Line Rehabilitation Program. *Logist. Transp. Rev.*, June 1985, *21*(2), pp. 161–72.   [G: Canada]

Wachs, M. The Politicization of Transit Subsidy Policy in America. In *Jansen, G. R. M.; Nijkamp, P. and Ruijgrok, C. J., eds.*, 1985, pp. 353–66.   [G: U.S.]

Walters, Stephen J. K. Reciprocity, Rebating, and Regulation. *Southern Econ. J.*, January 1985, *51*(3), pp. 766–75.   [G: U.S.]

Wang Chiang, Judy S. and Friedlaender, Ann F. Truck Technology and Efficient Market Structure. *Rev. Econ. Statist.*, May 1985, *67*(2), pp. 250–58.   [G: U.S.]

Waters, W. G., II. Transportation Policies and the Western Transition. *Can. Public Policy*, Supplement July 1985, *11*(3), pp. 339–43.
                    [G: Canada]

Webber, Melvin M. Urban Programs: Transportation and Housing: Commentary. In *Quigley, J. M. and Rubinfeld, D. L., eds.*, 1985, pp. 304–07.   [G: U.S.]

Williams, Harold R. and Mount, Randall I. Theory and Empirical Foundation for Energy Policy Designed to Promote U.S. Motor Gasoline Conservation. *Amer. Econ.*, Spring 1985, *29*(1), pp. 60–66.   [G: U.S.]

Winston, Clifford. Conceptual Development: in the Economics of Transportation: An Interpretive Survey. *J. Econ. Lit.*, March 1985, *23*(1), pp. 57–94.   [G: U.S.]

van Wissen, L.; Golob, T. F. and Smit, J. G. Determination of Differences among Household Mobility Patterns. In *Jansen, G. R. M.; Nijkamp, P. and Ruijgrok, C. J., eds.*, 1985, pp. 211–25.   [G: Netherlands]

Witte, Hermann. Intermodal Evaluation of Transport Policy Measures. *Int. J. Transport Econ.*, October 1985, *12*(3), pp. 273–82.
                    [G: W. Germany]

Wood, Wallace R. Discretionary Spending and Railroad Costing Bias. *Logist. Transp. Rev.*, June 1985, *21*(2), pp. 99–114.   [G: U.S.]

Wray, William D. NYK and the Commercial Diplomacy of the Far Eastern Freight Conference, 1896–1956. In *Yui, T. and Nakagawa, K., eds.*, 1985, pp. 279–305.
                    [G: Selected Countries]

Wray, William D. NYK and the Commercial Diplomacy of the Far Eastern Freight Conference, 1896–1956: Response. In *Yui, T. and Nakagawa, K., eds.*, 1985, pp. 310–11.
                    [G: Selected Countries]

Yamada, Tetsuji. The Probable Effects of Introducing a Sectional Fare System into New York City Subway. *Int. J. Transport Econ.*, October 1985, *12*(3), pp. 315–31.   [G: U.S.]

Yui, Tsunehiko. Business History of Shipping: Introduction. In *Yui, T. and Nakagawa, K., eds.*, 1985, pp. ix–xxix.   [G: Japan]

616 Industrial Policy

6160 Industrial Policy

Adams, F. Gerard. Empirical Analysis of Industrial Policies: The Challenges. In *Adams, F. G., ed.*, 1985, pp. 1–13.

Adams, F. Gerard. Empirical Evaluation of Industrial Policy: An Appraisal. In *Adams, F. G., ed.*, 1985, pp. 211–27.   [G: U.S.]

Adams, F. Gerard and Duggal, Vijaya G. General versus Industry-Specific Industrial Policies: Quantifying the National and Sectoral Impacts. In *Adams, F. G., ed.*, 1985, pp. 31–47.
                    [G: U.S.]

Adams, F. Gerard; Klein, Lawrence R. and Duggal, Vijaya G. The Effects of Foreign Export-Promotion Policies on the United States: Macro Model Simulations. In *Adams, F. G., ed.*, 1985, pp. 67–84.   [G: U.S.]

Adams, F. Gerard, et al. Industrial-Policy Impacts on the Steel Industry: A Simulation Study. In *Adams, F. G., ed.*, 1985, pp. 85–132.   [G: U.S.]

Adams, Walter and Brock, James W. Industrial Policy and Trade Unions. *J. Econ. Issues*, June 1985, *19*(2), pp. 497–505.   [G: U.S.]

Agarwal, Suraj Mal. Electronics in India: Past Strategies and Future Possibilities. *World Devel.*, March 1985, *13*(3), pp. 273–92.
                    [G: India]

Alézard, Gérald. Transnational Activity and Domestic Recovery. In *Zukin, S., ed.*, 1985, pp. 239–45.   [G: France]

Allen, Christopher S. and Rishikof, Harvey. Tale Thrice Told: A Review of Industrial Policy Proposals. *J. Policy Anal. Manage.*, Winter 1985, *4*(2), pp. 239–49.   [G: U.S.]

Attali, Bernard. Reindustrializing France through Urban and Regional Development. In *Zukin, S., ed.*, 1985, pp. 179–84.   [G: France]

Balassa, Bela. French Industrial Policy under the Socialist Government. *Amer. Econ. Rev.*, May 1985, *75*(2), pp. 315–19.   [G: France]

Bar-El, Raphael. Industrial Dispersion as an Instrument for the Achievement of Development Goals. *Econ. Geogr.*, July 1985, *61*(3), pp. 205–22.   [G: Brazil]

Bartlett, Bruce. America's New Ideology: "Industrial Policy": With Neo-Keynesianism Joining Supply-Side Economics in History's Dust-bin,

It's Splitting Economists. *Amer. J. Econ. Soc.*, January 1985, *44*(1), pp. 1–7.   [G: U.S.]

Bellon, Bertrand. Strengths and Weaknesses of French Industry. In *Zukin, S., ed.*, 1985, pp. 141–51.   [G: France]

Benson, Bruce L. Free Market Congestion Tolls: A Correction [Spatial Price Theory and an Efficient Congestion Toll Established by the Free Market]. *Econ. Inquiry*, April 1985, *23*(2), pp. 361–62.

Berger, Suzanne. The Socialists and the *patronat:* The Dilemmas of Co-existence in a Mixed Economy. In *Machin, H. and Wright, V., eds.*, 1985, pp. 225–44.   [G: France]

Boltho, Andrea. Was Japan's Industrial Policy Successful? *Cambridge J. Econ.*, June 1985, *9*(2), pp. 187–201.   [G: Japan]

Borrus, Michael and Zysman, John. Industrial Development Policy in Japan. In *Nanto, D. K., ed.*, 1985, pp. 143–67.   [G: Japan]

Borrus, Michael and Zysman, John. Japan's Industrial Policy and Its Pattern of Trade. In *Nanto, D. K., ed.*, 1985, pp. 13–22.   [G: Japan]

Bower, Joseph L. Restructuring Petrochemicals: A Comparative Study of Business and Government Strategy to Deal with a Declining Sector of the Economy. In *Scott, B. R. and Lodge, G. C., eds.*, 1985, pp. 263–300.   [G: U.S.; OECD]

Brown, William S. Industrial Policy and Corporate Power. *J. Econ. Issues*, June 1985, *19*(2), pp. 487–96.   [G: U.S.]

Button, John. Australia's Industry Policy—Now and the Future. In *Scutt, J. A., ed.*, 1985, pp. 62–69.   [G: Australia]

Chaikin, Sol C. The Needs of the Labor-Intensive Sector. In *Zukin, S., ed.*, 1985, pp. 226–38.   [G: U.S.]

Chaney, Paul K. and Thakor, Anjan V. Incentive Effects of Benevolent Intervention: The Case of Government Loan Guarantees. *J. Public Econ.*, March 1985, *26*(2), pp. 169–89.   [G: U.S.]

Chisholm, Michael. De-industrialization and British Regional Policy. *Reg. Stud.*, August 1985, *19*(4), pp. 301–13.   [G: U.K.]

Chou, Tein-Chen. The Pattern and Strategy of Industrialization in Taiwan: Specialization and Offsetting Policy. *Devel. Econ.*, June 1985, *23*(2), pp. 138–57.   [G: Taiwan]

Chu, David K. Y. The Politico-economic Background to the Development of the Special Economic Zones. In *Wong, K. and Chu, D. K. Y., eds.*, 1985, pp. 25–39.   [G: China]

Corden, W. Max. Relationships between Macroeconomic and Industrial Policies. In *Corden, W. M.*, 1985, pp. 288–301.

Cutcher-Gershenfeld, Joel. Policy Strategies for Labor–Management Cooperation. In *Woodworth, W.; Meek, C. and Whyte, W. F., eds.*, 1985, pp. 245–60.   [G: U.S.]

Daly, Donald J. Microeconomic Performance: Interrelations between Trade and Industrial Policies. In *Conklin, D. W. and Courchene,*

T. J., eds., 1985, pp. 156–87.   [G: OECD; Canada]

Erber, Fabio Stefano. The Development of the 'Electonics Complex' and Government Policies in Brazil. *World Devel.*, March 1985, *13*(3), pp. 293–309.   [G: Brazil]

Esser, Klaus. Modification of the Industrialization Model in Latin America. *Cepal Rev.*, August 1985, (26), pp. 101–13.   [G: Latin America]

Feldstein, Martin. Is Industrial Policy the Answer? In *Adams, J., ed.*, 1985, pp. 217–26.   [G: U.S.]

Fisher, Peter S. Corporate Tax Incentives: The American Version of Industrial Policy. *J. Econ. Issues*, March 1985, *19*(1), pp. 1–19.   [G: U.S.]

Forrest, David. Privatisation. In *Atkinson, G. B. J., ed.*, 1985, pp. 101–21.   [G: U.K.]

Forsyth, David J. C. Government Policy, Market Structure and Choice of Technology in Egypt. In *James, J. and Watanabe, S., eds.*, 1985, pp. 137–82.   [G: Egypt]

Forsyth, P. J. Trade and Industry Policy. *Australian Econ. Rev.*, 3rd Quarter, Spring 1985, (71), pp. 70–81.   [G: Australia]

Friedman, Sheldon. A UAW Perspective on Industrial Policy, International Investment, and Trade. In *Zukin, S., ed.*, 1985, pp. 221–25.   [G: U.S.]

Galbraith, James K. Congress and the Industrial Policy Debate. In *Zukin, S., ed.*, 1985, pp. 99–106.   [G: U.S.]

Goldey, David. The Socialists and the *patronat:* The Dilemmas of Co-existence in a Mixed Economy: Comment. In *Machin, H. and Wright, V., eds.*, 1985, pp. 244–54.   [G: France]

Gould, Andrew and Keeble, David. New Firms and Rural Industrialization in East Anglia. In *Storey, D. J., ed.*, 1985, pp. 43–71.   [G: U.K.]

Green, Diana. Economic Policy & Policy-Making under the Mitterrand Presidency 1981–84: Industrial Policy: Comment. In *Machin, H. and Wright, V., eds.*, 1985, pp. 139–43.   [G: France]

Grunwald, Joseph. Mexico and the United States: Studies in Economic Interaction: Trade and Industry: Comments. In *Musgrave, P. B., ed.*, 1985, pp. 113–19.   [G: Mexico]

Guinchard, Philippe. Prix relatifs et désindustrialisation. (Relative Prices and Deindustrialisation. With English summary.) *Revue Écon.*, March 1985, *36*(2), pp. 367–82.   [G: Selected Countries]

Harrison, Bennett. Eight Theses on Crisis and Reindustrialization. In *Zukin, S., ed.*, 1985, pp. 60–69.   [G: U.S.]

Harrison, Bennett and Bluestone, Barry. Problems of Economic Deterioration. In *Woodworth, W.; Meek, C. and Whyte, W. F., eds.*, 1985, pp. 64–77.   [G: U.S.]

Hayden, F. Gregory; Kruse, Douglas C. and Williams, Steve C. Industrial Policy at the State Level in the United States. *J. Econ. Issues*, June 1985, *19*(2), pp. 383–96.   [G: U.S.]

Hill, Hal. Subcontracting, Technological Diffusion, and the Development of Small Enterprise in Philippine Manufacturing. *J. Devel. Areas,* January 1985, *19*(2), pp. 245–61.
[G: Philippines]

Hill, Richard Child and Negrey, Cynthia. The Politics of Industrial Policy in Michigan. In *Zukin, S., ed.,* 1985, pp. 119–38. [G: U.S.]

Hood, Neil and Young, Stephen. The United Kingdom and the Changing Economic World Order. In *Hochmuth, M. and Davidson, W., eds.,* 1985, pp. 99–129. [G: OECD; U.K.]

Jacobsson, Staffan. Technical Change and Industrial Policy: The Case of Computer Numerically Controlled Lathes in Argentina, Korea and Taiwan. *World Devel.,* March 1985, *13*(3), pp. 353–70. [G: Argentina; Korea; Taiwan; OECD]

Kaplinsky, Raphael. Does De-industrialisation Beget Industrialisation which Begets Re-industrialisation?: Review Article. In *Saith, A., ed.,* 1985, pp. 227–42. [G: Global]

Kaplinsky, Raphael. Does De-industrialisation Beget Industrialisation Which Begets Re-industrialisation? Review Article. *J. Devel. Stud.,* October 1985, *22*(1), pp. 227–42. [G: Global]

Keyder, Caglar. State and Industry in France, 1750–1914. *Amer. Econ. Rev.,* May 1985, *75*(2), pp. 308–14. [G: France]

Kim, Kwan S. Industrial Development in Mexico: Problems, Policy Issues, and Perspectives. In *Kim, K. S. and Ruccio, D. F., eds.,* 1985, pp. 205–26. [G: Mexico]

Klein, Lawrence R. World Trade Growth and Industrial Policy. In *Peeters, T.; Praet, P. and Reding, P., eds.,* 1985, pp. 111–30. [G: U.S.; OECD]

Klein, Lawrence R.; Bollino, Carlo Andrea and Fardoust, Shah. International Interactions of Industrial Policy: Simulations of the World Economy, 1982–1990. In *Adams, F. G., ed.,* 1985, pp. 15–30. [G: OECD]

Kobayashi, T. Japanese Industrial Policy: Competition and Cooperation. In *Langdon, R. and Rothwell, R., eds.,* 1985, pp. 115–22. [G: Japan]

Kontorovich, Vladimir. Industrial Policy and the Electrical-Machinery Industry: The Case of Transformers. In *Adams, F. G., ed.,* 1985, pp. 133–59. [G: U.S.]

Kreinin, Mordechai E. United States Trade and Possible Restrictions in High-Technology Products. *J. Policy Modeling,* Spring 1985, *7*(1), pp. 69–105. [G: U.S.; Japan; EEC; Canada]

Kubursi, A. A. Industrialisation in the Arab States of the Gulf: A Ruhr without Water. In *Niblock, T. and Lawless, R., eds.,* 1985, pp. 42–65. [G: OPEC]

Kuhn, Robert Lawrence. Industrial Policy versus Creative Management: The Search for Economic Direction. In *Konecci, E. B. and Kuhn, R. L., eds.,* 1985, pp. 82–89. [G: U.S.]

Lassila, Jaakko. Bankerna och industripolitiken. (Banks and Industrial Policy. With English summary.) *Ekon. Samfundets Tidskr.,* 1985, *38*(4), pp. 179–86. [G: Finland]

Lavoie, Don. Rebuilding America: A Blueprint for the New Economy: Review Article. *Comparative Econ. Stud.,* Fall 1985, *27*(3), pp. 99–113. [G: U.S.]

Levy, Santiago. Mexico and the United States: Studies in Economic Interaction: Trade and Industry: Comments. In *Musgrave, P. B., ed.,* 1985, pp. 109–12. [G: Mexico]

Lodge, George C. and Crum, William C. U.S. Competitiveness in the World Economy: The Pursuit of Remedies. In *Scott, B. R. and Lodge, G. C., eds.,* 1985, pp. 479–502. [G: U.S.]

Lorino, Philippe. French Industrial Policy and U.S. Industry. In *Zukin, S., ed.,* 1985, pp. 152–64. [G: France; U.S.]

Lustig, R. Jeffrey. The Politics of Shutdown: Community, Property, Corporatism. *J. Econ. Issues,* March 1985, *19*(1), pp. 123–52. [G: U.S.]

Lynd, Staughton. Options for Reindustrialization: Brownfield versus Greenfield Approaches. In *Woodworth, W.; Meek, C. and Whyte, W. F., eds.,* 1985, pp. 49–63. [G: U.S.]

Markusen, Ann R. Defense Spending as Industrial Policy. In *Zukin, S., ed.,* 1985, pp. 70–84. [G: U.S.]

Marlin, Matthew R. Industrial Revenue Bonds: Evolution of a Subsidy. *Growth Change,* January 1985, *16*(1), pp. 30–35. [G: U.S.]

Mayer, Colin. The Assessment: Recent Developments in Industrial Economics and Their Implications for Policy. *Oxford Rev. Econ. Policy,* Autumn 1985, *1*(3), pp. 1–24. [G: U.K.]

McGregor, Margaret A. and Schinasi, Katherine V. Positive Adjustment Policies toward Declining Industries in Japan. In *Nanto, D. K., ed.,* 1985, pp. 168–80. [G: Japan]

Meek, Christopher and Woodworth, Warner. Absentee Ownership, Industrial Decline, and Organizational Renewal. In *Woodworth, W.; Meek, C. and Whyte, W. F., eds.,* 1985, pp. 78–96. [G: U.S.]

Moberg, David. Problems of Industrial Plant Shutdowns. In *Woodworth, W.; Meek, C. and Whyte, W. F., eds.,* 1985, pp. 28–48. [G: U.S.]

Morris, Derek J. and Stout, D. K. Industrial Policy. In *Morris, D., ed.,* 1985, pp. 851–94. [G: U.K.]

Mortimore, Michael. The Subsidiary Role of Direct Foreign Investment in Industrialization: The Colombian Manufacturing Sector. *Cepal Rev.,* April 1985, (25), pp. 67–84. [G: Colombia]

Morvan, Yves. Economic Policy & Policy-Making under the Mitterrand Presidency, 1981–84: Industrial Policy. In *Machin, H. and Wright, V., eds.,* 1985, pp. 117–39. [G: France]

Mytelka, Lynn Krieger. Knowledge, Investment, and the Manufacturing Firm. In *Zukin, S., ed.,* 1985, pp. 85–89. [G: U.S.]

Nakao, Takeo. The Effects of Demonopolization on Economic Growth. *Can. J. Econ.,* August

1985, *18*(3), pp. 622–35.

Naughton, Barry. False Starts and Second Wind: Financial Reforms in China's Industrial System. In *Perry, E. J. and Wong, C., eds.*, 1985, pp. 223–52. [G: China]

Newby, Howard, et al. From Class Structure to Class Action: British Working-Class Politics in the 1980s. In *Roberts, B.; Finnegan, R. and Gallie, D., eds.*, 1985, pp. 86–102. [G: U.K.]

Ng, Yen-Tak and Chu, David K. Y. The Geographical Endowment of China's Special Economic Zones. In *Wong, K. and Chu, D. K. Y., eds.*, 1985, pp. 40–56. [G: China]

O'Connor, David C. The Computer Industry in the Third World: Policy Options and Constraints. *World Devel.*, March 1985, *13*(3), pp. 311–32. [G: LDCs; OECD]

Owen, Thomas C. The Russian Industrial Society and Tsarist Economic Policy, 1867–1905. *J. Econ. Hist.*, September 1985, *45*(3), pp. 587–606. [G: Russia]

Paci, Raffaele. Accumulation Process and Investment Incentives in a Vintage Investment Model: The Case of Sardinia. *Rivista Int. Sci. Econ. Com.*, July-Aug. 1985, *32*(7–8), pp. 765–94. [G: Italy]

Pasha, Hafiz A. and Bengali, Kaiser. Impact of Fiscal Incentives on Industrialisation in Backward Areas: A Case Study of Hub Chowki in Baluchistan. *Pakistan J. Appl. Econ.*, Summer 1985, *4*(1), pp. 1–16. [G: Pakistan]

Patrick, Hugh. Japanese Industrial Policy. In *Bornstein, M., ed.*, 1985, pp. 95–108. [G: Japan]

Petrei, A. Humberto and Tybout, James R. Argentina 1976–1981: la importancia de variar los niveles de subsidios financieros. (With English summary.) *Cuadernos Econ.*, April 1985, *22*(65), pp. 13–36. [G: Argentina]

Ponting, J. Rick and Waters, Nigel. The Impact of Public Policy on Locational Decision-making by Industrial Firms. *Can. Public Policy*, December 1985, *11*(4), pp. 731–44. [G: Canada]

Prywes, Menahem. Quantity and Quality of Capital Impacts on Productivity in the Chemical Industry: An Empirical Study. In *Adams, F. G., ed.*, 1985, pp. 161–79. [G: U.S.]

Ramstad, Yngve. Industrial Policy and Trade Unions: Comments. *J. Econ. Issues*, June 1985, *19*(2), pp. 507–11. [G: U.S.]

Reich, Robert B. Bailout: A Comparative Study in Law and Industrial Structure. *Yale J. Regul.*, 1985, *2*(2), pp. 163–224. [G: U.S.; U.K.; W. Germany; Japan]

Robertson, E. J. Developing the West's Manufacturing Potential: The Role of Provincial Governments. *Can. Public Policy*, Supplement July 1985, *11*(3), pp. 335–38. [G: Canada]

del Roccili, John A. and Luce, Priscilla. Regionalized Analysis of Industrial Policy. In *Adams, F. G., ed.*, 1985, pp. 49–65. [G: U.S.]

Roepstorff, Torben M. Industrial Development in Indonesia: Performance and Prospects. *Bull. Indonesian Econ. Stud.*, April 1985, *21*(1), pp. 32–61. [G: Indonesia]

Roessner, J. David. Prospects for a National Innovation Policy in the United States. In *Langdon, R. and Rothwell, R., eds.*, 1985, pp. 63–72. [G: U.S.]

Rosen, Corey. Financing Employee Ownership. In *Woodworth, W.; Meek, C. and Whyte, W. F., eds.*, 1985, pp. 261–75. [G: U.S.]

Salvatore, Dominick. The New Protectionism and the Threat to World Welfare: Editor's Introduction. *J. Policy Modeling*, Spring 1985, *7*(1), pp. 1–22. [G: U.S.; LDCs]

Scott, Bruce R. National Strategies: Key to International Competition. In *Scott, B. R. and Lodge, G. C., eds.*, 1985, pp. 71–143. [G: U.S.]

Secchi, Carlo. On the Role of Small and Medium-Sized Enterprises in the Improvement of the Production Structure of Developing Countries. *Cepal Rev.*, December 1985, (27), pp. 131–41. [G: Italy]

Sekiguchi, Sueo and Horiuchi, Toshihiro. Myth and Reality of Japan's Industrial Policies. *World Econ.*, December 1985, *8*(4), pp. 373–91. [G: Japan]

Sheehan, Michael F. Plant Closings and the Community: The Instrumental Value of Public Enterprise in Countering Corporate Flight. *Amer. J. Econ. Soc.*, October 1985, *44*(4), pp. 423–33. [G: U.S.]

Shelp, Ronald Kent. An Industrial Policy for a Service Economy. In *Zukin, S., ed.*, 1985, pp. 208–18. [G: France; U.S.]

Shirk, Susan L. The Politics of Industrial Reform. In *Perry, E. J. and Wong, C., eds.*, 1985, pp. 195–221. [G: China]

Singh, Manmohan. Finance and Development: Inaugural Address. In *Bandyopadhyay, R. and Khankhoje, D. P., eds.*, 1985, pp. ix–xiii. [G: LDCs]

Singh, Manmohan. Industry. In *Mongia, J. N., ed.*, 1985, pp. 67–115. [G: India]

Smith, David A. and Levine, Marc V. Political Limits on a Progressive Industrial Policy. In *Zukin, S., ed.*, 1985, pp. 48–59. [G: U.S.]

Snape, Richard H. Trade and Industry Policy: Comment. *Australian Econ. Rev.*, 3rd Quarter, Spring 1985, (71), pp. 82. [G: Australia]

Sood, Anil and Kohli, Harinder. Industrial Restructuring in Developing Countries. *Finance Develop.*, December 1985, *22*(4), pp. 46–49. [G: LDCs]

Soskice, David. The Nationalizations: An Initial Assessment, 1981–1984: Comment. In *Machin, H. and Wright, V., eds.*, 1985, pp. 169–72. [G: France]

Soulage, Bernard. Industrial Priorities in the Current French Plan. In *Zukin, S., ed.*, 1985, pp. 165–78. [G: France]

Spero, Joan Edelman. International Services, Information, and European Industrial Policy. In *Zukin, S., ed.*, 1985, pp. 203–07. [G: France]

Stauffer, Thomas R. Energy-intensive Industrialization in the Middle East. *Industry Devel.*, 1985, (14), pp. 1–35. [G: Middle East]

Stoffaës, Christian. Explaining French Strategy

in Electronics. **In** *Zukin, S., ed.*, 1985, pp. 187–94. **[G: France]**

Stoffaës, Christian. The Nationalizations: An Initial Assessment, 1981–1984. **In** *Machin, H. and Wright, V., eds.*, 1985, pp. 144–69.
[G: France]

Strobel, Frederick R. The U.S. Banking and Corporate Structure: Some Implications for Industrial Policy. *J. Econ. Issues*, June 1985, *19*(2), pp. 541–49. **[G: U.S.]**

Thurow, Lester C. Public Intervention in the Industry. The Case of the U.S.A. *Ann. Pub. Co-op. Econ.*, January–June 1985, *56*(1–2), pp. 41–49. **[G: U.S.]**

Thurow, Lester C. The Case for Industrial Policies in America. **In** *Shishido, T. and Sato, R., eds.*, 1985, pp. 225–59. **[G: U.S.]**

Tsurumi, Yoshi. Japan's Challenge to the United States: Industrial Policies and Corporate Strategies. **In** *Hochmuth, M. and Davidson, W., eds.*, 1985, pp. 39–79. **[G: U.S.; Japan]**

Tyler, William G. Effective Incentives for Domestic Market Sales and Exports: View of Anti-export Biases and Commercial Policy in Brazil, 1980–81. *J. Devel. Econ.*, August 1985, *18*(2–3), pp. 219–42. **[G: Brazil]**

Van den Panhuyzen, W. Japan's Industrial Policy: From Promotion to Protection. *Tijdschrift Econ. Manage.*, 1985, *30*(1), pp. 45–74.
[G: Japan]

Verma, R. P. S. and Verma, J. D. Small-scale Sector. **In** *Mongia, J. N., ed.*, 1985, pp. 117–51. **[G: India]**

Vernon, Raymond. The State-Owned Enterprise and Industrial Policy. **In** *Shishido, T. and Sato, R., eds.*, 1985, pp. 215–24.

Weinstein, Michael M. Job Impact Statements: A Lesson from the 1930s. *Challenge*, Sept./Oct. 1985, *28*(4), pp. 55–58. **[G: U.S.]**

Weintraub, Sidney. Trade and Structural Change. **In** *Musgrave, P. B., ed.*, 1985, pp. 79–107.
[G: Mexico; U.S.]

Wescott, Robert F. Industrial Policy and Optimization in the Coal Industry. **In** *Adams, F. G., ed.*, 1985, pp. 181–209. **[G: U.S.]**

Wolozin, Harold. Corporate Power in an Aging Economy: Labor Force Policy. *J. Econ. Issues*, June 1985, *19*(2), pp. 475–86. **[G: U.S.]**

Wong, Christine. Material Allocation and Decentralization: Impact of the Local Sector on Industrial Reform. **In** *Perry, E. J. and Wong, C., eds.*, 1985, pp. 253–78. **[G: China]**

Wong, Kwan-Yiu. Trends and Strategies of Industrial Development. **In** *Wong, K. and Chu, D. K. Y., eds.*, 1985, pp. 57–78. **[G: China]**

Wong, Kwan-Yiu and Chu, David K. Y. Export Processing Zones and Special Economic Zones as Locomotives of Export-Led Economic Growth. **In** *Wong, K. and Chu, D. K. Y., eds.*, 1985, pp. 1–24. **[G: Asia]**

Wong, Kwan-Yiu and Chu, David K. Y. The Investment Environment. **In** *Wong, K. and Chu, D. K. Y., eds.*, 1985, pp. 176–207.
[G: China; S. Korea; Hong Kong; Taiwan; Singapore]

Woodworth, Warner; Meek, Christopher and

Whyte, William Foote. Theory and Practice of Community Economic Reindustrialization. **In** *Woodworth, W.; Meek, C. and Whyte, W. F., eds.*, 1985, pp. 297–304. **[G: U.S.]**

Yarrow, George K. Strategic Issues in Industrial Policy. *Oxford Rev. Econ. Policy*, Autumn 1985, *1*(3), pp. 95–109.

Yeh, Anthony G. O. Physical Planning. **In** *Wong, K. and Chu, D. K. Y., eds.*, 1985, pp. 108–30. **[G: China]**

Yoshino, Michael Y. and Fong, Glenn R. The Very High Speed Integrated Circuit Program: Lessons for Industrial Policy. **In** *Scott, B. R. and Lodge, G. C., eds.*, 1985, pp. 176–84.
[G: U.S.]

Young, Michael K. Structurally Depressed and Declining Industries in Japan: A Case Study in Minimally Intrusive Industrial Policy. **In** *Nanto, D. K., ed.*, 1985, pp. 181–99.
[G: Japan]

Zhou, Shulian. New Advances in Science and Technology and Economic Management. *Chinese Econ. Stud.*, Fall 1985, *19*(1), pp. 17–25.
[G: China]

Zukin, Sharon. Industrial Policy as Post-Keynesian Politics: Basic Assumptions in the United States and France. **In** *Zukin, S., ed.*, 1985, pp. 3–47. **[G: U.S.; France]**

Zysman, John. Inflation and the Politics of Supply. **In** *Lindberg, L. N. and Maier, C. S., eds.*, 1985, pp. 140–71. **[G: W. Germany; U.K.; France; Japan; U.S.]**

619 Economics of Regulation

6190 Economics of Regulation

Abel, John D. Comment: Competing Technologies and Inconsistent Regulation. **In** *Noam, E. M., ed.*, 1985, pp. 332–37. **[G: U.S.]**

Abolafia, Mitchel Y. Self-regulation as Market Maintenance: An Organization Perspective. **In** *Noll, R. G., ed.*, 1985, pp. 312–43. **[G: U.S.]**

Ackerman, Bruce A. Integrating Themes and Ideas: Cost Benefit and the Constitution. **In** *Noll, R. G., ed.*, 1985, pp. 351–57.

Agarwal, Vinod B. and Deacon, Robert T. Price Controls, Price Dispersion and the Supply of Refined Petroleum Products. *Energy Econ.*, October 1985, *7*(4), pp. 210–19. **[G: U.S.]**

Amacher, Ryan, et al. The Behavior of Regulatory Activity over the Business Cycle: An Empirical Test. *Econ. Inquiry*, January 1985, *23*(1), pp. 7–19. **[G: U.S.]**

Anderson, Terry L. The Market Alternative for Hawaiian Water. *Natural Res. J.*, October 1985, *25*(4), pp. 893–910. **[G: U.S.]**

Arnould, Richard J. and Van Vorst, Charles B. Supply Responses to Market and Regulatory Forces in Health Care. **In** *Meyer, J. A., ed.*, 1985, pp. 107–31. **[G: U.S.]**

Ashford, Nicholas A. Regulation as a Stimulas for Technological Change. **In** *Langdon, R. and Rothwell, R., eds.*, 1985, pp. 171–78.

Ault, David E. and Rutman, Gilbert L. Freedom and Regulation: An Anthropological Critique of Free Market Ideology: Comment. In *Zerbe, R. O., Jr., ed.*, 1985, pp. 149–56.

Balassa, Bela. Prices, Incentives and Economic Growth. In *Balassa, B.*, 1985, pp. 3–23. [G: Global]

Barke, Richard. Regulation and Cooperation among Firms in Technical Standard-Setting. *J. Behav. Econ.*, Winter 1985, *14*, pp. 141–54. [G: U.S.]

Baron, David P. Noncooperative Regulation of a Nonlocalized Externality. *Rand J. Econ.*, Winter 1985, *16*(4), pp. 553–68. [G: U.S.]

Baron, David P. Regulation of Prices and Pollution under Incomplete Information. *J. Public Econ.*, November 1985, *28*(2), pp. 211–31.

Batra, R. N. The Future of the Debt Situation in the LDCs. In *Kaushik, S. K., ed.*, 1985, pp. 47–57. [G: U.S.]

Bench, Robert R. Deregulation—A Worldwide Phenomenon? In *Kaushik, S. K., ed.*, 1985, pp. 85–91.

Besen, Stanley M. and Johnson, Leland L. Regulation of Broadcast Station Ownership: Evidence and Theory. In *Noam, E. M., ed.*, 1985, pp. 364–89. [G: U.S.]

Bilmes, Jack. Freedom and Regulation: An Anthropological Critique of Free Market Ideology. In *Zerbe, R. O., Jr., ed.*, 1985, pp. 123–47.

Bilmes, Jack. Freedom and Regulation: An Anthropological Critique of Free Market Ideology: Rejoinder. In *Zerbe, R. O., Jr., ed.*, 1985, pp. 157–59.

Binder, John J. Measuring the Effects of Regulation with Stock Price Data. *Rand J. Econ.*, Summer 1985, *16*(2), pp. 167–83. [G: U.S.]

Bohm, Peter and Russell, Clifford S. Comparative Analysis of Alternative Policy Instruments. In *Kneese, A. V. and Sweeney, J. L., eds. Vol. 1*, 1985, pp. 395–460. [G: U.S.; Selected Countries]

Borrus, Michael and Zysman, John. Industrial Development Policy in Japan. In *Nanto, D. K., ed.*, 1985, pp. 143–67. [G: Japan]

Botein, Michael. The FCC's Regulation of the New Video Technologies: Backing and Filling on the Level Playing Field. In *Noam, E. M., ed.*, 1985, pp. 311–29. [G: U.S.]

Braeutigam, Ronald R. Efficient Pricing with Rivalry between a Railroad and a Pipeline. In *Daughety, A. F., ed.*, 1985, pp. 207–20.

Brants, Kees and Jankowski, Nick. Cable Television in the Low Countries. In *Negrine, R. M., ed.*, 1985, pp. 74–102. [G: Belgium; Netherlands]

Bresnahan, Timothy F. and Yao, Dennis A. The Nonpecuniary Costs of Automobile Emissions Standards. *Rand J. Econ.*, Winter 1985, *16*(4), pp. 437–55. [G: U.S.]

Brock, William A. and Evans, David S. The Economics of Regulatory Tiering. *Rand J. Econ.*, Autumn 1985, *16*(3), pp. 398–409.

Brown, Donald J. and Heal, Geoffrey M. The Optimality of Regulated Pricing: A General Equilibrium Analysis. In *Aliprantis, C. D.;*

Burkinshaw, O. and Rothman, N. J., eds., 1985, pp. 43–54.

Buell, Stephen G. and Guerard, John B., Jr. An Econometric Analysis of the Formal Regulatory Process. In *Brown, R. C., ed.*, 1985, pp. 15–38. [G: U.S.]

Caplow, Theodore. Conflicting Regulations: Six Small Studies and an Interpretation. In *Noll, R. G., ed.*, 1985, pp. 284–304.

Caron, André and Taylor, James R. Cable Television at the Crossroads: An Analysis of the Canadian Cable Scene. In *Negrine, R. M., ed.*, 1985, pp. 47–73. [G: Canada]

Cave, Martin. Financing British Broadcasting. *Lloyds Bank Rev.*, July 1985, (157), pp. 25–35. [G: U.K.]

Caves, Douglas W., et al. The Effect of New Entry on Productivity Growth in the U.S. Airline Industry 1947–1981. *Logist. Transp. Rev.*, December 1985, *21*(4), pp. 299–335. [G: U.S.]

Claybrook, Joan and Bollier, David. The Hidden Benefits of Regulation: Disclosing the Auto Safety Payoff. *Yale J. Regul.*, Fall 1985, *3*(1), pp. 87–131. [G: U.S.]

Cohen, Mark A. and Rubin, Paul H. Private Enforcement of Public Policy. *Yale J. Regul.*, Fall 1985, *3*(1), pp. 167–93. [G: U.S.]

Conrad, Klaus. The Use of Standards and Prices for Environment Protection and Their Impact on Costs. *Z. ges. Staatswiss. (JITE)*, September 1985, *141*(3), pp. 390–400.

Copeland, Basil L., Jr. and Severn, Alan K. Price Theory and Telecommunications Regulation: A Dissenting View. *Yale J. Regul.*, Fall 1985, *3*(1), pp. 53–85. [G: U.S.]

Cowhey, Peter F. and Aronson, Jonathan D. Trade in Communications and Data Processing. In *Stern, R. M., ed.*, 1985, pp. 256–90. [G: Canada; U.S.]

Crew, Michael A. and Kleindorfer, Paul R. Governance Structures for Natural Monopoly: A Comparative Institutional Assessment. *J. Behav. Econ.*, Winter 1985, *14*, pp. 117–40.

DeLong, James V. On Regulation and Legal Process: Comment. In *Noll, R. G., ed.*, 1985, pp. 136–40.

Derthick, Martha and Quirk, Paul J. Why the Regulators Chose to Deregulate. In *Noll, R. G., ed.*, 1985, pp. 200–231.

Domberger, Simon and Middleton, Julian. Franchising in Practice: The Case of Independent Television in the UK. *Fisc. Stud.*, February 1985, *6*(1), pp. 17–32. [G: U.K.]

Eckard, E. Woodrow, Jr. The Effects of State Automobile Dealer Entry Regulation on New Car Prices. *Econ. Inquiry*, April 1985, *23*(2), pp. 223–42. [G: U.S.]

Eckstein, Zvi and Eichenbaum, Martin S. Inventories and Quantity-Constrained Equilibria in Regulated Markets: The U.S. Petroleum Industry, 1947–1972. In *Sargent, T. J., ed.*, 1985, pp. 70–100. [G: U.S.]

Erickson, Edward W. Deregulation and Natural Gas Supply and Demand. In *Crew, M. A., ed.*, 1985, pp. 141–59. [G: U.S.]

Feldman, Roger and Begun, James W. The Welfare Cost of Quality Changes Due to Professional Regulation. *J. Ind. Econ.*, September 1985, *34*(1), pp. 17–32. [G: U.S.]

Fenili, Robert. The Impact of Decontrol on Gasoline Wholesalers and Retailers. *Contemp. Policy Issues*, Spring, Pt. 2, 1985, *3*(3), pp. 119–30. [G: U.S.]

Ferejohn, John A. The State in Politics: Comment. In *Noll, R. G., ed.*, 1985, pp. 105–10.

Fiorina, Morris P. Group Concentration and the Delegation of Legislative Authority. In *Noll, R. G., ed.*, 1985, pp. 175–97.

Fisher, Franklin M. The Financial Interest and Syndication Rules in Network Television: Regulatory Fantasy and Reality. In *[McGowan, J. J.]*, 1985, pp. 263–98. [G: U.S.]

Fournier, Gary M. Nonprice Competition and the Dissipation of Rents from Television Regulation. *Southern Econ. J.*, January 1985, *51*(3), pp. 754–65. [G: U.S.]

Friedman, Lawrence M. On Regulation and Legal Process. In *Noll, R. G., ed.*, 1985, pp. 111–35.

Geller, Henry. The Role of Future Regulation: Licensing, Spectrum Allocation, Content, Access, Common Carrier, and Rates. In *Noam, E. M., ed.*, 1985, pp. 283–310. [G: U.S.]

Groth, Philip G. Energy Development and Security and Supply-side Ideology: Oligopoly, Monopoly, and Imperfect Competition Make Fossil Fuel Regulation a Necessity. *Amer. J. Econ. Soc.*, April 1985, *44*(2), pp. 155–68. [G: U.S.; Germany; Japan]

Hammond, Elizabeth M. and Kay, John A. Insurance Regulation in the United Kingdom and the Federal Republic of Germany. In *Currie, D., ed.*, 1985, pp. 192–206. [G: U.K.; W. Germany]

Harrison, Glenn W. and McKee, Michael. Monopoly Behavior, Decentralized Regulation, and Contestable Markets: An Experimental Evaluation. *Rand J. Econ.*, Spring 1985, *16*(1), pp. 51–69.

Henley, John S. and Nyaw, Mee-Kau. A Reappraisal of the Capital Goods Sector in Hong Kong: The Case for Free Trade. *World Devel.*, June 1985, *13*(6), pp. 737–48. [G: Hong Kong]

Horvitz, Paul M. The Combination of Banking and Insurance: Implications for Regulation. *Growth Change*, October 1985, *16*(4), pp. 10–19. [G: U.S.]

Joskow, Paul L. Long Term Vertical Relationships and the Study of Industrial Organization and Government Regulation. *Z. ges. Staatswiss. (JITE)*, December 1985, *141*(4), pp. 586–93. [G: U.S.]

Keeley, Michael C. The Regulation of Bank Entry. *Fed. Res. Bank San Francisco Econ. Rev.*, Summer 1985, (3), pp. 5–13. [G: U.S.]

Kemp, Michael A. and Kirby, Ronald F. Government Policies Affecting Competition in Public Transportation. In *Lave, C. A., ed.*, 1985, pp. 277–98. [G: U.S.]

Kirzner, Israel M. The Perils of Regulation: A Market-Process Approach. In *Kirzner, I. M.*, 1985, pp. 119–49.

Lee, Moon H. and Bishara, Halim. Securities Regulation and Market Efficiency. *Int. Rev. Law Econ.*, December 1985, *5*(2), pp. 247–54. [G: Canada]

Levin, Harvey J. Comment: Antitrust, Concentration, and Competition. In *Noam, E. M., ed.*, 1985, pp. 390–96. [G: U.S.]

Libecap, Gary D. Regulatory Constraints on Oil and Gas Production on Forest Service and BLM Lands. In *Deacon, R. T. and Johnson, M. B., eds.*, 1985, pp. 135–48. [G: U.S.]

Litan, Robert E. Evaluating and Controlling the Risks of Financial Product Deregulation. *Yale J. Regul.*, Fall 1985, *3*(1), pp. 1–52. [G: U.S.]

Lloyd, P. J. The Economics of Regulation of Alcohol Distribution and Consumption in Victoria. *Australian Econ. Rev.*, 1st Quarter 1985, (69), pp. 16–29. [G: Australia]

Logan, Robert G. Trade in Communications and Data Processing: Comments. In *Stern, R. M., ed.*, 1985, pp. 299–303. [G: Canada; U.S.]

Lowi, Theodore J. The State in Politics: The Relation between Policy and Administration. In *Noll, R. G., ed.*, 1985, pp. 67–105.

MacLennan, Carol. A Wide Angle on Regulation: Comment. In *Noll, R. G., ed.*, 1985, pp. 160–71. [G: U.S.]

Mai, Chao-cheng. Optimum Location and Theory of the Firm under a Regulatory Constraint. *J. Reg. Sci.*, August 1985, *25*(3), pp. 453–61.

Matthews, Steven and Postlewaite, Andrew. Quality Testing and Disclosure. *Rand J. Econ.*, Autumn 1985, *16*(3), pp. 328–40.

Mayer, Colin. The Assessment: Recent Developments in Industrial Economics and Their Implications for Policy. *Oxford Rev. Econ. Policy*, Autumn 1985, *1*(3), pp. 1–24. [G: U.K.]

Meyer, Robert A. Regulation of the Firm Based on Imperfect Information. *Quart. Rev. Econ. Bus.*, Summer 1985, *25*(2), pp. 7–17.

Moore, Thomas Gale. An Agenda for Regulatory Reform. In *Boaz, D. and Crane, E. H., eds.*, 1985, pp. 145–63. [G: U.S.]

Moore, Thomas Gale. Antitrust and Economic Efficiency: Introduction. *J. Law Econ.*, May 1985, *28*(2), pp. 245–46.

Myers, Stewart C.; Kolbe, A. Lawrence and Tye, William B. Inflation and Rate of Return Regulation. In *Keeler, T. E., ed.*, 1985, pp. 83–119. [G: U.S.]

Nader, Laura and Nader, Claire. A Wide Angle on Regulation: An Anthropological Perspective. In *Noll, R. G., ed.*, 1985, pp. 141–60. [G: U.S.]

Negrine, Ralph. Cable Television in Great Britain. In *Negrine, R. M., ed.*, 1985, pp. 103–33. [G: U.K.]

Nelson, Forrest D. and Noll, Roger G. Policymakers' Preferences for Alternative Allocations of the Broadcast Spectrum. In *[McGowan, J. J.]*, 1985, pp. 241–62. [G: U.S.]

Noam, Eli M. Economies of Scale and Regulation

in CATV. In *Crew, M. A., ed.*, 1985, pp. 95–110. [G: U.S.]

Noam, Eli M. Economies of Scale in Cable Television: A Multiproduct Analysis. In *Noam, E. M., ed.*, 1985, pp. 93–120. [G: U.S.]

Noll, Roger G. Government Regulatory Behavior: A Multidisciplinary Survey and Synthesis. In *Noll, R. G., ed.*, 1985, pp. 9–63.

Noll, Roger G. Self-Regulation as Market Maintenance: Comment. In *Noll, R. G., ed.*, 1985, pp. 343–47. [G: U.S.]

Owen, Bruce M. Interest Groups and the Political Economy of Regulation. In *Meyer, J. A., ed.*, 1985, pp. 26–52. [G: U.S.]

Pacey, Patricia L. Cable Television in a Less Regulated Market. *J. Ind. Econ.*, September 1985, *34*(1), pp. 81–91. [G: U.S.]

Palay, Thomas M. Avoiding Regulatory Constraints: Contracting Safeguards and the Role of Informal Agreements. *J. Law, Econ., Organ.*, Spring 1985, *1*(1), pp. 155–75. [G: U.S.]

Parkman, Allen M. The Multiplier in English Fatal Accident Cases: What Happens When Judges Teach Judges Economics. *Int. Rev. Law Econ.*, December 1985, *5*(2), pp. 187–97. [G: U.K.; U.S.]

Phillips, Almarin and Roberts, Gary L. Borrowing from Peter to Pay Paul: More on Departures of Price from Marginal Cost. In *[McGowan, J. J.]*, 1985 report, pp. 299–307.

Pustay, Michael W. A Comparison of Pre- and Post-reform Motor Carrier Service to Small Communities. *Growth Change*, January 1985, *16*(1), pp. 47–54. [G: U.S.]

Riker, William H. Group Concentration and the Delegation of Legislative Authority: Comment. In *Noll, R. G., ed.*, 1985, pp. 197–99.

Rose, Nancy L. The Incidence of Regulatory Rents in the Motor Carrier Industry. *Rand J. Econ.*, Autumn 1985, *16*(3), pp. 299–318. [G: U.S.]

Schacht, Michael and Hoffman, Rolf-Rüdiger. Cable Television in West Germany. In *Negrine, R. M., ed.*, 1985, pp. 164–85. [G: W. Germany]

Scott, W. Richard. Conflicting Regulations: Comment. In *Noll, R. G., ed.*, 1985, pp. 304–11.

Selznick, Philip. Integrating Themes and Ideas: Focusing Organizational Research on Regulation. In *Noll, R. G., ed.*, 1985, pp. 363–67.

Sharp, Stephen A. Comment: The Regulatory Setting. In *Noam, E. M., ed.*, 1985, pp. 330–31.

Shepsle, Kenneth A. Why the Regulators Chose to Deregulate: Comment. In *Noll, R. G., ed.*, 1985, pp. 231–37.

Shleifer, Andrei. A Theory of Yardstick Competition. *Rand J. Econ.*, Autumn 1985, *16*(3), pp. 319–27.

Slovic, Paul; Fischhoff, Baruch and Lichtenstein, Sarah. Regulation of Risk: A Psychological Perspective. In *Noll, R. G., ed.*, 1985, pp. 241–78. [G: U.S.]

Smith, J. Barry and Sims, W. A. The Impact of Pollution Charges on Productivity Growth in Canadian Brewing. *Rand J. Econ.*, Autumn 1985, *16*(3), pp. 410–23. [G: Canada]

Sohl, Jeffrey E. An Application of Quadratic Programming to the Deregulation of Natural Gas. In *Harker, P. T., ed.*, 1985, pp. 196–207. [G: U.S.]

Sparkes, Vernone. Cable Television in the United States: A Story of Continuing Growth and Change. In *Negrine, R. M., ed.*, 1985, pp. 15–46. [G: U.S.]

Staiger, Robert W. and Richardson, Barbara C. A Discounting Framework for Regulatory Impact Analysis. *Policy Sci.*, March 1985, *18*(1), pp. 33–54.

Thurow, Lester C. The Politics of Deregulation; Evolution of the Major Banks and the Financial Intermediaries in the U.S.A. *Rev. Econ. Cond. Italy*, Sept.-Dec. 1985, (3), pp. 353–62. [G: U.S.]

Tracey, Michael. Television and Cable Policy in Japan: An Essay. In *Negrine, R. M., ed.*, 1985, pp. 196–211. [G: Japan]

Tucci, Gianrocco. Regulation and "Contestability" in Formulating an Air Transport Policy for the European Community. *Rivista Polit. Econ.*, Suppl. Dec. 1985, *76*, pp. 219–39. [G: EEC]

Utton, Albert E. In Search of an Integrating Principle for Interstate Water Law: Regulation versus the Market Place. *Natural Res. J.*, October 1985, *25*(4), pp. 985–1004. [G: U.S.]

Vietor, Richard H. K. and Davidson, Dekkers L. Economics and Politics of Deregulation: The Issue of Telephone Access Charges. *J. Policy Anal. Manage.*, Fall 1985, *5*(1), pp. 3–22. [G: U.S.]

Waverman, Leonard. Trade in Communications and Data Processing: Comments. In *Stern, R. M., ed.*, 1985, pp. 291–98. [G: Canada; U.S.]

Williams, Stephen F. The Law of Prior Appropriation: Possible Lessons for Hawaii. *Natural Res. J.*, October 1985, *25*(4), pp. 911–34. [G: U.S.]

Wilson, James Q. Integrating Themes and Ideas: Neglected Areas of Research on Regulation. In *Noll, R. G., ed.*, 1985, pp. 357–63.

Winett, Richard A. Regulation of Risk: Comment. In *Noll, R. G., ed.*, 1985, pp. 278–83. [G: U.S.]

Wolken, John D. and Navratil, Frank J. The Choice of Regulatory Regime: A Logit Analysis of Credit Union Chartering. *Quart. Rev. Econ. Bus.*, Spring 1985, *25*(1), pp. 40–57. [G: U.S.]

Ziemes, Georg. The Averch/Johnson Effect in a Simple Oligopoly Model. *Z. ges. Staatswiss. (JITE)*, September 1985, *141*(3), pp. 444–51.

620 ECONOMICS OF TECHNOLOGICAL CHANGE

621 Technological Change; Innovation; Research and Development

6210 General

Aida, Shuhei. A Concept of Eco-technology: Technological Approaches to Complexity. In

Aida, S., et al., 1985, pp. 245–51.

Arrow, Kenneth J. Classificatory Notes on the Production and Transmission of Technological Knowledge. In *Arrow, K. J. (I)*, 1985, pp. 297–306.

Benoit, Jean-Pierre. Innovation and Imitation in a Duopoly. *Rev. Econ. Stud.*, January 1985, 52(1), pp. 99–106.

Bentsen, Lloyd. Technology Venturing: A Visionary Challenge for Prosperity, Security, and Opportunities. In *Konecci, E. B. and Kuhn, R. L., eds.*, 1985, pp. 45–50. [G: U.S.]

Bergson, Abram. Gorbachev Calls for Intensive Growth. *Challenge*, Nov./Dec. 1985, 28(5), pp. 11–14. [G: U.S.S.R.]

Bhalla, A. S. and Fluitman, A. G. Science and Technology Indicators and Socio-economic Development. *World Devel.*, February 1985, 13(2), pp. 177–90.

Bhattacharya, Gautam. Technology Transfer, Licensing and the Speed of Endogenous Technological Change. *J. Econ. Dynam. Control*, December 1985, 9(4), pp. 423–56.

Binswanger, Hans P. and Pingali, Prabhu L. Population Growth and Technological Change in Agriculture. In *Davis, T. J., ed.*, 1985, pp. 62–89.

Caswell, Margriet and Zilberman, David. The Choice of Irrigation Technologies in California. *Amer. J. Agr. Econ.*, May 1985, 67(2), pp. 224–34. [G: U.S.]

Cave, Jonathan A. K. A Further Comment on Preemptive Patenting and the Persistence of Monopoly. *Amer. Econ. Rev.*, March 1985, 75(1), pp. 256–58.

Chase, Richard X. A Theory of Socioeconomic Change: Entropic Processes, Technology, and Evolutionary Development. *J. Econ. Issues*, December 1985, 19(4), pp. 797–823.

Chrysomilides, G. S. Technology Cycles in Agricultural Productivity in Canada. *Amer. Econ. Rev.*, Spring 1985, 29(1), pp. 32–40. [G: Canada]

Coates, Joseph F. Scenarios Part Two: Alternative Futures. In *Mendell, J. S., ed.*, 1985, pp. 21–46. [G: U.S.]

Dams, Theodor. Moral Responsibility and Agricultural Research: Comment. In *[Heidhues, T.]*, 1985, pp. 84–87. [G: U.S.]

Davidson, Frank P. Joint Technology Venturing: New Institutional Arrangements, The Next Steps. In *Konecci, E. B. and Kuhn, R. L., eds.*, 1985, pp. 199–204. [G: U.S.]

Dodson, D. Keith. The Roles of Private and Public Sectors in Large-scale Public Works. In *Konecci, E. B. and Kuhn, R. L., eds.*, 1985, pp. 192–98. [G: U.S.]

Egan, John J. Industry and Government in Space: Making the Long-term Commitment. In *Konecci, E. B. and Kuhn, R. L., eds.*, 1985, pp. 144–63. [G: U.S.]

Elzinga, Kenneth G. Religion, Culture, and Technology: Comment. In *Block, W.; Brennan, G. and Elzinga, K., eds.*, 1985, pp. 322–29.

Evenson, Robert E. Equity Implications of Public Policy in an Unstable Agricultural Economy:
Discussion. *Amer. J. Agr. Econ.*, May 1985, 67(2), pp. 441–42. [G: U.S.; LDCs]

Feder, Gershon and Slade, Roger. The Role of Public Policy in the Diffusion of Improved Agricultural Technology. *Amer. J. Agr. Econ.*, May 1985, 67(2), pp. 423–28. [G: U.S.; LDCs]

Fox, Glenn. Is the United States Really Underinvesting in Agricultural Research? *Amer. J. Agr. Econ.*, November 1985, 67(4), pp. 806–12. [G: U.S.]

Friedman, David. Religion, Culture, and Technology: Comment. In *Block, W.; Brennan, G. and Elzinga, K., eds.*, 1985, pp. 313–21.

Fudenberg, Drew and Tirole, Jean. Preemption and Rent Equilization in the Adoption of New Technology. *Rev. Econ. Stud.*, July 1985, 52(3), pp. 383–401.

Gilly, Mary C. and Zeithaml, Valarie A. The Elderly Consumer and Adoption of Technologies. *J. Cons. Res.*, December 1985, 12(3), pp. 353–47. [G: U.S.]

Goisis, Gianandrea. Domanda variabile, prezzi dei fattori e scelta degli assetti produttivi: alcuni recenti contributi. (Variability of Demand, Prices of Inputs and Choice of Technologies: Some Recent Contributions. With English summary.) *Rivista Int. Sci. Econ. Com.*, May 1985, 32(5), pp. 467–80.

Goldsmith, Maurice. The Sunrise Industries beyond the 1980s: Discussion. In *Wells, N., ed.*, 1985, pp. 50–53.

Harris, Christopher J. and Vickers, John. Perfect Equilibrium in a Model of a Race. *Rev. Econ. Stud.*, April 1985, 52(2), pp. 193–209.

Hirshey, Mark and Weygandt, Jerry J. Amortization Policy for Advertising and Research and Development Expenditures. *J. Acc. Res.*, Spring 1985, 23(1), pp. 326–35. [G: U.S.]

Hoffman, Kurt. Microelectronics, International Competition and Development Strategies: The Unavoidable Issues—Editor's Introduction. *World Devel.*, March 1985, 13(3), pp. 263–72.

Horstmann, Ignatius J.; MacDonald, Glenn M. and Slivinski, Alan D. Patents as Information Transfer Mechanisms: To Patent or (Maybe) Not to Patent. *J. Polit. Econ.*, October 1985, 93(5), pp. 837–58.

Huffman, Wallace E. Human Capital, Adaptive Ability, and the Distributional Implications of Agricultural Policy. *Amer. J. Agr. Econ.*, May 1985, 67(2), pp. 429–34. [G: U.S.]

Hull, Cordell W. Financial and Investment Perspectives on Technology Venturing: A Private-Sector View. In *Konecci, E. B. and Kuhn, R. L., eds.*, 1985, pp. 74–81. [G: U.S.]

Inman, Bobby Ray. Technology Venturing: Collaborative Efforts. In *Konecci, E. B. and Kuhn, R. L., eds.*, 1985, pp. 51–58. [G: U.S.]

Just, Richard E. and Zilberman, David. Risk Aversion, Technology Choice, and Equity Effects of Agricultural Policy. *Amer. J. Agr. Econ.*, May 1985, 67(2), pp. 435–40. [G: U.S.]

Kaganovich, Mikhail. Efficiency of Sliding Plans in a Linear Model with Time-Dependent Technology. *Rev. Econ. Stud.*, October 1985, 52(4), pp. 691–702.

Kanter, Rosabeth Moss. Providing the Corporate Environment to Foster Innovation. In *Federal Reserve Bank of Atlanta (I)*, 1985, pp. 111–22.

Kantrow, Alan M. America's Industrial Renaissance. In *Federal Reserve Bank of Atlanta (I)*, 1985, pp. 97–110. [G: U.S.]

Kenward, Michael. The Sunrise Industries beyond the 1980s: Discussion. In *Wells, N., ed.*, 1985, pp. 54–56.

Klusoň, Václav. Innovations and Planned Management. *Czech. Econ. Pap.*, 1985, 23, pp. 39–54.

Kozmetsky, George. Technology Venturing: The New American Response to the Changing Economy. In *Konecci, E. B. and Kuhn, R. L., eds.*, 1985, pp. 3–13. [G: U.S.]

Kubačka, Jozef. Optimal Size of Industrial Enterprises—An Important Factor of Intensification of the Reproduction Process. *Czech. Econ. Digest.*, September 1985, (6), pp. 72–86. [G: Czechoslovakia]

Langdon, Richard and Rothwell, Roy. Design and Innovation: Policy and Management: Introduction. In *Langdon, R. and Rothwell, R., eds.*, 1985, pp. xi–xxi.

Leontief, Wassily. Machines and Man. In *Leontief, W.*, 1985, pp. 187–99. [G: U.S.]

Liebeler, Wesley J. Antitrust and Economic Efficiency: Comment. *J. Law Econ.*, May 1985, 28(2), pp. 335–43.

Lipsey, Robert E. and Kravis, Irving B. The Competitive Position of U.S. Manufacturing Firms. *Banca Naz. Lavoro Quart. Rev.*, June 1985, (153), pp. 127–54. [G: U.S.]

Lowe, Julian. Science Parks in the UK. *Lloyds Bank Rev.*, April 1985, (156), pp. 31–42. [G: U.S.; U.K.]

Lunghini, Giorgio. Marx sulle macchine: note di lettura. (Marx on Machinery. With English summary.) *Rivista Int. Sci. Econ. Com.*, June 1985, 32(6), pp. 517–24.

MacMurray, Robert R. Technological Change in a Society in Transition: Work in Progress on a Unified Reference Work in Early American Patent History. *J. Econ. Hist.*, June 1985, 45(2), pp. 299–303. [G: U.S.]

Matzner, Egon. Technological and Institutional Innovation. *Ann. Pub. Co-op. Econ.*, January–June 1985, 56(1–2), pp. 71–80. [G: Austria]

McDowell, George R. The Political Economy of Extension Program Design: Institutional Maintenance Issues in the Organization and Delivery of Extension Programs. *Amer. J. Agr. Econ.*, November 1985, 67(4), pp. 717–25. [G: U.S.]

Melody, William H. The Information Society: Implications for Economic Institutions and Market Theory. *J. Econ. Issues*, June 1985, 19(2), pp. 523–39.

Miliaev, V. and Khachaturian, A. Specialized Innovative Organizations (The Experience of CMEA Countries). *Prob. Econ.*, May 1985, 28(1), pp. 56–71. [G: CMEA]

Mishan, Ezra J. Religion, Culture, and Technology: Reply. In *Block, W.; Brennan, G. and Elzinga, K., eds.*, 1985, pp. 330–40.

Mishan, Ezra J. Religion, Culture, and Technology. In *Block, W.; Brennan, G. and Elzinga, K., eds.*, 1985, pp. 279–312.

Mokyr, Joel. The Industrial Revolution and the New Economic History. In *Mokyr, J., ed.*, 1985, pp. 1–51. [G: U.K.]

Monzani, Pierre. Innovation et nouveautés au XVIIIe siècle. (Innovation and Novelties in the 18th Century. With English summary.) *Écon. Soc.*, October 1985, 19(10), pp. 57–70. [G: France]

Müller, Harald. Western Policies: U.S. Energy Policy. In *Rode, R. and Jacobsen, H.-D., eds.*, 1985, pp. 200–212. [G: U.S.; CMEA]

Nagy, Joseph G. The Overall Rate of Return to Agricultural Research and Extension Investments in Pakistan. *Pakistan J. Appl. Econ.*, Summer 1985, 4(1), pp. 17–28. [G: Pakistan]

Ordover, Janusz A. and Willig, Robert D. Antitrust for High-Technology Industries: Assessing Research Joint Ventures and Mergers. *J. Law Econ.*, May 1985, 28(2), pp. 311–33.

Peterson, Willis. Equity Implications of Public Policy in an Unstable Agricultural Economy: Discussion. *Amer. J. Agr. Econ.*, May 1985, 67(2), pp. 443–45. [G: U.S.; LDCs]

Reinganum, Jennifer F. Corrigendum [Dynamic Games of Innovation]. *J. Econ. Theory*, February 1985, 35(1), pp. 196–97.

Reinganum, Jennifer F. Innovation and Industry Evolution. *Quart. J. Econ.*, February 1985, 100(1), pp. 81–99.

Rohlíček, Rudolf. Prospects and Certainty. *Czech. Econ. Digest.*, September 1985, (6), pp. 24–32. [G: U.S.S.R.; Czechoslovakia]

Ruttan, Vernon W. Moral Responsibility and Agricultural Research. In *[Heidhues, T.]*, 1985, pp. 66–83. [G: U.S.]

Solo, Robert. Across the Industrial Divide: A Review Article. *J. Econ. Issues*, September 1985, 19(3), pp. 829–36. [G: U.S.]

Storey, D. J. Small Firms in Regional Economic Development: The Implications for Policy. In *Storey, D. J., ed.*, 1985, pp. 219–29. [G: U.K.]

Sunley, Emil M. Private/Public Venturing Activities and Opportunities. In *Konecci, E. B. and Kuhn, R. L., eds.*, 1985, pp. 171–84. [G: U.S.]

Teitel, Simón. Indicadores de ciencia y tecnología, tamaño de país y desarrollo económico: una comparación internacional. (With English summary.) *Desarrollo Econ.*, Oct.-Dec. 1985, 25(99), pp. 329–49.

Thorsrud, Einar. Work and Technology. In *Gustavsson, B.; Karlsson, J. C. and Raftegard, C.*, 1985, pp. 57–60.

Toye, John. *Dirigisme* and Development Economics. *Cambridge J. Econ.*, March 1985, 9(1), pp. 1–14.

Vickers, John. Pre-emptive Patenting, Joint Ventures, and the Persistence of Oligopoly. *Int.*

J. Ind. Organ., September 1985, *3*(3), pp. 261–73.

Vitta, Paul B. New Technologies and Their Implications for Developing Countries: Outlines of Possible Policy Responses. *Can. J. Devel. Stud.*, 1985, *6*(2), pp. 241–55. **[G: LDCs]**

Zuscovitch, Ehud. La dynamique du développement des technologies: Éléments d'un cadre conceptuel. (The Economic Dynamics of Technologies Development. With English summary.) *Revue Écon.*, September 1985, *36*(5), pp. 897–915.

Zykov, Iu. Socioeconomic Forecasting of Scientific and Technical Progress. *Prob. Econ.*, April 1985, *27*(12), pp. 17–33.

6211 Technological Change and Innovation

Adekanye, Tomilayo O. Innovation and Rural Women in Nigeria: Cassava Processing and Food Production. In *Ahmed, I., ed.*, 1985, pp. 252–83. **[G: Nigeria]**

Adelstein, Richard P. and Peretz, Steven I. The Competition of Technologies in Markets for Ideas: Copyright and Fair Use in Evolutionary Perspective. *Int. Rev. Law Econ.*, December 1985, *5*(2), pp. 209–38. **[G: U.S.]**

Agarwal, Bina. Women and Technological Change in Agriculture: The Asian and African Experience. In *Ahmed, I., ed.*, 1985, pp. 67–114. **[G: India; Africa; Asia]**

Ahmed, Iftikhar. Technology and Rural Women: Conclusions. In *Ahmed, I., ed.*, 1985, pp. 327–41. **[G: LDCs]**

Albin, Peter S. Job Design, Control Technology, and Technical Change. *J. Econ. Issues*, September 1985, *19*(3), pp. 703–30.

Alfthan, Torkel. Developing Skills for Technological Change: Some Policy Issues. *Int. Lab. Rev.*, Sept.-Oct. 1985, *124*(5), pp. 517–29. **[G: OECD; LDCs]**

Altmann, Franz-Lothar. East–West Relations in Energy, Agriculture and Technology: Comments. In *Saunders, C. T., ed.*, 1985, pp. 242–46. **[G: U.S.S.R.; OECD]**

Amsden, Alice H. The Division of Labour Is Limited by the Rate of Growth of the Market: The Taiwan Machine Tool Industry in the 1970s. *Cambridge J. Econ.*, September 1985, *9*(3), pp. 271–84. **[G: Taiwan]**

Anderson, William P. Synfuels Development in the USA: Case Studies of National Environmental Feasibility and Local Socioeconomic Impacts: Technical Review of the U.S. Case Studies: I. In *Lakshmanan, T. R. and Johansson, B., eds.*, 1985, pp. 111–17. **[G: U.S.]**

Antonelli, Cristiano. The Diffusion of an Organizational Innovation: International Data Telecommunications and Multinational Industrial Firms. *Int. J. Ind. Organ.*, March 1985, *3*(1), pp. 109–18. **[G: OECD]**

Ashford, Nicholas A. Regulation as a Stimulas for Technological Change. In *Langdon, R. and Rothwell, R., eds.*, 1985, pp. 171–78.

Aubert, Jean-Eric. The Approach of Design and Concepts of Innovation Policy. In *Langdon,*

R. and Rothwell, R., eds., 1985, pp. 164–70.

Bailey, Kenneth W. Palay Area Response in the Philippines under Conditions of Technical Change. *Philippine Econ. J.*, 1985, *24*(4), pp. 302–21. **[G: Philippines]**

Baily, Martin Neil and Chakrabarti, Alok K. Innovation and Productivity in U.S. Industry. *Brookings Pap. Econ. Act.*, 1985, (2), pp. 609–32. **[G: U.S.]**

Balasubramanyam, V. N. Foreign Direct Investment and the International Transfer of Technology. In *Greenaway, D., ed.*, 1985, pp. 159–81. **[G: LDCs]**

Baldwin, G. B. The Appraisal of Rural Water Supplies: Reply [Why Present Value Calculations Should Not Be Used in Choosing Rural Water Supply Technology]. *World Devel.*, Oct./Nov. 1985, *13*(10/11), pp. 1179–80. **[G: LDCs]**

Baranson, Jack and Roark, Robin. Trends in North–South Transfer of High Technology. In *Rosenberg, N. and Frischtak, C., eds.*, 1985, pp. 24–42. **[G: LDCs; MDCs]**

Bartlett, Bruce. The Entrepreneurial Imperative. In *Boaz, D. and Crane, E. H., eds.*, 1985, pp. 75–90. **[G: U.S.]**

Basberg, Bjørn L. Technological Transformation in the Norwegian Whaling Industry in the Interwar Period. *Scand. Econ. Hist. Rev.*, 1985, *33*(2), pp. 83–107. **[G: Norway]**

Bednarzik, Robert W. The Impact of Microelectronics on Employment: Japan's Experience. *Mon. Lab. Rev.*, September 1985, *108*(9), pp. 45–48. **[G: Japan]**

Bhaduri, Amit. Technological Change and Rural Women: A Conceptual Analysis. In *Ahmed, I., ed.*, 1985, pp. 15–26.

Bhagwati, Jagdish N. Technology and Employment. In *Bhagwati, J. N. (II)*, 1985, pp. 229–30.

Bhagwati, Jagdish N. The Choice of Technology. In *Bhagwati, J. N. (II)*, 1985, pp. 231–36.

Bhagwati, Jagdish N. and Srinivasan, T. N. The Ranking of Policy Interventions under Factor Market Imperfections: The Case of Sector-Specific Sticky Wages and Unemployment. In *Bhagwati, J. N. (II)*, 1985, pp. 250–67.

Black, Andrew P. Technical Change, Product Quality and Market Structure in the West German Automobile Industry. *Stud. Econ.*, 1985, *40*(26), pp. 41–63. **[G: W. Germany]**

Bowles, Samuel; Gordon, David M. and Weisskopf, Thomas E. In Defense of the "Social Model." *Challenge*, May/June 1985, *28*(2), pp. 57–59. **[G: U.S.]**

Bowman, Mary Jean. Education, Population Trends and Technological Change. *Econ. Educ. Rev.*, 1985, *4*(1), pp. 29–44. **[G: Global]**

Brada, Josef C. Soviet–Western Trade and Technology Transfer: An Economic Overview. In *Parrott, B., ed.*, 1985, pp. 3–34. **[G: U.S.S.R.; OECD]**

Brada, Josef C. and Hoffman, Dennis L. The Productivity Differential between Soviet and Western Capital and the Benefits of Technology Imports to the Soviet Economy. *Quart.*

Rev. Econ. Bus., Spring 1985, *25*(1), pp. 6–18. **[G: U.S.S.R.]**

Braunstein, Yale M. and White, Lawrence J. Setting Technical Compatibility Standards: An Economic Analysis. *Antitrust Bull.*, Summer 1985, *30*(2), pp. 337–55.

Brooks, Harvey. Technology as a Factor in U.S. Competitiveness. In *Scott, B. R. and Lodge, G. C., eds.*, 1985, pp. 328–56. **[G: U.S.; OECD]**

Bruland, Kristine. Say's Law and the Single-Factor Explanation of British Industrialization: A Comment [The Cause of the Industrial Revolution: A Brief 'Single-Factor' Argument]. *J. Europ. Econ. Hist.*, Spring 1985, *14*(1), pp. 187–91. **[G: U.K.]**

Bruton, Henry J. On the Production of a National Technology. In *James, J. and Watanabe, S., eds.*, 1985, pp. 81–115.

Buckley, Peter J. New Forms of International Industrial Co-operation. In *Buckley, P. J. and Casson, M.*, 1985, pp. 39–59. **[G: LDCs; MDCs]**

Burgan, John U. Cyclical Behavior of High Tech Industries. *Mon. Lab. Rev.*, May 1985, *108*(5), pp. 9–15. **[G: U.S.]**

Buttel, Frederick H.; Kenney, Martin and Kloppenburg, Jack, Jr. From Green Revolution to Biorevolution: Some Observations on the Changing Technological Bases of Economic Transformation in the Third World. *Econ. Develop. Cult. Change*, October 1985, *34*(1), pp. 31–55. **[G: LDCs]**

Bykov, Alexandr. East–West Technology Transfers: Now and in the Future. In *Saunders, C. T., ed.*, 1985, pp. 231–42. **[G: U.S.; CMEA]**

Campbell, Robert W. Satellite Communications in the USSR. *Soviet Econ.*, Oct.-Dec. 1985, *1*(4), pp. 313–39. **[G: U.S.S.R.]**

Campbell, Robert W. Technology Transfer in the Soviet Energy Sector. In *Parrott, B., ed.*, 1985, pp. 141–68. **[G: U.S.S.R.]**

Carnoy, Martin. High Technology and International Labour Markets. *Int. Lab. Rev.*, Nov.-Dec. 1985, *124*(6), pp. 643–59. **[G: LDCs; OECD]**

Carr, Marilyn. Technologies for Rural Women: Impact and Dissemination. In *Ahmed, I., ed.*, 1985, pp. 115–53. **[G: Africa]**

Carré, Denis. Les modalités de la concurrence internationale et les performances des secteurs industriels français. (The International Competition and the Performance of French Industries. With English summary.) *L'Actual. Econ.*, March 1985, *61*(1), pp. 51–72. **[G: France]**

Casey, Tom. Linking Innovation Thoery to Innovation Policy. In *Langdon, R. and Rothwell, R., eds.*, 1985, pp. 179–87.

Cavusgil, S. Tamer. Mutinational Corporations and the Management of Technology Transfers. In *Samli, A. C., ed.*, 1985, pp. 217–29.

Cherviakov, Igor' and Nikht, Lotar. The Most Important Factor for Accelerating Scientific and Technical Progress. *Soviet E. Europ. For-*

eign Trade, Winter 1985-86, *21*(4), pp. 29–36. **[G: CMEA]**

Choi, Jai-Young and Yu, Eden S. H. Technical Progress, Terms of Trade and Welfare under Variable Returns to Scale. *Economica*, August 1985, *52*(207), pp. 365–77.

Chudnovsky, Daniel. La difusión de tecnologías de punta en la Argentina: el caso de las máquinas herramientas con control numérico, el CAD/CAM y los robots. (With English summary.) *Desarrollo Econ.*, January-March 1985, *24*(96), pp. 483–515. **[G: Argentina]**

Cingano, Francesco. La banca negli anni '90: evoluzione tecnoligica e professionalità. (The Bank in the Nineties: Technological Evolution and Professionalism. With English summary.) *Bancaria*, April 1985, *41*(4), pp. 411–18. **[G: Italy]**

Collins, Susan M. Technical Progress in a Three-Country Ricardian Model with a Continuum of Goods. *J. Int. Econ.*, August 1985, *19*(1/2), pp. 171–79.

Contractor, Farok J. Licensing versus Foreign Direct Investment in U.S. Corporate Strategy: An Analysis of Aggregate U.S. Data. In *Rosenberg, N. and Frischtak, C., eds.*, 1985, pp. 277–320. **[G: U.S.]**

Cooper, Julian M. Western Technology and the Soviet Defense Industry. In *Parrott, B., ed.*, 1985, pp. 169–202. **[G: U.S.S.R.]**

Crawford, Eric W. and Lassiter, Gregory C. Constraints on Oxen Cultivation in the Sahel: Comment. *Amer. J. Agr. Econ.*, August 1985, *67*(3), pp. 684–85. **[G: W. Africa]**

Daly, Donald J. Technology Transfer and Canada's Competitive Performance. In *Stern, R. M., ed.*, 1985, pp. 304–33. **[G: Canada]**

Date-Bah, Eugenia. Technologies for Rural Women of Ghana: Role of Socio-Cultural Factors. In *Ahmed, I., ed.*, 1985, pp. 211–51. **[G: Ghana]**

Daughety, Andrew F.; Nelson, Forrest D. and Vigdor, William R. An Econometric Analysis of the Cost and Production Structure of the Trucking Industry. In *Daughety, A. F., ed.*, 1985, pp. 65–95. **[G: U.S.]**

David, Paul A. Clio and the Economics of QWERTY. *Amer. Econ. Rev.*, May 1985, *75*(2), pp. 332–37. **[G: U.S.; U.K.]**

De Mattia, Renato. The Forces at Work in the Evolution of Payment Systems in the 1980s. *J. Bank Res.*, Winter 1985, *15*(4), pp. 211–21. **[G: Italy]**

DeBrock, Lawrence M. and Masson, Robert T. Sooner or Later? Inventive Rivalry and Welfare. *Int. J. Ind. Organ.*, December 1985, *3*(4), pp. 421–38.

Deger, Saadet and Sen, Somnath. Technology Transfer and Arms Production in Developing Countries. *Industry Devel.*, 1985, (15), pp. 1–18. **[G: LDCs]**

DeKoker, Neil. Labor–Management Relations for Survival. In *Dennis, B. D., ed.*, 1985, pp. 576–77. **[G: U.S.]**

Delgado, Christopher L. and McIntire, John. Constraints on Oxen Cultivation in the Sahel:

Reply. *Amer. J. Agr. Econ.*, August 1985, 67(3), pp. 686–87.   **[G: W. Africa]**

Diwan, Romesh and Kallianpur, Renu. Biological Technology and Land Productivity: Fertilizers and Food Production in India. *World Devel.*, May 1985, 13(5), pp. 627–38.   **[G: India]**

Diwan, Romesh and Leonardson, Nirjhar J. Productivity, Technical Change and Capital–Labor Substitution in Indian Industry. *Indian J. Quant. Econ.*, 1985, 1(2), pp. 1–16.
        [G: India]

Dotsey, Michael. Is There an Operational Interest Rate Rule? *Amer. Econ. Rev.*, June 1985, 75(3), pp. 552–56.

Dow, Gregory K. Internal Bargaining and Strategic Innovation in the Theory of the Firm. *J. Econ. Behav. Organ.*, September 1985, 6(3), pp. 301–20.

Drugge, Sten E. Nonneutral Technical Change and Regional Wage Differentials: A Comment. *J. Reg. Sci.*, February 1985, 25(1), pp. 135–36.   **[G: U.S.]**

Dungan, Peter and Younger, Arthur. New Technology and Unemployment: A Simulation of Macroeconomic Impacts and Responses in Canada. *J. Policy Modeling*, Winter 1985, 7(4), pp. 595–619.   **[G: Canada]**

Dupont, Serge and Diener, Steven G. The Future of Energy Conservation and Alternative Energies: Opportunities and Barriers. *Can. Public Policy*, Supplement July 1985, 11(3), pp. 443–54.   **[G: Canada]**

Edquist, Charles. Technology and Work in Sugar Cane Harvesting in Capitalist Jamaica and Socialist Cuba 1958–1983. In *Gustavsson, B.; Karlsson, J. C. and Raftegard, C.*, 1985, pp. 71–82.   **[G: Cuba; Jamaica]**

Eltis, Walter. Ricardo on Machinery and Technological Unemployment. In *Caravale, G. A.*, *ed.*, 1985, pp. 257–84.

Englmann, Frank C. Pasinetti on the Choice of Technique: A Note. *Cambridge J. Econ.*, March 1985, 9(1), pp. 85–88.

Enos, John L. A Game-Theoretic Approach to Choice of Technology in Developing Countries. In *James, J. and Watanabe, S., eds.*, 1985, pp. 47–80.

Epstein, Eugene. Innovation and Economic Growth. In *Federal Reserve Bank of Atlanta (I)*, 1985, pp. 89–95.   **[G: U.S.]**

Epstein, Larry G. and Yatchew, Adonis John. The Empirical Determination of Technology and Expectations: A Simplified Procedure. *J. Econometrics*, February 1985, 27(2), pp. 235–58.   **[G: U.S.]**

Erdilek, Asim. International Technology Transfer in the Middle East. In *Kaynak, E., ed. (II)*, 1985, pp. 85–99.   **[G: Middle East]**

Erdilek, Asim and Rapoport, Alan. Conceptual and Measurement Problems in International Technology Transfer: A Critical Analysis. In *Samli, A. C., ed.*, 1985, pp. 249–61.

Fakiolas, T. Basic Causes of Soviet Industry's Low International Competitiveness. *J. Econ. Stud.*, 1985, 12(5), pp. 39–52.   **[G: U.S.S.R.]**

Farrell, Carlyle and Funk, Thomas. The Deter-

mination of Ex-Ante Returns to Agricultural Research: The Case of Plant Biotechnology in Canada. *Can. J. Agr. Econ.*, March 1985, 33(1), pp. 67–81.   **[G: Canada]**

Farrell, Joseph and Saloner, Garth. Standardization, Compatability, and Innovation. *Rand J. Econ.*, Spring 1985, 16(1), pp. 70–83.

Foray, Dominique. Innovation majeure et transformation des structures productives: Une étude de cas: Le procédé de coulée en moule plein en fonderie. (Major Innovation and Changes in the Productive Structures of Casting Industry: The Fullmold Casting Process. With English summary.) *Revue Écon.*, September 1985, 36(5), pp. 1081–1116.

Forsyth, David J. C. Government Policy, Market Structure and Choice of Technology in Egypt. In *James, J. and Watanabe, S., eds.*, 1985, pp. 137–82.   **[G: Egypt]**

François, Jean-Paul. Recherche-développement et échanges techniques avec l'étranger dans l'industrie française: Une étude statistique. (Research and Development Expenditures and Foreign Technological Payments in French Industry. With English summary.) *Revue Écon.*, September 1985, 36(5), pp. 1043–80.
        [G: France]

Fransman, Martin. Conceptualising Technical Change in the Third World in the 1980s: An Interpretive Survey. *J. Devel. Stud.*, July 1985, 21(4), pp. 572–652.   **[G: LDCs]**

Franzmeyer, Fritz. Wirtschaftliche Aspekte der technologischen Entwicklung in den USA und in Japan: Herausforderung für die EG und ihre Mitgliedstaaten. (Economic Aspects of Technological Developments in the USA and Japan: A Challenge for the EEC and Its Member States. With English Summary.) *Konjunkturpolitik*, 1985, 31(4/5), pp. 261–84.   **[G: U.S.; Japan; EEC]**

Freeman, Orville. The Family Farm: A Success Story with Global Implications. In *Didsbury, H. F., Jr., ed.*, 1985, pp. 135–46.

Friedlaender, Ann F. and Bruce, Sharon Schur. Augmentation Effects and Technical Change in the Regulated Trucking Industry, 1974–1979. In *Daughety, A. F., ed.*, 1985, pp. 29–63.   **[G: U.S.]**

Garonna, Paolo. Controlling the Dynamics of Technological Change in the Industrial Labour Markets. *Econ. Lavoro*, Jan.-Mar. 1985, 19(1), pp. 137–42.   **[G: W. Europe; U.S.; Japan]**

Gatignon, Hubert and Robertson, Thomas S. A Propositional Inventory for New Diffusion Research. *J. Cons. Res.*, March 1985, 11(4), pp. 849–67.

Gaudin, Thierry. Definition of Innovation Policies. In *Sweeney, G., ed.*, 1985, pp. 11–47.
        [G: OECD]

Gehrels, Franz. Allocations, Outputs and Rentals in General Equilibrium with a Limiting Factor. *Rivista Int. Sci. Econ. Com.*, April 1985, 32(4), pp. 323–41.

Gelauff, George M. M.; Wennekers, Sander R. M. and de Jong, André H. M. A Putty-Clay Model with Three Factors of Production

and Partly Endogenous Technical Progress. *De Economist*, 1985, *133*(3), pp. 327–51.
[G: Netherlands]

Ghosh, Dipak. A Disequilibrium Interpretation of Kaldor's Technical Progress Function. *Bull. Econ. Res.*, January 1985, *37*(1), pp. 69–73.

Ginzberg, Eli. How to Think about Technology. In *Ginzberg, E.*, 1985, pp. 403–16.

Ginzberg, Eli. The Mechanization of Work. In *Ginzberg, E.*, 1985, pp. 431–45.

Goddard, J. B., et al. The Impact of New Information Technology on Urban and Regional Structure in Europe. In *Thwaites, A. T. and Oakey, R. P., eds.*, 1985, pp. 215–41.
[G: W. Europe; U.K.]

Goodman, S. E. Technology Transfer and the Development of the Soviet Computer Industry. In *Parrott, B., ed.*, 1985, pp. 117–40.
[G: U.S.S.R.]

Granstrand, Ove and Sigurdson, Jon. Innovation Policies in East Asia and Some Implications for Western Europe. In *Langdon, R. and Rothwell, R., eds.*, 1985, pp. 137–63.
[G: Hong Kong; S. Korea; Taiwan; Singapore; Japan]

Grossman, Gene M. and Razin, Assaf. Direct Foreign Investment and the Choice of Technique under Uncertainty. *Oxford Econ. Pap.*, December 1985, *37*(4), pp. 606–20.

Grossman, Gene M. and Shapiro, Carl. Normative Issues Raised by International Trade in Technology Services. In *Stern, R. M., ed.*, 1985, pp. 83–113. [G: OECD]

Guillerme, Jacques. "Invention" et "innovation" dans l'art du projet. ("Invention" and "Innovation" in Architectural Projects. With English summary.) *Écon. Soc.*, October 1985, *19*(10), pp. 71–87. [G: France]

Gupta, Kanhaya L. Money and the Bias of Technical Progress. *Appl. Econ.*, February 1985, *17*(1), pp. 87–93. [G: India]

Hagen, Everett E. More on the Employment Effects of Innovation: More than a Response [Technological Disemployment and Economic Growth]. *J. Devel. Econ.*, January–February 1985, *17*(1–2), pp. 163–73.

Hall, P. H. and Heffernan, Shelagh A. More on the Employment Effects of Innovation [Technological Disemployment and Economic Growth]. *J. Devel. Econ.*, January–February 1985, *17*(1–2), pp. 151–62.

Hanson, Philip. Soviet Assimilation of Western Technology. In *Parrott, B., ed.*, 1985, pp. 63–81. [G: U.S.S.R.]

Harris, Christopher J. and Vickers, John. Patent Races and the Persistence of Monopoly. In *Geroski, P. A.; Phlips, L. and Ulph, A., eds.*, 1985, pp. 93–113.

Harris, Martha Caldwell. Japan's International Technology Transfers. In *Nanto, D. K., ed.*, 1985, pp. 114–42. [G: Japan; U.S.]

Haug, Frigga. Automatization as a Field of Contradictions. In *Gustavsson, B.; Karlsson, J. C. and Raftegard, C.*, 1985, pp. 83–92.

Hayami, Yujiro and Kikuchi, Masao. Agricultural Technology and Income Distribution: Two In-

donesian Villages Viewed from the Japanese Experience. In *Ohkawa, K. and Ranis, G., eds.*, 1985, pp. 91–109. [G: Indonesia; Japan]

Heinsohn, Gunnar and Steiger, Otto. Technical Progress and Monetary Production: An Explanation. *Écon. Soc.*, August 1985, *19*(8), pp. 85–98.

Heyer, Nelson O. Managing Human Resources in a High Technology Enterprise. In *Niehaus, R. J., ed.*, 1985, pp. 45–66. [G: U.S.]

Hieneman, Bruce D., et al. Technology Transfer from Japan to Southeast Asia. In *Samli, A. C., ed.*, 1985, pp. 143–53. [G: Japan; S.E. Asia]

Hill, Hal. Subcontracting, Technological Diffusion, and the Development of Small Enterprise in Philippine Manufacturing. *J. Devel. Areas*, January 1985, *19*(2), pp. 245–61.
[G: Philippines]

Hoffman, Kurt. Clothing, Chips and Competitive Advantage: The Impact of Microelectronics on Trade and Production in the Garment Industry. *World Devel.*, March 1985, *13*(3), pp. 371–92. [G: LDCs]

Holliday, George D. Western Technology Transfer to the Soviet Automotive Industry. In *Parrott, B., ed.*, 1985, pp. 82–116.
[G: U.S.S.R.; OECD; Czechoslovakia; Hungary]

Honadle, George H.; Silverman, Jerry M. and Mickelwait, Donald R. Implementing Rural Development Projects: Technical Assistance Shortcomings. In *Morss, E. R. and Gow, D. D., eds.*, 1985, pp. 83–106. [G: LDCs]

Hordijk, Leen. Synfuels Development in the USA: Case Studies of National Environmental Feasibility and Local Socioeconomic Impacts: Technical Review of the U.S. Case Studies: II. In *Lakshmanan, T. R. and Johansson, B., eds.*, 1985, pp. 118–24. [G: U.S.]

Houttuin, G. Demand Oriented Instruments in Innovation Policy: Government Procurement and Regulation. In *Sweeney, G., ed.*, 1985, pp. 152–66. [G: OECD]

Houttuin, G. Venture Capitalism. In *Sweeney, G., ed.*, 1985, pp. 189–96. [G: OECD]

Iakovets, Iu. The National Economic Effect of Fundamentally New Technology. *Prob. Econ.*, August 1985, *28*(4), pp. 68–83.

Ingrao, Bruna and Piacentini, Paolo. Automazione flessibile e robotica: prospettive di ricerca sui processi di diffusione. (Flexible Automation and Robotics: Prospects for a Research on the Processes of Diffusion. With English summary.) *Econ. Lavoro*, July–Sept. 1985, *19*(3), pp. 57–74.

Inotai, András. East–West Relations in Energy, Agriculture and Technology: Comments. In *Saunders, C. T., ed.*, 1985, pp. 246–51.
[G: CMEA]

Ishikawa, Akihiro. Participation and the Effect of New Technology upon Work: The Case of Small- and Medium-scale Manufacturing Firms in Tokyo. *Econ. Anal. Worker's Manage.*, 1985, *19*(3), pp. 295–305. [G: Japan]

Jacobsson, Staffan. Technical Change and Industrial Policy: The Case of Computer Numerically

Controlled Lathes in Argentina, Korea and Taiwan. *World Devel.*, March 1985, *13*(3), pp. 353–70. **[G: Argentina; Korea; Taiwan; OECD]**

James, Jeffrey. The Role of Appropriate Technology in a Redistributive Development Strategy. In *James, J. and Watanabe, S., eds.*, 1985, pp. 116–33.

James, Jeffrey and Watanabe, Susumu. Technology, Institutions and Government Policies: Introduction. In *James, J. and Watanabe, S., eds.*, 1985, pp. 1–15.

Jha, L. K. Multinationals as a Source of Technology for Developing Countries. In *Jha, L. K.*, 1985, pp. 23–33. **[G: Global]**

Jha, L. K. Technology and Development. In *Jha, L. K.*, 1985, pp. 1–22. **[G: India]**

Jones, Barry O. Science and Technology—Managing Australia's Opportunities. In *Scutt, J. A., ed.*, 1985, pp. 103–14. **[G: Australia]**

Joskow, Paul L. and Rose, Nancy L. The Effects of Technological Change, Experience, and Environmental Regulation on the Construction Cost of Coal-burning Generating Units. *Rand J. Econ.*, Spring 1985, *16*(1), pp. 1–27. **[G: U.S.]**

Judd, Kenneth L. On the Performance of Patents. *Econometrica*, May 1985, *53*(3), pp. 567–85.

Kaplan, D. E. The Diffusion of Microelectronic Technology in South African Manufacturing Industry: The Case of Computer Aided Design. *J. Stud. Econ. Econometrics*, November 1985, (23), pp. 67–98. **[G: S. Africa]**

Kaplinsky, Raphael. Comparative Advantage by Design. In *Langdon, R. and Rothwell, R., eds.*, 1985, pp. 44–62. **[G: OECD]**

Kaplinsky, Raphael. Electronics-based Automation Technologies and the Onset of Systemofacture: Implications for Third World Industrialization. *World Devel.*, March 1985, *13*(3), pp. 423–39. **[G: LDCs]**

Karmeshu; Bhargava, S. C. and Jain, V. P. A Rationale for Law of Technological Substitution [A Simple Substitution Model of Technological Change]. *Reg. Sci. Urban Econ.*, February 1985, *15*(1), pp. 137–41.

Katsoulacos, Y. The Effect of Innovation in the Long-run: Ricardo and the Traverse. *Greek Econ. Rev.*, December 1985, *7*(3), pp. 242–54.

Katz, Jorge M. Domestic Technolgical Innovations and Dynamic Comparative Advantages: Further Reflections on a Comparative Care-Study Program. In *Rosenberg, N. and Frischtak, C., eds.*, 1985, pp. 127–66. **[G: Latin America]**

Kaynak, Erdener. Transfer of Technology from Developed to Developing Countries: Some Insights from Turkey. In *Samli, A. C., ed.*, 1985, pp. 155–76. **[G: OECD; LDCs]**

Kerdoun, A. Technology Transfers from Developed Countries to Developing Countries: Some Problems. *Indian J. Quant. Econ.*, 1985, *1*(2), pp. 125–28.

Khavina, S. Bourgeois Economists on Scientific and Technical Progress under Socialism. *Prob.*

Econ., January 1985, *27*(9), pp. 42–61. **[G: U.S.S.R.]**

Kibria, Muhammad G. and Tisdell, Clement A. Operating Capital and Productivity Patterns in Jute Weaving in Bangladesh. *J. Devel. Econ.*, May–June 1985, *18*(1), pp. 133–52. **[G: Bangladesh]**

Kirim, Arman S. Reconsidering Patents and Economic Development: A Case Study of the Turkish Pharmaceutical Industry. *World Devel.*, February 1985, *13*(2), pp. 219–36. **[G: Turkey]**

Klein, K. K. Economics of Biotechnology in Animal Production. *Can. J. Agr. Econ.*, August 1985, *32*, pp. 36–47.

Klodt, Henning. Kapitalgebundener technischer Fortschritt: Ein Überblick. (Embodied Technical Change: A Survey. With English summary.) *Weltwirtsch. Arch.*, 1985, *121*(1), pp. 151–70.

Knaus, William A. Medical Care and Medical Technology: The Need for New Understanding. In *Ginzberg, E., ed.*, 1985, pp. 70–88. **[G: U.S.]**

Kodras, Janet E. and Brown, Lawrence A. The Dissemination of Public Sector Innovations with Relevance to Regional Change in the United States. In *Thwaites, A. T. and Oakey, R. P., eds.*, 1985, pp. 195–214. **[G: U.S.]**

Konecci, Eugene B., et al. Initiatives for Transforming the American Economy. In *Konecci, E. B. and Kuhn, R. L., eds.*, 1985, pp. 21–42. **[G: U.S.]**

Koopmans, Tjalling C. Alternative Futures with or without Constraints on the Energy Technology Mix. In *Koopmans, T. C.*, 1985, pp. 251–61. **[G: U.S.]**

Kopp, Raymond J. and Smith, V. Kerry. The Measurement on Non-neutral Technological Change. *Int. Econ. Rev.*, February 1985, *26*(1), pp. 135–59. **[G: U.S.]**

Kosenko, Rustan and Samli, A. Coskun. China's Four Modernizations Program and Technology Transfer. In *Samli, A. C., ed.*, 1985, pp. 107–31. **[G: China]**

Kouri, Pentti J. K.; Braga de Macedo, Jorge and Viscio, Albert J. A Vintage Model of Supply Applied to French Manufacturing. *Economia (Portugal)*, January 1985, *9*(1), pp. 159–93. **[G: France]**

Krasovskii, V. Intensification of the Economy and the Capital Intensity of Production. *Prob. Econ.*, February 1985, *27*(10), pp. 3–22. **[G: U.S.S.R.]**

Kregel, J. A. Post-Keynesian Distribution Theory in Relation to Growth and Technical Progress. *Écon. Appl.*, 1985, *38*(2), pp. 375–88.

Krier, James E. and Gillette, Clayton P. The Un-easy Case for Technological Optimism. *Mich. Law Rev.*, December 1985, *84*(3), pp. 405–29.

Krokhotkin, A. Soviet–Hungarian Cooperation in the Development of Agroindustry. *Soviet E. Europ. Foreign Trade*, Winter 1985-86, *21*(4), pp. 37–40. **[G: U.S.S.R.; Hungary]**

Krugman, Paul R. A 'Technology Gap' Model of International Trade. In *Jungenfelt, K. and*

Hague, D. [Sir], eds., 1985, pp. 35–49.

Kümmel, Reiner and Strassl, W. Changing Energy Prices, Information Technology, and Industrial Growth. In *van Gool, W. and Bruggink, J. J. C., eds.*, 1985, pp. 175–94.
[G: W. Germany; U.S.]

Kümmel, Reiner, et al. Technical Progress and Energy Dependent Production Functions. *Z. Nationalökon.*, 1985, *45*(3), pp. 285–311.
[G: U.S.; W. Germany]

Kuprevich, R. The "Tsvetmetpromeksport" All-Union Association. *Soviet E. Europ. Foreign Trade*, Winter 1985-86, *21*(4), pp. 68–78.
[G: U.S.S.R.]

Laister, Peter. Electronics and Communications. In *Wells, N., ed.*, 1985, pp. 35–40.

Lall, Sanjaya. Trade in Technology by a Slowly Industrializing Country: India. In *Rosenberg, N. and Frischtak, C., eds.*, 1985, pp. 45–76.
[G: India]

Lee, Robert H. and Waldman, Donald M. The Diffusion of Innovations in Hospitals: Some Econometric Considerations. *J. Health Econ.*, December 1985, *4*(4), pp. 373–80. [G: U.S.]

Leinfellner, Werner. A Cyclic Model of Innovations. *Rivista Int. Sci. Econ. Com.*, September 1985, *32*(9), pp. 849–63.

Leonard-Barton, Dorothy. Experts as Negative Opinion Leaders in the Diffusion of a Technological Innovation. *J. Cons. Res.*, March 1985, *11*(4), pp. 914–26. [G: U.S.]

Leslie, Derek. Real Wage Growth, Technical Change and Competition in the Labor Market. *Rev. Econ. Statist.*, November 1985, *67*(4), pp. 640–47. [G: U.S.]

Levin, Henry M. Costs and Cost-Effectiveness of Computer-Assisted Instruction. In *Augenblick, J., ed.*, 1985, pp. 71–85. [G: U.S.]

Levin, Richard C. Innovation and Productivity in U.S. Industry: Comment. *Brookings Pap. Econ. Act.*, 1985, (2), pp. 633–37. [G: U.S.]

Levin, Sharon G.; Levin, Stanford L. and Meisel, John B. Intermarket Differences in the Early Diffusion of an Innovation. *Southern Econ. J.*, January 1985, *51*(3), pp. 672–80. [G: U.S.]

Linsenmayer, Tadd. ILO Examines Impact of Technology on Worker Safety and Health. *Mon. Lab. Rev.*, August 1985, *108*(8), pp. 46–47. [G: OECD]

Lynn, Leonard H. Technology Transfer to Japan: What We Know, What We Need to Know, and What We Know that May Not Be So. In *Rosenberg, N. and Frischtak, C., eds.*, 1985, pp. 255–76. [G: Japan]

Macarov, David. Planning for a Probability: The Almost-Workless World. *Int. Lab. Rev.*, Nov.-Dec. 1985, *124*(6), pp. 629–42.

Magee, Stephen P. The Appropriability Theory of the Multinational Corporation. In *Adams, J., ed.*, 1985, pp. 436–50. [G: Global]

Malish, Anton F. Soviet Trade in Agricultural Commodities and Technology. In *Parrott, B., ed.*, 1985, pp. 203–40. [G: U.S.S.R.; U.S.]

Malotke, Joseph F. Automation and Its Impact on the Labor Force and the GM–UAW Saturn

Project. In *Dennis, B. D., ed.*, 1985, pp. 568–69. [G: U.S.]

Mandell, Marvin B. Monitoring and Evaluating New Managerial Technologies. In *Samli, A. C., ed.*, 1985, pp. 263–83.

Mansfield, Edwin. How Rapidly Does New Industrial Technology Leak Out? *J. Ind. Econ.*, December 1985, *34*(2), pp. 217–23.
[G: U.S.]

Marco, Luc V. A. Entrepreneur et innovation: les sources françaises de Joseph Schumpeter. (The Entrepreneur and Innovation: The French Heritage of Joseph Schumpeter. With English summary.) *Écon. Soc.*, October 1985, *19*(10), pp. 89–106.

Marsden, Lorna R. Technological Change: Bad or Good? Comments. In *Economic Council of Canada.*, 1985, pp. 93–97. [G: U.S.]

Marshall, M. Technological Change and Local Economic Strategy in the West Midlands. *Reg. Stud.*, October 1985, *19*(6), pp. 570–78.
[G: U.K.]

Maurer, Martin. Technological Retardation. The Decline of the Swiss Watch Industry. *Z. Wirtschaft. Sozialwissen.*, 1985, *105*(6), pp. 661–82. [G: Switzerland]

McCulloch, Rachel. Normative Issues Raised by International Trade in Technology Services: Comments. In *Stern, R. M., ed.*, 1985, pp. 114–18. [G: OECD]

McHugh, Richard. The Potential for Private Cost-increasing Technological Innovation under a Tax-based, Economic Incentive Pollution Control Policy. *Land Econ.*, February 1985, *61*(1), pp. 58–64.

McNeill, Desmond. The Appraisal of Rural Water Supplies: Rejoinder [Why Present Value Calculations Should Not Be Used in Choosing Rural Water Supply Technology]. *World Devel.*, Oct./Nov. 1985, *13*(10/11), pp. 1181.
[G: LDCs]

McNeill, Desmond. The Appraisal of Rural Water Supplies [Why Present Value Calculations Should Not Be Used in Choosing Rural Water Supply Technology]. *World Devel.*, Oct./Nov. 1985, *13*(10/11), pp. 1175–78. [G: LDCs]

Merrill, Stephen A. The United States and the New Technological Competition. In *Yochelson, J. N., ed.*, 1985, pp. 45–76. [G: U.S.]

Michl, Thomas R. International Comparisons of Productivity Growth: Verdoorn's Law Revisited. *J. Post Keynesian Econ.*, Summer 1985, *7*(4), pp. 474–92. [G: OECD]

Miller, Edward McCarthy. On the Importance of the Embodiment of Technology Effect: A Comment on Denison's Growth Accounting Methodology. *J. Macroecon.*, Winter 1985, *7*(1), pp. 85–99.

Montes, Iván Lavados. The Role of the University in Integration. In *Gauhar, A., ed.*, 1985, 234–47. [G: Latin America]

Moroz, Andrew R. Technology Transfer and Canada's Competitive Performance: Comments. In *Stern, R. M., ed.*, 1985, pp. 339–44.
[G: Canada]

Moseley, Fred. Can the "Social Model" of Productivity Stand Scrutiny? *Challenge*, May/June 1985, *28*(2), pp. 55–57. **[G: U.S.]**

Mukas'ian, S.; Gaponenko, A. and Umanets, L. Social Aspects of Technological Obsolescence. *Prob. Econ.*, April 1985, *27*(12), pp. 34–48.

Mulligan, James G. A Stochastic Production Function for Machine Repair [A Microeconomic Production Function] [Returns to Scale and Substitutability in the Repairman Problem]. *Appl. Econ.*, June 1985, *17*(3), pp. 559–66.

Murphy, Kathleen J. Toward a U.S. Technology Agenda: Insights from Third-World Macroprojects. In *Konecci, E. B. and Kuhn, R. L., eds.*, 1985, pp. 117–133. **[G: U.S.; LDCs]**

Mytelka, Lynn Krieger. Stimulating Effective Technology Transfer: The Case of Textiles in Africa. In *Rosenberg, N. and Frischtak, C., eds.*, 1985, pp. 77–126. **[G: Ivory Coast; Kenya; Nigeria; Tanzania]**

Negandhi, Anant R. Peanut Philanthropy: Contributions of the Multinationals to the Host Countries' Economies. In *Takamiya, S. and Thurley, K., eds.*, 1985, pp. 59–78. **[G: Selected Countries]**

Nötzold, Jürgen. Economic Relations—Interdependence or Marginal Factor?: Technology Transfer. In *Rode, R. and Jacobsen, H.-D., eds.*, 1985, pp. 50–62. **[G: U.S.S.R.]**

Nyers, J. and Szatmári, T. The Exploitation of Licences and Economic Policy in Hungary. *Acta Oecon.*, 1985, *35*(3–4), pp. 377–91. **[G: Hungary]**

Nyers, J. and Szatmári, T. The Exploitation of Licences and Economic Policy in Hungary. *Acta Oecon.*, 1985, *35*(3–4), pp. 377–91. **[G: Hungary]**

Oakey, R. P. Innovation and Regional Growth in Small High Technology Firms: Evidence from Britain and the USA. In *Storey, D. J., ed.*, 1985, pp. 135–65. **[G: U.K.; U.S.]**

Olson, Dennis O. and Jonish, James. The Robustness of Translog Elasticity of Substitution Estimates and the Capital Energy Complementarity Controversy. *Quart. J. Bus. Econ.*, Winter 1985, *24*(1), pp. 21–35.

Oshiro, Kenji K. Mechanization of Rice Production in Japan. *Econ. Geogr.*, October 1985, *61*(4), pp. 323–31. **[G: Japan]**

Ouellette, Pierre and Lasserre, Pierre. Mesure de la productivité: la méthode de Divisia. (The Measurement of Productivity: The Method of Divisia. With English summary.) *L'Actual. Econ.*, December 1985, *61*(4), pp. 507–26.

Ozawa, Terutomo. Macroeconomic Factors Affecting Japan's Technology Inflows and Outflows: The Postwar Experience. In *Rosenberg, N. and Frischtak, C., eds.*, 1985, pp. 222–54. **[G: Japan]**

Paliwoda, Stanley J. and Liebrenz, Marilyn L. Technology Transfer to Eastern Europe. In *Samli, A. C., ed.*, 1985, pp. 55–85. **[G: E. Europe]**

Paliwoda, Stanley J. and Liebrenz, Marilyn L. Technology Transfer within Eastern Europe.

In *Samli, A. C., ed.*, 1985, pp. 87–106. **[G: CMEA]**

Palterovich, D. Conditions of Effectiveness of Adaptive Automation. *Prob. Econ.*, October 1985, *28*(6), pp. 40–59.

Pang, Eng Fong. Employment, Skills and Technology. In *Gustavsson, B.; Karlsson, J. C. and Raftegard, C.*, 1985, pp. 93–102.

Parrott, Bruce. Trade, Technology, and Soviet-American Relations: Conclusion. In *Parrott, B., ed.*, 1985, pp. 351–62. **[G: U.S.S.R.; U.S.]**

Pavitt, Keith. Technology Transfer among the Industrially Advanced Countries: An Overview. In *Rosenberg, N. and Frischtak, C., eds.*, 1985, pp. 3–23. **[G: OECD]**

Peitchinis, Stephen G. Technological Change: Bad or Good? In *Economic Council of Canada.*, 1985, pp. 83–93. **[G: U.S.]**

Perez, Carlota. Microelectronics, Long Waves and World Structural Change: New Perspectives for Developing Countries. *World Devel.*, March 1985, *13*(3), pp. 441–63.

Ranis, Gustav and Saxonhouse, Gary R. Determinants of Technology Choice: The Indian and Japanese Cotton Industries. In *Ohkawa, K. and Ranis, G., eds.*, 1985, pp. 135–54. **[G: India; Japan]**

Ranis, Gustav and Schive, Chi. Direct Foreign Investment in Taiwan's Development. In *Galenson, W., ed.*, 1985, pp. 85–137. **[G: Taiwan]**

Rao, D. S. Gundu; Bisaliah, S. and Krishnaswamy, H. S. Technical Change and Efficiency in Dryland Agriculture: An Econometric Study. *Margin*, July 1985, *17*(4), pp. 37–47. **[G: India]**

Rees, J.; Briggs, R. and Hicks, D. New Technology in the United States' Machinery Industry: Trends and Implications. In *Thwaites, A. T. and Oakey, R. P., eds.*, 1985, pp. 164–94. **[G: U.S.]**

Revell, Jack R. Payment Systems over the Next Decade. *J. Bank Res.*, Winter 1985, *15*(4), pp. 200–210.

Řiha, Ladislav. For Promotion and Application of Scientific and Technical Progress. *Czech. Econ. Digest.*, June 1985, (4), pp. 52–71. **[G: Czechoslovakia]**

Roddy, David J.; Simos, Evangelos O. and Triantis, John E. A Two-output, Multi-input Model of Exogenous and Endogenous Technological Change of the U.S. Economy. *Econ. Notes*, 1985, (2), pp. 118–31. **[G: U.S.]**

Roffe, P. UNCTAD: Code of Conduct on Transfer of Technology: Sixth Session of the U.N. Conference. *J. World Trade Law*, Nov.:Dec. 1985, *19*(6), pp. 669–72.

Rondinelli, Dennis A. Development Administration and American Foreign Assistance Policy: An Assessment of Theory and Practice in Aid. *Can. J. Devel. Stud.*, 1985, *6*(2), pp. 211–40. **[G: U.S.; LDCs]**

Rosegrant, Mark W.; Roumasset, James A. and Balisacan, Arsenio M. Biological Technology and Agricultural Policy: An Assessment of

Azolla in Philippine Rice Production. *Amer. J. Agr. Econ.*, November 1985, *67*(4), pp. 726–32.   **[G: Philippines]**

Rugman, Alan M. Normative Issues Raised by International Trade in Technology Services: Comments. In *Stern, R. M., ed.*, 1985, pp. 119–25.   **[G: OECD]**

Ruitenbeek, Jack. Economics of In-Situ Oilsands Production: Some Implications for Public Policy. *Can. Public Policy*, Supplement July 1985, *11*(3), pp. 407–14.   **[G: Canada]**

Salanti, Andrea. Prices of Production, Market Prices, and the Analysis of the Choice of Techniques. *Metroecon.*, February 1985, *37*(1), pp. 97–117.

Samli, A. Coskun. Technology Transfer to Third World Countries and Economic Development. In *Samli, A. C., ed.*, 1985, pp. 17–26.

Samli, A. Coskun. Technology Transfer: The General Model. In *Samli, A. C., ed.*, 1985, pp. 3–15.

Samli, A. Coskun and Gimpl, Martin L. Transferring Technology to Generate Effective Entrepreneurs in Less Developed Countries. In *Samli, A. C., ed.*, 1985, pp. 231–47.

Samli, A. Coskun and Walter, Jane H. A Technology Transfer Model to Third World Women toward Improving the Quality and Quantity of the Food Supply. In *Samli, A. C., ed.*, 1985, pp. 45–54.

Samli, A. Coskun and Yavas, Ugur. Reverse Technology Transfer: Demarketing Lessons from Less Developed Countries. In *Samli, A. C., ed.*, 1985, pp. 133–42.

Sánchez Chóliz, Julio. Eficiencia y control en las innovaciones. (With English summary.) *Revista Española Econ.*, 1985, *2*(2), pp. 291–305.

Sato, Ryuzo. Nothing New? An Historical Perspective on Japanese Technology Policy. In *Shishido, T. and Sato, R., eds.*, 1985, pp. 299–313.   **[G: Japan]**

Saxonhouse, Gary R. Technology Choice in Cotton Textile Manufacturing. In *Ohkawa, K. and Ranis, G., eds.*, 1985, pp. 212–35.   **[G: Selected Countries]**

Saxonhouse, Gary R. Technology Transfer and Canada's Competitive Performance: Comments. In *Stern, R. M., ed.*, 1985, pp. 334–38.   **[G: Canada]**

Saxonhouse, Gary R. and Ranis, Gustav. Technology Choice and the Quality Dimension in the Japanese Cotton Textile Industry. In *Ohkawa, K. and Ranis, G., eds.*, 1985, pp. 155–76.   **[G: Japan]**

Schive, Chi and Majumdar, Badiul A. Can Solow's Measure of Technical Change Be Applied to Cross-sectional Data? *J. Econ. Stud.*, 1985, *12*(5), pp. 58–61.

Segal, N. S. The Cambridge Phenomenon. *Reg. Stud.*, October 1985, *19*(6), pp. 563–70.   **[G: U.K.]**

Selan, Valerio. Technology versus Employment: A Distorted Problematic. *Rivista Polit. Econ.*, Suppl. Dec. 1985, *76*, pp. 145–73.

Shaw, Anthony B. Constraints on Agricultural Innovation Adoption. *Econ. Geogr.*, January 1985, *61*(1), pp. 25–45.   **[G: Guyana]**

Shishido, Toshio. Japanese Technological Development. In *Shishido, T. and Sato, R., eds.*, 1985, pp. 199–211.   **[G: Japan]**

Sickles, Robin C. A Nonlinear Multivariate Error Components Analysis of Technology and Specific Factor Productivity Growth with an Application to the U.S. Airlines. *J. Econometrics*, January 1985, *27*(1), pp. 61–78.   **[G: U.S.]**

Siggel, Eckhard. Learning by Consulting: A Model of Technology Transfer through Engineering Consulting Firms. *Can. J. Devel. Stud.*, 1985, *6*(1), pp. 27–44.

Sirgy, M. Joseph. Achievement Motivation, Technology Transfer, and National Development: A System Model. In *Samli, A. C., ed.*, 1985, pp. 193–216.

Sirgy, M. Joseph; Samli, A. Coskun and Bahn, Kenneth D. Personality, Culture, and Technology Transfer: A Parsonian Social System Perspective. In *Samli, A. C., ed.*, 1985, pp. 177–91.

Sit, Victor F. S. The Special Economic Zones of China: A New Type of Export Processing Zone? *Devel. Econ.*, March 1985, *23*(1), pp. 69–87.   **[G: China]**

Skomorokhin, Iakov. A Component of the Agroindustrial Complex. *Soviet E. Europ. Foreign Trade*, Winter 1985-86, *21*(4), pp. 41–49.   **[G: CMEA; Cuba]**

Smith, William. High Technology in Canadian Agriculture: A Science Council Perspective. *Can. J. Agr. Econ.*, August 1985, *32*, pp. 14–23.   **[G: Canada]**

Soete, Luc. International Diffusion of Technology, Industrial Development and Technological Leapfrogging. *World Devel.*, March 1985, *13*(3), pp. 409–22.

Soete, Luc and Patel, Pari. Recherche-développement importations de technologie et croissance Économique: Une tentative de comparaison internationale. (R-D, International Technology Imports and Economic Growth: An International Comparison. With English summary.) *Revue Écon.*, September 1985, *36*(5), pp. 975–1000.   **[G: OECD]**

Stankiewicz, Rikard. A New Role for Universities in Technological Innovation? In *Sweeney, G., ed.*, 1985, pp. 114–51.   **[G: OECD]**

Steedman, Ian. On the 'Impossibility' of Hicks-Neutral Technical Change. *Econ. J.*, September 1985, *95*(379), pp. 746–58.

Sterner, Thomas. Structural Change and Technology Choice: Energy Use in Mexican Manufacturing Industry, 1970–81. *Energy Econ.*, April 1985, *7*(2), pp. 77–86.   **[G: Mexico]**

Stevens, Yvette. Improved Technologies for Rural Women: Problems and Prospects in Sierra Leone. In *Ahmed, I., ed.*, 1985, pp. 284–326.   **[G: Sierra Leone]**

Stewart, D. F. Options for Cement Production in Papua New Guinea: A Study in Choice of Technology. *World Devel.*, May 1985, *13*(5), pp. 639–51.   **[G: Papua New Guinea]**

Stewart, Frances. Macro Policies for Appropriate Technology: An Introductory Classification. In

James, J. and Watanabe, S., eds., 1985, pp. 19–46.

Sullivan, B. C. Economics of Information Technology. *Int. J. Soc. Econ.*, 1985, *12*(1), pp. 37–53. [G: OECD]

Sullivan, Richard J. The Timing and Pattern of Technological Development in English Agriculture, 1611–1850. *J. Econ. Hist.*, June 1985, *45*(2), pp. 305–14. [G: U.K.]

Swann, G. M. P. Product Competition in Microprocessors. *J. Ind. Econ.*, September 1985, *34*(1), pp. 33–53. [G: U.S.]

Sweeney, G. P. Innovation is Entrepreneur-Led. In *Sweeney, G.*, ed., 1985, pp. 80–113. [G: OECD]

Taylor, Daniel B. and Young, Douglas L. The Influence of Technological Progress on the Long Run Farm Level Economics of Soil Conservation. *Western J. Agr. Econ.*, July 1985, *10*(1), pp. 63–76. [G: U.S.]

Taylor, Kenneth B. The Economic Impact of the Emerging Global Information Economy on Lesser Developed Nations. In *Didsbury, H. F., Jr.*, ed., 1985, pp. 147–63. [G: LDCs]

Thirtle, Colin G. Technological Change and the Productivity Slowdown in Field Crops: United States, 1939–78. *Southern J. Agr. Econ.*, December 1985, *17*(2), pp. 33–42. [G: U.S.]

Thirtle, Colin G. The Microeconomic Approach to Induced Innovation: A Reformulation of the Hayami and Ruttan Model. *Manchester Sch. Econ. Soc. Stud.*, September 1985, *53*(3), pp. 263–79. [G: U.S.]

Thomas, Morgan D. Regional Economic Development and the Role of Innovation and Technological Change. In *Thwaites, A. T. and Oakey, R. P.*, eds., 1985, pp. 13–35.

Thwaites, A. T. and Oakey, R. P. The Regional Economic Impact of Technological Change: Editorial Introduction. In *Thwaites, A. T. and Oakey, R. P.*, eds., 1985, pp. 1–12. [G: U.S.]

Tinbergen, Jan. Technology and Production Functions. *Rivista Int. Sci. Econ. Com.*, February 1985, *32*(2), pp. 107–17.

Toh, Mun Heng. Technical Change Elasticity of Factor Substitution, and Returns to Scale in Singapore Manufacturing Industries. *Singapore Econ. Rev.*, October 1985, *30*(2), pp. 36–56. [G: Singapore]

Ukaegbu, Chikwendu Christian. Are Nigerian Scientists and Engineers Effectively Utilized? Issues on the Deployment of Scientific and Technological Labor for National Development. *World Devel.*, April 1985, *13*(4), pp. 499–512. [G: Nigeria]

Unterweger, Peter. Appropriate Automation: Thoughts on Swedish Examples of Sociotechnical Innovation. In *Dennis, B. D.*, ed., 1985, pp. 569–73. [G: Sweden]

Vámos, Tibor. Problems and Responses in the Mirror of Technical Progress in Hungary during the Last Forty Years. *Acta Oecon.*, 1985, *34*(3/4), pp. 219–40. [G: Hungary]

Varshavskii, A. E. Models for Forecasting the Influence of Scientific and Technical Progress on Economic Growth. *Matekon*, Winter 1985-86, *22*(2), pp. 59–85. [G: U.S.S.R.]

Venables, Anthony J. The Economic Implications of a Discrete Technical Change. *Oxford Econ. Pap.*, June 1985, *37*(2), pp. 230–48.

Ventura-Dias, Vivianne. Modernisation, Production Organisation and Rural Women in Kenya. In *Ahmed, I.*, ed., 1985, pp. 157–210. [G: Kenya]

Vergani, Raffaello. Technology and Organization of Labour in the Venetian Copper Industry (16th–18th Centuries.) *J. Europ. Econ. Hist.*, Spring 1985, *14*(1), pp. 173–86. [G: Italy]

Vernon, Raymond. Technology's Effects on International Trade: A Look Ahead. In *Vernon, R.*, 1985, pp. 29–47. [G: OECD]

Walker, Thomas S. and Kshirsagar, K. G. The Village Impact of Machine Threshing and Implications for Technology Development in the Semi-arid Tropics of Peninsular India. *J. Devel. Stud.*, January 1985, *21*(2), pp. 215–31. [G: India]

Walter, Helmut. Sektorale Strukturpolitik als Gestaltungspolitik? Begründungen zur Technologie- und Forschungspolitik. (Shaping Economic Sectors by Structural Policy? Reasons for Technology- and Research-Policy. With English summary.) *Ifo-Studien*, 1985, *31*(1), pp. 69–86.

Watanabe, Susumu. Employment and Income Implications of the "Bio-revolution": A Speculative Note. *Int. Lab. Rev.*, May-June 1985, *124*(3), pp. 281–97. [G: LDCs; MDCs]

Watanabe, Susumu. The Patent System and Indigenous Technology Development in the Third World. In *James, J. and Watanabe, S.*, eds., 1985, pp. 217–57. [G: Selected Countries]

Waterson, Michael and Stoneman, Paul L. Employment, Technological Diffusion and Oligopoly. *Int. J. Ind. Organ.*, September 1985, *3*(3), pp. 327–44.

Weiner, Jonathan. Israel Innovates Energy Technology. In *Levinson, P. and Landau, P.*, eds., 1985, pp. 96–98. [G: Israel]

Weinrich, John E. The Dynamics of Managing the Change Process: A Persistent Challenge. *Rivista Int. Sci. Econ. Com.*, June 1985, *32*(6), pp. 551–70.

Wells, Louis T., Jr. Small-scale Manufacturing as a Competitive Advantage. In *Moran, T. H.*, ed., 1985, pp. 119–36. [G: Selected Countries]

Westphal, Larry E.; Kim, Linsu and Dahlman, Carl J. Reflections on the Republic of Korea's Acquisition of Technological Capability. In *Rosenberg, N. and Frischtak, C.*, eds., 1985, pp. 167–221. [G: S. Korea]

Whatley, Warren C. A History of Mechanization in the Cotton South: The Institutional Hypothesis. *Quart. J. Econ.*, November 1985, *100*(4), pp. 1191–1215. [G: U.S.]

White, John. External Development Finance and the Choice of Technology. In *James, J. and Watanabe, S.*, eds., 1985, pp. 183–216.

Whitehead, Ann. Effects of Technological Change

on Rural Women: A Review of Analysis and Concepts. In *Ahmed, I., ed.*, 1985, pp. 27–64. [G: LDCs]

Wicken, Olav. Learning, Inventions and Innovations: Productivity Increase and New Technology in an Industrial Firm. *Scand. Econ. Hist. Rev.*, 1985, 33(2), pp. 144–72. [G: Sweden]

Wijers, G. J. Innovation Policies: The Economic, Industrial and Institutional Setting. In *Sweeney, G., ed.*, 1985, pp. 1–10. [G: OECD]

Williams, Bruce. Prospects from the Sunrise. In *Wells, N., ed.*, 1985, pp. 24–27.

Williams, Martin. Technical Efficiency and Region: The U.S. Manufacturing Sector 1972–1977. *Reg. Sci. Urban Econ.*, August 1985, 15(3), pp. 459–75. [G: U.S.]

Williams, Ted. Synfuels Development in the USA: Case Studies of National Environmental Feasibility and Local Socioeconomic Impacts: The U.S. Synfuels Acceleration Program: An Environmental and Regional Impact Analysis. In *Lakshmanan, T. R. and Johansson, B., eds.*, 1985, pp. 77–99. [G: U.S.]

Wise, E. E. New Technology and Labor–Management Relations at Ford Motor Company. In *Dennis, B. D., ed.*, 1985, pp. 574–75. [G: U.S.]

Woods, John Edward. Okishio's Theorem and Fixed Capital. *Metroecon.*, June 1985, 37(2), pp. 187–97.

Zhou, Shulian. New Advances in Science and Technology and Economic Management. *Chinese Econ. Stud.*, Fall 1985, 19(1), pp. 17–25. [G: China]

Ziegler, Charles A. Innovation and the Imitative Entrepreneur. *J. Econ. Behav. Organ.*, June 1985, 6(2), pp. 103–21. [G: U.S.]

6212 Research and Development

Angelmar, Reinhard. Market Structure and Research Intensity in High-Technological-Opportunity Industries. *J. Ind. Econ.*, September 1985, 34(1), pp. 69–79. [G: U.S.; Canada; EEC]

Arrow, Kenneth J. Economic Welfare and the Allocation of Resources for Invention. In *Arrow, K. J. (I)*, 1985, pp. 104–19.

Balassa, Bela. French Industrial Policy under the Socialist Government. *Amer. Econ. Rev.*, May 1985, 75(2), pp. 315–19. [G: France]

Barke, Richard. Regulation and Cooperation among Firms in Technical Standard-Setting. *J. Behav. Econ.*, Winter 1985, 14, pp. 141–54. [G: U.S.]

Bhattacharya, Gautam. Strategic Learning and Entry-Equilibrium. *J. Econ. Dynam. Control*, October 1985, 9(2), pp. 195–223.

Bozeman, Barry and Link, Albert N. Public Support for Private R and D: The Case of the Research Tax Credit. *J. Policy Anal. Manage.*, Spring 1985, 4(3), pp. 370–82. [G: U.S.]

Britton, John N. H. Research and Development in the Canadian Economy: Sectoral, Ownership, Locational, and Policy Issues. In *Thwaites, A. T. and Oakey, R. P., eds.*, 1985, pp. 67–114. [G: Canada]

Brooks, Harvey. Technology as a Factor in U.S. Competitiveness. In *Scott, B. R. and Lodge, G. C., eds.*, 1985, pp. 328–56. [G: U.S.; OECD]

Burstall, Michael and Dunning, John H. International Investment in Innovation. In *Wells, N., ed.*, 1985, pp. 185–97. [G: OECD]

Buswell, R. J.; Easterbrook, R. P. and Morphet, C. S. Geography, Regions and Research and Development Activity: The Case of the United Kingdom. In *Thwaites, A. T. and Oakey, R. P., eds.*, 1985, pp. 36–66. [G: U.K.]

Carter, Colin A. High Technology in Agriculture and International Trade. *Can. J. Agr. Econ.*, August 1985, 32, pp. 24–35. [G: Canada]

Colton, R. M.; Ryan, T. M. and Senich, D. National Science Foundation Experiences in Stimulating Industrial Innovation. In *Langdon, R. and Rothwell, R., eds.*, 1985, pp. 103–14. [G: U.S.]

Culbertson, John D. Econometric Tests of the Market Structural Determinants of R&D Investment: Consistency of Absolute and Relative Firm Size Models. *J. Ind. Econ.*, September 1985, 34(1), pp. 101–08. [G: U.S.]

Culbertson, John D. and Mueller, Williard E. The Influence of Market Structure on Technological Performance in the Food-manufacturing Industries. *Rev. Ind. Organ.*, 1985, 2(1), pp. 40–54. [G: U.S.]

Daly, Donald J. Technology Transfer and Canada's Competitive Performance. In *Stern, R. M., ed.*, 1985, pp. 304–33. [G: Canada]

DeBrock, Lawrence M. Market Structure, Innovation, and Optimal Patent Life. *J. Law Econ.*, April 1985, 28(1), pp. 223–44.

Deshmukh, Sudhakar D. and Pliska, Stanley R. A Martingale Characterization of the Price of a Nonrenewable Resource with Decisions Involving Uncertainty. *J. Econ. Theory*, April 1985, 35(2), pp. 322–42.

Dhesi, Autar S. and Malhotra, Anju. Foreign Direct Investment in Manufacturing from an LDC: India. *Indian Econ. J.*, Jan.-Mar. 1985, 32(3), pp. 36–41. [G: India]

Dixon, Huw. Strategic Investment in an Industry with a Competitive Product Market. *J. Ind. Econ.*, June 1985, 33(4), pp. 483–99.

Doi, Noriyuki. Diversification and R&D Activity in Japanese Manufacturing Firms. *Managerial Dec. Econ.*, September 1985, 6(3), pp. 147–52. [G: Japan]

Engelhardt, Klaus. Conversion of Military Research and Development: Realism or Wishful Thinking? *Int. Lab. Rev.*, March-April 1985, 124(2), pp. 181–92.

Englander, A. Steven. The Interaction of Research and Training in Agricultural Development. In *Lundahl, M., ed.*, 1985, pp. 309–325.

Finger, Nachum and Mehrez, Abraham. The Role of Public Intervention in R&D. *Managerial Dec. Econ.*, September 1985, 6(3), pp. 172–77.

François, Jean-Paul. Recherche-développement et échanges techniques avec l'étranger dans l'industrie française: Une étude statistique.

(Research and Development Expenditures and Foreign Technological Payments in French Industry. With English summary.) *Revue Écon.*, September 1985, *36*(5), pp. 1043–80. [G: France]

Gallini, Nancy T. and Kotowitz, Yehuda. Optimal R and D Processes and Competition. *Economica*, August 1985, *52*(207), pp. 321–34.

Gallini, Nancy T. and Winter, Ralph A. Licensing in the Theory of Innovation. *Rand J. Econ.*, Summer 1985, *16*(2), pp. 237–52.

Ghemawat, Pankaj and Spence, A. Michael. Learning Curve Spillovers and Market Performance. *Quart. J. Econ.*, Supp. 1985, *100*, pp. 839–52.

Gibbs, D. C. and Edwards, A. The Diffusion of New Production Innovations in British Industry. In *Thwaites, A. T. and Oakey, R. P., eds.*, 1985, pp. 132–63. [G: U.K.]

Golosovskii, S. Robotics and Its Efficiency. *Prob. Econ.*, May 1985, *28*(1), pp. 72–87. [G: U.S.S.R.]

Gopalakrishnan, Chennat. Natural Gas from Seaweed: Is Near-term R and D Funding by the U.S. Gas Industry Warranted? *Energy J.*, October 1985, *6*(4), pp. 129–37. [G: U.S.]

Gordon, Ken. Technology Venturing: Private/Public Partnerships. In *Konecci, E. B. and Kuhn, R. L., eds.*, 1985, pp. 185–91. [G: U.S.]

Granstrand, Ove and Sigurdson, Jon. Innovation Policies in East Asia and Some Implications for Western Europe. In *Langdon, R. and Rothwell, R., eds.*, 1985, pp. 137–63. [G: Hong Kong; S. Korea; Taiwan; Singapore; Japan]

Guesnerie, Roger and Tirole, Jean. L'économie de la recherche-développement: Introduction à certains travaux théoriques. (The Economics of R-D: Introduction to the Pure Theory. With English summary.) *Revue Écon.*, September 1985, *36*(5), pp. 843–71.

Harris, Christopher J. and Vickers, John. Patent Races and the Persistence of Monopoly. *J. Ind. Econ.*, June 1985, *33*(4), pp. 461–81.

Harris, Martha Caldwell. Japan's International Technology Transfers. In *Nanto, D. K., ed.*, 1985, pp. 114–42. [G: Japan; U.S.]

Hewitt, Gary. Pitfalls in Using the Goldfeld–Quandt Test against Heteroscedasticity: A Comment [The Determinants of R&D Expenditures]. *Can. J. Econ.*, November 1985, *18*(4), pp. 898–903. [G: U.S.]

Hirsch, Seev and Bijaoui, Ilan. R&D Intensity and Export Performance: A Micro View. *Weltwirtsch. Arch.*, 1985, *121*(2), pp. 238–51. [G: Israel]

Hughes, Edward and McFetridge, Donald G. A Theoretical Analysis of Incremental Investment Incentives with an Application to the Case of Industrial R and D. *J. Public Econ.*, August 1985, *27*(3), pp. 311–29.

Hussenot, P. Management in the Public Sector. In *Rinnooy Kan, A. H. G., ed.*, 1985, pp. 179–88.

Juhl, Paulgeorg. Multinational Enterprises, Eco-

nomic Structure and International Competitiveness: The Federal Republic of Germany. In *Dunning, J. H., ed.*, 1985, pp. 127–54. [G: W. Germany]

Kalmbach, Peter and Kurz, Heinz D. Internationale Wettbewerbsfähigkeit und Technologieintensität—Eine Anwendung des Subsystem-Ansatzes. (International Competitiveness and the Technological Intensity of Production: An Application of the Sub-system Approach. With English summary.) *Ifo-Studien*, 1985, *31*(2), pp. 149–68. [G: W. Germany]

Kashik, Aleksei; Manukov, Viktor and Iakimov, Ianko. The International Division of Labor in Petroleum Seismic Prospecting. *Soviet E. Europ. Foreign Trade*, Winter 1985-86, *21*(4), pp. 50–57. [G: CMEA]

Katrak, Homi. Imported Technology, Enterprise Size and R&D in a Newly Industrializing Country: The Indian Experience. *Oxford Bull. Econ. Statist.*, August 1985, *47*(3), pp. 213–29. [G: India]

Katz, Michael L. and Shapiro, Carl. On the Licensing of Innovations. *Rand J. Econ.*, Winter 1985, *16*(4), pp. 504–20.

Kaufer, Erich. Economic Aspects: Discussion. In *Wells, N., ed.*, 1985, pp. 225–27.

Kay, John A. and Llewellyn Smith, Chris H. Science Policy and Public Spending. *Fisc. Stud.*, August 1985, *6*(3), pp. 14–23.

Kohn, Meir and Scott, John T. Scale Economies in Research and Development: A Reply. *J. Ind. Econ.*, March 1985, *33*(3), pp. 363.

Kollist, Ingrid and Searing, Marjory E. Government Policy toward High-Tech Industry. In *Zukin, S., ed.*, 1985, pp. 107–18. [G: U.S.]

Konecci, Eugene B., et al. Initiatives for Transforming the American Economy. In *Konecci, E. B. and Kuhn, R. L., eds.*, 1985, pp. 21–42. [G: U.S.]

Krupp, Helmar. Public Promotion of Innovation—Disappointments and Hopes. In *Sweeney, G., ed.*, 1985, pp. 48–79. [G: OECD]

Lafuente Félez, Alberto; Salas Fumás, Vicente and Yagüe Guillén, María Jesús. Formación de capital tecnológico en la industria española. (With English summary.) *Revista Española Econ.*, 1985, *2*(2), pp. 269–90. [G: Spain]

Lall, Sanjaya. Pharmaceuticals and the Third World Poor. In *Wells, N., ed.*, 1985, pp. 91–97.

Le Bas, Christian. La diffusion de l'innovation interne a la firme: Un survol de littérature et un modèle d'apprentissage technoligique. (The Intra-firm Diffusion of Innovation: A Survey and a Model of Technological Learning. With English summary.) *Revue Écon.*, September 1985, *36*(5), pp. 873–95.

Leontief, Wassily. On Assignment of Patent Rights on Inventions Made under Government Research Contracts. In *Leontief, W.*, 1985, pp. 216–22.

Levin, Richard C.; Cohen, Wesley M. and Mowery, David C. R&D Appropriability, Opportunity, and Market Structure: New Evidence on Some Schumpeterian Hypotheses. *Amer.*

Econ. Rev., May 1985, 75(2), pp. 20–24. **[G: U.S.]**

Link, Albert N. The Changing Composition of R&D. *Managerial Dec. Econ.*, June 1985, 6(2), pp. 125–28. **[G: U.S.]**

MacDonald, James M. R and D and the Directions of Diversification. *Rev. Econ. Statist.*, November 1985, 67(4), pp. 583–90. **[G: U.S.]**

Mace, John. Public Expenditure Policy, 1985–86: Education and Science. In *Cockle, P., ed.*, 1985, pp. 203–22. **[G: U.K.]**

Mairesse, Jacques and Cunéo, Philippe. Recherche-développement et performances des entreprises: Une étude éeconométrique sur données individuelles. (Research-Development and Firm Performance: An Econometric Study on Individual Data. With English summary.) *Revue Écon.*, September 1985, 36(5), pp. 1001–41. **[G: France]**

Malecki, Edward J. Public Sector Research and Development and Regional Economic Performance in the United States. In *Thwaites, A. T. and Oakey, R. P., eds.*, 1985, pp. 115–31. **[G: U.S.]**

Mansfield, Edwin and Switzer, Lorne. How Effective Are Canada's Direct Tax Incentives for R and D? *Can. Public Policy*, June 1985, 11(2), pp. 241–46. **[G: Canada]**

Matejić, Vlastimir and Kutlača, Djuro. Multicriteria Methodology for Efficient Evaluation and Ranking of R&D Project Proposals. In *Haimes, Y. Y. and Chankong, V., eds.*, 1985, pp. 524–31.

Mathews, Russell L. Programs and Policies. In *Mathews, R., et al.*, 1985, pp. 108–58. **[G: Australia]**

Meyer-Krahmer, Frieder. Innovation Behaviour and Regional Indigenous Potential. *Reg. Stud.*, October 1985, 19(6), pp. 523–34. **[G: W. Germany]**

Mohnen, Pierre and Nadiri, Ishaq. Demande de facteurs et recherche-développement: Estimations pour les États-Unis, le Japon, l'Allemagne et la France. (Factor Demands Research and Development: Estimates for the U.S., Japan, Germany and France. With English summary.) *Revue Écon.*, September 1985, 36(5), pp. 943–74. **[G: U.S.; Japan; W. Germany; France]**

Moroz, Andrew R. Technology Transfer and Canada's Competitive Performance: Comments. In *Stern, R. M., ed.*, 1985, pp. 339–44. **[G: Canada]**

Mukhopadhyay, Arun K. Returns to Scale in R&D and the Schumpeterian Hypothesis: A Comment. *J. Ind. Econ.*, March 1985, 33(3), pp. 359–61.

Mukhopadhyay, Arun K. Technological Progress and Change in Market Concentration in the U.S., 1963–77. *Southern Econ. J.*, July 1985, 52(1), pp. 141–49. **[G: U.S.]**

Mytelka, Lynn Krieger. Knowledge, Investment, and the Manufacturing Firm. In *Zukin, S., ed.*, 1985, pp. 85–89. **[G: U.S.]**

Oakey, R. P. Innovation and Regional Growth in Small High Technology Firms: Evidence

from Britain and the USA. In *Storey, D. J., ed.*, 1985, pp. 135–65. **[G: U.K.; U.S.]**

Oka, H. and Tanimitsu, T. A Short History of Mitsubishi Electric Corporation's Basic Philosophy of Semiconductor R & D and Its Related Human Resource Management. In *Niehaus, R. J., ed.*, 1985, pp. 173–86. **[G: Japan]**

Ormala, Erkki. A Research Laboratory as an Innovation Policy Instrument. In *Langdon, R. and Rothwell, R., eds.*, 1985, pp. 123–36. **[G: Finland]**

Owen, David. Pharmaceuticals among the Sunrise Industries: Speech to the Symposium Dinner. In *Wells, N., ed.*, 1985, pp. 1–9.

Pakes, Ariel. On Patents, R&D, and the Stock Market Rate of Return. *J. Polit. Econ.*, April 1985, 93(2), pp. 390–409. **[G: U.S.]**

Reinganum, Jennifer F. A Two-Stage Model of Research and Development with Endogenous Second-Mover Advantages. *Int. J. Ind. Organ.*, September 1985, 3(3), pp. 275–92.

Roessner, J. David. Prospects for a National Innovation Policy in the United States. In *Langdon, R. and Rothwell, R., eds.*, 1985, pp. 63–72. **[G: U.S.]**

Rothwell, Roy. Evaluation of Innovation Policy. In *Sweeney, G., ed.*, 1985, pp. 167–88.

Rothwell, Roy. Public Innovation Policy: To Have or to Have Not? In *Langdon, R. and Rothwell, R., eds.*, 1985 , pp. 188–208. **[G: OECD]**

Saint-Paul, Raymond and Barre, Rémi. La place de l'effort français de recherche-développement dans la compétition internationale. (With English summary.) *Revue Écon. Polit.*, Sept.-Oct. 1985, 95(5), pp. 568–77. **[G: U.S.; Japan; U.K.; France; W. Germany]**

Saxonhouse, Gary R. Technology Transfer and Canada's Competitive Performance: Comments. In *Stern, R. M., ed.*, 1985, pp. 334–38. **[G: Canada]**

Scarpa, Carlo. Innovazioni, esternalità e barriere all'entrata in mercati altamente innovativi. (Innovations, Externalities and Barriers to Entry in Highly Innovative Markets. With English summary.) *Ricerche Econ.*, Apr.-June 1985, 39(2), pp. 180–200.

Schankerman, Mark and Pakes, Ariel. Valeur et obsolescence des brevets: Une analyse des statistiques de renouvellement des brevets européens. (The Rate of Obsolescence and the Distribution of Patent Values: Some Evidence from European Patent Renewals. With English summary.) *Revue Écon.*, September 1985, 36(5), pp. 917–41. **[G: W. Germany; U.K.; France; Netherlands; Switzerland]**

Sekiguchi, Sueo and Horiuchi, Toshihiro. Myth and Reality of Japan's Industrial Policies. *World Econ.*, December 1985, 8(4), pp. 373–91. **[G: Japan]**

Seninger, Stephen F. Employment Cycles and Process Innovation in Regional Structural Change. *J. Reg. Sci.*, May 1985, 25(2), pp. 259–72.

Shapiro, Carl. Patent Licensing and R&D Rivalry. *Amer. Econ. Rev.*, May 1985, 75(2), pp. 25–30.

Smith, George Teeling. Politics and the Present Pattern. In *Wells, N., ed.*, 1985, pp. 64–75.
[G: OECD]

Soete, Luc and Patel, Pari. Recherche-développement importations de technologie et croissance Économique: Une tentative de comparaison internationale. (R-D, International Technology Imports and Economic Growth: An International Comparison. With English summary.) *Revue Écon.*, September 1985, *36*(5), pp. 975–1000.
[G: OECD]

Stankiewicz, Rikard. A New Role for Universities in Technological Innovation? In *Sweeney, G., ed.*, 1985, pp. 114–51.
[G: OECD]

Steinberg, Gerald M. Comparing Technological Risks in Large Scale National Projects. *Policy Sci.*, March 1985, *18*(1), pp. 79–93.
[G: U.S.]

Suzuki, Kazuyuki. Knowledge Capital and the Private Rate of Return to R and D in Japanese Manufacturing Industries. *Int. J. Ind. Organ.*, September 1985, *3*(3), pp. 293–305.
[G: Japan]

Swedenborg, Birgitta. Multinational Enterprises, Economic Structure and International Competitiveness: Sweden. In *Dunning, J. H., ed.*, 1985, pp. 217–48.
[G: Sweden]

Tsurumi, Yoshi. Japan's Challenge to the United States: Industrial Policies and Corporate Strategies. In *Hochmuth, M. and Davidson, W., eds.*, 1985, pp. 39–79.
[G: U.S.; Japan]

Vernon, Raymond. The Analytical Challenge. In *Hochmuth, M. and Davidson, W., eds.*, 1985, pp. 17–37.
[G: U.S.]

Watanabe, Susumu. The Patent System and Indigenous Technology Development in the Third World. In *James, J. and Watanabe, S., eds.*, 1985, pp. 217–57.
[G: Selected Countries]

Wells, Nicholas. Pharmaceuticals among the Sunrise Industries: Introduction. In *Wells, N., ed.*, 1985, pp. 10–17.
[G: U.K.]

Zopounidis, Constantin. Une méthode d'évaluation de la recherche-développement à partir des méthodes statistiques non paramétriques. (An Assessment Method of RD [Research Development] on the Basis of Non-parametric Statistical Methods. With English summary.) *Écon. Soc.*, June 1985, *19*(6), pp. 121–45.
[G: France]

630 INDUSTRY STUDIES

6300 General

Adams, F. Gerard. Empirical Evaluation of Industrial Policy: An Appraisal. In *Adams, F. G., ed.*, 1985, pp. 211–27. [G: U.S.]

Adams, F. Gerard and Duggal, Vijaya G. General versus Industry-Specific Industrial Policies: Quantifying the National and Sectoral Impacts. In *Adams, F. G., ed.*, 1985, pp. 31–47.
[G: U.S.]

Adams, F. Gerard; Klein, Lawrence R. and Duggal, Vijaya G. The Effects of Foreign Export-Promotion Policies on the United States: Macro

Model Simulations. In *Adams, F. G., ed.*, 1985, pp. 67–84. [G: U.S.]

Adams, Larry T. Changing Employment Patterns of Organized Workers. *Mon. Lab. Rev.*, February 1985, *108*(2), pp. 25–31. [G: U.S.]

Ahmad, Qazi Kholiquzzaman and Ahmed, Momtaz Uddin. A Review of Rural Non-farm Economic Activities in Bangladesh. In *Mukhopadhyay, S. and Chee, P. L., eds. (I)*, 1985, pp. 53–146. [G: Bangladesh]

Androuais, Anne. Les investissements japonais en Asie du sud-est: compléments ou concurrents de l'industrie au Japon. (With English summary.) *Revue Écon. Polit.*, May–June 1985, *95*(3), pp. 320–45. [G: Japan; S. E. Asia]

Armstrong, Warwick. The Social Origins of Industrial Growth: Canada, Argentina and Australia, 1870–1930. In *Platt, D. C. M. and di Tella, G., eds.*, 1985, pp. 76–94.
[G: Argentina; Australia; Canada]

Arrow, Kenneth J. Some Tests of the International Comparisons of Factor Efficiency with the CES Production Function: Reply. In *Arrow, K. J. (I)*, 1985, pp. 236–40.
[G: Selected Countries]

Arrow, Kenneth J., et al. Capital–Labor Substitution and Economic Efficiency. In *Arrow, K. J. (I)*, 1985, pp. 50–103.
[G: Selected Countries]

Asheghian, Parviz and Foote, William. In the Productivities of U.S. Multinationals in the Industrial Sector of the Canadian Economy. *Eastern Econ. J.*, April-June 1985, *11*(2), pp. 123–33. [G: Canada]

Ayeni, Bola. Interdependence Relations in Interaction Data: An Analysis of the Structure of the Nigerian Economy. In *Hutchinson, B. G.; Nijkamp, P. and Batty, M., eds.*, 1985, pp. 180–98. [G: Nigeria]

Ballantine, John W.; Cleveland, Frederick W. and Koeller, C. Timothy. Profit Differences and Corporate Power: Some Empirical Surprises. *J. Econ. Issues*, June 1985, *19*(2), pp. 355–64. [G: U.S.]

Batten, Dallas S. and Ott, Mack. The President's Proposed Corporate Tax Reforms: A Move toward Tax Neutrality. *Fed. Res. Bank St. Louis Rev.*, Aug./Sept. 1985, *67*(7), pp. 5–17.
[G: U.S.]

Baumol, William J.; Blackman, Sue Anne Batey and Wolff, Edward N. Unbalanced Growth Revisited: Asymptotic Stagnancy and New Evidence. *Amer. Econ. Rev.*, September 1985, *75*(4), pp. 806–17. [G: U.S.]

Benston, George J. The Validity of Profits-Structure Studies with Particular Reference to the FTC's Line of Business Data. *Amer. Econ. Rev.*, March 1985, *75*(1), pp. 37–67.
[G: U.S.]

Berger, Suzanne. The Socialists and the *patronat*: The Dilemmas of Co-existence in a Mixed Economy. In *Machin, H. and Wright, V., eds.*, 1985, pp. 225–44. [G: France]

Besley, Scott and Osteryoung, Jerome S. Survey of Current Practices in Establishing Trade-

Credit Limits. *Financial Rev.*, February 1985, *20*(1), pp. 70–82.

Bhagwati, Jagdish N. Why Does the Share of Manufacturing in GNP Rise with Development? [Transitional Growth and World Industrialisation]. In *Bhagwati, J. N. (II)*, 1985, pp. 79–81. [G: LDCs; MDCs]

Bittlingmayer, George. Did Antitrust Policy Cause the Great Merger Wave? *J. Law Econ.*, April 1985, *28*(1), pp. 77–118. [G: U.S.]

Blank, Rebecca M. and Rothschild, Emma. The Effect of United States Defence Spending on Employment and Output. *Int. Lab. Rev.*, Nov.-Dec. 1985, *124*(6), pp. 677–97. [G: U.S.]

Borrus, Michael and Zysman, John. Industrial Development Policy in Japan. In *Nanto, D. K., ed.*, 1985, pp. 143–67. [G: Japan]

Borum, Joan D. and Schlein, David. Bargaining Activity Light in Private Industry in 1985. *Mon. Lab. Rev.*, January 1985, *108*(1), pp. 13–26. [G: U.S.]

Boyer, Kenneth D. Is There a Principle for Defining Industries? Reply. *Southern Econ. J.*, October 1985, *52*(2), pp. 542–46.

Britton, John N. H. Research and Development in the Canadian Economy: Sectoral, Ownership, Locational, and Policy Issues. In *Thwaites, A. T. and Oakey, R. P., eds.*, 1985, pp. 67–114. [G: Canada]

Brown, Deborah J. and Pheasant, Jim. A Sharpe Portfolio Approach to Regional Economic Analysis. *J. Reg. Sci.*, February 1985, *25*(1), pp. 51–63. [G: U.S.]

Brundenius, Claes and Zimbalist, Andrew. Cuban Economic Growth One More Time: A Response to "Imbroglios." [Recent Studies on Cuban Economic Growth: A Review]. *Comparative Econ. Stud.*, Fall 1985, *27*(3), pp. 115–31. [G: Cuba]

Brundenius, Claes and Zimbalist, Andrew. Cuban Growth: A Final Worth [Cuban Economic Growth One More Time: A Response to Imbroglios]. *Comparative Econ. Stud.*, Winter 1985, *27*(4), pp. 83–84. [G: Cuba]

Brundenius, Claes and Zimbalist, Andrew. Recent Studies on Cuban Economic Growth: A Review. *Comparative Econ. Stud.*, Spring 1985, *27*(1), pp. 21–45. [G: Cuba]

Burgan, John U. Cyclical Behavior of High Tech Industries. *Mon. Lab. Rev.*, May 1985, *108*(5), pp. 9–15. [G: U.S.]

Cacnis, Demitrios G. The Translog Production Function and the Substitution of Factors of Production in England 1950–1976. *Greek Econ. Rev.*, August 1985, *7*(2), pp. 161–78. [G: U.K.]

Chan-Lee, James H. and Sutch, Helen. Profits and Rates of Return. *OECD Econ. Stud.*, Autumn 1985, (5), pp. 127–67. [G: OECD]

Chan, Paul and Lloyd, P. J. Analysis of Export–Import Instability in Peninsular Malaysia, 1960–80. *Singapore Econ. Rev.*, October 1985, *30*(2), pp. 1–16. [G: Malaysia]

Chaudhry, M. Ghaffar. The State and Development of Rural Industries in Pakistan. In *Muk-*

hopadhyay, S. and Chee, P. L., eds. (I), 1985, pp. 249–306. [G: Pakistan]

Chia, Siow Yue. The Role of Foreign Trade and Investment in the Development of Singapore. In *Galenson, W., ed.*, 1985, pp. 259–97. [G: Singapore]

Chiswick, Carmel U. The Elasticity of Substitution Revisited: The Effects of Secular Changes in Labor Force Structure. *J. Lab. Econ.*, October 1985, *3*(4), pp. 490–507. [G: U.S.]

Choe, Yang Boo. Development of Rural Non-farm Activities and Industries in Korea. In *Mukhopadhyay, S. and Chee, P. L., eds. (I)*, 1985, pp. 309–82. [G: S. Korea]

Chou, Tein-Chen. The Pattern and Strategy of Industrialization in Taiwan: Specialization and Offsetting Policy. *Devel. Econ.*, June 1985, *23*(2), pp. 138–57. [G: Taiwan]

Christainsen, G. B. and Tietenberg, T. H. Distributional and Macroeconomic Aspects of Environmental Policy. In *Kneese, A. V. and Sweeney, J. L., eds. Vol. 1*, 1985, pp. 345–93. [G: U.S.]

Chudnovsky, Daniel. La difusión de tecnologías de punta en la Argentina: el caso de las máquinas herramientas con control numérico, el CAD/CAM y los robots. (With English summary.) *Desarrollo Econ.*, January-March 1985, *24*(96), pp. 483–515. [G: Argentina]

Conde, Roberto Cortés. Some Notes on the Industrial Development of Argentina and Canada in the 1920s. In *Platt, D. C. M. and di Tella, G., eds.*, 1985, pp. 149–60. [G: Argentina; Canada]

Cox, David and Harris, Richard. Trade Liberalization and Industrial Organization: Some Estimates for Canada. *J. Polit. Econ.*, February 1985, *93*(1), pp. 115–45. [G: Canada]

Dogas, D. Market Power in a Bilateral Monopoly Model of Industry Wage Determination. *Appl. Econ.*, February 1985, *17*(1), pp. 149–64. [G: U.K.]

Driver, Ciaran; Kilpatrick, Andrew and Naisbitt, Barry. The Employment Effects of Changes in the Structure of UK Trade. *J. Econ. Stud.*, 1985, *12*(5), pp. 19–38. [G: U.K.]

Eckbo, B. Espen. Mergers and the Market Concentration Doctrine: Evidence from the Capital Market. *J. Bus.*, July 1985, *58*(3), pp. 325–49. [G: U.S.]

Fabella, Raul V. Rural Non-farm Activities in the Philippines: Composition, Growth and Seasonality. In *Mukhopadhyay, S. and Chee, P. L., eds. (I)*, 1985, pp. 495–589. [G: Philippines]

Fal'tsman, V. and Kornev, A. Reserves for Reducing the Investment Intensiveness of Industrial Capacities. *Prob. Econ.*, March 1985, *27*(11), pp. 23–38. [G: U.S.S.R.]

Feldman, Stanley J. and Palmer, Karen. Structural Change in the United States: Changing Input–Output Coefficients. *Bus. Econ.*, January 1985, *20*(1), pp. 38–54. [G: U.S.]

Fields, Gary S. Industrialization and Employment in Hong Kong, Singapore, and Taiwan. In *Gal-*

enson, W., ed., 1985, pp. 333–75.
[G: Hong Kong; Singapore; S. Korea; Taiwan]

Finger, J. Michael. Trade and the Structure of American Industry. In *Adams, J., ed.*, 1985, pp. 8–16. [G: U.S.]

Fothergill, Stephen and Gudgin, Graham. Ideology and Methods in Industrial Location Research. In *Massey, D. and Meegan, R., eds.*, 1985, pp. 92–115.

Fulco, Lawrence J. Productivity and Costs in 1984. *Mon. Lab. Rev.*, June 1985, *108*(6), pp. 40–43. [G: U.S.]

Fullerton, Don and Henderson, Yolanda Kodrzycki. Long-run Effects of the Accelerated Cost Recovery System. *Rev. Econ. Statist.*, August 1985, *67*(3), pp. 363–72. [G: U.S.]

Gálvez, Julio and Tybout, James R. Chile 1977–1981: impacto sobre las empresas chilenas de algunas reformas económicas e intentos de estabilización. (With English summary.) *Cuadernos Econ.*, April 1985, *22*(65), pp. 37–71. [G: Chile]

Gerard, M. and Vanden Berghe, C. Econometric Analysis of Sectoral Investment in Belgium (1956–1982). In *Weiserbs, D., ed.*, 1985, pp. 81–110. [G: Belgium]

Gillis, William R. and Shaffer, Ron E. Targeting Employment Opportunities toward Selected Workers. *Land Econ.*, November 1985, *61*(4), pp. 433–44. [G: U.S.]

Goldey, David. The Socialists and the *patronat:* The Dilemmas of Co-existence in a Mixed Economy: Comment. In *Machin, H. and Wright, V., eds.*, 1985, pp. 244–54. [G: France]

Guisinger, Stephen E. Investment Incentives and Performance Requirements: A Comparative Study of Country Policies. In *Guisinger, S. E., et al.*, 1985, pp. 1–55. [G: Global]

Habib, Ahsanul; Stahl, Charles and Alauddin, Mohammad. Inter-industry Analysis of Employment Linkages in Bangladesh. *Econ. Planning*, 1985, *19*(1), pp. 24–38. [G: Bangladesh]

Harrell, Louis and Fischer, Dale. The 1982 Mexican Peso Devaluation and Border Area Employment. *Mon. Lab. Rev.*, October 1985, *108*(10), pp. 25–32. [G: Mexico; U.S.]

Harris, Richard G. Canada/U.S. Trade and Investment Frictions: The U.S. View: Comments. In *Fretz, D.; Stern, R. and Whalley, J., eds.*, 1985, pp. 64–68. [G: Canada; U.S.]

Hill, Roger. Canada/U.S. Trade and Investment Frictions: The U.S. View: Comments. In *Fretz, D.; Stern, R. and Whalley, J., eds.*, 1985, pp. 69–71. [G: Canada; U.S.]

Hosley, Joan D. and Kennedy, James E. A Revision of the Index of Industrial Production. *Fed. Res. Bull.*, July 1985, *71*(7), pp. 487–501. [G: U.S.]

Hougland, James G., Jr. Industrial Sectors and Economic Outcomes: Experiences of Former CETA Participants. *Soc. Sci. Quart.*, December 1985, *66*(4), pp. 903–15. [G: U.S.]

Iatrov, S., et al. Planning the Fuel-Energy Com-

plex under Conditions of Intensification. *Prob. Econ.*, June 1985, *28*(2), pp. 25–39. [G: U.S.S.R.]

Jha, L. K. Importance of Competitiveness in Indian Industry. In *Jha, L. K.*, 1985, pp. 251–57. [G: India]

Jones, Derek C. The Cooperative Sector and Dualism in Command Economies: Theory and Evidence for the Case of Poland. In *Jones, D. C. and Svejnar, J., eds.*, 1985, pp. 195–218. [G: Poland]

Kádár, Béla. Hungarian Industrial Development in the Light of World Economic Changes. *Acta Oecon.*, 1985, *34*(3/4), pp. 241–62. [G: Hungary]

Kader, Ahmad A. Development Patterns among Countries Reexamined. *Devel. Econ.*, September 1985, *23*(3), pp. 199–220. [G: LDCs; MDCs]

Kaplinsky, Raphael. Does De-industrialisation Beget Industrialisation Which Begets Re-industrialisation? Review Article. *J. Devel. Stud.*, October 1985, *22*(1), pp. 227–42. [G: Global]

Kaplinsky, Raphael. Does De-industrialisation Beget Industrialisation which Begets Re-industrialisation?: Review Article. In *Saith, A., ed.*, 1985, pp. 227–42. [G: Global]

Keinath, William F., Jr. The Spatial Components of the Post-industrial Society. *Econ. Geogr.*, July 1985, *61*(3), pp. 223–40. [G: U.S.]

Keuning, Steven J. Segmented Development and the Way Profits Go: The Case of Indonesia. *Rev. Income Wealth*, December 1985, *31*(4), pp. 375–95. [G: Indonesia]

Klein, Christopher C. Is There a Principle for Defining Industries? Comment. *Southern Econ. J.*, October 1985, *52*(2), pp. 537–41.

Knight, Peter T. Financial Discipline and Structural Adjustment in Yugoslavia: Rehabilitation and Bankruptcy of Loss-making Enterprises. *Econ. Anal. Worker's Manage.*, 1985, *19*(1), pp. 101–26. [G: Yugoslavia]

Koo, Bohn-Young. The Role of Direct Foreign Investment in Korea's Recent Economic Growth. In *Galenson, W., ed.*, 1985, pp. 176–216. [G: S. Korea]

Kumar, P. Corporate Growth and Profitability in the Large Indian Companies. *Margin*, July 1985, *17*(4), pp. 32–36. [G: India]

Kunze, Kent. Hours at Work Increase Relative to Hours Paid. *Mon. Lab. Rev.*, June 1985, *108*(6), pp. 44–47. [G: U.S.]

Labus, Miroljub. Price Adjustment in the Labor-Managed Economy: Theory and Some Yugoslav Evidence. In *Jones, D. C. and Svejnar, J., eds.*, 1985, pp. 137–51. [G: Yugoslavia]

Lecraw, Donald J. Multinational Enterprises, Economic Structure and International Competitiveness: Singapore. In *Dunning, J. H., ed.*, 1985, pp. 379–405.
[G: Selected Countries; Singapore]

de Leeuw, Frank. An Indirect Technique for Measuring the Underground Economy. *Surv. Curr. Bus.*, April 1985, *65*(4), pp. 64–72. [G: U.S.]

Leslie, Derek. Productivity Growth in UK Manufacturing and Production Industries, 1948–68. *Appl. Econ.*, February 1985, *17*(1), pp. 1–16. [G: U.K.]

Liebermann, Yehoshua. The Role of Economic Analysis in Media-planning. *Managerial Dec. Econ.*, March 1985, *6*(1), pp. 33–40. [G: Israel]

Lim, Chee Peng. A Review of Rural Non-farm Activities in Malaysia. In *Mukhopadhyay, S. and Chee, P. L., eds. (I)*, 1985, pp. 383–493. [G: Malaysia]

Lin, Tzong-Biau and Mok, Victor. Trade, Foreign Investment, and Development in Hong Kong. In *Galenson, W., ed.*, 1985, pp. 219–56. [G: Hong Kong]

Lintner, John. Secular Patterns in the Financing of Corporations: Comment. In *Friedman, B. M., ed.*, 1985, pp. 75–80. [G: U.S.]

Mainardi, Stefano. Verso una misurazione dinamica del commercio intra-industriale. (Towards a Dynamic Measurement of Intra-industry Trade. With English summary.) *Giorn. Econ.*, Jan.-Feb. 1985, *44*(1–2), pp. 81–92.

Markusen, Ann R. and Teitz, Michael B. The World of Small Business: Turbulence and Survival. In *Storey, D. J., ed.*, 1985, pp. 193–218. [G: U.S.]

McGee, Robert T. State Unemployment Rates: What Explains the Differences? *Fed. Res. Bank New York Quart. Rev.*, Spring 1985, *10*(1), pp. 28–35. [G: U.S.]

McGregor, Margaret A. and Schinasi, Katherine V. Positive Adjustment Policies toward Declining Industries in Japan. In *Nanto, D. K., ed.*, 1985, pp. 168–80. [G: Japan]

de Melo, Jaime; Pascale, Ricardo and Tybout, James R. Microeconomic Adjustments in Uruguay during 1973–81: The Interplay of Real and Financial Shocks. *World Devel.*, August 1985, *13*(8), pp. 995–1015. [G: Uruguay]

Mesa-Lago, Carmelo and Perez-Lopez, Jorge. Imbroglios on the Cuban Economy: A Reply. *Comparative Econ. Stud.*, Spring 1985, *27*(1), pp. 47–83. [G: Cuba]

Mesa-Lago, Carmelo and Perez-Lopez, Jorge. The Endless Cuban Economy Saga: A Terminal Rebuttal [Recent Studies on Cuban Economic Growth: A Review]. *Comparative Econ. Stud.*, Winter 1985, *27*(4), pp. 67–82. [G: Cuba]

Mohabbat, Khan A. The Elasticities of Substitution of Inputs: A Case Study of Canada. *Weltwirtsch. Arch.*, 1985, *121*(3), pp. 541–52. [G: Canada]

Mukhopadhyay, Swapna and Lim, Chee Peng. Rural Non-farm Activities in the Asian Region: An Overview. In *Mukhopadhyay, S. and Chee, P. L., eds. (I)*, 1985, pp. 1–49. [G: Asia; LDCs]

Neumann, Manfred and Haid, Alfred. Concentration and Economic Performance: A Cross-Section Analysis of West German Industries. In *Schwalbach, J., ed.*, 1985, pp. 61–84. [G: W. Germany]

Ozawa, Terutomo. Multinational Enterprises, Economic Structure and International Competitiveness: Japan. In *Dunning, J. H., ed.*, 1985, pp. 155–85. [G: Japan]

Palma, Gabriel. External Disequilibrium and Internal Industrialization: Chile, 1914–1935. In *Abel, C. and Lewis, C. M., eds.*, 1985, pp. 318–38. [G: Chile]

Pasurka, Carl A., Jr. Environmental Control Costs and U.S. Effective Rates of Protection. *Public Finance Quart.*, April 1985, *13*(2), pp. 161–82. [G: U.S.; OECD]

Pauchard, A. Analysis of the Shares of Leading Companies in Switzerland. In *Meier, H. B., ed.*, 1985, pp. 135–77. [G: Switzerland]

Peterson, Milo O. Gross Product by Industry, 1984. *Surv. Curr. Bus.*, April 1985, *65*(4), pp. 20. [G: U.S.]

Petrei, A. Humberto and Tybout, James R. Microeconomic Adjustments in Argentina during 1976–81: The Importance of Changing Levels of Financial Subsidies. *World Devel.*, August 1985, *13*(8), pp. 949–67. [G: Argentina]

Raddock, Richard D. Revised Federal Reserve Rates of Capacity Utilization. *Fed. Res. Bull.*, October 1985, *71*(10), pp. 754–66. [G: U.S.]

Raffaelli, Cristina. On Modeling Structural Changes in Sectoral Wage Distribution in a Modern Input–Output Model. In *Smyshlyaev, A., ed.*, 1985, pp. 79–94. [G: Italy]

Raghupati, T., et al. Case Study on Rural Non-farm Activities in India. In *Mukhopadhyay, S. and Chee, P. L., eds. (II)*, 1985, pp. 3–74. [G: India]

Rao, B. Sudhakar. Rural Industrialisation and Rural Non-farm Employment in India. In *Mukhopadhyay, S. and Chee, P. L., eds. (I)*, 1985, pp. 147–248. [G: India]

Rettig, Rudi. Changes in Input Coefficients in the German Economy. In *Smyshlyaev, A., ed.*, 1985, pp. 141–50. [G: W. Germany]

Ruben, George. Modest Labor–Management Bargains Continue in 1984 Despite the Recovery. *Mon. Lab. Rev.*, January 1985, *108*(1), pp. 3–12. [G: U.S.]

Scott, Bruce R. National Strategies: Key to International Competition. In *Scott, B. R. and Lodge, G. C., eds.*, 1985, pp. 71–143. [G: U.S.]

Scott, Bruce R. U.S. Competitiveness: Concepts, Performance, and Implications. In *Scott, B. R. and Lodge, G. C., eds.*, 1985, pp. 13–70. [G: U.S.]

Segal, N. S. The Cambridge Phenomenon. *Reg. Stud.*, October 1985, *19*(6), pp. 563–70. [G: U.K.]

Seskin, Eugene P. Plant and Equipment Expenditures, First and Second Quarters and Second Half of 1985. *Surv. Curr. Bus.*, April 1985, *65*(4), pp. 21–25. [G: U.S.]

Seskin, Eugene P. and Sullivan, David F. Revised Estimates of New Plant and Equipment Expenditures in the United States, 1947–83. *Surv. Curr. Bus.*, February 1985, *65*(2), pp. 16–47. [G: U.S.]

Shaffer, Ron E. and Pulver, Glen C. Regional Variations in Capital Structure of New Small Businesses: The Wisconsin Case. In *Storey,*

D. J., ed., 1985, pp. 166–92.   [G: U.S.]

Sigit, Hananto and Asra, Abuzar. Indonesian Import Survey Analysis. In *Lim, D., ed.*, 1985, pp. 211–21.   [G: Indonesia; Selected Countries]

Singh, Manmohan. Industry. In *Mongia, J. N., ed.*, 1985, pp. 67–115.   [G: India]

Solnick, Loren M. The Effect of Blue-Collar Unions on White-Collar Wages and Fringe Benefits. *Ind. Lab. Relat. Rev.*, January 1985, *38*(2), pp. 236–43.   [G: U.S.]

Sood, Anil and Kohli, Harinder. Industrial Restructuring in Developing Countries. *Finance Develop.*, December 1985, *22*(4), pp. 46–49.   [G: LDCs]

Stern, Robert M. Canada–U.S. Trade and Investment Frictions: The U.S. View. In *Fretz, D.; Stern, R. and Whalley, J., eds.*, 1985, pp. 32–63.   [G: Canada; U.S.]

Svetanant, Prapant. Rural Non-farm Activities in Thailand: Comparative Case Studies in Irrigated and Rainfed Areas in the Northeast. In *Mukhopadhyay, S. and Chee, P. L., eds. (II)*, 1985, pp. 75–115.   [G: Thailand]

Taggart, Robert A., Jr. Secular Patterns in the Financing of U.S. Corporations. In *Friedman, B. M., ed.*, 1985, pp. 13–75.   [G: U.S.]

Thomson, Guy P. C. Protectionism and Industrialization in Mexico, 1821–1854: The Case of Puebla. In *Abel, C. and Lewis, C. M., eds.*, 1985, pp. 125–46.   [G: Mexico]

Thurow, Lester C. Public Intervention in the Industry. The Case of the U.S.A. *Ann. Pub. Co-op. Econ.*, January–June 1985, *56*(1–2), pp. 41–49.   [G: U.S.]

Tieber, Herbert. Public Enterprise and Employment Policy. *Ann. Pub. Co-op. Econ.*, January–June 1985, *56*(1–2), pp. 63–70.   [G: Austria]

Todd, Douglas. Factor Productivity Growth in Four EEC Countries, 1960–1981. *Cah. Écon. Bruxelles*, 3rd Trimester 1985, (107), pp. 279–325.   [G: Italy; France; W. Germany; U.K.]

Villani, Marco. Productivity and Purchasing Power Parity. *Econ. Notes*, 1985, (3), pp. 101–14.   [G: W. Europe; U.S.; Canada; Japan]

Vojta, Miloš. Occurrence and Use of Secondary Raw Materials in Czechoslovakian Industry during 1982. *Statist. J.*, December 1985, *3*(4), pp. 399–402.   [G: Czechoslovakia]

Warden, Gregory J. Is There a Principle for Defining Industries? Comment. *Southern Econ. J.*, October 1985, *52*(2), pp. 532–36.

Weck-Hannemann, Hannelore and Frey, Bruno S. Measuring the Shadow Economy: The Case of Switzerland. In *Gaertner, W. and Wenig, A., eds.*, 1985, pp. 76–104.   [G: Switzerland]

Weiss, Leonard W. Concentration and Price—A Possible Way Out of a Box. In *Schwalbach, J., ed.*, 1985, pp. 85–111.   [G: OECD]

Westaway, A. J. Econometric Analysis of Sectoral Investment in Belgium (1956–1982): Comment. In *Weiserbs, D., ed.*, 1985, pp. 111–13.   [G: Belgium]

Westphal, Larry E.; Kim, Linsu and Dahlman, Carl J. Reflections on the Republic of Korea's Acquisition of Technological Capability. In *Rosenberg, N. and Frischtak, C., eds.*, 1985, pp. 167–221.   [G: S. Korea]

Young, Michael K. Structurally Depressed and Declining Industries in Japan: A Case Study in Minimally Intrusive Industrial Policy. In *Nanto, D. K., ed.*, 1985, pp. 181–99.   [G: Japan]

Zong, Han. Reduce the Consumption of Materialized Labor. *Chinese Econ. Stud.*, Summer 1985, *18*(4), pp. 62–70.   [G: China]

631 Industry Studies: Manufacturing

6310 General

Afridi, Usman. Dynamics of Change in Pakistan's Large-Scale Manufacturing Sector. *Pakistan Devel. Rev.*, Autumn-Winter 1985, *24*(3/4), pp. 463–76.   [G: Pakistan]

Agarwal, Vinod B. and Morgan, W. Douglas. The Interindustry Effects of Tax and Expenditure Limitations: The California Case. *Growth Change*, April 1985, *16*(2), pp. 3–11.   [G: U.S.]

Ahmed, Meekal Aziz. Dynamics of Change in Pakistan's Large-Scale Manufacturing Sector: Comments. *Pakistan Devel. Rev.*, Autumn-Winter 1985, *24*(3/4), pp. 477–78.

Alam, Kazi F. The Influence of Tax Incentives on the Investment Decisions in U.K. Manufacturing. *METU*, 1985, *12*(3/4), pp. 301–16.   [G: U.K.]

Alam, Kazi F. and Stafford, L. W. T. Tax Incentives and Investment Policy: A Survey Report on the United Kingdom Manufacturing Industry. *Managerial Dec. Econ.*, March 1985, *6*(1), pp. 27–32.   [G: U.K.]

Amato, Louis and Wilder, Ronald P. The Effects of Firm Size on Profit Rates in U.S. Manufacturing. *Southern Econ. J.*, July 1985, *52*(1), pp. 181–90.   [G: U.S.]

Anandalingam, G. Government Policy and Industrial Investment in Cogeneration in the USA. *Energy Econ.*, April 1985, *7*(2), pp. 117–26.   [G: U.S.]

Arnaud-Ameller, Paule. Investissements directs et flux commerciaux compléments ou substituts? Le cas français 1968–1978. (With English summary.) *Revue Écon. Polit.*, May–June 1985, *95*(3), pp. 299–319.   [G: France]

Balassa, Bela. Trends in International Trade in Manufactured Goods and Structural Change in the Industrial Countries. In *Balassa, B.*, 1985, pp. 403–26.   [G: Global]

Balassa, Bela and Bauwens, Luc. Comparative Advantage in Manufactured Goods in a Multi-country, Multi-industry, and Multi-factor Model. In *Peeters, T.; Praet, P. and Reding, P., eds.*, 1985, pp. 31–52.   [G: Selected Countries]

Baldwin, John R. and Górecki, Paul K. The Determinants of Small Plant Market Share in Canadian Manufacturing Industries in the 1970s. *Rev. Econ. Statist.*, February 1985, *67*(1), pp. 156–61.   [G: Canada]

Baldwin, Robert E. and Parker, Stephen A. The Sectoral Adjustment Implications of Current U.S. Trends in Trade Competitiveness. In *Jungenfelt, K. and Hague, D. [Sir], eds.*, 1985, pp. 466–77. [G: U.S.]

Barbera, Anthony J. Determinants of Average Labor Productivity by U.S. Industry. *Amer. Econ.*, Spring 1985, *29*(1), pp. 41–52. [G: U.S.]

Barca, Fabrizio. Modifiche nella relatione fra scala produttiva ed efficienza economica e sviluppo della piccola impresa. (Changes in the Relations between Size and Economic Efficiency and Development of Small Company. With English summary.) *Econ. Lavoro*, Jan.-Mar. 1985, *19*(1), pp. 61–79. [G: Italy]

Barca, Fabrizio. Tendenze nella struttura dimensionale dell'industria italiana: una verifica empirica del "modello di specializzazione flessibile.". (Changes in the Size of Structure of the Italian Industry: a Test of the "Flexible Specialization Model." With English summary.) *Polit. Econ.*, April 1985, *1*(1), pp. 71–109. [G: Italy]

Barker, Terry S. Endogenising Input–Output Coefficients by Means of Industrial Submodels. In *Smyshlyaev, A., ed.*, 1985, pp. 183–92. [G: U.K.]

Bellon, Bertrand. Strengths and Weaknesses of French Industry. In *Zukin, S., ed.*, 1985, pp. 141–51. [G: France]

Benvignati, Anita M. An Empirical Investigation of International Transfer Pricing by U.S. Manufacturing Firms. In *Rugman, A. M. and Eden, L., eds.*, 1985, pp. 193–211. [G: U.S.]

Bhagwati, Jagdish N. and Cheh, John. LDC Exports: A Cross-Sectional Analysis. In *Bhagwati, J. N. (II),* 1985, pp. 157–66. [G: LDCs]

Biagioli, Mario. Contrattazione aziendale e differenziali retributivi interaziendali. (Workplace Bargaining and Wage Differentials among Firms. With English summary.) *Econ. Lavoro*, July-Sept. 1985, *19*(3), pp. 75–110. [G: Italy]

Bitar, Sergio. Crisis financiera e industrialización de América Latina. (With English summary.) *Desarrollo Econ.*, July-Sept. 1985, *25*(98), pp. 217–43. [G: Latin America]

Bitar, Sergio. Industrialización y crisis económica externa en América Latina. (Industrialization and External Economic Crisis in Latin America. With English summary.) *Colección Estud. CIEPLAN*, September 1985, (17), pp. 101–25. [G: Latin America]

Black, Boyd. Regional Earnings Convergence: The Case of Northern Ireland. *Reg. Stud.*, February 1985, *19*(1), pp. 1–7. [G: U.K.]

Blackley, Paul R. The Demand for Industrial Sites in a Metropolitan Area: Theory, Empirical Evidence, and Policy Implications. *J. Urban Econ.*, March 1985, *17*(2), pp. 247–61. [G: U.S.]

Block, Richard N. and McLennan, Kenneth. Structural Economic Change and Industrial Relations in the United States' Manufacturing Sectors and Transportation since 1973. In *Juris,*

H.; Thompson, M. and Daniels, W., eds., 1985, pp. 337–82. [G: U.S.]

Blumenfeld, Sue D. Public Utilities: Antitrust Law and Deregulation: Comment. In *Poole, R. W., Jr., ed.*, 1985, pp. 67–70. [G: U.S.]

Bodo, Giorgio and Giannini, Curzio. Average Working Time and the Influence of Contractual Hours: An Empirical Investigation for the Italian Industry (1970–1981). *Oxford Bull. Econ. Statist.*, May 1985, *47*(2), pp. 131–51. [G: Italy]

Bond, Eric W. and Guisinger, Stephen E. Investment Incentives as Tariff Substitutes: A Comprehensive Measure of Protection. *Rev. Econ. Statist.*, February 1985, *67*(1), pp. 91–97. [G: U.K.]

Bosworth, Barry P. Taxes and the Investment Recovery. *Brookings Pap. Econ. Act.*, 1985, (1), pp. 1–38. [G: U.S.]

Bosworth, Derek. Fuel Based Measures of Capital Utilisation. *Scot. J. Polit. Econ.*, February 1985, *32*(1), pp. 20–38. [G: U.K.]

Brada, Josef C. and Hoffman, Dennis L. The Productivity Differential between Soviet and Western Capital and the Benefits of Technology Imports to the Soviet Economy. *Quart. Rev. Econ. Bus.*, Spring 1985, *25*(1), pp. 6–18. [G: U.S.S.R.]

Braga de Macedo, Jorge. Labor and Investment Demand at the Firm Level: A Comparison of French, German and U.S. Manufacturing, 1970-79: Comment. *Europ. Econ. Rev.*, June-July 1985, *28*(1–2), pp. 237–41. [G: France; U.S.; W. Germany]

Brewer, H. L. and Moomaw, Ronald L. A Note on Population Size, Industrial Diversification, and Regional Economic Instability. *Urban Stud.*, August 1985, *22*(4), pp. 349–54. [G: U.S.]

Brunello, Giorgio. Labour Adjustment in Japanese Incorporated Enterprises: An Empirical Analysis for the Period 1965–1983. *Hitotsubashi J. Econ.*, December 1985, *26*(2), pp. 165–80. [G: Japan]

Brunner, Lawrence P.; Beladi, Hamid and Zuberi, Habib A. Inflation and Indexation: An Empirical Approach. *Southern Econ. J.*, July 1985, *52*(1), pp. 250–64. [G: U.S.]

Bühner, Rolf. Internal Organization and Returns: An Empirical Analysis of Large Diversified German Corporations. In *Schwalbach, J., ed.*, 1985, pp. 197–222. [G: W. Germany]

Button, K. J. Potential Differences in the Degree of X-Inefficiency between Industrial Sectors in the United Kingdom. *Quart. Rev. Econ. Bus.*, Autumn 1985, *25*(3), pp. 85–95. [G: U.K.]

Cameron, Norman E.; Dean, James M. and Good, Walter S. Western Transition in Manufacturing: A Perspective from Sectors in Manitoba. *Can. Public Policy*, Supplement July 1985, *11*(3), pp. 329–34. [G: Canada]

Cardani, Angelo M. Labor and Investment Demand at the Firm Level: A Comparison of French, German and U.S. Manufacturing, 1970-79: Comment. *Europ. Econ. Rev.*, June-

July 1985, 28(1–2), pp. 233–36. [G: France; U.S.; W. Germany]

Carnoy, Martin. High Technology and International Labour Markets. *Int. Lab. Rev.*, Nov.-Dec. 1985, 124(6), pp. 643–59. [G: LDCs; OECD]

Carré, Denis. Les modalités de la concurrence internationale et les performances des secteurs industriels français. (The International Competition and the Performance of French Industries. With English summary.) *L'Actual. Econ.*, March 1985, 61(1), pp. 51–72. [G: France]

Cassels, John. Manufacturing, Trade and the Far-sighted Manager in Britain. *World Econ.*, December 1985, 8(4), pp. 409–11. [G: U.K.]

Chaikin, Sol C. Trade, Investment, and Deindustrialization: Myth and Reality. In *Moran, T. H., ed.*, 1985, pp. 159–72. [G: U.S.]

Chall, Daniel E. New York City's "Skills Mismatch." *Fed. Res. Bank New York Quart. Rev.*, Spring 1985, 10(1), pp. 20–27. [G: U.S.]

Chappell, William F. and Cottle, Rex L. Sources of Concentration-related Profits. *Southern Econ. J.*, April 1985, 51(4), pp. 1031–37. [G: U.S.]

Chisholm, Michael. De-industrialization and British Regional Policy. *Reg. Stud.*, August 1985, 19(4), pp. 301–13. [G: U.K.]

Choe, Yang Boo and Lee, Dong Phil. Role and Characteristics of Very Small Industries in Rural Korea. In *Mukhopadhyay, S. and Chee, P. L., eds. (II)*, 1985, pp. 151–74. [G: S. Korea]

Ciccolo, John H., Jr. and Baum, Christopher F. Changes in the Balance Sheet of the U.S. Manufacturing Sector, 1926–1977. In *Friedman, B. M., ed.*, 1985, pp. 81–109. [G: U.S.]

Clark, Peter K. and Haltmaier, Jane T. The Labor Productivity Slowdown in the United States: Evidence from Physical Output Measures. *Rev. Econ. Statist.*, August 1985, 67(3), pp. 504–08. [G: U.S.]

Coates, J. H. UK Manufacturing Industry: Recession, Depression and Prospects for the Future. In *Meyer, F. V., ed.*, 1985, pp. 83–101. [G: U.K.]

Coomans, Gery. Note sur la transnationalisation de l'économie belge. (Note on the Transnationalisation of the Belgian Economy. With English summary.) *Écon. Soc.*, April 1985, 19(4), pp. 141–59. [G: Belgium]

Cornfield, Daniel B. Economic Segmentation and Expression of Labor Unrest: Striking versus Quitting in the Manufacturing Sector. *Soc. Sci. Quart.*, June 1985, 66(2), pp. 247–65. [G: U.S.]

Coughlin, Cletus C. and Watkins, Thomas G. The Impact of International Intra-firm Trade on Domestic Concentration Ratios. *Rev. Ind. Organ.*, 1985, 2(3), pp. 232–49. [G: U.S.]

Culem, Claudy and Chau, Nguyen T. M. Les performances relatives à l'exportation de produits manufacturés de l'EUBL au cours de la période 1970–1980. (With English summary.)

Cah. Écon. Bruxelles, 2nd Trimester 1985, (106), pp. 126–57. [G: EEC]

Daly, A.; Hitchens, D. M. W. N. and Wagner, Karin. Productivity, Machinery, and Skills in a Sample of British and German Manufacturing Plants: Results of a Pilot Inquiry. *Nat. Inst. Econ. Rev.*, February 1985, (111), pp. 48–61. [G: U.K.; W. Germany]

Daly, Donald J. Inflation, Inflation Accounting and Its Effect, Canadian Manufacturing, 1966–82. *Rev. Income Wealth*, December 1985, 31(4), pp. 355–74. [G: Canada]

Daly, Donald J. Technology Transfer and Canada's Competitive Performance. In *Stern, R. M., ed.*, 1985, pp. 304–33. [G: Canada]

Dar, Atul and DasGupta, Swapan. The Estimation of Production Functions: The CRES and CDE Approaches Applied to U.S. Manufacturing Data—A Comparative Study. *Appl. Econ.*, June 1985, 17(3), pp. 437–49. [G: U.S.]

Dasgupta, Sreemanta. Firm Size and Rate of Growth: An Empirical Analysis of Gibrat's Law. *Indian Econ. J.*, Oct.-Nov. 1985, 33(2), pp. 69–78. [G: India]

Deimezis, Nikitas. Analyse sectorielle de l'emploi dans l'industrie manufacturière belge. Perspectives à long terme. (With English summary.) *Cah. Écon. Bruxelles*, 2nd Trimester 1985, (106), pp. 192–216. [G: Belgium]

Demsetz, Harold and Lehn, Kenneth. The Structure of Corporate Ownership: Causes and Consequences. *J. Polit. Econ.*, December 1985, 93(6), pp. 1155–77. [G: U.S.]

Desai, Padma. Total Factor Productivity in Postwar Soviet Industry and Its Branches. *J. Compar. Econ.*, March 1985, 9(1), pp. 1–23. [G: U.S.S.R.]

DiLorenzo, Thomas J. The Origins of Antitrust: An Interest-Group Perspective. *Int. Rev. Law Econ.*, June 1985, 5(1), pp. 73–90. [G: U.S.]

Diwan, Romesh and Leonardson, Nirjhar J. Productivity, Technical Change and Capital–Labor Substitution in Indian Industry. *Indian J. Quant. Econ.*, 1985, 1(2), pp. 1–16. [G: India]

Doblin, Claire P. Patterns of Industrial Change in the Federal Republic of Germany. Part I: Flows of Manufacturing Output and Energy Input. In *Smyshlyaev, A., ed.*, 1985, pp. 73–78. [G: W. Germany]

Drach, Marcel. Le cycle de la relation État-entreprises en R.D.A. 1963–1983. *Écon. Soc.*, May 1985, 19(5), pp. 117–53. [G: E. Germany]

Dunning, John H. Multinational Enterprises and Industrial Restructuring in the UK. *Lloyds Bank Rev.*, October 1985, (158), pp. 1–19. [G: U.K.]

Ebel, Karl-H. Social and Labour Implications of Flexible Manufacturing Systems. *Int. Lab. Rev.*, March-April 1985, 124(2), pp. 133–45.

Ehrlich, Éva. The Size Structure of Manufacturing Establishments and Enterprises: An International Comparison. *J. Compar. Econ.*, September 1985, 9(3), pp. 267–95. [G: Europe; U.S.; Japan]

Elder, Harold W. An Economic Analysis of Factor

Usage and Workplace Regulation. *Southern Econ. J.*, October 1985, *52*(2), pp. 315–31. [G: U.S.]

Encarnation, Dennis J. and Wells, Louis T., Jr. Sovereignty en garde: Negotiating with Foreign Investors. *Int. Organ.*, Winter 1985, *39*(1), pp. 47–78. [G: India; Singapore; Philippines; Indonesia]

Epstein, Larry G. and Yatchew, Adonis John. The Empirical Determination of Technology and Expectations: A Simplified Procedure. *J. Econometrics*, February 1985, *27*(2), pp. 235–58. [G: U.S.]

Esser, Klaus. Modification of the Industrialization Model in Latin America. *Cepal Rev.*, August 1985, (26), pp. 101–13. [G: Latin America]

Fabella, Raul V. Rural Industry and Modernization. In *Mukhopadhyay, S. and Chee, P. L., eds. (II)*, 1985, pp. 117–50. [G: Philippines]

Faini, Riccardo and Schiantarelli, Fabio. A Unified Framework for Firms' Decisions Theoretical Analysis and Empirical Application to Italy 1970–1980. In *Weiserbs, D., ed.*, 1985, pp. 51–74. [G: Italy]

Faini, Riccardo and Schiantarelli, Fabio. Oligopolistic Models of Investment and Employment Decisions in a Regional Context: Theory and Empirical Evidence from a Putty–Clay Model. *Europ. Econ. Rev.*, March 1985, *27*(2), pp. 221–42. [G: Italy]

Fakiolas, T. Basic Causes of Soviet Industry's Low International Competitiveness. *J. Econ. Stud.*, 1985, *12*(5), pp. 39–52. [G: U.S.S.R.]

Farrow, Scott. Flexible Manufacturing: Market Structure and Market Failure. *J. Policy Anal. Manage.*, Summer 1985, *4*(4), pp. 583–87.

Fay, Jon A. and Medoff, James L. Labor and Output over the Business Cycle: Some Direct Evidence. *Amer. Econ. Rev.*, September 1985, *75*(4), pp. 638–55. [G: U.S.]

Ferleger, Louis. Capital Goods and Southern Economic Development. *J. Econ. Hist.*, June 1985, *45*(2), pp. 411–17. [G: U.S.]

Ferrão, João. Regional Variations in the Rate of Profit in Portuguese Industry. In *Hudson, R. and Lewis, J., eds.*, 1985, pp. 211–45. [G: Portugal]

Field, Alexander James. On the Unimportance of Machinery. *Exploration Econ. Hist.*, October 1985, *22*(4), pp. 378–401. [G: U.S.; U.K.]

Fieleke, Norman S. The Foreign Trade Deficit and American Industry. *New Eng. Econ. Rev.*, July/August 1985, pp. 43–52. [G: U.S.]

Foote, William and Asheghian, Parviz. X-Inefficiency and Interfirm Comparison of U.S. and Canadian Manufacturing Firms in Canada. *Quart. J. Bus. Econ.*, Autumn 1985, *24*(4), pp. 3–14. [G: U.S.; Canada]

Forsyth, David J. C. Government Policy, Market Structure and Choice of Technology in Egypt. In *James, J. and Watanabe, S., eds.*, 1985, pp. 137–82. [G: Egypt]

Forsyth, P. J. Trade and Industry Policy. *Australian Econ. Rev.*, 3rd Quarter, Spring 1985, (71), pp. 70–81. [G: Australia]

Fortune, J. Neill. Manufacturers' Aggregate Inventory Accumulation and Unfilled Orders. *J. Post Keynesian Econ.*, Spring 1985, *7*(3), pp. 324–31. [G: U.S.]

Foss, Murray F. Changing Utilization of Fixed Capital: An Element in Long-term Growth. *Mon. Lab. Rev.*, May 1985, *108*(5), pp. 3–8. [G: U.S.]

François, Jean-Paul. Recherche-développement et échanges techniques avec l'étranger dans l'industrie française: Une étude statistique. (Research and Development Expenditures and Foreign Technological Payments in French Industry. With English summary.) *Revue Écon.*, September 1985, *36*(5), pp. 1043–80. [G: France]

Frantzen, Dirk J. Cost Shifting and Price Flexibility in the Small Open Economy: A Disaggregated Study for Belgian Manufacturing. *Appl. Econ.*, February 1985, *17*(1), pp. 173–89. [G: Belgium]

Frantzen, Dirk J. Some Empirical Evidence on the Behaviour of Export and Domestic Prices in Belgian Manufacturing Industry. *Rech. Écon. Louvain*, 1985, *51*(1), pp. 29–49. [G: Belgium]

Frantzen, Dirk J. The Influence of Short-term Demand on the Mark-up in Belgian Manufacturing Industry. *Tijdschrift Econ. Manage.*, 1985, *30*(2), pp. 199–219. [G: Belgium]

Frantzen, Dirk J. The Pricing of Manufactures in an Open Economy: A Study of Belgium. *Cambridge J. Econ.*, December 1985, *9*(4), pp. 371–82. [G: Belgium]

Fritsch, Michael and Maas, Christof. Das Investitionsverhalten von Industriebetrieben. Ergebnisse aus einer Interviewstudie. (The Investment Behaviour of West German Industry—Results of an Interview Study. With English summary.) *Konjunkturpolitik*, 1985, *31*(1/2), pp. 52–78. [G: W. Germany]

Fulco, Lawrence J. The Decline in Productivity during the First Half of 1985. *Mon. Lab. Rev.*, December 1985, *108*(12), pp. 39–42. [G: U.S.]

Gallant, A. Ronald and Monahan, John F. Explicitly Infinite-Dimensional Bayesian Analysis of Production Technologies. *J. Econometrics*, Oct./Nov. 1985, *30*(1/2), pp. 171–201. [G: U.S.]

Garofalo, Gasper A. and Malhotra, Devinder M. The Impact of Changes in Input Prices on Net Investment in U.S. Manufacturing. *Atlantic Econ. J.*, December 1985, *13*(4), pp. 52–62. [G: U.S.]

Gereffi, Gary and Newfarmer, Richard S. International Oligopoly and Uneven Development: Some Lessons from Industrial Case Studies. In *Newfarmer, R. S., ed.*, 1985, pp. 385–444.

Gibbs, D. C. and Edwards, A. The Diffusion of New Production Innovations in British Industry. In *Thwaites, A. T. and Oakey, R. P., eds.*, 1985, pp. 132–63. [G: U.K.]

Giuliano, Giuseppe and Spaziani, F. M. Water Use Statistics in Industry. Experiences from Regional Surveys and Planning Studies in Italy.

Statist. J., May 1985, *3*(2), pp. 229–45.
[G: Italy]

Globerman, Steven. Multinational Enterprises, Economic Structure and International Competitiveness: Canada. In *Dunning, J. H., ed.*, 1985, pp. 187–215. [G: Canada]

Golosovskii, S. Robotics and Its Efficiency. *Prob. Econ.*, May 1985, *28*(1), pp. 72–87.
[G: U.S.S.R.]

van Gool, W. Towards a Physical Interpretation of Production Functions. In *van Gool, W. and Bruggink, J. J. C., eds.*, 1985, pp. 247–56.

Gordon, Myron J. The Postwar Growth in Monopoly Power. *J. Post Keynesian Econ.*, Fall 1985, *8*(1), pp. 3–13. [G: U.S.]

Gould, Andrew and Keeble, David. New Firms and Rural Industrialization in East Anglia. In *Storey, D. J., ed.*, 1985, pp. 43–71.
[G: U.K.]

Gregory, Mary; Lobban, Peter and Thomson, Andrew. Wage Settlements in Manufacturing, 1979–84: Evidence from the CBI Pay Databank. *Brit. J. Ind. Relat.*, November 1985, *23*(3), pp. 339–57. [G: U.K.]

Guinchard, Philippe. Prix relatifs et désindustrialisation. (Relative Prices and Deindustrialisation. With English summary.) *Revue Écon.*, March 1985, *36*(2), pp. 367–82.
[G: Selected Countries]

Gupta, Deepak. Productivity Trends and Factor Substitutability in Manufacturing Sector in Maharashtra. *Margin*, July 1985, *17*(4), pp. 62–70. [G: India]

Håkanson, Lars and Danielsson, Lars. Structural Adjustment in a Stagnating Economy: Regional Manufacturing Employment in Sweden, 1975–1980. *Reg. Stud.*, August 1985, *19*(4), pp. 329–42. [G: Sweden]

Hall, S. G., et al. Employment and Average Hours Worked in Manufacturing. *Brit. Rev. Econ. Issues*, Spring 1985, *7*(16), pp. 87–112.
[G: U.K.]

Halpern, Dan. The Structure of Industry in Israel. In *Levinson, P. and Landau, P., eds.*, 1985, pp. 73–74. [G: Israel]

Hamilton, Robert T. Closure Rates in Scottish Manufacturing Industries. *Scot. J. Polit. Econ.*, November 1985, *32*(3), pp. 333–42.
[G: U.K.]

Hamilton, Robert T. Interindustry Variation in Gross Entry Rates of 'Independent' and 'Dependent' Businesses. *Appl. Econ.*, April 1985, *17*(2), pp. 271–80. [G: U.K.]

Harris, R. I. D. Interrelated Demand for Factors of Production in the U.K. Engineering Industry, 1968–81. *Econ. J.*, December 1985, *95*(380), pp. 1049–68. [G: U.K.]

Harris, Richard and Taylor, Jim. The Measurement of Capacity Utilization. *Appl. Econ.*, October 1985, *17*(5), pp. 849–66. [G: U.K.]

Harrison, Bennett. Increasing Instability and Inequality in the "Revival" of the New England Economy. In *Richardson, H. W. and Turek, J. H., eds.*, 1985, pp. 123–49. [G: U.S.]

Harrison, Mark. Investment Mobilization and Capacity Completion in the Chinese and Soviet

Economies. *Econ. Planning*, 1985, *19*(2), pp. 56–75. [G: China; U.S.S.R.]

Hatzichronoglou, Thomas. Mutuations technologiques et compétitivité de l'industrie franç aise: dix constatations. (With English summary.) *Revue Écon. Polit.*, Sept.-Oct. 1985, *95*(5), pp. 578–95. [G: OECD]

Havrylyshyn, Oli and Civan, Engin. Intra-industry Trade among Developing Countries. *J. Devel. Econ.*, August 1985, *18*(2–3), pp. 253–71. [G: LDCs]

Hazledine, Tim. The Anatomy of Productivity Growth Slowdown and Recovery in Canadian Manufacturing, 1970–79. *Int. J. Ind. Organ.*, September 1985, *3*(3), pp. 307–25.
[G: Canada]

Heimler, Alberto. Cost, Prices and Income Distribution in Italian Industry. *Rivista Polit. Econ.*, Suppl. Dec. 1985, *76*, pp. 41–64.
[G: Italy]

Henley, John S. and Nyaw, Mee-Kau. A Reappraisal of the Capital Goods Sector in Hong Kong: The Case for Free Trade. *World Devel.*, June 1985, *13*(6), pp. 737–48.
[G: Hong Kong]

Herman, Arthur S. Productivity Reports: Productivity Increased in Many Industries in 1983. *Mon. Lab. Rev.*, March 1985, *108*(3), pp. 31–34. [G: U.S.]

Hewitt, Gary. Pitfalls in Using the Goldfeld–Quandt Test against Heteroscedasticity: A Comment [The Determinants of R&D Expenditures]. *Can. J. Econ.*, November 1985, *18*(4), pp. 898–903. [G: U.S.]

Hill, Charles W. L. Diversified Growth and Competition: The Experience of Twelve Large UK Firms. *Appl. Econ.*, October 1985, *17*(5), pp. 827–47. [G: U.K.]

Hill, Hal. Subcontracting, Technological Diffusion, and the Development of Small Enterprise in Philippine Manufacturing. *J. Devel. Areas*, January 1985, *19*(2), pp. 245–61.
[G: Philippines]

Hill, Roger. An Ontario Perspective on Trade Issues between Canada and the United States. In *Fretz, D.; Stern, R. and Whalley, J., eds.*, 1985 , pp. 478–94. [G: Canada; U.S.]

Hosek, William R. and Zahn, Frank. An Alternative Approach to the Estimation of the Real Rate of Interest. *J. Macroecon.*, Spring 1985, *7*(2), pp. 211–22. [G: U.S.]

Ilmakunnas, Pekka. Bayesian Estimation of Cost Functions with Stochastic or Exact Constraints on Parameters. *Int. Econ. Rev.*, February 1985, *26*(1), pp. 111–34. [G: U.S.]

Jakobsen, Arvid Stentoft. Changes in Factor Input Coefficients and the Leontief Paradox. In *Smyshlyaev, A., ed.*, 1985, pp. 105–17.
[G: Denmark]

James, John A. and Skinner, Jonathan S. The Resolution of the Labor-Scarcity Paradox. *J. Econ. Hist.*, September 1985, *45*(3), pp. 513–40. [G: U.S.; U.K.]

Jones, David R. Redundancy, Natural Turnover and the Paradox of Structural Change. *Bull.*

Econ. Res., January 1985, *37*(1), pp. 41–54.
[G: U.K.; New Zealand]

Jones, Derek C. and Svejnar, Jan. Participation, Profit Sharing, Worker Ownership and Efficiency in Italian Producer Cooperative. *Economica*, November 1985, *52*(208), pp. 449–65.
[G: Italy]

Juhl, Paulgeorg. Multinational Enterprises, Economic Structure and International Competitiveness: The Federal Republic of Germany. In *Dunning, J. H., ed.*, 1985, pp. 127–54.
[G: W. Germany]

Kaplan, D. E. The Diffusion of Microelectronic Technology in South African Manufacturing Industry: The Case of Computer Aided Design. *J. Stud. Econ. Econometrics*, November 1985, (23), pp. 67–98. **[G: S. Africa]**

Karier, Thomas M. Unions and Monopoly Profits. *Rev. Econ. Statist.*, February 1985, *67*(1), pp. 34–42. **[G: U.S.]**

Katrak, Homi. Imported Technology, Enterprise Size and R&D in a Newly Industrializing Country: The Indian Experience. *Oxford Bull. Econ. Statist.*, August 1985, *47*(3), pp. 213–29. **[G: India]**

Katz, Jorge M. Domestic Technolgical Innovations and Dynamic Comparative Advantages: Further Reflections on a Comparative Care-Study Program. In *Rosenberg, N. and Frischtak, C., eds.*, 1985, pp. 127–66.
[G: Latin America]

Kellman, Mitchell. The Crumbling Embargo? Evidence of OECD Cohesiveness from the Composition of Manufactured Exports to the USSR. *Comparative Econ. Stud.*, Summer 1985, *27*(2), pp. 53–70. **[G: OECD; U.S.S.R.]**

Kennan, John. The Duration of Contract Strikes in U.S. Manufacturing. *J. Econometrics*, April 1985, *28*(1), pp. 5–28. **[G: U.S.]**

Khan, Ashfaque H. and Ahmad, Mushtaq. Real Money Balances in the Production Function of a Developing Country. *Rev. Econ. Statist.*, May 1985, *67*(2), pp. 336–40. **[G: Pakistan]**

Kim, Kwan S. Industrial Development in Mexico: Problems, Policy Issues, and Perspectives. In *Kim, K. S. and Ruccio, D. F., eds.*, 1985, pp. 205–26. **[G: Mexico]**

King, Sandra L. and Williams, Harry B. Shift Work Pay Differentials and Practices in Manufacturing. *Mon. Lab. Rev.*, December 1985, *108*(12), pp. 26–33. **[G: U.S.]**

Kintis, Andreas A. Patterns and Sources of Growth in Greek Manufacturing. *Greek Econ. Rev.*, August 1985, *7*(2), pp. 144–60.
[G: Greece]

Koo, Bohn-Young. Multinational Enterprises, Economic Structure and International Competitiveness: Korea. In *Dunning, J. H., ed.*, 1985, pp. 281–307. **[G: S. Korea]**

Kooiman, Peter and Kloek, Teun. An Empirical Two Market Disequilibrium Model for Dutch Manufacturing. *Europ. Econ. Rev.*, December 1985, *29*(3), pp. 323–54. **[G: Netherlands]**

Kossov, V. Patterns in the Development of Heavy Industry (Methodological Problems). *Prob. Econ.*, September 1985, *28*(5), pp. 3–19.

Kouri, Pentti J. K.; Braga de Macedo, Jorge and Viscio, Albert J. A Vintage Model of Supply Applied to French Manufacturing. *Economia (Portugal)*, January 1985, *9*(1), pp. 159–93.
[G: France]

Kouri, Pentti J. K.; Braga de Macedo, Jorge and Viscio, Albert J. Profitability, Employment and Structural Adjustment in France. In *Melitz, J. and Wyplosz, C., eds.*, 1985, pp. 85–112. **[G: France]**

Kozlow, Ralph. Capital Expenditures by Majority-owned Foreign Affiliates of U.S. Companies, 1985. *Surv. Curr. Bus.*, March 1985, *65*(3), pp. 23–28. **[G: U.S.]**

Kreinin, Mordechai E. United States Trade and Possible Restrictions in High-Technology Products. *J. Policy Modeling*, Spring 1985, *7*(1), pp. 69–105. **[G: U.S.; Japan; EEC; Canada]**

Krüger, Hans-Peter. Comments [East–West Economic Relations: Expectations a Decade Ago and the Outcome] [East–West Economic Relations in the 1970s and 1980s]. In *Saunders, C. T., ed.*, 1985, pp. 131–34. **[G: OMEA; OECD]**

Kubo, Yuji. A Cross-country Comparison of Inter-industry Linkages and the Role of Imported Intermediate Inputs. *World Devel.*, December 1985, *13*(12), pp. 1287–98.
[G: Selected Countries]

Kuipers, S. K., et al. A Putty–Clay Vintage Model for Sectors of Industry in The Netherlands. *De Economist*, 1985, *133*(2), pp. 151–75.
[G: Netherlands]

Kulatilaka, Nalin. Tests on the Validity of Static Equilibrium Models. *J. Econometrics*, May 1985, *28*(2), pp. 253–68. **[G: U.S.]**

Kumar, Manmohan S. International Trade and Industrial Concentration. *Oxford Econ. Pap.*, March 1985, *37*(1), pp. 125–33. **[G: U.K.]**

Kumar, Rajendra; Sharma, R. C. and Phillip, P. J. Determinants of Industrial Production and Prices in India. *Indian Econ. J.*, Oct.-Nov. 1985, *33*(2), pp. 1–9. **[G: India]**

Kümmel, Reiner, et al. Technical Progress and Energy Dependent Production Functions. *Z. Nationalökon.*, 1985, *45*(3), pp. 285–311.
[G: U.S.; W. Germany]

Kushlin, V. I. The Development of the Production Apparatus and Investment Processes. *Prob. Econ.*, November 1985, *28*(7), pp. 33–47.
[G: U.S.S.R.]

Kwoka, John E., Jr. The Herfindahl Index in Theory and Practice. *Antitrust Bull.*, Winter 1985, *30*(4), pp. 915–47. **[G: U.S.]**

van de Laar, Aart. The Role of Industry in the Development of Pakistan. In *Jerve, A. M., ed.*, 1985, pp. 199–212. **[G: Pakistan]**

Lächler, Ulrich. The Elasticity of Substitution between Imported and Domestically Produced Goods in Germany. *Weltwirtsch. Arch.*, 1985, *121*(1), pp. 74–96. **[G: W. Germany]**

Lafay, Gérard. Spécialisation française: des handicaps structurels. (With English summary.) *Re-*

vue Écon. Polit., Sept.-Oct. 1985, *95*(5), pp. 627–39. [G: France; U.K.; U.S.; W. Germany; Japan]

Langhammer, Rolf J. and Hiemenz, Ulrich. Declining Competitiveness of EC Suppliers in ASEAN Markets: Singular Case or Symptom? *J. Common Market Stud.*, December 1985, *24*(2), pp. 105–19. [G: EEC; ASEAN]

Lee, Kyu Sik. Decentralization Trends of Employment Location and Spatial Policies in LDC Cities. *Urban Stud.*, April 1985, *22*(2), pp. 151–62. [G: Colombia]

Lennings, Manfred. Structural Problems of German Industry in International Comparison. In *Engels, W. and Pohl, H., eds.*, 1985, pp. 1–12. [G: Selected Countries]

Leontief, Wassily. An Alternative to Aggregation in Input–Output Analysis and National Accounts. In *Leontief, W.*, 1985, pp. 283–97. [G: U.S.]

Leslie, Derek. Real Wage Growth, Technical Change and Competition in the Labor Market. *Rev. Econ. Statist.*, November 1985, *67*(4), pp. 640–47. [G: U.S.]

Levcik, Friedrich and Stankovsky, Jan. East–West Economic Relations in the 1970s and 1980s. In *Saunders, C. T., ed.*, 1985, pp. 77–124. [G: CMEA; OECD]

Levy, David T. Specifying the Dynamics of Industry Concentration. *J. Ind. Econ.*, September 1985, *34*(1), pp. 55–68. [G: U.S.]

Levy, David T. The Transactions Cost Approach to Vertical Integration: An Empirical Examination. *Rev. Econ. Statist.*, August 1985, *67*(3), pp. 438–45. [G: U.S.]

Liebermann, Yehoshua and Zilberfarb, Ben-Zion. Price Adjustment Strategy under Conditions of High Inflation: An Empirical Examination. *J. Econ. Bus.*, August 1985, *37*(3), pp. 253–65. [G: Israel]

Lim, Chee Peng. The Role of Regional Development Authorities and Rural Non-farm Activities in Malaysia. In *Mukhopadhyay, S. and Chee, P. L., eds. (II)*, 1985, pp. 177–26. [G: Malaysia]

Lim, Chee Peng and Ling, Sieh Mei. Malaysia–Australia Trade. In *Lim, D., ed.*, 1985, pp. 23–38. [G: Malaysia; Australia]

Lim, Chee Peng and Ling, Sieh Mei. Malaysian Import Demand Analysis. In *Lim, D., ed.*, 1985, pp. 150–63. [G: Malaysia; Australia]

Lim, David. Australia–SEAN Trade. In *Lim, D., ed.*, 1985, pp. 2–13. [G: Australia; Selected Countries]

Lim, David. Australian Import Survey Analysis. In *Lim, D., ed.*, 1985, pp. 202–10. [G: Australia; ASEAN]

Lim, Hank. Singaporean Import Demand Analysis. In *Lim, D., ed.*, 1985, pp. 179–90. [G: Singapore]

Lindauer, David L. Regional Wage Determination and Economic Growth in Korea. *J. Econ. Devel.*, July 1985, *10*(1), pp. 129–41. [G: S. Korea]

Lipsey, Robert E. and Kravis, Irving B. The Competitive Position of U.S. Manufacturing Firms. *Banca Naz. Lavoro Quart. Rev.*, June

1985, (153), pp. 127–54. [G: U.S.]

Lloyd, Peter E. and Mason, C. M. Spatial Variations in New Firm Formation in the United Kingdom: Comparative Evidence from Merseyside, Greater Manchester and South Hampshire. In *Storey, D. J., ed.*, 1985, pp. 72–100. [G: U.K.]

Lloyd, Peter E. and Shutt, John. Recession and Restructuring in the North-west Region, 1975–82: The Implications of Recent Events. In *Massey, D. and Meegan, R., eds.*, 1985, pp. 16–60. [G: U.K.]

Louitri, Abdenbi. La validité empirique de la mesure catégorielle de diversification de Rumelt dans les groupes industriels français. (The Empirical Validity of Rumelt's Measure of Diversification in French Industrial Groups. With English summary.) *Écon. Soc.*, December 1985, *19*(12), pp. 205–24. [G: France]

Lustig, R. Jeffrey. The Politics of Shutdown: Community, Property, Corporatism. *J. Econ. Issues*, March 1985, *19*(1), pp. 123–52. [G: U.S.]

Lynk, Edward and Hartley, Keith. Input Demands and Elasticities in U.K. Defence Industries. *Int. J. Ind. Organ.*, March 1985, *3*(1), pp. 71–83. [G: U.K.]

MacDonald, James M. R and D and the Directions of Diversification. *Rev. Econ. Statist.*, November 1985, *67*(4), pp. 583–90. [G: U.S.]

Mairesse, Jacques. Profitability, Employment and Structural Adjustment in France: Comments. In *Melitz, J. and Wyplosz, C., eds.*, 1985, pp. 114–16. [G: France]

Mairesse, Jacques and Dormont, Brigitte. Labor and Investment Demand at the Firm Level: A Comparison of French, German and U.S. Manufacturing, 1970-79. *Europ. Econ. Rev.*, June-July 1985, *28*(1–2), pp. 201–31. [G: France; U.S.; W. Germany]

Mangan, J. and Stokes, L. Labour Demand in Australian Manufacturing: A Further Analysis. *S. Afr. J. Econ.*, June 1985, *53*(2), pp. 197–200. [G: Australia]

Marin, Dalia. Structural Change through Exchange Rate Policy. *Weltwirtsch. Arch.*, 1985, *121*(3), pp. 471–91. [G: Austria]

Marshall, M. Technological Change and Local Economic Strategy in the West Midlands. *Reg. Stud.*, October 1985, *19*(6), pp. 570–78. [G: U.K.]

McCombie, J. S. L. Increasing Returns and the Manufacturing Industries: Some Empirical Issues. *Manchester Sch. Econ. Soc. Stud.*, March 1985, *53*(1), pp. 55–75. [G: U.S.]

Meier, Peter. Erklärung konjunktureller Schwankungsintensitäten im Querschnitt von Produktionssektoren—eine empirische Analyse für die Schwiez. (The Intensity of Cyclical Fluctuations in Different Industries—An Empirical Analysis for Switzerland. With English summary.) *Schweiz. Z. Volkswirtsch. Statist.*, June 1985, *121*(2), pp. 115–38. [G: Switzerland]

de Melo, Jaime; Pascale, Ricardo and Tybout, James R. Uruguay 1973–1981: interrelación entre shocks financieros y reales. (With English summary.) *Cuadernos Econ.*, April 1985, 22(65), pp. 73–98. **[G: Uruguay]**

Merrill, Stephen A. The United States and the New Technological Competition. In *Yochelson, J. N., ed.,* 1985, pp. 45–76. **[G: U.S.]**

Michalet, Charles Albert and Chevallier, Thérèse. Multinational Enterprises, Economic Structure and International Competitiveness: France. In *Dunning, J. H., ed.,* 1985, pp. 91–125. **[G: OECD; France]**

Michl, Thomas R. International Comparisons of Productivity Growth: Verdoorn's Law Revisited. *J. Post Keynesian Econ.*, Summer 1985, 7(4), pp. 474–92. **[G: OECD]**

Mills, D. Quinn and Lovell, Malcolm R., Jr. Competitiveness: The Labor Dimension. In *Scott, B. R. and Lodge, G. C., eds.,* 1985, pp. 429–54. **[G: U.S.]**

Mills, David E. and Schumann, Laurence. Industry Structure with Fluctuating Demand. *Amer. Econ. Rev.*, September 1985, 75(4), pp. 758–67. **[G: U.S.]**

Miranda, Casimiro V., Jr. Philippines Import Demand Analysis. In *Lim, D., ed.,* 1985, pp. 164–78. **[G: Philippines; Australia; Japan; U.S.]**

Miranda, Casimiro V., Jr. Philippines Import Survey Analysis. In *Lim, D., ed.,* 1985, pp. 231–40. **[G: Philippines; Selected Countries]**

Modigliani, Franco. Changes in the Balance Sheet, 1926–1977: Comment. In *Friedman, B. M., ed.,* 1985, pp. 109–15. **[G: U.S.]**

Moghimzadeh, Mahmood and Kymn, Kern O. Energy–Capital and Energy–Labor: Complementarity and Substitutability. *Atlantic Econ. J.,* July 1985, 13(2), pp. 44–50. **[G: U.S.]**

Mohammad, Sharif and Whalley, John. Controls and the Intersectoral Terms of Trade: The Indian Case. *Econ. J.,* September 1985, 95(379), pp. 759–66. **[G: India]**

Mohnen, Pierre and Nadiri, Ishaq. Demande de facteurs et recherche-développement: Estimations pour les États-Unis, le Japon, l'Allemagne et la France. (Factor Demands Research and Development: Estimates for the U.S., Japan, Germany and France. With English summary.) *Revue Écon.*, September 1985, 36(5), pp. 943–74. **[G: U.S.; Japan; W. Germany; France]**

Moomaw, Ronald L. Firm Location and City Size: Reduced Productivity Advantages as a Factor in the Decline of Manufacturing in Urban Areas. *J. Urban Econ.,* January 1985, 17(1), pp. 73–89. **[G: U.S.]**

Moore, William J.; Newman, Robert J. and Cunningham, James. The Effect of the Extent of Unionism on Union and Nonunion Wages. *J. Lab. Res.,* Winter 1985, 6(1), pp. 21–44. **[G: U.S.]**

Moroz, Andrew R. Technology Transfer and Canada's Competitive Performance: Comments. In *Stern, R. M., ed.,* 1985, pp. 339–44. **[G: Canada]**

Morrison, Catherine J. On the Economic Interpretation and Measurement of Optimal Capacity Utilization with Anticipatory Expectations.

Rev. Econ. Stud., April 1985, 52(2), pp. 295–310. **[G: U.S.]**

Mortimore, Michael. The Subsidiary Role of Direct Foreign Investment in Industrialization: The Colombian Manufacturing Sector. *Cepal Rev.,* April 1985, (25), pp. 67–84. **[G: Colombia]**

Motamen, Homa and Schaller, C. Pattern of UK Fuel Use. *Energy Econ.,* October 1985, 7(4), pp. 221–30. **[G: U.K.]**

Mueller, Michael J. and Gorin, Daniel R. Informative Trends in Natural Resource Commodity Prices: A Comment. *J. Environ. Econ. Manage.,* March 1985, 12(1), pp. 89–95. **[G: U.S.]**

Muet, Pierre-Alain. A Unified Framework for Firm's Decisions: Theoretical Analysis and Empirical Application to Italy 1970–1981: Comment. In *Weiserbs, D., ed.,* 1985, pp. 75–79. **[G: Italy]**

Mukhopadhyay, Arun K. Technological Progress and Change in Market Concentration in the U.S., 1963–77. *Southern Econ. J.,* July 1985, 52(1), pp. 141–49. **[G: U.S.]**

Müller, Jürgen and Owen, Nicholas. The Effect of Trade on Plant Size. In *Schwalbach, J., ed.,* 1985, pp. 41–60. **[G: W. Germany]**

Myllyntaus, Timo. Initial Electrification in Three Main Branches of Finnish Industry, 1882–1920. *Scand. Econ. Hist. Rev.,* 1985, 33(2), pp. 122–43. **[G: Finland]**

Nakamura, Alice and Nakamura, Masao. Rational Expectations and the Firm's Dividend Behavior. *Rev. Econ. Statist.,* November 1985, 67(4), pp. 606–15. **[G: U.S.; Japan]**

Nakamura, Ryohei. Agglomeration Economies in Urban Manufacturing Industries: A Case of Japanese Cities. *J. Urban Econ.,* January 1985, 17(1), pp. 108–24. **[G: Japan]**

Naya, Seiji. The Role of Small-Scale Industries in Employment and Exports of Asian Developing Countries. *Hitotsubashi J. Econ.,* December 1985, 26(2), pp. 147–63. **[G: Asian LDCs]**

Neumann, Manfred; Böbel, Ingo and Haid, Alfred. Domestic Concentration, Foreign Trade, and Economic Performance. *Int. J. Ind. Organ.,* March 1985, 3(1), pp. 1–19. **[G: W. Germany]**

Nevalainen, Kari. The Use of Industrial Statistics to Estimate the Generation of Recycled and Waste Residuals in Finland. *Statist. J.,* May 1985, 3(2), pp. 161–74. **[G: Finland]**

Nicodano, Giovanna. Struttura finanziaria e decisioni d'investimento: una verifica econometrica. (Financial Structure and Investment Decisions: An Econometric Model. With English summary.) *Giorn. Econ.,* Mar.-Apr. 1985, 44(3–4), pp. 179–207. **[G: Italy]**

Nogués, Julio J. Distortions, Factor Proportions and Efficiency Losses: Argentina in the Latin American Scenario. *Weltwirtsch. Arch.,* 1985, 121(2), pp. 280–303. **[G: Argentina]**

Nugent, Jeffrey. The Potential for South–South Trade in Capital Goods Industries. *Industry Devel.,* 1985, (14), pp. 99–141. **[G: Global]**

O'Farrell, P. N. Employment Change in Manufacturing: The Case of Surviving Plants. *Urban Stud.*, February 1985, *22*(1), pp. 57–68. [G: U.K.]

O'Farrell, P. N. and Crouchley, R. An Industrial and Spatial Analysis of New Firm Formation in Ireland. In *Storey, D. J., ed.*, 1985, pp. 101–34. [G: Ireland]

Olson, Dennis O. and Jonish, James. The Robustness of Translog Elasticity of Substitution Estimates and the Capital Energy Complementarity Controversy. *Quart. J. Bus. Econ.*, Winter 1985, *24*(1), pp. 21–35.

Orléan, André. Spécialisation et taux de change: une vue d'ensemble. (International Specialization and Exchange Rates: A General View. With English summary.) *Écon. Soc.*, April 1985, *19*(4), pp. 67–94. [G: OECD]

Paci, Raffaele. Accumulation Process and Investment Incentives in a Vintage Investment Model: The Case of Sardinia. *Rivista Int. Sci. Econ. Com.*, July-Aug. 1985, *32*(7–8), pp. 765–94. [G: Italy]

Panas, E. E. An Empirical Examination of Alternative Error Specification in a Production Function: The Case of Greece. *Rivista Int. Sci. Econ. Com.*, July-Aug. 1985, *32*(7–8), pp. 751–64. [G: Greece]

Park, Se-Hark. North–South Comparison of the Sources of Change in Manufacturing Value Added, 1975–80: A Decomposition Analysis. *J. Devel. Stud.*, January 1985, *21*(2), pp. 205–14. [G: Global]

Pesaran, M. Hashem. Formation of Inflation Expectations in British Manufacturing Industries. *Econ. J.*, December 1985, *95*(380), pp. 948–75. [G: U.K.]

Petrei, A. Humberto and Tybout, James R. Argentina 1976–1981: la importancia de variar los niveles de subsidios financieros. (With English summary.) *Cuadernos Econ.*, April 1985, *22*(65), pp. 13–36. [G: Argentina]

Philips, Peter. A Note on the Apparent Constancy of the Racial Wage Gap in New Jersey Manufacturing, 1902 to 1979. *Rev. Black Polit. Econ.*, Spring 1985, *13*(4), pp. 71–76. [G: U.S.]

Pickford, Michael. A New Test for Manufacturing Industry Efficiency: An Analysis of the Results of Import License Tendering in New Zealand. *Int. J. Ind. Organ.*, June 1985, *3*(2), pp. 153–77. [G: New Zealand]

Pieplow, Rolf. Some Experience in the Planning of Input Coefficients. In *Smyshlyaev, A., ed.*, 1985, pp. 118–27. [G: E. Germany]

Pitt, Mark M. Estimating Industrial Energy Demand with Firm-Level Data: The Case of Indonesia. *Energy J.*, April 1985, *6*(2), pp. 25–39. [G: Indonesia]

Pløger, Ellen. The Effects of Structural Changes on Danish Energy Consumption. In *Smyshlyaev, A., ed.*, 1985, pp. 211–20. [G: Denmark]

Pomfret, Richard. The Trade Diversion Due to EC Enlargement: A Comment on Sawyer's Estimate [The Effects of the Second Enlargement of the EC on U.S. Exports to Europe]. *Welt-wirtsch. Arch.*, 1985, *121*(3), pp. 560–61. [G: EEC; U.S.]

Ponting, J. Rick and Waters, Nigel. The Impact of Public Policy on Locational Decision-making by Industrial Firms. *Can. Public Policy*, December 1985, *11*(4), pp. 731–44. [G: Canada]

Potestio, Paola. The Relationship between Working Hours and Employment in Italian Manufacturing Industry between 1965 and 1983. *Rivista Polit. Econ.*, Suppl. Dec. 1985, *76*, pp. 121–44. [G: Italy]

Prastacos, Poulicos P. and Brady, Raymond J. Industrial and Spatial Interdependency in Modeling: An Employment Forecasting Model for the Counties in the San Francisco Bay Region. *Ann. Reg. Sci.*, July 1985, *19*(2), pp. 17–28. [G: U.S.]

Pugel, Thomas A. Multinational Enterprises, Economic Structure and International Competitiveness: The United States. In *Dunning, J. H., ed.*, 1985, pp. 57–90. [G: U.S.]

Quataert, Jean H. The Shaping of Women's Work in Manufacturing: Guilds, Households, and the State in Central Europe, 1648–1870. *Amer. Hist. Rev.*, December 1985, *90*(5), pp. 1122–48. [G: Germany]

Rahmeyer, Fritz. Marktstruktur und industrielle Preisentwicklung. (Market Structure and Industrial Price Development. With English summary.) *Ifo-Studien*, 1985, *31*(4), pp. 295–330. [G: W. Germany]

Ranis, Gustav and Schive, Chi. Direct Foreign Investment in Taiwan's Development. In *Galenson, W., ed.*, 1985, pp. 85–137. [G: Taiwan]

Reddy, Nallapu N. Market Boundaries between Coal, Oil, and Natural Gas. *Rev. Ind. Organ.*, 1985, *2*(3), pp. 300–305. [G: U.S.]

Robertson, E. J. Developing the West's Manufacturing Potential: The Role of Provincial Governments. *Can. Public Policy*, Supplement July 1985, *11*(3), pp. 335–38. [G: Canada]

Roepstorff, Torben M. Industrial Development in Indonesia: Performance and Prospects. *Bull. Indonesian Econ. Stud.*, April 1985, *21*(1), pp. 32–61. [G: Indonesia]

Román, Zoltán. The Conditions of Market Competition in the Hungarian Industry. *Acta Oecon.*, 1985, *34*(1–2), pp. 79–97. [G: Hungary]

Rossana, Robert J. Buffer Stocks and Labor Demand: Further Evidence. *Rev. Econ. Statist.*, February 1985, *67*(1), pp. 16–26. [G: U.S.]

Rossi, Peter E. Comparison of Alternative Functional Forms in Production. *J. Econometrics*, Oct./Nov. 1985, *30*(1/2), pp. 345–61. [G: U.S.]

Sasaki, Komei. Regional Difference in Total Factor Productivity and Spatial Features: Empirical Analysis on the Basis of a Sectoral Translog Production Function. *Reg. Sci. Urban Econ.*, November 1985, *15*(4), pp. 489–516. [G: Japan]

Sawyer, W. Charles. The Effects of the Second Enlargement of the EC on U.S. Exports to

Europe: Reply. *Weltwirtsch. Arch.*, 1985, *121*(3), pp. 562–63. **[G: EEC; U.S.]**

Saxonhouse, Gary R. Technology Transfer and Canada's Competitive Performance: Comments. In *Stern, R. M., ed.*, 1985, pp. 334–38. **[G: Canada]**

Schmalensee, Richard. Do Markets Differ Much? *Amer. Econ. Rev.*, June 1985, *75*(3), pp. 341–51. **[G: U.S.]**

Schroeder, Gertrude E. The Slowdown in Soviet Industry, 1976–1982. *Soviet Econ.*, Jan.-Mar. 1985, *1*(1), pp. 42–74. **[G: U.S.S.R.]**

Segerson, Kathleen and Mount, Timothy D. A Non-homothetic Two-Stage Decision Model Using AIDS. *Rev. Econ. Statist.*, November 1985, *67*(4), pp. 630–39. **[G: U.S.]**

Seskin, Eugene P. and Sullivan, David F. Plant and Equipment Expenditures, of the Four Quarters of 1985. *Surv. Curr. Bus.*, September 1985, *65*(9), pp. 19–21. **[G: U.S.]**

Shoven, John B. Taxes and the Investment Recovery: Comment. *Brookings Pap. Econ. Act.*, 1985, (1), pp. 39–41. **[G: U.S.]**

Sider, Hal. Work-related Accidents and the Production Process. *J. Human Res.*, Winter 1985, *20*(1), pp. 47–63. **[G: U.S.]**

Sigit, Hananto and Asra, Abuzar. Indonesian Import Demand Analysis. In *Lim, D., ed.*, 1985, pp. 132–49. **[G: Indonesia; Australia]**

Silvapulla, Paramosathy and Phillips, Prue. Australian Import Demand Analysis. In *Lim, D., ed.*, 1985, pp. 108–31. **[G: Australia; Selected Countries]**

Silver, M. S. On the Measurement of Changes in Aggregate Concentration, Market Concentration and Diversification. *J. Ind. Econ.*, March 1985, *33*(3), pp. 349–52.

Silver, M. S. United Republic of Tanzania: Overall Concentration, Regional Concentration, and the Growth of the Parastatal Sector in the Manufacturing Industry. *Industry Devel.*, 1985, (15), pp. 19–36. **[G: Tanzania]**

Simonato, Rogelio E. El Argumento de la Industria Incipiente y las Políticas de Industrialización Selectivas. (Incipient Industry and Selective Industrialization Policies. With English summary.) *Económica (La Plata)*, Jan.-Apr. 1985, *31*(1), pp. 99–127. **[G: Argentina]**

Simões, Vitor Corado. Multinational Enterprises, Economic Structure and International Competitiveness: Portugal. In *Dunning, J. H., ed.*, 1985, pp. 337–78. **[G: Portugal]**

Smyth, David J. Quasi-fixity of Labour in United States Manufacturing. *Appl. Econ.*, April 1985, *17*(2), pp. 377–80. **[G: U.S.]**

Snape, Richard H. Trade and Industry Policy: Comment. *Australian Econ. Rev.*, 3rd Quarter, Spring 1985, (71), pp. 82. **[G: Australia]**

Soulage, Bernard. Industrial Priorities in the Current French Plan. In *Zukin, S., ed.*, 1985, pp. 165–78. **[G: France]**

Stagni, Anna. Sistemi dinamici di domanda di fattori: un'applicazione agli impieghi di energia nell'industria italiana. (Dynamic Factor Demand Systems: An Application to Energy Inputs in the Italian Industry. With English summary.) *Ricerche Econ.*, Jan.-Mar. 1985, *39*(1), pp. 5–28. **[G: Italy]**

Stauffer, Thomas R. Energy-intensive Industrialization in the Middle East. *Industry Devel.*, 1985, (14), pp. 1–35. **[G: Middle East]**

Sterner, Thomas. Structural Change and Technology Choice: Energy Use in Mexican Manufacturing Industry, 1970–81. *Energy Econ.*, April 1985, *7*(2), pp. 77–86. **[G: Mexico]**

Stevens, Benjamin H. Regional Cost Equalization and the Potential for Manufacturing Recovery in the Industrial North. In *Richardson, H. W. and Turek, J. H., eds.*, 1985, pp. 85–103. **[G: U.S.]**

Storey, D. J. Manufacturing Employment Change in Northern England 1965–78: The Role of Small Businesses. In *Storey, D. J., ed.*, 1985, pp. 6–42. **[G: U.K.]**

Storey, D. J. Small Firms in Regional Economic Development: The Implications for Policy. In *Storey, D. J., ed.*, 1985, pp. 219–29. **[G: U.K.]**

Stratton, Richard W. Monopoly, Monopsony, and Union Strength and Local Market Wage Differentials: Some Empirical Evidence on Their Impacts. *Amer. J. Econ. Soc.*, July 1985, *44*(3), pp. 305–18. **[G: U.S.]**

Strickland, Allyn D. Conglomerate Mergers, Mutual Forbearance Behavior and Price Competition. *Managerial Dec. Econ.*, September 1985, *6*(3), pp. 153–59. **[G: U.S.]**

Suarez-Villa, Luis. Urban Growth and Manufacturing Change in the United States–Mexico Borderlands: A Conceptual Framework and an Empirical Analysis. *Ann. Reg. Sci.*, November 1985, *19*(3), pp. 54–108. **[G: U.S.; Mexico]**

Sudarsanam, P. S. and Taffler, R. J. Industrial Classification in UK Capital Markets: A Test of Economic Homogeneity. *Appl. Econ.*, April 1985, *17*(2), pp. 291–308. **[G: U.K.]**

Sujan, I. and Oleksa, M. A Quarterly Econometric Model for Short-term Analysis of the Czech Economy. *Matekon*, Spring 1985, *21*(3), pp. 31–46. **[G: Czechoslovakia]**

Summers, Lawrence H. Taxes and the Investment Recovery: Comment. *Brookings Pap. Econ. Act.*, 1985, (1), pp. 42–44. **[G: U.S.]**

Suzuki, Kazuyuki. Knowledge Capital and the Private Rate of Return to R and D in Japanese Manufacturing Industries. *Int. J. Ind. Organ.*, September 1985, *3*(3), pp. 293–305. **[G: Japan]**

Sveikauskas, Leo; Townroe, Peter and Hansen, Eric. Intraregional Productivity Differences in São Paulo State Manufacturing Plants. *Weltwirtsch. Arch.*, 1985, *121*(4), pp. 722–40. **[G: Brazil]**

Swedenborg, Birgitta. Multinational Enterprises, Economic Structure and International Competitiveness: Sweden. In *Dunning, J. H., ed.*, 1985, pp. 217–48. **[G: Sweden]**

Symons, James S. V. Relative Prices and the Demand for Labour in British Manufacturing. *Economica*, February 1985, *52*(205), pp. 37–49. **[G: U.K.]**

Tambunlertchai, Somsak. Thai Import Survey

Analysis. In *Lim, D., ed.*, 1985, pp. 247–54.
[G: Thailand; Selected Countries]

Tambunlertchai, Somsak. Thailand Import Demand Analysis. In *Lim, D., ed.*, 1985, pp. 191–99.
[G: Australia; Thailand]

Tanzi, Vito and Iden, George. The Impact of Taxes on Wages: Reply. *Econ. Notes*, 1985, (2), pp. 175–78.
[G: U.S.]

Tervo, Hannu. Teollisuuden aluekehityksen uudet piirteet. (New Features in the Regional Development of Finnish Manufacturing. With English summary.) *Kansant. Aikak.*, 1985, *81*(3), pp. 314–25.
[G: Finland]

Todd, Douglas. Productive Performance in the West German Manufacturing Industry, 1970–80: A Farrell Frontier Characterisation. *J. Ind. Econ.*, March 1985, *33*(3), pp. 295–316.
[G: W. Germany]

Toh, Mun Heng. Technical Change Elasticity of Factor Substitution, and Returns to Scale in Singapore Manufacturing Industries. *Singapore Econ. Rev.*, October 1985, *30*(2), pp. 36–56.
[G: Singapore]

Truong, Truong P. Inter-fuel and Inter-factor Substitution in NSW Manufacturing Industry. *Econ. Rec.*, September 1985, *61*(174), pp. 644–53.
[G: Australia]

Tsao, Yuan. Growth without Productivity: Singapore Manufacturing in the 1970s. *J. Devel. Econ.*, Sept.-Oct. 1985, *19*(1/2), pp. 25–38.
[G: Singapore]

Twomey, Jim and Taylor, Jim. Regional Policy and the Interregional Movement of Manufacturing Industry in Great Britain. *Scot. J. Polit. Econ.*, November 1985, *32*(3), pp. 257–77.
[G: U.K.]

Tyers, Rodney and Phillips, Prue. Australia, ASEAN and Pacific Basin Merchandise Trade: Factor Composition and Performance in the 1970s. In *Lim, D., ed.*, 1985, pp. 78–106.
[G: Australia; ASEAN; Pacific Basin]

Tyler, William G. Effective Incentives for Domestic Market Sales and Exports: View of Anti-export Biases and Commercial Policy in Brazil, 1980–81. *J. Devel. Econ.*, August 1985, *18*(2–3), pp. 219–42.
[G: Brazil]

Van Den Bulcke, Daniel. Multinational Enterprises, Economic Structure and International Competitiveness: Belgium. In *Dunning, J. H., ed.*, 1985, pp. 249–80.
[G: Belgium]

Verma, R. P. S. and Verma, J. D. Small-scale Sector. In *Mongia, J. N., ed.*, 1985, pp. 117–51.
[G: India]

Vernardakis, Nikos. Capital Utilization, Its Determinants and Export Subsidies. *Greek Econ. Rev.*, August 1985, *7*(2), pp. 125–43.
[G: Greece]

Waagstein, Thorbjørn. Er industriens afkastningsgrad fejlvurderet? (Are Reported Profit Rates for the Danish Industry Misleading? With English summary.) *Nationaløkon. Tidsskr.*, 1985, *123*(1), pp. 94–103.
[G: Denmark]

Watanabe, Susumu. Employment and Income Implications of the "Bio-revolution": A Specu-

lative Note. *Int. Lab. Rev.*, May-June 1985, *124*(3), pp. 281–97.
[G: LDCs; MDCs]

Wells, Louis T., Jr. Small-scale Manufacturing as a Competitive Advantage. In *Moran, T. H., ed.*, 1985, pp. 119–36.
[G: Selected Countries]

Whitesell, Robert S. The Influence of Central Planning on the Economic Slowdown in the Soviet Union and Eastern Europe: A Comparative Production Function Analysis. *Economica*, May 1985, *52*(206), pp. 235–44.
[G: U.S.S.R.; E. Europe]

Williams, Bruce. Prospects from the Sunrise. In *Wells, N., ed.*, 1985, pp. 24–27.

Williams, Martin. Technical Efficiency and Region: The U.S. Manufacturing Sector 1972–1977. *Reg. Sci. Urban Econ.*, August 1985, *15*(3), pp. 459–75.
[G: U.S.]

Winiecki, Jan. Central Planning and Export Orientation in Manufactures. Theoretical Considerations on the Impact of System-Specific Features on Specialisation. *Econ. Notes*, 1985, (2), pp. 132–53.

Wong, Christine. Material Allocation and Decentralization: Impact of the Local Sector on Industrial Reform. In *Perry, E. J. and Wong, C., eds.*, 1985, pp. 253–78.
[G: China]

Wren-Lewis, Simon. The Quantification of Survey Data on Expectations. *Nat. Inst. Econ. Rev.*, August 1985, (113), pp. 39–49.
[G: U.K.]

Yamawaki, Hideki. International Trade and Foreign Direct Investment in West German Manufacturing Industries. In *Schwalbach, J., ed.*, 1985, pp. 247–86.
[G: W. Germany]

Yeats, Alexander J. On the Appropriate Interpretation of the Revealed Comparative Advantage Index: Implications of a Methodology Based on Industry Sector Analysis. *Weltwirtsch. Arch.*, 1985, *121*(1), pp. 61–73.
[G: Selected Countries]

Young, Kan H. The Relative Effects of Demand and Supply on Output Growth and Price Change. *Rev. Econ. Statist.*, May 1985, *67*(2), pp. 314–18.
[G: U.S.]

Yücelt, Ugur. Managerial Practices in the Middle East. In *Kaynak, E., ed. (II)*, 1985, pp. 113–26.
[G: Turkey]

6312 Metals (iron, steel, and other)

Adams, F. Gerard, et al. Industrial-Policy Impacts on the Steel Industry: A Simulation Study. In *Adams, F. G., ed.*, 1985, pp. 85–132.
[G: U.S.]

Bossong, Elizabeth A. Industry Perspective: The Steel Industry—Stagnation, Decay or Recovery? *Bus. Econ.*, July 1985, *20*(3), pp. 51–57.
[G: U.S.]

Browne, Lynn E. Autos—Another Steel? *New Eng. Econ. Rev.*, Nov./Dec. 1985, pp. 14–29.
[G: U.S.]

Browne, Lynn E. Steel—An Industry Beset on All Sides. *New Eng. Econ. Rev.*, May/June 1985, pp. 35–43.
[G: U.S.]

Duggan, James E. and Clem, Andrew G. Input Prices and Cost Inflation in Three Manufacturing Industries. *Mon. Lab. Rev.*, May 1985, *108*(5), pp. 16–21. **[G: U.S.]**

Evans, Peter B. Trends in United States Manufacturing Industry and Their Possible Implications for Latin American Industrialization: Case Studies of Steel, Electronics and Petrochemicals. *Industry Devel.*, 1985, (14), pp. 47–98. **[G: U.S.; Latin America]**

Foray, Dominique. Innovation majeure et transformation des structures productives: Une étude de cas: Le procédé de coulée en moule plein en fonderie. (Major Innovation and Changes in the Productive Structures of Casting Industry: The Fullmold Casting Process. With English summary.) *Revue Écon.*, September 1985, *36*(5), pp. 1081–1116.

Foster, Mark S. Giant of the West: Henry J. Kaiser and Regional Industrialization, 1930–1950. *Bus. Hist. Rev.*, Spring 1985, *59*(1), pp. 1–23. **[G: U.S.]**

Goldar, B. N. and Bharadwaj, Ranganath N. Determinants of Iron and Steel Exports. *Devel. Econ.*, March 1985, *23*(1), pp. 40–52. **[G: Selected Countries]**

Gruver, Gene W. and Sun, Yu. Variable Factors and Efficiency in the U.S. Steel Industry: A Production Frontier Analysis. *Appl. Econ.*, February 1985, *17*(1), pp. 117–33. **[G: U.S.]**

Holt, James. Trade Unionism in the British and U.S. Steel Industries, 1880–1914: A Comparative Study. In *Leab, D. J., ed.*, 1985, pp. 166–96. **[G: U.K.; U.S.]**

Inwood, Kris. Productivity Growth in Obsolescence: Charcoal Iron Revisited. *J. Econ. Hist.*, June 1985, *45*(2), pp. 293–98. **[G: Canada]**

Jones, Kent. Trade in Steel: Another Turn in the Protectionist Spiral. *World Econ.*, December 1985, *8*(4), pp. 393–408. **[G: EEC; U.S.]**

Kopp, Raymond J. and Smith, V. Kerry. The Measurement on Non-neutral Technological Change. *Int. Econ. Rev.*, February 1985, *26*(1), pp. 135–59. **[G: U.S.]**

Kreinin, Mordechai E. Wage Competitiveness in the U.S. Auto and Steel Industries. In *Adams, J., ed.*, 1985, pp. 174–88. **[G: U.S.]**

Kuprevich, R. The "Tsvetmetpromeksport" All-Union Association. *Soviet E. Europ. Foreign Trade*, Winter 1985-86, *21*(4), pp. 68–78. **[G: U.S.S.R.]**

Lager, Christian and Schöpp, Wolfgang. Estimation of Input–Output Coefficients Using Neoclassical Production Theory. In *Smyshlyaev, A., ed.*, 1985, pp. 151–61. **[G: Canada]**

Lawrence, Colin and Lawrence, Robert Z. Manufacturing Wage Dispersion: An End Game Interpretation. *Brookings Pap. Econ. Act.*, 1985, (1), pp. 47–106. **[G: U.S.]**

Lynd, Staughton. Options for Reindustrialization: Brownfield versus Greenfield Approaches. In *Woodworth, W.; Meek, C. and Whyte, W. F., eds.*, 1985, pp. 49–63. **[G: U.S.]**

Martin, David Dale. The Iron and Steel Industry: Transnational Control without TNCs? In *Newfarmer, R. S., ed.*, 1985, pp. 151–92. **[G: Selected Countries]**

Mueller, Hans. The Changing U.S. Position in the International Steel Market: Output, Trade, and Performance. In *Hochmuth, M. and Davidson, W., eds.*, 1985, pp. 213–62. **[G: U.S.; Global]**

Radetzki, Marian and Van Duyne, Carl. The Demand for Scrap and Primary Metal Ores after a Decline in Secular Growth. *Can. J. Econ.*, May 1985, *18*(2), pp. 435–49. **[G: U.S.]**

Roberts, Gerald. Aluminium. In *Roberts, G., ed.*, 1985, pp. 47–51. **[G: Global]**

Savage, John A. Growth and Success through Employee Motivation. In *Federal Reserve Bank of Atlanta (I)*, 1985, pp. 47–57. **[G: U.S.]**

Slade, Margaret E. Noninformative Trends in Natural Resource Commodity Prices: U-shaped Price Paths Exonerated: Reply [Trends in Natural-Resource Commodity Prices: An Analysis of the Time Domain]. *J. Environ. Econ. Manage.*, June 1985, *12*(2), pp. 181–92. **[G: U.S.]**

Smyshlyaev, Anatoli. An Econometric Model of the Soviet Iron and Steel Industry. In *Smyshlyaev, A., ed.*, 1985, pp. 197–209. **[G: U.S.S.R.]**

Solow, Robert M. Manufacturing Wage Dispersion: An End Game Interpretation: Comment. *Brookings Pap. Econ. Act.*, 1985, (1), pp. 107–10. **[G: U.S.]**

Stancu-Minasian, I. M., et al. Cybernetic System for the Control of Steel Batch Manufacturing Process in Electric Furnaces. *Econ. Computat. Cybern. Stud. Res.*, 1985, *20*(2), pp. 21–30.

Teräsvirta, Timo. Metalliteollisuustuotannon volyymin ennustaminen suhdannebarometrin avulla. (Forecasting the Output of the Metal and Engineering Industries Using the Finnish Business Survey. With English summary.) *Kansant. Aikak.*, 1985, *81*(3), pp. 288–97. **[G: Finland]**

Tsoukalis, Loukas and Strauss, Robert. Crisis and Adjustment in European Steel: Beyond Laisse-Faire. *J. Common Market Stud.*, March 1985, *23*(3), pp. 207–28. **[G: EEC]**

Voráček, Josef. Retrospective View of the Development of the Engineering and Electrical Engineering Industries and the Objectives up to 1990. *Czech. Econ. Digest.*, November 1985, (7), pp. 30–43. **[G: Czechoslovakia]**

Wachter, Michael L. Manufacturing Wage Dispersion: An End Game Interpretation: Comment. *Brookings Pap. Econ. Act.*, 1985, (1), pp. 110–15. **[G: U.S.]**

Walker, Alan; Noble, Iain and Westergaard, John. From Secure Employment to Labour Market Insecurity: The Impact of Redundancy on Older Workers in the Steel Industry. In *Roberts, B.; Finnegan, R. and Gallie, D., eds.*, 1985, pp. 319–37. **[G: U.K.]**

Wetter, Theresa. Trade Policy Developments in the Steel Sector. *J. World Trade Law*, Sept.-Oct. 1985, *19*(5), pp. 485–96. **[G: EEC; U.S.; Japan]**

Wright, Marcia. Iron and Regional History: Report on a Research Project in Southwestern Tanzania. *African Econ. Hist.*, 1985, *14*, pp. 147–65. **[G: Tanzania]**

Yamawaki, Hideki. Dominant Firm Pricing and Fringe Expansion: The Case of the U.S. Iron and Steel Industry, 1907–1930. *Rev. Econ. Statist.*, August 1985, *67*(3), pp. 429–37.
[G: U.S.]

6313 Machinery (tools, electrical equipment, computers, communication equipment, and appliances)

Adams, F. Gerard and Santarelli, Roberto. Econometric Modeling of Industries on the Microcomputer: A Model of the Italian Metal–Mechanical Industry. *Bus. Econ.*, April 1985, *20*(2), pp. 43–49. [G: Italy]

Agarwal, Suraj Mal. Electronics in India: Past Strategies and Future Possibilities. *World Devel.*, March 1985, *13*(3), pp. 273–92.
[G: India]

Amsden, Alice H. The Division of Labour Is Limited by the Rate of Growth of the Market: The Taiwan Machine Tool Industry in the 1970s. *Cambridge J. Econ.*, September 1985, *9*(3), pp. 271–84. [G: Taiwan]

Baker, Jonathan B. and Bresnahan, Timothy F. The Gains from Merger or Collusion in Product-differentiated Industries. *J. Ind. Econ.*, June 1985, *33*(4), pp. 427–44. [G: U.S.]

Bresnahan, Timothy F. Post-entry Competition in the Plain Paper Copier Market. *Amer. Econ. Rev.*, May 1985, *75*(2), pp. 15–19. [G: U.S.]

Cohen, Isaac. Workers' Control in the Cotton Industry: A Comparative Study of British and American Mule Spinning. *Labor Hist.*, Winter 1985, *26*(1), pp. 53–85. [G: U.S.; U.K.]

David, Paul A. Clio and the Economics of QWERTY. *Amer. Econ. Rev.*, May 1985, *75*(2), pp. 332–37. [G: U.S.; U.K.]

Davidson, William. The Information Technology Sector. In *Hochmuth, M. and Davidson, W., eds.*, 1985, pp. 293–332. [G: OECD]

Erber, Fabio Stefano. The Development of the 'Electonics Complex' and Government Policies in Brazil. *World Devel.*, March 1985, *13*(3), pp. 293–309. [G: Brazil]

Ernst, Dieter. Automation and the Worldwide Restructuring of the Electronics Industry: Strategic Implications for Developing Countries. *World Devel.*, March 1985, *13*(3), pp. 333–52.
[G: LDCs]

Evans, Peter B. Trends in United States Manufacturing Industry and Their Possible Implications for Latin American Industrialization: Case Studies of Steel, Electronics and Petrochemicals. *Industry Devel.*, 1985, (14), pp. 47–98.
[G: U.S.; Latin America]

Finan, William F. and LaMond, Annette M. Sustaining U.S. Competitiveness in Microelectronics: The Challenge to U.S. Policy. In *Scott, B. R. and Lodge, G. C., eds.*, 1985, pp. 144–75. [G: Japan; U.S.]

Friedman, Brian L. and Herman, Arthur S. Productivity Growth Low in the Oilfield Machinery Industry. *Mon. Lab. Rev.*, December 1985, *108*(12), pp. 34–38. [G: U.S.]

Goodman, S. E. Technology Transfer and the De-velopment of the Soviet Computer Industry. In *Parrott, B., ed.*, 1985, pp. 117–40.
[G: U.S.S.R.]

Grieco, Joseph M. Between Dependency and Autonomy: India's Experience with the International Computer Industry. In *Moran, T. H., ed.*, 1985, pp. 55–81. [G: India]

Harrington, James W., Jr. Intraindustry Structural Change and Location Change: U.S. Semiconductor Manufacturing, 1958–1980. *Reg. Stud.*, August 1985, *19*(4), pp. 343–52.
[G: U.S.]

Harrop, Jeffrey. Crisis in the Machine Tool Industry: A Policy Dilemma for the European Community. *J. Common Market Stud.*, September 1985, *24*(1), pp. 61–75. [G: EEC]

Hekman, John S. Branch Plant Location and the Product Cycle in Computer Manufacturing. *J. Econ. Bus.*, May 1985, *37*(2), pp. 89–102.
[G: U.S.]

Henneberger, J. Edwin and Herman, Arthur S. Productivity Growth Below Average in the Internal Combustion Engine Industry. *Mon. Lab. Rev.*, May 1985, *108*(5), pp. 22–26.
[G: U.S.]

Hirschhorn, Paul. Israeli Electronics on the Map. In *Levinson, P. and Landau, P., eds.*, 1985, pp. 75–79. [G: Israel]

Hoffman, Kurt. Microelectronics, International Competition and Development Strategies: The Unavoidable Issues—Editor's Introduction. *World Devel.*, March 1985, *13*(3), pp. 263–72.

Jacobsson, Staffan. Technical Change and Industrial Policy: The Case of Computer Numerically Controlled Lathes in Argentina, Korea and Taiwan. *World Devel.*, March 1985, *13*(3), pp. 353–70. [G: Argentina; Korea; Taiwan; OECD]

Jenkins, Rhys O. and West, Peter J. The International Tractor Industry and its Impact in Latin America. In *Newfarmer, R. S., ed.*, 1985, pp. 299–342. [G: Latin America]

Jenner, Faith S. and Trevor, Malcolm H. Personnel Management in Four U.K. Electronics Plants. In *Takamiya, S. and Thurley, K., eds.*, 1985, pp. 113–48. [G: U.K.; U.S.; Japan]

Kanamori, Hisao. Microelectronics and the Japanese Economy. In *Shishido, T. and Sato, R., eds.*, 1985, pp. 171–87. [G: Japan]

Kaplinsky, Raphael. Comparative Advantage by Design. In *Langdon, R. and Rothwell, R., eds.*, 1985, pp. 44–62. [G: OECD]

Kaplinsky, Raphael. Electronics-based Automation Technologies and the Onset of Systemofacture: Implications for Third World Industrialization. *World Devel.*, March 1985, *13*(3), pp. 423–39. [G: LDCs]

Khan, Shaheen and Nazir, Rauf. An Economic Analysis of Thresher Manufacturing Industry in Punjab. *Pakistan Econ. Soc. Rev.*, Summer 1985, *23*(1), pp. 1–23. [G: Pakistan]

Kheiman, S. A. The Development of Machine Building: Organizational and Structural Factors. *Prob. Econ.*, May 1985, *28*(1), pp. 3–23.
[G: U.S.S.R.]

Kobayashi, T. Japanese Industrial Policy: Competition and Cooperation. In *Langdon, R. and Rothwell, R., eds.*, 1985, pp. 115–22. [G: Japan]

Kollist, Ingrid and Searing, Marjory E. Government Policy toward High-Tech Industry. In *Zukin, S., ed.*, 1985, pp. 107–18. [G: U.S.]

Kontorovich, Vladimir. Industrial Policy and the Electrical-Machinery Industry: The Case of Transformers. In *Adams, F. G., ed.*, 1985, pp. 133–59. [G: U.S.]

Laister, Peter. Electronics and Communications. In *Wells, N., ed.*, 1985, pp. 35–40.

Lean, David F.; Ogur, Jonathan D. and Rogers, Robert P. Does Collusion Pay . . . Does Antiturst Work? *Southern Econ. J.*, January 1985, *51*(3), pp. 828–41. [G: U.S.]

Mairesse, Jacques and Cunéo, Philippe. Recherche-développement et performances des entreprises: Une étude éeconométrique sur données individuelles. (Research-Development and Firm Performance: An Econometric Study on Individual Data. With English summary.) *Revue Écon.*, September 1985, *36*(5), pp. 1001–41. [G: France]

Malecki, Edward J. Industrial Location and Corporate Organization in High Technology Industries. *Econ. Geogr.*, October 1985, *61*(4), pp. 345–69. [G: U.S.]

Maurer, Martin. Technological Retardation. The Decline of the Swiss Watch Industry. *Z. Wirtschaft. Sozialwissen.*, 1985, *105*(6), pp. 661–82. [G: Switzerland]

Miller, Robert R. Investment Incentives and Performance Requirements: Computers. In *Guisinger, S. E., et al.*, 1985, pp. 168–236. [G: Selected Countries]

Newfarmer, Richard S. International Oligopoly in the Electrical Industry. In *Newfarmer, R. S., ed.*, 1985, pp. 113–49. [G: Brazil; Selected Countries]

Nyström, Harry. Company Strategies for Designing and Marketing New Products in the Electrotechnical Industry. In *Langdon, R. and Rothwell, R., eds.*, 1985, pp. 18–26.

O'Connor, David C. The Computer Industry in the Third World: Policy Options and Constraints. *World Devel.*, March 1985, *13*(3), pp. 311–32. [G: LDCs; OECD]

Oakey, R. P. Innovation and Regional Growth in Small High Technology Firms: Evidence from Britain and the USA. In *Storey, D. J., ed.*, 1985, pp. 135–65. [G: U.K.; U.S.]

Rajalakshmi, K. Productivity in Electrical Machinery Industry in Leading States. *Indian Econ. Rev.*, July-Dec. 1985, *20*(2), pp. 269–81. [G: India]

Rees, J.; Briggs, R. and Hicks, D. New Technology in the United States' Machinery Industry: Trends and Implications. In *Thwaites, A. T. and Oakey, R. P., eds.*, 1985, pp. 164–94. [G: U.S.]

Sandhu, H. S. and Sodhi, T. S. Production Function Analysis for Engineering Goods Industry in Punjab—A Case Study. *Margin*, April 1985, *17*(3), pp. 66–74. [G: India]

Sharp, Daniel A. French Industrial Policy in the Office Automation Industry: A View from a French/American Firm. In *Zukin, S., ed.*, 1985, pp. 195–202. [G: France; U.S.]

Stoffaës, Christian. Explaining French Strategy in Electronics. In *Zukin, S., ed.*, 1985, pp. 187–94. [G: France]

Subrahmanian, K. K. Trends in Growth, Specialisation and Technological Dynamism of Indian Capital Goods Industries: An Overview. *Indian J. Quant. Econ.*, 1985, *1*(1), pp. 119–35. [G: India]

Swann, G. M. P. Product Competition in Microprocessors. *J. Ind. Econ.*, September 1985, *34*(1), pp. 33–53. [G: U.S.]

Toner, Bill. The Unionisation and Productivity Debate: An Employee Opinion Survey in Ireland. *Brit. J. Ind. Relat.*, July 1985, *23*(2), pp. 179–202. [G: Ireland]

Voráček, Josef. Retrospective View of the Development of the Engineering and Electrical Engineering Industries and the Objectives up to 1990. *Czech. Econ. Digest.*, November 1985, (7), pp. 30–43. [G: Czechoslovakia]

York, James D. Productivity Trends in the Machine Tool Accessories Industry. *Mon. Lab. Rev.*, June 1985, *108*(6), pp. 28–32. [G: U.S.]

Yoshino, Michael Y. and Fong, Glenn R. The Very High Speed Integrated Circuit Program: Lessons for Industrial Policy. In *Scott, B. R. and Lodge, G. C., eds.*, 1985, pp. 176–84. [G: U.S.]

6314 Transportation Equipment

Amin, Ash. Restructuring in Fiat and the Decentralization of Production into Southern Italy. In *Hudson, R. and Lewis, J., eds.*, 1985, pp. 155–91. [G: Italy; Europe]

Atkinson, Thomas R. Canada/U.S. Automotive Trade and Trade-policy Issues: Comments. In *Fretz, D.; Stern, R. and Whalley, J., eds.*, 1985, pp. 333–37. [G: Canada; U.S.]

Bellur, Venkatakrishna V. Factors Perceived as Important in Making Automobile Purchase Decision. *Liiketaloudellinen Aikak.*, 1985, *34*(3), pp. 219–36. [G: U.S.]

Bennett, Douglas C. and Sharpe, Kenneth E. The World Automobile Industry and its Implications. In *Newfarmer, R. S., ed.*, 1985, pp. 193–226. [G: Latin America; Selected Countries]

Berggren, Christian. Industrial Work, Technological Development and New Rationalization Strategies—The Case of the Swedish Automotive Industry. In *Gustavsson, B.; Karlsson, J. C. and Raftegard, C.*, 1985, pp. 61–69. [G: Sweden]

Berkovec, James. New Car Sales and Used Car Stocks: A Model of the Automobile Market. *Rand J. Econ.*, Summer 1985, *16*(2), pp. 195–214. [G: U.S.]

Black, Andrew P. Technical Change, Product Quality and Market Structure in the West German Automobile Industry. *Stud. Econ.*, 1985, *40*(26), pp. 41–63. [G: W. Germany]

Bresnahan, Timothy F. and Reiss, Peter C.

Dealer and Manufacturer Margins. *Rand J. Econ.*, Summer 1985, *16*(2), pp. 253–68.
[G: U.S.]

Bresnahan, Timothy F. and Yao, Dennis A. The Nonpecuniary Costs of Automobile Emissions Standards. *Rand J. Econ.*, Winter 1985, *16*(4), pp. 437–55. [G: U.S.]

Browne, Lynn E. Autos—Another Steel? *New Eng. Econ. Rev.*, Nov./Dec. 1985, pp. 14–29.
[G: U.S.]

Carbaugh, Robert and Wassink, Darwin. Joint Ventures, Voluntary Export Quotas, and Domestic Content Requirements. *Quart. J. Bus. Econ.*, Spring 1985, *24*(2), pp. 21–36.
[G: U.S.]

Claybrook, Joan and Bollier, David. The Hidden Benefits of Regulation: Disclosing the Auto Safety Payoff. *Yale J. Regul.*, Fall 1985, *3*(1), pp. 87–131. [G: U.S.]

Crandall, Robert W. What Have Auto-Import Quotas Wrought? *Challenge*, January/February 1985, *27*(6), pp. 40–47. [G: U.S.]

Cronin, M. R. Protection and Employment in the Motor Car Sector: A Further Comment. *Australian Econ. Pap.*, June 1985, *24*(44), pp. 225.

Doz, Yves. Automobiles: Shifts in International Competitiveness. In *Hochmuth, M. and Davidson, W., eds.*, 1985, pp. 189–212.
[G: Japan; U.S.]

Duggan, James E. and Clem, Andrew G. Input Prices and Cost Inflation in Three Manufacturing Industries. *Mon. Lab. Rev.*, May 1985, *108*(5), pp. 16–21. [G: U.S.]

Eckard, E. Woodrow, Jr. The Effects of State Automobile Dealer Entry Regulation on New Car Prices. *Econ. Inquiry*, April 1985, *23*(2), pp. 223–42. [G: U.S.]

Egan, John J. Industry and Government in Space: Making the Long-term Commitment. In *Konecci, E. B. and Kuhn, R. L., eds.*, 1985, pp. 144–63. [G: U.S.]

Färe, Rolf; Jansson, Leif and Lovell, C. A. Knox. Modelling Scale Economies with Ray-Homothetic Production Functions. *Rev. Econ. Statist.*, November 1985, *67*(4), pp. 624–29.
[G: U.S.]

Feenstra, Robert C. Automobile Prices and Protection: The U.S.–Japan Trade Restraint. *J. Policy Modeling*, Spring 1985, *7*(1), pp. 49–68. [G: U.S.; Japan]

Ferguson, G. J. W. A. and Mogridge, M. J. H. Is Car Ownership and Use Stagnating? Fuel Consumption Models and their Implications. In *Jansen, G. R. M.; Nijkamp, P. and Ruijgrok, C. J., eds.*, 1985, pp. 55–74. [G: U.K.; U.S.]

Fuhr, Joseph P., Jr. A Measurement of the Welfare Loss in the Terminal Equipment Market. *Rev. Ind. Organ.*, 1985, *2*(1), pp. 80–93.
[G: U.S.]

Hensher, David A. Empirical Vehicle Choice and Usage Models in the Household Sector: A Review. *Int. J. Transport Econ.*, October 1985, *12*(3), pp. 231–59. [G: U.S.; Australia; Israel]

Hochmuth, Milton. The Aerospace Industry. In *Hochmuth, M. and Davidson, W., eds.*, 1985, pp. 333–73. [G: U.K.; U.S.; France; W. Germany; Netherlands]

Holliday, George D. Western Technology Transfer to the Soviet Automotive Industry. In *Parrott, B., ed.*, 1985, pp. 82–116.
[G: U.S.S.R.; OECD; Czechoslovakia; Hungary]

Hood, Neil and Young, Stephen. Investment Incentives and Performance Requirements: The Automobile Industry. In *Guisinger, S. E., et al.*, 1985, pp. 96–167.
[G: Selected Countries]

Ilmakunnas, Pekka. Identification and Estimation of the Degree of Oligopoly Power in Industries Facing Domestic and Import Competition. In *Schwalbach, J., ed.*, 1985, pp. 287–308.
[G: W. Germany]

Jarrell, Gregg A. and Peltzman, Sam. The Impact of Product Recalls on the Wealth of Sellers. *J. Polit. Econ.*, June 1985, *93*(3), pp. 512–36.
[G: U.S.]

Jenkins, Rhys O. Internationalization of Capital and the Semi-industrialized Countries: The Case of the Motor Industry. *Rev. Radical Polit. Econ.*, Spring and Summer 1985, *17*(1/2), pp. 59–81. [G: LDCs]

Jones, Bryn. Controlling Production on the Shop Floor: The Role of State Administration and Regulation in the British and American Aerospace Industries. In *Tolliday, S. and Zeitlin, J., eds.*, 1985, pp. 219–55. [G: U.S.; U.K.]

Jones, Daniel T. and Womack, James P. Developing Countries and the Future of the Automobile Industry. *World Devel.*, March 1985, *13*(3), pp. 393–407. [G: Global]

Kahn, Mark L. Discussion: The 1984 Auto Negotiations. In *Dennis, B. D., ed.*, 1985, pp. 464–66. [G: U.S.]

Kappler, Frederick G. and Rutledge, Gary L. Expenditures for Abating Pollutant Emissions from Motor Vehicles, 1968–84. *Surv. Curr. Bus.*, July 1985, *65*(7), pp. 29–35. [G: U.S.]

Katz, Harry C. and Sabel, Charles F. Industrial Relations & Industrial Adjustment in the Car Industry. *Ind. Relat.*, Fall 1985, *24*(3), pp. 295–315. [G: Italy; U.K.; U.S.; W. Germany]

Kheiman, S. A. The Development of Machine Building: Organizational and Structural Factors. *Prob. Econ.*, May 1985, *28*(1), pp. 3–23.
[G: U.S.S.R.]

Kim, Jae-Cheol. The Market for "Lemons" Reconsidered: A Model of the Used Car Market with Asymmetric Information. *Amer. Econ. Rev.*, September 1985, *75*(4), pp. 836–43.

Kreinin, Mordechai E. Wage Competitiveness in the U.S. Auto and Steel Industries. In *Adams, J., ed.*, 1985, pp. 174–88. [G: U.S.]

Laffer, Arthur B., et al. A High Road for the American Automobile Industry. *World Econ.*, September 1985, *8*(3), pp. 267–86. [G: U.S.]

Lichtenstein, Nelson. UAW Bargaining Strategy and Shop-Floor Conflict: 1946–1970. *Ind. Relat.*, Fall 1985, *24*(3), pp. 360–81.
[G: U.S.]

Malecki, Edward J. Industrial Location and Corporate Organization in High Technology Industries. *Econ. Geogr.*, October 1985, *61*(4), pp. 345–69. [G: U.S.]

Mannering, Fred and Winston, Clifford. A Dynamic Empirical Analysis of Household Vehicle Ownership and Utilization. *Rand J. Econ.*, Summer 1985, *16*(2), pp. 215–36. [G: U.S.]

Marx, Thomas G. The Development of the Franchise Distribution System in the U.S. Automobile Industry. *Bus. Hist. Rev.*, Autumn 1985, *59*(3), pp. 465–74. [G: U.S.]

McCarthy, Patrick S. An Econometric Analysis of Automobile Transactions. *Int. J. Transport Econ.*, February 1985, *12*(1), pp. 71–92.
[G: U.S.]

Mertens, Yves and Ginsburgh, Victor. Product Differentiation and Price Discrimination in the European Community: The Case of Automobiles. *J. Ind. Econ.*, December 1985, *34*(2), pp. 151–66. [G: Belgium; France; W. Germany; Italy; U.K.]

Moran, Larry R. Motor Vehicles, Model Year 1985. *Surv. Curr. Bus.*, October 1985, *65*(10), pp. 29–31. [G: U.S.]

Moroz, Andrew R. Canada/U.S. Automotive Trade and Trade-policy Issues. In *Fretz, D.; Stern, R. and Whalley, J.*, eds., 1985, pp. 278–332. [G: Canada; U.S.]

Morrison, Catherine J. Primal and Dual Capacity Utilization: An Application to Productivity Measurement in the U.S. Automobile Industry. *J. Bus. Econ. Statist.*, October 1985, *3*(4), pp. 312–24. [G: U.S.]

Mowery, David C. and Rosenberg, Nathan. Government Policy, Technical Change, and Industrial Structure: The U.S. and Japanese Commercial Aircraft Industries, 1945–1983. In *Langdon, R. and Rothwell, R.*, eds., 1985, pp. 73–102. [G: Japan]

Norsworthy, J. R. and Zabala, Craig A. Effects of Worker Attitudes on Production Costs and the Value of Capital Input. *Econ. J.*, December 1985, *95*(380), pp. 992–1002. [G: U.S.]

Norsworthy, J. R. and Zabala, Craig A. Worker Attitudes, Worker Behavior, and Productivity in the U.S. Automobile Industry, 1959–1976. *Ind. Lab. Relat. Rev.*, July 1985, *38*(4), pp. 544–57. [G: U.S.]

Odaka, Konosuke. Is the Division of Labor Limited by the Extent of the Market? A Study of Automobile Parts Production in East and Southeast Asia. In *Ohkawa, K. and Ranis, G.*, eds., 1985, pp. 389–425. [G: E. Asia; S.E. Asia]

Ollerenshaw, Philip. An Economic History of Ulster 1820–1939: Industry, 1820–1914. In *Kennedy, L. and Ollerenshaw, P.*, eds., 1985, pp. 62–108. [G: U.K.]

Ostry, Bernard. Canada/U.S. Automotive Trade and Trade-policy Issues: Comments. In *Fretz, D.; Stern, R. and Whalley, J.*, eds., 1985, pp. 338–40. [G: Canada; U.S.]

Parry, Thomas G. Protection and Employment in the Motor Car Sector: A Note. *Australian Econ. Pap.*, June 1985, *24*(44), pp. 222–24.

Rajalakshmi, K. Production Function Analysis of Public Sector Transport Equipment Industry in India. *Indian Econ. J.*, Oct.-Nov. 1985, *33*(2), pp. 17–33. [G: India]

Ramamurti, Ravi. High Technology Exports by State Enterprises in LDCs: The Brazilian Aircraft Industry. *Devel. Econ.*, September 1985, *23*(3), pp. 254–80. [G: Brazil]

Runyon, Marvin. The Americanization of Japanese Management. In *Federal Reserve Bank of Atlanta (I)*, 1985, pp. 15–23. [G: U.S.]

Salter, Malcolm S.; Webber, Alan M. and Dyer, Davis. U.S. Competitiveness in Global Industries: Lessons from the Auto Industry. In *Scott, B. R. and Lodge, G. C.*, eds., 1985, pp. 185–229. [G: U.S.; Selected OECD]

Savoie, Ernest J. The 1984 Auto Contract: A Management Perspective. In *Dennis, B. D.*, ed., 1985, pp. 458–64. [G: U.S.]

Schwartz, Arthur R. Discussion: The 1984 Auto Negotiations. In *Dennis, B. D.*, ed., 1985, pp. 466–68. [G: U.S.]

Staiger, Robert W. and Richardson, Barbara C. A Discounting Framework for Regulatory Impact Analysis. *Policy Sci.*, March 1985, *18*(1), pp. 33–54.

Svidén, Ove. Automobile Usage in a Future Information Society. In *Langdon, R. and Rothwell, R.*, eds., 1985, pp. 27–43. [G: Sweden]

Tolliday, Steven. Government, Employers and Shop Floor Organisation in the British Motor Industry, 1939–69. In *Tolliday, S. and Zeitlin, J.*, eds., 1985, pp. 108–47. [G: U.K.]

Williams, Harry B. Wages at Motor Vehicle Plants Outpaced Those at Parts Factories. *Mon. Lab. Rev.*, May 1985, *108*(5), pp. 38–40. [G: U.S.]

Woodworth, Warner. Saving Jobs through Worker Buyouts. In *Woodworth, W.; Meek, C. and Whyte, W. F.*, eds., 1985, pp. 221–41. [G: U.S.]

Young, Howard. The 1984 Auto Negotiations: A UAW Perspective. In *Dennis, B. D.*, ed., 1985, pp. 454–57. [G: U.S.]

6315 Chemicals, Drugs, Plastics, Ceramics, Glass, Cement, and Rubber

Al-Jarbou, Abdulaziz S. Basic Industries Development by SABIC: Eight Years' Experience. *J. Energy Devel.*, Spring 1985, *10*(2), pp. 193–99. [G: Saudi Arabia]

Baily, Martin Neil and Chakrabarti, Alok K. Innovation and Productivity in U.S. Industry. *Brookings Pap. Econ. Act.*, 1985, (2), pp. 609–32. [G: U.S.]

Berlin, Hans and Jönsson, Bengt. Market Life, Age Structure and Renewal—An Analysis of Pharmaceutical Specialities and Substances in Sweden 1960–82. *Managerial Dec. Econ.*, December 1985, *6*(4), pp. 246–56. [G: Sweden]

Bosworth, Derek and Westaway, A. J. The Theory and Measurement of Capital Utilisation and Its Role in Modelling Investment. In *Weiserbs, D.*, ed., 1985, pp. 291–317. [G: U.K.]

Bower, Joseph L. Restructuring Petrochemicals: A Comparative Study of Business and Government Strategy to Deal with a Declining Sector of the Economy. In *Scott, B. R. and Lodge, G. C., eds.*, 1985, pp. 263–300.   [G: U.S.; OECD]

Buatsi, Seth N.; Pradhan, Suresh and Apasu, Yao. Human Resources, Managerial Perceptions, and the Global Marketing Behavior of Firms. In *Kaynak, E., ed. (I)*, 1985, pp. 183–96.   [G: U.K.]

Buckingham, A. C. Rubber. In *Roberts, G., ed.*, 1985, pp. 116–20.   [G: Global]

Burstall, Michael and Dunning, John H. International Investment in Innovation. In *Wells, N., ed.*, 1985, pp. 185–97.   [G: OECD]

Culyer, Tony. Economic Aspects: Discussion. In *Wells, N., ed.*, 1985, pp. 218–24.

Cunliffe, Peter. Chemicals and Pharmaceuticals. In *Wells, N., ed.*, 1985, pp. 41–49.

Denis, Jean-Emile and Poirier, René. The North American Chemical Industry in the Tokyo Round: Participation of Canadian and American Firms in the GATT Negotiation Process. *J. World Trade Law*, July:Aug. 1985, *19*(4), pp. 315–42.   [G: Canada; U.S.]

Duggan, James E. and Clem, Andrew G. Input Prices and Cost Inflation in Three Manufacturing Industries. *Mon. Lab. Rev.*, May 1985, *108*(5), pp. 16–21.   [G: U.S.]

Evans, Peter B. Trends in United States Manufacturing Industry and Their Possible Implications for Latin American Industrialization: Case Studies of Steel, Electronics and Petrochemicals. *Industry Devel.*, 1985, (14), pp. 47–98.   [G: U.S.; Latin America]

Filippello, A. Nicholas. The U.S. Chemical Industry—Restructuring for the Future. *Bus. Econ.*, October 1985, *20*(4), pp. 44–49.   [G: U.S.]

Førsund, Finn R.; Hjalmarsson, Lennart and Eitrheim, Øyvind. An Intercountry Comparison of Cement Production: The Short-run Production Function Approach. In *[Johansen, L.]*, 1985, pp. 11–42.   [G: Norway; Sweden; Denmark; Finland]

Garvey, Tom. The Role of the European Community. In *Wells, N., ed.*, 1985, pp. 76–90.   [G: EEC]

Georgakopoulos, Theodore A. Indirect Taxes and Industrial Exports in Greece: The Case of Cement. *Greek Econ. Rev.*, December 1985, *7*(3), pp. 255–67.   [G: Greece]

Gereffi, Gary. The Global Pharmaceutical Industry and its Impact in Latin America. In *Newfarmer, R. S., ed.*, 1985, pp. 259–97.   [G: Latin America]

Gereffi, Gary. The Renegotiation of Dependency and the Limits of State Autonomy in Mexico (1975–1982.) In *Moran, T. H., ed.*, 1985, pp. 83–106.   [G: Mexico; Selected Countries]

Gieringer, Dale H. The Safety and Efficacy of New Drug Approval. *Cato J.*, Spring/Summer 1985, *5*(1), pp. 177–201.   [G: U.S.]

Gray, H. Peter and Walter, Ingo. Investment Incentives and Performance Requirements: The Petrochemical Industry. In *Guisinger, S. E., et al.*, 1985, pp. 237–312.   [G: Selected Countries]

Gunnarsson, Christer. Growth and Stagnation in the Malaysian Rubber Smallholder Industry. In *Lundahl, M., ed.*, 1985, pp. 152–78.   [G: Malaysia]

Halpern, Dan. Chemicals, Rubber and Plastics. In *Levinson, P. and Landau, P., eds.*, 1985, pp. 107–12.   [G: Israel]

Hansén, Sten-Olof. Finlands läkemedelsindustri—möjligheter och problem. (The Finnish Pharmaceutical Industry—Possibilities and Problems. With English summary.) *Ekon. Samfundets Tidskr.*, 1985, *38*(1), pp. 22–33.   [G: Finland]

Janet, C.; Gorse, P. and Bouquery, J. M. Le rôle des grandes entreprises diversifiées du pétrole et de la chimie dans la production alimentaire. (Activities of Big Petrochemical and Chemical Diversified Firms in Food Production. With English summary.) *Écon. Soc.*, July 1985, *19*(7), pp. 243–84.   [G: France; U.S.]

Jarrell, Gregg A. and Peltzman, Sam. The Impact of Product Recalls on the Wealth of Sellers. *J. Polit. Econ.*, June 1985, *93*(3), pp. 512–36.   [G: U.S.]

Katz, Eliakim; Rosenberg, J. and Zilberfarb, Ben-Zion. The Demand for Liquid Assets and Involvement in Exports; Some Empirical Results. *Empirical Econ.*, 1985, *10*(2), pp. 125–29.   [G: Israel]

Kaufer, Erich. Economic Aspects: Discussion. In *Wells, N., ed.*, 1985, pp. 225–27.

Kirim, Arman S. Reconsidering Patents and Economic Development: A Case Study of the Turkish Pharmaceutical Industry. *World Devel.*, February 1985, *13*(2), pp. 219–36.   [G: Turkey]

Kubursi, A. A. Industrialisation in the Arab States of the Gulf: A Ruhr without Water. In *Niblock, T. and Lawless, R., eds.*, 1985, pp. 42–65.   [G: OPEC]

Lall, Sanjaya. Appropriate Pharmaceutical Policies in Developing Countries. *Managerial Dec. Econ.*, December 1985, *6*(4), pp. 226–33.   [G: LDCs]

Lall, Sanjaya. Pharmaceuticals and the Third World Poor. In *Wells, N., ed.*, 1985, pp. 91–97.

Levin, Richard C. Innovation and Productivity in U.S. Industry: Comment. *Brookings Pap. Econ. Act.*, 1985, (2), pp. 633–37.   [G: U.S.]

Maddox, John. The Public and Anti-science. In *Wells, N., ed.*, 1985, pp. 133–42.

Mairesse, Jacques and Cunéo, Philippe. Recherche-développement et performances des entreprises: Une étude éeconométrique sur données individuelles. (Research-Development and Firm Performance: An Econometric Study on Individual Data. With English summary.) *Revue Écon.*, September 1985, *36*(5), pp. 1001–41.   [G: France]

Mariner, Wendy K. The Potential Impact of Pharmaceutical and Vaccine Litigation. In *Baily, M. A. and Cikins, W. I., eds.*, 1985, pp. 43–68.   [G: U.S.]

McRae, James J. and Tapon, Francis. Some Empirical Evidence on Post-patent Barriers to Entry in the Canadian Pharmaceutical Industry. *J. Health Econ.*, March 1985, *4*(1), pp. 43–61. **[G: Canada]**

Montel, Jean-Jacques. Essai de modélisation économétrique du marché pharmaceutique. Modèle de part de marché. (Pharmaceutical Market. Econometric Modelisation Test Market Share Model. With English summary.) *Écon. Soc.*, December 1985, *19*(12), pp. 33–69. **[G: France]**

Münnich, Frank. The International Scene for Pharmaceuticals: Discussion. In *Wells, N., ed.*, 1985, pp. 111–13.

Nelson, Daniel. Origins of the Sit-Down Era: Worker Militancy and Innovation in the Rubber Industry, 1934–1938. In *Leab, D. J., ed.*, 1985, pp. 333–60. **[G: U.S.]**

Owen, David. Pharmaceuticals among the Sunrise Industries: Speech to the Symposium Dinner. In *Wells, N., ed.*, 1985, pp. 1–9.

Pettigrew, Andrew M. Examining Change in the Long-term Context of Culture and Politics. In *Pennings, J. M., et al.*, 1985, pp. 269–318. **[G: U.K.]**

Prywes, Menahem. Quantity and Quality of Capital Impacts on Productivity in the Chemical Industry: An Empirical Study. In *Adams, F. G., ed.*, 1985, pp. 161–79. **[G: U.S.]**

Reekie, W. Duncan. Pharmaceutical Pricing and Profits. In *Wells, N., ed.*, 1985, pp. 198–209. **[G: OECD]**

Reekie, W. Duncan and Allen, D. E. Generic Substitution in the UK Pharmaceutical Industry: A Markovian Analysis. *Managerial Dec. Econ.*, June 1985, *6*(2), pp. 93–101. **[G: U.K.]**

Roemer, Peter. Supply of Fertilizers in Europe with Special Reference to the Federal Republic of Germany. *Statist. J.*, December 1985, *3*(4), pp. 381–98. **[G: W. Germany]**

Scherer, F. M. Post-patent Barriers to Entry in the Pharmaceutical Industry. *J. Health Econ.*, March 1985, *4*(1), pp. 83–87. **[G: OECD]**

Schwalbach, Joachim. Multi-plant Operation Economies in the West German Beer and Cement Industries. In *Schwalbach, J., ed.*, 1985, pp. 167–95. **[G: W. Germany]**

Scott, D. R. and Reekie, W. Duncan. Competition in Atomistic and Oligopsonistic Markets: The South African Pharmaceutical Industry. *S. Afr. J. Econ.*, March 1985, *53*(1), pp. 39–54. **[G: S. Africa]**

Smith, George Teeling. Politics and the Present Pattern. In *Wells, N., ed.*, 1985, pp. 64–75. **[G: OECD]**

Stewart, D. F. Options for Cement Production in Papua New Guinea: A Study in Choice of Technology. *World Devel.*, May 1985, *13*(5), pp. 639–51. **[G: Papua New Guinea]**

Taylor, David. The Role of the Consumer Movement, and Its Challenge to the British Pharmaceutical Industry. In *Wells, N., ed.*, 1985, pp. 120–32. **[G: U.K.]**

Weiner, Jonathan. Israeli Biotech Firms: An Overview. In *Levinson, P. and Landau, P., eds.*, 1985, pp. 83–86. **[G: Israel]**

Wells, Nicholas. Pharmaceuticals among the Sunrise Industries: Introduction. In *Wells, N., ed.*, 1985, pp. 10–17. **[G: U.K.]**

Wescoe, Clarke. Factors in Pharmaceutical Investment. In *Wells, N., ed.*, 1985, pp. 210–17.

West, Peter J. International Expansion and Concentration of Tire Industry and Implications for Latin America. In *Newfarmer, R. S., ed.*, 1985, pp. 227–58. **[G: U.S.; OECD]**

Wing, Ron. Prospects for the 1990s. In *Wells, N., ed.*, 1985, pp. 98–107.

6316 Textiles, Leather, and Clothing

Anderson, Joan B. and Frantz, Roger S. Production Efficiency among Mexican Apparel Assembly Plants. *J. Devel. Areas*, April 1985, *19*(3), pp. 369–77. **[G: Mexico]**

Arpan, Jeffrey S. and Toyne, Brian. The U.S. Textile Industry: International Challenges and Strategies. In *Hochmuth, M. and Davidson, W., eds.*, 1985, pp. 263–92. **[G: Selected Countries]**

Baily, Martin Neil and Chakrabarti, Alok K. Innovation and Productivity in U.S. Industry. *Brookings Pap. Econ. Act.*, 1985, (2), pp. 609–32. **[G: U.S.]**

Bakht, Zaid. Handloom Industry in Bangladesh: A Review of Prospects and Problems. In *Mukhopadhyay, S. and Chee, P. L., eds. (II)*, 1985, pp. 357–88. **[G: Bangladesh]**

Danilin, V. I., et al. Measuring Enterprise Efficiency in the Soviet Union: A Stochastic Frontier Analysis. *Economica*, May 1985, *52*(206), pp. 225–33. **[G: U.S.S.R.]**

Das, Dilip K. Dismantling the Multifibre Arrangement? *J. World Trade Law*, January: February 1985, *19*(1), pp. 67–80. **[G: Global]**

Ebner, Michael H. The Passaic Strike of 1912 and the Two I.W.W.s. In *Leab, D. J., ed.*, 1985, pp. 254–68. **[G: U.S.]**

Fabella, Raul V. The Handloom Weaving Industry in La Union. In *Mukhopadhyay, S. and Chee, P. L., eds. (II)*, 1985, pp. 389–417. **[G: Philippines]**

Flaherty, Diane. Labor Control in the British Boot and Shoe Industry. *Ind. Relat.*, Fall 1985, *24*(3), pp. 339–59. **[G: U.K.]**

Halpern, Dan. The Clothing and Textile Industry. In *Levinson, P. and Landau, P., eds.*, 1985, pp. 113–14. **[G: Israel]**

Hamilton, Carl. Follies of Policies for Textile Imports in Western Europe. *World Econ.*, September 1985, *8*(3), pp. 219–34. **[G: W. Europe]**

Hoffman, Kurt. Clothing, Chips and Competitive Advantage: The Impact of Microelectronics on Trade and Production in the Garment Industry. *World Devel.*, March 1985, *13*(3), pp. 371–92. **[G: LDCs]**

Johnson, Merrill L. Postwar Industrial Development in the Southeast and the Pioneer Role of Labor-intensive Industry. *Econ. Geogr.*, January 1985, *61*(1), pp. 46–65. **[G: U.S.]**

Kibria, Muhammad G. and Tisdell, Clement A.

Operating Capital and Productivity Patterns in Jute Weaving in Bangladesh. *J. Devel. Econ.*, May–June 1985, *18*(1), pp. 133–52.
[G: Bangladesh]

Kibria, Muhammad G. and Tisdell, Clement A. Productivity Progress Parameters for Manufacturing in an LDC: The Startup or Learning Phase in Bangladesh Jute Mills. *Australian Econ. Pap.*, December 1985, *24*(45), pp. 370–79.
[G: Bangladesh]

Kibria, Muhammad G. and Tisdell, Clement A. Productivity, Progress and Learning: The Case of Jute Spinning in Bangladesh. *World Devel.*, Oct./Nov. 1985, *13*(10/11), pp. 1151–61.
[G: Bangladesh]

Lazonick, William and Brush, Thomas. The "Horndal Effect" in Early U.S. Manufacturing. *Exploration Econ. Hist.*, January 1985, *22*(1), pp. 53–96.
[G: U.S.]

Levin, Richard C. Innovation and Productivity in U.S. Industry: Comment. *Brookings Pap. Econ. Act.*, 1985, (2), pp. 633–37.
[G: U.S.]

Lloyd, P. J. The Australian Textile and Clothing Industry Group: Untoward Effects of Government Intervention. In *Jungenfelt, K. and Hague, D. [Sir], eds.*, 1985, pp. 485–522.
[G: Australia]

Lyons, John S. Vertical Integration in the British Cotton Industry, 1825–1850: A Revision. *J. Econ. Hist.*, June 1985, *45*(2), pp. 419–25.
[G: U.K.]

Mytelka, Lynn Krieger. Stimulating Effective Technology Transfer: The Case of Textiles in Africa. In *Rosenberg, N. and Frischtak, C., eds.*, 1985, pp. 77–126.
[G: Ivory Coast; Kenya; Nigeria; Tanzania]

Nehmer, Stanley and Love, Mark W. Textiles and Apparel: A Negotiated Approach to International Competition. In *Scott, B. R. and Lodge, G. C., eds.*, 1985, pp. 230–62.
[G: U.S.]

Ollerenshaw, Philip. An Economic History of Ulster 1820–1939: Industry, 1820–1914. In *Kennedy, L. and Ollerenshaw, P., eds.*, 1985, pp. 62–108.
[G: U.K.]

Phillips, William H. Southern Textile Mill Villages on the Eve of World War II: The Courtenay Mill of South Carolina. *J. Econ. Hist.*, June 1985, *45*(2), pp. 269–75.
[G: U.S.]

Ranis, Gustav and Saxonhouse, Gary R. Determinants of Technology Choice: The Indian and Japanese Cotton Industries. In *Ohkawa, K. and Ranis, G., eds.*, 1985, pp. 135–54.
[G: India; Japan]

Ray, Arthur J. Buying and Selling Hudson's Bay Company Furs in the Eighteenth Century. In *[Spry, I. M.]*, 1985, pp. 95–115.
[G: Canada]

Santos, Michael W. Community and Communism: The 1928 New Bedford Textile Strike. *Labor Hist.*, Spring 1985, *26*(2), pp. 230–49.
[G: U.S.]

Sarkar, Swapna and Sarkar, Debjani. A Study of Investment in the Jute Manufacturing Industry. *Indian Econ. J.*, Oct.-Nov. 1985, *33*(2), pp. 57–68.
[G: India]

Saxonhouse, Gary R. Technology Choice in Cotton Textile Manufacturing. In *Ohkawa, K. and Ranis, G., eds.*, 1985, pp. 212–35.
[G: Selected Countries]

Saxonhouse, Gary R. and Kiyokawa, Yukihiko. Supply and Demand for Quality Workers in Cotton Spinning in Japan and India. In *Ohkawa, K. and Ranis, G., eds.*, 1985, pp. 177–211.
[G: Japan; India]

Saxonhouse, Gary R. and Ranis, Gustav. Technology Choice and the Quality Dimension in the Japanese Cotton Textile Industry. In *Ohkawa, K. and Ranis, G., eds.*, 1985, pp. 155–76.
[G: Japan]

Shepherd, Geoffrey. Industrial Restructuring: The European Textile Industry. *Rev. Econ. Ind.*, 1st Trimester 1985, (31), pp. 68–78.
[G: EEC]

Sloan, Judith. The Regional Dimension of Structural Change: The Case of Textiles, Clothing and Footwear. *Australian Bull. Lab.*, December 1985, *12*(1), pp. 46–56.
[G: Australia]

Tussie, Diana. El GATT y el comercio Norte-Sur: el caso del sector textil. (With English summary.) *Desarrollo Econ.*, April–June 1985, *25*(97), pp. 85–106.
[G: Global]

Urdank, Albion M. Economic Decline in the English Industrial Revolution: The Gloucester Wool Trade, 1800–1840. *J. Econ. Hist.*, June 1985, *45*(2), pp. 427–33.
[G: U.K.]

Verma, P. C. Production Structure of Jute Industry in India. *Indian Econ. J.*, Oct.-Nov. 1985, *33*(2), pp. 123–30.
[G: India]

Viscusi, W. Kip. Cotton Dust Regulation: An OSHA Success Story? *J. Policy Anal. Manage.*, Spring 1985, *4*(3), pp. 325–43.
[G: U.S.]

Waldinger, Roger. Immigration and Industrial Change in the New York City Apparel Industry. In *Borjas, G. J. and Tienda, M., eds.*, 1985, pp. 323–49.
[G: U.S.]

Wolf, Martin. How to Unravel the Multi-fibre Arrangement. *World Econ.*, September 1985, *8*(3), pp. 235–48.
[G: Global]

Yamazawa, Ippei and Tambunlertchai, Somsak. Manufactured Exports and Developing Countries: The Thai Textile Industry and the Japanese Experience. In *Ohkawa, K. and Ranis, G., eds.*, 1985, pp. 369–88.
[G: Thailand; Japan]

6317 Forest Products, Lumber, Paper, and Printing and Publishing

Ahvenainen, Jorma. The Competitive Position of the Finnish Sawmill Industry in the 1920s and 1930s. *Scand. Econ. Hist. Rev.*, 1985, *33*(3), pp. 173–92.
[G: Finland]

Artto, Eero. Kilpailukyvystä ja siihen vaikuttavista tekijöistä. Tarkastelun kohteina paperiteollisuus ja kauppakorkeakoulu. (Competitiveness of Finnish Paper Industry and Competitiveness of Schools of Economics. With English summary.) *Liiketaloudellinen Aikak.*, 1985, *34*(4), pp. 411–21.
[G: Finland]

Brand, Horst and Bennett, Norman. Productivity Trends in Kitchen Cabinet Manufacturing.

Mon. Lab. Rev., March 1985, *108*(3), pp. 24–30. [G: U.S.]

Dasgupta, Ajit K. and Murty, M. N. Economic Evaluation of Water Pollution Abatement: A Case Study of Paper and Pulp Industry in India. *Indian Econ. Rev.*, July-Dec. 1985, *20*(2), pp. 231–67. [G: India]

Deacon, Robert T. The Simple Analytics of Forest Economics. In *Deacon, R. T. and Johnson, M. B., eds.*, 1985, pp. 275–302. [G: U.S.]

Dowdle, Barney and Hanke, Steve H. Public Timber Policy and the Wood-Products Industry. In *Deacon, R. T. and Johnson, M. B., eds.*, 1985, pp. 77–102. [G: U.S.]

Edquist, Andrew and Morris, Paul. Long-term Projections of the Consumption of Paper and Paper Products in Australia. *Rev. Marketing Agr. Econ.*, December 1985, *53*(3), pp. 157–71. [G: Australia]

Gilless, James Keith and Buongiorno, Joseph. Simulation of Future Trade in Wood Pulp between Canada and the United States. *Ann. Reg. Sci.*, July 1985, *19*(2), pp. 47–60. [G: U.S.; Canada]

Helmar, Michael D. and Yanagida, John F. Effects of Restrictions on Softwood Lumber and Plywood Trade in the Pacific Basin: Application of the Spatial Temporal Forest Products (STFP) Model. *J. Econ. Devel.*, December 1985, *10*(2), pp. 143–59. [G: U.S.; Canada; Japan]

Ilmakunnas, Pekka. Identification and Estimation of the Degree of Oligopoly Power in Industries Facing Domestic and Import Competition. In *Schwalbach, J., ed.*, 1985, pp. 287–308. [G: W. Germany]

Johnson, Ronald N. U.S. Forest Service Policy and Its Budget. In *Deacon, R. T. and Johnson, M. B., eds.*, 1985, pp. 103–33. [G: U.S.]

Kuuluvainen, Jari. Sahatukin kysyntä ja tarjonta Suomessa Ekonometrinen lyhyen aikavälin tarkastelu 1962–1981. (Demand for and Supply of Sawlogs in Finland. An Econometric Short Term Analysis, 1962–1981. With English summary.) *Kansant. Aikak.*, 1985, *81*(2), pp. 177–78. [G: Finland]

Liebowitz, S. J. Copying and Indirect Appropriability: Photocopying of Journals. *J. Polit. Econ.*, October 1985, *93*(5), pp. 945–57. [G: U.S.]

Löfgren, Karl-Gustaf. The Pricing of Pulpwood and Spatial Price Discrimination: Theory and Practice. *Europ. Rev. Agr. Econ.*, 1985, *12*(3), pp. 283–94.

Loikkanen, Heikki A.; Kuuluvainen, Jari and Salo, Jorma. Hintatekijät ja yksityismetsänomistajien ominaisuudet puuntarjontakäyttäytymisen selittäjinä: alustavia tuloksia. (Stumpage Prices and Owner Characteristics as Determinants of Timber Supply from Private Nonindustrial Forests: Preliminary Evidence form Finland. With English summary.) *Kansant. Aikak.*, 1985, *81*(2), pp. 189–216. [G: Finland]

Maki, Dennis R. Output Losses Due to Strikes: The Case of Sawmills in British Columbia. *Empirical Econ.*, 1985, *10*(2), pp. 121–24. [G: Canada]

Merrifield, David E. Imputed Rental Prices and Capital Stock Estimates for Equipment and Structures in the U.S. Lumber and Plywood Industries. *Appl. Econ.*, April 1985, *17*(2), pp. 243–56. [G: U.S.]

Merrifield, David E. and Haynes, Richard W. A Cost Analysis of the Lumber and Plywood Industries in Two Pacific Northwest Sub-regions. *Ann. Reg. Sci.*, November 1985, *19*(3), pp. 16–33. [G: U.S.]

Muraoka, Dennis D. and Watson, Richard B. Economic Issues in Federal Timber Sale Procedures. In *Deacon, R. T. and Johnson, M. B., eds.*, 1985, pp. 201–23. [G: U.S.]

Rosenband, Leonard N. Productivity and Labor Discipline in the Montgolfier Paper Mill, 1780–1805. *J. Econ. Hist.*, June 1985, *45*(2), pp. 435–43. [G: France]

Salmi, Timo; Dahlstedt, Roy and Luoma, Martti. Improving Firm-level Growth Estimates by Eliminating Cycles. *Liiketaloudellinen Aikak.*, 1985, *34*(4), pp. 383–410. [G: Finland]

Sandor, Richard L. Creation of a Plywood Futures Contract. In *Yamey, B. S.; Sandor, R. L. and Hindley, B.*, 1985, pp. 39–64. [G: U.S.]

Wallace, M. Long-term Projections of Wood-Based Panel Consumption in Australia. *Rev. Marketing Agr. Econ.*, December 1985, *53*(3), pp. 173–83. [G: Australia]

6318 Food Processing, Tobacco, and Beverages

Baker, Jonathan B. and Bresnahan, Timothy F. The Gains from Merger or Collusion in Product-Differentiated Industries. In *Geroski, P. A.; Phlips, L. and Ulph, A., eds.*, 1985, pp. 59–76. [G: U.S.]

Bingley, Pam; Burton, Michael and Strak, John. Inter- and Intra-sectoral Effects of Milk Quotas in the U.K. Milk Industry. *Europ. Rev. Agr. Econ.*, 1985, *12*(4), pp. 411–30. [G: U.K.]

Bishop, John A. and Yoo, Jang H. "Health Scare," Excise Taxes and Advertising Ban in the Cigarette Demand and Supply. *Southern Econ. J.*, October 1985, *52*(2), pp. 402–11. [G: U.S.]

Boussard, Jean Marc. Milk Quotas: Introduction. *Europ. Rev. Agr. Econ.*, 1985, *12*(4), pp. 325–33. [G: EEC]

Brown, Martin and Philips, Peter. The Evolution of Labor Market Structure: The California Canning Industry. *Ind. Lab. Relat. Rev.*, April 1985, *38*(3), pp. 392–407. [G: U.S.]

Bryan, Patrick E. The Question of Labor in the Sugar Industry of the Dominican Republic in the Late Nineteenth and Early Twentieth Centuries. In *Moreno Franginals, M.; Moya Pons, F. and Engerman, S. L., eds.*, 1985, pp. 235–51. [G: Dominican Republic]

Burrell, Alison. Price Uncertainty under EC Milk Quotas. *Europ. Rev. Agr. Econ.*, 1985, *12*(4), pp. 335–50. [G: EEC]

Burton, Michael. The Implementation of the EC Milk Quota. *Europ. Rev. Agr. Econ.*, 1985, *12*(4), pp. 461–71. [G: EEC]

del Castillo, José. The Formation of the Dominican Sugar Industry: From Competition to Monopoly, from National Semiproletariat to Foreign Proletariat. In *Moreno Franginals, M.; Moya Pons, F. and Engerman, S. L., eds.,* 1985, pp. 215–34. **[G: Dominican Republic]**

Cieślik, Jerzy. Food-processing Contracts with Developing Countries. *J. World Trade Law,* July:Aug. 1985, *19*(4), pp. 387–402.
[G: Selected LDCs]

Cioffi, Antonio, et al. An Evaluation of the Effects of the EC Quota System on the Italian Dairy Market. *Europ. Rev. Agr. Econ.,* 1985, *12*(4), pp. 389–400. **[G: Italy]**

Clark, Don P. Protection and Developing Country Exports: The Case of Vegetable Oils. *J. Econ. Stud.,* 1985, *12*(5), pp. 3–18.
[G: LDCs]

Cottino, A. and Morgan, Paul. Alcohol Policies: Italy. In *Grant, M., ed.,* 1985, pp. 83–92.
[G: Italy]

Culbertson, John D. and Mueller, Williard E. The Influence of Market Structure on Technological Performance in the Food-manufacturing Industries. *Rev. Ind. Organ.,* 1985, *2*(1), pp. 40–54. **[G: U.S.]**

van der Giessen, Leen B. and Post, Jaap H. Macro- and Micro-effects of the Super Levy in the Netherlands. *Europ. Rev. Agr. Econ.,* 1985, *12*(4), pp. 449–60. **[G: Netherlands]**

Gisser, Micha. Welfare Implications of Oligopoly in U.S. Food Manufacturing: Reply. *Amer. J. Agr. Econ.,* February 1985, *67*(1), pp. 146.
[G: U.S.]

Grant, M. Establishing Priorities for Action. In *Grant, M., ed.,* 1985, pp. 1–8.
[G: W. Europe]

Hallagan, William S. Contracting Problems and the Adoption of Regulatory Cartels. *Econ. Inquiry,* January 1985, *23*(1), pp. 37–56.
[G: U.S.]

Halpern, Dan. Israel's Food Industry. In *Levinson, P. and Landau, P., eds.,* 1985, pp. 124–26. **[G: Israel]**

Hattwick, Richard E. Gustavus Franklin Swift. *J. Behav. Econ.,* Summer 1985, *14*(2), pp. 131–53. **[G: U.S.]**

Henry, Mark S. and Schluter, Gerald. Measuring Backward and Forward Linkages in the U.S. Food and Fiber System. *Agr. Econ. Res.,* Fall 1985, *37*(4), pp. 33–39. **[G: U.S.]**

van Iwaarden, M. J. Public Health Aspects of the Marketing of Alcoholic Drinks. In *Grant, M., ed.,* 1985, pp. 45–55. **[G: Netherlands]**

Kelton, Christina M. L. Earnings Behavior in Food and Tobacco Manufacturing. *Rev. Ind. Organ.,* 1985, *2*(3), pp. 266–91. **[G: U.S.]**

Kenney, Genevieve M. Welfare Implications of Oligopoly in U.S. Food Manufacturing: Comment. *Amer. J. Agr. Econ.,* February 1985, *67*(1), pp. 144–45. **[G: U.S.]**

Klein, Herbert S. and Engerman, Stanley L. The Transition from Slave to Free Labor: Notes on a Comparative Economic Model. In *Moreno Franginals, M.; Moya Pons, F. and Engerman, S. L., eds.,* 1985, pp. 255–69.
[G: Caribbean; Brazil; U.S.]

Knight, Franklin W. Jamaican Migrants and the Cuban Sugar Industry, 1900–1934. In *Moreno Franginals, M.; Moya Pons, F. and Engerman, S. L., eds.,* 1985, pp. 94–114. **[G: Jamaica; Cuba]**

Lock, J. D. Measuring the Value of the Capital Stock by Direct Observation. *Rev. Income Wealth,* June 1985, *31*(2), pp. 127–38.
[G: Netherlands]

Lopez, Ramon E. Supply Response and Investment in the Canadian Food Processing Industry. *Amer. J. Agr. Econ.,* February 1985, *67*(1), pp. 40–48. **[G: Canada]**

Lynk, William J. The Price and Output of Beer Revisited [Interpreting Rising Concentration: The Case of Beer]. *J. Bus.,* October 1985, *58*(4), pp. 433–37. **[G: U.S.]**

Mackie, J. A. C. The Changing Political Economy of an Export Crop: The Case of Jember's Tobacco Industry. *Bull. Indonesian Econ. Stud.,* April 1985, *21*(1), pp. 112–39. **[G: Indonesia]**

Mäkelä, K. Alcohol Policies: Lessons from the Postwar Period. In *Grant, M., ed.,* 1985, pp. 9–22. **[G: Zambia; Mexico; U.K.]**

Mason, R. Hal. Investment Incentives and Performance Requirements: The International Food Processing Industry. In *Guisinger, S. E., et al.,* 1985, pp. 56–95.
[G: Selected Countries]

Mattei, Andrés A. Ramos. Technical Innovations and Social Change in the Sugar Industry of Puerto Rico, 1870–1880. In *Moreno Franginals, M.; Moya Pons, F. and Engerman, S. L., eds.,* 1985, pp. 158–78. **[G: Puerto Rico]**

Meagher, G. A., et al. ORANI-WINE: Tax Issues and the Australian Wine Industry. *Rev. Marketing Agr. Econ.,* August 1985, *53*(2), pp. 47–62. **[G: Australia]**

Meagher, G. A., et al. Special Purpose Versions of a General Purpose Multisectoral Model: Tax Issues and the Australian Wine Industry. In *Piggott, J. and Whalley, J., eds.,* 1985, pp. 283–92. **[G: Australia]**

Meek, Christopher and Woodworth, Warner. Worker–Community Collaboration and Ownership. In *Woodworth, W.; Meek, C. and Whyte, W. F., eds.,* 1985, pp. 195–220.
[G: U.S.]

Munk, Knud Jorgen. The Effect of Changes in Prices and Quotas: An Example of the Use of an Agricultural Sector Model Based on the Johansen Approach. *Europ. Rev. Agr. Econ.,* 1985, *12*(4), pp. 365–80. **[G: EEC]**

Muysken, Joan. Estimation of the Capacity Distribution of an Industry: The Swedish Dairy Industry 1964–1973. In *[Johansen, L.],* 1985, pp. 43–63. **[G: Sweden]**

Nowak, Jan and Romanowska, Hanna. Locational Patterns of the Food-Processing Industry in Poland. *Europ. Rev. Agr. Econ.,* 1985, *12*(3), pp. 233–46. **[G: Poland]**

Oskam, Arie J. A Super-Levy System for the Dairy Sector: Consequences and Alternatives. *Europ. Rev. Agr. Econ.,* 1985, *12*(4), pp. 431–48. **[G: EEC]**

Radfar, Mehran. The Effect of Advertising on

Total Consumption of Cigarettes in the U.K.: A Comment. *Europ. Econ. Rev.*, November 1985, *29*(2), pp. 225–31. [G: U.K.]

Ranada, Julie G. The Price Responsiveness of Energy Demand in the Philippine Food Processing Sector. *Philippine Rev. Econ. Bus.*, Sept./Dec. 1985, *22*(3/4), pp. 229–46. [G: Philippines]

Rasmussen, Svend and Nielsen, A. Hjortshøj. The Impact of Quotas on the Optimal Adjustment of Milk Production at the Farm Level. *Europ. Rev. Agr. Econ.*, 1985, *12*(4), pp. 351–64. [G: EEC]

Rieder, Peter. Experience with the Milk Quota System in Switzerland. *Europ. Rev. Agr. Econ.*, 1985, *12*(4), pp. 473–79. [G: Switzerland]

Sappington, David E. M. and Wernerfelt, Birger. To Brand or Not to Brand? A Theoretical and Empirical Question. *J. Bus.*, July 1985, *58*(3), pp. 279–93. [G: U.S.]

Sarmad, Khwaja. Evaluating the Operational Performance of Manufacturing Enterprises: An Evaluation Framework and Application to Pakistani Industry: Comments. *Pakistan Devel. Rev.*, Autumn-Winter 1985, *24*(3/4), pp. 718–19. [G: Pakistan]

Schmalensee, Richard. Econometric Diagnosis of Competitive Localization. *Int. J. Ind. Organ.*, March 1985, *3*(1), pp. 57–70. [G: U.S.]

Schneider, Dorothee. The New York Cigarmakers Strike of 1877. *Labor Hist.*, Summer 1985, *26*(3), pp. 325–52. [G: U.S.]

Schwalbach, Joachim. Multi-plant Operation Economies in the West German Beer and Cement Industries. In *Schwalbach, J., ed.*, 1985, pp. 167–95. [G: W. Germany]

Scott, Christopher D. Transnational Corporations, Comparative Advantage and Food Security in Latin America. In *Abel, C. and Lewis, C. M., eds.*, 1985, pp. 482–99. [G: Latin America]

Shaikh, Abdul Hafeez. Evaluating the Operational Performance of Manufacturing Enterprises: An Evaluation Framework and Application to Pakistani Industry. *Pakistan Devel. Rev.*, Autumn-Winter 1985, *24*(3/4), pp. 703–17. [G: Pakistan]

Shepherd, Philip L. Transnational Corporations and the International Cigarette Industry. In *Newfarmer, R. S., ed.*, 1985, pp. 63–112. [G: Selected Countries; U.S.]

Smith, J. Barry and Sims, W. A. The Impact of Pollution Charges on Productivity Growth in Canadian Brewing. *Rand J. Econ.*, Autumn 1985, *16*(3), pp. 410–23. [G: Canada]

Sullivan, Daniel. Testing Hypotheses about Firm Behavior in the Cigarette Industry. *J. Polit. Econ.*, June 1985, *93*(3), pp. 586–98. [G: U.S.]

Sumner, Daniel A. and Wohlgenant, Michael K. Effects of an Increase in the Federal Excise Tax on Cigarettes. *Amer. J. Agr. Econ.*, May 1985, *67*(2), pp. 235–42. [G: U.S.]

Thomson, Kenneth J. and Hubbard, Lionel J. Budgetary and Financial Effects of the EC Milk Quota System. *Europ. Rev. Agr. Econ.*, 1985, *12*(4), pp. 381–88. [G: EEC]

Tremblay, Victor J. A Reappraisal of Interpreting Rising Concentration: The Case of Beer. *J. Bus.*, October 1985, *58*(4), pp. 419–31. [G: U.S.]

Tremblay, Victor J. Strategic Groups and the Demand for Beer. *J. Ind. Econ.*, December 1985, *34*(2), pp. 183–98. [G: U.S.]

Walsh, B. M. Production of and International Trade in Alcoholic Drinks: Possible Public Health Implications. In *Grant, M., ed.*, 1985, pp. 23–44. [G: Global]

Whiting, Van R., Jr. Transnational Enterprise in the Food Processing Industry. In *Newfarmer, R. S., ed.*, 1985, pp. 343–83. [G: Mexico]

Wood, C. Martin, III. Optimizing the Decentralized Approach. In *Federal Reserve Bank of Atlanta (I)*, 1985, pp. 25–30. [G: U.S.]

Yfantopoulos, J. N. Alcohol Policies: Greece. In *Grant, M., ed.*, 1985, pp. 92–109. [G: Greece]

6319 Other Industries

Ariovich, G. The Economics of Diamond Price Movements. *Managerial Dec. Econ.*, December 1985, *6*(4), pp. 234–40. [G: Global]

Davies, Alun C. Rural Clockmaking in Eighteenth-Century Wales: Samuel Roberts of Llanfair Caereinion, 1755–1774. *Bus. Hist. Rev.*, Spring 1985, *59*(1), pp. 49–75. [G: U.K.]

Kornblith, Gary J. The Craftsman as Industrialist: Jonas Chickering and the Transformation of American Piano Making. *Bus. Hist. Rev.*, Autumn 1985, *59*(3), pp. 349–68. [G: U.S.]

Opaluch, James J. and Kashmanian, Richard M. Assessing the Viability of Marketable Permit Systems: An Application in Hazardous Waste Management. *Land Econ.*, August 1985, *61*(3), pp. 263–71. [G: U.S.]

Veloce, William and Zellner, Arnold. Entry and Empirical Demand and Supply Analysis for Competitive Industries. *J. Econometrics*, Oct./Nov. 1985, *30*(1/2), pp. 459–71. [G: Canada]

632 Industry Studies: Extractive Industries

6320 General

Brennan, Michael J. and Schwartz, Eduardo S. Evaluating Natural Resource Investments. *J. Bus.*, April 1985, *58*(2), pp. 135–57. [G: U.S.]

Crommelin, Michael. The Mineral Exploration and Production Regime within the Federal System. In *Drysdale, P. and Shibata, H., eds.*, 1985, pp. 90–104. [G: Australia]

Dienes, Leslie. The Energy System and Economic Imbalances in the USSR. *Soviet Econ.*, Oct.-Dec. 1985, *1*(4), pp. 340–72. [G: U.S.S.R.]

Emerson, Craig. Mining Taxation in Malaysia. *Singapore Econ. Rev.*, April 1985, *30*(1), pp. 34–55. [G: Malaysia]

Murakami, Katsutoshi and Nawashiro, Aoi. Issues and Problems in U.S.–Japan Energy Relations. In *Nanto, D. K., ed.*, 1985, pp. 102–13. [G: Japan; U.S.]

Reddy, Nallapu N. Market Boundaries between Coal, Oil, and Natural Gas. *Rev. Ind. Organ.*, 1985, 2(3), pp. 300–305. [G: U.S.]

Sakurai, Makoto. A Japanese Perspective on Resource Trade with Australia. In *Drysdale, P. and Shibata, H., eds.*, 1985, pp. 177–89. [G: Australia; Japan]

Shafer, Michael. Capturing the Mineral Multinationals: Advantage or Disadvantage? In *Moran, T. H., ed.*, 1985, pp. 25–53. [G: Zaire; Zambia]

Stollery, Kenneth R. Environmental Controls in Extractive Industries. *Land Econ.*, May 1985, 61(2), pp. 136–44.

Vernon, Raymond. Uncertainty in the Resource Industries: The Special Role of State-Owned Enterprises. In *Vernon, R.*, 1985, pp. 133–48. [G: LDCs]

Weiner, Jonathan. Israeli Energy Firms. In *Levinson, P. and Landau, P., eds.*, 1985, pp. 99–101. [G: Israel]

Yang, Chin-Wei and Labys, Walter C. A Sensitivity Analysis of the Linear Complementarity Programming Model: Appalachian Steam Coal and the Natural Gas Market. *Energy Econ.*, July 1985, 7(3), pp. 145–52. [G: U.S.]

6322 Mining (metal, coal, and other nonmetallic minerals)

Anderson, David L. Market Power and the Saskatchewan Potash Industry. *Can. Public Policy*, Supplement July 1985, 11(3), pp. 321–28. [G: Canada]

Appleton, William C. and Baker, Joe G. Unionization and Safety in Bituminous Deep Mines: Reply. *J. Lab. Res.*, Spring 1985, 6(2), pp. 217–20. [G: U.S.]

Ariovich, G. The Economics of Diamond Price Movements. *Managerial Dec. Econ.*, December 1985, 6(4), pp. 234–40. [G: Global]

Armstrong, Robert. The Quebec Asbestos Industry: Technological Change, 1878–1929. In *[Spry, I. M.]*, 1985, pp. 189–210. [G: Canada]

Ault, David E. and Rutman, Gilbert L. The Rural African and Gold Mining in Southern Africa, 1976–1980. *S. Afr. J. Econ.*, March 1985, 53(1), pp. 1–23. [G: S. Africa]

Becker, David G. Nonferrous Metals, Class Formation, and the State in Peru. In *Evans, P.; Rueschemeyer, D. and Stephens, E. H., eds.*, 1985, pp. 67–89. [G: Peru]

Bennett, James D. and Passmore, David L. Unions and Coal Mine Safety: Comment [The Effect of Unionization on Safety in Bituminous Deep Mines]. *J. Lab. Res.*, Spring 1985, 6(2), pp. 211–16. [G: U.S.]

Bradley, Paul G. Has the 'Economics of Exhaustible Resources' Advanced the Economics of Mining? In *Scott, A., ed.*, 1985, pp. 317–29. [G: Canada]

Braeutigam, Ronald R. Efficient Pricing with Rivalry between a Railroad and a Pipeline. In *Daughety, A. F., ed.*, 1985, pp. 207–20.

Brown, Gardner, Jr. Has the 'Economics of Exhaustible Resources' Advanced the Economics of Mining?: Comment. In *Scott, A., ed.*, 1985, pp. 329–33. [G: Canada]

Burns, Alan; Newby, Martin and Winterton, Jonathan. The Restructuring of the British Coal Industry. *Cambridge J. Econ.*, March 1985, 9(1), pp. 93–110. [G: U.K.]

Butler, Tom. Gold. In *Roberts, G., ed.*, 1985, pp. 84–89. [G: Global]

Cairns, Robert D. Nickel Depletion and Pricing: Further Considerations [User Costs versus Markups as Determinants of Prices in the Nickel Industry: Reply]. *J. Environ. Econ. Manage.*, December 1985, 12(4), pp. 395–96. [G: U.S.]

Campbell, Adrian and Warner, Malcolm. Changes in the Balance of Power in the British Mineworkers' Union: An Analysis of National Top-Office Elections, 1974–84. *Brit. J. Ind. Relat.*, March 1985, 23(1), pp. 1–24. [G: U.K.]

Campbell, Harry F. and Wrean, Douglas L. Deriving the Long-run Supply Curve for a Competitive Mining Industry: The Case of Saskatchewan Uranium. In *Scott, A., ed.*, 1985, pp. 290–309. [G: Canada]

Carruth, Alan A. and Oswald, Andrew J. Miners' Wages in Post-war Britain: An Application of a Model of Trade Union Behaviour. *Econ. J.*, December 1985, 95(380), pp. 1003–20. [G: U.K.]

Cloete, S. A. A Note on State Assistance to Marginal Gold Mines. *S. Afr. J. Econ.*, December 1985, 53(4), pp. 424–28. [G: S. Africa]

Cloete, S. A. The Structure of the International Supply of Coal—A Qualitative View. *J. Stud. Econ. Econometrics*, March 1985, (21), pp. 67–102.

Curzio, Alberto Quadrio. Dal rifiuto del numerario aureo ai prezzi quasi-ufficiali dell'oro. (From the Rejection of the Gold-Numeraire to Quasi-official Gold Prices. With English summary.) *Rivista Int. Sci. Econ. Com.*, Oct.-Nov. 1985, 32(10–11), pp. 965–87. [G: Global]

DePape, Denis. Alternatives to Single Project Mining Communities: A Critical Assessment. *Can. J. Agr. Econ.*, August 1985, 32, pp. 100–113. [G: Canada]

Dick, Rolf. Deep-Sea Mining versus Land-Based Mining: A Cost Comparison. In *Donges, J. B., ed.*, 1985, pp. 2–60. [G: U.S.]

Dow, Alexander. Prometheus in Canada: The Expansion of Metal Mining, 1900–1950. In *[Spry, I. M.]*, 1985, pp. 211–28. [G: Canada]

Edwards, Christine and Heery, Edmund. Formality and Informality in the Working of the National Coal Board's Incentive Scheme. *Brit. J. Ind. Relat.*, March 1985, 23(1), pp. 25–45. [G: U.K.]

Evan-Zohar, Chaim. The Diamond Industry. In

Levinson, P. and Landau, P., eds., 1985, pp. 90–93.   [G: Israel]

Farrow, Scott. Testing the Efficiency of Extraction from a Stock Resource. *J. Polit. Econ.*, June 1985, 93(3), pp. 452–87.   [G: U.S.]

Fishback, Price V. Discrimination on Nonwage Margins: Safety in the West Virginia Coal Industry, 1906–1925. *Econ. Inquiry*, October 1985, 23(4), pp. 651–69.   [G: U.S.]

Foders, Federico. Who Gains from Deep-Sea Mining? In *Donges, J. B., ed.*, 1985, pp. 336–69.   [G: Selected Countries]

Foders, Federico and Kim, Chungsoo. Impact of Deep-Sea Mining on the World Metal Markets: Manganese. In *Donges, J. B., ed.*, 1985, pp. 204–52.   [G: Selected Countries]

Foster, James C. *The Western Dilemma:* Miners, Silicosis, and Compensation. *Labor Hist.*, Spring 1985, 26(2), pp. 268–87.   [G: U.S.]

Gilbert, Christopher L. Futures Trading and the Welfare Evaluation of Commodity Price Stabilisation. *Econ. J.*, September 1985, 95(379), pp. 637–61.   [G: LDCs]

Godey, Ricardo A. Technical and Economic Efficiency of Peasant Miners in Bolivia. *Econ. Develop. Cult. Change*, October 1985, 34(1), pp. 103–20.   [G: Bolivia]

Gray, Edward C. Alternatives to Single Project Mining Communities: A Critical Assessment: Commentary. *Can. J. Agr. Econ.*, August 1985, 32, pp. 114–18.   [G: Canada]

Greasley, David. Wage Rates and Work Intensity in the South Wales Coalfield, 1874–1914. *Economica*, August 1985, 52(207), pp. 383–89.   [G: U.K.]

Halvorson, Alan L. Switching Regression Estimates of a Sequential Production Process: The Case of Underground Coal Mining. *Rev. Econ. Statist.*, February 1985, 67(1), pp. 161–65.   [G: U.S.]

Hausman, William J. British Coal: A Review Article. *J. Econ. Hist.*, September 1985, 45(3), pp. 712–15.   [G: U.K.]

Hirsch, Barry T. and Hausman, William J. Labour Productivity in the South Wales Coal Industry: Reply. *Economica*, August 1985, 52(207), pp. 391–94.   [G: U.K.]

Horesh, Edward and Joekes, Susan. The Impact of Primary Exports on the Ghanaian Economy: Linkages and Leakages from Mining and Cocoa 1956–69. In *Lundahl, M., ed.*, 1985, pp. 181–205.   [G: Ghana]

Kolstad, Charles D. and Wolak, Frank A., Jr. Strategy and Market Structure in Western Coal Taxation. *Rev. Econ. Statist.*, May 1985, 67(2), pp. 239–49.   [G: U.S.]

Kubursi, A. A. Industrialisation in the Arab States of the Gulf: A Ruhr without Water. In *Niblock, T. and Lawless, R., eds.*, 1985, pp. 42–65.   [G: OPEC]

Kuprevich, R. The "Tsvetmetpromeksport" All-Union Association. *Soviet E. Europ. Foreign Trade*, Winter 1985-86, 21(4), pp. 68–78.   [G: U.S.S.R.]

Lasserre, Pierre. Capacity Choice by Mines.

Can. *J. Econ.*, November 1985, 18(4), pp. 831–42.   [G: Canada]

Laux, Jeanne Kirk. Social Democracy and State Capital: Potash in Saskatchewan. In *[Spry, I. M.]*, 1985, pp. 141–55.   [G: Canada]

Lucas, Robert E. B. Mines and Migrants in South Africa. *Amer. Econ. Rev.*, December 1985, 75(5), pp. 1094–108.   [G: S. Africa]

Macleod, John D. S. The Mining Industry in the Federal System. In *Drysdale, P. and Shibata, H., eds.*, 1985, pp. 127–39.   [G: Australia]

Mashayekhi, Mina. The Present Legal Staus of Deep Sea-Bed Mining. *J. World Trade Law*, May:June 1985, 19(3), pp. 229–50.
          [G: Global]

Mueller, Michael J. and Gorin, Daniel R. Informative Trends in Natural Resource Commodity Prices: A Comment. *J. Environ. Econ. Manage.*, March 1985, 12(1), pp. 89–95.
          [G: U.S.]

Olewiler, Nancy. Deriving the Long-run Supply Curve for a Competitive Mining Industry: The Case of Saskatchewan Uranium: Comment. In *Scott, A., ed.*, 1985, pp. 310–16.
          [G: Canada]

Owen, A. D. Short-term Price Formation in the U.S. Uranium Market. *Energy J.*, July 1985, 6(3), pp. 37–49.   [G: U.S.]

Pachauri, R. K.; Chen, Chia-Yon and Srivastava, Leena. Coal Transportation System Modeling—The Case of Taiwan: A Comment. *Energy J.*, July 1985, 6(3), pp. 109–14.   [G: Taiwan]

Rafati, Reza. Impact of Deep-Sea Mining on the World Metal Markets: Nickel. In *Donges, J. B., ed.*, 1985, pp. 253–334.
          [G: Selected Countries]

Rafati, Reza. Impact of Deep-Sea Mining on the World Metal Markets: Cobalt. In *Donges, J. B., ed.*, 1985, pp. 62–112.
          [G: Selected Countries]

Randall, Robert W. British Company and Mexican Community: The English at Real del Monte, 1824–1849. *Bus. Hist. Rev.*, Winter 1985, 59(4), pp. 622–44.   [G: Mexico]

Roberts, Gerald. Copper. In *Roberts, G., ed.*, 1985, pp. 64–71.   [G: Global]

Roberts, Gerald. Lead. In *Roberts, G., ed.*, 1985, pp. 98–103.   [G: Global]

Roberts, Gerald. Nickel. In *Roberts, G., ed.*, 1985, pp. 111–15.   [G: Global]

Roberts, Gerald. Silver. In *Roberts, G., ed.*, 1985, pp. 121–24.   [G: Global]

Roberts, Gerald. Tin. In *Roberts, G., ed.*, 1985, pp. 154–59.   [G: Global]

Roberts, Gerald. Zinc. In *Roberts, G., ed.*, 1985, pp. 160–66.   [G: Global]

Rutledge, Ian and Wright, Phil. Coal Worldwide: The International Context of the British Miners' Strike. *Cambridge J. Econ.*, December 1985, 9(4), pp. 303–26.   [G: U.K.]

Slade, Margaret E. Noninformative Trends in Natural Resource Commodity Prices: U-shaped Price Paths Exonerated: Reply [Trends in Natural-Resource Commodity Prices: An Analysis of the Time Domain]. *J. Environ.*

Econ. Manage., June 1985, 12(2), pp. 181–92.
[G: U.S.]

Smith, Ben. Resource Markets and Resource Trade Issues. In *Drysdale, P. and Shibata, H., eds.*, 1985, pp. 203–17. [G: Australia]

Södersten, Bo. Mineral-Led Development: The Political Economy of Namibia. In *Lundahl, M., ed.*, 1985, pp. 206–17. [G: Namibia]

Solomon, Barry D. and Rubin, Barry M. Environmental Linkages in Regional Econometric Models: An Analysis of Coal Development in Western Kentucky. *Land Econ.*, February 1985, 61(1), pp. 43–57. [G: U.S.]

Soyster, A. L., et al. An Evaluation of the Competitiveness of the U.S. Coal Market. *Energy Econ.*, January 1985, 7(1), pp. 3–8. [G: U.S.]

Stauffer, Thomas R. Accounting for "Wasting Assets": Measurements of Income and Dependency in Oil-Rentier States. *J. Energy Devel.*, Autumn 1985, 11(1), pp. 69–93. [G: OPEC]

Stephens, Evelyne Huber and Stephens, John D. Bauxite and Democratic Socialism in Jamaica. In *Evans, P.; Rueschemeyer, D. and Stephens, E. H., eds.*, 1985, pp. 33–66.
[G: Jamaica; Selected Countries]

Stollery, Kenneth R. Productivity Change in Canadian Mining, 1957–1979. *Appl. Econ.*, June 1985, 17(3), pp. 543–58. [G: Canada]

Stollery, Kenneth R. User Costs versus Markups as Determinants of Prices in the Nickel Industry: Reply. *J. Environ. Econ. Manage.*, December 1985, 12(4), pp. 397–400. [G: U.S.]

Tanguay, A. Brian. Quebec's Asbestos Policy: A Preliminary Assessment. *Can. Public Policy*, June 1985, 11(2), pp. 227–40. [G: Canada]

Tarlock, A. Dan. The Making of Federal Coal Policy: Lessons for Public Lands Management from a Failed Program, an Essay and Review. *Natural Res. J.*, April 1985, 25(2), pp. 349–71. [G: U.S.]

Tyler, William G. Effective Incentives for Domestic Market Sales and Exports: View of Anti-export Biases and Commercial Policy in Brazil, 1980–81. *J. Devel. Econ.*, August 1985, 18(2–3), pp. 219–42. [G: Brazil]

Tzeng, Gwo-Hshiung. Coal Transportation System Modeling: The Case of Taiwan. *Energy J.*, January 1985, 6(1), pp. 145–56.
[G: Taiwan]

Vergani, Raffaello. Technology and Organization of Labour in the Venetian Copper Industry (16th–18th Centuries.) *J. Europ. Econ. Hist.*, Spring 1985, 14(1), pp. 173–86. [G: Italy]

Vernon, Raymond and Levy, Brian. State-Owned Enterprises in the World Economy: The Case of Iron Ore. In *Vernon, R.*, 1985, pp. 113–31. [G: Selected Countries]

Wagenhals, Gerhard. Impact of Deep-Sea Mining on the World Metal Markets: Copper. In *Donges, J. B., ed.*, 1985, pp. 113–203.
[G: Selected Countries]

Wagenhals, Gerhard. The Modeling of International Minerals' Supply: A Restricted Profit Maximization Approach. *Weltwirtsch. Arch.*, 1985, 121(3), pp. 492–500. [G: CIPEC; U.S.; Canada]

Wälde, Thomas. Third World Mineral Development in Crisis: The Impact of the Worldwide Recession on Legal Instruments Governing Third World Mineral Development. *J. World Trade Law*, January:February 1985, 19(1), pp. 3–33. [G: LDCs]

Webber, Barbara S. and Webber, David J. Promoting Economic Incentives for Environmental Protection in the Surface Mining Control and Reclamation Act of 1977: An Analysis of the Design and Implementation of Reclamation Performance Bonds. *Natural Res. J.*, April 1985, 25(2), pp. 389–414. [G: U.S.]

Weeks, James L. The Effect of Unionization on Safety in Bituminous Deep Mines: Comment. *J. Lab. Res.*, Spring 1985, 6(2), pp. 209–10.
[G: U.S.]

Wescott, Robert F. Industrial Policy and Optimization in the Coal Industry. In *Adams, F. G., ed.*, 1985, pp. 181–209. [G: U.S.]

Willett, Ken. Mining Taxation Issues in the Australian Federal System. In *Drysdale, P. and Shibata, H., eds.*, 1985, pp. 105–26.
[G: Australia]

Williams, K. G. and Fraser, R. W. State Taxation of the Iron Ore Industry in Western Australia. *Australian Econ. Rev.*, 1st Quarter 1985, (69), pp. 30–36. [G: Australia]

6323 Oil, Gas, and Other Fuels

Abbott, John R. White. Energy Futures. In *Roberts, G., ed.*, 1985, pp. 80–83. [G: Global]

Adelman, Morris A. An Unstable World Oil Market. *Energy J.*, January 1985, 6(1), pp. 17–22.

Adelman, Morris A. Western Hemisphere Perspectives: Oil and Natural Gas. *Contemp. Policy Issues*, Summer 1985, 3(4), pp. 3–12.
[G: OPEC; N. America; Latin America]

Agarwal, Vinod B. and Deacon, Robert T. Price Controls, Price Dispersion and the Supply of Refined Petroleum Products. *Energy Econ.*, October 1985, 7(4), pp. 210–19. [G: U.S.]

Ajami, Riad A. The Arabian American Oil Company (ARAMCO) and Saudi Society: A Study in Interaction. In *Kaynak, E., ed. (II)*, 1985, pp. 127–36. [G: Saudi Arabia]

Al-Jarbou, Abdulaziz S. Basic Industries Development by SABIC: Eight Years' Experience. *J. Energy Devel.*, Spring 1985, 10(2), pp. 193–99. [G: Saudi Arabia]

Al-Nasrawi, Abbas. OPEC and the Changing Structure of the World Oil Market. In *Kubursi, A. A. and Naylor, T., eds.*, 1985, pp. 19–30.
[G: OPEC; OECD]

Andersen, Arthur T. Industrial Organization in Oil Markets since the Embargo. *Rev. Ind. Organ.*, 1985, 2(2), pp. 194–216. [G: Global]

Atkinson, Lloyd C. The World Oil Market for the Balance of the 1980s: Stability or Turmoil? In *Kubursi, A. A. and Naylor, T., eds.*, 1985, pp. 31–41. [G: Global]

Baker, George. The Size of the Oil Industry in Mexico's Economy. *J. Energy Devel.*, Spring 1985, 10(2), pp. 213–30. [G: Mexico]

Barron, John M.; Loewenstein, Mark A. and Um-

beck, John R. Predatory Pricing: The Case of the Retail Gasoline Market. *Contemp. Policy Issues,* Spring, Pt. 2, 1985, *3*(3), pp. 131–39. [G: U.S.]

Barzelay, Michael and Pearson, Scott R. The Efficiency of Producing Alcohol for Energy in Brazil: Reply. *Econ. Develop. Cult. Change,* July 1985, *33*(4), pp. 857–63. [G: Brazil]

Boucher, Jacqueline and Smeers, Yves. Gas Trade in the European Community during the 1970s. *Energy Econ.,* April 1985, *7*(2), pp. 102–16. [G: EEC]

Boucher, Jacqueline and Smeers, Yves. Measuring the Consequences of the Take or Pay Clauses in Natural Gas Consuming Countries. In *Bjerkholt, O. and Offerdal, E., eds.,* 1985, pp. 123–39. [G: Belgium]

Bower, Joseph L. Restructuring Petrochemicals: A Comparative Study of Business and Government Strategy to Deal with a Declining Sector of the Economy. In *Scott, B. R. and Lodge, G. C., eds.,* 1985, pp. 263–300. [G: U.S.; OECD]

Broadman, Harry G. and Dunkerley, Joy. The Drilling Gap in Non-OPEC Developing Countries: The Role of Contractual and Fiscal Arrangements. *Natural Res. J.,* April 1985, *25*(2), pp. 415–28. [G: LDCs]

Broadman, Harry G.; Montgomery, W. David and Russell, Milton. Field Price Deregulation and the Carrier Status of Natural Gas Pipelines. *Energy J.,* April 1985, *6*(2), pp. 127–39. [G: U.S.]

Brown, Jonathan C. Why Foreign Oil Companies Shifted Their Production from Mexico to Venezuela during the 1920s. *Amer. Hist. Rev.,* April 1985, *90*(2), pp. 362–85. [G: Mexico; Venezuela]

Choucri, Nazli. Domestic Energy Pricing: Trends and Implications for the Arab World. *J. Energy Devel.,* Autumn 1985, *11*(1), pp. 27–68. [G: Middle East]

Clark, David, et al. Work and Marriage in the Offshore Oil Industry. *Int. J. Soc. Econ.,* 1985, *12*(2), pp. 36–47. [G: U.K.]

Clubley, Sally. The Gasoil Market. In *Roberts, G., ed.,* 1985, pp. 35–37. [G: U.K.; U.S.]

Copithorne, Lawrence and MacFadyen, Alan. Strategy for Energy Policy: Introduction. *Can. Public Policy,* Supplement July 1985, *11*(3), pp. 372–82. [G: Canada]

Cordes, Joseph J. and Galper, Harvey. Tax Shelter Activity: Lessons from Twenty Years of Evidence. *Nat. Tax J.,* September 1985, *38*(3), pp. 305–24. [G: U.S.]

Cramer, Curtis A. Horizontal Integration of the Natural Gas Pipeline Industry: An Exercise in Gas Pooling. *Rev. Ind. Organ.,* 1985, *2*(1), pp. 68–78. [G: U.S.]

Davison, Robert. A Note on Robert S. Pindyck's Paper "The Optimal Production of an Exhaustible Resource When Price Is Exogenous and Stochastic." *Scand. J. Econ.,* 1985, *87*(4), pp. 673–76.

Dixit, Avinash K. and Newbery, David M. G. Setting the Price of Oil in a Distorted Econ-

omy. *Econ. J.,* Supplement 1985, *95,* pp. 71–82. [G: Turkey]

Donnelly, William A. A State-Level, Variable Elasticity of Demand for Gasoline Model. *Int. J. Transport Econ.,* June 1985, *12*(2), pp. 193–202. [G: U.S.]

Dworin, Lowell and Kennedy, Michael. The Taxation of International Oil Production. *Nat. Tax J.,* March 1985, *38*(1), pp. 81–95. [G: U.S.]

Eckstein, Zvi and Eichenbaum, Martin S. Inventories and Quantity-Constrained Equilibria in Regulated Markets: The U.S. Petroleum Industry, 1947–1972. In *Sargent, T. J., ed.,* 1985, pp. 70–100. [G: U.S.]

El-Kuwaiz, Abdullah. Dynamics of Trade in Refined Petroleum Products between the Gulf Cooperation Council and Western Europe. *J. Energy Devel.,* Autumn 1985, *11*(1), pp. 5–11. [G: W. Europe; Middle East]

El-Kuwaiz, Abdullah. The Future of Oil Prices. In *Kubursi, A. A. and Naylor, T., eds.,* 1985, pp. 43–52. [G: OPEC; Global]

Elkan, Walter and Bishop, R. E. D. North Sea Oil: Responses to Employment Opportunities. *Energy Econ.,* April 1985, *7*(2), pp. 127–33. [G: U.K.]

Epple, Dennis. The Econometrics of Exhaustible Resource Supply: A Theory and an Application. In *Sargent, T. J., ed.,* 1985, pp. 143–200. [G: U.S.]

Erickson, Edward W. Deregulation and Natural Gas Supply and Demand. In *Crew, M. A., ed.,* 1985, pp. 141–59. [G: U.S.]

Frankel, P. H. Change and Continuity. *Energy J.,* October 1985, *6*(4), pp. 1–5. [G: OECD; OPEC]

Gilley, Otis W.; Karels, Gordon V. and Lyon, Randolph M. Joint Ventures and Offshore Oil Lease Sales. *Econ. Inquiry,* April 1985, *23*(2), pp. 321–39. [G: U.S.]

Gjølberg, Ole. Is the Spot Market for Oil Products Efficient? Some Rotterdam Evidence. *Energy Econ.,* October 1985, *7*(4), pp. 231–36. [G: Netherlands]

Gonzales, John J. The Relationship between Refined Product Imports and Refined Product Prices in the United States. *Energy J.,* July 1985, *6*(3), pp. 67–78. [G: U.S.]

Gopalakrishnan, Chennat. Natural Gas from Seaweed: Is Near-term R and D Funding by the U.S. Gas Industry Warranted? *Energy J.,* October 1985, *6*(4), pp. 129–37. [G: U.S.]

Griffin, James M. OPEC Behavior: A Test of Alternative Hypotheses. *Amer. Econ. Rev.,* December 1985, *75*(5), pp. 954–63. [G: OPEC]

Groth, Philip G. Energy Development and Security and Supply-side Ideology: Oligopoly, Monopoly, and Imperfect Competition Make Fossil Fuel Regulation a Necessity. *Amer. J. Econ. Soc.,* April 1985, *44*(2), pp. 155–68. [G: U.S.; Germany; Japan]

Halpern, Dan. Israeli Oil Exploration at the Crossroads. In *Levinson, P. and Landau, P., eds.,* 1985, pp. 102–06. [G: Israel]

Hann, Danny. Political and Bureaucratic Pressures on U.K. Oil Taxation Policy. *Scot. J. Po-*

lit. Econ., November 1985, *32*(3), pp. 278–95. [G: U.K.]

Hartshorn, Jack E. Government Sellers in a Restructured Crude Oil Market. In *Hawdon, D., ed.*, 1985, pp. 59–69.

Hay, George A. and Reynolds, Robert J. Competition and Antitrust in the Petroleum Industry: An Application of the Merger Guidelines. In *[McGowan, J. J.]*, 1985, pp. 15–48. [G: U.S.]

Hope, Chris and Gaskell, Phil. The Competitive Price of Oil: Some Results under Uncertainty. *Energy Econ.*, October 1985, *7*(4), pp. 289–96. [G: Global]

Hufbauer, Gary Clyde and Schott, Jeffrey J. The Soviet–European Gas Pipeline: A Case of Failed Sanction. In *Moran, T. H., ed.*, 1985, pp. 219–45. [G: U.S.; U.S.S.R.]

Itteilag, Richard L. An Analysis of Actual and Forecasted Conservation in the Residential Gas Space-Heating Market. In *Crew, M. A., ed.*, 1985, pp. 127–39. [G: U.S.]

Kaempfer, William H. and Min, Henry M., Jr. The Role of Oil in China's Economic Development, Growth, and Internationalization. *J. Energy Devel.*, Autumn 1985, *11*(1), pp. 13–26. [G: China]

Kashik, Aleksei; Manukov, Viktor and Iakimov, Ianko. The International Division of Labor in Petroleum Seismic Prospecting. *Soviet E. Europ. Foreign Trade*, Winter 1985-86, *21*(4), pp. 50–57. [G: CMEA]

Kearton, Lord. The Oil Industry. Some Personal Recollections and Opinions. In *Hawdon, D., ed.*, 1985, pp. 1–17.

Kosmo, Mark. OCS Leasing Policy: Its Effects on the Structure of the Petroleum Industry. *Energy J.*, January 1985, *6*(1), pp. 79–96.

Kyle, Albert S. The Pricing of Oil and Gas: Some Further Results: Discussion. *J. Finance*, July 1985, *40*(3), pp. 1018–20. [G: U.S.]

Landefeld, J. Steven and Hines, James R. National Accounting for Non-renewable Natural Resources in the Mining Industries. *Rev. Income Wealth*, March 1985, *31*(1), pp. 1–20. [G: U.S.]

Libecap, Gary D. and Wiggins, Steven N. The Influence of Private Contractual Failure on Regulation: The Case of Oil Field Unitization. *J. Polit. Econ.*, August 1985, *93*(4), pp. 690–714. [G: U.S.]

Lorentsen, Lorents and Roland, Kjell. Modelling the Crude Oil Market. Oil Prices in the Long Term. In *Bjerkholt, O. and Offerdal, E., eds.*, 1985, pp. 81–101.

Lorentsen, Lorents and Roland, Kjell. Norway's Export of Natural Gas to the European Gas Market. Policy Issues and Model Tools. In *Bjerkholt, O. and Offerdal, E., eds.*, 1985, pp. 103–22. [G: Norway; W. Europe]

Lorentsen, Lorents; Roland, Kjell and Aaheim, Asbjørn. Cost Structure and Profitability of North-Sea Oil and Gas Fields. In *Bjerkholt, O. and Offerdal, E., eds.*, 1985, pp. 143–76. [G: Norway; U.K.]

Lowinger, Thomas C.; Wihlborg, Clas and Will-

man, Elliott S. An Empirical Analysis of OPEC and Non-OPEC Behavior. *J. Energy Devel.*, Autumn 1985, *11*(1), pp. 119–40.

Mănescu, Manea. The Oil Industry—A Complex Cybernetics System. *Econ. Computat. Cybern. Stud. Res.*, 1985, *20*(3), pp. 3–20.

Mansell, Robert L. and Jordan, Barbara A. An Economic Evaluation of Methanol Blends in Canadian Markets. *Can. Public Policy*, Supplement July 1985, *11*(3), pp. 455–64. [G: Canada]

Martin, A. J. The Prediction of Strategic Reserves. In *Niblock, T. and Lawless, R., eds.*, 1985, pp. 16–39. [G: Global]

Masten, Scott E. and Crocker, Keith J. Efficient Adaptation in Long-term Contracts: Take-or-Pay Provisions for Natural Gas. *Amer. Econ. Rev.*, December 1985, *75*(5), pp. 1083–93. [G: U.S.]

McRae, Robert N. Petroleum Taxation: A Comparison Between Canada and the U.S. In *Bjerkholt, O. and Offerdal, E., eds.*, 1985, pp. 177–99. [G: Canada; U.S.]

Melese, François. Deregulation, Endogenous Expectations, and the Evolution of Industry Structure. *Southern Econ. J.*, January 1985, *51*(3), pp. 793–803.

Miller, John R. Petroleum Economics and Management. *J. Energy Devel.*, Spring 1985, *10*(2), pp. 165–72. [G: U.S.]

Miller, Merton H. and Upton, Charles W. The Pricing of Oil and Gas: Some Further Results. *J. Finance*, July 1985, *40*(3), pp. 1009–18. [G: U.S.]

Millsaps, Steven W. and Ott, Mack. Risk Aversion, Risk Sharing, and Joint Bidding: A Study of Outer Continental Shelf Petroleum Auctions. *Land Econ.*, November 1985, *61*(4), pp. 372–86. [G: U.S.]

Moody, Carlisle E.; Valentine, Patrick L. and Kruvant, William J. The GAO Natural Gas Supply Model. *Energy Econ.*, January 1985, *7*(1), pp. 49–57. [G: U.S.]

Mueller, Michael J. Scarcity and Ricardian Rents for Crude Oil. *Econ. Inquiry*, October 1985, *23*(4), pp. 703–24. [G: U.S.]

Murphy, Frederick H.; Toman, Michael A. and Weiss, Howard J. International Cooperation in Stockpiles and Tariffs for Coping with Oil Supply Disruptions. *J. Policy Modeling*, Winter 1985, *7*(4), pp. 649–72. [G: OECD]

Odell, Peter R. Back to Cheap Oil? *Lloyds Bank Rev.*, April 1985, (156), pp. 1–15. [G: OPEC]

Olmstead, Alan L. and Rhode, Paul. Rationing without Government: The West Coast Gas Famine of 1920. *Amer. Econ. Rev.*, December 1985, *75*(5), pp. 1044–55. [G: U.S.]

Penrose, Edith. Downstream Implications of Structural Change. In *Hawdon, D., ed.*, 1985, pp. 80–91.

Pindyck, Robert S. The Supply of Natural Gas Reserves in Alberta: Comment. In *Scott, A., ed.*, 1985, pp. 279–82. [G: Canada]

Pirog, Robert and Stamos, Stephen C. Energy Concentration: Implications for Energy Policy and Planning. *J. Econ. Issues*, June 1985, *19*(2), pp. 441–49. [G: U.S.]

Quirin, Brendan E. Issues in Canada/U.S. Energy Trade and Investment: A U.S. Perspective. In *Fretz, D.; Stern, R. and Whalley, J., eds.*, 1985, pp. 256–77. [G: Canada; U.S.]

Razavi, Hossein. Oil Production Policy and Economic Development in Mexico. *Energy J.*, April 1985, *6*(2), pp. 61–71. [G: Mexico]

Reid, Richard G. Standing the Test of Time. In *Hawdon, D., ed.*, 1985, pp. 52–58.

Rose, Adam. Modeling Energy Conservation Programs: An Application to Natural Gas Utilities. *Energy J.*, October 1985, *6*(4), pp. 87–103. [G: U.S.]

Rugman, Alan M. Transfer Pricing in the Canadian Petroleum Industry. In *Rugman, A. M. and Eden, L., eds.*, 1985, pp. 173–92. [G: Selected Countries]

Ruitenbeek, Jack. Economics of In-Situ Oilsands Production: Some Implications for Public Policy. *Can. Public Policy*, Supplement July 1985, *11*(3), pp. 407–14. [G: Canada]

Samii, Massood V. OPEC in an Interdependent Global Economy. *J. Energy Devel.*, Autumn 1985, *11*(1), pp. 95–103. [G: OPEC]

Saqqaf, Abdulaziz. Energy Production and Consumption in the Yemen Arab Republic. *J. Energy Devel.*, Autumn 1985, *11*(1), pp. 105–18. [G: Yemen]

Scarfe, Brian L. Canadian Energy Prospects: Natural Gas, Tar Sands, and Oil Policy. *Contemp. Policy Issues*, Summer 1985, *3*(4), pp. 13–24. [G: Canada]

Scarfe, Brian L. Financing Oil and Gas Exploration and Development Activity. *Can. Public Policy*, Supplement July 1985, *11*(3), pp. 402–06. [G: Canada]

Scarfe, Brian L. The National Energy Program after Three Years: An Economic Perspective. In *Kubursi, A. A. and Naylor, T., eds.*, 1985, pp. 83–116. [G: Canada]

Schreiner, Alette and Skoglund, Tor. Regional Impacts of Petroleum Activities in Norway. In *Bjerkholt, O. and Offerdal, E., eds.*, 1985, pp. 203–29. [G: Norway]

Seddighi, H. R. A General Equilibrium Framework for Optimal Planning in an Oil-producing Economy. *Energy Econ.*, July 1985, *7*(3), pp. 179–90.

Seymour, Ian. OPEC and Structural Change. In *Hawdon, D., ed.*, 1985, pp. 70–79.

Siegel, Daniel R. Estimating Potential Social Losses from Market Failure: Oil Exploration in Alberta. *Rand J. Econ.*, Winter 1985, *16*(4), pp. 537–52. [G: Canada]

Singer, S. Fred. Prospects for the World Oil Market. *Energy J.*, January 1985, *6*(1), pp. 13–16. [G: Global]

Snickars, F. and Johansson, B. The Development of Natural Gas Deposits in Western Siberia. In *Lakshmanan, T. R. and Johansson, B., eds.*, 1985, pp. 27–40. [G: U.S.S.R.]

Stevens, Paul. A Survey of Structural Change in the International Oil Industry 1945–1984. In *Hawdon, D., ed.*, 1985, pp. 18–51.

Stokes, Raymond G. The Oil Industry in Nazi Germany, 1936–1945. *Bus. Hist. Rev.*, Summer 1985, *59*(2), pp. 254–77. [G: Germany]

Taylor, M. E. C. The Taxation of Oil Companies. *Bull. Int. Fiscal Doc.*, April 1985, *39*(4), pp. 167–70. [G: Kenya]

Tellier, P. M. Canada's National Energy Policy. In *Kubursi, A. A. and Naylor, T., eds.*, 1985, pp. 73–81. [G: Canada]

Uffelmann, Maris. Hydrocarbon Supply Costs. *Can. Public Policy*, Supplement July 1985, *11*(3), pp. 397–401. [G: Canada]

Uhler, Russell S. The Supply of Natural Gas Reserves in Alberta. In *Scott, A., ed.*, 1985, pp. 263–79. [G: Canada]

Watkins, G. C. The Supply of Natural Gas Reserves in Alberta: Comment. In *Scott, A., ed.*, 1985, pp. 282–89. [G: Canada]

Watkins, G. C. and Waverman, Leonard. Canadian Natural Gas Export Pricing Behaviour. *Can. Public Policy*, Supplement July 1985, *11*(3), pp. 415–26. [G: Canada]

Whiteman, J. C. North Sea Oil. In *Morris, D., ed.*, 1985, pp. 829–50. [G: U.K.]

Wiggins, Steven N. and Libecap, Gary D. Oil Field Unitization: Contractual Failure in the Presence of Imperfect Information. *Amer. Econ. Rev.*, June 1985, *75*(3), pp. 368–85. [G: U.S.]

Wolfson, Mark A. Empirical Evidence of Incentive Problems and Their Mitigation in Oil and Gas Tax Shelter Programs. In *Pratt, J. W. and Zeckhauser, R. J., eds.*, 1985, pp. 101–25. [G: U.S.]

Wright, Jonathan. The Efficiency of Producing Alcohol for Energy in Brazil: Comment. *Econ. Develop. Cult. Change*, July 1985, *33*(4), pp. 851–56. [G: Brazil]

633 Industry Studies: Distributive Trades

6330 General

Cleveland, Douglas. It's Time to Retire the Import Penetration Ratio. *Challenge*, Sept./Oct. 1985, *28*(4), pp. 50–53. [G: U.S.]

Felli, Ernesto and Piersanti, Giovanni. Salari, prezzi e produttività nel commercio. (With English summary.) *Stud. Econ.*, 1985, *40*(27), pp. 141–76. [G: Italy]

Fenili, Robert. The Impact of Decontrol on Gasoline Wholesalers and Retailers. *Contemp. Policy Issues*, Spring, Pt. 2, 1985, *3*(3), pp. 119–30. [G: U.S.]

Pellegrini, Luca. The Distributive Trades in the Italian Economy: Some Remarks on the Decade 1970–80. *Rev. Econ. Cond. Italy*, May-Aug. 1985, (2), pp. 191–220. [G: Italy]

Rantala, Eero. Kaupan rakennemuutos ja kehitysnäkymät. (Structural Changes and Future Prospects in Domestic Trade in Finland. With English summary.) *Kansant. Aikak.*, 1985, *81*(2), pp. 123–30. [G: Finland]

Scott, Earl P. Lusaka's Informal Sector in National Economic Development. *J. Devel. Areas*, October 1985, *20*(1), pp. 71–99. [G: Zambia]

Yamazawa, Ippei and Kohama, Hirohisa. Trading Companies and the Expansion of Foreign Trade: Japan, Korea, and Thailand. In *Ohkawa, K. and Ranis, G., eds.*, 1985 , pp. 426–46. [G: Japan; S. Korea; Thailand]

6332 Wholesale Trade

Byrd, William. The Shanghai Market for the Means of Production: A Case Study of Reform in China's Material Supply System. *Comparative Econ. Stud.*, Winter 1985, 27(4), pp. 1–29. [G: China]

6333 Retail Trade

Bailey, Thomas. A Case Study of Immigrants in the Restaurant Industry. *Ind. Relat.*, Spring 1985, 24(2), pp. 205–21. [G: U.S.]

Balbinot, Pierangelo. Indicizzazione dei redditi e formazione dei prezzi nel settore commerciale: una verifica econometrica (Income Indexation and Price Formation in the Trade Sector. An Econometric Test. With English summary.) *Econ. Lavoro*, Oct.-Dec. 1985, 19(4), pp. 3–13. [G: Italy]

Barron, John M.; Loewenstein, Mark A. and Umbeck, John R. Predatory Pricing: The Case of the Retail Gasoline Market. *Contemp. Policy Issues*, Spring, Pt. 2, 1985, 3(3), pp. 131–39. [G: U.S.]

Benson, Bruce L. and Faminow, Merle D. An Alternative View of Pricing in Retail Food Markets. *Amer. J. Agr. Econ.*, May 1985, 67(2), pp. 296–306.

Carter, Michael J. and Carter, Susan B. Internal Labor Markets in Retailing: The Early Years. *Ind. Lab. Relat. Rev.*, July 1985, 38(4), pp. 586–98. [G: U.S.]

Centner, Terence J. Retail Food Cooperatives: Testing the "Small Is Beautiful" Hypothesis: Comment. *Amer. J. Agr. Econ.*, May 1985, 67(2), pp. 328–29. [G: U.S.]

Conners, Sandy B.; Samli, A. Coskun and Kaynak, Erdener. Transfer of Food Retail Technology into Less Developed Countries. In *Samli, A. C., ed.*, 1985, pp. 27–44. [G: LDCs]

Cotterill, Ronald W. Retail Food Cooperatives: Testing the "Small Is Beautiful" Hypothesis: Reply. *Amer. J. Agr. Econ.*, May 1985, 67(2), pp. 330. [G: U.S.]

Dawson, John A. Structural Change in European Retailing: The Polarization of Operating Scale. In *Kaynak, E., ed. (I)*, 1985, pp. 211–29. [G: W. Europe]

Eckard, E. Woodrow, Jr. The Effects of State Automobile Dealer Entry Regulation on New Car Prices. *Econ. Inquiry*, April 1985, 23(2), pp. 223–42. [G: U.S.]

Gerstner, Eitan. Sales: Demand-Supply Variation or Price Discrimination? *J. Econ. Bus.*, May 1985, 37(2), pp. 171–82. [G: U.S.]

Gripsrud, Geir and Gronhaug, Kjell. Structure and Strategy in Grocery Retailing: A Sociometric Approach. *J. Ind. Econ.*, March 1985, 33(3), pp. 339–47. [G: Norway]

Hogarty, Thomas F. Issues in Gasoline Marketing: Introduction. *Contemp. Policy Issues*, Spring, Pt. 2, 1985, 3(3), pp. 103–04. [G: U.S.]

Hollis, Mark C. Motivating Employees through Stock Ownership. In *Federal Reserve Bank of Atlanta (I)*, 1985, pp. 65–69. [G: U.S.]

Holstius, Karin. Retail Marketing of Convenience Goods in Finland: Special Offers Combining Customer and Retailer Benefit. *Liiketaloudellinen Aikak.*, 1985, 34(4), pp. 338–65. [G: Finland]

Honeycutt, T. Crawford. Competition in Controlled and Uncontrolled Gasoline Markets. *Contemp. Policy Issues*, Spring, Pt. 2, 1985, 3(3), pp. 105–18. [G: U.S.]

Judd, L. Lynn; Taylor, Raymond E. and Powell, Garth A. The Personal Characteristics of the Small Business Retailer: Do They Affect Store Profits and Retail Strategies? *J. Behav. Econ.*, Summer 1985, 14(2), pp. 59–75. [G: U.S.]

Kaynak, Erdener. Global Spread of Supermarkets: Some Experiences from Turkey. In *Kaynak, E., ed. (I)*, 1985, pp. 77–93. [G: Switzerland; Turkey]

Kooiman, Peter; van Dijk, Herman K. and Thurik, A. Roy. Likelihood Diagnostics and Bayesian Analysis of a Micro-Economic Disequilibrium Model for Retail Services. *J. Econometrics*, July/August 1985, 29(1/2), pp. 121–48. [G: Netherlands]

Levin, Sharon G.; Levin, Stanford L. and Meisel, John B. Intermarket Differences in the Early Diffusion of an Innovation. *Southern Econ. J.*, January 1985, 51(3), pp. 672–80. [G: U.S.]

Marcus, Bernard. Educating Managers and Employees. In *Federal Reserve Bank of Atlanta (I)*, 1985, pp. 75–79. [G: U.S.]

Marx, Thomas G. The Development of the Franchise Distribution System in the U.S. Automobile Industry. *Bus. Hist. Rev.*, Autumn 1985, 59(3), pp. 465–74. [G: U.S.]

Nooteboom, B. A Mark-up Model of Retail Margins. *Appl. Econ.*, August 1985, 17(4), pp. 647–67. [G: Netherlands; W. Germany]

Okabe, Atsuyuki; Asami, Yasushi and Miki, Fujio. Statistical Analysis of the Spatial Association of Convenience-Goods Stores by Use of a Random Clumping Model. *J. Reg. Sci.*, February 1985, 25(1), pp. 11–28. [G: Japan]

Ratchford, Brian T. and Brown, James R. A Study of Productivity Changes in Food Retailing. *Marketing Sci.*, Fall 1985, 4(4), pp. 292–311. [G: U.S.]

Reed, Michael R. and Robbins, Lynn W. The Relationship between Managerial Heuristics and Economics in Pricing Retail Meats. *Southern J. Agr. Econ.*, December 1985, 17(2), pp. 87–95. [G: U.S.]

Samiee, Saeed. Global Retail Strategy and Productivity Planning: Some International Comparisons. In *Kaynak, E., ed. (I)*, 1985, pp. 23–36.

Spranzi, Aldo. Modernisation and Efficiency of Italian Commerce. *Rev. Econ. Cond. Italy,*

May-Aug. 1985, (2), pp. 169–89.   [G: Italy; France]

Tsuchida, Shu. A Maximum Profit-Margin Vector in Retailing. (In Japanese. With English summary.) *Econ. Stud. Quart.*, April 1985, *36*(1), pp. 61–73.

634 Industry Studies: Construction

6340 Construction

Allen, Steven G. Why Construction Industry Productivity Is Declining. *Rev. Econ. Statist.*, November 1985, *67*(4), pp. 661–69.
    [G: U.S.]

Hekman, John S. Rental Price Adjustment and Investment in the Office Market. *Amer. Real Estate Urban Econ. Assoc. J.*, Spring 1985, *13*(1), pp. 32–47.   [G: U.S.]

Jenkins, Alexander W. The Analysis of Wage Formation with Application to Alberta Construction. *Appl. Econ.*, October 1985, *17*(5), pp. 907–21.   [G: Canada]

Johannes, James M.; Koch, Paul D. and Rasche, Robert H. Estimating Regional Construction Cost Differences: Theory and Evidence. *Managerial Dec. Econ.*, June 1985, *6*(2), pp. 70–79.   [G: U.S.]

Kaplan, D. E. The Diffusion of Microelectronic Technology in South African Manufacturing Industry: The Case of Computer Aided Design. *J. Stud. Econ. Econometrics*, November 1985, (23), pp. 67–98.   [G: S. Africa]

Lesse, Paul F. and Skowronski, Janislaw M. Stabilisation and Optimal Management in the Housing Industry. In *Batten, D. F. and Lesse, P. F., eds.*, 1985, pp. 47–68.

McKenna, J. A. and Rodger, Richard G. Control by Coercion: Employers' Associations and the Establishment of Industrial Order in the Building Industry of England and Wales, 1860–1914. *Bus. Hist. Rev.*, Summer 1985, *59*(2), pp. 203–31.   [G: U.K.]

Murphy, Kathleen J. Toward a U.S. Technology Agenda: Insights from Third-World Macroprojects. In *Konecci, E. B. and Kuhn, R. L., eds.*, 1985, pp. 117–133.   [G: U.S.; LDCs]

Noam, Eli M. A Local Regulator's Rewards for Conformity in Policy. *Public Choice*, 1985, *45*(3), pp. 291–302.   [G: U.S.]

Schriver, William R. and Bowlby, Roger L. Changes in Productivity and Composition of Output in Building Construction, 1972–1982. *Rev. Econ. Statist.*, May 1985, *67*(2), pp. 318–22.   [G: U.S.]

Stansell, Stanley R. and Mitchell, A. Cameron. The Impact of Credit Rationing on the Real Sector: A Study of the Effect of Mortgage Rates and Terms on Housing Starts. *Appl. Econ.*, October 1985, *17*(5), pp. 781–800. [G: U.S.]

Strassmann, W. Paul. Employment in Construction: Multicountry Estimates of Costs and Substitution Elasticities for Small Dwellings. *Econ. Develop. Cult. Change*, January 1985, *33*(2), pp. 395–414.   [G: LDCs]

Zijlstra, Jelle. The Construction Industry in a Macro-economic Fix. In *Zijlstra, J.*, 1985, pp. 163–69.   [G: Netherlands]

635 Industry Studies: Services and Related Industries

6350 General

Baldwin, Robert E. Negotiating about Trade and Investment in Services: Comments. In *Stern, R. M., ed.*, 1985, pp. 195–99.

Baumol, William J. Measurement of Output and Productivity in the Service Sector: Comment. In *Inman, R. P., ed.*, 1985, pp. 124–26.
    [G: U.S.]

Baumol, William J. Productivity Policy and the Service Sector. In *Inman, R. P., ed.*, 1985, pp. 301–17.

Behrman, Jere R. Services in the International Economy: Comment. In *Inman, R. P., ed.*, 1985, pp. 49–52.   [G: Selected Countries]

Bhagwati, Jagdish N. Splintering and Disembodiment of Services and Developing Nations. In *Bhagwati, J. N. (II)*, 1985, pp. 92–103.
    [G: LDCs; U.S.; U.K.]

Bhagwati, Jagdish N. Why Are Services Cheaper in the Poor Countries? In *Bhagwati, J. N. (II)*, 1985, pp. 82–91.

Deardorff, Alan V. Comparative Advantage and International Trade and Investment in Services. In *Stern, R. M., ed.*, 1985, pp. 39–71.

Duchêne, Gérard. Vers une réforme de la planification des services en URSS? (Towards a Reform in Planning for Services in U.S.S.R. With English summary.) *Écon. Soc.*, May 1985, *19*(5), pp. 15–42.   [G: U.S.S.R.]

Eckstein, Albert J. and Heien, Dale. Causes and Consequences of Service Sector Growth: The U.S. Experience. *Growth Change*, April 1985, *16*(2), pp. 12–17.   [G: U.S.]

Feketekuty, Geza. Negotiating about Trade and Investment in Services: Comments. In *Stern, R. M., ed.*, 1985, pp. 200–202.

Feketekuty, Geza. Negotiating Strategies for Liberalizing Trade and Investment in Services. In *Stern, R. M., ed.*, 1985, pp. 203–14.

Fuchs, Victor R. An Agenda for Research on the Service Sector. In *Inman, R. P., ed.*, 1985, pp. 319–25.

Gemmell, Norman. The Growth of Employment in Services: Egypt, 1960–75. *Devel. Econ.*, March 1985, *23*(1), pp. 53–68.   [G: Egypt]

Gibbs, Murray. Continuing the International Debate on Services. *J. World Trade Law*, May: June 1985, *19*(3), pp. 199–218.   [G: Global]

Ginzberg, Eli and Vojta, George J. The Service Sector of the U.S. Economy. In *Ginzberg, E.*, 1985, pp. 417–29.   [G: U.S.]

Grey, Rodney de C. Negotiating about Trade and Investment in Services. In *Stern, R. M., ed.*, 1985, pp. 181–94.

Harrison, Bennett. Increasing Instability and Inequality in the "Revival" of the New England Economy. In *Richardson, H. W. and Turek, J. H., eds.*, 1985, pp. 123–49.   [G: U.S.]

Holmström, Bengt R. The Provision of Services in a Market Economy. In *Inman, R. P., ed.*, 1985, pp. 183–213.

Hoppes, R. Bradley. Pooled Regression and Covariance Analysis of SMSA Selected Services: Earnings and Firm Size. *Reg. Sci. Persp.*, 1985, *15*(1), pp. 31–45.   [G: U.S.]

Hulten, Charles R. Measurement of Output and Productivity in the Service Sector: Comment. In *Inman, R. P., ed.*, 1985, pp. 127–30.
[G: U.S.]

Inman, Robert P. Managing the Service Economy: Prospects and Problems: Introduction and Overview. In *Inman, R. P., ed.*, 1985, pp. 1–24.

Jones, Ronald W. Comparative Advantage and International Trade and Investment in Services: Comments. In *Stern, R. M., ed.*, 1985, pp. 72–76.

Kendrick, John W. Measurement of Output and Productivity in the Service Sector. In *Inman, R. P., ed.*, 1985, pp. 111–23.   [G: U.S.]

Komarov, V. Effectiveness and the Intensification of the Nonproductive Sphere. *Prob. Econ.*, November 1985, *28*(7), pp. 68–83.
[G: U.S.S.R.]

Kravis, Irving B. Global Dimensions and Determinants of International Trade and Investment in Services: Comments. In *Stern, R. M., ed.*, 1985, pp. 169–75.   [G: U.S.; Canada; Japan; EEC]

Kravis, Irving B. Services in World Transactions. In *Inman, R. P., ed.*, 1985, pp. 135–60.
[G: Selected Countries]

Leveson, Irving. Services in the U.S. Economy. In *Inman, R. P., ed.*, 1985, pp. 89–102.
[G: U.S.]

Makhoul, Robert B. The Outlook for U.S.–Arab Trade in Services: The Insurance Industry. In *Czinkota, M. R. and Marciel, S., eds.*, 1985, pp. 263–68.   [G: U.S.; OPEC]

Malmgren, Harald B. Negotiating International Rules for Trade in Services. *World Econ.*, March 1985, *8*(1), pp. 11–26.   [G: Global]

Mann, Duncan. Services in the U.S. Economy: Comment. In *Inman, R. P., ed.*, 1985, pp. 103–04.   [G: U.S.]

Mansell, Robert L. The Service Sector and Western Economic Growth. *Can. Public Policy*, Supplement July 1985, *11*(3), pp. 354–60.
[G: Canada]

Marshall, J. N. Business Services, the Regions and Regional Policy. *Reg. Stud.*, August 1985, *19*(4), pp. 353–63.   [G: U.K.]

McCrae, James J. Can Growth in the Service Sector Rescue Western Canada? *Can. Public Policy*, Supplement July 1985, *11*(3), pp. 351–53.

Melvin, James R. Comparative Advantage and International Trade and Investment in Services: Comments. In *Stern, R. M., ed.*, 1985, pp. 77–82.

Norwood, Janet L. Measurement of Output and Productivity in the Service Sector: Comment. In *Inman, R. P., ed.*, 1985, pp. 131–33.
[G: U.S.]

Offe, Claus. The Growth of the Service Sector. In *Offe, C.*, 1985, pp. 101–28.

Paroush, Jacob. Notes on Partnerships in the Services Sector. *J. Econ. Behav. Organ.*, March 1985, *6*(1), pp. 79–87.

Patrick, Hugh. Services in the Japanese Economy: Comment. In *Inman, R. P., ed.*, 1985, pp. 84–88.   [G: Japan; OECD]

Peterson, George E. Pricing and Privatization of Public Services. In *Gramlich, E. M. and Ysander, B.-C., eds.*, 1985, pp. 137–72. [G: U.S.]

Postlewaite, Andrew. The Provision of Services in a Market Economy: Comment. In *Inman, R. P., ed.*, 1985, pp. 214–16.

Runyon, Herbert. The Services Industries: Employment, Productivity, and Inflation. *Bus. Econ.*, January 1985, *20*(1), pp. 55–63.
[G: U.S.]

Rutgaizer, V. and Teliukov, A. Improving the Methodology of the National Economic Accounting of Services. *Prob. Econ.*, March 1985, *27*(11), pp. 3–22.   [G: U.S.S.R.]

Sapir, André. North–South Issues in Trade in Services. *World Econ.*, March 1985, *8*(1), pp. 27–42.   [G: Global]

Saxonhouse, Gary R. Services in the Japanese Economy. In *Inman, R. P., ed.*, 1985, pp. 53–83.   [G: Japan; OECD]

Shelp, Ronald Kent. An Industrial Policy for a Service Economy. In *Zukin, S., ed.*, 1985, pp. 208–18.   [G: France; U.S.]

Spero, Joan Edelman. U.S. Trade Policy and International Service Transactions: Comment. In *Inman, R. P., ed.*, 1985, pp. 179–81.
[G: U.S.]

Stalson, Helena. U.S. Trade Policy and International Service Transactions. In *Inman, R. P., ed.*, 1985, pp. 161–78.   [G: U.S.]

Stern, Robert M. Global Dimensions and Determinants of International Trade and Investment in Services. In *Stern, R. M., ed.*, 1985, pp. 126–68.   [G: U.S.; Canada; Japan; EEC]

Summers, Robert. Services in the International Economy. In *Inman, R. P., ed.*, 1985, pp. 27–48.   [G: Selected Countries]

Swan, Neil M. The Service Sector: Engine of Growth? *Can. Public Policy*, Supplement July 1985, *11*(3), pp. 344–50.   [G: Canada]

Tessler, Andrew. Services. In *Meyer, F. V., ed.*, 1985, pp. 124–43.   [G: U.K.]

Walker, Richard A. Is There a Service Economy? The Changing Capitalist Division of Labor. *Sci. Soc.*, Spring 1985, *49*(1), pp. 42–83.

Wonnacott, Ronald J. Global Dimensions and Determinants of International Trade and Investment in Services: Comments. In *Stern, R. M., ed.*, 1985, pp. 176–80.   [G: U.S.; Canada; Japan; EEC]

6352 Electrical, Gas, Communication, and Information Services

Abel, John D. Comment: Competing Technologies and Inconsistent Regulation. In *Noam, E. M., ed.*, 1985, pp. 332–37.   [G: U.S.]

Agthe, Donald E. Revenue Effects from Changes

in a Declining Block Pricing Structure: Comment. *Land Econ.*, February 1985, *61*(1), pp. 79–80. [G: U.S.]

Aigner, Dennis J. The Residential Electricity Time-of-Use Pricing Experiments: What Have We Learned? In *Hausman, J. A. and Wise, D. A., eds.*, 1985, pp. 11–41. [G: U.S.]

Aigner, Dennis J. and Hirschberg, Joseph G. Commercial/Industrial Customer Response to Time-of-Use Electricity Prices: Some Experimental Results. *Rand J. Econ.*, Autumn 1985, *16*(3), pp. 341–55. [G: U.S.]

Albu, Cr. and Şerban, R. Numerical Results Concerning the Optimum Distribution of Electric and Thermal Charges between the Groups of a Thermoelectric Power Station. *Econ. Computat. Cybern. Stud. Res.*, 1985, *20*(4), pp. 29–32.

Andersson, Roland and Taylor, Lewis. Dimensioning Reserve Margins of Electrical Energy in Sweden. *Energy J.*, April 1985, *6*(2), pp. 41–60. [G: Sweden]

Andersson, Roland and Taylor, Lewis. The Investment Criteria of the Swedish Electricity Industry. *Energy Econ.*, January 1985, *7*(1), pp. 13–19. [G: Sweden]

Armstrong, Christopher and Nelles, H. V. The State and the Provision of Electricity in Canada and Australia, 1880–1965. In *Platt, D. C. M. and di Tella, G., eds.*, 1985, pp. 207–30. [G: Australia; Canada]

Baer, Walter S. Telephone and Cable Companies: Rivals or Partners in Video Distribution? In *Noam, E. M., ed.*, 1985, pp. 187–213. [G: U.S.; U.K.]

Barke, Richard. Regulation and Cooperation among Firms in Technical Standard-Setting. *J. Behav. Econ.*, Winter 1985, *14*, pp. 141–54. [G: U.S.]

Bernard, Keith. Deregulation in Telecommunications: A Comment. *Bus. Econ.*, October 1985, *20*(4), pp. 55–56. [G: U.S.]

Berry, William W. Total Deregulation of Electric Utilities: A Viable Policy Choice: Comment. In *Poole, R. W., Jr., ed.*, 1985, pp. 147–52. [G: U.S.]

Bertrand, Claude-Jean. Cable Television in France. In *Negrine, R. M., ed.*, 1985, pp. 134–63. [G: France]

Besen, Stanley M. and Johnson, Leland L. Regulation of Broadcast Station Ownership: Evidence and Theory. In *Noam, E. M., ed.*, 1985, pp. 364–89. [G: U.S.]

Borrus, Michael and Zysman, John. Industrial Development Policy in Japan. In *Nanto, D. K., ed.*, 1985, pp. 143–67. [G: Japan]

Boskin, Michael J.; Robinson, Marc S. and Ferron, Mark J. Economic Aspects of the Taxation of Decontrolled Natural Gas. *Nat. Tax J.*, June 1985, *38*(2), pp. 179–90. [G: U.S.]

Bosworth, Derek and Pugh, Clive. Industrial and Commercial Demand for Electricity by Time of Day. *Energy J.*, July 1985, *6*(3), pp. 101–07. [G: U.S.]

Botein, Michael. The FCC's Regulation of the New Video Technologies: Backing and Filling

on the Level Playing Field. In *Noam, E. M., ed.*, 1985, pp. 311–29. [G: U.S.]

Bower, Richard S. and Bower, Nancy L. Weather Normalization and Natural Gas Regulation. *Energy J.*, April 1985, *6*(2), pp. 101–15. [G: U.S.]

Bowie, Nolan A. Comment: Antitrust, Concentration, and Competition. In *Noam, E. M., ed.*, 1985, pp. 397–402. [G: U.S.]

Brants, Kees and Jankowski, Nick. Cable Television in the Low Countries. In *Negrine, R. M., ed.*, 1985, pp. 74–102. [G: Belgium; Netherlands]

Brotman, Stuart N. Comment: Analyzing the Critical, Unknown Factor. In *Noam, E. M., ed.*, 1985, pp. 180–86. [G: U.S.]

Brown, Stephen P. A. Consumers May Not Benefit from Wellhead Price Controls on Natural Gas. *Fed. Res. Bank Dallas Econ. Rev.*, July 1985, pp. 1–11. [G: U.S.]

Bubnys, Edward L. and Primeaux, Walter J., Jr. Rate-Base Valuation Methods and Firm Efficiency. *Managerial Dec. Econ.*, September 1985, *6*(3), pp. 167–71. [G: U.S.]

Burness, H. S.; Cummings, Ronald G. and Loose, Verne W. Scale Economies and Reliability in the Electric Power Industry. *Energy J.*, January 1985, *6*(1), pp. 157–68. [G: U.S.]

Caldwell, Geoffrey. Cable Television in Australia: A Study of Repose. In *Negrine, R. M., ed.*, 1985, pp. 186–95. [G: Australia]

Calley, Nicholas O.; Chambers, Donald R. and Woolridge, J. Randall. A Note on Standardized Unexpected Earnings: The Case of the Electric Utility Industry. *Financial Rev.*, February 1985, *20*(1), pp. 102–10. [G: U.S.]

Campbell, Robert W. Satellite Communications in the USSR. *Soviet Econ.*, Oct.-Dec. 1985, *1*(4), pp. 313–39. [G: U.S.S.R.]

Caron, André and Taylor, James R. Cable Television at the Crossroads: An Analysis of the Canadian Cable Scene. In *Negrine, R. M., ed.*, 1985, pp. 47–73. [G: Canada]

Caudill, Steven B. Modelling the Demand for Optional Classes of Local Measured Telephone Service. *Econ. Modelling*, January 1985, *2*(1), pp. 39–51. [G: U.S.]

Cave, Martin. Financing British Broadcasting. *Lloyds Bank Rev.*, July 1985, (157), pp. 25–35. [G: U.K.]

Chapman, C. B. and Cooper, Dale F. A Programmed Equity-Redemption Approach to the Finance of Public Projects. *Managerial Dec. Econ.*, June 1985, *6*(2), pp. 112–18.

Cohen, Linda. Private Contracting versus Public Regulation as a Solution to the Natural Monopoly Problem: Comment. In *Poole, R. W., Jr., ed.*, 1985, pp. 115–19. [G: U.S.]

Copeland, Basil L., Jr. and Severn, Alan K. Price Theory and Telecommunications Regulation: A Dissenting View. *Yale J. Regul.*, Fall 1985, *3*(1), pp. 53–85. [G: U.S.]

Cowhey, Peter F. and Aronson, Jonathan D. Trade in Communications and Data Processing. In *Stern, R. M., ed.*, 1985, pp. 256–90. [G: Canada; U.S.]

Cramer, Curtis A. Horizontal Integration of the Natural Gas Pipeline Industry: An Exercise in Gas Pooling. *Rev. Ind. Organ.*, 1985, 2(1), pp. 68–78. [G: U.S.]

Curien, Nicolas. Cost Allocation and Pricing Policy: The Case of French Telecommunications. In *Young, H. P., ed.*, 1985, pp. 167–78. [G: France]

Daly, Michael J. and Rao, P. Someshwar. Productivity, Scale Economies, and Technical Change in Ontario Hydro. *Southern Econ. J.*, July 1985, 52(1), pp. 167–80. [G: Canada]

Derthick, Martha and Quirk, Paul J. Why the Regulators Chose to Deregulate. In *Noll, R. G., ed.*, 1985, pp. 200–231.

Dobbs, Ian M. A Cost–Benefit Analysis of Combined Heat and Power. *Manchester Sch. Econ. Soc. Stud.*, September 1985, 53(3), pp. 241–62. [G: U.K.]

Domberger, Simon and Middleton, Julian. Franchising in Practice: The Case of Independent Television in the UK. *Fisc. Stud.*, February 1985, 6(1), pp. 17–32. [G: U.K.]

Donnelly, William A. A Note on 'The Residential Demand for Electricity: A Variant Parameters Approach.' *Appl. Econ.*, April 1985, 17(2), pp. 241–42. [G: U.S.]

Donnelly, William A. and Diesendorf, M. Variable Elasticity Models for Electricity Demand. *Energy Econ.*, July 1985, 7(3), pp. 159–62. [G: U.S.]

Färe, Rolf; Grosskopf, Shawna and Logan, J. The Relative Performance of Publicly Owned and Privately Owned Electric Utilities. *J. Public Econ.*, February 1985, 26(1), pp. 89–106. [G: U.S.]

Fisher, Franklin M. The Financial Interest and Syndication Rules in Network Television: Regulatory Fantasy and Reality. In *[McGowan, J. J.]*, 1985, pp. 263–98. [G: U.S.]

Fournier, Gary M. Nonprice Competition and the Dissipation of Rents from Television Regulation. *Southern Econ. J.*, January 1985, 51(3), pp. 754–65. [G: U.S.]

Garnham, Nicholas. Baumol's Disease: Audio-Visual Markets a Cure? *J. Cult. Econ.*, Supplement 1985, pp. 59–65. [G: U.S.; W. Europe]

Geller, Henry. The Role of Future Regulation: Licensing, Spectrum Allocation, Content, Access, Common Carrier, and Rates. In *Noam, E. M., ed.*, 1985, pp. 283–310. [G: U.S.]

Glakpe, Emmanuel and Fazzolare, Rocco. Economic Demand Analysis for Electricity in West Africa. *Energy J.*, January 1985, 6(1), pp. 137–44. [G: W. Africa]

Goddard, J. B., et al. The Impact of New Information Technology on Urban and Regional Structure in Europe. In *Thwaites, A. T. and Oakey, R. P., eds.*, 1985, pp. 215–41. [G: W. Europe; U.K.]

Goldsmith, Maurice. The Sunrise Industries beyond the 1980s: Discussion. In *Wells, N., ed.*, 1985, pp. 50–53.

Gordon, Richard L. The Rise and Fall of Oil Generation in the USA: A Study in Institutional

Adaptability. *Energy Econ.*, April 1985, 7(2), pp. 66–76. [G: U.S.]

Gottinger, Hans W. Dynamic Economic Strategies of Breeder Reactor Commitments. *Z. Wirtschaft. Sozialwissen.*, 1985, 105(1), pp. 1–15.

Griffin, James M. and Egan, Bruce L. Demand System Estimation in the Presence of Multiblock Tariffs: A Telecommunications Example. *Rev. Econ. Statist.*, August 1985, 67(3), pp. 520–24. [G: U.S.]

Guadagni, Alieto Aldo. La programación de las inversiones eléctricas y las actuales prioridades energéticas. (With English summary.) *Desarrollo Econ.*, July-Sept. 1985, 25(98), pp. 179–216. [G: Argentina]

Hayashi, Paul M.; Sevier, Melanie and Trapani, John M. Pricing Efficiency under Rate-of-Return Regulation: Some Empirical Evidence for the Electric Utility Industry. *Southern Econ. J.*, January 1985, 51(3), pp. 776–92. [G: U.S.]

Hazlett, Thomas. Private Contracting versus Public Regulation as a Solution to the Natural Monopoly Problem. In *Poole, R. W., Jr., ed.*, 1985, pp. 71–114. [G: U.S.]

Henderson, J. Stephen. Cost Estimation for Vertically Integrated Firms: The Case of Electricity. In *Crew, M. A., ed.*, 1985, pp. 75–94. [G: U.S.]

Henry, Jane B. The Economics of Pay-TV Media. In *Noam, E. M., ed.*, 1985, pp. 19–55. [G: U.S.]

Hertel, Thomas W. and Mount, Timothy D. The Pricing of Natural Resources in a Regional Economy. *Land Econ.*, August 1985, 61(3), pp. 229–43. [G: U.S.]

Hobbs, Benjamin F. Experiments in Multicriteria Decision Making and What We Can Learn from Them: An Example. In *Haimes, Y. Y. and Chankong, V., eds.*, 1985, pp. 400–23.

Hobbs, Benjamin F. and Schuler, Richard E. Evaluation of Electric Power Deregulation Using Network Models of Oligopolistic Spatial Markets. In *Harker, P. T., ed.*, 1985, pp. 208–54. [G: U.S.]

Hopley, John K. Comment: Telephone and Cable Issues. In *Noam, E. M., ed.*, 1985, pp. 214–20. [G: U.S.]

Houston, Douglas A. Revenue Effects from Changes in a Declining Block Pricing Structure: Reply. *Land Econ.*, February 1985, 61(1), pp. 81–82. [G: U.S.]

Hsiao, Cheng and Mountain, Dean C. Estimating the Short-run Income Elasticity of Demand for Electricity by Using Cross-sectional Categorized Data. *J. Amer. Statist. Assoc.*, June 1985, 80(390), pp. 259–65. [G: Canada]

Jackson, Charles L. Cable and Public Utility Regulation. In *Poole, R. W., Jr., ed.*, 1985, pp. 153–71. [G: U.S.]

Jones, S. Patricia. The Costs of Membership Aging in a Blue Cross and Blue Shield Plan. *Inquiry*, Summer 1985, 22(2), pp. 201–05.

Joskow, Paul L. Mixing Regulatory and Antitrust Policies in the Electric Power Industry: The

Price Squeeze and Retail Market Competition. In *[McGowan, J. J.]*, 1985, pp. 173–239. [G: U.S.]

Joskow, Paul L. The Residential Electricity Time-of-Use Pricing Experiments: What Have We Learned? Comment. In *Hausman, J. A. and Wise, D. A., eds.*, 1985, pp. 42–48. [G: U.S.]

Joskow, Paul L. Vertical Integration and Long-term Contracts: The Case of Coal-burning Electric Generating Plants. *J. Law, Econ., Organ.*, Spring 1985, *1*(1), pp. 33–80. [G: U.S.]

Joskow, Paul L. and Rose, Nancy L. The Effects of Technological Change, Experience, and Environmental Regulation on the Construction Cost of Coal-burning Generating Units. *Rand J. Econ.*, Spring 1985, *16*(1), pp. 1–27. [G: U.S.]

Jouhy, Ernest. New Media in the Third World. In *Noam, E. M., ed.*, 1985, pp. 416–39. [G: LDCs]

Kadir, Abdul. Electric Power in Indonesia's Fourth Five-Year Development Plan. *J. Energy Devel.*, Spring 1985, *10*(2), pp. 239–47. [G: Indonesia]

Kang, Kwang-Ha and Kendrick, David. The Tradeoff between Economies of Scale and Reliability in the Electric Power Industry. *J. Econ. Devel.*, July 1985, *10*(1), pp. 47–61. [G: S. Korea]

Karunaratne, N. D. The Information Revolution—Australia and the Developing Neighbours. *Econ. Int.*, May 1985, *38*(2), pp. 179–96. [G: Oceania]

Kaserman, David L. and Mayo, John W. Advertising and the Residential Demand for Electricity. *J. Bus.*, October 1985, *58*(4), pp. 399–408. [G: U.S.]

Keng, C. W. Kenneth. Forecasting Canadian Nuclear Power Station Construction Costs. *Energy Econ.*, October 1985, *7*(4), pp. 241–58. [G: Canada]

Knieps, Günther. Möglichkeiten des Wettbewerbs im schweizerischen Telekommunikationssektor. (The Role of Competition in the Swiss Telecommunications Sector. With English summary.) *Schweiz. Z. Volkswirtsch. Statist.*, December 1985, *121*(4), pp. 407–20. [G: Switzerland]

Le Diberder, Alain. No Culture-only Channels, but a More Important Role for the Audiovisual Media. *J. Cult. Econ.*, Supplement 1985, pp. 83–98. [G: U.S.; France]

Lee, Cheng F. and Primeaux, Walter J., Jr. Relative Importance of Current vs. Permanent Income for Payment Decisions in the Electric Utility Industry. *J. Behav. Econ.*, Winter 1985, *14*, pp. 83–97. [G: U.S.]

Levin, Harvey J. Comment: Antitrust, Concentration, and Competition. In *Noam, E. M., ed.*, 1985, pp. 390–96. [G: U.S.]

Levy, Jonathan D. and Pitsch, Peter K. Statistical Evidence of Substitutability among Video Delivery Systems. In *Noam, E. M., ed.*, 1985, pp. 56–92. [G: U.S.]

Lipartito, Kenneth. A Comparative Analysis of the Early History of the Southern and Northern Telephone Systems. In *Atack, J., ed.*, 1985, pp. 159–76. [G: U.S.]

Logan, Robert G. Trade in Communications and Data Processing: Comments. In *Stern, R. M., ed.*, 1985, pp. 299–303. [G: Canada; U.S.]

MacAvoy, Paul W. and Robinson, Kenneth. Losing by Judicial Policymaking: The First Year of the AT&T Divestiture. *Yale J. Regul.*, 1985, *2*(2), pp. 225–62. [G: U.S.]

Malecki, Edward J. Industrial Location and Corporate Organization in High Technology Industries. *Econ. Geogr.*, October 1985, *61*(4), pp. 345–69. [G: U.S.]

Mansouri, Avraham. Telecommunications in Israel. In *Levinson, P. and Landau, P., eds.*, 1985, pp. 155–56. [G: Israel]

McColl, G. D. Economic Issues Facing Electricity Supply Authorities. *Australian Econ. Rev.*, 4th Quarter 1985, (72), pp. 28–36. [G: Australia]

McNulty, Jean. Satellite Broadcasting in Northern Canada. In *[Spry, I. M.]*, 1985, pp. 281–99. [G: Canada]

Meyer, John R. and Tye, William B. The Regulatory Transition. *Amer. Econ. Rev.*, May 1985, *75*(2), pp. 46–51. [G: U.S.]

Militzer, Kenneth H. and Wolf, Martin H. Deregulation in Telecommunications. *Bus. Econ.*, July 1985, *20*(3), pp. 27–33. [G: U.S.]

Militzer, Kenneth H. and Wolf, Martin H. Deregulation in Telecommunications: A Reply. *Bus. Econ.*, October 1985, *20*(4), pp. 57–58. [G: U.S.]

Moore, William T. and Sartoris, William L. Dividends and Taxes: Another Look at the Electric Utility Industry. *Financial Rev.*, February 1985, *20*(1), pp. 1–20. [G: U.S.]

Mueller, Milton. The Information Revolution. In *Boaz, D. and Crane, E. H., eds.*, 1985, pp. 183–206. [G: U.S.]

Muller, R. A. and George, P. J. Northern Hydroelectric Development in an Optimal Expansion Program for Ontario Hydro. *Can. Public Policy*, September 1985, *11*(3), pp. 522–32. [G: Canada]

Mulligan, James G. An Econometric Assessment of Cost Savings from Coordination in U.S. Electric Power Generation: Comment. *Land Econ.*, May 1985, *61*(2), pp. 205–07. [G: U.S.]

Musgrove, A. R. de L. and Stocks, K. J. Electricity and Gas Supply in South-eastern Australia, 1980–2020. *Energy Econ.*, January 1985, *7*(1), pp. 37–48. [G: Australia]

Nadel, Mark S. Comment: Multichannel Video Competition. In *Noam, E. M., ed.*, 1985, pp. 174–79. [G: U.S.]

Negrine, Ralph. Cable Television and the Future of Broadcasting: Introduction. In *Negrine, R. M., ed.*, 1985, pp. 1–14. [G: Selected OECD]

Negrine, Ralph. Cable Television in Great Britain. In *Negrine, R. M., ed.*, 1985, pp. 103–33. [G: U.K.]

Nelson, Forrest D. and Noll, Roger G. Policymakers' Preferences for Alternative Allocations of the Broadcast Spectrum. In *[McGowan, J. J.]*, 1985, pp. 241–62. [G: U.S.]

Noam, Eli M. Economies of Scale and Regulation in CATV. In *Crew, M. A., ed.*, 1985, pp. 95–110. [G: U.S.]

Noam, Eli M. Economies of Scale in Cable Television: A Multiproduct Analysis. In *Noam, E. M., ed.*, 1985, pp. 93–120. [G: U.S.]

Noam, Eli M. Video Media Competition: Introduction. In *Noam, E. M., ed.*, 1985, pp. 1–16.

Noll, Roger G. "Let Them Make Toll Calls": A State Regulator's Lament. *Amer. Econ. Rev.*, May 1985, 75(2), pp. 52–56. [G: U.S.]

Norton, Seth W. Regulation and Systematic Risk: The Case of Electric Utilities. *J. Law Econ.*, October 1985, 28(3), pp. 671–86. [G: U.S.]

O'Connor, David C. The Computer Industry in the Third World: Policy Options and Constraints. *World Devel.*, March 1985, 13(3), pp. 311–32. [G: LDCs; OECD]

Ordover, Janusz A.; Sykes, A. O. and Willig, Robert D. Nonprice Anticompetitive Behavior by Dominant Firms toward the Producers of Complementary Products. In *[McGowan, J. J.]*, 1985, pp. 115–30. [G: U.S.]

Pacey, Patricia L. Cable Television in a Less Regulated Market. *J. Ind. Econ.*, September 1985, 34(1), pp. 81–91. [G: U.S.]

Peck, Stephen C. and Weyant, John P. Electricity Growth in the Future. *Energy J.*, January 1985, 6(1), pp. 23–43. [G: U.S.]

Pereira, M. V. F. and Pinto, L. M. V. G. Stochastic Optimization of a Multireservoir Hydroelectric System: A Decomposition Approach. *Water Resources Res.*, June 1985, 21(6), pp. 779–92. [G: Brazil]

Perrakis, Stylianos and Silva-Echenique, Julio. The Profitability and Risk of Television Stations in Canada. *Appl. Econ.*, August 1985, 17(4), pp. 745–59. [G: Canada]

Phillips, Almarin. The Reintegration of Telecommunications: An Interim View. In *Crew, M. A., ed.*, 1985, pp. 5–16. [G: U.S.]

Primeaux, Walter J., Jr. Total Deregulation of Electric Utilities: A Viable Policy Choice. In *Poole, R. W., Jr., ed.*, 1985, pp. 121–46. Experi [G: U.S.]

Radlauer, Marcy A.; Bauman, David S. and Chapel, Stephen W. Nuclear Construction Lead Times: Analysis of Past Trends and Outlook for the Future. *Energy J.*, January 1985, 6(1), pp. 45–62. [G: U.S.]

Reeb, Donald J. and Howe, Edward T. State and Local Taxation of Electric Utilities: A Study of the Record. In *Crew, M. A., ed.*, 1985, pp. 59–74. [G: U.S.]

Richter, Wolfram F. and Weimann, Joachim. Ramsey Pricing the Telephone Services of the Deutsche Bundespost. *Z. ges. Staatswiss. (JITE)*, December 1985, 141(4), pp. 516–24. [G: W. Germany]

Roy, Bernard and Bouyssou, Denis. Comparison of a Multi-attribute Utility and an Outranking Model Applied to a Nuclear Power Plant Siting Example. In *Haimes, Y. Y. and Chankong, V.,*

eds., 1985, pp. 482–94.

Samuel, Peter. Telecommunications: After the Bell Break-up. In *Poole, R. W., Jr., ed.*, 1985, pp. 177–203. [G: U.S.]

Savage, Christopher W. Antitrust Considerations Relating to the Distribution of Intangible Information Services. *Antitrust Bull.*, Winter 1985, 30(4), pp. 873–96. [G: U.S.]

Schacht, Michael and Hoffman, Rolf-Rüdiger. Cable Television in West Germany. In *Negrine, R. M., ed.*, 1985, pp. 164–85. [G: W. Germany]

Schäfer, Helmut. A European View of Competition and Control in a Multimedia Society. In *Noam, E. M., ed.*, 1985, pp. 405–15. [G: W. Europe]

Schwartz, David S. Idealism and Realism: An Institutionalist View of Corporate Power in the Regulated Utilities. *J. Econ. Issues*, June 1985, 19(2), pp. 311–31. [G: U.S.]

Sharkey, William W. Economic and Game-Theoretic Issues Associated with Cost Allocation in a Telecommunications Network. In *Young, H. P., ed.*, 1985, pp. 155–65.

Sharp, Stephen A. Comment: The Regulatory Setting. In *Noam, E. M., ed.*, 1985, pp. 330–31.

Shepsle, Kenneth A. Why the Regulators Chose to Deregulate: Comment. In *Noll, R. G., ed.*, 1985, pp. 231–37.

Shieh, Yeung-Nan. A Note on the Clarke and Shrestha Linear Space Model [Location and Input Mix Decisions for Energy Facilities]. *Reg. Sci. Urban Econ.*, February 1985, 15(1), pp. 131–35.

Shore, Haim. Corrections [Summer Time and Electricity Conservation: The Israeli Case]. *Energy J.*, January 1985, 6(1), pp. 169–70. [G: Israel]

Smiley, Robert. Management Compensation in Regulated Industries. In *Crew, M. A., ed.*, 1985, pp. 111–25. [G: U.S.]

de Sola Pool, Ithiel. Cable and Public Utility Regulation: Comment. In *Poole, R. W., Jr., ed.*, 1985, pp. 173–76. [G: U.S.]

Sparkes, Vernone. Cable Television in the United States: A Story of Continuing Growth and Change. In *Negrine, R. M., ed.*, 1985, pp. 15–46. [G: U.S.]

Spero, Joan Edelman. International Services, Information, and European Industrial Policy. In *Zukin, S., ed.*, 1985, pp. 203–07. [G: France]

Sullivan, B. C. Economics of Information Technology. *Int. J. Soc. Econ.*, 1985, 12(1), pp. 37–53. [G: OECD]

Sunley, Emil M. Private/Public Venturing Activities and Opportunities. In *Konecci, E. B. and Kuhn, R. L., eds.*, 1985, pp. 171–84. [G: U.S.]

Taylor, Kenneth B. The Economic Impact of the Emerging Global Information Economy on Lesser Developed Nations. In *Didsbury, H. F., Jr., ed.*, 1985, pp. 147–63. [G: LDCs]

Taylor, Lester D. The Residential Electricity

Time-of-Use Pricing Experiments: What Have We Learned? Comment. In *Hausman, J. A. and Wise, D. A., eds.*, 1985, pp. 49–50. [G: U.S.]

Teghem, J., Jr. and Kunsch, P. L. Multi-objective Decision Making under Uncertainty: An Example for Power System. In *Haimes, Y. Y. and Chankong, V., eds.*, 1985, pp. 443–56.

Temin, Peter and Peters, Geoffrey. Is History Stranger than Theory? The Origin of Telephone Separations. *Amer. Econ. Rev.*, May 1985, 75(2), pp. 324–27. [G: U.S.]

Thompson, Howard E. Estimating Return Deficiencies of Electric Utilities 1963–1981. In *Crew, M. A., ed.*, 1985, pp. 17–37.
[G: U.S.]

Thorpe, Kenneth. The Impact of Competing Technologies on Cable Television. In *Noam, E. M., ed.*, 1985, pp. 138–67. [G: U.S.]

Tracey, Michael. Television and Cable Policy in Japan: An Essay. In *Negrine, R. M., ed.*, 1985, pp. 196–211. [G: Japan]

Tsanacas, Demetri. The Transborder Data Flow in the New World Information Order: Privacy or Control. *Rev. Soc. Econ.*, December 1985, 43(3), pp. 357–70. [G: U.S.]

Varian, Hal R. Non-parametric Analysis of Optimizing Behavior with Measurement Error. *J. Econometrics*, Oct./Nov. 1985, 30(1/2), pp. 445–58. [G: U.S.]

Vernon, Jack. Discounting After-Tax Earnings with After-Tax Yields in Torts Settlements. *J. Risk Ins.*, December 1985, 52(4), pp. 696–703. [G: U.S.]

Vietor, Richard H. K. and Davidson, Dekkers L. Economics and Politics of Deregulation: The Issue of Telephone Access Charges. *J. Policy Anal. Manage.*, Fall 1985, 5(1), pp. 3–22.
[G: U.S.]

Waterman, David. Prerecorded Home Video and the Distribution of Theatrical Feature Films. In *Noam, E. M., ed.*, 1985, pp. 221–43.
[G: U.S.]

Waverman, Leonard. Trade in Communications and Data Processing: Comments. In *Stern, R. M., ed.*, 1985, pp. 291–98. [G: Canada; U.S.]

Webbink, Douglas W. Comment: Empirical Studies of Media Competition. In *Noam, E. M., ed.*, 1985, pp. 168–73. [G: U.S.]

White, Lawrence J. Antitrust and Video Markets: The Merger of Showtime and the Movie Channel as a Case Study. In *Noam, E. M., ed.*, 1985, pp. 338–63. [G: U.S.]

Wiggins, Patrick K. Telecommunications: After the Bell Break-up: Comment. In *Poole, R. W., Jr., ed.*, 1985, pp. 205–13. [G: U.S.]

Wildman, Steven S. and Owen, Bruce M. Program Competition, Diversity, and Multichannel Bundling in the New Video Industry. In *Noam, E. M., ed.*, 1985, pp. 244–73.
[G: U.S.]

Willard, Stephen Hopkins. A New Method of Calculating Copyright Liability for Cable Rebroadcasting of Distant Television Signals. *Yale Law J.*, May 1985, 94(6), pp. 1512–28. [G: U.S.]

Wirth, Michael O. and Bloch, Harry. The Broadcasters: The Future Role of Local Stations and the Three Networks. In *Noam, E. M., ed.*, 1985, pp. 121–37. [G: U.S.]

Woo, Chi-Keung. Demand for Electricity of Small Nonresidential Customers under Time-of-Use (TOU) Pricing. *Energy J.*, October 1985, 6(4), pp. 115–27. [G: U.S.]

Woodbury, John R. Comment: Welfare Analysis and the Video Marketplace. In *Noam, E. M., ed.*, 1985, pp. 274–79. [G: U.S.]

Zuker, R. C. and Pastor, M.-H. Financial Policies in the Canadian Electric Utility Sector: Origins, Practices, and Questions. *Can. Public Policy*, Supplement July 1985, 11(3), pp. 427–37. [G: Canada]

6353 Personal Services

Cummins, J. David and Harrington, Scott. Property-Liability Insurance Rate Regulation: Estimation of Underwriting Betas Using Quarterly Profit Data. *J. Risk Ins.*, March 1985, 52(1), pp. 16–43. [G: U.S.]

Huszagh, Sandra M. and Greene, Mark R. How Exporters View Credit Risk and FCIA Insurance—The Georgia Experience. *J. Risk Ins.*, March 1985, 52(1), pp. 117–32. [G: U.S.]

Jones, David D. Inflation Rates Implicit in Discounting Personal Injury Economic Losses. *J. Risk Ins.*, March 1985, 52(1), pp. 144–50.
[G: U.S.]

Schilling, Don. Estimating the Present Value of Future Income Losses: An Historical Simulation, 1900–1982. *J. Risk Ins.*, March 1985, 52(1), pp. 100–116. [G: U.S.]

Shaked, Israel. Measuring Prospective Probabilities of Insolvency: An Application to the Life Insurance Industry. *J. Risk Ins.*, March 1985, 52(1), pp. 59–80. [G: U.S.]

Walden, Michael L. The Whole Life Insurance Policy as an Options Package: An Empirical Investigation. *J. Risk Ins.*, March 1985, 52(1), pp. 44–58. [G: U.S.]

6354 Business and Legal Services

Eickhoff, Gerald E. Leveraging a Consulting Operation. In *Federal Reserve Bank of Atlanta (I)*, 1985, pp. 35–40. [G: U.S.]

Mangum, Garth; Mayall, Donald and Nelson, Kristin. The Temporary Help Industry: A Response to the Dual Internal Labor Market. *Ind. Lab. Relat. Rev.*, July 1985, 38(4), pp. 599–611. [G: U.S.]

6356 Insurance

Appel, David; Worrall, John D. and Butler, Richard J. Survivorship and the Size Distribution of the Property-Liability Insurance Industry. *J. Risk Ins.*, September 1985, 52(3), pp. 424–40. [G: U.S.]

Arnould, Richard J. and DeBrock, Lawrence M. The Effect of Provider Control of Blue Shield Plans on Health Care Markets. *Econ. Inquiry*, July 1985, 23(3), pp. 449–74. [G: U.S.]

Arrow, Kenneth J. The Implications of Transaction Costs and Adjustment Lags in Health Insurance [Uncertainty and the Welfare Economics of Medical Care]. In *Arrow, K. J. (II)*, 1985, pp. 51–55.

Arrow, Kenneth J. Theoretical Issues in Health Insurance. In *Arrow, K. J. (II)*, 1985, pp. 208–33.

Arrow, Kenneth J. Welfare Analysis of Changes in Health Coinsurance Rates. In *Arrow, K. J. (II)*, 1985, pp. 234–54.

Babbel, David F. The Price Elasticity of Demand for Whole Life Insurance. *J. Finance*, March 1985, *40*(1), pp. 225–39.   [G: U.S.]

Ben-Zion, Barry and Reddall, Ronald G. Life Expectancy and Actuarial Present Values: A Note to Forensic Economists. In *Zerbe, R. O., Jr., ed.*, 1985, pp. 161–71.

Blazenko, George. The Design of an Optimal Insurance Policy: Note. *Amer. Econ. Rev.*, March 1985, *75*(1), pp. 253–55.

Borscheid, Peter. The Establishment of the Life Insurance Business in Germany in the Nineteenth Century. In *Engels, W. and Pohl, H., eds.*, 1985, pp. 55–74.   [G: Germany]

Boyer, Marcel and Dionne, Georges. Sécurité routière: responsabilité pour négligence et tarification. Road Safety: Liability for Negligence and Pricing. With English summary.) *Can. J. Econ.*, November 1985, *18*(4), pp. 814–30.

Brady, Dennis; Brookshire, Michael and Cobb, William. The Development and Solution of a Tax-adjusted Model for Personal Injury Awards: A Response. *J. Risk Ins.*, September 1985, *52*(3), pp. 520–21.   [G: U.S.]

Briys, Eric P. and Loubergé, Henri. On the Theory of Rational Insurance Purchasing: A Note. *J. Finance*, June 1985, *40*(2), pp. 577–81.

Bronars, Stephen G. Fair Pricing of Unemployment Insurance Premiums. *J. Bus.*, January 1985, *58*(1), pp. 27–47.   [G: U.S.]

Brueckner, Jan K. A Simple Model of Mortgage Insurance. *Amer. Real Estate Urban Econ. Assoc. J.*, Summer 1985, *13*(2), pp. 129–42.

Cather, David A.; Gustavson, Sandra G. and Trieschmann, James S. A Profitability Analysis of Property-Liability Insurers Using Alternative Distribution Systems. *J. Risk Ins.*, June 1985, *52*(2), pp. 321–32.   [G: U.S.]

Cave, Jonathan A. K. Subsidy Equilibrium and Multiple-Option Insurance Markets. In *Scheffler, R. M. and Rossiter, L. F., eds.*, 1985, pp. 27–45.

Chamberlin, John R. Assessing the Fairness of Insurance Classifications. In *Zerbe, R. O., Jr., ed.*, 1985, pp. 65–87.   [G: U.S.]

Chang, Rosita P.; Lord, Blair M. and Rhee, S. Ghon. Inflation-caused Wealth-transfer: A Case of the Insurance Industry. *J. Risk Ins.*, December 1985, *52*(4), pp. 627–43. [G: U.S.]

Chang, Yang-Ming and Ehrlich, Issac. Insurance, Protection from Risk, and Risk-bearing. *Can. J. Econ.*, August 1985, *18*(3), pp. 574–86.

Clapp, John M. Quantity Competition in Spatial Markets with Incomplete Information. *Quart. J. Econ.*, May 1985, *100*(2), pp. 519–28.

Conrad, Douglas A.; Grembowski, David and Milgrom, Peter. Adverse Selection within Dental Insurance Markets. In *Scheffler, R. M. and Rossiter, L. F., eds.*, 1985, pp. 171–90. [G: U.S.]

Corkett, C. Earl. Minimizing Mortgage Loan Default Risks: Panel Presentation. In *Federal Home Loan Bank of San Francisco.*, 1985, pp. 70–77.   [G: U.S.]

Cresta, Jean-Paul. Tarification sur un marché monopolistique avec sélection adverse. (With English summary.) *Revue Écon. Polit.*, July-August 1985, *95*(4), pp. 397–413.

Crocker, Keith J. and Snow, Arthur. A Simple Tax Structure for Competitive Equilibrium and Redistribution in Insurance Markets with Asymmetric Information. *Southern Econ. J.*, April 1985, *51*(4), pp. 1142–50.

Crocker, Keith J. and Snow, Arthur. The Efficiency of Competitive Equilibria in Insurance Markets with Asymmetric Information. *J. Public Econ.*, March 1985, *26*(2), pp. 207–19.

Culyer, A. J. On Being Right or Wrong about the Welfare State. In *Bean, P.; Ferris, J. and Whynes, D., eds.*, 1985, pp. 122–41. [G: U.K.]

Daly, Michael J.; Rao, P. Someshwar and Geehan, Randall. Productivity, Scale Economies and Technical Progress in the Canadian Life Insurance Industry. *Int. J. Ind. Organ.*, September 1985, *3*(3), pp. 345–61.   [G: Canada]

Danzon, Patricia M. Liability and Liability Insurance for Medical Malpractice. *J. Health Econ.*, December 1985, *4*(4), pp. 309–31.   [G: U.S.]

Dionne, Georges and Lasserre, Pierre. Adverse Selection, Repeated Insurance Contracts and Announcement Strategy. *Rev. Econ. Stud.*, October 1985, *52*(4), pp. 719–23.

Dorfman, Mark. Insuring an Aging Society. *J. Risk Ins.*, March 1985, *52*(1), pp. 9–11. [G: U.S.]

Dowd, Bryan and Feldman, Roger. Biased Selection in Twin Cities Health Plans. In *Scheffler, R. M. and Rossiter, L. F., eds.*, 1985, pp. 253–71.   [G: U.S.]

Dubinsky, Alan J. and Yammarino, Francis J. Job-related Responses of Insurance Agents: A Multi-firm Investigation. *J. Risk Ins.*, September 1985, *52*(3), pp. 501–17.   [G: U.S.]

Ellis, Randall P. The Effect of Prior-Year Health Expenditures on Health Coverage Plan Choice. In *Scheffler, R. M. and Rossiter, L. F., eds.*, 1985, pp. 149–70.   [G: U.S.]

Fanara, Philip, Jr. and Greenberg, Warren. The Impact of Competition and Regulation on Blue Cross Enrollment of Non-group Individuals. *J. Risk Ins.*, June 1985, *52*(2), pp. 185–98. [G: U.S.]

Farley, Pamela J. and Monheit, Alan C. Selectivity in the Demand for Health Insurance and Health Care. In *Scheffler, R. M. and Rossiter, L. F., eds.*, 1985, pp. 231–48.   [G: U.S.]

Farley, Pamela J. and Wilensky, Gail R. Household Wealth and Health Insurance as Protection against Medical Risks. In *David, M. and*

Smeeding, T., eds., 1985, pp. 323–54.
[G: U.S.]

Felgran, Steven D. Banks as Insurance Agencies: Legal Constraints and Competitive Advances. *New Eng. Econ. Rev.*, Sept./Oct. 1985, pp. 34–49. [G: U.S.]

Field, Marilyn J. Comments on Policy Implications of Biased Selection in Health Insurance. In *Scheffler, R. M. and Rossiter, L. F., eds.*, 1985, pp. 249–52. [G: U.S.]

Fonkam, Azu'u. Insurance Law and Practice in Cameroon. *J. World Trade Law*, March:April 1985, *19*(2), pp. 136–46. [G: Cameroon]

Freifelder, Leonard R. Measuring the Impact of Merit Rating on Ratemaking Efficiency. *J. Risk Ins.*, December 1985, *52*(4), pp. 607–26.
[G: U.S.]

Freund, Deborah A. Improving the Medicare HMO Payment Formula to Deal with Biased Selection: Comments. In *Scheffler, R. M. and Rossiter, L. F., eds.*, 1985, pp. 123–26.
[G: U.S.]

Ginsburg, Paul B. Reflections on Biased Selection and Future Directions. In *Scheffler, R. M. and Rossiter, L. F., eds.*, 1985, pp. 275–80.
[G: U.S.]

Greenlick, Merwyn R. Medicare Capitation Payments to HMOs in Light of Regression toward the Mean in Health Care Costs: Comments. In *Scheffler, R. M. and Rossiter, L. F., eds.*, 1985, pp. 97–100. [G: U.S.]

Gustavson, Sandra G. Moving Insurance Education into the Computer Age. *J. Risk Ins.*, June 1985, *52*(2), pp. 301–10. [G: U.S.]

Hammond, Elizabeth M. and Kay, John A. Insurance Regulation in the United Kingdom and the Federal Republic of Germany. In *Currie, D., ed.*, 1985, pp. 192–206. [G: U.K.; W. Germany]

Hansmann, Henry. The Organization of Insurance Companies: Mutual versus Stock. *J. Law, Econ., Organ.*, Spring 1985, *1*(1), pp. 125–53.
[G: U.S.]

Harris, William G. Inflation Risk as a Determinant of the Discount Rate in Tort Settlements: Reply. *J. Risk Ins.*, September 1985, *52*(3), pp. 533–36. [G: U.S.]

Headon, Alvin E., Jr. and Headon, Sandra W. General Health Conditions and Medical Insurance Issues Concerning Black Women. *Rev. Black Polit. Econ.*, Fall-Winter 1985-86, *14*(2–3), pp. 183–97. [G: U.S.]

Hogarth, Robin M. and Kunreuther, Howard. Ambiguity and Insurance Decisions. *Amer. Econ. Rev.*, May 1985, *75*(2), pp. 386–90.
[G: U.S.]

Jaeger, Mireille. Un indicateur du prix des services d'assurance: application à l'analyse concurrentielle de l'assurance française depuis 1970. (A Price Indicator of Insurance Services: Application to a Competitive Analysis of the French Insurance Industry since 1970. With English summary.) *Écon. Soc.*, December 1985, *19*(12), pp. 5–32. [G: France]

Johns, Lucy; Derzon, Robert A. and Anderson, Maren D. Selective Contracting in California:

Early Effects and Policy Implications. *Inquiry*, Spring 1985, *22*(1), pp. 24–32. [G: U.S.]

Johnson, Larry J. and Phelps, John R. The Development and Solution of a Tax-adjusted Model for Personal Injury Awards: A Clarification. *J. Risk Ins.*, September 1985, *52*(3), pp. 518–19. [G: U.S.]

Kendall, Leon T. Mastering Mortgage Loan Portfolio Risks in Deregulated Markets: Panel Presentation. In *Federal Home Loan Bank of San Francisco.*, 1985, pp. 78–82. [G: U.S.]

Kimball, Spencer L. The Contest of "No Fault." *J. Risk Ins.*, December 1985, *52*(4), pp. 662–66. [G: U.S.]

Kochanowski, Paul S. and Young, Madelyn V. Deterrent Aspects of No-Fault Automobile Insurance: Some Empirical Findings. *J. Risk Ins.*, June 1985, *52*(2), pp. 269–88. [G: U.S.]

Krinsky, Itzhak. Mean–Variance Utility Functions, Flexible Functional Forms, and the Investment Behavior of Canadian Life Insurers. *J. Risk Ins.*, June 1985, *52*(2), pp. 241–68.
[G: Canada]

Kunreuther, Howard and Pauly, Mark V. Market Equilibrium with Private Knowledge: An Insurance Example. *J. Public Econ.*, April 1985, *26*(3), pp. 269–88.

Lambrinos, James. On the Use of Historical Data in the Estimation of Economic Losses. *J. Risk Ins.*, September 1985, *52*(3), pp. 464–76.
[G: U.S.]

Landau, Pinhas. Insurance—Survival Was the Name of the Game. In *Levinson, P. and Landau, P., eds.*, 1985, pp. 134–35. [G: Israel]

Lane, Julia and Glennon, Dennis. The Estimation of Age/Earnings Profiles in Wrongful Death and Injury Cases. *J. Risk Ins.*, December 1985, *52*(4), pp. 686–95. [G: U.S.]

Lee, D. Q. Insurance Aspects of Bushfire Disaster in South Australia. In *Healey, D. T.; Jarrett, F. G. and McKay, J. M., eds.*, 1985, pp. 57–73. [G: Australia]

Lee, Yoong-Sin. A Graphical Treatment of the Coinsurance Clause. *J. Risk Ins.*, December 1985, *52*(4), pp. 644–61. [G: U.S.]

Lubitz, James; Beebe, James and Riley, Gerald. Improving the Medicare HMO Payment Formula to Deal with Biased Selection. In *Scheffler, R. M. and Rossiter, L. F., eds.*, 1985, pp. 101–22. [G: U.S.]

Luft, Harold S.; Trauner, Joan B. and Maerki, Susan C. Adverse Selection in a Large, Multiple-Option Health Benefits Program: A Case Study of the California Public Employees' Retirement System. In *Scheffler, R. M. and Rossiter, L. F., eds.*, 1985, pp. 197–229.
[G: U.S.]

Mack, Thomas and Kulessa, Matthias. Reinsurance Decision Making and Expected Utility: Comment. *J. Risk Ins.*, June 1985, *52*(2), pp. 311.

Manning, Richard L.; Stephenson, Matilde K. and Todd, Jerry D. Information Technology in the Insurance Industry: A Forecast of Utilization and Impact. *J. Risk Ins.*, December 1985, *52*(4), pp. 711–22. [G: U.S.]

Marcus, Alan J. Spinoff/Terminations and the Value of Pension Insurance. *J. Finance*, July 1985, *40*(3), pp. 911–24. [G: U.S.]

Merville, Larry. Spinoff/Terminations and the Value of Pension Insurance: Discussion. *J. Finance*, July 1985, *40*(3), pp. 924–26. [G: U.S.]

Miller, Michael A. Age-related Reductions in Workers' Life Insurance. *Mon. Lab. Rev.*, September 1985, *108*(9), pp. 29–34. [G: U.S.]

Monheit, Alan C., et al. The Employed Uninsured and the Role of Public Policy. *Inquiry*, Winter 1985, *22*(4), pp. 348–64. [G: U.S.]

Moussa, H. An Alternative Solution to the Moral Hazard Problem and Some Sufficient Conditions for Its Absence. *Rech. Écon. Louvain*, 1985, *51*(2), pp. 181–94.

Neipp, Joachim and Zeckhauser, Richard J. Persistence in the Choice of Health Plans. In *Scheffler, R. M. and Rossiter, L. F., eds.*, 1985, pp. 47–72. [G: U.S.]

Neusser, Klaus. Portfolio Selection by Austrian Insurance Companies. *Empirica*, 1985, *12*(1), pp. 25–41. [G: Austria]

Newhouse, Joseph P. Household Wealth and Health Insurance as Protection against Medical Risks: Comment. In *David, M. and Smeeding, T., eds.*, 1985, pp. 354–58. [G: U.S.]

Ogunrinde, R. O. The Claim Settlement Provisions of the Nigerian Insurance Act of 1976: A Solution to What Problem? *J. World Trade Law*, March:April 1985, *19*(2), pp. 170–78. [G: Nigeria]

Outreville, J. François and Malouin, Jean-Louise. What Are the Major Journals That Members of ARIA Read? *J. Risk Ins.*, December 1985, *52*(4), pp. 723–33. [G: U.S.]

Outreville, J. François and Proulx, Carol. Fusions et économies de dimension sur le marché des assurances générales au Québec. (Mergers and Economies of Scale in the Quebec Property-Liability Insurance Industry. With English summary.) *L'Actual. Econ.*, September 1985, *61*(3), pp. 350–61. [G: Canada]

Palfrey, Thomas R. and Spatt, Chester S. Repeated Insurance Contracts and Learning. *Rand J. Econ.*, Autumn 1985, *16*(3), pp. 356–67.

Pauly, Mark V. What is Adverse about Adverse Selection? In *Scheffler, R. M. and Rossiter, L. F., eds.*, 1985, pp. 281–86. [G: U.S.]

Perry, Charles R. Paradise Not Found: The Case of Insurance Workers. *J. Lab. Res.*, Winter 1985, *6*(1), pp. 45–61. [G: U.S.]

Praetz, Peter. A Note on Economies of Scale in the United Kingdom Property-Liability Insurance Industry. *J. Risk Ins.*, June 1985, *52*(2), pp. 315–20. [G: U.K.]

Price, James R. and Mays, James W. Biased Selection in the Federal Employees Health Benefits Program. *Inquiry*, Spring 1985, *22*(1), pp. 67–77. [G: U.S.]

Price, James R. and Mays, James W. Selection and the Competitive Standing of Health Plans in a Multiple-Choice, Multiple-Insurer Mar-

ket. In *Scheffler, R. M. and Rossiter, L. F., eds.*, 1985, pp. 127–47. [G: U.S.]

Reynolds, Roger A. The Effect of Prior-Year Health Expenditures on Health Coverage Plan Choice: Adverse Selection within Dental Insurance Markets: Comments. In *Scheffler, R. M. and Rossiter, L. F., eds.*, 1985, pp. 191–93. [G: U.S.]

Rochet, Jean-Charles. Vers une tarification équitable de l'assurance? (Towards Equitable Insurance Tariffs. With English summary.) *L'Actual. Econ.*, December 1985, *61*(4), pp. 453–71.

Rodeno, Raymond A. Mortgage Insurance Risk: Implications for Mortgage Design and Pricing: Panel Presentation. In *Federal Home Loan Bank of San Francisco.*, 1985, pp. 84–88. [G: U.S.]

Rolph, John E.; Hammitt, James K. and Houchens, Robert L. Automobile Accident Compensation: Who Pays How Much How Soon? *J. Risk Ins.*, December 1985, *52*(4), pp. 667–85. [G: U.S.]

Sampson, Danny and Thomas, Howard. Reinsurance Decision Making and Expected Utility: Reply. *J. Risk Ins.*, June 1985, *52*(2), pp. 312–14.

Schallheim, James S. and McConnell, John J. A Model for the Determination of "Fair" Premiums on Lease Cancellation Insurance Policies. *J. Finance*, December 1985, *40*(5), pp. 1439–57.

Schlesinger, Harris. Choosing a Deductible for Insurance Contracts: Best or Worst Insurance Policy? *J. Risk Ins.*, September 1985, *52*(3), pp. 522–27.

Schlesinger, Harris and Doherty, Neil A. Incomplete Markets for Insurance: An Overview. *J. Risk Ins.*, September 1985, *52*(3), pp. 402–23.

Simpson, William A. Conforming Adjustable Mortgage Loans: Panel Presentation. In *Federal Home Loan Bank of San Francisco.*, 1985, pp. 90–96. [G: U.S.]

Smith, Barry D. The Effect of Life Insurance Underwriting Practices on Mortality Results. *J. Risk Ins.*, September 1985, *52*(3), pp. 441–63. [G: U.S.]

Smith, Michael L. and Witt, Robert C. An Economic Analysis of Retroactive Liability Insurance. *J. Risk Ins.*, September 1985, *52*(3), pp. 379–401. [G: U.S.]

Stowe, John D. and Watson, Collin J. A Multivariate Analysis of the Composition of Life Insurer Balance Sheets. *J. Risk Ins.*, June 1985, *52*(2), pp. 223–40. [G: U.S.; Canada]

Szpiro, George M. Optimal Insurance Coverage. *J. Risk Ins.*, December 1985, *52*(4), pp. 704–10.

Tauer, Loren W. Use of Life Insurance to Fund the Farm Purchase from Heirs. *Amer. J. Agr. Econ.*, February 1985, *67*(1), pp. 60–69. [G: U.S.]

Troy, John F. The Impact of Medicare Financing Reforms: A View from the Private Sector: Remarks. In *Employee Benefit Research Institute.*, 1985, pp. 57–62. [G: U.S.]

Troy, John F. The Impact of Medicare Financing Reforms: A View from the Private Sector. In *Employee Benefit Research Institute.*, 1985, pp. 45–57. [G: U.S.]

Venezian, Emilio C. Coding Errors and Classification Refinement. *J. Risk Ins.*, December 1985, *52*(4), pp. 734–42.

Venezian, Emilio C. Interactions in Insurance Classifications. *J. Risk Ins.*, December 1985, *52*(4), pp. 571–84. [G: U.S.]

Venezian, Emilio C. Ratemaking Methods and Profit Cycles in Property and Liability Insurance. *J. Risk Ins.*, September 1985, *52*(3), pp. 477–500. [G: U.S.]

Vernon, Jack. Inflation Risk as Determinant of the Discount Rate in Tort Settlements: Comment. *J. Risk Ins.*, September 1985, *52*(3), pp. 528–32. [G: U.S.]

Warshawsky, Mark. Life Insurance Savings and the After-Tax Life Insurance Rate of Return. *J. Risk Ins.*, December 1985, *52*(4), pp. 585–606. [G: U.S.]

Weiss, Mary. A Multivariate Analysis of Loss Reserving Estimates in Property-Liability Insurers. *J. Risk Ins.*, June 1985, *52*(2), pp. 199–221. [G: U.S.]

Welch, W. P. Health Care Utilization in HMO's: Results from Two National Samples. *J. Health Econ.*, December 1985, *4*(4), pp. 293–308. [G: U.S.]

Welch, W. P. Medicare Capitation Payments to HMOs in Light of Regression toward the Mean in Health Care Costs. In *Scheffler, R. M. and Rossiter, L. F., eds.*, 1985, pp. 75–96. [G: U.S.]

Wiatrowski, William J. Employee Income Protection against Short-term Disabilities. *Mon. Lab. Rev.*, February 1985, *108*(2), pp. 32–38. [G: U.S.]

Yett, Donald E., et al. Fee-Screen Reimbursement and Physician Fee Inflation. *J. Human Res.*, Spring 1985, *20*(2), pp. 278–91. [G: U.S.]

6357 Real Estate

Abelson, Peter W. House and Land Prices in Sydney: 1925 to 1970. *Urban Stud.*, December 1985, *22*(6), pp. 521–34. [G: Australia]

Asabere, Paul K. and Harvey, Barrie. Factors Influencing the Value of Urban Land: Evidence from Halifax-Dartmouth, Canada. *Amer. Real Estate Urban Econ. Assoc. J.*, Winter 1985, *13*(4), pp. 361–77. [G: Canada]

Barnett, Colin J. An Application of the Hedonic Price Model to the Perth Residential Land Market. *Econ. Rec.*, March 1985, *61*(172), pp. 476–81. [G: Australia]

Cordes, Joseph J. and Galper, Harvey. Tax Shelter Activity: Lessons from Twenty Years of Evidence. *Nat. Tax J.*, September 1985, *38*(3), pp. 305–24. [G: U.S.]

Dale-Johnson, David, et al. Valuation and Efficiency in the Market for Creatively Financed Houses. *Amer. Real Estate Urban Econ. Assoc.*

J., Winter 1985, *13*(4), pp. 388–403. [G: U.S.]

Eckart, Wolfgang. On the Land Assembly Problem. *J. Urban Econ.*, November 1985, *18*(3), pp. 364–78.

Elliott, Donald S., Jr.; Quinn, Michael A. and Mendelson, Robert E. Maintenance Behavior of Large-Scale Landlords and Theories of Neighborhood Succession. *Amer. Real Estate Urban Econ. Assoc. J.*, Winter 1985, *13*(4), pp. 424–45. [G: U.S.]

Fogler, H. Russell; Granito, Michael R. and Smith, Laurence R. A Theoretical Analysis of Real Estate Returns. *J. Finance*, July 1985, *40*(3), pp. 711–19. [G: U.S.]

Gamble, Hays B. and Downing, Roger H. The Relationship between Population Growth and Real Assessed Market Values: Note. *Growth Change*, July 1985, *16*(3), pp. 74–77. [G: U.S.]

Gau, George W. Public Information and Abnormal Returns in Real Estate Investment. *Amer. Real Estate Urban Econ. Assoc. J.*, Spring 1985, *13*(1), pp. 15–31. [G: Canada]

Goldberg, Michael A. American Real Estate and Urban Economics: A Canadian Perspective. *Amer. Real Estate Urban Econ. Assoc. J.*, Spring 1985, *13*(1), pp. 1–14. [G: Canada; U.S.]

Guy, Donald C.; Hysom, John L. and Ruth, Stephen R. The Effect of Subsidized Housing on Values of Adjacent Housing. *Amer. Real Estate Urban Econ. Assoc. J.*, Winter 1985, *13*(4), pp. 378–87. [G: U.S.]

Hekman, John S. Rental Price Adjustment and Investment in the Office Market. *Amer. Real Estate Urban Econ. Assoc. J.*, Spring 1985, *13*(1), pp. 32–47. [G: U.S.]

Henderson, J. Vernon. The Impact of Zoning Policies Which Regulate Housing Quality. *J. Urban Econ.*, November 1985, *18*(3), pp. 302–12.

Ling, David C. and Whinihan, Michael J. Valuing Depreciable Real Estate: A New Methodology. *Amer. Real Estate Urban Econ. Assoc. J.*, Summer 1985, *13*(2), pp. 181–94.

Ohkawara, Toru. Urban Residential Land Rent Function: An Alternative Muth–Mills Model [Economic Analysis of an Urban Housing Market]. *J. Urban Econ.*, November 1985, *18*(3), pp. 338–49. [G: Japan]

Rogers, Ronald C. and Owers, James E. The Investment Performance of Real Estate Limited Partnerships. *Amer. Real Estate Urban Econ. Assoc. J.*, Summer 1985, *13*(2), pp. 153–66. [G: U.S.]

Shilling, James D.; Benjamin, John D. and Sirmans, C. F. Contracts as Options: Some Evidence from Condominium Developments. *Amer. Real Estate Urban Econ. Assoc. J.*, Summer 1985, *13*(2), pp. 143–52. [G: U.S.]

Solt, Michael E. and Miller, Norman G. Managerial Incentives: Implications for the Financial Performance of Real Estate Investment Trusts. *Amer. Real Estate Urban Econ. Assoc. J.*, Winter 1985, *13*(4), pp. 404–23.   [G: U.S.]

Statman, Meir. A Theoretical Analysis of Real Estate Returns: Discussion. *J. Finance*, July 1985, *40*(3), pp. 719–21.   [G: U.S.]

6358 Entertainment, Recreation, and Tourism

Amoako-Adu, Ben; Marmer, Harry and Yagil, Joseph. The Efficiency of Certain Speculative Markets and Gambler Behavior. *J. Econ. Bus.*, December 1985, *37*(4), pp. 365–78.
[G: U.S.]

Arbel, Avner and Ravid, S. Abraham. On Recreation Demand: A Time-Series Approach. *Appl. Econ.*, December 1985, *17*(6), pp. 979–90.
[G: U.S.]

Bajic, Vladimir. Determinants of Theatre Going: The Effects on the Choice of Residential Location. *J. Cult. Econ.*, December 1985, *9*(2), pp. 60–70.   [G: Canada]

Baumol, Hilda and Baumol, William J. On the Cost Disease and Its True Policy Implications for the Arts. In *[Peacock, A.]*, 1985, pp. 67–77.

Baumol, Hilda and Baumol, William J. The Future of the Theater and the Cost Disease of the Arts. *J. Cult. Econ.*, Supplement 1985, pp. 7–31.   [G: U.S.]

Beck, Kirsten. Cultivating the Wasteland: The U.S. Cultural Cable Experience. *J. Cult. Econ.*, Supplement 1985, pp. 67–81.
[G: U.S.]

Bird, Richard M.; Bucovetsky, Meyer W. and Yatchew, Adonis John. Tax Incentives for Film Production: The Canadian Experience. *Public Finance Quart.*, October 1985, *13*(4), pp. 396–421.   [G: Canada]

Bolyard, Joan E. International Travel and Passenger Fares, 1984. *Surv. Curr. Bus.*, May 1985, *65*(5), pp. 14–17.   [G: U.S.]

Coughlin, Cletus C. and Erekson, O. Homer. Contributions to Intercollegiate Athletic Programs: Further Evidence. *Soc. Sci. Quart.*, March 1985, *66*(1), pp. 194–202.   [G: U.S.]

Crafts, N. F. R. Some Evidence of Insider Knowledge in Horse Race Betting in Britain. *Economica*, August 1985, *52*(207), pp. 295–304.
[G: U.K.]

Cymrot, Donald J. Does Competition Lessen Discrimination? Some Evidence. *J. Human Res.*, Fall 1985, *20*(4), pp. 605–12. [G: U.S.]

DeBoer, Larry. Is Rock 'n' Roll a Symptom of Baumol's Disease? *J. Cult. Econ.*, December 1985, *9*(2), pp. 48–59.   [G: U.S.]

Dolan, Robert C. and Schmidt, Robert M. Assessing the Competitive Effects of Major League Baseball's Reentry Draft. *Amer. Econ.*, Spring 1985, *29*(1), pp. 21–31.   [G: U.S.]

Dupuis, Xavier. The Microeconomics of the Performing Arts. *J. Cult. Econ.*, Supplement 1985, pp. 33–50.   [G: France]

Fong, Mo-Kwan Lee. Tourism: A Critical Review. In *Wong, K. and Chu, D. K. Y.*, *eds.*, 1985, pp. 79–88.   [G: China]

Fujii, Edwin T.; Khaled, Mohammed and Mak, James. An Almost Ideal Demand System for

Visitor Expenditures. *J. Transp. Econ. Policy*, May 1985, *19*(2), pp. 161–71.   [G: U.S.]

Fujii, Edwin T.; Khaled, Mohammed and Mak, James. The Exportability of Hotel Occupancy and Other Tourist Taxes. *Nat. Tax J.*, June 1985, *38*(2), pp. 169–77.   [G: U.S.]

Gapinski, James H. The Economics of Performing Shakespeare: Reply. *Amer. Econ. Rev.*, December 1985, *75*(5), pp. 1210–12.   [G: U.K.]

Gardini, Attilio. Una stima e una verifica statistica del modello differenziale di Rotterdam. (Analysis of Demand for Tourist Services in Italy: Statistical Estimate and Test of the Rotterdam Differential Model. With English summary.) *Statistica*, July-Sept. 1985, *45*(3), pp. 319–37.
[G: Italy]

Garnham, Nicholas. Baumol's Disease: Audio-Visual Markets a Cure? *J. Cult. Econ.*, Supplement 1985, pp. 59–65. [G: U.S.; W. Europe]

Geddert, Ronald L. and Semple, R. Keith. Locating a Major Hockey Franchise: Regional Considerations. *Reg. Sci. Persp.*, 1985, *15*(1), pp. 13–29.   [G: U.S.; Canada]

Gratton, Chris and Taylor, Peter. The Economics of Sport Sponsorship. *Nat. Westminster Bank Quart. Rev.*, August 1985, pp. 53–68.
[G: U.K.]

Guillard, Jean-Pierre. The Symphony as a Public Service: The Orchestra of Paris. *J. Cult. Econ.*, December 1985, *9*(2), pp. 35–47.
[G: France]

Halpern, Dan. Tourism. In *Levinson, P. and Landau, P.*, *eds.*, 1985, pp. 136–38.   [G: Israel]

Henderson, Peter A. and Bruggink, Thomas H. Will Running Baseball as a Business Ruin the Game? *Challenge*, March/April 1985, *28*(1), pp. 53–57.   [G: U.S.]

Hendon, William S. Economic Incentives: Theater and Cultural Programming. *J. Cult. Econ.*, Supplement 1985, pp. 117–34.

Hill, James Richard. The Threat of Free Agency and Exploitation in Professional Baseball: 1976–1979. *Quart. Rev. Econ. Bus.*, Winter 1985, *25*(4), pp. 68–82.   [G: U.S.]

Hirschman, Elizabeth C. and Pieros, Andrew, Jr. Relationships among Indicators of Success in Broadway Plays and Motion Pictures. *J. Cult. Econ.*, June 1985, *9*(1), pp. 35–63.
[G: U.S.]

Hodsoll, Frank. The National Endowment for the Arts and Cultural Economics: The Information Partnership. *J. Cult. Econ.*, June 1985, *9*(1), pp. 1–12.   [G: U.S.]

Jeffrey, D. Trends and Fluctuations in Visitor Flows to Yorkshire and Humberside Hotels: An Analysis of Daily Bed Occupancy Rates, 1982–1984. *Reg. Stud.*, October 1985, *19*(6), pp. 509–22.   [G: U.K.]

Lange, Mark, et al. Cost Functions for Symphony Orchestras. *J. Cult. Econ.*, December 1985, *9*(2), pp. 71–85.   [G: U.S.]

Le Diberder, Alain. No Culture-only Channels, but a More Important Role for the Audiovisual Media. *J. Cult. Econ.*, Supplement 1985, pp. 83–98.   [G: U.S.; France]

Møller, Michael and Nielsen, Neils Chr. Er tip-

pere rationelle? (The Efficiency of the Football Pools Markets. With English summary.) *Nationaløkon. Tidsskr.*, 1985, *123*(2), pp. 239–47.
[G: Denmark]

Morrison, Steven A. and Winston, Clifford. An Econometric Analysis of the Demand for Intercity Passenger Transportation. In *Keeler, T. E., ed.*, 1985, pp. 213–37. [G: U.S.]

Pacey, Patricia L. The Courts and College Football: New Playing Rules off the Field? *Amer. J. Econ. Soc.*, April 1985, *44*(2), pp. 145–54.
[G: U.S.]

Pacey, Patricia L. and Wickham, Elizabeth D. College Football Telecasts: Where Are They Going? *Econ. Inquiry*, January 1985, *23*(1), pp. 93–113. [G: U.S.]

Patton, Spiro G. Tourism and Local Economic Development: Factory Outlets and the Reading SMSA. *Growth Change*, July 1985, *16*(3), pp. 64–73. [G: U.S.]

Peacock, Alan. The Cost Disease: Analytical and Policy Aspects. *J. Cult. Econ.*, Supplement 1985, pp. 51–58.

Pescatrice, Donn R. An Intertrack Wagering Experiment. *Eastern Econ. J.*, April-June 1985, *11*(2), pp. 157–60. [G: U.S.]

Phillips, Richard A. and Silberman, Jonathan I. Forecasting Recreation Demand: An Application of the Travel Cost Model. *Rev. Reg. Stud.*, Winter 1985, *15*(1), pp. 20–25. [G: U.S.]

Pommerehne, Werner W. and Frey, Bruno S. Kunst: Was sagt der Ökonom dazu? (Arts—The Economist's Point of View. With English summary.) *Schweiz. Z. Volkswirtsch. Statist.*, June 1985, *121*(2), pp. 139–67. [G: Switzerland]

Pope, C. Arden, III and Stoll, John R. The Market Value of Ingress Rights for White-tailed Deer Hunting in Texas. *Southern J. Agr. Econ.*, July 1985, *17*(1), pp. 177–82.
[G: U.S.]

Scahill, Edward. The Determinants of Average Salaries in Professional Football. *Atlantic Econ. J.*, March 1985, *13*(1), pp. 103.

Scott, Frank A., Jr.; Long, James E. and Somppi, Ken. Salary vs. Marginal Revenue Product under Monopsony and Competition: The Case of Professional Basketball. *Atlantic Econ. J.*, September 1985, *13*(3), pp. 50–59. [G: U.S.]

Throsby, David and Withers, Glenn. What Price Culture? *J. Cult. Econ.*, December 1985, *9*(2), pp. 1–34. [G: Australia]

Wegg-Prosser, Victoria. A Twentieth Century Story: The BBC Television Series "All Our Working Lives": Essay Review. *Labor Hist.*, Fall 1985, *26*(4), pp. 577–82. [G: U.K.]

West, Edwin G. The Economics of Performing Shakespeare: Comment. *Amer. Econ. Rev.*, December 1985, *75*(5), pp. 1206–09.

Withers, Glenn. Artists' Subsidy of the Arts. *Australian Econ. Pap.*, December 1985, *24*(45), pp. 290–95. [G: Australia]

Zuber, Richard A.; Gandar, John M. and Bowers, Benny D. Beating the Spread: Testing the Efficiency of the Gambling Market for National Football League Games. *J. Polit. Econ.*, August 1985, *93*(4), pp. 800–806. [G: U.S.]

Austen-Smith, M. David and Jenkins, Stephen P. A Multiperiod Model of Nonprofit Enterprises. *Scot. J. Polit. Econ.*, June 1985, *32*(2), pp. 119–34. [G: U.K.]

Cain, James E. and Cain, A. Sue. An Economic Analysis of Accounting Decision Variables Used to Determine the Nature of Corporate Giving. *Quart. J. Bus. Econ.*, Autumn 1985, *24*(4), pp. 15–28. [G: U.S.]

Clotfelter, Charles T. Charitable Giving and Tax Legislation in the Reagan Era. *Law Contemp. Probl.*, Autumn 1985, *48*(4), pp. 197–212.
[G: U.S.]

Gapinski, James H. Do the Nonprofit Performing Arts Optimize? The Moral from Shakespeare. *Quart. Rev. Econ. Bus.*, Summer 1985, *25*(2), pp. 27–37. [G: U.K.]

Guillard, Jean-Pierre. The Symphony as a Public Service: The Orchestra of Paris. *J. Cult. Econ.*, December 1985, *9*(2), pp. 35–47.
[G: France]

Henrich, Amy L. Preferential Treatment of Charities under the Unemployment Insurance Laws. *Yale Law J.*, May 1985, *94*(6), pp. 1472–92.
[G: U.S.]

Hodsoll, Frank. The National Endowment for the Arts and Cultural Economics: The Information Partnership. *J. Cult. Econ.*, June 1985, *9*(1), pp. 1–12. [G: U.S.]

Jaffe, Eliezer D. Israel's Non-profit Sector: Problems and Prospects. In *Levinson, P. and Landau, P., eds.*, 1985, pp. 62–64. [G: Israel]

Kramer, Ralph M. The Welfare State and the Voluntary Sector: The Case of the Personal Social Services. In *Eisenstadt, S. N. and Ahimeir, O., eds.*, 1985, pp. 132–40. [G: Israel; Netherlands; U.K.; U.S.]

McElroy, Katherine Maddox and Siegfried, John J. The Effect of Firm Size on Corporate Philanthropy. *Quart. Rev. Econ. Bus.*, Summer 1985, *25*(2), pp. 18–26. [G: U.S.]

Moran, R. Allen. Queues: The Economic Theory of Screening and Human Service Productivity. *Southern Econ. J.*, October 1985, *52*(2), pp. 492–99. [G: U.S.]

Nunamaker, Thomas R. Using Data Envelopment Analysis to Measure the Efficiency of Non-profit Organizations: A Critical Evaluation. *Managerial Dec. Econ.*, March 1985, *6*(1), pp. 50–58.

Pitkänen, Eero. Julkisyhteisöjen talous liiketaloustieteen, erityisesti laskentatoimen tutkimuskohteena. (Research on the Economics of Public Organizations in Business Economics, Especially in Accounting and Finance. With English summary.) *Liiketaloudellinen Aikak.*, 1985, *34*(1), pp. 98–107. [G: Finland]

Pommerehne, Werner W. and Frey, Bruno S. Kunst: Was sagt der Ökonom dazu? (Arts—The Economist's Point of View. With English summary.) *Schweiz. Z. Volkswirtsch. Statist.*, June 1985, *121*(2), pp. 139–67. [G: Switzerland]

Reece, William S. and Zieschang, Kimberly D. Consistent Estimation of the Impact of Tax Deductibility on the Level of Charitable Contributions. *Econometrica*, March 1985, *53*(2), pp. 271–93. [G: U.S.]

Schiff, Jerald. Does Government Spending Crowd Out Charitable Contributions? *Nat. Tax J.*, December 1985, *38*(4), pp. 535–46. [G: U.S.]

Sullivan, Dennis H. Simultaneous Determination of Church Contributions and Church Attendance. *Econ. Inquiry*, April 1985, *23*(2), pp. 309–20. [G: U.S.]

Weiss, Jeffrey H. Can Donations Reduce a Donor's Welfare? *Public Choice*, 1985, *47*(2), pp. 337–47.

Zurawicka, Janina. Charity in Warsaw in the Second Half of the XIXth Century. *J. Europ. Econ. Hist.*, Fall 1985, *14*(2), pp. 319–30. [G: Poland]

640 ECONOMIC CAPACITY

641 Economic Capacity

6410 Economic Capacity

Bosworth, Derek. Fuel Based Measures of Capital Utilisation. *Scot. J. Polit. Econ.*, February 1985, *32*(1), pp. 20–38. [G: U.K.]

Burns, Michael E. and Mitchell, William F. Real Wages, Unemployment and Economic Policy in Australia. *Australian Econ. Pap.*, June 1985, *24*(44), pp. 1–23. [G: Australia]

Draper, Niek A. G. Exports of the Manufacturing Industry, an Econometric Analysis of the Significance of Capacity. *De Economist*, 1985, *133*(3), pp. 285–305. [G: Netherlands]

Fal'tsman, V. and Kornev, A. Reserves for Reducing the Investment Intensiveness of Industrial Capacities. *Prob. Econ.*, March 1985, *27*(11), pp. 23–38. [G: U.S.S.R.]

Feigenbaum, Susan and Willett, Thomas D. Domestic versus International Influences on Protectionist Pressures in the United States. In *Arndt, S. W.; Sweeney, R. J. and Willett, T. D., eds.*, 1985, pp. 181–90. [G: U.S.]

Foss, Murray F. Changing Utilization of Fixed Capital: An Element in Long-term Growth. *Mon. Lab. Rev.*, May 1985, *108*(5), pp. 3–8. [G: U.S.]

Gelauff, George M. M.; Wennekers, Sander R. M. and de Jong, André H. M. A Putty-Clay Model with Three Factors of Production and Partly Endogenous Technical Progress. *De Economist*, 1985, *133*(3), pp. 327–51. [G: Netherlands]

Harris, Richard and Taylor, Jim. The Measurement of Capacity Utilization. *Appl. Econ.*, October 1985, *17*(5), pp. 849–66. [G: U.K.]

Harrison, Mark. Investment Mobilization and Capacity Completion in the Chinese and Soviet Economies. *Econ. Planning*, 1985, *19*(2), pp. 56–75. [G: China; U.S.S.R.]

Hazari, Bharat R. and Bakalis, Steve. An Analysis of Capital Underutilization in Less Developed Countries—A Trade Theoretic Approach. *Devel. Econ.*, March 1985, *23*(1), pp. 3–15.

Jackson, John D. and Smyth, David J. Specifying Differential Cyclical Response in Economic Time Series: Capacity Utilization and Demand for Imports. *Econ. Modelling*, April 1985, *2*(2), pp. 149–61. [G: U.S.]

Kouri, Pentti J. K.; Braga de Macedo, Jorge and Viscio, Albert J. Profitability, Employment and Structural Adjustment in France. In *Melitz, J. and Wyplosz, C., eds.*, 1985, pp. 85–112. [G: France]

Lock, J. D. Measuring the Value of the Capital Stock by Direct Observation. *Rev. Income Wealth*, June 1985, *31*(2), pp. 127–38. [G: Netherlands]

Mairesse, Jacques. Profitability, Employment and Structural Adjustment in France: Comments. In *Melitz, J. and Wyplosz, C., eds.*, 1985, pp. 114–16. [G: France]

McElhattan, Rose. Inflation, Supply Shocks and the Stable-Inflation Rate of Capacity Utilization. *Fed. Res. Bank San Francisco Econ. Rev.*, Winter 1985, (1), pp. 45–63. [G: U.S.]

Morrison, Catherine J. On the Economic Interpretation and Measurement of Optimal Capacity Utilization with Anticipatory Expectations. *Rev. Econ. Stud.*, April 1985, *52*(2), pp. 295–310. [G: U.S.]

Morrison, Catherine J. Primal and Dual Capacity Utilization: An Application to Productivity Measurement in the U.S. Automobile Industry. *J. Bus. Econ. Statist.*, October 1985, *3*(4), pp. 312–24. [G: U.S.]

Parker, Ian. Harold Innis: Staples, Communications, and the Economics of Capacity, Overhead Costs, Rigidity, and Bias. In *[Spry, I. M.]*, 1985, pp. 73–93.

Raddock, Richard D. Revised Federal Reserve Rates of Capacity Utilization. *Fed. Res. Bull.*, October 1985, *71*(10), pp. 754–66. [G: U.S.]

Reynolds, Stanley S. Capacity, Output, and Sequential Entry: Comment. *Amer. Econ. Rev.*, September 1985, *75*(4), pp. 894–96.

Robinson, P. William. Capacity Constraints, Real Wages and the Role of the Public Sector in Creating Jobs. In *Kay, J., ed.*, 1985, pp. 40–50. [G: U.K.]

Spulber, Daniel F. Capacity, Output, and Sequential Entry: Reply. *Amer. Econ. Rev.*, September 1985, *75*(4), pp. 897–98.

Stark-Veltel, Gerd and Westphal, Uwe. Schzung des Produktionspotentials mit einem Putty-Clay-Ansatz. (A Putty-Clay Approach to the Estimation of Potential Output. With English summary.) *Ifo-Studien*, 1985, *31*(4), pp. 269–93. [G: W. Germany]

Thayer, Frederick C. The Crisis of Industrial Overcapacity: Avoiding Another Great Depression. In *Didsbury, H. F., Jr., ed.*, 1985, pp. 353–90. [G: U.S.]

Vernardakis, Nikos. Capital Utilization, Its Determinants and Export Subsidies. *Greek Econ. Rev.*, August 1985, *7*(2), pp. 125–43. [G: Greece]

Woodham, Douglas M. How Fast Can Europe

Grow? *Fed. Res. Bank New York Quart. Rev.*, Summer 1985, *10*(2), pp. 28–35.   [G: U.S.; W. Germany; U.K.]

700 Agriculture; Natural Resources

710 AGRICULTURE

7100 General

Ahmad, Alia. The Effect of Population Growth on a Peasant Economy: The Case of Bangladesh. In *Lundahl, M., ed.*, 1985, pp. 87–104.
[G: Bangladesh]

Ashton, John. Agricultural Markets and Prices. *Europ. Rev. Agr. Econ.*, 1985, *12*(1/2), pp. ix–xvi.   [G: EEC]

Austin, James; Fox, Jonathan and Kruger, Walter. The Role of the Revolutionary State in the Nicaraguan Food System. *World Devel.*, January 1985, *13*(1), pp. 15–40.
[G: Nicaragua]

Barker, Jonathan. Gaps in the Debates about Agriculture in Senegal, Tanzania and Mozambique. *World Devel.*, January 1985, *13*(1), pp. 59–76. [G: Senegal; Tanzania; Mozambique]

Barlow, Colin. Indonesian and Malayan Agricultural Development, 1870–1940. *Bull. Indonesian Econ. Stud.*, April 1985, *21*(1), pp. 81–111.   [G: Indonesia; Malaysia]

Belongia, Michael T. The Impact of Inflation on the Real Income of U.S. Farmers: Discussion. *Amer. J. Agr. Econ.*, May 1985, 67(2), pp. 398–99.   [G: U.S.]

Bharadwaj, Krishna. A Note on Commercialization in Agriculture. In *Raj, K. N., et al., eds.*, 1985, pp. 331–47.

Boserup, Ester. The Primary Sector in African Development. In *Lundahl, M., ed.*, 1985, pp. 56–65.   [G: Africa]

Bredahl, Maury E. The Effects of Inflation on the Welfare and Performance of Agriculture: Discussion [The Impact of Inflation on the Real Income of U.S. Farmers]. *Amer. J. Agr. Econ.*, May 1985, 67(2), pp. 400–401.   [G: U.S.]

Breimyer, Harold F. Agriculture and the Political Economy. *Challenge*, Nov./Dec. 1985, *28*(5), pp. 15–21.   [G: U.S.]

Breimyer, Harold F. Agriculture's Problem Is Rooted in Washington. *Challenge*, May/June 1985, *28*(2), pp. 53–54.   [G: U.S.]

Broder, Josef M. The Southern Agricultural Economics Association and Resident Instruction. *Southern J. Agr. Econ.*, July 1985, *17*(1), pp. 7–14.   [G: U.S.]

Broder, Josef M. and Deprey, Rodney P. Monetary Returns to Bachelors and Masters Degrees in Agricultural Economics. *Amer. J. Agr. Econ.*, August 1985, 67(3), pp. 666–73.
[G: U.S.]

Campagne, P. and Savané, M. A. Quel avenir pour les nouvelles stratégies alimentaires des paysanneries du Sahel? (What Future for the Food Strategies and Sahelian Peasants? With English summary.) *Écon. Soc.*, July 1985, *19*(7), pp. 23–45.   [G: Senegal]

Casas, Joseph. La stratégie agro-alimentaire de Cuba depuis 1959 et ses résultats. (Agri-Food Strategy and Results in Cuba since 1959. With English summary.) *Écon. Soc.*, July 1985, *19*(7), pp. 111–60.   [G: Cuba]

Chambers, Robert G. Credit Constraints, Interest Rates, and Agricultural Prices [Exchange Rates and U.S. Agriculture]. *Amer. J. Agr. Econ.*, May 1985, 67(2), pp. 390–95.
[G: U.S.]

Conner, J. Richard. Observations on Changes in Factors Influencing Agricultural Economics and Some Implications for the Profession. *Southern J. Agr. Econ.*, July 1985, *17*(1), pp. 1–6.   [G: U.S.]

Crom, Richard J. Range Economics Research (The National Interest). *Western J. Agr. Econ.*, July 1985, *10*(1), pp. 110–15.   [G: U.S.]

Darr, Todd and Gribbons, Gerry. How U.S. Exports Are Faring in the World Wheat Market. *Mon. Lab. Rev.*, October 1985, *108*(10), pp. 10–24.   [G: U.S.]

Davies, H. R. J. Natural Resources and Rural Development in Arid Lands: Case Studies from Sudan: Introduction. In *Davies, H. R. J., ed.*, 1985, pp. vii–x.   [G: Africa; Sudan]

Davis, Carlton G. Human Capital Needs of Black Land-Grant Institutions: Discussion. *Southern J. Agr. Econ.*, July 1985, *17*(1), pp. 71–73.
[G: U.S.]

Deane, Hugh. Mao's Rural Strategies: What Went Wrong? *Sci. Soc.*, Spring 1985, *49*(1), pp. 101–07.   [G: China]

Dhindsa, K. S. Some Aspects of Green Revolution—A Case Study. *Margin*, April 1985, *17*(3), pp. 50–54.   [G: India]

Englander, A. Steven. The Interaction of Research and Training in Agricultural Development. In *Lundahl, M., ed.*, 1985, pp. 309–325.

Figueroa, Manuel. Rural Development and Urban Food Programming. *Cepal Rev.*, April 1985, (25), pp. 111–27.   [G: Latin America]

Glassburner, Bruce. Macroeconomics and the Agricultural Sector. *Bull. Indonesian Econ. Stud.*, August 1985, *21*(2), pp. 51–73.
[G: Indonesia]

Goddard, E. The Future Role of the Agricultural Economist in Outlook Preparation. *Can. J. Agr. Econ.*, August 1985, *32*, pp. 86–99.

Guedry, Leo J., Jr. Teaching, Research, and Extension Programs at Predominantly Black Land-Grant Institutions: Discussion. *Southern J. Agr. Econ.*, July 1985, *17*(1), pp. 43–45.
[G: U.S.]

Hardaker, J. Brian. Beliefs and Values in Agricultural Economics Research. *Australian J. Agr. Econ.*, August 1985, *29*(2), pp. 97–106.

Harris, Harold M., Jr. Role of the Southern Agricultural Economics Association in Extension: Discussion. *Southern J. Agr. Econ.*, July 1985, *17*(1), pp. 27–29.   [G: U.S.]

Hartford, Kathleen. Hungarian Agriculture: A Model for the Socialist World? *World Devel.*, January 1985, *13*(1), pp. 123–50.
[G: Hungary]

Herrmann, Roland, et al. A Survey of Views of

Agricultural Economists in Europe. *Europ. Rev. Agr. Econ.*, 1985, *12*(3), pp. 295–311.
[G: W. Europe]

Holland, David and Carvalho, Joe. The Changing Mode of Production in American Agriculture: Emerging Conflicts in Agriculture's Role in the Reproduction of Advanced Capitalism. *Rev. Radical Polit. Econ.*, Winter 1985, *17*(4), pp. 1–27.
[G: U.S.]

Jackson, R. V. Growth and Deceleration in English Agriculture, 1660–1790. *Econ. Hist. Rev.*, *2nd Ser.*, August 1985, *38*(3), pp. 333–51.
[G: U.K.]

Joshi, P. C. Agriculture. In *Mongia, J. N., ed.*, 1985, pp. 25–66.
[G: India]

Kemenes, Egon. The Role and Pattern of Domestic Financing in the Process of Economic Development: Empirical Evidence. In *Gutowski, A.; Arnaudo, A. A. and Scharrer, H.-E., eds.*, 1985, pp. 29–41.
[G: LDCs]

Knutson, Ronald D. Role of the Southern Agricultural Economics Association in Extension. *Southern J. Agr. Econ.*, July 1985, *17*(1), pp. 17–25.
[G: U.S.]

Kohl, David M. The Southern Agricultural Economics Association and Resident Instruction: Discussion. *Southern J. Agr. Econ.*, July 1985, *17*(1), pp. 15–16.
[G: U.S.]

Krongkaew, Medhi. Agricultural Development, Rural Poverty, and Income Distribution in Thailand. *Devel. Econ.*, December 1985, *23*(4), pp. 325–46.
[G: Thailand]

Lee, Chinkook and Culver, David W. Agricultural Development in Three Asian Countries: A Comparative Analysis. *Agr. Econ. Res.*, Winter 1985, *37*(1), pp. 8–13.
[G: Japan; Korea; Taiwan]

Livingstone, Ian. Agricultural Development Strategy and Agricultural Pricing Policy in Malawi. In *Arhin, K.; Hesp, P. and van der Laan, L., eds.*, 1985, pp. 169–92.
[G: Malawi]

Lundahl, Mats. The Primary Sector in Economic Development: Proceedings of the Seventh Arne Ryde Symposium, Frostavallen, August 29–30 1983: Introduction. In *Lundahl, M., ed.*, 1985, pp. 1–39.

Mackintosh, Maureen. Economic Tactics: Commercial Policy and the Socialization of African Agriculture. *World Devel.*, January 1985, *13*(1), pp. 77–96.
[G: Africa]

Malassis, L. Politiques et stratégies alimentaires. (Policies and Food Strategies. With English summary.) *Écon. Soc.*, July 1985, *19*(7), pp. 3–22.

Mamalakis, Markos J. The Primary Sector: Composition and Functions. In *Lundahl, M., ed.*, 1985, pp. 43–55.

Mandle, Jay R. The Role of Agriculture in Self-Reliant Development. *Soc. Econ. Stud.*, June 1985, *34*(2), pp. 153–75.
[G: Caribbean]

McIntosh, Wm. Alex and Picou, J. Steven. Manpower Training and the Political Economy of Agriculture: CETA and the Texas Agricultural Environment. *Soc. Sci. Quart.*, June 1985, *66*(2), pp. 330–45.
[G: U.S.]

Mundle, Sudipto. The Agrarian Barrier to Indus-

trial Growth. In *Saith, A., ed.*, 1985, pp. 49–80.
[G: W. Europe; Japan; India]

Mundle, Sudipto. The Agrarian Barrier to Industrial Growth. *J. Devel. Stud.*, October 1985, *22*(1), pp. 49–80.
[G: W. Europe; Japan; India]

Munslow, Barry. Prospects for the Socialist Transition of Agriculture in Zimbabwe. *World Devel.*, January 1985, *13*(1), pp. 41–58.
[G: Zimbabwe]

Nabi, Ijaz and van de Laar, Aart. The Role of Agriculture in the Development of Pakistan. In *Jerve, A. M., ed.*, 1985, pp. 181–98.
[G: Pakistan]

Oshima, Harry T. Levels and Trends of Farm Families' Nonagricultural Incomes at Different Stages of Monsoon Development. *Philippine Rev. Econ. Bus.*, Sept./Dec. 1985, *22*(3/4), pp. 123–54.

Parks, Alfred L. and Robbins, Richard D. Human Capital Needs of Black Land-Grant Institutions. *Southern J. Agr. Econ.*, July 1985, *17*(1), pp. 61–69.
[G: U.S.]

Prokopenko, N. The Quality of Labor and Output in Agriculture. *Prob. Econ.*, July 1985, *28*(3), pp. 81–96.
[G: U.S.S.R.]

Rahman, Atiq. Agricultural Inputs in Bangladesh: Editor's Introduction. *Bangladesh Devel. Stud.*, Sept.-Dec. 1985, *13*(3&4), pp. iii–x.
[G: Bangladesh]

Raj, K. N. Essays on the Commercialization of Indian Agriculture: Introduction. In *Raj, K. N., et al., eds.*, 1985, pp. vii–xx.

Saith, Ashwani. Primitive Accumulation, Agrarian Reform and Socialist Transitions: An Argument. *J. Devel. Stud.*, October 1985, *22*(1), pp. 1–48.
[G: U.S.S.R.; LDCs; China]

Saith, Ashwani. Primitive Accumulation, Agrarian Reform and Socialist Transitions: An Argument. In *Saith, A., ed.*, 1985, pp. 1–48.
[G: U.S.S.R.; LDCs; China]

Sarris, Alexander H. Food Security and Agricultural Production Strategies under Risk in Egypt. *J. Devel. Econ.*, Sept.-Oct. 1985, *19*(1/2), pp. 85–111.
[G: Egypt]

Shammas, Carole. Black Women's Work and the Evolution of Plantation Society in Virginia. *Labor Hist.*, Winter 1985, *26*(1), pp. 5–28.
[G: U.S.]

Shaw, Anthony B. Constraints on Agricultural Innovation Adoption. *Econ. Geogr.*, January 1985, *61*(1), pp. 25–45.
[G: Guyana]

Starleaf, Dennis R.; Meyers, William H. and Womack, Abner W. The Impact of Inflation on the Real Income of U.S. Farmers. *Amer. J. Agr. Econ.*, May 1985, *67*(2), pp. 384–89.
[G: U.S.]

Strout, Alan M. Managing the Agricultural Transformation on Java: A Review of the *Survey Agro Ekonomi. Bull. Indonesian Econ. Stud.*, April 1985, *21*(1), pp. 62–80.
[G: Indonesia]

Suits, Daniel B. U.S. Farm Migration: An Application of the Harris–Todaro Model. *Econ. Develop. Cult. Change*, July 1985, *33*(4), pp. 815–28.
[G: U.S.]

Sullivan, Richard J. The Timing and Pattern of

Technological Development in English Agriculture, 1611–1850. *J. Econ. Hist.*, June 1985, *45*(2), pp. 305–14. **[G: U.K.]**

Thompson, Gary; Amon, Ricardo and Martin, Philip L. Mexicans or Tomatoes? Immigration and Imports. *J. Policy Anal. Manage.*, Summer 1985, *4*(4), pp. 603–05.
[G: Mexico; U.S.]

Thompson, Robert. Towards Agricultural Self-reliance in Grenada: An Alternative Model. In *Gomes, P. I., ed.*, 1985, pp. 123–53.
[G: Grenada]

Varga, Gy. Thirty Years of the Research Institute of Agrarian Economics. *Acta Oecon.*, 1985, *34*(3/4), pp. 374–81. **[G: Hungary]**

Veeman, Terrence S. and Veeman, Michele M. Western Canadian Agriculture: Prospects, Problems and Policy. *Can. Public Policy*, Supplement July 1985, *11*(3), pp. 301–09.
[G: Canada]

Williams, Thomas T. and Williamson, Handy, Jr. Teaching, Research, and Extension Programs at Predominantly Black Land-Grant Institutions. *Southern J. Agr. Econ.*, July 1985, *17*(1), pp. 31–41. **[G: U.S.]**

Wilson, Fiona. Women and Agricultural Change in Latin America: Some Concepts Guiding Research. *World Devel.*, September 1985, *13*(9), pp. 1017–35. **[G: Latin America]**

711 Agricultural Supply and Demand Analysis

7110 Agricultural Supply and Demand Analysis

Abedin, Joynal. Input Demand and Output Supply Elasticities for Rice in Bangladesh—A Study Based on Thakurgaon Farmers. *Bangladesh Devel. Stud.*, Sept.-Dec. 1985, *13*(3&4), pp. 111–25. **[G: Bangladesh]**

Abu Sin, M. E. Planners' and Participants' Perceptions of Development in the Semi-arid Lands of Sudan: A Case Study of the Khashm El Girba Scheme. In *Davies, H. R. J., ed.*, 1985, pp. 60–80. **[G: Sudan]**

Ackello-Ogutu, Christopher; Paris, Quirino and Williams, William A. Testing a von Liebig Crop Response Function against Polynomial Specifications. *Amer. J. Agr. Econ.*, November 1985, *67*(4), pp. 873–80. **[G: U.S.]**

Adamowicz, Wiktor L. and Manning, Travis W. The Measurement of Growth Rates from Time Series. *Can. J. Agr. Econ.*, July 1985, *33*(2), pp. 231–42. **[G: Canada]**

Adams, Richard H., Jr. Development and Structural Change in Rural Egypt, 1952 to 1982. *World Devel.*, June 1985, *13*(6), pp. 705–23.
[G: Egypt]

Adams, Richard M. and McCarl, Bruce A. Assessing the Benefits of Alternative Ozone Standards on Agriculture: The Role of Response Information. *J. Environ. Econ. Manage.*, September 1985, *12*(3), pp. 264–76. **[G: U.S.]**

Ahluwalia, Montek S. Rural Poverty, Agricultural Production, and Prices: A Reexamination. In *Mellor, J. W. and Desai, G. M., eds.*, 1985, pp. 59–75. **[G: India]**

Ahmed, Raisuddin. Growth and Equity in Indian Agriculture and a Few Paradigms from Bangladesh. In *Mellor, J. W. and Desai, G. M., eds.*, 1985, pp. 124–27. **[G: India; Bangladesh]**

Akhtar, Sajjad. Effects of the Timing and the Number of Sprays on Cotton Yields in Sind: An Exploratory Analysis. *Pakistan Devel. Rev.*, Summer 1985, *24*(2), pp. 173–81.
[G: Pakistan]

Alaouze, Chris M.; Read, Michael and Sturgess, N. H. A Statistical Analysis of a Pilot Survey of Salt-affected Dairy Farms. *Australian J. Agr. Econ.*, April 1985, *29*(1), pp. 49–62.
[G: Australia]

Albert, Bill. External Forces and the Transformation of Peruvian Coastal Agriculture, 1880–1930. In *Abel, C. and Lewis, C. M., eds.*, 1985, pp. 231–49. **[G: Peru]**

Anderson, Ronald W. and Wilkinson, M. Consumer Demand for Meat and the Evaluation of Agricultural Policy. *Empirical Econ.*, 1985, *10*(2), pp. 65–89. **[G: U.S.]**

Atkinson, Scott E.; Adams, Richard M. and Crocker, Thomas D. Optimal Measurement of Factors Affecting Crop Production: Maximum Likelihood Methods. *Amer. J. Agr. Econ.*, May 1985, *67*(2), pp. 414–18.
[G: U.S.]

Aylward, Justin. Sugar. In *Roberts, G., ed.*, 1985, pp. 134–46. **[G: Global]**

Bailey, DeeVon and Brorsen, B. Wade. Dynamics of Regional Fed Cattle Prices. *Western J. Agr. Econ.*, July 1985, *10*(1), pp. 126–33.
[G: U.S.]

Bailey, DeeVon and Brorsen, B. Wade. Hedging Carcass Beef to Reduce the Short-term Price Risk of Meat Packers. *Western J. Agr. Econ.*, December 1985, *10*(2), pp. 330–37.
[G: U.S.]

Bailey, Kenneth W. Palay Area Response in the Philippines under Conditions of Technical Change. *Philippine Econ. J.*, 1985, *24*(4), pp. 302–21. **[G: Philippines]**

Bailey, Kenneth W. and Womack, Abner W. Wheat Acreage Response: A Regional Econometric Investigation. *Southern J. Agr. Econ.*, December 1985, *17*(2), pp. 171–80.
[G: U.S.]

Bale, Malcolm D. Food Prices and the Poor in Developing Countries: Opening of the Discussion. *Europ. Rev. Agr. Econ.*, 1985, *12*(1/2), pp. 82–83. **[G: LDCs]**

Ball, V. Eldon. Output, Input, and Productivity Measurement in U.S. Agriculture, 1948-79. *Amer. J. Agr. Econ.*, August 1985, *67*(3), pp. 475–86. **[G: U.S.]**

Barzelay, Michael and Pearson, Scott R. The Efficiency of Producing Alcohol for Energy in Brazil: Reply. *Econ. Develop. Cult. Change*, July 1985, *33*(4), pp. 857–63. **[G: Brazil]**

Bautista, Romeo M. Effects of Trade and Exchange Rate Policies on Export Production Incentives in Philippine Agriculture. *Philippine Econ. J.*, 1985, *24*(2–3), pp. 87–115.
[G: Philippines]

Bebawi, F. F.; El-Hag, G. A. and Khogali,

M. M. The Production of Dura (Sorghum Vulgare) in Sudan and the Parasite Buda (Striga Hermonthica) In *Davies, H. R. J., ed.*, 1985, pp. 1–15. [G: Sudan]

Behrman, Jere R. and Murty, K. N. Market Impacts of Technological Change for Sorghum in Indian Near-Subsistence Agriculture. *Amer. J. Agr. Econ.*, August 1985, 67(3), pp. 539–49. [G: India]

Belbase, Krishna; Grabowski, Richard and Sanchez, Onesimo. The Marginal Productivity of Inputs and Agricultural Production in Nepal. *Pakistan Devel. Rev.*, Spring 1985, 24(1), pp. 51–60. [G: Nepal]

Belongia, Michael T. and Stone, Courtenay C. Would Lower Federal Deficits Increase U.S. Farm Exports? *Fed. Res. Bank St. Louis Rev.*, November 1985, 67(9), pp. 5–19. [G: U.S.]

Benson, Bruce L. and Faminow, Merle D. An Alternative View of Pricing in Retail Food Markets. *Amer. J. Agr. Econ.*, May 1985, 67(2), pp. 296–306.

Beresford, Melanie. Agriculture in the Transition to Socialism: The Case of South Vietnam. In *Lundahl, M., ed.*, 1985, pp. 370–95. [G: Vietnam]

Bertrand, Jean-Pierre and Green, Raùl H. Brésil et Thaïlande: stratégies agro-exportatrices, urbanisation et changements de l'alimentation de base. (Brazil and Thailand: Agro-export Oriented Strategies: Urbanisation and Food Consumption Models Change. With English summary.) *Écon. Soc.*, July 1985, 19(7), pp. 83–109. [G: Brazil; Thailand]

Birdsall, Nancy. A Population Perspective on Agricultural Development. In *Davis, T. J., ed.*, 1985, pp. 29–51. [G: Selected LDCs; Selected MDCs]

Booth, Anne. Accommodating a Growing Population in Javanese Agriculture. *Bull. Indonesian Econ. Stud.*, August 1985, 21(2), pp. 115–45. [G: Indonesia]

Boyd, Michael L. The Effect of Policy on System Performance: The Case of Yugoslav Agriculture. *Comparative Econ. Stud.*, Summer 1985, 27(2), pp. 1–23. [G: Yugoslavia]

Boyd, Milton S. and Brorsen, B. Wade. Dynamic Relationship of Weekly Prices in the United States Beef and Pork Marketing Channels. *Can. J. Agr. Econ.*, November 1985, 33(3), pp. 331–42. [G: U.S.]

Brandt, Loren. Chinese Agriculture and the International Economy, 1870–1930s: A Reassessment. *Exploration Econ. Hist.*, April 1985, 22(2), pp. 168–93. [G: China]

Brennan, John P. and Spohr, Lorraine J. A Note on the Effects on Yields of Shifts in the Australian Wheat Belt. *Australian J. Agr. Econ.*, December 1985, 29(3), pp. 235–43. [G: Australia]

Brorsen, B. Wade; Chavas, Jean-Paul and Grant, Warren R. A Dynamic Analysis of Prices in the U.S. Rice Marketing Channel. *J. Bus. Econ. Statist.*, October 1985, 3(4), pp. 362–69. [G: U.S.]

Brorsen, B. Wade and Grant, Warren R. Efficiency of Spatial Price Discovery for U.S. Rice under Different Farm Policies and Economic Conditions. *J. Policy Modeling*, Winter 1985, 7(4), pp. 621–33. [G: U.S.]

Brorsen, B. Wade; Grant, Warren R. and Chavas, Jean-Paul. Dynamic Relationships and Efficiency of Rice Byproduct Prices. *Agr. Econ. Res.*, Spring 1985, 37(2), pp. 15–26. [G: U.S.]

Brorsen, B. Wade, et al. Marketing Margins and Price Uncertainty: The Case of the U.S. Wheat Market. *Amer. J. Agr. Econ.*, August 1985, 67(3), pp. 521–28. [G: U.S.]

Brundenius, Claes and Zimbalist, Andrew. Cuban Economic Growth One More Time: A Response to "Imbroglios." [Recent Studies on Cuban Economic Growth: A Review]. *Comparative Econ. Stud.*, Fall 1985, 27(3), pp. 115–31. [G: Cuba]

Brundenius, Claes and Zimbalist, Andrew. Cuban Growth: A Final Worth [Cuban Economic Growth One More Time: A Response to Imbroglios]. *Comparative Econ. Stud.*, Winter 1985, 27(4), pp. 83–84. [G: Cuba]

Brundenius, Claes and Zimbalist, Andrew. Recent Studies on Cuban Economic Growth: A Review. *Comparative Econ. Stud.*, Spring 1985, 27(1), pp. 21–45. [G: Cuba]

Bryceson, Deborah Fahy. The Organization of Tanzanian Grain Marketing: Switching Roles of the Co-operative and the Parastatal. In *Arhin, K.; Hesp, P. and van der Laan, L., eds.*, 1985, pp. 53–78. [G: Tanzania]

Buckingham, A. C. Rubber. In *Roberts, G., ed.*, 1985, pp. 116–20. [G: Global]

Buckley, John. Soyabeans. In *Roberts, G., ed.*, 1985, pp. 125–33. [G: Global]

Buttel, Frederick H.; Kenney, Martin and Kloppenburg, Jack, Jr. From Green Revolution to Biorevolution: Some Observations on the Changing Technological Bases of Economic Transformation in the Third World. *Econ. Develop. Cult. Change*, October 1985, 34(1), pp. 31–55. [G: LDCs]

Canarella, Giorgio and Pollard, Stephen K. Price and Output Expectations in Agricultural Policy: The Case of Jamaica. *J. Econ. Devel.*, December 1985, 10(2), pp. 19–34. [G: Jamaica]

Carter, Colin A. High Technology in Agriculture and International Trade. *Can. J. Agr. Econ.*, August 1985, 32, pp. 24–35. [G: Canada]

Carter, Colin A. International Trade Opportunities for Canadian Agriculture. *Can. J. Agr. Econ.*, July 1985, 32, pp. 1–17. [G: Canada]

Caswell, Nim. Peasants, Peanuts and Politics: State Marketing in Senegal, 1966–80. In *Arhin, K.; Hesp, P. and van der Laan, L., eds.*, 1985, pp. 79–119. [G: Senegal]

Chambers, Robert G. Macroeconomics and U.S. Agricultural Policy: Commentary. In *Gardner, B. L., ed.*, 1985, pp. 253–56. [G: U.S.]

Chambers, Robert G.; Just, Richard E. and Moffitt, L. Joe. Estimation in Markets with Unobserved Price Barriers: An Application to the California Retail Milk Market. *Appl. Econ.*,

December 1985, *17*(6), pp. 991–1002.
[G: U.S.]

Chambers, Robert G. and Vasavada, Utpal. Testing Asset Fixity for Agriculture: Reply. *Amer. J. Agr. Econ.*, February 1985, *67*(1), pp. 139–40. [G: U.S.]

Chaudhary, Mohammad Aslam. Food Self-Sufficiency, Agricultural Adequacy and Impacts of Green Revolution in Pakistan. *Pakistan Econ. Soc. Rev.*, Winter 1985, *23*(2), pp. 95–112. [G: Pakistan]

Chisholm, Anthony H. and Tyers, Rodney. Agricultural Protection and Market Insulation Policies: Applications of a Dynamic Multisectoral Model. In *Piggott, J. and Whalley, J., eds.*, 1985, pp. 189–220. [G: Selected Countries]

Cliffe, Mark. Commodity Prices and World Economic Recovery. In *Meyer, F. V., ed.*, 1985, pp. 144–62. [G: OECD]

Coclanis, Peter A. Bitter Harvest: The South Carolina Low Country in Historic Perspective. *J. Econ. Hist.*, June 1985, *45*(2), pp. 251–59. [G: U.S.]

Cook, Christopher James. The Estimation of Aggregate Agricultural Output Responsiveness: A Case Study of Colombia. *Can. J. Devel. Stud.*, 1985, *6*(2), pp. 257–74. [G: Colombia]

Cornelisse, Peter A. and de Kruijk, Hans. Consumption and Trade of Wheat and Flour in Pakistan—The Role of Public and Private Sector. *Pakistan Devel. Rev.*, Summer 1985, *24*(2), pp. 151–71. [G: Pakistan]

Cornelisse, Peter A. and Kuijpers, Bart. On the Optimal Size of a Buffer Stock—The Case of Wheat in Pakistan. *Pakistan Devel. Rev.*, Autumn-Winter 1985, *24*(3/4), pp. 335–46.
[G: Pakistan]

Cornia, Giovanni Andrea. Farm Size, Land Yields and the Agricultural Production Function: An Analysis for Fifteen Developing Countries. *World Devel.*, April 1985, *13*(4), pp. 513–34. [G: Selected LDCs]

Cowan, C. A. Potatoes—The Influence of Age and Regional Differences on Preference for Size. *Irish J. Agr. Econ. Rural Soc.*, 1984-1985, *10*(2), pp. 119–27. [G: Ireland]

Cowan, C. A.; Griffiths, T. W. and Reid, S. N. A Survey of the Acceptability of Rashers by Consumers in the Dublin Area with Particular Reference to Salt Content. *Irish J. Agr. Econ. Rural Soc.*, 1984-1985, *10*(2), pp. 135–44.
[G: Ireland]

Cristini, Marcela. La oferta agropecuaria: el caso del trigo en la última década. (The Agropecuarian Supply: The Wheat Case in the Last Decade. With English summary.) *Económica (La Plata)*, Jan.-Apr. 1985, *31*(1), pp. 57–80.
[G: Argentina]

Cryde, Denise J. Input Interventions and Production Efficiency in Philippine Agriculture. *Philippine Rev. Econ. Bus.*, Mar./June 1985, *22*(1/2), pp. 83–108. [G: Philippines]

Csáki, Csaba. An Outlook of Food Supply and Demand in the CMEA Countries: Results of the IIASA/FAP Model System. *Acta Oecon.*, 1985, *35*(1–2), pp. 145–64. [G: CMEA]

Cuddy, John D. A. Commodity Trade. In *Preeg, E. H., ed.*, 1985, pp. 117–33. [G: LDCs; U.S.]

Dams, Theodor. Moral Responsibility and Agricultural Research: Comment. In *[Heidhues, T.]*, 1985, pp. 84–87. [G: U.S.]

Dantwala, M. L. Technology, Growth, and Equity in Agriculture. In *Mellor, J. W. and Desai, G. M., eds.*, 1985, pp. 110–23.
[G: India]

Davis, John and Kirk, Alan. Economic Aspects of Changing the Seasonality of Milk Production and Pricing. *Irish J. Agr. Econ. Rural Soc.*, 1984-1985, *10*(2), pp. 97–108. [G: Ireland]

De Maria, A. W. Grains. In *Roberts, G., ed.*, 1985, pp. 90–97. [G: Global]

Debertin, David L. Developing Realistic Agricultural Production Functions for Use in Undergraduate Classes. *Southern J. Agr. Econ.*, December 1985, *17*(2), pp. 207–14.

Diwan, Romesh and Kallianpur, Renu. Biological Technology and Land Productivity: Fertilizers and Food Production in India. *World Devel.*, May 1985, *13*(5), pp. 627–38. [G: India]

Dixon, Bruce L.; Garcia, Philip and Mjelde, James W. Primal versus Dual Methods for Measuring the Impact of Ozone on Cash Grain Farmers. *Amer. J. Agr. Econ.*, May 1985, *67*(2), pp. 402–06. [G: U.S.]

Dolenc, Vladimir. Optimal Price Policy of Buffer Stocks. *Z. ges. Staatswiss. (JITE)*, September 1985, *141*(3), pp. 401–12.

Dudal, R.; Higgins, G. M. and Kassam, A. H. Land, Food and Population in the Developing World. In *Davis, T. J., ed.*, 1985, pp. 5–28.
[G: LDCs]

Dunn, James and Heien, Dale. The Demand for Farm Output. *Western J. Agr. Econ.*, July 1985, *10*(1), pp. 13–22. [G: U.S.]

Eckstein, Zvi. The Dynamics of Agriculture Supply: A Reconsideration. *Amer. J. Agr. Econ.*, May 1985, *67*(2), pp. 204–14.

Edquist, Charles. Technology and Work in Sugar Cane Harvesting in Capitalist Jamaica and Socialist Cuba 1958–1983. In *Gustavsson, B.; Karlsson, J. C. and Raftegard, C.*, 1985, pp. 71–82. [G: Cuba; Jamaica]

Edwards, Clark. Productivity and Structure in U.S. Agriculture. *Agr. Econ. Res.*, Summer 1985, *37*(3), pp. 1–11. [G: U.S.]

Edwards, Clark. Testing Asset Fixity for U.S. Agriculture: Comment. *Amer. J. Agr. Econ.*, February 1985, *67*(1), pp. 136–38. [G: U.S.]

Epperson, James E. and Fletcher, Stanley M. Tandem Forecasting of Price and Probability—The Case of Watermelon. *Can. J. Agr. Econ.*, November 1985, *33*(3), pp. 375–85.
[G: U.S.]

Erickson, Elizabeth and House, Robert. Multiple Objective Analysis for a Spatial Market System: A Case Study of U.S. Agricultural Policy. In *Harker, P. T., ed.*, 1985, pp. 255–77.
[G: U.S.]

Evenson, Robert E. Output Supply and Input Demand Effects of High Yielding Rice and Wheat Varieties in North Indian Agriculture.

Indian J. Quant. Econ., 1985, *1*(1), pp. 85–96. [G: India]

Farrell, Carlyle and Funk, Thomas. The Determination of Ex-Ante Returns to Agricultural Research: The Case of Plant Biotechnology in Canada. *Can. J. Agr. Econ.*, March 1985, *33*(1), pp. 67–81. [G: Canada]

Faucher, Jean-Jacques and Schneider, Hartmut. Agricultural Crisis: Structural Constraints, Prices and Other Policy Issues. In *Rose, T., ed.*, 1985, pp. 50–65. [G: Sub-Saharan Africa]

Feinerman, E.; Bresler, E. and Dagan, G. Optimization of a Spatially Variable Resource: An Illustration for Irrigated Crops. *Water Resources Res.*, June 1985, *21*(6), pp. 793–800.

Ford, Lacy K. Self-Sufficiency, Cotton, and Economic Development in the South Carolina Upcountry, 1800–1860. *J. Econ. Hist.*, June 1985, *45*(2), pp. 261–67. [G: U.S.]

French, Ben C.; King, Gordon A. and Minami, Dwight D. Planting and Removal Relationships for Perennial Crops: An Application to Cling Peaches. *Amer. J. Agr. Econ.*, May 1985, *67*(2), pp. 215–23. [G: U.S.]

García, Fe Iglesias. The Development of Capitalism in Cuban Sugar Production, 1860–1900. In *Moreno Franginals, M.; Moya Pons, F. and Engerman, S. L., eds.*, 1985, pp. 54–75. [G: Cuba]

Gemmill, Gordon. Forward Contracts or International Buffer Stocks? A Study of Their Relative Efficiencies in Stabilising Commodity Export Earnings. *Econ. J.*, June 1985, *95*(378), pp. 400–417. [G: Selected LDCs]

Gemmill, Gordon. Optimal Hedging on Futures Markets for Commodity-exporting Nations. *Europ. Econ. Rev.*, March 1985, *27*(2), pp. 243–61. [G: LDCs]

Ghose, Ajit Kumar. Transforming Feudal Agriculture: Agrarian Change in Ethiopia since 1974. *J. Devel. Stud.*, October 1985, *22*(1), pp. 127–49. [G: Ethiopia]

Ghose, Ajit Kumar. Transforming Feudal Agriculture: Agrarian Change in Ethiopia since 1974. In *Saith, A., ed.*, 1985, pp. 127–49. [G: Ethiopia]

van der Giessen, Leen B. and Post, Jaap H. Macro- and Micro-effects of the Super Levy in the Netherlands. *Europ. Rev. Agr. Econ.*, 1985, *12*(4), pp. 449–60. [G: Netherlands]

Giles, David E. A.; Goss, Barry A. and Chin, Olive P. L. Intertemporal Allocation in the Corn and Soybean Markets with Rational Expectations. *Amer. J. Agr. Econ.*, November 1985, *67*(4), pp. 749–60. [G: U.S.]

Glassburner, Bruce. Macroeconomics and the Agricultural Sector. *Bull. Indonesian Econ. Stud.*, August 1985, *21*(2), pp. 51–73. [G: Indonesia]

Glenn, Marcia. International Trade Opportunities for Canadian Agriculture: Rapporteur's Report. *Can. J. Agr. Econ.*, July 1985, 32, pp. 18–23. [G: Canada]

Godfrey, Martin. Trade and Exchange Rate Policy: A Further Contribution to the Debate. In *Rose, T., ed.*, 1985, pp. 168–79. [G: Sub-Saharan Africa]

Goldsmith, Arthur. The Private Sector and Rural Development: Can Agribusiness Help the Small Farmer? *World Devel.*, Oct./Nov. 1985, *13*(10/11), pp. 1125–38. [G: LDCs]

Gordon, Alec and Shankleman, J. Coffee. In *Roberts, G., ed.*, 1985, pp. 59–63. [G: Global]

Grabowski, Richard and Sanchez, Onesimo. An Empirical Investigation of Optimal Scale and Factor Intensity: Philippine Agriculture 1948 to 1971. *Philippine Econ. J.*, 1985, *24*(2–3), pp. 132–42. [G: Philippines]

Grabowski, Richard and Sivan, David. The Price of Food, Labor Scarcity and the Real Wage: Egypt, 1950 to 1974. *Pakistan J. Appl. Econ.*, Winter 1985, *4*(2), pp. 93–99. [G: Egypt]

Griffin, Ronald C., et al. Scheduling Inputs with Production Functions: Optimal Nitrogen Programs for Rice. *Southern J. Agr. Econ.*, July 1985, *17*(1), pp. 159–68.

Grisley, William and Gitu, Kangethe W. A Translog Cost Analysis of Turkey Production in the Mid-Atlantic Region. *Southern J. Agr. Econ.*, July 1985, *17*(1), pp. 151–58. [G: U.S.]

Gürkan, A. Arslan. The Regional Structure of Agricultural Production in Turkey: A Multivariate Perspective. *METU*, 1985, *12*(1/2), pp. 27–47. [G: Turkey]

de Haen, Hartwig. Food Prices and the Poor in Developing Countries: Comment. *Europ. Rev. Agr. Econ.*, 1985, *12*(1/2), pp. 83–85. [G: LDCs]

Hall, Lana L. and Hall, Bruce F. Some Observations on the Efficiency of Animal Production in Hungary. *Comparative Econ. Stud.*, Winter 1985, *27*(4), pp. 85–95. [G: Hungary]

Hall, N. H. and Menz, K. M. Product Supply Elasticities for the Australian Broadacre Industries, Estimated with a Programming Model. *Rev. Marketing Agr. Econ.*, April 1985, *53*(1), pp. 6–13. [G: Australia]

Hamilton, Scott A.; McCarl, Bruce A. and Adams, Richard M. The Effect of Aggregate Response Assumptions on Environmental Impact Analyses. *Amer. J. Agr. Econ.*, May 1985, *67*(2), pp. 407–13. [G: U.S.]

Hartford, Kathleen. Socialist Agriculture Is Dead; Long Live Socialist Agriculture! Organizational Transformation in Rural China. In *Perry, E. J. and Wong, C., eds.*, pp. 31–61. [G: China]

Hayami, Yujiro and Kikuchi, Masao. Agricultural Technology and Income Distribution: Two Indonesian Villages Viewed from the Japanese Experience. In *Ohkawa, K. and Ranis, G., eds.*, 1985, pp. 91–109. [G: Indonesia; Japan]

Hayami, Yujiro and Kikuchi, Masao. Directions of Agrarian Change: A View from Villages in the Philippines. In *Mellor, J. W. and Desai, G. M., eds.*, 1985, pp. 132–48. [G: Philippines]

Hebbar, B. Gopalakrishna and Bisaliah, S. Output and Employment Elasticities of a Dominant Dryland Crop. *Margin*, April 1985, *17*(3), pp. 55–65. [G: India]

Henry, Mark S. and Schluter, Gerald. Measuring Backward and Forward Linkages in the U.S. Food and Fiber System. *Agr. Econ. Res.*, Fall 1985, *37*(4), pp. 33–39. [G: U.S.]

Hesse, Helmut. Export Restrictions as a Means of Avoiding "Critical Shortages." In [*Heidhues, T.*], 1985, pp. 195–213.

Hillman, Jimmye S. and Rothenberg, Robert A. Wider Implications of Protecting Japan's Rice Farmers. *World Econ.*, March 1985, *8*(1), pp. 43–62. [G: Japan]

Hirashima, S. Poverty as a Generation's Problem: A Note on the Japanese Experience. In *Mellor, J. W. and Desai, G. M., eds.*, 1985, pp. 149–60. [G: Japan]

Ho, Teresa J. Population Growth and Agricultural Productivity in Sub-Saharan Africa. In *Davis, T. J., ed.*, 1985, pp. 92–128. [G: Sub-Saharan Africa]

Horesh, Edward and Joekes, Susan. The Impact of Primary Exports on the Ghanaian Economy: Linkages and Leakages from Mining and Cocoa 1956–69. In *Lundahl, M., ed.*, 1985, pp. 181–205. [G: Ghana]

Hossain, Mahabub. Price Response of Fertilizer Demand in Bangladesh. *Bangladesh Devel. Stud.*, Sept.-Dec. 1985, *13*(3&4), pp. 41–66. [G: Bangladesh]

Hwa, Erh-Cheng. A Model of Price and Quantity Adjustments in Primary Commodity Markets. *J. Policy Modeling*, Summer 1985, *7*(2), pp. 305–38. [G: Global]

Ioannidis, Chris. The Effect of the Quota Policy on the Cattle Stock and Its Composition. *Europ. Rev. Agr. Econ.*, 1985, *12*(4), pp. 401–10. [G: EEC]

Jordan, Jeffery L, et al. Estimating Implicit Marginal Prices of Quality Characteristics of Tomatoes. *Southern J. Agr. Econ.*, December 1985, *17*(2), pp. 139–46. [G: U.S.]

Josling, Timothy E. Markets and Prices: Links between Agriculture and the General Economy. *Europ. Rev. Agr. Econ.*, 1985, *12*(1/2), pp. 1–11. [G: EEC]

Kalirajan, K. P. and Shand, R. T. Types of Education and Agricultural Productivity: A Quantitative Analysis of Tamil Nadu Rice Farming. *J. Devel. Stud.*, January 1985, *21*(2), pp. 232–43. [G: India]

Kawagoe, Toshihiko and Hayami, Yujiro. An Intercountry Comparison of Agricultural Production Efficiency. *Amer. J. Agr. Econ.*, February 1985, *67*(1), pp. 87–92. [G: Selected Countries]

Kawagoe, Toshihiko; Hayami, Yujiro and Ruttan, Vernon W. The Intercountry Agricultural Production Function and Productivity Differences among Countries. *J. Devel. Econ.*, Sept.-Oct. 1985, *19*(1/2), pp. 113–32. [G: Selected Countries]

Kerr, William A. The Changing Economics of the Western Livestock Industry. *Can. Public Policy*, Supplement July 1985, *11*(3), pp. 294–300. [G: Canada]

Kerr, William A. The Livestock Industry and Canadian Economic Development. *Can. J.*

Agr. Econ., July 1985, *32*, pp. 64–104. [G: Canada]

Khan, M. Mahmud. Labour Absorption and Unemployment in Rural Bangladesh. *Bangladesh Devel. Stud.*, Sept.-Dec. 1985, *13*(3&4), pp. 67–88. [G: Bangladesh]

Khan, Mamood Hasan. On the Optimal Size of a Buffer Stock—The Case of Wheat in Pakistan: Comments. *Pakistan Devel. Rev.*, Autumn-Winter 1985, *24*(3/4), pp. 337–48. [G: Pakistan]

Khan, Qaiser M. A Model of Endowment-constrained Demand for Food in an Agricultural Economy with Empirical Applications to Bangladesh. *World Devel.*, September 1985, *13*(9), pp. 1055–65. [G: Bangladesh]

Kikuchi, Masao and Hayami, Yujiro. Agricultural Growth against a Land-Resource Constraint: Japan, Taiwan, Korea, and the Philippines. In *Ohkawa, K. and Ranis, G., eds.*, 1985, pp. 67–90. [G: Japan; Taiwan; S. Korea; Philippines]

Kiss, István N. Agricultural and Livestock Production: Wine and Oxen. The Case of Hungary. In *Maczak, A.; Samsonowicz, H. and Burke, P., eds.*, 1985, pp. 84–96. [G: Hungary]

Klein, Herbert S. and Engerman, Stanley L. The Transition from Slave to Free Labor: Notes on a Comparative Economic Model. In *Moreno Franginals, M.; Moya Pons, F. and Engerman, S. L., eds.*, 1985, pp. 255–69. [G: Caribbean; Brazil; U.S.]

Klemme, Richard M. A Stochastic Dominance Comparison of Reduced Tillage Systems in Corn and Soybean Production under Risk. *Amer. J. Agr. Econ.*, August 1985, *67*(3), pp. 550–57. [G: U.S.]

Lachica-Sosa, Mary Ann Celeste. The Linear Programming Approach in the Derivation of a Food Price Index. *Philippine Econ. J.*, 1985, *24*(2–3), pp. 181–99. [G: Philippines]

LaFrance, Jeffrey T. and de Gorter, Harry. Regulation in a Dynamic Market: The U.S. Dairy Industry. *Amer. J. Agr. Econ.*, November 1985, *67*(4), pp. 821–32. [G: U.S.]

Lahiri, Ashok Kumar and Roy, Prannoy. Rainfall and Supply–Response: A Study of Rice in India. *J. Devel. Econ.*, August 1985, *18*(2–3), pp. 315–34. [G: India]

Lama de Espinosa, Jaime. Markets and Prices: Links between Agriculture and the General Economy: Opening of the Discussion. *Europ. Rev. Agr. Econ.*, 1985, *12*(1/2), pp. 12–14. [G: EEC]

Lányi, Kamilla. Hungarian Agriculture: Export Surplus or Superfluous Growth? (Contribution to the Development Strategy of Hungarian Agriculture). *Acta Oecon.*, 1985, *34*(3/4), pp. 299–315. [G: Hungary]

LeBlanc, Michael. The Effects of Natural Gas Decontrol on Fertilizer Demand, Production Costs, and Income in Agriculture. *Energy J.*, January 1985, *6*(1), pp. 117–35. [G: U.S.]

LeBlanc, Michael and Hrubovcak, James. The Effects of Interest Rates on Agricultural Machinery Investment. *Agr. Econ. Res.*, Summer

1985, 37(3), pp. 12–22. [G: U.S.]

Lee, David R. and Helmberger, Peter G. Estimating Supply Response in the Presence of Farm Programs. *Amer. J. Agr. Econ.*, May 1985, 67(2), pp. 193–203. [G: U.S.]

Lee, Jonq-Ying and Brown, Mark G. Coupon Redemption and the Demand for Frozen Concentrated Orange Juice: A Switching Regression Analysis. *Amer. J. Agr. Econ.*, August 1985, 67(3), pp. 647–53. [G: U.S.]

Lele, Uma. Terms of Trade, Agricultural Growth, and Rural Poverty in Africa. In *Mellor, J. W. and Desai, G. M., eds.*, 1985, pp. 161–80. [G: Sub-Saharan Africa]

Lipton, Michael. Education and Farm Efficiency: Comment. *Econ. Develop. Cult. Change*, October 1985, 34(1), pp. 167–68. [G: Nepal]

Loyns, R. M. A. The Livestock Industry and Canadian Economic Development: Rapporteur's Report. *Can. J. Agr. Econ.*, July 1985, 32, pp. 105–10. [G: Canada]

Lundahl, Mats. Agricultural Stagnation in Chile, 1930–55: A Result of Factor Market Imperfections? In *Lundahl, M., ed.*, 1985, pp. 105–30. [G: Chile]

MacArthur, J., et al. The Canadian Beef and Pork Sectors: New Found Relevance of Live Market Information. *Can. J. Agr. Econ.*, July 1985, 33(2), pp. 151–69. [G: Canada]

Macgregor, John. Philippines: Agricultural Sector/Inputs Project. In *Davis, T. J., ed.*, 1985, pp. 189–97. [G: Philippines]

Mackie, J. A. C. The Changing Political Economy of an Export Crop: The Case of Jember's Tobacco Industry. *Bull. Indonesian Econ. Stud.*, April 1985, 21(1), pp. 112–39. [G: Indonesia]

Mahmood, Muhammad. An Integrated Model of Production, Consumption and Export of Jute in Bangladesh. *Singapore Econ. Rev.*, April 1985, 30(1), pp. 56–67. [G: Bangladesh]

Makowski, Marek and Sosnowski, Janusz. A Decision Support System for Planning and Controlling Agricultural Production with a Decentralized Management Structure. In *Grauer, M.; Thompson, M. and Wierzbicki, A. P., eds.*, 1985, pp. 296–305.

Malish, Anton F. Soviet Trade in Agricultural Commodities and Technology. In *Parrott, B., ed.*, 1985, pp. 203–40. [G: U.S.S.R.; U.S.]

Marloie, Marcel. La stratégie alimentaire de la France au XIXᵉ siècle: quelles leçons pour aujourd'hui? (The French Food Strategy in the 19th Century: What Lessons at Now? With English summary.) *Écon. Soc.*, July 1985, 19(7), pp. 179–205. [G: France]

Marsh, John M. Monthly Price Premiums and Discounts between Steer Calves and Yearlings. *Amer. J. Agr. Econ.*, May 1985, 67(2), pp. 307–14. [G: U.S.]

Marsh, John M. and Brester, Gary W. Short-term Adjustments in Yellow Sheet Carcass Prices for Red Meats. *Amer. J. Agr. Econ.*, August 1985, 67(3), pp. 591–99. [G: U.S.]

Martin, William J. and Porter, Darrell. Testing for Changes in the Structure of the Demand for Meat in Australia. *Australian J. Agr. Econ.*,

April 1985, 29(1), pp. 16–31. [G: Australia]

Masud, Sharif M., et al. Impact of a More Intensive Insect Pest Infestation Level on Cotton Production: Texas High Plains. *Southern J. Agr. Econ.*, December 1985, 17(2), pp. 117–25. [G: U.S.]

Mathur, Subodh C. Rural Poverty and Agricultural Performance in India. *J. Devel. Stud.*, April 1985, 21(3), pp. 422–28. [G: India]

Mayne, D. Tea. In *Roberts, G., ed.*, 1985, pp. 147–53. [G: Global]

McIntosh, Curtis E. and Manchew, Patricia. Nutritional Needs, Food Availability and the Realism of Self-sufficiency. In *Gomes, P. I., ed.*, 1985, pp. 212–31. [G: Caribbean]

Medani, A. I. Food and Stabilization in Developing Africa. *World Devel.*, June 1985, 13(6), pp. 685–90. [G: Africa]

Mellor, John W. Determinants of Rural Poverty: The Dynamics of Production, Technology, and Price. In *Mellor, J. W. and Desai, G. M., eds.*, 1985, pp. 21–40. [G: LDCs]

Menkhaus, Dale J.; St. Clair, James S. and Hallingbye, Stig. A Reexamination of Consumer Buying Behavior for Beef, Pork, and Chicken. *Western J. Agr. Econ.*, July 1985, 10(1), pp. 116–25. [G: U.S.]

Mesa-Lago, Carmelo and Perez-Lopez, Jorge. Imbroglios on the Cuban Economy: A Reply. *Comparative Econ. Stud.*, Spring 1985, 27(1), pp. 47–83. [G: Cuba]

Mesa-Lago, Carmelo and Perez-Lopez, Jorge. The Endless Cuban Economy Saga: A Terminal Rebuttal [Recent Studies on Cuban Economic Growth: A Review]. *Comparative Econ. Stud.*, Winter 1985, 27(4), pp. 67–82. [G: Cuba]

Mitchell, Donald O. Trends in Grain Consumption in the Developing World, 1960–80. *Finance Develop.*, December 1985, 22(4), pp. 12–13. [G: LDCs]

Mody, Ashoka; Mundle, Sudipto and Raj, K. N. Resource Flows from Agriculture: Japan and India. In *Ohkawa, K. and Ranis, G., eds.*, 1985, pp. 266–93. [G: Japan; India]

Moghadam, Fatemeh E. An Evaluation of the Productive Performance of Agribusinesses: An Iranian Case Study. *Econ. Develop. Cult. Change*, July 1985, 33(4), pp. 755–76. [G: Iran]

Mohammad, Faiz. Farm Prices and the Green Revolution: Some Reflections on the Performance of Private Agricultural Markets in Pakistan. *Pakistan Devel. Rev.*, Summer 1985, 24(2), pp. 103–23. [G: Pakistan]

Mohammad, Sharif and Whalley, John. Controls and the Intersectoral Terms of Trade: The Indian Case. *Econ. J.*, September 1985, 95(379), pp. 759–66. [G: India]

Moock, Peter R. Education and Farm Efficiency: Reply. *Econ. Develop. Cult. Change*, October 1985, 34(1), pp. 169–72. [G: Nepal]

Morrisson, Christian. Agricultural Production and Government Policy in Burkina Faso and Mali. In *Rose, T., ed.*, 1985, pp. 66–77. [G: Burkina Faso; Mali]

Mukherjee, Mridula. Commercialization and

Agrarian Change in Pre-independence Punjab. In *Raj, K. N., et al., eds.*, 1985, pp. 51–104. [G: India]

Mules, T. J. Where There's Smoke There's Fire— An Apology and a Statement. *Rev. Marketing Agr. Econ.*, April 1985, 53(1), pp. 29–31.

Müller, A. L. Private Enterprise in Soviet Agriculture. *J. Stud. Econ. Econometrics*, November 1985, (23), pp. 51–66. [G: U.S.S.R.]

Myers, R. J.; Piggott, R. R. and MacAulay, T. G. Effects of Past Australian Wheat Price Policies on Key Industry Variables. *Australian J. Agr. Econ.*, April 1985, 29(1), pp. 1–15. [G: Australia]

Nagy, Joseph G. The Overall Rate of Return to Agricultural Research and Extension Investments in Pakistan. *Pakistan J. Appl. Econ.*, Summer 1985, 4(1), pp. 17–28. [G: Pakistan]

Nascimento, Jean-Claude and Raffinot, Marc. Politique de prix agricoles et comportement des producteurs: le cas de l'arachide au Sénégal. (Agricultural Pricing Policy and Primary Producers' Behavior: The Case of Senegal. With English summary.) *Revue Écon.*, July 1985, 36(4), pp. 779–96. [G: Senegal]

Nazarenko, V. I. European Countries with Centrally-planned Economies: Markets and Prices. *Europ. Rev. Agr. Econ.*, 1985, 12(1/2), pp. 17–26. [G: CMEA]

Ndulu, Benno J. and Msambichaka, Lucian A. Agricultural Sector Development in Tanzania 1961–82: Performance and Major Constraints. In *Lundahl, M., ed.*, 1985, pp. 352–69. [G: Tanzania]

Nguyen, Dung and Vo, Trang T. On Discarding Low Quality Produce. *Amer. J. Agr. Econ.*, August 1985, 67(3), pp. 614–18.

Nove, Alec. Soviet Peasantry in World War II. In *Linz, S. J., ed.*, 1985, pp. 77–90. [G: U.S.S.R.]

Önal, Hayri. Competitive Equilibrium Computations under Separated Demand Functions. *METU*, 1985, 12(3/4), pp. 333–42. [G: Turkey]

Ortmann, G. F. A Production Function Analysis of the South African Sugar Industry. *S. Afr. J. Econ.*, December 1985, 53(4), pp. 402–15. [G: S. Africa]

Osband, Kent. The Boll Weevil versus "King Cotton." *J. Econ. Hist.*, September 1985, 45(3), pp. 627–43. [G: U.S.]

Oskam, Arie J. A Super-Levy System for the Dairy Sector: Consequences and Alternatives. *Europ. Rev. Agr. Econ.*, 1985, 12(4), pp. 431–48. [G: EEC]

Osmani, S. R. Pricing and Distribution Policies for Agricultural Development in Bangladesh. *Bangladesh Devel. Stud.*, Sept.-Dec. 1985, 13(3&4), pp. 1–40. [G: Bangladesh]

Paarsch, Harry J. Micro-economic Models of Beef Supply. *Can. J. Econ.*, August 1985, 18(3), pp. 636–51.

Paige, Jeffery M. Cotton and Revolution in Nicaragua. In *Evans, P.; Rueschemeyer, D. and Stephens, E. H., eds.*, 1985, pp. 91–114. [G: Nicaragua]

Papanek, Gustav F. Agricultural Income Distribution and Employment in the 1970s. *Bull. Indonesian Econ. Stud.*, August 1985, 21(2), pp. 24–50. [G: Indonesia]

Parikh, Ashok. Some Aspects of Employment in Indian Agriculture. *World Devel.*, June 1985, 13(6), pp. 691–704. [G: India]

Paris, Quirino and Easter, Christopher D. A Programming Model with Stochastic Technology and Prices: The Case of Australian Agriculture. *Amer. J. Agr. Econ.*, February 1985, 67(1), pp. 120–29. [G: Australia]

Peebles, Gavin. Soviet-Style Agricultural Bonuses and Their Effect on Prices in China: A Search for Perversity and Its Consequences. *Hong Kong Econ. Pap.*, 1985, (16), pp. 40–53. [G: China]

Perkins, J. A. Rehearsal for Protectionism: Australian Wool Exports and German Agriculture, 1830–80. *Australian Econ. Hist. Rev.*, March 1985, 25(1), pp. 20–38. [G: Australia; Germany]

Perry, Douglas H. The Economics of Transmigrant Farming. *Bull. Indonesian Econ. Stud.*, December 1985, 21(3), pp. 104–17. [G: Indonesia]

Pickering, Donald C. Population and Food and Population Change and Development: Chairman's Comments. In *Davis, T. J., ed.*, 1985, pp. 52–54.

Pinstrup-Andersen, Per. Food Prices and the Poor in Developing Countries. *Europ. Rev. Agr. Econ.*, 1985, 12(1/2), pp. 69–81. [G: LDCs]

Pollard, H. J. The Erosion of Agriculture in an Oil Economy: The Case of Export Crop Production in Trinidad. *World Devel.*, July 1985, 13(7), pp. 819–35. [G: Trinidad]

Pollard, Stephen K. and Graham, Douglas H. Price Policy and Agricultural Export Performance in Jamaica. *World Devel.*, September 1985, 13(9), pp. 1067–75. [G: Jamaica]

Pollard, Stephen K. and Graham, Douglas H. The Performance of the Food-producing Sector in Jamaica, 1962–1979: A Policy Analysis. *Econ. Develop. Cult. Change*, July 1985, 33(4), pp. 731–54. [G: Jamaica]

Pollitt, Brian H. Towards the Socialist Transformation of Cuban Agriculture 1959–1982. In *Gomes, P. I., ed.*, 1985, pp. 154–72. [G: Cuba]

Porter, Darrell and Todd, Mike. The Effect of Carcass Quality on Beef Carcass Auction Prices. *Australian J. Agr. Econ.*, December 1985, 29(3), pp. 225–34. [G: Australia]

Prior-Willeard, Christopher. Meat. In *Roberts, G., ed.*, 1985, pp. 104–10. [G: Global]

Prokopenko, N. The Quality of Labor and Output in Agriculture. *Prob. Econ.*, July 1985, 28(3), pp. 81–96. [G: U.S.S.R.]

Qureshi, Sarfraz K. Domestic Terms of Trade and Public Policy for Agriculture in Pakistan. *Pakistan Devel. Rev.*, Autumn-Winter 1985, 24(3/4), pp. 363–79. [G: Pakistan]

Rao, D. S. Gundu; Bisaliah, S. and Krishnaswamy, H. S. Technical Change and Efficiency

in Dryland Agriculture: An Econometric Study. *Margin*, July 1985, *17*(4), pp. 37–47.
[G: India]

Rausser, Gordon C. Macroeconomics and U.S. Agricultural Policy. **In** *Gardner, B. L., ed.*, 1985, pp. 207–52. [G: U.S.]

Ravallion, Martin. The Information Efficiency of Traders' Price Expectations in a Bangladesh Price Market. *Oxford Bull. Econ. Statist.*, May 1985, *47*(2), pp. 171–84. [G: Bangladesh]

Ravallion, Martin. The Performance of Rice Markets in Bangladesh during the 1974 Famine. *Econ. J.*, March 1985, *95*(377), pp. 15–29.
[G: Bangladesh]

Richardson, James W. Methods for Measuring the Economic Impact of Ambient Pollutants on the Agricultural Sector: Discussion. *Amer. J. Agr. Econ.*, May 1985, *67*(2), pp. 421–22.
[G: U.S.]

Riordan, E. B. Estimation of a Bilateral Trade Model for a Food Processing Service: Obstacles to Trade in Deboned Beef. *Irish J. Agr. Econ. Rural Soc.*, 1984-1985, *10*(2), pp. 145–64.
[G: Ireland; U.K.]

Roberts, Gerald. Cocoa. **In** *Roberts, G., ed.*, 1985, pp. 52–58. [G: Global]

Roberts, Roland K. Transportation Costs in Econometric Models of State Agricultural Sectors: The Case of Beef in Hawaii. *Western J. Agr. Econ.*, July 1985, *10*(1), pp. 93–109.
[G: U.S.]

Roberts, Roland K. and Martin, William J. The Effects of Alternative Beef Import Quota Regimes on the Beef Industries of the Aggregate United States and Hawaii. *Western J. Agr. Econ.*, December 1985, *10*(2), pp. 230–44.
[G: U.S.]

Roe, Terry and Antonovitz, Frances. A Producer's Willingness to Pay for Information under Price Uncertainty: Theory and Application. *Southern Econ. J.*, October 1985, *52*(2), pp. 382–91. [G: U.S.]

Roe, Terry and Senauer, Benjamin. Simulating Alternative Foodgrain Price and Trade Policies: An Application for the Dominican Republic. *J. Policy Modeling*, Winter 1985, *7*(4), pp. 635–48. [G: Dominican Republic]

Roemer, Michael. Dutch Disease in Developing Countries: Swallowing Bitter Medicine. **In** *Lundahl, M., ed.*, 1985, pp. 234–52.
[G: LDCs]

Roemer, Peter. Supply of Fertilizers in Europe with Special Reference to the Federal Republic of Germany. *Statist. J.*, December 1985, *3*(4), pp. 381–98. [G: W. Germany]

Rosegrant, Mark W.; Roumasset, James A. and Balisacan, Arsenio M. Biological Technology and Agricultural Policy: An Assessment of Azolla in Philippine Rice Production. *Amer. J. Agr. Econ.*, November 1985, *67*(4), pp. 726–32. [G: Philippines]

Ruttan, Vernon W. Moral Responsibility and Agricultural Research. **In** *[Heidhues, T.]*, 1985, pp. 66–83. [G: U.S.]

Salem, Abdul. Domestic Terms of Trade and Public Policy for Agriculture in Pakistan: Com-

ments. *Pakistan Devel. Rev.*, Autumn-Winter 1985, *24*(3/4), pp. 380–83. [G: Pakistan]

Sangwan, S. S. Dynamics of Cropping Pattern in Haryana: A Supply Response Analysis. *Devel. Econ.*, June 1985, *23*(2), pp. 173–86.
[G: India]

Sarris, Alexander H. Food Security and Agricultural Production Strategies under Risk in Egypt. *J. Devel. Econ.*, Sept.-Oct. 1985, *19*(1/2), pp. 85–111. [G: Egypt]

Scheper, Wilhelm. Markets and Prices: Links between Agriculture and the General Economy: Comment. *Europ. Rev. Agr. Econ.*, 1985, *12*(1/2), pp. 14–15. [G: EEC]

Schinke, E. European Countries with Centrally-planned Economies: Markets and Prices: Comment. *Europ. Rev. Agr. Econ.*, 1985, *12*(1/2), pp. 28–29. [G: CMEA]

Schrader, Lee F.; Bessler, David A. and Preston, Warren. Egg Prices Revisited. *Southern J. Agr. Econ.*, December 1985, *17*(2), pp. 215–19. [G: U.S.]

Schultz, Robert W. and Marsh, John M. Steer and Heifer Price Differences in the Live Cattle and Carcass Markets. *Western J. Agr. Econ.*, July 1985, *10*(1), pp. 77–92. [G: U.S.]

Scott, Christopher D. Transnational Corporations, Comparative Advantage and Food Security in Latin America. **In** *Abel, C. and Lewis, C. M., eds.*, 1985, pp. 482–99.
[G: Latin America]

Seftel, Howard. Government Regulation and the Rise of the California Fruit Industry: The Entrepreneurial Attack on Fruit Pests, 1880–1920. *Bus. Hist. Rev.*, Autumn 1985, *59*(3), pp. 369–402. [G: U.S.]

Shaw, Anthony B. and da Costa, Richard C. Differential Levels of Technology Adoption and Returns to Scale in the Guyanese Rice Industry. *Can. J. Agr. Econ.*, March 1985, *33*(1), pp. 99–110. [G: Guyana]

Shonkwiler, J. Scott and Maddala, G. S. Modeling Expectations of Bounded Prices: An Application to the Market for Corn. *Rev. Econ. Statist.*, November 1985, *67*(4), pp. 697–702.
[G: U.S.]

Sicular, Terry. Rural Marketing and Exchange in the Wake of Recent Reforms. **In** *Perry, E. J. and Wong, C., eds.*, 1985, pp. 83–109.
[G: China]

Simpson, James R. and Steele, John T. Institutional Affiliation of Contributors to the *American Journal of Agricultural Economics*, 1973-83. *Amer. J. Agr. Econ.*, May 1985, *67*(2), pp. 325–27.

Smith, Joyotee and Umali, Gloria. Production Risk and Optimal Fertilizer Rates: A Random Coefficient Model. *Amer. J. Agr. Econ.*, August 1985, *67*(3), pp. 654–59.
[G: Philippines]

Snowdon, Brian. The Political Economy of the Ethiopian Famine. *Nat. Westminster Bank Quart. Rev.*, November 1985, pp. 41–55.
[G: Ethiopia]

Spalding, Rose J. Structural Barriers to Food Programming: An Analysis of the "Mexican Food

System." *World Devel.*, December 1985, *13*(12), pp. 1249–62. **[G: Mexico]**

Srinivasan, T. N. Agriculture Production, Relative Prices, Entitlements, and Poverty. In *Mellor, J. W. and Desai, G. M., eds.*, 1985, pp. 41–53. **[G: LDCs]**

Stavis, Benedict. Some Initial Results of China's New Agricultural Policies. *World Devel.*, December 1985, *13*(12), pp. 1299–1305. **[G: China]**

Štrougal, Lubomír. Scientific and Technical Progress—The Most Important Growth Factor in Agricultural Production. *Czech. Econ. Digest.*, March 1985, (2), pp. 3–34. **[G: Czechoslovakia]**

Szeskin, A. and Sternlicht, R. Analysis of Agricultural Developments. In *Levinson, P. and Landau, P., eds.*, 1985, pp. 115–23. **[G: Israel]**

Taylor, Timothy G. and Monson, Michael J. Dynamic Factor Demands for Aggregate Southeastern United States Agriculture. *Southern J. Agr. Econ.*, December 1985, *17*(2), pp. 1–9. **[G: U.S.]**

Taylor, Timothy G. and Shonkwiler, J. Scott. Interdependent Supply Functions and Revisional Price Expectations. *Can. J. Agr. Econ.*, November 1985, *33*(3), pp. 285–98. **[G: U.S.]**

Thirtle, Colin G. Technological Change and the Productivity Slowdown in Field Crops: United States, 1939–78. *Southern J. Agr. Econ.*, December 1985, *17*(2), pp. 33–42. **[G: U.S.]**

Thirtle, Colin G. The Microeconomic Approach to Induced Innovation: A Reformulation of the Hayami and Ruttan Model. *Manchester Sch. Econ. Soc. Stud.*, September 1985, *53*(3), pp. 263–79. **[G: U.S.]**

Thomas, Brinley. Food Supply in the United Kingdom during the Industrial Revolution. In *Mokyr, J., ed.*, 1985, pp. 137–50. **[G: U.K.]**

Tyers, Rodney and Anderson, Kym. Price, Trade and Welfare Effects of Agricultural Protection: The Case of East Asia. *Rev. Marketing Agr. Econ.*, December 1985, *53*(3), pp. 113–40. **[G: Japan; S. Korea; Taiwan]**

Unnevehr, Laurian J. The Costs of Squeezing Marketing Margins: Philippine Government Intervention in Rice Markets. *Devel. Econ.*, June 1985, *23*(2), pp. 158–72. **[G: Philippines]**

Walker, Thomas S. and Kshirsagar, K. G. The Village Impact of Machine Threshing and Implications for Technology Development in the Semi-arid Tropics of Peninsular India. *J. Devel. Stud.*, January 1985, *21*(2), pp. 215–31. **[G: India]**

Watanabe, Susumu. Employment and Income Implications of the "Bio-revolution": A Speculative Note. *Int. Lab. Rev.*, May-June 1985, *124*(3), pp. 281–97. **[G: LDCs; MDCs]**

Westcott, Paul C.; Hull, David B. and Green, Robert C. Relationships between Quarterly Corn Prices and Stocks. *Agr. Econ. Res.*, Winter 1985, *37*(1), pp. 1–7. **[G: U.S.]**

Wetzstein, Michael E. Methods for Measuring the Economic Impact of Ambient Pollutants on the Agricultural Sector: Discussion. *Amer.*

J. Agr. Econ., May 1985, *67*(2), pp. 419–20. **[G: U.S.]**

Whigham, Thomas L. Agriculture and the Upper Plata: The Tobacco Trade, 1780–1865. *Bus. Hist. Rev.*, Winter 1985, *59*(4), pp. 563–96. **[G: Argentina; Paraguay]**

Wilson-Smith, J. Cotton. In *Roberts, G., ed.*, 1985, pp. 72–79. **[G: Global]**

Wohlgenant, Michael K. Competitive Storage, Rational Expectations, and Short-Run Food Price Determination. *Amer. J. Agr. Econ.*, November 1985, *67*(4), pp. 739–48. **[G: U.S.]**

Wohlgenant, Michael K. Estimating Cross Elasticities of Demand for Beef. *Western J. Agr. Econ.*, December 1985, *10*(2), pp. 322–29. **[G: U.S.]**

Woś, Augustyn. European Countries with Centrally-planned Economies: Markets and Prices: Opening of the Discussion. *Europ. Rev. Agr. Econ.*, 1985, *12*(1/2), pp. 27–28. **[G: CMEA]**

Wright, Jonathan. The Efficiency of Producing Alcohol for Energy in Brazil: Comment. *Econ. Develop. Cult. Change*, July 1985, *33*(4), pp. 851–56. **[G: Brazil]**

Wyzan, Michael L. Soviet Agricultural Procurement Pricing: A Study in Perversity. *J. Compar. Econ.*, March 1985, *9*(1), pp. 24–45. **[G: U.S.S.R.]**

Yoon, Tae-Hee. Pakistan, SAL I (Agricultural Component). In *Davis, T. J., ed.*, 1985, pp. 174–78. **[G: Pakistan]**

Yotopoulos, Pan A. Middle-Income Classes and Food Crises: The "New" Food–Feed Competition. *Econ. Develop. Cult. Change*, April 1985, *33*(3), pp. 463–83. **[G: Global]**

Zheng, Tianxiang; Wei, Qingquan and Chu, David K. Y. Agricultural Land-Use Patterns and Export Potential. In *Wong, K. and Chu, D. K. Y., eds.*, 1985, pp. 89–107. **[G: China]**

712 Agricultural Situation and Outlook

7120 Agricultural Situation and Outlook

Akder, Halis. Reflections on Turkish Agriculture and Common Agricultural Policy. *METU*, 1985, *12*(3/4), pp. 343–51. **[G: Turkey; EEC]**

Alston, Lee J. and Ferrie, Joseph P. Labor Costs, Paternalism, and Loyalty in Southern Agriculture: A Constraint on the Growth of the Welfare State. *J. Econ. Hist.*, March 1985, *45*(1), pp. 95–117. **[G: U.S.]**

Belongia, Michael T. and Gilbert, R. Alton. The Farm Credit Crisis: Will It Hurt the Whole Economy? *Fed. Res. Bank St. Louis Rev.*, December 1985, *67*(10), pp. 5–15. **[G: U.S.]**

Bergmann, Theodor. Needs, Perspectives and Obstacles for Cooperation of Farmers in Highly Industrialized Economies. In *Bergmann, T. and Ogura, T. B., eds.*, 1985, pp. 131–45. **[G: W. Europe]**

Bovard, James. The Fat of the Land: What is the Farm Crisis? *Policy Rev.*, Spring 1985, (32), pp. 53. **[G: U.S.]**

Brhlovič, Gerhard. Changes in the Character of the Work of Cooperative Farmers. *Czech.*

Econ. Digest., June 1985, (4), pp. 24–41.
[G: Czechoslovakia]

Brockmann, C. Thomas. Women and Development in Northern Belize. *J. Devel. Areas*, July 1985, *19*(4), pp. 501–13. [G: Belize]

Brown, Lester R. and Wolf, Edward C. Origins of the African Food Crisis. *Challenge*, January/February 1985, *27*(6), pp. 50–52. [G: Africa]

Buttel, Frederick H.; Kenney, Martin and Kloppenburg, Jack, Jr. From Green Revolution to Biorevolution: Some Observations on the Changing Technological Bases of Economic Transformation in the Third World. *Econ. Develop. Cult. Change*, October 1985, *34*(1), pp. 31–55. [G: LDCs]

Bystrakov, Iu. Ecological Problems of the Agroindustrial Complex. *Prob. Econ.*, June 1985, *28*(2), pp. 50–64. [G: U.S.S.R.]

Carter, Colin A. and Loyns, R. M. A. The Prairie Grain Industry in Western Transition. *Can. Public Policy*, Supplement July 1985, *11*, pp. 290–93. [G: Canada]

Chataigner, J. Situation et perspectives de la production alimentaire en Côte-d'Ivoire. (Situation and Perspective of the Food Crop in Ivory Coast. With English summary.) *Écon. Soc.*, July 1985, *19*(7), pp. 57–81.
[G: Ivory Coast]

Craven, Gary. Role of High Technology as It Affects the Farm Management Consultant and Businessman. *Can. J. Agr. Econ.*, August 1985, *32*, pp. 10–13. [G: Canada]

Donges, Jürgen B. International Agricultural Policy: A Role for National Food Programmes?: Comment. In *[Heidhues, T.]*, 1985, pp. 286–88.

Dunn, Lucia F. Nonpecuniary Job Preferences and Welfare Losses among Migrant Agricultural Workers. *Amer. J. Agr. Econ.*, May 1985, *67*(2), pp. 257–65. [G: Mexico; U.S.]

Elam, Emmett W. and Holder, Shelby H. An Evaluation of the *Rice Outlook and Situation* Price Forecasts. *Southern J. Agr. Econ.*, December 1985, *17*(2), pp. 155–61. [G: U.S.]

Feder, Gershon; Just, Richard E. and Zilberman, David. Adoption of Agricultural Innovations in Developing Countries: A Survey. *Econ. Develop. Cult. Change*, January 1985, *33*(2), pp. 255–98. [G: LDCs]

Ghose, Ajit Kumar. Transforming Feudal Agriculture: Agrarian Change in Ethiopia since 1974. In *Saith, A., ed.*, 1985, pp. 127–49.
[G: Ethiopia]

Ghose, Ajit Kumar. Transforming Feudal Agriculture: Agrarian Change in Ethiopia since 1974. *J. Devel. Stud.*, October 1985, *22*(1), pp. 127–49. [G: Ethiopia]

Goddard, E. The Future Role of the Agricultural Economist in Outlook Preparation. *Can. J. Agr. Econ.*, August 1985, *32*, pp. 86–99.

Hall, Alan. Role of High Technology as It Affects the Extension Worker. *Can. J. Agr. Econ.*, August 1985, *32*, pp. 1–9. [G: Canada]

Hathaway, Dale E. Food Issues in North–South Relations. In *[Heidhues, T.]*, 1985, pp. 289–301.

Hayward, Brian. The Long Term Potential for Crop Production in Canada. *Can. J. Agr. Econ.*, July 1985, *32*, pp. 42–56.
[G: Canada]

Hedley, Douglas D. and Huff, H. Bruce. Utilization of Institutional and Quantitative Analysis in Outlook Preparation: Some Management Considerations. *Can. J. Agr. Econ.*, August 1985, *32*, pp. 60–69.

Imam, Syed Fakhar. Public Policy and Agricultural Transformation in Pakistan: Concluding Remarks. *Pakistan Devel. Rev.*, Autumn-Winter 1985, *24*(3/4), pp. 330–32. [G: Pakistan]

Insel, Barbara. A World Awash in Grain. *Foreign Aff.*, Spring 1985, *63*(4), pp. 892–911.
[G: Global]

Johnson, D. Gale. World Commodity Market Situation and Outlook. In *Gardner, B. L., ed.*, 1985, pp. 19–50. [G: U.S.; Global]

Johnson, Glenn L. The US Presidential World Food and Nutrition Study and Commission on World Hunger: Lessons for the United States and Other Countries. In *[Heidhues, T.]*, 1985, pp. 47–63.

Josling, Timothy E. International Agricultural Policy: A Role for National Food Programmes? In *[Heidhues, T.]*, 1985, pp. 273–85.

Josling, Timothy E. Markets and Prices: Links between Agriculture and the General Economy. *Europ. Rev. Agr. Econ.*, 1985, *12*(1/2), pp. 1–11. [G: EEC]

Kay, Cristóbal. Agrarian Change after Allende's Chile. In *Hojman, D. E., ed.*, 1985, pp. 97–113. [G: Chile]

Khan, Mahmood Hasan. Public Policy and Agricultural Transformation in Pakistan. *Pakistan Devel. Rev.*, Autumn-Winter 1985, *24*(3/4), pp. 305–29. [G: Pakistan]

Kirkpatrick, Colin H. Improving Food Security in Developing Countries: A Role for the IMF. *Banca Naz. Lavoro Quart. Rev.*, June 1985, (153), pp. 174–85. [G: LDCs]

Klein, K. K. Economics of Biotechnology in Animal Production. *Can. J. Agr. Econ.*, August 1985, *32*, pp. 36–47.

Krokhotkin, A. Soviet–Hungarian Cooperation in the Development of Agroindustry. *Soviet E. Europ. Foreign Trade*, Winter 1985-86, *21*(4), pp. 37–40. [G: U.S.S.R.; Hungary]

Kussmaul, Ann. Agrarian Change in Seventeenth-Century England: The Economic Historian as Paleontologist. *J. Econ. Hist.*, March 1985, *45*(1), pp. 1–30. [G: U.K.]

Labonne, Michel. Stratégies alimentaires: quelques principes de pratique. (Food Strategies: Some Practical Principles. With English summary.) *Écon. Soc.*, July 1985, *19*(7), pp. 161–77. [G: LDCs]

Lama de Espinosa, Jaime. Markets and Prices: Links between Agriculture and the General Economy: Opening of the Discussion. *Europ. Rev. Agr. Econ.*, 1985, *12*(1/2), pp. 12–14.
[G: EEC]

León, Carlos; Prudkin, Nora and Reboratti, Carlos. El conflicto entre producción sociedad y medio ambiente: la expansión agrícola en el sur de Salta. (With English summary.) *Desarrollo Econ.*, Oct.-Dec. 1985, *25*(99), pp. 399–420. **[G: Argentina]**

Lipton, Michael. Research and the Design of a Policy Frame for Agriculture. In *Rose, T., ed.*, 1985, pp. 78–93. **[G: Sub-Saharan Africa]**

Lu, Baifu and Yuan, Zhenyu. On Several Problems in the Current Situation with Regard to the Requisition and Procurement of Agricultural and Sideline Products. *Chinese Econ. Stud.*, Spring 1985, *18*(3), pp. 3–19.

[G: China]

Nazarenko, V. I. European Countries with Centrally-planned Economies: Markets and Prices. *Europ. Rev. Agr. Econ.*, 1985, *12*(1/2), pp. 17–26. **[G: CMEA]**

Nghiep, Le Thanh and Lynam, John K. The Impact of Improved Cassava Technology on Small Farming in Colombia. In *Ohkawa, K. and Ranis, G., eds.*, 1985, pp. 110–32.

[G: Colombia]

O'Brien, Patrick M. World Commodity Market Situation and Outlook: Commentary. In *Gardner, B. L., ed.*, 1985, pp. 51–55. **[G: U.S.; Global]**

Owens, Raymond E. The Agricultural Outlook for 1985. . .Little Promise Seen. *Fed. Res. Bank Richmond Econ. Rev.*, Jan./Feb. 1985, *71*(1), pp. 27–34. **[G: U.S.]**

Perry, Douglas H. The Economics of Transmigrant Farming. *Bull. Indonesian Econ. Stud.*, December 1985, *21*(3), pp. 104–17.

[G: Indonesia]

Petit, Michel. The US Presidential World Food and Nutrition Study and Commission on World Hunger: Lessons for the United States and Other Countries: Comment. In *[Heidhues, T.]*, 1985, pp. 64–65.

Pinstrup-Anderson, Per. Agricultural Project Design and Human Nutrition. In *Davis, T. J., ed.*, 1985, pp. 153–56.

Reutlinger, Shlomo. Food Security and Poverty in LDCs. *Finance Develop.*, December 1985, *22*(4), pp. 7–11. **[G: LDCs]**

Saith, Ashwani. The Distributional Dimensions of Revolutionary Transition: Ethiopia. *J. Devel. Stud.*, October 1985, *22*(1), pp. 150–79.

[G: Ethiopia]

Saith, Ashwani. The Distributional Dimensions of Revolutionary Transition: Ethiopia. In *Saith, A., ed.*, 1985, pp. 150–79. **[G: Ethiopia]**

Scheper, Wilhelm. Markets and Prices: Links between Agriculture and the General Economy: Comment. *Europ. Rev. Agr. Econ.*, 1985, *12*(1/2), pp. 14–15. **[G: EEC]**

Schinke, E. European Countries with Centrally-planned Economies: Markets and Prices: Comment. *Europ. Rev. Agr. Econ.*, 1985, *12*(1/2), pp. 28–29. **[G: CMEA]**

Schultz, Theodore W. The Economics of Poverty in Low-income Countries. In *Bapna, A., ed.*, 1985, pp. 137–49. **[G: LDCs]**

Simpson, G. M. Ethical Issues of High Technology in Agriculture. *Can. J. Agr. Econ.*, August 1985, *32*, pp. 48–59.

Skomorokhin, Iakov. A Component of the Agroindustrial Complex. *Soviet E. Europ. Foreign Trade*, Winter 1985-86, *21*(4), pp. 41–49.

[G: CMEA; Cuba]

Smith, William. High Technology in Canadian Agriculture: A Science Council Perspective. *Can. J. Agr. Econ.*, August 1985, *32*, pp. 14–23. **[G: Canada]**

Štrougal, Lubomír. Scientific and Technical Progress—The Most Important Growth Factor in Agricultural Production. *Czech. Econ. Digest.*, March 1985, (2), pp. 3–34.

[G: Czechoslovakia]

Veeman, Terrence S. and Veeman, Michele M. Western Canadian Agriculture: Prospects, Problems and Policy. *Can. Public Policy*, Supplement July 1985, *11*(3), pp. 301–09.

[G: Canada]

Viatte, Gérard. Agricultural Trade Policy Issues in the 1980s: Comment. In *[Heidhues, T.]*, 1985, pp. 266–69.

Walker, David. Critique of Current Outlook Practices. *Can. J. Agr. Econ.*, August 1985, *32*, pp. 70–76.

Warley, Thorald K. Agricultural Trade Policy Issues in the 1980s. In *[Heidhues, T.]*, 1985, pp. 248–65.

Wilson, Arthur. The Long Term Potential for Crop Production in Canada: Rapporteur's Report. *Can. J. Agr. Econ.*, July 1985, *32*, pp. 57–63. **[G: Canada]**

Woś, Augustyn. European Countries with Centrally-planned Economies: Markets and Prices: Opening of the Discussion. *Europ. Rev. Agr. Econ.*, 1985, *12*(1/2), pp. 27–28. **[G: CMEA]**

Wuyts, Marc. Money, Planning and Rural Transformation in Mozambique. *J. Devel. Stud.*, October 1985, *22*(1), pp. 180–207.

[G: Mozambique]

Wuyts, Marc. Money, Planning and Rural Transformation in Mozambique. In *Saith, A., ed.*, 1985, pp. 180–207. **[G: Mozambique]**

Yotopoulos, Pan A. Middle-Income Classes and Food Crises: The "New" Food–Feed Competition. *Econ. Develop. Cult. Change*, April 1985, *33*(3), pp. 463–83. **[G: Global]**

713 Agricultural Policy, Domestic and International

7130 Agricultural Policy, Domestic and International

Abdullah, A. A. The Fertilizer Subsidy—Cost and Return. *Bangladesh Devel. Stud.*, Sept.-Dec. 1985, *13*(3&4), pp. 141–46. **[G: Bangladesh]**

Akder, Halis. Reflections on Turkish Agriculture and Common Agricultural Policy. *METU*, 1985, *12*(3/4), pp. 343–51. **[G: Turkey; EEC]**

Anderson, Ronald W. and Wilkinson, M. Consumer Demand for Meat and the Evaluation of Agricultural Policy. *Empirical Econ.*, 1985, *10*(2), pp. 65–89. **[G: U.S.]**

Anderson, W. J. and Gellner, J. A. Canadian Agricultural Policy in the Export Sector. *Can. J. Agr. Econ.*, August 1985, *32*, pp. 170–85.

[G: Canada]

Andrews, Margaret S. Agricultural Terms of Trade and Distributional Perversities in a Neo-Ricardian Model. *J. Devel. Econ.*, January–February 1985, *17*(1–2), pp. 117–29.

Andrews, Margaret S. Profit, Rent, and the Terms of Trade: A Rejoinder [Agricultural Terms of Trade and Distributional Perversities in a Neo-Ricardian Model]. *J. Devel. Econ.*, January–February 1985, *17*(1–2), pp. 141–49.

Ayer, Harry W. Are Current Commodity Programs Outdated? Comments. *Western J. Agr. Econ.*, December 1985, *10*(2), pp. 279–81. [G: U.S.]

Baker, Greg and Mori, Hiroshi. Strawmen in Trade Protectionism: The Case of Citrus Import Quotas. *Western J. Agr. Econ.*, December 1985, *10*(2), pp. 338–43. [G: Japan; U.S.]

Bale, Malcolm D. Food Prices and the Poor in Developing Countries: Opening of the Discussion. *Europ. Rev. Agr. Econ.*, 1985, *12*(1/2), pp. 82–83. [G: LDCs]

Barker, Randolph. The Philippine Rice Program—Lessons for Agricultural Development. *Philippine Econ. J.*, 1985, *24*(2–3), pp. 116–31. [G: Philippines]

Barry, Peter J. Needed Changes in the Farmers Home Administration Lending Program. *Amer. J. Agr. Econ.*, May 1985, *67*(2), pp. 341–44. [G: U.S.]

Bates, Robert H. and Lien, Dau-Hsiang Donald. On the Operations of the International Coffee Agreement. *Int. Organ.*, Summer 1985, *39*(3), pp. 553–59. [G: U.S.; Europe; Brazil; Colombia; Kenya]

Beresford, Melanie. Agriculture in the Transition to Socialism: The Case of South Vietnam. In *Lundahl, M., ed.*, 1985, pp. 370–95. [G: Vietnam]

Berg, Alan. Bank Interventions in Nutrition. In *Davis, T. J., ed.*, 1985, pp. 145–52.

Berg, Elliot. The Potentials of the Private Sector in Sub-Saharan Africa. In *Rose, T., ed.*, 1985, pp. 135–44. [G: Sub-Saharan Africa]

Bergmann, Denis. Une stratégie exportatrice pour l'agriculture de la CEE. (An Export Strategy for the E.E.C. Farming. With English summary.) *Écon. Soc.*, July 1985, *19*(7), pp. 229–42. [G: EEC]

Bergmann, Theodor. Collective Farm Organization: The Soviet Experience and Its Lessons. In *Bergmann, T. and Ogura, T. B., eds.*, 1985, pp. 209–28. [G: U.S.S.R.]

Bertrand, Jean-Pierre and Green, Raùl H. Brésil et Thalande: stratégies agro-exportatrices, urbanisation et changements de l'alimentation de base. (Brazil and Thailand: Agro-export Oriented Strategies: Urbanisation and Food Consumption Models Change. With English summary.) *Écon. Soc.*, July 1985, *19*(7), pp. 83–109. [G: Brazil; Thailand]

Bhagwati, Jagdish N. Food Aid, Agricultural Production and Welfare. In *Bhagwati, J. N. (I)*, 1985, pp. 285–97.

Bingley, Pam; Burton, Michael and Strak, John. Inter- and Intra-sectoral Effects of Milk Quotas in the U.K. Milk Industry. *Europ. Rev. Agr.*

Econ., 1985, *12*(4), pp. 411–30. [G: U.K.]

Black, Jan Knippers. Ten Paradoxes of Rural Development: An Ecuadorian Case Study. *J. Devel. Areas*, July 1985, *19*(4), pp. 527–55. [G: Ecuador]

Blanchi, Claude. Senegal: Agricultural Policy Dialogue. In *Davis, T. J., ed.*, 1985, pp. 198–206. [G: Senegal]

Blecher, Marc. The Structure and Contradictions of Productive Relations in Socialist Agrarian 'Reform': A Framework for Analysis and the Chinese Case. *J. Devel. Stud.*, October 1985, *22*(1), pp. 104–26. [G: China]

Blecher, Marc. The Structure and Contradictions of Productive Relations in Socialist Agrarian 'Reform': A Framework for Analysis and the Chinese Case. In *Saith, A., ed.*, 1985, pp. 104–26. [G: China]

Boussard, Jean Marc. Milk Quotas: Introduction. *Europ. Rev. Agr. Econ.*, 1985, *12*(4), pp. 325–33. [G: EEC]

Bovard, James. The Fat of the Land: What is the Farm Crisis? *Policy Rev.*, Spring 1985, (32), pp. 53. [G: U.S.]

Boyd, Michael L. The Effect of Policy on System Performance: The Case of Yugoslav Agriculture. *Comparative Econ. Stud.*, Summer 1985, *27*(2), pp. 1–23. [G: Yugoslavia]

Breimyer, Harold F. Agriculture and the Political Economy. *Challenge*, Nov./Dec. 1985, *28*(5), pp. 15–21. [G: U.S.]

Brorsen, B. Wade and Grant, Warren R. Efficiency of Spatial Price Discovery for U.S. Rice under Different Farm Policies and Economic Conditions. *J. Policy Modeling*, Winter 1985, *7*(4), pp. 621–33. [G: U.S.]

Buchholz, Horst E. International Relationships in the World Beef Trade: Comment. In *[Heidhues, T.]*, 1985, pp. 189–91. [G: Selected Countries]

Bullock, J. Bruce. Prospects for Fundamental Change in Farm and Food Programs: Discussion. *Amer. J. Agr. Econ.*, May 1985, *67*(2), pp. 350–51. [G: U.S.]

Burcroff, Richard, II. Turkey: Agricultural Sector Adjustment Loan. In *Davis, T. J., ed.*, 1985, pp. 207–10. [G: Turkey]

Burrell, Alison. Price Uncertainty under EC Milk Quotas. *Europ. Rev. Agr. Econ.*, 1985, *12*(4), pp. 335–50. [G: EEC]

Burton, Michael. The Implementation of the EC Milk Quota. *Europ. Rev. Agr. Econ.*, 1985, *12*(4), pp. 461–71. [G: EEC]

Campagne, P. and Savané, M. A. Quel avenir pour les nouvelles stratégies alimentaires des paysanneries du Sahel? (What Future for the Food Strategies and Sahelian Peasants? With English summary.) *Écon. Soc.*, July 1985, *19*(7), pp. 23–45. [G: Senegal]

Campbell, Keith O. Changing Institutions, Processes and Issues in the Formation of Australian Agricultural Policy. *Australian J. Agr. Econ.*, December 1985, *29*(3), pp. 210–24. [G: Australia]

Canarella, Giorgio and Pollard, Stephen K. Price and Output Expectations in Agricultural Policy: The Case of Jamaica. *J. Econ. Devel.*, December 1985, *10*(2), pp. 19–34. **[G: Jamaica]**

Carter, Colin A. and Loyns, R. M. A. The Prairie Grain Industry in Western Transition. *Can. Public Policy*, Supplement July 1985, *11*, pp. 290–93. **[G: Canada]**

Carter, Michael R. Revisionist Lessons from the Peruvian Experience with Cooperative Agricultural Production. In *Jones, D. C. and Svejnar, J.*, eds., 1985, pp. 179–94. **[G: Peru]**

Casas, Joseph. La stratégie agro-alimentaire de Cuba depuis 1959 et ses résultats. (Agri-Food Strategy and Results in Cuba since 1959. With English summary.) *Écon. Soc.*, July 1985, *19*(7), pp. 111–60. **[G: Cuba]**

Caswell, Nim. Peasants, Peanuts and Politics: State Marketing in Senegal, 1966–80. In *Arhin, K.; Hesp, P. and van der Laan, L.*, eds., 1985, pp. 79–119. **[G: Senegal]**

Chambers, Robert G. Least-Cost Subsidization Alternatives. *Amer. J. Agr. Econ.*, May 1985, *67*(2), pp. 251–56.

Chambers, Robert G. Macroeconomics and U.S. Agricultural Policy: Commentary. In *Gardner, B. L.*, ed., 1985, pp. 253–56. **[G: U.S.]**

Chataigner, J. Situation et perspectives de la production alimentaire en Côte-d'Ivoire. (Situation and Perspective of the Food Crop in Ivory Coast. With English summary.) *Écon. Soc.*, July 1985, *19*(7), pp. 57–81. **[G: Ivory Coast]**

Chaudhary, Mohammad Aslam. Food Self-Sufficiency, Agricultural Adequacy and Impacts of Green Revolution in Pakistan. *Pakistan Econ. Soc. Rev.*, Winter 1985, *23*(2), pp. 95–112. **[G: Pakistan]**

Chino, Tetsuro. The Welfare Effects of Rice Policy and Its Nature in Japan. (In Japanese. With English summary.) *Econ. Stud. Quart.*, December 1985, *36*(3), pp. 216–30. **[G: Japan]**

Chisholm, Anthony H. and Tyers, Rodney. Agricultural Protection and Market Insulation Policies: Applications of a Dynamic Multisectoral Model. In *Piggott, J. and Whalley, J.*, eds., 1985, pp. 189–220. **[G: Selected Countries]**

Cioffi, Antonio, et al. An Evaluation of the Effects of the EC Quota System on the Italian Dairy Market. *Europ. Rev. Agr. Econ.*, 1985, *12*(4), pp. 389–400. **[G: Italy]**

Colclough, Christopher. Competing Paradigms—and Lack of Evidence—In the Analysis of African Development. In *Rose, T.*, ed., 1985, pp. 26–36. **[G: Nigeria; Ghana; Sudan; Tanzania; Senegal]**

Collins, Robert A. Expected Utility, Debt–Equity Structure, and Risk Balancing. *Amer. J. Agr. Econ.*, August 1985, *67*(3), pp. 627–29.

Colman, David. Imperfect Transmission of Policy Prices. *Europ. Rev. Agr. Econ.*, 1985, *12*(3), pp. 171–86. **[G: U.K.]**

Coper, Michael. In the Beginning There Was Interstate Trade... *Rev. Marketing Agr. Econ.*, December 1985, *53*(3), pp. 103–12. **[G: Australia]**

Corbet, Hugh. Agricultural Priorities after the To-

kyo Round Negotiations. In *[Heidhues, T.]*, 1985, pp. 235–47.

Cornelisse, Peter A. and de Kruijk, Hans. Consumption and Trade of Wheat and Flour in Pakistan—The Role of Public and Private Sector. *Pakistan Devel. Rev.*, Summer 1985, *24*(2), pp. 151–71. **[G: Pakistan]**

Cornelisse, Peter A. and Kuijpers, Bart. On the Optimal Size of a Buffer Stock—The Case of Wheat in Pakistan. *Pakistan Devel. Rev.*, Autumn-Winter 1985, *24*(3/4), pp. 335–46. **[G: Pakistan]**

Crecink, John C. Small Farm Research and Policy Implications: Discussion. *Southern J. Agr. Econ.*, July 1985, *17*(1), pp. 57–59. **[G: U.S.]**

Cristini, Marcela. La oferta agropecuaria: el caso del trigo en la última década. (The Agropecuarian Supply: The Wheat Case in the Last Decade. With English summary.) *Económica (La Plata)*, Jan.-Apr. 1985, *31*(1), pp. 57–80. **[G: Argentina]**

Cryde, Denise J. Input Interventions and Production Efficiency in Philippine Agriculture. *Philippine Rev. Econ. Bus.*, Mar./June 1985, *22*(1/2), pp. 83–108. **[G: Philippines]**

Csizmadia, Ernö. Recent Experiences of Cooperative Farming in Hungary. *Acta Oecon.*, 1985, *34*(1–2), pp. 1–11. **[G: Hungary]**

Dams, Theodor. Moral Responsibility and Agricultural Research: Comment. In *[Heidhues, T.]*, 1985, pp. 84–87. **[G: U.S.]**

Davies, H. R. J. Natural Resources and Rural Development in Arid Lands: Case Studies from Sudan: Introduction. In *Davies, H. R. J.*, ed., 1985, pp. vii–x. **[G: Africa; Sudan]**

Dawson, Anthony. In Defence of Food Aid: Some Answers to Its Critics. *Int. Lab. Rev.*, January–February 1985, *124*(1), pp. 17–30. **[G: LDCs]**

Deere, Carmen Diana. Rural Women and State Policy: The Latin American Agrarian Reform Experience. *World Devel.*, September 1985, *13*(9), pp. 1037–53. **[G: Latin America]**

Dobson, W. D. Will USDA Farm Programs Remain Highly Resistant to Change? *Amer. J. Agr. Econ.*, May 1985, *67*(2), pp. 331–35. **[G: U.S.]**

Dolenc, Vladimir. Optimal Price Policy of Buffer Stocks. *Z. ges. Staatswiss. (JITE)*, September 1985, *141*(3), pp. 401–12.

Donges, Jürgen B. International Agricultural Policy: A Role for National Food Programmes?: Comment. In *[Heidhues, T.]*, 1985, pp. 286–88.

Doye, Damona G. and Boehlje, Michael D. A Flat Rate Tax: Impacts on Representative Hog and Grain Farms. *Western J. Agr. Econ.*, December 1985, *10*(2), pp. 147–61. **[G: U.S.]**

Dubey, Vinod. Policy Based Lending and the World Bank. In *Davis, T. J.*, ed., 1985, pp. 166–73.

Duncan, Marvin. Statement to the U.S. Senate Committee on Agriculture, Nutrition, and Forestry, May 1, 1985. *Fed. Res. Bull.*, July 1985, *71*(7), pp. 504–08. **[G: U.S.]**

Edwards, Geoff. Frontiers in Agricultural Policy

Research: Discussion. *Rev. Marketing Agr. Econ.*, August 1985, 53(2), pp. 85–90.
[G: Australia]

Emerson, Robert D. Critical Issues in Agricultural Labor Markets. *Southern J. Agr. Econ.*, July 1985, 17(1), pp. 89–98. [G: U.S.]

Erickson, Elizabeth. Goal Tradeoffs for U.S. Agricultural Commodity Programs: An Application of Multiple Objective Analysis. In *Haimes, Y. Y. and Chankong, V., eds.*, 1985, pp. 430–42.

Erickson, Elizabeth and House, Robert. Multiple Objective Analysis for a Spatial Market System: A Case Study of U.S. Agricultural Policy. In *Harker, P. T., ed.*, 1985, pp. 255–77.
[G: U.S.]

Evenson, Robert E. Equity Implications of Public Policy in an Unstable Agricultural Economy: Discussion. *Amer. J. Agr. Econ.*, May 1985, 67(2), pp. 441–42. [G: U.S.; LDCs]

Faucher, Jean-Jacques and Schneider, Hartmut. Agricultural Crisis: Structural Constraints, Prices and Other Policy Issues. In *Rose, T., ed.*, 1985, pp. 50–65.
[G: Sub-Saharan Africa]

Feder, Gershon and Slade, Roger. The Role of Public Policy in the Diffusion of Improved Agricultural Technology. *Amer. J. Agr. Econ.*, May 1985, 67(2), pp. 423–28. [G: U.S.; LDCs]

Fennell, Rosemary. A Reconsideration of the Objectives of the Common Agricultural Policy. *J. Common Market Stud.*, March 1985, 23(3), pp. 257–76. [G: EEC]

Figueroa, Manuel. Rural Development and Urban Food Programming. *Cepal Rev.*, April 1985, (25), pp. 111–27. [G: Latin America]

FitzGerald, E. V. K. Agrarian Reform as a Model of Accumulation: The Case of Nicaragua since 1979. *J. Devel. Stud.*, October 1985, 22(1), pp. 208–26. [G: Nicaragua]

FitzGerald, E. V. K. Agrarian Reform as a Model of Accumulation: The Case of Nicaragua since 1979. In *Saith, A., ed.*, 1985, pp. 208–26.
[G: Nicaragua]

Folwell, R. J., et al. The Federal Hop Marketing Order and Volume-Control Behavior. *Agr. Econ. Res.*, Fall 1985, 37(4), pp. 17–32.
[G: U.S.]

Fox, Glenn. Is the United States Really Underinvesting in Agricultural Research? *Amer. J. Agr. Econ.*, November 1985, 67(4), pp. 806–12.
[G: U.S.]

Gardner, Bruce. Export Subsidies Are Still Irrational. *Agr. Econ. Res.*, Winter 1985, 37(1), pp. 17–19. [G: U.S.]

Gardner, Bruce. Structuring Incentives for Change in U.S. Farm Programs. *Amer. J. Agr. Econ.*, May 1985, 67(2), pp. 336–40.
[G: U.S.]

Gemmill, Gordon. Forward Contracts or International Buffer Stocks? A Study of Their Relative Efficiencies in Stabilising Commodity Export Earnings. *Econ. J.*, June 1985, 95(378), pp. 400–417. [G: Selected LDCs]

Georgakopoulos, Theodore A. and Paschos, Pan-

agiotis G. Greek Agriculture and the CAP. *Europ. Rev. Agr. Econ.*, 1985, 12(3), pp. 247–63. [G: Greece]

George, Aurelia. The Organization of Agricultural Cooperatives as a Pressure Group in Japan. In *Bergmann, T. and Ogura, T. B., eds.*, 1985, pp. 97–112. [G: Japan]

Ghebremedhin, Tesfa G. and Johnson, William M. Small Farm Research and Policy Implications. *Southern J. Agr. Econ.*, July 1985, 17(1), pp. 47–56. [G: U.S.]

Ghose, Ajit Kumar. Transforming Feudal Agriculture: Agrarian Change in Ethiopia since 1974. In *Saith, A., ed.*, 1985, pp. 127–49.
[G: Ethiopia]

Ghose, Ajit Kumar. Transforming Feudal Agriculture: Agrarian Change in Ethiopia since 1974. *J. Devel. Stud.*, October 1985, 22(1), pp. 127–49. [G: Ethiopia]

Gibson, Bill and McLeon, Darryl. Profit, Rent, and the Terms of Trade: A Reply [Terms of Trade Policy in a Model with Non-produced Means of Production] [Agricultural Terms of Trade and Distributional Perversities in a Neo-Ricardian Model]. *J. Devel. Econ.*, January–February 1985, 17(1–2), pp. 131–39.

van der Giessen, Leen B. and Post, Jaap H. Macro- and Micro-effects of the Super Levy in the Netherlands. *Europ. Rev. Agr. Econ.*, 1985, 12(4), pp. 449–60. [G: Netherlands]

Gilbert, Christopher L. Futures Trading and the Welfare Evaluation of Commodity Price Stabilisation. *Econ. J.*, September 1985, 95(379), pp. 637–61. [G: LDCs]

Goodwin, H. L., Jr. Critical Issues in Agricultural Labor Markets: Discussion. *Southern J. Agr. Econ.*, July 1985, 17(1), pp. 99–102.
[G: U.S.]

Grant, Wyn. Corporatism and the Public–Private Distinction. In *Lane, J.-E., ed.*, 1985, pp. 158–80. [G: U.K.]

Grindle, Merilee S. Rhetoric, Reality, and Self-Sufficiency: Recent Initiatives in Mexican Rural Development. *J. Devel. Areas*, January 1985, 19(2), pp. 171–84. [G: Mexico]

Grosskopf, Werner. Some Observations on Price Instability, Agricultural Trade Policy and the Food Consumer: Comment. In *[Heidhues, T.]*, 1985, pp. 133–34.

Gyenes, Antal. The Development of Farmers' Cooperatives in Hungary: Present Problems and Prospects. In *Bergmann, T. and Ogura, T. B., eds.*, 1985, pp. 229–41. [G: Hungary]

de Haen, Hartwig. Food Prices and the Poor in Developing Countries: Comment. *Europ. Rev. Agr. Econ.*, 1985, 12(1/2), pp. 83–85.
[G: LDCs]

Haen, Hartwig; de Johnson, Glenn L. and Tangermann, Stefan. Agriculture & International Relations: Analysis and Policy: Introduction. In *[Heidhues, T.]*, 1985, pp. 1–16.

Hallagan, William S. Contracting Problems and the Adoption of Regulatory Cartels. *Econ. Inquiry*, January 1985, 23(1), pp. 37–56.
[G: U.S.]

Hanson, Gregory D. and Eidman, Vernon R.

Agricultural Income Tax Expenditure—A Microeconomic Analysis. *Amer. J. Agr. Econ.*, May 1985, *67*(2), pp. 271–78. **[G: U.S.]**

Hardaker, J. Brian, et al. A Model of a Padi Farming Household in Central Java. *Bull. Indonesian Econ. Stud.*, December 1985, *21*(3), pp. 30–50. **[G: Indonesia]**

Harling, Kenneth F. and Thompson, Robert L. Government Intervention in Poultry Industries: A Cross-Country Comparison. *Amer. J. Agr. Econ.*, May 1985, *67*(2), pp. 243–50. **[G: Canada; W. Germany; U.K.]**

Harrison, Mark. Primary Accumulation in the Soviet Transition. *J. Devel. Stud.*, October 1985, *22*(1), pp. 81–103. **[G: U.S.S.R.]**

Harrison, Mark. Primary Accumulation in the Soviet Transition. In *Saith, A., ed.*, 1985, pp. 81–103. **[G: U.S.S.R.]**

Hartford, Kathleen. Socialist Agriculture Is Dead; Long Live Socialist Agriculture! Organizational Transformation in Rural China. In *Perry, E. J. and Wong, C., eds.*, pp. 31–61. **[G: China]**

Harvey, D. R. and Thomson, Kenneth J. Costs, Benefits and the Future of the Common Agricultural Policy. *J. Common Market Stud.*, September 1985, *24*(1), pp. 1–20. **[G: EEC]**

Hathaway, Dale E. Food Issues in North–South Relations. In *[Heidhues, T.]*, 1985, pp. 289–301.

Haynes, J. E. Rural Assistance Levels: The Influence of Policies and World Price Changes. *Australian J. Agr. Econ.*, April 1985, *29*(1), pp. 32–48. **[G: Australia]**

Henderson, Thomas H. and Patton, Michael Quinn. Agricultural Extension for Rural Transformation: The C.A.E.P. Model. In *Gomes, P. I., ed.*, 1985, pp. 194–211. **[G: Caribbean]**

Herruzo, A. Casimiro. Returns to Agricultural Research: The Case of Rice Breeding in Spain. *Europ. Rev. Agr. Econ.*, 1985, *12*(3), pp. 265–82. **[G: Spain]**

Hiemstra, Stephen J. Food Program Policy Initiatives in an Era of Farm Surpluses. *Amer. J. Agr. Econ.*, May 1985, *67*(2), pp. 345–49. **[G: U.S.]**

Hillman, Jimmye S. Evolution of American Agricultural Trade Policy and European Interaction. In *[Heidhues, T.]*, 1985, pp. 155–69. **[G: U.S.]**

Hillman, Jimmye S. and Rothenberg, Robert A. Wider Implications of Protecting Japan's Rice Farmers. *World Econ.*, March 1985, *8*(1), pp. 43–62. **[G: Japan]**

Hiraizumi, Kimio. Collectivization and Improvement of Agricultural Producers' Cooperative: The Hungarian Experience. In *Bergmann, T. and Ogura, T. B., eds.*, 1985, pp. 243–56. **[G: Hungary]**

Holzheu, Franz. Zur Diskussion über den Währungsausgleich auf dem EG-Agrarmarkt—Eine kritische Nachlese. (An Analytical Framework for Evaluating the Monetary Compensatory Amounts in the Common Agricultural Policy of the EC. With English summary.) *Ifo-Stu-*

dien, 1985, *31*(2), pp. 109–48. **[G: EEC]**

Huffman, Wallace E. Human Capital, Adaptive Ability, and the Distributional Implications of Agricultural Policy. *Amer. J. Agr. Econ.*, May 1985, *67*(2), pp. 429–34. **[G: U.S.]**

Huffman, Wallace E. and McNulty, Mark. Endogenous Local Public Extension Policy. *Amer. J. Agr. Econ.*, November 1985, *67*(4), pp. 761–68. **[G: U.S.]**

Imam, Syed Fakhar. Public Policy and Agricultural Transformation in Pakistan: Concluding Remarks. *Pakistan Devel. Rev.*, Autumn-Winter 1985, *24*(3/4), pp. 330–32. **[G: Pakistan]**

Insel, Barbara. A World Awash in Grain. *Foreign Aff.*, Spring 1985, *63*(4), pp. 892–911. **[G: Global]**

Ioannidis, Chris. The Effect of the Quota Policy on the Cattle Stock and Its Composition. *Europ. Rev. Agr. Econ.*, 1985, *12*(4), pp. 401–10. **[G: EEC]**

Isaacman, Allen. Chiefs, Rural Differentiation and Peasant Protest: The Mozambican Forced Cotton Regime 1938–1961. *African Econ. Hist.*, 1985, *14*, pp. 15–56. **[G: Mozambique]**

Jabara, Cathy L. Agricultural Pricing Policy in Kenya. *World Devel.*, May 1985, *13*(5), pp. 611–26. **[G: Kenya]**

Johnson, Stanley R., et al. Options for the 1985 Farm Bill: An Analysis and Evaluation. In *Gardner, B. L., ed.*, 1985, pp. 119–73. **[G: U.S.]**

Jordan, Robert S. Conclusions: The Global Interest or the National Interest: Must They Lead to Conflict or Can They Lead to Cooperation? In *Jordan, R. S., ed.*, 1985, pp. 151–66.

Josling, Timothy E. International Agricultural Policy: A Role for National Food Programmes? In *[Heidhues, T.]*, 1985, pp. 273–85.

Josling, Timothy E. Markets and Prices: Links between Agriculture and the General Economy. *Europ. Rev. Agr. Econ.*, 1985, *12*(1/2), pp. 1–11. **[G: EEC]**

Josling, Timothy E. The Repercussions of U.S. Agricultural Policies for the European Community: Commentary. In *Gardner, B. L., ed.*, 1985, pp. 345–49. **[G: U.S.; EEC]**

Just, Richard E. Automatic Adjustment Rules in Commodity Programs. In *Gardner, B. L., ed.*, 1985, pp. 355–77. **[G: U.S.]**

Just, Richard E. and Zilberman, David. Risk Aversion, Technology Choice, and Equity Effects of Agricultural Policy. *Amer. J. Agr. Econ.*, May 1985, *67*(2), pp. 435–40. **[G: U.S.]**

Kawamura, Yoshio. Dissolution of Rural People's Communes and the System of Responsibility of Agricultural Production in China. In *Bergmann, T. and Ogura, T. B., eds.*, 1985, pp. 323–36. **[G: China]**

Kay, Cristóbal. Agrarian Change after Allende's Chile. In *Hojman, D. E., ed.*, 1985, pp. 97–113. **[G: Chile]**

Keppler, Horst. Free Access to Supplies versus Restrictive Supply Policies: The Ability of LDCs to Control Commodity Markets. In *Weinblatt, J., ed.*, 1985, pp. 71–115. **[G: Selected LDCs]**

Khan, Mahmood Hasan. Public Policy and Agricultural Transformation in Pakistan. *Pakistan Devel. Rev.*, Autumn-Winter 1985, *24*(3/4), pp. 305–29. **[G: Pakistan]**

Khan, Mamood Hasan. On the Optimal Size of a Buffer Stock—The Case of Wheat in Pakistan: Comments. *Pakistan Devel. Rev.*, Autumn-Winter 1985, *24*(3/4), pp. 337–48. **[G: Pakistan]**

Kirkpatrick, Colin H. Improving Food Security in Developing Countries: A Role for the IMF. *Banca Naz. Lavoro Quart. Rev.*, June 1985, (153), pp. 174–85. **[G: LDCs]**

Klatzmann, Joseph. L'autosuffisance alimentaire, objectif réaliste? (Is Self-sufficiency in Food Supply a Realist Objective? With English summary.) *Écon. Soc.*, July 1985, *19*(7), pp. 47–55. **[G: LDCs]**

Knutson, Ronald D. Are Current Farm Commodity Programs Outdated? Arguments in the Negative. *Western J. Agr. Econ.*, December 1985, *10*(2), pp. 270–78. **[G: U.S.]**

Koester, Ulrich. Agricultural Market Intervention and International Trade. *Europ. Rev. Agr. Econ.*, 1985, *12*(1/2), pp. 87–99. **[G: EEC; U.S.]**

Kowalak, Tadeusz. Agricultural Cooperatives in Poland. In *Bergmann, T. and Ogura, T. B.*, eds., 1985, pp. 271–90. **[G: Poland]**

van de Laar, Aart. Interest Groups and Development. In *Jerve, A. M.*, ed., 1985, pp. 155–66. **[G: Pakistan]**

Labonne, Michel. Stratégies alimentaires: quelques principes de pratique. (Food Strategies: Some Practical Principles. With English summary.) *Écon. Soc.*, July 1985, *19*(7), pp. 161–77. **[G: LDCs]**

LaDue, Eddy. Needed Changes in the Farmers Home Administration Lending Programs: Discussion. *Amer. J. Agr. Econ.*, May 1985, *67*(2), pp. 352–53. **[G: U.S.]**

LaFrance, Jeffrey T. and de Gorter, Harry. Regulation in a Dynamic Market: The U.S. Dairy Industry. *Amer. J. Agr. Econ.*, November 1985, *67*(4), pp. 821–32. **[G: U.S.]**

Lama de Espinosa, Jaime. Markets and Prices: Links between Agriculture and the General Economy: Opening of the Discussion. *Europ. Rev. Agr. Econ.*, 1985, *12*(1/2), pp. 12–14. **[G: EEC]**

Lányi, Kamilla. Hungarian Agriculture: Export Surplus or Superfluous Growth? (Contribution to the Development Strategy of Hungarian Agriculture). *Acta Oecon.*, 1985, *34*(3/4), pp. 299–315. **[G: Hungary]**

Lee, David R. and Helmberger, Peter G. Estimating Supply Response in the Presence of Farm Programs. *Amer. J. Agr. Econ.*, May 1985, *67*(2), pp. 193–203. **[G: U.S.]**

Lee, Jonq-Ying and Brown, Mark G. Coupon Redemption and the Demand for Frozen Concentrated Orange Juice: A Switching Regression Analysis. *Amer. J. Agr. Econ.*, August 1985, *67*(3), pp. 647–53. **[G: U.S.]**

Lermer, George and Stanbury, W. T. Measuring the Cost of Redistributing Income by Means of Direct Regulation. *Can. J. Econ.*, February 1985, *18*(1), pp. 190–207. **[G: Canada]**

Levy, Victor. Cropping Pattern, Mechanization, Child Labor, and Fertility Behavior in a Farming Economy: Rural Egypt. *Econ. Develop. Cult. Change*, July 1985, *33*(4), pp. 777–91. **[G: Egypt]**

Lipton, Michael. Research and the Design of a Policy Frame for Agriculture. In *Rose, T.*, ed., 1985, pp. 78–93. **[G: Sub-Saharan Africa]**

Livingstone, Ian. Agricultural Development Strategy and Agricultural Pricing Policy in Malawi. In *Arhin, K.; Hesp, P. and van der Laan, L.*, eds., 1985, pp. 169–92. **[G: Malawi]**

Lowenberg-DeBoer, J. and Boehlje, Michael D. The Estate Tax Provision of the 1981 Economic Recovery Tax Act: Which Farmers Benefit? *Southern J. Agr. Econ.*, December 1985, *17*(2), pp. 77–86. **[G: U.S.]**

Lundborg, Per. The Distribution of Income in Brazil and Its Dependence on International and Domestic Agricultural Policies. In *Lundahl, M.*, ed., 1985, pp. 131–51. **[G: Brazil]**

Macgregor, John. Philippines: Agricultural Sector/Inputs Project. In *Davis, T. J.*, ed., 1985, pp. 189–97. **[G: Philippines]**

Malassis, L. Politiques et stratégies alimentaires. (Policies and Food Strategies. With English summary.) *Écon. Soc.*, July 1985, *19*(7), pp. 3–22.

Marloie, Marcel. La stratégie alimentaire de la France au XIXe siècle: quelles leçons pour aujourd'hui? (The French Food Strategy in the 19th Century: What Lessons at Now? With English summary.) *Écon. Soc.*, July 1985, *19*(7), pp. 179–205. **[G: France]**

Mauri, Arnaldo. The Role of Innovatory Financial Technologies in Promoting Rural Development in LDCs. *Rivista Int. Sci. Econ. Com.*, Oct.-Nov. 1985, *32*(10–11), pp. 989–1002. **[G: LDCs]**

McCalla, Alex F. U.S. Agricultural Policy: The 1985 Farm Legislation: Assessment from Outside the Beltway. In *Gardner, B. L.*, ed., 1985, pp. 174–94. **[G: U.S.]**

McDowell, George R. The Political Economy of Extension Program Design: Institutional Maintenance Issues in the Organization and Delivery of Extension Programs. *Amer. J. Agr. Econ.*, November 1985, *67*(4), pp. 717–25. **[G: U.S.]**

Melichar, Emanuel. Farm Financial Stress, Structure of Agriculture, and Public Policy: Commentary. In *Gardner, B. L.*, ed., 1985, pp. 113–16. **[G: U.S.]**

Monke, Eric A. International Agriculture and Trade Policies: Implications for the United States: Commentary. In *Gardner, B. L.*, ed., 1985, pp. 79–82. **[G: U.S.; Global]**

Monke, Eric A. and Taylor, Lester D. International Trade Constraints and Commodity Market Models: An Application to the Cotton Market. *Rev. Econ. Statist.*, February 1985, *67*(1), pp. 98–107. **[G: Global]**

Monterosso, Cesar D. B., et al. Grain Storage in Developing Areas: Location and Size of Facilities. *Amer. J. Agr. Econ.*, February 1985, 67(1), pp. 101–11. **[G: Brazil]**

Morrisson, Christian. Agricultural Production and Government Policy in Burkina Faso and Mali. In *Rose, T., ed.*, 1985, pp. 66–77.
[G: Burkina Faso; Mali]

Munk, Knud Jorgen. The Effect of Changes in Prices and Quotas: An Example of the Use of an Agricultural Sector Model Based on the Johansen Approach. *Europ. Rev. Agr. Econ.*, 1985, 12(4), pp. 365–80. **[G: EEC]**

Myers, R. J.; Piggott, R. R. and MacAulay, T. G. Effects of Past Australian Wheat Price Policies on Key Industry Variables. *Australian J. Agr. Econ.*, April 1985, 29(1), pp. 1–15.
[G: Australia]

Nascimento, Jean-Claude and Raffinot, Marc. Politique de prix agricoles et comportement des producteurs: le cas de l'arachide au Sénégal. (Agricultural Pricing Policy and Primary Producers' Behavior: The Case of Senegal. With English summary.) *Revue Écon.*, July 1985, 36(4), pp. 779–96. **[G: Senegal]**

Nathanson, R. and Weinblatt, J. The General Effect of Export Restrictions on Commodity Markets. In *Weinblatt, J., ed.*, 1985, pp. 10–50. **[G: LDCs; MDCs]**

Nazarenko, V. I. European Countries with Centrally-planned Economies: Markets and Prices. *Europ. Rev. Agr. Econ.*, 1985, 12(1/2), pp. 17–26. **[G: CMEA]**

Ndulu, Benno J. and Msambichaka, Lucian A. Agricultural Sector Development in Tanzania 1961–82: Performance and Major Constraints. In *Lundahl, M., ed.*, 1985, pp. 352–69.
[G: Tanzania]

Neale, Walter C. Indian Community Development, Local Government, Local Planning, and Rural Policy since 1950. *Econ. Develop. Cult. Change*, July 1985, 33(4), pp. 677–98.
[G: India]

Nichols, Wm. Patrick. A Farm Finance Proposal. *Challenge*, July/August 1985, 28(3), pp. 54–58.
[G: U.S.]

Nogués, Julio J. Agriculture and Developing Countries in the GATT. *World Econ.*, June 1985, 8(2), pp. 119–33. **[G: EEC]**

Ojala, Eric M. International Relationships in the World Beef Trade. In *[Heidhues, T.]*, 1985, pp. 172–88. **[G: Selected Countries]**

Oleson, B. T. Linkage of Agricultural Policy and Long Term Prospects in the International Grain Trade. *Can. J. Agr. Econ.*, August 1985, 32, pp. 186–206.

Orden, David. When Are Export Subsidies Rational? A Comment. *Agr. Econ. Res.*, Winter 1985, 37(1), pp. 14–16.

Oskam, Arie J. A Super-Levy System for the Dairy Sector: Consequences and Alternatives. *Europ. Rev. Agr. Econ.*, 1985, 12(4), pp. 431–48. **[G: EEC]**

Osmani, S. R. Pricing and Distribution Policies for Agricultural Development in Bangladesh. *Bangladesh Devel. Stud.*, Sept.-Dec. 1985, 13(3&4), pp. 1–40. **[G: Bangladesh]**

Otsuka, Keijiro and Hayami, Yujiro. Goals and

Consequences of Rice Policy in Japan, 1965-80. *Amer. J. Agr. Econ.*, August 1985, 67(3), pp. 529–38. **[G: Japan]**

Paarlberg, Philip L. When Are Export Subsidies Rational? A Reply. *Agr. Econ. Res.*, Winter 1985, 37(1), pp. 20–22. **[G: U.S.]**

Paris, Quirino. Sector Models with Explicit Expectations and Adjustments. *Statistica*, Oct.-Dec. 1985, 45(4), pp. 465–78.

Peck, Anne E. Commentary [Toward a Market Orientation: The Dilemma Facing Farm Policy in the 1980s] [Automatic Adjustment Rules in Commodity Programs]. In *Gardner, B. L., ed.*, 1985, pp. 382–85. **[G: U.S.]**

Peebles, Gavin. Soviet-Style Agricultural Bonuses and Their Effect on Prices in China: A Search for Perversity and Its Consequences. *Hong Kong Econ. Pap.*, 1985, (16), pp. 40–53.
[G: China]

Penn, J. B. U.S. Agricultural Policy: The 1985 Farm Legislation: Assessment from Inside the Beltway. In *Gardner, B. L., ed.*, 1985, pp. 195–200. **[G: U.S.]**

Perry, Douglas H. The Economics of Transmigrant Farming. *Bull. Indonesian Econ. Stud.*, December 1985, 21(3), pp. 104–17.
[G: Indonesia]

Peterson, Willis. Equity Implications of Public Policy in an Unstable Agricultural Economy: Discussion. *Amer. J. Agr. Econ.*, May 1985, 67(2), pp. 443–45. **[G: U.S.; LDCs]**

Petit, Michel. Agricultural Market Intervention and International Trade: Opening of the Discussion. *Europ. Rev. Agr. Econ.*, 1985, 12(1/2), pp. 100–101. **[G: EEC]**

Petit, Michel. Conflits entre stratégies agro-alimentaires: la confrontation entre les États-Unis et la Communauté Européenne. (Conflicts between Agri-Food Strategies: The Confrontation between the United States and the European Community. With English summary.) *Écon. Soc.*, July 1985, 19(7), pp. 208–28. **[G: U.S.; EEC]**

Petit, Michel. For an Analytical Political Economy: Relevance to the Study of Domestic and International Trade Agricultural Policies. In *[Heidhues, T.]*, 1985, pp. 31–44.

Petit, Michel. U.S.–EEC Confrontation in the International Trade of Agricultural Products: Consequences for Third Parties. *Can. J. Agr. Econ.*, August 1985, 32, pp. 146–69.
[G: U.S.; EEC]

Petzel, Todd E. Toward a Market Orientation: The Dilemma Facing Farm Policy in the 1980s. In *Gardner, B. L., ed.*, 1985, pp. 350–54.
[G: U.S.]

Picciotto, Robert. National Agricultural Research. *Finance Develop.*, June 1985, 22(2), pp. 45–48. **[G: LDCs]**

Pinstrup-Andersen, Per. Food Prices and the Poor in Developing Countries. *Europ. Rev. Agr. Econ.*, 1985, 12(1/2), pp. 69–81.
[G: LDCs]

Pivot, Catherine. Offices d'intervention et régulation contractuelle en agriculture. (With English summary.) *Revue Écon. Polit.*, January–

February 1985, *95*(1), pp. 66–86.

Pollard, Stephen K. and Graham, Douglas H. Price Policy and Agricultural Export Performance in Jamaica. *World Devel.*, September 1985, *13*(9), pp. 1067–75. **[G: Jamaica]**

Pollard, Stephen K. and Graham, Douglas H. The Performance of the Food-producing Sector in Jamaica, 1962–1979: A Policy Analysis. *Econ. Develop. Cult. Change*, July 1985, *33*(4), pp. 731–54. **[G: Jamaica]**

Pomfret, Richard. The Trade Diversion Due to EC Enlargement: A Comment on Sawyer's Estimate [The Effects of the Second Enlargement of the EC on U.S. Exports to Europe]. *Weltwirtsch. Arch.*, 1985, *121*(3), pp. 560–61. **[G: EEC; U.S.]**

Putterman, Louis. Extrinsic versus Intrinsic Problems of Agricultural Cooperation: Anti-incentivism in Tanzania and China. *J. Devel. Stud.*, January 1985, *21*(2), pp. 175–204. **[G: Tanzania; China]**

Putterman, Louis. The Restoration of the Peasant Household as Farm Production Unit in China: Some Incentive Theoretic Analysis. In *Perry, E. J. and Wong, C., eds.*, 1985, pp. 63–82. **[G: China]**

Quasem, Md. Abul. Impact of the New System of Distribution of Irrigation Machines in Bangladesh. *Bangladesh Devel. Stud.*, Sept.-Dec. 1985, *13*(3&4), pp. 127–40. **[G: Bangladesh]**

Qureshi, Sarfraz K. Domestic Terms of Trade and Public Policy for Agriculture in Pakistan. *Pakistan Devel. Rev.*, Autumn-Winter 1985, *24*(3/4), pp. 363–79. **[G: Pakistan]**

Radtke, Hans; Detering, Stan and Brokken, Ray F. A Comparison of Economic Impact Estimates for Changes in the Federal Grazing Fee: Secondary vs. Primary Data I/O Models. *Western J. Agr. Econ.*, December 1985, *10*(2), pp. 382–90. **[G: U.S.]**

Randall, Alan J. Commentary [Toward a Market Orientation: The Dilemma Facing Farm Policy in the 1980s] [Automatic Adjustment Rules in Commodity Programs]. In *Gardner, B. L., ed.*, 1985, pp. 378–81. **[G: U.S.]**

Rasmussen, Svend and Nielsen, A. Hjortshøj. The Impact of Quotas on the Optimal Adjustment of Milk Production at the Farm Level. *Europ. Rev. Agr. Econ.*, 1985, *12*(4), pp. 351–64. **[G: EEC]**

Rausser, Gordon C. Macroeconomics and U.S. Agricultural Policy. In *Gardner, B. L., ed.*, 1985, pp. 207–52. **[G: U.S.]**

Rawlins, Glenville. Measuring the Impact of I.R.D.P. II upon the Technical Efficiency Level of Jamaican Peasant Farmers. *Soc. Econ. Stud.*, June 1985, *34*(2), pp. 71–96. **[G: Jamaica]**

Regalado, Basilia M. Distributional Impacts of Selected Food Policies on Human Nutrition in the Philippines. *Philippine Econ. J.*, 1985, *24*(2–3), pp. 143–80. **[G: Philippines]**

Reutlinger, Shlomo. The Bank's Food Security Policy. In *Davis, T. J., ed.*, 1985, pp. 134–44.

Richardson, Bob. Frontiers in Agricultural Policy

Research: Discussion. *Rev. Marketing Agr. Econ.*, August 1985, *53*(2), pp. 91–94. **[G: Australia]**

Rieder, Peter. Experience with the Milk Quota System in Switzerland. *Europ. Rev. Agr. Econ.*, 1985, *12*(4), pp. 473–79. **[G: Switzerland]**

Riordan, E. B. Estimation of a Bilateral Trade Model for a Food Processing Service: Obstacles to Trade in Deboned Beef. *Irish J. Agr. Econ. Rural Soc.*, 1984-1985, *10*(2), pp. 145–64. **[G: Ireland; U.K.]**

Ritson, Christopher. Implications of Non-monetary Objectives in the Agricultural Policy of the European Community: Comment. In *[Heidhues, T.]*, 1985, pp. 150–51. **[G: EEC]**

Ritson, Christopher. Some Observations on Price Instability, Agricultural Trade Policy and the Food Consumer. In *[Heidhues, T.]*, 1985, pp. 117–32.

Roarty, Michael J. The EEC Common Agricultural Policy and Its Effects on Less-developed Countries. *Nat. Westminster Bank Quart. Rev.*, February 1985, pp. 2–17. **[G: EEC; LDCs]**

Roberts, Roland K. and Martin, William J. The Effects of Alternative Beef Import Quota Regimes on the Beef Industries of the Aggregate United States and Hawaii. *Western J. Agr. Econ.*, December 1985, *10*(2), pp. 230–44. **[G: U.S.]**

Robinson, Kenneth L. The Use of Agricultural Export Restrictions as an Instrument of Foreign Policy. In *[Heidhues, T.]*, 1985, pp. 214–28. **[G: Selected Countries]**

Roe, Terry and Senauer, Benjamin. Simulating Alternative Foodgrain Price and Trade Policies: An Application for the Dominican Republic. *J. Policy Modeling*, Winter 1985, *7*(4), pp. 635–48. **[G: Dominican Republic]**

Rose-Ackerman, Susan and Evenson, Robert E. The Political Economy of Agricultural Research and Extension: Grants, Votes, and Reapportionment. *Amer. J. Agr. Econ.*, February 1985, *67*(1), pp. 1–14. **[G: U.S.]**

Rosegrant, Mark W.; Roumasset, James A. and Balisacan, Arsenio M. Biological Technology and Agricultural Policy: An Assessment of Azolla in Philippine Rice Production. *Amer. J. Agr. Econ.*, November 1985, *67*(4), pp. 726–32. **[G: Philippines]**

Ruttan, Vernon W. Moral Responsibility and Agricultural Research. In *[Heidhues, T.]*, 1985, pp. 66–83. **[G: U.S.]**

Saith, Ashwani. Primitive Accumulation, Agrarian Reform and Socialist Transitions: An Argument. In *Saith, A., ed.*, 1985, pp. 1–48. **[G: U.S.S.R.; LDCs; China]**

Saith, Ashwani. Primitive Accumulation, Agrarian Reform and Socialist Transitions: An Argument. *J. Devel. Stud.*, October 1985, *22*(1), pp. 1–48. **[G: U.S.S.R.; LDCs; China]**

Salathe, Larry. Commodity Market Stabilization in Farm Programs: Commentary. In *Gardner, B. L., ed.*, 1985, pp. 277–82. **[G: U.S.]**

Salem, Abdul. Domestic Terms of Trade and Public Policy for Agriculture in Pakistan: Comments. *Pakistan Devel. Rev.*, Autumn-Winter 1985, *24*(3/4), pp. 380–83. **[G: Pakistan]**

Sarris, Alexander H. Food Security and Agricultural Production Strategies under Risk in Egypt. *J. Devel. Econ.*, Sept.-Oct. 1985, *19*(1/2), pp. 85–111. **[G: Egypt]**

Sawyer, W. Charles. The Effects of the Second Enlargement of the EC on U.S. Exports to Europe: Reply. *Weltwirtsch. Arch.*, 1985, *121*(3), pp. 562–63. **[G: EEC; U.S.]**

Scheper, Wilhelm. For an Analytical Political Economy: Relevance to the Study of Domestic and International Trade Agricultural Policies: Comment. In *[Heidhues, T.]*, 1985, pp. 45–46.

Scheper, Wilhelm. Markets and Prices: Links between Agriculture and the General Economy: Comment. *Europ. Rev. Agr. Econ.*, 1985, *12*(1/2), pp. 14–15. **[G: EEC]**

Schinke, E. European Countries with Centrally-planned Economies: Markets and Prices: Comment. *Europ. Rev. Agr. Econ.*, 1985, *12*(1/2), pp. 28–29. **[G: CMEA]**

Schmidt, Janet K. Some Issues in the Multilateral Management of Food Resources. In *Jordan, R. S., ed.*, 1985, pp. 65–95. **[G: U.S.]**

Schmitt, Günther. Agricultural Prices and Farm Incomes: Opening of the Discussion. *Europ. Rev. Agr. Econ.*, 1985, *12*(1/2), pp. 66–67.

Schmitt, Günther. Theodor Heidhues' Contribution to the Analysis of Agriculture and International Relations. In *[Heidhues, T.]*, 1985, pp. 17–28.

Schneider, Robert R. Food Subsidies: A Multiple Price Model. *Int. Monet. Fund Staff Pap.*, June 1985, *32*(2), pp. 289–316. **[G: LDCs]**

Schnittker, John A. U.S. Agricultural Policy: The 1985 Farm Legislation: A Synthesis. In *Gardner, B. L., ed.*, 1985, pp. 201–04. **[G: U.S.]**

Schuh, G. Edward. International Agriculture and Trade Policies: Implications for the United States. In *Gardner, B. L., ed.*, 1985, pp. 56–78. **[G: U.S.; Global]**

Seftel, Howard. Government Regulation and the Rise of the California Fruit Industry: The Entrepreneurial Attack on Fruit Pests, 1880–1920. *Bus. Hist. Rev.*, Autumn 1985, *59*(3), pp. 369–402. **[G: U.S.]**

Sen, S. R. A Strategy for Our Small Farms. *Indian Econ. Rev.*, Jan.-June 1985, *20*(1), pp. 143–58. **[G: India]**

Senauer, Benjamin. Food Program Policy Initiatives in an Era of Farm Surpluses: Discussion. *Amer. J. Agr. Econ.*, May 1985, *67*(2), pp. 354–55. **[G: U.S.]**

Shivakumar, J. Sudan: Agricultural Rehabilitation Program Credits. In *Davis, T. J., ed.*, 1985, pp. 179–88. **[G: Sudan]**

Sicular, Terry. Rural Marketing and Exchange in the Wake of Recent Reforms. In *Perry, E. J. and Wong, C., eds.*, 1985, pp. 83–109. **[G: China]**

Simpson, Ian G. Dynamic Aspects of Agricultural Policy: Intervention or Regulation? In *Lundahl, M., ed.*, 1985, pp. 273–90.

Smallwood, David M. and Blaylock, James R. Analysis of Food Stamp Program Participation and Food Expenditures. *Western J. Agr. Econ.*, July 1985, *10*(1), pp. 41–54. **[G: U.S.]**

Smith, Edward G.; Richardson, James W. and Knutson, Ronald D. Impact of Alternative Farm Programs on Different Size Cotton Farms in the Texas Southern High Plains: A Simulation Approach. *Western J. Agr. Econ.*, December 1985, *10*(2), pp. 365–74. **[G: U.S.]**

Smith, Ian. UNCTAD: Failure of the UN Sugar Conference. *J. World Trade Law*, May:June 1985, *19*(3), pp. 296–301. **[G: Global]**

Smith, William. High Technology in Canadian Agriculture: A Science Council Perspective. *Can. J. Agr. Econ.*, August 1985, *32*, pp. 14–23. **[G: Canada]**

Spalding, Rose J. Structural Barriers to Food Programming: An Analysis of the "Mexican Food System." *World Devel.*, December 1985, *13*(12), pp. 1249–62. **[G: Mexico]**

Spencer, John E. The European Economic Community: General Equilibrium Computations and the Economic Implications of Membership. In *Piggott, J. and Whalley, J., eds.*, 1985, pp. 119–42. **[G: EEC]**

Spriggs, John. Economic Analysis of the Western Grain Stabilization Program. *Can. J. Agr. Econ.*, July 1985, *33*(2), pp. 209–29. **[G: Canada]**

Stainer, Robin. Commodity Agreements. In *Roberts, G., ed.*, 1985, pp. 17–24. **[G: Global]**

Stanton, B. F. Farm Programs and Structural Issues: Commentary. In *Gardner, B. L., ed.*, 1985, pp. 321–28. **[G: U.S.]**

Stavis, Benedict. Some Initial Results of China's New Agricultural Policies. *World Devel.*, December 1985, *13*(12), pp. 1299–1305. **[G: China]**

Sumner, Daniel A. Farm Programs and Structural Issues. In *Gardner, B. L., ed.*, 1985, pp. 283–320. **[G: U.S.]**

Sumner, Daniel A. and Wohlgenant, Michael K. Effects of an Increase in the Federal Excise Tax on Cigarettes. *Amer. J. Agr. Econ.*, May 1985, *67*(2), pp. 235–42. **[G: U.S.]**

Tangermann, Stefan. The Repercussions of U.S. Agricultural Policies for the European Community. In *Gardner, B. L., ed.*, 1985, pp. 329–44. **[G: EEC; U.S.]**

Taniguchi, Nobukazu. Agricultural Production Cooperatives (LPG) in the German Democratic Republic (GDR). In *Bergmann, T. and Ogura, T. B., eds.*, 1985, pp. 257–70. **[G: E. Germany]**

Tarditi, Secondo. Agricultural Prices and Farm Incomes. *Europ. Rev. Agr. Econ.*, 1985, *12*(1/2), pp. 49–65.

Thomson, Kenneth J. and Hubbard, Lionel J. Budgetary and Financial Effects of the EC Milk Quota System. *Europ. Rev. Agr. Econ.*, 1985, *12*(4), pp. 381–88. **[G: EEC]**

Tomczak, Franciszek. Agricultural Prices and Farm Incomes: Comment. *Europ. Rev. Agr. Econ.*, 1985, *12*(1/2), pp. 67–68.

Tracy, Michael. Evolution of American Agricultural Trade Policy and European Interaction: Comment. In *[Heidhues, T.]*, 1985, pp. 170–71. [G: U.S.]

Tweeten, Luther. Are Current U.S. Farm Commodity Programs Outdated? Arguments in the Affirmative. *Western J. Agr. Econ.*, December 1985, *10*(2), pp. 259–69. [G: U.S.]

Tweeten, Luther. Farm Financial Stress, Structure of Agriculture, and Public Policy. In *Gardner, B. L., ed.*, 1985, pp. 83–112. [G: U.S.]

Tyers, Rodney. International Impacts of Protection: Model Structure and Results for EC Agricultural Policy. *J. Policy Modeling*, Summer 1985, *7*(2), pp. 219–51. [G: EEC]

Tyers, Rodney and Anderson, Kym. Price, Trade and Welfare Effects of Agricultural Protection: The Case of East Asia. *Rev. Marketing Agr. Econ.*, December 1985, *53*(3), pp. 113–40. [G: Japan; S. Korea; Taiwan]

Tyers, Rodney and Phillips, Prue. Australia, ASEAN and Pacific Basin Merchandise Trade: Factor Composition and Performance in the 1970s. In *Lim, D., ed.*, 1985, pp. 78–106. [G: Australia; ASEAN; Pacific Basin]

Unnevehr, Laurian J. The Costs of Squeezing Marketing Margins: Philippine Government Intervention in Rice Markets. *Devel. Econ.*, June 1985, *23*(2), pp. 158–72. [G: Philippines]

von Urff, Winfried. The Use of Agricultural Export Restrictions as an Instrument of Foreign Policy: Comment. In *[Heidhues, T.]*, 1985, pp. 229–31.

Vail, David. Revitalizing Rural Communities or Reviving Agrarian Myths? A Comment [A Geobased National Agricultural Policy for Rural Community Enhancement, Environmental Vitality, and Income Stabilization]. *J. Econ. Issues*, December 1985, *19*(4), pp. 995–1003. [G: U.S.]

Van Kooten, G. C. and Schmitz, Andrew. Commodity Price Stabilization: The Price Uncertainty Case. *Can. J. Econ.*, May 1985, *18*(2), pp. 426–34. [G: Canada]

Viatte, Gérard. Agricultural Market Intervention and International Trade: Comment. *Europ. Rev. Agr. Econ.*, 1985, *12*(1/2), pp. 101–03. [G: EEC]

Viatte, Gérard. Agricultural Trade Policy Issues in the 1980s: Comment. In *[Heidhues, T.]*, 1985, pp. 266–69.

Vogt, Donna U. Barter of Agriculture Commodities among Developing Countries. In *Fisher, B. S. and Harte, K. M., eds.*, 1985, pp. 120–55. [G: LDCs]

Wang, George C. and Hassler, James B. Econometric Investigation of the Dynamic Effects of the 1983 Payment-in-Kind Program on the Wheat Economy. *Western J. Agr. Econ.*, July 1985, *10*(1), pp. 23–31. [G: U.S.]

Warley, Thorald K. Agricultural Trade Policy Issues in the 1980s. In *[Heidhues, T.]*, 1985, pp. 248–65.

Weinschenck, Günther. Implications of Non-monetary Objectives in the Agricultural Policy of the European Community. In *[Heidhues, T.]*, 1985, pp. 135–49. [G: EEC]

Wenlin, Jia. Some Problems Concerning the Implementation of Lenin's Principles of Agricultural Cooperation. In *Bergmann, T. and Ogura, T. B., eds.*, 1985, pp. 305–22. [G: China]

Whipple, Glen D.; Powe, Charles and Gray, Morgan. An Economic Analysis of Selected U.S. Dairy Program Changes. *Southern J. Agr. Econ.*, December 1985, *17*(2), pp. 181–91. [G: U.S.]

White, Christine. Agricultural Planning, Pricing Policy and Co-operatives in Vietnam. *World Devel.*, January 1985, *13*(1), pp. 97–114. [G: Vietnam]

Woś, Augustyn. European Countries with Centrally-planned Economies: Markets and Prices: Opening of the Discussion. *Europ. Rev. Agr. Econ.*, 1985, *12*(1/2), pp. 27–28. [G: CMEA]

Wright, Brian D. Commodity Market Stabilization in Farm Programs. In *Gardner, B. L., ed.*, 1985, pp. 257–76. [G: U.S.]

Wuyts, Marc. Money, Planning and Rural Transformation in Mozambique. *J. Devel. Stud.*, October 1985, *22*(1), pp. 180–207. [G: Mozambique]

Wuyts, Marc. Money, Planning and Rural Transformation in Mozambique. In *Saith, A., ed.*, 1985, pp. 180–207. [G: Mozambique]

Wyzan, Michael L. Soviet Agricultural Procurement Pricing: A Study in Perversity. *J. Compar. Econ.*, March 1985, *9*(1), pp. 24–45. [G: U.S.S.R.]

Yokogawa, Hiroshi. Cooperation in Farming in Yugoslavia. In *Bergmann, T. and Ogura, T. B., eds.*, 1985, pp. 291–303. [G: Yugoslavia]

Yoon, Tae-Hee. Pakistan, SAL I (Agricultural Component). In *Davis, T. J., ed.*, 1985, pp. 174–78. [G: Pakistan]

Zheng, Tianxiang; Wei, Qingquan and Chu, David K. Y. Agricultural Land-Use Patterns and Export Potential. In *Wong, K. and Chu, D. K. Y., eds.*, 1985, pp. 89–107. [G: China]

714 Agricultural Finance

7140 Agricultural Finance

Ahmad, Qazi Kholiquzzaman and Hossain, Mahabub. An Evaluation of Selected Policies and Programmes for the Alleviation of Rural Poverty in Bangladesh. In *Islam, R., ed.*, 1985, pp. 67–98. [G: Bangladesh]

Anderson, Dennis and Khambata, Farida. Financing Small-Scale Industry and Agriculture in Developing Countries: The Merits and Limitations of "Commercial" Policies. *Econ. Develop. Cult. Change*, January 1985, *33*(2), pp. 349–71. [G: LDCs]

Anderson, Kim B. and Ikerd, John E. Whole Farm Risk-rating Microcomputer Model. *Southern J. Agr. Econ.*, July 1985, *17*(1), pp. 183–87.

Ashmead, Ralph. Economic Structure and Capital

Requirements for Agriculture. *Can. J. Agr. Econ.*, July 1985, *32*, pp. 24–38.
[G: Canada]

Bagnall, Herb and Aukes, Robert. Financial Reporting in Agriculture: In Need of a Reliable System. *Can. J. Agr. Econ.*, March 1985, *33*(1), pp. 83–98. [G: Canada]

Barry, Peter J. Needed Changes in the Farmers Home Administration Lending Program. *Amer. J. Agr. Econ.*, May 1985, *67*(2), pp. 341–44. [G: U.S.]

Belongia, Michael T. and Carraro, Kenneth C. The Status of Farm Lenders: An Assessment of Eighth District and National Trends. *Fed. Res. Bank St. Louis Rev.*, October 1985, *67*(8), pp. 17–27. [G: U.S.]

Belongia, Michael T. and Gilbert, R. Alton. The Farm Credit Crisis: Will It Hurt the Whole Economy? *Fed. Res. Bank St. Louis Rev.*, December 1985, *67*(10), pp. 5–15. [G: U.S.]

Bhatnagar, R. G. Integrated Structural, Institutional and Procedural Innovations Formulated by State Bank of India for Increasing Rural Lendings. In *Bandyopadhyay, R. and Khankhoje, D. P., eds.*, 1985, pp. 171–79.
[G: India]

Bhatnagar, R. G. Regional Rural Banks: A Critical Review. In *Bandyopadhyay, R. and Khankhoje, D. P., eds.*, 1985, pp. 147–51.
[G: India]

Bollman, Ray D. Economic Structure and Capital Requirements for Agriculture: Rapporteur's Report. *Can. J. Agr. Econ.*, July 1985, *32*, pp. 39–41. [G: Canada]

Bond, Gary E. and Thompson, Stanley R. Risk Aversion and the Recommended Hedging Ratio. *Amer. J. Agr. Econ.*, November 1985, *67*(4), pp. 870–72.

Breimyer, Harold F. Agriculture's Problem Is Rooted in Washington. *Challenge*, May/June 1985, *28*(2), pp. 53–54. [G: U.S.]

Buehler, John E. The Specific Role of Interest in Financial and Economic Analysis under Inflation: Discussion. *Amer. J. Agr. Econ.*, May 1985, *67*(2), pp. 396–97.

Burcroff, Richard, II. Turkey: Agricultural Sector Adjustment Loan. In *Davis, T. J., ed.*, 1985, pp. 207–10. [G: Turkey]

Collins, Robert A. Expected Utility, Debt–Equity Structure, and Risk Balancing. *Amer. J. Agr. Econ.*, August 1985, *67*(3), pp. 627–29.

Dubey, Vinod. Policy Based Lending and the World Bank. In *Davis, T. J., ed.*, 1985, pp. 166–73.

Feder, Gershon. The Relation between Farm Size and Farm Productivity: The Role of Family Labor, Supervision and Credit Constraints. *J. Devel. Econ.*, August 1985, *18*(2–3), pp. 297–313.

Gunter, Lewell, et al. Analysis of Economic Emergency Loan Allocations and Credit Market Expansion. *Southern J. Agr. Econ.*, December 1985, *17*(2), pp. 21–32. [G: U.S.]

Husain, S. Shahid. Proceedings of the Fifth Agriculture Sector Symposium: Population and Food: Closing Remarks. In *Davis, T. J., ed.*, 1985, pp. 220–26.

Klinefelter, Danny. Capital for the Agriculture of the Future: Discussion. *Southern J. Agr. Econ.*, July 1985, *17*(1), pp. 113–15.
[G: U.S.]

Kotwal, Ashok. The Role of Consumption Credit in Agricultural Tenancy. *J. Devel. Econ.*, August 1985, *18*(2–3), pp. 273–95.

LaDue, Eddy. Needed Changes in the Farmers Home Administration Lending Programs: Discussion. *Amer. J. Agr. Econ.*, May 1985, *67*(2), pp. 352–53. [G: U.S.]

LeBlanc, Michael and Hrubovcak, James. The Effects of Interest Rates on Agricultural Machinery Investment. *Agr. Econ. Res.*, Summer 1985, *37*(3), pp. 12–22. [G: U.S.]

Lee, John Gary; Brown, Deborah J. and Lovejoy, Stephen B. Stochastic Efficiency versus Mean-Variance Criteria as Predictors of Adoption of Reduced Tillage. *Amer. J. Agr. Econ.*, November 1985, *67*(4), pp. 839–45. [G: U.S.]

Mauri, Arnaldo. The Role of Innovatory Financial Technologies in Promoting Rural Development in LDCs. *Rivista Int. Sci. Econ. Com.*, Oct.-Nov. 1985, *32*(10–11), pp. 989–1002.
[G: LDCs]

Melichar, Emanuel. Farm Financial Stress, Structure of Agriculture, and Public Policy: Commentary. In *Gardner, B. L., ed.*, 1985, pp. 113–16. [G: U.S.]

Melichar, Emanuel. Statement to the U.S. House Subcommittee on Economic Stabilization of the Committee on Banking, Finance and Urban Affairs, October 23, 1985. *Fed. Res. Bull.*, December 1985, *71*(12), pp. 941–44.
[G: U.S.]

Melichar, Emanuel. Statement to the U.S. Senate Committee on Agriculture, Nutrition, and Forestry, March 20, 1985. *Fed. Res. Bull.*, May 1985, *71*(5), pp. 306–08. [G: U.S.]

Mody, Ashoka; Mundle, Sudipto and Raj, K. N. Resource Flows from Agriculture: Japan and India. In *Ohkawa, K. and Ranis, G., eds.*, 1985, pp. 266–93. [G: Japan; India]

Nepal Rastra Bank. Priority Sector Credit: Objectives, Policies and Programmes. In *Bandyopadhyay, R. and Khankhoje, D. P., eds.*, 1985, pp. 203–13. [G: Nepal]

Nichols, Wm. Patrick. A Farm Finance Proposal. *Challenge*, July/August 1985, *28*(3), pp. 54–58.
[G: U.S.]

Partee, J. Charles. Statement to the Subcommittee on Agriculture and Transportation of the Joint Economic Committee, June 19, 1985. *Fed. Res. Bull.*, August 1985, *71*(8), pp. 614–18. [G: U.S.]

Partee, J. Charles. Statement to the U.S. Senate Subcommittee on Financial Institutions of the Committee on Banking, Housing, and Urban Affairs, April 26, 1985. *Fed. Res. Bull.*, June 1985, *71*(6), pp. 435–39. [G: U.S.]

Patil, R. K. and Patel, K. V. Rural Development: Organisation and Management Issues. In *Bandyopadhyay, R. and Khankhoje, D. P., eds.*, 1985, pp. 77–98. [G: India]

Pearson, Scott R.; Monke, Eric A. and Avillez, Francisco. Fontes de financiamento do investimento agrícola em Portugal. (With English summary.) *Economia (Portugal)*, May 1985, 9(2), pp. 233–56. [G: Portugal]

Pearson, Scott R.; Monke, Eric A. and Avillez, Francisco. Sources of Funds for Agricultural Investment in Portugal. *Food Res. Inst. Stud.*, 1985, 19(3), pp. 335–52. [G: Portugal]

Plaxico, James S. and Knowles, Glenn J. Capital for the Agriculture of the Future. *Southern J. Agr. Econ.*, July 1985, 17(1), pp. 103–11. [G: U.S.]

Schmiesing, Brian H., et al. Differential Pricing of Agricultural Operating Loans by Commercial Banks. *Western J. Agr. Econ.*, December 1985, 10(2), pp. 192–203. [G: U.S.]

Severn, Alan K. Anticipatory Hedging with Treasury Bills: The Case of a Bank for Cooperatives. *Western J. Agr. Econ.*, December 1985, 10(2), pp. 413–22. [G: U.S.]

Shah, A. C. Evolving Role of Banks in Rural Credit. In *Bandyopadhyay, R. and Khankhoje, D. P., eds.*, 1985, pp. 109–23. [G: India]

Shah, A. C. Innovations of Structural, Institutional and Procedural Concepts in Rural Finance Introduced by Bank of Baroda. In *Bandyopadhyay, R. and Khankhoje, D. P., eds.*, 1985, pp. 161–70. [G: India]

Shashua, Leon and Goldschmidt, Yaaqov. The Specific Role of Interest in Financial and Economic Analysis under Inflation: Real, Nominal, or a Combination of Both. *Amer. J. Agr. Econ.*, May 1985, 67(2), pp. 377–83.

Shivakumar, J. Sudan: Agricultural Rehabilitation Program Credits. In *Davis, T. J., ed.*, 1985, pp. 179–88. [G: Sudan]

Smith, Hilary H. Variable-Rate Loans: Where Does Agriculture Fit In? *Fed. Res. Bank Dallas Econ. Rev.*, November 1985, pp. 1–12. [G: U.S.]

Stover, Roger D.; Teas, R. Kenneth and Gardner, Roy J. Agricultural Lending Decision: A Multiattribute Analysis. *Amer. J. Agr. Econ.*, August 1985, 67(3), pp. 513–20. [G: U.S.]

Tabasso, Luigi. I problemi finanziari della cooperazione agricola. (Financial Problems of Agricultural Cooperation. With English summary.) *Bancaria*, December 1985, 41(12), pp. 1243–48. [G: Italy]

Tauer, Loren W. Use of Life Insurance to Fund the Farm Purchase from Heirs. *Amer. J. Agr. Econ.*, February 1985, 67(1), pp. 60–69. [G: U.S.]

Teranishi, Juro. Government Credit to the Banking System: Rural Banks in Nineteenth Century Japan and the Postwar Philippines. In *Ohkawa, K. and Ranis, G., eds.*, 1985, pp. 294–310. [G: Japan; Philippines]

Thingalaya, N. K. Rural Financing: Syndicate Bank's Experience. In *Bandyopadhyay, R. and Khankhoje, D. P., eds.*, 1985, pp. 153–59. [G: India]

Thingalaya, N. K.; Khankhoje, D. P. and Godse, V. T. Systems and Procedures in Rural Banking: Some Operational Aspects. In *Bandyopa-*

dhyay, R. and Khankhoje, D. P., eds., 1985, pp. 99–108. [G: India]

Todd, Richard M. Taking Stock of the Farm Credit System: Riskier for Farm Borrowers. *Fed. Res. Bank Minn. Rev.*, Fall 1985, 9(4), pp. 14–24. [G: U.S.]

Tweeten, Luther. Farm Financial Stress, Structure of Agriculture, and Public Policy. In *Gardner, B. L., ed.*, 1985, pp. 83–112. [G: U.S.]

Wilson, Paul N. and Gundersen, Carl E. Financial Risk in Cotton Production. *Southern J. Agr. Econ.*, December 1985, 17(2), pp. 199–206. [G: U.S.]

715 Agricultural Markets and Marketing; Cooperatives

7150 Agricultural Markets and Marketing; Cooperatives

Albert, Bill. External Forces and the Transformation of Peruvian Coastal Agriculture, 1880–1930. In *Abel, C. and Lewis, C. M., eds.*, 1985, pp. 231–49. [G: Peru]

Anderson, Ronald W. Some Determinants of the Volatility of Futures Prices. *J. Futures Markets*, Fall 1985, 5(3), pp. 331–48. [G: U.S.]

Arhin, Kwame. The Ghana Cocoa Marketing Board and the Farmer. In *Arhin, K.; Hesp, P. and van der Laan, L., eds.*, 1985, pp. 37–52. [G: Ghana]

Arnould, Eric J. Evaluating Regional Economic Development: Results of a Marketing System Analysis in Zinder Province, Niger Republic. *J. Devel. Areas*, January 1985, 19(2), pp. 209–44. [G: Niger]

Aylward, Justin. Sugar. In *Roberts, G., ed.*, 1985, pp. 134–46. [G: Global]

Bailey, DeeVon and Richardson, James W. Analysis of Selected Marketing Strategies: A Whole-Farm Simulation Approach. *Amer. J. Agr. Econ.*, November 1985, 67(4), pp. 813–20.

Barichello, Richard R. and Glenday, Graham. The Tax Expenditure of Agricultural Marketing Quota Deductibility. *Can. J. Agr. Econ.*, November 1985, 33(3), pp. 263–84. [G: Canada]

Bautista, Romeo M. Does Increasing Agricultural Exports Raise Income Instability? An Empirical Note. *Philippine Rev. Econ. Bus.*, Sept./Dec. 1985, 22(3/4), pp. 247–58. [G: Philippines]

Baxter, Jennefer; Conine, Thomas E., Jr. and Tamarkin, Maurry. On Commodity Market Risk Premiums: Additional Evidence. *J. Futures Markets*, Spring 1985, 5(1), pp. 121–25. [G: U.S.]

Behrman, Jere R. and Murty, K. N. Market Impacts of Technological Change for Sorghum in Indian Near-Subsistence Agriculture. *Amer. J. Agr. Econ.*, August 1985, 67(3), pp. 539–49. [G: India]

Berck, Peter and Cecchetti, Stephen G. Portfolio Diversification, Futures Markets, and Uncertain Consumption Prices. *Amer. J. Agr. Econ.*, August 1985, 67(3), pp. 497–507.

Berck, Peter and Perloff, Jeffrey M. A Dynamic Analysis of Marketing Orders, Voting, and Welfare. *Amer. J. Agr. Econ.*, August 1985, 67(3), pp. 487–96.

Berg, Elliot. The Potentials of the Private Sector in Sub-Saharan Africa. In *Rose, T., ed.*, 1985, pp. 135–44. **[G: Sub-Saharan Africa]**

Bigman, David and Goldfarb, David. Efficiency and Efficient Trading Rules for Food and Feed Grains in the World Commodity Markets: The Israeli Experience. *J. Futures Markets*, Spring 1985, 5(1), pp. 1–10. **[G: Israel]**

Bird, Peter J. W. N. Dependency and Efficiency in the London Terminal Markets. *J. Futures Markets*, Fall 1985, 5(3), pp. 433–46. **[G: U.K.]**

Bond, Gary E. and Thompson, Stanley R. Risk Aversion and the Recommended Hedging Ratio. *Amer. J. Agr. Econ.*, November 1985, 67(4), pp. 870–72.

Bond, Gary E.; Thompson, Stanley R. and Geldard, Jane M. Basis Risk and Hedging Strategies for Australian Wheat Exports. *Australian J. Agr. Econ.*, December 1985, 29(3), pp. 199–209. **[G: Australia]**

Brandt, Jon A. Forecasting and Hedging: An Illustration of Risk Reduction in the Hog Industry. *Amer. J. Agr. Econ.*, February 1985, 67(1), pp. 24–31. **[G: U.S.]**

Brhlovič, Gerhard. Changes in the Character of the Work of Cooperative Farmers. *Czech. Econ. Digest.*, June 1985, (4), pp. 24–41. **[G: Czechoslovakia]**

Brorsen, B. Wade, et al. Marketing Margins and Price Uncertainty: The Case of the U.S. Wheat Market. *Amer. J. Agr. Econ.*, August 1985, 67(3), pp. 521–28. **[G: U.S.]**

Brown, Stewart L. A Reformulation of the Portfolio Model of Hedging. *Amer. J. Agr. Econ.*, August 1985, 67(3), pp. 508–12. **[G: U.S.]**

Bryceson, Deborah Fahy. The Organization of Tanzanian Grain Marketing: Switching Roles of the Co-operative and the Parastatal. In *Arhin, K.; Hesp, P. and van der Laan, L., eds.*, 1985, pp. 53–78. **[G: Tanzania]**

Buccola, Steven T. Pricing Efficiency in Centralized and Noncentralized Markets. *Amer. J. Agr. Econ.*, August 1985, 67(3), pp. 583–90. **[G: U.S.]**

Buccola, Steven T. and Subaei, Abdelbagi. Optimal Market Pools for Agricultural Cooperatives. *Amer. J. Agr. Econ.*, February 1985, 67(1), pp. 70–80. **[G: U.S.]**

Buckingham, A. C. Rubber. In *Roberts, G., ed.*, 1985, pp. 116–20. **[G: Global]**

Buckley, John. Soyabeans. In *Roberts, G., ed.*, 1985, pp. 125–33. **[G: Global]**

Campbell, Robert B. and Turnovsky, Stephen J. An Analysis of the Stabilizing and Welfare Effects of Intervention in Spot and Futures Markets. *J. Public Econ.*, November 1985, 28(2), pp. 165–209.

Canarella, Giorgio and Pollard, Stephen K. Efficiency of Commodity Futures: A Vector Autoregression Analysis. *J. Futures Markets*, Spring 1985, 5(1), pp. 57–76. **[G: U.S.]**

Carter, Colin A. Hedging Opportunities for Canadian Grains. *Can. J. Agr. Econ.*, March 1985, 33(1), pp. 37–45. **[G: Canada]**

Carter, Colin A. International Trade Opportunities for Canadian Agriculture. *Can. J. Agr. Econ.*, July 1985, 32, pp. 1–17. **[G: Canada]**

Carter, Colin A. and Loyns, R. M. A. Hedging Feedlot Cattle: A Canadian Perspective. *Amer. J. Agr. Econ.*, February 1985, 67(1), pp. 32–39. **[G: U.S.; Canada]**

Caswell, Nim. Peasants, Peanuts and Politics: State Marketing in Senegal, 1966–80. In *Arhin, K.; Hesp, P. and van der Laan, L., eds.*, 1985, pp. 79–119. **[G: Senegal]**

Centner, Terence J. Retail Food Cooperatives: Testing the "Small Is Beautiful" Hypothesis: Comment. *Amer. J. Agr. Econ.*, May 1985, 67(2), pp. 328–29. **[G: U.S.]**

Choi, Jin W. and Longstaff, Francis A. Pricing Options on Agricultural Futures: An Application of the Constant Elasticity of Variance Option Pricing Model. *J. Futures Markets*, Summer 1985, 5(2), pp. 247–58. **[G: U.S.]**

Conners, Sandy B.; Samli, A. Coskun and Kaynak, Erdener. Transfer of Food Retail Technology into Less Developed Countries. In *Samli, A. C., ed.*, 1985, pp. 27–44. **[G: LDCs]**

Coper, Michael. In the Beginning There Was Interstate Trade... *Rev. Marketing Agr. Econ.*, December 1985, 53(3), pp. 103–12. **[G: Australia]**

Cornelisse, Peter A. and de Kruijk, Hans. Consumption and Trade of Wheat and Flour in Pakistan—The Role of Public and Private Sector. *Pakistan Devel. Rev.*, Summer 1985, 24(2), pp. 151–71. **[G: Pakistan]**

Cotterill, Ronald W. Retail Food Cooperatives: Testing the "Small Is Beautiful" Hypothesis: Reply. *Amer. J. Agr. Econ.*, May 1985, 67(2), pp. 330. **[G: U.S.]**

Davis, John and Kirk, Alan. Economic Aspects of Changing the Seasonality of Milk Production and Pricing. *Irish J. Agr. Econ. Rural Soc.*, 1984-1985, 10(2), pp. 97–108. **[G: Ireland]**

De Maria, A. W. Grains. In *Roberts, G., ed.*, 1985, pp. 90–97. **[G: Global]**

Drummond, Ian M. Marketing Boards in the White Dominions, with Special Reference to Australia and Canada. In *Platt, D. C. M. and di Tella, G., eds.*, 1985, pp. 194–206. **[G: Australia; Canada; New Zealand]**

Duvvury, Nata. Tobacco Trading and Forms of Market Organization: A Case Study of Guntur District. In *Raj, K. N., et al., eds.*, 1985, pp. 273–305. **[G: India]**

Ellis, J. C. Fundamental Supply and Demand Factors in the Grain Futures Markets. In *Roberts, G., ed.*, 1985, pp. 38–44. **[G: U.S.; EEC]**

Filippi-Wilhelm, Laurence. Traders and Marketing Boards in Upper Volta: Ten Years of State Intervention in Agricultural Marketing, 1968–78. In *Arhin, K.; Hesp, P. and van der Laan, L., eds.*, 1985, pp. 120–48. **[G: Upper Volta]**

Folwell, R. J., et al. The Federal Hop Marketing

Order and Volume-Control Behavior. *Agr. Econ. Res.*, Fall 1985, *37*(4), pp. 17–32. [G: U.S.]

Garrido Egido, Leovigildo. Agricultural Cooperation in Spain: The Agricultural Production in Common. In *Bergmann, T. and Ogura, T. B.*, eds., 1985, pp. 31–42. [G: Spain]

Gillis, K. G., et al. The Prospects for Export of Primal Beef Cuts to California. *Can. J. Agr. Econ.*, July 1985, *33*(2), pp. 171–94. [G: Canada; U.S.]

Gisser, Micha. Welfare Implications of Oligopoly in U.S. Food Manufacturing: Reply. *Amer. J. Agr. Econ.*, February 1985, *67*(1), pp. 146. [G: U.S.]

Glenn, Marcia. International Trade Opportunities for Canadian Agriculture: Rapporteur's Report. *Can. J. Agr. Econ.*, July 1985, *32*, pp. 18–23. [G: Canada]

Gordon, Alec and Shankleman, J. Coffee. In *Roberts, G., ed.*, 1985, pp. 59–63. [G: Global]

Grant, Wyn. Corporatism and the Public–Private Distinction. In *Lane, J.-E., ed.*, 1985, pp. 158–80. [G: U.K.]

Gusev, P. The Development of the Process of Socialization of Collective Farm Production. *Prob. Econ.*, January 1985, *27*(9), pp. 81–100. [G: U.S.S.R.]

Hallagan, William S. Contracting Problems and the Adoption of Regulatory Cartels. *Econ. Inquiry*, January 1985, *23*(1), pp. 37–56. [G: U.S.]

Halpern, Dan. Israel's Food Industry. In *Levinson, P. and Landau, P., eds.*, 1985, pp. 124–26. [G: Israel]

Hauser, Robert J.; Beaulieu, Jeffrey and Baumel, C. Phillip. Impacts of Inland Waterway User Fees on Grain Transportation and Implied Barge Rate Elasticities. *Logist. Transp. Rev.*, March 1985, *21*(1), pp. 37–55. [G: U.S.]

Hauser, Robert J. and Neff, David. Pricing Options on Agricultural Futures: Departures from Traditional Theory. *J. Futures Markets*, Winter 1985, *5*(4), pp. 539–77. [G: U.S.]

Hayenga, Marvin L., et al. A Carcass Merit Pricing System for the Pork Industry. *Amer. J. Agr. Econ.*, May 1985, *67*(2), pp. 315–19. [G: U.S.]

Hayward, Brian. The Grain Trader and Market Outlook Usefulness. *Can. J. Agr. Econ.*, August 1985, *32*, pp. 77–85.

Hesp, Paul and van der Laan, Laurens. Marketing Boards in Tropical Africa: A Survey. In *Arhin, K.; Hesp, P. and van der Laan, L.*, eds., 1985, pp. 1–36. [G: Africa]

Hollier, Graham P. Examining Allegations of Exploitation and Inefficiency in Rural Marketing Systems: Some Evidence from West Cameroon. *J. Devel. Areas*, April 1985, *19*(3), pp. 393–416. [G: Cameroon]

Holmen, Hans. Agricultural Co-operatives in the Rural Development of Egypt: A Comment. *Ann. Pub. Co-op. Econ.*, Oct.-Dec. 1985, *56*(4), pp. 553–64. [G: Egypt]

Idachaba, Francis Sulemanu. Commodity Boards

in Nigeria: A Crisis of Identity. In *Arhin, K.; Hesp, P. and van der Laan, L.*, eds., 1985, pp. 149–68. [G: Nigeria]

Jabara, Cathy L. Agricultural Pricing Policy in Kenya. *World Devel.*, May 1985, *13*(5), pp. 611–26. [G: Kenya]

Jordan, Jeffery L, et al. Estimating Implicit Marginal Prices of Quality Characteristics of Tomatoes. *Southern J. Agr. Econ.*, December 1985, *17*(2), pp. 139–46. [G: U.S.]

Kenney, Genevieve M. Welfare Implications of Oligopoly in U.S. Food Manufacturing: Comment. *Amer. J. Agr. Econ.*, February 1985, *67*(1), pp. 144–45. [G: U.S.]

Kerr, William A. The Livestock Industry and Canadian Economic Development. *Can. J. Agr. Econ.*, July 1985, *32*, pp. 64–104. [G: Canada]

Knoeber, Charles R. and Baumer, David L. Understanding Retained Patronage Refunds in Agricultural Cooperatives: Reply. *Amer. J. Agr. Econ.*, February 1985, *67*(1), pp. 135. [G: U.S.]

Lee, Jonq-Ying and Brown, Mark G. Coupon Redemption and the Demand for Frozen Concentrated Orange Juice: A Switching Regression Analysis. *Amer. J. Agr. Econ.*, August 1985, *67*(3), pp. 647–53. [G: U.S.]

Livingstone, Ian. Agricultural Development Strategy and Agricultural Pricing Policy in Malawi. In *Arhin, K.; Hesp, P. and van der Laan, L.*, eds., 1985, pp. 169–92. [G: Malawi]

Loyns, R. M. A. The Livestock Industry and Canadian Economic Development: Rapporteur's Report. *Can. J. Agr. Econ.*, July 1985, *32*, pp. 105–10. [G: Canada]

Maberly, Edwin D. Testing Futures Market Efficiency—A Restatement. *J. Futures Markets*, Fall 1985, *5*(3), pp. 425–32. [G: U.S.]

MacArthur, J., et al. The Canadian Beef and Pork Sectors: New Found Relevance of Live Market Information. *Can. J. Agr. Econ.*, July 1985, *33*(2), pp. 151–69. [G: Canada]

Mackie, J. A. C. The Changing Political Economy of an Export Crop: The Case of Jember's Tobacco Industry. *Bull. Indonesian Econ. Stud.*, April 1985, *21*(1), pp. 112–39. [G: Indonesia]

Marsh, John M. Monthly Price Premiums and Discounts between Steer Calves and Yearlings. *Amer. J. Agr. Econ.*, May 1985, *67*(2), pp. 307–14. [G: U.S.]

Mayne, D. Tea. In *Roberts, G., ed.*, 1985, pp. 147–53. [G: Global]

McFadden, Daniel; Winston, Clifford and Boersch-Supan, Axel. Joint Estimation of Freight Transportation Decisions under Nonrandom Sampling. In *Daughety, A. F., ed.*, 1985, pp. 137–57. [G: U.S.]

Melnick, Rafi and Shalit, Haim. Estimating the Market for Tomatoes. *Amer. J. Agr. Econ.*, August 1985, *67*(3), pp. 573–82. [G: Israel]

Miller, Stephen E. Simple and Multiple Cross-hedging of Millfeeds. *J. Futures Markets*, Spring 1985, *5*(1), pp. 21–28. [G: U.S.]

Mohammad, Faiz. Farm Prices and the Green Revolution: Some Reflections on the Performance of Private Agricultural Markets in Pakistan. *Pakistan Devel. Rev.*, Summer 1985, 24(2), pp. 103–23. **[G: Pakistan]**

Monterosso, Cesar D. B., et al. Grain Storage in Developing Areas: Location and Size of Facilities. *Amer. J. Agr. Econ.*, February 1985, 67(1), pp. 101–11. **[G: Brazil]**

Motsinger, L. R.; Epperson, James E. and Mizelle, W. O., Jr. Temporal Allocation Alternatives for Southeastern Red Delicious Apples. *Southern J. Agr. Econ.*, July 1985, 17(1), pp. 131–138. **[G: U.S.]**

Myers, R. J.; Piggott, R. R. and MacAulay, T. G. Effects of Past Australian Wheat Price Policies on Key Industry Variables. *Australian J. Agr. Econ.*, April 1985, 29(1), pp. 1–15. **[G: Australia]**

Nagaraj, K. Marketing Structures for Paddy and Arecanut in South Kanara: A Comparison of Markets in a Backward Agricultural District. In *Raj, K. N., et al., eds.,* 1985, pp. 247–72. **[G: India]**

Nelson, Ray D. Forward and Futures Contracts as Preharvest Commodity Marketing Instruments. *Amer. J. Agr. Econ.*, February 1985, 67(1), pp. 15–23. **[G: U.S.]**

Nguyen, Dung and Vo, Trang T. On Discarding Low Quality Produce. *Amer. J. Agr. Econ.*, August 1985, 67(3), pp. 614–18.

Oellermann, Charles M. and Farris, Paul L. Futures or Cash: Which Market Leads Live Beef Cattle Prices? *J. Futures Markets,* Winter 1985, 5(4), pp. 529–38. **[G: U.S.]**

Peck, Anne E. The Economic Role of Traditional Commodity Futures Markets. In *Peck, A. E., ed. (II),* 1985, pp. 1–81. **[G: Canada; U.S.; Argentina; Australia]**

Plato, Gerald. Valuing American Options on Commodity Futures Contracts. *Agr. Econ. Res.*, Spring 1985, 37(2), pp. 1–14. **[G: U.S.; Europe]**

Pluhar, Darwin M.; Shafer, Carl E. and Sporleder, Thomas L. The Systematic Downward Bias in Live Cattle Futures: A Further Evaluation. *J. Futures Markets,* Spring 1985, 5(1), pp. 11–20. **[G: U.S.]**

Prior-Willeard, Christopher. Meat. In *Roberts, G., ed.,* 1985, pp. 104–10. **[G: Global]**

Purcell, Wayne D. and Hudson, Michael A. The Economic Roles and Implications of Trade in Livestock Futures. In *Peck, A. E., ed. (I),* 1985, pp. 329–76. **[G: U.S.]**

Putterman, Louis and DiGiorgio, Marie. Choice and Efficiency in a Model of Democratic Semicollective Agriculture. *Oxford Econ. Pap.,* March 1985, 37(1), pp. 1–21.

Ratchford, C. Brice. Understanding Retained Patronage Refunds in Agricultural Cooperatives: Comment. *Amer. J. Agr. Econ.*, February 1985, 67(1), pp. 133–34. **[G: U.S.]**

Ravallion, Martin. The Information Efficiency of Traders' Price Expectations in a Bangladesh Price Market. *Oxford Bull. Econ. Statist.,* May 1985, 47(2), pp. 171–84. **[G: Bangladesh]**

Reed, Michael R. and Robbins, Lynn W. The Relationship between Managerial Heuristics

and Economics in Pricing Retail Meats. *Southern J. Agr. Econ.*, December 1985, 17(2), pp. 87–95. **[G: U.S.]**

Roberts, Gerald. Cocoa. In *Roberts, G., ed.,* 1985, pp. 52–58. **[G: Global]**

Salathe, Larry. Commodity Market Stabilization in Farm Programs: Commentary. In *Gardner, B. L., ed.,* 1985, pp. 277–82. **[G: U.S.]**

Schultz, Robert W. and Marsh, John M. Steer and Heifer Price Differences in the Live Cattle and Carcass Markets. *Western J. Agr. Econ.*, July 1985, 10(1), pp. 77–92. **[G: U.S.]**

Schwart, Robert B., Jr. The Impact of Component Pricing of Soybeans and Milk: Comment. *Amer. J. Agr. Econ.*, November 1985, 67(4), pp. 881–82. **[G: U.S.]**

Sell, Friedrich L. and Schmidt, Felix. Risikominderung durch Terminkontraktmärkte. Empirische Evidenz für sogenannte "Kernrohstoffe." (With English summary.) *Z. Wirtschaft. Sozialwissen.,* 1985, 105(4), pp. 481–505. **[G: U.K.]**

Sicular, Terry. Rural Marketing and Exchange in the Wake of Recent Reforms. In *Perry, E. J. and Wong, C., eds.,* 1985, pp. 83–109. **[G: China]**

Spriggs, John and Sigurdson, Dale. Seller Cooperation in an Oligopoly–Monopsony Market: An Analysis Involving Experimental Economics. *Can. J. Agr. Econ.*, November 1985, 33(3), pp. 359–73. **[G: Global]**

Stanton, B. F. Farm Programs and Structural Issues: Commentary. In *Gardner, B. L., ed.,* 1985, pp. 321–28. **[G: U.S.]**

Strohmaier, Jay S. and Dahl, Reynold P. Price Relationships between Wheat Futures Markets: Implications for Hedging. *Food Res. Inst. Stud.,* 1985, 19(3), pp. 265–92. **[G: U.S.]**

Sumner, Daniel A. Farm Programs and Structural Issues. In *Gardner, B. L., ed.,* 1985, pp. 283–320. **[G: U.S.]**

Unnevehr, Laurian J. The Costs of Squeezing Marketing Margins: Philippine Government Intervention in Rice Markets. *Devel. Econ.,* June 1985, 23(2), pp. 158–72. **[G: Philippines]**

White, Christine. Agricultural Planning, Pricing Policy and Co-operatives in Vietnam. *World Devel.,* January 1985, 13(1), pp. 97–114. **[G: Vietnam]**

Wills, Robert L. Evaluating Price Enhancement by Processing Cooperatives. *Amer. J. Agr. Econ.*, May 1985, 67(2), pp. 183–92. **[G: U.S.]**

Wilson-Smith, J. Cotton. In *Roberts, G., ed.,* 1985, pp. 72–79. **[G: Global]**

Wright, Brian D. Commodity Market Stabilization in Farm Programs. In *Gardner, B. L., ed.,* 1985, pp. 257–76. **[G: U.S.]**

Zahiu, Letiţia and Manole, V. Optimal Size of Sheep Breeding Farms in the Agricultural Production Cooperatives in County Constanţa. *Econ. Computat. Cybern. Stud. Res.,* 1985, 20(3), pp. 33–38. **[G: Romania]**

7151 Corporate Agriculture

Acosta, Yvonne and Casimir, Jean. Social Origins of the Counter-plantation System in St. Lucia. In *Gomes, P. I., ed.*, 1985, pp. 34–59. [G: St. Lucia]

Altmann, Franz-Lothar. East–West Relations in Energy, Agriculture and Technology: Comments. In *Saunders, C. T., ed.*, 1985, pp. 242–46. [G: U.S.S.R.; OECD]

Babb, Emerson M. Agribusiness Simulators for Management Training. *Southern J. Agr. Econ.*, December 1985, 17(2), pp. 193–97.

Ethridge, Don E.; Roy, Sugit K. and Myers, David W. A Markov Chain Analysis of Structural Changes in the Texas High Plains Cotton Ginning Industry. *Southern J. Agr. Econ.*, December 1985, 17(2), pp. 11–20. [G: U.S.]

Freeman, Orville. The Family Farm: A Success Story with Global Implications. In *Didsbury, H. F., Jr., ed.*, 1985, pp. 135–46.

Goldsmith, Arthur. The Private Sector and Rural Development: Can Agribusiness Help the Small Farmer? *World Devel.*, Oct./Nov. 1985, 13(10/11), pp. 1125–38. [G: LDCs]

Hardt, John P. and Gold, Donna L. Agricultural Trade: U.S.A. and U.S.S.R. In *Saunders, C. T., ed.*, 1985, pp. 217–30. [G: U.S.; U.S.S.R.]

Inotai, András. East–West Relations in Energy, Agriculture and Technology: Comments. In *Saunders, C. T., ed.*, 1985, pp. 246–51. [G: CMEA]

Janet, C.; Gorse, P. and Bouquery, J. M. Le rôle des grandes entreprises diversifiées du pétrole et de la chimie dans la production alimentaire. (Activities of Big Petrochemical and Chemical Diversified Firms in Food Production. With English summary.) *Écon. Soc.*, July 1985, 19(7), pp. 243–84. [G: France; U.S.]

Johnson, Ronald N. Retail Price Controls in the Dairy Industry: A Political Coalition Argument. *J. Law Econ.*, April 1985, 28(1), pp. 55–75.

Klein, K. K. Economics of Biotechnology in Animal Production. *Can. J. Agr. Econ.*, August 1985, 32, pp. 36–47.

Mahmood, Muhammad. An Integrated Model of Production, Consumption and Export of Jute in Bangladesh. *Singapore Econ. Rev.*, April 1985, 30(1), pp. 56–67. [G: Bangladesh]

Marsh, John M. and Brester, Gary W. Short-term Adjustments in Yellow Sheet Carcass Prices for Red Meats. *Amer. J. Agr. Econ.*, August 1985, 67(3), pp. 591–99. [G: U.S.]

Moghadam, Fatemeh E. An Evaluation of the Productive Performance of Agribusinesses: An Iranian Case Study. *Econ. Develop. Cult. Change*, July 1985, 33(4), pp. 755–76. [G: Iran]

Muysken, Joan. Estimation of the Capacity Distribution of an Industry: The Swedish Dairy Industry 1964–1973. In *[Johansen, L.]*, 1985, pp. 43–63. [G: Sweden]

Scott, Christopher D. The Decline of an Export Industry, or the Growth of Peruvian Sugar

Consumption in the Long Run. *J. Devel. Stud.*, January 1985, 21(2), pp. 253–81. [G: Peru]

Sleeman, Michael. The Agri-business Bourgeoisie of Barbados and Martinique. In *Gomes, P. I., ed.*, 1985, pp. 15–33. [G: Caribbean]

Van Kooten, G. C. and Schmitz, Andrew. Commodity Price Stabilization: The Price Uncertainty Case. *Can. J. Econ.*, May 1985, 18(2), pp. 426–34. [G: Canada]

Whipple, Glen D.; Powe, Charles and Gray, Morgan. An Economic Analysis of Selected U.S. Dairy Program Changes. *Southern J. Agr. Econ.*, December 1985, 17(2), pp. 181–91. [G: U.S.]

Wilson, Hoyt G. and Kagan, Albert. Economics of Optimization of Fat Levels in Turkey Diets. *Can. J. Agr. Econ.*, March 1985, 33(1), pp. 3–21. [G: U.S.]

716 Farm Management

7160 Farm Management

Aage, Hans. The State and the Kolkhoznik. *Econ. Anal. Worker's Manage.*, 1985, 19(2), pp. 131–46. [G: U.S.S.R.]

Abdullah, A. A. The Fertilizer Subsidy—Cost and Return. *Bangladesh Devel. Stud.*, Sept.-Dec. 1985, 13(3&4), pp. 141–46. [G: Bangladesh]

Abedin, Joynal. Input Demand and Output Supply Elasticities for Rice in Bangladesh—A Study Based on Thakurgaon Farmers. *Bangladesh Devel. Stud.*, Sept.-Dec. 1985, 13(3&4), pp. 111–25. [G: Bangladesh]

Ackello-Ogutu, Christopher; Paris, Quirino and Williams, William A. Testing a von Liebig Crop Response Function against Polynomial Specifications. *Amer. J. Agr. Econ.*, November 1985, 67(4), pp. 873–80. [G: U.S.]

Adachi, Kyoichiro. Ideology, Present State and Problems of Yamagishikai. In *Bergmann, T. and Ogura, T. B., eds.*, 1985, pp. 113–30. [G: Japan]

Alaouze, Chris M.; Read, Michael and Sturgess, N. H. A Statistical Analysis of a Pilot Survey of Salt-affected Dairy Farms. *Australian J. Agr. Econ.*, April 1985, 29(1), pp. 49–62. [G: Australia]

Allen, Douglas W. Evidence of 'Tax' Farming: Tests Using Differential Land Assessments for BC Farms. *Can. Public Policy*, December 1985, 11(4), pp. 659–64. [G: Canada]

Almås, Reidar. New Forms of Cooperation in Norwegian Agriculture. In *Bergmann, T. and Ogura, T. B., eds.*, 1985, pp. 43–57. [G: Norway]

Anderson, Kim B. and Ikerd, John E. Whole Farm Risk-rating Microcomputer Model. *Southern J. Agr. Econ.*, July 1985, 17(1), pp. 183–87.

Aslam, Mian M. Size–Productivity Relationship in Pakistan's Agriculture in the Seventies: Comments. *Pakistan Devel. Rev.*, Autumn-Winter 1985, 24(3/4), pp. 360–61. [G: Pakistan]

Atwood, Joseph A. Demonstration of the Use of

Lower Partial Moments to Improve Safety-First Probability Limits. *Amer. J. Agr. Econ.*, November 1985, *67*(4), pp. 787–93.

Bagnall, Herb and Aukes, Robert. Financial Reporting in Agriculture: In Need of a Reliable System. *Can. J. Agr. Econ.*, March 1985, *33*(1), pp. 83–98.   [G: Canada]

Barichello, Richard R. and Glenday, Graham. The Tax Expenditure of Agricultural Marketing Quota Deductibility. *Can. J. Agr. Econ.*, November 1985, *33*(3), pp. 263–84.
[G: Canada]

Barthélemy, Denis. Propriété foncière et agriculture d'entreprise. (With English summary.) *Revue Écon. Polit.*, July-August 1985, *95*(4), pp. 484–501.

Batte, Marvin T. and Sonka, Steven T. Before- and After-Tax Size Economies: An Example for Cash Grain Production in Illinois. *Amer. J. Agr. Econ.*, August 1985, *67*(3), pp. 600–608.   [G: U.S.]

Batterham, R. L. A Note on Maximizing Utility in Quadratic Programming Models for Farm Planning. *Rev. Marketing Agr. Econ.*, April 1985, *53*(1), pp. 25–28.

Baumann, Hannelore and Kinsey, Jean. The Value of Price Information in the Profitability of Hog Sales. *Europ. Rev. Agr. Econ.*, 1985, *12*(3), pp. 187–205.   [G: W. Germany]

Belbase, Krishna and Grabowski, Richard. Technical Efficiency in Nepalese Agriculture. *J. Devel. Areas*, July 1985, *19*(4), pp. 515–25.
[G: Nepal]

Belbase, Krishna; Grabowski, Richard and Sanchez, Onesimo. The Marginal Productivity of Inputs and Agricultural Production in Nepal. *Pakistan Devel. Rev.*, Spring 1985, *24*(1), pp. 51–60.   [G: Nepal]

Berck, Peter and Perloff, Jeffrey M. A Dynamic Analysis of Marketing Orders, Voting, and Welfare. *Amer. J. Agr. Econ.*, August 1985, *67*(3), pp. 487–96.

Bergmann, Denis. Une stratégie exportatrice pour l'agriculture de la CEE. (An Export Strategy for the E.E.C. Farming. With English summary.) *Écon. Soc.*, July 1985, *19*(7), pp. 229–42.   [G: EEC]

Bergmann, Theodor. Collective Farm Organization: The Soviet Experience and Its Lessons. In *Bergmann, T. and Ogura, T. B., eds.*, 1985, pp. 209–28.   [G: U.S.S.R.]

Bergmann, Theodor. Needs, Perspectives and Obstacles for Cooperation of Farmers in Highly Industrialized Economies. In *Bergmann, T. and Ogura, T. B., eds.*, 1985, pp. 131–45.
[G: W. Europe]

Bhaduri, Amit. Class Relations and Commercialization in Indian Agriculture: A Study in the Post-independence Agrarian Reforms of Uttar Pradesh. In *Raj, K. N., et al., eds.*, 1985, pp. 306–18.   [G: India]

Bhattacharya, Neeladri. Agricultural Labour and Production: Central and South–East Punjab, 1870–1940. In *Raj, K. N., et al., eds.*, 1985, pp. 105–62.   [G: India]

Bigsten, Arne. What Do Smallholders Do for a Living? Some Evidence from Kenya. In *Lundahl, M., ed.*, 1985, pp. 66–83.   [G: Kenya]

Binswanger, Hans P. and Pingali, Prabhu L. Population Growth and Technological Change in Agriculture. In *Davis, T. J., ed.*, 1985, pp. 62–89.

Boggess, William G.; Anaman, Kwabena A. and Hanson, Gregory D. Importance, Causes, and Management Responses to Farm Risks: Evidence form Florida and Alabama. *Southern J. Agr. Econ.*, December 1985, *17*(2), pp. 105–16.   [G: U.S.]

Boggess, William G.; Cardelli, Dino J. and Barfield, C. S. A Bioeconomic Simulation Approach to Multi-species Insect Management. *Southern J. Agr. Econ.*, December 1985, *17*(2), pp. 43–55.   [G: U.S.]

Boussard, Jean Marc. Is Agricultural Production Responsive to Prices? *Europ. Rev. Agr. Econ.*, 1985, *12*(1/2), pp. 31–44.

Boyle, G. E. Measures of Real Farm Income: a Note. *Irish J. Agr. Econ. Rural Soc.*, 1984-1985, *10*(2), pp. 129–34.   [G: Ireland]

Boyle, G. E. and Collier, Paul. The Relationship between Expectations and Actual Outcomes: An Analysis of Data from Farmer Intentions' Surveys for Ireland. *Irish J. Agr. Econ. Rural Soc.*, 1984-1985, *10*(2), pp. 109–17.
[G: Ireland]

Bradford, G. L. and Debertin, David L. Establishing Linkages between Economic Theory and Enterprise Budgeting for Teaching and Extension Programs. *Southern J. Agr. Econ.*, December 1985, *17*(2), pp. 221–30.

Brandes, Wilhelm. The Complex Dynamics of Farm Growth. Comment. In *[Heidhues, T.]*, 1985, pp. 112–131.

Brandt, Jon A. Forecasting and Hedging: An Illustration of Risk Reduction in the Hog Industry. *Amer. J. Agr. Econ.*, February 1985, *67*(1), pp. 24–31.   [G: U.S.]

Brown, William J. and Schoney, Richard A. Calculating Least-Cost Machinery Size for Grain Farms Using Electronic Spreadsheets and Microcomputers. *Can. J. Agr. Econ.*, March 1985, *33*(1), pp. 47–65.   [G: Canada]

Brownschidle, Terry. A Generalized Stochastic Dominance Approach to Analyze Financial Decisions. In *Brown, R. C., ed.*, 1985, pp. 3–14.   [G: U.S.]

Buckwell, Allan. Is Agricultural Production Responsive to Prices? Comment. *Europ. Rev. Agr. Econ.*, 1985, *12*(1/2), pp. 46–47.

Burger, Kees. Is Agricultural Production Responsive to Prices? Opening of the Discussion. *Europ. Rev. Agr. Econ.*, 1985, *12*(1/2), pp. 45–46.

Canarella, Giorgio and Pollard, Stephen K. Price and Output Expectations in Agricultural Policy: The Case of Jamaica. *J. Econ. Devel.*, December 1985, *10*(2), pp. 19–34. [G: Jamaica]

Carter, Michael R. Revisionist Lessons from the Peruvian Experience with Cooperative Agricultural Production. In *Jones, D. C. and Svejnar, J., eds.*, 1985, pp. 179–94.
[G: Peru]

Chaudhry, M. Ghaffar; Gill, Manzoor A. and Chaudhry, Ghulam Mustafa. Size–Productivity Relationship in Pakistan's Agriculture in the Seventies. *Pakistan Devel. Rev.*, Autumn-Winter 1985, *24*(3/4), pp. 349–59. **[G: Pakistan]**

Chavas, Jean-Paul; Kliebenstein, James and Crenshaw, Thomas D. Modeling Dynamic Agricultural Production Response: The Case of Swine Production. *Amer. J. Agr. Econ.*, August 1985, *67*(3), pp. 636–46. **[G: U.S.]**

Chopra, Kanchan. Substitution and Complementarity between Inputs in Paddy Cultivation. *J. Quant. Econ.*, July 1985, *1*(2), pp. 315–32. **[G: India]**

Chrysomilides, G. S. Technology Cycles in Agricultural Productivity in Canada. *Amer. Econ.*, Spring 1985, *29*(1), pp. 32–40. **[G: Canada]**

Cochran, Mark J.; Robison, Lindon J. and Lodwick, Weldon. Improving the Efficiency of Stochastic Dominance Techniques Using Convex Set Stochastic Dominance. *Amer. J. Agr. Econ.*, May 1985, *67*(2), pp. 289–95. **[G: U.S.]**

Collender, Robert N. and Zilberman, David. Land Allocation under Uncertainty for Alternative Specifications of Return Distributions. *Amer. J. Agr. Econ.*, November 1985, *67*(4), pp. 779–86.

Collins, Robert A. Expected Utility, Debt–Equity Structure, and Risk Balancing. *Amer. J. Agr. Econ.*, August 1985, *67*(3), pp. 627–29.

Cornia, Giovanni Andrea. Farm Size, Land Yields and the Agricultural Production Function: An Analysis for Fifteen Developing Countries. *World Devel.*, April 1985, *13*(4), pp. 513–34. **[G: Selected LDCs]**

Crawford, Eric W. and Lassiter, Gregory C. Constraints on Oxen Cultivation in the Sahel: Comment. *Amer. J. Agr. Econ.*, August 1985, *67*(3), pp. 684–85. **[G: W. Africa]**

Crecink, John C. Small Farm Research and Policy Implications: Discussion. *Southern J. Agr. Econ.*, July 1985, *17*(1), pp. 57–59. **[G: U.S.]**

Crouch, Glen J. and Skowronski, Janislaw M. Identification of Stock and System Parameters in a Pareto Harvesting Game of Two Players. In *Batten, D. F. and Lesse, P. F., eds.*, 1985, pp. 105–16.

Csizmadia, Ernö. Recent Experiences of Cooperative Farming in Hungary. *Acta Oecon.*, 1985, *34*(1–2), pp. 1–11. **[G: Hungary]**

Curley, Michael D. and Gift, Richard E. Investment Incentives and Rural Conflict: The Case of South Vietnam. *J. Devel. Areas*, October 1985, *20*(1), pp. 49–70. **[G: Vietnam]**

Day, Richard H. The Complex Dynamics of Farm Growth. In *[Heidhues, T.]*, 1985, pp. 91–111.

Debertin, David L. and Pagoulatos, Angelos. Optimal Management Strategies for Alfalfa Production within a Total Farm Plan. *Southern J. Agr. Econ.*, December 1985, *17*(2), pp. 127–37. **[G: U.S.]**

Delgado, Christopher L. and McIntire, John. Constraints on Oxen Cultivation in the Sahel: Reply. *Amer. J. Agr. Econ.*, August 1985, *67*(3), pp. 686–87. **[G: W. Africa]**

Diwan, Romesh and Kallianpur, Renu. Biological Technology and Land Productivity: Fertilizers and Food Production in India. *World Devel.*, May 1985, *13*(5), pp. 627–38. **[G: India]**

Doran, Howard E. "Small" or "Large" Farm: Some Methodological Considerations. *Amer. J. Agr. Econ.*, February 1985, *67*(1), pp. 130–32.

Drynan, Ross G. A Generalised Maximin Approach to Imprecise Objective Function Coefficients in Linear Programs. *Australian J. Agr. Econ.*, August 1985, *29*(2), pp. 142–48.

Dülfer, Eberhard. Some Principal Problems of Cooperative Promotion in Developing Countries. In *Bergmann, T. and Ogura, T. B., eds.*, 1985, pp. 189–203. **[G: LDCs]**

Dunn, James and Heien, Dale. The Demand for Farm Output. *Western J. Agr. Econ.*, July 1985, *10*(1), pp. 13–22. **[G: U.S.]**

Dyson-Hudson, Neville. Pastoral Production Systems and Livestock Development Projects: An East African Perspective. In *Cernea, M. M., ed.*, 1985, pp. 157–86. **[G: E. Africa]**

Ethridge, Don E.; Roy, Sugit K. and Myers, David W. A Markov Chain Analysis of Structural Changes in the Texas High Plains Cotton Ginning Industry. *Southern J. Agr. Econ.*, December 1985, *17*(2), pp. 11–20. **[G: U.S.]**

Falatoonzadeh, Hamid; Conner, J. Richard and Pope, Rulon D. Risk Management Strategies to Reduce Net Income Variability for Farmers. *Southern J. Agr. Econ.*, July 1985, *17*(1), pp. 117–30. **[G: U.S.]**

Färe, Rolf; Grabowski, Richard and Grosskopf, Shawna. Technical Efficiency of Philippine Agriculture. *Appl. Econ.*, April 1985, *17*(2), pp. 205–14. **[G: Philippines]**

Feder, Gershon. The Relation between Farm Size and Farm Productivity: The Role of Family Labor, Supervision and Credit Constraints. *J. Devel. Econ.*, August 1985, *18*(2–3), pp. 297–313.

Feder, Gershon; Just, Richard E. and Zilberman, David. Adoption of Agricultural Innovations in Developing Countries: A Survey. *Econ. Develop. Cult. Change*, January 1985, *33*(2), pp. 255–98. **[G: LDCs]**

Folayan, Adekunle. Rural Accessibility Theory of Agricultural Productivity. *Int. J. Transport Econ.*, June 1985, *12*(2), pp. 165–74.

Freeman, Orville. The Family Farm: A Success Story with Global Implications. In *Didsbury, H. F., Jr., ed.*, 1985, pp. 135–46.

French, Ben C.; King, Gordon A. and Minami, Dwight D. Planting and Removal Relationships for Perennial Crops: An Application to Cling Peaches. *Amer. J. Agr. Econ.*, May 1985, *67*(2), pp. 215–23. **[G: U.S.]**

Fuller, Richard H. Schooling, Social Class and Productivity: A Study of Rice Farmers in Northeastern Bangladesh. *Bangladesh Devel. Stud.*, Sept.-Dec. 1985, *13*(3&4), pp. 89–110. **[G: Bangladesh]**

Garcia-Ramon, M. Dolores. Agricultural Change in an Industrializing Area: The Case of the Tarragona Area. In *Hudson, R. and Lewis, J., eds.*, 1985, pp. 140–54. **[G: Spain]**

Garrido Egido, Leovigildo. Agricultural Cooperation in Spain: The Agricultural Production in Common. In *Bergmann, T. and Ogura, T. B., eds.*, 1985, pp. 31–42.   [G: Spain]

Ghebremedhin, Tesfa G. and Johnson, William M. Small Farm Research and Policy Implications. *Southern J. Agr. Econ.*, July 1985, *17*(1), pp. 47–56.   [G: U.S.]

Glassburner, Bruce. Macroeconomics and the Agricultural Sector. *Bull. Indonesian Econ. Stud.*, August 1985, *21*(2), pp. 51–73.
        [G: Indonesia]

Grant, Dwight. Theory of the Firm with Joint Price and Output Risk and a Forward Market. *Amer. J. Agr. Econ.*, August 1985, *67*(3), pp. 630–35.

Greene, Catherine R., et al. An Economic Analysis of Soybean Integrated Pest Management. *Amer. J. Agr. Econ.*, August 1985, *67*(3), pp. 567–72.   [G: U.S.]

Griffin, Ronald C., et al. Scheduling Inputs with Production Functions: Optimal Nitrogen Programs for Rice. *Southern J. Agr. Econ.*, July 1985, *17*(1), pp. 159–68.

Grisley, William and Gitu, Kangethe W. A Translog Cost Analysis of Turkey Production in the Mid-Atlantic Region. *Southern J. Agr. Econ.*, July 1985, *17*(1), pp. 151–58.   [G: U.S.]

Grisley, William and Kellogg, Earl D. Farmers' Subjective Probabilities in Northern Thailand: Reply. *Amer. J. Agr. Econ.*, February 1985, *67*(1), pp. 149–52.   [G: Thailand]

Guha, Sumit. Some Aspects of Rural Economy in the Deccan 1820–1940. In *Raj, K. N., et al., eds.*, 1985, pp. 210–46.   [G: India]

Gunnarsson, Christer. Growth and Stagnation in the Malaysian Rubber Smallholder Industry. In *Lundahl, M., ed.*, 1985, pp. 152–78.
        [G: Malaysia]

Gyenes, Antal. The Development of Farmers' Cooperatives in Hungary: Present Problems and Prospects. In *Bergmann, T. and Ogura, T. B., eds.*, 1985, pp. 229–41.   [G: Hungary]

Hall, Darwin C. and Moffitt, L. Joe. Application of the Economic Threshold for Interseasonal Pest Control. *Western J. Agr. Econ.*, December 1985, *10*(2), pp. 223–29.   [G: U.S.]

Hall, Lana L. and Hall, Bruce F. Some Observations on the Efficiency of Animal Production in Hungary. *Comparative Econ. Stud.*, Winter 1985, *27*(4), pp. 85–95.   [G: Hungary]

Hardaker, J. Brian, et al. A Model of a Padi Farming Household in Central Java. *Bull. Indonesian Econ. Stud.*, December 1985, *21*(3), pp. 30–50.   [G: Indonesia]

Harmon, W. L., et al. No-Till Technology: Impacts on Farm Income, Energy Use and Groundwater Depletion in the Plains. *Western J. Agr. Econ.*, July 1985, *10*(1), pp. 134–46.
        [G: U.S.]

Hartford, Kathleen. Socialist Agriculture Is Dead; Long Live Socialist Agriculture! Organizational Transformation in Rural China. In *Perry, E. J. and Wong, C., eds.*, pp. 31–61.
        [G: China]

Hedlund, Stefan. On the Socialisation of Labour in Rural Cooperation. In *Lundahl, M., ed.*, 1985, pp. 329–51.   [G: Israel]

Heimlich, Ralph E. Landownership and the Adoption of Minimum Tillage: Comment. *Amer. J. Agr. Econ.*, August 1985, *67*(3), pp. 679–81.   [G: U.S.]

Herruzo, A. Casimiro. Returns to Agricultural Research: The Case of Rice Breeding in Spain. *Europ. Rev. Agr. Econ.*, 1985, *12*(3), pp. 265–82.   [G: Spain]

Hiraizumi, Kimio. Collectivization and Improvement of Agricultural Producers' Cooperative: The Hungarian Experience. In *Bergmann, T. and Ogura, T. B., eds.*, 1985, pp. 243–56.
        [G: Hungary]

Hossain, Mahabub. Price Response of Fertilizer Demand in Bangladesh. *Bangladesh Devel. Stud.*, Sept.-Dec. 1985, *13*(3&4), pp. 41–66.
        [G: Bangladesh]

Jobin, Jacques. The Components of Farm Income Instability on the Prairies. *Can. J. Agr. Econ.*, November 1985, *33*(3), pp. 299–313.
        [G: Canada]

Johnson, Thomas G.; Brown, William J. and O'Grady, Kevin. A Multivariate Analysis of Factors Influencing Farm Machinery Purchase Decisions. *Western J. Agr. Econ.*, December 1985, *10*(2), pp. 294–306.   [G: Canada]

Just, Richard E. and Candler, Wilfred. Production Functions and Rationality of Mixed Cropping. *Europ. Rev. Agr. Econ.*, 1985, *12*(3), pp. 207–31.   [G: Nigeria]

Kallianpur, Renu and Diwan, Romesh. Productivity Growth: Scale and Technology Analysis of Panjab Wheat Farms. *Indian J. Quant. Econ.*, 1985, *1*(1), pp. 61–84.   [G: India]

Kawagoe, Toshihiko and Hayami, Yujiro. An Intercountry Comparison of Agricultural Production Efficiency. *Amer. J. Agr. Econ.*, February 1985, *67*(1), pp. 87–92.
        [G: Selected Countries]

Kawamura, Yoshio. Dissolution of Rural People's Communes and the System of Responsibility of Agricultural Production in China. In *Bergmann, T. and Ogura, T. B., eds.*, 1985, pp. 323–36.   [G: China]

Klemme, Richard M. A Stochastic Dominance Comparison of Reduced Tillage Systems in Corn and Soybean Production under Risk. *Amer. J. Agr. Econ.*, August 1985, *67*(3), pp. 550–57.   [G: U.S.]

Knight, Tom; Johnson, Stanley R. and Finley, Robert M. Farmers' Subjective Probabilities in Northern Thailand: Comment. *Amer. J. Agr. Econ.*, February 1985, *67*(1), pp. 147–48.
        [G: Thailand]

Kotwal, Ashok. The Role of Consumption Credit in Agricultural Tenancy. *J. Devel. Econ.*, August 1985, *18*(2–3), pp. 273–95.

Kowalak, Tadeusz. Agricultural Cooperatives in Poland. In *Bergmann, T. and Ogura, T. B., eds.*, 1985, pp. 271–90.   [G: Poland]

LeBlanc, Michael. The Effects of Natural Gas Decontrol on Fertilizer Demand, Production Costs, and Income in Agriculture. *Energy J.*, January 1985, *6*(1), pp. 117–35.   [G: U.S.]

Lee, John Gary; Brown, Deborah J. and Lovejoy, Stephen B. Stochastic Efficiency versus Mean-Variance Criteria as Predictors of Adoption of Reduced Tillage. *Amer. J. Agr. Econ.*, November 1985, *67*(4), pp. 839–45.　　[G: U.S.]

Lee, Linda K. and Stewart, William H. Landownership and the Adoption of Minimum Tillage: Reply. *Amer. J. Agr. Econ.*, August 1985, *67*(3), pp. 682–83.　　[G: U.S.]

Levy, Victor. Cropping Pattern, Mechanization, Child Labor, and Fertility Behavior in a Farming Economy: Rural Egypt. *Econ. Develop. Cult. Change*, July 1985, *33*(4), pp. 777–91.　　[G: Egypt]

Lipton, Michael. Education and Farm Efficiency: Comment. *Econ. Develop. Cult. Change*, October 1985, *34*(1), pp. 167–68.　　[G: Nepal]

Lowenberg-DeBoer, J. and Boehlje, Michael D. The Estate Tax Provision of the 1981 Economic Recovery Tax Act: Which Farmers Benefit? *Southern J. Agr. Econ.*, December 1985, *17*(2), pp. 77–86.　　[G: U.S.]

Lucas, Robert E. B. The Lucas Model Misconstrued: Rebuttal [Sharing, Monitoring, and Incentives: Marshallian Misallocation Reassessed]. *World Devel.*, February 1985, *13*(2), pp. 243.

Lucas, Robert E. B. The Puzzle of Sharecropping: A Piece Refitted. *World Devel.*, February 1985, *13*(2), pp. 237–38.

Makowski, Marek and Sosnowski, Janusz. A Decision Support System for Planning and Controlling Agricultural Production with a Decentralized Management Structure. In *Grauer, M.; Thompson, M. and Wierzbicki, A. P., eds.*, 1985, pp. 296–305.

McIntire, John and Delgado, Christopher L. Statistical Significance of Indicators of Efficiency and Incentives: Examples from West African Agriculture. *Amer. J. Agr. Econ.*, November 1985, *67*(4), pp. 733–38.　　[G: Burkina Faso; Niger]

Melichar, Emanuel. Farm Financial Stress, Structure of Agriculture, and Public Policy: Commentary. In *Gardner, B. L., ed.*, 1985, pp. 113–16.　　[G: U.S.]

Michalowski, W. An Experiment with Zionts—Wallenius and Steuer Interactive Programming Methods. In *Haimes, Y. Y. and Chankong, V., eds.*, 1985, pp. 424–29.

Moghadam, Fatemeh E. An Evaluation of the Productive Performance of Agribusinesses: An Iranian Case Study. *Econ. Develop. Cult. Change*, July 1985, *33*(4), pp. 755–76.　　[G: Iran]

Moock, Peter R. Education and Farm Efficiency: Reply. *Econ. Develop. Cult. Change*, October 1985, *34*(1), pp. 169–72.　　[G: Nepal]

Müller, A. L. Private Enterprise in Soviet Agriculture. *J. Stud. Econ. Econometrics*, November 1985, (23), pp. 51–66.　　[G: U.S.S.R.]

Munk, Knud Jorgen. The Effect of Changes in Prices and Quotas: An Example of the Use of an Agricultural Sector Model Based on the Johansen Approach. *Europ. Rev. Agr. Econ.*, 1985, *12*(4), pp. 365–80.　　[G: EEC]

Musser, Wesley N., et al. A Mathematical Programming Model for Vegetable Rotations. *Southern J. Agr. Econ.*, July 1985, *17*(1), pp. 169–76.

Nascimento, Jean-Claude and Raffinot, Marc. Politique de prix agricoles et comportement des producteurs: le cas de l'arachide au Sénégal. (Agricultural Pricing Policy and Primary Producers' Behavior: The Case of Senegal. With English summary.) *Revue Écon.*, July 1985, *36*(4), pp. 779–96.　　[G: Senegal]

Nghiep, Le Thanh and Lynam, John K. The Impact of Improved Cassava Technology on Small Farming in Colombia. In *Ohkawa, K. and Ranis, G., eds.*, 1985, pp. 110–32.　　[G: Colombia]

Ogura, Takekazu, et al. Cooperative Organizations in Agricultural Production in Japan. In *Bergmann, T. and Ogura, T. B., eds.*, 1985, pp. 71–95.　　[G: Japan]

Oshiro, Kenji K. Mechanization of Rice Production in Japan. *Econ. Geogr.*, October 1985, *61*(4), pp. 323–31.　　[G: Japan]

Otiman, P. Optimizing the Location of Crop Fields. *Econ. Computat. Cybern. Stud. Res.*, 1985, *20*(4), pp. 79–82.

Paris, Quirino. Sector Models with Explicit Expectations and Adjustments. *Statistica*, Oct.-Dec. 1985, *45*(4), pp. 465–78.

Patrick, George R., et al. Risk Perceptions and Management Responses: Producer-generated Hypotheses for Risk Modeling. *Southern J. Agr. Econ.*, December 1985, *17*(2), pp. 231–38.　　[G: U.S.]

Philogène, Bernard J. R. Utilisation et réglementation des pesticides dans le Tiers Monde: problèmes et perspectives en Afrique. (With English summary.) *Can. J. Devel. Stud.*, 1985, *6*(2), pp. 275–88.　　[G: Ivory Coast]

Pingali, Prabhu L. and Carlson, Gerald A. Human Capital, Adjustments in Subjective Probabilities, and the Demand for Pest Controls. *Amer. J. Agr. Econ.*, November 1985, *67*(4), pp. 853–61.　　[G: U.S.]

Plant, Richard E.; Mangel, Marc and Flynn, Lawrence E. Multiseasonal Management of an Agricultural Pest II: The Economic Optimization Problem. *J. Environ. Econ. Manage.*, March 1985, *12*(1), pp. 45–61.

Putterman, Louis. The Restoration of the Peasant Household as Farm Production Unit in China: Some Incentive Theoretic Analysis. In *Perry, E. J. and Wong, C., eds.*, 1985, pp. 63–82.　　[G: China]

Quibria, M. G. and Rashid, Salim. The Puzzle of the Lucas Model: A Reply [Sharing, Monitoring, and Incentives: Marshallian Misallocation Reassessed]. *World Devel.*, February 1985, *13*(2), pp. 239–42.

Rambaud, Placide. The Invention of the Family Cooperative of Work in Rural France. In *Bergmann, T. and Ogura, T. B., eds.*, 1985, pp. 11–29.　　[G: France]

Rasmussen, Svend and Nielsen, A. Hjortshøj. The Impact of Quotas on the Optimal Adjustment of Milk Production at the Farm Level.

Europ. Rev. Agr. Econ., 1985, *12*(4), pp. 351–64. **[G: EEC]**

Rawlins, Glenville. Measuring the Impact of I.R.D.P. II upon the Technical Efficiency Level of Jamaican Peasant Farmers. *Soc. Econ. Stud.*, June 1985, *34*(2), pp. 71–96. **[G: Jamaica]**

Ray, Subhash C. Measurement and Test of Efficiency of Farms in Linear Programming Models: A Study of West Bengal Farms. *Oxford Bull. Econ. Statist.*, November 1985, *47*(4), pp. 371–86. **[G: India]**

Reddy, M. Atchi. The Commercialization of Agriculture in Nellore District 1850–1916: Effects on Wages, Employment and Tenancy. In *Raj, K. N., et al., eds.*, 1985, pp. 163–83. **[G: India]**

Rieder, Peter. Experience with the Milk Quota System in Switzerland. *Europ. Rev. Agr. Econ.*, 1985, *12*(4), pp. 473–79. **[G: Switzerland]**

Rook, Sarah P. and Carlson, Gerald A. Participation Pest Management Groups. *Amer. J. Agr. Econ.*, August 1985, *67*(3), pp. 563–66. **[G: U.S.]**

Rosegrant, Mark W. and Roumasset, James A. The Effect of Fertiliser on Risk: A Heteroscedastic Production Function with Measurable Stochastic Inputs. *Australian J. Agr. Econ.*, August 1985, *29*(2), pp. 107–21. **[G: Philippines]**

Rosenzweig, Mark R. and Wolpin, Kenneth I. Specific Experience, Household Structure, and Intergenerational Transfers: Farm Family Land and Labor Arraangements in Developing Countries. *Quart. J. Econ.*, Supp. 1985, *100*, pp. 961–87. **[G: India]**

Rosner, M. and Shur, S. The Integration of Agriculture and Industry in Cooperative Villages: The Experience of the Kibbutz. In *Bergmann, T. and Ogura, T. B., eds.*, 1985, pp. 59–70. **[G: Israel]**

Saidi, Khosrow. Rural Cooperatives in the Third World between State and Peasants. In *Bergmann, T. and Ogura, T. B., eds.*, 1985, pp. 179–88. **[G: LDCs]**

Salathe, Larry. Commodity Market Stabilization in Farm Programs: Commentary. In *Gardner, B. L., ed.*, 1985, pp. 277–82. **[G: U.S.]**

Saliba, Bonnie Colby. Soil Productivity and Farmers' Erosion Control Incentives—A Dynamic Modeling Approach. *Western J. Agr. Econ.*, December 1985, *10*(2), pp. 354–64.

Sampath, Rajan K. Efficiency and Equity Implications of Irrigation Water Distribution Policy. *Margin*, July 1985, *17*(4), pp. 48–61. **[G: India]**

Segarra, Eduardo; Kramer, Randall A. and Taylor, Daniel B. A Stochastic Programming Analysis of the Farm Level Implications of Soil Erosion Control. *Southern J. Agr. Econ.*, December 1985, *17*(2), pp. 147–54. **[G: U.S.]**

Sen, Chiranjib. Commercialization, Class Relations and Agricultural Performance in Uttar Pradesh: A Note on Bhaduri's Hypothesis. In *Raj, K. N., et al., eds.*, 1985, pp. 319–30. **[G: India]**

Sen, S. R. A Strategy for Our Small Farms. *Indian Econ. Rev.*, Jan.-June 1985, *20*(1), pp. 143–58. **[G: India]**

Shaw, Anthony B. Constraints on Agricultural Innovation Adoption. *Econ. Geogr.*, January 1985, *61*(1), pp. 25–45. **[G: Guyana]**

Shaw, Anthony B. and da Costa, Richard C. Differential Levels of Technology Adoption and Returns to Scale in the Guyanese Rice Industry. *Can. J. Agr. Econ.*, March 1985, *33*(1), pp. 99–110. **[G: Guyana]**

Shonkwiler, J. Scott and Hinckley, Suzanne. A Generalized Supply Response/Factor Demand Model and Its Application to the Feeder Cattle Market. *Western J. Agr. Econ.*, December 1985, *10*(2), pp. 245–53. **[G: U.S.]**

Short, Cameron and McNeill, Roger. Tractor Costs and Canadian Tax Policy. *Can. J. Agr. Econ.*, November 1985, *33*(3), pp. 343–58. **[G: Canada]**

Skowronski, Janislaw M. Competitive Differential Game of Harvesting Uncertain Resources. In *Batten, D. F. and Lesse, P. F., eds.*, 1985, pp. 87–103.

Smith, Edward G.; Richardson, James W. and Knutson, Ronald D. Impact of Alternative Farm Programs on Different Size Cotton Farms in the Texas Southern High Plains: A Simulation Approach. *Western J. Agr. Econ.*, December 1985, *10*(2), pp. 365–74. **[G: U.S.]**

Smith, Joyotee and Umali, Gloria. Production Risk and Optimal Fertilizer Rates: A Random Coefficient Model. *Amer. J. Agr. Econ.*, August 1985, *67*(3), pp. 654–59. **[G: Philippines]**

Stanton, B. F. Farm Programs and Structural Issues: Commentary. In *Gardner, B. L., ed.*, 1985, pp. 321–28. **[G: U.S.]**

Sumner, Daniel A. Farm Programs and Structural Issues. In *Gardner, B. L., ed.*, 1985, pp. 283–320. **[G: U.S.]**

Szabó-Medgyesi, Éva. Non-agricultural Activities of Agricultural Enterprises in Hungary. *Acta Oecon.*, 1985, *34*(3/4), pp. 361–74. **[G: Hungary]**

Taniguchi, Nobukazu. Agricultural Production Cooperatives (LPG) in the German Democratic Republic (GDR). In *Bergmann, T. and Ogura, T. B., eds.*, 1985, pp. 257–70. **[G: E. Germany]**

Taylor, Daniel B. and Young, Douglas L. The Influence of Technological Progress on the Long Run Farm Level Economics of Soil Conservation. *Western J. Agr. Econ.*, July 1985, *10*(1), pp. 63–76. **[G: U.S.]**

Taylor, Timothy G. and Monson, Michael J. Dynamic Factor Demands for Aggregate Southeastern United States Agriculture. *Southern J. Agr. Econ.*, December 1985, *17*(2), pp. 1–9. **[G: U.S.]**

Travers, S. Lee. Getting Rich through Diligence: Peasant Income after the Reforms. In *Perry,*

E. J. and Wong, C., eds., 1985, pp. 111–30. [G: China]

Tweeten, Luther. Farm Financial Stress, Structure of Agriculture, and Public Policy. In *Gardner, B. L., ed.*, 1985, pp. 83–112. [G: U.S.]

Van Kooten, G. C. and Arthur, Louise M. The Theory of the Farm Household: An Application to Saskatchewan. *Can. J. Agr. Econ.*, March 1985, *33*(1), pp. 23–35. [G: Canada]

Vanzetti, David and Quiggin, John. A Comparative Analysis of Agricultural Tractor Investment Models. *Australian J. Agr. Econ.*, August 1985, *29*(2), pp. 122–41. [G: Australia]

Vyas, Vijay Shankar and Jagannathan, N. Vijay. Cooperation in Farm Production: Conditions of Viability. In *Bergmann, T. and Ogura, T. B., eds.*, 1985, pp. 169–78. [G: India]

Wenlin, Jia. Some Problems Concerning the Implementation of Lenin's Principles of Agricultural Cooperation. In *Bergmann, T. and Ogura, T. B., eds.*, 1985, pp. 305–22. [G: China]

Wetzstein, Michael E., et al. An Evalution of Integrated Pest Management with Heterogeneous Participation. *Western J. Agr. Econ.*, December 1985, *10*(2), pp. 344–53. [G: U.S.]

Whan, I. F. and Hammer, G. L. The Cost of Delay in Harvesting Wheat. *Rev. Marketing Agr. Econ.*, April 1985, *53*(1), pp. 14–24. [G: Australia]

Whyte, William Foote. Working with Small Farmers and Agricultural Cooperatives in Latin America. In *Bergmann, T. and Ogura, T. B., eds.*, 1985, pp. 153–68. [G: Latin America]

Wilson, Hoyt G. and Kagan, Albert. Economics of Optimization of Fat Levels in Turkey Diets. *Can. J. Agr. Econ.*, March 1985, *33*(1), pp. 3–21. [G: U.S.]

Wilson, Paul N. and Eidman, Vernon R. Dominant Enterprise Size in the Swine Production Industry. *Amer. J. Agr. Econ.*, May 1985, *67*(2), pp. 279–88. [G: U.S.]

Wilson, Paul N. and Gundersen, Carl E. Financial Risk in Cotton Production. *Southern J. Agr. Econ.*, December 1985, *17*(2), pp. 199–206. [G: U.S.]

Wright, Brian D. Commodity Market Stabilization in Farm Programs. In *Gardner, B. L., ed.*, 1985, pp. 257–76. [G: U.S.]

Yokogawa, Hiroshi. Cooperation in Farming in Yugoslavia. In *Bergmann, T. and Ogura, T. B., eds.*, 1985, pp. 291–303. [G: Yugoslavia]

Zahiu, Letiţia and Manole, V. Optimal Size of Sheep Breeding Farms in the Agricultural Production Cooperatives in County Constanţa. *Econ. Computat. Cybern. Stud. Res.*, 1985, *20*(3), pp. 33–38. [G: Romania]

717 Land Reform and Land Use

7170 General

Chicoine, David L. and Hendricks, A. Donald. Evidence on Farm Use Value Assessment, Tax Shifts, and State School Aid. *Amer. J. Agr. Econ.*, May 1985, *67*(2), pp. 266–70. [G: U.S.]

D'Agata, Antonio. Produzione congiunta e ordine de fertilità: una nota. (With English summary.) *Econ. Polít.*, August 1985, *2*(2), pp. 245–48.

Edwards, Clark. Productivity and Structure in U.S. Agriculture. *Agr. Econ. Res.*, Summer 1985, *37*(3), pp. 1–11. [G: U.S.]

Edwards, Clark; Smith, Matthew G. and Peterson, R. Neal. The Changing Distribution of Farms by Size: A Markov Analysis. *Agr. Econ. Res.*, Fall 1985, *37*(4), pp. 1–16. [G: U.S.]

Heimlich, Ralph E. Landownership and the Adoption of Minimum Tillage: Comment. *Amer. J. Agr. Econ.*, August 1985, *67*(3), pp. 679–81. [G: U.S.]

van de Laar, Aart. Interest Groups and Development. In *Jerve, A. M., ed.*, 1985, pp. 155–66. [G: Pakistan]

Lee, Linda K. and Stewart, William H. Landownership and the Adoption of Minimum Tillage: Reply. *Amer. J. Agr. Econ.*, August 1985, *67*(3), pp. 682–83. [G: U.S.]

Pope, C. Arden, III. Agricultural Productive and Consumptive Use Components of Rural Land Values in Texas. *Amer. J. Agr. Econ.*, February 1985, *67*(1), pp. 81–86. [G: U.S.]

Putterman, Louis. The Restoration of the Peasant Household as Farm Production Unit in China: Some Incentive Theoretic Analysis. In *Perry, E. J. and Wong, C., eds.*, 1985, pp. 63–82. [G: China]

Randall, Alan J. and Castle, Emery N. Land Resources and Land Markets. In *Kneese, A. V. and Sweeney, J. L., eds. Vol. 2*, 1985, pp. 571–620.

Shaw, Anthony B. Constraints on Agricultural Innovation Adoption. *Econ. Geogr.*, January 1985, *61*(1), pp. 25–45. [G: Guyana]

7171 Land Ownership and Tenure; Land Reform

Acosta, Yvonne and Casimir, Jean. Social Origins of the Counter-plantation System in St. Lucia. In *Gomes, P. I., ed.*, 1985, pp. 34–59. [G: St. Lucia]

Adams, Richard H., Jr. Development and Structural Change in Rural Egypt, 1952 to 1982. *World Devel.*, June 1985, *13*(6), pp. 705–23. [G: Egypt]

Alberts, Tom. Peru—20 Years of Agrarian Reform. In *Lundahl, M., ed.*, 1985, pp. 291–308. [G: Peru]

Ali, M. Shaukat. Rural Poverty and Anti-poverty Policies in Pakistan. In *Islam, R., ed.*, 1985, pp. 175–99. [G: Pakistan]

Allen, Franklin. On the Fixed Nature of Sharecropping Contracts. *Econ. J.*, March 1985, *95*(377), pp. 30–48.

Bardhan, Pranab K. Agricultural Development and Land Tenancy in a Peasant Economy: Reply. *Amer. J. Agr. Econ.*, August 1985, *67*(3), pp. 691–92. [G: India]

Bhaduri, Amit. Class Relations and Commercialization in Indian Agriculture: A Study in the

Post-independence Agrarian Reforms of Uttar Pradesh. In *Raj, K. N., et al., eds.*, 1985, pp. 306–18.   [G: India]

Bhagwati, Jagdish N. Gunnar Myrdal [Need for Reforms in Underdeveloped Countries]. In *Bhagwati, J. N. (II)*, 1985, pp. 306–12.

Booth, Anne. Accommodating a Growing Population in Javanese Agriculture. *Bull. Indonesian Econ. Stud.*, August 1985, *21*(2), pp. 115–45.   [G: Indonesia]

Boxley, Robert F. Farmland Ownership and Distribution of Land Earnings. *Agr. Econ. Res.*, Fall 1985, *37*(4), pp. 40–44.   [G: U.S.]

Cain, Mead. Errata: On the Relationship between Landholding and Fertility. *Population Stud.*, July 1985, *39*(2), pp. 192.   [G: LDCs]

Cain, Mead. On the Relationship between Landholding and Fertility. *Population Stud.*, March 1985, *39*(1), pp. 5–15.   [G: LDCs]

Canto, Victor A. Property Rights, Land Reform, and Economic Well-being. *Cato J.*, Spring/Summer 1985, *5*(1), pp. 51–66.   [G: Mexico; Chile; Jamaica; El Salvador]

Datta, Samar K. and Nugent, Jeffrey B. Agricultural Development and Land Tenancy in a Peasant Economy: Comment. *Amer. J. Agr. Econ.*, August 1985, *67*(3), pp. 688–90.
[G: India]

Deere, Carmen Diana. Rural Women and State Policy: The Latin American Agrarian Reform Experience. *World Devel.*, September 1985, *13*(9), pp. 1037–53.   [G: Latin America]

Doran, Howard E. "Small" or "Large" Farm: Some Methodological Considerations. *Amer. J. Agr. Econ.*, February 1985, *67*(1), pp. 130–32.

Eswaran, Mukesh and Kotwal, Ashok. A Theory of Contractual Structure in Agriculture. *Amer. Econ. Rev.*, June 1985, *75*(3), pp. 352–67.

Feder, Gershon. The Relation between Farm Size and Farm Productivity: The Role of Family Labor, Supervision and Credit Constraints. *J. Devel. Econ.*, August 1985, *18*(2–3), pp. 297–313.

FitzGerald, E. V. K. Agrarian Reform as a Model of Accumluation: The Case of Nicaragua since 1979. *J. Devel. Stud.*, October 1985, *22*(1), pp. 208–26.   [G: Nicaragua]

FitzGerald, E. V. K. Agrarian Reform as a Model of Accumulation: The Case of Nicaragua since 1979. In *Saith, A., ed.*, 1985, pp. 208–26.
[G: Nicaragua]

Garcia-Ramon, M. Dolores. Agricultural Change in an Industrializing Area: The Case of the Tarragona Area. In *Hudson, R. and Lewis, J., eds.*, 1985, pp. 140–54.   [G: Spain]

Gomes, P. I. Plantation Dominance and Rural Dependence in Dominica. In *Gomes, P. I., ed.*, 1985, pp. 60–75.   [G: Dominica]

Gomes, P. I. Rural Development in the Caribbean: Introduction. In *Gomes, P. I., ed.*, 1985, pp. ix–xxi.   [G: Caribbean]

Gómez, Plácido. The History and Adjudication of the Common Lands of Spanish and Mexican Land Grants. *Natural Res. J.*, October 1985, *25*(4), pp. 1039–80.   [G: Mexico; U.S.]

Guha, Sumit. Some Aspects of Rural Economy in the Deccan 1820–1940. In *Raj, K. N., et al., eds.*, 1985, pp. 210–46.   [G: India]

Jodha, N. S. Population Growth and the Decline of Common Property Resources in Rajasthan, India. *Population Devel. Rev.*, June 1985, *11*(2), pp. 247–64.   [G: India]

Kaplan, Howard M. Farmland as a Portfolio Investment. *J. Portfol. Manage.*, Winter 1985, *11*(2), pp. 73–78.   [G: U.S.]

Kay, Cristóbal. Agrarian Change after Allende's Chile. In *Hojman, D. E., ed.*, 1985, pp. 97–113.   [G: Chile]

Kotwal, Ashok. The Role of Consumption Credit in Agricultural Tenancy. *J. Devel. Econ.*, August 1985, *18*(2–3), pp. 273–95.

Lucas, Robert E. B. The Lucas Model Misconstrued: Rebuttal [Sharing, Monitoring, and Incentives: Marshallian Misallocation Reassessed]. *World Devel.*, February 1985, *13*(2), pp. 243.

Lucas, Robert E. B. The Puzzle of Sharecropping: A Piece Refitted. *World Devel.*, February 1985, *13*(2), pp. 237–38.

Lundahl, Mats. Agricultural Stagnation in Chile, 1930–55: A Result of Factor Market Imperfections? In *Lundahl, M., ed.*, 1985, pp. 105–30.
[G: Chile]

Mangahas, Mahar. Rural Poverty and Operation Land Transfer in the Philippines. In *Islam, R., ed.*, 1985, pp. 201–41.   [G: Philippines]

Marshall, Woodville K. Peasant Development in the West Indies since 1838. In *Gomes, P. I., ed.*, 1985, pp. 1–14.   [G: Caribbean]

Miller, Barbara D. and Wozny, James A. Land Tenure Patterns in Bangladesh: Implications for the Revenue and Distributional Effects of Changes in Land Taxation. *J. Devel. Areas*, July 1985, *19*(4), pp. 459–81.
[G: Bangladesh]

Mosley, Paul. Achievements and Contradictions of the Peruvian Agrarian Reform: A Regional Perspective. *J. Devel. Stud.*, April 1985, *21*(3), pp. 440–48.   [G: Peru]

Nabi, Ijaz. Rural Factor Market Imperfections and the Incidence of Tenancy in Agriculture. *Oxford Econ. Pap.*, June 1985, *37*(2), pp. 319–29.   [G: Pakistan]

Neale, Walter C. Property in Land as Cultural Imperialism: Or, Why Ethnocentric Ideas Won't Work in India and Africa. *J. Econ. Issues*, December 1985, *19*(4), pp. 951–58.
[G: India; Africa]

Ogura, Takekazu, et al. Cooperative Organizations in Agricultural Production in Japan. In *Bergmann, T. and Ogura, T. B., eds.*, 1985, pp. 71–95.   [G: Japan]

Padhi, Sakti. Property in Land, Land Market and Tenancy Relations in the Colonial Period: A Review of Theoretical Categories and Study of a Zamindari District. In *Raj, K. N., et al., eds.*, 1985, pp. 1–50.   [G: India]

Parikh, Ashok. Some Aspects of Employment in Indian Agriculture. *World Devel.*, June 1985, *13*(6), pp. 691–704.   [G: India]

Pemberton, Carlisle. Economic Behaviour of

Peasants in Tobago. In *Gomes, P. I., ed.*, 1985, pp. 76–102. [G: Trinidad and Tobago]

Pollard, Stephen K. and Graham, Douglas H. The Performance of the Food-producing Sector in Jamaica, 1962–1979: A Policy Analysis. *Econ. Develop. Cult. Change*, July 1985, *33*(4), pp. 731–54. [G: Jamaica]

Quan, Nguyen T. and Koo, Anthony Y. C. Concentration of Land Holdings: An Empirical Exploration of Kuznets' Conjecture. *J. Devel. Econ.*, May–June 1985, *18*(1), pp. 101–17.

Quibria, M. G. and Rashid, Salim. The Puzzle of the Lucas Model: A Reply [Sharing, Monitoring, and Incentives: Marshallian Misallocation Reassessed]. *World Devel.*, February 1985, *13*(2), pp. 239–42.

Ramsay, Ansil. Population Pressure, Mechanization, and Landlessness in Central Thailand. *J. Devel. Areas*, April 1985, *19*(3), pp. 351–68. [G: Thailand]

Reddy, M. Atchi. The Commercialization of Agriculture in Nellore District 1850–1916: Effects on Wages, Employment and Tenancy. In *Raj, K. N., et al., eds.*, 1985, pp. 163–83. [G: India]

Robison, Lindon J.; Lins, David A. and VenKataraman, Ravi. Cash Rents and Land Values in U.S. Agriculture. *Amer. J. Agr. Econ.*, November 1985, *67*(4), pp. 794–805. [G: U.S.]

Rosenzweig, Mark R. and Wolpin, Kenneth I. Specific Experience, Household Structure, and Intergenerational Transfers: Farm Family Land and Labor Arraangements in Developing Countries. *Quart. J. Econ.*, Supp. 1985, *100*, pp. 961–87. [G: India]

Rudoph, Richard L. Agricultural Structure and Proto-Industrialization in Russia: Economic Development with Unfree Labor. *J. Econ. Hist.*, March 1985, *45*(1), pp. 47–69. [G: U.S.S.R.]

Scott, Anthony D. and Johnson, James. Property Rights: Developing the Characteristics of Interests in Natural Resources. In *Scott, A., ed.*, 1985, pp. 376–403. [G: Canada; U.S.]

Sen, Chiranjib. Commercialization, Class Relations and Agricultural Performance in Uttar Pradesh: A Note on Bhaduri's Hypothesis. In *Raj, K. N., et al., eds.*, 1985, pp. 319–30. [G: India]

Sen, S. R. A Strategy for Our Small Farms. *Indian Econ. Rev.*, Jan.-June 1985, *20*(1), pp. 143–58. [G: India]

Sigit, Hananto. Income Distribution and Household Characteristics. *Bull. Indonesian Econ. Stud.*, December 1985, *21*(3), pp. 51–68. [G: Indonesia]

Smith, Vernon L. Property Rights: Developing the Characteristics of Interests in Natural Resources: Comment. In *Scott, A., ed.*, 1985, pp. 403–21. [G: Canada; U.S.]

Solberg, Carl E. Land Tenure and Land Settlement: Policy and Patterns in the Canadian Prairies and the Argentine Pampas, 1880–1930. In *Platt, D. C. M. and di Tella, G., eds.*, 1985, pp. 53–75. [G: Argentina; Canada]

Swepston, Lee and Plant, Roger. International

Standards and the Protection of the Land Rights of Indigenous and Tribal Populations. *Int. Lab. Rev.*, January–February 1985, *124*(1), pp. 91–106.

Tauer, Loren W. Use of Life Insurance to Fund the Farm Purchase from Heirs. *Amer. J. Agr. Econ.*, February 1985, *67*(1), pp. 60–69. [G: U.S.]

Veramallay, Ashton I. Agricultural Development through Agrarian Reform in Guyana. *Atlantic Econ. J.*, December 1985, *13*(4), pp. 82. [G: Guyana]

Weiman, David F. The Economic Emancipation of the Non-slaveholding Class: Upcountry Farmers in the Georgia Cotton Economy. *J. Econ. Hist.*, March 1985, *45*(1), pp. 71–93. [G: U.S.]

Whatley, Warren C. A History of Mechanization in the Cotton South: The Institutional Hypothesis. *Quart. J. Econ.*, November 1985, *100*(4), pp. 1191–1215. [G: U.S.]

Wickramasekara, Piyasiri. An Evaluation of Policies and Programmes for the Alleviation of Poverty in Sri Lanka. In *Islam, R., ed.*, 1985, pp. 243–86. [G: Sri Lanka]

7172 Land Development; Land Use; Irrigation Policy

Abu Sin, M. E. Planners' and Participants' Perceptions of Development in the Semi-arid Lands of Sudan: A Case Study of the Khashm El Girba Scheme. In *Davies, H. R. J., ed.*, 1985, pp. 60–80. [G: Sudan]

Al-Awad, A. A.; Mohammed, Y. A. and El-Tayeb, S. A. The Impact of Improved Rural Water Supplies on the Environment: The Case of East Kordofan District. In *Davies, H. R. J., ed.*, 1985, pp. 16–29. [G: Sudan]

Allen, Douglas W. Evidence of 'Tax' Farming: Tests Using Differential Land Assessments for BC Farms. *Can. Public Policy*, December 1985, *11*(4), pp. 659–64. [G: Canada]

Amigues, Jean-Pierre. Ressource épuisable contre ressource renouvelable: le cas du gravier et du vin dans le Bordelais. (Exhaustible Resources versus Non Exhaustible Resources: The Case of Gravel and Vineyard in the Bordelais. With English summary.) *L'Actual. Econ.*, March 1985, *61*(1), pp. 5–23. [G: France]

Bagadion, Benjamin U. and Korten, Frances F. Developing Irrigators' Organizations: A Learning Process Approach. In *Cernea, M. M., ed.*, 1985, pp. 52–90. [G: Philippines]

Belongia, Michael T. Factors behind the Rise and Fall of Farmland Prices: A Preliminary Assessment. *Fed. Res. Bank St. Louis Rev.*, Aug./Sept. 1985, *67*(7), pp. 18–24. [G: U.S.]

Bergstrom, John C.; Dillman, B. L. and Stoll, John R. Public Environmental Amenity Benefits of Private Land: The Case of Prime Agricultural Land. *Southern J. Agr. Econ.*, July 1985, *17*(1), pp. 139–49. [G: U.S.]

Binswanger, Hans P. and Pingali, Prabhu L. Population Growth and Technological Change in Agriculture. In *Davis, T. J., ed.*, 1985, pp. 62–89.

Bowen, R. L. and Young, Robert A. Financial and Economic Irrigation Net Benefit Functions for Egypt's Northern Delta. *Water Resources Res.*, September 1985, *21*(9), pp. 1329–35.
[G: Egypt]

Bystrakov, Iu. Ecological Problems of the Agroindustrial Complex. *Prob. Econ.*, June 1985, *28*(2), pp. 50–64. [G: U.S.S.R.]

Caswell, Margriet and Zilberman, David. The Choice of Irrigation Technologies in California. *Amer. J. Agr. Econ.*, May 1985, *67*(2), pp. 224–34. [G: U.S.]

Ciriacy-Wantrup, S. V. Conceptual Problems in Projecting the Demand for Land and Water. In *Ciriacy-Wantrup, S. V.*, 1985, pp. 149–75.
[G: U.S.]

Ciriacy-Wantrup, S. V. The "New" Competition for Land and Some Implications for Public Policy. In *Ciriacy-Wantrup, S. V.*, 1985, pp. 247–59. [G: U.S.]

Cory, Dennis C. and Willis, Mary B. Contagion Externalities and the Conversion of Low-Intensity Land Uses on the Urban Fringe. *Ann. Reg. Sci.*, July 1985, *19*(2), pp. 77–92. [G: U.S.]

Coward, E. Walter, Jr. Technical and Social Change in Currently Irrigated Regions: Rules, Roles, and Rehabilitation. In *Cernea, M. M., ed.*, 1985, pp. 27–51. [G: Selected LDCs]

Dunford, Richard W.; Marti, Carole E. and Mittelhammer, Ronald C. A Case Study of Rural Land Prices at the Urban Fringe Including Subjective Buyer Expectations. *Land Econ.*, February 1985, *61*(1), pp. 10–16.

Ellis, John R.; Lacewell, Ronald D. and Reneau, Duane R. Estimated Economic Impact from Adoption of Water-Related Agricultural Technology. *Western J. Agr. Econ.*, December 1985, *10*(2), pp. 307–21. [G: U.S.]

Feinerman, E.; Bresler, E. and Dagan, G. Optimization of a Spatially Variable Resource: An Illustration for Irrigated Crops. *Water Resources Res.*, June 1985, *21*(6), pp. 793–800.

Fortmann, Louise. Seasonal Dimensions of Rural Social Organisation. *J. Devel. Stud.*, April 1985, *21*(3), pp. 377–89. [G: Botswana]

Freeman, David M. and Lowdermilk, Max L. Middle-Level Organizational Linkages in Irrigation Projects. In *Cernea, M. M., ed.*, 1985, pp. 91–118. [G: Selected LDCs]

Genovese, Frank C. Land Value Taxation in Developing Countries: The Case of Jamaica: Comments. In *Lewis, S. R., Jr., ed.*, 1985, pp. 79–81. [G: Jamaica]

Glenn, Jane Matthews. Approaches to the Protection of Agricultural Land in Quebec and Ontario: Highways and Byways. *Can. Public Policy*, December 1985, *11*(4), pp. 665–76.
[G: Canada]

Griffin, Ronald C. and Perry, Gregory M. Volumetric Pricing of Agricultural Water Supplies: A Case Study. *Water Resources Res.*, July 1985, *21*(7), pp. 944–50. [G: U.S.]

Hatch, L. Upton, et al. Optimal Irrigation Pivot Location on Irregularly Shaped Fields. *Southern J. Agr. Econ.*, December 1985, *17*(2), pp. 163–70. [G: U.S.]

Hecht, Susanna B. Environment, Development and Politics: Capital Accumulation and the Livestock Sector in Eastern Amazonia. *World Devel.*, June 1985, *13*(6), pp. 663–84.
[G: Brazil]

Hirashima, S. Poverty as a Generation's Problem: A Note on the Japanese Experience. In *Mellor, J. W. and Desai, G. M., eds.*, 1985, pp. 149–60. [G: Japan]

Holland, Daniel M. Land Value Taxation in Developing Countries: The Case of Jamaica. In *Lewis, S. R., Jr., ed.*, 1985, pp. 53–78.
[G: Jamaica]

Horn, Walter. Coase's Theorem and the Speculative Withholding of Land. *Land Econ.*, May 1985, *61*(2), pp. 208–12.

Kikuchi, Masao and Hayami, Yujiro. Agricultural Growth against a Land-Resource Constraint: Japan, Taiwan, Korea, and the Philippines. In *Ohkawa, K. and Ranis, G., eds.*, 1985, pp. 67–90. [G: Japan; Taiwan; S. Korea; Philippines]

Lahiri, Ashok Kumar and Roy, Prannoy. Rainfall and Supply–Response: A Study of Rice in India. *J. Devel. Econ.*, August 1985, *18*(2–3), pp. 315–34. [G: India]

Lebergott, Stanley. The Demand for Land: The United States, 1820–1860. *J. Econ. Hist.*, June 1985, *45*(2), pp. 181–212. [G: U.S.]

Leistritz, F. Larry; Wiedrich, Garland D. and Vreugdenhil, Harvey G. Effects of Energy Development on Agricultural Land Values. *Western J. Agr. Econ.*, December 1985, *10*(2), pp. 204–15. [G: U.S.]

Lemoine, Pierre H. and Gotsch, Carl H. Water Resource Development in the Salinas Valley: Economics and Hydrology in a Closed Control Model. *Food Res. Inst. Stud.*, 1985, *19*(3), pp. 293–333. [G: U.S.]

Lovejoy, Stephen B.; Lee, John Gary and Beasley, David B. Muddy Water and American Agriculture: How to Best Control Sedimentation from Agricultural Land? *Water Resources Res.*, August 1985, *21*(8), pp. 1065–68. [G: U.S.]

Manning, Travis W. and Anderson, Wayne. The Repayment of Water Development Costs. *Can. J. Agr. Econ.*, August 1985, *32*, pp. 119–32. [G: Canada]

Martellaro, Joseph A. Water as a Resource in the Third World. *J. Econ. Devel.*, July 1985, *10*(1), pp. 7–28. [G: LDCs]

McCarl, Bruce A. and Ross, Mark. The Cost Borne by Electricity Consumers under Expanded Irrigation from the Columbia River. *Water Resources Res.*, September 1985, *21*(9), pp. 1319–28.

Murshid, K. A. S. Is There a 'Structural' Constraint to Capacity Utilisation of Deep Tube-Wells? *Bangladesh Devel. Stud.*, Sept.-Dec. 1985, *13*(3&4), pp. 147–54. [G: Bangladesh]

Nieswiadomy, Michael. The Demand for Irrigation Water in the High Plains of Texas, 1957–80. *Amer. J. Agr. Econ.*, August 1985, *67*(3), pp. 619–26. [G: U.S.]

Pines, David and Sadka, Efraim. Zoning, First-Best, Second-Best, and Third-Best Criteria for

Allocating Land for Roads. *J. Urban Econ.*, March 1985, *17*(2), pp. 167–83.

Quasem, Md. Abul. Impact of the New System of Distribution of Irrigation Machines in Bangladesh. *Bangladesh Devel. Stud.*, Sept.-Dec. 1985, *13*(3&4), pp. 127–40. **[G: Bangladesh]**

Sampath, Rajan K. Efficiency and Equity Implications of Irrigation Water Distribution Policy. *Margin*, July 1985, *17*(4), pp. 48–61.
[G: India]

Sattar, M. A. and Bhuiyan, S. I. Constraints to Low Utilization of Deep Tubewell Water in a Selected Tubewell Project in Bangladesh. *Bangladesh Devel. Stud.*, Sept.-Dec. 1985, *13*(3&4), pp. 155–66. **[G: Bangladesh]**

Scudder, Thayer. A Sociological Framework for the Analysis of New Land Settlements. In *Cernea, M. M., ed.*, 1985, pp. 121–53.
[G: Selected LDCs]

Segarra, Eduardo; Kramer, Randall A. and Taylor, Daniel B. A Stochastic Programming Analysis of the Farm Level Implications of Soil Erosion Control. *Southern J. Agr. Econ.*, December 1985, *17*(2), pp. 147–54. **[G: U.S.]**

Simmie, James. Corporatism and Planning. In *Grant, W., ed.*, 1985, pp. 174–201.
[G: U.K.]

Solberg, Carl E. Land Tenure and Land Settlement: Policy and Patterns in the Canadian Prairies and the Argentine Pampas, 1880–1930. In *Platt, D. C. M. and di Tella, G., eds.*, 1985, pp. 53–75. **[G: Argentina; Canada]**

Spurlock, Stan R. Issues in Agricultural Land Markets: An Empirical Perspective: Discussion. *Southern J. Agr. Econ.*, July 1985, *17*(1), pp. 85–87. **[G: U.S.]**

Tew, Bernard V., et al. Market Failure in Multiphase Electric Power Development for Agricultural Irrigation. *Southern J. Agr. Econ.*, December 1985, *17*(2), pp. 57–65. **[G: U.S.]**

Tiwari, Padma Nath. An Investigation into Agricultural Land Acquisition: A Case Study of Palawan. *Philippine Rev. Econ. Bus.*, Mar./June 1985, *22*(1/2), pp. 109–20. **[G: Philippines]**

Vaidyanathan, A. Water Control Institutions and Agriculture: A Comparative Perspective. *Indian Econ. Rev.*, Jan.-June 1985, *20*(1), pp. 25–83.

Vail, David. Revitalizing Rural Communities or Reviving Agrarian Myths? A Comment [A Geobased National Agricultural Policy for Rural Community Enhancement, Environmental Vitality, and Income Stabilization]. *J. Econ. Issues*, December 1985, *19*(4), pp. 995–1003.
[G: U.S.]

Vaillancourt, François and Monty, Luc. The Effect of Agricultural Zoning on Land Prices, Quebec, 1975–1981. *Land Econ.*, February 1985, *61*(1), pp. 36–42. **[G: Canada]**

Vandeveer, Lonnie R. Issues in Agricultural Land Markets: An Empirical Perspective. *Southern J. Agr. Econ.*, July 1985, *17*(1), pp. 75–84.
[G: U.S.]

Veloz, Alberto, et al. The Economics of Erosion Control in a Subtropical Watershed: A Dominican Case. *Land Econ.*, May 1985, *61*(2), pp.

145–55. **[G: Dominican Republic]**

Wiltshaw, Desmond G. The Supply of Land. *Urban Stud.*, February 1985, *22*(1), pp. 49–56.

Wright, Robert. A Critique of the ECE Draft Standard International Classification of Land Use. *Statist. J.*, December 1985, *3*(4), pp. 403–11.

Young, David A. The Repayment of Water Development Costs: Commentary. *Can. J. Agr. Econ.*, August 1985, *32*, pp. 133–36.
[G: Canada]

Zalin, Giovanni. L'irrigazione dell'alto agro e il recupero fondiario e agricolo dell'antica "companea" veronese. The Irrigation of Alto Agro and the Reclamation of the Land and Agriculture of Veronese Campanea. With English summary.) *Rivista Int. Sci. Econ. Com.*, December 1985, *32*(12), pp. 1141–53. **[G: Italy]**

Zheng, Tianxiang; Wei, Qingquan and Chu, David K. Y. Agricultural Land-Use Patterns and Export Potential. In *Wong, K. and Chu, D. K. Y., eds.*, 1985, pp. 89–107. **[G: China]**

Ziemer, Rod F., et al. Differential Assessment and Agricultural Land Use in the South. *Rev. Reg. Stud.*, Winter 1985, *15*(1), pp. 46–57.
[G: U.S.]

718 Rural Economics

7180 Rural Economics

Adams, Richard H., Jr. Development and Structural Change in Rural Egypt, 1952 to 1982. *World Devel.*, June 1985, *13*(6), pp. 705–23.
[G: Egypt]

Adekanye, Tomilayo O. Innovation and Rural Women in Nigeria: Cassava Processing and Food Production. In *Ahmed, I., ed.*, 1985, pp. 252–83. **[G: Nigeria]**

Adeyemo, Remi. A New Dimension in the Participatory Role of Self-managed Co-operative Unions in Development Projects. *Econ. Anal. Worker's Manage.*, 1985, *19*(3), pp. 317–25.
[G: Nigeria]

Agarwal, Bina. Women and Technological Change in Agriculture: The Asian and African Experience. In *Ahmed, I., ed.*, 1985, pp. 67–114. **[G: India; Africa; Asia]**

Ahluwalia, Montek S. Rural Poverty, Agricultural Production, and Prices: A Reexamination. In *Mellor, J. W. and Desai, G. M., eds.*, 1985, pp. 59–75. **[G: India]**

Ahmad, Alia. The Effect of Population Growth on a Peasant Economy: The Case of Bangladesh. In *Lundahl, M., ed.*, 1985, pp. 87–104.
[G: Bangladesh]

Ahmad, Qazi Kholiquzzaman and Ahmed, Momtaz Uddin. A Review of Rural Non-farm Economic Activities in Bangladesh. In *Mukhopadhyay, S. and Chee, P. L., eds. (I)*, 1985, pp. 53–146. **[G: Bangladesh]**

Ahmad, Qazi Kholiquzzaman and Hossain, Mahabub. An Evaluation of Selected Policies and Programmes for the Alleviation of Rural Poverty in Bangladesh. In *Islam, R., ed.*, 1985, pp. 67–98. **[G: Bangladesh]**

Ahmed, Iftikhar. Technology and Rural Women: Conclusions. In *Ahmed, I., ed.*, 1985, pp. 327–41. **[G: LDCs]**

Ahmed, Momtaz Uddin. Institutional Framework Concerning Promotion of Rural Industries in Bangladesh: An Evaluation. In *Mukhopadhyay, S. and Chee, P. L., eds. (II)*, 1985, pp. 227–301. **[G: Bangladesh]**

Ahmed, Raisuddin. Growth and Equity in Indian Agriculture and a Few Paradigms from Bangladesh. In *Mellor, J. W. and Desai, G. M., eds.*, 1985, pp. 124–27. **[G: India; Bangladesh]**

Al-Awad, A. A.; Mohammed, Y. A. and El-Tayeb, S. A. The Impact of Improved Rural Water Supplies on the Environment: The Case of East Kordofan District. In *Davies, H. R. J., ed.*, 1985, pp. 16–29. **[G: Sudan]**

Alberts, Tom. Peru—20 Years of Agrarian Reform. In *Lundahl, M., ed.*, 1985, pp. 291–308. **[G: Peru]**

Ali, M. Shaukat. Rural Poverty and Anti-poverty Policies in Pakistan. In *Islam, R., ed.*, 1985, pp. 175–99. **[G: Pakistan]**

Åsberg, Rodney and Jerve, Alf Morten. Poverty in Pakistan. In *Jerve, A. M., ed.*, 1985, pp. 231–46. **[G: Pakistan]**

Bagadion, Benjamin U. and Korten, Frances F. Developing Irrigators' Organizations: A Learning Process Approach. In *Cernea, M. M., ed.*, 1985, pp. 52–90. **[G: Philippines]**

Bakht, Zaid. Handloom Industry in Bangladesh: A Review of Prospects and Problems. In *Mukhopadhyay, S. and Chee, P. L., eds. (II)*, 1985, pp. 357–88. **[G: Bangladesh]**

Bandyopadhyay, D. An Evaluation of Policies and Programmes for the Alleviation of Rural Poverty in India. In *Islam, R., ed.*, 1985, pp. 99–151. **[G: India]**

Bandyopadhyay, D. Rural Development. In *Mongia, J. N., ed.*, 1985, pp. 517–38. **[G: India]**

Banskota, Mahesh. Anti-poverty Policies in Rural Nepal. In *Islam, R., ed.*, 1985, pp. 153–74. **[G: Nepal]**

Bar-El, Raphael. Industrial Dispersion as an Instrument for the Achievement of Development Goals. *Econ. Geogr.*, July 1985, *61*(3), pp. 205–22. **[G: Brazil]**

Bardhan, Pranab K. Agricultural Development and Land Tenancy in a Peasant Economy: Reply. *Amer. J. Agr. Econ.*, August 1985, *67*(3), pp. 691–92. **[G: India]**

Bardhan, Pranab K. Poverty and "Trickle-Down" in Rural India: A Quantitative Analysis. In *Mellor, J. W. and Desai, G. M., eds.*, 1985, pp. 75–94. **[G: India]**

Bhaduri, Amit. Technological Change and Rural Women: A Conceptual Analysis. In *Ahmed, I., ed.*, 1985, pp. 15–26.

Bhatnagar, R. G. Regional Rural Banks. In *Bandyopadhyay, R. and Khankhoje, D. P., eds.*, 1985, pp. 181–84. **[G: India]**

Bhatnagar, R. G. Regional Rural Banks: A Critical Review. In *Bandyopadhyay, R. and Khankhoje, D. P., eds.*, 1985, pp. 147–51. **[G: India]**

Bigsten, Arne. What Do Smallholders Do for a

Living? Some Evidence from Kenya. In *Lundahl, M., ed.*, 1985, pp. 66–83. **[G: Kenya]**

Black, Jan Knippers. Ten Paradoxes of Rural Development: An Ecuadorian Case Study. *J. Devel. Areas*, July 1985, *19*(4), pp. 527–55. **[G: Ecuador]**

Blair, Harry W. Participation, Public Policy, Political Economy and Development in Rural Bangladesh, 1958–85. *World Devel.*, December 1985, *13*(12), pp. 1231–47. **[G: Bangladesh]**

Blecher, Marc. Inequality and Socialism in Rural China: A Conceptual Note. *World Devel.*, January 1985, *13*(1), pp. 115–21. **[G: China]**

Bliss, Christopher. A Note on the Price Variable. In *Mellor, J. W. and Desai, G. M., eds.*, 1985, pp. 18–20.

Booth, Alan R. Homestead, State, and Migrant Labor in Colonial Swaziland. *African Econ. Hist.*, 1985, *14*, pp. 107–45. **[G: Swaziland]**

Bowonder, B., et al. Energy Use in Eight Rural Communities in India. *World Devel.*, December 1985, *13*(12), pp. 1263–86. **[G: India]**

Boyer, George R. An Economic Model of the English Poor Law circa 1780–1834. *Exploration Econ. Hist.*, April 1985, *22*(2), pp. 129–67. **[G: U.K.]**

Campagne, P. and Savané, M. A. Quel avenir pour les nouvelles stratégies alimentaires des paysanneries du Sahel? (What Future for the Food Strategies and Sahelian Peasants? With English summary.) *Écon. Soc.*, July 1985, *19*(7), pp. 23–45. **[G: Senegal]**

Carr, Marilyn. Technologies for Rural Women: Impact and Dissemination. In *Ahmed, I., ed.*, 1985, pp. 115–53. **[G: Africa]**

Catanese, Anthony V. Third World Rural Poverty: Field Observations and Solutions and Some Operating Principles for Religious Groups. *Int. J. Soc. Econ.*, 1985, *12*(6/7), pp. 68–79. **[G: Guatemala; Honduras; Haiti]**

Cernea, Michael M. Alternative Units of Social Organization Sustaining Afforestation Strategies. In *Cernea, M. M., ed.*, 1985, pp. 267–93. **[G: Pakistan; Selected LDCs]**

Cernea, Michael M. Sociological Knowledge for Development Projects. In *Cernea, M. M., ed.*, 1985, pp. 3–21. **[G: LDCs]**

Chambers, Robert. Shortcut Methods of Gathering Social Information for Rural Development Projects. In *Cernea, M. M., ed.*, 1985, pp. 399–415. **[G: LDCs]**

Chaudhry, M. Ghaffar. The State and Development of Rural Industries in Pakistan. In *Mukhopadhyay, S. and Chee, P. L., eds. (I)*, 1985, pp. 249–306. **[G: Pakistan]**

Choe, Yang Boo. Development of Rural Non-farm Activities and Industries in Korea. In *Mukhopadhyay, S. and Chee, P. L., eds. (I)*, 1985, pp. 309–82. **[G: S. Korea]**

Choe, Yang Boo and Lee, Dong Phil. Role and Characteristics of Very Small Industries in Rural Korea. In *Mukhopadhyay, S. and Chee, P. L., eds. (II)*, 1985, pp. 151–74. **[G: S. Korea]**

Cook, Cynthia C. Social Analysis in Rural Road

Projects. In *Cernea, M. M., ed.*, 1985, pp. 297–321. **[G: Selected LDCs]**

Coward, E. Walter, Jr. Technical and Social Change in Currently Irrigated Regions: Rules, Roles, and Rehabilitation. In *Cernea, M. M., ed.*, 1985, pp. 27–51. **[G: Selected LDCs]**

Craig, Susan. Political Patronage and Community Resistance: Village Councils in Trinidad and Tobago. In *Gomes, P. I., ed.*, 1985, pp. 173–93. **[G: Trinidad and Tobago]**

Curley, Michael D. and Gift, Richard E. Investment Incentives and Rural Conflict: The Case of South Vietnam. *J. Devel. Areas*, October 1985, *20*(1), pp. 49–70. **[G: Vietnam]**

Curry, Robert L., Jr. Mineral-based Growth and Development-generated Socioeconomic Problems in Botswana: Rural Inequality, Water Scarcity, Food Insecurity, and Foreign Dependence Challenge New Governing Class. *Amer. J. Econ. Soc.*, July 1985, *44*(3), pp. 319–36. **[G: Botswana]**

Dantwala, M. L. Technology, Growth, and Equity in Agriculture. In *Mellor, J. W. and Desai, G. M., eds.*, 1985, pp. 110–23. **[G: India]**

Date-Bah, Eugenia. Technologies for Rural Women of Ghana: Role of Socio-Cultural Factors. In *Ahmed, I., ed.*, 1985, pp. 211–51. **[G: Ghana]**

Datta, Samar K. and Nugent, Jeffrey B. Agricultural Development and Land Tenancy in a Peasant Economy: Comment. *Amer. J. Agr. Econ.*, August 1985, *67*(3), pp. 688–90. **[G: India]**

Desai, Gunvant M. Trends in Rural Poverty in India: An Interpretation of Dharm Narain. In *Mellor, J. W. and Desai, G. M., eds.*, 1985, pp. 1–6. **[G: India]**

Dhindsa, K. S. Some Aspects of Green Revolution—A Case Study. *Margin*, April 1985, *17*(3), pp. 50–54. **[G: India]**

Durant-Gonzalez, Victoria. Higglering: Rural Women and the Internal Market System in Jamaica. In *Gomes, P. I., ed.*, 1985, pp. 103–22. **[G: Jamaica]**

Dyson-Hudson, Neville. Pastoral Production Systems and Livestock Development Projects: An East African Perspective. In *Cernea, M. M., ed.*, 1985, pp. 157–86. **[G: E. Africa]**

Eswaran, Mukesh and Kotwal, Ashok. A Theory of Two-Tier Labor Markets in Agrarian Economies. *Amer. Econ. Rev.*, March 1985, *75*(1), pp. 162–77.

Evans, Scott. Recent Changes in Rural Employment. *Australian Bull. Lab.*, December 1985, *12*(1), pp. 57–72. **[G: Australia]**

Fabella, Raul V. Rural Industry and Modernization. In *Mukhopadhyay, S. and Chee, P. L., eds. (II)*, 1985, pp. 117–50. **[G: Philippines]**

Fabella, Raul V. Rural Non-farm Activities in the Philippines: Composition, Growth and Seasonality. In *Mukhopadhyay, S. and Chee, P. L., eds. (I)*, 1985, pp. 495–589. **[G: Philippines]**

Fabella, Raul V. The Handloom Weaving Industry in La Union. In *Mukhopadhyay, S. and Chee, P. L., eds. (II)*, 1985, pp. 389–417. **[G: Philippines]**

Fong, Chan-Onn. Integrated Population-Development Program Performance: The Malaysian Felda Experience. *J. Devel. Areas*, January 1985, *19*(2), pp. 149–69. **[G: Malaysia]**

Ford, Lacy K. Self-Sufficiency, Cotton, and Economic Development in the South Carolina Upcountry, 1800–1860. *J. Econ. Hist.*, June 1985, *45*(2), pp. 261–67. **[G: U.S.]**

Fortmann, Louise. Seasonal Dimensions of Rural Social Organisation. *J. Devel. Stud.*, April 1985, *21*(3), pp. 377–89. **[G: Botswana]**

Franklin, David L. and Vial de Valdés, Isabel. Estrategias nutricionales de los hogares pobres. (With English summary.) *Cuadernos Econ.*, August 1985, *22*(66), pp. 247–65. **[G: Panama]**

Freeman, David M. and Lowdermilk, Max L. Middle-Level Organizational Linkages in Irrigation Projects. In *Cernea, M. M., ed.*, 1985, pp. 91–118. **[G: Selected LDCs]**

Gaiha, Raghav. Poverty, Technology and Infrastructure in Rural India. *Cambridge J. Econ.*, September 1985, *9*(3), pp. 221–43. **[G: India]**

Ghosh, Dipak. A Lewisian Model of Dual Economy with Rural–Urban Migration. *Scot. J. Polit. Econ.*, February 1985, *32*(1), pp. 95–106.

Goldsmith, Arthur. The Private Sector and Rural Development: Can Agribusiness Help the Small Farmer? *World Devel.*, Oct./Nov. 1985, *13*(10/11), pp. 1125–38. **[G: LDCs]**

Gomes, P. I. Plantation Dominance and Rural Dependence in Dominica. In *Gomes, P. I., ed.*, 1985, pp. 60–75. **[G: Dominica]**

Gomes, P. I. Rural Development in the Caribbean: Postscript: Conclusions and Policy Implications. In *Gomes, P. I., ed.*, 1985, pp. 232–39. **[G: Caribbean]**

Gomes, P. I. Rural Development in the Caribbean: Introduction. In *Gomes, P. I., ed.*, 1985, pp. ix–xxi. **[G: Caribbean]**

Gow, David D. and Morss, Elliott R. Implementing Rural Development Projects: Ineffective Information Systems. In *Morss, E. R. and Gow, D. D., eds.*, 1985, pp. 175–97. **[G: LDCs]**

Gow, David D. and Van Sant, Jerry. Implementing Rural Development Projects: Decentralization and Participation: Concepts in Need of Implementation Strategies. In *Morss, E. R. and Gow, D. D., eds.*, 1985, pp. 107–47. **[G: LDCs]**

Grabowski, Richard and Sivan, David. The Price of Food, Labor Scarcity and the Real Wage: Egypt, 1950 to 1974. *Pakistan J. Appl. Econ.*, Winter 1985, *4*(2), pp. 93–99. **[G: Egypt]**

Griffin, Keith. Rural Poverty in Asia: Analysis and Policy Alternatives. In *Islam, R., ed.*, 1985, pp. 29–65. **[G: LDCs]**

Grindle, Merilee S. Rhetoric, Reality, and Self-Sufficiency: Recent Initiatives in Mexican Rural Development. *J. Devel. Areas*, January 1985, *19*(2), pp. 171–84. **[G: Mexico]**

Harris, G. T. A Note on Rural Unemployment:

A Study of Four Northern New South Wales Towns. *Rev. Marketing Agr. Econ.*, August 1985, 53(2), pp. 63–73. [G: Australia]

Hayami, Yujiro and Kikuchi, Masao. Agricultural Technology and Income Distribution: Two Indonesian Villages Viewed from the Japanese Experience. In *Ohkawa, K. and Ranis, G., eds.*, 1985, pp. 91–109. [G: Indonesia; Japan]

Hayami, Yujiro and Kikuchi, Masao. Directions of Agrarian Change: A View from Villages in the Philippines. In *Mellor, J. W. and Desai, G. M., eds.*, 1985, pp. 132–48.
[G: Philippines]

Henderson, Thomas H. and Patton, Michael Quinn. Agricultural Extension for Rural Transformation: The C.A.E.P. Model. In *Gomes, P. I., ed.*, 1985, pp. 194–211.
[G: Caribbean]

Hilton, R. H. A Crisis of Feudalism. In *Aston, T. H. and Philpin, C. H. E., eds.*, 1985, pp. 119–37.

Hirashima, S. Poverty as a Generation's Problem: A Note on the Japanese Experience. In *Mellor, J. W. and Desai, G. M., eds.*, 1985, pp. 149–60. [G: Japan]

Honadle, George H.; Silverman, Jerry M. and Mickelwait, Donald R. Implementing Rural Development Projects: Technical Assistance Shortcomings. In *Morss, E. R. and Gow, D. D., eds.*, 1985, pp. 83–106. [G: LDCs]

Honadle, George H.; Walker, S. Tjip and Silverman, Jerry M. Implementing Rural Development Projects: Dealing with Institutional and Organizational Realities. In *Morss, E. R. and Gow, D. D., eds.*, 1985, pp. 33–63.
[G: LDCs]

Hughes, R. D. A Model of Rural Non-agricultural Activity in South Africa. *J. Stud. Econ. Econometrics*, March 1985, (21), pp. 41–66.
[G: S. Africa]

Hussain, Syed Akmal. Structure of Rural Income in Pakistan: Some Preliminary Estimates: Comments. *Pakistan Devel. Rev.*, Autumn-Winter 1985, 24(3/4), pp. 401–03.
[G: Pakistan]

Isaacman, Allen. Chiefs, Rural Differentiation and Peasant Protest: The Mozambican Forced Cotton Regime 1938–1961. *African Econ. Hist.*, 1985, 14, pp. 15–56. [G: Mozambique]

Islam, Rizwanul and Lee, Eddy. Strategies for Alleviating Poverty in Rural Asia. In *Islam, R., ed.*, 1985, pp. 1–27. [G: Asia]

Iyengar, N. Srinivasa and Indrakant, S. Pattern of Asset Holdings in Rural Andhra Pradesh: A Comparative Study. *Indian J. Quant. Econ.*, 1985, 1(1), pp. 97–117. [G: India]

Jain, A. K. Determinants of Regional Variations in Infant Mortality in Rural India. *Population Stud.*, November 1985, 39(3), pp. 407–24.
[G: India]

Jerve, Alf Morten; Tobiesen, Per and Åsberg, Rodney. Rural Energy. In *Jerve, A. M., ed.*, 1985, pp. 321–26. [G: Pakistan]

Jodha, N. S. Population Growth and the Decline of Common Property Resources in Rajasthan,

India. *Population Devel. Rev.*, June 1985, 11(2), pp. 247–64. [G: India]

Kennedy, Líam. An Economic History of Ulster 1820–1939: The Rural Economy, 1820–1914. In *Kennedy, L. and Ollerenshaw, P., eds.*, 1985, pp. 1–61. [G: U.K.]

Keyfitz, Nathan. An East Javanese Village in 1953 and 1985: Observations on Development. *Population Devel. Rev.*, December 1985, 11(4), pp. 695–719. [G: Indonesia]

Khan, M. Mahmud. Labour Absorption and Unemployment in Rural Bangladesh. *Bangladesh Devel. Stud.*, Sept.-Dec. 1985, 13(3&4), pp. 67–88. [G: Bangladesh]

Khan, Qaiser M. A Model of Endowment-constrained Demand for Food in an Agricultural Economy with Empirical Applications to Bangladesh. *World Devel.*, September 1985, 13(9), pp. 1055–65. [G: Bangladesh]

Kielstra, Nico. The Rural Languedoc: Periphery to "Relictual Space." In *Hudson, R. and Lewis, J., eds.*, 1985, pp. 246–62. [G: France]

King, Russell, et al. Return Migration and Rural Economic Change: A South Italian Case Study. In *Hudson, R. and Lewis, J., eds.*, 1985, pp. 101–122. [G: Italy]

Kottak, Conrad Phillip. When People Don't Come First: Some Sociological Lessons from Completed Projects. In *Cernea, M. M., ed.*, 1985, pp. 325–56. [G: LDCs]

Krongkaew, Medhi. Agricultural Development, Rural Poverty, and Income Distribution in Thailand. *Devel. Econ.*, December 1985, 23(4), pp. 325–46. [G: Thailand]

Kumar, Shubh K. The Income Approach to Measuring Poverty: A Note on Human Welfare below the Line. In *Mellor, J. W. and Desai, G. M., eds.*, 1985, pp. 54–58.

Lázniěková, Anna. Overcoming Social Disparities between the Urban and Rural Population in Socialist Society. *Czech. Econ. Digest.*, August 1985, (5), pp. 45–58. [G: Czechoslovakia]

Lele, Uma. Terms of Trade, Agricultural Growth, and Rural Poverty in Africa. In *Mellor, J. W. and Desai, G. M., eds.*, 1985, pp. 161–80.
[G: Sub-Saharan Africa]

Levy, Victor. Cropping Pattern, Mechanization, Child Labor, and Fertility Behavior in a Farming Economy: Rural Egypt. *Econ. Develop. Cult. Change*, July 1985, 33(4), pp. 777–91.
[G: Egypt]

Lim, Chee Peng. A Review of Rural Non-farm Activities in Malaysia. In *Mukhopadhyay, S. and Chee, P. L., eds. (I)*, 1985, pp. 383–493.
[G: Malaysia]

Lim, Chee Peng. A Survey of Bumiputra RNA Entrepreneurs in Peninsular Malaysia. In *Mukhopadhyay, S. and Chee, P. L., eds. (II)*, 1985, pp. 305–55. [G: Malaysia]

Lim, Chee Peng. The Role of Regional Development Authorities and Rural Non-farm Activities in Malaysia. In *Mukhopadhyay, S. and Chee, P. L., eds. (II)*, 1985, pp. 177–26.
[G: Malaysia]

Logan, Bernard I. Evaluating Public Policy Costs in Rural Development Planning: The Example of Health Care in Sierra Leone. *Econ. Geogr.*, April 1985, *61*(2), pp. 144–57.

[G: Sierra Leone]

Mangahas, Mahar. Rural Poverty and Operation Land Transfer in the Philippines. In *Islam, R., ed.*, 1985, pp. 201–41. [G: Philippines]

Mangahas, Mahar. The Data on Indian Poverty and the Poverty of ASEAN Data. In *Mellor, J. W. and Desai, G. M., eds.*, 1985, pp. 128–31. [G: ASEAN; India]

Marloie, Marcel. La stratégie alimentaire de la France au XIXe siècle: quelles leçons pour aujourd'hui? (The French Food Strategy in the 19th Century: What Lessons at Now? With English summary.) *Écon. Soc.*, July 1985, *19*(7), pp. 179–205. [G: France]

Marshall, Woodville K. Peasant Development in the West Indies since 1838. In *Gomes, P. I., ed.*, 1985, pp. 1–14. [G: Caribbean]

Mathur, Subodh C. Rural Poverty and Agricultural Performance in India. *J. Devel. Stud.*, April 1985, *21*(3), pp. 422–28. [G: India]

Mellor, John W. Determinants of Rural Poverty: The Dynamics of Production, Technology, and Price. In *Mellor, J. W. and Desai, G. M., eds.*, 1985, pp. 21–40. [G: LDCs]

Mellor, John W. and Desai, Gunvant M. Agricultural Change and Rural Poverty: A Synthesis. In *Mellor, J. W. and Desai, G. M., eds.*, 1985, pp. 192–210. [G: India; LDCs]

Miller, Barbara D. and Wozny, James A. Land Tenure Patterns in Bangladesh: Implications for the Revenue and Distributional Effects of Changes in Land Taxation. *J. Devel. Areas*, July 1985, *19*(4), pp. 459–81.

[G: Bangladesh]

Mitra, Gautam Kumar and Reddy, M. Surender. Rural Electrification and Distribution Benefits in Andhra Pradesh—A Case Study. *Margin*, October 1985, *18*(1), pp. 31–39. [G: India]

Mohammad, Faiz and Badar, Ghulam. Structure of Rural Income in Pakistan: Some Preliminary Estimates. *Pakistan Devel. Rev.*, Autumn-Winter 1985, *24*(3/4), pp. 385–400.

[G: Pakistan]

Morss, Elliott R.; Crawford, Paul R. and Owens, Gene M. Implementing Rural Development Projects: Personnel Constraints. In *Morss, E. R. and Gow, D. D., eds.*, 1985, pp. 65–81. [G: LDCs]

Morss, Elliott R.; Gow, David D. and Nordlinger, Christopher W. Implementing Rural Development Projects: Sustaining Project Benefits. In *Morss, E. R. and Gow, D. D., eds.*, 1985, pp. 217–43. [G: LDCs]

Morss, Elliott R. and Honadle, George H. Implementing Rural Development Projects: Differing Agendas. In *Morss, E. R. and Gow, D. D., eds.*, 1985, pp. 199–215. [G: LDCs]

Morss, Elliott R. and Van Sant, Jerry. Implementing Rural Development Projects: Timing. In *Morss, E. R. and Gow, D. D., eds.*, 1985, pp. 149–74. [G: LDCs]

Mukhopadhyay, Swapna and Lim, Chee Peng. Rural Non-farm Activities in the Asian Region: An Overview. In *Mukhopadhyay, S. and Chee,*

P. L., eds. (I), 1985, pp. 1–49. [G: Asia; LDCs]

Nabi, Ijaz. Rural Factor Market Imperfections and the Incidence of Tenancy in Agriculture. *Oxford Econ. Pap.*, June 1985, *37*(2), pp. 319–29. [G: Pakistan]

Neale, Walter C. Indian Community Development, Local Government, Local Planning, and Rural Policy since 1950. *Econ. Develop. Cult. Change*, July 1985, *33*(4), pp. 677–98.

[G: India]

Noronha, Raymond and Spears, John S. Sociological Variables in Forestry Project Design. In *Cernea, M. M., ed.*, 1985, pp. 227–66.

[G: Selected LDCs]

Nutley, S. D. Planning Options for the Improvement of Rural Accessibility: Use of the Time-Space Approach. *Reg. Stud.*, February 1985, *19*(1), pp. 37–50. [G: U.K.]

Oshima, Harry T. Levels and Trends of Farm Families' Nonagricultural Incomes at Different Stages of Monsoon Development. *Philippine Rev. Econ. Bus.*, Sept./Dec. 1985, 22(3/4), pp. 123–54.

Papanek, Gustav F. Agricultural Income Distribution and Employment in the 1970s. *Bull. Indonesian Econ. Stud.*, August 1985, *21*(2), pp. 24–50. [G: Indonesia]

Parthasarathy, G. Dharm Narain's Approach to Rural Poverty: Critical Issues. In *Mellor, J. W. and Desai, G. M., eds.*, 1985, pp. 181–85. [G: India; LDCs]

Patil, R. K. and Patel, K. V. Rural Development: Organisation and Management Issues. In *Bandyopadhyay, R. and Khankhoje, D. P., eds.*, 1985, pp. 77–98. [G: India]

Pearson, Scott R.; Monke, Eric A. and Avillez, Francisco. Fontes de financiamento do investimento agrícola em Portugal. (With English summary.) *Economia (Portugal)*, May 1985, *9*(2), pp. 233–56. [G: Portugal]

Pemberton, Carlisle. Economic Behaviour of Peasants in Tobago. In *Gomes, P. I., ed.*, 1985, pp. 76–102. [G: Trinidad and Tobago]

Pitt, Mark M. and Rosenzweig, Mark R. Health and Nutrient Consumption across and within Farm Households. *Rev. Econ. Statist.*, May 1985, *67*(2), pp. 212–23. [G: Indonesia]

Pollnac, Richard B. Social and Cultural Characteristics in Small-scale Fishery Development. In *Cernea, M. M., ed.*, 1985, pp. 189–223.

[G: Selected LDCs]

Pope, C. Arden, III. Agricultural Productive and Consumptive Use Components of Rural Land Values in Texas. *Amer. J. Agr. Econ.*, February 1985, *67*(1), pp. 81–86. [G: U.S.]

Pugliese, Enrico. Farm Workers in Italy: Agricultural Working Class, Landless Peasants, or Clients of the Welfare State? In *Hudson, R. and Lewis, J., eds.*, 1985, pp. 123–39.

[G: Italy]

Raghupati, T., et al. Case Study on Rural Non-farm Activities in India. In *Mukhopadhyay, S. and Chee, P. L., eds. (II)*, 1985, pp. 3–74.

[G: India]

Ramsay, Ansil. Population Pressure, Mechaniza-

tion, and Landlessness in Central Thailand. *J. Devel. Areas*, April 1985, *19*(3), pp. 351–68.
[G: Thailand]

Rao, B. Sudhakar. Rural Industrialisation and Rural Non-farm Employment in India. In *Mukhopadhyay, S. and Chee, P. L., eds. (I)*, 1985, pp. 147–248. [G: India]

Rao, C. H. Hanumantha; Gupta, Devendra B. and Sharma, P. S. Infrastructural Development and Rural Poverty in India: A Cross-Sectional Analysis. In *Mellor, J. W. and Desai, G. M., eds.*, 1985, pp. 95–109. [G: India]

Ray, Ranjan. A Dynamic Analysis of Expenditure Patterns in Rural India. *J. Devel. Econ.*, December 1985, *19*(3), pp. 283–97. [G: India]

Ray, Ranjan. Evaluating Expenditure Inequality Using Alternative Social Welfare Functions: A Case Study of Rural India. *Indian Econ. Rev.*, July-Dec. 1985, *20*(2), pp. 171–90. [G: India]

Rosenzweig, Mark R. and Wolpin, Kenneth I. Specific Experience, Household Structure, and Intergenerational Transfers: Farm Family Land and Labor Arraangements in Developing Countries. *Quart. J. Econ.*, Supp. 1985, *100*, pp. 961–87. [G: India]

Rosner, M. and Shur, S. The Integration of Agriculture and Industry in Cooperative Villages: The Experience of the Kibbutz. In *Bergmann, T. and Ogura, T. B., eds.*, 1985, pp. 59–70. [G: Israel]

Safilios-Rothschild, Constantina. The Persistence of Women's Invisibility in Agriculture: Theoretical and Policy Lessons from Lesotho and Sierra Leone. *Econ. Develop. Cult. Change*, January 1985, *33*(2), pp. 299–317.
[G: Lesotho; Sierra Leone]

Saidi, Khosrow. Rural Cooperatives in the Third World between State and Peasants. In *Bergmann, T. and Ogura, T. B., eds.*, 1985, pp. 179–88. [G: LDCs]

Saini, Balwant Singh. Barefoot Architects: A Training Program for Building in the Third World. In *Lea, J. P. and Courtney, J. M., eds.*, 1985, pp. 97–100.

Saith, Ashwani. The Distributional Dimensions of Revolutionary Transition: Ethiopia. *J. Devel. Stud.*, October 1985, *22*(1), pp. 150–79.
[G: Ethiopia]

Saith, Ashwani. The Distributional Dimensions of Revolutionary Transition: Ethiopia. In *Saith, A., ed.*, 1985, pp. 150–79. [G: Ethiopia]

Sarkar, B. N. Development Prospects in Rural West Bengal. *Margin*, January 1985, *17*(2), pp. 88–101. [G: India]

Schaefer, Donald and Schmitz, Mark D. The Parker–Gallman Sample and Wealth Distributions for the Antebellum South: A Comment [Notes on the Wealth Distribution of Farm Households in the United States, 1860: A New Look at Two Manuscript Census Samples]. *Exploration Econ. Hist.*, April 1985, *22*(2), pp. 220–26. [G: U.S.]

Scudder, Thayer. A Sociological Framework for the Analysis of New Land Settlements. In *Cernea, M. M., ed.*, 1985, pp. 121–53.
[G: Selected LDCs]

Sen, Amartya. Dharm Narain on Poverty: Concepts and Broader Issues. In *Mellor, J. W. and Desai, G. M., eds.*, 1985, pp. 7–17.
[G: Bangladesh; India]

Sharma, D. P. Explaining Poverty in India. *Margin*, January 1985, *17*(2), pp. 47–59.
[G: India]

Sidorova, M. Reducing Differences in the Living Standards of the Urban and Rural Population. *Prob. Econ.*, September 1985, *28*(5), pp. 32–47. [G: U.S.S.R.]

Srinivasan, T. N. Agriculture Production, Relative Prices, Entitlements, and Poverty. In *Mellor, J. W. and Desai, G. M., eds.*, 1985, pp. 41–53. [G: LDCs]

Stevens, Yvette. Improved Technologies for Rural Women: Problems and Prospects in Sierra Leone. In *Ahmed, I., ed.*, 1985, pp. 284–326.
[G: Sierra Leone]

Strout, Alan M. Managing the Agricultural Transformation on Java: A Review of the *Survey Agro Ekonomi. Bull. Indonesian Econ. Stud.*, April 1985, *21*(1), pp. 62–80. [G: Indonesia]

Svetanant, Prapant. Rural Non-farm Activities in Thailand: Comparative Case Studies in Irrigated and Rainfed Areas in the Northeast. In *Mukhopadhyay, S. and Chee, P. L., eds. (II)*, 1985, pp. 75–115. [G: Thailand]

Thakur, D. S. A Survey of Literature on Rural Poverty in India. *Margin*, April 1985, *17*(3), pp. 32–49. [G: India]

Thingalaya, N. K. Rural Financing: Syndicate Bank's Experience. In *Bandyopadhyay, R. and Khankhoje, D. P., eds.*, 1985, pp. 153–59.
[G: India]

Travers, S. Lee. Getting Rich through Diligence: Peasant Income after the Reforms. In *Perry, E. J. and Wong, C., eds.*, 1985, pp. 111–30.
[G: China]

Uphoff, Norman. Fitting Projects to People. In *Cernea, M. M., ed.*, 1985, pp. 359–95.
[G: Ghana; Mexico; Nepal; Sri Lanka]

Vail, David. Revitalizing Rural Communities or Reviving Agrarian Myths? A Comment [A Geobased National Agricultural Policy for Rural Community Enhancement, Environmental Vitality, and Income Stabilization]. *J. Econ. Issues*, December 1985, *19*(4), pp. 995–1003.
[G: U.S.]

Van Kooten, G. C. and Arthur, Louise M. The Theory of the Farm Household: An Application to Saskatchewan. *Can. J. Agr. Econ.*, March 1985, *33*(1), pp. 23–35. [G: Canada]

Van Sant, Jerry and Crawford, Paul R. Implementing Rural Development Projects: Coping with Political, Economic, Environmental, and Institutional Constraints. In *Morss, E. R. and Gow, D. D., eds.*, 1985, pp. 1–32.
[G: LDCs]

Ventura-Dias, Vivianne. Modernisation, Production Organisation and Rural Women in Kenya. In *Ahmed, I., ed.*, 1985, pp. 157–210.
[G: Kenya]

Vyas, Vijay Shankar. Poverty, Agrarian Structure, and Policy Options: A Note. In *Mellor, J. W.*

and Desai, G. M., eds., 1985, pp. 186–91.
[G: India; LDCs]

Walker, Thomas S. and Kshirsagar, K. G. The Village Impact of Machine Threshing and Implications for Technology Development in the Semi-arid Tropics of Peninsular India. *J. Devel. Stud.*, January 1985, *21*(2), pp. 215–31.
[G: India]

van de Walle, Dominique. Population Growth and Poverty: Another Look at the Indian Time Series Data. *J. Devel. Stud.*, April 1985, *21*(3), pp. 429–39. [G: India]

Weekes-Vagliani, Winifred. Women, Food and Rural Development. In *Rose, T., ed.*, 1985, pp. 104–10. [G: Sub-Saharan Africa]

Whitehead, Ann. Effects of Technological Change on Rural Women: A Review of Analysis and Concepts. In *Ahmed, I., ed.*, 1985, pp. 27–64. [G: LDCs]

Whyte, William Foote. Working with Small Farmers and Agricultural Cooperatives in Latin America. In *Bergmann, T. and Ogura, T. B., eds.*, 1985, pp. 153–68.
[G: Latin America]

Wickramasekara, Piyasiri. An Evaluation of Policies and Programmes for the Alleviation of Poverty in Sri Lanka. In *Islam, R., ed.*, 1985, pp. 243–86. [G: Sri Lanka]

Wignaraja, Ponna. Towards a New Praxis of Rural Development. *Ann. Pub. Co-op. Econ.*, January–June 1985, *56*(1–2), pp. 121–43.
[G: LDCs]

Wright, Marcia. Iron and Regional History: Report on a Research Project in Southwestern Tanzania. *African Econ. Hist.*, 1985, *14*, pp. 147–65. [G: Tanzania]

Wunder, Heide. Peasant Organization and Class Conflict in Eastern and Western Germany. In *Aston, T. H. and Philpin, C. H. E., eds.*, 1985, pp. 91–100. [G: W. Germany]

Yang, Donghyu. The Parker–Gallman Sample and Wealth Distributions for the Antebellum South: A Reply [Notes on the Wealth Distribution of Farm Households in the United States, 1860: A New Look at Two Manuscript Census Samples]. *Exploration Econ. Hist.*, April 1985, *22*(2), pp. 227–32. [G: U.S.]

720 NATURAL RESOURCES

7200 General

Aida, Shuhei. A Concept of Eco-technology: Technological Approaches to Complexity. In *Aida, S., et al.*, 1985, pp. 245–51.

Brouwer, Floor; Hafkamp, Wim and Nijkamp, Peter. Achievements in Modeling Environmental and Resource Issues. *Ricerche Econ.*, Oct.-Dec. 1985, *39*(4), pp. 491–515.

Gerelli, Emilio. Entropy and "The End of the World." *Ricerche Econ.*, Oct.-Dec. 1985, *39*(4), pp. 435–38.

Hägerstrand, Torsten. Time-Geography: Focus on the Corporeality of Man, Society, and Environment. In *Aida, S., et al.*, 1985, pp. 193–216.

Morey, Edward R. Desertification from an Economic Perspective. *Ricerche Econ.*, Oct.-Dec. 1985, *39*(4), pp. 550–60.

Southgate, Douglas and Runge, Carlisle Ford. Toward an Economic Model of Deforestation and Social Change in Amazonia. *Ricerche Econ.*, Oct.-Dec. 1985, *39*(4), pp. 561–67.
[G: S. America]

Swaney, James A. Economics, Ecology, and Entropy. *J. Econ. Issues*, December 1985, *19*(4), pp. 853–65.

721 Natural Resources

7210 General

Abrams, Burton A. The Expansion of Fishery Jurisdiction: Fishery Interests and Congressional Voting. *Marine Resource Econ.*, 1985, *2*(2), pp. 143–52. [G: U.S.]

Acheson, James M. The Maine Lobster Market: Between Market and Hierarchy. *J. Law, Econ., Organ.*, Fall 1985, *1*(2), pp. 385–98.
[G: U.S.]

Al-Qunaibet, Mohammad H. and Johnston, Richard S. Municipal Demand for Water in Kuwait: Methodological Issues and Empirical Results. *Water Resources Res.*, April 1985, *21*(4), pp. 433–38. [G: Kuwait]

Allen, Julia C. Wood Energy and Preservation of Woodlands in Semi-arid Developing Countries: The Case of Dodoma Region, Tanzania. *J. Devel. Econ.*, Sept.-Oct. 1985, *19*(1/2), pp. 59–84. [G: Tanzania]

Amigues, Jean-Pierre. Ressource épuisable contre ressource renouvelable: le cas du gravier et du vin dans le Bordelais. (Exhaustible Resources versus Non Exhaustible Resources: The Case of Gravel and Vineyard in the Bordelais. With English summary.) *L'Actual. Econ.*, March 1985, *61*(1), pp. 5–23. [G: France]

Anderson, James L. Market Interactions between Aquaculture and the Common-Property Commercial Fishery. *Marine Resource Econ.*, 1985, *2*(1), pp. 1–24. [G: U.S.]

Anderson, James L. Private Aquaculture and Commercial Fisheries: Bioeconomics of Salmon Ranching. *J. Environ. Econ. Manage.*, December 1985, *12*(4), pp. 353–70.

Anderson, Lee G. Potential Economic Benefits from Gear Restrictions and License Limitation in Fisheries Regulation. *Land Econ.*, November 1985, *61*(4), pp. 409–18.

Anderson, Lee G. The Economical Management of Multispecies Fisheries: Comment. *Land Econ.*, August 1985, *61*(3), pp. 319–22.

Anderson, Terry L. Reforming Resource Policy: Toward Free Market Environmentalism. In *Boaz, D. and Crane, E. H., eds.*, 1985, pp. 247–71. [G: U.S.]

Anderson, Terry L. The Market Alternative for Hawaiian Water. *Natural Res. J.*, October 1985, *25*(4), pp. 893–910. [G: U.S.]

Arrow, Kenneth J. and Chang, Sheldon. Optimal Pricing, Use, and Exploration of Uncertain Natural Resource Stocks. In *Arrow, K. J. (II)*, 1985, pp. 255–66.

Babiker, A. A.; Musnad, H. A. and Shaddad, M. Z. Wood Resources and Their Use in the Nuba Mountains. In *Davies, H. R. J., ed.,* 1985, pp. 30–59. **[G: Sudan]**

Baldwin, G. B. The Appraisal of Rural Water Supplies: Reply [Why Present Value Calculations Should Not Be Used in Choosing Rural Water Supply Technology]. *World Devel.,* Oct./Nov. 1985, *13*(10/11), pp. 1179–80. **[G: LDCs]**

Basberg, Bjørn L. Technological Transformation in the Norwegian Whaling Industry in the Interwar Period. *Scand. Econ. Hist. Rev.,* 1985, *33*(2), pp. 83–107. **[G: Norway]**

Batten, David F. and Lesse, Paul F. Modelling the Supply–Demand Dynamics of a Slowly Renewable Resource. In *Batten, D. F. and Lesse, P. F., eds.,* 1985, pp. 69–83.

Bentick, B. L. The Impact of the Fires on South Australian State Forests. In *Healey, D. T.; Jarrett, F. G. and McKay, J. M., eds.,* 1985, pp. 132–49. **[G: Australia]**

Berck, Peter and Bible, Thomas. Wood Products Futures Markets and the Reservation Price of Timber. *J. Futures Markets,* Fall 1985, *5*(3), pp. 311–16. **[G: U.S.]**

Berck, Peter and Perloff, Jeffrey M. The Commons as a Natural Barrier to Entry: Why There Are So Few Fish Farms. *Amer. J. Agr. Econ.,* May 1985, *67*(2), pp. 360–63.

Boserup, Ester. The Primary Sector in African Development. In *Lundahl, M., ed.,* 1985, pp. 56–65. **[G: Africa]**

Boskin, Michael J., et al. New Estimates of the Value of Federal Mineral Rights and Land. *Amer. Econ. Rev.,* December 1985, *75*(5), pp. 923–36. **[G: U.S.]**

Bowen, R. L. and Young, Robert A. Financial and Economic Irrigation Net Benefit Functions for Egypt's Northern Delta. *Water Resources Res.,* September 1985, *21*(9), pp. 1329–35. **[G: Egypt]**

Bowes, Michael D. and Krutilla, John V. Multiple Use Management of Public Forestlands. In *Kneese, A. V. and Sweeney, J. L., eds. Vol. 2,* 1985, pp. 531–69. **[G: U.S.]**

Boyd, Roy and Daniels, Barbara J. Capital Gains Treatment of Timber Income: Incidence and Welfare Implications. *Land Econ.,* November 1985, *61*(4), pp. 354–62. **[G: U.S.]**

Bradbury, J. J. International Movements and Crises in Resource Oriented Companies: The case of INCO in the Nickel Sector. *Econ. Geogr.,* April 1985, *61*(2), pp. 129–43. **[G: Canada; Guatemala; Indonesia]**

Braden, John B. Uncertainty and Open Access: Implications from the Repeated Prisoners' Dilemma Game. *Amer. J. Agr. Econ.,* May 1985, *67*(2), pp. 356–59.

Bradley, Paul G. Has the 'Economics of Exhaustible Resources' Advanced the Economics of Mining? In *Scott, A., ed.,* 1985, pp. 317–29. **[G: Canada]**

Brennan, Michael J. and Schwartz, Eduardo S. Evaluating Natural Resource Investments. *J. Bus.,* April 1985, *58*(2), pp. 135–57. **[G: U.S.]**

Bresnahan, Timothy F. and Suslow, Valerie Y. Inventories as an Asset: The Volatility of Copper Prices. *Int. Econ. Rev.,* June 1985, *26*(2), pp. 409–24. **[G: U.K.]**

Bromley, Daniel W. Resources and Economic Development: An Institutionalist Perspective. *J. Econ. Issues,* September 1985, *19*(3), pp. 779–96.

Brookshire, David S.; Watts, Gary L. and Merrill, James L. Current Issues in the Quantification of Federal Reserved Water Rights. *Water Resources Res.,* November 1985, *21*(11), pp. 1777–84. **[G: U.S.]**

Brown, Gardner, Jr. Has the 'Economics of Exhaustible Resources' Advanced the Economics of Mining?: Comment. In *Scott, A., ed.,* 1985, pp. 329–33. **[G: Canada]**

Brown, Martin. Price Prospects for Some Leading Mineral Exports. In *Rose, T., ed.,* 1985, pp. 149–54. **[G: Sub-Saharan Africa]**

Bruggink, Thomas H. Monopoly Pricing as a Consumer Exaction in the Public Utility Sector: Monopoly Welfare Loss and Regulation in the Municipal Water Industry. *Amer. J. Econ. Soc.,* April 1985, *44*(2), pp. 229–39. **[G: U.S.]**

Burn, Donald H. and McBean, Edward A. Optimization Modeling of Water Quality in an Uncertain Environment. *Water Resources Res.,* July 1985, *21*(7), pp. 934–40. **[G: Canada]**

Cairns, Robert D. Nickel Depletion and Pricing: Further Considerations [User Costs versus Markups as Determinants of Prices in the Nickel Industry: Reply]. *J. Environ. Econ. Manage.,* December 1985, *12*(4), pp. 395–96. **[G: U.S.]**

Cairns, Robert D. Reform of Exhaustible Resource Taxation. *Can. Public Policy,* December 1985, *11*(4), pp. 649–58.

Campbell, Harry F. and Lindner, R. K. A Model of Mineral Exploration and Resource Taxation. *Econ. J.,* March 1985, *95*(377), pp. 146–60.

Campbell, Harry F. and Lindner, R. K. Mineral Exploration and the Neutrality of Rent Royalties. *Econ. Rec.,* March 1985, *61*(172), pp. 445–49.

Campbell, Harry F. and Wrean, Douglas L. Deriving the Long-run Supply Curve for a Competitive Mining Industry: The Case of Saskatchewan Uranium. In *Scott, A., ed.,* 1985, pp. 290–309. **[G: Canada]**

Caponera, Dante A. Patterns of Cooperation in International Water Law: Principles and Institutions. *Natural Res. J.,* July 1985, *25*(3), pp. 563–87. **[G: Global]**

Cassing, James H. and Warr, Peter G. The Distributional Impact of a Resource Boom. *J. Int. Econ.,* May 1985, *18*(3/4), pp. 301–19.

Caswell, Margriet and Zilberman, David. The Choice of Irrigation Technologies in California. *Amer. J. Agr. Econ.,* May 1985, *67*(2), pp. 224–34. **[G: U.S.]**

Cernea, Michael M. Alternative Units of Social Organization Sustaining Afforestation Strategies. In *Cernea, M. M., ed.*, 1985, pp. 267–93. [G: Pakistan; Selected LDCs]

Charles, Anthony T. and Munro, Gordon R. Irreversible Investment and Optimal Fisheries Management: A Stochastic Analysis. *Marine Resource Econ.*, 1985, *1*(3), pp. 247–64.

Chasis, Sarah. The Coastal Zone Management Act: A Protective Mandate. *Natural Res. J.*, January 1985, *25*(1), pp. 21–30. [G: U.S.]

Ciriacy-Wantrup, S. V. Benefit–Cost Analysis and Public Resource Development. In *Ciriacy-Wantrup, S. V.*, 1985, pp. 135–47.

Ciriacy-Wantrup, S. V. "Common Property" as a Concept in Natural Resources Policy. In *Ciriacy-Wantrup, S. V.*, 1985, pp. 25–37.
[G: U.S.]

Ciriacy-Wantrup, S. V. Conceptual Problems in Projecting the Demand for Land and Water. In *Ciriacy-Wantrup, S. V.*, 1985, pp. 149–75.
[G: U.S.]

Ciriacy-Wantrup, S. V. Cost Allocation in Relation to Western Water Policies. In *Ciriacy-Wantrup, S. V.*, 1985, pp. 177–97. [G: U.S.]

Ciriacy-Wantrup, S. V. Criteria and Conditions for Public and Private Ownership of Range Resources. In *Ciriacy-Wantrup, S. V.*, 1985, pp. 51–57.
[G: U.S.]

Ciriacy-Wantrup, S. V. Multiple Use as a Concept for Water and Range Policy. In *Ciriacy-Wantrup, S. V.*, 1985, pp. 277–88. [G: U.S.]

Ciriacy-Wantrup, S. V. Natural Resources in Economic Growth: The Role of Institutions and Policies. In *Ciriacy-Wantrup, S. V.*, 1985, pp. 293–304. [G: India]

Ciriacy-Wantrup, S. V. Philosophy and Objectives of Watershed Policy. In *Ciriacy-Wantrup, S. V.*, 1985, pp. 105–16.

Ciriacy-Wantrup, S. V. The Economics of Environmental Policy. In *Ciriacy-Wantrup, S. V.*, 1985, pp. 39–50.

Ciriacy-Wantrup, S. V. Water Economics: Relations to Law and Policy. In *Ciriacy-Wantrup, S. V.*, 1985, pp. 77–103. [G: U.S.]

Ciriacy-Wantrup, S. V. Water Policy and Economic Optimizing: Some Conceptual Problems in Water Research. In *Ciriacy-Wantrup, S. V.*, 1985, pp. 67–76. [G: U.S.]

Ciriacy-Wantrup, S. V. Water Quality, a Problem for the Economist. In *Ciriacy-Wantrup, S. V.*, 1985, pp. 117–28.

Clark, Colin W. Modelling Fishermen and Regulator Behaviour in Schooling and Search Fisheries: Comment. In *Scott, A., ed.*, 1985, pp. 171–72.

Clark, Colin W. The Effect of Fishermen's Quotas on Expected Catch Rates. *Marine Resource Econ.*, 1985, *1*(4), pp. 419–27.

Clark, Colin W.; Munro, Gordon R. and Charles, Anthony T. Fisheries, Dynamics, and Uncertainty. In *Scott, A., ed.*, 1985, pp. 99–120.

Clark, Colin W., et al. Optimal Capacity Decisions in a Developing Fishery. *Marine Resource Econ.*, 1985, *2*(1), pp. 25–53.
[G: Australia]

Coate, Roger A. The International Seabed Authority: Progressive Development or Creative

Camouflage? In *Jordan, R. S., ed.*, 1985, pp. 99–131.

Cochran, Richard and Cotton, Arthur W. Municipal Water Demand Study, Oklahoma City and Tulsa, Oklahoma. *Water Resources Res.*, July 1985, *21*(7), pp. 941–43. [G: U.S.]

Conrad, Jon M. Management of a Multiple Cohort Fishery: Reply. *Amer. J. Agr. Econ.*, August 1985, *67*(3), pp. 676–78. [G: U.S.]

Conrad, Robert F. and Gillis, Malcolm. Progress and Poverty in Developing Countries: Rents and Resource Taxation. In *Lewis, S. R., Jr., ed.*, 1985, pp. 25–47.

Contant, Cheryl K. and Ortolano, Leonard. Evaluating a Cumulative Impact Assessment Approach. *Water Resources Res.*, September 1985, *21*(9), pp. 1313–18. [G: U.S.]

Copes, Parzival. The Market as a Commons: Open Access vs. Price Adjustment. *De Economist*, 1985, *133*(2), pp. 225–31.

Copithorne, Lawrence; MacFadyen, Alan and Bell, Bruce. Revenue Sharing and the Efficient Valuation of Natural Resources. *Can. Public Policy*, Supplement July 1985, *11*(3), pp. 465–78. [G: Canada]

Cory, Dennis C. and Martin, William E. Valuing Wildlife for Efficient Multiple Use: Elk versus Cattle. *Western J. Agr. Econ.*, December 1985, *10*(2), pp. 282–93. [G: U.S.]

Crabbe, Philippe J. Turgot's *Brief on Mines and Quaries:* An Early Economic Analysis of Mineral Land Tenure. *Natural Res. J.*, April 1985, *25*(2), pp. 267–73. [G: France]

Crommelin, Michael. The Mineral Exploration and Production Regime within the Federal System. In *Drysdale, P. and Shibata, H., eds.*, 1985, pp. 90–104. [G: Australia]

Crouch, Glen J. and Skowronski, Janislaw M. Identification of Stock and System Parameters in a Pareto Harvesting Game of Two Players. In *Batten, D. F. and Lesse, P. F., eds.*, 1985, pp. 105–16.

Crutchfield, Stephen R. The Impact of Groundfish Imports on the United States Fishing Industry: An Empirical Analysis. *Can. J. Agr. Econ.*, July 1985, *33*(2), pp. 195–207.
[G: U.S.]

Crutchfield, Stephen R. and Gates, John M. The Impact of Extended Fishery Jurisdiction on the New England Otter Trawl Fleet. *Marine Resource Econ.*, 1985, *2*(2), pp. 153–73.
[G: U.S.]

Cuddy, John D. A. Commodity Trade. In *Preeg, E. H., ed.*, 1985, pp. 117–33. [G: LDCs; U.S.]

Cummings, Ronald G. The Contemporary Setting for Water Management in the West: An Overview. *Water Resources Res.*, November 1985, *21*(11), pp. 1749–50. [G: U.S.]

Dacey, Robert J. Public Works and Their Impacts on Infrastructure and the National Economy. In *Konecci, E. B. and Kuhn, R. L., eds.*, 1985, pp. 134–41. [G: U.S.]

Dandy, G. C. An Approximate Method for the Analysis of Uncertainty in Benefit–Cost Ratios.

Water Resources Res., March 1985, *21*(3), pp. 267–71. **[G: U.S.]**

Daniel, Philip. Minerals in Sub-Saharan Africa— Problems and Prospects. **In** *Rose, T., ed.*, 1985, pp. 145–48. **[G: Sub-Saharan Africa]**

Dasgupta, Partha. Evolution of Market Structure in a Dominant Firm Model with Exhaustible Resources: Comment. **In** *Scott, A., ed.*, 1985, pp. 257–59.

Dasgupta, Partha. Resource Allocation Rules and Long-Range Planning: Comment. **In** *Scott, A., ed.*, 1985, pp. 150–52.

Davison, Robert. A Note on Robert S. Pindyck's Paper "The Optimal Production of an Exhaustible Resource When Price Is Exogenous and Stochastic." *Scand. J. Econ.*, 1985, *87*(4), pp. 673–76.

Deacon, Robert T. The Simple Analytics of Forest Economics. **In** *Deacon, R. T. and Johnson, M. B., eds.*, 1985, pp. 275–302. **[G: U.S.]**

Deacon, Robert T. and Johnson, M. Bruce. For-estlands: Public and Private: Introduction. **In** *Deacon, R. T. and Johnson, M. B., eds.*, 1985, pp. 1–22. **[G: U.S.]**

Deshmukh, Sudhakar D. and Pliska, Stanley R. A Martingale Characterization of the Price of a Nonrenewable Resource with Decisions Involving Uncertainty. *J. Econ. Theory*, April 1985, *35*(2), pp. 322–42.

DeVoretz, Don and Schwindt, Richard. Harvesting Canadian Fish and Rents: A Partial Review of the Report of the Commission on Canadian Pacific Fisheries Policy. *Marine Resource Econ.*, 1985, *1*(4), pp. 347–67. **[G: Canada]**

Dick, Rolf. Deep-Sea Mining versus Land-Based Mining: A Cost Comparison. **In** *Donges, J. B., ed.*, 1985, pp. 2–60. **[G: U.S.]**

Dnes', Antony W. Rent Seeking Behaviour and Open Access Fishing. *Scot. J. Polit. Econ.*, June 1985, *32*(2), pp. 159–70.

Dowdle, Barney and Hanke, Steve H. Public Timber Policy and the Wood-Products Industry. **In** *Deacon, R. T. and Johnson, M. B., eds.*, 1985, pp. 77–102. **[G: U.S.]**

Driessen, T. S. H. and Tijs, Stef H. The Cost Gap Method and Other Cost Allocation Methods for Multipurpose Water Projects. *Water Resources Res.*, October 1985, *21*(10), pp. 1469–75.

Drynan, Ross G. and Sandiford, Frances. Incorporating Economic Objectives in Goal Programs for Fishery Management. *Marine Resource Econ.*, 1985, *2*(2), pp. 175–95. **[G: U.K.]**

Drysdale, Peter. Federalism and Resource Development: The Australian Case: Summary and Comment. **In** *Drysdale, P. and Shibata, H., eds.*, 1985, pp. 218–41. **[G: Australia]**

Drysdale, Peter and Shibata, Hirofumi. Federalism and Resource Development: The Australian Case: Perspectives. **In** *Drysdale, P. and Shibata, H., eds.*, 1985, pp. 15–24. **[G: Australia]**

DuMars, Charles T. The State as a Participant of Water Markets: Appropriate Roles for Congress and the Courts. *Water Resources Res.*,

November 1985, *21*(11), pp. 1771–75. **[G: U.S.]**

Dunstan, G. Sources and Uses of Bushfire Appeal Funds. **In** *Healey, D. T.; Jarrett, F. G. and McKay, J. M., eds.*, 1985, pp. 41–56. **[G: Australia]**

Ehrnrooth, Gay. Skogsindustrins synvinkel. (The Viewpoint of the Forest Industry. With English summary.) *Ekon. Samfundets Tidskr.*, 1985, *38*(4), pp. 189–90. **[G: Finland]**

Ellis, John R.; Lacewell, Ronald D. and Reneau, Duane R. Estimated Economic Impact from Adoption of Water-Related Agricultural Technology. *Western J. Agr. Econ.*, December 1985, *10*(2), pp. 307–21. **[G: U.S.]**

Epple, Dennis. The Econometrics of Exhaustible Resource Supply: A Theory and an Application. **In** *Sargent, T. J., ed.*, 1985, pp. 143–200. **[G: U.S.]**

Ervasti, Seppo. Metsä 2000 -ohjelma—Suomen metsä- ja puutalouden kehittämisen suuntaviivat. (The Forest 2000 Programme—Guidelines for the Development of Finnish Forestry and Forest Industry. With English summary.) *Kansant. Aikak.*, 1985, *81*(2), pp. 171–76. **[G: Finland]**

Eswaran, Mukesh and Lewis, Tracy R. Evolution of Market Structure in a Dominant Firm Model with Exhaustible Resources. **In** *Scott, A., ed.*, 1985, pp. 242–57.

Eswaran, Mukesh and Lewis, Tracy R. Exhaustible Resources and Alternative Equilibrium Concepts. *Can. J. Econ.*, August 1985, *18*(3), pp. 459–73.

Faber, Malte and Proops, John L. R. Interdisciplinary Research between Economists and Physical Scientists: Retrospect and Prospect. *Kyklos*, 1985, *38*(4), pp. 599–616.

Farrow, Scott. Testing the Efficiency of Extraction from a Stock Resource. *J. Polit. Econ.*, June 1985, *93*(3), pp. 452–87. **[G: U.S.]**

Fedra, Kurt. A Modular Interactive Simulation System for Eutrophication and Regional Development. *Water Resources Res.*, February 1985, *21*(2), pp. 143–52. **[G: Austria]**

Feitel'man, N. The Management of Natural Resource Utilization. *Prob. Econ.*, January 1985, *27*(9), pp. 62–80. **[G: U.S.S.R.]**

Field, Barry C. The Optimal Commons. *Amer. J. Agr. Econ.*, May 1985, *67*(2), pp. 364–67.

Finnell, Gilbert L., Jr. Intergovernmental Relationships in Coastal Land Management. *Natural Res. J.*, January 1985, *25*(1), pp. 31–60. **[G: U.S.]**

Flåm, Sjur D. and Stensland, Gunnar. Exploration and Taxation: Some Normative Issues. *Energy Econ.*, October 1985, *7*(4), pp. 237–40. **[G: Norway]**

Fodella, Gianni. De-centralization of Economic Activity for Local Resource Development. *Rivista Int. Sci. Econ. Com.*, February 1985, *32*(2), pp. 183–95. **[G: OECD; LDCs]**

Foders, Federico. Who Gains from Deep-Sea Mining? **In** *Donges, J. B., ed.*, 1985, pp. 336–69. **[G: Selected Countries]**

Forkosch, Morris D. Halt the New Satellite Giveaway. *Amer. J. Econ. Soc.*, April 1985, *44*(2), pp. 196–98.   [G: U.S.]

Freeman, A. Myrick, III. Supply Uncertainty, Option Price, and Option Value. *Land Econ.*, May 1985, *61*(2), pp. 176–81.

Freeman, A. Myrick, III. The Sign and Size of Option Value: Reply. *Land Econ.*, February 1985, *61*(1), pp. 78.

Gale, James R. and Merz, Thomas E. The Opportunity Cost of an Abundant Resource: The Case of Water Diverted from the Great Lakes to the Ogallala Aquifer Region. *Reg. Sci. Persp.*, 1985, *15*(1), pp. 3–12.   [G: U.S.]

Gale, Richard P. Federal Management of Forests and Marine Fisheries: A Comparative Analysis of Renewable Resource Management. *Natural Res. J.*, April 1985, *25*(2), pp. 275–315.
                                                    [G: U.S.]

Gamponia, Villamor and Mendelsohn, Robert. The Taxation of Exhaustible Resources. *Quart. J. Econ.*, February 1985, *100*(1), pp. 165–81.
                                                    [G: U.S.]

Gardner, B. Delworth. Forestlands: Public and Private: Foreword. In *Deacon, R. T. and Johnson, M. B., eds.*, 1985, pp. xix–xxvii.

Gardner, Richard L. and Young, Robert A. An Economic Evaluation of the Colorado River Basin Salinity Control Program. *Western J. Agr. Econ.*, July 1985, *10*(1), pp. 1–12. [G: U.S.]

Gilley, Otis W.; Karels, Gordon V. and Lyon, Randolph M. Joint Ventures and Offshore Oil Lease Sales. *Econ. Inquiry*, April 1985, *23*(2), pp. 321–39.   [G: U.S.]

Giuliano, Giuseppe and Spaziani, F. M. Water Use Statistics in Industry. Experiences from Regional Surveys and Planning Studies in Italy. *Statist. J.*, May 1985, *3*(2), pp. 229–45.
                                                    [G: Italy]

Goldie, L. F. E. Equity and the International Management of Transboundary Resources. *Natural Res. J.*, July 1985, *25*(3), pp. 665–99.
                                                    [G: Global]

Goldman, Marshall I. Economics of Environment and Renewable Resources in Socialist Systems: Russia. In *Kneese, A. V. and Sweeney, J. L., eds. Vol. 2*, 1985, pp. 725–45. [G: U.S.S.R.]

Gordon, Scott and Stegemann, Klaus. The Market as a Commons: Is Catching Customers Like Catching Fish? *De Economist*, 1985, *133*(2), pp. 218–24.

Griffin, Ronald C. and Perry, Gregory M. Volumetric Pricing of Agricultural Water Supplies: A Case Study. *Water Resources Res.*, July 1985, *21*(7), pp. 944–50.   [G: U.S.]

Grobey, John H. Politics versus Bioeconomics: Salmon Fishery and Forestry Values in Conflict. In *Deacon, R. T. and Johnson, M. B., eds.*, 1985, pp. 169–200.   [G: U.S.]

Gross, Amnon and Zahavi, Jacob. Evaluating Alternative Investment Programs for the Mediterranean–Dead Sea Project. *Water Resources Res.*, July 1985, *21*(7), pp. 905–16. [G: U.S.]

Gunnarsson, Christer. Growth and Stagnation in the Malaysian Rubber Smallholder Industry. In *Lundahl, M., ed.*, 1985, pp. 152–78.
                                                    [G: Malaysia]

Guruswamy, Lakshman. Environmental Management in a North Sea Coastal Zone: Law, Institutions and Policy. *Natural Res. J.*, January 1985, *25*(1), pp. 233–42.   [G: U.K.; W. Germany]

Gutman, Pablo. Teoría económica y problemática ambiental: un diálogo difícil. (With English summary.) *Desarrollo Econ.*, April–June 1985, *25*(97), pp. 46–70.

Hakogi, Masumi. Trade Restrictions and Trade Promotion: Comments. In *Saunders, C. T., ed.*, 1985, pp. 309–12.   [G: CMEA; OECD]

Haley, David L. The Forest Tenure System as a Constraint on Efficient Timber Management: Problems and Solutions. *Can. Public Policy*, Supplement July 1985, *11*(3), pp. 315–20.
                                                    [G: Canada]

Hannesson, Rögnvaldur. Inefficiency through Government Regulations: The Case of Norway's Fishery Policy. *Marine Resource Econ.*, 1985, *2*(2), pp. 115–41.   [G: Norway]

Hannesson, Rögnvaldur. The Effects of a Fishermen's Monopoly in the Market for Unprocessed Fish. *Marine Resource Econ.*, 1985, *2*(1), pp. 75–85.

Hansen, Lars Peter; Epple, Dennis and Roberds, William. Linear-Quadratic Duopoly Models of Resource Depletion. In *Sargent, T. J., ed.*, 1985, pp. 101–42.

Harris, Stuart. State and Federal Objectives and Policies for the Use and Development of Resources. In *Drysdale, P. and Shibata, H., eds.*, 1985, pp. 67–89.   [G: Australia]

Harrison, Craig S. A Marine Sanctuary in the Northwestern Hawaiian Islands: An Idea Whose Time Has Come. *Natural Res. J.*, April 1985, *25*(2), pp. 317–47.   [G: U.S.]

Hassan, J. A. The Growth and Impact of the British Water Industry in the Nineteenth Century. *Econ. Hist. Rev., 2nd Ser.*, November 1985, *38*(4), pp. 531–47.   [G: U.K.]

Hatch, J. H. and Jarrett, F. G. The Economics of Fire Control/Suppression. In *Healey, D. T.; Jarrett, F. G. and McKay, J. M., eds.*, 1985, pp. 89–115.   [G: Australia]

Healey, Derek T. The Economics of Bushfires: The South Australian Experience: Introduction. In *Healey, D. T.; Jarrett, F. G. and McKay, J. M., eds.*, 1985, pp. 1–13.
                                                    [G: Australia]

Heaps, Terry. The Taxation of Nonreplenishable Natural Resources Revisited. *J. Environ. Econ. Manage.*, March 1985, *12*(1), pp. 14–27.

Heaps, Terry and Helliwell, John F. The Taxation of Natural Resources. In *Auerbach, A. J. and Feldstein, M., eds.*, 1985, pp. 421–72.

Hecht, Susanna B. Environment, Development and Politics: Capital Accumulation and the Livestock Sector in Eastern Amazonia. *World Devel.*, June 1985, *13*(6), pp. 663–84.
                                                    [G: Brazil]

Herrick, Christopher and Jordan, Robert S. United States Policy and the Management of Marine Minerals. In *Jordan, R. S., ed.*, 1985, pp. 133–50.   [G: U.S.]

Hertel, Thomas W. and Mount, Timothy D. The

Pricing of Natural Resources in a Regional Economy. *Land Econ.*, August 1985, *61*(3), pp. 229–43. [G: U.S.]

Hildreth, Richard G. and Johnson, Ralph W. CZM in California, Oregon, and Washington. *Natural Res. J.*, January 1985, *25*(1), pp. 103–65. [G: U.S.]

Hillman, Arye L. and Long, Ngo Van. Monopolistic Recycling of Oil Revenue and Intertemporal Bias in Oil Depletion and Trade. *Quart. J. Econ.*, August 1985, *100*(3), pp. 597–624.

Hof, John G.; Marose, Robin K. and King, David A. Potential Pitfalls in Renewable Resource Decision Making That Utilizes Convex Combinations of Discrete Alternatives. *Western J. Agr. Econ.*, December 1985, *10*(2), pp. 391–400.

Hof, John G., et al. An Analysis of Joint Costs in a Managed Forest Ecosystem. *J. Environ. Econ. Manage.*, December 1985, *12*(4), pp. 338–52. [G: U.S.]

Howard, Theodore E. Estate Planning for Nonindustrial Forest Owners. *Land Econ.*, November 1985, *61*(4), pp. 363–71. [G: U.S.]

Howe, Charles W. Natural Resources: Perspectives, Problems and Policy Guidelines. *Ricerche Econ.*, Oct.-Dec. 1985, *39*(4), pp. 439–66. [G: Global]

Hrezo, Margaret S. and Hrezo, William E. From Antagonist to Cooperative Federalism on Water Resources Development: A Model for Reconciling Federal, State, and Local Programs, Policies, and Planning. *Amer. J. Econ. Soc.*, April 1985, *44*(2), pp. 199–214. [G: U.S.]

Hsiao, Yu-Mong. Management of a Multiple Cohort Fishery: Comment. *Amer. J. Agr. Econ.*, August 1985, *67*(3), pp. 674–75. [G: U.S.]

Johansson, Per-Olov and Löfgren, Karl-Gustaf. A Bargaining Approach to the Modeling of the Swedish Roundwood Market. *Land Econ.*, February 1985, *61*(1), pp. 65–75.

Johnson, David. The Short-term Economic Effects of Environmental Constraints on Forest Industries. *Rev. Marketing Agr. Econ.*, December 1985, *53*(3), pp. 149–56. [G: Australia]

Johnson, Ronald N. Restraint under Open Access: Are Voluntary Incentives Sufficient or Is Coercion Required?: Discussion. *Amer. J. Agr. Econ.*, May 1985, *67*(2), pp. 373–76.

Johnson, Ronald N. U.S. Forest Service Policy and Its Budget. In *Deacon, R. T. and Johnson, M. B., eds.*, 1985, pp. 103–33. [G: U.S.]

Jordan, Robert S. Conclusions: The Global Interest or the National Interest: Must They Lead to Conflict or Can They Lead to Cooperation? In *Jordan, R. S., ed.*, 1985, pp. 151–66.

Just, Richard E. and Zilberman, David. Income Distributional Implications of Water Policy Decisions. *Western J. Agr. Econ.*, December 1985, *10*(2), pp. 170–82.

Kabir, M. and Ridler, N. B. The Demand for Atlantic Salmon in Canada: Reply. *Can. J. Agr. Econ.*, July 1985, *33*(2), pp. 247–49. [G: Canada]

Kahn, James R. and Kemp, W. Michael. Eco-

nomic Losses Associated with the Degradation of an Ecosystem: The Case of Submerged Aquatic Vegetation in Chesapeake Bay. *J. Environ. Econ. Manage.*, September 1985, *12*(3), pp. 246–63. [G: U.S.]

Kaitala, Veijo and Hämäläinen, Raimo. On the Role of Dynamics and Information in International Negotiations: The Case of Fishery Management. In *Grauer, M.; Thompson, M. and Wierzbicki, A. P., eds.*, 1985, pp. 212–21.

Kalt, Joseph P. and Otten, Anthony L. A Note on Nonrenewable Resource Extraction under Discontinuous Price Policy. *J. Environ. Econ. Manage.*, December 1985, *12*(4), pp. 371–81.

Kamien, Morton; Levhari, David and Mirman, Leonard J. Dynamic Model of Fishing: The Relationship to Conjectural Variations. *J. Environ. Econ. Manage.*, December 1985, *12*(4), pp. 308–21.

Karpoff, Jonathan M. Non-pecuniary Benefits in Commercial Fishing: Empirical Findings from the Alaska Salmon Fisheries. *Econ. Inquiry*, January 1985, *23*(1), pp. 159–74. [G: U.S.]

Karpoff, Jonathan M. Time, Capital Intensity, and the Cost of Fishing Effort. *Western J. Agr. Econ.*, December 1985, *10*(2), pp. 254–58.

Kennedy, John and Watkins, Jim. The Impact of Quotas on the Southern Bluefin Tuna Fishery. *Australian J. Agr. Econ.*, April 1985, *29*(1), pp. 63–83. [G: Australia]

Keppler, Horst. Free Access to Supplies versus Restrictive Supply Policies: The Ability of LDCs to Control Commodity Markets. In *Weinblatt, J., ed.*, 1985, pp. 71–115. [G: Selected LDCs]

Koopmans, Tjalling C. Proof for a Case where Discounting Advances the Doomsday. In *Koopmans, T. C.*, 1985, pp. 187–90.

Koopmans, Tjalling C. Some Observations on 'Optimal' Economic Growth and Exhaustible Resources. In *Koopmans, T. C.*, 1985, pp. 163–79.

Koopmans, Tjalling C. The Transition from Exhaustible to Renewable or Inexhaustible Resources. In *Koopmans, T. C.*, 1985, pp. 263–71.

Krautkraemer, Jeffrey A. Optimal Growth, Resource Amenities, and the Preservation of Natural Environments. *Rev. Econ. Stud.*, January 1985, *52*(1), pp. 153–70.

Kuuluvainen, Jari. Sahatukin kysyntä ja tarjonta Suomessa Ekonometrinen lyhyen aikavälin tarkastelu 1962–1981. (Demand for and Supply of Sawlogs in Finland. An Econometric Short Term Analysis, 1962–1981. With English summary.) *Kansant. Aikak.*, 1985, *81*(2), pp. 177–78. [G: Finland]

van de Laar, Aart and Jerve, Alf Morten. Water Supply and Sanitation. In *Jerve, A. M., ed.*, 1985, pp. 347–52. [G: Pakistan]

Landefeld, J. Steven and Hines, James R. National Accounting for Non-renewable Natural Resources in the Mining Industries. *Rev. Income Wealth*, March 1985, *31*(1), pp. 1–20. [G: U.S.]

Landry, Stephanie. State Immunity from the

Dormant Commerce Clause: Extension of the Market-Participant Doctrine from State Purchase and Sale of Goods and Services to Natural Resources. *Natural Res. J.*, April 1985, 25(2), pp. 515–46. **[G: U.S.]**

Lasserre, Pierre. Capacity Choice by Mines. *Can. J. Econ.*, November 1985, 18(4), pp. 831–42. **[G: Canada]**

Lasserre, Pierre. Discovery Costs as a Measure of Rent. *Can. J. Econ.*, August 1985, 18(3), pp. 474–83. **[G: Canada]**

Lasserre, Pierre. Exhaustible Resource Extraction with Capital. In *Scott, A., ed.*, 1985, pp. 176–95.

Lee, D. Q. Insurance Aspects of Bushfire Disaster in South Australia. In *Healey, D. T.; Jarrett, F. G. and McKay, J. M., eds.*, 1985, pp. 57–73. **[G: Australia]**

Lemeshev, M. Ia. Scientific-Technical Progress and Nature. *Prob. Econ.*, July 1985, 28(3), pp. 18–31.

Lemoine, Pierre H. and Gotsch, Carl H. Water Resource Development in the Salinas Valley: Economics and Hydrology in a Closed Control Model. *Food Res. Inst. Stud.*, 1985, 19(3), pp. 293–333. **[G: U.S.]**

Lewis, H. V. Comments on the Council's View of the Forest Industry. *Can. Public Policy*, Supplement July 1985, 11(3), pp. 310–14. **[G: Canada]**

Lewis, Stephen R., Jr. Progress and Poverty in Developing Countries: Rents and Resource Taxation: Comments. In *Lewis, S. R., Jr., ed.*, 1985, pp. 49–51.

Lewis, Tracy R. A Note on Mining with Investment in Capital [The Effect of Capital Intensity on the Optimal Rate of Extraction of a Mineral Deposit]. *Can. J. Econ.*, August 1985, 18(3), pp. 665–67.

Lewis, Tracy R. and Slade, Margaret E. The Effects of Price Controls, Taxes, and Subsidies on Exhaustible Resource Production. In *Scott, A., ed.*, 1985, pp. 203–27.

Libecap, Gary D. Regulatory Constraints on Oil and Gas Production on Forest Service and BLM Lands. In *Deacon, R. T. and Johnson, M. B., eds.*, 1985, pp. 135–48. **[G: U.S.]**

Lichtenberg, Erik and Zilberman, David. Efficient Regulation of Environmental Health Risks: The Case of Groundwater Contamination in California. *Ricerche Econ.*, Oct.-Dec. 1985, 39(4), pp. 540–49. **[G: U.S.]**

Lin, Biing-Hwan and Williams, Nancy A. The Demand for Atlantic Salmon in Canada: A Comment. *Can. J. Agr. Econ.*, July 1985, 33(2), pp. 243–46. **[G: Canada]**

Loikkanen, Heikki A.; Kuuluvainen, Jari and Salo, Jorma. Hintatekijät ja yksityismetsänomistajien ominaisuudet puuntarjontakäyttäytymisen selittäjinä: alustavia tuloksia. (Stumpage Prices and Owner Characteristics as Determinants of Timber Supply from Private Nonindustrial Forests: Preliminary Evidence form Finland. With English summary.) *Kansant. Aikak.*, 1985, 81(2), pp. 189–216. **[G: Finland]**

Long, Ngo Van and Sinn, Hans-Werner. Surprise Price Shifts, Tax Changes and the Supply Behaviour of Resource Extracting Firms. *Australian Econ. Pap.*, December 1985, 24(45), pp. 278–89.

Loomis, John; Walsh, Richard G. and McKean, John R. The Opportunity Costs of Redwood National Park: Comment and Elaboration. *Contemp. Policy Issues*, Winter 1984-85, 3(2), pp. 103–07. **[G: U.S.]**

Loucks, Daniel P.; Kindler, Janusz and Fedra, Kurt. Interactive Water Resources Modeling and Model Use: An Overview. *Water Resources Res.*, February 1985, 21(2), pp. 95–102.

Lukaszewicz, Aleksander. Trade Restrictions and Trade Promotion: Comments. In *Saunders, C. T., ed.*, 1985, pp. 312–14. **[G: CMEA; OECD]**

Lundahl, Mats. The Primary Sector in Economic Development: Proceedings of the Seventh Arne Ryde Symposium, Frostavallen, August 29–30 1983: Introduction. In *Lundahl, M., ed.*, 1985, pp. 1–39.

Macleod, John D. S. The Mining Industry in the Federal System. In *Drysdale, P. and Shibata, H., eds.*, 1985, pp. 127–39. **[G: Australia]**

Maidment, David R.; Miaou, Shaw-Pin and Crawford, Melba M. Transfer Function Models of Daily Urban Water Use. *Water Resources Res.*, April 1985, 21(4), pp. 425–32. **[G: U.S.]**

Mamalakis, Markos J. The Primary Sector: Composition and Functions. In *Lundahl, M., ed.*, 1985, pp. 43–55.

Mangel, Marc and Plant, Richard E. Regulatory Mechanisms and Information Processing in Uncertain Fisheries. *Marine Resource Econ.*, 1985, 1(4), pp. 389–418.

Manning, Travis W. and Anderson, Wayne. The Repayment of Water Development Costs. *Can. J. Agr. Econ.*, August 1985, 32, pp. 119–32. **[G: Canada]**

Marston, Geoffrey. The Newfoundland Offshore Jurisdictional Dispute—A Postcript. *J. World Trade Law*, July:Aug. 1985, 19(4), pp. 423–25. **[G: Canada]**

Martellaro, Joseph A. Taiwan: A Country Experience in Energy. *Econ. Int.*, Aug./Nov. 1985, 38(3/4), pp. 351–67. **[G: Taiwan]**

Martellaro, Joseph A. Water as a Resource in the Third World. *J. Econ. Devel.*, July 1985, 10(1), pp. 7–28. **[G: LDCs]**

Mashayekhi, Mina. The Present Legal Staus of Deep Sea-Bed Mining. *J. World Trade Law*, May:June 1985, 19(3), pp. 229–50. **[G: Global]**

Mason, Charles F. On Scale Economies and Exhaustible Resource Markets. *Rev. Ind. Organ.*, 1985, 2(2), pp. 144–59.

Masten, Scott E. and Crocker, Keith J. Efficient Adaptation in Long-term Contracts: Take-or-Pay Provisions for Natural Gas. *Amer. Econ. Rev.*, December 1985, 75(5), pp. 1083–93. **[G: U.S.]**

McBain, Helen. Towards a Viable Water Utility

in Jamaica. *Soc. Econ. Stud.*, March 1985, *34*(1), pp. 77–96. [G: Jamaica]

McCarl, Bruce A. and Brokken, Ray F. An Economic Analysis of Alternative Grazing Fee Systems. *Amer. J. Agr. Econ.*, November 1985, *67*(4), pp. 769–78.

McCarl, Bruce A. and Ross, Mark. The Cost Borne by Electricity Consumers under Expanded Irrigation from the Columbia River. *Water Resources Res.*, September 1985, *21*(9), pp. 1319–28.

McKay, Jennifer M. Community Adoption of Bushfire Mitigation Measures in the Adelaide Hills. In *Healey, D. T.; Jarrett, F. G. and McKay, J. M., eds.*, 1985, pp. 116–131. [G: Australia]

McKay, Jennifer M. Community Participation in Volunteer Fire-fighting in the Adelaide Hills. In *Healey, D. T.; Jarrett, F. G. and McKay, J. M., eds.*, 1985, pp. 74–88. [G: Australia]

McKelvey, Robert. Decentralized Regulation of a Common Property Renewable Resource Industry with Irreversible Investment. *J. Environ. Econ. Manage.*, December 1985, *12*(4), pp. 287–307.

McMillan, Melville L. Western Transition: The Economic Future of the West: Introduction. *Can. Public Policy*, Supplement July 1985, *11*(3), pp. 268–82. [G: Canada]

McNeill, Desmond. The Appraisal of Rural Water Supplies [Why Present Value Calculations Should Not Be Used in Choosing Rural Water Supply Technology]. *World Devel.*, Oct./Nov. 1985, *13*(10/11), pp. 1175–78. [G: LDCs]

McNeill, Desmond. The Appraisal of Rural Water Supplies: Rejoinder [Why Present Value Calculations Should Not Be Used in Choosing Rural Water Supply Technology]. *World Devel.*, Oct./Nov. 1985, *13*(10/11), pp. 1181. [G: LDCs]

Medvedev, Boris. Conserving Material Resources. *Soviet E. Europ. Foreign Trade*, Winter 1985-86, *21*(4), pp. 58–67. [G: CMEA]

Melese, François. Deregulation, Endogenous Expectations, and the Evolution of Industry Structure. *Southern Econ. J.*, January 1985, *51*(3), pp. 793–803.

Mercer, Lloyd J. and Morgan, W. Douglas. Conservation Using a Rate of Return Decision Rule: Some Examples from California Municipal Water Departments. *Water Resources Res.*, July 1985, *21*(7), pp. 927–33. [G: U.S.]

de Meza, David and de Möhr, Ernst. Price Deregulation and the Production of Depletable Resources. *Int. Econ. Rev.*, February 1985, *26*(1), pp. 213–18. [G: U.S.]

Mickwitz, Gosta. Låt bologen köpa in skogar. (Let Companies Buy Forests. With English summary.) *Ekon. Samfundets Tidskr.*, 1985, *38*(3), pp. 123–24. [G: Finland]

Miller, Merton H and Upton, Charles W. A Test of the Hotelling Valuation Principle. *J. Polit. Econ.*, February 1985, *93*(1), pp. 1–25. [G: U.S.]

Mirman, Leonard J. and Spulber, Daniel F. Fishery Regulation with Harvest Uncertainty.

Int. Econ. Rev., October 1985, *26*(3), pp. 731–46.

Mitra, Tapan and Wan, Henry Y., Jr. Some Theoretical Results on the Economics of Forestry. *Rev. Econ. Stud.*, April 1985, *52*(2), pp. 263–82.

Morgan, D. R. and Goulter, I. C. Optimal Urban Water Distribution Design. *Water Resources Res.*, May 1985, *21*(5), pp. 642–52. [G: U.S.]

Moussavian, Mohammed H. Growth Rates with an Exhaustible Resource and Home Goods. *J. Int. Econ.*, May 1985, *18*(3/4), pp. 281–99.

Mueller, Michael J. and Gorin, Daniel R. Informative Trends in Natural Resource Commodity Prices: A Comment. *J. Environ. Econ. Manage.*, March 1985, *12*(1), pp. 89–95. [G: U.S.]

Mules, T. J. An Input–Output Analysis of the Ash Wednesday Bushfires. In *Healey, D. T.; Jarrett, F. G. and McKay, J. M., eds.*, 1985, pp. 15–27. [G: Australia]

Mullen, John K. and Menz, Fredric C. The Effect of Acidification Damages on the Economic Value of the Adirondack Fishery to New York Anglers. *Amer. J. Agr. Econ.*, February 1985, *67*(1), pp. 112–19. [G: U.S.]

Munro, Gordon R. and Scott, Anthony D. The Economics of Fisheries Management. In *Kneese, A. V. and Sweeney, J. L., eds. Vol. 2*, 1985, pp. 623–76. [G: Canada; Selected Countries]

Muraoka, Dennis D. and Watson, Richard B. Economic Issues in Federal Timber Sale Procedures. In *Deacon, R. T. and Johnson, M. B., eds.*, 1985, pp. 201–23. [G: U.S.]

Muraro, Gilberto. Contents and Methods of Environmental Economics: Introduction to the Readings. *Ricerche Econ.*, Oct.-Dec. 1985, *39*(4), pp. 425–34. [G: OECD]

Murota, Takeshi. Heat Economy of the Water Planet Earth: Part II/Revision and Some New Results. *Hitotsubashi J. Econ.*, December 1985, *26*(2), pp. 181–85. [G: U.K.; Japan]

Nanda, Shibanarayan. More on Externality in the Fishery: A Discussion of Economic Efficiency. *Indian Econ. J.*, Apr.-June 1985, *32*(4), pp. 19–28.

Napier, Ted L.; Goe, W. Richard and Carter, Michael V. Reservoir Impacts: A Synthesis of a 10-Year Research Project. *Water Resources Res.*, June 1985, *21*(6), pp. 801–07. [G: U.S.]

Nathanson, R. and Weinblatt, J. The General Effect of Export Restrictions on Commodity Markets. In *Weinblatt, J., ed.*, 1985, pp. 10–50. [G: LDCs; MDCs]

Neher, Philip A. Resource Allocation Rules and Long-Range Planning. In *Scott, A., ed.*, 1985, pp. 130–50.

Nelson, Robert H. Mythology Instead of Analysis: The Story of Public Forest Management. In *Deacon, R. T. and Johnson, M. B., eds.*, 1985, pp. 23–76. [G: U.S.]

Nelson, Robert H. and Pugliaresi, Lucian. Timber Harvest Policy Issues on the O & C Lands. In *Deacon, R. T. and Johnson, M. B., eds.*,

1985, pp. 149–68.   [G: U.S.]

Newman, David H.; Gilbert, Charles B. and Hyde, William F. The Optimal Forest Rotation with Evolving Prices. *Land Econ.*, November 1985, *61*(4), pp. 347–53.

Noronha, Raymond and Spears, John S. Sociological Variables in Forestry Project Design. In *Cernea, M. M., ed.*, 1985, pp. 227–66.
[G: Selected LDCs]

Nunn, Susan Christopher. The Political Economy of Institutional Change: A Distribution Criterion for Acceptance of Groundwater Rules. *Natural Res. J.*, October 1985, *25*(4), pp. 867–92.   [G: U.S.]

Okada, Norio. Cost Allocation in Multipurpose Reservoir Development: The Japanese Experience. In *Young, H. P., ed.*, 1985, pp. 193–205.   [G: Japan]

Oldak, P. G. Balanced Natural Resource Utilization and Economic Growth. *Prob. Econ.*, July 1985, *28*(3), pp. 3–17.   [G: U.S.S.R.]

Olewiler, Nancy. Deriving the Long-run Supply Curve for a Competitive Mining Industry: The Case of Saskatchewan Uranium: Comment. In *Scott, A., ed.*, 1985, pp. 310–16.
[G: Canada]

Orosel, Gerhard O. Infinite Horizon Rational Expectations Equilibrium in a Competitive Market for an Exhaustible Resource. *Int. Econ. Rev.*, October 1985, *26*(3), pp. 701–20.

Osterfeld, David. Resources, People, and the Neomalthusian Fallacy. *Cato J.*, Spring/Summer 1985, *5*(1), pp. 67–102.   [G: Global]

Parks, Richard W. and Cox, Judith. The Economic Implications of Log Export Restrictions: Analysis of Existing and Proposed Legislation. In *Deacon, R. T. and Johnson, M. B., eds.*, 1985, pp. 247–73.   [G: Japan; U.S.]

Pendley, William Perry. Offshore Oil Drilling. *Policy Rev.*, Fall 1985, (34), pp. 82–83.
[G: U.S.]

Pindyck, Robert S. The Measurement of Monopoly Power in Dynamic Markets. *J. Law Econ.*, April 1985, *28*(1), pp. 193–222.

Pindyck, Robert S. The Supply of Natural Gas Reserves in Alberta: Comment. In *Scott, A., ed.*, 1985, pp. 279–82.   [G: Canada]

Plummer, Mark L. The Sign and Size of Option Value: Comment. *Land Econ.*, February 1985, *61*(1), pp. 76–77.

Pollnac, Richard B. Social and Cultural Characteristics in Small-scale Fishery Development. In *Cernea, M. M., ed.*, 1985, pp. 189–223.
[G: Selected LDCs]

Pooley, F. G. H. State and Federal Attitudes to Foreign Investment and Its Regulation. In *Drysdale, P. and Shibata, H., eds.*, 1985, pp. 140–50.   [G: Australia]

Pope, C. Arden, III and Stoll, John R. The Market Value of Ingress Rights for White-tailed Deer Hunting in Texas. *Southern J. Agr. Econ.*, July 1985, *17*(1), pp. 177–82.
[G: U.S.]

Prince, Raymond and Rosser, J. Barkley, Jr. Some Implications of Delayed Environmental Costs for Benefit Cost Analysis: A Study of Re-switching in the Western Coal Lands. *Growth Change*, April 1985, *16*(2), pp. 18–25.
[G: U.S.]

Quirk, James. Consumer Surplus under Uncertainty: An Application to Dam–Reservoir Projects. *Water Resources Res.*, September 1985, *21*(9), pp. 1307–12.

Rabinovich, B. The Effectiveness of Natural Resource Utilization. *Prob. Econ.*, December 1985, *28*(8), pp. 21–41.

Rafati, Reza. Impact of Deep-Sea Mining on the World Metal Markets: Cobalt. In *Donges, J. B., ed.*, 1985, pp. 62–112.
[G: Selected Countries]

Ragozin, David L. and Brown, Gardner, Jr. Harvest Policies and Nonmarket Valuation in a Predator–Prey System. *J. Environ. Econ. Manage.*, June 1985, *12*(2), pp. 155–68.

Ranck, Edward L. On the Incidence of Ad Valorem Severance Taxes. *Nat. Tax J.*, June 1985, *38*(2), pp. 241–45.

Randall, Alan J. and Castle, Emery N. Land Resources and Land Markets. In *Kneese, A. V. and Sweeney, J. L., eds. Vol. 2*, 1985, pp. 571–620.

Reinganum, Jennifer F. and Stokey, Nancy L. Oligopoly Extraction of a Common Property Natural Resource: The Importance of the Period of Commitment in Dynamic Games. *Int. Econ. Rev.*, February 1985, *26*(1), pp. 161–73.

Renninger, John P. The United States and Multilateral Resource Management: Issues in Energy, Food, and Marine Minerals: A Conference Report. In *Jordan, R. S., ed.*, 1985, pp. xiii–xix.   [G: U.S.]

Richardson, James W. Methods for Measuring the Economic Impact of Ambient Pollutants on the Agricultural Sector: Discussion. *Amer. J. Agr. Econ.*, May 1985, *67*(2), pp. 421–22.
[G: U.S.]

Roberts, Gerald. Copper. In *Roberts, G., ed.*, 1985, pp. 64–71.   [G: Global]

Roberts, Gerald. Lead. In *Roberts, G., ed.*, 1985, pp. 98–103.   [G: Global]

Roberts, Gerald. Nickel. In *Roberts, G., ed.*, 1985, pp. 111–15.   [G: Global]

Roberts, Gerald. Tin. In *Roberts, G., ed.*, 1985, pp. 154–59.   [G: Global]

Roberts, Gerald. Zinc. In *Roberts, G., ed.*, 1985, pp. 160–66.   [G: Global]

Roemer, Michael. Dutch Disease in Developing Countries: Swallowing Bitter Medicine. In *Lundahl, M., ed.*, 1985, pp. 234–52.
[G: LDCs]

Runge, Carlisle Ford. The Innovation of Rules and the Structure of Incentives in Open Access Resources. *Amer. J. Agr. Econ.*, May 1985, *67*(2), pp. 368–72.

Saila, S. B.; Lorda, E. and Walker, H. A. The Analysis of Parameter Error Propagation in Simple Fishery Models. *Marine Resource Econ.*, 1985, *1*(3), pp. 235–46.

Saliba, Bonnie Colby. Soil Productivity and Farmers' Erosion Control Incentives—A Dynamic Modeling Approach. *Western J. Agr. Econ.*, December 1985, *10*(2), pp. 354–64.

Samples, Karl C. and Bishop, Richard C. Estimating the Value of Variations in Anglers' Success Rates: An Application of the Multiple-Site Travel Cost Method. *Marine Resource Econ.*, 1985, 2(1), pp. 55–74. [G: U.S.]

Samuelson, Larry. Transfer Pricing in Exhaustible Resource Markets. In *Rugman, A. M. and Eden, L., eds.*, 1985, pp. 98–116.

Sander, William. The State of Economic Analysis in Water Resources Planning. *Amer. J. Econ. Soc.*, January 1985, 44(1), pp. 121–28.
[G: U.S.]

Schaeffers, Hans. Design of Computer Support for Multicriteria and Multiperson Decisions in Regional Water Resources Planning. In *Fandel, G. and Spronk, J., eds.*, 1985, pp. 245–66.

Schefold, Bertram. Ecological Problems as a Challenge to Classical and Keynesian Economics. *Metroecon.*, February 1985, 37(1), pp. 21–61. [G: Global]

Schefter, J. E. and David, E. L. Estimating Residential Water Demand under Multi-part Tariffs Using Aggregate Data. *Land Econ.*, August 1985, 61(3), pp. 272–80. [G: U.S.]

Schniepp, Mark. The Economic Consequences of the Setaside Program in the Douglas Fir Region of the Pacific Northwest. In *Deacon, R. T. and Johnson, M. B., eds.*, 1985, pp. 225–45. [G: U.S.]

Schworm, William. Exhaustible Resource Extraction with Capital: Comment. In *Scott, A., ed.*, 1985, pp. 195–202.

Scott, Anthony D. Progress in Natural Resource Economics: Introduction. In *Scott, A., ed.*, 1985, pp. 1–13.

Scott, Anthony D. The State and Property: Water Rights in Western Canada. In *[Spry, I. M.]*, 1985, pp. 157–88. [G: Canada]

Scott, Anthony D. and Johnson, James. Property Rights: Developing the Characteristics of Interests in Natural Resources. In *Scott, A., ed.*, 1985, pp. 376–403. [G: Canada; U.S.]

Scott, Norman. From Non-conventional to New Instruments of Trade Promotion? In *Saunders, C. T., ed.*, 1985, pp. 265–86. [G: CMEA; OECD]

Seddighi, H. R. A General Equilibrium Framework for Optimal Planning in an Oil-producing Economy. *Energy Econ.*, July 1985, 7(3), pp. 179–90.

Shabman, Leonard A. and Capps, Oral, Jr. Benefit Taxation for Environmental Improvement: A Case Example from Virginia's Soft Crab Fishery. *Land Econ.*, November 1985, 61(4), pp. 398–408. [G: U.S.]

Shafer, Michael. Capturing the Mineral Multinationals: Advantage or Disadvantage? In *Moran, T. H., ed.*, 1985, pp. 25–53. [G: Zaire; Zambia]

Shahrokh, Fereidoon and Labys, Walter C. A Commodity-regional Model of West Virginia. *J. Reg. Sci.*, August 1985, 25(3), pp. 383–411. [G: U.S.]

Shaldina, G. E. The Intensification of Natural Resource Utilization and the Reproduction of Resources. *Prob. Econ.*, June 1985, 28(2), pp. 80–92. [G: U.S.S.R.]

Shechter, Mordechai. An Anatomy of a Groundwater Contamination Episode. *J. Environ. Econ. Manage.*, March 1985, 12(1), pp. 72–88. [G: U.S.]

Shim, Jae K. A Spatial Equilibrium Analysis of Southern Pine Lumber Pricing and Allocation. *Ann. Reg. Sci.*, March 1985, 19(1), pp. 61–76. [G: U.S.]

Sinden, J. A. and Jones, A. D. Eucalypt Dieback and Stocking Rates in Southern New England, New South Wales. *Australian J. Agr. Econ.*, August 1985, 29(2), pp. 149–56.
[G: Australia]

Skowronski, Janislaw M. Competitive Differential Game of Harvesting Uncertain Resources. In *Batten, D. F. and Lesse, P. F., eds.*, 1985, pp. 87–103.

Slade, Margaret E. Noninformative Trends in Natural Resource Commodity Prices: U-shaped Price Paths Exonerated: Reply [Trends in Natural-Resource Commodity Prices: An Analysis of the Time Domain]. *J. Environ. Econ. Manage.*, June 1985, 12(2), pp. 181–92. [G: U.S.]

Smith, Ben. Resource Markets and Resource Trade Issues. In *Drysdale, P. and Shibata, H., eds.*, 1985, pp. 203–17. [G: Australia]

Smith, J. Barry. A Discrete Model of Replenishable Resource Management under Uncertainty. *Marine Resource Econ.*, 1985, 1(3), pp. 283–308.

Smith, V. Kerry. Supply Uncertainty, Option Price, and Indirect Benefit Estimation. *Land Econ.*, August 1985, 61(3), pp. 303–07.

Smith, V. Kerry. The Effects of Price Controls, Taxes, and Subsidies on Exhaustible Resource Production: Comment. In *Scott, A., ed.*, 1985, pp. 227–41.

Smith, Vernon L. Property Rights: Developing the Characteristics of Interests in Natural Resources: Comment. In *Scott, A., ed.*, 1985, pp. 403–21. [G: Canada; U.S.]

Södersten, Bo. Mineral-Led Development: The Political Economy of Namibia. In *Lundahl, M., ed.*, 1985, pp. 206–17. [G: Namibia]

Spulber, Daniel F. Fisheries, Dynamics, and Uncertainty: Comment. In *Scott, A., ed.*, 1985, pp. 120–29.

Spulber, Daniel F. The Multicohort Fishery under Uncertainty. *Marine Resource Econ.*, 1985, 1(3), pp. 265–82.

Stainer, Robin. Commodity Agreements. In *Roberts, G., ed.*, 1985, pp. 17–24. [G: Global]

Stollery, Kenneth R. User Costs versus Markups as Determinants of Prices in the Nickel Industry: Reply. *J. Environ. Econ. Manage.*, December 1985, 12(4), pp. 397–400. [G: U.S.]

Strong, Sam M. Rational Expectations and Weekly Price Variations of the Queensland Mud Crab. *Rev. Marketing Agr. Econ.*, December 1985, 53(3), pp. 141–48.
[G: Australia]

Sumi, Kazuo and Hanayama, Ken. Existing Institutional Arrangements and Implications for

Management of Tokyo Bay. *Natural Res. J.*, January 1985, *25*(1), pp. 167–93. **[G: Japan]**

Sutinen, Jon G. and Andersen, Peder. The Economics of Fisheries Law Enforcement. *Land Econ.*, November 1985, *61*(4), pp. 387–97.

Swan, Neil M. Competing Models of Western Growth: Continued Specialization in Resources or Greater Diversification. *Can. Public Policy*, Supplement July 1985, *11*(3), pp. 283–89. **[G: Canada]**

Swan, Neil M. and Slater, David W. Reflections on Western Transition. *Can. Public Policy*, Supplement July 1985, *11*(3), pp. 365–70. **[G: Canada]**

Swierzbinski, Joseph. Statistical Methods Applicable to Selected Problems in Fisheries Biology and Economics. *Marine Resource Econ.*, 1985, *1*(3), pp. 209–33.

Tarlock, A. Dan. An Overview of the Law of Groundwater Management. *Water Resources Res.*, November 1985, *21*(11), pp. 1751–66. **[G: U.S.]**

Tarlock, A. Dan. The Making of Federal Coal Policy: Lessons for Public Lands Management from a Failed Program, an Essay and Review. *Natural Res. J.*, April 1985, *25*(2), pp. 349–71. **[G: U.S.]**

Taylor, Timothy G. and Prochaska, Fred J. Fishing Power Functions in Aggregate Bioeconomic Models. *Marine Resource Econ.*, 1985, *2*(1), pp. 87–107. **[G: U.S.]**

Teeguarden, Dennis E. and Thomas, David. A Public Corporation Model for Federal Forest Land Management. *Natural Res. J.*, April 1985, *25*(2), pp. 373–87. **[G: U.S.]**

Texler, Jiří. Environment in Economic Theory and Practice. *Czech. Econ. Pap.*, 1985, *23*, pp. 151–54. **[G: Czechoslovakia]**

Thomson, Norm. The South Australian Bushfire Cost to Government. In *Healey, D. T.; Jarrett, F. G. and McKay, J. M.*, eds., 1985, pp. 28–40. **[G: Australia]**

Tisdell, Clement A. Conserving and Planting Trees on Farms: Lessons from Australian Cases. *Rev. Marketing Agr. Econ.*, December 1985, *53*(3), pp. 185–94. **[G: Australia]**

Townsend, Ralph E. On "Capital-stuffing" in Regulated Fisheries. *Land Econ.*, May 1985, *61*(2), pp. 195–97.

Tussing, Arlon R. Oil Prices Are Still Too High. *Energy J.*, January 1985, *6*(1), pp. 9–12. **[G: Global]**

Tyers, Rodney and Phillips, Prue. Australia, ASEAN and Pacific Basin Merchandise Trade: Factor Composition and Performance in the 1970s. In *Lim, D.*, ed., 1985, pp. 78–106. **[G: Australia; ASEAN; Pacific Basin]**

Uhler, Russell S. The Supply of Natural Gas Reserves in Alberta. In *Scott, A.*, ed., 1985, pp. 263–79. **[G: Canada]**

Utton, Albert E. Alternatives and Uncertainties in Interstate Groundwater Law. *Water Resources Res.*, November 1985, *21*(11), pp. 1767–70. **[G: U.S.]**

Utton, Albert E. In Search of an Integrating Principle for Interstate Water Law: Regulation versus the Market Place. *Natural Res. J.*, October 1985, *25*(4), pp. 985–1004. **[G: U.S.]**

Vaidyanathan, A. Water Control Institutions and Agriculture: A Comparative Perspective. *Indian Econ. Rev.*, Jan.-June 1985, *20*(1), pp. 25–83.

Valencia Mark J. and Jaafar, Abu Bakar. Environmental Management of the Malacca/Singapore Straits: Legal and Institutional Issues. *Natural Res. J.*, January 1985, *25*(1), pp. 195–232. **[G: Malaysia; Indonesia; Singapore]**

Waelti, John J. Cost Sharing for Federal Water Projects: Trends and Implications. *Water Resources Res.*, February 1985, *21*(2), pp. 153–58. **[G: U.S.]**

Wagenhals, Gerhard. The Modeling of International Minerals' Supply: A Restricted Profit Maximization Approach. *Weltwirtsch. Arch.*, 1985, *121*(3), pp. 492–500. **[G: CIPEC; U.S.; Canada]**

Wälde, Thomas. Third World Mineral Development in Crisis: The Impact of the Worldwide Recession on Legal Instruments Governing Third World Mineral Development. *J. World Trade Law*, January:February 1985, *19*(1), pp. 3–33. **[G: LDCs]**

Walker, John L. The Opportunity Cost of the Redwood National Park: Reply. *Contemp. Policy Issues*, Winter 1984-85, *3*(2), pp. 108–09. **[G: U.S.]**

Walker, P. A. and Kelly, P. C. Coordination of Land-related Data Initiatives at the Federal Level in Australia. *J. Econ. Soc. Meas.*, July 1985, *13*(2), pp. 199–208. **[G: Australia]**

Wallace, M. Long-term Projections of Wood-Based Panel Consumption in Australia. *Rev. Marketing Agr. Econ.*, December 1985, *53*(3), pp. 173–83. **[G: Australia]**

Ward, Frank A. Income Distribution Issues and Natural Resource Policy: Welfare Effects of Nonfederal Water Plans. *Western J. Agr. Econ.*, December 1985, *10*(2), pp. 187–91.

Watkins, G. C. The Supply of Natural Gas Reserves in Alberta: Comment. In *Scott, A.*, ed., 1985, pp. 282–89. **[G: Canada]**

Webber, Barbara S. and Webber, David J. Promoting Economic Incentives for Environmental Protection in the Surface Mining Control and Reclamation Act of 1977: An Analysis of the Design and Implementation of Reclamation Performance Bonds. *Natural Res. J.*, April 1985, *25*(2), pp. 389–414. **[G: U.S.]**

Wescoat, James L., Jr. On Water Conservation and Reform of the Prior Appropriation Doctrine in Colorado. *Econ. Geogr.*, January 1985, *61*(1), pp. 3–24. **[G: U.S.]**

Wilen, James E. Bioeconomics of Renewable Resource Use. In *Kneese, A. V. and Sweeney, J. L.*, eds. Vol. 1, 1985, pp. 61–124.

Wilen, James E. Modelling Fishermen and Regulator Behaviour in Schooling and Search Fisheries. In *Scott, A.*, ed., 1985, pp. 153–70.

Wilen, James E. Towards a Theory of the Regulated Fishery. *Marine Resource Econ.*, 1985, *1*(4), pp. 369–88.

Willett, Keith. Net Benefit Functions, Discounting, and the Optimal Time Horizon for Extracting Non-replenishable Resources. *Energy Econ.*, July 1985, *7*(3), pp. 163–67.

Willett, Ken. Mining Taxation Issues in the Australian Federal System. **In** *Drysdale, P. and Shibata, H., eds.*, 1985, pp. 105–26.
[G: Australia]

Williams, Martin. Estimating Urban Residential Demand for Water under Alternative Price Measures. *J. Urban Econ.*, September 1985, *18*(2), pp. 213–25.
[G: U.S.]

Williams, Stephen F. The Law of Prior Appropriation: Possible Lessons for Hawaii. *Natural Res. J.*, October 1985, *25*(4), pp. 911–34.
[G: U.S.]

Wilson, James A. The Economical Management of Multispecies Fisheries: Reply. *Land Econ.*, August 1985, *61*(3), pp. 323–26.

Wolf, Michael Allan. Accommodating Tensions in the Coastal Zone: An Introduction and Overview. *Natural Res. J.*, January 1985, *25*(1), pp. 7–19.
[G: U.S.]

Worthington, Virginia E.; Burt, Oscar R. and Brustkern, Richard L. Optimal Management of a Confined Groundwater System. *J. Environ. Econ. Manage.*, September 1985, *12*(3), pp. 229–45.
[G: U.S.]

Yeh, William W-G. Resevoir Management and Operations Models: A State-of-the-Art Review. *Water Resources Res.*, December 1985, *21*(12), pp. 1797–1818.
[G: U.S.]

Young, David A. The Repayment of Water Development Costs: Commentary. *Can. J. Agr. Econ.*, August 1985, *32*, pp. 133–36.
[G: Canada]

Young, Robert A. and Gray, S. Lee. Input–Output Models, Economic Surplus, and the Evaluation of State or Regional Water Plans. *Water Resources Res.*, December 1985, *21*(12), pp. 1819–23.

Young, Robert A. and Haveman, Robert H. Economics of Water Resources: A Survey. **In** *Kneese, A. V. and Sweeney, J. L., eds. Vol. 2*, 1985, pp. 465–529.
[G: U.S.]

7211 Recreational Aspects of Natural Resources

Batie, Sandra S. and Mabbs-Zeno, Carl C. Opportunity Costs of Preserving Coastal Wetlands: A Case Study of a Recreational Housing Development. *Land Econ.*, February 1985, *61*(1), pp. 1–9.

Bockstael, Nancy E. and Strand, Ivar E. Distributional Issues and Nonmarket Benefit Measurement. *Western J. Agr. Econ.*, December 1985, *10*(2), pp. 162–69.
[G: U.S.]

Boyle, Kevin J.; Bishop, Richard C. and Welsh, Michael P. Starting Point Bias in Contingent Valuation Bidding Games. *Land Econ.*, May 1985, *61*(2), pp. 188–94.

Caulkins, Peter P.; Bishop, Richard C. and Bouwes, Nicolaas W. Omitted Cross-Price Variable Biases in the Linear Travel Cost Model: Correcting Common Misperceptions. *Land Econ.*, May 1985, *61*(2), pp. 182–87.

Cory, Dennis C. Income–Time Endowments,

Distributive Equity, and the Valuation of Natural Environments. *Western J. Agr. Econ.*, December 1985, *10*(2), pp. 183–86.

Crocker, Thomas D. On the Value of the Condition of a Forest Stock. *Land Econ.*, August 1985, *61*(3), pp. 244–54.
[G: U.S.]

Delforce, Robert J. and Hardaker, J. Brian. An Experiment in Multiattribute Utility Theory. *Australian J. Agr. Econ.*, December 1985, *29*(3), pp. 179–98.
[G: Australia]

Fisher, Anthony C. and Krutilla, John V. Economics of Nature Preservation. **In** *Kneese, A. V. and Sweeney, J. L., eds. Vol. 1*, 1985, pp. 165–89.

Freeman, A. Myrick, III. Methods for Assessing the Benefits of Environmental Programs. **In** *Kneese, A. V. and Sweeney, J. L., eds. Vol. 1*, 1985, pp. 223–70.

Greenley, Douglas A.; Walsh, Richard G. and Young, Robert A. Option Value: Empirical Evidence from a Case Study of Recreation and Water Quality: Reply. *Quart. J. Econ.*, February 1985, *100*(1), pp. 295–99.
[G: U.S.]

Johnson, Ronald N. U.S. Forest Service Policy and Its Budget. **In** *Deacon, R. T. and Johnson, M. B., eds.*, 1985, pp. 103–33.
[G: U.S.]

Kahn, James R. and Kemp, W. Michael. Economic Losses Associated with the Degradation of an Ecosystem: The Case of Submerged Aquatic Vegetation in Chesapeake Bay. *J. Environ. Econ. Manage.*, September 1985, *12*(3), pp. 246–63.
[G: U.S.]

Keith, John E. and Lyon, Kenneth S. Valuing Wildlife Management: A Utah Deer Herd. *Western J. Agr. Econ.*, December 1985, *10*(2), pp. 216–22.
[G: U.S.]

McConnell, Kenneth E. The Economics of Outdoor Recreation. **In** *Kneese, A. V. and Sweeney, J. L., eds. Vol. 2*, 1985, pp. 677–722.
[G: U.S.]

Mitchell, Robert Cameron and Carson, Richard T. Option Value: Empirical Evidence from a Case Study of Recreation and Water Quality: Comment. *Quart. J. Econ.*, February 1985, *100*(1), pp. 291–94.
[G: U.S.]

Morey, Edward R. Characteristics, Consumer Surplus, and New Activities: A Proposed Ski Area. *J. Public Econ.*, March 1985, *26*(2), pp. 221–36.
[G: U.S.]

Phillips, Richard A. and Silberman, Jonathan I. Forecasting Recreation Demand: An Application of the Travel Cost Model. *Rev. Reg. Stud.*, Winter 1985, *15*(1), pp. 20–25.
[G: U.S.]

Samples, Karl C. A Note on the Existence of Starting Point Bias in Iterative Bidding Games. *Western J. Agr. Econ.*, July 1985, *10*(1), pp. 32–40.
[G: U.S.]

Seller, Christine; Stoll, John R. and Chavas, Jean-Paul. Validation of Empirical Measures of Welfare Change: A Comparison of Nonmarket Techniques. *Land Econ.*, May 1985, *61*(2), pp. 156–75.
[G: U.S.]

Smith, V. Kerry and Desvousges, William H. The Generalized Travel Cost Model and Water Quality Benefits: A Reconsideration. *Southern*

Econ. J., October 1985, *52*(2), pp. 371–81.
[G: U.S.]

Sutherland, Ronald J. and Walsh, Richard G.
Effect of Distance on the Preservation Value
of Water Quality. *Land Econ.*, August 1985,
61(3), pp. 281–91. [G: U.S.]

722 Conservation and Pollution

7220 Conservation and Pollution

Abel, Richard L. Risk as an Arena of Struggle.
Mich. Law Rev., February 1985, *83*(4), pp.
772–812. [G: U.S.; U.K.]

Abelson, Peter W. and Markandya, A. The Inter-
pretation of Capitalized Hedonic Prices in a
Dynamic Environment. *J. Environ. Econ.
Manage.*, September 1985, *12*(3), pp. 195–206.

Adams, Richard M. and McCarl, Bruce A. Assessing the Benefits of Alternative Ozone Standards on Agriculture: The Role of Response
Information. *J. Environ. Econ. Manage.*, September 1985, *12*(3), pp. 264–76. [G: U.S.]

Albin, Tom and Paulson, Steve. Environmental
and Economic Interests in Canada and the
United States. In *Schmandt, J. and Roderick,
H., eds.*, 1985, pp. 138–67. [G: Canada;
U.S.]

Allen, Julia C. Wood Energy and Preservation
of Woodlands in Semi-arid Developing Countries: The Case of Dodoma Region, Tanzania.
J. Devel. Econ., Sept.-Oct. 1985, *19*(1/2), pp.
59–84. [G: Tanzania]

Anderson, Lee G. Potential Economic Benefits
from Gear Restrictions and License Limitation
in Fisheries Regulation. *Land Econ.*, November 1985, *61*(4), pp. 409–18.

Anderson, Terry L. Reforming Resource Policy:
Toward Free Market Environmentalism. In
Boaz, D. and Crane, E. H., eds., 1985, pp.
247–71. [G: U.S.]

Anderson, William P. Synfuels Development in
the USA: Case Studies of National Environmental Feasibility and Local Socioeconomic
Impacts: Technical Review of the U.S. Case
Studies: I. In *Lakshmanan, T. R. and Johansson, B., eds.*, 1985, pp. 111–17. [G: U.S.]

Andrews, Richard N. L. Agency Responses to
NEPA: A Comparison and Implications. In
Kury, C., ed., 1985, pp. 122–43. [G: U.S.]

Arrow, Kenneth J. and Fisher, Anthony C. Environmental Preservation, Uncertainty, and Irreversibility. In *Arrow, K. J. (II)*, 1985, pp.
165–73.

Atkinson, Scott E. Marketable Pollution Permits
and Acid Rain Externalities: A Reply. *Can. J.
Econ.*, August 1985, *18*(3), pp. 676–79.
[G: U.S.; Canada]

**Atkinson, Scott E.; Adams, Richard M. and
Crocker, Thomas D.** Optimal Measurement
of Factors Affecting Crop Production: Maxi-
mum Likelihood Methods. *Amer. J. Agr.
Econ.*, May 1985, *67*(2), pp. 414–18.
[G: U.S.]

**Atkinson, Scott E.; Crocker, Thomas D. and
Murdock, Robert G.** Have Priors in Aggregate

Air Pollution Epidemiology Dictated Posteriors? *J. Urban Econ.*, May 1985, *17*(3), pp. 319–
34. [G: U.S.]

Awad, A. Safi El Din. Islamic Jurisprudence and
Environmental Planning: Comments. *J. Res.
Islamic Econ.*, Summer 1985, *3*(1), pp. 83–86.

Barnett, Harold C. The Allocation of Superfund,
1981–1983. *Land Econ.*, August 1985, *61*(3),
pp. 255–62. [G: U.S.]

Baron, David P. Noncooperative Regulation of a
Nonlocalized Externality. *Rand J. Econ.*, Winter 1985, *16*(4), pp. 553–68. [G: U.S.]

Baron, David P. Regulation of Prices and Pollution under Incomplete Information. *J. Public
Econ.*, November 1985, *28*(2), pp. 211–31.

Bartov, B. Political–Economic Problems in the
Interaction between Society and Nature. *Prob.
Econ.*, June 1985, *28*(2), pp. 65–79.
[G: U.S.S.R.]

Batie, Sandra S. and Mabbs-Zeno, Carl C. Opportunity Costs of Preserving Coastal Wetlands: A Case Study of a Recreational Housing
Development. *Land Econ.*, February 1985,
61(1), pp. 1–9.

Beazley, Ronald. Conservation Decision-Making:
A Rationalization. In *Kury, C., ed.*, 1985, pp.
1–16.

**Bergstrom, John C.; Dillman, B. L. and Stoll,
John R.** Public Environmental Amenity Benefits of Private Land: The Case of Prime Agricultural Land. *Southern J. Agr. Econ.*, July 1985,
17(1), pp. 139–49. [G: U.S.]

**Bogárdi, István; Bárdossy, Andras and Duck-
stein, Lucien.** Trade-off between Cost and Efficiency of Pollution Control. In *Haimes, Y. Y.
and Chankong, V., eds.*, 1985, pp. 515–23.

Bohm, Peter and Russell, Clifford S. Comparative Analysis of Alternative Policy Instruments.
In *Kneese, A. V. and Sweeney, J. L., eds. Vol.
1*, 1985, pp. 395–460. [G: U.S.;
Selected Countries]

Bolton, Roger. Conservation and Fuel Switching
in Sweden: Review of the Swedish Case Study.
In *Lakshmanan, T. R. and Johansson, B., eds.*,
1985, pp. 163–73. [G: Sweden]

Bowes, Michael D. and Krutilla, John V. Multiple
Use Management of Public Forestlands. In
*Kneese, A. V. and Sweeney, J. L., eds. Vol.
2*, 1985, pp. 531–69. [G: U.S.]

Braulke, Michael and Endres, Alfred. On the
Economics of Effluent Charges. *Can. J. Econ.*,
November 1985, *18*(4), pp. 891–97.

Bresnahan, Timothy F. and Yao, Dennis A. The
Nonpecuniary Costs of Automobile Emissions
Standards. *Rand J. Econ.*, Winter 1985, *16*(4),
pp. 437–55. [G: U.S.]

Britton, Barbara; Albin, Tom and Paulson, Steve.
The U.S. Policy Response to Acid Rain. In
Schmandt, J. and Roderick, H., eds., 1985,
pp. 116–37. [G: U.S.]

Brown, Gardner, Jr. Preserving Endangered
Species and Other Biological Resources. *Ricerche Econ.*, Oct.-Dec. 1985, *39*(4), pp. 516–
25. [G: Global]

Bruckner, Don. National Security and the National Environmental Policy Act. *Natural Res.*

J., April 1985, 25(2), pp. 467–79. [G: U.S.]

Bystrakov, Iu. Ecological Problems of the Agroindustrial Complex. *Prob. Econ.*, June 1985, 28(2), pp. 50–64. [G: U.S.S.R.]

Caldwell, Lynton K. Binational Responsibilities for a Shared Environment. In *Doran, C. F. and Sigler, J. H., eds.*, 1985, pp. 203–30.
[G: U.S.; Canada]

Charles, Anthony T. and Munro, Gordon R. Irreversible Investment and Optimal Fisheries Management: A Stochastic Analysis. *Marine Resource Econ.*, 1985, 1(3), pp. 247–64.

Christainsen, G. B. and Tietenberg, T. H. Distributional and Macroeconomic Aspects of Environmental Policy. In *Kneese, A. V. and Sweeney, J. L., eds. Vol. 1*, 1985, pp. 345–93.
[G: U.S.]

Ciriacy-Wantrup, S. V. Conservation and Resource Programming. In *Ciriacy-Wantrup, S. V.*, 1985, pp. 261–68.

Ciriacy-Wantrup, S. V. Conservation of the California Tule Elk: A Socioeconomic Study of a Survival Problem. In *Ciriacy-Wantrup, S. V.*, 1985, pp. 231–46. [G: U.S.]

Ciriacy-Wantrup, S. V. Economics and Policies of Resource Conservation. In *Ciriacy-Wantrup, S. V.*, 1985, pp. 207–30.

Ciriacy-Wantrup, S. V. Social Objectives of Conservation of Natural Resources with Particular Reference to Taxation of Forests. In *Ciriacy-Wantrup, S. V.*, 1985, pp. 269–76. [G: U.S.]

Ciriacy-Wantrup, S. V. Water Quality, a Problem for the Economist. In *Ciriacy-Wantrup, S. V.*, 1985, pp. 117–28.

Conrad, Jon M. Residuals Management: Disposal of Sewage Sludge in the New York Bight. *Marine Resource Econ.*, 1985, 1(4), pp. 321–45.
[G: U.S.]

Conrad, Klaus. The Use of Standards and Prices for Environment Protection and Their Impact on Costs. *Z. ges. Staatswiss. (JITE)*, September 1985, 141(3), pp. 390–400.

Cornes, Richard and Sandler, Todd. Externalities, Expectations, and Pigouvian Taxes. *J. Environ. Econ. Manage.*, March 1985, 12(1), pp. 1–13.

Crocker, Thomas D. On the Value of the Condition of a Forest Stock. *Land Econ.*, August 1985, 61(3), pp. 244–54. [G: U.S.]

Dasgupta, Ajit K. and Murty, M. N. Economic Evaluation of Water Pollution Abatement: A Case Study of Paper and Pulp Industry in India. *Indian Econ. Rev.*, July-Dec. 1985, 20(2), pp. 231–67. [G: India]

DeRidder, Kim J. The Nature and Effects of Acid Rain: A Comparison of Assessments. In *Schmandt, J. and Roderick, H., eds.*, 1985, pp. 31–60. [G: Canada]

Dixon, Bruce L.; Garcia, Philip and Mjelde, James W. Primal versus Dual Methods for Measuring the Impact of Ozone on Cash Grain Farmers. *Amer. J. Agr. Econ.*, May 1985, 67(2), pp. 402–06. [G: U.S.]

Dresch, Stephen P. The Potential Contributions of Mutually Consistent, Sectorally Disaggregated National Economic Models to Analyses of National Environmental Policies and Global Environmental Interdependence. In *Smyshlyaev, A., ed.*, 1985, pp. 51–60.

Dreyfus, Daniel A. and Ingram, Helen M. The National Environmental Policy Act: A View of Intent and Practice. In *Kury, C., ed.*, 1985, pp. 49–67. [G: U.S.]

Dutkowsky, Donald and Menz, Fredric C. A Cost Function for Neutralizing Acidic Adirondack Surface Waters. *J. Environ. Econ. Manage.*, September 1985, 12(3), pp. 277–85.
[G: U.S.]

Egel, Robert. Canada's Acid Rain Policy: Federal and Provincial Roles. In *Schmandt, J. and Roderick, H., eds.*, 1985, pp. 95–115.
[G: Canada]

Elliott, E. Donald; Ackerman, Bruce A. and Millian, John C. Toward a Theory of Statutory Evolution: The Federalization of Environmental Law. *J. Law, Econ., Organ.*, Fall 1985, 1(2), pp. 313–40. [G: U.S.]

Endres, Alfred. Effluent Charges and Environmental Damage: A Further Clarification. *Oxford Econ. Pap.*, December 1985, 37(4), pp. 703–04.

Endres, Alfred. Market Incentives for Pollution Control. *Ricerche Econ.*, Oct.-Dec. 1985, 39(4), pp. 526–39. [G: U.S.]

Faber, Malte. A Biophysical Approach to the Economy Entropy, Environment and Resources. In *van Gool, W. and Bruggink, J. J. C., eds.*, 1985, pp. 315–37.

Feitel'man, N. The Management of Natural Resource Utilization. *Prob. Econ.*, January 1985, 27(9), pp. 62–80. [G: U.S.S.R.]

Fisher, Anthony C. and Krutilla, John V. Economics of Nature Preservation. In *Kneese, A. V. and Sweeney, J. L., eds. Vol. 1*, 1985, pp. 165–89.

Førsund, Finn R. Input–Output Models, National Economic Models, and the Environment. In *Kneese, A. V. and Sweeney, J. L., eds. Vol. 1*, 1985, pp. 325–41. [G: Norway]

Foshee, Andrew W. and McNeil, Douglas W. Superfund Financing: Revenue Predictability versus Incentives. *Atlantic Econ. J.*, December 1985, 13(4), pp. 93. [G: U.S.]

Frankel, Marvin. Amenity Changes, Property Values, and Hedonic Prices in a Closed City. *J. Environ. Econ. Manage.*, June 1985, 12(2), pp. 117–31.

Freeman, A. Myrick, III. Methods for Assessing the Benefits of Environmental Programs. In *Kneese, A. V. and Sweeney, J. L., eds. Vol. 1*, 1985, pp. 223–70.

Frey, Bruno S.; Schneider, Friedrich and Pommerehne, Werner W. Economists' Opinions on Environmental Policy Instruments: Analysis of a Survey. *J. Environ. Econ. Manage.*, March 1985, 12(1), pp. 62–71. [G: Austria; France; W. Germany; Switzerland; U.S.]

Friesema, H. Paul and Culhane, Paul J. Social Impacts, Politics, and the Environmental Impact Statement Process. In *Kury, C., ed.*, 1985, pp. 144–61. [G: U.S.]

Gale, Richard P. Federal Management of Forests

and Marine Fisheries: A Comparative Analysis of Renewable Resource Management. *Natural Res. J.*, April 1985, 25(2), pp. 275–315. [G: U.S.]

Gallagher, David R. and Smith, V. Kerry. Measuring Values for Environmental Resources under Uncertainty. *J. Environ. Econ. Manage.*, June 1985, 12(2), pp. 132–43.

Goldman, Marshall I. Economics of Environment and Renewable Resources in Socialist Systems: Russia. In *Kneese, A. V. and Sweeney, J. L., eds. Vol. 2*, 1985, pp. 725–45. [G: U.S.S.R.]

Gollop, Frank M. and Roberts, Mark J. Cost-minimizing Regulation of Sulfur Emissions: Regional Gains in Electric Power. *Rev. Econ. Statist.*, February 1985, 67(1), pp. 81–90. [G: U.S.]

Grobey, John H. Politics versus Bioeconomics: Salmon Fishery and Forestry Values in Conflict. In *Deacon, R. T. and Johnson, M. B., eds.*, 1985, pp. 169–200. [G: U.S.]

Gutman, Pablo. Teoría económica y problemática ambiental: un diálogo difícil. (With English summary.) *Desarrollo Econ.*, April–June 1985, 25(97), pp. 46–70.

Hall, Darwin C. and Moffitt, L. Joe. Application of the Economic Threshold for Interseasonal Pest Control. *Western J. Agr. Econ.*, December 1985, 10(2), pp. 223–29. [G: U.S.]

Hamilton, Scott A.; McCarl, Bruce A. and Adams, Richard M. The Effect of Aggregate Response Assumptions on Environmental Impact Analyses. *Amer. J. Agr. Econ.*, May 1985, 67(2), pp. 407–13. [G: U.S.]

Hannon, B. M. Time Value in Ecosystems. In *van Gool, W. and Bruggink, J. J. C., eds.*, 1985, pp. 261–85.

Harford, Jon D. Monitoring and Budget Maximization in the Control of Pollution: Comment. *Econ. Inquiry*, April 1985, 23(2), pp. 357–60.

Harrison, Craig S. A Marine Sanctuary in the Northwestern Hawaiian Islands: An Idea Whose Time Has Come. *Natural Res. J.*, April 1985, 25(2), pp. 317–47. [G: U.S.]

Heberlein, Thomas A. Some Observations on Alternative Mechanisms for Public Involvement: The Hearing, Public Opinion Poll, the Workshop and the Quasi-experiment. In *Kury, C., ed.*, 1985, pp. 106–21.

Hecht, Susanna B. Environment, Development and Politics: Capital Accumulation and the Livestock Sector in Eastern Amazonia. *World Devel.*, June 1985, 13(6), pp. 663–84. [G: Brazil]

Hendrickson, Chris T. and McMichael, Francis Clay. Controlling Contradictions among Regulations: Note. *Amer. Econ. Rev.*, September 1985, 75(4), pp. 876–77. [G: U.S.]

Homer, Pierce. Lessons from the Great Lakes Water Quality Agreements. In *Schmandt, J. and Roderick, H., eds.*, 1985, pp. 193–210. [G: U.S.; Canada]

Hordijk, Leen. Synfuels Development in the USA: Case Studies of National Environmental Feasibility and Local Socioeconomic Impacts: Technical Review of the U.S. Case Studies:

II. In *Lakshmanan, T. R. and Johansson, B., eds.*, 1985, pp. 118–24. [G: U.S.]

Hutchison, S. Blair. Bringing Resource Conservation into the Main Stream of American Thought. In *Kury, C., ed.*, 1985, pp. 17–35. [G: U.S.]

Ilgen, Thomas L. Between Europe and America, Ottawa and the Provinces: Regulating Toxic Substances in Canada. *Can. Public Policy*, September 1985, 11(3), pp. 578–90. [G: Canada]

Ingram, Helen M. Information Channels and Environmental Decision Making. In *Kury, C., ed.*, 1985, pp. 86–105. [G: U.S.]

Itteilag, Richard L. An Analysis of Actual and Forecasted Conservation in the Residential Gas Space-Heating Market. In *Crew, M. A., ed.*, 1985, pp. 127–39. [G: U.S.]

Jackson, Henry M. Environmental Policy and the Congress. In *Kury, C., ed.*, 1985, pp. 36–48. [G: U.S.]

Jackson, Ray. Advent of a New Era: The Conserver Society. In *[Spry, I. M.]*, 1985, pp. 301–17. [G: Canada]

James, David. Environmental Economics, Industrial Process Models, and Regional-Residuals Management Models. In *Kneese, A. V. and Sweeney, J. L., eds. Vol. 1*, 1985, pp. 271–324.

Janssen, Ron and Nijkamp, Peter. A Multiple Criteria Evaluation Typology of Environmental Management Problems. In *Haimes, Y. Y. and Chankong, V., eds.*, 1985, pp. 495–514.

Janssen, Ron; Nijkamp, Peter and Voogd, Henk. A Methodology for Multiple Criteria Environmental Plan Evaluation. In *Fandel, G. and Spronk, J., eds.*, 1985, pp. 347–60.

Johansson, B. and Snickars, F. Conservation and Fuel Switching in Sweden: Large-scale Introduction of Energy Supply Systems: Issues, Methods, and Models in Sweden. In *Lakshmanan, T. R. and Johansson, B., eds.*, 1985, pp. 125–62. [G: Sweden]

Kahn, James R. and Kemp, W. Michael. Economic Losses Associated with the Degradation of an Ecosystem: The Case of Submerged Aquatic Vegetation in Chesapeake Bay. *J. Environ. Econ. Manage.*, September 1985, 12(3), pp. 246–63. [G: U.S.]

Kappler, Frederick G. and Rutledge, Gary L. Expenditures for Abating Pollutant Emissions from Motor Vehicles, 1968–84. *Surv. Curr. Bus.*, July 1985, 65(7), pp. 29–35. [G: U.S.]

Khachaturov, T. Nature Conservation in European Socialist Countries. *Prob. Econ.*, September 1985, 28(5), pp. 48–68. [G: CMEA]

Khodorkovskaia, S. The Effectiveness of Protection of the Atmosphere. *Prob. Econ.*, March 1985, 27(11), pp. 59–74. [G: U.S.S.R.]

Kinscherff, Paul. The International Joint Commission: The Role It Might Play. In *Schmandt, J. and Roderick, H., eds.*, 1985, pp. 174–92. [G: Canada; U.S.]

Kneese, Allen V. Environmental Economics. *Ricerche Econ.*, Oct.-Dec. 1985, 39(4), pp. 467–82. [G: U.S.]

Kneese, Allen V. and Schulze, William D. Ethics

and Environmental Economics. In *Kneese, A. V. and Sweeney, J. L., eds. Vol. 1*, 1985, pp. 191–220.

Kohn, Robert E. A General Equilibrium Analysis of the Optimal Number of Firms in a Polluting Industry. *Can. J. Econ.*, May 1985, *18*(2), pp. 347–54.

Kornbluh, Hy; Crowfoot, James and Cohen-Rosenthal, Edward. Worker Participation in Energy and Natural Resources Conservation. *Int. Lab. Rev.*, Nov.-Dec. 1985, *124*(6), pp. 737–54. [G: U.S.]

Krautkraemer, Jeffrey A. Optimal Growth, Resource Amenities, and the Preservation of Natural Environments. *Rev. Econ. Stud.*, January 1985, *52*(1), pp. 153–70.

Kunreuther, Howard and Miller, Louis. Interactive Computer Modeling for Policy Analysis: The Flood Hazard Problem. *Water Resources Res.*, February 1985, *21*(2), pp. 105–13.

Lam, Kin-Che and Hsu, Steve S. I. Environmental Considerations. In *Wong, K. and Chu, D. K. Y., eds.*, 1985, pp. 159–75. [G: China]

Lee, Dwight R. Rent-seeking and Its Implications for Pollution Taxation. *Southern Econ. J.*, January 1985, *51*(3), pp. 731–44.

Lemeshev, M. Ia. Scientific-Technical Progress and Nature. *Prob. Econ.*, July 1985, *28*(3), pp. 18–31.

Leontief, Wassily. Environmental Repercussions and the Economic Structure: An Input–Output Approach. In *Leontief, W.*, 1985, pp. 326–46. [G: U.S.]

Leontief, Wassily. National Income, Economic Structure, and Environmental Externalities. In *Leontief, W.*, 1985, pp. 347–58.

Lewandowski, A.; Rogowski, T. and Kręglewski, T. A Trajectory-Oriented Extension of DIDASS and Its Applications. In *Grauer, M.; Thompson, M. and Wierzbicki, A. P., eds.*, 1985, pp. 261–68.

Lewandowski, A.; Rogowski, T. and Kręglewski, T. Application of DIDASS Methodology to a Flood Control Problem—Numerical Experiments. In *Grauer, M.; Thompson, M. and Wierzbicki, A. P., eds.*, 1985, pp. 325–28.

Lichtenberg, Erik and Zilberman, David. Efficient Regulation of Environmental Health Risks: The Case of Groundwater Contamination in California. *Ricerche Econ.*, Oct.-Dec. 1985, *39*(4), pp. 540–49. [G: U.S.]

Liroff, Richard A. NEPA Litigation in the 1970s: A Deluge or a Dribble? In *Kury, C., ed.*, 1985, pp. 162–77. [G: U.S.]

Llewellyn, Othman A. Islamic Jurisprudence and Environmental Planning: Rejoinder. *J. Res. Islamic Econ.*, Summer 1985, *3*(1), pp. 87–90.

Lonergan, S. C. Tar Sands Development in Canada: A Case Study of Environmental Monitoring: Resource Extraction in Canada: Modeling the Regional Impacts. In *Lakshmanan, T. R. and Johansson, B., eds.*, 1985, pp. 41–61. [G: Canada]

Loucks, Daniel P.; Kindler, Janusz and Fedra, Kurt. Interactive Water Resources Modeling and Model Use: An Overview. *Water Resources Res.*, February 1985, *21*(2), pp. 95–102.

Lundqvist, Lars. Tar Sands Development in Canada: A Case Study of Environmental Monitoring: On Canadian Energy Impact Assessments. In *Lakshmanan, T. R. and Johansson, B., eds.*, 1985, pp. 62–71. [G: Canada]

Maddox, John. The Public and Anti-science. In *Wells, N., ed.*, 1985, pp. 133–42.

Mäler, Karl-Göran. Welfare Economics and the Environment. In *Kneese, A. V. and Sweeney, J. L., eds. Vol. 1*, 1985, pp. 3–60.

Mantell, Edmund H. On the Economics and the Politics of Environmental Protection: Policy Conflicts Can Be Mitigated by Selective Enforcement and Tax-financed Subsidies. *Amer. J. Econ. Soc.*, October 1985, *44*(4), pp. 435–47.

McGartland, Albert M. and Oates, Wallace E. Marketable Permits for the Prevention of Environmental Deterioration. *J. Environ. Econ. Manage.*, September 1985, *12*(3), pp. 207–28. [G: U.S.]

McHugh, Richard. The Potential for Private Cost-increasing Technological Innovation under a Tax-based, Economic Incentive Pollution Control Policy. *Land Econ.*, February 1985, *61*(1), pp. 58–64.

Medvedev, Boris. Conserving Material Resources. *Soviet E. Europ. Foreign Trade*, Winter 1985-86, *21*(4), pp. 58–67. [G: CMEA]

Mel'nik, L. G. The Ecological Components in the Life of an Enterprise. *Prob. Econ.*, June 1985, *28*(2), pp. 40–49. [G: U.S.S.R.]

Melachrinoudis, Emanuel and Cullinane, Thomas P. Locating an Undesirable Facility within a Geographical Region Using the MAXIMUM Criterion. *J. Reg. Sci.*, February 1985, *25*(1), pp. 115–27. [G: U.S.]

de Meza, David. Effluent Charges and Environmental Damage: A Clarification. *Oxford Econ. Pap.*, December 1985, *37*(4), pp. 700–02.

Mohai, Paul. Public Concern and Elite Involvement in Environmental–Conservation Issues. *Soc. Sci. Quart.*, December 1985, *66*(4), pp. 820–38. [G: U.S.]

Morriss, Andrew. Supporting Structures for Resolving Environmental Disputes among Friendly Neighbors. In *Schmandt, J. and Roderick, H., eds.*, 1985, pp. 211–45. [G: U.S.; Canada]

Mullen, John K. and Menz, Fredric C. The Effect of Acidification Damages on the Economic Value of the Adirondack Fishery to New York Anglers. *Amer. J. Agr. Econ.*, February 1985, *67*(1), pp. 112–19. [G: U.S.]

Muraro, Gilberto. Contents and Methods of Environmental Economics: Introduction to the Readings. *Ricerche Econ.*, Oct.-Dec. 1985, *39*(4), pp. 425–34. [G: OECD]

Nabi, Ijaz and van de Laar, Aart. Protection of the Environment. In *Jerve, A. M., ed.*, 1985, pp. 353–58. [G: Pakistan]

Norgaard, Richard B. Environmental Economics: An Evolutionary Critique and a Plea for Pluralism. *J. Environ. Econ. Manage.*, December

1985, *12*(4), pp. 382–94.

O'Byrne, Patricia Habuda; Nelson, Jon P. and Seneca, Joseph J. Housing Values, Census Estimates, Disequilibrium, and the Environmental Cost of Airport Noise: A Case Study of Atlanta. *J. Environ. Econ. Manage.*, June 1985, *12*(2), pp. 169–78.   [G: U.S.]

Oates, Wallace E. The Environment and the Economy: Environmental Policy at the Crossroads. In *Quigley, J. M. and Rubinfeld, D. L., eds.*, 1985, pp. 311–45.   [G: U.S.]

Oates, Wallace E. and McGartland, Albert M. Marketable Pollution Permits and Acid Rain Externalities: A Comment and Some Further Evidence. *Can. J. Econ.*, August 1985, *18*(3), pp. 668–75.   [G: Canada; U.S.]

Oldak, P. G. Balanced Natural Resource Utilization and Economic Growth. *Prob. Econ.*, July 1985, *28*(3), pp. 3–17.   [G: U.S.S.R.]

Opaluch, James J. and Kashmanian, Richard M. Assessing the Viability of Marketable Permit Systems: An Application in Hazardous Waste Management. *Land Econ.*, August 1985, *61*(3), pp. 263–71.   [G: U.S.]

Papps, Ivy E. Controlling and Monitoring Pollution: A Comment on "The Criminal Waste Discharger." *Scot. J. Polit. Econ.*, June 1985, *32*(2), pp. 171–80.

Pashigian, B. Peter. Environmental Regulation: Whose Self-interests Are Being Protected? *Econ. Inquiry*, October 1985, *23*(4), pp. 551–84.   [G: U.S.]

Pasurka, Carl A., Jr. Environmental Control Costs and U.S. Effective Rates of Protection. *Public Finance Quart.*, April 1985, *13*(2), pp. 161–82.   [G: U.S.; OECD]

Phaup, Marvin. Regulation and the Use of Knowledge. *Challenge*, January/February 1985, *27*(6), pp. 56–57.   [G: U.S.]

Pitt, Mark M. Equity, Externalities and Energy Subsidies: The Case of Kerosene in Indonesia. *J. Devel. Econ.*, April 1985, *17*(3), pp. 201–17.   [G: Indonesia]

Plant, Richard E.; Mangel, Marc and Flynn, Lawrence E. Multiseasonal Management of an Agricultural Pest II: The Economic Optimization Problem. *J. Environ. Econ. Manage.*, March 1985, *12*(1), pp. 45–61.

Plooy, L. H. E. C. International Comparison of Industrial Pollution Control Costs. *Statist. J.*, March 1985, *3*(1), pp. 55–68.
                            [G: Selected MDCs]

Portney, Paul R. Regional Issues: Commentary. In *Quigley, J. M. and Rubinfeld, D. L., eds.*, 1985, pp. 364–68.   [G: U.S.]

Prichard, Clark. Institutional Issues in the Siting of Low Level Radioactive Waste Facilities. *Rev. Reg. Stud.*, Winter 1985, *15*(1), pp. 1–6.
                                [G: U.S.]

Prince, Raymond. A Note on Environmental Risk and the Rate of Discount: Comment. *J. Environ. Econ. Manage.*, June 1985, *12*(2), pp. 179–80.

Randall, Alan. Benefit Cost Analysis of Environmental Program Alternatives: Economics, Political Philosophy and the Policy Process. *Ri-*

cerche Econ., Oct.-Dec. 1985, *39*(4), pp. 483–90.

Ratick, Samuel J. Assessing the Environmental Consequences of Large-scale Energy Projects. In *Lakshmanan, T. R. and Johansson, B., eds.*, 1985, pp. 233–55.   [G: U.S.; U.S.S.R.; Sweden]

Reiss, Albert J., Jr. Compliance without Coercion. *Mich. Law Rev.*, February 1985, *83*(4), pp. 813–19.   [G: U.S.]

Robison, H. David. Who Pays for Industrial Pollution Abatement? *Rev. Econ. Statist.*, November 1985, *67*(4), pp. 702–06.   [G: U.S.]

Schefold, Bertram. Ecological Problems as a Challenge to Classical and Keynesian Economics. *Metroecon.*, February 1985, *37*(1), pp. 21–61.   [G: Global]

Schmandt, Jurgen. Acid Rain and Friendly Neighbors: The Policy Dispute between Canada and the United States: Conclusions. In *Schmandt, J. and Roderick, H., eds.*, 1985, pp. 246–51.   [G: U.S.; Canada]

Schmandt, Jurgen; Roderick, Hilliard and Morriss, Andrew. Acid Rain Is Different. In *Schmandt, J. and Roderick, H., eds.*, 1985, pp. 7–30.   [G: Canada; U.S.]

Segarra, Eduardo; Kramer, Randall A. and Taylor, Daniel B. A Stochastic Programming Analysis of the Farm Level Implications of Soil Erosion Control. *Southern J. Agr. Econ.*, December 1985, *17*(2), pp. 147–54.
                                [G: U.S.]

Segerson, Kathleen. Unilateral Transfrontier Pollution: The Role of Economic Interdependence. *Land Econ.*, February 1985, *61*(1), pp. 83–87.

Shabman, Leonard A. and Capps, Oral, Jr. Benefit Taxation for Environmental Improvement: A Case Example from Virginia's Soft Crab Fishery. *Land Econ.*, November 1985, *61*(4), pp. 398–408.   [G: U.S.]

Shechter, Mordechai. An Anatomy of a Groundwater Contamination Episode. *J. Environ. Econ. Manage.*, March 1985, *12*(1), pp. 72–88.   [G: U.S.]

Siebert, Horst. Spatial Aspects of Environmental Economics. In *Kneese, A. V. and Sweeney, J. L., eds. Vol. 1*, 1985, pp. 125–64.

Simpson, G. M. Ethical Issues of High Technology in Agriculture. *Can. J. Agr. Econ.*, August 1985, *32*, pp. 48–59.

Slovic, Paul; Fischhoff, Baruch and Lichtenstein, Sarah. Regulation of Risk: A Psychological Perspective. In *Noll, R. G., ed.*, 1985, pp. 241–78.   [G: U.S.]

Smith, J. Barry and Sims, W. A. The Impact of Pollution Charges on Productivity Growth in Canadian Brewing. *Rand J. Econ.*, Autumn 1985, *16*(3), pp. 410–23.   [G: Canada]

Smith, V. Kerry and Desvousges, William H. The Generalized Travel Cost Model and Water Quality Benefits: A Reconsideration. *Southern Econ. J.*, October 1985, *52*(2), pp. 371–81.
                                [G: U.S.]

Smith, V. Kerry and Gilbert, Carol C. S. The Valuation of Environmental Risks Using Hedonic Wage Models. In *David, M. and Smeeding, T., eds.*, 1985, pp. 359–85.   **[G: U.S.]**

Solomon, Barry D. and Rubin, Barry M. Environmental Linkages in Regional Econometric Models: An Analysis of Coal Development in Western Kentucky. *Land Econ.*, February 1985, *61*(1), pp. 43–57.   **[G: U.S.]**

Spulber, Daniel F. Effluent Regulation and Long-run Optimality. *J. Environ. Econ. Manage.*, June 1985, *12*(2), pp. 103–16.

Stewart, Robert B. and Wilshusen, Katherine. U.S.–Canadian Negotiations on Acid Rain. In *Schmandt, J. and Roderick, H., eds.*, 1985, pp. 61–90.   **[G: U.S.; Canada]**

Stollery, Kenneth R. Environmental Controls in Extractive Industries. *Land Econ.*, May 1985, *61*(2), pp. 136–44.

Sullivan, Timothy J. Regional Issues: Commentary. In *Quigley, J. M. and Rubinfeld, D. L., eds.*, 1985, pp. 369–72.   **[G: U.S.]**

Sutherland, Ronald J. and Walsh, Richard G. Effect of Distance on the Preservation Value of Water Quality. *Land Econ.*, August 1985, *61*(3), pp. 281–91.   **[G: U.S.]**

Sutinen, Jon G. and Andersen, Peder. The Economics of Fisheries Law Enforcement. *Land Econ.*, November 1985, *61*(4), pp. 387–97.

Takayama, T. Conservation and Fuel Switching in Sweden: The Swedish Case Study Compared with Experiences in the USA and Japan. In *Lakshmanan, T. R. and Johansson, B., eds.*, 1985, pp. 174–84.   **[G: U.S.; Sweden; Japan]**

Taylor, Daniel B. and Young, Douglas L. The Influence of Technological Progress on the Long Run Farm Level Economics of Soil Conservation. *Western J. Agr. Econ.*, July 1985, *10*(1), pp. 63–76.   **[G: U.S.]**

Thomas, Vinod. Evaluating Pollution Control: The Case of São Paulo, Brazil. *J. Devel. Econ.*, Sept.-Oct. 1985, *19*(1/2), pp. 133–46.   **[G: Brazil]**

Tietenberg, T. H. The Valuation of Environmental Risks Using Hedonic Wage Models: Comment. In *David, M. and Smeeding, T., eds.*, 1985, pp. 385–91.   **[G: U.S.]**

Tollan, Arne. The Convention on Long-range Transboundary Air Pollution. *J. World Trade Law*, Nov.:Dec. 1985, *19*(6), pp. 615–21.

Tsuru, Shigeto. Economics of Environment and Renewable Resources in Socialist Systems: China. In *Kneese, A. V. and Sweeney, J. L., eds. Vol. 2*, 1985, pp. 746–49.   **[G: China]**

Vail, David. Revitalizing Rural Communities or Reviving Agrarian Myths? A Comment [A Geobased National Agricultural Policy for Rural Community Enhancement, Environmental Vitality, and Income Stabilization]. *J. Econ. Issues*, December 1985, *19*(4), pp. 995–1003.   **[G: U.S.]**

Veloz, Alberto, et al. The Economics of Erosion Control in a Subtropical Watershed: A Dominican Case. *Land Econ.*, May 1985, *61*(2), pp. 145–55.   **[G: Dominican Republic]**

Viscusi, W. Kip. Environmental Policy Choice with an Uncertain Chance of Irreversibility.

J. Environ. Econ. Manage., March 1985, *12*(1), pp. 28–44.

Wassermann, Ursula. Disposal of Radioactive Waste. *J. World Trade Law*, July:Aug. 1985, *19*(4), pp. 425–28.   **[G: OECD]**

Watson, William D. Tar Sands Development in Canada: A Case Study of Environmental Monitoring: Technical Review of the Canadian Case Study. In *Lakshmanan, T. R. and Johansson, B., eds.*, 1985, pp. 72–76.   **[G: Canada]**

Webber, Barbara S. and Webber, David J. Promoting Economic Incentives for Environmental Protection in the Surface Mining Control and Reclamation Act of 1977: An Analysis of the Design and Implementation of Reclamation Performance Bonds. *Natural Res. J.*, April 1985, *25*(2), pp. 389–414.   **[G: U.S.]**

Wengert, Norman. Citizen Participation: Practice in Search of a Theory. In *Kury, C., ed.*, 1985, pp. 68–85.

Wescoat, James L., Jr. On Water Conservation and Reform of the Prior Appropriation Doctrine in Colorado. *Econ. Geogr.*, January 1985, *61*(1), pp. 3–24.   **[G: U.S.]**

Wetzstein, Michael E. Methods for Measuring the Economic Impact of Ambient Pollutants on the Agricultural Sector: Discussion. *Amer. J. Agr. Econ.*, May 1985, *67*(2), pp. 419–20.   **[G: U.S.]**

Wetzstein, Michael E., et al. An Evalution of Integrated Pest Management with Heterogeneous Participation. *Western J. Agr. Econ.*, December 1985, *10*(2), pp. 344–53.   **[G: U.S.]**

Willett, Keith. Environmental Quality Standards: A General Equilibrium Analysis. *Managerial Dec. Econ.*, March 1985, *6*(1), pp. 41–49.

Winett, Richard A. Regulation of Risk: Comment. In *Noll, R. G., ed.*, 1985, pp. 278–83.   **[G: U.S.]**

Wittman, Donald. Pigovian Taxes Which Work in the Small-Number Case. *J. Environ. Econ. Manage.*, June 1985, *12*(2), pp. 144–54.

Wittman, Donald. Should Compensation Be Based on Costs or Benefits? *Int. Rev. Law Econ.*, December 1985, *5*(2), pp. 173–85.   **[G: U.S.]**

Yandle, Bruce. Unions and Environmental Regulation. *J. Lab. Res.*, Fall 1985, *6*(4), pp. 429–36.   **[G: U.S.]**

Young, Robert A. and Haveman, Robert H. Economics of Water Resources: A Survey. In *Kneese, A. V. and Sweeney, J. L., eds. Vol. 2*, 1985, pp. 465–529.   **[G: U.S.]**

Zinser, Lee D., et al. Effects of Rising Relative Energy Prices on Soil Erosion and Its Control. *Amer. J. Agr. Econ.*, August 1985, *67*(3), pp. 558–62.   **[G: U.S.]**

723 Energy

7230 Energy

Adelman, Morris A. An Unstable World Oil Market. *Energy J.*, January 1985, *6*(1), pp. 17–22.

Adelman, Morris A. Western Hemisphere Per-

spectives: Oil and Natural Gas. *Contemp. Policy Issues,* Summer 1985, *3*(4), pp. 3–12.
[G: OPEC; N. America; Latin America]

Afanasjew, Michail. East–West Cooperation in Energy. In *Saunders, C. T., ed.,* 1985, pp. 201–16. [G: U.S.S.R.; OECD]

Agarwal, Vinod B. and Deacon, Robert T. Price Controls, Price Dispersion and the Supply of Refined Petroleum Products. *Energy Econ.,* October 1985, *7*(4), pp. 210–19. [G: U.S.]

Aigner, Dennis J. The Residential Electricity Time-of-Use Pricing Experiments: What Have We Learned? In *Hausman, J. A. and Wise, D. A., eds.,* 1985, pp. 11–41. [G: U.S.]

Aiyagari, S. Rao and Riezman, Raymond G. Embargoes and Supply Shocks in a Market with a Dominant Seller. In *Sargent, T. J., ed.,* 1985, pp. 14–40.

Al-Dabbagh, Abdullah Taher. The Influence of Oil Revenues on U.S.–Arab Trade: Possible Changes in Arab Imports. In *Czinkota, M. R. and Marciel, S., eds.,* 1985, pp. 269–97.
[G: U.S.; Middle East]

Al-Nasrawi, Abbas. OPEC and the Changing Structure of the World Oil Market. In *Kubursi, A. A. and Naylor, T., eds.,* 1985, pp. 19–30.
[G: OPEC; OECD]

Al-Rumaihi, Mohammed. The Social Impact of Higher Oil Revenues on the Gulf Region. In *Kubursi, A. A. and Naylor, T., eds.,* 1985, pp. 53–58. [G: Persian Gulf]

Al-Sadik, A. T. National Accounting and Income Illusion of Petroleum Exports: The Case of the Arab Gulf Co-operation Council Members (AGCC) In *Niblock, T. and Lawless, R., eds.,* 1985, pp. 86–115. [G: OPEC]

Albu, Cr. and Şerban, R. Numerical Results Concerning the Optimum Distribution of Electric and Thermal Charges between the Groups of a Thermoelectric Power Station. *Econ. Computat. Cybern. Stud. Res.,* 1985, *20*(4), pp. 29–32.

Allen, Julia C. Wood Energy and Preservation of Woodlands in Semi-arid Developing Countries: The Case of Dodoma Region, Tanzania. *J. Devel. Econ.,* Sept.-Oct. 1985, *19*(1/2), pp. 59–84. [G: Tanzania]

Altmann, Franz-Lothar. East–West Relations in Energy, Agriculture and Technology: Comments. In *Saunders, C. T., ed.,* 1985, pp. 242–46. [G: U.S.S.R.; OECD]

Anandalingam, G. Government Policy and Industrial Investment in Cogeneration in the USA. *Energy Econ.,* April 1985, *7*(2), pp. 117–26.
[G: U.S.]

Anderson, William P. Synfuels Development in the USA: Case Studies of National Environmental Feasibility and Local Socioeconomic Impacts: Technical Review of the U.S. Case Studies: I. In *Lakshmanan, T. R. and Johansson, B., eds.,* 1985, pp. 111–17. [G: U.S.]

Andersson, Roland and Taylor, Lewis. Dimensioning Reserve Margins of Electrical Energy in Sweden. *Energy J.,* April 1985, *6*(2), pp. 41–60. [G: Sweden]

Andersson, Roland and Taylor, Lewis. The In-

vestment Criteria of the Swedish Electricity Industry. *Energy Econ.,* January 1985, *7*(1), pp. 13–19. [G: Sweden]

Arnoux, L. A. The Value of Energy / The Energy of Value. In *van Gool, W. and Bruggink, J. J. C., eds.,* 1985, pp. 343–79.

Arrow, Kenneth J. The Economic Cost to Western Europe of Restricted Availability of Oil Imports: A Linear Programming Computation. In *Arrow, K. J. (II),* 1985, pp. 1–8.

Aslaksen, Iulie and Bjerkholt, Olav. Certainty Equivalence Procedures in the Macroeconomic Planning of an Oil Economy. In *Bjerkholt, O. and Offerdal, E., eds.,* 1985, pp. 283–318.
[G: Norway]

Atkinson, Lloyd C. The World Oil Market for the Balance of the 1980s: Stability or Turmoil? In *Kubursi, A. A. and Naylor, T., eds.,* 1985, pp. 31–41. [G: Global]

Bailey, Richard. UK Energy Options. *Nat. Westminster Bank Quart. Rev.,* August 1985, pp. 30–41. [G: U.K.]

Balassa, Bela. Structural Adjustment Policies in Developing Economies. In *Balassa, B.,* 1985, pp. 63–88. [G: LDCs]

Barber, William J. Recreating the Science and Art of Political Economy: Lessons from the Energy Crisis. In *Schorr, P., ed.,* 1985, pp. 73–87. [G: U.S.]

Barzelay, Michael and Pearson, Scott R. The Efficiency of Producing Alcohol for Energy in Brazil: Reply. *Econ. Develop. Cult. Change,* July 1985, *33*(4), pp. 857–63. [G: Brazil]

Bergan, Roar and Offerdal, Erik. Using the Oil Revenues: A Long Run Perspective. In *Bjerkholt, O. and Offerdal, E., eds.,* 1985, pp. 249–82. [G: Norway]

Bergström, Clas; Loury, Glenn C. and Persson, Mats. Embargo Threats and the Management of Emergency Reserves. *J. Polit. Econ.,* February 1985, *93*(1), pp. 26–42.

Berndt, Ernst R. From Technocracy to Net Energy Analysis: Engineers, Economists, and Recurring Energy Theories of Value. In *Scott, A., ed.,* 1985, pp. 337–67. [G: U.S.]

Berndt, Ernst R. and Botero, German. Energy Demand in the Transportation Sector of Mexico. *J. Devel. Econ.,* April 1985, *17*(3), pp. 219–38. [G: Mexico]

Bethkenhagen, Jochen. The Impact of Energy on East–West Trade: Retrospect and Prospects. In *Saunders, C. T., ed.,* 1985, pp. 179–99.
[G: U.S.S.R.; OECD; CMEA]

Bolton, Roger. Conservation and Fuel Switching in Sweden: Review of the Swedish Case Study. In *Lakshmanan, T. R. and Johansson, B., eds.,* 1985, pp. 163–73. [G: Sweden]

Boquist, John A. and Long, Michael S. Capital Equilibrium for the Energy Industry, 1977-2000. *Econ. Notes,* 1985, (1), pp. 104–47.
[G: U.S.]

Bosworth, Derek. Fuel Based Measures of Capital Utilisation. *Scot. J. Polit. Econ.,* February 1985, *32*(1), pp. 20–38. [G: U.K.]

Bosworth, Derek and Pugh, Clive. Industrial and Commercial Demand for Electricity by Time of Day. *Energy J.*, July 1985, *6*(3), pp. 101–07. **[G: U.S.]**

Boucher, Jacqueline and Smeers, Yves. Measuring the Consequences of the Take or Pay Clauses in Natural Gas Consuming Countries. In *Bjerkholt, O. and Offerdal, E., eds.*, 1985, pp. 123–39. **[G: Belgium]**

Boucher, Jacqueline and Smeers, Yves. Programmation mathématique et modélisation énergétique. (Mathematical Programming and Energy Modelling. With English summary.) *L'Actual. Econ.*, March 1985, *61*(1), pp. 24–50.

Bower, Richard S. and Bower, Nancy L. Weather Normalization and Natural Gas Regulation. *Energy J.*, April 1985, *6*(2), pp. 101–15. **[G: U.S.]**

Bowonder, B., et al. Energy Use in Eight Rural Communities in India. *World Devel.*, December 1985, *13*(12), pp. 1263–86. **[G: India]**

Broadman, Harry G.; Montgomery, W. David and Russell, Milton. Field Price Deregulation and the Carrier Status of Natural Gas Pipelines. *Energy J.*, April 1985, *6*(2), pp. 127–39. **[G: U.S.]**

Brooks, David B. Energy Conservation and Energy Strategy: A Connection Not Made. *Can. Public Policy*, Supplement July 1985, *11*(3), pp. 438–42. **[G: Canada]**

Bruggink, J. J. C. The Theory of Economic Growth and Thermodynamical Laws. In *van Gool, W. and Bruggink, J. J. C., eds.*, 1985, pp. 135–45.

Bryant, J. Economics, Equilibrium and Thermodynamics. In *van Gool, W. and Bruggink, J. J. C., eds.*, 1985, pp. 197–221. **[G: U.K.; OECD]**

Burgess, David F. Canada/U.S. Energy Issues: A Canadian Perspective. In *Fretz, D.; Stern, R. and Whalley, J., eds.*, 1985, pp. 213–51. **[G: Canada; U.S.]**

Cameron, Trudy Ann. A Nested Logit Model of Energy Conservation Activity by Owners of Existing Single Family Dwellings. *Rev. Econ. Statist.*, May 1985, *67*(2), pp. 205–11. **[G: U.S.]**

Cameron, Trudy Ann. From Technocracy to Net Energy Analysis: Engineers, Economists, and Recurring Energy Theories of Value: Comment. In *Scott, A., ed.*, 1985, pp. 370–75. **[G: U.S.]**

Campbell, Robert W. Technology Transfer in the Soviet Energy Sector. In *Parrott, B., ed.*, 1985, pp. 141–68. **[G: U.S.S.R.]**

Campbell, Robert W. The Origins of the Soviet Oil Crisis, 1970–1985: Comments. *Soviet Econ.*, Apr.-June 1985, *1*(2), pp. 142–45. **[G: U.S.S.R.]**

Cappelen, Adne; Offerdal, Erik and Strøm, Steinar. Oil Revenues and the Norwegian Economy in the Seventies. In *Bjerkholt, O. and Offerdal, E., eds.*, 1985, pp. 35–62. **[G: Norway]**

Carpenter, Edwin H. and Durham, Cathy. Again, Federal Tax Credits Are Found Effec-

tive: A Reply. *Energy J.*, July 1985, *6*(3), pp. 127–28. **[G: U.S.]**

Cartucho Pereira, Paulo. A procura energia no Plano Energético Nacional—Apreciação crítica. (With English summary.) *Economia (Portugal)*, May 1985, *9*(2), pp. 301–15. **[G: Portugal]**

Castanias, Richard P. A Test of the OPEC Cartel Hypothesis: 1974–1983: Discussion. *J. Finance*, July 1985, *40*(3), pp. 1006–08. **[G: OPEC]**

Chalmers, James A. Synfuels Development in the USA: Case Studies of National Environmental Feasibility and Local Socioeconomic Impacts: The Cumulative Impacts Task Force Experience in Colorado. In *Lakshmanan, T. R. and Johansson, B., eds.*, 1985, pp. 100–110. **[G: U.S.]**

Chiesa, Gabriella. Oil Shock, Saving, Investment and Trade Balance: The Role of Short Run Rigidity versus Long Run Flexibility. An Intertemporal Approach. *Econ. Int.*, February 1985, *38*(1), pp. 1–20.

Choucri, Nazli. Domestic Energy Pricing: Trends and Implications for the Arab World. *J. Energy Devel.*, Autumn 1985, *11*(1), pp. 27–68. **[G: Middle East]**

Cloete, S. A. The Structure of the International Supply of Coal—A Qualitative View. *J. Stud. Econ. Econometrics*, March 1985, (21), pp. 67–102.

Coker, Christopher. Eastern Europe and the Middle East: The Forgotten Dimension of Soviet Policy. In *Cassen, R., ed.*, 1985, pp. 46–67. **[G: CMEA; Middle East]**

Common, Michael S. The Distributional Implications of Higher Energy Prices in the UK. *Appl. Econ.*, June 1985, *17*(3), pp. 421–36. **[G: U.K.]**

Copithorne, Lawrence and MacFadyen, Alan. Strategy for Energy Policy: Introduction. *Can. Public Policy*, Supplement July 1985, *11*(3), pp. 372–82. **[G: Canada]**

Copithorne, Lawrence; MacFadyen, Alan and Bell, Bruce. Revenue Sharing and the Efficient Valuation of Natural Resources. *Can. Public Policy*, Supplement July 1985, *11*(3), pp. 465–78. **[G: Canada]**

Cruz, Alejandro. Latin American Energy Cooperation and Its Extension to Other Developing Countries. *J. Energy Devel.*, Spring 1985, *10*(2), pp. 273–83. **[G: Latin America]**

Cumming, Peter A. Federal–Provincial Fiscal Arrangements and the Search for Fiscal Equity through Reformulation of the Equalization Program. In *Courchene, T. J.; Conklin, D. W. and Cook, G. C. A., eds. Vol. 1*, 1985, pp. 96–124. **[G: Canada]**

Dahl, Carol A. Do Gasoline Demand Elasticities Vary? Reply. *Land Econ.*, May 1985, *61*(2), pp. 201–04. **[G: Selected Countries]**

De Gleria, Silvana. Prodotto netto ed energia netta (ovvero: dogma fisiocratico e dogma energetico). (With English summary.) *Econ. Polít.*, August 1985, *2*(2), pp. 187–213.

Despraries, P. C. Oil and Rival Energy Sources.

Energy J., October 1985, *6*(4), pp. 23–28.
[G: OECD; OPEC]

Deutsch, Edwin. Energy and Employment: An Investigation of the Austrian Economy. In *van Gool, W. and Bruggink, J. J. C., eds.*, 1985, pp. 119–33. [G: Austria]

Dienes, Leslie. The Energy System and Economic Imbalances in the USSR. *Soviet Econ.*, Oct.-Dec. 1985, *1*(4), pp. 340–72.
[G: U.S.S.R.]

Dixit, Avinash K. and Newbery, David M. G. Setting the Price of Oil in a Distorted Economy. *Econ. J.*, Supplement 1985, *95*, pp. 71–82. [G: Turkey]

Dobbs, Ian M. A Cost–Benefit Analysis of Combined Heat and Power. *Manchester Sch. Econ. Soc. Stud.*, September 1985, *53*(3), pp. 241–62. [G: U.K.]

Doblin, Claire P. Patterns of Industrial Change in the Federal Republic of Germany. Part I: Flows of Manufacturing Output and Energy Input. In *Smyshlyaev, A., ed.*, 1985, pp. 73–78. [G: W. Germany]

Donnelly, William A. A State-Level, Variable Elasticity of Demand for Gasoline Model. *Int. J. Transport Econ.*, June 1985, *12*(2), pp. 193–202. [G: U.S.]

Donnelly, William A. Electricity Demand Modelling. In *Batten, D. F. and Lesse, P. F., eds.*, 1985, pp. 179–95. [G: Australia]

Dupont, Pierre. Substitutions énergie-travail dans le modèle de prix de Statistique Canada. (Energy-Labour Substitutions in the Price Model of Statistic Canada [Using Exogenous Elasticities to Induce Factor Substitution Input–Output Price Models]. With English summary.) *L'Actual. Econ.*, March 1985, *61*(1), pp. 112–26. [G: Canada]

Dupont, Serge and Diener, Steven G. The Future of Energy Conservation and Alternative Energies: Opportunities and Barriers. *Can. Public Policy*, Supplement July 1985, *11*(3), pp. 443–54. [G: Canada]

Eck, Theodore R. A U.S. Industry Perspective on Oil Consumption Trends. In *Czinkota, M. R. and Marciel, S., eds.*, 1985, pp. 79–85. [G: U.S.]

Eckstein, Zvi and Eichenbaum, Martin S. Inventories and Quantity-Constrained Equilibria in Regulated Markets: The U.S. Petroleum Industry, 1947–1972. In *Sargent, T. J., ed.*, 1985, pp. 70–100. [G: U.S.]

Eckstein, Zvi and Eichenbaum, Martin S. Oil Supply Disruptions and the Optimal Tariff in a Dynamic Stochastic Equilibrium Model. In *Sargent, T. J., ed.*, 1985, pp. 41–69.

Edmonds, James A. and Reilly, John. Time and Uncertainty: Analytic Paradigms and Policy Requirements. In *van Gool, W. and Bruggink, J. J. C., eds.*, 1985, pp. 287–313.

El-Kuwaiz, Abdullah. The Future of Oil Prices. In *Kubursi, A. A. and Naylor, T., eds.*, 1985, pp. 43–52. [G: OPEC; Global]

Erdösi, Pal. The Role of Energy Intensity in Economic Development. In *Smyshlyaev, A., ed.*, 1985, pp. 221–24.

Erickson, Edward W. Deregulation and Natural Gas Supply and Demand. In *Crew, M. A., ed.*, 1985, pp. 141–59. [G: U.S.]

Erickson, Edward W. Prospects for a Tighter World Oil Market. *Energy J.*, January 1985, *6*(1), pp. 3–7. [G: Global]

Ernst, Maurice. The Origins of the Soviet Oil Crisis, 1970–1985: Comments. *Soviet Econ.*, Apr.-June 1985, *1*(2), pp. 136–41.
[G: U.S.S.R.]

Escovar Salom, Ramón. Venezuela: The Oil Boom and the Debt Crisis. In *Duran, E., ed.*, 1985, pp. 120–29. [G: Venezuela]

Falk, James E. and McCormick, Garth P. Computational Aspects of the International Coal Trade Model. In *Harker, P. T., ed.*, 1985, pp. 73–117.

Farzin, Y. Hossein. The Economics of Natural Gas Utilization in Developing Countries: Methodology. *Energy J.*, July 1985, *6*(3), pp. 91–99.

Fender, John. Oil in a Dynamic Two Good Model. *Oxford Econ. Pap.*, June 1985, *37*(2), pp. 249–63.

Fenili, Robert. The Impact of Decontrol on Gasoline Wholesalers and Retailers. *Contemp. Policy Issues*, Spring, Pt. 2, 1985, *3*(3), pp. 119–30. [G: U.S.]

Frankel, P. H. Change and Continuity. *Energy J.*, October 1985, *6*(4), pp. 1–5. [G: OECD; OPEC]

Galer, G. S. Scenario Planning in the Context of International Energy Development. In *Niblock, T. and Lawless, R., eds.*, 1985, pp. 74–81. [G: Selected Countries]

Garbacz, Christopher. Residential Demand for Fuelwood. *Energy Econ.*, July 1985, *7*(3), pp. 191–93. [G: U.S.]

Garbacz, Christopher. Residential Fuel Oil Demand: A Micro-based National Model. *Appl. Econ.*, August 1985, *17*(4), pp. 669–74.
[G: U.S.]

Gellerson, Mark. The Economics of Small Hydro Power. *Pakistan Econ. Soc. Rev.*, Summer 1985, *23*(1), pp. 25–39. [G: Pakistan]

Gheorghe, A. Paradigms in Energy/Time Relationship. In *van Gool, W. and Bruggink, J. J. C., eds.*, 1985, pp. 81–102.

Ghirardi, André. Trends of Energy Use in Brazil: Is Self-sufficiency in Sight? *J. Energy Devel.*, Spring 1985, *10*(2), pp. 173–91. [G: Brazil]

Gholamnezhad, Hamid. 1995: The Turning Point in Oil Prices. In *Didsbury, H. F., Jr., ed.*, 1985, pp. 296–314.

Glakpe, Emmanuel and Fazzolare, Rocco. Economic Demand Analysis for Electricity in West Africa. *Energy J.*, January 1985, *6*(1), pp. 137–44. [G: W. Africa]

van Gool, W. Physics, Thermodynamics, Economics, Energy Analysis, and Time. In *van Gool, W. and Bruggink, J. J. C., eds.*, 1985, pp. 149–53.

van Gool, W. Towards a Physical Interpretation of Production Functions. In *van Gool, W. and Bruggink, J. J. C., eds.*, 1985, pp. 247–56.

Gopalakrishnan, Chennat. Natural Gas from

Seaweed: Is Near-term R and D Funding by the U.S. Gas Industry Warranted? *Energy J.*, October 1985, *6*(4), pp. 129–37. **[G: U.S.]**

Gordon, Richard L. The Rise and Fall of Oil Generation in the USA: A Study in Institutional Adaptability. *Energy Econ.*, April 1985, *7*(2), pp. 66–76. **[G: U.S.]**

Gottinger, Hans W. Dynamic Economic Strategies of Breeder Reactor Commitments. *Z. Wirtschaft. Sozialwissen.*, 1985, *105*(1), pp. 1–15.

Grauer, Manfred. Multiple Criteria Analysis in Energy Planning and Policy Assessment. In *Fandel, G. and Spronk, J., eds.*, 1985 , pp. 382–99.

Grauer, Manfred; Messner, Sabine and Strubegger, Manfred. An Integrated Programming Package for Multiple-Criteria Decision Analysis. In *Grauer, M.; Thompson, M. and Wierzbicki, A. P., eds.*, 1985, pp. 248–60. **[G: Selected Countries]**

Green, Christopher J. An Empirical Note on the Fiscal Accommodation of an Oil Price Increase. *Appl. Econ.*, February 1985, *17*(1), pp. 107–15. **[G: U.K.]**

Griffin, Ronald C.; Lacewell, Ronald D. and Collins, Glenn S. Impacts of Substituting Plant Oils for Diesel Fuel. *Western J. Agr. Econ.*, December 1985, *10*(2), pp. 401–12. **[G: U.S.]**

Groth, Philip G. Energy Development and Security and Supply-side Ideology: Oligopoly, Monopoly, and Imperfect Competition Make Fossil Fuel Regulation a Necessity. *Amer. J. Econ. Soc.*, April 1985, *44*(2), pp. 155–68. **[G: U.S.; Germany; Japan]**

Guadagni, Alieto Aldo. La programación de las inversiones eléctricas y las actuales prioridades energéticas. (With English summary.) *Desarrollo Econ.*, July-Sept. 1985, *25*(98), pp. 179–216. **[G: Argentina]**

Gustafson, Thane. The Origins of the Soviet Oil Crisis, 1970–1985. *Soviet Econ.*, Apr.-June 1985, *1*(2), pp. 103–35. **[G: U.S.S.R.]**

Haberler, Gottfried. Oil, Inflation, Recession and the International Monetary System. In *Haberler, G.*, 1985, pp. 335–47.

Hakogi, Masumi. Trade Restrictions and Trade Promotion: Comments. In *Saunders, C. T., ed.*, 1985, pp. 309–12. **[G: CMEA; OECD]**

Halpern, Dan. Israeli Oil Exploration at the Crossroads. In *Levinson, P. and Landau, P., eds.*, 1985, pp. 102–06. **[G: Israel]**

Hamilton, James D. Historical Causes of Postwar Oil Shocks and Recessions. *Energy J.*, January 1985, *6*(1), pp. 97–116. **[G: U.S.]**

Hammond, Elizabeth M.; Helm, Dieter R. and Thompson, David J. British Gas: Options for Privatisation. *Fisc. Stud.*, November 1985, *6*(4), pp. 1–20. **[G: U.K.]**

Hannon, B. M. Time Value in Ecosystems. In *van Gool, W. and Bruggink, J. J. C., eds.*, 1985, pp. 261–85.

Hanson, Gregory D. Financial Analysis of a Proposed Large-Scale Ethanol Cogeneration Proj-

ect. *Southern J. Agr. Econ.*, December 1985, *17*(2), pp. 67–76. **[G: U.S.]**

Hartshorn, Jack E. Government Sellers in a Restructured Crude Oil Market. In *Hawdon, D., ed.*, 1985, pp. 59–69.

Hassanain, Mahjoob A. Future Prospect for Alternative Sources of Energy. *J. Energy Devel.*, Spring 1985, *10*(2), pp. 231–37. **[G: W. Europe; U.S.; Japan]**

Hawdon, David. Survey of Oil Price Expectations 22/23 March 1984. In *Hawdon, D., ed.*, 1985, pp. 106–12. **[G: OPEC]**

Heaps, Terry and Helliwell, John F. The Taxation of Natural Resources. In *Auerbach, A. J. and Feldstein, M., eds.*, 1985, pp. 421–72.

Helliwell, John F., et al. Energy and the National Economy: An Overview of the MACE Model. In *Scott, A., ed.*, 1985, pp. 17–85. **[G: Canada]**

Helliwell, John F., et al. Energy Deregulation and Uncertain World Oil Prices: What Are the Connections? *Can. Public Policy*, Supplement July 1985, *11*(3), pp. 479–91. **[G: Canada]**

Hirst, Eric and Goeltz, Richard. Estimating Energy Savings Due to Conservation Programmes: The BPA Residential Weatherization Pilot Programme. *Energy Econ.*, January 1985, *7*(1), pp. 20–28. **[G: U.S.]**

Hochman, Eithan and Zilberman, David. Optimal Exploitation of Energy Resources: Solar Power and Electricity Generation in below Sea Level Basins. *J. Environ. Econ. Manage.*, December 1985, *12*(4), pp. 322–37.

Hogan, William W. Energy and Economy: Global Interdependences. *Energy J.*, October 1985, *6*(4), pp. 7–21. **[G: Global]**

Hogarty, Thomas F. Issues in Gasoline Marketing: Introduction. *Contemp. Policy Issues*, Spring, Pt. 2, 1985, *3*(3), pp. 103–04. **[G: U.S.]**

Honeycutt, T. Crawford. Competition in Controlled and Uncontrolled Gasoline Markets. *Contemp. Policy Issues*, Spring, Pt. 2, 1985, *3*(3), pp. 105–18. **[G: U.S.]**

Hope, Chris and Gaskell, Phil. The Competitive Price of Oil: Some Results under Uncertainty. *Energy Econ.*, October 1985, *7*(4), pp. 289–96. **[G: Global]**

Hordijk, Leen. Synfuels Development in the USA: Case Studies of National Environmental Feasibility and Local Socioeconomic Impacts: Technical Review of the U.S. Case Studies: II. In *Lakshmanan, T. R. and Johansson, B., eds.*, 1985, pp. 118–24. **[G: U.S.]**

Hsiao, Frank S. T. and Hsiao, Mei-Chu Wang. Elasticities, Ratios, and Energy Modelling. *Energy Econ.*, July 1985, *7*(3), pp. 153–58. **[G: U.K.]**

Hua, Chang-i. Energy-Related Boom Towns: Problems, Causes, Policies, and Modeling. In *Lakshmanan, T. R. and Johansson, B., eds.*, 1985, pp. 215–32.

Hubbard, R. Glenn and Weiner, Robert J. Modeling Oil Price Fluctuations and International Stockpile Coordination. *J. Policy Modeling*, Summer 1985, *7*(2), pp. 339–59. **[G: OECD]**

Hughes-Cromwick, Ellen L. Nairobi Households and Their Energy Use: An Economic Analysis of Consumption Patterns. *Energy Econ.*, October 1985, *7*(4), pp. 265–78. **[G: Kenya]**

Iatrov, S., et al. Planning the Fuel-Energy Complex under Conditions of Intensification. *Prob. Econ.*, June 1985, *28*(2), pp. 25–39. **[G: U.S.S.R.]**

Inotai, András. East–West Relations in Energy, Agriculture and Technology: Comments. In *Saunders, C. T., ed.*, 1985, pp. 246–51. **[G: CMEA]**

Iqbal, Mahmood. Estimates of Gasoline Demand in Pakistan. *Pakistan J. Appl. Econ.*, Summer 1985, *4*(1), pp. 35–45. **[G: Pakistan]**

Islam, Saiful. Effect of an Essential Input on Isoquants and Substitution Elasticities. *Energy Econ.*, July 1985, *7*(3), pp. 194–96.

Jerve, Alf Morten; Tobiesen, Per and Åsberg, Rodney. Rural Energy. In *Jerve, A. M., ed.*, 1985, pp. 321–26. **[G: Pakistan]**

Johansson, B. and Snickars, F. Conservation and Fuel Switching in Sweden: Large-scale Introduction of Energy Supply Systems: Issues, Methods, and Models in Sweden. In *Lakshmanan, T. R. and Johansson, B., eds.*, 1985, pp. 125–62. **[G: Sweden]**

Jones, Aubrey. Sources of Energy for the Twenty-first Century. In *Wells, N., ed.*, 1985, pp. 28–34. **[G: Global]**

Jorgenson, Dale W. The Great Transition: Energy and Economic Change. In *Shishido, T. and Sato, R., eds.*, 1985, pp. 260–86. **[G: OECD]**

Joskow, Paul L. The Residential Electricity Time-of-Use Pricing Experiments: What Have We Learned? Comment. In *Hausman, J. A. and Wise, D. A., eds.*, 1985, pp. 42–48. **[G: U.S.]**

Kadekodi, Gopal K. A Welfare Approach to Energy Pricing: A Case Study for India. *Energy J.*, July 1985, *6*(3), pp. 1–19. **[G: India]**

Kadir, Abdul. Electric Power in Indonesia's Fourth Five-Year Development Plan. *J. Energy Devel.*, Spring 1985, *10*(2), pp. 239–47. **[G: Indonesia]**

Kang, Kwang-Ha and Kendrick, David. The Tradeoff between Economies of Scale and Reliability in the Electric Power Industry. *J. Econ. Devel.*, July 1985, *10*(1), pp. 47–61. **[G: S. Korea]**

Kaser, Michael. Energy Trade within COMECON. In *[Levcik, F.]*, 1985, pp. 215–30. **[G: COMECON; CMEA]**

Kaserman, David L. and Mayo, John W. Advertising and the Residential Demand for Electricity. *J. Bus.*, October 1985, *58*(4), pp. 399–408. **[G: U.S.]**

Kearton, Lord. The Oil Industry. Some Personal Recollections and Opinions. In *Hawdon, D., ed.*, 1985, pp. 1–17.

Keng, C. W. Kenneth. Forecasting Canadian Nuclear Power Station Construction Costs. *Energy Econ.*, October 1985, *7*(4), pp. 241–58. **[G: Canada]**

Kessler, Richard J. No Fuel for Development:

United States Policy toward Managing International Energy Resources. In *Jordan, R. S., ed.*, 1985, pp. 21–42.

Khadduri, Walid. Oil in International Trade in the 1980s. In *Czinkota, M. R. and Marciel, S., eds.*, 1985, pp. 59–69. **[G: OPEC]**

Kharbanda, V. P. and Qureshi, M. A. Biogas Development in India and the PRC. *Energy J.*, July 1985, *6*(3), pp. 51–65. **[G: India]**

Khosla, S. L. Energy. In *Mongia, J. N., ed.*, 1985, pp. 417–51. **[G: India]**

Kim, Sunwoong. Models of Energy–Economy Interactions for Developing Countries: A Survey. *J. Energy Devel.*, Autumn 1985, *11*(1), pp. 141–64.

Kiraly, Julia and Lovei, Laszlo. Energy Consumption in Hungary: An Ex Post Analysis. *Energy J.*, July 1985, *6*(3), pp. 115–25. **[G: Hungary]**

Klein, Lawrence R. Energy and the National Economy: An Overview of the MACE Model: Comment. In *Scott, A., ed.*, 1985, pp. 85–89. **[G: Canada]**

Kogane, Yoshihiro. Economic Growth before and after the Oil Crisis and the Possibility of Deindustrialization. In *Didsbury, H. F., Jr., ed.*, 1985, pp. 267–95. **[G: Japan; W. Europe; U.S.]**

Kok, M. and Lootsma, F. A. Pairwise Comparisons in a Multi-objective Energy Model. In *Haimes, Y. Y. and Chankong, V., eds.*, 1985, pp. 457–74.

Koopmans, Tjalling C. Alternative Futures with or without Constraints on the Energy Technology Mix. In *Koopmans, T. C.*, 1985, pp. 251–61. **[G: U.S.]**

Kornbluh, Hy; Crowfoot, James and Cohen-Rosenthal, Edward. Worker Participation in Energy and Natural Resources Conservation. *Int. Lab. Rev.*, Nov.-Dec. 1985, *124*(6), pp. 737–54. **[G: U.S.]**

Koshal, Rajindar K. and Koshal, Manjulika. Energy Alternatives for Railways: Some Experience from Indian Railways. *Int. J. Transport Econ.*, June 1985, *12*(2), pp. 185–91. **[G: India]**

Kosmo, Mark. OCS Leasing Policy: Its Effects on the Structure of the Petroleum Industry. *Energy J.*, January 1985, *6*(1), pp. 79–96.

Kouri, Pentti J. K.; Braga de Macedo, Jorge and Viscio, Albert J. Profitability, Employment and Structural Adjustment in France. In *Melitz, J. and Wyplosz, C., eds.*, 1985, pp. 85–112. **[G: France]**

Köves, András. Some Questions of Energy Policy in East European Countries: Energy Supply and Foreign Economic Policy. *Acta Oecon.*, 1985, *35*(3–4), pp. 345–57. **[G: CMEA]**

Kubursi, A. A. Industrialisation in the Arab States of the Gulf: A Ruhr without Water. In *Niblock, T. and Lawless, R., eds.*, 1985, pp. 42–65. **[G: OPEC]**

Kümmel, Reiner and Strassl, W. Changing Energy Prices, Information Technology, and Industrial Growth. In *van Gool, W. and Brug-*

gink, J. J. C., eds., 1985, pp. 175–94.
[G: W. Germany; U.S.]

Kümmel, Reiner, et al. Technical Progress and Energy Dependent Production Functions. *Z. Nationalökon.*, 1985, *45*(3), pp. 285–311.
[G: U.S.; W. Germany]

Kyle, Albert S. The Pricing of Oil and Gas: Some Further Results: Discussion. *J. Finance*, July 1985, *40*(3), pp. 1018–20. [G: U.S.]

Lakshmanan, T. R. National and Regional Models for Economic Assessment of Energy Projects. In *Lakshmanan, T. R. and Johansson, B., eds.*, 1985, pp. 187–214.

Lakshmanan, T. R. and Johansson, B. Consequences of Energy Developments: An Approach to Assessment and Management. In *Lakshmanan, T. R. and Johansson, B., eds.*, 1985, pp. 1–24.

Lakshmanan, T. R. and Johansson, B. Energy Decisions and Models: Review and Prospects. In *Lakshmanan, T. R. and Johansson, B., eds.*, 1985, pp. 305–17. [G: U.S.; Canada; U.S.S.R.; Sweden]

Landsberg, Hans H. Energy in Transition: A View from 1960. *Energy J.*, April 1985, *6*(2), pp. 1–18. [G: U.S.]

Lantzke, U. International Energy Strategy in a North–South Context. In *Bapna, A., ed.*, 1985, pp. 117–30. [G: Global]

LeBlanc, Michael. The Effects of Natural Gas Decontrol on Fertilizer Demand, Production Costs, and Income in Agriculture. *Energy J.*, January 1985, *6*(1), pp. 117–35. [G: U.S.]

Leistritz, F. Larry; Wiedrich, Garland D. and Vreugdenhil, Harvey G. Effects of Energy Development on Agricultural Land Values. *Western J. Agr. Econ.*, December 1985, *10*(2), pp. 204–15. [G: U.S.]

Lesourd, Jean-Baptiste. Energy and Resources as Production Factors in Process Industries. *Energy Econ.*, July 1985, *7*(3), pp. 138–44.

Libecap, Gary D. Regulatory Constraints on Oil and Gas Production on Forest Service and BLM Lands. In *Deacon, R. T. and Johnson, M. B., eds.*, 1985, pp. 135–48. [G: U.S.]

Libecap, Gary D. and Wiggins, Steven N. The Influence of Private Contractual Failure on Regulation: The Case of Oil Field Unitization. *J. Polit. Econ.*, August 1985, *93*(4), pp. 690–714. [G: U.S.]

Lin, An-loh; Botsas, Eleftherios N. and Monroe, Scott A. State Gasoline Consumption in the USA: An Econometric Analysis. *Energy Econ.*, January 1985, *7*(1), pp. 29–36. [G: U.S.]

Loderer, Claudio. A Test of the OPEC Cartel Hypothesis: 1974–1983. *J. Finance*, July 1985, *40*(3), pp. 991–1006. [G: OPEC]

Lonergan, S. C. Tar Sands Development in Canada: A Case Study of Environmental Monitoring: Resource Extraction in Canada: Modeling the Regional Impacts. In *Lakshmanan, T. R. and Johansson, B., eds.*, 1985, pp. 41–61.
[G: Canada]

Lorentsen, Lorents and Roland, Kjell. Norway's Export of Natural Gas to the European Gas Market. Policy Issues and Model Tools. In

Bjerkholt, O. and Offerdal, E., eds., 1985, pp. 103–22. [G: Norway; W. Europe]

Loviscek, Anthony and Crowley, Frederick. Energy Prices and Municipal Bond Ratings: Are Interregional Terms of Trade Shifting? *J. Energy Devel.*, Spring 1985, *10*(2), pp. 201–12. [G: U.S.]

Lowinger, Thomas C.; Wihlborg, Clas and Willman, Elliott S. An Empirical Analysis of OPEC and Non-OPEC Behavior. *J. Energy Devel.*, Autumn 1985, *11*(1), pp. 119–40.

Lowinger, Thomas C.; Wihlborg, Clas and Willman, Elliott S. OPEC in World Financial Markets: Oil Prices and Interest Rates. *J. Int. Money Finance*, June 1985, *4*(2), pp. 253–66.
[G: OECD; OPEC]

Lukaszewicz, Aleksander. Comments [The Global Environment and Its Impact on Soviet and East European Economies] [The Impact of Energy on East–West Trade: Retrospect and Prospects]. In *Saunders, C. T., ed.*, 1985, pp. 135–36. [G: OECD; CMEA; U.S.S.R.]

Lukaszewicz, Aleksander. Trade Restrictions and Trade Promotion: Comments. In *Saunders, C. T., ed.*, 1985, pp. 312–14. [G: CMEA; OECD]

Lundqvist, Lars. Tar Sands Development in Canada: A Case Study of Environmental Monitoring: On Canadian Energy Impact Assessments. In *Lakshmanan, T. R. and Johansson, B., eds.*, 1985, pp. 62–71. [G: Canada]

Maachou, Abdelkader. Petroleum Policies of the Arab Countries and Their Relations with the Industrialised Countries. In *Kubursi, A. A. and Naylor, T., eds.*, 1985, pp. 61–71.
[G: Persian Gulf; OECD]

Mairesse, Jacques. Profitability, Employment and Structural Adjustment in France: Comments. In *Melitz, J. and Wyplosz, C., eds.*, 1985, pp. 114–16. [G: France]

Manne, Alan S. and Preckel, Paul V. A Three-Region Intertemporal Model of Energy, International Trade and Capital Flows. In *Manne, A. S., ed.*, 1985, pp. 56–74. [G: OECD; OPEC; LDCs]

Mansell, Robert L. and Jordan, Barbara A. An Economic Evaluation of Methanol Blends in Canadian Markets. *Can. Public Policy*, Supplement July 1985, *11*(3), pp. 455–64.
[G: Canada]

Marston, Geoffrey. The Newfoundland Offshore Jurisdictional Dispute—A Postscript. *J. World Trade Law*, July:Aug. 1985, *19*(4), pp. 423–25. [G: Canada]

Martellaro, Joseph A. Taiwan: A Country Experience in Energy. *Econ. Int.*, Aug./Nov. 1985, *38*(3/4), pp. 351–67. [G: Taiwan]

Martellaro, Joseph A. Water as a Resource in the Third World. *J. Econ. Devel.*, July 1985, *10*(1), pp. 7–28. [G: LDCs]

Martin, A. J. The Prediction of Strategic Reserves. In *Niblock, T. and Lawless, R., eds.*, 1985, pp. 16–39. [G: Global]

McCarl, Bruce A. and Ross, Mark. The Cost Borne by Electricity Consumers under Expanded Irrigation from the Columbia River.

Water Resources Res., September 1985, *21*(9), pp. 1319–28.

McColl, G. D. Economic Issues Facing Electricity Supply Authorities. *Australian Econ. Rev.*, 4th Quarter 1985, (72), pp. 28–36. **[G: Australia]**

McHale, Thomas R. Oil, the Financial Assets of the Arabian Gulf, and the World Economy. In *Czinkota, M. R. and Marciel, S., eds.*, 1985, pp. 86–97. **[G: OPEC]**

McRae, Robert N. A Survey of Canadian Energy Policy: 1974–1983. *Energy J.*, October 1985, *6*(4), pp. 49–64. **[G: Canada]**

Medvedev, Boris. Conserving Material Resources. *Soviet E. Europ. Foreign Trade*, Winter 1985-86, *21*(4), pp. 58–67. **[G: CMEA]**

Melese, François. Deregulation, Endogenous Expectations, and the Evolution of Industry Structure. *Southern Econ. J.*, January 1985, *51*(3), pp. 793–803.

Melese, François and Michel, Philippe. Deregulation as a Switch of Regime: Price Effects Using a Modified Hotelling Rule. *Energy Econ.*, April 1985, *7*(2), pp. 93–101.

Miernyk, William H. Energy Constraints and Economic Development in the Northeast. In *Richardson, H. W. and Turek, J. H., eds.*, 1985, pp. 104–22. **[G: U.S.]**

Miller, Ellen M. Pass-through Lags in Fuel Adjustment Clauses and Firm Performance. *Atlantic Econ. J.*, December 1985, *13*(4), pp. 91–92.

Miller, John R. Petroleum Economics and Management. *J. Energy Devel.*, Spring 1985, *10*(2), pp. 165–72. **[G: U.S.]**

Miller, Merton H and Upton, Charles W. A Test of the Hotelling Valuation Principle. *J. Polit. Econ.*, February 1985, *93*(1), pp. 1–25. **[G: U.S.]**

Miller, Merton H. and Upton, Charles W. The Pricing of Oil and Gas: Some Further Results. *J. Finance*, July 1985, *40*(3), pp. 1009–18. **[G: U.S.]**

Millsaps, Steven W. and Ott, Mack. Risk Aversion, Risk Sharing, and Joint Bidding: A Study of Outer Continental Shelf Petroleum Auctions. *Land Econ.*, November 1985, *61*(4), pp. 372–86. **[G: U.S.]**

Moghimzadeh, Mahmood and Kymn, Kern O. Energy–Capital and Energy–Labor: Complementarity and Substitutability. *Atlantic Econ. J.*, July 1985, *13*(2), pp. 44–50. **[G: U.S.]**

Mogridge, M. J. H. Transport, Land Use and Energy Interaction. *Urban Stud.*, December 1985, *22*(6), pp. 481–92. **[G: France; U.K.]**

Moody, Carlisle E.; Valentine, Patrick L. and Kruvant, William J. The GAO Natural Gas Supply Model. *Energy Econ.*, January 1985, *7*(1), pp. 49–57. **[G: U.S.]**

Mork, Knut Anton. Flexibility in Intercommodity Substitution May Sharpen Price Fluctuations. *Quart. J. Econ.*, May 1985, *100*(2), pp. 447–63.

Motamen, Homa. The Wealth Effect of North Sea Oil. In *Bjerkholt, O. and Offerdal, E., eds.*, 1985, pp. 231–47. **[G: U.K.]**

Motamen, Homa and Schaller, C. Pattern of UK

Fuel Use. *Energy Econ.*, October 1985, *7*(4), pp. 221–30. **[G: U.K.]**

Mountain, Dean C. Productivity and Energy Price Differentials. *Reg. Sci. Urban Econ.*, August 1985, *15*(3), pp. 477–89. **[G: Canada]**

Mountain, Dean C. The Contribution of Changing Energy and Import Prices to Changing Average Labor Productivity: A Profit Formulation for Canada. *Quart. J. Econ.*, August 1985, *100*(3), pp. 651–75. **[G: Canada]**

Müller, Friedemann. Economic Relations—Interdependence or Marginal Factor?: Energy. In *Rode, R. and Jacobsen, H.-D., eds.*, 1985, pp. 73–85. **[G: U.S.S.R.]**

Müller, Harald. Western Policies: U.S. Energy Policy. In *Rode, R. and Jacobsen, H.-D., eds.*, 1985, pp. 200–212. **[G: U.S.; CMEA]**

Muller, R. A. and George, P. J. Northern Hydroelectric Development in an Optimal Expansion Program for Ontario Hydro. *Can. Public Policy*, September 1985, *11*(3), pp. 522–32. **[G: Canada]**

Murakami, Katsutoshi and Nawashiro, Aoi. Issues and Problems in U.S.–Japan Energy Relations. In *Nanto, D. K., ed.*, 1985, pp. 102–13. **[G: Japan; U.S.]**

Murphy, Frederick H.; Toman, Michael A. and Weiss, Howard J. International Cooperation in Stockpiles and Tariffs for Coping with Oil Supply Disruptions. *J. Policy Modeling*, Winter 1985, *7*(4), pp. 649–72. **[G: OECD]**

Musgrove, A. R. de L. and Stocks, K. J. Electricity and Gas Supply in South-eastern Australia, 1980–2020. *Energy Econ.*, January 1985, *7*(1), pp. 37–48. **[G: Australia]**

Myllyntaus, Timo. Initial Electrification in Three Main Branches of Finnish Industry, 1882–1920. *Scand. Econ. Hist. Rev.*, 1985, *33*(2), pp. 122–43. **[G: Finland]**

Nelson, Charles R. and Peck, Stephen C. The NERC Fan: A Retrospective Analysis of the NERC Summary Forecasts. *J. Bus. Econ. Statist.*, July 1985, *3*(3), pp. 179–87. **[G: U.S.]**

Nielsen, Søren Bo. Valutakursvirkninger af olieprisstigninger. (The Impact of Oil Price Increases on Exchange Rate. With English summary.) *Nationaløkon. Tidsskr.*, 1985, *123*(1), pp. 50–63. **[G: U.S.; OPEC; U.K.; Japan]**

Nijkamp, Peter. Regional Information Systems and Impact Analyses for Large-scale Energy Developments. In *Lakshmanan, T. R. and Johansson, B., eds.*, 1985, pp. 257–69.

Nishimiya, Ryoichi. Input–Output Techniques in the Japanese Econometric Model. In *Smyshlyaev, A., ed.*, 1985, pp. 173–81. **[G: Japan]**

Odell, Peter R. Back to Cheap Oil? *Lloyds Bank Rev.*, April 1985, (156), pp. 1–15. **[G: OPEC]**

Ohtani, Kazuhiro and Katayama, Sei-ichi. An Alternative Gradual Switching Regression Model and Its Application. *Econ. Stud. Quart.*, August 1985, *36*(2), pp. 148–53. **[G: Japan]**

Okada, Norio. Cost Allocation in Multipurpose Reservoir Development: The Japanese Experience. In *Young, H. P., ed.*, 1985, pp. 193–205. **[G: Japan]**

Olson, Dennis O. and Jonish, James. The Robustness of Translog Elasticity of Substitution Estimates and the Capital Energy Complementarity Controversy. *Quart. J. Bus. Econ.*, Winter 1985, *24*(1), pp. 21–35.

Peck, Stephen C. and Weyant, John P. Electricity Growth in the Future. *Energy J.*, January 1985, *6*(1), pp. 23–43.   [G: U.S.]

Peerenboom, James P. and Foell, Wesley K. A Decision Analysis Approach to Energy System Expansion Planning. *Energy J.*, July 1985, *6*(3), pp. 21–36.   [G: U.S.]

Penrose, Edith. Downstream Implications of Structural Change. In *Hawdon, D., ed.*, 1985, pp. 80–91.

Pepper, M. P. G. Multivariate Box–Jenkins Analysis: A Case Study in UK Energy Demand Forecasting. *Energy Econ.*, July 1985, *7*(3), pp. 168–78.   [G: U.K.]

Pereira, M. V. F. and Pinto, L. M. V. G. Stochastic Optimization of a Multireservoir Hydroelectric System: A Decomposition Approach. *Water Resources Res.*, June 1985, *21*(6), pp. 779–92.   [G: Brazil]

Petersen, H. Craig. Solar versus Conservation Tax Credits. *Energy J.*, July 1985, *6*(3), pp. 129–35.   [G: U.S.]

Pirog, Robert and Stamos, Stephen C. Energy Concentration: Implications for Energy Policy and Planning. *J. Econ. Issues*, June 1985, *19*(2), pp. 441–49.   [G: U.S.]

Pitt, Mark M. Equity, Externalities and Energy Subsidies: The Case of Kerosene in Indonesia. *J. Devel. Econ.*, April 1985, *17*(3), pp. 201–17.   [G: Indonesia]

Pitt, Mark M. Estimating Industrial Energy Demand with Firm-Level Data: The Case of Indonesia. *Energy J.*, April 1985, *6*(2), pp. 25–39.   [G: Indonesia]

Pløger, Ellen. The Effects of Structural Changes on Danish Energy Consumption. In *Smyshlyaev, A., ed.*, 1985, pp. 211–20.

               [G: Denmark]

Plourde, Andre and Ryan, David. On the Use of Double-Log Forms in Energy Demand Analysis. *Energy J.*, October 1985, *6*(4), pp. 105–13.

Polzin, Paul K. The Specification of Price in Studies of Consumer Demand under Block Price Scheduling: Reply. *Land Econ.*, August 1985, *61*(3), pp. 330–31.

Proops, John L. R. Thermodynamics and Economics: From Analogy to Physical Functioning. In *van Gool, W. and Bruggink, J. J. C., eds.*, 1985, pp. 155–74.

Prosser, Richard D. Demand Elasticities in OECD: Dynamical Aspects. *Energy Econ.*, January 1985, *7*(1), pp. 9–12.   [G: OECD]

Qadir, Asghar. Energy Policy: An Optimal Allocation Approach: Comments. *Pakistan Devel. Rev.*, Autumn-Winter 1985, *24*(3/4), pp. 561–63.   [G: Pakistan]

Quirin, Brendan E. Issues in Canada/U.S. Energy Trade and Investment: A U.S. Perspective. In *Fretz, D.; Stern, R. and Whalley, J., eds.*, 1985, pp. 256–77.   [G: Canada; U.S.]

Rabl, A. Optimizing Investment Levels for Energy Conservation: Individual versus Social Perspective and the Role of Uncertainty. *Energy Econ.*, October 1985, *7*(4), pp. 259–64.

Radlauer, Marcy A.; Bauman, David S. and Chapel, Stephen W. Nuclear Construction Lead Times: Analysis of Past Trends and Outlook for the Future. *Energy J.*, January 1985, *6*(1), pp. 45–62.   [G: U.S.]

Ranada, Julie G. The Price Responsiveness of Energy Demand in the Philippine Food Processing Sector. *Philippine Rev. Econ. Bus.*, Sept./Dec. 1985, *22*(3/4), pp. 229–46.

               [G: Philippines]

Ratick, Samuel J. Assessing the Environmental Consequences of Large-scale Energy Projects. In *Lakshmanan, T. R. and Johansson, B., eds.*, 1985, pp. 233–55.   [G: U.S.; U.S.S.R.; Sweden]

Reddy, Nallapu N. Market Boundaries between Coal, Oil, and Natural Gas. *Rev. Ind. Organ.*, 1985, *2*(3), pp. 300–305.   [G: U.S.]

Reid, Richard G. Standing the Test of Time. In *Hawdon, D., ed.*, 1985, pp. 52–58.

Reilly, John and Edmonds, Jae. Changing Climate and Energy Modeling: A Review. *Energy J.*, July 1985, *6*(3), pp. 137–54.

Rettig, Rudi. Changes in Input Coefficients in the German Economy. In *Smyshlyaev, A., ed.*, 1985, pp. 141–50.   [G: W. Germany]

Riaz, Tariq. Energy Policy: An Optimal Allocation Approach. *Pakistan Devel. Rev.*, Autumn-Winter 1985, *24*(3/4), pp. 551–60.

               [G: Pakistan]

Roemer, Michael. Dutch Disease in Developing Countries: Swallowing Bitter Medicine. In *Lundahl, M., ed.*, 1985, pp. 234–52.

               [G: LDCs]

Rose, Adam. Modeling Energy Conservation Programs: An Application to Natural Gas Utilities. *Energy J.*, October 1985, *6*(4), pp. 87–103.

               [G: U.S.]

Ruitenbeek, Jack. Economics of In-Situ Oilsands Production: Some Implications for Public Policy. *Can. Public Policy*, Supplement July 1985, *11*(3), pp. 407–14.   [G: Canada]

Rutledge, Ian and Wright, Phil. Coal Worldwide: The International Context of the British Miners' Strike. *Cambridge J. Econ.*, December 1985, *9*(4), pp. 303–26.   [G: U.K.]

Sakurai, Makoto. A Japanese Perspective on Resource Trade with Australia. In *Drysdale, P. and Shibata, H., eds.*, 1985, pp. 177–89.

               [G: Australia; Japan]

Saqqaf, Abdulaziz. Energy Production and Consumption in the Yemen Arab Republic. *J. Energy Devel.*, Autumn 1985, *11*(1), pp. 105–18.

               [G: Yemen]

Sargent, Thomas J. Energy, Foresight, and Strategy. In *Sargent, T. J., ed.*, 1985, pp. 1–13.

Scarfe, Brian L. Canadian Energy Prospects: Natural Gas, Tar Sands, and Oil Policy. *Contemp. Policy Issues*, Summer 1985, *3*(4), pp. 13–24.

               [G: Canada]

Scarfe, Brian L. Financing Oil and Gas Exploration and Development Activity. *Can. Public*

Policy, Supplement July 1985, *11*(3), pp. 402–06. [G: Canada]

Scarfe, Brian L. The National Energy Program after Three Years: An Economic Perspective. In *Kubursi, A. A. and Naylor, T., eds.*, 1985, pp. 83–116. [G: Canada]

Schefold, Bertram. Ecological Problems as a Challenge to Classical and Keynesian Economics. *Metroecon.*, February 1985, *37*(1), pp. 21–61. [G: Global]

Schipper, Lee and Ketoff, Andrea N. Residential Energy Use in the OECD. *Energy J.*, October 1985, *6*(4), pp. 65–85. [G: OECD]

Schwartz, S. L.; Fuller, J. D. and Ziemba, W. T. Long-run Effects of the Canadian National Energy Agreements. *Energy J.*, January 1985, *6*(1), pp. 63–77. [G: Canada]

Scott, Anthony D. From Technocracy to Net Energy Analysis: Engineers, Economists, and Recurring Energy Theories of Value: Comment. In *Scott, A., ed.*, 1985, pp. 367–70. [G: U.S.]

Scott, Norman. From Non-conventional to New Instruments of Trade Promotion? In *Saunders, C. T., ed.*, 1985, pp. 265–86. [G: CMEA; OECD]

Sebold, Frederick D. and Fox, Eric W. Realized Savings from Residential Conservation Activity. *Energy J.*, April 1985, *6*(2), pp. 73–88. [G: U.S.]

Segerson, Kathleen and Mount, Timothy D. A Non-homothetic Two-Stage Decision Model Using AIDS. *Rev. Econ. Statist.*, November 1985, *67*(4), pp. 630–39. [G: U.S.]

Seymour, Ian. OPEC and Structural Change. In *Hawdon, D., ed.*, 1985, pp. 70–79.

Sharpe, Ron. An Optimum Economic/Energy Land-Use Transportation Model. In *Hutchinson, B. G.; Nijkamp, P. and Batty, M., eds.*, 1985, pp. 50–66.

Shasharin, G. Atomic Energy. *Prob. Econ.*, October 1985, *28*(6), pp. 60–73. [G: U.S.S.R.]

Shebelev, Ia. V. Using Discounted Costs to Evaluate the Effectiveness of Economic Measures in Atomic Energy. *Matekon*, Fall 1985, *22*(1), pp. 91–110.

Shelby, Richard. A U.S. Policy Perspective on Oil Consumption Trends. In *Czinkota, M. R. and Marciel, S., eds.*, 1985, pp. 70–78. [G: U.S.; OPEC]

Shin, Jeong-Shik. Perception of Price When Price Information Is Costly: Evidence from Residential Electricity Demand. *Rev. Econ. Statist.*, November 1985, *67*(4), pp. 591–98. [G: U.S.]

Shore, Haim. Corrections [Summer Time and Electricity Conservation: The Israeli Case]. *Energy J.*, January 1985, *6*(1), pp. 169–70. [G: Israel]

Sigurjonsson, Birgir Bjørn. A Comparative Study of the Macroeconomic Performance of Some Energy-Rich and Some Energy-Poor Economies. In *Bjerkholt, O. and Offerdal, E., eds.*, 1985, pp. 63–77. [G: OECD]

Singer, S. Fred. Prospects for the World Oil Market. *Energy J.*, January 1985, *6*(1), pp. 13–16. [G: Global]

Slesser, M. The Use of Dynamic Energy Analysis in Energy Planning. In *van Gool, W. and Bruggink, J. J. C., eds.*, 1985, pp. 239–46. [G: U.K.]

Smith, V. Kerry and Hill, Lawrence J. Validating Allocation Functions in Energy Models: An Experimental Methodology. *Energy J.*, October 1985, *6*(4), pp. 29–47.

Snickars, F. and Johansson, B. The Development of Natural Gas Deposits in Western Siberia. In *Lakshmanan, T. R. and Johansson, B., eds.*, 1985, pp. 27–40. [G: U.S.S.R.]

Sohl, Jeffrey E. An Application of Quadratic Programming to the Deregulation of Natural Gas. In *Harker, P. T., ed.*, 1985, pp. 196–207. [G: U.S.]

Solomon, Barry D. and Rubin, Barry M. Environmental Linkages in Regional Econometric Models: An Analysis of Coal Development in Western Kentucky. *Land Econ.*, February 1985, *61*(1), pp. 43–57. [G: U.S.]

Solow, John L. General Equilibrium Incidence of Energy Taxation. *Southern Econ. J.*, April 1985, *51*(4), pp. 1018–30. [G: U.S.]

Stagni, Anna. Sistemi dinamici di domanda di fattori: un'applicazione agli impieghi di energia nell'industria italiana. (Dynamic Factor Demand Systems: An Application to Energy Inputs in the Italian Industry. With English summary.) *Ricerche Econ.*, Jan.-Mar. 1985, *39*(1), pp. 5–28. [G: Italy]

Stamos, Stephen C. Energy Policy: Planning. *Rev. Radical Polit. Econ.*, Spring and Summer 1985, *17*(1/2), pp. 241–52. [G: U.S.]

Steeg, Helga. Role of The International Energy Agency. *World Econ.*, June 1985, *8*(2), pp. 189–93. [G: OECD]

Sterner, Thomas. Structural Change and Technology Choice: Energy Use in Mexican Manufacturing Industry, 1970–81. *Energy Econ.*, April 1985, *7*(2), pp. 77–86. [G: Mexico]

Stevens, Paul. A Survey of Structural Change in the International Oil Industry 1945–1984. In *Hawdon, D., ed.*, 1985, pp. 18–51.

Stevens, T. H.; Adams, G. and Willis, C. The Specification of Price in Studies of Consumer Demand under Block Price Scheduling: Comment. *Land Econ.*, August 1985, *61*(3), pp. 327–29.

Ströbele, Wolfgang. An Economist's Definition of the Energy Problem: On the Optimal Intertemporal Allocation of Exergy. In *van Gool, W. and Bruggink, J. J. C., eds.*, 1985, pp. 61–78.

Sunley, Emil M. Private/Public Venturing Activities and Opportunities. In *Konecci, E. B. and Kuhn, R. L., eds.*, 1985, pp. 171–84. [G: U.S.]

Takayama, T. Conservation and Fuel Switching in Sweden: The Swedish Case Study Compared with Experiences in the USA and Japan. In *Lakshmanan, T. R. and Johansson, B., eds.*, 1985, pp. 174–84. [G: U.S.; Sweden; Japan]

Tarlock, A. Dan. The Making of Federal Coal Policy: Lessons for Public Lands Management from a Failed Program, an Essay and Review. *Natural Res. J.*, April 1985, *25*(2), pp. 349–71.   [G: U.S.]

Taylor, Lester D. The Residential Electricity Time-of-Use Pricing Experiments: What Have We Learned? Comment. In *Hausman, J. A. and Wise, D. A., eds.*, 1985, pp. 49–50.
                                                    [G: U.S.]

Teghem, J., Jr. and Kunsch, P. L. Multi-objective Decision Making under Uncertainty: An Example for Power System. In *Haimes, Y. Y. and Chankong, V., eds.*, 1985, pp. 443–56.

Tellier, P. M. Canada's National Energy Policy. In *Kubursi, A. A. and Naylor, T., eds.*, 1985, pp. 73–81.   [G: Canada]

Tempest, Paul. International Energy Policy: The Conflict of Investment Needs and Market Signals. *Energy J.*, April 1985, *6*(2), pp. 19–24.
                                                  [G: Global]

Tew, Bernard V., et al. Market Failure in Multiphase Electric Power Development for Agricultural Irrigation. *Southern J. Agr. Econ.*, December 1985, *17*(2), pp. 57–65. [G: U.S.]

Thoresen, Per E. The Relationship between Standard of Living, Production and Energy Consumption. In *van Gool, W. and Bruggink, J. J. C., eds.*, 1985, pp. 103–18.   [G: U.S.; Selected Countries]

Truong, Truong P. Inter-fuel and Inter-factor Substitution in NSW Manufacturing Industry. *Econ. Rec.*, September 1985, *61*(174), pp. 644–53.   [G: Australia]

Tussing, Arlon R. Oil Prices Are Still Too High. *Energy J.*, January 1985, *6*(1), pp. 9–12.
                                                  [G: Global]

Uffelmann, Maris. Hydrocarbon Supply Costs. *Can. Public Policy*, Supplement July 1985, *11*(3), pp. 397–401.   [G: Canada]

Uri, Noel D. and Hassanein, Saad A. Testing for Stability: Motor Gasoline Demand and Distillate Fuel Oil Demand. *Energy Econ.*, April 1985, *7*(2), pp. 87–92.   [G: U.S.]

de Vries, Bert. Energy and Time in the Economic and Physical Sciences. In *van Gool, W. and Bruggink, J. J. C., eds.*, 1985, pp. 381–83.

Wang, Young-Doo; Tannian, Francis X. and Solano, Paul L. A Residential Energy Market Model: An Econometric Analysis. *J. Reg. Sci.*, May 1985, *25*(2), pp. 215–39.
                                                    [G: U.S.]

Wassermann, Ursula. Energy: A Buyer's Market. *J. World Trade Law*, January:February 1985, *19*(1), pp. 62–67.   [G: Global]

Watkins, G. C. and Waverman, Leonard. Canadian Natural Gas Export Pricing Behaviour. *Can. Public Policy*, Supplement July 1985, *11*(3), pp. 415–26.   [G: Canada]

Watson, William D. Tar Sands Development in Canada: A Case Study of Environmental Monitoring: Technical Review of the Canadian Case Study. In *Lakshmanan, T. R. and Johansson, B., eds.*, 1985, pp. 72–76.   [G: Canada]

Weiner, Jonathan. Israel Innovates Energy Technology. In *Levinson, P. and Landau, P., eds.*, 1985, pp. 96–98.   [G: Israel]

Weiner, Jonathan. Israel's Energy Economy. In *Levinson, P. and Landau, P., eds.*, 1985, pp. 94–95.   [G: Israel]

Weiner, Jonathan. Israeli Energy Firms. In *Levinson, P. and Landau, P., eds.*, 1985, pp. 99–101.   [G: Israel]

Wendt, E. Allan. Oil Products Prospects for an Open Trading Regime. *J. Energy Devel.*, Autumn 1985, *11*(1), pp. 1–4.   [G: OECD]

Whalley, John. Canada/U.S. Energy Issues: A Canadian Perspective: Comments. In *Fretz, D.; Stern, R. and Whalley, J., eds.*, 1985, pp. 252–55.   [G: Canada; U.S.]

Whiteman, J. C. North Sea Oil. In *Morris, D., ed.*, 1985, pp. 829–50.   [G: U.K.]

van Wijnbergen, Sweder. Oil Discoveries, Intertemporal Adjustment and Public Policy. In *Bjerkholt, O. and Offerdal, E., eds.*, 1985, pp. 3–33.   [G: Norway]

van Wijnbergen, Sweder. Optimal Capital Accumulation and the Allocation of Investment between Traded and Nontraded Sectors in Oil-producing Countries. *Scand. J. Econ.*, 1985, *87*(1), pp. 89–101.   [G: LDCs]

Wijnbergen, Sweder. Optimal Taxation of Imported Energy under Price Uncertainty. *Oxford Econ. Pap.*, March 1985, *37*(1), pp. 83–92.

Wilbanks, T. J. and Lee, R. Policy Analysis in Theory and Practice. In *Lakshmanan, T. R. and Johansson, B., eds.*, 1985, pp. 273–303.

Williams, Harold R. and Mount, Randall I. Theory and Empirical Foundation for Energy Policy Designed to Promote U.S. Motor Gasoline Conservation. *Amer. Econ.*, Spring 1985, *29*(1), pp. 60–66.   [G: U.S.]

Williams, Ted. Synfuels Development in the USA: Case Studies of National Environmental Feasibility and Local Socioeconomic Impacts: The U.S. Synfuels Acceleration Program: An Environmental and Regional Impact Analysis. In *Lakshmanan, T. R. and Johansson, B., eds.*, 1985, pp. 77–99.   [G: U.S.]

Wirl, Franz and Infanger, Gerd. The Prospects of Energy Conservation: A Different Approach to the Fuel Demand for Space Heating. *Empirica*, 1985, *12*(2), pp. 227–45.   [G: Austria]

Woo, Chi-Keung. An Application of the Expenditure Function in Electricity Pricing: Optimal Residential Time-of-Use Rate Option. *Energy J.*, April 1985, *6*(2), pp. 89–99.

Wright, Jonathan. The Efficiency of Producing Alcohol for Energy in Brazil: Comment. *Econ. Develop. Cult. Change*, July 1985, *33*(4), pp. 851–56.   [G: Brazil]

Yang, Bong M. Do Gasoline Demand Elasticities Vary? Comment. *Land Econ.*, May 1985, *61*(2), pp. 198–200. [G: Selected Countries]

Yang, Chin-Wei and Labys, Walter C. A Sensitivity Analysis of the Linear Complementarity Programming Model: Appalachian Steam Coal and the Natural Gas Market. *Energy Econ.*, July 1985, *7*(3), pp. 145–52.   [G: U.S.]

Yu, Eden S. H. and Choi, Jai-Young. The Causal Relationship between Energy and GNP: An International Comparison. *J. Energy Devel.*, Spring 1985, *10*(2), pp. 249–72.   [G: U.S.; U.K.; Poland; S. Korea; Philippines]

Zinser, Lee D., et al. Effects of Rising Relative Energy Prices on Soil Erosion and Its Control. *Amer. J. Agr. Econ.*, August 1985, *67*(3), pp. 558–62.   [G: U.S.]

Zubkov, A. Avenues toward Energy-saving Economic Development for the European CMEA Member Nations. *Prob. Econ.*, August 1985, *28*(4), pp. 19–36.   [G: CMEA]

Zuckerman, John V. Commercialization of Solar Thermal Power Generation: Policy Issues. *Natural Res. J.*, Supp. Oct. 1985, pp. 1145–57.   [G: U.S.]

Zuker, R. C. and Pastor, M.-H. Financial Policies in the Canadian Electric Utility Sector: Origins, Practices, and Questions. *Can. Public Policy*, Supplement July 1985, *11*(3), pp. 427–37.   [G: Canada]

730 ECONOMIC GEOGRAPHY

731 Economic Geography

7310 Economic Geography

Allen, Peter M. Towards a New Science of Complex Systems. In *Aida, S., et al.*, 1985, pp. 268–97.

Bar-El, Raphael. Industrial Dispersion as an Instrument for the Achievement of Development Goals. *Econ. Geogr.*, July 1985, *61*(3), pp. 205–22.   [G: Brazil]

Bartik, Timothy J. Business Location Decisions in the United States: Estimates of the Effects of Unionization, Taxes, and Other Characteristics of States. *J. Bus. Econ. Statist.*, January 1985, *3*(1), pp. 14–22.   [G: U.S.]

Bennett, R. J. and Haining, R. P. Spatial Structure and Spatial Interaction: Modelling Approaches to the Statistical Analysis of Geographical Data. *J. Roy. Statist. Soc.*, 1985, *148*(1), pp. 1–27.   [G: U.S.; U.K.]

Brambilla, Francesco. Un'analisi del valore dei fabbricati residenziali verso una nuova teoria della localizzazione. (An Analysis of the Value of Residential Buildings. Towards a New Theory of Localization. With English summary.) *Giorn. Econ.*, July-Aug. 1985, *44*(7–8), pp. 375–87.   [G: Italy]

Brown, Lawrence A. and Jones, John Paul, III. Spatial Variation in Migration Processes and Development: A Costa Rican Example of Conventional Modeling Augmented by the Expansion Method. *Demography*, August 1985, *22*(3), pp. 326–52.   [G: Costa Rica]

Buswell, R. J.; Easterbrook, R. P. and Morphet, C. S. Geography, Regions and Research and Development Activity: The Case of the United Kingdom. In *Thwaites, A. T. and Oakey, R. P., eds.*, 1985, pp. 36–66.   [G: U.K.]

Clark, Gordon L. The Spatial Division of Labor

and Wage and Price Controls of the Nixon Administration. *Econ. Geogr.*, April 1985, *61*(2), pp. 113–28.   [G: U.S.]

Couclelis, Helen. Prior Structure and Spatial Interaction. In *Hutchinson, B. G.; Nijkamp, P. and Batty, M., eds.*, 1985, pp. 162–79.

Cremer, Helmuth; de Kerchove, Anne-Marie and Thisse, Jacques-François. An Economic Theory of Public Facilities in Space. *Math. Soc. Sci.*, June 1985, *9*(3), pp. 249–62.

Fischer, Manfred M. and Nijkamp, Peter. Categorical Data and Choice Analysis in a Spatial Context. In *Hutchinson, B. G.; Nijkamp, P. and Batty, M., eds.*, 1985, pp. 1–30.

Foggin, Peter M. Canadian Geographers and International Development Studies. *Can. J. Devel. Stud.*, 1985, *6*(2), pp. 313–22.   [G: Canada]

Fothergill, Stephen and Gudgin, Graham. Ideology and Methods in Industrial Location Research. In *Massey, D. and Meegan, R., eds.*, 1985, pp. 92–115.

Fotheringham, A. Stewart. Modeling Firms' Locational Choices and Core-Periphery Growth. *Growth Change*, January 1985, *16*(1), pp. 13–16.

Gould, Andrew and Keeble, David. New Firms and Rural Industrialization in East Anglia. In *Storey, D. J., ed.*, 1985, pp. 43–71.   [G: U.K.]

Hägerstrand, Torsten. Time-Geography: Focus on the Corporeality of Man, Society, and Environment. In *Aida, S., et al.*, 1985, pp. 193–216.

Hall, Randolph W. Heuristics for Selecting Facility Locations. *Logist. Transp. Rev.*, December 1985, *21*(4), pp. 353–73.   [G: U.S.]

Hanjoul, Pierre and Thisse, Jacques-François. Localisation de la firme sur un réseau. (The Location of a Firm on a Network. With English summary.) *Revue Écon.*, January 1985, *36*(1), pp. 63–101.

Hannon, B. M. Time Value in Ecosystems. In *van Gool, W. and Bruggink, J. J. C., eds.*, 1985, pp. 261–85.

Keinath, William F., Jr. The Spatial Components of the Post-industrial Society. *Econ. Geogr.*, July 1985, *61*(3), pp. 223–40.   [G: U.S.]

Lloyd, Peter E. and Mason, C. M. Spatial Variations in New Firm Formation in the United Kingdom: Comparative Evidence from Merseyside, Greater Manchester and South Hampshire. In *Storey, D. J., ed.*, 1985, pp. 72–100.   [G: U.K.]

Massey, Doreen and Meegan, Richard. Politics and Methods: Contrasting Studies in Industrial Geography: Introduction: The Debate. In *Massey, D. and Meegan, R., eds.*, 1985, pp. 1–12.

Massey, Doreen and Meegan, Richard. Postscript: Doing Research. In *Massey, D. and Meegan, R., eds.*, 1985, pp. 169–74.

Mathur, V. K. Location Theory of the Firm under Price Uncertainty: Some New Conclusions.

Reg. Sci. Urban Econ., November 1985, *15*(4), pp. 597–98.

Melachrinoudis, Emanuel and Cullinane, Thomas P. Locating an Undesirable Facility within a Geographical Region Using the MAXI-MUM Criterion. *J. Reg. Sci.*, February 1985, *25*(1), pp. 115–27. [G: U.S.]

Mirakhor, Abbas and Khalili, A. Optimum Location and the Theory of Production: An Extension. *Reg. Sci. Persp.*, 1985, *15*(1), pp. 63–74.

Nutley, S. D. Planning Options for the Improvement of Rural Accessibility: Use of the Time-Space Approach. *Reg. Stud.*, February 1985, *19*(1), pp. 37–50. [G: U.K.]

Okabe, Atsuyuki; Asami, Yasushi and Miki, Fujio. Statistical Analysis of the Spatial Association of Convenience-Goods Stores by Use of a Random Clumping Model. *J. Reg. Sci.*, February 1985, *25*(1), pp. 11–28. [G: Japan]

Park, Siyoung. Quality of Life in Illinois Counties. *Growth Change*, October 1985, *16*(4), pp. 56–69. [G: U.S.]

Sayer, Andrew and Morgan, Kevin. A Modern Industry in a Declining Region: Links between Method, Theory and Policy. In *Massey, D. and Meegan, R., eds.*, 1985, pp. 147–68.

Schoenberger, Erica. Foreign Manufacturing Investment in the United States: Competitive Strategies and International Location. *Econ. Geogr.*, July 1985, *61*(3), pp. 241–59. [G: U.S.]

Storper, Michael. Oligopoly and the Product Cycle: Essentialism in Economic Geography. *Econ. Geogr.*, July 1985, *61*(3), pp. 260–82.

Swaney, James A. and Ward, Frank A. Optimally Locating a National Public Facility: An Empirical Application of Consumer Surplus Theory. *Econ. Geogr.*, April 1985, *61*(2), pp. 172–80. [G: U.S.]

Tobin, Roger L. and Friesz, Terry L. A New Look at Spatially Competitive Facility Location Models. In *Harker, P. T., ed.*, 1985, pp. 1–19.

Trent, Roger B.; Stout-Wiegand, Nancy and Smith, Dennis K. Attitudes toward New Development in Three Appalachian Counties. *Growth Change*, October 1985, *16*(4), pp. 70–86. [G: U.S.]

Wheeler, James O. and Brown, Catherine L. The Metropolitan Corporate Hierarchy in the U.S. South, 1960–1980. *Econ. Geogr.*, January 1985, *61*(1), pp. 66–78. [G: U.S.]

Wilder, Margaret G. Site and Situation Determinants of Land Use Change: An Empirical Example. *Econ. Geogr.*, October 1985, *61*(4), pp. 332–44. [G: U.S.]

Yadav, Hanuman Singh. Real Income and Income Potential Surface in India. *Indian Econ. J.*, Apr.-June 1985, *32*(4), pp. 8–16. [G: India]

Zanetto, Gabriele. Primo Lanzoni, ovvero l'economia come antitesi all'ambientalismo nel pensiero geografico ottocentesco. (Primo Lanzoni, Economics and Naturalism in Geographical Thought. With English summary.) *Ricerche Econ.*, Jan.-Mar. 1985, *39*(1), pp. 70–103.

800 Manpower; Labor; Population

8000 General

Dankert, Philip R. Recent Publications. *Ind. Lab. Relat. Rev.*, April 1985, *38*(3), pp. 438–51.

MaCurdy, Thomas E. Reading List in Economics of Labor: Labor Economics II: Stanford University. *Amer. Econ.*, Fall 1985, *29*(2), pp. 70–74.

Marshall, Ray. Labor in a Free Society. In *Taitte, W. L., ed.*, 1985, pp. 203–33.

Mincer, Jacob. Reading List in Economics of Labor: Columbia University, Population and Labor Economics: Labor Mobility, Human Capital, Demand for Labor, Wage Structures. *Amer. Econ.*, Fall 1985, *29*(2), pp. 88–91.

Mueser, Peter. Reading List in Economics of Labor: The Johns Hopkins University Department of Political Economy 18.351 Labor Economics. *Amer. Econ.*, Fall 1985, *29*(2), pp. 86–87.

Ormiston, Michael B. Reading List in Economics of Labor: Texas A&M University. *Amer. Econ.*, Fall 1985, *29*(2), pp. 77–81.

Pencavel, John. Reading List in Economics of Labor: Labor Economics I: Stanford University. *Amer. Econ.*, Fall 1985, *29*(2), pp. 67–70.

Reynolds, Morgan O. Reading List in Economics of Labor: Texas A&M University. *Amer. Econ.*, Fall 1985, *29*(2), pp. 82–86.

Swanson, Dorothy. Annual Bibliography on American Labor History, 1983: Periodicals, Dissertations, and Research in Progress. *Labor Hist.*, Winter 1985, *26*(1), pp. 103–17.

Wegg-Prosser, Victoria. A Twentieth Century Story: The BBC Television Series "All Our Working Lives": Essay Review. *Labor Hist.*, Fall 1985, *26*(4), pp. 577–82. [G: U.K.]

Welch, Finis. Reading List in Economics of Labor: Recommended Readings: UCLA. *Amer. Econ.*, Fall 1985, *29*(2), pp. 74–77.

810 MANPOWER TRAINING AND DEVELOPMENT; LABOR FORCE AND SUPPLY

811 Manpower Training and Development

8110 Manpower Training and Development

Achio, Françoise. Forecasts of Skilled-Manpower Needs in the Ivory Coast: An Evaluation of Methods and Results. In *Youdi, R. V. and Hinchliffe, K., eds.*, 1985, pp. 211–28. [G: Ivory Coast]

Albin, Peter S. Job Design, Control Technology, and Technical Change. *J. Econ. Issues*, September 1985, *19*(3), pp. 703–30.

Alfthan, Torkel. Developing Skills for Technological Change: Some Policy Issues. *Int. Lab. Rev.*, Sept.-Oct. 1985, *124*(5), pp. 517–29. [G: OECD; LDCs]

Anderson, Bernard E. Job Search and Job Programs. *Challenge*, July/August 1985, *28*(3), pp. 51–53. [G: U.S.]

Anderson, Elijah. The Social Context of Youth Employment Programs. In *Betsey, C. L.; Hollister, R. G., Jr. and Papageorgiou, M. R., eds.*, 1985, pp. 348–66. [G: U.S.]

Ashenfelter, Orley and Card, David. Using the Longitudinal Structure of Earnings to Estimate the Effect of Training Programs. *Rev. Econ. Statist.*, November 1985, *67*(4), pp. 648–60. [G: U.S.]

Asher, Shigeko M. and Inoue, Ken. Industrial Manpower Development in Japan. *Finance Develop.*, September 1985, *22*(3), pp. 23–26. [G: Japan]

Bassi, Laurie J. Evaluating Alternative Job Creation Strategies. *Econ. Inquiry*, October 1985, *23*(4), pp. 671–90. [G: U.S.]

Blaug, Mark. Education: Comments. In *Worswick, G. D. N., ed.*, 1985, pp. 19–31. [G: U.K.]

Burbridge, Lynn C. Black Women in Employment and Training Programs. *Rev. Black Polit. Econ.*, Fall-Winter 1985-86, *14*(2–3), pp. 97–114. [G: U.S.]

Cantor, Leonard. A Coherent Approach to the Education and Training of the 16–19 Age Group. In *Worswick, G. D. N., ed.*, 1985, pp. 13–24. [G: U.K.]

Carmichael, H. Lorne. Wage Profiles, Layoffs, and Specific Training: Comment. *Int. Econ. Rev.*, October 1985, *26*(3), pp. 747–51.

Carter, Charles. Implications for Policy and Research. In *Worswick, G. D. N., ed.*, 1985, pp. 7–10. [G: U.K.]

Casey, Bernard and Bruche, Gert. Active Labor Market Policy: An International Overview. *Ind. Relat.*, Winter 1985, *24*(1), pp. 37–61. [G: W. Europe; U.S.]

Cavin, Edward S. and Maynard, Rebecca. Short-term Indicators of Employment Program Performance: Evidence from the Supported Work Program. *J. Human Res.*, Summer 1985, *20*(3), pp. 331–45. [G: U.S.]

Cavin, Edward S. and Stafford, Frank P. Efficient Provision of Employment Service Outputs: A Production Frontier Analysis. *J. Human Res.*, Fall 1985, *20*(4), pp. 484–503. [G: U.S.]

Chapman, Bruce. Continuity and Change: Labour Market Programs and Education Expenditure. *Australian Econ. Rev.*, 3rd Quarter, Spring 1985, (71), pp. 98–112. [G: Australia]

Cohen, Suleiman I. A Cost–Benefit Analysis of Industrial Training. *Econ. Educ. Rev.*, 1985, *4*(4), pp. 327–39. [G: Malaysia]

Dale, Charles and Gilroy, Curtis. Enlistments in the All-Volunteer Force: Note. *Amer. Econ. Rev.*, June 1985, *75*(3), pp. 547–51. [G: U.S.]

Delaney-LeBlanc, Madeleine. Women and Education: Branching Out: Comments. In *Economic Council of Canada.*, 1985, pp. 54–58. [G: Canada]

Dougherty, C. R. S. Manpower Forecasting and Manpower-Development Planning in the United Kingdom. In *Youdi, R. V. and Hinchliffe, K., eds.*, 1985, pp. 75–98. [G: U.K.]

Elmore, Richard F. Knowledge Development under the Youth Employment and Demonstration Projects Act, 1977–1981. In *Betsey, C. L.; Hollister, R. G., Jr. and Papageorgiou, M. R., eds.*, 1985, pp. 281–347. [G: U.S.]

Englander, Frederick. The Author Replies: We Still Need to Demonstrate Program Effectiveness [Helping Ex-offenders Enter the Labor Market]. *Mon. Lab. Rev.*, April 1985, *108*(4), pp. 49–50.

Fisher, Norman. Continuity and Change: Labour Market Programs and Education Expenditure: Comment. *Australian Econ. Rev.*, 3rd Quarter, Spring 1985, (71), pp. 113–14. [G: Australia]

Ford, Hugh. Training: Comment. In *Worswick, G. D. N., ed.*, 1985, pp. 79–80. [G: U.K.]

Gaskell, Jane. Women and Education: Branching Out. In *Economic Council of Canada.*, 1985, pp. 43–54. [G: Canada]

Ginzberg, Eli. A Policy for Disadvantaged Youth. In *Ginzberg, E.*, 1985, pp. 655–67. [G: U.S.]

Ginzberg, Eli. Manpower Policy: Retrospect and Prospect. In *Ginzberg, E.*, 1985, pp. 615–35. [G: U.S.]

Glynn, Dermot. Training: Comment. In *Worswick, G. D. N., ed.*, 1985, pp. 80–86. [G: U.K.]

Harper, Harriett. Black Women and the Job Training Partnership Act. *Rev. Black Polit. Econ.*, Fall-Winter 1985-86, *14*(2–3), pp. 115–29.

Hashimoto, Masanori. Firm-specific Human Capital: Rejoinder [Wage Profiles, Layoffs, and Specific Training]. *Int. Econ. Rev.*, October 1985, *26*(3), pp. 753–54.

Haveman, Robert H. and Saks, Daniel H. Transatlantic Lessons for Employment and Training Policy. *Ind. Relat.*, Winter 1985, *24*(1), pp. 20–36. [G: U.S.; W. Europe]

Heckman, James J. and Robb, Richard, Jr. Alternative Methods for Evaluating the Impact of Interventions: An Overview. *J. Econometrics*, Oct./Nov. 1985, *30*(1/2), pp. 239–67.

Hougland, James G., Jr. Industrial Sectors and Economic Outcomes: Experiences of Former CETA Participants. *Soc. Sci. Quart.*, December 1985, *66*(4), pp. 903–15. [G: U.S.]

d'Iribarne, Alain. Developments in Vocational Training in France in the Past Twenty Years. In *Worswick, G. D. N., ed.*, 1985, pp. 52–67. [G: France]

Ivanov, I. V. Skilled-Manpower Planning, Forecasting and Training in the USSR. In *Youdi, R. V. and Hinchliffe, K., eds.*, 1985, pp. 153–72. [G: U.S.S.R.]

Ivanova, R. Curtailment of Manual Labor—A Key Social and Economic Task. *Prob. Econ.*, August 1985, *28*(4), pp. 49–67. [G: U.S.S.R.]

Jackson, Roy. Training: Comment. In *Worswick, G. D. N., ed.*, 1985, pp. 86–90. [G: U.K.]

Jeffries, John M. Education and Training: Discussion. *Rev. Black Polit. Econ.*, Fall-Winter 1985-86, *14*(2–3), pp. 131–37.

Jones, Ian S. Skill Formation and Pay Relativities.

In *Worswick, G. D. N., ed.*, 1985, pp. 25–39.   [G: U.K.; W. Germany; Switzerland]

Josefowicz, A.; Kluczynski, J. and Obrebski, T. Manpower and Education Planning and Policy Experience in Poland, 1960–80. In *Youdi, R. V. and Hinchliffe, K., eds.*, 1985, pp. 135–52.   [G: Poland]

Kanawaty, George. Training for a Changing World: Some General Reflections. *Int. Lab. Rev.*, July-Aug. 1985, *124*(4), pp. 401–09.

Kogan, Maurice. Education: Comments. In *Worswick, G. D. N., ed.*, 1985, pp. 135–38.   [G: U.K.]

Landymore, P. J. A. Education and Industry Since the War. In *Morris, D., ed.*, 1985, pp. 690–717.   [G: U.K.; EEC]

Lattimore, Pamela K. and Witte, Ann D. Programs to Aid Ex-offenders: We Don't Know 'Nothing Works' [Helping Ex-offenders Enter the Labor Market]. *Mon. Lab. Rev.*, April 1985, *108*(4), pp. 46–48.

Maclure, Stuart. The Responsiveness of the Education System to Change. In *Worswick, G. D. N., ed.*, 1985, pp. 113–29.   [G: U.K.]

Main, Brian G. M. School-leaver Unemployment and the Youth Opportunities Programme in Scotland. *Oxford Econ. Pap.*, September 1985, *37*(3), pp. 426–47.

McIntosh, Wm. Alex and Picou, J. Steven. Manpower Training and the Political Economy of Agriculture: CETA and the Texas Agricultural Environment. *Soc. Sci. Quart.*, June 1985, *66*(2), pp. 330–45.   [G: U.S.]

McKinney, Fred. JTPA, Black Employment, and Occupational Change: Separating Out Cyclical Changes from Program Changes. *Rev. Black Polit. Econ.*, Summer 1985, *14*(1), pp. 75–87.   [G: U.S.]

Nelson, Valerie and Turner, Charles F. Estimates of Effects of Employment and Training Programs Derived from National Longitudinal Surveys and Continuous Longitudinal Manpower Survey. In *Betsey, C. L.; Hollister, R. G., Jr. and Papageorgiou, M. R., eds.*, 1985, pp. 254–80.   [G: U.S.]

Peston, Maurice. Training: Comment. In *Worswick, G. D. N., ed.*, 1985, pp. 76–79.   [G: U.K.]

Pettersson, Lars. Engineer Training in Sweden during the Postwar Period in the Context of Technical and Structural Change. *Scand. Econ. Hist. Rev.*, 1985, *33*(2), pp. 108–21.   [G: Sweden]

Phan-Thuy, N. Employment and Training Schemes for Rural Youth: Learning from Experience. *Int. Lab. Rev.*, July-Aug. 1985, *124*(4), pp. 435–46.

Prais, S. J. What Can We Learn from the German System of Education and Vocational Training? In *Worswick, G. D. N., ed.*, 1985, pp. 40–51.   [G: W. Germany]

Rehn, Gösta. Swedish Active Labor Market Policy: Retrospect and Prospect. *Ind. Relat.*, Winter 1985, *24*(1), pp. 62–89.   [G: Sweden]

Russell, Russ. A Comparison of the Youth Training Scheme in the United Kingdom with the Vocational Foundation Training Year in Germany. In *Worswick, G. D. N., ed.*, 1985, pp. 68–75.   [G: U.K.; W. Germany]

Saini, Balwant Singh. Barefoot Architects: A Training Program for Building in the Third World. In *Lea, J. P. and Courtney, J. M., eds.*, 1985, pp. 97–100.

Saleh, Mamdouh. Retrospective Evaluation of Forecasting Methods for Qualified-Manpower Needs for Egypt. In *Youdi, R. V. and Hinchliffe, K., eds.*, 1985, pp. 175–93.   [G: Egypt]

Simms, Margaret C. The Participation of Young Women in Employment and Training Programs. In *Betsey, C. L.; Hollister, R. G., Jr. and Papageorgiou, M. R., eds.*, 1985, pp. 462–85.   [G: U.S.]

Sloan, Judith. Continuity and Change: Labour Market Programs and Education Expenditure: Comment. *Australian Econ. Rev.*, 3rd Quarter, Spring 1985, (71), pp. 114–15.   [G: Australia]

Sloan, Judith. Training or Wages: An Evaluation of the Kirby Report. *Australian Bull. Lab.*, June 1985, *11*(3), pp. 142–53.   [G: Australia]

Stanton, David. Education: Comments. In *Worswick, G. D. N., ed.*, 1985, pp. 138–40.   [G: U.K.]

Taylor, Patricia A. Institutional Job Training and Inequality. *Soc. Sci. Quart.*, March 1985, *66*(1), pp. 67–78.   [G: U.S.]

Thompson, Velma Montoya. Efficient Retraining during Unemployment. *J. Behav. Econ.*, Summer 1985, *14*(2), pp. 121–28.   [G: U.S.]

Tímár, János. Manpower and Educational Planning in Hungary. In *Youdi, R. V. and Hinchliffe, K., eds.*, 1985, pp. 119–34.   [G: Hungary]

Turner, Charles F. Standardized Data Collection for Large-scale Program Evaluation: An Assessment of the YEDPA-SAS Experience. In *Betsey, C. L.; Hollister, R. G., Jr. and Papageorgiou, M. R., eds.*, 1985, pp. 193–219.   [G: U.S.]

Weiss, Yoram. The Effect of Labor Unions on Investment in Training: A Dynamic Model. *J. Polit. Econ.*, October 1985, *93*(5), pp. 994–1007.

Wilensky, Harold L. Nothing Fails Like Success: The Evaluation-Research Industry and Labor Market Policy. *Ind. Relat.*, Winter 1985, *24*(1), pp. 1–19.   [G: U.S.; Sweden]

Williams, Gareth. Education: Comments. In *Worswick, G. D. N., ed.*, 1985, pp. 131–35.   [G: U.K.]

Worswick, G. D. N. Education and Economic Performance: Introduction. In *Worswick, G. D. N., ed.*, 1985, pp. 1–6.

812 Occupation

8120 Occupation

Achio, Françoise. Forecasts of Skilled-Manpower Needs in the Ivory Coast: An Evaluation of Methods and Results. In *Youdi, R. V. and Hinchliffe, K., eds.*, 1985, pp. 211–28.   [G: Ivory Coast]

Alfthan, Torkel. Developing Skills for Technological Change: Some Policy Issues. *Int. Lab. Rev.,* Sept.-Oct. 1985, *124*(5), pp. 517–29.
[G: OECD; LDCs]

Anker, Richard and Hein, Catherine. Why Third World Urban Employers Usually Prefer Men. *Int. Lab. Rev.,* January–February 1985, *124*(1), pp. 73–90. [G: LDCs]

Bazzoli, Gloria J. Does Educational Indebtedness Affect Physician Specialty Choice? *J. Health Econ.,* March 1985, *4*(1), pp. 1–19. [G: U.S.]

Beller, Andrea H. Changes in the Sex Composition of U.S. Occupations, 1960–1981. *J. Human Res.,* Spring 1985, *20*(2), pp. 235–50.
[G: U.S.]

Birdsall, Nancy and Fox, M. Louise. Why Males Earn More: Location and Training of Brazilian Schoolteachers. *Econ. Develop. Cult. Change,* April 1985, *33*(3), pp. 533–56. [G: Brazil]

Blank, Rebecca M. and Rothschild, Emma. The Effect of United States Defence Spending on Employment and Output. *Int. Lab. Rev.,* Nov.-Dec. 1985, *124*(6), pp. 677–97.
[G: U.S.]

Blomqvist, Ake G. Unemployment of the Educated and Emigration of Post-Secondary Graduates from the LDCs. *Pakistan Devel. Rev.,* Autumn-Winter 1985, *24*(3/4), pp. 643–54.
[G: LDCs]

Booton, Lavonne A. and Lane, Julia. Hospital Market Structure and the Return to Nursing Education. *J. Human Res.,* Spring 1985, *20*(2), pp. 184–96. [G: U.S.]

Boulet, Jac-André. Occupational Diversification of Women in the Workplace. In *Economic Council of Canada.,* 1985, pp. 31–37.
[G: Canada]

Browne, Lynn E. Structural Change and Dislocated Workers. *New Eng. Econ. Rev.,* January/February 1985, pp. 15–30. [G: U.S.]

Bruggink, Thomas H., et al. Direct and Indirect Effects of Unionization on the Wage Levels of Nurses: A Case Study of New Jersey Hospitals. *J. Lab. Res.,* Fall 1985, *6*(4), pp. 405–16. [G: U.S.]

Buchanan, R. A. Institutional Proliferation in the British Engineering Profession, 1847–1914. *Econ. Hist. Rev., 2nd Ser.,* February 1985, *38*(1), pp. 42–60. [G: U.K.]

Buckley, John E. Wage Differences among Workers in the Same Job and Establishment. *Mon. Lab. Rev.,* March 1985, *108*(3), pp. 11–16.
[G: U.S.]

Burstein, Philip L. and Cromwell, Jerry. Relative Incomes and Rates of Return for U.S. Physicians. *J. Health Econ.,* March 1985, *4*(1), pp. 63–78. [G: U.S.]

Cain, Pamela Stone. Prospects for Pay Equity in a Changing Economy. In *Hartmann, H. I., ed.,* 1985, pp. 137–65. [G: U.S.]

Carvajal, Manuel J. and Geithman, David T. Income, Human Capital and Sex Discrimination: Some Evidence from Costa Rica, 1963 and 1973. *J. Econ. Devel.,* July 1985, *10*(1), pp. 89–115. [G: Costa Rica]

Cassis, Y. Bankers in English Society in the Late Nineteenth Century. *Econ. Hist. Rev., 2nd Ser.,* May 1985, *38*(2), pp. 210–29.
[G: U.K.]

Chambers, Jay G. Patterns of Compensation of Public and Private School Teachers. *Econ. Educ. Rev.,* 1985, *4*(4), pp. 291–310.
[G: U.S.]

Clancy, Patrick. Symposium on "Equality of Opportunity in Irish Schools": Editorial Introduction. *Econ. Soc. Rev.,* January 1985, *16*(2), pp. 77–82. [G: Ireland]

Clark, David, et al. Work and Marriage in the Offshore Oil Industry. *Int. J. Soc. Econ.,* 1985, *12*(2), pp. 36–47. [G: U.K.]

Cohen, Suleiman I. The Labour Force Matrix of Pakistan: Selected Applications. *Pakistan Devel. Rev.,* Autumn-Winter 1985, *24*(3/4), pp. 565–84. [G: Pakistan]

Congdon, Peter. Heterogeneity and Timing Effects in Occupational Mobility: A General Model. *Oxford Bull. Econ. Statist.,* November 1985, *47*(4), pp. 347–69. [G: Ireland]

Culler, Steven D. and Bazzoli, Gloria J. The Moonlighting Decisions of Resident Physicians. *J. Health Econ.,* September 1985, *4*(3), pp. 283–92. [G: U.S.]

Davidson, Marilyn and Cooper, Cary. Women Managers: Work, Stress and Marriage. *Int. J. Soc. Econ.,* 1985, *12*(2), pp. 17–25.
[G: U.K.]

Davis, Carlton G. Human Capital Needs of Black Land-Grant Institutions: Discussion. *Southern J. Agr. Econ.,* July 1985, *17*(1), pp. 71–73.
[G: U.S.]

Debeauvais, Michel and Psacharopoulos, George. Forecasting the Needs for Qualified Manpower: Towards an Evaluation. In *Youdi, R. V. and Hinchliffe, K., eds.,* 1985, pp. 11–31. [G: Selected LDCs]

Delaney-LeBlanc, Madeleine. Women and Education: Branching Out: Comments. In *Economic Council of Canada.,* 1985, pp. 54–58.
[G: Canada]

Dougherty, C. R. S. Manpower Forecasting and Manpower-Development Planning in the United Kingdom. In *Youdi, R. V. and Hinchliffe, K., eds.,* 1985, pp. 75–98. [G: U.K.]

Dussault, Gilles. La politique de la délégation des actes professionnels au Québec. (With English summary.) *Can. Public Policy,* June 1985, *11*(2), pp. 218–26. [G: Canada]

Eastaugh, Steven R. The Impact of the Nurse Training Act on the Supply of Nurses, 1974–1983. *Inquiry,* Winter 1985, *22*(4), pp. 404–17. [G: U.S.]

Eberts, Randall W. and Stone, Joe A. Wages, Fringe Benefits, and Working Conditions: An Analysis of Compensating Differentials. *Southern Econ. J.,* July 1985, *52*(1), pp. 274–80.
[G: U.S.]

England, Paula. Occupational Segregation: Rejoinder [The Failure of Human Capital Theory to Explain Occupational Sex Segregation]. *J. Human Res.,* Summer 1985, *20*(3), pp. 441–43. [G: U.S.]

Filippello, A. Nicholas. Where Do Business

Economists Go from Here? *Bus. Econ.*, January 1985, *20*(1), pp. 12–16.

Flakierski, Henryk. Economic Reform & Income Distribution: A Case Study of Hungary and Poland. *Eastern Europ. Econ.*, Fall-Winter 1985-86, *24*(1–2), pp. iii–194.

Fløystad, Gunnar. The Labour Force Matrix of Pakistan: Selected Applications: Comments. *Pakistan Devel. Rev.*, Autumn-Winter 1985, *24*(3/4), pp. 585. [G: Pakistan]

Fujii, Edwin T. and Mak, James. On the Relative Economic Progress of U.S.-born Filipino Men. *Econ. Develop. Cult. Change*, April 1985, *33*(3), pp. 557–73. [G: U.S.]

Fulbright, Karen. The Myth of the Double-Advantage: Black Female Managers. *Rev. Black Polit. Econ.*, Fall-Winter 1985-86, *14*(2–3), pp. 33–45. [G: U.S.]

Gaskell, Jane. Women and Education: Branching Out. In *Economic Council of Canada.*, 1985, pp. 43–54. [G: Canada]

Gershuny, J. I. and Miles, I. D. Towards a New Social Economics. In *Roberts, B.; Finnegan, R. and Gallie, D.*, *eds.*, 1985, pp. 24–47. [G: U.K.]

Ginzberg, Eli. Ginzberg's Theory: A Retrospective View. In *Ginzberg, E.*, 1985, pp. 83–101.

Glenn, Evelyn Nakano. Racial Ethnic Women's Labor: The Intersection of Race, Gender and Class Oppression. *Rev. Radical Polit. Econ.*, Fall 1985, *17*(3), pp. 86–108. [G: U.S.]

Greenhalgh, Christine A. and Stewart, Mark B. The Occupational Status and Mobility of British Men and Women. *Oxford Econ. Pap.*, March 1985, *37*(1), pp. 40–71. [G: U.K.]

Hansen, Richard B. A Test of the Hansen–Weisbrod–Strauss Model of Faculty Salaries. *Atlantic Econ. J.*, September 1985, *13*(3), pp. 33–40. [G: U.S.]

Hansen, Richard B. On the Relationship between Human Capital and Productivity in the Case of Academic Economists. *Quart. Rev. Econ. Bus.*, Autumn 1985, *25*(3), pp. 96–104. [G: U.S.]

Hight, Joseph E. Review of Manpower Forecasts and Changes in Occupational Structure in the United States of America. In *Youdi, R. V. and Hinchliffe, K.*, *eds.*, 1985, pp. 99–115. [G: U.S.]

Hunter, Gregory S. The Development of Bankers: Career Patterns and Corporate Form at the Manhattan Company, 1799–1842. In *Atack, J.*, *ed.*, 1985, pp. 59–77. [G: U.S.]

Isuani, Ernesto A. Universalización de la seguridad social en América Latina: límites estructurales y cambios necesarios. (With English summary.) *Desarrollo Econ.*, April–June 1985, *25*(97), pp. 71–84. [G: Latin America]

Ivanov, I. V. Skilled-Manpower Planning, Forecasting and Training in the USSR. In *Youdi, R. V. and Hinchliffe, K.*, *eds.*, 1985, pp. 153–72. [G: U.S.S.R.]

Ivanova, R. Curtailment of Manual Labor—A Key Social and Economic Task. *Prob. Econ.*, August 1985, *28*(4), pp. 49–67. [G: U.S.S.R.]

Jones, Ian S. Skill Formation and Pay Relativities. In *Worswick, G. D. N.*, *ed.*, 1985, pp. 25–39. [G: U.K.; W. Germany; Switzerland]

Josefowicz, A.; Kluczynski, J. and Obrebski, T. Manpower and Education Planning and Policy Experience in Poland, 1960–80. In *Youdi, R. V. and Hinchliffe, K.*, *eds.*, 1985, pp. 135–52. [G: Poland]

Khan, M. Ali. Unemployment of the Educated and Emigration of Post-Secondary Graduates from the LDCs: Comments. *Pakistan Devel. Rev.*, Autumn-Winter 1985, *24*(3/4), pp. 655–56.

King, Russell; Strachan, Alan and Mortimer, Jill. The Urban Dimension of European Return Migration: The Case of Bari, Southern Italy. *Urban Stud.*, June 1985, *22*(3), pp. 219–35. [G: Italy]

Kunin, Roslyn. Occupational Diversification of Women in the Workplace: Comments. In *Economic Council of Canada.*, 1985, pp. 36–40. [G: Canada]

Laband, David N. and Lentz, Bernard F. Favorite Sons: Intergenerational Wealth Transfers among Politicians. *Econ. Inquiry*, July 1985, *23*(3), pp. 395–414. [G: U.S.]

Lancaster, Tony and Chesher, Andrew. Residuals, Tests and Plots with a Job Matching Illustration. *Ann. INSEE*, July-Dec. 1985, (59/60), pp. 47–70.

Lehrer, Evelyn L. and Stokes, Houston. Determinants of the Female Occupational Distribution: A Log-Linear Probability Analysis. *Rev. Econ. Statist.*, August 1985, *67*(3), pp. 395–404. [G: U.S.]

Lewis, Donald E. The Sources of Changes in the Occupational Segregation of Australian Women. *Econ. Rec.*, December 1985, *61*(175), pp. 719–36. [G: Australia]

Lewis, P. E. T. and Vella, F. G. M. Economic Factors Affecting the Number of Engineering Graduates in Australia. *Australian Econ. Pap.*, June 1985, *24*(44), pp. 66–75. [G: Australia]

Link, Charles R. and Settle, Russell F. Labor Supply Responses of Licensed Practical Nurses: A Partial Solution to a Nurse Shortage? *J. Econ. Bus.*, February 1985, *37*(1), pp. 49–57. [G: U.S.]

Lyson, Thomas A. Race and Sex Segregation in the Occupational Structures of Southern Employers. *Soc. Sci. Quart.*, June 1985, *66*(2), pp. 281–95. [G: U.S.]

Madhavan, M. C.; Green, Louis C. and Jung, Ken. A Note on Black–White Wage Disparity. *Rev. Black Polit. Econ.*, Spring 1985, *13*(4), pp. 39–50. [G: U.S.]

Malveaux, Julianne. The Economic Interests of Black and White Women: Are They Similar? *Rev. Black Polit. Econ.*, Summer 1985, *14*(1), pp. 5–27. [G: U.S.]

Mayhew, Ken. Employee Behaviour. In *Morris, D.*, *ed.*, 1985, pp. 86–111. [G: U.K.]

McKinney, Fred. JTPA, Black Employment, and Occupational Change: Separating Out Cyclical Changes from Program Changes. *Rev. Black*

Polit. Econ., Summer 1985, *14*(1), pp. 75–87.
[G: U.S.]

McPherson, Michael S. The State of Academic Labor Markets. In *Smith, B. L. R., ed.*, 1985, pp. 57–83. [G: U.S.]

Medoff, Marshall H. Discrimination and the Occupational Progress of Blacks since 1950. *Amer. J. Econ. Soc.*, July 1985, *44*(3), pp. 295–303.
[G: U.S.]

Medoff, Marshall H. The Effect of the Equal Rights Amendment on the Economic Status of Women. *Atlantic Econ. J.*, September 1985, *13*(3), pp. 60–68. [G: U.S.]

Mellor, Earl F. Weekly Earnings in 1983: A Look at More Than 200 Occupations. *Mon. Lab. Rev.*, January 1985, *108*(1), pp. 54–59.
[G: U.S.]

Miller, Paul W. and Volker, Paul A. Economic Progress in Australia: An Analysis of Occupational Mobility. *Econ. Rec.*, March 1985, *61*(172), pp. 463–75. [G: Australia]

Miller, Paul W. and Volker, Paul A. On the Determination of Occupational Attainment and Mobility. *J. Human Res.*, Spring 1985, *20*(2), pp. 197–213. [G: Australia]

Nieuwenhuysen, John. Towards Flexibility in Academic Labour Markets? *Australian Bull. Lab.*, March 1985, *11*(2), pp. 71–81.
[G: Australia]

Parks, Alfred L. and Robbins, Richard D. Human Capital Needs of Black Land-Grant Institutions. *Southern J. Agr. Econ.*, July 1985, *17*(1), pp. 61–69. [G: U.S.]

Paul, Jean-Jacques. Basic Concepts and Methods Used in Forecasting Skilled-Manpower Requirements in France. In *Youdi, R. V. and Hinchliffe, K., eds.*, 1985, pp. 35–56.
[G: France]

Pearce, James E. and Gunther, Jeffrey W. Illegal Immigration from Mexico: Effects on the Texas Economy. *Fed. Res. Bank Dallas Econ. Rev.*, September 1985, pp. 1–14. [G: U.S.]

Polachek, Solomon William. Occupation Segregation: A Defense of Human Capital Predictions [The Failure of Human Capital Theory to Explain Occupational Sex Segregation]. *J. Human Res.*, Summer 1985, *20*(3), pp. 437–40.
[G: U.S.]

Polachek, Solomon William. Occupational Segregation: Reply [The Failure of Human Capital Theory to Explain Occupational Sex Segregation]. *J. Human Res.*, Summer 1985, *20*(3), pp. 444. [G: U.S.]

Prieser, Carl. Occupational Salary Levels for White-Collar Workers, 1985. *Mon. Lab. Rev.*, October 1985, *108*(10), pp. 44–46. [G: U.S.]

Rugumyamheto, J. A. Manpower Forecasting in the United Republic of Tanzania. In *Youdi, R. V. and Hinchliffe, K., eds.*, 1985, pp. 229–46. [G: Tanzania]

Sackey, James A. and Sackey, Thywill E. Secondary School Students' Employment Aspirations and Expectations and the Barbados Labour Market. *Soc. Econ. Stud.*, September 1985, *34*(3), pp. 211–58. [G: Barbados]

Saleh, Mamdouh. Retrospective Evaluation of

Forecasting Methods for Qualified-Manpower Needs for Egypt. In *Youdi, R. V. and Hinchliffe, K., eds.*, 1985, pp. 175–93. [G: Egypt]

Scarpat, Orlando. Il conflitto tra efficienza ed equità nei differenziali salariali per qualifica. (The Conflict between Efficiency and Fairness in Occupational Wage Differentials. With English summary.) *Rivista Int. Sci. Econ. Com.*, May 1985, *32*(5), pp. 453–65.

Schmitt, Donald G. Tips: The Mainstay of Many Hotel Workers' Pay. *Mon. Lab. Rev.*, July 1985, *108*(7), pp. 50–51. [G: U.S.]

Scott, Frank A., Jr.; Long, James E. and Somppi, Ken. Salary vs. Marginal Revenue Product under Monopsony and Competition: The Case of Professional Basketball. *Atlantic Econ. J.*, September 1985, *13*(3), pp. 50–59. [G: U.S.]

Sharma, R. A. Industrial Entrepreneurship in India, 1961–1963. *Indian Econ. J.*, Oct.-Nov. 1985, *33*(2), pp. 79–92. [G: India]

Sheffrin, Steven M. Mobility and Efficiency in the Job Market for Economists. *Econ. Educ. Rev.*, 1985, *4*(4), pp. 311–20. [G: U.S.]

Silvestri, George T. and Lukasiewicz, John M. Occupational Employment Projections: The 1984–95 Outlook. *Mon. Lab. Rev.*, November 1985, *108*(11), pp. 42–57. [G: U.S.]

Singelmann, Joachim and Tienda, Marta. The Process of Occupational Change in a Service Society: The Case of the United States, 1960–80. In *Roberts, B.; Finnegan, R. and Gallie, D., eds.*, 1985, pp. 48–67. [G: U.S.]

Stewart, A.; Blackburn, R. M. and Prandy, K. Gender and Earnings: The Failure of Market Explanations. In *Roberts, B.; Finnegan, R. and Gallie, D., eds.*, 1985, pp. 280–98. [G: U.K.]

Tessaring, Manfred. An Evaluation of Labour-Market and Educational Forecasts in the Federal Republic of Germany. In *Youdi, R. V. and Hinchliffe, K., eds.*, 1985, pp. 57–74.

Theeuwes, Jules, et al. Estimation of Optimal Human Capital Accumulation Parameters for the Netherlands. *Europ. Econ. Rev.*, November 1985, *29*(2), pp. 233–57. [G: Netherlands]

Tienda, Marta and Guhleman, Patricia. The Occupational Position of Employed Hispanic Women. In *Borjas, G. J. and Tienda, M., eds.*, 1985, pp. 243–73. [G: U.S.]

Tímár, János. Manpower and Educational Planning in Hungary. In *Youdi, R. V. and Hinchliffe, K., eds.*, 1985, pp. 119–34.
[G: Hungary]

Tinbergen, Jan. Constraints on Production Functions: Essential vs. Non-essential Factors. In *Tinbergen, J.*, 1985, pp. 25–34. [G: U.S.]

Tinbergen, Jan. Production Functions with Several Factors. In *Tinbergen, J.*, 1985, pp. 20–24. [G: U.S.]

Tinbergen, Jan. The Role of Occupational Status in Income Formation. In *Tinbergen, J.*, 1985, pp. 78–84. [G: U.S.]

Tinbergen, Jan and Kol, Jacob. Market-Determined and Residual Incomes—Some Dilemmas. In *Tinbergen, J.*, 1985, pp. 3–19.
[G: U.S.; Japan]

Verma, M. C. Review of Skilled-Manpower Forecasts in India. In *Youdi, R. V. and Hinchliffe, K., eds.*, 1985, pp. 194–210. [G: India]

de la Viña, Lynda Y. Female Occupational Distribution: Treiman and Terrell Revisited. *Soc. Sci. Quart.*, September 1985, *66*(3), pp. 680–86. [G: U.S.]

Wassall, Gregory H. and Alper, Neil O. Occupational Characteristics of Artists: A Statistical Analysis. *J. Cult. Econ.*, June 1985, *9*(1), pp. 13–34. [G: U.S.]

Whelan, Christopher T. and Whelan, Brendan J. "Equality of Opportunity in Irish Schools": A Reassessment. *Econ. Soc. Rev.*, January 1985, *16*(2), pp. 103–14. [G: Ireland]

Williams, Harry B. Wages at Motor Vehicle Plants Outpaced Those at Parts Factories. *Mon. Lab. Rev.*, May 1985, *108*(5), pp. 38–40. [G: U.S.]

Wilson, Robert Andrew. A Longer Perspective on Rates of Return. *Scot. J. Polit. Econ.*, June 1985, *32*(2), pp. 191–98. [G: U.K.]

Winn, Conrad. Affirmative Action and Visible Minorities: Eight Premises in Quest of Evidence. *Can. Public Policy*, December 1985, *11*(4), pp. 684–700.

Withers, Glenn. Artists' Subsidy of the Arts. *Australian Econ. Pap.*, December 1985, *24*(45), pp. 290–95. [G: Australia]

Zarkin, Gary A. Occupational Choice: An Application to the Market for Public School Teachers. *Quart. J. Econ.*, May 1985, *100*(2), pp. 409–46. [G: U.S.]

813 Labor Force

8130 General

Abowd, John M. and Zellner, Arnold. Estimating Gross Labor-Force Flows. *J. Bus. Econ. Statist.*, July 1985, *3*(3), pp. 254–83. [G: U.S.]

Adams, Larry T. Changing Employment Patterns of Organized Workers. *Mon. Lab. Rev.*, February 1985, *108*(2), pp. 25–31. [G: U.S.]

Agrafiotis, G. K. Fitting the Lognormal Distribution to Censored Labour Wastage Data. *Math. Soc. Sci.*, December 1985, *10*(3), pp. 269–274.

Albelda, Randy. "Nice Work If You Can Get It": Segmentation of White and Black Women Workers in the Post-War Period. *Rev. Radical Polit. Econ.*, Fall 1985, *17*(3), pp. 72–85. [G: U.S.]

Alter, George C. and Becker, William E. Estimating Lost Future Earnings Using the New Worklife Tables. *Mon. Lab. Rev.*, February 1985, *108*(2), pp. 39–42. [G: U.S.]

Anker, Richard and Hein, Catherine. Why Third World Urban Employers Usually Prefer Men. *Int. Lab. Rev.*, January–February 1985, *124*(1), pp. 73–90. [G: LDCs]

Bailey, David and Parikh, Ashok. An Analysis of Duration of Unemployment: 1967–1979. *Empirical Econ.*, 1985, *10*(3), pp. 131–41. [G: U.K.]

Barrère-Maurisson, Marie-Agnès; Battagliola, Françoise and Daune-Richard, Anne-Marie. The Course of Women's Careers and Family

Life. In *Roberts, B.; Finnegan, R. and Gallie, D., eds.*, 1985, pp. 431–58. [G: France]

Bean, Frank D.; Swicegood, C. Gray and King, Allan G. Role Incompatibility and the Relationship between Fertility and Labor Supply among Hispanic Women. In *Borjas, G. J. and Tienda, M., eds.*, 1985, pp. 221–42. [G: U.S.]

Ben-Porath, Yoram and Gronau, Reuben. Jewish Mother Goes to Work: Trends in the Labor Force Participation of Women in Israel, 1955–1980. *J. Lab. Econ.*, Part 2 January 1985, *3*(1), pp. S310–27. [G: Israel]

Bettio, Francesca. The Unremoved Constraint: Job Sex-Typing and Female Participation, 1901–1981. *Stud. Econ.*, 1985, *40*(27), pp. 77–122. [G: Italy]

Blau, David M. The Effects of Economic Development on Life Cycle Wage Rates and Labor Supply Behavior in Malaysia. *J. Devel. Econ.*, Sept.-Oct. 1985, *19*(1/2), pp. 163–85. [G: Malaysia]

Bradbury, Katharine L. Prospects for Growth in New England: The Labor Force. *New Eng. Econ. Rev.*, Sept./Oct. 1985, pp. 50–60. [G: U.S.]

Brown, Clair. An Institutional Model of Wives' Work Decisions. *Ind. Relat.*, Spring 1985, *24*(2), pp. 182–204. [G: U.S.]

Brown, Richard K. Attitudes to Work, Occupational Identity and Industrial Change. In *Roberts, B.; Finnegan, R. and Gallie, D., eds.*, 1985, pp. 461–75. [G: U.K.]

Brown, William. The Effect of Recent Changes in the World Economy on British Industrial Relations. In *Juris, H.; Thompson, M. and Daniels, W., eds.*, 1985, pp. 151–75. [G: U.K.]

Browne, Lynn E. Structural Change and Dislocated Workers. *New Eng. Econ. Rev.*, January/February 1985, pp. 15–30. [G: U.S.]

Chalmers, James A. and Greenwood, Michael J. The Regional Labor Market Adjustment Process: Determinants of Changes in Rates of Labor Force Participation, Unemployment, and Migration. *Ann. Reg. Sci.*, March 1985, *19*(1), pp. 1–17. [G: U.S.]

Chaudhry, M. Ghaffar. The State and Development of Rural Industries in Pakistan. In *Mukhopadhyay, S. and Chee, P. L., eds. (I)*, 1985, pp. 249–306. [G: Pakistan]

Chiswick, Carmel U. The Elasticity of Substitution Revisited: The Effects of Secular Changes in Labor Force Structure. *J. Lab. Econ.*, October 1985, *3*(4), pp. 490–507. [G: U.S.]

Cohen, Suleiman I. The Labour Force Matrix of Pakistan: Selected Applications. *Pakistan Devel. Rev.*, Autumn-Winter 1985, *24*(3/4), pp. 565–84. [G: Pakistan]

Colombino, Ugo and De Stavola, Bianca. A Model of Female Labor Supply in Italy Using Cohort Data. *J. Lab. Econ.*, Part 2 January 1985, *3*(1), pp. S275–92. [G: Italy]

Corpeleijn, A. W. F. Labour Force Participation of Young Women in the Netherlands: An Analysis of Flow Data. *Statist. J.*, December 1985, 3(4), pp. 353–62.   [G: Netherlands]

David-McNeil, Jeannine. The Changing Economic Status of the Female Labour Force in Canada. In *Economic Council of Canada.*, 1985, pp. 1–8.   [G: Canada]

Dougherty, C. R. S. Manpower Forecasting and Manpower-Development Planning in the United Kingdom. In *Youdi, R. V. and Hinchliffe, K., eds.*, 1985, pp. 75–98.   [G: U.K.]

Dungan, Peter and Younger, Arthur. New Technology and Unemployment: A Simulation of Macroeconomic Impacts and Responses in Canada. *J. Policy Modeling*, Winter 1985, 7(4), pp. 595–619.   [G: Canada]

Ermisch, John F. Work, Jobs and Social Policy. In *Klein, R. and O'Higgins, M., ed.*, 1985, pp. 59–71.   [G: U.K.]

Fabella, Raul V. Rural Non-farm Activities in the Philippines: Composition, Growth and Seasonality. In *Mukhopadhyay, S. and Chee, P. L., eds. (I)*, 1985, pp. 495–589.   [G: Philippines]

Fields, Gary S. and Jakubson, George. Labor Market Analysis Using SIPP. *J. Econ. Soc. Meas.*, December 1985, 13(3–4), pp. 281–86.   [G: U.S.]

Fitzpatrick, Sheila. Postwar Soviet Society: The "Return to Normalcy," 1945–1953. In *Linz, S. J., ed.*, 1985, pp. 129–56.   [G: U.S.S.R.]

Flaim, Paul O. and Hogue, Carma R. Measuring Labor Force Flows: A Special Conference Examines the Problems. *Mon. Lab. Rev.*, July 1985, 108(7), pp. 7–17.   [G: U.S.]

Flaim, Paul O. and Sehgal, Ellen. Displaced Workers of 1979–83: How Well Have They Fared? *Mon. Lab. Rev.*, June 1985, 108(6), pp. 3–16.   [G: U.S.]

Flakierski, Henryk. Economic Reform & Income Distribution: A Case Study of Hungary and Poland. *Eastern Europ. Econ.*, Fall-Winter 1985-86, 24(1–2), pp. iii–194.

Fløystad, Gunnar. The Labour Force Matrix of Pakistan: Selected Applications: Comments. *Pakistan Devel. Rev.*, Autumn-Winter 1985, 24(3/4), pp. 585.   [G: Pakistan]

Franz, Wolfgang. An Economic Analysis of Female Work Participation, Education, and Fertility: Theory and Empirical Evidence for the Federal Republic of Germany. *J. Lab. Econ.*, Part 2 January 1985, 3(1), pp. S218–34.
                                   [G: W. Germany]

Fullerton, Howard N., Jr. Erratum [The 1995 Labor Force: BLS' Latest Projections]. *Mon. Lab. Rev.*, December 1985, 108(12), pp. 33.
                                          [G: U.S.]

Fullerton, Howard N., Jr. The 1995 Labor Force: BLS' Latest Projections. *Mon. Lab. Rev.*, November 1985, 108(11), pp. 17–25.   [G: U.S.]

Funaba, Takuji. The Labor Supply of Married Women. (In Japanese. With English summary.) *Osaka Econ. Pap.*, March 1985, 34(4), pp. 16–22.   [G: Japan]

Gabin, Nancy. Women Workers and the UAW in the Post-World War II Period: 1945–1954. In *Leab, D. J., ed.*, 1985, pp. 407–32.
                                          [G: U.S.]

Galasi, Péter and Sziráczki, György. State Regulation, Enterprise Behaviour and the Labour Market in Hungary, 1968–83. *Cambridge J. Econ.*, September 1985, 9(3), pp. 203–19.
                                       [G: Hungary]

Ginzberg, Eli. Reentry of Women to the Labor Force: A Fifteen-Country Perspective. In *Ginzberg, E.*, 1985, pp. 269–73.

Ginzberg, Eli. Returnees: Cross-National Research. In *Ginzberg, E.*, 1985, pp. 251–67.
    [G: W. Germany; France; Sweden; U.K.; U.S.]

Ginzberg, Eli. Women in the Work Force. In *Ginzberg, E.*, 1985, pp. 245–49.

Gordon, Ian R. and Molho, Ian. Women in the Labour Markets of the London Region: A Model of Dependence and Constraint. *Urban Stud.*, October 1985, 22(5), pp. 367–86.
                                          [G: U.K.]

Greenhalgh, Christine A. and Stewart, Mark B. The Occupational Status and Mobility of British Men and Women. *Oxford Econ. Pap.*, March 1985, 37(1), pp. 40–71.   [G: U.K.]

Gregory, R. G.; McMahon, P. J. and Whittingham, B. Women in the Australian Labor Force: Trends, Causes, and Consequences. *J. Lab. Econ.*, Part 2 January 1985, 3(1), pp. S293–309.   [G: Australia]

Gustafsson, Siv and Jacobsson, Roger. Trends in Female Labor Force Participation in Sweden. *J. Lab. Econ.*, Part 2 January 1985, 3(1), pp. S256–74.   [G: Sweden]

Gustman, Alan L. and Steinmeier, Thomas L. The 1983 Social Security Reforms and Labor Supply Adjustments of Older Individuals in the Long Run. *J. Lab. Econ.*, April 1985, 3(2), pp. 237–53.   [G: U.S.]

Hamel, Harvey R. and Tucker, John T. Implementing the Levitan Commission's Recommendations to Improve Labor Data. *Mon. Lab. Rev.*, February 1985, 108(2), pp. 16–24.
                                          [G: U.S.]

Hartog, Joop and Theeuwes, Jules. The Emergence of the Working Wife in Holland. *J. Lab. Econ.*, Part 2 January 1985, 3(1), pp. S235–55.   [G: Holland]

Hausman, Jerry A. The Econometrics of Nonlinear Budget Sets. *Econometrica*, November 1985, 53(6), pp. 1255–82.   [G: U.S.]

Haveman, Robert H. and Wolfe, Barbara L. The Effect of Disability Transfers on Work Effort: Research Results and Their Use in Policy Decisions. In *[Recktenwald, H. C.]*, 1985, pp. 261–78.   [G: OECD]

Hernandez Iglesias, Feliciano and Riboud, Michelle. Trends in Labor Force Participation of Spanish Women: An Interpretive Essay. *J. Lab. Econ.*, Part 2 January 1985, 3(1), pp. S201–17.   [G: Spain]

Hersch, Joni. Allocation of Time and Human Energy and Its Effects on Productivity. *Appl. Econ.*, October 1985, 17(5), pp. 867–84.
                                          [G: U.S.]

Hight, Joseph E. Review of Manpower Forecasts and Changes in Occupational Structure in the United States of America. In *Youdi, R. V. and*

Hinchliffe, K., eds., 1985, pp. 99–115.
[G: U.S.]

Hoem, Jan M. Weighting, Misclassification, and Other Issues in the Analysis of Survey Samples of Life Histories. In *Heckman, J. J. and Singer, B., eds.*, 1985, pp. 249–93.

Honig, Marjorie. Partial Retirement among Women [Partial Retirement as a Separate Mode of Retirement Behavior]. *J. Human Res.*, Fall 1985, *20*(4), pp. 613–21. [G: U.S.]

Honig, Marjorie and Hanoch, Giora. Partial Retirement as a Separate Mode of Retirement Behavior. *J. Human Res.*, Winter 1985, *20*(1), pp. 21–46. [G: U.S.]

Iakovleva, E. Overcoming Social and Economic Differences in Labor. *Prob. Econ.*, December 1985, *28*(8), pp. 3–20. [G: U.S.S.R.]

Ikemoto, Yukio. Income Distribution in Malaysia: 1957–80. *Devel. Econ.*, December 1985, *23*(4), pp. 347–67. [G: Malaysia]

Ivanova, R. Curtailment of Manual Labor—A Key Social and Economic Task. *Prob. Econ.*, August 1985, *28*(4), pp. 49–67. [G: U.S.S.R.]

Jones, Barbara A. P. Black Women and Labor Force Participation: An Analysis of Sluggish Growth Rates. *Rev. Black Polit. Econ.*, Fall-Winter 1985-86, *14*(2–3), pp. 11–31.
[G: U.S.]

Josefowicz, A.; Kluczynski, J. and Obrebski, T. Manpower and Education Planning and Policy Experience in Poland, 1960–80. In *Youdi, R. V. and Hinchliffe, K., eds.*, 1985, pp. 135–52. [G: Poland]

Joshi, Heather E.; Layard, Richard and Owen, Susan J. Why Are More Women Working in Britain? *J. Lab. Econ.*, Part 2 January 1985, *3*(1), pp. S147–76. [G: U.K.]

Kleber, Wolfgang. Labor Force Change in Germany since 1882: A Life Cycle Perspective. *Exploration Econ. Hist.*, January 1985, *22*(1), pp. 97–126. [G: W. Germany]

Lee, Bun Song and McElwain, Adrienne M. An Empirical Investigation of Female Labor-Force Participation, Fertility, Age at Marriage, and Wages in Korea. *J. Devel. Areas*, July 1985, *19*(4), pp. 483–99. [G: S. Korea]

Lee, Kyu Sik. Decentralization Trends of Employment Location and Spatial Policies in LDC Cities. *Urban Stud.*, April 1985, *22*(2), pp. 151–62. [G: Colombia]

Leuthold, Jane H. Labor Supply with an Endogenous Tax Rate. *Public Finance*, 1985, *40*(1), pp. 82–92. [G: U.S.]

Leuthold, Jane H. Work Incentives and the Two-Earner Deduction. *Public Finance Quart.*, January 1985, *13*(1), pp. 63–73. [G: U.S.]

Levy, Michel Louis. Rapport salarial et transition dé ographique. (With English summary.) *Revue Écon. Polit.*, Sept.-Oct. 1985, *95*(5), pp. 555–67. [G: OECD]

Lewis, Philip E. T. Substitution between Young and Adult Workers in Australia. *Australian Econ. Pap.*, June 1985, *24*(44), pp. 115–26.
[G: Australia]

Lillydahl, Jane H. and Singell, Larry D. The Spatial Variation in Unemployment and La-

bour Force Participation Rates of Male and Female Workers. *Reg. Stud.*, October 1985, *19*(5), pp. 459–69. [G: U.K.]

Lim, Chee Peng. A Review of Rural Non-farm Activities in Malaysia. In *Mukhopadhyay, S. and Chee, P. L., eds. (I)*, 1985, pp. 383–493.
[G: Malaysia]

Linke, R. D.; Oertel, L. M. and Kelsey, N. J. M. Participation and Equity in Higher Education: A Preliminary Report on the Socioeconomic Profile of Higher Education Students in South Australia, 1974–1984. *Australian Bull. Lab.*, June 1985, *11*(3), pp. 124–41.
[G: Australia]

Linsenmayer, Tadd. ILO Adopts New Standards on Health Services, Labor Data. *Mon. Lab. Rev.*, December 1985, *108*(12), pp. 43–47.

Lundberg, Shelly J. The Added Worker Effect. *J. Lab. Econ.*, Part 1 January 1985, *3*(1), pp. 11–37. [G: U.S.]

Lundberg, Shelly J. Tied Wage–Hours Offers and the Endogeneity of Wages. *Rev. Econ. Statist.*, August 1985, *67*(3), pp. 405–10. [G: U.S.]

Macarov, David. Planning for a Probability: The Almost-Workless World. *Int. Lab. Rev.*, Nov.-Dec. 1985, *124*(6), pp. 629–42.

MaCurdy, Thomas E. Interpreting Empirical Models of Labor Supply in an Intertemporal Framework with Uncertainty. In *Heckman, J. J. and Singer, B., eds.*, 1985, pp. 111–55.
[G: U.S.]

Marsden, Lorna R. Technological Change: Bad or Good? Comments. In *Economic Council of Canada.*, 1985, pp. 93–97. [G: U.S.]

Michael, Robert T. Consequences of the Rise in Female Labor Force Participation Rates. Questions and Probes. *J. Lab. Econ.*, Part 2 January 1985, *3*(1), pp. S117–46. [G: U.S.]

Mincer, Jacob. Intercountry Comparisons of Labor Force Trends and of Related Developments: An Overview. *J. Lab. Econ.*, Part 2 January 1985, *3*(1), pp. S1–32.
[G: Selected Countries]

Moy, Joyanna. Recent Trends in Unemployment and the Labor Force, 10 Countries. *Mon. Lab. Rev.*, August 1985, *108*(8), pp. 9–22.
[G: OECD]

Murphy, Kevin J. Geographic Differences in U.S. Unemployment Rates: A Variance Decomposition Approach. *Econ. Inquiry*, January 1985, *23*(1), pp. 135–58. [G: U.S.]

de Neubourg, Chris. Part-Time Work: An International Quantitative Comparison. *Int. Lab. Rev.*, Sept.-Oct. 1985, *124*(5), pp. 559–76.
[G: OECD]

O'Boyle, Edward J. On Reconstructing the Foundations of Policy toward the Unemployed. *Rev. Soc. Econ.*, December 1985, *43*(3), pp. 325–44.

Ofer, Gur and Vinokur, Aaron. Work and Family Roles of Soviet Women: Historical Trends and Cross-Section Analysis. *J. Lab. Econ.*, Part 2 January 1985, *3*(1), pp. S328–54.
[G: U.S.S.R.]

Paul, Jean-Jacques. Basic Concepts and Methods Used in Forecasting Skilled-Manpower Re-

quirements in France. In *Youdi, R. V. and Hinchliffe, K., eds.*, 1985, pp. 35–56.
[G: France]

Peitchinis, Stephen G. Technological Change: Bad or Good? In *Economic Council of Canada.*, 1985, pp. 83–93. [G: U.S.]

Personick, Valerie A. A Second Look at Industry Output and Employment Trends through 1995. *Mon. Lab. Rev.*, November 1985, *108*(11), pp. 26–41. [G: U.S.]

Peters, R. W. and Petridis, A. Employment, the Labour Force and Unemployment in Australia: A Disaggregated Approach. *Australian Econ. Rev.*, 4th Quarter 1985, (72), pp. 51–67.
[G: Australia]

Quester, Aline O. and Greene, William H. The Labor Market Experience of Black and White Wives in the Sixties and Seventies. *Soc. Sci. Quart.*, December 1985, *66*(4), pp. 854–66.
[G: U.S.]

Rabeau, Yves. Le marché du travail: quelques perspectives d'avenir. (The Labour Marker: Some Prospects. With English summary.) *L'Actual. Econ.*, March 1985, *61*(1), pp. 127–42.

Rehn, Gösta. Swedish Active Labor Market Policy: Retrospect and Prospect. *Ind. Relat.*, Winter 1985, *24*(1), pp. 62–89. [G: Sweden]

Reimers, Cordelia W. Cultural Differences in Labor Force Participation among Married Women. *Amer. Econ. Rev.*, May 1985, *75*(2), pp. 251–55. [G: U.S.]

Rein, Martin. Women, Employment and Social Welfare. In *Klein, R. and O'Higgins, M., ed.*, 1985, pp. 37–58. [G: Sweden; U.K.; U.S.; W. Germany]

Riboud, Michelle. An Analysis of Women's Labor Force Participation in France: Cross-Section Estimates and Time-Series Evidence. *J. Lab. Econ.*, Part 2 January 1985, *3*(1), pp. S177–200. [G: France]

Robins, Philip K. A Comparison of the Labor Supply Findings from the Four Negative Income Tax Experiments. *J. Human Res.*, Fall 1985, *20*(4), pp. 567–82. [G: U.S.]

Robinson, Chris and Tomes, Nigel. More on the Labour Supply of Canadian Women. *Can. J. Econ.*, February 1985, *18*(1), pp. 156–63.
[G: Canada]

Romani, Claudine. Dinamiche dell'occupazione industriale nella crisi: un confronto tra Francia e Germania. (Dynamics of Industrial Employment in the Crisis: A Comparison France–Germany. With English summary.) *Econ. Lavoro*, Apr.-June 1985, *19*(2), pp. 35–48.
[G: France; W. Germany]

Rones, Philip L. Technical Note: Revisions in Hispanic Population and Labor Force Data. *Mon. Lab. Rev.*, March 1985, *108*(3), pp. 43–44.
[G: U.S.]

Rones, Philip L. Using the CPS to Track Retirement Trends among Older Men. *Mon. Lab. Rev.*, February 1985, *108*(2), pp. 46–49.
[G: U.S.]

Ryscavage, Paul M. and Bregger, John E. New Household Survey and the CPS: A Look at

Labor Force Differences. *Mon. Lab. Rev.*, September 1985, *108*(9), pp. 3–12. [G: U.S.]

Saleh, Mamdouh. Retrospective Evaluation of Forecasting Methods for Qualified-Manpower Needs for Egypt. In *Youdi, R. V. and Hinchliffe, K., eds.*, 1985, pp. 175–93.
[G: Egypt]

Santiago, Carlos E. and Rossiter, Rosemary. A Multiple Time-Series Analysis of Labor Supply and Earnings in Economic Development. *J. Devel. Econ.*, April 1985, *17*(3), pp. 259–75.
[G: Puerto Rico]

Scoville, James G. The Labor Market in Prerevolutionary Iran. *Econ. Develop. Cult. Change*, October 1985, *34*(1), pp. 143–55. [G: Iran]

Sethuraman, S. V. The Informal Sector in Indonesia: Policies and Prospects. *Int. Lab. Rev.*, Nov.-Dec. 1985, *124*(6), pp. 719–35.
[G: Indonesia]

Shimada, Haruo. International Trade and Labour Market Adjustment: The Case of Japan. *Econ. Lavoro*, July-Sept. 1985, *19*(3), pp. 3–30.
[G: Japan]

Shimada, Haruo and Higuchi, Yoshio. An Analysis of Trends in Female Labor Force Participation in Japan. *Econ. Lavoro*, Apr.-June 1985, *19*(2), pp. 3–18. [G: Japan]

Shimada, Haruo and Higuchi, Yoshio. An Analysis of Trends in Female Labor Force Participation in Japan. *J. Lab. Econ.*, Part 2 January 1985, *3*(1), pp. S355–74. [G: Japan]

Silvestri, George T. and Lukasiewicz, John M. Occupational Employment Projections: The 1984–95 Outlook. *Mon. Lab. Rev.*, November 1985, *108*(11), pp. 42–57. [G: U.S.]

Smith, James P. and Ward, Michael P. Time-Series Growth in the Female Labor Force. *J. Lab. Econ.*, Part 2 January 1985, *3*(1), pp. S59–90. [G: U.S.]

Smith, Shirley J. Estimating Lost Future Earnings Using the New Worklife Tables: A Comment [Using the Appropriate Worklife Estimate in Court Proceedings]. *Mon. Lab. Rev.*, February 1985, *108*(2), pp. 42. [G: U.S.]

Smith, Shirley J. Revised Worklife Tables Reflect 1979–80 Experience. *Mon. Lab. Rev.*, August 1985, *108*(8), pp. 23–30. [G: U.S.]

Smyth, David J. The Effects of Unemployment Insurance on the Supply of Labor: Does the Dole Cause Unemployment? In *Terny, G. and Culyer, A. J., eds.*, 1985, pp. 143–55.
[G: U.S.]

Stelcner, Morton and Breslaw, Jon. Income Taxes and the Labor Supply of Married Women in Quebec. *Southern Econ. J.*, April 1985, *51*(4), pp. 1053–72. [G: Canada]

Stevans, Lonnie K.; Register, Charles and Grimes, Paul. Race and the Discouraged Female Worker: A Question of Labor Force Attachment. *Rev. Black Polit. Econ.*, Summer 1985, *14*(1), pp. 89–97. [G: U.S.]

Stone, John Owen. Youth Unemployment in Australia. *Nat. Westminster Bank Quart. Rev.*, May 1985, pp. 3–11. [G: Australia]

Thomson, Peter. Sources of Local Employment Information: A Comparison of Census of Employment Data with 1981 Population Census Workplace Data. *J. Econ. Soc. Meas.*, April 1985, *13*(1), pp. 39–48.   [G: U.K.]

Tienda, Marta and Glass, Jennifer. Household Structure and Labor Force Participation of Black, Hispanic, and White Mothers. *Demography*, August 1985, *22*(3), pp. 381–94.
[G: U.S.]

Tímár, János. Time and Work Time: Certain Problems with the Time Basis of Social Reproduction in Hungary. In *[Levcik, F.]*, 1985, pp. 137–48.   [G: Hungary]

Tomoda, Shizue. Measuring Female Labour Activities in Asian Developing Countries: A Time-Allocation Approach. *Int. Lab. Rev.*, Nov.-Dec. 1985, *124*(6), pp. 661–76.
[G: Bangladesh; Nepal; Indonesia; Philippines]

Tyree, Andrea. Tracking a Ghost To Test a Theory. *Soc. Sci. Quart.*, September 1985, *66*(3), pp. 668–74.   [G: Selected MDCs]

Urban, Jan. Population Trends and Employment in the European CMEA Countries. *Czech. Econ. Digest.*, June 1985, (4), pp. 42–51.
[G: CMEA]

Verma, M. C. Review of Skilled-Manpower Forecasts in India. In *Youdi, R. V. and Hinchliffe, K., eds.*, 1985, pp. 194–210.   [G: India]

de la Viña, Lynda Y. Female Occupational Distribution: Treiman and Terrell Revisited. *Soc. Sci. Quart.*, September 1985, *66*(3), pp. 680–86.   [G: U.S.]

Vincens, Jean. Emploi—chômage. (With English summary.) *Revue Écon. Polit.*, Sept.-Oct. 1985, *95*(5), pp. 684–94.   [G: OECD]

Viren, Matti. Determination of Employment with Wage and Price Speculation. *Scand. J. Econ.*, 1985, *87*(3), pp. 537–53.   [G: Finland]

Ward, Kathryn B. and Pampel, Fred C. More on the Meaning of the Effect of the Sex Ratio on Female Labor Force Participation. *Soc. Sci. Quart.*, September 1985, *66*(3), pp. 675–79.
[G: Selected MDCs]

Ward, Kathryn B. and Pampel, Fred C. Structural Determinants of Female Labor Force Participation in Developed Nations, 1955–75. *Soc. Sci. Quart.*, September 1985, *66*(3), pp. 654–67.   [G: Selected MDCs]

Weser, L. Wilhelm. Medium-term Employment Perspectives in the Federal Republic of Germany (Conference on Medium-term Economic Assessment from 10 to 12 September 1984 in Stockholm). *Econ. Lavoro*, July-Sept. 1985, *19*(3), pp. 121–28.   [G: W. Germany]

Yatchew, Adonis John. Labor Supply in the Presence of Taxes: An Alternative Specification. *Rev. Econ. Statist.*, February 1985, *67*(1), pp. 27–33.   [G: U.S.]

Young, Anne McDougall. One-fourth of the Adult Labor Force Are College Graduates. *Mon. Lab. Rev.*, February 1985, *108*(2), pp. 43–46.
[G: U.S.]

Yue, Guangzhao. Employment, Wages and Social Security in China. *Int. Lab. Rev.*, July-Aug. 1985, *124*(4), pp. 411–22.   [G: China]

Zietz, Joachim. A Pre-estimation Sample Separa-

tion Method for a Labor Market in Disequilibrium. *J. Macroecon.*, Winter 1985, *7*(1), pp. 51–67.   [G: U.S.]

8131 Agriculture

Agarwal, Bina. Women and Technological Change in Agriculture: The Asian and African Experience. In *Ahmed, I., ed.*, 1985, pp. 67–114.   [G: India; Africa; Asia]

Bandyopadhyay, D. An Evaluation of Policies and Programmes for the Alleviation of Rural Poverty in India. In *Islam, R., ed.*, 1985, pp. 99–151.   [G: India]

Bhattacharya, Neeladri. Agricultural Labour and Production: Central and South–East Punjab, 1870–1940. In *Raj, K. N., et al., eds.*, 1985, pp. 105–62.   [G: India]

Birdsall, Nancy. A Population Perspective on Agricultural Development. In *Davis, T. J., ed.*, 1985, pp. 29–51.   [G: Selected LDCs; Selected MDCs]

Broder, Josef M. and Deprey, Rodney P. Monetary Returns to Bachelors and Masters Degrees in Agricultural Economics. *Amer. J. Agr. Econ.*, August 1985, *67*(3), pp. 666–73.
[G: U.S.]

Domar, Evsey D. and Machina, Mark J. The Profitability of Serfdom: A Reply [On the Profitability of Russian Serfdom]. *J. Econ. Hist.*, December 1985, *45*(4), pp. 960–62.

Durant-Gonzalez, Victoria. Higglering: Rural Women and the Internal Market System in Jamaica. In *Gomes, P. I., ed.*, 1985, pp. 103–22.   [G: Jamaica]

Edquist, Charles. Technology and Work in Sugar Cane Harvesting in Capitalist Jamaica and Socialist Cuba 1958–1983. In *Gustavsson, B.; Karlsson, J. C. and Raftegard, C.*, 1985, pp. 71–82.   [G: Cuba; Jamaica]

Emerson, Robert D. Critical Issues in Agricultural Labor Markets. *Southern J. Agr. Econ.*, July 1985, *17*(1), pp. 89–98.   [G: U.S.]

Garcia-Ramon, M. Dolores. Agricultural Change in an Industrializing Area: The Case of the Tarragona Area. In *Hudson, R. and Lewis, J., eds.*, 1985, pp. 140–54.   [G: Spain]

Goodwin, H. L., Jr. Critical Issues in Agricultural Labor Markets: Discussion. *Southern J. Agr. Econ.*, July 1985, *17*(1), pp. 99–102.
[G: U.S.]

Hebbar, B. Gopalakrishna and Bisaliah, S. Output and Employment Elasticities of a Dominant Dryland Crop. *Margin*, April 1985, *17*(3), pp. 55–65.   [G: India]

Khan, M. Mahmud. Labour Absorption and Unemployment in Rural Bangladesh. *Bangladesh Devel. Stud.*, Sept.-Dec. 1985, *13*(3&4), pp. 67–88.   [G: Bangladesh]

Nove, Alec. Soviet Peasantry in World War II. In *Linz, S. J., ed.*, 1985, pp. 77–90.
[G: U.S.S.R.]

Papanek, Gustav F. Agricultural Income Distribution and Employment in the 1970s. *Bull. Indonesian Econ. Stud.*, August 1985, *21*(2), pp. 24–50.   [G: Indonesia]

Parikh, Ashok. Some Aspects of Employment in Indian Agriculture. *World Devel.*, June 1985, *13*(6), pp. 691–704.   [G: India]

Pickering, Donald C. Population and Food and Population Change and Development: Chairman's Comments. In *Davis, T. J., ed.*, 1985, pp. 52–54.

Pollitt, Brian H. Towards the Socialist Transformation of Cuban Agriculture 1959–1982. In *Gomes, P. I., ed.*, 1985, pp. 154–72.
[G: Cuba]

Pugliese, Enrico. Farm Workers in Italy: Agricultural Working Class, Landless Peasants, or Clients of the Welfare State? In *Hudson, R. and Lewis, J., eds.*, 1985, pp. 123–39.
[G: Italy]

Shammas, Carole. Black Women's Work and the Evolution of Plantation Society in Virginia. *Labor Hist.*, Winter 1985, *26*(1), pp. 5–28.
[G: U.S.]

Toumanoff, Peter G. The Profitability of Serfdom: A Comment [On the Profitability of Russian Serfdom]. *J. Econ. Hist.*, December 1985, *45*(4), pp. 955–59.

Travers, S. Lee. Getting Rich through Diligence: Peasant Income after the Reforms. In *Perry, E. J. and Wong, C., eds.*, 1985, pp. 111–30.
[G: China]

8132 Manufacturing

Afridi, Usman. Dynamics of Change in Pakistan's Large-Scale Manufacturing Sector. *Pakistan Devel. Rev.*, Autumn-Winter 1985, *24*(3/4), pp. 463–76.   [G: Pakistan]

Ahmed, Meekal Aziz. Dynamics of Change in Pakistan's Large-Scale Manufacturing Sector: Comments. *Pakistan Devel. Rev.*, Autumn-Winter 1985, *24*(3/4), pp. 477–78.

Carruth, Alan A. and Oswald, Andrew J. Miners' Wages in Post-war Britain: An Application of a Model of Trade Union Behaviour. *Econ. J.*, December 1985, *95*(380), pp. 1003–20.
[G: U.K.]

Cornfield, Daniel B. Economic Segmentation and Expression of Labor Unrest: Striking versus Quitting in the Manufacturing Sector. *Soc. Sci. Quart.*, June 1985, *66*(2), pp. 247–65.
[G: U.S.]

Deimezis, Nikitas. Analyse sectorielle de l'emploi dans l'industrie manufacturière belge. Perspectives à long terme. (With English summary.) *Cah. Écon. Bruxelles*, 2nd Trimester 1985, (106), pp. 192–216.   [G: Belgium]

Driver, Ciaran; Kilpatrick, Andrew and Naisbitt, Barry. The Employment Effects of Changes in the Structure of UK Trade. *J. Econ. Stud.*, 1985, *12*(5), pp. 19–38.   [G: U.K.]

Ebel, Karl-H. Social and Labour Implications of Flexible Manufacturing Systems. *Int. Lab. Rev.*, March-April 1985, *124*(2), pp. 133–45.

King, Sandra L. and Williams, Harry B. Shift Work Pay Differentials and Practices in Manufacturing. *Mon. Lab. Rev.*, December 1985, *108*(12), pp. 26–33.   [G: U.S.]

Lawrence, Colin and Lawrence, Robert Z. Man-

ufacturing Wage Dispersion: An End Game Interpretation. *Brookings Pap. Econ. Act.*, 1985, (1), pp. 47–106.   [G: U.S.]

Lee, Kyu Sik. Decentralization Trends of Employment Location and Spatial Policies in LDC Cities. *Urban Stud.*, April 1985, *22*(2), pp. 151–62.   [G: Colombia]

Lindauer, David L. Regional Wage Determination and Economic Growth in Korea. *J. Econ. Devel.*, July 1985, *10*(1), pp. 129–41.
[G: S. Korea]

Mangan, J. and Stokes, L. Labour Demand in Australian Manufacturing: A Further Analysis. *S. Afr. J. Econ.*, June 1985, *53*(2), pp. 197–200.   [G: Australia]

O'Farrell, P. N. Employment Change in Manufacturing: The Case of Surviving Plants. *Urban Stud.*, February 1985, *22*(1), pp. 57–68.
[G: U.K.]

Saxonhouse, Gary R. and Kiyokawa, Yukihiko. Supply and Demand for Quality Workers in Cotton Spinning in Japan and India. In *Ohkawa, K. and Ranis, G., eds.*, 1985, pp. 177–211.   [G: Japan; India]

Solow, Robert M. Manufacturing Wage Dispersion: An End Game Interpretation: Comment. *Brookings Pap. Econ. Act.*, 1985, (1), pp. 107–10.   [G: U.S.]

Wachter, Michael L. Manufacturing Wage Dispersion: An End Game Interpretation: Comment. *Brookings Pap. Econ. Act.*, 1985, (1), pp. 110–15.   [G: U.S.]

Waldinger, Roger. Immigration and Industrial Change in the New York City Apparel Industry. In *Borjas, G. J. and Tienda, M., eds.*, 1985, pp. 323–49.   [G: U.S.]

Walker, Alan; Noble, Iain and Westergaard, John. From Secure Employment to Labour Market Insecurity: The Impact of Redundancy on Older Workers in the Steel Industry. In *Roberts, B.; Finnegan, R. and Gallie, D., eds.*, 1985, pp. 319–37.   [G: U.K.]

8133 Service

Carter, Michael J. and Carter, Susan B. Internal Labor Markets in Retailing: The Early Years. *Ind. Lab. Relat. Rev.*, July 1985, *38*(4), pp. 586–98.   [G: U.S.]

Eckstein, Albert J. and Heien, Dale. Causes and Consequences of Service Sector Growth: The U.S. Experience. *Growth Change*, April 1985, *16*(2), pp. 12–17.   [G: U.S.]

Gemmell, Norman. The Growth of Employment in Services: Egypt, 1960–75. *Devel. Econ.*, March 1985, *23*(1), pp. 53–68.   [G: Egypt]

McKinney, Fred. Employment Implications of a Changing Health-Care System. *Rev. Black Polit. Econ.*, Fall-Winter 1985-86, *14*(2–3), pp. 199–215.

Pellegrini, Luca. The Distributive Trades in the Italian Economy: Some Remarks on the Decade 1970–80. *Rev. Econ. Cond. Italy*, May-Aug. 1985, (2), pp. 191–220.   [G: Italy]

Rutgaizer, V. and Teliukov, A. Improving the Methodology of the National Economic Accounting of Services. *Prob. Econ.*, March 1985, 27(11), pp. 3–22. **[G: U.S.S.R.]**

Silberberg, Eugene. Race, Recent Entry, and Labor Market Participation. *Amer. Econ. Rev.*, December 1985, 75(5), pp. 1168–77.
[G: U.S.]

Tessler, Andrew. Services. In *Meyer, F. V., ed.*, 1985, pp. 124–43. **[G: U.K.]**

Wolff, Edward N. The Disappearance of Domestic Servants and the Underground Economy. In *Gaertner, W. and Wenig, A., eds.*, 1985, pp. 316–29. **[G: U.S.]**

8134 Professional

Agarwal, Vinod B. and Winkler, Donald R. United States Immigration Policy and Indirect Immigration of Professionals. *Econ. Educ. Rev.*, 1985, 4(1), pp. 1–16. **[G: U.S.]**

Aronson, Robert L. Unionism among Professional Employees in the Private Sector. *Ind. Lab. Relat. Rev.*, April 1985, 38(3), pp. 352–64.
[G: U.S.]

Booton, Lavonne A. and Lane, Julia. Hospital Market Structure and the Return to Nursing Education. *J. Human Res.*, Spring 1985, 20(2), pp. 184–96. **[G: U.S.]**

Bruggink, Thomas H., et al. Direct and Indirect Effects of Unionization on the Wage Levels of Nurses: A Case Study of New Jersey Hospitals. *J. Lab. Res.*, Fall 1985, 6(4), pp. 405–16. **[G: U.S.]**

Buchanan, R. A. Institutional Proliferation in the British Engineering Profession, 1847–1914. *Econ. Hist. Rev., 2nd Ser.*, February 1985, 38(1), pp. 42–60. **[G: U.K.]**

Eastaugh, Steven R. The Impact of the Nurse Training Act on the Supply of Nurses, 1974–1983. *Inquiry*, Winter 1985, 22(4), pp. 404–17. **[G: U.S.]**

Frank, Richard G. Pricing and Location of Physician Services in Mental Health. *Econ. Inquiry*, January 1985, 23(1), pp. 115–33. **[G: U.S.]**

Harris, Jeffrey. Competition and Equilibrium as a Driving Force in the Health Services Sector: Comment. In *Inman, R. P., ed.*, 1985, pp. 268–72.

Lewis, P. E. T. and Vella, F. G. M. Economic Factors Affecting the Number of Engineering Graduates in Australia. *Australian Econ. Pap.*, June 1985, 24(44), pp. 66–75. **[G: Australia]**

Ley, Robert D. and Wines, William A. The Economics of Teachers' Strikes in Minnesota in 1981. *Econ. Educ. Rev.*, 1985, 4(1), pp. 57–65. **[G: U.S.]**

Link, Charles R. and Settle, Russell F. Labor Supply Responses of Licensed Practical Nurses: A Partial Solution to a Nurse Shortage? *J. Econ. Bus.*, February 1985, 37(1), pp. 49–57. **[G: U.S.]**

Megdal, Sharon Bernstein and Ransom, Michael R. Longitudinal Changes at a Large Public University: What Response to Equal Pay Legislation? *Amer. Econ. Rev.*, May 1985, 75(2), pp. 271–74. **[G: U.S.]**

Pettersson, Lars. Engineer Training in Sweden

during the Postwar Period in the Context of Technical and Structural Change. *Scand. Econ. Hist. Rev.*, 1985, 33(2), pp. 108–21.
[G: Sweden]

Saini, Balwant Singh. Barefoot Architects: A Training Program for Building in the Third World. In *Lea, J. P. and Courtney, J. M., eds.*, 1985, pp. 97–100.

Saltzman, Gregory M. Bargaining Laws as a Cause and Consequence of the Growth of Teacher Unionism. *Ind. Lab. Relat. Rev.*, April 1985, 38(3), pp. 335–51. **[G: U.S.]**

Satterthwaite, Mark A. Competition and Equilibrium as a Driving Force in the Health Services Sector. In *Inman, R. P., ed.*, 1985, pp. 239–67.

Sheffrin, Steven M. Mobility and Efficiency in the Job Market for Economists. *Econ. Educ. Rev.*, 1985, 4(4), pp. 311–20. **[G: U.S.]**

Tímár, János. Manpower and Educational Planning in Hungary. In *Youdi, R. V. and Hinchliffe, K., eds.*, 1985, pp. 119–34.
[G: Hungary]

Ukaegbu, Chikwendu Christian. Are Nigerian Scientists and Engineers Effectively Utilized? Issues on the Deployment of Scientific and Technological Labor for National Development. *World Devel.*, April 1985, 13(4), pp. 499–512. **[G: Nigeria]**

Willner, Johan. Professional Associations and Their Members: A Study of the Market for Professional Services When Ability and Size Are Independent. *Int. J. Ind. Organ.*, June 1985, 3(2), pp. 179–95.

Zarkin, Gary A. Occupational Choice: An Application to the Market for Public School Teachers. *Quart. J. Econ.*, May 1985, 100(2), pp. 409–46. **[G: U.S.]**

8135 Government Employees

Atwater, D. M.; Bres, E. S., III and Niehaus, Richard J. Human Resources Supply–Demand Policy Analysis Models. In *Niehaus, R. J., ed.*, 1985, pp. 92–120. **[G: U.S.]**

Bacharach, Samuel B.; Mitchell, Stephen M. and Malanowski, Rose. Strategic Choice and Collective Action: Organizational Determinants of Teachers Militancy. In *Lipsky, D. B., ed.*, 1985, pp. 197–222. **[G: U.S.]**

Bosanquet, Nick. Welfare Needs, Welfare Jobs and Efficiency. In *Klein, R. and O'Higgins, M., ed.*, 1985, pp. 186–203. **[G: U.K.]**

Charnes, A., et al. A Goal Programming System for the Management of the U.S. Navy's Sea–Shore Rotation Program. In *Niehaus, R. J., ed.*, 1985, pp. 145–72. **[G: U.S.]**

Delaney, John Thomas. Unionism, Bargaining Spillovers, and Teacher Compensation. In *Lipsky, D. B., ed.*, 1985, pp. 111–42. **[G: U.S.]**

Gerhart, Paul F. and Drotning, John E. The Effectiveness of Public Sector Impasse Procedures: A Six State Study. In *Lipsky, D. B., ed.*, 1985, pp. 143–95. **[G: U.S.]**

Gurdon, Michael A. The Emergence of Co-determination in Australian Government Employment. *Int. Lab. Rev.*, July-Aug. 1985, *124*(4), pp. 465–78.

Jackson, Peter M. Fiscal Containment and Local Government Finance in the U.K. In *Gramlich, E. M. and Ysander, B.-C., eds.*, 1985, pp. 175–228. [G: U.K.]

Leonard, Herman B. The Federal Civil Service Retirement System: An Analysis of Its Financial Condition and Current Reform Proposals. In *Wise, D. A., ed.*, 1985, pp. 399–438. [G: U.S.]

Murrell, Peter. The Size of Public Employment: An Empirical Study. *J. Compar. Econ.*, December 1985, *9*(4), pp. 424–37. [G: OECD]

Niehaus, Richard J.; Schinnar, A. P. and Walters, L. C. Productivity and Organizational Economies of Personnel Services. In *Niehaus, R. J., ed.*, 1985, pp. 187–214. [G: U.S.]

Owen, John D. Changing from a Rotating to a Permanent Shift System in the Detroit Police Department: Effects on Employee Attitudes and Behavior. In *Dennis, B. D., ed.*, 1985, pp. 484–89. [G: U.S.]

Page, Edward. From *l'État* to Big Government. In *Rose, R.*, 1985, pp. 97–125. [G: France]

Parry, Richard. Britain: Stable Aggregates, Changing Composition. In *Rose, R.*, 1985, pp. 54–96. [G: U.K.]

Peters, B. Guy. Administrative Change and the Grace Commission. In *Levine, C. H., ed.*, 1985, pp. 19–39. [G: U.S.]

Peters, B. Guy. Sweden: The Explosion of Public Employment. In *Rose, R.*, 1985, pp. 203–27. [G: Sweden]

Peters, B. Guy. The United States: Absolute Change and Relative Stability. In *Rose, R.*, 1985, pp. 228–61. [G: U.S.]

Pignatelli, Andrea Cendali. Italy: The Development of a Late Developing State. In *Rose, R.*, 1985, pp. 163–201. [G: Italy]

Rose, Richard. The Significance of Public Employment. In *Rose, R.*, 1985, pp. 1–53. [G: Selected OECD]

Samuelson, Paul A. The Federal Civil Service Retirement System: An Analysis of Its Financial Condition and Current Reform Proposals: Comment. In *Wise, D. A., ed.*, 1985, pp. 438–43. [G: U.S.]

Schleck, Robert W. Reforming Federal Pension Programs. In *Harriss, C. L., ed.*, 1985, pp. 85–100. [G: U.S.]

Schmidt, Klaus-Dieter and Rose, Richard. Germany: The Expansion of an Active State. In *Rose, R.*, 1985, pp. 126–62. [G: W. Germany]

Wade, Robert. The Market for Public Office: Why the Indian State Is Not Better at Development. *World Devel.*, April 1985, *13*(4), pp. 467–97.

8136 Construction

Strassmann, W. Paul. Employment in Construction: Multicountry Estimates of Costs and Substitution Elasticities for Small Dwellings. *Econ. Develop. Cult. Change*, January 1985, *33*(2), pp. 395–414. [G: LDCs]

820 LABOR MARKETS; PUBLIC POLICY

8200 General

Carnoy, Martin. High Technology and International Labour Markets. *Int. Lab. Rev.*, Nov.-Dec. 1985, *124*(6), pp. 643–59. [G: LDCs; OECD]

Crane, Maurice A. Labor History Materials in the G. Robert Vincent Voice Library, Michigan State University. *Labor Hist.*, Spring 1985, *26*(2), pp. 288–90. [G: U.S.]

Maxwell, Nan L. Survey of Labor Economics Textbooks. *J. Econ. Educ.*, Spring 1985, *16*(2), pp. 147–56.

Storper, Michael. Disequilibrium and Dynamics in Metropolitan Economic Development in the Third World: Reply. *Reg. Stud.*, February 1985, *19*(1), pp. 51–57. [G: LDCs]

Storper, Michael. Response to Professor Vining's 'Query' [Who Benefits from Industrial Decentralization? Social Power in the Labour Market, Income Distribution and Spatial Policy in Brazil]. *Reg. Stud.*, April 1985, *19*(2), pp. 164. [G: Brazil]

Vining, Daniel R. Industrial Decentralization in Brazil: A Query [Who Benefits from Industrial Decentralization? Social Power in the Labour Market, Income Distribution and Spatial Policy in Brazil]. *Reg. Stud.*, April 1985, *19*(2), pp. 163–64. [G: Brazil]

821 Labor Economics

8210 Labor Economics: Theory and Empirical Studies Illustrating Theory

Adams, James D. Permanent Differences in Unemployment and Permanent Wage Differentials. *Quart. J. Econ.*, February 1985, *100*(1), pp. 29–56. [G: U.S.]

Adler, Moshe. Stardom and Talent. *Amer. Econ. Rev.*, March 1985, *75*(1), pp. 208–12.

Afxentiou, P. C. Opportunity Costs and Collective Bargaining. *S. Afr. J. Econ.*, December 1985, *53*(4), pp. 381–92.

Ahsan, Syed M. and Ali, Ali A. G. Income Taxation, Migration, and Work Incentives in a Dual Economy Model. *Devel. Econ.*, March 1985, *23*(1), pp. 16–39.

Aizenman, Joshua. Wage Flexibility and Openness. *Quart. J. Econ.*, May 1985, *100*(2), pp. 539–50.

Aizenman, Joshua and Frenkel, Jacob A. Optimal Wage Indexation, Foreign Exchange Intervention, and Monetary Policy. *Amer. Econ. Rev.*, June 1985, *75*(3), pp. 402–23.

Akerlof, George A. Discriminatory, Status-based Wages among Tradition-oriented, Stochastically Trading Coconut Producers. *J. Polit. Econ.*, April 1985, *93*(2), pp. 265–76.

Alao, Nurudeen. Urban Unemployment Equilibrium in LDCs: A Perspective. *Reg. Stud.*, June 1985, *19*(3), pp. 185–92. [G: LDCs]

Albaek, Karsten. Løntilskud og læringebeskæftigelse. (Wage-Subsidies and Employment of

Apprentices in Denmark. With English summary.) *Nationaløkon. Tidsskr.*, 1985, *123*(2), pp. 176–93.   [G: Denmark]

Andersen, Per Kragh. Statistical Models for Longitudinal Labor Market Data Based on Counting Processes. In *Heckman, J. J. and Singer, B., eds.*, 1985, pp. 294–307.

Andersen, Torben M. Arbejdstidsforkortelse som konjunkturpolitisk instrument. (Shortening of Working Hours as an Instrument in Stabilization Policy. With English summary.) *Nationaløkon. Tidsskr.*, 1985, *123*(2), pp. 145–59.   [G: Netherlands]

Antel, John J. Costly Employment Contract Renegotiation and the Labor Mobility of Young Men. *Amer. Econ. Rev.*, December 1985, *75*(5), pp. 976–91.   [G: U.S.]

Aoki, Masahiko. Dynamics of Unemployment, Vacancies and Real Wages with Trade Unions: Comment. *Scand. J. Econ.*, 1985, *87*(2), pp. 404–07.

Appelbaum, Eileen. Employment and the Distribution of Earned Income. *J. Post Keynesian Econ.*, Summer 1985, *7*(4), pp. 594–602.

Arnott, Richard J. and Stiglitz, Joseph E. Labor Turnover, Wage Structures, and Moral Hazard: The Inefficiency of Competitive Markets. *J. Lab. Econ.*, October 1985, *3*(4), pp. 434–62.

Arrow, Kenneth J. Models of Job Discrimination. In *Arrow, K. J. (II)*, 1985, pp. 89–111.

Arrow, Kenneth J. Some Mathematical Models of Race Discrimination in the Labor Market. In *Arrow, K. J. (II)*, 1985, pp. 112–29.

Arrow, Kenneth J. The Theory of Discrimination. In *Arrow, K. J. (II)*, 1985, pp. 143–64.

Asimakopulos, Athanasios. The Foundations of Unemployment Theory: A Comment. *J. Post Keynesian Econ.*, Spring 1985, *7*(3), pp. 352–62.

Auerbach, Alan J. The Riskiness of Private Pensions: Comment. In *Wise, D. A., ed.*, 1985, pp. 375–78.

Azariadis, Costas and Cooper, Russell. Nominal Wage–Price Rigidity as a Rational Expectations Equilibrium. *Amer. Econ. Rev.*, May 1985, *75*(2), pp. 31–35.

Azariadis, Costas and Cooper, Russell. Predetermined Prices and the Allocation of Social Risks. *Quart. J. Econ.*, May 1985, *100*(2), pp. 495–518.

Balducci, Renato. Economia di partecipazione e accumulazione. (Share Economy and Accumulation. With English summary.) *Giorn. Econ.*, Nov.-Dec. 1985, *44*(11–12), pp. 639–50.

Barron, John M.; Bishop, John and Dunkelberg, William C. Employer Search: The Interviewing and Hiring of New Employees. *Rev. Econ. Statist.*, February 1985, *67*(1), pp. 43–52.   [G: U.S.]

Barron, John M. and Loewenstein, Mark A. On Employer-specific Information and Internal Labor Markets. *Southern Econ. J.*, October 1985, *52*(2), pp. 431–45.   [G: U.S.]

Benassy, Jean-Pascal. A Non-Walrasian Model of Employment with Partial Price Flexibility and Indexation. In *Feiwel, G. R., ed. (I)*, 1985, pp. 184–96.

Benderly, Jason and Zwick, Burton. Money, Unemployment and Inflation. *Rev. Econ. Statist.*, February 1985, *67*(1), pp. 139–43.   [G: U.S.]

Benería, Lourdes. Meditations on Ivan Illich's Gender. In *Gustavsson, B.; Karlsson, J. C. and Raftegard, C.*, 1985, pp. 121–29.

Bental, Benjamin; Ben-Zion, Uri and Wenig, Alois. Macroeconomic Policy and the Shadow Economy. In *Gaertner, W. and Wenig, A., eds.*, 1985, pp. 179–93.

Betson, David and van der Gaag, Jacques. Measuring the Benefits of Income Maintenance Programs. In *David, M. and Smeeding, T., eds.*, 1985, pp. 215–33.   [G: U.S.]

Bhagwati, Jagdish N. Reflections on Unemployment Models in Development Theory. In *Bhagwati, J. N. (II)*, 1985, pp. 237–49.

Bhagwati, Jagdish N. and Srinivasan, T. N. The Ranking of Policy Interventions under Factor Market Imperfections: The Case of Sector-Specific Sticky Wages and Unemployment. In *Bhagwati, J. N. (II)*, 1985, pp. 250–67.

Black, Dan A. and Parker, Darrell F. The Division of Union Rents. *J. Lab. Res.*, Summer 1985, *6*(3), pp. 281–88.

Black, J. M. and Bulkley, George. Wage-Employments Contracts When There Is a Constraint on the Firm's Profit Level in Each State. *Scot. J. Polit. Econ.*, November 1985, *32*(3), pp. 328–32.

Blank, Rebecca M. The Impact of State Economic Differentials on Household Welfare and Labor Force Behavior. *J. Public Econ.*, October 1985, *28*(1), pp. 25–58.   [G: U.S.]

Blau, David M. Self-Employment and Self-Selection in Developing Country Labor Markets. *Southern Econ. J.*, October 1985, *52*(2), pp. 351–63.   [G: Malaysia]

Blomquist, N. Sören. Labour Supply in a Two-Period Model: The Effect of a Nonlinear Progressive Income Tax. *Rev. Econ. Stud.*, July 1985, *52*(3), pp. 515–24.

Blomquist, N. Sören. The Wage Rate Tax—An Alternative to the Income Tax? In *Førsund, F. R. and Honkapohja, S., eds.*, 1985, pp. 171–87.

Bodo, Giorgio and Giannini, Curzio. Average Working Time and the Influence of Contractual Hours: An Empirical Investigation for the Italian Industry (1970–1981). *Oxford Bull. Econ. Statist.*, May 1985, *47*(2), pp. 131–51.   [G: Italy]

Bolle, Friedel. Natural and Optimal Unemployment. *Z. ges. Staatswiss. (JITE)*, June 1985, *141*(2), pp. 256–68.

Bornstein, Morris. Unemployment in Capitalist Regulated Market Economies and in Socialist Centrally Planned Economies. In *Bornstein, M., ed.*, 1985, pp. 337–44.

Bowles, Samuel. The Production Process in a Competitive Economy: Walrasian, Neo-Hobbesian, and Marxian Models. *Amer. Econ. Rev.*, March 1985, *75*(1), pp. 16–36.

Broady, Donald. Work and Education. In *Gus-*

tavsson, B.; Karlsson, J. C. and Raftegard, C., 1985, pp. 151–57.

Brown, Clair. An Institutional Model of Wives' Work Decisions. *Ind. Relat.*, Spring 1985, *24*(2), pp. 182–204. [G: U.S.]

Brown, Murray and Wolfstetter, Elmar. A Micro Theory of Layoffs and Involuntary Unemployment. *Metroecon.*, February 1985, *37*(1), pp. 1–19.

Brown, Murray and Wolfstetter, Elmar. Under- and Overemployment in Optimal Layoff Contracts. *Z. Nationalökon.*, 1985, *45*(2), pp. 101–14.

Browning, Edgar K. A Critical Appraisal of Hausman's Welfare Cost Estimates. *J. Polit. Econ.*, October 1985, *93*(5), pp. 1025–34. [G: U.S.]

Browning, Edgar K. The Marginal Social Security Tax on Labor. *Public Finance Quart.*, July 1985, *13*(3), pp. 227–51. [G: U.S.]

Browning, Martin J.; Deaton, Angus and Irish, Margaret. A Profitable Approach to Labor Supply and Commodity Demands over the Life-Cycle. *Econometrica*, May 1985, *53*(3), pp. 503–43. [G: U.K.]

Buiter, Willem H. The Real Wage Gap and Employment: Comments. In *Melitz, J. and Wyplosz, C., eds.*, 1985, pp. 71–80. [G: France; U.S.; EEC]

Bull, Clive. Eqilibrium Unemployment as a Worker Discipline Device: Comment. *Amer. Econ. Rev.*, September 1985, *75*(4), pp. 890–91.

Bulow, Jeremy I. and Landsman, Wayne. The Relationship between Wages and Benefits. In *Wise, D. A., ed.*, 1985, pp. 379–94. [G: U.S.]

Burdett, Kenneth; Kiefer, Nicholas M. and Sharma, Sunil. Layoffs and Duration Dependence in a Model of Turnover. *J. Econometrics*, April 1985, *28*(1), pp. 51–69. [G: U.S.]

Burdett, Kenneth and Ondrich, Jan I. How Changes in Labor Demand Affect Unemployed Workers. *J. Lab. Econ.*, Part 1 January 1985, *3*(1), pp. 1–10.

Burns, Michael E. and Mitchell, William F. Real Wages, Unemployment and Economic Policy in Australia. *Australian Econ. Pap.*, June 1985, *24*(44), pp. 1–23. [G: Australia]

Burtless, Gary and Moffitt, Robert. The Joint Choice of Retirement Age and Postretirement Hours of Work. *J. Lab. Econ.*, April 1985, *3*(2), pp. 209–36. [G: U.S.]

Calmfors, Lars. Trade Unions, Wage Formation and Macroeconomic Stability—An Introduction. *Scand. J. Econ.*, 1985, *87*(2), pp. 143–59. [G: W. Europe; U.S.]

Calmfors, Lars. Work Sharing, Employment and Wages. *Europ. Econ. Rev.*, April 1985, *27*(3), pp. 293–309.

Calmfors, Lars and Horn, Henrik. Classical Unemployment, Accommodation Policies and Adjustment of Real Wages. *Scand. J. Econ.*, 1985, *87*(2), pp. 234–61.

Calvo, Guillermo A. The Inefficiency of Unemployment: The Supervision Perspective.

Quart. J. Econ., May 1985, *100*(2), pp. 373–87.

Cameron, Samuel. Family Labour Supply Models: An Expository Account of a Simple Case. *Rivista Int. Sci. Econ. Com.*, July-Aug. 1985, *32*(7–8), pp. 625–33.

Cameron, Samuel. Inter-industry Variations in the Wage-Rates of Adult Male Manual Workers. *Scot. J. Polit. Econ.*, November 1985, *32*(3), pp. 296–314.

Campbell, Tim S. and Kracaw, William A. The Market for Managerial Labor Services and Capital Market Equilibrium. *J. Finan. Quant. Anal.*, September 1985, *20*(3), pp. 277–97.

Canzoneri, Matthew B. and Underwood, John M. Wage Contracting, Exchange Rate Volatility, and Exchange Intervention Policy. In *Bhandari, J. S., ed.*, 1985, pp. 247–71.

Capen, Margaret M.; Cohn, Elchanan and Ellson, Richard Wayne. Labour Supply Effects of Unemployment Insurance Benefits. *Appl. Econ.*, February 1985, *17*(1), pp. 73–85. [G: U.S.]

Cappelli, Peter. Theory Construction in IR and Some Implications for Research. *Ind. Relat.*, Winter 1985, *24*(1), pp. 90–112. [G: U.S.; U.K.]

Carlberg, Michael. Makroökonomische Effekte einer Arbeitszeitverkürzung. (With English summary.) *Z. Wirtschaft. Sozialwissen.*, 1985, *105*(1), pp. 17–32.

Carline, Derek. Trade Unions and Wages. In *Carline, D., et al.*, 1985, pp. 186–232. [G: U.K.; U.S.]

Carmichael, H. Lorne. Can Unemployment Be Involuntary? Comment [Equilibrium Unemployment as a Worker Discipline Device]. *Amer. Econ. Rev.*, December 1985, *75*(5), pp. 1213–14.

Carmichael, H. Lorne. Wage Profiles, Layoffs, and Specific Training: Comment. *Int. Econ. Rev.*, October 1985, *26*(3), pp. 747–51.

Carmichael, Jeffrey; Fahrer, Jerome and Hawkins, John. Some Macroeconomic Implications of Wage Indexation: A Survey. In *Argy, V. E. and Neville, J. W., eds.*, 1985, pp. 78–102.

Carnoy, Martin. Education and the Changing American Workplace. In *Gustavsson, B.; Karlsson, J. C. and Raftegard, C.*, 1985, pp. 159–70. [G: U.S.]

Chamberlain, Gary. Heterogeneity, Omitted Variable Bias, and Duration Dependence. In *Heckman, J. J. and Singer, B., eds.*, 1985, pp. 3–38.

Chang, Yang-Ming and Ehrlich, Isaac. On the Economics of Compliance with the Minimum Wage Law. *J. Polit. Econ.*, February 1985, *93*(1), pp. 84–91.

Cherry, Robert. Textbook Treatments of Minimum-Wage Legislation. *Rev. Black Polit. Econ.*, Spring 1985, *13*(4), pp. 25–38.

Choudhri, Ehsan U. and Ferris, J. Stephen. Wage and Price Contracts in a Macro Model with Information Costs. *Can. J. Econ.*, November 1985, *18*(4), pp. 766–83.

Christiansen, Vidar. The Choice of Excise Taxes

When Savings and Labour Decisions Are Distorted. *J. Public Econ.*, October 1985, *28*(1), pp. 95–110.

Cole, William E. and Sanders, Richard D. Internal Migration and Urban Employment in the Third World. *Amer. Econ. Rev.*, June 1985, *75*(3), pp. 481–94. **[G: Mexico; India; Colombia; Nigeria]**

Coles, Jeffrey Link and Harte-Chen, Paul. Real Wage Indices. *J. Lab. Econ.*, July 1985, *3*(3), pp. 317–36. **[G: U.S.]**

Colombino, Ugo. A Model of Married Women's Labour Supply with Systematic and Random Disequilibrium Components. *Ricerche Econ.*, Apr.-June 1985, *39*(2), pp. 165–79. **[G: Italy]**

Congdon, Peter. Heterogeneity and Timing Effects in Occupational Mobility: A General Model. *Oxford Bull. Econ. Statist.*, November 1985, *47*(4), pp. 347–69. **[G: Ireland]**

Cooke, William N. Toward a General Theory of Industrial Relations. In *Lipsky, D. B., ed.*, 1985, pp. 223–52.

Cooper, Russell. Worker Asymmetric Information and Employment Distortions. *J. Lab. Econ.*, April 1985, *3*(2), pp. 188–208.

Corden, W. Max and Findlay, Ronald F. Urban Unemployment, Intersectoral Capital Mobility and Development Policy. In *Corden, W. M.*, 1985, pp. 73–93.

Cornell, Lasse; Karlsson, Jan Ch. and Lindqvist, Ulla. Missing Concepts of Work. In *Gustavsson, B.; Karlsson, J. C. and Raftegard, C.*, 1985, pp. 15–25.

Cowell, Frank A. Tax Evasion with Labour Income. *J. Public Econ.*, February 1985, *26*(1), pp. 19–34.

Craig, Christine, et al. Economic, Social and Political Factors in the Operation of the Labour Market. In *Roberts, B.; Finnegan, R. and Gallie, D., eds.*, 1985, pp. 105–23.

Currie, David. Overlapping Wage Contracts and Exchange Rate Overshooting. *Greek Econ. Rev.*, April 1985, *7*(1), pp. 71–81.

Curry, Leslie. Inefficiencies in the Geographical Operation of Labour Markets. *Reg. Stud.*, June 1985, *19*(3), pp. 203–15.

Cymrot, Donald J. Earnings Growth and Pension Coverage: Comment. *Southern Econ. J.*, April 1985, *51*(4), pp. 1245–48. **[G: U.S.]**

Dagsvik, John; Jovanovic, Boyan and Shepard, Andrea. A Foundation for Three Popular Assumptions in Job-matching Models. *J. Lab. Econ.*, October 1985, *3*(4), pp. 403–20. **[G: U.S.]**

Dahlkvist, Mats. Work and Culture. In *Gustavsson, B.; Karlsson, J. C. and Raftegard, C.*, 1985, pp. 105–09.

Darby, Michael R.; Haltiwanger, John C. and Plant, Mark W. Unemployment Rate Dynamics and Persistent Unemployment under Rational Expectations. *Amer. Econ. Rev.*, September 1985, *75*(4), pp. 614–37. **[G: U.S.]**

Darity, William A., Jr. On Involuntary Unemployment and Increasing Returns. *J. Post Keynesian Econ.*, Spring 1985, *7*(3), pp. 363–72.

Davidson, Paul. Liquidity and Not Increasing Returns Is the Ultimate Source of Unemployment Equilibrium. *J. Post Keynesian Econ.*, Spring 1985, *7*(3), pp. 373–84.

Dawkins, Peter and Wooden, Mark. Labour Utilization and Wage Inflation in Australia: An Empirical Examination. *Econ. Rec.*, June 1985, *61*(173), pp. 516–21. **[G: Australia]**

De Bruyne, Guido. Union Militancy, External Shocks and the Accommodation Dilemma: Comment. *Scand. J. Econ.*, 1985, *87*(2), pp. 352–54.

De Gijsel, Peter. A Microeconomic Analysis of Black Labour Demand and Supply. In *Gaertner, W. and Wenig, A., eds.*, 1985, pp. 218–26.

De Stavola, Bianca and Poli, Irene. Un'analisi longitudinale dell'offerta di lavoro giovanile. (A Longitudinal Study of Youth Labour Market. With English summary.) *Statistica*, July-Sept. 1985, *45*(3), pp. 403–19. **[G: Italy]**

De Vroey, Michel. La théorie du salaire de Marx: une critique hétérodoxe. (Marx's Theory of Wages: An Heterodox Criticism. With English summary.) *Revue Écon.*, May 1985, *36*(3), pp. 451–80.

Dehez, Pierre. Monopolistic Equilibrium and Involuntary Unemployment. *J. Econ. Theory*, June 1985, *36*(1), pp. 160–65.

Diamond, Peter A. and Mirrlees, James A. Insurance Aspects of Pensions. In *Wise, D. A., ed.*, 1985, pp. 317–43.

Dickens, William T. and Lang, Kevin. A Test of Dual Labor Market Theory. *Amer. Econ. Rev.*, September 1985, *75*(4), pp. 792–805. **[G: U.S.]**

Djajić, Slobodan. Human Capital, Minimum Wage and Unemployment: A Harris–Todaro Model of a Developed Open Economy. *Economica*, November 1985, *52*(208), pp. 491–508.

Dogas, D. Market Power in a Bilateral Monopoly Model of Industry Wage Determination. *Appl. Econ.*, February 1985, *17*(1), pp. 149–64. **[G: U.K.]**

Domínguez Martínez, José M. and Sánchez Maldonado, José. La política de dirección de la demanda y la inestabilidad de la curva de Phillips: Una visión de conjunto. (With English summary.) *Revista Española Econ.*, 1985, *2*(2), pp. 203–67.

Dorsey, Stuart. Earnings Growth and Pension Coverage: Reply. *Southern Econ. J.*, April 1985, *51*(4), pp. 1249–51. **[G: U.S.]**

Dowell, Richard. Risk Preference and the Work–Leisure Trade-off. *Econ. Inquiry*, October 1985, *23*(4), pp. 691–701.

Drazen, Allan. Cyclical Determinants of the Natural Level of Economic Activity. *Int. Econ. Rev.*, June 1985, *26*(2), pp. 387–97.

Driffill, John. Macroeconomic Stabilization Policy and Trade Union Behaviour as a Repeated Game. *Scand. J. Econ.*, 1985, *87*(2), pp. 300–326.

Drugge, Sten E. Factor Mobility, the Elasticity of Substitution and Interregional Wage Differentials. *Ann. Reg. Sci.*, November 1985, *19*(3), pp. 34–39.

Dunlevy, James A. Factor Endowments, Heterogeneous Labor and North–South Migration. *Southern Econ. J.*, October 1985, *52*(2), pp. 446–59.   [G: U.S.]

Dye, Ronald A. Optimal Length of Labor Contracts. *Int. Econ. Rev.*, February 1985, *26*(1), pp. 251–70.

Easley, David; Kiefer, Nicholas M. and Possen, Uri. An Equilibrium Analysis of Optimal Unemployment Insurance and Taxation. *Quart. J. Econ.*, Supp. 1985, *100*, pp. 989–1010.

Eden, Benjamin. Indexation and Related Issues: A Review Essay. *J. Monet. Econ.*, September 1985, *16*(2), pp. 259–66.

Eden, Benjamin. Trading Uncertainty, Enforcement and Labor Unions. *Econ. Inquiry*, October 1985, *23*(4), pp. 637–50.

Edgecombe Robb, Roberta. Equal-Pay Policy. In *Economic Council of Canada.*, 1985, pp. 61–70.   [G: Canada]

Eichner, Alfred S. An Anthropogenic Approach to Labor Economics. In *Eichner, A. S.*, 1985, pp. 75–97.

Eichner, Alfred S. Stagflation: Explaining the Inexplicable. In *Eichner, A. S.*, 1985, pp. 113–50.   [G: U.S.]

Ellis, Christopher J. and Fender, John. Wage Bargaining in a Macroeconomic Model with Rationing. *Quart. J. Econ.*, August 1985, *100*(3), pp. 625–50.

England, Paula and Norris, Bahar. Comparable Worth: A New Doctrine of Sex Discrimination. *Soc. Sci. Quart.*, September 1985, *66*(3), pp. 629–43.   [G: U.S.]

England, Paula and Norris, Bahar. Comparable Worth: Rejoinder. *Soc. Sci. Quart.*, September 1985, *66*(3), pp. 650–53.   [G: U.S.]

Estrin, Saul and Svejnar, Jan. Explanations of Earnings in Yugoslavia: The Capital and Labour Schools Compared. *Econ. Anal. Worker's Manage.*, 1985, *19*(1), pp. 1–12.
                                    [G: Yugoslavia]

Eswaran, Mukesh and Kotwal, Ashok. A Theory of Two-Tier Labor Markets in Agrarian Economies. *Amer. Econ. Rev.*, March 1985, *75*(1), pp. 162–77.

Ethier, Wilfred J. International Trade and Labor Migration. *Amer. Econ. Rev.*, September 1985, *75*(4), pp. 691–707.

Eyerman, Ron. Work—A Contested Concept. In *Gustavsson, B.; Karlsson, J. C. and Raftegard, C.*, 1985, pp. 27–31.

Fandel, Günter. On the Applicability of Game-Theoretic Bargaining Methods to a Wage Bargaining Problem. In *Fandel, G. and Spronk, J.*, eds., 1985, pp. 317–36.
                                    [G: W. Germany]

Farmer, Roger E. A. Implicit Contracts with Asymmetric Information and Bankruptcy: The Effect of Interest Rates on Layoffs. *Rev. Econ. Stud.*, July 1985, *52*(3), pp. 427–42.
                                    [G: U.S.]

Feenberg, Daniel. The Relationship between Wages and Benefits: Comment. In *Wise,*

D. A., ed., 1985, pp. 394–97.   [G: U.S.]

Fender, John. Counterinflationary Policy in a Unionised Economy with Nonsynchronised Wage Setting: Comment. *Scand. J. Econ.*, 1985, *87*(2), pp. 379–81.

Ferri, Piero. Wage Dynamics and Instability Processes. *Econ. Notes*, 1985, (3), pp. 35–48.

Fischer, Stanley. Macroeconomic Stabilization Policy and Trade Union Behaviour as a Repeated Game: Comment. *Scand. J. Econ.*, 1985, *87*(2), pp. 327–31.

FitzRoy, Felix R. and Hart, Robert A. Hours, Layoffs and Unemployment Insurance Funding: Theory and Practice in an International Perspective. *Econ. J.*, September 1985, *95*(379), pp. 700–713.

Fon, Vincy; Boulier, Bryan L. and Goldfarb, Robert S. The Firm's Demand for Daily Hours of Work: Some Implications. *Atlantic Econ. J.*, March 1985, *13*(1), pp. 36–42.

Frank, Jeff. Search and Contracting—Efficiency and Inefficiency. *Oxford Econ. Pap.*, March 1985, *37*(1), pp. 72–82.

Frank, Jeff. Trade Union Efficiency and Overemployment with Seniority Wage Scales. *Econ. J.*, December 1985, *95*(380), pp. 1021–34.

Fuhrmann, Wilfried. Tatsächliche und erwartete Nominallohnsatzänderungen in einem einfachen keynesianischen Modell. (Actual and Expected Changes of the Nominal Wage Rate in a Simple Keynesian Model. With English summary.) *Jahr. Nationalökon. Statist.*, March 1985, *200*(2), pp. 137–52.

Funaba, Takuji. The Labor Supply of Married Women. (In Japanese. With English summary.) *Osaka Econ. Pap.*, March 1985, *34*(4), pp. 16–22.   [G: Japan]

Gang, Ira N. and Gangapadhyay, Shubhashis. A Note on Optimal Policies in Dual Economies. *Quart. J. Econ.*, Supp. 1985, *100*, pp. 1067–71.

Garen, John E. Worker Heterogeneity, Job Screening, and Firm Size. *J. Polit. Econ.*, August 1985, *93*(4), pp. 715–39.   [G: U.S.]

Gärtner, Manfred. Strikes and the Real Wage-Employment Nexus: A Hicksian Analysis of Industrial Disputes and Pay. *J. Lab. Res.*, Summer 1985, *6*(3), pp. 323–36.
                                    [G: W. Germany]

German, Israel. Disequilibrium Dynamics and the Stability of Quasi Equilibria. *Quart. J. Econ.*, August 1985, *100*(3), pp. 571–96.

Ginsburgh, Victor, et al. Macroeconomic Policy in the Presence of an Irregular Sector. In *Gaertner, W. and Wenig, A.*, eds., 1985, pp. 194–217.

Golbe, Devra L. Imperfect Signalling, Affirmative Action, and Black–White Wage Differentials. *Southern Econ. J.*, January 1985, *51*(3), pp. 842–48.

Gordon, Roger H. Incentive Effects of Pensions: Comment. In *Wise, D. A., ed.*, 1985, pp. 278–82.

Gottschalk, Peter and Maloney, Tim. Involuntary Terminations, Unemployment, and Job Matching: A Test of Job Search Theory. *J. Lab. Econ.*,

April 1985, *3*(2), pp. 109–23.   [G: U.S.]

Graham, Andrew W. M. Inflation and Unemployment. In *Morris, D., ed.*, 1985, pp. 217–48.
[G: U.K.]

Graves, Philip E. and Knapp, Thomas A. Hedonic Analysis in a Spatial Context: Theoretical Problems in Valuing Location-Specific Amenities. *Econ. Rec.*, December 1985, *61*(175), pp. 737–43.

Green, Jerry R. The Riskiness of Private Pensions. In *Wise, D. A., ed.*, 1985, pp. 357–75.

Grellet, Gérard. La monnaie est-elle à l'origine du chômage? (Is Money Generating Unemployment? With English summary.) *Écon. Appl.*, 1985, *38*(1), pp. 301–08.

Gröschel, Ulrich. Risikobewältigung durch Güter- und Arbeitsmarktkontrakte. (Contracts on Labour and Commodity Markets and the Allocation of Risk. With English Summary.) *Konjunkturpolitik*, 1985, *31*(4/5), pp. 300–317.

Grossbard-Shechtman, Amyra. Marriage Squeezes and the Marriage Market. In *Davis, K., ed.*, 1985, pp. 375–95.   [G: U.S.]

Grout, Paul A. A Theoretical Approach to the Effect of Trade Union Immunities on Investment and Employment. *Econ. J.*, Supplement 1985, *95*, pp. 96–101.

Gunning, James Patrick. Causes of Unemployment: The Austrian Perspective. *Hist. Polit. Econ.*, Summer 1985, *17*(2), pp. 223–44.

Gustavsson, BengtOve; Karlsson, Jan Ch. and Räftegård, Curt. Work in the 1980s: Emancipation and Derogation: Introduction. In *Gustavsson, B.; Karlsson, J. C. and Raftegard, C.*, 1985, pp. 1–5.

Gylfason, Thorvaldur. Counterinflationary Policy in a Unionised Economy with Nonsynchronised Wage Setting: Comment. *Scand. J. Econ.*, 1985, *87*(2), pp. 382–85.

Gylfason, Thorvaldur. Workers versus Government—Who Adjusts to Whom? Comment. *Scand. J. Econ.*, 1985, *87*(2), pp. 293–97.
[G: Norway; U.K.]

Hahn, Frank H. Fix-Price Models: A Survey of Recent Empirical Work: Comment. In *Arrow, K. J. and Honkapohja, S., eds.*, 1985, pp. 368–78.

Hall, S. G., et al. Employment and Average Hours Worked in Manufacturing. *Brit. Rev. Econ. Issues*, Spring 1985, *7*(16), pp. 87–112.
[G: U.K.]

Hallwirth, Volker. Reallohn und Beschäftigung—Ein Ansatz zum Test der klassischen Grenzproduktivitätstheorie der Arbeit. (The Marginal Productivity Relationship of Wages and Employment—A Specification of an Empirical Test. With English summary.) *Jahr. Nationalökon. Statist.*, March 1985, *200*(2), pp. 153–72.
[G: W. Germany]

Halperin, Robert and Tzur, Joseph. Monetary Compensation and Nontaxable Employee Benefits: An Analytical Perspective. *Accounting Rev.*, October 1985, *60*(4), pp. 670–80.

Halperin, Robert and Tzur, Joseph. The Effects of Nontaxable Employee Benefits on Employer Profits and Employee Work Effort. *Nat. Tax*

J., March 1985, *38*(1), pp. 65–79.

Hansen, Gary D. Indivisible Labor and the Business Cycle. *J. Monet. Econ.*, November 1985, *16*(3), pp. 309–27.

Hansson, Ingemar. Tax Evasion and Government Policy. In *Gaertner, W. and Wenig, A., eds.*, 1985, pp. 285–300.

Hanushek, Eric A. and Quigley, John M. Life-Cycle Earning Capacity and the OJT Investment Model. *Int. Econ. Rev.*, June 1985, *26*(2), pp. 365–85.   [G: U.S.]

Hartman, David G. The Economics of Incremental Incentive Programs: The Example of Employment Subsidies. *Public Finance Quart.*, October 1985, *13*(4), pp. 375–95.

Harvey, Philip. The Value-creating Capacity of Skilled Labor in Marxian Economics. *Rev. Radical Polit. Econ.*, Spring and Summer 1985, *17*(1/2), pp. 83–102.

Hashimoto, Masanori. Firm-specific Human Capital: Rejoinder [Wage Profiles, Layoffs, and Specific Training]. *Int. Econ. Rev.*, October 1985, *26*(3), pp. 753–54.

Haug, Frigga. Automatization as a Field of Contradictions. In *Gustavsson, B.; Karlsson, J. C. and Raftegard, C.*, 1985, pp. 83–92.

Hausman, Daniel M. Classical Wage Theory and the Causal Complications of Explaining Distribution. In *Pitt, J. C., ed.*, 1985, pp. 171–97.

Hausman, Jerry A. Taxes and Labor Supply. In *Auerbach, A. J. and Feldstein, M., eds.*, 1985, pp. 213–63.   [G: U.S.]

Heckman, James A. and Singer, Burton. Erratum [Econometric Duration Analysis]. *J. Econometrics*, January 1985, *27*(1), pp. 137–38.

Heckman, James J. and Robb, Richard, Jr. Alternative Methods for Evaluating the Impact of Interventions. In *Heckman, J. J. and Singer, B., eds.*, 1985, pp. 156–245.

Heckman, James J. and Sedlacek, Guilherme. Heterogeneity, Aggregation, and Market Wage Functions: An Empirical Model of Self-selection in the Labor Market. *J. Polit. Econ.*, December 1985, *93*(6), pp. 1077–1125.
[G: U.S.]

Heckman, James J. and Singer, Burton. Social Science Duration Analysis. In *Heckman, J. J. and Singer, B., eds.*, 1985, pp. 39–110.
[G: U.S.]

Heijke, Johannes A. M., et al. A Model of the Dutch Labour Market (AMO-K). *De Economist*, 1985, *133*(4), pp. 484–526.
[G: Netherlands]

Henry, S. G. B.; Payne, J. M. and Trinder, C. Real Wages and Unemployment: A Rejoinder [Labour Market Equilibrium in an Open Economy]. *Oxford Econ. Pap.*, June 1985, *37*(2), pp. 344–45.   [G: U.K.]

Henry, S. G. B.; Payne, J. M. and Trinder, C. Unemployment and Real Wages: The Role of Unemployment, Social Security Benefits and Unionisation [Labour Market Equilibrium in an Open Economy] [Unions Real Wages and Employment]. *Oxford Econ. Pap.*, June 1985, *37*(2), pp. 330–38.   [G: U.K.]

Hersch, Joni. Allocation of Time and Human En-

ergy and Its Effects on Productivity. *Appl. Econ.*, October 1985, *17*(5), pp. 867–84.
[G: U.S.]

Hersoug, Tor. Workers versus Government—Who Adjusts to Whom? *Scand. J. Econ.*, 1985, *87*(2), pp. 270–92. [G: Norway]

Hillier, Brian. Unemployment Benefits and Labor Supply: A Note on the Theoretical Foundations. *Weltwirtsch. Arch.*, 1985, *121*(2), pp. 315–20.

Hoem, Jan M. Weighting, Misclassification, and Other Issues in the Analysis of Survey Samples of Life Histories. In *Heckman, J. J. and Singer, B., eds.*, 1985, pp. 249–93.

Hofler, Richard A. and Polachek, Solomon William. A New Approach for Measuring Wage Ignorance in the Labor Market. *J. Econ. Bus.*, August 1985, *37*(3), pp. 267–76. [G: U.S.]

Holmlund, Bertil. Wages and Employment under Trade Unionism: Microeconomic Models and Macroeconomic Applications: Comment. *Scand. J. Econ.*, 1985, *87*(2), pp. 228–33.
[G: Sweden]

Holmlund, Bertil and Lang, Harald. Quit Behavior under Imperfect Information: Searching, Moving, Learning. *Econ. Inquiry*, July 1985, *23*(3), pp. 383–93.

Horn, Gustav and Möller, Joachim. Keynesianische oder Klassische Arbeitslosigkeit in der Bundesrepublik Deutschland? Empirische überprüfung eines Mengenrationierungsmodells mittels Kalman–Verfahren für den Zeitraum 1970–1982. (Keynesian or Classical Unemployment in the Federal Republic of Germany? Empirical Test of a Quantity Rationing Model Applying the Kalman Approach with Data from 1970 to 1982. With English summary.) *Ifo-Studien*, 1985, *31*(3), pp. 203–38.
[G: W. Germany]

Horvat, Branko. The Prospects for Disalienation of Work. In *Gustavsson, B.; Karlsson, J. C. and Raftegard, C.*, 1985, pp. 235–39.

Hosios, Arthur J. Unemployment and Recruitment with Heterogeneous Labor. *J. Lab. Econ.*, April 1985, *3*(2), pp. 175–87.

Hughes, Gordon and McCormick, Barry. An Empirical Analysis of On-the-Job Search and Job Mobility. *Manchester Sch. Econ. Soc. Stud.*, March 1985, *53*(1), pp. 76–95. [G: U.K.]

Humphrey, Thomas M. The Early History of the Phillips Curve. *Fed. Res. Bank Richmond Econ. Rev.*, Sept./Oct. 1985, *71*(5), pp. 17–24.

Humphrey, Thomas M. The Evolution and Policy Implications of Phillips Curve Analysis. *Fed. Res. Bank Richmond Econ. Rev.*, Mar./Apr. 1985, *71*(2), pp. 3–22.

Hunt, Janet C.; Hill, C. R. and Kiker, B. F. The Effect of Taxation on Labour Supply: The Case of Moonlighting. *Appl. Econ.*, October 1985, *17*(5), pp. 897–905. [G: U.S.]

Imam, M. Hasan and Whalley, John. Incidence Analysis of a Sector-specific Minimum Wage in a Two-Sector Harris–Todaro Model. *Quart. J. Econ.*, February 1985, *100*(1), pp. 207–24.
[G: Mexico]

Inman, Robert P. Managing the Service Economy: Prospects and Problems: Introduction and Overview. In *Inman, R. P., ed.*, 1985, pp. 1–24.

Ioannides, Yannis M. and Pissarides, Christopher A. Monopsony and the Lifetime Relation between Wages and Productivity. *J. Lab. Econ.*, Part 1 January 1985, *3*(1), pp. 91–100.

Ippolito, Richard A. Income Tax Policy and Lifetime Labor Supply. *J. Public Econ.*, April 1985, *26*(3), pp. 327–47. [G: U.S.]

Isachsen, Arne Jon; Samuelson, Sven Ove and Strøm, Steinar. The Behavior of Tax Evaders. In *Gaertner, W. and Wenig, A., eds.*, 1985, pp. 227–44. [G: Norway]

Jackman, Richard. Counterinflationary Policy in a Unionised Economy with Nonsynchronised Wage Setting. *Scand. J. Econ.*, 1985, *87*(2), pp. 357–78.

Johnes, Geraint. Error Removal, Loss Reduction and External Effects in the Theory of Strikes. *Australian Econ. Pap.*, December 1985, *24*(45), pp. 310–25.

Johnson, George E. The Economic Theory of Trade Unions—An Introductory Survey: Comment. *Scand. J. Econ.*, 1985, *87*(2), pp. 194–96. [G: U.S.; U.K.]

Johnson, William R. The Social Efficiency of Fixed Wages. *Quart. J. Econ.*, February 1985, *100*(1), pp. 101–18.

Jonung, Lars. Classical Unemployment, Accommodation Policies and Adjustment of Real Wages: Comment. *Scand. J. Econ.*, 1985, *87*(2), pp. 262–66.

Juster, F. Thomas. Measuring the Benefits of Income Maintenance Programs: Comment. In *David, M. and Smeeding, T., eds.*, 1985, pp. 234–38. [G: U.S.]

Kagawa, Akio and Kuga, Kiyoshi. Some Fundamentals of the Implicit Contract Theory. *Econ. Stud. Quart.*, April 1985, *36*(1), pp. 81–86.

Kahn, Charles M. Optimal Severance Pay with Incomplete Information. *J. Polit. Econ.*, June 1985, *93*(3), pp. 435–51.

Kahn, Charles M. and Scheinkman, José A. Optimal Employment Contracts with Bankruptcy Constraints. *J. Econ. Theory*, April 1985, *35*(2), pp. 343–65.

Kannappan, Subbiah. Urban Employment and the Labor Market in Developing Nations. *Econ. Develop. Cult. Change*, July 1985, *33*(4), pp. 699–730. [G: LDCs]

Keeley, Michael C. and Robins, Philip K. Government Programs, Job Search Requirements, and the Duration of Unemployment. *J. Lab. Econ.*, July 1985, *3*(3), pp. 337–62. [G: U.S.]

Kemp, Murray C. and Shimomura, Koji. Do Labour Unions Drive Out Capital? *Econ. J.*, December 1985, *95*(380), pp. 1087–90.

Kiefer, Nicholas M. Specification Diagnostics Based on Laguerre Alteratives for Econometric Models of Duration. *J. Econometrics*, April 1985, *28*(1), pp. 135–54. [G: U.S.]

Kierzkowski, Henryk. Insiders and Outsiders in Wage Determination: Comment. *Scand. J. Econ.*, 1985, *87*(2), pp. 429–31.

Kierzkowski, Henryk. Workers versus Government—Who Adjusts to Whom? Comment. *Scand. J. Econ.*, 1985, *87*(2), pp. 298–99.

Killingsworth, Mark R. Substitution and Output Effects on Labor Demand: Theory and Policy Applications. *J. Human Res.*, Winter 1985, *20*(1), pp. 142–52. **[G: U.S.]**

Killingsworth, Mark R. The Economics of Comparable Worth: Analytical, Empirical, and Policy Questions. In *Hartmann, H. I., ed.*, 1985, pp. 86–115.

Kornai, János. Fix-Price Models: A Survey of Recent Empirical Work: Comment. In *Arrow, K. J. and Honkapohja, S., eds.*, 1985, pp. 379–90.

Koskela, Erkki and Virén, Matti. Consumption Function, Labour Supply Rationing and Borrowing Constraints. *Oxford Econ. Pap.*, September 1985, *37*(3), pp. 500–509.

[G: Finland]

Kregel, J. A. Harrod and Keynes: Increasing Returns, the Theory of Employment and Dynamic Economics. In *Harcourt, G. C., ed.*, 1985, pp. 66–88.

Krugman, Paul R. The Real Wage Gap and Employment. In *Melitz, J. and Wyplosz, C., eds.*, 1985, pp. 51–69. **[G: France; U.S.; EEC]**

Kuhn, Peter. Union Productivity Effects and Economic Efficiency. *J. Lab. Res.*, Summer 1985, *6*(3), pp. 229–48.

Laffond, Gilbert and Lesourne, Jacques. Un exemple d'auto-organisation: la création de capacités professionnelles par le marché du travail. (An Example of Self-organization: The Creation of Professional Abilities by the Labour Market of Professional Abilities by the Labour Market. With English summary.) *Écon. Appl.*, 1985, *38*(3/4), pp. 767–88.

Laffont, Jean-Jacques. Fix-Price Models: A Survey of Recent Empirical Work. In *Arrow, K. J. and Honkapohja, S., eds.*, 1985, pp. 328–67.

Lancaster, Tony. Simultaneous Equations Models in Applied Search Theory. *J. Econometrics*, April 1985, *28*(1), pp. 113–26. **[G: U.K.]**

Lantz, Göran. Work and Power. In *Gustavsson, B.; Karlsson, J. C. and Raftegard, C.*, 1985, pp. 205–15.

Lapp, John S. Mandatory Retirement as a Clause in an Employment Insurance Contract. *Econ. Inquiry*, January 1985, *23*(1), pp. 69–92.

[G: U.S.]

Lawrence, Colin and Lawrence, Robert Z. Manufacturing Wage Dispersion: An End Game Interpretation. *Brookings Pap. Econ. Act.*, 1985, (1), pp. 47–106. **[G: U.S.]**

Layard, Richard. Classical Unemployment, Accommodation Policies and Adjustment of Real Wages: Comment. *Scand. J. Econ.*, 1985, *87*(2), pp. 267–69.

Layard, Richard and Nickell, Stephen. Unemployment, Real Wages, and Aggregate Demand in Europe, Japan and the United States. *Carnegie-Rochester Conf. Ser. Public Policy*, Autumn 1985, *23*, pp. 143–202. **[G: France; U.K.; W. Germany; Japan; U.S.]**

Layard, Richard and Nickell, Stephen. The Causes of British Unemployment. *Nat. Inst. Econ. Rev.*, February 1985, (111), pp. 62–85.

[G: U.K.]

Lazear, Edward P. Incentive Effects of Pensions. In *Wise, D. A., ed.*, 1985, pp. 253–78.

Le Pen, Claude. Emplois publics et distribution des revenus. (Public Employment and Distribution of Income. With English summary.) *Revue Écon.*, July 1985, *36*(4), pp. 715–39.

[G: France]

Léonard, Daniel. Monopoly Unionism: Note. *Amer. Econ. Rev.*, March 1985, *75*(1), pp. 246–49.

Leontief, Wassily. The Pure Theory of the Guaranteed Annual Wage Contract. In *Leontief, W.*, 1985, pp. 108–15.

Leslie, Derek. The Economics of Cash Limits as a Method of Pay Determination. *Econ. J.*, September 1985, *95*(379), pp. 662–78.

Lesourne, Jacques. Le marché et l'auto-organisation. (Market and Self-Organization. With English summary.) *Écon. Appl.*, 1985, *38*(3/4), pp. 663–701.

Lesueur, J.-Y. Théorie des contrats implicites et théorie du chômage. (With English summary.) *Revue Écon. Polit.*, July-August 1985, *95*(4), pp. 414–41.

Levačić, Rosalind. Supply Side Economics. In *Atkinson, G. B. J., ed.*, 1985, pp. 133–53.

[G: U.K.]

Liedman, Sven-Erik. The Concept of Work. In *Gustavsson, B.; Karlsson, J. C. and Raftegard, C.*, 1985, pp. 9–13.

Lindbeck, Assar and Snower, Dennis J. Explanations of Unemployment. *Oxford Rev. Econ. Policy*, Summer 1985, *1*(2), pp. 34–59.

Lubrano, Michel. Some Aspects of Prior Elicitation Problems in Disequilibrium Models. *J. Econometrics*, July/August 1985, *29*(1/2), pp. 165–72. **[G: U.S.]**

Lundberg, Shelly J. The Added Worker Effect. *J. Lab. Econ.*, Part 1 January 1985, *3*(1), pp. 11–37. **[G: U.S.]**

Lundberg, Shelly J. Tied Wage–Hours Offers and the Endogeneity of Wages. *Rev. Econ. Statist.*, August 1985, *67*(3), pp. 405–10. **[G: U.S.]**

MacDonald, Glenn M. and Markusen, James R. A Rehabilitation of Absolute Advantage. *J. Polit. Econ.*, April 1985, *93*(2), pp. 277–97.

Macpherson, C. B. Notes on Work and Power. In *Gustavsson, B.; Karlsson, J. C. and Raftegard, C.*, 1985, pp. 241–44.

MaCurdy, Thomas E. Interpreting Empirical Models of Labor Supply in an Intertemporal Framework with Uncertainty. In *Heckman, J. J. and Singer, B., eds.*, 1985, pp. 111–55.

[G: U.S.]

Maier, Gunther. Cumulative Causation and Selectivity in Labour Market Oriented Migration Caused by Imperfect Information. *Reg. Stud.*, June 1985, *19*(3), pp. 231–41.

Malcomson, James M. Incomplete Contracts and Involuntary Unemployment. *Oxford Econ. Pap.*, June 1985, *37*(2), pp. 196–209.

Malinvaud, Edmond. The Real Wage Gap and

Employment: Comments. In *Melitz, J. and Wyplosz, C., eds.*, 1985, pp. 81–83.
[G: France; U.S.; EEC]

Marion, Gérald. La détermination des salaires et le chômage naturel dans la perspective de prospection du marché du travail. (Wages and Natural Rate of Unemployment in a Job Search Perspective. With English summary.) *L'Actual. Econ.*, September 1985, *61*(3), pp. 330–49. [G: Canada]

Marston, Richard C. and Turnovsky, Stephen J. Imported Materials Prices, Wage Policy, and Macro-economic Stabilization. *Can. J. Econ.*, May 1985, *18*(2), pp. 273–84.

Marston, Richard C. and Turnovsky, Stephen J. Macroeconomic Stabilization through Taxation and Indexation: The Use of Firm-Specific Information. *J. Monet. Econ.*, November 1985, *16*(3), pp. 375–95.

Marston, Stephen T. Two Views of the Geographic Distribution of Unemployment. *Quart. J. Econ.*, February 1985, *100*(1), pp. 57–79. [G: U.S.]

Marty, Alvin L. Karni on Optimal Wage Indexation: A Correction. *J. Polit. Econ.*, August 1985, *93*(4), pp. 824–25.

Mayhew, Ken. Employee Behaviour. In *Morris, D., ed.*, 1985, pp. 86–111. [G: U.K.]

McCallum, John. Wage Gaps, Factor Shares and Real Wages. *Scand. J. Econ.*, 1985, *87*(2), pp. 436–59. [G: U.S.; W. Europe; Japan; Canada]

McDonald, Ian M. and Solow, Robert M. Wages and Employment in a Segmented Labor Market. *Quart. J. Econ.*, November 1985, *100*(4), pp. 1115–41.

McElroy, Marjorie B. The Joint Determination of Household Membership and Market Work: The Case of Young Men. *J. Lab. Econ.*, July 1985, *3*(3), pp. 293–316.

Merton, Robert C. Insurance Aspects of Pensions: Comment. In *Wise, D. A., ed.*, 1985, pp. 343–56.

Meyer, Margaret A. Asymmetric Information and Labor Contracts: A Survey. *Revista Española Econ.*, 1985, *2*(2), pp. 347–64.

de Meza, David and Perlman, Morris. Increasing Returns and the Foundation of Unemployment Theory. *J. Post Keynesian Econ.*, Spring 1985, *7*(3), pp. 385–94.

Minford, Patrick. Unemployment and Real Wages: The Role of Unemployment, Social Security Benefits and Unionisation [Labour Market Equilibrium in an Open Economy]: Reply. *Oxford Econ. Pap.*, June 1985, *37*(2), pp. 339–43. [G: U.K.]

Mishel, Lawrence. Unions, Monopolies, and the Marshallian Rules: An Institutionalist Appraisal. In *Lipsky, D. B., ed.*, 1985, pp. 69–109. [G: U.S.]

Miyazaki, Hajime and Neary, Hugh M. Output, Work Hours and Employment in the Short Run of a Labour-managed Firm. *Econ. J.*, December 1985, *95*(380), pp. 1035–48.

Montgomery, Edward and Shaw, Kathryn. Long-term Contracts, Expectations and Wage Iner-

tia. *J. Monet. Econ.*, September 1985, *16*(2), pp. 209–26.

Montgomery, Mark and Wilson, Charles A. On the Dynamic Response of a Firm to an Employment Subsidy with a Fixed Threshold. *J. Econ. Dynam. Control*, December 1985, *9*(4), pp. 405–22.

Moore, John. Optimal Labour Contracts When Workers Have a Variety of Privately Observed Reservation Wages. *Rev. Econ. Stud.*, January 1985, *52*(1), pp. 37–67.

Moreh, J. Human Capital and Learning by Doing. *Metroecon.*, October 1985, *37*(3), pp. 307–29. [G: U.S.]

Morgan, Peter B. Distributions of the Duration and Value of Job Search with Learning. *Econometrica*, September 1985, *53*(5), pp. 1199–1232.

Mori, Pier Angelo. Licenziamenti temporanei e forza-lavoro permanente. (Temporary Lay-offs and Permanent Work-force. With English summary.) *Ricerche Econ.*, Jan.-Mar. 1985, *39*(1), pp. 104–20.

Moss, Richard Loring and Curtis, Thomas D. The Economics of Flextime. *J. Behav. Econ.*, Summer 1985, *14*(2), pp. 95–114. [G: U.S.]

Mueser, Peter. A Note on Simultaneous Equations Models of Migration and Employment Growth. *Southern Econ. J.*, October 1985, *52*(2), pp. 516–22.

Mumy, Gene E. The Role of Taxes and Social Security in Determining the Structure of Wages and Pensions. *J. Polit. Econ.*, June 1985, *93*(3), pp. 574–85. [G: U.S.]

Musgrove, Philip. Why Everything Takes 2. . . . Times as Long as Expected. *Amer. Econ. Rev.*, March 1985, *75*(1), pp. 250–52.

Nakamura, Alice and Nakamura, Masao. Dynamic Models of the Labor Force Behavior of Married Women Which Can Be Estimated Using Limited Amounts of Past Information. *J. Econometrics*, March 1985, *27*(3), pp. 273–98. [G: U.S.]

Nalebuff, Barry and Zeckhauser, Richard J. Pensions and the Retirement Decision. In *Wise, D. A., ed.*, 1985, pp. 283–316. [G: U.S.]

Naqib, Fadle M. Some Redistributive Aspects of Social Security and Their Impact on the Supply of Labor. *Public Finance*, 1985, *40*(2), pp. 230–46.

Narendranathan, Wiji and Nickell, Stephen. Modelling the Process of Job Search. *J. Econometrics*, April 1985, *28*(1), pp. 29–49. [G: U.S.]

Nickell, Stephen. The Determinants of Equilibrium Unemployment in Britain: A Reply. *Econ. J.*, March 1985, *95*(377), pp. 196–98.

Nickell, Stephen. Understanding Unemployment. *Empirica*, 1985, *12*(2), pp. 147–61.

Nishijima, Masuyuki. Firm Specific Labor and Wage Structure. (In Japanese. With English summary.) *Econ. Stud. Quart.*, August 1985, *36*(2), pp. 154–68.

Offe, Claus. The Growth of the Service Sector. In *Offe, C.*, 1985, pp. 101–28.

Offe, Claus. Three Perspectives on the Problem

of Unemployment. In *Offe, C.*, 1985, pp. 80–100.

Offe, Claus. Work: The Key Sociological Category? In *Offe, C.*, 1985, pp. 129–50.

Offe, Claus and Berger, Johannes. The Future of the Labour Market. In *Offe, C.*, 1985, pp. 52–79.

Offe, Claus and Hinrichs, Karl. The Political Economy of the Labour Market. In *Offe, C.*, 1985, pp. 10–51.

Oi, Walter Y. Unemployment, Real Wages, and Aggregate Demand in Europe, Japan and the United States: Comments on the Layard–Nickell Model of Unemployment and Real Wages. *Carnegie-Rochester Conf. Ser. Public Policy*, Autumn 1985, *23*, pp. 203–09.   [G: France; U.K.; W. Germany; Japan; U.S.]

Oswald, Andrew J. The Economic Theory of Trade Unions: An Introductory Survey. *Scand. J. Econ.*, 1985, *87*(2), pp. 160–93.   [G: U.S.; U.K.]

Oswald, Andrew J. Wages and Employment under Trade Unionism: Microeconomic Models and Macroeconomic Applications: Comment. *Scand. J. Econ.*, 1985, *87*(2), pp. 226–27.   [G: Sweden]

Pang, Eng Fong. Employment, Skills and Technology. In *Gustavsson, B.; Karlsson, J. C. and Raftegard, C.*, 1985, pp. 93–102.

Pemberton, James. A Model of Wage and Employment Dynamics with Endogenous Preferences. *Oxford Econ. Pap.*, September 1985, *37*(3), pp. 448–65.

Pemberton, James. Unemployment. In *Atkinson, G. B. J.*, ed., 1985, pp. 1–33.   [G: U.K.]

Pencavel, John. Wages and Employment under Trade Unionism: Microeconomic Models and Macroeconomic Applications. *Scand. J. Econ.*, 1985, *87*(2), pp. 197–225.   [G: Sweden]

Perry, Motty and Solon, Gary R. Wage Bargaining, Labor Turnover, and the Business Cycle: A Model with Asymmetric Information. *J. Lab. Econ.*, October 1985, *3*(4), pp. 421–33.

Phaneuf, Louis. Rigidités de prix contractuelles, anticipations rationnelles et cycle économique. (Contractual Price Rigidities, Rational Expectations and the Business Cycle. With English summary.) *L'Actual. Econ.*, June 1985, *61*(2), pp. 252–73.

Phelps, Edmund S. Dynamics of Unemployment, Vacancies and Real Wages with Trade Unions: Comment. *Scand. J. Econ.*, 1985, *87*(2), pp. 408–10.

Phelps, Edmund S. Union Militancy, External Shocks and the Accommodation Dilemma: Comment. *Scand. J. Econ.*, 1985, *87*(2), pp. 355–56.

Pini, Paolo. La natura della disoccupazione nei modelli dei contratti impliciti: alcune considerazioni introduttive di ordine teorico. (The Nature of Unemployment in Implicits Contract Models: Some Introductory Note. With English summary.) *Econ. Lavoro*, Apr.-June 1985, *19*(2), pp. 19–33.

Pissarides, Christopher A. Dynamics of Unemployment, Vacancies and Real Wages with

Trade Unions. *Scand. J. Econ.*, 1985, *87*(2), pp. 386–403.

Pissarides, Christopher A. Job Search and the Functioning of Labour Markets. In *Carline, D., et al.*, 1985, pp. 159–85.

Pissarides, Christopher A. Short-run Equilibrium Dynamics of Unemployment Vacancies, and Real Wages. *Amer. Econ. Rev.*, September 1985, *75*(4), pp. 676–90.

Pissarides, Christopher A. Taxes, Subsidies, and Equilibrium Unemployment. *Rev. Econ. Stud.*, January 1985, *52*(1), pp. 121–33.

Poli, Irene. A Bayesian Non-parametric Estimate for Multivariate Regression. *J. Econometrics*, May 1985, *28*(2), pp. 171–82.   [G: Italy]

Price, Simon. The Determinants of Equilibrium Unemployment in Britain: A Comment. *Econ. J.*, March 1985, *95*(377), pp. 189–95.   [G: U.K.]

Putterman, Louis. On the Interdependence of Labor Supplies in Producers' Cooperatives. In *Jones, D. C. and Svejnar, J.*, eds., 1985, pp. 87–105.

Quester, Aline O. and Utgoff, Kathleen. Comparable Worth: Another View. *Soc. Sci. Quart.*, September 1985, *66*(3), pp. 644–49.   [G: U.S.]

Quinzii, Martine and Rochet, Jean-Charles. Multidimensional Signalling. *J. Math. Econ.*, 1985, *14*(3), pp. 261–84.

Ramb, Bernd-Thomas. Arbeitsangebotseffekte regulierter Beschäftigungszeitverkürzungen. (Labor Supply Effects of Regulated Employment Time Reductions. With English summary.) *Z. Wirtschaft. Sozialwissen.*, 1985, *105*(1), pp. 33–49.

Ranney, Susan I. The Labour Market in a Dual Economy: Another Look at Colonial Rhodesia. *J. Devel. Stud.*, July 1985, *21*(4), pp. 505–24.   [G: Zimbabwe]

Rau, Nicholas. The Microeconomic Theory of the Trade Union: A Comment. *Econ. J.*, June 1985, *95*(378), pp. 480–82.

Renault, Eric and Lesourne, Jacques. Auto-organisation et dispersion géographique des marchés. (Self-Organization and Markets Geographical Distribution. With English summary.) *Écon. Appl.*, 1985, *38*(3/4), pp. 703–38.

Riveros, Luis A. Determinación de salarios y eficiencia del mercado laboral en la década del 70. (With English summary.) *Cuadernos Econ.*, April 1985, *22*(65), pp. 123–43.   [G: Chile]

Rødseth, Asbjørn. Dynamics of Wages and Trade in a Fixed-Exchange-Rate Economy. *Scand. J. Econ.*, 1985, *87*(1), pp. 120–36.

Rose-Lizée, Ruth. Towards Equity: Directions for Future Research: Panel Discussion. In *Economic Council of Canada.*, 1985, pp. 127–31.

Rosen, Sherwin. Implicit Contracts: A Survey. *J. Econ. Lit.*, September 1985, *23*(3), pp. 1144–75.

Rosen, Sherwin. The Structure of Uncertainty and the Use of Nontransferable Pensions as a Mobility-Reduction Device: Comment. In

Wise, D. A., ed., 1985, pp. 248–51.

Roth, Alvin E. Common and Conflicting Interests in Two-sided Matching Markets. *Europ. Econ. Rev.*, February 1985, 27(1), pp. 75–96. [G: U.S.]

Rozen, Marvin E. Labor Markets, Wage Policy, and Macroeconomic Equilibrium: A Review Article of Annable's *The Price of Industrial Labor. J. Econ. Issues*, March 1985, 19(1), pp. 153–74. [G: U.S.]

Sah, Raaj Kumar and Stiglitz, Joseph E. The Social Cost of Labor and Project Evaluation: A General Approach. *J. Public Econ.*, November 1985, 28(2), pp. 135–63.

Saikkonen, Pentti and Teräsvirta, Timo. Modelling the Dynamic Relationship between Wages and Prices in Finland. *Scand. J. Econ.*, 1985, 87(1), pp. 102–19. [G: Finland]

Salituro, Bruno. La teoria dei contratti impliciti, la rigidità salariale e la disoccupazione involontaria: una sintesi dei risultati. (With English summary.) *Econ. Polit.*, April 1985, 2(1), pp. 31–53.

Saloner, Garth. Old Boy Networks as Screening Mechanisms. *J. Lab. Econ.*, July 1985, 3(3), pp. 255–67.

Samuelson, Larry. Implicit Contracts with Heterogeneous Labor. *J. Lab. Econ.*, Part 1 January 1985, 3(1), pp. 70–90.

Sánchez Chóliz, Julio. Eficiencia y control en las innovaciones. (With English summary.) *Revista Española Econ.*, 1985, 2(2), pp. 291–305.

Sawyer, Malcolm C. On the Nature of the Phillips Curve. *Brit. Rev. Econ. Issues*, Spring 1985, 7(16), pp. 63–86.

Scarpat, Orlando. Il conflitto tra efficienza ed equità nei differenziali salariali per qualifica. (The Conflict between Efficiency and Fairness in Occupational Wage Differentials. With English summary.) *Rivista Int. Sci. Econ. Com.*, May 1985, 32(5), pp. 453–65.

Schmidt-Sørensen, Jan Beyer and Søndergaard, Jørgen. Beskæftigelsesvirkninger af en arbejdstidsforkortelse. (Employment Consequences of a Shortening of Working Hours. With English summary.) *Nationaløkon. Tidsskr.*, 1985, 123(2), pp. 160–75.

Schultze, Charles L. Microeconomic Efficiency and Nominal Wage Stickiness. *Amer. Econ. Rev.*, March 1985, 75(1), pp. 1–15.

Schulz, Norbert and Stahl, Konrad. Localisation des oligopoles et marchés du travail locaux. (Oligopolistic Industry Location and Local Labor Markets. With English summary.) *Revue Écon.*, January 1985, 36(1), pp. 103–34.

Schwab, Robert M. Pay-as-You-Go versus Advance-funded Public Pension Systems under Imperfect Capital Markets. *Public Finance Quart.*, July 1985, 13(3), pp. 269–91.

Schwartz, Harvey A. What Do We Know about Statistical Discrimination? In *Brown, R. C., ed.*, 1985, pp. 153–91. [G: U.S.]

Scitovsky, Tibor. Pricetakers' Plenty: A Neglected Benefit of Capitalism. *Kyklos*, 1985, 38(4), pp. 517–36.

Seater, John J. Testing Equilibrium Models of the Business Cycle: The Case of the Labor Market. *Rev. Econ. Statist.*, November 1985, 67(4), pp. 670–75. [G: U.S.]

Seninger, Stephen F. Vacancy Transfers and Job Restructuring in Regional Labor Markets. *Reg. Sci. Urban Econ.*, August 1985, 15(3), pp. 435–48.

Shah, Anup R. Wage/Job Security Contracts and Unionism. *Southern Econ. J.*, January 1985, 51(3), pp. 849–59. [G: U.K.]

Shapiro, Carl and Stiglitz, Joseph E. Can Unemployment Be Involuntary? Reply [Equilibrium Unemployment as a Worker Discipline Device]. *Amer. Econ. Rev.*, December 1985, 75(5), pp. 1215–17.

Shapiro, Carl and Stiglitz, Joseph E. Equilibrium Unemployment as a Worker Discipline Device: Reply. *Amer. Econ. Rev.*, September 1985, 75(4), pp. 892–93.

Shen, T. Y. Worker Motivation and X-Efficiency. *Kyklos*, 1985, 38(3), pp. 392–411.

Siebert, W. Stanley; Bertrand, Philip V. and Addison, John T. The Political Model of Strikes: A New Twist. *Southern Econ. J.*, July 1985, 52(1), pp. 23–33. [G: U.S.]

Silberberg, Eugene. Race, Recent Entry, and Labor Market Participation. *Amer. Econ. Rev.*, December 1985, 75(5), pp. 1168–77. [G: U.S.]

Skott, Peter. Increasing Returns and Involuntary Unemployment: Is There a Connection? *J. Post Keynesian Econ.*, Spring 1985, 7(3), pp. 395–402.

Sloane, Peter J. Discrimination in the Labour Market. In *Carline, D., et al.*, 1985, pp. 78–158. [G: U.K.; U.S.; Selected Countries]

Smith, V. Kerry and Gilbert, Carol C. S. The Valuation of Environmental Risks Using Hedonic Wage Models. In *David, M. and Smeeding, T., eds.*, 1985, pp. 359–85. [G: U.S.]

Smyth, David J. Quasi-fixity of Labour in United States Manufacturing. *Appl. Econ.*, April 1985, 17(2), pp. 377–80. [G: U.S.]

Smyth, David J. The Effects of Unemployment Insurance on the Supply of Labor: Does the Dole Cause Unemployment? In *Terny, G. and Culyer, A. J., eds.*, 1985, pp. 143–55. [G: U.S.]

Snower, Dennis J. Insiders and Outsiders in Wage Determination: Comment. *Scand. J. Econ.*, 1985, 87(2), pp. 432–35.

Söderström, Hans Tson. Union Militancy, External Shocks and the Accommodation Dilemma. *Scand. J. Econ.*, 1985, 87(2), pp. 335–51.

Solow, Robert M. Insiders and Outsiders in Wage Determination. *Scand. J. Econ.*, 1985, 87(2), pp. 411–28.

Solow, Robert M. Manufacturing Wage Dispersion: An End Game Interpretation: Comment. *Brookings Pap. Econ. Act.*, 1985, (1), pp. 107–10. [G: U.S.]

Sondermann, Dieter. Keynesian Unemployment as Non-Walrasian Equilibria. In *Feiwel, G. R., ed. (I)*, 1985, pp. 197–215.

Sproule, Robert A. An Optimal Allocation of Labor Supply and Savings under Interest-Rate

Uncertainty: An Extension. *Bull. Econ. Res.*, May 1985, *37*(2), pp. 115–22.

Sproule, Robert A. Tax Evasion and Labor Supply under Imperfect Information about Individual Parameters of the Tax System. *Public Finance*, 1985, *40*(3), pp. 441–56.

Steedman, Ian. Heterogeneous Labour, Money Wages, and Marx's Theory. *Hist. Polit. Econ.*, Winter 1985, *17*(4), pp. 551–74.

Steinherr, Alfred. Income Distribution and Employment in the European Communities 1960–1982. *Z. Wirtschaft. Sozialwissen.*, 1985, *105*(2/3), pp. 223–69. **[G: EEC; U.S.; Japan]**

Stemp, Peter J. The Effects on the Economy of Changing Unemployment Benefits and Pensions. *Australian Econ. Pap.*, June 1985, *24*(44), pp. 127–41. **[G: Australia]**

Stiassny, Alfred. The Austrian Phillips Curve Reconsidered. *Empirica*, 1985, *12*(1), pp. 43–65. **[G: Austria]**

Stiglitz, Joseph E. Equilibrium Wage Distribution. *Econ. J.*, September 1985, *95*(379), pp. 595–618.

Strand, Jon. Work Effort and Search Subsidies with Long-run Equilibrium Contracts. *Europ. Econ. Rev.*, December 1985, *29*(3), pp. 387–406.

Takeshima, Masao. Optimal Labour Contract under Asymmetric Information. *Keio Econ. Stud.*, 1985, *22*(1), pp. 65–85.

Thorsrud, Einar. Work and Technology. In *Gustavsson, B.; Karlsson, J. C. and Raftegard, C.*, 1985, pp. 57–60.

Tietenberg, T. H. The Valuation of Environmental Risks Using Hedonic Wage Models: Comment. In *David, M. and Smeeding, T., eds.*, 1985, pp. 385–91. **[G: U.S.]**

Tímár, János. Time and Work Time: Certain Problems with the Time Basis of Social Reproduction in Hungary. In *[Levcik, F.]*, 1985, pp. 137–48. **[G: Hungary]**

Tinbergen, Jan. The Allocation of Workers to Jobs. In *Tinbergen, J.*, 1985, pp. 123–30.

Torr, C. S. W. Involuntary Unemployment and Equilibrium. *S. Afr. J. Econ.*, March 1985, *53*(1), pp. 82–84.

Trivedi, Pravin K. and Baker, G. M. Equilibrium Unemployment in Australia: Concepts and Measurement. *Econ. Rec.*, September 1985, *61*(174), pp. 629–43. **[G: Australia]**

Tsang, Mun C. and Levin, Henry M. The Economics of Overeducation. *Econ. Educ. Rev.*, 1985, *4*(2), pp. 93–104.

Tuma, Nancy Brandon. Effects of Labor Market Structure on Job Shift Patterns. In *Heckman, J. J. and Singer, B., eds.*, 1985, pp. 327–63. **[G: U.S.]**

Ueshima, Yasuhiro. Business Fluctuations and Employment Adjustments. (In Japanese. With English summary.) *Econ. Stud. Quart.*, December 1985, *36*(3), pp. 231–46.

Van Wijnbergen, Sweder. Oil Price Shocks, Unemployment, Investment and the Current Account: An Intertemporal Disequilibrium Analysis. *Rev. Econ. Stud.*, October 1985, *52*(4), pp. 627–45.

Vincens, Jean. Réel, nominal, monétaire: Keynes et les salaires relatifs. (Real, Nominal and Monetary: Keynes and Relative Wages. With English summary.) *Écon. Appl.*, 1985, *38*(1), pp. 237–64.

Virén, Matti. Determination of Employment with Wage and Price Speculation. *Scand. J. Econ.*, 1985, *87*(3), pp. 537–53. **[G: Finland]**

Viscusi, W. Kip. The Structure of Uncertainty and the Use of Nontransferable Pensions as a Mobility-Reduction Device. In *Wise, D. A., ed.*, 1985, pp. 223–48.

Vizeu, Maria Clementina. Inflação tradicional num modelo de desequilíbrio. (With English summary.) *Economia (Portugal)*, October 1985, *9*(3), pp. 467–84.

Vroman, S. B. No-Help-Wanted Signs and the Duration of Job Search. *Econ. J.*, September 1985, *95*(379), pp. 767–73.

Wachter, Michael L. Manufacturing Wage Dispersion: An End Game Interpretation: Comment. *Brookings Pap. Econ. Act.*, 1985, (1), pp. 110–15. **[G: U.S.]**

Wadensjö, Eskil. Wage Gaps, Factor Shares and Real Wages: Comment. *Scand. J. Econ.*, 1985, *87*(2), pp. 460–62. **[G: U.S.; W. Europe; Japan]**

Waller, William S. and Chow, Chee W. The Self-selection and Effort Effects Standard-based Employment Contracts: A Framework and Some Empirical Evidence. *Accounting Rev.*, July 1985, *60*(3), pp. 458–76.

Wallman, Sandra. Employment, Live lihood and the Organisation of Resources: What Is Work Really About? In *Gustavsson, B.; Karlsson, J. C. and Raftegard, C.*, 1985, pp. 45–53.

Warr, Peter G. Sub-optimal Saving and the Shadow Price of Labor: The Public Good Argument. *J. Devel. Econ.*, April 1985, *17*(3), pp. 239–57.

Waterson, Michael and Stoneman, Paul L. Employment, Technological Diffusion and Oligopoly. *Int. J. Ind. Organ.*, September 1985, *3*(3), pp. 327–44.

Weiss, Yoram. The Effect of Labor Unions on Investment in Training: A Dynamic Model. *J. Polit. Econ.*, October 1985, *93*(5), pp. 994–1007.

Weitzman, Martin L. Increasing Returns and the Foundations of Unemployment Theory: An Explanation. *J. Post Keynesian Econ.*, Spring 1985, *7*(3), pp. 403–09.

Weitzman, Martin L. The Simple Macroeconomics of Profit Sharing. *Amer. Econ. Rev.*, December 1985, *75*(5), pp. 937–53.

Wessels, Walter J. The Effects of Unions on Employment and Productivity: An Unresolved Contradiction. *J. Lab. Econ.*, Part 1 January 1985, *3*(1), pp. 101–08.

Williams, Donald R. A Comment on the Appropriateness of Fixed Effects Assumptions. *Quart. J. Bus. Econ.*, Winter 1985, *24*(1), pp. 93–100.

Williamson, Jeffrey G. The Historical Content of the Classical Labor Surplus Model. *Popula-*

tion Devel. Rev., June 1985, *11*(2), pp. 171–91. [G: U.K.]

Willner, Johan. Professional Associations and Their Members: A Study of the Market for Professional Services When Ability and Size Are Independent. *Int. J. Ind. Organ.*, June 1985, *3*(2), pp. 179–95.

Wolfe, John R. A Model of Declining Health and Retirement. *J. Polit. Econ.*, December 1985, *93*(6), pp. 1258–67. [G: U.S.]

Wolfstetter, Elmar. Optimale Arbeitsverträge bei asymmetrischer Information: Ein Beitrag zur Theorie der Arbeitslosigkeit. (With English summary.) *Z. Wirtschaft. Sozialwissen.*, 1985, *105*(4), pp. 433–58.

Wren-Lewis, Simon. Private Sector Earnings and Excess Demand from 1966 to 1980. *Oxford Bull. Econ. Statist.*, February 1985, *47*(1), pp. 1–18. [G: U.K.]

Yatchew, Adonis John. Labor Supply in the Presence of Taxes: An Alternative Specification. *Rev. Econ. Statist.*, February 1985, *67*(1), pp. 27–33. [G: U.S.]

Zarkin, Gary A. Occupational Choice: An Application to the Market for Public School Teachers. *Quart. J. Econ.*, May 1985, *100*(2), pp. 409–46. [G: U.S.]

Zietz, Joachim. A Pre-estimation Sample Separation Method for a Labor Market in Disequilibrium. *J. Macroecon.*, Winter 1985, *7*(1), pp. 51–67. [G: U.S.]

822 Public Policy; Role of Government

8220 General

Anthony, Douglas. Managing Workforce Reduction: Japan. In *Cross, M., ed.*, 1985, pp. 91–129. [G: Japan]

Balassa, Bela. Prices, Incentives and Economic Growth. In *Balassa, B.*, 1985, pp. 3–23. [G: Global]

Balassa, Bela. Public Finance and Social Policy—Explanation of Trends and Developments: The Case of Developing Countries. In *Terny, G. and Culyer, A. J., eds.*, 1985, pp. 41–58. [G: LDCs]

Balassa, Bela. The Economic Consequences of Social Policies in the Industrial Countries. In *Balassa, B.*, 1985, pp. 44–59. [G: EEC; U.S.]

Barrett, Jerome T. The FMCS Contribution to Nonlabor Dispute Resolution. *Mon. Lab. Rev.*, August 1985, *108*(8), pp. 31–34. [G: U.S.]

Cain, Glen G. Welfare Economics of Policies toward Women. *J. Lab. Econ.*, Part 2 January 1985, *3*(1), pp. S375–96. [G: U.S.]

Casey, Bernard and Bruche, Gert. Active Labor Market Policy: An International Overview. *Ind. Relat.*, Winter 1985, *24*(1), pp. 37–61. [G: W. Europe; U.S.]

Deery, Stephen; Brooks, Ray and Morris, Alan. Redundancy and Public Policy in Australia. *Australian Bull. Lab.*, June 1985, *11*(3), pp. 154–77. [G: Australia]

Delaney, John Thomas; Lewin, David and Soc-

kell, Donna. The NLRA at Fifty: A Research Appraisal and Agenda. *Ind. Lab. Relat. Rev.*, October 1985, *39*(1), pp. 46–75. [G: U.S.]

Donges, Jürgen B. Chronic Unemployment in Western Europe Forever? *World Econ.*, December 1985, *8*(4), pp. 353–72. [G: W. Europe]

Flanagan, Thomas. Policy-making by Exegesis: The Abolition of 'Mandatory Retirement' in Manitoba. *Can. Public Policy*, March 1985, *11*(1), pp. 40–53. [G: Canada]

Gross, James A. Conflicting Statutory Purposes: Another Look at Fifty Years of NLRB Law Making. *Ind. Lab. Relat. Rev.*, October 1985, *39*(1), pp. 7–18. [G: U.S.]

d'Harmant François, Antonio and Brunetta, Renato. La cassa integrazione guadagni: l'evoluzione economico-normativa, le ipotesi di riforma e la loro efficacia di razionalizzazione. (The Temporary Unemployment Fund in Italy. A Survey of Its Historical and Institutional Evolution. Some Hypotheses of Reform and Their Efficacy. With English summary.) *Econ. Lavoro*, Oct.-Dec. 1985, *19*(4), pp. 35–67. [G: Italy]

Hart, Robert A. Wage Supplements through Collective Agreement or Statutory Requirement? *Kyklos*, 1985, *38*(1), pp. 20–42. [G: OECD]

Kalula, E. The Influence of International Labour Standards on Zambian Legislation. *Int. Lab. Rev.*, Sept.-Oct. 1985, *124*(5), pp. 593–609. [G: Zambia]

Lehrer, Susan. Protective Labor Legislation for Women. *Rev. Radical Polit. Econ.*, Spring and Summer 1985, *17*(1/2), pp. 187–200. [G: U.S.]

Marsden, David. Chronicle: Industrial Relations in the United Kingdom, April–July 1985. *Brit. J. Ind. Relat.*, November 1985, *23*(3), pp. 449–58. [G: U.K.]

Mayer, Jean. The Concept of the Right to Work in International Standards and the Legislation of ILO Member States. *Int. Lab. Rev.*, March-April 1985, *124*(2), pp. 225–42.

Moore, William J. and Newman, Robert J. The Effects of Right-to-Work Laws: A Review of the Literature. *Ind. Lab. Relat. Rev.*, July 1985, *38*(4), pp. 571–85. [G: U.S.]

Morgenstern, Felice. The Importance, in Practice, of Conflicts of Labour Law. *Int. Lab. Rev.*, March-April 1985, *124*(2), pp. 119–31.

Norwood, Janet L. One Hundred Years of the Bureau of Labor Statistics. *Mon. Lab. Rev.*, July 1985, *108*(7), pp. 3–6. [G: U.S.]

Rehn, Gösta. Swedish Active Labor Market Policy: Retrospect and Prospect. *Ind. Relat.*, Winter 1985, *24*(1), pp. 62–89. [G: Sweden]

Rojot, Jacques. The 1984 Revision of the OECD Guidelines for Multinational Enterprises. *Brit. J. Ind. Relat.*, November 1985, *23*(3), pp. 379–97. [G: OECD; LDCs]

Rottenberg, Simon. Job Protection in Urban Mass Transit. *Cato J.*, Spring/Summer 1985, *5*(1), pp. 239–58. [G: U.S.]

Sethuraman, S. V. The Informal Sector in Indonesia: Policies and Prospects. *Int. Lab. Rev.*,

Nov.-Dec. 1985, *124*(6), pp. 719–35.
[G: Indonesia]

Taylor, Vic and Yerbury, Di. Managing Workforce Reduction: Australia. In *Cross, M., ed.*, 1985, pp. 130–63. [G: Australia]

Tomlins, Christopher L. The New Deal, Collective Bargaining, and the Triumph of Industrial Pluralism. *Ind. Lab. Relat. Rev.*, October 1985, *39*(1), pp. 19–34. [G: U.S.]

Wilensky, Harold L. Nothing Fails Like Success: The Evaluation-Research Industry and Labor Market Policy. *Ind. Relat.*, Winter 1985, *24*(1), pp. 1–19. [G: U.S.; Sweden]

8221 Wages and Hours

Chang, Yang-Ming and Ehrlich, Isaac. On the Economics of Compliance with the Minimum Wage Law. *J. Polit. Econ.*, February 1985, *93*(1), pp. 84–91.

Cherry, Robert. Textbook Treatments of Minimum-Wage Legislation. *Rev. Black Polit. Econ.*, Spring 1985, *13*(4), pp. 25–38.

Dabscheck, Braham and Niland, John. Australian Industrial Relations and the Shift to Centralism. In *Juris, H.; Thompson, M. and Daniels, W., eds.*, 1985, pp. 41–72. [G: Australia]

Dawkins, Peter. Penalty Rates and the Review of the Principles. *Australian Bull. Lab.*, June 1985, *11*(3), pp. 178–88. [G: Australia]

Forster, Colin. An Economic Consequence of Mr Justice Higgins. *Australian Econ. Hist. Rev.*, September 1985, *25*(2), pp. 95–111.
[G: Australia]

Forster, Colin. Unemployment and Minimum Wages in Australia, 1900–1930. *J. Econ. Hist.*, June 1985, *45*(2), pp. 383–88. [G: Australia]

Helby, Peter. Er ungdomsløn et egnet middel mod ungdomsarbejdsløshed? (Would a Youth Subminimal Wage Be Effective against Youth Employment? With English summary.) *Nationaløkon. Tidsskr.*, 1985, *123*(2), pp. 194–205. [G: Denmark]

Hojman, David E. The Phillips Curve and Minimum Wage Rates in LDC's: The Brazilian Experience. *J. Econ. Devel.*, December 1985, *10*(2), pp. 161–69. [G: Brazil]

Koziara, Karen Shallcross. Comparable Worth: Organizational Dilemmas. *Mon. Lab. Rev.*, December 1985, *108*(12), pp. 13–16.
[G: U.S.]

McDonald, Nicholas. Regulating Hours of Work in the Road Haulage Industry: The Case for Social Criteria. *Int. Lab. Rev.*, Sept.-Oct. 1985, *124*(5), pp. 577–92. [G: EEC; U.S.]

Nelson, Richard R. State Labor Legislation Enacted in 1984. *Mon. Lab. Rev.*, January 1985, *108*(1), pp. 27–42. [G: U.S.]

Norwood, Janet L. Perspectives on Comparable Worth: An Introduction to the Numbers. *Mon. Lab. Rev.*, December 1985, *108*(12), pp. 3–4.
[G: U.S.]

Rozen, Marvin E. Labor Markets, Wage Policy, and Macroeconomic Equilibrium: A Review Article of Annable's *The Price of Industrial Labor. J. Econ. Issues*, March 1985, *19*(1), pp. 153–74. [G: U.S.]

Rustici, Thomas. A Public Choice View of the Minimum Wage. *Cato J.*, Spring/Summer 1985, *5*(1), pp. 103–31. [G: U.S.; Puerto Rico]

Sauramo, Pekka and Solttila, Heikki. Minimipalkat ja nuorisotyöttömyys Suomessa 1965–1981. (Minimum Wages and Youth Unemployment in Finland 1965–1981. With English summary.) *Kansant. Aikak.*, 1985, *81*(4), pp. 384–94. [G: Finland]

Sellier, Francois. Economic Change and Industrial Relations in France. In *Juris, H.; Thompson, M. and Daniels, W., eds.*, 1985, pp. 177–209. [G: France]

Solon, Gary R. The Minimum Wage and Teenage Employment: A Reanalysis with Attention to Serial Correlation and Seasonality. *J. Human Res.*, Spring 1985, *20*(2), pp. 292–97.
[G: U.S.]

Van Alstyne, William W. The Second Death of Federalism. *Mich. Law Rev.*, June 1985, *83*(7), pp. 1709–33. [G: U.S.]

8222 Workmen's Compensation and Vocational Rehabilitation

Berkowitz, Edward D. and Berkowitz, Monroe. Challenges to Workers' Compensation: An Historical Analysis. In *Worrall, J. D. and Appel, D., eds.*, 1985, pp. 158–79. [G: U.S.]

Butler, Richard J. and Worrall, John D. Work Injury Compensation and the Duration of Nonwork Spells. *Econ. J.*, September 1985, *95*(379), pp. 714–24. [G: U.S.]

Elder, Harold W. An Economic Analysis of Factor Usage and Workplace Regulation. *Southern Econ. J.*, October 1985, *52*(2), pp. 315–31.
[G: U.S.]

Englander, Valerie. Treatment and Comparison Groups, Once Again—And the Birth of a "New" Evaluation Criteria, a Rejoinder. *Amer. Econ.*, Fall 1985, *29*(2), pp. 63–64. [G: U.S.]

Ganguly, Pradeep and Van De Verg, Eric. Application of Categorical Data Analysis to Workers' Compensation Insurance Rates. *Atlantic Econ. J.*, March 1985, *13*(1), pp. 104. [G: U.S.]

Gogol, Daniel. The Much Greater Profitablity of New York Workers' Compensation Risks with Higher Modifications. *J. Risk Ins.*, March 1985, *52*(1), pp. 151–56. [G: U.S.]

Haveman, Robert H. and Wolfe, Barbara L. The Effect of Disability Transfers on Work Effort: Research Results and Their Use in Policy Decisions. In *[Recktenwald, H. C.]*, 1985, pp. 261–78. [G: OECD]

Larson, Lloyd W. and Burton, John F., Jr. Special Funds in Workers' Compensation. In *Worrall, J. D. and Appel, D., eds.*, 1985, pp. 117–57. [G: U.S.]

Leigh, J. Paul. Analysis of Workers' Compensation Using Data on Individuals. *Ind. Relat.*, Spring 1985, *24*(2), pp. 247–56. [G: U.S.]

Miller, Arye L. Compensation for Personal Injury under Social Security. *Int. Lab. Rev.*, March-April 1985, *124*(2), pp. 193–205.
[G: Netherlands; New Zealand]

Nowak, Laura. Comparison Groups, Program Costs, and Evaluation Criteria in B/C Analyses—Final Reply. *Amer. Econ.*, Fall 1985, 29(2), pp. 65–66. [G: U.S.]

Price, Daniel N. The 1984 Amendments to the Longshore and Harbor Workers' Compensation Act. *Soc. Sec. Bull.*, April 1985, 48(4), pp. 39–40. [G: U.S.]

Ruser, John W. Workers' Compensation Insurance, Experience-rating, and Occupational Injuries. *Rand J. Econ.*, Winter 1985, 16(4), pp. 487–503. [G: U.S.]

Tinsley, La Verne C. Workers' Compensation: 1984 State Enactments. *Mon. Lab. Rev.*, January 1985, 108(1), pp. 49–53. [G: U.S.]

Victor, Richard B. Experience Rating and Workplace Safety. In *Worrall, J. D. and Appel, D., eds.*, 1985, pp. 71–88. [G: U.S.]

Williams, C. Arthur, Jr. Minimum Weekly Workers' Compensation Benefits. In *Worrall, J. D. and Appel, D., eds.*, 1985, pp. 89–116. [G: U.S.]

Worrall, John D. and Appel, David. Some Benefit Issues in Workers' Compensation. In *Worrall, J. D. and Appel, D., eds.*, 1985, pp. 1–18. [G: U.S.]

Worrall, John D. and Butler, Richard J. Benefits and Claim Duration. In *Worrall, J. D. and Appel, D., eds.*, 1985, pp. 57–70. [G: U.S.]

8223 Factory Act and Safety Legislation

Abel, Richard L. Risk as an Arena of Struggle. *Mich. Law Rev.*, February 1985, 83(4), pp. 772–812. [G: U.S.; U.K.]

Bartel, Ann P. and Thomas, Lacy Glenn. Direct and Indirect Effects of Regulation: A New Look at OSHA's Impact. *J. Law Econ.*, April 1985, 28(1), pp. 1–25. [G: U.S.]

Bartel, Ann P. and Thomas, Lacy Glenn. The Costs and Benefits of OSHA-Induced Investments in Employee Safety and Health. In *Worrall, J. D. and Appel, D., eds.*, 1985, pp. 41–56. [G: U.S.]

Bartrip, Peter. Success or Failure? The Prosecution of the Early Factory Acts [The Successful Prosecution of the Factory Acts, 1833–55]. *Econ. Hist. Rev., 2nd Ser.*, August 1985, 38(3), pp. 423–27. [G: U.K.]

Dickens, William T. Occupational Safety and Health and "Irrational" Behavior: A Preliminary Analysis. In *Worrall, J. D. and Appel, D., eds.*, 1985, pp. 19–40. [G: U.S.]

Elder, Harold W. An Economic Analysis of Factor Usage and Workplace Regulation. *Southern Econ. J.*, October 1985, 52(2), pp. 315–31. [G: U.S.]

Fishback, Price V. Discrimination on Nonwage Margins: Safety in the West Virginia Coal Industry, 1906–1925. *Econ. Inquiry*, October 1985, 23(4), pp. 651–69. [G: U.S.]

Ilgen, Thomas L. Between Europe and America, Ottawa and the Provinces: Regulating Toxic Substances in Canada. *Can. Public Policy*, September 1985, 11(3), pp. 578–90. [G: Canada]

McCaffrey, David P., et al. Modeling Complex-

ity: Using Dynamic Simulation to Link Regression and Case Studies. *J. Policy Anal. Manage.*, Winter 1985, 4(2), pp. 196–216.

Nardinelli, Clark. The Successful Prosecution of the Factory Acts: A Suggested Explanation. *Econ. Hist. Rev., 2nd Ser.*, August 1985, 38(3), pp. 428–30. [G: U.K.]

Nelson, Richard R. State Labor Legislation Enacted in 1984. *Mon. Lab. Rev.*, January 1985, 108(1), pp. 27–42. [G: U.S.]

Peacock, A. E. Factory Act Prosecutions: A Hidden Consensus? [The Successful Prosecution of the Factory Acts, 1833–55]. *Econ. Hist. Rev., 2nd Ser.*, August 1985, 38(3), pp. 431–36. [G: U.K.]

Schuster, Michael and Rhodes, Susan. The Impact of Overtime Work on Industrial Accident Rates. *Ind. Relat.*, Spring 1985, 24(2), pp. 234–46. [G: U.S.]

Viscusi, W. Kip. Cotton Dust Regulation: An OSHA Success Story? *J. Policy Anal. Manage.*, Spring 1985, 4(3), pp. 325–43. [G: U.S.]

8224 Unemployment Insurance

Adams, James D. Permanent Differences in Unemployment and Permanent Wage Differentials. *Quart. J. Econ.*, February 1985, 100(1), pp. 29–56. [G: U.S.]

Aho, C. Michael. U.S. Labor-Market Adjustment and Import Restrictions. In *Preeg, E. H., ed.*, 1985, pp. 87–112. [G: U.S.]

Ambachtsheer, Keith P. "Pensions in the American Economy": A Review Article. *J. Portfol. Manage.*, Spring 1985, 11(3), pp. 77–78. [G: U.S.]

Arndt, Sven W. U.S. Labor-Market Adjustment and Import Restrictions: Comment. In *Preeg, E. H., ed.*, 1985, pp. 113–15. [G: U.S.]

Banting, Keith G. Federalism and Income Security: Themes and Variations. In *Courchene, T. J.; Conklin, D. W. and Cook, G. C. A., eds. Vol. 1*, 1985, pp. 253–76. [G: Canada]

Bronars, Stephen G. Fair Pricing of Unemployment Insurance Premiums. *J. Bus.*, January 1985, 58(1), pp. 27–47. [G: U.S.]

Bryce, R. B. The Canadian Economy in the 1930s: Unemployment Relief under Bennett and Mackenzie King. In *[Spry, I. M.]*, 1985, pp. 7–26. [G: Canada]

Capen, Margaret M.; Cohn, Elchanan and Ellson, Richard Wayne. Labour Supply Effects of Unemployment Insurance Benefits. *Appl. Econ.*, February 1985, 17(1), pp. 73–85. [G: U.S.]

Choate, Pat and Carey, Dennis C. An IRA for Structural Unemployment. *Challenge*, Nov./Dec. 1985, 28(5), pp. 57–59. [G: U.S.]

Cohn, Elchanan and Capen, Margaret M. The Distribution of Unemployment Insurance Benefits by Income and Earnings Classes. *Rev. Soc. Econ.*, April 1985, 43(1), pp. 24–36. [G: U.S.]

Cottle, Rex L. and Macaulay, Hugh H. Property Rights and Unemployment Insurance Reserves. *Policy Sci.*, September 1985, 18(2), pp. 127–39. [G: U.S.]

Davis, Evan H. and Dilnot, Andrew W. The Restructuring of National Insurance Contributions in the 1985 Budget. *Fisc. Stud.*, May 1985, *6*(2), pp. 51–60.   [G: U.K.]

Easley, David; Kiefer, Nicholas M. and Possen, Uri. An Equilibrium Analysis of Optimal Unemployment Insurance and Taxation. *Quart. J. Econ.*, Supp. 1985, *100*, pp. 989–1010.

Euvrard, Françoise. L'indemnisation du Chomage: Un Essai de Comparaison internationale. (With English summary.) In *Terny, G. and Culyer, A. J., eds.*, 1985, pp. 67–82.
          [G: France; U.K.; W. Germany; Canada; Sweden]

FitzRoy, Felix R. and Hart, Robert A. Hours, Layoffs and Unemployment Insurance Funding: Theory and Practice in an International Perspective. *Econ. J.*, September 1985, *95*(379), pp. 700–713.

García de Blas, Antonio. Unemployment Benefits in Spain and Other European OECD Countries. *Int. Lab. Rev.*, March-April 1985, *124*(2), pp. 147–61.   [G: Spain; OECD]

Henrich, Amy L. Preferential Treatment of Charities under the Unemployment Insurance Laws. *Yale Law J.*, May 1985, *94*(6), pp. 1472–92.
          [G: U.S.]

Henry, S. G. B.; Payne, J. M. and Trinder, C. Real Wages and Unemployment: A Rejoinder [Labour Market Equilibrium in an Open Economy]. *Oxford Econ. Pap.*, June 1985, *37*(2), pp. 344–45.   [G: U.K.]

Henry, S. G. B.; Payne, J. M. and Trinder, C. Unemployment and Real Wages: The Role of Unemployment, Social Security Benefits and Unionisation [Labour Market Equilibrium in an Open Economy] [Unions Real Wages and Employment]. *Oxford Econ. Pap.*, June 1985, *37*(2), pp. 330–38.   [G: U.K.]

Hicks, Peter. A National System for Parental Leave: Comments. In *Economic Council of Canada.*, 1985, pp. 28–29.   [G: Canada]

Hillier, Brian. Unemployment Benefits and Labor Supply: A Note on the Theoretical Foundations. *Weltwirtsch. Arch.*, 1985, *121*(2), pp. 315–20.

Lang, Graeme. Regional Variations in Worksharing: The Case of Newfoundland. *Can. Public Policy*, March 1985, *11*(1), pp. 54–63.
          [G: Canada]

Mendelson, Michael. Rationalization of Income Security in Canada. In *Courchene, T. J.; Conklin, D. W. and Cook, G. C. A., eds. Vol. 1*, 1985, pp. 229–52.

Micklewright, John. Fiction versus Fact: Unemployment Benefits in Britain. *Nat. Westminster Bank Quart. Rev.*, May 1985, pp. 52–62.
          [G: U.K.]

Micklewright, John. On Earnings-related Unemployment Benefits and Their Relation to Earnings. *Econ. J.*, March 1985, *95*(377), pp. 133–45.   [G: U.K.]

Miller, Paul W. and Volker, Paul A. Unemployment Insurance Eligibility Rights: Evidence from a Comparison of Australia and Canada.

J. Macroecon., Spring 1985, *7*(2), pp. 223–35.
          [G: Australia; Canada]

Minford, Patrick. Unemployment and Real Wages: The Role of Unemployment, Social Security Benefits and Unionisation [Labour Market Equilibrium in an Open Economy]: Reply. *Oxford Econ. Pap.*, June 1985, *37*(2), pp. 339–43.   [G: U.K.]

Moffitt, Robert. Unemployment Insurance and the Distribution of Unemployment Spells. *J. Econometrics*, April 1985, *28*(1), pp. 85–101.
          [G: U.S.]

Narendranathan, Wiji; Nickell, Stephen and Stern, J. Unemployment Benefits Revisited. *Econ. J.*, June 1985, *95*(378), pp. 307–29.
          [G: U.K.]

Pal, Leslie A. Maternity Benefits and Unemployment Insurance: A Question of Policy Design. *Can. Public Policy*, September 1985, *11*(3), pp. 551–60.   [G: Canada]

Price, Daniel N. Unemployment Insurance, Then and Now, 1935–1985. *Soc. Sec. Bull.*, October 1985, *48*(10), pp. 22–32.   [G: U.S.]

Reno, Virginia P. and Price, Daniel N. Relationship between the Retirement, Disability, and Unemployment Insurance Programs: The U.S. Experience. *Soc. Sec. Bull.*, May 1985, *48*(5), pp. 24–37.   [G: U.S.]

Rosbrow, James M. Unemployment Insurance System Marks Its 50th Anniversary. *Mon. Lab. Rev.*, September 1985, *108*(9), pp. 21–28.
          [G: U.S.]

Rowlatt, Don. The Social-Security System in the 1990s: Comments. In *Courchene, T. J.; Conklin, D. W. and Cook, G. C. A., eds. Vol. 1*, 1985, pp. 277–83.   [G: Canada]

Runner, Diana. Changes in Unemployment Insurance Legislation during 1984. *Mon. Lab. Rev.*, January 1985, *108*(1), pp. 43–48.
          [G: U.S.]

Smyth, David J. The Effects of Unemployment Insurance on the Supply of Labor: Does the Dole Cause Unemployment? In *Terny, G. and Culyer, A. J., eds.*, 1985, pp. 143–55.
          [G: U.S.]

Solon, Gary R. Work Incentive Effects of Taxing Unemployment Benefits. *Econometrica*, March 1985, *53*(2), pp. 295–306.   [G: U.S.]

Stemp, Peter J. The Effects on the Economy of Changing Unemployment Benefits and Pensions. *Australian Econ. Pap.*, June 1985, *24*(44), pp. 127–41.   [G: Australia]

Sweet, Morris L. Managing Workforce Reduction: The United States of America and Canada. In *Cross, M., ed.*, 1985, pp. 6–66.
          [G: Canada; U.S.]

Townson, Monica. A National System for Parental Leave. In *Economic Council of Canada.*, 1985, pp. 21–28.   [G: Canada]

8225 Government Employment Policies (including employment services)

Abedian, I. and Standish, B. Poor Whites and the Role of the State: The Evidence. *S. Afr. J. Econ.*, June 1985, *53*(2), pp. 141–65.
          [G: S. Africa]

Bassi, Laurie J. Evaluating Alternative Job Creation Strategies. *Econ. Inquiry,* October 1985, *23*(4), pp. 671–90. [G: U.S.]

Bekemans, Léonce. Job Creation Schemes in Europe: A Review. *Int. J. Soc. Econ.,* 1985, *12*(1), pp. 27–36. [G: EEC]

Bosch, Gerhard. Managing Workforce Reduction: West Germany. In *Cross, M., ed.,* 1985, pp. 164–98. [G: W. Germany]

Burtless, Gary. Are Targeted Wage Subsidies Harmful? Evidence from a Wage Voucher Experiment. *Ind. Lab. Relat. Rev.,* October 1985, *39*(1), pp. 105–14. [G: U.S.]

Cavin, Edward S. and Maynard, Rebecca. Short-term Indicators of Employment Program Performance: Evidence from the Supported Work Program. *J. Human Res.,* Summer 1985, *20*(3), pp. 331–45. [G: U.S.]

Cavin, Edward S. and Stafford, Frank P. Efficient Provision of Employment Service Outputs: A Production Frontier Analysis. *J. Human Res.,* Fall 1985, *20*(4), pp. 484–503. [G: U.S.]

Chapman, Bruce. Continuity and Change: Labour Market Programs and Education Expenditure. *Australian Econ. Rev.,* 3rd Quarter, Spring 1985, (71), pp. 98–112. [G: Australia]

Choate, Pat and Carey, Dennis C. An IRA for Structural Unemployment. *Challenge,* Nov./Dec. 1985, *28*(5), pp. 57–59. [G: U.S.]

Daniel, W. W. Managing Workforce Reduction: The United Kingdom. In *Cross, M., ed.,* 1985, pp. 67–90. [G: U.K.]

Derrier, Jean-François. Public Works Programmes in Rwanda: Conditions for Popular Participation. *Int. Lab. Rev.,* Sept.-Oct. 1985, *124*(5), pp. 611–21. [G: Rwanda]

Fisher, Norman. Continuity and Change: Labour Market Programs and Education Expenditure: Comment. *Australian Econ. Rev.,* 3rd Quarter, Spring 1985, (71), pp. 113–14. [G: Australia]

Galasi, Péter and Sziráczki, György. State Regulation, Enterprise Behaviour and the Labour Market in Hungary, 1968–83. *Cambridge J. Econ.,* September 1985, *9*(3), pp. 203–19. [G: Hungary]

Gillis, William R. and Shaffer, Ron E. Targeting Employment Opportunities toward Selected Workers. *Land Econ.,* November 1985, *61*(4), pp. 433–44. [G: U.S.]

Ginzberg, Eli. Manpower Policy: Retrospect and Prospect. In *Ginzberg, E.,* 1985, pp. 615–35. [G: U.S.]

Gregory, R. G. and Smith, Ralph E. Unemployment, Inflation and Job Creation Policies in Australia. In *Argy, V. E. and Neville, J. W., eds.,* 1985, pp. 325–45. [G: Australia]

Hartman, David G. The Economics of Incremental Incentive Programs: The Example of Employment Subsidies. *Public Finance Quart.,* October 1985, *13*(4), pp. 375–95.

Haveman, Robert H. and Saks, Daniel H. Transatlantic Lessons for Employment and Training Policy. *Ind. Relat.,* Winter 1985, *24*(1), pp. 20–36. [G: U.S.; W. Europe]

Johnson, Terry R.; Dickinson, Katherine P. and West, Richard W. An Evaluation of the Impact of ES Referrals on Applicant Earnings. *J. Human Res.,* Winter 1985, *20*(1), pp. 117–37. [G: U.S.]

Lang, Graeme. Regional Variations in Worksharing: The Case of Newfoundland. *Can. Public Policy,* March 1985, *11*(1), pp. 54–63. [G: Canada]

Leonard, Jonathan S. Affirmative Action as Earnings Redistribution: The Targeting of Compliance Reviews. *J. Lab. Econ.,* July 1985, *3*(3), pp. 363–84.

Montgomery, Mark and Wilson, Charles A. On the Dynamic Response of a Firm to an Employment Subsidy with a Fixed Threshold. *J. Econ. Dynam. Control,* December 1985, *9*(4), pp. 405–22.

Nickell, Stephen. The Government's Policy for Jobs: An Analysis. *Oxford Rev. Econ. Policy,* Summer 1985, *1*(2), pp. 98–115. [G: U.K.]

O'Boyle, Edward J. On Reconstructing the Foundations of Policy toward the Unemployed. *Rev. Soc. Econ.,* December 1985, *43*(3), pp. 325–44.

Piliawsky, Monte. The Impact of Black Mayors on the Black Community: The Case of New Orleans' Ernest Morial. *Rev. Black Polit. Econ.,* Spring 1985, *13*(4), pp. 5–23. [G: U.S.]

Robinson, P. William. Capacity Constraints, Real Wages and the Role of the Public Sector in Creating Jobs. In *Kay, J., ed.,* 1985, pp. 40–50. [G: U.K.]

Robinson, P. William. Capacity Constraints, Real Wages and the Role of the Public Sector in Creating Jobs. *Fisc. Stud.,* May 1985, *6*(2), pp. 40–50. [G: U.K.]

Romagnoli, Gian Cesare. Les entreprises a participation d'etat dans la politique de l'emploi. (The Role of Enterprises with State Share Holdings in Employment Policy. With English summary.) *Ann. Pub. Co-op. Econ.,* Oct.-Dec. 1985, *56*(4), pp. 485–95. [G: Italy]

Sloan, Judith. Continuity and Change: Labour Market Programs and Education Expenditure: Comment. *Australian Econ. Rev.,* 3rd Quarter, Spring 1985, (71), pp. 114–15. [G: Australia]

Sloan, Judith. Training or Wages: An Evaluation of the Kirby Report. *Australian Bull. Lab.,* June 1985, *11*(3), pp. 142–53. [G: Australia]

Steinherr, Alfred. Investment or Employment Subsidies for Rapid Employment Creation in the European Economic Community? In *Weiserbs, D., ed.,* 1985, pp. 145–80. [G: OECD]

Sweet, Morris L. Managing Workforce Reduction: The United States of America and Canada. In *Cross, M., ed.,* 1985, pp. 6–66. [G: Canada; U.S.]

Taylor, Patricia A. Institutional Job Training and Inequality. *Soc. Sci. Quart.,* March 1985, *66*(1), pp. 67–78. [G: U.S.]

Thurow, Lester C. Public Intervention in the Industry. The Case of the U.S.A. *Ann. Pub. Co-*

op. Econ., January–June 1985, *56*(1–2), pp. 41–49. [G: U.S.]

Walker, Alan. Policies for Sharing the Job Shortage: Reducing or Redistributing Unemployment? In *Klein, R. and O'Higgins, M., ed.*, 1985, pp. 166–85. [G: U.K.]

Warburton, Peter J. Investment or Employment Subsidies for Rapid Employment Creation in the EEC: Comment. In *Weiserbs, D., ed.*, 1985, pp. 181–82. [G: OECD]

Willis, K. G. Estimating the Benefits of Job Creation from Local Investment Subsidies. *Urban Stud.*, April 1985, *22*(2), pp. 163–77.
[G: U.K.]

Wilson, Robert Andrew. Public Expenditure Policy, 1985–86: Employment. In *Cockle, P., ed.*, 1985, pp. 153–85. [G: U.K.]

Wiltshaw, Desmond G. Jobs and Local Authority Subsidies. *Urban Stud.*, October 1985, *22*(5), pp. 433–37. [G: U.K.]

8226 Employment in the Public Sector

Bixby, Ann Kallman. Benefits and Beneficiaries under Public Employee Retirement Systems, 1981 and 1982. *Soc. Sec. Bull.*, April 1985, *48*(4), pp. 41–45. [G: U.S.]

Blank, Rebecca M. An Analysis of Workers' Choice between Employment in the Public and Private Sectors. *Ind. Lab. Relat. Rev.*, January 1985, *38*(2), pp. 211–24. [G: U.S.]

Cameron, Samuel. The Supply and Demand for Police Manpower in England and Wales. *Public Finance*, 1985, *40*(3), pp. 447–62.
[G: U.K.]

Cappelli, Peter. Fair Wages and the Industrial Civil Service. *Scot. J. Polit. Econ.*, February 1985, *32*(1), pp. 55–66. [G: U.K.]

Chapman, Bruce J. Sex and Location Differences in Wages in the Australian Public Service. *Australian Econ. Pap.*, December 1985, *24*(45), pp. 296–309. [G: Australia]

Dale, Charles. An Interdisciplinary Approach to Predicting Military Performance. *Atlantic Econ. J.*, September 1985, *13*(3), pp. 92.
[G: U.S.]

Dale, Charles and Gilroy, Curtis. The Outlook for Army Recruiting. *Eastern Econ. J.*, April–June 1985, *11*(2), pp. 107–22. [G: U.S.]

Dunson, Bruce H. Pay, Experience, and Productivity: The Government-Sector Case. *J. Human Res.*, Winter 1985, *20*(1), pp. 153–60.
[G: U.S.]

Farrell, John B. Establishment Survey Incorporates March 1984 Employment Benchmarks. *Mon. Lab. Rev.*, August 1985, *108*(8), pp. 39–41. [G: U.S.]

Fisk, Donald M. Productivity Trends in the Federal Government. *Mon. Lab. Rev.*, October 1985, *108*(10), pp. 3–9. [G: U.S.]

Goldenberg, Edie N. The Grace Commission and Civil Service Reform: Seeking a Common Understanding. In *Levine, C. H., ed.*, 1985, pp. 69–94. [G: U.S.]

Grosskopf, Shawna; Hayes, Kathy J. and Kennedy, Thomas E. Supply and Demand Effects

of Underfunding of Pensions on Public Employee Wages. *Southern Econ. J.*, January 1985, *51*(3), pp. 745–53. [G: U.S.]

Gurdon, Michael A. The Emergence of Co-determination in Australian Government Employment. *Int. Lab. Rev.*, July-Aug. 1985, *124*(4), pp. 465–78.

Hirsch, Werner Z. and Rufolo, Anthony M. Economic Effects of Residence Laws on Municipal Police. *J. Urban Econ.*, May 1985, *17*(3), pp. 335–48. [G: U.S.]

Hoggart, Keith. Welsh Local Authority Employment since 1979: Political Party Effects in District Councils. *Reg. Stud.*, October 1985, *19*(5), pp. 447–57. [G: U.K.]

Horne, David K. Modeling Army Enlistment Supply for the All-Volunteer Force. *Mon. Lab. Rev.*, August 1985, *108*(8), pp. 35–39.
[G: U.S.]

Irfan, Mohammad and Ahmed, Meekal Aziz. Real Wages in Pakistan: Structure and Trends, 1970–84. *Pakistan Devel. Rev.*, Autumn-Winter 1985, *24*(3/4), pp. 423–37. [G: Pakistan]

Jackson, Peter M. Fiscal Containment and Local Government Finance in the U.K. In *Gramlich, E. M. and Ysander, B.-C., eds.*, 1985, pp. 175–228. [G: U.K.]

Khan, M. Fahim. Real Wages in Pakistan: Structure and Trends, 1970–84: Comments. *Pakistan Devel. Rev.*, Autumn-Winter 1985, *24*(3/4), pp. 438–40. [G: Pakistan]

Le Pen, Claude. Emplois publics et distribution des revenus. (Public Employment and Distribution of Income. With English summary.) *Revue Écon.*, July 1985, *36*(4), pp. 715–39.
[G: France]

Leonard, Herman B. The Federal Civil Service Retirement System: An Analysis of Its Financial Condition and Current Reform Proposals. In *Wise, D. A., ed.*, 1985, pp. 399–438.
[G: U.S.]

Levine, Charles H. The Unfinished Agenda for Civil Service Reform *Implications of the Grace Commission Report:* Introduction. In *Levine, C. H., ed.*, 1985, pp. 1–14. [G: U.S.]

McGregor, Eugene B., Jr. The Grace Commission's Challenge to Public Personnel Administration. In *Levine, C. H., ed.*, 1985, pp. 43–59. [G: U.S.]

Murrell, Peter. The Size of Public Employment: An Empirical Study. *J. Compar. Econ.*, December 1985, *9*(4), pp. 424–37. [G: OECD]

Page, Edward. From *l'État* to Big Government. In *Rose, R.*, 1985, pp. 97–125. [G: France]

Parry, Richard. Britain: Stable Aggregates, Changing Composition. In *Rose, R.*, 1985, pp. 54–96. [G: U.K.]

Peters, B. Guy. Administrative Change and the Grace Commission. In *Levine, C. H., ed.*, 1985, pp. 19–39. [G: U.S.]

Peters, B. Guy. Sweden: The Explosion of Public Employment. In *Rose, R.*, 1985, pp. 203–27.
[G: Sweden]

Peters, B. Guy. The United States: Absolute Change and Relative Stability. In *Rose, R.*, 1985, pp. 228–61. [G: U.S.]

Pignatelli, Andrea Cendali. Italy: The Development of a Late Developing State. In *Rose, R.*, 1985, pp. 163–201. [G: Italy]

Rein, Martin. The Social Welfare Labour Market. In *Eisenstadt, S. N. and Ahimeir, O., eds.*, 1985, pp. 109–31. [G: Israel; U.S.; W. Europe]

Rein, Martin. Women, Employment and Social Welfare. In *Klein, R. and O'Higgins, M., ed.*, 1985, pp. 37–58. [G: Sweden; U.K.; U.S.; W. Germany]

Rose, Richard. The Significance of Public Employment. In *Rose, R.*, 1985, pp. 1–53. [G: Selected OECD]

Rosen, Bernard. Civil Service Reform: Are the Constraints Impenetrable? In *Levine, C. H., ed.*, 1985, pp. 102–114. [G: U.S.]

Samuelson, Paul A. The Federal Civil Service Retirement System: An Analysis of Its Financial Condition and Current Reform Proposals: Comment. In *Wise, D. A., ed.*, 1985, pp. 438–43. [G: U.S.]

Schmidt, Klaus-Dieter and Rose, Richard. Germany: The Expansion of an Active State. In *Rose, R.*, 1985, pp. 126–62. [G: W. Germany]

Theeuwes, Jules, et al. Estimation of Optimal Human Capital Accumulation Parameters for the Netherlands. *Europ. Econ. Rev.*, November 1985, *29*(2), pp. 233–57. [G: Netherlands]

Trinder, C. and Biswas, Rajiv. Public Services Pay in the 1980s. *Nat. Inst. Econ. Rev.*, May 1985, (112), pp. 31–34. [G: U.K.]

823 Labor Mobility; National and International Migration

8230 Labor Mobility; National and International Migration

Adams, John W. and Kaskoff, Alice Bee. Wealth and Migration in Massachusetts and Maine: 1771–1798. *J. Econ. Hist.*, June 1985, *45*(2), pp. 363–68. [G: U.S.]

Adelman, Irma. Shadow Households and Competing Auspices: Migration Behavior in the Philippines: Discussion. *J. Devel. Econ.*, January–February 1985, *17*(1–2), pp. 27–28. [G: Philippines]

Agarwal, Vinod B. and Winkler, Donald R. United States Immigration Policy and Indirect Immigration of Professionals. *Econ. Educ. Rev.*, 1985, *4*(1), pp. 1–16. [G: U.S.]

Ahsan, Syed M. and Ali, Ali A. G. Income Taxation, Migration, and Work Incentives in a Dual Economy Model. *Devel. Econ.*, March 1985, *23*(1), pp. 16–39.

Al-Qudsi, Sulayman S. Earnings Differences in the Labor Market of the Arab Gulf States: The Case of Kuwait. *J. Devel. Econ.*, May–June 1985, *18*(1), pp. 119–32. [G: Kuwait; United Arab Emirates; Bahrain; Saudi Arabia; Qatar]

Alao, Nurudeen. Urban Unemployment Equilibrium in LDCs: A Perspective. *Reg. Stud.*, June 1985, *19*(3), pp. 185–92. [G: LDCs]

Amrhein, Carl G. and MacKinnon, R. D. An Elementary Simulation Model of the Job Matching Process within an Interregional Setting. *Reg. Stud.*, June 1985, *19*(3), pp. 193–202.

Ault, David E. and Rutman, Gilbert L. The Rural African and Gold Mining in Southern Africa, 1976–1980. *S. Afr. J. Econ.*, March 1985, *53*(1), pp. 1–23. [G: S. Africa]

Bailey, Thomas. A Case Study of Immigrants in the Restaurant Industry. *Ind. Relat.*, Spring 1985, *24*(2), pp. 205–21. [G: U.S.]

Bhagwati, Jagdish N. International Migration and Investment. In *Bhagwati, J. N. (I)*, 1985, pp. 299–302.

Bhagwati, Jagdish N. Taxation and International Migration: Recent Policy Issues. In *Bhagwati, J. N. (I)*, 1985, pp. 347–61. [G: U.S.; LDCs]

Bhagwati, Jagdish N. The Brain Drain: International Resource Flow Accounting, Compensation, Taxation and Related Policy Proposals. In *Bhagwati, J. N. (I)*, 1985, pp. 303–46. [G: Selected LDCs; U.S.; Canada]

Bhagwati, Jagdish N. and Krugman, Paul R. The Decision to Migrate: A Survey. In *Bhagwati, J. N. (I)*, 1985, pp. 362–82. [G: Selected LDCs; U.S.; Canada]

Bhattacharyya, Bharati. The Role of Family Decision in Internal Migration: The Case of India. *J. Devel. Econ.*, May–June 1985, *18*(1), pp. 51–66. [G: India]

Bilsborrow, R. E. and Winegarden, C. R. Landholding, Rural Fertility and Internal Migration in Developing Countries: Econometric Evidence from Cross-National Data. *Pakistan Devel. Rev.*, Summer 1985, *24*(2), pp. 125–49. [G: LDCs]

Blomqvist, Ake G. Unemployment of the Educated and Emigration of Post-Secondary Graduates from the LDCs. *Pakistan Devel. Rev.*, Autumn-Winter 1985, *24*(3/4), pp. 643–54. [G: LDCs]

Borjas, George J. Assimilation, Changes in Cohort Quality, and the Earnings of Immigrants. *J. Lab. Econ.*, October 1985, *3*(4), pp. 463–89. [G: U.S.]

Briggs, Vernon M., Jr. Employment Trends and Contemporary Immigration Policy. In *Glazer, N., ed.*, 1985, pp. 135–60. [G: U.S.]

Brown, Lawrence A. and Jones, John Paul, III. Spatial Variation in Migration Processes and Development: A Costa Rican Example of Conventional Modeling Augmented by the Expansion Method. *Demography*, August 1985, *22*(3), pp. 326–52. [G: Costa Rica]

Brown, Lawrence A. and Lawson, Victoria A. Rural-destined Migration in Third World Settings: A Neglected Phenomenon? *Reg. Stud.*, October 1985, *19*(5), pp. 415–32. [G: Costa Rica]

Browning, Harley L. and Rodríguez, Nestor. The Migration of Mexican Indocumentados as a Settlement Process: Implications for Work. In *Borjas, G. J. and Tienda, M., eds.*, 1985, pp. 277–97. [G: U.S.]

Bustamante, Jorge A. Mexican Migration to the

United States: De Facto Rules. In *Musgrave, P. B., ed.*, 1985, pp. 185–205. [**G: Mexico; U.S.**]

Caces, Fe, et al. Shadow Households and Competing Auspices: Migration Behavior in the Philippines. *J. Devel. Econ.*, January–February 1985, *17*(1–2), pp. 5–25. [**G: Philippines**]

Chalmers, James A. and Greenwood, Michael J. The Regional Labor Market Adjustment Process: Determinants of Changes in Rates of Labor Force Participation, Unemployment, and Migration. *Ann. Reg. Sci.*, March 1985, *19*(1), pp. 1–17. [**G: U.S.**]

Chaudhuri, Pradipta. The Impact of Forced Commerce on the Pattern of Emigration from Orissa, 1901–21. In *Raj, K. N., et al., eds.*, 1985, pp. 184–209. [**G: India**]

Chiswick, Barry R. and Miller, Paul W. Immigrant Generation and Income in Australia. *Econ. Rec.*, June 1985, *61*(173), pp. 540–53. [**G: Australia**]

Cole, William E. and Sanders, Richard D. Internal Migration and Urban Employment in the Third World. *Amer. Econ. Rev.*, June 1985, *75*(3), pp. 481–94. [**G: Mexico; India; Colombia; Nigeria**]

Corden, W. Max and Findlay, Ronald F. Urban Unemployment, Intersectoral Capital Mobility and Development Policy. In *Corden, W. M.*, 1985, pp. 73–93.

Dunlevy, James A. Factor Endowments, Heterogeneous Labor and North–South Migration. *Southern Econ. J.*, October 1985, *52*(2), pp. 446–59. [**G: U.S.**]

Dunn, Lucia F. Nonpecuniary Job Preferences and Welfare Losses among Migrant Agricultural Workers. *Amer. J. Agr. Econ.*, May 1985, *67*(2), pp. 257–65. [**G: Mexico; U.S.**]

Emerson, Robert D. Critical Issues in Agricultural Labor Markets. *Southern J. Agr. Econ.*, July 1985, *17*(1), pp. 89–98. [**G: U.S.**]

Evers, Gerard H. M. and van der Veen, Anne. A Simultaneous Non-linear Model for Labour Migration and Commuting. *Reg. Stud.*, June 1985, *19*(3), pp. 217–29. [**G: Netherlands**]

Frey, William H. Mover Destination Selectivity and the Changing Suburbanization of Metropolitan Whites and Blacks. *Demography*, May 1985, *22*(2), pp. 223–43. [**G: U.S.**]

Fuchs, Lawrence H. The Search for a Sound Immigration Policy: A Personal View. In *Glazer, N., ed.*, 1985, pp. 17–48. [**G: U.S.**]

Fuller, Theodore D.; Lightfoot, Paul and Kamnuansilpa, Peerasit. Rural–Urban Mobility in Thailand: A Decision-making Approach. *Demography*, November 1985, *22*(4), pp. 565–79. [**G: Thailand**]

Galenson, David W. Errata [Population Turnover in the British West Indies in the Late Seventeenth Century]. *J. Econ. Hist.*, September 1985, *45*(3), pp. 719. [**G: Barbados**]

Galenson, David W. Population Turnover in the English West Indies in the Late Seventeenth Century: A Comparative Perspective. *J. Econ. Hist.*, June 1985, *45*(2), pp. 227–35. [**G: Barbados**]

de la Garza, Rodolfo O. Mexican Americans, Mexican Immigrants, and Immigration Reform. In *Glazer, N., ed.*, 1985, pp. 93–105. [**G: U.S.**]

Goodwin, H. L., Jr. Critical Issues in Agricultural Labor Markets: Discussion. *Southern J. Agr. Econ.*, July 1985, *17*(1), pp. 99–102. [**G: U.S.**]

Gordon, Ian R. The Cyclical Interaction between Regional Migration, Employment and Unemployment: A Time Series Analysis for Scotland. *Scot. J. Polit. Econ.*, June 1985, *32*(2), pp. 135–58. [**G: U.K.**]

Goss, Ernst P. and Schoening, Niles C. The Migration Propensities of Workers in High Tech Occupations. *Atlantic Econ. J.*, July 1985, *13*(2), pp. 87–88. [**G: U.S.**]

Grant, E. Kenneth and Vanderkamp, John. Migrant Information and the Remigration Decision: Further Evidence. *Southern Econ. J.*, April 1985, *51*(4), pp. 1202–15. [**G: Canada**]

Greenwood, Michael J. Human Migration: Theory, Models, and Empirical Studies. *J. Reg. Sci.*, November 1985, *25*(4), pp. 521–44. [**G: U.S.**]

Greenwood, Michael J. and McDowell, John M. U.S. Immigration Reform: Policy Issues and Economic Analysis. *Contemp. Policy Issues*, Spring, Pt. 1, 1985, *3*(3), pp. 59–75. [**G: U.S.**]

Grubb, Farley. The Incidence of Servitude in Trans-Atlantic Migration, 1771–1804. *Exploration Econ. Hist.*, July 1985, *22*(3), pp. 316–39.

Grubb, Farley. The Market for Indentured Immigrants: Evidence on the Efficiency of Forward-Labor Contracting in Philadelphia, 1745–1773. *J. Econ. Hist.*, December 1985, *45*(4), pp. 855–68. [**G: U.S.**]

Hamlin, Alan P. Capital and Labour Movements in the European Community: Comment. In *Weiserbs, D., ed.*, 1985, pp. 285–87. [**G: EEC**]

Hansen, Bent. Wage Differentials in Italy and Egypt. The Incentive to Migrate before World War I. *J. Europ. Econ. Hist.*, Fall 1985, *14*(2), pp. 347–60. [**G: Italy; Egypt**]

Harwood, Edwin. How Should We Enforce Immigration Law? In *Glazer, N., ed.*, 1985, pp. 73–91. [**G: U.S.**]

Herzog, Henry W., Jr.; Hofler, Richard A. and Schlottmann, Alan M. Life on the Frontier: Migrant Information, Earnings and Past Mobility. *Rev. Econ. Statist.*, August 1985, *67*(3), pp. 373–82. [**G: U.S.**]

Hill, John K. The Economic Impact of Tighter U.S. Border Security. *Fed. Res. Bank Dallas Econ. Rev.*, July 1985, pp. 12–20. [**G: U.S.**]

Hughes, Gordon and McCormick, Barry. An Empirical Analysis of On-the-Job Search and Job Mobility. *Manchester Sch. Econ. Soc. Stud.*, March 1985, *53*(1), pp. 76–95. [**G: U.K.**]

Hughes, Gordon and McCormick, Barry. Migration Intentions in the U.K.: Which Households Want to Migrate and Which Succeed? *Econ.*

J., Supplement 1985, *95*, pp. 113–23.
[G: U.K.]

Hunt, Janet C. and Kau, James B. Migration and Wage Growth: A Human Capital Approach. *Southern Econ. J.*, January 1985, *51*(3), pp. 697–710. [G: U.S.]

Isserman, Andrew M., et al. Forecasting Interstate Migration with Limited Data: A Demographic-Economic Approach. *J. Amer. Statist. Assoc.*, June 1985, *80*(390), pp. 277–85.
[G: U.S.]

Kannappan, Subbiah. Urban Employment and the Labor Market in Developing Nations. *Econ. Develop. Cult. Change*, July 1985, *33*(4), pp. 699–730. [G: LDCs]

Keleş, Ruşen. The Effects of External Migration on Regional Development in Turkey. In *Hudson, R. and Lewis, J., eds.*, 1985, pp. 54–75.
[G: Turkey]

Khan, M. Ali. Unemployment of the Educated and Emigration of Post-Secondary Graduates from the LDCs: Comments. *Pakistan Devel. Rev.*, Autumn-Winter 1985, *24*(3/4), pp. 655–56.

King, Russell; Strachan, Alan and Mortimer, Jill. The Urban Dimension of European Return Migration: The Case of Bari, Southern Italy. *Urban Stud.*, June 1985, *22*(3), pp. 219–35.
[G: Italy]

King, Russell, et al. Return Migration and Rural Economic Change: A South Italian Case Study. In *Hudson, R. and Lewis, J., eds.*, 1985, pp. 101–122. [G: Italy]

Kirwan, Frank. Migration and Emigrants' Remittances: Theory and Evidence from the Middle East. In *Lundahl, M., ed.*, 1985, pp. 253–70.
[G: Jordan]

Knight, Franklin W. Jamaican Migrants and the Cuban Sugar Industry, 1900–1934. In *Moreno Franginals, M.; Moya Pons, F. and Engerman, S. L., eds.*, 1985, pp. 94–114. [G: Jamaica; Cuba]

van de Laar, Aart and Ask, Karin. Aspects of International Labour Migration. In *Jerve, A. M., ed.*, 1985, pp. 223–29. [G: Pakistan]

Landale, Nancy S. and Guest, Avery M. Constraints, Satisfaction, and Residential Mobility: Speare's Model Reconsidered. *Demography*, May 1985, *22*(2), pp. 199–222. [G: U.S.]

Light, Ivan. Immigrant Entrepreneurs in America: Koreans in Los Angeles. In *Glazer, N., ed.*, 1985, pp. 161–78. [G: U.S.]

Lucas, Robert E. B. Migration amongst the Botswana. *Econ. J.*, June 1985, *95*(378), pp. 358–82. [G: Botswana]

Lucas, Robert E. B. Mines and Migrants in South Africa. *Amer. Econ. Rev.*, December 1985, *75*(5), pp. 1094–108. [G: S. Africa]

Lucas, Robert E. B. and Stark, Oded. Motivations to Remit: Evidence from Botswana. *J. Polit. Econ.*, October 1985, *93*(5), pp. 901–18.
[G: Botswana]

Lundahl, Mats. International Migration, Remittances and Real Incomes: Effects on the Source Country. *Scand. J. Econ.*, 1985, *87*(4), pp. 647–57.

Madhavan, M. C. Indian Emigrants: Numbers, Characteristics, and Economic Impact. *Population Devel. Rev.*, September 1985, *11*(3), pp. 457–81. [G: India]

Maier, Gunther. Cumulative Causation and Selectivity in Labour Market Oriented Migration Caused by Imperfect Information. *Reg. Stud.*, June 1985, *19*(3), pp. 231–41.

Manson, Donald M.; Espenshade, Thomas J. and Muller, Thomas. Mexican Immigration to Southern California: Issues of Job Competition and Worker Mobility. *Rev. Reg. Stud.*, Spring 1985, *15*(2), pp. 21–33. [G: U.S.; Mexico]

Marston, Stephen T. Two Views of the Geographic Distribution of Unemployment. *Quart. J. Econ.*, February 1985, *100*(1), pp. 57–79. [G: U.S.]

Mayes, David G. Capital and Labour Movements in the European Community. In *Weiserbs, D., ed.*, 1985, pp. 257–83. [G: EEC]

McManus, Walter S. Labor Market Assimilation of Immigrants: The Importance of Language Skills. *Contemp. Policy Issues*, Spring, Pt. 1, 1985, *3*(3), pp. 77–89. [G: U.S.]

Miller, Harris N. "The Right Thing to Do": A History of Simpson–Mazzoli. In *Glazer, N., ed.*, 1985, pp. 49–71. [G: U.S.]

Mincer, Jacob. The Effect of Immigrants on Natives' Incomes through the Use of Capital: Discussion. *J. Devel. Econ.*, January–February 1985, *17*(1–2), pp. 95–97. [G: U.S.]

Mines, Richard and Kaufman, Michael. Mexican Immigrants: The Labor Market Issue. In *Musgrave, P. B., ed.*, 1985, pp. 207–28.
[G: Mexico; U.S.]

Mueser, Peter. A Note on Simultaneous Equations Models of Migration and Employment Growth. *Southern Econ. J.*, October 1985, *52*(2), pp. 516–22.

Muller, Thomas. Economic Effects of Immigration. In *Glazer, N., ed.*, 1985, pp. 109–33.
[G: U.S.]

O'Loughlin, John. The Geographic Distribution of Foreigners in West Germany. *Reg. Stud.*, August 1985, *19*(4), pp. 365–77.
[G: W. Germany]

Pearce, James E. and Gunther, Jeffrey W. Illegal Immigration from Mexico: Effects on the Texas Economy. *Fed. Res. Bank Dallas Econ. Rev.*, September 1985, pp. 1–14. [G: U.S.]

Reynolds, Clark W. and McCleery, Robert K. Modeling U.S.—Mexico Economic Linkages. *Amer. Econ. Rev.*, May 1985, *75*(2), pp. 217–22. [G: U.S.; Mexico]

Richards, Alan. Mexico and the United States: Studies in Economic Interaction: Labor Markets: Comments. In *Musgrave, P. B., ed.*, 1985, pp. 229–34. [G: Mexico; U.S.]

Richter, Kerry. Nonmetropolitan Growth in the Late 1970s: The End of the Turnaround? *Demography*, May 1985, *22*(2), pp. 245–63.
[G: U.S.]

Robinson, D. The Economic System in the UK: Government and Pay. In *Morris, D., ed.*, 1985, pp. 333–65. [G: U.K.]

Rogers, Rosemarie. Migration Theory and Prac-

tice. In *Connor, W., ed.,* 1985, pp. 161–204.
[G: Mexico; U.S.; Selected Countries]

Sabato, Hilda. La formación del mercado de trabajo en Buenos Aires, 1850–1880. (With English summary.) *Desarrollo Econ.,* January–March 1985, *24*(96), pp. 561–92.
[G: Argentina]

Sandefur, Gary D. Variations in Interstate Migration of Men across the Early Stages of the Life Cycle. *Demography,* August 1985, *22*(3), pp. 353–66.
[G: U.S.]

Sassen-Koob, Saskia. Changing Composition and Labor Market Location of Hispanic Immigrants in New York City, 1960–1980. In *Borjas, G. J. and Tienda, M., eds.,* 1985, pp. 299–322.
[G: U.S.]

Schaeffer, Peter. Human Capital Accumulation and Job Mobility. *J. Reg. Sci.,* February 1985, *25*(1), pp. 103–14.

Schuck, Peter H. Immigration Law and the Problem of Community. In *Glazer, N., ed.,* 1985, pp. 285–307.
[G: U.S.]

Seccareccia, Mario S. Immigration and Business Cycles: Pauper Migration to Canada, 1815–1874. In *[Spry, I. M.],* 1985, pp. 117–38.
[G: Canada]

Sehgal, Ellen. Foreign Born in the U.S. Labor Market: The Results of a Special Survey. *Mon. Lab. Rev.,* July 1985, *108*(7), pp. 18–24.
[G: U.S.]

Simon, Julian L. and Heins, A. James. The Effect of Immigrants on Natives' Incomes through the Use of Capital. *J. Devel. Econ.,* January–February 1985, *17*(1–2), pp. 75–93.   [G: U.S.]

Stark, Oded and Bloom, David E. The New Economics of Labor Migration. *Amer. Econ. Rev.,* May 1985, *75*(2), pp. 173–78.

Stott, Richard. British Immigrants and the American "Work Ethic" in the Mid-Nineteenth Century. *Labor Hist.,* Winter 1985, *26*(1), pp. 86–102.
[G: U.S.; U.K.]

Straubhaar, Thomas. Der Zahlungsbilanzeffekt der Devisentransfers ausgewanderter Arbeitskräfte für ihre Herkunftsländer. (The Balance of Payments Effect for Their Home Country of Migrant Workers' Remittances. With English summary.) *Jahr. Nationalökon. Statist.,* May 1985, *200*(3), pp. 280–97.   [G: Greece; Spain; Portugal; Turkey]

Suits, Daniel B. U.S. Farm Migration: An Application of the Harris–Todaro Model. *Econ. Develop. Cult. Change,* July 1985, *33*(4), pp. 815–28.
[G: U.S.]

Tabuchi, Takatoshi. Time-Series Modeling of Gross Migration and Dynamic Equilibrium. *J. Reg. Sci.,* February 1985, *25*(1), pp. 65–83.
[G: U.S.; Japan]

Talafha, Hussain. Emigration and Wage Differentials Facing the Jordanian Workers. *METU,* 1985, *12*(3/4), pp. 317–32.   [G: Jordan; Saudi Arabia]

Talafha, Hussain. The Effects of Workers' Remittances on the Jordanian Economy. *METU,* 1985, *12*(1/2), pp. 119–30.   [G: Jordan]

Thompson, Gary; Amon, Ricardo and Martin, Philip L. Mexicans or Tomatoes? Immigration

and Imports. *J. Policy Anal. Manage.,* Summer 1985, *4*(4), pp. 603–05.   [G: Mexico; U.S.]

Toepfer, Helmuth. The Economic Impact of Returned Emigrants in Trabzon, Turkey. In *Hudson, R. and Lewis, J., eds.,* 1985, pp. 76–100.
[G: Turkey]

Vining, Daniel R. The Growth of Core Urban Regions in Developing Countries. *Population Devel. Rev.,* September 1985, *11*(3), pp. 495–514.   [G: LDCs; MDCs]

Wadycki, Walter J. Single-Place Alternative Opportunities in an Economic Model of Migration. *Ann. Reg. Sci.,* July 1985, *19*(2), pp. 10–16.   [G: U.S.]

Waldinger, Roger. Immigrant Enterprise and the Structure of the Labour Market. In *Roberts, B.; Finnegan, R. and Gallie, D., eds.,* 1985, pp. 213–28.   [G: U.S.]

Waldinger, Roger. Immigration and Industrial Change in the New York City Apparel Industry. In *Borjas, G. J. and Tienda, M., eds.,* 1985 , pp. 323–49.   [G: U.S.]

Webb, Michael A. Migration and Education Subsidies by Governments: A Game-theoretic Analysis. *J. Public Econ.,* March 1985, *26*(2), pp. 249–62.

Webb, Michael A. The Brain Drain and Education Opportunity in Less Developed Countries. *Eastern Econ. J.,* April–June 1985, *11*(2), pp. 145–55.   [G: LDCs]

Weiner, Myron. On International Migration and International Relations. *Population Devel. Rev.,* September 1985, *11*(3), pp. 441–55.

Williams, Donald R. Technical Note: Employment in Recession and Recovery: A Demographic Flow Analysis. *Mon. Lab. Rev.,* March 1985, *108*(3), pp. 35–42.   [G: U.S.]

Withers, Glenn and Pope, David. Immigration and Unemployment. *Econ. Rec.,* June 1985, *61*(173), pp. 554–63.   [G: Australia]

Wooton, Ian. Labour Migration in a Model of North–South Trade. *Econ. Modelling,* October 1985, *2*(4), pp. 339–46.

824 Labor Market Studies, Wages, Employment

8240 General

Amrhein, Carl G. and MacKinnon, R. D. An Elementary Simulation Model of the Job Matching Process within an Interregional Setting. *Reg. Stud.,* June 1985, *19*(3), pp. 193–202.

Andrews, M. J., et al. Models of the UK Economy and the Real Wage–Employment Debate. *Nat. Inst. Econ. Rev.,* May 1985, (112), pp. 41–52.
[G: U.K.]

Antel, John J. Costly Employment Contract Renegotiation and the Labor Mobility of Young Men. *Amer. Econ. Rev.,* December 1985, *75*(5), pp. 976–91.   [G: U.S.]

Broer, D. P. and Siebrand, J. C. A Macroeconomic Disequilibrium Model of Product Market and Labour Market for the Netherlands. *Appl. Econ.*, August 1985, *17*(4), pp. 633–46. [G: Netherlands]

Burtless, Gary. Are Targeted Wage Subsidies Harmful? Evidence from a Wage Voucher Experiment. *Ind. Lab. Relat. Rev.*, October 1985, *39*(1), pp. 105–14. [G: U.S.]

Carter, Michael J. and Carter, Susan B. Internal Labor Markets in Retailing: The Early Years. *Ind. Lab. Relat. Rev.*, July 1985, *38*(4), pp. 586–98. [G: U.S.]

Challen, D. W. Wages, Unemployment and Inflation. In *Argy, V. E. and Neville, J. W., eds.*, 1985, pp. 346–69. [G: Australia]

Dabscheck, Braham and Niland, John. Australian Industrial Relations and the Shift to Centralism. In *Juris, H.; Thompson, M. and Daniels, W., eds.*, 1985, pp. 41–72. [G: Australia]

Dickens, William T. and Lang, Kevin. A Test of Dual Labor Market Theory. *Amer. Econ. Rev.*, September 1985, *75*(4), pp. 792–805. [G: U.S.]

Duncan, Greg J. and Hill, Daniel H. An Investigation of the Extent and Consequences of Measurement Error in Labor-Economic Survey Data. *J. Lab. Econ.*, October 1985, *3*(4), pp. 508–32. [G: U.S.]

Fay, Jon A. and Medoff, James L. Labor and Output over the Business Cycle: Some Direct Evidence. *Amer. Econ. Rev.*, September 1985, *75*(4), pp. 638–55. [G: U.S.]

Fields, Gary S. and Jakubson, George. Labor Market Analysis Using SIPP. *J. Econ. Soc. Meas.*, December 1985, *13*(3–4), pp. 281–86. [G: U.S.]

Fitzpatrick, Sheila. Postwar Soviet Society: The "Return to Normalcy," 1945–1953. In *Linz, S. J., ed.*, 1985, pp. 129–56. [G: U.S.S.R.]

Gallie, Duncan. Directions for the Future. In *Roberts, B.; Finnegan, R. and Gallie, D., eds.*, 1985, pp. 512–30.

George, Kenneth D. and Shorey, John. Manual Workers, Good Jobs and Structured Internal Labour Markets. *Brit. J. Ind. Relat.*, November 1985, *23*(3), pp. 425–47. [G: U.K.]

Ginsburgh, Victor. Can a Real Wage Decrease Cure Unemployment? A General Equilibrium Analysis for Belgium. *Rech. Écon. Louvain*, 1985, *51*(3–4), pp. 381–86. [G: Belgium]

Gordon, Ian R. and Molho, Ian. Women in the Labour Markets of the London Region: A Model of Dependence and Constraint. *Urban Stud.*, October 1985, *22*(5), pp. 367–86. [G: U.K.]

Griliches, Zvi. Income-Maintenance Policy and Work Effort: Learning from Experiments and Labor-Market Studies: Comment. In *Hausman, J. A. and Wise, D. A., eds.*, 1985, pp. 137–38.

Hall, S. G., et al. Employment and Average Hours Worked in Manufacturing. *Brit. Rev. Econ. Issues*, Spring 1985, *7*(16), pp. 87–112. [G: U.K.]

Hanoch, Giora and Honig, Marjorie. "True" Age Profiles of Earnings: Adjusting for Censoring

and for Period and Cohort Effects. *Rev. Econ. Statist.*, August 1985, *67*(3), pp. 383–94. [G: U.S.]

Harrison, Bennett. Increasing Instability and Inequality in the "Revival" of the New England Economy. In *Richardson, H. W. and Turek, J. H., eds.*, 1985, pp. 123–49. [G: U.S.]

Hougland, James G., Jr. Industrial Sectors and Economic Outcomes: Experiences of Former CETA Participants. *Soc. Sci. Quart.*, December 1985, *66*(4), pp. 903–15. [G: U.S.]

Isachsen, Arne Jon and Strøm, Steinar. The Size and Growth of the Hidden Economy in Norway. *Rev. Income Wealth*, March 1985, *31*(1), pp. 21–38. [G: Norway]

Jones, Ian S. Skill Formation and Pay Relativities. In *Worswick, G. D. N., ed.*, 1985, pp. 25–39. [G: U.K.; W. Germany; Switzerland]

Jones, Stephen G. The Worksharing Debate in Western Europe. *Nat. Westminster Bank Quart. Rev.*, February 1985, pp. 30–41. [G: EEC]

King, Sandra L. and Williams, Harry B. Shift Work Pay Differentials and Practices in Manufacturing. *Mon. Lab. Rev.*, December 1985, *108*(12), pp. 26–33. [G: U.S.]

Kooreman, Peter and Kapteyn, Arie. The Systems Approach to Household Labor Supply in the Netherlands. *De Economist*, 1985, *133*(1), pp. 21–42. [G: Netherlands]

Levy, Michel Louis. Rapport salarial et transition dé ographique. (With English summary.) *Revue Écon. Polit.*, Sept.-Oct. 1985, *95*(5), pp. 555–67. [G: OECD]

Lin, Vivian. Women Factory Workers in Asian Export Processing Zones. In *Utrecht, E., ed.*, 1985, pp. 159–219. [G: Asia]

Macarov, David. The Prospect of Work in the Western Context. In *Didsbury, H. F., Jr., ed.*, 1985, pp. 76–108.

Marsden, David. Chronicle: Industrial Relations in the United Kingdom, August–November 1984: Statistical Background to the Industrial Relations Scene. *Brit. J. Ind. Relat.*, March 1985, *23*(1), pp. 139–58. [G: U.K.]

Mayhew, Ken. Reforming the Labour Market. *Oxford Rev. Econ. Policy*, Summer 1985, *1*(2), pp. 60–79. [G: U.K.]

McGavin, P. A. The Australian Labour Market, March 1985. *Australian Bull. Lab.*, March 1985, *11*(2), pp. 57–70. [G: Australia]

McGavin, P. A. and Kain, Peter. The Australian Labour Market September 1985. *Australian Bull. Lab.*, September 1985, *11*(4), pp. 193–211. [G: Australia]

McKinney, Fred. Employment Implications of a Changing Health-Care System. *Rev. Black Polit. Econ.*, Fall-Winter 1985-86, *14*(2–3), pp. 199–215. [G: U.S.]

McPherson, Michael S. The State of Academic Labor Markets. In *Smith, B. L. R., ed.*, 1985, pp. 57–83. [G: U.S.]

Meng, Ronald. An Empirical Test for Labor Market Segmentation of Males in Canada. *Ind.*

Relat., Spring 1985, *24*(2), pp. 280–87.
[G: Canada]

Myatt, Anthony. The Real Wage Employment Relationship: A Comment on the Time-Series Approach. *Appl. Econ.*, December 1985, *17*(6), pp. 947–53.
[G: Canada]

Nakamura, Alice and Nakamura, Masao. Dynamic Models of the Labor Force Behavior of Married Women Which Can Be Estimated Using Limited Amounts of Past Information. *J. Econometrics*, March 1985, *27*(3), pp. 273–98.
[G: U.S.]

Nelson, Valerie and Turner, Charles F. Estimates of Effects of Employment and Training Programs Derived from National Longitudinal Surveys and Continuous Longitudinal Manpower Survey. **In** *Betsey, C. L.; Hollister, R. G., Jr. and Papageorgiou, M. R., eds.*, 1985, pp. 254–80.
[G: U.S.]

Nickell, Stephen. The Government's Policy for Jobs: An Analysis. *Oxford Rev. Econ. Policy*, Summer 1985, *1*(2), pp. 98–115. [G: U.K.]

Niehaus, Richard J. Organizational Human Resource Policy Analysis in the 1980s. **In** *Niehaus, R. J., ed.*, 1985, pp. 1–44.

Oswald, Andrew J. and Turnbull, Peter J. Pay and Employment Determination in Britain: What Are Labour 'Contracts' Really Like? *Oxford Rev. Econ. Policy*, Summer 1985, *1*(2), pp. 80–97. [G: U.K.]

Paricio, Joaquina and Quesada, Javier. Wages and Employment in the Spanish Economy: Behavior and Trends during the Crisis. *Z. Wirtschaft. Sozialwissen.*, 1985, *105*(2/3), pp. 341–56. [G: Spain]

Pastore, José and Skidmore, Thomas E. Brazilian Labor Relations: A New Era? **In** *Juris, H.; Thompson, M. and Daniels, W., eds.*, 1985, pp. 73–113. [G: Brazil]

Pestieau, Pierre. Belgium's Irregular Economy. **In** *Gaertner, W. and Wenig, A., eds.*, 1985, pp. 144–60. [G: Belgium]

Petersen, Jørn Henrik. Alderspensionering, befolkningsudvikling og omfordeling mellem generationerne. (Old-age Pension, Fertility Behavior and Intergenerational Redistribution. With English summary.) *Nationaløkon. Tidsskr.*, 1985, *123*(3), pp. 298–318.
[G: Denmark]

Peterson, Richard B. Economic and Political Impacts on the Swedish Model of Industrial Relations. **In** *Juris, H.; Thompson, M. and Daniels, W., eds.*, 1985, pp. 301–36. [G: Sweden]

Potestio, Paola. The Relationship between Working Hours and Employment in Italian Manufacturing Industry between 1965 and 1983. *Rivista Polit. Econ.*, Suppl. Dec. 1985, *76*, pp. 121–44. [G: Italy]

Riveros, Luis A. Determinación de salarios y eficiencia del mercado laboral en la década del 70. (With English summary.) *Cuadernos Econ.*, April 1985, *22*(65), pp. 123–43.
[G: Chile]

Robinson, Chris and Tomes, Nigel. More on the Labour Supply of Canadian Women. *Can. J.*

Econ., February 1985, *18*(1), pp. 156–63.
[G: Canada]

Rose, Richard. Getting By in Three Economies: The Resources of the Official, Unofficial and Domestic Economies. **In** *Lane, J.-E., ed.*, 1985, pp. 103–41. [G: OECD]

Rosen, Sherwin. Income-Maintenance Policy and Work Effort: Learning from Experiments and Labor-Market Studies: Comment. **In** *Hausman, J. A. and Wise, D. A., eds.*, 1985, pp. 134–37. [G: U.S.]

Salvati, Michele. The Italian Inflation. **In** *Lindberg, L. N. and Maier, C. S., eds.*, 1985, pp. 509–63. [G: Italy; U.K.; France; W. Germany]

Schmähl, Winfried. Auswirkungen verkürzter Wochenarbeitszeit und vermehrter Teilzeitarbeit auf die Finanzlage der gesetzlichen Rentenversicherung in der Bundesrepublik Deutschland. (Effects of Reduced Weekly Working Time and Increased Part Time Work on the Budget of the Social Retirement System in the Federal Republic of Germany. With English Summary.) *Konjunkturpolitik*, 1985, *31*(4/5), pp. 285–99. [G: W. Germany]

Shah, Anup R. Wage/Job Security Contracts and Unionism. *Southern Econ. J.*, January 1985, *51*(3), pp. 849–59. [G: U.K.]

Sider, Hal. Work-related Accidents and the Production Process. *J. Human Res.*, Winter 1985, *20*(1), pp. 47–63. [G: U.S.]

Smith, James D. Market Motives in the Informal Economy. **In** *Gaertner, W. and Wenig, A., eds.*, 1985, pp. 161–77. [G: U.S.]

Stafford, Frank P. Income-Maintenance Policy and Work Effort: Learning from Experiments and Labor-Market Studies. **In** *Hausman, J. A. and Wise, D. A., eds.*, 1985, pp. 95–134.
[G: U.S.]

Stein, Bruno. Subterranean Labor Markets: A Conceptual Analysis. **In** *Gaertner, W. and Wenig, A., eds.*, 1985, pp. 37–44.

Steinherr, Alfred. Income Distribution and Employment in the European Communities 1960–1982. *Z. Wirtschaft. Sozialwissen.*, 1985, *105*(2/3), pp. 223–69. [G: EEC; U.S.; Japan]

Taira, Koji and Levine, Solomon B. Japan's Industrial Relations: A Social Compact Emerges. **In** *Juris, H.; Thompson, M. and Daniels, W., eds.*, 1985, pp. 247–300. [G: Japan]

Turek, Joseph H. The Northeast in a National Context: Background Trends in Population, Income, and Employment. **In** *Richardson, H. W. and Turek, J. H., eds.*, 1985, pp. 28–65. [G: U.S.]

Vose, W. J. Wiehahn and Riekert Revisited: A Review of Prevailing Black Labour Conditions in South Africa. *Int. Lab. Rev.*, July-Aug. 1985, *124*(4), pp. 447–64.

Waldinger, Roger. Immigrant Enterprise and the Structure of the Labour Market. **In** *Roberts, B.; Finnegan, R. and Gallie, D., eds.*, 1985, pp. 213–28. [G: U.S.]

Watanabe, Susumu. Employment and Income Implications of the "Bio-revolution": A Speculative Note. *Int. Lab. Rev.*, May-June 1985, *124*(3), pp. 281–97.   [G: LDCs; MDCs]

8241 Geographic Labor Market Studies

Bradbury, Katharine L. Prospects for Growth in New England: The Labor Force. *New Eng. Econ. Rev.*, Sept./Oct. 1985, pp. 50–60.
[G: U.S.]

Brown, Martin and Philips, Peter. The Evolution of Labor Market Structure: The California Canning Industry. *Ind. Lab. Relat. Rev.*, April 1985, *38*(3), pp. 392–407.   [G: U.S.]

Cebula, Richard J. Interstate per Capital Real Income Differentials. *Atlantic Econ. J.*, September 1985, *13*(3), pp. 97.   [G: U.S.]

Doolittle, Fred C. Adjustments in Buffalo's Labor Market. *Fed. Res. Bank New York Quart. Rev.*, Winter 1985-86, *10*(4), pp. 28–37.
[G: U.S.]

Drugge, Sten E. Nonneutral Technical Change and Regional Wage Differentials: A Comment. *J. Reg. Sci.*, February 1985, *25*(1), pp. 135–36.   [G: U.S.]

Gordon, Ian R. The Cyclical Sensitivity of Regional Employment and Unemployment Differentials. *Reg. Stud.*, April 1985, *19*(2), pp. 95–110.   [G: U.K.]

Green, A. E. Unemployment Duration in the Recession: The Local Labour Market Area Scale. *Reg. Stud.*, April 1985, *19*(2), pp. 111–29.
[G: U.K.]

Green, A. E. and Coombes, M. G. Local Unemployment Rates: Statistical Sensitivities and Policy Implications. *Reg. Stud.*, June 1985, *19*(3), pp. 268–73.   [G: U.K.]

Kleiner, Morris M. Metropolitan Area Labour Market Changes: Determinants and Comparisons by Industry. *Reg. Stud.*, April 1985, *19*(2), pp. 131–38.   [G: U.S.]

Macauley, Molly K. Estimation and Recent Behavior of Urban Population and Employment Density Gradients. *J. Urban Econ.*, September 1985, *18*(2), pp. 251–60.   [G: U.S.]

Maxwell, Philip. Growth, Decline and Structural Change: A Study of Regional Labour Markets in Australia 1971–1981. *Urban Stud.*, December 1985, *22*(6), pp. 493–505.   [G: Australia]

Santoni, G. J. Local Area Labor Statistics—A Phantom Army of the Unemployed? *Fed. Res. Bank St. Louis Rev.*, April 1985, *67*(4), pp. 5–14.   [G: U.S.]

8242 Wage, Hours, and Fringe Benefit Studies

Abowd, John M. and Killingsworth, Mark R. Employment, Wages, and Earnings of Hispanics in the Federal and Nonfederal Sectors: Methodological Issues and Their Empirical Consequences. In *Borjas, G. J. and Tienda, M., eds.,* 1985, pp. 77–125.   [G: U.S.]

Abraham, Katharine G. Shifting Norms in Wage Determination: Comment. *Brookings Pap. Econ. Act.*, 1985, (2), pp. 600–605. [G: U.S.]

Adamache, Killard W. and Sloan, Frank A. Fringe Benefits: To Tax or Not to Tax? *Nat.*

Tax J., March 1985, *38*(1), pp. 47–64.
[G: U.S.]

Adams, James D. Permanent Differences in Unemployment and Permanent Wage Differentials. *Quart. J. Econ.*, February 1985, *100*(1), pp. 29–56.   [G: U.S.]

Adiseshiah, Malcolm S. Wages and Incomes. In *Mongia, J. N., ed.,* 1985, pp. 349–84.
[G: India; Selected Countries]

Al-Qudsi, Sulayman S. Earnings Differences in the Labor Market of the Arab Gulf States: The Case of Kuwait. *J. Devel. Econ.*, May–June 1985, *18*(1), pp. 119–32.   [G: Kuwait; United Arab Emirates; Bahrain; Saudi Arabia; Qatar]

Aldabe, Hernán. The Impact of Social Security on Savings and Development: Comment. In *Mesa-Lago, C., ed.,* 1985, pp. 241–43.
[G: Chile]

Ambachtsheer, Keith P. "Pensions in the American Economy": A Review Article. *J. Portfol. Manage.*, Spring 1985, *11*(3), pp. 77–78.
[G: U.S.]

Anderson, Kathryn H. and Burkhauser, Richard V. The Retirement–Health Nexus: A New Measure of an Old Puzzle. *J. Human Res.*, Summer 1985, *20*(3), pp. 315–30.   [G: U.S.]

Anthony, Douglas. Managing Workforce Reduction: Japan. In *Cross, M., ed.,* 1985, pp. 91–129.   [G: Japan]

Arellano, José-Pablo. The Impact of Social Security on Savings and Development. In *Mesa-Lago, C., ed.,* 1985, pp. 217–40.   [G: Chile]

Armstrong, Muriel. Towards Equity: Summary of Proceedings. In *Economic Council of Canada.*, 1985, pp. 137–45.   [G: Canada]

Artis, Michael J. and Lewis, M. K. Inflation in the United Kingdom. In *Argy, V. E. and Neville, J. W., eds.,* 1985, pp. 200–220.
[G: U.K.]

Atwater, D. M.; Bres, E. S., III and Niehaus, Richard J. Human Resources Supply–Demand Policy Analysis Models. In *Niehaus, R. J., ed.,* 1985, pp. 92–120.   [G: U.S.]

Auerbach, Alan J. The Riskiness of Private Pensions: Comment. In *Wise, D. A., ed.,* 1985, pp. 375–78.

Banerjee, Biswajit and Knight, J. B. Caste Discrimination in the Indian Urban Labour Market. *J. Devel. Econ.*, April 1985, *17*(3), pp. 277–307.   [G: India]

Barron, John M.; Bishop, John and Dunkelberg, William C. Employer Search: The Interviewing and Hiring of New Employees. *Rev. Econ. Statist.*, February 1985, *67*(1), pp. 43–52.
[G: U.S.]

Barry, Janis. Women Production Workers: Low Pay and Hazardous Work. *Amer. Econ. Rev.*, May 1985, *75*(2), pp. 262–65.   [G: U.S.]

Beechey, Veronica and Perkins, Teresa. Conceptualising Part-Time Work. In *Roberts, B.; Finnegan, R. and Gallie, D., eds.,* 1985, pp. 246–63.   [G: U.K.]

Behrman, Jere R. and Birdsall, Nancy. The Quality of Schooling: Reply. *Amer. Econ. Rev.*, December 1985, *75*(5), pp. 1202–05. [G: Brazil]

Behrman, Jere R. and Tarbman, Paul. Intergenerational Earnings Mobility in the United States: Some Estimates and a Test of Becker's Intergenerational Endowments Model. *Rev. Econ. Statist.*, February 1985, *67*(1), pp. 144–51. [G: U.S.]

Behrman, Jere R.; Wolfe, Barbara L. and Blau, David M. Human Capital and Earnings Distribution in a Developing Country: The Case of Prerevolutionary Nicaragua. *Econ. Develop. Cult. Change*, October 1985, *34*(1), pp. 1–29. [G: Nicaragua]

Bell, Carolyn Shaw. Comparable Worth: How Do We Know It Will Work? *Mon. Lab. Rev.*, December 1985, *108*(12), pp. 5–12. [G: U.S.]

Ben-Porath, Yoram and Gronau, Reuben. Jewish Mother Goes to Work: Trends in the Labor Force Participation of Women in Israel, 1955–1980. *J. Lab. Econ.*, Part 2 January 1985, *3*(1), pp. S310–27. [G: Israel]

Berger, Mark C. The Effect of Cohort Size on Earnings Growth: A Reexamination of the Evidence. *J. Polit. Econ.*, June 1985, *93*(3), pp. 561–73. [G: U.S.]

Berger, Mark C. and Hirsch, Barry T. Veteran Status as a Screening Device during the Vietnam Era. *Soc. Sci. Quart.*, March 1985, *66*(1), pp. 79–89. [G: U.S.]

Bergmann, Barbara R. The Economic Case for Comparable Worth. In *Hartmann, H. I., ed.*, 1985, pp. 71–85. [G: U.S.]

Bettio, Francesca. The Secular Decrease of Sex-Linked Wage Differentials: A Case of Non Competition. *Econ. Lavoro*, July-Sept. 1985, *19*(3), pp. 31–56. [G: W. Europe; U.S.]

Bhattacherjee, Debashish. A Note on Caste Discrimination in a Bombay Automobile Firm. *Ind. Relat.*, Winter 1985, *24*(1), pp. 155–59. [G: India]

Biagioli, Mario. Contrattazione aziendale e differenziali retributivi interaziendali. (Workplace Bargaining and Wage Differentials among Firms. With English summary.) *Econ. Lavoro*, July-Sept. 1985, *19*(3), pp. 75–110. [G: Italy]

Bils, Mark J. Real Wages over the Business Cycle: Evidence from Panel Data. *J. Polit. Econ.*, August 1985, *93*(4), pp. 666–89. [G: U.S.]

Birdsall, Nancy and Fox, M. Louise. Why Males Earn More: Location and Training of Brazilian Schoolteachers. *Econ. Develop. Cult. Change*, April 1985, *33*(3), pp. 533–56. [G: Brazil]

Black, Boyd. Regional Earnings Convergence: The Case of Northern Ireland. *Reg. Stud.*, February 1985, *19*(1), pp. 1–7. [G: U.K.]

Blau, David M. Self-Employment and Self-Selection in Developing Country Labor Markets. *Southern Econ. J.*, October 1985, *52*(2), pp. 351–63. [G: Malaysia]

Blau, David M. The Effects of Economic Development on Life Cycle Wage Rates and Labor Supply Behavior in Malaysia. *J. Devel. Econ.*, Sept.-Oct. 1985, *19*(1/2), pp. 163–85. [G: Malaysia]

Block, Walter. Towards Equity: Directions for Future Research: Panel Discussion. In *Economic Council of Canada.*, 1985, pp. 119–21. [G: Canada]

Boamah, Daniel O. Wage Formation, Employment and Output in Barbados. *Soc. Econ. Stud.*, December 1985, *34*(4), pp. 199–218. [G: Barbados]

Bodie, Zvi. Labor Compensation and the Structure of Private Pension Plans: Evidence for Contractual versus Spot Labor Markets: Comment. In *Wise, D. A., ed.*, 1985, pp. 85–87. [G: U.S.]

Bodie, Zvi. Pensions and the Labor Market: A Starting Point (The Mouse Can Roar): Comment. In *Wise, D. A., ed.*, 1985, pp. 50–53. [G: U.S.]

Bodo, Giorgio and Giannini, Curzio. Average Working Time and the Influence of Contractual Hours: An Empirical Investigation for the Italian Industry (1970–1981). *Oxford Bull. Econ. Statist.*, May 1985, *47*(2), pp. 131–51. [G: Italy]

Boissiere, M.; Knight, J. B. and Sabot, R. H. Earnings, Schooling, Ability, and Cognitive Skills. *Amer. Econ. Rev.*, December 1985, *75*(5), pp. 1016–30. [G: Kenya; Tanzania]

Booton, Lavonne A. and Lane, Julia. Hospital Market Structure and the Return to Nursing Education. *J. Human Res.*, Spring 1985, *20*(2), pp. 184–96. [G: U.S.]

Borjas, George J. Assimilation, Changes in Cohort Quality, and the Earnings of Immigrants. *J. Lab. Econ.*, October 1985, *3*(4), pp. 463–89. [G: U.S.]

Bourguignon, François and Morrisson, Christian. Une analyse de décomposition de l'inégalite des revenus individuels en France. (A Decomposition Analysis of Income Inequality in France. With English summary.) *Revue Écon.*, July 1985, *36*(4), pp. 741–77. [G: France]

Bradshaw, Jonathan. Social Security Policy and Assumptions about Patterns of Work. In *Klein, R. and O'Higgins, M., ed.*, 1985, pp. 204–15. [G: U.K.]

Brinner, Roger E. and Kline, Kenneth J. A New Market Realism: Wage Moderation. *Challenge*, Sept./Oct. 1985, *28*(4), pp. 27–29. [G: U.S.]

Brockway, George P. Executive Salaries and Their Justification. *J. Post Keynesian Econ.*, Winter 1984–85, *7*(2), pp. 168–76.

Brown, Martin and Philips, Peter. The Evolution of Labor Market Structure: The California Canning Industry. *Ind. Lab. Relat. Rev.*, April 1985, *38*(3), pp. 392–407. [G: U.S.]

Brown, William. The Effect of Recent Changes in the World Economy on British Industrial Relations. In *Juris, H.; Thompson, M. and Daniels, W., eds.*, 1985, pp. 151–75. [G: U.K.]

Bruggink, Thomas H., et al. Direct and Indirect Effects of Unionization on the Wage Levels of Nurses: A Case Study of New Jersey Hospitals. *J. Lab. Res.*, Fall 1985, *6*(4), pp. 405–16. [G: U.S.]

Brush, Brian C. and Crane, Steven E. The Effect of Market Power on the Fringe Benefit Share of Labor Compensation. *Quart. J. Bus. Econ.*,

Autumn 1985, *24*(4), pp. 70–84.   [G: U.S.]

Buchele, Robert and Aldrich, Mark. How Much Difference Would Comparable Worth Make? *Ind. Relat.*, Spring 1985, *24*(2), pp. 222–33.
[G: U.S.]

Buckley, John E. Wage Differences among Workers in the Same Job and Establishment. *Mon. Lab. Rev.*, March 1985, *108*(3), pp. 11–16.
[G: U.S.]

Buiter, Willem H. The Real Wage Gap and Employment: Comments. In *Melitz, J. and Wyplosz, C., eds.*, 1985, pp. 71–80. [G: France; U.S.; EEC]

Bulow, Jeremy I. and Landsman, Wayne. The Relationship between Wages and Benefits. In *Wise, D. A., ed.*, 1985, pp. 379–94.
[G: U.S.]

Burbridge, Lynn C. Black Women in Employment and Training Programs. *Rev. Black Polit. Econ.*, Fall-Winter 1985-86, *14*(2–3), pp. 97–114.   [G: U.S.]

Burtless, Gary. Social Security, Health Status, and Retirement: Comment. In *Wise, D. A., ed.*, 1985, pp. 181–91.   [G: U.S.]

Byrne, Dennis M. and Stratton, Richard W. The Impact of Family Disruption on the Earnings of Children. *Soc. Sci. Quart.*, December 1985, *66*(4), pp. 924–32.   [G: U.S.]

Cain, Pamela Stone. Prospects for Pay Equity in a Changing Economy. In *Hartmann, H. I., ed.*, 1985, pp. 137–65.   [G: U.S.]

Cameron, Samuel. Inter-industry Variations in the Wage-Rates of Adult Male Manual Workers. *Scot. J. Polit. Econ.*, November 1985, *32*(3), pp. 296–314.

Cameron, Samuel. Marriage and the Distribution of Employment Incomes. *Appl. Econ.*, February 1985, *17*(1), pp. 33–40.

Capen, Margaret M.; Cohn, Elchanan and Ellson, Richard Wayne. Labour Supply Effects of Unemployment Insurance Benefits. *Appl. Econ.*, February 1985, *17*(1), pp. 73–85.
[G: U.S.]

Cappelli, Peter. Fair Wages and the Industrial Civil Service. *Scot. J. Polit. Econ.*, February 1985, *32*(1), pp. 55–66.   [G: U.K.]

Carline, Derek. Trade Unions and Wages. In *Carline, D., et al.*, 1985, pp. 186–232.
[G: U.K.; U.S.]

Carliner, Geoffrey and McKee, Michael J. Designing a Tax Incentive Scheme: The Case of a Wage TIP. *J. Policy Anal. Manage.*, Summer 1985, *4*(4), pp. 501–15.   [G: U.S.]

Carruth, Alan A. and Oswald, Andrew J. Miners' Wages in Post-war Britain: An Application of a Model of Trade Union Behaviour. *Econ. J.*, December 1985, *95*(380), pp. 1003–20.
[G: U.K.]

Carvajal, Manuel J. and Geithman, David T. Income, Human Capital and Sex Discrimination: Some Evidence from Costa Rica, 1963 and 1973. *J. Econ. Devel.*, July 1985, *10*(1), pp. 89–115.   [G: Costa Rica]

Caves, Richard E. Income Distribution and Labor Relations. In *Moran, T. H., ed.*, 1985, pp. 173–98.   [G: U.S.]

Chambers, Jay G. Patterns of Compensation of Public and Private School Teachers. *Econ. Educ. Rev.*, 1985, *4*(4), pp. 291–310.
[G: U.S.]

Chang, Yang-Ming and Ehrlich, Isaac. On the Economics of Compliance with the Minimum Wage Law. *J. Polit. Econ.*, February 1985, *93*(1), pp. 84–91.

Chapman, Bruce J. Sex and Location Differences in Wages in the Australian Public Service. *Australian Econ. Pap.*, December 1985, *24*(45), pp. 296–309.   [G: Australia]

Chapman, Bruce J. and Harding, J. Ross. Sex Differences in Earnings: An Analysis of Malaysian Wage Data. *J. Devel. Stud.*, April 1985, *21*(3), pp. 362–76.   [G: Malaysia]

Chaykowski, Richard P. and Beach, Charles M. Prizes in an Industrial Union Environment. *J. Lab. Res.*, Spring 1985, *6*(2), pp. 181–98.
[G: Canada]

Chirikos, Thomas N. and Nestel, Gilbert. Further Evidence on the Economic Effects of Poor Health. *Rev. Econ. Statist.*, February 1985, *67*(1), pp. 61–69.   [G: U.S.]

Chiswick, Barry R. and Miller, Paul W. Immigrant Generation and Income in Australia. *Econ. Rec.*, June 1985, *61*(173), pp. 540–53.
[G: Australia]

Choe, Yang Boo. Development of Rural Non-farm Activities and Industries in Korea. In *Mukhopadhyay, S. and Chee, P. L., eds. (I)*, 1985, pp. 309–82.   [G: S. Korea]

Christofides, Louis N. The Impact of Controls on Wage Contract Duration. *Econ. J.*, March 1985, *95*(377), pp. 161–68.   [G: Canada]

Christofides, Louis N. and Wilton, David A. Wage Determination in the Aftermath of Controls. *Economica*, February 1985, *52*(205), pp. 51–64.   [G: Canada]

Clark, Gordon L. The Spatial Division of Labor and Wage and Price Controls of the Nixon Administration. *Econ. Geogr.*, April 1985, *61*(2), pp. 113–28.   [G: U.S.]

Coe, David T. Nominal Wages, the Nairu and Wage Flexibility. *OECD Econ. Stud.*, Autumn 1985, (5), pp. 87–126.   [G: OECD]

Cohen, Suleiman I. Rates of Returns to Education and the Determinants of Earnings in Pakistan: Comments. *Pakistan Devel. Rev.*, Autumn-Winter 1985, *24*(3/4), pp. 681–83.
[G: Pakistan]

Coles, Jeffrey Link and Harte-Chen, Paul. Real Wage Indices. *J. Lab. Econ.*, July 1985, *3*(3), pp. 317–36.   [G: U.S.]

Collier, Paul and Knight, J. B. Seniority Payments, Quit Rates, and Internal Labour Markets in Britain and Japan. *Oxford Bull. Econ. Statist.*, February 1985, *47*(1), pp. 19–32.
[G: U.K.; Japan]

Colombino, Ugo and De Stavola, Bianca. A Model of Female Labor Supply in Italy Using Cohort Data. *J. Lab. Econ.*, Part 2 January 1985, *3*(1), pp. S275–92.   [G: Italy]

Corcoran, Mary E. and Courant, Paul N. Sex Role Socialization and Labor Market Outcomes. *Amer. Econ. Rev.*, May 1985, 75(2), pp. 275–78. [G: U.S.]

Cotton, Jeremiah. A Comparative Analysis of Black–White and Mexican-American–White Male Wage Differentials. *Rev. Black Polit. Econ.*, Spring 1985, 13(4), pp. 51–69. [G: U.S.]

Cotton, Jeremiah. More on the "Cost" of Being a Black or Mexican American Male Worker. *Soc. Sci. Quart.*, December 1985, 66(4), pp. 867–85. [G: U.S.]

Coulombe, Serge and Lavoie, Marc. Les francophones dans la ligue nationale de hockey: une analyse économique de la discrimination (Francophones in the National Hockey League: A Comment Followed by an Economic Analysis of Discrimination. With English summary.) *L'Actual. Econ.*, March 1985, 61(1), pp. 73–92. [G: Canada]

Crafts, N. F. R. English Workers' Real Wages during the Industrial Revolution: Some Remaining Problems. *J. Econ. Hist.*, March 1985, 45(1), pp. 139–44. [G: U.K.]

Craig, Christine; Garnsey, Elizabeth and Rubery, Jill. Labour Market Segmentation and Women's Employment: A Case-Study from the United Kingdom. *Int. Lab. Rev.*, May-June 1985, 124(3), pp. 267–80. [G: U.K.]

Cymrot, Donald J. Earnings Growth and Pension Coverage: Comment. *Southern Econ. J.*, April 1985, 51(4), pp. 1245–48. [G: U.S.]

Datta, Ramesh C. Schooling, Experience and Earnings: An Empirical Analysis. *Margin*, January 1985, 17(2), pp. 60–73. [G: India]

David-McNeil, Jeannine. The Changing Economic Status of the Female Labour Force in Canada. In *Economic Council of Canada.*, 1985, pp. 1–8. [G: Canada]

Davila, Alberto E. and Mattila, J. Peter. Do Workers Earn Less along the U.S.–Mexico Border? *Soc. Sci. Quart.*, June 1985, 66(2), pp. 310–18. [G: U.S.]

Davis, Evan H. and Dilnot, Andrew W. The Restructuring of National Insurance Contributions in the 1985 Budget. *Fisc. Stud.*, May 1985, 6(2), pp. 51–60. [G: U.K.]

Dawkins, Peter. Penalty Rates and the Review of the Principles. *Australian Bull. Lab.*, June 1985, 11(3), pp. 178–88. [G: Australia]

Dawkins, Peter. The Australian Labour Market, June 1985. *Australian Bull. Lab.*, June 1985, 11(3), pp. 105–23. [G: Australia]

Dawkins, Peter and Blandy, Richard. Labour Costs and the Future of the Accord. *Australian Econ. Rev.*, 2nd Quarter 1985, (70), pp. 37–50. [G: Australia]

Dawkins, Peter and Wooden, Mark. Labour Utilization and Wage Inflation in Australia: An Empirical Examination. *Econ. Rec.*, June 1985, 61(173), pp. 516–21. [G: Australia]

De Gijsel, Peter. A Microeconomic Analysis of Black Labour Demand and Supply. In *Gaertner, W. and Wenig, A., eds.*, 1985, pp. 218–26.

DeFina, Robert H. Union–Nonunion Wage Differentials and the Functional Distribution of Income: Some Simulation Results from a General Equilibrium Model. *J. Lab. Res.*, Summer 1985, 6(3), pp. 263–79.

Deutsch, Antal. Review of "Building Better Pensions for Canadians." *Can. Public Policy*, September 1985, 11(3), pp. 617–22. [G: Canada]

Diamond, Peter A. and Mirrlees, James A. Insurance Aspects of Pensions. In *Wise, D. A., ed.*, 1985, pp. 317–43.

Dogas, D. Market Power in a Bilateral Monopoly Model of Industry Wage Determination. *Appl. Econ.*, February 1985, 17(1), pp. 149–64. [G: U.K.]

Donovan, Edmund T. The Retirement Equity Act of 1984: A Review. *Soc. Sec. Bull.*, May 1985, 48(5), pp. 38–44. [G: U.S.]

Dooley, Martin and Gottschalk, Peter. The Increasing Proportion of Men with Low Earnings in the United States. *Demography*, February 1985, 22(1), pp. 25–34. [G: U.S.]

Dorsey, Stuart. Earnings Growth and Pension Coverage: Reply. *Southern Econ. J.*, April 1985, 51(4), pp. 1249–51. [G: U.S.]

Dulude, Louise. Fringe Benefits and the Female Workforce. In *Economic Council of Canada.*, 1985, pp. 71–78. [G: Canada]

Duncan, Gregory M. and Leigh, Duane E. The Endogeneity of Union Status: An Empirical Test. *J. Lab. Econ.*, July 1985, 3(3), pp. 385–402.

Dye, Richard F. Payroll Tax Effects on Wage Growth. *Eastern Econ. J.*, April-June 1985, 11(2), pp. 89–100. [G: U.S.]

Eaton, Peter J. The Quality of Schooling: Comment. *Amer. Econ. Rev.*, December 1985, 75(5), pp. 1195–1201. [G: Brazil]

Eberts, Randall W. and Stone, Joe A. Wages, Fringe Benefits, and Working Conditions: An Analysis of Compensating Differentials. *Southern Econ. J.*, July 1985, 52(1), pp. 274–80. [G: U.S.]

Edgecombe Robb, Roberta. Equal-Pay Policy. In *Economic Council of Canada.*, 1985, pp. 61–70. [G: Canada]

Ellis, Randall P. The Effect of Prior-Year Health Expenditures on Health Coverage Plan Choice. In *Scheffler, R. M. and Rossiter, L. F., eds.*, 1985, pp. 149–70. [G: U.S.]

Ellwood, David T. Pensions and the Labor Market: A Starting Point (The Mouse Can Roar). In *Wise, D. A., ed.*, 1985, pp. 19–49. [G: U.S.]

Estrin, Saul and Svejnar, Jan. Explanations of Earnings in Yugoslavia: The Capital and Labour Schools Compared. *Econ. Anal. Worker's Manage.*, 1985, 19(1), pp. 1–12. [G: Yugoslavia]

Fagan, Christine A. Fringe Benefits and the Female Workforce: Comments. In *Economic Council of Canada.*, 1985, pp. 79–81. [G: Canada]

Feenberg, Daniel. The Relationship between Wages and Benefits: Comment. In *Wise, D. A., ed.*, 1985, pp. 394–97. [G: U.S.]

Ferber, Marianne A. and Green, Carole A. Homemakers' Imputed Wages: Results of the

Heckman Technique Compared with Women's Own Estimates. *J. Human Res.*, Winter 1985, *20*(1), pp. 90–99. [G: U.S.]

Ferrara, Peter J. Private Alternatives to Social Security: The Experience of Other Countries: Comment. In *Ferrara, P. J., ed.*, 1985, pp. 113–15. [G: U.K.]

Ferrara, Peter J. Social Security and the Super IRA: A Populist Proposal. In *Ferrara, P. J., ed.*, 1985, pp. 193–220. [G: U.S.]

Feuille, Peter; Delaney, John Thomas and Hendricks, Wallace. Police Bargaining, Arbitration, and Fringe Benefits. *J. Lab. Res.*, Winter 1985, *6*(1), pp. 1–20. [G: U.S.]

Fields, Gary S. Industrialization and Employment in Hong Kong, Singapore, and Taiwan. In *Galenson, W., ed.*, 1985, pp. 333–75. [G: Hong Kong; Singapore; S. Korea; Taiwan]

Filer, Randall K. Male–Female Wage Differences: The Importance of Compensating Differentials. *Ind. Lab. Relat. Rev.*, April 1985, *38*(3), pp. 426–37. [G: U.S.]

FitzRoy, Felix R. and Kraft, Kornelius. Unionization, Wages and Efficiency: Theories and Evidence from the U.S. and West Germany. *Kyklos*, 1985, *38*(4), pp. 537–54. [G: U.S.; W. Germany]

Flaim, Paul O. and Sehgal, Ellen. Displaced Workers of 1979–83: How Well Have They Fared? *Mon. Lab. Rev.*, June 1985, *108*(6), pp. 3–16. [G: U.S.]

Foster, James C. *The Western Dilemma:* Miners, Silicosis, and Compensation. *Labor Hist.*, Spring 1985, *26*(2), pp. 268–87. [G: U.S.]

Franz, Wolfgang. An Economic Analysis of Female Work Participation, Education, and Fertility: Theory and Empirical Evidence for the Federal Republic of Germany. *J. Lab. Econ.*, Part 2 January 1985, *3*(1), pp. S218–34. [G: W. Germany]

Fredland, J. Eric and Little, Roger D. Socioeconomic Status of World War II Veterans by Race: An Empirical Test of the Bridging Hypothesis. *Soc. Sci. Quart.*, September 1985, *66*(3), pp. 533–51. [G: U.S.]

Freeman, Richard B. Unions, Pensions, and Union Pension Funds. In *Wise, D. A., ed.*, 1985, pp. 89–118. [G: U.S.]

Fuchs, Victor R. Determinants of Pension Benefits: Comment. In *Wise, D. A., ed.*, 1985, pp. 153–57. [G: U.S.]

Fujii, Edwin T. and Mak, James. On the Relative Economic Progress of U.S.-born Filipino Men. *Econ. Develop. Cult. Change*, April 1985, *33*(3), pp. 557–73. [G: U.S.]

Fulco, Lawrence J. Productivity and Costs in 1984. *Mon. Lab. Rev.*, June 1985, *108*(6), pp. 40–43. [G: U.S.]

García de Blas, Antonio. Unemployment Benefits in Spain and Other European OECD Countries. *Int. Lab. Rev.*, March-April 1985, *124*(2), pp. 147–61. [G: Spain; OECD]

Garcia-Ramon, M. Dolores. Agricultural Change in an Industrializing Area: The Case of the Tarragona Area. In *Hudson, R. and Lewis, J., eds.*, 1985, pp. 140–54. [G: Spain]

Garen, John E. The Trade-off between Wages and Wage Growth. *J. Human Res.*, Fall 1985, *20*(4), pp. 522–39. [G: U.S.]

Garen, John E. Worker Heterogeneity, Job Screening, and Firm Size. *J. Polit. Econ.*, August 1985, *93*(4), pp. 715–39. [G: U.S.]

Gärtner, Manfred. Political and Industrial Change in a Model of Trade Union Militancy and Real Wage Growth. *Rev. Econ. Statist.*, May 1985, *67*(2), pp. 322–27. [G: W. Germany]

Gärtner, Manfred. Strikes and the Real Wage–Employment Nexus: A Hicksian Analysis of Industrial Disputes and Pay. *J. Lab. Res.*, Summer 1985, *6*(3), pp. 323–36. [G: W. Germany]

Ginsburg, Helen. Flexible and Partial Retirement for Norwegian and Swedish Workers. *Mon. Lab. Rev.*, October 1985, *108*(10), pp. 33–43. [G: Norway; Sweden]

Gleason, Sandra E. Comparable Worth: Some Questions Still Unanswered. *Mon. Lab. Rev.*, December 1985, *108*(12), pp. 17–18. [G: U.S.]

Glynn, Sean; Booth, Alan and Howells, Peter. NEH, NEH, NEH and the 'Keynesian Solution' [Unemployment in the 1930s: The Keynesian Solution Reconsidered]. *Australian Econ. Hist. Rev.*, September 1985, *25*(2), pp. 149–57. [G: U.K.]

Goldenberg, Edie N. The Grace Commission and Civil Service Reform: Seeking a Common Understanding. In *Levine, C. H., ed.*, 1985, pp. 69–94. [G: U.S.]

Goodman, John C. Private Alternatives to Social Security: The Experience of Other Countries. In *Ferrara, P. J., ed.*, 1985, pp. 103–12. [G: U.K.]

Gordon, Roger H. Incentive Effects of Pensions: Comment. In *Wise, D. A., ed.*, 1985, pp. 278–82.

Green, Francis; Hadjimatheou, George and Smail, Robin. Fringe Benefit Distribution in Britain. *Brit. J. Ind. Relat.*, July 1985, *23*(2), pp. 261–80. [G: U.K.]

Green, Jerry R. The Riskiness of Private Pensions. In *Wise, D. A., ed.*, 1985, pp. 357–75.

Gregory, Mary; Lobban, Peter and Thomson, Andrew. Wage Settlements in Manufacturing, 1979–84: Evidence from the CBI Pay Databank. *Brit. J. Ind. Relat.*, November 1985, *23*(3), pp. 339–57. [G: U.K.]

Gregory, R. G.; McMahon, P. J. and Whittingham, B. Women in the Australian Labor Force: Trends, Causes, and Consequences. *J. Lab. Econ.*, Part 2 January 1985, *3*(1), pp. S293–309. [G: Australia]

Grubb, David B. Ability and Power over Production in the Distribution of Earnings. *Rev. Econ. Statist.*, May 1985, *67*(2), pp. 188–94. [G: W. Europe; U.S.; Australia]

Guha, Sumit. Some Aspects of Rural Economy in the Deccan 1820–1940. In *Raj, K. N., et al., eds.*, 1985, pp. 210–46. [G: India]

Gustafson, Elizabeth F. and Hadley, Lawrence H. An Empirical Analysis of the Distributional Effects of Inflation on Wage Income by Occupation: 1969–1977. *Quart. J. Bus. Econ.*, Autumn 1985, *24*(4), pp. 29–43. [G: U.S.]

Gustafsson, Siv and Jacobsson, Roger. Trends in Female Labor Force Participation in Sweden. *J. Lab. Econ.*, Part 2 January 1985, *3*(1), pp. S256–74. [G: Sweden]

Gustman, Alan L. and Steinmeier, Thomas L. The Effect of Partial Retirement on the Wage Profiles of Older Workers. *Ind. Relat.*, Spring 1985, *24*(2), pp. 257–65. [G: U.S.]

Hamel, Harvey R. Technical Note: New Data Series on Involuntary Part-Time Work. *Mon. Lab. Rev.*, March 1985, *108*(3), pp. 42–43. [G: U.S.]

Hamermesh, Daniel S. Substitution between Different Categories of Labour, Relative Wages and Youth Unemployment. *OECD Econ. Stud.*, Autumn 1985, (5), pp. 57–85. [G: OECD]

Hancock, Keith and Richardson, Sue. Discount Rates and the Distribution of Lifetime Earnings. *J. Human Res.*, Summer 1985, *20*(3), pp. 346–60. [G: Australia]

Hannah, Leslie. Why Employer-based Pension Plans? The Case of Britain. *J. Econ. Hist.*, June 1985, *45*(2), pp. 347–54. [G: U.K.]

Hansen, Richard B. A Test of the Hansen–Weisbrod–Strauss Model of Faculty Salaries. *Atlantic Econ. J.*, September 1985, *13*(3), pp. 33–40. [G: U.S.]

Hanushek, Eric A. and Quigley, John M. Life-Cycle Earning Capacity and the OJT Investment Model. *Int. Econ. Rev.*, June 1985, *26*(2), pp. 365–85. [G: U.S.]

Hart, Robert A. Wage Supplements through Collective Agreement or Statutory Requirement? *Kyklos*, 1985, *38*(1), pp. 20–42. [G: OECD]

Hartmann, Heidi I.; Roos, Patricia A. and Treiman, Donald J. An Agenda for Basic Research on Comparable Worth. In *Hartmann, H. I., ed.*, 1985, pp. 3–33. [G: U.S.]

Hartog, Joop and Theeuwes, Jules. The Emergence of the Working Wife in Holland. *J. Lab. Econ.*, Part 2 January 1985, *3*(1), pp. S235–55. [G: Holland]

Hashimoto, Masanori and Raisian, John. Employment Tenure and Earnings Profiles in Japan and the United States. *Amer. Econ. Rev.*, September 1985, *75*(4), pp. 721–35. [G: Japan; U.S.]

Hatton, T. J. Unemployment in the 1930s and the 'Keynesian Solution': Some Notes of Dissent. *Australian Econ. Hist. Rev.*, September 1985, *25*(2), pp. 129–48. [G: U.K.]

Hausman, Jerry A. and Wise, David A. Social Security, Health Status, and Retirement. In *Wise, D. A., ed.*, 1985, pp. 159–81. [G: U.S.]

Heckman, James J. and Sedlacek, Guilherme. Heterogeneity, Aggregation, and Market Wage Functions: An Empirical Model of Self-selection in the Labor Market. *J. Polit. Econ.*, December 1985, *93*(6), pp. 1077–1125. [G: U.S.]

Henderson, A. G. A Comparison of Japanese and Australian Labour Markets. *Australian Bull. Lab.*, December 1985, *12*(1), pp. 22–45. [G: Australia; Japan]

Hernandez Iglesias, Feliciano and Riboud, Michelle. Trends in Labor Force Participation of Spanish Women: An Interpretive Essay. *J. Lab. Econ.*, Part 2 January 1985, *3*(1), pp. S201–17. [G: Spain]

Hersch, Joni. Effect of Housework on Earnings of Husbands and Wives: Evidence from Full-Time Piece Rate Workers. *Soc. Sci. Quart.*, March 1985, *66*(1), pp. 210–17. [G: U.S.]

Hersch, Joni and Stone, Joe A. "New and Improved" Estimates of Qualification Discrimination. *Southern Econ. J.*, October 1985, *52*(2), pp. 484–91. [G: U.S.]

Herzog, Henry W., Jr.; Hofler, Richard A. and Schlottmann, Alan M. Life on the Frontier: Migrant Information, Earnings and Past Mobility. *Rev. Econ. Statist.*, August 1985, *67*(3), pp. 373–82. [G: U.S.]

Hicks, Peter. A National System for Parental Leave: Comments. In *Economic Council of Canada.*, 1985, pp. 28–29. [G: Canada]

Hochmuth, Milton. Revitalizing American Industry: Analysis and Summary. In *Hochmuth, M. and Davidson, W., eds.*, 1985, pp. 375–95. [G: Selected Countries]

Hofler, Richard A. and Polachek, Solomon William. A New Approach for Measuring Wage Ignorance in the Labor Market. *J. Econ. Bus.*, August 1985, *37*(3), pp. 267–76. [G: U.S.]

Hojman, David E. The Phillips Curve and Minimum Wage Rates in LDC's: The Brazilian Experience. *J. Econ. Devel.*, December 1985, *10*(2), pp. 161–69. [G: Brazil]

Holden, Karen C. Maintaining Faculty Vitality through Early Retirement Options. In *Clark, S. M. and Lewis, D. R., eds.*, 1985, pp. 224–44. [G: U.S.]

Hosay, Cynthia K. The Impact of Medicare Reform on the Private Sector: Remarks. In *Employee Benefit Research Institute.*, 1985, pp. 72–77. [G: U.S.]

Hosay, Cynthia K. The Impact of Medicare Reform on the Private Sector. In *Employee Benefit Research Institute.*, 1985, pp. 65–72. [G: U.S.]

Hu, Sheng-Cheng. The Growth in Pension Saving. In *Hendershott, P. H., ed.*, 1985, pp. 235–66. [G: U.S.]

Hunt, Janet C.; Hill, C. R. and Kiker, B. F. The Effect of Taxation on Labour Supply: The Case of Moonlighting. *Appl. Econ.*, October 1985, *17*(5), pp. 897–905. [G: U.S.]

Hunt, Janet C. and Kau, James B. Migration and Wage Growth: A Human Capital Approach. *Southern Econ. J.*, January 1985, *51*(3), pp. 697–710. [G: U.S.]

Hylleberg, Svend and Paldam, Martin. Price and Wages in the OECD Area 1913–1980—A Study of the Time Series Evidence. *Z. Wirtschaft.*

Sozialwissen., 1985, *105*(2/3), pp. 193–221.
[G: OECD]

Ignagni, Karen. Organized Labor's Perspective on Rising Health Costs. In *Dennis, B. D., ed.*, 1985, pp. 473–76. [G: U.S.]

Ippolito, Richard A. The Economic Function of Underfunded Pension Plans. *J. Law Econ.*, October 1985, *28*(3), pp. 611–51. [G: U.S.]

Ippolito, Richard A. The Labor Contract and True Economic Pension Liabilities. *Amer. Econ. Rev.*, December 1985, *75*(5), pp. 1031–43. [G: U.S.]

Irfan, Mohammad and Ahmed, Meekal Aziz. Real Wages in Pakistan: Structure and Trends, 1970–84. *Pakistan Devel. Rev.*, Autumn-Winter 1985, *24*(3/4), pp. 423–37. [G: Pakistan]

Isaac, J. E. Continuity and Change in Australian Wages Policy: Comment. *Australian Econ. Rev.*, 3rd Quarter, Spring 1985, (71), pp. 68–69. [G: Australia]

Jenkins, Alexander W. The Analysis of Wage Formation with Application to Alberta Construction. *Appl. Econ.*, October 1985, *17*(5), pp. 907–21. [G: Canada]

Johnson, George E. Investment in and Returns from Education. In *Hendershott, P. H., ed.*, 1985, pp. 267–95. [G: U.S.]

Johnson, William G. and Lambrinos, James. Wage Discrimination against Handicapped Men and Women. *J. Human Res.*, Spring 1985, *20*(2), pp. 264–77. [G: U.S.]

Katz, Avery and Mankiw, N. Gregory. How Should Fringe Benefits Be Taxed? *Nat. Tax J.*, March 1985, *38*(1), pp. 37–46. [G: U.S.]

Kelton, Christina M. L. Earnings Behavior in Food and Tobacco Manufacturing. *Rev. Ind. Organ.*, 1985, *2*(3), pp. 266–91. [G: U.S.]

Khan, M. Fahim. Real Wages in Pakistan: Structure and Trends, 1970–84: Comments. *Pakistan Devel. Rev.*, Autumn-Winter 1985, *24*(3/4), pp. 438–40. [G: Pakistan]

Khan, Shahrukh Rafi and Irfan, Mohammad. Rates of Returns to Education and the Determinants of Earnings in Pakistan. *Pakistan Devel. Rev.*, Autumn-Winter 1985, *24*(3/4), pp. 671–80. [G: Pakistan]

Kiker, B. F. and Heath, Julia A. The Effect of Socioeconomic Background on Earnings: A Comparison by Race. *Econ. Educ. Rev.*, 1985, *4*(1), pp. 45–55. [G: U.S.]

Killingsworth, Mark R. The Economics of Comparable Worth: Analytical, Empirical, and Policy Questions. In *Hartmann, H. I., ed.*, 1985, pp. 86–115.

Kirwan, Frank. Migration and Emigrants' Remittances: Theory and Evidence from the Middle East. In *Lundahl, M., ed.*, 1985, pp. 253–70. [G: Jordan]

Koeller, C. Timothy. Wages, Trade Union Activity, and the Political Environment of Unionism: A Simultaneous Equation Model. *J. Lab. Res.*, Spring 1985, *6*(2), pp. 147–65. [G: U.S.]

Kolluri, Bharat R. and Piette, Michael J. The Determinants of the Salaries of Chief Academic Administrators. *Atlantic Econ. J.*, July 1985, *13*(2), pp. 61–68. [G: U.S.]

Kotlikoff, Laurence J. and Wise, David A. Labor Compensation and the Structure of Private Pension Plans: Evidence for Contractual versus Spot Labor Markets. In *Wise, D. A., ed.*, 1985, pp. 55–85. [G: U.S.]

Koziara, Karen Shallcross. Comparable Worth: Organizational Dilemmas. *Mon. Lab. Rev.*, December 1985, *108*(12), pp. 13–16. [G: U.S.]

Kreinin, Mordechai E. Wage Competitiveness in the U.S. Auto and Steel Industries. In *Adams, J., ed.*, 1985, pp. 174–88. [G: U.S.]

Krugman, Paul R. The Real Wage Gap and Employment. In *Melitz, J. and Wyplosz, C., eds.*, 1985, pp. 51–69. [G: France; U.S.; EEC]

Kumar, Pradeep and Stengos, Thanasis. Measuring the Union Relative Wage Impact: A Methodological Note. *Can. J. Econ.*, February 1985, *18*(1), pp. 182–89. [G: Canada]

Kunze, Kent. Hours at Work Increase Relative to Hours Paid. *Mon. Lab. Rev.*, June 1985, *108*(6), pp. 44–47. [G: U.S.]

Lacombe, John J., II and Conley, James R. Major Agreements in 1984 Provide Record Low Wage Increases. *Mon. Lab. Rev.*, April 1985, *108*(4), pp. 39–45. [G: U.S.]

Lancaster, Tony. Simultaneous Equations Models in Applied Search Theory. *J. Econometrics*, April 1985, *28*(1), pp. 113–26. [G: U.K.]

Lane, Julia and Glennon, Dennis. The Estimation of Age/Earnings Profiles in Wrongful Death and Injury Cases. *J. Risk Ins.*, December 1985, *52*(4), pp. 686–95. [G: U.S.]

Lawrence, Colin and Lawrence, Robert Z. Manufacturing Wage Dispersion: An End Game Interpretation. *Brookings Pap. Econ. Act.*, 1985, (1), pp. 47–106. [G: U.S.]

Layard, Richard and Nickell, Stephen. Unemployment, Real Wages, and Aggregate Demand in Europe, Japan and the United States. *Carnegie-Rochester Conf. Ser. Public Policy*, Autumn 1985, 23, pp. 143–202. [G: France; U.K.; W. Germany; Japan; U.S.]

Layard, Richard and Nickell, Stephen. The Causes of British Unemployment. *Nat. Inst. Econ. Rev.*, February 1985, (111), pp. 62–85. [G: U.K.]

Lazear, Edward P. Incentive Effects of Pensions. In *Wise, D. A., ed.*, 1985, pp. 253–78.

Lázničková, Anna. Overcoming Social Disparities between the Urban and Rural Population in Socialist Society. *Czech. Econ. Digest.*, August 1985, (5), pp. 45–58. [G: Czechoslovakia]

Lee, Bun Song and McElwain, Adrienne M. An Empirical Investigation of Female Labor-Force Participation, Fertility, Age at Marriage, and Wages in Korea. *J. Devel. Areas*, July 1985, *19*(4), pp. 483–99. [G: S. Korea]

Leigh, J. Paul. The Effects of Unemployment and the Business Cycle on Absenteeism. *J. Econ. Bus.*, May 1985, *37*(2), pp. 159–70. [G: U.S.]

Leonard, Herman B. The Federal Civil Service Retirement System: An Analysis of Its Financial Condition and Current Reform Proposals.

In *Wise, D. A., ed.*, 1985, pp. 399–438.
[G: U.S.]

Leslie, Derek. Real Wage Growth, Technical Change and Competition in the Labor Market. *Rev. Econ. Statist.*, November 1985, 67(4), pp. 640–47. [G: U.S.]

Leuthold, Jane H. Labor Supply with an Endogenous Tax Rate. *Public Finance*, 1985, 40(1), pp. 82–92. [G: U.S.]

Levin, William R. The False Promise of Worker Capitalism: Congress and the Leveraged Employee Stock Ownership Plan. *Yale Law J.*, November 1985, 95(1), pp. 148–73.
[G: U.S.]

Lin, Chung-cheng and Chu, Yun-peng. Further Evidence of Cohort Size Effects on Earnings: The Case of Taiwan. *J. Econ. Devel.*, December 1985, 10(2), pp. 101–21. [G: Taiwan]

Lindauer, David L. Regional Wage Determination and Economic Growth in Korea. *J. Econ. Devel.*, July 1985, 10(1), pp. 129–41.
[G: S. Korea]

Lindert, Peter H. and Williamson, Jeffrey G. English Workers' Real Wages: Reply. *J. Econ. Hist.*, March 1985, 45(1), pp. 145–53.
[G: U.K.]

Logue, Dennis E. The Usefulness of the Wind-Up Measure of Pension Liabilities: A Labor Market Perspective: Discussion. *J. Finance*, July 1985, 40(3), pp. 940–42. [G: U.S.]

Lorence, Jon. Establishment Size and Metropolitan Earnings Inequality: An Examination of Lydall's Managerial Hierarchy Hypothesis. *Soc. Sci. Quart.*, December 1985, 66(4), pp. 886–902. [G: U.S.]

Lucas, Robert E. B. Mines and Migrants in South Africa. *Amer. Econ. Rev.*, December 1985, 75(5), pp. 1094–108. [G: S. Africa]

Luft, Harold S.; Trauner, Joan B. and Maerki, Susan C. Adverse Selection in a Large, Multiple-Option Health Benefits Program: A Case Study of the California Public Employees' Retirement System. In *Scheffler, R. M. and Rossiter, L. F., eds.*, 1985, pp. 197–229.
[G: U.S.]

Lundberg, Shelly J. Tied Wage–Hours Offers and the Endogeneity of Wages. *Rev. Econ. Statist.*, August 1985, 67(3), pp. 405–10. [G: U.S.]

MacDonald, Glenn M. and Robinson, Chris. Cautionary Tails about Arbitrary Deletion of Observations; or, Throwing the Variance Out with the Bathwater. *J. Lab. Econ.*, April 1985, 3(2), pp. 124–52. [G: U.S.]

Macphee, Ian. Poor Nation of the Pacific: The Labour Market. In *Scutt, J. A., ed.*, 1985, pp. 75–92. [G: Australia]

MaCurdy, Thomas E. Interpreting Empirical Models of Labor Supply in an Intertemporal Framework with Uncertainty. In *Heckman, J. J. and Singer, B., eds.*, 1985, pp. 111–55.
[G: U.S.]

Madden, Janice Fanning. Urban Wage Gradients: Empirical Evidence. *J. Urban Econ.*, November 1985, 18(3), pp. 291–301. [G: U.S.]

Madhavan, M. C.; Green, Louis C. and Jung, Ken. A Note on Black–White Wage Disparity.

Rev. Black Polit. Econ., Spring 1985, 13(4), pp. 39–50. [G: U.S.]

Malinvaud, Edmond. The Real Wage Gap and Employment: Comments. In *Melitz, J. and Wyplosz, C., eds.*, 1985, pp. 81–83.
[G: France; U.S.; EEC]

Mallia, Linda Baylis. Human Resource Planning in a Decentralized Market Driven Environment. In *Niehaus, R. J., ed.*, 1985, pp. 67–76. [G: U.S.]

Malveaux, Julianne. Comparable Worth and Its Impact on Black Women. *Rev. Black Polit. Econ.*, Fall-Winter 1985-86, 14(2–3), pp. 47–62. [G: U.S.]

Maranto, Cheryl L. Union Effects on Human Capital Investments and Returns. *J. Human Res.*, Summer 1985, 20(3), pp. 453–62.
[G: U.S.]

Marion, Gérald. La détermination des salaires et le chômage naturel dans la perspective de prospection du marché du travail. (Wages and Natural Rate of Unemployment in a Job Search Perspective. With English summary.) *L'Actual. Econ.*, September 1985, 61(3), pp. 330–49. [G: Canada]

Marsden, David. Youth Pay in Britain Compared with France, and FR Germany since 1966. *Brit. J. Ind. Relat.*, November 1985, 23(3), pp. 399–414. [G: France; U.K.; W. Germany]

Maurer, Martin. Technological Retardation. The Decline of the Swiss Watch Industry. *Z. Wirtschaft. Sozialwissen.*, 1985, 105(6), pp. 661–82. [G: Switzerland]

Maxfield, Linda Drazga and Reno, Virginia P. Distribution of Income Sources of Recent Retirees: Findings from the New Beneficiary Survey. *Soc. Sec. Bull.*, January 1985, 48(1), pp. 7–13. [G: U.S.]

Maxwell, Nan L. The Retirement Experience: Psychological and Financial Linkages to the Labor Market. *Soc. Sci. Quart.*, March 1985, 66(1), pp. 22–33. [G: U.S.]

McArthur, Leslie Zebrowitz. Social Judgment Biases in Comparable Worth Analysis. In *Hartmann, H. I., ed.*, 1985, pp. 53–70. [G: U.S.]

McCallum, John. Wage Gaps, Factor Shares and Real Wages. *Scand. J. Econ.*, 1985, 87(2), pp. 436–59. [G: U.S.; W. Europe; Japan; Canada]

McManus, Walter S. Labor Market Assimilation of Immigrants: The Importance of Language Skills. *Contemp. Policy Issues*, Spring, Pt. 1, 1985, 3(3), pp. 77–89. [G: U.S.]

McManus, Walter S. Labor Market Costs of Language Disparity: An Interpretation of Hispanic Earnings Differences. *Amer. Econ. Rev.*, September 1985, 75(4), pp. 818–27. [G: U.S.]

Medoff, Marshall H. The Effect of the Equal Rights Amendment on the Economic Status of Women. *Atlantic Econ. J.*, September 1985, 13(3), pp. 60–68. [G: U.S.]

Megdal, Sharon Bernstein and Ransom, Michael R. Longitudinal Changes at a Large Public University: What Response to Equal Pay Legislation? *Amer. Econ. Rev.*, May 1985, 75(2), pp. 271–74. [G: U.S.]

Mellor, Earl F. Weekly Earnings in 1983: A Look at More Than 200 Occupations. *Mon. Lab. Rev.*, January 1985, 108(1), pp. 54–59. [G: U.S.]

Merton, Robert C. Insurance Aspects of Pensions: Comment. In *Wise, D. A., ed.*, 1985, pp. 343–56.

Miller, Michael A. Age-related Reductions in Workers' Life Insurance. *Mon. Lab. Rev.*, September 1985, 108(9), pp. 29–34. [G: U.S.]

Mills, D. Quinn and Lovell, Malcolm R., Jr. Competitiveness: The Labor Dimension. In *Scott, B. R. and Lodge, G. C., eds.*, 1985, pp. 429–54. [G: U.S.]

Mincer, Jacob. Intercountry Comparisons of Labor Force Trends and of Related Developments: An Overview. *J. Lab. Econ.*, Part 2 January 1985, 3(1), pp. S1–32. [G: Selected Countries]

Mitchell, Daniel J. B. Shifting Norms in Wage Determination. *Brookings Pap. Econ. Act.*, 1985, (2), pp. 575–99. [G: U.S.]

Mitchell, Daniel J. B. Wage Flexibility in the United States: Lessons from the Past. *Amer. Econ. Rev.*, May 1985, 75(2), pp. 36–40. [G: U.S.]

Mitchell, Daniel J. B. Wage Flexibility: Then and Now. *Ind. Relat.*, Spring 1985, 24(2), pp. 266–79. [G: U.S.]

Mitchell, Mark L.; Wallace, Myles S. and Warner, John T. Real Wages over the Business Cycle: Some Further Evidence. *Southern Econ. J.*, April 1985, 51(4), pp. 1162–73. [G: U.S.]

Mitchell, Olivia S. and Fields, Gary S. Rewards for Continued Work: The Economic Incentives for Postponing Retirement. In *David, M. and Smeeding, T., eds.*, 1985, pp. 269–86. [G: U.S.]

Moore, William J. and Newman, Robert J. The Effects of Right-to-Work Laws: A Review of the Literature. *Ind. Lab. Relat. Rev.*, July 1985, 38(4), pp. 571–85. [G: U.S.]

Moore, William J.; Newman, Robert J. and Cunningham, James. The Effect of the Extent of Unionism on Union and Nonunion Wages. *J. Lab. Res.*, Winter 1985, 6(1), pp. 21–44. [G: U.S.]

Mosk, Carl and Nakata, Yoshi-Fumi. The Age-Wage Profile and Structural Change in the Japanese Labor Market for Males, 1964–1982. *J. Human Res.*, Winter 1985, 20(1), pp. 100–116. [G: Japan]

Moss, Richard Loring and Curtis, Thomas D. The Economics of Flextime. *J. Behav. Econ.*, Summer 1985, 14(2), pp. 95–114. [G: U.S.]

Mstislavskii, P. The Dynamics of Labor Productivity and Wages. *Prob. Econ.*, May 1985, 28(1), pp. 38–55. [G: U.S.S.R.]

Muller, Thomas. Economic Effects of Immigration. In *Glazer, N., ed.*, 1985, pp. 109–33. [G: U.S.]

Mumy, Gene E. and Manson, William D. The Relative Importance of Tax and Agency Incen-

tives to Offer Pensions: A Test Using the Impact of ERISA. *Public Finance Quart.*, October 1985, 13(4), pp. 464–85. [G: U.S.]

Munnell, Alicia H. Social Security, Private Pensions and Saving. In *Terny, G. and Culyer, A. J., eds.*, 1985, pp. 157–70.

Myers, Robert J. Income of Social Security Beneficiaries as Affected by Earnings Test and Income Taxes on Benefits. *J. Risk Ins.*, June 1985, 52(2), pp. 289–300. [G: U.S.]

Nalebuff, Barry and Zeckhauser, Richard J. Pensions and the Retirement Decision. In *Wise, D. A., ed.*, 1985, pp. 283–316. [G: U.S.]

Nieuwenhuysen, John. Towards Flexibility in Academic Labour Markets? *Australian Bull. Lab.*, March 1985, 11(2), pp. 71–81. [G: Australia]

Norwood, Janet L. Perspectives on Comparable Worth: An Introduction to the Numbers. *Mon. Lab. Rev.*, December 1985, 108(12), pp. 3–4. [G: U.S.]

O'Brien, Anthony. The Cyclical Sensitivity of Wages [The Changing Cyclical Behavior of Wages and Prices: 1890–1976] [Cross-Country and Cross-Temporal Differences in Inflation Responsiveness]. *Amer. Econ. Rev.*, December 1985, 75(5), pp. 1124–32. [G: U.S.]

O'Brien, Richard F. Health Care Cost Containment: An Employer's Perspective. In *Dennis, B. D., ed.*, 1985, pp. 468–73. [G: U.S.]

O'Neill, June. The Trend in the Male–Female Wage Gap in the United States. *J. Lab. Econ.*, Part 2 January 1985, 3(1), pp. S91–116. [G: U.S.]

Oi, Walter Y. Unemployment, Real Wages, and Aggregate Demand in Europe, Japan and the United States: Comments on the Layard–Nickell Model of Unemployment and Real Wages. *Carnegie-Rochester Conf. Ser. Public Policy*, Autumn 1985, 23, pp. 203–09. [G: France; U.K.; W. Germany; Japan; U.S.]

Owen, John D. Changing from a Rotating to a Permanent Shift System in the Detroit Police Department: Effects on Employee Attitudes and Behavior. In *Dennis, B. D., ed.*, 1985, pp. 484–89. [G: U.S.]

Papanek, Gustav F. Agricultural Income Distribution and Employment in the 1970s. *Bull. Indonesian Econ. Stud.*, August 1985, 21(2), pp. 24–50. [G: Indonesia]

Pesando, James E. The Usefulness of the Wind-Up Measure of Pension Liabilities: A Labor Market Perspective. *J. Finance*, July 1985, 40(3), pp. 927–40. [G: U.S.]

Peters, B. Guy. Administrative Change and the Grace Commission. In *Levine, C. H., ed.*, 1985, pp. 19–39. [G: U.S.]

Philips, Peter. A Note on the Apparent Constancy of the Racial Wage Gap in New Jersey Manufacturing, 1902 to 1979. *Rev. Black Polit. Econ.*, Spring 1985, 13(4), pp. 71–76. [G: U.S.]

Pike, Maureen. The Employment Response to Equal Pay Legislation. *Oxford Econ. Pap.*, June 1985, 37(2), pp. 304–18. [G: U.K.]

Poli, Irene. A Bayesian Non-parametric Estimate

for Multivariate Regression. *J. Econometrics*, May 1985, *28*(2), pp. 171–82. [G: Italy]

Porter, Michael G. The Labour of Liberalisation. In *Scutt, J. A., ed.*, 1985, pp. 37–61. [G: Australia]

Porter, Philip K. and Scully, Gerald W. Potential Earnings, Post-schooling Investment and Returns to Human Capital. *Econ. Educ. Rev.*, 1985, *4*(2), pp. 87–92. [G: U.S.]

Price, Richard and Mills, Edwin S. Race and Residence in Earnings Determination. *J. Urban Econ.*, January 1985, *17*(1), pp. 1–18. [G: U.S.]

Prieser, Carl. Occupational Salary Levels for White-Collar Workers, 1985. *Mon. Lab. Rev.*, October 1985, *108*(10), pp. 44–46. [G: U.S.]

Quinn, Joseph F. Retirement Income Rights as a Component of Wealth in the United States. *Rev. Income Wealth*, September 1985, *31*(3), pp. 223–36. [G: U.S.]

Quinn, Joseph F. Rewards for Continued Work: The Economic Incentives for Postponing Retirement: Comment. In *David, M. and Smeeding, T., eds.*, 1985, pp. 286–92. [G: U.S.]

Raffaelli, Cristina. On Modeling Structural Changes in Sectoral Wage Distribution in a Modern Input–Output Model. In *Smyshlyaev, A., ed.*, 1985, pp. 79–94. [G: Italy]

Rao, M. J. Manohar and Datta, Ramesh C. Human Capital and Hierarchy. *Econ. Educ. Rev.*, 1985, *4*(1), pp. 67–76. [G: India]

Ratti, Ronald A. The Effects of Inflation Surprises and Uncertainty on Real Wages. *Rev. Econ. Statist.*, May 1985, *67*(2), pp. 309–14. [G: U.S.]

Reddy, M. Atchi. The Commercialization of Agriculture in Nellore District 1850–1916: Effects on Wages, Employment and Tenancy. In *Raj, K. N., et al., eds.*, 1985, pp. 163–83. [G: India]

Rees, Albert. Unions, Pensions, and Union Pension Funds: Comment. In *Wise, D. A., ed.*, 1985, pp. 118–21. [G: U.S.]

Reid, Clifford E. The Effect of Residential Location on the Wages of Black Women and White Women. *J. Urban Econ.*, November 1985, *18*(3), pp. 350–63. [G: U.S.]

Reimers, Cordelia W. A Comparative Analysis of the Wages of Hispanics, Blacks, and Non-Hispanic Whites. In *Borjas, G. J. and Tienda, M., eds.*, 1985, pp. 27–75. [G: U.S.]

Riboud, Michelle. An Analysis of Women's Labor Force Participation in France: Cross-Section Estimates and Time-Series Evidence. *J. Lab. Econ.*, Part 2 January 1985, *3*(1), pp. S177–200. [G: France]

Robinson, D. The Economic System in the UK: Government and Pay. In *Morris, D., ed.*, 1985, pp. 333–65. [G: U.K.]

Rosen, Sherwin. The Structure of Uncertainty and the Use of Nontransferable Pensions as a Mobility-Reduction Device: Comment. In *Wise, D. A., ed.*, 1985, pp. 248–51.

Rosenbaum, James E. Jobs, Job Status, and Women's Gains from Affirmative Action: Implications for Comparable Worth. In *Hartmann,*

H. I., ed., 1985, pp. 116–36. [G: U.S.]

Rosendre R., Francisco. Tipo de cambio y salarios reales: consideraciones sobre el caso chileno. (With English summary.) *Cuadernos Econ.*, December 1985, *22*(67), pp. 343–55. [G: Chile]

Rosenthal, Neal H. The Shrinking Middle Class: Myth or Reality? *Mon. Lab. Rev.*, March 1985, *108*(3), pp. 3–10. [G: U.S.]

Rossana, Robert J. Buffer Stocks and Labor Demand: Further Evidence. *Rev. Econ. Statist.*, February 1985, *67*(1), pp. 16–26. [G: U.S.]

Rotherham, James A. The Railroad Retirement Program: A Case Study in the Deficit Dilemma. *Public Budg. Finance*, Autumn 1985, *5*(3), pp. 40–57. [G: U.S.]

Sadowski, Dieter and Schittenhelm, Rainer. Tax Subsidies and the Intra-organizational Trading of Fringe Benefits: An Economic Model Building Approach. In *Niehaus, R. J., ed.*, 1985, pp. 121–44. [G: W. Germany]

Samuelson, Paul A. The Federal Civil Service Retirement System: An Analysis of Its Financial Condition and Current Reform Proposals: Comment. In *Wise, D. A., ed.*, 1985, pp. 438–43. [G: U.S.]

Santiago, Carlos E. and Rossiter, Rosemary. A Multiple Time-Series Analysis of Labor Supply and Earnings in Economic Development. *J. Devel. Econ.*, April 1985, *17*(3), pp. 259–75. [G: Puerto Rico]

Scahill, Edward. The Determinants of Average Salaries in Professional Football. *Atlantic Econ. J.*, March 1985, *13*(1), pp. 103.

Scherer, Peter. Continuity and Change in Australian Wages Policy. *Australian Econ. Rev.*, 3rd Quarter, Spring 1985, (71), pp. 53–67. [G: Australia]

Schleck, Robert W. Reforming Federal Pension Programs. In *Harriss, C. L., ed.*, 1985, pp. 85–100. [G: U.S.]

Schmidt-Sørensen, Jan Beyer and Søndergaard, Jørgen. Beskæftigelsesvirkninger af en arbejdstidsforkortelse. (Employment Consequences of a Shortening of Working Hours. With English summary.) *Nationaløkon. Tidsskr.*, 1985, *123*(2), pp. 160–75.

Schmitt, Donald G. Tips: The Mainstay of Many Hotel Workers' Pay. *Mon. Lab. Rev.*, July 1985, *108*(7), pp. 50–51. [G: U.S.]

Schor, Juliet B. Changes in the Cyclical Pattern of Rural Wages: Evidence from Nine Countries, 1955–80. *Econ. J.*, June 1985, *95*(378), pp. 452–68. [G: OECD]

Schultz, T. Paul. Changing World Prices, Women's Wages, and the Fertility Transition: Sweden, 1860–1910. *J. Polit. Econ.*, December 1985, *93*(6), pp. 1126–54. [G: Sweden]

Schwab, Donald P. Job Evaluation Research and Research Needs. In *Hartmann, H. I., ed.*, 1985, pp. 37–52.

Schwartz, Harvey A. What Do We Know about Statistical Discrimination? In *Brown, R. C., ed.*, 1985, pp. 153–91. [G: U.S.]

Schwenk, Albert E. Introducing New Weights for the Employment Cost Index. *Mon. Lab. Rev.*,

June 1985, *108*(6), pp. 22–27.   [G: U.S.]

Scott, Frank A., Jr.; Long, James E. and Somppi, Ken. Salary vs. Marginal Revenue Product under Monopsony and Competition: The Case of Professional Basketball. *Atlantic Econ. J.,* September 1985, *13*(3), pp. 50–59. [G: U.S.]

Sehgal, Ellen. Employment Problems and Their Effect on Family Income, 1979–83. *Mon. Lab. Rev.,* August 1985, *108*(8), pp. 42–43.
    [G: U.S.]

Sellier, Francois. Economic Change and Industrial Relations in France. In *Juris, H.; Thompson, M. and Daniels, W., eds.,* 1985, pp. 177–209.   [G: France]

Shah, Anup R. Are Wage Incentives and Unionism Importance Determinants of Job Tenure? *Oxford Econ. Pap.,* December 1985, *37*(4), pp. 643–58.   [G: U.K.]

Shah, Anup R. Does Education Act as a Screening Device for Certain British Occupations? *Oxford Econ. Pap.,* March 1985, *37*(1), pp. 118–24.   [G: U.K.]

Shapiro, David and Sandell, Steven H. Age Discrimination in Wages and Displaced Older Men. *Southern Econ. J.,* July 1985, *52*(1), pp. 90–102.   [G: U.S.]

Shimada, Haruo and Higuchi, Yoshio. An Analysis of Trends in Female Labor Force Participation in Japan. *J. Lab. Econ.,* Part 2 January 1985, *3*(1), pp. S355–74.   [G: Japan]

Simpson, Wayne. The Impact of Unions on the Structure of Canadian Wages: An Empirical Analysis with Microdata. *Can. J. Econ.,* February 1985, *18*(1), pp. 164–81.   [G: Canada]

Smeeding, Timothy M. The Scientific Potential of SIPP: Its Content and Methods Regarding Fringe Benefits, Noncash Income, and Value of Government Services. *J. Econ. Soc. Meas.,* December 1985, *13*(3–4), pp. 287–94.
    [G: U.S.]

Smith, James P. and Ward, Michael P. Time-Series Growth in the Female Labor Force. *J. Lab. Econ.,* Part 2 January 1985, *3*(1), pp. S59–90.   [G: U.S.]

Smith, V. Kerry and Gilbert, Carol C. S. The Valuation of Environmental Risks Using Hedonic Wage Models. In *David, M. and Smeeding, T., eds.,* 1985, pp. 359–85. [G: U.S.]

Solmon, Lewis C. Quality of Education and Economic Growth. *Econ. Educ. Rev.,* 1985, *4*(4), pp. 273–90.   [G: Global]

Solnick, Loren M. The Effect of Blue-Collar Unions on White-Collar Wages and Fringe Benefits. *Ind. Lab. Relat. Rev.,* January 1985, *38*(2), pp. 236–43.   [G: U.S.]

Solow, Robert M. Manufacturing Wage Dispersion: An End Game Interpretation: Comment. *Brookings Pap. Econ. Act.,* 1985, (1), pp. 107–10.   [G: U.S.]

Stelcner, Morton and Breslaw, Jon. Income Taxes and the Labor Supply of Married Women in Quebec. *Southern Econ. J.,* April 1985, *51*(4), pp. 1053–72.   [G: Canada]

Stewart, A.; Blackburn, R. M. and Prandy, K. Gender and Earnings: The Failure of Market Explanations. In *Roberts, B.; Finnegan, R. and*

Gallie, D., eds., 1985, pp. 280–98. [G: U.K.]

Stone, Joe A. Determinants of Administrators' Salaries in Public Schools: Differences for Men and Women. *Econ. Educ. Rev.,* 1985, *4*(2), pp. 105–09.   [G: U.S.]

Stratton, Richard W. Monopoly, Monopsony, and Union Strength and Local Market Wage Differentials: Some Empirical Evidence on Their Impacts. *Amer. J. Econ. Soc.,* July 1985, *44*(3), pp. 305–18.   [G: U.S.]

Stricker, Frank. Affluence for Whom?—Another Look at Prosperity and the Working Classes in the 1920s. In *Leab, D. J., ed.,* 1985, pp. 288–316.   [G: U.S.]

Talafha, Hussain. Emigration and Wage Differentials Facing the Jordanian Workers. *METU,* 1985, *12*(3/4), pp. 317–32.   [G: Jordan; Saudi Arabia]

Tanzi, Vito and Iden, George. The Impact of Taxes on Wages: Reply. *Econ. Notes,* 1985, (2), pp. 175–78.   [G: U.S.]

Taubman, Paul. Determinants of Pension Benefits. In *Wise, D. A., ed.,* 1985, pp. 123–53.
    [G: U.S.]

Taylor, Patricia A. and Gwartney-Gibbs, Patricia A. Economic Segmentation, Inequality, and the North–South Earnings Gap. *Rev. Reg. Stud.,* Spring 1985, *15*(2), pp. 43–53.
    [G: U.S.]

Tessaring, Manfred. An Evaluation of Labour-Market and Educational Forecasts in the Federal Republic of Germany. In *Youdi, R. V. and Hinchliffe, K., eds.,* 1985, pp. 57–74.

Theeuwes, Jules, et al. Estimation of Optimal Human Capital Accumulation Parameters for the Netherlands. *Europ. Econ. Rev.,* November 1985, *29*(2), pp. 233–57.   [G: Netherlands]

Thiry, Bernard. La discrimination salariale entre hommes et femmes sur le marché du travail en France. (Wage Discrimination between Men and Women in the Labor Market in France. With English summary.) *Ann. INSEE,* Apr.-June 1985, (58), pp. 39–68. [G: France]

Tietenberg, T. H. The Valuation of Environmental Risks Using Hedonic Wage Models: Comment. In *David, M. and Smeeding, T., eds.,* 1985, pp. 385–91.   [G: U.S.]

Tímár, János. Time and Work Time: Certain Problems with the Time Basis of Social Reproduction in Hungary. In *[Levcik, F.],* 1985, pp. 137–48.   [G: Hungary]

Tinbergen, Jan. Determinants of Manager Incomes. In *Tinbergen, J.,* 1985, pp. 85–100.
    [G: OECD]

Tinbergen, Jan. The Role of Occupational Status in Income Formation. In *Tinbergen, J.,* 1985, pp. 78–84.   [G: U.S.]

Tinbergen, Jan and Wegner, Eckhard. On a Macroeconomic Model of Income Formation. In *Tinbergen, J.,* 1985, pp. 69–77.
    [G: Switzerland]

Tokman, Victor E. Wages and Employment in International Recessions: Recent Latin American Experience. In *Kim, K. S. and Ruccio, D. F., eds.,* 1985, pp. 74–95.
    [G: Latin America]

Townson, Monica. A National System for Parental Leave. In *Economic Council of Canada.*, 1985, pp. 21–28. [G: Canada]

Travers, S. Lee. Getting Rich through Diligence: Peasant Income after the Reforms. In *Perry, E. J. and Wong, C., eds.*, 1985, pp. 111–30. [G: China]

Trinder, C. and Biswas, Rajiv. Public Services Pay in the 1980s. *Nat. Inst. Econ. Rev.*, May 1985, (112), pp. 31–34. [G: U.K.]

Tucker, Irvin B., III. Use of the Decomposition Technique to Test the Educational Screening Hypothesis. *Econ. Educ. Rev.*, 1985, 4(4), pp. 321–26. [G: U.S.]

Uthoff B., Andras and Pollack E., Molly. Dinámica de salarios y precios en Costa Rica 1976–1983. (With English summary.) *Cuadernos Econ.*, December 1985, 22(67), pp. 443–73. [G: Costa Rica]

Verbon, Harry A. A. and van Winden, Frans A. A. M. Public Pensions and Political Decision-making. *De Economist*, 1985, 133(4), pp. 527–44. [G: Netherlands]

Vernon, Jack. Discounting After-Tax Earnings with After-Tax Yields in Torts Settlements. *J. Risk Ins.*, December 1985, 52(4), pp. 696–703. [G: U.S.]

Viscusi, W. Kip. The Structure of Uncertainty and the Use of Nontransferable Pensions as a Mobility-Reduction Device. In *Wise, D. A., ed.*, 1985, pp. 223–48.

Vroman, Wayne. Cost-of-Living Escalators and Price–Wage Linkages in the U.S. Economy, 1968–1980. *Ind. Lab. Relat. Rev.*, January 1985, 38(2), pp. 225–35. [G: U.S.]

Wachter, Michael L. Manufacturing Wage Dispersion: An End Game Interpretation: Comment. *Brookings Pap. Econ. Act.*, 1985, (1), pp. 110–15. [G: U.S.]

Wadensjö, Eskil. Wage Gaps, Factor Shares and Real Wages: Comment. *Scand. J. Econ.*, 1985, 87(2), pp. 460–62. [G: U.S.; W. Europe; Japan]

Wadhwani, Sushil B. Wage Inflation in the United Kingdom. *Economica*, May 1985, 52(206), pp. 195–207. [G: U.K.]

Wassall, Gregory H. and Alper, Neil O. Occupational Characteristics of Artists: A Statistical Analysis. *J. Cult. Econ.*, June 1985, 9(1), pp. 13–34. [G: U.S.]

Weisskopf, Thomas E.; Bowles, Samuel and Gordon, David M. Two Views of Capitalist Stagnation: Underconsumption and Challenges to Capitalist Control. *Sci. Soc.*, Fall 1985, 49(3), pp. 259–86. [G: U.S.]

Wiatrowski, William J. Employee Income Protection against Short-term Disabilities. *Mon. Lab. Rev.*, February 1985, 108(2), pp. 32–38. [G: U.S.]

Williams, Harry B. Wages at Motor Vehicle Plants Outpaced Those at Parts Factories. *Mon. Lab. Rev.*, May 1985, 108(5), pp. 38–40. [G: U.S.]

Winn, Conrad. Affirmative Action and Visible Minorities: Eight Premises in Quest of Evidence.

Can. Public Policy, December 1985, 11(4), pp. 684–700.

Wise, David A. Pensions, Labor, and Individual Choice: Overview. In *Wise, D. A., ed.*, 1985, pp. 1–17. [G: U.S.]

Withers, Glenn. Artists' Subsidy of the Arts. *Australian Econ. Pap.*, December 1985, 24(45), pp. 290–95. [G: Australia]

Wolfe, Barbara L., et al. The Contribution of Income Transfers to Lagging Economic Performance: The United States and the Netherlands in the 1970s. In *Terny, G. and Culyer, A. J., eds.*, 1985, pp. 109–21. [G: U.S.; Netherlands]

Worrall, John D. and Butler, Richard J. Benefits and Claim Duration. In *Worrall, J. D. and Appel, D., eds.*, 1985, pp. 57–70. [G: U.S.]

Wren-Lewis, Simon. Private Sector Earnings and Excess Demand from 1966 to 1980. *Oxford Bull. Econ. Statist.*, February 1985, 47(1), pp. 1–18. [G: U.K.]

Yamada, Narumi. Working Time in Japan: Recent Trends and Issues. *Int. Lab. Rev.*, Nov.-Dec. 1985, 124(6), pp. 699–718. [G: Japan]

Yue, Guangzhao. Employment, Wages and Social Security in China. *Int. Lab. Rev.*, July-Aug. 1985, 124(4), pp. 411–22. [G: China]

Yuskavage, Robert E. Employment and Employee Compensation in the 1977 Input–Output Accounts. *Surv. Curr. Bus.*, November 1985, 65(11), pp. 11–25. [G: U.S.]

Zabalza, Anton and Tzannatos, Zafaris. The Effect of Britain's Anti-discriminatory Legislation on Relative Pay and Employment. *Econ. J.*, September 1985, 95(379), pp. 679–99. [G: U.K.]

Zhao, Lukuan. The Problem of Reforming the Wage System in Our Country. *Chinese Econ. Stud.*, Spring 1985, 18(3), pp. 35–54. [G: China]

8243 Employment Studies; Unemployment and Vacancies; Retirements and Quits

Abella, Rosalie S. Equality in Employment. In *Economic Council of Canada.*, 1985, pp. 109–17. [G: Canada]

Abowd, John M. and Killingsworth, Mark R. Employment, Wages, and Earnings of Hispanics in the Federal and Nonfederal Sectors: Methodological Issues and Their Empirical Consequences. In *Borjas, G. J. and Tienda, M., eds.*, 1985, pp. 77–125. [G: U.S.]

Abowd, John M. and Zellner, Arnold. Estimating Gross Labor-Force Flows. *J. Bus. Econ. Statist.*, July 1985, 3(3), pp. 254–83. [G: U.S.]

Achio, Françoise. Forecasts of Skilled-Manpower Needs in the Ivory Coast: An Evaluation of Methods and Results. In *Youdi, R. V. and Hinchliffe, K., eds.*, 1985, pp. 211–28. [G: Ivory Coast]

Adams, Larry T. Changing Employment Patterns of Organized Workers. *Mon. Lab. Rev.*, February 1985, 108(2), pp. 25–31. [G: U.S.]

Agrafiotis, G. K. Fitting the Lognormal Distribution to Censored Labour Wastage Data. *Math.*

Soc. Sci., December 1985, *10*(3), pp. 269–274.

Ahmad, Qazi Kholiquzzaman and Ahmed, Momtaz Uddin. A Review of Rural Non-farm Economic Activities in Bangladesh. In *Mukhopadhyay, S. and Chee, P. L., eds. (I)*, 1985, pp. 53–146. [G: Bangladesh]

Aitkin, Murray and Healey, Robert. Statistical Modelling of Unemployment Rates from the EEC Labour Force Survey. *J. Roy. Statist. Soc.*, 1985, *148*(1), pp. 45–56. [G: U.K.; France]

Akerlof, George A. and Yellen, Janet L. Unemployment through the Filter of Memory. *Quart. J. Econ.*, August 1985, *100*(3), pp. 747–73. [G: U.S.]

Albaek, Karsten. Løntilskud og læringebeskæftigelse. (Wage-Subsidies and Employment of Apprentices in Denmark. With English summary.) *Nationaløkon. Tidsskr.*, 1985, *123*(2), pp. 176–93. [G: Denmark]

Alt, James E. Political Parties, World Demand, and Unemployment: Domestic and International Sources of Economic Activity. *Amer. Polit. Sci. Rev.*, December 1985, *79*(4), pp. 1016–40. [G: OECD]

Anderson, Bernard E. Job Search and Job Programs. *Challenge*, July/August 1985, *28*(3), pp. 51–53. [G: U.S.]

Anderson, Kathryn H. The Effect of Mandatory Retirement on Mortality. *J. Econ. Bus.*, February 1985, *37*(1), pp. 81–88. [G: U.S.]

Anthony, Douglas. Managing Workforce Reduction: Japan. In *Cross, M., ed.*, 1985, pp. 91–129. [G: Japan]

Armstrong, Harvey W. and Taylor, Jim. Spatial Variations in the Male Unemployment Inflow Rate. *Appl. Econ.*, February 1985, *17*(1), pp. 41–54. [G: U.K.]

Ault, David E. and Rutman, Gilbert L. The Rural African and Gold Mining in Southern Africa, 1976–1980. *S. Afr. J. Econ.*, March 1985, *53*(1), pp. 1–23. [G: S. Africa]

Auray, J. P., et al. Assessing the Effects of Unemployment on Health Services Use in a Specific Group: A Research Proposal. In *Westcott, G.; Svensson, P.-G. and Zollner, H. F. K., eds.*, 1985, pp. 335–45. [G: France]

Backus, David and Driffill, John. Policy Credibility and Unemployment in the U.K. In *Currie, D., ed.*, 1985, pp. 3–16. [G: U.K.]

Bailey, David and Parikh, Ashok. An Analysis of Duration of Unemployment: 1967–1979. *Empirical Econ.*, 1985, *10*(3), pp. 131–41. [G: U.K.]

Baker, G. M. and Trivedi, Pravin K. Estimation of Unemployment Duration from Grouped Data: A Comparative Study. *J. Lab. Econ.*, April 1985, *3*(2), pp. 153–74. [G: Australia]

Barker, F. S. and Döckel, J. A. The Relationship between Unemployment and Vacancies in South Africa. *S. Afr. J. Econ.*, December 1985, *53*(4), pp. 416–23. [G: S. Africa]

Barron, John M. and Bishop, John. Extensive Search, Intensive Search, and Hiring Costs: New Evidence on Employer Hiring Activity.

Econ. Inquiry, July 1985, *23*(3), pp. 363–82. [G: U.S.]

Barron, John M.; Bishop, John and Dunkelberg, William C. Employer Search: The Interviewing and Hiring of New Employees. *Rev. Econ. Statist.*, February 1985, *67*(1), pp. 43–52. [G: U.S.]

Bazzoli, Gloria J. The Early Retirement Decision: New Empirical Evidence on the Influence of Health. *J. Human Res.*, Spring 1985, *20*(2), pp. 214–34. [G: U.S.]

Bednarzik, Robert W. The Impact of Microelectronics on Employment: Japan's Experience. *Mon. Lab. Rev.*, September 1985, *108*(9), pp. 45–48. [G: Japan]

Bell, R. T. Issue in South African Unemployment. *S. Afr. J. Econ.*, March 1985, *53*(1), pp. 24–38. [G: S. Africa]

Ben-Porath, Yoram and Gronau, Reuben. Jewish Mother Goes to Work: Trends in the Labor Force Participation of Women in Israel, 1955–1980. *J. Lab. Econ.*, Part 2 January 1985, *3*(1), pp. S310–27. [G: Israel]

Benderly, Jason and Zwick, Burton. Money, Unemployment and Inflation. *Rev. Econ. Statist.*, February 1985, *67*(1), pp. 139–43. [G: U.S.]

Bettio, Francesca. The Unremoved Constraint: Job Sex-Typing and Female Participation, 1901–1981. *Stud. Econ.*, 1985, *40*(27), pp. 77–122. [G: Italy]

Bhagwati, Jagdish N. Technology and Employment. In *Bhagwati, J. N. (II)*, 1985, pp. 229–30.

Bhagwati, Jagdish N. What Do Commissars Do? In *Bhagwati, J. N. (II)*, 1985, pp. 210–15. [G: China]

Björklund, Anders. Unemployment and Mental Health: Some Evidence from Panel Data. *J. Human Res.*, Fall 1985, *20*(4), pp. 469–83. [G: Sweden]

Blanchard, Olivier J., et al. Occupazione e crescita in europa: un intervento su due fronti. (Employment and Growth in Europe: A Two-Handed Approach. With English summary.) *Giorn. Econ.*, Nov.-Dec. 1985, *44*(11–12), pp. 585–618. [G: W. Europe]

Blank, Rebecca M. An Analysis of Workers' Choice between Employment in the Public and Private Sectors. *Ind. Lab. Relat. Rev.*, January 1985, *38*(2), pp. 211–24. [G: U.S.]

Blank, Rebecca M. and Rothschild, Emma. The Effect of United States Defence Spending on Employment and Output. *Int. Lab. Rev.*, Nov.-Dec. 1985, *124*(6), pp. 677–97. [G: U.S.]

Boamah, Daniel O. Wage Formation, Employment and Output in Barbados. *Soc. Econ. Stud.*, December 1985, *34*(4), pp. 199–218. [G: Barbados]

Bodie, Zvi. Labor Compensation and the Structure of Private Pension Plans: Evidence for Contractual versus Spot Labor Markets: Comment. In *Wise, D. A., ed.*, 1985, pp. 85–87. [G: U.S.]

Bodie, Zvi. Pensions and the Labor Market: A Starting Point (The Mouse Can Roar): Com-

ment. In *Wise, D. A., ed.*, 1985, pp. 50–53.
[G: U.S.]

Bosanquet, Nick. Welfare Needs, Welfare Jobs and Efficiency. In *Klein, R. and O'Higgins, M., ed.*, 1985, pp. 186–203. [G: U.K.]

Bosch, Gerhard. Managing Workforce Reduction: West Germany. In *Cross, M., ed.*, 1985, pp. 164–98. [G: W. Germany]

Bradshaw, Jonathan. Social Security Policy and Assumptions about Patterns of Work. In *Klein, R. and O'Higgins, M., ed.*, 1985, pp. 204–15.
[G: U.K.]

Braga de Macedo, Jorge. Labor and Investment Demand at the Firm Level: A Comparison of French, German and U.S. Manufacturing, 1970-79: Comment. *Europ. Econ. Rev.*, June-July 1985, *28*(1–2), pp. 237–41. [G: France; U.S.; W. Germany]

Breakwell, Glynis M. Young People In and Out of Work. In *Roberts, B.; Finnegan, R. and Gallie, D., eds.*, 1985, pp. 490–501.[G: U.K.]

Brenner, M. Harvey. Economic Change and Mortality by Cause in Selected European Countries: Special Reference to Behaviour Health Risks, Emphasising Alcohol Consumption. In *Westcott, G.; Svensson, P.-G. and Zollner, H. F. K., eds.*, 1985, pp. 143–80.
[G: OECD]

Brenner, Sten Olof, et al. Job Insecurity and Unemployment: Effects on Health and Wellbeing and an Evaluation of Coping Measures. In *Westcott, G.; Svensson, P.-G. and Zollner, H. F. K., eds.*, 1985, pp. 325–34.
[G: Sweden]

Briggs, Vernon M., Jr. Employment Trends and Contemporary Immigration Policy. In *Glazer, N., ed.*, 1985, pp. 135–60. [G: U.S.]

Brinkmann, Christian. Health Problems in the Initial Phase of Unemployment: Some Research Findings and Policy Implications. In *Westcott, G.; Svensson, P.-G. and Zollner, H. F. K., eds.*, 1985, pp. 273–91.
[G: W. Germany]

Brittan, Samuel. Back to Full Employment: The Economic Aspect. *Nat. Westminster Bank Quart. Rev.*, May 1985, pp. 41–51.
[G: U.K.]

Britton, Andrew J. C. Unemployment and the Structure of Labour Demand. *Nat. Westminster Bank Quart. Rev.*, May 1985, pp. 32–40.
[G: U.K.]

Browne, Lynn E. Structural Change and Dislocated Workers. *New Eng. Econ. Rev.*, January/February 1985, pp. 15–30. [G: U.S.]

Brunello, Giorgio. Labour Adjustment in Japanese Incorporated Enterprises: An Empirical Analysis for the Period 1965–1983. *Hitotsubashi J. Econ.*, December 1985, *26*(2), pp. 165–80. [G: Japan]

Buiter, Willem H. The Real Wage Gap and Employment: Comments. In *Melitz, J. and Wyplosz, C., eds.*, 1985, pp. 71–80. [G: France; U.S.; EEC]

Burdett, Kenneth; Kiefer, Nicholas M. and Sharma, Sunil. Layoffs and Duration Dependence in a Model of Turnover. *J. Econometrics*, April 1985, *28*(1), pp. 51–69. [G: U.S.]

Burgan, John U. Cyclical Behavior of High Tech Industries. *Mon. Lab. Rev.*, May 1985, *108*(5), pp. 9–15. [G: U.S.]

Burtless, Gary. Social Security, Health Status, and Retirement: Comment. In *Wise, D. A., ed.*, 1985, pp. 181–91. [G: U.S.]

Burtless, Gary and Moffitt, Robert. The Joint Choice of Retirement Age and Postretirement Hours of Work. *J. Lab. Econ.*, April 1985, *3*(2), pp. 209–36. [G: U.S.]

Cardani, Angelo M. Labor and Investment Demand at the Firm Level: A Comparison of French, German and U.S. Manufacturing, 1970-79: Comment. *Europ. Econ. Rev.*, June-July 1985, *28*(1–2), pp. 233–36. [G: France; U.S.; W. Germany]

Carlino, Gerald A. Declining City Productivity and the Growth of Rural Regions: A Test of Alternative Explanations. *J. Urban Econ.*, July 1985, *18*(1), pp. 11–27. [G: U.S.]

Carr-Hill, Roy A. Whither (Research on) Unemployment? In *Roberts, B.; Finnegan, R. and Gallie, D., eds.*, 1985, pp. 338–50.

Cave, George. Youth Joblessness and Race: Evidence from the 1980 Census. In *Betsey, C. L.; Hollister, R. G., Jr. and Papageorgiou, M. R., eds.*, 1985, pp. 367–409. [G: U.S.]

Chaikin, Sol C. The Needs of the Labor-Intensive Sector. In *Zukin, S., ed.*, 1985, pp. 226–38.
[G: U.S.]

Chall, Daniel E. New York City's "Skills Mismatch." *Fed. Res. Bank New York Quart. Rev.*, Spring 1985, *10*(1), pp. 20–27. [G: U.S.]

Cheema, Aftab Ahmad and Malik, Muhammad Hussain. Changes in Consumption Patterns and Employment under Alternative Income Distributions in Pakistan. *Pakistan Devel. Rev.*, Spring 1985, *24*(1), pp. 1–22.
[G: Pakistan]

Choate, Pat and Carey, Dennis C. An IRA for Structural Unemployment. *Challenge*, Nov./Dec. 1985, *28*(5), pp. 57–59. [G: U.S.]

Choe, Yang Boo. Development of Rural Non-farm Activities and Industries in Korea. In *Mukhopadhyay, S. and Chee, P. L., eds. (I)*, 1985, pp. 309–82. [G: S. Korea]

Choe, Yang Boo and Lee, Dong Phil. Role and Characteristics of Very Small Industries in Rural Korea. In *Mukhopadhyay, S. and Chee, P. L., eds. (II)*, 1985, pp. 151–74.
[G: S. Korea]

Christainsen, G. B. and Tietenberg, T. H. Distributional and Macroeconomic Aspects of Environmental Policy. In *Kneese, A. V. and Sweeney, J. L., eds. Vol. 1*, 1985, pp. 345–93.
[G: U.S.]

Clark, Peter B. Inflation and Unemployment in the United States: Recent Experience and Policies. In *Argy, V. E. and Neville, J. W., eds.*, 1985, pp. 221–48. [G: U.S.]

Clogg, Clifford C. and Shockey, James W. The Effect of Changing Demographic Composition on Recent Trends in Underemployment. *De-*

mography, August 1985, *22*(3), pp. 395–414. [G: U.S.]

Collis, Clive and Mallier, Anthony T. Employment Change in Coventry, 1971–78: A Shift–Share Approach. *Brit. Rev. Econ. Issues*, Autumn 1985, *7*(17), pp. 51–85. [G: U.K.]

Colwill, Nina L. Towards Equity: Directions for Future Research: Panel Discussion. In *Economic Council of Canada.*, 1985, pp. 121–24.

Cooke, William N. The Rising Toll of Discrimination against Union Activists. *Ind. Relat.*, Fall 1985, *24*(3), pp. 421–42. [G: U.S.]

Corcoran, Mary E. and Hill, Martha S. Reoccurrence of Unemployment among Adult Men. *J. Human Res.*, Spring 1985, *20*(2), pp. 165–83. [G: U.S.]

Craig, Christine; Garnsey, Elizabeth and Rubery, Jill. Labour Market Segmentation and Women's Employment: A Case-Study from the United Kingdom. *Int. Lab. Rev.*, May-June 1985, *124*(3), pp. 267–80. [G: U.K.]

Cronin, M. R. Protection and Employment in the Motor Car Sector: A Further Comment. *Australian Econ. Pap.*, June 1985, *24*(44), pp. 225.

Cross, Michael. Managing Workforce Reduction: Introduction. In *Cross, M., ed.*, 1985, pp. 1–5. [G: OECD]

Daniel, W. W. Managing Workforce Reduction: The United Kingdom. In *Cross, M., ed.*, 1985, pp. 67–90. [G: U.K.]

Darby, Michael R.; Haltiwanger, John C. and Plant, Mark W. Unemployment Rate Dynamics and Persistent Unemployment under Rational Expectations. *Amer. Econ. Rev.*, September 1985, *75*(4), pp. 614–37. [G: U.S.]

David-McNeil, Jeannine. The Changing Economic Status of the Female Labour Force in Canada. In *Economic Council of Canada.*, 1985, pp. 1–8. [G: Canada]

Dawkins, Peter. The Australian Labour Market, June 1985. *Australian Bull. Lab.*, June 1985, *11*(3), pp. 105–23. [G: Australia]

Debeauvais, Michel and Psacharopoulos, George. Forecasting the Needs for Qualified Manpower: Towards an Evaluation. In *Youdi, R. V. and Hinchliffe, K., eds.*, 1985, pp. 11–31. [G: Selected LDCs]

DeFreitas, Gregory. Ethnic Differentials in Unemployment among Hispanic Americans. In *Borjas, G. J. and Tienda, M., eds.*, 1985, pp. 127–57. [G: U.S.]

Deimezis, Nikitas. Analyse sectorielle de l'emploi dans l'industrie manufacturière belge. Perspectives à long terme. (With English summary.) *Cah. Écon. Bruxelles*, 2nd Trimester 1985, (106), pp. 192–216. [G: Belgium]

Devens, Richard M., Jr.; Leon, Carol Boyd and Sprinkle, Debbie L. Employment and Unemployment in 1984: A Second Year of Strong Growth in Jobs. *Mon. Lab. Rev.*, February 1985, *108*(2), pp. 3–15. [G: U.S.]

Diamond, Peter A. and Mirrlees, James A. Insurance Aspects of Pensions. In *Wise, D. A., ed.*, 1985, pp. 317–43.

Donges, Jürgen B. Chronic Unemployment in

Western Europe Forever? *World Econ.*, December 1985, *8*(4), pp. 353–72. [G: W. Europe]

Dooley, David and Catalano, Ralph. Does Economic Change Increase Mental Disorder?: A Synthesis of Recent Research. In *Westcott, G.; Svensson, P.-G. and Zollner, H. F. K., eds.*, 1985, pp. 57–86.

Dooley, David and Catalano, Ralph. Why the Economy Predicts Help Seeking: A Test of Competing Explanations. In *Westcott, G.; Svensson, P.-G. and Zollner, H. F. K., eds.*, 1985, pp. 205–29. [G: U.S.]

Dougherty, C. R. S. Manpower Forecasting and Manpower-Development Planning in the United Kingdom. In *Youdi, R. V. and Hinchliffe, K., eds.*, 1985, pp. 75–98. [G: U.K.]

Driver, Ciaran; Kilpatrick, Andrew and Naisbitt, Barry. The Employment Effects of Changes in the Structure of UK Trade. *J. Econ. Stud.*, 1985, *12*(5), pp. 19–38. [G: U.K.]

Eckstein, Albert J. and Heien, Dale. Causes and Consequences of Service Sector Growth: The U.S. Experience. *Growth Change*, April 1985, *16*(2), pp. 12–17. [G: U.S.]

Efremov, Aleksandr. The Effects of Disarmament on Employment in the USSR. *Int. Lab. Rev.*, July-Aug. 1985, *124*(4), pp. 423–34.

Elkan, Walter and Bishop, R. E. D. North Sea Oil: Responses to Employment Opportunities. *Energy Econ.*, April 1985, *7*(2), pp. 127–33. [G: U.K.]

Ellwood, David T. Pensions and the Labor Market: A Starting Point (The Mouse Can Roar). In *Wise, D. A., ed.*, 1985, pp. 19–49. [G: U.S.]

Elmore, Richard F. Knowledge Development under the Youth Employment and Demonstration Projects Act, 1977–1981. In *Betsey, C. L.; Hollister, R. G., Jr. and Papageorgiou, M. R., eds.*, 1985, pp. 281–347. [G: U.S.]

Eriksson, Tor. Taoustiede työllisyyspolitiikan apuna. (Economics and Employment Policy. With English summary.) *Kansant. Aikak.*, 1985, *81*(4), pp. 404–17. [G: Finland]

Ermisch, John F. Work, Jobs and Social Policy. In *Klein, R. and O'Higgins, M., ed.*, 1985, pp. 59–71. [G: U.K.]

Estrin, Saul. The Role of Producer Co-operatives in Employment Creation. *Econ. Anal. Worker's Manage.*, 1985, *19*(4), pp. 345–84. [G: OECD]

Euvrard, Françoise. L'indemnisation du Chomage: Un Essai de Comparaison internationale. (With English summary.) In *Terny, G. and Culyer, A. J., eds.*, 1985, pp. 67–82. [G: France; U.K.; W. Germany; Canada; Sweden]

Evans, Scott. Recent Changes in Rural Employment. *Australian Bull. Lab.*, December 1985, *12*(1), pp. 57–72. [G: Australia]

Fabella, Raul V. Rural Industry and Modernization. In *Mukhopadhyay, S. and Chee, P. L., eds. (II)*, 1985, pp. 117–50. [G: Philippines]

Fabella, Raul V. Rural Non-farm Activities in the Philippines: Composition, Growth and Seasonality. In *Mukhopadhyay, S. and Chee, P. L.*, *eds. (I)*, 1985, pp. 495–589. [G: Philippines]

Fair, Ray C. Excess Labor and the Business Cycle. *Amer. Econ. Rev.*, March 1985, 75(1), pp. 239–45. [G: U.S.]

Falter, Jürgen W., et al. Hat Arbeitslosigkeit tatsächlich den Aufstieg des Nationalsozialismus bewirkt? Eine Überprüfung der Analyse von Frey und Weck. (Did Unemployment Really Cause the Rise of National Socialism? With English summary.) *Jahr. Nationalökon. Statist.*, March 1985, 200(2), pp. 121–36.
[G: Germany]

Farrell, John B. Establishment Survey Incorporates March 1984 Employment Benchmarks. *Mon. Lab. Rev.*, August 1985, 108(8), pp. 39–41. [G: U.S.]

Fernandez, Roberto M. Hispanic Youth in the Labor Market: An Analysis of High School and Beyond. In *Betsey, C. L.; Hollister, R. G., Jr. and Papageorgiou, M. R., eds.*, 1985, pp. 410–61. [G: U.S.]

Fields, Gary S. Industrialization and Employment in Hong Kong, Singapore, and Taiwan. In *Galenson, W., ed.*, 1985, pp. 333–75.
[G: Hong Kong; Singapore; S. Korea; Taiwan]

FitzRoy, Felix R. and Hart, Robert A. Hours, Layoffs and Unemployment Insurance Funding: Theory and Practice in an International Perspective. *Econ. J.*, September 1985, 95(379), pp. 700–713.

Flaim, Paul O. and Hogue, Carma R. Measuring Labor Force Flows: A Special Conference Examines the Problems. *Mon. Lab. Rev.*, July 1985, 108(7), pp. 7–17. [G: U.S.]

Flaim, Paul O. and Sehgal, Ellen. Displaced Workers of 1979–83: How Well Have They Fared? *Mon. Lab. Rev.*, June 1985, 108(6), pp. 3–16. [G: U.S.]

Flanagan, Thomas. Policy-making by Exegesis: The Abolition of 'Mandatory Retirement' in Manitoba. *Can. Public Policy*, March 1985, 11(1), pp. 40–53. [G: Canada]

Foreman-Peck, James S. Seedcorn or Chaff? New Firm Formation and the Performance of the Interwar Economy. *Econ. Hist. Rev., 2nd Ser.*, August 1985, 38(3), pp. 402–22. [G: U.K.]

Forster, Colin. Unemployment and Minimum Wages in Australia, 1900–1930. *J. Econ. Hist.*, June 1985, 45(2), pp. 383–88. [G: Australia]

Franz, Wolfgang. An Economic Analysis of Female Work Participation, Education, and Fertility: Theory and Empirical Evidence for the Federal Republic of Germany. *J. Lab. Econ.*, Part 2 January 1985, 3(1), pp. S218–34.
[G: W. Germany]

Franz, Wolfgang. Challenges to the German Economy 1973–1983. Supply Shocks, Investment Slowdown, Inflation Variability and the Underutilization of Labor. *Z. Wirtschaft. Sozialwissen.*, 1985, 105(2/3), pp. 407–30.
[G: W. Germany]

Fraser, Colin; Marsh, Catherine and Jobling, Ray. Political Responses to Unemployment. In *Roberts, B.; Finnegan, R. and Gallie, D.,*

eds., 1985, pp. 351–64. [G: U.K.]

Friedman, Sheldon. Negotiated Approaches to Job Security. In *Dennis, B. D., ed.*, 1985, pp. 553–57. [G: U.S.]

Galasi, Péter and Sziráczki, György. State Regulation, Enterprise Behaviour and the Labour Market in Hungary, 1968–83. *Cambridge J. Econ.*, September 1985, 9(3), pp. 203–19.
[G: Hungary]

Galbraith, J. A. Valuing Pensions (Annuities) with Different Types of Inflation Protection in Total Compensation Comparisons: A Note. *Can. J. Econ.*, November 1985, 18(4), pp. 810–13.
[G: Canada]

Garside, W. R. The Failure of the 'Radical Alternative': Public Works, Deficit Finance and British Interwar Unemployment. *J. Europ. Econ. Hist.*, Sept.-Dec. 1985, 14(3), pp. 537–55. [G: U.K.]

Garside, W. R. and Hatton, T. J. Keynesian Policy and British Unemployment in the 1930s [Unemployment in Interwar Britain: A Case for Re-learning the Lessons of the 1930s?]. *Econ. Hist. Rev., 2nd Ser.*, February 1985, 38(1), pp. 83–88. [G: U.K.]

Gemmell, Norman. The Growth of Employment in Services: Egypt, 1960–75. *Devel. Econ.*, March 1985, 23(1), pp. 53–68. [G: Egypt]

Gillis, William R. and Shaffer, Ron E. Targeting Employment Opportunities toward Selected Workers. *Land Econ.*, November 1985, 61(4), pp. 433–44. [G: U.S.]

Ginsburg, Helen. Flexible and Partial Retirement for Norwegian and Swedish Workers. *Mon. Lab. Rev.*, October 1985, 108(10), pp. 33–43.
[G: Norway; Sweden]

Glynn, Sean and Booth, Alan. Building Counterfactual Pyramids [Keynesian Policy and British Unemployment in the 1930s] [Unemployment in Interwar Britain: A Case for Re-learning the Lessons of the 1930s?]. *Econ. Hist. Rev., 2nd Ser.*, February 1985, 38(1), pp. 89–94.
[G: U.K.]

Gordon, Ian R. The Cyclical Interaction between Regional Migration, Employment and Unemployment: A Time Series Analysis for Scotland. *Scot. J. Polit. Econ.*, June 1985, 32(2), pp. 135–58. [G: U.K.]

Gordon, Ian R. The Cyclical Sensitivity of Regional Employment and Unemployment Differentials. *Reg. Stud.*, April 1985, 19(2), pp. 95–110. [G: U.K.]

Gottschalk, Peter and Maloney, Tim. Involuntary Terminations, Unemployment, and Job Matching: A Test of Job Search Theory. *J. Lab. Econ.*, April 1985, 3(2), pp. 109–23. [G: U.S.]

Green, A. E. Unemployment Duration in the Recession: The Local Labour Market Area Scale. *Reg. Stud.*, April 1985, 19(2), pp. 111–29.
[G: U.K.]

Green, A. E. and Coombes, M. G. Local Unemployment Rates: Statistical Sensitivities and Policy Implications. *Reg. Stud.*, June 1985, 19(3), pp. 268–73. [G: U.K.]

Gregory, R. G. and Smith, Ralph E. Unemployment, Inflation and Job Creation Policies in

Australia. In *Argy, V. E. and Neville, J. W.*, eds., 1985, pp. 325–45. [G: Australia]

Grönberg, Rolf and Rahmeyer, Fritz. Preis- und Mengenanpassungen in den Konjunkturzyklen der Bundesrepublik Deutschland, 1963–1981. (Price and Quantity Adjustments in the Business Cycles of the Federal Republic of Germany, 1963–1981. With English summary.) *Jahr. Nationalökon. Statist.*, May 1985, *200*(3), pp. 239–61. [G: W. Germany]

Gross, Bertram and Singh, Kusum. Global Unemployment: Challenge to Futurists. In *Didsbury, H. F., Jr., ed.*, 1985, pp. 35–59.

Gustafsson, Siv and Jacobsson, Roger. Trends in Female Labor Force Participation in Sweden. *J. Lab. Econ.*, Part 2 January 1985, *3*(1), pp. S256–74. [G: Sweden]

Habib, Ahsanul; Stahl, Charles and Alauddin, Mohammad. Inter-industry Analysis of Employment Linkages in Bangladesh. *Econ. Planning*, 1985, *19*(1), pp. 24–38.
[G: Bangladesh]

Håkanson, Lars and Danielsson, Lars. Structural Adjustment in a Stagnating Economy: Regional Manufacturing Employment in Sweden, 1975–1980. *Reg. Stud.*, August 1985, *19*(4), pp. 329–42. [G: Sweden]

Hallwirth, Volker. Reallohn und Beschäftigung—Ein Ansatz zum Test der klassischen Grenzproduktivitätstheorie der Arbeit. (The Marginal Productivity Relationship of Wages and Employment—A Specification of an Empirical Test. With English summary.) *Jahr. Nationalökon. Statist.*, March 1985, *200*(2), pp. 153–72.
[G: W. Germany]

Hamada, Koichi. Lessons from the Macroeconomic Performance of the Japanese Economy. In *Argy, V. E. and Neville, J. W.*, eds., 1985, pp. 181–99. [G: Japan]

Hamel, Harvey R. and Tucker, John T. Implementing the Levitan Commission's Recommendations to Improve Labor Data. *Mon. Lab. Rev.*, February 1985, *108*(2), pp. 16–24.
[G: U.S.]

Hamermesh, Daniel S. Substitution between Different Categories of Labour, Relative Wages and Youth Unemployment. *OECD Econ. Stud.*, Autumn 1985, (5), pp. 57–85.
[G: OECD]

Harrell, Louis and Fischer, Dale. The 1982 Mexican Peso Devaluation and Border Area Employment. *Mon. Lab. Rev.*, October 1985, *108*(10), pp. 25–32. [G: Mexico; U.S.]

Harris, C. C.; Lee, R. M. and Morris, Lydia D. Redundancy in Steel: Labour-Market Behaviour, Local Social Networks and Domestic Organisation. In *Roberts, B.; Finnegan, R. and Gallie, D.*, eds., 1985, pp. 154–66. [G: U.K.]

Harris, G. T. A Note on Rural Unemployment: A Study of Four Northern New South Wales Towns. *Rev. Marketing Agr. Econ.*, August 1985, *53*(2), pp. 63–73. [G: Australia]

Harris, Richard G. Jobs and Free Trade. In *Conklin, D. W. and Courchene, T. J.*, eds., 1985, pp. 188–203. [G: Canada]

Harrison, Bennett and Bluestone, Barry. Prob-

lems of Economic Deterioration. In *Woodworth, W.; Meek, C. and Whyte, W. F.*, eds., 1985, pp. 64–77. [G: U.S.]

Hashemzadeh, Nozar and Long, Burl F. Cyclical Aspects of Black Unemployment: An Empirical Analysis. *Rev. Reg. Stud.*, Winter 1985, *15*(1), pp. 7–19. [G: U.S.]

Hashimoto, Masanori and Raisian, John. Employment Tenure and Earnings Profiles in Japan and the United States. *Amer. Econ. Rev.*, September 1985, *75*(4), pp. 721–35.
[G: Japan; U.S.]

Hatton, T. J. The British Labor Market in the 1920s: A Test of the Search–Turnover Approach. *Exploration Econ. Hist.*, July 1985, *22*(3), pp. 257–70. [G: U.K.]

Hausman, Jerry A. and Watson, Mark W. Errors in Variables and Seasonal Adjustment Procedures. *J. Amer. Statist. Assoc.*, September 1985, *80*(391), pp. 531–40. [G: U.S.]

Hausman, Jerry A. and Wise, David A. Social Security, Health Status, and Retirement. In *Wise, D. A.*, ed., 1985, pp. 159–81.
[G: U.S.]

Haveman, Robert H. and Wolfe, Barbara L. The Effect of Disability Transfers on Work Effort: Research Results and Their Use in Policy Decisions. In *[Recktenwald, H. C.]*, 1985, pp. 261–78. [G: OECD]

Heckman, James J. and Singer, Burton. Social Science Duration Analysis. In *Heckman, J. J. and Singer, B.*, eds., 1985, pp. 39–110.
[G: U.S.]

Hekman, John S. Branch Plant Location and the Product Cycle in Computer Manufacturing. *J. Econ. Bus.*, May 1985, *37*(2), pp. 89–102.
[G: U.S.]

Helby, Peter. Er ungdomsløn et egnet middel mod ungdomsarbejdsløshed? (Would a Youth Subminimal Wage Be Effective against Youth Employment? With English summary.) *Nationaløkon. Tidsskr.*, 1985, *123*(2), pp. 194–205. [G: Denmark]

Henderson, A. G. A Comparison of Japanese and Australian Labour Markets. *Australian Bull. Lab.*, December 1985, *12*(1), pp. 22–45.
[G: Australia; Japan]

Henry, S. G. B.; Payne, J. M. and Trinder, C. Real Wages and Unemployment: A Rejoinder [Labour Market Equilibrium in an Open Economy]. *Oxford Econ. Pap.*, June 1985, *37*(2), pp. 344–45. [G: U.K.]

Henry, S. G. B.; Payne, J. M. and Trinder, C. Unemployment and Real Wages: The Role of Unemployment, Social Security Benefits and Unionisation [Labour Market Equilibrium in an Open Economy] [Unions Real Wages and Employment]. *Oxford Econ. Pap.*, June 1985, *37*(2), pp. 330–38. [G: U.K.]

Hernandez Iglesias, Feliciano and Riboud, Michelle. Trends in Labor Force Participation of Spanish Women: An Interpretive Essay. *J. Lab. Econ.*, Part 2 January 1985, *3*(1), pp. S201–17. [G: Spain]

Heyer, Nelson O. Managing Human Resources in a High Technology Enterprise. In *Niehaus*,

R. J., ed., 1985, pp. 45–66.   [G: U.S.]

Hicks, Peter. A National System for Parental Leave: Comments. In *Economic Council of Canada.*, 1985, pp. 28–29.   [G: Canada]

Hight, Joseph E. Review of Manpower Forecasts and Changes in Occupational Structure in the United States of America. In *Youdi, R. V. and Hinchliffe, K., eds.*, 1985, pp. 99–115.
[G: U.S.]

Hill, John K. The Economic Impact of Tighter U.S. Border Security. *Fed. Res. Bank Dallas Econ. Rev.*, July 1985, pp. 12–20.   [G: U.S.]

Hoffman, Emily P. Fertility and Female Employment. *Quart. Rev. Econ. Bus.*, Spring 1985, 25(1), pp. 85–95.   [G: U.S.]

Holden, Karen C. Maintaining Faculty Vitality through Early Retirement Options. In *Clark, S. M. and Lewis, D. R., eds.*, 1985, pp. 224–44.   [G: U.S.]

Honig, Marjorie. Partial Retirement among Women [Partial Retirement as a Separate Mode of Retirement Behavior]. *J. Human Res.*, Fall 1985, 20(4), pp. 613–21.   [G: U.S.]

Honig, Marjorie and Hanoch, Giora. Partial Retirement as a Separate Mode of Retirement Behavior. *J. Human Res.*, Winter 1985, 20(1), pp. 21–46.   [G: U.S.]

Horn, Gustav and Möller, Joachim. Keynesianische oder Klassische Arbeitslosigkeit in der Bundesrepublik Deutschland? Empirische überprüfung eines Mengenrationierungsmodells mittels Kalman–Verfahren für den Zeitraum 1970–1982. (Keynesian or Classical Unemployment in the Federal Republic of Germany? Empirical Test of a Quantity Rationing Model Applying the Kalman Approach with Data from 1970 to 1982. With English summary.) *Ifo-Studien*, 1985, 31(3), pp. 203–38.
[G: W. Germany]

Howenstine, Ned G. U.S. Affiliates of Foreign Companies: Operations in 1983. *Surv. Curr. Bus.*, November 1985, 65(11), pp. 36–50.
[G: U.S.]

Hudson, John. Inflation and Unemployment Aversion. *Econ. J.*, Supplement 1985, 95, pp. 148–50.   [G: U.K.]

Huskey, Lee. The Hidden Dynamic in the Growth of Frontier Regions: Import Substitution. *Growth Change*, October 1985, 16(4), pp. 43–55.   [G: U.S.]

Ippolito, Richard A. Income Tax Policy and Lifetime Labor Supply. *J. Public Econ.*, April 1985, 26(3), pp. 327–47.   [G: U.S.]

Isuani, Ernesto A. Social Security and Public Assistance. In *Mesa-Lago, C., ed.*, 1985, pp. 89–102.   [G: Latin America]

Isuani, Ernesto A. Universalización de la seguridad social en América Latina: límites estructurales y cambios necesarios. (With English summary.) *Desarrollo Econ.*, April–June 1985, 25(97), pp. 71–84.   [G: Latin America]

Janlert, Urban. Unemployment and Health. In *Westcott, G.; Svensson, P.-G. and Zollner, H. F. K., eds.*, 1985, pp. 7–26.   [G: U.K.; Sweden; Finland]

Jenkins, Richard. Black Workers in the Labour Market: The Price of Recession. In *Roberts, B.; Finnegan, R. and Gallie, D., eds.*, 1985, pp. 169–83.   [G: U.K.]

Jha, L. K. Unemployment. In *Jha, L. K.*, 1985, pp. 53–59.   [G: India]

Johnson, Kenneth P. and Friedenberg, Howard L. Regional and State Projections of Income, Employment, and Population to the Year 2000. *Surv. Curr. Bus.*, May 1985, 65(5), pp. 39–63.   [G: U.S.]

Johnson, Merrill L. Postwar Industrial Development in the Southeast and the Pioneer Role of Labor-intensive Industry. *Econ. Geogr.*, January 1985, 61(1), pp. 46–65.   [G: U.S.]

Johnson, Willene A. Women and Self-Employment in Urban Tanzania. *Rev. Black Polit. Econ.*, Fall-Winter 1985-86, 14(2–3), pp. 245–57.   [G: Tanzania]

Jones, Barbara A. P. Black Women and Labor Force Participation: An Analysis of Sluggish Growth Rates. *Rev. Black Polit. Econ.*, Fall-Winter 1985-86, 14(2–3), pp. 11–31.
[G: U.S.]

Jones, David R. Redundancy, Natural Turnover and the Paradox of Structural Change. *Bull. Econ. Res.*, January 1985, 37(1), pp. 41–54.
[G: U.K.; New Zealand]

Jones, David R. and MacKay, R. Ross. Unemployment in Wales: The Implications of Government Priorities. *Nat. Westminster Bank Quart. Rev.*, May 1985, pp. 74–84.
[G: U.K.]

Jones, M. E. F. Regional Employment Multipliers, Regional Policy, and Structural Change in Interwar Britain. *Exploration Econ. Hist.*, October 1985, 22(4), pp. 417–39.   [G: U.K.]

Jones, M. E. F. The Regional Impact of an Overvalued Pound in the 1920s. *Econ. Hist. Rev.*, 2nd Ser., August 1985, 38(3), pp. 393–401.
[G: U.K.]

Jones, Stephen G. The Worksharing Debate in Western Europe. *Nat. Westminster Bank Quart. Rev.*, February 1985, pp. 30–41.
[G: EEC]

Jordan, Bill. Unemployment and the Recovery: The Future of Labour Utilisation. In *Meyer, F. V., ed.*, 1985, pp. 183–212.   [G: OECD; U.K.]

Josefowicz, A.; Kluczynski, J. and Obrebski, T. Manpower and Education Planning and Policy Experience in Poland, 1960–80. In *Youdi, R. V. and Hinchliffe, K., eds.*, 1985, pp. 135–52.   [G: Poland]

Joshi, Heather E.; Layard, Richard and Owen, Susan J. Why Are More Women Working in Britain? *J. Lab. Econ.*, Part 2 January 1985, 3(1), pp. S147–76.   [G: U.K.]

Kasarda, John D. Urban Change and Minority Opportunities. In *Peterson, P. E., ed.*, 1985, pp. 33–67.   [G: U.S.]

Katz, Arnold. Growth and Regional Variations in Unemployment in Yugoslavia: 1965–1980. In *Jones, D. C. and Svejnar, J., eds.*, 1985, pp. 153–77.   [G: Yugoslavia]

Keeley, Michael C. and Robins, Philip K. Government Programs, Job Search Requirements, and the Duration of Unemployment. *J. Lab. Econ.*, July 1985, *3*(3), pp. 337–62. [G: U.S.]

Kestenbaum, Bert. The Measurement of Early Retirement. *J. Amer. Statist. Assoc.*, March 1985, *80*(389), pp. 38–45. [G: U.S.]

Kiefer, Nicholas M. Evidence on the Role of Education in Labor Turnover. *J. Human Res.*, Summer 1985, *20*(3), pp. 445–52. [G: U.S.]

Kiefer, Nicholas M.; Lundberg, Shelly J. and Neumann, George R. How Long Is a Spell of Unemployment? Illusions and Biases in the Use of CPS Data. *J. Bus. Econ. Statist.*, April 1985, *3*(2), pp. 118–28. [G: U.S.]

Kieselbach, Thomas. The Contribution of Psychology to the Realm of Unemployment in the Community: Intervention and Research Concepts. In *Westcott, G.; Svensson, P.-G. and Zollner, H. F. K., eds.*, 1985, pp. 367–82. [G: W. Germany]

Kotlikoff, Laurence J. and Wise, David A. Labor Compensation and the Structure of Private Pension Plans: Evidence for Contractual versus Spot Labor Markets. In *Wise, D. A., ed.*, 1985, pp. 55–85. [G: U.S.]

Krugman, Paul R. The Real Wage Gap and Employment. In *Melitz, J. and Wyplosz, C., eds.*, 1985, pp. 51–69. [G: France; U.S.; EEC]

Lancaster, Tony and Chesher, Andrew. Residuals, Tests and Plots with a Job Matching Illustration. *Ann. INSEE*, July-Dec. 1985, (59/60), pp. 47–70.

Lang, Graeme. Regional Variations in Worksharing: The Case of Newfoundland. *Can. Public Policy*, March 1985, *11*(1), pp. 54–63. [G: Canada]

Laulan, Yves M. Unemployment in France. *Nat. Westminster Bank Quart. Rev.*, May 1985, pp. 21–31. [G: France]

Layard, Richard and Nickell, Stephen. Unemployment, Real Wages, and Aggregate Demand in Europe, Japan and the United States. *Carnegie-Rochester Conf. Ser. Public Policy*, Autumn 1985, *23*, pp. 143–202. [G: France; U.K.; W. Germany; Japan; U.S.]

Layard, Richard and Nickell, Stephen. The Causes of British Unemployment. *Nat. Inst. Econ. Rev.*, February 1985, (111), pp. 62–85. [G: U.K.]

Le Pen, Claude. Emplois publics et distribution des revenus. (Public Employment and Distribution of Income. With English summary.) *Revue Écon.*, July 1985, *36*(4), pp. 715–39. [G: France]

Lee, Robert H. and Hadley, Jack. The Demand for Residents. *J. Health Econ.*, December 1985, *4*(4), pp. 357–71. [G: U.S.]

Leigh, J. Paul. The Effects of Unemployment and the Business Cycle on Absenteeism. *J. Econ. Bus.*, May 1985, *37*(2), pp. 159–70. [G: U.S.]

León, Francisco. Social Security and Public Assistance: Comment. In *Mesa-Lago, C., ed.*, 1985, pp. 102–08. [G: Latin America]

Leonard, Herman B. The Federal Civil Service Retirement System: An Analysis of Its Financial Condition and Current Reform Proposals. In *Wise, D. A., ed.*, 1985, pp. 399–438. [G: U.S.]

Leonard, Jonathan S. Affirmative Action as Earnings Redistribution: The Targeting of Compliance Reviews. *J. Lab. Econ.*, July 1985, *3*(3), pp. 363–84.

Leonard, Jonathan S. The Effect of Unions on the Employment of Blacks, Hispanics, and Women. *Ind. Lab. Relat. Rev.*, October 1985, *39*(1), pp. 115–32. [G: U.S.]

Leonard, Jonathan S. What Promises Are Worth: The Impact of Affirmative Action Goals. *J. Human Res.*, Winter 1985, *20*(1), pp. 3–20. [G: U.S.]

Lesourne, Jacques. Social Values, Political Goals, and Economic Systems: The Issue of Employment in European Societies. In *Didsbury, H. F., Jr., ed.*, 1985, pp. 60–75.

Lewin-Epstein, Noah. Neighborhoods, Local Labor Markets, and Employment Opportunities for White and Nonwhite Youth. *Soc. Sci. Quart.*, March 1985, *66*(1), pp. 163–71. [G: U.S.]

Lewis, Jane. Work, Women and Welfare. In *Klein, R. and O'Higgins, M., ed.*, 1985, pp. 216–22. [G: U.K.]

Lillydahl, Jane H. and Singell, Larry D. The Spatial Variation in Unemployment and Labour Force Participation Rates of Male and Female Workers. *Reg. Stud.*, October 1985, *19*(5), pp. 459–69. [G: U.K.]

Little, Jane Sneddon. Foreign Direct Investment in New England. *New Eng. Econ. Rev.*, March/April 1985, pp. 48–57. [G: U.S.]

Lloyd, Peter E. and Shutt, John. Recession and Restructuring in the North-west Region, 1975–82: The Implications of Recent Events. In *Massey, D. and Meegan, R., eds.*, 1985, pp. 16–60. [G: U.K.]

Lundberg, Shelly J. The Added Worker Effect. *J. Lab. Econ.*, Part 1 January 1985, *3*(1), pp. 11–37. [G: U.S.]

Lynch, Lisa M. State Dependency in Youth Unemployment: A Lost Generation? *J. Econometrics*, April 1985, *28*(1), pp. 71–84. [G: U.K.]

Lynd, Staughton. Options for Reindustrialization: Brownfield versus Greenfield Approaches. In *Woodworth, W.; Meek, C. and Whyte, W. F., eds.*, 1985, pp. 49–63. [G: U.S.]

MacDonald, Martha. Towards Equity: Directions for Future Research: Panel Discussion. In *Economic Council of Canada.*, 1985, pp. 124–27.

Main, Brian G. M. School-leaver Unemployment and the Youth Opportunities Programme in Scotland. *Oxford Econ. Pap.*, September 1985, *37*(3), pp. 426–47.

Mairesse, Jacques and Dormont, Brigitte. Labor and Investment Demand at the Firm Level: A Comparison of French, German and U.S. Manufacturing, 1970-79. *Europ. Econ. Rev.*, June-July 1985, *28*(1–2), pp. 201–31. [G: France; U.S.; W. Germany]

Malinvaud, Edmond. The Real Wage Gap and Employment: Comments. In *Melitz, J. and Wyplosz, C., eds.*, 1985, pp. 81–83. **[G: France; U.S.; EEC]**

Malkas, Tapani. Health Effects of Unemployment and National Health Policy in Finland. In *Westcott, G.; Svensson, P.-G. and Zollner, H. F. K., eds.*, 1985, pp. 357–65. **[G: Finland]**

Mangan, J. and Stokes, L. Labour Demand in Australian Manufacturing: A Further Analysis. *S. Afr. J. Econ.*, June 1985, *53*(2), pp. 197–200. **[G: Australia]**

Mangum, Garth; Mayall, Donald and Nelson, Kristin. The Temporary Help Industry: A Response to the Dual Internal Labor Market. *Ind. Lab. Relat. Rev.*, July 1985, *38*(4), pp. 599–611. **[G: U.S.]**

Mare, Robert D. and Winship, Christopher. School Enrollment, Military Enlistment, and the Transition to Work: Implications for the Age Pattern of Employment. In *Heckman, J. J. and Singer, B., eds.*, 1985, pp. 364–99. **[G: U.S.]**

Marsden, Lorna R. Technological Change: Bad or Good? Comments. In *Economic Council of Canada.*, 1985, pp. 93–97. **[G: U.S.]**

Marshall, J. N. Business Services, the Regions and Regional Policy. *Reg. Stud.*, August 1985, *19*(4), pp. 353–63. **[G: U.K.]**

Marshall, Ray. The American Industrial Relations System in a Time of Change. *J. Econ. Educ.*, Spring 1985, *16*(2), pp. 85–97. **[G: U.S.; EEC; Japan]**

Marston, Stephen T. Two Views of the Geographic Distribution of Unemployment. *Quart. J. Econ.*, February 1985, *100*(1), pp. 57–79. **[G: U.S.]**

Martin, Roderick and Wallace, Judith. Women and Unemployment: Activities and Social Contact. In *Roberts, B.; Finnegan, R. and Gallie, D., eds.*, 1985, pp. 417–30. **[G: U.K.]**

Mason, Greg. The Manitoba Basic Annual Income Data Base. *Can. Public Policy*, March 1985, *11*(1), pp. 113–14. **[G: Canada]**

Massey, Doreen and Meegan, Richard. Profits and Job Loss. In *Massey, D. and Meegan, R., eds.*, 1985, pp. 119–43.

Mayer, Francine and Roy, Paul-Martel. Aspects dynamiques de la structure du chômage au Québec. (Dynamic Aspects of the Structure of Unemployment in Quebec. With English summary.) *L'Actual. Econ.*, June 1985, *61*(2), pp. 200–219. **[G: Canada]**

Mayhew, Ken. Employee Behaviour. In *Morris, D., ed.*, 1985, pp. 86–111. **[G: U.K.]**

McDonald, John F. The Intensity of Land Use in Urban Employment Sectors: Chicago 1956–1970. *J. Urban Econ.*, November 1985, *18*(3), pp. 261–77. **[G: U.S.]**

McGee, Robert T. State Unemployment Rates: What Explains the Differences? *Fed. Res. Bank New York Quart. Rev.*, Spring 1985, *10*(1), pp. 28–35. **[G: U.S.]**

McKee, Lorna and Bell, Colin. Marital and Family Relations in Times of Male Unemployment. In *Roberts, B.; Finnegan, R. and Gallie, D., eds.*, 1985, pp. 387–99. **[G: U.K.]**

Meek, Christopher. Labor–Management Committee Outcomes: The Jamestown Case. In *Woodworth, W.; Meek, C. and Whyte, W. F., eds.*, 1985, pp. 141–59. **[G: U.S.]**

Merton, Robert C. Insurance Aspects of Pensions: Comment. In *Wise, D. A., ed.*, 1985, pp. 343–56.

Micklewright, John. Fiction versus Fact: Unemployment Benefits in Britain. *Nat. Westminster Bank Quart. Rev.*, May 1985, pp. 52–62. **[G: U.K.]**

Mier, Robert and Giloth, Robert. Hispanic Employment Opportunities: A Case of Internal Labor Markets and Weak-tied Social Networks. *Soc. Sci. Quart.*, June 1985, *66*(2), pp. 296–309. **[G: U.S.]**

Mieszkowski, Peter. The Differential Effect of the Foreign Trade Deficit on Regions in the United States. In *Quigley, J. M. and Rubinfeld, D. L., eds.*, 1985, pp. 346–63. **[G: U.S.]**

Miller, Paul W. and Volker, Paul A. Economic Progress in Australia: An Analysis of Occupational Mobility. *Econ. Rec.*, March 1985, *61*(172), pp. 463–75. **[G: Australia]**

Miller, Paul W. and Volker, Paul A. Unemployment Insurance Eligibility Rights: Evidence from a Comparison of Australia and Canada. *J. Macroecon.*, Spring 1985, *7*(2), pp. 223–35. **[G: Australia; Canada]**

Mills, D. Quinn and Lovell, Malcolm R., Jr. Competitiveness: The Labor Dimension. In *Scott, B. R. and Lodge, G. C., eds.*, 1985, pp. 429–54. **[G: U.S.]**

Mills, Edwin S. Open Housing Laws as Stimulus to Central City Employment. *J. Urban Econ.*, March 1985, *17*(2), pp. 184–88. **[G: U.S.]**

Minford, Patrick. Unemployment and Real Wages: The Role of Unemployment, Social Security Benefits and Unionisation [Labour Market Equilibrium in an Open Economy]: Reply. *Oxford Econ. Pap.*, June 1985, *37*(2), pp. 339–43. **[G: U.K.]**

Mitchell, Mark L.; Wallace, Myles S. and Warner, John T. Real Wages over the Business Cycle: Some Further Evidence. *Southern Econ. J.*, April 1985, *51*(4), pp. 1162–73. **[G: U.S.]**

Mitchell, Olivia S. and Fields, Gary S. Rewards for Continued Work: The Economic Incentives for Postponing Retirement. In *David, M. and Smeeding, T., eds.*, 1985, pp. 269–86. **[G: U.S.]**

Moberg, David. Problems of Industrial Plant Shutdowns. In *Woodworth, W.; Meek, C. and Whyte, W. F., eds.*, 1985, pp. 28–48. **[G: U.S.]**

Moffitt, Robert. Unemployment Insurance and the Distribution of Unemployment Spells. *J. Econometrics*, April 1985, *28*(1), pp. 85–101. **[G: U.S.]**

Mohabbat, Khan A. and Arshanapalli, Gangadhar. Unemployment, Inflation and Compensation Growth—A Case Study of Italy, 1970–

1980. *Econ. Int.*, May 1985, *38*(2), pp. 214–21. [G: Italy]

Montuschi, Luisa. Los Sectores Claves para el Trabajo Asalariado en la Economía Argentina 1963–1970. (The Key Sectors for the Labor Force in the Argentine Economy. With English summary.) *Económica (La Plata)*, Jan.-Apr. 1985, *31*(1), pp. 81–98. [G: Argentina]

Morris, Derek J. and Sinclair, Peter. The Assessment: The Unemployment Problems in the 1980's. *Oxford Rev. Econ. Policy*, Summer 1985, *1*(2), pp. 1–19. [G: U.K.]

Morris, Lydia D. Renegotiation of the Domestic Division of Labour in the Context of Male Redundancy. In *Roberts, B.; Finnegan, R. and Gallie, D., eds.*, 1985, pp. 400–416. [G: U.K.]

Morris, Lydia D. Responses to Redundancy: Labour-Market Experience, Domestic Organisation and Male Social Networks. *Int. J. Soc. Econ.*, 1985, *12*(2), pp. 5–16. [G: U.K.]

Motley, Brian. Whither the Unemployment Rate? *Fed. Res. Bank San Francisco Econ. Rev.*, Spring 1985, (2), pp. 40–54. [G: U.S.]

Moy, Joyanna. Recent Trends in Unemployment and the Labor Force, 10 Countries. *Mon. Lab. Rev.*, August 1985, *108*(8), pp. 9–22. [G: OECD]

Murgatroyd, Linda G. and Urry, John. The Class and Gender Restructuring of the Lancaster Economy, 1950–80. In *Roberts, B.; Finnegan, R. and Gallie, D., eds.*, 1985, pp. 68–85. [G: U.K.]

Murphy, Kevin J. Geographic Differences in U.S. Unemployment Rates: A Variance Decomposition Approach. *Econ. Inquiry*, January 1985, *23*(1), pp. 135–58. [G: U.S.]

Murphy, Kevin J. Unemployment Dispersion and the Allocative Efficiency of the Labor Market. *J. Macroecon.*, Fall 1985, *7*(4), pp. 509–22. [G: U.S.]

Myers, Robert J. Income of Social Security Beneficiaries as Affected by Earnings Test and Income Taxes on Benefits. *J. Risk Ins.*, June 1985, *52*(2), pp. 289–300. [G: U.S.]

Nalebuff, Barry and Zeckhauser, Richard J. Pensions and the Retirement Decision. In *Wise, D. A., ed.*, 1985, pp. 283–316. [G: U.S.]

Narendranathan, Wiji; Nickell, Stephen and Metcalf, D. An Investigation into the Incidence and Dynamic Structure of Sickness and Unemployment in Britain, 1965–75. *J. Roy. Statist. Soc.*, 1985, *148*(3), pp. 254–67. [G: U.K.]

Narendranathan, Wiji; Nickell, Stephen and Stern, J. Unemployment Benefits Revisited. *Econ. J.*, June 1985, *95*(378), pp. 307–29. [G: U.K.]

Neck, Reinhard. On the Effects of Disinflationary Policies on Unemployment and Inflation: A Simulation Study with Keynesian and Monetarist Models for Austria. *Z. Wirtschaft. Sozialwissen.*, 1985, *105*(2/3), pp. 357–86. [G: Austria]

de Neubourg, Chris. Part-Time Work: An International Quantitative Comparison. *Int. Lab.*

Rev., Sept.-Oct. 1985, *124*(5), pp. 559–76. [G: OECD]

de Neubourg, Chris. The Origin and Insignificance of Labour Market Imperfections in the Netherlands: Another Note on the Specification of the UV Curve 1955-1980. *De Economist*, 1985, *133*(1), pp. 64–77. [G: Netherlands]

Neuburger, Henry. Why Is Unemployment So High? *Nat. Westminster Bank Quart. Rev.*, May 1985, pp. 12–20. [G: W. Europe; U.S.]

Nickell, Stephen. The Determinants of Equilibrium Unemployment in Britain: A Reply. *Econ. J.*, March 1985, *95*(377), pp. 196–98.

Nogués, Julio J. Distortions, Factor Proportions and Efficiency Losses: Argentina in the Latin American Scenario. *Weltwirtsch. Arch.*, 1985, *121*(2), pp. 280–303. [G: Argentina]

Novak, Michael. Morality of the Market: Religious and Economic Perspectives: Overview. In *Block, W.; Brennan, G. and Elzinga, K., eds.*, 1985, pp. 567–87. [G: U.S.]

Novek, Joel. University Graduates, Jobs, and University–Industry Linkages. *Can. Public Policy*, June 1985, *11*(2), pp. 180–95. [G: Canada]

O'Farrell, P. N. Employment Change in Manufacturing: The Case of Surviving Plants. *Urban Stud.*, February 1985, *22*(1), pp. 57–68. [G: U.K.]

O'Neill, June. The Trend in the Male–Female Wage Gap in the United States. *J. Lab. Econ.*, Part 2 January 1985, *3*(1), pp. S91–116. [G: U.S.]

Odaka, Konosuke. Is the Division of Labor Limited by the Extent of the Market? A Study of Automobile Parts Production in East and Southeast Asia. In *Ohkawa, K. and Ranis, G., eds.*, 1985, pp. 389–425. [G: E. Asia; S.E. Asia]

Offe, Claus. The Growth of the Service Sector. In *Offe, C.*, 1985, pp. 101–28.

Offe, Claus. Three Perspectives on the Problem of Unemployment. In *Offe, C.*, 1985, pp. 80–100.

Offe, Claus, et al. Interest Diversity and Trade Union Unity. In *Offe, C.*, 1985, pp. 151–69. [G: W. Germany]

Oi, Walter Y. Unemployment, Real Wages, and Aggregate Demand in Europe, Japan and the United States: Comments on the Layard–Nickell Model of Unemployment and Real Wages. *Carnegie-Rochester Conf. Ser. Public Policy*, Autumn 1985, *23*, pp. 203–09. [G: France; U.K.; W. Germany; Japan; U.S.]

Ondrich, Jan I. The Initial Conditions Problem in Work History Data. *Rev. Econ. Statist.*, August 1985, *67*(3), pp. 441–21. [G: U.S.]

Packard, Michael. Company Policies and Attitudes toward Older Workers. *Soc. Sec. Bull.*, May 1985, *48*(5), pp. 45–46. [G: U.S.]

Pahl, R. E. and Wallace, C. D. Forms of Work and Privatisation on the Isle of Sheppey. In *Roberts, B.; Finnegan, R. and Gallie, D., eds.*, 1985, pp. 368–86. [G: U.K.]

Pang, Eng Fong. Employment, Skills and Technology. In *Gustavsson, B.; Karlsson, J. C. and Raftegard, C.*, 1985, pp. 93–102.

Parry, Thomas G. Protection and Employment in the Motor Car Sector: A Note. *Australian Econ. Pap.*, June 1985, *24*(44), pp. 222–24.

Paul, Jean-Jacques. Basic Concepts and Methods Used in Forecasting Skilled-Manpower Requirements in France. In *Youdi, R. V. and Hinchliffe, K., eds.*, 1985, pp. 35–56. [G: France]

Peitchinis, Stephen G. Technological Change: Bad or Good? In *Economic Council of Canada.*, 1985, pp. 83–93. [G: U.S.]

Pellegrini, Luca. The Distributive Trades in the Italian Economy: Some Remarks on the Decade 1970–80. *Rev. Econ. Cond. Italy*, May-Aug. 1985, (2), pp. 191–220. [G: Italy]

Pemberton, James. Unemployment. In *Atkinson, G. B. J., ed.*, 1985, pp. 1–33. [G: U.K.]

Personick, Valerie A. A Second Look at Industry Output and Employment Trends through 1995. *Mon. Lab. Rev.*, November 1985, *108*(11), pp. 26–41. [G: U.S.]

Peters, R. W. and Petridis, A. Employment, the Labour Force and Unemployment in Australia: A Disaggregated Approach. *Australian Econ. Rev.*, 4th Quarter 1985, (72), pp. 51–67. [G: Australia]

Platt, Stephen. Suicidal Behaviour and Unemployment: A Literature Review. In *Westcott, G.; Svensson, P.-G. and Zollner, H. F. K., eds.*, 1985, pp. 87–132. [G: Global]

Popay, Jennie. Responding to Unemployment at a Local Level. In *Westcott, G.; Svensson, P.-G. and Zollner, H. F. K., eds.*, 1985, pp. 383–99. [G: U.K.]

Portney, Paul R. Regional Issues: Commentary. In *Quigley, J. M. and Rubinfeld, D. L., eds.*, 1985, pp. 364–68. [G: U.S.]

Price, Simon. The Determinants of Equilibrium Unemployment in Britain: A Comment. *Econ. J.*, March 1985, *95*(377), pp. 189–95. [G: U.K.]

Quinn, Joseph F. Rewards for Continued Work: The Economic Incentives for Postponing Retirement: Comment. In *David, M. and Smeeding, T., eds.*, 1985, pp. 286–92. [G: U.S.]

Rabeau, Yves. Le marché du travail: quelques perspectives d'avenir. (The Labour Marker: Some Prospects. With English summary.) *L'Actual. Econ.*, March 1985, *61*(1), pp. 127–42.

Raghupati, T., et al. Case Study on Rural Non-farm Activities in India. In *Mukhopadhyay, S. and Chee, P. L., eds. (II)*, 1985, pp. 3–74. [G: India]

Rao, B. Sudhakar. Rural Industrialisation and Rural Non-farm Employment in India. In *Mukhopadhyay, S. and Chee, P. L., eds. (I)*, 1985, pp. 147–248. [G: India]

Ratti, Ronald A. Sectoral Employment Variability and Unexpected Inflation. *Rev. Econ. Statist.*, May 1985, *67*(2), pp. 278–83. [G: U.S.]

Rehn, Gösta. Swedish Active Labor Market Policy: Retrospect and Prospect. *Ind. Relat.*, Winter 1985, *24*(1), pp. 62–89. [G: Sweden]

Rein, Martin. The Social Welfare Labour Market. In *Eisenstadt, S. N. and Ahimeir, O., eds.*, 1985, pp. 109–31. [G: Israel; U.S.; W. Europe]

Reno, Virginia P. and Price, Daniel N. Relationship between the Retirement, Disability, and Unemployment Insurance Programs: The U.S. Experience. *Soc. Sec. Bull.*, May 1985, *48*(5), pp. 24–37. [G: U.S.]

Riboud, Michelle. An Analysis of Women's Labor Force Participation in France: Cross-Section Estimates and Time-Series Evidence. *J. Lab. Econ.*, Part 2 January 1985, *3*(1), pp. S177–200. [G: France]

Rives, Janet M. and Turner, Keith K. Industrial Distributions and Aggregate Unemployment Rates of Men and Women. *Soc. Sci. Quart.*, December 1985, *66*(4), pp. 916–23. [G: U.S.]

Robinson, Olive. The Changing Labour Market: The Phenomenon of Part-time Employment in Britain. *Nat. Westminster Bank Quart. Rev.*, November 1985, pp. 19–29. [G: U.K.]

Rones, Philip L. Using the CPS to Track Retirement Trends among Older Men. *Mon. Lab. Rev.*, February 1985, *108*(2), pp. 46–49. [G: U.S.]

Rosen, Sherwin. The Structure of Uncertainty and the Use of Nontransferable Pensions as a Mobility-Reduction Device: Comment. In *Wise, D. A., ed.*, 1985, pp. 248–51.

Ross, Russell T. Improved Labour Market Information: Beyond Unemployment Statistics. *Australian Bull. Lab.*, September 1985, *11*(4), pp. 236–45. [G: Australia]

Rossana, Robert J. Buffer Stocks and Labor Demand: Further Evidence. *Rev. Econ. Statist.*, February 1985, *67*(1), pp. 16–26. [G: U.S.]

Rosser, Mike J. and Mallier, Anthony T. Part-Time Employment. Some Lessons from the British Case. *Econ. Lavoro*, Oct.-Dec. 1985, *19*(4), pp. 69–83. [G: U.K.]

Rugumyamheto, J. A. Manpower Forecasting in the United Republic of Tanzania. In *Youdi, R. V. and Hinchliffe, K., eds.*, 1985, pp. 229–46. [G: Tanzania]

Ryscavage, Paul M. and Bregger, John E. New Household Survey and the CPS: A Look at Labor Force Differences. *Mon. Lab. Rev.*, September 1985, *108*(9), pp. 3–12. [G: U.S.]

Sabato, Hilda. La formación del mercado de trabajo en Buenos Aires, 1850–1880. (With English summary.) *Desarrollo Econ.*, January-March 1985, *24*(96), pp. 561–92. [G: Argentina]

Salais, Robert. La formation du chomage comme catégorie: le moment des années 1930. (The Forming of Unemployment as a Category during the Thirties. With English summary.) *Revue Écon.*, March 1985, *36*(2), pp. 321–65. [G: France]

Samson, Lucie. A Study of the Impact of Sectoral Shifts on Aggregate Unemployment in Canada. *Can. J. Econ.*, August 1985, *18*(3), pp. 518–30. [G: Canada]

Samuelson, Paul A. The Federal Civil Service

Retirement System: An Analysis of Its Financial Condition and Current Reform Proposals: Comment. In *Wise, D. A., ed.*, 1985, pp. 438–43. [G: U.S.]

Santiago, Carlos E. and Rossiter, Rosemary. A Multiple Time-Series Analysis of Labor Supply and Earnings in Economic Development. *J. Devel. Econ.*, April 1985, *17*(3), pp. 259–75. [G: Puerto Rico]

Santoni, G. J. Local Area Labor Statistics—A Phantom Army of the Unemployed? *Fed. Res. Bank St. Louis Rev.*, April 1985, *67*(4), pp. 5–14. [G: U.S.]

Sassen-Koob, Saskia. Changing Composition and Labor Market Location of Hispanic Immigrants in New York City, 1960–1980. In *Borjas, G. J. and Tienda, M., eds.*, 1985, pp. 299–322. [G: U.S.]

Sauramo, Pekka and Solttila, Heikki. Minimipalkat ja nuorisotyöttömyys Suomessa 1965–1981. (Minimum Wages and Youth Unemployment in Finland 1965–1981. With English summary.) *Kansant. Aikak.*, 1985, *81*(4), pp. 384–94. [G: Finland]

Saxonhouse, Gary R. and Kiyokawa, Yukihiko. Supply and Demand for Quality Workers in Cotton Spinning in Japan and India. In *Ohkawa, K. and Ranis, G., eds.*, 1985, pp. 177–211. [G: Japan; India]

Schmitt, Donald G. Today's Pension Plans: How Much Do They Pay? *Mon. Lab. Rev.*, December 1985, *108*(12), pp. 19–25. [G: U.S.]

Schreiner, Alette and Skoglund, Tor. Regional Impacts of Petroleum Activities in Norway. In *Bjerkholt, O. and Offerdal, E., eds.*, 1985, pp. 203–29. [G: Norway]

Scoville, James G. The Labor Market in Prerevolutionary Iran. *Econ. Develop. Cult. Change*, October 1985, *34*(1), pp. 143–55. [G: Iran]

Sehgal, Ellen. Employment Problems and Their Effect on Family Income, 1979–83. *Mon. Lab. Rev.*, August 1985, *108*(8), pp. 42–43. [G: U.S.]

Selan, Valerio. Technology versus Employment: A Distorted Problematic. *Rivista Polit. Econ.*, Suppl. Dec. 1985, *76*, pp. 145–73.

Shah, Anup R. Are Wage Incentives and Unionism Importance Determinants of Job Tenure? *Oxford Econ. Pap.*, December 1985, *37*(4), pp. 643–58. [G: U.K.]

Shank, Susan Elizabeth. Changes in Regional Unemployment over the Last Decade. *Mon. Lab. Rev.*, March 1985, *108*(3), pp. 17–23. [G: U.S.]

Shank, Susan Elizabeth. Employment Rose in the First Half of 1985 as the Recovery Entered Its Third Year. *Mon. Lab. Rev.*, August 1985, *108*(8), pp. 3–8. [G: U.S.]

Shaw, R. Paul. The Burden of Unemployment in Canada. *Can. Public Policy*, June 1985, *11*(2), pp. 143–60. [G: Canada]

Sheets, Robert G.; Smith, Russell L. and Voytek, Kenneth P. Corporate Disinvestment and Metropolitan Manufacturing Job Loss. *Soc. Sci. Quart.*, March 1985, *66*(1), pp. 218–26. [G: U.S.]

Sherman, Sally R. Reported Reasons Retired Workers Left Their Last Job: Findings from the New Beneficiary Survey. *Soc. Sec. Bull.*, March 1985, *48*(3), pp. 22–30. [G: U.S.]

Shieh, Yeung-Nan. A Note on Lee's Model of Intraurban Employment Location. *J. Urban Econ.*, September 1985, *18*(2), pp. 196–98.

Shimada, Haruo and Higuchi, Yoshio. An Analysis of Trends in Female Labor Force Participation in Japan. *J. Lab. Econ.*, Part 2 January 1985, *3*(1), pp. S355–74. [G: Japan]

Sider, Hal. Unemployment Duration and Incidence: 1968–82. *Amer. Econ. Rev.*, June 1985, *75*(3), pp. 461–72. [G: U.S.]

Silvestri, George T. and Lukasiewicz, John M. Occupational Employment Projections: The 1984–95 Outlook. *Mon. Lab. Rev.*, November 1985, *108*(11), pp. 42–57. [G: U.S.]

Singelmann, Joachim and Tienda, Marta. The Process of Occupational Change in a Service Society: The Case of the United States, 1960–80. In *Roberts, B.; Finnegan, R. and Gallie, D., eds.*, 1985, pp. 48–67. [G: U.S.]

Sloan, Judith. The Australian Labour Market December 1985. *Australian Bull. Lab.*, December 1985, *12*(1), pp. 3–21. [G: Australia]

Smith, Shirley J. Revised Worklife Tables Reflect 1979–80 Experience. *Mon. Lab. Rev.*, August 1985, *108*(8), pp. 23–30. [G: U.S.]

Solon, Gary R. The Minimum Wage and Teenage Employment: A Reanalysis with Attention to Serial Correlation and Seasonality. *J. Human Res.*, Spring 1985, *20*(2), pp. 292–97. [G: U.S.]

Spinelli, Franco. Protectionism and Real Wage Rigidity: A Discussion of the Macroeconomic Literature. *J. Policy Modeling*, Spring 1985, *7*(1), pp. 157–80. [G: U.K.]

Spruit, Ingeborg P. Employment, Unemployment and Health in Families in Leiden (the Netherlands). In *Westcott, G.; Svensson, P.-G. and Zollner, H. F. K., eds.*, 1985, pp. 231–59. [G: Netherlands]

St. Antoine, Theodore J. The Revision of Employment-at-Will Enters a New Phase. In *Dennis, B. D., ed.*, 1985, pp. 563–67. [G: U.S.]

Steece, Bert M. and Wood, Steven. A Test for the Equivalence of k ARMA Models. *Empirical Econ.*, 1985, *10*(1), pp. 1–11. [G: U.S.]

Stelcner, Morton and Breslaw, Jon. Income Taxes and the Labor Supply of Married Women in Quebec. *Southern Econ. J.*, April 1985, *51*(4), pp. 1053–72. [G: Canada]

Stephenson, Stanley P., Jr. Labor Market Turnover and Joblessness for Hispanic Youth. In *Borjas, G. J. and Tienda, M., eds.*, 1985, pp. 193–218. [G: U.S.]

Sternlieb, George and Hughes, James W. The National Economy and the Northeast: A Context for Discussion. In *Richardson, H. W. and Turek, J. H., eds.*, 1985, pp. 66–84. [G: U.S.]

Stevans, Lonnie K.; Register, Charles and Grimes, Paul. Race and the Discouraged Female Worker: A Question of Labor Force Attachment. *Rev. Black Polit. Econ.*, Summer

1985, *14*(1), pp. 89–97.　　　　　[G: U.S.]

Stevens, Benjamin H. Regional Cost Equalization and the Potential for Manufacturing Recovery in the Industrial North. In *Richardson, H. W. and Turek, J. H., eds.*, 1985, pp. 85–103.
　　　　　[G: U.S.]

Stieber, Jack. Recent Developments in Employment-at-Will. In *Dennis, B. D., ed.*, 1985, pp. 557–63.　　　　　[G: U.S.]

Stokes, Graham. Epidemiological Studies of the Psychological Response to Economic Instability in England: A Summary. In *Westcott, G.; Svensson, P.-G. and Zollner, H. F. K., eds.*, 1985, pp. 133–42.　　　　　[G: U.K.]

Stolz, Peter. (Empirical Research on the Relation of Registered to Self-declared Unemployment in Switzerland. With English summary.) *Schweiz. Z. Volkswirtsch. Statist.*, December 1985, *121*(4), pp. 391–406.　[G: Switzerland]

Stone, John Owen. Youth Unemployment in Australia. *Nat. Westminster Bank Quart. Rev.*, May 1985, pp. 3–11.　　　[G: Australia]

Storey, D. J. Manufacturing Employment Change in Northern England 1965–78: The Role of Small Businesses. In *Storey, D. J., ed.*, 1985, pp. 6–42.　　　　　[G: U.K.]

Stricker, Frank. Affluence for Whom?—Another Look at Prosperity and the Working Classes in the 1920s. In *Leab, D. J., ed.*, 1985, pp. 288–316.　　　　　[G: U.S.]

Svensson, Per-Gunnar and Zöllner, Herbert. Health Policy Implications of Unemployment: Introduction. In *Westcott, G.; Svensson, P.-G. and Zollner, H. F. K., eds.*, 1985, pp. 1–6.

Svetanant, Prapant. Rural Non-farm Activities in Thailand: Comparative Case Studies in Irrigated and Rainfed Areas in the Northeast. In *Mukhopadhyay, S. and Chee, P. L., eds. (II)*, 1985, pp. 75–115.　　　　　[G: Thailand]

Sweet, Morris L. Managing Workforce Reduction: The United States of America and Canada. In *Cross, M., ed.*, 1985, pp. 6–66.
　　　　　[G: Canada; U.S.]

Symons, James S. V. Relative Prices and the Demand for Labour in British Manufacturing. *Economica*, February 1985, *52*(205), pp. 37–49.　　　　　[G: U.K.]

Taylor, Vic and Yerbury, Di. Managing Workforce Reduction: Australia. In *Cross, M., ed.*, 1985, pp. 130–63.　　　[G: Australia]

Tessler, Andrew. Services. In *Meyer, F. V., ed.*, 1985, pp. 124–43.　　　　　[G: U.K.]

Thomann, Klaus-Dieter. Some Results of Medical Research in the Frankfurt/Main Employment Office. In *Westcott, G.; Svensson, P.-G. and Zollner, H. F. K., eds.*, 1985, pp. 293–98.
　　　　　[G: W. Germany]

Thomson, Peter. Sources of Local Employment Information: A Comparison of Census of Employment Data with 1981 Population Census Workplace Data. *J. Econ. Soc. Meas.*, April 1985, *13*(1), pp. 39–48.　　　[G: U.K.]

Thury, Gerhard. Seasonal Adjustment by Signal Extraction. *Empirica*, 1985, *12*(2), pp. 191–207.　　　　　[G: Austria]

Tinbergen, Jan. The Allocation of Workers to Jobs. In *Tinbergen, J.*, 1985, pp. 123–30.

Tokman, Victor E. The Impact of Social Security on Employment: Comment. In *Mesa-Lago, C., ed.*, 1985, pp. 279–84.　　[G: Colombia; Mexico; Venezuela]

Tokman, Victor E. Wages and Employment in International Recessions: Recent Latin American Experience. In *Kim, K. S. and Ruccio, D. F., eds.*, 1985, pp. 74–95.
　　　　　[G: Latin America]

Townsend, Alan and Peck, Francis. An Approach to the Analysis of Redundancies in the UK (Post-1976): Some Methodological Problems and Policy Implications. In *Massey, D. and Meegan, R., eds.*, 1985, pp. 64–87.
　　　　　[G: U.K.]

Townson, Monica. A National System for Parental Leave. In *Economic Council of Canada.*, 1985, pp. 21–28.　　　　　[G: Canada]

Trivedi, Pravin K. and Baker, G. M. Equilibrium Unemployment in Australia: Concepts and Measurement. *Econ. Rec.*, September 1985, *61*(174), pp. 629–43.　　[G: Australia]

Trivedi, Pravin K. A Note on Estimating Unemployment Duration. *Australian Econ. Rev.*, 1st Quarter 1985, (69), pp. 37–41. [G: Australia]

Tuma, Nancy Brandon. Effects of Labor Market Structure on Job Shift Patterns. In *Heckman, J. J. and Singer, B., eds.*, 1985, pp. 327–63.
　　　　　[G: U.S.]

Turner, Charles F. Standardized Data Collection for Large-scale Program Evaluation: An Assessment of the YEDPA-SAS Experience. In *Betsey, C. L.; Hollister, R. G., Jr. and Papageorglou, M. R., eds.*, 1985, pp. 193–219.
　　　　　[G: U.S.]

Turner, Robert; Bostyn, Anne-Marie and Wight, Daniel. The Work Ethic in a Scottish Town with Declining Employment. In *Roberts, B.; Finnegan, R. and Gallie, D., eds.*, 1985, pp. 476–89.　　　　　[G: U.K.]

Tzannatos, Zafaris and Zabalza, Anton. The Effect of Sex Antidiscriminatory Legislation on the Variability of Female Employment in Britain. *Appl. Econ.*, December 1985, *17*(6), pp. 1117–34.　　　　　[G: U.K.]

Van Dijk, Jouke and Folmer, Hendrik. Entry of the Unemployment into Employment: Theory, Methodology, and Dutch Experience. *Reg. Stud.*, June 1985, *19*(3), pp. 243–56.
　　　　　[G: Netherlands]

Vincens, Jean. Emploi—chômage. (With English summary.) *Revue Écon. Polit.*, Sept.-Oct. 1985, *95*(5), pp. 684–94.　　　[G: OECD]

Virén, Matti. Determination of Employment with Wage and Price Speculation. *Scand. J. Econ.*, 1985, *87*(3), pp. 537–53.　　　[G: Finland]

Viscusi, W. Kip. The Structure of Uncertainty and the Use of Nontransferable Pensions as a Mobility-Reduction Device. In *Wise, D. A., ed.*, 1985, pp. 223–48.

Walby, Sylvia. Approaches to the Study of Gender Relations in Unemployment and Employment. In *Roberts, B.; Finnegan, R. and Gallie, D., eds.*, 1985, pp. 264–79.　　[G: EEC; U.K.]

Waldinger, Roger. Immigration and Industrial Change in the New York City Apparel Industry. In *Borjas, G. J. and Tienda, M., eds.,* 1985 , pp. 323–49.   [G: U.S.]

Walker, Alan. Policies for Sharing the Job Shortage: Reducing or Redistributing Unemployment? In *Klein, R. and O'Higgins, M., ed.,* 1985, pp. 166–85.   [G: U.K.]

Walker, Alan; Noble, Iain and Westergaard, John. From Secure Employment to Labour Market Insecurity: The Impact of Redundancy on Older Workers in the Steel Industry. In *Roberts, B.; Finnegan, R. and Gallie, D., eds.,* 1985, pp. 319–37.   [G: U.K.]

Walker, Richard A. Is There a Service Economy? The Changing Capitalist Division of Labor. *Sci. Soc.,* Spring 1985, *49*(1), pp. 42–83.

Ward, Robin. Minority Settlement and the Local Economy. In *Roberts, B.; Finnegan, R. and Gallie, D., eds.,* 1985, pp. 198–212.

          [G: U.K.]

Warr, Peter. Twelve Questions about Unemployment and Health. In *Roberts, B.; Finnegan, R. and Gallie, D., eds.,* 1985, pp. 302–18.

          [G: U.K.]

Wasylenko, Michael and McGuire, Therese J. Jobs and Taxes: The Effect of Business Climate on States' Employment Growth Rates. *Nat. Tax J.,* December 1985, *38*(4), pp. 497–511.

          [G: U.S.]

Watkins, Stephen. Recession and Health—A Literature Review. In *Westcott, G.; Svensson, P.-G. and Zollner, H. F. K., eds.,* 1985, pp. 27–56.   [G: U.S.; U.K.]

Watkins, Stephen J. Recession and Health—The Policy Implications. In *Westcott, G.; Svensson, P.-G. and Zollner, H. F. K., eds.,* 1985, pp. 347–56.

Weinstein, Michael M. Job Impact Statements: A Lesson from the 1930s. *Challenge,* Sept./Oct. 1985, *28*(4), pp. 55–58.   [G: U.S.]

Westcott, Gill. The Effect of Unemployment on the Health of Workers in a UK Steel Town: Preliminary Results. In *Westcott, G.; Svensson, P.-G. and Zollner, H. F. K., eds.,* 1985, pp. 261–71.   [G: U.K.]

Westergård-Nielsen, Niels. Regional arbejdsløshed i Danmark 1948–78. (Regional Unemplooyment in Denmark, 194878. With English summary.) *Nationaløkon. Tidsskr.,* 1985, *123*(2), pp. 206–19.   [G: Denmark]

Williams, Donald R. Technical Note: Employment in Recession and Recovery: A Demographic Flow Analysis. *Mon. Lab. Rev.,* March 1985, *108*(3), pp. 35–42.   [G: U.S.]

Willis, K. G. Estimating the Benefits of Job Creation from Local Investment Subsidies. *Urban Stud.,* April 1985, *22*(2), pp. 163–77.

          [G: U.K.]

Willms, Manfred and Karsten, Ingo. Government Policies towards Inflation and Unemployment in West Germany. In *Argy, V. E. and Neville, J. W., eds.,* 1985, pp. 153–80.

          [G: W. Germany]

Wilson, Richard R. The Impact of Social Security

on Employment. In *Mesa-Lago, C., ed.,* 1985, pp. 245–78.   [G: Colombia; Mexico; Venezuela]

Wilson, Robert Andrew. Public Expenditure Policy, 1985–86: Employment. In *Cockle, P., ed.,* 1985, pp. 153–85.   [G: U.K.]

Wilson, William Julius. The Urban Underclass in Advanced Industrial Society. In *Peterson, P. E., ed.,* 1985, pp. 129–60.   [G: U.S.]

Wise, David A. Pensions, Labor, and Individual Choice: Overview. In *Wise, D. A., ed.,* 1985, pp. 1–17.   [G: U.S.]

Withers, Glenn and Pope, David. Immigration and Unemployment. *Econ. Rec.,* June 1985, *61*(173), pp. 554–63.   [G: Australia]

Wolff, Edward N. The Disappearance of Domestic Servants and the Underground Economy. In *Gaertner, W. and Wenig, A., eds.,* 1985, pp. 316–29.   [G: U.S.]

Woodworth, Warner. Achieving Labor–Management Joint Action. In *Woodworth, W.; Meek, C. and Whyte, W. F., eds.,* 1985, pp. 121–39.   [G: U.S.]

Woodworth, Warner. Saving Jobs through Worker Buyouts. In *Woodworth, W.; Meek, C. and Whyte, W. F., eds.,* 1985, pp. 221–41.   [G: U.S.]

Wren-Lewis, Simon. Private Sector Earnings and Excess Demand from 1966 to 1980. *Oxford Bull. Econ. Statist.,* February 1985, *47*(1), pp. 1–18.   [G: U.K.]

Yuskavage, Robert E. Employment and Employee Compensation in the 1977 Input–Output Accounts. *Surv. Curr. Bus.,* November 1985, *65*(11), pp. 11–25.   [G: U.S.]

Zabalza, Anton and Tzannatos, Zafaris. The Effect of Britain's Anti-discriminatory Legislation on Relative Pay and Employment. *Econ. J.,* September 1985, *95*(379), pp. 679–99.

          [G: U.K.]

Zietz, Joachim. A Pre-estimation Sample Separation Method for a Labor Market in Disequilibrium. *J. Macroecon.,* Winter 1985, *7*(1), pp. 51–67.   [G: U.S.]

825 Productivity Studies: Labor, Capital, and Total Factor

8250 Productivity Studies: Labor, Capital, and Total Factor

Ali, M. Shaukat. Contribution of Education towards Labor Productivity: A Cross-Country Study. *Pakistan Econ. Soc. Rev.,* Summer 1985, *23*(1), pp. 41–54.

Allen, Steven G. Why Construction Industry Productivity Is Declining. *Rev. Econ. Statist.,* November 1985, *67*(4), pp. 661–69.

          [G: U.S.]

Amin, Ash. Restructuring in Fiat and the Decentralization of Production into Southern Italy. In *Hudson, R. and Lewis, J., eds.,* 1985, pp. 155–91.   [G: Italy; Europe]

Armstrong, Robert. The Quebec Asbestos Industry: Technological Change, 1878–1929. In *[Spry, I. M.],* 1985, pp. 189–210.

          [G: Canada]

Arpan, Jeffrey S. and Toyne, Brian. The U.S. Textile Industry: International Challenges and Strategies. In *Hochmuth, M. and Davidson, W., eds.*, 1985, pp. 263–92.
[G: Selected Countries]

Arrow, Kenneth J. Knowledge, Productivity, and Practice. In *Arrow, K. J. (I)*, 1985, pp. 191–99.

Arrow, Kenneth J. The Economic Implications of Learning by Doing. In *Arrow, K. J. (I)*, 1985, pp. 157–80.

Asheghian, Parviz and Foote, William. In the Productivities of U.S. Multinationals in the Industrial Sector of the Canadian Economy. *Eastern Econ. J.*, April-June 1985, *11*(2), pp. 123–33. [G: Canada]

Athanasopoulos, Christos N. Productivity Standard: For a Healthier Global Economy. In *Didsbury, H. F., Jr., ed.*, 1985, pp. 239–50. [G: U.S.]

Barbera, Anthony J. Determinants of Average Labor Productivity by U.S. Industry. *Amer. Econ.*, Spring 1985, *29*(1), pp. 41–52. [G: U.S.]

Barnett, C. Long-term Industrial Performance in the UK: The Role of Education and Research, 1850–1939. In *Morris, D., ed.*, 1985, pp. 668–89. [G: OECD]

Baumol, William J. Measurement of Output and Productivity in the Service Sector: Comment. In *Inman, R. P., ed.*, 1985, pp. 124–26. [G: U.S.]

Baumol, William J. Productivity Policy and the Service Sector. In *Inman, R. P., ed.*, 1985, pp. 301–17.

Booth, Douglas E. The Problems of Corporate Bureaucracy and the Producer Cooperative as an Alternative. *Rev. Soc. Econ.*, December 1985, *43*(3), pp. 298–315. [G: U.S.]

Bowles, Samuel; Gordon, David M. and Weisskopf, Thomas E. In Defense of the "Social Model." *Challenge*, May/June 1985, *28*(2), pp. 57–59. [G: U.S.]

Brand, Horst and Bennett, Norman. Productivity Trends in Kitchen Cabinet Manufacturing. *Mon. Lab. Rev.*, March 1985, *108*(3), pp. 24–30. [G: U.S.]

Branson, William H. International Comparison of the Sources of Productivity Slowdown, 1973-1982: Comment. *Europ. Econ. Rev.*, June-July 1985, *28*(1–2), pp. 193–95. [G: OECD]

Bronfenbrenner, Martin. An Essay on Negative Screening. In *Shishido, T. and Sato, R., eds.*, 1985, pp. 188–98. [G: Japan]

Bryant, J. Economics, Equilibrium and Thermodynamics. In *van Gool, W. and Bruggink, J. J. C., eds.*, 1985, pp. 197–221. [G: U.K.; OECD]

Cacnis, Demitrios G. The Translog Production Function and the Substitution of Factors of Production in England 1950–1976. *Greek Econ. Rev.*, August 1985, *7*(2), pp. 161–78. [G: U.K.]

Caves, Douglas W., et al. The Effect of New Entry on Productivity Growth in the U.S. Airline Industry 1947–1981. *Logist. Transp. Rev.*, De-

cember 1985, *21*(4), pp. 299–335. [G: U.S.]

Clark, Peter K. and Haltmaier, Jane T. The Labor Productivity Slowdown in the United States: Evidence from Physical Output Measures. *Rev. Econ. Statist.*, August 1985, *67*(3), pp. 504–08. [G: U.S.]

Comanor, William S. and Miyao, Takahiro. The Organization and Relative Productivity of Japanese and American Industry. *Managerial Dec. Econ.*, June 1985, *6*(2), pp. 88–92. [G: Japan; U.S.]

Daly, A.; Hitchens, D. M. W. N. and Wagner, Karin. Productivity, Machinery, and Skills in a Sample of British and German Manufacturing Plants: Results of a Pilot Inquiry. *Nat. Inst. Econ. Rev.*, February 1985, (111), pp. 48–61. [G: U.K.; W. Germany]

Daly, Michael J.; Rao, P. Someshwar and Geehan, Randall. Productivity, Scale Economies and Technical Progress in the Canadian Life Insurance Industry. *Int. J. Ind. Organ.*, September 1985, *3*(3), pp. 345–61. [G: Canada]

Daughety, Andrew F.; Nelson, Forrest D. and Vigdor, William R. An Econometric Analysis of the Cost and Production Structure of the Trucking Industry. In *Daughety, A. F., ed.*, 1985, pp. 65–95. [G: U.S.]

Davidson, Lawrence S. and Fratianni, Michele. Economic Growth in the 1970s and Beyond. *Econ. Notes*, 1985, (3), pp. 17–34. [G: U.S.]

Deimezis, Nikitas. Analyse sectorielle de l'emploi dans l'industrie manufacturière belge. Perspectives à long terme. (With English summary.) *Cah. Écon. Bruxelles*, 2nd Trimester 1985, (106), pp. 192–216. [G: Belgium]

Diwan, Romesh and Leonardson, Nirjhar J. Productivity, Technical Change and Capital–Labor Substitution in Indian Industry. *Indian J. Quant. Econ.*, 1985, *1*(2), pp. 1–16. [G: India]

Dolishny, M. I. Regional Programmes for Improving Labour Productivity: An Example from the Western Ukraine. *Int. Lab. Rev.*, May-June 1985, *124*(3), pp. 323–33. [G: U.S.S.R.]

Dungan, Peter and Younger, Arthur. New Technology and Unemployment: A Simulation of Macroeconomic Impacts and Responses in Canada. *J. Policy Modeling*, Winter 1985, *7*(4), pp. 595–619. [G: Canada]

Dunson, Bruce H. Pay, Experience, and Productivity: The Government-Sector Case. *J. Human Res.*, Winter 1985, *20*(1), pp. 153–60. [G: U.S.]

Dworkin, James B. and Ahlburg, Dennis A. Unions and Productivity: A Review of the Research. In *Lipsky, D. B., ed.*, 1985, pp. 51–68. [G: U.S.]

Elias, Victor J. La productividad del sector público en la Argentina. (The Productivity of the Public Sector in Argentina. With English summary.) *Económica (La Plata)*, May-Dec. 1985, *31*(2–3), pp. 133–45.

Faini, Riccardo. International Comparison of the Sources of Productivity Slowdown, 1973-1982: Comment. *Europ. Econ. Rev.*, June-July 1985, *28*(1–2), pp. 197–200. [G: OECD]

Fair, Ray C. Excess Labor and the Business Cycle. *Amer. Econ. Rev.*, March 1985, 75(1), pp. 239–45. [G: U.S.]

Fay, Jon A. and Medoff, James L. Labor and Output over the Business Cycle: Some Direct Evidence. *Amer. Econ. Rev.*, September 1985, 75(4), pp. 638–55. [G: U.S.]

Ferri, Piero. Domanda di lavoro e produttività: scenari a confronto. (Demand for Labour and Productivity: A Comparison of Scenarios. With English summary.) *Econ. Lavoro*, Jan.-Mar. 1985, 19(1), pp. 51–60. [G: EEC; U.S.; Japan]

Fisk, Donald M. Productivity Trends in the Federal Government. *Mon. Lab. Rev.*, October 1985, 108(10), pp. 3–9. [G: U.S.]

Foss, Murray F. Changing Utilization of Fixed Capital: An Element in Long-term Growth. *Mon. Lab. Rev.*, May 1985, 108(5), pp. 3–8. [G: U.S.]

Freeman, Kenneth D., et al. The Total Factor Productivity of the Canadian Class I Railways: 1956–1981. *Logist. Transp. Rev.*, September 1985, 21(3), pp. 249–76. [G: Canada]

Friedlaender, Ann F. and Bruce, Sharon Schur. Augmentation Effects and Technical Change in the Regulated Trucking Industry, 1974–1979. In *Daughety, A. F., ed.*, 1985, pp. 29–63. [G: U.S.]

Friedman, Brian L. and Herman, Arthur S. Productivity Growth Low in the Oilfield Machinery Industry. *Mon. Lab. Rev.*, December 1985, 108(12), pp. 34–38. [G: U.S.]

Fulco, Lawrence J. Productivity and Costs in 1984. *Mon. Lab. Rev.*, June 1985, 108(6), pp. 40–43. [G: U.S.]

Fulco, Lawrence J. The Decline in Productivity during the First Half of 1985. *Mon. Lab. Rev.*, December 1985, 108(12), pp. 39–42. [G: U.S.]

Garonna, Paolo. Controlling the Dynamics of Technological Change in the Industrial Labour Markets. *Econ. Lavoro*, Jan.-Mar. 1985, 19(1), pp. 137–42. [G: W. Europe; U.S.; Japan]

Ginzberg, Eli. Work and Workers: Transatlantic Comparisons. In *Ginzberg, E.*, 1985, pp. 465–74. [G: U.S.; W. Europe]

Gordon, Roger H. Incentive Effects of Pensions: Comment. In *Wise, D. A., ed.*, 1985, pp. 278–82.

Graddy, Duane B. and Hall, Gary. Unionization and Productivity in Commercial Banking. *J. Lab. Res.*, Summer 1985, 6(3), pp. 249–62. [G: U.S.]

Greasley, David. Wage Rates and Work Intensity in the South Wales Coalfield, 1874–1914. *Economica*, August 1985, 52(207), pp. 383–89. [G: U.K.]

Greytak, David and Blackley, Paul R. Labor Productivity and Local Industry Size: Further Issues in Assessing Agglomeration Economies. *Southern Econ. J.*, April 1985, 51(4), pp. 1121–29. [G: U.S.]

Gupta, Deepak. Productivity Trends and Factor Substitutability in Manufacturing Sector in Ma-

harashtra. *Margin*, July 1985, 17(4), pp. 62–70. [G: India]

Havighurst, Robert J. Aging and Productivity: The Case of Older Faculty. In *Clark, S. M. and Lewis, D. R., eds.*, 1985, pp. 98–111. [G: U.S.]

Hazledine, Tim. The Anatomy of Productivity Growth Slowdown and Recovery in Canadian Manufacturing, 1970–79. *Int. J. Ind. Organ.*, September 1985, 3(3), pp. 307–25. [G: Canada]

Heimler, Alberto. Cost, Prices and Income Distribution in Italian Industry. *Rivista Polit. Econ.*, Suppl. Dec. 1985, 76, pp. 41–64. [G: Italy]

Helliwell, John F.; Sturm, Peter H. and Salou, Gérard. International Comparison of the Sources of Productivity Slowdown, 1973-1982. *Europ. Econ. Rev.*, June-July 1985, 28(1–2), pp. 157–91. [G: OECD]

Henneberger, J. Edwin and Herman, Arthur S. Productivity Growth Below Average in the Internal Combustion Engine Industry. *Mon. Lab. Rev.*, May 1985, 108(5), pp. 22–26. [G: U.S.]

Herman, Arthur S. Productivity Reports: Productivity Increased in Many Industries in 1983. *Mon. Lab. Rev.*, March 1985, 108(3), pp. 31–34. [G: U.S.]

Hirsch, Barry T. and Hausman, William J. Labour Productivity in the South Wales Coal Industry: Reply. *Economica*, August 1985, 52(207), pp. 391–94. [G: U.K.]

Hulten, Charles R. Measurement of Output and Productivity in the Service Sector: Comment. In *Inman, R. P., ed.*, 1985, pp. 127–30. [G: U.S.]

Inwood, Kris. Productivity Growth in Obsolescence: Charcoal Iron Revisited. *J. Econ. Hist.*, June 1985, 45(2), pp. 293–98. [G: Canada]

Jerome, Robert T., Jr. Estimates of Sources of Growth in Bulgaria, Greece, and Yugoslavia, 1950–1980. *Comparative Econ. Stud.*, Fall 1985, 27(3), pp. 31–82. [G: Bulgaria; Greece; Yugoslavia]

Jonsson, Ernst. A Model of a Non–budget-maximizing Bureau. In *Lane, J.-E., ed.*, 1985, pp. 70–82. [G: Sweden]

Junge, Georg. The Impact of Swiss Taxation on Economic Growth. *Schweiz. Z. Volkswirtsch. Statist.*, March 1985, 121(1), pp. 23–34. [G: Switzerland]

Kallianpur, Renu and Diwan, Romesh. Productivity Growth: Scale and Technology Analysis of Panjab Wheat Farms. *Indian J. Quant. Econ.*, 1985, 1(1), pp. 61–84. [G: India]

Kawagoe, Toshihiko and Hayami, Yujiro. An Intercountry Comparison of Agricultural Production Efficiency. *Amer. J. Agr. Econ.*, February 1985, 67(1), pp. 87–92. [G: Selected Countries]

Kendrick, John W. Measurement of Output and Productivity in the Service Sector. In *Inman, R. P., ed.*, 1985, pp. 111–23. [G: U.S.]

Khan, Shaheen and Nazir, Rauf. An Economic Analysis of Thresher Manufacturing Industry in Punjab. *Pakistan Econ. Soc. Rev.*, Summer 1985, *23*(1), pp. 1–23. **[G: Pakistan]**

Kibria, Muhammad G. and Tisdell, Clement A. Productivity Progress Parameters for Manufacturing in an LDC: The Startup or Learning Phase in Bangladesh Jute Mills. *Australian Econ. Pap.*, December 1985, *24*(45), pp. 370–79. **[G: Bangladesh]**

Kibria, Muhammad G. and Tisdell, Clement A. Productivity, Progress and Learning: The Case of Jute Spinning in Bangladesh. *World Devel.*, Oct./Nov. 1985, *13*(10/11), pp. 1151–61. **[G: Bangladesh]**

Kim, Moshe. Total Factor Productivity in Bus Transport. *J. Transp. Econ. Policy*, May 1985, *19*(2), pp. 173–82. **[G: Israel]**

Kintis, Andreas A. Patterns and Sources of Growth in Greek Manufacturing. *Greek Econ. Rev.*, August 1985, *7*(2), pp. 144–60. **[G: Greece]**

Klein, Herbert S. and Engerman, Stanley L. The Transition from Slave to Free Labor: Notes on a Comparative Economic Model. In *Moreno Franginals, M.; Moya Pons, F. and Engerman, S. L., eds.*, 1985, pp. 255–69. **[G: Caribbean; Brazil; U.S.]**

Kuhn, Peter. Union Productivity Effects and Economic Efficiency. *J. Lab. Res.*, Summer 1985, *6*(3), pp. 229–48.

Lazear, Edward P. Incentive Effects of Pensions. In *Wise, D. A., ed.*, 1985, pp. 253–78.

Lazonick, William and Brush, Thomas. The "Horndal Effect" in Early U.S. Manufacturing. *Exploration Econ. Hist.*, January 1985, *22*(1), pp. 53–96. **[G: U.S.]**

Leslie, Derek. Real Wage Growth, Technical Change and Competition in the Labor Market. *Rev. Econ. Statist.*, November 1985, *67*(4), pp. 640–47. **[G: U.S.]**

Macphee, Ian. Poor Nation of the Pacific: The Labour Market. In *Scutt, J. A., ed.*, 1985, pp. 75–92. **[G: Australia]**

Maineri, Bruno. Alla ricerca di un metodo per calcolare la produttività nelle aziende di credito. E' il mercato ad imporre l'adozione di nuovi strumenti manageriali. La sperimentazione del Sistema BAI nella realtà italiana. (A System for Measuring Productivity of Banks. With English summary.) *Bancaria*, June 1985, *41*(6), pp. 629–38. **[G: Italy]**

Marin, Dalia. Structural Change through Exchange Rate Policy. *Weltwirtsch. Arch.*, 1985, *121*(3), pp. 471–91. **[G: Austria]**

Matlin, I. S.; Akhundova, T. A. and Kurkina, O. M. A Study of the Relationship between Balance in the Goods Market, Capital-Intensity, and Labor Productivity Based on a Dynamic Input–Output Model. *Matekon*, Spring 1985, *21*(3), pp. 63–80. **[G: U.S.S.R.]**

McMillion, Charles W. The Global Economy Requires Greater U.S. Productivity. In *Didsbury, H. F., Jr., ed.*, 1985, pp. 251–64. **[G: U.S.]**

Mills, D. Quinn and Lovell, Malcolm R., Jr. Competitiveness: The Labor Dimension. In *Scott, B. R. and Lodge, G. C., eds.*, 1985, pp. 429–54. **[G: U.S.]**

Mohnen, Pierre and Nadiri, Ishaq. Demande de facteurs et recherche-développement: Estimations pour les États-Unis, le Japon, l'Allemagne et la France. (Factor Demands Research and Development: Estimates for the U.S., Japan, Germany and France. With English summary.) *Revue Écon.*, September 1985, *36*(5), pp. 943–74. **[G: U.S.; Japan; W. Germany; France]**

Moseley, Fred. Can the "Social Model" of Productivity Stand Scrutiny? *Challenge*, May/June 1985, *28*(2), pp. 55–57. **[G: U.S.]**

Mountain, Dean C. Productivity and Energy Price Differentials. *Reg. Sci. Urban Econ.*, August 1985, *15*(3), pp. 477–89. **[G: Canada]**

Mountain, Dean C. The Contribution of Changing Energy and Import Prices to Changing Average Labor Productivity: A Profit Formulation for Canada. *Quart. J. Econ.*, August 1985, *100*(3), pp. 651–75. **[G: Canada]**

Mstislavskii, P. The Dynamics of Labor Productivity and Wages. *Prob. Econ.*, May 1985, *28*(1), pp. 38–55. **[G: U.S.S.R.]**

Musgrove, Philip. Why Everything Takes 2.71828 . . . Times as Long as Expected. *Amer. Econ. Rev.*, March 1985, *75*(1), pp. 250–52.

Niccoli, Alberto. Efficiency of Microeconomic Income Distribution and Global Productivity Differentials. *Rivista Polit. Econ.*, Suppl. Dec. 1985, *76*, pp. 65–119. **[G: Italy]**

Niehaus, Richard J.; Schinnar, A. P. and Walters, L. C. Productivity and Organizational Economies of Personnel Services. In *Niehaus, R. J., ed.*, 1985, pp. 187–214. **[G: U.S.]**

Norsworthy, J. R. and Zabala, Craig A. Effects of Worker Attitudes on Production Costs and the Value of Capital Input. *Econ. J.*, December 1985, *95*(380), pp. 992–1002. **[G: U.S.]**

Norsworthy, J. R. and Zabala, Craig A. Worker Attitudes, Worker Behavior, and Productivity in the U.S. Automobile Industry, 1959–1976. *Ind. Lab. Relat. Rev.*, July 1985, *38*(4), pp. 544–57. **[G: U.S.]**

Norwood, Janet L. Measurement of Output and Productivity in the Service Sector: Comment. In *Inman, R. P., ed.*, 1985, pp. 131–33. **[G: U.S.]**

Obeng, Kofi. Bus Transit Cost, Productivity and Factor Substitution. *J. Transp. Econ. Policy*, May 1985, *19*(2), pp. 183–203. **[G: U.S.]**

Ouellette, Pierre and Lasserre, Pierre. Mesure de la productivité: la méthode de Divisia. (The Measurement of Productivity: The Method of Divisia. With English summary.) *L'Actual. Econ.*, December 1985, *61*(4), pp. 507–26.

Ovsienko, Iu. V., et al. On the Relationship between Labor Productivity, Household Income, and Prices. *Matekon*, Summer 1985, *21*(4), pp. 3–22.

Owen, John D. Changing from a Rotating to a Permanent Shift System in the Detroit Police Department: Effects on Employee Attitudes and Behavior. In *Dennis, B. D., ed.*, 1985, pp. 484–89. **[G: U.S.]**

Peterson, Richard B. and Tracy, Lane. Problem Solving in American Collective Bargaining: A

Review and Assessment. In *Lipsky, D. B., ed.*, 1985, pp. 1–50.   [G: U.S.]

Prywes, Menahem. Quantity and Quality of Capital Impacts on Productivity in the Chemical Industry: An Empirical Study. In *Adams, F. G., ed.*, 1985, pp. 161–79.   [G: U.S.]

Rabeau, Yves. Le marché du travail: quelques perspectives d'avenir. (The Labour Marker: Some Prospects. With English summary.) *L'Actual. Econ.*, March 1985, *61*(1), pp. 127–42.

Rajalakshmi, K. Production Function Analysis of Public Sector Transport Equipment Industry in India. *Indian Econ. J.*, Oct.-Nov. 1985, *33*(2), pp. 17–33.   [G: India]

Rajalakshmi, K. Productivity in Electrical Machinery Industry in Leading States. *Indian Econ. Rev.*, July-Dec. 1985, *20*(2), pp. 269–81.   [G: India]

Rao, B. Sudhakar. Rural Industrialisation and Rural Non-farm Employment in India. In *Mukhopadhyay, S. and Chee, P. L., eds. (I)*, 1985, pp. 147–248.   [G: India]

Ratchford, Brian T. and Brown, James R. A Study of Productivity Changes in Food Retailing. *Marketing Sci.*, Fall 1985, *4*(4), pp. 292–311.   [G: U.S.]

Reskin, Barbara F. Aging and Productivity: Careers and Results. In *Clark, S. M. and Lewis, D. R., eds.*, 1985, pp. 86–97.   [G: U.S.]

Roddy, David J.; Simos, Evangelos O. and Triantis, John E. A Two-output, Multi-input Model of Exogenous and Endogenous Technological Change of the U.S. Economy. *Econ. Notes*, 1985, (2), pp. 118–31.   [G: U.S.]

Román, Zoltán. Productivity Growth and Its Slowdown in the Hungarian Economy. *Acta Oecon.*, 1985, *35*(1–2), pp. 81–104.
[G: Hungary]

Rosenband, Leonard N. Productivity and Labor Discipline in the Montgolfier Paper Mill, 1780–1805. *J. Econ. Hist.*, June 1985, *45*(2), pp. 435–43.   [G: France]

Samiee, Saeed. Global Retail Strategy and Productivity Planning: Some International Comparisons. In *Kaynak, E., ed. (I)*, 1985, pp. 23–36.

Sasaki, Komei. Regional Difference in Total Factor Productivity and Spatial Features: Empirical Analysis on the Basis of a Sectoral Translog Production Function. *Reg. Sci. Urban Econ.*, November 1985, *15*(4), pp. 489–516.
[G: Japan]

Saxena, A. N. Productivity. In *Mongia, J. N., ed.*, 1985, pp. 385–416.   [G: India]

Simon, Herbert A. Japan's Emerging Multinationals: Foreward. In *Takamiya, S. and Thurley, K., eds.*, 1985, pp. 3–12.

Soete, Luc and Patel, Pari. Recherche-développement importations de technologie et croissance Économique: Une tentative de comparaison internationale. (R-D, International Technology Imports and Economic Growth: An International Comparison. With English summary.) *Revue Écon.*, September 1985, *36*(5), pp. 975–1000.   [G: OECD]

Stollery, Kenneth R. Productivity Change in Canadian Mining, 1957–1979. *Appl. Econ.*, June 1985, *17*(3), pp. 543–58.   [G: Canada]

Suzuki, Kazuyuki. Knowledge Capital and the Private Rate of Return to R and D in Japanese Manufacturing Industries. *Int. J. Ind. Organ.*, September 1985, *3*(3), pp. 293–305.
[G: Japan]

Sveikauskas, Leo; Townroe, Peter and Hansen, Eric. Intraregional Productivity Differences in São Paulo State Manufacturing Plants. *Weltwirtsch. Arch.*, 1985, *121*(4), pp. 722–40.
[G: Brazil]

Tinbergen, Jan. Marginal Productivity of Labor Categories in Japan and the United States. In *Shishido, T. and Sato, R., eds.*, 1985, pp. 149–58.   [G: Japan; U.S.]

Todd, Douglas. Factor Productivity Growth in Four EEC Countries, 1960–1981. *Cah. Écon. Bruxelles*, 3rd Trimester 1985, (107), pp. 279–325.   [G: Italy; France; W. Germany; U.K.]

Todd, Douglas. Productive Performance in the West German Manufacturing Industry, 1970–80: A Farrell Frontier Characterisation. *J. Ind. Econ.*, March 1985, *33*(3), pp. 295–316.
[G: W. Germany]

Toner, Bill. The Unionisation and Productivity Debate: An Employee Opinion Survey in Ireland. *Brit. J. Ind. Relat.*, July 1985, *23*(2), pp. 179–202.   [G: Ireland]

Tsao, Yuan. Growth without Productivity: Singapore Manufacturing in the 1970s. *J. Devel. Econ.*, Sept.-Oct. 1985, *19*(1/2), pp. 25–38.
[G: Singapore]

Tsurumi, Yoshi. Japan's Challenge to the United States: Industrial Policies and Corporate Strategies. In *Hochmuth, M. and Davidson, W., eds.*, 1985, pp. 39–79.   [G: U.S.; Japan]

Verma, P. C. Production Structure of Jute Industry in India. *Indian Econ. J.*, Oct.-Nov. 1985, *33*(2), pp. 123–30.   [G: India]

Wachter, Kenneth W. and Becker, Richard A. Are Productive People to Be Found? Robust Analysis of Sparse Two-Way Tables. *J. Amer. Statist. Assoc.*, June 1985, *80*(390), pp. 266–76.   [G: U.S.]

Walker, Richard A. Is There a Service Economy? The Changing Capitalist Division of Labor. *Sci. Soc.*, Spring 1985, *49*(1), pp. 42–83.

Warren, Ronald S., Jr. The Effect of Unionization on Labor Productivity: Some Time-Series Evidence. *J. Lab. Res.*, Spring 1985, *6*(2), pp. 199–207.   [G: U.S.]

Weisskopf, Thomas E.; Bowles, Samuel and Gordon, David M. Two Views of Capitalist Stagnation: Underconsumption and Challenges to Capitalist Control. *Sci. Soc.*, Fall 1985, *49*(3), pp. 259–86.   [G: U.S.]

Wessels, Walter J. The Effects of Unions on Employment and Productivity: An Unresolved Contradiction. *J. Lab. Econ.*, Part 1 January 1985, *3*(1), pp. 101–08.

Worswick, G. D. N. Education and Economic Performance: Introduction. In *Worswick, G. D. N., ed.*, 1985, pp. 1–6.

York, James D. Productivity Trends in the Ma-

chine Tool Accessories Industry. *Mon. Lab. Rev.*, June 1985, *108*(6), pp. 28–32.
[G: U.S.]

826 Labor Markets: Demographic Characteristics

8260 Labor Markets: Demographic Characteristics

Abedian, I. and Standish, B. Poor Whites and the Role of the State: The Evidence. *S. Afr. J. Econ.*, June 1985, *53*(2), pp. 141–65.
[G: S. Africa]

Abowd, John M. and Killingsworth, Mark R. Employment, Wages, and Earnings of Hispanics in the Federal and Nonfederal Sectors: Methodological Issues and Their Empirical Consequences. In *Borjas, G. J. and Tienda, M., eds.*, 1985, pp. 77–125.
[G: U.S.]

Albelda, Randy. "Nice Work If You Can Get It": Segmentation of White and Black Women Workers in the Post-War Period. *Rev. Radical Polit. Econ.*, Fall 1985, *17*(3), pp. 72–85.
[G: U.S.]

Anderson, Bernard E. Job Search and Job Programs. *Challenge*, July/August 1985, *28*(3), pp. 51–53.
[G: U.S.]

Anderson, Elijah. The Social Context of Youth Employment Programs. In *Betsey, C. L.; Hollister, R. G., Jr. and Papageorgiou, M. R., eds.*, 1985, pp. 348–66.
[G: U.S.]

Anker, Richard and Hein, Catherine. Why Third World Urban Employers Usually Prefer Men. *Int. Lab. Rev.*, January–February 1985, *124*(1), pp. 73–90.
[G: LDCs]

Armstrong, Harvey W. and Taylor, Jim. Spatial Variations in the Male Unemployment Inflow Rate. *Appl. Econ.*, February 1985, *17*(1), pp. 41–54.
[G: U.K.]

Armstrong, Muriel. Towards Equity: Summary of Proceedings. In *Economic Council of Canada.*, 1985, pp. 137–45.
[G: Canada]

Ask, Karin. The Position of Women and Women as a Target Group for Development Assistance. In *Jerve, A. M., ed.*, 1985, pp. 327–45.
[G: Pakistan; Norway]

Becker, Gary S. Human Capital, Effort, and the Sexual Division of Labor. *J. Lab. Econ.*, Part 2 January 1985, *3*(1), pp. S33–58.
[G: U.S.]

Ben-Porath, Yoram and Gronau, Reuben. Jewish Mother Goes to Work: Trends in the Labor Force Participation of Women in Israel, 1955–1980. *J. Lab. Econ.*, Part 2 January 1985, *3*(1), pp. S310–27.
[G: Israel]

Berger, Mark C. The Effect of Cohort Size on Earnings Growth: A Reexamination of the Evidence. *J. Polit. Econ.*, June 1985, *93*(3), pp. 561–73.
[G: U.S.]

Blau, David M. The Effects of Economic Development on Life Cycle Wage Rates and Labor Supply Behavior in Malaysia. *J. Devel. Econ.*, Sept.-Oct. 1985, *19*(1/2), pp. 163–85.
[G: Malaysia]

Boily, Nicole. Daycare and Public Policy: Comments. In *Economic Council of Canada.*, 1985, pp. 16–18.
[G: Canada]

Borjas, George J. and Tienda, Marta. Hispanics in the U.S. Economy: Introduction. In *Borjas, G. J. and Tienda, M., eds.*, 1985, pp. 1–24.
[G: U.S.]

Boulet, Jac-André. Occupational Diversification of Women in the Workplace. In *Economic Council of Canada.*, 1985, pp. 31–37.
[G: Canada]

Bourguignon, François and Morrisson, Christian. Une analyse de décomposition de l'inégalite des revenus individuels en France. (A Decomposition Analysis of Income Inequality in France. With English summary.) *Revue Écon.*, July 1985, *36*(4), pp. 741–77.
[G: France]

Breakwell, Glynis M. Young People In and Out of Work. In *Roberts, B.; Finnegan, R. and Gallie, D., eds.*, 1985, pp. 490–501.
[G: U.K.]

Brockmann, C. Thomas. Women and Development in Northern Belize. *J. Devel. Areas*, July 1985, *19*(4), pp. 501–13.
[G: Belize]

Brown, Clair. An Institutional Model of Wives' Work Decisions. *Ind. Relat.*, Spring 1985, *24*(2), pp. 182–204.
[G: U.S.]

Byrne, Dennis M. and Stratton, Richard W. The Impact of Family Disruption on the Earnings of Children. *Soc. Sci. Quart.*, December 1985, *66*(4), pp. 924–32.
[G: U.S.]

Cain, Glen G. Welfare Economics of Policies toward Women. *J. Lab. Econ.*, Part 2 January 1985, *3*(1), pp. S375–96.
[G: U.S.]

Cain, Pamela Stone. Prospects for Pay Equity in a Changing Economy. In *Hartmann, H. I., ed.*, 1985, pp. 137–65.
[G: U.S.]

Cantor, Leonard. A Coherent Approach to the Education and Training of the 16–19 Age Group. In *Worswick, G. D. N., ed.*, 1985, pp. 13–24.
[G: U.K.]

Cave, George. Youth Joblessness and Race: Evidence from the 1980 Census. In *Betsey, C. L.; Hollister, R. G., Jr. and Papageorgiou, M. R., eds.*, 1985, pp. 367–409.
[G: U.S.]

Clogg, Clifford C. and Shockey, James W. The Effect of Changing Demographic Composition on Recent Trends in Underemployment. *Demography*, August 1985, *22*(3), pp. 395–414.
[G: U.S.]

Colombino, Ugo and De Stavola, Bianca. A Model of Female Labor Supply in Italy Using Cohort Data. *J. Lab. Econ.*, Part 2 January 1985, *3*(1), pp. S275–92.
[G: Italy]

Corpeleijn, A. W. F. Labour Force Participation of Young Women in the Netherlands: An Analysis of Flow Data. *Statist. J.*, December 1985, *3*(4), pp. 353–62.
[G: Netherlands]

Cotter, Diane M. Work-related Deaths Dropped Sharply during 1983, BLS Survey Finds. *Mon. Lab. Rev.*, September 1985, *108*(9), pp. 41–44.
[G: U.S.]

Cotton, Jeremiah. More on the "Cost" of Being a Black or Mexican American Male Worker. *Soc. Sci. Quart.*, December 1985, *66*(4), pp. 867–85.
[G: U.S.]

Craig, Christine; Garnsey, Elizabeth and Rubery, Jill. Labour Market Segmentation and Women's Employment: A Case-Study from the

United Kingdom. *Int. Lab. Rev.*, May-June 1985, *124*(3), pp. 267–80. [G: U.K.]

David-McNeil, Jeannine. The Changing Economic Status of the Female Labour Force in Canada. In *Economic Council of Canada.*, 1985, pp. 1–8. [G: Canada]

De Stavola, Bianca and Poli, Irene. Un'analisi longitudinale dell'offerta di lavoro giovanile. (A Longitudinal Study of Youth Labour Market. With English summary.) *Statistica*, July-Sept. 1985, *45*(3), pp. 403–19. [G: Italy]

DeFreitas, Gregory. Ethnic Differentials in Unemployment among Hispanic Americans. In *Borjas, G. J. and Tienda, M., eds.*, 1985, pp. 127–57. [G: U.S.]

Dulude, Louise. Fringe Benefits and the Female Workforce. In *Economic Council of Canada.*, 1985, pp. 71–78. [G: Canada]

Dumas, Cécile. Unfamiliar Sources of Data from Statistics Canada. In *Economic Council of Canada.*, 1985, pp. 149–55. [G: Canada]

Elmore, Richard F. Knowledge Development under the Youth Employment and Demonstration Projects Act, 1977–1981. In *Betsey, C. L.; Hollister, R. G., Jr. and Papageorgiou, M. R., eds.*, 1985, pp. 281–347. [G: U.S.]

Fagan, Christine A. Fringe Benefits and the Female Workforce: Comments. In *Economic Council of Canada.*, 1985, pp. 79–81. [G: Canada]

Farley, Reynolds. Understanding Racial Differences and Trends: How SIPP Can Assist. *J. Econ. Soc. Meas.*, December 1985, *13*(3–4), pp. 245–61. [G: U.S.]

Fernandez, Roberto M. Hispanic Youth in the Labor Market: An Analysis of High School and Beyond. In *Betsey, C. L.; Hollister, R. G., Jr. and Papageorgiou, M. R., eds.*, 1985, pp. 410–61. [G: U.S.]

Finch, Janet. Work, the Family and the Home: A More Egalitarian Future? *Int. J. Soc. Econ.*, 1985, *12*(2), pp. 26–35.

Flaim, Paul O. and Sehgal, Ellen. Displaced Workers of 1979–83: How Well Have They Fared? *Mon. Lab. Rev.*, June 1985, *108*(6), pp. 3–16. [G: U.S.]

Ford, Hugh. Training: Comment. In *Worswick, G. D. N., ed.*, 1985, pp. 79–80. [G: U.K.]

Franz, Wolfgang. An Economic Analysis of Female Work Participation, Education, and Fertility: Theory and Empirical Evidence for the Federal Republic of Germany. *J. Lab. Econ.*, Part 2 January 1985, *3*(1), pp. S218–34. [G: W. Germany]

Fuchs, Victor R. Determinants of Pension Benefits: Comment. In *Wise, D. A., ed.*, 1985, pp. 153–57. [G: U.S.]

Funaba, Takuji. The Labor Supply of Married Women. (In Japanese. With English summary.) *Osaka Econ. Pap.*, March 1985, *34*(4), pp. 16–22. [G: Japan]

Gabin, Nancy. Women Workers and the UAW in the Post-World War II Period: 1945–1954. In *Leab, D. J., ed.*, 1985, pp. 407–32. [G: U.S.]

Ginzberg, Eli. A Policy for Disadvantaged Youth. In *Ginzberg, E.*, 1985, pp. 655–67. [G: U.S.]

Glenn, Evelyn Nakano. Racial Ethnic Women's Labor: The Intersection of Race, Gender and Class Oppression. *Rev. Radical Polit. Econ.*, Fall 1985, *17*(3), pp. 86–108. [G: U.S.]

Glynn, Dermot. Training: Comment. In *Worswick, G. D. N., ed.*, 1985, pp. 80–86. [G: U.K.]

Gordon, Ian R. and Molho, Ian. Women in the Labour Markets of the London Region: A Model of Dependence and Constraint. *Urban Stud.*, October 1985, *22*(5), pp. 367–86. [G: U.K.]

Greenhalgh, Christine A. and Stewart, Mark B. The Occupational Status and Mobility of British Men and Women. *Oxford Econ. Pap.*, March 1985, *37*(1), pp. 40–71. [G: U.K.]

Greenhalgh, Susan. Sexual Stratification: The Other Side of "Growth with Equity" in East Asia. *Population Devel. Rev.*, June 1985, *11*(2), pp. 265–314. [G: E. Asia]

Gregory, R. G.; McMahon, P. J. and Whittingham, B. Women in the Australian Labor Force: Trends, Causes, and Consequences. *J. Lab. Econ.*, Part 2 January 1985, *3*(1), pp. S293–309. [G: Australia]

Griliches, Zvi. Income-Maintenance Policy and Work Effort: Learning from Experiments and Labor-Market Studies: Comment. In *Hausman, J. A. and Wise, D. A., eds.*, 1985, pp. 137–38.

Gustafsson, Siv and Jacobsson, Roger. Trends in Female Labor Force Participation in Sweden. *J. Lab. Econ.*, Part 2 January 1985, *3*(1), pp. S256–74. [G: Sweden]

Gustman, Alan L. and Steinmeier, Thomas L. The Effect of Partial Retirement on the Wage Profiles of Older Workers. *Ind. Relat.*, Spring 1985, *24*(2), pp. 257–65. [G: U.S.]

Gustman, Alan L. and Steinmeier, Thomas L. The 1983 Social Security Reforms and Labor Supply Adjustments of Older Individuals in the Long Run. *J. Lab. Econ.*, April 1985, *3*(2), pp. 237–53. [G: U.S.]

Hamermesh, Daniel S. Substitution between Different Categories of Labour, Relative Wages and Youth Unemployment. *OECD Econ. Stud.*, Autumn 1985, (5), pp. 57–85. [G: OECD]

Hansen, W. Lee. Changing Demography of Faculty in Higher Education. In *Clark, S. M. and Lewis, D. R., eds.*, 1985, pp. 27–54. [G: U.S.]

Hartog, Joop and Theeuwes, Jules. The Emergence of the Working Wife in Holland. *J. Lab. Econ.*, Part 2 January 1985, *3*(1), pp. S235–55. [G: Holland]

Hendry, Joy. Japan: Culture versus Industrialization as Determinant of Marital Patterns. In *Davis, K., ed.*, 1985, pp. 197–222. [G: Japan; Selected Countries]

Hernandez Iglesias, Feliciano and Riboud, Michelle. Trends in Labor Force Participation of Spanish Women: An Interpretive Essay. *J. Lab. Econ.*, Part 2 January 1985, *3*(1), pp. S201–17. [G: Spain]

Hicks, Peter. A National System for Parental Leave: Comments. In *Economic Council of Canada.*, 1985, pp. 28–29. [G: Canada]

Hoffman, Emily P. Fertility and Female Employment. *Quart. Rev. Econ. Bus.*, Spring 1985, 25(1), pp. 85–95. [G: U.S.]

Iams, Howard M. Characteristics of the Longest Job for New Retired Workers: Findings from the New Beneficiary Survey. *Soc. Sec. Bull.*, March 1985, 48(3), pp. 5–21. [G: U.S.]

Jackson, Roy. Training: Comment. In *Worswick, G. D. N.*, ed., 1985, pp. 86–90. [G: U.K.]

Joshi, Heather E.; Layard, Richard and Owen, Susan J. Why Are More Women Working in Britain? *J. Lab. Econ.*, Part 2 January 1985, 3(1), pp. S147–76. [G: U.K.]

Keeley, Michael C. and Robins, Philip K. Government Programs, Job Search Requirements, and the Duration of Unemployment. *J. Lab. Econ.*, July 1985, 3(3), pp. 337–62. [G: U.S.]

Krashinsky, Michael. Daycare and Public Policy. In *Economic Council of Canada.*, 1985, pp. 9–16. [G: Canada]

Kunin, Roslyn. Occupational Diversification of Women in the Workplace: Comments. In *Economic Council of Canada.*, 1985, pp. 36–40. [G: Canada]

Leuthold, Jane H. Work Incentives and the Two-Earner Deduction. *Public Finance Quart.*, January 1985, 13(1), pp. 63–73. [G: U.S.]

Lewin-Epstein, Noah. Neighborhoods, Local Labor Markets, and Employment Opportunities for White and Nonwhite Youth. *Soc. Sci. Quart.*, March 1985, 66(1), pp. 163–71. [G: U.S.]

Lewis, Jane. Work, Women and Welfare. In *Klein, R. and O'Higgins, M.*, ed., 1985, pp. 216–22. [G: U.K.]

Lewis, Philip E. T. Substitution between Young and Adult Workers in Australia. *Australian Econ. Pap.*, June 1985, 24(44), pp. 115–26. [G: Australia]

Lillydahl, Jane H. and Singell, Larry D. The Spatial Variation in Unemployment and Labour Force Participation Rates of Male and Female Workers. *Reg. Stud.*, October 1985, 19(5), pp. 459–69. [G: U.K.]

Lin, Chung-cheng and Chu, Yun-peng. Further Evidence of Cohort Size Effects on Earnings: The Case of Taiwan. *J. Econ. Devel.*, December 1985, 10(2), pp. 101–21. [G: Taiwan]

Lin, Vivian. Women Factory Workers in Asian Export Processing Zones. In *Utrecht, E.*, ed., 1985, pp. 159–219. [G: Asia]

Linke, R. D.; Oertel, L. M. and Kelsey, N. J. M. Participation and Equity in Higher Education: A Preliminary Report on the Socioeconomic Profile of Higher Education Students in South Australia, 1974–1984. *Australian Bull. Lab.*, June 1985, 11(3), pp. 124–41. [G: Australia]

Lynch, Lisa M. State Dependency in Youth Unemployment: A Lost Generation? *J. Econometrics*, April 1985, 28(1), pp. 71–84. [G: U.K.]

Mare, Robert D. and Winship, Christopher. School Enrollment, Military Enlistment, and the Transition to Work: Implications for the Age Pattern of Employment. In *Heckman, J. J. and Singer, B.*, eds., 1985, pp. 364–99. [G: U.S.]

Marsden, David. Youth Pay in Britain Compared with France, and FR Germany since 1966. *Brit. J. Ind. Relat.*, November 1985, 23(3), pp. 399–414. [G: France; U.K.; W. Germany]

Marsden, Lorna R. Technological Change: Bad or Good? Comments. In *Economic Council of Canada.*, 1985, pp. 93–97. [G: U.S.]

Mayer, Francine and Roy, Paul-Martel. Aspects dynamiques de la structure du chômage au Québec. (Dynamic Aspects of the Structure of Unemployment in Quebec. With English summary.) *L'Actual. Econ.*, June 1985, 61(2), pp. 200–219. [G: Canada]

McElroy, Marjorie B. The Joint Determination of Household Membership and Market Work: The Case of Young Men. *J. Lab. Econ.*, July 1985, 3(3), pp. 293–316.

McKee, Lorna and Bell, Colin. Marital and Family Relations in Times of Male Unemployment. In *Roberts, B.; Finnegan, R. and Gallie, D.*, eds., 1985, pp. 387–99. [G: U.K.]

Meng, Ronald. An Empirical Test for Labor Market Segmentation of Males in Canada. *Ind. Relat.*, Spring 1985, 24(2), pp. 280–87. [G: Canada]

Michael, Robert T. Consequences of the Rise in Female Labor Force Participation Rates: Questions and Probes. *J. Lab. Econ.*, Part 2 January 1985, 3(1), pp. S117–46. [G: U.S.]

Miller, Paul W. and Volker, Paul A. Economic Progress in Australia: An Analysis of Occupational Mobility. *Econ. Rec.*, March 1985, 61(172), pp. 463–75. [G: Australia]

Mincer, Jacob. Intercountry Comparisons of Labor Force Trends and of Related Developments: An Overview. *J. Lab. Econ.*, Part 2 January 1985, 3(1), pp. S1–32. [G: Selected Countries]

Morris, Lydia D. Renegotiation of the Domestic Division of Labour in the Context of Male Redundancy. In *Roberts, B.; Finnegan, R. and Gallie, D.*, eds., 1985, pp. 400–416. [G: U.K.]

Morris, Lydia D. Responses to Redundancy: Labour-Market Experience, Domestic Organisation and Male Social Networks. *Int. J. Soc. Econ.*, 1985, 12(2), pp. 5–16. [G: U.K.]

Mosk, Carl and Nakata, Yoshi-Fumi. The Age-Wage Profile and Structural Change in the Japanese Labor Market for Males, 1964–1982. *J. Human Res.*, Winter 1985, 20(1), pp. 100–116. [G: Japan]

Nakamura, Alice and Nakamura, Masao. Dynamic Models of the Labor Force Behavior of Married Women Which Can Be Estimated Using Limited Amounts of Past Information. *J. Econometrics*, March 1985, 27(3), pp. 273–98. [G: U.S.]

Nelson, Valerie and Turner, Charles F. Estimates of Effects of Employment and Training Programs Derived from National Longitudinal

Surveys and Continuous Longitudinal Manpower Survey. In *Betsey, C. L.; Hollister, R. G., Jr. and Papageorgiou, M. R., eds.*, 1985, pp. 254–80. [G: U.S.]

de Neubourg, Chris. Part-Time Work: An International Quantitative Comparison. *Int. Lab. Rev.*, Sept.-Oct. 1985, *124*(5), pp. 559–76. [G: OECD]

Ofer, Gur and Vinokur, Aaron. Work and Family Roles of Soviet Women: Historical Trends and Cross-Section Analysis. *J. Lab. Econ.*, Part 2 January 1985, *3*(1), pp. S328–54. [G: U.S.S.R.]

Packard, Michael. Company Policies and Attitudes toward Older Workers. *Soc. Sec. Bull.*, May 1985, *48*(5), pp. 45–46. [G: U.S.]

Peitchinis, Stephen G. Technological Change: Bad or Good? In *Economic Council of Canada.*, 1985, pp. 83–93. [G: U.S.]

Peston, Maurice. Training: Comment. In *Worswick, G. D. N., ed.*, 1985, pp. 76–79. [G: U.K.]

Pickup, L. Women's Travel Needs in a Period of Rising Female Employment. In *Jansen, G. R. M.; Nijkamp, P. and Ruijgrok, C. J., eds.*, 1985, pp. 97–113. [G: U.K.]

Pike, Maureen. The Employment Response to Equal Pay Legislation. *Oxford Econ. Pap.*, June 1985, *37*(2), pp. 304–18. [G: U.K.]

Quester, Aline O. and Greene, William H. The Labor Market Experience of Black and White Wives in the Sixties and Seventies. *Soc. Sci. Quart.*, December 1985, *66*(4), pp. 854–66. [G: U.S.]

Rabeau, Yves. Le marché du travail: quelques perspectives d'avenir. (The Labour Marker: Some Prospects. With English summary.) *L'Actual. Econ.*, March 1985, *61*(1), pp. 127–42.

Reimers, Cordelia W. A Comparative Analysis of the Wages of Hispanics, Blacks, and Non-Hispanic Whites. In *Borjas, G. J. and Tienda, M., eds.*, 1985, pp. 27–75. [G: U.S.]

Reimers, Cordelia W. Cultural Differences in Labor Force Participation among Married Women. *Amer. Econ. Rev.*, May 1985, *75*(2), pp. 251–55. [G: U.S.]

Rein, Martin. The Social Welfare Labour Market. In *Eisenstadt, S. N. and Ahimeir, O., eds.*, 1985, pp. 109–31. [G: Israel; U.S.; W. Europe]

Reno, Virginia P. and Grad, Susan. Economic Security, 1935–85. *Soc. Sec. Bull.*, December 1985, *48*(12), pp. 5–20.

Riboud, Michelle. An Analysis of Women's Labor Force Participation in France: Cross-Section Estimates and Time-Series Evidence. *J. Lab. Econ.*, Part 2 January 1985, *3*(1), pp. S177–200. [G: France]

Rives, Janet M. and Turner, Keith K. Industrial Distributions and Aggregate Unemployment Rates of Men and Women. *Soc. Sci. Quart.*, December 1985, *66*(4), pp. 916–23. [G: U.S.]

Roberts, Ceridwen. Research on Women in the Labour Market: The Context and Scope of the Women and Employment Survey. In *Roberts, B.; Finnegan, R. and Gallie, D., eds.*, 1985, pp. 232–45. [G: U.K.]

Rosen, Sherwin. Income-Maintenance Policy and Work Effort: Learning from Experiments and Labor-Market Studies: Comment. In *Hausman, J. A. and Wise, D. A., eds.*, 1985, pp. 134–37. [G: U.S.]

Rosenbloom, Sandra. The Growth of Non-traditional Families: A Challenge to Traditional Planning Approaches. In *Jansen, G. R. M.; Nijkamp, P. and Ruijgrok, C. J., eds.*, 1985, pp. 75–96. [G: U.S.; Netherlands]

Russell, Russ. A Comparison of the Youth Training Scheme in the United Kingdom with the Vocational Foundation Training Year in Germany. In *Worswick, G. D. N., ed.*, 1985, pp. 68–75. [G: U.K.; W. Germany]

Ryscavage, Paul M. and Bregger, John E. New Household Survey and the CPS: A Look at Labor Force Differences. *Mon. Lab. Rev.*, September 1985, *108*(9), pp. 3–12. [G: U.S.]

Santiago, Carlos E. and Rossiter, Rosemary. A Multiple Time-Series Analysis of Labor Supply and Earnings in Economic Development. *J. Devel. Econ.*, April 1985, *17*(3), pp. 259–75. [G: Puerto Rico]

Sassen-Koob, Saskia. Changing Composition and Labor Market Location of Hispanic Immigrants in New York City, 1960–1980. In *Borjas, G. J. and Tienda, M., eds.*, 1985, pp. 299–322. [G: U.S.]

Sehgal, Ellen. Foreign Born in the U.S. Labor Market: The Results of a Special Survey. *Mon. Lab. Rev.*, July 1985, *108*(7), pp. 18–24. [G: U.S.]

Shank, Susan Elizabeth. Employment Rose in the First Half of 1985 as the Recovery Entered Its Third Year. *Mon. Lab. Rev.*, August 1985, *108*(8), pp. 3–8. [G: U.S.]

Shimada, Haruo and Higuchi, Yoshio. An Analysis of Trends in Female Labor Force Participation in Japan. *J. Lab. Econ.*, Part 2 January 1985, *3*(1), pp. S355–74. [G: Japan]

Shimada, Haruo and Higuchi, Yoshio. An Analysis of Trends in Female Labor Force Participation in Japan. *Econ. Lavoro*, Apr.-June 1985, *19*(2), pp. 3–18. [G: Japan]

Sigit, Hananto. Income Distribution and Household Characteristics. *Bull. Indonesian Econ. Stud.*, December 1985, *21*(3), pp. 51–68. [G: Indonesia]

Simms, Margaret C. The Participation of Young Women in Employment and Training Programs. In *Betsey, C. L.; Hollister, R. G., Jr. and Papageorgiou, M. R., eds.*, 1985, pp. 462–85. [G: U.S.]

Sloane, Peter J. Discrimination in the Labour Market. In *Carline, D., et al.*, 1985, pp. 78–158. [G: U.K.; U.S.; Selected Countries]

Smith, James P. and Ward, Michael P. Time-Series Growth in the Female Labor Force. *J. Lab. Econ.*, Part 2 January 1985, *3*(1), pp. S59–90. [G: U.S.]

Smith, Marvin M. Early Labor Market Experiences of Youth and Subsequent Wages. *Amer.*

J. Econ. Soc., October 1985, *44*(4), pp. 391–400. [G: U.S.]

Smith, Shirley J. Estimating Lost Future Earnings Using the New Worklife Tables: A Comment [Using the Appropriate Worklife Estimate in Court Proceedings]. *Mon. Lab. Rev.*, February 1985, *108*(2), pp. 42. [G: U.S.]

Smith, Shirley J. Revised Worklife Tables Reflect 1979–80 Experience. *Mon. Lab. Rev.*, August 1985, *108*(8), pp. 23–30. [G: U.S.]

Solon, Gary R. The Minimum Wage and Teenage Employment: A Reanalysis with Attention to Serial Correlation and Seasonality. *J. Human Res.*, Spring 1985, *20*(2), pp. 292–97. [G: U.S.]

Stafford, Frank P. Income-Maintenance Policy and Work Effort: Learning from Experiments and Labor-Market Studies. In *Hausman, J. A. and Wise, D. A., eds.*, 1985, pp. 95–134. [G: U.S.]

Stelcner, Morton and Breslaw, Jon. Income Taxes and the Labor Supply of Married Women in Quebec. *Southern Econ. J.*, April 1985, *51*(4), pp. 1053–72. [G: Canada]

Stephenson, Stanley P., Jr. Labor Market Turnover and Joblessness for Hispanic Youth. In *Borjas, G. J. and Tienda, M., eds.*, 1985, pp. 193–218. [G: U.S.]

Stevans, Lonnie K.; Register, Charles and Grimes, Paul. Race and the Discouraged Female Worker: A Question of Labor Force Attachment. *Rev. Black Polit. Econ.*, Summer 1985, *14*(1), pp. 89–97. [G: U.S.]

Stoddart, Jennifer. Towards Equity: Directions for Future Research: Panel Discussion. In *Economic Council of Canada.*, 1985, pp. 131–34.

Stone, John Owen. Youth Unemployment in Australia. *Nat. Westminster Bank Quart. Rev.*, May 1985, pp. 3–11. [G: Australia]

Taubman, Paul. Determinants of Pension Benefits. In *Wise, D. A., ed.*, 1985, pp. 123–53. [G: U.S.]

Tienda, Marta and Glass, Jennifer. Household Structure and Labor Force Participation of Black, Hispanic, and White Mothers. *Demography*, August 1985, *22*(3), pp. 381–94. [G: U.S.]

Tienda, Marta and Guhleman, Patricia. The Occupational Position of Employed Hispanic Women. In *Borjas, G. J. and Tienda, M., eds.*, 1985, pp. 243–73. [G: U.S.]

Tomoda, Shizue. Measuring Female Labour Activities in Asian Developing Countries: A Time-Allocation Approach. *Int. Lab. Rev.*, Nov.-Dec. 1985, *124*(6), pp. 661–76.
[G: Bangladesh; Nepal; Indonesia; Philippines]

Townson, Monica. A National System for Parental Leave. In *Economic Council of Canada.*, 1985, pp. 21–28. [G: Canada]

Turner, Charles F. Standardized Data Collection for Large-scale Program Evaluation: An Assessment of the YEDPA-SAS Experience. In *Betsey, C. L.; Hollister, R. G., Jr. and Papageorgiou, M. R., eds.*, 1985, pp. 193–219. [G: U.S.]

Tyree, Andrea. Tracking a Ghost To Test a Theory. *Soc. Sci. Quart.*, September 1985, *66*(3), pp. 668–74. [G: Selected MDCs]

Ward, Kathryn B. and Pampel, Fred C. More on the Meaning of the Effect of the Sex Ratio on Female Labor Force Participation. *Soc. Sci. Quart.*, September 1985, *66*(3), pp. 675–79. [G: Selected MDCs]

Ward, Kathryn B. and Pampel, Fred C. Structural Determinants of Female Labor Force Participation in Developed Nations, 1955–75. *Soc. Sci. Quart.*, September 1985, *66*(3), pp. 654–67. [G: Selected MDCs]

Williams, Donald R. Technical Note: Employment in Recession and Recovery: A Demographic Flow Analysis. *Mon. Lab. Rev.*, March 1985, *108*(3), pp. 35–42. [G: U.S.]

Wise, David A. Pensions, Labor, and Individual Choice: Overview. In *Wise, D. A., ed.*, 1985, pp. 1–17. [G: U.S.]

Wolozin, Harold. Corporate Power in an Aging Economy: Labor Force Policy. *J. Econ. Issues*, June 1985, *19*(2), pp. 475–86. [G: U.S.]

Young, Anne McDougall. New Monthly Data Series on School Age Youth. *Mon. Lab. Rev.*, July 1985, *108*(7), pp. 49–50. [G: U.S.]

Young, Anne McDougall. One-fourth of the Adult Labor Force Are College Graduates. *Mon. Lab. Rev.*, February 1985, *108*(2), pp. 43–46. [G: U.S.]

830 TRADE UNIONS; COLLECTIVE BARGAINING; LABOR–MANAGEMENT RELATIONS

8300 General

Brundage, David. The Producing Classes and the Saloon: Denver in the 1880s. *Labor Hist.*, Winter 1985, *26*(1), pp. 29–52. [G: U.S.]

Dubofsky, Melvyn. Give Us That Old Time Labor History: Philip S. Foner and the American Worker: Essay Review. *Labor Hist.*, Winter 1985, *26*(1), pp. 118–37.

Macphee, Ian. Poor Nation of the Pacific: The Labour Market. In *Scutt, J. A., ed.*, 1985, pp. 75–92. [G: Australia]

Macpherson, C. B. The Prospects of Economic and Industrial Democracy. In *Macpherson, C. B.*, 1985, pp. 35–43.

Marsden, David. Chronicle: Industrial Relations in the United Kingdom December 1984–March 1985. *Brit. J. Ind. Relat.*, July 1985, *23*(2), pp. 309–20. [G: U.K.]

Martin, Andrew. Wages, Profits, and Investment in Sweden. In *Lindberg, L. N. and Maier, C. S., eds.*, 1985, pp. 403–66. [G: Sweden]

Rojot, Jacques. The 1984 Revision of the OECD Guidelines for Multinational Enterprises. *Brit. J. Ind. Relat.*, November 1985, *23*(3), pp. 379–97. [G: OECD; LDCs]

831 Trade Unions

8310 Trade Unions

Aaron, Benjamin. The Changing Law of Fair Representation: The State of the Law: An Overview. **In** *McKelvey, J. T., ed.*, 1985, pp. 15–46. **[G: U.S.]**

Abraham, Katharine G. and Medoff, James L. Length of Service and Promotions in Union and Nonunion Work Groups. *Ind. Lab. Relat. Rev.*, April 1985, *38*(3), pp. 408–20. **[G: U.S.]**

Adams, Larry T. Changing Employment Patterns of Organized Workers. *Mon. Lab. Rev.*, February 1985, *108*(2), pp. 25–31. **[G: U.S.]**

Adams, Roy J. Should Works Councils Be Used as Industrial Relations Policy? *Mon. Lab. Rev.*, July 1985, *108*(7), pp. 25–29. **[G: U.S.; Canada]**

Adams, Walter and Brock, James W. Industrial Policy and Trade Unions. *J. Econ. Issues*, June 1985, *19*(2), pp. 497–505. **[G: U.S.]**

Addison, John T. What Do Unions Really Do? A Review Article. *J. Lab. Res.*, Spring 1985, *6*(2), pp. 127–46. **[G: U.S.]**

Ahern, Robert W. Labor–Management Structures in the Large City. **In** *Woodworth, W.; Meek, C. and Whyte, W. F., eds.*, 1985, pp. 161–78. **[G: U.S.]**

Ahiauzu, Augustine I. Ideology, Culture, and Trade Union Behavior: The Nigerian Case. *Devel. Econ.*, September 1985, *23*(3), pp. 281–95. **[G: Nigeria]**

Albeda, W. Recent Trends in Collective Bargaining in the Netherlands. *Int. Lab. Rev.*, January–February 1985, *124*(1), pp. 49–60. **[G: Netherlands]**

Aoki, Masahiko. Dynamics of Unemployment, Vacancies and Real Wages with Trade Unions: Comment. *Scand. J. Econ.*, 1985, *87*(2), pp. 404–07.

Appleton, William C. and Baker, Joe G. Unionization and Safety in Bituminous Deep Mines: Reply. *J. Lab. Res.*, Spring 1985, *6*(2), pp. 217–20. **[G: U.S.]**

Aronson, Robert L. Unionism among Professional Employees in the Private Sector. *Ind. Lab. Relat. Rev.*, April 1985, *38*(3), pp. 352–64. **[G: U.S.]**

Bacharach, Samuel B.; Mitchell, Stephen M. and Malanowski, Rose. Strategic Choice and Collective Action: Organizational Determinants of Teachers Militancy. **In** *Lipsky, D. B., ed.*, 1985, pp. 197–222. **[G: U.S.]**

Bain, George Sayers and Elias, Peter. Trade Union Membership in Great Britain: An Individual-Level Analysis. *Brit. J. Ind. Relat.*, March 1985, *23*(1), pp. 71–92. **[G: U.K.]**

Baird, Charles W. Labor Law and the First Amendment. *Cato J.*, Spring/Summer 1985, *5*(1), pp. 203–18. **[G: U.S.]**

Barbash, Jack. The Theory of Industrial Unionism. **In** *Dennis, B. D., ed.*, 1985, pp. 648–54. **[G: U.S.]**

Bennett, James D. and Passmore, David L. Unions and Coal Mine Safety: Comment [The Effect of Unionization on Safety in Bituminous Deep Mines]. *J. Lab. Res.*, Spring 1985, *6*(2), pp. 211–16. **[G: U.S.]**

Bernstein, Irving. The Historical Significance of the CIO. **In** *Dennis, B. D., ed.*, 1985, pp. 654–58. **[G: U.S.]**

Biagioli, Mario. Contrattazione aziendale e differenziali retributivi interaziendali. (Workplace Bargaining and Wage Differentials among Firms. With English summary.) *Econ. Lavoro*, July-Sept. 1985, *19*(3), pp. 75–110. **[G: Italy]**

Black, Dan A. and Parker, Darrell F. The Division of Union Rents. *J. Lab. Res.*, Summer 1985, *6*(3), pp. 281–88.

Blum, Albert A. and Thompson, Mark. Workers of the World Disunited. *Challenge*, Nov./Dec. 1985, *28*(5), pp. 32–37. **[G: U.S.; Mexico]**

Booth, Alison L. The Free Rider Problem and a Social Custom Model of Trade Union Membership. *Quart. J. Econ.*, February 1985, *100*(1), pp. 253–61.

Brinker, Paul A. Violence by U.S. Labor Unions. *J. Lab. Res.*, Fall 1985, *6*(4), pp. 417–27. **[G: U.S.]**

Brown, Martin and Philips, Peter. The Evolution of Labor Market Structure: The California Canning Industry. *Ind. Lab. Relat. Rev.*, April 1985, *38*(3), pp. 392–407. **[G: U.S.]**

Bruggink, Thomas H., et al. Direct and Indirect Effects of Unionization on the Wage Levels of Nurses: A Case Study of New Jersey Hospitals. *J. Lab. Res.*, Fall 1985, *6*(4), pp. 405–16. **[G: U.S.]**

Calmfors, Lars. Trade Unions, Wage Formation and Macroeconomic Stability—An Introduction. *Scand. J. Econ.*, 1985, *87*(2), pp. 143–59. **[G: W. Europe; U.S.]**

Calmfors, Lars. Work Sharing, Employment and Wages. *Europ. Econ. Rev.*, April 1985, *27*(3), pp. 293–309.

Calmfors, Lars and Horn, Henrik. Classical Unemployment, Accommodation Policies and Adjustment of Real Wages. *Scand. J. Econ.*, 1985, *87*(2), pp. 234–61.

Campbell, Adrian and Warner, Malcolm. Changes in the Balance of Power in the British Mineworkers' Union: An Analysis of National Top-Office Elections, 1974–84. *Brit. J. Ind. Relat.*, March 1985, *23*(1), pp. 1–24. **[G: U.K.]**

Campero, Guillermo and Cortázar, René. Lógicas de acción sindical en Chile. (Logics of Trade Union Action in Chile. With English summary.) *Colección Estud. CIEPLAN*, 1985, (18), pp. 5–37. **[G: Chile]**

Carline, Derek. Trade Unions and Wages. **In** *Carline, D., et al.*, 1985, pp. 186–232. **[G: U.K.; U.S.]**

Carnoy, Martin. Education and the Changing American Workplace. **In** *Gustavsson, B.; Karlsson, J. C. and Raftegard, C.*, 1985, pp. 159–70. **[G: U.S.]**

Carruth, Alan A. and Oswald, Andrew J. Miners' Wages in Post-war Britain: An Application of a Model of Trade Union Behaviour. *Econ. J.*, December 1985, *95*(380), pp. 1003–20. **[G: U.K.]**

Chacko, Thomas I. Member Participation in Union Activities: Perceptions of Union Priorities, Performance, and Satisfaction. *J. Lab.*

Res., Fall 1985, *6*(4), pp. 363–73. [G: U.S.]

Chaykowski, Richard P. and Beach, Charles M. Prizes in an Industrial Union Environment. *J. Lab. Res.*, Spring 1985, *6*(2), pp. 181–98. [G: Canada]

Chermesh, Ran. Strikes as Social Problems: A Social Problem Matrix Approach. *Brit. J. Ind. Relat.*, July 1985, *23*(2), pp. 281–307. [G: Israel]

Chowdhury, Gopa and Nickell, Stephen. Hourly Earnings in the United States: Another Look at Unionization, Schooling, Sickness, and Unemployment Using PSID Data. *J. Lab. Econ.*, Part 1 January 1985, *3*(1), pp. 38–69. [G: U.S.]

Christensen, Andrea S. What Employers Can Do about DFR Suits. In *McKelvey, J. T., ed.*, 1985, pp. 117–27. [G: U.S.]

Cohen, Isaac. Workers' Control in the Cotton Industry: A Comparative Study of British and American Mule Spinning. *Labor Hist.*, Winter 1985, *26*(1), pp. 53–85. [G: U.S.; U.K.]

Contini, Giovanni. Politics, Law and Shop Floor Bargaining in Postwar Italy. In *Tolliday, S. and Zeitlin, J., eds.*, 1985, pp. 192–218. [G: Italy]

Cooke, William N. The Rising Toll of Discrimination against Union Activists. *Ind. Relat.*, Fall 1985, *24*(3), pp. 421–42. [G: U.S.]

Craft, James A.; Abboushi, Suhail and Labovitz, Trudy. Concession Bargaining and Unions: Impacts and Implications. *J. Lab. Res.*, Spring 1985, *6*(2), pp. 167–80. [G: U.S.]

Crouch, Colin. Conditions for Trade Union Wage Restraint. In *Lindberg, L. N. and Maier, C. S., eds.*, 1985, pp. 105–39. [G: OECD]

De Bruyne, Guido. Union Militancy, External Shocks and the Accommodation Dilemma: Comment. *Scand. J. Econ.*, 1985, *87*(2), pp. 352–54.

DeFina, Robert H. Union–Nonunion Wage Differentials and the Functional Distribution of Income: Some Simulation Results from a General Equilibrium Model. *J. Lab. Res.*, Summer 1985, *6*(3), pp. 263–79.

Delamotte, Yves. Managerial and Supervisory Staff in a Changing World. *Int. Lab. Rev.*, January–February 1985, *124*(1), pp. 1–16. [G: W. Germany; Italy; France; U.K.; Sweden]

Delaney, John Thomas. Unionism, Bargaining Spillovers, and Teacher Compensation. In *Lipsky, D. B., ed.*, 1985, pp. 111–42. [G: U.S.]

Dickens, William T. and Leonard, Jonathan S. Accounting for the Decline in Union Membership, 1950–1980. *Ind. Lab. Relat. Rev.*, April 1985, *38*(3), pp. 323–34. [G: U.S.]

Dogas, D. Market Power in a Bilateral Monopoly Model of Industry Wage Determination. *Appl. Econ.*, February 1985, *17*(1), pp. 149–64. [G: U.K.]

Doyle, Philip M. Area Wage Surveys Shed Light on Declines in Unionization. *Mon. Lab. Rev.*, September 1985, *108*(9), pp. 13–20. [G: U.S.]

Driffill, John. Macroeconomic Stabilization Policy

and Trade Union Behaviour as a Repeated Game. *Scand. J. Econ.*, 1985, *87*(2), pp. 300–326.

Dubofsky, Melvyn. The Origins of Western Working-Class Radicalism, 1890–1905. In *Leab, D. J., ed.*, 1985, pp. 230–53. [G: U.S.]

Dubois, Pierre. Quindici anni di nuove forme di organizzazione del lavoro in Francia: Dagli scioperi per il miglioramento delle condizioni di lavoro alla legislazione sul "diritto di espressione" dei lavoratori. (Fifteen Years of New Labour Organization Experiences in France. With English summary.) *Econ. Lavoro*, Jan.-Mar. 1985, *19*(1), pp. 37–49. [G: France]

Duncan, Gregory M. and Leigh, Duane E. The Endogeneity of Union Status: An Empirical Test. *J. Lab. Econ.*, July 1985, *3*(3), pp. 385–402.

Dworkin, James B. and Ahlburg, Dennis A. Unions and Productivity: A Review of the Research. In *Lipsky, D. B., ed.*, 1985, pp. 51–68. [G: U.S.]

Eden, Benjamin. Trading Uncertainty, Enforcement and Labor Unions. *Econ. Inquiry*, October 1985, *23*(4), pp. 637–50.

Edwards, Christine and Heery, Edmund. Formality and Informality in the Working of the National Coal Board's Incentive Scheme. *Brit. J. Ind. Relat.*, March 1985, *23*(1), pp. 25–45. [G: U.K.]

Edwards, Harry T. The Duty of Fair Representation: A View from the Bench. In *McKelvey, J. T., ed.*, 1985, pp. 93–105. [G: U.S.]

Egolf, Jeremy R. The Limits of Shop Floor Struggle: Workers vs. the Bedaux System at Willapa Harbor Lumber Mills, 1933–35. *Labor Hist.*, Spring 1985, *26*(2), pp. 195–229. [G: U.S.]

Eisenhammer, John S. Trade Unions and Economic Policy: Comment. In *Machin, H. and Wright, V., eds.*, 1985, pp. 279–83. [G: France]

Epstein, Richard A. Agency Costs, Employment Contracts, and Labor Unions. In *Pratt, J. W. and Zeckhauser, R. J., eds.*, 1985, pp. 127–48.

Erd, Rainer and Scherrer, Christoph. Unions—Caught between Structural Competition and Temporary Solidarity: A Critique of Contemporary Marxist Analysis of Trade Unions in Germany. *Brit. J. Ind. Relat.*, March 1985, *23*(1), pp. 115–31. [G: W. Germany]

Evans, Stephen. The Use of Injunctions in Industrial Disputes. *Brit. J. Ind. Relat.*, March 1985, *23*(1), pp. 133–37. [G: U.K.]

Fender, John. Counterinflationary Policy in a Unionised Economy with Nonsynchronised Wage Setting: Comment. *Scand. J. Econ.*, 1985, *87*(2), pp. 379–81.

Ferman, Louis A. and Klingel, Sally. On the Shop Floor: The Implications of Unions and Employers Seeking to Foster Employee Involvement. In *Dennis, B. D., ed.*, 1985, pp. 631–36. [G: U.S.]

Feuille, Peter; Delaney, John Thomas and Hendricks, Wallace. Police Bargaining, Arbitration, and Fringe Benefits. *J. Lab. Res.*, Winter 1985, *6*(1), pp. 1–20.   [G: U.S.]

Feuille, Peter; Delaney, John Thomas and Hendricks, Wallace. The Impact of Interest Arbitration on Police Contracts. *Ind. Relat.*, Spring 1985, *24*(2), pp. 161–81.   [G: U.S.]

Fields, Mitchell W. and Thacker, James W. The Impact of Survey Feedback upon Member Perceptions of the Union. In *Dennis, B. D., ed.*, 1985, pp. 477–83.   [G: U.S.]

Fischer, Ben. Collective Bargaining and Fifty Years of the CIO. In *Dennis, B. D., ed.*, 1985, pp. 659–64.

Fischer, Stanley. Contracts, Credibility and Disinflation. In *Argy, V. E. and Neville, J. W., eds.*, 1985, pp. 39–59.   [G: U.S.]

Fischer, Stanley. Macroeconomic Stabilization Policy and Trade Union Behaviour as a Repeated Game: Comment. *Scand. J. Econ.*, 1985, *87*(2), pp. 327–31.

FitzRoy, Felix R. and Kraft, Kornelius. Unionization, Wages and Efficiency: Theories and Evidence from the U.S. and West Germany. *Kyklos*, 1985, *38*(4), pp. 537–54.   [G: U.S.; W. Germany]

Frank, Jeff. Trade Union Efficiency and Overemployment with Seniority Wage Scales. *Econ. J.*, December 1985, *95*(380), pp. 1021–34.

Freeman, Joshua. Delivering the Goods: Industrial Unionism during World War II. In *Leab, D. J., ed.*, 1985, pp. 383–406.   [G: U.S.]

Freeman, Richard B. Unions, Pensions, and Union Pension Funds. In *Wise, D. A., ed.*, 1985, pp. 89–118.   [G: U.S.]

Friedman, Sheldon. A UAW Perspective on Industrial Policy, International Investment, and Trade. In *Zukin, S., ed.*, 1985, pp. 221–25.
[G: U.S.]

Gabin, Nancy. Women Workers and the UAW in the Post-World War II Period: 1945–1954. In *Leab, D. J., ed.*, 1985, pp. 407–32.
[G: U.S.]

Gärtner, Manfred. Political and Industrial Change in a Model of Trade Union Militancy and Real Wage Growth. *Rev. Econ. Statist.*, May 1985, *67*(2), pp. 322–27.
[G: W. Germany]

Gerhart, Paul F. and Drotning, John E. The Effectiveness of Public Sector Impasse Procedures: A Six State Study. In *Lipsky, D. B., ed.*, 1985, pp. 143–95.   [G: U.S.]

Gitelman, H. M. Adolph Strasser and the Origins of Pure and Simple Unionism. In *Leab, D. J., ed.*, 1985, pp. 153–65.   [G: U.S.]

Goldberg, Marshall. The UAW–Ford Career Services and Reemployment Assistance Centers: New Ventures in Service Delivery to Unionized Workers. In *Dennis, B. D., ed.*, 1985, pp. 527–34.

Graddy, Duane B. and Hall, Gary. Unionization and Productivity in Commercial Banking. *J. Lab. Res.*, Summer 1985, *6*(3), pp. 249–62.
[G: U.S.]

Grout, Paul A. A Theoretical Approach to the Effect of Trade Union Immunities on Invest-

ment and Employment. *Econ. J.*, Supplement 1985, *95*, pp. 96–101.

Gurdon, Michael A. Equity Participation by Employees: The Growing Debate in West Germany. *Ind. Relat.*, Winter 1985, *24*(1), pp. 113–29.   [G: W. Germany]

Gylfason, Thorvaldur. Counterinflationary Policy in a Unionised Economy with Nonsynchronised Wage Setting: Comment. *Scand. J. Econ.*, 1985, *87*(2), pp. 382–85.

Gylfason, Thorvaldur. Workers versus Government—Who Adjusts to Whom? Comment. *Scand. J. Econ.*, 1985, *87*(2), pp. 293–97.
[G: Norway; U.K.]

Hansen, Gary B. Industrial Relations Research Association: Proceedings of the 1985 Spring Meeting: Discussion: EDTP. In *Dennis, B. D., ed.*, 1985, pp. 548–53.   [G: U.S.]

Harris, Howell. The Snares of Liberalism? Politicians, Bureaucrats, and the Shaping of Federal Labour Relations Policy in the United States, ca. 1915–47. In *Tolliday, S. and Zeitlin, J., eds.*, 1985, pp. 148–91.   [G: U.S.]

Henry, S. G. B.; Payne, J. M. and Trinder, C. Real Wages and Unemployment: A Rejoinder [Labour Market Equilibrium in an Open Economy]. *Oxford Econ. Pap.*, June 1985, *37*(2), pp. 344–45.   [G: U.K.]

Henry, S. G. B.; Payne, J. M. and Trinder, C. Unemployment and Real Wages: The Role of Unemployment, Social Security Benefits and Unionisation [Labour Market Equilibrium in an Open Economy] [Unions Real Wages and Employment]. *Oxford Econ. Pap.*, June 1985, *37*(2), pp. 330–38.   [G: U.K.]

Hersoug, Tor. Workers versus Government— Who Adjusts to Whom? *Scand. J. Econ.*, 1985, *87*(2), pp. 270–92.   [G: Norway]

Hills, Stephen M. Erratum [The Attitudes of Union and Nonunion Male Workers toward Union Representation: Review Article]. *Ind. Lab. Relat. Rev.*, July 1985, *38*(4), pp. 639.
[G: U.S.]

Hills, Stephen M. The Attitudes of Union and Nonunion Male Workers toward Union Representation. *Ind. Lab. Relat. Rev.*, January 1985, *38*(2), pp. 179–94.   [G: U.S.]

Holmlund, Bertil. Wages and Employment under Trade Unionism: Microeconomic Models and Macroeconomic Applications: Comment. *Scand. J. Econ.*, 1985, *87*(2), pp. 228–33.
[G: Sweden]

Holt, James. Trade Unionism in the British and U.S. Steel Industries, 1880–1914: A Comparative Study. In *Leab, D. J., ed.*, 1985, pp. 166–96.   [G: U.K.; U.S.]

Horowitz, Joel. Los trabajadores ferroviarios en la Argentina (1920–1943). La formación de una elite obrera. (With English summary.) *Desarrollo Econ.*, Oct.-Dec. 1985, *25*(99), pp. 421–46.   [G: Argentina]

Hunt, Janet C. and White, Rudolph A. The Effects of Management Practices on Union Election Returns. *J. Lab. Res.*, Fall 1985, *6*(4), pp. 389–403.   [G: U.S.]

Hunt, Janet C.; White, Rudolph A. and Moore,

T. A. State Employee Bargaining Legislation. *J. Lab. Res.*, Winter 1985, 6(1), pp. 63–76. [G: U.S.]

Ignagni, Karen. Organized Labor's Perspective on Rising Health Costs. In *Dennis, B. D., ed.,* 1985, pp. 473–76. [G: U.S.]

Ippolito, Richard A. The Economic Function of Underfunded Pension Plans. *J. Law Econ.*, October 1985, 28(3), pp. 611–51. [G: U.S.]

Isaac, J. E. Continuity and Change in Australian Wages Policy: Comment. *Australian Econ. Rev.*, 3rd Quarter, Spring 1985, (71), pp. 68–69. [G: Australia]

Isacowitz, Roy. Labor Trends in 1984. In *Levinson, P. and Landau, P., eds.,* 1985, pp. 65–69. [G: Israel]

Jackman, Richard. Counterinflationary Policy in a Unionised Economy with Nonsynchronised Wage Setting. *Scand. J. Econ.*, 1985, 87(2), pp. 357–78.

Jackson, Roy. Training: Comment. In *Worswick, G. D. N., ed.,* 1985, pp. 86–90. [G: U.K.]

Jacobi, Otto. World Economic Changes and Industrial Relations in the Federal Republic of Germany. In *Juris, H.; Thompson, M. and Daniels, W., eds.,* 1985, pp. 211–46. [G: W. Germany]

Jacobs, David. In Society: New Representational Roles for Labor and Management. In *Dennis, B. D., ed.,* 1985, pp. 624–31. [G: U.S.]

Jenkins, Alexander W. The Analysis of Wage Formation with Application to Alberta Construction. *Appl. Econ.*, October 1985, 17(5), pp. 907–21. [G: Canada]

Johnes, Geraint. Error Removal, Loss Reduction and External Effects in the Theory of Strikes. *Australian Econ. Pap.*, December 1985, 24(45), pp. 310–25.

Johnson, George E. The Economic Theory of Trade Unions—An Introductory Survey: Comment. *Scand. J. Econ.*, 1985, 87(2), pp. 194–96. [G: U.S.; U.K.]

Jones, James E., Jr. The Changing Law of Fair Representation: The Duty in Other Forums: Time for a Midcourse Correction? In *McKelvey, J. T., ed.,* 1985, pp. 223–72. [G: U.S.]

Jones, Robert A. The Changing Structure of Industrial Relations in South Africa. *Managerial Dec. Econ.*, December 1985, 6(4), pp. 217–25. [G: S. Africa]

Jones, Robert A. The Emergence of Shop-Floor Trade Union Power in South Africa. *Managerial Dec. Econ.*, September 1985, 6(3), pp. 160–66. [G: S. Africa]

Jonung, Lars. Classical Unemployment, Accommodation Policies and Adjustment of Real Wages: Comment. *Scand. J. Econ.*, 1985, 87(2), pp. 262–66.

Karier, Thomas M. Unions and Monopoly Profits. *Rev. Econ. Statist.*, February 1985, 67(1), pp. 34–42. [G: U.S.]

Katz, Harry C. and Sabel, Charles F. Industrial Relations & Industrial Adjustment in the Car Industry. *Ind. Relat.*, Fall 1985, 24(3), pp. 295–315. [G: Italy; U.K.; U.S.; W. Germany]

Kemp, Murray C. and Shimomura, Koji. Do La-

bour Unions Drive Out Capital? *Econ. J.*, December 1985, 95(380), pp. 1087–90.

Kessler-Harris, Alice. Organizing the Unorganizable: Three Jewish Women and Their Union. In *Leab, D. J., ed.,* 1985, pp. 269–87. [G: U.S.]

Kierzkowski, Henryk. Insiders and Outsiders in Wage Determination: Comment. *Scand. J. Econ.*, 1985, 87(2), pp. 429–31.

Kierzkowski, Henryk. Workers versus Government—Who Adjusts to Whom? Comment. *Scand. J. Econ.*, 1985, 87(2), pp. 298–99.

Klein, David Y. Exhaustion of Internal Union Remedies after *Clayton* and *Bowen.* In *McKelvey, J. T., ed.,* 1985, pp. 70–84. [G: U.S.]

Knight, Thomas R. Toward a Contingency Theory of the Grievance-Arbitration System. In *Lipsky, D. B., ed.,* 1985, pp. 269–318. [G: U.S.]

Koeller, C. Timothy. Wages, Trade Union Activity, and the Political Environment of Unionism: A Simultaneous Equation Model. *J. Lab. Res.*, Spring 1985, 6(2), pp. 147–65. [G: U.S.]

Kokkelenberg, Edward C. and Sockell, Donna. Union Membership in the United States, 1973–1981. *Ind. Lab. Relat. Rev.*, July 1985, 38(4), pp. 497–543. [G: U.S.]

Kuhn, Peter. Union Productivity Effects and Economic Efficiency. *J. Lab. Res.*, Summer 1985, 6(3), pp. 229–48.

Kumar, Pradeep and Stengos, Thanasis. Measuring the Union Relative Wage Impact: A Methodological Note. *Can. J. Econ.*, February 1985, 18(1), pp. 182–89. [G: Canada]

Lande, Robert H. and Zerbe, Richard O., Jr. Reducing Unions' Monopoly Power: Costs and Benefits. *J. Law Econ.*, May 1985, 28(2), pp. 297–310. [G: U.S.]

Lawler, John J. and West, Robin. Impact of Union-Avoidance Strategy in Representation Elections. *Ind. Relat.*, Fall 1985, 24(3), pp. 406–20. [G: U.S.]

Layard, Richard. Classical Unemployment, Accommodation Policies and Adjustment of Real Wages: Comment. *Scand. J. Econ.*, 1985, 87(2), pp. 267–69.

Layard, Richard and Nickell, Stephen. The Causes of British Unemployment. *Nat. Inst. Econ. Rev.*, February 1985, (111), pp. 62–85. [G: U.K.]

Leab, Daniel J. "United We Eat": The Creation and Organization of the Unemployed Councils in 1930. In *Leab, D. J., ed.,* 1985, pp. 317–32. [G: U.S.]

Leigh, Duane E. The Determinants of Workers' Union Status: Evidence from the National Longitudinal Surveys. *J. Human Res.*, Fall 1985, 20(4), pp. 555–66. [G: U.S.]

Léonard, Daniel. Monopoly Unionism: Note. *Amer. Econ. Rev.*, March 1985, 75(1), pp. 246–49.

Leonard, Jonathan S. The Effect of Unions on the Employment of Blacks, Hispanics, and Women. *Ind. Lab. Relat. Rev.*, October 1985, 39(1), pp. 115–32. [G: U.S.]

Lewin, David. The Effects of Regulation on Public

Sector Labor Relations: Theory and Evidence. *J. Lab. Res.*, Winter 1985, 6(1), pp. 77–95. [G: U.S.]

Lichtenstein, Nelson. UAW Bargaining Strategy and Shop-Floor Conflict: 1946–1970. *Ind. Relat.*, Fall 1985, 24(3), pp. 360–81. [G: U.S.]

Lipsitz, Richard. The Changing Law of Fair Representation: The State of the Law: New Substantive and Procedural Areas. In *McKelvey, J. T., ed.*, 1985, pp. 47–69. [G: U.S.]

Maki, Dennis R. A Note on Money Wages, Prices, Controls, and Trade Unions in Canada. *Appl. Econ.*, February 1985, 17(1), pp. 165–72. [G: Canada]

Maranto, Cheryl L. Union Effects on Human Capital Investments and Returns. *J. Human Res.*, Summer 1985, 20(3), pp. 453–62. [G: U.S.]

Marginson, Paul. The Multidivisional Firm and Control over the Work Process. *Int. J. Ind. Organ.*, March 1985, 3(1), pp. 37–56. [G: U.K.]

Marin, Bernd. Austria—The Paradigm Case of Liberal Corporatism? In *Grant, W., ed.*, 1985, pp. 89–125. [G: Austria]

Marsden, David. Chronicle: Industrial Relations in the United Kingdom, April–July 1985. *Brit. J. Ind. Relat.*, November 1985, 23(3), pp. 449–58. [G: U.K.]

Martin, Charles H. The International Labor Defense and Black America. *Labor Hist.*, Spring 1985, 26(2), pp. 165–94. [G: U.S.]

Martin, James E. Employee Characteristics and Representation Election Outcomes. *Ind. Lab. Relat. Rev.*, April 1985, 38(3), pp. 365–76. [G: U.S.]

Martin, James E. and Magenau, John M. An Analysis of Factors Related to the Accuracy of Steward Predictions of Membership Views. In *Dennis, B. D., ed.*, 1985, pp. 490–96. [G: U.S.]

Marx, Karl. La lutte pour le bill de dix heures. (Struggle over the Ten Hours' Bill. Strikes [1853]. With English summary.) *Écon. Soc.*, November 1985, 19(11), pp. 113–24.

Masters, Marick F. Federal-Employee Unions and Political Action. *Ind. Lab. Relat. Rev.*, July 1985, 38(4), pp. 612–28. [G: U.S.]

Masters, Marick F. and Delaney, John Thomas. The Causes of Union Political Involvement: A Longitudinal Analysis. *J. Lab. Res.*, Fall 1985, 6(4), pp. 341–62. [G: U.S.]

Mayer, Jean. The Concept of the Right to Work in International Standards and the Legislation of ILO Member States. *Int. Lab. Rev.*, March-April 1985, 124(2), pp. 225–42.

Mayhew, Ken. Reforming the Labour Market. *Oxford Rev. Econ. Policy*, Summer 1985, 1(2), pp. 60–79. [G: U.K.]

Mills, D. Quinn and Lovell, Malcolm R., Jr. Enhancing Competitiveness: The Contribution of Employee Relations. In *Scott, B. R. and Lodge, G. C., eds.*, 1985, pp. 455–78. [G: U.S.]

Minford, Patrick. Unemployment and Real Wages: The Role of Unemployment, Social Security Benefits and Unionisation [Labour Market Equilibrium in an Open Economy]: Reply. *Oxford Econ. Pap.*, June 1985, 37(2), pp. 339–43. [G: U.K.]

Mishel, Lawrence. Unions, Monopolies, and the Marshallian Rules: An Institutionalist Appraisal. In *Lipsky, D. B., ed.*, 1985, pp. 69–109. [G: U.S.]

Mitchell, Daniel J. B. Concession Bargaining and Wage Determination. *Bus. Econ.*, July 1985, 20(3), pp. 45–50. [G: U.S.]

Montgomery, David. Workers' Control of Machine Production in the Nineteenth Century. In *Leab, D. J., ed.*, 1985, pp. 107–31. [G: U.S.]

Montgomery, Edward and Shaw, Kathryn. Long-term Contracts, Expectations and Wage Inertia. *J. Monet. Econ.*, September 1985, 16(2), pp. 209–26.

Moore, William J. and Newman, Robert J. The Effects of Right-to-Work Laws: A Review of the Literature. *Ind. Lab. Relat. Rev.*, July 1985, 38(4), pp. 571–85. [G: U.S.]

Moore, William J.; Newman, Robert J. and Cunningham, James. The Effect of the Extent of Unionism on Union and Nonunion Wages. *J. Lab. Res.*, Winter 1985, 6(1), pp. 21–44. [G: U.S.]

Morgenstern, Felice. The Importance, in Practice, of Conflicts of Labour Law. *Int. Lab. Rev.*, March-April 1985, 124(2), pp. 119–31.

Murphy, Cait. Labor Pains. *Policy Rev.*, Fall 1985, (34), pp. 76–80. [G: U.S.]

Nelson, Daniel. Origins of the Sit-Down Era: Worker Militancy and Innovation in the Rubber Industry, 1934–1938. In *Leab, D. J., ed.*, 1985, pp. 333–60. [G: U.S.]

Newman, Harold R. The Changing Law of Fair Representation: The State of the Law: The Duty in the Public Sector. In *McKelvey, J. T., ed.*, 1985, pp. 85–92. [G: U.S.]

Nugent, Angela. Organizing Trade Unions to Combat Disease: The Workers' Health Bureau, 1921–1928. *Labor Hist.*, Summer 1985, 26(3), pp. 423–46. [G: U.S.]

O'Connor, Robert. Workers Co-operatives—Their Employment Potential. *Ann. Pub. Co-op. Econ.*, Oct.-Dec. 1985, 56(4), pp. 539–51. [G: Europe]

Offe, Claus and Hinrichs, Karl. The Political Economy of the Labour Market. In *Offe, C.*, 1985, pp. 10–51.

Offe, Claus and Wiesenthal, Helmut. Two Logics of Collective Action. In *Offe, C.*, 1985, pp. 170–220.

Offe, Claus, et al. Interest Diversity and Trade Union Unity. In *Offe, C.*, 1985, pp. 151–69. [G: W. Germany]

Oswald, Andrew J. The Economic Theory of Trade Unions: An Introductory Survey. *Scand. J. Econ.*, 1985, 87(2), pp. 160–93. [G: U.S.; U.K.]

Oswald, Andrew J. Wages and Employment under Trade Unionism: Microeconomic Models and Macroeconomic Applications: Comment.

Scand. J. Econ., 1985, 87(2), pp. 226–27.
[G: Sweden]
Oswald, Andrew J. and Turnbull, Peter J. Pay and Employment Determination in Britain: What Are Labour 'Contracts' Really Like? *Oxford Rev. Econ. Policy*, Summer 1985, *1*(2), pp. 80–97.
[G: U.K.]
Oswald, Rudy. Statement on U.S. Aims at the World Trade Ministers' Meeting: A Labor View. In *Adams, J., ed.*, 1985, pp. 78–84.
[G: U.S.]
Pankert, Alfred. Recent Developments in Labour Relations in the Industrialised Market Economy Countries: Some Bench-Marks. *Int. Lab. Rev.*, Sept.-Oct. 1985, *124*(5), pp. 531–44.
[G: OECD]
Pascoe, Thomas J. and Collins, Richard J. UAW–Ford Employee Development and Training Program: Overview of Operations and Structure. In *Dennis, B. D., ed.*, 1985, pp. 519–26.
[G: U.S.]
Patterson, Henry. An Economic History of Ulster 1820–1939: Industrial Labour and the Labour Movement, 1820–1914. In *Kennedy, L. and Ollerenshaw, P., eds.*, 1985, pp. 158–83.
[G: U.K.]
Pencavel, John. Wages and Employment under Trade Unionism: Microeconomic Models and Macroeconomic Applications. *Scand. J. Econ.*, 1985, 87(2), pp. 197–225. [G: Sweden]
Perry, Charles R. Paradise Not Found: The Case of Insurance Workers. *J. Lab. Res.*, Winter 1985, *6*(1), pp. 45–61. [G: U.S.]
Phelps, Edmund S. Dynamics of Unemployment, Vacancies and Real Wages with Trade Unions: Comment. *Scand. J. Econ.*, 1985, 87(2), pp. 408–10.
Phelps, Edmund S. Union Militancy, External Shocks and the Accommodation Dilemma: Comment. *Scand. J. Econ.*, 1985, 87(2), pp. 355–56.
Pihkala, Erkki. USA:n henkilöstö rahastot. (Employee Ownership Plans in the United States. With English summary.) *Liiketaloudellinen Aikak.*, 1985, *34*(4), pp. 439–50. [G: U.S.]
Pinelli, Cesare. Il ruolo dei sindacati nell'amministrazione centrale dello stato. (The Role of Unions in the Public Administration in Italy: Some Notes. With English summary.) *Econ. Lavoro*, July-Sept. 1985, *19*(3), pp. 111–20.
[G: Italy]
Pissarides, Christopher A. Dynamics of Unemployment, Vacancies and Real Wages with Trade Unions. *Scand. J. Econ.*, 1985, 87(2), pp. 386–403.
Pohjola, Matti. Macroeconomic Stabilization Policy and Trade Union Behaviour as a Repeated Game: Comment. *Scand. J. Econ.*, 1985, 87(2), pp. 332–34.
Popay, Jennie. Responding to Unemployment at a Local Level. In *Westcott, G.; Svensson, P.-G. and Zollner, H. F. K., eds.*, 1985, pp. 383–99. [G: U.K.]
Rabin, Robert J. The Changing Law of Fair Representation: The Duty in Other Forums: Fair Representation in Arbitration. In *McKelvey,*

J. T., ed., 1985, pp. 173–207. [G: U.S.]
Ramstad, Yngve. Industrial Policy and Trade Unions: Comments. *J. Econ. Issues*, June 1985, *19*(2), pp. 507–11. [G: U.S.]
Rau, Nicholas. The Microeconomic Theory of the Trade Union: A Comment. *Econ. J.*, June 1985, *95*(378), pp. 480–82.
Rees, Albert. Unions, Pensions, and Union Pension Funds: Comment. In *Wise, D. A., ed.*, 1985, pp. 118–21. [G: U.S.]
Reynolds, Peter J. Measuring the Influence of Trade Unions. *Brit. Rev. Econ. Issues*, Autumn 1985, *7*(17), pp. 39–49. [G: U.K.]
Rose, Joseph B. and Chaison, Gary N. The State of the Unions: United States and Canada. *J. Lab. Res.*, Winter 1985, *6*(1), pp. 97–111.
[G: U.S.; Canada]
Saltzman, Gregory M. Bargaining Laws as a Cause and Consequence of the Growth of Teacher Unionism. *Ind. Lab. Relat. Rev.*, April 1985, *38*(3), pp. 335–51. [G: U.S.]
Savoie, Ernest J. Current Developments and Future Agenda in Union–Management Cooperation in Training and Retraining of Workers. In *Dennis, B. D., ed.*, 1985, pp. 535–48.
[G: U.S.]
Scherer, Peter. Continuity and Change in Australian Wages Policy. *Australian Econ. Rev.*, 3rd Quarter, Spring 1985, (71), pp. 53–67.
[G: Australia]
Schneider, Dorothee. The New York Cigarmakers Strike of 1877. *Labor Hist.*, Summer 1985, *26*(3), pp. 325–52. [G: U.S.]
Schuster, Michael. Models of Cooperation and Change in Union Settings. *Ind. Relat.*, Fall 1985, *24*(3), pp. 382–94. [G: U.S.]
Seal, W. B. On the Nature of the Firm and Trades Unions: A Critique of the Property Rights Literature. *Brit. Rev. Econ. Issues*, Spring 1985, *7*(16), pp. 47–61.
Sellier, Francois. Economic Change and Industrial Relations in France. In *Juris, H.; Thompson, M. and Daniels, W., eds.*, 1985, pp. 177–209. [G: France]
Shah, Anup R. A Macro Model with Trade Unions. *J. Macroecon.*, Spring 1985, *7*(2), pp. 175–94.
Shah, Anup R. Are Wage Incentives and Unionism Importance Determinants of Job Tenure? *Oxford Econ. Pap.*, December 1985, *37*(4), pp. 643–58. [G: U.K.]
Shah, Anup R. Wage/Job Security Contracts and Unionism. *Southern Econ. J.*, January 1985, *51*(3), pp. 849–59. [G: U.K.]
Siebert, W. Stanley; Bertrand, Philip V. and Addison, John T. The Political Model of Strikes: A New Twist. *Southern Econ. J.*, July 1985, *52*(1), pp. 23–33. [G: U.S.]
Simpson, Wayne. The Impact of Unions on the Structure of Canadian Wages: An Empirical Analysis with Microdata. *Can. J. Econ.*, February 1985, *18*(1), pp. 164–81. [G: Canada]
Snower, Dennis J. Insiders and Outsiders in Wage Determination: Comment. *Scand. J. Econ.*, 1985, 87(2), pp. 432–35.
Sockell, Donna. Attitudes, Behavior, and Em-

ployee Ownership: Some Preliminary Data. *Ind. Relat.*, Winter 1985, *24*(1), pp. 130–38. [G: U.S.]

Söderström, Hans Tson. Union Militancy, External Shocks and the Accommodation Dilemma. *Scand. J. Econ.*, 1985, *87*(2), pp. 335–51.

Solnick, Loren M. The Effect of Blue-Collar Unions on White-Collar Wages and Fringe Benefits. *Ind. Lab. Relat. Rev.*, January 1985, *38*(2), pp. 236–43. [G: U.S.]

Solow, Robert M. Insiders and Outsiders in Wage Determination. *Scand. J. Econ.*, 1985, *87*(2), pp. 411–28.

Solow, Robert M. Manufacturing Wage Dispersion: An End Game Interpretation: Comment. *Brookings Pap. Econ. Act.*, 1985, (1), pp. 107–10. [G: U.S.]

Story, Christopher. The Labour Cartels: Has Anything Really Changed? *Nat. Westminster Bank Quart. Rev.*, May 1985, pp. 63–73. [G: U.K.]

Stratton, Richard W. Monopoly, Monopsony, and Union Strength and Local Market Wage Differentials: Some Empirical Evidence on Their Impacts. *Amer. J. Econ. Soc.*, July 1985, *44*(3), pp. 305–18. [G: U.S.]

Summers, Clyde W. Measuring the Union's Duty to the Individual: An Analytic Framework. In *McKelvey, J. T., ed.*, 1985, pp. 145–69. [G: U.S.]

Swanson, Dorothy. Annual Bibliography on American Labor History, 1984: Periodicals, Dissertations, and Research in Progress. *Labor Hist.*, Fall 1985, *26*(4), pp. 546–68. [G: U.S.]

Tabellini, Guido. Accomodative Monetary Policy and Central Bank Reputation. *Giorn. Econ.*, July-Aug. 1985, *44*(7–8), pp. 389–425.

Taira, Koji and Levine, Solomon B. Japan's Industrial Relations: A Social Compact Emerges. In *Juris, H.; Thompson, M. and Daniels, W., eds.*, 1985, pp. 247–300. [G: Japan]

Terry, Michael. Combine Committees: Developments of the 1970s. *Brit. J. Ind. Relat.*, November 1985, *23*(3), pp. 359–78. [G: U.K.]

Thakur, C. P. Labour and Industrial Relations. In *Mongia, J. N., ed.*, 1985, pp. 315–48. [G: India]

Thompson, Mark. Restraint and Labour Relations: The Case of British Columbia. *Can. Public Policy*, June 1985, *11*(2), pp. 171–79. [G: Canada]

Tobias, Paul H. The Changing Law of Fair Representation: The Parties: The Plaintiff's Perception of Litigation. In *McKelvey, J. T., ed.*, 1985, pp. 128–44. [G: U.S.]

Tolliday, Steven. Government, Employers and Shop Floor Organisation in the British Motor Industry, 1939–69. In *Tolliday, S. and Zeitlin, J., eds.*, 1985, pp. 108–47. [G: U.K.]

Toner, Bill. The Unionisation and Productivity Debate: An Employee Opinion Survey in Ireland. *Brit. J. Ind. Relat.*, July 1985, *23*(2), pp. 179–202. [G: Ireland]

Truesdale, John C. The NLRB and the Duty. In *McKelvey, J. T., ed.*, 1985, pp. 208–22. [G: U.S.]

Venturini, Patrick. Workers' and Employers' Roles in a New Corporate Culture. In *Zukin, S., ed.*, 1985, pp. 246–52. [G: France]

Verma, Anil. Relative Flow of Capital to Union and Nonunion Plants within a Firm. *Ind. Relat.*, Fall 1985, *24*(3), pp. 395–405. [G: U.S.]

Waldman, Seymour M. The Changing Law of Fair Representation: The Parties: A Union Advocate's View. In *McKelvey, J. T., ed.*, 1985, pp. 109–16. [G: U.S.]

Warren, Ronald S., Jr. The Effect of Unionization on Labor Productivity: Some Time-Series Evidence. *J. Lab. Res.*, Spring 1985, *6*(2), pp. 199–207. [G: U.S.]

Weeks, James L. The Effect of Unionization on Safety in Bituminous Deep Mines: Comment. *J. Lab. Res.*, Spring 1985, *6*(2), pp. 209–10. [G: U.S.]

Weiss, Yoram. The Effect of Labor Unions on Investment in Training: A Dynamic Model. *J. Polit. Econ.*, October 1985, *93*(5), pp. 994–1007.

Wessels, Walter J. The Effects of Unions on Employment and Productivity: An Unresolved Contradiction. *J. Lab. Econ.*, Part 1 January 1985, *3*(1), pp. 101–08.

Whiteside, Noel. Public Policy and Port Labour Reform: The Dock Decasualisation Issue, 1910–50. In *Tolliday, S. and Zeitlin, J., eds.*, 1985, pp. 75–107. [G: U.K.]

Wilson, Frank L. Trade Unions and Economic Policy. In *Machin, H. and Wright, V., eds.*, 1985, pp. 255–78. [G: France]

Worthman, Paul B. Black Workers and Labor Unions in Birmingham, Alabama, 1897–1904. In *Leab, D. J., ed.*, 1985, pp. 197–229. [G: U.S.]

Yandle, Bruce. Unions and Environmental Regulation. *J. Lab. Res.*, Fall 1985, *6*(4), pp. 429–36. [G: U.S.]

Zeitlin, Jonathan. Shop Floor Bargaining and the State: A Contradictory Relationship. In *Tolliday, S. and Zeitlin, J., eds.*, 1985, pp. 1–45.

Zieger, Robert H. Toward the History of the CIO: A Bibliographical Report. *Labor Hist.*, Fall 1985, *26*(4), pp. 485–516. [G: U.S.]

832 Collective Bargaining

8320 General

Aaron, Benjamin. The Changing Law of Fair Representation: The State of the Law: An Overview. In *McKelvey, J. T., ed.*, 1985, pp. 15–46. [G: U.S.]

Aaron, Benjamin. The NLRB, Labor Courts, and Industrial Tribunals: A Selective Comparison. *Ind. Lab. Relat. Rev.*, October 1985, *39*(1), pp. 35–45.

Adams, Roy J. Industrial Relations and the Economic Crisis: Canada Moves Toward Europe. In *Juris, H.; Thompson, M. and Daniels, W., eds.*, 1985, pp. 115–49. [G: OECD]

Bazerman, Max H. Norms of Distributive Justice in Interest Arbitration. *Ind. Lab. Relat. Rev.*,

July 1985, *38*(4), pp. 558–70.

Bazerman, Max H. and Farber, Henry S. Arbitrator Decision Making: When Are Final Offers Important? *Ind. Lab. Relat. Rev.*, October 1985, *39*(1), pp. 76–89. [G: U.S.]

Beare, John B. Uncertainty and Front-End Loading of Labor Agreements. *J. Lab. Res.*, Winter 1985, *6*(1), pp. 113–17. [G: U.S.]

Becker, William E. Maintaining Faculty Vitality through Collective Bargaining. In *Clark, S. M. and Lewis, D. R.*, eds., 1985, pp. 198–223. [G: U.S.]

Block, Richard N. Discussion: The NLRA at Age Fifty. In *Dennis, B. D.*, ed., 1985, pp. 615–17. [G: U.S.]

Borum, Joan D. and Schlein, David. Bargaining Activity Light in Private Industry in 1985. *Mon. Lab. Rev.*, January 1985, *108*(1), pp. 13–26. [G: U.S.]

Brown, William. The Effect of Recent Changes in the World Economy on British Industrial Relations. In *Juris, H.; Thompson, M. and Daniels, W.*, eds., 1985, pp. 151–75. [G: U.K.]

Calmfors, Lars. The Roles of Stabilization Policy and Wage Setting for Macroeconomic Stability—The Experiences of Economies with Centralized Bargaining. *Kyklos*, 1985, *38*(3), pp. 329–47. [G: W. Europe]

Christensen, Andrea S. What Employers Can Do about DFR Suits. In *McKelvey, J. T.*, ed., 1985, pp. 117–27. [G: U.S.]

Contini, Giovanni. Politics, Law and Shop Floor Bargaining in Postwar Italy. In *Tolliday, S. and Zeitlin, J.*, eds., 1985, pp. 192–218. [G: Italy]

Cornfield, Daniel B. Economic Segmentation and Expression of Labor Unrest: Striking versus Quitting in the Manufacturing Sector. *Soc. Sci. Quart.*, June 1985, *66*(2), pp. 247–65. [G: U.S.]

Craver, Charles B. The NLRA at Fifty: From Youthful Exuberance to Middle-Aged Complacency. In *Dennis, B. D.*, ed., 1985, pp. 604–15. [G: U.S.]

Crouch, Colin. Conditions for Trade Union Wage Restraint. In *Lindberg, L. N. and Maier, C. S.*, eds., 1985, pp. 105–39. [G: OECD]

Crouch, Colin. Corporatism in Industrial Relations: A Formal Model. In *Grant, W.*, ed., 1985, pp. 63–88.

Cutcher-Gershenfeld, Joel. Reconceiving the Web of Labor–Management Relations. In *Dennis, B. D.*, ed., 1985, pp. 637–45. [G: U.S.]

Delamotte, Yves. Managerial and Supervisory Staff in a Changing World. *Int. Lab. Rev.*, January–February 1985, *124*(1), pp. 1–16. [G: W. Germany; Italy; France; U.K.; Sweden]

Delaney, John Thomas; Lewin, David and Sockell, Donna. The NLRA at Fifty: A Research Appraisal and Agenda. *Ind. Lab. Relat. Rev.*, October 1985, *39*(1), pp. 46–75. [G: U.S.]

Dolton, Peter J. and Treble, John C. On "Final Offer" and "Not Quite Compulsory" Arbitration. *Scot. J. Polit. Econ.*, June 1985, *32*(2),

pp. 181–90. [G: U.S.; U.K.]

Edwards, Harry T. The Duty of Fair Representation: A View from the Bench. In *McKelvey, J. T.*, ed., 1985, pp. 93–105. [G: U.S.]

Epstein, Richard A. Agency Costs, Employment Contracts, and Labor Unions. In *Pratt, J. W. and Zeckhauser, R. J.*, eds., 1985, pp. 127–48.

FitzRoy, Felix R. and Kraft, Kornelius. Unionization, Wages and Efficiency: Theories and Evidence from the U.S. and West Germany. *Kyklos*, 1985, *38*(4), pp. 537–54. [G: U.S.; W. Germany]

Gallie, Duncan. *Les lois Auroux:* The Reform of French Industrial Relations? In *Machin, H. and Wright, V.*, eds., 1985, pp. 205–21. [G: France]

George, B. Glenn. Collective Bargaining in Chapter 11 and Beyond. *Yale Law J.*, December 1985, *95*(2), pp. 300–346. [G: U.S.]

Gross, James A. Conflicting Statutory Purposes: Another Look at Fifty Years of NLRB Law Making. *Ind. Lab. Relat. Rev.*, October 1985, *39*(1), pp. 7–18. [G: U.S.]

Harris, Howell. The Snares of Liberalism? Politicians, Bureaucrats, and the Shaping of Federal Labour Relations Policy in the United States, ca. 1915–47. In *Tolliday, S. and Zeitlin, J.*, eds., 1985, pp. 148–91. [G: U.S.]

Hart, Robert A. Wage Supplements through Collective Agreement or Statutory Requirement? *Kyklos*, 1985, *38*(1), pp. 20–42. [G: OECD]

Hiltrop, Jean M. Dispute Settlement and Mediation: Data from Britain. *Ind. Relat.*, Winter 1985, *24*(1), pp. 139–46. [G: U.K.]

Jacobi, Otto. World Economic Changes and Industrial Relations in the Federal Republic of Germany. In *Juris, H.; Thompson, M. and Daniels, W.*, eds., 1985, pp. 211–46. [G: W. Germany]

Jones, James E., Jr. The Changing Law of Fair Representation: The Duty in Other Forums: Time for a Midcourse Correction? In *McKelvey, J. T.*, ed., 1985, pp. 223–72. [G: U.S.]

Jones, Robert A. The Emergence of Shop-Floor Trade Union Power in South Africa. *Managerial Dec. Econ.*, September 1985, *6*(3), pp. 160–66. [G: S. Africa]

Klein, David Y. Exhaustion of Internal Union Remedies after *Clayton* and *Bowen*. In *McKelvey, J. T.*, ed., 1985, pp. 70–84. [G: U.S.]

Knight, Thomas R. Toward a Contingency Theory of the Grievance-Arbitration System. In *Lipsky, D. B.*, ed., 1985, pp. 269–318. [G: U.S.]

Lipsitz, Richard. The Changing Law of Fair Representation: The State of the Law: New Substantive and Procedural Areas. In *McKelvey, J. T.*, ed., 1985, pp. 47–69. [G: U.S.]

Marsden, David. *Les lois Auroux:* The Reform of French Industrial Relations?: Comment. In *Machin, H. and Wright, V.*, eds., 1985, pp. 221–24. [G: France]

Marsden, David. Chronicle: Industrial Relations in the United Kingdom, April–July 1985. *Brit.*

J. Ind. Relat., November 1985, *23*(3), pp. 449–58. [G: U.K.]

Mayer, Jean. The Concept of the Right to Work in International Standards and the Legislation of ILO Member States. *Int. Lab. Rev.*, March-April 1985, *124*(2), pp. 225–42.

Mills, D. Quinn and Lovell, Malcolm R., Jr. Enhancing Competitiveness: The Contribution of Employee Relations. In *Scott, B. R. and Lodge, G. C., eds.,* 1985, pp. 455–78. [G: U.S.]

Mitchell, Daniel J. B. Wage Flexibility: Then and Now. *Ind. Relat.*, Spring 1985, *24*(2), pp. 266–79. [G: U.S.]

Morgenstern, Felice. The Importance, in Practice, of Conflicts of Labour Law. *Int. Lab. Rev.*, March-April 1985, *124*(2), pp. 119–31.

Nash, Peter G. The NLRA at Age Fifty. In *Dennis, B. D., ed.,* 1985, pp. 600–603. [G: U.S.]

Newby, Martin. A Further Note on the Distribution of Strike Duration. *J. Roy. Statist. Soc.*, 1985, *148*(4), pp. 350–56.

Offe, Claus and Wiesenthal, Helmut. Two Logics of Collective Action. In *Offe, C.,* 1985, pp. 170–220.

Oswald, Andrew J. and Turnbull, Peter J. Pay and Employment Determination in Britain: What Are Labour 'Contracts' Really Like? *Oxford Rev. Econ. Policy*, Summer 1985, *1*(2), pp. 80–97. [G: U.K.]

Page, Leonard R. The Rise, Decline, and Resurrection of American Labor Law: A Critical Assessment of the NLRA at Age Fifty. In *Dennis, B. D., ed.,* 1985, pp. 594–600. [G: U.S.]

Pankert, Alfred. Recent Developments in Labour Relations in the Industrialised Market Economy Countries: Some Bench-Marks. *Int. Lab. Rev.*, Sept.-Oct. 1985, *124*(5), pp. 531–44. [G: OECD]

Pastore, José and Skidmore, Thomas E. Brazilian Labor Relations: A New Era? In *Juris, H.; Thompson, M. and Daniels, W., eds.,* 1985, pp. 73–113. [G: Brazil]

Peterson, Richard B. Economic and Political Impacts on the Swedish Model of Industrial Relations. In *Juris, H.; Thompson, M. and Daniels, W., eds.,* 1985, pp. 301–36. [G: Sweden]

Plowman, David H. National Tripartism: The Case of the Ministry of Labour Advisory Council 1953–1960. *Australian Bull. Lab.*, September 1985, *11*(4), pp. 246–56. [G: Australia]

Rabin, Robert J. The Changing Law of Fair Representation: The Duty in Other Forums: Fair Representation in Arbitration. In *McKelvey, J. T., ed.,* 1985, pp. 173–207. [G: U.S.]

Reid, Alastair. Dilution, Trade Unionism and the State in Britain during the First World War. In *Tolliday, S. and Zeitlin, J., eds.,* 1985, pp. 46–74. [G: U.K.]

Rizzi, Dino. A Tax-based Incomes Policy Involving Payroll Taxation: Theoretical and Empirical Analyses. *Rivista Int. Sci. Econ. Com.*, July-Aug. 1985, *32*(7–8), pp. 679–700. [G: Italy]

Ruben, George. Modest Labor–Management Bargains Continue in 1984 Despite the Recovery.

Mon. Lab. Rev., January 1985, *108*(1), pp. 3–12. [G: U.S.]

Sellier, Francois. Economic Change and Industrial Relations in France. In *Juris, H.; Thompson, M. and Daniels, W., eds.,* 1985, pp. 177–209. [G: France]

Shalev, Michael. Labor Relations and Class Conflict: A Critical Survey of the Contributions of John R. Commons. In *Lipsky, D. B., ed.,* 1985, pp. 319–63. [G: U.S.]

Shirom, Arie. Tactical Planning of Collective Bargaining: A Facet-Theoretic Approach. In *Lipsky, D. B., ed.,* 1985, pp. 253–67.

Smith, Graham F. The High Court and Industrial Relations in the 1980s. *Australian Bull. Lab.*, March 1985, *11*(2), pp. 82–101. [G: Australia]

Summers, Clyde W. Measuring the Union's Duty to the Individual: An Analytic Framework. In *McKelvey, J. T., ed.,* 1985, pp. 145–69. [G: U.S.]

Taira, Koji and Levine, Solomon B. Japan's Industrial Relations: A Social Compact Emerges. In *Juris, H.; Thompson, M. and Daniels, W., eds.,* 1985, pp. 247–300. [G: Japan]

Terry, Michael. Combine Committees: Developments of the 1970s. *Brit. J. Ind. Relat.*, November 1985, *23*(3), pp. 359–78. [G: U.K.]

Thakur, C. P. Labour and Industrial Relations. In *Mongia, J. N., ed.,* 1985, pp. 315–48. [G: India]

Thompson, Mark and Juris, Hervey A. The Response of Industrial Relations to Economic Change. In *Juris, H.; Thompson, M. and Daniels, W., eds.,* 1985, pp. 383–407. [G: OECD]

Tobias, Paul H. The Changing Law of Fair Representation: The Parties: The Plaintiff's Perception of Litigation. In *McKelvey, J. T., ed.,* 1985, pp. 128–44. [G: U.S.]

Tomlins, Christopher L. The New Deal, Collective Bargaining, and the Triumph of Industrial Pluralism. *Ind. Lab. Relat. Rev.*, October 1985, *39*(1), pp. 19–34. [G: U.S.]

Truesdale, John C. The NLRB and the Duty. In *McKelvey, J. T., ed.,* 1985, pp. 208–22. [G: U.S.]

Vroman, Wayne. Cost-of-Living Escalators and Price–Wage Linkages in the U.S. Economy, 1968–1980. *Ind. Lab. Relat. Rev.*, January 1985, *38*(2), pp. 225–35. [G: U.S.]

Waldman, Seymour M. The Changing Law of Fair Representation: The Parties: A Union Advocate's View. In *McKelvey, J. T., ed.,* 1985, pp. 109–16. [G: U.S.]

Wheeler, Hoyt N. Toward an Integrative Theory of Industrial Conflict. In *Rowland, K. M. and Ferris, G. R., eds.,* 1985, pp. 231–70.

Youngblood, Stuart A. and Bierman, Leonard. Due Process and Employment-At-Will: A Legal and Behavioral Analysis. In *Rowland, K. M. and Ferris, G. R., eds.,* 1985, pp. 185–230. [G: U.S.]

Zeitlin, Jonathan. Shop Floor Bargaining and the State: A Contradictory Relationship. In *Tolliday, S. and Zeitlin, J., eds.,* 1985, pp. 1–45.

8321 Collective Bargaining in the Private Sector

Abraham, Katharine G. Shifting Norms in Wage Determination: Comment. *Brookings Pap. Econ. Act.*, 1985, (2), pp. 600–605. [G: U.S.]

Albeda, W. Recent Trends in Collective Bargaining in the Netherlands. *Int. Lab. Rev.*, January–February 1985, *124*(1), pp. 49–60.
[G: Netherlands]

Aronson, Robert L. Unionism among Professional Employees in the Private Sector. *Ind. Lab. Relat. Rev.*, April 1985, *38*(3), pp. 352–64.
[G: U.S.]

Block, Richard N. and McLennan, Kenneth. Structural Economic Change and Industrial Relations in the United States' Manufacturing Sectors and Transportation since 1973. In *Juris, H.; Thompson, M. and Daniels, W., eds.*, 1985, pp. 337–82. [G: U.S.]

Brinner, Roger E. and Kline, Kenneth J. A New Market Realism: Wage Moderation. *Challenge*, Sept./Oct. 1985, *28*(4), pp. 27–29. [G: U.S.]

Cappelli, Peter. Competitive Pressures and Labor Relations in the Airline Industry. *Ind. Relat.*, Fall 1985, *24*(3), pp. 316–38. [G: U.S.]

Cappelli, Peter. Plant-Level Concession Bargaining. *Ind. Lab. Relat. Rev.*, October 1985, *39*(1), pp. 90–104. [G: U.S.]

Cooke, William N. The Failure to Negotiate First Contracts: Determinants and Policy Implications. *Ind. Lab. Relat. Rev.*, January 1985, *38*(2), pp. 163–78. [G: U.S.]

Cooke, William N. The Rising Toll of Discrimination against Union Activists. *Ind. Relat.*, Fall 1985, *24*(3), pp. 421–42. [G: U.S.]

Craft, James A.; Abboushi, Suhail and Labovitz, Trudy. Concession Bargaining and Unions: Impacts and Implications. *J. Lab. Res.*, Spring 1985, *6*(2), pp. 167–80. [G: U.S.]

Cullen, Donald E. Recent Trends in Collective Bargaining in the United States. *Int. Lab. Rev.*, May-June 1985, *124*(3), pp. 299–322.
[G: U.S.]

Dabscheck, Braham and Niland, John. Australian Industrial Relations and the Shift to Centralism. In *Juris, H.; Thompson, M. and Daniels, W., eds.*, 1985, pp. 41–72. [G: Australia]

Doyle, Philip M. Area Wage Surveys Shed Light on Declines in Unionization. *Mon. Lab. Rev.*, September 1985, *108*(9), pp. 13–20.
[G: U.S.]

Ebner, Michael H. The Passaic Strike of 1912 and the Two I.W.W.s. In *Leab, D. J., ed.*, 1985, pp. 254–68. [G: U.S.]

Evans, Stephen. The Use of Injunctions in Industrial Disputes. *Brit. J. Ind. Relat.*, March 1985, *23*(1), pp. 133–37. [G: U.K.]

Eyraud, François and Tchobanian, Robert. The Auroux Reforms and Company Level Industrial Relations in France. *Brit. J. Ind. Relat.*, July 1985, *23*(2), pp. 241–59. [G: France]

Fandel, Günter. On the Applicability of Group Decision Making Concepts to Wage Bargaining. In *Haimes, Y. Y. and Chankong, V., eds.*, 1985, pp. 532–48. [G: W. Germany]

Fandel, Günter. On the Applicability of Game-Theoretic Bargaining Methods to a Wage Bargaining Problem. In *Fandel, G. and Spronk, J., eds.*, 1985, pp. 317–36.
[G: W. Germany]

Fine, Sidney. Frank Murphy, the Thornhill Decision, and Picketing as Free Speech. In *Leab, D. J., ed.*, 1985, pp. 361–82. [G: U.S.]

Fischer, Ben. Collective Bargaining and Fifty Years of the CIO. In *Dennis, B. D., ed.*, 1985, pp. 659–64.

Friedman, Sheldon. Negotiated Approaches to Job Security. In *Dennis, B. D., ed.*, 1985, pp. 553–57. [G: U.S.]

Gärtner, Manfred. Strikes and the Real Wage–Employment Nexus: A Hicksian Analysis of Industrial Disputes and Pay. *J. Lab. Res.*, Summer 1985, *6*(3), pp. 323–36.
[G: W. Germany]

Gregory, Mary; Lobban, Peter and Thomson, Andrew. Wage Settlements in Manufacturing, 1979–84: Evidence from the CBI Pay Databank. *Brit. J. Ind. Relat.*, November 1985, *23*(3), pp. 339–57. [G: U.K.]

Gutman, Herbert G. Trouble on the Railroads in 1873–1874: Prelude to the 1877 Crisis? In *Leab, D. J., ed.*, 1985, pp. 132–52. [G: U.S.]

Hansen, Gary B. Industrial Relations Research Association: Proceedings of the 1985 Spring Meeting: Discussion: EDTP. In *Dennis, B. D., ed.*, 1985, pp. 548–53. [G: U.S.]

Hernández Álvarez, Oscar and Lucena, Héctor. Political and Economic Determinants of Collective Bargaining in Venezuela. *Int. Lab. Rev.*, May-June 1985, *124*(3), pp. 363–76.
[G: Venezuela]

Jones, Bryn. Controlling Production on the Shop Floor: The Role of State Administration and Regulation in the British and American Aerospace Industries. In *Tolliday, S. and Zeitlin, J., eds.*, 1985, pp. 219–55. [G: U.S.; U.K.]

Jones, Robert A. The Changing Structure of Industrial Relations in South Africa. *Managerial Dec. Econ.*, December 1985, *6*(4), pp. 217–25. [G: S. Africa]

Kahn, Mark L. Discussion: The 1984 Auto Negotiations. In *Dennis, B. D., ed.*, 1985, pp. 464–66. [G: U.S.]

Katz, Harry C. and Sabel, Charles F. Industrial Relations & Industrial Adjustment in the Car Industry. *Ind. Relat.*, Fall 1985, *24*(3), pp. 295–315. [G: Italy; U.K.; U.S.; W. Germany]

Kennan, John. The Duration of Contract Strikes in U.S. Manufacturing. *J. Econometrics*, April 1985, *28*(1), pp. 5–28. [G: U.S.]

Lacombe, John J., II and Conley, James R. Major Agreements in 1984 Provide Record Low Wage Increases. *Mon. Lab. Rev.*, April 1985, *108*(4), pp. 39–45. [G: U.S.]

Lang, Graeme. Regional Variations in Worksharing: The Case of Newfoundland. *Can. Public Policy*, March 1985, *11*(1), pp. 54–63.
[G: Canada]

Lash, Scott. The End of Neo-corporatism? The Breakdown of Centralised Bargaining in Sweden. *Brit. J. Ind. Relat.*, July 1985, *23*(2), pp. 215–39. [G: Sweden]

Lawler, John J. and West, Robin. Impact of Union-Avoidance Strategy in Representation Elections. *Ind. Relat.*, Fall 1985, *24*(3), pp. 406–20. [G: U.S.]

Lawrence, Colin and Lawrence, Robert Z. Manufacturing Wage Dispersion: An End Game Interpretation. *Brookings Pap. Econ. Act.*, 1985, (1), pp. 47–106. [G: U.S.]

Lichtenstein, Nelson. UAW Bargaining Strategy and Shop-Floor Conflict: 1946–1970. *Ind. Relat.*, Fall 1985, *24*(3), pp. 360–81. [G: U.S.]

MacInnes, John. Conjuring up Consultation: The Role and Extent of Joint Consultation in Postwar Private Manufacturing Industry. *Brit. J. Ind. Relat.*, March 1985, *23*(1), pp. 93–113. [G: U.K.]

Maki, Dennis R. Output Losses Due to Strikes: The Case of Sawmills in British Columbia. *Empirical Econ.*, 1985, *10*(2), pp. 121–24. [G: Canada]

McKersie, Robert B. New Dimensions in Industrial Relations. In *Dennis, B. D., ed.*, 1985, pp. 645–48. [G: U.S.]

Mitchell, Daniel J. B. Concession Bargaining and Wage Determination. *Bus. Econ.*, July 1985, *20*(3), pp. 45–50. [G: U.S.]

Mitchell, Daniel J. B. Shifting Norms in Wage Determination. *Brookings Pap. Econ. Act.*, 1985, (2), pp. 575–99. [G: U.S.]

Nelson, Daniel. Origins of the Sit-Down Era: Worker Militancy and Innovation in the Rubber Industry, 1934–1938. In *Leab, D. J., ed.*, 1985, pp. 333–60. [G: U.S.]

O'Brien, Richard F. Health Care Cost Containment: An Employer's Perspective. In *Dennis, B. D., ed.*, 1985, pp. 468–73. [G: U.S.]

Pascoe, Thomas J. and Collins, Richard J. UAW–Ford Employee Development and Training Program: Overview of Operations and Structure. In *Dennis, B. D., ed.*, 1985, pp. 519–26. [G: U.S.]

Peterson, Richard B. and Tracy, Lane. Problem Solving in American Collective Bargaining: A Review and Assessment. In *Lipsky, D. B., ed.*, 1985, pp. 1–50. [G: U.S.]

Piott, Steven L. The Chicago Teamsters' Strike of 1902: A Community Confronts the Beef Trust. *Labor Hist.*, Spring 1985, *26*(2), pp. 250–67. [G: U.S.]

Rodgers, Robert C. and Stieber, Jack. Employee Discharge in the 20th Century: A Review of the Literature. *Mon. Lab. Rev.*, September 1985, *108*(9), pp. 35–41. [G: U.S.]

Saikkonen, Pentti and Taräsvirta, Timo. Modelling the Dynamic Relationship between Wages and Prices in Finland. *Scand. J. Econ.*, 1985, *87*(1), pp. 102–19. [G: Finland]

Santos, Michael W. Community and Communism: The 1928 New Bedford Textile Strike. *Labor Hist.*, Spring 1985, *26*(2), pp. 230–49. [G: U.S.]

Savoie, Ernest J. The 1984 Auto Contract: A Management Perspective. In *Dennis, B. D., ed.*, 1985, pp. 458–64. [G: U.S.]

Schneider, Dorothee. The New York Cigarmakers

Strike of 1877. *Labor Hist.*, Summer 1985, *26*(3), pp. 325–52. [G: U.S.]

Schwartz, Arthur R. Discussion: The 1984 Auto Negotiations. In *Dennis, B. D., ed.*, 1985, pp. 466–68. [G: U.S.]

Siebert, W. Stanley; Bertrand, Philip V. and Addison, John T. The Political Model of Strikes: A New Twist. *Southern Econ. J.*, July 1985, *52*(1), pp. 23–33. [G: U.S.]

Takamiya, Makoto. Conclusions and Policy Implications. In *Takamiya, S. and Thurley, K., eds.*, 1985, pp. 183–201. [G: U.K.; U.S.; Japan]

Tolliday, Steven. Government, Employers and Shop Floor Organisation in the British Motor Industry, 1939–69. In *Tolliday, S. and Zeitlin, J., eds.*, 1985, pp. 108–47. [G: U.K.]

Wachter, Michael L. Manufacturing Wage Dispersion: An End Game Interpretation: Comment. *Brookings Pap. Econ. Act.*, 1985, (1), pp. 110–15. [G: U.S.]

Wolkinson, Benjamin W. The Impact of the *Collyer* Policy of Deferral: An Empirical Study. *Ind. Lab. Relat. Rev.*, April 1985, *38*(3), pp. 377–91. [G: U.S.]

Wood, John [Sir]. Last Offer Arbitration. *Brit. J. Ind. Relat.*, November 1985, *23*(3), pp. 415–24. [G: Canada; U.S.]

Young, Howard. The 1984 Auto Negotiations: A UAW Perspective. In *Dennis, B. D., ed.*, 1985, pp. 454–57. [G: U.S.]

8322 Collective Bargaining in the Public Sector

Bacharach, Samuel B.; Mitchell, Stephen M. and Malanowski, Rose. Strategic Choice and Collective Action: Organizational Determinants of Teachers Militancy. In *Lipsky, D. B., ed.*, 1985, pp. 197–222. [G: U.S.]

Benjamin, Ernst. Collective Bargaining in Public Higher Education. In *Dennis, B. D., ed.*, 1985, pp. 514–19. [G: U.S.]

Cappelli, Peter. Fair Wages and the Industrial Civil Service. *Scot. J. Polit. Econ.*, February 1985, *32*(1), pp. 55–66. [G: U.K.]

Champlin, Frederic C. and Bognanno, Mario F. "Chilling" under Arbitration and Mixed Strike–Arbitration Regimes. *J. Lab. Res.*, Fall 1985, *6*(4), pp. 375–87. [G: U.S.]

Chelius, James R. and Extejt, Marian M. The Narcotic Effect of Impasse-Resolution Procedures. *Ind. Lab. Relat. Rev.*, July 1985, *38*(4), pp. 629–38. [G: U.S.]

Córdova, Efrén. Strikes in the Public Service: Some Determinants and Trends. *Int. Lab. Rev.*, March-April 1985, *124*(2), pp. 163–79.

Cullen, Donald E. Recent Trends in Collective Bargaining in the United States. *Int. Lab. Rev.*, May-June 1985, *124*(3), pp. 299–322. [G: U.S.]

Delaney, John Thomas. Unionism, Bargaining Spillovers, and Teacher Compensation. In *Lipsky, D. B., ed.*, 1985, pp. 111–42. [G: U.S.]

Feuille, Peter; Delaney, John Thomas and Hendricks, Wallace. Police Bargaining, Arbitration, and Fringe Benefits. *J. Lab. Res.*, Winter 1985, *6*(1), pp. 1–20. [G: U.S.]

Feuille, Peter; Delaney, John Thomas and Hendricks, Wallace. The Impact of Interest Arbitration on Police Contracts. *Ind. Relat.*, Spring 1985, *24*(2), pp. 161–81. [G: U.S.]

Gerhart, Paul F. and Drotning, John E. The Effectiveness of Public Sector Impasse Procedures: A Six State Study. In *Lipsky, D. B., ed.*, 1985, pp. 143–95. [G: U.S.]

Hunt, Janet C.; White, Rudolph A. and Moore, T. A. State Employee Bargaining Legislation. *J. Lab. Res.*, Winter 1985, *6*(1), pp. 63–76. [G: U.S.]

Kelly, Aidan and Brannick, Teresa. The Strike-Proneness of Public Sector Organisations. *Econ. Soc. Rev.*, July 1985, *16*(4), pp. 251–71. [G: Ireland]

Kruger, Daniel H. Interest Arbitration Revisited. In *Dennis, B. D., ed.*, 1985, pp. 497–514. [G: U.S.]

Leslie, Derek. The Economics of Cash Limits as a Method of Pay Determination. *Econ. J.*, September 1985, *95*(379), pp. 662–78.

Lewin, David. The Effects of Regulation on Public Sector Labor Relations: Theory and Evidence. *J. Lab. Res.*, Winter 1985, *6*(1), pp. 77–95. [G: U.S.]

Ley, Robert D. and Wines, William A. The Economics of Teachers' Strikes in Minnesota in 1981. *Econ. Educ. Rev.*, 1985, *4*(1), pp. 57–65. [G: U.S.]

Martin, James E. Employee Characteristics and Representation Election Outcomes. *Ind. Lab. Relat. Rev.*, April 1985, *38*(3), pp. 365–76. [G: U.S.]

Martin, James E. and Smith, Richard L. Appropriate Bargaining Units for State Employees: Potential Impacts for Labor Relations and Public Administration. *J. Lab. Res.*, Summer 1985, *6*(3), pp. 289–305. [G: U.S.]

Murphy, Michael J. The Impact of Collective Bargaining on School Management and Governance. In *Augenblick, J., ed.*, 1985, pp. 47–58. [G: U.S.]

Murphy, Michael J. The Impact of Collective Bargaining on School Management and Governance. *Public Budg. Finance*, Spring 1985, *5*(1), pp. 3–14. [G: U.S.]

Newman, Harold R. The Changing Law of Fair Representation: The State of the Law: The Duty in the Public Sector. In *McKelvey, J. T., ed.*, 1985, pp. 85–92. [G: U.S.]

Saltzman, Gregory M. Bargaining Laws as a Cause and Consequence of the Growth of Teacher Unionism. *Ind. Lab. Relat. Rev.*, April 1985, *38*(3), pp. 335–51. [G: U.S.]

Stark, David. The Micropolitics of the Firm and the Macropolitics of Reform: New Forms of Workplace Bargaining in Hungarian Enterprises. In *Evans, P.; Rueschemeyer, D. and Stephens, E. H., eds.*, 1985, pp. 247–73. [G: Hungary]

Tanimoto, Helene S. and Inaba, Gail F. State Employee Bargaining: Policy and Organization. *Mon. Lab. Rev.*, April 1985, *108*(4), pp. 51–55. [G: U.S.]

Wasilewski, Edward. BLS Expands Collective

Bargaining Series for State and Local Government. *Mon. Lab. Rev.*, May 1985, *108*(5), pp. 36–38. [G: U.S.]

Wood, John [Sir]. Last Offer Arbitration. *Brit. J. Ind. Relat.*, November 1985, *23*(3), pp. 415–24. [G: Canada; U.S.]

Woodbury, Stephen A. The Scope of Bargaining and Bargaining Outcomes in the Public Schools. *Ind. Lab. Relat. Rev.*, January 1985, *38*(2), pp. 195–210. [G: U.S.]

833 Labor–Management Relations

8330 General

Aaron, Benjamin. The NLRB, Labor Courts, and Industrial Tribunals: A Selective Comparison. *Ind. Lab. Relat. Rev.*, October 1985, *39*(1), pp. 35–45.

Abraham, Katharine G. and Medoff, James L. Length of Service and Promotions in Union and Nonunion Work Groups. *Ind. Lab. Relat. Rev.*, April 1985, *38*(3), pp. 408–20. [G: U.S.]

Anthony, P. D. The Metamorphosis of Management, from Villain to Hero. In *Gustavsson, B.; Karlsson, J. C. and Raftegard, C.*, 1985, pp. 111–20.

Arvey, Richard D. and Jones, Allen P. The Use of Discipline in Organizational Settings: A Framework for Future Research. In *Cummings, L. L. and Staw, B. M., eds.*, 1985, pp. 367–408.

Balducci, Renata. Economia di partecipazione e accumulazione. (Share Economy and Accumulation. With English summary.) *Giorn. Econ.*, Nov.-Dec. 1985, *44*(11–12), pp. 639–50.

Blomqvist, Kai. Cooperative Enterprise and New Relationships between Capital and Labour. *Ann. Pub. Co-op. Econ.*, January–June 1985, *56*(1–2), pp. 93–110.

Brunello, Giorgio. Labour Adjustment in Japanese Incorporated Enterprises: An Empirical Analysis for the Period 1965–1983. *Hitotsubashi J. Econ.*, December 1985, *26*(2), pp. 165–80. [G: Japan]

Cappelli, Peter. Theory Construction in IR and Some Implications for Research. *Ind. Relat.*, Winter 1985, *24*(1), pp. 90–112. [G: U.S.; U.K.]

Cooke, William N. Toward a General Theory of Industrial Relations. In *Lipsky, D. B., ed.*, 1985, pp. 223–52.

Covick, Owen. The Hancock Report on Australia's Industrial Relations System. *Australian Econ. Pap.*, December 1985, *24*(45), pp. 242–57. [G: Australia]

Dahlkvist, Mats. Work and Culture. In *Gustavsson, B.; Karlsson, J. C. and Raftegard, C.*, 1985, pp. 105–09.

Delamotte, Yves. Managerial and Supervisory Staff in a Changing World. *Int. Lab. Rev.*, January–February 1985, *124*(1), pp. 1–16. [G: W. Germany; Italy; France; U.K.; Sweden]

Delaney, John Thomas; Lewin, David and Soc-

kell, Donna. The NLRA at Fifty: A Research Appraisal and Agenda. *Ind. Lab. Relat. Rev.*, October 1985, *39*(1), pp. 46–75. **[G: U.S.]**

Dubois, Pierre. Quindici anni di nuove forme di organizzazione del lavoro in Francia: Dagli scioperi per il miglioramento delle condizioni di lavoro alla legislazione sul "diritto di espressione" dei lavoratori. (Fifteen Years of New Labour Organization Experiences in France. With English summary.) *Econ. Lavoro*, Jan.-Mar. 1985, *19*(1), pp. 37–49. **[G: France]**

Edwards, Christine and Heery, Edmund. Formality and Informality in the Working of the National Coal Board's Incentive Scheme. *Brit. J. Ind. Relat.*, March 1985, *23*(1), pp. 25–45. **[G: U.K.]**

Eidem, Rolf. The Power of Economics and the Economics of Power. In *Gustavsson, B.; Karlsson, J. C. and Raftegard, C.*, 1985, pp. 217–24.

Eldridge, John. Industrial Democracy at Enterprise Level: Problems and Prospects. In *Matthews, R. C. O., ed.*, 1985, pp. 204–18.

Eyerman, Ron. Work—A Contested Concept. In *Gustavsson, B.; Karlsson, J. C. and Raftegard, C.*, 1985, pp. 27–31.

Folger, Robert and Belew, Janet. Nonreactive Measurement: A Focus for Research on Absenteeism and Occupational Stress. In *Cummings, L. L. and Staw, B. M., eds.*, 1985, pp. 129–70.

Gallie, Duncan. *Les lois Auroux:* The Reform of French Industrial Relations? In *Machin, H. and Wright, V., eds.*, 1985, pp. 205–21. **[G: France]**

Galtung, Johan. Work, Needs and Three Cultures. In *Gustavsson, B.; Karlsson, J. C. and Raftegard, C.*, 1985, pp. 131–38.

Gould, Carol C. Economic Justice, Self-management, and the Principle of Reciprocity. In *Kipnis, K. and Meyers, D. T., eds.*, 1985, pp. 202–16.

Gross, James A. Conflicting Statutory Purposes: Another Look at Fifty Years of NLRB Law Making. *Ind. Lab. Relat. Rev.*, October 1985, *39*(1), pp. 7–18. **[G: U.S.]**

Haug, Frigga. Automatization as a Field of Contradictions. In *Gustavsson, B.; Karlsson, J. C. and Raftegard, C.*, 1985, pp. 83–92.

Hedlund, Stefan. On the Socialisation of Labour in Rural Cooperation. In *Lundahl, M., ed.*, 1985, pp. 329–51. **[G: Israel]**

Hodson, Randy. Workers' Comparisons and Job Satisfaction. *Soc. Sci. Quart.*, June 1985, *66*(2), pp. 266–80.

Horvat, Branko. The Prospects for Disalienation of Work. In *Gustavsson, B.; Karlsson, J. C. and Raftegard, C.*, 1985, pp. 235–39.

Hulin, Charles L. and Roznowski, Mary. Organizational Technologies: Effects on Organizations' Characteristics and Individuals' Responses. In *Cummings, L. L. and Staw, B. M., eds.*, 1985, pp. 39–85.

Jones, Derek C. The Cooperative Sector and Dualism in Command Economies: Theory and Evidence for the Case of Poland. In *Jones,*

D. C. and Svejnar, J., eds., 1985, pp. 195–218. **[G: Poland]**

Jones, Derek C. and Svejnar, Jan. Advances in the Economic Analysis of Participatory and Labor-Managed Firms: Introduction. In *Jones, D. C. and Svejnar, J., eds.*, 1985, pp. xi–xiv.

Kantrow, Alan M. America's Industrial Renaissance. In *Federal Reserve Bank of Atlanta (I)*, 1985, pp. 97–110. **[G: U.S.]**

Kotzorek, Andreas. Zur Häufigkeit arbeitsrechtlicher Prozesse in der Bundesrepublik Deutschland—Eine ökonomische Analyse. (On the Litigation Rate of Labor Cases in West Germany. With English summary.) *Z. ges. Staatswiss. (JITE)*, June 1985, *141*(2), pp. 312–35. **[G: W. Germany]**

Kuhn, David and Martinko, Mark. The Management of Organization Behavior. In *Damjanovic, M. and Voich, D., Jr., eds.*, 1985, pp. 279–99. **[G: U.S.]**

Lantz, Göran. Work and Power. In *Gustavsson, B.; Karlsson, J. C. and Raftegard, C.*, 1985, pp. 205–15.

Lash, Scott. The End of Neo-corporatism? The Breakdown of Centralised Bargaining in Sweden. *Brit. J. Ind. Relat.*, July 1985, *23*(2), pp. 215–39. **[G: Sweden]**

Macarov, David. The Prospect of Work in the Western Context. In *Didsbury, H. F., Jr., ed.*, 1985, pp. 76–108.

Macpherson, C. B. Notes on Work and Power. In *Gustavsson, B.; Karlsson, J. C. and Raftegard, C.*, 1985, pp. 241–44.

Maital, Shlomo and Meltz, Noah M. Labor and Management Attitudes toward a New Social Contract: A Comparison of Canada and the United States. In *Maital, S. and Lipnowski, I., eds.*, 1985, pp. 193–206. **[G: U.S.; Canada]**

Marin, Bernd. Austria—The Paradigm Case of Liberal Corporatism? In *Grant, W., ed.*, 1985, pp. 89–125. **[G: Austria]**

Marsden, David. *Les lois Auroux:* The Reform of French Industrial Relations?: Comment. In *Machin, H. and Wright, V., eds.*, 1985, pp. 221–24. **[G: France]**

Mills, D. Quinn. Seniority versus Ability in Promotion Decisions. *Ind. Lab. Relat. Rev.*, April 1985, *38*(3), pp. 421–25. **[G: U.S.]**

Mills, D. Quinn and Lovell, Malcolm R., Jr. Enhancing Competitiveness: The Contribution of Employee Relations. In *Scott, B. R. and Lodge, G. C., eds.*, 1985, pp. 455–78. **[G: U.S.]**

Moe, Terry M. Control and Feedback in Economic Regulation: The Case of the NLRB. *Amer. Polit. Sci. Rev.*, December 1985, *79*(4), pp. 1094–116. **[G: U.S.]**

Pang, Eng Fong. Employment, Skills and Technology. In *Gustavsson, B.; Karlsson, J. C. and Raftegard, C.*, 1985, pp. 93–102.

Pankert, Alfred. Recent Developments in Labour Relations in the Industrialised Market Economy Countries: Some Bench-Marks. *Int. Lab. Rev.*, Sept.-Oct. 1985, *124*(5), pp. 531–44. **[G: OECD]**

Shackleton, J. R. Is Workers' Self-management the Answer? In *Bornstein, M., ed.*, 1985, pp. 141–52.

Shalev, Michael. Labor Relations and Class Conflict: A Critical Survey of the Contributions of John R. Commons. In *Lipsky, D. B., ed.*, 1985, pp. 319–63. [G: U.S.]

Sheridan, James A. A Discussion of Value-Added Human Resource Management and Planning. In *Niehaus, R. J., ed.*, 1985, pp. 215–229.

Smith, Graham F. The High Court and Industrial Relations in the 1980s. *Australian Bull. Lab.*, March 1985, *11*(2), pp. 82–101. [G: Australia]

Spurling, Graham. Industry and Human Resources. In *Scutt, J. A., ed.*, 1985, pp. 70–74. [G: Australia]

Story, Christopher. The Labour Cartels: Has Anything Really Changed? *Nat. Westminster Bank Quart. Rev.*, May 1985, pp. 63–73. [G: U.K.]

Stymne, B. Reorganization of Work: Causes and Effects. In *Rinnooy Kan, A. H. G., ed.*, 1985, pp. 93–113.

Šuvaković, Đorđe. Modeliranje raspodele u samouprovnoj privredi i jugoslovenski program stabilizacije. (The Rule of Distribution in a Self-managed Economy and the Yugoslav Programme of Stabilization. With English summary.) *Econ. Anal. Worker's Manage.*, 1985, *19*(2), pp. 181–94. [G: Yugoslavia]

Taira, Koji and Levine, Solomon B. Japan's Industrial Relations: A Social Compact Emerges. In *Juris, H.; Thompson, M. and Daniels, W., eds.*, 1985, pp. 247–300. [G: Japan]

Thakur, C. P. Labour and Industrial Relations. In *Mongia, J. N., ed.*, 1985, pp. 315–48. [G: India]

Thomas, Henk. The Dynamics of Social Ownership: Some Considerations in the Perspective of the Mondragon Experience. *Econ. Anal. Worker's Manage.*, 1985, *19*(2), pp. 147–60. [G: Spain]

Thorsrud, Einar. Work and Technology. In *Gustavsson, B.; Karlsson, J. C. and Raftegard, C.*, 1985, pp. 57–60.

Vanek, Jaroslav. The Participatory Economy. In *Bornstein, M., ed.*, 1985, pp. 131–40.

Wallman, Sandra. Employment, Live lihood and the Organisation of Resources: What Is Work Really About? In *Gustavsson, B.; Karlsson, J. C. and Raftegard, C.*, 1985, pp. 45–53.

8331 Labor–Management Relations in the Private Sector

Adams, Roy J. Should Works Councils Be Used as Industrial Relations Policy? *Mon. Lab. Rev.*, July 1985, *108*(7), pp. 25–29. [G: U.S.; Canada]

Ahern, Robert W. Labor–Management Structures in the Large City. In *Woodworth, W.; Meek, C. and Whyte, W. F., eds.*, 1985, pp. 161–78. [G: U.S.]

Albin, Peter S. Job Design, Control Technology, and Technical Change. *J. Econ. Issues*, Sep-

tember 1985, *19*(3), pp. 703–30.

Alexander, Kenneth O. Worker Ownership and Participation in the Context of Social Change: Progress Is Slow and Difficult, But It Need Not Wait upon Massive Redistribution of Wealth. *Amer. J. Econ. Soc.*, July 1985, *44*(3), pp. 337–47. [G: U.S.]

Allen, P. T. and Stephenson, G. M. The Relationship of Inter-group Understanding and Interparty Friction in Industry. *Brit. J. Ind. Relat.*, July 1985, *23*(2), pp. 203–13.

Amin, Ash. Restructuring in Fiat and the Decentralization of Production into Southern Italy. In *Hudson, R. and Lewis, J., eds.*, 1985, pp. 155–91. [G: Italy; Europe]

Berggren, Christian. Industrial Work, Technological Development and New Rationalization Strategies—The Case of the Swedish Automotive Industry. In *Gustavsson, B.; Karlsson, J. C. and Raftegard, C.*, 1985, pp. 61–69. [G: Sweden]

Bilson, R. E. A Workers' Charter: What Do We Mean by Rights? [Workers' Rights and Freedoms]. *Can. Public Policy*, December 1985, *11*(4), pp. 749–55.

Blasi, Joseph. Labor Policy and the Changing Role of Government. In *Woodworth, W.; Meek, C. and Whyte, W. F., eds.*, 1985, pp. 277–96. [G: U.S.]

Bowles, Samuel; Gordon, David M. and Weisskopf, Thomas E. In Defense of the "Social Model." *Challenge*, May/June 1985, *28*(2), pp. 57–59. [G: U.S.]

Bronfenbrenner, Martin. An Essay on Negative Screening. In *Shishido, T. and Sato, R., eds.*, 1985, pp. 188–98. [G: Japan]

Carnoy, Martin. High Technology and International Labour Markets. *Int. Lab. Rev.*, Nov.-Dec. 1985, *124*(6), pp. 643–59. [G: LDCs; OECD]

Caves, Richard E. Income Distribution and Labor Relations. In *Moran, T. H., ed.*, 1985, pp. 173–98. [G: U.S.]

Chermesh, Ran. Strikes as Social Problems: A Social Problem Matrix Approach. *Brit. J. Ind. Relat.*, July 1985, *23*(2), pp. 281–307. [G: Israel]

Collier, Paul and Knight, J. B. Seniority Payments, Quit Rates, and Internal Labour Markets in Britain and Japan. *Oxford Bull. Econ. Statist.*, February 1985, *47*(1), pp. 19–32. [G: U.K.; Japan]

Cutcher-Gershenfeld, Joel. Policy Strategies for Labor–Management Cooperation. In *Woodworth, W.; Meek, C. and Whyte, W. F., eds.*, 1985, pp. 245–60. [G: U.S.]

Cutcher-Gershenfeld, Joel. Reconceiving the Web of Labor–Management Relations. In *Dennis, B. D., ed.*, 1985, pp. 637–45. [G: U.S.]

Cutcher-Gershenfeld, Joel. The Emergence of Community Labor-Management Cooperation. In *Woodworth, W.; Meek, C. and Whyte, W. F., eds.*, 1985, pp. 99–120. [G: U.S.]

Deery, Stephen; Brooks, Ray and Morris, Alan. Redundancy and Public Policy in Australia.

Australian Bull. Lab., June 1985, *11*(3), pp. 154–77.   [G: Australia]

Defourney, Jacques; Estrin, Saul and Jones, Derek C. The Effects of Workers' Participation on Enterprise Performance: Empirical Evidence from French Cooperatives. *Int. J. Ind. Organ.*, June 1985, *3*(2), pp. 197–217.
                                     [G: France]

DeKoker, Neil. Labor–Management Relations for Survival. In *Dennis, B. D., ed.*, 1985, pp. 576–77.   [G: U.S.]

Drago, Robert. New Use of an Old Technology: The Growth of Worker Participation. *J. Post Keynesian Econ.*, Winter 1984–85, *7*(2), pp. 153–67.

Düll, Klaus. L'analisi delle nuove forme di organizzazione del lavoro–elementi di confronto a livello internazionale (risultati degli study su casi tedeschi, francesi e italiani). (The Analysis of New Forms of Work Organisation International Comparative Aspects [Results of Case-Studies from the Federal Republic of Germany, France and Italy]. With English summary.) *Econ. Lavoro*, Apr.-June 1985, *19*(2), pp. 49–64.   [G: W. Germany; France; Italy]

Ebel, Karl-H. Social and Labour Implications of Flexible Manufacturing Systems. *Int. Lab. Rev.*, March-April 1985, *124*(2), pp. 133–45.

Edquist, Charles. Technology and Work in Sugar Cane Harvesting in Capitalist Jamaica and Socialist Cuba 1958–1983. In *Gustavsson, B.; Karlsson, J. C. and Raftegard, C.*, 1985, pp. 71–82.   [G: Cuba; Jamaica]

Egolf, Jeremy R. The Limits of Shop Floor Struggle: Workers vs. the Bedaux System at Willapa Harbor Lumber Mills, 1933–35. *Labor Hist.*, Spring 1985, *26*(2), pp. 195–229.   [G: U.S.]

Eyraud, François and Tchobanian, Robert. The Auroux Reforms and Company Level Industrial Relations in France. *Brit. J. Ind. Relat.*, July 1985, *23*(2), pp. 241–59.   [G: France]

Ferman, Louis A. and Klingel, Sally. On the Shop Floor: The Implications of Unions and Employers Seeking to Foster Employee Involvement. In *Dennis, B. D., ed.*, 1985, pp. 631–36.
                                     [G: U.S.]

Flaherty, Diane. Labor Control in the British Boot and Shoe Industry. *Ind. Relat.*, Fall 1985, *24*(3), pp. 339–59.   [G: U.K.]

Friedman, Sheldon. Negotiated Approaches to Job Security. In *Dennis, B. D., ed.*, 1985, pp. 553–70.   [G: U.S.]

Furubotn, Eirik G. Codetermination, Productivity Gains, and the Economics of the Firm. *Oxford Econ. Pap.*, March 1985, *37*(1), pp. 22–39.

Ginzberg, Eli. The Inevitability of Manpower Waste in Large Organizations. In *Ginzberg, E.*, 1985, pp. 519–24.

Goldberg, Marshall. The UAW–Ford Career Services and Reemployment Assistance Centers: New Ventures in Service Delivery to Unionized Workers. In *Dennis, B. D., ed.*, 1985, pp. 527–34.   [G: U.S.]

Gurdon, Michael A. Equity Participation by Employees: The Growing Debate in West Germany. *Ind. Relat.*, Winter 1985, *24*(1), pp. 113–29.   [G: W. Germany]

Gustavsen, Bjørn. A Decade with Employee Representation on Company Boards: Experiences and Prospects for the Future. In *Gustavsson, B.; Karlsson, J. C. and Raftegard, C.*, 1985, pp. 225–34. [G: Sweden; Norway; Denmark]

Hansen, Gary B. Industrial Relations Research Association: Proceedings of the 1985 Spring Meeting: Discussion: EDTP. In *Dennis, B. D., ed.*, 1985, pp. 548–53.   [G: U.S.]

Hollis, Mark C. Motivating Employees through Stock Ownership. In *Federal Reserve Bank of Atlanta (I)*, 1985, pp. 65–69.   [G: U.S.]

Inumaru, Kazuo F. Le relazioni industriali e l'incentivazione del lavoro in Giappone. (The Industrial Relations and Labour Improvements in Japan. With English summary.) *Econ. Lavoro*, Jan.-Mar. 1985, *19*(1), pp. 5–35.
                                     [G: Japan]

Ippolito, Richard A. The Labor Contract and True Economic Pension Liabilities. *Amer. Econ. Rev.*, December 1985, *75*(5), pp. 1031–43.
                                     [G: U.S.]

Ishikawa, Akihiro. Participation and the Effect of New Technology upon Work: The Case of Small- and Medium-scale Manufacturing Firms in Tokyo. *Econ. Anal. Worker's Manage.*, 1985, *19*(3), pp. 295–305.   [G: Japan]

Jacobs, David. In Society: New Representational Roles for Labor and Management. In *Dennis, B. D., ed.*, 1985, pp. 624–31.   [G: U.S.]

Jacobsen, Thomas H. Innovation through Experimentation. In *Federal Reserve Bank of Atlanta (I)*, 1985, pp. 81–87.   [G: U.S.]

Jenner, Faith S. and Trevor, Malcolm H. Personnel Management in Four U.K. Electronics Plants. In *Takamiya, S. and Thurley, K., eds.*, 1985, pp. 113–48. [G: U.K.; U.S.; Japan]

Jones, Derek C. and Svejnar, Jan. Participation, Profit Sharing, Worker Ownership and Efficiency in Italian Producer Cooperative. *Economica*, November 1985, *52*(208), pp. 449–65.
                                     [G: Italy]

Jones, Robert A. The Changing Structure of Industrial Relations in South Africa. *Managerial Dec. Econ.*, December 1985, *6*(4), pp. 217–25.   [G: S. Africa]

Kahn, Mark L. Discussion: The 1984 Auto Negotiations. In *Dennis, B. D., ed.*, 1985, pp. 464–66.   [G: U.S.]

Kaynak, Erdener. International Business in the Middle East. In *Kaynak, E., ed. (II)*, 1985, pp. 3–18.

Kobayashi, Noritake. The Patterns of Management Style Developing in Japanese Multinationals in the 1980s. In *Takamiya, S. and Thurley, K., eds.*, 1985, pp. 229–64.   [G: Japan; U.S.; U.K.; W. Germany; France]

Kornbluh, Hy; Crowfoot, James and Cohen-Rosenthal, Edward. Worker Participation in Energy and Natural Resources Conservation. *Int. Lab. Rev.*, Nov.-Dec. 1985, *124*(6), pp. 737–54.   [G: U.S.]

Koshiro, Kazutoshi. Foreign Direct Investment and Industrial Relations: Japanese Experience after the Oil Crisis. In *Takamiya, S. and Thurley, K., eds.*, 1985, pp. 205–27.   [G: Japan; Selected Countries]

Levin, William R. The False Promise of Worker Capitalism: Congress and the Leveraged Employee Stock Ownership Plan. *Yale Law J.*, November 1985, *95*(1), pp. 148–73.
[G: U.S.]

Lin, Vivian. Women Factory Workers in Asian Export Processing Zones. In *Utrecht, E., ed.*, 1985, pp. 159–219.   [G: Asia]

Linsenmayer, Tadd. ILO Examines Impact of Technology on Worker Safety and Health. *Mon. Lab. Rev.*, August 1985, *108*(8), pp. 46–47.   [G: OECD]

MacInnes, John. Conjuring up Consultation: The Role and Extent of Joint Consultation in Postwar Private Manufacturing Industry. *Brit. J. Ind. Relat.*, March 1985, *23*(1), pp. 93–113.
[G: U.K.]

Malotke, Joseph F. Automation and Its Impact on the Labor Force and the GM–UAW Saturn Project. In *Dennis, B. D., ed.*, 1985, pp. 568–69.   [G: U.S.]

Marcus, Bernard. Educating Managers and Employees. In *Federal Reserve Bank of Atlanta.*, 1985, pp. 75–79.   [G: U.S.]

Marshall, Ray. The American Industrial Relations System in a Time of Change. *J. Econ. Educ.*, Spring 1985, *16*(2), pp. 85–97.   [G: U.S.; EEC; Japan]

McKenna, J. A. and Rodger, Richard G. Control by Coercion: Employers' Associations and the Establishment of Industrial Order in the Building Industry of England and Wales, 1860–1914. *Bus. Hist. Rev.*, Summer 1985, *59*(2), pp. 203–31.   [G: U.K.]

McKersie, Robert B. New Dimensions in Industrial Relations. In *Dennis, B. D., ed.*, 1985, pp. 645–48.   [G: U.S.]

Meek, Christopher. Labor–Management Committee Outcomes: The Jamestown Case. In *Woodworth, W.; Meek, C. and Whyte, W. F., eds.*, 1985, pp. 141–59.   [G: U.S.]

Meek, Christopher and Woodworth, Warner. Absentee Ownership, Industrial Decline, and Organizational Renewal. In *Woodworth, W.; Meek, C. and Whyte, W. F., eds.*, 1985, pp. 78–96.   [G: U.S.]

Meek, Christopher and Woodworth, Warner. Worker–Community Collaboration and Ownership. In *Woodworth, W.; Meek, C. and Whyte, W. F., eds.*, 1985, pp. 195–220.
[G: U.S.]

Mitchell, Daniel J. B. Wage Flexibility in the United States: Lessons from the Past. *Amer. Econ. Rev.*, May 1985, *75*(2), pp. 36–40.
[G: U.S.]

Mitchell, William F. and Watts, Martin. Efficiency under Capitalist Production: A Critique and Reformulation. *Rev. Radical Polit. Econ.*, Spring and Summer 1985, *17*(1/2), pp. 212–20.

Moseley, Fred. Can the "Social Model" of Productivity Stand Scrutiny? *Challenge*, May/June 1985, *28*(2), pp. 55–57.   [G: U.S.]

Niehaus, Richard J. Organizational Human Resource Policy Analysis in the 1980s. In *Niehaus, R. J., ed.*, 1985, pp. 1–44.

Norsworthy, J. R. and Zabala, Craig A. Effects of Worker Attitudes on Production Costs and the Value of Capital Input. *Econ. J.*, December 1985, *95*(380), pp. 992–1002.   [G: U.S.]

Norsworthy, J. R. and Zabala, Craig A. Worker Attitudes, Worker Behavior, and Productivity in the U.S. Automobile Industry, 1959–1976. *Ind. Lab. Relat. Rev.*, July 1985, *38*(4), pp. 544–57.   [G: U.S.]

Oka, H. and Tanimitsu, T. A Short History of Mitsubishi Electric Corporation's Basic Philosophy of Semiconductor R & D and Its Related Human Resource Management. In *Niehaus, R. J., ed.*, 1985, pp. 173–86.   [G: Japan]

Pascoe, Thomas J. and Collins, Richard J. UAW–Ford Employee Development and Training Program: Overview of Operations and Structure. In *Dennis, B. D., ed.*, 1985, pp. 519–26.   [G: U.S.]

Rehmus, Charles M. The Changing Role of Universities in Industrial Relations Training. In *Dennis, B. D., ed.*, 1985, pp. 591–94.
[G: U.S.]

Reitsperger, Wolf. Personnel Policy and Employee Satisfaction. In *Takamiya, S. and Thurley, K., eds.*, 1985, pp. 149–81.   [G: U.S.; U.K.; Japan]

Rosen, Corey. Financing Employee Ownership. In *Woodworth, W.; Meek, C. and Whyte, W. F., eds.*, 1985, pp. 261–75.   [G: U.S.]

Runyon, Marvin. The Americanization of Japanese Management. In *Federal Reserve Bank of Atlanta (1)*, 1985, pp. 15–23.   [G: U.S.]

Russell, Raymond. Employee Ownership and Internal Governance. *J. Econ. Behav. Organ.*, September 1985, *6*(3), pp. 217–41. [G: U.S.]

Sacks, Stephen R. The Yugoslav Firm. In *Bornstein, M., ed.*, 1985, pp. 153–73.
[G: Yugoslavia]

Savage, John A. Growth and Success through Employee Motivation. In *Federal Reserve Bank of Atlanta (1)*, 1985, pp. 47–57.   [G: U.S.]

Savoie, Ernest J. Current Developments and Future Agenda in Union–Management Cooperation in Training and Retraining of Workers. In *Dennis, B. D., ed.*, 1985, pp. 535–48.
[G: U.S.]

Schuster, Michael. Models of Cooperation and Change in Union Settings. *Ind. Relat.*, Fall 1985, *24*(3), pp. 382–94.   [G: U.S.]

Schwartz, Arthur R. Discussion: The 1984 Auto Negotiations. In *Dennis, B. D., ed.*, 1985, pp. 466–68.   [G: U.S.]

Seal, W. B. On the Nature of the Firm and Trades Unions: A Critique of the Property Rights Literature. *Brit. Rev. Econ. Issues*, Spring 1985, *7*(16), pp. 47–61.

Shahandeh, Behrouz. Drug and Alcohol Abuse in the Workplace: Consequences and Countermeasures. *Int. Lab. Rev.*, March-April 1985, *124*(2), pp. 207–23.

Smith, Stephen C. Political Behavior as an Economic Externality: Econometric Evidence on the Relationship between Ownership and Decision Making Participation in U.S. Firms and Participation in Community Affairs. In *Jones, D. C. and Svejnar, J., eds.*, 1985, pp. 123–36.   [G: U.S.]

Sockell, Donna. Attitudes, Behavior, and Employee Ownership: Some Preliminary Data. *Ind. Relat.*, Winter 1985, *24*(1), pp. 130–38.   [G: U.S.]

Sperry, Charles W. What Makes Mondragon Work? *Rev. Soc. Econ.*, December 1985, *43*(3), pp. 345–56.   [G: Spain]

St. Antoine, Theodore J. The Revision of Employment-at-Will Enters a New Phase. In *Dennis, B. D., ed.*, 1985, pp. 563–67.   [G: U.S.]

Stepina, Lee P. and Kircher, Kraig. Environmental Influences on the Development of U.S. Labor–Management Relations. In *Damjanovic, M. and Voich, D., Jr., eds.*, 1985, pp. 64–94.   [G: U.S.]

Stieber, Jack. Recent Developments in Employment-at-Will. In *Dennis, B. D., ed.*, 1985, pp. 557–63.   [G: U.S.]

Tomita, Teruhiko. Japanese Management as Applied in the Philippines. *Philippine Rev. Econ. Bus.*, Mar./June 1985, *22*(1/2), pp. 23–57.   [G: Philippines]

Tushman, Michael L. and Romanelli, Elaine. Organizational Evolution: A Metamorphosis Model of Convergence and Reorientation. In *Cummings, L. L. and Staw, B. M., eds.*, 1985, pp. 171–222.   [G: U.S.]

Unterweger, Peter. Appropriate Automation: Thoughts on Swedish Examples of Sociotechnical Innovation. In *Dennis, B. D., ed.*, 1985, pp. 569–73.   [G: Sweden]

Venturini, Patrick. Workers' and Employers' Roles in a New Corporate Culture. In *Zukin, S., ed.*, 1985, pp. 246–52.   [G: France]

Wells, Joel R., Jr. Customer and Employee Feedback. In *Federal Reserve Bank of Atlanta (I)*, 1985, pp. 31–34.   [G: U.S.]

Whyte, William Foote and Blasi, Joseph. The Potential of Employee Ownership. In *Woodworth, W.; Meek, C. and Whyte, W. F., eds.*, 1985, pp. 181–94.   [G: U.S.]

Williamson, Oliver E. Employee Ownership and Internal Governance: A Perspective. *J. Econ. Behav. Organ.*, September 1985, *6*(3), pp. 243–45.

Wingren, Gustaf. Everyday Life in Europe and the Effect of the 'Protestant Work Ethic.' In *Gustavsson, B.; Karlsson, J. C. and Raftegard, C.*, 1985, pp. 139–47.

Wise, E. E. New Technology and Labor–Management Relations at Ford Motor Company. In *Dennis, B. D., ed.*, 1985, pp. 574–75.   [G: U.S.]

Wolozin, Harold. Corporate Power in an Aging Economy: Labor Force Policy. *J. Econ. Issues*, June 1985, *19*(2), pp. 475–86.   [G: U.S.]

Wood, C. Martin, III. Optimizing the Decentralized Approach. In *Federal Reserve Bank of Atlanta (I)*, 1985, pp. 25–30.   [G: U.S.]

Woodworth, Warner. Achieving Labor–Management Joint Action. In *Woodworth, W.; Meek,*

C. and Whyte, W. F., eds., 1985, pp. 121–39.   [G: U.S.]

Woodworth, Warner. Promethean Industrial Relations: Labor, ESOPs, and the Boardroom. In *Dennis, B. D., ed.*, 1985, pp. 618–24.   [G: U.S.]

Woodworth, Warner. Saving Jobs through Worker Buyouts. In *Woodworth, W.; Meek, C. and Whyte, W. F., eds.*, 1985, pp. 221–41.   [G: U.S.]

Woodworth, Warner; Meek, Christopher and Whyte, William Foote. Theory and Practice of Community Economic Reindustrialization. In *Woodworth, W.; Meek, C. and Whyte, W. F., eds.*, 1985, pp. 297–304.   [G: U.S.]

Yamada, Narumi. Working Time in Japan: Recent Trends and Issues. *Int. Lab. Rev.*, Nov.-Dec. 1985, *124*(6), pp. 699–718.   [G: Japan]

Young, Howard. The 1984 Auto Negotiations: A UAW Perspective. In *Dennis, B. D., ed.*, 1985, pp. 454–57.   [G: U.S.]

Youngblood, Stuart A. and Bierman, Leonard. Due Process and Employment-At-Will: A Legal and Behavioral Analysis. In *Rowland, K. M. and Ferris, G. R., eds.*, 1985, pp. 185–230.   [G: U.S.]

8332 Labor–Management Relations in the Public Sector

Aage, Hans. The State and the Kolkhoznik. *Econ. Anal. Worker's Manage.*, 1985, *19*(2), pp. 131–46.   [G: U.S.S.R.]

Bacharach, Samuel B.; Mitchell, Stephen M. and Malanowski, Rose. Strategic Choice and Collective Action: Organizational Determinants of Teachers Militancy. In *Lipsky, D. B., ed.*, 1985, pp. 197–222.   [G: U.S.]

Charnes, A., et al. A Goal Programming System for the Management of the U.S. Navy's Sea–Shore Rotation Program. In *Niehaus, R. J., ed.*, 1985, pp. 145–72.   [G: U.S.]

Damjanovic, Mijat. The System and Process of Decision Making in Organizations of Associated Labor. In *Damjanovic, M. and Voich, D., Jr., eds.*, 1985, pp. 159–77.   [G: Yugoslavia]

Eberts, Randall W. and Stone, Joe A. Wages, Fringe Benefits, and Working Conditions: An Analysis of Compensating Differentials. *Southern Econ. J.*, July 1985, *52*(1), pp. 274–80.   [G: U.S.]

Ferner, Anthony. Political Constraints and Management Strategies: The Case of Working Practices in British Rail. *Brit. J. Ind. Relat.*, March 1985, *23*(1), pp. 47–70.   [G: U.K.]

Gerhart, Paul F. and Drotning, John E. The Effectiveness of Public Sector Impasse Procedures: A Six State Study. In *Lipsky, D. B., ed.*, 1985, pp. 143–95.   [G: U.S.]

Hoch, Róbert. The Maxi and Mini (Reflections on the Hungarian Debate on Large Firms). *Acta Oecon.*, 1985, *35*(3–4), pp. 251–67.   [G: Hungary]

Klimentov, G. A. What Is Impeding the Potential of Collective Labor? *Prob. Econ.*, May 1985, *28*(1), pp. 24–37.   [G: U.S.S.R.]

Lewin, David. The Effects of Regulation on Public Sector Labor Relations: Theory and Evidence. *J. Lab. Res.*, Winter 1985, *6*(1), pp. 77–95. [G: U.S.]

Martin, James E. and Smith, Richard L. Appropriate Bargaining Units for State Employees: Potential Impacts for Labor Relations and Public Administration. *J. Lab. Res.*, Summer 1985, *6*(3), pp. 289–305. [G: U.S.]

Matic, Milan. Leadership Motivation and Communication: The Yugoslav Experience. In *Damjanovic, M. and Voich, D., Jr., eds.*, 1985, pp. 246–78. [G: Yugoslavia]

Owen, John D. Changing from a Rotating to a Permanent Shift System in the Detroit Police Department: Effects on Employee Attitudes and Behavior. In *Dennis, B. D., ed.*, 1985, pp. 484–89. [G: U.S.]

Petschnig, Mária. Causes of Difficulties in Changing the Normal State of the Hungarian Economy. *Acta Oecon.*, 1985, *35*(3–4), pp. 235–50. [G: Hungary]

Popovic, Slavoljub. The Control Mechanism in Managing Organizations of Associated Labor. In *Damjanovic, M. and Voich, D., Jr., eds.*, 1985, pp. 343–65. [G: Yugoslavia]

Ratkovic, Radoslav. Fundamentals of the Yugoslav Political Socialist Self-Management System. In *Damjanovic, M. and Voich, D., Jr., eds.*, 1985, pp. 10–20. [G: Yugoslavia]

Stark, David. The Micropolitics of the Firm and the Macropolitics of Reform: New Forms of Workplace Bargaining in Hungarian Enterprises. In *Evans, P.; Rueschemeyer, D. and Stephens, E. H., eds.*, 1985, pp. 247–73. [G: Hungary]

Strahinjic, Caslav. Organizations of Associated Labor and Other Forms of Self-management Organizations in Yugoslavia. In *Damjanovic, M. and Voich, D., Jr., eds.*, 1985, pp. 95–123. [G: Yugoslavia]

Thompson, Mark. Restraint and Labour Relations: The Case of British Columbia. *Can. Public Policy*, June 1985, *11*(2), pp. 171–79. [G: Canada]

840 DEMOGRAPHIC ECONOMICS

841 Demographic Economics

8410 Demographic Economics

Adams, John W. and Kaskoff, Alice Bee. Wealth and Migration in Massachusetts and Maine: 1771–1798. *J. Econ. Hist.*, June 1985, *45*(2), pp. 363–68. [G: U.S.]

Adelman, Irma. Shadow Households and Competing Auspices: Migration Behavior in the Philippines: Discussion. *J. Devel. Econ.*, January–February 1985, *17*(1–2), pp. 27–28. [G: Philippines]

Adelman, Irma. The Influence of Rapid Rural–Urban Migration on Korean National Fertility Levels: Discussion. *J. Devel. Econ.*, January–February 1985, *17*(1–2), pp. 73–74. [G: S. Korea]

Ahmad, Alia. The Effect of Population Growth on a Peasant Economy: The Case of Bangladesh. In *Lundahl, M., ed.*, 1985, pp. 87–104. [G: Bangladesh]

Alao, Nurudeen. Urban Unemployment Equilibrium in LDCs: A Perspective. *Reg. Stud.*, June 1985, *19*(3), pp. 185–92. [G: LDCs]

Alho, Juha M. and Spencer, Bruce D. Uncertain Population Forecasting. *J. Amer. Statist. Assoc.*, June 1985, *80*(390), pp. 306–14. [G: U.S.]

Ali, Karamat. Determinants of Fertility in Developing Countries. *Pakistan Econ. Soc. Rev.*, Summer 1985, *23*(1), pp. 65–83. [G: LDCs]

Allman, James. Conjugal Unions in Rural and Urban Haiti. *Soc. Econ. Stud.*, March 1985, *34*(1), pp. 27–57. [G: Haiti]

Amrhein, Carl G. and MacKinnon, R. D. An Elementary Simulation Model of the Job Matching Process within an Interregional Setting. *Reg. Stud.*, June 1985, *19*(3), pp. 193–202.

Anderson, Barbara A. and Silver, Brian D. Demographic Consequences of World War II on the Non-Russian Nationalities of the USSR. In *Linz, S. J., ed.*, 1985, pp. 207–42. [G: U.S.S.R.]

Anderson, Barbara A. and Silver, Brian D. Estimating Census Undercount from School Enrollment Data: An Application to the Soviet Censuses of 1959 and 1970. *Demography*, May 1985, *22*(2), pp. 289–308. [G: U.S.S.R.]

Anderson, John E. Estimating Generalized Urban Density Functions. *J. Urban Econ.*, July 1985, *18*(1), pp. 1–10. [G: U.S.]

Anderton, Douglas L. and Bean, Lee L. Birth Spacing and Fertility Limitation: A Behavioral Analysis of a Nineteenth Century Frontier Population. *Demography*, May 1985, *22*(2), pp. 169–83. [G: U.S.]

Auerbach, Alan J. and Kotlikoff, Laurence J. Simulating Alternative Social Security Responses to the Demographic Transition. *Nat. Tax J.*, June 1985, *38*(2), pp. 153–68. [G: U.S.]

Bailar, Barbara A. Estimating the Population in a Census Year: 1980 and Beyond: Comment. *J. Amer. Statist. Assoc.*, March 1985, *80*(389), pp. 109–14. [G: U.S.]

Bane, Mary Jo and Welsh, James. SIPP's Potential Contributions to Policy Research on Children. *J. Econ. Soc. Meas.*, December 1985, *13*(3–4), pp. 273–79. [G: U.S.]

Bean, Frank D.; Swicegood, C. Gray and King, Allan G. Role Incompatibility and the Relationship between Fertility and Labor Supply among Hispanic Women. In *Borjas, G. J. and Tienda, M., eds.*, 1985, pp. 221–42. [G: U.S.]

de Beer, Joop. A Time Series Model for Cohort Data. *J. Amer. Statist. Assoc.*, September 1985, *80*(391), pp. 525–30. [G: Netherlands]

Behrman, Jere R. and Tarbman, Paul. Intergenerational Earnings Mobility in the United States: Some Estimates and a Test of Becker's Intergenerational Endowments Model. *Rev.*

Econ. Statist., February 1985, *67*(1), pp. 144–51. [G: U.S.]

Bell, Carolyn Shaw. SIPP and the Female Condition. *J. Econ. Soc. Meas.*, December 1985, *13*(3–4), pp. 263–71. [G: U.S.]

Beller, Andrea H. and Graham, John W. Variations in the Economic Well-Being of Divorced Women and Their Children: The Role of Child Support Income. In *David, M. and Smeeding, T., eds.*, 1985, pp. 471–506. [G: U.S.]

Ben-Porath, Yoram and Gronau, Reuben. Jewish Mother Goes to Work: Trends in the Labor Force Participation of Women in Israel, 1955–1980. *J. Lab. Econ.*, Part 2 January 1985, *3*(1), pp. S310–27. [G: Israel]

Bhagwati, Jagdish N. International Migration and Investment. In *Bhagwati, J. N. (I)*, 1985, pp. 299–302.

Bhagwati, Jagdish N. Taxation and International Migration: Recent Policy Issues. In *Bhagwati, J. N. (I)*, 1985, pp. 347–61. [G: U.S.; LDCs]

Bhattacharyya, Bharati. The Role of Family Decision in Internal Migration: The Case of India. *J. Devel. Econ.*, May–June 1985, *18*(1), pp. 51–66. [G: India]

Bierens, Herman J. and Hoever, Roy. Population Forecasting at the City Level: An Econometric Approach. *Urban Stud.*, February 1985, *22*(1), pp. 83–90. [G: U.S.]

Bilsborrow, R. E. and Winegarden, C. R. Landholding, Rural Fertility and Internal Migration in Developing Countries: Econometric Evidence from Cross-National Data. *Pakistan Devel. Rev.*, Summer 1985, *24*(2), pp. 125–49. [G: LDCs]

Birdsall, Nancy. A Population Perspective on Agricultural Development. In *Davis, T. J., ed.*, 1985, pp. 29–51. [G: Selected LDCs; Selected MDCs]

Black, Robert W. Instead of the 1986 Census: The Potential Contribution of Enhanced Electoral Registers. *J. Roy. Statist. Soc.*, 1985, *148*(4), pp. 287–306. [G: U.K.]

Bois, Guy. Against the Neo-Malthusian Orthodoxy. In *Aston, T. H. and Philpin, C. H. E., eds.*, 1985, pp. 107–18.

Bongaarts, John and Greenhalgh, Susan. An Alternative to the One-Child Policy in China. *Population Devel. Rev.*, December 1985, *11*(4), pp. 585–617. [G: China]

Booth, Anne. Accommodating a Growing Population in Javanese Agriculture. *Bull. Indonesian Econ. Stud.*, August 1985, *21*(2), pp. 115–45. [G: Indonesia]

Bose, Ashish and Narain, Vir. Population. In *Mongia, J. N., ed.*, 1985, pp. 1–24. [G: India]

Boserup, Ester. Economic and Demographic Interrelationships in Sub-Saharan Africa. *Population Devel. Rev.*, September 1985, *11*(3), pp. 383–97. [G: Sub-Saharan Africa]

Botero, Giovanni. Giovanni Botero on the Forces Governing Population Growth. *Population Devel. Rev.*, June 1985, *11*(2), pp. 335–40.

Boulding, Kenneth E. World Development Report 1984: Review Symposium: Comment.

Bowman, Mary Jean. Education, Population Trends and Technological Change. *Econ. Educ. Rev.*, 1985, *4*(1), pp. 29–44. [G: Global]

Bradbury, Katharine L. Prospects for Growth in New England: The Labor Force. *New Eng. Econ. Rev.*, Sept./Oct. 1985, pp. 50–60. [G: U.S.]

Brenner, Robert. Agrarian Class Structure and Economic Development in Pre-industrial Europe. In *Aston, T. H. and Philpin, C. H. E., eds.*, 1985, pp. 10–63.

Brenner, Robert. The Agrarian Roots of European Capitalism. In *Aston, T. H. and Philpin, C. H. E., eds.*, 1985, pp. 213–327.

Briggs, Vernon M., Jr. Employment Trends and Contemporary Immigration Policy. In *Glazer, N., ed.*, 1985, pp. 135–60. [G: U.S.]

Broome, John. The Economic Value of Life. *Economica*, August 1985, *52*(207), pp. 281–94.

Broström, Göran. Practical Aspects on the Estimation of the Parameters in Coale's Model for Marital Fertility. *Demography*, November 1985, *22*(4), pp. 625–31.

Brown, Lawrence A. and Jones, John Paul, III. Spatial Variation in Migration Processes and Development: A Costa Rican Example of Conventional Modeling Augmented by the Expansion Method. *Demography*, August 1985, *22*(3), pp. 326–52. [G: Costa Rica]

Brown, Lawrence A. and Lawson, Victoria A. Rural-destined Migration in Third World Settings: A Neglected Phenomenon? *Reg. Stud.*, October 1985, *19*(5), pp. 415–32. [G: Costa Rica]

Caces, Fe, et al. Shadow Households and Competing Auspices: Migration Behavior in the Philippines. *J. Devel. Econ.*, January–February 1985, *17*(1–2), pp. 5–25. [G: Philippines]

Cain, Mead. Errata: On the Relationship between Landholding and Fertility. *Population Stud.*, July 1985, *39*(2), pp. 192. [G: LDCs]

Cain, Mead. On the Relationship between Landholding and Fertility. *Population Stud.*, March 1985, *39*(1), pp. 5–15. [G: LDCs]

Caldwell, John C.; Reddy, P. H. and Caldwell, Pat. Educational Transition in Rural South India. *Population Devel. Rev.*, March 1985, *11*(1), pp. 29–51. [G: India]

Cameron, Samuel. Marriage and the Distribution of Employment Incomes. *Appl. Econ.*, February 1985, *17*(1), pp. 33–40.

Carlson, Elwood D. Couples without Children: Premarital Cohabitation in France. In *Davis, K., ed.*, 1985, pp. 113–30. [G: France]

Carlson, Elwood D. The Impact of International Migration upon the Timing of Marriage and Childbearing. *Demography*, February 1985, *22*(1), pp. 61–72. [G: Australia]

Castañeda, Tarsicio. Determinantes del descenso de la mortalidad infantil en Chile: 1975–1982. *Cuadernos Econ.*, August 1985, *22*(66), pp. 195–214. [G: Chile]

Charlton, Martin; Openshaw, Stan and Wymer,

Colin. Some New Classifications of Census Enumeration Districts in Britain: A Poor Man's ACORN. *J. Econ. Soc. Meas.*, April 1985, *13*(1), pp. 69–96. **[G: U.K.]**

Chernichovsky, Dov. Socioeconomic and Demographic Aspects of School Enrollment and Attendance in Rural Botswana. *Econ. Develop. Cult. Change*, January 1985, *33*(2), pp. 319–32. **[G: Botswana]**

Chiswick, Barry R. and Miller, Paul W. Immigrant Generation and Income in Australia. *Econ. Rec.*, June 1985, *61*(173), pp. 540–53. **[G: Australia]**

Chu, David K. Y. Population Growth and Related Issues. In *Wong, K. and Chu, D. K. Y., eds.*, 1985, pp. 131–39. **[G: China]**

Clark, Colin W. World Development Research 1984: Review Symposium: Review. *Population Devel. Rev.*, March 1985, *11*(1), pp. 120–26.

Clarkson, L. A. An Economic History of Ulster 1820–1939: Population Change and Urbanisation, 1821–1911. In *Kennedy, L. and Ollerenshaw, P., eds.*, 1985, pp. 137–57. **[G: U.K.]**

Clausen, A. W. Population Growth and Economic and Social Development. *J. Econ. Educ.*, Summer 1985, *16*(3), pp. 165–76.

Clogg, Clifford C. and Shockey, James W. The Effect of Changing Demographic Composition on Recent Trends in Underemployment. *Demography*, August 1985, *22*(3), pp. 395–414. **[G: U.S.]**

Coale, Ansley J. Estimating the Expectation of Life at Old Ages: Comments. *Population Stud.*, November 1985, *39*(3), pp. 507–09. **[G: Selected Countries]**

Coale, Ansley J.; John, A. Meredith and Richards, Toni. Calculation of Age-specific Fertility Schedules from Tabulations of Parity in Two Censuses. *Demography*, November 1985, *22*(4), pp. 611–23. **[G: China; Korea]**

Cohn, Raymond L. Deaths of Slaves in the Middle Passage. *J. Econ. Hist.*, September 1985, *45*(3), pp. 685–92. **[G: U.K.; France; Portugal; U.S.; Netherlands]**

Colombino, Ugo and De Stavola, Bianca. A Model of Female Labor Supply in Italy Using Cohort Data. *J. Lab. Econ.*, Part 2 January 1985, *3*(1), pp. S275–92. **[G: Italy]**

Compton, P. A. Rising Mortality in Hungary. *Population Stud.*, March 1985, *39*(1), pp. 71–86. **[G: Hungary]**

Cooper, J. P. In Search of Agrarian Capitalism. In *Aston, T. H. and Philpin, C. H. E., eds.*, 1985, pp. 138–91.

Corman, Hope and Grossman, Michael. Determinants of Neonatal Mortality Rates in the U.S.: A Reduced Form Model. *J. Health Econ.*, September 1985, *4*(3), pp. 213–36. **[G: U.S.]**

Daly, Herman E. Marx and Malthus in Northeast Brazil: A Note on the World's Largest Class Difference in Fertility and Its Recent Trends. *Population Stud.*, July 1985, *39*(2), pp. 329–38. **[G: Brazil]**

Datta, Pranati. Inter-state Migration in India.

Margin, October 1985, *18*(1), pp. 69–82. **[G: India]**

David, Martin. The Design and Development of SIPP: Introduction. *J. Econ. Soc. Meas.*, December 1985, *13*(3–4), pp. 215–24. **[G: U.S.]**

Davis, Kingsley. The Future of Marriage. In *Davis, K., ed.*, 1985, pp. 25–52. **[G: Selected Countries]**

Davis, Kingsley. The Meaning and Significance of Marriage in Contemporary Society. In *Davis, K., ed.*, 1985, pp. 1–21.

De Vos, Susan. An Old-Age Security Incentive for Children in the Philippines and Taiwan. *Econ. Develop. Cult. Change*, July 1985, *33*(4), pp. 793–814. **[G: Philippines; Taiwan]**

Demeny, Paul. Bucharest, Mexico City, and Beyond. *Population Devel. Rev.*, March 1985, *11*(1), pp. 99–106.

Denham, Chris. The 1981 Census in Retrospect. *J. Econ. Soc. Meas.*, April 1985, *13*(1), pp. 5–17. **[G: U.K.]**

Denton, Frank T. and Spencer, Byron G. Prospective Changes in Population and Their Implications for Government Expenditures. In *Courchene, T. J.; Conklin, D. W. and Cook, G. C. A., eds. Vol. 1*, 1985, pp. 44–95. **[G: Canada]**

Dholakia, Ruby Roy; Kindra, G. S. and Pangotra, Prem. Marketing of Birth Control in LDCs: With Special References to India. *Can. J. Devel. Stud.*, 1985, *6*(1), pp. 147–59. **[G: India]**

Dinkel, R. H. The Seeming Paradox of Increasing Mortality in a Highly Industralized Nation: The Example of the Soviet Union. *Population Stud.*, March 1985, *39*(1), pp. 87–97. **[G: U.S.S.R.]**

Dixon, Daryl and Foster, Chris. The Age Composition of Australian Taxpayers. *Australian Tax Forum*, Summer 1985, *2*(4), pp. 439–50. **[G: Australia]**

Dudal, R.; Higgins, G. M. and Kassam, A. H. Land, Food and Population in the Developing World. In *Davis, T. J., ed.*, 1985, pp. 5–28. **[G: LDCs]**

Duncan, Greg J. A Framework for Tracking Family Relationships over Time. *J. Econ. Soc. Meas.*, December 1985, *13*(3–4), pp. 237–43. **[G: U.S.]**

Duncan, Greg J. and Hoffman, Saul D. A Reconsideration of the Economic Consequences of Marital Dissolution. *Demography*, November 1985, *22*(4), pp. 485–97. **[G: U.S.]**

Duncan, Greg J. and Hoffman, Saul D. Economic Consequences of Marital Instability. In *David, M. and Smeeding, T., eds.*, 1985, pp. 427–67. **[G: U.S.]**

Dyson, Tim and Murphy, Mike. The Onset of Fertility Transition. *Population Devel. Rev.*, September 1985, *11*(3), pp. 399–440. **[G: LDCs; MDCs]**

Easterlin, Richard A. World Development Report 1984: Review. *Population Devel. Rev.*, March 1985, *11*(1), pp. 113–19.

Eckstein, Zvi and Wolpin, Kenneth I. Endogenous Fertility and Optimal Population Size.

J. Public Econ., June 1985, 27(1), pp. 93–106.

Edmonston, Barry; Goldberg, Michael A. and Mercer, John. Urban Form in Canada and the United States: An Examination of Urban Density Gradients. *Urban Stud.*, June 1985, 22(3), pp. 209–17. **[G: Canada; U.S.]**

Ericksen, Eugene P. and Kadane, Joseph B. Estimating the Population in a Census Year: 1980 and Beyond: Rejoinder. *J. Amer. Statist. Assoc.*, March 1985, 80(389), pp. 129–31.
[G: U.S.]

Ericksen, Eugene P. and Kadane, Joseph B. Estimating the Population in a Census Year: 1980 and Beyond. *J. Amer. Statist. Assoc.*, March 1985, 80(389), pp. 98–109. **[G: U.S.]**

Ermisch, John F. and Overton, Elizabeth. Minimal Household Units: A New Approach to the Analysis of Household Formation. *Population Stud.*, March 1985, 39(1), pp. 33–54.
[G: U.K.]

Espenshade, Thomas J. Marriage Trends in America: Estimates, Implications, and Underlying Causes. *Population Devel. Rev.*, June 1985, 11(2), pp. 193–245. **[G: U.S.]**

Espenshade, Thomas J. The Recent Decline of American Marriage: Blacks and Whites in Comparative Perspective. In *Davis, K., ed.,* 1985, pp. 53–90. **[G: U.S.]**

Espenshade, Thomas J. and Wolf, Douglas A. SIPP Data on Marriage, Separation, Divorce, and Remarriage: Problems, Opportunities, and Recommendations. *J. Econ. Soc. Meas.*, December 1985, 13(3–4), pp. 229–36. **[G: U.S.]**

Evers, Gerard H. M. and van der Veen, Anne. A Simultaneous Non-linear Model for Labour Migration and Commuting. *Reg. Stud.*, June 1985, 19(3), pp. 217–29. **[G: Netherlands]**

Farley, Reynolds. Understanding Racial Differences and Trends: How SIPP Can Assist. *J. Econ. Soc. Meas.*, December 1985, 13(3–4), pp. 245–61. **[G: U.S.]**

Fay, Robert E. Estimating the Population in a Census Year: 1980 and Beyond: Comment. *J. Amer. Statist. Assoc.*, March 1985, 80(389), pp. 114–16. **[G: U.S.]**

Fellegi, I. P. Estimating the Population in a Census Year: 1980 and Beyond: Comment. *J. Amer. Statist. Assoc.*, March 1985, 80(389), pp. 116–19. **[G: U.S.]**

Feshbach, Murray. The Age Structure of Soviet Population: Preliminary Analysis of Unpublished Data. *Soviet Econ.*, Apr.-June 1985, 1(2), pp. 177–93. **[G: U.S.S.R.]**

Finch, Janet. Work, the Family and the Home: A More Egalitarian Future? *Int. J. Soc. Econ.*, 1985, 12(2), pp. 26–35.

Finkle, Jason L. and Crane, Barbara B. Ideology and Politics at Mexico City: The United States at the 1984 International Conference on Population. *Population Devel. Rev.*, March 1985, 11(1), pp. 1–28.

Fitzpatrick, Sheila. Postwar Soviet Society: The "Return to Normalcy," 1945–1953. In *Linz, S. J., ed.,* 1985, pp. 129–56. **[G: U.S.S.R.]**

Fong, Chan-Onn. Integrated Population-Development Program Performance: The Malaysian

Felda Experience. *J. Devel. Areas,* January 1985, 19(2), pp. 149–69. **[G: Malaysia]**

Franz, Wolfgang. An Economic Analysis of Female Work Participation, Education, and Fertility: Theory and Empirical Evidence for the Federal Republic of Germany. *J. Lab. Econ.*, Part 2 January 1985, 3(1), pp. S218–34.
[G: W. Germany]

Frey, William H. Mover Destination Selectivity and the Changing Suburbanization of Metropolitan Whites and Blacks. *Demography*, May 1985, 22(2), pp. 223–43. **[G: U.S.]**

Friedlander, Dor, et al. Socio-economic Characteristics and Life Expectancies in Nineteenth-Century England: A District Analysis. *Population Stud.*, March 1985, 39(1), pp. 137–51.
[G: U.K.]

Fuchs, Lawrence H. The Search for a Sound Immigration Policy: A Personal View. In *Glazer, N., ed.,* 1985, pp. 17–48. **[G: U.S.]**

Fügedi, Eric. The Demographic Landscape of East-central Europe. In *Mączak, A.; Samsonowicz, H. and Burke, P., eds.,* 1985, pp. 47–58. **[G: E. Europe]**

Fuller, Theodore D.; Lightfoot, Paul and Kamnuansilpa, Peerasit. Rural–Urban Mobility in Thailand: A Decision-making Approach. *Demography*, November 1985, 22(4), pp. 565–79. **[G: Thailand]**

Fuller, Theodore D.; Lightfoot, Paul and Kamnuansilpa, Peerasit. Toward Migration Management: A Field Experiment in Thailand. *Econ. Develop. Cult. Change*, April 1985, 33(3), pp. 601–21. **[G: Thailand]**

Galenson, David W. Errata [Population Turnover in the British West Indies in the Late Seventeenth Century]. *J. Econ. Hist.*, September 1985, 45(3), pp. 719. **[G: Barbados]**

Galenson, David W. Population Turnover in the English West Indies in the Late Seventeenth Century: A Comparative Perspective. *J. Econ. Hist.*, June 1985, 45(2), pp. 227–35.
[G: Barbados]

Gallaway, Lowell and Vedder, Richard. Migration Efficiency Ratios and the Optimal Distribution of Population. *Growth Change*, January 1985, 16(1), pp. 3–7.

Galloway, P. R. Annual Variations in Deaths by Age, Deaths by Cause, Prices, and Weather in London 1670 to 1830. *Population Stud.*, November 1985, 39(3), pp. 487–505. **[G: U.K.]**

Gamble, Hays B. and Downing, Roger H. The Relationship between Population Growth and Real Assessed Market Values: Note. *Growth Change*, July 1985, 16(3), pp. 74–77.
[G: U.S.]

Garfinkel, Irwin. Variations in the Economic Well-Being of Divorced Women and Their Children: The Role of Child Support Income: Comment. In *David, M. and Smeeding, T., eds.,* 1985, pp. 506–09. **[G: U.S.]**

de la Garza, Rodolfo O. Mexican Americans, Mexican Immigrants, and Immigration Reform. In *Glazer, N., ed.,* 1985, pp. 93–105.
[G: U.S.]

Gaspari, K. Celeste and Woolf, Arthur G. In-

come, Public Works, and Mortality in Early Twentieth-Century American Cities. *J. Econ. Hist.*, June 1985, *45*(2), pp. 355–61.
[G: U.S.]

Ghosh, Dipak. A Lewisian Model of Dual Economy with Rural–Urban Migration. *Scot. J. Polit. Econ.*, February 1985, *32*(1), pp. 95–106.

Glazer, Nathan. Clamor at the Gates: The New American Immigration: Conclusion. In *Glazer, N., ed.*, 1985, pp. 311–15. **[G: U.S.]**

Glazer, Nathan. Clamor at the Gates: The New American Immigration: Introduction. In *Glazer, N., ed.*, 1985, pp. 3–13. **[G: U.S.]**

Glazer, Nathan. Immigrants and Education. In *Glazer, N., ed.*, 1985, pp. 213–39. **[G: U.S.]**

Gmelch, George and Gmelch, Sharon Bohn. The Cross-Channel Migration of Irish Travellers. *Econ. Soc. Rev.*, July 1985, *16*(4), pp. 287–96. **[G: Ireland; U.K.]**

Goldscheider, Frances Kobrin and DaVanzo, Julie. Living Arrangements and the Transition to Adulthood. *Demography*, November 1985, *22*(4), pp. 545–63. **[G: U.S.]**

Goldstein, Joshua S. Basic Human Needs: The Plateau Curve. *World Devel.*, May 1985, *13*(5), pp. 595–609.

Graham, John W. and Beller, Andrea H. A Note on the Number and Living Arrangements of Women with Children under 21 from an Absent Father: Revised Estimates from the April 1979 and 1982 Current Population Surveys. *J. Econ. Soc. Meas.*, July 1985, *13*(2), pp. 209–14. **[G: U.S.]**

Grant, E. Kenneth and Vanderkamp, John. Migrant Information and the Remigration Decision: Further Evidence. *Southern Econ. J.*, April 1985, *51*(4), pp. 1202–15. **[G: Canada]**

Greenwood, Michael J. Human Migration: Theory, Models, and Empirical Studies. *J. Reg. Sci.*, November 1985, *25*(4), pp. 521–44.
[G: U.S.]

Greenwood, Michael J. and McDowell, John M. U.S. Immigration Reform: Policy Issues and Economic Analysis. *Contemp. Policy Issues,* Spring, Pt. 1, 1985, *3*(3), pp. 59–75.
[G: U.S.]

Grossbard-Shechtman, Amyra. Marriage Squeezes and the Marriage Market. In *Davis, K., ed.*, 1985, pp. 375–95. **[G: U.S.]**

Gupta, Kanhaya L. Foreign Capital, Income Inequality, Demographic Pressures, Savings and Growth in Developing Countries: A Cross Country Analysis. *J. Econ. Devel.*, July 1985, *10*(1), pp. 63–88. **[G: LDCs]**

Gwatkin, Davidson R. The State of the World's Population Movement: Implications of the 1984 Mexico City Conference. *World Devel.*, April 1985, *13*(4), pp. 557–69.

Haag, G. and Weidlich, W. A Stochastic Migration Model and Its Application to Canadian Data. In *Aubin, J.-P.; Saari, D. and Sigmund, K., eds.*, 1985, pp. 177–91. **[G: Canada]**

Hadley, Garland R. Interstate Migration, Income and Public School Expenditures: An Update of an Experiment. *Public Choice*, 1985, *46*(2), pp. 207–14. **[G: U.S.]**

Haines, Michael R. Inequality and Childhood Mortality: A Comparison of England and Wales, 1911, and the United States, 1900. *J. Econ. Hist.*, December 1985, *45*(4), pp. 885–912. **[G: U.K.; U.S.]**

Hallam, H. E. Age at First Marriage and Age at Death in the Lincolnshire Fenland, 1252–1478. *Population Stud.*, March 1985, *39*(1), pp. 55–69. **[G: U.K.]**

Hamermesh, Daniel S. Expectations, Life Expectancy, and Economic Behavior. *Quart. J. Econ.*, May 1985, *100*(2), pp. 389–408.
[G: U.S.]

Hansen, Morris H. Estimating the Population in a Census Year: 1980 and Beyond: Comment. *J. Amer. Statist. Assoc.*, March 1985, *80*(389), pp. 119–22. **[G: U.S.]**

Harbert, Lloyd and Scandizzo, Pasquale L. Distribución de alimentos e intervención en la nutrición: el caso de Chile. (With English summary.) *Cuadernos Econ.*, August 1985, *22*(66), pp. 215–46. **[G: Chile]**

Hardin, Garrett. World Development Report 1984: Review Symposium: Comment. *Population Devel. Rev.*, March 1985, *11*(1), pp. 132–35.

Hartog, Joop and Theeuwes, Jules. The Emergence of the Working Wife in Holland. *J. Lab. Econ.*, Part 2 January 1985, *3*(1), pp. S235–55. **[G: Holland]**

Harwood, Edwin. How Should We Enforce Immigration Law? In *Glazer, N., ed.*, 1985, pp. 73–91. **[G: U.S.]**

Hauser, Philip M. Estimating the Population in a Census Year: 1980 and Beyond: Comment. *J. Amer. Statist. Assoc.*, March 1985, *80*(389), pp. 122–23. **[G: U.S.]**

Haynes, Stephen E.; Phillips, Llad and Votey, Harold L., Jr. An Econometric Test of Structural Change in the Demographic Transition. *Scand. J. Econ.*, 1985, *87*(3), pp. 554–67.
[G: Finland; Norway; Sweden; U.K.]

Heckman, James J.; Hotz, V. Joseph and Walker, James R. New Evidence on the Timing and Spacing of Births. *Amer. Econ. Rev.*, May 1985, *75*(2), pp. 179–84. **[G: Sweden]**

Hendershott, Patric H. and Smith, Mark. Household Formations. In *Hendershott, P. H., ed.*, 1985, pp. 183–203. **[G: U.S.]**

Henderson, J. Vernon. Population Composition of Cities: Restructuring the Tiebout Model. *J. Public Econ.*, July 1985, *27*(2), pp. 131–56.
[G: U.S.]

Hendry, Joy. Japan: Culture versus Industrialization as Determinant of Marital Patterns. In *Davis, K., ed.*, 1985, pp. 197–222. **[G: Japan; Selected Countries]**

Herberger, L. and Bretz, M. The Use of Population Censuses as Multi-subject Data Bases in the Federal Republic of Germany. *Statist. J.*, March 1985, *3*(1), pp. 115–33.
[G: W. Germany]

Hilton, R. H. A Crisis of Feudalism. In *Aston, T. H. and Philpin, C. H. E., eds.*, 1985, pp. 119–37.

Hilton, R. H. The Brenner Debate: Introduction.

In *Aston, T. H. and Philpin, C. H. E., eds.,* 1985, pp. 1–9.

Hirschman, Charles. Premarital Socioeconomic Roles and the Timing of Family Formation: A Comparative Study of Five Asian Societies. *Demography,* February 1985, 22(1), pp. 35–59.
[G: Korea; Taiwan; Sri Lanka; Indonesia; Malaysia]

Ho, Teresa J. Population Growth and Agricultural Productivity in Sub-Saharan Africa. In *Davis, T. J., ed.,* 1985, pp. 92–128. [G: Sub-Saharan Africa]

Hobcraft, J. N.; McDonald, John W. and Rutstein, S. O. Demographic Determinants of Infant and Early Child Mortality: A Comparative Analysis. *Population Stud.,* November 1985, 39(3), pp. 363–85. [G: LDCs]

Hoffman, Emily P. Fertility and Female Employment. *Quart. Rev. Econ. Bus.,* Spring 1985, 25(1), pp. 85–95. [G: U.S.]

Hogan, Dennis P. and Kertzer, David I. Migration Patterns during Italian Urbanization, 1865–1921. *Demography,* August 1985, 22(3), pp. 309–25. [G: Italy]

Huffman, Sandra L. Response to Determinants of Natural Fertility Reconsidered. *Population Stud.,* March 1985, 39(1), pp. 163–68.
[G: Bangladesh]

Hughes, Gordon and McCormick, Barry. Migration Intentions in the U.K.: Which Households Want to Migrate and Which Succeed? *Econ. J.,* Supplement 1985, 95, pp. 113–23.
[G: U.K.]

Hunt, Gary L. and Greenwood, Michael J. Econometrically Accounting for Identities and Restrictions in Models of Interregional Migration: Further Thoughts. *Reg. Sci. Urban Econ.,* November 1985, 15(4), pp. 605–14.
[G: U.S.]

Hussain, Syeda Abida. Reporting Masculinity Ratio in Pakistan: A Triumph of Anthropology and Economics over Biology: Concluding Remarks. *Pakistan Devel. Rev.,* Autumn-Winter 1985, 24(3/4), pp. 297–303. [G: Pakistan]

Isserman, Andrew M., et al. Forecasting Interstate Migration with Limited Data: A Demographic-Economic Approach. *J. Amer. Statist. Assoc.,* June 1985, 80(390), pp. 277–85.
[G: U.S.]

Jackson, Marvin R. Comparing the Balkan Demographic Experience, 1860 to 1970. *J. Europ. Econ. Hist.,* Fall 1985, 14(2), pp. 223–72.
[G: Bulgaria; Yugoslavia; Hungary; Greece; Romania]

Jäggi, Stefan. Karl Marx und die Malthusianische Bevölkerungstheorie. (Karl Marx and the Malthusian Population Theory. With English summary.) *Schweiz. Z. Volkswirtsch. Statist.,* June 1985, 121(2), pp. 95–113.

Jain, A. K. Determinants of Regional Variations in Infant Mortality in Rural India. *Population Stud.,* November 1985, 39(3), pp. 407–24.
[G: India]

James, William H. Commentary: Black and White Birth Weights. *Demography,* February 1985, 22(1), pp. 143. [G: U.S.]

Jenkins, Stephen P. The Implications of 'Stochastic' Demographic Assumptions for Models of the Distribution of Inherited Wealth. *Bull. Econ. Res.,* September 1985, 37(3), pp. 231–44.

Jensen, Eric. Desired Fertility, the "Up to God" Response, and Sample Selection Bias. *Demography,* August 1985, 22(3), pp. 445–54.
[G: Guatemala; India]

Jodha, N. S. Population Growth and the Decline of Common Property Resources in Rajasthan, India. *Population Devel. Rev.,* June 1985, 11(2), pp. 247–64. [G: India]

John, Jürgen. Economic Instability and Health: Infant Mortality and Suicide Reconsidered. In *Westcott, G.; Svensson, P.-G. and Zollner, H. F. K., eds.,* 1985, pp. 181–204.
[G: W. Germany]

Johnson, Kenneth P. and Friedenberg, Howard L. Regional and State Projections of Income, Employment, and Population to the Year 2000. *Surv. Curr. Bus.,* May 1985, 65(5), pp. 39–63. [G: U.S.]

Johnson, Nan E. and Lean, Suewen. Relative Income, Race, and Fertility. *Population Stud.,* March 1985, 39(1), pp. 99–112. [G: U.S.]

Jones, Jo Ann, et al. Nonmarital Childbearing: Divergent Legal and Social Concerns. *Population Devel. Rev.,* December 1985, 11(4), pp. 677–93. [G: U.S.]

Joshi, Heather E.; Layard, Richard and Owen, Susan J. Why Are More Women Working in Britain? *J. Lab. Econ.,* Part 2 January 1985, 3(1), pp. S147–76. [G: U.K.]

Kallgren, Joyce K. Politics, Welfare, and Change: The Single-Child Family in China. In *Perry, E. J. and Wong, C., eds.,* 1985, pp. 131–56.
[G: China]

Kannappan, Subbiah. Urban Employment and the Labor Market in Developing Nations. *Econ. Develop. Cult. Change,* July 1985, 33(4), pp. 699–730. [G: LDCs]

Kazi, Shahnaz and Sathar, Zeba A. Differences in Household Characteristics by Income Distribution in Pakistan. *Pakistan Devel. Rev.,* Autumn-Winter 1985, 24(3/4), pp. 657–67.
[G: Pakistan]

Kelley, Allen C. Population and Development: Controversy and Reconciliation. *J. Econ. Educ.,* Summer 1985, 16(3), pp. 177–88.

Keyfitz, Nathan. An East Javanese Village in 1953 and 1985: Observations on Development. *Population Devel. Rev.,* December 1985, 11(4), pp. 695–719. [G: Indonesia]

Khan, Akhtar Hasan. Literacy Transition and Female Nuptiality: Implications for Fertility in Pakistan: Comments. *Pakistan Devel. Rev.,* Autumn-Winter 1985, 24(3/4), pp. 601–03.
[G: Pakistan]

Kim, Young J. On the Dynamics of Population with Two Age Groups. *Demography,* August 1985, 22(3), pp. 455–68.

Kipnis, Baruch A. Graph Analysis of Metropolitan Residential Mobility: Methodology and Theoretical Implications. *Urban Stud.,* April 1985, 22(2), pp. 179–87. [G: Israel]

Klatzmann, Joseph. L'autosuffisance alimentaire, objectif réaliste? (Is Self-sufficiency in Food Supply a Realist Objective? With English summary.) *Écon. Soc.*, July 1985, *19*(7), pp. 47–55. [G: LDCs]

Krakover, Shaul. Spatio-Temporal Structure of Population Growth in Urban Regions: The Cases of Tel-Aviv and Haifa, Israel. *Urban Stud.*, August 1985, *22*(4), pp. 317–28. [G: Israel]

Krishnamoorthy, S. and Kulkarni, P. M. Mortality Levels and Family Fertility Goals: Comment. *Demography*, November 1985, *22*(4), pp. 633–34.

Krotki, Karol J. Differences in Household Characteristics by Income Distribution in Pakistan: Comments. *Pakistan Devel. Rev.*, Autumn-Winter 1985, *24*(3/4), pp. 668–69. [G: Pakistan]

Krotki, Karol J. Reported Masculinity Ratio in Pakistan: A Triumph of Anthropology and Economics over Biology. *Pakistan Devel. Rev.*, Autumn-Winter 1985, *24*(3/4), pp. 267–97. [G: Pakistan]

Kuper, Adam. African Marriage in an Impinging World: The Case of Southern Africa. In *Davis, K., ed.*, 1985, pp. 253–71. [G: Africa]

Kussmaul, Ann. Agrarian Change in Seventeenth-Century England: The Economic Historian as Paleontologist. *J. Econ. Hist.*, March 1985, *45*(1), pp. 1–30. [G: U.K.]

Labonne, Michel. Stratégies alimentaires: quelques principes de pratique. (Food Strategies: Some Practical Principles. With English summary.) *Écon. Soc.*, July 1085, *19*(7), pp 161–77. [G: LDCs]

Landale, Nancy S. and Guest, Avery M. Constraints, Satisfaction, and Residential Mobility: Speare's Model Reconsidered. *Demography*, May 1985, *22*(2), pp. 199–222. [G: U.S.]

Langsten, R. Determinants of Natural Fertility in Rural Bangladesh Reconsidered. *Population Stud.*, March 1985, *39*(1), pp. 153–61. [G: Bangladesh]

Laslett, Peter. Gregory King, Robert Malthus and the Origins of English Social Realism. *Population Stud.*, November 1985, *39*(3), pp. 351–62.

Lazer, William. Threats and Opportunities in the Demographic Transition. In *Mendell, J. S., ed.*, 1985, pp. 159–70. [G: U.S.]

Le Roy Ladurie, Emmanuel. Agrarian Class Structure and Economic Development in Pre-industrial Europe: A Reply. In *Aston, T. H. and Philpin, C. H. E., eds.*, 1985, pp. 101–06.

Lee, Bun Song and Farber, Stephen C. The Influence of Rapid Rural–Urban Migration on Korean National Fertility Levels. *J. Devel. Econ.*, January–February 1985, *17*(1–2), pp. 47–71. [G: Korea]

Lee, Bun Song and Pol, Louis. A Comparison of Fertility Adaptation between Mexican Immigrants to the U.S. and Internal Migrants in Mexico. *Contemp. Policy Issues*, Spring, Pt. 1, 1985, *3*(3), pp. 91–101. [G: U.S.; Mexico]

Lee, Ronald D. Inverse Projection and Back Projection: A Critical Appraisal, and Comparative Results for England, 1539 to 1871. *Population Stud.*, July 1985, *39*(2), pp. 233–48. [G: U.K.]

Lee, Ronald D. World Development Report 1984: Review Symposium: Review. *Population Devel. Rev.*, March 1985, *11*(1), pp. 127–30.

Lehrer, Evelyn L. Log-linear Probability Models: An Application to the Analysis of Timing of First Birth. *Appl. Econ.*, June 1985, *17*(3), pp. 477–89. [G: U.S.]

Lehrer, Evelyn L. and Kawasaki, Seiichi. Child Care Arrangements and Fertility: An Analysis of Two-Earner Households. *Demography*, November 1985, *22*(4), pp. 499–513. [G: U.S.]

Leibenstein, Harvey. World Development Report 1984: Review Symposium: Comment. *Population Devel. Rev.*, March 1985, *11*(1), pp. 135–37.

Leigh, J. Paul. Divorce as a Risky Prospect. *Appl. Econ.*, April 1985, *17*(2), pp. 309–20. [G: U.S.]

Leppel, Karen. Income Effects on Marriage and Household Formation: A Paradox Resolved. *Atlantic Econ. J.*, July 1985, *13*(2), pp. 89.

Levy, Victor. Cropping Pattern, Mechanization, Child Labor, and Fertility Behavior in a Farming Economy: Rural Egypt. *Econ. Develop. Cult. Change*, July 1985, *33*(4), pp. 777–91. [G: Egypt]

Lewbel, Arthur. A Unified Approach to Incorporating Demographic or Other Effects into Demand Systems. *Rev. Econ. Stud.*, January 1985, *52*(1), pp. 1–18.

Lichter, Daniel T. Racial Concentration and Segregation across U.S. Counties, 1950–1980. *Demography*, November 1985, *22*(4), pp. 603–09. [G: U.S.]

Light, Ivan. Immigrant Entrepreneurs in America: Koreans in Los Angeles. In *Glazer, N., ed.*, 1985, pp. 161–78. [G: U.S.]

Lin, Chung-cheng and Chu, Yun-peng. Further Evidence of Cohort Size Effects on Earnings: The Case of Taiwan. *J. Econ. Devel.*, December 1985, *10*(2), pp. 101–21. [G: Taiwan]

Listgengurt, F. and Portianskii, I. The Large City under Conditions of Transition to an Intensive Economy. *Prob. Econ.*, November 1985, *28*(7), pp. 84–98. [G: U.S.S.R.]

Long, John F. Migration and the Phases of Population Redistribution. *J. Devel. Econ.*, January–February 1985, *17*(1–2), pp. 29–42.

Lucas, Robert E. B. Migration amongst the Botswana. *Econ. J.*, June 1985, *95*(378), pp. 358–82. [G: Botswana]

Lucas, Robert E. B. and Stark, Oded. Motivations to Remit: Evidence from Botswana. *J. Polit. Econ.*, October 1985, *93*(5), pp. 901–18. [G: Botswana]

Macauley, Molly K. Estimation and Recent Behavior of Urban Population and Employment Density Gradients. *J. Urban Econ.*, September 1985, *18*(2), pp. 251–60. [G: U.S.]

Madhavan, M. C. Indian Emigrants: Numbers, Characteristics, and Economic Impact. *Popula-*

tion Devel. Rev., September 1985, *11*(3), pp. 457–81. [G: India]

Mahmood, Naushin and Khan, Zubeda. Literacy Transition and Female Nuptiality: Implications for Fertility in Pakistan. *Pakistan Devel. Rev.*, Autumn-Winter 1985, *24*(3/4), pp. 589–600. [G: Pakistan]

Manson, Donald M.; Espenshade, Thomas J. and Muller, Thomas. Mexican Immigration to Southern California: Issues of Job Competition and Worker Mobility. *Rev. Reg. Stud.*, Spring 1985, *15*(2), pp. 21–33. [G: U.S.; Mexico]

Masters, R. J. The Scottish Experience in 1981: A Guide to the Future? *J. Econ. Soc. Meas.*, April 1985, *13*(1), pp. 19–28. [G: U.K.]

Matthiessen, Poul Christian. Befolkningsudviklingen, samfundsstruktukren og den offentlige sektor. (Economic and Social Implications of the Decline of Fertility in Denmark. With English summary.) *Nationaløkon. Tidsskr.*, 1985, *123*(3), pp. 281–97. [G: Denmark]

McDonald, John F. and South, David W. A Comparison of Two Methods to Project Regional and State Populations for the U.S. *Ann. Reg. Sci.*, November 1985, *19*(3), pp. 40–53. [G: U.S.]

McElroy, Marjorie B. The Joint Determination of Household Membership and Market Work: The Case of Young Men. *J. Lab. Econ.*, July 1985, *3*(3), pp. 293–316.

Menken, Jane. Age and Fertility: How Late Can You Wait? *Demography*, November 1985, *22*(4), pp. 469–83. [G: U.S.]

Mercer, A. J. Smallpox and Epidemiological–Demographic Change in Europe: The Role of Vaccination. *Population Stud.*, July 1985, *39*(2), pp. 287–307. [G: OECD]

Merrick, Thomas W. The Effect of Piped Water on Early Childhood Mortality in Urban Brazil, 1970 to 1976. *Demography*, February 1985, *22*(1), pp. 1–24. [G: Brazil]

Meyer, Judith W. and Speare, Alden, Jr. Distinctively Elderly Mobility: Types and Determinants. *Econ. Geogr.*, January 1985, *61*(1), pp. 79–88. [G: U.S.]

Michael, Robert T. and Tuma, Nancy Brandon. Entry into Marriage and Parenthood by Young Men and Women: The Influence of Family Background. *Demography*, November 1985, *22*(4), pp. 515–44. [G: U.S.]

Miller, Harris N. "The Right Thing to Do": A History of Simpson–Mazzoli. In *Glazer, N., ed.*, 1985, pp. 49–71. [G: U.S.]

Milne, William J. and Foot, David K. Econometrically Accounting for Identities and Restrictions in Models of Interregional Migration: A Comment. *Reg. Sci. Urban Econ.*, November 1985, *15*(4), pp. 599–603. [G: U.S.]

Mincer, Jacob. Intercountry Comparisons of Labor Force Trends and of Related Developments: An Overview. *J. Lab. Econ.*, Part 2 January 1985, *3*(1), pp. S1–32. [G: Selected Countries]

Mincer, Jacob. Migration and the Phases of Population Redistribution: Discussion. *J. Devel.*

Econ., January–February 1985, *17*(1–2), pp. 43–45.

Miranda, Armindo. Population Policies and Programmes. In *Jerve, A. M., ed.*, 1985, pp. 311–19. [G: Pakistan]

Mitra, S. On Estimating the Expectation of Life at Old Ages: Reply. *Population Stud.*, November 1985, *39*(3), pp. 511–12. [G: Selected Countries]

Modell, John. Historical Reflections on American Marriage. In *Davis, K., ed.*, 1985, pp. 181–96. [G: U.S.]

Mohan, Rakesh. Urbanization in India's Future. *Population Devel. Rev.*, December 1985, *11*(4), pp. 619–45. [G: India]

Moynihan, Daniel Patrick. We Can't Avoid Family Policy Much Longer. *Challenge*, Sept./Oct. 1985, *28*(4), pp. 9–17. [G: U.S.]

Muller, Thomas. Economic Effects of Immigration. In *Glazer, N., ed.*, 1985, pp. 109–33. [G: U.S.]

Murphy, Mike. Demographic and Socio-economic Influences on Recent British Marital Breakdown Patterns. *Population Stud.*, November 1985, *39*(3), pp. 441–60. [G: U.K.]

Nair, P. S. Estimation of Period-Specific Gross Migration Flows from Limited Data: Bi-proportional Adjustment Approach. *Demography*, February 1985, *22*(1), pp. 133–42. [G: India]

Nath, V. Urbanization. In *Mongia, J. N., ed.*, 1985, pp. 585–615. [G: India]

Nerlove, Marc; Razin, Assaf and Sadka, Efraim. Population Size: Individual Choice and Social Optima. *Quart. J. Econ.*, May 1985, *100*(2), pp. 321–34.

Nerlove, Marc; Razin, Assaf and Sadka, Efraim. 'The Old Age Security Hypothesis' Reconsidered. *J. Devel. Econ.*, August 1985, *18*(2–3), pp. 243–52. [G: LDCs]

Nguiagain, Titus. Trends and Patterns of Internal Migration in the Philippines, 1970–80. *Philippine Econ. J.*, 1985, *24*(4), pp. 234–62. [G: Philippines]

Nistal-Moret, Benjamín. Problems in the Social Structure of Slavery in Puerto Rico during the Process of Abolition, 1872. In *Moreno Fraginals, M.; Moya Pons, F. and Engerman, S. L., eds.*, 1985, pp. 141–57. [G: Puerto Rico]

Norris, Peter and Jones, Kelvyn. Planning Applications of Area Classification: Some Examples from Hampshire. *J. Econ. Soc. Meas.*, April 1985, *13*(1), pp. 97–111. [G: U.K.]

Nugent, Jeffrey B. The Old-Age Security Motive for Fertility. *Population Devel. Rev.*, March 1985, *11*(1), pp. 75–97.

O'Loughlin, John. The Geographic Distribution of Foreigners in West Germany. *Reg. Stud.*, August 1985, *19*(4), pp. 365–77. [G: W. Germany]

Ofer, Gur and Vinokur, Aaron. Work and Family Roles of Soviet Women: Historical Trends and Cross-Section Analysis. *J. Lab. Econ.*, Part 2 January 1985, *3*(1), pp. S328–54. [G: U.S.S.R.]

Olsen, Randall J. and Farkas, George. Conception Intervals and the Substitution of Fertility over Time. *J. Econometrics*, April 1985, *28*(1), pp. 103–12. [G: U.S.]

Osterfeld, David. Resources, People, and the Neomalthusian Fallacy. *Cato J.*, Spring/Summer 1985, *5*(1), pp. 67–102. [G: Global]

Pamuk, Elsie R. Social Class Inequality in Mortality from 1921 to 1972 in England and Wales. *Population Stud.*, March 1985, *39*(1), pp. 17–31. [G: U.K.]

Parillón, Cutberto, et al. Clasificación funcional de la desnutrición en Panamá. (With English summary.) *Cuadernos Econ.*, August 1985, *22*(66), pp. 307–27. [G: Panama]

Parr, John B. A Population-Density Approach to Regional Spatial Structure. *Urban Stud.*, August 1985, *22*(4), pp. 289–303. [G: U.S.; U.K.]

Parr, John B. The Form of the Regional Density Function. *Reg. Stud.*, October 1985, *19*(6), pp. 535–46. [G: U.K.; U.S.; Canada]

Passel, Jeffrey S. Estimating the Population in a Census Year: 1980 and Beyond: Comment. *J. Amer. Statist. Assoc.*, March 1985, *80*(389), pp. 123–24. [G: U.S.]

Paul, Satya. On the Estimation of Continuous Equivalent Adult Scales. *Indian Econ. Rev.*, Jan.-June 1985, *20*(1), pp. 117–42. [G: India]

Pearce, James E. and Gunther, Jeffrey W. Illegal Immigration from Mexico: Effects on the Texas Economy. *Fed. Res. Bank Dallas Econ. Rev.*, September 1985, pp. 1–14. [G: U.S.]

Pebley, Anne R., et al. Intra-uterine Mortality and Maternal Nutritional Status in Rural Bangladesh. *Population Stud.*, November 1985, *30*(3), pp. 125–40. [G: Bangladesh]

Peraita de Grado, Carlos. Análisis microeconómico de los determinantes del tamaño de la familia en Tenerife. (With English summary.) *Revista Española Econ.*, 1985, *2*(2), pp. 321–32. [G: Spain]

Peres, Yochanan and Pasternack, Rachel. The Importance of Marriage for Socialization: A Comparison of Achievements and Social Adjustment between Offspring of One- and Two-Parent Families in Israel. In *Davis, K., ed.*, 1985, pp. 157–78. [G: Israel]

Petersen, Jørn Henrik. Alderspensionering, befolkningsudvikling og omfordeling mellem generationerne. (Old-age Pension, Fertility Behavior and Intergenerational Redistribution. With English summary.) *Nationaløkon. Tidsskr.*, 1985, *123*(3), pp. 298–318. [G: Denmark]

Pickering, Donald C. Population and Food and Population Change and Development: Chairman's Comments. In *Davis, T. J., ed.*, 1985, pp. 52–54.

Pison, G. and Langaney, A. The Level and Age Pattern of Mortality in Bandafassi (Eastern Senegal): Results from a Small-Scale and Intensive Multi-round Survey. *Population Stud.*, November 1985, *39*(3), pp. 387–405. [G: Senegal]

Pitchford, J. D. External Effects of Population Growth. *Oxford Econ. Pap.*, June 1985, *37*(2), pp. 264–81.

Pollak, Robert A. A Transaction Cost Approach to Families and Households. *J. Econ. Lit.*, June 1985, *23*(2), pp. 581–608.

Poos, L. R. The Rural Population of Essex in the Later Middle Ages. *Econ. Hist. Rev., 2nd Ser.*, November 1985, *38*(4), pp. 515–30. [G: U.K.]

Postan, M. M. and Hatcher, John. Population and Class Relations in Feudal Society. In *Aston, T. H. and Philpin, C. H. E., eds.*, 1985, pp. 64–78.

Poston, Dudley L., Jr., et al. Modernization and Childlessness in the States of Mexico. *Econ. Develop. Cult. Change*, April 1985, *33*(3), pp. 503–19. [G: Mexico]

Pressat, Roland. Historical Perspectives on the Population of the Soviet Union. *Population Devel. Rev.*, June 1985, *11*(2), pp. 315–34. [G: U.S.S.R.]

Preston, Samuel H. Estimating the Population in a Census Year: 1980 and Beyond: Comment. *J. Amer. Statist. Assoc.*, March 1985, *80*(389), pp. 124–25. [G: U.S.]

Ray, Ranjan. Prices, Children and Inequality: Further Evidence for the United Kingdom, 1965–82. *Econ. J.*, December 1985, *95*(380), pp. 1069–77. [G: U.K.]

Repetto, Robert. Population Policy after Mexico City: Reality vs. Ideology. *Challenge*, July/August 1985, *28*(3), pp. 41–46. [G: U.S.]

Retherford, R. D. A Theory of Marital Fertility Transition. *Population Stud.*, July 1985, *39*(2), pp. 249–68.

Reynolds, Clark W. and McCleery, Robert K. Modeling U.S.—Mexico Economic Linkages. *Amer. Econ. Rev.*, May 1985, *75*(2), pp. 217–22. [G: U.S.; Mexico]

Rhind, David. Successors to the Census of Population. *J. Econ. Soc. Meas.*, April 1985, *13*(1), pp. 29–38. [G: U.K.]

Richter, Kerry. Nonmetropolitan Growth in the Late 1970s: The End of the Turnaround? *Demography*, May 1985, *22*(2), pp. 245–63. [G: U.S.]

Rickson, R. E.; Parlange, J.-Y. and Guilfoyle, M. J. Mortality Levels and Family Fertility Goals: A Reply. *Demography*, November 1985, *22*(4), pp. 635–37.

Ritschl, Albrecht. On the Stability of the Steady State When Population Is Decreasing. *Z. Nationalökon.*, 1985, *45*(2), pp. 161–70.

Robins, Philip K. and Dickinson, Katherine P. Child Support and Welfare Dependence: A Multinomial Logit Analysis. *Demography*, August 1985, *22*(3), pp. 367–80. [G: U.S.]

Rogers, Rosemarie. Migration Theory and Practice. In *Connor, W., ed.*, 1985, pp. 161–204. [G: Mexico; U.S.; Selected Countries]

Rolph, John E. Estimating the Population in a Census Year: 1980 and Beyond: Comment. *J. Amer. Statist. Assoc.*, March 1985, *80*(389), pp. 125–26. [G: U.S.]

Rose, Peter I. Asian Americans: From Pariahs to Paragons. In *Glazer, N., ed.*, 1985, pp. 181–212. [G: U.S.]

Rosenzweig, Mark R. and Schultz, T. Paul. The

Demand for and Supply of Births: Fertility and Its Life Cycle Consequences. *Amer. Econ. Rev.*, December 1985, 75(5), pp. 992–1015. [G: U.S.]

Ryder, N. B. The Structure of Pregnancy Intervals by Planning Status. *Population Stud.*, July 1985, 39(2), pp. 193–211. [G: U.S.]

Samuelson, Paul A. Modes of Thought in Economics and Biology. *Amer. Econ. Rev.*, May 1985, 75(2), pp. 166–72.

Sandefur, Gary D. Variations in Interstate Migration of Men across the Early Stages of the Life Cycle. *Demography*, August 1985, 22(3), pp. 353–66. [G: U.S.]

Sander, William. Women, Work, and Divorce. *Amer. Econ. Rev.*, June 1985, 75(3), pp. 519–23. [G: U.S.]

Sawhill, Isabel V. Economic Consequences of Marital Instability: Comment. In *David, M. and Smeeding, T.*, eds., 1985, pp. 467–70. [G: U.S.]

Schapiro, Morton Owen. A General Dynamic Model of 19th Century U.S. Population Change. *Econ. Modelling*, October 1985, 2(4), pp. 347–56. [G: U.S.]

Schoen, Robert, et al. Marriage and Divorce in Twentieth Century American Cohorts. *Demography*, February 1985, 22(1), pp. 101–14. [G: U.S.]

Schuck, Peter H. Immigration Law and the Problem of Community. In *Glazer, N., ed.*, 1985, pp. 285–307. [G: U.S.]

Schultz, T. Paul. Changing World Prices, Women's Wages, and the Fertility Transition: Sweden, 1860–1910. *J. Polit. Econ.*, December 1985, 93(6), pp. 1126–54. [G: Sweden]

Seccareccia, Mario S. Immigration and Business Cycles: Pauper Migration to Canada, 1815–1874. In *[Spry, I. M.]*, 1985, pp. 117–38. [G: Canada]

Sedransk, J. Estimating the Population in a Census Year: 1980 and Beyond: Comment. *J. Amer. Statist. Assoc.*, March 1985, 80(389), pp. 126–27. [G: U.S.]

Seiver, Daniel A. Trend and Variation in the Seasonality of U.S. Fertility, 1947–1976. *Demography*, February 1985, 22(1), pp. 89–100. [G: U.S.]

Selwyn, Percy. Costs and Benefits of a Modest Proposal. *World Devel.*, May 1985, 13(5), pp. 653–58. [G: Ireland]

Shefer, Daniel and Primo, Niki. The Determinants of Household Migration into and out of Distressed Neighborhoods. *Urban Stud.*, August 1985, 22(4), pp. 339–47. [G: Israel]

Shimada, Haruo and Higuchi, Yoshio. An Analysis of Trends in Female Labor Force Participation in Japan. *J. Lab. Econ.*, Part 2 January 1985, 3(1), pp. S355–74. [G: Japan]

Sibley, David. Travelling People in England: Regional Comparisons. *Reg. Stud.*, April 1985, 19(2), pp. 139–47. [G: U.K.]

Siddiqui, Khalil A. Fertility Preferences and Contraceptive Use in Pakistan: Comments. *Paki-*

stan Devel. Rev., Autumn-Winter 1985, 24(3/4), pp. 617–18. [G: Pakistan]

Sidorova, M. Reducing Differences in the Living Standards of the Urban and Rural Population. *Prob. Econ.*, September 1985, 28(5), pp. 32–47. [G: U.S.S.R.]

Simon, Julian L. The War on People. *Challenge*, March/April 1985, 28(1), pp. 50–53.

Simon, Julian L. and Steinmann, Gunter. On the Optimum Theoretical Rate of Population Growth. *Jahr. Nationalökon. Statist.*, September 1985, 200(5), pp. 508–31.

Singh, Susheela; Casterline, B. and Cleland, J. G. The Proximate Determinants of Fertility: Sub-national Variations. *Population Stud.*, March 1985, 39(1), pp. 113–35. [G: LDCs]

Skerry, Peter. The Ambiguity of Mexican American Politics. In *Glazer, N., ed.*, 1985, pp. 241–57. [G: U.S.]

Smith, James E. A Familistic Religion in a Modern Society. In *Davis, K., ed.*, 1985, pp. 273–98. [G: U.S.]

Smith, James P. and Ward, Michael P. Time-Series Growth in the Female Labor Force. *J. Lab. Econ.*, Part 2 January 1985, 3(1), pp. S59–90. [G: U.S.]

Smith, Stanley K. and Fishkind, Henry H. Elderly Migration into Rapidly Growing Areas: A Time Series Approach. *Rev. Reg. Stud.*, Spring 1985, 15(2), pp. 11–20. [G: U.S.]

Soomro, Ghulam Yasin and Farooqui, M. Naseem Iqbal. Fertility Preferences and Contraceptive Use in Pakistan. *Pakistan Devel. Rev.*, Autumn-Winter 1985, 24(3/4), pp. 605–16. [G: Pakistan]

Spanier, Graham B. Cohabitation in the 1980s: Recent Changes in the United States. In *Davis, K., ed.*, 1985, pp. 91–111. [G: U.S.]

Stanfield, Jacqueline B. Research on Wife/Mother Role Strain in Dual Career Families: Its Present State Has Laid an Adequate Basis for Representative Empirical Studies. *Amer. J. Econ. Soc.*, July 1985, 44(3), pp. 355–63. [G: U.S.]

Stark, Oded and Bloom, David E. The New Economics of Labor Migration. *Amer. Econ. Rev.*, May 1985, 75(2), pp. 173–78.

Staroverov, O. V. Surveys and Aggregation in Markov Models. *Matekon*, Summer 1985, 21(4), pp. 79–103. [G: U.S.S.R.]

Stott, Richard. British Immigrants and the American "Work Ethic" in the Mid-Nineteenth Century. *Labor Hist.*, Winter 1985, 26(1), pp. 86–102. [G: U.S.; U.K.]

Stycos, J. Mayone; Sayed, Hussein Abdel-Aziz and Avery, Roger. An Evaluation of the Population and Development Program in Egypt. *Demography*, August 1985, 22(3), pp. 431–43. [G: Egypt]

Tabuchi, Takatoshi. Time-Series Modeling of Gross Migration and Dynamic Equilibrium. *J. Reg. Sci.*, February 1985, 25(1), pp. 65–83. [G: U.S.; Japan]

Tarascio, Vincent J. Keynes, Population, and Equity Prices. *J. Post Keynesian Econ.*, Spring 1985, 7(3), pp. 303–10. [G: U.S.]

Tayman, Jeff and Schafer, Edward. The Impact of Coefficient Drift and Measurement Error on the Accuracy of Ratio-Correlation Population Estimates. *Rev. Reg. Stud.*, Spring 1985, 15(2), pp. 3–10. [G: U.S.]

Teitelbaum, Michael S. Forced Migration: The Tragedy of Mass Expulsions. In *Glazer, N., ed.*, 1985, pp. 261–83. [G: Vietnam; Uganda; Cuba; Israel]

Tienda, Marta and Glass, Jennifer. Household Structure and Labor Force Participation of Black, Hispanic, and White Mothers. *Demography*, August 1985, 22(3), pp. 381–94. [G: U.S.]

Tinbergen, Jan. World Development Report 1984: Review Symposium: Comment. *Population Devel. Rev.*, March 1985, 11(1), pp. 137–38.

Torche, Arístides. Una evaluación económica del Programa Nacional de Alimentación Complementaria (PNAC). (With English summary.) *Cuadernos Econ.*, August 1985, 22(66), pp. 175–93. [G: Chile]

Trussell, James and Wilson, C. Sterility in a Population with Natural Fertility. *Population Stud.*, July 1985, 39(2), pp. 269–86. [G: U.K.]

Trussell, James, et al. Determinants of Birth-Interval Length in the Philippines, Malaysia, and Indonesia: A Hazard-Model Analysis. *Demography*, May 1985, 22(2), pp. 145–68. [G: Philippines; Malaysia; Indonesia]

Tukey, John W. Estimating the Population in a Census Year: 1980 and Beyond: Comment. *J. Amer. Statist. Assoc.*, March 1985, 80(389), pp. 127–28. [G: U.S.]

Turek, Joseph H. The Northeast in a National Context: Background Trends in Population, Income, and Employment. In *Richardson, H. W. and Turek, J. H., eds.*, 1985, pp. 28–65. [G: U.S.]

Upp, Melinda. Demographic and Socioeconomic Aspects of Aging. *Soc. Sec. Bull.*, May 1985, 48(5), pp. 46–47. [G: U.S.]

Urban, Jan. Population Trends and Employment in the European CMEA Countries. *Czech. Econ. Digest.*, June 1985, (4), pp. 42–51. [G: CMEA]

Vining, Daniel R. The Growth of Core Urban Regions in Developing Countries. *Population Devel. Rev.*, September 1985, 11(3), pp. 495–514. [G: LDCs; MDCs]

Wadycki, Walter J. Single-Place Alternative Opportunities in an Economic Model of Migration. *Ann. Reg. Sci.*, July 1985, 19(2), pp. 10–16. [G: U.S.]

van de Walle, Dominique. Population Growth and Poverty: Another Look at the Indian Time Series Data. *J. Devel. Stud.*, April 1985, 21(3), pp. 429–39. [G: India]

Watkins, Susan Cotts and Menken, Jane. Famines in Historical Perspective. *Population Devel. Rev.*, December 1985, 11(4), pp. 647–75. [G: Bangladesh]

Watts, Harold W. The Scientific Potential of SIPP

for Analysis of Living Arrangements for Families and Households. *J. Econ. Soc. Meas.*, December 1985, 13(3–4), pp. 225–27. [G: U.S.]

Weiner, Myron. On International Migration and International Relations. *Population Devel. Rev.*, September 1985, 11(3), pp. 441–55.

Weiss, Yoram and Willis, Robert J. Children as Collective Goods and Divorce Settlements. *J. Lab. Econ.*, July 1985, 3(3), pp. 268–92.

Wenig, Alois. Übervölkerung—eine Kriegsursache? Einige Anmerkungen zur Bevölkerungslehre von Thomas Robert Malthus. (Overpopulation—A Cause for War? With English summary.) *Kyklos*, 1985, 38(3), pp. 365–91. [G: Europe]

Wilcox-Gök, Virginia L. Mother's Education, Health Practices and Children's Health Needs: A Variance Components Model. *Rev. Econ. Statist.*, November 1985, 67(4), pp. 706–10. [G: U.S.]

Willcox, Walter. Walter Willcox on the Expansion of Europe and Its Influence on Population. *Population Devel. Rev.*, September 1985, 11(3), pp. 515–27. [G: Europe]

Williamson, Jeffrey G. The Historical Content of the Classical Labor Surplus Model. *Population Devel. Rev.*, June 1985, 11(2), pp. 171–91. [G: U.K.]

Wolf, Margery. Marriage, Family, and the State in Contemporary China. In *Davis, K., ed.*, 1985, pp. 223–51. [G: China]

Wolfson, Margaret. Population and Poverty in Sub-Saharan Africa. In *Rose, T., ed.*, 1985, pp. 94–103. [G: Sub-Saharan Africa]

Wong, George Y. and Mason, William M. The Hierarchical Logistic Regression Model for Multilevel Analysis. *J. Amer. Statist. Assoc.*, September 1985, 80(391), pp. 513–24. [G: LDCs]

Woodbury, Stephen A. The Dilemma of American Immigration: A Review Article. *J. Human Res.*, Winter 1985, 20(1), pp. 138–41. [G: U.S.]

Woods, Robert. The Effects of Population Redistribution on the Level of Mortality in Nineteenth-Century England and Wales. *J. Econ. Hist.*, September 1985, 45(3), pp. 645–51. [G: U.K.]

Yamada, Tadashi. Causal Relationships between Infant Mortality and Fertility in Developed and Less Developed Countries. *Southern Econ. J.*, October 1985, 52(2), pp. 364–70. [G: LDCs; MDCs]

Yamaguchi, Mitoshi. Interrelationships between Population and Economic Growth. *Kobe Univ. Econ.*, 1985, (31), pp. 15–32.

Yotopoulos, Pan A. Middle-Income Classes and Food Crises: The "New" Food–Feed Competition. *Econ. Develop. Cult. Change*, April 1985, 33(3), pp. 463–83. [G: Global]

Zeng, Yi; Vaupel, James W. and Yashin, Anatoli I. Marriage and Fertility in China: A Graphical Analysis. *Population Devel. Rev.*, December 1985, 11(4), pp. 721–36. [G: China]

Zylberberg, André. Migration Equilibrium with Price Rigidity: The Harris and Todaro Model

Revisited. *J. Econ. Theory*, December 1985, 37(2), pp. 281–309.

850 HUMAN CAPITAL; VALUE OF HUMAN LIFE

851 Human Capital; Value of Human Life

8510 Human Capital; Value of Human Life

Ali, M. Shaukat. Contribution of Education towards Labor Productivity: A Cross-Country Study. *Pakistan Econ. Soc. Rev.*, Summer 1985, 23(1), pp. 41–54.

Alter, George C. and Becker, William E. Estimating Lost Future Earnings Using the New Worklife Tables. *Mon. Lab. Rev.*, February 1985, 108(2), pp. 39–42. [G: U.S.]

Balassa, Bela. Public Finance and Social Policy—Explanation of Trends and Developments: The Case of Developing Countries. In *Terny, G. and Culyer, A. J.*, eds., 1985, pp. 41–58. [G: LDCs]

Bates, Timothy. Entrepreneur Human Capital Endowments and Minority Business Viability. *J. Human Res.*, Fall 1985, 20(4), pp. 540–54. [G: U.S.]

Becker, Gary S. Human Capital, Effort, and the Sexual Division of Labor. *J. Lab. Econ.*, Part 2 January 1985, 3(1), pp. S33–58. [G: U.S.]

Behrman, Jere R. and Birdsall, Nancy. The Quality of Schooling: Reply. *Amer. Econ. Rev.*, December 1985, 75(5), pp. 1202–05. [G: Brazil]

Behrman, Jere R. and Tarbman, Paul. Intergenerational Earnings Mobility in the United States: Some Estimates and a Test of Becker's Intergenerational Endowments Model. *Rev. Econ. Statist.*, February 1985, 67(1), pp. 144–51. [G: U.S.]

Behrman, Jere R.; Wolfe, Barbara L. and Blau, David M. Human Capital and Earnings Distribution in a Developing Country: The Case of Prerevolutionary Nicaragua. *Econ. Develop. Cult. Change*, October 1985, 34(1), pp. 1–29. [G: Nicaragua]

Berger, Mark C. and Hirsch, Barry T. Veteran Status as a Screening Device during the Vietnam Era. *Soc. Sci. Quart.*, March 1985, 66(1), pp. 79–89. [G: U.S.]

Bhagwati, Jagdish N. Education, Class Structure and Income Equality. In *Bhagwati, J. N. (II)*, 1985, pp. 170–204. [G: India]

Bhagwati, Jagdish N. and Bharadwaj, Ranganath N. Human Capital and the Pattern of Foreign Trade: The Indian Case. In *Bhagwati, J. N. (II)*, 1985, pp. 104–34. [G: India]

Blakemore, Arthur E. and Low, Stuart A. Public Expenditures on Higher Education and Their Impact on Enrollment Patterns. *Appl. Econ.*, April 1985, 17(2), pp. 331–40. [G: U.S.]

Blau, Francine D. and Kahn, Lawrence M. On Estimating Discrimination in the Economy: Comment. *Southern Econ. J.*, April 1985, 51(4), pp. 1221–26. [G: U.S.]

Blaug, Mark. Where Are We Now in the Economics of Education? *Econ. Educ. Rev.*, 1985, 4(1), pp. 17–28.

Blomqvist, Ake G. Unemployment of the Educated and Emigration of Post-Secondary Graduates from the LDCs. *Pakistan Devel. Rev.*, Autumn-Winter 1985, 24(3/4), pp. 643–54. [G: LDCs]

Boissiere, M.; Knight, J. B. and Sabot, R. H. Earnings, Schooling, Ability, and Cognitive Skills. *Amer. Econ. Rev.*, December 1985, 75(5), pp. 1016–30. [G: Kenya; Tanzania]

Booton, Lavonne A. and Lane, Julia. Hospital Market Structure and the Return to Nursing Education. *J. Human Res.*, Spring 1985, 20(2), pp. 184–96. [G: U.S.]

Bowman, Mary Jean. Education, Population Trends and Technological Change. *Econ. Educ. Rev.*, 1985, 4(1), pp. 29–44. [G: Global]

Broady, Donald. Work and Education. In *Gustavsson, B.; Karlsson, J. C. and Raftegard, C.*, 1985, pp. 151–57.

Broder, Josef M. and Deprey, Rodney P. Monetary Returns to Bachelors and Masters Degrees in Agricultural Economics. *Amer. J. Agr. Econ.*, August 1985, 67(3), pp. 666–73. [G: U.S.]

Bronfenbrenner, Martin. An Essay on Negative Screening. In *Shishido, T. and Sato, R.*, eds., 1985, pp. 188–98. [G: Japan]

Buatsi, Seth N.; Pradhan, Suresh and Apasu, Yao. Human Resources, Managerial Perceptions, and the Global Marketing Behavior of Firms. In *Kaynak, E.*, ed. (I), 1985, pp. 183–96. [G: U.K.]

Carnoy, Martin. Education and the Changing American Workplace. In *Gustavsson, B.; Karlsson, J. C. and Raftegard, C.*, 1985, pp. 159–70. [G: U.S.]

Carvajal, Manuel J. and Geithman, David T. Income, Human Capital and Sex Discrimination: Some Evidence from Costa Rica, 1963 and 1973. *J. Econ. Devel.*, July 1985, 10(1), pp. 89–115. [G: Costa Rica]

Chapman, Bruce J. and Harding, J. Ross. Sex Differences in Earnings: An Analysis of Malaysian Wage Data. *J. Devel. Stud.*, April 1985, 21(3), pp. 362–76. [G: Malaysia]

Chiswick, Carmel U. The Elasticity of Substitution Revisited: The Effects of Secular Changes in Labor Force Structure. *J. Lab. Econ.*, October 1985, 3(4), pp. 490–507. [G: U.S.]

Chowdhury, Gopa and Nickell, Stephen. Hourly Earnings in the United States: Another Look at Unionization, Schooling, Sickness, and Unemployment Using PSID Data. *J. Lab. Econ.*, Part 1 January 1985, 3(1), pp. 38–69. [G: U.S.]

Cohen, Suleiman I. Rates of Returns to Education and the Determinants of Earnings in Pakistan: Comments. *Pakistan Devel. Rev.*, Autumn-Winter 1985, 24(3/4), pp. 681–83. [G: Pakistan]

Collier, Paul and Knight, J. B. Seniority Payments, Quit Rates, and Internal Labour Markets in Britain and Japan. *Oxford Bull. Econ. Statist.*, February 1985, 47(1), pp. 19–32. [G: U.K.; Japan]

Congdon, Peter. Heterogeneity and Timing Effects in Occupational Mobility: A General Model. *Oxford Bull. Econ. Statist.*, November 1985, *47*(4), pp. 347–69. **[G: Ireland]**

Darity, William A., Jr. and Williams, Rhonda M. Peddlers Forever? Culture, Competition, and Discrimination. *Amer. Econ. Rev.*, May 1985, *75*(2), pp. 256–61. **[G: U.S.]**

Datta, Ramesh C. Schooling, Experience and Earnings: An Empirical Analysis. *Margin*, January 1985, *17*(2), pp. 60–73. **[G: India]**

Deger, Saadet. Human Resources, Government Education Expenditure, and the Military Burden in Less Developed Countries. *J. Devel. Areas*, October 1985, *20*(1), pp. 37–48. **[G: LDCs]**

Dickens, William T. and Lang, Kevin. A Test of Dual Labor Market Theory. *Amer. Econ. Rev.*, September 1985, *75*(4), pp. 792–805. **[G: U.S.]**

Dillingham, Alan E. The Influence of Risk Variable Definition on Value-of-Life Estimates. *Econ. Inquiry*, April 1985, *23*(2), pp. 277–94. **[G: U.S.]**

Djajić, Slobodan. Human Capital, Minimum Wage and Unemployment: A Harris–Todaro Model of a Developed Open Economy. *Economica*, November 1985, *52*(208), pp. 491–508.

Eaton, Peter J. The Quality of Schooling: Comment. *Amer. Econ. Rev.*, December 1985, *75*(5), pp. 1195–1201. **[G: Brazil]**

England, Paula. Occupational Segregation: Rejoinder [The Failure of Human Capital Theory to Explain Occupational Sex Segregation]. *J. Human Res.*, Summer 1985, *20*(3), pp. 441–43. **[G: U.S.]**

England, Richard W. Public School Finance in the United States: Historical Trends and Contending Interpretations. *Rev. Radical Polit. Econ.*, Spring and Summer 1985, *17*(1/2), pp. 129–55. **[G: U.S.]**

Estrin, Saul and Svejnar, Jan. Explanations of Earnings in Yugoslavia: The Capital and Labour Schools Compared. *Econ. Anal. Worker's Manage.*, 1985, *19*(1), pp. 1–12. **[G: Yugoslavia]**

Fredland, J. Eric and Little, Roger D. Socioeconomic Status of World War II Veterans by Race: An Empirical Test of the Bridging Hypothesis. *Soc. Sci. Quart.*, September 1985, *66*(3), pp. 533–51. **[G: U.S.]**

Fuller, Richard H. Schooling, Social Class and Productivity: A Study of Rice Farmers in Northeastern Bangladesh. *Bangladesh Devel. Stud.*, Sept.-Dec. 1985, *13*(3&4), pp. 89–110. **[G: Bangladesh]**

Garen, John E. The Trade-off between Wages and Wage Growth. *J. Human Res.*, Fall 1985, *20*(4), pp. 522–39. **[G: U.S.]**

Ginzberg, Eli. Ginzberg's Theory: A Retrospective View. In *Ginzberg, E.*, 1985, pp. 83–101.

Ginzberg, Eli. Manpower Policy: Retrospect and Prospect. In *Ginzberg, E.*, 1985, pp. 615–35. **[G: U.S.]**

Ginzberg, Eli. Understanding Human Resources: Perspectives, People, and Policy: Afterword: Gleanings and Challenges. In *Ginzberg, E.*, 1985, pp. 683–89.

Háber, Judit. What Are We Trained For? In *Gustavsson, B.; Karlsson, J. C. and Raftegard, C.*, 1985, pp. 171–78. **[G: Hungary]**

Hancock, Keith and Richardson, Sue. Discount Rates and the Distribution of Lifetime Earnings. *J. Human Res.*, Summer 1985, *20*(3), pp. 346–60. **[G: Australia]**

Hansen, Richard B. On the Relationship between Human Capital and Productivity in the Case of Academic Economists. *Quart. Rev. Econ. Bus.*, Autumn 1985, *25*(3), pp. 96–104. **[G: U.S.]**

Hanushek, Eric A. and Quigley, John M. Life-Cycle Earning Capacity and the OJT Investment Model. *Int. Econ. Rev.*, June 1985, *26*(2), pp. 365–85. **[G: U.S.]**

Hart, Robert A. Wage Supplements through Collective Agreement or Statutory Requirement? *Kyklos*, 1985, *38*(1), pp. 20–42. **[G: OECD]**

Hashimoto, Masanori. Firm-specific Human Capital: Rejoinder [Wage Profiles, Layoffs, and Specific Training]. *Int. Econ. Rev.*, October 1985, *26*(3), pp. 753–54.

Heckman, James J. and Robb, Richard, Jr. Alternative Methods for Evaluating the Impact of Interventions. In *Heckman, J. J. and Singer, B.*, eds., 1985, pp. 156–245.

Heyer, Nelson O. Managing Human Resources in a High Technology Enterprise. In *Niehaus, R. J.*, ed., 1985, pp. 45–66. **[G: U.S.]**

Holmer, Jan. The Swedish University Providing Corporate Further Education for Blue and White Collar Industrial Workers. In *Gustavsson, B.; Karlsson, J. C. and Raftegard, C.*, 1985, pp. 179–91. **[G: Sweden]**

Hunt, Janet C. and Kau, James B. Migration and Wage Growth: A Human Capital Approach. *Southern Econ. J.*, January 1985, *51*(3), pp. 697–710. **[G: U.S.]**

Johnson, George E. Investment in and Returns from Education. In *Hendershott, P. H.*, ed., 1985, pp. 267–95. **[G: U.S.]**

Jones, David D. Inflation Rates Implicit in Discounting Personal Injury Economic Losses. *J. Risk Ins.*, March 1985, *52*(1), pp. 144–50. **[G: U.S.]**

Kalirajan, K. P. and Shand, R. T. Types of Education and Agricultural Productivity: A Quantitative Analysis of Tamil Nadu Rice Farming. *J. Devel. Stud.*, January 1985, *21*(2), pp. 232–43. **[G: India]**

Kamalich, Richard F. and Polachek, Solomon William. On Estimating Discrimination in the Economy: Reply. *Southern Econ. J.*, April 1985, *51*(4), pp. 1227–29. **[G: U.S.]**

Kemmerer, Frances and Wagner, Alan P. The Economics of Educational Reform. *Econ. Educ. Rev.*, 1985, *4*(2), pp. 111–21. **[G: U.S.]**

Khan, M. Ali. Unemployment of the Educated and Emigration of Post-Secondary Graduates from the LDCs: Comments. *Pakistan Devel.*

Rev., Autumn-Winter 1985, *24*(3/4), pp. 655–56.

Khan, Shahrukh Rafi and Irfan, Mohammad. Rates of Returns to Education and the Determinants of Earnings in Pakistan. *Pakistan Devel. Rev.*, Autumn-Winter 1985, *24*(3/4), pp. 671–80. **[G: Pakistan]**

Kiefer, Nicholas M. Evidence on the Role of Education in Labor Turnover. *J. Human Res.*, Summer 1985, *20*(3), pp. 445–52. **[G: U.S.]**

Kiker, B. F. and Heath, Julia A. The Effect of Socioeconomic Background on Earnings: A Comparison by Race. *Econ. Educ. Rev.*, 1985, *4*(1), pp. 45–55. **[G: U.S.]**

Kodde, David A. and Ritzen, Josef M. M. The Demand for Education under Capital Market Imperfections. *Europ. Econ. Rev.*, August 1985, *28*(3), pp. 347–62.

Lehrer, Evelyn L. and Stokes, Houston. Determinants of the Female Occupational Distribution: A Log-Linear Probability Analysis. *Rev. Econ. Statist.*, August 1985, *67*(3), pp. 395–404. **[G: U.S.]**

Lobdell, Jared C. "Musquapsink?..." the Economics of Property Rights in Already-Granted College Degrees. *Eastern Econ. J.*, July-Sept. 1985, *11*(3), pp. 283–90.

Main, Brian G. M. School-leaver Unemployment and the Youth Opportunities Programme in Scotland. *Oxford Econ. Pap.*, September 1985, *37*(3), pp. 426–47.

Manning, Richard. Optimal Human and Physical Capital Accumulation in a Fixed-Coefficients Economy. *Australian Econ. Pap.*, December 1985, *24*(45), pp. 258–70.

Maranto, Cheryl L. Union Effects on Human Capital Investments and Returns. *J. Human Res.*, Summer 1985, *20*(3), pp. 453–62. **[G: U.S.]**

Mathiesen, Anders. Wage-Labour and Polarization within Vocational Education in Denmark 1960–1980. In *Gustavsson, B.; Karlsson, J. C. and Raftegard, C.*, 1985, pp. 193–202. **[G: Denmark]**

Meckling, William H. Three Reflections on Performance Rewards and Higher Education. *J. Acc. Econ.*, April 1985, *7*(1–3), pp. 247–51. **[G: U.S.]**

Miller, Ted R. A Cost–Benefit Analysis of the 55 MPH Speed Limit: Comment. *Southern Econ. J.*, October 1985, *52*(2), pp. 547–49. **[G: U.S.]**

Mishan, Ezra J. Consistency in the Valuation of Life: A Wild Goose Chase? In *Paul, E. F.; Paul, J. and Miller, F. D., Jr., eds.*, 1985, pp. 152–67.

Moreh, J. Human Capital and Learning by Doing. *Metroecon.*, October 1985, *37*(3), pp. 307–29. **[G: U.S.]**

Niehaus, Richard J. Organizational Human Resource Policy Analysis in the 1980s. In *Niehaus, R. J., ed.*, 1985, pp. 1–44.

Pingali, Prabhu L. and Carlson, Gerald A. Human Capital, Adjustments in Subjective Probabilities, and the Demand for Pest Controls.

Amer. J. Agr. Econ., November 1985, *67*(4), pp. 853–61. **[G: U.S.]**

Pogue, Thomas F. and Sgontz, L. G. Human Capital Transfers: Implications for Equity in Social Security Systems. *Rev. Soc. Econ.*, April 1985, *43*(1), pp. 37–52. **[G: U.S.]**

Polachek, Solomon William. Occupation Segregation: A Defense of Human Capital Predictions [The Failure of Human Capital Theory to Explain Occupational Sex Segregation]. *J. Human Res.*, Summer 1985, *20*(3), pp. 437–40. **[G: U.S.]**

Polachek, Solomon William. Occupational Segregation: Reply [The Failure of Human Capital Theory to Explain Occupational Sex Segregation]. *J. Human Res.*, Summer 1985, *20*(3), pp. 444. **[G: U.S.]**

Porter, Philip K. and Scully, Gerald W. Potential Earnings, Post-schooling Investment and Returns to Human Capital. *Econ. Educ. Rev.*, 1985, *4*(2), pp. 87–92. **[G: U.S.]**

Prais, S. J. and Wagner, Karin. Schooling Standards in England and Germany: Some Summary Comparisons Bearing on Economic Performance. *Nat. Inst. Econ. Rev.*, May 1985, (112), pp. 53–76. **[G: U.K.; W. Germany]**

Psacharopoulos, George. Returns to Education: A Further International Update and Implications. *J. Human Res.*, Fall 1985, *20*(4), pp. 583–604. **[G: Selected Countries]**

Quah, Euston. Human Capital Investment and the Economics of Washing Hair: A Theoretical Treatment. *Indian Econ. J.*, Apr.-June 1985, *32*(4), pp. 55–57.

Rao, M. J. Manohar and Datta, Ramesh C. Human Capital and Hierarchy. *Econ. Educ. Rev.*, 1985, *4*(1), pp. 67–76. **[G: India]**

Rosenbaum, James E. Jobs, Job Status, and Women's Gains from Affirmative Action: Implications for Comparable Worth. In *Hartmann, H. I., ed.*, 1985, pp. 116–36. **[G: U.S.]**

Schaeffer, Peter. Human Capital Accumulation and Job Mobility. *J. Reg. Sci.*, February 1985, *25*(1), pp. 103–14.

Schilling, Don. Estimating the Present Value of Future Income Losses: An Historical Simulation, 1900–1982. *J. Risk Ins.*, March 1985, *52*(1), pp. 100–116. **[G: U.S.]**

Shah, Anup R. Does Education Act as a Screening Device for Certain British Occupations? *Oxford Econ. Pap.*, March 1985, *37*(1), pp. 118–24. **[G: U.K.]**

Sheridan, James A. A Discussion of Value-Added Human Resource Management and Planning. In *Niehaus, R. J., ed.*, 1985, pp. 215–229.

Siebert, W. Stanley. Developments in the Economics of Human Capital. In *Carline, D., et al.*, 1985, pp. 5–77. **[G: U.K.; U.S.]**

Singell, Larry D. and McNown, Robert F. A Cost–Benefit Analysis of the 55 MPH Speed Limit: Reply. *Southern Econ. J.*, October 1985, *52*(2), pp. 550–53. **[G: U.S.]**

Solmon, Lewis C. Quality of Education and Economic Growth. *Econ. Educ. Rev.*, 1985, *4*(4), pp. 273–90. **[G: Global]**

Steinberg, Stephen. Human Capital: A Critique.

Rev. Black Polit. Econ., Summer 1985, *14*(1), pp. 67–74. **[G: U.S.]**

Tessaring, Manfred. An Evaluation of Labour-Market and Educational Forecasts in the Federal Republic of Germany. In *Youdi, R. V. and Hinchliffe, K., eds.*, 1985, pp. 57–74.

Theeuwes, Jules, et al. Estimation of Optimal Human Capital Accumulation Parameters for the Netherlands. *Europ. Econ. Rev.*, November 1985, *29*(2), pp. 233–57. **[G: Netherlands]**

Tinbergen, Jan. Optimal Education, Occupation, and Income Distribution in a Simplistic Model. In *Tinbergen, J.*, 1985, pp. 168–73.
[G: Netherlands]

Tinbergen, Jan. The Role of Occupational Status in Income Formation. In *Tinbergen, J.*, 1985, pp. 78–84. **[G: U.S.]**

Tinbergen, Jan and Wegner, Eckhard. On a Macroeconomic Model of Income Formation. In *Tinbergen, J.*, 1985, pp. 69–77.
[G: Switzerland]

Tomes, Nigel. Religion and the Earnings Function. *Amer. Econ. Rev.*, May 1985, *75*(2), pp. 245–50. **[G: U.S.; Canada]**

Tsang, Mun C. and Levin, Henry M. The Economics of Overeducation. *Econ. Educ. Rev.*, 1985, *4*(2), pp. 93–104.

Tucker, Irvin B., III. Use of the Decomposition Technique to Test the Educational Screening Hypothesis. *Econ. Educ. Rev.*, 1985, *4*(4), pp. 321–26. **[G: U.S.]**

Usher, Dan. The Value of Life for Decision Making in the Public Sector. In *Paul, E. F.; Paul, J. and Miller, F. D., Jr., eds.*, 1985, pp. 168–91.

Vernon, Jack. Discounting After-Tax Earnings with After-Tax Yields in Torts Settlements. *J. Risk Ins.*, December 1985, *52*(4), pp. 696–703.
[G: U.S.]

Webb, Michael A. Migration and Education Subsidies by Governments: A Game-theoretic Analysis. *J. Public Econ.*, March 1985, *26*(2), pp. 249–62.

Webb, Michael A. The Brain Drain and Education Opportunity in Less Developed Countries. *Eastern Econ. J.*, April-June 1985, *11*(2), pp. 145–55. **[G: LDCs]**

Weiss, Andrew. Education as a Test: An Elementary Exposition. *Econ. Educ. Rev.*, 1985, *4*(2), pp. 123–28.

Wilson, Robert Andrew. A Longer Perspective on Rates of Return. *Scot. J. Polit. Econ.*, June 1985, *32*(2), pp. 191–98. **[G: U.K.]**

900 Welfare Programs; Consumer Economics; Urban and Regional Economics

910 WELFARE; HEALTH; EDUCATION

9100 General

Abel-Smith, Brian. The Major Problems of the Welfare State: Defining the Issues. In *Eisen-* *stadt, S. N. and Ahimeir, O., eds.*, 1985, pp. 31–43. **[G: U.S.; W. Europe]**

Aharoni, Yair. Social Services: At What Costs? In *Eisenstadt, S. N. and Ahimeir, O., eds.*, 1985, pp. 262–71. **[G: Israel]**

Andreatta, Benjamino. Public Intervention for Redistributive Ends. The Social Services Sector. *Ann. Pub. Co-op. Econ.*, January–June 1985, *56*(1–2), pp. 25–39.

Arellano, José-Pablo. Meeting Basic Needs: The Trade-off between the Quality and Coverage of the Programs. *J. Devel. Econ.*, May–June 1985, *18*(1), pp. 87–99. **[G: Chile]**

Armour, Philip K. and Coughlin, Richard M. Social Control and Social Security: Theory and Research on Capitalist and Communist Nations. *Soc. Sci. Quart.*, December 1985, *66*(4), pp. 770–88. **[G: CMEA; OECD]**

Babeau, André. Finances Publiques et Politiques Sociales: Leurs Evolutions et Développements dans les Economies de Marché. (With English summary.) In *Terny, G. and Culyer, A. J., eds.*, 1985, pp. 21–39. **[G: OECD]**

Balassa, Bela. Public Finance and Social Policy—Explanation of Trends and Developments: The Case of Developing Countries. In *Terny, G. and Culyer, A. J., eds.*, 1985, pp. 41–58.
[G: LDCs]

Bar-Yosef, Rivka. Welfare and Integration in Israel. In *Eisenstadt, S. N. and Ahimeir, O., eds.*, 1985, pp. 247–61. **[G: Israel]**

Bhagwati, Jagdish N. Class Structure, Poverty and Redistribution. In *Bhagwati, J. N. (II)*, 1985, pp. 167–69.

Bhagwati, Jagdish N. Gunnar Myrdal [Need for Reforms in Underdeveloped Countries]. In *Bhagwati, J. N. (II)*, 1985, pp. 306–12.

Bosanquet, Nick. Welfare Needs, Welfare Jobs and Efficiency. In *Klein, R. and O'Higgins, M., ed.*, 1985, pp. 186–203. **[G: U.K.]**

Bradshaw, Jonathan. A Defence of Social Security. In *Bean, P.; Ferris, J. and Whynes, D., eds.*, 1985, pp. 227–56. **[G: U.K.]**

Burkett, John P. Systemic Influences on the Physical Quality of Life: A Bayesian Analysis of Cross-sectional Data. *J. Compar. Econ.*, June 1985, *9*(2), pp. 145–63.

Byatt, Ian. Market and Non-market Alternatives in the Public Supply of Public Services: British Experience with Privatization. In *Forte, F. and Peacock, A., eds.*, 1985, pp. 203–11.
[G: U.K.]

Flora, Peter. On the History and Current Problems of the Welfare State. In *Eisenstadt, S. N. and Ahimeir, O., eds.*, 1985, pp. 11–30. **[G: U.S.; W. Europe]**

Gadó, Ottó. Perspectives on and Limits to Public Finance for the Financing of Social Policy Goals in Socialist Economies (The Example of Hungary). In *Terny, G. and Culyer, A. J., eds.*, 1985, pp. 271–77. **[G: Hungary]**

Gillion, Colin and Hemming, Richard. Social Expenditure in the United Kingdom in a Comparative Context: Trends, Explanations and Projections. In *Klein, R. and O'Higgins, M., ed.*, 1985, pp. 22–36. **[G: U.K.; OECD]**

Goodin, Robert E. Vulnerabilities and Responsibilities: An Ethical Defense of the Welfare State. *Amer. Polit. Sci. Rev.*, September 1985, 79(3), pp. 775–87.

Haveman, Robert H. Does the Welfare State Increase Welfare? Reflections on Hidden Negatives and Observed Positives. *De Economist*, 1985, 133(4), pp. 445–66. [G: U.S.; Netherlands]

Johansen, Lars Nørby and Kolberg, Jon Eivind. Welfare State Regression in Scandinavia? The Development of the Scandinavian Welfare States from 1970 to 1980. In *Eisenstadt, S. N. and Ahimeir, O., eds.*, 1985, pp. 143–76. [G: Scandinavia]

Jurković, Pero. A New Approach to Financing Social Services in a Socialist Self-Managing Country. In *Terny, G. and Culyer, A. J., eds.*, 1985, pp. 279–89. [G: Yugoslavia]

Kienzl, Heinz. The Welfare State—The Case of Austria. In *Eisenstadt, S. N. and Ahimeir, O., eds.*, 1985, pp. 177–81. [G: Austria]

Kiss, Otto; Mencl, Karel and Ulman, Václav. Social Consumption and Social Development Planning. *Czech. Econ. Digest.*, August 1985, (5), pp. 27–44. [G: Czechoslovakia]

Klein, Rudolf and O'Higgins, Michael. Conclusions: Social Policy after Incrementalism. In *Klein, R. and O'Higgins, M., ed.*, 1985, pp. 223–30. [G: U.K.]

Konukiewitz, Manfred and Wollmann, Hellmut. Urban Innovation: A Response to Deficiencies of the Intervention and Welfare State? In *Clark, T. N., ed.*, 1985, pp. 327–39. [G: W. Germany]

Kulcsár, Kálmán. Public Finance and Social Policy—Explanation of Trends and Developments: The Case of Socialist Economies. In *Terny, G. and Culyer, A. J., eds.*, 1985, pp. 59–65.

Levy, Baruch. Social Welfare Policy and the Advancement of the Disadvantaged. In *Eisenstadt, S. N. and Ahimeir, O., eds.*, 1985, pp. 272–79. [G: Israel]

Manning, Ian. Continuity and Change in Australian Economic Policy: The Social Welfare Services. *Australian Econ. Rev.*, 3rd Quarter, Spring 1985, (71), pp. 116–29. [G: Australia]

Mathews, Russell L. Programs and Policies. In *Mathews, R., et al.*, 1985, pp. 108–58. [G: Australia]

Musgrave, Richard A. Perspectives on and Limits to Public Finance for the Financing of Social Policy in Market Economies. In *Terny, G. and Culyer, A. J., eds.*, 1985, pp. 261–70.

O'Higgins, Michael. Welfare, Redistribution, and Inequality—Disillusion, Illusion, and Reality. In *Bean, P.; Ferris, J. and Whynes, D., eds.*, 1985, pp. 162–79. [G: U.K.]

Peterson, Wallace C. The U.S. "Welfare State" and the Conservative Counterrevolution. *J. Econ. Issues*, September 1985, 19(3), pp. 601–41. [G: U.S.]

Pinker, Robert. Social Welfare and the Thatcher Administration. In *Bean, P.; Ferris, J. and*

Whynes, D., eds., 1985, pp. 183–205. [G: U.K.]

Rein, Martin. Women, Employment and Social Welfare. In *Klein, R. and O'Higgins, M., ed.*, 1985, pp. 37–58. [G: Sweden; U.K.; U.S.; W. Germany]

Saunders, Peter and Klau, Friedrich. The Role of the Public Sector: Causes and Consequences of the Growth of Government. *OECD Econ. Stud.*, Spring 1985, (4), pp. 5–239. [G: OECD]

Taylor-Gooby, Peter. The Politics of Welfare: Public Attitudes and Behaviour. In *Klein, R. and O'Higgins, M., ed.*, 1985, pp. 72–91. [G: U.K.]

911 General Welfare Programs

9110 General Welfare Programs

Aaron, Henry J. Social Science Analysis and the Formulation of Public Policy: Illustrations of What the President "Knows" and How He Comes to "Know" It: Comment. In *Hausman, J. A. and Wise, D. A., eds.*, 1985, pp. 272–77.

Akin, John S., et al. The Impact of Federal Transfer Programs on the Nutrient Intake of Elderly Individuals. *J. Human Res.*, Summer 1985, 20(3), pp. 383–404. [G: U.S.]

Allén, Tuovi. Vähennykset tuloverotuksessa—tulonsiirtopolitiikan jatke? (Deductions in Personal Income Taxation—Substitutes for Government Transfer Programmes? With English summary.) *Kansant. Aikak.*, 1985, 81(1), pp. 65–72.

Banting, Keith G. Federalism and Income Security: Themes and Variations. In *Courchene, T. J.; Conklin, D. W. and Cook, G. C. A., eds. Vol. 1*, 1985, pp. 253–76. [G: Canada]

Baum, Sandra R. and Schwartz, Saul. The Fairness Test for Student-Aid Cuts. *Challenge*, May/June 1985, 28(2), pp. 39–46. [G: U.S.]

Beller, Andrea H. and Graham, John W. Variations in the Economic Well-Being of Divorced Women and Their Children: The Role of Child Support Income. In *David, M. and Smeeding, T., eds.*, 1985, pp. 471–506. [G: U.S.]

Betson, David and van der Gaag, Jacques. Measuring the Benefits of Income Maintenance Programs. In *David, M. and Smeeding, T., eds.*, 1985, pp. 215–33. [G: U.S.]

Boily, Nicole. Daycare and Public Policy: Comments. In *Economic Council of Canada.*, 1985, pp. 16–18. [G: Canada]

Bradshaw, Jonathan. Social Security Policy and Assumptions about Patterns of Work. In *Klein, R. and O'Higgins, M., ed.*, 1985, pp. 204–15. [G: U.K.]

Butler, J. S.; Ohls, James C. and Posner, Barbara. The Effect of the Food Stamp Program on the Nutrient Intake of the Eligible Elderly. *J. Human Res.*, Summer 1985, 20(3), pp. 405–20. [G: U.S.]

Caniglia, Alan S. Do Recipients Necessarily Prefer Cash Grants to Excise Subsidies? *Public*

Finance Quart., October 1985, *13*(4), pp. 422–35.

Capps, Oral, Jr. and Kramer, Randall A. Analysis of Food Stamp Participation Using Qualitative Choice Models. *Amer. J. Agr. Econ.*, February 1985, *67*(1), pp. 49–59. [G: U.S.]

Coe, Richard D. Nonparticipation in the SSI Program by the Eligible Elderly. *Southern Econ. J.*, January 1985, *51*(3), pp. 891–97.
[G: U.S.]

Conlisk, John. Technical Problems in Social Experimentation: Cost versus Ease of Analysis: Comment. In *Hausman, J. A. and Wise, D. A., eds.*, 1985, pp. 208–14.

Courant, Paul N. Distributional Programs: Education and Antipoverty: Commentary. In *Quigley, J. M. and Rubinfeld, D. L., eds.*, 1985, pp. 148–53. [G: U.S.]

Danziger, Sheldon and Feaster, Daniel. Income Transfers and Poverty in the 1980s. In *Quigley, J. M. and Rubinfeld, D. L., eds.*, 1985, pp. 89–117. [G: U.S.]

Danziger, Sheldon and Gottschalk, Peter. The Poverty of Losing Ground. *Challenge*, May/June 1985, *28*(2), pp. 32–38. [G: U.S.]

Davis, Evan H.; Dilnot, Andrea W. and Kay, John A. The Social Security Green Paper. *Fisc. Stud.*, August 1985, *6*(3), pp. 1–8. [G: U.K.]

Denton, Frank T.; Robb, A. Leslie and Spencer, Byron G. Shelter Allowances in a General Equilibrium Setting: A Model and Some Simulations. *J. Urban Econ.*, July 1985, *18*(1), pp. 47–72. [G: Canada]

Disney, Richard. Public Expenditure Policy, 1985–86: Social Security. In *Cockle, P., ed.*, 1985, pp. 121–51. [G: U.K.]

Donaldson, Thomas. The Feasibility of Welfare Rights in Less Developed Countries: Comment: Trading Justice for Bread. In *Kipnis, K. and Meyers, D. T., eds.*, 1985, pp. 226–28.
[G: LDCs]

Espenshade, Thomas J. The Recent Decline of American Marriage: Blacks and Whites in Comparative Perspective. In *Davis, K., ed.*, 1985, pp. 53–90. [G: U.S.]

Fraker, Thomas; Moffitt, Robert and Wolf, Douglas. Effective Tax Rates and Guarantees in the AFDC Program, 1967–1982. *J. Human Res.*, Spring 1985, *20*(2), pp. 251–63.
[G: U.S.]

Garfinkel, Irwin. Variations in the Economic Well-Being of Divorced Women and Their Children: The Role of Child Support Income: Comment. In *David, M. and Smeeding, T., eds.*, 1985, pp. 506–09. [G: U.S.]

Goodin, Robert E. Erring on the Side of Kindness in Social Welfare Policy. *Policy Sci.*, September 1985, *18*(2), pp. 141–56. [G: U.S.]

Griliches, Zvi. Income-Maintenance Policy and Work Effort: Learning from Experiments and Labor-Market Studies: Comment. In *Hausman, J. A. and Wise, D. A., eds.*, 1985, pp. 137–38.

Gruen, Fred H. Australian Government Policy on Retirement Incomes. *Econ. Rec.*, September 1985, *61*(174), pp. 613–21. [G: Australia]

Grundmann, Herman F. Adult Assistance Programs under the Social Security Act. *Soc. Sec. Bull.*, October 1985, *48*(10), pp. 10–21.
[G: U.S.]

Gwartney, James and McCaleb, Thomas S. Have Antipoverty Programs Increased Poverty? *Cato J.*, Spring/Summer 1985, *5*(1), pp. 1–16.
[G: U.S.]

Hamermesh, Daniel S. and Johannes, James M. Food Stamps as Money: The Macroeconomics of a Transfer Program. *J. Polit. Econ.*, February 1985, *93*(1), pp. 205–13. [G: U.S.]

Hannon, Joan Underhill. Poor Relief Policy in Antebellum New York State: The Rise and Decline of the Poorhouse. *Exploration Econ. Hist.*, July 1985, *22*(3), pp. 233–56.
[G: U.S.]

Hanushek, Eric A. Distributional Programs: Education and Antipoverty: Commentary. In *Quigley, J. M. and Rubinfeld, D. L., eds.*, 1985, pp. 154–60. [G: U.S.]

Harbert, Lloyd and Scandizzo, Pasquale L. Distribución de alimentos e intervención en la nutrición: el caso de Chile. (With English summary.) *Cuadernos Econ.*, August 1985, *22*(66), pp. 215–46. [G: Chile]

Hausman, Jerry A. and Wise, David A. Technical Problems in Social Experimentation: Cost versus Ease of Analysis. In *Hausman, J. A. and Wise, D. A., eds.*, 1985, pp. 187–208.
[G: U.S.]

Hollonbeck, Darrell; Ohls, James C. and Posner, Barbara. The Effects of Cashing Out Food Stamps on Food Expenditures. *Amer. J. Agr. Econ.*, August 1985, *67*(3), pp. 609–13.
[G: U.S.]

Ingberg, Mikael. Offentliga transfereringar och konjunkturpolitiken. (Public Transfers and Stabilization Policy. With English summary.) *Ekon. Samfundets Tidskr.*, 1985, *38*(2), pp. 97–112. [G: Finland]

Ingram, Gregory K. Housing Behavior and the Experimental Housing-Allowance Program: What Have We Learned? Comment. In *Hausman, J. A. and Wise, D. A., eds.*, 1985, pp. 87–94. [G: U.S.]

Isuani, Ernesto A. Social Security and Public Assistance. In *Mesa-Lago, C., ed.*, 1985, pp. 89–102. [G: Latin America]

Janowitz, Morris. Youth and the Welfare State in the United States. In *Eisenstadt, S. N. and Ahimeir, O., eds.*, 1985, pp. 93–108.
[G: U.S.]

Juster, F. Thomas. Measuring the Benefits of Income Maintenance Programs: Comment. In *David, M. and Smeeding, T., eds.*, 1985, pp. 234–38. [G: U.S.]

Kodras, Janet E. and Brown, Lawrence A. The Dissemination of Public Sector Innovations with Relevance to Regional Change in the United States. In *Thwaites, A. T. and Oakey, R. P., eds.*, 1985, pp. 195–214. [G: U.S.]

Konukiewitz, Manfred. Taming the Housing Market. In *Lane, J.-E., ed.*, 1985, pp. 181–98.
[G: W. Germany]

Krashinsky, Michael. Daycare and Public Policy.

In *Economic Council of Canada.*, 1985, pp. 9–16. [G: Canada]

Lee, Dwight R. The Politics of Poverty and the Poverty of Politics. *Cato J.*, Spring/Summer 1985, *5*(1), pp. 17–35. [G: U.S.]

León, Francisco. Social Security and Public Assistance: Comment. In *Mesa-Lago, C., ed.*, 1985, pp. 102–08. [G: Latin America]

Levitan, Sar A. The Evolving Welfare System. In *Dennis, B. D., ed.*, 1985, pp. 577–86. [G: U.S.]

Lynn, Laurence E., Jr. Social Science Analysis and the Formulation of Public Policy: Illustrations of What the President "Knows" and How He Comes to "Know" It: Comment. In *Hausman, J. A. and Wise, D. A., eds.*, 1985, pp. 277–78.

MacDonald, Maurice. Government Welfare Benefits and the Social Safety Net. *J. Post Keynesian Econ.*, Fall 1985, *8*(1), pp. 47–65. [G: U.S.]

MacDonald, Maurice. The Role of Multiple Benefits in Maintaining the Social Safety Net: The Case of Food Stamps. *J. Human Res.*, Summer 1985, *20*(3), pp. 421–36. [G: U.S.]

Maisel, Sherman. The Agenda for Metropolitan Housing Policies. In *Quigley, J. M. and Rubinfeld, D. L., eds.*, 1985, pp. 224–52. [G: U.S.]

McCall, John J. Welfare Reform: Cost Reductions or Increased Work Incentives. In *Kipnis, K. and Meyers, D. T., eds.*, 1985, pp. 190–201. [G: U.S.]

McFadden, Daniel. Technical Problems in Social Experimentation: Cost versus Ease of Analysis: Comment. In *Hausman, J. A. and Wise, D. A., eds.*, 1985, pp. 214–18.

Mendelson, Michael. Rationalization of Income Security in Canada. In *Courchene, T. J.; Conklin, D. W. and Cook, G. C. A., eds. Vol. 1*, 1985, pp. 229–52.

Miller, S. M. Defend and Change: The Welfare System in the Longer Run. In *Dennis, B. D., ed.*, 1985, pp. 586–90. [G: U.S.]

Miller, Victor J. Recent Changes in Federal Grants and State Budgets. In *Lewin, M. E., ed.*, 1985, pp. 44–64. [G: U.S.]

Moffitt, Robert. Evaluating the Effects of Changes in AFDC: Methodological Issues and Challenges. *J. Policy Anal. Manage.*, Summer 1985, *4*(4), pp. 537–53. [G: U.S.]

Moynihan, Daniel Patrick. We Can't Avoid Family Policy Much Longer. *Challenge*, Sept./Oct. 1985, *28*(4), pp. 9–17. [G: U.S.]

Mundel, David S. The Use of Information in the Policy Process: Are Social-Policy Experiments Worthwhile? In *Hausman, J. A. and Wise, D. A., eds.*, 1985, pp. 251–56.

Nathan, Richard P. Reagan and the Cities: How to Meet the Challenge. *Challenge*, Sept./Oct. 1985, *28*(4), pp. 4–8. [G: U.S.]

Nickel, James W. The Feasibility of Welfare Rights in Less Developed Countries. In *Kipnis, K. and Meyers, D. T., eds.*, 1985, pp. 217–25. [G: LDCs]

Questiaux, Nicole. Family Policy in France. In *Eisenstadt, S. N. and Ahimeir, O., eds.*, 1985, pp. 237–43. [G: France]

Quigley, John M. Housing Behavior and the Experimental Housing-Allowance Program: What Have We Learned? Comment. In *Hausman, J. A. and Wise, D. A., eds.*, 1985, pp. 75–86.

Quigley, John M. and Rubinfeld, Daniel L. Domestic Priorities in Our Federal System. In *Quigley, J. M. and Rubinfeld, D. L., eds.*, 1985, pp. 381–95. [G: U.S.]

Rahn, Sheldon L. and McCready, Douglas L. Note on Social Service Provision in Canada [Privatized Social Service Systems: Lessons from Ontario Children's Services]. *Can. Public Policy*, September 1985, *11*(3), pp. 625–28. [G: Canada]

Reeder, William J. The Benefits and Costs of the Section 8 Existing Housing Program. *J. Public Econ.*, April 1985, *26*(3), pp. 349–77. [G: U.S.]

Roberts, Russell D. Recipient Preferences and the Design of Government Transfer Programs. *J. Law Econ.*, April 1985, *28*(1), pp. 27–54. [G: U.S.]

Robins, Philip K. A Comparison of the Labor Supply Findings from the Four Negative Income Tax Experiments. *J. Human Res.*, Fall 1985, *20*(4), pp. 567–82. [G: U.S.]

Robins, Philip K. and Dickinson, Katherine P. Child Support and Welfare Dependence: A Multinomial Logit Analysis. *Demography*, August 1985, *22*(3), pp. 367–80. [G: U.S.]

Rosen, Harvey S. Housing Behavior and the Experimental Housing-Allowance Program: What Have We Learned? In *Hausman, J. A. and Wise, D. A., eds.*, 1985, pp. 55–75. [G: U.S.]

Rosen, Sherwin. Income-Maintenance Policy and Work Effort: Learning from Experiments and Labor-Market Studies: Comment. In *Hausman, J. A. and Wise, D. A., eds.*, 1985, pp. 134–37. [G: U.S.]

Ross, Jo Anne B. Fifty Years of Service to Children and Their Families. *Soc. Sec. Bull.*, October 1985, *48*(10), pp. 5–9. [G: U.S]

Rowlatt, Don. The Social-Security System in the 1990s: Comments. In *Courchene, T. J.; Conklin, D. W. and Cook, G. C. A., eds. Vol. 1*, 1985, pp. 277–83. [G: Canada]

Sayeed, Adil. The Canada Assistance Plan: Some Background. In *Courchene, T. J.; Conklin, D. W. and Cook, G. C. A., eds. Vol. 2*, 1985, pp. 276–310. [G: Canada]

Schneider, Robert R. Food Subsidies: A Multiple Price Model. *Int. Monet. Fund Staff Pap.*, June 1985, *32*(2), pp. 289–316. [G: LDCs]

Schwab, Robert M. The Benefits of In-Kind Government Programs. *J. Public Econ.*, July 1985, *27*(2), pp. 195–210. [G: U.S.]

Smallwood, David M. and Blaylock, James R. Analysis of Food Stamp Program Participation and Food Expenditures. *Western J. Agr. Econ.*, July 1985, *10*(1), pp. 41–54. [G: U.S.]

Stafford, Frank P. Income-Maintenance Policy and Work Effort: Learning from Experiments and Labor-Market Studies. In *Hausman, J. A.*

and Wise, D. A., eds., 1985, pp. 95–134.
[G: U.S.]

Stern, David. Distributional Programs: Education and Antipoverty: Commentary. In *Quigley, J. M. and Rubinfeld, D. L., eds.*, 1985, pp. 161–72. [G: U.S.]

Stromsdorfer, Ernst W. Social Science Analysis and the Formulation of Public Policy: Illustrations of What the President "Knows" and How He Comes to "Know" It. In *Hausman, J. A. and Wise, D. A., eds.*, 1985, pp. 257–72.

Struyk, Raymond J. Administering Social Welfare: The Reagan Record. *J. Policy Anal. Manage.*, Summer 1985, *4*(4), pp. 481–500.
[G: U.S.]

Taylor, Joan Kennedy. Deregulating the Poor. In *Boaz, D. and Crane, E. H., eds.*, 1985, pp. 223–45. [G: U.S.]

Torche, Arístides. Una evaluación económica del Programa Nacional de Alimentación Complementaria (PNAC). (With English summary.) *Cuadernos Econ.*, August 1985, *22*(66), pp. 175–93. [G: Chile]

Valdés, Alberto. Subsidios alimentarios en países en desarrollo: estimaciones de sus costos y efectos distributivos. (With English summary.) *Cuadernos Econ.*, August 1985, *22*(66), pp. 329–36. [G: LDCs]

Weale, Albert. Why Are We Waiting? The Problem of Unresponsiveness in the Public Social Services. In *Klein, R. and O'Higgins, M., ed.*, 1985, pp. 150–65. [G: U.K.]

Weaver, R. Kent. Controlling Entitlements. In *Chubb, J. E. and Peterson, P. E., eds.*, 1985, pp. 307–41. [G: U.S.]

Weinberg, Daniel H. Filling the "Poverty Gap": Multiple Transfer Program Participation. *J. Human Res.*, Winter 1985, *20*(1), pp. 64–89.
[G: U.S.]

Wickramasekara, Piyasiri. An Evaluation of Policies and Programmes for the Alleviation of Poverty in Sri Lanka. In *Islam, R., ed.*, 1985, pp. 243–86. [G: Sri Lanka]

Williams, Oliver P. Governmental Intervention into Local Economies under Market Conditions: The Case of Urban Renewal. In *Lane, J.-E., ed.*, 1985, pp. 142–57. [G: U.S.]

Wilson, Thomas. The Unwithered Welfare State. In *[Peacock, A.]*, 1985, pp. 78–93. [G: U.K.]

Wolch, Jennifer R. Distributional Programs: Education and Antipoverty: Commentary. In *Quigley, J. M. and Rubinfeld, D. L., eds.*, 1985, pp. 173–80. [G: U.S.]

Wolfe, Barbara L., et al. The Contribution of Income Transfers to Lagging Economic Performance: The United States and the Netherlands in the 1970s. In *Terny, G. and Culyer, A. J., eds.*, 1985, pp. 109–21. [G: U.S.; Netherlands]

912 Economics of Education

9120 Economics of Education

Agarwal, Vinod B. and Winkler, Donald R. Foreign Demand for United States Higher Education:

tion: A Study of Developing Countries in the Eastern Hemisphere. *Econ. Develop. Cult. Change*, April 1985, *33*(3), pp. 623–44.
[G: U.S.]

Anderson, R. D. School Attendance in Nineteenth-Century Scotland: A Reply [Education and the State in Nineteenth-Century Scotland]. *Econ. Hist. Rev., 2nd Ser.*, May 1985, *38*(2), pp. 282–86. [G: Scotland]

Åsberg, Rodney. Primary Education. In *Jerve, A. M., ed.*, 1985, pp. 281–97. [G: Pakistan]

Augenblick, John. Elementary and Secondary Education: Issues in Budgeting and Financial Management. In *Augenblick, J., ed.*, 1985, pp. vii–ix.

Avnimelech, Moria. Education in Israel: Problems in Funding and Curricula. In *Levinson, P. and Landau, P., eds.*, 1985, pp. 58–61.

Bacharach, Samuel B.; Mitchell, Stephen M. and Malanowski, Rose. Strategic Choice and Collective Action: Organizational Determinants of Teachers Militancy. In *Lipsky, D. B., ed.*, 1985, pp. 197–222. [G: U.S.]

Bara, S. and Miăiţă, N. V. Methods and Techniques of Objective Assessment of the Student's Personality. *Econ. Computat. Cybern. Stud. Res.*, 1985, *20*(4), pp. 53–56.

Barnett, C. Long-term Industrial Performance in the UK: The Role of Education and Research, 1850–1939. In *Morris, D., ed.*, 1985, pp. 668–89. [G: OECD]

Bartlett, Katharine T. The Role of Cost in Educational Decisionmaking for the Handicapped Child. *Law Contemp. Probl.*, Spring 1985, *48*(2), pp. 7–62. [G: U.S.]

Baum, Sandra R. and Schwartz, Saul. The Fairness Test for Student-Aid Cuts. *Challenge*, May/June 1985, *28*(2), pp. 39–46. [G: U.S.]

Becker, William E. Maintaining Faculty Vitality through Collective Bargaining. In *Clark, S. M. and Lewis, D. R., eds.*, 1985, pp. 198–223.
[G: U.S.]

Bee, Malcolm and Dolton, Peter J. Costs and Economies of Scale in UK Private Schools. *Appl. Econ.*, April 1985, *17*(2), pp. 281–90.
[G: U.K.]

Bee, Malcolm and Dolton, Peter J. Educational Production in Independent Secondary Schools. *Bull. Econ. Res.*, January 1985, *37*(1), pp. 27–40. [G: U.K.]

Behrman, Jere R. and Birdsall, Nancy. The Quality of Schooling: Reply. *Amer. Econ. Rev.*, December 1985, *75*(5), pp. 1202–05. [G: Brazil]

Benjamin, Ernst. Collective Bargaining in Public Higher Education. In *Dennis, B. D., ed.*, 1985, pp. 514–19. [G: U.S.]

Benson, Charles S. State Government Contributions to the Public Schools. In *Augenblick, J., ed.*, 1985, pp. 11–23. [G: U.S.]

Bhagwati, Jagdish N. Education, Class Structure and Income Equality. In *Bhagwati, J. N. (II)*, 1985, pp. 170–204. [G: India]

Birdsall, Nancy. Public Inputs and Child Schooling in Brazil. *J. Devel. Econ.*, May–June 1985, *18*(1), pp. 67–86. [G: Brazil]

Blakemore, Arthur E. and Low, Stuart A. Public

Expenditures on Higher Education and Their Impact on Enrollment Patterns. *Appl. Econ.*, April 1985, *17*(2), pp. 331–40. **[G: U.S.]**

Blaug, Mark. Education: Comments. In *Worswick, G. D. N., ed.*, 1985, pp. 19–31. **[G: U.K.]**

Blaug, Mark. Where Are We Now in the Economics of Education? *Econ. Educ. Rev.*, 1985, *4*(1), pp. 17–28.

Boily, Nicole. Daycare and Public Policy: Comments. In *Economic Council of Canada.*, 1985, pp. 16–18. **[G: Canada]**

Boissiere, M.; Knight, J. B. and Sabot, R. H. Earnings, Schooling, Ability, and Cognitive Skills. *Amer. Econ. Rev.*, December 1985, *75*(5), pp. 1016–30. **[G: Kenya; Tanzania]**

Bolick, Clint. Solving the Education Crisis: Market Alternatives and Parental Choice. In *Boaz, D. and Crane, E. H., eds.*, 1985, pp. 207–21. **[G: U.S.]**

Broder, Josef M.; Tew, Bernard V. and Williams, Jeffrey R. Effective Learning in Large Classes through Risk Management. *Southern J. Agr. Econ.*, December 1985, *17*(2), pp. 97–103. **[G: U.S.]**

Butler, Richard J. and Monk, David H. The Cost of Public Schooling in New York State: The Role of Scale and Efficiency in 1978–79. *J. Human Res.*, Summer 1985, *20*(3), pp. 361–82. **[G: U.S.]**

Caldwell, John C.; Reddy, P. H. and Caldwell, Pat. Educational Transition in Rural South India. *Population Devel. Rev.*, March 1985, *11*(1), pp. 29–51. **[G: India]**

Cameron, David. Postsecondary Education: Some Thoughts on the Position of the Government of Canada. In *Courchene, T. J.; Conklin, D. W. and Cook, G. C. A., eds. Vol. 1*, 1985, pp. 315–22. **[G: Canada]**

Cantor, Leonard. A Coherent Approach to the Education and Training of the 16–19 Age Group. In *Worswick, G. D. N., ed.*, 1985, pp. 13–24. **[G: U.K.]**

Carter, Charles. Implications for Policy and Research. In *Worswick, G. D. N., ed.*, 1985, pp. 7–10. **[G: U.K.]**

Chambers, Jay G. Patterns of Compensation of Public and Private School Teachers. *Econ. Educ. Rev.*, 1985, *4*(4), pp. 291–310. **[G: U.S.]**

Chapman, Bruce. Continuity and Change: Labour Market Programs and Education Expenditure. *Australian Econ. Rev.*, 3rd Quarter, Spring 1985, (71), pp. 98–112. **[G: Australia]**

Chernichovsky, Dov. Socioeconomic and Demographic Aspects of School Enrollment and Attendance in Rural Botswana. *Econ. Develop. Cult. Change*, January 1985, *33*(2), pp. 319–32. **[G: Botswana]**

Chicoine, David L. and Hendricks, A. Donald. Evidence on Farm Use Value Assessment, Tax Shifts, and State School Aid. *Amer. J. Agr. Econ.*, May 1985, *67*(2), pp. 266–70. **[G: U.S.]**

Choo, Eng Ung and Wedley, William C. Optimal Criterion Weights in Multicriteria Decision

Making. In *Haimes, Y. Y. and Chankong, V., eds.*, 1985, pp. 345–57. **[G: Canada]**

Clancy, Patrick. Symposium on "Equality of Opportunity in Irish Schools": Editorial Introduction. *Econ. Soc. Rev.*, January 1985, *16*(2), pp. 77–82. **[G: Ireland]**

Cohen, Suleiman I. The Labour Force Matrix of Pakistan: Selected Applications. *Pakistan Devel. Rev.*, Autumn-Winter 1985, *24*(3/4), pp. 565–84. **[G: Pakistan]**

Cohn, Elchanan. Implementation of Federal Chapter 2 Block Grants to Education in South Carolina. *Econ. Educ. Rev.*, 1985, *4*(3), pp. 215–25. **[G: U.S.]**

Conte, Michael A. Do Wealth Neutralizing Matching Grants Neutralize the Effects of Wealth? *Rev. Econ. Statist.*, August 1985, *67*(3), pp. 508–14. **[G: U.S.]**

Coughlin, Cletus C. and Erekson, O. Homer. Contributions to Intercollegiate Athletic Programs: Further Evidence. *Soc. Sci. Quart.*, March 1985, *66*(1), pp. 194–202. **[G: U.S.]**

Courant, Paul N. Distributional Programs: Education and Antipoverty: Commentary. In *Quigley, J. M. and Rubinfeld, D. L., eds.*, 1985, pp. 148–53. **[G: U.S.]**

Deger, Saadet. Human Resources, Government Education Expenditure, and the Military Burden in Less Developed Countries. *J. Devel. Areas*, October 1985, *20*(1), pp. 37–48. **[G: LDCs]**

Delaney, John Thomas. Unionism, Bargaining Spillovers, and Teacher Compensation. In *Lipsky, D. B., ed.*, 1985, pp. 111–42. **[G: U.S.]**

Delaney-LeBlanc, Madeleine. Women and Education: Branching Out: Comments. In *Economic Council of Canada.*, 1985, pp. 54–58. **[G: Canada]**

Dolan, Robert C.; Jung, Clarence R., Jr. and Schmidt, Robert M. Evaluating Educational Inputs in Undergraduate Education. *Rev. Econ. Statist.*, August 1985, *67*(3), pp. 514–20. **[G: U.S.]**

Eastaugh, Steven R. The Impact of the Nurse Training Act on the Supply of Nurses, 1974–1983. *Inquiry*, Winter 1985, *22*(4), pp. 404–17. **[G: U.S.]**

Eaton, Peter J. The Quality of Schooling: Comment. *Amer. Econ. Rev.*, December 1985, *75*(5), pp. 1195–1201. **[G: Brazil]**

Eberts, Randall W. and Stone, Joe A. Male–Female Differences in Promotions: EEO in Public Education. *J. Human Res.*, Fall 1985, *20*(4), pp. 504–21. **[G: U.S.]**

Egbert, Robert L.; Kluender, Mary M. and Roach, James L. Rural Elementary School Districts in Nebraska: Their Application for ECIA Funds as Related to Demographic and Economic Issues. *Econ. Educ. Rev.*, 1985, *4*(3), pp. 189–95. **[G: U.S.]**

Elmore, Richard F. Implementation of Chapter 2 in Washington State. *Econ. Educ. Rev.*, 1985, *4*(3), pp. 245–52. **[G: U.S.]**

England, Richard W. Public School Finance in the United States: Historical Trends and Contending Interpretations. *Rev. Radical Polit.*

Econ., Spring and Summer 1985, *17*(1/2), pp. 129–55. [G: U.S.]

Eyler, Janet. Implementation of Chapter 2 in Tennessee. *Econ. Educ. Rev.*, 1985, *4*(3), pp. 227–35. [G: U.S.]

Fisher, Norman. Continuity and Change: Labour Market Programs and Education Expenditure: Comment. *Australian Econ. Rev.*, 3rd Quarter, Spring 1985, (71), pp. 113–14.
[G: Australia]

Fligstein, Neil and Fernandez, Roberto M. Educational Transitions of Whites and Mexican-Americans. In *Borjas, G. J. and Tienda, M.*, eds., 1985, pp. 161–92. [G: U.S.]

Fløystad, Gunnar. The Labour Force Matrix of Pakistan: Selected Applications: Comments. *Pakistan Devel. Rev.*, Autumn-Winter 1985, *24*(3/4), pp. 585. [G: Pakistan]

Ford, Hugh. Training: Comment. In *Worswick, G. D. N.*, ed., 1985, pp. 79–80. [G: U.K.]

Forget, Claude E. Educational Policy Goals for Canada: Major Trade-offs and Other Issues. In *Courchene, T. J.; Conklin, D. W. and Cook, G. C. A.*, eds. Vol. 1, 1985, pp. 299–314.
[G: Canada]

Gaskell, Jane. Women and Education: Branching Out. In *Economic Council of Canada.*, 1985, pp. 43–54. [G: Canada]

Glazer, Nathan. Immigrants and Education. In *Glazer, N.*, ed., 1985, pp. 213–39. [G: U.S.]

Glynn, Dermot. Training: Comment. In *Worswick, G. D. N.*, ed., 1985, pp. 80–86.
[G: U.K.]

Gold, Steven D. State Aid for Local Schools: Trends and Prospects. In *Augenblick, J.*, ed., 1985, pp. 24–34. [G: U.S.]

Goodman, Richard H. Providing Adequate Resources for Public Elementary and Secondary Schools. In *Augenblick, J.*, ed., 1985, pp. 35–46. [G: U.S.]

Graham, John F. Funding of Universities of Canada. In *Courchene, T. J.; Conklin, D. W. and Cook, G. C. A.*, eds. Vol. 1, 1985, pp. 323–34. [G: Canada]

Grant, Rudolph W. and Paul, Una M. Perceptions of Caribbean Regional Integration: A Comparative Study of the Perceptions of Caribbean Teacher Trainees. *Soc. Econ. Stud.*, March 1985, *34*(1), pp. 1–26. [G: Guyana]

Greaney, Vincent and Kellaghan, Thomas. Factors Related to Level of Educational Attainment in Ireland. *Econ. Soc. Rev.*, January 1985, *16*(2), pp. 141–56. [G: Ireland]

Greenhalgh, Susan. Sexual Stratification: The Other Side of "Growth with Equity" in East Asia. *Population Devel. Rev.*, June 1985, *11*(2), pp. 265–314. [G: E. Asia]

Guedry, Leo J., Jr. Teaching, Research, and Extension Programs at Predominantly Black Land-Grant Institutions: Discussion. *Southern J. Agr. Econ.*, July 1985, *17*(1), pp. 43–45.
[G: U.S.]

Háber, Judit. What Are We Trained For? In *Gustavsson, B.; Karlsson, J. C. and Raftegard, C.*, 1985, pp. 171–78. [G: Hungary]

Hadley, Garland R. Interstate Migration, Income and Public School Expenditures: An Update of an Experiment. *Public Choice*, 1985, *46*(2), pp. 207–14. [G: U.S.]

Hansen, W. Lee. Changing Demography of Faculty in Higher Education. In *Clark, S. M. and Lewis, D. R.*, eds., 1985, pp. 27–54.
[G: U.S.]

Hanushek, Eric A. Distributional Programs: Education and Antipoverty: Commentary. In *Quigley, J. M. and Rubinfeld, D. L.*, eds., 1985, pp. 154–60. [G: U.S.]

Havighurst, Robert J. Aging and Productivity: The Case of Older Faculty. In *Clark, S. M. and Lewis, D. R.*, eds., 1985, pp. 98–111.
[G: U.S.]

Hentschke, Guilbert C. Emerging Roles of School District Administrators: Implications for Planning, Budgeting, and Management. *Public Budg. Finance*, Spring 1985, *5*(1), pp. 15–26.
[G: U.S.]

Hentschke, Guilbert C. Emerging Roles of School District Administrators: Implications for Planning, Budgeting, and Management. In *Augenblick, J.*, ed., 1985, pp. 59–70. [G: U.S.]

High, Jack. State Education: Have Economists Made a Case? *Cato J.*, Spring/Summer 1985, *5*(1), pp. 305–23.

Hochmaulová, Daniela. Education of Young People in Czechoslovakia. *Czech. Econ. Digest.*, December 1985, (8), pp. 39–43.
[G: Czechoslovakia]

Hodgin, Robert F. and Weed, Norman L. An Inquiry into Performance Quality Effects on Consumer Attitudes: The Case of Education. *J. Behav. Econ.*, Summer 1985, *14*(2), pp. 43–58. [G: U.S.]

Holden, Karen C. Maintaining Faculty Vitality through Early Retirement Options. In *Clark, S. M. and Lewis, D. R.*, eds., 1985, pp. 224–44. [G: U.S.]

Holmer, Jan. The Swedish University Providing Corporate Further Education for Blue and White Collar Industrial Workers. In *Gustavsson, B.; Karlsson, J. C. and Raftegard, C.*, 1985, pp. 179–91. [G: Sweden]

Hough, J. R. A Note on Economies of Scale in Schools. *Appl. Econ.*, February 1985, *17*(1), pp. 143–44. [G: Canada]

d'Iribarne, Alain. Developments in Vocational Training in France in the Past Twenty Years. In *Worswick, G. D. N.*, ed., 1985, pp. 52–67. [G: France]

Jackson, Roy. Training: Comment. In *Worswick, G. D. N.*, ed., 1985, pp. 86–90. [G: U.K.]

Janowitz, Morris. Youth and the Welfare State in the United States. In *Eisenstadt, S. N. and Ahimeir, O.*, eds., 1985, pp. 93–108.
[G: U.S.]

Jha, L. K. Education in Economic Development. In *Jha, L. K.*, 1985, pp. 258–66. [G: India]

Johnson, Eldon L. Some Development Lessons from the Early Land-Grant Colleges. *J. Devel. Areas*, January 1985, *19*(2), pp. 139–48.
[G: LDCs; U.S.]

Johnson, George E. Investment in and Returns from Education. In *Hendershott, P. H., ed.*, 1985, pp. 267–95. [G: U.S.]

Johnson, James W. The Computer Revolution and Graduate Education. In *Smith, B. L. R., ed.*, 1985, pp. 97–119. [G: U.S.]

Josefowicz, A.; Kluczynski, J. and Obrebski, T. Manpower and Education Planning and Policy Experience in Poland, 1960–80. In *Youdi, R. V. and Hinchliffe, K., eds.*, 1985, pp. 135–52. [G: Poland]

Jud, G. Donald. A Further Note on Schools and Housing Values. *Amer. Real Estate Urban Econ. Assoc. J.*, Winter 1985, *13*(4), pp. 452–62. [G: U.S.]

Kalirajan, K. P. and Shand, R. T. Types of Education and Agricultural Productivity: A Quantitative Analysis of Tamil Nadu Rice Farming. *J. Devel. Stud.*, January 1985, *21*(2), pp. 232–43. [G: India]

Katzman, Martin T. Implementation of Chapter 2 of ECIA in Texas. *Econ. Educ. Rev.*, 1985, *4*(3), pp. 237–43. [G: U.S.]

Kearney, C. Philip. Michigan's Experience with Federal Education Block Grant. *Econ. Educ. Rev.*, 1985, *4*(3), pp. 181–88. [G: U.S.]

Kemmerer, Frances and Wagner, Alan P. The Economics of Educational Reform. *Econ. Educ. Rev.*, 1985, *4*(2), pp. 111–21. [G: U.S.]

Khan, Akhtar Hasan. Literacy Transition and Female Nuptiality: Implications for Fertility in Pakistan: Comments. *Pakistan Devel. Rev.*, Autumn-Winter 1985, *24*(3/4), pp. 601–03. [G: Pakistan]

Kiker, B. F. and Heath, Julia A. The Effect of Socioeconomic Background on Earnings: A Comparison by Race. *Econ. Educ. Rev.*, 1985, *4*(1), pp. 45–55. [G: U.S.]

Kirst, Michael W. The New Agenda for Education: A Perspective for Policymakers. In *Augenblick, J., ed.*, 1985, pp. 1–10. [G: U.S.]

Kodde, David A. and Ritzen, Josef M. M. The Demand for Education under Capital Market Imperfections. *Europ. Econ. Rev.*, August 1985, *28*(3), pp. 347–62.

Kogan, Maurice. Education: Comments. In *Worswick, G. D. N., ed.*, 1985, pp. 135–38. [G: U.K.]

Krashinsky, Michael. Daycare and Public Policy. In *Economic Council of Canada.*, 1985, pp. 9–16. [G: Canada]

Kumar, Ramesh C. Economies of Scale in School Operation—A Reply. *Appl. Econ.*, February 1985, *17*(1), pp. 145–48. [G: Canada]

Kuriloff, Peter J. The Distributive and Education Consequences of Chapter 2 Block Grants in Pennsylvania. *Econ. Educ. Rev.*, 1985, *4*(3), pp. 197–214. [G: U.S.]

Landymore, P. J. A. Education and Industry Since the War. In *Morris, D., ed.*, 1985, pp. 690–717. [G: U.K.; EEC]

Lankford, Ralph Hamilton. Efficiency and Equity in the Provision of Public Education. *Rev. Econ. Statist.*, February 1985, *67*(1), pp. 70–80. [G: U.S.]

Lankford, Ralph Hamilton. Preferences of Citizens for Public Expenditures on Elementary and Secondary Education. *J. Econometrics*, January 1985, *27*(1), pp. 1–20. [G: U.S.]

Layard, Richard and Petoussis, Emmanuel. Overseas Students' Fees and the Demand for Education. *Appl. Econ.*, October 1985, *17*(5), pp. 805–16. [G: U.K.]

Levin, Henry M. Are Block Grants the Answaer to the Federal Role in Education? *Econ. Educ. Rev.*, 1985, *4*(3), pp. 261–69. [G: U.S.]

Levin, Henry M. Costs and Cost-Effectiveness of Computer-Assisted Instruction. In *Augenblick, J., ed.*, 1985, pp. 71–85. [G: U.S.]

Levin, Henry M. Costs and Cost-Effectiveness of Computer-assisted Instruction. *Public Budg. Finance*, Spring 1985, *5*(1), pp. 27–42. [G: U.S.]

Lewis, P. E. T. and Vella, F. G. M. Economic Factors Affecting the Number of Engineering Graduates in Australia. *Australian Econ. Pap.*, June 1985, *24*(44), pp. 66–75. [G: Australia]

Ley, Robert D. and Wines, William A. The Economics of Teachers' Strikes in Minnesota in 1981. *Econ. Educ. Rev.*, 1985, *4*(1), pp. 57–65. [G: U.S.]

Lichtenstein, Peter M. Radical Liberalism and Radical Education: A Synthesis and Critical Evaluation of Illich, Freire, and Dewey. *Amer. J. Econ. Soc.*, January 1985, *44*(1), pp. 39–53.

Linke, R. D.; Oertel, L. M. and Kelsey, N. J. M. Participation and Equity in Higher Education: A Preliminary Report on the Socioeconomic Profile of Higher Education Students in South Australia, 1974–1984. *Australian Bull. Lab.*, June 1985, *11*(3), pp. 124–41. [G: Australia]

Lipton, Michael. Education and Farm Efficiency: Comment. *Econ. Develop. Cult. Change*, October 1985, *34*(1), pp. 167–68. [G: Nepal]

Lobdell, Jared C. "Musquapsink?..." the Economics of Property Rights in Already-Granted College Degrees. *Eastern Econ. J.*, July-Sept. 1985, *11*(3), pp. 283–90.

Lumsden, Keith and Scott, Alex. Public Funding of Universities: Effects on Economics I Students. In *[Peacock, A.]*, 1985, pp. 105–24. [G: U.K.]

Lynch, Kathleen. An Analysis of Some Presuppositions Underlying the Concepts of Meritocracy and Ability as Presented in Greaney and Kellaghan's Study. *Econ. Soc. Rev.*, January 1985, *16*(2), pp. 83–102. [G: Ireland]

Mace, John. Public Expenditure Policy, 1985–86: Education and Science. In *Cockle, P., ed.*, 1985, pp. 203–22. [G: U.K.]

Maclure, Stuart. The Responsiveness of the Education System to Change. In *Worswick, G. D. N., ed.*, 1985, pp. 113–29. [G: U.K.]

Mahmood, Naushin and Khan, Zubeda. Literacy Transition and Female Nuptiality: Implications for Fertility in Pakistan. *Pakistan Devel. Rev.*, Autumn-Winter 1985, *24*(3/4), pp. 589–600. [G: Pakistan]

Martinez-Vazquez, Jorge and Seaman, Bruce A. Private Schooling and the Tiebout Hypothesis.

Public Finance Quart., July 1985, *13*(3), pp. 293–318.

Mason, D. M. School Attendance in Nineteenth-Century Scotland [Education and the State in Nineteenth-Century Scotland]. *Econ. Hist. Rev.*, *2nd Ser.*, May 1985, *38*(2), pp. 276–81. **[G: Scotland]**

Mathiesen, Anders. Wage-Labour and Polarization within Vocational Education in Denmark 1960–1980. In *Gustavsson, B.; Karlsson, J. C. and Raftegard, C.*, 1985, pp. 193–202. **[G: Denmark]**

McPherson, Michael S. The State of Academic Labor Markets. In *Smith, B. L. R.*, *ed.*, 1985, pp. 57–83. **[G: U.S.]**

Megdal, Sharon Bernstein. A Note on "Estimating School District Expenditure Functions under Conditions of Closed-End Matching Aid": Closed-End Matching Aid in the Context of a Two-Part Tariff. *J. Urban Econ.*, January 1985, *17*(1), pp. 19–29. **[G: U.S.]**

Melck, Antony. On Subsidizing Education with Block Grants. *Econ. Educ. Rev.*, 1985, *4*(3), pp. 253–59. **[G: U.S.]**

Miller, Ralph. Human Resource Development: The Role of Education. In *Rose, T.*, *ed.*, 1985, pp. 124–34. **[G: Sub-Saharan Africa]**

Mingat, Alain and Psacharopoulos, George. Financing Education in Sub-Saharan Africa. *Finance Develop.*, March 1985, *22*(1), pp. 35–38. **[G: Sub-Saharan Africa]**

Mingat, Alain and Tan, Jee-Peng. On Equity in Education Again: An International Comparison. *J. Human Res.*, Spring 1985, *20*(2), pp. 298–308. **[G: Global]**

Moock, Peter R. Education and Farm Efficiency: Reply. *Econ. Develop. Cult. Change*, October 1985, *34*(1), pp. 169–72. **[G: Nepal]**

Murnane, Richard J. An Economist's Look at Federal and State Education Policies. In *Quigley, J. M. and Rubinfeld, D. L.*, *eds.*, 1985, pp. 118–47. **[G: U.S.]**

Murnane, Richard J.; Newstead, Stuart and Olsen, Randall J. Comparing Public and Private Schools: The Puzzling Role of Selectivity Bias. *J. Bus. Econ. Statist.*, January 1985, *3*(1), pp. 23–35. **[G: U.S.]**

Murphy, Michael J. The Impact of Collective Bargaining on School Management and Governance. *Public Budg. Finance*, Spring 1985, *5*(1), pp. 3–14. **[G: U.S.]**

Murphy, Michael J. The Impact of Collective Bargaining on School Management and Governance. In *Augenblick, J.*, *ed.*, 1985, pp. 47–58. **[G: U.S.]**

Nair, D. Prabhakaran. Demand-Supply Imbalance of Higher Education in Kerala. *Margin*, October 1985, *18*(1), pp. 83–91. **[G: India]**

Nevin, Edward. The Finance of University Academic Departments. *Appl. Econ.*, October 1985, *17*(5), pp. 761–79. **[G: U.K.]**

Novek, Joel. University Graduates, Jobs, and University–Industry Linkages. *Can. Public Policy*, June 1985, *11*(2), pp. 180–95. **[G: Canada]**

Olneck, Michael R. Critique of Questions Pertain-

ing to Education in SIPP. *J. Econ. Soc. Meas.*, December 1985, *13*(3–4), pp. 299–304. **[G: U.S.]**

Peled, Elad. Welfare Policy in Israel: The Domain of Education. In *Eisenstadt, S. N. and Ahimeir, O.*, *eds.*, 1985, pp. 280–88. **[G: Israel]**

Pelissero, John P. Welfare and Education Aid to Cities: An Analysis of State Responsiveness to Needs. *Soc. Sci. Quart.*, June 1985, *66*(2), pp. 444–52. **[G: U.S.]**

Peston, Maurice. Training: Comment. In *Worswick, G. D. N.*, *ed.*, 1985, pp. 76–79. **[G: U.K.]**

Postlethwaite, T. Neville. The Bottom Half in Lower Secondary Schooling. In *Worswick, G. D. N.*, *ed.*, 1985, pp. 93–100. **[G: Selected Countries]**

Prais, S. J. What Can We Learn from the German System of Education and Vocational Training? In *Worswick, G. D. N.*, *ed.*, 1985, pp. 40–51. **[G: W. Germany]**

Prais, S. J. and Wagner, Karin. Schooling Standards in England and Germany: Some Summary Comparisons Bearing on Economic Performance. *Nat. Inst. Econ. Rev.*, May 1985, (112), pp. 53–76. **[G: U.K.; W. Germany]**

Psacharopoulos, George. Educational Research and Policy Development at the World Bank. *Indian J. Quant. Econ.*, 1985, *1*(2), pp. 119–24.

Psacharopoulos, George. Returns to Education: A Further International Update and Implications. *J. Human Res.*, Fall 1985, *20*(4), pp. 583–604. **[G: Selected Countries]**

Raftery, Adrian E. and Hout, Michael. Does Irish Education Approach the Meritocratic Ideal? A Logistic Analysis. *Econ. Soc. Rev.*, January 1985, *16*(2), pp. 115–40. **[G: Ireland]**

Reskin, Barbara F. Aging and Productivity: Careers and Results. In *Clark, S. M. and Lewis, D. R.*, *eds.*, 1985, pp. 86–97. **[G: U.S.]**

Rose, James. Implementation of Federal ECIA Block Grants to Education in Colorado. *Econ. Educ. Rev.*, 1985, *4*(3), pp. 171–79. **[G: U.S.]**

Roth, Alvin E. The College Admissions Problem Is Not Equivalent to the Marriage Problem. *J. Econ. Theory*, August 1985, *36*(2), pp. 277–88.

Russell, Russ. A Comparison of the Youth Training Scheme in the United Kingdom with the Vocational Foundation Training Year in Germany. In *Worswick, G. D. N.*, *ed.*, 1985, pp. 68–75. **[G: U.K.; W. Germany]**

Sackey, James A. and Sackey, Thywill E. Secondary School Students' Employment Aspirations and Expectations and the Barbados Labour Market. *Soc. Econ. Stud.*, September 1985, *34*(3), pp. 211–58. **[G: Barbados]**

Schwartz, J. Brad. Student Financial Aid and the College Enrollment Decision: The Effects of Public and Private Grants and Interest Subsidies. *Econ. Educ. Rev.*, 1985, *4*(2), pp. 129–44.

Sexton, Thomas R. and Weinstein, Joan B. Student Recruiting: Linear Programming as Problem-Solver and Heuristic. *J. Policy Anal. Manage.*, Summer 1985, *4*(4), pp. 597–603.

Shah, Anup R. Does Education Act as a Screening Device for Certain British Occupations? *Oxford Econ. Pap.*, March 1985, *37*(1), pp. 118–24. [G: U.K.]

Shorten, Sarah J. The Funding of Postsecondary Education: Proposals of the Canadian Association of University Teachers. **In** *Courchene, T. J.; Conklin, D. W. and Cook, G. C. A., eds. Vol. 1*, 1985, pp. 335–39. [G: Canada]

Slater, David W. Public Support of Postsecondary Education. **In** *Courchene, T. J.; Conklin, D. W. and Cook, G. C. A., eds. Vol. 1*, 1985, pp. 287–98. [G: Canada]

Sloan, Judith. Continuity and Change: Labour Market Programs and Education Expenditure: Comment. *Australian Econ. Rev.*, 3rd Quarter, Spring 1985, (71), pp. 114–15. [G: Australia]

Smith, Bruce L. R. Graduate Education in the United States. **In** *Smith, B. L. R., ed.*, 1985, pp. 1–30. [G: U.S.]

Snyder, Robert G. Some Indicators of the Condition of Graduate Education in the Sciences. **In** *Smith, B. L. R., ed.*, 1985, pp. 31–55. [G: U.S.]

Solmon, Lewis C. Quality of Education and Economic Growth. *Econ. Educ. Rev.*, 1985, *4*(4), pp. 273–90. [G: Global]

Stankiewicz, Rikard. A New Role for Universities in Technological Innovation? **In** *Sweeney, G., ed.*, 1985, pp. 114–51. [G: OECD]

Stanton, David. Education: Comments. **In** *Worswick, G. D. N., ed.*, 1985, pp. 138–40. [G: U.K.]

Stern, David. Distributional Programs: Education and Antipoverty: Commentary. **In** *Quigley, J. M. and Rubinfeld, D. L., eds.*, 1985, pp. 161–72. [G: U.S.]

Stone, Joe A. Determinants of Administrators' Salaries in Public Schools: Differences for Men and Women. *Econ. Educ. Rev.*, 1985, *4*(2), pp. 105–09. [G: U.S.]

Taylor, Terry. A Value-added Student Assessment Model: Northeast Missouri State University. *Econ. Educ. Rev.*, 1985, *4*(4), pp. 341–50. [G: U.S.]

Taylor, William X. Productivity and Educational Values. **In** *Worswick, G. D. N., ed.*, 1985, pp. 101–12. [G: U.K.]

Tilak, Jandhyala B. G. and Verghese, N. V. Educational Planning at District Level: An Exercise on Gurgaon District (Haryana). *Margin*, April 1985, *17*(3), pp. 75–96. [G: India]

Tímár, János. Manpower and Educational Planning in Hungary. **In** *Youdi, R. V. and Hinchliffe, K., eds.*, 1985, pp. 119–34. [G: Hungary]

Tridimas, George. Economic Theory and the Allocation of Public Expenditures in Greece. *Greek Econ. Rev.*, April 1985, *7*(1), pp. 34–52. [G: Greece]

Valencia, Richard R. Public School Closures and Policy Issues: Financial and Social Implica-

tions. *Public Budg. Finance*, Spring 1985, *5*(1), pp. 43–53. [G: U.S.]

Verma, M. C. Review of Skilled-Manpower Forecasts in India. **In** *Youdi, R. V. and Hinchliffe, K., eds.*, 1985, pp. 194–210. [G: India]

Watson, William G. Some Questions of Principle. *Can. Public Policy*, March 1985, *11*(1), pp. 118–25. [G: Canada]

Watts, Michael. School District Inputs and Biased Estimation of Educational Production Functions. *J. Econ. Educ.*, Fall 1985, *16*(4), pp. 281–85. [G: U.S.]

Webb, Michael A. Migration and Education Subsidies by Governments: A Game-theoretic Analysis. *J. Public Econ.*, March 1985, *26*(2), pp. 249–62.

Webb, Michael A. The Brain Drain and Education Opportunity in Less Developed Countries. *Eastern Econ. J.*, April-June 1985, *11*(2), pp. 145–55. [G: LDCs]

Wedeman, Sara Capen; Passman, Vicki Fay and Day, James Merideth. Education Block Grants: Introduction to the Debate. *Econ. Educ. Rev.*, 1985, *4*(3), pp. 163–70. [G: U.S.]

West, Edwin G. Public Aid to Ontario's Independent Schools. *Can. Public Policy*, December 1985, *11*(4), pp. 701–10. [G: Canada]

West, Edwin G. The Demise of "Free" Education. *Challenge*, January/February 1985, *27*(6), pp. 26–32. [G: U.S.]

West, Edwin G. The Real Costs of Tuition Tax Credits. *Public Choice*, 1985, *46*(1), pp. 61–70. [G: U.S.]

Wetzel, James N. Transferable Property Rights to Education. *Land Econ.*, May 1985, *61*(2), pp. 213–16.

Whelan, Christopher T. and Whelan, Brendan J. "Equality of Opportunity in Irish Schools": A Reassessment. *Econ. Soc. Rev.*, January 1985, *16*(2), pp. 103–14. [G: Ireland]

Wilkerson, Margaret B. A Report on the Educational Status of Black Women during the UN Decade of Women, 1976–85. *Rev. Black Polit. Econ.*, Fall-Winter 1985-86, *14*(2–3), pp. 83–96. [G: U.S.]

Willenbrock, F. Karl. The Status of Engineering Education in the United States. **In** *Smith, B. L. R., ed.*, 1985, pp. 85–96. [G: U.S.]

Williams, Gareth. Education: Comments. **In** *Worswick, G. D. N., ed.*, 1985, pp. 131–35. [G: U.K.]

Williams, Ross A. The Economic Determinants of Private Schooling in Australia. *Econ. Rec.*, September 1985, *61*(174), pp. 622–28. [G: Australia]

Williams, Thomas T. and Williamson, Handy, Jr. Teaching, Research, and Extension Programs at Predominantly Black Land-Grant Institutions. *Southern J. Agr. Econ.*, July 1985, *17*(1), pp. 31–41. [G: U.S.]

Wilson, Linda S. The Capital Facilities Dilemma in the American Graduate School. **In** *Smith, B. L. R., ed.*, 1985, pp. 121–49. [G: U.S.]

Wolch, Jennifer R. Distributional Programs: Education and Antipoverty: Commentary. **In** *Quig-*

ley, J. M. and Rubinfeld, D. L., eds., 1985, pp. 173–80. **[G: U.S.]**

Woodbury, Stephen A. The Scope of Bargaining and Bargaining Outcomes in the Public Schools. *Ind. Lab. Relat. Rev.*, January 1985, 38(2), pp. 195–210. **[G: U.S.]**

Worswick, G. D. N. Education and Economic Performance: Introduction. In *Worswick, G. D. N., ed.*, 1985, pp. 1–6.

Young, Anne McDougall. New Monthly Data Series on School Age Youth. *Mon. Lab. Rev.*, July 1985, 108(7), pp. 49–50. **[G: U.S.]**

Zarkin, Gary A. Occupational Choice: An Application to the Market for Public School Teachers. *Quart. J. Econ.*, May 1985, 100(2), pp. 409–46. **[G: U.S.]**

913 Economics of Health (including medical subsidy programs)

9130 Economics of Health (including medical subsidy programs)

Akin, John S., et al. Determinants of Infant Feeding: A Household Production Approach. *Econ. Develop. Cult. Change*, October 1985, 34(1), pp. 57–81. **[G: Philippines]**

Akin, John S., et al. The Impact of Federal Transfer Programs on the Nutrient Intake of Elderly Individuals. *J. Human Res.*, Summer 1985, 20(3), pp. 383–404. **[G: U.S.]**

Albert, James H. Bayesian Estimation Methods for Incomplete Two-Way Contingency Tables Using Prior Beliefs of Association. In *Bernardo, J. M., et al., eds.*, 1985, pp. 589–602.

Anderson, Gerard F. and Steinberg, Earl P. Predicting Hospital Readmissions in the Medicare Population. *Inquiry*, Fall 1985, 22(3), pp. 251–58. **[G: U.S.]**

Anderson, Kathryn H. and Burkhauser, Richard V. The Retirement–Health Nexus: A New Measure of an Old Puzzle. *J. Human Res.*, Summer 1985, 20(3), pp. 315–30. **[G: U.S.]**

Andreasen, Alan R. Consumer Responses to Dissatisfaction in Loose Monopolies. *J. Cons. Res.*, September 1985, 12(2), pp. 135–41.
[G: U.S.]

Arnould, Richard J. and DeBrock, Lawrence M. The Effect of Provider Control of Blue Shield Plans on Health Care Markets. *Econ. Inquiry*, July 1985, 23(3), pp. 449–74. **[G: U.S.]**

Arnould, Richard J. and Van Vorst, Charles B. Supply Responses to Market and Regulatory Forces in Health Care. In *Meyer, J. A., ed.*, 1985, pp. 107–31. **[G: U.S.]**

Arrow, Kenneth J. Problems of Resource Allocation in United States Medical Care. In *Arrow, K. J. (II)*, 1985, pp. 70–88. **[G: U.S.]**

Arrow, Kenneth J. The Implications of Transaction Costs and Adjustment Lags in Health Insurance [Uncertainty and the Welfare Economics of Medical Care]. In *Arrow, K. J. (II)*, 1985, pp. 51–55.

Arrow, Kenneth J. Theoretical Issues in Health Insurance. In *Arrow, K. J. (II)*, 1985, pp. 208–33.

Arrow, Kenneth J. Uncertainty and the Welfare Economics of Medical Care. In *Arrow, K. J. (II)*, 1985, pp. 15–50.

Arrow, Kenneth J. Welfare Analysis of Changes in Health Coinsurance Rates. In *Arrow, K. J. (II)*, 1985, pp. 234–54.

Atkinson, Scott E.; Crocker, Thomas D. and Murdock, Robert G. Have Priors in Aggregate Air Pollution Epidemiology Dictated Posteriors? *J. Urban Econ.*, May 1985, 17(3), pp. 319–34. **[G: U.S.]**

Auray, J. P., et al. Assessing the Effects of Unemployment on Health Services Use in a Specific Group: A Research Proposal. In *Westcott, G.; Svensson, P.-G. and Zollner, H. F. K., eds.*, 1985, pp. 335–45. **[G: France]**

Bartlett, Katharine T. The Role of Cost in Educational Decisionmaking for the Handicapped Child. *Law Contemp. Probl.*, Spring 1985, 48(2), pp. 7–62. **[G: U.S.]**

Bazzoli, Gloria J. Does Educational Indebtedness Affect Physician Specialty Choice? *J. Health Econ.*, March 1985, 4(1), pp. 1–19. **[G: U.S.]**

Bazzoli, Gloria J. The Early Retirement Decision: New Empirical Evidence on the Influence of Health. *J. Human Res.*, Spring 1985, 20(2), pp. 214–34. **[G: U.S.]**

Becker, Edmund R. and Sloan, Frank A. Hospital Ownership and Performance. *Econ. Inquiry*, January 1985, 23(1), pp. 21–36. **[G: U.S.]**

Beigel, Allen and Kettel, Louis J. Current Strategies for Containing Health Care Expenditures: Voluntary Efforts by Providers. In *Christianson, J. B. and Smith, K. R., eds.*, 1985, pp. 76–84. **[G: U.S.]**

Bénard, Jean. Capital Humain et Optimum de Second Rang. Le Cas des Dépenses de Sante. In *Terny, G. and Culyer, A. J., eds.*, 1985, pp. 319–35.

Berg, Alan. Bank Interventions in Nutrition. In *Davis, T. J., ed.*, 1985, pp. 145–52.

Birch, Stephen and Maynard, Alan. Public Expenditure Policy, 1985–86: Health and Personal Social Services. In *Cockle, P., ed.*, 1985, pp. 223–42. **[G: U.K.]**

Björklund, Anders. Unemployment and Mental Health: Some Evidence from Panel Data. *J. Human Res.*, Fall 1985, 20(4), pp. 469–83.
[G: Sweden]

Blendon, Robert J. Public Choices for the 1990s: An Uncertain Look into America's Future. In *Ginzberg, E., ed.*, 1985, pp. 5–27. **[G: U.S.]**

Boland, Peter. Questioning Assumptions about Preferred Provider Arrangements. *Inquiry*, Summer 1985, 22(2), pp. 132–41. **[G: U.S.]**

Booton, Lavonne A. and Lane, Julia. Hospital Market Structure and the Return to Nursing Education. *J. Human Res.*, Spring 1985, 20(2), pp. 184–96. **[G: U.S.]**

Brenner, M. Harvey. Economic Change and Mortality by Cause in Selected European Countries: Special Reference to Behaviour Health Risks, Emphasising Alcohol Consumption. In *Westcott, G.; Svensson, P.-G. and Zollner, H. F. K., eds.*, 1985, pp. 143–80.
[G: OECD]

Brenner, Sten Olof, et al. Job Insecurity and Unemployment: Effects on Health and Wellbeing and an Evaluation of Coping Measures. In *Westcott, G.; Svensson, P.-G. and Zollner, H. F. K., eds.*, 1985, pp. 325–34.
[G: Sweden]

Brewster, Alan C., et al. MEDISGRPS: A Clinically Based Approach to Classifying Hospital Patients at Admission. *Inquiry*, Winter 1985, 22(4), pp. 377–87. [G: U.S.]

Breyer, Friedrich. Die Fallpauschale als Vergütung für Krankenhausleistungen. Idee, Formen und vermutete Auswirkungen. (With English summary.) *Z. Wirtschaft. Sozialwissen.*, 1985, 105(6), pp. 743–67.

Brinkmann, Christian. Health Problems in the Initial Phase of Unemployment: Some Research Findings and Policy Implications. In *Westcott, G.; Svensson, P.-G. and Zollner, H. F. K., eds.*, 1985, pp. 273–91.
[G: W. Germany]

Broome, John. The Economic Value of Life. *Economica*, August 1985, 52(207), pp. 281–94.

Brown, E. Richard; Cousineau, Michael R. and Price, Walter T. Competing for Medi-Cal Business: Why Hospitals Did, and Did Not, Get Contracts. *Inquiry*, Fall 1985, 22(3), pp. 237–50. [G: U.S.]

Brown, John Prather. Alternatives to tsm Balsent System of Litigation for Personal Injury. In *Baily, M. A. and Cikins, W. I., eds.*, 1985, pp. 69–79. [G: U.S.]

Brown, Jonathan Betz and Saltman, Richard B. Health Capital in the United States: A Strategic Perspective. *Inquiry*, Summer 1985, 22(2), pp. 122–31. [G: U.S.]

Brown, Lawrence D. The Managerial Imperative and Organizational Innovation in Health Services. In *Ginzberg, E., ed.*, 1985, pp. 28–47.
[G: U.S.]

Bruun, K. E. Alcohol Policies: Sweden. In *Grant, M., ed.*, 1985, pp. 114–19. [G: Sweden; U.K.]

Bruun, K. E. Formulating Comprehensive National Alcohol Policies. In *Grant, M., ed.*, 1985, pp. 137–42.

Burke, Sheila P. Medicare Reform: Where Will the Emphasis Be in Congress and the Administration? In *Employee Benefit Research Institute.*, 1985, pp. 7–17. [G: U.S.]

Burstein, Philip L. and Cromwell, Jerry. Relative Incomes and Rates of Return for U.S. Physicians. *J. Health Econ.*, March 1985, 4(1), pp. 63–78. [G: U.S.]

Butler, J. S.; Ohls, James C. and Posner, Barbara. The Effect of the Food Stamp Program on the Nutrient Intake of the Eligible Elderly. *J. Human Res.*, Summer 1985, 20(3), pp. 405–20. [G: U.S.]

Butterfield, John. Adding Life to Years. In *Wells, N., ed.*, 1985, pp. 152–58.

Caplovitz, David. Concepts, Indices and Contexts. In *Smith, R. B., ed.*, 1985, pp. 193–240.
[G: U.S.]

Capron, Alexander Morgan. Allocating Finite Resources: Questions of Equity and Access. In *Lewin, M. E., ed.*, 1985, pp. 7–25. [G: U.S.]

Castañeda, Tarsicio. Determinantes del descenso de la mortalidad infantil en Chile: 1975–1982. *Cuadernos Econ.*, August 1985, 22(66), pp. 195–214. [G: Chile]

Cave, Jonathan A. K. Subsidy Equilibrium and Multiple-Option Insurance Markets. In *Scheffler, R. M. and Rossiter, L. F., eds.*, 1985, pp. 27–45.

Chachere, Bernadette. Health Issues: Discussion II. *Rev. Black Polit. Econ.*, Fall-Winter 1985-86, 14(2–3), pp. 235–38.

Chirikos, Thomas N. and Nestel, Gilbert. Further Evidence on the Economic Effects of Poor Health. *Rev. Econ. Statist.*, February 1985, 67(1), pp. 61–69. [G: U.S.]

Chollet, Deborah J. Liability Rules and Health Care Costs. In *Baily, M. A. and Cikins, W. I., eds.*, 1985, pp. 22–27. [G: U.S.]

Christianson, Jon B. Current Strategies for Containing Health Care Expenditures: Increased Competition Over Prices and Premiums. In *Christianson, J. B. and Smith, K. R., eds.*, 1985, pp. 52–75. [G: U.S.]

Christianson, Jon B. Current Strategies for Containing Health Care Expenditures: Summary and Interpretation. In *Christianson, J. B. and Smith, K. R., eds.*, 1985, pp. 108–10.
[G: U.S.]

Christianson, Jon B. The Concern About Containment of Health Care Expenditures. In *Christianson, J. B. and Smith, K. R., eds.*, 1985, pp. 1–10. [G: U.S.]

Christianson, Jon B. and Smith, Kenneth R. Options in the Design of Competitive-Bidding Processes for Indigent Medical Care. *Contemp. Policy Issues*, Winter 1984-85, 3(2), pp. 55–68. [G: U.S.]

Cohen, Steven B. and Burt, Vicki L. Data Collection Frequency Effect in the National Medical Care Expenditure Survey. *J. Econ. Soc. Meas.*, July 1985, 13(2), pp. 125–51. [G: U.S.]

Conlisk, John. Technical Problems in Social Experimentation: Cost versus Ease of Analysis: Comment. In *Hausman, J. A. and Wise, D. A., eds.*, 1985, pp. 208–14.

Conrad, Douglas A., et al. All-Payer Rate Regulation: An Analysis of Hospital Response. In *Lewin, M. E., ed.*, 1985, pp. 65–84.
[G: U.S.]

Conrad, Douglas A.; Grembowski, David and Milgrom, Peter. Adverse Selection within Dental Insurance Markets. In *Scheffler, R. M. and Rossiter, L. F., eds.*, 1985, pp. 171–90.
[G: U.S.]

Corman, Hope and Grossman, Michael. Determinants of Neonatal Mortality Rates in the U.S.: A Reduced Form Model. *J. Health Econ.*, September 1985, 4(3), pp. 213–36.
[G: U.S.]

Cottino, A. and Morgan, Paul. Alcohol Policies: Italy. In *Grant, M., ed.*, 1985, pp. 83–92.
[G: Italy]

Coyte, Peter C. The Market for Medical Services and Physicians: An Application of Hedonic

Price Theory. *Can. J. Econ.*, May 1985, *18*(2), pp. 377–94.

Coyte, Peter C. The Operation of the Hospital Sector: Towards a Diagnosis. *Southern Econ. J.*, January 1985, *51*(3), pp. 655–71.

Culler, Steven D. and Bazzoli, Gloria J. The Moonlighting Decisions of Resident Physicians. *J. Health Econ.*, September 1985, *4*(3), pp. 283–92.   [G: U.S.]

Cullis, John G. and Jones, Philip R. National Health Service Waiting Lists: A Discussion of Competing Explanations and a Policy Proposal. *J. Health Econ.*, June 1985, *4*(2), pp. 119–35.   [G: U.S.]

Culyer, A. J. On Being Right or Wrong about the Welfare State. In *Bean, P.; Ferris, J. and Whynes, D., eds.*, 1985, pp. 122–41.   [G: U.K.]

Curtin, Philip D. Medical Knowledge and Urban Planning in Tropical Africa. *Amer. Hist. Rev.*, June 1985, *90*(3), pp. 594–613.
                    [G: Tropical Africa]

Danzon, Patricia M. Liability and Liability Insurance for Medical Malpractice. *J. Health Econ.*, December 1985, *4*(4), pp. 309–31. [G: U.S.]

Danzon, Patricia M. The Medical Malpractice System: Facts and Reforms. In *Baily, M. A. and Cikins, W. I., eds.*, 1985, pp. 28–35.
                    [G: U.S.]

Dionne, Georges and Contandriopoulos, André-Pierre. Doctors and Their Workshops: A Review Article. *J. Health Econ.*, March 1985, *4*(1), pp. 21–33.

Dobbs, Ian M. Shadow Prices, Consistency and the Value of Life. *J. Public Econ.*, July 1985, *27*(2), pp. 177–93.

Doll, Richard. Risk Factors in Health Care. In *Wells, N., ed.*, 1985, pp. 143–51.   [G: U.K.]

Donabedian, Avedis. The Epidemiology of Quality. *Inquiry*, Fall 1985, *22*(3), pp. 282–92.
                    [G: U.S.]

Dooley, David and Catalano, Ralph. Does Economic Change Increase Mental Disorder?: A Synthesis of Recent Research. In *Westcott, G.; Svensson, P.-G. and Zollner, H. F. K., eds.*, 1985, pp. 57–86.

Dooley, David and Catalano, Ralph. Why the Economy Predicts Help Seeking: A Test of Competing Explanations. In *Westcott, G.; Svensson, P.-G. and Zollner, H. F. K., eds.*, 1985, pp. 205–29.   [G: U.S.]

Dowd, Bryan and Feldman, Roger. Biased Selection in Twin Cities Health Plans. In *Scheffler, R. M. and Rossiter, L. F., eds.*, 1985, pp. 253–71.   [G: U.S.]

Dranove, David. An Empirical Study of a Hospital-based Home Care Program. *Inquiry*, Spring 1985, *22*(1), pp. 59–66.   [G: U.S.]

Dranove, David and Cone, Kenneth. Do State Rate Setting Regulations Really Lower Hospital Expenses? *J. Health Econ.*, June 1985, *4*(2), pp. 159–65.   [G: U.S.]

Duan, Naihua, et al. A Survey of the Literature on Selectivity Bias as it Pertains to Health Care Markets: Comments. In *Scheffler, R. M. and Rossiter, L. F., eds.*, 1985, pp. 19–24.

Dussault, Gilles. La politique de la délégation des actes professionnels au Québec. (With English summary.) *Can. Public Policy*, June 1985, *11*(2), pp. 218–26.   [G: Canada]

Eastaugh, Steven R. The Impact of the Nurse Training Act on the Supply of Nurses, 1974–1983. *Inquiry*, Winter 1985, *22*(4), pp. 404–17.   [G: U.S.]

Eeckhoudt, Louis; Lebrun, T. and Sailly, J. C. Risk-aversion and Physicians' Medical Decision-making. *J. Health Econ.*, September 1985, *4*(3), pp. 273–81.

Ellis, Randall P. The Effect of Prior-Year Health Expenditures on Health Coverage Plan Choice. In *Scheffler, R. M. and Rossiter, L. F., eds.*, 1985, pp. 149–70.   [G: U.S.]

Etheredge, Lynn. Health Care Financing in 1990, or What Will Happen on the San Andreas Fault? In *Ginzberg, E., ed.*, 1985, pp. 89–107.
                    [G: U.S.]

Fanara, Philip, Jr. and Greenberg, Warren. Factors Affecting the Adoption of Prospective Reimbursement Programs by State Governments. In *Meyer, J. A., ed.*, 1985, pp. 144–56.   [G: U.S.]

Fanara, Philip, Jr. and Greenberg, Warren. The Impact of Competition and Regulation on Blue Cross Enrollment of Non-group Individuals. *J. Risk Ins.*, June 1985, *52*(2), pp. 185–98.
                    [G: U.S.]

Farley, Pamela J. and Monheit, Alan C. Selectivity in the Demand for Health Insurance and Health Care. In *Scheffler, R. M. and Rossiter, L. F., eds.*, 1985, pp. 231–48.   [G: U.S.]

Farley, Pamela J. and Wilensky, Gail R. Household Wealth and Health Insurance as Protection against Medical Risks. In *David, M. and Smeeding, T., eds.*, 1985, pp. 323–54.
                    [G: U.S.]

Feldman, Roger and Begun, James W. The Welfare Cost of Quality Changes Due to Professional Regulation. *J. Ind. Econ.*, September 1985, *34*(1), pp. 17–32.   [G: U.S.]

Feldman, Roger; Jensen, Gail and Dowd, Bryan. What Are Employers Doing to Create a Competitive Market for Health Care in the Twin Cities? *Contemp. Policy Issues*, Winter 1984-85, *3*(2), pp. 69–88.   [G: U.S.]

Ferguson, Brian S. Physician Objectives and Resource Allocation. *J. Health Econ.*, March 1985, *4*(1), pp. 35–42.

Fickling, William A., Jr. Succeeding by Anticipating Trends. In *Federal Reserve Bank of Atlanta (I)*, 1985, pp. 59–64.   [G: U.S.]

Field, Marilyn J. Comments on Policy Implications of Biased Selection in Health Insurance. In *Scheffler, R. M. and Rossiter, L. F., eds.*, 1985, pp. 249–52.   [G: U.S.]

Finkler, Merton D. Changes in Certificate-of-Need Laws: Read the Fine Print. In *Meyer, J. A., ed.*, 1985, pp. 132–43.   [G: U.S.]

Fleming, Steven T.; Kobrinski, Edward J. and Long, Michael J. A Multidimensional Analysis of the Impact of High-Cost Hospitalization. *Inquiry*, Summer 1985, *22*(2), pp. 178–87.

Foster, James C. *The Western Dilemma:* Miners,

Silicosis, and Compensation. *Labor Hist.*, Spring 1985, *26*(2), pp. 268–87.   [G: U.S.]

Foster, Richard W. Cost-shifting under Cost Reimbursement and Prospective Payments. *J. Health Econ.*, September 1985, *4*(3), pp. 261–71.

Frank, Beryl. Social Security in Latin America: Trends and Outlook: Comment. In *Mesa-Lago, C., ed.*, 1985, pp. 84–87.

[G: Latin America]

Frank, Richard G. A Model of State Expenditures on Mental Health Services. *Public Finance Quart.*, July 1985, *13*(3), pp. 319–38.

[G: U.S.]

Frank, Richard G. Pricing and Location of Physician Services in Mental Health. *Econ. Inquiry*, January 1985, *23*(1), pp. 115–33.   [G: U.S.]

Frank, Richard G. and Welch, W. P. The Competitive Effects of HMOs: A Review of the Evidence. *Inquiry*, Summer 1985, *22*(2), pp. 148–61.

Franklin, David L. and Vial de Valdés, Isabel. Estrategias nutricionales de los hogares pobres. (With English summary.) *Cuadernos Econ.*, August 1985, *22*(66), pp. 247–65.

[G: Panama]

Frech, H. E., III. The Property Rights Theory of the Firm: Some Evidence from the U.S. Nursing Home Industry. *Z. ges. Staatswiss. (JITE)*, March 1985, *141*(1), pp. 146–66.

[G: U.S.]

Freund, Deborah A. Improving the Medicare HMO Payment Formula to Deal with Biased Selection: Comments. In *Scheffler, R. M. and Rossiter, L. F., eds.*, 1985, pp. 123–26.

[G: U.S.]

Freund, Deborah A., et al. Analysis of Length-of-Stay Differences between Investor-owned and Voluntary Hospitals. *Inquiry*, Spring 1985, *22*(1), pp. 33–44.   [G: U.S.]

Gäfgen, Gérard. The Property Rights Theory of the Firm: Some Evidence from the U.S. Nursing Home Industry: Comment. *Z. ges. Staatswiss. (JITE)*, March 1985, *141*(1), pp. 167–69.

Gaspari, K. Celeste and Woolf, Arthur G. Income, Public Works, and Mortality in Early Twentieth-Century American Cities. *J. Econ. Hist.*, June 1985, *45*(2), pp. 355–61.

[G: U.S.]

Gensheimer, Cynthia Francis. Reform of the Individual Income Tax: Effects on Tax Preferences for Medical Care. In *Meyer, J. A., ed.*, 1985, pp. 53–66.   [G: U.S.]

Gieringer, Dale H. The Safety and Efficacy of New Drug Approval. *Cato J.*, Spring/Summer 1985, *5*(1), pp. 177–201.   [G: U.S.]

Ginsburg, Paul B. Macroexperiments versus Microexperiments for Health Policy: Comment. In *Hausman, J. A. and Wise, D. A., eds.*, 1985, pp. 170–72.

Ginsburg, Paul B. Reflections on Biased Selection and Future Directions. In *Scheffler, R. M. and Rossiter, L. F., eds.*, 1985, pp. 275–80.

[G: U.S.]

Ginzberg, Eli. The Restructuring of U.S. Health Care. *Inquiry*, Fall 1985, *22*(3), pp. 272–81.

[G: U.S.]

Ginzberg, Eli. The U.S. Health Care System: A Look to the 1990s: Directions for Policy. In *Ginzberg, E., ed.*, 1985, pp. 108–13.

[G: U.S.]

Goldsmith, Jeff Charles. The Changing Role of the Hospital. In *Ginzberg, E., ed.*, 1985, pp. 48–69.   [G: U.S.]

Goldstein, Joshua S. Basic Human Needs: The Plateau Curve. *World Devel.*, May 1985, *13*(5), pp. 595–609.

Grant, M. Alcohol Policies: National and International Approaches: Strengthening the Links. In *Grant, M., ed.*, 1985, pp. 143–47.

Grant, M. Establishing Priorities for Action. In *Grant, M., ed.*, 1985, pp. 1–8.

[G: W. Europe]

Greenberg, Warren. Demand, Supply, and Information in Health Care and Other Industries. In *Meyer, J. A., ed.*, 1985, pp. 96–106.

[G: U.S.]

Greene, Vernon L. Current Strategies for Containing Health Care Expenditures: Government Imposed Controls on Expenditures. In *Christianson, J. B. and Smith, K. R., eds.*, 1985, pp. 38–51.   [G: U.S.]

Greenlick, Merwyn R. Medicare Capitation Payments to HMOs in Light of Regression toward the Mean in Health Care Costs: Comments. In *Scheffler, R. M. and Rossiter, L. F., eds.*, 1985, pp. 97–100.   [G: U.S.]

Gutiérrez, Alvaro Castro. Alternative Strategies to the Social Security Crisis: Socialist, Market and Mixed Approaches: Comment. In *Mesa-Lago, C., ed.*, 1985, pp. 362–65.   [G: Chile; Costa Rica; Cuba]

Hanft, Ruth S. Physicians and Hospitals: Changing Dynamics. In *Lewin, M. E., ed.*, 1985, pp. 99–114.   [G: U.S.]

Harbert, Lloyd and Scandizzo, Pasquale L. Distribución de alimentos e intervención en la nutrición: el caso de Chile. (With English summary.) *Cuadernos Econ.*, August 1985, *22*(66), pp. 215–46.   [G: Chile]

Harris, Jeffrey. Competition and Equilibrium as a Driving Force in the Health Services Sector: Comment. In *Inman, R. P., ed.*, 1985, pp. 268–72.

Harris, Jeffrey E. Macroexperiments versus Microexperiments for Health Policy. In *Hausman, J. A. and Wise, D. A., eds.*, 1985, pp. 145–70.

Harris, Ralph. The Importance of a Market Economy. In *Wells, N., ed.*, 1985, pp. 175–84.

Hausman, Jerry A. and Wise, David A. Technical Problems in Social Experimentation: Cost versus Ease of Analysis. In *Hausman, J. A. and Wise, D. A., eds.*, 1985, pp. 187–208.

[G: U.S.]

Haveman, Robert H. and Wolfe, Barbara L. Income, Inequality, and Uncertainty: Differences between the Disabled and Nondisabled. In *David, M. and Smeeding, T., eds.*, 1985, pp. 293–319.   [G: U.S.]

Havighurst, Clark C. The Debate over Health

Care Cost-Containment Regulation: The Issues and the Interests. In *Meyer, J. A., ed.*, 1985, pp. 9–25. [G: U.S.]

Haynes, Robin. Regional Anomalies in Hospital Bed Use in England and Wales. *Reg. Stud.*, February 1985, *19*(1), pp. 19–27. [G: U.K.]

Headon, Alvin E., Jr. and Headon, Sandra W. General Health Conditions and Medical Insurance Issues Concerning Black Women. *Rev. Black Polit. Econ.*, Fall-Winter 1985-86, *14*(2–3), pp. 183–97. [G: U.S.]

Hellinger, Fred J. Recent Evidence on Case-based Systems for Setting Hospital Rates. *Inquiry*, Spring 1985, *22*(1), pp. 78–91.
[G: U.S.]

Hemenway, David. The Smoldering Issue of Fire Fatalities. *J. Policy Anal. Manage.*, Summer 1985, *4*(4), pp. 593–97.

Hillman, Diane G. Current Strategies for Containing Health Care Expenditures: Strategies in the Fifty States. In *Christianson, J. B. and Smith, K. R., eds.*, 1985, pp. 85–107.
[G: U.S.]

Hornbrook, Mark C. and Monheit, Alan C. The Contribution of Case-Mix Severity to the Hospital Cost-Output Relation. *Inquiry*, Fall 1985, *22*(3), pp. 259–71. [G: U.S.]

Horton, Susan. The Determinants of Nutrient Intake: Results from Western India. *J. Devel. Econ.*, Sept.-Oct. 1985, *19*(1/2), pp. 147–62.
[G: India]

Hosay, Cynthia K. The Impact of Medicare Reform on the Private Sector. In *Employee Benefit Research Institute.*, 1985, pp. 65–72.
[G: U.S.]

Hosay, Cynthia K. The Impact of Medicare Reform on the Private Sector: Remarks. In *Employee Benefit Research Institute.*, 1985, pp. 72–77. [G: U.S.]

Huffman, Sandra L. Response to Determinants of Natural Fertility Reconsidered. *Population Stud.*, March 1985, *39*(1), pp. 163–68.
[G: Bangladesh]

Hunsaker, Ann T. The Federal Government's Perspective on Litigation and Health Care Costs. In *Baily, M. A. and Cikins, W. I., eds.*, 1985, pp. 11–21. [G: U.S.]

Hurley, Rosalinde. Balancing Risks and Benefits: Discussion. In *Wells, N., ed.*, 1985, pp. 159–60.

Ignagni, Karen. Organized Labor's Perspective on Rising Health Costs. In *Dennis, B. D., ed.*, 1985, pp. 473–76. [G: U.S.]

van Iwaarden, M. J. Public Health Aspects of the Marketing of Alcoholic Drinks. In *Grant, M., ed.*, 1985, pp. 45–55. [G: Netherlands]

Jackson, Beryl B. Health Issues: Discussion I. *Rev. Black Polit. Econ.*, Fall-Winter 1985-86, *14*(2–3), pp. 227–34. [G: U.S.]

Jamal, Haroon. Highlights from National Survey on Drug Abuse: 1982. *Pakistan Econ. Soc. Rev.*, Winter 1985, *23*(2), pp. 135–49.
[G: Pakistan]

Janlert, Urban. Unemployment and Health. In *Westcott, G.; Svensson, P.-G. and Zollner,*

H. F. K., eds., 1985, pp. 7–26. [G: U.K.; Sweden; Finland]

John, Jürgen. Economic Instability and Health: Infant Mortality and Suicide Reconsidered. In *Westcott, G.; Svensson, P.-G. and Zollner, H. F. K., eds.*, 1985, pp. 181–204.
[G: W. Germany]

Johns, Lucy; Anderson, Maren D. and Derzon, Robert A. Selective Contracting in California: Experience in the Second Year. *Inquiry*, Winter 1985, *22*(4), pp. 335–47. [G: U.S.]

Johns, Lucy; Derzon, Robert A. and Anderson, Maren D. Selective Contracting in California: Early Effects and Policy Implications. *Inquiry*, Spring 1985, *22*(1), pp. 24–32. [G: U.S.]

Johnson, Glenn L. The US Presidential World Food and Nutrition Study and Commission on World Hunger: Lessons for the United States and Other Countries. In *[Heidhues, T.]*, 1985, pp. 47–63.

Jones, David D. Inflation Rates Implicit in Discounting Personal Injury Economic Losses. *J. Risk Ins.*, March 1985, *52*(1), pp. 144–50.
[G: U.S.]

Jones-Lee, M. W.; Hammerton, M. and Philips, P. R. The Value of Safety: Results of a National Sample Survey. *Econ. J.*, March 1985, *95*(377), pp. 49–72. [G: U.K.]

Jones, S. Patricia. The Costs of Membership Aging in a Blue Cross and Blue Shield Plan. *Inquiry*, Summer 1985, *22*(2), pp. 201–05.

Joskow, Paul L. The Stochastic Determinants of Hospital-Bed Supply: Reply [The Effects of Competition and Regulation on Hospital Bed Supply and the Reservation Quality of the Hospital]. *J. Health Econ.*, June 1985, *4*(2), pp. 183–85. [G: U.S.]

Kadanc, Joseph B. Toward Evaluating the Cost-Effectiveness of Medical and Social Experiments: Comment. In *Hausman, J. A. and Wise, D. A., eds.*, 1985, pp. 246–47. [G: U.S.]

Keating, B. Cost Shifting: A Reply [Cost Shifting: An Empirical Examination of Hospital Bureaucracy]. *Appl. Econ.*, October 1985, *17*(5), pp. 803. [G: U.S.]

Kieselbach, Thomas. The Contribution of Psychology to the Realm of Unemployment in the Community: Intervention and Research Concepts. In *Westcott, G.; Svensson, P.-G. and Zollner, H. F. K., eds.*, 1985, pp. 367–82.
[G: W. Germany]

Knaus, William A. Medical Care and Medical Technology: The Need for New Understanding. In *Ginzberg, E., ed.*, 1985, pp. 70–88.
[G: U.S.]

Knickman, James R. and Foltz, Anne-Marie. A Statistical Analysis of Reasons for East–West Differences in Hospital Use. *Inquiry*, Spring 1985, *22*(1), pp. 45–58. [G: U.S.]

Komlos, John. Stature and Nutrition in the Habsburg Monarchy: The Standard of Living and Economic Development in the Eighteenth Century. *Amer. Hist. Rev.*, December 1985, *90*(5), pp. 1149–61. [G: Europe]

van de Laar, Aart and Åsberg, Rodney. Public

Health. In *Jerve, A. M., ed.*, 1985, pp. 299–310. [G: Pakistan]

van de Laar, Aart and Jerve, Alf Morten. Water Supply and Sanitation. In *Jerve, A. M., ed.*, 1985, pp. 347–52. [G: Pakistan]

Langsten, R. Determinants of Natural Fertility in Rural Bangladesh Reconsidered. *Population Stud.*, March 1985, 39(1), pp. 153–61. [G: Bangladesh]

Lave, Judith R. Cost Containment Policies in Long-term Care. *Inquiry*, Spring 1985, 22(1), pp. 7–23. [G: U.S.]

Lave, Judith R. Is Compression Occurring in DRG Prices? *Inquiry*, Summer 1985, 22(2), pp. 142–47. [G: U.S.]

Law, Ron. Public Policy and Health-Care Delivery: A Practitioner's Perspective. *Rev. Black Polit. Econ.*, Fall-Winter 1985-86, 14(2–3), pp. 217–25. [G: U.S.]

Lee, Hau L. and Cohen, Morris A. A Multinomial Logit Model for the Spatial Distribution of Hospital Utilization. *J. Bus. Econ. Statist.*, April 1985, 3(2), pp. 159–68. [G: U.S.]

Lee, Robert H. and Hadley, Jack. The Demand for Residents. *J. Health Econ.*, December 1985, 4(4), pp. 357–71. [G: U.S.]

Lee, Robert H. and Waldman, Donald M. The Diffusion of Innovations in Hospitals: Some Econometric Considerations. *J. Health Econ.*, December 1985, 4(4), pp. 373–80. [G: U.S.]

Leonard-Barton, Dorothy. Experts as Negative Opinion Leaders in the Diffusion of a Technological Innovation. *J. Cons. Res.*, March 1985, 11(4), pp. 914–26. [G: U.S.]

Leu, Robert E. and Frey, René L. Budget Incidence, Demographic Change, and Health Policy in Switzerland. In *Terny, G. and Culyer, A. J., eds.*, 1985, pp. 225–38. [G: Switzerland]

Levi, Isaac. Common Causes, Smoking, and Lung Cancer. In *Campbell, R. and Sowden, L., eds.*, 1985, pp. 234–47.

Lewin, Marion Ein. Financing Care for the Poor and Underinsured: An Overview. In *Lewin, M. E., ed.*, 1985, pp. 26–43. [G: U.S.]

Lewin, Marion Ein. The Health Policy Agenda: Introduction. In *Lewin, M. E., ed.*, 1985, pp. 1–6. [G: U.S.]

Link, Charles R. and Settle, Russell F. Labor Supply Responses of Licensed Practical Nurses: A Partial Solution to a Nurse Shortage? *J. Econ. Bus.*, February 1985, 37(1), pp. 49–57. [G: U.S.]

Lloyd, P. J. The Economics of Regulation of Alcohol Distribution and Consumption in Victoria. *Australian Econ. Rev.*, 1st Quarter 1985, (69), pp. 16–29. [G: Australia]

Logan, Bernard I. Evaluating Public Policy Costs in Rural Development Planning: The Example of Health Care in Sierra Leone. *Econ. Geogr.*, April 1985, 61(2), pp. 144–57. [G: Sierra Leone]

Long, Stephen H. Medicare Reform: What Are the Options? In *Employee Benefit Research Institute.*, 1985, pp. 1–6. [G: U.S.]

Lubitz, James; Beebe, James and Riley, Gerald.

Improving the Medicare HMO Payment Formula to Deal with Biased Selection. In *Scheffler, R. M. and Rossiter, L. F., eds.*, 1985, pp. 101–22. [G: U.S.]

Luft, Harold S. From Policy Question to Empirical Answers. *J. Health Econ.*, December 1985, 4(4), pp. 381–86. [G: U.S.]

Luft, Harold S. and Maerki, Susan C. Competitive Potential of Hospitals and Their Neighbors. *Contemp. Policy Issues*, Winter 1984-85, 3(2), pp. 89–102. [G: U.S.]

Luft, Harold S.; Trauner, Joan B. and Maerki, Susan C. Adverse Selection in a Large, Multiple-Option Health Benefits Program: A Case Study of the California Public Employees' Retirement System. In *Scheffler, R. M. and Rossiter, L. F., eds.*, 1985, pp. 197–229. [G: U.S.]

Maddala, G. S. A Survey of the Literature on Selectivity Bias as it Pertains to Health Care Markets. In *Scheffler, R. M. and Rossiter, L. F., eds.*, 1985, pp. 3–18.

Mäkelä, K. Alcohol Policies: Lessons from the Postwar Period. In *Grant, M., ed.*, 1985, pp. 9–22. [G: Zambia; Mexico; U.K.]

Malkas, Tapani. Health Effects of Unemployment and National Health Policy in Finland. In *Westcott, G.; Svensson, P.-G. and Zollner, H. F. K., eds.*, 1985, pp. 357–65. [G: Finland]

Marder, William D. and Zuckerman, Stephen. Competition and Medical Groups: A Survivor Analysis. *J. Health Econ.*, June 1985, 4(2), pp. 167–76. [G: U.S.]

Mariner, Wendy K. The Potential Impact of Pharmaceutical and Vaccine Litigation. In *Baily, M. A. and Cikins, W. I., eds.*, 1985, pp. 43–68. [G: U.S.]

Marquis, M. Susan. Cost-sharing and Provider Choice. *J. Health Econ.*, June 1985, 4(2), pp. 137–57. [G: U.S.]

Martin, James B., et al. A Computer-aided System for Planning Acute Care Bed Need in Michigan. *Inquiry*, Fall 1985, 22(3), pp. 316–25. [G: U.S.]

Martin, Stephen and Goddeeris, John. Policy and Structural Change in the Health Care Industry. *Antitrust Bull.*, Winter 1985, 30(4), pp. 949–74. [G: U.S.]

Maynard, Alan. Welfare: Who Pays? In *Bean, P.; Ferris, J. and Whynes, D., eds.*, 1985, pp. 142–61. [G: U.K.]

McCarthy, Thomas R. The Competitive Nature of the Primary-Care Physician Services Market. *J. Health Econ.*, June 1985, 4(2), pp. 93–117. [G: U.S.]

McFadden, Daniel. Technical Problems in Social Experimentation: Cost versus Ease of Analysis: Comment. In *Hausman, J. A. and Wise, D. A., eds.*, 1985, pp. 214–18.

McGreevey, William Paul. The Impact of Social Security on Income Distribution: Comment. In *Mesa-Lago, C., ed.*, 1985, pp. 209–15. [G: Brazil]

McIntosh, Curtis E. and Manchew, Patricia. Nutritional Needs, Food Availability and the Realism of Self-sufficiency. In *Gomes, P. I., ed.*, 1985, pp. 212–31. [G: Caribbean]

McKinney, Fred. Employment Implications of a Changing Health-Care System. *Rev. Black Polit. Econ.*, Fall-Winter 1985-86, *14*(2–3), pp. 199–215. [G: U.S.]

Mendell, Jay S. Forecasting Through Understanding Changes in Human Consciousness: Applications to Health Care Public Relations. In *Mendell, J. S., ed.*, 1985, pp. 91–98. [G: U.S.]

Mercer, A. J. Smallpox and Epidemiological-Demographic Change in Europe: The Role of Vaccination. *Population Stud.*, July 1985, *39*(2), pp. 287–307. [G: OECD]

Merrill, Jeffrey; Jackson, Catherine and Reuter, James. Factors That Affect the HMO Enrollment Decision: A Tale of Two Cities. *Inquiry*, Winter 1985, *22*(4), pp. 388–95. [G: U.S.]

Mesa-Lago, Carmelo. Alternative Strategies to the Social Security Crisis: Socialist, Market and Mixed Approaches. In *Mesa-Lago, C., ed.*, 1985, pp. 311–61. [G: Chile; Costa Rica; Cuba]

Meyer, Jack A. Health Care Policy: Historical Background and Recent Developments. In *Meyer, J. A., ed.*, 1985, pp. 1–8. [G: U.S.]

Miller, Karen E., et al. Patient Characteristics and the Demand for Care in Two Freestanding Emergency Centers. *Inquiry*, Winter 1985, *22*(4), pp. 418–25. [G: U.S.]

Miller, Victor J. Recent Changes in Federal Grants and State Budgets. In *Lewin, M. E., ed.*, 1985, pp. 44–64. [G: U.S.]

Monheit, Alan C., et al. The Employed Uninsured and the Role of Public Policy. *Inquiry*, Winter 1985, *22*(4), pp. 348–64. [G: U.S.]

Morey, Richard C.; Capettini, Robert and Dittman, David A. Pareto Rate Setting Strategies: An Application to Medicaid Drug Reimbursement. *Policy Sci.*, September 1985, *18*(2), pp. 169–200. [G: U.S.]

Mosteller, Frederick and Weinstein, Milton C. Toward Evaluating the Cost-Effectiveness of Medical and Social Experiments. In *Hausman, J. A. and Wise, D. A., eds.*, 1985, pp. 221–46. [G: U.S.]

Mueller, Curt D. Waiting for Physicians' Services: Model and Evidence. *J. Bus.*, April 1985, *58*(2), pp. 173–90. [G: U.S.]

Mulligan, James G. The Stochastic Determinants of Hospital-Bed Supply [The Effects of Competition and Regulation on Hospital Bed Supply and the Reservation Quality of the Hospital]. *J. Health Econ.*, June 1985, *4*(2), pp. 177–81. [G: U.S.]

Munnell, Alicia H. Ensuring Entitlement to Health Care Services. *New Eng. Econ. Rev.*, Nov./Dec. 1985, pp. 30–40. [G: U.S.]

Munnell, Alicia H. Paying for the Medicare Program. *New Eng. Econ. Rev.*, January/February 1985, pp. 46–61. [G: U.S.]

Musgrove, Philip. Food Needs and Absolute Poverty in Urban South America. *Rev. Income Wealth*, March 1985, *31*(1), pp. 63–83. [G: S. America]

Musgrove, Philip. Reflexiones sobre la demanda por salud en América Latina. (With English summary.) *Cuadernos Econ.*, August 1985, *22*(66), pp. 293–305. [G: Latin America]

Mussey, Sol. Actuarial Status of the HI and SMI Trust Funds. *Soc. Sec. Bull.*, June 1985, *48*(6), pp. 32–40. [G: U.S.]

Myers, Robert J. Income of Social Security Beneficiaries as Affected by Earnings Test and Income Taxes on Benefits. *J. Risk Ins.*, June 1985, *52*(2), pp. 289–300. [G: U.S.]

Narendranathan, Wiji; Nickell, Stephen and Metcalf, D. An Investigation into the Incidence and Dynamic Structure of Sickness and Unemployment in Britain, 1965–75. *J. Roy. Statist. Soc.*, 1985, *148*(3), pp. 254–67. [G: U.K.]

Neelakanta, B. C. Improving Efficiency in Hospitals: An Economic Outlook. *Indian Econ. J.*, Apr.-June 1985, *32*(4), pp. 39–44.

Neipp, Joachim and Zeckhauser, Richard J. Persistence in the Choice of Health Plans. In *Scheffler, R. M. and Rossiter, L. F., eds.*, 1985, pp. 47–72. [G: U.S.]

Newhouse, Joseph P. Household Wealth and Health Insurance as Protection against Medical Risks: Comment. In *David, M. and Smeeding, T., eds.*, 1985, pp. 354–58. [G: U.S.]

Nugent, Angela. Organizing Trade Unions to Combat Disease: The Workers' Health Bureau, 1921–1928. *Labor Hist.*, Summer 1985, *26*(3), pp. 423–46. [G: U.S.]

Nyman, John A. Prospective and 'Cost-Plus' Medicaid Reimbursement, Excess Medicaid Demand, and the Quality of Nursing Home Care. *J. Health Econ.*, September 1985, *4*(3), pp. 237–59. [G: U.S.]

O'Brien, Richard F. Health Care Cost Containment: An Employer's Perspective. In *Dennis, B. D., ed.*, 1985, pp. 468–73. [G: U.S.]

Orr, Lawrence L. Macroexperiments versus Microexperiments for Health Policy: Comment. In *Hausman, J. A. and Wise, D. A., eds.*, 1985, pp. 172–81.

Parillón, Cutberto, et al. Clasificación funcional de la desnutrición en Panama. (With English summary.) *Cuadernos Econ.*, August 1985, *22*(66), pp. 307–27. [G: Panama]

Pauly, Mark V. Reflections on Using Physician Agents to Minimize the Cost of Health. *J. Health Econ.*, March 1985, *4*(1), pp. 79–81.

Pauly, Mark V. What is Adverse about Adverse Selection? In *Scheffler, R. M. and Rossiter, L. F., eds.*, 1985, pp. 281–86. [G: U.S.]

Pebley, Anne R., et al. Intra-uterine Mortality and Maternal Nutritional Status in Rural Bangladesh. *Population Stud.*, November 1985, *39*(3), pp. 425–40. [G: Bangladesh]

Petit, Michel. The US Presidential World Food and Nutrition Study and Commission on World Hunger: Lessons for the United States and Other Countries: Comment. In *[Heidhues, T.]*, 1985, pp. 64–65.

Phelps, Charles E. Taxing Health Insurance: How Much Is Enough? *Contemp. Policy Issues*, Winter 1984-85, *3*(2), pp. 47–54. [G: U.S.]

Pinstrup-Anderson, Per. Agricultural Project Design and Human Nutrition. In *Davis, T. J., ed.*, 1985, pp. 153–56.

Pitt, Mark M. and Rosenzweig, Mark R. Health and Nutrient Consumption across and within Farm Households. *Rev. Econ. Statist.*, May 1985, 67(2), pp. 212–23. [G: Indonesia]

Platt, Stephen. Suicidal Behaviour and Unemployment: A Literature Review. In *Westcott, G.; Svensson, P.-G. and Zollner, H. F. K., eds.*, 1985, pp. 87–132. [G: Global]

Porter, John E. The Effects of Litigation on Health Care Costs: A Congressional Perspective. In *Baily, M. A. and Cikins, W. I., eds.*, 1985, pp. 36–42. [G: U.S.]

Price, James R. and Mays, James W. Biased Selection in the Federal Employees Health Benefits Program. *Inquiry*, Spring 1985, 22(1), pp. 67–77. [G: U.S.]

Price, James R. and Mays, James W. Selection and the Competitive Standing of Health Plans in a Multiple-Choice, Multiple-Insurer Market. In *Scheffler, R. M. and Rossiter, L. F., eds.*, 1985, pp. 127–47. [G: U.S.]

Prottas, Jeffrey M. The Structure and Effectiveness of the U.S. Organ Porcurement System. *Inquiry*, Winter 1985, 22(4), pp. 365–76. [G: U.S.]

Quisumbing, Ma. Agnes R. Food Demand Parameters and Their Application to Nutrition Policy Simulation. *Philippine Rev. Econ. Bus.*, Sept./Dec. 1985, 22(3/4), pp. 177–213. [G: Philippines]

Ram, Rati. The Role of Real Income Level and Income Distribution in Fulfillment of Basic Needs. *World Devel.*, May 1985, 13(5), pp. 589–94. [G: LDCs]

Reeder, C. E. and Nelson, Arthur A. The Differential Impact of Copayment on Drug Use in a Medicaid Population. *Inquiry*, Winter 1985, 22(4), pp. 396–403. [G: U.S.]

Regalado, Basilia M. Distributional Impacts of Selected Food Policies on Human Nutrition in the Philippines. *Philippine Econ. J.*, 1985, 24(2–3), pp. 143–80. [G: Philippines]

Reinhardt, Uwe E. The Theory of Physician-induced Demand Reflections after a Decade. *J. Health Econ.*, June 1985, 4(2), pp. 187–93.

Renn, Steven C., et al. The Effects of Ownership and System Affiliation on the Economic Performance of Hospitals. *Inquiry*, Fall 1985, 22(3), pp. 219–36. [G: U.S.]

Reutlinger, Shlomo. Food Security and Poverty in LDCs. *Finance Develop.*, December 1985, 22(4), pp. 7–11. [G: LDCs]

Reynolds, Roger A. The Effect of Prior-Year Health Expenditures on Health Coverage Plan Choice: Adverse Selection within Dental Insurance Markets: Comments. In *Scheffler, R. M. and Rossiter, L. F., eds.*, 1985, pp. 191–93. [G: U.S.]

Rice, Thomas and McCall, Nelda. The Extent of Ownership and the Characteristics of Medicare Supplemental Policies. *Inquiry*, Summer 1985, 22(2), pp. 188–200. [G: U.S.]

Robinson, James C. and Luft, Harold S. The Impact of Hospital Market Structure on Patient Volume, Average Length of Stay, and the Cost of Care. *J. Health Econ.*, December 1985, 4(4), pp. 333–56. [G: U.S.]

Rodríguez Grossi, Jorge. El acceso a la salud, la eficacia hospitalaria y la distribución de los beneficios de la salud pública. (With English summary.) *Cuadernos Econ.*, August 1985, 22(66), pp. 267–91. [G: Chile]

Rootman, I. Using Health Promotion to Reduce Alcohol Problems. In *Grant, M., ed.*, 1985, pp. 57–81. [G: U.S.; W. Europe]

Rother, John C. Medicare Reform: Where the Emphasis Should Be: Remarks. In *Employee Benefit Research Institute.*, 1985, pp. 84–87. [G: U.S.]

Rother, John C. Medicare Reform: Where the Emphasis Should Be. In *Employee Benefit Research Institute.*, 1985, pp. 79–84. [G: U.S.]

Ružičková, Zdenka and Seidl, Vladimír. Economic Aspects of Health and Sickness. *Czech. Econ. Digest.*, November 1985, (7), pp. 61–76. [G: Czechoslovakia]

Sahota, Gian Singh. Financial Analysis of a Development Project. *Indian J. Quant. Econ.*, 1985, 1(1), pp. 1–31. [G: Nepal]

Satterthwaite, Mark A. Competition and Equilibrium as a Driving Force in the Health Services Sector. In *Inman, R. P., ed.*, 1985, pp. 239–67.

Schaafsma, Joseph. Cost Shifting: An Empirical Examination of Hospital Bureaucracy—A Comment. *Appl. Econ.*, October 1985, 17(5), pp. 801–02. [G: U.S.]

Schuster, Michael and Rhodes, Susan. The Impact of Overtime Work on Industrial Accident Rates. *Ind. Relat.*, Spring 1985, 24(2), pp. 234–46. [G: U.S.]

Scott, G. W. S. Health Care in the 1990s: Comments. In *Courchene, T. J.; Conklin, D. W. and Cook, G. C. A., eds. Vol. 2*, 1985, pp. 58–65. [G: Canada]

Seidman, Robert L. and Frank, Richard G. Hospital Responses to Incentives in Alternative Reimbursement Systems. *J. Behav. Econ.*, Winter 1985, 14, pp. 155–80. [G: U.S.]

Shahandeh, Behrouz. Drug and Alcohol Abuse in the Workplace: Consequences and Countermeasures. *Int. Lab. Rev.*, March-April 1985, 124(2), pp. 207–23.

Shaughnessy, Peter W. and Tynan, Eileen A. The Use of Swing Beds in Rural Hospitals. *Inquiry*, Fall 1985, 22(3), pp. 303–15. [G: U.S.]

Shaughnessy, Peter W., et al. Nursing Home Case-Mix Differences between Medicare and Non-Medicare and between Hospital-based and Freestanding Patients. *Inquiry*, Summer 1985, 22(2), pp. 162–77. [G: U.S.]

Shaul, D'vora Ben. Israeli Health Services. In *Levinson, P. and Landau, P., eds.*, 1985, pp. 144–46. [G: Israel]

Shechter, Mordechai. An Anatomy of a Groundwater Contamination Episode. *J. Environ. Econ. Manage.*, March 1985, 12(1), pp. 72–88. [G: U.S.]

Shleifer, Andrei. A Theory of Yardstick Competition. *Rand J. Econ.*, Autumn 1985, *16*(3), pp. 319–27.

Shukla, Ramesh K. Admissions Monitoring and Scheduling to Improve Work Flow in Hospitals. *Inquiry*, Spring 1985, *22*(1), pp. 92–101. **[G: U.S.]**

Sider, Hal. Work-related Accidents and the Production Process. *J. Human Res.*, Winter 1985, *20*(1), pp. 47–63. **[G: U.S.]**

Silberberg, Eugene. Nutrition and the Demand for Tastes. *J. Polit. Econ.*, October 1985, *93*(5), pp. 881–900. **[G: U.S.]**

Smith, Christopher J. and Hanham, Robert Q. Regional Change and Problem Drinking in the United States, 1970–1978. *Reg. Stud.*, April 1985, *19*(2), pp. 149–62. **[G: U.S.]**

Smith, Kenneth R. Current Strategies for Containing Health Care Expenditures: The Implications of Effective Expenditure Containment. In *Christianson, J. B. and Smith, K. R., eds.*, 1985, pp. 11–20. **[G: U.S.]**

Smith, V. Kerry and Gilbert, Carol C. S. The Valuation of Environmental Risks Using Hedonic Wage Models. In *David, M. and Smeeding, T., eds.*, 1985, pp. 359–85. **[G: U.S.]**

Sommers, Paul M. Drinking Age and the 55 MPH Speed Limit. *Atlantic Econ. J.*, March 1985, *13*(1), pp. 43–48. **[G: U.S.]**

Spruit, Ingeborg P. Employment, Unemployment and Health in Families in Leiden (the Netherlands). In *Westcott, G.; Svensson, P.-G. and Zollner, H. F. K., eds.*, 1985, pp. 231–59. **[G: Netherlands]**

Stano, Miron. An Analysis of the Evidence on Competition in the Physician Services Markets. *J. Health Econ.*, September 1985, *4*(3), pp. 197–211. **[G: U.S.]**

Stano, Miron, et al. The Effects of Physician Availability on Fees and the Demand for Doctors' Services. *Atlantic Econ. J.*, July 1985, *13*(2), pp. 51–60. **[G: U.S.]**

Stark, Fortney H. The Politics of Medicare Reform Options. In *Employee Benefit Research Institute.*, 1985, pp. 95–101. **[G: U.S.]**

Stevenson, H. Michael and Williams, Alan Paul. Physicians and Medicare: Professional Ideology and Canadian Health Care Policy. *Can. Public Policy*, September 1985, *11*(3), pp. 504–21. **[G: Canada]**

Stoddart, Greg L. Rationalizing the Health-Care System. In *Courchene, T. J.; Conklin, D. W. and Cook, G. C. A., eds. Vol. 2*, 1985, pp. 3–39. **[G: Canada]**

Stokes, Graham. Epidemiological Studies of the Psychological Response to Economic Instability in England: A Summary. In *Westcott, G.; Svensson, P.-G. and Zollner, H. F. K., eds.*, 1985, pp. 133–42. **[G: U.K.]**

Sulkunen, P. International Aspects of the Prevention of Alcohol Problems: Research Experiences and Perspectives. In *Grant, M., ed.*, 1985, pp. 121–36.

Svensson, Per-Gunnar and Zöllner, Herbert. Health Policy Implications of Unemployment: Introduction. In *Westcott, G.; Svensson,*

P.-G. and Zollner, H. F. K., eds., 1985, pp. 1–6.

Tamburi, Giovanni. Social Security in Latin America: Trends and Outlook. In *Mesa-Lago, C., ed.*, 1985, pp. 57–84. **[G: Latin America]**

Teulade, René. The Role of Mutual Benefit Societies and Insurance Funds in Today's Economic and Social Policy. *Ann. Pub. Co-op. Econ.*, January–June 1985, *56*(1–2), pp. 81–91. **[G: France]**

Thomann, Klaus-Dieter. Some Results of Medical Research in the Frankfurt/Main Employment Office. In *Westcott, G.; Svensson, P.-G. and Zollner, H. F. K., eds.*, 1985, pp. 293–98. **[G: W. Germany]**

Thomsen, Carsten Krogsgaard. En empirisk model for kommunernes sygehusforbrug. (An Empirical Model of Hospital Consumption in Denmark. With English summary.) *Nationaløkon. Tidsskr.*, 1985, *123*(1), pp. 77–93. **[G: Denmark]**

Thurow, Lester C. Public Expenditures and the Elderly. *Eastern Econ. J.*, Jan.-Mar. 1985, *11*(1), pp. 42–50. **[G: U.S.]**

Tietenberg, T. H. The Valuation of Environmental Risks Using Hedonic Wage Models: Comment. In *David, M. and Smeeding, T., eds.*, 1985, pp. 385–91. **[G: U.S.]**

Torche, Arístides. Una evaluación económica del Programa Nacional de Alimentación Complementaria (PNAC). (With English summary.) *Cuadernos Econ.*, August 1985, *22*(66), pp. 175–93. **[G: Chile]**

Tridimas, George. Economic Theory and the Allocation of Public Expenditures in Greece. *Greek Econ. Rev.*, April 1985, *7*(1), pp. 34–52. **[G: Greece]**

Troy, John F. The Impact of Medicare Financing Reforms: A View from the Private Sector: Remarks. In *Employee Benefit Research Institute.*, 1985, pp. 57–62. **[G: U.S.]**

Troy, John F. The Impact of Medicare Financing Reforms: A View from the Private Sector. In *Employee Benefit Research Institute.*, 1985, pp. 45–57. **[G: U.S.]**

Ugalde, Antonio. The Integration of Health Care Programs into a National Health Service. In *Mesa-Lago, C., ed.*, 1985, pp. 109–42. **[G: Ecuador; Colombia; Honduras]**

Ullmann, Steven G. The Impact of Quality on Cost in the Provision of Long-term Care. *Inquiry*, Fall 1985, *22*(3), pp. 293–302. **[G: U.S.]**

Ullmann, Steven G. and Holtmann, A. G. Economies of Scope, Ownership, and Nursing Home Costs. *Quart. Rev. Econ. Bus.*, Winter 1985, *25*(4), pp. 83–94. **[G: U.S.]**

Usher, Dan. Income, Inequality, and Uncertainty: Differences between the Disabled and Nondisabled: Comment. In *David, M. and Smeeding, T., eds.*, 1985, pp. 319–21. **[G: U.S.]**

Valencia, Richard R. The Effects of Litigation on Health Care Costs: Introductional Implications. In *Baily, M. A. and Cikins, W. I., eds.*,

1985 T1Baily, Mary Ann, pp. 1–107.
[G: U.S.]

Virts, John R. and Wilson, George W. The Determinants of Rising Health Care Costs: Some Empirical Assessments. In *Meyer, J. A., ed.,* 1985, pp. 67–95. [G: U.S.]

Viscusi, W. Kip. Consumer Behavior and the Safety Effects of Product Safety Regulation. *J. Law Econ.,* October 1985, *28*(3), pp. 527–53. [G: U.S.]

Vladeck, Bruce C. The Dilemma between Competition and Community Service. *Inquiry,* Summer 1985, *22*(2), pp. 115–21. [G: U.S.]

Vladeck, Bruce C. The Static Dynamics of Long-term Care Policy. In *Lewin, M. E., ed.,* 1985, pp. 115–26. [G: U.S.]

Vogel, Ronald J. Current Strategies for Containing Health Care Expenditures: Government Imposed Regulation of Prices, Revenues and the Utilization of Services. In *Christianson, J. B. and Smith, K. R., eds.,* 1985, pp. 21–37. [G: U.S.]

Vogel, Ronald J. Health-Care Competition: Introduction. *Contemp. Policy Issues,* Winter 1984-85, *3*(2), pp. 42–46. [G: U.S.]

Wagner, Judith L. DRGs and Other Payment Groupings: The Impact on Medical Practice and Technology. In *Lewin, M. E., ed.,* 1985, pp. 85–98. [G: U.S.]

Wald, I.; Morawski, J. and Moskalewicz, J. Alcohol Policies: Poland. In *Grant, M., ed.,* 1985, pp. 109–13. [G: Poland]

Walsh, B. M. Production of and International Trade in Alcoholic Drinks: Possible Public Health Implications. In *Grant, M., ed.,* 1985, pp. 23–44. [G: Global]

Warr, Peter. Twelve Questions about Unemployment and Health. In *Roberts, B.; Finnegan, R. and Gallie, D., eds.,* 1985, pp. 302–18. [G: U.K.]

Watkins, Stephen. Recession and Health—A Literature Review. In *Westcott, G.; Svensson, P.-G. and Zollner, H. F. K., eds.,* 1985, pp. 27–56. [G: U.S.; U.K.]

Watkins, Stephen J. Recession and Health—The Policy Implications. In *Westcott, G.; Svensson, P.-G. and Zollner, H. F. K., eds.,* 1985, pp. 347–56.

Watson, William G. Health Care and Federalism. In *Courchene, T. J.; Conklin, D. W. and Cook, G. C. A., eds. Vol. 2,* 1985, pp. 40–57. [G: Canada]

Weisbrod, Burton A. America's Health-Care Dilemma. *Challenge,* Sept./Oct. 1985, *28*(4), pp. 30–34. [G: U.S.]

Welch, W. P. Health Care Utilization in HMO's: Results from Two National Samples. *J. Health Econ.,* December 1985, *4*(4), pp. 293–308. [G: U.S.]

Welch, W. P. Medicare Capitation Payments to HMOs in Light of Regression toward the Mean in Health Care Costs. In *Scheffler, R. M. and Rossiter, L. F., eds.,* 1985, pp. 75–96. [G: U.S.]

Wells, Nicholas. Balancing Risks and Benefits:

Discussion. In *Wells, N., ed.,* 1985, pp. 161–65.

Westcott, Gill. The Effect of Unemployment on the Health of Workers in a UK Steel Town: Preliminary Results. In *Westcott, G.; Svensson, P.-G. and Zollner, H. F. K., eds.,* 1985, pp. 261–71. [G: U.K.]

Wilcox-Gök, Virginia L. Mother's Education, Health Practices and Children's Health Needs: A Variance Components Model. *Rev. Econ. Statist.,* November 1985, *67*(4), pp. 706–10. [G: U.S.]

Wilensky, Gail R. SIPP and Health Care Issues. *J. Econ. Soc. Meas.,* December 1985, *13*(3–4), pp. 295–98.

Willcocks, A. J. In Defence of the National Health Service. In *Bean, P.; Ferris, J. and Whynes, D., eds.,* 1985, pp. 257–71. [G: U.K.]

Williams, Karen. Medicare Reform: Impact of Changes in Eligibility. In *Employee Benefit Research Institute.,* 1985, pp. 37–44. [G: U.S.]

Wilson, L. S. The Socialization of Medical Insurance in Canada. *Can. J. Econ.,* May 1985, *18*(2), pp. 355–76. [G: Canada]

Wlodarczyk, W. Cezary. Health Status, Health Service and Socio Economic Development of Provinces in Poland. In *Westcott, G.; Svensson, P.-G. and Zollner, H. F. K., eds.,* 1985, pp. 299–324. [G: Poland]

Wolfe, John R. A Model of Declining Health and Retirement. *J. Polit. Econ.,* December 1985, *93*(6), pp. 1258–67. [G: U.S.]

Wood, Donna J. The Strategic Use of Public Policy: Business Support for the 1906 Food and Drug Act. *Bus. Hist. Rev.,* Autumn 1985, *59*(3), pp. 403–32. [G: U.S.]

Yett, Donald E., et al. Fee-Screen Reimbursement and Physician Fee Inflation. *J. Human Res.,* Spring 1985, *20*(2), pp. 278–91. [G: U.S.]

Yfantopoulos, J. N. Alcohol Policies: Greece. In *Grant, M., ed.,* 1985, pp. 92–109. [G: Greece]

Zschock, Dieter K. The Integration of Health Care Programs into a National Health Service: Comment. In *Mesa-Lago, C., ed.,* 1985, pp. 142–46. [G: Ecuador; Colombia; Honduras]

Zweifel, Peter. Individual Choice in Social Health Insurance: A Curb on Inflation in the Health Care Sector? Evidence from Switzerland. In *Terny, G. and Culyer, A. J., eds.,* 1985, pp. 303–18. [G: Switzerland]

914 Economics of Poverty

9140 Economics of Poverty

Abedian, I. and Standish, B. Poor Whites and the Role of the State: The Evidence. *S. Afr. J. Econ.,* June 1985, *53*(2), pp. 141–65. [G: S. Africa]

Ahluwalia, Montek S. Rural Poverty, Agricultural Production, and Prices: A Reexamination. In *Mellor, J. W. and Desai, G. M., eds.,* 1985, pp. 59–75. [G: India]

Ahmad, Qazi Kholiquzzaman and Hossain, Ma-

habub. An Evaluation of Selected Policies and Programmes for the Alleviation of Rural Poverty in Bangladesh. In *Islam, R., ed.*, 1985, pp. 67–98.   [G: Bangladesh]

Ahmed, Osman Sheikh and Field, Alfred J., Jr. Potential Effects of Income-Redistribution Policies on the Final Pattern of Income Distribution: The Case of Kenya. *J. Devel. Areas*, October 1985, *20*(1), pp. 1–21.   [G: Kenya]

Ahmed, Raisuddin. Growth and Equity in Indian Agriculture and a Few Paradigms from Bangladesh. In *Mellor, J. W. and Desai, G. M., eds.*, 1985, pp. 124–27.   [G: India; Bangladesh]

Airaksinen, Timo. Hegel on Poverty and Violence. In *Kipnis, K. and Meyers, D. T., eds.*, 1985, pp. 42–58.

Ali, M. Shaukat. Rural Poverty and Anti-poverty Policies in Pakistan. In *Islam, R., ed.*, 1985, pp. 175–99.   [G: Pakistan]

Anand, Sudhir and Kanbur, S. M. R. Poverty under the Kuznets Process. *Econ. J.*, Supplement 1985, *95*, pp. 42–50.

Åsberg, Rodney and Jerve, Alf Morten. Poverty in Pakistan. In *Jerve, A. M., ed.*, 1985, pp. 231–46.   [G: Pakistan]

Asiama, Seth Opuni. The Rich Slum-Dweller: A Problem of Unequal Access. *Int. Lab. Rev.*, May-June 1985, *124*(3), pp. 353–62.

[G: LDCs; Ghana]

Axinn, June. Hegel on Poverty and Violence: Comment: Explorations of the Definition of Poverty. In *Kipnis, K. and Meyers, D. T., eds.*, 1985, pp. 59–64.   [G: U.S.]

Azmon, Yael. The Protest of a Disadvantaged Population in a Welfare State. In *Eisenstadt, S. N. and Ahimeir, O., eds.*, 1985, pp. 289–301.   [G: Israel]

Bale, Malcolm D. Food Prices and the Poor in Developing Countries: Opening of the Discussion. *Europ. Rev. Agr. Econ.*, 1985, *12*(1/2), pp. 82–83.   [G: LDCs]

Bandyopadhyay, D. An Evaluation of Policies and Programmes for the Alleviation of Rural Poverty in India. In *Islam, R., ed.*, 1985, pp. 99–151.   [G: India]

Bane, Mary Jo and Welsh, James. SIPP's Potential Contributions to Policy Research on Children. *J. Econ. Soc. Meas.*, December 1985, *13*(3–4), pp. 273–79.   [G: U.S.]

Banskota, Mahesh. Anti-poverty Policies in Rural Nepal. In *Islam, R., ed.*, 1985, pp. 153–74.

[G: Nepal]

Bardhan, Pranab K. Poverty and "Trickle-Down" in Rural India: A Quantitative Analysis. In *Mellor, J. W. and Desai, G. M., eds.*, 1985, pp. 75–94.   [G: India]

Basu, Kaushik. Poverty Measurement: A Decomposition of the Normalization Axion [Cardinal Utility, Utilitarianism and a Class of Invariance Axioms in Welfare Analysis] [Poverty: An Ordinal Approach to Measurement]. *Econometrica*, November 1985, *53*(6), pp. 1439–43.

Beller, Andrea H. and Graham, John W. Variations in the Economic Well-Being of Divorced Women and Their Children: The Role of Child Support Income. In *David, M. and Smeeding,*

T., eds., 1985, pp. 471–506.   [G: U.S.]

Berrebi, Z. M. and Silber, Jacques. Income Inequality Indices and Deprivation: A Generalization [Relative Deprivation and the Gini Coefficient]. *Quart. J. Econ.*, August 1985, *100*(3), pp. 807–10.

Blank, Rebecca M. The Impact of State Economic Differentials on Household Welfare and Labor Force Behavior. *J. Public Econ.*, October 1985, *28*(1), pp. 25–58.   [G: U.S.]

Bliss, Christopher. A Note on the Price Variable. In *Mellor, J. W. and Desai, G. M., eds.*, 1985, pp. 18–20.

Boyer, George R. An Economic Model of the English Poor Law circa 1780–1834. *Exploration Econ. Hist.*, April 1985, *22*(2), pp. 129–67.   [G: U.K.]

Brownlee, Helen. Poverty Traps. *Australian Tax Forum*, Winter 1985, *2*(2), pp. 161–72.

[G: Australia]

Brunner, Karl. The Poverty of Nations. *Cato J.*, Spring/Summer 1985, *5*(1), pp. 37–49.

Brunner, Karl. The Poverty of Nations. *Bus. Econ.*, January 1985, *20*(1), pp. 5–11.

Chape, A. Urban Poverty and Economic Decline: A Liverpool Perspective. *Reg. Stud.*, February 1985, *19*(1), pp. 63–65.   [G: U.K.]

Corcoran, Mary E., et al. Myth and Reality: The Causes and Persistence of Poverty. *J. Policy Anal. Manage.*, Summer 1985, *4*(4), pp. 516–36.   [G: U.S.]

Courant, Paul N. Distributional Programs: Education and Antipoverty: Commentary. In *Quigley, J. M. and Rubinfeld, D. L., eds.*, 1985, pp. 148–53.   [G: U.S.]

Dantwala, M. L. Technology, Growth, and Equity in Agriculture. In *Mellor, J. W. and Desai, G. M., eds.*, 1985, pp. 110–23.

[G: India]

Danziger, Sheldon and Feaster, Daniel. Income Transfers and Poverty in the 1980s. In *Quigley, J. M. and Rubinfeld, D. L., eds.*, 1985, pp. 89–117.   [G: U.S.]

Danziger, Sheldon and Gottschalk, Peter. The Impact of Budget Cuts and Economic Conditions on Poverty. *J. Policy Anal. Manage.*, Summer 1985, *4*(4), pp. 587–93.   [G: U.S.]

Danziger, Sheldon and Gottschalk, Peter. The Poverty of Losing Ground. *Challenge*, May/June 1985, *28*(2), pp. 32–38.   [G: U.S.]

Desai, Gunvant M. Trends in Rural Poverty in India: An Interpretation of Dharm Narain. In *Mellor, J. W. and Desai, G. M., eds.*, 1985, pp. 1–6.   [G: India]

Duncan, Greg J. and Hoffman, Saul D. Economic Consequences of Marital Instability. In *David, M. and Smeeding, T., eds.*, 1985, pp. 427–67.   [G: U.S.]

Fogel, Richard L. Homelessness: A Complex Problem and the Federal Response: A Report on Intergovernmental Relations and Human Resources of the Committee on Intergovernmental Relations and Human Resources of the Committee on Government Operations. *Amer. J. Econ. Soc.*, October 1985, *44*(4), pp. 385–89.   [G: U.S.]

Franklin, David L. and Vial de Valdés, Isabel. Estrategias nutricionales de los hogares pobres. (With English summary.) *Cuadernos Econ.*, August 1985, 22(66), pp. 247–65.
[G: Panama]

Gaiha, Raghav. Poverty, Technology and Infrastructure in Rural India. *Cambridge J. Econ.*, September 1985, 9(3), pp. 221–43.
[G: India]

Garfinkel, Irwin. Variations in the Economic Well-Being of Divorced Women and Their Children: The Role of Child Support Income: Comment. In *David, M. and Smeeding, T., eds.*, 1985, pp. 506–09. [G: U.S.]

Gilbert, Geoffrey N. The *Morning Chronicle*, Poor Laws, and Political Economy. *Hist. Polit. Econ.*, Winter 1985, 17(4), pp. 507–21.

Gottschalk, Peter and Danziger, Sheldon. A Framework for Evaluating the Effects of Economic Growth and Transfers on Poverty. *Amer. Econ. Rev.*, March 1985, 75(1), pp. 153–61.
[G: U.S.]

Griffin, Keith. Rural Poverty in Asia: Analysis and Policy Alternatives. In *Islam, R., ed.*, 1985, pp. 29–65. [G: LDCs]

Griliches, Zvi. Income-Maintenance Policy and Work Effort: Learning from Experiments and Labor-Market Studies: Comment. In *Hausman, J. A. and Wise, D. A., eds.*, 1985, pp. 137–38.

Gupta, Sanjeev. Poverty. In *Mongia, J. N., ed.*, 1985, pp. 495–516. [G: India]

Gwartney, James and McCaleb, Thomas S. Have Antipoverty Programs Increased Poverty? *Cato J.*, Spring/Summer 1985, 5(1), pp. 1–16.
[G: U.S.]

de Haen, Hartwig. Food Prices and the Poor in Developing Countries: Comment. *Europ. Rev. Agr. Econ.*, 1985, 12(1/2), pp. 83–85.
[G: LDCs]

Hagenaars, Aldi J. M. and van Praag, Bernard M. S. A Synthesis of Poverty Line Definitions. *Rev. Income Wealth*, June 1985, 31(2), pp. 139–54. [G: EEC]

Hannon, Joan Underhill. Poor Relief Policy in Antebellum New York State: The Rise and Decline of the Poorhouse. *Exploration Econ. Hist.*, July 1985, 22(3), pp. 233–56. [G: U.S.]

Hanushek, Eric A. Distributional Programs: Education and Antipoverty: Commentary. In *Quigley, J. M. and Rubinfeld, D. L., eds.*, 1985, pp. 154–60. [G: U.S.]

Herber, Bernard P. The State and Distribution: A Historical Look at Egalitarianism in the United States. In *[Recktenwald, H. C.]*, 1985, pp. 333–45. [G: U.S.]

Hirsch, Barry T. Poverty, Transfers, and Economic Growth. *Public Finance Quart.*, January 1985, 13(1), pp. 81–98. [G: U.S.]

Islam, Rizwanul and Lee, Eddy. Strategies for Alleviating Poverty in Rural Asia. In *Islam, R., ed.*, 1985, pp. 1–27. [G: Asia]

Iyengar, N. Srinivasa and Gopalakrishna, Mallika. Appropriate Criteria for the Measurement of Levels of Living. *Indian Econ. Rev.*, July-Dec. 1985, 20(2), pp. 191–229. [G: India]

James, Jeffrey. The Role of Appropriate Technology in a Redistributive Development Strategy. In *James, J. and Watanabe, S., eds.*, 1985, pp. 116–33.

Kapteyn, Arie; van de Geer, Sara and van de Stadt, Huib. The Impact of Changes in Income and Family Composition on Subjective Measures of Well-Being. In *David, M. and Smeeding, T., eds.*, 1985, pp. 35–64.
[G: Netherlands]

Kemal, A. R. Changes in Poverty and Income Inequality in Pakistan during the 1970s: Comments. *Pakistan Devel. Rev.*, Autumn-Winter 1985, 24(3/4), pp. 420–22. [G: Pakistan]

Kidd, Alan J. 'Outcast Manchester': Voluntary Charity, Poor Relief and the Casual Poor 1860–1905. In *Kidd, A. J. and Roberts, K. W.*, 1985, pp. 48–73. [G: U.K.]

de Kruijk, Hans and van Leeuwen, Myrna. Changes in Poverty and Income Inequality in Pakistan during the 1970s. *Pakistan Devel. Rev.*, Autumn-Winter 1985, 24(3/4), pp. 407–19. [G: Pakistan]

Kumar, Shubh K. The Income Approach to Measuring Poverty: A Note on Human Welfare below the Line. In *Mellor, J. W. and Desai, G. M., eds.*, 1985, pp. 54–58.

Lee, Dwight R. The Politics of Poverty and the Poverty of Politics. *Cato J.*, Spring/Summer 1985, 5(1), pp. 17–35. [G: U.S.]

Leiser, Burton M. Vagrancy, Loitering, and Economic Justice. In *Kipnis, K. and Meyers, D. T., eds.*, 1985, pp. 149–60. [G: U.S.]

Lele, Uma. Terms of Trade, Agricultural Growth, and Rural Poverty in Africa. In *Mellor, J. W. and Desai, G. M., eds.*, 1985, pp. 161–80.
[G: Sub-Saharan Africa]

Lewin, Marion Ein. Financing Care for the Poor and Underinsured: An Overview. In *Lewin, M. E., ed.*, 1985, pp. 26–43. [G: U.S.]

Lipton, Michael. A Problem in Poverty Measurement. *Math. Soc. Sci.*, August 1985, 10(1), pp. 91–97.

MacDonald, Maurice. Government Welfare Benefits and the Social Safety Net. *J. Post Keynesian Econ.*, Fall 1985, 8(1), pp. 47–65.
[G: U.S.]

MacDonald, Maurice. The Role of Multiple Benefits in Maintaining the Social Safety Net: The Case of Food Stamps. *J. Human Res.*, Summer 1985, 20(3), pp. 421–36. [G: U.S.]

Malveaux, Julianne. The Economic Interests of Black and White Women: Are They Similar? *Rev. Black Polit. Econ.*, Summer 1985, 14(1), pp. 5–27. [G: U.S.]

Mangahas, Mahar. Rural Poverty and Operation Land Transfer in the Philippines. In *Islam, R., ed.*, 1985, pp. 201–41. [G: Philippines]

Mangahas, Mahar. The Data on Indian Poverty and the Poverty of ASEAN Data. In *Mellor, J. W. and Desai, G. M., eds.*, 1985, pp. 128–31. [G: ASEAN; India]

Martin, Rex. Poverty and Welfare in Rawl's Theory of Justice: On the Just Response to Needs. In *Kipnis, K. and Meyers, D. T., eds.*, 1985, pp. 161–75.

Mellor, John W. Determinants of Rural Poverty: The Dynamics of Production, Technology, and Price. In *Mellor, J. W. and Desai, G. M., eds.*, 1985, pp. 21–40. **[G: LDCs]**

Mellor, John W. and Desai, Gunvant M. Agricultural Change and Rural Poverty: A Synthesis. In *Mellor, J. W. and Desai, G. M., eds.*, 1985, pp. 192–210. **[G: India; LDCs]**

Moynihan, Daniel Patrick. We Can't Avoid Family Policy Much Longer. *Challenge*, Sept./Oct. 1985, *28*(4), pp. 9–17. **[G: U.S.]**

Musgrove, Philip. Food Needs and Absolute Poverty in Urban South America. *Rev. Income Wealth*, March 1985, *31*(1), pp. 63–83. **[G: S. America]**

Naqvi, Syed Nawab Haider and Qadir, Asghar. Incrementalism and Structural Change: A Technical Note. *Pakistan Devel. Rev.*, Summer 1985, *24*(2), pp. 87–102.

Parillón, Cutberto, et al. Clasificación funcional de la desnutrición en Panama. (With English summary.) *Cuadernos Econ.*, August 1985, *22*(66), pp. 307–27. **[G: Panama]**

Parthasarathy, G. Dharm Narain's Approach to Rural Poverty: Critical Issues. In *Mellor, J. W. and Desai, G. M., eds.*, 1985, pp. 181–85. **[G: India; LDCs]**

Pinstrup-Andersen, Per. Food Prices and the Poor in Developing Countries. *Europ. Rev. Agr. Econ.*, 1985, *12*(1/2), pp. 69–81. **[G: LDCs]**

Rao, C. II. Hanumantha; Gupta, Devendra B. and Sharma, P. S. Infrastructural Development and Rural Poverty in India: A Cross-Sectional Analysis. In *Mellor, J. W. and Desai, G. M., eds.*, 1985, pp. 95–109. **[G: India]**

Rosen, Sherwin. Income-Maintenance Policy and Work Effort: Learning from Experiments and Labor-Market Studies: Comment. In *Hausman, J. A. and Wise, D. A., eds.*, 1985, pp. 134–37. **[G: U.S.]**

Ross, Jo Anne B. Fifty Years of Service to Children and Their Families. *Soc. Sec. Bull.*, October 1985, *48*(10), pp. 5–9. **[G: U.S.]**

Saith, Ashwani. The Distributional Dimensions of Revolutionary Transition: Ethiopia. *J. Devel. Stud.*, October 1985, *22*(1), pp. 150–79. **[G: Ethiopia]**

Saith, Ashwani. The Distributional Dimensions of Revolutionary Transition: Ethiopia. In *Saith, A., ed.*, 1985, pp. 150–79. **[G: Ethiopia]**

Sawhill, Isabel V. Economic Consequences of Marital Instability: Comment. In *David, M. and Smeeding, T., eds.*, 1985, pp. 467–70. **[G: U.S.]**

Scoville, Orlin J. Relief and Rehabilitation in Kampuchea. *J. Devel. Areas*, October 1985, *20*(1), pp. 23–36. **[G: Kampuchea]**

Sen, Amartya. A Sociological Approach to the Measurement of Poverty: A Reply [Poor, Relatively Speaking]. *Oxford Econ. Pap.*, December 1985, *37*(4), pp. 669–76.

Sen, Amartya. Dharm Narain on Poverty: Concepts and Broader Issues. In *Mellor, J. W. and Desai, G. M., eds.*, 1985, pp. 7–17. **[G: Bangladesh; India]**

Sharma, D. P. Explaining Poverty in India. *Margin*, January 1985, *17*(2), pp. 47–59. **[G: India]**

Simms, Margaret C. Black Women Who Head Families: An Economic Struggle. *Rev. Black Polit. Econ.*, Fall-Winter 1985-86, *14*(2–3), pp. 141–51. **[G: U.S.]**

Srinivasan, T. N. Agriculture Production, Relative Prices, Entitlements, and Poverty. In *Mellor, J. W. and Desai, G. M., eds.*, 1985, pp. 41–53. **[G: LDCs]**

Stafford, Frank P. Income-Maintenance Policy and Work Effort: Learning from Experiments and Labor-Market Studies. In *Hausman, J. A. and Wise, D. A., eds.*, 1985, pp. 95–134. **[G: U.S.]**

Stern, David. Distributional Programs: Education and Antipoverty: Commentary. In *Quigley, J. M. and Rubinfeld, D. L., eds.*, 1985, pp. 161–72. **[G: U.S.]**

Taylor, Joan Kennedy. Deregulating the Poor. In *Boaz, D. and Crane, E. H., eds.*, 1985, pp. 223–45. **[G: U.S.]**

Thakur, D. S. A Survey of Literature on Rural Poverty in India. *Margin*, April 1985, *17*(3), pp. 32–49. **[G: India]**

Townsend, Peter. A Sociological Approach to the Measurement of Poverty—A Rejoinder [Poor, Relatively Speaking]. *Oxford Econ. Pap.*, December 1985, *37*(4), pp. 659–68.

Vyas, Vijay Shankar. Poverty, Agrarian Structure, and Policy Options: A Note. In *Mellor, J. W. and Desai, G. M., eds.*, 1985, pp. 186–91. **[G: India; LDCs]**

Watts, Harold W. The Impact of Changes in Income and Family Composition on Subjective Measures of Well-Being: Comment. In *David, M. and Smeeding, T., eds.*, 1985, pp. 64–67. **[G: Netherlands]**

Weinberg, Daniel H. Filling the "Poverty Gap": Multiple Transfer Program Participation. *J. Human Res.*, Winter 1985, *20*(1), pp. 64–89. **[G: U.S.]**

Wickramasekara, Piyasiri. An Evaluation of Policies and Programmes for the Alleviation of Poverty in Sri Lanka. In *Islam, R., ed.*, 1985, pp. 243–86. **[G: Sri Lanka]**

Wolch, Jennifer R. Distributional Programs: Education and Antipoverty: Commentary. In *Quigley, J. M. and Rubinfeld, D. L., eds.*, 1985, pp. 173–80. **[G: U.S.]**

Wolfson, Margaret. Population and Poverty in Sub-Saharan Africa. In *Rose, T., ed.*, 1985, pp. 94–103. **[G: Sub-Saharan Africa]**

Woodward, Donald. "Swords into Ploughshares": Recycling in Pre-industrial England. *Econ. Hist. Rev.*, *2nd Ser.*, May 1985, *38*(2), pp. 175–91. **[G: U.K.]**

Yotopoulos, Pan A. Middle-Income Classes and Food Crises: The "New" Food–Feed Competition. *Econ. Develop. Cult. Change*, April 1985, *33*(3), pp. 463–83. **[G: Global]**

Zurawicka, Janina. Charity in Warsaw in the Second Half of the XIXth Century. *J. Europ. Econ. Hist.*, Fall 1985, *14*(2), pp. 319–30. **[G: Poland]**

915 Social Security

9150 Social Security

Aaron, Henry J. The Distributional Impact of Social Security: Comment. In *Wise, D. A., ed.*, 1985, pp. 215–21. [G: U.S.]

Aldabe, Hernán. The Impact of Social Security on Savings and Development: Comment. In *Mesa-Lago, C., ed.*, 1985, pp. 241–43.
[G: Chile]

Allén, Tuovi. Vähennykset tuloverotuksessa—tulonsiirtopolitiikan jatke? (Deductions in Personal Income Taxation—Substitutes for Government Transfer Programmes? With English summary.) *Kansant. Aikak.*, 1985, *81*(1), pp. 65–72.

Arellano, José-Pablo. The Impact of Social Security on Savings and Development. In *Mesa-Lago, C., ed.*, 1985, pp. 217–40. [G: Chile]

Auerbach, Alan J. and Kotlikoff, Laurence J. Simulating Alternative Social Security Responses to the Demographic Transition. *Nat. Tax J.*, June 1985, *38*(2), pp. 153–68.
[G: U.S.]

Balassa, Bela. The Economic Consequences of Social Policies in the Industrial Countries. In *Balassa, B.*, 1985, pp. 44–59. [G: EEC; U.S.]

Ballantyne, Harry C. Actuarial Status of the OASI and DI Trust Funds. *Soc. Sec. Bull.*, June 1985, *48*(6), pp. 27–31. [G: U.S.]

Banting, Keith G. Federalism and Income Security: Themes and Variations. In *Courchene, T. J.; Conklin, D. W. and Cook, G. C. A., eds. Vol. 1*, 1985, pp. 253–76. [G: Canada]

Barron, Erma W. The Role of Research and Statistics in the Development of Social Security. *Soc. Sec. Bull.*, November 1985, *48*(11), pp. 5–21. [G: U.S.]

Bondar, Joseph. Effects of OASDI Benefit Increase, December 1984. *Soc. Sec. Bull.*, July 1985, *48*(7), pp. 44–47. [G: U.S.]

Borzutzky, Silvia. Politics and Social Security Reform. In *Mesa-Lago, C., ed.*, 1985, pp. 285–304. [G: Brazil; Chile; Argentina]

Boskin, Michael J. and Hurd, Michael D. Indexing Social Security Benefits: A Separate Price Index for the Elderly? *Public Finance Quart.*, October 1985, *13*(4), pp. 436–49. [G: U.S.]

Boskin, Michael J. and Kotlikoff, Laurence J. Public Debt and United States Saving: A New Test of the Neutrality Hypothesis. *Carnegie-Rochester Conf. Ser. Public Policy*, Autumn 1985, *23*, pp. 55–86. [G: U.S.]

Browning, Edgar K. The Marginal Social Security Tax on Labor. *Public Finance Quart.*, July 1985, *13*(3), pp. 227–51. [G: U.S.]

Burkhauser, Richard V. and Turner, John A. Is the Social Security Payroll Tax a Tax? *Public Finance Quart.*, July 1985, *13*(3), pp. 253–67.
[G: U.S.]

Burtless, Gary. Social Security, Health Status, and Retirement: Comment. In *Wise, D. A., ed.*, 1985, pp. 181–91. [G: U.S.]

Burtless, Gary and Moffitt, Robert. The Joint

Choice of Retirement Age and Postretirement Hours of Work. *J. Lab. Econ.*, April 1985, *3*(2), pp. 209–36. [G: U.S.]

Butler, Stuart and Germanis, Peter. Achieving a Political Strategy for Reform. In *Ferrara, P. J., ed.*, 1985, pp. 159–69. [G: U.S.]

Carmichael, Jeffrey and Plowman, Kathleen. Income Provision in Old Age. *Australian Econ. Rev.*, 3rd Quarter, Spring 1985, (71), pp. 130–44. [G: Australia]

Chernick, Howard and Reschovsky, Andrew. The Taxation of Social Security. *Nat. Tax J.*, June 1985, *38*(2), pp. 141–52. [G: U.S.]

Collins, Katharine P. and Erfle, Anne. Social Security Disability Benefits Reform Act of 1984: Legislative History and Summary of Provisions. *Soc. Sec. Bull.*, April 1985, *48*(4), pp. 5–32. [G: U.S.]

Crank, Sandy. The Evolution of Privacy and Disclosure Policy in the Social Security Administration. *Soc. Sec. Bull.*, June 1985, *48*(6), pp. 7–13. [G: U.S]

Cronin, Michael A. Fifty Years of Operations in the Social Security Administration. *Soc. Sec. Bull.*, June 1985, *48*(6), pp. 14–26. [G: U.S.]

Danziger, Sheldon. Inflation Vulnerability, Income, and Wealth of the Elderly, 1969–1979: Comment. In *David, M. and Smeeding, T., eds.*, 1985, pp. 172–77. [G: U.S.]

David, Martin and Menchik, Paul L. The Effect of Social Security on Lifetime Wealth Accumulation and Bequests. *Economica*, November 1985, *52*(208), pp. 421–34. [G: U.S.]

Davis, Evan H.; Dilnot, Andrea W. and Kay, John A. The Social Security Green Paper. *Fisc. Stud.*, August 1985, *6*(3), pp. 1–8. [G: U.K.]

Davis, Evan H. and Dilnot, Andrew W. The Restructuring of National Insurance Contributions in the 1985 Budget. In *Kay, J., ed.*, 1985, pp. 51–60. [G: U.S.]

Disney, Richard. Public Expenditure Policy, 1985–86: Social Security. In *Cockle, P., ed.*, 1985, pp. 121–51. [G: U.K.]

Donovan, Edmund T. The Retirement Equity Act of 1984: A Review. *Soc. Sec. Bull.*, May 1985, *48*(5), pp. 38–44. [G: U.S.]

Dye, Richard F. Influencing Retirement Behavior: Untangling the Effects of Income Taxation of Social Security Benefits. *J. Policy Anal. Manage.*, Fall 1985, *5*(1), pp. 150–54. [G: U.S.]

Dye, Richard F. Payroll Tax Effects on Wage Growth. *Eastern Econ. J.*, April-June 1985, *11*(2), pp. 89–100. [G: U.S.]

Eckstein, Zvi; Eichenbaum, Martin S. and Peled, Dan. Uncertain Lifetimes and the Welfare Enhancing Properties of Annuity Markets and Social Security. *J. Public Econ.*, April 1985, *26*(3), pp. 303–26.

Fauvel, Yvon. Théorie du cycle de vie et rentes publiques. (Life Cycle Theory and Public Pension Plans. With English summary.) *L'Actual. Econ.*, June 1985, *61*(2), pp. 220–38.

Feldstein, Martin. The Optimal Level of Social Security Benefits. *Quart. J. Econ.*, May 1985, *100*(2), pp. 303–20.

Ferrara, Peter J. Private Alternatives to Social

Security: The Experience of Other Countries: Comment. In *Ferrara, P. J., ed.*, 1985, pp. 113–15. **[G: U.K.]**

Ferrara, Peter J. Rates of Return Promised by Social Security to Today's Young Workers: Comment. In *Ferrara, P. J., ed.*, 1985, pp. 33–36. **[G: U.S.]**

Ferrara, Peter J. Social Security and the Super IRA: A Populist Proposal. In *Ferrara, P. J., ed.*, 1985, pp. 193–220. **[G: U.S.]**

Ferrara, Peter J. Social Security Reform: Some Theoretical Considerations. In *Ferrara, P. J., ed.*, 1985, pp. 173–89.

Ferrara, Peter J. Social Security Reform: The Super IRA. In *Boaz, D. and Crane, E. H., eds.*, 1985, pp. 51–73. **[G: U.S.]**

Ferrara, Peter J. Social Security: Myths and Realities: Comment. In *Ferrara, P. J., ed.*, 1985, pp. 69–70. **[G: U.S.]**

Ferrara, Peter J. Social Security: Prospects for Real Reform: Introduction. In *Ferrara, P. J., ed.*, 1985, pp. 1–9. **[G: U.S.]**

Ferrara, Peter J. Supply-Side Effects of Social Insurance: Comment. In *Ferrara, P. J., ed.*, 1985, pp. 83–87. **[G: U.S.]**

Ferrara, Peter J. The National Commission's Failure to Achieve Real Reform: Comment. In *Ferrara, P. J., ed.*, 1985, pp. 49–58. **[G: U.S.]**

Ferrara, Peter J. The Political Foundations of Social Security. In *Ferrara, P. J., ed.*, 1985, pp. 89–97. **[G: U.S.]**

Ferrara, Peter J. and Lott, John R., Jr. Rates of Return Promised by Social Security to Today's Young Workers. In *Ferrara, P. J., ed.*, 1985, pp. 13–32. **[G: U.S.]**

Frank, Beryl. Social Security in Latin America: Trends and Outlook: Comment. In *Mesa-Lago, C., ed.*, 1985, pp. 84–87. **[G: Latin America]**

Freeman, Gary P. Statecraft and Social Security Policy and Crisis: A Comparison of Latin America and the United States: Comment. In *Mesa-Lago, C., ed.*, 1985, pp. 51–56. **[G: Latin America; U.S.]**

Galbraith, J. A. Valuing Pensions (Annuities) with Different Types of Inflation Protection in Total Compensation Comparisons: A Note. *Can. J. Econ.*, November 1985, *18*(4), pp. 810–13. **[G: Canada]**

Ginsburg, Helen. Flexible and Partial Retirement for Norwegian and Swedish Workers. *Mon. Lab. Rev.*, October 1985, *108*(10), pp. 33–43. **[G: Norway; Sweden]**

Ginzberg, Eli. The Social Security System. In *Ginzberg, E.*, 1985, pp. 309–21. **[G: U.S.]**

Goodman, John C. Private Alternatives to Social Security: The Experience of Other Countries. In *Ferrara, P. J., ed.*, 1985, pp. 103–12. **[G: U.K.]**

Gruen, Fred H. Australian Government Policy on Retirement Incomes. *Econ. Rec.*, September 1985, *61*(174), pp. 613–21. **[G: Australia]**

Grundmann, Herman F. Adult Assistance Programs under the Social Security Act. *Soc. Sec.*

Bull., October 1985, *48*(10), pp. 10–21. **[G: U.S.]**

Gustman, Alan L. and Steinmeier, Thomas L. The 1983 Social Security Reforms and Labor Supply Adjustments of Older Individuals in the Long Run. *J. Lab. Econ.*, April 1985, *3*(2), pp. 237–53. **[G: U.S.]**

Gutiérrez, Alvaro Castro. Alternative Strategies to the Social Security Crisis: Socialist, Market and Mixed Approaches: Comment. In *Mesa-Lago, C., ed.*, 1985, pp. 362–65. **[G: Chile; Costa Rica; Cuba]**

Hamermesh, Daniel S. Expectations, Life Expectancy, and Economic Behavior. *Quart. J. Econ.*, May 1985, *100*(2), pp. 389–408. **[G: U.S.]**

Hammond, Elizabeth M. and Morris, C. Nick. Matrimonial Property Law, Independent Taxation and Pensions: A Search for Consistency. *Fisc. Stud.*, November 1985, *6*(4), pp. 57–65. **[G: U.K.]**

Harding, Ann. Tax Reform, Equity, and Social Security. *Australian Tax Forum*, Winter 1985, *2*(2), pp. 223–38. **[G: Australia]**

Hausman, Jerry A. The Econometrics of Nonlinear Budget Sets. *Econometrica*, November 1985, *53*(6), pp. 1255–82. **[G: U.S.]**

Hausman, Jerry A. and Wise, David A. Social Security, Health Status, and Retirement. In *Wise, D. A., ed.*, 1985, pp. 159–81. **[G: U.S.]**

Hubbard, R. Glenn. Personal Taxation, Pension Wealth, and Portfolio Composition. *Rev. Econ. Statist.*, February 1985, *67*(1), pp. 53–60. **[G: U.S.]**

Hubbard, R. Glenn. Social Security, Liquidity Constraints, and Pre-retirement Consumption. *Southern Econ. J.*, October 1985, *52*(2), pp. 471–83.

Hurd, Michael D. and Shoven, John B. Inflation Vulnerability, Income, and Wealth of the Elderly, 1969–1979. In *David, M. and Smeeding, T., eds.*, 1985, pp. 125–72. **[G: U.S.]**

Hurd, Michael D. and Shoven, John B. The Distributional Impact of Social Security. In *Wise, D. A., ed.*, 1985, pp. 193–215. **[G: U.S.]**

Iams, Howard M. Characteristics of the Longest Job for New Retired Workers: Findings from the New Beneficiary Survey. *Soc. Sec. Bull.*, March 1985, *48*(3), pp. 5–21. **[G: U.S.]**

Ingberg, Mikael. Offentliga transfereringar och konjunkturpolitiken. (Public Transfers and Stabilization Policy. With English summary.) *Ekon. Samfundets Tidskr.*, 1985, *38*(2), pp. 97–112. **[G: Finland]**

Irick, Christine. Income of New Retired Workers by Social Security Benefit Levels: Findings from the New Beneficiary Survey. *Soc. Sec. Bull.*, May 1985, *48*(5), pp. 7–23. **[G: U.S.]**

Isuani, Ernesto A. Social Security and Public Assistance. In *Mesa-Lago, C., ed.*, 1985, pp. 89–102. **[G: Latin America]**

Isuani, Ernesto A. Universalización de la seguridad social en América Latina: límites estructurales y cambios necesarios. (With English summary.) *Desarrollo Econ.*, April–June 1985, *25*(97), pp. 71–84. **[G: Latin America]**

Jonsson, Ernst. A Model of a Non–budget-maximizing Bureau. In *Lane, J.-E., ed.*, 1985, pp. 70–82. **[G: Sweden]**

Jonsson, Ernst. Budget-making with the Aid of an Equation Relating to Cost-determining Factors. *Public Finance*, 1985, *40*(2), pp. 210–19. **[G: Sweden]**

Kestenbaum, Bert. The Measurement of Early Retirement. *J. Amer. Statist. Assoc.*, March 1985, *80*(389), pp. 38–45. **[G: U.S.]**

León, Francisco. Social Security and Public Assistance: Comment. In *Mesa-Lago, C., ed.*, 1985, pp. 102–08. **[G: Latin America]**

Lesnoy, Selig D. and Leimer, Dean R. Social Security and Private Saving: Theory and Historical Evidence. *Soc. Sec. Bull.*, January 1985, *48*(1), pp. 14–30. **[G: U.S.]**

Loh, Choon Cheong and Veall, Michael R. A Note on Social Security and Private Savings in Singapore. *Public Finance*, 1985, *40*(2), pp. 299–304. **[G: Singapore]**

Lomasky, Loren E. Is Social Security Politically Untouchable? *Cato J.*, Spring/Summer 1985, *5*(1), pp. 157–75. **[G: U.S.]**

Malloy, James M. Statecraft and Social Security Policy and Crisis: A Comparison of Latin America and the United States. In *Mesa-Lago, C., ed.*, 1985, pp. 19–50. **[G: Latin America; U.S.]**

Mattei, Aurelio. Epargne et sécurité sociale. (Saving and Social Security. With English summary.) *Schweiz. Z. Volkswirtsch. Statist.*, March 1985, *121*(1), pp. 45–60. **[G: Switzerland]**

Maxfield, Linda Drazga. Income of New Retired Workers by Age at First Benefit Receipt: Findings from the New Beneficiary Survey. *Soc. Sec. Bull.*, July 1985, *48*(7), pp. 7–26. **[G: U.S.]**

Maxfield, Linda Drazga and Reno, Virginia P. Distribution of Income Sources of Recent Retirees: Findings from the New Beneficiary Survey. *Soc. Sec. Bull.*, January 1985, *48*(1), pp. 7–13. **[G: U.S.]**

McGreevey, William Paul. The Impact of Social Security on Income Distribution: Comment. In *Mesa-Lago, C., ed.*, 1985, pp. 209–15. **[G: Brazil]**

McSteen, Martha A. Fifty Years of Social Security. *Soc. Sec. Bull.*, August 1985, *48*(8), pp. 36–44. **[G: U.S.]**

Mendelson, Michael. Rationalization of Income Security in Canada. In *Courchene, T. J.; Conklin, D. W. and Cook, G. C. A., eds. Vol. 1*, 1985, pp. 229–52.

Mesa-Lago, Carmelo. Alternative Strategies to the Social Security Crisis: Socialist, Market and Mixed Approaches. In *Mesa-Lago, C., ed.*, 1985, pp. 311–61. **[G: Chile; Costa Rica; Cuba]**

Mesa-Lago, Carmelo. The Crisis of Social Security and Health Care: Introduction. In *Mesa-Lago, C., ed.*, 1985, pp. 1–17. **[G: Latin America]**

Miller, Arye L. Compensation for Personal Injury under Social Security. *Int. Lab. Rev.*, March-April 1985, *124*(2), pp. 193–205. **[G: Netherlands; New Zealand]**

Moynihan, Daniel Patrick. We Can't Avoid Family Policy Much Longer. *Challenge*, Sept./Oct. 1985, *28*(4), pp. 9–17. **[G: U.S.]**

Mumy, Gene E. The Role of Taxes and Social Security in Determining the Structure of Wages and Pensions. *J. Polit. Econ.*, June 1985, *93*(3), pp. 574–85. **[G: U.S.]**

Munnell, Alicia H. Social Security and the Budget. *New Eng. Econ. Rev.*, July/August 1985, pp. 5–18. **[G: U.S.]**

Munnell, Alicia H. Social Security, Private Pensions and Saving. In *Terny, G. and Culyer, A. J., eds.*, 1985, pp. 157–70.

Musgrove, Philip. The Impact of Social Security on Income Distribution. In *Mesa-Lago, C., ed.*, 1985, pp. 185–208. **[G: Latin America]**

Mussey, Sol. Actuarial Status of the HI and SMI Trust Funds. *Soc. Sec. Bull.*, June 1985, *48*(6), pp. 32–40. **[G: U.S.]**

Naqib, Fadle and Stollery, Kenneth R. The Effects of Alternative Public Pension Financing on Capital Formation: Consumption versus Payroll Taxes. *Economica*, May 1985, *52*(206), pp. 257–61.

Naqib, Fadle M. Some Redistributive Aspects of Social Security and Their Impact on the Supply of Labor. *Public Finance*, 1985, *40*(2), pp. 230–46.

Nelson, William J., Jr. Employment Covered under the Social Security Program, 1935–84. *Soc. Sec. Bull.*, April 1985, *48*(4), pp. 33–39. **[G: U.S.]**

Owens, Jeffrey and Roberti, Paolo. The Financing of Social Security Systems: International Comparisons: Trends and Policy Issues. In *Terny, G. and Culyer, A. J., eds.*, 1985, pp. 3–20. **[G: OECD]**

Parrott, Alec L. The System That Lost Its Way: Social Security Reform in the United Kingdom. *Int. Lab. Rev.*, Sept.-Oct. 1985, *124*(5), pp. 545–58. **[G: U.K.]**

Perelman, Sergio and Pestieau, Pierre. Social Allowances and Household Saving. In *Terny, G. and Culyer, A. J., eds.*, 1985, pp. 123–42. **[G: OECD]**

Podger, A. S. Income Provision in Old Age: Comment. *Australian Econ. Rev.*, 3rd Quarter, Spring 1985, (71), pp. 145–46. **[G: Australia]**

Pogue, Thomas F. and Sgontz, L. G. Human Capital Transfers: Implications for Equity in Social Security Systems. *Rev. Soc. Econ.*, April 1985, *43*(1), pp. 37–52. **[G: U.S.]**

Porter, Michael G. Income Provision in Old Age: Comment. *Australian Econ. Rev.*, 3rd Quarter, Spring 1985, (71), pp. 146–47. **[G: Australia]**

Price, Thomas E. Fifty Years Ago. *Soc. Sec. Bull.*, July 1985, *48*(7), pp. 5–6. **[G: U.S.]**

Quinn, Joseph F. Retirement Income Rights as a Component of Wealth in the United States. *Rev. Income Wealth*, September 1985, *31*(3), pp. 223–36. **[G: U.S.]**

Ranson, David. Criteria for Reforming Social Security. In *Ferrara, P. J., ed.*, 1985, pp. 139–55. [G: U.S.]

Reno, Virginia P. and Grad, Susan. Economic Security, 1935–85. *Soc. Sec. Bull.*, December 1985, *48*(12), pp. 5–20.

Reno, Virginia P. and Price, Daniel N. Relationship between the Retirement, Disability, and Unemployment Insurance Programs: The U.S. Experience. *Soc. Sec. Bull.*, May 1985, *48*(5), pp. 24–37. [G: U.S.]

Rezende, Fernando. The Financing of Social Security Pensions: Principles, Current Issues and Trends: Comment. In *Mesa-Lago, C., ed.*, 1985, pp. 178–83. [G: Latin America]

Roberts, Paul Craig. Social Security: Myths and Realities. In *Ferrara, P. J., ed.*, 1985, pp. 59–67. [G: U.S.]

Robertson, A. Haeworth. The National Commission's Failure to Achieve Real Reform. In *Ferrara, P. J., ed.*, 1985, pp. 37–48. [G: U.S.]

Romer, Paul M. Public Debt Policies and United States Saving: A Comment. *Carnegie-Rochester Conf. Ser. Public Policy*, Autumn 1985, *23*, pp. 87–89. [G: U.S.]

Rosenberg, Mark B. Politics and Social Security Reform: Comment. In *Mesa-Lago, C., ed.*, 1985, pp. 304–10. [G: Brazil; Chile; Argentina; Uruguay]

Rotherham, James A. The Railroad Retirement Program: A Case Study in the Deficit Dilemma. *Public Budg. Finance*, Autumn 1985, *5*(3), pp. 40–57. [G: U.S.]

Rowlatt, Don. The Social-Security System in the 1990s: Comments. In *Courchene, T. J.; Conklin, D. W. and Cook, G. C. A., eds. Vol. 1,* 1985, pp. 277–83. [G: Canada]

Rüegg, Walter. Social Rights or Social Responsibilities? The Case of Switzerland. In *Eisenstadt, S. N. and Ahimeir, O., eds.*, 1985, pp. 183–99. [G: Switzerland]

Sammartino, Frank J. and Kasten, Richard A. The Distributional Consequences of Taxing Social Security Benefits: Current Law and Alternative Schemes. *J. Post Keynesian Econ.*, Fall 1985, *8*(1), pp. 28–46. [G: U.S.]

Schmähl, Winfried. Auswirkungen verkürzter Wochenarbeitszeit und vermehrter Teilzeitarbeit auf die Finanzlage der gesetzlichen Rentenversicherung in der Bundesrepublik Deutschland. (Effects of Reduced Weekly Working Time and Increased Part Time Work on the Budget of the Social Retirement System in the Federal Republic of Germany. With English Summary). *Konjunkturpolitik*, 1985, *31*(4/5), pp. 285–99. [G: W. Germany]

Seidl, Vladimír and Pråša, Ladislav. Changes in the Social Security System in 1970–1985. *Czech. Econ. Digest.*, September 1985, (6), pp. 58–71. [G: Czechoslovakia]

Seidman, Laurence S. A General Equilibrium Critique of Feldstein's Social Security Estimate. *Eastern Econ. J.*, April-June 1985, *11*(2), pp. 101–05. [G: U.S.]

Sherman, Sally R. Assets of New Retired-Worker Beneficiaries: Findings from the New Beneficiary Survey. *Soc. Sec. Bull.*, July 1985, *48*(7), pp. 27–43. [G: U.S.]

Sherman, Sally R. Attitudes of the American Public toward Social Security. *Soc. Sec. Bull.*, November 1985, *48*(11), pp. 22–23. [G: U.S.]

Shibata, Hirofumi. Financing and the Politics of Financing Social Security Programs: An Analysis and Proposals for Reform. In *Terny, G. and Culyer, A. J., eds.*, 1985, pp. 291–302.

Shimono, Keiko and Tachibanaki, Toshiaki. Lifetime Income and Public Pension: An Analysis of the Effect on Redistribution Using a Two-Period Analysis. *J. Public Econ.*, February 1985, *26*(1), pp. 75–87.

Sjöberg, Björn. Reforming the Swedish Social Security System. *Int. Lab. Rev.*, January–February 1985, *124*(1), pp. 61–72. [G: Sweden]

Sjoblom, Kriss. Voting for Social Security. *Public Choice*, 1985, *45*(3), pp. 225–40. [G: U.S.]

Springer, Philip B. Home Equity Conversion Plans as a Source of Retirement Income. *Soc. Sec. Bull.*, September 1985, *48*(9), pp. 10–19. [G: U.S.]

Tamburi, Giovanni. Social Security in Latin America: Trends and Outlook. In *Mesa-Lago, C., ed.*, 1985, pp. 57–84. [G: Latin America]

Thornborrow, Nancy. Social Security's Effect on Retirement Assets. *Quart. J. Bus. Econ.*, Spring 1985, *24*(2), pp. 51–72. [G: U.S.]

Thullen, Peter. The Financing of Social Security Pensions: Principles, Current Issues and Trends. In *Mesa-Lago, C., ed.*, 1985, pp. 147–77. [G: Latin America]

Thurow, Lester C. Public Expenditures and the Elderly. *Eastern Econ. J.*, Jan.-Mar. 1985, *11*(1), pp. 42–50. [G: U.S.]

Tokman, Victor E. The Impact of Social Security on Employment: Comment. In *Mesa-Lago, C., ed.*, 1985, pp. 279–84. [G: Colombia; Mexico; Venezuela]

Ture, Norman B. Supply-Side Effects of Social Insurance. In *Ferrara, P. J., ed.*, 1985, pp. 71–81. [G: U.S.]

van Velthoven, Ben and van Winden, Frans A. A. M. Towards a Politico-economic Theory of Social Security. *Europ. Econ. Rev.*, March 1985, *27*(2), pp. 263–89.

Verbon, Harry A. A. Measuring the Redistributive Impact of Public Pensions. *De Economist*, 1985, *133*(1), pp. 87–98. [G: Netherlands]

Verbon, Harry A. A. On the Independence of Financing Methods and Redistributive Aspects of Pensions Plans. *Public Finance*, 1985, *40*(2), pp. 280–90.

Weaver, Carolyn L. The Economics and Politics of the Emergence of Social Security: Some Implications for Reform. In *Ferrara, P. J., ed.*, 1985, pp. 117–36. [G: U.S.]

Wilson, Richard R. The Impact of Social Security on Employment. In *Mesa-Lago, C., ed.*, 1985, pp. 245–78. [G: Colombia; Mexico; Venezuela]

Wiseman, Jack. Genesis, Aims and Goals of Social Policy. In *Terny, G. and Culyer, A. J., eds.*, 1985, pp. 93–106.

Yue, Guangzhao. Employment, Wages and Social Security in China. *Int. Lab. Rev.*, July-Aug. 1985, *124*(4), pp. 411–22. [G: China]

916 Economics of Law; Economics of Crime

9160 Economics of Law; Economics of Crime

Aaron, Benjamin. The Changing Law of Fair Representation: The State of the Law: An Overview. In *McKelvey, J. T., ed.*, 1985, pp. 15–46. [G: U.S.]

Adelstein, Richard P. and Peretz, Steven I. The Competition of Technologies in Markets for Ideas: Copyright and Fair Use in Evolutionary Perspective. *Int. Rev. Law Econ.*, December 1985, *5*(2), pp. 209–38. [G: U.S.]

Allison, Theodore E. Statement to the U.S. House Subcommittee on Consumer Affairs and Coinage of the Committee on Banking, Finance and Urban Affairs, June 18, 1985. *Fed. Res. Bull.*, August 1985, *71*(8), pp. 613–14. [G: U.S.]

Allison, Theodore E. Statement to the U.S. House Subcommittee on Financial Institutions Supervision, Regulation and Insurance of the Committee on Banking, Finance and Urban Affairs, April 4, 1985. *Fed. Res. Bull.*, June 1985, *71*(6), pp. 422–23. [G: U.S.]

Appleton, Lynn M. Explaining Laws' Making and Their Enforcement in the American States. *Soc. Sci. Quart.*, December 1985, *66*(4), pp. 839–53. [G: U.S.]

Aranson, Peter H. Judicial Control of the Political Branches: Public Purpose and Public Law. *Cato J.*, Winter 1985, *4*(3), pp. 719–82. [G: U.S.]

Armitage, Thomas C. Economic Efficiency as a Legal Norm. In *Zerbe, R. O., Jr., ed.*, 1985, pp. 1–27.

Awad, A. Safi El Din. Islamic Jurisprudence and Environmental Planning: Comments. *J. Res. Islamic Econ.*, Summer 1985, *3*(1), pp. 83–86.

Baysinger, Barry D. and Butler, Henry N. The Role of Corporate Law in the Theory of the Firm. *J. Law Econ.*, April 1985, *28*(1), pp. 179–91. [G: U.S.]

Beilock, Richard. Are Truckers Forced to Speed? *Logist. Transp. Rev.*, September 1985, *21*(3), pp. 277–91. [G: U.S.]

Benjamini, Yael and Maital, Shlomo. Optimal Tax Evasion and Optimal Tax Evasion Policy: Behavioral Aspects. In *Gaertner, W. and Wenig, A., eds.*, 1985, pp. 245–64. [G: Israel]

Blades, Derek W. Crime: What Should Be Recorded in the National Accounts; and What Difference Would It Make? In *Gaertner, W. and Wenig, A., eds.*, 1985, pp. 45–58. [G: U.S.]

Bone, John. On Substituting a Socially Costless Penalty for Costly Crime. *Int. Rev. Law Econ.*, December 1985, *5*(2), pp. 239–46.

Breit, William and Elzinga, Kenneth G. Private Antitrust Enforcement: The New Learning. *J. Law Econ.*, May 1985, *28*(2), pp. 405–43. [G: U.S.]

Brenner, Gabrielle A. Why Did Inheritance Laws Change? *Int. Rev. Law Econ.*, June 1985, *5*(1), pp. 91–106. [G: U.K.]

Brezinski, Horst. The Second Economy in the Soviet Union and Its Implications for Economic Policy. In *Gaertner, W. and Wenig, A., eds.*, 1985, pp. 362–76. [G: U.S.S.R.]

Broesterhuizen, G. A. A. M. The Unobserved Economy and the National Accounts in the Netherlands: A Sensitivity Analysis. In *Gaertner, W. and Wenig, A., eds.*, 1985, pp. 105–26. [G: Netherlands]

Brown, John Prather. Alternatives to tsm Balsent System of Litigation for Personal Injury. In *Baily, M. A. and Cikins, W. I., eds.*, 1985, pp. 69–79. [G: U.S.]

Brunet, Edward. Measuring the Costs of Civil Justice. *Mich. Law Rev.*, February 1985, *83*(4), pp. 916–38. [G: U.S.]

Buck, Andrew J.; Hakim, Simon and Spiegel, Uriel. The Natural Rate of Crime by Type of Community. *Rev. Soc. Econ.*, October 1985, *43*(2), pp. 245–59. [G: U.S.]

Burnside, Alec. Enforcement of EEC Competition Law by Interim Measures: The *Ford* Case. *J. World Trade Law*, January:February 1985, *19*(1), pp. 34–53. [G: EEC]

Burrows, Paul. Efficiency Levels, Efficiency Gains and Alternative Nuisance Remedies. *Int. Rev. Law Econ.*, June 1985, *5*(1), pp. 59–71.

Calande, Pauline E. State Incorporation of Federal Law: A Response to the Demise of Implied Federal Rights of Action. *Yale Law J.*, April 1985, *94*(5), pp. 1144–63. [G: U.S.]

Castan, Ron. Self-policing by Advisers in Taxation. *Australian Tax Forum*, Autumn 1985, *2*(1), pp. 79–83.

Chollet, Deborah J. Liability Rules and Health Care Costs. In *Baily, M. A. and Cikins, W. I., eds.*, 1985, pp. 22–27. [G: U.S.]

Christensen, Andrea S. What Employers Can Do about DFR Suits. In *McKelvey, J. T., ed.*, 1985, pp. 117–27. [G: U.S.]

Ciriacy-Wantrup, S. V. Water Economics: Relations to Law and Policy. In *Ciriacy-Wantrup, S. V.*, 1985, pp. 77–103. [G: U.S.]

Cloninger, Dale O. An Analysis of the Effect of Illegal Corporate Activity on Share Value. *J. Behav. Econ.*, Summer 1985, *14*(2), pp. 1–13.

Coffee, John C., Jr. The Unfaithful Champion: The Plaintiff as Monitor in Shareholder Litigation. *Law Contemp. Probl.*, Summer 1985, *48*(3), pp. 5–81. [G: U.S.]

Cowell, Frank A. Public Policy and Tax Evasion: Some Problems. In *Gaertner, W. and Wenig, A., eds.*, 1985, pp. 273–84.

Cowell, Frank A. The Economic Analysis of Tax Evasion. *Bull. Econ. Res.*, September 1985, *37*(3), pp. 163–93.

Cox, James D. and Munsinger, Harry L. Bias in the Boardroom: Psychological Foundations and Legal Implications of Corporate Cohesion. *Law Contemp. Probl.*, Summer 1985, *48*(3), pp. 83–135. [G: U.S.]

Crain, W. Mark; Tollison, Robert D. and Kimenyi, S. Mwangi. Litigation, the Business

Cycle, and Government Growth. *Z. ges. Staatswiss. (JITE)*, September 1985, *141*(3), pp. 435–43. [G: U.S.]

Crane, Steven E. and Nourzad, Farrokh. Time Value of Money and Income Tax Evasion under Risk-averse Behavior: Theoretical Analysis and Empirical Evidence. *Public Finance*, 1985, *40*(3), pp. 481–94. [G: U.S.]

Dalton, Clare. An Essay in the Deconstruction of Contract Doctrine. *Yale Law J.*, April 1985, *94*(5), pp. 997–1114.

Danzon, Patricia M. Liability and Liability Insurance for Medical Malpractice. *J. Health Econ.*, December 1985, *4*(4), pp. 309–31. [G: U.S.]

Danzon, Patricia M. The Medical Malpractice System: Facts and Reforms. In *Baily, M. A. and Cikins, W. I., eds.*, 1985, pp. 28–35. [G: U.S.]

Davies, S. J. Classes and Police in Manchester 1829–1880. In *Kidd, A. J. and Roberts, K. W.*, 1985, pp. 26–47. [G: U.K.]

De Alessi, Louis. Property Rights and the Judiciary. *Cato J.*, Winter 1985, *4*(3), pp. 805–11. [G: U.S.]

De Gijsel, Peter. A Microeconomic Analysis of Black Labour Demand and Supply. In *Gaertner, W. and Wenig, A., eds.*, 1985, pp. 218–26.

DeSouza, Patrick J. Regulating Fraud in Military Procurement: A Legal Process Model. *Yale Law J.*, December 1985, *95*(2), pp. 390–413. [G: U.S.]

Deutsch, Joseph; Hakim, Simon and Weinblatt, J. Errata [Interjurisdictional Criminal Mobility: A Theoretical Perspective]. *Urban Stud.*, August 1985, *22*(4), pp. 288.

Deutsch, Joseph; Hakim, Simon and Weinblatt, J. Errata [Interjurisdictional Criminal Mobility: A Theoretical Perspective]. *Urban Stud.*, December 1985, *22*(6), pp. 460.

Dixon, Daryl. Tax Avoidance and Withholding Tax. *Australian Tax Forum*, Autumn 1985, *2*(1), pp. 33–52. [G: Australia]

Dorn, James A. Economic Liberties and the Judiciary. *Cato J.*, Winter 1985, *4*(3), pp. 661–87.

Edwards, Harry T. The Duty of Fair Representation: A View from the Bench. In *McKelvey, J. T., ed.*, 1985, pp. 93–105. [G: U.S.]

Englander, Frederick. The Author Replies: We Still Need to Demonstrate Program Effectiveness [Helping Ex-offenders Enter the Labor Market]. *Mon. Lab. Rev.*, April 1985, *108*(4), pp. 49–50.

Epstein, Richard A. Judicial Review: Reckoning on Two Kinds of Error. *Cato J.*, Winter 1985, *4*(3), pp. 711–18. [G: U.S.]

Farnsworth, E. Allan. Your Loss or My Gain? The Dilemma of the Disgorgement Principle in Breach of Contract. *Yale Law J.*, May 1985, *94*(6), pp. 1339–93. [G: U.S.]

Fayle, Richard D. Controlling Abusive Tax Shelters. *Australian Tax Forum*, Autumn 1985, *2*(1), pp. 53–69. [G: Australia]

Fisher, Vickie L. Recent Innovations in State Tax Compliance Programs. *Nat. Tax J.*, September 1985, *38*(3), pp. 565–71. [G: U.S.]

Gaertner, Wulf and Wenig, Alois. The Economics of the Shadow Economy: Introduction. In *Gaertner, W. and Wenig, A., eds.*, 1985, pp. iii–xii.

Galasi, Péter. Peculiarities and Limits of the Second Economy in Socialism (the Hungarian Case). In *Gaertner, W. and Wenig, A., eds.*, 1985, pp. 353–61. [G: Hungary]

Gammie, Malcomb J. The Implications of *Furniss v Dawson. Fisc. Stud.*, August 1985, *6*(3), pp. 51–65. [G: U.K.]

Garth, Bryant G.; Nagel, Ilene H. and Plager, Sheldon J. Empirical Research and the Shareholder Derivative Suit: Toward a Better-informed Debate. *Law Contemp. Probl.*, Summer 1985, *48*(3), pp. 137–59. [G: U.S.]

George, Edward I. and Wecker, William E. Estimating Damages in a Class Action Litigation. *J. Bus. Econ. Statist.*, April 1985, *3*(2), pp. 132–39.

Giertz, J. Fred and Nardulli, Peter F. Prison Overcrowding. *Public Choice*, 1985, *46*(1), pp. 71–78. [G: U.S.]

Ginsburgh, Victor, et al. Macroeconomic Policy in the Presence of an Irregular Sector. In *Gaertner, W. and Wenig, A., eds.*, 1985, pp. 194–217.

Gleizal, J.-J. Critique du droit et théorie de la régulation. (Critique of Law and the Theory of Regulation. With English summary.) *Écon. Soc.*, January 1985, *19*(1), pp. 91–101.

Goetz, Charles J. Contractual Remedies and the Normative Acceptability of State-imposed Coercion [Mistaken Judicial Activism: Proposed Constraints on Creditor Remedies]. *Cato J.*, Winter 1985, *4*(3), pp. 075–80.

Goldberg, Victor P. Economic Aspects of Bankruptcy Law: Comment. *Z. ges. Staatswiss. (JITE)*, March 1985, *141*(1), pp. 99–103.

Goldberg, Victor P. Relational Exchange, Contract Law, and the *Boomer* Problem. *Z. ges. Staatswiss. (JITE)*, December 1985, *141*(4), pp. 570–75.

Graetz, Michael J. and Wilde, Louis L. The Economics of Tax Compliance: Fact and Fantasy. *Nat. Tax J.*, September 1985, *38*(3), pp. 355–63. [G: U.S.]

Gutmann, Peter M. The Subterranean Economy, Redux. In *Gaertner, W. and Wenig, A., eds.*, 1985, pp. 2–18. [G: U.S.]

Hanke, Steve H. Rules versus Cost–Benefit Analysis in the Common Law: A Comment. *Cato J.*, Winter 1985, *4*(3), pp. 893–96.

Hansson, Ingemar. Tax Evasion and Government Policy. In *Gaertner, W. and Wenig, A., eds.*, 1985, pp. 285–300.

Harris, Peter. Difficult Cases and the Display of Authority. *J. Law, Econ., Organ.*, Spring 1985, *1*(1), pp. 209–21. [G: U.S.]

Harris, William G. Inflation Risk as a Determinant of the Discount Rate in Tort Settlements: Reply. *J. Risk Ins.*, September 1985, *52*(3), pp. 533–36. [G: U.S.]

Hartmann, Charles J. and Renas, Stephen M. Anglo-American Privacy Law: An Economic Analysis. *Int. Rev. Law Econ.*, December

1985, 5(2), pp. 133–52.   [G: U.S.; U.K.]

Harwood, Edwin. How Should We Enforce Immigration Law? In *Glazer, N., ed.*, 1985, pp. 73–91.   [G: U.S.]

Hax, Herbert. Economic Aspects of Bankruptcy Law. *Z. ges. Staatswiss. (JITE)*, March 1985, *141*(1), pp. 80–98.

Hay, George A. Anti-trust and Economic Theory: Some Observations from the U.S. Experience. *Fisc. Stud.*, February 1985, *6*(1), pp. 59–69.   [G: U.S.]

Hay, George A. Vertical Restraints. *Fisc. Stud.*, August 1985, *6*(3), pp. 37–50.   [G: U.S.]

Hill, John K. The Economic Impact of Tighter U.S. Border Security. *Fed. Res. Bank Dallas Econ. Rev.*, July 1985, pp. 12–20.   [G: U.S.]

Hirsch, Werner Z. and Rufolo, Anthony M. Economic Effects of Residence Laws on Municipal Police. *J. Urban Econ.*, May 1985, *17*(3), pp. 335–48.   [G: U.S.]

Howard, Jeffrey H. Applying the Antitrust Laws to Local Governments: Congress Changes the Approach. *Antitrust Bull.*, Winter 1985, *30*(4), pp. 745–90.   [G: U.S.]

Howell, H. Wayne. State Securities Regulation of Tax Shelters. *Nat. Tax J.*, September 1985, *38*(3), pp. 339–43.   [G: U.S.]

Hunsaker, Ann T. The Federal Government's Perspective on Litigation and Health Care Costs. In *Baily, M. A. and Cikins, W. I., eds.*, 1985, pp. 11–21.   [G: U.S.]

Jacob, Herbert. Policy Responses to Crime. In *Peterson, P. E., ed.*, 1985, pp. 225–52.   [G: U.S.]

Jarrell, Gregg A. The Wealth Effects of Litigation by Targets: Do Interests Diverge in a Merge? *J. Law Econ.*, April 1985, *28*(1), pp. 151–77.

Jones, James E., Jr. The Changing Law of Fair Representation: The Duty in Other Forums: Time for a Midcourse Correction? In *McKelvey, J. T., ed.*, 1985, pp. 223–72.   [G: U.S.]

Kadane, Joseph B. Is Victimization Chronic? A Bayesian Analysis of Multinomial Missing Data. *J. Econometrics*, July/August 1985, *29*(1/2), pp. 47–67.   [G: U.S.]

Kaplan, Steven E. and Reckers, Philip M. J. A Study of Tax Evasion Judgments. *Nat. Tax J.*, March 1985, *38*(1), pp. 97–102.   [G: U.S.]

Kaprelian, Mark A. Privity Revisited: Tort Recovery by a Commercial Buyer for a Defective Product's Self-Inflicted Damage. *Mich. Law Rev.*, December 1985, *84*(3), pp. 517–40.   [G: U.S.]

van Kempen, Jan M. The Business Purpose Test: The Dutch Approach. *Fisc. Stud.*, August 1985, *6*(3), pp. 66–76.   [G: Netherlands]

Kimball, Spencer L. The Contest of "No Fault." *J. Risk Ins.*, December 1985, *52*(4), pp. 662–66.   [G: U.S.]

Klein, Benjamin and Saft, Lester F. The Law and Economics of Franchise Tying Contracts. *J. Law Econ.*, May 1985, *28*(2), pp. 345–61.   [G: U.S.]

Klein, David Y. Exhaustion of Internal Union Remedies after *Clayton* and *Bowen*. In *McKelvey, J. T., ed.*, 1985, pp. 70–84.   [G: U.S.]

Kneebone, Susan. Estoppel as the Basis of Judicial Review: R v Inland Revenue Commissioners ex parte Preston [1985] 2 WLR 836. *Australian Tax Forum*, Spring 1985, *2*(3), pp. 349–62.   [G: U.K.]

Kotzorek, Andreas. Zur Häufigkeit arbeitsrechtlicher Prozesse in der Bundesrepublik Deutschland—Eine ökonomische Analyse. (On the Litigation Rate of Labor Cases in West Germany. With English summary.) *Z. ges. Staatswiss. (JITE)*, June 1985, *141*(2), pp. 312–35.   [G: W. Germany]

Krapp, Thea. The Limitation Convention for International Sale of Goods. *J. World Trade Law*, July:Aug. 1985, *19*(4), pp. 343–72.   [G: Global]

Kronman, Anthony T. Contract Law and the State of Nature. *J. Law, Econ., Organ.*, Spring 1985, *1*(1), pp. 5–32.

de Lacharrière, Guy Ladreit. Case for a Tribunal to Assist in Settling Trade Disputes. *World Econ.*, December 1985, *8*(4), pp. 339–52.   [G: Global]

Landau, C. E. Recent Australian Legislation and Case-Law on Sex Equality at Work. *Int. Lab. Rev.*, May-June 1985, *124*(3), pp. 335–51.   [G: Australia]

Langfeldt, Enno. Is a Growing Unobserved Sector Undermining Monetary Policy in the Federal Republic of Germany? In *Gaertner, W. and Wenig, A., eds.*, 1985, pp. 301–14.   [G: W. Germany]

Lattimore, Pamela K. and Witte, Ann D. Programs to Aid Ex-offenders: We Don't Know 'Nothing Works' [Helping Ex-offenders Enter the Labor Market]. *Mon. Lab. Rev.*, April 1985, *108*(4), pp. 46–48.

Lave, Charles A. Speeding, Coordination, and the 55 MPH Limit. *Amer. Econ. Rev.*, December 1985, *75*(5), pp. 1159–64.   [G: U.S.]

Layson, Stephen K. Homicide and Deterrence: A Reexamination of the United States Time-Series Evidence. *Southern Econ. J.*, July 1985, *52*(1), pp. 68–89.   [G: U.S.]

Lee, Dwight R. Policing Cost, Evasion Cost, and the Optimal Speed Limit. *Southern Econ. J.*, July 1985, *52*(1), pp. 34–45.

Leiser, Burton M. Vagrancy, Loitering, and Economic Justice. In *Kipnis, K. and Meyers, D. T., eds.*, 1985, pp. 149–60.   [G: U.S.]

Liebeler, Wesley J. A Property Rights Approach to Judicial Decision Making. *Cato J.*, Winter 1985, *4*(3), pp. 783–804.   [G: U.S.]

Liebowitz, S. J. Copying and Indirect Appropriability: Photocopying of Journals. *J. Polit. Econ.*, October 1985, *93*(5), pp. 945–57.   [G: U.S.]

Lindenberg, Siegwart and de Vos, Henk. The Limits of Solidarity: Relational Contracting in Perspective and Some Criticism of Traditional Sociology. *Z. ges. Staatswiss. (JITE)*, December 1985, *141*(4), pp. 558–69.

Lipsitz, Richard. The Changing Law of Fair Representation: The State of the Law: New Substantive and Procedural Areas. In *McKelvey, J. T., ed.*, 1985, pp. 47–69.   [G: U.S.]

Llewellyn, Othman A. Islamic Jurisprudence and

Environmental Planning: Rejoinder. *J. Res. Islamic Econ.*, Summer 1985, *3*(1), pp. 87–90.

Lui, Francis T. An Equilibrium Queuing Model of Bribery. *J. Polit. Econ.*, August 1985, *93*(4), pp. 760–81.

Macneil, Ian R. Reflections on Relational Contract. *Z. ges. Staatswiss. (JITE)*, December 1985, *141*(4), pp. 541–46.

Mariner, Wendy K. The Potential Impact of Pharmaceutical and Vaccine Litigation. In *Baily, M. A. and Cikins, W. I., eds.*, 1985, pp. 43–68. [G: U.S.]

Markovits, Richard S. The Functions, Allocative Efficiency, and Legality of Tie-ins: A Comment. *J. Law Econ.*, May 1985, *28*(2), pp. 387–404. [G: U.S.]

Mathis, Edward J. and Zech, Charles E. The Community Demand for Police Officers: Relative to the Maximum Base Salary, Citizen Wants Tend to Be Elastic. *Amer. J. Econ. Soc.*, October 1985, *44*(4), pp. 401–10. [G: U.S.]

McDonald, Donogh C. Trade Data Discrepancies and the Incentive to Smuggle: An Empirical Analysis. *Int. Monet. Fund Staff Pap.*, December 1985, *32*(4), pp. 668–92. [G: LDCs]

McManus, Walter S. Estimates of the Deterrent Effect of Capital Punishment: The Importance of the Researcher's Prior Beliefs. *J. Polit. Econ.*, April 1985, *93*(2), pp. 417–25. [G: U.S.]

Müller-Graff, Peter-Christian. Long-term Business Relations: Conflicts and the Law. *Z. ges. Staatswiss. (JITE)*, December 1985, *141*(4), pp. 547–57.

Newman, Harold R. The Changing Law of Fair Representation: The State of the Law: The Duty in the Public Sector. In *McKelvey, J. T., ed.*, 1985, pp. 85–92. [G: U.S.]

Norman, Neville. The Economics of Tax Ploision and Corporate Tax Integration. *Australian Tax Forum*, Autumn 1985, *2*(1), pp. 71–77.

O'Hare, Michael. Copyright: When Is Monopoly Efficient? *J. Policy Anal. Manage.*, Spring 1985, *4*(3), pp. 407–18.

O'Higgins, Michael. The Relationship between the Formal and Hidden Economies: An Exploratory Analysis for Four Countries. In *Gaertner, W. and Wenig, A., eds.*, 1985, pp. 127–43. [G: Canada; U.S.; U.K.; W. Germany]

Ogus, Anthony. Legislation, the Courts and the Demand for Compensation. In *Matthews, R. C. O., ed.*, 1985, pp. 151–67.

Pacey, Patricia L. The Courts and College Football: New Playing Rules off the Field? *Amer. J. Econ. Soc.*, April 1985, *44*(2), pp. 145–54. [G: U.S.]

Page, Talbot and Ricci, Paolo F. A Cost–Benefit Perspective for Risk Assessment. In *Ricci, P. F., ed.*, 1985, pp. 37–65.

Paul, Ellen Frankel. Public Use: A Vanishing Limitation on Governmental Takings. *Cato J.*, Winter 1985, *4*(3), pp. 835–51.

Pestieau, Pierre. Belgium's Irregular Economy. In *Gaertner, W. and Wenig, A., eds.*, 1985, pp. 144–60. [G: Belgium]

Peterson, Laura Bennett. Comment on Antitrust Remedies [Detrebling Antitrust Damages] [Private Antitrust Enforcement: The New Learning]. *J. Law Econ.*, May 1985, *28*(2), pp. 483–88. [G: U.S.]

Pilon, Roger. Legislative Activism, Judicial Activism, and the Decline of Private Sovereignty. *Cato J.*, Winter 1985, *4*(3), pp. 813–33. [G: U.S.]

Porter, John E. The Effects of Litigation on Health Care Costs: A Congressional Perspective. In *Baily, M. A. and Cikins, W. I., eds.*, 1985, pp. 36–42. [G: U.S.]

Rabin, Robert J. The Changing Law of Fair Representation: The Duty in Other Forums: Fair Representation in Arbitration. In *McKelvey, J. T., ed.*, 1985, pp. 173–207. [G: U.S.]

Reed, Mike. An Alternative View of the Underground Economy. *J. Econ. Issues*, June 1985, *19*(2), pp. 567–73.

Richardson, Ivor L. M. Appellate Court Responsibilities and Tax Avoidance. *Australian Tax Forum*, Autumn 1985, *2*(1), pp. 3–20. [G: New Zealand]

Rizzo, Mario J. Rules versus Cost–Benefit Analysis in the Common Law. *Cato J.*, Winter 1985, *4*(3), pp. 865–84.

Robinson, Glen O. Rizzo on Rules: A Comment [Rules versus Cost–Benefit Analysis in the Common Law]. *Cato J.*, Winter 1985, *4*(3), pp. 885–91.

Roessler, Frieder. The Scope, Limits and Function of the GATT Legal System. *World Econ.*, September 1985, *8*(3), pp. 287–98. [G: Global]

Roin, Kathleen Leslie. Due Process Limits on State Estate Taxation: An Analogy to the State Corporate Income Tax. *Yale Law J.*, April 1985, *94*(5), pp. 1229–51. [G: U.S.]

Romano, Roberta. Law as a Product: Some Pieces of the Incorporation Puzzle. *J. Law, Econ., Organ.*, Fall 1985, *1*(2), pp. 225–83. [G: U.S.]

Roper, Brian A. The Economics of Penological Policy: The Restoration of Equilibrium in a Social Market. *Int. J. Soc. Econ.*, 1985, *12*(1), pp. 54–76. [G: U.K.]

Rosenberg, D. and Shavell, Steven. A Model in Which Suits Are Brought for Their Nuisance Value. *Int. Rev. Law Econ.*, June 1985, *5*(1), pp. 3–13. [G: U.S.; U.K.]

Rottenberg, Simon. Mistaken Judicial Activism: Proposed Constraints on Creditor Remedies. *Cato J.*, Winter 1985, *4*(3), pp. 959–74. [G: U.S.]

Rowley, Charles K. Supreme Court Economic Review. *Int. Rev. Law Econ.*, June 1985, *5*(1), pp. 107–19. [G: U.S.]

Rowley, Charles K. The Relationship between Economics, Politics and the Law in the Formation of Public Policy. In *Matthews, R. C. O., ed.*, 1985, pp. 127–50.

Rubin, Paul H. Some Notes on Methodology in Law and Economics. In *Zerbe, R. O., Jr., ed.*, 1985, pp. 29–39.

Samuels, Warren J. Some Considerations Which

May Lead Lawmakers to Modify a Policy When Adopting It as Law: Comment. *Z. ges. Staatswiss. (JITE)*, March 1985, *141*(1), pp. 58–61.

Scalia, Antonin. Economic Affairs as Human Affairs. *Cato J.*, Winter 1985, *4*(3), pp. 703–10.
[G: U.S.]

Schlicht, Ekkehart. The Shadow Economy and Morals: A Note. In *Gaertner, W. and Wenig, A., eds.*, 1985, pp. 265–71.

Semkow, Brian W. Social Insurance and Tort Liability. *Int. Rev. Law Econ.*, December 1985, *5*(2), pp. 153–71.

Shavell, Steven. Uncertainty over Causation and the Determination of Civil Liability. *J. Law Econ.*, October 1985, *28*(3), pp. 587–609.

Shughart, William F., II and Tollison, Robert D. Corporate Chartering: An Exploration in the Economics of Legal Change. *Econ. Inquiry*, October 1985, *23*(4), pp. 585–99.
[G: U.S.]

Siegan, Bernard H. Economic Liberties and the Constitution: Protection at the State Level. *Cato J.*, Winter 1985, *4*(3), pp. 689–702.
[G: U.S.]

Simon, Marilyn J.; Wolf, Robert G. and Perloff, Jeffrey M. Product Safety, Liability Rules and Retailer Bankruptcy. *Southern Econ. J.*, April 1985, *51*(4), pp. 1130–41.

Skinner, Jonathan S. and Slemrod, Joel B. An Economic Perspective on Tax Evasion. *Nat. Tax J.*, September 1985, *38*(3), pp. 345–53.
[G: U.S.]

Skolka, Jiri. The Parallel Economy in Austria. In *Gaertner, W. and Wenig, A., eds.*, 1985, pp. 60–75.
[G: Austria]

Smith, James D. Market Motives in the Informal Economy. In *Gaertner, W. and Wenig, A., eds.*, 1985, pp. 161–77.
[G: U.S.]

St. Antoine, Theodore J. The Revision of Employment-at-Will Enters a New Phase. In *Dennis, B. D., ed.*, 1985, pp. 563–67.
[G: U.S.]

Stein, Bruno. Subterranean Labor Markets: A Conceptual Analysis. In *Gaertner, W. and Wenig, A., eds.*, 1985, pp. 37–44.

Stieber, Jack. Recent Developments in Employment-at-Will. In *Dennis, B. D., ed.*, 1985, pp. 557–63.
[G: U.S.]

Summers, Clyde W. Measuring the Union's Duty to the Individual: An Analytic Framework. In *McKelvey, J. T., ed.*, 1985, pp. 145–69.
[G: U.S.]

Summers, Robert S. Some Considerations Which May Lead Lawmakers to Modify a Policy When Adopting It as Law. *Z. ges. Staatswiss. (JITE)*, March 1985, *141*(1), pp. 41–57.

Sutinen, Jon G. and Andersen, Peder. The Economics of Fisheries Law Enforcement. *Land Econ.*, November 1985, *61*(4), pp. 387–97.

Thomas, Ewart A. C. On Calculating Optimal Contributory Negligence Rules. *Soc. Choice Welfare*, May 1985, *2*(1), pp. 65–85.

Tobias, Paul H. The Changing Law of Fair Representation: The Parties: The Plaintiff's Perception of Litigation. In *McKelvey, J. T., ed.*, 1985, pp. 128–44.
[G: U.S.]

Trengove, Chris D. Measuring the Hidden Economy. *Australian Tax Forum*, Autumn 1985, *2*(1), pp. 85–95.
[G: U.S.]

Truesdale, John C. The NLRB and the Duty. In *McKelvey, J. T., ed.*, 1985, pp. 208–22.
[G: U.S.]

Valencia, Richard R. The Effects of Litigation on Health Care Costs: Introductional Implications. In *Baily, M. A. and Cikins, W. I., eds.*, 1985 T1Baily, Mary Ann, pp. 1–107.
[G: U.S.]

Van Alstyne, William W. The Second Death of Federalism. *Mich. Law Rev.*, June 1985, *83*(7), pp. 1709–33.
[G: U.S.]

Veljanovski, Cento G. Organized Futures Contracting. *Int. Rev. Law Econ.*, June 1985, *5*(1), pp. 25–38.

Veljanovski, Cento G. The Role of Economics in the Common Law. In *Zerbe, R. O., Jr., ed.*, 1985, pp. 41–64.

Vernon, Jack. Inflation Risk as Determinant of the Discount Rate in Tort Settlements: Comment. *J. Risk Ins.*, September 1985, *52*(3), pp. 528–32.
[G: U.S.]

Waldman, Seymour M. The Changing Law of Fair Representation: The Parties: A Union Advocate's View. In *McKelvey, J. T., ed.*, 1985, pp. 109–16.
[G: U.S.]

Weck-Hannemann, Hannelore and Frey, Bruno S. Measuring the Shadow Economy: The Case of Switzerland. In *Gaertner, W. and Wenig, A., eds.*, 1985, pp. 76–104. [G: Switzerland]

Wescoat, James L., Jr. On Water Conservation and Reform of the Prior Appropriation Doctrine in Colorado. *Econ. Geogr.*, January 1985, *61*(1), pp. 3–24.
[G: U.S.]

Wittman, Donald. Should Compensation Be Based on Costs or Benefits? *Int. Rev. Law Econ.*, December 1985, *5*(2), pp. 173–85.
[G: U.S.]

Wolff, Edward N. The Disappearance of Domestic Servants and the Underground Economy. In *Gaertner, W. and Wenig, A., eds.*, 1985, pp. 316–29.
[G: U.S.]

Yamashita, Robert C. and Park, Peter. The Politics of Race: The Open Door, Ozawa and the Case of the Japanese in America. *Rev. Radical Polit. Econ.*, Fall 1985, *17*(3), pp. 135–56.
[G: U.S.]

917 Economics of Minorities; Economics of Discrimination

9170 Economics of Minorities; Economics of Discrimination

Abella, Rosalie S. Equality in Employment. In *Economic Council of Canada.*, 1985, pp. 109–17.
[G: Canada]

Abowd, John M. and Killingsworth, Mark R. Employment, Wages, and Earnings of Hispanics in the Federal and Nonfederal Sectors: Methodological Issues and Their Empirical Consequences. In *Borjas, G. J. and Tienda, M., eds.*, 1985, pp. 77–125.
[G: U.S.]

Adekanye, Tomilayo O. Innovation and Rural Women in Nigeria: Cassava Processing and

Food Production. In *Ahmed, I., ed.*, 1985, pp. 252–83. **[G: Nigeria]**

Agarwal, Bina. Women and Technological Change in Agriculture: The Asian and African Experience. In *Ahmed, I., ed.*, 1985, pp. 67–114. **[G: India; Africa; Asia]**

Ahmed, Iftikhar. Technology and Rural Women: Conclusions. In *Ahmed, I., ed.*, 1985, pp. 327–41. **[G: LDCs]**

Akerlof, George A. Discriminatory, Status-based Wages among Tradition-oriented, Stochastically Trading Coconut Producers. *J. Polit. Econ.*, April 1985, *93*(2), pp. 265–76.

Akin, John S., et al. Determinants of Infant Feeding: A Household Production Approach. *Econ. Develop. Cult. Change*, October 1985, *34*(1), pp. 57–81. **[G: Philippines]**

Al-Qudsi, Sulayman S. Earnings Differences in the Labor Market of the Arab Gulf States: The Case of Kuwait. *J. Devel. Econ.*, May–June 1985, *18*(1), pp. 119–32. **[G: Kuwait; United Arab Emirates; Bahrain; Saudi Arabia; Qatar]**

Albelda, Randy. "Nice Work If You Can Get It": Segmentation of White and Black Women Workers in the Post-War Period. *Rev. Radical Polit. Econ.*, Fall 1985, *17*(3), pp. 72–85. **[G: U.S.]**

Albers, Patricia C. Autonomy and Dependency in the Lives of Dakota Women: A Study in Historical Change. *Rev. Radical Polit. Econ.*, Fall 1985, *17*(3), pp. 109–34. **[G: U.S.]**

Allison, Caroline. Health and Education for Development: African Women's Status and Prospects. In *Rose, T., ed.*, 1985, pp. 111–23. **[G: Sub-Saharan Africa]**

Anderson, Elijah. Race and Neighborhood Transition. In *Peterson, P. E., ed.*, 1985, pp. 99–127. **[G: U.S.]**

Anker, Richard and Hein, Catherine. Why Third World Urban Employers Usually Prefer Men. *Int. Lab. Rev.*, January–February 1985, *124*(1), pp. 73–90. **[G: LDCs]**

Armstrong, Muriel. Towards Equity: Summary of Proceedings. In *Economic Council of Canada.*, 1985, pp. 137–45. **[G: Canada]**

Arrow, Kenneth J. Models of Job Discrimination. In *Arrow, K. J. (II)*, 1985, pp. 89–111.

Arrow, Kenneth J. Some Mathematical Models of Race Discrimination in the Labor Market. In *Arrow, K. J. (II)*, 1985, pp. 112–29.

Arrow, Kenneth J. The Theory of Discrimination. In *Arrow, K. J. (II)*, 1985, pp. 143–64.

Ask, Karin. The Position of Women and Women as a Target Group for Development Assistance. In *Jerve, A. M., ed.*, 1985, pp. 327–45. **[G: Pakistan; Norway]**

Banerjee, Biswajit and Knight, J. B. Caste Discrimination in the Indian Urban Labour Market. *J. Devel. Econ.*, April 1985, *17*(3), pp. 277–307. **[G: India]**

Baron, Harold M. Racism Transformed: The Implications of the 1960s. *Rev. Radical Polit. Econ.*, Fall 1985, *17*(3), pp. 10–33. **[G: U.S.]**

Barrère-Maurisson, Marie-Agnès; Battagliola, Françoise and Daune-Richard, Anne-Marie. The Course of Women's Careers and Family Life. In *Roberts, B.; Finnegan, R. and Gallie, D., eds.*, 1985, pp. 431–58. **[G: France]**

Barry, Janis. Women Production Workers: Low Pay and Hazardous Work. *Amer. Econ. Rev.*, May 1985, *75*(2), pp. 262–65. **[G: U.S.]**

Bates, Timothy. Entrepreneur Human Capital Endowments and Minority Business Viability. *J. Human Res.*, Fall 1985, *20*(4), pp. 540–54. **[G: U.S.]**

Bates, Timothy. Impact of Preferential Procurement Policies on Minority-owned Businesses. *Rev. Black Polit. Econ.*, Summer 1985, *14*(1), pp. 51–65. **[G: U.S.]**

Bean, Frank D.; Swicegood, C. Gray and King, Allan G. Role Incompatibility and the Relationship between Fertility and Labor Supply among Hispanic Women. In *Borjas, G. J. and Tienda, M., eds.*, 1985, pp. 221–42. **[G: U.S.]**

Becker, Gary S. Human Capital, Effort, and the Sexual Division of Labor. *J. Lab. Econ.*, Part 2 January 1985, *3*(1), pp. S33–58. **[G: U.S.]**

Beechey, Veronica and Perkins, Teresa. Conceptualising Part-Time Work. In *Roberts, B.; Finnegan, R. and Gallie, D., eds.*, 1985, pp. 246–63. **[G: U.K.]**

Bell, Carolyn Shaw. Comparable Worth: How Do We Know It Will Work? *Mon. Lab. Rev.*, December 1985, *108*(12), pp. 5–12. **[G: U.S.]**

Bell, Carolyn Shaw. SIPP and the Female Condition. *J. Econ. Soc. Meas.*, December 1985, *13*(3–4), pp. 263–71. **[G: U.S.]**

Beller, Andrea H. Changes in the Sex Composition of U.S. Occupations, 1960–1981. *J. Human Res.*, Spring 1985, *20*(2), pp. 235–50. **[G: U.S.]**

Beller, Andrea H. and Graham, John W. Variations in the Economic Well-Being of Divorced Women and Their Children: The Role of Child Support Income. In *David, M. and Smeeding, T., eds.*, 1985, pp. 471–506. **[G: U.S.]**

Benería, Lourdes. Meditations on Ivan Illich's Gender. In *Gustavsson, B.; Karlsson, J. C. and Raftegard, C.*, 1985, pp. 121–29.

Berg, Alan. Improving Nutrition: The Bank's Experience. *Finance Develop.*, June 1985, *22*(2), pp. 32–35. **[G: Brazil; Indonesia; Colombia; India]**

Bergmann, Barbara R. The Economic Case for Comparable Worth. In *Hartmann, H. I., ed.*, 1985, pp. 71–85. **[G: U.S.]**

Betsey, Charles L. Employment Issues: Discussion. *Rev. Black Polit. Econ.*, Fall-Winter 1985-86, *14*(2–3), pp. 71–77.

Bettio, Francesca. The Secular Decrease of Sex-Linked Wage Differentials: A Case of Non Competition. *Econ. Lavoro*, July-Sept. 1985, *19*(3), pp. 31–56. **[G: W. Europe; U.S.]**

Bettio, Francesca. The Unremoved Constraint: Job Sex-Typing and Female Participation, 1901–1981. *Stud. Econ.*, 1985, *40*(27), pp. 77–122. **[G: Italy]**

Bhaduri, Amit. Technological Change and Rural Women: A Conceptual Analysis. In *Ahmed, I., ed.*, 1985, pp. 15–26.

Bhattacherjee, Debashish. A Note on Caste Discrimination in a Bombay Automobile Firm. *Ind. Relat.*, Winter 1985, *24*(1), pp. 155–59. [G: India]

Birdsall, Nancy and Fox, M. Louise. Why Males Earn More: Location and Training of Brazilian Schoolteachers. *Econ. Develop. Cult. Change*, April 1985, *33*(3), pp. 533–56. [G: Brazil]

Black, Harold A. and Schweitzer, Robert L. Black-controlled Credit Unions: A Comparative Analysis. *J. Finan. Res.*, Fall 1985, *8*(3), pp. 193–202.

Blau, Francine D. and Kahn, Lawrence M. On Estimating Discrimination in the Economy: Comment. *Southern Econ. J.*, April 1985, *51*(4), pp. 1221–26. [G: U.S.]

Block, Walter. Towards Equity: Directions for Future Research: Panel Discussion. In *Economic Council of Canada.*, 1985, pp. 119–21. [G: Canada]

Borjas, George J. and Tienda, Marta. Hispanics in the U.S. Economy: Introduction. In *Borjas, G. J. and Tienda, M., eds.*, 1985, pp. 1–24. [G: U.S.]

Boston, Thomas D. Racial Inequality and Class Stratification: A Contribution to a Critique of Black Conservatism. *Rev. Radical Polit. Econ.*, Fall 1985, *17*(3), pp. 46–71. [G: U.S.]

Boulet, Jac-André. Occupational Diversification of Women in the Workplace. In *Economic Council of Canada.*, 1985, pp. 31–37. [G: Canada]

Brockmann, C. Thomas. Women and Development in Northern Belize. *J. Devel. Areas*, July 1985, *19*(4), pp. 501–13. [G: Belize]

Brown, Clair. An Institutional Model of Wives' Work Decisions. *Ind. Relat.*, Spring 1985, *24*(2), pp. 182–204. [G: U.S.]

Browning, Harley L. and Rodríguez, Nestor. The Migration of Mexican Indocumentados as a Settlement Process: Implications for Work. In *Borjas, G. J. and Tienda, M., eds.*, 1985, pp. 277–97. [G: U.S.]

Buchele, Robert and Aldrich, Mark. How Much Difference Would Comparable Worth Make? *Ind. Relat.*, Spring 1985, *24*(2), pp. 222–33. [G: U.S.]

Burbridge, Lynn C. Black Women in Employment and Training Programs. *Rev. Black Polit. Econ.*, Fall-Winter 1985-86, *14*(2–3), pp. 97–114. [G: U.S.]

Cain, Glen G. Welfare Economics of Policies toward Women. *J. Lab. Econ.*, Part 2 January 1985, *3*(1), pp. S375–96. [G: U.S.]

Cain, Pamela Stone. Prospects for Pay Equity in a Changing Economy. In *Hartmann, H. I., ed.*, 1985, pp. 137–65. [G: U.S.]

Carr, Marilyn. Technologies for Rural Women: Impact and Dissemination. In *Ahmed, I., ed.*, 1985, pp. 115–53. [G: Africa]

Carter, Michael J. and Carter, Susan B. Internal Labor Markets in Retailing: The Early Years. *Ind. Lab. Relat. Rev.*, July 1985, *38*(4), pp. 586–98. [G: U.S.]

Carvajal, Manuel J. and Geithman, David T. Income, Human Capital and Sex Discrimination: Some Evidence from Costa Rica, 1963 and 1973. *J. Econ. Devel.*, July 1985, *10*(1), pp. 89–115. [G: Costa Rica]

Cave, George. Youth Joblessness and Race: Evidence from the 1980 Census. In *Betsey, C. L.; Hollister, R. G., Jr. and Papageorgiou, M. R., eds.*, 1985, pp. 367–409. [G: U.S.]

Chang, Harry. Toward a Marxist Theory of Racism: Two Essays. *Rev. Radical Polit. Econ.*, Fall 1985, *17*(3), pp. 34–45. [G: U.S.]

Chapman, Bruce J. and Harding, J. Ross. Sex Differences in Earnings: An Analysis of Malaysian Wage Data. *J. Devel. Stud.*, April 1985, *21*(3), pp. 362–76. [G: Malaysia]

Cherry, Robert. Textbook Treatments of Minimum-Wage Legislation. *Rev. Black Polit. Econ.*, Spring 1985, *13*(4), pp. 25–38.

Clark, David, et al. Work and Marriage in the Offshore Oil Industry. *Int. J. Soc. Econ.*, 1985, *12*(2), pp. 36–47. [G: U.K.]

Cole, John A., et al. Black Banks: A Survey and Analysis of the Literature. *Rev. Black Polit. Econ.*, Summer 1985, *14*(1), pp. 29–50. [G: U.S.]

Colwill, Nina L. Towards Equity: Directions for Future Research: Panel Discussion. In *Economic Council of Canada.*, 1985, pp. 121–24.

Corcoran, Mary E. and Courant, Paul N. Sex Role Socialization and Labor Market Outcomes. *Amer. Econ. Rev.*, May 1985, *75*(2), pp. 275–78. [G: U.S.]

Corpeleijn, A. W. F. Labour Force Participation of Young Women in the Netherlands: An Analysis of Flow Data. *Statist. J.*, December 1985, *3*(4), pp. 353–62. [G: Netherlands]

Cotton, Jeremiah. A Comparative Analysis of Black–White and Mexican-American–White Male Wage Differentials. *Rev. Black Polit. Econ.*, Spring 1985, *13*(4), pp. 51–69. [G: U.S.]

Cotton, Jeremiah. More on the "Cost" of Being a Black or Mexican American Male Worker. *Soc. Sci. Quart.*, December 1985, *66*(4), pp. 867–85. [G: U.S.]

Coulombe, Serge and Lavoie, Marc. Les francophones dans la ligue nationale de hockey: une analyse économique de la discrimination (Francophones in the National Hockey League: A Comment Followed by an Economic Analysis of Discrimination. With English summary.) *L'Actual. Econ.*, March 1985, *61*(1), pp. 73–92. [G: Canada]

Craig, Christine; Garnsey, Elizabeth and Rubery, Jill. Labour Market Segmentation and Women's Employment: A Case-Study from the United Kingdom. *Int. Lab. Rev.*, May-June 1985, *124*(3), pp. 267–80. [G: U.K.]

Cymrot, Donald J. Does Competition Lessen Discrimination? Some Evidence. *J. Human Res.*, Fall 1985, *20*(4), pp. 605–12. [G: U.S.]

Darity, William A., Jr. and Williams, Rhonda M. Peddlers Forever? Culture, Competition, and Discrimination. *Amer. Econ. Rev.*, May 1985, *75*(2), pp. 256–61. [G: U.S.]

Date-Bah, Eugenia. Technologies for Rural Women of Ghana: Role of Socio-Cultural Fac-

tors. In *Ahmed, I., ed.*, 1985, pp. 211–51.
[G: Ghana]

David-McNeil, Jeannine. The Changing Economic Status of the Female Labour Force in Canada. In *Economic Council of Canada.*, 1985, pp. 1–8. [G: Canada]

Davidson, Marilyn and Cooper, Cary. Women Managers: Work, Stress and Marriage. *Int. J. Soc. Econ.*, 1985, *12*(2), pp. 17–25.
[G: U.K.]

Davis, Carlton G. Human Capital Needs of Black Land-Grant Institutions: Discussion. *Southern J. Agr. Econ.*, July 1985, *17*(1), pp. 71–73.
[G: U.S.]

Deere, Carmen Diana. Rural Women and State Policy: The Latin American Agrarian Reform Experience. *World Devel.*, September 1985, *13*(9), pp. 1037–53. [G: Latin America]

DeFreitas, Gregory. Ethnic Differentials in Unemployment among Hispanic Americans. In *Borjas, G. J. and Tienda, M., eds.*, 1985, pp. 127–57. [G: U.S.]

Dulude, Louise. Fringe Benefits and the Female Workforce. In *Economic Council of Canada.*, 1985, pp. 71–78. [G: Canada]

Duncan, Greg J. and Hoffman, Saul D. A Reconsideration of the Economic Consequences of Marital Dissolution. *Demography*, November 1985, *22*(4), pp. 485–97. [G: U.S.]

Durant-Gonzalez, Victoria. Higglering: Rural Women and the Internal Market System in Jamaica. In *Gomes, P. I., ed.*, 1985, pp. 103–22. [G: Jamaica]

Dymski, Gary. The Political Economy of Race and Class: Introduction. *Rev. Radical Polit. Econ.*, Fall 1985, *17*(3), pp. 1 0. [G: U.S.]

Eberts, Randall W. and Stone, Joe A. Male–Female Differences in Promotions: EEO in Public Education. *J. Human Res.*, Fall 1985, *20*(4), pp. 504–21. [G: U.S.]

Eden, Benjamin. Trading Uncertainty, Enforcement and Labor Unions. *Econ. Inquiry*, October 1985, *23*(4), pp. 637–50.

Edgecombe Robb, Roberta. Equal-Pay Policy. In *Economic Council of Canada.*, 1985, pp. 61–70. [G: Canada]

England, Paula. Occupational Segregation: Rejoinder [The Failure of Human Capital Theory to Explain Occupational Sex Segregation]. *J. Human Res.*, Summer 1985, *20*(3), pp. 441–43. [G: U.S.]

England, Paula and Norris, Bahar. Comparable Worth: A New Doctrine of Sex Discrimination. *Soc. Sci. Quart.*, September 1985, *66*(3), pp. 629–43. [G: U.S.]

England, Paula and Norris, Bahar. Comparable Worth: Rejoinder. *Soc. Sci. Quart.*, September 1985, *66*(3), pp. 650–53. [G: U.S.]

Espenshade, Thomas J. The Recent Decline of American Marriage: Blacks and Whites in Comparative Perspective. In *Davis, K., ed.*, 1985, pp. 53–90. [G: U.S.]

Fagan, Christine A. Fringe Benefits and the Female Workforce: Comments. In *Economic Council of Canada.*, 1985, pp. 79–81.
[G: Canada]

Farley, Reynolds. Understanding Racial Differences and Trends: How SIPP Can Assist. *J. Econ. Soc. Meas.*, December 1985, *13*(3–4), pp. 245–61. [G: U.S.]

Feiner, Susan F. and Morgan, Barbara A. Discrimination: The Case of Economics Textbooks. *Challenge*, Nov./Dec. 1985, *28*(5), pp. 52–54. [G: U.S.]

Ferber, Marianne A. and Green, Carole A. Homemakers' Imputed Wages: Results of the Heckman Technique Compared with Women's Own Estimates. *J. Human Res.*, Winter 1985, *20*(1), pp. 90–99. [G: U.S.]

Fernandez, Roberto M. Hispanic Youth in the Labor Market: An Analysis of High School and Beyond. In *Betsey, C. L.; Hollister, R. G., Jr. and Papageorgiou, M. R., eds.*, 1985, pp. 410–61. [G: U.S.]

Filer, Randall K. Male–Female Wage Differences: The Importance of Compensating Differentials. *Ind. Lab. Relat. Rev.*, April 1985, *38*(3), pp. 426–37. [G: U.S.]

Finch, Janet. Work, the Family and the Home: A More Egalitarian Future? *Int. J. Soc. Econ.*, 1985, *12*(2), pp. 26–35.

Fishback, Price V. Discrimination on Nonwage Margins: Safety in the West Virginia Coal Industry, 1906–1925. *Econ. Inquiry*, October 1985, *23*(4), pp. 651–69. [G: U.S.]

Fligstein, Neil and Fernandez, Roberto M. Educational Transitions of Whites and Mexican-Americans. In *Borjas, G. J. and Tienda, M., eds.*, 1985, pp. 161–92. [G: U.S.]

Fujii, Edwin T. and Mak, James. On the Relative Economic Progress of U.S.-born Filipino Men. *Econ. Develop. Cult. Change*, April 1985, *33*(3), pp. 557–73. [G: U.S.]

Fulbright, Karen. The Myth of the Double-Advantage: Black Female Managers. *Rev. Black Polit. Econ.*, Fall-Winter 1985-86, *14*(2–3), pp. 33–45. [G: U.S.]

Gabin, Nancy. Women Workers and the UAW in the Post-World War II Period: 1945–1954. In *Leab, D. J., ed.*, 1985, pp. 407–32.
[G: U.S.]

Garfinkel, Irwin. Variations in the Economic Well-Being of Divorced Women and Their Children: The Role of Child Support Income: Comment. In *David, M. and Smeeding, T., eds.*, 1985, pp. 506–09. [G: U.S.]

Gaskell, Jane. Women and Education: Branching Out. In *Economic Council of Canada.*, 1985, pp. 43–54. [G: Canada]

Gastwirth, Joseph L. Measurement of Economic Distance between Blacks and Whites: Comment. *J. Bus. Econ. Statist.*, October 1985, *3*(4), pp. 405–07.

Ginzberg, Eli. American Democracy and the Negro. In *Ginzberg, E.*, 1985, pp. 355–65.
[G: U.S.]

Ginzberg, Eli. Reentry of Women to the Labor Force: A Fifteen-Country Perspective. In *Ginzberg, E.*, 1985, pp. 269–73.

Ginzberg, Eli. Returnees: Cross-National Re-

search. In *Ginzberg, E.*, 1985, pp. 251–67.
[G: W. Germany; France; Sweden; U.K.; U.S.]

Ginzberg, Eli. Women in the Work Force. In *Ginzberg, E.*, 1985, pp. 245–49.

Gleason, Sandra E. Comparable Worth: Some Questions Still Unanswered. *Mon. Lab. Rev.*, December 1985, *108*(12), pp. 17–18.
[G: U.S.]

Glenn, Evelyn Nakano. Racial Ethnic Women's Labor: The Intersection of Race, Gender and Class Oppression. *Rev. Radical Polit. Econ.*, Fall 1985, *17*(3), pp. 86–108. [G: U.S.]

Golbe, Devra L. Imperfect Signalling, Affirmative Action, and Black–White Wage Differentials. *Southern Econ. J.*, January 1985, *51*(3), pp. 842–48.

Goodman, Allen C. A Note on Neighborhood Size and the Measurement of Segregation Indices. *J. Reg. Sci.*, August 1985, *25*(3), pp. 471–76.
[G: U.S.]

Greenhalgh, Susan. Sexual Stratification: The Other Side of "Growth with Equity" in East Asia. *Population Devel. Rev.*, June 1985, *11*(2), pp. 265–314. [G: E. Asia]

Grigsby, J. Eugene, III and Hruby, Mary L. A Review of the Status of Black Renters, 1970–1980. *Rev. Black Polit. Econ.*, Spring 1985, *13*(4), pp. 77–91.

Grossbard-Shechtman, Amyra. Marriage Squeezes and the Marriage Market. In *Davis, K.*, ed., 1985, pp. 375–95. [G: U.S.]

Harper, Harriett. Black Women and the Job Training Partnership Act. *Rev. Black Polit. Econ.*, Fall-Winter 1985-86, *14*(2–3), pp. 115–29.

Hartmann, Heidi I.; Roos, Patricia A. and Treiman, Donald J. An Agenda for Basic Research on Comparable Worth. In *Hartmann, H. I.*, ed., 1985, pp. 3–33. [G: U.S.]

Hashemzadeh, Nozar and Long, Burl F. Cyclical Aspects of Black Unemployment: An Empirical Analysis. *Rev. Reg. Stud.*, Winter 1985, *15*(1), pp. 7–19. [G: U.S.]

Headon, Alvin E., Jr. and Headon, Sandra W. General Health Conditions and Medical Insurance Issues Concerning Black Women. *Rev. Black Polit. Econ.*, Fall-Winter 1985-86, *14*(2–3), pp. 183–97. [G: U.S.]

Hersch, Joni and Stone, Joe A. "New and Improved" Estimates of Qualification Discrimination. *Southern Econ. J.*, October 1985, *52*(2), pp. 484–91. [G: U.S.]

Hershfield, David C. Attacking Housing Discrimination: Economic Power of the Military in Desegregating Off-Base Rental Housing. *Amer. J. Econ. Soc.*, January 1985, *44*(1), pp. 23–28.
[G: U.S.]

Hirschman, Elizabeth C. Primitive Aspects of Consumption in Modern American Society. *J. Cons. Res.*, September 1985, *12*(2), pp. 142–54. [G: U.S.]

Hoffman, Emily P. Fertility and Female Employment. *Quart. Rev. Econ. Bus.*, Spring 1985, *25*(1), pp. 85–95. [G: U.S.]

Ikemoto, Yukio. Income Distribution in Malaysia:

1957–80. *Devel. Econ.*, December 1985, *23*(4), pp. 347–67. [G: Malaysia]

Jackson, Beryl B. Health Issues: Discussion I. *Rev. Black Polit. Econ.*, Fall-Winter 1985-86, *14*(2–3), pp. 227–34. [G: U.S.]

Jackson, Ralph W.; McDaniel, Stephen W. and Rao, C. P. Food Shopping and Preparation: Psychographic Differences of Working Wives and Housewives. *J. Cons. Res.*, June 1985, *12*(1), pp. 110–13. [G: U.S.]

Jeffries, John M. Education and Training: Discussion. *Rev. Black Polit. Econ.*, Fall-Winter 1985-86, *14*(2–3), pp. 131–37.

Jenkins, Richard. Black Workers in the Labour Market: The Price of Recession. In *Roberts, B.; Finnegan, R. and Gallie, D.*, eds., 1985, pp. 169–83. [G: U.K.]

Johnson, Nan E. and Lean, Suewen. Relative Income, Race, and Fertility. *Population Stud.*, March 1985, *39*(1), pp. 99–112. [G: U.S.]

Johnson, Willene A. Women and Self-Employment in Urban Tanzania. *Rev. Black Polit. Econ.*, Fall-Winter 1985-86, *14*(2–3), pp. 245–57. [G: Tanzania]

Johnson, William G. and Lambrinos, James. Wage Discrimination against Handicapped Men and Women. *J. Human Res.*, Spring 1985, *20*(2), pp. 264–77. [G: U.S.]

Jones, Barbara A. P. Black Women and Labor Force Participation: An Analysis of Sluggish Growth Rates. *Rev. Black Polit. Econ.*, Fall-Winter 1985-86, *14*(2–3), pp. 11–31.
[G: U.S.]

Kain, John F. Black Suburbanization in the Eighties: A New Beginning or a False Hope? In *Quigley, J. M. and Rubinfeld, D. L.*, eds., 1985, pp. 253–84. [G: U.S.]

Kamalich, Richard F. and Polachek, Solomon William. On Estimating Discrimination in the Economy: Reply. *Southern Econ. J.*, April 1985, *51*(4), pp. 1227–29. [G: U.S.]

Kasarda, John D. Urban Change and Minority Opportunities. In *Peterson, P. E.*, ed., 1985, pp. 33–67. [G: U.S.]

Kessler-Harris, Alice. Organizing the Unorganizable: Three Jewish Women and Their Union. In *Leab, D. J.*, ed., 1985, pp. 269–87.
[G: U.S.]

Killingsworth, Mark R. The Economics of Comparable Worth: Analytical, Empirical, and Policy Questions. In *Hartmann, H. I.*, ed., 1985, pp. 86–115.

Koziara, Karen Shallcross. Comparable Worth: Organizational Dilemmas. *Mon. Lab. Rev.*, December 1985, *108*(12), pp. 13–16.
[G: U.S.]

Kunin, Roslyn. Occupational Diversification of Women in the Workplace: Comments. In *Economic Council of Canada.*, 1985, pp. 36–40.
[G: Canada]

Land, Hilary and Rose, Hilary. Compulsory Altruism for Some or an Altruistic Society for All? In *Bean, P.; Ferris, J. and Whynes, D.*, eds., 1985, pp. 74–96. [G: U.K.]

Landau, C. E. Recent Australian Legislation and Case-Law on Sex Equality at Work. *Int. Lab.*

Rev., May-June 1985, *124*(3), pp. 335–51. [G: Australia]

Leahy, Peter J. Are Racial Factors Important for the Allocation of Mortgage Money? A Quasi-experimental Approach to an Aspect of Discrimination. *Amer. J. Econ. Soc.*, April 1985, *44*(2), pp. 185–96. [G: U.S.]

Lee, Barrett A. Racially Mixed Neighborhoods during the 1970s: Change or Stability? *Soc. Sci. Quart.*, June 1985, *66*(2), pp. 346–64. [G: U.S.]

Lee, Barrett A.; Spain, Daphne and Umberson, Debra J. Neighborhood Revitalization and Racial Change: The Case of Washington, D.C. *Demography*, November 1985, *22*(4), pp. 581–602. [G: U.S.]

Lee, Bun Song and McElwain, Adrienne M. An Empirical Investigation of Female Labor-Force Participation, Fertility, Age at Marriage, and Wages in Korea. *J. Devel. Areas*, July 1985, *19*(4), pp. 483–99. [G: S. Korea]

Lehrer, Susan. Protective Labor Legislation for Women. *Rev. Radical Polit. Econ.*, Spring and Summer 1985, *17*(1/2), pp. 187–200. [G: U.S.]

Leonard, Jonathan S. Affirmative Action as Earnings Redistribution: The Targeting of Compliance Reviews. *J. Lab. Econ.*, July 1985, *3*(3), pp. 363–84.

Leonard, Jonathan S. The Effect of Unions on the Employment of Blacks, Hispanics, and Women. *Ind. Lab. Relat. Rev.*, October 1985, *39*(1), pp. 115–32. [G: U.S.]

Leonard, Jonathan S. What Promises Are Worth: The Impact of Affirmative Action Goals. *J. Human Res.*, Winter 1985, *20*(1), pp. 3–20. [G: U.S.]

Lewin-Epstein, Noah. Neighborhoods, Local Labor Markets, and Employment Opportunities for White and Nonwhite Youth. *Soc. Sci. Quart.*, March 1985, *66*(1), pp. 163–71. [G: U.S.]

Lewis, Donald E. The Sources of Changes in the Occupational Segregation of Australian Women. *Econ. Rec.*, December 1985, *61*(175), pp. 719–36. [G: Australia]

Lewis, Jane. Work, Women and Welfare. In *Klein, R. and O'Higgins, M., ed.*, 1985, pp. 216–22. [G: U.K.]

Lichter, Daniel T. Racial Concentration and Segregation across U.S. Counties, 1950–1980. *Demography*, November 1985, *22*(4), pp. 603–09. [G: U.S.]

Light, Ivan. Immigrant Entrepreneurs in America: Koreans in Los Angeles. In *Glazer, N., ed.*, 1985, pp. 161–78. [G: U.S.]

Lin, Vivian. Women Factory Workers in Asian Export Processing Zones. In *Utrecht, E., ed.*, 1985, pp. 159–219. [G: Asia]

Lorenz, Wilhelm. Drei neoklassische Modelle der Diskriminierung. Eine vergleichende Darstellung. (With English summary.) *Z. Wirtschaft. Sozialwissen.*, 1985, *105*(4), pp. 459–79.

Lucas, Robert E. B. Mines and Migrants in South Africa. *Amer. Econ. Rev.*, December 1985, *75*(5), pp. 1094–108. [G: S. Africa]

Lundahl, Mats. Errata: Economic Effects of a Trade and Investment Boycott against South Africa. *Scand. J. Econ.*, 1985, *87*(1), pp. 142. [G: S. Africa]

Lyson, Thomas A. Race and Sex Segregation in the Occupational Structures of Southern Employers. *Soc. Sci. Quart.*, June 1985, *66*(2), pp. 281–95. [G: U.S.]

MacDonald, Martha. Towards Equity: Directions for Future Research: Panel Discussion. In *Economic Council of Canada.*, 1985, pp. 124–27.

Madhaven, M. C.; Green, Louis C. and Jung, Ken. A Note on Black–White Wage Disparity. *Rev. Black Polit. Econ.*, Spring 1985, *13*(4), pp. 39–50. [G: U.S.]

Malveaux, Julianne. Comparable Worth and Its Impact on Black Women. *Rev. Black Polit. Econ.*, Fall-Winter 1985-86, *14*(2–3), pp. 47–62. [G: U.S.]

Malveaux, Julianne. The Economic Interests of Black and White Women: Are They Similar? *Rev. Black Polit. Econ.*, Summer 1985, *14*(1), pp. 5–27. [G: U.S.]

Malveaux, Julianne. You Have Struck a Rock: A Note on the Status of Black Women in South Africa. *Rev. Black Polit. Econ.*, Fall-Winter 1985-86, *14*(2–3), pp. 277–84. [G: S. Africa]

Malveaux, Julianne and Simms, Margaret C. A Legislative/Policy Agenda to Improve the Status of Black Women. *Rev. Black Polit. Econ.*, Fall-Winter 1985-86, *14*(2–3), pp. 297–300.

Marable, Manning. Black Power in Chicago: An Historical Overview of Class Stratification and Electoral Politics in a Black Urban Community. *Rev. Radical Polit. Econ.*, Fall 1985, *17*(3), pp. 157–82. [G: U.S.]

Marsden, Lorna R. Technological Change: Bad or Good? Comments. In *Economic Council of Canada.*, 1985, pp. 93–97. [G: U.S.]

Martin, Charles H. The International Labor Defense and Black America. *Labor Hist.*, Spring 1985, *26*(2), pp. 165–94. [G: U.S.]

Martin, Roderick and Wallace, Judith. Women and Unemployment: Activities and Social Contact. In *Roberts, B.; Finnegan, R. and Gallie, D., eds.*, 1985, pp. 417–30. [G: U.K.]

Mason, Beverly J. Jamaican Working-Class Women: Producers and Reproducers. *Rev. Black Polit. Econ.*, Fall-Winter 1985-86, *14*(2–3), pp. 259–75.

Mayer, Neil S. The Impacts of Lending, Race, and Ownership on Rental Housing Rehabilitation. *J. Urban Econ.*, May 1985, *17*(3), pp. 349–74. [G: U.S.]

McAdoo, Harriette Pipes. Strategies Used by Black Single Mothers against Stress. *Rev. Black Polit. Econ.*, Fall-Winter 1985-86, *14*(2–3), pp. 153–66. [G: U.S.]

McArthur, Leslie Zebrowitz. Social Judgment Biases in Comparable Worth Analysis. In *Hartmann, H. I., ed.*, 1985, pp. 53–70. [G: U.S.]

McKinney, Fred. Employment Implications of a Changing Health-Care System. *Rev. Black Polit. Econ.*, Fall-Winter 1985-86, *14*(2–3), pp. 199–215. [G: U.S.]

McKinney, Fred. JTPA, Black Employment, and Occupational Change: Separating Out Cyclical Changes from Program Changes. *Rev. Black Polit. Econ.*, Summer 1985, *14*(1), pp. 75–87. [G: U.S.]

McManus, Walter S. Labor Market Costs of Language Disparity: An Interpretation of Hispanic Earnings Differences. *Amer. Econ. Rev.*, September 1985, *75*(4), pp. 818–27. [G: U.S.]

Medoff, Marshall H. Discrimination and the Occupational Progress of Blacks since 1950. *Amer. J. Econ. Soc.*, July 1985, *44*(3), pp. 295–303. [G: U.S.]

Medoff, Marshall H. The Effect of the Equal Rights Amendment on the Economic Status of Women. *Atlantic Econ. J.*, September 1985, *13*(3), pp. 60–68. [G: U.S.]

Megdal, Sharon Bernstein and Ransom, Michael R. Longitudinal Changes at a Large Public University: What Response to Equal Pay Legislation? *Amer. Econ. Rev.*, May 1985, *75*(2), pp. 271–74. [G: U.S.]

Michael, Robert T. and Tuma, Nancy Brandon. Entry into Marriage and Parenthood by Young Men and Women: The Influence of Family Background. *Demography*, November 1985, *22*(4), pp. 515–44. [G: U.S.]

Mier, Robert and Giloth, Robert. Hispanic Employment Opportunities: A Case of Internal Labor Markets and Weak-tied Social Networks. *Soc. Sci. Quart.*, June 1985, *66*(2), pp. 296–309. [G: U.S.]

Mills, Edwin S. Open Housing Laws as Stimulus to Central City Employment. *J. Urban Econ.*, March 1985, *17*(2), pp. 184–88. [G: U.S.]

Muller, Thomas. Economic Effects of Immigration. In *Glazer, N., ed.*, 1985, pp. 109–33. [G: U.S.]

Muth, Richard F. Urban Programs: Transportation and Housing: Commentary. In *Quigley, J. M. and Rubinfeld, D. L., eds.*, 1985, pp. 297–303. [G: U.S.]

Nash, Gary B. The Failure of Female Factory Labor in Colonial Boston. In *Leab, D. J., ed.*, 1985, pp. 42–65. [G: U.S.]

Norwood, Janet L. Perspectives on Comparable Worth: An Introduction to the Numbers. *Mon. Lab. Rev.*, December 1985, *108*(12), pp. 3–4. [G: U.S.]

O'Neill, June. The Trend in the Male–Female Wage Gap in the United States. *J. Lab. Econ.*, Part 2 January 1985, *3*(1), pp. S91–116. [G: U.S.]

Orfield, Gary. Ghettoization and Its Alternatives. In *Peterson, P. E., ed.*, 1985, pp. 161–93. [G: U.S.]

Ostas, James R. Reduced Form Coefficients, Structural Coefficients, and Mortgage Redlining. *Amer. Real Estate Urban Econ. Assoc. J.*, Spring 1985, *13*(1), pp. 76–92. [G: U.S.]

Oudijk, Corrine. Research on the Position of Women in the Netherlands. *Statist. J.*, December 1985, *3*(4), pp. 363–74. [G: Netherlands]

Pal, Leslie A. Maternity Benefits and Unemployment Insurance: A Question of Policy Design. *Can. Public Policy*, September 1985, *11*(3), pp. 551–60. [G: Canada]

Parks, Alfred L. and Robbins, Richard D. Human Capital Needs of Black Land-Grant Institutions. *Southern J. Agr. Econ.*, July 1985, *17*(1), pp. 61–69. [G: U.S.]

Peitchinis, Stephen G. Technological Change: Bad or Good? In *Economic Council of Canada.*, 1985, pp. 83–93. [G: U.S.]

Peterson, Paul E. The New Urban Reality: Introduction: Technology, Race, and Urban Policy. In *Peterson, P. E., ed.*, 1985, pp. 1–29. [G: U.S.]

Philips, Peter. A Note on the Apparent Constancy of the Racial Wage Gap in New Jersey Manufacturing, 1902 to 1979. *Rev. Black Polit. Econ.*, Spring 1985, *13*(4), pp. 71–76. [G: U.S.]

Piliawsky, Monte. The Impact of Black Mayors on the Black Community: The Case of New Orleans' Ernest Morial. *Rev. Black Polit. Econ.*, Spring 1985, *13*(4), pp. 5–23. [G: U.S.]

Polachek, Solomon William. Occupation Segregation: A Defense of Human Capital Predictions [The Failure of Human Capital Theory to Explain Occupational Sex Segregation]. *J. Human Res.*, Summer 1985, *20*(3), pp. 437–40. [G: U.S.]

Polachek, Solomon William. Occupational Segregation: Reply [The Failure of Human Capital Theory to Explain Occupational Sex Segregation]. *J. Human Res.*, Summer 1985, *20*(3), pp. 444. [G: U.S.]

Price, Richard and Mills, Edwin S. Race and Residence in Earnings Determination. *J. Urban Econ.*, January 1985, *17*(1), pp. 1–18. [G: U.S.]

Quataert, Jean H. The Shaping of Women's Work in Manufacturing: Guilds, Households, and the State in Central Europe, 1648–1870. *Amer. Hist. Rev.*, December 1985, *90*(5), pp. 1122–48. [G: Germany]

Quester, Aline O. and Greene, William H. The Labor Market Experience of Black and White Wives in the Sixties and Seventies. *Soc. Sci. Quart.*, December 1985, *66*(4), pp. 854–66. [G: U.S.]

Quester, Aline O. and Utgoff, Kathleen. Comparable Worth: Another View. *Soc. Sci. Quart.*, September 1985, *66*(3), pp. 644–49. [G: U.S.]

Reid, Clifford E. The Effect of Residential Location on the Wages of Black Women and White Women. *J. Urban Econ.*, November 1985, *18*(3), pp. 350–63. [G: U.S.]

Reimers, Cordelia W. A Comparative Analysis of the Wages of Hispanics, Blacks, and Non-Hispanic Whites. In *Borjas, G. J. and Tienda, M., eds.*, 1985, pp. 27–75. [G: U.S.]

Rein, Martin. The Social Welfare Labour Market. In *Eisenstadt, S. N. and Ahimeir, O., eds.*, 1985, pp. 109–31. [G: Israel; U.S.; W. Europe]

Rein, Martin. Women, Employment and Social Welfare. In *Klein, R. and O'Higgins, M., ed.*,

1985, pp. 37–58. [G: Sweden; U.K.; U.S.; W. Germany]

Roberts, Ceridwen. Research on Women in the Labour Market: The Context and Scope of the Women and Employment Survey. In *Roberts, B.; Finnegan, R. and Gallie, D., eds.*, 1985, pp. 232–45. [G: U.K.]

Rose-Lizée, Ruth. Towards Equity: Directions for Future Research: Panel Discussion. In *Economic Council of Canada.*, 1985, pp. 127–31.

Rosenbaum, James E. Jobs, Job Status, and Women's Gains from Affirmative Action: Implications for Comparable Worth. In *Hartmann, H. I., ed.*, 1985, pp. 116–36. [G: U.S.]

Saegert, Joel; Hoover, Robert J. and Hilger, Marye Tharp. Characteristics of Mexican American Consumers. *J. Cons. Res.*, June 1985, *12*(1), pp. 104–09. [G: U.S.]

Safilios-Rothschild, Constantina. The Persistence of Women's Invisibility in Agriculture: Theoretical and Policy Lessons from Lesotho and Sierra Leone. *Econ. Develop. Cult. Change*, January 1985, *33*(2), pp. 299–317.
[G: Lesotho; Sierra Leone]

Sander, William. Women, Work, and Divorce. *Amer. Econ. Rev.*, June 1985, *75*(3), pp. 519–23. [G: U.S.]

Sassen-Koob, Saskia. Changing Composition and Labor Market Location of Hispanic Immigrants in New York City, 1960–1980. In *Borjas, G. J. and Tienda, M., eds.*, 1985, pp. 299–322. [G: U.S.]

Schwab, Donald P. Job Evaluation Research and Research Needs. In *Hartmann, H. I., ed.*, 1985, pp. 37–52.

Schwartz, Harvey A. What Do We Know about Statistical Discrimination? In *Brown, R. C., ed.*, 1985, pp. 153–91. [G: U.S.]

Scott, Frank A., Jr.; Long, James E. and Somppi, Ken. Salary vs. Marginal Revenue Product under Monopsony and Competition: The Case of Professional Basketball. *Atlantic Econ. J.*, September 1985, *13*(3), pp. 50–59. [G: U.S.]

Scott, Gloria L. Development Issues: Discussion. *Rev. Black Polit. Econ.*, Fall-Winter 1985-86, *14*(2–3), pp. 285–88.

Shapiro, David and Sandell, Steven H. Age Discrimination in Wages and Displaced Older Men. *Southern Econ. J.*, July 1985, *52*(1), pp. 90–102. [G: U.S.]

Shear, William B. and Yezer, Anthony M. J. Discrimination in Urban Housing Finance: An Empirical Study across Cities. *Land Econ.*, August 1985, *61*(3), pp. 292–302. [G: U.S.]

Sibley, David. Travelling People in England: Regional Comparisons. *Reg. Stud.*, April 1985, *19*(2), pp. 139–47. [G: U.K.]

Silberberg, Eugene. Race, Recent Entry, and Labor Market Participation. *Amer. Econ. Rev.*, December 1985, *75*(5), pp. 1168–77.
[G: U.S.]

Simms, Margaret C. Black Women Who Head Families: An Economic Struggle. *Rev. Black Polit. Econ.*, Fall-Winter 1985-86, *14*(2–3), pp. 141–51. [G: U.S.]

Simms, Margaret C. The Participation of Young

Women in Employment and Training Programs. In *Betsey, C. L.; Hollister, R. G., Jr. and Papageorgiou, M. R., eds.*, 1985, pp. 462–85. [G: U.S.]

Sloane, Peter J. Discrimination in the Labour Market. In *Carline, D., et al.*, 1985, pp. 78–158. [G: U.K.; U.S.; Selected Countries]

Stanfield, Jacqueline B. Research on Wife/Mother Role Strain in Dual Career Families: Its Present State Has Laid an Adequate Basis for Representative Empirical Studies. *Amer. J. Econ. Soc.*, July 1985, *44*(3), pp. 355–63. [G: U.S.]

Steinberg, Stephen. Human Capital: A Critique. *Rev. Black Polit. Econ.*, Summer 1985, *14*(1), pp. 67–74. [G: U.S.]

Stephenson, Stanley P., Jr. Labor Market Turnover and Joblessness for Hispanic Youth. In *Borjas, G. J. and Tienda, M., eds.*, 1985, pp. 193–218. [G: U.S.]

Stevans, Lonnie K.; Register, Charles and Grimes, Paul. Race and the Discouraged Female Worker: A Question of Labor Force Attachment. *Rev. Black Polit. Econ.*, Summer 1985, *14*(1), pp. 89–97. [G: U.S.]

Stevens, Yvette. Improved Technologies for Rural Women: Problems and Prospects in Sierra Leone. In *Ahmed, I., ed.*, 1985, pp. 284–326.
[G: Sierra Leone]

Stewart, A.; Blackburn, R. M. and Prandy, K. Gender and Earnings: The Failure of Market Explanations. In *Roberts, B.; Finnegan, R. and Gallie, D., eds.*, 1985, pp. 280–98. [G: U.K.]

Stoddart, Jennifer. Towards Equity: Directions for Future Research: Panel Discussion. In *Economic Council of Canada.*, 1985, pp. 131–34.

Szymanski, Al. The Structure of Race. *Rev. Radical Polit. Econ.*, Winter 1985, *17*(4), pp. 106–20.

Taylor, Patricia A. Institutional Job Training and Inequality. *Soc. Sci. Quart.*, March 1985, *66*(1), pp. 67–78. [G: U.S.]

Thiry, Bernard. La discrimination salariale entre hommes et femmes sur le marché du travail en France. (Wage Discrimination between Men and Women in the Labor Market in France. With English summary.) *Ann. INSEE*, Apr.-June 1985, (58), pp. 39–68. [G: France]

Tienda, Marta and Glass, Jennifer. Household Structure and Labor Force Participation of Black, Hispanic, and White Mothers. *Demography*, August 1985, *22*(3), pp. 381–94.
[G: U.S.]

Tienda, Marta and Guhleman, Patricia. The Occupational Position of Employed Hispanic Women. In *Borjas, G. J. and Tienda, M., eds.*, 1985, pp. 243–73. [G: U.S.]

Tomoda, Shizue. Measuring Female Labour Activities in Asian Developing Countries: A Time-Allocation Approach. *Int. Lab. Rev.*, Nov.-Dec. 1985, *124*(6), pp. 661–76.
[G: Bangladesh; Nepal; Indonesia; Philippines]

Tzannatos, Zafaris and Zabalza, Anton. The Effect of Sex Antidiscriminatory Legislation on the Variability of Female Employment in Britain. *Appl. Econ.*, December 1985, *17*(6), pp. 1117–34. [G: U.K.]

Vaughn, John C. Minority Students in Graduate Education. In *Smith, B. L. R., ed.,* 1985, pp. 151–68. [G: U.S.]

Ventura-Dias, Vivianne. Modernisation, Production Organisation and Rural Women in Kenya. In *Ahmed, I., ed.,* 1985, pp. 157–210.
[G: Kenya]

de la Viña, Lynda Y. Female Occupational Distribution: Treiman and Terrell Revisited. *Soc. Sci. Quart.,* September 1985, *66*(3), pp. 680–86. [G: U.S.]

Vinod, H. D. Measurement of Economic Distance between Blacks and Whites: Reply. *J. Bus. Econ. Statist.,* October 1985, *3*(4), pp. 408–09.

Vinod, H. D. Measurement of Economic Distance between Blacks and Whites. *J. Bus. Econ. Statist.,* January 1985, *3*(1), pp. 78–88.

Vogel-Polsky, Eliane. Positive Action Programmes for Women: 2. Practical Application. *Int. Lab. Rev.,* July-Aug. 1985, *124*(4), pp. 385–99.

Vogel-Polsky, Eliane. Positive Action Programmes for Women. *Int. Lab. Rev.,* May-June 1985, *124*(3), pp. 253–65.
[G: W. Europe]

Vose, W. J. Wiehahn and Riekert Revisited: A Review of Prevailing Black Labour Conditions in South Africa. *Int. Lab. Rev.,* July-Aug. 1985, *124*(4), pp. 447–64.

Walby, Sylvia. Approaches to the Study of Gender Relations in Unemployment and Employment. In *Roberts, B.; Finnegan, R. and Gallie, D., eds.,* 1985, pp. 264–79. [G: EEC; U.K.]

Waldinger, Roger. Immigrant Enterprise and the Structure of the Labour Market. In *Roberts, B.; Finnegan, R. and Gallie, D., eds.,* 1985, pp. 213–28. [G: U.S.]

Wallace, Phyllis A. A Research Agenda on the Economic Status of Black Women. *Rev. Black Polit. Econ.,* Fall-Winter 1985-86, *14*(2–3), pp. 293–95.

Ward, Robin. Minority Settlement and the Local Economy. In *Roberts, B.; Finnegan, R. and Gallie, D., eds.,* 1985, pp. 198–212.
[G: U.K.]

Weekes-Vagliani, Winifred. Women, Food and Rural Development. In *Rose, T., ed.,* 1985, pp. 104–10. [G: Sub-Saharan Africa]

Whitehead, Ann. Effects of Technological Change on Rural Women: A Review of Analysis and Concepts. In *Ahmed, I., ed.,* 1985, pp. 27–64. [G: LDCs]

Wilkerson, Margaret B. A Report on the Educational Status of Black Women during the UN Decade of Women, 1976–85. *Rev. Black Polit. Econ.,* Fall-Winter 1985-86, *14*(2–3), pp. 83–96. [G: U.S.]

Wilson, Fiona. Women and Agricultural Change in Latin America: Some Concepts Guiding Research. *World Devel.,* September 1985, *13*(9), pp. 1017–35. [G: Latin America]

Wilson, William Julius. The Urban Underclass in Advanced Industrial Society. In *Peterson, P. E., ed.,* 1985, pp. 129–60. [G: U.S.]

Winn, Conrad. Affirmative Action and Visible Minorities: Eight Premises in Quest of Evidence. *Can. Public Policy,* December 1985, *11*(4), pp. 684–700.

Winsberg, Morton D. Flight from the Ghetto: The Migration of Middle Class and Highly Educated Blacks into White Urban Neighborhoods. *Amer. J. Econ. Soc.,* October 1985, *44*(4), pp. 411–21. [G: U.S.]

Worthman, Paul B. Black Workers and Labor Unions in Birmingham, Alabama, 1897–1904. In *Leab, D. J., ed.,* 1985, pp. 197–229.
[G: U.S.]

Yamashita, Robert C. and Park, Peter. The Politics of Race: The Open Door, Ozawa and the Case of the Japanese in America. *Rev. Radical Polit. Econ.,* Fall 1985, *17*(3), pp. 135–56.
[G: U.S.]

Zabalza, Anton and Tzannatos, Zafaris. The Effect of Britain's Anti-discriminatory Legislation on Relative Pay and Employment. *Econ. J.,* September 1985, *95*(379), pp. 679–99.
[G: U.K.]

918 Economics of Aging

9180 Economics of Aging

Akin, John S., et al. The Impact of Federal Transfer Programs on the Nutrient Intake of Elderly Individuals. *J. Human Res.,* Summer 1985, *20*(3), pp. 383–404. [G: U.S.]

Anderson, Kathryn H. The Effect of Mandatory Retirement on Mortality. *J. Econ. Bus.,* February 1985, *37*(1), pp. 81–88. [G: U.S.]

Anderson, Kathryn H. and Burkhauser, Richard V. The Retirement–Health Nexus: A New Measure of an Old Puzzle. *J. Human Res.,* Summer 1985, *20*(3), pp. 315–30. [G: U.S.]

Bazzoli, Gloria J. The Early Retirement Decision: New Empirical Evidence on the Influence of Health. *J. Human Res.,* Spring 1985, *20*(2), pp. 214–34. [G: U.S.]

Boskin, Michael J. and Hurd, Michael D. Indexing Social Security Benefits: A Separate Price Index for the Elderly? *Public Finance Quart.,* October 1985, *13*(4), pp. 436–49. [G: U.S.]

Burkhauser, Richard V.; Butler, J. S. and Wilkinson, James T. Estimating Changes in Well-Being across Life: A Realized vs. Comprehensive Income Approach. In *David, M. and Smeeding, T., eds.,* 1985, pp. 69–87.
[G: U.S.]

Burtless, Gary. Social Security, Health Status, and Retirement: Comment. In *Wise, D. A., ed.,* 1985, pp. 181–91. [G: U.S.]

Butler, J. S.; Ohls, James C. and Posner, Barbara. The Effect of the Food Stamp Program on the Nutrient Intake of the Eligible Elderly. *J. Human Res.,* Summer 1985, *20*(3), pp. 405–20. [G: U.S.]

Carmichael, Jeffrey and Plowman, Kathleen. Income Provision in Old Age. *Australian Econ. Rev.,* 3rd Quarter, Spring 1985, (71), pp. 130–44. [G: Australia]

Chernick, Howard and Reschovsky, Andrew. The

Taxation of Social Security. *Nat. Tax J.*, June 1985, *38*(2), pp. 141–52. [G: U.S.]

Coe, Richard D. Nonparticipation in the SSI Program by the Eligible Elderly. *Southern Econ. J.*, January 1985, *51*(3), pp. 891–97.
[G: U.S.]

Danziger, Sheldon. Inflation Vulnerability, Income, and Wealth of the Elderly, 1969–1979: Comment. In *David, M. and Smeeding, T., eds.*, 1985, pp. 172–77. [G: U.S.]

De Vos, Susan. An Old-Age Security Incentive for Children in the Philippines and Taiwan. *Econ. Develop. Cult. Change*, July 1985, *33*(4), pp. 793–814. [G: Philippines; Taiwan]

Fuchs, Victor R. Determinants of Pension Benefits: Comment. In *Wise, D. A., ed.*, 1985, pp. 153–57. [G: U.S.]

Gilly, Mary C. and Zeithaml, Valarie A. The Elderly Consumer and Adoption of Technologies. *J. Cons. Res.*, December 1985, *12*(3), pp. 353–47. [G: U.S.]

Ginsburg, Helen. Flexible and Partial Retirement for Norwegian and Swedish Workers. *Mon. Lab. Rev.*, October 1985, *108*(10), pp. 33–43. [G: Norway; Sweden]

Ginzberg, Eli. Life without Work: Does It Make Sense? In *Ginzberg, E.*, 1985, pp. 287–93.
[G: U.S.]

Ginzberg, Eli. Strategic Factors in the Adjustment of Older Persons. In *Ginzberg, E.*, 1985, pp. 277–85.

Ginzberg, Eli. The Elderly: An International Perspective. In *Ginzberg, E.*, 1985, pp. 323–36.

Gruen, Fred H. Australian Government Policy on Retirement Incomes. *Econ. Rec.*, September 1985, *61*(174), pp. 613–21. [G: Australia]

Grundmann, Herman F. Adult Assistance Programs under the Social Security Act. *Soc. Sec. Bull.*, October 1985, *48*(10), pp. 10–21.
[G: U.S.]

Hamermesh, Daniel S. Expectations, Life Expectancy, and Economic Behavior. *Quart. J. Econ.*, May 1985, *100*(2), pp. 389–408.
[G: U.S.]

Hausman, Jerry A. and Wise, David A. Social Security, Health Status, and Retirement. In *Wise, D. A., ed.*, 1985, pp. 159–81.
[G: U.S.]

Havighurst, Robert J. Aging and Productivity: The Case of Older Faculty. In *Clark, S. M. and Lewis, D. R., eds.*, 1985, pp. 98–111.
[G: U.S.]

Honig, Marjorie. Partial Retirement among Women [Partial Retirement as a Separate Mode of Retirement Behavior]. *J. Human Res.*, Fall 1985, *20*(4), pp. 613–21. [G: U.S.]

Honig, Marjorie and Hanoch, Giora. Partial Retirement as a Separate Mode of Retirement Behavior. *J. Human Res.*, Winter 1985, *20*(1), pp. 21–46. [G: U.S.]

Hurd, Michael D. and Shoven, John B. Inflation Vulnerability, Income, and Wealth of the Elderly, 1969–1979. In *David, M. and Smeeding, T., eds.*, 1985, pp. 125–72. [G: U.S.]

Iams, Howard M. Characteristics of the Longest Job for New Retired Workers: Findings from the New Beneficiary Survey. *Soc. Sec. Bull.*, March 1985, *48*(3), pp. 5–21. [G: U.S.]

Irick, Christine. Income of New Retired Workers by Social Security Benefit Levels: Findings from the New Beneficiary Survey. *Soc. Sec. Bull.*, May 1985, *48*(5), pp. 7–23. [G: U.S.]

Jones, S. Patricia. The Costs of Membership Aging in a Blue Cross and Blue Shield Plan. *Inquiry*, Summer 1985, *22*(2), pp. 201–05.

Judge, Ken and Knapp, Martin. Efficiency in the Production of Welfare: The Public and the Private Sectors Compared. In *Klein, R. and O'Higgins, M., ed.*, 1985, pp. 131–49.
[G: U.K.]

Lapp, John S. Mandatory Retirement as a Clause in an Employment Insurance Contract. *Econ. Inquiry*, January 1985, *23*(1), pp. 69–92.
[G: U.S.]

Lave, Judith R. Cost Containment Policies in Long-term Care. *Inquiry*, Spring 1985, *22*(1), pp. 7–23. [G: U.S.]

Lillard, Lee A. Estimating Changes in Well-Being across Life: A Realized vs. Comprehensive Income Approach: Comment. In *David, M. and Smeeding, T., eds.*, 1985, pp. 88–90.
[G: U.S.]

Maxfield, Linda Drazga and Reno, Virginia P. Distribution of Income Sources of Recent Retirees: Findings from the New Beneficiary Survey. *Soc. Sec. Bull.*, January 1985, *48*(1), pp. 7–13. [G: U.S.]

Maxwell, Nan L. The Retirement Experience: Psychological and Financial Linkages to the Labor Market. *Soc. Sci. Quart.*, March 1985, *66*(1), pp. 22–33. [G: U.S.]

Meyer, Judith W. and Speare, Alden, Jr. Distinctively Elderly Mobility: Types and Determinants. *Econ. Geogr.*, January 1985, *61*(1), pp. 79–88. [G: U.S.]

Miller, Michael A. Age-related Reductions in Workers' Life Insurance. *Mon. Lab. Rev.*, September 1985, *108*(9), pp. 29–34. [G: U.S.]

Packard, Michael. Company Policies and Attitudes toward Older Workers. *Soc. Sec. Bull.*, May 1985, *48*(5), pp. 45–46. [G: U.S.]

Podger, A. S. Income Provision in Old Age: Comment. *Australian Econ. Rev.*, 3rd Quarter, Spring 1985, (71), pp. 145–46. [G: Australia]

Porter, Michael G. Income Provision in Old Age: Comment. *Australian Econ. Rev.*, 3rd Quarter, Spring 1985, (71), pp. 146–47.
[G: Australia]

Reno, Virginia P. and Grad, Susan. Economic Security, 1935–85. *Soc. Sec. Bull.*, December 1985, *48*(12), pp. 5–20.

Reskin, Barbara F. Aging and Productivity: Careers and Results. In *Clark, S. M. and Lewis, D. R., eds.*, 1985, pp. 86–97.

Rones, Philip L. Using the CPS to Track Retirement Trends among Older Men. *Mon. Lab. Rev.*, February 1985, *108*(2), pp. 46–49.
[G: U.S.]

Rother, John C. Medicare Reform: Where the Emphasis Should Be. In *Employee Benefit Research Institute.*, 1985, pp. 79–84. [G: U.S.]

Rother, John C. Medicare Reform: Where the

Emphasis Should Be: Remarks. In *Employee Benefit Research Institute.*, 1985, pp. 84–87. [G: U.S.]

Schmitt, Donald G. Today's Pension Plans: How Much Do They Pay? *Mon. Lab. Rev.*, December 1985, *108*(12), pp. 19–25. [G: U.S.]

Shapiro, David and Sandell, Steven H. Age Discrimination in Wages and Displaced Older Men. *Southern Econ. J.*, July 1985, *52*(1), pp. 90–102. [G: U.S.]

Shaughnessy, Peter W., et al. Nursing Home Case-Mix Differences between Medicare and Non-Medicare and between Hospital-based and Freestanding Patients. *Inquiry*, Summer 1985, *22*(2), pp. 162–77. [G: U.S.]

Sherman, Sally R. Assets of New Retired-Worker Beneficiaries: Findings from the New Beneficiary Survey. *Soc. Sec. Bull.*, July 1985, *48*(7), pp. 27–43. [G: U.S.]

Skinner, Jonathan S. The Effect of Increased Longevity on Capital Accumulation. *Amer. Econ. Rev.*, December 1985, *75*(5), pp. 1143–50. [G: U.S.]

Springer, Philip B. Home Equity Conversion Plans as a Source of Retirement Income. *Soc. Sec. Bull.*, September 1985, *48*(9), pp. 10–19. [G: U.S.]

Taubman, Paul. Determinants of Pension Benefits. In *Wise, D. A.*, *ed.*, 1985, pp. 123–53. [G: U.S.]

Upp, Melinda. Demographic and Socioeconomic Aspects of Aging. *Soc. Sec. Bull.*, May 1985, *48*(5), pp. 46–47. [G: U.S.]

Weinrobe, Maurice. HELP Comes to Buffalo: A Review and Analysis of the Initial Equity Conversion Experience. *Housing Finance Rev.*, January 1985, *4*(1), pp. 537–48. [G: U.S.]

Williams, Alan Paul. Public Policy Aspects of the Economics of Aging (or The Economics of Dependence Revisited). In *[Peacock, A.]*, 1985, pp. 94–104.

920 CONSUMER ECONOMICS

921 Consumer Economics; Levels and Standards of Living

9210 General

Amine, Lyn S. and Cavusgil, S. Tamer. Consumer Market Environment in the Middle East. In *Kaynak, E.*, *ed.* *(II)*, 1985, pp. 163–76. [G: Middle East]

Andreasen, Alan R. Consumer Responses to Dissatisfaction in Loose Monopolies. *J. Cons. Res.*, September 1985, *12*(2), pp. 135–41. [G: U.S.]

Barnett, William A. The Minflex-Laurent Translog Flexible Functional Form. *J. Econometrics*, Oct./Nov. 1985, *30*(1/2), pp. 33–44.

Barnett, William A.; Lee, Yul W. and Wolfe, Michael D. The Three-Dimensional Global Properties of the Minflex Laurent, Generalized Leontief, and Translog Flexible Functional Forms. *J. Econometrics*, Oct./Nov. 1985, *30*(1/2), pp. 3–31.

Belk, Russell W. Materialism: Trait Aspects of Living in the Material World. *J. Cons. Res.*, December 1985, *12*(3), pp. 265–80. [G: U.S.]

Bennett, Jeff W. and Smith, Ben. The Estimation of Indifference Maps by Expected Utility Analysis. *Amer. J. Agr. Econ.*, November 1985, *67*(4), pp. 833–38.

Childers, Terry L.; Houston, Michael J. and Heckler, Susan E. Measurement of Individual Differences in Visual versus Verbal Information Processing. *J. Cons. Res.*, September 1985, *12*(2), pp. 125–34. [G: U.S.]

Coursey, Don L. A Normative Model of Behavior Based upon an Activity Hierarchy. *J. Cons. Res.*, June 1985, *12*(1), pp. 64–73.

David, Martin and Smeeding, Timothy M. Horizontal Equity, Uncertainty, and Economic Well-Being: Introduction. In *David, M. and Smeeding, T.*, *eds.*, 1985, pp. 1–6.

Deaton, Angus. Panel Data from Time Series of Cross-Sections. *J. Econometrics*, Oct./Nov. 1985, *30*(1/2), pp. 109–26.

Diewert, W. E. and Parkan, C. Tests for the Consistency of Consumer Data. *J. Econometrics*, Oct./Nov. 1985, *30*(1/2), pp. 127–47.

Gardner, Meryl Paula. Mood States and Consumer Behavior: A Critical Review. *J. Cons. Res.*, December 1985, *12*(3), pp. 281–300.

Gatignon, Hubert and Robertson, Thomas S. A Propositional Inventory for New Diffusion Research. *J. Cons. Res.*, March 1985, *11*(4), pp. 849–67.

Goering, Patricia A. Effects of Product Trial on Consumer Expectations, Demand, and Prices. *J. Cons. Res.*, June 1985, *12*(1), pp. 74–82.

Hirschman, Elizabeth C. Primitive Aspects of Consumption in Modern American Society. *J. Cons. Res.*, September 1985, *12*(2), pp. 142–54. [G: U.S.]

Hirschman, Elizabeth C. Scientific Style and the Conduct of Consumer Research. *J. Cons. Res.*, September 1985, *12*(2), pp. 225–39.

Hvidding, James M. On the Rationality of Household Inflation Expectations. *Quart. J. Bus. Econ.*, Summer 1985, *24*(3), pp. 41–66. [G: U.S.]

Késenne, Stefan. Substitution in Consumption: A Reply. *Europ. Econ. Rev.*, April 1985, *27*(3), pp. 395–96. [G: Belgium]

Kiss, Otto; Mencl, Karel and Ulman, Václav. Social Consumption and Social Development Planning. *Czech. Econ. Digest.*, August 1985, (5), pp. 27–44. [G: Czechoslovakia]

Kooreman, Peter. Substitution in Consumption; An Application to the Allocation of Time: A Comment. *Europ. Econ. Rev.*, April 1985, *27*(3), pp. 391–94. [G: Belgium]

Kula, Erhun. The Social Time Preference Rate for Portugal. *Economia (Portugal)*, October 1985, *9*(3), pp. 447–66. [G: Portugal]

Leontief, Wassily. National Income, Economic Structure, and Environmental Externalities. In *Leontief, W.*, 1985, pp. 347–58.

Levy, Frank. Happiness, Affluence, and Altruism in the Postwar Period. In *David, M. and*

Smeeding, T., eds., 1985, pp. 7–29.
[G: U.S.]

Meyer, Robert J. and Sathi, Arvind. A Multiattribute Model of Consumer Choice during Product Learning. *Marketing Sci.*, Winter 1985, *4*(1), pp. 41–61.

Moschis, George P. The Role of Family Communication in Consumer Socialization of Children and Adolescents. *J. Cons. Res.*, March 1985, *11*(4), pp. 898–913.

Painton, Scott and Gentry, James W. Another Look at the Impact of Information Presentation Format. *J. Cons. Res.*, September 1985, *12*(2), pp. 240–44.
[G: U.S.]

Peterson, Robert A.; Albaum, Gerald and Beltramini, Richard F. A Meta-Analysis of Effect Sizes in Consumer Behavior Experiments. *J. Cons. Res.*, June 1985, *12*(1), pp. 97–103.
[G: U.S.]

Pickering, J. F. Giving in the Church of England: An Econometric Analysis. *Appl. Econ.*, August 1985, *17*(4), pp. 6360.
[G: U.K.]

Pollak, Robert A. A Transaction Cost Approach to Families and Households. *J. Econ. Lit.*, June 1985, *23*(2), pp. 581–608.

Porter, Philip K. and Slottje, Daniel J. A Comprehensive Analysis of Inequality in the Size Distribution of Income for the United States, 1952–1981. *Southern Econ. J.*, October 1985, *52*(2), pp. 412–21.
[G: U.S.]

Rainwater, Lee. Happiness, Affluence, and Altruism in the Postwar Period: Comment. In *David, M. and Smeeding, T., eds.*, 1985, pp. 29–33.
[G: U.S.]

Rook, Dennis W. The Ritual Dimension of Consumer Behavior. *J. Cons. Res.*, December 1985, *12*(3), pp. 251–64.

Samli, A. Coskun and Walter, Jane H. A Technology Transfer Model to Third World Women toward Improving the Quality and Quantity of the Food Supply. In *Samli, A. C., ed.*, 1985, pp. 45–54.

Slemrod, Joel B. A General Equilibrium Model of Taxation that Uses Micro-unit Data: With an Application to the Impact of Instituting a Flat-Rate Income Tax. In *Piggott, J. and Whalley, J., eds.*, 1985, pp. 221–52.
[G: U.S.]

Smith, Ruth Ann and Houston, Michael J. A Psychometric Assessment of Measures of Scripts in Consumer Memory. *J. Cons. Res.*, September 1985, *12*(2), pp. 214–24.
[G: U.S.]

van de Stadt, Huib; Kapteyn, Arie and van de Geer, Sara. The Relativity of Utility: Evidence from Panel Data. *Rev. Econ. Statist.*, May 1985, *67*(2), pp. 179–87.
[G: Netherlands]

Thaler, Richard. Mental Accounting and Consumer Choice. *Marketing Sci.*, Summer 1985, *4*(3), pp. 199–214.

Thistle, Paul D. An Experimental Study of Consumer Demand Using Rats: Comment. *J. Behav. Econ.*, Summer 1985, *14*(2), pp. 115–19.

Woronoff, Jon. Japan's Structural Shift from Exports to Domestic Demand. In *Nanto, D. K., ed.*, 1985, pp. 64–78.
[G: Japan]

9211 Living Standards, Composition of Overall Expenditures, and Empirical Consumption and Savings Studies

Abadia, Antonio. Income Distribution and Composition of Consumer Demand in the Spanish Economy. *Europ. Econ. Rev.*, October 1985, *29*(1), pp. 1–13.
[G: Spain]

Abel, Andrew B. Precautionary Saving and Accidental Bequests. *Amer. Econ. Rev.*, September 1985, *75*(4), pp. 777–91.
[G: U.S.]

Abelson, Peter W. Measures of Economic Welfare: Discussion and Application to Sydney. *Australian Econ. Pap.*, June 1985, *24*(44), pp. 95–114.

Aldabe, Hernán. The Impact of Social Security on Savings and Development: Comment. In *Mesa-Lago, C., ed.*, 1985, pp. 241–43.
[G: Chile]

Ali, M. Shaukat. Household Consumption and Saving Behaviour in Pakistan: An Application of the Extended Linear Expenditure System. *Pakistan Devel. Rev.*, Spring 1985, *24*(1), pp. 23–37.
[G: Pakistan]

Arellano, José-Pablo. Políticas para promover el ahorro en América Latina. (Saving Policies in Latin America. With English summary.) *Colección Estud. CIEPLAN*, September 1985, (17), pp. 127–51.
[G: Latin America]

Arellano, José-Pablo. The Impact of Social Security on Savings and Development. In *Mesa-Lago, C., ed.*, 1985, pp. 217–40. [G: Chile]

Auerbach, Alan J. Saving in the U.S.: Some Conceptual Issues. In *Hendershott, P. H., ed.*, 1985, pp. 15–38.
[G: U.S.]

Ballard, Charles L. and Goulder, Larry H. Consumption Taxes, Foresight, and Welfare: A Computable General Equilibrium Analysis. In *Piggott, J. and Whalley, J., eds.*, 1985, pp. 253–82.
[G: U.S.]

Barbour, G. Jeffrey; Beladi, Hamid and Severson, Robert F. Empirical Testing of the Life Cycle Hypothesis. *Atlantic Econ. J.*, December 1985, *13*(4), pp. 71–74.
[G: U.S.]

Basmann, R. L., et al. On Deviations between Neoclassical and GFT-Based True Cost-of-Living Indexes Derived from the Same Demand Function System. *J. Econometrics*, Oct./Nov. 1985, *30*(1/2), pp. 45–66.

Belk, Russell W. and Pollay, Richard W. Images of Ourselves: The Good Life in Twentieth Century Advertising. *J. Cons. Res.*, March 1985, *11*(4), pp. 887–97.
[G: U.S.]

Beller, Andrea H. and Graham, John W. Variations in the Economic Well-Being of Divorced Women and Their Children: The Role of Child Support Income. In *David, M. and Smeeding, T., eds.*, 1985, pp. 471–506.
[G: U.S.]

Benabou, Roland. Le modèle d'optimisation dynamique de la consommation et de l'offre de travail: un test sur données françaises. (The Model of Dynamic Optimisation on Consumption and Labour Supply: A Test on French Data. With English summary.) *Ann. INSEE*, Jan.-Mar. 1985, (57), pp. 75–97. [G: France]

Berliant, Marcus and Strauss, Robert P. The

Horizontal and Vertical Equity Characteristics of the Federal Individual Income Tax, 1966–1977. In *David, M. and Smeeding, T., eds.,* 1985, pp. 179–211. [G: U.S.]

Bernanke, Ben. Adjustment Costs, Durables, and Aggregate Consumption. *J. Monet. Econ.,* January 1985, *15*(1), pp. 41–68. [G: U.S.]

Bernheim, B. Douglas; Shleifer, Andrei and Summers, Lawrence H. The Strategic Bequest Motive. *J. Polit. Econ.,* December 1985, *93*(6), pp. 1045–76. [G: U.S.]

Bhagwati, Jagdish N. Savings and the Foreign Trade Regime. In *Bhagwati, J. N. (I),* 1985, pp. 277–84. [G: India]

Blinder, Alan S. and Deaton, Angus. The Time Series Consumption Function Revisited. *Brookings Pap. Econ. Act.,* 1985, (2), pp. 465–511. [G: U.S.]

Blumin, Stuart M. The Hypothesis of Middle-Class Formation in Nineteenth-Century America: A Critique and Some Proposals. *Amer. Hist. Rev.,* April 1985, *90*(2), pp. 299–338. [G: U.S.]

Bollerslev, Tim and Hylleberg, Svend. A Note on the Relation between Consumers' Expenditure and Income in the United Kingdom. *Oxford Bull. Econ. Statist.,* May 1985, *47*(2), pp. 153–70. [G: U.K.]

Boroooah, Vani K. Consumers' Expenditure Estimates Using the Rotterdam Model: An Application to the United Kingdom, 1954–81. *Appl. Econ.,* August 1985, *17*(4), pp. 675–88. [G: U.K.]

Boroooah, Vani K. and Sharpe, D. R. Household Income, Consumption and Savings in the United Kingdom, 1966–82. *Scot. J. Polit. Econ.,* November 1985, *32*(3), pp. 234–56. [G: U.K.]

Boskin, Michael J. and Kotlikoff, Laurence J. Public Debt and United States Saving: A New Test of the Neutrality Hypothesis. *Carnegie-Rochester Conf. Ser. Public Policy,* Autumn 1985, *23*, pp. 55–86. [G: U.S.]

Bouchal, Milan. Trends in Private Cash Holdings. *Czech. Econ. Digest.,* June 1985, (4), pp. 85–95. [G: Czechoslovakia]

Brookshire, David S., et al. A Test of the Expected Utility Model: Evidence from Earthquake Risks. *J. Polit. Econ.,* April 1985, *93*(2), pp. 369–89. [G: U.S.]

Browning, Martin J.; Deaton, Angus and Irish, Margaret. A Profitable Approach to Labor Supply and Commodity Demands over the Life-Cycle. *Econometrica,* May 1985, *53*(3), pp. 503–43. [G: U.K.]

Burbridge, John B. and Robb, A. Leslie. Evidence on Wealth-Age Profiles in Canadian Cross-Section Data. *Can. J. Econ.,* November 1985, *18*(4), pp. 854–75. [G: Canada]

Burkhauser, Richard V.; Butler, J. S. and Wilkinson, James T. Estimating Changes in Well-Being across Life: A Realized vs. Comprehensive Income Approach. In *David, M. and Smeeding, T., eds.,* 1985, pp. 69–87. [G: U.S.]

Cameron, Trudy Ann. A Nested Logit Model of

Energy Conservation Activity by Owners of Existing Single Family Dwellings. *Rev. Econ. Statist.,* May 1985, *67*(2), pp. 205–11. [G: U.S.]

Capps, Oral, Jr. and Kramer, Randall A. Analysis of Food Stamp Participation Using Qualitative Choice Models. *Amer. J. Agr. Econ.,* February 1985, *67*(1), pp. 49–59. [G: U.S.]

Chiappori, Pierre-André. Distribution of Income and the "Law of Demand." *Econometrica,* January 1985, *53*(1), pp. 109–27. [G: Selected Countries]

Chul, Song Lee. International Double Taxation of Inheritances and Gifts: Republic of Korea. In *International Fiscal Association (II),* 1985, pp. 513–17. [G: S. Korea]

Clements, R. T. Savings in New Zealand during Inflationary Times: Measurement, Determinants, and Implications. *J. Bus. Econ. Statist.,* July 1985, *3*(3), pp. 188–208. [G: New Zealand]

Coles, Jeffrey Link and Harte-Chen, Paul. Real Wage Indices. *J. Lab. Econ.,* July 1985, *3*(3), pp. 317–36. [G: U.S.]

Cox, Donald and Raines, Fredric. Interfamily Transfers and Income Redistribution. In *David, M. and Smeeding, T., eds.,* 1985, pp. 393–421. [G: U.S.]

Cullity, Maurice C. International Double Taxation of Inheritances and Gifts: Canada. In *International Fiscal Association (II),* 1985, pp. 293–96. [G: Canada]

Danziger, Sheldon. Inflation Vulnerability, Income, and Wealth of the Elderly, 1969–1979: Comment. In *David, M. and Smeeding, T., eds.,* 1985, pp. 172–77. [G: U.S.]

Darian, Jean C. Family Resources and Buyer Behavior. In *Brown, R. C., ed.,* 1985, pp. 257–67.

Darrat, Ali F. Inflation, Its Variability and Consumers' Behavior in a Developing Economy. *Econ. Int.,* Aug./Nov. 1985, *38*(3/4), pp. 309–17. [G: Morocco]

David, Martin and Menchik, Paul L. The Effect of Social Security on Lifetime Wealth Accumulation and Bequests. *Economica,* November 1985, *52*(208), pp. 421–34. [G: U.S.]

Deblauwe, R. La double imposition internationale des successions et donations: Belgique. (International Double Taxation of Inheritances and Gifts: Belgium. With English summary.) In *International Fiscal Association (II),* 1985, pp. 269–91. [G: Belgium]

Derrick, Frederick W. and Wolken, John D. The Effects of Price Aggregation Bias in Systems of Demand Equations. *J. Bus. Econ. Statist.,* October 1985, *3*(4), pp. 325–31. [G: U.S.]

Diamond, Peter A. The Economics of Saving: A Survey of Recent Contributions: Comment. In *Arrow, K. J. and Honkapohja, S., eds.,* 1985, pp. 295–306. [G: U.S.]

Díaz, Francisco Gil. Investment and Debt. In *Musgrave, P. B., ed.,* 1985, pp. 3–32. [G: Mexico]

Dietsch, Michel. Les imperfections des marchés financiers et l'effet d'éviction directe de la dette publique: Le cas de la France. (Imperfect Financial Markets and the Crowding Out Effect of Public Debt: The French Case. With English summary.) *Écon. Soc.*, September 1985, *19*(9), pp. 81–108. **[G: France]**

Dilnot, Andrew W.; Kay, John A. and Morris, Nick. The UK Tax System, Structure and Progressivity, 1948–1982. In *Førsund, F. R. and Honkapohja, S., eds.*, 1985, pp. 52–67. **[G: U.K.]**

Drechsler, László and Horváth, Piroska. Some Problems of the Measurement of Total Consumption in Hungary. *Rev. Income Wealth*, June 1985, *31*(2), pp. 171–87. **[G: Hungary]**

Duncan, Greg J. and Hoffman, Saul D. A Reconsideration of the Economic Consequences of Marital Dissolution. *Demography*, November 1985, *22*(4), pp. 485–97. **[G: U.S.]**

Duncan, Greg J. and Hoffman, Saul D. Economic Consequences of Marital Instability. In *David, M. and Smeeding, T., eds.*, 1985, pp. 427–67. **[G: U.S.]**

Edwards, P. S. A. International Double Taxation of Inheritances and Gifts: Hong Kong. In *International Fiscal Association (II)*, 1985, pp. 397–412. **[G: Hong Kong]**

El-Sheikh, S. Consumption and Credit in a Less Developed Country: An Econometric Analysis of Egypt. *Empirical Econ.*, 1985, *10*(3), pp. 143–61. **[G: Egypt]**

Erickson, Gary M. and Johansson, Johny K. The Role of Price in Multi-attribute Product Evaluations. *J. Cons. Res.*, September 1985, *12*(2), pp. 195–99. **[G: U.S.]**

Espenshade, Thomas J. The Recent Decline of American Marriage: Blacks and Whites in Comparative Perspective. In *Davis, K., ed.*, 1985, pp. 53–90. **[G: U.S.]**

Farley, Pamela J. and Wilensky, Gail R. Household Wealth and Health Insurance as Protection against Medical Risks. In *David, M. and Smeeding, T., eds.*, 1985, pp. 323–54. **[G: U.S.]**

Ferrara, Peter J. Rates of Return Promised by Social Security to Today's Young Workers: Comment. In *Ferrara, P. J., ed.*, 1985, pp. 33–36. **[G: U.S.]**

Ferrara, Peter J. and Lott, John R., Jr. Rates of Return Promised by Social Security to Today's Young Workers. In *Ferrara, P. J., ed.*, 1985, pp. 13–32. **[G: U.S.]**

Ferrari, Camillo. Il risparmio per l'oggi e per il domani: problemi di formazione, di remunerazione, di investimento. (Saving for Today and for Tomorrow: The Formation, Remuneration and Investment of Savings. With English summary.) *Bancaria*, January 1985, *41*(1), pp. 32–44. **[G: Italy]**

Flamm, Kenneth. Mexico and the United States: Studies in Economic Interaction: Finance: Comments. In *Musgrave, P. B., ed.*, 1985, pp. 71–76. **[G: Mexico]**

Flavin, Marjorie. Excess Sensitivity of Consumption to Current Income: Liquidity Constraints or Myopia? *Can. J. Econ.*, February 1985, *18*(1), pp. 117–36. **[G: U.S.]**

Flowers, Marilyn R. Owner-occupied Housing, the CPI, and Indexing. *Public Finance Quart.*, January 1985, *13*(1), pp. 74–80.

Fortune, Peter and Ortmeyer, David L. The Roles of Relative Prices, Interest Rates, and Bequests in the Consumption Function. *J. Macroecon.*, Summer 1985, *7*(3), pp. 381–400. **[G: U.S.]**

Frank, Robert H. The Demand for Unobservable and Other Nonpositional Goods. *Amer. Econ. Rev.*, March 1985, *75*(1), pp. 101–16. **[G: U.S.]**

Friedman, Benjamin M. Saving, Investment, and Government Deficits in the 1980s. In *Scott, B. R. and Lodge, G. C., eds.*, 1985, pp. 395–428. **[G: U.S.; OECD]**

Fry, Vanessa C. and Pashardes, Panos. Distributional Aspects of Inflation: Who Has Suffered Most? *Fisc. Stud.*, November 1985, *6*(4), pp. 21–29. **[G: U.K.]**

Garfinkel, Irwin. Variations in the Economic Well-Being of Divorced Women and Their Children: The Role of Child Support Income: Comment. In *David, M. and Smeeding, T., eds.*, 1985, pp. 506–09. **[G: U.S.]**

Gillioz, Pierre. La double imposition internationale des successions et donations: Suisse. (International Double Taxation of Inheritances and Gifts: Switzerland. With English summary.) In *International Fiscal Association (II)*, 1985, pp. 547–61. **[G: Switzerland]**

Giovannini, Alberto. Saving and the Real Interest Rate in LDCs. *J. Devel. Econ.*, August 1985, *18*(2–3), pp. 197–217. **[G: LDCs]**

Glatzer, Wolfgang and Berger, Regina. Household Composition, Social Networks and Household Production. In *Gaertner, W. and Wenig, A., eds.*, 1985, pp. 330–51. **[G: W. Germany]**

Glennon, Dennis. An Examination of the Stability of the Gross Private Saving Rate. *Quart. J. Bus. Econ.*, Autumn 1985, *24*(4), pp. 44–53. **[G: U.S.]**

Goldberg, Sanford H.; Stapper, Erik J. and Carlson, George N. International Double Taxation of Inheritances and Gifts: United States. In *International Fiscal Association (II)*, 1985, pp. 337–47. **[G: U.S.]**

Gramlich, Edward M. A Comparison of Measures of Horizontal Inequity: Comment. In *David, M. and Smeeding, T., eds.*, 1985, pp. 264–68. **[G: U.S.]**

Green, Gordon. Estimating After-Tax Income Using Survey and Administrative Data. *Statist. J.*, March 1985, *3*(1), pp. 85–113. **[G: U.S.]**

Hall, Robert E. The Time Series Consumption Function Revisited: Comment. *Brookings Pap. Econ. Act.*, 1985, (2), pp. 512–13. **[G: U.S.]**

Harboe, Einar. International Double Taxation of Inheritances and Gifts: Norway. In *International Fiscal Association (II)*, 1985, pp. 453–57. **[G: Norway]**

Haveman, Robert H. and Wolfe, Barbara L. Income, Inequality, and Uncertainty: Differences between the Disabled and Nondisabled. In *Da-*

vid, M. and Smeeding, T., eds., 1985, pp. 293–319. [G: U.S.]

Havlik, Peter. A Comparison of Purchasing Power Parity and Consumption Levels in Austria and Czechoslovakia. J. Compar. Econ., June 1985, 9(2), pp. 178–90. [G: Austria; Czechoslovakia]

Hayashi, Fumio. The Effect of Liquidity Constraints on Consumption: A Cross-sectional Analysis. Quart. J. Econ., February 1985, 100(1), pp. 183–206. [G: U.S.]

Hayashi, Fumio. The Permanent Income Hypothesis and Consumption Durability: Analysis Based on Japanese Panel Data. Quart. J. Econ., November 1985, 100(4), pp. 1083–1113. [G: Japan]

Heien, Dale and Dunn, James. The True Cost-of-Living Index with Changing Preferences. J. Bus. Econ. Statist., October 1985, 3(4), pp. 332–43. [G: U.S.]

Helbich, Franz. Internationale Doppelbesteuerung bei Erbschaften und Schenkungen: Österreich. (International Double Taxation of Inheritances and Gifts: Austria. With English summary.) In International Fiscal Association (II), 1985, pp. 253–67. [G: Austria]

Hendershott, Patric H. and Peek, Joe. Household Saving: An Econometric Investigation. In Hendershott, P. H., ed., 1985, pp. 63–100. [G: U.S.]

Hewitt, Daniel. Demand for National Public Goods: Estimates from Surveys. Econ. Inquiry, July 1985, 23(3), pp. 487–506. [G: U.S.]

Hoem, Jan M. Weighting, Misclassification, and Other Issues in the Analysis of Survey Samples of Life Histories. In Heckman, J. J. and Singer, B., eds., 1985, pp. 249–93.

Holden, K. and Peel, D. A. Surprises in the Consumption Function, Incomplete Current Information, and Moving Average Errors: A Note [Stochastic Implications of the Life Cycle Permanent Income Hypothesis: Theory and Evidence]. Econ. J., March 1985, 95(377), pp. 183–88. [G: U.K.]

Horton, Susan. The Determinants of Nutrient Intake: Results from Western India. J. Devel. Econ., Sept.-Oct. 1985, 19(1/2), pp. 147–62. [G: India]

Hsiao, Cheng and Mountain, Dean C. Estimating the Short-run Income Elasticity of Demand for Electricity by Using Cross-sectional Categorized Data. J. Amer. Statist. Assoc., June 1985, 80(390), pp. 259–65. [G: Canada]

Hubbard, R. Glenn. The Time Series Consumption Function Revisited: Comment. Brookings Pap. Econ. Act., 1985, (2), pp. 514–19. [G: U.S.]

Hurd, Michael D. and Shoven, John B. Inflation Vulnerability, Income, and Wealth of the Elderly, 1969–1979. In David, M. and Smeeding, T., eds., 1985, pp. 125–72. [G: U.S.]

Husby, Ralph D. The Nonlinear Consumption Function Twelve Years Later. Atlantic Econ. J., July 1985, 13(2), pp. 82. [G: U.S.]

Iqbal, Munawar. Zakah, Moderation and Aggre-

gate Consumption in an Islamic Economy. J. Res. Islamic Econ., Summer 1985, 3(1), pp. 45–61.

Iyengar, N. Srinivasa and Gopalakrishna, Mallika. Appropriate Criteria for the Measurement of Levels of Living. Indian Econ. Rev., July-Dec. 1985, 20(2), pp. 191–229. [G: India]

Iyengar, N. Srinivasa and Suryanarayana, M. H. An Analysis of Economic Size Distributions of Consumption. J. Quant. Econ., January 1985, 1(1), pp. 125–34. [G: India]

Janáček, Kamil. On Selected Issues of the Long-Run Projections of the Living Standard. Czech. Econ. Pap., 1985, 23, pp. 75–89. [G: Czechoslovakia]

Jírava, Miroslav. Raising the Living Standard—The Aim and Prerequisite for Building an Advanced Socialist Society. Czech. Econ. Digest., August 1985, (5), pp. 3–26. [G: Czechoslovakia]

Jones, H. G. Consumer Behaviour. In Morris, D., ed., 1985, pp. 29–52. [G: U.K.]

Jones, J. F. Avery. International Double Taxation of Inheritances and Gifts: United Kingdom. In International Fiscal Association (II), 1985, pp. 519–35. [G: U.K.]

Kane, Edward J. Microeconomic Evidence on the Composition of Household Savings in Recent Years. In Hendershott, P. H., ed., 1985, pp. 101–49. [G: U.S.]

Kapteyn, Arie; van de Geer, Sara and van de Stadt, Huib. The Impact of Changes in Income and Family Composition on Subjective Measures of Well-Being. In David, M. and Smeeding, T., eds., 1985, pp. 35–64. [G: Netherlands]

Kay, John A. Changes in Tax Progressivity, 1951-85. Fisc. Stud., May 1985, 6(2), pp. 61–66. [G: U.K.]

Kazi, Shahnaz and Sathar, Zeba A. Differences in Household Characteristics by Income Distribution in Pakistan. Pakistan Devel. Rev., Autumn-Winter 1985, 24(3/4), pp. 657–67. [G: Pakistan]

Keeler, James P.; James, William L. and Abdel-Ghany, Mohamed. The Relative Size of Windfall Income and the Permanent Income Hypothesis. J. Bus. Econ. Statist., July 1985, 3(3), pp. 209–15. [G: U.S.]

Keller, W. J. and van Driel, J. Differential Consumer Demand Systems. Europ. Econ. Rev., April 1985, 27(3), pp. 375–90. [G: Netherlands]

Kennally, Gerard. Committed and Discretionary Saving of Households. Nat. Inst. Econ. Rev., May 1985, (112), pp. 35–40. [G: U.K.]

King, Mervyn. The Economics of Saving: A Survey of Recent Contributions. In Arrow, K. J. and Honkapohja, S., eds., 1985, pp. 227–94.

Komlos, John. Stature and Nutrition in the Habsburg Monarchy: The Standard of Living and Economic Development in the Eighteenth Century. Amer. Hist. Rev., December 1985, 90(5), pp. 1149–61. [G: Europe]

Koskela, Erkki and Virén, Matti. Consumption Function, Labour Supply Rationing and Bor-

rowing Constraints. *Oxford Econ. Pap.*, September 1985, *37*(3), pp. 500–509.
[G: Finland]

Koskela, Erkki and Virén, Matti. On the Role of Inflation in Consumption Function. *Weltwirtsch. Arch.*, 1985, *121*(2), pp. 252–60.
[G: U.K.]

Kremer, Claude and Elvinger, Jacques. La double imposition internationale des successions et donations: Luxembourg. (International Double Taxation of Inheritances and Gifts: Luxemburg. With English summary.) In *International Fiscal Association (II)*, 1985, pp. 441–51.
[G: Luxemburg]

Krotki, Karol J. Differences in Household Characteristics by Income Distribution in Pakistan: Comments. *Pakistan Devel. Rev.*, Autumn-Winter 1985, *24*(3/4), pp. 668–69.
[G: Pakistan]

Kurz, Mordecai. Heterogeneity in Savings Behavior: A Comment. In *Arrow, K. J. and Honkapohja, S., eds.*, 1985, pp. 307–27. [G: U.S.]

Lampreave, José L. International Double Taxation of Inheritances and Gifts: Spain. In *International Fiscal Association (II)*, 1985, pp. 321–35.
[G: Spain]

Langston, Donald; Rasmussen, David W. and Simmons, James C. A Note on Geographic Living Cost Differentials. *Land Econ.*, August 1985, *61*(3), pp. 314–18. [G: U.S.]

Lazer, William. Threats and Opportunities in the Demographic Transition. In *Mendell, J. S., ed.*, 1985, pp. 159–70. [G: U.S.]

Lázniěková, Anna. Overcoming Social Disparities between the Urban and Rural Population in Socialist Society. *Czech. Econ. Digest.*, August 1985, (5), pp. 45–58. [G: Czechoslovakia]

Lenti, Libero. Lo zoccolo duro dell'inflazione. (The Hard Core of Inflation. With English summary.) *Rivista Int. Sci. Econ. Com.*, March 1985, *32*(3), pp. 201–06. [G: Italy]

Lesnoy, Selig D. and Leimer, Dean R. Social Security and Private Saving: Theory and Historical Evidence. *Soc. Sec. Bull.*, January 1985, *48*(1), pp. 14–30. [G: U.S.]

Lethaus, Hans J. Internationale Doppelbesteuerung bei Erbschaften und Schenkungen: Deutschland. (International Double Taxation of Inheritances and Gifts: Germany. With English summary.) In *International Fiscal Association (II)*, 1985, pp. 227–45. [G: Germany]

Lillard, Lee A. Estimating Changes in Well-Being across Life: A Realized vs. Comprehensive Income Approach: Comment. In *David, M. and Smeeding, T., eds.*, 1985, pp. 88–90.
[G: U.S.]

Loh, Choon Cheong and Veall, Michael R. A Note on Social Security and Private Savings in Singapore. *Public Finance*, 1985, *40*(2), pp. 299–304. [G: Singapore]

Lopes, Antonio. Scelte di portafoglio delle famiglie, finanziamento del tesoro ed aspettative inflazionistiche in Italia (1979–1983). (With English summary.) *Stud. Econ.*, 1985, *40*(25), pp. 29–70. [G: Italy]

MacDonald, Ronald and Peel, D. A. Involuntary

Saving, Unanticipated Inflation and the Rationality of Expectations Formation: Some Empirical Evidence. *Weltwirtsch. Arch.*, 1985, *121*(3), pp. 553–59. [G: W. Europe; Canada; U.S.]

Mankiw, N. Gregory; Rotemberg, Julio J. and Summers, Lawrence H. Intertemporal Substitution in Macroeconomics. *Quart. J. Econ.*, February 1985, *100*(1), pp. 225–51.
[G: U.S.]

Mann, Arthur J. Economic Development, Income Distribution, and Real Income Levels: Puerto Rico, 1953–1977. *Econ. Develop. Cult. Change*, April 1985, *33*(3), pp. 485–502.
[G: Puerto Rico]

Marzorati, Osvaldo J. International Double Taxation of Inheritances and Gifts: Argentina. In *International Fiscal Association (II)*, 1985, pp. 247–52. [G: Argentina]

Matlin, I. S.; Akhundova, T. A. and Kurkina, O. M. A Study of the Relationship between Balance in the Goods Market, Capital-Intensity, and Labor Productivity Based on a Dynamic Input–Output Model. *Matekon*, Spring 1985, *21*(3), pp. 63–80. [G: U.S.S.R.]

Mattei, Aurelio. Epargne et sécurité sociale. (Saving and Social Security. With English summary.) *Schweiz. Z. Volkswirtsch. Statist.*, March 1985, *121*(1), pp. 45–60.
[G: Switzerland]

Matthews, Kent. Private Sector Expenditure in the Inter-war Period: An Integrated Portfolio Approach. *Manchester Sch. Econ. Soc. Stud.*, March 1985, *53*(1), pp. 23–44. [G: U.K.]

Mayr, Siegfried. International Double Taxation of Inheritances and Gifts: Italy. In *International Fiscal Association (II)*, 1985, pp. 413–22. [G: Italy]

McAdoo, Harriette Pipes. Strategies Used by Black Single Mothers against Stress. *Rev. Black Polit. Econ.*, Fall-Winter 1985-86, *14*(2–3), pp. 153–66. [G: U.S.]

Mehdizadeh, Mostafa. The Effect of Liquid Assets on the Consumption Function of a Less Developed Economy, a Note. *Amer. Econ.*, Spring 1985, *29*(1), pp. 78–79. [G: Iran]

Menchik, Paul L. Interfamily Transfers and Income Redistribution: Comment. In *David, M. and Smeeding, T., eds.*, 1985, pp. 421–25.
[G: U.S.]

de Ménil, Georges and Sastre, José. Transfer Policies, Income, and Employment in France. In *de Ménil, G. and Westphal, U., eds.*, 1985, pp. 23–58. [G: France]

Modigliani, Franco and Jappelli, Tullio. Politica fiscale e risparmio in Italia: l'esperienza dell'ultimo secolo. (Fiscal Policy and Saving in Italy: The Experience of the Last Century. With English summary.) *Giorn. Econ.*, Sept.-Oct. 1985, *44*(9–10), pp. 475–518.

Modigliani, Franco; Jappelli, Tullio and Pagona, Marco. The Impact of Fiscal Policy and Inflation on National Saving: The Italian Case. *Banca Naz. Lavoro Quart. Rev.*, June 1985, (153), pp. 91–126. [G: Italy]

Montgomery, Edward. An Ordered Probit Analysis of Saving Behavior. *Quart. Rev. Econ. Bus.*, Autumn 1985, *25*(3), pp. 22–35.   [G: U.S.]

Monticelli, Carlo. La teoria della funzione del consumo con aspettative razionali e il caso italiano. (With English summary.) *Stud. Econ.*, 1985, *40*(26), pp. 15–39.   [G: Italy]

Morciano, Michele. Il ruolo delle aspettative e della domanda nella formazione dei prezzi al consumo. (Effects of Expectations and Demand on Retail Prices. With English summary.) *Ricerche Econ.*, Jan.-Mar. 1985, *39*(1), pp. 40–69.   [G: Italy]

Munnell, Alicia H. Social Security, Private Pensions and Saving. In *Terny, G. and Culyer, A. J., eds.*, 1985, pp. 157–70.

Murty, G. V. S. N. Prices and Inequalities in a Developing Economy: The Case of India. *J. Devel. Stud.*, July 1985, *21*(4), pp. 533–47.   [G: India]

Najjar, Annette and Marcelle, Hazel. Estimating a National Savings Series for Trinidad and Tobago: 1970–1983. *Soc. Econ. Stud.*, December 1985, *34*(4), pp. 165–97.   [G: Trinidad and Tobago]

Nellor, David C. L. Tax Policy, Regulated Interest Rates, and Saving. *World Devel.*, June 1985, *13*(6), pp. 725–36.   [G: LDCs]

Neutmann, Wolf-Dieter and Sander, Uwe. Transfer Policies, Income, and Employment in Germany. In *de Ménil, G. and Westphal, U., eds.*, 1985, pp. 59–96. [G: W. Germany]

Newhouse, Joseph P. Household Wealth and Health Insurance as Protection against Medical Risks: Comment. In *David, M. and Smeeding, T., eds.*, 1985, pp. 354–58.   [G: U.S.]

Nicholas, Nick L. Methodological Issues Raised in the Measurement of Family Decision-Making Processes. In *Brown, R. C., ed.*, 1985, pp. 269–73.

Nielsen, Thøger. International Double Taxation of Inheritances and Gifts: Denmark. In *International Fiscal Association (II)*, 1985, pp. 305–319.   [G: Denmark]

Nissan, Edward and Caveny, Regina. Quality of Life Indicators for Selected South American Nations. *Atlantic Econ. J.*, September 1985, *13*(3), pp. 93.   [G: Latin America]

Norris, Keith. Taxes, Transfers, and the Social Wage in Australia 1975–84. *Australian Bull. Lab.*, September 1985, *11*(4), pp. 212–35.   [G: Australia]

Ortiz Amaya, Bernardo and Gonzalez Parada, Hernan Alberto. La double imposition internationale des successions et donations: Colombie. (International Double Taxation of Inheritances and Gifts: Colombia. With English summary.) In *International Fiscal Association (II)*, 1985, pp. 297–303.   [G: Colombia]

Ortmeyer, David L. A Portfolio Model of Korean Household Saving Behavior, 1962–1976. *Econ. Develop. Cult. Change*, April 1985, *33*(3), pp. 575–99.   [G: Korea]

Ortmeyer, David L. and Fortune, Peter. An Application of the Life-Cycle Linear Expenditure System to the South Korean Household Sector,

1962–1976. *J. Devel. Econ.*, August 1985, *18*(2–3), pp. 361–79.   [G: S. Korea]

Otsuka, Masatami. International Double Taxation of Inheritances and Gifts: Japan. In *International Fiscal Association (II)*, 1985, pp. 423–40.   [G: Japan]

Owen, P. Dorian. Systems Testing of Wealth-Aggregation Restrictions in an Integrated Model of Expenditure and Asset Behaviour. *Appl. Econ.*, December 1985, *17*(6), pp. 1099–1115.   [G: U.K.]

Pandit, B. L. Saving Behaviour and Choice of Assets of Indian Households. *Indian Econ. Rev.*, Jan.-June 1985, *20*(1), pp. 85–116.   [G: India]

Park, Siyoung. Quality of Life in Illinois Counties. *Growth Change*, October 1985, *16*(4), pp. 56–69.   [G: U.S.]

Paroutsas, Athanasios D. International Double Taxation of Inheritances and Gifts: Greece. In *International Fiscal Association (II)*, 1985, pp. 379–95.   [G: Greece]

Patterson, Kerry D. Income Adjustments and the Role of Consumers' Durables in Some Leading Consumption Functions. *Econ. J.*, June 1985, *95*(378), pp. 469–79.   [G: U.K.]

Paul, Satya. On the Estimation of Continuous Equivalent Adult Scales. *Indian Econ. Rev.*, Jan.-June 1985, *20*(1), pp. 117–42. [G: India]

Perelman, Sergio and Pestieau, Pierre. Social Allowances and Household Saving. In *Terny, G. and Culyer, A. J., eds.*, 1985, pp. 123–42.   [G: OECD]

Peres, Yochanan and Pasternack, Rachel. The Importance of Marriage for Socialization: A Comparison of Achievements and Social Adjustment between Offspring of One- and Two-Parent Families in Israel. In *Davis, K., ed.*, 1985, pp. 157–78.   [G: Israel]

Pestieau, Pierre. Belgium's Irregular Economy. In *Gaertner, W. and Wenig, A., eds.*, 1985, pp. 144–60.   [G: Belgium]

Pitelis, Christos N. The Effects of Life Assurance and Pension Funds on Other Savings: The Postwar UK Experience. *Bull. Econ. Res.*, September 1985, *37*(3), pp. 213–29.   [G: U.K.]

Plotnick, Robert D. A Comparison of Measures of Horizontal Inequity. In *David, M. and Smeeding, T., eds.*, 1985, pp. 239–63.   [G: U.S.]

Prebble, John. International Double Taxation of Inheritances and Gifts: New Zealand. In *International Fiscal Association (II)*, 1985, pp. 459–70.   [G: New Zealand]

Ray, Ranjan. Evaluating Expenditure Inequality Using Alternative Social Welfare Functions: A Case Study of Rural India. *Indian Econ. Rev.*, July-Dec. 1985, *20*(2), pp. 171–90. [G: India]

Ray, Ranjan. Prices, Children and Inequality: Further Evidence for the United Kingdom, 1965–82. *Econ. J.*, December 1985, *95*(380), pp. 1069–77.   [G: U.K.]

Ray, Ranjan. Specification and Time Series Estimation of Dynamic Gorman Polar Form Demand Systems. *Europ. Econ. Rev.*, April 1985, 27(3), pp. 357–74. [G: U.K.]

Reece, William S. and Zieschang, Kimberly D. Consistent Estimation of the Impact of Tax Deductibility on the Level of Charitable Contributions. *Econometrica*, March 1985, 53(2), pp. 271–93. [G: U.S.]

Reid, Bradford G. Aggregate Consumption and Deficit Financing: An Attempt to Separate Permanent from Transitory Effects. *Econ. Inquiry*, July 1985, 23(3), pp. 475–86. [G: U.S.]

Ring, Raymond J., Jr. Variability of Inflation and Income across Income Classes. *Soc. Sci. Quart.*, March 1985, 66(1), pp. 203–09. [G: U.S.]

Romer, Paul M. Public Debt Policies and United States Saving: A Comment. *Carnegie-Rochester Conf. Ser. Public Policy*, Autumn 1985, 23, pp. 87–89. [G: U.S.]

Rose, Richard. Getting By in Three Economies: The Resources of the Official, Unofficial and Domestic Economies. In *Lane, J.-E., ed.*, 1985, pp. 103–41. [G: OECD]

Saarinen, Ola. International Double Taxation of Inheritances and Gifts: Finland. In *International Fiscal Association (II)*, 1985, pp. 349–63. [G: Finland]

Sarantis, Nicholas. Fiscal Policies and Consumer Behaviour in Western Europe. *Kyklos*, 1985, 38(2), pp. 233–48. [G: W. Europe]

Sarantis, Nicholas. Government Deficits and Personal Expenditure in the E.E.C. *Rivista Int. Sci. Econ. Com.*, July-Aug. 1985, 32(7–8), pp. 723–34. [G: EEC]

Sawhill, Isabel V. Economic Consequences of Marital Instability: Comment. In *David, M. and Smeeding, T., eds.*, 1985, pp. 467–70. [G: U.S.]

Schwarz, L. D. The Standard of Living in the Long Run: London, 1700–1860. *Econ. Hist. Rev., 2nd Ser.*, February 1985, 38(1), pp. 24–41. [G: U.K.]

Seater, John J. and Mariano, Roberto S. New Tests of the Life Cycle and Tax Discounting Hypotheses. *J. Monet. Econ.*, March 1985, 15(2), pp. 195–215. [G: U.S.]

Sherman, Sally R. Assets of New Retired-Worker Beneficiaries: Findings from the New Beneficiary Survey. *Soc. Sec. Bull.*, July 1985, 48(7), pp. 27–43. [G: U.S.]

Silberberg, Eugene. Nutrition and the Demand for Tastes. *J. Polit. Econ.*, October 1985, 93(5), pp. 881–900. [G: U.S.]

Skinner, Jonathan S. The Effect of Increased Longevity on Capital Accumulation. *Amer. Econ. Rev.*, December 1985, 75(5), pp. 1143–50. [G: U.S.]

Skinner, Jonathan S. Variable Lifespan and the Intertemporal Elasticity of Consumption. *Rev. Econ. Statist.*, November 1985, 67(4), pp. 616–23. [G: U.S.]

Smith, Donald J. A Comment on IRAs and Keoghs. *Nat. Tax J.*, March 1985, 38(1), pp. 111–12. [G: U.S.]

Smith, James D. Market Motives in the Informal Economy. In *Gaertner, W. and Wenig, A.,*

eds., 1985, pp. 161–77. [G: U.S.]

Smith, James D. Wealth, Realized Income, and the Measure of Well-Being: Comment. In *David, M. and Smeeding, T., eds.*, 1985, pp. 117–24. [G: U.S.]

Sørensen, Christen. Real indkomstbeskatning. (Taxation of Real Income. With English summary.) *Nationaløkon. Tidsskr.*, 1985, 123(2), pp. 220–38. [G: Iceland; Norway; Sweden]

Spanier, Graham B. Cohabitation in the 1980s: Recent Changes in the United States. In *Davis, K., ed.*, 1985, pp. 91–111. [G: U.S.]

Spranzi, Aldo. Modernisation and Efficiency of Italian Commerce. *Rev. Econ. Cond. Italy*, May-Aug. 1985, (2), pp. 169–89. [G: Italy; France]

Srinivasan, T. N. The Horizontal and Vertical Equity Characteristics of the Federal Individual Income Tax, 1966–1977: Comment. In *David, M. and Smeeding, T., eds.*, 1985, pp. 212–14. [G: U.S.]

Steuerle, C. Eugene. Wealth, Realized Income, and the Measure of Well-Being. In *David, M. and Smeeding, T., eds.*, 1985, pp. 91–117. [G: U.S.]

Stewart, Douglas B. and Venieris, Yiannis P. Sociopolitical Instability and the Behavior of Savings in Less-Developed Countries. *Rev. Econ. Statist.*, November 1985, 67(4), pp. 557–63. [G: LDCs]

Stricker, Frank. Affluence for Whom?—Another Look at Prosperity and the Working Classes in the 1920s. In *Leab, D. J., ed.*, 1985, pp. 288–316. [G: U.S.]

Stuart, O. D. J. Are Business and Consumer Surveys Still of Value? *J. Stud. Econ. Economet-rics*, November 1985, (23), pp. 29–50.

Testi, Angela. Alcune considerazioni sul ruolo della ricchezza nella funzione aggregata del consumo. (Analysis of the Role of Wealth in the Consumption Function. With English summary.) *Econ. Int.*, February 1985, 38(1), pp. 91–120. [G: Italy]

Thomsen, Carsten Krogsgaard. En empirisk model for kommunernes sygehusforbrug. (An Empirical Model of Hospital Consumption in Denmark. With English summary.) *Nationaløkon. Tidsskr.*, 1985, 123(1), pp. 77–93. [G: Denmark]

Thornborrow, Nancy. Social Security's Effect on Retirement Assets. *Quart. J. Bus. Econ.*, Spring 1985, 24(2), pp. 51–72. [G: U.S.]

Tiwari, S. G. Government Services in Relation to Total Consumption of the Population in Asian and Pacific Countries, with Special Reference to India. *Rev. Income Wealth*, June 1985, 31(2), pp. 189–200. [G: India]

von Tunzelmann, G. N. The Standard of Living Debate and Optimal Economic Growth. In *Mokyr, J., ed.*, 1985, pp. 207–26. [G: U.K.]

Usher, Dan. Income, Inequality, and Uncertainty: Differences between the Disabled and Nondisabled: Comment. In *David, M. and Smeeding, T., eds.*, 1985, pp. 319–21. [G: U.S.]

de Vin, Willem E. International Double Taxation

of Inheritances and Gifts: Netherlands. In *International Fiscal Association (II)*, 1985, pp. 471–91. [G: Netherlands]

Waller, Erik. International Double Taxation of Inheritances and Gifts: Sweden. In *International Fiscal Association (II)*, 1985, pp. 537–45. [G: Sweden]

Watts, Harold W. The Impact of Changes in Income and Family Composition on Subjective Measures of Well-Being: Comment. In *David, M. and Smeeding, T., eds.*, 1985, pp. 64–67. [G: Netherlands]

Yoneda, Kimimaru. A Note on Income Distribution in Indonesia. *Devel. Econ.*, December 1985, *23*(4), pp. 414–22. [G: Indonesia]

Zellner, Arnold and Moulton, Brent R. Bayesian Regression Diagnostics with Applications to International Consumption and Income Data. *J. Econometrics*, July/August 1985, *29*(1/2), pp. 187–211. [G: LDCs; MDCs]

Zieba, Andrzej. Maximum Principle for Speculative Money Balances. In *Gaertner, W. and Wenig, A., eds.*, 1985, pp. 389–91.

9212 Expenditure Patterns and Consumption of Specific Items

Abadia, Antonio. Income Distribution and Composition of Consumer Demand in the Spanish Economy. *Europ. Econ. Rev.*, October 1985, *29*(1), pp. 1–13. [G: Spain]

Agthe, Donald E. Revenue Effects from Changes in a Declining Block Pricing Structure: Comment. *Land Econ.*, February 1985, *61*(1), pp. 79–80. [G: U.S.]

Aigner, Dennis J. The Residential Electricity Time-of-Use Pricing Experiments: What Have We Learned? In *Hausman, J. A. and Wise, D. A., eds.*, 1985, pp. 11–41. [G: U.S.]

Akin, John S., et al. Determinants of Infant Feeding: A Household Production Approach. *Econ. Develop. Cult. Change*, October 1985, *34*(1), pp. 57–81. [G: Philippines]

Al-Qunaibet, Mohammad H. and Johnston, Richard S. Municipal Demand for Water in Kuwait: Methodological Issues and Empirical Results. *Water Resources Res.*, April 1985, *21*(4), pp. 433–38. [G: Kuwait]

Alcordo, Eduard A. and Johnson, Lester W. An Alternative Approach to the Specification of Approximate Demand Systems. *Australian Econ. Pap.*, December 1985, *24*(45), pp. 380–93. [G: Australia]

Ali, M. Shaukat. Household Consumption and Saving Behaviour in Pakistan: An Application of the Extended Linear Expenditure System. *Pakistan Devel. Rev.*, Spring 1985, *24*(1), pp. 23–37. [G: Pakistan]

Allen, Chris T. and Madden, Thomas J. A Closer Look at Classical Conditioning. *J. Cons. Res.*, December 1985, *12*(3), pp. 301–15. [G: U.S.]

Anderson, Ronald W. and Wilkinson, M. Consumer Demand for Meat and the Evaluation of Agricultural Policy. *Empirical Econ.*, 1985, *10*(2), pp. 65–89. [G: U.S.]

Arbel, Avner and Ravid, S. Abraham. On Recreation Demand: A Time-Series Approach. *Appl. Econ.*, December 1985, *17*(6), pp. 979–90. [G: U.S.]

Askanas, Benedykt and Laski, Kazimierz. Consumer Prices and Private Consumption in Poland and Austria. *J. Compar. Econ.*, June 1985, *9*(2), pp. 164–77. [G: Poland; Austria]

Attfield, Clifford L. F. Homogeneity and Endogeneity in Systems of Demand Equations. *J. Econometrics*, February 1985, *27*(2), pp. 197–209. [G: U.K.]

Attfield, Clifford L. F. and Browning, Martin J. A Differential Demand System, Rational Expectations and the Life Cycle Hypothesis. *Econometrica*, January 1985, *53*(1), pp. 31–48. [G: U.K.]

Baanders, A.; Kremer-Nass, J. and Ruijgrok, C. J. Income Decline and Travel Behaviour: Some Recent Dutch Findings and Research Orientations. In *Jansen, G. R. M.; Nijkamp, P. and Ruijgrok, C. J., eds.*, 1985, pp. 37–53. [G: Netherlands]

Babiker, A. A.; Musnad, H. A. and Shaddad, M. Z. Wood Resources and Their Use in the Nuba Mountains. In *Davies, H. R. J., ed.*, 1985, pp. 30–59. [G: Sudan]

Bechtel, Gordon G. Generalizing the Rasch Model for Consumer Rating Scales. *Marketing Sci.*, Winter 1985, *4*(1), pp. 62–73. [G: U.S.]

Bellur, Venkatakrishna V. Factors Perceived as Important in Making Automobile Purchase Decision. *Liiketaloudellinen Aikak.*, 1985, *34*(3), pp. 219–36. [G: U.S.]

Berkovec, James. New Car Sales and Used Car Stocks: A Model of the Automobile Market. *Rand J. Econ.*, Summer 1985, *16*(2), pp. 195–214. [G: U.S.]

Berndt, Ernst R. and Botero, German. Energy Demand in the Transportation Sector of Mexico. *J. Devel. Econ.*, April 1985, *17*(3), pp. 219–38. [G: Mexico]

Bertrand, Jean-Pierre and Green, Raùl H. Brésil et Thalande: stratégies agro-exportatrices, urbanisation et changements de l'alimentation de base. (Brazil and Thailand: Agro-export Oriented Strategies: Urbanisation and Food Consumption Models Change. With English summary.) *Écon. Soc.*, July 1985, *19*(7), pp. 83–109. [G: Brazil; Thailand]

Bierley, Calvin; McSweeney, Frances K. and Vannieuwkerk, Renee. Classical Conditioning of Preferences for Stimuli. *J. Cons. Res.*, December 1985, *12*(3), pp. 316–23. [G: U.S.]

Bingen, Georges and Dewatripont, Mathias. Vérification empirique de la théorie du consommateur: quelques testes emboîtés et non emboîtés. (With English summary.) *Cah. Écon. Bruxelles*, 1st Trimester 1985, (105), pp. 3–40. [G: Belgium]

Bly, P. H. Effects of the Recession on Travel Expenditure and Travel Patterns. In *Jansen, G. R. M.; Nijkamp, P. and Ruijgrok, C. J., eds.*, 1985, pp. 15–36. [G: OECD]

Boroooh, Vani K. Consumers' Expenditure Estimates Using the Rotterdam Model: An Appli-

cation to the United Kingdom, 1954–81. *Appl. Econ.*, August 1985, *17*(4), pp. 675–88.
[G: U.K.]

Bower, Richard S. and Bower, Nancy L. Weather Normalization and Natural Gas Regulation. *Energy J.*, April 1985, *6*(2), pp. 101–15.
[G: U.S.]

Bowonder, B., et al. Energy Use in Eight Rural Communities in India. *World Devel.*, December 1985, *13*(12), pp. 1263–86. [G: India]

Brueckner, Jan K. A Note on the Determinants of Metropolitan Airline Traffic. *Int. J. Transport Econ.*, June 1985, *12*(2), pp. 175–84.
[G: U.S.]

Bruun, K. E. Alcohol Policies: Sweden. In *Grant, M., ed.*, 1985, pp. 114–19. [G: Sweden; U.K.]

Cameron, Trudy Ann and White, K. J. Demand Models Incorporating Price Differences across Political Boundaries. *Ann. Reg. Sci.*, March 1985, *19*(1), pp. 50–60. [G: U.S.]

Canlas, Dante B. Estimating Price and Income Elasticities of the Demand for Food: A Philippine Illustration. *Philippine Rev. Econ. Bus.*, Sept./Dec. 1985, *22*(3/4), pp. 215–28.
[G: Philippines]

Capps, Oral, Jr.; Tedford, John R. and Havlicek, Joseph, Jr. Household Demand for Convenience and Nonconvenience Foods. *Amer. J. Agr. Econ.*, November 1985, *67*(4), pp. 862–69. [G: U.S.]

Carpenter, Edwin H. and Durham, Cathy. Again, Federal Tax Credits Are Found Effective: A Reply. *Energy J.*, July 1985, *6*(3), pp. 127–28. [G: U.S.]

Caudill, Steven B. Modelling the Demand for Optional Classes of Local Measured Telephone Service. *Econ. Modelling*, January 1985, *2*(1), pp. 39–51. [G: U.S.]

Cheema, Aftab Ahmad and Malik, Muhammad Hussain. Changes in Consumption Patterns and Employment under Alternative Income Distributions in Pakistan. *Pakistan Devel. Rev.*, Spring 1985, *24*(1), pp. 1–22.
[G: Pakistan]

Chesher, Andrew; Lancaster, Tony and Irish, Margaret. On Detecting the Failure of Distributional Assumptions. *Ann. INSEE*, July-Dec. 1985, (59/60), pp. 7–45.

Cochran, Richard and Cotton, Arthur W. Municipal Water Demand Study, Oklahoma City and Tulsa, Oklahoma. *Water Resources Res.*, July 1985, *21*(7), pp. 941–43. [G: U.S.]

Common, Michael S. The Distributional Implications of Higher Energy Prices in the UK. *Appl. Econ.*, June 1985, *17*(3), pp. 421–36.
[G: U.K.]

Coondoo, Dipankar and Majumder, Amita. Performance of the Linear Expenditure System and Its Modifications with Nonlinear Price Functions on Indian Data. *J. Quant. Econ.*, July 1985, *1*(2), pp. 299–313. [G: India]

Cornelisse, Peter A. and de Kruijk, Hans. Consumption and Trade of Wheat and Flour in Pakistan—The Role of Public and Private Sec-

tor. *Pakistan Devel. Rev.*, Summer 1985, *24*(2), pp. 151–71. [G: Pakistan]

Cote, Joseph A.; McCullough, James and Reilly, Michael. Effects of Unexpected Situations on Behavior–Intention Differences: A Garbology Analysis. *J. Cons. Res.*, September 1985, *12*(2), pp. 188–94. [G: U.S.]

Cottino, A. and Morgan, Paul. Alcohol Policies: Italy. In *Grant, M., ed.*, 1985, pp. 83–92.
[G: Italy]

Cowan, C. A. Potatoes—The Influence of Age and Regional Differences on Preference for Size. *Irish J. Agr. Econ. Rural Soc.*, 1984-1985, *10*(2), pp. 119–27. [G: Ireland]

Cowan, C. A.; Griffiths, T. W. and Reid, S. N. A Survey of the Acceptability of Rashers by Consumers in the Dublin Area with Particular Reference to Salt Content. *Irish J. Agr. Econ. Rural Soc.*, 1984-1985, *10*(2), pp. 135–44.
[G: Ireland]

Crutchfield, Stephen R. The Impact of Groundfish Imports on the United States Fishing Industry: An Empirical Analysis. *Can. J. Agr. Econ.*, July 1985, *33*(2), pp. 195–207.
[G: U.S.]

Csáki, Csaba. An Outlook of Food Supply and Demand in the CMEA Countries: Results of the IIASA/FAP Model System. *Acta Oecon.*, 1985, *35*(1–2), pp. 145–64. [G: CMEA]

Dahl, Carol A. Do Gasoline Demand Elasticities Vary? Reply. *Land Econ.*, May 1985, *61*(2), pp. 201–04. [G: Selected Countries]

Deacon, Robert T. and Sonstelie, Jon. Rationing by Waiting and the Value of Time: Results from a Natural Experiment. *J. Polit. Econ.*, August 1985, *93*(4), pp. 627–47. [G: U.S.]

Derrick, Frederick W. and Wolken, John D. The Effects of Price Aggregation Bias in Systems of Demand Equations. *J. Bus. Econ. Statist.*, October 1985, *3*(4), pp. 325–31. [G: U.S.]

Donnelly, William A. A Note on 'The Residential Demand for Electricity: A Variant Parameters Approach.' *Appl. Econ.*, April 1985, *17*(2), pp. 241–42. [G: U.S.]

Donnelly, William A. A State-Level, Variable Elasticity of Demand for Gasoline Model. *Int. J. Transport Econ.*, June 1985, *12*(2), pp. 193–202. [G: U.S.]

Donnelly, William A. Electricity Demand Modelling. In *Batten, D. F. and Lesse, P. F., eds.*, 1985, pp. 179–95. [G: Australia]

Donnelly, William A. and Diesendorf, M. Variable Elasticity Models for Electricity Demand. *Energy Econ.*, July 1985, *7*(3), pp. 159–62.
[G: U.S.]

Doxsey, Lawrence B. Demand for Unlimited Use Transit Passes: A Rejoinder. *J. Transp. Econ. Policy*, September 1985, *19*(3), pp. 307–11.
[G: U.S.]

Dynarski, Mark R. and Sheffrin, Steven M. Housing Purchases and Transitory Income: A Study with Panel Data. *Rev. Econ. Statist.*, May 1985, *67*(2), pp. 195–204. [G: U.S.]

El-Sheikh, S. Consumption and Credit in a Less Developed Country: An Econometric Analysis of Egypt. *Empirical Econ.*, 1985, *10*(3), pp. 143–61. [G: Egypt]

Eshghi, Abdolreza and Sheth, Jagdish N. The Globalization of Consumption Patterns: An Empirical Investigation. In *Kaynak, E., ed. (I)*, 1985, pp. 133–48. [G: Brazil; France; Japan; U.S.]

Feehan, James P. Provincial Government Taxation of Clothing and Footwear: Revenue and Equity Aspects. *Can. Public Policy*, March 1985, *11*(1), pp. 26–39. [G: Canada]

Ferguson, G. J. W. A. and Mogridge, M. J. H. Is Car Ownership and Use Stagnating? Fuel Consumption Models and their Implications. In *Jansen, G. R. M.; Nijkamp, P. and Ruijgrok, C. J., eds.*, 1985, pp. 55–74. [G: U.K.; U.S.]

Ferris, James M. Interrelationships among Public Spending Preferences: A Micro Analysis. *Public Choice*, 1985, *45*(2), pp. 139–53.
[G: U.S.]

Fortune, Peter and Ortmeyer, David L. The Roles of Relative Prices, Interest Rates, and Bequests in the Consumption Function. *J. Macroecon.*, Summer 1985, 7(3), pp. 381–400.
[G: U.S.]

Fujii, Edwin T.; Khaled, Mohammed and Mak, James. An Almost Ideal Demand System for Visitor Expenditures. *J. Transp. Econ. Policy*, May 1985, *19*(2), pp. 161–71. [G: U.S.]

Garbacz, Christopher. Residential Demand for Fuelwood. *Energy Econ.*, July 1985, 7(3), pp. 191–93. [G: U.S.]

Garbacz, Christopher. Residential Fuel Oil Demand: A Micro-based National Model. *Appl. Econ.*, August 1985, *17*(4), pp. 669–74.
[G: U.S.]

Gardini, Attilio. Una stima e una verifica statistica del modello differenziale di Rotterdam. (Analysis of Demand for Tourist Services in Italy: Statistical Estimate and Test of the Rotterdam Differential Model. With English summary.) *Statistica*, July-Sept. 1985, *45*(3), pp. 319–37.
[G: Italy]

Giles, David E. A. and Hampton, Peter. An Engel Curve Analysis of Household Expenditure in New Zealand. *Econ. Rec.*, March 1985, *61*(172), pp. 450–62. [G: Australia]

Gilly, Mary C. and Zeithaml, Valarie A. The Elderly Consumer and Adoption of Technologies. *J. Cons. Res.*, December 1985, *12*(3), pp. 353–47. [G: U.S.]

Glakpe, Emmanuel and Fazzolare, Rocco. Economic Demand Analysis for Electricity in West Africa. *Energy J.*, January 1985, *6*(1), pp. 137–44. [G: W. Africa]

Goodwin, P. B. and Layzell, A. D. Longitudinal Analysis for Public Transport Policy Issues. In *Jansen, G. R. M.; Nijkamp, P. and Ruijgrok, C. J., eds.*, 1985, pp. 185–200. [G: U.K.]

Grant, M. Establishing Priorities for Action. In *Grant, M., ed.*, 1985, pp. 1–8.
[G: W. Europe]

Grigsby, J. Eugene, III and Hruby, Mary L. A Review of the Status of Black Renters, 1970–1980. *Rev. Black Polit. Econ.*, Spring 1985, *13*(4), pp. 77–91.

Guseman, Patricia K. and Sapp, Stephen G. Regional Trends in U.S. Food Consumption: Population Scale, Composition, and Income Effects. *Rev. Reg. Stud.*, Spring 1985, *15*(2), pp. 34–42. [G: U.S.]

Hall, Graham and Lloyd, Tony. The Usefulness of Hedonic Prices to the Consumers' Association. *Appl. Econ.*, April 1985, *17*(2), pp. 191–203. [G: U.K.]

Hansen, Gerd. Die Nachfrage nach nichtdauerhaften Gütern—Eine Schätzung anhand des "Almost-Ideal-Demand-System." (The Demand for Nondurables: An Example of the "Almost-Ideal-Demand System." With English summary.) *Jahr. Nationalökon. Statist.*, January 1985, *200*(1), pp. 27–40.
[G: W. Germany]

Hardaker, J. Brian, et al. A Model of a Padi Farming Household in Central Java. *Bull. Indonesian Econ. Stud.*, December 1985, *21*(3), pp. 30–50. [G: Indonesia]

Hausman, Jerry A. The Econometrics of Nonlinear Budget Sets. *Econometrica*, November 1985, *53*(6), pp. 1255–82. [G: U.S.]

Heckman, James A. and Singer, Burton. Erratum [Econometric Duration Analysis]. *J. Econometrics*, January 1985, *27*(1), pp. 137–38.

Hensher, David A. Empirical Vehicle Choice and Usage Models in the Household Sector: A Review. *Int. J. Transport Econ.*, October 1985, *12*(3), pp. 231–59. [G: U.S.; Australia; Israel]

Hirst, Eric and Goeltz, Richard. Estimating Energy Savings Due to Conservation Programmes: The BPA Residential Weatherization Pilot Programme. *Energy Econ.*, January 1985, 7(1), pp. 20–28. [G: U.S.]

Hodgin, Robert F. and Weed, Norman L. An Inquiry into Performance Quality Effects on Consumer Attitudes: The Case of Education. *J. Behav. Econ.*, Summer 1985, *14*(2), pp. 43–58. [G: U.S.]

Hollonbeck, Darrell; Ohls, James C. and Posner, Barbara. The Effects of Cashing Out Food Stamps on Food Expenditures. *Amer. J. Agr. Econ.*, August 1985, *67*(3), pp. 609–13.
[G: U.S.]

Holtgrefe, A. A. I. Stagnation and Public Transport in the Netherlands: Demand, Cost, Supply and Planning. In *Jansen, G. R. M.; Nijkamp, P. and Ruijgrok, C. J., eds.*, 1985, pp. 335–51. [G: Netherlands]

Houston, Douglas A. Revenue Effects from Changes in a Declining Block Pricing Structure: Reply. *Land Econ.*, February 1985, *61*(1), pp. 81–82. [G: U.S.]

Huang, Chung L. and Raunikar, Robert. Effect of Consigned Income on Food Expenditures. *Can. J. Agr. Econ.*, November 1985, *33*(3), pp. 315–29. [G: U.S.]

Huang, Kuo S. Monthly Demand Relationships of U.S. Meat Commodities. *Agr. Econ. Res.*, Summer 1985, *37*(3), pp. 23–29. [G: U.S.]

Hughes-Cromwick, Ellen L. Nairobi Households and Their Energy Use: An Economic Analysis of Consumption Patterns. *Energy Econ.*, October 1985, 7(4), pp. 265–78. [G: Kenya]

Ingram, Gregory K. Housing Behavior and the Experimental Housing-Allowance Program: What Have We Learned? Comment. In *Hausman, J. A. and Wise, D. A., eds.*, 1985, pp. 87–94. [G: U.S.]

Iqbal, Mahmood. Estimates of Gasoline Demand in Pakistan. *Pakistan J. Appl. Econ.*, Summer 1985, *4*(1), pp. 35–45. [G: Pakistan]

Itteilag, Richard L. An Analysis of Actual and Forecasted Conservation in the Residential Gas Space-Heating Market. In *Crew, M. A., ed.*, 1985, pp. 127–39. [G: U.S.]

van Iwaarden, M. J. Public Health Aspects of the Marketing of Alcoholic Drinks. In *Grant, M., ed.*, 1985, pp. 45–55. [G: Netherlands]

Johansen, Leif. Richard Stone's Contributions to Economics. *Scand. J. Econ.*, 1985, *87*(1), pp. 4–32.

Johnson, Richard D. and Levin, Irwin P. More than Meets the Eye: The Effect of Missing Information on Purchase Evaluations. *J. Cons. Res.*, September 1985, *12*(2), pp. 169–77. [G: U.S.]

Joskow, Paul L. The Residential Electricity Time-of-Use Pricing Experiments: What Have We Learned? Comment. In *Hausman, J. A. and Wise, D. A., eds.*, 1985, pp. 42–48. [G: U.S.]

Kabir, M. and Ridler, N. B. The Demand for Atlantic Salmon in Canada: Reply. *Can. J. Agr. Econ.*, July 1985, *33*(2), pp. 247–49. [G: Canada]

Kaserman, David L. and Mayo, John W. Advertising and the Residential Demand for Electricity. *J. Bus.*, October 1985, *58*(4), pp. 399–408. [G: U.S.]

Khan, Qaiser M. A Model of Endowment-constrained Demand for Food in an Agricultural Economy with Empirical Applications to Bangladesh. *World Devel.*, September 1985, *13*(9), pp. 1055–65. [G: Bangladesh]

Kovács, Ilona. International Comparison of Consumption Patterns by Cluster Analysis. *Acta Oecon.*, 1985, *35*(3–4), pp. 313–26. [G: OECD]

Kroes, E. P. and Sheldon, R. J. Stated Preference Techniques in Measuring Travel Elasticities. In *Jansen, G. R. M.; Nijkamp, P. and Ruijgrok, C. J., eds.*, 1985, pp. 201–10.

Kugler, Peter. Autoregressive Modelling of Consumption, Income, Inflation, and Interest Rate Data: A Multicountry Study. *Empirical Econ.*, 1985, *10*(1), pp. 37–50. [G: U.S.; U.K.; W. Germany; France]

Lankford, Ralph Hamilton. Preferences of Citizens for Public Expenditures on Elementary and Secondary Education. *J. Econometrics*, January 1985, *27*(1), pp. 1–20. [G: U.S.]

Le Diberder, Alain. No Culture-only Channels, but a More Important Role for the Audiovisual Media. *J. Cult. Econ.*, Supplement 1985, pp. 83–98. [G: U.S.; France]

Lemmon, Richard C. Investment in Consumer Durables. In *Hendershott, P. H., ed.*, 1985, pp. 205–34. [G: U.S.]

Leu, Robert E. and Frey, René L. Budget Inci-

dence, Demographic Change, and Health Policy in Switzerland. In *Terny, G. and Culyer, A. J., eds.*, 1985, pp. 225–38. [G: Switzerland]

Levy, Jonathan D. and Pitsch, Peter K. Statistical Evidence of Substitutability among Video Delivery Systems. In *Noam, E. M., ed.*, 1985, pp. 56–92. [G: U.S.]

Lewbel, Arthur. A Unified Approach to Incorporating Demographic or Other Effects into Demand Systems. *Rev. Econ. Stud.*, January 1985, *52*(1), pp. 1–18.

Lin, An-loh; Botsas, Eleftherios N. and Monroe, Scott A. State Gasoline Consumption in the USA: An Econometric Analysis. *Energy Econ.*, January 1985, *7*(1), pp. 29–36. [G: U.S.]

Lin, Biing-Hwan and Williams, Nancy A. The Demand for Atlantic Salmon in Canada: A Comment. *Can. J. Agr. Econ.*, July 1985, *33*(2), pp. 243–46. [G: Canada]

Lippert, Alice A. Trip Expenditure Comparisons from 1972–73 to 1980–81. *Mon. Lab. Rev.*, July 1985, *108*(7), pp. 46–48. [G: U.S.]

Loken, Barbara and Hoverstad, Ronald. Relationships between Information Recall and Subsequent Attitudes: Some Exploratory Findings. *J. Cons. Res.*, September 1985, *12*(2), pp. 155–68. [G: U.S.]

Mäkelä, K. Alcohol Policies: Lessons from the Postwar Period. In *Grant, M., ed.*, 1985, pp. 9–22. [G: Zambia; Mexico; U.K.]

Mankiw, N. Gregory. Consumer Durables and the Real Interest Rate. *Rev. Econ. Statist.*, August 1985, *67*(3), pp. 353–62. [G: U.S.]

Mannering, Fred and Winston, Clifford. A Dynamic Empirical Analysis of Household Vehicle Ownership and Utilization. *Rand J. Econ.*, Summer 1985, *16*(2), pp. 215–36. [G: U.S.]

Martin, William J. and Porter, Darrell. Testing for Changes in the Structure of the Demand for Meat in Australia. *Australian J. Agr. Econ.*, April 1985, *29*(1), pp. 16–31. [G: Australia]

McCarthy, Patrick S. An Econometric Analysis of Automobile Transactions. *Int. J. Transport Econ.*, February 1985, *12*(1), pp. 71–92. [G: U.S.]

Menkhaus, Dale J.; St. Clair, James S. and Hallingbye, Stig. A Reexamination of Consumer Buying Behavior for Beef, Pork, and Chicken. *Western J. Agr. Econ.*, July 1985, *10*(1), pp. 116–25. [G: U.S.]

Mitchell, Donald O. Trends in Grain Consumption in the Developing World, 1960–80. *Finance Develop.*, December 1985, *22*(4), pp. 12–13. [G: LDCs]

Mitchell, Ivor. Correlates of Consumer Shopping Behaviour in the Cooperative Socialist Republic of Guyana. *Soc. Econ. Stud.*, June 1985, *34*(2), pp. 26–68. [G: Guyana]

Mondal, S. K. Measurement of Utility, Social Welfare and Taxation—A Cardinal Approach. *Margin*, July 1985, *17*(4), pp. 80–89. [G: India]

Morgan, James N. Comparing Static and Dynamic Estimates of Behavioral Responses to Changes in Family Composition or Income.

J. Cons. Res., June 1985, *12*(1), pp. 83–89.
[G: U.S.]

Morrison, Steven A. and Winston, Clifford. An Econometric Analysis of the Demand for Intercity Passenger Transportation. In *Keeler, T. E., ed.*, 1985, pp. 213–37. [G: U.S.]

Musgrove, Philip. Food Needs and Absolute Poverty in Urban South America. *Rev. Income Wealth*, March 1985, *31*(1), pp. 63–83.
[G: S. America]

Musgrove, Philip. Household Food Consumption in the Dominican Republic: Effects of Income, Price, and Family Size. *Econ. Develop. Cult. Change*, October 1985, *34*(1), pp. 83–101.
[G: Dominican Republic]

Myers, Dowell. Wives' Earnings and Rising Costs of Homeownership. *Soc. Sci. Quart.*, June 1985, *66*(2), pp. 319–29. [G: U.S.]

Nelson, Charles R. and Peck, Stephen C. The NERC Fan: A Retrospective Analysis of the NERC Summary Forecasts. *J. Bus. Econ. Statist.*, July 1985, *3*(3), pp. 179–87. [G: U.S.]

Ohsfeldt, Robert L. and Smith, Barton A. Estimating the Demand for Heterogeneous Goods. *Rev. Econ. Statist.*, February 1985, *67*(1), pp. 165–71.

Oliver, Richard L. and Bearden, William O. Crossover Effects in the Theory of Reasoned Action: A Moderating Influence Attempt. *J. Cons. Res.*, December 1985, *12*(3), pp. 324–40. [G: U.S.]

Ornstein, Stanley I. and Hanssens, Dominique M. Alcohol Control Laws and the Consumption of Distilled Spirits and Beer. *J. Cons. Res.*, September 1985, *12*(2), pp. 200–213.
[G: U.S.]

Ortmeyer, David L. and Fortune, Peter. An Application of the Life-Cycle Linear Expenditure System to the South Korean Household Sector, 1962–1976. *J. Devel. Econ.*, August 1985, *18*(2–3), pp. 361–79. [G: S. Korea]

Peck, Stephen C. and Weyant, John P. Electricity Growth in the Future. *Energy J.*, January 1985, *6*(1), pp. 23–43. [G: U.S.]

Pepper, M. P. G. Multivariate Box–Jenkins Analysis: A Case Study in UK Energy Demand Forecasting. *Energy Econ.*, July 1985, *7*(3), pp. 168–78. [G: U.K.]

Phillips, Richard A. and Silberman, Jonathan I. Forecasting Recreation Demand: An Application of the Travel Cost Model. *Rev. Reg. Stud.*, Winter 1985, *15*(1), pp. 20–25. [G: U.S.]

Pitt, Mark M. Equity, Externalities and Energy Subsidies: The Case of Kerosene in Indonesia. *J. Devel. Econ.*, April 1985, *17*(3), pp. 201–17. [G: Indonesia]

Pitt, Mark M. and Rosenzweig, Mark R. Health and Nutrient Consumption across and within Farm Households. *Rev. Econ. Statist.*, May 1985, *67*(2), pp. 212–23. [G: Indonesia]

Plourde, Andre and Ryan, David. On the Use of Double-Log Forms in Energy Demand Analysis. *Energy J.*, October 1985, *6*(4), pp. 105–13.

Pollard, Stephen K. and Graham, Douglas H. The Performance of the Food-producing Sector in Jamaica, 1962–1979: A Policy Analysis. *Econ. Develop. Cult. Change*, July 1985, *33*(4), pp. 731–54. [G: Jamaica]

Polzin, Paul K. The Specification of Price in Studies of Consumer Demand under Block Price Scheduling: Reply. *Land Econ.*, August 1985, *61*(3), pp. 330–31.

Prosser, Richard D. Demand Elasticities in OECD: Dynamical Aspects. *Energy Econ.*, January 1985, *7*(1), pp. 9–12. [G: OECD]

Quigley, John M. Housing Behavior and the Experimental Housing-Allowance Program: What Have We Learned? Comment. In *Hausman, J. A. and Wise, D. A., eds.*, 1985, pp. 75–86.

Quisumbing, Ma. Agnes R. Food Demand Parameters and Their Application to Nutrition Policy Simulation. *Philippine Rev. Econ. Bus.*, Sept./Dec. 1985, *22*(3/4), pp. 177–213.
[G: Philippines]

Radfar, Mehran. The Effect of Advertising on Total Consumption of Cigarettes in the U.K.: A Comment. *Europ. Econ. Rev.*, November 1985, *29*(2), pp. 225–31. [G: U.K.]

Ray, Ranjan. A Dynamic Analysis of Expenditure Patterns in Rural India. *J. Devel. Econ.*, December 1985, *19*(3), pp. 283–97. [G: India]

Regalado, Basilia M. Distributional Impacts of Selected Food Policies on Human Nutrition in the Philippines. *Philippine Econ. J.*, 1985, *24*(2–3), pp. 143–80. [G: Philippines]

Rosen, Harvey S. Housing Behavior and the Experimental Housing-Allowance Program: What Have We Learned? In *Hausman, J. A. and Wise, D. A., eds.*, 1985, pp. 55–75.
[G: U.S.]

Rossi, Nicola. Commodity Aggregation in Applied Demand Analysis: A Note. *Statistica*, July–Sept. 1985, *45*(3), pp. 421–26. [G: Italy]

Samples, Karl C. and Bishop, Richard C. Estimating the Value of Variations in Anglers' Success Rates: An Application of the Multiple-Site Travel Cost Method. *Marine Resource Econ.*, 1985, *2*(1), pp. 55–74. [G: U.S.]

Schefter, J. E. and David, E. L. Estimating Residential Water Demand under Multi-part Tariffs Using Aggregate Data. *Land Econ.*, August 1985, *61*(3), pp. 272–80. [G: U.S.]

Schipper, Lee and Ketoff, Andrea N. Residential Energy Use in the OECD. *Energy J.*, October 1985, *6*(4), pp. 65–85. [G: OECD]

Scott, Christopher D. The Decline of an Export Industry, or the Growth of Peruvian Sugar Consumption in the Long Run. *J. Devel. Stud.*, January 1985, *21*(2), pp. 253–81. [G: Peru]

Sebold, Frederick D. and Fox, Eric W. Realized Savings from Residential Conservation Activity. *Energy J.*, April 1985, *6*(2), pp. 73–88.
[G: U.S.]

Shin, Jeong-Shik. Perception of Price When Price Information Is Costly: Evidence from Residential Electricity Demand. *Rev. Econ. Statist.*, November 1985, *67*(4), pp. 591–98.
[G: U.S.]

Shore, Haim. Corrections [Summer Time and Electricity Conservation: The Israeli Case].

Energy J., January 1985, *6*(1), pp. 169–70. [G: Israel]

Singleton, Kenneth J. Testing Specifications of Economic Agents' Intertemporal Optimum Problems in the Presence of Alternative Models. *J. Econometrics*, Oct./Nov. 1985, *30*(1/2), pp. 391–413. [G: U.S.]

Sinha, Arun Kumar. On a Probabilistic Model of Purchasing Behavior. In *Brown, R. C., ed.*, 1985, pp. 225–29. [G: India]

Smallwood, David M. and Blaylock, James R. Analysis of Food Stamp Program Participation and Food Expenditures. *Western J. Agr. Econ.*, July 1985, *10*(1), pp. 41–54. [G: U.S.]

Smith, Christopher J. and Hanham, Robert Q. Regional Change and Problem Drinking in the United States, 1970–1978. *Reg. Stud.*, April 1985, *19*(2), pp. 149–62. [G: U.S.]

Stevens, T. H.; Adams, G. and Willis, C. The Specification of Price in Studies of Consumer Demand under Block Price Scheduling: Comment. *Land Econ.*, August 1985, *61*(3), pp. 327–29.

Sullivan, Dennis H. Simultaneous Determination of Church Contributions and Church Attendance. *Econ. Inquiry*, April 1985, *23*(2), pp. 309–20. [G: U.S.]

Svidén, Ove. Automobile Usage in a Future Information Society. In *Langdon, R. and Rothwell, R., eds.*, 1985, pp. 27–43. [G: Sweden]

Swamy, Gurushri and Binswanger, Hans P. Flexible Consumer Demand Functions and Linear Estimation: Reply. *Amer. J. Agr. Econ.*, February 1985, *67*(1), pp. 143. [G: India]

Szakolczai, György, et al. Using Classical Models to Analyze Demand to Develop a Retail Price Policy in Hungary. *Matekon*, Spring 1985, *21*(3), pp. 3–30. [G: Hungary]

Taylor, Lester D. The Residential Electricity Time-of-Use Pricing Experiments: What Have We Learned? Comment. In *Hausman, J. A. and Wise, D. A., eds.*, 1985, pp. 49–50. [G: U.S.]

Tremblay, Victor J. Strategic Groups and the Demand for Beer. *J. Ind. Econ.*, December 1985, *34*(2), pp. 183–98. [G: U.S.]

Uri, Noel D. and Hassanein, Saad A. Testing for Stability: Motor Gasoline Demand and Distillate Fuel Oil Demand. *Energy Econ.*, April 1985, *7*(2), pp. 87–92. [G: U.S.]

Wald, I.; Morawski, J. and Moskalewicz, J. Alcohol Policies: Poland. In *Grant, M., ed.*, 1985, pp. 109–13. [G: Poland]

Wang, Young-Doo; Tannian, Francis X. and Solano, Paul L. A Residential Energy Market Model: An Econometric Analysis. *J. Reg. Sci.*, May 1985, *25*(2), pp. 215–39. [G: U.S.]

Webbink, Douglas W. Comment: Empirical Studies of Media Competition. In *Noam, E. M., ed.*, 1985, pp. 168–73. [G: U.S.]

White, Peter R. Demand for Unlimited Use Transit Passes: A Comment. *J. Transp. Econ. Policy*, September 1985, *19*(3), pp. 305–07. [G: U.S.; U.K.]

Williams, Harold R. and Mount, Randall I. Theory and Empirical Foundation for Energy Pol-

icy Designed to Promote U.S. Motor Gasoline Conservation. *Amer. Econ.*, Spring 1985, *29*(1), pp. 60–66. [G: U.S.]

Williams, Martin. Estimating Urban Residential Demand for Water under Alternative Price Measures. *J. Urban Econ.*, September 1985, *18*(2), pp. 213–25. [G: U.S.]

Winer, Russell S. A Price Vector Model of Demand for Consumer Durables: Preliminary Developments. *Marketing Sci.*, Winter 1985, *4*(1), pp. 74–90. [G: U.S.]

Wirl, Franz and Infanger, Gerd. The Prospects of Energy Conservation: A Different Approach to the Fuel Demand for Space Heating. *Empirica*, 1985, *12*(2), pp. 227–45. [G: Austria]

Wohlgenant, Michael K. Flexible Consumer Demand Functions and Linear Estimation: Comment. *Amer. J. Agr. Econ.*, February 1985, *67*(1), pp. 141–42. [G: India]

Woods, Walter A.; Chéron, Emmanuel J. and Kim, Dong Man. Strategic Implications of Differences in Consumer Purposes for Purchasing in Three Global Markets. In *Kaynak, E., ed. (I)*, 1985, pp. 155–70. [G: Canada; S. Korea; U.S.]

Woodward, Donald. "Swords into Ploughshares": Recycling in Pre-industrial England. *Econ. Hist. Rev., 2nd Ser.*, May 1985, *38*(2), pp. 175–91. [G: U.K.]

Yang, Bong M. Do Gasoline Demand Elasticities Vary? Comment. *Land Econ.*, May 1985, *61*(2), pp. 198–200. [G: Selected Countries]

Yfantopoulos, J. N. Alcohol Policies: Greece. In *Grant, M., ed.*, 1985, pp. 92–109. [G: Greece]

Zaichkowsky, Judith Lynne. Measuring the Involvement Construct. *J. Cons. Res.*, December 1985, *12*(3), pp. 341–52. [G: U.S.]

9213 Consumer Protection

Agege, Charles O. Dumping of Dangerous American Products Overseas: Should Congress Sit and Watch? *J. World Trade Law*, July:Aug. 1985, *19*(4), pp. 403–10. [G: LDCs; U.S.]

Appleton, Lynn M. Explaining Laws' Making and Their Enforcement in the American States. *Soc. Sci. Quart.*, December 1985, *66*(4), pp. 839–53. [G: U.S.]

Boddewyn, Jean J. Global Perspectives on Advertising Control. In *Kaynak, E., ed. (I)*, 1985, pp. 37–51. [G: Global]

Chollet, Deborah J. Liability Rules and Health Care Costs. In *Baily, M. A. and Cikins, W. I., eds.*, 1985, pp. 22–27. [G: U.S.]

Claybrook, Joan and Bollier, David. The Hidden Benefits of Regulation: Disclosing the Auto Safety Payoff. *Yale J. Regul.*, Fall 1985, *3*(1), pp. 87–131. [G: U.S.]

Cohen, Mark A. and Rubin, Paul H. Private Enforcement of Public Policy. *Yale J. Regul.*, Fall 1985, *3*(1), pp. 167–93. [G: U.S.]

Cooper, Russell and Ross, Thomas W. Product Warranties and Double Moral Hazard. *Rand J. Econ.*, Spring 1985, *16*(1), pp. 103–13.

Farnsworth, E. Allan. Your Loss or My Gain?

The Dilemma of the Disgorgement Principle in Breach of Contract. *Yale Law J.*, May 1985, *94*(6), pp. 1339–93. [G: U.S.]

George, Edward I. and Wecker, William E. Estimating Damages in a Class Action Litigation. *J. Bus. Econ. Statist.*, April 1985, *3*(2), pp. 132–39.

Gieringer, Dale H. The Safety and Efficacy of New Drug Approval. *Cato J.*, Spring/Summer 1985, *5*(1), pp. 177–201. [G: U.S.]

Hall, Graham and Lloyd, Tony. The Usefulness of Hedonic Prices to the Consumers' Association. *Appl. Econ.*, April 1985, *17*(2), pp. 191–203. [G: U.K.]

Hurley, Rosalinde. Balancing Risks and Benefits: Discussion. In *Wells, N., ed.*, 1985, pp. 159–60.

Kaprelian, Mark A. Privity Revisited: Tort Recovery by a Commercial Buyer for a Defective Product's Self-Inflicted Damage. *Mich. Law Rev.*, December 1985, *84*(3), pp. 517–40. [G: U.S.]

Kochanowski, Paul S. and Young, Madelyn V. Deterrent Aspects of No-Fault Automobile Insurance: Some Empirical Findings. *J. Risk Ins.*, June 1985, *52*(2), pp. 269–88. [G: U.S.]

Kunreuther, Howard; Sanderson, Warren and Vetschera, Rudolf. A Behavioral Model of the Adoption of Protective Activities. *J. Econ. Behav. Organ.*, March 1985, *6*(1), pp. 1–15. [G: U.S.]

Lave, Charles A. Speeding, Coordination, and the 55 MPH Limit. *Amer. Econ. Rev.*, December 1985, *75*(5), pp. 1159–64. [G: U.S.]

Lloyd, P. J. The Economics of Regulation of Alcohol Distribution and Consumption in Victoria. *Australian Econ. Rev.*, 1st Quarter 1985, (69), pp. 16–29. [G: Australia]

Loeb, Peter D. The Efficacy and Cost Effectiveness of Motor Vehicle Inspection Using Cross-Sectional Data—An Econometric Analysis. *Southern Econ. J.*, October 1985, *52*(2), pp. 500–509. [G: U.S.]

MacLennan, Carol. A Wide Angle on Regulation: Comment. In *Noll, R. G., ed.*, 1985, pp. 160–71. [G: U.S.]

Maddox, John. The Public and Anti-science. In *Wells, N., ed.*, 1985, pp. 133–42.

Maddox, Jon R. Products Liability in Europe: Towards a Regime of Strict Liability. *J. World Trade Law*, Sept.:Oct. 1985, *19*(5), pp. 508–21. [G: EEC]

Main, Timothy. An Economic Evaluation of Child Restraints. *J. Transp. Econ. Policy*, January 1985, *19*(1), pp. 23–40. [G: New Zealand]

Mariner, Wendy K. The Potential Impact of Pharmaceutical and Vaccine Litigation. In *Baily, M. A. and Cikins, W. I., eds.*, 1985, pp. 43–68. [G: U.S.]

Nader, Laura and Nader, Claire. A Wide Angle on Regulation: An Anthropological Perspective. In *Noll, R. G., ed.*, 1985, pp. 141–60. [G: U.S.]

Partee, J. Charles. Statement to the U.S. House Subcommittee on Telecommunications, Consumer Protection, and Finance of the Committee on Energy and Commerce, April 2, 1985. *Fed. Res. Bull.*, June 1985, *71*(6), pp. 409–12. [G: U.S.]

Simon, Marilyn J.; Wolf, Robert G. and Perloff, Jeffrey M. Product Safety, Liability Rules and Retailer Bankruptcy. *Southern Econ. J.*, April 1985, *51*(4), pp. 1130–41.

Slovic, Paul; Fischhoff, Baruch and Lichtenstein, Sarah. Regulation of Risk: A Psychological Perspective. In *Noll, R. G., ed.*, 1985, pp. 241–78. [G: U.S.]

Smith, Dolores S. Revision of the Board's Equal Credit Regulation: An Overview. *Fed. Res. Bull.*, December 1985, *71*(12), pp. 913–23. [G: U.S.]

Sommers, Paul M. Drinking Age and the 55 MPH Speed Limit. *Atlantic Econ. J.*, March 1985, *13*(1), pp. 43–48. [G: U.S.]

Stegemann, Klaus. Anti-dumping Policy and the Consumer. *J. World Trade Law*, Sept.:Oct. 1985, *19*(5), pp. 466–84. [G: U.S.; Canada]

Taylor, David. The Role of the Consumer Movement, and Its Challenge to the British Pharmaceutical Industry. In *Wells, N., ed.*, 1985, pp. 120–32. [G: U.K.]

Viscusi, W. Kip. Consumer Behavior and the Safety Effects of Product Safety Regulation. *J. Law Econ.*, October 1985, *28*(3), pp. 527–53. [G: U.S.]

Wells, Nicholas. Balancing Risks and Benefits: Discussion. In *Wells, N., ed.*, 1985, pp. 161–65.

Wiener, Joshua Lyle. Are Warranties Accurate Signals of Product Reliability? *J. Cons. Res.*, September 1985, *12*(2), pp. 245–50. [G: U.S.]

Winett, Richard A. Regulation of Risk: Comment. In *Noll, R. G., ed.*, 1985, pp. 278–83. [G: U.S.]

Wood, Donna J. The Strategic Use of Public Policy: Business Support for the 1906 Food and Drug Act. *Bus. Hist. Rev.*, Autumn 1985, *59*(3), pp. 403–32. [G: U.S.]

930 Urban Economics

9300 General

Bogucka, Maria. The Towns of East-central Europe from the Fourteenth to the Seventeenth Century. In *Mączak, A.; Samsonowicz, H. and Burke, P., eds.*, 1985, pp. 97–108. [G: E. Europe]

Botero, Giovanni. Giovanni Botero on the Forces Governing Population Growth. *Population Devel. Rev.*, June 1985, *11*(2), pp. 335–40.

Cawson, Alan. Corporatism and Local Politics. In *Grant, W., ed.*, 1985, pp. 126–47. [G: U.K.]

Ginzberg, Eli. In Praise of Cities. In *Ginzberg, E.*, 1985, pp. 539–48. [G: U.S.]

Ginzberg, Eli. New York City: Next Turn of the Wheel. In *Ginzberg, E.*, 1985, pp. 561–68.

Ginzberg, Eli. New York: A View from the Seine. In *Ginzberg, E.*, 1985, pp. 549–59. [G: U.S.]

Goldberg, Michael A. American Real Estate and

Urban Economics: A Canadian Perspective. *Amer. Real Estate Urban Econ. Assoc. J.,* Spring 1985, *13*(1), pp. 1–14. **[G: Canada; U.S.]**

Gramlich, Edward M. and Ysander, Bengt-Christer. Control of Local Government: Introduction. In *Gramlich, E. M. and Ysander, B.-C., eds.,* 1985, pp. 9–25.

Long, John F. Migration and the Phases of Population Redistribution. *J. Devel. Econ.,* January–February 1985, *17*(1–2), pp. 29–42.

Mincer, Jacob. Migration and the Phases of Population Redistribution: Discussion. *J. Devel. Econ.,* January–February 1985, *17*(1–2), pp. 43–45.

931 Urban Economics and Public Policy

9310 Urban Economics and Public Policy

Adler, Moshe. Street Parking: The Case for Communal Property. *Logist. Transp. Rev.,* December 1985, *21*(4), pp. 375–87.

Ahern, Robert W. Labor–Management Structures in the Large City. In *Woodworth, W.; Meek, C. and Whyte, W. F., eds.,* 1985, pp. 161–78. **[G: U.S.]**

Alao, Nurudeen. Urban Unemployment Equilibrium in LDCs: A Perspective. *Reg. Stud.,* June 1985, *19*(3), pp. 185–92. **[G: LDCs]**

de Almeida Vasconcelos, Pedro. Le travail informel urbain: Une évaluation de la littérature. (With English summary.) *Can. J. Devel. Stud.,* 1985, *6*(1), pp. 87–124. **[G: Latin America]**

Alperovich, Gershon. Erratum [The Size Distribution of Cities: On the Empirical Validity of the Rank-Size Rule]. *J. Urban Econ.,* January 1985, *17*(1), pp. 125. **[G: Selected MDCs; Selected LDCs]**

Alperovich, Gershon. Urban Spatial Structure and Income: New Estimates. *J. Urban Econ.,* November 1985, *18*(3), pp. 278–90. **[G: Israel]**

Amundsen, Eirik S. Moving Costs and the Microeconomics of Intra-urban Mobility. *Reg. Sci. Urban Econ.,* November 1985, *15*(4), pp. 573–83.

Anas, Alex. The Combined Equilibrium of Travel Networks and Residential Location Markets. *Reg. Sci. Urban Econ.,* February 1985, *15*(1), pp. 1–21.

Anderson, Elijah. Race and Neighborhood Transition. In *Peterson, P. E., ed.,* 1985, pp. 99–127. **[G: U.S.]**

Anderson, John E. Estimating Generalized Urban Density Functions. *J. Urban Econ.,* July 1985, *18*(1), pp. 1–10. **[G: U.S.]**

Anderson, John E. The Changing Structure of a City: Temporal Changes in Cubic Spline Urban Density Patterns. *J. Reg. Sci.,* August 1985, *25*(3), pp. 413–35. **[G: U.S.]**

Andersson, Roland and Samartin, Avelino. An Extension of Mohring's Model for Land Rent Distribution. *J. Urban Econ.,* September 1985, *18*(2), pp. 143–60. **[G: Sweden]**

Arrow, Kenneth J. Criteria, Institutions, and Function in Urban Development Decisions. In *Arrow, K. J. (II),* 1985, pp. 63–69.

Arrow, Kenneth J. The Effect of the Price System and Market on Urban Economic Development. In *Arrow, K. J. (II),* 1985, pp. 56–62.

Asabere, Paul K. and Harvey, Barrie. Factors Influencing the Value of Urban Land: Evidence from Halifax-Dartmouth, Canada. *Amer. Real Estate Urban Econ. Assoc. J.,* Winter 1985, *13*(4), pp. 361–77. **[G: Canada]**

Asiama, Seth Opuni. The Rich Slum-Dweller: A Problem of Unequal Access. *Int. Lab. Rev.,* May-June 1985, *124*(3), pp. 353–62. **[G: LDCs; Ghana]**

Bahl, Roy. Fiscal Problems of Cities in the Northeast. In *Richardson, H. W. and Turek, J. H., eds.,* 1985, pp. 150–63. **[G: U.S.]**

Barnett, Colin J. An Application of the Hedonic Price Model to the Perth Residential Land Market. *Econ. Rec.,* March 1985, *61*(172), pp. 476–81. **[G: Australia]**

Batten, David F. Conflict, Inertia, and Adaptive Learning in Urban Systems Modelling. In *Hutchinson, B. G.; Nijkamp, P. and Batty, M., eds.,* 1985, pp. 87–114.

Beguin, Hubert. A Property of the Rank-Size Distribution and Its Use in an Urban Hierarchy Context. *J. Reg. Sci.,* August 1985, *25*(3), pp. 437–41.

Bennett, R. J. Central City–City Region Fiscal Disparities in Austria: Estimates for 1979. *Urban Stud.,* February 1985, *22*(1), pp. 69–81. **[G: Austria]**

Benson, Bruce L. Free Market Congestion Tolls: A Correction [Spatial Price Theory and an Efficient Congestion Toll Established by the Free Market]. *Econ. Inquiry,* April 1985, *23*(2), pp. 361–62.

Benson, Virginia O. The Rise of the Independent Sector in Urban Land Development. *Growth Change,* July 1985, *16*(3), pp. 25–39. **[G: U.S.]**

Bentham, C. G. Which Areas Have the Worst Urban Problems? *Urban Stud.,* April 1985, *22*(2), pp. 119–31. **[G: U.K.]**

Berliant, Marcus. Equilibrium Models with Land: A Criticism and an Alternative. *Reg. Sci. Urban Econ.,* June 1985, *15*(2), pp. 325–40.

Berry, Brian J. L. Islands of Renewal in Seas of Decay. In *Peterson, P. E., ed.,* 1985, pp. 69–96. **[G: U.S.]**

Bierens, Herman J. and Hoever, Roy. Population Forecasting at the City Level: An Econometric Approach. *Urban Stud.,* February 1985, *22*(1), pp. 83–90. **[G: U.S.]**

Blackley, Paul R. The Demand for Industrial Sites in a Metropolitan Area: Theory, Empirical Evidence, and Policy Implications. *J. Urban Econ.,* March 1985, *17*(2), pp. 247–61. **[G: U.S.]**

Botha, D. J. J. The Differential Impact of a Change in the Rating System. *S. Afr. J. Econ.,* September 1985, *53*(3), pp. 258–63. **[G: S. Africa]**

Bradbury, Katharine L. and Ladd, Helen F. Changes in the Revenue-raising Capacity of

U.S. Cities, 1970–1982. *New Eng. Econ. Rev.*, March/April 1985, pp. 20–37. [G: U.S.]

Brambilla, Francesco. Un'analisi del valore dei fabbricati residenziali verso una nuova teoria della localizzazione. (An Analysis of the Value of Residential Buildings. Towards a New Theory of Localization. With English summary.) *Giorn. Econ.*, July-Aug. 1985, *44*(7–8), pp. 375–87. [G: Italy]

Brewer, H. L. and Moomaw, Ronald L. A Note on Population Size, Industrial Diversification, and Regional Economic Instability. *Urban Stud.*, August 1985, *22*(4), pp. 349–54. [G: U.S.]

Bristow, R. Some Questions on Unitary Development Plans—A Plain Man's Guide? *Reg. Stud.*, June 1985, *19*(3), pp. 263–68. [G: U.K.]

Bubis, Edward and Ruble, Blair A. The Impact of World War II on Leningrad. In *Linz, S. J., ed.*, 1985, pp. 189–206. [G: U.S.S.R.]

Büttler, Hans-Jürg. A Combined Linear/Non-linear Programming Model of Employment, Transportation, and Housing in an Urban Economy. In *Hutchinson, B. G.; Nijkamp, P. and Batty, M., eds.*, 1985, pp. 32–49.

Cain, Louis P. William Dean's Theory of Urban Growth: Chicago's Commerce and Industry, 1854–1871. *J. Econ. Hist.*, June 1985, *45*(2), pp. 241–49. [G: U.S.]

Carlino, Gerald A. Declining City Productivity and the Growth of Rural Regions: A Test of Alternative Explanations. *J. Urban Econ.*, July 1985, *18*(1), pp. 11–27. [G: U.S.]

Chall, Daniel E. New York City's "Skills Mismatch." *Fed. Res. Bank New York Quart. Rev.*, Spring 1985, *10*(1), pp. 20–27. [G: U.S.]

Chape, A. Urban Poverty and Economic Decline: A Liverpool Perspective. *Reg. Stud.*, February 1985, *19*(1), pp. 63–65. [G: U.K.]

Clark, Terry Nichols. Fiscal Strain: How Different Are Snow Belt and Sun Belt Cities? In *Peterson, P. E., ed.*, 1985, pp. 253–80. [G: U.S.]

Clark, Terry Nichols. The Fiscal Austerity and Urban Innovation Project. In *Clark, T. N., ed.*, 1985, pp. 357–63. [G: U.S.]

Clarke, Giles T. R. Jakarta, Indonesia; Planning to Solve Urban Conflicts. In *Lea, J. P. and Courtney, J. M., eds.*, 1985, pp. 35–58. [G: Indonesia]

Clarke, Susan E. and Rich, Michael J. Making Money Work: The New Urban Policy Arena. In *Clark, T. N., ed.*, 1985, pp. 101–15. [G: U.S.]

Clarkson, L. A. An Economic History of Ulster 1820–1939: Population Change and Urbanisation, 1821–1911. In *Kennedy, L. and Ollerenshaw, P., eds.*, 1985, pp. 137–57. [G: U.K.]

Congdon, Peter and Shepherd, John. Small-Area Social Change in Greater London: A Regression Approach to Measurement. *J. Econ. Soc. Meas.*, April 1985, *13*(1), pp. 49–67. [G: U.K.]

Corden, W. Max and Findlay, Ronald F. Urban Unemployment, Intersectoral Capital Mobility and Development Policy. In *Corden, W. M.*, 1985, pp. 73–93.

Cory, Dennis C. and Willis, Mary B. Contagion Externalities and the Conversion of Low-Intensity Land Uses on the Urban Fringe. *Ann. Reg. Sci.*, July 1985, *19*(2), pp. 77–92. [G: U.S.]

Couclelis, Helen. Prior Structure and Spatial Interaction. In *Hutchinson, B. G.; Nijkamp, P. and Batty, M., eds.*, 1985, pp. 162–79.

Courtney, John M. and Lea, John P. Lessons in Resolving the Conflicts. In *Lea, J. P. and Courtney, J. M., eds.*, 1985, pp. 101–07. [G: Philippines; Indonesia; India]

Curtin, Philip D. Medical Knowledge and Urban Planning in Tropical Africa. *Amer. Hist. Rev.*, June 1985, *90*(3), pp. 594–613. [G: Tropical Africa]

Dasgupta, M.; Frost, M. and Spence, N. Interaction between Urban Form and Mode Choice for the Work Journey: Manchester/Sheffield 1971–1981. *Reg. Stud.*, August 1985, *19*(4), pp. 315–28. [G: U.K.]

DeSalvo, Joseph S. A Model of Urban Household Behavior with Leisure Choice. *J. Reg. Sci.*, May 1985, *25*(2), pp. 159–74.

Deutsch, Joseph; Hakim, Simon and Weinblatt, J. Errata [Interjurisdictional Criminal Mobility: A Theoretical Perspective]. *Urban Stud.*, August 1985, *22*(4), pp. 288.

Deutsch, Joseph; Hakim, Simon and Weinblatt, J. Errata [Interjurisdictional Criminal Mobility: A Theoretical Perspective]. *Urban Stud.*, December 1985, *22*(6), pp. 460.

Dilger, Robert Jay. Eliminating the Deductibility of State and Local Taxes: Impacts on States and Cities. *Public Budg. Finance*, Winter 1985, *5*(4), pp. 75–90. [G: U.S.]

Downs, Anthony. The Future of Industrial Cities. In *Peterson, P. E., ed.*, 1985, pp. 281–94. [G: U.S.]

Eberts, Paul R. Fiscal Austerity and Its Consequences in Local Governments. In *Clark, T. N., ed.*, 1985, pp. 365–86. [G: U.S.]

Eberts, Paul R. and Kelly, Janet M. How Mayors Get Things Done: Community Politics and Mayors' Initiatives. In *Clark, T. N., ed.*, 1985, pp. 39–70. [G: U.S.]

Eckart, Wolfgang. On the Land Assembly Problem. *J. Urban Econ.*, November 1985, *18*(3), pp. 364–78.

Edmonston, Barry; Goldberg, Michael A. and Mercer, John. Urban Form in Canada and the United States: An Examination of Urban Density Gradients. *Urban Stud.*, June 1985, *22*(3), pp. 209–17. [G: Canada; U.S.]

Elliott, Donald S., Jr.; Quinn, Michael A. and Mendelson, Robert E. Maintenance Behavior of Large-Scale Landlords and Theories of Neighborhood Succession. *Amer. Real Estate Urban Econ. Assoc. J.*, Winter 1985, *13*(4), pp. 424–45. [G: U.S.]

Emmanuel, Dimitris. Urban Land Prices and Housing Distribution: Monopolistic Competition and the Myth of the 'Law' of Differential Rent. *Urban Stud.*, December 1985, *22*(6), pp. 461–80.

Figueroa, Manuel. Rural Development and Urban Food Programming. *Cepal Rev.*, April 1985, (25), pp. 111–27. **[G: Latin America]**

Fischer, Manfred M. and Nijkamp, Peter. Categorical Data and Choice Analysis in a Spatial Context. In *Hutchinson, B. G.; Nijkamp, P. and Batty, M., eds.*, 1985, pp. 1–30.

Frey, William H. Mover Destination Selectivity and the Changing Suburbanization of Metropolitan Whites and Blacks. *Demography*, May 1985, 22(2), pp. 223–43. **[G: U.S.]**

Fujita, Masahisa. Existence and Uniqueness of Equilibrium and Optimal Land Use: Boundary Rent Curve Approach. *Reg. Sci. Urban Econ.*, June 1985, 15(2), pp. 295–324.

Fujita, Masahisa. Towards General Equilibrium Models of Urban Land Use. *Revue Écon.*, January 1985, 36(1), pp. 135–67.

Fuller, Theodore D.; Lightfoot, Paul and Kamnuansilpa, Peerasit. Toward Migration Management: A Field Experiment in Thailand. *Econ. Develop. Cult. Change*, April 1985, 33(3), pp. 601–21. **[G: Thailand]**

Garnick, Daniel H. Patterns of Growth in Metropolitan and Nonmetropolitan Areas: An Update. *Surv. Curr. Bus.*, May 1985, 65(5), pp. 33–38. **[G: U.S.]**

Ginsburgh, Victor; Papageorgiou, Yorgo and Thisse, Jacques-François. On Existence and Stability of Spatial Equilibria and Steady-States. *Reg. Sci. Urban Econ.*, June 1985, 15(2), pp. 149–58.

Ginzberg, Eli. Urban Priorities. In *Ginzberg, E.*, 1985, pp. 669–74. **[G: U.S.]**

Ginzberg, Eli and Brecher, Charles. The Japanese Presence. In *Ginzberg, E.*, 1985, pp. 581–97. **[G: U.S.]**

Glenn, Jane Matthews. Approaches to the Protection of Agricultural Land in Quebec and Ontario: Highways and Byways. *Can. Public Policy*, December 1985, 11(4), pp. 665–76. **[G: Canada]**

Goldberg, Kalman and Scott, Robert C. City Sales and Property Tax Restructuring: Household and Business Incidence Effects. *Public Budg. Finance*, Autumn 1985, 5(3), pp. 89–98. **[G: U.S.]**

Goodman, Allen C. A Note on Neighborhood Size and the Measurement of Segregation Indices. *J. Reg. Sci.*, August 1985, 25(3), pp. 471–76. **[G: U.S.]**

Grieco, M. S. Corby: New Town Planning and Imbalanced Development. *Reg. Stud.*, February 1985, 19(1), pp. 9–18. **[G: U.K.]**

Gurr, Ted Robert and King, Desmond S. The Post-industrial City in Transition from Private to Public. In *Lane, J.-E., ed.*, 1985, pp. 271–93.

Hamer, Andrew. Urbanization Patterns in the Third World. *Finance Develop.*, March 1985, 22(1), pp. 39–42. **[G: LDCs]**

Harris, Britton. Urban Simulation Models in Regional Science. *J. Reg. Sci.*, November 1985, 25(4), pp. 545–67.

Hassan, J. A. The Growth and Impact of the British Water Industry in the Nineteenth Century. *Econ. Hist. Rev., 2nd Ser.*, November 1985, 38(4), pp. 531–47. **[G: U.K.]**

Hayes, Kathy. Congestion Measures for Local Public Goods in Metropolitan and Nonmetropolitan Cities. *Growth Change*, October 1985, 16(4), pp. 1–9. **[G: U.S.]**

Henderson, J. Vernon. Population Composition of Cities: Restructuring the Tiebout Model. *J. Public Econ.*, July 1985, 27(2), pp. 131–56. **[G: U.S.]**

Henward, Howard B., Jr. Metro Manila, Philippines: Conflicts and Illusions in Planning Urban Development. In *Lea, J. P. and Courtney, J. M., eds.*, 1985, pp. 19–33. **[G: Philippines]**

Hirsch, Werner Z. and Rufolo, Anthony M. Economic Effects of Residence Laws on Municipal Police. *J. Urban Econ.*, May 1985, 17(3), pp. 335–48. **[G: U.S.]**

Hogan, Dennis P. and Kertzer, David I. Migration Patterns during Italian Urbanization, 1865–1921. *Demography*, August 1985, 22(3), pp. 309–25. **[G: Italy]**

Jacob, Herbert. Policy Responses to Crime. In *Peterson, P. E., ed.*, 1985, pp. 225–52. **[G: U.S.]**

James, Franklin J. Economic Impacts of Private Reinvestment in Older Regional Shopping Centers. *Growth Change*, July 1985, 16(3), pp. 11–24. **[G: U.S.]**

Kannappan, Subbiah. Urban Employment and the Labor Market in Developing Nations. *Econ. Develop. Cult. Change*, July 1985, 33(4), pp. 699–730. **[G: LDCs]**

Kasarda, John D. Urban Change and Minority Opportunities. In *Peterson, P. E., ed.*, 1985, pp. 33–67. **[G: U.S.]**

King, Roger. Corporatism and the Local Economy. In *Grant, W., ed.*, 1985, pp. 202–28. **[G: U.K.]**

King, Russell; Strachan, Alan and Mortimer, Jill. The Urban Dimension of European Return Migration: The Case of Bari, Southern Italy. *Urban Stud.*, June 1985, 22(3), pp. 219–35. **[G: Italy]**

Kipnis, Baruch A. Graph Analysis of Metropolitan Residential Mobility: Methodology and Theoretical Implications. *Urban Stud.*, April 1985, 22(2), pp. 179–87. **[G: Israel]**

Kirlin, John J. Toward a Differentiated Theory of Federalism: Education and Housing Policy in the 1980s: Comment. In *Clark, T. N., ed.*, 1985, pp. 349–52. **[G: U.S.]**

Kleiner, Morris M. Metropolitan Area Labour Market Changes: Determinants and Comparisons by Industry. *Reg. Stud.*, April 1985, 19(2), pp. 131–38. **[G: U.S.]**

Knaap, Gerrit J. The Price Effects of Urban Growth Boundaries in Metropolitan Portland, Oregon. *Land Econ.*, February 1985, 61(1), pp. 26–35. **[G: U.S.]**

Konukiewitz, Manfred and Wollmann, Hellmut. Urban Innovation: A Response to Deficiencies of the Intervention and Welfare State? In *Clark, T. N., ed.*, 1985, pp. 327–39. **[G: W. Germany]**

Krakover, Shaul. Spatio-Temporal Structure of Population Growth in Urban Regions: The Cases of Tel-Aviv and Haifa, Israel. *Urban Stud.*, August 1985, *22*(4), pp. 317–28. [G: Israel]

Lakshmanan, A. and Rotner, E. Madras, India: Low-cost Approaches to Managing Development. In *Lea, J. P. and Courtney, J. M., eds.*, 1985, pp. 81–93. [G: India]

Lea, John P. and Courtney, John M. Conflict/Resolution and the Asian City: An Overview. In *Lea, J. P. and Courtney, J. M., eds.*, 1985, pp. 3–15. [G: Asia]

Leach, S. The Monitoring and Evaluation of Inner City Policy. *Reg. Stud.*, February 1985, *19*(1), pp. 59–63. [G: U.K.]

Lee, Barrett A. Racially Mixed Neighborhoods during the 1970s: Change or Stability? *Soc. Sci. Quart.*, June 1985, *66*(2), pp. 346–64. [G: U.S.]

Lee, Barrett A.; Spain, Daphne and Umberson, Debra J. Neighborhood Revitalization and Racial Change: The Case of Washington, D.C. *Demography*, November 1985, *22*(4), pp. 581–602. [G: U.S.]

Lee, Kyu Sik. Decentralization Trends of Employment Location and Spatial Policies in LDC Cities. *Urban Stud.*, April 1985, *22*(2), pp. 151–62. [G: Colombia]

Leonardi, Giorgio. A Stochastic Multi-stage Mobility Choice Model. In *Hutchinson, B. G.; Nijkamp, P. and Batty, M., eds.*, 1985, pp. 132–47.

Lerman, Steven R. Random Utility Models of Spatial Choice. In *Hutchinson, B. G.; Nijkamp, P. and Batty, M., eds.*, 1985, pp. 200–217.

Lesourne, Jacques. Les infrastructures de transport et la localisation des agents économiques: quelques évidences. (Transportation Infrastructures and Agents' Location: An Analysis of a Few Simple Facts. With English summary.) *Revue Écon.*, January 1985, *36*(1), pp. 169–214.

van Lierop, Wal and Nijkamp, Peter. Choice of Model for Spatial Choices: A Methodological Framework. *Indian J. Quant. Econ.*, 1985, *1*(2), pp. 43–87.

Lindley, P. D. The Merseyside Task Force. *Reg. Stud.*, February 1985, *19*(1), pp. 69–74. [G: U.K.]

Listgengurt, F. and Portianskii, I. The Large City under Conditions of Transition to an Intensive Economy. *Prob. Econ.*, November 1985, *28*(7), pp. 84–98. [G: U.S.S.R.]

Liu, Ben-chieh. Mathis and Zech's 'Empirical Test' of Land Value and Taxation: A Critique of a Commendable but Unsuccessful Effort to Measure the Effects of a Basic Levy. *Amer. J. Econ. Soc.*, April 1985, *44*(2), pp. 137–43. [G: U.S.]

Macauley, Molly K. Estimation and Recent Behavior of Urban Population and Employment Density Gradients. *J. Urban Econ.*, September 1985, *18*(2), pp. 251–60. [G: U.S.]

Madden, Janice Fanning. Urban Wage Gradients: Empirical Evidence. *J. Urban Econ.*, November 1985, *18*(3), pp. 291–301. [G: U.S.]

Maeda, Hiroshi and Murakami, Shuta. Population's Urban Environment Evaluation Model and Its Application. *J. Risk Ins.*, June 1985, *52*(2), pp. 273–90. [G: Japan]

Mark, Jonathan H. and Goldberg, Michael A. Revisiting Neighbourhood Change from a Canadian Perspective: Some Supporting Evidence from Vancouver. *Ann. Reg. Sci.*, July 1985, *19*(2), pp. 29–46. [G: Canada]

Mathis, Edward J. and Zech, Charles E. It Raises Interesting Questions, But Its Logic Is Not Compelling: A Reply [The Economic Effects of Land Value Taxation: An Empirical Test]. *Amer. J. Econ. Soc.*, July 1985, *44*(3), pp. 351–53. [G: U.S.]

McDonald, John F. The Intensity of Land Use in Urban Employment Sectors: Chicago 1956–1970. *J. Urban Econ.*, November 1985, *18*(3), pp. 261–77. [G: U.S.]

McGuire, Therese J. Are Local Property Taxes Important in the Intrametropolitan Location Decisions of Firms? An Empirical Analysis of the Minneapolis–St. Paul Metropolitan Area. *J. Urban Econ.*, September 1985, *18*(2), pp. 226–34. [G: U.S.]

Meek, Christopher. Labor–Management Committee Outcomes: The Jamestown Case. In *Woodworth, W.; Meek, C. and Whyte, W. F., eds.*, 1985, pp. 141–59. [G: U.S.]

Meek, Christopher and Woodworth, Warner. Worker–Community Collaboration and Ownership. In *Woodworth, W.; Meek, C. and Whyte, W. F., eds.*, 1985, pp. 195–220. [G: U.S.]

Menezes, Braz O. Calcutta, India: Conflict or Consistency? In *Lea, J. P. and Courtney, J. M., eds.*, 1985, pp. 61–78. [G: India]

Mills, David E. Indivisibilities and Development Timing: The Shopping-Center Problem. *Reg. Sci. Urban Econ.*, February 1985, *15*(1), pp. 23–40.

Mills, Edwin S. Open Housing Laws as Stimulus to Central City Employment. *J. Urban Econ.*, March 1985, *17*(2), pp. 184–88. [G: U.S.]

Mirucki, Jean. City Rank–Size Hypothesis and the Soviet Urban System: 1897–1979. *Atlantic Econ. J.*, July 1985, *13*(2), pp. 90. [G: U.S.S.R.]

Moberg, David. Problems of Industrial Plant Shutdowns. In *Woodworth, W.; Meek, C. and Whyte, W. F., eds.*, 1985, pp. 28–48. [G: U.S.]

Mohan, Rakesh. Urbanization in India's Future. *Population Devel. Rev.*, December 1985, *11*(4), pp. 619–45. [G: India]

Moomaw, Ronald L. Firm Location and City Size: Reduced Productivity Advantages as a Factor in the Decline of Manufacturing in Urban Areas. *J. Urban Econ.*, January 1985, *17*(1), pp. 73–89. [G: U.S.]

Muth, Richard F. Models of Land-Use, Housing, and Rent: An Evaluation. *J. Reg. Sci.*, November 1985, *25*(4), pp. 593–606. [G: U.S.]

Nagel, Stuart S. Optimally Allocating Federal

Money to Cities. *Public Budg. Finance,* Winter 1985, *5*(4), pp. 39–50. [G: U.S.]

Nakamura, Ryohei. Agglomeration Economies in Urban Manufacturing Industries: A Case of Japanese Cities. *J. Urban Econ.,* January 1985, *17*(1), pp. 108–24. [G: Japan]

Nath, V. Urbanization. In *Mongia, J. N., ed.,* 1985, pp. 585–615. [G: India]

Nathan, Richard P. Reagan and the Cities: How to Meet the Challenge. *Challenge,* Sept./Oct. 1985, *28*(4), pp. 4–8. [G: U.S.]

Nelson, Arthur C. A Unifying View of Greenbelt Influences on Regional Land Values and Implications for Regional Planning Policy. *Growth Change,* April 1985, *16*(2), pp. 43–48.

Nelson, Arthur C. Demand, Segmentation, and Timing Effects of an Urban Containment Program on Urban Fringe Land Values. *Urban Stud.,* October 1985, *22*(5), pp. 439–43. [G: U.S.]

Norton, A. The Functions of Metropolitan Government in Seven Western Democracies. *Reg. Stud.,* June 1985, *19*(3), pp. 257–62. [G: W. Europe; Canada]

Oates, Wallace E. The Environment and the Economy: Environmental Policy at the Crossroads. In *Quigley, J. M. and Rubinfeld, D. L., eds.,* 1985, pp. 311–45. [G: U.S.]

Orfield, Gary. Ghettoization and Its Alternatives. In *Peterson, P. E., ed.,* 1985, pp. 161–93. [G: U.S.]

Othick, John. The Economic History of Ulster: A Perspective. In *Kennedy, L. and Ollerenshaw, P., eds.,* 1985, pp. 224–40. [G: U.K.]

de Palma, André and Lefèvre, Claude. Residential Change and Economic Choice Behavior. *Reg. Sci. Urban Econ.,* August 1985, *15*(3), pp. 421–34.

Papageorgiou, Yorgo and Thisse, Jacques-François. Agglomeration as Spatial Interdependence between Firms and Households. *J. Econ. Theory,* October 1985, *37*(1), pp. 19–31.

Parkinson, M. H. and Wilks, S. R. M. Testing Partnership to Destruction in Liverpool. *Reg. Stud.,* February 1985, *19*(1), pp. 65–69. [G: U.K.]

Parr, John B. A Note on the Size Distribution of Cities over Time. *J. Urban Econ.,* September 1985, *18*(2), pp. 199–212. [G: Selected Countries]

Parr, John B. A Population-Density Approach to Regional Spatial Structure. *Urban Stud.,* August 1985, *22*(4), pp. 289–303. [G: U.S.; U.K.]

Pasha, Hafiz A. Welfare Consequences of Building Height Controls. *Pakistan J. Appl. Econ.,* Winter 1985, *4*(2), pp. 69–92. [G: Saudi Arabia]

Peterson, George E. Pricing and Privatization of Public Services. In *Gramlich, E. M. and Ysander, B.-C., eds.,* 1985, pp. 137–72. [G: U.S.]

Peterson, Paul E. The New Urban Reality: Introduction: Technology, Race, and Urban Policy. In *Peterson, P. E., ed.,* 1985, pp. 1–29. [G: U.S.]

Peterson, Paul E. and Wong, Kenneth K. Toward a Differentiated Theory of Federalism: Education and Housing Policy in the 1980s. In *Clark, T. N., ed.,* 1985, pp. 301–24. [G: U.S.]

Pines, David. Profit Maximizing Developers and the Optimal Provision of Local Public Good in a Closed System of a Few Cities. *Revue Écon.,* January 1985, *36*(1), pp. 45–62.

Pines, David and Sadka, Efraim. Zoning, First-Best, Second-Best, and Third-Best Criteria for Allocating Land for Roads. *J. Urban Econ.,* March 1985, *17*(2), pp. 167–83.

Platt, D. C. M. The Financing of City Expansion: Buenos Aires and Montreal Compared, 1880–1914. In *Platt, D. C. M. and di Tella, G., eds.,* 1985, pp. 139–48. [G: Argentina; Canada]

Ratcliffe, Barrie M. The Business Elite and the Development of Paris: Intervention in Ports and Entrepôts, 1814–1834. *J. Europ. Econ. Hist.,* Spring 1985, *14*(1), pp. 95–142. [G: France]

Reid, Clifford E. The Effect of Residential Location on the Wages of Black Women and White Women. *J. Urban Econ.,* November 1985, *18*(3), pp. 350–63. [G: U.S.]

Rothenberg, Jerome. Regional Issues: Commentary. In *Quigley, J. M. and Rubinfeld, D. L., eds.,* 1985, pp. 373–77. [G: U.S.]

Roy, John R. and Lesse, Paul F. Information Flows and Decision-Making in Urban Models. In *Hutchinson, B. G.; Nijkamp, P. and Batty, M., eds.,* 1985, pp. 67–86.

Santerre, Rexford E. Spatial Differences in the Demands for Local Public Goods. *Land Econ.,* May 1985, *61*(2), pp. 119–28. [G: U.S.]

Saunders, Peter. Corporatism and Urban Service Provision. In *Grant, W., ed.,* 1985, pp. 148–73. [G: Australia; U.K.]

Savitch, H. V. Boom and Bust in the New York Region: Implications for Government Policy. In *Richardson, H. W. and Turek, J. H., eds.,* 1985, pp. 164–85. [G: U.S.]

Schweizer, Urs. Theory of City System Structure. *Reg. Sci. Urban Econ.,* June 1985, *15*(2), pp. 159–80.

Scott, Earl P. Lusaka's Informal Sector in National Economic Development. *J. Devel. Areas,* October 1985, *20*(1), pp. 71–99. [G: Zambia]

Segedinov, A. Development of the Urban Infrastructure. *Prob. Econ.,* August 1985, *28*(4), pp. 37–48.

Seley, John E. and Wolpert, Julian. The Savings/Harm Tableau for Social Impact Assessment of Retrenchment Policies. *Econ. Geogr.,* April 1985, *61*(2), pp. 158–71.

Sheets, Robert G.; Smith, Russell L. and Voytek, Kenneth P. Corporate Disinvestment and Metropolitan Manufacturing Job Loss. *Soc. Sci. Quart.,* March 1985, *66*(1), pp. 218–26. [G: U.S.]

Shefer, Daniel and Primo, Niki. The Determinants of Household Migration into and out of Distressed Neighborhoods. *Urban Stud.,* August 1985, *22*(4), pp. 339–47. [G: Israel]

Shieh, Yeung-Nan. A Note on Lee's Model of

Intraurban Employment Location. *J. Urban Econ.*, September 1985, *18*(2), pp. 196–98.

Sidorova, M. Reducing Differences in the Living Standards of the Urban and Rural Population. *Prob. Econ.*, September 1985, *28*(5), pp. 32–47. [G: U.S.S.R.]

Solomon, D. The Site Value Tax: An Evaluation. *S. Afr. J. Econ.*, September 1985, *53*(3), pp. 248–57. [G: S. Africa]

Southwick, Lawrence, Jr. and Butler, Richard J. Fire Department Demand and Supply in Large Cities. *Appl. Econ.*, December 1985, *17*(6), pp. 1043–64. [G: U.S.]

Stokes, Charles J. Do Urban Tax Rates Converge? They Do in Cities Alike in Population, Settlement Density and Dependence on Non-property Tax Revenues. *Amer. J. Econ. Soc.*, January 1985, *44*(1), pp. 29–38. [G: U.S.]

Suarez-Villa, Luis. Urban Growth and Manufacturing Change in the United States–Mexico Borderlands: A Conceptual Framework and an Empirical Analysis. *Ann. Reg. Sci.*, November 1985, *19*(3), pp. 54–108. [G: U.S.; Mexico]

Sullivan, Arthur M. The General-Equilibrium Effects of the Residential Property Tax: Incidence and Excess Burden. *J. Urban Econ.*, September 1985, *18*(2), pp. 235–50.

Sullivan, Arthur M. The Pricing of Urban Services and the Spatial Distribution of Residence. *Land Econ.*, February 1985, *61*(1), pp. 17–25.

Sullivan, Timothy J. Regional Issues: Commentary. In *Quigley, J. M. and Rubinfeld, D. L., eds.*, 1985, pp. 369–72. [G: U.S.]

Titman, Sheridan. Urban Land Prices under Uncertainty. *Amer. Econ. Rev.*, June 1985, *75*(3), pp. 505–14.

Tsuneki, Atsushi. On the Neutrality of Local Public Bond in a Spatial Economy. *Econ. Stud. Quart.*, April 1985, *36*(1), pp. 46–52.

Vining, Daniel R. The Growth of Core Urban Regions in Developing Countries. *Population Devel. Rev.*, September 1985, *11*(3), pp. 495–514. [G: LDCs; MDCs]

Wallman, Sandra. Structures of Informality: Variation in Local Style and the Scope for Unofficial Economic Organisation in London. In *Roberts, B.; Finnegan, R. and Gallie, D., eds.*, 1985, pp. 184–97. [G: U.K.]

Ward, Peter and Melligan, Stephen. Urban Renovation and the Impact upon Low Income Families in Mexico City. *Urban Stud.*, June 1985, *22*(3), pp. 199–207. [G: Mexico]

Weber, James S. and Sen, Ashish K. On the Sensitivity of Maximum Likelihood Estimates of Gravity Model Parameters. In *Hutchinson, B. G.; Nijkamp, P. and Batty, M., eds.*, 1985, pp. 148–61.

Wheeler, James O. and Brown, Catherine L. The Metropolitan Corporate Hierarchy in the U.S. South, 1960–1980. *Econ. Geogr.*, January 1985, *61*(1), pp. 66–78. [G: U.S.]

Wildasin, David E. Income Taxes and Urban Spatial Structure. *J. Urban Econ.*, November 1985, *18*(3), pp. 313–33.

Wilder, Margaret G. Site and Situation Determinants of Land Use Change: An Empirical Ex-

ample. *Econ. Geogr.*, October 1985, *61*(4), pp. 332–44. [G: U.S.]

Williams, Martin. Estimating Urban Residential Demand for Water under Alternative Price Measures. *J. Urban Econ.*, September 1985, *18*(2), pp. 213–25. [G: U.S.]

Williams, Oliver P. Governmental Intervention into Local Economies under Market Conditions: The Case of Urban Renewal. In *Lane, J.-E., ed.*, 1985, pp. 142–57.

Willis, K. G. Estimating the Benefits of Job Creation from Local Investment Subsidies. *Urban Stud.*, April 1985, *22*(2), pp. 163–77. [G: U.K.]

Wilson, John D. Optimal Property Taxation in the Presence of Interregional Capital Mobility. *J. Urban Econ.*, July 1985, *18*(1), pp. 73–89.

Wilson, William Julius. The Urban Underclass in Advanced Industrial Society. In *Peterson, P. E., ed.*, 1985, pp. 129–60. [G: U.S.]

Wiltshaw, Desmond G. The Supply of Land. *Urban Stud.*, February 1985, *22*(1), pp. 49–56.

Wolkoff, Michael J. Chasing a Dream: The Use of Tax Abatements to Spur Urban Economic Development. *Urban Stud.*, August 1985, *22*(4), pp. 305–15. [G: U.S.]

Woodworth, Warner; Meek, Christopher and Whyte, William Foote. Theory and Practice of Community Economic Reindustrialization. In *Woodworth, W.; Meek, C. and Whyte, W. F., eds.*, 1985, pp. 297–304. [G: U.S.]

Young, William. The Application of an Elimination-by-Aspects Model to Urban Location Decisions. In *Hutchinson, B. G.; Nijkamp, P. and Batty, M., eds.*, 1985, pp. 218–34. [G: Australia]

Zorn, Peter M. Capitalization, Population Movement, and the Local Public Sector: A Probabilistic Analysis. *J. Urban Econ.*, March 1985, *17*(2), pp. 189–207. [G: U.S.]

932 Housing Economics

9320 Housing Economics (including nonurban housing)

Abelson, Peter W. House and Land Prices in Sydney: 1925 to 1970. *Urban Stud.*, December 1985, *22*(6), pp. 521–34. [G: Australia]

Abelson, Peter W. and Markandya, A. The Interpretation of Capitalized Hedonic Prices in a Dynamic Environment. *J. Environ. Econ. Manage.*, September 1985, *12*(3), pp. 195–206.

Agarwal, Vinod B. and Philips, Richard A. The Effects of Assumption Financing across Housing Price Categories. *Amer. Real Estate Urban Econ. Assoc. J.*, Spring 1985, *13*(1), pp. 48–57. [G: U.S.]

Ahmad, Nuzhat. Biases in Tax Assessment of Residential Properties in Karachi. *Pakistan J. Appl. Econ.*, Winter 1985, *4*(2), pp. 53–67. [G: Pakistan]

Alm, James; Follain, James R. and Beeman, Mary Anne. Tax Expenditures and Other Programs to Stimulate Housing: Do We Need More? *J. Urban Econ.*, September 1985, *18*(2), pp. 180–95. [G: U.S.]

Alperovich, Gershon. Urban Spatial Structure and Income: New Estimates. *J. Urban Econ.*, November 1985, *18*(3), pp. 278–90. [G: Israel]

Amundsen, Eirik S. Moving Costs and the Microeconomics of Intra-urban Mobility. *Reg. Sci. Urban Econ.*, November 1985, *15*(4), pp. 573–83.

Anas, Alex. Modeling the Dynamic Evolution of Land Use in Response to Transportation Improvement Policies. In *Jansen, G. R. M.; Nijkamp, P. and Ruijgrok, C. J., eds.,* 1985, pp. 227–36. [G: U.S.]

Anderson, John E. On Testing the Convexity of Hedonic Price Functions. *J. Urban Econ.*, November 1985, *18*(3), pp. 334–37.

Andrikopoulos, Andreas A. and Brox, James A. Predicting Intra-Urban Residential Location Preferences: An Application of the Dynamic Generalized Linear Expenditure System. *Urban Stud.*, August 1985, *22*(4), pp. 329–37. [G: Canada]

Arellano, José-Pablo. Meeting Basic Needs: The Trade-off between the Quality and Coverage of the Programs. *J. Devel. Econ.*, May–June 1985, *18*(1), pp. 87–99. [G: Chile]

Asabere, Paul K. and Colwell, Peter F. The Relative Lot Size Hypothesis: An Empirical Note. *Urban Stud.*, August 1985, *22*(4), pp. 355–57. [G: U.S.]

Asiama, Seth Opuni. The Rich Slum-Dweller: A Problem of Unequal Access. *Int. Lab. Rev.*, May-June 1985, *124*(3), pp. 353–62. [G: LDCs; Ghana]

Bailey, Stephen J. The Relationship between Cities' Housing Rents and Block Grant. *Urban Stud.*, June 1985, *22*(3), pp. 237–48. [G: U.K.]

Bajic, Vladimir. Housing-Market Segmentation and Demand for Housing Attributes: Some Empirical Findings. *Amer. Real Estate Urban Econ. Assoc. J.*, Spring 1985, *13*(1), pp. 58–75. [G: Canada]

Behring, Karin and Goldrian, Georg. The IFO Housing Market Model. In *Stahl, K., ed.,* 1985, pp. 119–43. [G: W. Germany]

Bender, Bruce and Hwang, Hae-shin. Hedonic Housing Price Indices and Secondary Employment Centers. *J. Urban Econ.*, January 1985, *17*(1), pp. 90–107. [G: U.S.]

Berry, Brian J. L. Islands of Renewal in Seas of Decay. In *Peterson, P. E., ed.,* 1985, pp. 69–96. [G: U.S.]

Brambilla, Francesco. Un'analisi del valore dei fabbricati residenziali verso una nuova teoria della localizzazione. (An Analysis of the Value of Residential Buildings. Towards a New Theory of Localization. With English summary.) *Giorn. Econ.*, July-Aug. 1985, *44*(7–8), pp. 375–87. [G: Italy]

Brookshire, David S., et al. A Test of the Expected Utility Model: Evidence from Earthquake Risks. *J. Polit. Econ.*, April 1985, *93*(2), pp. 369–89. [G: U.S.]

Brown, Barbara. Location and Housing Demand. *J. Urban Econ.*, January 1985, *17*(1), pp. 30–41.

Brownstone, David; Englund, Peter and Persson, Mats. Effects of the Swedish 1983–85 Tax Reform on the Demand for Owner-occupied Housing: A Microsimulation Approach. *Scand. J. Econ.*, 1985, *87*(4), pp. 625–46. [G: Sweden]

Burnell, James D. Industrial Land Use, Externalities, and Residential Location. *Urban Stud.*, October 1985, *22*(5), pp. 399–408.

Cassel, Eric and Mendelsohn, Robert. The Choice of Functional Forms for Hedonic Price Equations: Comment. *J. Urban Econ.*, September 1985, *18*(2), pp. 135–42. [G: U.S.]

Chall, Daniel E. Housing Reform in New Jersey: The *Mount Laurel* Decision. *Fed. Res. Bank New York Quart. Rev.*, Winter 1985-86, *10*(4), pp. 19–27. [G: U.S.]

Chun, Dong Hoon and Linneman, Peter. An Empirical Analysis of the Determinants of Intrajurisdictional Property Tax Payment Inequities. *J. Urban Econ.*, July 1985, *18*(1), pp. 90–102. [G: U.S.]

Ciriacy-Wantrup, S. V. The "New" Competition for Land and Some Implications for Public Policy. In *Ciriacy-Wantrup, S. V.,* 1985, pp. 247–59. [G: U.S.]

Dale-Johnson, David, et al. Valuation and Efficiency in the Market for Creatively Financed Houses. *Amer. Real Estate Urban Econ. Assoc. J.*, Winter 1985, *13*(4), pp. 388–403. [G: U.S.]

Dániel, Zsuzsa. The Effect of Housing Allocation on Social Inequality in Hungary. *J. Compar. Econ.*, December 1985, *9*(4), pp. 391–409. [G: Hungary]

DeBoer, Larry. Resident Age and Housing Search: Evidence from Hedonic Residuals. *Urban Stud.*, October 1985, *22*(5), pp. 445–51. [G: U.S.]

DeBorger, B. L. Benefits and Consumption Effects of Public Housing Programs in Belgium: Some Aggregate Results. *Urban Stud.*, October 1985, *22*(5), pp. 409–19. [G: Belgium]

Denton, Frank T.; Robb, A. Leslie and Spencer, Byron G. Shelter Allowances in a General Equilibrium Setting: A Model and Some Simulations. *J. Urban Econ.*, July 1985, *18*(1), pp. 47–72. [G: Canada]

DeSalvo, Joseph S. A Model of Urban Household Behavior with Leisure Choice. *J. Reg. Sci.*, May 1985, *25*(2), pp. 159–74.

Diamond, Douglas B., Jr. and Smith, Barton A. Simultaneity in the Market for Housing Characteristics. *J. Urban Econ.*, May 1985, *17*(3), pp. 280–92.

Doling, John; Karn, Valerie and Stafford, Bruce. How Far Can Privatization Go? Owner-Occupation and Mortgage Default. *Nat. Westminster Bank Quart. Rev.*, August 1985, pp. 42–52. [G: U.K.]

Doti, James and Adibi, Essie. A Residential Building Investment Model at the Local Level. *Quart. J. Bus. Econ.*, Spring 1985, *24*(2), pp. 88–103. [G: U.S.]

849

Dubin, Robin A. Transportation Costs and the Residential Location Decision: A New Approach. *J. Urban Econ.*, January 1985, *17*(1), pp. 58–72.

Durning, Dan and Quigley, John M. On the Distributional Implications of Mortgage Revenue Bonds and Creative Finance. *Nat. Tax J.*, December 1985, *38*(4), pp. 513–23.   [G: U.S.]

Dynarski, Mark R. Housing Demand and Disequilibrium. *J. Urban Econ.*, January 1985, *17*(1), pp. 42–57.   [G: U.S.]

Dynarski, Mark R. and Sheffrin, Steven M. Housing Purchases and Transitory Income: A Study with Panel Data. *Rev. Econ. Statist.*, May 1985, *67*(2), pp. 195–204.   [G: U.S.]

Eckart, Wolfgang. On the Land Assembly Problem. *J. Urban Econ.*, November 1985, *18*(3), pp. 364–78.

Edmonds, Radcliffe G., Jr. Some Evidence on the Intertemporal Stability of Hedonic Price Functions. *Land Econ.*, November 1985, *61*(4), pp. 445–51.   [G: Japan]

Eilbott, Peter and Binkowski, Edward S. The Determinants of SMSA Homeownership Rates. *J. Urban Econ.*, May 1985, *17*(3), pp. 293–304.   [G: U.S.]

Emmanuel, Dimitris. Urban Land Prices and Housing Distribution: Monopolistic Competition and the Myth of the 'Law' of Differential Rent. *Urban Stud.*, December 1985, *22*(6), pp. 461–80.

Engle, Robert F.; Lilien, David M. and Watson, Mark. A Dynamic Model of Housing Price Determination. *J. Econometrics,* June 1985, *28*(3), pp. 307–26.   [G: U.S.]

Englund, Peter. Taxation of Capital Gains on Owner-occupied Homes: Accrual vs Realization. *Europ. Econ. Rev.*, April 1985, *27*(3), pp. 311–34.

Evans, Richard D.; Maris, Brian A. and Weinstein, Robert I. Expected Loss and Mortgage Default Risk. *Quart. J. Bus. Econ.*, Winter 1985, *24*(1), pp. 75–92.   [G: U.S.]

Fallis, George and Smith, Lawrence B. Price Effects of Rent Control on Controlled and Uncontrolled Rental Housing in Toronto: A Hedonic Index Approach. *Can. J. Econ.*, August 1985, *18*(3), pp. 652–59.   [G: Canada]

Fallis, George and Smith, Lawrence B. Rent Control in Toronto: Tentant Rationing and Tenant Benefits. *Can. Public Policy*, September 1985, *11*(3), pp. 543–50.   [G: Canada]

Färe, Rolf and Yoon, Bong Joon. On Capital–Land Substitution in Urban Housing Production. *J. Urban Econ.*, July 1985, *18*(1), pp. 119–24.   [G: U.S.]

Fleming, M. C. and Nellis, J. G. The Application of Hedonic Indexing Methods: A Study of House Prices in the United Kingdom. *Statist. J.*, September 1985, *3*(3), pp. 249–70.   [G: U.K.]

Flowers, Marilyn R. Owner-occupied Housing, the CPI, and Indexing. *Public Finance Quart.*, January 1985, *13*(1), pp. 74–80.

Follain, James R. and Jimenez, Emmanuel. Estimating the Demand for Housing Characteris-

tics: A Survey and Critique. *Reg. Sci. Urban Econ.*, February 1985, *15*(1), pp. 77–107.   [G: U.S.; Korea; Colombia]

Follain, James R. and Jimenez, Emmanuel. The Demand for Housing Characteristics in Developing Countries. *Urban Stud.*, October 1985, *22*(5), pp. 421–32.   [G: Colombia; S. Korea; Philippines]

Frankel, Marvin. Amenity Changes, Property Values, and Hedonic Prices in a Closed City. *J. Environ. Econ. Manage.*, June 1985, *12*(2), pp. 117–31.

Fujita, Masahisa. Existence and Uniqueness of Equilibrium and Optimal Land Use: Boundary Rent Curve Approach. *Reg. Sci. Urban Econ.*, June 1985, *15*(2), pp. 295–324.

Gahvari, Firouz. Taxation of Housing, Capital Accumulation, and Welfare: A Study in Dynamic Tax Reform. *Public Finance Quart.*, April 1985, *13*(2), pp. 132–60.   [G: U.S.]

Gerber, Robert I. Existence and Description of Housing Market Equilibrium. *Reg. Sci. Urban Econ.*, August 1985, *15*(3), pp. 383–401.

Gerking, Shelby and Dickie, Mark. Systematic Assessment Error and Intrajurisdiction Property Tax Capitalization: Comment. *Southern Econ. J.*, January 1985, *51*(3), pp. 886–90.   [G: U.S.]

Goldberg, Michael A. Urban Programs: Transportation and Housing: Commentary. In *Quigley, J. M. and Rubinfeld, D. L., eds.*, 1985, pp. 285–93.   [G: Canada; U.S.]

Goldner, William. Housing Affordability: A Regional Perspective. In *Hutchinson, B. G.; Nijkamp, P. and Batty, M., eds.*, 1985, pp. 311–26.   [G: U.S.]

Goodman, Allen C. and Kawai, Masahiro. Length-of-Residence Discounts and Rental Housing Demand: Theory and Evidence. *Land Econ.*, May 1985, *61*(2), pp. 93–105.   [G: U.S.]

Gordon, Ian R. and Molho, Ian. Women in the Labour Markets of the London Region: A Model of Dependence and Constraint. *Urban Stud.*, October 1985, *22*(5), pp. 367–86.   [G: U.K.]

Grigsby, J. Eugene, III and Hruby, Mary L. A Review of the Status of Black Renters, 1970–1980. *Rev. Black Polit. Econ.*, Spring 1985, *13*(4), pp. 77–91.

Guasch, J. Luis and Marshall, Robert C. Age of Rental Housing Units and Vacancy Characteristics: A Filtering Explanation. *Reg. Sci. Urban Econ.*, August 1985, *15*(3), pp. 403–19.   [G: U.S.]

Guasch, J. Luis and Marshall, Robert C. An Analysis of Vacancy Patterns in the Rental Housing Market. *J. Urban Econ.*, March 1985, *17*(2), pp. 208–29.   [G: U.S.]

Guy, Donald C.; Hysom, John L. and Ruth, Stephen R. The Effect of Subsidized Housing on Values of Adjacent Housing. *Amer. Real Estate Urban Econ. Assoc. J.*, Winter 1985, *13*(4), pp. 378–87.   [G: U.S.]

Hamilton, Bob and Whalley, John. Tax Treatment of Housing in a Dynamic Sequenced

General Equilibrium Model. *J. Public Econ.*, July 1985, *27*(2), pp. 157–75. [G: Canada]

Hamilton, Bruce W. and Schwab, Robert M. Expected Appreciation in Urban Housing Markets. *J. Urban Econ.*, July 1985, *18*(1), pp. 103–18. [G: U.S.]

Henderson, J. Vernon. The Impact of Zoning Policies Which Regulate Housing Quality. *J. Urban Econ.*, November 1985, *18*(3), pp. 302–12.

Hershfield, David C. Attacking Housing Discrimination: Economic Power of the Military in Desegregating Off-Base Rental Housing. *Amer. J. Econ. Soc.*, January 1985, *44*(1), pp. 23–28. [G: U.S.]

Hohm, Charles F. A Profile of Landlords: Demographic, Economic, and Social Characteristics. *Growth Change*, January 1985, *16*(1), pp. 36–46. [G: U.S.]

Ihlanfeldt, Keith and Silberman, Jonathan I. Differential Response to Change: The Case of Home Purchase. *J. Urban Econ.*, March 1985, *17*(2), pp. 127–44. [G: U.S.]

Ingram, Gregory K. Housing Behavior and the Experimental Housing-Allowance Program: What Have We Learned? Comment. In *Hausman, J. A. and Wise, D. A., eds.*, 1985, pp. 87–94. [G: U.S.]

Jimenez, Emmanuel. Urban Squatting and Community Organization in Developing Countries. *J. Public Econ.*, June 1985, *27*(1), pp. 69–92.

Jud, G. Donald. A Further Note on Schools and Housing Values. *Amer. Real Estate Urban Econ. Assoc. J.*, Winter 1985, *13*(4), pp. 452–62. [G: U.S.]

Judge, Ken and Knapp, Martin. Efficiency in the Production of Welfare: The Public and the Private Sectors Compared. In *Klein, R. and O'Higgins, M., ed.*, 1985, pp. 131–49. [G: U.K.]

Kain, John F. Black Suburbanization in the Eighties: A New Beginning or a False Hope? In *Quigley, J. M. and Rubinfeld, D. L., eds.*, 1985, pp. 253–84. [G: U.S.]

Kain, John F. and Apgar, William C., Jr. The Harvard Urban Development Simulation Model. In *Stahl, K., ed.*, 1985, pp. 27–71. [G: U.S.]

Kanemoto, Yoshitsugu. Housing as an Asset and the Effects of Property Taxation on the Residential Development Process. *J. Urban Econ.*, March 1985, *17*(2), pp. 145–66.

Kirlin, John J. Toward a Differentiated Theory of Federalism: Education and Housing Policy in the 1980s: Comment. In *Clark, T. N., ed.*, 1985, pp. 349–52. [G: U.S.]

Konukiewitz, Manfred. Taming the Housing Market. In *Lane, J.-E., ed.*, 1985, pp. 181–98. [G: W. Germany]

Korn, Francis and de la Torre, Lidia. La vivienda en Buenos Aires 1887–1914. (With English summary.) *Desarrollo Econ.*, July-Sept. 1985, *25*(98), pp. 245–58. [G: Argentina]

Landale, Nancy S. and Guest, Avery M. Constraints, Satisfaction, and Residential Mobility: Speare's Model Reconsidered. *Demography*,

May 1985, *22*(2), pp. 199–222. [G: U.S.]

Leeds, Michael A. Property Values and Pension Underfunding in the Local Public Sector. *J. Urban Econ.*, July 1985, *18*(1), pp. 34–46. [G: U.S.]

Lesse, Paul F. and Skowronski, Janislaw M. Stabilisation and Optimal Management in the Housing Industry. In *Batten, D. F. and Lesse, P. F., eds.*, 1985, pp. 47–68.

Ley, David. Work-Residence Relations for Head Office Employees in an Inflating Housing Market. *Urban Stud.*, February 1985, *22*(1), pp. 21–38. [G: Canada]

van Lierop, Wal. Residential Mobility with a Probit Model. In *Hutchinson, B. G.; Nijkamp, P. and Batty, M., eds.*, 1985, pp. 235–48. [G: Netherlands]

Lin, Chuan. Labor Mobility and the Incidence of the Residential Property Tax: A Comment. *J. Urban Econ.*, July 1985, *18*(1), pp. 28–33.

Linneman, Peter. An Economic Analysis of the Homeownership Decision. *J. Urban Econ.*, March 1985, *17*(2), pp. 230–46. [G: U.S.]

Loikkanen, Heikki A. On Availability Discrimination under Rent Control. *Scand. J. Econ.*, 1985, *87*(3), pp. 500–520.

MacDonald, John F. Expectations and Urban Housing Prices [The Dynamics of Neighborhood Change]. *Urban Stud.*, December 1985, *22*(6), pp. 543–49. [G: U.S.]

Maisel, Sherman. The Agenda for Metropolitan Housing Policies. In *Quigley, J. M. and Rubinfeld, D. L., eds.*, 1985, pp. 224–52. [G: U.S.]

Mark, Jonathan H. and Goldberg, Michael A. House Prices: Under RRAPS? *Can. Public Policy*, March 1985, *11*(1), pp. 16–25. [G: Canada]

Mayer, Neil S. The Impacts of Lending, Race, and Ownership on Rental Housing Rehabilitation. *J. Urban Econ.*, May 1985, *17*(3), pp. 349–74. [G: U.S.]

McCallum, Douglas and Benjamin, Stan. Low-Income Urban Housing in the Third World: Broadening the Economic Perspective. *Urban Stud.*, August 1985, *22*(4), pp. 277–87. [G: U.S.]

McConney, Mary E. An Empirical Look at Housing Rehabilitation as a Spatial Process. *Urban Stud.*, February 1985, *22*(1), pp. 39–48. [G: U.S.]

McConney, Mary E. Errata [An Empirical Look at Housing Rehabilitation as a Spatial Process]. *Urban Stud.*, August 1985, *22*(4), pp. 288. [G: U.S.]

Meador, Mark. The Effects of Federally Sponsored Credit on Housing Markets: Some Evidence from Multivariate Exogeneity Tests. *Housing Finance Rev.*, January 1985, *4*(1), pp. 505–15. [G: U.S.]

Mongia, J. N. Housing and Urban Renewal. In *Mongia, J. N., ed.*, 1985, pp. 539–83. [G: India]

Muth, Richard F. Urban Programs: Transportation and Housing: Commentary. In *Quigley,*

J. M. and Rubinfeld, D. L., eds., 1985, pp. 297–303. **[G: U.S.]**

Myers, Dowell. Wives' Earnings and Rising Costs of Homeownership. *Soc. Sci. Quart.*, June 1985, *66*(2), pp. 319–29. **[G: U.S.]**

Nelson, Arthur C. Demand, Segmentation, and Timing Effects of an Urban Containment Program on Urban Fringe Land Values. *Urban Stud.*, October 1985, *22*(5), pp. 439–43. **[G: U.S.]**

Nijkamp, Peter; Rima, A. and van Wissen, L. Spatial Mobility in Models for Structural Urban Dynamics. In *Jansen, G. R. M.; Nijkamp, P. and Ruijgrok, C. J., eds.*, 1985, pp. 121–40.

Nothaft, Frank E. Survey of Home-Seller Finance, 1983. *Fed. Res. Bull.*, October 1985, *71*(10), pp. 767–75. **[G: U.S.]**

O'Byrne, Patricia Habuda; Nelson, Jon P. and Seneca, Joseph J. Housing Values, Census Estimates, Disequilibrium, and the Environmental Cost of Airport Noise: A Case Study of Atlanta. *J. Environ. Econ. Manage.*, June 1985, *12*(2), pp. 169–78. **[G: U.S.]**

Ohkawara, Toru. Urban Residential Land Rent Function: An Alternative Muth–Mills Model [Economic Analysis of an Urban Housing Market]. *J. Urban Econ.*, November 1985, *18*(3), pp. 338–49. **[G: Japan]**

Ostas, James R. Reduced Form Coefficients, Structural Coefficients, and Mortgage Redlining. *Amer. Real Estate Urban Econ. Assoc. J.*, Spring 1985, *13*(1), pp. 76–92.

Ozanne, Larry and Malpezzi, Stephen. The Efficacy of Hedonic Estimation with the Annual Housing Survey: Evidence from the Demand Experiment. *J. Econ. Soc. Meas.*, July 1985, *13*(2), pp. 153–72. **[G: U.S.]**

Palash, Carl J. and Stoddard, Robert B. ARMs: Their Financing Rate and Impact on Housing. *Fed. Res. Bank New York Quart. Rev.*, Autumn 1985, *10*(3), pp. 39–49. **[G: U.S.]**

Pasha, Hafiz A. Welfare Consequences of Building Height Controls. *Pakistan J. Appl. Econ.*, Winter 1985, *4*(2), pp. 69–92. **[G: Saudi Arabia]**

Peiser, Richard B. and Smith, Lawrence B. Homeownership Returns, Tenure Choice and Inflation. *Amer. Real Estate Urban Econ. Assoc. J.*, Winter 1985, *13*(4), pp. 343–60. **[G: U.S.]**

Pesando, James E. and Turnbull, Stuart M. The Time Path of Homeowner's Equity under Different Mortgage Instruments: A Simulation Study. *Housing Finance Rev.*, January 1985, *4*(1), pp. 483–504. **[G: Canada]**

Peterson, Paul E. and Wong, Kenneth K. Toward a Differentiated Theory of Federalism: Education and Housing Policy in the 1980s. In *Clark, T. N., ed.*, 1985, pp. 301–24. **[G: U.S.]**

Pickles, Andrew and Davies, Richard. The Longitudinal Analysis of Housing Careers. *J. Reg. Sci.*, February 1985, *25*(1), pp. 85–101. **[G: U.S.]**

Pines, David; Sadka, Efraim and Sheshinski, Eytan. The Normative and Positive Aspects of the Taxation of Imputed Rent on Owner-occu-

pied Housing. *J. Public Econ.*, June 1985, *27*(1), pp. 1–23.

Pinfield, Lawrence T. and Etherington, Lois D. Housing Strategies of Resource Firms in Western Canada. *Can. Public Policy*, March 1985, *11*(1), pp. 93–106. **[G: Canada]**

Plaut, Steven E. Tenure Decisions, Mortgage Interest, and the Spatial Distribution of Household Demand: A Theoretical Analysis. *Reg. Sci. Urban Econ.*, February 1985, *15*(1), pp. 65–76.

Porell, Frank W. One Man's Ceiling Is Another Man's Floor: Landlord/Manager Residency and Housing Condition. *Land Econ.*, May 1985, *61*(2), pp. 106–18. **[G: U.S.]**

Price, Richard and Mills, Edwin S. Race and Residence in Earnings Determination. *J. Urban Econ.*, January 1985, *17*(1), pp. 1–18. **[G: U.S.]**

Quigley, John M. Consumer Choice of Dwelling, Neighborhood, and Public Services. *Reg. Sci. Urban Econ.*, February 1985, *15*(1), pp. 41–63. **[G: U.S.]**

Quigley, John M. Housing Behavior and the Experimental Housing-Allowance Program: What Have We Learned? Comment. In *Hausman, J. A. and Wise, D. A., eds.*, 1985, pp. 75–86.

Randall, Alan J. and Castle, Emery N. Land Resources and Land Markets. In *Kneese, A. V. and Sweeney, J. L., eds. Vol. 2*, 1985, pp. 571–620.

Reeder, William J. The Benefits and Costs of the Section 8 Existing Housing Program. *J. Public Econ.*, April 1985, *26*(3), pp. 349–77. **[G: U.S.]**

Robinson, Ray; O'Sullivan, Tony and Le Grand, Julian. Inequality and Housing. *Urban Stud.*, June 1985, *22*(3), pp. 249–56. **[G: U.K.]**

Rosen, Harvey S. Housing Behavior and the Experimental Housing-Allowance Program: What Have We Learned? In *Hausman, J. A. and Wise, D. A., eds.*, 1985, pp. 55–75. **[G: U.S.]**

Rosen, Harvey S. Housing Subsidies: Effects on Housing Decisions, Efficiency, and Equity. In *Auerbach, A. J. and Feldstein, M., eds.*, 1985, pp. 375–420. **[G: OECD]**

Rudel, Thomas K. Changes in Access to Homeownership during the 1970s. *Ann. Reg. Sci.*, March 1985, *19*(1), pp. 37–49. **[G: U.S.]**

Salo, Sinikka. Miten rahoitustekijät vaikuttavat kotitalouksien asuntojen kysyntään? (What Is the Influence of Financial Market Conditions on the Demand for Housing? With English summary.) *Kansant. Aikak.*, 1985, *81*(4), pp. 418–28. **[G: Finland]**

Santerre, Rexford E. Spatial Differences in the Demands for Local Public Goods. *Land Econ.*, May 1985, *61*(2), pp. 119–28. **[G: U.S.]**

Schoettle, Ferdinand P. A Three-Sector Model for Real Property Tax Incidence. *J. Public Econ.*, August 1985, *27*(3), pp. 355–70. **[G: U.S.]**

Schwab, Robert M. Renovation and Mobility: An Application of the Theory of Rationing. *Southern Econ. J.*, July 1985, *52*(1), pp. 203–15.

Schwab, Robert M. The Benefits of In-Kind Government Programs. *J. Public Econ.*, July 1985, 27(2), pp. 195–210. [G: U.S.]

Scotchmer, Suzanne. Hedonic Prices and Cost/Benefit Analysis. *J. Econ. Theory*, October 1985, 37(1), pp. 55–75.

Shah, Anup R. and Rees, Hedley. The Distribution of Housing Tenure in Britain. *Manchester Sch. Econ. Soc. Stud.*, September 1985, 53(3), pp. 296–314. [G: U.K.]

Shear, William B. and Yezer, Anthony M. J. Discrimination in Urban Housing Finance: An Empirical Study across Cities. *Land Econ.*, August 1985, 61(3), pp. 292–302. [G: U.S.]

Sillince, J. A. A. The Housing Market of the Budapest Urban Region, 1949–1983. *Urban Stud.*, April 1985, 22(2), pp. 141–49. [G: Hungary]

Sørensen, Rune J. Economic Relations between City and Suburban Governments. In *Lane, J.-E., ed.*, 1985, pp. 83–99. [G: Sweden]

Southworth, Frank. On Household Travel Circuit Benefits and Their Locational Implications. In *Hutchinson, B. G.; Nijkamp, P. and Batty, M., eds.*, 1985, pp. 116–31.

Springer, Philip B. Home Equity Conversion Plans as a Source of Retirement Income. *Soc. Sec. Bull.*, September 1985, 48(9), pp. 10–19. [G: U.S.]

Stahl, Konrad. Microeconomic Analysis of Housing Markets: Towards a Conceptual Framework. In *Stahl, K., ed.*, 1985, pp. 1–26.

Stansell, Stanley R. and Mitchell, A. Cameron. The Impact of Credit Rationing on the Real Sector: A Study of the Effect of Mortgage Rates and Terms on Housing Starts. *Appl. Econ.*, October 1985, 17(5), pp. 781–800. [G: U.S.]

Stutzer, Michael J. and Roberds, William. Adjustable Rate Mortgages: Increasing Efficiency More than Housing Activity. *Fed. Res. Bank Minn. Rev.*, Summer 1985, 9(3), pp. 10–20. [G: U.S.]

Sullivan, Arthur M. The Pricing of Urban Services and the Spatial Distribution of Residence. *Land Econ.*, February 1985, 61(1), pp. 17–25.

Swenarton, Mark and Taylor, Sandra. The Scale and Nature of the Growth of Owner-Occupation in Britain between the Wars. *Econ. Hist. Rev., 2nd Ser.*, August 1985, 38(3), pp. 373–92. [G: U.K.]

Tanzer, Ellen P. The Effect on Housing Quality of Reducing the Structure Tax Rate. *J. Urban Econ.*, May 1985, 17(3), pp. 305–18. [G: U.S.]

Thom, Rodney. The Relationship between Housing Starts and Mortgage Availability. *Rev. Econ. Statist.*, November 1985, 67(4), pp. 693–96. [G: U.S.]

Todt, Horst. Postscript: The Evolution of Housing Market Analysis: A Historical Perspective. In *Stahl, K., ed.*, 1985, pp. 192–97.

Varady, David P. and Lipton, S. Gregory. Neighborhood Conservation and Population Stabilization: Lessons from the Urban Homesteading Demonstration. *Reg. Sci. Persp.*, 1985, 15(1), pp. 75–80. [G: U.S.]

Vitaliano, Donald F. The Short-run Supply of

Housing Services under Rent Control. *Urban Stud.*, December 1985, 22(6), pp. 535–42. [G: U.S.]

van Vliet, Willem. Housing Policy as a Planning Tool. *Urban Stud.*, April 1985, 22(2), pp. 105–17. [G: Israel]

Ward, Peter and Melligan, Stephen. Urban Renovation and the Impact upon Low Income Families in Mexico City. *Urban Stud.*, June 1985, 22(3), pp. 199–207. [G: Mexico]

Wegener, Michael. The Dortmund Housing Market Model: A Monte Carlo Simulation of a Regional Housing Market. In *Stahl, K., ed.*, 1985, pp. 144–91. [G: W. Germany]

Weinrobe, Maurice. HELP Comes to Buffalo: A Review and Analysis of the Initial Equity Conversion Experience. *Housing Finance Rev.*, January 1985, 4(1), pp. 537–48. [G: U.S.]

Welham, P. J. Reform of Tax Reliefs for Owner-Occupation. *J. Econ. Stud.*, 1985, 12(4), pp. 30–40. [G: U.K.]

Whalley, Diane. Hedonic Price Functions and Progressive Neighborhood Improvement: A Theoretical Exploration. *Math. Soc. Sci.*, December 1985, 10(3), pp. 275–79.

Wheaton, William C. Life-Cycle Theory, Inflation, and the Demand for Housing. *J. Urban Econ.*, September 1985, 18(2), pp. 161–79.

Whitehead, Christine M. E. and Klcinman, Mark. The Private Rented Sector: A Characteristics Approach. *Urban Stud.*, December 1985, 22(6), pp. 507–20. [G: U.K.]

Wiesmeth, Hans. Fixprice Equilibria in a Rental Housing Market. In *Stahl, K., ed.*, 1985, pp. 72–118.

Willis, K. C. The Economics of Rationing by Waiting. *Indian J. Quant. Econ.*, 1985, 1(2), pp. 17–42. [G: U.K.]

Wolfson, Mark A. Tax, Incentive, and Risk-sharing Issues in the Allocation of Property Rights: The Generalized Lease-or-Buy Problem. *J. Bus.*, April 1985, 58(2), pp. 159–71.

Yeh, Anthony G. O. Physical Planning. In *Wong, K. and Chu, D. K. Y., eds.*, 1985, pp. 108–30. [G: China]

Yi, Chin-chun. Urban Housing Satisfaction in a Transitional Society: A Case Study in Taichung, Taiwan. *Urban Stud.*, February 1985, 22(1), pp. 1–12. [G: Taiwan]

You, Jong Keun and Falk, Laurence H. Estimation of the Countercyclical Effect of Mortgage Interest Subsidies. In *Brown, R. C., ed.*, 1985, pp. 231–48. [G: U.S.]

Yu, Fu-Lai and Li, Si-Ming. The Welfare Cost of Hong Kong's Public Housing Programme. *Urban Stud.*, April 1985, 22(2), pp. 133–40. [G: Hong Kong]

933 Urban Transportation Economics

9330 Urban Transportation Economics

Anas, Alex. Modeling the Dynamic Evolution of Land Use in Response to Transportation Improvement Policies. In *Jansen, G. R. M.; Nijkamp, P. and Ruijgrok, C. J., eds.*, 1985, pp. 227–36. [G: U.S.]

Anas, Alex. The Combined Equilibrium of Travel Networks and Residential Location Markets. *Reg. Sci. Urban Econ.*, February 1985, *15*(1), pp. 1–21.

Baanders, A.; Kremer-Nass, J. and Ruijgrok, C. J. Income Decline and Travel Behaviour: Some Recent Dutch Findings and Research Orientations. In *Jansen, G. R. M.; Nijkamp, P. and Ruijgrok, C. J., eds.*, 1985, pp. 37–53. [G: Netherlands]

van den Berg, L. and Klaassen, L. H. Economic Cycles, Spatial Cycles and Transportation Structures in Urban Areas. In *Jansen, G. R. M.; Nijkamp, P. and Ruijgrok, C. J., eds.*, 1985, pp. 259–73. [G: Netherlands]

Button, K. J. and O'Donnell, K. J. An Examination of the Cost Structures Associated with Providing Urban Bus Services in Britain. *Scot. J. Polit. Econ.*, February 1985, *32*(1), pp. 67–81. [G: U.K.]

Cervero, Robert. Deregulating Urban Transportation. *Cato J.*, Spring/Summer 1985, *5*(1), pp. 219–38. [G: U.S.]

Chaudry-Shah, Anwar M. Provincial Transportation Grants to Alberta Cities: Structure, Evaluation and a Proposal for an Alternate Design. In *Brown, R. C., ed.*, 1985, pp. 59–107. [G: Canada]

Chu, David K. Y. Forecasting Future Transportation Demand and the Planned Road Network. In *Wong, K. and Chu, D. K. Y., eds.*, 1985, pp. 140–58. [G: China]

Dasgupta, M.; Frost, M. and Spence, N. Interaction between Urban Form and Mode Choice for the Work Journey: Manchester/Sheffield 1971–1981. *Reg. Stud.*, August 1985, *19*(4), pp. 315–28. [G: U.K.]

de Dios Ortúzar, Juan and Donoso, Patricio. Modal Choice Modelling for Several Alternatives: Application of Disaggregate Demand Models in Santiago, Chile. In *Hutchinson, B. G.; Nijkamp, P. and Batty, M., eds.*, 1985, pp. 249–61. [G: Chile; U.K.]

Doxsey, Lawrence B. Demand for Unlimited Use Transit Passes: A Rejoinder. *J. Transp. Econ. Policy*, September 1985, *19*(3), pp. 307–11. [G: U.S.]

Dubin, Robin A. Transportation Costs and the Residential Location Decision: A New Approach. *J. Urban Econ.*, January 1985, *17*(1), pp. 58–72.

Echols, James C. Use of Private Companies to Provide Public Transportation Services in Tidewater Virginia. In *Lave, C. A., ed.*, 1985, pp. 79–100. [G: U.S.]

Else, Peter K. Optimal Pricing and Subsidies for Scheduled Transport Services. *J. Transp. Econ. Policy*, September 1985, *19*(3), pp. 263–79. [G: U.K.]

Evans, Andrew. Equalising Grants for Public Transport Subsidy. *J. Transp. Econ. Policy*, May 1985, *19*(2), pp. 105–38. [G: U.K.]

Giuliano, Genevieve and Teal, Roger F. Privately Provided Commuter Bus Services: Experiences, Problems, and Prospects. In *Lave, C. A., ed.*, 1985, pp. 151–79. [G: U.S.]

Glaister, Stephen. Competition on an Urban Bus Route. *J. Transp. Econ. Policy*, January 1985, *19*(1), pp. 65–82. [G: U.K.]

Glaister, Stephen. Competition on an Urban Bus Route: A Rejoinder. *J. Transp. Econ. Policy*, September 1985, *19*(3), pp. 317–19. [G: U.K.]

Goedman, J.; van de Hoef, G. and Timmerman, F. Transportation and Urban Form. In *Jansen, G. R. M.; Nijkamp, P. and Ruijgrok, C. J., eds.*, 1985, pp. 275–93. [G: Netherlands]

Goldberg, Michael A. Urban Programs: Transportation and Housing: Commentary. In *Quigley, J. M. and Rubinfeld, D. L., eds.*, 1985, pp. 285–93. [G: Canada; U.S.]

Gomez-Ibañez, Jose A. The Federal Role in Urban Transportation. In *Quigley, J. M. and Rubinfeld, D. L., eds.*, 1985, pp. 183–223. [G: U.S.]

Gomez-Ibañez, Jose A. Transportation Policy as a Tool for Shaping Metropolitan Development. In *Keeler, T. E., ed.*, 1985, pp. 55–81. [G: U.S.]

Goodwin, P. B. and Layzell, A. D. Longitudinal Analysis for Public Transport Policy Issues. In *Jansen, G. R. M.; Nijkamp, P. and Ruijgrok, C. J., eds.*, 1985, pp. 185–200. [G: U.K.]

Guria, Jagadish C. and Gollin, Anthony E. A. Influence of Income and Public Transit Accessibility on the Modal Choice Behaviour of the New Zealand Labour Force. *Int. J. Transport Econ.*, October 1985, *12*(3), pp. 301–13. [G: New Zealand]

Hall, P. Urban Transportation: Paradoxes for the 1980s. In *Jansen, G. R. M.; Nijkamp, P. and Ruijgrok, C. J., eds.*, 1985, pp. 367–75.

Hilton, George W. The Rise and Fall of Monopolized Transit. In *Lave, C. A., ed.*, 1985, pp. 31–48. [G: U.S.]

Holtgrefe, A. A. I. Stagnation and Public Transport in the Netherlands: Demand, Cost, Supply and Planning. In *Jansen, G. R. M.; Nijkamp, P. and Ruijgrok, C. J., eds.*, 1985, pp. 335–51. [G: Netherlands]

Hutchinson, Bruce. Contingency Table Analysis and Urban Travel Accounts. In *Hutchinson, B. G.; Nijkamp, P. and Batty, M., eds.*, 1985, pp. 343–56. [G: Canada]

Izraeli, Oded and McCarthy, Thomas R. Variations in Travel Distance, Travel Time and Modal Choice among SMSAs. *J. Transp. Econ. Policy*, May 1985, *19*(2), pp. 139–60. [G: U.S.]

Johnson, Christine M. and Pikarsky, Milton. Toward Fragmentation: The Evolution of Public Transportation in Chicago. In *Lave, C. A., ed.*, 1985, pp. 49–77. [G: U.S.]

Keeler, Theodore E. Urban Programs: Transportation and Housing: Commentary. In *Quigley, J. M. and Rubinfeld, D. L., eds.*, 1985, pp. 294–96. [G: U.S.]

Kemp, Michael A. and Kirby, Ronald F. Government Policies Affecting Competition in Public Transportation. In *Lave, C. A., ed.*, 1985, pp. 277–98. [G: U.S.]

Koppelman, Frank S. and Rose, Geoffrey. Geographic Transfer of Travel Choice Models: Evaluation and Procedures. In *Hutchinson, B. G.; Nijkamp, P. and Batty, M., eds.*, 1985, pp. 272–309.

Kroes, E. P. and Sheldon, R. J. Stated Preference Techniques in Measuring Travel Elasticities. In *Jansen, G. R. M.; Nijkamp, P. and Ruijgrok, C. J., eds.*, 1985, pp. 201–10.

Kutter, E. New Targets for Transport Facilities Planning. In *Jansen, G. R. M.; Nijkamp, P. and Ruijgrok, C. J., eds.*, 1985, pp. 377–88. [G: W. Germany]

Lave, Charles A. The Private Challenge to Public Transportation—An Overview. In *Lave, C. A., ed.*, 1985, pp. 1–29. [G: U.S.]

Leonardi, Giorgio. A Stochastic Multi-stage Mobility Choice Model. In *Hutchinson, B. G.; Nijkamp, P. and Batty, M., eds.*, 1985, pp. 132–47.

Loeb, Peter D. The Efficacy and Cost Effectiveness of Motor Vehicle Inspection Using Cross-Sectional Data—An Econometric Analysis. *Southern Econ. J.*, October 1985, *52*(2), pp. 500–509. [G: U.S.]

Mackett, Roger. Forecasting the Long Term Effects of Increases in the Cost of Travel. In *Hutchinson, B. G.; Nijkamp, P. and Batty, M., eds.*, 1985, pp. 327–42. [G: U.K.]

Mason, Charles F. and Train, Kenneth E. A Route Forecasting Method for the Portland Area. In *Keeler, T. E., ed.*, 1985, pp. 239–59. [G: U.S.]

Meyer, M. D. Urban Transportation Planning in the United States: Current Trends and Future Directions. In *Jansen, G. R. M.; Nijkamp, P. and Ruijgrok, C. J., eds.*, 1985, pp. 313–22.

Mogridge, M. J. H. Transport, Land Use and Energy Interaction. *Urban Stud.*, December 1985, *22*(6), pp. 481–92. [G: France; U.K.]

Mohring, Herbert. Profit Maximization, Cost Minimization, and Pricing for Congestion-prone Facilities. *Logist. Transp. Rev.*, March 1985, *21*(1), pp. 27–36.

Monkman, Neil and Shortreed, John. Transport Impacts of Changing Household Structure. In *Hutchinson, B. G.; Nijkamp, P. and Batty, M., eds.*, 1985, pp. 357–71. [G: Canada]

Morlok, Edward K. and Viton, Philip A. Recent Experience with Successful Private Transit in Large U.S. Cities. In *Lave, C. A., ed.*, 1985, pp. 121–49. [G: U.S.]

Morlok, Edward K. and Viton, Philip A. The Comparative Costs of Public and Private Providers of Mass Transit. In *Lave, C. A., ed.*, 1985, pp. 233–53. [G: U.K.; U.S.; Australia]

Nash, C. A. Competition on an Urban Bus Route: A Comment. *J. Transp. Econ. Policy*, September 1985, *19*(3), pp. 313–17. [G: U.K.]

Nijkamp, Peter; Rima, A. and van Wissen, L. Spatial Mobility in Models for Structural Urban Dynamics. In *Jansen, G. R. M.; Nijkamp, P. and Ruijgrok, C. J., eds.*, 1985, pp. 121–40.

Obeng, Kofi. Bus Transit Cost, Productivity and Factor Substitution. *J. Transp. Econ. Policy*, May 1985, *19*(2), pp. 183–203. [G: U.S.]

Orski, C. Kenneth. Redesigning Local Transpor-

tation Service. In *Lave, C. A., ed.*, 1985, pp. 255–75. [G: U.S.]

Orski, C. Kenneth. The Private Challenge to Public Transportation. In *Lave, C. A., ed.*, 1985, pp. 311–31. [G: U.S.]

de Palma, André and Lefèvre, Claude. Residential Change and Economic Choice Behavior. *Reg. Sci. Urban Econ.*, August 1985, *15*(3), pp. 421–34.

Pickrell, Don H. Rising Deficits and the Uses of Transit Subsidies in the United States. *J. Transp. Econ. Policy*, September 1985, *19*(3), pp. 281–98. [G: U.S.]

Pickup, L. Women's Travel Needs in a Period of Rising Female Employment. In *Jansen, G. R. M.; Nijkamp, P. and Ruijgrok, C. J., eds.*, 1985, pp. 97–113. [G: U.K.]

Recker, W. W. and Kitamura, R. Activity-based Travel Analysis. In *Jansen, G. R. M.; Nijkamp, P. and Ruijgrok, C. J., eds.*, 1985, pp. 157–83. [G: U.S.]

Rosenbloom, Sandra. The Growth of Non-traditional Families: A Challenge to Traditional Planning Approaches. In *Jansen, G. R. M.; Nijkamp, P. and Ruijgrok, C. J., eds.*, 1985, pp. 75–96. [G: U.S.; Netherlands]

Rosenbloom, Sandra. The Taxi in the Urban Transport System. In *Lave, C. A., ed.*, 1985, pp. 181–213. [G: U.S.]

Roth, Gabriel. The Overseas Experience. In *Lave, C. A., ed.*, 1985, pp. 215–31. [G: Australia]

Rottenberg, Simon. Job Protection in Urban Mass Transit. *Cato J.*, Spring/Summer 1985, *5*(1), pp. 239–58. [G: U.S.]

Sharpe, Ron. An Optimum Economic/Energy Land-Use Transportation Model. In *Hutchinson, B. G.; Nijkamp, P. and Batty, M., eds.*, 1985, pp. 50–66.

Simpson, Anthony U. Implications of Efficiency Incentives on Use of Private Sector Contracting by the Public Transit Industry. In *Lave, C. A., ed.*, 1985, pp. 299–309.

Sinha, H. K.; Khanna, S. K. and Arora, M. G. Choice of Urban Transport Modes for Work Trips. In *Hutchinson, B. G.; Nijkamp, P. and Batty, M., eds.*, 1985, pp. 262–71. [G: India]

Small, Kenneth A. Transportation and Urban Change. In *Peterson, P. E., ed.*, 1985, pp. 197–223. [G: U.S.]

Southworth, Frank. On Household Travel Circuit Benefits and Their Locational Implications. In *Hutchinson, B. G.; Nijkamp, P. and Batty, M., eds.*, 1985, pp. 116–31.

Tolley, George, et al. Transportation Policy and Economic Development for the Northeastern Cities. In *Clark, T. N., ed.*, 1985, pp. 271–95. [G: U.S.]

Wachs, M. The Politicization of Transit Subsidy Policy in America. In *Jansen, G. R. M.; Nijkamp, P. and Ruijgrok, C. J., eds.*, 1985, pp. 353–66. [G: U.S.]

Walder, Jay H. Private Commuter Vans in New York. In *Lave, C. A., ed.*, 1985, pp. 101–19. [G: U.S.]

Webber, Melvin M. Urban Programs: Transportation and Housing: Commentary. In *Quigley, J. M. and Rubinfeld, D. L., eds.*, 1985, pp. 304–07. [G: U.S.]

White, Peter R. Demand for Unlimited Use Transit Passes: A Comment. *J. Transp. Econ. Policy*, September 1985, *19*(3), pp. 305–07. [G: U.S.; U.K.]

Wildasin, David E. Income Taxes and Urban Spatial Structure. *J. Urban Econ.*, November 1985, *18*(3), pp. 313–33.

van Wissen, L.; Golob, T. F. and Smit, J. G. Determination of Differences among Household Mobility Patterns. In *Jansen, G. R. M.; Nijkamp, P. and Ruijgrok, C. J., eds.*, 1985, pp. 211–25. [G: Netherlands]

Yamada, Tetsuji. The Probable Effects of Introducing a Sectional Fare System into New York City Subway. *Int. J. Transport Econ.*, October 1985, *12*(3), pp. 315–31. [G: U.S.]

940 REGIONAL ECONOMICS

941 Regional Economics

9410 General

Atkinson, Scott E. Marketable Pollution Permits and Acid Rain Externalities: A Reply. *Can. J. Econ.*, August 1985, *18*(3), pp. 676–79. [G: U.S.; Canada]

Attali, Bernard. Reindustrializing France through Urban and Regional Development. In *Zukin, S., ed.*, 1985, pp. 179–84. [G: France]

Beigie, Carl E. and Stewart, James K. An Ontario Perspective on Canadian Trade Options. In *Conklin, D. W. and Courchene, T. J., eds.*, 1985, pp. 77–94. [G: Canada]

Coffey, William J. and Polese, Mario. Local Development: Conceptual Bases and Policy Implications. *Reg. Stud.*, April 1985, *19*(2), pp. 85–93.

Greenwood, Michael J. Human Migration: Theory, Models, and Empirical Studies. *J. Reg. Sci.*, November 1985, *25*(4), pp. 521–44. [G: U.S.]

Harris, Britton. Urban Simulation Models in Regional Science. *J. Reg. Sci.*, November 1985, *25*(4), pp. 545–67.

Hertel, Thomas W. and Mount, Timothy D. The Pricing of Natural Resources in a Regional Economy. *Land Econ.*, August 1985, *61*(3), pp. 229–43. [G: U.S.]

Klaassen, L. H. The Accessibility of Rural Areas. *Int. J. Transport Econ.*, June 1985, *12*(2), pp. 157–63.

Leven, Charles L. Regional Development Analysis and Policy. *J. Reg. Sci.*, November 1985, *25*(4), pp. 569–92. [G: U.S.; Selected Countries]

Lynd, Staughton. Options for Reindustrialization: Brownfield versus Greenfield Approaches. In *Woodworth, W.; Meek, C. and Whyte, W. F., eds.*, 1985, pp. 49–63. [G: U.S.]

Massey, Doreen and Meegan, Richard. Politics and Methods: Contrasting Studies in Industrial Geography: Introduction: The Debate. In *Massey, D. and Meegan, R., eds.*, 1985, pp. 1–12.

Massey, Doreen and Meegan, Richard. Postscript: Doing Research. In *Massey, D. and Meegan, R., eds.*, 1985, pp. 169–74.

Parr, John B. The Form of the Regional Density Function. *Reg. Stud.*, October 1985, *19*(6), pp. 535–46. [G: U.K.; U.S.; Canada]

Scarfe, Brian L. A Western Perspective on Canadian Trade Options. In *Conklin, D. W. and Courchene, T. J., eds.*, 1985, pp. 95–103. [G: Canada]

Smith, Murray G. and Steger, Debra P. Canada's Constitutional Quandary: The Federal/Provincial Dimension in International Economic Agreements. In *Conklin, D. W. and Courchene, T. J., eds.*, 1985, pp. 362–79. [G: Canada]

Whyte, William Foote. New Approaches to Industrial Development and Community Development. In *Woodworth, W.; Meek, C. and Whyte, W. F., eds.*, 1985, pp. 15–27. [G: U.S.]

9411 Theory of Regional Economics

Alperovich, Gershon and Katz, Eliakim. Rent Gradient under Uncertainty. *Urban Stud.*, June 1985, *22*(3), pp. 257–61.

Anderson, Simon. Product Choice with Economies of Scope. *Reg. Sci. Urban Econ.*, June 1985, *15*(2), pp. 277–94.

Arvan, Lanny and Moses, Leon N. A Model of the Firm in Time and Space. *J. Econ. Dynam. Control*, September 1985, *9*(1), pp. 77–100.

Bartik, Timothy J. Business Location Decisions in the United States: Estimates of the Effects of Unionization, Taxes, and Other Characteristics of States. *J. Bus. Econ. Statist.*, January 1985, *3*(1), pp. 14–22. [G: U.S.]

Beckmann, Martin J. A Model of Perfect Competition in Spatial Markets. *Rivista Int. Sci. Econ. Com.*, May 1985, *32*(5), pp. 413–19.

Beckmann, Martin J. Spatial Price Policy and the Demand for Transportation. *J. Reg. Sci.*, August 1985, *25*(3), pp. 367–71.

Bennett, R. J. and Haining, R. P. Spatial Structure and Spatial Interaction: Modelling Approaches to the Statistical Analysis of Geographical Data. *J. Roy. Statist. Soc.*, 1985, *148*(1), pp. 1–27. [G: U.S.; U.K.]

Blaga, I., et al. Modelling of Territorial Development within the General Cybernetic System of National Economy. *Econ. Computat. Cybern. Stud. Res.*, 1985, *20*(2), pp. 5–14. [G: Romania]

Borenstein, Severin. Price Discrimination in Free-Entry Markets. *Rand J. Econ.*, Autumn 1985, *16*(3), pp. 380–97.

Burgat, Paul and Jeanrenaud, Claude. Consequences d'une perequation tarifaire spatiale du point de vue du bien-etre et de la redistribution des revenus. (Consequences of Interregional Cross Subsidization with Regard to Welfare and Redistribution. With English summary.) *Public Finance*, 1985, *40*(1), pp. 64–81.

Casson, Mark. Multinationals and Intermediate Product Trade. In *Buckley, P. J. and Casson, M.,* 1985, pp. 144–71.

Corden, W. Max and Findlay, Ronald F. Urban Unemployment, Intersectoral Capital Mobility and Development Policy. In *Corden, W. M.,* 1985, pp. 73–93.

Cremer, Helmuth; de Kerchove, Anne-Marie and Thisse, Jacques-François. An Economic Theory of Public Facilities in Space. *Math. Soc. Sci.,* June 1985, *9*(3), pp. 249–62.

Curry, Leslie. Inefficiencies in the Geographical Operation of Labour Markets. *Reg. Stud.,* June 1985, *19*(3), pp. 203–15.

Czamanski, Daniel Z. and Fogel, Smadar. Industrial Location and the Divorce of Management and Ownership. *Ann. Reg. Sci.,* March 1985, *19*(1), pp. 77–86.

Das, Chandrasekhar and Verma, Anil. A Heuristic Method for Finding the Optimal Location and Size of Facilities with Variable Demands. *Logist. Transp. Rev.,* June 1985, *21*(2), pp. 115–31.

Drugge, Sten E. Factor Mobility, the Elasticity of Substitution and Interregional Wage Differentials. *Ann. Reg. Sci.,* November 1985, *19*(3), pp. 34–39.

Evers, Gerard H. M. and van der Veen, Anne. A Simultaneous Non-linear Model for Labour Migration and Commuting. *Reg. Stud.,* June 1985, *19*(3), pp. 217–29. [G: Netherlands]

Faini, Riccardo and Schiantarelli, Fabio. Oligopolistic Models of Investment and Employment Decisions in a Regional Context: Theory and Empirical Evidence from a Putty–Clay Model. *Europ. Econ. Rev.,* March 1985, *27*(2), pp. 221–42. [G: Italy]

Fothergill, Stephen and Gudgin, Graham. Ideology and Methods in Industrial Location Research. In *Massey, D. and Meegan, R., eds.,* 1985, pp. 92–115.

Fotheringham, A. Stewart. Modeling Firms' Locational Choices and Core-Periphery Growth. *Growth Change,* January 1985, *16*(1), pp. 13–16.

Garhart, Robert, Jr. The Role of Error Structure in Simulations on Regional Input–Output Analysis. *J. Reg. Sci.,* August 1985, *25*(3), pp. 353–66.

Gee, J. M. A. Competitive Pricing for a Spatial Industry. *Oxford Econ. Pap.,* September 1985, *37*(3), pp. 466–85.

Ginsburgh, Victor; Papageorgiou, Yorgo and Thisse, Jacques-François. On Existence and Stability of Spatial Equilibria and Steady-States. *Reg. Sci. Urban Econ.,* June 1985, *15*(2), pp. 149–58.

Graves, Philip E. and Knapp, Thomas A. Hedonic Analysis in a Spatial Context: Theoretical Problems in Valuing Location-Specific Amenities. *Econ. Rec.,* December 1985, *61*(175), pp. 737–43.

Greenhut, Melvin L.; Ohta, Hiroshi and Sailors, Joel. Reverse Dumping: A Form of Spatial Price Discrimination. *J. Ind. Econ.,* December 1985, *34*(2), pp. 167–81.

Greenhut, Melvin L., et al. An Anomaly in the Service Industry: The Effect of Entry on Fees. *Econ. J.,* March 1985, *95*(377), pp. 169–77.

Greytak, David and Blackley, Paul R. Labor Productivity and Local Industry Size: Further Issues in Assessing Agglomeration Economies. *Southern Econ. J.,* April 1985, *51*(4), pp. 1121–29. [G: U.S.]

Hanjoul, Pierre and Thisse, Jacques-François. Localisation de la firme sur un réseau. (The Location of a Firm on a Network. With English summary.) *Revue Écon.,* January 1985, *36*(1), pp. 63–101.

Harker, Patrick T. Investigating the Use of the Core as a Solution Concept in Spatial Price Equilibrium Games. In *Harker, P. T., ed.,* 1985, pp. 41–72.

Harris, Curtis C., Jr. and Nadji, Mehrzad. The Spatial Content of the Arrow–Debreu General Equilibrium System. *J. Reg. Sci.,* February 1985, *25*(1), pp. 1–10.

Hashimoto, Hideo. A Spatial Nash Equilibrium Model. In *Harker, P. T., ed.,* 1985, pp. 20–40.

Hashimoto, Hideo. Transshipments and Inventories in the Takayama–Judge Model. *Reg. Sci. Urban Econ.,* August 1985, *15*(3), pp. 365–81.

Higani, Yoshiro. On the 'Exclusion Theorem.' *Reg. Sci. Urban Econ.,* August 1985, *15*(3), pp. 449–58.

Horstmann, Ignatius J. and Slivinski, Alan D. Location Models as Models of Product Choice. *J. Econ. Theory,* August 1985, *36*(2), pp. 367–86.

Hurter, Arthur P., Jr. and Lederer, Phillip J. Spatial Duopoly with Discriminatory Pricing. *Reg. Sci. Urban Econ.,* November 1985, *15*(4), pp. 541–53.

Hurter, Arthur P., Jr. and Martinich, Joseph S. Input Price Uncertainty and the Production-location Decision: A Critique and Synthesis. *Reg. Sci. Urban Econ.,* November 1985, *15*(4), pp. 591–96.

Kanemoto, Yoshitsugu and Mera, Koichi. General Equilibrium Analysis of the Benefits of Large Transportation Improvements. *Reg. Sci. Urban Econ.,* August 1985, *15*(3), pp. 343–63.

Karlson, Stephen H. Spatial Competition with Location-dependent costs. *J. Reg. Sci.,* May 1985, *25*(2), pp. 201–14.

Karmeshu; Bhargava, S. C. and Jain, V. P. A Rationale for Law of Technological Substitution [A Simple Substitution Model of Technological Change]. *Reg. Sci. Urban Econ.,* February 1985, *15*(1), pp. 137–41.

Katz, Joseph L. and Burford, Roger L. Shortcut Formulas for Output, Income and Employment Multipliers. *Ann. Reg. Sci.,* July 1985, *19*(2), pp. 61–76. [G: U.S.]

Klein, Christopher C.; Rifkin, Edward J. and Uri, Noel D. A Note on Defining Geographic Markets. *Reg. Sci. Urban Econ.,* February 1985, *15*(1), pp. 109–19. [G: U.S.]

Kusumoto, Sho-Ichiro. Leontief Technology and the Location of the Firm in a Weber Triangle-specific Localization Theorem. *J. Reg. Sci.,* August 1985, 25(3), pp. 443–51.

Lerman, Steven R. Random Utility Models of Spatial Choice. In *Hutchinson, B. G.; Nijkamp, P. and Batty, M., eds.*, 1985, pp. 200–217.

Lesourne, Jacques. Les infrastructures de transport et la localisation des agents économiques: quelques évidences. (Transportation Infrastructures and Agents' Location: An Analysis of a Few Simple Facts. With English summary.) *Revue Écon.*, January 1985, 36(1), pp. 169–214.

van Lierop, Wal and Nijkamp, Peter. Choice of Model for Spatial Choices: A Methodological Framework. *Indian J. Quant. Econ.*, 1985, 1(2), pp. 43–87.

MacLeod, W. Bentley. On the Non-existence of Equilibria in Differentiated Product Models. *Reg. Sci. Urban Econ.*, June 1985, 15(2), pp. 245–62.

Mai, Chao-cheng. Optimum Location and Theory of the Firm under a Regulatory Constraint. *J. Reg. Sci.*, August 1985, 25(3), pp. 453–61.

Martinich, Joseph S. and Hurter, Arthur P., Jr. Price Uncertainty, Factor Substitution, and the Locational Bias of Business Taxes. *J. Reg. Sci.*, May 1985, 25(2), pp. 175–90.

Mathur, V. K. Location Theory of the Firm under Price Uncertainty: Some New Conclusions. *Reg. Sci. Urban Econ.*, November 1985, 15(4), pp. 597–98.

Melvin, James R. The Regional Economic Consequences of Tariffs and Domestic Transportation Costs. *Can. J. Econ.*, May 1985, 18(2), pp. 237–57.

Mills, David E. Indivisibilities and Development Timing: The Shopping-Center Problem. *Reg. Sci. Urban Econ.*, February 1985, 15(1), pp. 23–40.

Mirakhor, Abbas and Khalili, A. Optimum Location and the Theory of Production: An Extension. *Reg. Sci. Persp.*, 1985, 15(1), pp. 63–74.

Moore, Craig L.; Karaska, Gerald J. and Hill, Joanne M. The Impact of the Banking System on Regional Analyses. *Reg. Stud.*, February 1985, 19(1), pp. 29–35. [G: U.S.]

Nelson, Arthur C. A Unifying View of Greenbelt Influences on Regional Land Values and Implications for Regional Planning Policy. *Growth Change*, April 1985, 16(2), pp. 43–48.

Neven, Damien J. Two Stage (Perfect) Equilibrium in Hotelling's Model. *J. Ind. Econ.*, March 1985, 33(3), pp. 317–25.

de Palma, André, et al. The Principle of Minimum Differentiation Holds under Sufficient Heterogeneity. *Econometrica*, July 1985, 53(4), pp. 767–81.

Pang, Jong-Shi and Lin, Yuh-Yang. A Dual Conjugate Gradient Method for the Single-Commodity Spatial Price Equilibrium Problem. In *Harker, P. T., ed.*, 1985, pp. 136–57.

Persky, Joseph J. and Tam, Mo-Yin S. The Optimal Convergence of Regional Incomes. *J. Reg. Sci.*, August 1985, 25(3), pp. 337–51.

Pinto, James V. Loria and Location Theory. *Ricerche Econ.*, Apr.-June 1985, 39(2), pp. 221–32.

ten Raa, Thijs and Berliant, Marcus. General Competitive Equilibrium of the Spatial Economy: Two Teasers. *Reg. Sci. Urban Econ.*, November 1985, 15(4), pp. 585–90.

Randall, Alan J. and Castle, Emery N. Land Resources and Land Markets. In *Kneese, A. V. and Sweeney, J. L., eds. Vol. 2*, 1985, pp. 571–620.

Renault, Eric and Lesourne, Jacques. Auto-organisation et dispersion géographique des marchés. (Self-Organization and Markets Geographical Distribution. With English summary.) *Écon. Appl.*, 1985, 38(3/4), pp. 703–38.

Richardson, Harry W. Input–Output and Economic Base Multipliers: Looking Backward and Forward. *J. Reg. Sci.*, November 1985, 25(4), pp. 607–61.

Richardson, Harry W. Regional Development Theories. In *Richardson, H. W. and Turek, J. H., eds.*, 1985, pp. 8–27.

Sappington, David E. M. and Wernerfelt, Birger. To Brand or Not to Brand? A Theoretical and Empirical Question. *J. Bus.*, July 1985, 58(3), pp. 279–93. [G: U.S.]

Sayer, Andrew and Morgan, Kevin. A Modern Industry in a Declining Region: Links between Method, Theory and Policy. In *Massey, D. and Meegan, R., eds.*, 1985, pp. 147–68.

Schmalensee, Richard. Econometric Diagnosis of Competitive Localization. *Int. J. Ind. Organ.*, March 1985, 3(1), pp. 57–70. [G: U.S.]

Schöler, Klaus. The Welfare Effects of Spatial Competition under Sequential Market Entry. *Southern Econ. J.*, July 1985, 52(1), pp. 265–73.

Schulz, Norbert and Stahl, Konrad. Localisation des oligopoles et marchés du travail locaux. (Oligopolistic Industry Location and Local Labor Markets. With English summary.) *Revue Écon.*, January 1985, 36(1), pp. 103–34.

Schulz, Norbert and Stahl, Konrad. On the Non-existence of Oligopolistic Equilibria in Differentiated Products Spaces. *Reg. Sci. Urban Econ.*, June 1985, 15(2), pp. 229–43.

Schwab, Robert M. Regional Effects of Investment Incentives. *J. Urban Econ.*, September 1985, 18(2), pp. 125–34. [G: U.S.]

Schweizer, Urs. Theory of City System Structure. *Reg. Sci. Urban Econ.*, June 1985, 15(2), pp. 159–80.

Seninger, Stephen F. Employment Cycles and Process Innovation in Regional Structural Change. *J. Reg. Sci.*, May 1985, 25(2), pp. 259–72.

Seninger, Stephen F. Vacancy Transfers and Job Restructuring in Regional Labor Markets. *Reg. Sci. Urban Econ.*, August 1985, 15(3), pp. 435–48.

Shieh, Yeung-Nan. A Note on the Clarke and Shrestha Linear Space Model [Location and Input Mix Decisions for Energy Facilities]. *Reg. Sci. Urban Econ.*, February 1985, 15(1), pp. 131–35.

Shieh, Yeung-Nan. K. H. Rau and the Economic

Law of Market Areas. *J. Reg. Sci.*, May 1985, 25(2), pp. 191–99.

Shieh, Yeung-Nan. On the Space Cost Curve and Industrial Location: Reply and a Further Analysis. *Ann. Reg. Sci.*, July 1985, 19(2), pp. 95–99.

Siebert, Horst. Spatial Aspects of Environmental Economics. In *Kneese, A. V. and Sweeney, J. L., eds. Vol. 1*, 1985, pp. 125–64.

Smith, Tony E. and Friesz, Terry L. Spatial Market Equilibria with Flow-Dependent Supply and Demand: The Single Commodity Case. *Reg. Sci. Urban Econ.*, June 1985, 15(2), pp. 181–218.

Stahl, Konrad. Existence of Equilibria in Spatial Economies: Presentation. *Reg. Sci. Urban Econ.*, June 1985, 15(2), pp. 143–47.

Steiner, Michael. Old Industrial Areas: A Theoretical Approach. *Urban Stud.*, October 1985, 22(5), pp. 387–98.

Stephan, G. Edward and Dorman, Dan. Testing Size–Density Relationships without Ratio-Variables, Multicollinearity, Logarithmic Transformations, or Regression Analysis. *J. Reg. Sci.*, August 1985, 25(3), pp. 427–35.

Stevens, Benjamin H. Location of Economic Activities: The JRS Contribution to the Research Literature. *J. Reg. Sci.*, November 1985, 25(4), pp. 663–85.

Swaney, James A. and Ward, Frank A. Optimally Locating a National Public Facility: An Empirical Application of Consumer Surplus Theory. *Econ. Geogr.*, April 1985, 61(2), pp. 172–80. [G: U.S.]

Teboul, René. Le circuit comme représentation de l'espace économique (une relecture de l'oeuvre de Pierre de Boisguilbert). (With English summary.) *Revue Écon. Polit.*, Mar.–Apr. 1985, 95(2), pp. 117–33.

Thomas, Morgan D. Regional Economic Development and the Role of Innovation and Technological Change. In *Thwaites, A. T. and Oakey, R. P., eds.*, 1985, pp. 13–35.

Tobin, Roger L. General Spatial Price Equilibria: Sensitivity Analysis for Variational Inequality and Nonlinear Complementarity Formulations. In *Harker, P. T., ed.*, 1985, pp. 158–95.

Tobin, Roger L. and Friesz, Terry L. A New Look at Spatially Competitive Facility Location Models. In *Harker, P. T., ed.*, 1985, pp. 1–19.

Tsuchida, Shu. A Maximum Profit-Margin Vector in Retailing. (In Japanese. With English summary.) *Econ. Stud. Quart.*, April 1985, 36(1), pp. 61–73.

Waterson, Michael. Locational Mobility and Welfare. *Econ. J.*, September 1985, 95(379), pp. 774–77.

Watson, John Keith. A Behavioral Analysis of Negative Price Reactions in Spatial Markets. *Southern Econ. J.*, January 1985, 51(3), pp. 882–85.

Weinberg, Jakob. Bertrand Oligopoly in a Spatial Context: The Case of Quantity Independent Transportation Costs. *Reg. Sci. Urban Econ.*,

June 1985, 15(2), pp. 263–75.

Weskamp, Anita. Existence of Spatial Cournot Equilibria. *Reg. Sci. Urban Econ.*, June 1985, 15(2), pp. 219–27.

West, Douglas S.; Von Hohenbalken, Balder and Kroner, Kenneth. Tests of Intraurban Central Place Theories. *Econ. J.*, March 1985, 95(377), pp. 101–17. [G: Canada]

Wolff, Reiner. Efficient Growth of an Agglomerating Regional Economy. *Reg. Sci. Urban Econ.*, November 1985, 15(4), pp. 555–72.

Young, William. The Application of an Elimination-by-Aspects Model to Urban Location Decisions. In *Hutchinson, B. G.; Nijkamp, P. and Batty, M., eds.*, 1985, pp. 218–34. [G: Australia]

Yu, Eden S. H. and Ingene, Charles A. Resource Allocation with Factor Price Differentials under Price Uncertainty. *Southern Econ. J.*, October 1985, 52(2), pp. 460–70.

Ziegler, Joseph A. On the Space Cost Curve and Industrial Location: Comment. *Ann. Reg. Sci.*, July 1985, 19(2), pp. 93–94.

9412 Regional Economic Studies

Abelson, Peter W. Measures of Economic Welfare: Discussion and Application to Sydney. *Australian Econ. Pap.*, June 1985, 24(44), pp. 95–114.

Agarwal, Vinod B. and Morgan, W. Douglas. The Interindustry Effects of Tax and Expenditure Limitations: The California Case. *Growth Change*, April 1985, 16(2), pp. 3–11. [G: U.S.]

Alden, J. D. and Awang, A. H. Regional Development Planning in Malaysia. *Reg. Stud.*, October 1985, 19(6), pp. 495–508. [G: Malaysia]

Amin, Ash. Restructuring in Fiat and the Decentralization of Production into Southern Italy. In *Hudson, R. and Lewis, J., eds.*, 1985, pp. 155–91. [G: Italy; Europe]

Armstrong, Harvey W. and Taylor, Jim. Regional Policy. In *Atkinson, G. B. J., ed.*, 1985, pp. 35–61. [G: U.K.]

Arnould, Eric J. Evaluating Regional Economic Development: Results of a Marketing System Analysis in Zinder Province, Niger Republic. *J. Devel. Areas*, January 1985, 19(2), pp. 209–44. [G: Niger]

Baer, Donald E. Economic Relations between Latin America and Miami. In *Jorge, A.; Salazar-Carrillo, J. and Diaz-Pou, F., eds.*, 1985, pp. 221–23. [G: U.S.]

Bahl, Roy. Fiscal Problems of Cities in the Northeast. In *Richardson, H. W. and Turek, J. H., eds.*, 1985, pp. 150–63. [G: U.S.]

Bailey, DeeVon and Brorsen, B. Wade. Dynamics of Regional Fed Cattle Prices. *Western J. Agr. Econ.*, July 1985, 10(1), pp. 126–33. [G: U.S.]

Balasubramanyam, V. N. and Rothschild, R. Free Port Zones in the United Kingdom. *Lloyds Bank Rev.*, October 1985, (158), pp. 20–31. [G: U.K.]

Bar-El, Raphael. Industrial Dispersion as an Instrument for the Achievement of Development Goals. *Econ. Geogr.*, July 1985, *61*(3), pp. 205–22.   [G: Brazil]

Barkley, David L. and Helander, Peter E. Commercial Bank Loans and Non-metropolitan Economic Activity: A Question of Causality. *Rev. Reg. Stud.*, Winter 1985, *15*(1), pp. 26–32.   [G: U.S.]

Black, Boyd. Regional Earnings Convergence: The Case of Northern Ireland. *Reg. Stud.*, February 1985, *19*(1), pp. 1–7.   [G: U.K.]

Blackley, Paul R. The Demand for Industrial Sites in a Metropolitan Area: Theory, Empirical Evidence, and Policy Implications. *J. Urban Econ.*, March 1985, *17*(2), pp. 247–61.
                                          [G: U.S.]

Blank, Rebecca M. The Impact of State Economic Differentials on Household Welfare and Labor Force Behavior. *J. Public Econ.*, October 1985, *28*(1), pp. 25–58.   [G: U.S.]

Bourque, Philip J. The Infrastructure Gap. *Growth Change*, January 1985, *16*(1), pp. 17–23.   [G: U.S.]

Bradbury, Katharine L. Prospects for Growth in New England: The Labor Force. *New Eng. Econ. Rev.*, Sept./Oct. 1985, pp. 50–60.
                                          [G: U.S.]

Brewer, H. L. and Moomaw, Ronald L. A Note on Population Size, Industrial Diversification, and Regional Economic Instability. *Urban Stud.*, August 1985, *22*(4), pp. 349–54.
                                          [G: U.S.]

Bromley, Rosemary D. F. and Morgan, Richard H. The Effects of Enterprise Zone Policy: Evidence from Swansea. *Reg. Stud.*, October 1985, *19*(5), pp. 403–13.   [G: U.K.]

Brown, Deborah J. and Pheasant, Jim. A Sharpe Portfolio Approach to Regional Economic Analysis. *J. Reg. Sci.*, February 1985, *25*(1), pp. 51–63.   [G: U.S.]

Buswell, R. J.; Easterbrook, R. P. and Morphet, C. S. Geography, Regions and Research and Development Activity: The Case of the United Kingdom. In *Thwaites, A. T. and Oakey, R. P., eds.*, 1985, pp. 36–66.   [G: U.K.]

Cain, Louis P. William Dean's Theory of Urban Growth: Chicago's Commerce and Industry, 1854–1871. *J. Econ. Hist.*, June 1985, *45*(2), pp. 241–49.   [G: U.S.]

Cameron, Norman E.; Dean, James M. and Good, Walter S. Western Transition in Manufacturing: A Perspective from Sectors in Manitoba. *Can. Public Policy*, Supplement July 1985, *11*(3), pp. 329–34.   [G: Canada]

Carlino, Gerald A. Declining City Productivity and the Growth of Rural Regions: A Test of Alternative Explanations. *J. Urban Econ.*, July 1985, *18*(1), pp. 11–27.   [G: U.S.]

Chall, Daniel E. New York City's "Skills Mismatch." *Fed. Res. Bank New York Quart. Rev.*, Spring 1985, *10*(1), pp. 20–27.   [G: U.S.]

Chalmers, James A. and Greenwood, Michael J. The Regional Labor Market Adjustment Process: Determinants of Changes in Rates of Labor Force Participation, Unemployment, and

Migration. *Ann. Reg. Sci.*, March 1985, *19*(1), pp. 1–17.   [G: U.S.]

Chisholm, Michael. De-industrialization and British Regional Policy. *Reg. Stud.*, August 1985, *19*(4), pp. 301–13.   [G: U.K.]

Civardi, Marisa Bottiroli. La distribuzione personale dei redditi: analisi delle diseguaglianze entor e tra le regioni. (Personal Income Distribution: An Analysis of Internal and Interregional Inequalities. With English summary.) *Ricerche Econ.*, July-Sept. 1985, *39*(3), pp. 337–56.
                                          [G: Italy]

Clark, Gordon L. The Spatial Division of Labor and Wage and Price Controls of the Nixon Administration. *Econ. Geogr.*, April 1985, *61*(2), pp. 113–28.   [G: U.S.]

Clarkson, L. A. An Economic History of Ulster 1820–1939: Population Change and Urbanisation, 1821–1911. In *Kennedy, L. and Ollerenshaw, P., eds.*, 1985, pp. 137–57.   [G: U.K.]

Cocheba, Donald J.; Gilmer, Robert W. and Mack, Richard S. Data Refinement Recommendations and Their Impact on a Study of the Tennessee Valley: Measuring Changes in Service Sector Activity. *Growth Change*, October 1985, *16*(4), pp. 20–42.   [G: U.S.]

Coclanis, Peter A. Bitter Harvest: The South Carolina Low Country in Historic Perspective. *J. Econ. Hist.*, June 1985, *45*(2), pp. 251–59.
                                          [G: U.S.]

Collis, Clive and Mallier, Anthony T. Employment Change in Coventry, 1971–78: A Shift–Share Approach. *Brit. Rev. Econ. Issues*, Autumn 1985, *7*(17), pp. 51–85.   [G: U.K.]

Connaughton, John E. and Madsen, Ronald A. State and Regional Impact of the 1981–82 Recession. *Growth Change*, July 1985, *16*(3), pp. 1–10.   [G: U.S.]

Cromley, Robert G. and Green, Milford B. Joint Venture Activity Patterns of U.S. Firms, 1972–1979. *Growth Change*, July 1985, *16*(3), pp. 40–53.   [G: U.S.]

Cruz, Robert D. Forecasting the Economic Interaction between Latin America and Miami. In *Jorge, A.; Salazar-Carrillo, J. and Diaz-Pou, F., eds.*, 1985, pp. 165–80.   [G: U.S.; Latin America]

Dienes, Leslie. Economic and Strategic Position of the Soviet Far East. *Soviet Econ.*, Apr.-June 1985, *1*(2), pp. 146–76.   [G: U.S.S.R.]

Docwra, George and Strong, Sam M. Road Fund Allocation: An Analysis of Decision Criteria. *Int. J. Transport Econ.*, October 1985, *12*(3), pp. 283–300.   [G: Australia]

Dolishny, M. I. Regional Programmes for Improving Labour Productivity: An Example from the Western Ukraine. *Int. Lab. Rev.*, May-June 1985, *124*(3), pp. 323–33.   [G: U.S.S.R.]

Doolittle, Fred C. Adjustments in Buffalo's Labor Market. *Fed. Res. Bank New York Quart. Rev.*, Winter 1985-86, *10*(4), pp. 28–37.
                                          [G: U.S.]

Drugge, Sten E. Nonneutral Technical Change and Regional Wage Differentials: A Comment. *J. Reg. Sci.*, February 1985, *25*(1), pp. 135–36.   [G: U.S.]

Dunlevy, James A. Factor Endowments, Heterogeneous Labor and North–South Migration. *Southern Econ. J.*, October 1985, 52(2), pp. 446–59. [G: U.S.]

Eberstein, Isaac W.; Wrigley, J. Michael and Serow, William J. An Examination of the Utility of Ecological and Economic Base Approaches to Regional Structures. *Soc. Sci. Quart.*, March 1985, 66(1), pp. 34–49. [G: U.S.]

Eskelinen, Heikki. International Integration and Regional Economic Development: The Finnish Experience. *J. Common Market Stud.*, March 1985, 23(3), pp. 229–55. [G: EEC; Finland]

Faini, Riccardo. Incentivi e poccole e medie imprese nel mezzogiorno. (Incentives and Small Firms in the Mezzogiorno. With English summary.) *Ricerche Econ.*, July-Sept. 1985, 39(3), pp. 318–36. [G: Italy]

Ferleger, Louis. Capital Goods and Southern Economic Development. *J. Econ. Hist.*, June 1985, 45(2), pp. 411–17. [G: U.S.]

Ferrão, João. Regional Variations in the Rate of Profit in Portuguese Industry. In *Hudson, R. and Lewis, J., eds.*, 1985, pp. 211–45. [G: Portugal]

Fodella, Gianni. De-centralization of Economic Activity for Local Resource Development. *Rivista Int. Sci. Econ. Com.*, February 1985, 32(2), pp. 183–95. [G: OECD; LDCs]

Fong, Mo-Kwan Lee. Tourism: A Critical Review. In *Wong, K. and Chu, D. K. Y., eds.*, 1985, pp. 79–88. [G: China]

Foster, Mark S. Giant of the West: Henry J. Kaiser and Regional Industrialization, 1930–1950. *Bus. Hist. Rev.*, Spring 1985, 59(1), pp. 1–23. [G: U.S.]

Gale, James R. and Merz, Thomas E. The Opportunity Cost of an Abundant Resource: The Case of Water Diverted from the Great Lakes to the Ogallala Aquifer Region. *Reg. Sci. Persp.*, 1985, 15(1), pp. 3–12. [G: U.S.]

Gamble, Hays B. and Downing, Roger H. The Relationship between Population Growth and Real Assessed Market Values: Note. *Growth Change*, July 1985, 16(3), pp. 74–77. [G: U.S.]

Garnick, Daniel H. Patterns of Growth in Metropolitan and Nonmetropolitan Areas: An Update. *Surv. Curr. Bus.*, May 1985, 65(5), pp. 33–38. [G: U.S.]

Geddert, Ronald L. and Semple, R. Keith. Locating a Major Hockey Franchise: Regional Considerations. *Reg. Sci. Persp.*, 1985, 15(1), pp. 13–29. [G: U.S.; Canada]

Gibbs, D. C. and Edwards, A. The Diffusion of New Production Innovations in British Industry. In *Thwaites, A. T. and Oakey, R. P., eds.*, 1985, pp. 132–63. [G: U.K.]

Goddard, J. B., et al. The Impact of New Information Technology on Urban and Regional Structure in Europe. In *Thwaites, A. T. and Oakey, R. P., eds.*, 1985, pp. 215–41. [G: W. Europe; U.K.]

Goode, Frank M. The Use of Microdata to Measure Employment Changes in Small Communi-ties. *J. Econ. Soc. Meas.*, July 1985, 13(2), pp. 187–97. [G: U.S.]

Gordon, Ian R. The Cyclical Interaction between Regional Migration, Employment and Unemployment: A Time Series Analysis for Scotland. *Scot. J. Polit. Econ.*, June 1985, 32(2), pp. 135–58. [G: U.K.]

Gordon, Ian R. The Cyclical Sensitivity of Regional Employment and Unemployment Differentials. *Reg. Stud.*, April 1985, 19(2), pp. 95–110. [G: U.K.]

Gould, Andrew and Keeble, David. New Firms and Rural Industrialization in East Anglia. In *Storey, D. J., ed.*, 1985, pp. 43–71. [G: U.K.]

Green, A. E. Unemployment Duration in the Recession: The Local Labour Market Area Scale. *Reg. Stud.*, April 1985, 19(2), pp. 111–29. [G: U.K.]

Greytak, David and Blackley, Paul R. Labor Productivity and Local Industry Size: Further Issues in Assessing Agglomeration Economies. *Southern Econ. J.*, April 1985, 51(4), pp. 1121–29. [G: U.S.]

Gripsrud, Geir and Gronhaug, Kjell. Structure and Strategy in Grocery Retailing: A Sociometric Approach. *J. Ind. Econ.*, March 1985, 33(3), pp. 339–47. [G: Norway]

Gürkan, A. Arslan. The Regional Structure of Agricultural Production in Turkey: A Multivariate Perspective. *METU*, 1985, 12(1/2), pp. 27–47. [G: Turkey]

Guseman, Patricia K. and Sapp, Stephen G. Regional Trends in U.S. Food Consumption: Population Scale, Composition, and Income Effects. *Rev. Reg. Stud.*, Spring 1985, 15(2), pp. 34–42. [G: U.S.]

Håkanson, Lars and Danielsson, Lars. Structural Adjustment in a Stagnating Economy: Regional Manufacturing Employment in Sweden, 1975–1980. *Reg. Stud.*, August 1985, 19(4), pp. 329–42. [G: Sweden]

Hall, Randolph W. Heuristics for Selecting Facility Locations. *Logist. Transp. Rev.*, December 1985, 21(4), pp. 353–73. [G: U.S.]

Harrell, Louis and Fischer, Dale. The 1982 Mexican Peso Devaluation and Border Area Employment. *Mon. Lab. Rev.*, October 1985, 108(10), pp. 25–32. [G: Mexico; U.S.]

Harrington, James W., Jr. Intraindustry Structural Change and Location Change: U.S. Semiconductor Manufacturing, 1958–1980. *Reg. Stud.*, August 1985, 19(4), pp. 343–52. [G: U.S.]

Harrison, Bennett. Increasing Instability and Inequality in the "Revival" of the New England Economy. In *Richardson, H. W. and Turek, J. H., eds.*, 1985, pp. 123–49. [G: U.S.]

Harrison, Bennett and Bluestone, Barry. Problems of Economic Deterioration. In *Woodworth, W.; Meek, C. and Whyte, W. F., eds.*, 1985, pp. 64–77. [G: U.S.]

Hebbert, Michael. Regional Autonomy and Economic Action in the First Catalan Government, 1980–1984. *Reg. Stud.*, October 1985, 19(5), pp. 433–45. [G: Spain]

Hekman, John S. Branch Plant Location and the Product Cycle in Computer Manufacturing. *J. Econ. Bus.*, May 1985, *37*(2), pp. 89–102. [G: U.S.]

Helms, L. Jay. The Effect of State and Local Taxes on Economic Growth: A Time Series–Cross Section Approach. *Rev. Econ. Statist.*, November 1985, *67*(4), pp. 574–82. [G: U.S.]

Hill, Richard Child and Negrey, Cynthia. The Politics of Industrial Policy in Michigan. In *Zukin, S., ed.*, 1985, pp. 119–38. [G: U.S.]

Hoggart, Keith. Welsh Local Authority Employment since 1979: Political Party Effects in District Councils. *Reg. Stud.*, October 1985, *19*(5), pp. 447–57. [G: U.K.]

Hoppes, R. Bradley. Pooled Regression and Covariance Analysis of SMSA Selected Services: Earnings and Firm Size. *Reg. Sci. Persp.*, 1985, *15*(1), pp. 31–45. [G: U.S.]

Hunt, Gary L. and Greenwood, Michael J. Econometrically Accounting for Identities and Restrictions in Models of Interregional Migration: Further Thoughts. *Reg. Sci. Urban Econ.*, November 1985, *15*(4), pp. 605–14. [G: U.S.]

Huskey, Lee. The Hidden Dynamic in the Growth of Frontier Regions: Import Substitution. *Growth Change*, October 1985, *16*(4), pp. 43–55. [G: U.S.]

Hutchinson, William K. Import Substitution, Structural Change, and Regional Economic Growth in the United States: The Northeast, 1870–1910. *J. Econ. Hist.*, June 1985, *45*(2), pp. 319–25. [G: U.S.]

Jeffrey, D. Trends and Fluctuations in Visitor Flows to Yorkshire and Humberside Hotels: An Analysis of Daily Bed Occupancy Rates, 1982–1984. *Reg. Stud.*, October 1985, *19*(6), pp. 509–22. [G: U.K.]

Johannes, James M.; Koch, Paul D. and Rasche, Robert H. Estimating Regional Construction Cost Differences: Theory and Evidence. *Managerial Dec. Econ.*, June 1985, *6*(2), pp. 70–79. [G: U.S.]

Johnson, D. S. The Northern Ireland Economy, 1914–39. In *Kennedy, L. and Ollerenshaw, P., eds.*, 1985, pp. 184–223. [G: U.K.]

Johnson, Kenneth P. and Friedenberg, Howard L. Regional and State Projections of Income, Employment, and Population to the Year 2000. *Surv. Curr. Bus.*, May 1985, *65*(5), pp. 39–63. [G: U.S.]

Johnson, Merrill L. Postwar Industrial Development in the Southeast and the Pioneer Role of Labor-intensive Industry. *Econ. Geogr.*, January 1985, *61*(1), pp. 46–65. [G: U.S.]

Jones, David R. and MacKay, R. Ross. Unemployment in Wales: The Implications of Government Priorities. *Nat. Westminster Bank Quart. Rev.*, May 1985, pp. 74–84. [G: U.K.]

Jones, M. E. F. Regional Employment Multipliers, Regional Policy, and Structural Change in Interwar Britain. *Exploration Econ. Hist.*, October 1985, *22*(4), pp. 417–39. [G: U.K.]

Katz, Arnold. Growth and Regional Variations in

Unemployment in Yugoslavia: 1965–1980. In *Jones, D. C. and Svejnar, J., eds.*, 1985, pp. 153–77. [G: Yugoslavia]

Keinath, William F., Jr. The Spatial Components of the Post-industrial Society. *Econ. Geogr.*, July 1985, *61*(3), pp. 223–40. [G: U.S.]

Keleş, Ruşen. The Effects of External Migration on Regional Development in Turkey. In *Hudson, R. and Lewis, J., eds.*, 1985, pp. 54–75. [G: Turkey]

Kennedy, Líam. An Economic History of Ulster 1820–1939: The Rural Economy, 1820–1914. In *Kennedy, L. and Ollerenshaw, P., eds.*, 1985, pp. 1–61. [G: U.K.]

Kerr, William A. The Changing Economics of the Western Livestock Industry. *Can. Public Policy*, Supplement July 1985, *11*(3), pp. 294–300. [G: Canada]

Kielstra, Nico. The Rural Languedoc: Periphery to "Relictual Space." In *Hudson, R. and Lewis, J., eds.*, 1985, pp. 246–62. [G: France]

Kim, Tschangho John and Kim, Jong Gie. Issues in Building a National Transportation Development Model: Experience from a Korean Application. *Ann. Reg. Sci.*, March 1985, *19*(1), pp. 18–36. [G: S. Korea]

Klein, Christopher C.; Rifkin, Edward J. and Uri, Noel D. A Note on Defining Geographic Markets. *Reg. Sci. Urban Econ.*, February 1985, *15*(1), pp. 109–19. [G: U.S.]

Kodras, Janet E. and Brown, Lawrence A. The Dissemination of Public Sector Innovations with Relevance to Regional Change in the United States. In *Thwaites, A. T. and Oakey, R. P., eds.*, 1985, pp. 195–214. [G: U.S.]

Kofman, Eleonore. Dependent Development in Corisca. In *Hudson, R. and Lewis, J., eds.*, 1985, pp. 263–83. [G: France]

Kuehn, John A. and Bender, Lloyd D. Nonmetropolitan Economic Bases and Their Policy Implications. *Growth Change*, January 1985, *16*(1), pp. 24–29. [G: U.S.]

Langston, Donald; Rasmussen, David W. and Simmons, James C. A Note on Geographic Living Cost Differentials. *Land Econ.*, August 1985, *61*(3), pp. 314–18. [G: U.S.]

Lee, Kyu Sik. Decentralization Trends of Employment Location and Spatial Policies in LDC Cities. *Urban Stud.*, April 1985, *22*(2), pp. 151–62. [G: Colombia]

Lichter, Daniel T. Racial Concentration and Segregation across U.S. Counties, 1950–1980. *Demography*, November 1985, *22*(4), pp. 603–09. [G: U.S.]

Lichty, Richard W.; Steinnes, Donald N. and Vose, David A. Strategic Planning of Economic Development Based on an Analysis of the Extent and Pattern of Importation. *Reg. Sci. Persp.*, 1985, *15*(1), pp. 46–62. [G: U.S.]

Lim, Chee Peng. The Role of Regional Development Authorities and Rural Non-farm Activities in Malaysia. In *Mukhopadhyay, S. and Chee, P. L., eds. (II)*, 1985, pp. 177–26. [G: Malaysia]

Lin, An-loh. A Note on Testing for Regional Homogeneity of a Parameter. *J. Reg. Sci.*, February

1985, *25*(1), pp. 129–34.   [G: U.S.]
Lindauer, David L. Regional Wage Determination and Economic Growth in Korea. *J. Econ. Devel.*, July 1985, *10*(1), pp. 129–41.
          [G: S. Korea]
Lindblad, Jan Thomas. Economic Change in Southeast Kalimantan 1880–1940. *Bull. Indonesian Econ. Stud.*, December 1985, *21*(3), pp. 69–103.   [G: Indonesia]
Little, Jane Sneddon. Foreign Direct Investment in New England. *New Eng. Econ. Rev.*, March/April 1985, pp. 48–57.   [G: U.S.]
Lloyd, Peter E. and Mason, C. M. Spatial Variations in New Firm Formation in the United Kingdom: Comparative Evidence from Merseyside, Greater Manchester and South Hampshire. In *Storey, D. J., ed.,* 1985, pp. 72–100.
          [G: U.K.]
Lloyd, Peter E. and Shutt, John. Recession and Restructuring in the North-west Region, 1975–82: The Implications of Recent Events. In *Massey, D. and Meegan, R., eds.,* 1985, pp. 16–60.   [G: U.K.]
Loviscek, Anthony and Crowley, Frederick. Energy Prices and Municipal Bond Ratings: Are Interregional Terms of Trade Shifting? *J. Energy Devel.*, Spring 1985, *10*(2), pp. 201–12.
          [G: U.S.]
Lyons, Thomas P. China's Cellular Economy: A Test of the Fragmentation Hypothesis. *J. Compar. Econ.*, June 1985, *9*(2), pp. 125–44.
          [G: China]
Madden, J. R.; Challen, D. W. and Hagger, A. J. The Grants Commission's Relativities Proposals: Effects on the State Economies—A Reply. *Australian Econ. Pap.*, June 1985, *24*(44), pp. 218–21.   [G: Australia]
Malecki, Edward J. Industrial Location and Corporate Organization in High Technology Industries. *Econ. Geogr.*, October 1985, *61*(4), pp. 345–69.   [G: U.S.]
Malecki, Edward J. Public Sector Research and Development and Regional Economic Performance in the United States. In *Thwaites, A. T. and Oakey, R. P., eds.,* 1985, pp. 115–31.   [G: U.S.]
Mansell, Robert L. The Service Sector and Western Economic Growth. *Can. Public Policy,* Supplement July 1985, *11*(3), pp. 354–60.
          [G: Canada]
Markusen, Ann R. and Teitz, Michael B. The World of Small Business: Turbulence and Survival. In *Storey, D. J., ed.,* 1985, pp. 193–218.   [G: U.S.]
Marshall, J. N. Business Services, the Regions and Regional Policy. *Reg. Stud.*, August 1985, *19*(4), pp. 353–63.   [G: U.K.]
Marshall, M. Technological Change and Local Economic Strategy in the West Midlands. *Reg. Stud.*, October 1985, *19*(6), pp. 570–78.
          [G: U.K.]
Marston, Stephen T. Two Views of the Geographic Distribution of Unemployment. *Quart. J. Econ.*, February 1985, *100*(1), pp. 57–79.   [G: U.S.]
Martin, R. L. Monetarism Masquerading as Re-

gional Policy? The Government's New System of Regional Aid. *Reg. Stud.*, August 1985, *19*(4), pp. 379–88.   [G: U.S.]
Mathews, Russell L. The Grants Commission's Relativities Proposals: A Comment. *Australian Econ. Pap.*, June 1985, *24*(44), pp. 214–17.
          [G: Australia]
Maxwell, Philip. Growth, Decline and Structural Change: A Study of Regional Labour Markets in Australia 1971–1981. *Urban Stud.*, December 1985, *22*(6), pp. 493–505.   [G: Australia]
McAuley, Alastair. Soviet Development Policy in Central Asia. In *Cassen, R., ed.,* 1985, pp. 299–318.   [G: U.S.S.R.]
McCrae, James J. Can Growth in the Service Sector Rescue Western Canada? *Can. Public Policy,* Supplement July 1985, *11*(3), pp. 351–53.
McDonald, John F. and South, David W. A Comparison of Two Methods to Project Regional and State Populations for the U.S. *Ann. Reg. Sci.*, November 1985, *19*(3), pp. 40–53.
          [G: U.S.]
McGee, Robert T. State Unemployment Rates: What Explains the Differences? *Fed. Res. Bank New York Quart. Rev.*, Spring 1985, *10*(1), pp. 28–35.   [G: U.S.]
McGuire, Therese J. Are Local Property Taxes Important in the Intrametropolitan Location Decisions of Firms? An Empirical Analysis of the Minneapolis–St. Paul Metropolitan Area. *J. Urban Econ.*, September 1985, *18*(2), pp. 226–34.   [G: U.S.]
McMillan, Melville L. Western Transition: The Economic Future of the West: Introduction. *Can. Public Policy,* Supplement July 1985, *11*(3), pp. 260–62.   [G: Canada]
Meek, Christopher and Woodworth, Warner. Absentee Ownership, Industrial Decline, and Organizational Renewal. In *Woodworth, W.; Meek, C. and Whyte, W. F., eds.,* 1985, pp. 78–96.   [G: U.S.]
Merrifield, David E. and Haynes, Richard W. A Cost Analysis of the Lumber and Plywood Industries in Two Pacific Northwest Sub-regions. *Ann. Reg. Sci.*, November 1985, *19*(3), pp. 16–33.   [G: U.S.]
Meyer-Krahmer, Frieder. Innovation Behaviour and Regional Indigenous Potential. *Reg. Stud.,* October 1985, *19*(6), pp. 523–34.
          [G: W. Germany]
Miernyk, William H. Energy Constraints and Economic Development in the Northeast. In *Richardson, H. W. and Turek, J. H., eds.,* 1985, pp. 104–22.   [G: U.S.]
Mieszkowski, Peter. The Differential Effect of the Foreign Trade Deficit on Regions in the United States. In *Quigley, J. M. and Rubinfeld, D. L., eds.,* 1985, pp. 346–63.   [G: U.S.]
Milne, William J. and Foot, David K. Econometrically Accounting for Identities and Restrictions in Models of Interregional Migration: A Comment. *Reg. Sci. Urban Econ.*, November 1985, *15*(4), pp. 599–603.   [G: U.S.]
Moomaw, Ronald L. Firm Location and City Size: Reduced Productivity Advantages as a Factor

in the Decline of Manufacturing in Urban Areas. *J. Urban Econ.*, January 1985, *17*(1), pp. 73–89. [G: U.S.]

Moore, William J. and Newman, Robert J. The Effects of Right-to-Work Laws: A Review of the Literature. *Ind. Lab. Relat. Rev.*, July 1985, *38*(4), pp. 571–85. [G: U.S.]

Mosley, Paul. Achievements and Contradictions of the Peruvian Agrarian Reform: A Regional Perspective. *J. Devel. Stud.*, April 1985, *21*(3), pp. 440–48. [G: Peru]

Mountain, Dean C. Productivity and Energy Price Differentials. *Reg. Sci. Urban Econ.*, August 1985, *15*(3), pp. 477–89. [G: Canada]

Murgatroyd, Linda G. and Urry, John. The Class and Gender Restructuring of the Lancaster Economy, 1950–80. In *Roberts, B.; Finnegan, R. and Gallie, D., eds.*, 1985, pp. 68–85. [G: U.K.]

Murphy, Kevin J. Unemployment Dispersion and the Allocative Efficiency of the Labor Market. *J. Macroecon.*, Fall 1985, *7*(4), pp. 509–22. [G: U.S.]

Nakamura, Ryohei. Agglomeration Economies in Urban Manufacturing Industries: A Case of Japanese Cities. *J. Urban Econ.*, January 1985, *17*(1), pp. 108–24. [G: Japan]

Neale, Walter C. Indian Community Development, Local Government, Local Planning, and Rural Policy since 1950. *Econ. Develop. Cult. Change*, July 1985, *33*(4), pp. 677–98. [G: India]

Ng, Yen-Tak and Chu, David K. Y. The Geographical Endowment of China's Special Economic Zones. In *Wong, K. and Chu, D. K. Y., eds.*, 1985, pp. 40–56. [G: China]

Nikolinakos, Marios. Transnationalization of Production, Location of Industry and the Deformation of Regional Development in Peripheral Countries: The Case of Greece. In *Hudson, R. and Lewis, J., eds.*, 1985, pp. 192–210. [G: Greece]

Norris, Peter and Jones, Kelvyn. Planning Applications of Area Classification: Some Examples from Hampshire. *J. Econ. Soc. Meas.*, April 1985, *13*(1), pp. 97–111. [G: U.K.]

Nowak, Jan and Romanowska, Hanna. Locational Patterns of the Food-Processing Industry in Poland. *Europ. Rev. Agr. Econ.*, 1985, *12*(3), pp. 233–46. [G: Poland]

O'Farrell, P. N. and Crouchley, R. An Industrial and Spatial Analysis of New Firm Formation in Ireland. In *Storey, D. J., ed.*, 1985, pp. 101–34. [G: Ireland]

Oakey, R. P. Innovation and Regional Growth in Small High Technology Firms: Evidence from Britain and the USA. In *Storey, D. J., ed.*, 1985, pp. 135–65. [G: U.K.; U.S.]

Oates, Wallace E. and McGartland, Albert M. Marketable Pollution Permits and Acid Rain Externalities: A Comment and Some Further Evidence. *Can. J. Econ.*, August 1985, *18*(3), pp. 668–75. [G: Canada; U.S.]

Okabe, Atsuyuki; Asami, Yasushi and Miki, Fujio. Statistical Analysis of the Spatial Association of Convenience-Goods Stores by Use of a Random Clumping Model. *J. Reg. Sci.*, February 1985, *25*(1), pp. 11–28. [G: Japan]

Pachauri, R. K.; Chen, Chia-Yon and Srivastava, Leena. Coal Transportation System Modeling—The Case of Taiwan: A Comment. *Energy J.*, July 1985, *6*(3), pp. 109–14. [G: Taiwan]

Paci, Raffaele. Accumulation Process and Investment Incentives in a Vintage Investment Model: The Case of Sardinia. *Rivista Int. Sci. Econ. Com.*, July-Aug. 1985, *32*(7–8), pp. 765–94. [G: Italy]

Parr, John B. A Note on the Size Distribution of Cities over Time. *J. Urban Econ.*, September 1985, *18*(2), pp. 199–212. [G: Selected Countries]

Parr, John B. A Population-Density Approach to Regional Spatial Structure. *Urban Stud.*, August 1985, *22*(4), pp. 289–303. [G: U.S.; U.K.]

Pasha, Hafiz A. and Bengali, Kaiser. Impact of Fiscal Incentives on Industrialisation in Backward Areas: A Case Study of Hub Chowki in Baluchistan. *Pakistan J. Appl. Econ.*, Summer 1985, *4*(1), pp. 1–16. [G: Pakistan]

Pearce, James E. and Gunther, Jeffrey W. Illegal Immigration from Mexico: Effects on the Texas Economy. *Fed. Res. Bank Dallas Econ. Rev.*, September 1985, pp. 1–14. [G: U.S.]

Persky, Joseph J. and Tam, Mo-Yin S. The Optimal Convergence of Regional Incomes. *J. Reg. Sci.*, August 1985, *25*(3), pp. 337–51.

Petrović, Radivoj and Stojanović, Sonja. Prilog višekriterijumskom rangiranju regiona. (Multi-criteria Ranking of Economic Regions. With English summary.) *Econ. Anal. Worker's Manage.*, 1985, *19*(4), pp. 395–434. [G: Yugoslavia]

Ponting, J. Rick and Waters, Nigel. The Impact of Public Policy on Locational Decision-making by Industrial Firms. *Can. Public Policy*, December 1985, *11*(4), pp. 731–44. [G: Canada]

Portney, Paul R. Regional Issues: Commentary. In *Quigley, J. M. and Rubinfeld, D. L., eds.*, 1985, pp. 364–68. [G: U.S.]

Pugliese, Enrico. Farm Workers in Italy: Agricultural Working Class, Landless Peasants, or Clients of the Welfare State? In *Hudson, R. and Lewis, J., eds.*, 1985, pp. 123–39. [G: Italy]

Raghupati, T., et al. Case Study on Rural Non-farm Activities in India. In *Mukhopadhyay, S. and Chee, P. L., eds. (II)*, 1985, pp. 3–74. [G: India]

Rees, J.; Briggs, R. and Hicks, D. New Technology in the United States' Machinery Industry: Trends and Implications. In *Thwaites, A. T. and Oakey, R. P., eds.*, 1985, pp. 164–94. [G: U.S.]

Rees, R. David. Is There Still a National Economic Case for Regional Policy? *Reg. Stud.*, October 1985, *19*(5), pp. 471–75. [G: U.K.]

Richardson, David and Rubinstein, Danny. West Bank and Gaza—Economy. In *Levinson, P. and Landau, P., eds.*, 1985, pp. 54–57. [G: Israel]

Richardson, Harry W. Regional Policy in a "Slowth" Economy. In *Richardson, H. W. and Turek, J. H., eds.*, 1985, pp. 243–63.
[G: U.S.]

Richardson, Harry W. and Turek, Joseph H. The Scope and Limits of Federal Intervention. In *Richardson, H. W. and Turek, J. H., eds.*, 1985, pp. 211–42.
[G: U.S.]

Rizzo, Ilde. Regional Disparities and Decentralization as Determinants of Public-Sector Expenditure Growth in Italy (1960–81). In *Forte, F. and Peacock, A., eds.*, 1985, pp. 65–82.
[G: Italy]

Roberts, P. W. Mobile Manufacturing Firms: Locational Choice and Some Policy Implications. *Reg. Stud.*, October 1985, *19*(5), pp. 475–81.
[G: U.K.]

Robertson, E. J. Developing the West's Manufacturing Potential: The Role of Provincial Governments. *Can. Public Policy*, Supplement July 1985, *11*(3), pp. 335–38. [G: Canada]

Sagers, Matthew J. The Soviet Periphery: Economic Development of Belorussia. *Soviet Econ.*, July-Sept. 1985, *1*(3), pp. 261–84.
[G: U.S.S.R.]

Sasaki, Komei. Regional Difference in Total Factor Productivity and Spatial Features: Empirical Analysis on the Basis of a Sectoral Translog Production Function. *Reg. Sci. Urban Econ.*, November 1985, *15*(4), pp. 489–516.
[G: Japan]

Savitch, H. V. Boom and Bust in the New York Region: Implications for Government Policy. In *Richardson, H. W. and Turek, J. H., eds.*, 1985, pp. 164–85. [G: U.S.]

Scarfe, Brian L. Financing Oil and Gas Exploration and Development Activity. *Can. Public Policy*, Supplement July 1985, *11*(3), pp. 402–06. [G: Canada]

Scarfe, Brian L. Prospects and Policies for Western Canadian Growth. *Can. Public Policy*, Supplement July 1985, *11*(3), pp. 361–64.
[G: Canada]

Schreiner, Alette and Skoglund, Tor. Regional Impacts of Petroleum Activities in Norway. In *Bjerkholt, O. and Offerdal, E., eds.*, 1985, pp. 203–29. [G: Norway]

Schwab, Robert M. Regional Effects of Investment Incentives. *J. Urban Econ.*, September 1985, *18*(2), pp. 125–34. [G: U.S.]

Schweikart, Larry. Antebellum Southern Bankers: Origins and Mobility. In *Atack, J., ed.*, 1985, pp. 79–103. [G: U.S.]

Segal, N. S. The Cambridge Phenomenon. *Reg. Stud.*, October 1985, *19*(6), pp. 563–70.
[G: U.K.]

Shaffer, Ron E. and Pulver, Glen C. Regional Variations in Capital Structure of New Small Businesses: The Wisconsin Case. In *Storey, D. J., ed.*, 1985, pp. 166–92. [G: U.S.]

Shank, Susan Elizabeth. Changes in Regional Unemployment over the Last Decade. *Mon. Lab. Rev.*, March 1985, *108*(3), pp. 17–23.
[G: U.S.]

Shim, Jae K. A Spatial Equilibrium Analysis of Southern Pine Lumber Pricing and Allocation.

Ann. Reg. Sci., March 1985, *19*(1), pp. 61–76. [G: U.S.]

Silver, M. S. United Republic of Tanzania: Overall Concentration, Regional Concentration, and the Growth of the Parastatal Sector in the Manufacturing Industry. *Industry Devel.*, 1985, (15), pp. 19–36. [G: Tanzania]

Sloan, Judith. The Regional Dimension of Structural Change: The Case of Textiles, Clothing and Footwear. *Australian Bull. Lab.*, December 1985, *12*(1), pp. 46–56. [G: Australia]

Snickars, F. and Johansson, B. The Development of Natural Gas Deposits in Western Siberia. In *Lakshmanan, T. R. and Johansson, B., eds.*, 1985, pp. 27–40. [G: U.S.S.R.]

Söderberg, Johan. Regional Economic Disparity and Dynamics, 1840–1914: A Comparison between France, Great Britain, Prussia, and Sweden. *J. Europ. Econ. Hist.*, Fall 1985, *14*(2), pp. 273–96. [G: France; U.K.; Sweden; Prussia]

Solomon, Barry D. and Rubin, Barry M. Environmental Linkages in Regional Econometric Models: An Analysis of Coal Development in Western Kentucky. *Land Econ.*, February 1985, *61*(1), pp. 43–57. [G: U.S.]

Sternlieb, George and Hughes, James W. The National Economy and the Northeast: A Context for Discussion. In *Richardson, H. W. and Turek, J. H., eds.*, 1985, pp. 66–84.
[G: U.S.]

Stevens, Benjamin H. Regional Cost Equalization and the Potential for Manufacturing Recovery in the Industrial North. In *Richardson, H. W. and Turek, J. H., eds.*, 1985, pp. 85–103.
[G: U.S.]

Storey, D. J. Manufacturing Employment Change in Northern England 1965–78: The Role of Small Businesses. In *Storey, D. J., ed.*, 1985, pp. 6–42. [G: U.K.]

Storey, D. J. Small Firms in Regional Economic Development: The Implications for Policy. In *Storey, D. J., ed.*, 1985, pp. 219–29.
[G: U.K.]

Storper, Michael. Disequilibrium and Dynamics in Metropolitan Economic Development in the Third World: Reply. *Reg. Stud.*, February 1985, *19*(1), pp. 51–57. [G: LDCs]

Storper, Michael. Response to Professor Vining's 'Query' [Who Benefits from Industrial Decentralization? Social Power in the Labour Market, Income Distribution and Spatial Policy in Brazil]. *Reg. Stud.*, April 1985, *19*(2), pp. 164.
[G: Brazil]

Stutzer, Michael J. The Statewide Economic Impact of Small-Issue Industrial Revenue Bonds. *Fed. Res. Bank Minn. Rev.*, Spring 1985, *9*(2), pp. 2–13. [G: U.S.]

Sveikauskas, Leo; Townroe, Peter and Hansen, Eric. Intraregional Productivity Differences in São Paulo State Manufacturing Plants. *Weltwirtsch. Arch.*, 1985, *121*(4), pp. 722–40.
[G: Brazil]

Svetanant, Prapant. Rural Non-farm Activities in Thailand: Comparative Case Studies in Irrigated and Rainfed Areas in the Northeast. In

Mukhopadhyay, S. and Chee, P. L., eds. (II), 1985, pp. 75–115. [G: Thailand]

Swan, Neil M. Competing Models of Western Growth: Continued Specialization in Resources or Greater Diversification. *Can. Public Policy,* Supplement July 1985, *11*(3), pp. 283–89. [G: Canada]

Swan, Neil M. The Service Sector: Engine of Growth? *Can. Public Policy,* Supplement July 1985, *11*(3), pp. 344–50. [G: Canada]

Swan, Neil M. and Slater, David W. Reflections on Western Transition. *Can. Public Policy,* Supplement July 1985, *11*(3), pp. 365–70. [G: Canada]

Swann, G. M. P. Product Competition in Microprocessors. *J. Ind. Econ.,* September 1985, *34*(1), pp. 33–53. [G: U.S.]

Tabuchi, Takatoshi. Time-Series Modeling of Gross Migration and Dynamic Equilibrium. *J. Reg. Sci.,* February 1985, *25*(1), pp. 65–83. [G: U.S.; Japan]

Taylor, Patricia A. and Gwartney-Gibbs, Patricia A. Economic Segmentation, Inequality, and the North–South Earnings Gap. *Rev. Reg. Stud.,* Spring 1985, *15*(2), pp. 43–53. [G: U.S.]

Tervo, Hannu. Teollisuuden aluekehityksen uudet piirteet. (New Features in the Regional Development of Finnish Manufacturing. With English summary.) *Kansant. Aikak.,* 1985, *81*(3), pp. 314–25. [G: Finland]

Tewari, Amitabh. Regional Disparities: A Study of Uttar Pradesh. *Margin,* January 1985, *17*(2), pp. 74–87. [G: India]

Thwaites, A. T. and Oakey, R. P. The Regional Economic Impact of Technological Change: Editorial Introduction. In *Thwaites, A. T. and Oakey, R. P., eds.,* 1985, pp. 1–12. [G: U.S.]

Toepfer, Helmuth. The Economic Impact of Returned Emigrants in Trabzon, Turkey. In *Hudson, R. and Lewis, J., eds.,* 1985, pp. 76–100. [G: Turkey]

Townsend, Alan and Peck, Francis. An Approach to the Analysis of Redundancies in the UK (Post-1976): Some Methodological Problems and Policy Implications. In *Massey, D. and Meegan, R., eds.,* 1985, pp. 64–87. [G: U.K.]

Tremblay, Rodrigue. A Quebec Perspective on Canadian Trade Options. In *Conklin, D. W. and Courchene, T. J., eds.,* 1985, pp. 57–76. [G: Canada]

Trent, Roger B.; Stout-Wiegand, Nancy and Smith, Dennis K. Attitudes toward New Development in Three Appalachian Counties. *Growth Change,* October 1985, *16*(4), pp. 70–86. [G: U.S.]

Turek, Joseph H. The Northeast in a National Context: Background Trends in Population, Income, and Employment. In *Richardson, H. W. and Turek, J. H., eds.,* 1985, pp. 28–65. [G: U.S.]

Twomey, Jim and Taylor, Jim. Regional Policy and the Interregional Movement of Manufacturing Industry in Great Britain. *Scot. J. Polit.*

Econ., November 1985, *32*(3), pp. 257–77. [G: U.K.]

Tzeng, Gwo-Hshiung. Coal Transportation System Modeling: The Case of Taiwan. *Energy J.,* January 1985, *6*(1), pp. 145–56. [G: Taiwan]

Uri, Noel D.; Howell, John and Rifkin, Edward J. On Defining Geographic Markets. *Appl. Econ.,* December 1985, *17*(6), pp. 959–77. [G: U.S.]

Vaughan, Roger J. State Policies for Promoting Economic Development: The Case of New York State. In *Richardson, H. W. and Turek, J. H., eds.,* 1985, pp. 186–210. [G: U.S.]

Veeman, Terrence S. and Veeman, Michele M. Western Canadian Agriculture: Prospects, Problems and Policy. *Can. Public Policy,* Supplement July 1985, *11*(3), pp. 301–09. [G: Canada]

Vihriälä, Vesa. Alueellisesta rahapolitiikasta. (On Regional Monetary Policy. With English summary.) *Kansant. Aikak.,* 1985, *81*(3), pp. 255–65. [G: Finland]

Vining, Daniel R. Industrial Decentralization in Brazil: A Query [Who Benefits from Industrial Decentralization? Social Power in the Labour Market, Income Distribution and Spatial Policy in Brazil]. *Reg. Stud.,* April 1985, *19*(2), pp. 163–64. [G: Brazil]

Wallman, Sandra. Structures of Informality: Variation in Local Style and the Scope for Unofficial Economic Organisation in London. In *Roberts, B.; Finnegan, R. and Gallie, D., eds.,* 1985, pp. 184–97. [G: U.K.]

Wasylenko, Michael and McGuire, Therese J. Jobs and Taxes: The Effect of Business Climate on States' Employment Growth Rates. *Nat. Tax J.,* December 1985, *38*(4), pp. 497–511. [G: U.S.]

Waters, W. G., II. Transportation Policies and the Western Transition. *Can. Public Policy,* Supplement July 1985, *11*(3), pp. 339–43. [G: Canada]

Williams, Martin. Technical Efficiency and Region: The U.S. Manufacturing Sector 1972–1977. *Reg. Sci. Urban Econ.,* August 1985, *15*(3), pp. 459–75. [G: U.S.]

Williams, Steven D. and Brinker, William J. A Survey of Foreign Firms Recently Locating in Tennessee. *Growth Change,* July 1985, *16*(3), pp. 54–63. [G: U.S.]

Wlodarczyk, W. Cezary. Health Status, Health Service and Socio Economic Development of Provinces in Poland. In *Westcott, G.; Svensson, P.-G. and Zollner, H. F. K., eds.,* 1985, pp. 299–324. [G: Poland]

Wong, Kwan-Yiu. Trends and Strategies of Industrial Development. In *Wong, K. and Chu, D. K. Y., eds.,* 1985, pp. 57–78. [G: China]

Wong, Kwan-Yiu and Chu, David K. Y. The Investment Environment. In *Wong, K. and Chu, D. K. Y., eds.,* 1985, pp. 176–207. [G: China; S. Korea; Hong Kong; Taiwan; Singapore]

Woodworth, Warner. Achieving Labor–Management Joint Action. In *Woodworth, W.; Meek,*

C. and Whyte, W. F., eds., 1985, pp. 121–39. [G: U.S.]

Yadav, Hanuman Singh. Real Income and Income Potential Surface in India. *Indian Econ. J.*, Apr.-June 1985, *32*(4), pp. 8–16. [G: India]

Yang, Chin-Wei and Labys, Walter C. A Sensitivity Analysis of the Linear Complementarity Programming Model: Appalachian Steam Coal and the Natural Gas Market. *Energy Econ.*, July 1985, *7*(3), pp. 145–52. [G: U.S.]

Young, Robert A. and Gray, S. Lee. Input–Output Models, Economic Surplus, and the Evaluation of State or Regional Water Plans. *Water Resources Res.*, December 1985, *21*(12), pp. 1819–23.

Zimmer, Terese S. Regional Input into Centralized Economic Planning: The Case of Soviet Central Asia. *Policy Sci.*, September 1985, *18*(2), pp. 111–26. [G: U.S.S.R.]

Zukin, Sharon. Markets and Politics in France's Declining Regions. *J. Policy Anal. Manage.*, Fall 1985, *5*(1), pp. 40–57. [G: France]

9413 Regional Economic Models and Forecasts

Agarwal, Vinod B. and Morgan, W. Douglas. The Interindustry Effects of Tax and Expenditure Limitations: The California Case. *Growth Change*, April 1985, *16*(2), pp. 3–11. [G: U.S.]

Allen, Peter M. Towards a New Science of Complex Systems. In *Aida, S., et al.*, 1985, pp. 268–97.

Batten, David F. and Martellato, D. Classical versus Modern Approaches to Interregional Input–Output Analysis. *Ann. Reg. Sci.*, November 1985, *19*(3), pp. 1–15.

Bennett, R. J. and Haining, R. P. Spatial Structure and Spatial Interaction: Modelling Approaches to the Statistical Analysis of Geographical Data. *J. Roy. Statist. Soc.*, 1985, *148*(1), pp. 1–27. [G: U.S.; U.K.]

Bolton, Roger. Conservation and Fuel Switching in Sweden: Review of the Swedish Case Study. In *Lakshmanan, T. R. and Johansson, B., eds.*, 1985, pp. 163–73. [G: Sweden]

Bolton, Roger. Regional Econometric Models. *J. Reg. Sci.*, November 1985, *25*(4), pp. 495–520. [G: U.S.]

Brewer, H. L. Measures of Diversification: Predictors of Regional Economic Instability. *J. Reg. Sci.*, August 1985, *25*(3), pp. 463–70. [G: U.S.]

Finch, Robert A. and Henry, Mark S. An Interindustry Approach to Financing Small Port Development and Maintenance. *Growth Change*, April 1985, *16*(2), pp. 26–33. [G: U.S.]

Fischer, Manfred M. and Nijkamp, Peter. Categorical Data and Choice Analysis in a Spatial Context. In *Hutchinson, B. G.; Nijkamp, P. and Batty, M., eds.*, 1985, pp. 1–30.

Freeman, Daniel; Alperovich, Gershon and Weksler, Itzhak. Inter-regional Input–Output Model—The Israeli Case. *Appl. Econ.*, June 1985, *17*(3), pp. 381–93. [G: Israel]

Friesz, Terry L. and Harker, Patrick T. Freight

Network Equilibrium: A Review of the State of the Art. In *Daughety, A. F., ed.*, 1985, pp. 161–206. [G: U.S.]

Giarratani, Frank and Soeroso. A Neoclassical Model of Regional Growth in Indonesia. *J. Reg. Sci.*, August 1985, *25*(3), pp. 373–82. [G: Indonesia]

Gilless, James Keith and Buongiorno, Joseph. Simulation of Future Trade in Wood Pulp between Canada and the United States. *Ann. Reg. Sci.*, July 1985, *19*(2), pp. 47–60. [G: U.S.; Canada]

Gould, B. W. and Kulshreshtha, S. N. An Input–Output Analysis of the Impacts of Increased Export Demand for Saskatchewan Products. *Can. J. Agr. Econ.*, July 1985, *33*(2), pp. 127–49. [G: Canada]

Hertel, Thomas W. Partial vs. General Equilibrium Analysis and Choice of Functional Form: Implications for Policy Modeling. *J. Policy Modeling*, Summer 1985, *7*(2), pp. 281–303. [G: U.S.]

Hua, Chang-i. Energy-Related Boom Towns: Problems, Causes, Policies, and Modeling. In *Lakshmanan, T. R. and Johansson, B., eds.*, 1985, pp. 215–32.

James, David. Environmental Economics, Industrial Process Models, and Regional-Residuals Management Models. In *Kneese, A. V. and Sweeney, J. L., eds. Vol. 1*, 1985, pp. 271–324.

Johansson, B. and Snickars, F. Conservation and Fuel Switching in Sweden: Large-scale Introduction of Energy Supply Systems: Issues, Methods, and Models in Sweden. In *Lakshmanan, T. R. and Johansson, B., eds.*, 1985, pp. 125–62. [G: Sweden]

Jones, M. E. F. The Regional Impact of an Overvalued Pound in the 1920s. *Econ. Hist. Rev.*, 2nd Ser., August 1985, *38*(3), pp. 393–401. [G: U.K.]

Jones, Philip C.; Saigal, Romesh and Schneider, Michael. Demand Homotopies for Computing Nonlinear and Multi-commodity Spatial Equilibria. In *Harker, P. T., ed.*, 1985, pp. 118–35.

Jones, Rich; Whalley, John and Wigle, Randall. Regional Impacts of Tariffs in Canada: Preliminary Results from a Small Dimensional Numerical General Equilibrium Model. In *Piggott, J. and Whalley, J., eds.*, 1985, pp. 175–88. [G: Canada]

Katz, Joseph L. and Burford, Roger L. Shortcut Formulas for Output, Income and Employment Multipliers. *Ann. Reg. Sci.*, July 1985, *19*(2), pp. 61–76. [G: U.S.]

Kruś, Lech. An Interactive Method for Decision Support in a Two-Person Game with an Example from Regional Planning. In *Grauer, M.; Thompson, M. and Wierzbicki, A. P., eds.*, 1985, pp. 336–43.

Kuehn, John A.; Procter, Michael H. and Braschler, Curtis H. Comparisons of Multipliers from Input–Output and Economic Base Models. *Land Econ.*, May 1985, *61*(2), pp. 129–35. [G: U.S.]

Lakshmanan, T. R. National and Regional Models for Economic Assessment of Energy Projects. In *Lakshmanan, T. R. and Johansson, B., eds.*, 1985, pp. 187–214.

Liew, Chong K. and Liew, Chung J. Measuring the Development Impact of a Transportation System: A Simplified Approach. *J. Reg. Sci.*, May 1985, 25(2), pp. 241–58.   [G: U.S.]

Lonergan, S. C. Tar Sands Development in Canada: A Case Study of Environmental Monitoring: Resource Extraction in Canada: Modeling the Regional Impacts. In *Lakshmanan, T. R. and Johansson, B., eds.*, 1985, pp. 41–61.
[G: Canada]

Lundqvist, Lars. Tar Sands Development in Canada: A Case Study of Environmental Monitoring: On Canadian Energy Impact Assessments. In *Lakshmanan, T. R. and Johansson, B., eds.*, 1985, pp. 62–71.   [G: Canada]

Madden, Moss. Demographic–Economic Analysis in a Multi-zonal Region: A Case Study of Nordrhein–Westfalen. *Reg. Sci. Urban Econ.*, November 1985, 15(4), pp. 517–40.
[G: W. Germany]

Netzer, Dick. 1985 Projections of the New York Metropolitan Region Study. *Amer. Econ. Rev.*, May 1985, 75(2), pp. 114–19.   [G: U.S.]

Nijkamp, Peter. Regional Information Systems and Impact Analyses for Large-scale Energy Developments. In *Lakshmanan, T. R. and Johansson, B., eds.*, 1985, pp. 257–69.

Pigozzi, Bruce Wm. and Hinojosa, Rene C. Regional Input–Output Inverse Coefficients Adjusted from National Tables. *Growth Change*, January 1985, 16(1), pp. 8–12.   [G: U.S.]

Prastacos, Poulicos P. and Brady, Raymond J. Industrial and Spatial Interdependency in Modeling: An Employment Forecasting Model for the Counties in the San Francisco Bay Region. *Ann. Reg. Sci.*, July 1985, 19(2), pp. 17–28.   [G: U.S.]

Ratick, Samuel J. Assessing the Environmental Consequences of Large-scale Energy Projects. In *Lakshmanan, T. R. and Johansson, B., eds.*, 1985, pp. 233–55.   [G: U.S.; U.S.S.R.; Sweden]

Ratner, Jonathan B. and Kinal, Terrence W. A Comparison of Alternative Approaches to Regional Forecasting as Applied to New York State. In *Richardson, H. W. and Turek, J. H., eds.*, 1985, pp. 264–83.   [G: U.S.]

Richardson, Harry W. Input–Output and Economic Base Multipliers: Looking Backward and Forward. *J. Reg. Sci.*, November 1985, 25(4), pp. 607–61.

del Roccili, John A. and Luce, Priscilla. Regionalized Analysis of Industrial Policy. In *Adams, F. G., ed.*, 1985, pp. 49–65.   [G: U.S.]

Roy, Bernard and Bouyssou, Denis. An Example of Comparison of Two Decision-Aid Models. In *Fandel, G. and Spronk, J., eds.*, 1985, pp. 361–81.

Schaeffers, Hans. Design of Computer Support for Multicriteria and Multiperson Decisions in Regional Water Resources Planning. In *Fandel, G. and Spronk, J., eds.*, 1985, pp. 245–66.

Shahrokh, Fereidoon and Labys, Walter C. A Commodity-regional Model of West Virginia. *J. Reg. Sci.*, August 1985, 25(3), pp. 383–411.
[G: U.S.]

Soule, Mason H. and Taaffe, Robert N. Mathematical Programming Approaches to the Planning of Siberian Regional Economic Development: A Nonmathematical Survey. *Soviet Econ.*, Jan.-Mar. 1985, 1(1), pp. 75–98.
[G: U.S.S.R.]

Takayama, T. Conservation and Fuel Switching in Sweden: The Swedish Case Study Compared with Experiences in the USA and Japan. In *Lakshmanan, T. R. and Johansson, B., eds.*, 1985, pp. 174–84.   [G: U.S.; Sweden; Japan]

Tatarević, Ljiljana. Dvoregionalni međusektorski model jugoslovenske privrede. (Two regional Intersectional Model of Yugoslav Economy. With English summary.) *Econ. Anal. Worker's Manage.*, 1985, 19(2), pp. 205–21.
[G: Yugoslavia]

Treyz, George I. and Stevens, Benjamin H. The TRS Regional Modelling Methodology. *Reg. Stud.*, October 1985, 19(6), pp. 547–62.
[G: U.S.]

Weber, James S. and Sen, Ashish K. On the Sensitivity of Gravity Model Forecasts. *J. Reg. Sci.*, August 1985, 25(3), pp. 317–36.

**Topical Guide
To Classification Schedule**

TOPICAL GUIDE TO CLASSIFICATION SCHEDULE

This index refers to the subject index *group, category,* or *subcategory* in which the listed topic may be found. The subject index classifications include, in most cases, related topics as well. The term *category* generally indicates that the topic may be found in all of the *subcategories* of the 3-digit code; the term *group,* indicates that the topics may be found in all of the *subcategories* in the 2-digit code. The classification schedule (p. xxxiii) serves to refer the user to cross references.

ABSENTEEISM: 8240

ACCELERATOR: 0233

ACCOUNTING: firm, 5410; national income, 2210, 2212; social, 2250

ADMINISTERED PRICES: theory, 0226; empirical studies, 6110; industry, 6354

ADMINISTRATION: 513 category; business, 5131; and planning, programming, and budgeting: national, 5132, 3226, state and local, 3241; public, 5132

ADVERTISING: industry, 6354; and marketing, 5310

AFFLUENT SOCIETY: 0510, 0110

AGENT THEORY, 0228

AGING: economics of, 9180

AGGREGATION: 2118; in input-output analysis, 2220; from micro to macro, 0220, 0230

AGREEMENTS: collective, 832 category; commodity, 4220, 7130; international trade, 4220

AGRIBUSINESS: *see* CORPORATE AGRICULTURE

AGRICULTURAL: commodity exchanges, 3132, 7150; cooperatives, 7150; credit, 7140; research and innovation, 621 category; employment, 8131; marketing, 7150; outlook, 7120; productivity, 7110, 7160; situation, 7120; supply and demand analysis, 7110; surpluses, 7130

AGRICULTURE: 710 group; government programs and policy, 7130; and development, 7100, 1120

AIR TRANSPORTATION: 6150

AIRPORT: 6150, 9410

AIRCRAFT MANUFACTURING: 6314

ALLOCATION: welfare aspects, 0242; and general equilibrium, 0210

ALUMINUM INDUSTRY: 6312

ANCIENT ECONOMIC HISTORY: 043 category

ANCIENT ECONOMIC THOUGHT: 0311; individuals, 0322

ANTITRUST POLICY: 6120

APPLIANCE INDUSTRY: 6313

APPRENTICESHIP: 8110

ARBITRATION: labor, 832 category

ASSISTANCE: foreign, 4430

ATOMIC ENERGY: conservation and pollution, 7220; industries, 6352, 7230

AUCTION MARKETS: theory, 0227

AUSTRIAN SCHOOL: 0315; individuals, 0322

AUTOMATION: employment: empirical studies, 8243, theory, 8210

AUTOMOBILE MANUFACTURING: 6314

BALANCE OF PAYMENTS: 431 category; accounting, 4310; empirical studies, 4313; theory, 4312

BANK FOR INTERNATIONAL SETTLEMENTS: 4320

BANKS: central, 3116; commercial, 3120; investment, 3140; other, 3140; portfolios, 3120; savings and loan, 3140; savings, 3140; supervision and regulation of, 3120, 3140, 3116

BARGAINING: collective, 832 category; theory, 0262

BAYESIAN ANALYSIS: 2115

BENEFIT–COST ANALYSIS: theory 0242; applied, see individual fields

BEQUESTS: empirical, 9211; theoretical, 0243

BEVERAGE INDUSTRIES: 6318

BIBLIOGRAPHY: 0110; see also the GENERAL heading under each subject

BIOGRAPHY: businessmen, 040 group; history of thought, 0322

BOND MARKET: 3132

BOOK PUBLISHING: 6352

BOYCOTTS, LABOR: 833 category; 832 category

BRAIN DRAIN: 8230, 8410

BRAND PREFERENCE: 5310; and consumers, 9212

BREAK-EVEN ANALYSIS: 5120

BRETTON WOODS AGREEMENT: 4320

BUDGETS: consumers, 9211; governments: theory, 3212, national studies, 3226, state and local studies, 3241

BUILDING: construction industry, 6340; materials industry, 6317

LABOR TURNOVER: 8243

LABOR UNIONS: *see* TRADE UNIONS

LAND: development and use, 7172; ownership and tenure, 7171; reform, 7171; taxes, 3242

LAUSANNE SCHOOL: 0316; individuals, 0322

LAW AND CRIME, ECONOMICS OF: 9160

LEASE–PURCHASE DECISIONS: 5210

LEATHER MANUFACTURING: 6316

LEISURE: and living standards, 9210; theory of, 8210; and utility, 0222

LENDING: international (public), 4430; (private) 4330

LESS DEVELOPED COUNTRIES: *see* COUNTRY STUDIES

LICENSING: 6120

LIFE-CYCLE THEORY: 0232

LINEAR AND NONLINEAR PROGRAMMING: 2135

LIQUIDITY PREFERENCE: 3112

LIVESTOCK: 7110; marketing of, 7150

LIVING STANDARDS: studies, 9211; rural, 7180

LOANABLE FUNDS THEORY OF INTEREST: 3112

LOCATION ECONOMICS: 9411, 7310

LUMBER INDUSTRY: 6317

MACHINE TOOLS MANUFACTURING: 6313

MACHINERY MANUFACTURING: 6313

MANAGEMENT: of farm, 7160; of firm, 5120; of personnel, 5130

MANAGERIAL ECONOMICS: 5120

MANPOWER TRAINING: 8110

MANUFACTURING INDUSTRIES: 631 category

MARGINAL: cost, 0223; efficiency of capital, 0224; productivity, 0224

MARGINALISM: 0315, 0360

MARKET: equilibrium, 0225; 0226; research, 5310; structure, 6110

MARKETING: 5310

MARKOV CHAIN: 2114

MARSHALLIAN SCHOOL: 0315; individuals, 0322

MARXIST SCHOOL: 0317; for individuals belonging to this group, 0322

MASS TRANSIT: 6150; urban, 9330

MATHEMATICAL PROGRAMMING: 2135

MATHEMATICAL METHODS AND MODELS: 213 category, 0115

MEDICAL CARE: *see* HEALTH, ECONOMICS OF

MEDICAL SUBSIDY PROGRAMS: 9130

MEDIEVAL: economic thought, 0311; individuals, 0322; economic history, 043 category

MERCANTILISTS: 0313; for individuals belonging to this group, 0322

MERCHANT MARINE: 6150

MERGERS: 6110; government policy toward, 6120

METAL MANUFACTURING: 6312

METHODS: 0115; experimental economic methods, 215 category

METHODOLOGY OF ECONOMICS: 0360

METROPOLITAN PLANNING STUDIES: *see* REGIONAL PLANNING

METROPOLITANIZATION: 9310

MICRODATA: 2290

MIGRATION: of labor, 8230; of population, 8410

MILITARY PROCUREMENT: 1140

MINERALS: 7210; energy producing minerals, 7230

MINING INDUSTRIES: 632 category, 7210; energy producing mining, 7320

MINORITIES: 9170

MOBILITY: *see* MIGRATION

MONETARY: growth theory, 1114; policy, 3116; theories of cycles, 3112, 1310; theory, 3112

MONEY: demand for, 3112; markets, 3130, 3132; supply of, 3112

MONOPOLISTIC COMPETITION: 0226

MONOPOLY: 0226; control of, 6120

MONOPSONY: 0226

MONTE CARLO METHOD: 2112

MORBIDITY RATES: 8410

MORTALITY RATES: 8410

MORTGAGE MARKET: 3152, 9320

MOTIVATION: consumer, 0222; and marketing, 5310; profit maximization, 0223, 5140

MOTION PICTURE INDUSTRY: 6358

MULTINATIONAL CORPORATION: 4420

MULTIPLIER: 0232; balanced budget, 3212; foreign trade, 4112; investment, 0233

MULTICOLLINEARITY: 2113

MULTIVARIATE ANALYSIS: 2114

NATALITY RATES: 8410

NATIONAL INCOME: accounting, 2212; distribution of, 2213; international comparisons of, 1230; theory and procedures, 2210

NATIONAL WEALTH: 2240

NATIONALIZATION OF INDUSTRY: domestic, 6140; foreign, 4420

NATURAL GAS: conservation, 7230; industry, 6320, 7230; resources, 7230; utilities, 6130, 7230

NATURAL RESOURCES: 7210; conservation, 7220; and population, 8410; recreational aspects, 7211; energy producing resources, 7230

NEGATIVE INCOME TAX: studies, 3230, 9140, 9110; theory, 3212

NEOCLASSICAL SCHOOL: 0315; individuals, 0322

NEW INTERNATIONAL ECONOMIC ORDER: 400 group

NEWSPAPER PUBLISHING: 6317

NON-MARXIST SOCIALISM: 0317, 0321

NON-PROFIT ORGANIZATIONS: 6360

NUTRITION: 9130

OCCUPATION: classification, 8120; safety, 8223; wage differentials, 8120, 8210, 8242